# The Norton Anthology
# of World Masterpieces

## FIFTH EDITION

### VOLUME 1

## VOLUME 1

MASTERPIECES OF THE ANCIENT WORLD • Knox

MASTERPIECES OF THE MIDDLE AGES • McGalliard

MASTERPIECES OF THE RENAISSANCE • Pasinetti

## VOLUME 2

MASTERPIECES OF THE ENLIGHTENMENT • Hugo/Spacks

MASTERPIECES OF THE NINETEENTH CENTURY:
VARIETIES OF ROMANTICISM • Hugo/Spacks

MASTERPIECES OF THE NINETEENTH CENTURY:
REALISM, NATURALISM, AND THE NEW POETRY • Wellek

MASTERPIECES OF THE TWENTIETH CENTURY:
VARIETIES OF MODERNISM • Douglas/Lawall

MASTERPIECES OF THE TWENTIETH CENTURY:
CONTEMPORARY EXPLORATIONS • Lawall

## A COMPANION VOLUME

MASTERPIECES OF THE ORIENT
Edited by G. L. Anderson

# The Norton Anthology
# of World Masterpieces

## FIFTH EDITION

Maynard Mack, *General Editor*

Bernard M. W. Knox

John C. McGalliard

P. M. Pasinetti

Howard E. Hugo

Patricia Meyer Spacks

René Wellek

Kenneth Douglas

Sarah Lawall

## VOLUME 1
*Literature of Western Culture through the Renaissance*

W · W · NORTON & COMPANY · *New York* · *London*

Copyright © 1985, 1979, 1973, 1965, 1956
by W. W. Norton & Company, Inc.
All rights reserved.
Printed in the United States of America.

The text of this book is composed in Electra, with display type set in Bernhard
Modern. Composition by Vail-Ballou. Manufacturing by R. R. Donnelley. Book
design by Antonina Krass.

**Library of Congress Cataloging in Publication Data**
Main entry under title:

The Norton anthology of world masterpieces.

Includes indexes.
Contents: v. 1. Literature of Western culture through the Renaissance—
v. 2. Literature of Western culture since the Renaissance.
1. Literature Collections.    I. Mack, Maynard, 1909–
            PN6014.N66    1985    808.8    84-18882

ISBN 0-393-95428-5 {V.1}
ISBN 0-393-95432-3 {PBK.:V.1}

Since this page cannot legibly accommodate all the copyright notices, the
following pages constitute an extension of the copyright page.

W. W. Norton & Company, Inc., 500 Fifth Avenue, New York, N.Y. 10110
W. W. Norton & Company Ltd., 37 Great Russell Street, London WC1B 3NU

4567890

v

# Contents

# Masterpieces of the Middle Ages

# Masterpieces of the Renaissance

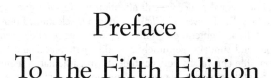

# Preface
# To The Fifth Edition

The Fifth Edition of the *Norton Anthology of World Masterpieces* is a new book throughout.

Every selection has been carefully reconsidered, both for its intrinsic interest to today's students and for its contribution to their understanding of the author and period from which it comes, as well as its representation of the ever-broadening cultural tradition that in these latter years of the twentieth century we all share.

Introductions and notes have been extensively revised—in many cases entirely rewritten—to bring them into line with the best critical scholarship of the 1980s, but also, and most particularly, to guarantee their clarity and attractiveness for current student readers. In the same interest, introductions to individual selections now appear as headnotes, placed immediately before the work to which they refer, and all suggested lists of supplementary reading have been annotated to help students find their way about. Both volumes of the anthology, it is hardly necessary to add, have been entirely redesigned and reset to produce a work rich in content but easy for student and teacher to handle and read.

The same principles have determined our Fifth Edition selections. On the advice of our users, a few have been dropped, some have been expanded or curtailed, many have been added. Our representation of the Ancient World now contains, for instance, the *Odyssey*—complete—in the sensitive translation of Robert Fitzgerald. It also contains the three plays of Aeschylus's great trilogy, the *Oresteia*, in a new translation by Robert Fagles, greeted by reviewers generally as a triumph. To Fagles we have also turned for the most faithful as well as most readable renderings of *Oedipus the King* and *Antigone* that this century has yet produced. Other vitalizing changes for the Ancient World include a liberal selection from Ovid's *Metamorphoses* in a rollicking English by Rolfe Humphries that admirably suits the witty genius of that Roman poet; and a shift, for our selections from the *Aeneid*, to the new Robert Fitzgerald version that we have been awaiting for some time. Though Virgil is the most difficult of all Latin poets to translate, this version comes closer than any other to catching the authentic Virgilian tone.

Improvements no less striking appear throughout the book. One of the most notable is the result of our success in obtaining the use of John Ciardi's hitherto unavailable translation of Dante. Acceptable English versions of the *Divine Comedy* abound, and we have in the past printed more than one of them ourselves. But for reading pleasure, and for the indispensable sense that what one is reading is not a treatise but a great poem, Ciardi easily tops all. We are proud to be permitted to offer here a work of such distinction.

With almost equal pride, we call attention to our inclusion of Madame de la Fayette's *The Princess of Clèves* among our selections from the early literature of the Enlightenment. This is a pioneering psychological novel of great depth and subtlety, genuinely a world masterpiece, and by English readers too little known. By college students, in particular, a more sensitive appreciation of the struggles, oppressions, and aspirations of the lives of women may be had from such imaginative explorations as are found in *The Princess of Clèves*, *Madame Bovary*, and *Hedda Gabler* than from any number of theoretical treatises. It is by imagination, not argument, that empathy is learned.

Equally inspired enlargements in this edition, we believe, are the four brilliant short pieces in the medieval section bringing to vivid life the fortitude and laughter of the Celtic and Nordic peoples; the addition to the Enlightenment period of selections from Samuel Johnson's *The History of Rasselas, Prince of Abyssinia*, providing a fascinating counterpoint not only with Voltaire's *Candide*, published the same year, but with the *Confessions* of Rousseau; the generous space allotted in this edition to the poetry of Baudelaire, again a dramatic opening into aspects of nineteenth-century thought and feeling that do not become explicit, though often implicit, in the plays and narratives of the time; and—a particularly valuable accession from this point of view—Frederick Douglass's autobiographical narrative of his life as a slave. This work has the double virtue of being a factual account of kinds of experience not met with in our other nineteenth-century offerings and at the same time a serious work of art, thoughtfully and skilfully shaped by a master hand.

As the foregoing statements will, we hope, make clear, the Norton Anthology of World Literature has never aspired to be either a grab-bag or an encyclopaedia. It is a teaching instrument. From its first edition in 1956, it has been a carefully planned whole, each of its parts designed and executed by a recognized authority in that field, but changing steadily with the times and with the needs and preferences of the hundreds of teachers who year after year have insisted on nothing but the best for their students, and, by generously pooling their classroom experiences with ours, have guided us in our efforts to deliver it. Like the syllabus of every sound multiple-division course, the anthology offers more than any class can master in a single year, in order to leave options for the individual teacher and provide supplementary outside reading (often not available in the college library in sufficient copies) for those who wish it. On the other hand, we have been careful not to overwhelm the student new to world literature with masses of material unrelated except by their appearance between the same covers.

We have equally taken pains to make our selections from any given period or culture truly representative. We include both Shakespeare's *Hamlet* and Marlowe's *The Tragedy of Dr. Faustus* in our Renaissance section, for example, because these two plays sum up the complex sensibility of that era more fully than any other two works now extant, and at the same time have an unmatched pertinence for us. Today's students, growing up in a nuclear world they never made and burdened with a life-or-death imperative to "set it right," identify more readily with Shakespeare's young prince, similarly burdened and like them a university student, than with any other character in literature. Nor are they unmindful of that Faustian thrust to power in humankind which helps create the threat of annihilation we all face and which is so richly and unforgettably depicted from differing perspectives in Marlowe's play and Goethe's dramatic poem. On the same grounds, and also because we intend this book to be an effective teaching instrument offering many interconnections, we include not merely the magical and folktale side of Greek literature, represented in the *Odyssey*, but the fiercely realist and "heroic" side represented by that greatest of epic poems, the *Iliad*, without which such later works as Milton's *Paradise Lost* and Pope's *Rape of the Lock* cannot be understood. For the *Iliad* in this fifth edition, however, our own experience as well as consultation with our users has dictated a return to the translation of Richmond Lattimore, which, deprived though it is of a certain "nobility" by the informalization of twentieth century English, can nevertheless flash into electric moments:

> Honor then the gods, Achilleus, and take pity upon me
> remembering your father, yet I am still more pitiful;
> I have gone through what no other mortal on earth has gone through;
> I put my lips to the hands of the man who has killed my children.

Nowhere, we believe, is our determination to do full justice to the complexities of a given period while at the same time opening new horizons to class discussion more apparent than in our treatment in this fifth edition of the literature of our own century. Here we offer for the first time a movie script, Jean Renoir's *Grand Illusion*, from which one of the greatest films of our time (some think the very greatest) was made. With or without the picture produced from it, it is a fascinating text for close study, an exercise not only for the visual imagination but for the moral sense. We offer also in this section (as with Douglass's slave narrative earlier) some important windows opening on experiences and ways of life which are not part of the cultural tradition students brought up on the American continent usually know best: Yukio Mishima's grim but brilliant "Patriotism," R. K. Narayan's "Emden," and Wole Soyinka's hilarious yet poignant *The Lion and the Jewel*.

To clarify further the development of twentieth-century literature, we have Other authors new to the anthology in this edition are Samuel Beckett (*Endgame*), Doris Lessing ("To Room Nineteen"), Gabriel García Márquez ("Death Constant Beyond Love"), and Alain Robbe-Grillet ("The Secret Room"). Authors restored from earlier editions by popular request are Ralph Ellison ("King of the Bingo Game"), Federico García Lorca ("Lament for [the Matador] Ignacio Sanchez Mejias"), Rainer Maria Rilke (*Duino Elegies*, 1 and 10, and "Archaic Torso of Apollo"), and Alexander Solzhenitsyn ("Matryona's Home"). Needless to say, in making these additions we have not scanted the earlier great innovators like Proust in fiction, without whom the course of the twentieth-century novel is unintelligible, Pirandello and Brecht in drama, or Yeats and Eliot in modern verse.

To clarify further the development of twentieth-century literature, we have made what we believe will be for most students a helpful division between

# The Norton Anthology of World Masterpieces

## FIFTH EDITION

### VOLUME 1

# Masterpieces of the
# Ancient World

This section represents, not the ancient world as a whole, but the most significant area and period of ancient man's development. The area is the Mediterranean basin, and the period the twelve hundred years from, roughly, 800 B.C. to A.D. 400. In this place and time ancient man laid the intellectual and religious foundations of the modern Western outlook.

The literature of the ancient world, which, whether or not we are acquainted with it, is still the background of our institutions, attitudes, and thought, was written in three languages—Hebrew, Greek, and Latin. The peoples who spoke these languages created their civilizations independently in place and time, but the development of the Mediterranean area into one economic and political unit brought them into contact with one another and produced a fusion of their typical attitudes that is the basis of all subsequent Western thought. This process of independent development, interaction, and final fusion is represented in the arrangement of this section: In the last part of it the three separate lines converge, and they finally meet in the figure of St. Augustine, who had the intellectual honesty and curiosity of the Greek at his best, the social seriousness and sense of order of the Roman, and the Hebrew's feeling of man's inadequacy and God's omnipotent justice.

### THE ANCIENT WORLD

Though Rome at the height of her power was to extend her rule northward through France as far as Britain and eastward to the Euphrates, the ancient world was centered on the Mediterranean Sea—"We live around the sea," said the Greek philosopher Socrates, "like frogs around a pond." Climate and basic crops were (and still are) similar over most of the area: a dry hot summer and a comparatively mild winter, more favorable to sheep and goats than cattle, to vine and olive rather than cereal crops. Though metal was mined and worked, what we know as heavy industry did not exist; coal and oil were not exploited for energy, and the war galleys were propelled by sail and human oarsmen, the armies moved on foot. All the advanced civilizations of the ancient world depended for their existence on a slave class to do their heavy work, on the land, in the mines, and in the house; this institution, widely varied in its forms—peasants tied to the land as in Egypt, bought slaves as in Greece and Rome, or men enslaved for debt as in Greece and Israel—lasted until the end of the ancient world, to be gradually replaced in

Europe by the feudal system with a peasantry technically free but in practice working the land for the benefit of an overlord.

Civilization began, not on the shores of the Mediterranean, but east and south of that sea: in Babylon and Egypt. Ancient civilization was based on agriculture and it flourished first in regions where the soil gave rich rewards: in the valley of the Nile, where annual floods left large tracts of land moist and fertile under the Egyptian sun and in the valleys of the Euphrates and Tigris rivers, which flowed through the "Fertile Crescent," the land now known as Iraq and Iran. Great cities—Thebes and Memphis in Egypt, Babylon and Nineveh in the Fertile Crescent—came into being as centers for the complicated administration of the irrigated fields; supported by the surplus the land produced, they became centers also for government, religion, and culture. Civilization begins with cities; the word itself is derived from a Latin word which means "citizen." As far back as 3000 B.C. the pharaohs of Egypt began to build their splendid temples and gigantic pyramids, as well as to record their political acts and religious beliefs in hieroglyphic script; the Sumerians, Babylonians, and Assyrians began to build the palaces and temples of Babylon, as well as to record their laws in cuneiform script on clay tablets.

These civilizations were already immemorially old when Israel, Greece and, later, Rome became conscious of their national character and destiny, yet it was to the younger nations that the future belonged. Babylon, Nineveh, and Egypt as the centuries went by were all but lost to the memory of mankind; the pyramids and the Sphinx remained but it was not until the nineteenth century A.D. that the hieroglyphic writing of the Egyptians and the cuneiform records of Babylon and Nineveh were deciphered and their contents read again after a lapse of thousands of years. The cultural history of the ancient world came to medieval Europe in the languages not of Babylon and Egypt but in Hebrew, Greek, and Latin.

### THE HEBREWS

There was, of course, contact between the old civilizations and the new. The Hebrews, in fact, early in their history, spent some years as government slaves in Egypt before their Exodus, their migration, under the leadership of Moses, through the Sinai desert to Palestine. This new home of the Hebrews was of no particular strategic importance, and their record is not that of an imperial people. In their period of independence, from their beginnings as a pastoral tribe to their high point as a kingdom with a splendid capital in Jerusalem, they accomplished little of note in the political or military spheres; their later history was a bitter and unsuccessful struggle for freedom against a series of foreign masters—Babylonian, Greek, and Roman.

After the period of expansion and prosperity under the great kings, David and Solomon (1005–925 B.C.), the kingdom fell apart again into warring factions, which called in outside powers; the melancholy end of a long period of internal and external struggle was the destruction of the cities and the deportation of the population to Babylon (586 B.C.). This period of exile (it ended in 539 when Cyrus, the Persian conqueror of Babylon, released the Hebrews from bondage) was a formative period for Hebrew religious thought, which was enriched and refined by the teachings of the prophet Ezekiel and the unknown prophet known as the Second Isaiah (pp. 16, 62). The return to Palestine was crowned by the rebuilding of the Temple and the creation of the canonical version of the Pentateuch or Torah, the first five books of the Old Testament; the religious legacy of the Hebrew people was now codified for future generations. But the independent state of Israel was not destined to last long. By 300 B.C. the Macedonian successors of Alexander the Great had encroached on its borders and prerogatives; in spite of a heroic resistance, the territory eventually became part of a Hellenistic Greek-speaking kingdom and, finally, was absorbed by the Roman Empire. A desperate revolt against Rome was crushed in A.D. 70 by the emperor Titus (on the arch of Titus in Rome a relief shows the legionaries carrying the menorah, the seven-branched candlestick, in Titus' triumph); a second revolt, against the emperor Hadrian (A.D. 131–134) resulted in the final extermination or removal from Palestine of the Hebrew people. Henceforward, they were the people of the *diaspora*, the "scattering": religious communities in the great cities of the ancient world maintaining local cohesion and universal religious solidarity but stateless, as they were to be all through the centuries until the re-creation, in our time, of the state of Israel.

The political history of the ancient Hebrews ended in a series of disasters; in the field of the arts they left behind them no painting or sculpture and little or no secular literature—no drama, for example, no epic poetry. What they did leave us is a religious literature, written down probably between the eighth and second centuries B.C., which is informed by an attitude different from that of any other nation of the ancient world. It is founded on the idea of one God, the creator of all things, all-powerful and just—a conception of the divine essence and the government of the universe so simple that to us, who have inherited it, it seems obvious. But in its time it was so revolutionary that it made the Hebrews a nation apart, sometimes laughed at, sometimes feared, but always alien.

### THE GREEKS

The origin of the peoples who eventually produced the great literature of the eighth to the fourth centuries B.C. is still a mystery. The language they spoke clearly belongs to the great Indo-European family (which includes the Germanic, Celtic, Italic, and Sanskrit language groups) but many of the ancient Greek words and place names have terminations which are definitely not Indo-European—the word for sea (*thalassa*), for example. The Greeks of historic times were presumably a blend of the native tribes and the Indo-European invaders, en route from the European landmass.

In the last hundred years archaeology has given us a clearer picture than our forefathers had of the level of civilization in early Greece. The second millennium B.C. saw a brilliant culture, called Minoan after the mythical king Minos, flourishing on the large island of Crete, and the citadel of Mycenae and the palace at Pylos show that mainland Greece, in that same period, had centers of wealth and power unsuspected before the excavators discovered the gold masks of the buried kings and the clay tablets covered with strange signs. The decipherment of these signs (published in 1953) revealed that the language of these Myceneans was an early form of Greek. It must have been the memory of these rich kingdoms that inspired Homer's vision of "Mycenae rich in gold" and the splendid armed hosts that assembled for the attack on Troy.

It was a blurred memory (Homer does not remember the writing, for example, nor the detailed bureaucratic accounting recorded on the tablets) and this is easy to understand: some time in the last century of the millennium the great palaces were destroyed by fire; with them disappeared not only the arts and skills which had created Mycenean wealth but even the system of writing. For the next few hundred poverty-stricken years the Greeks were illiterate and so no written evidence survives for what, in view of our ignorance about so many aspects of it, we call the Dark Age of Greece.

One thing we do know about it: it produced a body of oral epic poetry which was the raw material Homer shaped into the two great poems, the *Iliad* and *Odyssey*. These Homeric poems, which seem from internal evidence to date from the eighth century B.C. (which is incidentally, or perhaps not incidentally, the century in which the Greeks learned how to write again), played in the subsequent development of Greek civilization the same role that the Old Testament writings had played in Palestine: they became the basis of an education and therefore of a whole culture. Not only did the great characters of the epic serve as models of conduct for later generations of Greeks, but the figures of the Olympian gods retained, in the prayers, poems, and sculpture of the succeeding centuries, the shapes and attributes set down by Homer. The difference between the Greek and the Hebrew hero, between Achilles and Joseph, for example, is remarkable, but the difference between "the God of Abraham and of Isaac" and the Olympians who interfere capriciously in the lives of Hector and Achilles is an unbridgeable chasm. The two conceptions of the power that governs the universe are irreconcilable; and in fact the struggle between them ended, not in synthesis, but in the complete victory of the one and the disappearance of the other. The Greek conception of the nature of the gods and of their relation to man is so alien to us that it is difficult for the modern reader to take it seriously. The Hebrew basis of European Christianity has made it almost impossible for us to imagine a god who can be feared and laughed at, blamed and admired, and still sincerely worshiped. Yet all these are proper attitudes toward the gods on Olympus; they are all implicit in Homer's poems.

The Hebrew conception of God is clearly an expression of an emphasis on those aspects of the universe which imply a harmonious order. The elements of disorder in the universe are, in the story of Creation, blamed on man, and in all Hebrew literature the evidences of disorder are something the writer tries to reconcile with an *a priori* assumption of an all-powerful, just God; he never tampers with the fundamental datum. Just as clearly, the Greeks conceived their gods as an expression of the disorder of the world in which they lived; the Olympian gods, like the natural forces of sea and sky, follow their own will even to the extreme of conflict with each other, and always with a sublime disregard for the human beings who may be affected by the results of their actions. It is true that they are all subjects of a single more powerful god, Zeus, but his authority over them is based only on superior strength; though he cannot be openly resisted, he can be temporarily deceived by his fellow Olympians. And Zeus, although by virtue of his superior power his will is finally accomplished in the matter of Achilles' wrath, knows limits to his power too; he cannot save the life of his son the Lycian hero Sarpedon. Behind Zeus stands the mysterious power of Fate, to which even he must bow.

Such gods as these, representing as they do the blind forces of the universe which man cannot control, are not thought of as connected with morality. Morality is a human creation, and though the gods may approve of it, they are not bound by it. And violent as they are, they cannot feel the ultimate consequence of violence; death is a human fear, just as the courage to face it is a human quality. There is a double standard, one for gods, one for men, and the inevitable consequence is that our real admiration and sympathy is directed not toward the gods but toward the men. With Hector, and even with Achilles at his worst, we can sympathize; but the gods, though they may excite terror or laughter, can never have our sympathy; we could as easily sympathize with the blizzard or the force of gravity. Homer imposed on Greek literature the anthropocentric emphasis which is its distinguishing mark and its great contribution to the Western mind; though the gods are ever-present characters in the incidents of his poem, his true concern, first and last, is with men and women.

## THE CITY-STATES OF GREECE

The stories told in the Homeric poems are set in the age of the Trojan War, which archaeologists (those, that is, who believe that it happened at all) date to the twelfth century B.C. Though the poems do perhaps preserve some faded memories of the Mycenaean age, there is no doubt that the poems as we have them are the creation of later centuries, the tenth to the eighth B.C., the so-called Dark Age which succeeded the collapse (or destruction) of Mycenaean civilization. This was the time of the final settlement of the Greek peoples, an age of invasion and migration, which saw the foundation and growth of many small independent cities. The geography of the Greek peninsula and its scattered islands encouraged this fragmentation: the Greek cities never lost sight of their common Hellenic heritage but it was not enough to unite them except in the face of unmistakable and overwhelming danger, and even then only partially and for a short time. They differed from each other in custom, political constitution, and even dialect: their relations with each other were those of rivals and fierce competitors.

In these cities, constantly at war with each other in the pursuit of more productive land for growing populations, the kings of Homeric society gave way to aristocratic oligarchies, which maintained a strangle hold on the land and the economy of which it was the base. An important safety valve was colonization; in the eighth and seventh centuries B.C. landless men founded new cities (always near the sea and generally owing little or no allegiance to the home base) all over the Mediterranean coast—in Spain, southern France (Marseilles, Nice, and Antibes were all Greek cities), in South Italy (Naples), Sicily (Syracuse), North Africa (Cyrene), all along the coast of Asia Minor (Smyrna, Miletus), and even on the Black Sea as far as Russian Crimea. Many of these new outposts of Greek civilization experienced a faster economic and cultural development than the older cities of the mainland. It was in the cities founded on the Asian coast that the Greeks adapted to their own language the Phoenician system of writing (adding signs for the vowels to create the first efficient alphabet); its first use was probably for commercial records and transactions, but as literacy became a general condition all over the Greek world in the course of the seventh century B.C. treaties and political decrees were inscribed on stone and literary works written on rolls of paper made from the Egyptian papyrus plant.

## ATHENS AND SPARTA

By the beginning of the fifth century B.C. the two most prominent city-states were Athens and Sparta; these two cities led the combined Greek resistance to the Persian invasion of Europe in the years 490 to 479 B.C. The defeat of the solid Persian power by the divided and insignificant Greek cities surprised the world and inspired in Greece, and particularly in Athens, a confidence that knew no bounds.

Athens was at this time a democracy, the first in Western history. It was a direct, not a representative, democracy, for the number of free citizens was small enough to permit the exercise of power by a meeting of the citizens as a body in assembly. Athens' power lay in the fleet with which she had played her decisive part in the struggle against Persia, and with this fleet she rapidly became the leader of a naval alliance which included most of the islands of the Aegean Sea and many Greek cities on the coast of Asia Minor. Sparta, on the other hand, was a totalitarian state, rigidly conservative in government and policy, in which the individual citizen was reared and trained by the state for the state's business, war. The Spartan land army was consequently superior to any other in Greece, and the Spartans controlled, by direct rule or by alliance, the majority of the city-states of the Peloponnese.

These two cities, allies for the war of liberation against Persia, became enemies when the external danger was eliminated. The middle years of the fifth century were disturbed by indecisive hostilities between them and haunted by the probability of full-scale war to come; as the years went by this war came to be accepted as "inevitable" by both sides, and in 431 B.C. it began. It was to end in 404 B.C. with the total defeat of Athens.

Before the beginning of this disastrous war Athenian democracy provided its citizens with a cultural and political environment that was without precedent in the ancient world. The institutions of Athens encouraged the maximum development of the individual's capacities and at the same time inspired the maximum devotion to the interests of the community. It was a moment in history of delicate and precarious balance between the freedom of the individual and the demands of the state. Its uniqueness was emphasized by the complete lack of balance in Sparta, where the necessities of the state annihilated the individual as a creative and independent being. It was the proud boast of the Athenians that without sacrificing the cultural amenities of civilized life they could yet when called upon surpass in policy and war their adversary, whose citizen body was an army in constant training. The Athenians were, in this respect as in others, a nation of amateurs. "The individual Athenian," said Pericles in the speech that is at once the panegyric of Athenian democracy and its epitaph, "in his own person seems to have the power of adapting himself to the most varied forms of action with the utmost versatility and grace." But the freedom of the individual did not, in Athens' great days, produce anarchy. "While we are . . . unconstrained in our private intercourse," Pericles had observed earlier in his speech, "a spirit of reverence pervades our public acts."

This balance of individual freedom and communal unity was not destined to outlast the century. It went down, with Athens, in the war. Under the mounting pressure of the long conflict, the Athenians lost the "spirit of reverence" that Pericles saw as the stabilizing factor in Athenian democracy. They subordinated all considerations to the immediate interest of the city and surpassed their enemy in the logical ferocity of their actions; they finally fell victims to leaders who carried the process one step further and subordinated all considerations to their own private interest. The war years saw the decay of that freedom in unity which is celebrated in Pericles' speech; by the end of the fifth century Athens was divided internally as well as defeated externally. The individual citizen no longer thought of himself and Athens as one and the same; the balance was gone forever.

One of the solvents of traditional values was an intellectual revolution which was taking place in the advanced Athenian democracy of the last half of the fifth century, a critical evaluation of accepted ideas in every sphere of thought and action. It stemmed from innovations in education. Democratic institutions had created a demand for an education that would prepare men for public life, especially by training them in the art of public speaking. The demand was met by the appearance of the professional teacher, the Sophist, as he was called, who taught, for a handsome fee, not only the techniques of public speaking but also the subjects which gave a man something to talk about—government, ethics, literary criticism, even astronomy. The curriculum of the Sophists, in fact, marks the first appearance in European civilization of the liberal education, just as they themselves were the first professors.

The Sophists were great teachers, but like most teachers they had little or no control over the results of their teaching. Their methods placed an inevitable emphasis on effective presentation of a point of view, to the detriment, and if necessary the exclusion, of anything which might make it less convincing. They produced a generation that had been trained to see both sides of any question and to argue the weaker side as effectively as the stronger, the false as effectively as the true; to argue inferentially from probability in the absence of concrete evidence; to appeal to the audience's sense of its own advantage rather than to accepted moral standards; and to justify individual defiance of general prejudice and even of law by the distinction between "nature" and "convention." These methods dominated the thinking of the Athenians of the last half of the century. The emphasis on the technique of effective presentation of both sides of any case encouraged a relativistic point of view and finally produced a cynical mood which denied the existence of any absolute standards. The canon of probability (which implies an appeal to human reason as the supreme authority) became a critical weapon for an attack on myth and on traditional conceptions of the gods; it had its constructive side, too, for it was the base for historical reconstruction of the unrecorded past and of the theoretical outline of the stages in mankind's progress from savagery to civilization. The rhetorical appeal to the self-inter-

est of the audience, to expediency, became the method of the political leaders of the wartime democracy and the fundamental doctrine of new theories
of power-politics: these theories served as cynical justification for the increasing severity of the measures Athens took to terrorize her rebellious subjects.
The distinction between "nature" and "convention" is the source of the
doctrine of the superman, who breaks free of the conventional restraints of
society and acts according to the law of his own "nature." The new spirit in
Athens has magnificent achievements to its credit, but it undermined old
solid moral convictions. At its roots was a supreme confidence in the human
intelligence and a secular view of man's position in the universe that is best
expressed in the statement of Protagoras, the most famous of the Sophists:
"Man is the measure of all things."

### THE DECLINE OF THE CITY-STATE

In the last half of the fifth century the whole traditional basis of individual
conduct, the unity and cohesion of the city-state, was undermined, gradually at first by the critical approach of the Sophists and their pupils, and then
rapidly, as the war accelerated the process of moral disintegration. "In peace
and prosperity," says Thucydides, "both states and individuals are actuated
by higher motives . . . but war, which takes away the comfortable provision
of daily life, is a hard master, and tends to assimilate men's characters to
their conditions." The war brought to Athens the rule of the new politicians
who, schooled in the doctrine of the new power-politics, initiated savage
reprisals against Athens' rebellious subject-allies and launched the city on
an expansionist course which ended in disaster in Sicily (411 B.C.). Seven
years later Athens, her last fleet gone, surrendered to the Spartans. A pro-
Spartan antidemocratic regime, the Thirty Tyrants, was installed, but soon
overthrown; Athens became a democracy again but the confidence and unity
of Athens' great age were gone forever. Community and individual were no
longer one, and the individual, cast on his own resources for guidance,
found only conflicting attitudes which he could not refer to any absolute
standards. The mood of postwar Athens oscillated between a fanatic,
unthinking reassertion of traditional values and a weary cynicism which wanted
only to be left alone. The only thing common to the two extremes was a
distrust of intelligence.

In the disillusioned gloom of the years of defeat the Athenians began to feel
more and more exasperation with a voice they had been listening to for
many years, the voice of Socrates, a stonemason who for most of his adult
life had made it his business to discuss with his fellow citizens the great issues
of which the Athenians were now so weary—the nature of justice, of truth,
of piety. Unlike the Sophists, he did not lecture nor did he charge a fee; his
method was dialectic, the search for truth by a process of questions and
answers, and his dedication to his mission had kept him poor. But the initial
results of his discussions were often infuriatingly like the results of sophistic
teaching. By questions and answers he succeeded in exposing the illogicality
of his opponent's position, but Socrates did not often provide a substitute for
the erroneous belief he had destroyed. Yet it is clear that he did believe in
absolute standards, and what is more, he believed they could be discovered
by a process of logical inquiry and supported by logical proof. His ethics

rested on an intellectual basis. The resentment against him, which came to a head in 399 B.C., is partly explained by the fact that he satisfied neither extreme of the postwar mood. He questioned the old standards in order to establish new, and he refused to let the Athenians live in peace, for he preached that it was every man's duty to think his way through to the truth. In this last respect he was the prophet of the new age; for him the city and the accepted code were no substitute for the task of self-examination which each individual must set himself and carry through to a conclusion. The characteristic statement of the old Athens was public, in the assembly or the theater; Socrates proclaimed the right and duty of each individual to work out his own salvation and made clear his distrust of public life: "he who will fight for the right . . . must have a private station and not a public one."

The Athenians sentenced him to death on a charge of impiety; they hoped, no doubt, that he would go into exile to escape execution but he remained, as he put it himself, at his post, and they were forced to have the sentence carried out. If they thought they were finished with him, they were sadly mistaken. In the next century Athens became the center for a large group of philosophical schools, all of them claiming to develop and interpret the ideas of Socrates.

The century that followed his death saw the exhaustion of the Greek city-states in constant internecine warfare. Politically and economically bankrupt, they fell under the power of the kingdom of Macedon, in the north, whose king, Philip, combined a ferocious energy with a cynicism which enabled him to take full advantage of the corrupt governments of the city-states. Greek liberty ended at the battle of Chaeronea in 338 B.C., and Philip's son Alexander inherited a powerful army and the political control of all Greece. He led his Macedonian and Greek armies against Persia, and in a few brilliant campaigns became master of an empire which extended into Egypt in the south and to the borders of India in the east. He died at Babylon in 323 B.C., and his empire broke up into a number of independent kingdoms ruled by his generals; but the results of his fantastic achievements were more durable than might have been expected. Into the newly conquered territories came thousands of Greeks who wished to escape from the political futility and economic crisis of the homeland. Wherever they went they took with them their language, their culture, and their typical buildings, the gymnasium and the theater. At Alexandria in Egypt, for example, a Greek library was formed to preserve the texts of Greek literature for the scholars who edited them, a school of Greek poetry flourished, Greek mathematicians and geographers made new advances in science. The Middle East became, as far as the cities were concerned, a Greek-speaking area; and when, some two or three centuries later, the first accounts of Jesus' life and teaching were written down, they were written in Greek, the language on which the cultural homogeneity of the whole area was based.

## ROME

When Alexander died at Babylon in 323 B.C., the Italian city of Rome, situated on the Tiber in the western coastal plain, was engaged in a struggle for the control of central Italy. Less than a hundred years later (269 B.C.) Rome, in control of the whole Italian peninsula, was drawn into a hundred-year war against the Phoenician city of Carthage, on the West African coast, from which she emerged mistress of the western Mediterranean. At the end of the first century B.C., in spite of a series of civil wars fought with savage vindictiveness and on a continental scale, Rome was the capital of an empire which stretched from the Straits of Gibraltar to the frontiers of Palestine. This empire gave peace and orderly government to the Mediterranean area for the next two centuries, and for two centuries after that maintained a desperate but losing battle against the invading savage tribes moving in from the north and east. When it finally went down, it left behind it the ideal of the world-state, an ideal which was to be reconstituted as a reality by the medieval church, which ruled from the same center, Rome, and with a spiritual authority as great as the secular authority it replaced.

The achievements of the Romans, not only their conquests but also their success in consolidating the conquests and organizing the conquered, are best understood in the light of the Roman character. Unlike the Greek, the Roman was above all a practical man. He might have no aptitude for pure mathematics, but he could build an aqueduct to last two thousand years; he was not notable as a political theorist, but he organized a complicated yet stable federation which held Italy loyal to him in the presence of invading armies. He was conservative to the core; his strongest authority was *mos maiorum*, the custom of his predecessors; a monument of this conservatism, the great body of Roman law, is one of his greatest contributions to Western civilization. The quality he most admired was *gravitas*, seriousness of attitude and purpose, and his highest words of commendation were "manliness," "industry," "discipline." Pericles, in his funeral speech, praised the Athenian for his adaptability, versatility, and grace; this would have seemed strange praise to a Roman, whose idea of personal and civic virtue was different. "By her ancient custom and her men the Roman state stands," says Ennius the Roman poet, in a line which by its metrical heaviness emphasizes the stability implied in the key word "stands": *moribus antiquis res stat Romana virisque.*

Greek history begins, not with a king, a battle, or the founding of a city, but with an epic poem; the literary achievement preceded the political by many centuries. The Romans, on the other hand, had conquered half the world before they began to write. The stimulus to the creation of Latin literature was the Greek literature which the Romans discovered when, in the second century B.C., they assumed political responsibility for Greece and the Near East. Latin literature began with a translation of the *Odyssey*, made by a Greek prisoner of war, and with the exception of satire, until Latin literature became Christian, the model was always Greek. The Latin writer (especially the poet) borrowed wholesale from his Greek original, not furtively, but openly and proudly, as a tribute to the master from whom he had learned. But this frank acknowledgment of indebtedness should not blind us to the fact that Latin literature is original, and sometimes profoundly so. This is true above all of Virgil, who chose as his theme the coming of the Trojan prince Aeneas to Italy, where he was to found a city from which, in the fullness of time, would come "the Latin race, . . . and the walls of lofty Rome."

When Virgil was born in 70 B.C. the Roman republic, which had conquered and now governed the Mediterranean world, had barely recovered from one civil war and was drifting inexorably toward another. The institutions of the city-state proved inadequate for world government. The civil conflict which had disrupted the republic for more than a hundred years ended finally in the establishment of a powerful executive. Although the Senate, which had been the controlling body of the republic, retained an impressive share of the power, the new arrangement developed inevitably toward autocracy, the rule of the executive, the emperor, as he was called once the system was stabilized. The first of the long line of Roman emperors who gave stable government to the Roman world during the first two centuries A.D. was Octavius, known generally by his title, Augustus. He had made his way cautiously through the intrigues and bloodshed that followed the murder of his uncle Julius Caesar in 44 B.C., until by 31 B.C., he controlled the western half of the empire. In that year he fought a decisive battle with the ruler of the eastern half of the empire, Mark Antony, who was supported by Cleopatra, queen of Egypt. Octavius' victory at Actium united the empire under one authority and ushered in an age of peace and reconstruction.

For the next two hundred years the successors of Augustus, the Roman emperors, ruled the ancient world with only occasional disturbances, most of them confined to Rome, where emperors who flagrantly abused their immense power—Nero, for example—were overthrown by force. The second half of this period was described by Gibbon, the great historian of imperial Rome, as the period "in the history of the world during which the condition of the human race was most happy and prosperous." The years A.D. 96–180, those of the "five good emperors," were in fact remarkable: this was the longest period of peace that has ever been enjoyed by the inhabitants of the area (which included Britain, France, all southern Europe, the Middle East, and the whole of North Africa). Trade and agriculture flourished and the cities, with their public baths, theaters, and libraries, offered all the amenities of civilized life. Yet there was apparent, especially in the literature of the second century, a spiritual emptiness; Petronius's *Satyricon* paints a sardonic portrait of the vulgar display and intellectual poverty of the newly rich who can think only in terms of money and possessions. The old religion offered no comfort to those who looked beyond mere material ends; it had been too closely knit into the fabric of the independent city-state and was inadequate for a time in which men were citizens of the world. New religions arose or were imported from the East, universal religions which made their appeal to all nations and classes: the worship of the Egyptian goddess Isis, of the Persian god Mithras, who offered bliss in the life to come, and of the Hebrew prophet Jesus Christ, crucified in Jerusalem and risen from the dead. This was the religion which, working underground, often suppressed (there was a persecution of the Christians under Nero in the first century, another under the last of the "good emperors" Marcus Aurelius in the second), finally triumphed and became the official and later the exclusive religion of the Roman world. As the empire in the third and fourth centuries disintegrated under the never-ending invasions by barbarian tribes from the north, the Church, with its center and spiritual head in Rome, converted the new inhabitants and so made possible the preservation of much of that Latin and Greek literature which was to serve the European Middle Ages

# THE OLD TESTAMENT

The religious attitudes of the Hebrews appear in the story that they told of the creation of the world and of man. This creation is the work of one God, who is omnipotent and omniscient, and who creates a perfect and harmonious order. The disorder which we see all around us, physical and moral, is not God's creation but Adam's; it is the consequence of man's disobedience. The story not only reconciles the undeniable existence of evil and disorder in the world with the conception of God's infinite justice, it also attributes to man himself an independence of God, free will, which in this case he had used for evil. The Hebrew God is not limited in His power by other deities, who oppose His will (as in the Greek stories of Zeus and his undisciplined family); His power over inanimate nature is infinite; in all the range of His creation there is only one being able to resist Him—man.

Since God is all-powerful, even this resistance on Adam's part is in some mysterious way a manifestation of God's will; how this can be is not explained by the story, and we are left with the mystery that still eludes us, the coexistence of God's prescient power and man's unrestricted free will.

The story of the Fall of Man ends with a situation in which Adam has earned for himself and his descendants a short life of sorrow relieved only by death. It was the achievement of later Hebrew teachers to carry the story on and develop a concept of a God who is as merciful as He is just, who watches tenderly over the destinies of the creatures who have rebelled against Him, and brings about the possibility of atonement and full reconciliation.

Adam's son Cain is the first man to shed human blood, but though God drives him out to be a wanderer on the face of the earth, He does not kill him, and the brand on Cain's forehead, while it marks him as a murderer, also protects his life—no man is to touch him. Later when the descendants of Adam grow so wicked that God is sorry He has created the human race, He decides to destroy it by sending a universal flood. But He spares one man, Noah, with his family, to beget a new human race, on which God pins His hopes. His rainbow in the sky reminds men of His promise that He will never again let loose the waters. But men do not learn their lesson: they start to build a tower high enough to reach to Heaven, and God is afraid that if they succeed they will then recognize no limit to their ambitions. Yet He does not destroy them; He merely frustrates their purpose by depriving them of their common language.

And yet Man must eventually atone for Adam's act; human guilt must be wiped out by sacrifice. The development of this idea was extended over centuries of thought and suffering. For the Christians, it reached its culmination in the figure of Christ, the Son of God, who as a man pays the full measure due in human suffering and human death. But the idea of the one who suffers for all had long been a major theme in Hebrew religious literature. Not only did there emerge slowly a concept of the Hebrews as a chosen nation that suffers for the rest, but individual figures of Hebrew history and imagination embodied this theme in the form of the story of the suffering servant whose suffering brings relief to his fellow men and ultimate glory to himself. This is the idea behind the story of Joseph.

Joseph, his father's favorite son, has a sense of his own great destiny, confirmed by his dreams, which represent him as the first of all his race. He is indeed to be the first, but to become so he must also be the last. He is sold into slavery by his brothers; the savior is rejected by those whom he is to save, as the Hebrews were rejected by their neighbors and as they rejected their own prophets.

With the loss of his liberty, Joseph's trials have only begun. In Egypt after making a new and successful life for himself, he is thrown into prison on a false accusation. He interprets the dream of Pharaoh's butler, who promises, if his interpretation is correct, to secure his release; the butler is restored to freedom and royal favor, but, as is the way of the world, forgets his promise and leaves his comforter in jail. Joeseph stays in prison two more years but finally obtains his freedom and becomes Pharaoh's most trusted adviser. When his brothers come from starving Palestine and bow down before him asking for help, he saves them; not only does he give them grain but he also provides a home for his people in Egypt. "I am Joseph your brother, whom ye sold into Egypt," he says to them when he reveals his identity. "God sent me before you to preserve you a posterity in the earth, and to save your lives by a great deliverance."

One of the essential points of this story, and the whole conception of the suffering servant, is the distinction which it emphasizes between an external, secular standard of good and a spiritual, religious standard. In the eyes of the average person, prosperity and righteousness are connected, if not identified; and the sufferer is felt to be one whose misfortune must be explained as a punishment for his wickedness. This feeling is strong in ancient (especially in Greek) literature, but we should not be unduly complacent about our superiority to the ancients in this respect, for the attitude is still with us. It is in fact a basic assumption of the competitive society—the view, seldom expressed but strongly rooted, that the plight of the unfortunate is the result of their own laziness, the wealth of the rich the reward of superior virtue.

The writer of the Joseph story sees in the unfortunate sufferer the savior who is the instrument of God's will; it is because of what he suffers that the sun and the moon and the eleven stars will bow down to Joseph. Yet the story does not emphasize the sufferings of Joseph; he is pictured rather as the man of action who through native ability and divine protection turns the injuries done him into advantages. We are not made to feel the torment in his soul; when he weeps it is because of the memory of what he had suffered and his yearning for his youngest brother, and he is in full control of the situation. And his reward in the things of this world is great. Not only does he reveal himself as the savior of his nation, but he becomes rich and powerful beyond his brothers' dreams, and in a great kingdom. The spiritual and secular standards are at the end of the story combined; Joseph's suffering is neatly balanced by his worldly reward.

## JOB

Later Hebrew writers developed a sadder and profounder view. The greatest literary masterpiece of the Old Testament, the Book of Job, is also concerned with the inadequacy of worldly standards of happiness and righteousness, but the suffering of Job is so overwhelming and so magnificently expressed, that even with our knowledge of its purpose and its meaning it seems excessive. Joseph suffered slavery, exile, and imprisonment, but turned them all to account; Job loses his family and wealth in a series of calamities, which strike one on the other like hammer blows, and is then plagued with a loathsome disease. Unlike Joseph, he is old; he cannot adapt himself and rise above adverse circumstances, and he no longer wishes to live. Except for one thing. He wishes to understand the reason for his suffering.

For his friends the explanation is simple. With the blindness of men who know no standards other than those of this world, they are sure that Job's misfortune must be the result of some wickedness on his part. But Job is confident in his righteousness; his torture is as much mental as physical; he cannot reconcile the fact of his innocence with the calamities that have come upon him with all the decisive suddenness of the hand of God.

The full explanation is never given to him, but it is given to the reader in the two opening chapters of the book. This prologue to the dramatic section of the work gives us the knowledge which is hidden from the participants in the ensuing dialogue; the writer uses the method characteristic of Greek tragedy—irony, the deeper understanding of the dramatic spoken word which is based on the superior knowledge of the audience. The prologue explains God's motive in allowing Job to suffer. It is an important one: God intends to use Job as a demonstration to His skeptical subordinate, Satan, of the fact that a human being can retain faith in God's justice in the face of the greatest imaginable suffering. This motive, which Job does not know and which is never revealed to him, gives to the dialogue between Job and his friends its suspense and its importance; God has rested His case, that humanity is capable of keeping faith in divine justice, against all appearances to the contrary, on this one man.

The arguments of Job's friends are based on the worldly equation, success = virtue. They attempt to undermine Job's faith, not in God, but in himself. ". . . who ever perished, being innocent?" asks Eliphaz, "or where were the righteous cut off?" Job's misfortune is a proof that he must have sinned; all he has to do is to admit his guilt and ask God for pardon, which he will surely receive. He refuses to accept this easy way out, and we know that he is right. In fact, we know from the prologue that he has been selected for misfortune not because he has sinned, but precisely because of his outstanding virtue. "There is none like him in the earth," God says, "a perfect and an upright man, one that feareth God, and escheweth evil." What Job must do is to persevere not only in his faith in God's justice but also in the conviction of his own innocence. He must believe the illogical, accept a paradox. His friends are offering him an easy way out, one which seems to be the way of humility and submission. But it is a false way. And God finally tells them so. "The Lord said to Eliphaz the Temanite, My wrath is kindled against thee, and against thy two friends: for ye have not spoken of me the thing that is right, as my servant Job hath."

Job's confidence in his own righteousness is not pride, but intellectual honesty. He sees that the problem is much harder than his friends imagine; to let them persuade him of his own guilt would lighten his mental burden by answering the question which tortures him, but his intelligence will not let him yield. Like Oedipus, he refuses to stop short of the truth; he even uses the same words: "let me alone, that I may speak, and let come on me what will." He finally expresses his understanding and acceptance of the paradox involved in the combination of his suffering with his innocence, but he does so with a human independence and dignity. "Though he slay me, yet will I trust in him: but I will maintain mine own ways before him." He sums up his case with a detailed account of the righteousness of his ways, and it is clear that this account is addressed not only to his three friends but also to God. "My desire is, that the Almighty would answer me," he says. His friends are silenced by the majesty and firmness of his statement, they "ceased to answer Job, because he was righteous in his own eyes," but God is moved to reply.

The magnificent poetry of that reply, the voice out of the whirlwind, still does not give Job the full explanation, God's motive in putting him to the torture. It is a triumphant proclamation of God's power and also of His justice, and it silences Job, who accepts it as a sufficient answer. That God does not reveal the key to the riddle even to the man who has victoriously stood the test and vindicated His faith in humanity is perhaps the most significant point in the poem. It suggests that there is not and never will be an explanation of human suffering that man's intelligence can comprehend. The sufferer must, like Job, cling to his faith in himself and in God; he must accept the inexplicable fact that his own undeserved suffering is the working of God's justice.

### THE PROPHETS

In the last days of Israel's independence, before conquerors overran the land and transported the population to captivity in the East (an exile mourned in Psalm 137—"By the rivers of Babylon . . ."), a series of prophets reproved the children of Israel for their transgressions and foretold the wrath to come, the end of the kingdom of Israel, and, beyond that, the overthrow of the neighboring kingdoms. The prophet was a man who believed himself to be the spokesman of God, the messenger of a terrifying vision. The horror of the vision of destruction was often too heavy a load for the human mind, and the disbelief and mockery of his hearers tipped the precarious balance so that what might have been merely a strange urgency came often close to madness. The vision of things to come was expressed in magnificent but disconnected images which to the workaday mind of the man in the street seemed only to confirm the suspicion that the prophet was deranged. Amos, Nahum, Jeremiah, and many others poured out their charged and clotted imagery of catastrophe to an unbelieving people.

The prophets were not always messengers of doom; it is in the words of an unnamed prophet (whose writings are included in the Book of Isaiah) that the theme of the one who suffers for others finds its most profound and moving expression. In the earlier versions the sufferer has it all made up to him in the end: Job, like Joseph, has his reward. Job's suffering is greater than Joseph's and it is clear that the writer of the Book of Job shows, alike in the speeches and in the ironic framework of the whole, a profounder understanding of the nature and meaning of suffering than the narrator of the story of Joseph, but like Joseph, Job lives to see the end of his troubles and has his material reward. "The Lord gave Job twice as much as he had before. . . . After this lived Job an hundred and forty years, and saw his sons, and his sons' sons, even four generations."

But in the Song of the Suffering Servant there is no recompense in this life: the suffering ends in death. In this deeper vision there is no reconciliation between the standards of this world and the standards of the higher authority behind the suffering. The one who is to save Israel and the world is not well favored like Joseph: "he hath no form nor comeliness." Nor is he, like Job, "the greatest of all the men of the east"; he is "despised and rejected of men." He suffers for his fellow men: "the Lord hath laid on him the iniquity of us all." His suffering knows no limit but death; he is oppressed and afflicted, imprisoned and executed. "He was cut off out of the land of the living" and "he made his grave with the wicked."

The circumstances described here are familiar from other cultures than the Hebrew; they are found in the primitive ritual of many peoples, and ceremonial relics of them still existed in civilized fifth-century Athens. In certain primitive societies, to rid the group of guilt a scapegoat was chosen, who was declared responsible for the misdeeds of all, and who was then mocked, beaten, driven out of the community, and killed. The scapegoat was hated and despised as the embodiment of the guilt of the whole community; his death was the most ignominious imaginable. The memory of some such primitive ritual is unmistakable in the Hebrew song; but its meaning has been utterly changed. It is precisely in the figure of the hated and suffering scapegoat that the Hebrew prophet sees the savior of mankind—an innocent sufferer, "he had done no violence, neither was any deceit in his mouth"— and he sees this without visible confirmation; there is no recognition by the brothers, no vindication by a voice out of the whirlwind. It is the highest expression of the Hebrew vision at its saddest and most profound, this portrayal of the savior who comes not in pomp and power but in suffering and meekness, who dies rejected and despised, and who atones for human sin and makes "intercession for the transgressors."

The student will find good background in *The Cambridge History of the Bible*, edited by R. R. Ackroyd and C. F. Evans, vol. I (1970). R. H. Rowley, *The Growth of the Old Testament* (1950), concentrates on the Old Testament; the New Testament is explored historically in M. S. Enslin, *Christian Beginnings* (1938), and C. K. Barrett, *The New Testament Background: Selected Documents* (1956).

# The Old Testament[1]

*Genesis 1–3. [The Creation—The Fall]*

1. In the beginning God created the heaven and the earth. And the earth was without form, and void; and darkness was upon the face of the deep. And the Spirit of God moved upon the face of the waters.

And God said, Let there be light: and there was light. And God saw the light, that it was good and God divided the light from the darkness. And God called the light Day, and the darkness he called Night. And the evening and the morning were the first day.

And God said, Let there be a firmament in the midst of the waters,[2] and let it divide the waters from the waters. And God made the firmament, and divided the waters which were under the firmament from the waters which were above the firmament: and it was so. And God called the firmament Heaven. And the evening and the morning were the second day.

And God said, Let the waters under the heaven be gathered together unto one place, and let the dry land appear: and it was so. And God called the dry land Earth; and the gathering together of the waters called he Seas: and God saw that it was good. And God said, Let the earth bring forth grass, the herb yielding seed, and the fruit tree yielding fruit after his kind, whose seed is in itself, upon the earth: and it was so. And the earth brought forth grass, and herb yielding seed after his kind, and the tree yielding fruit, whose seed was in itself, after his kind: and God saw that it was good. And the evening and the morning were the third day.

And God said, Let there be lights in the firmament of the heaven to divide the day from the night; and let them be for signs, and for seasons, and for days, and years: and let them be for lights in the firmament of the heaven to give light upon the earth: and it was so. And God made two great lights; the greater light to rule the day, and the lesser light to rule the night: he made the stars also. And God set them in the firmament of the heaven to give light upon the earth, and to rule over the day and over the night, and to divide the light from the darkness: and God saw that it was good. And the evening and the morning were the fourth day. And God said, Let the waters bring forth abundantly the moving creature that hath life, and fowl that may fly above the earth in the open firmament of heaven. And God created great whales, and every living creature that moveth, which the waters brought forth abundantly, after their kind, and every

---

1. The text of these selections is that of the King James, or Authorized, Version.    2. The firmament is the sky, which seen from below has the appearance of a ceiling; the waters above it are those which come down in the form of rain.

winged fowl after his kind: and God saw that it was good. And God blessed them, saying, Be fruitful, and multiply, and fill the waters in the seas, and let fowl multiply in the earth. And the evening and the morning were the fifth day.

And God said, Let the earth bring forth the living creature after his kind, cattle, and creeping thing, and beast of the earth after his kind: and it was so. And God made the beast of the earth after his kind, and cattle after their kind, and everything that creepeth upon the earth after his kind: and God saw that it was good.

And God said, Let us make man in our image, after our likeness: and let them have dominion over the fish of the sea, and over the fowl of the air, and over the cattle, and over all the earth, and over every creeping thing that creepeth upon the earth. So God created man in his own image, in the image of God created he him; male and female created he them. And God blessed them, and God said unto them, Be fruitful, and multiply, and replenish the earth, and subdue it: and have dominion over the fish of the sea, and over the fowl of the air, and over every living thing that moveth upon the earth.

And God said, Behold, I have given you every herb bearing seed, which is upon the face of all the earth, and every tree, in which is the fruit of a tree yielding seed; to you it shall be for meat. And to every beast of the earth, and to every fowl of the air, and to every thing that creepeth upon the earth, wherein there is life, I have given every green herb for meat: and it was so. And God saw every thing that he had made, and, behold, it was very good. And the evening and the morning were the sixth day.

2. Thus the heavens and the earth were finished, and all the host of them. And on the seventh day God ended his work which he had made; and he rested on the seventh day from all his work which he had made. And God blessed the seventh day, and sanctified it: because that in it he had rested from all his work which God created and made.

These are generations of the heavens and of the earth when they were created,[3] in the day that the Lord God made the earth and the heavens, and every plant of the field before it was in the earth, and every herb of the field before it grew: for the Lord God had not caused it to rain upon the earth, and there was not a man to till the ground. But there went up a mist from the earth, and watered the whole face of the ground. And the Lord God formed man of the dust of the ground, and breathed into his nostrils the breath of life; and man became a living soul.

3. This is the beginning of a different account of the Creation, which does not agree in all respects with the first.

And the Lord God planted a garden eastward in Eden; and there he put the man whom he had formed. And out of the ground made the Lord God to grow every tree that is pleasant to the sight, and good for food; the tree of life also in the midst of the garden, and the tree of knowledge of good and evil. And a river went out of Eden to water the garden; and from thence it was parted, and became into four heads. The name of the first is Pison: that is. it which compasseth the whole land of Havilah, where there is gold; and the gold of that land is good: there is bdellium and the onyx stone. And the name of the second river is Gihon: the same is it that compasseth the whole land of Ethiopia. And the name of the third river is Hiddekel: that is it which goeth toward the east of Assyria. And the fourth river is Euphrates. And the Lord God took the man, and put him into the garden of Eden to dress it and to keep it. And the Lord God commanded the man, saying, Of every tree of the garden thou mayest freely eat: but of the tree of the knowledge of good and evil, thou shalt not eat of it: for in the day that thou eatest thereof thou shalt surely die.

And the Lord God said, It is not good that the man should be alone; I will make him an help meet for him. And out of the ground the Lord God formed every beast of the field, and every fowl of the air; and brought them unto Adam to see what he would call them: and whatsoever Adam called every living creature, that was the name thereof. And Adam gave names to all cattle, and to the fowl of the air, and to every beast of the field; but for Adam there was not found an help meet for him. And the Lord God caused a deep sleep to fall upon Adam, and he slept: and he took one of his ribs, and closed up the flesh instead thereof; and the rib, which the Lord God had taken from man, made he a woman, and brought her unto the man. And Adam said, This is now bone of my bones, and flesh of my flesh: she shall be called Woman, because she was taken out of Man. Therefore shall a man leave his father and his mother, and shall cleave unto his wife: and they shall be one flesh. And they were both naked, the man and his wife, and were not ashamed.

3. Now the serpent was more subtil than any beast of the field which the Lord God had made. And he said unto the woman, Yea, hath God said, Ye shall not eat of every tree of the garden? And the woman said unto the serpent, We may eat of the fruit of the trees of the garden: but of the fruit of the tree which is in the midst of the garden, God hath said, Ye shall not eat of it, neither shall ye touch it, lest ye die. And the serpent said unto the woman, Ye shall not surely die: for God doth know that in the day ye eat thereof, then your eyes shall be opened, and ye shall be as gods, knowing good and evil. And when the woman saw that the tree was good for food, and that it was pleasant to the eyes, and a tree to be desired to make

one wise, she took the fruit thereof, and did eat, and gave also unto her husband with her; and he did eat. And the eyes of them both were opened, and they knew that they were naked; and they sewed fig leaves together, and made themselves aprons. And they heard the voice of the Lord God walking in the garden in the cool of the day: and Adam and his wife hid themselves from the presence of the Lord God amongst the trees of the garden. And the Lord God called unto Adam, and said unto him, Where art thou? And he said, I heard thy voice in the garden, and I was afraid, because I was naked; and I hid myself. And he said, Who told thee that thou wast naked? Hast thou eaten of the tree, whereof I commanded thee that thou shouldest not eat? And the man said, The woman whom thou gavest to be with me, she gave me of the tree, and I did eat. And the Lord God said unto the woman, What is this that thou hast done? And the woman said, The serpent beguiled me, and I did eat. And the Lord God said unto the serpent, Because thou hast done this, thou art cursed above all cattle, and above every beast of the field; upon thy belly shalt thou go, and dust shalt thou eat all the days of thy life: and I will put enmity between thee and the woman, and between thy seed and her seed; it shall bruise thy head, and thou shalt bruise his heel. Unto the woman he said, I will greatly multiply thy sorrow and thy conception; in sorrow thou shalt bring forth children; and thy desire shall be to thy husband, and he shall rule over thee. And unto Adam he said, Because thou hast hearkened unto the voice of thy wife, and hast eaten of the tree, of which I commanded thee, saying, Thou shalt not eat of it: cursed is the ground for thy sake; in sorrow shalt thou eat of it all the days of thy life; thorns also and thistles shall it bring forth to thee; and thou shalt eat the herb of the field; in the sweat of thy face shalt thou eat bread, till thou return unto the ground; for out of it wast thou taken: for dust thou art, and unto dust shalt thou return. And Adam called his wife's name Eve; because she was the mother of all living. Unto Adam also and to his wife did the Lord God make coats of skins, and clothed them.

And the Lord God said, Behold, the man is become as one of us, to know good and evil: and now, lest he put forth his hand, and take also of the tree of life, and eat, and live forever: therefore the Lord God sent him forth from the garden of Eden, to till the ground from whence he was taken. So he drove out the man; and he placed at the east of the garden of Eden Cherubims, and a flaming sword which turned every way, to keep the way of the tree of life.

### Genesis 4. [The First Murder]

4. And Adam knew Eve his wife; and she conceived, and bare Cain, and said, I have gotten a man from the Lord. And she again bare his brother Abel. And Abel was a keeper of sheep, but Cain was

a tiller of the ground. And in process of time it came to pass, that
Cain brought of the fruit of the ground an offering unto the Lord.
And Abel, he also brought of the firstlings of his flock and of the fat
thereof. And the Lord had respect unto Abel and to his offering: But
unto Cain and to his offering he had not respect. And Cain was very
wroth, and his countenance fell. And the Lord said unto Cain, Why
art thou wroth? and why is thy countenance fallen? If thou doest
well, shalt thou not be accepted? and if thou doest not well, sin lieth
at the door. And unto thee shall be his desire, and thou shall rule
over him.[4] And Cain talked with Abel his brother: and it came to
pass, when they were in the field, that Cain rose up against Abel his
brother, and slew him.

And the Lord said unto Cain, Where is Abel thy brother? And he
said, I know not: Am I my brother's keeper? And he said, What hast
thou done? the voice of thy brother's blood crieth unto me from the
ground. And now art thou cursed from the earth, which hath opened
her mouth to receive thy brother's blood from thy hand; When thou
tillest the ground, it shall not henceforth yield unto thee her strength;
a fugitive and a vagabond shalt thou be in the earth. And Cain said
unto the Lord, My punishment is greater than I can bear. Behold,
thou hast driven me out this day from the face of the earth; and from
thy face shall I be hid; and I shall be a fugitive and a vagabond in
the earth; and it shall come to pass, that every one that findeth me
shall slay me. And the Lord said unto him, Therefore whosoever
slayeth Cain, vengeance shall be taken on him sevenfold. And the
Lord set a mark upon Cain, lest any finding him should kill him.

### Genesis 6–9. [The Flood]

6. . . . And God saw that the wickedness of man was great in the
earth, and that every imagination of the thoughts of his heart was
only evil continually. And it repented the Lord that he had made
man on the earth, and it grieved him at his heart. And the Lord said,
I will destroy man whom I have created from the face of the earth;
both man, and beast, and the creeping thing, and the fowls of the
air; for it repenteth me that I have made them. But Noah found
grace in the eyes of the Lord.

These are the generations of Noah: Noah was a just man and
perfect in his generations, and Noah walked with God. And Noah
begat three sons, Shem, Ham, and Japheth.

The earth also was corrupt before God, and the earth was filled
with violence. And God looked upon the earth, and, behold, it was
corrupt; for all flesh had corrupted his way upon the earth. And God

4. An obscure sentence. It seems to mean something like: "It (i.e., sin) shall be eager for you,
but you must master it."

said unto Noah, The end of all flesh is come before me; for the earth is filled with violence through them; and, behold, I will destroy them with the earth. Make thee an ark of gopher wood;[5] rooms shalt thou make in the ark, and shalt pitch it within and without with pitch. And this is the fashion which thou shalt make it of: The length of the ark shall be three hundred cubits,[6] the breadth of it fifty cubits, and the height of it thirty cubits. A window[7] shalt thou make to the ark, and in a cubit shalt thou finish it above; and the door of the ark shalt thou set in the side thereof; with lower, second, and third stories shalt thou make it. And, behold, I, even I, do bring a flood of waters upon the earth, to destroy all flesh, wherein is the breath of life, from under heaven; and every thing that is in the earth shall die. But with thee will I establish my covenant; and thou shalt come into the ark, thou, and thy sons, and thy wife, and thy sons' wives with thee. And of every living thing of all flesh, two of every sort shalt thou bring into the ark, to keep them alive with thee; they shall be male and female. Of fowls after their kind, and of cattle after their kind, of every creeping thing of the earth after his kind, two of every sort shall come unto thee, to keep them alive. And take thou unto thee of all food that is eaten, and thou shalt gather it to thee; and it shall be for food for thee, and for them. Thus did Noah; according to all that God commanded him, so did he.

7. . . . And Noah was six hundred years old when the flood of waters was upon the earth. And Noah went in, and his sons, and his wife, and his sons' wives with him, into the ark, because of the waters of the flood. Of clean beasts, and of beasts that are not clean, and of fowls, and of everything that creepeth upon the earth, There went in two and two unto Noah into the ark, the male and the female, as God had commanded Noah. And it came to pass after seven days, that the waters of the flood were upon the earth. In the six hundredth year of Noah's life, in the second month, the seventeenth day of the month, the same day were all the fountains of the great deep broken up, and the windows of heaven were opened. And the rain was upon the earth forty days and forty nights. In the selfsame day entered Noah, and Shem, and Ham, and Japheth, the sons of Noah, and Noah's wife, and the three wives of his sons with them, into the ark; They, and every beast after his kind, and all the cattle after their kind, and every creeping thing that creepeth upon the earth after his kind, and every fowl after his kind, every bird of every sort. And they went in unto Noah into the ark, two and two of all flesh, wherein is the breath of life. And they that went in, went in male and female of all flesh, as God had commanded him, and the Lord shut him in.

5. Cypress.    6. A Hebrew measure of length, about one and a half feet.    7. The text is obscure; it may refer to a skylight in the roof.

And the flood was forty days upon the earth; and the waters increased, and bare up the ark, and it was lift up above the earth. And the waters prevailed, and were increased greatly upon the earth; and the ark went upon the face of the waters. And the waters prevailed exceedingly upon the earth; and all the high hills, that were under the whole heaven, were covered. Fifteen cubits upward did the waters prevail; and the mountains were covered. And all flesh died that moved upon the earth, both of fowl, and of cattle, and of beast, and of every creeping thing that creepeth upon the earth, and every man: All in whose nostrils was the breath of life, of all that was in the dry land, died. And every living substance was destroyed which was upon the face of the ground, both man, and cattle, and the creeping things, and the fowl of the heaven; and they were destroyed from the earth, and Noah only remained alive, and they that were with him in the ark. And the waters prevailed upon the earth an hundred and fifty days.

8. And God remembered Noah, and every living thing, and all the cattle that was with him in the ark: and God made a wind to pass over the earth, and the waters assuaged; The fountains also of the deep and the windows of heaven were stopped, and the rain from heaven was restrained; And the waters returned from off the earth continually: and after the end of the hundred and fifty days the waters were abated. And the ark rested in the seventh month, on the seventeenth day of the month, upon the mountains of Ararat. And the waters decreased continually until the tenth month: in the tenth month, on the first day of the month, were the tops of the mountains seen.

And it came to pass at the end of forty days, that Noah opened the window of the ark which he had made: And he sent forth a raven, which went forth to and fro, until the waters were dried up from off the earth. Also he sent forth a dove from him, to see if the waters were abated from off the face of the ground; But the dove found no rest for the sole of her foot, and she returned unto him into the ark, for the waters were on the face of the whole earth: then he put forth his hand, and took her, and pulled her in unto him into the ark. And he stayed yet another seven days; and again he sent forth the dove out of the ark; And the dove came in to him in the evening; and, lo, in her mouth was an olive leaf plucked off: so Noah knew that the waters were abated from off the earth. And he stayed yet other seven days; and sent forth the dove; which returned not again unto him any more.

And it came to pass in the six hundredth and first year, in the first month, the first day of the month, the waters were dried up from off the earth: and Noah removed the covering of the ark, and looked, and, behold, the face of the ground was dry. And in the second month, on the seven and twentieth day of the month, was the earth dried.

And God spake unto Noah, saying, Go forth of the ark, thou, and thy wife, and thy sons, and thy sons' wives with thee. Bring forth with thee every living thing that is with thee, of all flesh, both of fowl, and of cattle, and of every creeping thing that creepeth upon the earth; that they may breed abundantly in the earth, and be fruitful, and multiply upon the earth. And Noah went forth, and his sons, and his wife, and his sons' wives with him: Every beast, every creeping thing, and every fowl, and whatsoever creepeth upon the earth, after their kinds, went forth out of the ark. And Noah builded an altar unto the Lord; and took of every clean beast, and of every clean fowl, and offered burnt offerings on the altar. And the Lord smelled a sweet savour; and the Lord said in his heart, I will not again curse the ground any more for man's sake; for the imagination of man's heart is evil from his youth; neither will I again smite any more every thing living, as I have done. While the earth remaineth, seedtime and harvest, and cold and heat, and summer and winter, and day and night shall not cease.

9. And God blessed Noah and his sons, and said unto them, Be fruitful, and multiply, and replenish the earth. And the fear of you and the dread of you shall be upon every beast of the earth, and upon every fowl of the air, upon all that moveth upon the earth, and upon all the fishes of the sea; into your hand are they delivered. Every moving thing that liveth shall be meat for you; even as the green herb have I given you all things. But flesh with the life thereof, which is the blood thereof, shall ye not eat.[8] And surely your blood of your lives will I require; at the hand of every beast will I require it, and at the hand of man; at the hand of every man's brother will I require the life of man. Whoso sheddeth man's blood, by man shall his blood be shed, for in the image of God made he man. And you, be ye fruitful, and multiply; bring forth abundantly in the earth, and multiply therein.

And God spake unto Noah, and to his sons with him, saying, And I, behold, I establish my covenant with you, and with your seed after you; And with every living creature that is with you, of the fowl, of the cattle, and of every beast of the earth with you; from all that go out of the ark, to every beast of the earth. And I will establish my covenant with you; neither shall all flesh be cut off any more by the waters of a flood; neither shall there any more be a flood to destroy the earth. And God said, This is the token of the covenant which I

---

8. This sentence refers to the dietary laws: blood was drained from the slaughtered animal.

make between me and you and every living creature that is with you, for perpetual generations: I do set my bow in the cloud, and it shall be for a token of a covenant between me and the earth. And it shall come to pass, when I bring a cloud over the earth, that the bow shall be seen in the cloud: And I will remember my covenant, which is between me and you and every living creature of all flesh; and the waters shall no more become a flood to destroy all flesh. And the bow shall be in the cloud; and I will look upon it, that I may remember the everlasting covenant between God and every living creature of all flesh that is upon the earth. And God said unto Noah, This is the token of the covenant, which I have established between me and all flesh that is upon the earth.

### Genesis 11. [The Origin of Languages]

11. And the whole earth was of one language, and of one speech. And it came to pass, as they[9] journeyed from the east, that they found a plain in the land of Shinar;[1] and they dwelt there. And they said one to another, Go to, let us make brick, and burn them throughly. And they had brick for stone, and slime[2] had they for mortar. And they said, Go to, let us build us a city and a tower,[3] whose top may reach unto heaven; and let us make us a name, lest we be scattered abroad upon the face of the whole earth. And the Lord came down to see the city and the tower, which the children of men builded. And the Lord said, Behold, the people is one, and they have all one language; and this they begin to do: and now nothing will be restrained from them, which they have imagined to do. Go to, let us go down, and there confound their language, that they may not understand one another's speech. So the Lord scattered them abroad from thence upon the face of all the earth: and they left off to build the city. Therefore is the name of it called Babel;[4] because the Lord did there confound the language of all the earth: and from thence did the Lord scatter them abroad upon the face of all the earth.

### Genesis 37–46. [The Story of Joseph]

37. . . . Joseph, being seventeen years old, was feeding the flock with his brethren; and the lad was with the sons of Bilhah, and with the sons of Zilpah, his father's wives: and Joseph brought unto his father their evil report.[5] Now Israel loved Joseph more than all his children, because he was the son of his old age: and he made him a coat of many colours. And when his brethren saw that their father

9. The human race.　　1. In Mesopotamia.　　2. Bitumen.　　3. This story is based on the Babylonian practice of building temples in the form of terraced pyramids (ziggurats). 4. Babylon.　　5. Joseph reported their misdeeds. *Father:* Israel.

loved him more than all his brethren, they hated him, and could not speak peaceably unto him.

And Joseph dreamed a dream, and he told it his brethren: and they hated him yet the more. And he said unto them, Hear, I pray you, this dream which I have dreamed: for, behold, we were binding sheaves in the field, and, lo, my sheaf arose, and also stood upright; and, behold, your sheaves stood round about, and made obeisance to my sheaf. And his brethren said to him, Shalt thou indeed reign over us? or shalt thou indeed have dominion over us? And they hated him yet the more for his dreams, and for his words.

And he dreamed yet another dream, and told it his brethren, and said, Behold, I have dreamed a dream more; and, behold, the sun and the moon and the eleven stars made obeisance to me. And he told it to his father, and to his brethren: and his father rebuked him, and said unto him, What is this dream that thou hast dreamed? Shall I and thy mother and thy brethren indeed come to bow down ourselves to thee to the earth? And his brethren envied him; but his father observed the saying.

And his brethren went to feed their father's flock in Shechem. And Israel said unto Joseph, Do not thy brethren feed the flock in Shechem? come, and I will send thee unto them. And he said to him, Here am I. And he said to him, Go, I pray thee, see whether it be well with thy brethren, and well with the flocks; and bring me word again. So he sent him out of the vale of Hebron, and he came to Shechem.

And a certain man found him, and, behold, he was wandering in the field: and the man asked him, saying, What seekest thou? And he said, I seek my brethren: tell me, I pray thee, where they feed their flocks. And the man said, They are departed hence; for I heard them say, Let us go to Dothan. And Joseph went after his brethren, and found them in Dothan. And when they saw him afar off, even before he came near unto them, they conspired against him to slay him. And they said one to another, Behold, this dreamer cometh. Come now therefore, and let us slay him, and cast him into some pit, and we will say, Some evil beast hath devoured him: and we shall see what will become of his dreams. And Reuben heard it, and he delivered him out of their hands; and said, Let us not kill him. And Reuben said unto them, Shed no blood, but cast him into this pit that is in the wilderness, and lay no hand upon him; that he might rid him out of their hands, to deliver him to his father again.

And it came to pass, when Joseph was come unto his brethren, that they stripped Joseph out of his coat, his coat of many colours that was on him; and they took him, and cast him into a pit: and the pit was empty, there was no water in it. And they sat down to eat bread: and they lifted up their eyes and looked, and, behold, a com-

pany of Ishmeelites came from Gilead with their camels bearing spi-
cery and balm and myrrh, going to carry it down to Egypt. And
Judah said unto his brethren, What profit is it if we slay our brother,
and conceal his blood? Come, and let us sell him to the Ishmeelites,
and let not our hand be upon him; for he is our brother and our
flesh. And his brethren were content. Then there passed by Midi-
anites merchantmen;[6] and they[7] drew and lifted up Joseph out of the
pit, and sold Joseph to the Ishmeelites for twenty pieces of silver: and
they[8] brought Joseph into Egypt.

And Reuben returned unto the pit; and, behold, Joseph was not
in the pit; and he rent his clothes. And he returned unto his brethren, and said, The child is not; and I, whither shall I go? And they
took Joseph's coat, and killed a kid of the goats, and dipped the coat
in the blood; and they sent the coat of many colours, and they brought
it to their father; and said, This have we found: know now whether
it be thy son's coat or no. And he knew it, and said, It is my son's
coat; an evil beast hath devoured him; Joseph is without doubt rent
in pieces. And Jacob rent his clothes, and put sackcloth upon his
loins, and mourned for his son many days. And all his sons and all
his daughters rose up to comfort him; but he refused to be comforted;
and he said, For I will go down into the grave unto my son mourning. Thus his father wept for him. . . .

39. And Joseph was brought down to Egypt; and Potiphar, an
officer of Pharaoh, captain of the guard, an Egyptian, bought him
of the hands of the Ishmeelites, which had brought him down thither.
And the Lord was with Joseph, and he was a prosperous man; and
he was in the house of his master the Egyptian. And his master saw
that the Lord was with him, and that the Lord made all he did to
prosper in his hand. And Joseph found grace in his sight, and he
served him: and he made him overseer over his house, and all that
he had he put into his hand. And it came to pass from the time that
he had made him overseer in his house, and over all that he had,
that the Lord blessed the Egyptian's house for Joseph's sake; and the
blessing of the Lord was upon all that he had in the house, and in
the field. And he left all that he had in Joseph's hand; and he knew
not ought he had, save the bread which he did eat. And Joseph was
a goodly person, and well favoured.

And it came to pass after these things, that his master's wife cast
her eyes upon Joseph; and she said, Lie with me. But he refused,
and said unto his master's wife, Behold, my master wotteth not what
is with me in the house, and he hath committed all that he hath to

6. The confusion in this passage may be due to the fact that the version we have is a composite
of two different versions.     7. The brothers.     8. The Ishmeelites.

my hand; there is none greater in this house than I; neither hath he
kept back any thing from me but thee, because thou art his wife: how
then can I do this great wickedness, and sin against God? And it
came to pass, as she spake to Joseph day by day, that he hearkened
not unto her, to lie by her, or to be with her. And it came to pass
about this time, that Joseph went into the house to do his business;
and there was none of the men of the house there within. And she
caught him by his garment, saying, Lie with me: and he left his
garment in her hand, and fled and got him out. And it came to pass,
when she saw that he had left his garment in her hand, and was fled
forth, that she called unto the men of her house, and spoke unto
them, saying, See, he hath brought in an Hebrew unto us to mock
us; he came in unto me to lie with me, and I cried with a loud voice:
and it came to pass, when he heard that I lifted up my voice and
cried, that he left his garment with me, and fled, and got him out.
And she laid up his garment by her, until his lord came home. And
she spake unto him according to these words, saying, The Hebrew
servant, which thou hast brought unto us, came in unto me to mock
me: and it came to pass, as I lifted up my voice and cried, that he
left his garment with me, and fled out. And it came to pass, when
his master heard the words of his wife, which she spake unto him,
saying, After this manner did thy servant to me; that his wrath was
kindled. And Joseph's master took him, and put him into the prison,
a place where the king's prisoners were bound: and he was there in
the prison.

But the Lord was with Joseph, and showed him mercy, and gave
him favour in the sight of the keeper of the prison. And the keeper
of the prison committed to Joseph's hand all the prisoners that were
in the prison; and whatsoever they did there, he was the doer of it.
The keeper of the prison looked not to any thing that was under his
hand; because the Lord was with him, and that which he did, the
Lord made it to prosper.

40. And it came to pass after these things that the butler of the
king of Egypt and his baker had offended their lord the king of Egypt.
And Pharaoh was wroth against two of his officers, against the chief
of the butlers, and against the chief of the bakers. And he put them
in ward in the house of the captain of the guard, into the prison, the
place where Joseph was bound. And the captain of the guard charged
Joseph with them, and he served them: and they continued a season
in ward.

And they dreamed a dream both of them, each man his dream in
one night, each man according to the interpretation of his dream,
the butler and the baker of the king of Egypt, which were bound in
the prison. And Joseph came in unto them in the morning, and

looked upon them, and, behold, they were sad. And he asked Pharaoh's officers that were with him in the ward of his lord's house, saying, Wherefore look ye so sadly to day? And they said unto him, We have dreamed a dream, and there is no interpreter of it. And Joseph said unto them, Do not interpretations belong to God? tell me them, I pray you. And the chief butler told his dream to Joseph, and said to him, In my dream, behold, a vine was before me; and in the vine were three branches: and it was as though it budded, and her blossoms shot forth; and the clusters thereof brought forth ripe grapes: and Pharaoh's cup was in my hand: and I took the grapes, and pressed them into Pharaoh's cup, and I gave the cup into Pharaoh's hand. And Joseph said unto him, This is the interpretation of it: the three branches are three days: yet within three days shall Pharaoh lift up thine head, and restore thee unto thy place: and thou shalt deliver Pharaoh's cup into his hand, after the former manner when thou wast his butler. But think on me when it shall be well with thee, and shew kindness, I pray thee, unto me, and make mention of me unto Pharaoh, and bring me out of this house: for indeed I was stolen away out of the land of the Hebrews: and here also have I done nothing that they should put me into the dungeon. When the chief baker saw that the interpretation was good, he said unto Joseph, I also was in my dream, and, behold, I had three white baskets on my head: and in the uppermost basket there was of all manner of bakemeats for Pharaoh; and the birds did eat them out of the basket upon my head. And Joseph answered and said, This is the interpretation thereof: the three baskets are three days: yet within three days shall Pharaoh lift up thy head from off thee, and shall hang thee on a tree; and the birds shall eat thy flesh from off thee.

And it came to pass the third day, which was Pharaoh's birthday, that he made a feast unto all his servants: and he lifted up the head of the chief butler and of the chief baker among his servants. And he restored the chief butler unto his butlership again; and he gave the cup into Pharaoh's hand. But he hanged the chief baker: as Joseph had interpreted to them. Yet did not the chief butler remember Joseph, but forgat him.

41. And it came to pass at the end of two full years, that Pharaoh dreamed: and, behold, he stood by the river. And, behold, there came up out of the river seven well favoured kine[9] and fatfleshed; and they fed in a meadow. And, behold, seven other kine came up after them out of the river, ill favoured and leanfleshed; and stood by the other kine upon the brink of the river. And the ill favoured and leanfleshed kine did eat up the seven well favoured and fat kine.

9. Cattle.

So Pharaoh awoke. And he slept and dreamed the second time: and, behold, seven ears of corn came up upon one stalk, rank[1] and good. And, behold, seven thin ears and blasted with the east wind sprung up after them. And the seven thin ears devoured the seven rank and full ears. And Pharaoh awoke, and, behold, it was a dream. And it came to pass in the morning that his spirit was troubled; and he sent and called for all the magicians of Egypt, and all the wise men thereof: and Pharaoh told them his dream; but there was none that could interpret them unto Pharaoh.

Then spake the chief butler unto Pharaoh, saying, I do remember my faults this day: Pharaoh was wroth with his servants, and put me in ward in the captain of the guard's house, both me and the chief baker: and we dreamed a dream in one night, I and he; we dreamed each man according to the interpretation of his dream. And there was there with us a young man, an Hebrew, servant to the captain of the guard; and we told him, and he interpreted to us our dreams; to each man according to his dream he did interpret. And it came to pass, as he interpreted to us, so it was; me he restored unto mine office, and him he hanged.

Then Pharaoh sent and called Joseph, and they brought him hastily out of the dungeon: and he shaved himself, and changed his raiment, and came in unto Pharaoh. And Pharaoh said unto Joseph, I have dreamed a dream, and there is none that can interpret it: and I have heard say of thee that thou canst understand a dream to interpret it. And Joseph answered Pharaoh, saying, It is not in me: God shall give Pharaoh an answer of peace. And Pharaoh said unto Joseph, In my dream, behold, I stood upon the bank of the river; and, behold, there came up out of the river seven kine, fatfleshed and well favoured; and they fed in a meadow; and, behold, seven other kine came up after them, poor and very ill favoured and leanfleshed, such as I never saw in all the land of Egypt for badness: and the lean and the ill favoured kine did eat up the first seven fat kine; and when they had eaten them up, it could not be known that they had eaten them; but they were still ill favoured, as at the beginning. So I awoke. And I saw in my dream, and, behold, seven ears came up in one stalk, full and good: and, behold, seven ears, withered, thin, and blasted with the east wind, sprung up after them: and the thin ears devoured the seven good ears: and I told this unto the magicians; but there was none that could declare it to me.

And Joseph said unto Pharaoh, The dream of Pharaoh is one: God hath shewed Pharaoh what he is about to do. The seven good kine are seven years; and the seven good ears are seven years: the dream is one. And the seven thin and ill favoured kine that came up after

1. Fat.

them are seven years; and the seven empty ears blasted with the east wind shall be seven years of famine. This is the thing which I have spoken unto Pharaoh: what God is about to do he sheweth unto Pharaoh. Behold, there come seven years of great plenty throughout all the land of Egypt: and there shall arise after them seven years of famine; and all the plenty shall be forgotten in the land of Egypt; and the famine shall consume the land; and the plenty shall not be known in the land by reason of that famine following; for it shall be very grievous. And for that the dream was doubled unto Pharaoh twice; it is because the thing is established by God, and God will shortly bring it to pass. Now therefore let Pharaoh look out a man discreet and wise, and set him over the land of Egypt. Let Pharaoh do this, and let him appoint officers over the land, and take up the fifth part of the land[2] of Egypt in the seven plenteous years. And let them gather all the food of those good years that come, and lay up corn under the hand of Pharaoh, and let them keep food in the cities. And that food shall be for store to the land against the seven years of famine, which shall be in the land of Egypt; that the land perish not through the famine.

And the thing was good in the eyes of Pharaoh, and in the eyes of all his servants. And Pharaoh said unto his servants, Can we find such a one as this is, a man in whom the Spirit of God is? And Pharaoh said unto Joseph, Forasmuch as God hath shewed thee all this, there is none so discreet and wise as thou art: thou shalt be over my house, and according unto thy word shall all my people be ruled: only in the throne will I be greater than thou. And Pharaoh said unto Joseph, See, I have set thee over all the land of Egypt. And Pharaoh took off his ring from his hand, and put it upon Joseph's hand, and arrayed him in vestures of fine linen, and put a gold chain about his neck; and he made him to ride in the second chariot which he had; and they cried before him, Bow the knee: and he made him ruler over all the land of Egypt. And Pharaoh said unto Joseph, I am Pharaoh, and without thee shall no man lift his hand or foot in all the land of Egypt. And Pharaoh called Joseph's name Zaphnath-paaneah; and he gave him to wife Asenath the daughter of Poti-pherah priest of On. And Joseph went out over all the land of Egypt.

And Joseph was thirty years old when he stood before Pharaoh king of Egypt. And Joseph went out from the presence of Pharaoh, and went throughout all the land of Egypt. And in the seven plenteous years the earth brought forth by handfuls. And he gathered up all the food of the seven years, which were in the land of Egypt, and laid up the food in the cities: the food of the field, which was round about every city, laid he up in the same. And Joseph gathered corn

2. I.e., of the crop.

as the sand of the sea, very much, until he left numbering; for it was without number. And unto Joseph were born two sons before the years of famine came, which Asenath the daughter of Poti-pherah priest of On bare unto him. And Joseph called the name of the first born Manasseh:[3] For God, said he, hath made me forget all my toil, and all my father's house. And the name of the second called he Ephraim:[4] For God hath caused me to be fruitful in the land of my affliction.

And the seven years of plenteousness, that was in the land of Egypt, were ended. And the seven years of dearth began to come, according as Joseph had said: and the dearth was in all lands; but in all the land of Egypt there was bread. And when all the land of Egypt was famished, the people cried to Pharaoh for bread: and Pharaoh said unto all the Egyptians, Go unto Joseph; what he saith to you, do. And the famine was over all the face of the earth. And Joseph opened all the storehouses, and sold unto the Egyptians; and the famine waxed sore in the land of Egypt. And all countries came into Egypt to Joseph for to buy corn; because that the famine was so sore in all lands.

42.  Now when Jacob saw that there was corn in Egypt, Jacob said unto his sons, Why do ye look one upon another? And he said, Behold, I have heard that there is corn in Egypt: get you down thither, and buy for us from thence; that we may live, and not die.

And Joseph's ten brethren went down to buy corn in Egypt. But Benjamin, Joseph's brother, Jacob sent not with his brethren; for he said, Lest peradventure mischief befall him. And the sons of Israel came to buy corn among those that came: for the famine was in the land of Canaan. And Joseph was the governor over the land, and he it was that sold to all the people of the land: and Joseph's brethren came, and bowed down themselves before him with their faces to the earth. And Joseph saw his brethren, and he knew them, but made himself strange unto them, and spake roughly unto them; and he said unto them, Whence come ye? And they said, From the land of Canaan to buy food. And Joseph knew his brethren, but they knew not him. And Joseph remembered the dreams which he dreamed of them, and said unto them, Ye are spies; to see the nakedness of the land ye are come. And they said unto him, Nay, my lord, but to buy food are thy servants come. We are all one man's sons; we are true men, thy servants are no spies. And he said unto them, Nay, but to see the nakedness of the land ye are come. And they said, Thy servants are twelve brethren, the sons of one man in the land of Canaan; and, behold, the youngest is this day with our father, and one is not. And Joseph said unto them, That is it that I spake unto

---

3. Meaning "causing to forget."    4. Meaning "fruitfulness."

you, saying, Ye are spies: Hereby ye shall be proved: By the life of
Pharaoh ye shall not go forth hence, except your youngest brother
come hither. Send one of you, and let him fetch your brother, and
ye shall be kept in prison, that your words may be proved, whether
there be any truth in you: or else by the life of Pharaoh surely ye are
spies. And he put them all together into ward three days. And Joseph
said unto them the third day, This do, and live; for I fear God: if ye
be true men, let one of your brethren be bound in the house of your
prison: go ye, carry corn for the famine of your houses: but bring
your youngest brother unto me; so shall your words be verified, and
ye shall not die. And they did so.

  And they said one to another, We are verily guilty concerning our
brother, in that we saw the anguish of his soul, when he besought
us, and we would not hear; therefore is this distress come upon us.
And Reuben answered them, saying, Spake I not unto you, saying,
Do not sin against the child; and ye would not hear? therefore, behold,
also his blood is required. And they knew not that Joseph understood
them; for he spake unto them by an interpreter. And he turned himself about from them, and wept; and returned to them again, and
communed with them, and took from them Simeon, and bound
him before their eyes.

  Then Joseph commanded to fill their sacks with corn, and to restore
every man's money into his sack, and to give them provision for the
way: and thus did he unto them. And they laded their asses with the
corn, and departed thence. And as one of them opened his sack to
give his ass provender in the inn, he espied his money; for, behold,
it was in his sack's mouth. And he said unto his brethren, My money
is restored; and, lo, it is even in my sack: and their heart failed them,
and they were afraid, saying one to another, What is this that God
hath done unto us?

  And they came unto Jacob their father unto the land of Canaan,
and told him all that befell unto them; saying, The man, who is lord
of the land, spake roughly to us, and took us for spies of the country.
And we said unto him, We are true men; we are no spies: we be
twelve brethren, sons of our father; one is not, and the youngest is
this day with our father in the land of Canaan. And the man, the
lord of the country, said unto us, Hereby shall I know that ye are
true men; leave one of your brethren here with me, and take food
for the famine of your households, and be gone: and bring your
youngest brother unto me: then shall I know that ye are no spies, but
that ye are true men: so will I deliver you your brother, and ye shall
traffick in the land.

  And it came to pass as they emptied their sacks, that, behold,
every man's bundle of money was in his sack: and when both they
and their father saw the bundles of money, they were afraid. And

Jacob their father said unto them, Me have ye bereaved of my children: Joseph is not, and Simeon is not, and ye will take Benjamin away: all these things are against me.

And Reuben spake unto his father, saying, Slay my two sons, if I bring him not to thee: deliver him into my hand, and I will bring him to thee again. And he said, My son shall not go down with you; for his brother is dead, and he is left alone: if mischief befall him by the way in the which ye go, then shall ye bring down my gray hairs with sorrow to the grave.

43. And the famine was sore in the land. And it came to pass, when they had eaten up the corn which they had brought out of Egypt, their father said unto them, Go again, buy us a little food. And Judah spake unto him, saying, The man did solemnly protest unto us, saying, Ye shall not see my face, except your brother be with you. If thou wilt send our brother with us, we will go down and buy thee food: but if thou wilt not send him, we will not go down: for the man said unto us, Ye shall not see my face, except your brother be with you. And Israel said, Wherefore dealt ye so ill with me, as to tell the man whether ye had yet a brother? And they said, The man asked us straitly of our state, and of our kindred, saying, Is your father yet alive? have ye another brother? and we told him according to the tenor of these words: could we certainly know that he would say, Bring your brother down? And Judah said unto Israel his father, Send the lad with me, and we will arise and go; that we may live, and not die, both we, and thou, and also our little ones. I will be surety for him; of my hand shalt thou require him: if I bring him not unto thee, and set him before thee, then let me bear the blame for ever: for except we had lingered, surely now we had returned this second time. And their father Israel said unto them, If it must be so now, do this; take of the best fruits in the land in your vessels, and carry down the man a present, a little balm, and a little honey, spices, and myrrh, nuts, and almonds: and take double money in your hand: and the money that was brought again in the mouth of your sacks, carry it again in your hand; peradventure it was an oversight: take also your brother, and arise, go again unto the man: and God Almighty give you mercy before the man, that he may send away your other brother, and Benjamin. If I be bereaved of my children, I am bereaved.

And the men took that present, and they took double money in their hand, and Benjamin; and rose up, and went down to Egypt, and stood before Joseph. And when Joseph saw Benjamin with them, he said to the ruler of his house, Bring these men home, and slay,[5]

5. Kill an animal for meat.

and make ready; for these men shall dine with me at noon. And the man did as Joseph bade; and the man brought the men into Joseph's house. And the men were afraid, because they were brought into Joseph's house; and they said, Because of the money that was returned in our sacks at the first time are we brought in; that he may seek occasion against us, and fall upon us, and take us for bondmen, and our asses. And they came near to the steward of Joseph's house, and they communed with him at the door of the house, and said, O sir, we came indeed down at the first time to buy food; and it came to pass, when we came to the inn, that we opened our sacks, and behold, every man's money was in the mouth of his sack, our money in full weight: and we have brought it again in our hand. And other money have we brought down in our hands to buy food: we cannot tell who put our money in our sacks. And he said, Peace be to you, fear not: your God, and the God of your father, hath given you treasure in your sacks: I had your money. And he brought Simeon out unto them. And the man brought the men into Joseph's house, and gave them water, and they washed their feet; and he gave their asses provender. And they made ready the present against Joseph came at noon: for they heard that they should eat bread there.

And when Joseph came home, they brought him the present which was in their hand into the house, and bowed themselves to him to the earth. And he asked them of their welfare, and said, Is your father well, the old man of whom ye spoke? Is he yet alive? And they answered, Thy servant our father is in good health, he is yet alive. And they bowed down their heads, and made obeisance. And he lifted up his eyes, and saw his brother Benjamin, his mother's son, and said, Is this your younger brother, of whom ye spoke unto me? And he said, God be gracious unto thee, my son. And Joseph made haste; for his bowels did yearn upon his brother: and he sought where to weep; and he entered into his chamber, and wept there. And he washed his face, and went out, and refrained himself and said, Set on bread. And they set on for him by himself, and for them by themselves, and for the Egyptians, which did eat with him, by themselves: because the Egyptians might not eat bread with the Hebrews; for that is an abomination unto the Egyptians. And they sat before him, the firstborn according to his birthright, and the youngest according to his youth: and the men marvelled one at another. And he took and sent messes[6] unto them from before him: but Benjamin's mess was five times so much as any of theirs. And they drank, and were merry with him.

44. And he commanded the steward of his house, saying, Fill the men's sacks with food, as much as they can carry, and put every

6. Portions.

man's money in his sack's mouth. And put my cup, the silver cup,
in the sack's mouth of the youngest, and his corn money. And he
did according to the word that Joseph had spoken. As soon as the
morning was light, the men were sent away, they and their asses.
And when they were gone out of the city, and not yet far off, Joseph
said unto his steward, Up, follow after the men; and when thou dost
overtake them, say unto them, Wherefore have ye rewarded evil for
good? Is not this it in which my lord drinketh, and whereby indeed
he divineth?[7] ye have done evil in so doing.

And he overtook them, and he spake unto them these same words.
And they said unto him, Wherefore saith my lord these words? God
forbid that thy servants should do according to this thing: behold,
the money, which we found in our sacks' mouths, we brought again
unto thee out of the land of Canaan: how then should we steal out
of thy lord's house silver or gold? With whomsoever of thy servants
it be found, both let him die, and we also will be my lord's bondmen. And he said, Now also let it be according unto your words: he
with whom it is found shall be my servant; and ye shall be blameless.
Then they speedily took down every man his sack to the ground, and
opened every man his sack. And he searched, and began at the eldest, and left at the youngest: and the cup was found in Benjamin's
sack. Then they rent their clothes, and laded every man his ass, and
returned to the city.

And Judah and his brethren came to Joseph's house; for he was
yet there: and they fell before him on the ground. And Joseph said
unto them, What deed is this that ye have done? wot ye not that
such a man as I can certainly divine? And Judah said, What shall
we say unto my lord? what shall we speak? or how shall we clear
ourselves? God hath found out the iniquity of thy servants: behold,
we are my lord's servants, both we, and he also with whom the cup
is found. And he said, God forbid that I should do so: but the man
in whose hand the cup is found, he shall be my servant; and as for
you, get you up in peace unto your father.

Then Judah came near unto him, and said, Oh my lord, let thy
servant, I pray thee, speak a word in my lord's ears, and let not thine
anger burn against thy servant: for thou art even as Pharaoh. My lord
asked his servants, saying, Have ye a father, or a brother? And we
said unto my lord, We have a father, an old man, and a child of his
old age, a little one; and his brother is dead, and he alone is left of
his mother, and his father loveth him. And thou saidst unto thy
servants, Bring him down unto me, that I may set mine eyes upon
him. And we said unto my lord, The lad cannot leave his father: for
if he should leave his father, his father would die. And thou saidst

7. Joseph's servant is to claim that this is the cup Joseph uses for clairvoyance: the diviner stared
into a cup of water and foretold the future.

unto thy servants, Except your youngest brother come down with you, ye shall see my face no more. And it came to pass when we came up unto thy servant my father, we told him the words of my lord. And our father said, Go again, and buy us a little food. And we said, We cannot go down: if our youngest brother be with us, then will we go down: for we may not see the man's face, except our youngest brother be with us. And thy servant my father said unto us, Ye know that my wife bare me two sons; and the one went out from me, and I said, Surely he is torn in pieces; and I saw him not since: and if ye take this also from me, and mischief befall him, ye shall bring down my gray hairs with sorrow to the grave. Now therefore when I come to thy servant my father, and the lad be not with us; seeing that his life is bound up in the lad's life; it shall come to pass, when he seeth that the lad is not with us, that he will die: and thy servants shall bring down the gray hairs of thy servant our father with sorrow to the grave. For thy servant became surety for the lad unto my father, saying, If I bring him not unto thee, then I shall bear the blame to my father for ever. Now therefore, I pray thee, let thy servant abide instead of the lad a bondman to my lord; and let the lad go up with his brethren. For how shall I go up to my father, and the lad be not with me? lest peradventure I see the evil that shall come on my father.

45. Then Joseph could not refrain himself before all them that stood by him; and he cried, Cause every man to go out from me. And there stood no man with him, while Joseph made himself known unto his brethren. And he wept aloud: and the Egyptians and the house of Pharaoh heard. And Joseph said unto his brethren, I am Joseph; doth my father yet live? And his brethren could not answer him; for they were troubled at his presence. And Joseph said unto his brethren, Come near to me, I pray you. And they came near. And he said, I am Joseph your brother, whom ye sold into Egypt. Now therefore be not grieved, nor angry with yourselves, that ye sold me hither: for God did send me before you to preserve life. For these two years hath the famine been in the land: and yet there are five years, in the which there shall neither be earing nor harvest. And God sent me before you to preserve you a posterity in the earth, and to save your lives by a great deliverance. So now it was not you that sent me hither, but God: and he hath made me a father to Pharaoh, and lord of all his house, and a ruler throughout all the land of Egypt. Haste ye, and go up to my father, and say unto him, Thus saith thy son Joseph, God hath made me lord of all Egypt: come down unto me, tarry not: and thou shalt dwell in the land of Goshen, and thou shalt be near unto me, thou, and thy children, and thy children's children, and thy flocks, and thy herds, and all thou hast:

and there will I nourish thee; for yet there are five years of famine; lest thou, and thy household, and all that thou hast, come to poverty. And, behold, your eyes see, and the eyes of my brother Benjamin, that it is my mouth that speaketh unto you. And ye shall tell my father of all my glory in Egypt, and of all that ye have seen; and ye shall haste and bring down my father hither. And he fell upon his brother Benjamin's neck, and wept; and Benjamin wept upon his neck. Moreover he kissed all his brethren, and wept upon them: and after that his brethren talked with him.

And the fame thereof was heard in Pharaoh's house, saying, Joseph's brethren are come: and it pleased Pharaoh well, and his servants. And Pharaoh said unto Joseph, Say unto thy brethren, This do ye; lade your beasts, and go, get you unto the land of Canaan; and take your father and your households, and come unto me: and I will give you the good of the land of Egypt, and ye shall eat the fat of the land. Now thou art commanded, this do ye; take you wagons out of the land of Egypt for your little ones, and for your wives, and bring your father, and come. Also regard not your stuff; for the good of all the land of Egypt is yours. And the children of Israel did so: and Joseph gave them wagons, according to the commandment of Pharaoh, and gave them provision for the way. To all of them he gave each man changes of raiment; but to Benjamin he gave three hundred pieces of silver, and five changes of raiment. And to his father he sent after this manner; ten asses laden with the good things of Egypt, and ten she-asses laden with corn and bread and meat for his father by the way. So he sent his brethren away, and they departed: and he said unto them, See that ye fall not out by the way.

And they went up out of Egypt, and came into the land of Canaan unto Jacob their father, and told him, saying, Joseph is yet alive, and he is governor over all the land of Egypt. And Jacob's heart fainted, for he believed them not. And they told him all the words of Joseph, which he had said unto them: and when he saw the wagons which Joseph had sent to carry him, the spirit of Jacob their father revived. And Israel said, It is enough; Joseph my son is yet alive: I will go and see him before I die.

46. And Israel took his journey with all that he had, and came to Beer-sheba, and offered sacrifices unto the God of his father Isaac. And God spake unto Israel in the visions of the night, and said, Jacob, Jacob. And he said, Here am I. And he said, I am God, the God of thy father: fear not to go down into Egypt; for I will there make of thee a great nation: I will go down with thee into Egypt; and I will also surely bring thee up again: and Joseph shall put his hand upon thine eyes. And Jacob rose up from Beer-sheba: and the sons of Israel carried Jacob their father, and their little ones, and their

wives, in the wagons which Pharaoh had sent to carry him. And they took their cattle, and their goods, which they had gotten in the land of Canaan, and came into Egypt, Jacob, and all his seed with him: his sons, and his sons' sons with him, his daughters, and his sons' daughters, and all his seed brought he with him into Egypt.

## Job[8]

1. There was a man in the land of Uz whose name was Job, and that man was perfect and upright, and one that feared God, and eschewed evil. And there were born unto him seven sons and three daughters. His substance also was seven thousand sheep, and three thousand camels, and five hundred yoke of oxen, and five hundred she asses, and a very great household; so that this man was the greatest of all the men of the east. And his sons went and feasted in their houses, every one his day;[9] and sent and called for their three sisters to eat and to drink with them. And it was so, when the days of their feasting were gone about, that Job sent and sanctified them, and rose up early in the morning, and offered burnt offerings according to the number of them all: for Job said, It may be that my sons have sinned, and cursed God in their hearts. Thus did Job continually.

Now there was a day when the sons of God came to present themselves before the Lord, and Satan came also among them. And the Lord said unto Satan, Whence comest thou? Then Satan answered the Lord, and said, From going to and fro in the earth, and from walking up and down in it. And the Lord said unto Satan, Hast thou considered my servant Job, that there is none like him in the earth, a perfect and an upright man, one that feareth God, and escheweth evil? Then Satan answered the Lord, and said, Doth Job fear God for nought? Hast not thou made an hedge about him, and about his house, and about all that he hath on every side? thou hast blessed the work of his hands, and his substance is increased in the land. But put forth thine hand now, and touch all that he hath, and he will curse thee to thy face. And the Lord said unto Satan, Behold, all that he hath is in thy power; only upon himself put not forth thine hand. So Satan went forth from the presence of the Lord.

And there was a day when his sons and his daughters were eating and drinking wine in their eldest brother's house: and there came a messenger unto Job, and said, The oxen were plowing, and the asses feeding beside them: and the Sabeans fell upon them, and took them away; yea, they have slain the servants with the edge of the sword; and I only am escaped alone to tell thee. While he was yet speaking, there came also another, and said, The fire of God is fallen from heaven, and hath burned up the sheep, and the servants, and con-

8. Chapters 1–14, 29–31, 38–42.    9. In rotation at each son's house.

sumed them; and I only am escaped alone to tell thee. While he was yet speaking, there came also another, and said, The Chaldeans made out three bands,[1] and fell upon the camels, and have carried them away, yea, and slain the servants with the edge of the sword; and I only am escaped alone to tell thee. While he was yet speaking, there came also another, and said, Thy sons and thy daughters were eating and drinking wine in their eldest brother's house: and, behold, there came a great wind from the wilderness, and smote the four corners of the house, and it fell upon the young men, and they are dead; and I only am escaped alone to tell thee.

Then Job arose and rent his mantle,[2] and shaved his head, and fell down upon the ground, and worshipped, and said, Naked came I out of my mother's womb, and naked shall I return thither: the Lord gave, and the Lord hath taken away; blessed be the name of the Lord. In all this Job sinned not, nor charged God foolishly.

2. Again there was a day when the sons of God came to present themselves before the Lord, and Satan came also among them to present himself before the Lord. And the Lord said unto Satan, From whence comest thou? And Satan answered the Lord, and said, From going to and fro in the earth, and from walking up and down in it. And the Lord said unto Satan, Hast thou considered my servant Job, that there is none like him in the earth, a perfect and an upright man, one that feareth God, and escheweth evil? and still he holdeth fast his integrity, although thou movedst me against him, to destroy him without cause. And Satan answered the Lord, and said, Skin for skin, yea, all that a man hath will he give for his life. But put forth thine hand now, and touch his bone and his flesh, and he will curse thee to thy face. And the Lord said unto Satan, Behold, he is in thine hand; but save his life.

So went Satan forth from the presence of the Lord, and smote Job with sore boils from the sole of his foot unto his crown. And he took him a potsherd to scrape himself withal; and he sat down among the ashes.

Then said his wife unto him, Dost thou still retain thine integrity? curse God, and die. But he said unto her, Thou speakest as one of the foolish women speaketh. What? shall we receive good at the hand of God, and shall we not receive evil? In all this did not Job sin with his lips.

Now when Job's three friends heard of all this evil that was come upon him, they came every one from his own place; Eliphaz the Temanite, and Bildad the Shuhite, and Zophar the Naamathite: for they had made an appointment together to come to mourn with him

1. Split up into three groups.    2. Tore his cloak.

and to comfort him. And when they lifted up their eyes afar off, and knew him not, they lifted up their voice, and wept; and they rent every one his mantle, and sprinkled dust upon their heads toward heaven. So they sat down with him upon the ground seven days and seven nights, and none spake a word unto him: for they saw that his grief was very great.

3. After this opened Job his mouth, and cursed his day. And Job spake, and said, Let the day perish wherein I was born, and the night in which it was said, There is a man child conceived. Let that day be darkness; let not God regard it from above, neither let the light shine upon it. Let darkness and the shadow of death stain it; let a cloud dwell upon it; let the blackness of the day terrify it. As for that night, let darkness seize upon it; let it not be joined unto the days of the year, let it not come into the number of the months. Lo, let that night be solitary, let no joyful voice come therein. Let them curse it that curse the day,[3] who are ready to raise up their mourning. Let the stars of the twilight thereof be dark; let it look for light, but have none; neither let it see the dawning of the day: because it shut not up the doors of my mother's womb, nor hid sorrow from mine eyes. Why died I not from the womb? Why did I not give up the ghost when I came out of the belly? Why did the knees prevent[4] me? or why the breasts that I should suck? For now should I have lain still and been quiet, I should have slept: then had I been at rest, with kings and counsellors of the earth, which built desolate places for themselves; or with princes that had gold, who filled their houses with silver: or as an hidden untimely birth I had not been; as infants which never saw light. There the wicked cease from troubling; and there the weary be at rest. There the prisoners rest together; they hear not the voice of the oppressor. The small and great are there; and the servant is free from his master. Wherefore is light given to him that is in misery, and life unto the bitter in soul; which long for death, but it cometh not; and dig for it more than for hid treasures; which rejoice exceedingly, and are glad, when they can find the grave? Why is light given to a man whose way is hid, and whom God hath hedged in? For my sighing cometh before I eat, and my roarings are poured out like the waters. For the thing which I greatly feared is come upon me, and that which I was afraid of is come unto me. I was not in safety, neither had I rest, neither was I quiet; yet trouble came.

4. Then Eliphaz the Temanite answered and said, If we assay to commune with thee, wilt thou be grieved? But who can withhold

3. Sorcerers, magicians. A more literal translation of the next clause would read, "who are ready to rouse up leviathan," a dragon that was thought to produce darkness.    4. Receive.

himself from speaking? Behold, thou hast instructed many, and thou hast strengthened the weak hands. Thy words have upholden him that was falling, and thou hast strengthened the feeble knees. But now it is come upon thee, and thou faintest; it toucheth thee, and thou art troubled. Is not this thy fear, thy confidence, thy hope, and the uprightness of thy ways?[5] Remember, I pray thee, who ever perished, being innocent? or where were the righteous cut off? Even as I have seen, they that plow iniquity, and sow wickedness, reap the same. By the blast of God they perish, and by the breath of his nostrils are they consumed. The roaring of the lion, and the voice of the fierce lion, and the teeth of the young lions, are broken. The old lion perisheth for lack of prey, and the stout lion's whelps are scattered abroad. Now a thing was secretly brought to me, and mine ear received a little thereof. In thoughts from the visions of the night, when deep sleep falleth on men, fear came upon me, and trembling, which made all my bones to shake. Then a spirit passed before my face; the hair of my flesh stood up: It stood still, but I could not discern the form thereof: an image was before mine eyes, there was silence, and I heard a voice, saying, Shall mortal man be more just than God? Shall a man be more pure than his maker? Behold, he put no trust in his servants; and his angels he charged with folly: How much less in them that dwell in houses of clay, whose foundation is in the dust, which are crushed before the moth? They are destroyed from morning to evening: they perish for ever without any regarding it. Doth not their excellency which is in them go away? They die, even without wisdom.

5. Call now, if there be any that will answer thee; and to which of the saints wilt thou turn? For wrath killeth the foolish man, and envy slayeth the silly one. I have seen the foolish taking root: but suddenly I cursed his habitation. His children are far from safety, and they are crushed in the gate, neither is there any to deliver them. Whose harvest the hungry eateth up, and taketh it even out of the thorns, and the robber swalloweth up their substance. Although affliction cometh not forth of the dust, neither doth trouble spring out of the ground; yet man is born unto trouble, as the sparks fly upward. I would seek unto God, and unto God would I commit my cause: which doeth great things and unsearchable; marvellous things without number: who giveth rain upon the earth, and sendeth waters upon the fields: to set up on high those that be low; that those which mourn may be exalted to safety. He disappointeth the devices of the crafty, so that their hands cannot perform their enterprise. He taketh the wise in their own craftiness: and the counsel of the froward is

5. A more literal translation of this sentence would read, "Is not thy fear of God thy confidence, and thy hope the uprightness of thy ways?"

carried headlong. They meet with darkness in the daytime, and grope in the noonday as in the night. But he saveth the poor from the sword, from their mouth, and from the hand of the mighty. So the poor hath hope, and iniquity stoppeth her mouth. Behold, happy is the man whom God correcteth: therefore despise not thou the chastening of the Almighty: for he maketh sore, and bindeth up: he woundeth, and his hands make whole. He shall deliver thee in six troubles: yea, in seven there shall no evil touch thee. In famine he shall redeem thee from death: and in war from the power of the sword. Thou shalt be hid from the scourge of the tongue: neither shalt thou be afraid of destruction when it cometh. At destruction and famine thou shalt laugh: neither shalt thou be afraid of the beasts of the earth. For thou shalt be in league with the stones of the field: and the beasts of the field shall be at peace with thee. And thou shalt know that thy tabernacle[6] shall be in peace; and thou shalt visit thy habitation, and shalt not sin. Thou shalt know also that thy seed shall be great, and thine offspring as the grass of the earth. Thou shalt come to thy grave in a full age, like as a shock of corn cometh in in his season. Lo this, we have searched it, so it is; hear it, and know thou it for thy good.

6. But Job answered and said, Oh that my grief were thoroughly weighed, and my calamity laid in the balances together! For now it would be heavier than the sand of the sea: therefore my words are swallowed up.[7] For the arrows of the Almighty are within me, the poison whereof drinketh up my spirit: the terrors of God do set themselves in array against me. Doth the wild ass bray when he hath grass? or loweth the ox over his fodder?[8] Can that which is unsavoury be eaten without salt? or is there any taste in the white of an egg? The things that my soul refused to touch are as my sorrowful meat.[9] Oh that I might have my request; and that God would grant me the thing that I long for! Even that it would please God to destroy me; that he would let loose his hand, and cut me off! Then should I yet have comfort; yea, I would harden myself in sorrow: let him not spare; for I have not concealed[1] the words of the Holy One. What is my strength, that I should hope? and what is mine end, that I should prolong my life? Is my strength the strength of stones? or is my flesh of brass? Is not my help in me? and is wisdom driven quite from me?[2] To him that is afflicted pity should be shewed from his friend; but he forsaketh the fear of the Almighty. My brethren have dealt

6. Tent.    7. A more literal translation of this clause would read, "therefore have my words been rash." Job recognizes the exaggeration of his first outburst.    8. Animals do not complain without reason; therefore when a rational man complains, he must have some justification for it. 9. More literally, "My soul refuseth to touch them, they are as loathsome meat to me." He is referring to the statements of his friends.    1. More literally, "denied."    2. More literally, "Is not my help within me gone, and is not wisdom driven quite away from me."

deceitfully as a brook, and as the stream of brooks they pass away; which are blackish by reason of the ice, and wherein the snow is hid: what time they wax warm, they vanish: when it is hot, they are consumed out of their place. The paths of their way are turned aside; they go to nothing, and perish. The troops of Tema looked, the companies of Sheba waited for them. They were confounded because they had hoped;[3] they came thither, and were ashamed. For now ye are nothing; ye see my casting down, and are afraid. Did I say, Bring unto me? or, Give a reward for me of your substance? or, Deliver me from the enemy's hand? or, Redeem me from the hand of the mighty? Teach me, and I will hold my tongue: and cause me to understand wherein I have erred. How forcible are right words! But what doth your arguing reprove? Do ye imagine to reprove words, and the speeches of one that is desperate, which are as wind? Yea, ye overwhelm the fatherless, and ye dig a pit for your friend. Now therefore be content, look upon me; for it is evident unto you if I lie. Return, I pray you, let it not be iniquity; yea, return again, my righteousness is in it. Is there iniquity in my tongue? Cannot my taste discern perverse things?

7. Is there not an appointed time to man upon earth? Are not his days also like the days of an hireling? As a servant earnestly desireth the shadow,[4] and as an hireling looketh for the reward of his work: so am I made to possess months of vanity, and wearisome nights are appointed to me. When I lie down, I say, When shall I arise, and the night be gone? and I am full of tossings to and fro unto the dawning of the day. My flesh is clothed with worms and clods of dust; my skin is broken, and become loathsome. My days are swifter than a weaver's shuttle, and are spent without hope. O remember that my life is wind: mine eye shall no more see good. The eye of him that hath seen me shall see me no more: thine eyes are upon me, and I am not. As the cloud is consumed and vanisheth away: so he that goeth down to the grave shall come up no more. He shall return no more to his house, neither shall his place know him any more. Therefore I will not refrain my mouth; I will speak in the anguish of my spirit; I will complain in the bitterness of my soul. Am I a sea, or a whale, that thou settest a watch over me?[5] When I say, My bed shall comfort me, my couch shall ease my complaint; then thou scarest me with dreams, and terrifiest me through visions: so that my soul chooseth strangling, and death rather than my life. I loathe it; I would not live alway: let me alone; for my days are vanity.

---

3. The caravans reached the springs they had counted on and found them dry.    4. Evening, the end of the working day.    5. Job, now addressing God directly, compares his situation with that of the sea monster whom a god fought against in the Babylonian myth. He reproves God for exerting His power against anything as small as himself.

What is man, that thou shouldest magnify him? and that thou shouldest set thine heart upon him? and that thou shouldest visit him every morning, and try him every moment? How long wilt thou not depart from me, nor let me alone till I swallow down my spittle?[6] I have sinned; what shall I do unto thee, O thou preserver[7] of men? Why hast thou set me as a mark against thee, so that I am a burden to myself? And why dost thou not pardon my transgression, and take away mine iniquity? For now shall I sleep in the dust; and thou shalt seek me in the morning, but I shall not be.

8. Then answered Bildad the Shuhite, and said, How long wilt thou speak these things? and how long shall the words of thy mouth be like a strong wind? Doth God pervert judgment? or doth the Almighty pervert justice? If thy children have sinned against him, and he have cast them away for their transgression; if thou wouldest seek unto God betimes, and make thy supplication to the Almighty; if thou wert pure and upright; surely now he would awake for thee, and make the habitation of thy righteousness prosperous. Though thy beginning was small, yet thy latter end should greatly increase. For enquire, I pray thee, of the former age, and prepare thy self to the search of their fathers: (For we are but of yesterday, and know nothing, because our days upon earth are a shadow:) shall not they teach thee, and tell thee, and utter words out of their heart? Can the rush grow up without mire?[8] Can the flag grow without water? Whilst it is yet in his greenness, and not cut down, it withereth before any other herb. So are the paths of all that forget God; and the hypocrite's hope shall perish: whose hope shall be cut off, and whose trust shall be a spider's web. He shall lean upon his house, but it shall not stand: he shall hold it fast, but it shall not endure. He is green before the sun, and his branch shooteth forth in his garden. His roots are wrapped about the heap, and seeth the place of stones. If he destroy him from his place, then it shall deny him, saying, I have not seen thee. Behold, this is the joy of his way, and out of the earth shall others grow. Behold, God will not cast away a perfect man, neither will he help the evil doers: till he fill thy mouth with laughing, and thy lips with rejoicing. They that hate thee shall be clothed with shame; and the dwelling place of the wicked shall come to nought.

9. Then Job answered and said, I know it is of a truth: but how should man be just with God? If he will contend with him, he cannot answer him one of a thousand.[9] He is wise in heart, and mighty in strength: who hath hardened himself against him, and hath pros-

6. Even for a moment.    7. More literally, "watcher."    8. The papyrus which grows rapidly when the Nile is high, But withers at once when the waters go down.    9. One of a thousand questions.

pered? Which removeth the mountains, and they know not: which overturneth them in his anger. Which shaketh the earth out of her place, and the pillars thereof tremble. Which commandeth the sun, and it riseth not; and sealeth up the stars. Which alone spreadeth out the heavens, and treadeth upon the waves of the sea. Which maketh Arcturus, Orion, and Pleiades, and the chambers of the south. Which doeth great things past finding out; yea, and wonders without number. Lo, he goeth by me, and I see him not: he passeth on also, but I perceive him not. Behold, he taketh away, who can hinder him? Who will say unto him, What doest thou? If God will not withdraw his anger, the proud helpers do stoop under him. How much less shall I answer him, and choose out my words to reason with him? Whom, though I were righteous, yet would I not answer, but I would make supplication to my judge. If I had called, and he had answered me; yet would I not believe that he had hearkened unto my voice. For he breaketh me with a tempest, and multiplieth my wounds without cause. He will not suffer me to take my breath, but filleth me with bitterness. If I speak of strength, lo, he is strong: and if of judgment, who shall set me a time to plead? If I justify myself, mine own mouth shall condemn me: if I say, I am perfect, it shall also prove me perverse. Though I were perfect, yet would I not know my soul: I would despise my life. This is one thing, there- fore I said it, He destroyeth the perfect and the wicked. If the scourge slay suddenly, he will laugh at the trial of the innocent. The earth is given into the hand of the wicked: he covereth the faces of the judges thereof; if not, where, and who is he? Now my days are swifter than a post:[1] they flee away, they see no good. They are passed away as the swift ships: as the eagle that hasteth to the prey. If I say, I will forget my complaint, I will leave off my heaviness, and comfort myself: I am afraid of all my sorrows, I know that thou wilt not hold me innocent. If I be wicked, why then labour I in vain? If I wash myself with snow water, and make my hands never so clean; yet shalt thou plunge me in the ditch, and mine own clothes abhor me. For he is not a man, as I am, that I should answer him, and we should come together in judgment. Neither is there any daysman[2] betwixt us, that might lay his hand upon us both. Let him take his rod away from me, and let not his fear terrify me: then would I speak, and not fear him; but it is not so with me.

10. My soul is weary of my life; I will leave my complaint upon[3] myself; I will speak in the bitterness of my soul. I will say unto God, Do not condemn me; shew me wherefore thou contendest with me. Is it good unto thee that thou shouldest oppress, that thou shouldest

1. Courier.    2. Arbitrator.    3. On behalf of. *Leave:* Give free course to.

despise the work of thine hands, and shine upon the counsel of the wicked? Hath thou eyes of flesh? or seest thou as man seeth? Are thy days as the days of man? Are thy years as man's days,[4] that thou enquirest after mine iniquity, and searchest after my sin? Thou knowest that I am not wicked; and there is none that can deliver out of thine hand. Thine hands have made me and fashioned me together round about; yet thou dost destroy me. Remember, I beseech thee, that thou hast made me as the clay; and wilt thou bring me into dust again? Hast thou not poured me out as milk and curdled me like cheese? Thou hast clothed me with skin and flesh, and hast fenced me with bones and sinews. Thou hast granted me life and favour, and thy visitation hath preserved my spirit. And these things hast thou hid in thine heart: I know that this is with thee.[5] If I sin, then thou markest me, and thou wilt not acquit me from mine iniquity. If I be wicked, woe unto me; and if I be righteous, yet will I not lift up my head. I am full of confusion; therefore see thou mine affliction; for it increaseth. Thou huntest me as a fierce lion: and again thou shewest thyself marvellous upon me. Thou renewest thy witnesses against me,[6] and increasest thine indignation upon me; changes and war are against me. Wherefore then hast thou brought me forth out of the womb? Oh that I had given up the ghost, and no eye had seen me! I should have been as though I had not been; I should have been carried from the womb to the grave. Are not my days few? Cease then, and let me alone, that I may take comfort a little before I go whence I shall not return, even to the land of darkness and the shadow of death: a land of darkness, as darkness itself; and of the shadow of death, without any order, and where the light is as darkness.

11. Then answered Zophar the Naamathite, and said, Should not the multitude of words be answered? And should a man full of talk be justified? Should thy lies make men hold their peace? And when thou mockest, shall no man make thee ashamed? For thou hast said, My doctrine is pure, and I am clean in thine eyes. But oh that God would speak, and open his lips against thee; and that he would shew thee the secrets of wisdom, that they are double to that which is! Know therefore that God exacteth of thee less than thine iniquity deserveth. Canst thou by searching find out God? Canst thou find out the Almighty unto perfection? It is as high as heaven; what canst thou do? Deeper than hell; what canst thou know? The measure thereof is longer than the earth, and broader than the sea. If he cut off, and shut up, or gather together,[7] then who can hinder him? For

---

**4.** Is your time, like man's, short, so that you have to judge hastily?   **5.** The meaning is: "My destruction (this) is your purpose." Job accuses God of planning his destruction while showing favor to him.   **6.** His afflictions, which prove (to his friends) his guilt.   **7.** For judgment.

he knoweth vain men: he seeth wickedness also; will he not then consider it? For vain man would be wise, though man be born like a wild ass's colt. If thou prepare thine heart, and stretch out thine hands toward him; if iniquity be in thine hand, put it far away, and let not wickedness dwell in thy tabernacles. For then shalt thou lift up thy face without spot; yea, thou shalt be stedfast, and shalt not fear: because thou shalt forget thy misery, and remember it as waters that pass away: and thine age shall be clearer than the noonday; thou shalt shine forth, thou shalt be as the morning. And thou shalt be secure, because there is hope; yea, thou shalt dig about thee,[8] and thou shalt take thy rest in safety. Also thou shalt lie down, and none shall make thee afraid; yea, many shall make suit unto thee. But the eyes of the wicked shall fail, and they shall not escape, and their hope shall be as the giving up of the ghost.

12. And Job answered and said, No doubt but ye are the people, and wisdom shall die with you. But I have understanding as well as you; I am not inferior to you: yea, who knoweth not such things as these? I am as one mocked of his neighbour, who calleth upon God, and he answered him: the just upright man is laughed to scorn. He that is ready to slip with his feet is as a lamp despised in the thought of him that is at ease. The tabernacles of robbers prosper, and they that provoke God are secure; into whose hand God bringeth abundantly. But ask now the beasts, and they shall teach thee; and the fowls of the air, and they shall tell thee: or speak to the earth, and it shall teach thee: and the fishes of the sea shall declare unto thee. Who knoweth not in all these that the hand of the Lord hath wrought this? In whose hand is the soul of every living thing, and the breath of all mankind. Doth not the ear try words? and the mouth taste his meat? With the ancient is wisdom; and in length of days understanding. With him is wisdom and strength, he hath counsel and understanding. Behold, he breaketh down, and it cannot be built again: he shutteth up a man, and there can be no opening. Behold, he withholdeth the waters, and they dry up: also he sendeth them out, and they overturn the earth. With him is strength and wisdom: the deceived and the deceiver are his. He leadeth counsellors away spoiled, and maketh the judges fools. He looseth the bond of kings, and girdeth their loins with a girdle. He leadeth princes away spoiled, and overthroweth the mighty. He removeth away the speech of the trusty, and taketh away the understanding of the aged. He poureth contempt upon princes, and weakeneth the strength of the mighty. He discovereth deep things out of darkness, and bringeth out to light the shadow of death. He increaseth the nations, and destroyeth them: he

8. Search. The master inspects his property before retiring.

enlargeth the nations, and straiteneth them again.[9] He taketh away the heart of the chief of the people of the earth, and causeth them to wander in a wilderness where there is no way. They grope in the dark without light, and he maketh them to stagger like a drunken man.

13. Lo, mine eye hath seen all this, mine ear hath heard and understood it. What ye know, the same do I know also: I am not inferior unto you. Surely I would speak to the Almighty, and I desire to reason with God. But ye are forgers of lies, ye are all physicians of no value. O that ye would altogether hold your peace! and it should be your wisdom. Hear now my reasoning, and hearken to the pleadings of my lips. Will ye speak wickedly for God? and talk deceitfully for him? Will ye accept[1] his person? Will ye contend for God? Is it good that he should search you out? or as one man mocketh another, do ye so mock him? He will surely reprove you, if ye do secretly accept persons.[2] Shall not his excellency make you afraid? and his dread fall upon you? Your remembrances[3] are like unto ashes, your bodies to bodies of clay. Hold your peace, let me alone, that I may speak, and let come on me what will. Wherefore do I take my flesh in my teeth,[4] and put my life in mine hand? Though he slay me, yet will I trust in him: but I will maintain mine own ways before him. He also shall be my salvation: for an hypocrite shall not come before him. Hear diligently my speech, and my declaration with your ears. Behold now, I have ordered my cause; I know that I shall be justified. Who is he that will plead with me?[5] for now, if I hold my tongue, I shall give up the ghost. Only do not two things unto me: then will I not hide myself from thee.[6] Withdraw thine hand far from me: and let not thy dread make me afraid. Then call thou, and I will answer: or let me speak, and answer thou me. How many are mine iniquities and sins? Make me to know my transgression and my sin. Wherefore hidest thou thy face, and holdest me for thine enemy? Wilt thou break a leaf driven to and fro? and wilt thou pursue the dry stubble? For thou writest bitter things against me, and makest me to possess the iniquities of my youth. Thou puttest my feet also in the stocks, and lookest narrowly unto all my paths; thou settest a print upon the heels of my feet. And he, as a rotten thing, consumeth, as a garment that is moth eaten.

14. Man that is born of a woman is of few days, and full of trouble. He cometh forth like a flower, and is cut down: he fleeth also as

9. Contracts their boundaries.     1. Respect.     2. This phrase seems to mean something like, "back the winning side for personal reasons."     3. Memorable sayings.     4. Like a wild beast at bay, defending its life with its teeth.     5. Accuse me.     6. He now addresses himself directly to God.

a shadow, and continueth not. And dost thou open thine eyes upon such an one, and bringest me into judgment with thee? Who can bring a clean thing out of an unclean? not one. Seeing his days are determined, the number of his months are with thee, thou hast appointed his bounds that he cannot pass; turn from him, that he may rest, till he shall accomplish, as an hireling, his day. For there is hope of a tree, if it be cut down, that it will sprout again, and that the tender branch thereof will not cease. Though the root thereof wax old in the earth, and the stock thereof die in the ground; yet through the scent of water it will bud, and bring forth boughs like a plant. But man dieth, and wasteth away: yea, man giveth up the ghost, and where is he? As the waters fail from the sea, and the flood decayeth and drieth up: so man lieth down, and riseth not: till the heavens be no more, they shall not awake, nor be raised out of their sleep. O that thou wouldest hide me in the grave, that thou wouldest keep me secret, until thy wrath be past, that thou wouldest appoint me a set time, and remember me! If a man die, shall he live again? All the days of my appointed time will I wait, till my change[7] come. Thou shalt call, and I will answer thee: thou wilt have a desire to[8] the work of thine hands. For now thou numberest my steps: dost thou not watch over my sin? My transgression is sealed up in a bag, and thou sewest up mine iniquity. And surely the mountain falling cometh to nought, and the rock is removed out of his place. The waters wear the stones: thou washest away the things which grow out of the dust of the earth; and thou destroyest the hope of man. Thou prevailest for ever against him, and he passeth; thou changest his countenance, and sendest him away. His sons come to honour, and he knoweth it not; and they are brought low, but he perceiveth it not of them. But his flesh upon him shall have pain, and his soul within him shall mourn.

29. Moreover Job continued his parable, and said, Oh that I were as in months past, as in the days when God preserved me; when his candle shined upon my head, and when by his light I walked through darkness; as I was in the days of my youth, when the secret of God was upon my tabernacle; when the Almighty was yet with me, when my children were about me; when I washed my steps with butter and the rock poured me out rivers of oil; when I went out to the gate[9] through the city, when I prepared my seat in the street! The young men saw me, and hid themselves: and the aged arose, and stood up. The princes refrained talking, and laid their hand on their mouth. The nobles held their peace, and their tongue cleaved to the roof of their mouth. When the ear heard me, then it blessed me; and when

7. Release.   8. For.   9. The town meeting place and law court was just inside the gate.

the eye saw me, it gave witness to me: because I delivered the poor
that cried, and the fatherless, and him that had none to help him.
The blessing of him that was ready to perish came upon me: and I
caused the widow's heart to sing for joy. I put on righteousness, and
it clothed me: my judgment was as a robe and a diadem. I was eyes
to the blind, and feet was I to the lame. I was a father to the poor:
and the cause which I knew not I searched out. And I brake the jaws
of the wicked, and plucked the spoil out of his teeth. Then I said, I
shall die in my nest, and I shall multiply my days as the sand. My
root was spread out by the waters, and the dew lay all night upon my
branch. My glory was fresh in me, and my bow was renewed in my
hand. Unto me men gave ear, and waited, and kept silence at my
counsel. After my words they spake not again; and my speech dropped
upon them. And they waited for me as for the rain; and they opened
their mouth wide as for the latter rain. If I laughed on them, they
believed it not; and the light of my countenance they cast not down.
I chose out their way, and sat chief, and dwelt as a king in the army,
as one that comforteth the mourners.

30. But now they that are younger than I have me in derision,
whose fathers I would have disdained to have set with the dogs of my
flock. Yea, whereto might the strength of their hands profit me,[1] in
whom old age was perished? For want and famine they were solitary;
fleeing into the wilderness in former time desolate and waste. Who
cut up mallows by the bushes, and juniper roots for their meat. They
were driven forth from among men, (they cried after them as after a
thief;) to dwell in the cliffs of the valleys, in caves of the earth, and
in the rocks. Among the bushes they brayed; under the nettles they
were gathered together. They were children of fools, yea, children
of base men: they were viler than the earth. And now am I their
song, yea, I am their byword. They abhor me, they flee far from me,
and spare not to spit in my face. Because he hath loosed my cord,
and afflicted me, they have also let loose the bridle before me. Upon
my right hand rise the youth; they push away my feet, and they raise
up against me the ways of their destruction. They mar my path, they
set forward my calamity, they have no helper. They came upon me
as a wide breaking in of waters: in the desolation they rolled themselves upon me. Terrors are turned upon me: they pursue my soul
as the wind: and my welfare passeth away as a cloud. And now my
soul is poured out upon[2] me; the days of affliction have taken hold
upon me. My bones are pierced in me in the night season: and my
sinews take no rest. By the great force of my disease is my garment
changed: it bindeth me about as the collar of my coat. He hath cast

1. They were too old to work.    2. Within.

me into the mire, and I am become like dust and ashes. I cry unto thee, and thou dost not hear me: I stand up, and thou regardest me not. Thou art become cruel to me: with thy strong hand thou opposest thyself against me. Thou liftest me up to the wind; thou causest me to ride upon it, and dissolvest my substance. For I know that thou wilt bring me to death, and to the house appointed for all living. Howbeit he will not stretch out his hand to the grave, though they cry in his destruction. Did not I weep for him that was in trouble? Was not my soul grieved for the poor? When I looked for good, then evil came unto me: and when I waited for light, there came darkness. My bowels boiled, and rested not: the days of affliction prevented me. I went mourning without the sun: I stood up, and I cried in the congregation. I am a brother to dragons, and a companion to owls. My skin is black upon me, and my bones are burned with heat. My harp also is turned to mourning, and my organ[3] into the voice of them that weep.

31. I made a covenant with mine eyes; why then should I think upon a maid? For what portion of God is there from above? and what inheritance of the Almighty from on high? Is not destruction to the wicked? and a strange punishment to the workers of iniquity? Doth not he see my ways, and count all my steps? If I have walked with vanity, or if my foot hath hasted to deceit; let me be weighed in an even balance, that God may know mine integrity. If my step hath turned out of the way, and mine heart walked after mine eyes, and if any blot hath cleaved to mine hands; then let me sow, and let another eat; yea, let my offspring be rooted out. If mine heart have been deceived by a woman, or if I have laid wait at my neighbour's door; then let my wife grind unto another, and let others bow down upon her. For this is an heinous crime; yea, it is an iniquity to be punished by the judges. For it is a fire that consumeth to destruction, and would root out all mine increase.

If I did despise the cause of my manservant or of my maidservant, when they contended with me; what then shall I do when God riseth up? and when he visiteth, what shall I answer him? Did not he that made me in the womb make him? and did not one fashion us in the womb? If I have withheld the poor from their desire, or have caused the eyes of the widow to fail; or have eaten my morsel myself alone, and the fatherless hath not eaten thereof; (For from my youth he was brought up with me, as with a father, and I have guided her from my mother's womb;) if I have seen any perish for want of clothing, or any poor without covering; if his loins have not blessed me, and if he were not warmed with the fleece of my sheep; if I have lifted

3. Pipe.

up my hand against the fatherless, when I saw my help in the gate:[4] then let mine arm fall from my shoulder blade, and mine arm be broken from the bone. For destruction from God was a terror to me, and by reason of his highness I could not endure. If I have made gold my hope, or have said to the fine gold, Thou art my confidence; if I rejoiced because my wealth was great, and because mine hand had gotten much; if I beheld the sun when it shined, or the moon walking in brightness; and my heart hath been secretly enticed, or my mouth hath kissed my hand:[5] this also were an iniquity to be punished by the judge: for I should have denied the God that is above.

If I rejoiced at the destruction of him that hated me, or lifted up myself when evil found him: neither have I suffered my mouth to sin by wishing a curse to his soul. If the men of my tabernacle said not, Oh that we had of his flesh! We cannot be satisfied. The stranger did not lodge in the street: but I opened my doors to the traveller. If I covered my transgressions as Adam, by hiding mine iniquity in my bosom: did I fear a great multitude, or did the contempt of families terrify me, that I kept silence, and went not out of the door? Oh that one would hear me! Behold, my desire is, that the Almighty would answer me, and that mine adversary had written a book. Surely I would take it upon my shoulder, and bind it as a crown to me. I would declare unto him the number of my steps; as a prince would I go near unto him. If my land cry against me, or that the furrows likewise thereof complain; if I have eaten the fruits thereof without money, or have caused the owners thereof to lose their life: let thistles grow instead of wheat, and cockle instead of barley. The words of Job are ended.

38. Then the Lord answered Job out of the whirlwind, and said, Who is this that darkeneth counsel by words without knowledge? Gird up now thy loins like a man; for I will demand of thee, and answer thou me. Where wast thou when I laid the foundations of the earth? Declare, if thou hast understanding. Who hath laid the measures thereof, if thou knowest? or who hath stretched the line upon it? Whereupon are the foundations thereof fastened? or who laid the corner stone thereof; when the morning stars sang together, and all the sons of God shouted for joy? Or who shut up the sea with doors, when it brake forth, as if it had issued out of the womb? When I made the cloud the garment thereof, and thick darkness a swaddlingband for it, and brake up for it my decreed place,[6] and set bars and doors, and said, Hitherto shalt thou come, but no further: and here shall thy proud waves be stayed? Hast thou commanded the

---

4. The gate is the court; the clause means, "when I had influence in the court."     5. Idolatrous acts of worship of the sun and moon.     6. The broken coastline.

morning since thy days; and caused the dayspring[7] to know his place; that it might take hold of the ends of the earth, that the wicked might be shaken out of it? It is turned as clay to the seal;[8] and they[9] stand as a garment. And from the wicked their light is withholden, and the high arm shall be broken. Hast thou entered into the springs of the sea? or hast thou walked in the search of the depth? Have the gates of death been opened unto thee? or hast thou seen the doors of the shadow of death? Hast thou perceived the breadth of the earth? Declare if thou knowest it all. Where is the way where light dwelleth? And as for darkness, where is the place thereof, that thou shouldest take it to the bound thereof, and that thou shouldest know the paths to the house thereof? Knowest thou it, because thou wast then born? or because the number of thy days is great? Hast thou entered into the treasures of the snow? or hast thou seen the treasures of the hail, which I have reserved against the time of trouble, against the day of battle and war? By what way is the light parted, which scattereth the east wind upon the earth? Who hath divided a watercourse for the overflowing of waters, or a way for the lightning of thunder; to cause it to rain on the earth, where no man is; on the wilderness, wherein there is no man; to satisfy the desolate and waste ground; and to cause the bud of the tender herb to spring forth? Hath the rain a father? or who hath begotten the drops of dew? Out of whose womb came the ice? And the hoary frost of heaven, who hath gendered it? The waters are hid as with a stone, and the face of the deep is frozen. Canst thou bind the sweet influences of Pleiades, or loose the bands of Orion? Canst thou bring forth Mazzaroth[1] in his season? or canst thou guide Arcturus with his sons? Knowest thou the ordinances of heaven? Canst thou set the dominion thereof in the earth? Canst thou lift up thy voice to the clouds, that abundance of waters may cover thee? Canst thou send lightnings, that they may go, and say unto thee, Here we are? Who hath put wisdom in the inward parts? or who hath given understanding to the heart? Who can number the clouds in wisdom? or who can stay the bottles of heaven, when the dust groweth into hardness, and the clods cleave fast together? Wilt thou hunt the prey for the lion? or fill the appetite of the young lion, when they couch in their dens, and abide in the covert to lie in wait? Who provideth for the raven his food? when his young ones cry unto God, they wander for lack of meat.

39. Knowest thou the time when the wild goats of the rock bring forth? or canst thou mark when the hinds do calve? Canst thou number the months that they fulfil? or knowest thou the time when they

---

7. Dawn.     8. More literally, "changed as clay under the seal."     9. All things. God is describing the moment of the creation of the universe.     1. Meaning disputed; it may be a name for the signs of the zodiac, or for some particular constellation.

bring forth? They bow themselves, they bring forth their young ones, they cast out their sorrows. Their young ones are in good liking, they grow up with corn; they go forth, and return not unto them. Who hath sent out the wild ass free? or who hath loosed the bands of the wild ass? Whose house I have made the wilderness, and the barren land his dwellings. He scorneth the multitude of the city, neither regardeth he the crying of the driver. The range of the mountains is his pasture, and he searcheth after every green thing. Will the unicorn[2] be willing to serve thee, or abide by thy crib? Canst thou bind the unicorn with his band in the furrow? or will he harrow the valleys after thee? Wilt thou trust him, because his strength is great? or wilt thou leave thy labour to him? Wilt thou believe him, that he will bring home thy seed, and gather it into thy barn? Gavest thou the goodly wings unto the peacocks? or wings and feathers unto the ostrich? Which leaveth her eggs in the earth, and warmeth them in dust, and forgetteth that the foot may crush them, or that the wild beast may break them. She is hardened against her young ones, as though they were not her's: her labour is in vain without fear;[3] because God hath deprived her of wisdom, neither hath he imparted to her understanding. What time she lifteth up herself on high, she scorneth the horse and his rider. Hast thou given the horse strength? Hast thou clothed his neck with thunder? Canst thou make him afraid as a grasshopper? The glory of his nostrils is terrible. He paweth in the valley, and rejoiceth in his strength: he goeth on to meet the armed men. He mocketh at fear, and is not affrighted; neither turneth he back from the sword. The quiver rattleth against him, the glittering spear and the shield. He swalloweth the ground with fierceness and rage: neither believeth he that it is the sound of the trumpet. He saith among the trumpets, Ha, ha; and he smelleth the battle afar off, the thunder of the captains, and the shouting. Doth the hawk fly by thy wisdom, and stretch her wings toward the south? Doth the eagle mount up at thy command, and make her nest on high? She dwelleth and abideth on the rock, upon the crag of the rock, and the strong place. From thence she seeketh the prey, and her eyes behold afar off. Her young ones also suck up blood: and where the slain are, there is she.

40. Moreover the Lord answered Job, and said, Shall he that contendeth with the Almighty instruct him? He that reproveth God, let him answer it.

Then Job answered the Lord, and said, Behold, I am vile; what shall I answer thee? I will lay mine hand upon my mouth. Once have I spoken; but I will not answer: yea, twice; but I will proceed no further.

---

2. The Hebrew has "wild ox."    3. Though her labor is in vain, she is without fear.

Then answered the Lord unto Job out of the whirlwind, and said, Gird up thy loins now like a man: I will demand of thee, and declare thou unto me. Wilt thou also disannul my judgment? Wilt thou condemn me, that thou mayest be righteous? Hast thou an arm like God: or canst thou thunder with a voice like him? Deck thyself now with majesty and excellency; and array thyself with glory and beauty. Cast abroad the rage of thy wrath: and behold every one that is proud, and abase him. Look on every one that is proud, and bring him low; and tread down the wicked in their place. Hide them in the dust together; and bind their faces in secret. Then will I also confess unto thee that thine own right hand can save thee.

Behold now behemoth,[4] which I made with thee; he eateth grass as an ox. Lo now, his strength is in his loins, and his force is in the navel of his belly. He moveth his tail like a cedar: the sinews of his stone[5] are wrapped together. His bones are as strong pieces of brass; his bones are like bars of iron. He is the chief of the ways of God: he that made him can make his sword to approach unto him. Surely the mountains bring him forth food, where all the beasts of the field play. He lieth under the shady trees, in the covert of the reed, and fens. The shady trees cover him with their shadow; the willows of the brook compass him about. Behold, he drinketh up a river, and hasteth not: he trusteth that he can draw up Jordan into his mouth. He taketh it with his eyes:[6] his nose pierceth through snares.

41. Canst thou draw out leviathan[7] with an hook? or his tongue with a cord which thou lettest down? Canst thou put an hook into his nose? or bore his jaw through with a thorn? Will he make many supplications unto thee? will he speak soft words unto thee? Will he make a covenant with thee? wilt thou take him for a servant for ever? Wilt thou play with him as with a bird? or wilt thou bind him for thy maidens? Shall the companions make a banquet of him? Shall they part him among the merchants? Canst thou fill his skin with barbed irons? or his head with fish spears? Lay thine hand upon him, remember the battle, do no more. Behold, the hope of him is in vain: shall not one be cast down even at the sight of him? None is so fierce that dare stir him up: who then is able to stand before me? Who hath prevented[8] me, that I should repay him? Whatsoever is under the whole heaven is mine. I will not conceal his parts, nor his power, nor his comely proportion. Who can discover the face of his garment?[9] or who can come to him with his double bridle? Who can open the doors of his face? His teeth are terrible round about. His scales are his pride, shut up together as with a close seal. One is so

---

4. Generally identified with the hippopotamus.    5. More literally, "thighs."    6. Obscure in the original; probably, "None can attack him in the eyes."    7. Here probably the crocodile. 8. Given anything to me first.    9. His scales. *Discover:* strip off.

near to another, that no air can come between them. They are joined
one to another, they stick together, that they cannot be sundered. By
his neesings[1] a light doth shine, and his eyes are like the eyelids of
the morning. Out of his mouth go burning lamps, and sparks of fire
leap out. Out of his nostrils goeth smoke, as out of a seething pot or
caldron. His breath kindleth coals, and a flame goeth out of his
mouth. In his neck remaineth strength, and sorrow is turned into
joy before him. The flakes of his flesh are joined together: they are
firm in themselves; they cannot be moved. His heart is as firm as a
stone; yea, as hard as a piece of the nether millstone. When he
raiseth up himself, the mighty are afraid: by reason of breakings they
purify themselves.[2] The sword of him that layeth at him cannot hold:
the spear, the dart, nor the habergeon. He esteemeth iron as straw,
and brass as rotten wood. The arrow cannot make him flee: sling-
stones are turned with him into stubble. Darts are counted as stubble: he laugheth at the shaking of a spear. Sharp stones are under
him: he spreadeth sharp pointed things upon the mire. He maketh
the deep to boil like a pot: he maketh the sea like a pot of ointment.
He maketh a path to shine after him; one would think the deep to be
hoary.[3] Upon earth there is not his like, who is made without fear.
He beholdeth all high things: he is a king over all the children of
pride.

42. Then Job answered the Lord, and said, I know that thou canst
do every thing, and that no thought can be withholden from thee.
Who is he that hideth counsel without knowledge? Therefore have I
uttered that I understood not; things too wonderful for me, which I
knew not. Hear, I beseech thee, and I will speak: I will demand of
thee, and declare thou unto me. I have heard of thee by the hearing
of the ear: but now mine eye seeth thee. Wherefore I abhor myself,
and repent in dust and ashes.

And it was so, that after the Lord had spoken these words unto
Job, the Lord said to Eliphaz the Temanite, My wrath is kindled
against thee, and against thy two friends: for ye have not spoken of
me the thing that is right, as my servant Job hath. Therefore take
unto you now seven bullocks and seven rams, and go to my servant
Job, and offer up for yourselves a burnt offering; and my servant Job
shall pray for you: for him will I accept: lest I deal with you after
your folly, in that ye have not spoken of me the thing which is right,
like my servant Job. So Eliphaz the Temanite and Bildad the Shuhite and Zophar the Naamathite went, and did according as the Lord
commanded them: the Lord also accepted Job. And the Lord turned

1. His breath (compare, "sneeze"). The vapor exhaled by the crocodile appears luminous in the
sunlight.  2. A corrupt text. The clause probably should read, "in consternation they are beside
themselves."  3. White (with foam).

the captivity[4] of Job, when he prayed for his friends: also the Lord gave Job twice as much as he had before. Then came there unto him all his brethren, and all his sisters, and all they that had been of his acquaintance before, and did eat bread with him in his house: and they bemoaned him, and comforted him over all the evil that the Lord had brought upon him: every man also gave him a piece of money, and every one an earring of gold. So the Lord blessed the latter end of Job more than his beginning: for he had fourteen thousand sheep, and six thousand camels, and a thousand yoke of oxen, and a thousand she asses. He had also seven sons and three daughters. And he called the name of the first, Jemima; and the name of the second, Kezia; and the name of the third, Kerenhappuch. And in all the land were no women found so fair as the daughters of Job: and their father gave them inheritance among their brethren. After this lived Job an hundred and forty years, and saw his sons, and his sons' sons, even four generations. So Job died, being old and full of days.

## Psalm 8

1. O Lord our Lord, how excellent is thy name in all the earth! who hast set thy glory above the heavens.

2. Out of the mouth of babes and sucklings hast thou ordained strength because of thine enemies, that thou mightest still the enemy and the avenger.

3. When I consider thy heavens, the work of thy fingers, the moon and the stars, which thou hast ordained;

4. What is man, that thou art mindful of him? and the son of man, that thou visitest him?

5. For thou hast made him a little lower than the angels, and hast crowned him with glory and honour.

6. Thou madest him to have dominion over the works of thy hands; thou hast put all things under his feet:

7. All sheep and oxen, yea, and the beasts of the field;

8. The fowl of the air, and the fish of the sea, and whatsoever passeth through the paths of the seas.

9. O Lord our Lord, how excellent is thy name in all the earth!

## Psalm 19

1. The heavens declare the glory of God; and the firmament sheweth his handywork.

2. Day unto day uttereth speech, and night unto night sheweth knowledge.

---

4. Put an end to the suffering.

3. There is no speech nor language, where their voice is not heard.

4. Their line is gone out through all the earth, and their words to the end of the world. In them hath he set a tabernacle for the sun,

5. Which is as a bridegroom coming out of his chamber, and rejoiceth as a strong man to run a race.

6. His going forth is from the end of the heaven, and his circuit unto the ends of it: and there is nothing hid from the heat thereof.

7. The law of the Lord is perfect, converting the soul: the testimony of the Lord is sure, making wise the simple.

8. The statutes of the Lord are right, rejoicing the heart: the commandment of the Lord is pure, enlightening the eyes.

9. The fear of the Lord is clean, enduring for ever: the judgments of the Lord are true and righteous altogether.

10. More to be desired are they than gold, yea, than much fine gold: sweeter also than honey and the honeycomb.

11. Moreover by them is thy servant warned: and in keeping of them there is great reward.

12. Who can understand his errors? cleanse thou me from secret faults.

13. Keep back thy servant also from presumptuous sins; let them not have dominion over me: then shall I be upright, and I shall be innocent from the great transgression.

14. Let the words of my mouth, and the meditation of my heart, be acceptable in thy sight, O Lord, my strength, and my redeemer.

## Psalm 23

1. The Lord is my shepherd; I shall not want.

2. He maketh me to lie down in green pastures: he leadeth me beside the still waters.

3. He restoreth my soul: he leadeth me in the paths of righteousness for his name's sake.

4. Yea, though I walk through the valley of the shadow of death, I will fear no evil: for thou art with me; thy rod and thy staff they comfort me.

5. Thou preparest a table before me in the presence of mine enemies: thou anointest my head with oil; my cup runneth over.

6. Surely goodness and mercy shall follow me all the days of my life: and I will dwell in the house of the Lord for ever.

## Psalm 104

1. Bless the Lord, O my soul. O Lord my God, thou art very great; thou art clothed with honour and majesty.

2. Who coverest thyself with light as with a garment: who stretchest out the heavens like a curtain:

3. Who layeth the beams of his chambers in the waters: who maketh the clouds his chariot: who walketh upon the wings of the wind:

4. Who maketh his angels spirits; his ministers a flaming fire:

5. Who laid the foundations of the earth, that it should not be removed for ever.

6. Thou coveredst it with the deep as with a garment: the waters stood above the mountains.

7. At thy rebuke they fled; at the voice of thy thunder they hasted away.

8. They go up by the mountains; they go down by the valleys unto the place which thou hast founded for them.

9. Thou hast set a bound that they may not pass over; that they turn not again to cover the earth.

10. He sendeth the springs into the valleys, which run among the hills.

11. They give drink to every beast of the field: the wild asses quench their thirst.

12. By them shall the fowls of the heaven have their habitation, which sing among the branches.

13. He watereth the hills from his chambers: the earth is satisfied with the fruit of thy works.

14. He causeth the grass to grow for the cattle, and herb for the service of man: that he may bring forth food out of the earth;

15. And wine that maketh glad the heart of man, and oil to make his face to shine, and bread which strengtheneth man's heart.

16. The trees of the Lord are full of sap; the cedars of Lebanon, which he hath planted;

17. Where the birds make their nests: as for the stork, the fir trees are her house.

18. The high hills are a refuge for the wild goats; and the rocks for the conies.

19. He appointed the moon for seasons: the sun knoweth his going down.

20. Thou makest darkness, and it is night: wherein all the beasts of the forest do creep forth.

21. The young lions roar after their prey, and seek their meat from God.

22. The sun ariseth, they gather themselves together, and lay them down in their dens.

23. Man goeth forth unto his work and to his labour until the evening.

24. O Lord, how manifold are thy works! in wisdom hast thou made them all: the earth is full of thy riches.

25. So is this great and wide sea, wherein are things creeping innumerable, both small and great beasts.

26. There go the ships: there is that leviathan, whom thou hast made to play therein.

27. These wait all upon thee; that thou mayest give them their meat in due season.

28. That thou givest them they gather: thou openest thine hand, they are filled with good.

29. Thou hidest thy face, they are troubled: thou takest away their breath, they die, and return to their dust.

30. Thou sendest forth thy spirit, they are created: and thou renewest the face of the earth.

31. The glory of the Lord shall endure for ever: the Lord shall rejoice in his works.

32. He looketh on the earth, and it trembleth: he toucheth the hills, and they smoke.

33. I will sing unto the Lord as long as I live: I will sing praise to my God while I have my being.

34. My meditation of him shall be sweet: I will be glad in the Lord.

35. Let the sinners be consumed out of the earth, and let the wicked be no more. Bless thou the Lord, O my soul. Praise ye the Lord.

### Psalm 137

1. By the rivers of Babylon,[5] there we sat down, yea, we wept, when we remembered Zion.

2. We hanged our harps upon the willows in the midst thereof.

3. For there they that carried us away captive required of us a song; and they that wasted us required of us mirth, saying, Sing us one of the songs of Zion.

4. How shall we sing the Lord's song in a strange land?

5. If I forget thee, O Jerusalem, let my right hand forget her cunning.

6. If I do not remember thee, let my tongue cleave to the roof of my mouth; if I prefer not Jerusalem above my chief joy.

7. Remember, O Lord, the children of Edom[6] in the day of Jerusalem; who said, Rase it, rase it, even to the foundation thereof.

8. O daughter of Babylon, who art to be destroyed; happy shall he be, that rewardeth thee as thou hast served us.

9. Happy shall he be, that taketh and dasheth thy little ones against the stones.

---

5. On the river Euphrates. Jerusalem was captured and sacked by the Babylonians in 586 B.C. The Jews were taken away into captivity in Babylon.    6. The Edomites helped the Babylonians to capture Jerusalem.

*Isaiah 52–53. [The Song of the Suffering Servant]*

52:13. Behold, my servant shall deal prudently, he shall be exalted and extolled, and be very high.

14. As many were astonied at thee; his visage was so marred more than any man, and his form more than the sons of men:

15. So shall he sprinkle many nations; the kings shall shut their mouths at him: for that which had not been told them shall they see; and that which they had not heard shall they consider.

53:1. Who hath believed our report? and to whom is the arm of the Lord revealed?

2. For he shall grow up before him as a tender plant, and as a root out of a dry ground: he hath no form nor comeliness; and when we shall see him, there is no beauty that we should desire him.

3. He is despised and rejected of men; a man of sorrows, and acquainted with grief: and we hid as it were our faces from him; he was despised, and we esteemed him not.

4. Surely he hath borne our griefs, and carried our sorrows: yet we did esteem him stricken, smitten of God, and afflicted.

5. But he was wounded for our transgressions, he was bruised for our iniquities: the chastisement of our peace was upon him; and with his stripes we are healed.

6. All we like sheep have gone astray; we have turned every one to his own way; and the Lord hath laid on him the iniquity of us all.

7. He was oppressed, and he was afflicted, yet he opened not his mouth: he is brought as a lamb to the slaughter, and as a sheep before her shearers is dumb, so he openeth not his mouth.

8. He was taken from prison and from judgment: and who shall declare his generation? for he was cut off out of the land of the living: for the transgression of my people was he stricken.

9. And he made his grave with the wicked, and with the rich[7] in his death; because he had done no violence, neither was any deceit in his mouth.

10. Yet it pleased the Lord to bruise him; he hath put him to grief: when thou shalt make his soul an offering for sin, he shall see his seed, he shall prolong his days, and the pleasure of the Lord shall prosper in his hand.

11. He shall see the travail of his soul, and shall be satisfied: by his knowledge shall my righteous servant justify many; for he shall bear their iniquities.

12. Therefore will I divide him a portion with the great, and he shall divide the spoil with the strong; because he hath poured out his

---

7. Some editors emend the Hebrew to give the meaning, "evildoers."

soul unto death: and he was numbered with the transgressors; and he bare the sin of many, and made intercession for the transgressors.

---

# HOMER

Greek literature begins with two masterpieces, the *Iliad* and the *Odyssey*, which cannot be accurately dated (the conjectural dates range over three centuries), and which are attributed to a poet, Homer, about whom nothing is known except his name. The Greeks believed that he was blind, perhaps because the bard Demodokos in the *Odyssey* was blind (see p. 265) and seven different cities put forward claims to be his birthplace. They are all in what the Greeks called Ionia, the Western coast of Asia Minor, which was heavily settled by Greek colonists. It does seem likely that he came from this area: the *Iliad* contains several accurate descriptions of natural features of the Ionian landscape and, on the other hand, his grasp of the geography of mainland, especially western, Greece is unsure. But even this is a guess, and all the other stories the Greeks told about him are obvious inventions.

The two great epics which have made his name supreme among poets may have been fixed in something like their present form before the art of writing was in general use in Greece; it is certain that they were intended not for reading but for oral recitation. The earliest stages of their composition date from long before the beginnings of Greek literacy—the late eighth century B.C.: the poems exhibit the unmistakable characteristics of oral composition.

The oral poet had at his disposal not reading and writing, but a vast and intricate system of metrical formulas—phrases which would fit in at different places in the line—and a repertoire of standard scenes (the arming of the warrior, the battle of two champions) as well as the known outline of the story. Of course he could and did invent new phrases and scenes as he recited—but his base was the immense poetic reserve created by many generations of singers before him. When he told again for his hearers the old story of Achilles and his wrath, he was recreating a traditional story which had been recited, with differences, additions, and improvements, by a long line of predecessors: the poem was not, in the modern sense, his creation, still less an expression of his personality. Consequently there is no trace of his identity to be found in it: the poet remains as hidden behind the action and speech of his characters as if he were a dramatist.

The poems as we have them, however, are unlike most of the oral literature we know from other times and places. The poetic organization of each of the two epics, the subtle interrelationship of the parts which creates their structural and emotional unity, suggests that they owe their present form to the shaping hand of a single poet, the architect who selected from the enormous wealth of the oral tradition and fused what he took with original material to create, perhaps with the aid of the new medium of writing, the two magnificently ordered poems known as the *Iliad* and the *Odyssey*.

### THE ILIAD

Of these two the *Iliad* is perhaps the earlier. Its subject is war; its characters
are men in battle and women whose fate depends on the outcome. The war
is fought by the Achaeans* against the Trojans for the recovery of Helen,
the wife of the Achaean chieftain Menelaus; the combatants are heroes who
in their chariots engage in individual duels before the supporting lines of
infantry and archers. This romantic war aim and the outmoded military
technique suggest to the modern reader a comparison with chivalrous
engagements between medieval knights—a vision of individual prowess in
combat which the nostalgia of our mechanized age contrasts sentimentally
with the mass slaughter of modern war. But there is no sentimentality in
Homer's description of battle. "Patroclus went up to him and drove a spear
into his right jaw; he thus hooked him by the teeth and the spear pulled him
over the rim of his car. As one who sits at the end of some jutting rock and
draws a strong fish out of the sea with a hook and line—even so with his
spear did he pull Thestor all gaping from his chariot; he threw him down on
his face and he died while falling." This is meticulously accurate; there is
no attempt to suppress the ugliness of Thestor's death. The bare, careful
description creates the true nightmare quality of battle, in which men perform monstrous actions with the same matter-of-fact efficiency they display
in their normal occupations; and the simile reproduces the grotesque
appearance of violent death—the simple spear thrust takes away Thestor's
dignity as a human being even before it takes his life. He is gaping, like a
fish on the hook.

The simile does something else too. The comparison of Patroclus to an
angler emphasizes another aspect of battle, its excitement. Homer's lines
here combine two contrary emotions, the human revulsion from the horror
of violent death and the human attraction to the excitement of violent action.
This passage is typical of the poem as a whole. Everywhere in it we are
conscious of these two poles, of war's ugly brutality and its "terrible beauty."
The poet accepts violence as a basic factor in human life, and accepts it
without sentimentality; for it is equally sentimental to pretend that war is not
ugly and to pretend that it does not have its beauty. Three thousand years
have not changed the human condition in this respect; we are still both
lovers and victims of the will to violence, and as long as we are, Homer will
be read as its greatest interpreter.

The *Iliad* describes the events of a few weeks in the ten-year siege of Troy.
The particular subject of the poem, as its first line announces, is the anger
of Achilles, the bravest of the Achaean chieftains encamped outside the city.
Achilles is a man who lives by and for violence, who is creative and alive
only in violent action. He knows that he will be killed if he stays before
Troy, but rather than decay, as he would decay, in peace, he accepts that

---

*The transcription of Greek names is, unfortunately, a game with no rules. It used to be the
convention that Greek names would be spelled according to the form they were given in Latin
(and as they appear in our selections from Virgil and Ovid): Achaeans, Achilles. Recently it has
become fashionable to stay closer to the Greek—Akhaians, Akhilleus; this is the system followed
by Fitzgerald for the *Odyssey*. Lattimore in our selections from the *Iliad* chooses something in
between: Achaians, Achilleus. For the introduction it seems best to use the Latin forms which
have been standard in English verse and prose for many centuries.

certainty. His inadequacy for peace is shown by the fact that even in war the violence of his temper makes him a man apart and alone. His anger cuts him off from his commander and his fellow princes; to spite them he withdraws from the fighting, the only context in which his life has any meaning. He is brought back into it at last by the death of his one real friend, Patroclus; the consequences of his wrath and withdrawal fall heavily on the Achaeans, but most heavily on himself.

The great champion of the Trojans, Hector, fights bravely, but reluctantly; war, for him, is a necessary evil, and he thinks nostalgically of the peaceful past, though he has little hope of peace to come. His pre-eminence in peace is emphasized by the tenderness of his relations with his wife and child and also by his kindness to Helen, the cause of the war which he knows in his heart will bring his city to destruction. We see Hector always against the background of the patterns of civilized life—the rich city with its temples and palaces, the continuity of the family. Achilles' background is the discord of the armed camp on the shore, his loneliness, and his certainty of early death. The duel between these two men is the inevitable crisis of the poem, and just as inevitable is Hector's defeat and death. For against Achilles in his native element of violence nothing can stand.

At the climactic moment of Hector's death, as everywhere in the poem, Homer's firm control of his material preserves the balance in which our contrary emotions are held; pity for Hector does not entirely rob us of sympathy for Achilles. His brutal words to the dying Hector and the insults he inflicts on his corpse are the mark of the savage, but we are never allowed to forget that this inflexible hatred is the expression of his love for Patroclus. And the final book of the poem shows us an Achilles whose iron heart is moved at last; he is touched by the sight of Hector's father clasping in suppliance the terrible hands that have killed so many of his sons. He remembers that he has a father, and that he will never see him again; Achilles and Priam, the slayer and the father of the slain, weep together:

> . . . and the two remembered, as Priam sat huddled
> at the feet of Achilleus and wept close for manslaughtering Hektor
> and Achilleus wept now for his own father, now again
> for Patroklos. The sound of their mourning moved in the house.

Achilles gives Hector's body to Priam for honorable burial. His anger has run its full course and been appeased; it has brought death, first to the Achaeans and then to the Trojans, to Patroclus and to Hector, and so to Achilles himself, for his death is fated to come "soon after Hector's." The violence to which he is dedicated will finally destroy him too.

This tragic action is the center of the poem, but it is surrounded by scenes which remind us that the organized destruction of war, though an integral part of human life, is only a part of it. Except for Achilles, whose worship of violence falters only in the final moment of pity for his enemy's father and his own, the yearning for peace and its creative possibilities is never far below the surface. This is most poignantly expressed by the scenes which take place in Troy, especially the farewell between Hector and Andromache;

but it is made clear that the Achaeans too are conscious of what they have sacrificed. Early in the poem, when Agamemnon, the Achaean commander, tests the morale of his troops by suggesting that the war be abandoned, they rush for the ships so eagerly and with such heartfelt relief that their commanders are hard put to it to stop them. These two poles of the human condition, war and peace, with their corresponding aspects of human nature, the destructive and the creative, are implicit in every situation and statement of the poem, and they are put before us, in symbolic form, in the shield which the god Hephaestus makes for Achilles. Its emblem is an image of human life as a whole. Here are two cities, one at peace and one at war. In one a marriage is celebrated and a quarrel settled by process of law; the other is besieged by a hostile army and fights for its existence. Scenes of violence—peaceful shepherds slaughtered in an ambush, Death dragging away a corpse by its foot—are balanced by scenes of plowing, harvesting, work in the vineyard and on the pasture, a green on which youths and maidens dance. And around the outermost rim of the shield runs "the might of the Ocean stream," a river which is at once the frontier of the known and the imagined world and the barrier between the quick and the dead. The shield of Achilles is the total background for the tragic violence of the central figures; it provides a frame which gives the wrath of Achilles and the death of Hector their just proportion and true significance.

### THE ODYSSEY

The other Homeric epic, the *Odyssey*, is concerned with the peace which followed the war, and in particular with the return of the heroes who survived. Its subject is the long drawn out return of one of the heroes, Odysseus of Ithaca, who had come farther than most (all the way from western Greece) and who was destined to spend ten years wandering in unknown seas before he returned to his rocky kingdom. When Odysseus' wanderings began, Achilles had already received, at the hands of Apollo, the death which he had chosen, and which was the only appropriate end for his fatal and magnificent violence. Odysseus chose life, and his outstanding quality is a probing and versatile intelligence, which, combined with long experience, keeps him safe and alive through the trials and dangers of twenty years of war and seafaring. To stay alive he has to do things that Achilles would never have done, and use an ingenuity and experience that Achilles did not possess; but his life is just as much a struggle. Troy has fallen, but "there is no discharge in the war." The way back is as perilous as the ten-year siege.

The opening lines of the poem state the theme:

> Sing in me, Muse, and through me tell the story
> of that man skilled in all ways of contending
> the wanderer, harried for years on end,
> after he plundered the stronghold
> on the proud height of Troy.
>              He saw the townlands
> and learned the minds of many distant men,
> and weathered many bitter nights and days

in his deep heart at sea, while he fought only
to save his life. . . .

In this world it is a struggle even to stay alive, and it is a struggle for which Odysseus is naturally endowed. But his objective is not life at any price. Where honor demands, he can be soberly courageous in the face of death (as on Circe's island, where he goes alone and against his mate's advice to save his sailors), and he can even be led into foolhardiness by his insatiable curiosity (as in the expedition to see the island of the Cyclopes). Much as he clings to life, it must be life with honor; what he is trying to preserve is not just existence but a worldwide reputation. His name has become a byword for successful courage and intelligence, and he must not betray it. When he reveals his identity at the palace of the Phaeacians, he speaks of his fame in an objective manner, as if it were something apart from himself.

> I am Laertes' son, Odysseus.
>     Men hold me
> formidable for guile in peace and war:
> this fame has gone abroad to the sky's rim.

This is not boasting, but a calm recognition of the qualities and achievements for which he stands, and to which he must be true.

Ironically enough, to be true to his reputation, he is often forced to conceal his name. In the Cyclopes' cave, he calls himself "Nobody," in order to assure his escape, and it is clear how hard he finds this denial of his reputation when, out of the cave and on board ship, he insists on telling Polyphemus his name. Not only does this reassertion of his identity bring himself, his ship, and his crew back within reach of Polyphemus' arm, but it also enables the blinded giant to call down on his enemy the wrath of his father Poseidon, who, from this point on, musters the full might of the sea against Odysseus' return. Warned by the consequences of this boastful revelation of his name, he conceals his identity even from the hospitable Phaeacians, until his emotional reaction to the singer's tale of Troy gives him away. And when he finally returns home, to a palace full of violent suitors for his wife's hand who think that he is dead and who have presumed so far that they will kill him if they now find out that he is alive, he has to become Nobody again; he disguises himself as an old dirty beggar, to flatter and fawn on his enemies for bread in his own house.

The trials of the voyage home are not just physical obstacles to his return, they are also temptations. Odysseus is tempted, time after time, to forget his identity, to secede from the life of struggle and constant vigilance for which his name stands. The lotus flower which makes a man forget home and family is the most obvious form of temptation; it occurs early in the voyage and is easily resisted. But he is offered more attractive bait. Circe gives him a life of ease and self-indulgence on an enchanted island; his resistance has by this time been lowered, and he stays a full year before his sailors remonstrate with him and remind him of his home. At the Phaeacian palace where he tells the story of his voyages, he is offered the love of a young princess, Nausicaa, and her hand in marriage by her father Alkinoös—a new life in a

richer kingdom than his rocky Ithaca. The Sirens tempt him to live in the
memory of the glorious past. "Come here, famous Odysseus," they sing,
"great glory of the Achaeans, and hear our song. . . . For we know all that
at broad Troy the Argives and the Trojans suffered by the will of the gods."
If he had not been bound to the mast, he would have gone to hear and join
the dead men whose bones rot on the Sirens' island. Calypso, the goddess
with whom he spent seven years, longing all the time to escape, offers him
the greatest temptation of all, immortality. If he will stay as her husband, he
will live forever, a life of ease and tranquility, like that of the gods. Odysseus
refuses this too; he prefers the human condition, with all its struggle, its
disappointments, and its inevitable end. And the end, death, is an ever-
present temptation. It is always near him; at the slightest slackening of effort,
the smallest failure of intelligence, the first weakness of will, death will bring
him release from his trials. But he hangs on tenaciously, and, toward the
end of his ordeals, he is sent living to the world of the dead to see for himself
what death means. It is dark and comfortless; Homer's land of the dead is
the most frightening picture of the afterlife in European literature. Odysseus
talks to the dead and any illusion he had about death as repose is shattered
when he comforts the shade of Achilles with talk of his everlasting glory and
hears him reply.

> Let me hear no smooth talk
> of death from you, Odysseus, light
> of councils.
> Better, I say, to break sod as a farm
> hand
> for some poor country man, on iron
> rations,
> than lord it over all the exhausted
> dead.

When he hears these words Odysseus does not yet understand their full
significance (that he, the living man, will taste the depths of degradation,
not as a serf, but as a despised beggar, mocked and manhandled in his own
palace), but he is prepared now to face everything that may be necessary, to
push on without another look behind.

In this scene Homer brings his two great prototypes face to face, and poses
the tragic fury of Achilles against the mature intelligence of Odysseus. There
can be little doubt where his sympathy lies. Against the dark background of
Achilles' regret for life lost the figure of Odysseus shines more warmly: a
man dedicated to life, accepting its limitations and making full use of its
possibilities, a man who is destined to endure to the end and be saved. He
finds in the end the home and the peace he fought for, his wife faithful, a
son worthy of his name ready to succeed him, and the knowledge that the
death which must come at last will be gentle.

> Then a seaborne death
> soft as this hand of mist will come
> upon you

when you are wearied out with rich
   old age,
your country folk in blessed peace
   around you.

A very short but thoughtful discussion of the basic themes of the two poems
is found in J. Griffin, *Homer* (1980). Richmond Lattimore, *The Iliad of
Homer* (1951), provides in the introduction the best available short analysis
of Homeric poetry. H. W. Clarke, *The Art of the Odyssey* (1967), a literary
analysis of the poem, explores the pattern of its unity.


# The Iliad[1]

## *Book I*

### [THE QUARREL OF ACHILLEUS AND AGAMEMNON]

Sing, goddess,[2] the anger of Peleus' son Achilleus
and its devastation, which put pains thousandfold upon the
   Achaians,[3]
hurled in their multitudes to the house of Hades strong souls
of heroes, but gave their bodies to be the delicate feasting
of dogs, of all birds, and the will of Zeus was accomplished          5
since that time when first there stood in division of conflict
Atreus' son[4] the lord of men and brilliant Achilleus.
   What god was it then set them together in bitter collision?
Zeus' son and Leto's, Apollo, who in anger at the king drove
the foul pestilence along the host, and the people perished,          10
since Atreus' son had dishonoured Chryses,[5] priest of Apollo,
when he came beside the fast ships of the Achaians to ransom
back his daughter, carrying gifts beyond count and holding
in his hands wound on a staff of gold the ribbons of Apollo
who strikes from afar, and supplicated all the Achaians,              15
but above all Atreus' two sons,[6] the marshals of the people:
'Sons of Atreus and you other strong-greaved[7] Achaians,
to you may the gods grant who have their homes on Olympos
Priam's city[8] to be plundered and a fair homecoming thereafter,
but may you give me back my own daughter and take the ransom,   20
giving honour to Zeus' son who strikes from afar, Apollo.'
   Then all the rest of the Achaians cried out in favour
that the priest be respected and the shining ransom be taken;
yet this pleased not the heart of Atreus' son Agamemnon,

1. Translated by Richmond Lattimore.    2. The Muse, inspiration for epic poetry.    3. The
Greeks. Homer also calls them Danaans and Argives.    4. Agamemnon, the commander of the
Greek army.    5. His daughter is called Chryseis, and the place where he lives, Chryse.
6. Agamemnon and his brother Menelaos.    7. The greave is a piece of armor which fits over
the leg below the knee.    8. Priam was king of Troy. *Olympos*: The mountain in northern
Greece which was supposed to be the home of the gods.

but harshly he drove him away with a strong order upon him:        25
'Never let me find you again, old sir, near our hollow
ships, neither lingering now nor coming again hereafter,
for fear your staff and the god's ribbons help you no longer.
The girl I will not give back; sooner will old age come upon her
in my own house, in Argos, far from her own land, going        30
up and down by the loom and being in my bed as my companion.
So go now, do not make me angry; so you will be safer.'
     So he spoke, and the old man in terror obeyed him
and went silently away beside the murmuring sea beach.
Over and over the old man prayed as he walked in solitude        35
to King Apollo, whom Leto of the lovely hair bore: 'Hear me,
lord of the silver bow who set your power about Chryse
and Killa the sacrosanct, who are lord in strength over Tenedos,[9]
Smintheus,[1] if ever it pleased your heart that I built your temple,
if ever it pleased you that I burned all the rich thigh pieces        40
of bulls, of goats, then bring to pass this wish I pray for:
let your arrows make the Danaans[2] pay for my tears shed.'
     So he spoke in prayer, and Phoibos Apollo heard him,
and strode down along the pinnacles of Olympos, angered
in his heart, carrying across his shoulders the bow and the hooded 45
quiver; and shafts clashed on the shoulders of the god walking
angrily. He came as night comes down and knelt then
apart and opposite the ships and let go an arrow.
Terrible was the clash that rose from the bow of silver.
First he went after the mules and the circling hounds, then let go  50
a tearing arrow against the men themselves and struck them.
The corpse fires burned everywhere and did not stop burning.
     Nine days up and down the host ranged the god's arrows,
but on the tenth Achilleus called the people to assembly;
a thing put into his mind by the goddess of the white arms, Hera,[3]
who had pity upon the Danaans when she saw them dying.        56
Now when they were all assembled in one place together,
Achilleus of the swift feet stood up among them and spoke forth:
'Son of Atreus, I believe now that straggling backwards
we must make our way home if we can even escape death,        60
if fighting now must crush the Achaians and the plague likewise.
No, come, let us ask some holy man, some prophet,
even an interpreter of dreams, since a dream also
comes from Zeus, who can tell why Phoibos Apollo is so angry,
if for the sake of some vow, some hecatomb[4] he blames us,        65

9. An island off the Trojan coast. *Chryse and Killa:* cities near Troy.    1. A cult name of Apollo,
probably a reference to his role as the destroyer of field mice. The Greek *sminthos* means
"mouse."    2. Greeks.    3. Sister and wife of Zeus, the father of the gods; she was hostile to
the Trojans.    4. Strictly, the word denotes a sacrifice of a hundred animals, but it is often used
to refer to smaller offerings.

if given the fragrant smoke of lambs, of he goats, somehow
he can be made willing to beat the bane aside from us.'
    He spoke thus and sat down again, and among them stood up
Kalchas, Thestor's son, far the best of the bird interpreters,          69
who knew all things that were, the things to come and the things
        past,
who guided into the land of Ilion[5] the ships of the Achaians
through that seercraft of his own that Phoibos Apollo gave him.
He in kind intention toward all stood forth and addressed them:
'You have bidden me, Achilleus beloved of Zeus, to explain to
you this anger of Apollo the lord who strikes from afar. Then          75
I will speak; yet make me a promise and swear before me
readily by word and work of your hands to defend me,
since I believe I shall make a man angry who holds great kingship
over the men of Argos, and all the Achaians obey him.
For a king when he is angry with a man beneath him is too strong,
and suppose even for the day itself he swallow down his anger,          81
he still keeps bitterness that remains until its fulfilment
deep in his chest. Speak forth then, tell me if you will protect me.'
    Then in answer again spoke Achilleus of the swift feet:
'Speak, interpreting whatever you know, and fear nothing.          85
In the name of Apollo beloved of Zeus to whom you, Kalchas,
make your prayers when you interpret the gods' will to the Danaans,
no man so long as I am alive above earth and see daylight
shall lay the weight of his hands on you beside the hollow ships,
not one of all the Danaans, even if you mean Agamemnon,          90
who now claims to be far the greatest of all the Achaians.'
    At this the blameless seer took courage again and spoke forth:
'No, it is not for the sake of some vow or hecatomb he blames us,
but for the sake of his priest whom Agamemnon dishonoured
and would not give him back his daughter nor accept the ransom.
Therefore the archer sent griefs against us and will send them          96
still, nor sooner thrust back the shameful plague from the Danaans
until we give the glancing-eyed girl back to her father
without price, without ransom, and lead also a blessed hecatomb
to Chryse; thus we might propitiate and persuade him.'          100
    He spoke thus and sat down again, and among them stood up
Atreus' son the hero wide-ruling Agamemnon
raging, the heart within filled black to the brim with anger
from beneath, but his two eyes showed like fire in their blazing.
First of all he eyed Kalchas bitterly and spoke to him:          105
'Seer of evil: never yet have you told me a good thing.
Always the evil things are dear to your heart to prophesy,

5. Troy.

but nothing excellent have you said nor ever accomplished.
Now once more you make divination to the Danaans, argue
forth your reason why he who strikes from afar afflicts them,       110
because I for the sake of the girl Chryseis would not take the shining
ransom; and indeed I wish greatly to have her
in my own house; since I like her better than Klytaimnestra
my own wife, for in truth she is no way inferior,
neither in build nor stature nor wit, nor in accomplishment.        115
Still I am willing to give her back, if such is the best way.
I myself desire that my people be safe, not perish.
Find me then some prize that shall be my own, lest I only
among the Argives go without, since that were unfitting;
you are all witnesses to this thing, that my prize goes elsewhere.'  120
    Then in answer again spoke brilliant swift-footed Achilleus:
'Son of Atreus, most lordly, greediest for gain of all men,
how shall the great-hearted Achaians give you a prize now?
There is no great store of things lying about I know of.
But what we took from the cities by storm has been distributed;     125
it is unbecoming for the people to call back things once given.
No, for the present give the girl back to the god; we Achaians
thrice and four times over will repay you, if ever Zeus gives
into our hands the strong-walled citadel of Troy to be plundered.'
    Then in answer again spoke powerful Agamemnon:                  130
'Not that way, good fighter though you be, godlike Achilleus,
strive to cheat, for you will not deceive, you will not persuade me.
What do you want? To keep your own prize and have me sit here
lacking one? Are you ordering me to give this girl back?
Either the great-hearted Achaians shall give me a new prize         135
chosen according to my desire to atone for the girl lost,
or else if they will not give me one I myself shall take her,
your own prize, or that of Aias, or that of Odysseus,[6]
going myself in person; and he whom I visit will be bitter.
Still, these are things we shall deliberate again hereafter.        140
come, now, we must haul a black ship down to the bright sea,
and assemble rowers enough for it, and put on board it
the hecatomb, and the girl herself, Chryseis of the fair cheeks,
and let there be one responsible man in charge of her,
either Aias or Idomeneus or brilliant Odysseus,                     145
or you yourself, son of Peleus, most terrifying of all men,
to reconcile by accomplishing sacrifice the archer.'
    Then looking darkly at him Achilleus of the swift feet spoke:
'O wrapped in shamelessness, with your mind forever on profit,
how shall any one of the Achaians readily obey you                  150

6. The most subtle and crafty of the Greeks. Aias: Ajax, the bravest of the Greeks after Achilleus.

either to go on a journey or to fight men strongly in battle?
I for my part did not come here for the sake of the Trojan
spearmen to fight against them, since to me they have done nothing.
Never yet have they driven away my cattle or my horses,
never in Phthia[7] where the soil is rich and men grow great did they
spoil my harvest, since indeed there is much that lies between us, 156
the shadowy mountains and the echoing sea; but for your sake,
o great shamelessness, we followed, to do you favour,
you with the dog's eyes, to win your honour and Menelaos'[8]
from the Trojans. You forget all this or else you care nothing.    160
And now my prize you threaten in person to strip from me,
for whom I laboured much, the gift of the sons of the Achaians.
never, when the Achaians sack some well-founded citadel
of the Trojans, do I have a prize that is equal to your prize.
Always the greater part of the painful fighting is the work of    165
my hands; but when the time comes to distribute the booty
yours is far the greater reward, and I with some small thing
yet dear to me go back to my ships when I am weary with fighting.
Now I am returning to Phthia, since it is much better
to go home again with my curved ships, and I am minded no longer
to stay here dishonoured and pile up your wealth and your luxury.'

    Then answered him in turn the lord of men Agamemnon:    172
'Run away by all means if your heart drives you. I will not
entreat you to stay here for my sake. There are others with me
who will do me honour, and above all Zeus of the counsels.    175
To me you are the most hateful of all the kings whom the gods love.
Forever quarrelling is dear to your heart, and wars and battles;
and if you are very strong indeed, that is a god's gift.
Go home then with your own ships and your own companions,
be king over the Myrmidons.[9] I care nothing about you.    180
I take no account of your anger. But here is my threat to you.
Even as Phoibos Apollo is taking away my Chryseis,
I shall convey her back in my own ship, with my own
followers; but I shall take the fair-cheeked Briseis,
your prize, I myself going to your shelter, that you may learn well185
how much greater I am than you, and another man may shrink back
from likening himself to me and contending against me.'

    So he spoke. And the anger came on Peleus' son, and within
his shaggy breast the heart was divided two ways, pondering
whether to draw from beside his thigh the sharp sword driving    190
away all those who stood between and kill the son of Atreus,
or else to check the spleen within and keep down his anger

---

7. Achilleus' home in northern Greece.    8. The aim of the expedition was to recapture Helen,
the wife of Menelaos, who had run off to Troy with Priam's son Paris.    9. The name of Achilleus' people.

Now as he weighed in mind and spirit these two courses
and was drawing from its scabbard the great sword, Athene[1] descended
from the sky. For Hera the goddess of the white arms sent her,        195
who loved both men equally in her heart and cared for them.
The goddess standing behind Peleus' son caught him by the fair hair,
appearing to him only, for no man of the others saw her.
Achilleus in amazement turned about, and straightway
knew Pallas Athene and the terrible eyes shining.                     200
He uttered winged words and addressed her: 'Why have you come
        now,
o child of Zeus of the aegis,[2] once more? Is it that you may see
the outrageousness of the son of Atreus Agamemnon?
Yet will I tell you this thing, and I think it shall be accomplished.
By such acts of arrogance he may even lose his own life.'             205
    Then in answer the goddess grey-eyed Athene spoke to him:
'I have come down to stay your anger—but will you obey me?—
from the sky; and the goddess of the white arms Hera sent me,
who loves both of you equally in her heart and cares for you.         209
Come then, do not take your sword in your hand, keep clear of
        fighting,
though indeed with words you may abuse him, and it will be that
        way.
And this also will I tell you and it will be a thing accomplished.
Some day three times over such shining gifts shall be given you
by reason of this outrage. Hold your hand then, and obey us.'
    Then in answer again spoke Achilleus of the swift feet:            215
'Goddess, it is necessary that I obey the word of you two,
angry though I am in my heart. So it will be better.
If any man obeys the gods, they listen to him also.'
    He spoke, and laid his heavy hand on the silver sword hilt
and thrust the great blade back into the scabbard nor disobeyed       220
the word of Athene. And she went back again to Olympos
to the house of Zeus of the aegis with the other divinities.
    But Peleus' son once again in words of derision
spoke to Atreides,[3] and did not yet let go of his anger:
'You wine sack, with a dog's eyes, with a deer's heart. Never         225
once have you taken courage in your heart to arm with your people
for battle, or go into ambuscade with the best of the Achaians.
No, for in such things you see death. Far better to your mind
is it, all along the widespread host of the Achaians
to take away the gifts of any man who speaks up against you.          230

1. A goddess, daughter of Zeus, a patron of human ingenuity and resourcefulness, whether exemplified by handicrafts, such as spinning, or by skill in human relations, such as her favorite among the Greeks, Odysseus, possessed. She supported the Greek side in the war.    2. A terrible shield with which Zeus (or any other god to whom it was entrusted) stirred up storms or threw panic into human beings.    3. Son of Atreus, i.e., Agamemnon.

King who feed on your people, since you rule nonentities;
otherwise, son of Atreus, this were your last outrage.
But I will tell you this and swear a great oath upon it:
in the name of this sceptre, which never again will bear leaf nor
branch, now that it has left behind the cut stump in the moun-
    tains,                                                                            235
nor shall it ever blossom again, since the bronze blade stripped
bark and leafage, and now at last the sons of the Achaians
carry it in their hands in state when they administer
the justice of Zeus. And this shall be a great oath before you:
some day longing for Achilleus will come to the sons of the Achai-
    ans,
all of them. Then stricken at heart though you be, you will be able
to do nothing, when in their numbers before man-slaughtering Hektor[4]
they drop and die. And then you will eat out the heart within you
in sorrow, that you did no honour to the best of the Achaians.'
    Thus spoke Peleus' son and dashed to the ground the sceptre    245
studded with golden nails, and sat down again. But Atreides
raged still on the other side, and between them Nestor
the fair-spoken rose up, the lucid speaker of Pylos,[5]
from whose lips the streams of words ran sweeter than honey.
In his time two generations of mortal men had perished,            250
those who had grown up with him and they who had been born to
these in sacred Pylos, and he was king in the third age.
He in kind intention toward both stood forth and addressed them:
'Oh, for shame. Great sorrow comes on the land of Achaia.
Now might Priam and the sons of Priam in truth be happy,           255
and all the rest of the Trojans be visited in their hearts with gladness,
were they to hear all this wherein you two are quarrelling,
you, who surpass all Danaans in council, in fighting.
Yet be persuaded. Both of you are younger than I am.
Yes, and in my time I have dealt with better men than              260
you are, and never once did they disregard me. Never
yet have I seen nor shall see again such men as these were,
men like Peirithoös, and Dryas, shepherd of the people,
Kaineus and Exadios, godlike Polyphemos,
or Theseus,[6] Aigeus' son, in the likeness of the immortals.      265
These were the strongest generation of earth-born mortals,
the strongest, and they fought against the strongest, the beast men
living within the mountains, and terribly they destroyed them.
I was of the company of these men, coming from Pylos,
a long way from a distant land, since they had summoned me.        270
And I fought single-handed, yet against such men no one

---

4. Son of Priam; the foremost warrior of the Trojans.    5. On the western shore of the
Peloponnese.    6. Names of heroes of an older generation.

of the mortals now alive upon earth could do battle. And also
these listened to the counsels I have and heeded my bidding.
Do you also obey, since to be persuaded is better.
You, great man that you are, yet do not take the girl away        275
but let her be, a prize as the sons of the Achaians gave her first. Nor,
son of Peleus, think to match your strength with
the king, since never equal with the rest is the portion of honour
of the sceptred king to whom Zeus gives magnificence. Even
though you are the stronger man, and the mother who bore you[7]
    was immortal,                                                 280
yet is this man greater who is lord over more than you rule.
Son of Atreus, give up your anger; even I entreat you
to give over your bitterness against Achilleus, he who
stands as a great bulwark of battle over all the Achaians.

    Then in answer again spoke powerful Agamemnon:               285
'Yes, old sir, all this you have said is fair and orderly.
Yet here is a man who wishes to be above all others,
who wishes to hold power over all, and to be lord of
all, and give them their orders, yet I think one will not obey him.
And if the everlasting gods have made him a spearman,           290
yet they have not given him the right to speak abusively.'

    Then looking at him darkly brilliant Achilleus answered him:
'So must I be called of no account and a coward
if I must carry out every order you may happen to give me.
Tell other men to do these things, but give me no more          295
commands, since I for my part have no intention to obey you.
And put away in your thoughts this other thing I tell you.
With my hands I will not fight for the girl's sake, neither
with you nor any other man, since you take her away who gave her.
But of all the other things that are mine beside my fast black   300
ship, you shall take nothing away against my pleasure.
Come, then, only try it, that these others may see also;
instantly your own black blood will stain my spearpoint.'

    So these two after battling in words of contention
stood up, and broke the assembly beside the ships of the Achaians.
Peleus' son went back to his balanced ships and his shelter      306
with Patroklos, Menoitios' son, and his own companions.
But the son of Atreus drew a fast ship down to the water
and allotted into it twenty rowers and put on board it
the hecatomb for the god and Chryseis of the fair cheeks         310
leading her by the hand. And in charge went crafty Odysseus.
    These then putting out went over the ways of the water

---

7. Achilleus' mother was Thetis, a sea nymph. She was married to a mortal, Peleus (Achilleus' father), but later left humankind and went to live with her father, Nereus, in the depths of the Aegean Sea.

while Atreus' son told his people to wash off their defilement.
And they washed it away and threw the washings into the salt sea.
Then they accomplished perfect hecatombs to Apollo,                    315
of bulls and goats along the beach of the barren salt sea.
The savour of the burning swept in circles to the bright sky.
   Thus these were busy about the army. But Agamemnon
did not give up his anger and the first threat he made to Achilleus,
but to Talthybios he gave his orders and Eurybates                     320
who were heralds and hard-working henchmen to him: 'Go now
to the shelter of Peleus' son Achilleus, to bring back
Briseis of the fair cheeks leading her by the hand. And if he
will not give her, I must come in person to take her
with many men behind me, and it will be the worse for him.'            325
   He spoke and sent them forth with this strong order upon them.
They went against their will beside the beach of the barren
salt sea, and came to the shelters and the ships of the Myrmidons.
The man himself they found beside his shelter and his black ship
sitting. And Achilleus took no joy at all when he saw them.            330
These two terrified and in awe of the king stood waiting
quietly, and did not speak a word at all nor question him.
But he knew the whole matter in his own heart, and spoke first:
'Welcome, heralds, messengers of Zeus and of mortals.
Draw near. You are not to blame in my sight but Agamemnon             335
who sent the two of you here for the sake of the girl Briseis.
Go then, illustrious Patroklos, and bring the girl forth
and give her to these to be taken away. Yet let them be witnesses
in the sight of the blessed gods, in the sight of mortal
men, and of this cruel king, if ever hereafter                         340
there shall be need of me to beat back the shameful destruction
from the rest. For surely in ruinous heart he makes sacrifice
and has not wit enough to look behind and before him
that the Achaians fighting beside their ships shall not perish.'
   So he spoke, and Patroklos obeyed his beloved companion.          345
He led forth from the hut Briseis of the fair cheeks and gave her
to be taken away; and they walked back beside the ships of the Achai-
       ans,
and the woman all unwilling went with them still. But Achilleus
weeping went and sat in sorrow apart from his companions
beside the beach of the grey sea looking out on the infinite water. 350
Many times stretching forth his hands he called on his mother:
'Since, my mother, you bore me to be a man with a short life,
therefore Zeus of the loud thunder on Olympos should grant me
honour at least. But now he has given me not even a little.
Now the son of Atreus, powerful Agamemnon,                            355
has dishonoured me, since he has taken away my prize and keeps it.'

So he spoke in tears and the lady his mother heard him
as she sat in the depths of the sea at the side of her aged father,
and lightly she emerged like a mist from the grey water.
She came and sat beside him as he wept, and stroked him          360
with her hand and called him by name and spoke to him: 'Why
    then,
child, do you lament? What sorrow has come to your heart now?
Tell me, do not hide it in your mind, and thus we shall both know.'
    Sighing heavily Achilleus of the swift feet answered her:
'You know; since you know why must I tell you all this?          365
We went against Thebe, the sacred city of Eëtion,[8]
and the city we sacked, and carried everything back to this place,
and the sons of the Achaians made a fair distribution
and for Atreus' son they chose out Chryseis of the fair cheeks.
Then Chryses, priest of him who strikes from afar, Apollo,       370
came beside the fast ships of the bronze-armoured Achaians to ran-
    som
back his daughter, carrying gifts beyond count and holding
in his hands wound on a staff of gold the ribbons of Apollo
who strikes from afar, and supplicated all the Achaians,
but above all Atreus' two sons, the marshals of the people.      375
Then all the rest of the Achaians cried out in favour
that the priest be respected and the shining ransom be taken;
yet this pleased not the heart of Atreus' son Agamemnon,
but harshly he sent him away with a strong order upon him.
The old man went back again in anger, but Apollo                 380
listened to his prayer, since he was very dear to him, and let go
the wicked arrow against the Argives. And now the people
were dying one after another while the god's shafts ranged
everywhere along the wide host of the Achaians, till the seer
knowing well the truth interpreted the designs of the archer.    385
It was I first of all urged then the god's appeasement;
and the anger took hold of Atreus' son, and in speed standing
he uttered his threat against me, and now it is a thing accomplished.
For the girl the glancing-eyed Achaians are taking to Chryse
in a fast ship, also carrying to the king[9] presents. But even  390
now the heralds went away from my shelter leading
Briseus' daughter, whom the sons of the Achaians gave me.
You then, if you have power to, protect your own son, going
to Olympos and supplicating Zeus, if ever before now
either by word you comforted Zeus' heart or by action.           395
Since it is many times in my father's halls I have heard you
making claims, when you said you only among the immortals

8. King of the Kilikians, and father of Hektor's wife Andromache. *Thebe* was the Kilikian capital city.    9. Apollo.

beat aside shameful destruction from Kronos' son the dark-misted,[1]
that time when all the other Olympians sought to bind him,
Hera and Poseidon[2] and Pallas Athene. Then you,                        400
goddess, went and set him free from his shackles, summoning
in speed the creature of the hundred hands to tall Olympos,
that creature the gods name Briareus,[3] but all men
Aigaios' son, but he is far greater in strength than his father.
He rejoicing in the glory of it sat down by Kronion,[4]                   405
and the rest of the blessed gods were frightened and gave up binding
          him.
Sit beside him and take his knees and remind him of these things
now, if perhaps he might be willing to help the Trojans,
and pin the Achaians back against the ships and the water,
dying, so that thus they may all have profit of their own king,          410
that Atreus' son wide-ruling Agamemnon may recognize
his madness, that he did no honour to the best of the Achaians.'

     Thetis answered him then letting the tears fall: 'Ah me,
my child. Your birth was bitterness. Why did I raise you?
If only you could sit by your ship untroubled, not weeping,              415
since indeed your lifetime is to be short, of no length.
Now it has befallen that your life must be brief and bitter
beyond all men's. To a bad destiny I bore you in my chambers.
But I will go to cloud-dark Olympos and ask this
thing of Zeus who delights in the thunder. Perhaps he will do it.  420
Do you therefore continuing to sit by your swift ships
be angry at the Achaians and stay away from all fighting.
For Zeus went to the blameless Aithiopians at the Ocean[5]
yesterday to feast, and the rest of the gods went with him.
On the twelfth day he will be coming back to Olympos,                    425
and then I will go for your sake to the house of Zeus, bronze-
          founded,
and take him by the knees and I think I can persuade him.'

     So speaking she went away from that place and left him
sorrowing in his heart for the sake of the fair-girdled woman
whom they were taking by force against his will. But Odysseus      430
meanwhile drew near to Chryse conveying the sacred hecatomb.
These when they were inside the many-hollowed harbour
took down and gathered together the sails and stowed them in the
          black ship
let down mast by the forestays, and settled it into the mast crutch
easily, and rowed her in with oars to the mooring.                       435

---

1. Zeus is the god of the sky, who brings rain and sunshine.    2. Brother of Zeus; god of the
sea.    3. A giant, son of Poseidon.    4. Zeus.    5. The river which was believed to encircle
the whole world. The Ethiopians were thought to live at the extreme edges of the world.

They threw over the anchor stones and made fast the stern cables
and themselves stepped out on to the break of the sea beach,
and led forth the hecatomb to the archer Apollo,
and Chryseis herself stepped forth from the sea-going vessel.
Odysseus of the many designs guided her to the altar                    440
and left her in her father's arms and spoke a word to him:
'Chryses, I was sent here by the lord of men Agamemnon
to lead back your daughter and accomplish a sacred hecatomb
to Apollo on behalf of the Danaans, that we may propitiate
the lord who has heaped unhappiness and tears on the Argives.'          445
   He spoke, and left her in his arms. And he received gladly
his beloved child. And the men arranged the sacred hecatomb
for the god in orderly fashion around the strong-founded altar.
Next they washed their hands and took up the scattering barley.
Standing among them with lifted arms Chryses prayed in a great
      voice:                                                            450
'Hear me, lord of the silver bow, who set your power about
Chryse and Killa the sacrosanct, who are lord in strength over
Tenedos; if once before you listened to my prayers,
and did me honour and smote strongly the host of the Achaians,
so one more time bring to pass the wish that I pray for.                455
Beat aside at last the shameful plague from the Danaans.'
   So he spoke in prayer, and Phoibos Apollo heard him.
And when all had made prayer and flung down the scattering barley
first they drew back the victims' heads and slaughtered them and
      skinned them,
and cut away the meat from the thighs and wrapped them in fat,          460
making a double fold, and laid shreds of flesh upon them.
The old man burned these on a cleft stick and poured the gleaming
wine over, while the young men with forks in their hands stood
      about him.
But when they had burned the thigh pieces and tasted the vitals,
they cut all the remainder into pieces and spitted them                 465
and roasted all carefully and took off the pieces.
Then after they had finished the work and got the feast ready
they feasted, nor was any man's hunger denied a fair portion.
But when they had put away their desire for eating and drinking,
the young men filled the mixing bowls with pure wine, passing
a portion to all, when they had offered drink in the goblets.           471
All day long they propitiated the god with singing,
chanting a splendid hymn to Apollo, these young Achaians,
singing to the one who works from afar, who listened in gladness.
   Afterwards when the sun went down and darkness came
      onward                                                            475
they lay down and slept beside the ship's stern cables.

But when the young Dawn showed again with her rosy fingers,
they put forth to sea toward the wide camp of the Achaians.
And Apollo who works from afar sent them a favouring stern wind.
They set up the mast again and spread on it the white sails,          480
and the wind blew into the middle of the sail, and at the cutwater
a blue wave rose and sang strongly as the ship went onward.
She ran swiftly cutting across the swell her pathway.
But when they had come back to the wide camp of the Achaians
they hauled the black ship up on the mainland, high up          485
on the sand, and underneath her they fixed the long props.
Afterwards they scattered to their own ships and their shelters.

   But that other still sat in anger beside his swift ships,
Peleus' son divinely born, Achilleus of the swift feet.
Never now would he go to assemblies where men win glory,          490
never more into battle, but continued to waste his heart out
sitting there, though he longed always for the clamour and fighting.

   But when the twelfth dawn after this day appeared, the gods who
live forever came back to Olympos all in a body
and Zeus led them; nor did Thetis forget the entreaties          495
of her son, but she emerged from the sea's waves early
in the morning and went up to the tall sky and Olympos.
She found Kronos' broad-browed son apart from the others
sitting upon the highest peak of rugged Olympos.
She came and sat beside him with her left hand embracing          500
his knees, but took him underneath the chin with her right hand[6]
and spoke in supplication to lord Zeus son of Kronos:
'Father Zeus, if ever before in word or action
I did you favour among the immortals, now grant what I ask for.
Now give honour to my son short-lived beyond all other          505
mortals. Since even now the lord of men Agamemnon
dishonours him, who has taken away his prize and keeps it.
Zeus of the counsels, lord of Olympos, now do him honour.
So long put strength into the Trojans, until the Achaians
give my son his rights, and his honour is increased among them.' 510

   She spoke thus. But Zeus who gathers the clouds made no answer
but sat in silence a long time. And Thetis, as she had taken
his knees, clung fast to them and urged once more her question:
'Bend your head and promise me to accomplish this thing,
or else refuse it, you have nothing to fear, that I may know          515
by how much I am the most dishonoured of all gods.'

   Deeply disturbed Zeus who gathers the clouds answered her:
'This is a disastrous matter when you set me in conflict
with Hera, and she troubles me with recriminations.

---

6. The posture of the suppliant, who by this physical pressure emphasized his desperation and
the urgency of the request. Zeus was above all other gods the protector of suppliants.

Since even as things are, forever among the immortals                    520
she is at me and speaks of how I help the Trojans in battle.
Even so, go back again now, go away, for fear she
see us. I will look to these things that they be accomplished.
See then, I will bend my head that you may believe me.
For this among the immortal gods is the mightiest witness                    525
I can give, and nothing I do shall be vain nor revocable
nor a thing unfulfilled when I bend my head in assent to it.'
    He spoke, the son of Kronos, and nodded his head with the dark
        brows,
and the immortally anointed hair of the great god
swept from his divine head, and all Olympos was shaken.                    530
    So these two who had made their plans separated, and Thetis
leapt down again from shining Olympos into the sea's depth,
but Zeus went back to his own house, and all the gods rose up
from their chairs to greet the coming of their father, not one had
        courage
to keep his place as the father advanced, but stood up to greet
        him.                    535
Thus he took his place on the throne; yet Hera was not
ignorant, having seen how he had been plotting counsels
with Thetis the silver-footed, the daughter of the sea's ancient,[7]
and at once she spoke revilingly to Zeus son of Kronos:
'Treacherous one, what god has been plotting counsels with you? 540
Always it is dear to your heart in my absence to think of
secret things and decide upon them. Never have you patience
frankly to speak forth to me the thing that you purpose.'
    Then to her the father of gods and men made answer:
'Hera, do not go on hoping that you will hear all my                    545
thoughts, since these will be too hard for you, though you are my
        wife.
And thought that it is right for you to listen to, no one
neither man nor any immortal shall hear it before you.
But anything that apart from the rest of the gods I wish to
plan, do not always question each detail nor probe me.'                    550
    Then the goddess the ox-eyed lady Hera answered:
'Majesty, son of Kronos, what sort of thing have you spoken?
Truly too much in time past I have not questioned nor probed you,
but you are entirely free to think out whatever pleases you.
Now, though, I am terribly afraid you were won over                    555
by Thetis the silver-footed, the daughter of the sea's ancient.
For early in the morning she sat beside you and took your
knees, and I think you bowed your head in assent to do honour

7. Nereus.

to Achilleus, and to destroy many beside the ships of the Achaians.'
    Then in return Zeus who gathers the clouds made answer:   560
'Dear lady, I never escape you, you are always full of suspicion.
Yet thus you can accomplish nothing surely, but be more
distant from my heart than ever, and it will be the worse for you.
If what you say is true, then that is the way I wish it.
But go then, sit down in silence, and do as I tell you,   565
for fear all the gods, as many as are on Olympos, can do nothing
if I come close and lay my unconquerable hands upon you.'
    He spoke, and the goddess the ox-eyed lady Hera was frightened
and went and sat down in silence wrenching her heart to obedience,
and all the Uranian[8] gods in the house of Zeus were troubled.   570
Hephaistos[9] the renowned smith rose up to speak among them,
to bring comfort to his beloved mother, Hera of the white arms:
'This will be a disastrous matter and not endurable
if you two are to quarrel thus for the sake of mortals
and bring brawling among the gods. There will be no pleasure   575
in the stately feast at all, since vile things will be uppermost.
And I entreat my mother, though she herself understands it,
to be ingratiating toward our father Zeus, that no longer
our father may scold her and break up the quiet of our feasting.
For if the Olympian who handles the lightning should be   580
minded to hurl us out of our places, he is far too strong for any.
Do you therefore approach him again with words made gentle,
and at once the Olympian will be gracious again to us.'
    He spoke, and springing to his feet put a two-handled goblet
into his mother's hands and spoke again to her once more:   585
'Have patience, my mother, and endure it, though you be saddened,
for fear that, dear as you are, I see you before my own eyes
struck down, and then sorry though I be I shall not be able
to do anything. It is too hard to fight against the Olympian.
There was a time once before now I was minded to help you,   590
and he caught me by the foot and threw me from the magic thresh-
    old,
and all day long I dropped helpless, and about sunset
I landed in Lemnos, and there was not much life left in me.
After that fall it was the Sintian men[1] who took care of me.'
He spoke, and the goddess of the white arms Hera smiled at him,  595
and smiling she accepted the goblet out of her son's hand.
Thereafter beginning from the left he poured drinks for the other
gods, dipping up from the mixing bowl the sweet nectar.[2]
But among the blessed immortals uncontrollable laughter

---

8. The Greek word *uranos* means "sky," "heaven."   9. The patron god of craftsmen, especially
workers in metal.   1. The ancient inhabitants of Lemnos, an island in the Aegean Sea.
2. The drink of the gods.

went up as they saw Hephaistos bustling about the palace.                    600
    Thus thereafter the whole day long until the sun went under
they feasted, nor was anyone's hunger denied a fair portion,
nor denied the beautifully wrought lyre in the hands of Apollo
nor the antiphonal sweet sound of the Muses singing.[3]
    Afterwards when the light of the flaming sun went under                    605
they went away each one to sleep in his home where
for each one the far-renowned strong-handed Hephaistos
had built a house by means of his craftsmanship and cunning.
Zeus the Olympian and lord of the lightning went to
his own bed, where always he lay when sweet sleep came on him   610
Going up to the bed he slept and Hera of the gold throne beside
    him.

[The Greeks, in spite of Achilleus' withdrawal, continued to fight.
They did not suffer immoderately from Achilleus' absence; on the
contrary, they pressed the Trojans so hard that Hektor, the Trojan
leader, after rallying his men, returned to the city to urge the Trojans
to offer special prayers and sacrifices to the gods.]

## Book VI

### [THE MEETING OF HEKTOR AND ANDROMACHE]

   . . . Now as Hektor had come to the Skaian gates[4] and the oak
    tree,
all the wives of the Trojans and their daughters came running about
    him
to ask after their sons, after their brothers and neighbours,
their husbands; and he told them to pray to the immortals,                    240
all, in turn; but there were sorrows in store for many.
    Now he entered the wonderfully built palace of Priam.
This was fashioned with smooth-stone cloister walks, and within it
were embodied fifty sleeping chambers of smoothed stone
built so as to connect with each other; and within these slept                245
each beside his own wedded wife, the sons of Priam.
In the same inner court on the opposite side, to face these,
lay the twelve close smooth-stone sleeping chambers of his daughters
built so as to connect with each other; and within these slept,
each by his own modest wife, the lords of the daughters of Priam. 250
There there came to meet Hektor his bountiful mother[5]
with Laodike, the loveliest looking of all her daughters.
She clung to his hand and called him by name and spoke to him:
'Why then,

3. The nine Muses were goddesses of the arts, and the source of artistic inspiration.    4. One
of the entrances to Troy.    5. Hekabe (Hecuba).

child, have you come here and left behind the bold battle?
Surely it is these accursed sons of the Achaians who wear you        255
out, as they fight close to the city, and the spirit stirred you
to return, and from the peak of the citadel lift your hands, praying
to Zeus. But stay while I bring you honey-sweet wine, to pour out
a libation to father Zeus and the other immortals
first, and afterwards if you will drink yourself, be strengthened.     260
In a tired man, wine will bring back his strength to its bigness,
in a man tired as you are tired, defending your neighbours.'
    Tall Hektor of the shining helm spoke to her answering:
'My honoured mother, lift not to me the kindly sweet wine,
for fear you stagger my strength and make me forget my courage;        265
and with hands unwashed I would take shame to pour the glittering
wine to Zeus; there is no means for a man to pray to the dark-misted
son of Kronos, with blood and muck all spattered upon him.
But go yourself to the temple of the spoiler Athene,
assembling the ladies of honour, and with things to be sacrificed,      270
and take a robe, which seems to you the largest and loveliest
in the great house, and that which is far your dearest possession.
Lay this along the knees of Athene the lovely haired. Also
promise to dedicate within the shrine twelve heifers,
yearlings, never broken, if only she will have pity                     275
on the town of Troy, and the Trojan wives, and their innocent chil-
    dren,
if she will hold back from sacred Ilion the son of Tydeus,[6]
that wild spear-fighter, the strong one who drives men to thoughts of
    terror.
So go yourself to the temple of the spoiler Athene,
while I go in search of Paris,[7] to call him, if he will listen        280
to anything I tell him. How I wish at this moment the earth might
open beneath him. The Olympian let him live, a great sorrow
to the Trojans, and high-hearted Priam, and all of his children.
If only I could see him gone down to the house of the Death God,
then I could say my heart had forgotten its joyless affliction.'        285
    So he spoke, and she going into the great house called out
to her handmaidens, who assembled throughout the city the high-
    born
women; while she descended into the fragrant store-chamber.
There lay the elaborately wrought robes the work of Sidonian
women, whom Alexandros[8] himself, the godlike, had brought
    home                                                          290

---

6. Diomedes, one of the Greek champions, who has just distinguished himself in the fighting.
7. Hektor's brother. His seduction and abduction of Helen, the wife of Menelaos, is the cause of
the war.    8. Another name for Paris. *Sidonian:* Sidon was a Phoenician city on the coast of
what is now Lebanon.

from the land of Sidon, crossing the wide sea, on that journey
when he brought back also gloriously descended Helen.
Hekabe lifted out one and took it as gift to Athene,
that which was the loveliest in design and the largest,
and shone like a star. It lay beneath the others. She went on        295
her way, and a throng of noble women hastened about her.
    When these had come to Athene's temple on the peak of the cit-
        adel,
Theano of the fair cheeks opened the door for them, daughter
of Kisseüs, and wife of Antenor, breaker of horses,
she whom the Trojans had established to be Athene's priestess.       300
With a wailing cry all lifted up their hands to Athene,
and Theano of the fair cheeks taking up the robe laid it
along the knees of Athene the lovely haired, and praying
she supplicated the daughter of powerful Zeus: 'O lady,
Athene, our city's defender, shining among goddesses:               305
break the spear of Diomedes, and grant that the man be
hurled on his face in front of the Skaian gates; so may we instantly
        dedicate within your shrine twelve heifers,
yearlings, never broken, if only you will have pity
on the town of Troy, and the Trojan wives, and their innocent chil-
        dren.'                                                      310
    She spoke in prayer, but Pallas Athene turned her head from her.
    So they made their prayer to the daughter of Zeus the powerful.
But Hektor went away to the house of Alexandros,
a splendid place he had built himself, with the men who at that time
were the best men for craftsmanship in the generous Troad,[9]      315
who had made him a sleeping room and a hall and a courtyard
near the houses of Hektor and Priam, on the peak of the citadel.
There entered Hektor beloved of Zeus, in his hand holding
the eleven-cubit-long[1] spear, whose shaft was tipped with a shining
bronze spearhead, and a ring of gold was hooped to hold it.        320
He found the man in his chamber busy with his splendid armour,
the corselet and the shield, and turning in his hands the curved bow,
while Helen of Argos was sitting among her attendant women
directing the magnificent work done by her handmaidens.
    But Hektor saw him, and in words of shame he rebuked him:[2]   325
'Strange man! It is not fair to keep in your heart this coldness.
The people are dying around the city and around the steep wall
as they fight hard; and it is for you that this war with its clamour
has flared up about our city. You yourself would fight with another

---

9. The soil of the Trojan plain (Troad) was fertile.    1. The Greek word translated as "cubit"
means "the length of the forearm."    2. Paris, like Achilleus, was sulking at home. He had been
worsted in a duel with Menelaos, but the goddess Aphrodite saved him from the consequences of
his defeat and brought him to his house in Troy. Paris was hated by his countrymen as the cause
of the war.

whom you saw anywhere hanging back from the hateful encoun-
    ter.                                                                                330
Up then, to keep our town from burning at once in the hot fire.'
    Then in answer the godlike Alexandros spoke to him:
'Hektor, seeing you have scolded me rightly, not beyond measure,
therefore I will tell, and you in turn understand and listen.
It was not so much in coldness and bitter will toward the Trojans 335
that I sat in my room, but I wished to give myself over to sorrow.
But just now with soft words my wife was winning me over
and urging me into the fight, and that way seems to me also
the better one. Victory passes back and forth between men.
Come then, wait for me now while I put on my armour of battle, 340
or go, and I will follow, and I think I can overtake you.'
    He spoke, but Hektor of the shining helm gave him no answer,
but Helen spoke to him in words of endearment: 'Brother
by marriage to me, who am a nasty bitch evil-intriguing,
how I wish that on that day when my mother first bore me          345
the foul whirlwind of the storm had caught me away and swept me
to the mountain, or into the wash of the sea deep-thundering
where the waves would have swept me away before all these things
had happened.
Yet since the gods had brought it about that these vile things must
    be,
I wish I had been the wife of a better man than this is,          350
one who knew modesty and all things of shame that men say.
But this man's heart is no steadfast thing, nor yet will it be so
ever hereafter; for that I think he shall take the consequence.
But come now, come in and rest on this chair, my brother,
since it is on your heart beyond all that the hard work has fallen 355
for the sake of dishonoured me and the blind act of Alexandros,
us two, on whom Zeus set a vile destiny, so that hereafter
we shall be made into things of song for the men of the future.'
    Then tall Hektor of the shining helm answered her: 'Do not, Helen,
make me sit with you, though you love me. You will not persuade
    me.                                                               360
Already my heart within is hastening me to defend
the Trojans, who when I am away long greatly to have me.
Rather rouse this man, and let himself also be swift to action
so he may overtake me while I am still in the city.
For I am going first to my own house, so I can visit             365
my own people, my beloved wife and my son, who is little,
since I do not know if ever again I shall come back this way,
or whether the gods will strike me down at the hands of the Achai-
    ans.'
    So speaking Hektor of the shining helm departed

and in speed made his way to his own well-established dwelling,       370
but failed to find in the house Andromache of the white arms;
for she, with the child, and followed by one fair-robed attendant,
had taken her place on the tower in lamentation, and tearful.
When he saw no sign of his perfect wife within the house, Hektor
stopped in his way on the threshold and spoke among the hand-
        maidens:                                                                     375
Come then, tell me truthfully as you may, handmaidens:
where has Andromache of the white arms gone? Is she
with any of the sisters of her lord or the wives of his brothers?
Or has she gone to the house of Athene, where all the other
lovely-haired women of Troy propitiate the grim goddess?'       380
    Then in turn the hard-working housekeeper gave him an answer:
'Hecktor, since you have urged me to tell you the truth, she is not
with any of the sisters of her lord or the wives of his brothers,
nor has she gone to the house of Athene, where all the other
lovely-haired women of Troy propitiate the grim goddess,       385
but she has gone to the great bastion of Ilion, because she heard that
the Trojans were losing, and great grew the strength of the Achaians.
Therefore she has gone in speed to the wall, like a woman
gone mad, and a nurse attending her carries the baby.'
    So the housekeeper spoke, and Hektor hastened from his home 390
backward by the way he had come through the well-laid streets. So
as he had come to the gates on his way through the great city,
the Skaian gates, whereby he would issue into the plain, there
at last his own generous wife came running to meet him,
Andromache, the daughter of high-hearted Eëtion;       395
Eëtion, who had dwelt underneath wooded Plakos,
in Thebe below Plakos, lord over the Kilikian people.
It was his daughter who was given to Hektor of the bronze helm.
She came to him there, and beside her went an attendant carrying
the boy in the fold of her bosom, a little child, only a baby,       400
Hektor's son, the admired, beautiful as a star shining,
whom Hektor called Skamandrios, but all of the others
Astyanax[3]—lord of the city; since Hektor alone saved Ilion.
Hektor smiled in silence as he looked on his son, but she,
Andromache, stood close beside him, letting her tears fall,       405
and clung to his hand and called him by name and spoke to him:
        'Dearest,
your own great strength will be your death, and you have no pity
on your little son, nor on me, ill-starred, who soon must be your
        widow;
for presently the Achaians, gathering together,

3.  The name does literally mean "lord of the city." *Skamandrios*: After the Trojan river Skaman-
der.

will set upon you and kill you; and for me it would be far better      410
to sink into the earth when I have lost you, for there is no other
consolation for me after you have gone to your destiny—
only grief; since I have no father, no honoured mother.
It was brilliant Achilleus who slew my father, Eëtion,
when he stormed the strong-founded citadel of the Kilikians,      415
Thebe of the towering gates. He killed Eëtion
but did not strip his armour, for his heart respected the dead man,
but burned the body in all its elaborate war-gear
and piled a grave mound over it, and the nymphs of the mountains,
daughters of Zeus of the aegis, planted elm trees about it.      420
And they who were my seven brothers in the great house all went
upon a single day down into the house of the death god,
for swift-footed brilliant Achilleus slaughtered all of them
as they were tending their white sheep and their lumbering oxen;
and when he had led my mother, who was queen under wooded
     Plakos,      425
here, along with all his other possessions, Achilleus
released her again, accepting ransom beyond count, but Artemis[4]
of the showering arrows struck her down in the halls of her father.
Hektor, thus you are father to me, and my honoured mother,
you are my brother, and you it is who are my young husband.      430
Please take pity upon me then, stay here on the rampart,
that you may not leave your child an orphan, your wife a widow,
but draw your people up by the fig tree, there where the city
is openest to attack, and where the wall may be mounted.
Three times their bravest came that way, and fought there to storm
     it      435
about the two Aiantes and renowned Idomeneus,
about the two Atreidai[5] and the fighting son of Tydeus.
Either some man well skilled in prophetic arts had spoken,
or the very spirit within themselves had stirred them to the onslaught.'
     Then tall Hektor of the shining helm answered her: 'All these      440
things are in my mind also, lady; yet I would feel deep shame
before the Trojans, and the Trojan women with trailing garments,
if like a coward I were to shrink aside from the fighting;
and the spirit will not let me, since I have learned to be valiant
and to fight always among the foremost ranks of the Trojans,      445
winning for my own self great glory, and for my father.
For I know this thing well in my heart, and my mind knows it:
there will come a day when sacred Ilion shall perish,
and Priam, and the people of Priam of the strong ash spear.

---

4. A virgin goddess, dispenser of natural and painless death to women.      5. The sons of Atreus.
*Aiantes:* There were two Greek warriors called Aias (Ajax). *Idomeneus:* A hero from Crete.

But it is not so much the pain to come of the Trojans                    450
that troubles me, not even of Priam the king nor Hekabe,
not the thought of my brothers who in their numbers and valour
shall drop in the dust under the hands of men who hate them,
as troubles me the thought of you, when some bronze-armoured
Achaian leads you off, taking away your day of liberty,                    455
in tears; and in Argos you must work at the loom of another,
and carry water from the spring Messeis or Hypereia,[6]
all unwilling, but strong will be the necessity upon you;
and some day seeing you shedding tears a man will say of you:
"This is the wife of Hektor, who was ever the bravest fighter                    460
of the Trojans, breakers of horses, in the days when they fought
    about Ilion."
so will one speak of you; and for you it will be yet a fresh grief,
to be widowed of such a man who could fight off the day of your
    slavery.
But may I be dead and the piled earth hide me under before I
hear you crying and know by this that they drag you captive.'                    465
    So speaking glorious Hektor held out his arms to his baby,
who shrank back to his fair-girdled nurse's bosom
screaming, and frightened at the aspect of his own father,
terrified as he saw the bronze and the crest with its horse-hair,
nodding dreadfully, as he thought, from the peak of the helmet.                    470
Then his beloved father laughed out, and his honoured mother,
and at once glorious Hektor lifted from his head the helmet
and laid it in all its shining upon the ground. Then taking
up his dear son he tossed him about in his arms, and kissed him,
and lifted his voice in prayer to Zeus and the other immortals:                    475
'Zeus, and you other immortals, grant that this boy, who is my son,
may be as I am, pre-eminent among the Trojans,
great in strength, as am I, and rule strongly over Ilion;
and some day let them say of him: "He is better by far than his
    father,"
as he comes in from the fighting; and let him kill his enemy                    480
and bring home the blooded spoils, and delight the heart of his
    mother.'
    So speaking he set his child again in the arms of his beloved
wife, who took him back again to her fragrant bosom
smiling in her tears; and her husband saw, and took pity upon her,
and stroked her with his hand, and called her by name and spoke to
    her:                    485
'Poor Andromache! Why does your heart sorrow so much for me?
No man is going to hurl me to Hades, unless it is fated,

---

6. One in central, the other in northern, Greece.

but as for fate, I think that no man yet has escaped it
once it has taken its first form, neither brave man nor coward.
Go therefore back to our house, and take up your own work,          490
the loom and the distaff, and see to it that your handmaidens
ply their work also; but the men must see to the fighting,
all men who are the people of Ilion, but I beyond others.'
   So glorious Hektor spoke and again took up the helmet
with its crest of horse-hair, while his beloved wife went home-
     ward,                                                       495
turning to look back on the way, letting the live tears fall.
And as she came in speed into the well-settled household
of Hektor the slayer of men, she found numbers of handmaidens
within, and her coming stirred all of them into lamentation.
So they mourned in his house over Hektor while he was living   500
still, for they thought he would never again come back from the
     fighting
alive, escaping the Achaian hands and their violence.
   But Paris in turn did not linger long in his high house,
but when he had put on his glorious armour with bronze elaborate
he ran in the confidence of his quick feet through the city.      505
As when some stalled horse who has been corn-fed at the manger
breaking free of his rope gallops over the plain in thunder
to his accustomed bathing place in a sweet-running river
and in the pride of his strength holds high his head, and the mane
     floats
over his shoulders; sure of his glorious strength, the quick knees   510
carry him to the loved places and the pasture of horses;
so from uttermost Pergamos[7] came Paris, the son of
Priam, shining in all his armour of war as the sun shines,
laughing aloud, and his quick feet carried him; suddenly thereafter
he came on brilliant Hektor, his brother, where he yet lingered   515
before turning away from the place where he had talked with his
     lady.
It was Alexandros the godlike who first spoke to him:
'Brother, I fear that I have held back your haste, by being
slow on the way, not coming in time, as you commanded me.'
   Then tall Hektor of the shining helm spoke to him in answer:   520
'Strange man! There is no way that one, giving judgment in fairness,
could dishonour your work in battle, since you are a strong man.
But of your own accord you hang back, unwilling. And my heart
is grieved in its thought, when I hear shameful things spoken about
     you
by the Trojans, who undergo hard fighting for your sake.          525

---

7. The citadel of Troy.

Let us go now; some day hereafter we will make all right
with the immortal gods in the sky, if Zeus ever grant it,
setting up to them in our houses the wine-bowl of liberty
after we have driven out of Troy the strong-greaved Achaians.'

[The Trojans rallied successfully and went over to the offensive.
They drove the Greeks back to the light fortifications they had built
around their beached ships. The Trojans lit their watchfires on the
plain, ready to deliver the attack in the morning.]

## Book VIII

### [THE EVE OF BATTLE]

. . . So with hearts made high these sat night-long by the outworks
of battle, and their watchfires blazed numerous about them.
As when in the sky the stars about the moon's shining                    555
are seen in all their glory, when the air has fallen to stillness,
and all the high places of the hills are clear, and the shoulders
  outjutting,
and the deep ravines, as endless bright air spills from the heavens
and all the stars are seen, to make glad the heart of the shepherd;
such in their numbers blazed the watchfires the Trojans were burning                                                          560
between the waters of Xanthos[8] and the ships, before Ilion.
A thousand fires were burning there in the plain, and beside each
one sat fifty men in the flare of the blazing firelight.
And standing each beside his chariot, champing white barley
and oats, the horses waited for the dawn to mount to her high
  place.                                                        565

## Book IX

### [THE EMBASSY TO ACHILLEUS]

So the Trojans held their night watches. Meanwhile immortal
Panic, companion of cold Terror, gripped the Achaians
as all their best were stricken with grief that passes endurance.
As two winds rise to shake the sea where the fish swarm, Boreas
and Zephyros, north wind and west, that blow from Thraceward,[9]  5
suddenly descending, and the darkened water is gathered
to crests, and far across the salt water scatters the seaweed;
so the heart in the breast of each Achaian was troubled.
And the son of Atreus, stricken at heart with the great sorrow,
went among his heralds the clear-spoken and told them              10
to summon calling by name each man into the assembly

8. One of the rivers of the Trojan plain.   9. Thrace was the region northwest of Troy.

but with no outcry, and he himself was at work with the foremost.
They took their seats in assembly, dispirited, and Agamemnon
stood up before them, shedding tears, like a spring dark-running
that down the face of a rock impassable drips its dim water.                 15
So, groaning heavily, Agamemnon spoke to the Argives:
'Friends, who are leaders of the Argives and keep their counsel:
Zeus son of Kronos has caught me badly in bitter futility.
He is hard: who before this time promised me and consented
that I might sack strong-walled Ilion and sail homeward.                     20
Now he has devised a vile deception and bids me go back
to Argos in dishonour having lost many of my people.
Such is the way it will be pleasing to Zeus, who is too strong,
who before now has broken the crests of many cities
and will break them again, since his power is beyond all others.             25
Come then, do as I say, let us all be won over; let us
run away with our ships to the beloved land of our fathers
since no longer now shall we capture Troy of the wide ways.'
    So he spoke, and all of them stayed stricken to silence.
For some time the sons of the Achaians said nothing in sorrow;              30
but at long last Diomedes of the great war cry addressed them:
'Son of Atreus: I will be first to fight with your folly,
as is my right, lord, in this assembly; then do not be angered.
I was the first of the Danaans whose valour you slighted
and said I was unwarlike and without courage.[1] The young men             35
of the Argives know all these things, and the elders know it.
The son of devious-devising Kronos has given you
gifts in two ways: with the sceptre he gave you honour beyond all,
but he did not give you a heart, and of all power this is the greatest.
Sir, sir, can you really believe the sons of the Achaians                   40
are so unwarlike and so weak of their hearts as you call them?
But if in truth your own heart is so set upon going,
go. The way is there, and next to the water are standing
your ships that came—so many of them!—with you from Mykenai,[2]
and yet the rest of the flowing-haired Achaians will stay here             45
until we have sacked the city of Troy; let even these also
run away with their ships to the beloved land of their fathers,
still we two, Sthenelos[3] and I, will fight till we witness
the end of Ilion; for it was with God that we made our way hither.'
    So he spoke, and all the sons of the Achaians shouted                   50
acclaim for the word of Diomedes, breaker of horses.
And now Nestor the horseman stood forth among them and spoke to
        them:
'Son of Tydeus,[4] beyond others you are strong in battle,

---

1. This happened during Agamemnon's review of his forces before the battle.   2. Mycenae, a
city near Argos.   3. The companion of Diomedes.   4. Diomedes.

and in counsel also are noblest among all men of your own age.
Not one man of all the Achaians will belittle your words nor          55
speak against them. Yet you have not made complete your argu-
      ment,
since you are a young man still and could even be my own son
and my youngest born of all; yet still you argue in wisdom
with the Argive kings, since all you have spoken was spoken fairly.
But let me speak, since I can call myself older than you are,          60
and go through the whole matter, since there is none who can dis-
      honour
the thing I say, not even powerful Agamemnon.
Out of all brotherhood, outlawed, homeless shall be that man
who longs for all the horror of fighting among his own people.
But now let us give way to the darkness of night, and let us          65
make ready our evening meal; and let the guards severally
take their stations by the ditch we have dug outside the ramparts.[5]
This I would enjoin upon our young men; but thereafter
do you, son of Atreus, take command, since you are our kingliest.
Divide a feast among the princes; it befits you, it is not            70
unbecoming. Our shelters are filled with wine that the Achaian
ships carry day by day from Thrace across the wide water.
All hospitality is for you; you are lord over many.
When many assemble together follow him who advises
the best counsel, for in truth there is need for all the Achaians     75
of good close counsel, since now close to our ships the enemy
burn their numerous fires. What man could be cheered to see this?
Here is the night that will break our army, or else will preserve it.'

    So he spoke, and they listened hard to him, and obeyed him,
and the sentries went forth rapidly in their armour, gathering        80
about Nestor's son Thrasymedes, shepherd of the people,
and about Askalaphos and Ialmenos, sons both of Ares,[6]
about Meriones and Aphareus and Deïpyros
and about the son of Kreion, Lykomedes the brilliant.
There were seven leaders of the sentinels, and with each one a
      hundred                                                         85
fighting men followed gripping in their hands the long spears.
They took position in the space between the ditch and the rampart,
and there they kindled their fires and each made ready his supper.

    But the son of Atreus led the assembled lords of the Achaians
to his own shelter, and set before them the feast in abundance.       90
They put their hands to the good things that lay ready before them.
But when they had put away their desire for eating and drinking,
the aged man began to weave his counsel before them

5. The Greeks are now besieged beside their ships; Zeus' promise to Thetis is being fulfilled.
6. God of war.

first, Nestor, whose advice had shown best before this.
He in kind intention toward all stood forth and addressed them:    95
'Son of Atreus, most lordly and king of men, Agamemnon,
with you I will end, with you I will make my beginning, since you
are lord over many people, and Zeus has given into your hand
the sceptre and rights of judgment, to be king over the people.
It is yours therefore to speak a word, yours also to listen,         100
and grant the right to another also, when his spirit stirs him
to speak for our good. All shall be yours when you lead the way. Still
I will speak in the way it seems best to my mind, and no one
shall have in his mind any thought that is better than this one
that I have in my mind either now or long before now            105
ever since that day, illustrious, when you went from the shelter of
angered Achilleus, taking by force the girl Briseis
against the will of the rest of us, since I for my part
urged you strongly not to, but you, giving way to your proud heart's
anger, dishonoured a great man, one whom the immortals         110
honour, since you have taken his prize and keep it. But let us
even now think how we can make this good and perusade him
with words of supplication and with the gifts of friendship.'
    Then in turn the lord of men Agamemnon spoke to him:
Aged sir, this was no lie when you spoke of my madness.          115
I was mad, I myself will not deny it. Worth many
fighters is that man whom Zeus in his heart loves, as now
he has honoured this man and beaten down the Achaian people.
But since I was mad, in the persuasion of my heart's evil,
I am willing to make all good, and give back gifts in abundance.   120
Before you all I will count off my gifts in their splendour:
seven unfired tripods; ten talents' weight of gold;[7] twenty
shining cauldrons; and twelve horses, strong, race-competitors
who have won prizes in the speed of their feet. That man would not
      be
poor in possessions, to whom were given all these have won me,    125
nor be unpossessed of dearly honoured gold, were he given
all the prizes these single-foot horses have won for me.
I will give him seven women of Lesbos,[8] the work of whose hands is
blameless, whom when he himself captured strong-founded Lesbos
I chose, and who in their beauty surpassed the races of women.    130
I will give him these, and with them shall go the one I took from
      him,
the daughter of Briseus. And to all this I will swear a great oath
that I never entered into her bed and never lay with her

---

7. An enormous sum; the talent was the largest measure of weight. *Unfired:* Unused, brand new.
*Tripods:* Three-footed kettles; such metal equipment was rare and highly valued.    8. A large
island off the coast of what is now Turkey.

as is natural for human people, between men and women.
All these gifts shall be his at once; but again, if hereafter         135
the gods grant that we storm and sack the great city of Priam,
let him go to his ship and load it deep as he pleases
with gold and bronze, when we Achaians divide the war spoils,
and let him choose for himself twenty of the Trojan women
who are the loveliest of all after Helen of Argos.                    140
And if we come back to Achaian Argos, pride of the tilled land,
he may be my son-in-law; I will honour him with Orestes
my growing son, who is brought up there in abundant luxury.
Since, as I have three daughters there in my strong-built castle,
Chrysothemis and Laodike and Iphianassa,                              145
let him lead away the one of these that he likes, with no bride-price,
to the house of Peleus, and with the girl I will grant him as dowry
many gifts, such as no man ever gave with his daughter.
I will grant to him seven citadels, strongly settled:
Kardamyle, and Enope, and Hire of the grasses,                        150
Pherai the sacrosanct, and Antheia deep in the meadows,
with Aipeia the lovely and Pedasos of the vineyards.
All these lie near the sea, at the bottom of sandy Pylos,
and men live among them rich in cattle and rich in sheepflocks,
who will honour him as if he were a god with gifts given             155
and fulfil his prospering decrees underneath his sceptre.
All this I will bring to pass for him, if he changes from his anger.
Let him give way. For Hades[9] gives not way, and is pitiless,
and therefore he among all the gods is most hateful to mortals.
And let him yield place to me, inasmuch as I am the kinglier          160
and inasmuch as I can call myself born the elder.'
     Thereupon the Gerenian[1] horseman Nestor answered him:
'Son of Atreus, most lordly and king of men, Agamemnon,
none could scorn any longer these gifts you offer to Achilleus
the king. Come, let us choose and send some men, who in all
          speed                                                        165
will go to the shelter of Achilleus, the son of Peleus;
or come, the men on whom my eye falls, let these take the duty.
First of all let Phoinix,[2] beloved of Zeus, be their leader,
and after him take Aias the great, and brilliant Odysseus,
and of the heralds let Odios and Eurybates go with them.             170
Bring also water for their hands, and bid them keep words of good
          omen,
so we may pray to Zeus, son of Kronos, if he will have pity.'
     So he spoke, and the word he spoke was pleasing to all of them.

---

9. The god who rules the underworld.   1. From Gerena, the city in southwestern Greece
where Nestor was brought up.   2. He is especially suited for this embassy since he was tutor to
the young Achilleus.

And the heralds brought water at once, and poured it over
their hands, and the young men filled the mixing-bowl with pure
    wine                                                                            175
and passed it to all, pouring first a libation in goblets.
Then when they had poured out wine, and drunk as much as their
    hearts wished,
they set out from the shelter of Atreus' son, Agamemnon.
And the Gerenian horseman Nestor gave them much instruction,
looking eagerly at each, and most of all at Odysseus,                    180
to try hard, so that they might win over the blameless Peleion.[3]

    So these two walked along the strand of the sea deep-thundering
with many prayers to the holder and shaker of the earth, that they
might readily persuade the great heart of Aiakides.[4]
Now they came beside the shelters and ships of the Myrmidons      185
and they found Achilleus delighting his heart in a lyre, clear-sound-
    ing,
splendid and carefully wrought, with a bridge of silver upon it,
which he won out of the spoils when he ruined Eëtion's city.
With this he was pleasuring his heart, and singing of men's fame,
as Patroklos was sitting over against him, alone, in silence,               190
watching Aiakides and the time he would leave off singing.
Now these two came forward, as brilliant Odysseus led them,
and stood in his presence. Achilleus rose to his feet in amazement
holding the lyre as it was, leaving the place where he was sitting.
In the same way Patroklos, when he saw the men come, stood up.
And in greeting Achilleus the swift of foot spoke to them:              196
'Welcome. You are my friends who have come, and greatly I need
    you,
who even to this my anger are dearest of all the Achaians.'

    So brilliant Achilleus spoke, and guided them forward,
and caused them to sit down on couches with purple coverlets       200
and at once called over to Patrokles who was not far from him:
'Son of Menoitios, set up a mixing-bowl that is bigger,
and mix us stronger drink, and make ready a cup for each man,
since these who have come beneath my roof are the men that I love
    best.'

    So he spoke, and Patroklos obeyed his beloved companion,         205
and tossed down a great chopping-block into the firelight,
and laid upon it the back of a sheep, and one of a fat goat,
with the chine of a fatted pig edged thick with lard, and for him
Automedon[5] held the meats, and brilliant Achilleus carved them,

---

3. Son of Peleus, i.e., Achilleus.    4. Descendant of Aiakos (father of Peleus), i.e., Achilleus.
*Holder and shaker:* Poseidon, who was believed to be responsible for earthquakes.    5. The charioteer of Achilleus.

and cut it well into pieces and spitted them, as meanwhile     210
Menoitios' son, man like a god, made the fire blaze greatly.
But when the fire had burned itself out, and the flames had died
     down,
he scattered the embers apart, and extended the spits across them
lifting them to the andirons, and sprinkled the meats with divine salt.
Then when he had roasted all, and spread the food on the platters,
Patroklos took the bread and set it out on a table     216
in fair baskets, while Achilleus served the meats. Thereafter
he himself sat over against the godlike Odysseus
against the further wall, and told his companion, Patroklos,
to sacrifice to the gods; and he threw the firstlings[6] in the fire.     220
They put their hands to the good things that lay ready before them.
But when they had put aside their desire for eating and drinking,
Aias nodded to Phoinix, and brilliant Odysseus saw it,
and filled a cup with wine, and lifted it to Achilleus:
'Your health, Achilleus. You have no lack of your equal portion  225
either within the shelter of Atreus' son, Agamemnon,
nor here now in your own. We have good things in abundance
to feast on; here it is not the desirable feast we think of,
but a trouble all too great, beloved of Zeus, that we look on
and are afraid. There is doubt if we save our strong-benched ves-
     sels     230
or if they will be destroyed, unless you put on your war strength.
The Trojans in their pride, with their far-renowned companions,
have set up an encampment close by the ships and the rampart,
and lit many fires along their army, and think no longer
of being held, but rather to drive in upon the black ships.     235
And Zeus, son of Kronos, lightens upon their right hand, showing
     them
portents of good, while Hektor in the huge pride of his strength rages
irresistibly, reliant on Zeus, and gives way to no one
neither god nor man, but the strong fury has descended upon him.
He prays now that the divine Dawn will show most quickly,     240
since he threatens to shear the uttermost horns from the ship-sterns,
to light the ships themselves with ravening fire, and to cut down
the Achaians themselves as they stir from the smoke beside them.
All this I fear terribly in my heart, lest immortals
accomplish all these threats, and lest for us it be destiny     245
to die here in Troy, far away from horse-pasturing Argos.
Up, then! if you are minded, late though it be, to rescue
the afflicted sons of the Achaians from the Trojan onslaught.
It will be an affliction to you hereafter, there will be no remedy

6. The portion of the meat reserved for the gods.

found to heal the evil thing when it has been done. No, before-
      hand                                                                          250
take thought to beat the evil day aside from the Danaans.
Dear friend, surely thus your father Peleus advised you
that day when he sent you away to Agamemnon from Phthia:
"My child, for the matter of strength, Athene and Hera will give it
if it be their will, but be it yours to hold fast in your bosom          255
the anger of the proud heart, for consideration is better.
Keep from the bad complication of quarrel, and all the more for this
the Argives will honour you, both their younger men and their eld-
      ers." '
So the old man advised, but you have forgotten. Yet even now
stop, and give way from the anger that hurts the heart. Agamem-
      non                                                                            260
offers you worthy recompense if you change from your anger.
Come then, if you will, listen to me, while I count off for you
all the gifts in his shelter that Agamemnon has promised:
Seven unfired tripods; ten talents' weight of gold; twenty
shining cauldrons; and twelve horses, strong, race-competitors      265
who have won prize in the speed of their feet. That man would not
      be
poor in possessions, to whom were given all these have won him,
nor be unpossessed of dearly honoured gold, were he given
all the prizes Agamemnon's horses won in their speed for him.
He will give you seven women of Lesbos, the work of whose hands
is blameless, whom when you yourself captured strong-founded
      Lesbos                                                                         271
he chose, and who in their beauty surpassed the races of women.
He will give you these, and with them shall go the one he took from
      you,
the daughter of Briseus. And to all this he will swear a great oath
that he never entered into her bed and never lay with her              275
as is natural for human people, between men and women.
All these gifts shall be yours at once; but again, if hereafter
the gods grant that we storm and sack the great city of Priam,
you may go to your ship and load it deep as you please with
gold and bronze, when we Achaians divide the war spoils,            280
and you may choose for yourself twenty of the Trojan women,
who are the loveliest of all after Helen of Argos.
And if we come back to Achaian Argos, pride of the tilled land,
you could be his son-in-law; he would honour you with Orestes,
his growing son, who is brought up there in abundant luxury.      285
Since, as he has three daughters there in his strong-built castle,
Chrysothemis and Laodike and Iphianassa,

you may lead away the one of these that you like, with no bride-
     price,
to the house of Peleus; and with the girl he will grant you as dowry
many gifts, such as no man ever gave with his daughter.            290
He will grant you seven citadels, strongly settled:
Kardamyle and Enope and Hire of the grasses,
Pherai the sacrosanct, and Antheia deep in the meadows,
with Aipeia the lovely, and Pedasos of the vineyards.
All these lie near the sea, at the bottom of sandy Pylos,           295
and men live among them rich in cattle and rich in sheepflocks,
who will honour you as if you were a god with gifts given
and fulfil your prospering decrees underneath your sceptre.
All this he will bring to pass for you, if you change from your anger.
But if the son of Atreus is too much hated in your heart,           300
himself and his gifts, at least take pity on all the other
Achaians, who are afflicted along the host, and will honour you
as a god. You may win very great glory among them.
For now you might kill Hektor, since he would come very close to
     you
with the wicked fury upon him, since he thinks there is not his equal
among the rest of the Danaans the ships carried hither.'           306
     Then in answer to him spoke Achilleus of the swift feet:
'Son of Laertes and seed of Zeus, resourceful Odysseus:
without consideration for you I must make my answer,
the way I think, and the way it will be accomplished, that you may
     not                                                           310
come one after another, and sit by me, and speak softly.
For as I detest the doorways of Death, I detest that man, who
hides one thing in the depths of his heart, and speaks forth another.
But I will speak to you the way it seems best to me: neither
do I think the son of Atreus, Agamemnon, will persuade me,         315
nor the rest of the Danaans, since there was no gratitude given
for fighting incessantly forever against your enemies.
Fate is the same for the man who holds back, the same if he fights
     hard.
We are all held in a single honour, the brave with the weaklings.
A man dies still if he has done nothing, as one who has done much.
Nothing is won for me, now that my heart has gone through its
     afflictions                                                   321
in forever setting my life on the hazard of battle.
For as to her unwinged young ones the mother bird brings back
morsels, wherever she can find them, but as for herself it is suffering,
such was I, as I lay through all the many nights unsleeping,       325
such as I wore through the bloody days of the fighting,

striving with warriors for the sake of these men's women.
But I say that I have stormed from my ships twelve cities
of men, and by land eleven more through the generous Troad.
From all these we took forth treasures, goodly and numerous,          330
and we would bring them back, and give them to Agamemnon,
Atreus' son; while he, waiting back beside the swift ships,
would take them, and distribute them little by little, and keep many.
All the other prizes of honour he gave the great men and the princes
are held fast by them, but from me alone of all the Achaians          335
he has taken and keeps the bride of my heart. Let him lie beside her
and be happy. Yet why must the Argives fight with the Trojans?
And why was it the son of Atreus assembled and led here
these people? Was it not for the sake of lovely-haired Helen?
Are the sons of Atreus alone among mortal men the ones          340
who love their wives? Since any who is a good man, and careful,
loves her who is his own and cares for her, even as I now
loved this one from my heart, though it was my spear that won her.
Now that he has deceived me and taken from my hands my prize of
     honour,          344
let him try me no more. I know him well. He will not persuade me.
Let him take counsel with you, Odysseus, and the rest of the princes
how to fight the ravening fire away from his vessels.
Indeed, there has been much hard work done even without me;
he has built himself a wall and driven a ditch about it,
making it great and wide, and fixed the sharp stakes inside it.          350
Yet even so he cannot hold the strength of manslaughtering
Hektor; and yet when I was fighting among the Achaians
Hektor would not drive his attack beyond the wall's shelter
but would come forth only so far as the Skaian gates and the oak
     tree.
There once he endured me alone, and barely escaped my onslaught.
But, now I am unwilling to fight against brilliant Hektor,          356
tomorrow, when I have sacrificed to Zeus and to all gods,
and loaded well my ships, and rowed out on to the salt water,
you will see, if you have a mind to it and if it concerns you,
my ships in the dawn at sea on the Hellespont where the fish swarm
and my men manning them with good will to row. If the glorious 361
shaker of the earth should grant us a favouring passage
on the third day thereafter we might raise generous Phthia.
I have many possessions there that I left behind when I came here
on this desperate venture, and from here there is more gold, and red
     bronze,          365
and fair-girdled women, and grey iron I will take back;
all that was allotted to me. But my prize: he who gave it,
powerful Agamemnon, son of Atreus, has taken it back again

outrageously. Go back and proclaim to him all that I tell you,
openly, so other Achaians may turn against him in anger                    370
if he hopes yet one more time to swindle some other Danaan,
wrapped as he is forever in shamelessness; yet he would not,
bold as a dog though he be, dare look in my face any longer.
I will join with him in no counsel, and in no action.
He cheated me and he did me hurt. Let him not beguile me                   375
with words again. This is enough for him. Let him of his own will
be damned, since Zeus of the counsels has taken his wits away from
         him.
I hate his gifts. I hold him light as the strip of a splinter.
Not if he gave me ten times as much, and twenty times over
as he possesses now, not if more should come to him from else-
         where,                                                            380
or give all that is brought in to Orchomenos,[7] all that is brought in
to Thebes of Egypt, where the greatest possessions lie up in the houses,
Thebes of the hundred gates, where through each of the gates two
         hundred
fighting men come forth to war with horses and chariots;
not if he gave me gifts as many as the sand or the dust is,                385
not even so would Agamemnon have his way with my spirit
until he had made good to me all this heartrending insolence.
Nor will I marry a daughter of Atreus' son, Agamemnon,
not if she challenged Aphrodite the golden for loveliness,
not if she matched the work of her hands with grey-eyed Athene;            390
not even so will I marry her; let him pick some other Achaian,
one who is to his liking and is kinglier than I am.
For if the gods will keep me alive and I win homeward,
Peleus himself will presently arrange a wife for me.
There are many Achaian girls in the land of Hellas and Phthia,             395
daughters of great men who hold strong places in guard. And of these
any one that I please I might make my beloved lady.
And the great desire in my heart drives me rather in that place
to take a wedded wife in marriage, the bride of my fancy,
to enjoy with her the possessions won by aged Peleus. For not             400
worth the value of my life are all the possessions they fable
were won for Ilion, that strong-founded citadel, in the old days
when there was peace, before the coming of the sons of the Achai-
         ans;
not all that the stone doorsill of the Archer holds fast within it,
of Phoibos Apollo in Pytho[8] of the rocks. Of possessions                405
cattle and fat sheep are things to be had for the lifting,

---

7. Great city north of Athens.     8. Apollo's shrine at Delphi. The treasures consisted of offerings made to the god by grateful worshipers.

and tripods can be won, and the tawny high heads of horses,
but a man's life cannot come back again, it cannot be lifted
nor captured again by force, once it has crossed the teeth's barrier.
For my mother Thetis the goddess of the silver feet tells me          410
I carry two sorts of destiny toward the day of my death. Either,
if I stay here and fight beside the city of the Trojans,
my return home is gone, but my glory shall be everlasting;
but if I return home to the beloved land of my fathers,
the excellence of my glory is gone, but there will be a long life     415
left for me, and my end in death will not come to me quickly.
And this would be my counsel to others also, to sail back
home again, since no longer shall you find any term set
on the sheer city of Ilion, since Zeus of the wide brows has strongly
held his own hand over it, and its people are made bold.              420
     Do you go back therefore to the great men of the Achaians,
and take them this message, since such is the privilege of the princes:
that they think out in their minds some other scheme that is better,
which might rescue their ships, and the people of the Achaians
who man the hollow ships, since this plan will not work for them 425
which they thought of by reason of my anger. Let Phoinix
remain here with us and sleep here, so that tomorrow
he may come with us in our ships to the beloved land of our fathers,
if he will; but I will never use force to hold him.'
     So he spoke, and all of them stayed stricken to silence          430
in amazement at his words. He had spoken to them very strongly.
But at long last Phoinix the aged horseman spoke out
in a stormburst of tears, and fearing for the ships of the Achaians:
'If it is going home, glorious Achilleus, you ponder
in your heart, and are utterly unwilling to drive the obliterating   435
fire from the fast ships, since anger has descended on your spirit,
how then shall I, dear child, be left in this place behind you
all alone? Peleus the aged horseman sent me forth with you
on that day when he sent you from Phthia to Agamemnon
a mere child, who knew nothing yet of the joining of battle          440
nor of debate where men are made pre-eminent. Therefore
he sent me along with you to teach you of all these matters,
to make you a speaker of words and one who accomplished in action.
Therefore apart from you, dear child, I would not be willing
to be left behind, not were the god in person to promise            445
he would scale away my old age and make me a young man blossom-
          ing
as I was that time when I first left Hellas, the land of fair women,
running from the hatred of Ormenos' son Amyntor,
my father; who hated me for the sake of a fair-haired mistress.
For he made love to her himself, and dishonoured his own wife, 450

my mother; who was forever taking my knees and entreating me
to lie with this mistress instead so that she would hate the old man.
I was persuaded and did it; and my father when he heard of it
    straightway
called down his curses, and invoked against me the dreaded furies[9]
that I might never have any son born of my seed to dandle    455
on my knees; and the divinities, Zeus of the underworld[1]
and Persephone the honoured goddess, accomplished his curses.
Then I took it into my mind to cut him down with the sharp bronze,
but some one of the immortals checked my anger, reminding me
of rumour among the people and men's maledictions repeated,    460
that I might not be called a parricide among the Achaians.
But now no more could the heart in my breast be ruled entirely
to range still among these halls when my father was angered.
Rather it was the many kinsmen and cousins about me
who held me closed in the house, with supplications repeated,    465
and slaughtered fat sheep in their numbers, and shambling horn-
    curved
cattle, and numerous swine with the fat abundant upon them
were singed and stretched out across the flame of Hephaistos,
and much wine was drunk that was stored in the jars of the old man.
Nine nights they slept nightlong in their places beside me,    470
and they kept up an interchange of watches, and the fire was never
put out; one below the gate of the strong-closed courtyard,
and one in the ante-chamber before the doors of the bedroom.
But when the tenth night had come to me in its darkness,
then I broke the close-compacted doors of the chamber    475
and got away, and overleapt the fence of the courtyard
lightly, unnoticed by the guarding men and the women servants.
Then I fled far away through the wide spaces of Hellas
and came as far as generous Phthia, mother of sheepflocks,
and to lord Peleus, who accepted me with a good will    480
and gave me his love, even as a father loves his own son
who is a single child brought up among many possessions.
He made me a rich man, and granted me many people,
and I lived, lord over the Dolopes, in remotest Phthia,
and, godlike Achilleus, I made you all that you are now,    485
and loved you out of my heart, for you would not go with another
out to any feast, nor taste any food in your own halls
until I had set you on my knees, and cut little pieces
from the meat, and given you all you wished, and held the wine for
    you.
And many times you soaked the shirt that was on my body    490

9. A avenging spirits, particularly concerned with crimes committed by kinsmen against
kinsmen.   1. The god Hades. *Persephone:* Wife of Hades.

with wine you would spit up in the troublesomeness of your childhood.
So I have suffered much through you, and have had much trouble,
thinking always how the gods would not bring to birth any children
of my own; so that it was you, godlike Achilleus, I made
my own child, so that some day you might keep hard affliction from
 me.                                                               495
Then, Achilleus, beat down your great anger. It is not
yours to have a pitiless heart. The very immortals
can be moved; their virtue and honour and strength are greater than
 ours are,
and yet with sacrifices and offerings for endearment,
with libations and with savour men turn back even the immortals
in supplication, when any man does wrong and transgresses.        501
For there are also the spirits of Prayer, the daughters of great Zeus,
and they are lame of their feet, and wrinkled, and cast their eyes
 sidelong,
who toil on their way left far behind by the spirit of Ruin:
but she, Ruin, is strong and sound on her feet, and therefore      505
far outruns all Prayers, and wins into every country
to force men astray; and the Prayers follow as healers after her.
If a man venerates these daughters of Zeus as they draw near,
such a man they bring great advantage, and hear his entreaty;
but if a man shall deny them, and stubbornly with a harsh word     510
refuse, they go to Zeus, son of Kronos, in supplication
that Ruin may overtake this man, that he be hurt, and punished.
So, Achilleus: grant, you also, that Zeus' daughters be given
their honour, which, lordly though they be, curbs the will of others.
Since, were he not bringing gifts and naming still more hereafter, 515
Atreus' son; were he to remain still swollen with rancour,
even I would not bid you throw your anger aside, nor
defend the Argives, though they needed you sorely. But see now,
he offers you much straightway, and has promised you more hereafter;
he has sent the best men to you to supplicate you, choosing them  520
out of the Achaian host, those who to yourself are the dearest
of all the Argives. Do not you make vain their argument
nor their footsteps, though before this one could not blame your
 anger.
Thus it was in the old days also, the deeds that we hear of         524
from the great men, when the swelling anger descended upon them.
The heroes would take gifts; they would listen, and be persuaded.
For I remember this action of old, it is not a new thing,
and how it went; you are all my friends, I will tell it among you.
   The Kouretes and the steadfast Aitolians were fighting

and slaughtering one another about the city of Kalydon,[2]                    530
the Aitolians in lovely Kalydon's defence, the Kouretes
furious to storm and sack it in war. For Artemis,
she of the golden chair, had driven this evil upon them,
angered that Oineus[3] had not given the pride of the orchards
to her, first fruits; the rest of the gods were given due sacrifice,                    535
but alone to this daughter of great Zeus he had given nothing.
He had forgotten, or had not thought, in his hard delusion,
and in wrath at his whole mighty line the Lady of Arrows
sent upon them the fierce wild boar with the shining teeth, who
after the way of his kind did much evil to the orchards of Oineus. 540
For he ripped up whole tall trees from the ground and scattered them
        headlong
roots and all, even to the very flowers of the orchard.
The son of Oineus killed this boar, Meleagros, assembling
together many hunting men out of numerous cities
with their hounds; since the boar might not have been killed by a
        few men,                    545
so huge was he, and had put many men on the sad fire for burning.
But the goddess again made a great stir of anger and crying
battle, over the head of the boar and the bristling boar's hide,
between Kouretes and the high-hearted Aitolians. So long
as Meleagros lover of battle stayed in the fighting                    550
it went the worse for the Kouretes, and they could not even
hold their ground outside the wall, though they were so many.
But when the anger came upon Meleagros, such anger
as wells in the hearts of others also, though their minds are careful,
he, in the wrath of his heart against his own mother, Althaia,                    555
lay apart with his wedded bride, Kleopatra the lovely,
daughter of sweet-stepping Marpessa,[4] child of Euenos,
and Idas, who was the strongest of all men upon earth
in his time; for he even took up the bow to face the King's onset,
Phoibos Apollo, for the sake of the sweet-stepping maiden;                    560
a girl her father and honoured mother had named in their palace
Alkyone, sea-bird, as a by-name, since for her sake
her mother with the sorrow-laden cry of a sea-bird
wept because far-reaching Phoibos Apollo had taken her;[5]
with this Kleopatra he lay mulling his heart-sore anger,                    565

2. A city in northwest Greece. The Kouretes and Aitolians were the local tribes, once allied, now
at odds.    3. King of Kalydon.    4. The story to which Homer alludes runs as follows: Idas,
the famous archer, carried off and married Marpessa, daughter of Euenos. Apollo also had been
her suitor, and he overtook Idas and carried off Marpessa. Idas defied Apollo to combat, but Zeus
decided that the choice was up to Marpessa, who preferred Idas. They gave their daughter Kleopatra the nickname Alkyone (compare "halcyon"), the name of a sea-bird that is supposed to
mourn for its mate, to commemorate the time when Marpessa, carried off by Apollo, mourned
for Idas.    5. Marpessa.

raging by reason of his mother's curses, which she called down
from the gods upon him, in deep grief for the death of her brother,[6]
and many times beating with her hands on the earth abundant
she called on Hades and on honoured Persephone, lying
at length along the ground, and the tears were wet on her bosom, 570
to give death to her son; and Erinys,[7] the mist-walking,
she of the heart without pity, heard her out of the dark places.
Presently there was thunder about the gates, and the sound rose
of towers under assault, and the Aitolian elders
supplicated him, sending their noblest priests of the immortals,      575
to come forth and defend them; they offered him a great gift:
wherever might lie the richest ground in lovely Kalydon,
there they told him to choose out a piece of land, an entirely
good one, of fifty acres, the half of it to be vineyard
and the half of it unworked ploughland of the plain to be fur-
     rowed.                                                           580
And the aged horseman Oineus again and again entreated him,
and took his place at the threshold of the high-vaulted chamber
and shook against the bolted doors, pleading with his own son.
And again and again his honoured mother and his sisters
entreated him, but he only refused the more; then his own friends
who were the most honoured and dearest of all entreated him;        580
but even so they could not persuade the heart within him
until, as the chamber was under close assault, the Kouretes
were mounting along the towers and set fire to the great city.
And then at last his wife, the fair-girdled bride, supplicated       590
Meleagros, in tears, and rehearsed in their numbers before him
all the sorrows that come to men when their city is taken:
they kill the men, and the fire leaves the city in ashes,
and strangers lead the children away and the deep-girdled women.
And the heart, as he listened to all this evil, was stirred within
     him                                                             595
and he rose, and went, and closed his body in shining armour.
So he gave way in his own heart, and drove back the day of evil
from the Aitolians; yet these no longer would make good
their many and gracious gifts; yet he drove back the evil from them.
     Listen, then; do not have such a thought in your mind; let not 600
the spirit within you turn you that way, dear friend. It would be
     worse
to defend the ships after they are burning. No, with gifts promised
go forth. The Achaians will honour you as they would an immortal.
But if without gifts you go into the fighting where men perish,

6. In the course of the battles Meleagros had killed one of his mother's brothers.    7. The
personified spirit of vengeance, a Fury (compare "furies," Book IX, 1. 454).

your honour will no longer be as great, though you drive back the
    battle.'                                                         605
    Then in answer to him spoke Achilleus of the swift feet:
'Phoinix my father, aged, illustrious, such honour is a thing
I need not. I think I am honoured already in Zeus' ordinance
which will hold me here beside my curved ships as long as life's wind
stays in my breast, as long as my knees have their spring beneath
    me.                                                              610
And put away in your thoughts this other thing I tell you.
Stop confusing my heart with lamentation and sorrow
for the favour of great Atreides. It does not become you
to love this man, for fear you turn hateful to me, who love you.
It should be your pride with me to hurt whoever shall hurt me.   615
Be king equally with me; take half of my honour.
There men will carry back the message; you stay here and sleep here
in a soft bed, and we shall decide tomorrow, as dawn shows,
whether to go back home again or else to remain here.'
    He spoke, and, saying nothing, nodded with his brows to Patroklos
to make up a neat bed for Phoinix, so the others might presently
think of going home from his shelter. The son of Telamon,
Aias the godlike, saw it, and now spoke his word among them:
'Son of Laertes and seed of Zeus, resourceful Odysseus:
let us go. I think that nothing will be accomplished             625
by argument on this errand; it is best to go back quickly
and tell this story, though it is not good, to the Danaans
who sit there waiting for us to come back, seeing that Achilleus
has made savage the proud-hearted spirit within his body.
He is hard, and does not remember that friends' affection        630
wherein we honoured him by the ships, far beyond all others.
Pitiless. And yet a man takes from his brother's slayer
the blood price, or the price for a child who was killed, and the guilty
one, when he has largely repaid, stays still in the country,
and the injured man's heart is curbed, and his pride, and his
    anger                                                           635
when he has taken the price; but the gods put in your breast a spirit
not to be placated, bad, for the sake of one single
girl. Yet now we offer you seven, surpassingly lovely,
and much beside these. Now make gracious the spirit within you.
Respect your own house; see, we are under the same roof with
    you,                                                            640
from the multitude of the Danaans, we who desire beyond all
others to have your honour and love, out of all the Achaians.'
    Then in answer to him spoke Achilleus of the swift feet:
'Son of Telamon, seed of Zeus, Aias, lord of the people:

all that you have said seems spoken after my own mind.        645
Yet still the heart in me swells up in anger, when I remember
the disgrace that he wrought upon me before the Argives,
the son of Atreus, as if I were some dishonoured vagabond.
Do you then go back to him, and take him this message:
that I shall not think again of the bloody fighting        650
until such time as the son of wise Priam, Hektor the brilliant,
comes all the way to the ships of the Myrmidons, and their shelters,
slaughtering the Argives, and shall darken with fire our vessels.
But around my own shelter, I think, and beside my black ship
Hektor will be held, though he be very hungry for battle.'        655
    He spoke, and they taking each a two-handled cup poured out
a libation, then went back to their ships, and Odysseus led them.
Now Patroklos gave the maids and his followers orders
to make up without delay a neat bed for Phoinix.
And these obeyed him and made up the bed as he had commanded,
laying fleeces on it, and a blanket, and a sheet of fine linen.        661
There the old man lay down and waited for the divine Dawn.
But Achilleus slept in the inward corner of the strong-built shelter,
and a woman lay beside him, one he had taken from Lesbos,
Phorbas' daughter, Diomede of the fair colouring.        665
In the other corner Patroklos went to bed; with him also
was a girl, Iphis the fair-girdled, whom brilliant Achilleus
gave him, when he took sheer Skyros, Enyeus' citadel.
    Now when these had come back to the shelters of Agamemnon,
the sons of the Achaians greeted them with their gold cups        670
uplifted, one after another, standing, and asked them questions.
And the first to question them was the lord of men, Agamemnon:
'Tell me, honoured Odysseus, great glory of the Achaians:
is he willing to fight the ravening fire away from our vessels,
or did he refuse, and does the anger still hold his proud heart?'        675
    Then long-suffering great Odysseus spoke to him in answer:
'Son of Atreus, most lordly, king of men, Agamemnon.
That man will not quench his anger, but still more than ever
is filled with rage. He refuses you and refuses your presents.
He tells you yourself to take counsel among the Argives        680
how to save your ships, and the people of the Achaians.
And he himself has threatened that tomorrow as dawn shows
he will drag down his strong-benched, oarswept ships to the water.
He said it would be his counsel to others also, to sail back
home again, since no longer will you find any term set        685
on the sheer city of Ilion, since Zeus of the wide brows has strongly
held his own hand over it, and its people are made bold.
So he spoke. There are these to attest it who went there with me
also, Aias, and the two heralds, both men of good counsel.

But aged Phoinix stayed there for the night, as Achilleus urged
    him,                                                                                  690
so he might go home in the ships to the beloved land of his fathers
if Phoinix will; but he will never use force to persuade him.'
    So he spoke, and all of them stayed stricken to silence
in amazement at his words. He had spoken to them very strongly.
For a long time the sons of the Achaians said nothing, in sorrow, 695
but at long last Diomedes of the great war cry spoke to them:
'Son of Atreus, most lordly and king of men, Agamemnon,
I wish you had not supplicated the blameless son of Peleus
with innumerable gifts offered. He is a proud man without this,
and now you have driven him far deeper into his pride. Rather    700
we shall pay him no more attention, whether he comes in with us
or stays away. He will fight again, whenever the time comes
that the heart in his body urges him to, and the god drives him.
Come then, do as I say, and let us all be won over.
Go to sleep, now that the inward heart is made happy              705
with food and drink, for these are the strength and courage within
    us.
But when the lovely dawn shows forth with rose fingers, Atreides,
rapidly form before our ships both people and horses
stirring them on, and yourself be ready to fight in the foremost.'
    So he spoke, and all the kings gave him their approval,           710
acclaiming the word of Diomedes, breaker of horses.
Then they poured a libation, and each man went to his shelter,
where they went to their beds and took the blessing of slumber.

[After Achilleus' refusal, the situation of the Greeks worsened rapidly. Agamemnon, Diomedes, and Odysseus were all wounded. The
Trojans breached the stockade and fought beside the ships. Patroklos
tried to bring Achilleus to the aid of the Greeks, but the most he
could obtain was permission for himself to fight, clad in Achilleus'
armor, at the head of the Myrmidons. He turned the tide of battle
and drove the Trojans back to their walls, only to fall himself through
the direct intervention of Apollo. Hektor stripped Achilleus' armor
from the body. A fierce fight for the body itself ended in partial
success for the Greeks; they took Patroklos' body but had to retreat to
their camp, with the Trojans at their heels.]

## Book XVIII

### [THE ARMING OF ACHILLEUS]

So these fought on in the likeness of blazing fire. Meanwhile,
Antilochos[8] came, a swift-footed messenger, to Achilleus,

8. A son of Nestor.

and found him sitting in front of the steep-horned ships, thinking
over in his heart of things which had now been accomplished.
Disturbed, Achilleus spoke to the spirit in his own great heart:        5
'Ah me, how is it that once again the flowing-haired Achaians
are driven out of the plain on their ships in fear and confusion?
May the gods not accomplish vile sorrows upon the heart in me
in the way my mother once made it clear to me, when she told me
how while I yet lived the bravest of all the Myrmidons        10
must leave the light of the sun beneath the hands of the Trojans.
Surely, then, the strong son of Menoitios[9] has perished.
Unhappy! and yet I told him, once he had beaten the fierce fire
off, to come back to the ships, not fight in strength against Hektor.'
    Now as he was pondering this in his heart and his spirit,        15
meanwhile the son of stately Nestor was drawing near him
and wept warm tears, and gave Achilleus his sorrowful message:
'Ah me, son of valiant Peleus; you must hear from me
the ghastly message of a thing I wish never had happened.
Patroklos has fallen, and now they are fighting over his body        20
which is naked. Hektor of the shining helm has taken his armour.'
    He spoke, and the black cloud of sorrow closed on Achilleus.
In both hands he caught up the grimy dust, and poured it
over his head and face, and fouled his handsome countenance,
and the black ashes were scattered over his immortal tunic.        25
And he himself, mightily in his might, in the dust lay
at length, and took and tore at his hair with his hands, and defiled
    it.
And the handmaidens Achilleus and Patroklos had taken
captive, stricken at heart cried out aloud, and came running
out of doors about valiant Achilleus, and all of them        30
beat their breasts with their hands, and the limbs went slack in each
    of them.
On the other side Antilochos mourned with him, letting the tears
    fall,
and held the hands of Achilleus as he grieved in his proud heart,
fearing Achilleus might cut his throat with the iron. He cried out
terribly, aloud, and the lady his mother heard him        35
as she sat in the depths of the sea at the side of her aged father,
and she cried shrill in turn, and the goddesses gathered about her,
all who along the depth of the sea were daughters of Nereus.
For Glauke was there, Kymodoke and Thaleia,
Nesaie and Speio and Thoë, and ox-eyed Halia;        40
Kymothoë was there, Aktaia and Limnoreia,
Melite and Iaira, Amphithoë and Agauë,

9. Patroklos.

Doto and Proto, Dynamene and Pherousa,
Dexamene and Amphinome and Kallianeira;
Doris and Panope and glorious Galateia, 45
Nemertes and Apseudes and Kallianassa;
Klymene was there, Ianeira and Ianassa,
Maira and Oreithyia and lovely-haired Amatheia,
and the rest who along the depth of the sea were daughters of Ner-
    eus.
The silvery cave was filled with these, and together all of them 50
beat their breasts, and among them Thetis led out the threnody:
'Hear me, Nereids, my sisters; so you may all know
well all the sorrows that are in my heart, when you hear of them
    from me.
Ah me, my sorrow, the bitterness in this best of child-bearing,
since I gave birth to a son who was without fault and powerful, 55
conspicuous among heroes; and he shot up like a young tree,
and I nurtured him, like a tree grown in the pride of the orchard.
I sent him away with the curved ships into the land of Ilion
to fight with the Trojans; but I shall never again receive him
won home again to his country and into the house of Peleus. 60
Yet while I see him live and he looks on the sunlight, he has
sorrows, and though I go to him I can do nothing to help him.
Yet I shall go, to look on my dear son, and to listen
to the sorrow that has come to him as he stays back from the fight-
    ing.'
    So she spoke, and left the cave, and the others together 65
went with her in tears, and about them the wave of the water
was broken. Now these, when they came to the generous Troad,
followed each other out on the sea-shore, where close together
the ships of the Myrmidons were hauled up about swift Achilleus.
There as he sighed heavily the lady his mother stood by him 70
and cried out shrill and aloud, and took her son's head in her arms,
    then
sorrowing for him she spoke to him in winged words: 'Why then,
child, do you lament? What sorrow has come to your heart now?
Speak out, do not hide it. These things are brought to accomplish-
    ment
through Zeus: in the way that you lifted your hands and prayed
    for, 75
that all the sons of the Achaians be pinned on their grounded vessels
by reason of your loss, and suffer things that are shameful.'
    Then sighing heavily Achilleus of the swift feet answered her:
'My mother, all these things the Olympian[1] brought to accomplish-
    ment.

1. Zeus.

But what pleasure is this to me, since my dear companion has
    perished,                                                                    80
Patroklos, whom I loved beyond all other companions,
as well as my own life. I have lost him, and Hektor, who killed him,
has stripped away that gigantic armour, a wonder to look on
and splendid, which the gods gave Peleus, a glorious present,
on that day they drove you to the marriage bed of a mortal.         85
I wish you had gone on living then with the other goddesses
of the sea, and that Peleus had married some mortal woman.
As it is, there must be on your heart a numberless sorrow
for your son's death, since you can never again receive him
won home again to his country; since the spirit within does not drive
    me                                                                         90
to go on living and be among men, except on condition
that Hektor first be beaten down under my spear, lose his life
and pay the price for stripping Patroklos, the son of Menoitios.'
    Then in turn Thetis spoke to him, letting the tears fall:
'Then I must lose you soon, my child, by what you are saying,     95
since it is decreed your death must come soon after Hektor's.'
    Then deeply disturbed Achilleus of the swift feet answered her:
'I must die soon, then; since I was not to stand by my companion
when he was killed. And now, far away from the land of his fathers,
he has perished, and lacked my fighting strength to defend him.  100
Now, since I am not going back to the beloved land of my fathers,
since I was no light of safety to Patroklos, nor to my other
companions, who in their numbers went down before glorious Hek-
    tor,
but sit here beside my ships, a useless weight on the good land,
I, who am such as no other of the bronze-armoured Achaians     105
in battle, though there are others also better in council—
why, I wish that strife would vanish away from among gods and
    mortals,
and gall, which makes a man grow angry for all his great mind,
that gall of anger that swarms like smoke inside of a man's heart
and becomes a thing sweeter to him by far than the dripping of
    honey.                                                                     110
So it was here that the lord of men Agamemnon angered me.
Still, we will let all this be a thing of the past, and for all our
sorrow beat down by force the anger deeply within us.
Now I shall go, to overtake that killer of a dear life,
Hektor; then I will accept my own death, at whatever            115
time Zeus wishes to bring it about, and the other immortals.
For not even the strength of Herakles[2] fled away from destruction,

2. Or Hercules, son of Zeus by a mortal woman; pursued by the jealousy of Hera, he was forced
to undertake twelve great labors and finally died in agony from the effects of a poisoned garment.

although he was dearest of all to lord Zeus, son of Kronos,
but his fate beat him under, and the wearisome anger of Hera.
So I likewise, if such is the fate which has been wrought for me,    120
shall lie still, when I am dead. Now I must win excellent glory,
and drive some one of the women of Troy, or some deep-girdled
Dardanian[3] woman, lifting up to her soft cheeks both hands
to wipe away the close bursts of tears in her lamentation,
and learn that I stayed too long out of the fighting. Do not         125
hold me back from the fight, though you love me. You will not
        persuade me.'
    In turn the goddess Thetis of the silver feet answered him:
'Yes, it is true, my child, this is no cowardly action,
to beat aside sudden death from your afflicted companions.
Yet, see now, your splendid armour, glaring and brazen,              130
is held among the Trojans, and Hektor of the shining helmet
wears it on his own shoulders, and glories in it. Yet I think
he will not glory for long, since his death stands very close to him.
Therefore do not yet go into the grind of the war god,
not before with your own eyes you see me come back to you.           135
For I am coming to you at dawn and as the sun rises
bringing splendid armour to you from the lord Hephaistos.'
    So she spoke, and turned, and went away from her son,
and turning now to her sisters of the sea she spoke to them:
'Do you now go back into the wide fold of the water                  140
to visit the ancient of the sea and the house of our father,
and tell him everything. I am going to tall Olympos
and to Hephaistos, the glorious smith, if he might be willing
to give me for my son renowned and radiant armour.'
    She spoke, and they plunged back beneath the wave of the water,
while she the goddess Thetis of the silver feet went onward          146
to Olympos, to bring back to her son the glorious armour.
    So her feet carried her to Olympos; meanwhile the Achaians
with inhuman clamour before the attack of manslaughtering Hektor
fled until they were making for their own ships and the Hellespont;
nor could the strong-greaved Achaians have dragged the body          151
of Patroklos, henchman of Achilleus, from under the missiles,
for once again the men and the horses came over upon him,
and Hektor, Priam's son, who fought like a flame in his fury.
Three times from behind glorious Hektor caught him                   155
by the feet, trying to drag him, and called aloud on the Trojans.
Three times the two Aiantes with their battle-fury upon them
beat him from the corpse, but he, steady in the confidence of his
        great strength,
kept making, now a rush into the crowd, or again at another time

3. Trojan.

stood fast, with his great cry, but gave not a bit of ground back-
        ward.                                                          160
And as herdsmen who dwell in the fields are not able to frighten
a tawny lion in his great hunger away from a carcass,
so the two Aiantes, marshals of men, were not able
to scare Hektor, Priam's son, away from the body.
And now he would have dragged it away and won glory forever    165
had not swift wind-footed Iris[4] come running from Olympos
with a message for Peleus' son to arm. She came secretly
from Zeus and the other gods, since it was Hera who sent her.
She came and stood close to him and addressed him in winged words:
'Rise up, son of Peleus, most terrifying of all men.          170
Defend Patroklos, for whose sake the terrible fighting
stands now in front of the ships. They are destroying each other;
the Achaians fight in defence over the fallen body
while the others, the Trojans, are rushing to drag the corpse off
to windy Ilion, and beyond all glorious Hektor                175
rages to haul it away, since the anger within him is urgent
to cut the head from the soft neck and set it on sharp stakes.
Up, then, lie here no longer; let shame come into your heart, lest
Patroklos become sport for the dogs of Troy to worry,
your shame, if the body goes from here with defilement upon it.' 180
     Then in turn Achilleus of the swift feet answered her:
'Divine Iris, what god sent you to me with a message?'
     Then in turn swift wind-footed Iris spoke to him:
'Hera sent me, the honoured wife of Zeus; but the son of
Kronos, who sits on high, does not know this, nor any other   185
immortal, of all those who dwell by the snows of Olympos.'
     Then in answer to her spoke Achilleus of the swift feet:
'How shall I go into the fighting? They have my armour.
And my beloved mother told me I must not be armoured,
not before with my own eyes I see her come back to me.        190
She promised she would bring magnificent arms from Hephaistos.
Nor do I know of another whose glorious armour I could wear
unless it were the great shield of Telamonian[5] Aias.
But he himself wears it, I think, and goes in the foremost
of the spear-fight over the body of fallen Patroklos.'        195
     Then in turn swift wind-footed Iris spoke to him:
'Yes, we also know well how they hold your glorious armour.
But go to the ditch, and show yourself as you are to the Trojans,
if perhaps the Trojans might be frightened, and give way
from their attack, and the fighting sons of the Achaians get wind 200
again after hard work. There is little breathing space in the fighting.'

4. Messenger of the gods, particularly of Hera.     5. The more famous of the two heroes called
Aias (Ajax) was the son of Telamon.

So speaking Iris of the swift feet went away from him;
but Achilleus, the beloved of Zeus, rose up, and Athene
swept about his powerful shoulders the fluttering aegis;
and she, the divine among goddesses, about his head circled          205
a golden cloud, and kindled from it a flame far-shining.
As when a flare goes up into the high air from a city
from an island far away, with enemies fighting about it
who all day long are in the hateful division of Ares[6]
fighting from their own city, but as the sun goes down signal        210
fires blaze out one after another, so that the glare goes
pulsing high for men of the neighbouring islands to see it,
in case they might come over in ships to beat off the enemy;
so from the head of Achilleus the blaze shot into the bright air.
He went from the wall and stood by the ditch, nor mixed with the
      other                                                          215
Achaians, since he followed the close command of his mother.
There he stood, and shouted, and from her place Pallas Athene
gave cry, and drove an endless terror upon the Trojans.
As loud as comes the voice that is screamed out by a trumpet
by murderous attackers who beleaguer a city,                         220
so then high and clear went up the voice of Aiakides.[7]
But the Trojans, when they heard the brazen voice of Aiakides,
the heart was shaken in all, and the very floating-maned horses
turned their chariots about, since their hearts saw the coming afflic-
      tions.
The charioteers were dumbfounded as they saw the unwearied
      dangerous                                                      225
fire that played above the head of great-hearted Peleion
blazing, and kindled by the goddess grey-eyed Athene.
Three times across the ditch brilliant Achilleus gave his great cry,
and three times the Trojans and their renowned companions were
      routed.
There at that time twelve of the best men among them perished       230
upon their own chariots and spears. Meanwhile the Achaians
gladly pulled Patroklos out from under the missiles
and set him upon a litter, and his own companions about him
stood mourning, and along with them swift-footed Achilleus
went, letting fall warm tears as he saw his steadfast companion      235
lying there on a carried litter and torn with the sharp bronze,
the man he had sent off before with horses and chariot
into the fighting; who never again came home to be welcomed.
      Now the lady Hera of the ox eyes drove the unwilling
weariless sun god to sink in the depth of the Ocean,                 240

6. The god of war.     7. Achilleus, grandson of Aiakos.

and the sun went down, and the brilliant Achaians gave over
their strong fighting, and the doubtful collision of battle.
    The Trojans on the other side moved from the strong encounter
in their turn, and unyoked their running horses from under the char-
        iots,
and gathered into assembly before taking thought for their supper.
They stood on their feet in assembly, nor did any man have the
        patience                                                            246
to sit down, but the terror was on them all, seeing that Achilleus
had appeared, after he had stayed so long from the difficult fighting.
First to speak among them was the careful Poulydamas,
Panthöos' son, who alone of them looked before and behind
        him.[8]                                                             250
He was companion to Hektor, and born on the same night with
        him,
but he was better in words, the other with the spear far better.
He in kind intention toward all stood forth and addressed them:
'Now take careful thought, dear friends; for I myself urge you
to go back into the city and not wait for the divine dawn            255
in the plain beside the ships. We are too far from the wall now.
While this man was still angry with great Agamemnon,
for all that time the Achaians were easier men to fight with.
For I also used then to be one who was glad to sleep out
near their ships, and I hoped to capture the oarswept vessels.       260
But now I terribly dread the swift-footed son of Peleus.
So violent is the valour in him, he will not be willing
to stay here in the plain, where now Achaians and Trojans
from either side sunder between them the wrath of the war god.
With him, the fight will be for the sake of our city and women.      265
Let us go into the town; believe me; thus it will happen.
For this present, immortal night has stopped the swift-footed
son of Peleus, but if he catches us still in this place
tomorrow, and drives upon us in arms, a man will be well
aware of him, be glad to get back into sacred Ilion,                 270
the man who escapes; there will be many Trojans the vultures
and dogs will feed on. But let such a word be out of my hearing!
If all of us will do as I say, though it hurts us to do it,
this night we will hold our strength in the market place, and the
        great walls
and the gateways, and the long, smooth-planed, close-joined gate
        timbers                                                             275
that close to fit them shall defend our city. Then, early
in the morning, under dawn, we shall arm ourselves in our war gear

8. He was a prophet; he knew the past and foresaw the future.

and take stations along the walls. The worse for him, if he endea-
    vours
to come away from the ships and fight us here for our city.
Back he must go to his ships again, when he wears out the strong
    necks                                                              280
of his horses, driving them at a gallop everywhere by the city.
His valour will not give him leave to burst in upon us
nor sack our town. Sooner the circling dogs will feed on him.'
    Then looking darkly at him Hektor of the shining helm spoke:
'Poulydamas, these things that you argue please me no longer       285
when you tell us to go back again and be cooped in our city.
Have you not all had your glut of being fenced in our outworks?
There was a time when mortal men would speak of the city
of Priam as a place with much gold and much bronze. But now
the lovely treasures that lay away in our houses have vanished,      290
and many possessions have been sold and gone into Phrygia
and into Maionia the lovely, when great Zeus was angry.
But now, when the son of devious-devising Kronos has given
me the winning of glory by the ships, to pin the Achaians
on the sea, why, fool, no longer show these thoughts to our people.
Not one of the Trojans will obey you. I shall not allow it.          296
Come, then, do as I say and let us all be persuaded.
Now, take your supper by positions along the encampment,
and do not forget your watch, and let every man be wakeful.
And if any Trojan is strongly concerned about his possessions,       300
let him gather them and give them to the people, to use them in
    common.
It is better for one of us to enjoy them than for the Achaians.
In the morning, under dawn, we shall arm ourselves in our war gear
and waken the bitter god of war by the hollow vessels.
If it is true that brilliant Achilleus is risen beside their         305
ships, then the worse for him if he tries it, since I for my part
will not run from him out of the sorrowful battle, but rather
stand fast, to see if he wins the great glory, or if I can win it.
The war god is impartial. Before now he has killed the killer.'
    So spoke Hektor, and the Trojans thundered to hear him;         310
fools, since Pallas Athene had taken away the wits from them.
They gave their applause to Hektor in his counsel of evil,
but none to Poulydamas, who had spoken good sense before them.
They took their supper along the encampment. Meanwhile the
    Achaians
mourned all night in lamentation over Patroklos.                     315
Peleus' son led the thronging chant of their lamentation,
and laid his manslaughtering hands over the chest of his dear friend
with outbursts of incessant grief. As some great bearded lion

when some man, a deer hunter, has stolen his cubs away from him
out of the close wood; the lion comes back too late, and is
    anguished,                                320
and turns into many valleys quartering after the man's trail
on the chance of finding him, and taken with bitter anger;
so he, groaning heavily, spoke out to the Myrmidons:
'Ah me. It was an empty word I cast forth on that day
when in his halls I tried to comfort the hero Menoitios.     325
I told him I would bring back his son in glory to Opous[9]
with Ilion sacked, and bringing his share of war spoils allotted.
But Zeus does not bring to accomplishment all thoughts in men's
    minds.
Thus it is destiny for us both to stain the same soil
here in Troy; since I shall never come home, and my father,   330
Peleus the aged rider, will not welcome me in his great house,
nor Thetis my mother, but in this place the earth will receive me.
But seeing that it is I, Patroklos, who follow you underground,
I will not bury you till I bring to this place the armour
and the head of Hektor, since he was your great-hearted murderer.
Before your burning pyre I shall behead twelve glorious   336
children of the Trojans, for my anger over your slaying.
Until then, you shall lie where you are in front of my curved ships
and beside you women of Troy and deep-girdled Dardanian women
shall sorrow for you night and day and shed tears for you, those
    whom                                   340
you and I worked hard to capture by force and the long spear
in days when we were storming the rich cities of mortals.'
    So speaking brilliant Achilleus gave orders to his companions
to set a great cauldron across the fire, so that with all speed
they could wash away the clotted blood from Patroklos.     345
They set up over the blaze of the fire a bath-water cauldron
and poured water into it and put logs underneath and kindled them.
The fire worked on the swell of the cauldron, and the water heated.
But when the water had come to a boil in the shining bronze, then
they washed the body and anointed it softly with olive oil   350
and stopped the gashes in his body with stored-up unguents
and laid him on a bed, and shrouded him in a thin sheet
from head to foot, and covered that over with a white mantle.
    Then all night long, gathered about Achilleus of the swift feet,
the Myrmidons mourned for Patroklos and lamented over him.   355
But Zeus spoke to Hera, who was his wife and his sister:
'So you have acted, then, lady Hera of the ox eyes.
You have roused up Achilleus of the swift feet. It must be then

---

9. Ancient city on the eastern coast of the Greek mainland and home of Menoitios, father of
Patroklos.

that the flowing-haired Achaians are born of your own generation.'
  Then the goddess the ox-eyed lady Hera answered him:          360
'Majesty, son of Kronos, what sort of thing have you spoken?
Even one who is mortal will try to accomplish his purpose
for another, though he be a man and knows not such wisdom as we
      do.
As for me then, who claim I am highest of all the goddesses,
both ways, since I am eldest born and am called your consort,     365
yours, and you in turn are lord over all the immortals,
how could I not weave sorrows for the men of Troy, when I hate
      them?'
  Now as these two were saying things like this to each other,
Thetis of the silver feet came to the house of Hephaistos,
imperishable, starry, and shining among the immortals,           370
built in bronze for himself by the god of the dragging footsteps.[1]
She found him sweating as he turned here and there to his bellows
busily, since he was working on twenty tripods
which were to stand against the wall of his strong-founded dwelling.
And he had set golden wheels underneath the base of each one     375
so that of their own motion they could wheel into the immortal
gathering, and return to his house: a wonder to look at.
These were so far finished, but the elaborate ear handles
were not yet on. He was forging these, and beating the chains out.
As he was at work on this in his craftsmanship and his cunning   380
meanwhile the goddess Thetis the silver-footed drew near him.
Charis[2] of the shining veil saw her as she came forward,
she, the lovely goddess the renowned strong-armed one had married.
She came, and caught her hand and called her by name and spoke
      to her:
'Why is it, Thetis of the light robes, you have come to our house
      now?                                                        385
We honour you and love you; but you have not come much before
      this.
But come in with me, so I may put entertainment before you.'
  She spoke, and, shining among divinities, led the way forward
and made Thetis sit down in a chair that was wrought elaborately
and splendid with silver nails, and under it was a footstool.    390
She called to Hephaistos the renowned smith and spoke a word to
      him:
'Hephaistos, come this way; here is Thetis, who has need of you.'
  Hearing her the renowned smith of the strong arms answered her:
'Then there is a goddess we honour and respect in our house.
She saved me when I suffered much at the time of my great fall   395

─────────────

1. Hephaistos was lame.    2. Her name means "grace," "beauty."

through the will of my own brazen-faced mother, who wanted
to hide me, for being lame. Then my soul would have taken much
    suffering
had not Eurynome and Thetis caught me and held me,
Eurynome, daughter of Ocean, whose stream bends back in a cir-
    cle.[3]
With them I worked nine years as a smith, and wrought many
    intricate                                                    400
things; pins that bend back, curved clasps, cups, necklaces working
there in the hollow of the cave, and the stream of Ocean around us
went on forever with its foam and its murmur. No other
among the gods or among mortal men knew about us
except Eurynome and Thetis. They knew, since they saved me.   405
Now she has come into our house; so I must by all means
do everything to give recompense to lovely-haired Thetis
for my life. Therefore set out before her fair entertainment
while I am putting away my bellows and all my instruments.'
    He spoke, and took the huge blower off from the block of the anvil
limping; and yet his shrunken legs moved lightly beneath him.   411
He set the bellows away from the fire, and gathered and put away
all the tools with which he worked in a silver strongbox.
Then with a sponge he wiped clean his forehead, and both hands,
and his massive neck and hairy chest, and put on a tunic,        415
and took up a heavy stick in his hand, and went to the doorway
limping. And in support of their master moved his attendants.
These are golden, and in appearance like living young women.
There is intelligence in their hearts, and there is speech in them
and strength, and from the immortal gods they have learned how to
    do things.                                                  420
These stirred nimbly in support of their master, and moving
near to where Thetis sat in her shining chair, Hephaistos
caught her by the hand and called her by name and spoke a word to
    her:
'Why is it, Thetis of the light robes, you have come to our house
    now?
We honour you and love you; but you have not come much before
    this.                                                       425
Speak forth what is in your mind. My heart is urgent to do it
if I can, and if it is a thing that can be accomplished.'
    Then in turn Thetis answered him, letting the tears fall:
'Hephaistos, is there among all the goddesses on Olympos
one who in her heart has endured so many grim sorrows            430
as the griefs Zeus, son of Kronos, has given me beyond others?

3. Since the river Ocean was supposed to surround the earth.

Of all the other sisters of the sea he gave me to a mortal,
to Peleus, Aiakos' son, and I had to endure mortal marriage
though much against my will. And now he, broken by mournful
old age, lies away in his halls. Yet I have other troubles.          435
For since he has given me a son to bear and to raise up
conspicuous among heroes, and he shot up like a young tree,
I nurtured him, like a tree grown in the pride of the orchard.
I sent him away in the curved ships to the land of Ilion
to fight with the Trojans; but I shall never again receive him       440
won home again to his country and into the house of Peleus.
Yet while I see him live and he looks on the sunlight, he has
sorrows, and though I go to him I can do nothing to help him.
And the girl the sons of the Achaians chose out for his honour
powerful Agamemnon took her away again out of his hands.             445
For her his heart has been wasting in sorrow; but meanwhile the
        Trojans
pinned the Achaians against their grounded ships, and would not
let them win outside, and the elders of the Argives entreated
my son, and named the many glorious gifts they would give him.
But at that time he refused himself to fight the death from them;    450
nevertheless he put his own armour upon Patroklos
and sent him into the fighting, and gave many men to go with him.
All day they fought about the Skaian Gates, and on that day
they would have stormed the city, if only Phoibos Apollo
had not killed the fighting son of Menoitios there in the first
        ranks                                                        455
after he had wrought much damage, and given the glory to Hektor.
Therefore now I come to your knees; so might you be willing
to give me for my short-lived son a shield and a helmet
and two beautiful greaves fitted with clasps for the ankles
and a corselet. What he had was lost with his steadfast companion
when the Trojans killed him. Now my son lies on the ground, heart
sorrowing.'
    Hearing her the renowned smith of the strong arms answered her:
'Do not fear. Let not these things be a thought in your mind.
And I wish that I could hide him away from death and its sorrow
at that time when his hard fate comes upon him, as surely            465
as there shall be fine armour for him, such as another
man out of many men shall wonder at, when he looks on it.'
    So he spoke, and left her there, and went to his bellows.
He turned these toward the fire and gave them their orders for work-
        ing.
And the bellows, all twenty of them, blew on the crucibles,          470
from all directions blasting forth wind to blow the flames high
now as he hurried to be at this place and now at another,

wherever Hephaistos might wish them to blow, and the work went
    forward.
He cast on the fire bronze which is weariless, and tin with it
and valuable gold, and silver, and thereafter set forth                    475
upon its standard the great anvil, and gripped in one hand
the ponderous hammer, while in the other he grasped the pincers.
    First of all he forged a shield that was huge and heavy,
elaborating it about, and threw around it a shining
triple rim that glittered, and the shield strap was cast of silver.        480
There were five folds composing the shield itself, and upon it
he elaborated many things in his skill and craftsmanship
    He made the earth upon it, and the sky, and the sea's water,
and the tireless sun, and the moon waxing into her fullness,
and on it all the constellations that festoon the heavens,                 485
the Pleiades and the Hyades and the strength of Orion
and the Bear,[4] whom men give also the name of the Wagon,
who turns about in a fixed place and looks at Orion
and she alone is never plunged in the wash of the Ocean.
    On it he wrought in all their beauty two cities of mortal              490
men. And there were marriages in one, and festivals.
They were leading the brides along the city from their maiden cham-
    bers
under the flaring of torches, and the loud bride song was arising.
The young men followed the circles of the dance, and among them
the flutes and lyres kept up their clamour as in the meantime             495
the women standing each at the door of her court admired them.
The people were assembled in the market place, where a quarrel
had arisen, and two men were disputing over the blood price
for a man who had been killed. One man promised full restitution
in a public statement, but the other refused and would accept
    nothing.                                                               500
Both then made for an arbitrator, to have a decision;
and people were speaking up on either side, to help both men.
But the heralds kept the people in hand, as meanwhile the elders
were in session on benches of polished stone in the sacred circle
and held in their hands the staves of the heralds who lift their
    voices.                                                                505
The two men rushed before these, and took turns speaking their
    cases,
and between them lay on the ground two talents of gold, to be given
to that judge who in this case spoke the straightest opinion.

---

4. The Big Dipper, which never descends below the horizon. It is a female bear (Ursa Major),
hence "she" in l. 489. *Pleiades, Hyades, Orion:* All constellations; Orion was a giant hunter of
Greek myth.

But around the other city were lying two forces of armed men
shining in their war gear. For one side counsel was divided        510
whether to storm and sack, or share between both sides the property
and all the possessions the lovely citadel held hard within it.
But the city's people were not giving way, and armed for an ambush.
Their beloved wives and their little children stood on the rampart
to hold it, and with them the men with age upon them, but
    meanwhile                                                      515
the others went out. And Ares led them, and Pallas Athene.
These were gold, both, and golden raiment upon them, and they
    were
beautiful and huge in their armour, being divinities,
and conspicuous from afar, but the people around them were smaller.
These, when they were come to the place that was set for their
    ambush,                                                        520
in a river, where there was a watering place for all animals,
there they sat down in place shrouding themselves in the bright bronze.
But apart from these were sitting two men to watch for the rest of
    them.
and waiting until they could see the sheep and the shambling cattle,
who appeared presently, and two herdsmen went along with them
playing happily on pipes, and took no thought of the treachery.    526
Those others saw them, and made a rush, and quickly thereafter
cut off on both sides the herds of cattle and the beautiful
flocks of shining sheep, and killed the shepherds upon them.
But the other army, as soon as they heard the uproar arising        530
from the cattle, as they sat in their councils, suddenly mounted
behind their light-foot horses, and went after, and soon overtook
    them.
These stood their ground and fought a battle by the banks of the
    river,
and they were making casts at each other with their spears bronze-
    headed;
and Hate was there with Confusion among them, and Death the
    destructive;                                                   535
she was holding a live man with a new wound, and another
one unhurt, and dragged a dead man by the feet through the car-
    nage.
The clothing upon her shoulders showed strong red with the men's
    blood.
All closed together like living men and fought with each other
and dragged away from each other the corpses of those who had
    fallen.                                                        540
    He made upon it a soft field, the pride of the tilled land,

wide and triple-ploughed, with many ploughmen upon it
who wheeled their teams at the turn and drove them in either direc-
     tion.
And as these making their turn would reach he end-strip of the field,
a man would come up to them at this point and hand them a
     flagon                                                                                        545
of honey-sweet wine, and they would turn again to the furrows
in their haste to come again to the end-strip of the deep field.
The earth darkened behind them and looked like earth that has been
     ploughed
though it was gold. Such was the wonder of the shield's forging.
     He made on it the precinct of a king, where the labourers        550
were reaping, with the sharp reaping hooks in their hands. Of the
     cut swathes
some fell along the lines of reaping, one after another,
while the sheaf-binders caught up others and tied them with bind-
     ropes.
There were three sheaf-binders who stood by, and behind them
were children picking up the cut swathes, and filled their arms with
     them                                                                                       555
and carried and gave them always; and by them the king in silence
and holding his staff stood near the line of the reapers, happily.
And apart and under a tree the heralds made a feast ready
and trimmed a great ox they had slaughtered. Meanwhile the women
scattered, for the workmen to eat, abundant white barley.          560
     He made on it a great vineyard heavy with clusters,
lovely and in gold, but the grapes upon it were darkened
and the vines themselves stood out through poles of silver. About
     them
he made a field-ditch of dark metal, and drove all around this
a fence of tin; and there was only one path to the vineyard,        565
and along it ran the grape-bearers for the vineyards' stripping.
Young girls and young men, in all their light-hearted innocence,
carried the kind, sweet fruit away in their woven baskets,
and in their midst a youth with a singing lyre played charmingly
upon it for them, and sang the beautiful song for Linos[5]         570
in a light voice, and they followed him, and with singing and whis-
     tling
and light dance-steps of their feet kept time to the music.
     He made upon it a herd of horn-straight oxen. The cattle
were wrought of gold and of tin, and thronged in speed and with
     lowing
out of the dung of the farmyard to a pasturing place by a sounding

---

5. An ancient folk song commemorating Linos, the favorite of Apollo.

river, and beside the moving field of a reed bed.                                576
The herdmen were of gold who went along with the cattle,
four of them, and nine dogs shifting their feet followed them.
But among the foremost of the cattle two formidable lions
had caught hold of a bellowing bull, and he with loud lowings        580
was dragged away, as the dogs and the young men went in pursuit of
     him.
But the two lions, breaking open the hide of the great ox,
gulped the black blood and the inward guts, as meanwhile the herds-
     men
were in the act of setting and urging the quick dogs on them.
But they, before they could get their teeth in, turned back from the
     lions,                                                                              585
but would come and take their stand very close, and bayed, and kept
     clear.
     And the renowned smith of the strong arms made on it a meadow
large and in a lovely valley for the glimmering sheepflocks,
with dwelling places upon it, and covered shelters, and sheepfolds.
     And the renowned smith of the strong arms made elaborate on
     it                                                                                   590
a dancing floor, like that which once in the wide spaces of Knossos
Daidalos built for Ariadne[6] of the lovely tresses.
And there were young men on it and young girls, sought for their
     beauty
with gifts of oxen, dancing, and holding hands at the wrist. These
wore, the maidens long light robes, but the men wore tunics           595
of finespun work and shining softly, touched with olive oil.
And the girls wore fair garlands on their heads, while the young men
carried golden knives that hung from sword-belts of silver.
At whiles on their understanding feet they would run very lightly,
as when a potter crouching makes trial of his wheel, holding          600
it close in his hands, to see if it will run smooth. At another
time they would form rows, and run, rows crossing each other.
And around the lovely chorus of dancers stood a great multitude
happily watching, while among the dancers two acrobats
led the measures of song and dance revolving among them.              605
     He made on it the great strength of the Ocean River
which ran around the uttermost rim of the shield's strong structure.
     Then after he had wrought this shield, which was huge and heavy,
he wrought for him a corselet brighter than fire in its shining,
and wrought him a helmet, massive and fitting close to his tem-       610
     ples,

6. Daughter of Minos king of Crete. *Knossos:* In Crete, the site of the great "palace of Minos."
*Daidalos:* The "fabulous artificer" who built the labyrinth and, with his son Icarus, escaped from
Crete on wings.

lovely and intricate work, and laid a gold top-ridge along it,
and out of pliable tin wrought him leg-armour. Thereafter
when the renowned smith of the strong arms had finished the armour
he lifted it and laid it before the mother of Achilleus.
And she like a hawk came sweeping down from the snows of
    Olympos                                                                        615
and carried with her the shining armour, the gift of Hephaistos.

## Book XIX

### [ACHILLEUS RETURNS TO THE BATTLE]

    Now Dawn the yellow-robed arose from the river of Ocean
to carry her light to men and to immortals. And Thetis
came to the ships and carried with her the gifts of Hephaistos.
She found her beloved son lying in the arms of Patroklos
crying shrill, and his companions in their numbers about him                    5
mourned. She, shining among divinities, stood there beside them.
She clung to her son's hand and called him by name and spoke to
    him:
'My child, now, though we grieve for him, we must let this man lie
dead, in the way he first was killed through the gods' designing.
Accept rather from me the glorious arms of Hephaistos,                          10
so splendid, and such as no man has ever worn on his shoulders.'
    The goddess spoke so, and set down the armour on the ground
before Achilleus, and all its elaboration clashed loudly.
Trembling took hold of all the Myrmidons. None had the courage
to look straight at it. They were afraid of it. Only Achilleus                  15
looked, and as he looked the anger came harder upon him
and his eyes glittered terribly under his lids, like sunflare.
He was glad, holding in his hands the shining gifts of Hephaistos.
But when he had satisfied his heart with looking at the intricate
armour, he spoke to his mother and addressed her in winged
    words:                                                                      20
My mother, the god has given me these weapons; they are such
as are the work of immortals. No mortal man could have made them.
Therefore now I shall arm myself in them. Yet I am sadly
afraid, during this time, for the warlike son of Menoitios
that flies might get into the wounds beaten by bronze in his body             25
and breed worms in them, and these make foul the body, seeing
that the life is killed in him, and that all his flesh may be rotted.'
    In turn the goddess Thetis the silver-footed answered him:
'My child, no longer let these things be a care in your mind.
I shall endeavour to drive from him the swarming and fierce
    things,                                                                      30
those flies, which feed upon the bodies of men who have perished;

and although he lie here till a year has gone to fulfilment,
still his body shall be as it was, or firmer than ever.
Go then and summon into assembly the fighting Achaians,
and unsay your anger against Agamemnon, shepherd of the people,
and arm at once for the fighting, and put your war strength upon
  you.'                                                                       36

  She spoke so, and drove the strength of great courage into him;
and meanwhile through the nostrils of Patroklos she distilled
ambrosia and red nectar, so that his flesh might not spoil.

  But he, brilliant Achilleus, walked along by the sea-shore           40
crying his terrible cry, and stirred up the fighting Achaians.
And even those who before had stayed where the ships were assembled,
they who were helmsmen of the ships and handled the steering oar,
they who were stewards among the ships and dispensers of rations,
even these came then to assembly, since now Achilleus                  45
had appeared, after staying so long from the sorrowful battle.
And there were two who came limping among them, henchmen of
  Ares
both, Tydeus' son the staunch in battle, and brilliant Odysseus,
leaning on spears, since they had the pain of their wounds yet upon
  them,
and came and took their seats in the front rank of these assembled.
And last of them came in the lord of men Agamemnon                     51
with a wound on him, seeing that Koön, the son of Antenor,
had stabbed him with the bronze edge of the spear in the strong
  encounter.
But now, when all the Achaians were in one body together,
Achilleus of the swift feet stood up before them and spoke to
  them:                                                                        55
'Son of Atreus, was this after all the better way for
both, for you and me, that we, for all our hearts' sorrow,
quarrelled together for the sake of a girl in soul-perishing hatred?
I wish Artemis had killed her beside the ships with an arrow
on that day when I destroyed Lyrnessos and took her.                   60
For thus not all these too many Achaians would have bitten
the dust, by enemy hands, when I was away in my anger.
This way was better for the Trojans and Hektor; yet I think
the Achaians will too long remember this quarrel between us.
Still, we will let all this be a thing of the past, though it hurts us,  65
and beat down by constraint the anger that rises inside us.
Now I am making an end of my anger. It does not become me
unrelentingly to rage on. Come, then! The more quickly
drive on the flowing-haired Achaians into the fighting,
so that I may go up against the Trojans, and find out                  70

if they still wish to sleep out beside the ships. I think rather
they will be glad to rest where they are, whoever among them
gets away with his life from the fury of our spears' onset.'
   He spoke, and the strong-greaved Achaians were pleasured to hear
     him
and how the great-hearted son of Peleus unsaid his anger.      75
Now among them spoke forth the lord of men Agamemnon
from the place where he was sitting, and did not stand up among
     them:
'Fighting men and friends, o Danaans, henchmen of Ares:
it is well to listen to the speaker, it is not becoming
to break in on him. This will be hard for him, though he be able. 80
How among the great murmur of people shall anyone listen
or speak either? A man, though he speak very clearly, is baffled.
I shall address the son of Peleus; yet all you other
Argives listen also, and give my word careful attention.
This is the word the Achaians have spoken often against me     85
and found fault with me in it, yet I am not responsible
but Zeus is, and Destiny, and Erinys the mist-walking
who in assembly caught my heart in the savage delusion
on that day I myself stripped from him the prize of Achilleus.
Yet what could I do? It is the god who accomplishes all things.   90
Delusion is the elder daughter of Zeus, the accursed
who deludes all; her feet are delicate and they step not
on the firm earth, but she walks the air above men's heads
and leads them astray. She has entangled others before me.
Yes, for once Zeus even was deluded, though men say      95
he is the highest one of gods and mortals. Yet Hera
who is female deluded even Zeus in her craftiness
on that day when in strong wall-circled Thebe Alkmene[7]
was at her time to bring forth the strength of Herakles. Therefore
Zeus spoke forth and made a vow before all the immortals:    100
"Hear me, all you gods and all you goddesses: hear me
while I speak forth what the heart within my breast urges.
This day Eileithyia[8] of women's child-pains shall bring forth
a man to the light who, among the men sprung of the generation
of my blood, shall be lord over all those dwelling about him."   105
Then in guileful intention the lady Hera said to him:
"You will be a liar, not put fulfilment on what you have spoken.
Come, then, lord of Olympos, and swear before me a strong oath
that he shall be lord over all those dwelling about him
who this day shall fall between the feet of a woman,[9]    110
that man who is born of the blood of your generation." So Hera

---

7. Mortal woman who, though married to Amphitryon, King of Thebes, was pregnant by Zeus.
8. The goddess who presided over human birth.   9. Be born.

spoke. And Zeus was entirely unaware of her falsehood,
but swore a great oath, and therein lay all his deception.
But Hera in a flash of speed left the horn of Olympos
and rapidly came to Argos of Achaia, where she knew                    115
was the mighty wife of Sthenelos, descended of Perseus.[1]
And she was carrying a son, and this was the seventh month for her,
but she brought him sooner into the light, and made him premature,
and stayed the childbirth of Alkmene, and held back the birth pangs.
She went herself and spoke the message to Zeus, son of Kronos:    120
"Father Zeus of the shining bolt, I will tell you a message
for your heart. A great man is born, who will be lord over the Argives,
Eurystheus,[2] son of Sthenelos, of the seed of Perseus,
your generation. It is not unfit that he should rule over
the Argives." She spoke, and the sharp sorrow struck at his deep
        heart.                                                         125
He caught by the shining hair of her head the goddess Delusion
in the anger of his heart, and swore a strong oath, that never
after this might Delusion, who deludes all, come back
to Olympos and the starry sky. So speaking, he whirled her
about in his hand and slung her out of the starry heaven,             130
and presently she came to men's establishments. But Zeus
would forever grieve over her each time that he saw his dear son
doing some shameful work of the tasks that Eurystheus set him.
So I in my time, when tall Hektor of the shining helm
was forever destroying the Argives against the sterns of their ves-
        sels,                                                         135
could not forget Delusion, the way I was first deluded.
But since I was deluded and Zeus took my wits away from me,
I am willing to make all good and give back gifts in abundance.
Rise up, then, to the fighting and rouse the rest of the people.
Here am I, to give you all those gifts, as many                      140
as brilliant Odysseus yesterday went to your shelter and promised.
Or if you will, hold back, though you lean hard into the battle,
while my followers take the gifts from my ship and bring them
to you, so you may see what I give to comfort your spirit.'
    Then in answer to him spoke Achilleus of the swift feet:         145
'Son of Atreus, most lordly and king of men, Agamemnon,
the gifts are yours to give if you wish, and as it is proper,
or to keep with yourself. But now let us remember our joy in war-
        craft,
immediately, for it is not fitting to stay here and waste time
nor delay, since there is still a big work to be done.                150
So can a man see once more Achilleus among the front fighters

1. A son of Zeus.   2. He became king of Argos, and taskmaster of Hercules, who performed
twelve great labors for him.

with the bronze spear wrecking the Trojan battalions. Therefore
let each of you remember this and fight his antagonist.'
   Then in answer to him spoke resourceful Odysseus:
'Not that way, good fighter that you are, godlike Achilleus.                155
Do not drive the sons of the Achaians on Ilion when they are hun-
     gry,
to fight against the Trojans, since not short will be the time
of battle, once the massed formations of men have encountered
together, with the god inspiring fury in both sides.
Rather tell the men of Achaia here by their swift ships,                   160
to take food and wine, since these make fighting fury and warcraft.
For a man will not have strength to fight his way forward all day
long until the sun goes down if he is starved for food. Even
though in his heart he be very passionate for the battle,
yet without his knowing it his limbs will go heavy, and hunger            165
and thirst will catch up with him and cumber his knees as he moves
     on.
But when a man has been well filled with wine and with eating
and then does battle all day long against the enemy,
why, then the heart inside him is full of cheer, nor do his limbs
get weary, until all are ready to give over the fighting.                 170
Come then, tell your men to scatter and bid them get ready
a meal; and as for the gifts, let the lord of men Agamemnon
bring them to the middle of our assembly so all the Achaians
can see them before their eyes, so your own heart may be pleasured.
And let him stand up before the Argives and swear an oath to you
that he never entered into her bed and never lay with her[3]              176
as is natural for people, my lord, between men and women.
And by this let the spirit in your own heart be made gracious.
After that in his own shelter let him appease you
with a generous meal, so you will lack nothing of what is due you.
And you, son of Atreus, after this be more righteous to another          181
man. For there is no fault when even one who is a king
appeases a man, when the king was the first one to be angry.'
   Then in turn the lord of men Agamemnon answered him:
'Hearing what you have said, son of Laertes, I am pleased with
     you.                                                                  185
Fairly have you gone through everything and explained it.
And all this I am willing to swear to, and my heart urges me,
and I will not be forsworn before the gods. Let Achilleus
stay here the while, though he lean very hard toward the work of the
     war god,
and remain the rest of you all here assembled, until the gifts come

3. Briseis.

back from my shelter and while we cut our oaths[4] of fidelity.      191
And for you yourself, Odysseus, I give you this errand, this order,
that you choose out excellent young men of all the Achaians
and bring the gifts back here from my ships, all that you promised
yesterday to Achilleus, and bring the women back also.      195
And in the wide host of the Achaians let Talthybios[5] make ready
a boar for me, and dedicate it to Zeus and Helios.'[6]
      Then in answer to him spoke Achilleus of the swift feet:
'Son of Atreus, most lordly and king of men, Agamemnon,
at some other time rather you should busy yourself about these
      things,      200
when there is some stopping point in the fighting, at some time
when there is not so much fury inside of my heart. But now
as things are they lie there torn whom the son of Priam
Hektor has beaten down, since Zeus was giving him glory,
and then you urge a man to eating. No, but I would now      205
drive forward the sons of the Achaians into the fighting
starving and unfed, and afterwards when the sun sets
make ready a great dinner, when we have paid off our defilement.
But before this, for me at least, neither drink nor food shall
go down my very throat, since my companion has perished      210
and lies inside my shelter torn about with the cutting
bronze, and turned against the forecourt while my companions
mourn about him. Food and drink mean nothing to my heart
but blood does, and slaughter, and the groaning of men in the hard
      work.'
      Then in answer to him spoke resourceful Odysseus:      215
'Son of Peleus, Achilleus, far greatest of the Achaians,
you are stronger than I am and greater by not a little
with the spear, yet I in turn might overpass you in wisdom
by far, since I was born before you and have learned more things.
Therefore let your heart endure to listen to my words.      220
When there is battle men have suddenly their fill of it
when the bronze scatters on the ground the straw in most numbers
and the harvest is most thin, when Zeus has poised his balance,
Zeus, who is administrator to men in their fighting.
There is no way the Achaians can mourn a dead man by denying 225
the belly. Too many fall day by day, one upon another,
and how could anyone find breathing space from his labour?
No, but we must harden our hearts and bury the man who
dies, when we have wept over him on the day, and all those
who are left about from the hateful work of war must remember      230
food and drink, so that afterwards all the more strongly

4. "Cut" refers to the killing of the animals sacrificed to seal the oath.   5. Agamemnon's
herald.   6. The sun.

we may fight on forever relentless against our enemies
with the weariless bronze put on about our bodies. Let one not
wait longing for any other summons to stir on the people.
This summons now shall be an evil on anyone left behind                235
by the ships of the Argives. Therefore let us drive on together
and wake the bitter war god on the Trojans, breakers of horses.'

    He spoke, and went away with the sons of glorious Nestor,
with Meges, the son of Phyleus, and Meriones, and Thoas,
and Lykomedes, the son of Kreion, and Melanippos. These went
on their way to the shelter of Atreus' son Agamemnon.                  241
No sooner was the order given than the thing had been done.
They brought back seven tripods from the shelter, those Agamem-
    non
had promised, and twenty shining cauldrons, twelve horses. They
    brought back
immediately the seven women the work of whose hands was            245
blameless, and the eighth of them was Briseis of the fair cheeks.
Odysseus weighed out ten full talents of gold and led them
back, and the young men of the Achaians carried the other gifts.
They brought these into the midst of assembly, and Agamemnon
stood up, and Talthybios in voice like an immortal                     250
stood beside the shepherd of the people with the boar in his hands.
Atreus' son laid hands upon his work-knife, and drew it
from where it hung ever beside the great sheath of his war sword,
and cut first hairs away from the boar, and lifting his hands up
to Zeus, prayed, while all the Argives stayed fast at their places     255
in silence and in order of station, and listened to their king.
He spoke before them in prayer gazing into the wide sky:
'Let Zeus first be my witness, highest of the gods and greatest,
and Earth, and Helios the Sun, and Furies, who underground
avenge dead men, when any man has sworn to a falsehood,            260
that I have never laid a hand on the girl Briseis
on pretext to go to bed with her, or for any other
reason, but she remained, not singled out, in my shelter.
If any of this is falsely sworn, may the gods give me many            264
griefs, all that they inflict on those who swear falsely before them.'

    So he spoke, and with pitiless bronze he cut the boar's throat.
Talthybios whirled the body about, and threw it in the great reach
of the grey sea, to feed the fishes. Meanwhile Achilleus
stood up among the battle-fond Achaians, and spoke to them:
'Father Zeus, great are the delusions with which you visit men.     270
Without you, the son of Atreus could never have stirred so
the heart inside my breast, nor taken the girl away from me
against my will, and be in helplessness. No, but Zeus somehow
wished that death should befall great numbers of the Achaians.

Go now and take your dinner, so we may draw on the battle.'      275
    So he spoke, and suddenly broke up the assembly.
Now these scattered away each man to his own ship. Meanwhile
the great-hearted Myrmidons disposed of the presents.
They went on their way carrying them to the ship of godlike
        Achilleus,                                              279
and stowed the gifts in the shelters, and let the women be settled,
while proud henchmen drove the horses into Achilleus' horse-herd.
    And now, in the likeness of golden Aphrodite, Briseis
when she saw Patroklos lying torn with sharp bronze, folding
him in her arms cried shrilly above him and with her hands tore
at her breasts and her soft throat and her beautiful forehead.      285
The woman like the immortals mourning for him spoke to him:
'Patroklos, far most pleasing to my heart in its sorrows,
I left you here alive when I went away from the shelter,
but now I come back, lord of the people, to find you have fallen.
So evil in my life takes over from evil forever.                290
The husband on whom my father and honoured mother bestowed
        me
I saw before my city lying torn with the sharp bronze,
and my three brothers, whom a single mother bore with me
and who were close to me, all went on one day to destruction.
And yet you would not let me, when swift Achilleus had cut down
my husband, and sacked the city of godlike Mynes, you would not
let me sorrow, but said you would make me godlike Achilleus'
wedded lawful wife, that you would take me back in the ships
to Phthia, and formalize my marriage among the Myrmidons.
Therefore I weep your death without ceasing. You were kind
        always.'                                               300
    So she spoke, lamenting, and the women sorrowed around her
grieving openly for Patroklos, but for her own sorrows
each. But the lords of Achaia were gathered about Achilleus
beseeching him to eat, but he with a groan denied them:
'I beg of you, if any dear companion will listen               305
to me, stop urging me to satisfy the heart in me
with food and drink, since this strong sorrow has come upon me.
I will hold out till the sun goes down and endure, though it be hard.'
    So he spoke, and caused the rest of the kings to scatter;
but the two sons of Atreus stayed with him, and brilliant Odys-
        seus,                                                  310
and Nestor, and Idomeneus, and the aged charioteer, Phoinix,
comforting him close in his sorrow, yet his heart would not
be comforted, till he went into the jaws of the bleeding battle.
Remembering Patroklos he sighed much for him, and spoke aloud:
'There was a time, ill fated, o dearest of all my companions,      315

when you yourself would set the desirable dinner before me
quickly and expertly, at the time the Achaians were urgent
to carry sorrowful war on the Trojans, breakers of horses.
But now you lie here torn before me, and my heart goes starved
for meat and drink, though they are here beside me, by reason　　320
of longing for you. There is nothing worse than this I could suffer,
not even if I were to hear of the death of my father
who now, I think, in Phthia somewhere lets fall a soft tear
for bereavement of such a son, for me, who now in a strange land
make war upon the Trojans for the sake of accursed Helen;　　325
or the death of my dear son, who is raised for my sake in Skyros[7]
now, if godlike Neoptolemos is still one of the living.
Before now the spirit inside my breast was hopeful
that I alone should die far away from horse-pasturing Argos
here in Troy; I hoped you would win back again to Phthia　　330
so that in a fast black ship you could take my son back
from Skyros to Phthia, and show him all my possessions,
my property, my serving men, my great high-roofed house.
For by this time I think that Peleus must altogether
have perished, or still keeps a little scant life in sorrow　　335
for the hatefulness of old age and because he waits ever from me
the evil message, for the day he hears I have been killed.'

So he spoke, mourning, and the elders lamented around him
remembering each those he had left behind in his own halls.
The son of Kronos took pity on them as he watched them
　　　mourning　　340
and immediately spoke in winged words to Athene:
'My child, have you utterly abandoned the man of your choice?
Is there no longer deep concern in your heart for Achilleus?
Now he has sat down before the steep horned ships and is mourning
for his own beloved companion, while all the others　　345
have gone to take their dinner, but he is fasting and unfed.
Go then to him and distil nectar inside his chest, and delicate
ambrosia, so the weakness of hunger will not come upon him.'

Speaking so, he stirred Athene, who was eager before this,
and she in the likeness of a wide-winged, thin-crying　　350
hawk plummeted from the sky through the bright air. Now the
　　　Achaians
were arming at once along the encampment. She dropped the deli-
　　　cate
ambrosia and the nectar inside the breast of Achilleus
softly, so no sad weakness of hunger would come on his knees,
and she herself went back to the close house of her powerful　　355

7. An island in the North Aegean.

father, while they were scattering out away from the fast ships.
As when in their thickness the snowflakes of Zeus come fluttering
cold beneath the blast of the north wind born in the bright sky,
so now in their thickness the pride of the helms bright shining
were carried out from the ships, and shields massive in the middle
and the corselets strongly hollowed and the ash spears were worn
     forth.
The shining swept to the sky and all earth was laughing about them
under the glitter of bronze and beneath their feet stirred the thunder
of men, within whose midst brilliant Achilleus helmed him.
A clash went from the grinding of his teeth, and his eyes glowed   365
as if they were the stare of a fire, and the heart inside him
was entered with sorrow beyond endurance. Raging at the Trojans
he put on the gifts of the god, that Hephaistos wrought him with
     much toil.
   First he placed along his legs the fair greaves linked with
silver fastenings to hold the greaves at the ankles.                370
Afterward he girt on about his chest the corselet,
and across his shoulders slung the sword with the nails of silver,
a bronze sword, and caught up the great shield, huge and heavy
next, and from it the light glimmered far, as from the moon.
And as when from across water a light shines to mariners           375
from a blazing fire, when the fire is burning high in the mountains
in a desolate steading, as the mariners are carried unwilling
by storm winds over the fish-swarming sea, far away from their loved
     ones;
so the light from the fair elaborate shield of Achilleus
shot into the high air. And lifting the helm he set it             380
massive upon his head, and the helmet crested with horse-hair
shone like a star, the golden fringes were shaken about it
which Hephaistos had driven close along the horn of the helmet.
And brilliant Achilleus tried himself in his armour, to see
if it fitted close, and how his glorious limbs ran within it,      385
and the armour became as wings and upheld the shepherd of the
     people.
Next he pulled out from its standing place the spear of his father,
huge, heavy, thick, which no one else of all the Achaians
could handle, but Achilleus alone knew how to wield it,
the Pelian ash spear which Cheiron had brought to his father       390
from high on Pelion,[8] to be death for fighters in battle.
Automedon and Alkimos, in charge of the horses,
yoked them, and put the fair breast straps about them, and forced
     the bits home

---

8. A heavily wooded mountain in central Greece. *Cheiron:* A centaur famous as a wise teacher.

between their jaws, and pulled the reins back against the compacted
chariot seat, and one, Automedon, took up the shining                    395
whip caught close in his hand and vaulted up to the chariot,
while behind him Achilleus helmed for battle took his stance
shining in all his armour like the sun when he crosses above us,
and cried in a terrible voice on the horses of his father:
'Xanthos, Balios, Bay and Dapple, famed sons of Podarge,                 400
take care to bring in another way your charioteer back
to the company of the Danaans, when we give over fighting,
not leave him to lie fallen there, as you did to Patroklos.'
     Then from beneath the yoke the gleam-footed horse answered him,
Xanthos, and as he spoke bowed his head, so that all the mane            405
fell away from the pad and swept the ground by the cross-yoke;
the goddess of the white arms, Hera, had put a voice in him:
'We shall still keep you safe for this time, o hard Achilleus.
And yet the day of your death is near, but it is not we
who are to blame, but a great god and powerful Destiny.                  410
For it was not because we were slow, because we were careless,
that the Trojans have taken the armour from the shoulders of Patrok-
     los,
but it was that high god,[9] the child of lovely-haired Leto,
who killed him among the champions and gave the glory to Hektor.
But for us, we two could run with the blast of the west wind             415
who they say is the lightest of all things; yet still for you
there is destiny to be killed in force by a god and a mortal.'[1]
     When he had spoken so the Furies stopped the voice in him,[2]
but deeply disturbed, Achilleus of the swift feet answered him:
'Xanthos, why do you prophesy my death? This is not for you.             420
I myself know well it is destined for me to die here
far from my beloved father and mother. But for all that
I will not stop till the Trojans had had enough of my fighting.'
     He spoke, and shouting held on in the foremost his single-foot
     horses.

     [Achilleus' return to the fighting brought terror to the Trojans,
and turned the battle into a rout in which Achilleus killed every
Trojan that crossed his path. As he pursued Agenor, Apollo tricked
him by rescuing his intended victim (he spirited him away in a mist)
and assumed Agenor's shape to lead Achilleus away from the walls
of Troy. The Trojans took refuge in the city, all except Hektor.]

---

9. Apollo.    1. Achilleus will eventually fall by the hand of Paris as a result of the intervention
of Apollo.    2. One of the functions of these goddesses was to ensure that all the creatures of the
universe observed their proper limits.

## Book XXII

### [THE DEATH OF HEKTOR]

So along the city the Trojans, who had run like fawns, dried
the sweat off from their bodies and drank and slaked their thirst,
    leaning
along the magnificent battlements. Meanwhile the Achaians
sloping their shields across their shoulders came close to the rampart.
But his deadly fate held Hektor shackled, so that he stood fast     5
in front of Ilion and the Skaian gates. Now Phoibos
Apollo spoke aloud to Peleion: 'Why, son of Peleus,
do you keep after me in the speed of your feet, being mortal
while I am an immortal god? Even yet you have not
seen that I am a god, but strain after me in your fury.     10
Now hard fighting with the Trojans whom you stampeded means
    nothing
to you. They are crowded in the city, but you bent away here.
You will never kill me. I am not one who is fated.'
    Deeply vexed Achilleus of the swift feet spoke to him:
'You have balked me, striker from afar, most malignant of all
    gods,     15
when you turned me here away from the rampart, else many Trojans
would have caught the soil in their teeth before they got back into
    Ilion.
Now you have robbed me of great glory, and rescued these people
lightly, since you have no retribution to fear hereafter.
Else I would punish you, if only the strength were in me.'     20
    He spoke, and stalked away against the city, with high thoughts
in mind, and in tearing speed, like a racehorse with his chariot
who runs lightly as he pulls the chariot over the flat land.
Such was the action of Achilleus in feet and quick knees.
    The aged Priam was the first of all whose eyes saw him     25
as he swept across the flat land in full shining, like that star
which comes on in the autumn and whose conspicuous brightness
far outshines the stars that are numbered in the night's darkening,
the star they give the name of Orion's Dog,[3] which is brightest
among the stars, and yet is wrought as a sign of evil     30
and brings on the great fever for unfortunate mortals.
Such was the flare of the bronze that girt his chest in his running.
The old man groaned aloud and with both hands high uplifted
beat his head, and groaned amain, and spoke supplicating
his beloved son, who there still in front of the gateway     35

---

3. Sirius, the "dog star," in the constellation *Canis Major.*

stood fast in determined fury to fight with Achilleus.
The old man stretching his hands out called pitifully to him:
'Hektor, beloved child, do not wait the attack of this man
alone, away from the others. You might encounter your destiny
beaten down by Peleion, since he is far stronger than you are.          40
A hard man: I wish he were as beloved of the immortal
as loved by me. Soon he would lie dead, and the dogs and the vul-
     tures
would eat him, and bitter sorrow so be taken from my heart.
He has made me desolate of my sons, who were brave and many.
He killed them, or sold them away among the far-lying islands.          45
Even now there are two sons, Lykaon and Polydoros,[4]
whom I cannot see among the Trojans pent up in the city,
sons Laothoë[5] a princess among women bore to me.
But if these are alive somewhere in the army, then I can
set them free for bronze and gold; it is there inside, since           50
Altes[6] the aged and renowned gave much with his daughter.
But if they are dead already and gone down to the house of Hades,
it is sorrow to our hearts, who bore them, myself and their mother,
but to the rest of the people a sorrow that will be fleeting
beside their sorrow for you, if you go down before Achilleus.          55
Come then inside the wall, my child, so that you can rescue
the Trojans and the women of Troy, neither win the high glory
for Peleus' son, and yourself be robbed of your very life. Oh, take
pity on me, the unfortunate still alive, still sentient
but ill-starred, whom the father, Kronos' son, on the threshold of
     old age                                                            60
will blast with hard fate, after I have looked upon evils
and seen my sons destroyed and my daughters dragged away captive
and the chambers of marriage wrecked and the innocent children
     taken
and dashed to the ground in the hatefulness of war, and the wives
of my sons dragged off by the accursed hands of the Achaians.          65
And myself last of all, my dogs in front of my doorway
will rip me raw, after some man with stroke of the sharp bronze
spear, or with spearcast, has torn the life out of my body;
those dogs I raised in my halls to be at my table, to guard my
gates, who will lap my blood in the savagery of their anger            70
and then lie down in my courts. For a young man all is decorous
when he is cut down in battle and torn with the sharp bronze, and
     lies there
dead, and though dead still all that shows about him is beautiful;
but when an old man is dead and down, and the dogs mutilate

---

4. Both already killed by Achilleus in the fighting outside the city.    5. Priam, in oriental style,
has more than one wife.    6. Father of Laothoë.

the grey head and the grey beard and the parts that are secret,            75
this, for all sad mortality, is the sight most pitiful.'
    So the old man spoke, and in his hands seizing the grey hairs
tore them from his head, but could not move the spirit in Hektor.
And side by side with him his mother in tears was mourning
and laid the fold of her bosom bare and with one hand held out         80
a breast, and wept her tears for him and called to him in winged
        words:
'Hektor, my child, look upon these and obey, and take pity
on me, if ever I gave you the breast to quiet your sorrow.
Remember all these things, dear child, and from inside the wall
beat off this grim man. Do not go out as champion against him,         85
o hard one; for if he kills you I can no longer
mourn you on the death-bed, sweet branch, o child of my bearing,
nor can your generous wife mourn you, but a big way from us
beside the ships of the Argives the running dogs will feed on you.'
    So these two in tears and with much supplication called out         90
to their dear son, but could not move the spirit in Hektor,
but he awaited Achilleus as he came on, gigantic.
But as a snake waits for a man by his hole, in the mountains,
glutted with evil poisons, and the fell venom has got inside him,
and coiled about the hole he stares malignant, so Hektor              95
would not give ground but kept unquenched the fury within him
and sloped his shining shield against the jut of the bastion.
Deeply troubled he spoke to his own great-hearted spirit:
'Ah me! If I go now inside the wall and the gateway,
Poulydamas will be first to put a reproach upon me,                   100
since he tried to make me lead the Trojans inside the city
on that accursed night when brilliant Achilleus rose up,
and I would not obey him, but that would have been far better.
Now, since by my own recklessness I have ruined my people,
I feel shame before the Trojans and the Trojan women with trail-
        ing                                                           105
robes, that someone who is less of a man than I will say of me:
"Hektor believed in his own strength and ruined his people."
Thus they will speak; and as for me, it would be much better
at that time, to go against Achilleus, and slay him, and come back,
or else be killed by him in glory in front of the city.              110
Or if again I set down my shield massive in the middle
and my ponderous helm, and lean my spear up against the rampart
and go out as I am to meet Achilleus the blameless
and promise to give back Helen, and with her all her possessions,
all those things that once in the hollow ships Alexandros
brought back to Troy, and these were the beginning of the quarrel;
to give these to Atreus' sons to take away, and for the Achaians

also to divide up all that is hidden within the city,
and take an oath thereafter for the Trojans in conclave
not to hide anything away, but distribute all of it,                         120
as much as the lovely citadel keeps guarded within it;
yet still, why does the heart within me debate on these things?
I might go up to him, and he take no pity upon me
nor respect my position, but kill me naked so, as if I were
a woman, once I stripped my armour from me. There is no     125
way any more from a tree or a rock to talk to him gently
whispering like a young man and a young girl, in the way
a young man and a young maiden whisper together.
Better to bring on the fight with him as soon as it may be.
We shall see to which one the Olympian grants the glory.'    130
    So he pondered, waiting, but Achilleus was closing upon him
in the likeness of the lord of battles, the helm-shining warrior,
and shaking from above his shoulder the dangerous Pelian
ash spear, while the bronze that closed about him was shining
like the flare of blazing fire or the sun in its rising.              135
And the shivers took hold of Hektor when he saw him, and he could
    no longer
stand his ground there, but left the gates behind, and fled, fright-
    ened,
and Peleus' son went after him in the confidence of his quick feet.
As when a hawk in the mountains who moves lightest of things flying
makes his effortless swoop for a trembling dove, but she slips away
from beneath and flies and he shrill screaming close after her     141
plunges for her again and again, heart furious to take her;
so Achilleus went straight for him in fury, but Hektor
fled away under the Trojan wall and moved his knees rapidly.
They raced along by the watching point and the windy fig tree     145
always away from under the wall and along the wagon-way
and came to the two sweet-running well springs. There there are
    double
springs of water that jet up, the springs of whirling Skamandros.
One of these runs hot water and the steam on all sides
of it rises as if from a fire that was burning inside it.              150
But the other in the summer-time runs water that is like hail
or chill snow or ice that forms from water. Beside these
in this place, and close to them, are the washing-hollows
of stone, and magnificent, where the wives of the Trojans and their
    lovely
daughters washed the clothes to shining, in the old days              155
when there was peace, before the coming of the sons of the Achai-
    ans.
They ran beside these, one escaping, the other after him.

It was a great man who fled, but far better he who pursued him
rapidly, since here was no festal beast, no ox-hide
they strove for, for these are prizes that are given men for their
     running.                                                                                                            160
No, they ran for the life of Hektor, breaker of horses.
As when about the turnposts racing single-foot horses
run at full speed, when a great prize is laid up for their winning,
at tripod or a woman, in games for a man's funeral,
so these two swept whirling about the city of Priam                                        165
in the speed of their feet, while all the gods were looking upon them.
First to speak among them was the father of gods and mortals:
'Ah me, this is a man beloved whom now my eyes watch
being chased around the wall; my heart is mourning for Hektor
who has burned in my honour many thigh pieces of oxen                              170
on the peaks of Ida[7] with all her folds, or again on the uttermost
part of the citadel, but now the brilliant Achilleus
drives him in speed of his feet around the city of Priam.
Come then, you immortals, take thought and take counsel, whether
to rescue this man or whether to make him, for all his valour,              175
go down under the hands of Achilleus, the son of Peleus.
     Then in answer the goddess grey-eyed Athene spoke to him:
'Father of the shining blot, dark misted, what is this you said?
Do you wish to bring back a man who is mortal, one long since
doomed by his destiny, from ill-sounding death and release him? 180
Do it, then; but not all the rest of us gods shall approve you.'
     Then Zeus the gatherer of the clouds spoke to her in answer:
'Tritogeneia,[8] dear daughter, do not lose heart; for I say this
not in outright anger, and my meaning toward you is kindly.
Act as your purpose would have you do, and hold back no
     longer.'                                                                                                          185
     So he spoke, and stirred on Athene, who was eager before this,
and she went in a flash of speed down the pinnacles of Olympos.
     But swift Achilleus kept unremittingly after Hektor,
chasing him, as a dog in the mountains who has flushed from his
     covert
a deer's fawn follows him through the folding ways and the valleys,
and though the fawn crouched down under a bush and be hidden
he keeps running and noses him out until he comes on him;
so Hektor could not lose himself from swift-footed Peleion.
If ever he made a dash right on for the gates of Dardanos
to get quickly under the strong-built bastions, endeavouring              195
that they from above with missiles thrown might somehow defend
     him,

7. The great mountain range near Troy.    8. A title of Athene; its origin and meaning are
unknown.

each time Achilleus would get in front and force him to turn back
into the plain, and himself kept his flying course next the city.
As in a dream a man is not able to follow one who runs
from him, nor can the runner escape, nor the other pursue him,    200
so he could not run him down in his speed, nor the other get clear.
How then could Hektor have escaped the death spirits, had not
Apollo, for this last and uttermost time, stood by him
close, and driven strength into him, and made his knees light?
But brilliant Achilleus kept shaking his head at his own people    205
and would not let them throw their bitter projectiles at Hektor
for fear the thrower might win the glory, and himself come second.
But when for the fourth time they had come around to the well
        springs
then the Father balanced his golden scales, and in them
he set two fateful portions of death, which lays men prostrate,    210
one for Achilleus, and one for Hektor, breaker of horses,
and balanced it by the middle; and Hektor's death-day was heavier
and dragged downward toward death, and Phoibos Apollo forsook
        him.
But the goddess grey-eyed Athene came now to Peleion
and stood close beside him and addressed him in winged words:
        'Beloved                                                   215
of Zeus, shining Achilleus, I am hopeful now that you and I
will take back great glory to the ships of the Achaians, after
we have killed Hektor, for all his slakeless fury for battle.
Now there is no way for him to get clear away from us,
not though Apollo who strikes from afar should be willing to
        undergo                                                    220
much, and wallow before our father Zeus of the aegis.
Stand you here then and get your wind again, while I go
to this man and persuade him to stand up to you in combat.'
    So spoke Athene, and he was glad at heart, and obeyed her,
and stopped, and stood leaning on his bronze-barbed ash spear.
        Meanwhile                                                  225
Athene left him there, and caught up with brilliant Hektor,
and likened herself in form and weariless voice to Deïphobos.[9]
She came now and stood close to him and addressed him in winged
        words:
'Dear brother, indeed swift-footed Achilleus is using you roughly
and chasing you on swift feet around the city of Priam.            230
Come on, then; let us stand fast against him and beat him back from
        us.'
    Then tall Hektor of the shining helm answered her: 'Deïphobos,

---

9. One of Hektor's brothers.

before now you were dearest to me by far of my brothers,
of all those who were sons of Priam and Hekabe, and now
I am minded all the more within my heart to honour you,          235
you who dared for my sake, when your eyes saw me, to come forth
from the fortifications, while the others stand fast inside them.'
    Then in turn the goddess grey-eyed Athene answered him:
'My brother, it is true our father and the lady our mother, taking
my knees in turn, and my companions about me, entreated          240
that I stay within, such was the terror upon all of them.
But the heart within me was worn away by hard sorrow for you.
But now let us go straight on and fight hard, let there be no sparing
of our spears, so that we can find out whether Achilleus
will kill us both and carry our bloody war spoils back            245
to the hollow ships, or will himself go down under your spear.'
    So Athene spoke and led him on by beguilement.
Now as the two in their advance were come close together,
first of the two to speak was tall helm-glittering Hektor:
'Son of Peleus, I will no longer run from you, as before this      250
I fled three times around the great city of Priam, and dared not
stand to your onfall. But now my spirit in turn has driven me
to stand and face you. I must take you now, or I must be taken.
Come then, shall we swear before the gods? For these are the highest
who shall be witnesses and watch over our agreements.             255
Brutal as you are I will not defile you, if Zeus grants
to me that I can wear you out, and take the life from you.
But after I have stripped your glorious armour, Achilleus,
I will give your corpse back to the Achaians. Do you do likewise.'
    Then looking darkly at him swift-footed Achilleus answered:   260
'Hektor, argue me no arguments. I cannot forgive you.
As there are no trustworthy oaths between men and lions,
nor wolves and lambs have spirit that can be brought to agreement
but forever these hold feelings of hate for each other,
so there can be no love between you and me, nor shall there be    265
oaths between us, but one or the other must fall before then
to glut with his blood Ares the god who fights under the shield's
        guard.
Remember every valour of yours, for now the need comes
hardest upon you to be a spearman and a bold warrior.
There shall be no more escape for you, but Pallas Athene          270
will kill you soon by my spear. You will pay in a lump for all those
sorrows of my companions you killed in your spear's fury.'
    So he spoke, and balanced the spear far shadowed, and threw it;
but glorious Hektor kept his eyes on him, and avoided it,
for he dropped, watchful, to his knee, and the bronze spear flew over
        his shoulder                                             275

and stuck in the ground, but Pallas Athene snatched it, and gave it
back to Achilleus, unseen by Hektor shepherd of the people.
But now Hektor spoke out to the blameless son of Peleus:
'You missed; and it was not, o Achilleus like the immortals,
from Zeus that you knew my destiny; but you thought so; or    280
    rather
you are someone clever in speech and spoke to swindle me,
to make me afraid of you and forget my valour and war strength.
You will not stick your spear in my back as I run away from you
but drive it into my chest as I storm straight in against you;
if the god gives you that; and now look out for my brazen    285
spear. I wish it might be taken full length in your body.
And indeed the war would be a lighter thing for the Trojans
if you were dead, seeing that you are their greatest affliction.'
    So he spoke, and balanced the spear far shadowed, and threw it,
and struck the middle of Peleïdes' shield, nor missed it,    290
but the spear was driven far back from the shield, and Hektor was
    angered
because his swift weapon had been loosed from his hand in a vain
    . cast.
He stood discouraged, and had no other ash spear; but lifting
his voice he called aloud on Deïphobos of the pale shield,
and asked him for a long spear, but Deïphobos was not near him. 295
And Hektor knew the truth inside his heart, and spoke aloud:
'No use. Here at last the gods have summoned me deathward.
I thought Deïphobos the hero was here close beside me,
but he is behind the wall and it was Athene cheating me,
and now evil death is close to me, and no longer far away,    300
and there is no way out. So it must long since have been pleasing
to Zeus, and Zeus' son who strikes from afar, this way; though before
    this
they defended me gladly. But now my death is upon me.
Let me at least not die without a struggle, inglorious,
but do some big thing first, that men to come shall know of it.'   305
    So he spoke, and pulling out the sharp sword that was slung
at the hollow of his side, huge and heavy, and gathering
himself together, he made his swoop, like a high-flown eagle
who launches himself out of the murk of the clouds on the flat land
to catch away a tender lamb or a shivering hare; so    310
Hektor made his swoop, swinging his sharp sword, and Achilleus
charged, the heart within him loaded with savage fury.
In front of his chest the beautiful elaborate great shield
covered him, and with the glittering helm with four horns
he nodded; the lovely golden fringes were shaken about it    315
which Hephaistos had driven close along the horn of the helmet.

And as a star moves among stars in the night's darkening,
Hesper,[1] who is the fairest star who stands in the sky, such
was the shining from the pointed spear Achilleus was shaking
in his right hand with evil intention toward brilliant Hektor.          320
He was eyeing Hektor's splendid body, to see where it might best
give way, but all the rest of the skin was held in the armour,
brazen and splendid, he stripped when he cut down the strength of
     Patroklos;
yet showed where the collar-bones hold the neck from the shoulders,
the throat, where death of the soul comes most swiftly; in this
     place                                                             325
brilliant Achilleus drove the spear as he came on in fury,
and clean through the soft part of the neck the spearpoint was driven.
Yet the ash spear heavy with bronze did not sever the windpipe,
so that Hektor could still make exchange of words spoken.
But he dropped in the dust, and brilliant Achilles vaunted above
     him:                                                             330
'Hektor, surely you thought as you killed Patroklos you would be
safe, and since I was far away you thought nothing of me,
o fool, for an avenger was left, far greater than he was,
behind him and away by the hollow ships. And it was I;
and I have broken your strength; on you the dogs and the vul-
     tures                                                            335
shall feed and foully rip you; the Achaians will bury Patroklos.'
     In his weakness Hektor of the shining helm spoke to him:
'I entreat you, by your life, by your knees, by your parents,
do not let the dogs feed on me by the ships of the Achaians,
but take yourself the bronze and gold that are there in abun-
     dance,                                                           340
those gifts that my father and the lady my mother will give you,
and give my body to be taken home again, so that the Trojans
and the wives of the Trojans may give me in death my rite of burn-
     ing.'
     But looking darkly at him swift-footed Achilleus answered:
'No more entreating of me, you dog, by knees or parents.             345
I wish only that my spirit and fury would drive me
to hack your meat away and eat it raw for the things that
you have done to me. So there is no one who can hold the dogs off
from your head, not if they bring here and set before me ten times
and twenty times the ransom, and promise more in addition,           350
not if Priam son of Dardanos should offer to weigh out
your bulk in gold; not even so shall the lady your mother
who herself bore you lay you on the death-bed and mourn you:

1. The evening star.

no, but the dogs and the birds will have you all for their feasting.'
    Then, dying, Hektor of the shining helmet spoke to him:     355
'I know you well as I look upon you, I know that I could not
persuade you, since indeed in your breast is a heart of iron.
Be careful now; for I might be made into the gods' curse
upon you, on that day when Paris and Phoibos Apollo
destroy you in the Skaian gates, for all your valour.'     360
    He spoke, and as he spoke the end of death closed in upon him,
and the soul fluttering free of the limbs went down into Death's
    house
mourning her destiny, leaving youth and manhood behind her.
Now though he was a dead man brilliant Achilleus spoke to him:
'Die: and I will take my own death at whatever time     365
Zeus and the rest of the immortals choose to accomplish it.'
    He spoke, and pulled the brazen spear from the body, and laid it
on one side, and stripped away from the shoulders the bloody
armour. And the other sons of the Achaians came running about
    him,
and gazed upon the stature and on the imposing beauty     370
of Hektor; and none stood beside him who did not stab him;
and thus they would speak one to another, each looking at his neigh-
    bour:
'See now, Hektor is much softer to handle than he was
when he set the ships ablaze with the burning firebrand.'
    So as they stood beside him they would speak, and stab him.     375
But now, when he had despoiled the body, swift-footed brilliant
Achilleus stood among the Achaians and addressed them in winged
    words:
'Friends, who are leaders of the Argives and keep their counsel:
since the gods have granted me the killing of this man
who has done us much damage, such as not all the others to-
    gether     380
have done, come, let us go in armour about the city
to see if we can find out what purpose is in the Trojans,
whether they will abandon their high city, now that this man
has fallen, or are minded to stay, though Hektor lives no longer.
Yet still, why does the heart within me debate on these things?     385
There is a dead man who lies by the ships, unwept, unburied:
Patroklos: and I will not forget him, never so long as
I remain among the living and my knees have their spring beneath
    me.
And though the dead forget the dead in the house of Hades,
even there I shall still remember my beloved companion.     390
But now, you young men of the Achaians, let us go back, singing
a victory song, to our hollow ships; and take this with us.

We have won ourselves enormous fame; we have killed the great
    Hektor
whom the Trojans glorified as if he were a god in their city.'
    He spoke, and now thought of shameful treatment for glorious
        Hektor.                                                        395
In both of his feet at the back he made holes by the tendons
in the space between ankle and heel, and drew thongs of ox-hide through
    them,
and fastened them to the chariot so as to let the head drag,
and mounted the chariot, and lifted the glorious armour inside it,
then whipped the horses to a run, and they winged their way
    unreluctant.                                                      400
A cloud of dust rose where Hektor was dragged, his dark hair was
    falling
about him, and all that head that was once so handsome was tum-
    bled
in the dust; since by this time Zeus had given him over
to his enemies, to be defiled in the land of his fathers.
    So all his head was dragged in the dust; and now his mother      405
tore out her hair, and threw the shining veil far from her
and raised a great wail as she looked upon her son; and his father
beloved groaned pitifully, and all his people about him
were taken with wailing and lamentation all through the city.
It was most like what would have happened, if all lowering          410
Ilion had been burning top to bottom in fire.
His people could scarcely keep the old man in his impatience
from storming out of the Dardanian gates; he implored them all,
and wallowed in the muck before them calling each man
and naming him by his name: 'Give way, dear friends,                415
and let me alone though you care for me, leave me to go out
from the city and make my way to the ships of the Achaians.
I must be suppliant to this man, who is harsh and violent,
and he might have respect for my age and take pity upon it
since I am old, and his father also is old, as I am,                420
Peleus, who begot and reared him to be an affliction
on the Trojans. He has given us most sorrow, beyond all others,
such is the number of my flowering sons he has cut down.
But for all of these I mourn not so much, in spite of my sorrow,
as for one, Hektor, and the sharp grief for him will carry me
    downward                                                         425
into Death's house. I wish he had died in my arms, for that way
we two, I myself and his mother who bore him unhappy,
might so have glutted ourselves with weeeping for him and mourn-
    ing.'
    So he spoke, in tears, and beside him mourned the citizens.

But for the women of Troy Hekabe led out the thronging                    430
chant of sorrow: 'Child, I am wretched. What shall my life be
in my sorrows, now you are dead, who by day and in the night
were my glory in the town, and to all of the Trojans
and the women of Troy a blessing throughout their city. They adored
          you
as if you were a god, since in truth you were their high honour      435
while you lived. Now death and fate have closed in upon you.'
     So she spoke in tears but the wife of Hektor had not yet
heard: for no sure messenger had come to her and told her
how her husband had held his ground there outside the gates;
but she was weaving a web in the inner room of the high house,    440
a red folding robe, and inworking elaborate figures.
She called out through the house to her lovely-haired handmaidens
to set a great cauldron over the fire, so that there would be
hot water for Hektor's bath as he came back out of the fighting;
poor innocent, nor knew how, far from waters for bathing,             445
Pallas Athene had cut him down at the hands of Achilleus.
She heard from the great bastion the noise of mourning and sorrow.
Her limbs spun, and the shuttle dropped from her hand to the ground.
     Then
she called aloud to her lovely-haired handmaidens: 'Come here.
Two of you come with me, so I can see what has happened.             450
I heard the voice of Hektor's honoured mother; within me
my own heart rising beats in my mouth, my limbs under me
are frozen. Surely some evil is near for the children of Priam.
May what I say come never close to my ear; yet dreadfully
I fear that great Achilleus might have cut off bold Hektor           455
alone, away from the city, and be driving him into the flat land,
might put an end to that bitter pride of courage, that always
was on him, since he would never stay back where the men were in
          numbers
but break far out in front, and give way in his fury to no man.'
     So she spoke, and ran out of the house like a raving woman      460
with pulsing heart, and her two handmaidens went along with her.
But when she came to the bastion and where the men were gathered
she stopped, staring, on the wall; and she saw him
being dragged in front of the city, and the running horses
dragged him at random toward the hollow ships of the Achaians.  465
The darkness of night misted over the eyes of Andromache.
She fell backward, and gasped the life breath from her, and far off
threw from her head the shining gear that ordered her headdress,
the diadem and the cap, and the holding-band woven together,
and the circlet, which Aphrodite the golden once had given her    470
on that day when Hektor of the shining helmet led her forth

from the house of Eëtion, and gave numberless gifts to win her.
And about her stood thronging her husband's sisters and the wives of
    his brothers
and these, in her despair for death, held her up among them.
But she, when she breathed again and the life was gathered back into
    her,                                                                                         475
lifted her voice among the women of Troy in mourning:
'Hektor, I grieve for you. You and I were born to a single
destiny, you in Troy in the house of Priam, and I
in Thebe, underneath the timbered mountain of Plakos
in the house of Eëtion, who cared for me when I was little,        480
ill-fated he, I ill-starred. I wish he had never begotten me.
Now you go down to the house of Death in the secret places
of the earth, and left me here behind in the sorrow of mourning,
a widow in your house, and the boy is only a baby
who was born to you and me, the unfortunate. You cannot help
    him,                                                                                        485
Hektor, any more, since you are dead. Nor can he help you.
Though he escape the attack of the Achaians with all its sorrows,
yet all his days for your sake there will be hard work for him
and sorrows, for others will take his lands away from him. The day
of bereavement leaves a child with no agemates to befriend him.   490
He bows his head before every man, his cheeks are bewept, he
goes, needy, a boy among his father's companions,
and tugs at this man by the mantle, that man by the tunic,
and they pity him, and one gives him a tiny drink from a goblet,
enough to moisten his lips, not enough to moisten his palate.    495
But one whose parents are living beats him out of the banquet
hitting him with his fists and in words also abuses him:
"Get out, you! Your father is not dining among us."
And the boy goes away in tears to his widowed mother,
Astyanax, who in days before on the knees of his father          500
would eat only the marrow or the flesh of sheep that was fattest.
And when sleep would come upon him and he was done with his
    playing,
he would go to sleep in a bed, in the arms of his nurse, in a soft
bed, with his heart given all its fill of luxury.
Now, with his dear father gone, he has much to suffer:           505
he, whom the Trojans have called Astyanax, lord of the city,
since it was you alone who defended the gates and the long walls.
But now, beside the curving ships, far away from your parents,
the writhing worms will feed, when the dogs have had enough of
    you,
on your naked corpse, though in your house there is clothing laid
    up                                                                                           510

that is fine-textured and pleasant, wrought by the hands of women.
But all of these I will burn up in the fire's blazing,
no use to you, since you will never be laid away in them;
but in your honour, from the men of Troy and the Trojan women.'
   So she spoke, in tears; and the women joined in her mourn-
     ing.                                               515

[Achilleus buried Patroklos, and the Greeks celebrated the dead
hero's fame with athletic games, for which Achilleus gave the prizes.]

## Book XXIV

### [ACHILLEUS AND PRIAM]

And the games broke up, and the people scattered to go away, each
    man
to his fast-running ship, and the rest of them took thought of their
    dinner
and of sweet sleep and its enjoyment; only Achilleus
wept still as he remembered his beloved companion, nor did sleep
who subdues all come over him, but he tossed from one side to the
    other                                               5
in longing for Patroklos, for his manhood and his great strength
and all the action he had seen to the end with him, and the hard-
    ships
he had suffered; the wars of men; hard crossing of the big waters.
Remembering all these things he let fall the swelling tears, lying
sometimes along his side, sometimes on his back, and now again  10
prone on his face; then he would stand upright, and pace turning
in distraction along the beach of the sea, nor did dawn rising
escape him as she brightened across the sea and the beaches.
Then, when he had yoked running horses under the chariot
he would fasten Hektor behind the chariot, so as to drag him,  15
and draw him three times around the tomb of Menoitios' fallen
son, then rest again in his shelter, and throw down the dead man
and leave him to lie sprawled on his face in the dust. But Apollo
had pity on him, though he was only a dead man, and guarded
the body from all ugliness, and hid all of it under the golden  20
aegis, so that it might not be torn when Achilleus dragged it.
   So Achilleus in his standing fury outraged great Hektor.
The blessed gods as they looked upon him were filled with compas-
    sion
and kept urging clear-sighted Argeïphontes[2] to steal the body.
There this was pleasing to all the others, but never to Hera  25

2. A title of Hermes (its meaning is disputed). Hermes was the messenger of Zeus, and was also renowned for his trickery and thieving.

nor Poseidon, nor the girl of the grey eyes,[3] who kept still
their hatred for sacred Ilion as in the beginning,
and for Priam and his people, because of the delusion of Paris[4]
who insulted the goddesses when they came to him in his courtyard
and favoured her who supplied the lust that led to disaster.          30
But now, as it was the twelfth dawn after the death of Hektor,
Phoibos Apollo spoke his word out among the immortals:
'You are hard, you gods, and destructive. Now did not Hektor
burn thigh pieces of oxen and unblemished goats in your honour?
Now you cannot bring yourselves to save him, though he is only     35
a corpse, for his wife to look upon, his child and his mother
and Priam his father, and his people, who presently thereafter
would burn his body in the fire and give him his rites of burial.
No, you gods; your desire is to help this cursed Achilleus
within whose breast there are no feelings of justice, nor can      40
his mind be bent, but his purposes are fierce, like a lion
who when he has given way to his own great strength and his haughty
spirit, goes among the flocks of men, to devour them.
So Achilleus has destroyed pity, and there is not in him
any shame; which does much harm to men but profits them also.  45
For a man must some day lose one who was ever closer
than this; a brother from the same womb, or a son. And yet
he weeps for him, and sorrows for him, and then it is over,
for the Destinies put in mortal men the heart of endurance.
But this man, now he has torn the heart of life from great Hektor,  50
ties him to his horses and drags him around his beloved compa-
        nion's
tomb; and nothing is gained thereby for his good, or his honour.
Great as he is, let him take care not to make us angry;
for see, he does dishonour to the dumb earth in his fury.'
    Then bitterly Hera of the white arms answered him, saying:     55
'What you have said could be true, lord of the silver bow, only
if you give Hektor such pride of place as you give to Achilleus.
But Hektor was mortal, and suckled at the breast of a woman,
while Achilleus is the child of a goddess, one whom I myself
nourished and brought up and gave her as bride to her husband     60
Peleus, one dear to the hearts of the immortals, for you all
went, you gods, to the wedding; and you too feasted among them
and held your lyre, o friend of the evil, faithless forever.'
    In turn Zeus who gathers the clouds spoke to her in answer:
'Hera, be not utterly angry with the gods, for there shall not     65
be the same pride of place given both. Yet Hektor also

---

3. Athene.    4. He was appointed judge in a contest of beauty between Aphrodite, Hera, and
Athene. All three goddesses offered bribes, but Aphrodite's promise to give him Helen proved the
most attractive.

was loved by the gods, best of all the mortals in Ilion.
I loved him too. He never failed of gifts to my liking.
Never yet has my altar gone without fair sacrifice,
the smoke and the savour of it, since that is our portion of hon-
     our.                                                                                      70
The stealing of him we will dismiss, for it is not possible
to take bold Hektor secretly from Achilleus, since always
his mother is near him night and day; but it would be better if one
of the gods would summon Thetis here to my presence
so that I can say a close word to her, and see that Achilleus      75
is given gifts by Priam and gives back the body of Hektor.'
     He spoke, and Iris storm-footed sprang away with the message,
and at a point between Samos and Imbros[5] of the high cliffs
plunged in the dark water, and the sea crashed moaning about her.
She plummeted to sea floor like a lead weight which, mounted      80
along the horn of an ox[6] who ranges the fields, goes downward
and takes death with it to the raw-ravening fish. She found Thetis
inside the hollow of her cave, and gathered about her
sat the rest of the sea goddesses, and she in their midst
was mourning the death of her blameless son, who so soon was
     destined                                                                              85
to die in Troy of the rich soil, far from the land of his fathers.
Iris the swift-foot came close beside her and spoke to her:
'Rise, Thetis. Zeus whose purposes are infinite calls you.'
     In turn Thetis the goddess, the silver-footed, answered her:
'What does he, the great god, want with me? I feel shamefast      90
to mingle with the immortals, and my heart is confused with sor-
     rows.
But I will go. No word shall be in vain, if he says it.'
     So she spoke, and shining among the divinities took up
her black veil, and there is no darker garment. She went
on her way, and in front of her rapid wind-footed Iris             95
guided her, and the wave of the water opened about them.
They stepped out on the dry land and swept to the sky. There they
     found
the son of Kronos of the wide brows, and gathered about him
sat all the rest of the gods, the blessed, who live forever.
She sat down beside Zeus father, and Athene made a place for
     her.                                                                                   100
Hera put into her hand a beautiful golden goblet
and spoke to her to comfort her, and Thetis accepting drank from it.
The father of gods and men began the discourse among them:
'You have come to Olympos, divine Thetis, for all your sorrow,

5. Two islands in the north Aegean.    6. A lure for big fish.

with an unforgotten grief in your heart. I myself know this.           105
But even so I will tell you why I summoned you hither.
For nine days there has risen a quarrel among the immortals
over the body of Hektor, and Achilleus, stormer of cities.
They keep urging clear-sighted Argeïphontes to steal the body,
but I still put upon Achilleus the honour that he has, guarding      110
your reverence and your love for me into time afterwards. Go then
in all speed to the encampment and give to your son this message:
tell him that the gods frown upon him, that beyond all other
immortals I myself am angered that in his heart's madness
he holds Hektor beside the curved ships and did not give him        115
back. Perhaps in fear of me he will give back Hektor.
Then I will send Iris to Priam of the great heart, with an order
to ransom his dear son, going down to the ships of the Achaians
and bringing gifts to Achilleus which might soften his anger.'
     He spoke and the goddess silver-foot Thetis did not disobey
          him                                                        120
but descended in a flash of speed from the peaks of Olympos
and made her way to the shelter of her son, and there found him
in close lamentation, and his beloved companions about him
were busy at their work and made ready the morning meal, and there
stood a great fleecy sheep being sacrificed in the shelter.         125
His honoured mother came close to him and sat down beside him,
and stroked him with her hand and called him by name and spoke
          to him:
'My child, how long will you go on eating your heart out in sorrow
and lamentation, and remember neither your food nor going
to bed? It is a good thing even to lie with a woman                 130
in love. For you will not be with me long, but already
death and powerful destiny stand closely above you.
But listen hard to me, for I come from Zeus with a message.
He says that the gods frown upon you, that beyond all other
immortals he himself is angered that in your heart's madness        135
you hold Hektor beside the curved ships and did not redeem him.
Come, then, give him up and accept ransom for the body.'
     Then in turn Achilleus of the swift feet answered her:
'So be it. He can bring the ransom and take off the body,
if the Olympian himself so urgently bids it.'                       140
     So, where the ships were drawn together, the son and his mother
conversed at long length in winged words. But the son of Kronos
stirred Iris to go down to sacred Ilion, saying:
'Go forth, Iris the swift, leaving your place on Olympos,
and go to Priam of the great heart within Ilion, tell him           145
to ransom his dear son, going down to the ships of the Achaians
and bringing gifts to Achilleus which might soften his anger:

alone, let no other man of the Trojans go with him, but only
let one elder herald attend him, one who can manage
the mules and the easily running wagon, so he can carry          150
the dead man, whom great Achilleus slew, back to the city.
Let death not be a thought in his heart, let him have no fear;
such an escort shall I send to guide him, Argeïphontes
who shall lead him until he brings him to Achilleus. And after
he has brought him inside the shelter of Achilleus, neither          155
will the man himself kill him, but will hold back all the others,
for he is no witless man nor unwatchful, nor is he wicked,
but will in all kindness spare one who comes to him as a suppliant.'
    He spoke, and storm-footed Iris swept away with the message
and came to the house of Priam. There she found outcry and
    mourning.          160
The sons sitting around their father inside the courtyard
made their clothes sodden with their tears, and among them the old
    man
sat veiled, beaten into his mantle. Dung lay thick
on the head and neck of the aged man, for he had been rolling
in it, he had gathered and smeared it on with his hands. And his
    daughters          165
all up and down the house and the wives of his sons were mourning
as they remembered all those men in their numbers and valour
who lay dead, their lives perished at the hands of the Argives.
The messenger of Zeus stood beside Priam and spoke to him
in a small voice, and yet the shivers took hold of his body:          170
'Take heart, Priam, son of Dardanos, do not be frightened.
I come to you not eyeing you with evil intention
but with the purpose of good toward you. I am a messenger
of Zeus, who far away cares much for you and is pitiful.
The Olympian orders you to ransom Hektor the brilliant,          175
to bring gifts to Achilleus which may soften his anger:
alone, let no other man of the Trojans go with you, but only
let one elder herald attend you, one who can manage
the mules and the easily running wagon, so he can carry
the dead man, whom great Achilleus slew, back to the city.          180
Let death not be a thought in your heart, you need have no fear,
such an escort shall go with you to guide you, Argeïphontes
who will lead you till he brings you to Achilleus. And after
he has brought you inside the shelter of Achilleus, neither
will the man himself kill you but will hold back all the others;          185
for he is no witless man nor unwatchful, nor is he wicked
but will in all kindness spare one who comes to him as a suppliant.'
    So Iris the swift-footed spoke and went away from him.
Thereupon he ordered his sons to make ready the easily rolling

mule wagon, and to fasten upon it the carrying basket.                190
He himself went into the storeroom, which was fragrant
and of cedar, and high-ceilinged, with many bright treasures inside
    it.
He called out to Hekabe his wife, and said to her:
'Dear wife, a messenger came to me from Zeus on Olympos,
that I must go to the ships of the Achaians and ransom my dear
    son,                                                              195
bringing gifts to Achilleus which may soften his anger.
Come then, tell me. What does it seem best to your own mind
for me to do? My heart, my strength are terribly urgent
that I go there to the ships within the wide army of the Achaians.'
    So he spoke, and his wife cried out aloud, and answered him:     200
'Ah me, where has that wisdom gone for which you were famous
in time before, among outlanders and those you rule over?
How can you wish to go alone to the ships of the Achaians
before the eyes of a man who has slaughtered in such numbers
such brave sons of yours? The heart in you is iron. For if          205
he has within his grasp and lays eyes upon you, that man
who is savage and not to be trusted will not take pity upon you
nor have respect for your rights. Let us sit apart in our palace
now, and weep for Hektor, and the way at the first strong Destiny
spun with his life line when he was born, when I gave birth to
    him,                                                             210
that the dogs with their shifting feet should feed on him, far from his
    parents,
gone down before a stronger man; I wish I could set teeth
in the middle of his liver and eat it. That would be vengeance
for what he did to my son; for he slew him when he was no coward
but standing before the men of Troy and the deep-girdled women 215
of Troy, with no thought in his mind of flight or withdrawal.'
    In turn the aged Priam, the godlike, answered her saying:
'Do not hold me back when I would be going, neither yourself be
a bird of bad omen in my palace. You will not persuade me.
If it had been some other who ordered me, one of the mortals,      220
one of those who are soothsayers, or priests, or diviners,
I might have called it a lie and we might rather have rejected it.
But now, for I myself heard the god and looked straight upon her,
I am going, and this word shall not be in vain. If it is my destiny
to die there by the ships of the bronze-armoured Achaians,          225
then I wish that. Achilleus can slay me at once, with my own son
caught in my arms, once I have my fill of mourning above him.'
    He spoke, and lifted back the fair covering of his clothes-chest
and from inside took out twelve robes surpassingly lovely
and twelve mantles to be worn single, as many blankets,            230

as many great white cloaks, also the same number of tunics.
He weighed and carried out ten full talents of gold, and brought forth
two shining tripods, and four cauldrons, and brought out a goblet
of surpassing loveliness that the men of Thrace had given him
when he went to them with a message, but now the old man spared
    not                                                                          235
even this in his halls, so much was it his heart's desire
to ransom back his beloved son. But he drove off the Trojans
all from his cloister walks, scolding them with words of revilement:
'Get out, you failures, you disgraces. Have you not also
mourning of your own at home that you come to me with your
    sorrows?                                                                     240
Is it not enough that Zeus, son of Kronos, has given me sorrow
in losing the best of my sons? You also shall be aware of this
since you will be all the easier for the Achaians to slaughter
now he is dead. But, for myself, before my eyes look
upon this city as it is destroyed and its people are slaughtered,          245
my wish is to go sooner down to the house of the death god.'
    He spoke, and went after the men with a stick, and they fled out-
        side
before the fury of the old man. He was scolding his children
and cursing Helenos, and Paris, Agathon the brilliant,
Pammon and Antiphonos, Polites of the great war cry,                        250
Deïphobos and Hippothoös and proud Dios. There were nine
sons to whom now the old man gave orders and spoke to them roughly:
'Make haste, wicked children, my disgraces. I wish all of you
had been killed beside the running ships in the place of Hektor.
Ah me, for my evil destiny. I have had the noblest                          255
of sons in Troy, but I say not one of them is left to me,
Mestor like a god and Troilos whose delight was in horses,
and Hektor, who was a god among men, for he did not seem like
one who was child of a mortal man, but of a god. All these
Ares has killed, and all that are left me are the disgraces,                260
the liars and the dancers, champions of the chorus, the plunderers
of their own people in their land of lambs and kids. Well then,
will you not get my wagon ready and be quick about it,
and put all these things on it, so we can get on with our journey?'
    So he spoke, and they in terror at the old man's scolding                 265
hauled out the easily running wagon for mules, a fine thing
new-fabricated, and fastened the carrying basket upon it.
They took away from its peg the mule yoke made of boxwood
with its massive knob, well fitted with guiding rings, and brought
    forth
the yoke lashing (together with the yoke itself) of nine cubits             270
and snugged it well into place upon the smooth-polished wagonpole

at the foot of the beam, then slipped the ring over the peg, and
    lashed it
with three turns on either side to the knob, and afterwards
fastened it all in order and secured it under a hooked guard.
Then they carried out and piled into the smooth-polished mule
    wagon                                                                                275
all the unnumbered spoils to be given for the head of Hektor,
then yoked the powerful-footed mules who pulled in the harness
and whom the Mysians[7] gave once as glorious presents to Priam;
but for Priam they led under the yoke those horses the old man
himself had kept, and cared for them at his polished manger.      280
    Now in the high house the yoking was done for the herald
and Priam, men both with close counsels in their minds. And now
    came
Hekabe with sorrowful heart and stood close beside them
carrying in her right hand the kind, sweet wine in a golden
goblet, so that before they went they might pour a drink-offering. 285
She stood in front of the horses, called Priam by name and spoke to
    him:
'Here, pour a libation to Zeus father, and pray you may come back
home again from those who hate you, since it seems the spirit
within you drives you upon the ships, though I would not have it.
Make your prayer then to the dark-misted, the son of Kronos      290
on Ida, who looks out on all the Troad, and ask him
for a bird of omen, a rapid messenger, which to his own mind
is dearest of all birds and his strength is the biggest, one seen
on the right, so that once your eyes have rested upon him
you can trust in him and go to the ships of the fast-mounted
    Danaans.                                                                             295
But if Zeus of the wide brows will not grant you his own messenger,
then I, for one, would never urge you on nor advise you
to go to the Argive ships, for all your passion to do it.'
    Then in answer to her again spoke Priam the godlike:
'My lady, I will not disregard this wherein you urge me.          300
It is well to lift hands to Zeus and ask if he will have mercy.'
    The old man spoke, and told the housekeeper who attended them
to pour unstained water over his hands. She standing beside them
and serving them held the washing-bowl in her hands, and a pitcher.
He washed his hands and took the cup from his wife. He stood
    up                                                                                          305
in the middle of the enclosure, and prayed, and poured the wine out
looking up into the sky, and gave utterance and spoke, saying:
'Father Zeus, watching over us from Ida, most high, most honoured:

---

7. A people of central Asia Minor.

grant that I come to Achilleus for love and pity; but send me
a bird of omen, a rapid messenger which to your own mind          310
is dearest of all birds and his strength is biggest, one seen
on the right, so that once my eyes have rested upon him
I may trust in him and go to the ships of the fast-mounted Danaans.'
   So he spoke in prayer, and Zeus of the counsels heard him.
Straightway he sent down the most lordly of birds, an eagle,       315
the dark one, the marauder, called as well the black eagle.
And as big as is the build of the door to a towering chamber
in the house of a rich man, strongly fitted with bars, of such size
was the spread of his wings on either side. He swept through the city
appearing on the right hand, and the people looking upon him       320
were uplifted and the hearts made glad in the breasts of all of them.
   Now in urgent haste the old man mounted into his chariot
and drove out though the forecourt and the thundering close. Before
      him
the mules hauled the wagon on its four wheels, Idaios
the sober-minded driving them, and behind him the horses           325
came on as the old man laid the lash upon them and urged them
rapidly through the town, and all his kinsmen were following
much lamenting, as if he went to his death. When the two men
had gone down through the city, and out, and come to the flat land,
the rest of them turned back to go to Ilion, the sons              330
and the sons-in-law. And Zeus of the wide brows failed not to notice
the two as they showed in the plain. He saw the old man and took
      pity
upon him, and spoke directly to his beloved son, Hermes:
'Hermes, for to you beyond all other gods it is dearest
to be man's companion, and you listen to whom you will, go
      now                                                          335
on your way, and so guide Priam inside the hollow ships
of the Achaians, that no man shall see him, none be aware of him,
of the other Danaans, till he has come to the son of Peleus.'
   He spoke, nor disobeyed him the courier, Argeïphontes.
Immediately he bound upon his feet the fair sandals                340
golden and immortal, that carried him over the water
as over the dry land of the main abreast of the wind's blast.
He caught up the staff, with which he mazes the eyes of those mor-
      tals
whose eyes he would maze, or wakes again the sleepers. Holding
this in his hands, strong Argeïphontes winged his way onward       345
until he came suddenly to Troy and the Hellespont, and there
walked on, and there took the likeness of a young man, a noble,
with beard new grown, which is the most graceful time of young
      manhood.

Now then the two had driven past the great tomb of Ilos[8]
they stayed their mules and horses to water them in the river,          350
for by this time darkness had descended on the land; and the herald
made out Hermes, who was coming toward them at a short distance.
He lifted his voice and spoke aloud to Priam: 'Take thought,
son of Dardanos. Here is work for a mind that is careful.
I see a man; I think he will presently tear us to pieces.          355
Come then, let us run away with our horses, or if not, then
clasp his knees and entreat him to have mercy upon us.'
    So he spoke, and the old man's mind was confused, he was badly
frightened, and the hairs stood up all over his gnarled body
and he stood staring, but the kindly god himself coming closer          360
took the old man's hand, and spoke to him and asked him a question:
'Where, my father, are you thus guiding your mules and horses
through the immortal night while other mortals are sleeping?
Have you no fear of the Achaians whose wind is fury,
who hate you, who are your enemies, and are near? For if one          365
of these to see you, how you are conveying so many
treasures through the swift black night, what then could you think
        of?
You are not young yourself, and he who attends you is aged
for beating off any man who might pick a quarrel with you.
But I will do you no harm myself, I will even keep off          370
another who would. You seem to me like a beloved father.'
    In answer to him again spoke aged Priam the godlike:
'Yes, in truth, dear child, all this is much as you tell me;
yet still there is some god who has held his hand above me,
who sent such a wayfarer as you to meet me, an omen          375
of good, for such you are by your form, your admired beauty
and the wisdom in your mind. Your parents are fortunate in you.'
    Then in turn answered him the courier Argeïphontes:
'Yes, old sir, all this that you said is fair and orderly.
But come, tell me this thing and recite it to me accurately.          380
Can it be you convey these treasures in all their numbers and beauty
to outland men, so that they can be still kept safe for you?
Or are all of you by now abandoning sacred Ilion
in fear, such a one was he who died, the best man among you,
your son; who was never wanting when you fought against the
        Achaians.'          385
    In answer to him again spoke aged Priam the godlike:
'But who are you, o best of men, and who are your parents?
Since you spoke of my ill-starred son's death, and with honour.'
    Then in turn answered him the courier Argeïphontes:

8. The tomb of Priam's grandfather, a landmark on the Trojan plain.

'You try me out, aged sir. You ask me of glorious Hektor        390
whom many a time my eyes have seen in the fighting where men
        win
glory, as also on that time when he drove back the Argives
on their ships and kept killing them with the stroke of the sharp
        bronze,
and we stood by and wondered at him; for then Achilleus
would not let us fight by reason of his anger at Agamemnon.     395
For I am Achilleus' henchman, and the same strong-wrought vessel
brought us here; and I am a Myrmidon, and my father
is Polyktor; a man of substance, but aged, as you are.
He has six sons beside, and I am the seventh, and I shook
lots with the others, and it was my lot to come on this venture.   400
But now I have come to the plain away from the ships, for at day-
        break
the glancing-eyed Achaians will do battle around the city.
They chafe from sitting here too long, nor have the Achaians'
kings the strength to hold them back as they break for the fighting.'
        In answer to him again spoke aged Priam the godlike:        405
'If then you are henchman to Peleïd Achilleus,
come, tell me the entire truth, and whether my son lies
still beside the ships, or whether by now he has been hewn
limb from limb and thrown before the dogs by Achilleus.'
        Then in turn answered him the courier Argeïphontes:        410
'Aged sir, neither have any dogs eaten him, nor have
the birds, but he lies yet beside the ship of Achilleus
at the shelters, and as he was; now here is the twelfth dawn
he has lain there, nor does his flesh decay, nor do worms feed
on him, they who devour men who have fallen in battle.         415
It is true, Achilleus drags him at random around his beloved
companion's tomb, as dawn on dawn appears, yet he cannot
mutilate him; you yourself can see when you go there
how fresh with dew he lies, and the blood is all washed from him,
nor is there any corruption, and all the wounds have been closed
        up                                                          420
where he was struck, since many drove the bronze in his body.
So it is that the blessed immortals care for your son, though
he is nothing but a dead man; because in their hearts they loved
        him.'
        He spoke, and the old man was made joyful and answered him,
        saying:
'My child, surely it is good to give the immortals                425
their due gifts; because my own son, if ever I had one,
never forgot in his halls the gods who live on Olympos.
Therefore they remembered him even in death's stage. Come, then,

accept at my hands this beautiful drinking-cup, and give me
protection for my body, and with the gods' grace be my escort          430
until I make my way to the shelter of the son of Peleus.'
   In turn answered him the courier Argeïphontes:
'You try me out, aged sir, for I am young, but you will not
persuade me, telling me to accept your gifts when Achilleus
does not know. I fear him at heart and have too much reverence   435
to rob him. Such a thing might be to my sorrow hereafter.
But I would be your escort and take good care of you, even
till I came to glorious Argos in a fast ship or following
on foot, and none would fight you because he despised your escort.'
   The kind god spoke, and sprang up behind the horses and into   440
the chariot, and rapidly caught in his hands the lash and the guide
      reins.
and breathed great strength into the mules and horses. Now after
they had got to the fortifications about the ships, and the ditch, there
were sentries, who had just begun to make ready their dinner,
but about these the courier Argeïphontes drifted                       445
sleep, on all, and quickly opened the gate, and shoved back
the door-bars, and brought in Priam and the glorious gifts on the
      wagon.
But when they had got to the shelter of Peleus' son: a towering
shelter the Myrmidons had built for their king, hewing
the timbers of pine, and they made a roof of thatch above it           450
shaggy with grass that they had gathered out of the meadows;
and around it made a great courtyard for their king, with hedgepoles
set close together; the gate was secured by a single door-piece
of pine, and three Achaians could ram it home in its socket
and three could pull back and open the huge door-bar; three other
Achaians, that is, but Achilleus all by himself could close it.        456
At this time Hermes, the kind god, opened the gate for the old man
and brought in the glorious gifts for Peleus' son, the swift-footed,
and dismounted to the ground from behind the horses, and spoke
      forth:
'Aged sir, I who came to you am a god immortal,                        460
Hermes. My father sent me down to guide and go with you.
But now I am going back again, and I will not go in
before the eyes of Achilleus, for it would make others angry
for an immortal god so to face mortal men with favour.
But go you in yourself and clasp the knees of Peleion                  465
and entreat him in the name of his father, the name of his mother
of the lovely hair, and his child, and so move the spirit within him.'
   So Hermes spoke, and went away to the height of Olympos,
but Priam vaulted down to the ground from behind the horses
and left Idaios where he was, for he stayed behind, holding            470

in hand the horses and mules. The old man made straight for the
    dwelling
where Achilleus the beloved of Zeus was sitting. He found him
inside, and his companions were sitting apart, as two only
Automedon the hero and Alkimos, scion of Ares,
were busy beside him. He had just now got through with his
    dinner,                                                      475
with eating and drinking, and the table still stood by. Tall Priam
came in unseen by the other men and stood close beside him
and caught the knees of Achilleus in his arms, and kissed the hands
that were dangerous and manslaughtering and had killed so many
of his sons. As when dense disaster closes on one who has
    murdered                                                     480
a man in his own land, and he comes to the country of others,
to a man of substance, and wonder seizes on those who behold him,
so Achilleus wondered as he looked on Priam, a godlike
man, and the rest of them wondered also, and looked at each other.
But now Priam spoke to him in the words of a suppliant:        485
'Achilleus like the gods, remember your father, one who
is of years like mine, and on the door-sill of sorrowful old age.
And they who dwell nearby encompass him and afflict him,
nor is there any to defend him against the wrath, the destruction.
Yet surely he, when he hears of you and that you are still living,  490
is gladdened within his heart and all his days he is hopeful
that he will see his beloved son come home from the Troad.
But for me, my destiny was evil. I have had the noblest
of sons in Troy, but I say not one of them is left to me.
Fifty were my sons, when the sons of the Achaians came here.   495
Nineteen were born to me from the womb of a single mother,
and other women bore the rest in my palace; and of these
violent Ares broke the strength in the knees of most of them,
but one was left me who guarded my city and people, that one
you killed a few days since as he fought in defence of his country, 500
Hektor; for whose sake I come now to the ships of the Achaians
to win him back from you, and I bring you gifts beyond number.
Honour then the gods, Achilleus, and take pity upon me
remembering your father, yet I am still more pitiful;
I have gone through what no other mortal on earth has gone
    through;                                                     505
I put my lips to the hands of the man who has killed my children.'
    So he spoke, and stirred in the other a passion of grieving
for his own father. He took the old man's hand and pushed him
gently away, and the two remembered, as Priam sat huddled
at the feet of Achilleus and wept close for manslaughtering Hek-
    tor                                                          510

and Achilleus wept now for his own father, now again
for Patroklos. The sound of their mourning moved in the house.
    Then
when great Achilleus had taken full satisfaction in sorrow
and the passion for it had gone from his mind and body, thereafter
he rose from his chair, and took the old man by the hand, and set
    him                                                            515
on his feet again, in pity for the grey head and the grey beard,
and spoke to him and addressed him in winged words: 'Ah, unlucky,
surely you have had much evil to endure in your spirit.
How could you dare to come alone to the ships of the Achaians
and before my eyes, when I am one who have killed in such
    numbers                                                        520
such brave sons of yours? The heart in you is iron. Come, then,
and sit down upon this chair, and you and I will even let
our sorrows lie still in the heart for all our grieving. There is not
any advantage to be won from grim lamentation.
Such is the way the gods spun life for unfortunate mortals,        525
that we live in unhappiness, but the gods themselves have no sor-
    rows.
There are two urns that stand on the door-sill of Zeus. They are
    unlike
for the gifts they bestow: an urn of evils, an urn of blessings.
If Zeus who delights in thunder mingles these and bestows them
on man, he shifts, and moves now in evil, again in good fortune, 530
But when Zeus bestows from the urn of sorrows, he makes a failure
of man, and the evil hunger drives him over the shining
earth, and he wanders respected neither of gods nor mortals.
Such were the shining gifts given by the gods to Peleus
from his birth, who outshone all men beside for his riches         535
and pride of possession, and was lord over the Myrmidons. Thereto
the gods bestowed an immortal wife on him, who was mortal.
But even on him the god piled evil also. There was not
any generation of strong sons born to him in his great house
but a single all-untimely child he had, and I give him             540
no care as he grows old, since far from the land of my fathers
I sit here in Troy, and bring nothing but sorrow to you and your
    children.
And you, old sir, we are told you prospered once; for as much as
Lesbos, Makar's hold,[9] confines to the north above it
and Phrygia from the north confines, and enormous Hellespont,     545
of these, old sir, you were lord once in your wealth and your chil-
    dren.

9. Makar was the legendary first king of Lesbos, a large and fertile island of the coast of Asia
Minor.

But now the Uranian gods brought us, an affliction upon you,
forever there is fighting about your city, and men killed.
But bear up, nor mourn endlessly in your heart, for there is not
anything to be gained from grief for your son; you will never        550
bring him back; sooner you must go through yet another sorrow.'
     In answer to him again spoke aged Priam the godlike:
'Do not, beloved of Zeus, make me sit on a chair while Hektor
lies yet forlorn among the shelters; rather with all speed
give him back, so my eyes may behold him, and accept the
          ransom                                                     555
we bring you, which is great. You may have joy of it, and go back
to the land of your own fathers, since once you have permitted me
to go on living myself and continue to look on the sunlight.'
     Then looking darkly at him spoke swift-footed Achilleus:
'No longer stir me up, old sir. I myself am minded                   560
to give Hektor back to you. A messenger came to me from Zeus,
my mother, she who bore me, the daughter of the sea's ancient.
I know you, Priam, in my heart, and it does not escape me
that some god led you to the running ships of the Achaians.
For no mortal would dare come to our encampment, not even            565
one strong in youth. He could not get by the pickets, he could not
lightly unbar the bolt that secures our gateway. Therefore
you must not further make my spirit move in my sorrows,
for fear, old sir, I might not let you alone in my shelter,
suppliant as you are; and be guilty before the god's orders.'        570
     He spoke, and the old man was frightened and did as he told him.
The son of Peleus bounded to the door of the house like a lion,
nor went alone, but the two henchmen followed attending,
the hero Automedon and Alkimos, those whom Achilleus
honoured beyond all companions after Patroklos dead. These two 575
now set free from under the yoke the mules and the horses,
and led inside the herald, the old king's crier, and gave him
a chair to sit in, then from the smooth-polished mule wagon
lifted out the innumerable spoils for the head of Hektor,
but left inside it two great cloaks and a finespun tunic             580
to shroud the corpse in when they carried him home. Then Achil-
          leus
called out to his serving-maids to wash the body and anoint it
all over; but take it first aside, since otherwise Priam
might see his son and in the heart's sorrow not hold in his anger
at the sight, and the deep heart in Achilleus be shaken to anger;    585
that he might not kill Priam and be guilty before the god's orders.
Then when the serving-maids had washed the corpse and anointed
          it
with olive oil, they threw a fair great cloak and a tunic

about him, and Achilleus himself lifted him and laid him
on a litter, and his friends helped him lift it to the smooth-pol-
     ished                                                                590
mule wagon. He groaned then, and called by name on his beloved
     companion:
'Be not angry with me, Patroklos, if you discover,
though you be in the house of Hades, that I give back great Hektor
to his loved father, for the ransom he gave me was not unworthy.
I will give you your share of the spoils, as much as is fitting.'     595
    So spoke great Achilleus and went back into the shelter
and sat down on the elaborate couch from which he had risen,
against the inward wall, and now spoke his word to Priam:
'Your son is given back to you, aged sir, as you asked it.
He lies on a bier. When dawn shows you yourself shall see him    600
as you take him away. Now you and I must remember our supper.
For even Niobe,[1] she of the lovely tresses, remembered
to eat, whose twelve children were destroyed in her palace,
six daughters, and six sons in the pride of their youth, whom Apollo
killed with arrows from his silver bow, being angered             605
with Niobe, and shaft-showering Artemis killed the daughters;
because Niobe likened herself to Leto[2] of the fair colouring
and said Leto had borne only two, she herself had borne many;
but the two, though they were only two, destroyed all those others.
Nine days long they lay in their blood, nor was there anyone      610
to bury them, for the son of Kronos made stones out of
the people; but on the tenth day the Uranian gods buried them.
But she remembered to eat when she was worn out with weeping.
And now somewhere among the rocks, in the lonely mountains,
in Sipylos,[3] where they say is the resting place of the goddesses  615
who are nymphs, and dance beside the waters of Acheloios,
there, stone still,[4] she broods on the sorrows that the gods gave her.
Come then, we also, aged magnificent sir, must remember
to eat, and afterwards you may take your beloved son back
to Ilion, and mourn for him; and he will be much lamented.'       620
    So spoke fleet Achilleus and sprang to his feet and slaughtered
a gleaming sheep, and his friends skinned it and butchered it fairly,
And cut up the meat expertly into small pieces, and spitted them,
and roasted all carefully and took off the pieces.
Automedon took the bread and set it out on the table             625
in fair baskets, while Achilleus served the meats. And thereon

---

1. Wife of Amphion, one of the two founders of the great Greek city of Thebes.   2. Mother of
Apollo and Artemis.   3. A mountain in Asia Minor. The legend is thought to have had its
origin in a rock face which resembled a weeping woman, like Niobe, who wept inconsolably for
the loss of her children.   4. She was changed into a rock. *Acheloios:* The river near Mount
Sipylos in Asia Minor.

168 **Homer**

they put their hands to the good things that lay ready before them.
But when they had put aside their desire for eating and drinking,
Priam, son of Dardanos, gazed upon Achilleus, wondering
at his size and beauty, for he seemed like an outright vision          630
of gods. Achilleus in turn gazed on Dardanian Priam
and wondered, as he saw his brave looks and listened to him talking.
But when they had taken their fill of gazing one on the other,
first of the two to speak was the aged man, Priam the godlike:
'Give me, beloved of Zeus, a place to sleep presently, so that          635
we may even go to bed and take the pleasure of sweet sleep.
For my eyes have not closed underneath my lids since that time
when my son lost his life beneath your hands, but always
I have been grieving and brooding over my numberless sorrows
and wallowed in the muck about my courtyard's enclosure.              640
Now I have tasted food again and have let the gleaming
wine go down my throat. Before, I had tasted nothing.'
    He spoke, and Achilleus ordered his serving-maids and compan-
        ions
to make a bed in the porch's shelter and to lay upon it
fine underbedding of purple, and spread blankets above it             645
and fleecy robes to be an over-all covering. The maid-servants
went forth from the main house, and in their hands held torches,
and set to work, and presently had two beds made. Achilleus
of the swift feet now looked at Priam and said, sarcastic:
'Sleep outside, aged sir and good friend, for fear some Achaian        650
might come in here on a matter of counsel, since they keep coming
and sitting by me and making plans; as they are supposed to.
But if one of these come through the fleeting black night should
        notice you,
he would go straight and tell Agamemnon, shepherd of the people,
and there would be delay in the ransoming of the body.                655
But come, tell me this and count off for me exactly
how many days you intend for the burial of great Hektor.
Tell me, so I myself shall stay still and hold back the people.'
    In answer to him again spoke aged Priam the godlike:
'If you are willing that we accomplish a complete funeral             660
for great Hektor, this, Achilleus, is what you could do and give
me pleasure. For you know surely how we are penned in our city,
and wood is far to bring in from the hills, and the Trojans are fright-
        ened
badly. Nine days we would keep him in our palace and mourn him,
and bury him on the tenth day, and the people feast by him,           665
and on the eleventh day we would make the grave-barrow for him,
and on the twelfth day fight again; if so we must do.'
    Then in turn swift-footed brilliant Achilleus answered him:

'Then all this, aged Priam, shall be done as you ask it.
I will hold off our attack for as much time as you bid me.'          670
    So he spoke, and took the aged king by the right hand
at the wrist, so that his heart might have no fear. Then these two,
Priam and the herald who were both men of close counsel,
slept in the place outside the house, in the porch's shelter;
but Achilleus slept in the inward corner of the strong-built shel-
        ter,                                                         675
and at his side lay Briseis of the fair colouring.
    Now the rest of the gods and men who were lords of chariots
slept nightlong, with the easy bondage of slumber upon them,
only sleep had not caught Hermes the kind god, who pondered
now in his heart the problem of how to escort King Priam            680
from the ships and not be seen by the devoted gate-wardens.
He stood above his head and spoke a word to him, saying:
'Aged sir, you can have no thought of evil from the way
you sleep still among your enemies now Achilleus has left you
unharmed. You have ransomed now your dear son and given much
        for him.                                                     685
But the sons you left behind would give three times as much ransom
for you, who are alive, were Atreus' son Agamemnon
to recognize you, and all the other Achaians learn of you.'
    He spoke, and the old man was afraid, and wakened his herald,
and lightly Hermes harnessed for them the mules and the horses   690
and himself drove them through the encampment. And no man
        knew of them.
But when they came to the crossing-place of the fair-running river,
of whirling Xanthos, a stream whose father was Zeus the immortal,
there Hermes left them and went away to the height of Olympos,
and dawn, she of the yellow robe, scattered over all earth,         695
and they drove their horses on to the city with lamentation
and clamour, while the mules drew the body. Nor was any other
aware of them at the first, no man, no fair-girdled woman,
only Kassandra, a girl like Aphrodite the golden,
who had gone up to the height of the Pergamos. She saw            700
her dear father standing in the chariot, his herald and crier
with him. She saw Hektor drawn by the mules on a litter.
She cried out then in sorrow and spoke to the entire city:
'Come, men of Troy and Trojan women; look upon Hektor
if ever before you were joyful when you saw him come back liv-
        ing                                                          705
from battle; for he was a great joy to his city, and all his people.'
    She spoke, and there was no man left there in all the city
nor woman, but all were held in sorrow passing endurance.
They met Priam beside the gates as he brought the dead in.

First among them were Hektor's wife and his honoured mother          710
who tore their hair, and ran up beside the smooth-rolling wagon,
and touched his head. And the multitude, wailing, stood there about
    them.
And now and there in front of the gates they would have lamented
all day till the sun went down and let fall their tears for Hektor,
except that the old man spoke from the chariot to his people:          715
'Give me way to get through with my mules; then afterwards
you may sate yourselves with mourning, when I have him inside the
    palace.'
    So he spoke, and they stood apart and made way for the wagon.
And when they had brought him inside the renowned house, they
    laid him
then on a carved bed, and seated beside him the singers          720
who were to lead the melody in the dirge, and the singers
chanted the song of sorrow, and the women were mourning beside
    them.
Andromache of the white arms led the lamentation
of the women, and held in her arms the head of manslaughtering
    Hektor:
'My husband, you were lost young from life, and have left me          725
a widow in your house, and the boy is only a baby
who was born to you and me, the unhappy. I think he will never
come of age, for before then head to heel this city
will be sacked, for you, its defender, are gone, you who guarded
the city, and the grave wives, and the innocent children,          730
wives who before long must go away in the hollow ships,
and among them I shall also go, and you, my child, follow
where I go, and there do much hard work that is unworthy
of you, drudgery for a hard master; or else some Achaian
will take you by hand and hurl you from the tower[5] into horrible          735
death, in anger because Hektor once killed his brother,
or his father, or his son; there were so many Achaians
whose teeth bit the vast earth, beaten down by the hands of Hektor.
Your father was no merciful man in the horror of battle.
Therefore your people are grieving for you all through their city,          740
Hektor, and you left for your parents mourning and sorrow
beyond words, but for me passing all others is left the bitterness
and the pain, for you did not die in bed, and stretch your arms to
    me,
nor tell me some last intimate word that I could remember
always, all the nights and days of my weeping for you.'          745
    So she spoke in tears, and the women were mourning about her.

5. After the fall of Troy Astyanax was, in fact, hurled from the walls.

Now Hekabe led out the thronging chant of their sorrow:
'Hektor, of all my sons the dearest by far to my spirit;
while you still lived for me you were dear to the gods, and even
in the stage of death they cared about you still. There were others 750
of my sons whom at times swift-footed Achilleus captured,
and he would sell them as slaves far across the unresting salt water
into Samos, and Imbros, and Lemnos in the gloom of the mists.
      You,
when he had taken your life with the thin edge of the bronze sword,
he dragged again and again around his beloved companion's        755
tomb, Patroklos', whom you killed, but even so did not
bring him back to life. Now you lie in the palace, handsome
and fresh with dew, in the likeness of one whom he of the silver
bow, Apollo, has attacked and killed with his gentle arrows.'

      So she spoke, in tears, and wakened the endless mourning.        760
Third and last Helen led the song of sorrow among them:
'Hektor, of all my lord's brothers dearest by far to my spirit:
my husband is Alexandros, like an immortal, who brought me
here to Troy; and I should have died before I came with him;
and here now is the twentieth year upon me since I came        765
from the place where I was, forsaking the land of my fathers. In this
      time
I have never heard a harsh saying from you, nor an insult.
No, but when another, one of my lord's brothers or sisters, a fair-
      robed
wife of some brother, would say a harsh word to me in the palace,
or my lord's mother—but his father was gentle always, a father        770
indeed—then you would speak and put them off and restrain them
by your own gentleness of heart and your gentle words. Therefore
I mourn for you in sorrow of heart and mourn myself also
and my ill luck. There was no other in all the wide Troad
who was kind to me, and my friend; all others shrank when they saw
      me.'        775

      So she spoke in tears, and the vast populace grieved with her.
Now Priam the aged king spoke forth his word to his people:
'Now, men of Troy, bring timber into the city, and let not
your hearts fear a close ambush of the Argives. Achilleus
promised me, as he sent me on my way from the black ships,        780
that none should do us injury until the twelfth dawn comes.'

      He spoke, and they harnessed to the wagons their mules and their
      oxen
and presently were gathered in front of the city. Nine days
they spent bringing in an endless supply of timber. But when
the tenth dawn had shown forth with her light upon mortals,        785
they carried out bold Hektor, weeping, and set the body

aloft a towering pyre for burning. And set fire to it.
But when the young dawn showed again with her rosy fingers,
the people gathered around the pyre of illustrious Hektor.
But when all were gathered to one place and assembled together,   790
first with gleaming wine they put out the pyre that was burning,
all where the fury of the fire still was in force, and thereafter
the brothers and companions of Hektor gathered the white bones
up, mourning, as the tears swelled and ran down their cheeks. Then
they laid what they had gathered up in a golden casket            795
and wrapped this about with soft robes of purple, and presently
put it away in the hollow of the grave, and over it
piled huge stones laid close together. Lightly and quickly
they piled up the grave-barrow, and on all sides were set watchmen
for fear the strong-greaved Achaians might too soon set upon them.
They piled up the grave-barrow and went away, and thereafter      801
assembled in a fair gathering and held a glorious
feast within the house of Priam, king under God's hand.
    Such was their burial of Hektor, breaker of horses.

# The Odyssey[1]

## *Book I*

### A GODDESS INTERVENES

Sing in me, Muse, and through me tell the story
of that man skilled in all ways of contending,
the wanderer, harried for years on end,
after he plundered the stronghold
on the proud height of Troy.
                                       He saw the townlands        5
and learned the minds of many distant men,
and weathered many bitter nights and days
in his deep heart at sea, while he fought only
to save his life, to bring his shipmates home.
But not by will nor valor could he save them,                     10
for their own recklessness destroyed them all—
children and fools, they killed and feasted on
the cattle of Lord Hêlios,[2] the Sun,
and he who moves all day through heaven
took from their eyes the dawn of their return.

Of these adventures, Muse, daughter of Zeus,
tell us in our time, lift the great song again.

1. Translated by Robert Fitzgerald.    2. This is described in Book XII.

Begin when all the rest who left behind them
headlong death in battle or at sea
had long ago returned,[3] while he alone still hungered
for home and wife. Her ladyship Kalypso[4]
clung to him in her sea-hollowed caves—
a nymph, immortal and most beautiful,
who craved him for her own.
                And when long years and seasons
wheeling brought around that point of time                    25
ordained for him to make his passage homeward,
trials and dangers, even so, attended him
even in Ithaka,[5] near those he loved.
Yet all the gods had pitied Lord Odysseus,
all but Poseidon, raging cold and rough[6]
against the brave king till he came ashore
at last on his own land.
              But now that god
had gone far off among the sunburnt races,
most remote of men, at earth's two verges,
in sunset lands and lands of the rising sun,                    35
to be regaled by smoke of thighbones burning,
haunches of rams and bulls, a hundred fold.
He lingered delighted at the banquet side.

In the bright hall of Zeus upon Olympos
the other gods were all at home, and Zeus,                    40
the father of gods and men, made conversation.
For he had meditated on Aigísthos,[7] dead
by the hand of Agamémnon's son, Orestês,
and spoke his thought aloud before them all:
"My word, how mortals take the gods to task!                    45
All their afflictions come from us, we hear.
And what of their own failings? Greed and folly
double the suffering in the lot of man.
See how Aigísthos, for his double portion,
stole Agamémnon's wife and killed the soldier                    50
on his homecoming day. And yet Aigísthos
knew that his own doom lay in this. We gods
had warned him, sent down Hermês Argeiphontês,[8]
our most observant courier, to say:
'Don't kill the man, don't touch his wife,                    55

3. From the siege of Troy.    4. Her name is formed from a Greek verb which means "cover,
hide."    5. An island off the northwest coast of Greece, Odysseus' home.    6. The reason for
his rage is given by Zeus below in lines 87–90.    7. The story of Agamémnon's return and death
will be told in detail later, in Book XI.    8. Both the meaning and origin of this epithet are
uncertain.

or face a reckoning with Orestês
the day he comes of age and wants his patrimony.'
Friendly advice—but would Aigísthos take it?
Now he has paid the reckoning in full."
The grey-eyed goddess Athena replied to Zeus:                    60
"O Majesty, O Father of us all,
that man is in the dust indeed, and justly.
So perish all who do what he had done.
But my own heart is broken for Odysseus,
the master mind of war, so long a castaway                       65
upon an island in the running sea;
a wooded island, in the sea's middle,
and there's a goddess in the place, the daughter
of one whose baleful mind knows all the deeps
of the blue sea—Atlas,[9] who holds the columns                 70
that bear from land the great thrust of the sky.
His daughter will not let Odysseus go,
poor mournful man; she keeps on coaxing him
with her beguiling talk, to turn his mind
from Ithaka. But such desire is in him                           75
merely to see the hearthsmoke leaping upward
from his own island, that he longs to die.
Are you not moved by this, Lord of Olympos?
Had you no pleasure from Odysseus' offerings
beside the Argive[1] ships, on Troy's wide seaboard?             80
O Zeus, what do you hold against him now?"

To this the summoner of cloud replied:
"My child, what strange remarks you let escape you.
Could I forget that kingly man, Odysseus?
There is no mortal half so wise; no mortal                       85
gave so much to the lords of open sky.
Only the god who laps the land in water,
Poseidon, bears the fighter an old grudge
since he poked out the eye of Polyphêmos,[2]
brawniest of the Kyklopês. Who bore
that giant lout? Thoösa, daughter of Phorkys,
an offshore sea lord: for this nymph had lain
with Lord Poseidon in her hollow caves.
Naturally, the god, after the blinding,
mind you, he does not kill the man;                              95

---

9. A Titan, whose punishment for his part in the war against Zeus was to hold up the sky on his shoulders. His daughter is Kalypso, who lives on the island of Ogýgia.    1. One of the collective names for the Greeks fighting at Troy.    2. He had one central eye in his forehead. The encounter with Kyklopês (or Cyclops) will be told in detail in Book IX.

he only buffets him away from home.
But come now, we are all at leisure here,
let us take up this matter of his return.
How should he sail? Poseidon must relent,
for being quarrelsome will get him nowhere,                    100
one god, flouting the will of all the gods."

The grey-eyed goddess Athena answered him:

"O Majesty, O Father of us all,
if it now please the blissful gods
that wise Odysseus reach his home again,                    105
let the Wayfinder, Hermês, cross the sea
to the island of Ogýgia; let him tell
our fixed intent to the nymph with pretty braids,
and let the steadfast man depart for home.
For my part, I shall visit Ithaka                    110
to put more courage in the son, and rouse him
to call an assembly of the islanders,
Akhaian[3] gentlemen with flowing hair.
He must warn off that wolf pack of the suitors
who prey upon his flocks and dusky cattle.                    115
I'll send him to the mainland then, to Sparta
by the sand beach of Pylos; let him find
news of his dear father where he may
and win his own renown about the world."

She bent to tie her beautiful sandals on,                    120
ambrosial, golden, that carry her over water
or over endless land on the wings of the wind, and took the great haft
    of her spear in hand—
that bronzeshod spear this child of Power can use
to break in wrath long battle lines of fighters.                    125

Flashing down from Olympos' height she went
to stand in Ithaka, before the Manor,
just at the doorsill of the court. She seemed
a family friend, the Taphian[4] captain, Mentês,
waiting, with a light hand on her spear.                    130
Before her eyes she found the lusty suitors
casting dice inside the gate, at ease
on hides of oxen—oxen they had killed.

3. Another of the collective names for the Greeks.    4. The name of a nearby sea-faring people.

Their own retainers made a busy sight
with houseboys, mixing bowls of water and wine,                    135
or sopping water up in sponges, wiping
tables to be placed about in hall,
or butchering whole carcasses for roasting.

Long before anyone else, the prince Telémakhos
now caught sight of Athena—for he, too,                           140
was sitting there, unhappy among the suitors,
a boy, daydreaming. What if his great father
came from the unknown world and drove these men
like dead leaves through the place, recovering
honor and lordship in his own domains?                            145
Then he who dreamed in the crowd gazed out at Athena.

Straight to the door he came, irked with himself
to think a visitor had been kept there waiting,
and took her right hand, grasping with his left
her tall bronze-bladed spear. Then he said warmly:                150

"Greetings, stranger! Welcome to our feast.
There will be time to tell your errand later."

He led the way, and Pallas Athena followed
into the lofty hall. The boy reached up
and thrust her spear high in a polished rack                      155
against a pillar, where tough spear on spear
of the old soldier, his father, stood in order.
Then, shaking out a splendid coverlet,
he seated her on a throne with footrest—all
finely carved—and drew his painted armchair                       160
near her, at a distance from the rest.
To be amid the din, the suitors' riot
would ruin his guest's appetite, he thought,
and he wished privacy to ask for news
about his father, gone for years.
                              A maid
brought them a silver finger bowl and filled it
out of a beautiful spouting golden jug,
then drew a polished table to their side.
The larder mistress with her tray came by
and served them generously. A carver lifted                       170
cuts of each roast meat to put on trenchers
before the two. He gave them cups of gold,

and these the steward as he went his rounds
filled and filled again.
            Now came the suitors,
young bloods trooping in to their own seats                                    175
on thrones or easy chairs. Attendants poured
water over their fingers, while the maids
piled baskets full of brown loaves near at hand,
and houseboys brimmed the bowls with wine.
Now they laid hands upon the ready feast                                       180
and thought of nothing more. Not till desire
for food and drink had left them were they mindful
of dance and song, that are the grace of feasting.
A herald gave a shapely cithern harp
to Phêmios, whom they compelled[5] to sing—
and what a storm he plucked upon the strings
for prelude! High and clear the song arose.

Telémakhos now spoke to grey-eyed Athena,
his head bent close, so no one else might hear:

"Dear guest, will this offend you, if I speak?                                 190
It is easy for these men to like these things,
harping and song; they have an easy life,
scot free, eating the livestock of another—
a man whose bones are rotting somewhere now,
white in the rain on dark earth where they lie,                                195
or tumbling in the groundswell of the sea.
If he returned, if these men ever saw him,
faster legs they'd pray for, to a man,
and not more wealth in handsome robes or gold.
But he is lost; he came to grief and perished,                                 200
and there's no help for us in someone's hoping
he still may come; that sun has long gone down.
But tell me now and put it for me clearly—
who are you? Where do you come from? Where's your home
and family? What kind of ship is yours,                                        205
and what course brought you here? Who are your sailors?
I don't suppose you walked here on the sea.
Another thing—this too I ought to know—
is Ithaka new to you, or were you ever
a guest here in the old days? Far and near                                     210
friends knew this house; for he whose home it was
had much acquaintance in the world."

5. He belonged to the household of Odysseus.

To this
the grey-eyed goddess answered:
"As you ask,
I can account most clearly for myself.
Mentês I'm called, son of the veteran                                    215
Ankhíalos; I rule seafaring Taphos.
I came by ship, with a ship's company,
sailing the winedark sea for ports of call
on alien shores—to Témesê, for copper,
bringing bright bars of iron in exchange.                                 220
My ship is moored on a wild strip of coast
in Reithron Bight, under the wooded mountain.
Years back, my family and yours were friends,
as Lord Laërtês[6] knows; ask when you see him.
I hear the old man comes to town no longer,                               225
stays up country, ailing, with only one
old woman to prepare his meat and drink
when pain and stiffness take him in the legs
from working on his terraced plot, his vineyard.
As for my sailing here—                                                   230
the tale was that your father had come home,
therefore I came. I see the gods delay him.
but never in this world is Odysseus dead—
only detained somewhere on the wide sea,
upon some island, with wild islanders;                                    235
savages, they must be, to hold him captive.
Well, I will forecast for you, as the gods
put the strong feeling in me—I see it all,
and I'm no prophet, no adept in bird-signs.
He will not, now, be long away from Ithaka,                               240
his father's dear land; though he be in chains
he'll scheme a way to come; he can do anything.

But tell me this now, make it clear to me:
You must be, by your looks, Odysseus' boy?
The way your head is shaped, the fine eyes—yes,                           245
how like him! We took meals like this together
many a time, before he sailed for Troy
with all the lords of Argos in the ships.
I have not seen him since, nor has he seen me."

And thoughtfully Telémakhos replied:                                      250

6. Father of Odysseus.

"Friend, let me put it in the plainest way.
My mother says I am his son: I know not
surely. Who has known his own engendering?
I wish at least I had some happy man
as father, growing old in his own house—          255
but unknown death and silence are the fate
of him that, since you ask, they call my father."

Then grey-eyed Athena said:
                    "The gods decreed
no lack of honor in this generation:
such is the son Penélopê bore in you.              260
But tell me now, and make this clear to me:
what gathering, what feast is this? Why here?
A wedding? Revel? At the expense of all?
Not that, I think. How arrogant they seem,
these gluttons, making free here in your house!    265
A sensible man would blush to be among them."

To this Telémakhos answered:

"Friend, now that you ask about these matters,
our house was always princely, a great house,
as long as he of whom we speak remained here.      270
But evil days the gods have brought upon it,
making him vanish, as they have, so strangely.
Were his death known, I could not feel such pain—
if he had died of wounds in Trojan country
or in the arms of friends, after the war.          275
They would have made a tomb for him, the Akhaians,
and I should have all honor as his son.
Instead, the whirlwinds got him, and no glory.
He's gone, no sign, no word of him; and I inherit
trouble and tears—and not for him alone,           280
the gods have laid such other burdens on me.
For now the lords of the islands,
Doulíkhion and Samê, wooded Zakynthos,[7]
and rocky Ithaka's young lords as well,
are here courting my mother; and they use          285
our house as if it were a house to plunder.
Spurn them she dare not, though she hates that marriage,
nor can she bring herself to choose among them.

---

7. Islands close to Ithaka.

Meanwhile they eat their way through all we have,
and when they will, they can demolish me."                              290

Pallas Athena was disturbed, and said:

"Ah, bitterly you need Odysseus, then!
High time he came back to engage these upstarts.
I wish we saw him standing helmeted
there in the doorway, holding shield and spear,                         295
looking the way he did when I first knew him.
That was at our house, where he drank and feasted
after he left Ephyra, homeward bound
from a visit to the son of Mérmeris, Ilos.
He took his fast ship down the gulf that time                           300
for a fatal drug to dip his arrows in
and poison the bronze points; but young Ilos
turned him away, fearing the gods' wrath.
My father gave it, for he loved him well.
I wish these men could meet the man of those days!                      305
They'd know their fortune quickly: a cold bed.
Aye! but it lies upon the gods' great knees
whether he can return and force a reckoning
in his own house, or not.
                            If I were you,
I should take steps to make these men disperse.                         310
Listen, now, and attend to what I say:
at daybreak call the islanders to assembly
and speak your will, and call the gods to witness:
the suitors must go scattering to their homes.
Then here's a course for you, if you agree:                             315
get a sound craft afloat with twenty oars
and go abroad for news of your lost father—
perhaps a traveller's tale, or rumored fame
issued from Zeus abroad in the world of men.
Talk to that noble sage at Pylos, Nestor,                               320
then go to Meneláos, the red-haired king
at Sparta, last man home of all the Akhaians.
Stay a full year. You may learn he's alive
and coming home; or else you may hear nothing,
or learn that he is dead and gone. If so,                               325
then you can come back to your own dear country
and raise a mound for him, and burn his gear,
with all the funeral honors due the man,
and give your mother to another husband.

When you have done all this, or seen it done,                    330
it will be time to ponder
concerning these contenders in your house—
how you should kill them, outright or by guile.
You need not bear this insolence of theirs,
you are a child no longer. Have you heard                        335
what glory young Orestês won
when he cut down that two-faced man, Aigísthos,
for killing his illustrious father?
Dear friend, you are tall and well set up, I see;
be brave—you, too—men in times to come                          340
will speak of you respectfully.
                         Now I must join my ships;
my crew will grumble if I keep them waiting.
Look to yourself; remember what I told you."
Telémakhos replied:
                         "Friend, you have done me
kindness, like a father to his son,                              345
and I shall not forget your counsel ever.
You must get back to sea, I know, but come
take a hot bath, and rest; accept a gift
to make your heart lift up when you embark—
some precious thing, and beautiful, from me,                     350
a keepsake, such as dear friends give their friends."

But the grey-eyed goddess Athena answered him:

"Do not delay me, for I love the sea ways.
As for the gift your heart is set on giving,
let me accept it on my passage home,                             355
and you shall have a choice gift in exchange."

With this Athena left him
as a bird rustles upward, off and gone.
But as she went she put new spirit in him,
a new dream of his father, clearer now,                          360
so that he marvelled to himself
divining that a god had been his guest.
Then godlike in his turn he joined the suitors.

The famous minstrel still sang on before them,
and they sat still and listened, while he sang                   365
that bitter song, the Homecoming of Akhaians—
how by Athena's will they fared from Troy;
and in her high room careful Penélopê,

Ikários' daughter, heeded the holy song.
She came, then, down the long stairs of her house,                    370
this beautiful lady, with two maids in train
attending her as she approached the suitors;
and near a pillar of the roof she paused,
her shining veil drawn over across her cheeks,
the two girls close to her and still,                                 375
and through her tears spoke to the noble minstrel:
"Phêmios, other spells you know, high deeds
of gods and heroes, as the poets tell them;
let these men hear some other, while they sit
silent and drink their wine. But sing no more                        380
this bitter tale that wears my heart away.
It opens in me again the wound of longing
for one incomparable, ever in my mind—
his fame all Hellas[8] knows, and midland Argos."

But Telémakhos intervened and said to her:                           385

"Mother, why do you grudge our own dear minstrel
joy of song, wherever his thought may lead?
Poets are not to blame, but Zeus who gives
what fate he pleases to adventurous men.
Here is no reason for reproof: to sing                               390
the news of the Danaans![9] Men like best
a song that rings like morning on the ear.
But you must nerve yourself and try to listen.
Odysseus was not the only one at Troy
never to know the day of his homecoming.                             395
Others, how many others, lost their lives!"

The lady gazed in wonder and withdrew,
her son's clear wisdom echoing in her mind.
But when she had mounted to her rooms again
with her two handmaids, then she fell to weeping                     400
for Odysseus, her husband. Grey-eyed Athena
presently cast a sweet sleep on her eyes.

Meanwhile the din grew loud in the shadowy hall
as every suitor swore to lie beside her,
but Telémakhos turned now and spoke to them:                         405

"You suitors of my mother! Insolent men,
now we have dined, let us have entertainment

8. The ancient name for Greece.    9. Another name for the Greeks as a whole.

and no more shouting. There can be no pleasure
so fair as giving heed to a great minstrel
like ours, whose voice itself is pure delight.                410
At daybreak we shall sit down in assembly
and I shall tell you—take it as you will—
you are to leave this hall. Go feasting elsewhere,
consume your own stores. Turn and turn about,
use one another's houses. If you choose                      420
to slaughter one man's livestock and pay nothing,
this is rapine; and by the eternal gods
I beg Zeus you shall get what you deserve:
a slaughter here, and nothing paid for it!"

By now their teeth seemed fixed in their under-lips,         425
Telémakhos' bold speaking stunned them so.
Antínoös, Eupeithês' son, made answer:

"Telémakhos, no doubt the gods themselves
are teaching you this high and mighty manner.
Zeus forbid you should be king in Ithaka,                    430
though you are eligible as your father's son."

Telémakhos kept his head and answered him:

"Antínoös, you may not like my answer,
but I would happily be king, if Zeus
conferred the prize. Or do you think it wretched?            435
I shouldn't call it bad at all. A king
will be respected, and his house will flourish.
But there are eligible men enough,
heaven knows, on the island, young and old,
and one of them perhaps may come to power                    440
after the death of King Odysseus.
All I insist on is that I rule our house
and rule the slaves my father won for me."

Eurýmakhos, Pólybos' son, replied:

"Telémakhos, it is on the gods' great knees                  445
who will be king in sea-girt Ithaka.
But keep your property, and rule your house,
and let no man, against your will, make havoc
of your possessions, while there's life on Ithaka.
But now, my brave young friend,                              450
a question or two about the stranger.

Where did your guest come from? Of what country?
Where does he say his home is, and his family?
Has he some message of your father's coming,
or business of his own, asking a favor?                              455
He left so quickly that one hadn't time
to meet him, but he seemed a gentleman."

Telémakhos made answer, cool enough:

"Eurýmakhos, there's no hope for my father.
I would not trust a message, if one came,                           460
nor any forecaster my mother invites
to tell by divination of time to come.
My guest, however, was a family friend,
Mentês, son of Ankhíalos.
He rules the Taphian people of the sea."                            465

So said Telémakhos, though in his heart
he knew his visitor had been immortal.
But now the suitors turned to play again
with dance and haunting song. They stayed till nightfall,
indeed black night came on them at their pleasure,                  470
and half asleep they left, each for his home.

Telémakhos' bedroom was above the court,
a kind of tower, with a view all round;
here he retired to ponder in the silence,
while carrying brands of pine alight beside him                     475
Eurýkleia went padding, sage and old.
Her father had been Ops, Peisênor's son,
and she had been a purchase of Laërtês
when she was still a blossoming girl. He gave
the price of twenty oxen for her, kept her                          480
as kindly in his house as his own wife,
though, for the sake of peace, he never touched her.
No servant loved Telémakhos as she did,
she who had nursed him in his infancy.
So now she held the light, as he swung open                         485
the door of his neat freshly painted chamber.
There he sat down, pulling his tunic off,
and tossed it into the wise old woman's hands.
She folded it and smoothed it, and then hung it
beside the inlaid bed upon a bar;                                   490
then, drawing the door shut by its silver handle
she slid the catch in place and went away.

And all night long, wrapped in the finest fleece,
he took in thought the course Athena gave him.

## Book II

### A HERO'S SON AWAKENS

When primal Dawn spread on the eastern sky
her fingers of pink light, Odysseus' true son
stood up, drew on his tunic and his mantle,
slung on a sword-belt and a new-edged sword,
tied his smooth feet into good rawhide sandals,                    5
and left his room, a god's brilliance upon him.
He found the criers with clarion voices and told them
to muster the unshorn Akhaians in full assembly.
The call sang out, and the men came streaming in;
and when they filled the assembly ground, he entered,              10
spear in hand, with two quick hounds at heel;
Athena lavished on him a sunlit grace
that held the eye of the multitude. Old men
made way for him as he took his father's chair.

Now Lord Aigýptios, bent down and sage with years,                15
opened the assembly. This man's son
had served under the great Odysseus, gone
in the decked ships with him to the wild horse country
of Troy—a spearman, Antiphos by name.
The ravenous Kyklops in the cave destroyed him                    20
last in his feast of men. Three other sons
the old man had, and one, Eurýnomos,
went with the suitors; two farmed for their father;
but even so the old man pined, remembering
the absent one, and a tear welled up as he spoke:                 25

"Hear me, Ithakans! Hear what I have to say.
No meeting has been held here since our king,
Odysseus, left port in the decked ships.
Who finds occasion for assembly, now?
one of the young men? one of the older lot?                       30
Has he had word our fighters are returning—
news to report if he got wind of it—
or is it something else, touching the realm?
The man has vigor, I should say; more power to him.
Whatever he desires, may Zeus fulfill it."                        35

The old man's words delighted the son of Odysseus,
who kept his chair no longer but stood up,

eager to speak, in the midst of all the men.
The crier, Peisênor, master of debate,
brought him the staff and placed it in his hand;[1]                    40
then the boy touched the old man's shoulder, and said:

"No need to wonder any more, Sir,
who called this session. The distress is mine.
As to our troops returning, I have no news—
news to report if I got wind of it—                                   45
nor have I public business to propose;
only my need, and the trouble of my house—
the troubles.
            My distinguished father is lost,
who ruled among you once, mild as a father,
and there is now this greater evil still:                             50
my home and all I have are being ruined.
Mother wanted no suitors, but like a pack
they came—sons of the best men here among them—
lads with no stomach for an introduction
to Ikários, her father across the sea;                                55
he would require a wedding gift, and give her
to someone who found favor in her eyes.
No; these men spend their days around our house
killing our beeves and sheep and fatted goats,
carousing, soaking up our good dark wine,                             60
not caring what they do. They squander everything.
We have no strong Odysseus to defend us,
and as to putting up a fight ourselves—
we'd only show our incompetence in arms.
Expel them, yes, if I only had the power;                             65
the whole thing's out of hand, insufferable.
My house is being plundered: is this courtesy?
Where is your indignation? Where is your shame?
Think of the talk in the islands all around us,
and fear the wrath of the gods,                                       70
or they may turn, and send you some devilry.
Friends, by Olympian Zeus and holy Justice
that holds men in assembly and sets them free,
make an end of this! Let me lament in peace
my private loss. Or did my father, Odysseus,                         75
ever do injury to the armed Akhaians?
Is this your way of taking it out on me,
giving free rein to these young men?

1. As in the assembly in Book I of the *Iliad*, the man who is given the floor to speak has a staff, the symbol of authority, placed in his hand by the herald.

I might as well-might better—see my treasure
and livestock taken over by you all;                                    80
then, if you fed on them, I'd have some remedy,
and when we met, in public, in the town,
I'd press my claim; you might make restitution.
This way you hurt me when my hands are tied."

And in hot anger now he threw the staff to the ground,         85
his eyes grown bright with tears. A wave of sympathy
ran through the crowd, all hushed; and no one there
had the audacity to answer harshly
except Antínoös, who said:
                                          "What high and mighty
talk, Telémakhos! Control your temper.
You want to shame us, and humiliate us,
but you should know the suitors are not to blame—
it is your own dear, incomparably cunning mother.
For three years now—and it will soon be four—
she has been breaking the hearts of the Akhaians,              95
holding out hope to all, and sending promises
to each man privately[2]—but thinking otherwise.

Here is an instance of her trickery:
she had her great loom standing in the hall
and the fine warp of some vast fabric on it;                        100
we were attending her, and she said to us:
'Young men, my suitors, now my lord is dead,
let me finish my weaving before I marry,
or else my thread will have been spun in vain.
It is a shroud I weave for Lord Laërtês,                               105
when cold death comes to lay him on his bier.
The country wives would hold me in dishonor
if he, with all his fortune, lay unshrouded.'
We have men's hearts; she touched them; we agreed.
So every day she wove on the great loom—                         110
but every night by torchlight she unwove it;
and so for three years she deceived the Akhaians.
But when the seasons brought the fourth around,
one of her maids, who knew the secret, told us;
we found her unraveling the splendid shroud.                       115
She had to finish then, although she hated it.

Now here is the suitors' answer—
you and all the Akhaians, mark it well:

2. Her tactic is to divide the suitors and so put off the day that they will unanimously demand a decision.

dismiss your mother from the house, or make her marry
the man her father names and she prefers.                    120
Does she intend to keep us dangling forever?
She may rely too long on Athena's gifts—
talent in handicraft and a clever mind;
so cunning—history cannot show the like
among the ringleted ladies of Akhaia,                        125
Mykênê with her coronet, Alkmênê, Tyro.[3]
Wits like Penélopê's never were before,
but this time—well, she made poor use of them.
For here are suitors eating up your property
as long as she holds out—a plan some god                     130
put in her mind. She makes a name for herself,
but you can feel the loss it means for you.
Our own affairs can wait; we'll never go anywhere else,
until she takes an Akhaian to her liking."

But clear-headed Telémakhos replied:                         135

"Antínoös, can I banish against her will
the mother who bore me and took care of me?
My father is either dead or far away,
but dearly I should pay for this
at Ikários' hands, if ever I sent her back.                  140
The powers of darkness would requite it, too,
my mother's parting curse would call hell's furies[4]
to punish me, along with the scorn of men.
No: I can never give the word for this.
But if your hearts are capable of shame,                     145
leave my great hall, and take your dinner elsewhere,
consume your own stores. Turn and turn about,
use one another's houses. If you choose
to slaughter one man's livestock and pay nothing,
this is rapine; and by the eternal gods                      150
I beg Zeus you shall get what you deserve:
a slaughter here, and nothing paid for it!"

Now Zeus who views the wide world sent a sign to him,
launching a pair of eagles[5] from a mountain crest
in gliding flight down the soft blowing wind,                155
wing-tip to wing-tip quivering taut, companions,

---

3. Famous ladies of the past (Alkmênê was the mother of Herakles): Odysseus sees the ghosts of
Tyro and Alkmênê in the lower world in Book IX.    4. *Erinyes* is the Greek word for these
creatures who avenge injured parents, especially (since they themselves are female) a mother.
They appear as the chorus in the final play of the *Oresteia*.    5. The royal bird, the emblem of
Zeus.

till high above the assembly of many voices
they wheeled, their dense wings beating, and in havoc
dropped on the heads of the crowd—a deathly omen—
wielding their talons, tearing cheeks and throats;                    160
then veered away on the right hand through the city.
Astonished, gaping after the birds, the men
felt their heartsflood, foreboding things to come.
And now they heard the old lord Halithersês,
son of Mastóridês, keenest among the old                              165
at reading birdflight into accurate speech;
in his anxiety for them, he rose and said:

'Hear me, Ithakans! Hear what I have to say,
and may I hope to open the suitors' eyes
to the black wave towering over them. Odysseus                        170
will not be absent from his family long:
he is already near, carrying in him
a bloody doom for all these men, and sorrow
for many more on our high seamark, Ithaka.
Let us think how to stop it; let the suitors                          175
drop their suit; they had better, without delay.
I am old enough to know a sign when I see one,
and I say all has come to pass for Odysseus
as I foretold when the Argives massed on Troy,
and he, the great tactician, joined the rest.                         180
My forecast was that after nineteen years,
many blows weathered, all his shipmates lost,
himself unrecognized by anyone,
he would come home. I see this all fulfilled."

But Pólybos' son, Eurýmakhos, retorted:                               185

"Old man, go tell the omens for your children
at home, and try to keep them out of trouble.
I am more fit to interpret this than you are.
Bird life aplenty is found in the sunny air,
not all of it significant. As for Odysseus,                           190
he perished far from home. You should have perished with him—
then we'd be spared this nonsense in assembly,
as good as telling Telémakhos to rage on;
do you think you can gamble on a gift from him?
Here is what I foretell, and it's quite certain:                      195
if you, with what you know of ancient lore,
encourage bitterness in this young man,
it means, for him, only the more frustration—

he can do nothing whatever with two eagles—
and as for you, old man, we'll fix a penalty                    200
that you will groan to pay.
Before the whole assembly I advise Telémakhos
to send his mother to her father's house;
let them arrange her wedding there, and fix
a portion[6] suitable for a valued daughter.
Until he does this, courtship is our business,
vexing though it may be; we fear no one,
certainly not Telémakhos, with his talk;
and we care nothing for your divining, uncle,
useless talk; you win more hatred by it.                       210
We'll share his meat, no thanks or fee to him,
as long as she delays and maddens us.
It is a long, long time we have been waiting
in rivalry for this beauty. We could have gone
elsewhere and found ourselves very decent wives."              215

Clear-headed Telémakhos replied to this:

"Eurýmakhos, and noble suitors all,
I am finished with appeals and argument.
The gods know, and the Akhaians know, these things.
But give me a fast ship and a crew of twenty                   220
who will see me through a voyage, out and back.
I'll go to sandy Pylos then to Sparta,
for news of Father since he sailed from Troy—
some traveller's tale, perhaps, or rumored fame
issued from Zeus himself into the world.                       225
If he's alive, and beating his way home,
I might hold out for another weary year;
but if they tell me that he's dead and gone,
then I can come back to my own dear country
and raise a mound for him, and burn his gear,                  230
with all the funeral honors that befit him,
and give my mother to another husband."

The boy sat down in silence. Next to stand
was Mentor, comrade in arms of the prince Odysseus,
an old man now. Odysseus left him authority                    235
over his house and slaves, to guard them well.
In his concern, he spoke to the assembly:

6. I.e. a dowry. In other passages (e.g., VIII. 327) it is the suitors who offer gifts to the bride's
father. Such a cultural amalgam, customs from different periods or places side by side, is characteristic of oral epic traditions.

"Hear me, Ithakans! Hear what I have to say.
Let no man holding scepter as a king
be thoughtful, mild, kindly, or virtuous;                    240
let him be cruel, and practice evil ways;
it is so clear that no one here remembers
how like a gentle father Odysseus ruled you.
I find it less revolting that the suitors
carry their malice into violent acts;                        245
at least they stake their lives
when they go pillaging the house of Odysseus—
their lives upon it, he will not come again.
What sickens me is to see the whole community
sitting still, and never a voice or a hand raised            250
against them—a mere handful compared with you."

Leókritos, Euênor's son, replied to him:

"Mentor, what mischief are you raking up?
Will this crowd risk the sword's edge over a dinner?
Suppose Odysseus himself indeed                              255
came in and found the suitors at his table:
he might be hot to drive them out. What then?
Never would he enjoy his wife again—
the wife who loves him well; he'd only bring down
abject death on himself against those odds.                  260
Madness, to talk of fighting in either case.
Now let all present go about their business!
Halithersês and Mentor will speed the traveller;
they can help him: they were his father's friends.
I rather think he will be sitting here                       265
a long time yet, waiting for news of Ithaka;
that seafaring he spoke of is beyond him."

On this note they were quick to end their parley.
The assembly broke up; everyone went home—
the suitors home to Odysseus' house again.                   270
But Telémakhos walked down along the shore
and washed his hands in the foam of the grey sea,
then said this prayer:
                "O god of yesterday,
guest in our house, who told me to take ship
on the hazy sea for news of my lost father,                  275
listen to me, be near me:
the Akhaians only wait, or hope to hinder me,
the damned insolent suitors most of all."

Athena was nearby and came to him,
putting on Mentor's figure and his tone,                    280
the warm voice in a lucid flight of words:

"You'll never be fainthearted or a fool,
Telémakhos, if you have your father's spirit;
he finished what he cared to say,
and what he took in hand he brought to pass.               285
The sea routes will yield their distances
to his true son, Penélopê's true son,—
I doubt another's luck would hold so far.
The son is rare who measures with his father,
and one in a thousand is a better man,                     290
but you will have the sap and wit
and prudence—for you get that from Odysseus—
to give you a fair chance of winning through.
So never mind the suitors and their ways,
there is no judgment in them, neither do they              295
know anything of death and the black terror
close upon them—doom's day on them all.
You need not linger over going to sea.
I sailed beside your father in the old days,
I'll find a ship for you, and help you sail her.           300
So go on home, as if to join the suitors,
but get provisions ready in containers—
wine in two-handled jugs and barley meal,
the staying power of oarsmen,
in skin bags, watertight. I'll go the rounds               305
and call a crew of volunteers together.
Hundreds of ships are beached on sea-girt Ithaka;
let me but choose the soundest, old or new,
we'll rig her and take her out on the broad sea."

This was the divine speech Telmakhos heard                 310
from Athena, Zeus's daughter. He stayed no longer,
but took his heartache home,
and found the robust suitors there at work,
skinning goats and roasting pigs in the courtyard.
Antínoös came straight over, laughing at him,             315
and took him by the hand with a bold greeting:
"High-handed Telémakhos, control your temper!
Come on, get over it, no more grim thoughts,
but feast and drink with me, the way you used to.
The Akhaians will attend to all you ask for—             320

ship, crew, and crossing to the holy land
of Pylos, for the news about your father."

Telémakhos replied with no confusion:

"Antínoös, I cannot see myself again
taking a quiet dinner in this company.                                    325
Isn't it enough that you could strip my house
under my very nose when I was young?
Now that I know, being grown, what others say,
I understand it all, and my heart is full.
I'll bring black doom upon you if I can—                                  330
either in Pylos, if I go, or in this country.
And I will go, go all the way, if only
as someone's passenger. I have no ship,
no oarsmen: and it suits you that I have none."

Calmly he drew his hand from Antínoös' hand.                              335
At this the suitors, while they dressed their meat,
began to exchange loud mocking talk about him.
One young toplofty gallant set the tone:
                              "Well, think of that!
Telémakhos has a mind to murder us.
He's going to lead avengers out of Pylos,                                 340
or Sparta, maybe; oh, he's wild to do it.
Or else he'll try the fat land of Ephyra—
he can get poison there, and bring it home,
doctor the wine jar and dispatch us all."

Another took the cue:

                              "Well now, who knows?                       345
He might be lost at sea, just like Odysseus,
knocking around in a ship, far from his friends.
And what a lot of trouble that would give us,
making the right division of his things!
We'd keep his house as dowry for his mother—                             350
his mother and the man who marries her."

That was the drift of it. Telémakhos
went on through to the storeroom of his father,
a great vault where gold and bronze lay piled
along with chests of clothes, and fragrant oil.                           355
And there were jars of earthenware in rows

holding an old wine,
mellow, unmixed, and rare; cool stood the jars
against the wall, kept for whatever day                          360
Odysseus, worn by hardships, might come home.
The double folding doors were tightly locked
and guarded, night and day, by the serving woman,
Eurýkleia, grand-daughter of Peisênor,
in all her duty vigilant and shrewd.                             365
Telémakhos called her to the storeroom, saying:

"Nurse, get a few two-handled travelling jugs
filled up with wine—the second best, not that
you keep for your unlucky lord and king,
hoping he may have slipped away from death                       370
and may yet come again—royal Odysseus.
Twelve amphorai will do; seal them up tight.
And pour out barely into leather bags—
twenty bushels of barley meal ground fine.
Now keep this to yourself! Collect these things,                 375
and after dark, when mother has retired
and gone upstairs to bed, I'll come for them.
I sail to sandy Pylos, then to Sparta,
to see what news there is of Father's voyage."

His loving nurse Eurýkleia gave a cry,                           380
and tears sprang to her eyes as she wailed softly:

"Dear child, whatever put this in your head?
Why do you want to go so far in the world—
and you our only darling? Lord Odysseus
died in some strange place, far from his homeland.               385
Think how, when you have turned your back, these men
will plot to kill you and share all your things!
Stay with your own, dear, do. Why should you suffer
hardship and homelessness on the wild sea?"

But seeing all clear, Telémakhos replied:                        390

"Take heart, Nurse, there's a god behind this plan.
And you must swear to keep it from my mother,
until the eleventh day, or twelfth, or till
she misses me, or hears that I am gone.
She must not tear her lovely skin lamenting."                    395

So the old woman vowed by all the gods,
and vowed again, to carry out his wishes;

then she filled up the amphorai with wine
and sifted barely meal into leather bags.
Telémakhos rejoined the suitors.

                     Meanwhile                              400
the goddess with grey eyes had other business:
disguised as Telémakhos, she roamed the town
taking each likely man aside and telling him:
"Meet us at nightfall at the ship!" Indeed,
she asked Noêmon, Phronios' wealthy son,                              405
to lend her a fast ship, and he complied.
Now when at sundown shadows crossed the lanes
she dragged the cutter to the sea and launched it,
fitted out with tough seagoing gear,
and tied it up, away at the harbor's edge.                              410
The crewmen gathered, sent there by the goddess.
Then it occurred to the grey-eyed goddess Athena
to pass inside the house of the hero Odysseus,
showering a sweet drowsiness on the suitors,
whom she had presently wandering in their wine;                              415
and soon, as they could hold their cups no longer,
they straggled off to find their beds in town,
eyes heavy-lidded, laden down with sleep.
Then to Telémakhos the grey-eyed goddess
appeared again with Mentor's form and voice.                              420
calling him out of the lofty emptied hall:
"Telémakhos, your crew of fighting men
is ready at the oars, and waiting for you;
come on, no point in holding up the sailing."

And Pallas Athena turned like the wind, running                              425
ahead of him. He followed in her footsteps
down to the seaside, where they found the ship,
and oarsmen with flowing hair at the water's edge.
Telmakhos, now strong in the magic, cried:

"Come with me, friends, and get our rations down!                              430
They are all packed at home, and my own mother
knows nothing!—only one maid was told."

He turned and led the way, and they came after,
carried and stowed all in the well-trimmed ship
as the dear son of Odysseus commanded.                              435
Telémakhos then stepped aboard; Athena
took her position aft, and he sat by her.
The two stroke oars cast off the stern hawsers

and vaulted over the gunnels to their benches.
Grey-eyed Athena stirred them a following wind,                    440
soughing from the north-west on the winedark sea,
and as he felt the wind, Telémakhos
called to all hands to break out mast and sail.
They pushed the fir mast high and stepped it firm
amidships in the box, made fast the forestays,                     445
then hoisted up the white sail on its halyards
until the wind caught, booming in the sail;
and a flushing wave sang backward from the bow
on either side, as the ship got way upon her,
holding her steady course.
Now they made all secure in the fast black ship,                   450
and, setting out the winebowls all a-brim,
they made libation to the gods,

                              the undying, the ever-new,
most of all to the grey-eyed daughter of Zeus.


## Book III

### THE LORD OF THE WESTERN APPROACHES

The sun rose on the flawless brimming sea
into a sky all brazen—all one brightening
for gods immortal and for mortal men
on plowlands kind with grain.

                              And facing sunrise
the voyagers now lay off Pylos town,                                5
compact stronghold of Neleus.[7] On the shore
black bulls were being offered by the people
to the blue-maned god[8] who makes the islands tremble:
nine congregations, each five hundred strong,
led out nine bulls apiece to sacrifice,                            10
taking the tripes to eat, while on their altars
thighbones in fat lay burning for the god.
Here they put in, furled sail, and beached the ship;
but Telémakhos hung back in disembarking,
so that Athena turned and said:                                    15

"Not the least shyness, now, Telémakhos.
You came across the open sea for this—
to find out where the great earth hides your father
and what the doom was that he came upon.
Go to old Nestor, master charioteer,                               20

---

7. Mortal son of the god Poseidon and father of Nestor.    8. Poseidon.

so we may broach the storehouse of his mind.
Ask him with courtesy, and in his wisdom
he will tell you history and no lies."
But clear-headed Telémakhos replied:

"Mentor, how can I do it, how approach him?                    25
I have no practice in elaborate speeches, and
for a young man to interrogate an old man
seems disrespectful—"

                    But the grey-eyed goddess said:
"Reason and heart will give you words, Telémakhos;
and a spirit will counsel others. I should say                    30
the gods were never indifferent to your life."

She went on quickly, and he followed her
to where the men of Pylos had their altars.
Nestor appeared enthroned among his sons,
while friends around them skewered the red beef                    35
or held it scorching. When they saw the strangers
a hail went up, and all that crowd came forward
calling out invitations to the feast.
Peisístratos in the lead, the young prince,
caught up their hands in his and gave them places                    40
on curly lambskins flat on the sea sand
near Thrasymêdês, his brother, and his father;
he passed them bits of the food of sacrifice,
and, pouring wine in a golden cup,
he said to Pallas Athena, daughter of Zeus:                    45

"Friend, I must ask you to invoke Poseidon:
you find us at this feast, keep in his honor.
Make the appointed offering then, and pray,
and give the honeyed winecup to your friend
so he may do the same. He, too,                    50
must pray to the gods on whom all men depend,
but he is just my age, you are the senior,
so here, I give the goblet first to you."

And he put the cup of sweet wine in her hand.
Athena liked his manners, and the equity                    55
that gave her precedence with the cup of gold,
so she besought Poseidon at some length:
"Earthshaker, listen and be well disposed.
Grant your petitioners everything they ask:

above all, honor to Nestor and his sons;                                    60
second, to every man of Pylos town
a fair gift in exchange for this hekatomb;[9]
third, may Telémakhos and I perform
the errand on which last night we put to sea."

This was the prayer of Athena—                                             65
granted in every particular by herself.
She passed the beautiful wine cup to Telémakhos,
who tipped the wine and prayed as she had done.
Meanwhile the spits were taken off the fire,
portions of crisp meat for all. They feasted,                              70
and when they had eaten and drunk their fill, at last
they heard from Nestor, prince of charioteers:

"Now is the time," he said, "for a few questions,
now that our young guests have enjoyed their dinner.
Who are you, strangers? Where are you sailing from,                        75
and where to, down the highways of sea water?
Have you some business here? or are you, now,
reckless wanderers of the sea, like those corsairs
who risk their lives to prey on other men?"

Clear-headed Telémakhos responded cheerfully,                              80
for Athena gave him heart. By her design
his quest for news about his father's wandering
would bring him fame in the world's eyes. So he said:

"Nestor, pride of Akhaians, Neleus' son,
you ask where we are from, and I can tell you:                             85
our home port is under Mount Neion, Ithaka.
We are not here on Ithakan business, though,
but on my own. I want news of my father,
Odysseus, known for his great heart, and I
will comb the wide world for it. People say                                90
he fought along with you when Troy was taken.
As to the other men who fought that war,
we know where each one died, and how he died;
but Zeus allotted my father death and mystery.
No one can say for sure where he was killed,                               95
whether some hostile landsmen or the sea,
the stormwaves on the deep sea, got the best of him.
And this is why I come to you for help.

9. Strictly, the word denotes a sacrifice of a hundred animals, but it is often used to refer to smaller offerings.

Tell me of his death, sir, if perhaps
you witnessed it, or have heard some wanderer                           100
tell the tale. The man was born for trouble.
Spare me no part of it for kindness' sake,
but put the scene before me as you saw it.
If ever Odysseus my noble father
served you by promise kept or work accomplished                        105
in the land of Troy, where you Akhaians suffered,
recall those things for me the way they were."

Then Nestor, prince of charioteers, made answer:

"Dear friend, you take me back to all the trouble
we went through in that country, we Akhaians:                          110
rough days aboard ship on the cloudy sea
cruising away for pillage after Akhilleus;
rough days of battle around Priam's town.
Our losses, then—so many good men gone:[1]
Arês' great Aias lies there, Akhilleus lies there,                     115
Patróklos, too, the wondrous counselor,
and my own strong and princely son, Antílokhos—
fastest man of them all, and a born fighter.
Other miseries, and many, we endured there.
Could any mortal man tell the whole story?                             120
Not if you stayed five years or six to hear
how hard it was for the flower of the Akhaians;
you'd go home weary, and the tale untold.
Think: we were there nine years, and we tried everything,
all stratagems against them,                                           125
up to the bitter end that Zeus begrudged us.
And as to stratagems, no man would claim
Odysseus' gift for those. He had no rivals,
your father, at the tricks of war.
                              Your father?
Well, I must say I marvel at the sight of you:                         130
your manner of speech couldn't be more like his;
one would say No; no boy could speak so well.
And all that time at Ilion,[2] he and I
were never at odds in council or assembly—
saw things the same way, had one mind between us                       135
in all the good advice we gave the Argives.

1. Nestor, who was the oldest of the warriors at the siege of Troy, lists the great heroes who fall
there: Akhilleus, the bravest of the Akhaians; Patroklos, his closest friend; Aias, who committed
suicide because the armor of the dead Akhilleus, a prize awarded to the bravest after Akhilleus,
was given to Odysseus. Odysseus will meet the ghosts of Akhilleus and Aias in the Underworld
(Book XI). Priam, King of Troy, was killed when the city fell.    2. Troy.

But when we plundered Priam's town and tower
and took to the ships, God scattered the Akhaians.
He had a mind to make homecoming hard for them,
seeing they would not think straight nor behave,                    140
or some would not. So evil days came on them,
and she who had been angered,[3]
Zeus's dangerous grey-eyed daughter, did it,
starting a fight between the sons of Atreus.[4]
First they were fools enough to call assembly                       145
at sundown, unheard of hour;
the Akhaian soldiers turned out, soaked with wine,
to hear talk, talk about it from their commanders:
Meneláos harangued them to get organized—
time to ride home on the sea's broad back, he said;
but Agamémnon wouldn't hear of it. He wanted                        150
to hold the troops, make sacrifice, a hekatomb,
something to pacify Athena's rage.
Folly again, to think that he could move her.
Will you change the will of the everlasting gods
in a night or a day's time?                                         155
The two men stood there hammering at each other
until the army got to its feet with a roar,
and no decision, wanting it both ways.
That night no one slept well, everyone cursing
someone else. Here was the bane from Zeus.                          160
At dawn we dragged our ships to the lordly water,
stowed aboard all our plunder
and the slave women in their low hip girdles.
But half the army elected to stay behind
with Agamémnon as their corps commander;                            165
the other half embarked and pulled away.
We made good time, the huge sea smoothed before us,
and held our rites when we reached Ténedos,[5]
being wild for home. But Zeus, not willing yet,
now cruelly set us at odds a second time,                           170
and one lot turned, put back in the rolling ships,
under command of the subtle captain, Odysseus;
their notion was to please Lord Agamémnon.
Not I. I fled, with every ship I had;
I knew fate had some devilment brewing there.                       175

3. Athena. The Trojan princess Cassandra took refuge in Athena's temple when the Akhaians captured Troy, but she was raped by Aias (not the great Aias but another chieftain of the same name). Athena was angry not just with him, but with the whole Akhaian army because they did not punish him.    4. Meneláos and Agamémnon.    5. An island off the coast, southwest of Troy.

Diomêdês roused his company and fled, too,
and later Meneláos, the red-haired captain,
caught up with us at Lesbos,
while we mulled over the long sea route, unsure
whether to lay our course northward of Khios,                    180
keeping the Isle of Psyria off to port,
or inside Khios, coasting by windy Mimas.[6]
We asked for a sign from heaven, and the sign came
to cut across the open sea to Euboia,
and lose no time putting our ills behind us.                     185
The wind freshened astern, and the ships ran
before the wind on paths of the deep sea fish,
making Geraistos before dawn. We thanked Poseidon
with many a charred thighbone for that crossing.
On the fourth day, Diomêdês'[7] company                          190
under full sail put in at Argos port,
and I held on for Pylos. The fair wind,
once heaven set it blowing, never failed.

So this, dear child, was how I came from Troy,
and saw no more of the others, lost or saved.                    195
But you are welcome to all I've heard since then
at home; I have no reason to keep it from you.
The Myrmidon[8] spearfighters returned, they say,
under the son of lionhearted Akhilleus;
and so did Poias' great son, Philoktêtês.[9]                     200
Idómeneus[1] brought his company back to Krete;
the sea took not a man from him, of all
who lived through the long war.
And even as far away as Ithaka
you've heard of Agamémnon—how he came                            205
home, how Aigísthos waited to destroy him
but paid a bitter price for it in the end.
That is a good thing, now, for a man to leave
a son behind him, like the son who punished
Aigísthos for the murder of his great father.                    210
You, too, are tall and well set-up, I see;

**6.** In their frail ships and without benefit of compass, Greek sailors preferred to hug the shore: the normal route would have been inside (i.e., to the east) of the island of Khios, past the headland of Mimas on the coast of Asia Minor, and across the Aegean along the island chain of the Cyclades. But Nestor is in a hurry; he goes northward of Khios and directly across the northern Aegean to Geraistos on the long island of Euboia, which hugs the coast of the Greek mainland. **7.** One of the Greek champions: his home was Argos. **8.** The tribal contingent led by Akhilleus, whose son, Neoptolemos, came to Troy to avenge his father: it was he who killed Priam on the altar in his palace. **9.** He had been abandoned on a desert island by the Greeks because he fell sick of a loathsome disease; cured, he was brought to Troy for the final assault. **1.** Leader of the Greek troops from Krete.

be brave, you too, so men in times to come
will speak well of you."

        Then Telémakhos said:

"Nestor, pride of Akhaians, Neleus' son,
that was revenge, and far and wide the Akhaians          215
will tell the tale in song for generations.
I wish the gods would buckle his arms on me!
I'd be revenged for outrage
on my insidious and brazen enemies.
But no such happy lot was given to me                    220
or to my father. Still, I must hold fast."

To this Lord Nestor of Gerênia said:

"My dear young friend, now that you speak of it,
I hear a crowd of suitors for your mother
lives with you, uninvited, making trouble.                225
Now tell me how you take this. Do the people
side against you, hearkening to some oracle?
Who knows, your father might come home someday
alone or backed by troops, and have it out with them
If grey-eyed Athena loved you                             230
the way she did Odysseus in the old days,
in Troy country, where we all went through so much—
never have I seen the gods help any man
as openly as Athena did your father—
well, as I say, if she cared for you that way,            235
there would be those to quit this marriage game."

But prudently Telémakhos replied:

"I can't think what you say will ever happen, sir.
It is a dazzling hope. But not for me.
It could not be—even if the gods willed it."             240
At this grey-eyed Athena broke in, saying:

"What strange talk you permit yourself, Telémakhos.
A god could save the man by simply wishing it—
from the farthest shore in the world.
If I were he, I should prefer to suffer                   245
years at sea, and then be safe at home;
better that than a knife at my hearthside
where Agamémnon found it—killed by adulterers.

Though as for death, of course all men must suffer it:
the gods may love a man, but they can't help him                    250
when cold death comes to lay him on her bier."

Telémakhos replied:

"Mentor, grievously though we miss my father, why
go on as if that homecoming could happen?                    255
You know the gods had settled it already,
years ago, when dark death came for him.
But there is something else I imagine Nestor
can tell us, knowing as he does the ways of men.
They say his rule goes back over three generations,                    260
so long, so old, it seems death cannot touch him.
Nestor, Neleus' son, true sage, say how
did the Lord of the Great Plains, Agamémnon, die?
What was the trick Aigísthos used
to kill the better man? And Meneláos,                    265
where was he? Not at Argos in Akhaia,
but blown off course, held up in some far country,
is that what gave the killer nerve to strike?"

Lord Nestor of Gerênia made answer:

"Well, now, my son, I'll tell you the whole story.                    270
You know, yourself, what would have come to pass
if red-haired Meneláos, back from Troy,
had caught Aigísthos in that house alive.
There would have been no burial mound for him,
but dogs and carrion birds to huddle on him                    275
in the fields beyond the wall, and not a soul
bewailing him, for the great wrong he committed.
While we were hard-pressed in the war at Troy
he stayed safe inland in the grazing country,
making light talk to win Agamémnon's queen.                    280
But the Lady Klytaimnéstra, in the first days,
rebuffed him, being faithful still;
then, too, she had at hand as her companion
a minstrel Agamémnon left attending her,
charged with her care, when he took ship for Troy.                    285
Then came the fated hour when she gave in.
Her lover tricked the poet and marooned him
on a bare island for the seabirds' picking,
and took her home, as he and she desired.
Many thighbones he burned on the gods' altars                    290

and many a woven and golden ornament
hung to bedeck them, in his satisfaction;
he had not thought life held such glory for him.


Now Meneláos and I sailed home together
on friendly terms, from Troy,                                    295
but when we came off Sunion Point[2] in Attika,
the ships still running free, Onêtor's son
Phrontis, the steersman of Meneláos' ship,
fell over with a death grip on the tiller:
some unseen arrow from Apollo hit him.[3]                        300
No man handled a ship better than he did
in a high wind and sea, so Meneláos
put down his longing to get on, and landed
to give this man full honor in funeral.
His own luck turned then. Out on the winedark sea               305
in the murmuring hulls again, he made Cape Malea,[4]
but Zeus who views the wide world sent a gloom
over the ocean, and a hawling gale
came on with seas increasing, mountainous,
parting the ships and driving half toward Krete[5]              310
where the Kydonians live by Iardanos river.
Off Gortyn's coastline in the misty sea there
a reef, a razorback, cuts through the water,
and ever westerly piles up a pounding
surf along the left side, going toward Phaistos—               315
big seas buffeted back by the narrow stone.
They were blown here, and fought in vain for sea room;
the ships kept going in to their destruction,
slammed on the reef. The crews were saved. But now
those five that weathered it got off to southward,             320
taken by wind and current on to Egypt;
and there Meneláos stayed. He made a fortune
in sea traffic among those distant races,
but while he did so, the foul crime was planned
and carried out in Argos by Aigísthos,                         325
who ruled over golden Mykênai[6] seven years.
Seven long years, with Agamémnon dead,
he held the people down, before the vengeance.

2. The southern cape of Attica: They would round this to go toward the Peloponnese.    3. A
formula for a sudden death which has no obvious explanation. (For women the arrow comes from
Artemis.)    4. The most westerly of the three capes in which the Peloponnese ends. Meneláos
would have to round it to get into a harbor for Sparta. It is still a place of storms.    5. Meneláos
is blown southeast, toward Egypt where he eventually arrives. Gortyn and Phaistos (site of a
Minoan palace) are inland from the south coast of Crete.    6. Argos and Mykênai are close to
each other and Homer sometimes does not discriminate between them.

But in the eighth year, back from exile in Attika,
Orestês killed the snake who killed his father.                    330
He gave his hateful mother and her soft man
a tomb together, and proclaimed the funeral day
a festal day for all the Argive people.
That day Lord Meneláos of the great war cry
made port with all the gold his ships could carry.                 335
And this should give you pause, my son:
don't stay too long away from home, leaving
your treasure there, and brazen suitors near;
they'll squander all you have or take it from you,
and then how will your journey serve?                              340
I urge you, though, to call on Meneláos,
he being but lately home from distant parts
in the wide world. A man could well despair
of getting home at all, if the winds blew him
over the Great South Sea—that weary waste,                         345
even the wintering birds delay
one winter more before the northward crossing.
Well, take your ship and crew and go by water,
or if you'd rather go by land, here are
horses, a car, and my own sons for company                         350
as far as the ancient land of Lakedaimon[7]
and Meneláos, the red-haired captain there.
Ask him with courtesy, and in his wisdom
he will tell you history and no lies."
While Nestor talked, the sun went down the sky                     355
and gloom came on the land,
and now the grey-eyed goddess Athena said:

"Sir, this is all most welcome and to the point,
but why not slice the bulls' tongues[8] now, and mix
libations for Poseidon and the gods?                               360
Then we can all retire; high time we did;
the light is going under the dark world's rim,
better not linger at the sacred feast."

When Zeus' daughter spoke, they turned to listen,
and soon the squires brought water for their hands,                365
while stewards filled the winebowls and poured out
a fresh cup full for every man. The company
stood up to fling the tongues and a shower of wine
over the flames, then drank their thirst away.

7. Sparta.   8. The tongue was one of the parts of the meat reserved for the gods; it was thrown
on the fire.

Now finally Telémakhos and Athena                          370
bestirred themselves, turning away to the ship,
but Nestor put a hand on each, and said:

"Now Zeus forbid, and the other gods as well,
that you should spend the night on board, and leave me
as though I were some pauper without a stitch,     375
no blankets in his house, no piles of rugs,
no sleeping soft for host or guest! Far from it!
I have all these, blankets and deep-piled rugs,
and while I live the only son of Odysseus
will never make his bed on a ship's deck—          380
no, not while sons of mine are left at home
to welcome any guest who comes to us."

The grey-eyed goddess Athena answered him:

"You are very kind, sir, and Telémakhos
should do as you ask. That is the best thing.      385
He will go with you, and will spend the night
under your roof. But I must join our ship
and talk to the crew, to keep their spirits up,
since I'm the only senior in the company.
The rest are boys who shipped for friendship's sake,     390
no older than Telémakhos, any of them.
Let me sleep out, then, by the black hull's side,
this night at least. At daybreak I'll be off
to see the Kaukonians about a debt they owe me,
an old one and no trifle. As for your guest,     395
send him off in a car,[9] with one of your sons,
and give him thoroughbreds, a racing team."

Even as she spoke, Athena left them—seeming
a seahawk, in a clap of wings,—and all
the Akhaians of Pylos town looked up astounded.     400
Awed then by what his eyes had seen, the old man
took Telémakhos' hand and said warmly:

"My dear child, I can have no fears for you,
no doubt about your conduct or your heart,
if, at your age, the gods are your companions.     405
Here we had someone from Olympos—clearly
the glorious daughter of Zeus, his third child,

9. A horse-drawn chariot.

who held your father dear among the Argives.
O, Lady, hear me! Grant an illustrious name
to me and to my children and my dear wife!                    410
A noble heifer shall be yours in sacrifice,
one that no man has ever yoked or driven;
my gift to you—her horns all sheathed in gold."

So he ended, praying; and Athena heard him.
Then Nestor of Gerênia led them all,                    415
his sons and sons-in-law, to his great house;
and in they went to the famous hall of Nestor,
taking their seats on thrones and easy chairs,
while the old man mixed water in a wine bowl
with sweet red wine, mellowed eleven years                    420
before his housekeeper uncapped the jar.
He mixed and poured his offering, repeating
prayers to Athena, daughter of royal Zeus.
The others made libation, and drank deep,
then all the company went to their quarters,                    425
and Nestor of Gerênia showed Telémakhos
under the echoing eastern entrance hall
to a fine bed near the bed of Peisístratos,
captain of spearmen, his unmarried son.
Then he lay down in his own inner chamber                    430
where his dear faithful wife had smoothed his bed.

When Dawn spread out her finger tips of rose,
Lord Nestor of Gerênia, charioteer,
left his room for a throne of polished stone,
white and gleaming as though with oil, that stood                    435
before the main gate of the palace; Neleus here
had sat before him—masterful in kingship,
Neleus, long ago a prey to death, gone down
to the night of the underworld.
So Nestor held his throne and scepter now,                    440
lord of the western approaches to Akhaia.
And presently his sons came out to join him,
leaving the palace: Ekhéphron and Stratíos,
Perseus and Arêtós and Thrasymêdês,
and after them the prince Peisístratos,                    445
bringing Telémakhos along with him.
Seeing all present, the old lord Nestor said:

"Dear sons, here is my wish, and do it briskly
to please the gods, Athena first of all,

my guest in daylight at our holy feast.                              450
One of you must go for a young heifer
and have the cowherd lead her from the pasture.
another call on Lord Telémakhos' ship
to invite his crewmen, leaving two behind;
and someone else again send for the goldsmith,                       455
Laerkés, to gild the horns.
The rest stay here together. Tell the servants
a ritual feast will be prepared in hall.
Tell them to bring seats, firewood and fresh water."

Before he finished, they were about these errands.                   460
The heifer came from pasture,
the crewmen of Telémakhos from the ship,
the smith arrived, bearing the tools of his trade—
hammer and anvil, and the precision tongs
he handled fiery gold with,—and Athena                               465
came as a god comes, numinous, to the rites.

The smith now gloved each horn in a pure foil
beaten out of the gold that Nestor gave him—
a glory and delight for the goddess' eyes—
while Ekhéphron and Stratíos held the horns.                         470
Arêtós brought clear lustral water[1]
in a bowl quivering with freshcut flowers,
a basket of barley in his other hand.
Thrasymêdês, who could stand his ground in war,
stood ready, with a sharp two-bladed axe,                            475
for the stroke of sacrifice, and Perseus
held a bowl for the blood. And now Nestor,
strewing the barley grains, and water drops,
pronounced his invocation to Athena
and burned a pinch of bristles from the victim.
When prayers were said and all the grain was scattered
great-hearted Thrasymêdês in a flash
swung the axe, at one blow cutting through
the neck tendons. The heifer's spirit failed.
Then all the women gave a wail of joy[2]—                            485
daughters, daughters-in-law, and the Lady Eurydíkê,
Klymémnos' eldest daughter. But the men
still held the heifer, shored her up
from the wide earth where the living go their ways,
until Peisístratos cut her throat across,                            490

1. Water for sprinkling.    2. The ritual cry at the moment of sacrifice.

the black blood ran, and life ebbed from her marrow.
The carcass now sank down, and they disjointed
shoulder and thigh bone, wrapping them in fat,
two layers, folded, with raw strips of flesh.
These offerings Nestor burned on the split-wood fire                495
and moistened with red wine. His sons took up
five-tined forks in their hands, while the altar flame
ate through the bones, and bits of tripe went round.
Then came the carving of the quarters, and they spitted
morsels of lean meat on the long sharp tines                        500
and broiled them at arm's length upon the fire.

Polykástê, a fair girl, Nestor's youngest,
had meanwhile given a bath to Telémakhos—
bathing him first, then rubbing him with oil.
She held fine clothes and a cloak to put around him                 505
when he came godlike from the bathing place;
then out he went to take his place with Nestor.
When the best cuts were broiled and off the spits,
they all sat down to banquet. Gentle squires
kept every golden wine cup brimming full.
And so they feasted to their heart's content,
until the prince of charioteers commanded:

"Sons, harness the blood mares for Telémakhos;
hitch up the car, and let him take the road."

They swung out smartly to do the work, and hooked                   515
the handsome horses to a chariot shaft.
The mistress of the stores brought up provisions
of bread and wine, with victuals fit for kings,
and Telémakhos stepped up on the painted car.
Just at his elbow stood Peisístratos,
captain of spearmen, reins in hand. He gave
a flick to the horses, and with streaming manes
they ran for the open country. The tall town
of Pylos sank behind them in the distance,
as all day long they kept the harness shaking.                      525

The sun was low and shadows crossed the lanes
when they arrived at Phêrai. There Dióklês,
son of Ortílokhos whom Alpheios fathered,
welcomed the young men, and they slept the night.
But up when the young Dawn's finger tips of rose                    530
opened in the east, they hitched the team

once more to the painted car,
and steered out eastward through the echoing gate,
whipping their fresh horses into a run.
That day they made the grainlands of Lakedaimon,                    535
where, as the horses held to a fast clip,
they kept on to their journey's end. Behind them
the sun went down and all the roads grew dark.


## Book IV

### THE RED-HAIRED KING AND HIS LADY

By vales and sharp ravines in Lakedaimon
the travellers drove to Meneláos' mansion,
and found him at a double wedding feast
for son and daughter.
                    Long ago at Troy
he pledged her to the heir[3] of great Akhilleus,                    5
breaker of men—a match the gods had ripened;
so he must send her with a chariot train
to the town and glory of the Myrmidons.
And that day, too, he brought Alektor's daughter
to marry his tall scion, Megapénthês,                                10
born of a slave girl during the long war—
for the gods had never after granted Helen
a child to bring into the sunlit world
after the first, rose-lipped Hermionê,
a girl like the pale-gold goddess Aphroditê.                         15

Down the great hall in happiness they feasted,
neighbors of Meneláos, and his kin,
for whom a holy minstrel harped and sang;
and two lithe tumblers moved out on the song
with spins and handsprings through the company.                     20
Now when Telémakhos and Nestor's son
pulled up their horses at the main gate,
one of the king's companions in arms, Eteóneus,
going outside, caught sight of them. He turned
and passed through court and hall to tell the master,               25
stepping up close to get his ear. Said he:

"Two men are here—two strangers, Meneláos,
but nobly born Akhaians, they appear.

3. His son Neoptolemos. Akhilleus asks for news of him from Odysseus in the lower world.

What do you say, shall we unhitch their team,
or send them on to someone free to receive them?"                    30

The red-haired captain answered him in anger:

"You were no idiot before, Eteóneus,
but here you are talking like a child of ten.
Could we have made it home again—and Zeus
gave us no more hard roving!—if other men                    35
had never fed us, given us lodging?
                              Bring
these men to be our guests: unhitch their team!"

Eteóneus left the long room like an arrow,
calling equerries after him, on the run.
Outside, they freed the sweating team from harness,                    40
stabled the horses, tied them up, and showered
bushels of wheat and barley in the feed box;
then leaned the chariot pole
against the gleaming entry wall of stone
and took the guests in. What a brilliant place                    45
that mansion of the great prince seemed to them!
A-glitter everywhere, as though with fiery
points of sunlight, lusters of the moon.
The young men gazed in joy before they entered
into a room of polished tubs to bathe.                    50
Maidservants gave them baths, anointed them,
held out fresh tunics, cloaked them warm; and soon
they took tall thrones beside the son of Atreus.
Here a maid tipped out water for their hands
from a golden pitcher into a silver bowl,                    55
and set a polished table near at hand;
the larder mistress with her tray of loaves
and savories came, dispensing all her best,
and then a carver heaped their platters high
with various meats, and put down cups of gold.                    60
Now said the red-haired captain, Meneláos,
gesturing:

          "Welcome; and fall to; in time,
when you have supped, we hope to hear your names,
forebears and families—in your case, it seems,
no anonymities, but lordly men.                    65
Lads like yourselves are not base born."

                                    At this,
he lifted in his own hands the king's portion,
a chine of beef, and set it down before them.
Seeing all ready then, they took their dinner;
but when they had feasted well,                                    70
Telémakhos could not keep still, but whispered,
his head bent close, so the others might not hear:

"My dear friend, can you believe your eyes?—
the murmuring hall, how luminous it is
with bronze, gold, amber, silver, and ivory!                       75
This is the way the court of Zeus must be,
inside, upon Olympos. What a wonder!"

But splendid Meneláos had overheard him
and spoke out on the instant to them both:

"Young friends, no mortal man can vie with Zeus.                   80
His home and all his treasures are for ever.
But as for men, it may well be that few
have more than I. How painfully I wandered
before I brought it home! Seven years at sea,
Kypros, Phoinikia, Egypt, and still farther                        85
among the sun-burnt races.
I saw the men of Sidon and Arabia
and Libya, too, where lambs are horned at birth.
In every year they have three lambing seasons,
so no man, chief or shepherd, ever goes                            90
hungry for want of mutton, cheese, or milk—
all year at milking time there are fresh ewes.
But while I made my fortune on those travels
a stranger killed my brother, in cold blood,—
tricked blind, caught in the web of his deadly queen.              95
What pleasure can I take, then, being lord
over these costly things?
You must have heard your fathers tell my story,
whoever your fathers are; you must know of my life,
the anguish I once had, and the great house                        100
full of my treasure, left in desolation.
How gladly I should live one third as rich
to have my friends back safe at home!—my friends
who died on Troy's wide seaboard, far
from the grazing lands of Argos.                                   105
But as things are, nothing but grief is left me
for those companionns. While I sit at home

sometimes hot tears come, and I revel in them,
or stop before the surfeit makes me shiver.
And there is one I miss more than the other                110
dead I mourn for; sleep and food alike
grow hateful when I think of him. No soldier
took on so much, went through so much, as Odysseus.
That seems to have been his destiny, and this mine—
to feel each day the emptiness of his absence,              115
ignorant, even, whether he lived or died.
How his old father and his quiet wife,
Penélopê, must miss him still!
And Telémakhos, whom he left as a new-born child."

Now hearing these things said, the boy's heart rose        120
in a long pang for his father, and he wept,
holding his purple mantle with both hands
before his eyes. Menláos knew him now,
and so fell silent with uncertainty
whether to let him speak and name his father             125
in his own time, or to inquire, and prompt him.
And while he pondered, Helen came
out of her scented chamber, a moving grace
like Artemis,[4] straight as a shaft of gold.
Beside her came Adrastê, to place her armchair,           130
Alkippê, with a rug of downy wool,
and Phylo, bringing a silver basket, once
given by Alkandrê, the wife of Pólybos,
in the treasure city, Thebes of distant Egypt.
He gave two silver bathtubs to Meneláos                   135
and a pair of tripods, with ten pure gold bars,
and she, then, made these beautiful gifts to Helen:
a golden distaff, and the silver basket
rimmed in hammered gold, with wheels to run on.
So Phylo rolled it in to stand beside her,                140
heaped with fine spun stuff, and cradled on it
the distaff swathed in dusky violet wool.
Reclining in her light chair with its footrest,
Helen gazed at her husband and demanded:

"Meneláos, my lord, have we yet heard                     145
our new guests introduce themselves? Shall I
dissemble what I feel? No, I must say it.
Never, anywhere, have I seen so great a likeness

4. A virgin goddess, sister of Apollo. She was associated with wild animals, and women called on
her for help in childbirth.

in man or woman—but it is truly strange!
This boy must be the son of Odysseus,                          150
Telémakhos, the child he left at home
that year the Akhaian host made war on Troy—
daring all for the wanton that I was."

And the red-haired captain, Meneláos, answered:

"My dear, I see the likeness as well as you do.                 155
Odysseus' hands and feet were like this boy's;
his head, and hair, and the glinting of his eyes.
Not only that, but when I spoke, just now,
of Odysseus' years of toil on my behalf
and all he had to endure—the boy broke down                    160
and wept into his cloak."

                    Now Nestor's son,
Peisístratos, spoke up in answer to him:

"My lord marshal, Meneláos, son of Atreus,
this is that hero's son as you surmise,
but he is gentle, and would be ashamed                         165
to clamor for attention before your grace
whose words have been so moving to us both.
Nestor, Lord of Gerênia, sent me with him
as guide and escort; he had wished to see you,
to be advised by you or assisted somehow.                      170
A father far from home means difficulty
for an only son, with no one else to help him;
so with Telémakhos:
his father left the house without defenders."

The king with flaming hair now spoke again:                    175

"His son, in my house! How I loved the man,
And how he fought through hardship for my sake!
I swore I'd cherish him above all others
if Zeus, who views the wide world, gave us passage
homeward across the sea in the fast ships.                     180
I would have settled him in Argos, brought him
over with herds and household out of Ithaka,
his child and all his people. I could have cleaned out
one of my towns to be his new domain.
And so we might have been together often                       185
in feasts and entertainments, never parted

till the dark mist of death lapped over one of us.
But God himself must have been envious,
to batter the bruised man so that he alone
should fail in his return."                                                    190


A twinging ache of grief rose up in everyone,
and Helen of Argos wept, the daughter of Zeus, [5]
Telémakhos and Meneláos wept,
and tears came to the eyes of Nestor's son—
remembering, for his part, Antílokhos,                                       195
whom the son of shining Dawn had killed in battle.
But thinking of that brother, he broke out:


"O son of Atreus, when we spoke of you
at home, and asked about you, my old father
would say you have the clearest mind of all.                                  200
If it is not too much to ask, then, let us not
weep away these hours after supper;
I feel we should not: Dawn will soon be here!
You understand, I would not grudge a man
right mourning when he comes to death and doom:                              205
what else can one bestow on the poor dead?—
a lock of hair sheared, and a tear let fall.
For that matter, I, too,
lost someone in the war at Troy—my brother,
and no mean soldier, whom you must have known,                               210
although I never did,—Antílokhos.
He ranked high as a runner and fighting man."


The red-haired captain Meneláos answered:


"My lad, what you have said is only sensible,
and you did well to speak. Yes, that was worthy                              215
a wise man and an older man than you are:
you speak for all the world like Nestor's son.
How easily one can tell the man whose father
had true felicity, marrying and begetting!
And that was true of Nestor, all his days,                                    220
down to his sleek old age in peace at home,
with clever sons, good spearmen into the bargain.
Come, we'll shake off this mourning mood of ours
and think of supper. Let the men at arms

5. Helen was the daughter of Leda, whom Zeus seduced in the shape of a swan.

rinse our hands again! There will be time
for a long talk with Telémakhos in the morning." 225

The hero Meneláos' companion in arms,
Asphalion, poured water for their hands,
and once again they touched the food before them.
But now it entered Helen's mind 230
to drop into the wine that they were drinking
an anodyne, mild magic of forgetfulness.
Whoever drank this mixture in the wine bowl
would be incapable of tears that day—
though he should lose mother and father both, 235
or see, with his own eyes, a son or brother
mauled by weapons of bronze at his own gate.
The opiate of Zeus's daughter bore
this canny power. It had been supplied her
by Polydamna, mistress of Lord Thôn, 240
in Egypt,[6] where the rich plantations grow
herbs of all kinds, maleficent and healthful;
and no one else knows medicine as they do,
Egyptian heirs of Paian, the healing god.
She drugged the wine, then, had it served, and said— 245
taking again her part in the conversation—

"O Meneláos, Atreus' royal son,
and you that are great heroes' sons, you know
how Zeus gives all of us in turn
good luck and bad luck, being all powerful. 250
So take refreshment, take your ease in hall,
and cheer the time with stories. I'll begin.
Not that I think of naming, far less telling,
every feat of that rugged man, Odysseus,
but here is something that he dared to do 255
at Troy, where you Akhaians endured the war.
He had, first, given himself an outrageous beating
and thrown some rags on—like a household slave—
then slipped into that city of wide lanes
among his enemies. So changed, he looked
as never before upon the Akhaian beachhead, 260
but like a beggar, merged in the townspeople;
and no one there remarked him. But I knew him—
even as he was, I knew him,
and questioned him. How shrewdly he put me off!

6. The Greeks had great respect for Egyptian doctors, and Egyptian papyri document their skill
as surgeons and their expertise with drugs.

But in the end I bathed him and anointed him,                265
put a fresh cloak around him, and swore an oath
not to give him away as Odysseus to the Trojans,
till he got back to camp where the long ships lay.
He spoke up then, and told me
all about the Akhaians, and their plans—                     270
then sworded many Trojans through the body
on his way out with what he learned of theirs.
The Trojan women raised a cry—but my heart
sang—for I had come round, long before,
to dreams of sailing home, and I repented                    275
the mad day Aphroditê
drew me away from my dear fatherland,
forsaking all—child, bridal bed, and husband—
a man without defect in form or mind."

Replied the red-haired captain, Meneláos:                    280

"An excellent tale, my dear, and most becoming.
In my life I have met, in many countries,
foresight and wit in many first rate men,
but never have I seen one like Odysseus
for steadiness and a stout heart. Here, for instance,        285
is what he did—had the cold nerve to do—
inside the hollow horse, where we were waiting,
picked men all of us, for the Trojan slaughter,
when all of a sudden, you came by—I dare say
drawn by some superhuman                                     290
power that planned an exploit for the Trojans;
and Deïphobos,[7] that handsome man, came with you.
Three times you walked around it, patting it everywhere,
and called by name the flower of our fighters,
making your voice sound like their wives, calling.           295
Diomêdês and I crouched in the center
along with Odysseus; we could hear you plainly;
and listening, we two were swept
by waves of longing—to reply, or go.
Odysseus fought us down, despite our craving,                300
and all the Akhaians kept their lips shut tight,
all but Antiklos. Desire moved his throat
to hail you, but Odysseus' great hands clamped
over his jaws, and held. So he saved us all,
till Pallas Athena led you away at last."                    305

7. A Trojan prince whom Helen married after Paris was killed in battle.

Then clear-headed Telémakhos addressed him:

"My lord marshal, Meneláos, son of Atreus,
all the more pity, since these valors
could not defend him from annihilation—
not if his heart were iron in his breast.                                    310
But will you not dismiss us for the night now?
Sweet sleep will be a pleasure, drifting over us."

He said no more, but Helen called the maids
and sent them to make beds, with purple rugs
piled up, and sheets outspread, and fleecy                                   315
coverlets, in the porch inside the gate.
The girls went out with torches in their hands,
and presently a squire led the guests—
Telémakhos and Nestor's radiant son—
under the entrance colonnade, to bed.                                        320
Then deep in the great mansion, in his chamber,
Meneláos went to rest, and Helen,
queenly in her long gown, lay beside him.

When the young Dawn with finger tips of rose
made heaven bright, the deep-lunged man of battle                            325
stood up, pulled on his tunic and his mantle,
slung on a swordbelt and a new edged sword,
tied his smooth feet into fine rawhide sandals
and left his room, a god's brilliance upon him.
He sat down by Telémakhos, asking gently:                                     330

"Telémakhos, why did you come, sir, riding
the sea's broad back to reach old Lakedaimon?
A public errand or private? Why, precisely?"

Telémakhos replied:

"My lord marshal Meneláos, son of Atreus,                                    335
I came to hear what news you had of Father.
My house, my good estates are being ruined.
Each day my mother's bullying suitors come
to slaughter flocks of mine and my black cattle;
enemies crowd our home. And this is why                                      340
I come to you for news of him who owned it.
Tell me of his death, sir, if perhaps
you witnessed it, or have heard some wanderer
tell the tale. The man was born for trouble.

Spare me no part for kindness' sake; be harsh;                    345
but put the scene before me as you saw it.
If ever Odysseus my noble father
served you by promise kept or work accomplished
in the land of Troy, where you Akhaians suffered,
recall those things for me the way they were."                    350
Stirred now to anger, Meneláos said:

"Intolerable—that soft men, as those are,
should think to lie in that great captain's bed.
Fawn in a lion's lair! As if a doe
put down her litter of sucklings there, while she                 355
quested a glen or cropped some grassy hollow.
Ha! Then the lord returns to his own bed
and deals out wretched doom on both alike.
So will Odysseus deal out doom on these.
O Father Zeus, Athena, and Apollo!                                360
I pray he comes as once he was, in Lesbos,
when he stood up to wrestle Philomeleidês—[8]
champion and Island King—
and smashed him down. How the Akhaians cheered!
If only that Odysseus met the suitors,                            365
they'd have their consummation, a cold bed!
Now for your questions, let me come to the point.
I would not misreport it for you; let me
tell you what the Ancient of the Sea,
who is infallible, said to me—every word.                         370

During my first try at a passage homeward
the gods detained me, tied me down to Egypt—
for I had been too scant in hekatombs,
and gods will have the rules each time remembered.
There is an island washed by the open sea                         375
lying off Nile mouth—seamen call it Pharos—
distant a day's sail in a clean hull
with a brisk land breeze behind. It has a harbor,
a sheltered bay, where shipmasters
take on dark water for the outward voyage.                        380
Here the gods held me twenty days becalmed.
No winds came up, seaward escorting winds
for ships that ride the sea's broad back, and so
my stores and men were used up; we were failing
had not one goddess intervened in pity—                           385

8. A king of Lesbos who challenged all comers to wrestle with him.

Eidothea, daughter of Proteus,
the Ancient of the Sea. How I distressed her!
I had been walking out alone that day—
my sailors, thin-bellied from the long fast,
were off with fish hooks, angling on the shore—                    390
then she appeared to me, and her voice sang:

'What fool is here, what drooping dunce of dreams?
Or can it be, friend, that you love to suffer?
How can you linger on this island, aimless
and shiftless, while your people waste away?'                    395

To this I quickly answered:

                    'Let me tell you,
goddess, whatever goddess you may be,
these doldrums are no will of mine. I take it
the gods who own broad heaven are offended.
Why don't you tell me—since the gods know everything—                    400
who has me pinned down here?
How am I going to make my voyage home?'

Now she replied in her immortal beauty:

'I'll put it for you clearly as may be, friend.
The Ancient of the Salt Sea haunts this place,                    405
immortal Proteus of Egypt; all the deeps
are known to him; he serves under Poseidon,
and is, they say, my father.
If you could take him by surprise and hold him,
he'd give you course and distance for your sailing                    410
homeward across the cold fish-breeding sea.
And should you wish it, noble friend, he'd tell you
all that occurred at home, both good and evil,
while you were gone so long and hard a journey.'

To this I said:

                    'But you, now—you must tell me                    415
how I can trap this venerable sea-god.
He will elude me if he takes alarm;
no man—god knows—can quell a god with ease.'
That fairest of unearthly nymphs replied:

'I'll tell you this, too, clearly as may be.                    420
When the sun hangs at high noon in heaven,

the Ancient glides ashore under the Westwind,
hidden by shivering glooms on the clear water,
and rests in caverns hollowed by the sea.
There flippered seals, brine children, shining come      425
from silvery foam in crowds to lie around him,
exhaling rankness from the deep sea floor.
Tomorrow dawn I'll take you to those caves
and bed you down there. Choose three officers
for company—brave men they had better be—              430
the old one has strange powers, I must tell you.
He goes amid the seals to check their number,
and when he sees them all, and counts them all,
he lies down like a shepherd with his flock.
Here is your opportunity: at this point                  435
gather yourselves, with all your heart and strength,
and tackle him before he bursts away.
He'll make you fight—for he can take the forms
of all the beasts, and water, and blinding fire;
but you must hold on, even so, and crush him             440
until he breaks the silence. When he does,
he will be in that shape you saw asleep.
Relax your grip, then, set the Ancient free,
and put your questions, hero:
Who is the god so hostile to you,                        445
and how will you go home on the fish-cold sea.'

At this she dove under a swell and left me.
Back to the ships in the sandy cove I went,
my heart within me like a high surf running;
but there I joined my men once more                      450
at supper, as the sacred Night came on,
and slept at last beside the lapping water.
When Dawn spread out her finger tips of rose
I started, by the sea's wide level ways,
praying the gods for help, and took along               455
three lads I counted on in any fight.
Meanwhile the nereid[9] swam from the lap of Ocean
laden with four sealskins, new flayed
for the hoax she thought of playing on her father.
In the sand she scooped out hollows for our bodies       460
and sat down, waiting. We came close to touch her,
and, bedding us, she threw the sealskins over us—
a strong disguise; oh, yes, terribly strong

9. Sea nymph.

as I recall the stench of those damned seals.
Would any man lie snug with a sea monster?                    465
But here the nymph, again, came to our rescue,
dabbing ambrosia under each man's nose—
a perfume drowning out the bestial odor.
So there we lay with beating hearts all morning
while seals came shoreward out of ripples, jostling          470
to take their places, flopping on the sand.
At noon the Ancient issued from the sea
and held inspection, counting off the sea-beasts.
We were the first he numbered; he went by,
detecting nothing. When at last he slept                     475
we gave a battlecry and plunged for him,
locking our hands behind him. But the old one's
tricks were not knocked out of him; far from it.
First he took on a whiskered lion's shape,
a serpent then; a leopard; a great boar;                     480
then sousing water; then a tall green tree.
Still we hung on, by hook or crook, through everything,
until the Ancient saw defeat, and grimly
opened his lips to ask me:

                        'Son of Atreus,
who counselled you to this? A god: what god?                 485
Set a trap for me, overpower me—why?'

He bit if off, then, and I answered:

                        'Old one,
you know the reason—why feign not to know?
High and dry so long upon this island
I'm at my wits' end, and my heart is sore.                   490
You gods know everything; now you can tell me:
which of the immortals chained me here?
And how will I get home on the fish-cold sea?'

He made reply at once:

                        'You should have paid
honor to Zeus and the other gods, performing                 495
a proper sacrifice before embarking:
that was your short way home on the winedark sea.
You may not see your friends, your own fine house,
or enter your own land again,
unless you first remount the Nile in flood                   500

and pay your hekatomb to the gods of heaven.
Then, and then only,
the gods will grant the passage you desire.'

Ah, how my heart sank, hearing this—
hearing him send me back on the cloudy sea                            505
in my own track, the long hard way of Egypt.
Neverheless, I answered him and said:

'Ancient, I shall do all as you command.
But tell me, now, the others—
had they a safe return, all those Akhaians                           510
who stayed behind when Nestor and I left Troy?
Or were there any lost at sea—what bitterness!—
any who died in camp, after the war?'

To this he said:

                    'For you to know these things
goes beyond all necessity, Meneláos.                                 515
Why must you ask?—you should not know my mind,
and you will grieve to learn it, I can tell you.
Many there were who died, many remain,
but two high officers alone were lost—
on the passage home, I mean; you saw the war.                        520
One is alive, a castaway at sea;
the other, Aias,[1] perished with all hands—
though first Poseidon landed him on Gyrai
promontory, and saved him from the ocean.
Despite Athena's hate, he had lived on,                              525
but the great sinner in his insolence
yelled that the gods' will and the sea were beaten,
and this loud brag came to Poseidon's ears.
He swung the trident in his massive hands
and in one shock from top to bottom split                            530
that promontory, toppling into the sea
the fragment where the great fool sat.
So the vast ocean had its will with Aias,
drunk in the end on salt spume as he drowned.
Meanwhile your brother[2] left that doom astern                      535
in his decked ships—the Lady Hera[3] saved him;

---

1. The Lesser Aias, the one who raped Cassandra in Athene's temple. The other Aias, the great warrior of the *Iliad*, committed suicide at Troy when the award of valor, Akhilleus' armor, was given to Odysseus instead of to him. Odysseus meets his ghost in the lower world (Book XI). 2. Agamémnon.    3. The wife and sister of Zeus.

but as he came round Malea
a fresh squall caught him, bearing him away
over the cold sea, groaning in disgust,
to the Land's End of Argos, where Thyestês          540
lived in the days of old, and then his son,
Aigísthos. Now, again, return seemed easy:
the high gods wound the wind into the east,
and back he sailed, this time to his own coast.
He went ashore and kissed the earth in joy,          545
hot tears blinding his eyes at sight of home.
But there were eyes that watched him from a height—
a lookout, paid two bars of gold to keep
vigil the year round for Aigísthos' sake,
that he should be forewarned, and Agamémnon's          550
furious valor sleep unroused.
Now this man with his news ran to the tyrant,
who made his crooked arrangements in a flash,
stationed picked men at arms, a score of men
in hiding; set a feast in the next room;          555
then he went out with chariots and horses
to hail the king and welcome him to evil.
He led him in to banquet, all serene,
and killed him, like an ox felled at the trough;
and not a man of either company          560
survived that ambush in Aigísthos' house.'

Before the end my heart was broken down.
I slumped on the trampled sand and cried aloud,
caring no more for life or the light of day,
and rolled there weeping, till my tears were spent.          565

'No more, no more; how long must you persist?
Nothing is gained by grieving so. How soon
can you return to Argos? You may take him
alive there still—or else meanwhile Orestês          570
will have despatched him. You'll attend the feast.'

At this my heart revived, and I recovered
the self command to question him once more:

'Of two companions now I know. The third?
Tell me his name, the one marooned at sea;          575
living, you say, or dead? Even in pain
I wish to hear.'

And this is all he answered:

'Laërtês' son, whose home is Ithaka.
I saw him weeping, weeping on an island.
The nymph Kalypso has him, in her hall.                                    580
No means of faring home are left him now;
no ship with oars, and no ship's company
to pull him on the broad back of the sea.
As to your own destiny, prince Meneláos,
you shall not die in the bluegrass land of Argos;                          585
rather the gods intend you for Elysion[4]
with golden Rhadamanthos at the world's end,
where all existence is a dream of ease.
Snowfall is never known there, neither long
frost of winter, nor torrential rain,                                      590
but only mild and lulling airs from Ocean
bearing refreshment for the souls of men—
the West Wind always blowing.
                                        For the gods
hold you, as Helen's lord, a son of Zeus.'

At this he dove under a swell and left me,                                 595
and I went back to the ship with my companions,
feeling my heart's blood in me running high;
but in the long hull's shadow, near the sea,
we supped again as sacred Night came on
and slept at last beside the lapping water.                                600

When Dawn spread out her finger tips of rose,
in first light we launched on the courtly breakers,
setting up masts and yards in the well-found ships;
went all on board, and braced on planks athwart
oarsmen in line dipped oars in the grey sea.                               605
Soon I drew in to the great stream fed by heaven[5]
and, laying by, slew bulls in the proper number,
until the immortal gods were thus appeased;
then heaped a death mound on that shore against
all-quenching time for Agamémnon's honor,                                  610
and put to sea once more. The gods sent down
a sternwind for a racing passage homeward.

So ends the story. Now you must stay with me
and be my guest eleven or twelve days more.

4. A paradise reserved for a few of the heroes who were related to gods (Menelaos is married to Helen, daughter of Zeus). *Rhadamanthos* was son of Zeus.     5. The river Nile.

I'll send you on your way with gifts, and fine ones:                    615
three chariot horses, and a polished car;
a hammered cup, too, so that all your days,
tipping the red wine for the deathless gods,
you will remember me."

Telémakhos answered:

"Lord, son of Atreus, no, you must not keep me.                    620
Not that a year with you would be too long:
I never could be homesick here—I find
your tales and all you say so marvellous.
But time hangs heavy on my shipmates' hands
at holy Pylos, if you make me stay.                                       625
As for your gift, now, let it be some keepsake.
Horses I cannot take to Ithaka;
let me bestow them back on you, to serve
your glory here. My lord, you rule wide country,
rolling and rich with clover, galingale                                   630
and all the grains: red wheat and hoary barley.
At home we have no level runs or meadows,
but highland, goat land—prettier than plains, though.
Grasses, and pasture land, are hard to come by
upon the islands tilted in the sea,                                       635
and Ithaka is the island of them all."

At this the deep-lunged man of battle smiled.
Then he said kindly, patting the boy's hand:

"You come of good stock, lad. That was well spoken.
I'll change the gift, then—as indeed I can.                              640
Let me see what is costliest and most beautiful
of all the precious things my house contains:
a wine bowl, mixing bowl, all wrought of silver,
but rimmed with hammered gold. Let this be yours.
It is Hephaistos'[6] work, given me by Phaidimos,                        645
captain and king of Sidon. He received me
during my travels. Let it be yours, I say."

This was their discourse on that morning. Meanwhile
guests were arriving at the great lord's house,
bringing their sheep, and wine, the ease of men,                        650

---

6. The smith-god, who made Akhilleus' armor. He was married to the goddess Aphrodite.

with loaves their comely kerchiefed women sent,
to make a feast in hall.
                              At that same hour,
before the distant manor of Odysseus,
the suitors were competing at the discus throw
and javelin, on a measured field they used,                            655
arrogant lords at play. The two best men,
Antínoös and Eurýmakhos, presided.
Now Phronios' son, Noêmon, came to see them
with a question for Antínoös. He said:

"Do any of us know, or not, Antínoös,                                  660
what day Telémakhos will be home from Pylos?
He took my ship, but now I need it back
to make a cruise to Elis, where the plains are.
I have a dozen mares at pasture there
with mule colts yet unweaned. My notion is                             665
to bring one home and break him in for labor."
His first words made them stare—for they knew well
Telémakhos could not have gone to Pylos,
but inland with his flocks, or to the swineherd.
Eupeithês' son, Antínoös, quickly answered:                            670

"Tell the story straight. He sailed? Who joined him—
a crew he picked up here in Ithaka,
or his own slaves? He might have done it that way.
And will you make it clear
whether he took the ship against your will?                            675
Did he ask for it, did you lend it to him?"

Now said the son of Phronios in reply:

"Lent it to him, and freely. Who would not,
when a prince of that house asked for it, in trouble?
Hard to refuse the favor, it seems to me.                              680
As for his crew, the best men on the island,
after ourselves, went with him. Mentor I noted
going aboard—or a god who looked like Mentor.
The strange thing is, I saw Lord Mentor here
in the first light yesterday—although he sailed                        685
five days ago for Pylos."

                       Turning away,
Noêmon took the path to his father's house,

leaving the two men there, baffled and hostile.
They called the rest in from the playing field
and made them all sit down, so that Antínoös                           690
could speak out from the stormcloud of his heart,
swollen with anger; and his eyes blazed:

"A bad business. Telémakhos had the gall
to make that crossing, though we said he could not.
So the young cub rounds up a first rate crew                          695
in spite of all our crowd, and puts to sea.
What devilment will he be up to next time?—
Zeus blast the life out of him before he's grown!
Just give me a fast ship and twenty men;
I'll intercept him, board him in the strait                            700
between the crags of Samê and this island.
He'll find his sea adventure after his father
swamping work in the end!"

                         They all cried "Aye!"
and "After him!" and trailed back to the manor.

Now not much time went by before Penélopê                             705
learned what was afoot among the suitors.
Medôn the crier told her. He had been
outside the wall, and heard them in the court
conspiring. Into the house and up the stairs
he ran to her with his news upon his tongue—                          710
but at the door Penélopê met him, crying:

"Why have they sent you up here now? To tell
the maids of King Odysseus—'Leave your spinning:
Time to go down and slave to feed those men?'
I wish this were the last time they came feasting,                    715
counting me or consorting here! The last!
Each day you crowd this house like wolves
to eat away my brave son's patrimony.
When you were boys, did your own fathers tell you
nothing of what Odysseus was for them?                                720
In word and act impeccable, disinterested
toward all the realm—though it is king's justice
to hold one man abhorred and love another;
no man alive could say Odysseus wronged him.
But your own hearts—how different!—and your deeds!                    725
How soon are benefactions all forgotten!"

Now Medôn, the alert and cool man, answered:

"I wish that were the worst of it, my Lady,
but they intend something more terrible—
may Zeus forfend and spare us!                                    730
They plan to drive the keen bronze through Telémakhos
when he comes home. He sailed away, you know,
to hallowed Pylos and old Lakedaimon
for news about his father."

                        Her knees failed,
and her heart failed as she listened to the words,             735
and all her power of speech went out of her.
Tears came; but the rich voice could not come.
Only after a long while she made answer:

"Why has my child left me? He had no need
of those long ships on which men shake out sail               740
to tug like horses, breasting miles of sea.
Why did he go? Must he, too, be forgotten?"

Then Medôn, the perceptive man, replied:

"A god moved him—who knows?—or his own heart
sent him to learn, at Pylos, if his father                        745
roams the wide world still, or what befell him."

He left her then, and went down through the house.
And now the pain around her heart benumbed her;
chairs were a step away, but far beyond her;
she sank down on the door sill of the chamber,                750
wailing, and all her women young and old
made a low murmur of lament around her,
until at last she broke out through her tears:

"Dearest companions, what has Zeus given me?
Pain—more pain than any living woman.                         755
My lord, my lion heart, gone, long ago—
the bravest man, and best, of the Danaans,
famous through Hellas and the Argive midlands—
and now the squalls have blown my son, my dear one,
an unknown boy, southward. No one told me.                   760
O brute creatures, not one soul would dare
to wake me from my sleep; you knew
the hour he took the black ship out to sea!

If I had seen that sailing in his eyes
he should have stayed with me, for all his longing,                765
stayed—or left me dead in the great hall.
Go, someone, now, and call old Dólios,
the slave my father gave me before I came,
my orchard keeper—tell him to make haste
and put these things before Laërtês; he                          770
may plan some kind of action; let him come
to cry shame on these ruffians who would murder
Odysseus' son and heir, and end his line!"

The dear old nurse, Eurýkleia, answered her:

"Sweet mistress, have my throat cut without mercy               775
or what you will; it's true, I won't conceal it,
I knew the whole thing; gave him his provisions;
grain and sweet wine I gave, and a great oath
to tell you nothing till twelve days went by,
or till you heard of it yourself, or missed him;                 780
he hoped you would not tear your skin lamenting.
Come, bathe and dress your loveliness afresh,
and go to the upper rooms with all your maids
to ask help from Athena, Zeus's daughter.
She it will be who saves this boy from death.                    785
Spare the old man this further suffering;
the blissful gods cannot so hate his line,
heirs of Arkêsios;[7] one will yet again
be lord of the tall house and the far fields."

She hushed her weeping in this way, and soothed her.            790
The Lady Penélopê arose and bathed,
dressing her body in her freshest linen,
filled a basket with barley, and led her maids
to the upper rooms, where she besought Athena:

"Tireless child of Zeus, graciously hear me!                    795
If ever Odysseus burned at our altar fire
thighbones of beef or mutton in sacrifice,
remember it for my sake! Save my son!
Shield him, and make the killers go astray!"

She ended with a cry, and the goddess heard her.               800
Now voices rose from the shadowy hall below
where the suitors were assuring one another:

7. Father of Laërtês, Odysseus' father.

"Our so-long-courted Queen is even now
of a mind to marry one of us, and knows
nothing of what is destined for her son."                    805
Of what was destined they in fact knew nothing,
but Antínoös addressed them in a whisper:

"No boasting—are you mad?—and no loud talk:
someone might hear it and alarm the house.
Come along now, be quiet, this way; come,                    810
we'll carry out the plan our hearts are set on."

Picking out twenty of the strongest seamen,
he led them to a ship at the sea's edge,
and down they dragged her into deeper water,
stepping a mast in her, with furled sails,                    815
and oars a-trail from thongs looped over thole pins,
ready all; then tried the white sail, hoisting,
while men at arms carried their gear aboard.
They moored the ship some way off shore, and left her
to take their evening meal there, waiting for night to come.   820

Penélopê at that hour in her high chamber
lay silent, tasting neither food nor drink,
and thought of nothing but her princely son—
could he escape, or would they find and kill him?—
her mind turning at bay, like a cornered lion                  825
in whom fear comes as hunters close the ring.
But in her sick thought sweet sleep overtook her,
and she dozed off, her body slack and still.

Now it occurred to the grey-eyed goddess Athena
to make a figure of dream in a woman's form—                   830
Iphthimê, great Ikários' other daughter,
whom Eumêlos of Phêrai took as bride.
The goddess sent this dream to Odysseus' house
to quiet Penélopê and end her grieving.
So, passing by the strap-slit through the door,[8]             835
the image came a-gliding down the room
to stand at her bedside and murmur to her:

"Sleepest thou, sorrowing Penélopê?
The gods whose life is ease no longer suffer thee

8. As we would say "through the keyhole." The inside bolt could by closed from outside by means
of a strap which came through a slit in the door.

to pine and weep, then; he returns unharmed,                    840
thy little one; no way hath he offended."

Then pensive Penélopê made this reply,
slumbering sweetly in the gates of dream:

"Sister, hast thou come hither? Why? Aforetime
never wouldst come, so far away thy dwelling.                    845
And am I bid be done with all my grieving?
But see what anguish hath my heart and soul!
My lord, my lion heart, gone, long ago—
the bravest man, and best, of the Danaans,
famous through Hellas and the Argive midlands—                   850
and now my son, my dear one, gone seafaring,
a child, untrained in hardship or in council.
Aye, 'tis for him I weep, more than his father!
Aye, how I tremble for him, lest some blow
befall him at men's hands or on the sea!                         855
Cruel are they and many who plot against him,
to take his life before he can return."

Now the dim phantom spoke to her once more:

"Lift up thy heart, and fear not overmuch.
For by his side one goes whom all men else                       860
invoke as their defender, one so powerful—
Pallas Athena; in thy tears she pitied thee
and now hath sent me that I so assure thee."

Then said Penélopê the wise:

                                        "If thou art
numinous and hast ears for divine speech,                        865
O tell me, what of Odysseus, man of woe?
Is he alive still somewhere, seeth he day light still?
Or gone in death to the sunless underworld?"

The dim phantom said only this in answer:

"Of him I may not tell thee in this discourse,                   870
alive or dead. And empty words are evil."
The wavering form withdrew along the doorbolt
into a draft of wind, and out of sleep
Penélopê awoke, in better heart
for that clear dream in the twilight of the night.               875

Meanwhile the suitors had got under way,
planning the death plunge for Telémakhos.
Between the Isles of Ithaka and Samê
the sea is broken by an islet, Asteris,
with access to both channels from a cove.                    880
In ambush here that night the Akhaians lay.


## Book V

### SWEET NYMPH AND OPEN SEA

Dawn came up from the couch of her reclining,
leaving her lord Tithonos'[9] brilliant side
with fresh light in her arms for gods and men.
And the master of heaven and high thunder, Zeus,
went to his place among the gods assembled                    5
hearing Athena tell Odysseus' woe.
For she, being vexed that he was still sojourning
in the sea chambers of Kalypso, said:

"O Father Zeus and gods in bliss forever,
let no man holding scepter as a king                         10
think to be mild, or kind, or virtuous;
let him be cruel, and practice evil ways,
for those Odysseus ruled cannot remember
the fatherhood and mercy of his reign.
Meanwhile he lives and grieves upon that island             15
in thralldom to the nymph; he cannot stir,
cannot fare homeward, for no ship is left him,
fitted with oars—no crewmen or companions
to pull him on the broad back of the sea.
And now murder is hatched on the high sea                    20
against his son, who sought news of his father
in the holy lands of Pylos and Lakedaimon."
To this the summoner of cloud replied:

"My child, what odd complaints you let escape you.
Have you not, you yourself, arranged this matter—            25
as we all know—so that Odysseus
will bring these men to book, on his return?
And are you not the one to give Telémakhos
a safe route for sailing? Let his enemies
encounter no one and row home again."                        30

9. A mortal man whom Eos, the dawn goddess, took for her husband.

He turned then to his favorite son and said:

"Hermês, you have much practice on our missions,
go make it known to the softly-braided nymph
that we, whose will is not subject to error,            35
order Odysseus home; let him depart.
But let him have no company, gods or men,
only a raft that he must lash together,
and after twenty days, worn out at sea,
he shall make land upon the garden isle,
Skhería,[1] of our kinsmen, the Phaiákians.         40
Let these men take him to their hearts in honor
and berth him in a ship, and send him home,
with gifts of garments, gold, and bronze—
so much he had not counted on from Troy
could he have carried home his share of plunder.    45
His destiny is to see his friends again
under his own roof, in his father's country."

No words were lost on Hermês the Wayfinder,
who bent to tie his beautiful sandals on,
ambrosial, golden, that carry him over water        50
or over endless land in a swish of the wind,
and took the wand with which he charms asleep—
or when he wills, awake—the eyes of men.
So wand in hand he paced into the air,
shot from Pieria[2] down, down to sea level,        55
and veered to skim the swell. A gull patrolling
between the wave crests of the desolate sea
will dip to catch a fish, and douse his wings;
no higher above the whitecaps Hermês flew
until the distant island lay ahead,        60
then rising shoreward from the violet ocean
he stepped up to the cave. Divine Kalypso,
the mistress of the isle, was now at home.
Upon her hearthstone a great fire blazing
scented the farthest shores with cedar smoke        65
and smoke of thyme, and singing high and low
in her sweet voice, before her loom a-weaving,
she passed her golden shuttle to and fro.
A deep wood grew outside, with summer leaves
of alder and black poplar, pungent cypress.        70
Ornate birds here rested their stretched wings—

---

1. Later Greeks identified it as the island of Corcyra (modern Corfu) off the northwest coast of mainland Greece.    2. The vicinity of Mount Olympus.

horned owls, falcons, cormorants—long-tongued
beachcombing birds, and followers of the sea.
Around the smoothwalled cave a crooking vine
held purple clusters under ply of green;                          75
and four springs, bubbling up near one another
shallow and clear, took channels here and there
through beds of violets and tender parsley.
Even a god who found this place
would gaze, and feel his heart beat with delight:    .             80
so Hermês did; but when he had gazed his fill
he entered the wide cave. Now face to face
the magical Kalypso recognized him,
as all immortal gods know one another
on sight—though seeming strangers, far from home.                  85
But he saw nothing of the great Odysseus,
who sat apart, as a thousand times before,
and racked his own heart groaning, with eyes wet
scanning the bare horizon of the sea.
Kalypso, lovely nymph, seated her guest                            90
in a bright chair all shimmering, and asked:

"O Hermês, ever with your golden wand,
what brings you to my island?
Your awesome visits in the past were few.
Now tell me what request you have in mind;                         95
for I desire to do it, if I can,
and if it is a proper thing to do.
But wait a while, and let me serve my friend."

She drew a table of ambrosia near him
and stirred a cup of ruby-colored nectar—                          100
food and drink for the luminous Wayfinder,
who took both at his leisure, and replied:[3]

"Goddess to god, you greet me, questioning me?
Well, here is truth for you in courtesy.
Zeus made me come, and not my inclination;                         105
who cares to cross that tract of desolation,
the bitter sea, all mortal towns behind
where gods have beef and honors from mankind?
But it is not to be thought of—and no use—
for any god to elude the will of Zeus.                             110

3. The translator puts Hermes' speech into rhymed couplets; there is no rhyme in the original
Greek.

He notes your friend, most ill-starred by renown
of all the peers who fought for Priam's town—
nine years of war they had, before great Troy was down.
Homing, they wronged the goddess with grey eyes,
who made a black wind blow and the seas rise,                          115
in which his troops were lost, and all his gear,
while easterlies and current washed him here.
Now the command is: send him back in haste.
His life may not in ex exile go to waste.
His destiny, his homecoming, is at hand,                               120
when he shall see his dearest, and walk on his own land."

That goddess most divinely made
shuddered before him, and her warm voice rose:

"Oh you vile gods, in jealousy supernal!
You hate it when we choose to lie with men—                            125
immortal flesh by some dear mortal side.
So radiant Dawn once took to bed Orion
until you easeful gods grew peevish at it,
and holy Artemis, Artemis throned in gold,
hunted him down in Delos with her arrows.                              130
Then Dêmêtêr of the tasseled tresses yielded
to Iasion, mingling and making love
in a furrow three times plowed;[4] but Zeus found out
and killed him with a white-hot thunderbolt.
So now you grudge me, too, my mortal friend.                           135
But it was I who saved him—saw him straddle
his own keel board, the one man left afloat
when Zeus rent wide his ship with chain lightning
and overturned him in the winedark sea.
Then all his troops were lost, his good companions,                    140
but wind and current washed him here to me.
I fed him, loved him, sang that he should not die
nor grow old, ever, in all the days to come.
But now there's no eluding Zeus's will.
If this thing be ordained by him, I say                                145
so be it, let the man strike out alone
on the vast water. Surely I cannot 'send' him.
I have no long-oared ships, no company
to pull him on the broad back of the sea.
My counsel he shall have, and nothing hidden,                          150
to help him homeward without harm."

---

4. Demeter was the goddess associated with the growth of the crops, especially wheat.

To this the Wayfinder made answer briefly:

"Thus you shall send him, then. And show more grace
in your obedience, or be chastised by Zeus."

The strong god glittering left her as he spoke,                    155
and now her ladyship, having given heed
to Zeus's mandate, went to find Odysseus
in his stone seat to seaward—tear on tear
brimming his eyes. The sweet days of his life time
were running out in anguish over his exile,                        160
for long ago the nymph had ceased to please.
Though he fought shy of her and her desire,
he lay with her each night, for she compelled him.
But when day came he sat on the rocky shore
and broke his own heart groaning, with eyes wet                    165
scanning the bare horizon of the sea.
Now she stood near him in her beauty, saying:

"O forlorn man, be still.
Here you need grieve no more; you need not feel
your life consumed here; I have pondered it,                       170
and I shall help you go.
Come and cut down high timber for a raft
or flatboat; make her broad-beamed, and decked over,
so you can ride her on the misty sea.
Stores I shall put aboard for you—bread, water,                    175
and ruby-colored wine, to stay your hunger—
give you a seacloak and a following wind
to help you homeward without harm—provided
the gods who rule wide heaven wish it so.
Stronger than I they are, in mind and power."                      180

For all he had endured, Odysseus shuddered.
But when he spoke, his words went to the mark:

"After these years, a helping hand? O goddess,
what guile is hidden here?
A raft, you say, to cross the Western Ocean,                       185
rough water, and unknown? Seaworthy ships
that glory in god's wind will never cross it.
I take no raft you grudge me out to sea.
Or yield me first a great oath, if I do,
to work no more enchantment to my harm."                           190

At this the beautiful nymph Kalypso smiled
and answered sweetly, laying her hand upon him:

"What a dog you are! And not for nothing learned,
having the wit to ask this thing of me!
My witness then be earth and sky                                    195
and dripping Styx[5] that I swear by—
the gay gods cannot swear more seriously—
I have no further spells to work against you.
But what I shall devise, and what I tell you,
will be the same as if your need were mine.                         200
Fairness is all I think of. There are hearts
made of cold iron—but my heart is kind."

Swiftly she turned and led him to her cave,
and they went in, the mortal and immortal.
He took the chair left empty now by Hermês,                         205
where the divine Kalypso placed before him
victuals and drink of men; then she sat down
facing Odysseus, while her serving maid
brought nectar and ambrosia to her side.
Then each one's hands went out on each one's feast                  210
until they had had their pleasure; and she said:

"Son of Laërtês, versatile Odysseus,
after these years with me, you still desire
your old home? Even so, I wish you well.
If you could see it all, before you go—                             215
all the adversity you face at sea—
you would stay here, and guard this house, and be
immortal—though you wanted her forever,
that bride for whom you pine each day.
Can I be less desirable than she is?                                220
Less interesting? Less beautiful? Can mortals
compare with goddesses in grace and form?"

To this the strategist Odysseus answered:

"My lady goddess, here is no cause for anger.
My quiet Penélopê—how well I know—                                  225
would seem a shade before your majesty,
death and old age being unknown to you,
while she must die. Yet, it is true, each day

5. One of the rivers of the Underworld.

I long for home, long for the sight of home.
If any god has marked me out again                      230
for shipwreck, my tough heart can undergo it.
What hardship have I not long since endured
at sea, in battle! Let the trial come."


Now as he spoke the sun set, dusk drew on,
and they retired, this pair, to the inner cave          235
to revel and rest softly, side by side.


When Dawn spread out her finger tips of rose
Odysseus pulled his tunic and his cloak on,
while the sea nymph dressed in a silvery gown
of subtle tissue, drew about her waist                  240
a golden belt, and veiled her head, and then
took thought for the great-hearted hero's voyage.
A brazen axehead first she had to give him,
two-bladed, and agreeable to the palm
with a smooth-fitting haft of olive wood;               245
next a well-polished adze; and then she led him
to the island's tip where bigger timber grew—
besides the alder and poplar, tall pine trees,
long dead and seasoned, that would float him high.
Showing him in that place her stand of timber           250
the loveliest of nymphs took her way home.
Now the man fell to chopping; when he paused
twenty tall trees were down. He lopped the branches,
split the trunks, and trimmed his puncheons true.
Meanwhile Kalypso brought him an auger tool             255
with which he drilled through all his planks, then drove
stout pins to bolt them, fitted side by side.
A master shipwright, building a cargo vessel,
lays down a broad and shallow hull; just so
Odysseus shaped the bottom of his craft.                260
He made his decking fast to close-set ribs
before he closed the side with longer planking,
then cut a mast pole, and a proper yard,
and shaped a steering oar to hold her steady.
He drove long strands of willow in all the seams        265
to keep out waves, and ballasted with logs.
As for a sail, the lovely nymph Kalypso
brought him a cloth so he could make that, too.
Then he ran up his rigging—halyards, braces—
and hauled the boat on rollers to the water.            270

This was the fourth day, when he had all ready;
on the fifth day, she sent him out to sea.
But first she bathed him, gave him a scented cloak,
and put on board a skin of dusky wine
with water in a bigger skin, and stores—                                    275
boiled meats and other victuals—in a bag.
Then she conjured a warm landbreeze to blowing—
joy for Odysseus when he shook out sail!
Now the great seaman, leaning on his oar,
steered all the night unsleeping, and his eyes                             280
picked out the Pleiadês, the laggard Ploughman,[6]
and the Great Bear, that some have called the Wain,[7]
pivoting in the sky before Orion;
of all the night's pure figures, she alone
would never bathe or dip in the Ocean stream.[8]                           285
These stars the beautiful Kalypso bade him
hold on his left hand as he crossed the main.
Seventeen nights and days in the open water
he sailed, before a dark shoreline appeared;
Skhería then came slowly into view                                         290
like a rough shield of bull's hide on the sea.

But now the god of earthquake,[9] storming home
over the mountains of Asia from the Sunburned land,
sighted him far away. The god grew sullen
and tossed his great head, muttering to himself:                           295
"Here is a pretty cruise! While I was gone,
the gods have changed their minds about Odysseus.
Look at him now, just offshore of that island
that frees him from the bondage of his exile!
Still I can give him a rough ride in, and will."                           300

Brewing high thunderheads, he churned the deep
with both hands on his trident—called up wind
from every quarter, and sent a wall of rain
to blot out land and sea in torrential night.
Hurricane winds now struck from the South and East                         305
shifting North West in a great spume of seas,
on which Odysseus' knees grew slack, his heart
sickened, and he said within himself:

"Rag of man that I am, is this the end of me?
I fear the goddess told it all too well—                                   310

---

**6.** The constellation Boötes (which means "ploughman"). *Pleiadês*: A cluster of stars in the constellation Taurus.     **7.** The Big Dipper.     **8.** It is visible all year long.     **9.** Poseidon.

predicting great adversity at sea
and far from home. Now all things bear her out:
the whole rondure of heaven hooded so
by Zeus in woeful cloud, and the sea raging
under such winds. I am going down, that's sure.          315
How lucky those Danaans were who perished
on Troy's wide seaboard, serving the Atreidai!
Would God I, too, had died there—met my end
that time the Trojans made so many casts at me
when I stood by Akhilleus after death.                   320
I should have had a soldier's burial
and praise from the Akhaians—not this choking
waiting for me at sea, unmarked and lonely."

A great wave drove at him with toppling crest
spinning him round, in one tremendous blow,              325
and he went plunging overboard, the oar-haft
wrenched from his grip. A gust that came on howling
at the same instant broke his mast in two,
hurling his yard and sail far out to leeward.
Now the big wave a long time kept him under,             330
helpless to surface, held by tons of water,
tangled, too, by the seacloak of Kalypso.
Long, long, until he came up spouting brine,
with streamlets gushing from his head and beard;
but still bethought him, half-drowned as he was,         335
to flounder for the boat and get a handhold
into the bilge—to crouch there, foiling death.
Across the foaming water, to and fro,
the boat careered like a ball of tumbleweed
blown on the autumn plains, but intact still.            340
So the winds drove this wreck over the deep,
East Wind and North Wind, then South Wind and West,
coursing each in turn to the brutal harry.

But Ino saw him—Ino, Kadmos' daughter,
slim-legged, lovely, once an earthling girl,             345
now in the seas a nereid, Leukothea.
Touched by Odysseus' painful buffeting
she broke the surface, like a diving bird,
to rest upon the tossing raft and say:

"O forlorn man, I wonder                                 350
why the Earthshaker, Lord Poseidon, holds
this fearful grudge—father of all your woes.

He will not drown you, though, despite his rage.
You seem clear-headed still; do what I tell you.
Shed that cloak, let the gale take your craft,                     355
and swim for it—swim hard to get ashore
upon Skhería, yonder,
where it is fated that you find a shelter.
Here: make my veil your sash; it is not mortal;
you cannot, now, be drowned or suffer harm.              360
Only, the instant you lay hold of earth,
discard it, cast it far, far out from shore
in the winedark sea again, and turn away."

After she had bestowed her veil, the nereid
dove like a gull to windward                                               365
where a dark waveside closed over her whiteness.
But in perplexity Odysseus
said to himself, his great heart laboring:

"O damned confusion! Can this be a ruse
to trick me from the boat for some god's pleasure?      370
No I'll not swim; with my own eyes I saw
how far the land lies that she called my shelter.
Better to do the wise thing, as I see it.
While this poor planking holds, I stay aboard;
I may ride out the pounding of the storm,                      375
or if she cracks up, take to the water then;
I cannot think it through a better way."

But even while he pondered and decided,
the god of earthquake heaved a wave against him
high as a rooftree and of awful gloom.                            380
A gust of wind, hitting a pile of chaff,
will scatter all the parched stuff far and wide;
just so, when this gigantic billow struck
the boat's big timbers flew apart. Odysseus
clung to a single beam, like a jockey riding,                   385
meanwhile stripping Kalypso's cloak away;
then he slung round his chest the veil of Ino
and plunged headfirst into the sea. His hands
went out to stroke, and he gave a swimmer's kick.
But the strong Earthshaker had him under his eye,      390
and nodded as he said:

                    "Go on, go on;
wander the high seas this way, take your blows,

before you join that race the gods have nurtured.[1]
Nor will you grumble, even then, I think,
for want of trouble."

               Whipping his glossy team                    395
he rode off to his glorious home at Aigai.[2]
But Zeus's daughter Athena countered him:
she checked the course of all the winds but one,
commanding them, "Be quiet and go to sleep."
Then sent a long swell running under a norther          400
to bear the prince Odysseus, back from danger,
to join the Phaiákians, people of the sea.

Two nights, two days, in the solid deep-sea swell
he drifted, many times awaiting death,
until with shining ringlets in the East                 405
the dawn confirmed a third day, breaking clear
over a high and windless sea; and mounting
a rolling wave he caught a glimpse of land.
What a dear welcome thing life seems to children
whose father, in the extremity, recovers                410
after some weakening and malignant illness:
his pangs are gone, the gods have delivered him.
So dear and welcome to Odysseus
the sight of land, of woodland, on that morning.
It made him swim again, to get a foothold               415
on solid ground. But when he came in earshot
he heard the trampling roar of sea on rock,
where combers, rising shoreward, thudded down
on the sucking ebb—all sheeted with salt foam.
Here were no coves or harborage or shelter,             420
only steep headlands, rockfallen reefs and crags.
Odysseus' knees grew slack, his heart faint,
a heaviness came over him, and he said:
"A cruel turn, this. Never had I thought
to see this land, but Zeus has let me see it—           425
and let me, too, traverse the Western Ocean—
only to find no exit from these breakers.
Here are sharp rocks off shore, and the sea a smother
rushing around them; rock face rising sheer
from deep water; nowhere could I stand up                430
on my two feet and fight free of the welter.
No matter how I try it, the surf may throw me

1. The Phaiákians, favored by the gods.    2. An island off Euboia, which gave its name to the
Aegean Sea.

against the cliffside; no good fighting there.
If I swim down the coast, outside the breakers,
I may find shelving shore and quiet water—                          435
but what if another gale comes on to blow?
Then I go cursing out to sea once more.
Or then again, some shark of Amphitritê's[3]
may hunt me, sent by the genius of the deep.
I know how he who makes earth tremble hates me."                    440

During this meditation a heavy surge
was taking him, in fact, straight on the rocks.
He had been flayed there, and his bones broken,
had not grey-eyed Athena instructed him:
he gripped a rock-ledge with both hands in passing                  445
and held on, groaning, as the surge went by,
to keep clear of its breaking. Then the backwash
hit him, ripping him under and far out.
An octopus, when you drag one from his chamber,
comes up with suckers full of tiny stones:                          450
Odysseus left the skin of his great hands
torn on that rock-ledge as the wave submerged him.
And now at last Odysseus would have perished,
battered inhumanly, but he had the gift
of self-possession from grey-eyed Athena.                           455
So, when the backwash spewed him up again,
he swam out and along, and scanned the coast
for some landspit that made a breakwater.
Lo and behold, the mouth of a calm river
at length came into view, with level shores                         460
unbroken, free from rock, shielded from wind—
by far the best place he had found.
But as he felt the current flowing seaward
he prayed in his heart:

                    "O hear me, lord of the stream:
how sorely I depend upon your mercy!                                465
derelict as I am by the sea's anger.
Is he not sacred, even to the gods,
the wandering man who comes, as I have come,
in weariness before your knees, your waters?
Here is your servant; lord, have mercy on me."                      470

Now even as he prayed the tide at ebb
had turned, and the river god made quiet water,

3. A sea-goddess.

drawing him in to safety in the shallows.
His knees buckled, his arms gave way beneath him,
all vital force now conquered by the sea.                    475
Swollen from head to foot he was, and seawater
gushed from his mouth and nostrils. There he lay,
scarce drawing breath, unstirring, deathly spent.
In time, as air came back into his lungs
and warmth around his heart, he loosed the veil,           480
letting it drift away on the estuary
downstream to where a white wave took it under
and Ino's hands received it. Then the man
crawled to the river bank among the reeds
where, face down, he could kiss the soil of earth,          485
in his exhaustion murmuring to himself:

"What more can this hulk suffer? What comes now?
In vigil through the night here by the river
how can I not succumb, being weak and sick,
to the night's damp and hoarfrost of the morning?          490
The air comes cold from rivers before dawn.
But if I climb the slope and fall asleep
in the dark forest's undergrowth—supposing
cold and fatigue will go, and sweet sleep come—
I fear I make the wild beasts easy prey."                   495

But this seemed best to him, as he thought it over.
He made his way to a grove above the water
on open ground, and crept under twin bushes
grown from the same spot—olive and wild olive—
a thicket proof against the stinging wind                   500
or Sun's blaze, fine soever the needling sunlight;
nor could a downpour wet it through, so dense
those plants were interwoven. Here Odysseus
tunnelled, and raked together with his hands
a wide bed—for a fall of leaves was there,                  505
enough to save two men or maybe three
on a winter night, a night of bitter cold.
Odysseus' heart laughed when he saw his leaf-bed,
and down he lay, heaping more leaves above him.

A man in a distant field, no hearthfires near,            510
will hide a fresh brand in his bed of embers
to keep a spark alive for the next day;
so in the leaves Odysseus hid himself,
while over him Athena showered sleep

that his distress should end, and soon, soon.                    515
In quiet sleep she sealed his cherished eyes.


## Book VI

### THE PRINCESS AT THE RIVER

Far gone in weariness, in oblivion,
the noble and enduring man slept on;
but Athena in the night went down the land
of the Phaiákians, entering their city.
In days gone by, these men held Hypereia,[4]                      5
a country of wide dancing grounds, but near them
were overbearing Kyklopês, whose power
could not be turned from pillage. So the Phaiákians
migrated thence under Nausíthoös
to settle a New World across the sea,                             10
Skhería Island. That first captain walled
their promontory, built their homes and shrines,
and parcelled out the black land for the plow.
But he had gone down long ago to Death.
Alkínoös ruled, and Heaven gave him wisdom,                       15
so on this night the goddess, grey-eyed Athena,
entered the palace of Alkínoös
to make sure of Odysseus' voyage home.
She took her way to a painted bedchamber
where a young girl lay fast asleep—so fine                        20
in mould and feature that she seemed a goddess—
the daughter of Alkínoös Nausikaa.
On either side, as Graces[5] might have slept,
her maids were sleeping. The bright doors were shut,
but like a sudden stir of wind, Athena                            25
moved to the bedside of the girl, and grew
visible as the shipman Dymas' daughter,
a girl the princess' age, and her dear friend.
In this form grey-eyed Athena said to her:


"How so remiss, and yet thy mother's daughter?                    30
leaving thy clothes uncared for, Nausikaa,
when soon thou must have store of marriage linen,
and put thy minstrelsy in wedding dress!

4. An imaginary place, probably, and the one-eyed Kyklopes are certainly mythical but the migration under pressure and the founding of the new city (fortification, homes, temples, division of the land) suggests the atmosphere of the great age of Greek colonization (eighth century B.C.).
5. Goddesses (usually three) personifying charm and beauty.

Beauty, in these, will make the folk admire,
and bring thy father and gentle mother joy.                    35
Let us go washing in the shine of morning!
Beside thee will I drub, so wedding chests
will brim by evening. Maidenhood must end!
Have not the noblest born Phaiákians
paid court to thee, whose birth none can excel?                    40
Go beg thy sovereign father, even at dawn,
to have the mule cart and the mules brought round
to take thy body-linen, gowns and mantles.
Thou shouldst ride, for it becomes thee more,
the washing pools are found so far from home."                    45

On this word she departed, grey-eyed Athena,
to where the gods have their eternal dwelling—
as men say—in the fastness of Olympos.
Never a tremor of wind, or a splash of rain,
no errant snowflake comes to stain that heaven,                    50
so calm, so vaporless, the world of light.
Here, where the gay gods live their days of pleasure,
the grey-eyed one withdrew, leaving the princess.

And now Dawn took her own fair throne, awaking
the girl in the sweet gown, still charmed by dream.                    55
Down through the rooms she went to tell her parents,
whom she found still at home: her mother seated
near the great hearth among her maids—and twirling
out of her distaff yarn dyed like the sea—;
her father at the door, bound for a council                    60
of princes on petition of the gentry.
She went up close to him and softly said:
"My dear Papà, could you not send the mule cart
around for me—the gig with pretty wheels?
I must take all our things and get them washed                    65
at the river pools; our linen is all soiled.
And you should wear fresh clothing, going to council
with counselors and first men of the realm.
Remember your five sons at home: though two
are married, we have still three bachelor sprigs;                    70
they will have none but laundered clothes each time
they go to the dancing. See what I must think of!"

She had no word to say of her own wedding,
though her keen father saw her blush. Said he:

"No mules would I deny you, child, nor anything.                    75
Go along, now; the grooms will bring your gig
with pretty wheels and the cargo box upon it."

He spoke to the stableman, who soon brought round
the cart, low-wheeled and nimble;
harnessed the mules, and backed them in the traces.               80
Meanwhile the girl fetched all her soiled apparel
to bundle in the polished wagon box.
Her mother, for their luncheon, packed a hamper
with picnic fare, and filled a skin of wine,
and, when the princess had been handed up,                        85
gave her a golden bottle of olive oil
for softening girls' bodies, after bathing.
Nausikaa took the reins and raised her whip,
lashing the mules. What jingling! What a clatter!
But off they went in a ground-covering trot,                      90
with princess, maids, and laundry drawn behind.
By the lower river where the wagon came
were washing pools, with water all year flowing
in limpid spillways that no grime withstood.
The girls unhitched the mules, and sent them down                 95
along the eddying stream to crop sweet grass.
Then sliding out the chart's tail board, they took
armloads of clothing to the dusky water,
and trod them in the pits, making a race of it.
All being drubbed, all blemish rinsed away,                       100
they spread them, piece by piece, along the beach
whose pebbles had been laundered by the sea;
then took a dip themselves, and, all anointed
with golden oil, ate lunch beside the river
while the bright burning sun dried out their linen.               105
Princess and maids delighted in that feast;
then, putting off their veils,
they ran and passed a ball to a rhythmic beat,
Nausikaa flashing first with her white arms.

So Artemis goes flying after her arrows flown                     110
down some tremendous valley-side—
                              Taÿgetos, Erymanthos—[6]
chasing the mountain goats or ghosting deer,
with nymphs of the wild places flanking her;
and Lêto's[7] heart delights to see them running,                  115

6. Taÿgetos is the mountain range west of Sparta; *Erymanthos*, a mountain in Arcadia—both places rich in game.     7. Mother of Artemis and Apollo.

for, taller by a head than nymphs can be,
the goddess shows more stately, all being beautiful.
So one could tell the princess from the maids.

Soon it was time, she knew, for riding homeward—
mules to be harnessed, linen folded smooth—                         120
but the grey-eyed goddess Athena made her tarry,
so that Odysseus might behold her beauty
and win her guidance to the town.
                                   It happened
when the king's daughter threw her ball off line
and missed, and put it in the whirling stream,—                      125
at which they all gave such a shout, Odysseus
awoke and sat up, saying to himself:

"Now, by my life, mankind again! But who?
Savages, are they, strangers to courtesy?
Or gentle folk, who know and fear the gods?                          130
That was a lusty cry of tall young girls—
most like the cry of nymphs, who haunt the peaks,
and springs of brooks, and inland grassy places.
Or am I amid people of human speech?
Up again, man; and let me see for myself."                           135
He pushed aside the bushes, breaking off
with his great hand a single branch of olive,
whose leaves might shield him in his nakedness;
so came out rustling, like a mountain lion,
rain-drenched, wind-buffeted, but in his might at ease,              140
with burning eyes—who prowls among the herds
or flocks, or after game, his hungry belly
taking him near stout homesteads for his prey.
Odysseus had this look, in his rough skin
advancing on the girls with pretty braids;                           145
and he was driven on by hunger, too.
Streaked with brine, and swollen, he terrified them,
so that they fled, this way and that. Only
Alkínoös' daughter stood her ground, being given
a bold heart by Athena, and steady knees.                            150

She faced him, waiting. And Odysseus came,
debating inwardly what he should do:
embrace this beauty's knees in supplication?
or stand apart, and using honeyed speech,
inquire the way to town, and beg some clothing?                      155
In his swift reckoning, he thought it best

to trust in words to please her—and keep away;
he might anger the girl, touching her knees.
So he began, and let the soft words fall:

"Mistress: please: are you divine, or mortal?                    160
If one of those who dwell in the wide heaven,
you are most near to Artemis, I should say—
great Zeus's daughter—in your grace and presence.
If you are one of earth's inhabitants,
how blest your father, and your gentle mother,            165
blest all your kin. I know what happiness
must send the warm tears to their eyes, each time
they see their wondrous child go to the dancing!
But one man's destiny is more than blest—
he who prevails, and takes you as his bride.               170
Never have I laid eyes on equal beauty
in man or woman. I am hushed indeed.
So fair, one time, I thought a young palm tree
at Delos[8] near the altar of Apollo—
I had troops under me when I was there                    175
on the sea route that later brought me grief—
but that slim palm tree filled my heart with wonder:
never came shoot from earth so beautiful.
So now, my lady, I stand in awe so great
I cannot take your knees. And yet my case is desperate:   180
twenty days, yesterday, in the winedark sea,
on the ever-lunging swell, under gale winds,
getting away from the Island of Ogýgia.
And now the terror of Storm has left me stranded
upon this shore—with more blows yet to suffer,           185
I must believe, before the gods relent.
Mistress, do me a kindness!
After much weary toil, I come to you,
and you are the first soul I have seen—I know
no others here. Direct me to the town,                   190
give me a rag that I can throw around me,
some cloth or wrapping that you brought along.
And may the gods accomplish your desire:
a home, a husband, and harmonious
converse with him—the best thing in the world            195
being a strong house held in serenity
where man and wife agree. Woe to their enemies,
joy to their friends! But all this they know best."

8. A small island in the middle of the Aegean sea, the birthplace of Apollo and a center for his worship.

Then she of the white arms, Nausikaa, replied:

"Stranger, there is no quirk or evil in you                    200
that I can see. You know Zeus metes out fortune
to good and bad men as it pleases him.
Hardship he sent to you, and you must bear it.
But now that you have taken refuge here
you shall not lack for clothing, or any other                    205
comfort due to a poor man in distress.
The town lies this way, and the men are called
Phaiákians, who own the land and city.
I am daughter to the Prince Alkínoös,
by whom the power of our people stands."                    210
Turning, she called out to her maids-in-waiting:

"Stay with me! Does the sight of a man scare you?
Or do you take this one for an enemy?
Why, there's no fool so brash, and never will be,
as to bring war or pillage to this coast,                    215
for we are dear to the immortal gods,
living here, in the sea that rolls forever,
distant from other lands and other men.
No: this man is a castaway, poor fellow;
we must take care of him. Strangers and beggars                    220
come from Zeus: a small gift, then, is friendly.
Give our new guest some food and drink, and take him
into the river, out of the wind, to bathe."

They stood up now, and called to one another
to go on back. Quite soon they led Odysseus                    225
under the river bank, as they were bidden;
and there laid out a tunic, and a cloak,
and gave him olive oil in the golden flask.
"Here," they said, "go bathe in the flowing water."
But heard now from that kingly man, Odysseus:                    230

"Maids," he said, "keep away a little; let me
wash the brine from my own back, and rub on
plenty of oil. It is long since my anointing.
I take no bath, however, where you can see me—
naked before young girls with pretty braids."                    235

They left him, then, and went to tell the princess.
And now Odysseus, dousing in the river,
scrubbed the coat of brine from back and shoulders

and rinsed the clot of sea-spume from his hair;
got himself all rubbed down, from head to foot,                    240
then he put on the clothes the princess gave him.
Athena lent a hand, making him seem
taller, and massive too, with crisping hair
in curls like petals of wild hyacinth,
but all red-golden. Think of gold infused                          245
on silver by a craftsman, whose fine art
Hephaistos taught him, or Athena: one
whose work moves to delight: just so she lavished
beauty over Odysseus' head and shoulders.
Then he went down to sit on the sea beach                          250
in his new splendor. There the girl regarded him,
and after a time she said to the maids beside her:

"My gentlewomen, I have a thing to tell you.
The Olympian gods cannot be all averse
to this man's coming here among our islanders.                     255
Uncouth he seemed, I thought so, too, before;
but now he looks like one of heaven's people.
I wish my husband could be fine as he
and glad to stay forever on Skhería!

But have you given refreshment to our guest?"                      260

At this the maids, all gravely listening, hastened
to set out bread and wine before Odysseus,
and ah! how ravenously that patient man
took food and drink, his long fast at an end.

The princess Nausikaa now turned aside                             265
to fold her linens; in the pretty cart
she stowed them, put the mule team under harness,
mounted the driver's seat, and then looked down
to say with cheerful prompting to Odysseus:

"Up with you now, friend; back to town we go;                      270
and I shall send you in before my father
who is wondrous wise; there in our house with him
you'll meet the noblest of the Phaiákians.
You have good sense, I think; here's how to do it:
while we go through the countryside and farmland                   275
stay with my maids, behind the wagon, walking
briskly enough to follow where I lead.
But near the town—well, there's a wall with towers

around the Isle, and beautiful ship basins
right and left of the causeway of approach; 280
seagoing craft are beached beside the road
each on its launching ways. The agora,[9]
with fieldstone benches bedded in the earth,
lies either side Poseidon's shrine—for there
men are at work on pitch-black hulls and rigging, 285
cables and sails, and tapering of oars.
The archer's craft is not for the Phaiákians,
but ship designing, modes of oaring cutters
in which they love to cross the foaming sea.
From these fellows I will have no salty talk, 290
no gossip later. Plenty are insolent.
And some seadog might say, after we passed:
'Who is this handsome stranger trailing Nausikaa?
Where did she find him? Will he be her husband?
Or is she being hospitable to some rover 295
come off his ship from lands across the sea—
there being no lands nearer. A god, maybe?
a god from heaven, the answer to her prayer,
descending now—to make her his forever?
Better, if she's roamed and found a husband 300
somewhere else: none of our own will suit her,
though many come to court her, and those the best.'
This is the way they might make light of me.
And I myself should hold it shame
for any girl to flout her own dear parents, 305
taking up with a man, before her marriage.

Note well, now, what I say, friend, and your chances
are excellent for safe conduct from my father.
You'll find black poplars in a roadside park
around a meadow and fountain—all Athena's— 310
this within earshot of the city wall.
Go in there and sit down, giving us time
to pass through town and reach my father's house.
And when you can imagine we're at home, 315
then take the road into the city, asking
directions to the palace of Alkínoös.
You'll find it easily: any small boy
can take you there; no family has a mansion
half so grand as he does, being king. 320
As soon as you are safe inside, cross over

9. Place of assembly.

and go straight through into the mégaron[1]
to find my mother. She'll be there in firelight
before a column, with her maids in shadow,
spinning a wool dyed richly as the sea.                                    325
My father's great chair faces the fire, too;
there like a god he sits and takes his wine.
Go past him; cast yourself before my mother,
embrace her knees—and you may wake up soon
at home rejoicing, though your home be far.                                330
On Mother's feeling much depends; if she
looks on you kindly, you shall see your friends
under your own roof in your father's country."

At this she raised her glistening whip, lashing
the team into a run; they left the river                                   335
cantering beautifully, then trotted smartly.
But then she reined them in, and spared the whip,
so that her maids could follow with Odysseus.
The sun was going down when they went by
Athena's grove. Here, then, Odysseus rested,                               340
and lifted up his prayer to Zeus's daughter:

"Hear me, unwearied child of royal Zeus!
O listen to me now—thou so aloof
while the Earthshaker wrecked and battered me.
May I find love and mercy among these people."

He prayed for that, and Pallas Athena heard him—                           345
although in deference to her father's brother
she would not show her true form to Odysseus,
at whom Poseidon smoldered on
until the kingly man came home to his own shore.


## Book VII

### GARDENS AND FIRELIGHT

As Lord Odysseus prayed there in the grove
the girl rode on, behind her strapping team,
and came late to the mansion of her father,
where she reined in at the courtyard gate. Her brothers
awaited her like tall gods in the court,                                    5
circling to lead the mules away and carry
the laundered things inside. But she withdrew

---

1. The great hall of the palace.

to her own bedroom, where a fire soon shone,
kindled by her old nurse, Eurymedousa.
Years ago, from a raid on the continent,                          10
the rolling ships had brought this woman over
to be Alkínoös' share—fit spoil for him
whose realm hung on his word as on a god's.
And she had schooled the princess, Nausikaa,
whose fire she tended now, making her supper.                     15

Odysseus, when the time had passed, arose
and turned into the city. But Athena
poured a sea fog around him as he went—
her love's expedient, that no jeering sailor
should halt the man or challenge him for luck.                    20
Instead, as he set foot in the pleasant city,
the grey-eyed goddess came to him, in figure
a small girl child, hugging a water jug.
Confronted by her, Lord Odysseus asked:

"Little one, could you take me to the house                       25
of that Alkínoös, king among these people?
You see, I am a poor old stranger here;
my home is far away; here there is no one
known to me, in countryside or city."

The grey-eyed goddess Athena replied to him:                      30

"Oh yes, good grandfer, sir, I know, I'll show you
the house you mean; it is quite near my father's.
But come now, hush, like this, and follow me.
You must not stare at people, or be inquisitive.
They do not care for strangers in this neighborhood;              35
a foreign man will get no welcome here.
The only things they trust are the racing ships
Poseidon gave, to sail the deep blue sea
like white wings in the sky, or a flashing thought."

Pallas Athena turned like the wind, running                       40
ahead of him, and he followed in her footsteps.
And no seafaring men of Phaiákia
perceived Odysseus passing through their town:
the awesome one in pigtails barred their sight
with folds of sacred mist. And yet Odysseus                       45
gazed out marvelling at the ships and harbors,
public squares, and ramparts towering up

with pointed palisades along the top.
When they were near the mansion of the king,
grey-eyed Athena in the child cried out:                          50

"Here it is, grandfer, sir—that mansion house
you asked to see. You'll find our king and queen
at supper, but you must not be dismayed;
go in to them. A cheerful man does best
in every enterprise—even a stranger.                              55
You'll see our lady just inside the hall—
her name is Arêtê; her grandfather
was our good king Alkínoös' father—
Nausithoös by name, son of Poseidon
and Periboia. That was a great beauty,                            60
the daughter of Eurymedon, commander
of the Gigantês[2] in the olden days,
who led those wild things to their doom and his.
Poseidon then made love to Periboia,
and she bore Nausíthoös, Phaiákia's lord,                         65
whose sons in turn were Rhêxênor and Alkínoös.
Rhêxênor had no sons; even as a bridegroom
he fell before the silver bow of Apollo,
his only child a daughter, Arêtê.
When she grew up, Alkínoös married her                            70
and holds her dear. No lady in the world,
no other mistress of a man's household,
is honored as our mistress is, and loved,
by her own children, by Alkínoös,
and by the people. When she walks the town                       75
they murmur and gaze, as though she were a goddess.
No grace or wisdom fails in her; indeed
just men in quarrels come to her for equity.
Supposing, then, she looks upon you kindly,
the chances are that you shall see your friends                  80
under your own roof, in your father's country."

At this the grey-eyed goddess Athena left him
and left that comely land, going over sea
to Marathon, to the wide roadways of Athens
and her retreat in the stronghold of Erekhtheus.[3]              85
Odysseus, now alone before the palace,
meditated a long time before crossing

2. The Giants, an older race of gods who battled, unsuccessfully, against the Olympians.
3. King of Athens. *Marathon:* A village north of Athens near the coast. It was the site of the
famous battle at which the Athenians repulsed a Persian invasion force (490 B.C.).

the brazen threshold of the great coutryard.
High rooms he saw ahead, airy and luminous
as though with lusters of the sun and moon,                    90
bronze-paneled walls, at several distances,
making a vista, with an azure molding
of lapis lazuli. The doors were golden
guardians of the great room. Shining bronze
plated the wide door sill; the posts and lintel                    95
were silver upon silver; golden handles
curved on the doors, and golden, too, and silver
were sculptured hounds, flanking the entrance way,
cast by the skill and ardor of Hephaistos
to guard the prince Alkínoös's house—                    100
undying dogs that never could grow old.
Through all the rooms, as far as he could see,
tall chairs were placed around the walls, and strewn
with fine embroidered stuff made by the women.
Here were enthroned the leaders of Phaiákia                    105
drinking and dining, with abundant fare.
Here, too, were boys of gold on pedestals
holding aloft bright torches of pitch pine
to light the great rooms, and the night-time feasting.
And fifty maids-in-waiting of the household                    110
sat by the round mill, grinding yellow corn,
or wove upon their looms, or twirled their distaffs,
flickering like the leaves of a poplar tree;
while drops of oil glistened on linen weft.
Skillful as were the men of Phaiákia                    115
in ship handling at sea, so were these women
skilled at the loom, having this lovely craft
and artistry as talents from Athena.

To left and right, outside, he saw on orchard
closed by a pale—four spacious acres planted                    120
with trees in bloom or weighted down for picking:
pear trees, pomegranates, brilliant apples,
luscious figs, and olives ripe and dark.
Fruit never failed upon these trees: winter
and summer time they bore, for through the year                    125
the breathing Westwind ripened all in turn—
so one pear came to prime, and then another,
and so with apples, figs, and the vine's fruit
empurpled in the royal vineyard there.
Currants were dried at one end, on a platform                    130
bare to the sun, beyond the vintage arbors

and vats the vintners trod; while near at hand
were new grapes barely formed as the green bloom fell,
or half-ripe clusters, faintly coloring.
After the vines came rows of vegetables                                    135
of all the kinds that flourish in every season,
and through the garden plots and orchard ran
channels from one clear fountain, while another
gushed through a pipe under the courtyard entrance
to serve the house and all who came for water.                             140
These were the gifts of heaven to Alkínoös.

Odysseus, who had borne the barren sea,
stood in the gateway and surveyed this bounty.
He gazed his fill, then swiftly he went in.
The lords and nobles of Phaiákia
were tipping wine to the wakeful god, to Hermês—
a last libation before going to bed—
but down the hall Odysseus went unseen,
still in the cloud Athena cloaked him in,
until he reached Arêtê, and the king.                                      150
He threw his great hands round Arêtê's knees,
whereon the sacred mist hurled back;
they saw him; and the diners hushed amazed
to see an unknown man inside the palace.
Under their eyes Odysseus made his plea:                                   155

"Arêtê, admirable Rhêxênor's daughter,
here is a man bruised by adversity, thrown
upon your mercy and the king your husband's,
begging indulgence of this company—
may the gods' blessing rest on them! May life                              160
be kind to all! Let each one leave his children
every good thing this realm confers upon him!
But grant me passage to my father land.
My home and friends lie far. My life is pain."

He moved, then, toward the fire, and sat him down                          165
amid the ashes.[4] No one stirred or spoke
until Ekhenêos broke the spell—an old man,
eldest of the Phaiákians, an oracle,
versed in the laws and manners of old time.
He rose among them now and spoke out kindly:                               170

4. The fire, the hearth, was the sacred center of the home: the suppliant who sits there is, so to
speak, on consecrated ground and cannot be forcibly removed.

"Alkínoös, this will not pass for courtesy:
a guest abased in ashes at our hearth?
Everyone here awaits your word; so come, then,
lift the man up; give him a seat of honor,
a silver-studded chair. Then tell the stewards          175
we'll have another wine bowl for libation
to Zeus, lord of the lightning—advocate
of honorable petitioners. And supper
may be supplied our friend by the larder mistress."

Alkínoös, calm in power, heard him out,                 180
then took the great adventurer by the hand
and led him from the fire. Nearest his throne
the son whom he loved best, Laódamas,
had long held place; now the king bade him rise
and gave his shining chair to Lord Odysseus.            185
A serving maid poured water for his hands
from a gold pitcher into a silver bowl,
and spread a polished table at his side;
the mistress of provisions came with bread
and other victuals, generous with her store.            190
So Lord Odysseus drank, and tasted supper.
Seeing this done, the king in majesty
said to his squire:

                "A fresh bowl, Pontónoös;
we make libation to the lord of lightning,
who seconds honorable petitioners."                     195

Mixing the honey-hearted wine, Pontónoös
went on his rounds and poured fresh cups for all,
whereof when all had spilt they drank their fill.
Alkínoös then spoke to the company:

"My lords and leaders of Phaiákia:                      200
hear now, all that my heart would have me say.
Our banquet's ended, so you may retire,
but let our seniors gather in the morning
to give this guest a festal day, and make
fair offerings to the gods. In due course we            205
shall put our minds upon the means at hand
to take him safely, comfortably, well
and happily, with speed, to his own country,
distant though it may lie. And may no trouble

come to him here or on the way; his fate                              210
he shall pay out at home, even as the Spinners[5]
spun for him on the day his mother bore him.
If, as may be, he is some god, come down
from heaven's height, the gods are working strangely:
until now, they have shown themselves in glory                       215
only after great hekatombs—those figures
banqueting at our side, throned like ourselves.
Or if some traveller met them when alone
they bore no least disguise; we are their kin; Gigantês,
Kyklopês, rank no nearer gods than we."                              220

Odysseus' wits were ready, and he replied:

"Alkínoös, you may set your mind at rest.
Body and birth, a most unlikely god
am I, being all of earth and mortal nature.
I should say, rather, I am like those men                            225
who suffer the worst trials that you know,
and miseries greater yet, as I might tell you—
hundreds; indeed the gods could send no more.
You will indulge me if I finish dinner—?
grieved though I am to say it. There's no part                       230
of man more like a dog than brazen Belly,
crying to be remembered—and it must be—
when we are mortal weary and sick at heart;
and that is my condition. Yet my hunger
drives me to take this food, and think no more                       235
of my afflictions. Belly must be filled.
Be equally impelled, my lords, tomorrow
to berth me in a ship and send me home!
Rough years I've had; now may I see once more
my hall, my lands, my people before I die!"                          240

Now all who heard cried out assent to this:
the guest had spoken well; he must have passage.
Then tipping wine they drank their thirst away,
and one by one went homeward for the night.
So Lord Odysseus kept his place alone                                245
with Arêtê and the king Alkínoös
beside him, while the maids went to and fro
clearing away the wine cups and the tables.
Presently the ivory-skinned lady

5. The Fates, who spin the pattern of each individual; destiny.

turned to him—for she knew his cloak and tunic                    250
to be her own fine work, done with her maids—
and arrowy came her words upon the air:

"Friend, I, for one, have certain questions for you.
Who are you, and who has given you this clothing?
Did you not say you wandered here by sea?"                    255

The great tactician carefully replied:

"Ah, majesty, what labor it would be
to go through the whole story! All my years
of misadventures, given by those on high!
But this you ask about is quickly told:                    260
in mid-ocean lies Ogýgia, the island
haunt of Kalypso, Atlas' guileful daughter,
a lovely goddess and a dangerous one.
No one, no god or man, consorts with her;
but supernatural power brought me there                    265
to be her solitary guest: for Zeus
let fly with his bright bolt and split my ship,
rolling me over in the winedark sea.
There all my shipmates, friends were drowned, while I
hung on the keelboard of the wreck and drifted                    270
nine full days. Then in the dead of night
the gods brought me ashore upon Ogýgia
into her hands. The enchantress in her beauty
fed and caressed me, promised me I should be
immortal, youthful, all the days to come;                    275
but in my heart I never gave consent
though seven years detained. Immortal clothing
I had from her, and kept it wet with tears.
Then came the eighth year on the wheel of heaven
and word to her from Zeus, or a change of heart,                    280
so that she now commanded me to sail,
sending me out to sea on a craft I made
with timber and tools of hers. She gave me stores,
victuals and wine, a cloak divinely woven,
and made a warm land breeze come up astern.                    285
Seventeen days I sailed in the open water
before I saw your country's shore, a shadow
upon the sea rim. Then my heart rejoiced—
pitiable as I am! For blows aplenty
awaited me from the god who shakes the earth.                    290
Cross gales he blew, making me lose my bearings,

and heaved up seas beyond imagination—
huge and foundering seas. All I could do
was hold hard, groaning under every shock,
until my craft broke up in the hurricane.                              295
I kept afloat and swam your sea, or drifted,
taken by wind and current to this coast
where I went in on big swells running landward.
But cliffs and rock shoals made that place forbidding,
so I turned back, swimming off shore, and came            300
in the end to a river, to auspicious water,
with smooth beach and a rise that broke the wind.
I lay there where I fell till strength returned.
Then sacred night came on, and I went inland
to high ground and a leaf bed in a thicket.                        305
Heaven sent slumber in an endless tide
submerging my sad heart among the leaves.
That night and next day's dawn and noon I slept;
the sun went west; and then sweet sleep unbound me,
when I became aware of maids—your daughter's—         310
playing along the beach; the princess, too,
most beautiful. I prayed her to assist me,
and her good sense was perfect; one could hope
for no behavior like it from the young,
thoughtless as they most often are. But she                      315
gave me good provender and good red wine,
a river bath, and finally this clothing.
There is the bitter tale. These are the facts."

But in reply Alkínoös observed:

"Friend, my child's good judgment failed in this—      320
not to have brought you in her company home.
Once you approached her, you became her charge."
To this Odysseus tactfully replied:

"Sir, as to that, you should not blame the princess.
She did tell me to follow with her maids,                          325
but I would not. I felt abashed, and feared
the sight would somehow ruffle or offend you.
All of us on this earth are plagued by jealousy."

Alkínoös' answer was a declaration:

"Friend, I am not a man for trivial anger:                         330
better a sense of measure in everything.

No anger here. I say that if it should please
our father Zeus, Athena, and Apollo—
seeing the man you are, seeing your thoughts
are my own thoughts—my daughter should be yours          335
and you my son-in-law, if you remained.
A home, lands, riches you should have from me
if you could be contented here. If not,
by Father Zeus, let none of our men hold you!
On the contrary, I can assure you now                    340
of passage late tomorrow: while you sleep
my men will row you through the tranquil night
to your own land and home or where you please.
It may be, even, far beyond Euboia—[6]
called most remote by seamen of our isle                 345
who landed there, conveying Rhadamanthos
when he sought Títyos, the son of Gaia.
They put about, with neither pause nor rest,
and entered their home port the selfsame day.
But this you, too, will see: what ships I have,          350
how my young oarsmen send the foam a-scudding!"

Now joy welled up in the patient Lord Odysseus
who said devoutly in the warmest tones:

"O Father Zeus, let all this be fulfilled
as spoken by Alkínoös! Earth of harvests                 355
remember him! Return me to my homeland!"

In this manner they conversed with one another;
but the great lady called her maids, and sent them
to make a kingly bed, with purple rugs
piled up, and sheets outspread, and fleecy               360
coverlets, in an eastern colonnade.
The girls went out with torches in their hands,
swift at their work of bedmaking; returning
they whispered at the lord Odysseus' shoulder:

"Sir, you may come; your bed has been prepared."         365

How welcome the word "bed" came to his ears!
Now, then, Odysseus laid him down and slept

6. The long island which hugs the coast of Attica. *Rhadamanthos* was the son of Zeus by the
mortal Europa, and brother to King Minos of Krete. *Títyos* was a giant who tried to rape Leto,
the mother, by Zeus, of Apollo and Artemis. Later on (Book XI), Odysseus sees him in the
Underworld, eternally punished for his crime. Why Rhadamanthos went to see Títyos we have
no idea.

in luxury under the Porch of Morning,
while in his inner chamber Alkínoös
retired to rest where his dear consort lay.                               370

## Book VIII

### THE SONGS OF THE HARPER

Under the opening fingers of the dawn
Alkínoös, the sacred prince, arose,
and then arose Odysseus, raider of cities.
As the king willed, they went down by the shipways
to the assembly ground of the Phaiákians.                                 5
Side by side the two men took their ease there
on smooth stone benches. Meanwhile Pallas Athena
roamed through the byways of the town, contriving
Odysseus' voyage home—in voice and feature
the crier of the king Alkínoös                                            10
who stopped and passed the word to every man:

"Phaiákian lords and counselors, this way!
Come to assembly: learn about the stranger,
the new guest at the palace of Alkínoös—
a man the sea drove, but a comely man;                                    15
the gods' own light is on him."

                              She aroused them,
and soon the assembly ground and seats were filled
with curious men, a throng who peered and saw
the master mind of war, Laërtês' son.
Athena now poured out her grace upon him,                                 20
head and shoulders, height and mass—a splendor
awesome to the eyes of the Phaiákians;
she put him in a fettle to win the day,
mastering every trial they set to test him.
When all the crowd sat marshalled, quieted,                               25
Alkínoös addressed the full assembly:

"Hear me, lords and captains of the Phaiákians!
Hear what my heart would have me say!
Our guest and new friend—nameless to me still—
comes to my house after long wandering                                    30
in Dawn lands, or among the Sunset races.
Now he appeals to me for conveyance home.
As in the past, therefore, let us provide
passage, and quickly, for no guest of mine
languishes here for lack of it. Look to it:                                35

get a black ship afloat on the noble sea,
and pick our fastest sailer; draft a crew
of two and fifty from our younger townsmen—
men who have made their names at sea. Loop oars
well to your tholepins, lads, then leave the ship,                40
come to our house, fall to, and take your supper:
we'll furnish out a feast for every crewman.
These are your orders. As for my older peers
and princes of the realm, let them foregather
in festival for our friend in my great hall;                45
and let no man refuse. Call in our minstrel,
Demódokos, whom God made lord of song,
heart-easing, sing upon what theme he will."

He turned, led the procession, and those princes
followed, while his herald sought the minstrel.                50
Young oarsmen from the assembly chose a crew
of two and fifty, as the king commanded,
and these filed off along the waterside
to where the ship lay, poised above open water.
They hauled the black hull down to ride the sea,                55
rigging a mast and spar in the black ship,
with oars at trail from corded rawhide, all
seamanly; then tried the white sail, hoisting,
and moored her off the beach. Then going ashore
the crew went up to the great house of Alkínoös.                60
Here the enclosures, entrance ways, and rooms
were filled with men, young men and old, for whom
Alkínoös had put twelve sheep to sacrifice,
eight tuskers and a pair of shambling oxen.
These, now, they flayed and dressed to make their banquet.                65
The crier soon came, leading that man of song
whom the Muse cherished; by her gift he knew
the good of life, and evil—
for she who lent him sweetness made him blind.
Pontónoös fixed a studded chair for him                70
hard by a pillar amid the banqueters,
hanging the taut harp from a peg above him,
and guided up his hands upon the strings;
placed a bread basket at his side, and poured
wine in a cup, that he might drink his fill.                75
Now each man's hand went out upon the banquet.

In time, when hunger and thirst were turned away,
the Muse brought to the minstrel's mind a song
of heroes whose great fame rang under heaven:

the clash between Odysseus and Akhilleus,                     80
how one time they contended at the godfeast
raging, and the marshal, Agamémnon,
felt inward joy over his captains' quarrel;
for such had been foretold him by Apollo
at Pytho[7]—hallowed height—when the Akhaian        85
crossed that portal of rock to ask a sign—
in the old days when grim war lay ahead
for Trojans and Danaans, by God's will.
So ran the tale the minstrel sang. Odysseus
with massive hand drew his rich mantle down          90
over his brow, cloaking his face with it,
to make the Phaiákians miss the secret tears
that started to his eyes. How skillfully
he dried them when the song came to a pause!
threw back his mantle, spilt his gout of wine!       95
But soon the minstrel plucked his note once more
to please the Phaiákian lords, who loved the song;
then in his cloak Odysseus wept again.
His tears flowed in the mantle unperceived:
only Alkínoös, at his elbow, saw them,               100
and caught the low groan in the man's breathing.
At once he spoke to all the seafolk round him:

"Hear me, lords and captains of the Phaiákians.
Our meat is shared, our hearts are full of pleasure
from the clear harp tone that accords with feasting;  105
now for the field and track; we shall have trials
in the pentathlon. Let our guest go home
and tell his friends what champions we are
at boxing, wrestling, broadjump and foot racing."

On this he led the way and all went after.           110
The crier unslung and pegged the shining harp
and, taking Demódokos's hand,
led him along with all the rest—Phaiákian
peers, gay amateurs of the great games.
They gained the common, where a crowd was forming,   115
and many a young athlete now came forward
with seaside names like Tipmast, Tiderace, Sparwood,
Hullman, Sternman, Beacher and Pullerman,
Bluewater, Shearwater, Runningwake, Boardalee,
Seabelt, son of Grandfleet Shipwrightson;            120

7. The oracular shrine of Apollo at Delphi, high up on the mountain side.

Seareach stepped up, son of the Launching Master,
rugged as Arês[8] bane of men; his build
excelled all but the Prince Laódamas;
and Laódamas made entry with his brothers,
Halios and Klytóneus, sons of the king.                            125
The runners, first, must have their quarter mile.
All lined up tense; then Go! and down the track
they raised the dust in a flying bunch, strung out
longer and longer behind Prince Klytóneus.
By just so far as a mule team, breaking ground,                    130
will distance oxen, he left all behind
and came up to the crowd, an easy winner.
Then they made room for wrestling—grinding bouts
that Seareach won, pinning the strongest men;
then the broadjump; first place went to Seabelt;                   135
Sparwood gave the discus the mightiest fling,
and Prince Laódamas outboxed them all.
Now it was he, the son of Alkínoös,
who said when they had run through these diversions:

"Look here, friends, we ought to ask the stranger                  140
if he competes in something. He's no cripple;
look at his leg muscles and his forearms.
Neck like a bollard; strong as a bull, he seems;
and not old, though he may have gone stale under
the rough times he had. Nothing like the sea                       145
for wearing out the toughest man alive."

Then Seareach took him up at once, and said:

"Laódamas, you're right, by all the powers.
Go up to him, yourself, and put the question."

At this, Alkínoös' tall son advanced                               150
to the center ground, and there addressed Odysseus:

"Friend, Excellency, come join our competition,
if you are practiced, as you seem to be.
While a man lives he wins no greater honor
than footwork and the skill of hands can bring him.                155
Enter our games, then; ease your heart of trouble.
Your journey home is not far off, remember;
the ship is launched, the crew all primed for sea."

8. The Greek war-god.

Odysseus, canniest of men, replied:

"Laódamas, why do you young chaps challenge me?                    160
I have more on my mind than track and field—
hard days, and many, have I seen, and suffered.
I sit here at your field meet, yes; but only
as one who begs your king to send him home."

Now Seareach put his word in, and contentiously:                   165

"The reason being, as I see it, friend,
you never learned a sport, and have no skill
in any of the contests of fighting men.
You must have been the skipper of some tramp
that crawled from one port to the next, jam full               170
of chaffering hands: a tallier of cargoes,
itching for gold—not, by your looks, an athlete."

Odysseus frowned, and eyed him coldly, saying:

"That was uncalled for, friend, you talk like a fool.
The gods deal out no gift, this one or any—                        175
birth, brains, or speech—to every man alike.
In looks a man may be a shade, a specter,
and yet be master of speech so crowned with beauty
that people gaze at him with pleasure. Courteous,
sure of himself, he can command assemblies,                    180
and when he comes to town, the crowds gather.
A handsome man, contrariwise, may lack
grace and good sense in everything he says.
You now, for instance, with your fine physique—
a god's, indeed—you have an empty noddle.                      185
I find my heart inside my ribs aroused
by your impertinence. I am no stranger
to contests, as you fancy. I rated well
when I could count on youth and my two hands.
Now pain has cramped me, and my years of combat             190
hacking through ranks in war, and the bitter sea.
Aye. Even so I'll give your games a trial.
You spoke heart-wounding words. You shall be answered."

He leapt out, cloaked as he was, and picked a discus,
a rounded stone, more ponderous than those                     195
already used by the Phaiákian throwers,
and, whirling, let it fly from his great hand

with a low hum. The crowd went flat on the ground—
all those oar-pulling, seafaring Phaiákians—
under the rushing noise. The spinning disk                          200
soared out, light as a bird, beyond all others.
Disguised now as a Phaiákian, Athena
staked it and called out:

                    "Even a blind man,
friend, could judge this, finding with his fingers
one discus, quite alone, beyond the cluster.
Congratulations; this event is yours;                               205
not a man here can beat you or come near you."

That was a cheering hail, Odysseus thought,
seeing one friend there on the emulous field,
so, in relief, he turned among the Phaiákians
and said:

                    "Now come alongside that one, lads.            210
The next I'll send as far, I think, or farther.
Anyone else on edge for competition
try me now. By heaven, you angered me.
Racing, wrestling, boxing—I bar nothing
with any man except Laódamas,                                       215
for he's my host. Who quarrels with his host?
Only a madman—or no man at all—
would challenge his protector among strangers,
cutting the ground away under his feet.
Here are no others I will not engage,                               220
none but I hope to know what he is made of.
Inept at combat, am I? Not entirely.
Give me a smooth bow; I can handle it,
and I might well be first to hit my man
amid a swarm of enemies, though archers                             225
in company around me drew together.
Philoktêtês[9] alone, at Troy, when we
Akhaians took the bow, used to outshoot me.
Of men who now eat bread upon the earth
I hold myself the best hand with a bow—                             230
conceding mastery to the men of old,
Heraklês, or Eurýtos of Oikhalía,[1]

9. He inherited the bow of Herakles, which never missed its mark.    1. Eurýtos of Oikhalía (in
central Greece) challenged Apollo (also an archer) and was killed by the god. Eurýtos' bow was
given to Odysseus by his son Iphitos and it is with that bow that Odysseus will kill the suitors in
Book XXII.

heroes who vied with gods in bowmanship.
Eurýtos came to grief, it's true; old age
never crept over him in his long hall;                                    235
Apollo took his challenge ill, and killed him.
What then, the spear? I'll plant it like an arrow.
Only in sprinting, I'm afraid, I may
be passed by someone. Roll of the sea waves
wearied me, and the victuals in my ship                                   240
ran low; my legs are flabby."
                              When he finished,
the rest were silent, but Alkínoös answered:

"Friend, we take your challenge in good part,
for this man angered and affronted you
here at our peaceful games. You'd have us note                            245
the prowess that is in you, and so clearly,
no man of sense would ever cry it down!
Come, turn your mind, now, on a thing to tell
among your peers when you are home again,
dining in hall, beside your wife and children:                           250 •
I mean our prowess, as you may remember it,
for we, too, have our skills, given by Zeus,
and practiced from our father's time to this—
not in the boxing ring nor the palestra[2]
conspicuous, but in racing, land or sea;                                  255
and all our days we set great store by feasting,
harpers, and the grace of dancing choirs,
changes of dress, warm baths, and downy beds.
O master dancers of the Phaiákians!
Perform now: let our guest on his return                                  260
tell his companions we excel the world
in dance and song, as in our ships and running.
Someone go find the gittern[3] harp in hall
and bring it quickly to Demódokos!"

At the serene king's word, a squire ran                                   265
to bring the polished harp out of the palace,
and place was given to nine referees—
peers of the realm, masters of ceremony—
who cleared a space and smoothed a dancing floor.
The squire brought down, and gave Demódokos,                             270
the clear-toned harp; and centering on the minstrel
magic young dancers formed a circle

2. Wrestling ground.    3. Shaped like a guitar.

with a light beat, and stamp of feet. Beholding,
Odysseus marvelled at the flashing ring.

Now to his harp the blinded minstrel sang                              275
of Arês' dalliance with Aphroditê:
how hidden in Hephaistos' house they played
at love together, and the gifts of Arês,
dishonoring Hephaistos' bed—and how
the word that wounds the heart came to the master                     280
from Hêlios,[4] who had seen the two embrace;
and when he learned it, Lord Hephaistos went
with baleful calculation to his forge.
There mightily he armed his anvil block
and hammered out a chain, whose tempered links                        285
could not be sprung or bent; he meant that they should hold.
Those shackles fashioned, hot in wrath Hephaistos
climbed to the bower and the bed of love,
pooled all his net of chain around the bed posts
and swung it from the rafters overhead—                               290
light as a cobweb even gods in bliss
could not perceive, so wonderful his cunning.
Seeing his bed now made a snare, he feigned
a journey to the trim stronghold of Lemnos,[5]
the dearest of earth's towns to him. And Arês?                        295
Ah, golden Arês' watch had its reward
when he beheld the great smith leaving home.
How promptly to the famous door he came,
intent on pleasure with sweet Kythereia![6]
She, who had left her father's side but now,                          300
sat in her chamber when her lover entered;
and tenderly he pressed her hand and said:

"Come and lie down, my darling, and be happy!
Hephaistos is no longer here, but gone
to see his grunting[7] Sintian friends on Lemnos."                    305

As she, too, thought repose would be most welcome,
the pair went in to bed—into a shower
of clever chains, the netting of Hephaistos.
So trussed, they could not move apart, nor rise,
at last they knew there could be no escape,                           310

4. The sun, who sees everything.   5. An island off the coast of Asia Minor, the "dearest of
earth's towns" to Hephaistos because when Zeus threw him off Olympus (*Iliad*, I.590ff) he landed
on Lemnos and the inhabitants took care of him.   6. A title of Aphrodite.   7. The Sintians,
the inhabitants of Lemnos, do not speak Greek.

they were to see the glorious cripple now—
for Hêlios had spied for him, and told him;
so he turned back, this side of Lemnos Isle,
sick at heart, making his way homeward.
Now in the doorway of the room he stood                    315
while deadly rage took hold of him; his voice,
hoarse and terrible, reached all the gods:

"O Father Zeus, O gods in bliss forever,
here is indecorous entertainment for you,
Aphroditê, Zeus's daughter,                                320
caught in the act, cheating me, her cripple,
with Arês—devastating Arês.
Cleanlimbed beauty is her joy, not these
bandylegs I came into the world with:
no one to blame but the two gods who bred me![8]           325
Come see this pair entwining here
in my own bed! How hot it makes me burn!
I think they may not care to lie much longer,
pressing on one another, passionate lovers;
they'll have enough of bed together soon.                  330
And yet the chain that bagged them holds them down
till Father sends me back my wedding gifts—
all that I poured out for his damned pigeon,
so lovely, and so wanton."

                          All the others
were crowding in, now, to the brazen house—                335
Poseidon who embraces earth, and Hermês
the runner, and Apollo, lord of Distance.
The goddesses stayed home for shame; but these
munificences ranged there in the doorway,                  340
and irrepressible among them all
arose the laughter of the happy gods.
Gazing hard at Hephaistos' handiwork
the gods in turn remarked among themselves:

"No dash in adultery now."
                          "The tortoise tags the hare—
Hephaistos catches Arês—and Arês outran the wind."         345

"The lame god's craft has pinned him. Now shall he
pay what is due from gods taken in cuckoldry."

8. Zeus and Hera.

They made these improving remarks to one another,
but Apollo leaned aside to say to Hermês:
"Son of Zeus, beneficent Wayfinder,                              350
would you accept a coverlet of chain, if only
you lay by Aphroditê's golden side?"

To this the Wayfinder replied, shining:

"Would I not, though, Apollo of distances!
Wrap me in chains three times the weight of these,              355
come goddesses and gods to see the fun;
only let me lie beside the pale-golden one!"

The gods gave way again to peals of laughter,
all but Poseidon, and he never smiled,
but urged Hephaistos to unpinion Arês,                          360
saying emphatically, in a loud voice:
                              "Free him;
you will be paid, I swear; ask what you will;
he pays up every jot the gods decree."

To this the Great Gamelegs replied:

                              "Poseidon,
lord of the earth-surrounding sea, I should not                 365
swear to a scoundrel's honor. What have I
as surety from you, if Arês leaves me
empty-handed, with my empty chain?"

The Earth-shaker for answer urged again:

"Hephaistos, let us grant he goes, and leaves                   370
the fine unpaid; I swear, then, I shall pay it."

Then said the Great Gamelegs at last:

                              "No more;
you offer terms I cannot well refuse."

And down the strong god bent to set them free,
till disencumbered of their bond, the chain,                    375
the lovers leapt away—he into Thrace,[9]
while Aphroditê, laughter's darling, fled

9. The non-Greek territory to the North, where the war-god was supposed to be at home.

to Kypros[1] Isle and Paphos, to her meadow
and altar dim with incense. There the Graces
bathed and anointed her with golden oil—                              380
a bloom that clings upon immortal flesh alone—
and let her folds of mantle fall in glory.

So ran the song the minstrel sang.

                         Odysseus,
listening, found sweet pleasure in the tale,
among the Phaiákian mariners and oarsmen.                             385
And next Alkínoös called upon his sons,
Halios and Laódamas, to show
the dance no one could do as well as they—
handling a purple ball carven by Pólybos.
One made it shoot up under the shadowing clouds                      395
as he leaned backward; bounding high in air
the other cut its flight far off the ground—
and neither missed a step as the ball soared.
The next turn was to keep it low, and shuttling
hard between them, while the ring of boys                            395
gave them a steady stamping beat.
Odysseus now addressed Alkínoös:

"O majesty, model of all your folk,
your promise was to show me peerless dancers;
here is the promise kept. I am all wonder."                          400

At this Alkínoös in his might rejoicing
said to the seafarers of Phaiákia:

"Attend me now, Phiákian lords and captains:
our guest appears a clear-eyed man and wise.
Come, let him feel our bounty as he should.                          405
Here are twelve princes of the kingdom—lords
paramount, and I who make thirteen;
let each one bring a laundered cloak and tunic,
and add one bar of honorable gold.
Heap all our gifts together; load his arms;                          410
let him go joyous to our evening feast!
As for Seareach—why, man to man
he'll make amends, and handsomely; he blundered."
Now all as one acclaimed the king's good pleasure,

1. Cyprus, where Aphrodite had a famous shrine at Paphos.

and each one sent a squire to bring his gifts.                              415
Meanwhile Seareach found speech again, saying:

"My lord and model of us all, Alkínoös,
as you require of me, in satisfaction,
this broadsword of clear bronze goes to our guest.
Its hilt is silver, and the ringed sheath
of new-sawn ivory—a costly weapon."                                         420

He turned to give the broadsword to Odysseus,
facing him, saying blithely:

                              "Sir, my best
wishes, my respects; if I offended,
I hope the seawinds blow it out of mind.
God send you see your lady and your homeland                                425
soon again, after the pain of exile."

Odysseus, the great tactician, answered:

"My hand, friend; may the gods award you fortune.
I hope no pressing need comes on you ever
for this fine blade you give me in amends."                                 430

He slung it, glinting silver, from his shoulder,
as the light shone from sundown. Messengers
were bearing gifts and treasure to the palace,
where the king's sons received them all, and made
a glittering pile at their grave mother's side;                             435
then, as Alkínoös took his throne of power,
each went to his own high-backed chair in turn,
and said Alkínoös to Arêtê:

"Lady, bring here a chest, the finest one;
a clean cloak and tunic; stow these things;                                 440
and warm a cauldron for him. Let him bathe,
when he has seen the gifts of the Phaiákians,
and so dine happily to a running song.
My own wine-cup of gold intaglio
I'll give him, too; through all the days to come,                           445
tipping his wine to Zeus or other gods
in his great hall, he shall remember me."

Then said Arêtê to her maids:

"The tripod:
stand the great tripod legs about the fire."

They swung the cauldron on the fire's heart,                    450
poured water in, and fed the blaze beneath
until the basin simmered, cupped in flame.
The queen set out a rich chest from her chamber
and folded in the gifts—clothing and gold
given Odysseus by the Phaiákians;                               455
then she put in the royal cloak and tunic,
briskly saying to her guest:

                        "Now here, sir,
look to the lid yourself, and tie it down
against light fingers, if there be any,
on the black ship tonight while you are sleeping."              460

Noble Odysseus, expert in adversity,
battened the lid down with a lightning knot
learned, once, long ago, from the Lady Kirkê.[2]
And soon a call came from the Bathing Mistress
who led him to a hip-bath, warm and clear—                      465
a happy sight, and rare in his immersions
after he left Kalypso's home—where, surely,
the luxuries of a god were ever his.
When the bath maids had washed him, rubbed him down,
put a fresh tunic and a cloak around him,                       470
he left the bathing place to join the men
at wine in hall.

                        The princess Nausikaa,
exquisite figure, as of heaven's shaping,
waited beside a pillar as he passed
and said swiftly, with wonder in her look:                      475

"Fare well, stranger; in your land remember me
who met and saved you. It is worth your thought."

The man of all occasions now met this:

"Daughter of great Alkínoös, Nausikaa,
may Zeus the lord of thunder, Hera's consort,                   480
grant me daybreak again in my own country!

2. Or Circe. A divine sorceress on whose island Odysseus had spent some time during his travels
(see Book XII).

But there and all my days until I die
may I invoke you as I would a goddess,
princess, to whom I owe my life."

                              He left her
and went to take his place beside the king.                    485

Now when the roasts were cut, the winebowls full,
a herald led the minstrel down the room
amid the deference of the crowd, and paused
to seat him near a pillar in the center—
whereupon that resourceful man, Odysseus,                       490
carved out a quarter from his chine of pork,
crisp with fat, and called the blind man's guide:

"Herald! here, take this to Demódokos:
let him feast and be merry, with my compliments.
All men owe honor to the poets—honor                            495
and awe, for they are dearest to the Muse
who puts upon their lips the ways of life."

Gentle Demódokos took the proffered gift
and inwardly rejoiced. When all were served,
every man's hand went out upon the banquet,                     500
repelling hunger and thirst, until at length
Odysseus spoke again to the blind minstrel:

"Demódokos, accept my utmost praise.
The Muse, daughter of Zeus in radiance,
or else Apollo gave you skill to shape                          505
with such great style your songs of the Akhaians—
their hard lot, how they fought and suffered war.
You shared it, one would say, or heard it all.
Now shift your theme, and sing that wooden horse
Epeios built, inspired by Athena—                               510
the ambuscade Odysseus filled with fighters
and sent to take the inner town of Troy.
Sing only this for me, sing me this well,
and I shall say at once before the world
the grace of heaven has given us a song."                       515

The minstrel stirred, murmuring to the god, and soon
clear words and notes came one by one, a vision
of the Akhaians in their graceful ships
drawing away from shore: the torches flung

and shelters flaring: Argive soldiers crouched          520
in the close dark around Odysseus: and
the horse, tall on the assembly ground of Troy.
For when the Trojans pulled it in, themselves,
up to the citadel, they sat nearby
with long-drawn-out and hapless argument—          525
favoring, in the end, one course of three:
either to stave the vault with brazen axes,
or haul it to a cliff and pitch it down,
or else to save it for the gods, a votive glory—
the plan that could not but prevail.          530
For Troy must perish, as ordained, that day
she harbored the great horse of timber; hidden
the flower of Akhaia lay, and bore
slaughter and death upon the men of Troy.
He sang, then, of the town sacked by Akhaians          535
pouring down from the horse's hollow cave,
this way and that way raping the steep city,
and how Odysseus came like Arês to
the door of Deïphobos, with Meneláos,
and braved the desperate fight there—          540
conquering once more by Athena's power.

The splendid minstrel sang it.
                    And Odysseus
let the bright molten tears run down his cheeks,
weeping the way a wife mourns for her lord
on the lost field where he has gone down fighting          545
the day of wrath that came upon his children.
At sight of the man panting and dying there,
she slips down to enfold him, crying out;
then feels the spears, prodding her back and shoulders,
and goes bound into slavery and grief.          550
Piteous weeping wears away her cheeks:
but no more piteous than Odysseus' tears,
cloaked as they were, now, from the company.
Only Alkínoös, at his elbow, knew—
hearing the low sob in the man's breathing—          555
and when he knew, he spoke:

"Hear me, lords and captains of Phaiákia!
And let Demódokos touch his harp no more.
His theme has not been pleasing to all here.
During the feast, since our fine poet sang,          560
our guest has never left off weeping. Grief

seems fixed upon his heart. Break off the song!
Let everyone be easy, host and guest;
there's more decorum in a smiling banquet!
We had prepared here, on our friend's behalf,                565
safe conduct in a ship, and gifts to cheer him,
holding that any man with a grain of wit
will treat a decent suppliant like a brother.
Now by the same rule, friend, you must not be
secretive any longer! Come, in fairness,                     570
tell me the name you bore in that far country;
how were you known to family, and neighbors?
No man is nameless—no man, good or bad,
but gets a name in his first infancy,
none being born, unless a mother bears him!                  575
Tell me your native land, your coast and city—
sailing directions for the ships, you know—
for those Phaiákian ships of ours
that have no steersman, and no steering oar,
divining the crew's wishes, as they do,                      580
and knowing, as they do, the ports of call
about the world. Hidden in mist or cloud
they scud the open sea, with never a thought
of being in distress or going down.
There is, however, something I once heard                    585
Nausíthoös, my father, say: Poseidon
holds it against us that our deep sea ships
are sure conveyance for all passengers.
My father said, some day one of our cutters
homeward bound over the cloudy sea                           590
would be wrecked by the god, and a range of hills
thrown round our city. So, in his age, he said,
and let it be, or not, as the god please.
But come, now, put it for me clearly, tell me
the sea ways that you wandered, and the shores               595
you touched; the cities, and the men therein,
uncivilized, if such there were, and hostile,
and those godfearing who had kindly manners.
Tell me why you should grieve so terribly
over the Argives and the fall of Troy.                       600
That was all gods' work, weaving ruin there
so it should make a song for men to come!
Some kin of yours, then, died at Ilion,
some first rate man, by marriage near to you,
next your own blood most dear?                               605
Or some companion of congenial mind

and valor? True it is, a wise friend
can take a brother's place in our affection."

## Book IX

### NEW COASTS AND POSEIDON'S SON

Now this was the reply Odysseus made:
"Alkínoös, king and admiration of men,
how beautiful this is, to hear a minstrel
gifted as yours: a god he might be, singing!
There is no boon in life more sweet, I say,            5
then when a summer joy holds all the realm,
and banqueters sit listening to a harper
in a great hall, by rows of tables heaped
with bread and roast meat, while a steward goes
to dip up wine and brim your cups again.               10
Here is the flower of life, it seems to me!
But now you wish to know my cause for sorrow—
and thereby give me cause for more.

What shall I say first? What
shall I keep until the end?
The gods have tried me in a thousand ways.             15
But first my name: let that be known to you,
and if I pull away from pitiless death,
friendship will bind us, though my land lies far.

I am Laërtês' son, Odysseus.
                    Men hold me
formidable for guile in peace and war:                 20
this fame has gone abroad to the sky's rim.
My home is on the peaked sea-mark of Ithaka
under Mount Neion's wind-blown robe of leaves,
in sight of other islands—Doulíkhion,
Samê, wooded Zakynthos—Ithaka                          25
being most lofty in that coastal sea,
and northwest, while the rest lie east and south.
A rocky isle, but good for a boy's training;
I shall not see on earth a place more dear,
though I have been detained long by Kalypso,           30
loveliest among goddesses, who held me
in her smooth caves, to be her heart's delight,
as Kirkê of Aiaia, the enchantress,
desired me, and detained me in her hall.
But in my heart I never gave consent.                  35
Where shall a man find sweetness to surpass

his own home and his parents? In far lands
he shall not, though he find a house of gold.

What of my sailing, then, from Troy?
                              What of those years
of rough adventure, weathered under Zeus?                    40
The wind that carried west from Ilion
brought me to Ismaros, on the far shore,
a strongpoint on the coast of the Kikonês.[3]
I stormed that place and killed the men who fought.
Plunder we took, and we enslaved the women,                  45
to make division, equal shares to all—
but on the spot I told them: 'Back, and quickly!
Out to sea again!' My men were mutinous,
fools, on stores of wine. Sheep after sheep
they butchered by the surf, and shambling cattle,            50
feasting,—while fugitives went inland, running
to call to arms the main force of Kikonês.
This was an army, trained to fight on horseback
or, where the ground required, on foot. They came
with dawn over that terrain like the leaves                  55
and blades of spring. So doom appeared to us,
dark word of Zeus for us, our evil days.
My men stood up and made a fight of it—
backed on the ships, with lances kept in play,
from bright morning through the blaze of noon                60
holding our beach, although so far outnumbered;
but when the sun passed toward unyoking time,
then the Akhaians, one by one, gave way.
Six benches were left empty in every ship
that evening when we pulled away from death.                 65
And this new grief we bore with us to sea:
our precious lives we had, but not our friends.
No ship made sail next day until some shipmate
had raised a cry, three times, for each poor ghost
unfleshed by the Kikonês on that field.                      70
Now Zeus the lord of cloud roused in the north
a storm against the ships, and driving veils
of squall moved down like night on land and sea.
The bows went plunging at the gust; sails
cracked and lashed out strips in the big wind.               75
We saw death in that fury, dropped the yards,
unshipped the oars, and pulled for the nearest lee:

3. Allies of the Trojans, but Odysseus does not even mention this fact to excuse the piratical raid;
he did not think any excuse was needed.

then two long days and nights we lay offshore
worn out and sick at heart, tasting our grief,
until a third Dawn came with ringlets shining.          80
Then we put up our masts, hauled sail, and rested,
letting the steersmen and the breeze take over.

I might have made it safely home, that time,
but as I came round Malea[4] the current
took me out to sea, and from the north          85
a fresh gale drove me on, past Kythera.
Nine days I drifted on the teeming sea
before dangerous high winds. Upon the tenth
we came to the coastline of the Lotos Eaters,[5]
who live upon that flower. We landed there          90
to take on water. All ships' companies
mustered alongside for the mid-day meal.
Then I sent out two picked men and a runner
to learn what race of men that land sustained.
They fell in, soon enough, with Lotos Eaters,          95
who showed no will to do us harm, only
offering the sweet Lotos to our friends—
but those who ate this honeyed plant, the Lotos,
never cared to report, nor to return:
they longed to stay forever, browsing on          100
that native bloom, forgetful of their homeland.
I drove them, all three wailing, to the ships,
tied them down under their rowing benches,
and called the rest: 'All hands aboard;
come, clear the beach and no one taste          105
the Lotos, or you lose your hope of home.'
Filing in to their places by the rowlocks
my oarsmen dipped their long oars in the surf,
and we moved out again on our sea faring.
In the next land[6] we found were Kyklopês,          110
giants, louts, without a law to bless them.
In ignorance leaving the fruitage of the earth in mystery
to the immortal gods, they neither plow
nor sow by hand, nor till the ground, though grain—
wild wheat and barley—grows untended, and          115
wine-grapes, in clusters, ripen in heaven's rain.

---

**4.** The southeastern tip of the Peloponnese. *Kythera:* a large island off the headland.     **5.** It is
generally thought that this story contains some memory of early Greek contact with North Africa;
the north wind Odysseus describes would have taken him to the area of Cyrenaica, modern Libya.
Modern identifications of the lotos range from dates to hashish.     **6.** According to ancient tradition the Kyklopes lived in Sicily.

Kyklopês have no muster and no meeting,
no consultation or old tribal ways,
but each one dwells in his own mountain cave
dealing out rough justice to wife and child,                    120
indifferent to what the others do.
                                        Well, then:
across the wide bay from the mainland
there lies a desert island, not far out,
but still not close inshore. Wild goats in hundreds
breed there; and no human being comes                          125
upon the isle to startle them—no hunter
of all who ever tracked with hounds through forests
or had rough going over mountain trails.
The isle, unplanted and untilled, a wilderness,
pastures goats alone. And this is why:                         130
good ships like ours with cheekpaint[7] at the bows
are far beyond the Kyklopês. No shipwright
toils among them, shaping and building up
symmetrical trim hulls to cross the sea
and visit all the seaboard towns, as men do                    135
who go and come in commerce over water.
This isle—seagoing folk would have annexed it
and built their homestead on it: all good land,
fertile for every crop in season: lush
well-watered meads along the shore, vines in profusion,        140
prairie, clear for the plow, where grain would grow
chin high by harvest time, and rich sub-soil.
The island cover is landlocked, so you need
no hawsers out astern, bow-stones[8] or mooring:
run in and ride there till the day your crews                  145
chafe to be under sail and a fair wind blows.
You'll find good water flowing from a cavern
through dusky poplars into the upper bay.
Here we made harbor. Some god guided us
that night, for we could barely see our bows                   150
in the dense fog around us, and no moonlight
filtered through the overcast. No look-out,
nobody saw the island dead ahead,
nor even the great landward rolling billow
that took us in: we found ourselves in shallows,               155
keels grazing shore: so furled our sails
and disembarked where the low ripples broke.
There on the beach we lay, and slept till morning.

7. On a Greek ship an emblem (often shown as a huge eye on vase-paintings) was painted on the
bows.    8. A primitive anchor made up of a stone attached to a rope.

When Dawn spread out her finger tips of rose
we turned out marvelling, to tour the isle,                               160
while Zeus's shy nymph daughters flushed wild goats
down from the heights—a breakfast for my men.
We ran to fetch our hunting bows and long-shanked
lances from the ships, and in three companies
we took our shots. Heaven gave us game a-plenty:                         165
for every one of twelve ships in my squadron
nine goats fell to be shared; my lot was ten.
So there all day, until the sun went down,
we made our feast on meat galore, and wine—
wine from the ship, for our supply held out,                            170
so many jars were filled at Ísmaros
from stores of the Kikonês that we plundered.
We gazed, too, at Kyklopês Land, so near,
we saw their smoke, heard bleating from their flocks.
But after sundown, in the gathering dusk,                               175
we slept again above the wash of ripples.

When the young Dawn with finger tips of rose
came in the east, I called my men together
and made a speech to them:
                              'Old shipmates, friends,
the rest of you stand by; I'll make the crossing                        180
in my own ship, with my own company,
and find out what the mainland natives are—
for they may be wild savages, and lawless,
or hospitable and god-fearing men.'

At this I went aboard, and gave the word                                185
to cast off by the stern. My oarsmen followed,
filing in to their benches by the rowlocks,
and all in line dipped oars in the grey sea.

As we rowed on, and nearer to the mainland,
at one end of the bay, we saw a cavern                                  190
yawning above the water, screened with laurel,
and many rams and goats about the place
inside a sheepfold—made from slabs of stone
earthfast between tall trunks of pine and rugged
towering oak trees.
                      A prodigious man                                  195
slept in this cave alone, and took his flocks
to graze afield—remote from all companions,
knowing none but savage ways, a brute

so huge, he seemed no man at all of those
who eat good wheaten bread; but he seemed rather                    200
a shaggy mountain reared in solitude.
We beached there, and I told the crew
to stand by and keep watch over the ship;
as for myself I took my twelve best fighters
and went ahead. I had a goatskin full                    205
of that sweet liquor that Euanthês' son,
Maron, had given me. He kept Apollo's
holy grove at Ismaros; for kindness
we showed him there, and showed his wife and child,
he gave me seven shining golden talents[9]                    210
perfectly formed, a solid silver winebowl,
and then this liquor—twelve two-handled jars
of brandy, pure and fiery. Not a slave
in Maron's household knew this drink; only
he, his wife and the storeroom mistress knew;                    215
and they would put one cupful—ruby-colored,
honey-smooth—in twenty more of water,
but still the sweet scent hovered like a fume
over the winebowl. No man turned away
when cups of this came round.                    220
                              A wineskin full
I brought along, and victuals in a bag.
for in my bones I knew some towering brute
would be upon us soon—all outward power,
a wild man, ignorant of civility.

We climbed, then, briskly to the cave. But Kyklops                    225
had gone afield, to pasture his fat sheep,
so we looked round at everything inside:
a drying rack that sagged with cheeses, pens
crowded with lambs and kids, each in its class:
firstlings apart from middlings, and the 'dewdrops,'                    230
or newborn lambkins, penned apart from both.
And vessels full of whey were brimming there—
bowls of earthenware and pails of milking.
My men came pressing round me, pleading:
                              'Why not                    235
take these cheeses, get them stowed, come back,
throw open all the pens, and make a run for it?
We'll drive the kids and lambs aboard. We say
put out again on good salt water!'

9. Ingots of gold; the talent was a standard weight.

Ah,
how sound that was! Yet I refused, I wished                    240
to see the caveman, what he had to offer—
no pretty sight, it turned out, for my friends.
We lit a fire, burnt an offering,
and took some cheese to eat; then sat in silence
around the embers, waiting. When he came                       245
he had a load of dry boughs on his shoulder
to stoke his fire at suppertime. He damped it
with a great crash into that hollow cave,
and we all scattered fast to the far wall.
Then over the broad cavern floor he ushered                    250
the ewes he meant to milk. He left his rams
and he-goats in the yard outside, and swung
high overhead a slab of solid rock
to close the cave. Two dozen four-wheeled wagons,
with heaving wagon teams, could not have stirred               255
the tonnage of that rock from where he wedged it
over the doorsill. Next he took his seat
and milked his bleating ewes. A practiced job
he made of it, giving each ewe her suckling:
thickened his milk, then, into curds and whey,                 260
sieved out the curds to drip in withy baskets,
and poured the whey to stand in bowls
cooling until he drank it for his supper.
When all these chores were done, he poked the fire,
heaping on brushwood. In the glare he saw us.                  265

'Strangers,' he said, 'who are you? And where from?
What brings you here by sea ways—a fair traffic?
Or are you wandering rogues, who cast your lives
like dice, and ravage other folk by sea?'

We felt a pressure on our hearts, in dread                     270
of that deep rumble and that mighty man.
But all the same I spoke up in reply:
'We are from Troy, Akhaians, blown off course
by shifting gales on the Great South Sea;
homeward bound, but taking routes and ways                     275
uncommon; so the will of Zeus would have it.
We served under Agamémnon, son of Atreus—
the whole world knows what city
he laid waste, what armies he destroyed.
It was our luck to come here; here we stand,                   280
beholden for your help, or any gifts

you give[1]—as custom is to honor strangers.
We would entreat you, great Sir, have a care
for the gods' courtesy; Zeus will avenge
the unoffending guest.'
                              He answered this                    285
from his brute chest, unmoved:
                              'You are a ninny,
or else you come from the other end of nowhere,
telling me, mind the gods! We Kyklopês
care not a whistle for your thundering Zeus
or all the gods in bliss; we have more force by far.    290
I would not let you go for fear of Zeus—
you or your friends—unless I had a whim to.
Tell me, where was it, now, you left your ship—
around the point, or down the shore, I wonder?'

He thought he'd find out, but I saw through this,              295
and answered with a ready lie:
                              'My ship?
Poseidon Lord, who sets the earth a-tremble,
broke it up on the rocks at your land's end.
A wind from seaward served him, drove us there.
We are survivors, these good men and I.'                      300

Neither reply nor pity came from him,
but in one stride he clutched at my companions
and caught two in his hands like squirming puppies
to beat their brains out, spattering the floor.
Then he dismembered them and made his meal,                   305
gaping and crunching like a mountain lion—
everything: innards, flesh, and marrow bones.
We cried aloud, lifting our hands to Zeus,
powerless, looking on at this, appalled;
but Kyklops went on filling up his belly                      310
with manflesh and great gulps of whey,
then lay down like a mast among his sheep.
My heart beat high now at the chance of action,
and drawing the sharp sword from my hip I went
along his flank to stab him where the midriff              315
holds the liver. I had touched the spot
when sudden fear stayed me: if I killed him
we perished there as well, for we could never

---

1. It is the mark of civilized men in the *Odyssey*, like Meneláos and Alkínoös, that they welcome
the stranger and send him on his way with gifts.

move his ponderous doorway slab aside.
So we were left to groan and wait for morning.                    320

When the young Dawn with finger tips of rose
lit up the world, the Kyklops built a fire
and milked his handsome ewes, all in due order,
putting the sucklings to the mothers. Then,
his chores being all dispatched, he caught                         325
another brace of men to make his breakfast,
and whisked away his great door slab
to let his sheep go through—but he, behind,
reset the stone as one would cap a quiver.
There was a din of whistling as the Kyklops                        330
rounded his flock to higher ground, then stillness.
And now I pondered how to hurt him worst,
if but Athena granted what I prayed for.

Here are the means I thought would serve my turn:
a club, or staff, lay there along the fold—                        335
an olive tree, felled green and left to season
for Kyklops' hand. And it was like a mast
a lugger of twenty oars, broad in the beam—
a deep-sea going craft—might carry:
so long, so big around, it seemed. Now I                           340
chopped out a six foot section of this pole
and set it down before my men, who scraped it;
and when they had it smooth, I hewed again
to make a stake with pointed end. I held this
in the fire's heart and turned it, toughening it,                  345
then hid it, well back in the cavern, under
one of the dung piles in profusion there.
Now came the time to toss for it: who ventured
along with me? whose hand could bear to thrust
and grind that spike in Kyklops' eye, when mild                    350
sleep had mastered him? As luck would have it,
the men I would have chosen, won the toss—
four men, and I made five as captain.

At evening came the shepherd with his flock,
his woolly flock. The rams as well, this time,                     355
entered the cave: by some sheep-herding whim—
or a god's bidding—none were left outside.
He hefted his great boulder into place
and sat him down to milk the bleating ewes
in proper order, put the lambs to suck,                            360

and swiftly ran through all his evening chores.
Then he caught two more men and feasted on them.
My moment was at hand, and I went forward
holding an ivy bowl of my dark drink,
looking up, saying:
                    'Kyklops, try some wine.                    365
Here's liquor to wash down your scraps of men.
Taste it, and see the kind of drink we carried
under our planks. I meant it for an offering
if you would help us home. But you are mad,
unbearable, a bloody monster! After this,                     370
will any other traveller come to see you?'

He seized and drained the bowl, and it went down
so fiery and smooth he called for more:
'Give me another, thank you kindly. Tell me,
how are you called? I'll make a gift will please you.         375
Even Kyklopês know the wine-grapes grew
out of grassland and loam in heaven's rain,
but here's a bit of nectar and ambrosia!'

Three bowls I brought him and he poured them down.
I saw the fuddle and flush come over him,                     380
then I sang out in cordial tones:
                              'Kyklops,
you ask my honorable name? Remember
the gift you promised me, and I shall tell you.
My name is Nohbdy: mother, father, and friends,
everyone calls me Nohbdy.'

                    And he said:                               385
'Nohbdy's my meat, then, after I eat his friends.
Others come first. There's a noble gift, now.'

Even as he spoke, he reeled and tumbled backward,
his great head lolling to one side; and sleep
took him like any creature. Drunk, hiccuping,                 390
he dribbled streams of liquor and bits of men.

Now, by the gods, I drove my big hand spike
deep in the embers, charring it again,
and cheered my men along with battle talk
to keep their courage up: no quitting now.                    395
The pike of olive, green though it had been,
reddened and glowed as if about to catch.

I drew it from the coals and my four fellows
gave me a hand, lugging it near the Kyklops
as more than natural force nerved them; straight          400
forward they sprinted, lifted it, and rammed it
deep in his crater eye, and I leaned on it
turning it as a shipwright turns a drill
in planking, having men below to swing
the two-handled strap that spins it in the groove.        405
So with our brand we bored that great eye socket
while blood ran out around the red hot bar.
Eyelid and lash were seared; the pierced ball
hissed broiling, and the roots popped.

                              In a smithy
one sees a white-hot axehead or an adze                    410
plunged and wrung in a cold tub, screeching steam—
the way they make soft iron hale and hard—:
just so that eyeball hissed around the spike.
The Kyklops bellowed and the rock roared round him,
and we fell back in fear. Clawing his face                 415
he tugged the bloody spike out of his eye,
threw it away, and his wild hands went groping;
then he set up a howl for Kyklopês
who lived in caves on windy peaks nearby.
Some heard him; and they came by divers ways               420
to clump around outside and call:
                                    'What ails you,
Polyphêmos? Why do you cry so sore
in the starry night? You will not let us sleep.
Sure no man's driving off your flock? No man
has tricked you, ruined you?'
                              Out of the cave              425
the mammoth Polyphêmos roared in answer:
'Nohbdy, Nohbdy's tricked me, Nohbdy's ruined me!'

To this rough shout they made a sage reply;
'Ah well, if nobody has played you foul
there in your lonely bed, we are no use in pain            430
given by great Zeus. Let it be your father,
Poseidon Lord, to whom you pray.'
                              So saying
they trailed away. And I was filled with laughter
to see how like a charm the name deceived them.
Now Kyklops, wheezing as the pain came on him,             435
fumbled to wrench away the great doorstone

and squatted in the breach with arms thrown wide
for any silly beast or man who bolted—
hoping somehow I might be such a fool.
But I kept thinking how to win the game:                              440
death sat there huge; how could we slip away?
I drew on all my wits, and ran through tactics,
reasoning as a man will for dear life,
until a trick came—and it pleased me well.
The Kyklops' rams were handsome, fat, with heavy                       445
fleeces, a dark violet.

           Three abreast
I tied them silently together, twining
cords of willow from the ogre's bed;
then slung a man under each middle one
to ride there safely, shielded left and right.                        450
So three sheep could convey each man. I took
the woolliest ram, the choicest of the flock,
and hung myself under his kinky belly,
pulled up tight, with fingers twisted deep
in sheepskin ringlets for an iron grip.                               455
So, breathing hard, we waited until morning.

When Dawn spread out her finger tips of rose
the rams began to stir, moving for pasture,
and peals of bleating echoed round the pens
where dams with udders full called for a milking.                     460
Blinded, and sick with pain from his head wound,
the master stroked each ram, then let it pass,
but my men riding on the pectoral fleece
the giant's blind hands blundering never found.
Last of them all my ram, the leader, came,                            465
weighted by wool and me with my meditations.
The Kyklops patted him, and then he said:
'Sweet cousin ram, why lag behind the rest
in the night cave? You never linger so,
but graze before them all, and go afar                                470
to crop sweet grass, and take your stately way
leading along the streams, until at evening
you run to be the first one in the fold.
Why, now, so far behind? Can you be grieving
over your Master's eye? That carrion rogue                            475
and his accurst companions burnt it out
when he had conquered all my wits with wine.
Nohbdy will not get out alive, I swear.

Oh, had you brain and voice to tell
where he may be now, dodging all my fury!                               480
Bashed by this hand and bashed on this rock wall
his brains would strew the floor, and I should have
rest from the outrage Nohbdy worked upon me.'
He sent us into the open, then. Close by,
I dropped and rolled clear of the ram's belly,                          485
going this way and that to untie the men.
With many glances back, we rounded up
his fat, stiff-legged sheep to take aboard,
and drove them down to where the good ship lay.
We saw, as we came near, our fellows' faces                             490
shining; then we saw them turn to grief
tallying those who had not fled from death.
I hushed them, jerking head and eyebrows up,
and in a low voice told them: 'Load this herd;
move fast, and put the ship's head toward the breakers.'                495
They all pitched in at loading, then embarked
and struck their oars into the sea. Far out,
as far off shore as shouted words would carry,
I sent a few back to the adversary:
'O Kyklops! Would you feast on my companions?                           500
Puny, am I, in a Caveman's hands?
How do you like the beating that we gave you,
you damned cannibal? Eater of guests
under your roof! Zeus and the gods have paid you!'

The blind thing in his doubled fury broke                               505
a hilltop in his hands and heaved it after us.
Ahead of our black prow it struck and sank
whelmed in a spuming geyser, a giant wave
that washed the ship stern foremost back to shore.
I got the longest boathook out and stood                                510
fending us off, with furious nods to all
to put their backs into a racing stroke—
row, row, or perish. So the long oars bent
kicking the foam sternward, making head
until we drew away, and twice as far.                                   515
Now when I cupped my hands I heard the crew
in low voices protesting:
                    'Godsake, Captain!
Why bait the beast again? Let him alone!'
'That tidal wave he made on the first throw
all but beached us.'

'All but stove us in!'                                520

'Give him our bearing with your trumpeting,
he'll get the range and lob a boulder.'

                                        'Aye
He'll smash our timbers and our heads together!'

I would not heed them in my glorying spirit,
but let my anger flare and yelled:
                            'Kyklops,                 525
if ever mortal man inquire
how you were put to shame and blinded, tell him
Odysseus, raider of cities, took your eye:
Laërtês' son, whose home's on Ithaka!'

At this he gave a mighty sob and rumbled:             530
'Now comes the weird[2] upon me, spoken of old.
A wizard, grand and wondrous, lived here—Télemos,
a son of Eurymos; great length of days
he had in wizardry among the Kyklopês,
and these things he foretold for time to come:        535
my great eye lost, and at Odysseus' hands.
Always I had in mind some giant, armed
in giant force, would come against me here.
But this, but you—small, pitiful and twiggy—
you put me down with wine, you blinded me.            540
Come back, Odysseus, and I'll treat you well,
praying the god of earthquake to befriend you—
his son I am, for he by his avowal
fathered me, and, if he will, he may
heal me of this black wound—he and no other          545
of all the happy gods or mortal men.'

Few words I shouted in reply to him:
'If I could take your life I would and take
your time away, and hurl you down to hell!
The god of earthquake could not heal you there!'      550

At this he stretched his hands out in his darkness
toward the sky of stars, and prayed Poseidon:
'O hear me, lord, blue girdler of the islands,

2. Fate, destiny.

if I am thine indeed, and thou art father:
grant that Odysseus, raider of cities, never                         555
see his home: Laërtês' son, I mean,
who kept his hall on Ithaka. Should destiny
intend that he shall see his roof again
among his family in his father land,
far be that day, and dark the years between.                         560
Let him lose all companions, and return
under strange sail to bitter days at home.'

In these words he prayed, and the god heard him.
Now he laid hands upon a bigger stone
and wheeled around, titanic for the cast,                            565
to let it fly in the black-prowed vessel's track.
But it fell short, just aft the steering oar,
and whelming seas rose giant above the stone
to bear us onward toward the island.
                                              There
as we ran in we saw the squadron waiting,                            570
the trim ships drawn up side by side, and all
our troubled friends who waited, looking seaward.
We beached her, grinding keel in the soft sand,
and waded in, ourselves, on the sandy beach.
Then we unloaded all the Kyklops' flock                              575
to make division, share and share alike,
only my fighters voted that my ram,
the prize of all, should go to me. I slew him
by the sea side and burnt his long thighbones
to Zeus beyond the stormcloud, Kronos' son,                          580
who rules the world. But Zeus disdained my offering;
destruction for my ships he had in store
and death for those who sailed them, my companions.
Now all day long until the sun went down
we made our feast on mutton and sweet wine,                          585
till after sunset in the gathering dark
we went to sleep above the wash of ripples.

When the young Dawn with finger tips of rose
touched the world, I roused the men, gave orders
to man the ships, cast off the mooring lines;                        590
and filing in to sit beside the rowlocks
oarsmen in line dipped oars in the grey sea.
so we moved out, sad in the vast offing,
having our precious lives, but not our friends.

## Book X

### THE GRACE OF THE WITCH

We made our landfall on Aiolia Island,[3]
domain of Aiolos Hippotadês,
the wind king, dear to the gods who never die—
an isle adrift upon the sea, ringed round
with brazen ramparts on a sheer cliffside.                          5
Twelve children had old Aiolos at home—
six daughters and six lusty sons—and he
gave girls to boys to be their gentle brides;
now those lords, in their parents' company,
sup every day in hall—a royal feast                                10
with fumes of sacrifice and winds that pipe
'round hollow courts; and all the night they sleep
on beds of filigree beside their ladies.
Here we put in, lodged in the town and palace,
while Aiolos played host to me. He kept me                         15
one full month to hear the tale of Troy,
the ships and the return of the Akhaians,
all which I told him point by point in order.
When in return I asked his leave to sail
and asked provisioning, he stinted nothing,                        20
adding a bull's hide sewn from neck to tail
into a mighty bag, bottling storm winds;
for Zeus had long ago made Aiolos
warden of winds, to rouse or calm at will.
He wedged this bag under my afterdeck,                             25
lashing the neck with shining silver wire
so not a breath got through; only the west wind
he lofted for me in a quartering breeze
to take my squadron spanking home.
                                     No luck:
the fair wind failed us when our prudence failed.                  30
Nine days and nights we sailed without event,
till on the tenth we raised our land. We neared it,
and saw men building fires along the shore;
but now, being weary to the bone, I fell
into deep slumber; I had worked the sheet                          35
nine days alone, and given it to no one,

3. A moving island, the home of the king of the winds (whose name in Greek means "shifting,
changeable"). It has been located by modern geographers in the Lipari Islands of the Sicilian
coast. The great ancient geographer Eratosthenes was not so confident. He once said that we
would know exactly where Odysseus wandered after we had traced the leatherworker who made
the bag in which the winds were contained.

wishing to spill no wind on the homeward run.
But while I slept, the crew began to parley:
silver and gold, they guessed, were in that bag
bestowed on me by Aiolos' great heart;                              40
and one would glance at his benchmate and say:
'It never fails. He's welcome everywhere:
hail to the captain when he goes ashore!
He brought along so many presents, plunder
out of Troy, that's it. How about ourselves—                       45
his shipmates all the way. Nigh home we are
with empty hands. And who has gifts from Aiolos?
He has. I say we ought to crack that bag,
there's gold and silver, plenty, in that bag!'

Temptation had its way with my companions,                          50
and they untied the bag.
                        Then every wind
roared into hurricane; the ships went pitching
west with many cries; our land was lost.
Roused up, despairing in that gloom, I thought:
"Should I go overside for a quick finish                            55
or clench my teeth and stay among the living?"
Down in the bilge I lay, pulling my sea cloak
over my head, while the rough gale blew the ships
and rueful crews clear back to Aiolia.

We put ashore for water; then all hands                             60
gathered alongside for a mid-day meal.
When we had taken bread and drink, I picked
one soldier, and one herald, to go with me
and called again on Aiolos. I found him
at meat with his young princes and his lady,                        65
but there beside the pillars, in his portico,
we sat down silent at the open door.
The sight amazed them, and they all exclaimed:
'Why back again, Odysseus?'
                        'What sea fiend
rose in your path?'
                        'Did we not launch you well                70
for home, or for whatever land you chose?'

Out of my melancholy I replied:
'Mischief aboard and nodding at the tiller—
a damned drowse—did for me. Make good my loss,
dear friends! You have the power!'

                    Gently I pleaded,                          75
but they turned cold and still. Said Father Aiolos:
'Take yourself out of this island, creeping thing—
no law, no wisdom, lays it on me now
to help a man the blessed gods detest—
out! Your voyage here was cursed by heaven!'            80

He drove me from the place, groan as I would,
and comfortless we went again to sea,
days of it, till the men flagged at the oars—
no breeze, no help in sight, by our own folly—
six indistinguishable nights and days                   85
before we raised the Laistrygonian height
and far stronghold of Lamos.[4] In that land
the daybreak follows dusk, and so the shepherd
homing calls to the cowherd setting out;
and he who never slept could earn two wages,            90
tending oxen, pasturing silvery flocks,
where the low night path of the sun is near
the sun's path by day.[5] Here, then, we found
a curious bay with mountain walls of stone
to left and right, and reaching far inland,—            95
a narrow entrance opening from the sea
where cliffs converged as though to touch and close.
All of my squadron sheltered here, inside
the cavern of this bay.
                    Black prow by prow
those hulls were made fast in a limpid calm            100
without a ripple, stillness all around them.
My own black ship I chose to moor alone
on the sea side, using a rock for bollard;
and climbed a rocky point to get my bearings.
No farms, no cultivated land appeared,                 105
but puffs of smoke rose in the wilderness;
so I sent out two picked men and a herald
to learn what race of men this land sustained.

My party found a track—a wagon road
for bringing wood down from the heights to town;       110
and near the settlement they met a daughter
of Antiphatês the Laistrygon—a stalwart
young girl taking her pail to Artakía,

4. Presumably the founder of the city of the Laistrygonians, a race of man-eating giants.
5. Generally thought to be a confused reference to the short summer nights of the far north.

the fountain where these people go for water.
My fellows hailed her, put their questions to her:                    115
who might the king be? ruling over whom?
She waved her hand, showing her father's lodge,
so they approached it. In its gloom they saw
a woman like a mountain crag, the queen—
and loathed the sight of her. But she, for greeting,                    120
called from the meeting ground her lord and master,
Antiphatês, who came to drink their blood.
He seized one man and tore him on the spot,
making a meal of him; the other two
leaped out of doors and ran to join the ships.                    125
Behind, he raised the whole tribe howling, countless
Laistrygonês—and more than men they seemed,
gigantic when they gathered on the sky line
to shoot great boulders down from slings; and hell's own
crashing rose, and crying from the ships,                    130
as planks and men were smashed to bits—poor gobbets
the wildmen speared like fish and bore away.
But long before it ended in the anchorage—
havoc and slaughter—I had drawn my sword
and cut my own ship's cable. 'Men,' I shouted,                    135
'man the oars and pull till your hearts break
if you would put this butchery behind!'
The oarsmen rent the sea in mortal fear
and my ship spurted out of range, far out
from that deep canyon where the rest were lost.                    140
So we fared onward, and death fell behind,
and we took breath to grieve for our companions.

Our next landfall was on Aiaia, island
of Kirkê, dire beauty and divine,
sister of baleful Aiêtês, like him                    145
fathered by Hêlios the light of mortals
on Persê, child of the Ocean stream.
                                        We came
washed in our silent ship upon her shore,
and found a cove, a haven for the ship—
some god, invisible, conned us in. We landed,                    150
to lie down in that place two days and nights,
worn out and sick at heart, tasting our grief.
But when Dawn set another day a-shining
I took my spear and broadsword, and I climbed
a rocky point above the ship, for sight                    155
or sound of human labor. Gazing out

from that high place over a land of thicket,
oaks and wide watercourses, I could see
a smoke wisp from the woodland hall of Kirkê.
So I took counsel with myself: should I                            160
go inland scouting out that reddish smoke?
No: better not, I thought, but first return
to waterside and ship, and give the men
breakfast before I sent them to explore.
Now as I went down quite alone, and came                           165
a bowshot from the ship, some god's compassion
set a big buck in motion to cross my path—
a stag with noble antlers, pacing down
from pasture in the woods to the riverside,
as long thirst and the power of sun constrained him.               170
He started from the bush and wheeled: I hit him
square in the spine midway along his back
and the bronze point broke through it. In the dust
he fell and whinnied as life bled away.
I set one foot against him, pulling hard                           175
to wrench my weapon from the wound, then left it,
butt-end on the ground. I plucked some withies
and twined a double strand into a rope—
enough to tie the hocks of my huge trophy;
then pickaback I lugged him to the ship,                           180
leaning on my long spearshaft; I could not
haul that mighty carcass on one shoulder.
Beside the ship I let him drop, and spoke
gently and low to each man standing near:
'Come, friends, though hard beset, we'll not go down               185
into the House of Death before our time.
As long as food and drink remain aboard
let us rely on it, not die of hunger.'

At this those faces, cloaked in desolation
upon the waste sea beach, were bared;                              190
their eyes turned toward me and the mighty trophy,
lighting, foreseeing pleasure, one by one.
So hands were washed to take what heaven sent us.
And all that day until the sun went down
we had our fill of venison and wine,                               195
till after sunset in the gathering dusk
we slept at last above the line of breakers.
When the young Dawn with finger tips of rose
made heaven bright, I called them round and said:
'Shipmates, companions in disastrous time,                         200

O my dear friends, where Dawn lies,[6] and the West,
and where the great Sun, light of men, may go
under the earth by night, and where he rises—
of these things we know nothing. Do we know
any least thing to serve us now? I wonder.                                    205
All that I saw when I went up the rock
was one more island in the boundless main,
a low landscape, covered with woods and scrub,
and puffs of smoke ascending in mid-forest.'

They were all silent, but their hearts contracted,                           210
remembering Antiphatês the Laistrygon
and that prodigious cannibal, the Kyklops.
They cried out, and the salt tears wet their eyes.
But seeing our time for action lost in weeping,
I mustered those Akhaians under arms,                                        215
counting them off in two platoons, myself
and my godlike Eurýlokhos commanding.
We shook lots in a soldier's dogskin cap
and his came bounding out—valiant Eurýlokhos!—
So off he went, with twenty-two companions                                   220
weeping, as mine wept, too, who stayed behind.

In the wild wood they found an open glade,
around a smooth stone house—the hall of Kirkê—
and wolves and mountain lions lay there, mild
in her soft spell, fed on her drug of evil.                                  225
None would attack—oh, it was strange, I tell you—
but switching their long tails they faced our men
like hounds, who look up when their master comes
with tidbits for them—as he will—from table.
Humbly those wolves and lions with mighty paws                               230
fawned on our men—who met their yellow eyes
and feared them.
              In the entrance way they stayed
to listen there: inside her quiet house
they heard the goddess Kirkê.
                        Low she sang
in her beguiling voice, while on her loom                                    235
she wove ambrosial fabric sheer and bright,
by that craft known to the goddesses of heaven.
No one would speak, until Politês—most
faithful and likable of my officers, said:

6. In view of the immediately preceding lines, this can hardly be taken literally. It is possibly a
sailor's metaphorical way of saying, "We don't know where we are."

'Dear friends, no need for stealth: here's a young weaver          240
singing a pretty song to set the air
a-tingle on these lawns and paven courts.
Goddess she is, or lady. Shall we greet her?'

So reassured, they all cried out together,
and she came swiftly to the shining doors                         245
to call them in. All but Eurýlokhos—
who feared a snare—the innocents went after her.
On thrones she seated them, and lounging chairs,
while she prepared a meal of cheese and barley
and amber honey mixed with Pramnian wine,[7]                      250
adding her own vile pinch, to make them lose
desire or thought of our dear father land.
Scarce had they drunk when she flew after them
with her long stick and shut them in a pigsty—
bodies, voices, heads, and bristles, all                          255
swinish now, though minds were still unchanged.
So, squealing, in they went. And Kirkê tossed them
acorns, mast, and cornel berries—fodder
for hogs who rut and slumber on the earth.

Down to the ship Eurýlokhos came running                          260
to cry alarm, foul magic doomed his men!
But working with dry lips to speak a word
he could not, being so shaken; blinding tears
welled in his eyes; foreboding filled his heart.
When we were frantic questioning him, at last                     265
we heard the tale: our friends were gone. Said he:
'We went up through the oak scrub where you sent us,
Odysseus, glory of commanders,
until we found a palace in a glade,
a marble house on open ground, and someone                        270
singing before her loom a chill, sweet song—
goddess or girl, we could not tell. They hailed her,
and then she stepped through shining doors and said,
"Come, come in!" Like sheep they followed her,
but I saw cruel deceit, and stayed behind.                        275
Then all our fellows vanished. Not a sound,
and nothing stirred, although I watched for hours.'

When I heard this I slung my silver-hilted
broadsword on, and shouldered my long bow,

7. A harsh, dark wine.

and said, 'Come, take me back the way you came.'                    280
But he put both his hands around my knees
in desperate woe, and said in supplication:
'Not back there, O my lord! Oh, leave me here!
You, even you, cannot return, I know it,
I know you cannot bring away our shipmates;                          285
better make sail with these men, quickly too,
and save ourselves from horror while we may.'

But I replied:
                'By heaven, Eurýlokhos,
rest here then; take food and wine;
stay in the black hull's shelter. Let me go,                         290
as I see nothing for it but to go.'

I turned and left him, left the shore and ship,
and went up through the woodland hushed and shady
to find the subtle witch in her long hall.
But Hermês met me, with his golden wand,                             295
barring the way—a boy whose lip was downy
in the first bloom of manhood, so he seemed.
He took my hand and spoke as though he knew me:[8]

   'Why take the inland path alone,
   poor seafarer, by hill and dale                                  300
   upon this island all unknown?
   Your friends are locked in Kirkê's pale;
   all are become like swine to see;
   and if you go to set them free
   you go to stay, and never more make sail                         305
   for your old home upon Thaki.

   But I can tell you what to do
   to come unchanged from Kirkê's power
   and disenthrall your fighting crew:
   take with you to her bower                                       310
   as amulet, this plant I know—
   it will defeat her horrid show,
   so pure and potent is the flower;
   no mortal herb was ever so.

   Your cup with numbing drops of night                             315
   and evil, stilled of all remorse,

---

8. The four rhymed stanzas which follow are a translator's license; in the original there is no
change of meter and, of course, no rhyme. *Thaki*, below: Ithaka.

she will infuse to charm your sight;
but this great herb with holy force
will keep your mind and senses clear:
when she turns cruel, coming near                                      320
with her long stick to whip you out of doors,
then let your cutting blade appear,

Let instant death upon it shine,
and she will cower and yield her bed—
a pleasure you must not decline,                                       325
so may her lust and fear bestead
you and your friends, and break her spell;
but make her swear by heaven and hell
no witches' tricks, or else, your harness shed,
you'll be unmanned by her as well.'                                    330

He bent down glittering for the magic plant
and pulled it up, black root and milky flower—
a *molü* in the language of the gods—
fatigue and pain for mortals to uproot;
but gods do this, and everything, with ease.                           335

Then toward Olympos through the island trees
Hermês departed, and I sought out Kirkê,
my heart high with excitement, beating hard.
Before her mansion in the porch I stood
to call her, all being still. Quick as a cat                           340
she opened her bright doors and sighed a welcome;
then I strode after her with heavy heart
down the long hall, and took the chair she gave me,
silver-studded, intricately carved,
made with a low footrest. The lady Kirkê                               345
mixed me a golden cup of honeyed wine,
adding in mischief her unholy drug.
I drank, and the drink failed. But she came forward
aiming a stroke with her long stick, and whispered:
'Down in the sty and snore among the rest!'                            350

Without a word, I drew my sharpened sword
and in one bound held it against her throat.
She cried out, then slid under to take my knees,
catching her breath to say, in her distress:
'What champion, of what country, can you be?                           355
Where are your kinsmen and your city?
Are you not sluggish with my wine? Ah, wonder!

Never a mortal man that drank this cup
but when it passed his lips he had succumbed.
Hale must your heart be and your tempered will. 360
Odysseus then you are, O great contender,
of whom the glittering god with golden wand[9]
spoke to me ever, and foretold
the black swift ship would carry you from Troy.
Put up your weapon in the sheath. We two 365
shall mingle and make love upon our bed.
So mutual trust may come of play and love.'

To this I said:
         'Kirkê, am I a boy,
that you should make me soft and doting now?
Here in this house you turned my men to swine; 370
now it is I myself you hold, enticing
into your chamber, to your dangerous bed,
to take my manhood when you have me stripped.
I mount no bed of love with you upon it.
Or swear me first a great oath, if I do, 375
you'll work no more enchantment to my harm.'
She swore at once, outright, as I demanded,
and after she had sworn, and bound herself,
I entered Kirkê's flawless bed of love.

Presently in the hall her maids were busy, 380
the nymphs who waited upon Kirkê: four,
whose cradles were in fountains, under boughs,
or in the glassy seaward-gliding streams.
One came with richly colored rugs to throw
on seat and chairback, over linen covers; 385
a second pulled the tables out, all silver,
and loaded them with baskets all of gold;
a third mixed wine as tawny-mild as honey
in a bright bowl, and set out golden cups.
The fourth came bearing water, and lit a blaze 390
under a cauldron. By and by it bubbled,
and when the dazzling brazen vessel seethed
she filled a bathtub to my waist, and bathed me,
pouring a soothing blend on head and shoulder,
warming the soreness of my joints away. 395
When she had done, and smoothed me with sweet oil,
she put a tunic and a cloak around me

9. Hermes.

and took me to a silver-studded chair
with footrest, all elaborately carven.
Now came a maid to tip a golden jug                              400
of water into a silver finger bowl,
and draw a polished table to my side.
The larder mistress brought her tray of loaves
with many savory slices, and she gave
the best, to tempt me. But no pleasure came;                     405
I huddled with my mind elsewhere, oppressed.

Kirkê regarded me, as there I sat
disconsolate, and never touched a crust.
Then she stood over me and chided me:
'Why sit at table mute, Odysseus?                                410
Are you mistrustful of my bread and drink?
Can it be treachery that you fear again,
after the gods' great oath I swore for you?'
I turned to her at once, and said:
                                        'Kirkê,
where is the captain who could bear to touch                     415
this banquet, in my place? A decent man
would see his company before him first.
Put heart in me to eat and drink—you may,
by freeing my companions. I must see them.'

But Kirkê had already turned away.                               420
Her long staff in her hand, she left the hall
and opened up the sty, I saw her enter,
driving those men turned swine to stand before me.
She stroked them, each in turn, with some new chrism;
and then, behold! their bristles fell away,                      425
the coarse pelt grown upon them by her drug
melted away, and they were men again,
younger, more handsome, taller than before.
Their eyes upon me, each one took my hands,
and wild regret and longing pierced them through,                430
so the room rang with sobs, and even Kirkê
pitied that transformation. Exquisite
the goddess looked as she stood near me, saying:
'Son of Laërtês and the gods of old,
Odysseus, master mariner and soldier,                            435
go to the sea beach and sea-breasting ship;
drag it ashore, full length upon the land;
stow gear and stores in rock-holes under cover;
return; be quick; bring all your dear companions.'

Now, being a man, I could not help consenting.                    440
So I went down to the sea beach and the ship,
where I found all my other men on board,
weeping, in despair along the benches.
Sometimes in farmyards when the cows return
well fed from pasture to the barn, one sees                       445
the pens give way before the calves in tumult,
breaking through to cluster about mothers,
bumping together, bawling. Just that way
my crew poured round me when they saw me come—
their faces wet with tears as if they saw                         450
their homeland, and the crags of Ithaka,
even the very town where they were born.
And weeping still they all cried out in greeting:
'Prince, what joy this is, your safe return!
Now Ithaka seems here, and we in Ithaka!                          455
But tell us now, what death befell our friends?'

And, speaking gently, I replied:
'First we must get the ship high on the shingle,
and stow our gear and stores in clefts of rock
for cover. Then come follow me, to see                            460
your shipmates in the magic house of Kirkê
eating and drinking, endlessly regaled.'

They turned back, as commanded, to this work;
only one lagged, and tried to hold the others;
Eurýlokhos it was, who blurted out:                               465
'Where now, poor remnants? is it devil's work
you long for? Will you go to Kirkê's hall?
Swine, wolves, and lions she will make us all,
beasts of her courtyard, bound by her enchantment.
Remember those the Kyklops held, remember                         470
shipmates who made that visit with Odysseus!
The daring man! They died for his foolishness!'
When I heard this I had a mind to draw
the blade that swung against my side and chop him,
bowling his head upon the ground—kinsman[1]                       475
or no kinsman, close to me though he was.
But others came between, saying, to stop me,
'Prince, we can leave him, if you say the word;
let him stay here on guard. As for ourselves,
show us the way to Kirkê's magic hall.'                           480

1. Eurýlokhos was related to Odysseus by marriage.

So all turned inland, leaving shore and ship,
and Eurýlokhos—he, too, came on behind,
fearing the rough edge of my tongue. Meanwhile
at Kirkê's hands the rest were gently bathed,
anointed with sweet oil, and dressed afresh                    485
in tunics and new cloaks with fleecy linings.
We found them all at supper when we came.
But greeting their old friends once more, the crew
could not hold back their tears; and now again
the rooms rang with sobs. Then Kirkê, loveliest                490
of all immortals, came to counsel me:
'Son of Laërtês and the gods of old.
Odysseus, master mariner and soldier,
enough of weeping fits. I know—I, too—
what you endured upon the inhuman sea,                         495
what odds you met on land from hostile men.
Remain with me, and share my meat and wine;
restore behind your ribs those gallant hearts
that served you in the old days, when you sailed
from stony Ithaka. Now parched and spent,                      500
your cruel wandering is all you think of,
never of joy, after so many blows.'

As we were men we could not help consenting.
So day by day we lingered, feasting long
on roasts and wine, until a year grew fat.                     505
But when the passing months and wheeling seasons
brought the long summery days, the pause of summer,
my shipmates one day summoned me and said:
'Captain, shake off this trance, and think of home—
if home indeed awaits us,
                          if we shall ever see             510
your own well-timbered hall on Ithaka.'

They made me feel a pang, and I agreed.
That day, and all day long, from dawn to sundown,
we feasted on roast meat and ruddy wine,
and after sunset when the dusk came on                         515
my men slept in the shadowy hall, but I
went through the dark to Kirkê's flawless bed
and took the goddess' knees in supplication,
urging, as she bent to hear:
                          'O Kirkê,
now you must keep your promise; it is time.                    520
Help me make sail for home. Day after day

my longing quickens, and my company
give me no peace, but wear my heart away
pleading when you are not at hand to hear.'

The loveliest of goddesses replied:                                    525
'Son of Laërtês and the gods of old,
Odysseus, master mariner and soldier,
you shall not stay here longer against your will;
but home you may not go
unless you take a strange way round and come          530
to the cold homes of Death and pale Perséphonê.[2]
You shall hear prophecy from the rapt shade
of blind Teirêsias of Thebes,[3] forever
charged with reason even among the dead;
to him alone, of all the flitting ghosts,                         535
Perséphonê has given a mind undarkened.'

At this I felt a weight like stone within me,
and, moaning, pressed my length against the bed,
with no desire to see the daylight more.
But when I had wept and tossed and had my fill          540
of this despair, at last I answered her:
'Kirkê, who pilots me upon this journey?
No man has ever sailed to the land of Death.'

That loveliest of goddesses replied:
'Son of Laërtês and gods of old,                                  545
Odysseus, master of land ways and sea ways,
feel no dismay because you lack a pilot;
only set up your mast and haul your canvas
to the fresh blowing North; sit down and steer,
and hold that wind, even to the bourne of Ocean,          550
Perséphonê's deserted stand and grove,
dusky with poplars and the drooping willow.
Run through the tide-rip, bring your ship to shore,
land there, and find the crumbling homes of Death.
Here, toward the Sorrowing Water, run the streams     555
of Wailing, out of Styx, and quenchless Burning[4]—
torrents that join in thunder at the Rock.
Here then, great soldier, setting foot obey me:
dig a well shaft a forearm square; pour out

2. Queen of the underworld.    3. A blind prophet who figures prominently in the legends of
Thebes (he is a character in Sophocles' *Oedipus the King*).    4. Pyriphlegethon, a river of the
underworld, as are the Sorrowing Water (Acheron), the stream of Wailing (Cocytus), and the
Styx.

libations round it to the unnumbered dead:
sweet milk and honey, then sweet wine, and last
clear water, scattering handfulls of white barley.
Pray now, with all your heart, to the faint dead;
swear you will sacrifice your finest heifer,
at home in Ithaka, and burn for them                               565
her tenderest parts in sacrifice; and vow
to the lord Teirêsias, apart from all,
a black lamb, handsomest of all your flock—
thus to appease the nations of the dead.
Then slash a black ewe's throat, and a black ram,                 570
facing the gloom of Erebos;[5] but turn
your head away toward Ocean. You shall see, now
souls of the buried dead in shadowy hosts,
and now you must call out to your companions
to flay those sheep the bronze knife has cut down,                575
for offerings, burnt flesh to those below,
to sovereign Death and pale Perséphonê.
Meanwhile draw sword from hip, crouch down, ward off
the surging phantoms from the bloody pit
until you know the presence of Teirêsias.                         580
He will come soon, great captain; be it he
who gives you course and distance for your sailing
homeward across the cold fish-breeding sea.'

As the goddess ended, Dawn came stitched in gold.
Now Kirkê dressed me in my shirt and cloak,                       585
put on a gown of subtle tissue, silvery,
then wound a golden belt about her waist
and veiled her head in linen,
while I went through the hall to rouse my crew.
I bent above each one, and gently said:                           590
'Wake from your sleep; no more sweet slumber. Come,
we sail: the Lady Kirkê so ordains it.'
They were soon up, and ready at that word;
but I was not to take my men unharmed
from this place, even from this. Among them all                   595
the youngest was Elpênor—
no mainstay in a fight nor very clever—
and this one, having climbed on Kirkê's roof[6]
to taste the cool night, fell asleep with wine.
Waked by our morning voices, and the tramp                        600

5. The darkest region of the underworld, usually imagined as below the underworld itself but
here to the west.    6. A flat roof, and the coolest place to sleep.

of men below, he started up, but missed
his footing on the long steep backward ladder
and fell that height headlong. The blow smashed
the nape cord, and his ghost fled to the dark.
But I was outside, walking with the rest,                                605
saying:
              'Homeward you think we must be sailing
to our own land; no, elsewhere is the voyage
Kirkê has laid upon me. We must go
to the cold homes of Death and pale Perséphonê                           610
to hear Teirêsias tell of time to come.'

They felt so stricken, upon hearing this,
they sat down wailing loud, and tore their hair.
but nothing came of giving way to grief.
Down to the shore and ship at last we went,
bowed with anguish, cheeks all wet with tears,                           615
to find that Kirkê had been there before us
and tied nearby a black ewe and a ram:
she had gone by like air.
For who could see the passage of a goddess
unless she wished his mortal eyes aware?                                 620

## Book XI

### A GATHERING OF SHADES

We bore down on the ship at the sea's edge
and launched her on the salt immortal sea,
stepping our mast and spar in the black ship;
embarked the ram and ewe and went aboard
in tears, with bitter and sore dread upon us.                            5
But now a breeze came up for us astern—
a canvas-bellying landbreeze, hale shipmate
sent by the singing nymph with sun-bright hair;
so we made fast the braces, took our thwarts,
and let the wind and steersman work the ship                             10
with full sail spread all day above our coursing,
till the sun dipped, and all the ways grew dark
upon the fathomless unresting sea.
                          By night
our ship ran onward toward the Ocean's bourne,
the realm and region of the Men of Winter,[7]                           15

7. Although Homer usually places Hades below the earth, here he puts it across a great expanse
of sea, apparently in the far north.

hidden in mist and cloud. Never the flaming
eye of Hêlios lights on those men
at morning, when he climbs the sky of stars,
nor in descending earthward out of heaven;
ruinous night being rove[8] over those wretches.                20
We made the land, put ram and ewe ashore,
and took our way along the Ocean stream
to find the place foretold for us by Kirkê.
There Perimêdês and Eurýlokhos
pinioned the sacred beast. With my drawn blade        25
I spaded up the votive pit, and poured
libations round it to the unnumbered dead:
sweet milk and honey, then sweet wine, and last
clear water; and I scattered barley down.
Then I addressed the blurred and breathless dead,      30
vowing to slaughter my best heifer for them
before she calved, at home in Ithaka,
and burn the choice bits on the altar fire;
as for Teirêsias, I swore to sacrifice
a black lamb, handsomest of all our flock.              35
Thus to assuage the nations of the dead
I pledged these rites, then slashed the lamb and ewe,
letting their black blood stream into the wellpit.
Now the souls gathered, stirring out of Erebos,
brides and young men, and men grown old in pain,        40
and tender girls whose hearts were new to grief;
many were there, too, torn by brazen lanceheads,
battle-slim, bearing still their bloody gear.
From every side they came and sought the pit
with rustling cries; and I grew sick with fear.         45
But presently I gave command to my officers
to flay those sheep the bronze cut down, and make
burnt offerings of flesh to the gods below—
to sovereign Death, to pale Perséphonê.
Meanwhile I crouched with my drawn sword to keep        50
the surging phantoms from the bloody pit
till I should know the presence of Teirêsias.
One shade came first—Elpênor, of our company,
who lay unburied still on the wide earth
as we had left him—dead in Kirkê's hall,               55
untouched, unmourned, when other cares compelled us.
Now when I saw him there I wept for pity
and called out to him:

8. Stretched or spread.

'How is this, Elpênor,
how could you journey to the western gloom
swifter afoot than I in the black lugger?'                                    60

He sighed, and answered:
                              'Son of great Laërtês,
Odysseus, master mariner and soldier,
bad luck shadowed me, and no kindly power;
ignoble death I drank with so much wine.
I slept on Kirkê's roof, then could not see                                    65
the long steep backward ladder, coming down,
and fell that height. My neck bone, buckled under,
snapped, and my spirit found this well of dark.
Now hear the grace I pray for, in the name
of those back in the world, not here—your wife                                 70
and father, he who gave you bread in childhood,
and your own child, your only son, Telémakhos,
long ago left at home.
                        When you make sail
and put these lodgings of dim Death behind,
you will moor ship, I know, upon Aiaia Island;                                 75
there, O my lord, remember me, I pray,
do not abandon me unwept, unburied,
to tempt the gods' wrath, while you sail for home;
but fire my corpse, and all the gear I had,
and build a cairn for me above the breakers—                                   80
an unknown sailor's mark for men to come.
Heap up the mound there and implant upon it
the oar I pulled in life with my companions.'

He ceased, and I replied:
                            'Unhappy spirit,
I promise you the barrow and the burial.'                                      85

So we conversed, and grimly, at a distance,
with my long sword between, guarding the blood,
while the faint image of the lad spoke on.
Now came the soul of Antikleía, dead,
my mother, daughter of Autólykos,                                              90
dead now, though living still when I took ship
for holy Troy. Seeing this ghost I grieved,
but held her off, through pang on pang of tears,
till I should know the presence of Teirêsias.
Soon from the dark that prince of Thebes came forward                          95
bearing a golden staff; and he addressed me:

'Son of Laërtês and the gods of old,
Odysseus, master of land ways and sea ways,
why leave the blazing sun, O man of woe,
to see the cold dead and the joyless region?                    100
Stand clear, put up your sword;
let me but taste of blood, I shall speak true.'

At this I stepped aside, and in the scabbard
let my long sword ring home to the pommel silver,
as he bent down to the sombre blood. Then spoke                    105
the prince of those with gift of speech:[9]
                              'Great captain,
a fair wind and the honey lights of home
are all you seek. But anguish lies ahead;
the god who thunders on the land prepares it,
not to be shaken from your track, implacable,                    110
in rancor for the son whose eye you blinded.
One narrow strait may take you through his blows:
denial of yourself, restraint of shipmates.
When you make landfall on Thrinakia first
and quit the violet sea, dark on the land                    115
you'll find the grazing herds of Hêlios
by whom all things are seen, all speech is known.
Avoid those kine, hold fast to your intent,
and hard seafaring brings you all to Ithaka.
But if you raid the beeves, I see destruction                    120
for ship and crew. Though you survive alone,
bereft of all companions, lost for years,
under strange sail shall you come home, to find
your own house filled with trouble: insolent men
eating your livestock as they court your lady.                    125
Aye, you shall make those men atone in blood!
But after you have dealt out death—in open
combat or by stealth—to all the suitors,
go overland on foot, and take an oar,
until one day you come where men have lived                    130
with meat unsalted, never known the sea,
nor seen seagoing ships, with crimson bows
and oars that fledge light hulls for dipping flight.
The spot will soon be plain to you, and I
can tell you how: some passerby will say,                    135

---

9. Tiresias here predicts the future of Odysseus. Like many Greek prophecies, it contains alternatives. The second (l. 120ff.) is what happens. The journey inland to find a people who have never seen the sea (and so mistake an oar for a winnowing fan—l. 136) does not take place within the *Odyssey* itself.

"What winnowing fan is that upon your shoulder?"
Halt, and implant your smooth oar in the turf
and make fair sacrifice to Lord Poseidon:
a ram, a bull, a great buck boar; turn back,
and carry out pure hekatombs at home                              140
to all wide heaven's lords, the undying gods,
to each in order. Then a seaborne death
soft as this hand of mist will come upon you
when you are wearied out with rich old age,
your country folk in blessed peace around you.                    145
And all this shall be just as I foretell.'

When he had done, I said at once,
                              'Teirêsias,
my life runs on then as the gods have spun it.
But come, now, tell me this; make this thing clear:
I see my mother's ghost among the dead                            150
sitting in silence near the blood. Not once
has she glanced this way toward her son, nor spoken.
Tell me, my lord,
may she in some way come to know my presence?'

To this he answered:
                              'I shall make it clear              155
in a few words and simply. Any dead man
whom you allow to enter where the blood is
will speak to you, and speak the truth; but those
deprived will grow remote again and fade.'
When he had prophesied, Teirêsias' shade                          160
retired lordly to the halls of Death;
but I stood fast until my mother stirred,
moving to sip the black blood; then she knew me
and called out sorrowfully to me:
                              'Child,
how could you cross alive into this gloom                         165
at the world's end?—No sight for living eyes;
great currents run between, desolate waters,
the Ocean first, where no man goes a journey
without ship's timber under him.
                              Say, now,
is it from Troy, still wandering, after years,                    170
that you come here with ship and company?
Have you not gone at all to Ithaka?
Have you not seen your lady in your hall?'

She put these questions, and I answered her:
'Mother, I came here, driven to the land of death                    175
in want of prophecy from Teirêsias' shade;
nor have I yet coasted Akhaia's hills
nor touched my own land, but have had hard roving
since first I joined Lord Agamémnon's host
by sea for Ilion, the wild horse country,                    180
to fight the men of Troy.
But come now, tell me this, and tell me clearly,
what was the bane that pinned you down in Death?
Some ravaging long illness, or mild arrows
a-flying down one day from Artemis?                    185
Tell me of Father, tell me of the son
I left behind me; have they still my place,
my honors, or have other men assumed them?
Do they not say that I shall come no more?
And tell me of my wife: how runs her thought,                    190
still with her child, still keeping our domains,
or bride again to the best of the Akhaians?'

To this my noble mother quickly answered:
'Still with her child indeed she is, poor heart,
still in your palace hall. Forlorn her nights                    195
and days go by, her life used up in weeping.
But no man takes your honored place. Telémakhos
has care of all your garden plots and fields,
and holds the public honor of a magistrate,
feasting and being feasted. But your father                    200
is country bound and comes to town no more.
He owns no bedding, rugs, or fleecy mantles,
but lies down, winter nights, among the slaves,
rolled in old cloaks for cover, near the embers
Or when the heat comes at the end of summer,                    205
the fallen leaves, all round his vineyard plot,
heaped into windrows, make his lowly bed.
He lies now even so, with aching heart,
and longs for your return, while age comes on him.
So I, too, pined away, so doom befell me,                    210
not that the keen-eyed huntress[1] with her shafts
had marked me down and shot to kill me; not
that illness overtook me—no true illness
wasting the body to undo the spirit;

1. Artemis.

only my loneliness for you, Odysseus,                                     215
for your kind heart and counsel, gentle Odysseus,
took my own life away.'
                                    I bit my lip,
rising perplexed, with longing to embrace her,
and tried three times, putting my arms around her,
but she went sifting through my hands, impalpable          220
as shadows are, and wavering like a dream.
Now this embittered all the pain I bore,
and I cried in the darkness:
                                    'O my mother,
will you not stay, be still, here in my arms,
may we not, in this place of Death, as well,               225
hold one another, touch with love, and taste
salt tears' relief, the twinge of welling tears?
Or is this all hallucination, sent
against me by the iron queen, Perséphonê,
to make me groan again?'


                                    My noble mother        230
answered quickly:
                        'O my child—alas,
most sorely tried of men—great Zeus's daughter,
Perséphonê, knits no illusion for you.
All mortals meet this judgment when they die.
No flesh and bone are here, none bound by sinew,           235
since the bright-hearted pyre consumed them down—
the white bones long exanimate—to ash;
dreamlike the soul flies, insubstantial.
You must crave sunlight soon.
                                    Note all things strange
seen here, to tell your lady in after days.'               240


So went our talk; then other shadows came,
ladies in company, sent by Perséphonê—
consorts or daughters of illustrious men—
crowding about the black blood.
                                    I took thought
how best to separate and question them,                    245
and saw no help for it, but drew once more
the long bright edge of broadsword from my hip,
that none should sip the blood in company
but one by one, in order; so it fell
that each declared her lineage and name.                   250

Here was great loveliness of ghosts![2] I saw
before them all, that princess of great ladies,
Tyro,[3] Salmoneus' daughter, as she told me,
and queen to Krêtheus, a son of Aiolos.
She had gone daft for the river Enipeus,[4]                         255
most graceful of all running streams, and ranged
all day by Enipeus' limpid side,
whose form the foaming girdler of the islands,
the god who makes earth tremble, took and so
lay down with her where he sent flooding seaward,                   260
their bower a purple billow, arching round
to hide them in a sea-vale, god and lady.
Now when his pleasure was complete, the god
spoke to her softly, holding fast her hand:
'Dear mortal, go in joy! At the turn of seasons,                    265
winter to summer, you shall bear me sons;
no lovemaking of gods can be in vain.
Nurse our sweet children tenderly, and rear them.
Home with you now, and hold your tongue, and tell
no one your lover's name—though I am yours,                         270
Poseidon, lord of surf that makes earth tremble.'

He plunged away into the deep sea swell,
and she grew big with Pelias and Neleus,[5]
powerful vassals, in their time, of Zeus.
Pelias lived on broad Iolkos seaboard                               275
rich in flocks, and Neleus at Pylos.
As for the sons borne by that queen of women
to Krêtheus, their names were Aison,[6] Pherês,
and Amytháon, expert charioteer.
Next after her I saw Antiopê,                                       280
daughter of Ásopos.[7] She too could boast
a god for lover, having lain with Zeus
and borne two sons to him: Amphion and
Zêthos, who founded Thebes, the upper city,
and built the ancient citadel. They sheltered                       285
no life upon that plain, for all their power,
without a fortress wall.
                        And next I saw

2. There follows a "catalogue of women," a list of famous and beautiful women of former
times.   3. A queen of Thessaly; among her famous descendants were Nestor and Jason.
4. A river of Thessaly. Tyro had fallen in love with the rivergod; Poseidon, the "god who makes
earth tremble," assumed his shape.   5. Father of Nestor of Pylos.   6. Father of Jason, the
Argonaut.   7. A river in Boeotia, the territory of Thebes.

Amphitrion's true wife, Alkmênê, mother,
as all men know, of lionish Heraklês,
conceived when she lay close in Zeus's arms;                    290
and Megarê, high-hearted Kreon's daughter,
wife of Amphitrion's unwearying son.


I saw the mother of Oidipous, Epikastê,[8]
whose great unwitting deed it was
to marry her own son. He took that prize                        295
from a slain father; presently the gods
brought all to light that made the famous story.
But by their fearsome wills he kept his throne
in dearest Thebes, all through his evil days,
while she descended to the place of Death,                      300
god of the locked and iron door. Steep down
from a high rafter, throttled in her noose,
she swung, carried away by pain, and left him
endless agony from a mother's Furies.


And I saw Khloris, that most lovely lady,                       305
whom for her beauty in the olden time
Neleus wooed with countless gifts, and married.
She was the youngest daughter of Amphion,
son of Iasos. In those days he[9] held
power at Orkhómenos, over the Minyai.                           310
At Pylos then as queen she bore her children—
Nestor, Khromios, Periklýmenos,
and Pêro, too, who turned the heads of men
with her magnificence. A host of princes
from nearby lands came courting her; but Neleus                 315
would hear of no one, not unless the suitor
could drive the steers of giant Iphiklos
from Phylakê—longhorns, broad in the brow,
so fierce that one man only, a diviner,[1]
offered to round them up. But bitter fate                       320
saw him bound hand and foot by savage herdsmen.
Then days and months grew full and waned, the year
went wheeling round, the seasons came again,
before at last the power of Iphiklos,
relenting, freed the prisoner, who foretold                     325
all things to him. So Zeus's will was done.

8. Usually known as Jocasta. *Oidipous*: Oedipus.    9. Amphion (not the same Amphion who
founded Thebes, l. 284).    1. Named Melampus.

And I saw Lêda,[2] wife of Tyndareus,
upon whom Tyndareus had sired twins
indomitable: Kastor, tamer of horses,
and Polydeukês, best in the boxing ring.                    330
Those two live still, though life-creating earth
embraces them: even in the underworld
honored as gods by Zeus, each day in turn[3]
one comes alive, the other dies again.

Then after Lêda to my vision came                    335
the wife of Aloeus, Iphimedeia,
proud that she once had held the flowing sea[4]
and borne him sons, thunderers for a day,
the world-renowned Otos and Ephialtês.
Never were men on such a scale                    340
bred on the plowlands and the grainlands, never
so magnificent any, after Orion.[5]
At nine years old they towered nine fathoms tall,
nine cubits in the shoulders, and they promised
furor upon Olympos, heaven broken by battle cries,                    345
the day they met the gods in arms.

                              With Ossa's
mountain peak[6] they meant to crown Olympos
and over Ossa Pelion's forest pile
for footholds up the sky. As giants grown
they might have done it, but the bright son of Zeus[7]                    350
by Lêto of the smooth braid shot them down
while they were boys unbearded; no dark curls
clustered yet from temples to the chin.
Then I saw Phaidra,[8] Prokris; and Ariadnê,
daughter of Minos,[9] the grim king. Theseus took her                    355
aboard with him from Krete for the terraced land
of ancient Athens; but he had no joy of her.
Artemis killed her on the Isle of Dia
at a word from Dionysos.[1]

2. She bore Helen to Zeus; to her husband Tyndareus, she bore the two sons, Castor and Poly-
deuces, and Clytemnestra, who was to be the wife of Agamemnon.    3. They shared, as it were,
one immortality between them.    4. Poseidon.    5. The hunter who was, according to later
legend, transformed into the constellation which still bears his name; in Homer he is in the
underworld after his death (ll. 643ff.).    6. Ossa and Pelion are mountains near Olympus in
Thessaly.    7. Apollo, son of Zeus and Lêto.    8. The Cretan wife of Theseus of Athens, who
fell in love with her stepson Hippolytus. *Prokris:* the unfaithful wife of Cephalus, king of Athens.
*Ariadnê:* sister of Phaedra; she helped Theseus slay the Minotaur on Crete and escaped with him,
only to die on the island of Dia.    9. *Minos:* king of Crete, father of Phaedra and Ariadnê.
1. We have no other account of this version of the episode which explains why Dionysus wanted
Ariadnê killed; the prevalent version of the story in later times is that Dionysus carried Ariadnê off
to be his bride. *Maira:* a nymph of Artemis who broke her vow of chastity and was killed by the
goddess.

Maira, then,
and Klymênê, and that detested queen,                    360
Eríphylê,[2] who betrayed her lord for gold . . .
but how name all the women I beheld there,
daughters and wives of kings? The starry night
wanes long before I close.
                    Here, or aboard ship,
amid the crew, the hour for sleep has come.            365
Our sailing is the gods' affair and yours."[3]


Then he fell silent. Down the shadowy hall
the enchanted banqueters were still. Only
the queen with ivory pale arms, Arêtê, spoke,
saying to all the silent men:
                    "Phaiákians,                        370
how does he stand, now, in your eyes, this captain,
the look and bulk of him, the inward poise?
He is my guest, but each one shares that honor.
Be in no haste to send him on his way
or scant your bounty in his need. Remember             375
how rich, by heaven's will, your possessions are."


Then Ekhenêos, the old soldier, eldest
of all Phaiákians, added his word:
"Friends, here was nothing but our own thought spoken,
the mark hit square. Our duties to her majesty.      380
For what is to be said and done,
we wait upon Alkínoös' command."


At this the king's voice rang:
                    "I so command—
as sure as it is I who, while I live,
rule the sea rovers of Phaiákia. Our friend           385
longs to put out for home, but let him be
content to rest here one more day, until
I see all gifts bestowed. And every man
will take thought for his launching and his voyage,
I most of all, for I am master here."                 390


Odysseus, the great tactician, answered:
"Alkínoös, king and admiration of men,

2. Bribed with a golden necklace by Polynices, son of Oedipus, she persuaded her husband
Amphiaraus to take part in the attack on Thebes, where he was killed. *Klymênê:* some story must
have been attached to this name, but we do not know what it was.    3. Odysseus breaks off the
story of his wanderings, and we are transported back to the scene of the banqueting hall of the
Phaiakians.

even a year's delay, if you should urge it,
in loading gifts and furnishing for sea—
I too could wish it; better far that I                                    395
return with some largesse of wealth about me—
I shall be thought more worthy of love and courtesy
by every man who greets me home in Ithaka."
The king said:

                    "As to that, one word, Odysseus:
from all we see, we take you for no swindler—                            400
though the dark earth be patient of so many,
scattered everywhere, baiting their traps with lies
of old times and of places no one knows.
You speak with art, but your intent is honest.
The Argive troubles, and your own troubles,                              405
you told as a poet would, a man who knows the world.
But now come tell me this: among the dead
did you meet any of your peers, companions
who sailed with you and met their doom at Troy?
Here's a long night—an endless night—before us,                         410
and no time yet for sleep, not in this hall.
Recall the past deeds and the strange adventures.
I could stay up until the sacred Dawn
as long as you might wish to tell your story."


Odysseus the great tactician answered:                                   415
"Alkínoös, king and admiration of men,
there is a time for story telling; there is
also a time for sleep. But even so,
if, indeed, listening be still your pleasure,
I must not grudge my part. Other and sadder                              420
tales there are to tell, of my companions,
of some who came through all the Trojan spears,
clangor and groan of war,
only to find a brutal death at home—
and a bad wife behind it.

                    After Perséphonê,                                    425
icy and pale, dispersed the shades of women,
the soul of Agamémnon, son of Atreus,
came before me, sombre in the gloom,
and others gathered round, all who were with him
when death and doom struck in Aigísthos' hall.                           430
Sipping the black blood, the tall shade perceived me,
and cried out sharply, breaking into tears;
then tried to stretch his hands toward me, but could not,
being bereft of all the reach and power

he once felt in the great torque of his arms.                                    435
Gazing at him, and stirred, I wept for pity,
and spoke across to him:
                              'O son of Atreus,
illustrious Lord Marshal, Agamémnon,
what was the doom that brought you low in death?
Were you at sea, aboard ship, and Poseidon                                       440
blew up a wicked squall to send you under,
or were you cattle-raiding on the mainland
or in a fight for some strongpoint, or women,
when the foe hit you to your mortal hurt?'

But he replied at once:
                              'Son of Laërtês,                                    445
Odysseus, master of land ways and sea ways,
neither did I go down with some good ship
in any gale Poseidon blew, nor die
upon the mainland, hurt by foes in battle.
It was Aigísthos who designed my death,                                          450
he and my heartless wife, and killed me, after
feeding me, like an ox felled at the trough.
That was my miserable end—and with me
my fellows butchered, like so many swine
killed for some troop, or feast, or wedding banquet                              455
in a great landholder's household. In your day
you have seen men, and hundreds, die in war,
in the bloody press, or downed in single combat,
but these were murders you would catch your breath at:
think of us fallen, all our throats cut, winebowl                                460
brimming, tables laden on every side,
while blood ran smoking over the whole floor.
In my extremity I heard Kassandra,[4]
Priam's daughter, piteously crying
as the traitress Klytaimnéstra made to kill her                                  465
along with me. I heaved up from the ground
and got my hands around the blade, but she
eluded me, that whore. Nor would she close
my two eyes[5] as my soul swam to the underworld
or shut my lips. There is no being more fell,                                    470
more bestial than a wife in such an action,
and what an action that one planned!
The murder of her husband and her lord.
Great god, I thought my children and my slaves

4. She was part of Agamémnon's share of the booty at Troy.    5. I.e., give me a proper burial.

at least would give me welcome. But that woman,                      475
plotting a thing so low, defiled herself
and all her sex, all women yet to come,
even those few who may be virtuous.'
He paused then, and I answered:
                          'Foul and dreadful.
That was the way that Zeus who views the wide world                  480
vented his hatred on the sons of Atreus—
intrigues of women, even from the start.
                          Myriads
died by Helen's fault, and Klytaimnéstra
plotted against you half the world away.'

And he at once said:
                          'Let it be a warning                       485
even to you. Indulge a woman never,
and never tell her all you know. Some things
a man may tell, some he should cover up.
Not that I see a risk for you, Odysseus,
of death at your wife's hands. She is too wise,                      490
too clear-eyed, sees alternatives too well,
Penélopê, Ikários' daughter—
that young bride whom we left behind—think of it!—
when we sailed off to war. The baby boy
still cradled at her breast—now he must be                           495
a grown man, and a lucky one. By heaven,
you'll see him yet, and he'll embrace his father
with old fashioned respect, and rightly.
                          My own
lady never let me glut my eyes
on my own son, but bled me to death first.                           500
One thing I will advise, on second thought;
stow it away and ponder it.
                          Land your ship
in secret on your island; give no warning.
The day of faithful wives is gone forever.

But tell me, have you any word at all                                505
about my son's life? Gone to Orkhómenos
or sandy Pylos, can he be? Or waiting
with Meneláos in the plain of Sparta?
Death on earth has not yet taken Orestês.'

But I could only answer:
                          'Son of Atreus,                            510

why do you ask these questions of me? Neither
news of home have I, nor news of him,
alive or dead. And empty words are evil.'

So we exchanged our speech, in bitterness,
weighed down by grief, and tears welled in our eyes,                    515
when there appeared the spirit of Akhilleus,
son of Peleus; then Patróklos' shade,
and then Antílokhos,[6] and then Aias,
first among all the Danaans in strength
and bodily beauty, next to prince Akhilleus.                            520
Now that great runner, grandson of Aíakhos,[7]
recognized me and called across to me:
'Son of Laërtês and the gods of old,
Odysseus, master mariner and soldier,
old knife, what next? What greater feat remains                         525
for you to put your mind on, after this?
How did you find your way down to the dark
where these dimwitted dead are camped forever,
the after images of used-up men?'

                              I answered:
'Akhilleus, Peleus' son, strongest of all                               530
among the Akhaians, I had need of foresight
such as Teirêsias alone could give
to help me, homeward bound for the crags of Ithaka.
I have not yet coasted Akhaia, not yet
touched my land; my life is all adversity.                              535
But was there ever a man more blest by fortune
than you, Akhilleus? Can there ever be?
We ranked you with immortals in your lifetime,
we Argives did, and here your power is royal
among the dead men's shades. Think, then, Akhilleus:                    540
you need not be so pained by death.'
                              To this
he answered swiftly:
'Let me hear no smooth talk
of death from you, Odysseus, light of councils.
Better, I say, to break sod as a farm hand
for some poor country man, on iron rations,                             545
than lord it over all the exhausted dead.
Tell me, what news of the prince my son:[8] did he
come after me to make a name in battle

6. Son of Nestor.    7. Akhilleus.    8. Neoptólemos (the name means "new war").

or could it be he did not? Do you know
if rank and honor still belong to Peleus                             550
in the towns of the Myrmidons? Or now, may be,
Hellas and Phthia spurn him, seeing old age
fetters him, hand and foot. I cannot help him
under the sun's rays, cannot be that man
I was on Troy's wide seaboard, in those days                         555
when I made bastion for the Argives
and put an army's best men in the dust.
Were I but whole again, could I go now
to my father's house, one hour would do to make
my passion and my hands no man could hold                            560
hateful to any who shoulder him aside.'

Now when he paused I answered:
                                'Of all that—
of Peleus' life, that is—I know nothing;
but happily I can tell you the whole story
of Neoptólemos, as you require.                                      565
In my own ship I brought him out from Skyros[9]
to join the Akhaians under arms.
                                And I can tell you,
in every council before Troy thereafter
your son spoke first and always to the point;
no one but Nestor and I could out-debate him.                        570
And when we formed against the Trojan line
he never hung back in the mass, but ranged
far forward of his troops—no man could touch him
for gallantry. Aye, scores went down before him
in hard fights man to man. I shall not tell                          575
all about each, or name them all—the long
roster of enemies he put out of action,
taking the shock of charges on the Argives.
But what a champion his lance ran through
in Eurýpulos[1] the son of Télephos! Keteians                        580
in throngs around that captain also died—
all because Priam's gifts had won his mother
to send the lad to battle; and I thought
Memnon[2] alone in splendor ever outshone him.

But one fact more: while our picked Argive crew                      585
still rode that hollow horse Epeios built,

9. The Greeks were told by a prophet that Troy would fall only to the son of Achilles, who was
living on the rocky island of Skyros.    1. He came to the aid of the Trojans with a fresh army.
*Keteians*: The people of Eurýpulos, from Asia Minor.    2. Son of the dawn goddess, King of
the Ethiopians, and a Trojan ally.

and when the whole thing lay with me, to open
the trapdoor of the ambuscade or not,
at that point our Danaan lords and soldiers
wiped their eyes, and their knees began to quake,　590
all but Neoptólemos. I never saw
his tanned cheek change color or his hand
brush one tear away. Rather he prayed me,
hand on hilt, to sortie, and he gripped
his tough spear, bent on havoc for the Trojans.　595
And when we had pierced and sacked Priam's tall city
he loaded his choice plunder and embarked
with no scar on him; not a spear had grazed him
nor the sword's edge in close work—common wounds
one gets in war. Arês in his mad fits　600
knows no favorites.'

　　　　　　　But I said no more,
for he had gone off striding the field of asphodel,
the ghost of our great runner, Akhilleus Aikidês,[3]
glorying in what I told him of his son.

Now other souls of mournful dead stood by,　605
each with his troubled questioning, but one
remained alone, apart: the son of Télamon,
Aías, it was—the great shade burning still
because I had won favor on the beachhead
in rivalry over Akhilleus' arms.[4]
The Lady Thetis, mother of Akhilleus,
laid out for us the dead man's battle gear,
and Trojan children, with Athena,
named the Danaan fittest to own them. Would
god I had not borne the palm that day!　615
For earth took Aías then to hold forever,
the handsomest and, in all feats of war,
noblest of the Danaans after Akhilleus.
Gently therefore I called across to him:
'Aías, dear son of royal Télamon,　620
you would not then forget, even in death,
your fury with me over those accurst
calamitous arms?—and so they were, a bane
sent by the gods upon the Argive host.

---

3. Akhilleus is the son of Peleus, whose father was Aiakos.　4. After Akhilleus was killed by
the Trojan Paris, his mother Thetis offered his weapons as a prize to the Greek who had done
most harm to the Trojans. They were awarded to Odysseus. Ajax, after an attempt to kill Odysseus
and the two kings, Meneláos and Agamémnon, committed suicide.

For when you died by your own hand we lost                          625
a tower, formidable in war. All we Akhaians
mourn you forever, as we do Akhilleus;
and no one bears the blame but Zeus.
He fixed that doom for you because he frowned
on the whole expedition of our spearmen.                            630
My lord, come nearer, listen to our story!
Conquer your indignation and your pride.'

But he gave no reply, and turned away,
following other ghosts toward Erebos.
Who knows if in that darkness he might still                        635
have spoken, and I answered?
                                    But my heart
longed, after this, to see the dead elsewhere.
And now there came before my eyes Minos,
the son of Zeus, enthroned, holding a golden staff,
dealing out justice among ghostly pleaders                          640
arrayed about the broad doorways of Death.

And then I glimpsed Orion, the huge hunter,
gripping his club, studded with bronze, unbreakable,
with wild beasts he had overpowered in life
on lonely mountainsides, now brought to bay                         645
on fields of asphodel.
                          And I saw Títyos,
the son of Gaia, lying
abandoned over nine square rods of plain.
Vultures, hunched above him, left and right,
rifling his belly, stabbed into the liver,                          650
and he could never push them off.
                                    This hulk
had once committed rape of Zeus's mistress,
Léto, in her glory, when she crossed
the open grass of Panopeus toward Pytho.
Then I saw Tántalos[5] put to the torture:
in a cool pond he stood, lapped round by water
clear to the chin, and being athirst he burned
to slake his dry weasand with drink, though drink
he would not ever again. For when the old man
put his lips down to the sheet of water                             660
it vanished round his feet, gulped underground,
and black mud baked there in a wind from hell.

5. King of Lydia. He was the confidant of the gods and ate at their table, but he betrayed their secrets..

Boughs, too, drooped low above him, big with fruit,
pear trees, pomegranates, brilliant apples,
luscious figs, and olives, ripe and dark;                              665
but if he stretched his hand for one, the wind
under the dark sky tossed the bough beyond him.

Then Sísyphos[6] in torment I beheld
being roustabout to a tremendous boulder.
Leaning with both arms braced and legs driving,                        670
he heaved it toward a height, and almost over,
but then a Power spun him round and sent
the cruel boulder bounding again to the plain.
Whereon the man bent down again to toil,
dripping sweat, and the dust rose overhead.                            675
Next I saw manifest the power of Heraklês—
a phantom, this, for he himself has gone
feasting amid the gods, reclining soft
with Hêbê of the ravishing pale ankles,
daughter of Zeus and Hêra, shod in gold.                               680
But, in my vision, all the dead around him
cried like affrighted birds; like Night itself
he loomed with naked bow and nocked arrow
and glances terrible as continual archery.
My hackles rose at the gold swordbelt he wore                          685
sweeping across him: gorgeous intaglio
of savage bears, boars, lions with wildfire eyes,
swordfights, battle, slaughter, and sudden death—
the smith who had that belt in him, I hope
he never made, and never will make, another.                           690
The eyes of the vast figure rested on me,
and of a sudden he said in kindly tones:
'Son of Laërtês and the gods of old,
Odysseus, master mariner and soldier,
under a cloud, you too? Destined to grinding                           695
labors like my own in the sunny world?
Son of Kroníon Zeus or not, how many
days I sweated out, being bound in servitude
to a man far worse than I, a rough master![7]
He made me hunt this place one time                                    700
to get the watchdog of the dead: no more
perilous task, he thought, could be; but I

---

6. King of Corinth, the archetype of the liar and trickster. We do not know what misdeed he is being punished for in this passage.    7. Heraklês, son of Zeus, was made subject to the orders of Eurýstheus of Argos who ordered him to perform the twelve famous labors. One of them was to bring back from Hades the dog which guarded the gate.

brought back that beast, up from the underworld
Hermês and grey-eyed Athena showed the way.'

And Heraklês, down the vistas of the dead,                              705
faded from sight; but I stood fast, awaiting
other great souls who perished in times past.
I should have met, then, god-begotten Theseus[8]
and Peirithoös, whom both I longed to see,
but first came shades in thousands, rustling                           710
in a pandemonium of whispers, blown together,
and the horror took me that Perséphonê
had brought from darker hell some saurian death's head.
I whirled then, made for the ship, shouted to crewmen
to get aboard and cast off the stern hawsers,                          715
an order soon obeyed. They took their thwarts,
and the ship went leaping toward the stream of Ocean
first under oars, then with a following wind.

## Book XII

### SEA PERILS AND DEFEAT

The ship sailed on, out of the Ocean Stream,
riding a long swell on the open sea
for the Island of Aiaia.
                        Summering Dawn
has dancing grounds there, and the Sun his rising;[9]
but still by night we beached on a sand shelf                           5
and waded in beyond the line of breakers
to fall asleep, awaiting the Day Star.

When the young Dawn with finger tips of rose
made heaven bright, I sent shipmates to bring
Elpênor's body from the house of Kirkê.                                10
We others cut down timber on the foreland,
on a high point, and built his pyre of logs,
then stood by weeping while the flame burnt through
corse and equipment.
                        Then we heaped his barrow,
lifting a gravestone on the mound, and fixed                           15
his light but unwarped oar against the sky.
These were our rites in memory of him. Soon, then,
knowing us back from the Dark Land, Kirkê came

8. After his adventures in Krete, he went with his friend Perithoös to Hades to kidnap Perséphonê;
the venture failed, and the two heroes, imprisoned in Hades, were rescued by Heraklês.    9. This
places Kirkê's island in the east, whereas Odysseus' ship, when it was blown past Cape Malea, was
headed west. It is one more indication that Odyssean geography is highly imaginative.

freshly adorned for us, with handmaids bearing
loaves, roast meats, and ruby-colored wine.                                20
She stood among us in immortal beauty
jesting:

      'Hearts of oak, did you go down
alive into the homes of Death? One visit
finishes all men but yourselves, twice mortal!
Come, here is meat and wine, enjoy your feasting                          25
for one whole day; and in the dawn tomorrow
you shall put out to sea. Sailing directions,
landmarks, perils, I shall sketch for you, to keep you
from being caught by land or water
in some black sack of trouble.'

                 In high humor                    30
and ready for carousal, we agreed;
so all that day until the sun went down
we feasted on roast meat and good red wine,
till after sunset, at the fall of night,
the men dropped off to sleep by the stern hawsers.                        35
She took my hand then, silent in that hush,
drew me apart, made me sit down, and lay
beside me, softly questioning, as I told
all I had seen, from first to last.
                Then said the Lady Kirkê:

'So: all those trials are over.
                 Listen with care                  40
to this, now, and a god will arm your mind.
Square in your ship's path are Seirênês,[1] crying
beauty to bewitch men coasting by;
woe to the innocent who hears that sound!
He will not see his lady nor his children                                 45
in joy, crowding about him, home from sea;
the Seirênês will sing his mind away
on their sweet meadow lolling. There are bones
of dead men rotting in a pile beside them
and flayed skins shrivel around the spot.
                Steer wide;                      50
keep well to seaward; plug your oarsmen's ears
with beeswax kneaded soft; none of the rest
should hear that song.

---

1. Sirens.

But if you wish to listen,
let the men tie you in the lugger, hand
and foot, back to the mast, lashed to the mast,                    55
so you may hear those harpies' thrilling voices;
shout as you will, begging to be untied,
your crew must only twist more line around you
and keep their stroke up, till the singers fade.
What then? One of two courses you may take,                    60
and you yourself must weigh them. I shall not
plan the whole action for you now, but only
tell you of both.

        Ahead are beetling rocks
and dark blue glancing Amphitritê,[2] surging,
roars around them. Prowling Rocks,[3] or Drifters,                    65
the gods in bliss have named them—named them well.
Not even birds can pass them by, not even
the timorous doves that bear ambrosia
to Father Zeus; caught by downdrafts, they die
on rockwall smooth as ice.

        Each time, the Father                    70
wafts a new courier to make up his crew.

Still less can ships get searoom of these Drifters,
whose boiling surf, under high fiery winds,
carries tossing wreckage of ships and men.
Only one ocean-going craft, the far-famed                    75
Argo, made it, sailing from Aiêta;
but she, too, would have crashed on the big rocks
if Hêra had not pulled her through, for love
of Iêson, her captain.

        A second course
lies between headlands. One is a sharp mountain
piercing the sky, with stormcloud round the peak
dissolving never, not in the brightest summer,
to show heaven's azure there, nor in the fall.
No mortal man could scale it, nor so much
as land there, not with twenty hands and feet,                    85
so sheer the cliffs are—as of polished stone.
Midway that height, a cavern full of mist
opens toward Erebos and evening.[4] Skirting
this in the lugger, great Odysseus,

---

2. I.e., the sea.    3. Homer does not precisely identify them with the Symplegades, the
Clashing Rocks which came together and crushed whatever tried to pass between them. They
were thought of as located at the entrance to the Black Sea; the Argo passed safely through them
on its way to the land of the golden fleece. Homer's Prowling Rocks seem to be located, like Scylla
and Charybdis, near the straits between Sicily and Italy.    4. I.e., northwest.

your master bowman, shooting from the deck,                              90
would come short of the cavemouth with his shaft;
but that is the den of Skylla, where she yaps
abominably, a newborn whelp's cry,
though she is huge and monstrous. God or man,
no one could look on her in joy. Her legs—                               95
and there are twelve—are like great tentacles,
unjointed, and upon her serpent necks
are borne six heads like nightmares of ferocity,
with triple serried rows of fangs and deep
gullets of black death. Half her length, she sways                      100
her heads in air, outside her horrid cleft,
hunting the sea around that promontory
for dolphins, dogfish, or what bigger game
thundering Amphitritê feeds in thousands.
And no ship's company can claim                                         105
to have passed her without loss and grief; she takes,
from every ship, one man for every gullet.

The opposite point seems more a tongue of land
you'd touch with a good bowshot, at the narrows.
A great wild fig, a shaggy mass of leaves,                              110
grows on it, and Kharybdis lurks below
to swallow down the dark sea tide. Three times
from dawn to dusk she spews it up
and sucks it down again three times, whirling
maelstrom; if you come upon her then                                    115
the god who makes earth tremble could not save you.
No, hug the cliff of Skylla, take your ship
through on a racing stroke. Better to mourn
six men than lose them all, and the ship, too.'

So her advice ran; but I faced her, saying:                             120

'Only instruct me, goddess, if you will,
how, if possible, can I pass Kharybdis,
or fight off Skylla when she raids my crew?'

Swiftly that loveliest goddess answered me:

'Must you have battle in your heart forever?                            125
The bloody toil of combat? Old contender,
will you not yield to the immortal gods?
That nightmare cannot die, being eternal
evil itself—horror, and pain, and chaos;

there is no fighting her, no power can fight her,                    130
all that avails is flight.
               Lose headway there
along that rockface while you break out arms,
and she'll swoop over you, I fear, once more,
taking one man again for every gullet.
No, no, put all your backs into it, row on;                    135
invoke Blind Force, that bore this scourge of men,
to keep her from a second strike against you.

Then you will coast Thrinákis,[5] the island
where Hêlios' cattle graze, fine herds, and flocks
of goodly sheep. The herds and flocks are seven,                    140
with fifty beasts in each.
               No lambs are dropped,
or calves, and these fat cattle never die.
Immortal, too, their cowherds are—their shepherds—
Phaëthousa and Lampetía, sweetly braided
nymphs that divine Neaira bore                    145
to the overlord of high noon, Hêlios.
These nymphs their gentle mother bred and placed
upon Thrinákia, the distant land,
in care of flocks and cattle for their father.

Now give those kine a wide berth, keep your thoughts                    150
intent upon your course for home,
and hard seafaring brings you all to Ithaka.
But if you raid the beeves, I see destruction
for ship and crew.
               Rough years then lie between
you and your homecoming, alone and old,                    155
the one survivor, all companions lost.'

As Kirkê spoke, Dawn mounted her golden throne,
and on the first rays Kirkê left me, taking
her way like a great goddess up the island.
I made straight for the ship, roused up the men                    160
to get aboard and cast off at the stern.
They scrambled to their places by the rowlocks
and all in line dipped oars in the grey sea.
But soon an off-shore breeze blew to our liking—
a canvas-bellying breeze, a lusty shipmate                    165
sent by the singing nymph with sunbright hair.
So we made fast the braces, and we rested,

5. Later Greeks identified this island as Sicily.

letting the wind and steersman work the ship.
The crew being now silent before me, I
addressed them, sore at heart:

                  'Dear friends,          170
more than one man, or two, should know those things
Kirkê foresaw for us and shared with me,
so let me tell her forecast: then we die
with our eyes open, if we are going to die,
or know what death we baffle if we can. Seirênês     175
weaving a haunting song over the sea
we are to shun, she said, and their green shore
all sweet with clover; yet she urged that I
alone should listen to their song. Therefore
you are to tie me up, tight as a splint,         180
erect along the mast, lashed to the mast,
and if I shout and beg to be untied,
take more turns of the rope to muffle me.'

I rather dwelt on this part of the forecast,
while our good ship made time, bound outward down    185
the wind for the strange island of Seirênês.
Then all at once the wind fell, and a calm
came over all the sea, as though some power
lulled the swell.
            The crew were on their feet
briskly, to furl the sail, and stow it; then,        190
each in place, they poised the smooth oar blades
and sent the white foam scudding by. I carved
a massive cake of beeswax into bits
and rolled them in my hands until they softened—
no long task, for a burning heat came down        195
from Hêlios, lord of high noon. Going forward
I carried wax along the line, and laid it
thick on their ears. They tied me up then, plumb
amidships, back to the mast, lashed to the mast,
and took themselves again to rowing. Soon,       200
as we came smartly within hailing distance,
the two Seirênês, noting our fast ship
off their point, made ready, and they sang:

       *This way, oh turn your bows,*[6]
       *Akhaia's glory,*         205

---

6. Fitzgerald has turned the eight unrhymed lines of the original into a lyric poem. Here is a prose version of the Greek: "Draw near, illustrious Odysseus, flower of Akhaian chivalry, and

As all the world allows—
  Moor and be merry.

Sweet coupled airs we sing.
  No lonely seafarer
Holds clear of entering                    210
  Our green mirror.

Pleased by each purling note
  Like honey twining
From her throat and my throat,
  Who lies a-pining?                    215

Sea rovers here take joy
  Voyaging onward,
As from our song of Troy
Greybeard and rower-boy
  Goeth more learnèd.                    220

All feats on that great field
  In the long warfare,
Dark days the bright gods willed,
  Wounds you bore there,

Argos' old soldiery                    225
  On Troy beach teeming,
Charmed out of time we see.
No life on earth can be
  Hid from our dreaming.

The lovely voices in ardor appealing over the water        230
made me crave to listen, and I tried to say
'Untie me!' to the crew, jerking my brows;
but they bent steady to the oars. Then Perimêdês
got to his feet, he and Eurýlokhos,
and passed more line about, to hold me still.        235
So all rowed on, until the Seirênês
dropped under the sea rim, and their singing
dwindled away.
            My faithful company
rested on their oars now, peeling off

bring your ship to rest so that you may hear our voices. No seaman ever sailed his black ship past this spot without listening to the sweet tones that flow from our lips, and none that has listened has not been delighted and gone on a wiser man. For we know all that the Argives and Trojans suffered on the broad plain of Troy by the will of the gods, and we have foreknowledge of all that is going to happen on this fruitful earth."

the wax that I had laid thick on their ears;                    240
then set me free.
                    But scarcely had that island
faded in blue air than I saw smoke
and white water, with sound of waves in tumult—
a sound the men heard, and it terrified them.
Oars flew from their hands; the blades went knocking         245
wild alongside till the ship lost way,
with no oarblades to drive her through the water.


Well, I walked up and down from bow to stern,
trying to put heart into them, standing over
every oarsman, saying gently,


                    'Friends,                                   250
have we never been in danger before this?
More fearsome, is it now, than when the Kyklops
penned us in his cave? What power he had!
Did I not keep my nerve, and use my wits
to find a way out for us?
                    Now I say                                   255
by hook or crook this peril too shall be
something that we remember.
                    Heads up, lads!
We must obey the orders as I give them.
Get the oarshafts in your hands, and lay back
hard on your benches; hit these breaking seas.               260
Zeus help us pull away before we founder.
You at the tiller, listen, and take in
all that I say—the rudders are your duty;
keep her out of the combers and the smoke;
steer for that headland; watch the drift, or we              265
fetch up in the smother, and you drown us.'


That was all, and it brought them round to action.
But as I sent them on toward Skylla, I
told them nothing, as they could do nothing.
They would have dropped their oars again, in panic,          270
to roll for cover under the decking. Kirkê's
bidding against arms had slipped my mind,
so I tied on my cuirass and took up
two heavy spears, then made my way along
to the foredeck—thinking to see her first from there,       275
the monster of the grey rock, harboring
torment for my friends. I strained my eyes

upon that cliffside veiled in cloud, but nowhere
could I catch sight of her.
                              And all this time,
in travail, sobbing, gaining on the current,                    280
we rowed into the strait—Skylla to port
and on our starboard beam Kharybdis, dire
gorge of the salt sea tide. By heaven! when she
vomited, all the sea was like a cauldron
seething over intense fire, when the mixture                    285
suddenly heaves and rises.
                              The shot spume
soared to the landside heights, and fell like rain.

But when she swallowed the sea water down
we saw the funnel of the maelstrom, heard
the rock bellowing all around, and dark                         290
sand raged on the bottom far below.
My men all blanched against the gloom, our eyes
were fixed upon that yawning mouth in fear
of being devoured.
                              Then Skylla made her strike,
whisking six of my best men from the ship.                      295
I happened to glance aft at ship and oarsmen
and caught sight of their arms and legs, dangling
high overhead. Voices came down to me
in anguish, calling my name for the last time.

A man surfcasting on a point of rock                            300
for bass or mackerel, whipping his long rod
to drop the sinker and the bait far out,
will hook a fish and rip it from the surface
to dangle wriggling through the air:
                              so these
were borne aloft in spasms toward the cliff.                    305

She ate them as they shrieked there, in her den,
in the dire grapple, reaching still for me—
and deathly pity ran me through
at that sight—far the worst I ever suffered,
questing the passes of the strange sea.
                              We rowed on.                      310
The Rocks were now behind; Kharybdis, too,
and Skylla dropped astern.
                              Then we were coasting
the noble island of the god, where grazed

those cattle with wide brows, and bounteous flocks
of Hêlios, lord of noon, who rides high heaven.                     315

From the black ship far still at sea, I heard
the lowing of the cattle winding home
and sheep bleating; and heard, too, in my heart
the words of blind Teirêsias of Thebes
and Kirkê of Aiaia: both forbade me                                320
the island of the world's delight, the Sun.
So I spoke out in gloom to my companions:

'Shipmates, grieving and weary though you are,
listen: I had forewarning from Teirêsias
and Kirkê, too; both told me I must shun                           325
this island of the Sun, the world's delight.
Nothing but fatal trouble shall we find here.
Pull away, then, and put the land astern.'
That strained them to the breaking point, and, cursing,
Eurýlokhos cried out in bitterness:                                330

'Are you flesh and blood, Odysseus, to endure
more than a man can? Do you never tire?
God, look at you, iron is what you're made of.
Here we all are, half dead with weariness,
falling asleep over the oars, and you                              335
say "No landing"—no firm island earth
where we could make a quiet supper. No:
pull out to sea, you say, with night upon us—
just as before, but wandering now, and lost.
Sudden storms can rise at night and swamp                          340
ships without a trace.
                        Where is your shelter
if some stiff gale blows up from south or west—
the winds that break up shipping every time
when seamen flout the lord gods' will? I say
do as the hour demands and go ashore                               345
before black night comes down.
                        We'll make our supper
alongside, and at dawn put out to sea.'

Now when the rest said 'Aye' to this, I saw
the power of destiny devising ill.
Sharply I answered, without hesitation:                            350

'Eurýlokhos, they are with you to a man.
I am alone, outmatched.

Let this whole company
swear me a great oath: Any herd of cattle
or flock of sheep here found shall go unharmed;
no one shall slaughter out of wantonness 355
ram or heifer; all shall be content
with what the goddess Kirkê put aboard.'

They fell at once to swearing as I ordered,
and when the round of oaths had ceased, we found
a halfmoon bay to beach and moor the ship in, 360
with a fresh spring nearby. All hands ashore
went about skillfully getting up a meal.
Then, after thirst and hunger, those besiegers,
were turned away, they mourned for their companions
plucked from the ship by Skylla and devoured, 365
and sleep came soft upon them as they mourned.

In the small hours of the third watch, when stars
that shone out in the first dusk of evening
had gone down to their setting, a giant wind
blew from heaven, and clouds driven by Zeus 370
shrouded land and sea in a night of storm;
so, just as Dawn with finger tips of rose
touched the windy world, we dragged our ship
to cover in a grotto, a sea cave
where nymphs had chairs of rock and sanded floors. 375
I mustered all the crew and said:

'Old shipmates,
our stores are in the ship's hold, food and drink;
the cattle here are not for our provision,
or we pay dearly for it.
                    Fierce the god is
who cherishes these heifers and these sheep:
Hêlios; and no man avoids his eye.'

To this my fighters nodded. Yes. But now
we had a month of onshore gales, blowing
day in, day out—south winds, or south by east.
As long as bread and good red wine remained 385
to keep the men up, and appease their craving,
they would not touch the cattle. But in the end,
when all the barley in the ship was gone,
hunger drove them to scour the wild shore
with angling hooks, for fishes and sea fowl, 390

whatever fell into their hands; and lean days
wore their bellies thin.

                 The storms continued.
So one day I withdrew to the interior
to pray the gods in solitude, for hope
that one might show me some way of salvation.         395
Slipping away, I struck across the island
to a sheltered spot, out of the driving gale.
I washed my hands there, and made supplication
to the gods who own Olympos, all the gods—
but they, for answer, only closed my eyes        400
under slow drops of sleep.
                  Now on the shore Eurýlokhos
made his insidious plea:
                     'Comrades,' he said,
'You've gone through everything; listen to what I say.
All deaths are hateful to us, mortal wretches,
but famine is the most pitiful, the worst        405
end that a man can come to.
                    Will you fight it?
Come, we'll cut out the noblest of these cattle
for sacrifice to the gods who own the sky;
and once at home, in the old country of Ithaka,
if ever that day comes—        410
we'll build a costly temple and adorn it
with every beauty for the Lord of Noon.
But if he flares up over his heifers lost,
wishing our ship destroyed, and if the gods
make cause with him, why, then I say: Better        415
open your lungs to a big sea once for all
than waste to skin and bones on a lonely island!'

Thus Eurýlokhos; and they murmured 'Aye!'
trooping away at once to round up heifers.
Now, that day tranquil cattle with broad brows        420
were grazing near, and soon the men drew up
around their chosen beasts in ceremony.
They plucked the leaves that shone on a tall oak—
having no barley meal—to strew the victims,
performed the prayers and ritual, knifed the kine        425
and flayed each carcass, cutting thighbones free
to wrap in double folds of fat. These offerings,
with strips of meat, were laid upon the fire.
Then, as they had no wine, they made libation

with clear spring water, broiling the entrails first;                    430
and when the bones were burnt and tripes shared,
they spitted the carved meat.
                              Just then my slumber
left me in a rush, my eyes opened,
and I went down the seaward path. No sooner
had I caught sight of our black hull, than savory                    435
odors of burnt fat eddied around me;
grief took hold of me, and I cried aloud:

'O Father Zeus and gods in bliss forever,
you made me sleep away this day of mischief!
O cruel drowsing, in the evil hour!                    440
Here they sat, and a great work they contrived.'

Lampetía in her long gown meanwhile
had borne swift word to the Overlord of Noon:

'They have killed your kine.'

                              And the Lord Hêlios
burst into angry speech amid the immortals:                    445

'O Father Zeus and gods in bliss forever,
punish Odysseus' men! So overweening,
now they have killed my peaceful kine, my joy
at morning when I climbed the sky of stars,
and evening, when I bore westward from heaven.                    450
Restitution or penalty they shall pay—
and pay in full—or I go down forever
to light the dead men in the underworld.'

Then Zeus who drives the stormcloud made reply:

'Peace, Hêlios: shine on among the gods,                    455
shine over mortals in the fields of grain.
Let me throw down one white-hot bolt, and make
splinters of their ship in the winedark sea.'

—Kalypso later told me of this exchange,
as she declared that Hermês had told her.                    460
Well, when I reached the sea cave and the ship,
I faced each man, and had it out; but where
could any remedy be found? There was none.
The silken beeves of Hêlios were dead.

The gods, moreover, made queer signs appear:                        465
cowhides began to crawl, and beef, both raw
and roasted, lowed like kine upon the spits.

Now six full days my gallant crew could feast
upon the prime beef they had marked for slaughter
from Hêlios' herd; and Zeus, the son of Kronos,                     470
added one fine morning.
                        All the gales
had ceased, blown out, and with an offshore breeze
we launched again, stepping the mast and sail,
to make for the open sea. Astern of us
the island coastline faded, and no land                             475
showed anywhere, but only sea and heaven,
when Zeus Kroníon piled a thunderhead
above the ship, while gloom spread on the ocean.
we held our course, but briefly. Then the squall
struck whining from the west, with gale force, breaking             480
both forestays, and the mast came toppling aft
along the ship's length, so the running rigging
showered into the bilge.
                        On the after deck
the mast had hit the steersman a slant blow
bashing the skull in, knocking him overside,                        485
as the brave soul fled the body, like a diver.
With crack on crack of thunder, Zeus let fly
a bolt against the ship, a direct hit,
so that she bucked, in reeking fumes of sulphur,
and all the men were flung into the sea.                            490
They came up 'round the wreck, bobbing a while
like petrels on the waves.
                        No more seafaring
homeward for these, no sweet day of return;
the god had turned his face from them.
                                        I clambered
fore and aft my hulk until a comber                                 495
split her, keel from ribs, and the big timber
floated free; the mast, too, broke away.
A backstay floated dangling from it, stout
rawhide rope, and I used this for lashing
mast and keel together. These I straddled,                          500
riding the frightful storm.
                        Nor had I yet
seen the worst of it: for now the west wind

dropped, and a southeast gale came on—one more
twist of the knife—taking me north again,
straight for Kharybdis. All that night I drifted,                 505
and in the sunrise, sure enough, I lay
off Skylla mountain and Kharybdis deep.
There, as the whirlpool drank the tide, a billow
tossed me, and I sprang for the great fig tree,
catching on like a bat under a bough.                 510
Nowhere had I to stand, no way of climbing,
the root and bole being far below, and far
above my head the branches and their leaves,
massed, overshadowing Kharybdis pool.
But I clung grimly, thinking my mast and keel                 515
would come back to the surface when she spouted.
And ah! how long, with what desire, I waited!
till, at the twilight hour, when one who hears
and judges pleas in the marketplace all day
between contentious men, goes home to supper,                 520
the long poles at last reared from the sea.

Now I let go with hands and feet, plunging
straight into the foam beside the timbers,
pulled astride, and rowed hard with my hands
to pass by Skylla. Never could I have passed her                 525
had not the Father of gods and men, this time,
kept me from her eyes. Once through the strait,
nine days I drifted in the open sea
before I made shore, buoyed up by the gods,
upon Ogýia Isle. The dangerous nymph                 530
Kalypso lives and sings there, in her beauty,
and she received me, loved me.

                                    But why tell
the same tale that I told last night in hall
to you and to your lady? Those adventures
made a long evening, and I do not hold                 535
with tiresome repetition of a story."

## Book XIII

### ONE MORE STRANGE ISLAND

He ended it, and no one stirred or sighed
in the shadowy hall spellbound as they all were,
until Alkínoös answered:

                                    "When you came
here to my strong home, Odysseus, under
my tall roof, headwinds were left behind you.                                    5
Clear sailing shall you have now, homeward now,
however painful all the past.
                                    My lords,
ever my company, sharing the wine of Council,
the songs of the blind harper, hear me further:
garments are folded for our guest and friend                                    10
in the smooth chest, and gold
in various shaping of adornment lies
with other gifts, and many, brought by our peers;
let each man add his tripod and deep-bellied
cauldron: we'll make levy upon the realm                                    15
to pay us for the loss each bears in this."

Alkínoös had voiced their own hearts' wish.
All gave assent, then home they went to rest;
but young Dawn's finger tips of rose, touching
the world, roused them to make haste to the ship,                                    20
each with his gift of noble bronze. Alkínoös,
their ardent king, stepping aboard himself,
directed the stowing under the cross planks,
not to cramp the long pull of the oarsmen.
Going then to the great hall, lords and crew                                    25
prepared for feasting.
                                    As the gods' anointed,
Alkíoös made offering on their behalf—an ox
to Zeus beyond the stormcloud, Kronos' son,
who rules the world. They burnt the great thighbones
and feasted at their ease on fresh roast meat,                                    30
as in their midst the godlike harper sang—
Demódokos, honored by all that realm.
                                    Only Odysseus
time and again turned craning toward the sun,
impatient for day's end, for the open sea.
Just as a farmer's hunger grows, behind                                    35
the bolted plow and share, all day afield,
drawn by his team of winedark oxen: sundown
is benison for him, sending him homeward
stiff in the knees from weariness, to dine;
just so, the light on the sea rim gladdened Odysseus,                                    40
and as it dipped he stood among the Phaiákians,
turned to Alkínoös, and said:

"O king and admiration of your people,
give me fare well, and stain the ground with wine;
my blessings on you all! This hour brings                          45
fulfillment to the longing of my heart:
a ship for home, and gifts the gods of heaven
make so precious and so bountiful.

                              After this voyage
god grant I find my own wife in my hall
with everyone I love best, safe and sound!                         50
And may you, settled in your land, give joy
to wives and children; may the gods reward you
every way, and your realm be free of woe."


Then all the voices rang out, "Be it so!"
and "Well spoken!" and "Let our friend make sail!"                 55
Whereon Alkínoös gave command to his crier:


"Fill the winebowl, Pontónoös: mix and serve:
go the whole round, so may this company
invoke our Father Zeus, and bless our friend,
seaborne tonight and bound for his own country."                   60
Pontónoös mixed the honey-hearted wine
and went from chair to chair, filling the cups;
then each man where he sat poured out his offering
to the gods in bliss who own the sweep of heaven.
With gentle bearing Odysseus rose, and placed                      65
his double goblet in Arêtê's hands,
saying:


         "Great Queen, farewell;
be blest through all your days till age comes on you,
and death, last end for mortals, after age.
Now I must go my way. Live in felicity,                            70
and make this palace lovely for your children,
your countrymen, and your king, Alkínoös."


Royal Odysseus turned and crossed the door sill,
a herald at his right hand, sent by Alkónoös
to lead him to the sea beach and the ship.                         75
Arêtê, too, sent maids in waiting after him,
one with a laundered great cloak and a tunic,
a second balancing the crammed sea chest,
a third one bearing loaves and good red wine.
As soon as they arrived alongside, crewmen
took these things for stowage under the planks,

their victualling and drink; then spread a rug
and linen cover on the after deck,
where Lord Odysseus might sleep in peace.
Now he himself embarked, lay down, lay still,                    85
while oarsmen took their places at the rowlocks
all in order. They untied their hawser,
passing it through a drilled stone ring; then bent
forward at the oars and caught the sea
as one man, stroking.
                Slumber, soft and deep                    90
like the still sleep of death, weighed on his eyes
as the ship hove seaward.
                How a four horse team
whipped into a run on a straightaway
consumes the road, surging and surging over it!
So ran that craft and showed her heels to the swell,             95
her bow wave riding after, and her wake
on the purple night-sea foaming.
                Hour by hour
she held her pace; not even a falcon wheeling
downwind, swiftest bird, could stay abreast of her
in that most arrowy flight through open water,                   100
with her great passenger—godlike in counsel,
he that in twenty years had borne such blows
in his deep heart, breaking through ranks in war
and waves on the bitter sea.
                This night at last
he slept serene, his long-tried mind at rest.                    105

When on the East the sheer bright star arose
that tells of coming Dawn, the ship made landfall
and came up islandward in the dim of night.
Phorkys, the old sea baron, has a cave
here in the realm of Ithaka; two points                          110
of high rock, breaking sharply, hunch around it,
making a haven from the plunging surf
that gales at sea roll shoreward. Deep inside,
at mooring range, good ships can ride unmoored.
There, on the inmost shore, an olive tree                        115
throws wide its boughs over the bay; nearby
a cave of dusky light is hidden
for those immortal girls, the Naiadês.[7]
Within are winebowls hollowed in the rock

7. Nymphs of lake, river, and stream.

and amphorai; bees bring their honey here;                    120
and there are looms of stone, great looms, whereon
the weaving nymphs make tissues, richly dyed
as the deep sea is; and clear springs in the cavern
flow forever. Of two entrances,
one on the north allows descent of mortals,                   125
but beings out of light alone, the undying,
can pass by the south slit; no men come there.

This cove the sailors knew. Here they drew in,
and the ship ran half her keel's length up the shore,
she had such way on her from those great oarsmen.            130
Then from their benches forward on dry ground
they disembarked. They hoisted up Odysseus
unruffled on his bed, under his cover,
handing him overside still fast asleep,
to lay him on the sand; and they unloaded                     135
all those gifts the princes of Phaiákia
gave him, when by Athena's heart and will
he won his passage home. They bore this treasure
off the beach, and piled it close around
the roots of the olive tree, that no one passing              140
should steal Odysseus' gear before he woke.
That done, they pulled away on the homeward track.

But now the god that shakes the islands, brooding
over old threats of his against Odysseus,
approached Lord Zeus to learn his will. Said he:             145

"Father of gods, will the bright immortals ever
pay me respect again, if mortals do not?—
Phaiákians, too, my own blood kin?
                              I thought
Odysseus should in time regain his homeland;
I had no mind to rob him of that day—                         150
no, no; you promised it, being so inclined;
only I thought he should be made to suffer
all the way.
                    But now these islanders
have shipped him homeward, sleeping soft, and put him
on Ithaka, with gifts untold                                  155
of bronze and gold, and fine cloth to his shoulder.
Never from Troy had he borne off such booty
if he had got home safe with all his share."
Then Zeus who drives the stormcloud answered, sighing:

"God of horizons, making earth's underbeam                    160
tremble, why do you grumble so?
The immortal gods show you no less esteem,
and the rough consequence would make them slow
to let barbs fly at their eldest and most noble.
But if some mortal captain, overcome                          165
by his own pride of strength, cuts or defies you,
are you not always free to take reprisal?
Act as your wrath requires and as you will."

Now said Poseidon, god of earthquake:

                            "Aye,
god of the stormy sky, I should have taken                    170
vengeance, as you say, and on my own;
but I respect, and would avoid, your anger.
The sleek Phaiákian cutter, even now,
has carried out her mission and glides home
over the misty sea. Let me impale her,                        175
end her voyage, and end all ocean-crossing
with passengers, then heave a mass of mountain
in a ring around the city."

Now Zeus who drives the stormcloud said benignly:

"Here is how I should do it, little brother:                  180
when all who watch upon the wall have caught
sight of the ship, let her be turned to stone—
an island like a ship, just off the bay.
Mortals may gape at that for generations!
But throw no mountain round the sea port city."[8]           185

When he heard this, Poseidon, god of earthquake,
departed for Skhería, where the Phaiákians
are born and dwell. Their ocean-going ship
he saw already near, heading for harbor;
so up behind her swam the island-shaker                       190
and struck her into stone, rooted in stone, at one
blow of his palm,
                  then took to the open sea.

8. This translates a correction of the text made in antiquity by the Alexandrian scholar Aristophanes of Byzantium. But another great Alexandrian scholar, Aristarchus, defended the original text, which means "and throw a big mountain round." Zeus, in other words, approved of Poseidon's intention to cut the Phaiákians off from the sea altogether, and adds the proposal to turn the ship into a rock. It is a difficult question to decide, since Homer does not tell us what happened to the Phaiákians in the end.

Those famous ship handlers, the Phaiákians,
gazed at each other, murmuring in wonder;
you could have heard one say:

                          "Now who in thunder                    195
has anchored, moored that ship in the seaway,
when everyone could see her making harbor?"


The god had wrought a charm beyond their thought.
But soon Alkínoös made them hush, and told them:


"This present doom upon the ship—on me—                          200
my father prophesied in the olden time.
If we gave safe conveyance to all passengers
we should incur Poseidon's wrath, he said,
whereby one day a fair ship, manned by Phaiákians,
would come to grief at the god's hands; and great                205
mountains would hide our city from the sea.
So my old father forecast.
                          Use your eyes:
these things are even now being brought to pass.
Let all here abide by my decree:
                          We make
an end henceforth of taking, in our ships,                       210
castaways who may land upon Skhería;
and twelve choice bulls we dedicate at once
to Lord Poseidon, praying him of his mercy
not to heave up a mountain round our city."


In fearful awe they led the bulls to sacrifice                   215
and stood about the altar stone, those captains,
peers of Phaiákia, led by their king in prayer
to Lord Poseidon.


Meanwhile, on his island,
his father's shore, that kingly man, Odysseus,
awoke, but could not tell what land it was                       220
after so many years away; moreover,
Pallas Athena, Zeus's daughter, poured
a grey mist all around him, hiding him
from common sight—for she had things to tell him
and wished no one to know him, wife or townsmen,                 225
before the suitors paid up for their crimes.

The landscape then looked strange, unearthly strange
to the Lord Odysseus: paths by hill and shore,
glimpses of harbors, cliffs, and summer trees.
He stood up, rubbed his eyes, gazed at his homeland,                    230
and swore, slapping his thighs with both his palms,
then cried aloud:

        "What am I in for now?
Whose country have I come to this time? Rough
savages and outlaws, are they, or
godfearing people, friendly to castaways?                              235
Where shall I take these things? Where take myself,
with no guide, no directions? These should be
still in Phaiákian hands, and I uncumbered,
free to find some other openhearted
prince who might be kind and give me passage.                          240
I have no notion where to store this treasure;
first-comer's trove it is, if I leave it here.

My lords and captains of Phaiákia
were not those decent men they seemed, not honorable,
landing me in this unknown country—no,                                 245
by god, they swore to take me home to Ithaka
and did not! Zeus attend to their reward,
Zeus, patron of petitioners, who holds
all other mortals under his eye; he takes
payment from betrayers!
             I'll be busy.                                     250
I can look through my gear. I shouldn't wonder
if they pulled out with part of it on board."

He made a tally of his shining pile—
tripods, cauldrons, cloaks, and gold—and found
he lacked nothing at all.
          And then he wept,                                       255
despairing, for his own land, trudging down
beside the endless wash of the wide, wide sea,
weary and desolate as the sea. But soon
Athena came to him from the nearby air,
putting a young man's figure on—a shepherd,                            260
like a king's son, all delicately made.
She wore a cloak, in two folds off her shoulders,
and sandals bound upon her shining feet.
A hunting lance lay in her hands.
               At sight of her

Odysseus took heart, and he went forward                                        265
to greet the lad, speaking out fair and clear:

"Friend, you are the first man I've laid eyes on
here in this cove. Greetings. Do not feel
alarmed or hostile, coming across me; only
receive me into safety with my stores.                                          270
Touching your knees I ask it, as I might
ask grace of a god.
     O sir, advise me,
what is this land and realm, who are the people?
Is it an island all distinct, or part
of the fertile mainland, sloping to the sea?"                                   275

To this grey-eyed Athena answered:

        "Stranger,
you must come from the other end of nowhere,
else you are a great booby, having to ask
what place this is. It is no nameless country.
Why, everyone has heard of it, the nations                                      280
over on the dawn side, toward the sun,
and westerners in cloudy lands of evening.
No one would use this ground for training horses,
it is too broken, has no breadth of meadow;
but there is nothing meager about the soil,                                      285
the yield of grain is wondrous, and wine, too,
with drenching rains and dewfall.
       There's good pasture
for oxen and for goats, all kinds of timber,
and water all year long in the cattle ponds.
For these blessings, friend, the name of Ithaka                                 290
has made its way even as far as Troy—
and they say Troy lies far beyond Akhaia."

Now Lord Odysseus, the long-enduring,
laughed in his heart, hearing his land described
by Pallas Athena, daughter of Zeus who rules                                    295
the veering stormwind; and he answered her
with ready speech—not that he told the truth,
but, just as she did, held back what he knew,
weighing within himself at every step
what he made up to serve his turn.

        Said he:                          300

"Far away in Krete I learned of Ithaka—
in that broad island over the great ocean.
And here I am now, come myself to Ithaka!
Here is my fortune with me. I left my sons
an equal part, when I shipped out. I killed      305
Orsílokhos, the courier, son of Idómeneus.
This man could beat the best cross country runners
in Krete, but he desired to take away
my Trojan plunder, all I had fought and bled for,
cutting through ranks in war and the cruel sea.      310
Confiscation is what he planned; he knew
I had not cared to win his father's favor
as a staff officer in the field at Troy,
but led my own command.
                I acted: I
hit him with a spearcast from a roadside      315
as he came down from the open country. Murky
night shrouded all heaven and the stars.
I made that ambush with one man at arms.
We were unseen. I took his life in secret,
finished him off with my sharp sword. That night      320
skippered by gentlemen of Phoinikia;[9] I gave
all they could wish, out of my store of plunder,
for passage, and for landing me at Pylos
or Elis Town,[1] where the Epeioi are in power.      325
Contrary winds carried them willy-nilly
past that coast; they had no wish to cheat me,
but we were blown off course.
                Here, then, by night
we came, and made this haven by hard rowing.
All famished, but too tired to think of food,      330
each man dropped in his tracks after the landing,
and I slept hard, being wearied out. Before
I woke today, they put my things ashore
on the sand here beside me where I lay,
then reimbarked for Sidon, that great city.      335
Now they are far at sea, while I am left
forsaken here."

        At this the grey-eyed goddess
Athena smiled, and gave him a caress,
her looks being changed now, so she seemed a woman,

---

9. Phoenicia.     1. In the Western Peloponnese. *Epeioi:* The local tribe.

tall and beautiful and no doubt skilled                              340
at weaving splendid things. She answered briskly:

"Whoever gets around you must be sharp
and guileful as a snake; even a god
might bow to you in ways of dissimulation.
You! You chameleon!                                                  345
Bottomless bag of tricks! Here in your own country
would you not give your stratagems a rest
or stop spellbinding for an instant?

You play a part as if it were your own tough skin.

No more of this, though. Two of a kind, we are,                      350
contrivers, both. Of all men now alive
you are the best in plots and story telling.
My own fame is for wisdom among the gods—
deceptions, too.
                    Would even you have guessed
that I am Pallas Athena, daughter of Zeus,                           355
I that am always with you in times of trial,
a shield to you in battle, I who made
the Phaiákians befriend you, to a man?
Now I am here again to counsel with you—
but first to put away those gifts the Phaiákians                     360
gave you at departure—I planned it so.
Then I can tell you of the gall and wormwood
it is your lot to drink in your own hall.
Patience, iron patience, you must show;
so give it out to neither man nor woman                              365
that you are back from wandering. Be silent
under all injuries, even blows from men."

His mind ranging far, Odysseus answered:

"Can mortal man be sure of you on sight,
even a sage, O mistress of disguises?                                370
Once you were fond of me—I am sure of that—
years ago, when we Akhaians made
war, in our generation, upon Troy.
But after we had sacked the shrines of Priam
and put to sea, God scattered the Akhaians                           375
I never saw you after that, never
knew you aboard with me, to act as shield

354    HOMER

in grievous times—not till you gave me comfort
in the rich hinterland of the Phaiákians
and were yourself my guide into that city.                                    380

Hear me now in your father's name, for I
cannot believe that I have come to Ithaka.
It is some other land. You made that speech
only to mock me, and to take me in.
Have I come back in truth to my home island?"                                 385

To this the grey-eyed goddess Athena answered:

"Always the same detachment! That is why
I cannot fail you, in your evil fortune,
coolheaded, quick, well-spoken as you are!
Would not another wandering man, in joy,                                      390
make haste home to his wife and children? Not
you, not yet. Before you hear their story
you will have proof about your wife.
                                        I tell you,
she still sits where you left her, and her days
and nights go by forlorn, in lonely weeping.                                  395
For my part, never had I despaired; I felt
sure of your coming home, though all your men
should perish; but I never cared to fight
Poseidon, Father's brother, in his baleful
rage with you for taking his son's eye.                                       400

Now I shall make you see the shape of Ithaka.
Here is the cove the sea lord Phorkys owns,
there is the olive spreading out her leaves
over the inner bay, and there the cavern
dusky and lovely, hallowed by the feet                                        405
of those immortal girls, the Naiadês—
the same wide cave under whose vault you came
to honor them with hekatombs—and there
Mount Neion, with his forest on his back!"

She had dispelled the mist, so all the island                                 410
stood out clearly. Then indeed Odysseus'
heart stirred with joy. He kissed the earth,
and lifting up his hands prayed to the nymphs:

"O slim shy Naiadês, young maids of Zeus,
I had not thought to see you ever again!

O listen smiling                    415
to my gentle prayers, and we'll make offering
plentiful as in the old time, granted I
live, granted my son grows tall, by favor
of great Athena, Zeus's daughter,
who gives the winning fighter his reward!"                420

The grey-eyed goddess said directly:

"Courage;
and let the future trouble you no more.
We go to make a cache now, in the cave,
to keep your treasure hid. Then we'll consider
how best the present action may unfold."                425
The goddess turned and entered the dim cave,
exploring it for crannies, while Odysseus
carried up all the gold, the fire-hard bronze,
and well-made clothing the Phaiákians gave him.
Pallas Athena, daughter of Zeus the storm king,                430
placed them, and shut the cave mouth with a stone,
and under the old grey olive tree those two
sat down to work the suitors death and woe.
Grey-eyed Athena was the first to speak, saying:

"Son of Laërtês and the gods of old,                435
Odysseus, master of land ways and sea ways,
put your mind on a way to reach and strike
a crowd of brazen upstarts.
                        Three long years
they have played master in your house: three years
trying to win your lovely lady, making                440
gifts as though betrothed. And she? Forever
grieving for you, missing your return,
she has allowed them all to hope, and sent
messengers with promises to each—
though her true thoughts are fixed elsewhere."

                        At this                445
the man of ranging mind, Odysseus, cried:

"So hard beset! An end like Agamémnon's
might very likely have been mine, a bad end,
bleeding to death in my own hall. You forestalled it,
goddess, by telling me how the land lies.                450
Weave me a way to pay them back! And you, too,

take your place with me, breathe valor in me
the way you did that night when we Akhaians
unbound the bright veil from the brow of Troy!
O grey-eyed one, fire my heart and brace me!                                    455
I'll take on fighting men three hundred strong
if you fight at my back, immortal lady!"

The grey-eyed goddess Athena answered him:
"No fear but I shall be there; you'll go forward
under my arm when the crux comes at last.                                       460
And I foresee your vast floor stained with blood,
spattered with brains of this or that tall suitor
who fed upon your cattle.
                                    Now, for a while,
I shall transform you; not a soul will know you,
the clear skin of your arms and legs shriveled,                                 465
your chestnut hair all gone, your body dressed
in sacking that a man would gag to see,
and the two eyes, that were so brilliant, dirtied—
contemptible, you shall seem to your enemies,
as to the wife and son you left behind.                                         470

But join the swineherd first—the overseer
of all your swine, a good soul now as ever,
devoted to Penélopê and your son.
He will be found near Raven's Rock and the well
of Arethousa, where the swine are pastured,                                     475
rooting for acorns to their hearts' content,
drinking the dark still water. Boarflesh grows
pink and fat on that fresh diet. There
stay with him, and question him, while I
am off to the great beauty's land of Sparta,                                    480
to call your son Telémakhos home again—
for you should know, he went to the wide land
of Lakedaimon, Meneláos' country,
to learn if there were news of you abroad."

Odysseus answered:

                                    "Why not tell him, knowing                  485
my whole history, as you do? Must he
traverse the barren sea, he too, and live
in pain, while others feed on what is his?"

At this the grey-eyed goddess Athena said:

"No need for anguish on that lad's account.                      490
I sent him off myself, to make his name
in foreign parts—no hardship in the bargain,
taking his ease in Meneláos' mansion,
lapped in gold.
                    The young bucks here, I know,
lie in wait for him in a cutter, bent                            495
on murdering him before he reaches home.
I rather doubt they will. Cold earth instead
will take in her embrace a man or two
of those who fed so long on what is his."

Speaking no more, she touched him with her wand,                 500
shriveled the clear skin of his arms and legs,
made all his hair fall out, cast over him
the wrinkled hide of an old man, and bleared
both his eyes, that were so bright. Then she
clapped an old tunic, a foul cloak, upon him,                    505
tattered, filthy, stained by greasy smoke,
and over that a mangy big buck skin.
A staff she gave him, and a leaky knapsack
with no strap but a loop of string.
                                    Now then,                     510
their colloquy at an end, they went their ways—
Athena toward illustrious Lakedaimon
far over sea, to join Odysseus' son.

## Book XIV

### HOSPITALITY IN THE FOREST

He went up from the cove through wooded ground,
taking a stony trail into the high hills, where
the swineherd lived, according to Athena.
Of all Odysseus' field hands in the old days
this forester cared most for the estate;                          5
and now Odysseus found him
in a remote clearing, sitting inside the gate
of a stockade he built to keep the swine
while his great lord was gone.
                                    Working alone,
far from Penélopê and old Laërtês,                                10
he had put up a fieldstone hut and timbered it
with wild pear wood. Dark hearts of oak he split
and trimmed for a high palisade around it,
and built twelve sties adjoining in this yard

to hold the livestock. Fifty sows with farrows          15
were penned in each, bedded upon the earth,
while the boars lay outside—fewer by far,
as those well-fatted were for the suitors' table,
fine pork, sent by the swineherd every day.
Three hundred sixty now lay there at night,          20
guarded by dogs—four dogs like wolves, one each
for the four lads the swineherd reared and kept
as under-herdsmen.
              When Odysseus came,
the good servant sat shaping to his feet
oxhide for sandals, cutting the well-cured leather.          25
Three of his young men were afield, pasturing
herds in other woods; one he had sent
with a fat boar for tribute into town,
the boy to serve while the suitors got their fill.

The watch dogs, when they caught sight of Odysseus,          30
faced him, a snarling troop, and pelted out
viciously after him. Like a tricky beggar
he sat down plump, and dropped his stick. No use.
They would have rolled him in the dust and torn him
there by his own steading if the swineherd          35
had not sprung up and flung his leather down,
making a beeline for the open. Shouting,
throwing stone after stone,
he made them scatter; then turned to his lord
and said:
        "You might have got a ripping, man!          40
Two shakes more and a pretty mess for me
you could have called it, if you had the breath.
As though I had not trouble enough already,
given me by the gods, my master gone,
true king that he was. I hang on here,          45
still mourning for him, raising pigs of his
to feed foreigners, and who knows where the man is,
in some far country among strangers! Aye—
if he is living still, if he still sees the light of day.

Come to the cabin. You're a wanderer too.          50
You must eat something, drink some wine, and tell me
where you are from and the hard times you've seen."

The forester now led him to his hut
and made a couch for him, with tips of fir

piled for a mattress under a wild goat skin,                              55
shaggy and thick, his own bed covering.
                                        Odysseus,
in pleasure at this courtesy, gently said:

"May Zeus and all the gods give you your heart's desire
for taking me in so kindly, friend."

                              Eumaios—
O my swineherd!² —answered him:

                                  "Tush, friend,                          60
rudeness to a stranger is not decency,
poor though he may be, poorer than you.
                              All wanderers
and beggars come from Zeus. What we can give
is slight but well-meant—all we dare. You know
that is the way of slaves, who live in dread                              65
of masters—new ones like our own.
                              I told you
the gods, long ago, hindered our lord's return.
He had a fondness for me, would have pensioned me
with acres of my own, a house, a wife
that other men admired and courted; all                                   70
gifts good-hearted kings bestow for service,
for a life work the bounty of god has prospered—
for it does prosper here, this work I do.
Had he grown old in his own house, my master
would have rewarded me. But the man's gone.                               75
God curse the race of Helen and cut it down,
that wrung the strength out of the knees of many!
And he went, too—for the honor of Agamémnon
he took ship overseas for the wild horse country
of Troy, to fight the Trojans."

                              This being told.                            80
he tucked his long shirt up inside his belt
and strode into the pens for two young porkers.
He slaughtered them and singed them at the fire,
flayed and quartered them, and skewered the meat

2. This direct address by the poet to one of his characters is confined to Eumaios; it occurs frequently in connection with his name through Books XIV–XVII. A medieval commentator suggested that it showed a special affection for Eumaios on Homer's part, but since in the *Iliad* a similar form of address is used for five different characters (among them the god Apollo and the obscure Melanippos) this seems unlikely. In the case of Eumaios it may have been a formula devised to avoid hiatus (clashing vowels).

to broil it all; then gave it to Odysseus                            85
hot on the spits. He shook out barley meal,
took a winebowl of ivy wood and filled it,
and sat down facing him, with a gesture, saying:

"There is your dinner, friend, the pork of slaves.
Our fat shoats are all eaten by the suitors,                         90
cold-hearted men, who never spare a thought
for how they stand in the sight of Zeus. The gods
living in bliss are fond of no wrongdoing,
but honor discipline and right behavior.
Even the outcasts of the earth, who bring                            95
piracy from the sea, and bear off plunder
given by Zeus in shiploads—even those men
deep in their hearts tremble for heaven's eye.
But the suitors, now, have heard some word, some oracle
of my lord's death, being so unconcerned                            100
to pay court properly or to go about their business.
All they want is to prey on his estate,
proud dogs; they stop at nothing. Not a day
goes by, and not a night comes under Zeus,
but they make butchery of our beeves and swine—                     105
not one or two beasts at a time, either.
As for swilling down wine, they drink us dry.
Only a great domain like his could stand it—
greater than any on the dusky mainland
or here in Ithaka. Not twenty heroes                                110
in the whole world were as rich as he. I know:
I could count it all up: twelve herds in Elis,
as many flocks, as many herds of swine,
and twelve wide-ranging herds of goats, as well,
attended by his own men or by others—                               115
out at the end of the island, eleven herds
are scattered now, with good men looking after them,
and every herdsman, every day, picks out
a prize ram to hand over to those fellows.
I too as overseer, keeper of swine,                                 120
must go through all my boars and send the best."

While he ran on, Odysseus with zeal
applied himself to the meat and wine, but inwardly
his thought shaped woe and ruin for the suitors.
When he had eaten all that he desired                               125
and the cup he drank from had been filled again
with wine—a welcome sight—,
he spoke, and the words came light upon the air:

"Who is this lord who once acquired you,
so rich, so powerful, as you describe him?                    130
You think he died for Agamémnon's honor.
Tell me his name: I may have met someone
of that description in my time. Who knows?
Perhaps only the immortal gods could say
if I should claim to have seen him: I have roamed          135
about the world so long."

                    The swineherd answered
as one who held a place of trust:

                    "Well, man,
his lady and his son will put no stock
in any news of him brought by a rover.
Wandering men tell lies for a night's lodging,              140
for fresh clothing; truth doesn't interest them.
Every time some traveller comes ashore
he has to tell my mistress his pretty tale,
and she receives him kindly, questions him,
remembering her prince, while the tears run               145
down her cheeks—and that is as it should be
when a woman's husband has been lost abroad.
I suppose you, too, can work your story up
at a moment's notice, given a shirt or cloak.
No: long ago wild dogs and carrion                        150
birds, most like, laid bare his ribs on land
where life had left him. Or it may be, quick fishes
picked him clean in the deep sea, and his bones
lie mounded over in sand upon some shore.
One way or another, far from home he died,                155
a bitter loss, and pain, for everyone,
certainly for me. Never again shall I
have for my lot a master mild as he was
anywhere—not even with my parents
at home, where I was born and bred. I miss them           160
less than I do him—though a longing comes
to set my eyes on them in the old country.
No, it is the lost man I ache to think of—
Odysseus. And I speak the name respectfully,
even if he is not here. He loved me, cared for me.         165
I call him dear my lord, far though he be."

Now royal Odysseus, who had borne the long war,
spoke again:

       "Friend, as you are so dead sure
he will not come—and so mistrustful, too—
let me not merely talk, as others talk,
but swear to it: your lord is now at hand.          170
And I expect a gift for this good news
when he enters his own hall. Till then I would not
take a rag, no matter what my need.
I hate as I hate Hell's own gate that weakness       175
that makes a poor man into a flatterer.
Zeus be my witness, and the table garnished
for true friends, and Odysseus' own hearth—
by heaven, all I say will come to pass!
He will return, and he will be avenged               180
on any who dishonor his wife and son."

Eumaios— O my swineherd!—answered him:

"I take you at your word, then: you shall have
no good news gift from me. Nor will Odysseus         185
enter his hall. But peace! drink up your wine.
Let us talk now of other things. No more
imaginings. It makes me heavy-hearted
when someone brings my master back to mind—
my own true master.
                 No, by heaven,                      190
let us have no oaths! But if Odysseus
can come again god send he may! My wish
is that of Penélopê and old Laërtês
and Prince Telémakhos.
                    Ah, he's another
to be distressed about—Odysseus' child,             195
Telémakhos! By the gods' grace he grew
like a tough sapling, and I thought he'd be
no less a man than his great father—strong
and admirably made; but then someone,
god or man, upset him, made him rash,                200
so that he sailed away to sandy Pylos
to hear news of his father. Now the suitors
lie in ambush on his homeward track,
ready to cut away the last shoot of Arkêsios'[3]
line, the royal stock of Ithaka.
                       No good                        205
dwelling on it. Either he'll be caught
or else Kroníon's[4] hand will take him through.

3. Father of Laërtês, grandfather of Odysseus.   4. Zeus, son of Kronos.

Tell me, now, of your own trials and troubles.
And tell me truly first, for I should know,
who are you, where do you hail from, where's your home          210
and family? What kind of ship was yours,
and what course brought you here? Who are your sailors?
I don't suppose you walked here on the sea."

To this the master of improvisation answered:

"I'll tell you all that, clearly as I may.                      215
If we could sit here long enough, with meat
and good sweet wine, warm here, in peace and quiet
within doors, while the work of the world goes on—
I might take all this year to tell my story
and never end the tale of misadventures                         220
that wore my heart out, by the gods' will.

My native land is the wide seaboard of Krete
where I grew up. I had a wealthy father,
and many other sons were born to him
of his true lady. My mother was a slave,                        225
his concubine; but Kastor Hylákidês,
my father, treated me as a true born son.
High honor came to him in that part of Krete
for wealth and ease, and sons born for renown,
before the death-bearing Kêrês drew him down                    230
to the underworld. His avid sons thereafter
dividing up the property by lot
gave me a wretched portion, a poor house.
But my ability won me a wife
of rich family. Fool I was never called,                        235
nor turn-tail in a fight.
                          My strength's all gone,
but from the husk you may divine the ear
that stood tall in the old days. Misery owns me
now, but then great Arês and Athena
gave me valor and man-breaking power,                           240
whenever I made choice of men-at-arms
to set a trap with me for my enemies.
Never, as I am a man, did I fear Death
ahead, but went in foremost in the charge,
putting a spear through any man whose legs                      245
were not as fast as mine. That was my element,
war and battle. Farming I never cared for,
nor life at home, nor fathering fair children.

I reveled in long ships with oars; I loved
polished lances, arrows in the skirmish,                           250
the shapes of doom that others shake to see.
Carnage suited me; heaven put those things
in me somehow. Each to his own pleasure!
Before we young Akhaians shipped for Troy
I led men on nine cruises in corsairs                              255
to raid strange coasts, and had great luck, taking
rich spoils on the spot, and even more
in the division. So my house grew prosperous,
my standing therefore high among the Kretans.
Then came the day when Zeus who views the wide world              260
drew men's eyes upon that way accurst
that wrung the manhood from the knees of many!
Everyone pressed me, pressed King Idómeneus
to take command of ships for Ilion.
No way out; the country rang with talk of it.                     265
So we Akhaians had nine years of war.
In the tenth year we sacked the inner city,
Priam's town, and sailed for home; but heaven
dispersed the Akhaians. Evil days for me
were stored up in the hidden mind of Zeus.                        270
One month, no more, I stayed at home in joy
with children, wife, and treasure. Lust for action
drove me to go to sea then, in command
of ships and gallant seamen bound for Egypt.
Nine ships I fitted out; my men signed on                         275
and came to feast with me, as good shipmates,
for six full days. Many a beast I slaughtered
in the gods' honor, for my friends to eat.
Embarking on the seventh, we hauled sail
and filled away from Krete on a fresh north wind                  280
effortlessly, as boats will glide down stream.
All rigging whole and all hands well, we rested,
letting the wind and steersmen work the ships,
for five days; on the fifth we made the delta.[5]
I brought my squadron in to the river bank                        285
with one turn of the sweeps. There, heaven knows,
I told the men to wait and guard the ships
while I sent out patrols to rising ground.
But reckless greed carried them all away
to plunder the rich bottomlands; they bore off                    290
wives and children, killed what men they found.

5. Of the Nile.

When this news reached the city, all who heard it
came at dawn. On foot they came, and horsemen,
filling the river plain with dazzle of bronze;
and Zeus lord of lightning                                    295
threw my men into blind panic: no one dared
stand against that host closing around us.
Their scything weapons left our dead in piles,
but some they took alive, into forced labor.
And I—ah, how I wish that I had died                          300
in Egypt, on that field! So many blows
awaited me!— Well, Zeus himself inspired me;
I wrenched my dogskin helmet off my head,
dropped my spear, dodged out of my long shield,
ran for the king's chariot and swung on                       305
to embrace and kiss his knees. He pulled me up,
took pity on me, placed me on the footboards,
and drove home with me crouching there in tears.
Aye—for the troops, in battle fury still,
made one pass at me after another, pricking me                310
with spears, hoping to kill me. But he saved me,
for fear of the great wrath of Zeus that comes
when men who ask asylum are given death.

Seven years, then, my sojourn lasted there,
and I amassed a fortune, going about                          315
among the openhanded Egyptians.
But when the eighth came round, a certain
Phoinikian adventurer came too,
a plausible rat, who had already done
plenty of devilry in the world.

                              This fellow                     320
took me in completely with his schemes,
and led me with him to Phoinikia,
where he had land and houses. One full year
I stayed there with him, to the month and day,
and when fair weather came around again                       325
he took me in a deepsea ship for Libya,
pretending I could help in the cargo trade;
he meant, in fact, to trade me off, and get
a high price for me. I could guess the game
but had to follow him aboard. One day                         330
on course due west, off central Krete, the ship
caught a fresh norther, and we ran southward
before the wind while Zeus piled ruin ahead.

When Krete was out of sight astern, no land
anywhere to be seen, but sky and ocean,                                335
Kroníon put a dark cloud in the zenith
over the ship, and gloom spread on the sea.
With crack on crack of thunder, he let fly
a bolt against the ship, a direct hit,
so that she bucked, in sacred fumes of sulphur,                        340
and all the men were flung into the water.
They came up round the wreck, bobbing a while
like petrels on the waves. No homecoming
for these, from whom the god had turned his face!
Stunned in the smother as I was, yet Zeus                              345
put into my hands the great mast of the ship—
a way to keep from drowning. So I twined
my arms and legs around it in the gale
and stayed afloat nine days. On the tenth night,
a big surf cast me up in Thesprotia.[6]                                350
Pheidon the king there gave me refuge, nobly,
with no talk of reward. His son discovered me
exhausted and half dead with cold, and gave me
a hand to bear me up till he reached home
where he could clothe me in a shirt and cloak.                         355
In that king's house I heard news of Odysseus,
who lately was a guest there, passing by
on his way home, the king said; and he showed me
the treasure that Odysseus had brought:
bronze, gold, and iron wrought with heavy labor—                       360
in that great room I saw enough to last
Odysseus' heirs for ten long generations.
The man himself had gone up to Dodona[7]
to ask the spelling leaves of the old oak
the will of God: how to return, that is,                               365
to the rich realm of Ithaka, after so long
an absence—openly, or on the quiet.
And, tipping wine out, Pheidon swore to me
the ship was launched, the seaman standing by
to take Odysseus to his land at last.                                  370
But he had passage first for me: Thesprotians
were sailing, as luck had it, for Doulíkhion,[8]
the grain-growing island; there, he said,
they were to bring me to the king, Akastos.
Instead, that company saw fit to plot                                  375

6. On the west coast of the Greek mainland, north of Ithaka.     7. An oracle of Zeus. The
message of the god was supposed to come from the sacred oak, perhaps from the rushing of the
leaves in the wind.     8. An island off the west coast of Greece.

foul play against me; in my wretched life
there was to be more suffering.
                              At sea, then,
when land lay far astern, they sprang their trap.
They'd make a slave of me that day, stripping
cloak and tunic off me, throwing around me                    380
the dirty rags you see before you now.
At evening, off the fields of Ithaka,
they bound me, lashed me down under the decking
with stout ship's rope, while they all went ashore
in haste to make their supper on the beach.                   385
The gods helped me to pry the lashing loose
until it fell away. I wound my rags
in a bundle round my head and eased myself
down the smooth lading plank into the water,
up to the chin, then swam an easy breast stroke               390
out and around, putting that crew behind,
and went ashore in underbrush, a thicket,
where I lay still, making myself small.
They raised a bitter yelling, and passed by
several times. When further groping seemed                    395
useless to them, back to the ship they went
and out to sea again. The gods were with me,
keeping me hid; and with me when they brought me
here to the door of one who knows the world.
My destiny is yet to live awhile."                            400


The swineherd bowed and said:


                              "Ah well, poor drifter,
you've made me sad for you, going back over it,
all your hard life and wandering. That tale
about Odysseus, though, you might have spared me;
you will not make me believe that.                            405
Why must you lie, being the man you are,
and all for nothing?
                    I can see so well
what happened to my master, sailing home!
Surely the gods turned on him, to refuse him
death in the field, or in his friends' arms                   410
after he wound up the great war at Troy.
They would have made a tomb for him, the Akhaians,
and paid all honor to his son thereafter. No,
stormwinds made off with him. No glory came to him.

I moved here to the mountain with my swine.                    415
Never, now, do I go down to town
unless I am sent for by Penélopê
when news of some sort comes. But those who sit
around her go on asking the old questions—
a few who miss their master still,                             420
and those who eat his house up, and go free.
For my part, I have had no heart for inquiry
since one year an Aitolian[9] made a fool of me.
Exiled from land to land after some killing,
he turned up at my door; I took him in.                        425
My master he had seen in Krete, he said,
lodged with Idómeneus, while the long ships,
leaky from gales, were laid up for repairs.
But they were all to sail, he said, that summer,               430
or the first days of fall—hulls laden deep
with treasure, manned by crews of heroes.
                                        This time
you are the derelict the Powers bring.
Well, give up trying to win me with false news
or flattery. If I receive and shelter you,                     435
it is not for your tales but for your trouble,
and with an eye to Zeus, who guards a guest."

Then said that sly and guileful man, Odysseus:

"A black suspicious heart beats in your surely;
the man you are, not even an oath could change you.            440
Come then, we'll make a compact; let the gods
witness it from Olympos, where they dwell.
Upon your lord's homecoming, if he comes
here to this very hut, and soon—
then give me a new outfit, shirt and cloak,                    445
and ship me to Doulíkhion—I thought it
a pleasant island. But if Odysseus
fails to appear as I predict, then Swish!
let the slaves pitch me down from some high rock,
so the next poor man who comes will watch his tongue."         450

The forester gave a snort and answered:

                                        "Friend,
if I agreed to that, a great name
I should acquire in the world for goodness—

9. Aitolia is on the mainland, east of Ithaka.

at one stroke and forever: your kind host
who gave you shelter and the hand of friendship,                    455
only to take your life next day!
How confidently, after that, should I
address my prayers to Zeus, the son of Kronos!

It is time now for supper. My young herdsmen
should be arriving soon to set about it.                    460
We'll make a quiet feast here at our hearth."

At this point in their talk the swine had come
up to the clearing, and the drovers followed
to pen them for the night—the porkers squealing
to high heaven, milling around the yard.                    465
The swineherd then gave orders to his men:

"Bring in our best pig for a stranger's dinner.
A feast will do our hearts good, too; we know
grief and pain, hard scrabbling with our swine,
while the outsiders live on our labor."

                                        Bronze                    470
axe in hand, he turned to split up kindling,
while they drove in a tall boar, prime and fat,
planting him square before the fire. The gods,
as ever, had their due in the swineherd's thought,
for he it was who tossed the forehead bristles                    475
as a first offering on the flames, calling
upon the immortal gods to let Odysseus
reach his home once more.
                              Then he stood up
and brained the boar with split oak from the woodpile.
Life ebbed from the beast; they slaughtered him,                    480
singed the carcass, and cut out the joints.
Eumaios, taking flesh from every quarter,
put lean strips on the fat of sacrifice,
floured each one with barley meal, and cast it
into the blaze. The rest they sliced and skewered,                    485
roasted with care, then took it off the fire
and heaped it up on platters. Now their chief,
who knew best the amenities, rose to serve,
dividing all that meat in seven portions—
one to be set aside, with proper prayers,                    490
for the wood nymphs and Hermês, Maia's son;
the others for the company. Odysseus

he honored with long slices from the chine—
warming the master's heart. Odysseus looked at him
and said:

> "May you be dear to Zeus                                       495
> as you are dear to me for this, Eumaios,
> favoring with choice cuts a man like me."

And—O my swineherd!—you replied, Eumaios:

"Bless you, stranger, fall to and enjoy it
for what it is. Zeus grants us this or that,                     500
or else refrains from granting, as he wills;
all things are in his power."

> He cut and burnt
a morsel for the gods who are young forever,
tipped out some wine, then put it in the hands
of Odysseus, the old soldier, raider of cities,                  505
who sat at ease now with his meat before him.
As for the loaves, Mesaúlios dealt them out,
a yard boy, bought by the swineherd on his own,
unaided by his mistress or Laërtês,
from Taphians, while Odysseus was away.                          510
Now all hands reached for that array of supper,
until, when hunger and thirst were turned away
Mesaúlios removed the bread and, heavy
with food and drink, they settled back to rest.

Now night had come on, rough, with no moon,                      515
but a nightlong downpour setting in, the rainwind
blowing hard from the west. Odysseus
began to talk, to test the swineherd, trying
to put it in his head to take his cloak off
and lend it, or else urge the others to.                         520
He knew the man's compassion.
> "Listen," he said,
"Eumaios, and you others, here's a wishful
tale that I shall tell. The wine's behind it,
vaporing wine, that makes a serious man
break down and sing, kick up his heels and clown,                525
or tell some story that were best untold.
But not I'm launched, I can't stop now.
> Would god I felt
the hot blood in me that I had at Troy!

Laying an ambush near the walls one time,
Odysseus and Meneláos were commanders                      530
and I ranked third. I went at their request.
We worked in toward the bluffs and battlements
and, circling the town, got into canebreaks,
thick and high, a marsh where we took cover,
hunched under arms.

            The northwind dropped, and night     535
came black and wintry. A fine sleet descending
whitened the cane like hoarfrost, and clear ice
grew dense upon our shields. The other men,
all wrapt in blanket cloaks as well as tunics,
rested well, in shields up to their shoulder,                   540
but I had left my cloak with friends in camp,
foolhardy as I was. No chance of freezing hard,
I thought, so I wore kilts and a shield only.
But in the small hours of the third watch, when stars
that rise at evening go down to their setting,                  545
I nudged Odysseus, who lay close beside me;
he was alert then, listening, and I said:

'Son of Laërtês and the gods of old,
Odysseus, master mariner and soldier,
I cannot hold on long among the living.                         550
The cold is making a corpse of me. Some god
inveigled me to come without a cloak.
No help for it now; too late.'

            Next thing I knew
he had a scheme all ready in his mind—
and what a man he was for schemes and battles!                  555
Speaking under his breath to me, he murmured:

"Quiet; none of the rest should hear you.'

                  Then,
propping his head on his forearm, he said:

'Listen, lads, I had an ominous dream,
the point being how far forward from our ships                  560
and lines we've come. Someone should volunteer
to tell the corps commander, Agamémnon;
he may reinforce us from the base.'

             At this,

Thoas, jumped up, the young son of Andriamon,
put down his crimson cloak and headed off,                     565
running shoreward.
                        Wrapped in that man's cloak
how gratefully I lay in the bitter dark
until the dawn came stitched in gold! I wish
I had that sap and fiber in me now!"

Then—O my swineherd!—you replied, Eumaios:               570

"That was a fine story, and well told,
not a word out of place, not a pointless word.
No, you'll not sleep cold for lack of cover,
or any other comfort one should give
to a needy guest. However, in the morning,                     575
you must go flapping in the same old clothes.
Shirts and cloaks are few here; every man
has one change only. When our prince arrives,
the son of Odysseus, he will make you gifts—
cloak, tunic, everything—and grant you passage              580
wherever you care to go."

                        On this he rose
and placed the bed of balsam near the fire,
strewing sheepskins on top, and skins of goats.
Odysseus lay down. His host threw over him
a heavy blanket cloak, his own reserve                           585
against the winter wind when it came wild.
So there Odysseus dropped off to sleep,
while herdsmen slept nearby. But not the swineherd:
not in the hut could he lie down in peace,
but now equipped himself for the night outside;              590
and this rejoiced Odysseus' heart, to see him
care for the herd so, while his lord was gone.
He hung a sharp sword from his shoulder, gathered
a great cloak round him, close, to break the wind,
and pulled a shaggy goatskin on his head.                      595
Then, to keep at a distance dogs or men,
he took a sharpened lance, and went to rest
under a hollow rock where swine were sleeping
out of the wind and rain.

## Book XV

### HOW THEY CAME TO ITHAKA

                South into Lakedaimon
into the land where greens are wide for dancing
Athena went, to put in mind of home
her great-hearted hero's honored son,
rousing him to return.
                And there she found him                    5
with Nestor's lad in the late night at rest
under the portico of Meneláos,
the famous king. Stilled by the power of slumber
the son of Nestor lay, but honeyed sleep
had not yet taken in her arms Telémakhos.              10
All through the starlit night, with open eyes,
he pondered what he had heard about his father,
until at his bedside grey-eyed Athena
towered and said:

                "The brave thing now, Telémakhos,
would be to end this journey far from home.
All that you own you left behind
with men so lost to honor in your house
they may devour it all, shared out among them.
How will your journey save you then?
                                Go quickly
to the lord of the great war cry, Meneláos;
press him to send you back. You may yet find
the queen your mother in her rooms alone.
It seems her father and her kinsmen say
Eurýmakhos is the man for her to marry.
He has outdone the suitors, all the rest,             25
in gifts to her, and made his pledges double.
Check him, or he will have your lands and chattels[1]
in spite of you.
                You know a woman's pride
at bringing riches to the man she marries.
As to her girlhood husband, her first children,      30
he is forgotten, being dead—and they
no longer worry her.

1. The Greek could also mean: "Be careful she (Penélopê) doesn't carry off, against your will, some of your property," i.e., for her new husband. This would explain why Athena tells Telémakhos, in the following lines, to turn the property over to the maids he has most confidence in. The suggestion that Penélopê is planning to marry Eurýmakhos and take Telémakhos' property with her is not to be taken seriously; Athena uses it to get Telémakhos moving.

So act alone.
Go back; entrust your riches to the servant
worthiest in your eyes, until the gods
make known what beauty you yourself shall marry.                    35

This too I have to tell you: now take heed:
the suitors' ringleaders are hot for murder,
waiting in the channel between Ithaka
and Samê's rocky side; they mean to kill you
before you can set foot ashore. I doubt                             40
they'll bring it off. Dark earth instead
may take to her cold bed a few brave suitors
who preyed upon your cattle.
                              Bear well out
in your good ship, to eastward of the islands,
and sail again by night. Someone immortal                          45
who cares for you will make a fair wind blow.
Touch at the first beach, go ashore, and send
your ship and crew around to port by sea,
while you go inland to the forester,
your old friend, loyal keeper of the swine.                        50
Remain that night with him; send him to town
to tell your watchful mother Penélopê
that you are back from Pylos safe and sound."

With this Athena left him for Olympos.
He swung his foot across and gave a kick                           55
and said to the son of Nestor:

                              "Open your eyes,
Peisístratos. Get our team into harness.
We have a long day's journey."

                              Nestor's son
turned over and answered him:

                              "It is still night,
and no moon. Can we drive now? We can not,                         60
itch as we may for the road home. Dawn is near.
Allow the captain of spearmen, Meneláos,
time to pack our car with gifts and time
to speak a gracious word, sending us off.
A guest remembers all his days                                     65
that host who makes provision for him kindly."

The Dawn soon took her throne of gold, and Lord
Meneláos, clarion in battle,
rose from where he lay beside the beauty
of Helen with her shining hair. He strode                            70
into the hall nearby.
              Hearing him come,
Odysseus' son pulled on his snowy tunic
over the skin, gathered his long cape
about his breadth of shoulder like a captain,
the heir of King Odysseus. At the door                               75
he stood and said:

           "Lord Marshal, Meneláos,
send me home now to my own dear country:
longing has come upon me to go home."

The lord of the great war cry said at once:

"If you are longing to go home, Telémakhos,                          80
I would not keep you for the world, not I.
I'd think myself or any other host
as ill-mannered for over-friendliness
as for hostility.
           Measure is best in everything.
To send a guest packing, or cling to him                             85
when he's in haste—one sin equals the other.
'Good entertaining ends with no detaining.'
Only let me load your car with gifts
and fine ones, you shall see.
           I'll bid the women
set out breakfast from the larder stores;                            90
honor and appetite—we'll attend to both
before a long day's journey overland.
Or would you care to try the Argive midlands
and Hellas, in my company? I'll harness
my own team, and take you through the towns.                         95
Guests like ourselves no lord will turn away;
each one will make one gift, at least,
to carry home with us: tripod or cauldron
wrought in bronze, mule team, or golden cup."

Clearheaded Telémakhos replied:

                "Lord Marshal                         100

Meneláos, royal son of Atreus,
I must return to my own hearth. I left
no one behind as guardian of my property.
This going abroad for news of a great father—
heaven forbid it be my own undoing,                    105
or any precious thing be lost at home."

At this the tall king, clarion in battle,
called to his lady and her waiting women
to give them breakfast from the larder stores.
Eteóneus, the son of Boethoös, came                    110
straight from bed, from where he lodged nearby,
and Meneláos ordered a fire lit
for broiling mutton. The king's man obeyed.
Then down to the cedar chamber Meneláos
walked with Helen and Prince Megapénthês.               115
Amid the gold he had in that place lying
the son of Atreus picked a wine cup, wrought
with handles left and right, and told his son
to take a silver winebowl.
                        Helen lingered
near the deep coffers filled with gowns, her own        120
handiwork.
            Tall goddess among women,
she lifted out one robe of state so royal,
adorned and brilliant with embroidery,
deep in the chest it shimmered like a star.
Now all three turned back to the door to greet          125
Telémakhos. And red-haired Meneláos
cried out to him:

            "O prince Telémakhos,
may Hêra's Lord of Thunder see you home
and bring you to the welcome you desire!
Here are your gifts—perfect and precious things         130
I wish to make your own, out of my treasure."

And gently the great captain, son of Atreus,
handed him the goblet. Megapénthês
carried the winebowl glinting silvery
to set before him, and the Lady Helen                   135
drew near, so that he saw her cheek's pure line.
She held the gown and murmured:

"I, too,

bring you a gift, dear child, and here it is;
remember Helen's hands by this; keep it                         140
for your own bride, your joyful wedding day;
let your dear mother guard it in her chamber.
My blessing: may you come soon to your island,
home to your timbered hall."

                              So she bestowed it,
and happily he took it. These fine things                       145
Peisístratos packed well in the wicker carrier,
admiring every one. Then Meneláos
led the two guests in to take their seats
on thrones and easy chairs in the great hall.
Now came a maid to tip a golden jug                             150
of water over a silver finger bowl,
and drew the polished tables up beside them;
the larder mistress brought her tray of loaves,
with many savories to lavish on them;
viands were served by Eteóneus, and wine                       155
by Meneláos' son. Then every hand
reached out upon good meat and drink to take them,
driving away hunger and thirst. At last,
Telémakhos and Nestor's son led out
their team to harness, mounted their bright car,              160
and drove down under the echoing entrance way,
while red-haired Meneláos, Atreus' son,
walked alongside with a golden cup—
wine for the wayfarers to spill at parting.
Then by the tugging team he stood, and spoke                   165
over the horses' heads:
                         "Farewell, my lads.
Homage to Nestor, the benevolent king;
in my time he was fatherly to me,
when the flower of Akhaia warred on Troy."

Telémakhos made this reply:                                     170

"No fear
but we shall bear at least as far as Nestor
your messages, great king. How I could wish
to bring them home to Ithaka! If only
Odysseus were there, if he could hear me tell                  175
of all the courtesy I have had from you,
returning with your finery and your treasure."

Even as he spoke, a beat of wings went skyward
off to the right—a mountain eagle, grappling
a white goose in his talons, heavy prey                                      180
hooked from a farmyard. Women and men-at-arms
made hubbub, running up, as he flew over,
but then he wheeled hard right before the horses—
a sight that made the whole crowd cheer, with hearts
lifting in joy. Peisístratos called out:                                     185

"Read us the sign, O Meneláos, Lord
Marshal of armies! Was the god revealing
something thus to you, or to ourselves?"

At this the old friend of the god of battle
groped in his mind for the right thing to say,                               190
but regal Helen put in quickly:

"Listen:
I can tell you—tell what the omen means,
as light is given me, and as I see it
point by point fulfilled. The beaked eagle                                   195
flew from the wild mountain of his fathers
to take for prey the tame house bird. Just so,
Odysseus, back from his hard trials and wandering,
will soon come down in fury on his house.
He may be there today, and a black hour                                      200
he brings upon the suitors."

                         Telémakhos
gazed and said:

            "May Zeus, the lord of Hêra,
make it so! In far-off Ithaka, all my life,
I shall invoke you as a goddess, lady."

He let the whip fall, and the restive mares                                  205
broke forward at a canter through the town
into the open country.
                         All that day
they kept their harness shaking, side by side,
until at sundown when the roads grew dim
they made a halt at Pherai. There Dióklês                                    210
son of Ortílokhos whom Alpheios fathered,
welcomed the young men, and they slept the night.
Up when the young Dawn's finger tips of rose

opened in the east, they hitched the team
once more to the painted car                                          215
and steered out westward through the echoing gate,
whipping their fresh horses into a run.
Approaching Pylos Height at that day's end,
Telémakhos appealed to the son of Nestor:

"Could you, I wonder, do a thing I'll tell you,                       220
supposing you agree?
We take ourselves to be true friends—in age
alike, and bound by ties between our fathers,
and now by partnership in this adventure.
Prince, do not take me roundabout,                                    225
but leave me at the ship, else the old king
your father will detain me overnight
for love of guests, when I should be at sea."

The son of Nestor nodded, thinking swiftly
how best he could oblige his friend.                                  230
Here was his choice: to pull the team hard over
along the beach till he could rein them in
beside the ship. Unloading Meneláos'
royal keepsakes into the stern sheets,
he sang out:

                    "Now for action! Get aboard,                      235
and call your men, before I break the news
at home in hall to father. Who knows better
the old man's heart than I? If you delay,
he will not let you go, but he'll descend on you
in person and imperious; no turning                                   240
back with empty hands for him, believe me,
once his blood is up."

                    He shook the reins
to the lovely mares with long manes in the wind,
guiding them full tilt toward his father's hall.
Telémakhos called in the crew, and told them:

"Get everything shipshape aboard this craft;                          245
we pull out now, and put sea miles behind us."

The listening men obeyed him, climbing in
to settle on their benches by the rowlocks,
while he stood watchful by the stern. He poured out

offerings there, and prayers to Athena.                          250

Now a strange man came up to him, an easterner
fresh from spilling blood in distant Argos,
a hunted man. Gifted in prophecy,
he had as forebear that Melampous, wizard
who lived of old in Pylos, mother city                           255
of western flocks.
                    Melampous, a rich lord,[2]
had owned a house unmatched among the Pylians,
until the day came when king Neleus, noblest
in that age, drove him from his native land.
And Neleus for a year's term sequestered                         260
Melampous' fields and flocks, while he lay bound
hand and foot in the keep of Phylakos.
Beauty of Neleus' daughter put him there
and sombre folly the inbreaking Fury
thrust upon him. But he gave the slip                            265
to death, and drove the bellowing herd of Iphiklos
from Phylakê to Pylos, there to claim
the bride that ordeal won him from the king.
He led her to his brother's house, and went on
eastward into another land, the bluegrass                        270
plain of Argos. Destiny held for him
rule over many Argives. Here he married,
built a great manor house, fathered Antíphatês
and Mantios, commanders both, of whom
Antíphatês begot Oikleiês                                        275
and Oikleiês the firebrand Amphiaraos.
This champion the lord of stormcloud, Zeus,
and strong Apollo loved; nor had he ever
to cross the doorsill into dim old age.

2. The complicated story which follows (obscure in some of its details) gives us the genealogical
background of the young man who comes up to Telémakhos. His name, as we learn only at the
end of the genealogy, is Theoklýmenos, and he has an important role to play in the last part of
the *Odyssey*. He is a prophet, one who can interpret signs, foretell the future. This gift is hereditary: his ancestor Melampous had it (and so did another descendant of Melampous, Amphiaraos).
The brother of Melampous (who lived in Pylos under King Neleus, Nestor's father) asked for the
hand of Neleus' daughter: Neleus demanded as bride-price the herds of cattle of a neighboring
lord, Phylakos. Melampous tried to steal the cattle for his brother, was caught and imprisoned. In
prison he heard the worms in the roofbeams announce that the wood was almost eaten through
and predicted the collapse of the roof. Phylakos, impressed, released him, with the cattle; his
brother was given the bride. Melampous then left for Argos where he settled and prospered: one
of his great-grandsons was the prophet Amphiaraos who foresaw that if he joined the champions
who went to besiege Thebes (The Seven against Thebes) he would lose his life. But his wife
persuaded him to go: she had been bribed with a golden necklace by Polyneicês, son of Oedipus,
who was preparing to attack his brother, Eteoclês, now King of Thebes. Amphiaraos was the
grandson of Melampous' son Antíphatês; the other son of Melampous, Mantios, had a son called
Polypheidês (also a prophet) who moved to Hypereia (in the vicinity of Argos); his son Theoklýmenos now begs Telémakhos for a place in his ship, so that he can escape the relatives of a man
he has killed.

A woman, bought by trinkets, gave him over                    280
to be cut down in the assault on Thebes.
His sons were Alkmáon and Amphílokhos.
In the meantime Lord Mantios begot
Polypheidês, the prophet, and
Kleitos—famous name! For Dawn in silks                    285
of gold carried off Kleitos for his beauty
to live among the gods. But Polypheidês,
high-hearted and exalted by Apollo
above all men for prophecy, withdrew
to Hyperesia when his father angered him.                    290
He lived on there, foretelling to the world
the shape of things to come.
                                        His son it was,
Theoklýmenos, who came upon Telémakhos
as he poured out the red wine in the sand
near his trim ship, with prayer to Athena;                    295
and he called out, approaching:

                              "Friend, well met
here at libation before going to sea.
I pray you by the wine you spend, and by
your god, your own life, and your company;
enlighten me, and let the truth be known.                    300
Who are you? Of what city and what parents?"

Telémakhos turned to him and replied:

"Stranger, as truly as may be, I'll tell you.
I am from Ithaka, where I was born;
my father is, or he once was, Odysseus.                    305
But he's a long time gone, and dead, may be;
and that is what I took ship with my friends
to find out—for he left long years ago."

Said Theoklýmenos in reply:

"I too                    310
have had to leave my home. I killed a cousin.
In the wide grazing lands of Argos live
many kinsmen of his and friends in power,
great among the Akhaians. These I fled.
Death and vengeance at my back, as Fate                    315
has turned now, I came wandering overland.
Give me a plank aboard your ship, I beg,

or they will kill me. They are on my track."
Telémakhos made answer:

                                        "No two ways
about it. Will I pry you from our gunnel                                    320
when you are desperate to get to sea?
Come aboard; share what we have, and welcome."

He took the bronze-shod lance from the man's hand
and laid it down full-length on deck; then swung
his own weight after it aboard the cutter,                                  325
taking position aft, making a place
for Theoklýmenos near him. The stern lines
were slacked off, and Telémakhos commanded:

"Rig the mast; make sail!" Nimbly they ran
to push the fir pole high and step it firm                                  330
amidships in the box, make fast the forestays,
and hoist aloft the white sail on its halyards.
A following wind came down from grey-eyed Athena,
blowing brisk through heaven, and so steady
the cutter lapped up miles of salt blue sea,                                335
passing Krounoi abeam and Khalkis estuary[3]
at sundown when the sea ways all grew dark.
Then, by Athena's wind borne on, the ship
rounded Pheai by night and coasted Elis,
the green domain of the Epeioi; thence                                      340
he put her head north toward the running pack
of islets, wondering if by sailing wide
he sheered off Death, or would be caught.

                                        That night
Odysseus and the swineherd supped again
with herdsmen in their mountain hut. At ease                                345
when appetite and thirst were turned away,
Odysseus, while he talked, observed the swineherd
to see if he were hospitable still—
if yet again the man would make him stay
under his roof, or send him off to town.                                    350

"Listen," he said, "Eumaios; listen, lads.
At daybreak I must go and try my luck
around the port. I burden you too long.

3. The precise location of these places is disputed but the mention of Elis in line 339 shows that
they are all on the west coast of the Peloponnese, south of the Gulf of Corinth.

Direct me, put me on the road with someone.
Nothing else for it but to play the beggar                          355
in populous parts. I'll get a cup or loaf,
maybe, from some householder. If I go
as far as the great hall of King Odysseus
I might tell Queen Penélopê my news.
Or I can drift inside among the suitors                             360
to see what alms they give, rich as they are.
If they have whims, I'm deft in ways of service—
that I can say, and you may know for sure.
By grace of Hermês the Wayfinder, patron
of mortal tasks, the god who honors toil,                           365
no man can do a chore better than I can.
Set me to build a fire, or chop wood,
cook or carve, mix wine and serve—or anything
inferior men attend to for the gentry."

Now you were furious at this, Eumaios,                              370
and answered—O my swineherd!—

                              "Friend, friend,
how could this fantasy take hold of you?
You dally with your life, and nothing less,
if you feel drawn to mingle in that company—
reckless, violent, and famous for it                                375
out to the rim of heaven. Slaves
they have, but not like you. No—theirs are boys
in fresh cloaks and tunics, with pomade
ever on their sleek heads, and pretty faces.
These are their minions, while their tables gleam              380
and groan under big roasts, with loaves and wine.
Stay with us here. No one is burdened by you,
neither myself nor any of my hands.
Wait here until Odysseus' son returns.
You shall have clothing from him, cloak and tunic,             385
and passage where your heart desires to go."

The noble and enduring man replied:

"May you be dear to Zeus for this, Eumaios,
even as you are to me. Respite from pain
you give me—and from homelessness. In life                     390
there's nothing worse than knocking about the world,
no bitterness we vagabonds are spared
when the curst belly rages! Well, you master it

and me, making me wait for the king's son.
But now, come, tell me:                                    395
what of Odysseus' mother, and his father
whom he took leave of on the sill of age?
Are they under the sun's rays, living still,
or gone down long ago to lodge with Death?"

To this the rugged herdsman answered:                      400

"Aye,
that I can tell you; it is briefly told.
Laërtês lives, but daily in his hall
prays for the end of life and soul's delivery,
heartbroken as he is for a son long gone             405
and for his lady. Sorrow, when she died,
aged and enfeebled him like a green tree stricken;
but pining for her son, her brilliant son,
wore out her life
                    Would god no death so sad
might come to benefactors dear as she!               410
I loved always to ask and hear about her
while she lived, although she lived in sorrow.
For she had brought me up with her own daughter,
Princess Ktimenê, her youngest child.
We were alike in age and nursed as equals           415
nearly, till in the flower of our years
they gave her, married her, to a Samian prince,[4]
taking his many gifts. For my own portion
her mother gave new clothing, cloak and sandals,
and sent me to the woodland. Well she loved me.      420
Ah, how I miss that family! It is true
the blissful gods prosper my work; I have
meat and drink to spare for those I prize;
but so removed I am, I have no speech
with my sweet mistress, now that evil days           425
and overbearing men darken her house.
Tenants all hanker for good talk and gossip
around their lady, and a snack in hall,
a cup or two before they take the road
to their home acres, each one bearing home           430
some gift to cheer his heart."

                              The great tactician

4. From Same, a nearby island or town.

answered:

      "You were still a child, I see,
when exiled somehow from your parents' land.
Tell me, had it been sacked in war, the city
of spacious ways in which they made their home,       435
your father and your gentle mother? Or
were you kidnapped alone, brought here by sea
huddled with sheep in some foul pirate squadron,
to this landowner's hall? He paid your ransom?"

The master of the woodland answered:

                        "Friend,       440
now that you show an interest in that matter,
attend me quietly, be at your ease,
and drink your wine. These autumn nights are long,
ample for story-telling and for sleep.
You need not go to bed before the hour;       445
sleeping from dusk to dawn's a dull affair.
Let any other here who wished, though,
retire to rest. At daybreak let him breakfast
and take the king's own swine into the wilderness.
Here's a tight roof; we'll drink on, you and I,       450
and ease our hearts of hardships we remember,
sharing old times. In later days a man
can find a charm in old adversity,
exile and pain. As to your question, now:

A certain island, Syriê by name—       455
you may have heard the name—lies off Ortýgia[5]
due west, and holds the sunsets of the year.
Not very populous, but good for grazing
sheep and kine; rich too in wine and grain.
No dearth is ever known there, no disease       460
wars on the folk, of ills that plague mankind;
but when the townsmen reach old age, Apollo
with his longbow of silver comes, and Artemis,
showering arrows of mild death.
                       Two towns
divide the farmlands of that whole domain,       465

---

5. Another name for Delos, the central island of the Cyclades, but also the name of the central island of the city of Syracuse in Sicily. However, the fact that on Syrie there is no disease and that everyone there dies painlessly suggests that it is not located in this world at all—like Phaiákia, it is in Fairyland.

and both were ruled by Ktêsios, my father,
Orménos' heir, and a great godlike man.

Now one day some of those renowned seafaring
men, sea-dogs, Phoinikians, came ashore
with bags of gauds for trading. Father had                    470
in our household a woman of Phoinikia,
a handsome one, and highly skilled. Well, she
gave in to the seductions of those rovers.
One of them found her washing near the mooring
and lay with her, making such love to her                     475
as women in their frailty are confused by,
even the best of them.
                    In due course, then,
he asked her who she was and where she hailed from:
and nodding toward my father's roof, she said:

'I am of Sidon town, smithy of bronze                         480
for all the East. Arubas Pasha's daughter.
Taphian pirates caught me in a byway
and sold me into slavery overseas
in this man's home. He could afford my ransom.'

The sailor who had lain with her replied:                     485

'Why not ship out with us on the run homeward,
and see your father's high-roofed hall again,
your father and your mother? Still in Sidon
and still rich, they are said to be.'

                    She answered:

'It could be done, that, if you sailors take                  490
oath I'll be given passage home unharmed.'

Well, soon she had them swearing it all pat
as she desired, repeating every syllable,
whereupon she warned them:

                    'Not a word
about our meeting here! Never call out to me                  495
when any of you see me in the lane
or at the well. Some visitor might bear
tales to the old man. If he guessed the truth,
I'd be chained up, your lives would be in peril.

No: keep it secret. Hurry with your peddling,                              500
and when your hold is filled with livestock, send
a message to me at the manor hall.
Gold I'll bring, whatever comes to hand,
and something else, too, as my passage fee—
the master's child, my charge: a boy so high,                              505
bright for his age; he runs with me on errands.
I'd take him with me happily; his price
would be I know not what in sale abroad.'

Her bargain made, she went back to the manor.
But they were on the island all that year,                                 510
getting by trade a cargo of our cattle;
until, the ship at length being laden full,
ready for sea, they sent a messenger
to the Phoinkian woman. Shrewd he was,
this fellow who came round my father's hall,                               515
showing a golden chain all strung with amber,
a necklace. Maids in waiting and my mother
passed it from hand to hand, admiring it,
engaging they would buy it. But that dodger,
as soon as he had caught the woman's eye                                   520
and nodded, slipped away to join the ship.
She took my hand and led me through the court
into the portico. There by luck she found
winecups and tables still in place—for Father's
attendant counselors had dined just now                                    525
before they went to the assembly. Quickly
she hid three goblets in her bellying dress
to carry with her, while I tagged along
in my bewilderment. The sun went down
and all the lanes grew dark as we descended,                               530
skirting the harbor in our haste to where
those traders of Phoinikia held their ship.
All went aboard at once and put to sea,
taking the two of us. A favoring wind
blew from the power of heaven. We sailed on                                535
six nights and days without event. Then Zeus
the son of Kronos added one more noon—and sudden
arrows from Artemis pierced the woman's heart.
Stone-dead she dropped
into the sloshing bilge the way a tern                                     540
plummets; and the sailors heaved her over
as tender pickings for the seals and fish.
Now I was left in dread, alone, while wind

and current bore them on to Ithaka.
Laërtês purchased me. That was the way                            545
I first laid eyes upon this land."

                    Odysseus,

the kingly man, replied:

                              "You rouse my pity,
telling what you endured when you were young.
But surely Zeus put good alongside ill:
torn from your own far home, you had the luck            550
to come into a kind man's service, generous
with food and drink. And a good life you lead,
unlike my own, all spent in barren roaming
from one country to the next, till now."

So the two men talked on, into the night,                        555
leaving few hours for sleep before the Dawn
stepped up to her bright chair.
                              The ship now drifting
under the island lee, Telémakhos'
companions took in sail and mast, unshipped
the oars and rowed ashore. They moored her stern        560
by the stout hawser lines, tossed out the bow stones,
and waded in beyond the wash of ripples
to mix their wine and cook their morning meal.
When they had turned back hunger and thirst, Telémakhos
arose to give the order of the day.                              565

"Pull for the town," he said, "and berth our ship,
while I go inland across country. Later,
this evening, after looking at my farms,
I'll join you in the city. When day comes
I hope to celebrate our crossing, feasting                       570
everyone on good red meat and wine."

His noble passenger, Theoklýmenos,
now asked:

                    "What as to me, my dear young fellow,
where shall I go? Will I find lodging here
with some one of the lords of stony Ithaka?                      575
Or go straight to your mother's hall and yours?"

Telémakhos turned round to him and said:

"I should myself invite you to our hall
if things were otherwise; there'd be no lack
of entertainment for you. As it stands,                          580
no place could be more wretched for a guest
while I'm away. Mother will never see you;
she almost never shows herself at home
to the suitors there, but stays in her high chamber
weaving upon her loom. No, let me name                           585
another man for you to go to visit:
Eurýmakhos, the honored son of Pólybos.
In Ithaka they are dazzled by him now—
the strongest of their princes, bent on making
mother and all Odysseus' wealth his own.                         590
Zeus on Olympos only knows
if some dark hour for them will intervene."

The words were barely spoken, when a hawk,
Apollo's courier, flew up on the right,
clutching a dove and plucking her—so feathers                    595
floated down to the ground between Telémakhos
and the moored cutter. Theoklýmenos
called him apart and gripped his hand, whispering:

"A god spoke in this bird-sign on the right.
I knew it when I saw the hawk fly over us.                       600
There is no kinglier house than yours, Telémakhos,
here in the realm of Ithaka. Your family
will be in power forever."
                              The young prince,

clear in spirit, answered:

                              "Be it so,
friend, as you say. And may you know as well                     605
the friendship of my house, and many gifts
from me, so everyone my call you fortunate."

He called a trusted crewman named Peiraios,
and said to him:

                         "Peiraios, son of Klýtios,
can I rely on you again as ever, most                            610

of all the friends who sailed with me to Pylos?
Take this man home with you, take care of him,
treat him with honor, till I come."

                                   To this
Peiraios the good spearman answered:

"Aye,                                                              615
stay in the wild country while you will,
I shall be looking after him, Telémakhos.
He will not lack good lodging."
                                   Down to the ship
he turned, and boarded her, and called the others
to cast off the stern lines and come aboard.                       620
So the men climbed in to sit beside the rowlocks.
Telémakhos now tied his sandals on
and lifted his tough spear from the ship's deck;
hawsers were taken in, and they shoved off
to reach the town by way of the open sea                           625
as he commanded them—royal Odysseus'
own dear son, Telémakhos.
                                   On foot
and swiftly he went up toward the stockade
where swine were penned in hundreds, and at night
the guardian of the swine, the forester,                           630
slept under arms on duty for his masters.


## Book XVI

### FATHER AND SON

But there were two men in the mountain hut—
Odysseus and the swineherd. At first light
blowing their fire up, they cooked their breakfast
and sent their lads out, driving herds to root
in the tall timber.
                                   When Telémakhos came,              5
the wolvish troop of watchdogs only fawned on him
as he advanced. Odysseus heard them go
and heard the light crunch of a man's footfall—
at which he turned quickly to say:

                                   "Eumaios,
here is one of your crew come back, or maybe
another friend: the dogs are out there snuffling                    10

belly down; not one has even growled.
I can hear footsteps—"

                    But before he finished
his tall son stood at the door.
                    The swineherd
rose in surprise, letting a bowl and jug                          15
tumble from his fingers. Going forward,
he kissed the young man's head, his shining eyes
and both hands, while his own tears brimmed and fell.
Think of a man whose dear and only son,
born to him in exile, reared with labor,                          20
has lived ten years abroad and now returns:
how would that man embrace his son! Just so
the herdsman clapped his arms around Telémakhos
and covered him with kisses—for he knew
the lad had got away from death. He said:                         25

"Light of my days, Telémakhos,
you made it back! When you took ship for Pylos
I never thought to see you here again.
Come in, dear child, and let me feast my eyes;
here you are, home from the distant places!                       30
How rarely, anyway, you visit us,
your own men, and your own woods and pastures!
Always in the town, a man would think
you loved the suitors' company, those dogs!"

Telémakhos with his clear candor said:                            35

"I am with you, Uncle. See now, I have come
because I wanted to see you first, to hear from you
if Mother stayed at home—or is she married
off to someone, and Odysseus' bed
left empty for some gloomy spider's weaving?"                     40

Gently the forester replied to this:

"At home indeed your mother is, poor lady,
still in the women's hall. Her nights and days
are wearied out with grieving."

                    Stepping back
he took the bronze-shod lance, and the young prince             45

entered the cabin over the worn door stone.
Odysseus moved aside, yielding his couch,
but from across the room Telémakhos checked him:

"Friend, sit down; we'll find another chair
in our own hut. Here is the man to make one!"                50

The swineherd, when the quiet man sank down,
built a new pile of evergreens and fleeces—
a couch for the dear son of great Odysseus—
then gave them trenchers of good meat, left over
from the roast pork of yesterday, and heaped up          55
willow baskets full of bread, and mixed
an ivy bowl of honey-heated wine.
Then he in turn sat down, facing Odysseus,
their hands went out upon the meat and drink
as they fell to, ridding themselves of hunger,              60
until Telémakhos paused and said:

                              "Oh, Uncle,
what's your friend's home port? How did he come?
Who were the sailors brought him here to Ithaka?
I doubt if he came walking on the sea."

And you replied, Eumaios—O my swineherd—               65

"Son, the truth about him is soon told.
His home land, and a broad land, too, is Krete,
but he has knocked about the world, he says,
for years, as the Powers wove his life. Just now
he broke away from a shipload of Thesprotians          70
to reach my hut. I place him in your hands.
Act as you will. He wishes your protection."

The young man said:

                    "Eumaios, my protection!
The notion cuts me to the heart. How can I
receive your friend at home? I am not old enough       75
or trained in arms. Could I defend myself
if someone picked a fight with me?
                              Besides,
mother is in a quandary, whether to stay with me
as mistress of our household, honoring
her lord's bed, and opinion in the town,                    80

or take the best Akhaian who comes her way—
the one who offers most.
                              I'll undertake,
at all events, to clothe your friend for winter,
now he is with you. Tunic and cloak of wool,
a good broadsword, and sandals—these are his.                    85
I can arrange to send him where he likes
or you may keep him in your cabin here.
I shall have bread and wine sent up; you need not
feel any pinch on his behalf.
                                   Impossible
to let him stay in hall, among the suitors.                      90
They are drunk, drunk on impudence, they might
injure my guest—and how could I bear that?
How could a single man take on those odds?
Not even a hero could.
                          The suitors are too strong."

At this the noble and enduring man, Odysseus,                    95
addressed his son:

            "Kind prince, it may be fitting
for me to speak a word. All that you say
gives me an inward wound as I sit listening.
I mean this wanton game they play, these fellows,
riding roughshod over you in your own house,                    100
admirable as you are. But tell me,
are you resigned to being bled? The townsmen,
stirred up against you, are they, by some oracle?
Your brothers—can you say your brothers fail you?
A man should feel his kin, at least, behind him                 105
in any clash, when a real fight is coming.
If my heart were as young as yours, if I were
son of Odysseus, or the man himself,
I'd rather have my head cut from my shoulders
by some slashing adversary, if I                                110
brought no hurt upon that crew! Suppose
I went down, being alone, before the lot,
better, I say, to die at home in battle
than see these insupportable things, day after
day the stranger cuffed, the women slaves                       115
dragged here and there, shame in the lovely rooms,
the wine drunk up in rivers, sheer waste
of pointless feasting, never at an end!"
Telémakhos replied:

"Friend, I'll explain to you.
There is no rancor in the town against me,                                    120
no fault of brothers, whom a man should feel
behind him when a fight is in the making;
no, no—in our family the First Born
of Heaven, Zeus made single sons the rule.
Arkeísios had but one, Laërtês; he                                           125
in his turn fathered only one, Odysseus,
who left me in his hall alone, too young
to be of any use to him.
And so you see why enemies fill our house
in these days: all the princes of the islands,                               130
Doulíkhion, Samê, wooded Zakýnthos,
Ithaka, too—lords of our island rock—
eating our house up as they court my mother.
She cannot put an end to it; she dare not
bar the marriage that she hates; and they                                    135
devour all my substance and my cattle,
and who knows when they'll slaughter me as well?
It rests upon the gods' great knees.
                              Uncle,
go down at once and tell the Lady Penélopê
that I am back from Pylos, safe and sound.                                   140
I stay here meanwhile. You will give your message
and then return. Let none of the Akhaians
hear it; they have a mind to do me harm."

To this, Eumaios, you replied:

                              "I know.
But make this clear, now—should I not likewise                              145
call on Laërtês with your news? Hard hit
by sorrow though he was, mourning Odysseus,
he used to keep an eye upon his farm.
He had what meals he pleased, with his own folk.
But now no more, not since you sailed for Pylos;                            150
he has not taken food or drink, I hear,
sitting all day, blind to the work of harvest,
groaning, while the skin shrinks on his bones."

Telémakhos answered:

                              "One more misery,
but we had better leave it so.

If men could choose, and have their choice, in everything,        155
we'd have my father home.

                    Turn back
when you have done your errand, as you must,
not to be caught alone in the countryside.[6]
But wait—you may tell Mother
to send our old housekeeper on the quiet                            160
and quickly; she can tell the news to Grandfather."

The swineherd, roused, reached out to get his sandals,
tied them on, and took the road.

                              Who else
beheld this but Athena? From the air
she walked, taking the form of a tall woman,                       165
handsome and clever at her craft, and stood
beyond the gate in plain sight of Odysseus,
unseen, though, by Telémakhos, unguessed,
for not to everyone will gods appear.
Odysseus noticed her; so did the dogs,                             170
who cowered whimpering away from her. She only
nodded, signing to him with her brows,
a sign he recognized. Crossing the yard,
he passed out through the gate in the stockade
to face the goddess. There she said to him:                        175

"Son of Laërtês and gods of old,
Odysseus, master of land ways and sea ways,
dissemble to your son no longer now.
The time has come: tell him how you together
will bring doom on the suitors in the town.                        180
I shall not be far distant then, for I
myself desire battle."

                    Saying no more,
she tipped her golden wand upon the man,
making his cloak pure white, and the knit tunic
fresh around him. Lithe and young she made him,                    185
ruddy with sun, his jawline clean, the beard
no longer grey upon his chin. And she
withdrew when she had done.

6. The Greek says something more like: "and don't go wandering round the countryside after
him" (i.e., Laërtês).

Then Lord Odysseus
reappeared—and his son was thunderstruck.
Fear in his eyes, he looked down and away                               190
as though it were a god, and whispered:

"Stranger,
you are no longer what you were just now!
Your cloak is new; even your skin! You are
one of the gods who rule the sweep of heaven!
Be kind to us, we'll make you fair oblation                            195
and gifts of hammered gold. Have mercy on us!"

The noble and enduring man replied:

"No god. Why take me for a god? No, no.
I am that father whom your boyhood lacked
and suffered pain for lack of. I am he."                               200

Held back too long, the tears ran down his cheeks
as he embraced his son.
Only Telémakhos,
uncomprehending, wild
with incredulity, cried out:

"You cannot
be my father Odysseus! Meddling spirits
conceived this trick to twist the knife in me!                         205
no man of woman born could work these wonders
by his own craft, unless a god came into it
with ease to turn him young or old at will.
I swear you were in rags and old,
and here you stand like one of the immortals!"                         210

Odysseus brought his ranging mind to bear
and said:

"This is not princely, to be swept
away by wonder at your father's presence.
No other Odysseus will ever come,
for he and I are one, the same; his bitter                             215
fortune and his wanderings are mine.
Twenty years gone, and I am back again
on my own island.
As for my change of skin,

that is a charm Athena, Hope of Soldiers,[7]
uses as she will; she has the knack                                220
to make me seem a beggar man sometimes
and sometimes young, with finer clothes about me.
It is no hard thing for the gods of heaven
to glorify a man or bring him low."

When he had spoken, down he sat.
                        Then, throwing                    225
his arms around this marvel of a father
Telémakhos began to weep. Salt tears
rose from the wells of longing in both men,
and cries burst from both as keen and fluttering
as those of the great taloned hawk,                                230
whose nestlings farmers take before they fly.
So helplessly they cried, pouring out tears,
and might have gone on weeping so till sundown,
had not Telémakhos said:

              "Dear father! Tell me
what kind of vessel put you here ashore                             235
on Ithaka? Your sailors, who were they?
I doubt you made it, walking on the sea!"

Then said Odysseus, who had borne the barren sea:

"Only plain truth shall I tell you, child.
Great seafarers, the Phaiákians, gave me passage                    240
as they give other wanderers. By night
over the open ocean, while I slept,
they brought me in their cutter, set me down
on Ithaka, with gifts of bronze and gold
and stores of woven things. By the gods' will                       245
these lie all hidden in a cave. I came
to this wild place, directed by Athena,
so that we might lay plans to kill our enemies.
Count up the suitors for me, let me know
what men at arms are there, how many men.                           250
I must put all my mind to it, to see
if we two by ourselves can take them on
or if we should look round for help."

---

7. Athena was a warrior goddess.

Telémakhos
replied:

"O Father, all my life your fame                                    255
as a fighting man has echoed in my ears—
your skill with weapons and the tricks of war—
but what you speak of is a staggering thing,
beyond imagining, for me. How can two men
do battle with a houseful in their prime?                           260
For I must tell you this is no affair
of ten or even twice ten men, but scores,
throngs of them. You shall see, here and now.
The number from Doulíkhion alone
is fifty-two, picked men, with armorers,                            265
a half dozen; twenty-four came from Samê,
twenty from Zakýnthos; our own island
accounts for twelve, high-ranked, and their retainers,
Medôn the crier, and the Master Harper,
besides a pair of handymen at feasts.                               270
If we go in against all these
I fear we pay in salt blood for your vengeance.
You must think hard if you would conjure up
the fighting strength to take us through."

Odysseus
who had endured the long war and the sea                            275
answered:

"I'll tell you now.
Suppose Athena's arm is over us, and Zeus
her father's, must I rack my brains for more?"

Clearheaded Telémakhos looked hard and said:

"Those two are great defenders, no one doubts it,                   280
but throned in the serene clouds overhead;
other affairs of men and gods they have
to rule over."

And the hero answered:

"Before long they will stand to right and left of us
in combat, in the shouting, when the test comes—                   285
our nerve against the suitors' in my hall.
Here is your part: at break of day tomorrow
home with you, go mingle with our princes.

The swineherd later on will take me down
the port-side trail—a beggar, by my looks,                    290
hangdog and old. If they make fun of me
in my own coutryard, let your ribs cage up
your springing heart, no matter what I suffer,
no matter if they pull me by the heels
or practice shots at me, to drive me out.                     295
Look on, hold down your anger. You may even
plead with them, by heaven! in gentle terms
to quit their horseplay—not that they will heed you,
rash as they are, facing their day of wrath.
Now fix the next step in your mind.
                              Athena,                         300
counseling me, will give me word, and I
shall signal to you, nodding: at that point
round up all armor, lances, gear of war
left in our hall, and stow the lot away
back in the vaulted store room. When the suitors              305
miss those arms and question you, be soft
in what you say: answer:


                    'I thought I'd move them
out of the smoke. They seemed no longer those
bright arms Odysseus left us years ago
when he went off to Troy. Here where the fire's               310
hot breath came, they had grown black and drear.
One better reason, too, I had from Zeus:
Suppose a brawl starts up when you are drunk,
you might be crazed and bloody one another,
and that would strain your feat, your courtship. Tempered     315
iron can magnetize a man.'
                    Say that.
But put aside two broadswords and two spears
for our own use, two oxhide shields nearby
when we go into action. Pallas Athena
and Zeus All Provident will see you through,                  320
bemusing our young friends.
                    Now one thing more.
If son of mine you are and blood of mine,
let no one hear Odysseus is about.
Neither Laërtês, nor the swineherd here,
nor any slave, nor even Penélopê.                             325
But you and I alone must learn how far
the women are corrupted; we should know

how to locate good men among our hands,
the loyal and respectful, and the shirkers
who take you lightly, as alone and young."                    330

His admirable son replied:

                                    "Ah, Father,
even when danger comes I think you'll find
courage in me. I am not scatterbrained.
But as to checking on the field hands now,
I see no gain for us in that. Reflect,                        335
you make a long toil, that way, if you care
to look men in the eye at every farm,
while these gay devils in our hall at ease
eat up our flocks and herds, leaving us nothing.

As for the maids I say, Yes: make distinction                 340
between good girls and those who shame your house;
all that I shy away from is a scrutiny
of cottagers just now. The time for that
comes later—if in truth you have a sign
from Zeus the Stormking."

                              So their talk ran on,            345
while down the coast, and round toward Ithaka,
hove the good ship that had gone out to Pylos
bearing Telémakhos and his companions.
Into the wide bay waters, on to the dark land,
they drove her, hauled her up, took out the oars              350
and canvas for light-hearted squires to carry
homeward—as they carried, too, the gifts
of Meneláos round to Klýtios'[8] house.
But first they sped a runner to Penélopê.                     355
They knew that quiet lady must be told
the prince her son had come ashore, and sent
his good ship round to port; not one soft tear
should their sweet queen let fall.
                                    Both messengers,
crewman and swineherd—reached the outer gate                  360
in the same instant, bearing the same news,
and went in side by side to the king's hall.
He of the ship burst out among the maids:

---

8. The father of Peiraios (XV. 608), the man to whom Telémakhos entrusted his suppliant
Theoklýmenos.

"Your son's ashore this morning, O my Queen!"

But the swineherd calmly stood near Penélopê                365
whispering what her son had bade him tell
and what he had enjoined on her. No more.
When he had done, he left the place and turned
back to his steading in the hills.

                              By now,
sullen confusion weighed upon the suitors.                370
Out of the house, out of the court they went,
beyond the wall and gate, to sit in council.
Eurýmakhos, the son of Pólybos,
opened discussion:

                    "Friends, face up to it;
that young pup, Telémakhos, has done it;                375
he made the round trip, though we said he could not.
Well—now to get the best craft we can find
afloat, with oarsmen who can drench her bows,
and tell those on the island to come home."

He was yet speaking when Amphínomos,                380
craning seaward, spotted the picket ship
already in the roadstead under oars
with canvas brailed up; and this fresh arrival
made him chuckle. Then he told his friends:

"Too late for messages. Look, here they come                385
along the bay. Some god has brought them news,
or else they saw the cutter pass—and could not
overtake her."

                    On their feet at once,
the suitors took the road to the sea beach,
where, meeting the black ship, they hauled her in.                390
Oars and gear they left for their light-hearted
squires to carry, and all in company
made off for the assembly ground. All others,
young and old alike, they barred from sitting.
Eupeithês' son, Antínoös, made the speech:                395

"How the gods let our man escape a boarding,
that is the wonder.
                    We had lookouts posted

up on the heights all day in the sea wind,
and every hour a fresh pair of eyes;
at night we never slept ashore                                      400
but after sundown cruised the open water
to the southeast, patrolling until Dawn.
We were prepared to cut him off and catch him,
squelch him for good and all. The power of heaven
steered him the long way home.                                      405

Well, let this company plan his destruction,
and leave him no way out, this time. I see
our business here unfinished while he lives.
He knows, now, and he's no fool. Besides,
his people are all tired of playing up to us.                       410
I say, act now, before he brings the whole
body of Akhaians to assembly—
and he would leave no word unsaid, in righteous
anger speaking out before them all
of how we plotted murder, and then missed him.                      415
Will they commend us for that pretty work?
Take action now, or we are in for trouble;
we might be exiled, driven off our lands.
Let the first blow be ours.
If we move first, and get our hands on him                          420
far from the city's eye, on path or field,
then stores and livestock will be ours to share;
the house we may confer upon his mother—
and on the man who marries her. Decide
otherwise you may—but if, my friends,                               425
you want that boy to live and have his patrimony,
then we should eat no more of his good mutton,
come to this place no more.
                            Let each from his own hall
court her with dower gifts. And let her marry
the destined one, the one who offers most."                         430

He ended, and no sound was heard among them,
sitting all hushed, until at last the son
of Nísos Aretíadês arose—
Amphínomos.
                    He led the group of suitors
who came from grainlands on Doulíkhion,                             435
and he had lightness in his talk that pleased
Penélopê, for he meant no ill.
Now, in concern for them, he spoke:

"O Friends
I should not like to kill Telémakhos.
It is a shivery thing to kill a prince                    440
of royal blood.
                    We should consult the gods.
If Zeus hands down a ruling for that act,
then I shall say, 'Come one, come all,' and go
cut him down with my own hand—
but I say Halt, if gods are contrary."                    445

Now this proposal won them, and it carried.
Breaking their session up, away they went
to take their smooth chairs in Odysseus' house.
Meanwhile Penélopê the Wise,
decided, for her part, to make appearance                    450
before the valiant young men.
                    She knew now
they plotted her child's death in her own hall,
for once more Medôn, who had heard them, told her.
Into the hall that lovely lady came,
with maids attending, and approached the suitors,                    455
till near a pillar of the well-wrought roof
she paused, her shining veil across her cheeks,
and spoke directly to Antínoös:

                    "Infatuate,
steeped in evil! Yet in Ithaka they say
you were the best one of your generation                    460
in mind and speech. Not so, you never were.
Madman, why do you keep forever knitting
death for Telémakhos? Have you no piety
toward men dependent on another's mercy?
Before Lord Zeus, no sanction can be found                    465
for one such man to plot against another!
Or are you not aware that your own father
fled to us when the realm was up in arms
against him? He had joined the Taphian pirates
in ravaging Thesprotian folk, our friends.                    470
Our people would have raided *him*, then—breached
his heart, butchered his herds to feast upon—
only Odysseus took him in, and held
the furious townsmen off. It is Odysseus'
house you now consume, his wife you court,                    475
his son you kill, or try to kill. And me
you ravage now, and grieve. I call upon you

to make an end of it!—and your friends too!"

The son of Pólybos it was, Eurýmakhos,
who answered her with ready speech:

"My lady                                    480
Penélopê, wise daughter of Ikários,
you must shake off these ugly thoughts. I say
that man does not exist, nor will, who dares
lay hands upon your son Telémakhos,
while I live, walk the earth, and use my eyes.     485
The man's life blood, I swear,
will spurt and run out black around my lancehead!
For it is true of me, too, that Odysseus,
raider of cities, took me on his knees
and fed me often—tidbits and red wine.             490
Should not Telémakhos, therefore, be dear to me
above the rest of men? I tell the lad
he must not tremble for his life, at least
alone in the suitors' company. Heaven
deals death no man avoids."

Blasphemous lies                                   495
in earnest tones he told—the one who planned
the lad's destruction!

Silently the lady
made her way to her glowing upper chamber,
there to weep for her dear lord, Odysseus,
until grey-eyed Athena                             500
cast sweet sleep upon her eyes.

At fall of dusk
Odysseus and his son heard the approach
of the good forester. They had been standing
over the fire with a spitted pig,
a yearling. And Athena coming near                 505
with one rap of her wand made of Odysseus
an old old man again, with rags about him—
for if the swineherd knew his lord were there
he could not hold the news; Penélopê
would hear it from him.

Now Telémakhos                                     510
greeted him first:

"Eumaios, back again!
What was the talk in town? Are the tall suitors

home again, by this time, from their ambush,
or are they still on watch for my return?"

And you replied, Eumaios—O my swineherd:                    515

"There was no time to ask or talk of that;
I hurried through the town. Even while I spoke
my message, I felt driven to return.
A runner from your friends turned up, a crier,
who gave the news first to your mother. Ah!                 520
One thing I do know; with my own two eyes
I saw it. As I climbed above the town
to where the sky is cut by Hermês' ridge,
I saw a ship bound in for our own bay
with many oarsmen in it, laden down                         525
with sea provisioning and two-edged spears,
and I surmised those were the men.
                                    Who knows?"

Telémakhos, now strong with magic, smiled
across at his own father—but avoided
the swineherd's eye.
                        So when the pig was done,            530
the spit no longer to be turned, the table
garnished, everyone sat down to feast
on all the savory flesh he craved. And when
they had put off desire for meat and drink,
they turned to bed and took the gift of sleep.              535


## Book XVII

### THE BEGGAR AT THE MANOR

When the young Dawn came bright into the East
spreading her finger tips of rose, Telémakhos
the king's son, tied on his rawhide sandals
and took the lance that bore his handgrip. Burning
to be away, and on the path to town,                          5
he told the swineherd:

                        "Uncle, the truth is
I must go down myself into the city.
Mother must see me there, with her own eyes,
or she will weep and feel forsaken still,
and will not set her mind at rest. Your job                  10

will be to lead this poor man down to beg.
Some householder may want to dole him out
a loaf and pint. I have my own troubles.
Am I to care for every last man who comes?
And if he takes it badly—well, so much                          15
the worse for him. Plain truth is what I favor."

At once Odysseus the great tactician
spoke up briskly:

                    "Neither would I myself
care to be kept here, lad. A beggar man
fares better in the town. Let it be said                        20
I am not yet so old I must lay up
indoors and mumble, 'Aye, Aye' to a master.
Go on, then. As you say, my friend can lead me
as soon as I have had a bit of fire
and when the sun grows warmer. These old rags                   25
could be my death, outside on a frosty morning,
and the town is distant, so they say."

                                    Telémakhos
with no more words went out, and through the fence,
and down hill, going fast on the steep footing,
nursing woe for the suitors in his heart.                       30

Before the manor hall, he leaned his lance
against a great porch pillar and stepped in
across the door stone.
                    Old Eurýkleia
saw him first, for that day she was covering
handsome chairs nearby with clean fleeces.                      35
She ran to him at once, tears in her eyes;
and other maidservants of the old soldier
Odysseus gathered round to greet their prince,
kissing his head and shoulders.
                              Quickly, then,                    40
Penélopê the Wise, tall in her beauty
as Artemis or pale-gold Aphroditê,
appeared from her high chamber and came down
to throw her arms around her son. In tears
she kissed his head, kissed both his shining eyes,
then cried out, and her words flew:

                              "Back with me!                    45

Telémakhos, more sweet to me than sunlight!
I thought I should not see you again, ever,
after you took the ship that night to Pylos—
against my will, with not a word! you went
for news of your dear father. Tell me now                    50
of everything you saw!"

                    But he made answer:
"Mother, not now. You make me weep. My heart
already aches—I came near death at sea.
You must bathe, first of all, and change your dress,
and take your maids to the highest room to pray.            55
Pray, and burn offerings to the gods of heaven,
that Zeus may put his hand to our revenge.

I am off now to bring home from the square
a guest, a passenger I had. I sent him
yesterday with all my crew to town.                         60
Peiraios was to care for him, I said,
and keep him well, with honor, till I came."

She caught back the swift words upon her tongue.
Then softly she withdrew
to bathe and dress her body in fresh linen,                 65
and make her offerings to the gods of heaven,
praying Almighty Zeus
to put his hand to their revenge.

                    Telémakhos
had left the hall, taken his lance, and gone
with two quick hounds at heel into the town,                70
Athena's grace in his long stride
making the people gaze as he came near.
And suitors gathered, primed with friendly words,
despite the deadly plotting in their hearts—
but these, and all their crowd, he kept away from.          75
Next he saw sitting some way off, apart,
Mentor, with Antiphos and Halithersês,
friends of his father's house in years gone by.
Near these men he sat down, and told his tale
under their questioning.
                    His crewman, young Peiraios,             80
guided through town, meanwhile, into the Square,
the Argive exile, Theoklýmenos.
Telémakhos lost no time in moving toward him;
but first Peiraios had his say:

"Telémakhos,
you must send maids to me, at once, and let me                    85
turn over to you those gifts from Meneláos!"
The prince had pondered it, and said:

"Peiraios,
none of us knows how this affair will end.
Say one day our fine suitors, without warning,
draw upon me, kill me in our hall,                                90
and parcel out my patrimony—I wish
you, and no one of them, to have those things.
But if my hour comes, if I can bring down
bloody death on all that crew,
you will rejoice to send my gifts to me—                          95
and so will I rejoice!"

Then he departed,
leading his guest, the lonely stranger, home.

Over chair-backs in hall they dropped their mantles
and passed in to the polished tubs, where maids
poured out warm baths for them, anointed them,                    100
and pulled fresh tunics, fleecy cloaks around them.
Soon they were seated at their ease in hall.
A maid came by to tip a golden jug
over their fingers into a silver bowl
and drew a gleaming table up beside them.                         105
The larder mistress brought her tray of loaves
and savories, dispensing each.
                              In silence
across the hall, beside a pillar, propped
in a long chair, Telémakhos' mother
spun a fine wool yarn.
                    The young men's hands                         110
went out upon the good things placed before them,
and only when their hunger and thirst were gone
did she look up and say:

"Telémakhos,
what am I to do now? Return alone
and lie again on my forsaken bed—                                 115
sodden how often with my weeping
since that day when Odysseus put to sea

to join the Atreidai[9] before Troy?
                              Could you not
tell me, before the suitors fill our house,
what news you have of his return?"

                    He answered:                    120

"Now that you ask a second time, dear Mother,
here is the truth.
                    We went ashore at Pylos
to Nestor, lord and guardian of the West,
who gave me welcome in his towering hall.
So kind he was, he might have been my father          125
and I his long-lost son—so truly kind,
taking me in with his own honored sons.
But as to Odysseus' bitter fate,
living or dead, he had no news at all
from anyone on earth, he said. He sent me             130
overland in a strong chariot
to Atreus' son, the captain, Meneláos.
And I saw Helen there, for whom the Argives
fought, and the Trojans fought, as the gods willed.
Then Meneláos of the great war cry                    135
asked me my errand in that ancient land
of Lakedaimon. So I told our story,
and in reply he burst out:

                    'Intolerable!
That feeble men, unfit as those men are,
should think to lie in that great captain's bed,      140
fawns in the lion's lair! As if a doe
put down her litter of sucklings there, while she
sniffed at the glen or grazed a grassy hollow.
Ha! Then the lord returns to his own bed
and deals out wretched doom on both alike.            145

So will Odysseus deal out doom on these.
O Father Zeus, Athena, and Apollo!
I pray he comes as once he was, in Lesbos,
when he stood up to wrestle Philomeleidês—
champion and Island King—                             150
and smashed him down. How the Akhaians cheered!

9. The sons of Atreus, Agamémnon and Meneláos.

If that Odysseus could meet the suitors,
they'd have a quick reply, a stunning dowry!
Now for your questions, let me come to the point.
I would not misreport it for you; let me                          155
tell you what the Ancient of the Sea,
that infallible seer, told me.
                    On an island
your father lies and grieves. The Ancient saw him
held by a nymph, Kalypso, in her hall;
no means of sailing home remained to him,                          160
no ship with oars, and no ship's company
to pull him on the broad back of the sea.'

I had this from the lord marshal, Meneláos,
and when my errand in that place was done
I left for home. A fair breeze from the gods                       165
brought me swiftly back to our dear island."

The boy's tale made her heart stir in her breast,
but this was not all. Mother and son now heard
Theoklýmenos, the diviner, say:

"He does not see it clear:
                   O gentle lady,                       170
wife of Odysseus Laërtiadês,
listen to me, I can reveal this thing.
Zeus be my witness, and the table set
for strangers and the hearth to which I've come—
the lord Odysseus, I tell you,                                     175
is present now, already, on this island!
Quartered somewhere, or going about, he knows
what evil is afoot. He has it in him
to bring a black hour on the suitors. Yesterday,
still at the ship, I saw this in a portent.                        180
I read the sign aloud, I told Telémakhos'!"

The prudent queen, for her part, said:

                       "Stranger,
if only this came true—
our love would go to you, with many gifts;
aye, every man who passed would call you happy!"            185

So ran the talk between these three.

                              Meanwhile,
swaggering before Odysseus' hall,
the suitors were competing at the discus throw
and javelin, on the level measured field.
But when the dinner hour drew on, and beasts                         190
were being driven from the fields to slaughter—
as beasts were, every day—Medôn spoke out:
Medôn, the crier, whom the suitors liked;
he took his meat beside them.

                              "Men," he said,
"each one has had his work-out and his pleasure,                     195
come in to Hall now; time to make our feast.
Are discus throws more admirable than a roast
when the proper hour comes?"

                              At this reminder
they all broke up their games, and trailed away
into the gracious, timbered hall. There, first,                      200
they dropped their cloaks on chairs; then came their ritual:
putting great rams and fat goats to the knife—
pigs and a cow, too.
                    So they made their feast.

During these hours, Odysseus and the swineherd
were on their way out of the hills to town.                          205
The forester had got them started, saying:

"Friend, you have hopes, I know, of your adventure
into the heart of town today. My lord
wishes it so, not I. No, I should rather
you stood by here as guardian of our steading.                       210
But I owe reverence to my prince, and fear
he'll make my ears burn later if I fail.
A master's tongue has a rough edge. Off we go.
Part of the day is past; nightfall will be
early, and colder, too."
                         Odysseus,                                   220
who had it all timed in his head, replied:

"I know, as well as you do. Let's move on.
You lead the way—the whole way. Have you got
a staff, a lopped stick, you could let me use
to put my weight on when I slip? This path                           225
is hard going, they said."

                                              Over his shoulders
he slung his patched-up knapsack, an old bundle
tied with twine. Eumaios found a stick for him,
the kind he wanted, and the two set out,
leaving the boys and dogs to guard the place.                                    230
In this way good Eumaios led his lord
down to the city.

                              And it seemed to him
he led an old outcast, a beggar man,
leaning most painfully upon a stick,
his poor cloak, all in tatters, looped about him.                                235

Down by the stony trail they made their way
as far as Clearwater, not far from town—
a spring house where the people filled their jars.
Ithakos, Nêritos, and Polýktor[1] built it,
and round it on the humid ground a grove,                                        240
a circular wood of poplars grew. Ice cold
in runnels from a high rock ran the spring,
and over it there stood an altar stone
to the cool nymphs, where all men going by
laid offerings.

                       Well, here the son of Dólios                              245
crossed their path—Melánthios.

                                        He was driving
a string of choice goats for the evening meal,
with two goatherds beside him; and no sooner
had he laid eyes upon the wayfarers
than he began to growl and taunt them both                                       250
so grossly that Odysseus' heart grew hot:
"Here comes one scurvy type leading another!
God pairs them off together, every time.
Swineherd, where are you taking your new pig,
that stinking beggar there, licker of pots?                                      255
How many doorposts has he rubbed his back on
whining for garbage, where a noble guest
would rate a cauldron or a sword?

                                          Hand him
over to me, I'll make a farmhand of him,
a stall scraper, a fodder carrier! Whey                                          260
for drink will put good muscle on his shank!
No chance: he learned his dodges long ago—

1. Presumably the first rulers of Ithaka: Ithakos, who gave the island its name; Nêritos, whose
name was given to the mountain on Ithaka (IX. 22); and Polýktor, whose name may possibly
mean "having great possessions."

no honest sweat. He'd rather tramp the country
begging, to keep his hoggish belly full.
Well, I can tell you this for sure:                                265
in King Odysseus' hall, if he goes there,
footstools will fly around his head—good shots
from strong hands. Back and side, his ribs will catch it
on the way out!"

            And like a drunken fool
he kicked at Odysseus' hip as he passed by.                        270
Not even jogged off stride, or off the trail,
the Lord Odysseus walked along, debating
inwardly whether to whirl and beat
the life out of this fellow with his stick,
or toss him, brain him on the stony ground.                        275
Then he controlled himself, and bore it quietly.
Not so the swineherd.
                Seeing the man before him,
he raised his arms and cried:

                "Nymphs of the spring,
daughters of Zeus, if ever Odysseus
burnt you a thighbone in rich fat—a ram's                          280
or kid's thighbone, hear me, grant my prayer:
let our true lord come back, let heaven bring him
to rid the earth of these fine courtly ways
Melánthios picks up around the town—
all wine and wind! Bad shepherds ruin flocks!"                     285

Melánthios the goatherd answered:

               "Bless me!
The dog can snap: how he goes on! Some day
I'll take him in a slave ship overseas
and trade him for a herd!
            Old Silverbow
Apollo, if he shot clean through Telémakhos                        290
in hall today, what luck! Or let the suitors
cut him down!
          Odysseus died at sea;
no coming home for him."

              He flung this out
and left the two behind to come on slowly,

while he went hurrying to the king's hall.                        295
There he slipped in, and sat among the suitors,
beside the one he doted on—Eurýmakhos.
Then working servants helped him to his meat
and the mistress of the larder gave him bread.

Reaching the gate, Odysseus and the forester              300
halted and stood outside, for harp notes came
around them ripping on the air
as Phêmios picked out a song. Odysseus
caught his companion's arm and said:

                              "My friend,
here is the beautiful place—who could mistake it?       305
Here is Odysseus' hall: no hall like this!
See how one chamber grows out of another;
see how the court is tight with wall and coping;
no man at arms could break this gateway down!
Your banqueting young lords are here in force,          310
I gather, from the fumes of mutton roasting
and strum of harping—harping, which the gods
appoint sweet friend of feasts!"

                    And—O my swineherd!
you replied:

          "That was quick recognition;
but you are no numbskull—in this or anything.           315
Now we must plan this action. Will you take
leave of me here, and go ahead alone
to make your entrance now among the suitors?
Or do you choose to wait?—Let me go forward
and go in first.

          Do not delay too long;                          320
someone might find you skulking here outside
and take a club to you, or heave a lance.
Bear this in mind, I say."

                    The patient hero
Odysseus answered:

                    "Just what I was thinking.
You go in first, and leave me here a little.             325
But as for blows and missiles,
I am no tyro at these things. I learned
to keep my head in hardship—years of war
and years at sea. Let this new trial come.

The cruel belly, can you hide its ache?                                    330
How many bitter days it brings! Long ships
with good stout planks athwart—would fighters rig them
to ride the barren sea, except for hunger?
Seawolves—woe to their enemies!"

                           While he spoke
an old hound, lying near, pricked up his ears                              335
and lifted up his muzzle. This was Argos,
trained as a puppy by Odysseus,
but never taken on a hunt before
his master sailed for Troy. The young men, afterward,
hunted wild goats with him, and hare, and deer,                            340
but he had grown old in his master's absence.
Treated as rubbish now, he lay at last
upon a mass of dung before the gates—
manure of mules and cows, piled there until
fieldhands could spread it on the king's estate.                           345
Abandoned there, and half destroyed with flies,
old Argos lay.
           But when he knew he heard
Odysseus' voice nearby, he did his best
to wag his tail, nose down, with flattened ears,
having no strength to move nearer his master.                              350
And the man looked away,
wiping a salt tear from his cheek; but he
hid this from Eumaios. Then he said:

"I marvel that they leave this hound to lie
here on the dung pile;                                                     355
he would have been a fine dog, from the look of him,
though I can't say as to his power and speed
when he was young. You find the same good build
in house dogs, table dogs landowners keep
all for style."

          And you replied, Eumaios:                             360

"A hunter owned him—but the man is dead
in some far place. If this old hound could show
the form he had when Lord Odysseus left him,
going to Troy, you'd see him swift and strong.
He never shrank from any savage thing                                      365
he'd brought to bay in the deep woods; on the scent
no other dog kept up with him. Now misery
has him in leash. His owner died abroad,

and here the women slaves will take no care of him.
You know how servants are: without a master                    370
they have no will to labor, or excel.
For Zeus who views the wide world takes away
half the manhood of a man, that day
he goes into captivity and slavery."

Eumaios crossed the court and went straight forward           375
into the mégaron[2] among the suitors;
but death and darkness in that instant closed
the eyes of Argos, who had seen his master,
Odysseus, after twenty years.

                                        Long before anyone else
Telélmakhos caught sight of the grey woodsman                  380
coming from the door, and called him over
with a quick jerk of his head. Eumaios'
narrowed eyes made out an empty bench
beside the one the carver used—that servant
who had no respite, carving for the suitors.                   385
This bench he took possession of, and placed it
across the table from Telémakhos
for his own use. Then the two men were served
cuts from a roast and bread from a bread basket.

At no long interval, Odysseus came                             390
through his own doorway as a mendicant,
humped like a bundle of rags over his stick.
He settled on the inner ash wood sill,
leaning against the door jamb—cypress timber
the skilled carpenter planed years ago                         395
and set up with a plumbline.

                                        Now Telémakhos
took an entire loaf and a double handful
of roast meat; then he said to the forester:

"Give these to the stranger there. But tell him
to go among the suitors, on his own;                           400
he may beg all he wants. This hanging back
is no asset to a hungry man."

The swineherd rose at once, crossed to the door,
and halted by Odysseus.

2. The great hall.

"Friend," he said,
"Telémakhos is pleased to give you these,                              405
but he commands you to approach the suitors;
you may ask all you want from them. He adds,
your shyness is no asset to a beggar."
The great tactician, lifting up his eyes,
cried:
          "Zeus aloft! A blessing on Telémakhos!                       410
Let all things come to pass as he desires!"

Palms held out, in the beggar's gesture, he
received the bread and meat and put it down
before him on his knapsack—lowly table!—
then he fell to, devouring it. Meanwhile                               415
the harper in the great room sang a song.
Not till the man was fed did the sweet harper
end his singing—whereupon the company
made the walls ring again with talk.

                              Unseen,
Athena took her place beside Odysseus                                  420
whispering in his ear:

                    "Yes, try the suitors.
You may collect a few more loaves, and learn
who are the decent lads, and who are vicious—
although not one can be excused from death!"

So he appealed to them, one after another,                             425
going from left to right, with open palm,
as though his life time had been spent in beggary.
And they gave bread, for pity—wondering, though,
at the strange man. Who could this beggar be,
where did he come from? each would ask his neighbor;  430
till in their midst the goatherd, Melánthios,
raised his voice:

               "Hear just a word from me,
my lords who court our illustrious queen!
                              This man,
this foreigner, I saw him on the road;
the swineherd, here was leading him this way;          435
who, what, or whence he claims to be, I could not
say for sure."
          At this, Antínoös
turned on the swineherd brutally, saying:

                                        "You famous
breeder of pigs, why bring this fellow here?
Are we not plagued enough with beggars,                        440
foragers and such rats?
                    You find the company
too slow at eating up your lord's estate—
is that it? So you call this scarecrow in?"

The forester replied:

                        "Antínoös,
well born you are, but that was not well said.        445
Who would call in a foreigner?—unless
an artisan with skill to serve the realm,
a healer, or a prophet, or a builder
or one whose harp and song might give us joy.
All these are sought for on the endless earth,        450
but when have beggars come by invitation?
Who puts a field mouse in his granary? My lord,
you are a hard man, and you always were,
more so than others of this company—hard
on all Odysseus' people and on me.                    455
But this I can forget
as long as Penélopê lives on, the wise and tender
mistress of this hall; as long
as Prince Telémakhos—"

                    But he broke off
at a look from Telémakhos, who said:

                                "Be still.                460
Spare me a long-drawn answer to this gentleman.
With his unpleasantness, he will forever make
strife where he can—and goad the others on."

He turned and spoke out clearly to Antínoös:

"What fatherly concern you show me! Frighten        465
this unknown fellow, would you, from my hall
with words that promise blows—may God forbid it!
Give him a loaf. Am I a niggard? No,
I call on you to give. And spare your qualms
as to my mother's loss, or anyone's—                  470
your heart is all in feeding, not in giving."

Antínoös replied:

                    "What high and mighty
talk, Telémakhos! Control your temper,

If every suitor gave what I may give him,
he could be kept for months—kept out of sight!"

He reached under the table for the footstool
his shining feet had rested on—and this
he held up so that all could see his gift.

But all the rest gave alms,                                    480
enough to fill the beggar's pack with bread
and roast meat.
                So it looked as though Odysseus
had had his taste of what these men were like
and could return scot free to his own doorway—
but halting now before Antínoös                                485
he made a little speech to him. Said he:

"Give a mite, friend. I would not say, myself,
you are the worst man of the young Akhaians.
The noblest, rather; kingly, by your look;
therefore you'll give more bread than others do.                490
Let me speak well of you as I pass on
over the boundless earth!
                          I, too, you know,
had fortune once, lived well, stood well with men,
and gave alms, often, to poor wanderers
like this one that you see—aye, to all sorts,                   495
no matter in what dire want. I owned
servants—many, god knows—and all the rest
that goes with being prosperous, as they say.
But Zeus the son of Kronos brought me down.

No telling                                                      500
why he would have it, but he made me go
to Egypt with a company of rovers—
a long sail to the south—for my undoing.
Up the broad Nile and in to the river bank
I brought my dipping squadron. There, indeed,                   505
I told the men to stand guard at the ships;
I sent patrols out—out to rising ground;
but reckless greed carried my crews away
to plunder the Egyptian farms; they bore off
wives and children, killed what men they found.                 510
The news ran on the wind to the city, a night cry,
and sunrise brought both infantry and horsemen,
filling the river plain with dazzle of bronze;

then Zeus lord of lightning
threw my men into a blind panic; no one dared                    515
stand against that host closing around us.
Their scything weapons left our dead in piles,
but some they took alive, into forced labor,
myself among them. And they gave me, then,
to one Dmêtor, a traveller, son of Iasos,                        520
who ruled at Kypros.[3] He conveyed me there.
From that place, working northward, miserably—"

But here Antínoös broke in, shouting:

        "God!
What evil wind blew in this pest?
        Get over,
stand in the passage! Nudge my table, will you?               525
Egyptian whips are sweet
to what you'll come to here, you nosing rat,
making your pitch to everyone!
These men have bread to throw away on you
because it is not theirs. Who cares? Who spares                530
another's food, when he has more than plenty?"
With guile Odysseus drew away, then said:

"A pity that you have more looks than heart.
You'd grudge a pinch of salt from your own larder
to your own handy man. You sit here, fat                       535
on others' meat, and cannot bring yourself
to rummage out a crust of bread for me!"

Then anger made Antínoös' heart beat hard,
and, glowering under his brows, he answered:

        "Now!
You think you'll shuffle off and get away                      540
after that impudence? Oh, no you don't!"

The stool he let fly hit the man's right shoulder
on the packed muscle under the shoulder blade—
like solid rock, for all the effect one saw.
Odysseus only shook his head, containing                       545
thoughts of bloody work, as he walked on,
then sat, and dropped his loaded bag again
upon the door sill. Facing the whole crowd
he said, and eyed them all:

3. Cyprus.

"One word only,
my lords, and suitors of the famous queen.                          550
One thing I have to say.
There is no pain, no burden for the heart
when blows come to a man, and he defending
his own cattle—his own cows and lambs.
Here it was otherwise. Antínoös                                     555
hit me for being driven on by hunger—
how many bitter seas men cross for hunger!
If beggars interest the gods, if there are Furies
pent in the dark to avenge a poor man's wrong, then may
Antínoös meet his death before his wedding day!"                    560

Then said Eupithês' son, Antínoös:

                                    "Enough.
Eat and be quiet where you are, or shamble elsewhere,
unless you want these lads to stop your mouth
pulling you by the heels, or hands and feet,
over the whole floor, till your back is peeled!"                    565

But now the rest were mortified, and someone
spoke from the crowd of young bucks to rebuke him:

"A poor show, that—hitting this famished tramp—
bad business, if he happened to be a god.
You know they go in foreign guise, the gods do,                     570
looking like strangers, turning up
in towns and settlements to keep an eye
on manners, good or bad."

                        But at this notion
Antínoös only shrugged.
                        Telémakhos,
after the blow his father bore, sat still                           575
without a tear, though his heart felt the blow.
Slowly he shook his head from side to side,
containing murderous thoughts.
                        Penélopê
on the higher level of her room had heard
the blow, and knew who gave it. Now she murmured:                   580

"Would god you could be hit yourself, Antínoös—
hit by Apollo's bowshot!"

And Eurýnomê
her housekeeper, put in:

"He and no other?
If all we pray for came to pass, not one
would live till dawn!"

Her gentle mistress said:                        585
"Oh, Nan, they are a bad lot; they intend
ruin for all of us; but Antínoös
appears a blacker-hearted hound than any.
Here is a poor man come, a wanderer,
driven by want to beg his bread, and everyone          590
in hall gave bits, to cram his bag—only
Antínoös threw a stool, and banged his shoulder!"

So she described it, sitting in her chamber
among her maids—while her true lord was eating.
Then she called in the forester and said:              595

"Go to that man on my behalf, Eumaios,
and send him here, so I can greet and question him.
Abroad in the great world, he may have heard
rumors about Odysseus—may have known him!"

Then you replied—O swineherd!

                              "Ah, my queen,        600
if these Akhaian sprigs would hush their babble
the man could tell you tales to charm your heart.
Three days and nights I kept him in my hut;
he came straight off a ship, you know, to me.
There was no end to what he made me hear              605
of his hard roving; and I listened, eyes
upon him, as a man drinks in a tale
a minstrel sings—a minstrel taught by heaven
to touch the hearts of men. At such a song
the listener becomes rapt and still. Just so         610
I found myself enchanted by this man.
He claims an old tie with Odysseus, too—
in his home country, the Minoan land
of Krete. From Krete he came, a rolling stone
washed by the gales of life this way and that         615
to our own beach.
                    If he can be believed

he has news of Odysseus near at hand
alive, in the rich country of Thesprotia,
bringing a mass of treasure home."

Then wise Penélopê said again:                                        620

"Go call him, let him come here, let him tell
that tale again for my own ears.
                         Our friends
can drink their cups outside or stay in hall,
being so carefree. And why not? Their stores
lie intact in their homes, both food and drink,                      625
with only servants left to take a little.
But these men spend their days around our house
killing our beeves, our fat goats and our sheep,
carousing, drinking up our good dark wine;
sparing nothing, squandering everything.                             630
No champion like Odysseus takes our part.
Ah, if he comes again, no falcon ever
struck more suddenly than he will, with his son,
to avenge this outrage!"

                         The great hall below
at this point rang with a tremendous sneeze—                         635
"kchaou!" from Telémakhos—like an acclamation.
And laughter seized Penélopê.
                         Then quickly,
lucidly she went on:

                    "Go call the stranger
straight to me. Did you hear that, Eumaios?
My son's thundering sneeze at what I said!                            640
May death come of a sudden so; may death
relieve us, clean as that, of all the suitors!
Let me add one thing—do not overlook it—
if I can see this man has told the truth,
I promise him a warm new cloak and tunic."                           645

With all this in his head, the forester
went down the hall, and halted near the beggar,
saying aloud:

                    "Good father, you are called
by the wise mother of Telémakhos,

Penélopê. The queen, despite her troubles,                                    650
is moved by a desire to hear your tales
about her lord—and if she finds them true,
she'll see you clothed in what you need, a cloak
and a fresh tunic.
                    You may have your belly
full each day you go about this realm                                          655
begging. For all may give, and all they wish."

Now said Odysseus, the old soldier:

"Friend,
I wish this instant I could tell my facts
to the wise daughter of Ikários, Penélopê—                                     660
and I have much to tell about her husband;
we went through much together.
                                But just now
this hard crowd worries me. They are, you said
infamous to the very rim of heaven
for violent acts: and here, just now, this fellow                             665
gave me a bruise. What had I done to him?
But who would lift a hand for me? Telémakhos?
Anyone else?
              No; bid the queen be patient.
Let her remain till sundown in her room,
and then—if she will seat me near the fire—                                    670
inquire tonight about her lord's return.
My rags are sorry cover; you know that;
I showed my sad condition first to you."


The woodsman heard him out, and then returned;
but the queen met him on her threshold, crying:                               675


"Have you not brought him? Why? What is he thinking?
Has he some fear of overstepping? Shy
about these inner rooms? A hangdog beggar?"

To this you answered, friend Eumaios:

"No:                                                                           680
he reasons as another might, and well,
not to tempt any swordplay from these drunkards.
Be paitent, wait—he says—till darkness falls.
And, O my queen, for you too that is better:

better to be alone with him, and question him,                    685
and hear him out."
                    Penélopê replied:
"He is no fool; he sees how it could be.
Never were mortal men like these
for bullying and brainless arrogance!"

Thus she accepted what had been proposed,                    690
so he went back into the crowd. He joined
Telémakhos, and said at once in whispers—
his head bent, so that no one else might hear:

"Dear prince, I must go home to keep good watch
on hut and swine, and look to my own affairs.                    695
Everything here is in your hands. Consider
your own safety before the rest; take care
not to get hurt. Many are dangerous here.
May Zeus destroy them first, before we suffer!"

Telémakhos said:

                    "Your wish is mine, Uncle.                    700
Go when your meal is finished. Then come back
at dawn, and bring good victims for a slaughter.
Everything here is in my hands indeed—
and in the disposition of the gods."

Taking his seat on the smooth bench again,                    705
Eumaios ate and drank his fill, then rose
to climb the mountain trail back to his swine,
leaving the mégaron and court behind him
crowded with banqueters.
                    These had their joy
of dance and song, as day waned into evening.                    710

## Book XVIII

### BLOWS AND A QUEEN'S BEAUTY

Now a true scavenger came in—a public tramp
who begged around the town of Ithaka,
a by-word for his insatiable swag-belly,
feeding and drinking, dawn to dark. No pith
was in him, and no nerve, huge as he looked.                    5
Arnaios, as his gentle mother called him,

he had been nicknamed "Iros" by the young
for being ready to take messages.[4]
This fellow
thought he would rout Odysseus from his doorway,
growling at him:

"Clear out, grandfather,                                     10
or else be hauled out by the ankle bone.
See them all giving me the wink? That means,
'Go on and drag him out!' I hate to do it.
Up with you! Or would you like a fist fight?"

Odysseus only frowned and looked him over,         15
taking account of everything, then said:

"Master, I am no trouble to you here.
I offer no remarks. I grudge you nothing.
Take all you get, and welcome. Here is room
for two on this doorslab—or do you own it?         20
You are a tramp, I think, like me. Patience:
a windfall from the gods will come. But drop
that talk of using fists; it could annoy me.
Old as I am, I might just crack a rib
or split a lip for you. My life would go              25
even more peacefully, after tomorrow,
looking for no more visits here from you."

Iros the tramp grew red and hooted:

"Ho,
listen to him! The swine can talk your arm off,      30
like an old oven woman! With two punches
I'd knock him snoring, if I had a mind to—
and not a tooth left in his head, the same
as an old sow caught in the corn! Belt up!
And let this company see the way I do it             35
when we square off. Can you fight a fresher man?"

Under the lofty doorway, on the door sill
of wide smooth ash, they held this rough exchange.
And the tall full-blooded suitor, Antínoös,
overhearing, broke into happy laughter.              40
Then he said to the others:

4. The goddess Iris often served as messenger for the gods.

   "Oh, my friends,
no luck like this ever turned up before!
What a farce heaven has brought this house!
      The stranger
and Iros have had words, they brag of boxing!
Into the ring they go, and no more talk!"   45

All the young men got on their feet now, laughing,
to crowd around the ragged pair. Antínoös
called out:

   "Gentlemen, quiet! One more thing:
here are goat stomachs ready on the fire
to stuff with blood and fat, good supper pudding.   50
The man who wins this gallant bout
may step up here and take the one he likes.
And let him feast with us from this day on:
no other beggar will be admitted here
when we are at our wine."

     This pleased them all.   55
But now that wily man, Odysseus, muttered:

"An old man, an old hulk, has no business
fighting a young man, but my belly nags me;
nothing will do but I must take a beating.
Well, then, let every man here swear an oath   60
not to step in for Iros. No one throw
a punch for luck. I could be whipped that way."

So much the suitors were content to swear,
but after they reeled off their oaths, Telémakhos
put in a word to clinch it, saying:

     "Friend,   65
if you will stand and fight, as pride requires,
don't worry about a foul blow from behind.
Whoever hits you will take on the crowd.
You have my word as host; you have the word
of these two kings, Antínoös and Eurýmakhos—   70
a pair of thinking men."

     All shouted, "Aye!"
So now Odysseus made his shirt a belt
and roped his rags around his loins, baring

his hurdler's thighs and boxer's breadth of shoulder,
the dense rib-sheath and upper arms. Athena                              75
stood nearby to give him bulk and power,
while the young suitors watched with narrowed eyes—
and comments went around:

"By god, old Iros now retires."
                                        "Aye,
he asked for it, he'll get it—bloody, too."                              80

"The build this fellow had, under his rags!"
Panic made Iros' heart jump, but the yard-boys
hustled and got him belted by main force,
though all his blubber quivered now with dread.
Antínoös angry voice rang in his ears:                                   85

"You sack of guts, you might as well be dead,
might as well never have seen the light of day,
if this man makes you tremble! Chicken-heart,
afraid of an old wreck, far gone in misery!
Well, here is what I say—and what I'll do.                               90
If this ragpicker can outfight you, whip you,
I'll ship you out to that king in Epeíros,[5]
Ékhetos—he skins everyone alive.
Let him just cut your nose off and your ears
and pull your privy parts out by the roots                              95
to feed raw to his hunting dogs!"

                              Poor Iros
felt a new fit of shaking take his knees.
But the yard-boys pushed him out. Now both contenders
put their hands up. Royal Odysseus
pondered if he should hit him with all he had                          100
and drop the man dead on the spot, or only
spar, with force enough to knock him down.
Better that way, he thought—a gentle blow,
else he might give himself away.
                                        The two
were at close quarters now, and Iros lunged                            105
hitting the shoulder. Then Odysseus hooked him
under the ear and shattered his jaw bone,
so bright red blood came bubbling from his mouth,

5. Epirus, the mainland north of Ithaka. *Ékhetos:* All we know of him is what Homer tells us
here.

as down he pitched into the dust, bleating,
kicking against the ground, his teeth stove in.                    110
The suitors whooped and swung their arms, half dead
with pangs of laughter.
                    Then, by the ankle bone,
Odysseus hauled the fallen one outside,
crossing the courtyard to the gate, and piled him
against the wall. In his right hand he stuck                    115
his begging staff, and said:

                    "Here, take your post.
Sit here to keep the dogs and pigs away.
You can give up your habit of command
over poor waifs and beggarmen—you swab.
Another time you may not know what hit you."                    120

When he had slung his rucksack by the string
over his shoulder, like a wad of rags,
he sat down on the broad door sill again,
as laughing suitors came to flock inside;
and each young buck in passing gave him greeting,                    125
saying, maybe,

                    "Zeus fill your pouch for this!
May the gods grant your heart's desire!"

                              "Well done
to put that walking famine out of business."

"We'll ship him out to that king in Epeíros,
Ékhetos—he skins everyone alive."                    130

Odysseus found grim cheer in their good wishes—
his work had started well.
                    Now from the fire
his fat blood pudding came, deposited
before him by Antínoös—then, to boot,
two brown loaves from the basket, and some wine                    135
in a fine cup of gold. These gifts Amphínomos
gave him. Then he said:

                    "Here's luck, grandfather;
a new day; may the worst be over now."

Odysseus answered, and his mind ranged far:

"Amphínomos, your head is clear, I'd say;
so was your father's—or at least I've heard
good things of Nísos the Doulíkhion,
whose son you are, they tell me—an easy man.
And you seem gently bred.
                              In view of that,
I have a word to say to you, so listen.                    145

Of mortal creatures, all that breathe and move,
earth bears none frailer than mankind. What man
believes in woe to come, so long as valor
and tough knees are supplied him by the gods?
But when the gods in bliss bring miseries on,          150
then willy-nilly, blindly, he endures.
Our minds are as the days are, dark or bright,
blown over by the father of gods and men.

So I, too, in my time thought to be happy;
but far and rash I ventured, counting on            155
my own right arm, my father, and my kin;
behold me now.
                    No man should flout the law,
but keep in peace what gifts the gods may give.

I see you young blades living dangerously,
a household eaten up, a wife dishonored—               160
and yet the master will return, I tell you,
to his own place, and soon; for he is near.
So may some power take you out of this,
homeward, and softly, not to face that man
the hour he sets foot on his native ground.            165
Between him and the suitors I foretell
no quittance, no way out, unless by blood,
once he shall stand beneath his own roof-beam."

Gravely, when he had done, he made libation
and took a sip of honey-hearted wine,                  170
giving the cup, then, back into the hands
of the young nobleman. Amphínomos, for his part,
shaking his head, with chill and burdened breast,
turned in the great hall.
                              Now his heart foreknew
the wrath to come, but he could not take flight,       175
being by Athena bound there.
                                 Death would have him

broken by a spear thrown by Telémakhos.
So he sat down where he had sat before.

And now heart-prompting from the grey-eyed goddess
came to the quiet queen, Penélopê:                              180
a wish to show herself before the suitors;
for thus by fanning their desire again
Athena meant to set her beauty high
before her husband's eyes, before her son.
Knowing no reason, laughing confusedly,                         185
she said:

     "Eurýnomê, I have a craving
I never had at all—I would be seen
among those ruffians, hateful as they are.
I might well say a word, then, to my son,
for his own good—tell him to shun that crowd;                   190
for all their gay talk, they are bent on evil."

Mistress Eurýnomê replied:

        "Well said, child,
now is the time. Go down, and make it clear,
hold nothing back from him.
          But you must bathe
and put a shine upon your cheeks—not this way,                  195
streaked under your eyes and stained with tears.
You make it worse, being forever sad,
and now your boy's a bearded man! Remember
you prayed the gods to let you see him so."

Penélopê replied:

       "Eurýnomê,                                200
it is a kind thought, but I will not hear it—
to bathe and sleek with perfumed oil. No, no,
the gods forever took my sheen away
when my lord sailed for Troy in the decked ships.
Only tell my Autonoë to come,                                   205
and Hippodameía; they should be attending me
in hall, if I appear there. I could not
enter alone into that crowd of men."

At this the good old woman left the chamber
to tell the maids her bidding. But now too                      210

the grey-eyed goddess had her own designs.
Upon the quiet daughter of Ikários
she let clear drops of slumber fall, until
the queen lay back asleep, her limbs unstrung,
in her long chair. And while she slept the goddess          215
endowed her with immortal grace to hold
the eyes of the Akhaians. With ambrosia
she bathed her cheeks and throat and smoothed her brow—
ambrosia, used by flower-crowned Kythereia[6]
when she would join the rose-lipped Graces dancing.         220
Grandeur she gave her, too, in height and form,
and made her whiter than carved ivory.
touching her so, the perfect one was gone.
Now came the maids, bare-armed and lovely, voices
breaking into the room. The queen awoke                     225
and as she rubbed her cheek she sighed:

                                        "Ah, soft
that drowse I lay embraced in, pain forgot!
If only Artemis the Pure would give me
death as mild, and soon! No heart-ache more,
no wearing out my lifetime with desire                      230
and sorrow, mindful of my lord, good man
in all ways that he was, best of the Akhaians!"

She rose and left her glowing upper room,
and down the stairs, with her two maids in train,
this beautiful lady went before the suitors.                235
Then by a pillar of the solid roof
she paused, her shining veil across her cheek,
the two girls close to her and still;
and in that instant weakness took those men
in the knee joints, their hearts grew faint with lust;      240
not one but swore to god to lie beside her.
But speaking for her dear son's ears alone
she said:

          "Telémakhos, what has come over you?
Lightminded you were not, in all your boyhood.
Now you are full grown, come of age; a man                  245
from foreign parts might take you for the son
of royalty, to go by your good looks;
and have you no more thoughtfulness or manners?

6. Aphrodite.

How could it happen in our hall that you
permit the stranger to be so abused?          250
Here, in our house, a guest, can any man
suffer indignity, come by such injury?
What can this be for you but public shame?"

Telémakhos looked in her eyes and answered,
with his clear head and his discretion:          255

"Mother,
I cannot take it ill that you are angry.
I know the meaning of these actions now,
both good and bad. I had been young and blind.
How can I always keep to what is fair          260
while these sit here to put fear in me?—princes
from near and far whose interest is my ruin;
are any on my side?

              But you should know
the suitors did not have their way, matching
the stranger here and Iros—for the stranger          265
beat him to the ground.

              O Father Zeus!
Athena and Apollo! could I see
the suitors whipped like that! Courtyard and hall
strewn with our friends, too weak-kneed to get up,
chapfallen to their collarbones, the way          270
old Iros rolls his head there by the gate
as though he were pig-drunk! No energy
to stagger on his homeward path; no fight
left in his numb legs!"

              Thus Penélopê
reproached her son, and he replied. Now, interrupting,          275
Eurýmakhos called out to her:

              "Penélopê,
deep-minded queen, daughter of Ikários,
if all Akhaians in the land of Argos
only saw you now! What hundreds more
would join your suitors here to feast tomorrow!          280
Beauty like yours no woman had before,
or majesty, or mastery."

              She answered:

"Eurýmakhos, my qualities—I know—

my face, my figure, all were lost or blighted
when the Akhaians crossed the sea to Troy,                          285
Odysseus my lord among the rest.
If he returned, if he were here to care for me,
I might be happily renowned!
But grief instead heaven sent me—years of pain.
Can I forget?—the day he left this island,                          290
enfolding my right hand and wrist in his,
he said:

     'My lady, the Akhaian troops
will not easily make it home again
full strength, unhurt, from Troy. They say the Trojans
are fighters too; good lances and good bowmen,                       295
horsemen, charioteers—and those can be
decisive when a battle hangs in doubt.
So whether God will send me back, or whether
I'll be a captive there, I cannot tell.
Here, then, you must attend to everything.                           300
My parents in our house will be a care for you
as they are now, or more, while I am gone.
Wait for the beard to darken our boy's cheek;
then marry whom you will, and move away.'

The years he spoke of are now past; the night            305
comes when a bitter marriage overtakes me,
desolate as I am, deprived by Zeus
of all the sweets of life.

     How galling, too,
to see newfangled manners in my suitors!
Others who go to court a gentlewoman,                                310
daughter of a rich house, if they are rivals,
bring their own beeves and sheep along; her friends
ought to be feasted, gifts are due to her;
would any dare to live at her expense?"

Odysseus' heart laughed when he heard all this—             315
her sweet tones charming gifts out of the suitors
with talk of marriage, though she intended none.
Eupeithês' son, Antínoös, now addressed her:

"Ikários' daughter, O deep-minded queen!
If someone cares to make you gifts, accept them!                     320
It is no courtesy to turn gifts away.

But we go neither to our homes nor elsewhere
until of all Akhaians here you take
the best man for your lord."

                  Pleased at this answer,
every man sent a squire to fetch a gift—           325
Antínoös, a wide resplendent robe,
embroidered fine, and fastened with twelve brooches,
pins pressed into sheathing tubes of gold;
Eurýmakhos, a necklace, wrought in gold,
with sunray pieces of clear glinting amber.         330
Eurýdamas' men came back with pendants,
ear-drops in triple clusters of warm lights;
and from the hoard of Lord Polýktor's son,
Peisándros, came a band for her white throat,
jewelled adornment. Other wondrous things         335
were brought as gifts from the Akhaian princes.
Penélopê then mounted the stair again,
her maids behind, with treasure in their arms.

And now the suitors gave themselves to dancing,
to harp and haunting song, as night drew on;        340
black night indeed came on them at their pleasure.
But three torch fires were placed in the long hall
to give them light. On hand were stores of fuel,
dry seasoned chips of resinous wood, split up
by the bronze hatchet blade—these were mixed in      345
among the flames to keep them flaring bright;
each housemaid of Odysseus took her turn.

Now he himself, the shrewd and kingly man,
approached and told them:

                "Housemaids of Odysseus,
your master so long absent in the world,         350
go to the women's chambers, to your queen.
Attend her, make the distaff whirl, divert her,
stay in her room, comb wool for her.
                    I stand here
ready to tend these flares and offer light
to everyone. They cannot tire me out,         355
even if they wish to drink till Dawn.
I am a patient man."

              But the women giggled,

glancing back and forth—laughed in his face;
one one smooth girl, Melántho, spoke to him
most impudently. She was Dólios' daughter,                    360
taken as ward in childhood by Penélopê
who gave her playthings to her heart's content
and raised her as her own. Yet the girl felt
nothing for her mistress, no compunction,
but slept and made love with Eurýmakhos.                    365
Her bold voice rang now in Odysseus' ears:

"You must be crazy, punch drunk, you old goat.
Instead of going out to find a smithy
to sleep warm in—or a tavern bench—you stay
putting your oar in, amid all our men.                    370
Numbskull, not to be scared! The wine you drank
has clogged your brain, or are you always this way,
boasting like a fool? Or have you lost
your mind because you beat that tramp, that Iros?
Look out, or someone better may get up                    375
and give you a good knocking about the ears
to send you out all bloody."

                    But Odysseus
glared at her under his brows and said:

                                        "One minute:
let me tell Telémakhos how you talk
in hall, you slut; he'll cut your arms and legs off!"                    380

This hard shot took the women's breath away
and drove them quaking to their rooms, as though
knives were behind: they felt he spoke the truth.
So there he stood and kept the firelight high
and looked the suitors over, while his mind                    385
roamed far ahead to what must be accomplished.

They, for their part, could not now be still
or drop their mockery—for Athena wished
Odysseus mortified still more.
                                        Eurýmakhos,
the son of Pólybos, took up the baiting,                    390
angling for a laugh among his friends.

"Suitors of our distinguished queen," he said,
"hear what my heart would have me say.

                                   This man
comes with a certain aura of divinity
into Odysseus' hall. He shines.
                                   He shines                           395
around the noggin, like a flashing light.
having no hair at all to dim his lustre."

Then turning to Odysseus, raider of cities,
he went on:

          "Friend, you have a mind to work,
do you? Could I hire you to clear stones                               400
from wasteland for me—you'll be paid enough—
collecting boundary walls and planting trees?
I'd give you a bread ration every day,
a cloak to wrap in, sandals for your feet.
Oh no: you learned your dodges long ago—                              405
no honest sweat. You'd rather tramp the country
begging, to keep your hoggish belly full."

The master of many crafts replied:

                         "Eurýmakhos,
we two might try our hands against each other
in early summer when the days are long,                               410
in meadow grass, with one good scythe for me
and one as good for you: we'd cut our way
down a deep hayfield, fasting to late evening.
Or we could try our hands behind a plow,
driving the best of oxen—fat, well-fed,                               415
well-matched for age and pulling power, and say
four strips apiece of loam the share could break:
you'd see then if I cleft you a straight furrow.
Competition in arms? If Zeus Kroníon
roused up a scuffle now, give me a shield,                            420
two spears, a dogskin cap with plates of bronze
to fit my temples, and you'd see me go
where the first rank of fighters lock in battle.
There would be no more jeers about my belly.
You thick-skinned menace to all courtesy!                             425
You think you are a great man and a champion,
but up against few men, poor stuff, at that.
Just let Odysseus return, those doors
wide open as they are, you'd find too narrow
to suit you on your sudden journey out."                              430

Now fury mounted in Eurýmakhos,
who scowled and shot back:

                "Bundle of rags and lice!
By god, I'll make you suffer for your gall,
your insolent gabble before all our men."
He had his foot-stool out: but now Odysseus                      435
took to his hauches by Amphínomos' knees,
fearing Eurýmakhos' missile, as it flew.
It clipped a wine steward on the serving hand,
so that his pitcher dropped with a loud clang
while he fell backward, cursing, in the dust.                    440
In the shadowy hall a low sound rose—of suitors
murmuring to one another.

                "Ai!" they said,
"This vagabond would have done well to perish
somewhere else, and make us no such rumpus.
Here we are, quarreling over tramps; good meat             445
and wine forgotten; good sense gone by the board."

Telémakhos, his young heart high, put in:

"Bright souls, alight with wine, you can no longer
hide the cups you've taken.[7] Aye, some god
is goading you. Why not go home to bed?—                  450
I mean when you are moved to. No one jumps
at my command."

               Struck by his blithe manner,
the young men's teeth grew fixed in their under lips,
but now the son of Nísos, Lord Amphínomos
of Aretíadês, addressed them all:                                  455

"O friends, no ruffling replies are called for;
that was fair counsel.
            Hands off the stranger, now,
and hands off any other servant here
in the great house of King Odysseus. Come,
let my own herald wet our cups once more,                  460
we'll make an offering, and then to bed.
The stranger can be left behind in hall;
Telémakhos may care for him; he came

---

7. I.e., you can't hide the fact that you are drunk.

to Telémakhos' door, not ours."

                       This won them over.
The soldier Moulios, Doulíkhion herald,                  465
comrade in arms of Lord Amphínomos,
mixed the wine and served them all. They tipped out
drops for the blissful gods, and drank the rest,
and when they had drunk their thirst away
they trailed off homeward drowsily to bed.                470

## Book XIX

### RECOGNITIONS AND A DREAM

Now by Athena's side in the quiet hall
studying the ground for slaughter, Lord Odysseus
turned to Telémakhos.

               "The arms," he said.
"Harness and weapons must be out of sight
in the inner room. And if the suitors miss them,         5
be mild; just say 'I had a mind to move them
out of the smoke. They seemed no longer
the bright arms that Odysseus left at home
when he went off to Troy. Here where the fire's
hot breath came, they had grown black and drear.         10
One better reason struck me, too:
suppose a brawl starts up when you've been drinking—
you might in madness let each other's blood,
and that would stain your feast, your courtship.
                                 Iron
itself can draw men's hands.' "

                 Then he fell silent,         15
and Telémakhos obeyed his father's word.
He called Eurýkleia, the nurse, and told her:

"Nurse, go shut the women in their quarters
while I shift Father's armor back
to the inner rooms—these beautiful arms unburnished,      20
caked with black soot in his years abroad.
I was a child then. Well, I am not now.
I want them shielded from the draught and smoke."

And the old woman answered:

"It is time, child,
you took an interest in such things. I wish                    25
you'd put your mind on all your house and chattels.
But who will go along to hold a light?
You said no maids, no torch-bearers."

                              Telémakhos
looked at her and replied:

                    "Our friend here.
A man who shares my meat can bear a hand,              30
no matter how far he is from home."

                              He spoke so soldierly
her own speech halted on her tongue. Straight back
she went to lock the doors of the women's hall.
And now the two men sprang to work—father
and princely son, loaded with round helms            35
and studded bucklers, lifting the long spears,
while in their path Pallas Athena
held up a golden lamp of purest light.
Telémakhos at last burst out:

                    "Oh, Father,
here is a marvel! All around I see                    40
the walls and roof beams, pedestals and pillars,
lighted as though by white fire blazing near.
One of the gods of heaven is in this place!"

Then said Odysseus, the great tactician,

"Be still: keep still about it: just remember it.     45
The gods who rule Olympos make this light.
You may go off to bed now. Here I stay
to test your mother and her maids again.
Out of her long grief she will question me."
Telémakhos went across the hall and out              50
under the light of torches—crossed the court
to the tower chamber where he had always slept.
Here now again he lay, waiting for dawn,
while in the great hall by Athena's side
Odysseus waited with his mind on slaughter.         55

Presently Penélopê from her chamber
stepped in her thoughtful beauty.
                              So might Artemis

or golden Aphroditê have descended;
and maids drew to the hearth her own smooth chair
inlaid with silver whorls and ivory. The artisan            60
Ikmálios had made it, long before,
with a footrest in a single piece, and soft
upon the seat a heavy fleece was thrown.
Here by the fire the queen sat down. Her maids,
leaving their quarters, came with white arms bare           65
to clear the wine cups and the bread, and move
the trestle boards where men had lingered drinking.
Fiery ashes out of the pine-chip flares
they tossed, and piled on fuel for light and heat.
And now a second time Melántho's voice                      70
rang brazen in Odysseus' ears:


                         "Ah, stranger,
are you still here, so creepy, late at night
hanging about, looking the women over?
You old goat, go outside, cuddle your supper;
get out, or a torch may kindle you behind!"                 75


At this Odysseus glared under his brows
and said:


          "Little devil, why pitch into me again?
Because I go unwashed and wear these rags,
and make the rounds? But so I must, being needy;
that is the way a vagabond must live.                       80
And do not overlook this: in my time
I too had luck, lived well, stood well with men,
and gave alms, often, to poor wanderers
like him you see before you—aye, to all sorts,
no matter in what dire want. I owned                        85
servants—many, I say—and all the rest
that goes with what men call prosperity.
But Zeus the son of Kronos brought me down.
Mistress, mend your ways, or you may lose
all this vivacity of yours. What if her ladyship            90
were stirred to anger? What if Odysseus came?—
and I can tell you, there is hope of that—
or if the man is done for, still his son
lives to be reckoned with, by Apollo's will.
None of you can go wantoning on the sly                     95
and fool him now. He is too old for that."

Penélopê, being near enough to hear him,
spoke out sharply to her maid:

                              "Oh, shameless,
through and through! And do you think me blind,
blind to your conquest? It will cost your life.          100
You knew I waited—for you heard me say it—
waited to see this man in hall and question him
about my lord; I am so hard beset."

She turned away and said to the housekeeper:

"Eurýnomê, a bench, a spread of sheepskin,                105
to put my guest at ease. Now he shall talk
and listen, and be questioned."

                          Willing hands
brought a smooth bench, and dropped a fleece upon it.
Here the adventurer and king sat down;
then carefully Penélopê began:                            110

"Friend, let me ask you first of all:
who are you, where do you come from, of what nation
and parents were you born?"

                          And he replied:

"My lady, never a man in the wide world
should have a fault to find with you. Your name         115
has gone out under heaven like the sweet
honor of some god-fearing king, who rules
in equity over the strong: his black lands bear
both wheat and barely, fruit trees laden bright,
new lambs at lambing time—and the deep sea             120
gives great hauls of fish by his good strategy,
so that his folk fare well.
                          O my dear lady,
this being so, let it suffice to ask me
of other matters—not my blood, my homeland.
Do not enforce me to recall my pain.                    125
My heart is sore; but I must not be found
sitting in tears here, in another's house:
it is not well forever to be grieving.
One of the maids might say—or you might think—
I had got maudlin over cups of wine."                   130

And Penélopê replied:

"Stranger, my looks,
my face, my carriage, were soon lost or faded
when the Akhaians crossed the sea to Troy,
Odysseus my lord among the rest.
If he returned, if he were here to care for me,                    135
I might be happily renowned!
But grief instead heaven sent me—years of pain.
Sons of the noblest families on the islands,
Doulíkion, Samê, wooded Zakýnthos,
with native Ithakans, are here to court me,                    140
against my wish; and they consume this house.
Can I give proper heed to guest or suppliant
or herald on the realm's affairs?
                                   How could I?
wasted with longing for Odysseus, while here
they press for marriage.
                         Ruses served my turn
to draw the time out—first a close-grained web                    145
I had the happy thought to set up weaving
on my big loom in hall. I said, that day:
'Young men—my suitors, now my lord is dead,
let me finish my weaving before I marry,                    150
or else my thread will have been spun in vain.
It is a shroud I weave for Lord Laërtês
when cold Death comes to lay him on his bier.
The country wives would hold me in dishonor
if he, with all his fortune, lay unshrouded.'                    155
I reached their hearts that way, and they agreed.
So every day I wove on the great loom,
but every night by torchlight I unwove it;
and so for three years I deceived the Akhaians.
But when the seasons brought a fourth year on,                    160
as long months waned, and the long days were spent,
through impudent folly in the slinking maids
they caught me—clamored up to me at night;
I had no choice then but to finish it.
And now, as matters stand at last,                    165
I have no strength left to evade a marriage,
cannot find any further way; my parents
urge it upon me, and my son
will not stand by while they eat up his property.
He comprehends it, being a man full grown,                    170
able to oversee the kind of house

Zeus would endow with honor.
                              But you too
confide in me, tell me your ancestry.
You were not born of mythic oak or stone."

And the great master of invention answered:                    175

"O honorable wife of Lord Odysseus,
must you go on asking about my family?
Then I will tell you, though my pain
be doubled by it: and whose pain would not
if he had been away as long as I have                          180
and had hard roving in the world of men?
But I will tell you even so, my lady.

One of the great islands of the world
in midsea, in the winedark sea, is Krete:
spacious and rich and populous, with ninety                    185
cities and a mingling of tongues.
Akhaians there are found, along with Kretan
hillmen of the old stock, and Kydonians,
Dorians in three blood-lines, Pelasgians—
and one among their ninety towns is Knossos.[8]               190
Here lived King Minos whom great Zeus received
every ninth year in private council—Minos,
the father of my father, Deukálion.
Two sons Deukálion had: Idómeneus,
who went to join the Atreidai before Troy                      195
in the beaked ships of war; and then myself,
Aithôn by name—a stripling next my brother.
But I saw with my own eyes at Knossos once
Odysseus.
          Gales had caught him off Cape Malea,
driven him southward on the coast of Krete,                    200
when he was bound for Troy. At Ámnisos,
hard by the holy cave of Eileithuía,[9]
he lay to, and dropped anchor, in that open
and rough roadstead riding out the blow.
Meanwhile he came ashore, came inland, asking                  205
after Idómeneus: dear friends he said they were;

8. The site of the great palace discovered by Evans, who called the civilization which produced
it Minoan. It is impossible to extract historical fact from this confused account of the population
of Crete: Kydonians may be the inhabitants of the western end of the island; Dorians were the
people who, according to Greek belief, invaded Greece and destroyed the Mycenean palace-
civilizations (but Homer does not mention them elsewhere); Pelasgians were the pre-Greek inhabitants of the area.   9. Goddess of childbirth. *Ámnisos:* On the wash near Knossos.

but now ten mornings had already passed,
ten or eleven, since my brother sailed.
So I played host and took Odysseus home,
saw him well lodged and fed, for we had plenty;                    210
then I made requisitions—barley, wine,
and beeves for sacrifice—to give his company
abundant fare along with him.
                                        Twelve days
they stayed with us, the Akhaians, while that wind
out of the north shut everyone inside—                            215
even on land you could not keep your feet,
such fury was abroad. On the thirteenth,
when the gale dropped, they put to sea."

Now all these lies he made appear so truthful
she wept as she sat listening. The skin                           220
of her pale face grew moist the way pure snow
softens and glistens on the mountains, thawed
by Southwind after powdering from the West,
and, as the snow melts, mountain streams run full:
so her white cheeks were wetted by these tears                    225
shed for her lord—and he close by her side.
Imagine how his heart ached for his lady,
his wife in tears; and yet he never blinked;
his eyes might have been made of horn or iron
for all that she could see. He had this trick—                    230
wept, if he willed to, inwardly.
                                        Well, then,
as soon as her relieving tears were shed
she spoke once more:

                        "I think that I shall say, friend,
give me some proof, if it is really true
that you were host in that place to my husband                    235
with his brave men, as you declare. Come, tell me
the quality of his clothing, how he looked,
and some particular of his company."

Odysseus answered, and his mind ranged far:

"Lady, so long a time now lies between,                           240
it is hard to speak of it. Here is the twentieth year
since that man left the island of my father.
But I shall tell what memory calls to mind.
A purple cloak, and fleecy, he had on—

a double thick one. Then, he wore a brooch                        245
made of pure gold with twin tubes for the prongs,
and on the face a work of art: a hunting dog
pinning a spotted fawn in agony
between his forepaws—wonderful to see
how being gold, and nothing more, he bit                          250
the golden deer convulsed, with wild hooves flying.
Odysseus' shirt I noticed, too—a fine
closefitting tunic like dry onion skin,
so soft it was, and shiny.
                              Women there,
many of them, would cast their eyes on it.                        255
But I might add, for your consideration,
whether he brought these things from home, or whether
a shipmate gave them to him, coming aboard,
I have no notion: some regardful host
in another port perhaps it was. Affection                         260
followed him—there were few Akhaians like him.
And I too made him gifts: a good bronze blade,
a cloak with lining and a broidered shirt,
and sent him off in his trim ship with honor.
A herald, somewhat older than himself,                            265
he kept beside him; I'll describe this man:
round-shouldered, dusky, woolly-headed;
Eurýbatês, his name was—and Odysseus
gave him preferment over the officers.
He had a shrewd head, like the captain's own."                    270


Now hearing these details—minutely true—
she felt more strangely moved, and tears flowed
until she had tasted her salt grief again.
Then she found words to answer:

                              "Before this
you won my sympathy, but now indeed                               275
you shall be our respected guest and friend.
With my own hands I put that cloak and tunic
upon him—took them folded from their place—
and the bright brooch for ornament.
                              Gone now,
I will not meet the man again                                     280
returning to his own home fields. Unkind
the fate that sent him young in the long ship
to see that misery at Ilion, unspeakable!"

And the master improviser answered:

                                        "Honorable
wife of Odysseus Laërtiadês,                                    285
you need not stain your beauty with these tears,
nor wear yourself out grieving for your husband.
Not that I can blame you. Any wife
grieves for the man she married in her girlhood,
lay with in love, bore children to—though he          290
may be no prince like this Odysseus,
whom they compare even to the gods. But listen:
weep no more, and listen:
I have a thing to tell you, something true.
I heard but lately of your lord's return,                      295
heard that he is alive, not far away,
among Thesprótians in their green land
amassing fortune to bring home. His company
went down in shipwreck in the winedark sea
off the coast of Thrinákia. Zeus and Hêlios          300
held it against him that his men had killed
the kine of Hêlios. The crew drowned for this.
He rode the ship's keel. Big seas cast him up
on the island of Phaiákians, godlike men
who took him to their hearts. They honored him          305
with many gifts and a safe passage home,
or so they wished. Long since he should have been here,
but he thought better to restore his fortune
playing the vagabond about the world;
and no adventurer could beat Odysseus                    310
at living by his wits—no man alive.
I had this from King Phaidôn of Thesprótia;
and, tipping wine out, Phaidôn swore to me
the ship was launched, the seamen standing by
to bring Odysseus to his land at last,                          315
but I got out to sea ahead of him
by the king's order—as it chanced a freighter
left port for the grain bins of Doulíkhion.
Phaidôn, however, showed me Odysseus' treasure.
Ten generations of his heirs or more                           320
could live on what lay piled in that great room.
The man himself had gone up to Dodona
to ask the spelling leaves of the old oak
what Zeus would have him do—how to return to Ithaka
after so many years—by stealth or openly.                      335

You see, then, he is alive and well, and headed
homeward now, no more to be abroad
far from his island, his dear wife and son.
Here is my sworn word for it. Witness this,
god of the zenith, noblest of the gods,                                340
and Lord Odysseus' hearthfire, now before me:
I swear these things shall turn out as I say.
Between this present dark and one day's ebb,
after the wane, before the crescent moon,
Odysseus will come."

                    Penélopê,                                 345
the attentive queen, replied to him:

                        "Ah, stranger,
if what you say could ever happen!
You would soon know our love! Our bounty, too:
men would turn after you to call you blessed.
But my heart tells me what must be.                                    350
Odysseus will not come to me; no ship
will be prepared for you. We have no master
quick to receive and furnish out a guest
as Lord Odysseus was.
                Or did I dream him?

Maids, maids: come wash him, make a bed for him,                       355
bedstead and colored rugs and coverlets
to let him lie warm into the gold of Dawn.
In morning light you'll bathe him and anoint him
so that he'll take his place beside Telémakhos
feasting in hall. If there be one man there                            360
to bully or annoy him, that man wins
no further triumph here, burn though he may.
How will you understand me, friend, how find in me,
more than in common women, any courage
or gentleness, if you are kept in rags                                 365
and filthy at our feast? Men's lives are short.
The hard man and his cruelties will be
cursed behind his back, and mocked in death.
But one whose heart and ways are kind—of him
strangers will bear report to the wide world,                          370
and distant men will praise him."

                    Warily

Odysseus answered:

                    "Honorable lady,
wife of Odysseus Laërtiadês,
a weight of rugs and cover? Not for me.
I've had none since the day I saw the mountains          375
of Krete, white with snow, low on the sea line
fading behind me as the long oars drove me north.
Let me lie down tonight as I've lain often,
many a night unsleeping, many a time
afield on hard ground waiting for pure Dawn.          380
No: and I have no longing for a footbath
either; none of these maids will touch my feet,
unless there is an old one, old and wise,
one who has lived through suffering as I have:
I would not mind letting my feet be touched          385
by that old servant."

                    And Penélopê said:

"Dear guest, no foreign man so sympathetic
ever came to my house, no guest more likeable,
so wry and humble are the things you say.
I have an old maidservant ripe with years,          390
one who in her time nursed my lord. She took him
into her arms the hour his mother bore him.
Let her, then, wash your feet, though she is frail.
Come here, stand by me, faithful Eurýkleia,
and bathe—bathe your master, I almost said,          395
for they are of an age, and now Odysseus'
feet and hands would be enseamed like his.
Men grow old soon in hardship."

                    Hearing this,
the old nurse hid her face between her hands
and wept hot tears, and murmured:

                    "Oh, my child!          400
I can do nothing for you! How Zeus hated you,
no other man so much! No use, great heart,
O faithful heart, the rich thighbones you burnt
to Zeus who plays in lightning—and no man
ever gave more to Zeus—with all your prayers          405
for a green age, a tall son reared to manhood.
There is no day of homecoming for you.

Stranger, some women in some far off place
perhaps have mocked my lord when he'd be home
as now these strumpets mock you here. No wonder                    410
you would keep clear of all their whorishness
and have no bath. But here am I. The queen
Penélopê, Ikários' daughter, bids me;
so let me bathe your feet to serve my lady—
to serve you, too.

       My heart within me stirs,                               415
mindful of something. Listen to what I say:
strangers have come here, many through the years,
but no one ever came, I swear, who seemed
so like Odysseus—body, voice and limbs—
as you do."

       Ready for this, Odysseus answered:                          420
"Old woman, that is what they say. All who have seen
the two of us remark how like we are,
as you yourself have said, and rightly, too."

Then he kept still, while the old nurse filled up
her basin glittering in firelight; she poured                      425
cold water in, then hot.

       But Lord Odysseus
whirled suddenly from the fire to face the dark.
The scar: he had forgotten that. She must not
handle his scarred thigh, or the game was up.
But when she bared her lord's leg, bending near,                   430
she knew the groove at once.

       An old wound
a boar's white tusk inflicted, on Parnassos[1]
years ago. He had gone hunting there
in company with his uncles and Autólykos,
his mother's father—a great thief and swindler                     435
by Hermês' favor,[2] for Autólykos pleased him
with burnt offerings of sheep and kids. The god
acted as his accomplice. Well, Autólykos
on a trip to Ithaka
arrived just after his daughter's boy was born.                    440
In fact, he had no sooner finished supper
than Nurse Euríkleia put the baby down
in his own lap and said:

1. The mountain range above Apollo's oracular shrine at Delphi.   2. Hermes was not only the
messenger of the gods and the god who guided the dead down to the lower world, he was also the
god of the marketplace and so of trickery and swindling.

"It is for you, now,
to choose a name for him, your child's dear baby;
the answer to her prayers."

Autólykos replied:                                    445

"My son-in-law, my daughter, call the boy
by the name I tell you. Well you know, my hand
has been against the world of men and women;
odium[3] and distrust I've won. Odysseus
should be his given name. When he grows up,       450
when he comes visiting his mother's home
under Parnassos, where my treasures are,
I'll make him gifts and send him back rejoicing."

Odysseus in due course went for the gifts,
and old Autólykos and his sons embraced him     455
with welcoming sweet words; and Amphithéa,
his mother's mother, held him tight and kissed him,
kissed his head and his fine eyes.
                              The father
called on his noble sons to make a feast,
and going about it briskly they led in            460
an ox of five years, whom they killed and flayed
and cut in bits for roasting on the skewers
with skilled hands, with care; then shared it out.
So all the day until the sun went down
they feasted to their hearts' content. At evening, 465
after the sun was down and dusk had come,
they turned to bed and took the gift of sleep.

When the young Dawn spread in the eastern sky
her finger tips of rose, the men and dogs
went hunting, taking Odysseus. They climbed      470
Parnassos' rugged flank mantled in forest,
entering amid high windy folds at noon
when Hêlios beat upon the valley floor
and on the winding Ocean whence he came.
With hounds questing ahead, in open order,        475
the sons of Autólykos went down a glen,
Odysseus in the lead, behind the dogs,
pointing his long-shadowing spear.
                              Before them

3. The translator is reproducing a pun in the original Greek: Autólykos speaks of himself as
*odyssamenos*, one who is angry and gives cause for anger.

a great boar lay hid in undergrowth,
in a green thicket proof against the wind                          480
or sun's blaze, fine soever the needling sunlight,
impervious too to any rain, so dense
that cover was, heaped up with fallen leaves.
Patter of hounds' feet, men's feet, woke the boar
as they came up—and from his woody ambush              485
with razor back bristling and raging eyes
he trotted and stood at bay. Odysseus,
being on top of him, had the first shot,
lunging to stick him; but the boar
had already charged under the long spear.                      490
He hooked aslant with one white tusk and ripped out
flesh above the knee, but missed the bone.
Odysseus' second thrust went home by luck,
his bright spear passing through the shoulder joint;
and the beast fell, moaning as life pulsed away.              495
Autólykos' tall sons took up the wounded,
working skillfully over the Prince Odysseus
to bind his gash, and with a rune[4] they stanched
the dark flow of blood. Then downhill swiftly
they all repaired to the father's house, and there          500
tended him well—so well they soon could send him,
with Grandfather Autólykos' magnificent gifts,
rejoicing, over sea to Ithaka.
His father and the Lady Antikleía
welcomed him, and wanted all the news                          505
of how he got his wound; so he spun out
his tale, recalling how the boar's white tusk
caught him when he was hunting on Parnassos.

This was the scar the old nurse recognized;
she traced it under her spread hands, then let go,         510
and into the basin fell the lower leg
making the bronze clang, sloshing the water out.
Then joy and anguish seized her heart; her eyes
filled up with tears; her throat closed, and she whispered,
with hand held out to touch his chin:

                                        "Oh yes!                        515
You are Odysseus! Ah, dear child! I could not
see you until now—not till I knew
my master's very body with my hands!"

---

4. An incantation, primitive magic to stop the flow of blood.

Her eyes turned to Penélopê with desire
to make her lord, her husband, known—in vain,                    520
because Athena had bemused the queen,
so that she took no notice, paid no heed.
At the same time Odysseus' right hand
gripped the old throat; his hand pulled her near,
and in her ear he said:

               "Will you destroy me,                    525
nurse, who gave me milk at your own breast?
Now with a hard lifetime behind I've come
in the twentieth year home to my father's island.
You found me out, as the chance was given you.
Be quiet; keep it from the others, else                    530
I warn you, and I mean it, too,
if by my hand god brings the suitors down
I'll kill you, nurse or not, when the time comes—
when the time comes to kill the other women."
Euríkleia kept her wits and answered him:                    535

"Oh, what mad words are these you let escape you!
Child, you know my blood, my bones are yours;
no one could whip this out of me. I'll be
a woman turned to stone, iron I'll be.
And let me tell you too—mind now—if god                    540
cuts down the arrogant suitors by your hand,
I can report to you on all the maids,
those who dishonor you, and the innocent."

But in response the great tactician said:

"Nurse, no need to tell me tales of these.                    545
I will have seen them, each one, for myself.
Trust in the gods, be quiet, hold your peace."

Silent, the old nurse went to fetch more water,
her basin being all spilt.
            When she had washed
and rubbed his feet with golden oil, he turned,                    550
dragging his bench again to the fire side
for warmth, and hid the scar under his rags.
Penélopê broke the silence, saying:

                "Friend,
allow me one brief question more. You know,

the time for bed, sweet rest, is coming soon,                                    555
if only that warm luxury of slumber
would come to enfold us, in our trouble. But for me
my fate at night is anguish and no rest.
By day being busy, seeing to my work,
I find relief sometimes from loss and sorrow;                                    560
but when night comes and all the world's abed
I lie in mine alone, my heart thudding,
while bitter thoughts and fears crowd on my grief.
Think how Pandáreos' daughter,[5] pale forever,
sings as the nightingale in the new leaves                                       565
through those long quiet hours of night,
on some thick-flowering orchard bough in spring;
how she rills out and tilts her note, high now, now low,
mourning for Itylos whom she killed in madness—
her child, and her lord Zêthos' only child.                                      570
My forlorn thought flows variable as her song,
wondering: shall I stay beside my son
and guard my own things here, my maids, my hall,
to honor my lord's bed and the common talk?
Or had I best join fortunes with a suitor,                                       575
the noblest one, most lavish in his gifts?
Is it now time for that?
My son being still a callow boy forbade
marriage, or absence from my lord's domain;
but now the child is grown, grown up, a man,                                     580
he, too, begins to pray for my departure,
aghast at all the suitors gorge on.

                              Listen:
interpret me this dream: From a water's edge
twenty fat geese have come to feed on grain
beside my house. And I delight to see them.                                      585
But now a mountain eagle with great wings
and crooked beak storms in to break their necks
and strew their bodies here. Away he soars
into the bright sky; and I cry aloud—
all this in dream—I wail and round me gather                                     590
softly braided Akhaian women mourning
because the eagle killed my geese.
                              Then down

5. The reference is to one of the many Greek legends that explain the song of the nightingale. In this one (for another see note 8, XX. 68) the daughter of Pandáreos, a Cretan King, was married to Zêthos, King of Thebes. She had only one son; her sister-in-law Niobe had many. In a fit of jealousy she tried to kill Niobe's eldest son but by mistake (in the dark) killed her own son, Itylos, instead. Zeus changed her into a nightingale and she sings in mourning for Itylos.

out of the sky he drops to a cornice beam
with mortal voice telling me not to weep.
'Be glad,' says he, 'renowned Ikários' daughter:                    595
here is no dream but something real as day,
something about to happen. All those geese
were suitors, and the bird was I. See now,
I am no eagle but your lord come back
to bring inglorious death upon them all!'                          600
As he said this, my honeyed slumber left me.
Peering through half-shut eyes, I saw the geese
in hall, still feeding at the self-same trough."
The master of subtle ways and straight replied:

"My dear, how can you choose to read the dream                      605
differently? Has not Odysseus himself
shown you what is to come? Death to the suitors,
sure death, too. Not one escapes his doom."

Penélopê shook her head and answered:

                    "Friend,
many and many a dream is mere confusion,                           610
a cobweb of no consequence at all.
Two gates for ghostly dreams there are: one gateway
of honest horn, and one of ivory.
Issuing by the ivory gate are dreams
of glimmering illusion, fantasies,                                 615
but those that come through solid polished horn
may be borne out, if mortals only know them.
I doubt it came by horn, my fearful dream—
too good to be true, that, for my son and me.
But one thing more I wish to tell you: listen                      620
carefully. It is a black day, this that comes.
Odysseus' house and I are to be parted.
I shall decree a contest for the day.
We have twelve axe heads. In his time, my lord
could line them up, all twelve, at intervals                       625
like a ship's ribbing; then he'd back away
a long way off and whip an arrow through.[6]
Now I'll impose this trial on the suitors.

6. The nature of this archery contest is a puzzle that has never been satisfactorily solved. The axes were probably double-headed; the aperture through which the arrow passed must have been the socket in which the wooden handle fitted. If the twelve axe heads were lined up, fixed in the ground (Telémakhos later digs a trench for them) so that the empty sockets were on a straight line, an archer might be able to shoot through them. (When Odysseus finally does so, he is sitting down, XXI. 441.)

The one who easily handles and strings the bow
and shoots through all twelve axes I shall marry,          630
whoever he may be—then look my last
on this my first love's beautiful brimming house.
But I'll remember, though I dream it only."

Odysseus said:

                    "Dear honorable lady,
wife of Odysseus Laërtiadês,                              635
let there be no postponement of the trial.
Odysseus, who knows the shifts of combat,
will be here: aye, he'll be here long before
one of these lads can stretch or string that bow
or shoot to thread the iron!"

                              Grave and wise,            640
Penélopê replied:

                    "If you were willing
to sit with me and comfort me, my friend,
no tide of sleep would ever close my eyes.
But mortals cannot go forever sleepless.
This the undying gods decree for all                      645
who live and die on earth, kind furrowed earth.
Upstairs I go, then, to my single bed,
my sighing bed, wet with so many tears
after my Lord Odysseus took ship
to see that misery at Ilion, unspeakable.                 650
Let me rest there, you here. You can stretch out
on the bare floor, or else command a bed."

So she went up to her chamber softly lit,
accompanied by her maids. Once there, she wept
for Odysseus, her husband, till Athena                    655
cast sweet sleep upon her eyes.


## Book XX

### SIGNS AND A VISION

Outside in the entry way he made his bed—
raw oxhide spread on level ground, and heaped up
fleeces, left from sheep the Akhaians killed.
And when he had lain down, Eurýnomê
flung out a robe to cover him. Unsleeping                  5

the Lord Odysseus lay, and roved in thought
to the undoing of his enemies.
                              Now came a covey of women
laughing as they slipped out, arm in arm,
as many a night before, to the suitors' beds;
and anger took him like a wave to leap                                 10
into their midst and kill them, every one—
or should he let them all go hot to bed
one final night? His heart cried out within him
the way a brach[7] with whelps between her legs
would howl and bristle at a stranger—so                                15
the hackles of his heart rose at that laughter.
Knocking his breast he muttered to himself:

"Down; be steady. You've seen worse, that time
the Kyklops like a rockslide ate your men
while you looked on. Nobody, only guile,                               20
got you out of that cave alive."

                              His rage
held hard in leash, submitted to his mind,
while he himself rocked, rolling from side to side,
as a cook turns a sausage, big with blood
and fat, at a scorching blaze, without a pause,                        25
to broil it quick: so he rolled left and right,
casting about to see how he, alone,
against the false outrageous crowd of suitors
could press the fight.
                              And out of the night sky
Athena came to him; out of the nearby dark                             30
in body like a woman; came and stood
over his head to chide him:

                              "Why so wakeful,
most forlorn of men? Here is your home,
there lies your lady; and your son is here,
as fine as one could wish a son to be."                                35

Odysseus looked up and answered:

"Aye,
goddess, that much is true; but still
I have some cause to fret in this affair.

7. An obsolete word meaning "bitch."

I am one man; how can I whip those dogs?                    40
They are always here in force. Neither
is that the end of it, there's more to come.
If by the will of Zeus and by your will
I killed them all, where could I go for safety?
Tell me that!"

      And the grey-eyed goddess said:                    45

"Your touching faith! Another man would trust
some villainous mortal, with no brains—and what
am I? Your goddess-guardian to the end
in all your trials. Let it be plain as day:
if fifty bands of men surrounded us                    50
and every sword sang for your blood,
you could make off still with their cows and sheep.
Now you, too, go to sleep. This all night vigil
wearies the flesh. You'll come out soon enough
on the other side of trouble."

                  Raining soft                    55
sleep on his eyes, the beautiful one was gone
back to Olympos. Now at peace, the man
slumbered and lay still, but not his lady.
Wakeful again with all her cares, reclining
in the soft bed, she wept and cried aloud                    60
until she had had her fill of tears, then spoke
in prayer first to Artemis:

              "O gracious
divine lady Artemis, daughter of Zeus,
if you could only make an end now quickly,
let the arrow fly, stop my heart,                    65
or if some wind could take me by the hair
up into running cloud, to plunge in tides of Ocean,
as hurricane winds took Pandareos' daughters[8]
when they were left at home alone. The gods
had sapped their parents' lives. But Aphroditê                    70
fed those children honey, cheese, and wine,
and Hêra gave them looks and wit, and Artemis,
pure Artemis, gave lovely height, and wise
Athena made them practised in her arts—
till Aphroditê in glory walked on Olympos,                    75

8. These are the other daughters of Pandáreos; their fate was different from the one who married
Zêthos and became a nightingale (XIX. 564). They paid for the sin of their father who stole a
golden image from the temple of Hephaistos. Though the gods showered gifts on them, in the
end they were swept away to their deaths by the stormwinds.

begging for each a happy wedding day
from Zeus, the lightning's joyous king, who knows
all fate of mortals, fair and foul—
but even at that hour the cyclone winds
had ravished them away                                            80
to serve the loathsome Furies.
                                        Let me be
blown out by the Olympians! Shot by Artemis,
I still might go and see amid the shades
Odysseus in the rot of underworld.
No coward's eye should light by my consenting!                    85
Evil may be endured when our days pass
in mourning, heavy-hearted, hard beset,
if only sleep reign over nighttime, blanketing
the world's good and evil from our eyes.
But not for me: dreams too my demon sends me.                     90
Tonight the image of my lord came by
as I remember him with troops. O strange
exultation! I thought him real, and not a dream."


Now as the Dawn appeared all stitched in gold,
the queen's cry reached Odysseus at his waking,                   95
so that he wondered, half asleep: it seemed
she knew him, and stood near him! Then he woke
and picked his bedding up to stow away
on a chair in the mégaron. The oxhide pad
he took outdoors. There, spreading wide his arms,                100
he prayed:


          "O Father Zeus, if over land and water,
after adversity, you willed to bring me home,
let someone in the waking house give me good augury,
and a sign be shown, too, in the outer world."


He prayed thus, and the mind of Zeus in heaven                   105
heard him. He thundered out of bright Olympos
down from above the cloudlands, in reply—
a rousing peal for Odysseus. Then a token
came to him from a woman grinding flour
in the court nearby. His own handmills were there,               110
and twelve maids had the job of grinding out
whole grain and barley meal, the pith of men.
Now all the rest, their bushels ground, were sleeping;
one only, frail and slow, kept at it still.

She stopped, stayed her hand, and her lord heard　　　　115
the omen from her lips:

　　　　　　　　"Ah, Father Zeus
almighty over gods and men!
A great bang of thunder that was, surely,
out of the starry sky, and not a cloud in sight.
It is your nod to someone. Hear me, then,　　　　120
make what I say come true:
let this day be the last the suitors feed
so dainty in Odysseus' hall!
They've made me work my heart out till I drop,
grinding barley. May they feast no more!"　　　　125
The servant's prayer, after the cloudless thunder
of Zeus, Odysseus heard with lifting heart,
sure in his bones that vengeance was at hand.
Then other servants, wakening, came down
to build and light a fresh fire at the hearth.　　　　130
Telémakhos, clear-eyed as a god, awoke,
put on his shirt and belted on his sword,
bound rawhide sandals under his smooth feet,
and took his bronze-shod lance. He came and stood
on the broad sill of the doorway, calling Eurýkleia:　　　　135

"Nurse, dear Nurse, how did you treat our guest?
Had he a supper and a good bed? Has he lain
uncared for still? My mother is like that,
perverse for all her cleverness:
she'd entertain some riff-raff, and turn out　　　　140
a solid man."

　　　　　　　The old nurse answered him:
"I would not be so quick to accuse her, child.
He sat and drank here while he had a mind to;
food he no longer hungered for, he said—
for she did ask him. When he thought of sleeping,　　　　145
she ordered them to make a bed. Poor soul!
Poor gentleman! So humble and so miserable,
he would accept no bed with rugs to lie on,
but slept on sheepskins and a raw oxhide
in the entry way. We covered him ourselves."　　　　150

Telémakhos left the hall, hefting his lance,
with two swift flickering hounds for company,
to face the island Akhaians in the square;

and gently born Eurýkleia, the daughter
of Ops Peisenóridês, called to the maids:                         155

"Bestir yourselves! you have your brooms, go sprinkle
the rooms and sweep them, robe the chairs in red,
sponge off the tables till they shine.
Wash out the winebowls and two-handled cups.
You others go fetch water from the spring;                        160
no loitering; come straight back. Our company
will be here soon; morning is sure to bring them;
everyone has a holiday today."

The women ran to obey her—twenty girls
off to the spring with jars for dusky water,                      165
the rest at work inside. Then tall woodcutters
entered to split up logs for the hearth fire,
the water carriers returned; and on their heels
arrived the swineherd, driving three fat pigs,
chosen among his pens. In the wide court                          170
he let them feed, and said to Odysseus kindly:

"Friend, are they more respectful of you now,
or still insulting you?"

                              Replied Odysseus:
"The young men, yes. And may the gods requite
those insolent puppies for the game they play                     175
in a home not their own. They have no decency."

During this talk, Melánthios the goatherd
came in, driving goats for the suitors' feast,
with his two herdsmen. Under the portico
they tied the animals, and Melánthios                             180
looked at Odysseus with a sneer. Said he:

                                        "Stranger,
I see you mean to stay and turn our stomachs
begging in this hall. Clear out, why don't you?
Or will you have to taste a bloody beating
before you see the point? Your begging ways                       185
nauseate everyone. There are feasts elsewhere."

Odysseus answered not a word, but grimly
shook his head over his murderous heart.
A third man came up now: Philoítios

the cattle foreman, with an ox behind him                      190
and fat goats for the suitors. Ferrymen
had brought these from the mainland, as they bring
travellers, too—whoever comes along.
Philoítios tied the beasts under the portico
and joined the swineherd.

                "Who is this," he said,            195
"Who is the new arrival at the manor?
Akhaian? or what else does he claim to be?
Where are his family and fields of home?
Down on his luck, all right: carries himself like a captain.
How the immortal gods can change and drag us down      200
once they begin to spin dark days for us!—
Kings and commanders, too."

                Then he stepped over
and took Odysseus by the right hand, saying:

"Welcome, Sir. May good luck lie ahead
at the next turn. Hard times you're having, surely.       205
O Zeus! no god is more berserk in heaven
if gentle folk, whom you yourself begot,
you plunge in grief and hardship without mercy!
Sir, I began to sweat when I first saw you,
and tears came to my eyes, remembering                      210
Odysseus: rags like these he may be wearing
somewhere on his wanderings now—
I mean, if he's alive still under the sun.
But if he's dead and in the house of Death,
I mourn Odysseus. He entrusted cows to me                   215
in Kephallênia, when I was knee high,
and now his herds are numberless, no man else
ever had cattle multiply like grain.
But new men tell me I must bring my beeves
to feed them, who care nothing for our prince,             220
fear nothing from the watchful gods. They crave
partition of our lost king's land and wealth.
My own feelings keep going round and round
upon this tether: can I desert the boy
by moving, herds and all, to another country,             225
a new life among strangers? Yet it's worse
to stay here, in my old post, herding cattle
for upstarts.
             I'd have gone long since,

gone, taken service with another king; this shame
is no more to be borne; but I keep thinking                                230
my own lord, poor devil, still might come
and make a rout of suitors in his hall."

Odysseus, with his mind on action, answered:

"Herdsman, I make you out to be no coward
and no fool: I can see that for myself.                                     235
So let me tell you this. I swear by Zeus
all highest, by the table set for friends,
and by your king's hearthstone to which I've come,
Odysseus will return. You'll be on hand
to see, if you care to see it,                                              240
how those who lord it here will be cut down."

The cowman said:

            "Would god it all came true!
You'd see the fight that's in me!"

                        Then Eumaios
echoed him, and invoked the gods, and prayed
that his great-minded master should return.                                245
While these three talked, the suitors in the field
had come together plotting—what but death
for Telémakhos?—when from the left an eagle
crossed high with a rockdove in his claws.

Amphínomos got up. Said he, cutting them short:                            250

"Friends, no luck lies in that plan for us,
no luck, knifing the lad. Let's think of feasting."

A grateful thought, they felt, and walking on
entered the great hall of the hero Odysseus,
where they all dropped their cloaks on chairs or couches                   255
and made a ritual slaughter, knifing sheep,
fat goats and pigs, knifing the grass-fed steer.
Then tripes were broiled and eaten. Mixing bowls
were filled with wine. The swineherd passed out cups,
Philoítios, chief cowherd, dealt the loaves                                260
into the panniers, Melánthios poured wine,
and all their hands went out upon the feast.

Telémakhos placed his father to advantage
just at the door sill of the pillared hall,
setting a stool there and a sawed-off table,                    265
gave him a share of tripes, poured out his wine
in a golden cup, and said:

               "Stay here, sit down
to drink with our young friends. I stand between you
and any cutting word or cuffing hand
from any suitor. Here is no public house                        270
but the old home of Odysseus, my inheritance.
Hold your tongues then, gentlemen, and your blows,
and let no wrangling start, no scuffle either."

The others, disconcerted, bit their lips
at the ring in the young man's voice. Antínoös,                 275
Eupeithês' son, turned round to them and said:

"It goes against the grain, my lords, but still
I say we take this hectoring by Telémakhos.
You know Zeus balked at it, or else
we might have shut his mouth a long time past,
the silvery speaker."

              But Telémakhos                280
paid no heed to what Antínoös said.

Now public heralds wound through Ithaka
leading a file of beasts for sacrifice, and islanders
gathered under the shade trees of Apollo,
in the precinct of the Archer[9]—while in hall                  285
the suitors roasted mutton and fat beef
on skewers, pulling off the fragrant cuts;
and those who did the roasting served Odysseus
a portion equal to their own, for so
Telémakhos commanded.
              But Athena                      290
had no desire now to let the suitors
restrain themselves from wounding words and acts.
Laërtês' son again must be offended.
There was a scapegrace fellow in the crowd
named Ktésippos, a Samian, rich beyond                          295
all measure, arrogant with riches, early

---

9. An epithet of Apollo. See *Iliad*, Book I. The trees are in his open-air precinct.

and late a bidder for Odysseus' queen.
Now this one called attention to himself:

"Hear me, my lords, I have a thing to say.
Our friend has had his fair share from the start                    300
and that's polite; it would be most improper
if we were cold to guests of Telémakhos—
no matter what tramp turns up. Well then, look here,
let me throw in my own small contribution.
He must have prizes to confer, himself,                    305
on some brave bathman or another slave
here in Odysseus' house."

                    His hand went backward
and, fishing out a cow's foot from the basket,
he let it fly.
                    Odysseus rolled his head
to one side softly, ducking the blow, and smiled                    310
a crooked smile with teeth clenched. On the wall
the cow's foot struck and fell. Telémakhos
blazed up:

                    "Ktésippos, lucky for you, by heaven,
not to have hit him! He took care of himself,
else you'd have had my lance-head in your belly;                    315
no marriage, but a grave instead on Ithaka
for your father's pains.
                    You others, let me see
no more contemptible conduct in my house!
I've been awake to it for a long time—by now
I know what is honorable and what is not.                    320
Before, I was a child. I can endure it
while sheep are slaughtered, wine drunk up, and bread—
can one man check the greed of a hundred men?—
but I will suffer no more viciousness.
Granted you mean at last to cut me down:                    325
I welcome that—better to die than have
humiliation always before my eyes,
the stranger buffeted, and the serving women
dragged about, abused in a noble house."

They quieted, grew still, under his lashing,                    330
and after a long silence, Ageláos,
Damástor's son, spoke to them all:

"Friends, friends,
I hope no one will answer like a fishwife.
What has been said is true. Hands off this stranger,
he is no target, neither is any servant                          335
here in the hall of King Odysseus.
Let me say a word, though, to Telémakhos
and to his mother, if it please them both:
as long as hope remained in you to see
Odysseus, that great gifted man, again,                          340
you could not be reproached for obstinacy,
tying the suitors down here; better so,
if still your father fared the great sea homeward.
How plain it is, though, now, he'll come no more!
Go sit then by your mother, reason with her,                     345
tell her to take the best man, highest bidder,
and you can have and hold your patrimony,
feed on it, drink it all, while she
adorns another's house."

                          Keeping his head,
Telémakhos replied:

                          "By Zeus Almighty,                     350
Ageláos, and by my father's sufferings,
far from Ithaka, whether he's dead or lost,
I make no impediment to Mother's marriage.
'Take whom you wish,' I say, 'I'll add my dowry.'
But can I pack her off against her will                          355
from her own home? Heaven forbid!"

                          At this,
Pallas Athena touched off in the suitors
a fit of laughter, uncontrollable.
She drove them into nightmare, till they wheezed
and neighed as though with jaws no longer theirs,               360
while blood defiled their meat, and blurring tears
flooded their eyes, heart-sore with woe to come.
Then said the visionary, Theoklýmenos:

"O lost sad men, what terror is this you suffer?
Night shrouds you to the knees, your heads, your faces;         365
dry retch of death runs round like fire in sticks;
your cheeks are streaming; these fair walls and pedestals
are dripping crimson blood. And thick with shades
is the entry way, the courtyard thick with shades

passing athirst toward Erebos, into the dark,                    370
the sun is quenched in heaven, foul mist hems us in . . ."

The young men greeted this with shouts of laughter,
and Eurýmakhos, the son of Pólybos, crowed:

"The mind of our new guest has gone astray.
Hustle him out of doors, lads, into the sunlight;                    375
he finds it dark as night inside!"

The man of vision looked at him and said:

"When I need help, I'll ask for it, Eurýmakhos.
I have my eyes and ears, a pair of legs,
and a straight mind, still with me. These will do                    380
to take me out. Damnation and black night
I see arriving for yourselves: no shelter,
no defence for any in this crowd—
fools and vipers in the king's own hall."

With this he left that handsome room and went                    385
home to Peiraios, who received him kindly.
The suitors made wide eyes at one another
and set to work provoking Telémakhos
with jokes about his friends. One said, for instance:

"Telémakhos, no man is a luckier host                    390
when it comes to what the cat dragged in. What burning
eyes your beggar had for bread and wine!
But not for labor, not for a single heave—
he'd be a deadweight on a field. Then comes
this other, with his mumbo-jumbo. Boy,                    395
for your own good, I tell you, toss them both
into a slave ship for the Sikels.[1] That would pay you."

Telémakhos ignored the suitors' talk.
He kept his eyes in silence on his father,
awaiting the first blow. Meanwhile                    400
the daughter of Ikários, Penélopê,
had placed her chair to look across and down
on father and son at bay; she heard the crowd,
and how they laughed as they resumed their dinner,
a fragrant feast, for many beasts were slain—                    405
but as for supper, men supped never colder

---

1. The primitive (pre-Greek) inhabitants of Sicily.

than these, on what the goddess and the warrior
were even then preparing for the suitors,
whose treachery had filled that house with pain.


## Book XXI

### THE TEST OF THE BOW

Upon Penélopê, most worn in love and thought,
Athena cast a glance like a grey sea
lifting her. Now to bring the tough bow out and bring
the iron blades. Now try those dogs at archery
to usher bloody slaughter in.
                So moving stairward                    5
the queen took up a fine doorhook of bronze,
ivory-hafted, smooth in her clenched hand,
and led her maids down to a distant room,
a storeroom where the master's treasure lay:
bronze, bar gold, black iron forged and wrought.          10
In this place hung the double-torsion bow
and arrows in a quiver, a great sheaf—
quills of groaning.
              In the old time in Lakedaimon
her lord had got these arms from Íphitos,
Eurýtos' son. The two met in Messenia[2]                  15
at Ortílokhos' table, on the day
Odysseus claimed a debt owed by that realm—
sheep stolen by Messenians out of Ithaka
in their long ships, three hundred head, and herdsmen.
Seniors of Ithaka and his father sent him                 20
on that far embassy when he was young.
But Íphitos had come there tracking strays,
twelve shy mares, with mule colts yet unweaned.
And a fatal chase they led him over prairies
into the hands of Heraklês. That massive                  25
son of toil and mortal son of Zeus
murdered his guest[3] at wine in his own house—
inhuman, shameless in the sight of heaven—
to keep the mares and colts in his own grange.
Now Íphitos, when he knew Odysseus, gave him              30
the master bowman's arm; for old Eurýtos
had left it on his deathbed to his son.
In fellowship Odysseus gave a lance

---

2. A coastal district in the Western Peloponnese. *Íphitos*: Son of Eurýtos, king of Oekhalia in Thessaly. *Ortílokhos*: King of Pherai in Thessaly (see III. 528).   3. I.e., Íphitos.

and a sharp sword. But Heraklês killed Íphitos
before one friend could play host to the other.                    35
And Lord Odysseus would not take the bow
in the black ships to the great war at Troy.
As a keepsake he put it by:
it served him well at home in Ithaka.


Now the queen reached the storeroom door and halted.               40
Here was an oaken sill, cut long ago
and sanded clean and bedded true. Foursquare
the doorjambs and the shining doors were set
by the careful builder. Penélopê untied the strap
around the curving handle, pushed her hook                         45
into the slit, aimed at the bolts inside
and shot them back. Then came a rasping sound
as those bright doors the key had sprung gave way—
a bellow like a bull's vaunt in a meadow—
followed by her light footfall entering                            50
over the plank floor. Herb-scented robes
lay there in chests, but the lady's milkwhite arms
went up to lift the bow down from a peg
in its own polished bowcase.
                        Now Penélopê
sank down, holding the weapon on her knees,                        55
and drew her husband's great bow out, and sobbed
and bit her lip and let the salt tears flow.
Then back she went to face the crowded hall
tremendous bow in hand, and on her shoulder hung
the quiver spiked with coughing death. Behind her                  60
maids bore a basket full of axeheads, bronze
and iron implements for the master's game.
Thus in her beauty she approached the suitors,
and near a pillar of the solid roof
she paused, her shining veil across her cheeks,                    65
her maids on either hand and still,
then spoke to the banqueters:


                "My lords, hear me:
suitors indeed, you commandeered this house
to feast and drink in, day and night, my husband
being long gone, long out of mind. You found                       70
no justification for yourselves—none
except your lust to marry me. Stand up, then:
we now declare a contest for that prize.
Here is my lord Odysseus' hunting bow.

Bend and string it if you can. Who sends an arrow                75
through iron axe-helve sockets, twelve in line?
I join my life with his, and leave this place, my home,
my rich and beautiful bridal house, forever
to be remembered, though I dream it only."

Then to Eumaios:

                    "Carry the bow forward.                       80
Carry the blades."

                    Tears came to the swineherd's eyes
as he reached out for the big bow. He laid it
down at the suitors' feet. Across the room
the cowherd sobbed, knowing the master's weapon.
Antínoös growled, with a glance at both:

                              "Clods.                             85
They go to pieces over nothing.
                    You two, there,
why are you sniveling? To upset the woman
even more? Has she not pain enough
over her lost husband? *Sit down.*
Get on with dinner quietly, or cry about it                      90
outside, if you must. Leave us the bow.
A clean-cut game, it looks to me.
Nobody bends that bowstave easily
in this company. Is there a man here
made like Odysseus? I remember him                               95
from childhood: I can see him even now."

That was the way he played it, hoping inwardly
to span the great horn bow with corded gut
and drill the iron with his shot—he, Antínoös,
destined to be the first of all to savor                         100
blood from a biting arrow at his throat,
a shaft drawn by the fingers of Odysseus
whom he had mocked and plundered, leading on
the rest, his boon companions. Now they heard
a gay snort of laughter from Telémakhos,                         105
who said then brilliantly:

                    "A queer thing, that!
Has Zeus almighty made me a half-wit?
For all her spirit, Mother has given in,

promised to go off with someone—and
is that amusing? What am I cackling for?                    110
Step up, my lords, contend now for your prize.
There is no woman like her in Akhaia,
not in old Argos, Pylos, or Mykênê,
neither in Ithaka nor on the mainland,
and you all know it without praise of mine.                    115
Come on, no hanging back, no more delay
in getting the bow bent. Who's the winner?
I myself should like to try that bow.
Suppose I bend it and bring off the shot,
my heart will be less heavy, seeing the queen my mother                    120
go for the last time from this house and hall,
if I who stay can do my father's feat."

He moved out quickly, dropping his crimson cloak,
and lifted sword and sword belt from his shoulders.
His preparation was to dig a trench,                    125
heaping the earth in a long ridge beside it
to hold the blades half-bedded. A taut cord
aligned the socket rings. And no one there
but looked on wondering at his workmanship,
for the boy had never seen it done.

                        He took his stand then                    130
on the broad door sill to attempt the bow.
Three times he put his back into it and sprang it,
three times he had to slack off. Still he meant
to string that bow and pull for the needle shot.
A fourth try, and he had it all but strung—                    135
when a stiffening in Odysseus made him check.
Abruptly then he stopped and turned and said:

"Blast and damn it, must I be a milksop
all my life? Half-grown, all thumbs,
no strength or knack at arms, to defend myself                    140
if someone picks a fight with me.
                        Take over,
O my elders and betters, try the bow,
run off the contest."

                    And he stood the weapon
upright against the massy-timbered door
with one arrow across the horn aslant,                    145
then went back to his chair. Antínoös
gave the word:

              "Now one man at a time
rise and go forward. Round the room in order;
left to right from where they dip the wine."

As this seemed fair enough, upstood Leódês          150
the son of Oinops. This man used to find
visions for them in the smoke of sacrifice.
He kept his chair well back, retired by the winebowl,
for he alone could not abide their manners
but sat in shame for all the rest. Now it was he          155
who had first to confront the bow,
standing up on the broad door sill. He failed.
The bow unbending made his thin hands yield,
no muscle in them. He gave up and said:

"Friends, I cannot. Let the next man handle it.          160
Here is a bow to break the heart and spirit
of many strong men. Aye. And death is less
bitter than to live on and never have
the beauty that we came here laying siege to
so many days. Resolute, are you still,          165
to win Odysseus' lady Penélopê?
Pit yourselves against the bow, and look
among Akhaians for another's daughter.
Gifts will be enough to court and take her.
Let the best offer win."

              With this Leódês          170
thrust the bow away from him, and left it
upright against the massy-timbered door,
with one arrow aslant across the horn.
As he went down to his chair he heard Antínoös'
voice rising:

              "What is that you say?          175
It makes me burn. You cannot string the weapon,
so 'Here is a bow to break the heart and spirit
of many strong men.' Crushing thought!
You were not born—you never had it in you—
to pull that bow or let an arrow fly.          180
But here are men who can and will."

He called out to the goatherd, Melánthios:

"Kindle a fire there, be quick about it,

draw up a big bench with a sheepskin on it,
and bring a cake of lard out of the stores.                                185
Contenders from now on will heat and grease the bow.
We'll try it limber, and bring off the shot."

Melánthios darted out to light a blaze,
drew up a bench, threw a big sheepskin over it,
and brought a cake of lard. So one by one                                  190
the young men warmed and greased the bow for bending,
but not a man could string it. They were whipped.
Antínoös held off; so did Eurýmakhos,
suitors in chief, by far the ablest there.

Two men had meanwhile left the hall:                                       195
swineherd and cowherd, in companionship,
one downcast as the other. But Odysseus
followed them outdoors, outside the court,
and coming up said gently:

                         "You, herdsman,
and you, too, swineherd, I could say a thing to you,                       200
or should I keep it dark?
                         No, no; speak,
my heart tells me. Would you be men enough
to stand by Odysseus if he came back?
Suppose he dropped out of a clear sky, as I did?
Suppose some god should bring him?                                         205
Would you bear arms for him, or for the suitors?"

The cowherd said:

                         "Ah, let the master come!
Father Zeus, grant our old wish! Some courier
guide him back! Then judge what stuff is in me
and how I manage arms!"

                         Likewise Eumaios                                  210
fell to praying all heaven for his return,
so that Odysseus, sure at least of these,
told them:

                         "I am at home, for I am he.
I bore adversities, but in the twentieth year
I am ashore in my own land. I find                                         215
the two of you, alone among my people,

longed for my coming. Prayers I never heard
except your own that I might come again.
So now what is in store for you I'll tell you:
If Zeus brings down the suitors by my hand          220
I promise marriages to both, and cattle,
and houses built near mine. And you shall be
brothers-in-arms of my Telémakhos.
Here, let me show you something else, a sign
that I am he, that you can trust me, look:          225
this old scar from the tusk wound that I got
boar hunting on Parnassos—
Autólykos' sons and I."

                    Shifting his rags
he bared the long gash. Both men looked, and knew,
and threw their arms around the old soldier, weeping,          230
kissing his head and shoulders. He as well
took each man's head and hands to kiss, then said—
to cut it short, else they might weep till dark—

"Break off, no more of this.
Anyone at the door could see and tell them.          235
Drift back in, but separately at intervals
after me.
                    Now listen to your orders:
when the time comes, those gentlemen, to a man,
will be dead against giving me bow or quiver.
Defy them. Eumaios, bring the bow          240
and put it in my hands there at the door.
Tell the women to lock their own door tight.
Tell them if someone hears the shock of arms
or groans of men, in hall or court, not one
must show her face, but keep still at her weaving.          245
Philoítios, run to the outer gate and lock it.
Throw the cross bar and lash it."

                              He turned back
into the courtyard and the beautiful house
and took the stool he had before. They followed
one by one, the two hands loyal to him.          250

Eurýmakhos had now picked up the bow.
He turned it round, and turned it round
before the licking flame to warm it up,

but could not, even so, put stress upon it
to jam the loop over the tip
       though his heart groaned to bursting. 255
Then he said grimly:

     "Curse this day.
What gloom I feel, not for myself alone,
and not only because we lose that bride.
Women are not lacking in Akhaia,
in other towns, or on Ithaka. No, the worst    260
is humiliation—to be shown up for children
measured against Odysseus—we who cannot
even hitch the string over his bow.
What shame to be repeated of us, after us!"

Antínoös said:

    "Come to yourself. You know   265
that is not the way this business ends.
Today the islanders held holiday, a holy day,
no day to sweat over a bowstring.
        Keep your head.
Postpone the bow. I say we leave the axes
planted where they are. No one will take them.  270
No one comes to Odysseus' hall tonight.
Break out good wine and brim our cups again,
we'll keep the crooked bow safe overnight,
order the fattest goats Melánthios has
brought down tomorrow noon, and offer thighbones burning 275
to Apollo, god of archers,
while we try out the bow and make the shot."

As this appealed to everyone, heralds came
pouring fresh water for their hands, and boys
filled up the winebowls. Joints of meat went round,  280
fresh cuts for all, while each man made his offering,
tilting the red wine to the gods, and drank his fill.
Then spoke Odysseus, all craft and gall:

"My lords, contenders for the queen, permit me:
a passion in me moves me to speak out.    285
I put it to Eurýmakhos above all
and to that brilliant prince, Antínoös. Just now

how wise his counsel was, to leave the trial
and turn your thoughts to the immortal gods! Apollo
will give power tomorrow to whom he wills.                          290
But let me try my hand at the smooth bow!
Let me test my fingers and my pull
to see if any of the oldtime kick is there,
or if thin fare and roving took it out of me."

Now irritation beyond reason swept them all,                       295
since they were nagged by fear that he could string it.
Antínoös answered, coldly and at length:

"You bleary vagabond, no rag of sense is left you.
Are you not coddled here enough, at table
taking meat with gentlemen, your betters,                          300
denied nothing, and listening to our talk?
The sweet goad of wine has made you rave!
Here is the evil wine can do
to those who swig it down. Even the centaur                        305
Eurýtion,[4] in Peiríthoös' hall
among the Lapíthai, came to a bloody end
because of wine; wine ruined him: it crazed him,
drove him wild for rape in that great house.
The princes cornered him in fury, leaping on him                   310
to drag him out and crop his ears and nose.
Drink had destroyed his mind, and so he ended
in that mutilation—fool that he was.
Centaurs and men made war for this
but the drunkard first brought hurt upon himself.                  315

The tale applies to you: I promise you
great trouble if you touch that bow. You'll come by
no indulgence in our house; kicked down
into a ship's bilge, out to sea you go,
and nothing saves you. Drink, but hold your tongue.                320
Make no contention here with younger men."
At this the watchful queen Penélopê
interposed:

         "Antínoös, discourtesy
to a guest of Telémakhos—whatever guest—

---

4. The centaurs were half-horse, half-man. At a wedding in the house of the Lapíthai, their
human neighbors, they got drunk and tried to rape the women. A fight ensued; the great pediment
at Olympia presents this scene, and individual contests of Lapith and centaur are portrayed on the
Parthenon at Athens.

that is not handsome. What are you afraid of?                    325
Suppose this exile put his back into it
and drew the great bow of Odysseus—
could he then take me home to be his bride?
You know he does not imagine that! No one
need let that prospect weigh upon his dinner!                    330
How very, very improbable it seems."

It was Eurýmakhos who answered her:

"Penélopê, O daughter of Ikários,
most subtle queen, we are not given to fantasy.
No, but our ears burn at what men might say                    335
and women, too. We hear some jackal whispering:
'How far inferior to the great husband
her suitors are! Can't even budge his bow!
Think of it; and a beggar, out of nowhere,
strung it quick and made the needle shot!'                    340
That kind of disrepute we would not care for."

Penélopê replied, steadfast and wary:

"Eurýmakhos, you have no good repute
in this realm, nor the faintest hope of it—
men who abused a prince's house for years,                    345
consumed his wine and cattle. Shame enough.
Why hang your heads over a trifle now?
The stranger is a big man, well-compacted,
and claims to be of noble blood.
Ai!
Give him the bow, and let us have it out!                    350
What I can promise him I will:
if by the kindness of Apollo he prevails
he shall be clothed well and equipped.
A fine shirt and a cloak I promise him;
a lance for keeping dogs at bay, or men;                    355
a broadsword; sandals to protect his feet;
escort, and freedom to go where he will."

Telémakhos now faced her and said sharply:

"Mother, as to the bow and who may handle it
or not handle it, no man here                    360
has more authority than I do—not one lord
of our own stony Ithaka nor the islands lying

east toward Elis:[5] no one stops me if I choose
to give these weapons outright to my guest.
Return to your own hall. Tend your spindle.                      365
Tend your loom. Direct your maids at work.
This question of the bow will be for men to settle,
most of all for me. I am master here."

She gazed in wonder, turned, and so withdrew,
her son's clearheaded bravery in her heart.                      370
But when she had mounted to her rooms again
with all her women, then she fell to weeping
for Odysseus, her husband. Grey-eyed Athena
presently cast a sweet sleep on her eyes.

The swineherd had the horned bow in his hands              375
moving toward Odysseus, when the crowd
in the banquet hall broke into an ugly din,
shouts rising from the flushed young men:

                          "Ho! Where
do you think you are taking that, you smutty slave?"

"What is this dithering?"

                       "We'll toss you back alone                 380
among the pigs, for your own dogs to eat,
if bright Apollo nods and the gods are kind!"

He faltered, all at once put down the bow, and stood
in panic, buffeted by waves of cries,
hearing Telémakhos from another quarter                          385
shout:

"Go on, take him the bow!
                      Do you obey this pack?
You will be stoned back to your hills! Young as I am
my power is over you! I wish to God
I had as much the upper hand of these!                           390
There would be suitors pitched like dead rats
through our gate, for the evil plotted here!"

Telémakhos' frenzy struck someone as funny,
and soon the whole room roared with laughter at him,

5. In the Peloponnese. The Olympic Games were held in its territory.

so that all tension passed. Eumaios picked up                        395
bow and quiver, making for the door,
and there he placed them in Odysseus' hands.
Calling Eurýkleia to his side he said:

                              "Telémakhos
trusts you to take care of the women's doorway.
Lock it tight. If anyone inside                                      400
should hear the shock of arms or groans of men
in hall or court, not one must show her face,
but go on with her weaving."

                         The old woman
nodded and kept still. She disappeared
into the women's hall, bolting the door behind her.                  405
Philoítios left the house now at one bound,
catlike, running to bolt the courtyard gate.
A coil of deck-rope of papyrus fiber[6]
lay in the gateway; this he used for lashing,
and ran back to the same stool as before,                            410
fastening his eyes upon Odysseus.
                         And Odysseus took his time,
turning the bow, tapping it, every inch,
for borings that termites might have made
while the master of the weapon was abroad.
The suitors were now watching him, and some                          415
jested among themselves:

                    "A bow lover!"

"Dealer in old bows!"

                    "Maybe he has one like it
at home!"

          "Or has an itch to make one for himself."

"See how he handles it, the sly old buzzard!"

And one disdainful suitor added this:                                420

"May his fortune grow an inch for every inch he bends it!"

---

6. The fibers of a plant grown in Egypt, used, as here, for rope, later as writing material (paper).

But the man skilled in all ways of contending,
satisfied by the great bow's look and heft,
like a musician, like a harper, when
with quiet hand upon his instrument                               425
he draws between his thumb and forefinger
a sweet new string upon a peg: so effortlessly
Odysseus in one motion strung the bow.
Then slid his right hand down the cord and plucked it,
so the taut gut vibrating hummed and sang                         430
a swallow's note.
                    In the hushed hall it smote the suitors
and all their faces changed. Then Zeus thundered
overhead, one loud crack for a sign.
And Odysseus laughed within him that the son
of crooked-minded Kronos had flung that omen down.                435
He picked one ready arrow from his table
where it lay bare: the rest were waiting still
in the quiver for the young men's turn to come.
He nocked it, let it rest across the handgrip,
and drew the string and grooved butt of the arrow,               440
aiming from where he sat upon the stool.
                                        Now flashed
arrow from twanging bow clean as a whistle
through every socket ring, and grazed not one,
to thud with heavy brazen head beyond.
                                    Then quietly
Odysseus said:


                    "Telémakhos, the stranger                      445
you welcomed in your hall has not disgraced you.
I did not miss, neither did I take all day
stringing the bow. My hand and eye are sound,
not so contemptible as the young men say.
The hour has come to cook their lordships' mutton—               450
supper by daylight. Other amusements later,
with song and harping that adorn a feast."


He dropped his eyes and nodded, and the prince
Telémakhos, true son of King Odysseus,
belted his sword on, clapped hand to his spear,                  455
and with a clink and glitter of keen bronze
stood by his chair, in the forefront near his father.

## Book XXII

### DEATH IN THE GREAT HALL

Now shrugging off his rags the wiliest fighter of the islands[7]
leapt and stood on the broad door sill, his own bow in his
   hand.
He poured out at his feet a rain of arrows from the quiver
and spoke to the crowd:

"So much for that. Your clean-cut game is over.
Now watch me hit a target that no man has hit before,                  5
if I can make this shot. Help me, Apollo."


He drew to his fist the cruel head of an arrow for Antínoös
just as the young man leaned to lift his beautiful drinking cup,
embossed, two-handled, golden: the cup was in his fingers:
the wine was even at his lips: and did he dream of death?           10
How could he? In that revelry amid his throng of friends
who would imagine a single foe—though a strong foe indeed—
could dare to bring death's pain on him and darkness on his
   eyes?
Odysseus' arrow hit him under the chin
and punched up to the feathers through his throat.                  15


Backward and down he went, letting the winecup fall
from his shocked hand. Like pipes his nostrils jetted
crimson runnels, a river of mortal red,
and one last kick upset his table
knocking the bread and meat to soak in dusty blood.                 20
Now as they craned to see their champion where he lay
the suitors jostled in uproar down the hall,
everyone on his feet. Wildly they turned and scanned
the walls in the long room for arms; but not a shield,
not a good ashen spear was there for a man to take and throw.        25
All they could do was yell in outrage at Odysseus:

"Foul! to shoot at a man! That was your last shot!"


"Your own throat will be slit for this!"


7. In the account of the battle in the hall the translator occasionally, as here, uses a longer line than usual. There is no such variation of length in the original.

                              "Our finest lad is down!
You killed the best on Ithaka."

                         "Buzzards will tear your eyes out!"

For they imagined as they wished—that it was a wild shot,          30
an unintended killing—fools, not to comprehend
they were already in the grip of death.
But glaring under his brows Odysseus answered:

"You yellow dogs, you thought I'd never make it
home from the land of Troy. You took my house to plunder,          35
twisted my maids to serve your beds. You dared
bid for my wife while I was still alive.
Contempt was all you had for the gods who rule wide heaven,
contempt for what men say of you hereafter.
Your last hour has come. You die in blood."                        40

As they all took this in, sickly green fear
pulled at their entrails, and their eyes flickered
looking for some hatch or hideaway from death.
Eurýmakhos alone could speak. He said:

"If you are Odysseus of Ithaka come back,                          45
all that you say these men have done is true.
Rash actions, many here, more in the countryside.
But here he lies, the man who caused them all.
Antínoös was the ringleader, he whipped us on
to do these things. He cared less for a marriage                   50
than for the power Kroníon has denied him
as king of Ithaka. For that
he tried to trap your son and would have killed him.
He is dead now and has his portion. Spare
your own people. As for ourselves, we'll make                     55
restitution of wine and meat consumed,
and add, each one, a tithe of twenty oxen
with gifts of bronze and gold to warm your heart.
Meanwhile we cannot blame you for your anger."

Odysseus glowered under his black brows                            60
and said:

          "Not for the whole treasure of your fathers,
all you enjoy, lands, flocks, or any gold

put up by others, would I hold my hand.
There will be killing till the score is paid.
You forced yourselves upon this house. Fight your way out,          65
or run for it, if you think you'll escape death.
I doubt one man of you skins by."

They felt their knees fail, and their hearts—but heard
Eurýmakhos for the last time rallying them.

"Friends," he said, "the man is implacable.                         70
Now that he's got his hands on bow and quiver
he'll shoot from the big door stone there
until he kills us to the last man.

                              Fight, I say,
let's remember the joy of it. Swords out!
Hold up your tables to deflect his arrows.                          75
After me, everyone: rush him where he stands.
If we can budge him from the door, if we can pass
into the town, we'll call out men to chase him.
This fellow with his bow will shoot no more."

He drew his own sword as he spoke, a broadsword of fine
     bronze,                                                        80
honed like a razor on either edge. Then crying hoarse and
     loud
he hurled himself at Odysseus. But the kingly man let fly
an arrow at that instant, and the quivering feathered butt
sprang to the nipple of his breast as the barb stuck in his
     liver.
The bright broadsword clanged down. He lurched and fell
     aside,                                                         85
pitching across his table. His cup, his bread and meat,
were spilt and scattered far and wide, and his head slammed
     on the ground.
Revulsion, anguish in his heart, with both feet kicking out,
he downed his chair, while the shrouding wave of mist closed
     on his eyes.

Amphínomos now came running at Odysseus,                            90
broadsword naked in his hand. He thought to make
the great soldier give way at the door.
But with a spear throw from behind Telémakhos hit him
between the shoulders, and the lancehead drove
clear through his chest. He left his feet and fell                  95
forward, thudding, forehead against the ground.

Telémakhos swerved around him, leaving the long dark spear
planted in Amphínomos. If he paused to yank it out
someone might jump him from behind or cut him down with
   a sword
at the moment he bent over. So he ran—ran from the tables     100
to his father's side and halted, panting, saying:


"Father let me bring you a shield and spear,
a pair of spears, a helmet.
I can arm on the run myself; I'll give
outfits to Eumaios and this cowherd.     105
Better to have equipment."


         Said Odysseus:


"Run then, while I hold them off with arrows
as long as the arrows last. When all are gone
if I'm alone they can dislodge me."

            Quick
upon his father's word Telémakhos     110
ran to the room where spears and armor lay.
He caught up four light shields, four pairs of spears,
four helms of war high-plumed with flowing manes,
and ran back, loaded down, to his father's side.
He was the first to pull a helmet on     115
and slide his bare arm in a buckler strap.
The servants armed themselves, and all three took their stand
beside the master of battle.
          While he had arrows
he aimed and shot, and every shot brought down
one of his huddling enemies.
But when all barbs had flown from the bowman's fist,     120
he leaned his bow in the bright entry way
beside the door, and armed: a four-ply shield
hard on his shoulder, and a crested helm,
horsetailed, nodding stormy upon his head,
then took his tough and bronze-shod spears.
               The suitors     125
who held their feet, no longer under bowshot,
could see a window high in a recess of the wall,
a vent, lighting the passage to the storeroom.
This passage had one entry, with a door,

at the edge of the great hall's threshold, just outside.          130

Odysseus told the swineherd to stand over
and guard this door and passage. As he did so,
a suitor named Ageláos asked the others:

"Who will get a leg up on that window
and run to alarm the town? One sharp attack          135
and this fellow will never shoot again."

                              His answer
came from the goatherd, Melánthios:

                              "No chance, my lord.
The exit into the courtyard is too near them,
too narrow. One good man could hold that portal
against a crowd. No: let me scale the wall          140
and bring you arms out of the storage chamber.
Odysseus and his son put them indoors,
I'm sure of it; not outside."

                    The goatish goatherd
clambered up the wall, toes in the chinks,
and slipped through to the storeroom. Twelve light shields,          145
twelve spears he took, and twelve thick-crested helms,
and handed all down quickly to the suitors.
Odysseus, when he saw his adversaries
girded and capped and long spears in their hands
shaken at him, felt his knees go slack,          150
his heart sink, for the fight was turning grim.
He spoke rapidly to his son:

"Telémakhos, one of the serving women
is tipping the scales against us in this fight,
or maybe Melánthios."          155

                    But sharp and clear
Telémakhos said:

                    "It is my own fault, Father,
mine alone. The storeroom door—I left it
wide open. They were more alert than I.
Eumaios, go and lock that door,          160
and bring back word if a woman is doing this

or Melánthios, Dólios' son. More likely he."

Even as they conferred, Melánthios
entered the storeroom for a second load,
and the swineherd at the passage entry saw him.          165
He cried out to his lord:

                    "Son of Laërtês,
Odysseus, master mariner and soldier,
there he goes, the monkey, as we thought,
there he goes into the storeroom.
                         Let me hear your will:
put a spear through him—I hope I am the stronger—          170
or drag him here to pay for his foul tricks
against your house?"

              Odysseus said:

                         "Telémakhos and I
will keep these gentlemen in hall, for all their urge to leave.
You two go throw him into the storeroom, wrench his arms
and legs behind him, lash his hands and feet          175
to a plank, and hoist him up to the roof beams.
Let him live on there suffering at his leisure."

The two men heard him with appreciation
and ducked into the passage. Melánthios,
rummaging in the chamber, could not hear them          180
as they came up; nor could he see them freeze
like posts on either side the door.
He turned back with a handsome crested helmet
in one hand, in the other an old shield
coated with dust—a shield Laërtês bore          185
soldiering in his youth. It had lain there for years,
and the seams on strap and grip had rotted away.
As Melánthios came out the two men sprang,
jerked him backward by the hair, and threw him.
Hands and feet they tied with a cutting cord          190
behind him, so his bones ground in their sockets,
just as Laërtês' royal son commanded.
Then with a whip of rope they hoisted him
in agony up a pillar to the beams,
and—O my swineherd—you were the one to say:          195

"Watch through the night up there, Melánthios.
An airy bed is what you need.
You'll be awake to see the primrose Dawn
when she goes glowing from the streams of Ocean
to mount her golden throne.
                              No oversleeping                    200
the hour for driving goats to feed the suitors."

They stopped for helm and shield and left him there
contorted, in his brutal sling,
and shut the doors, and went to join Odysseus,
whose mind moved through the combat now to come.          205
Breathing deep, and snorting hard, they stood
four at the entry, facing two score men.
But now into the gracious doorway stepped
Zeus's daughter Athena. She wore the guise of Mentor,
and Odysseus appealed to her in joy:                      210

"O Mentor, join me in this fight! Remember
how all my life I've been devoted to you,
friend of my youth!"

                    For he guessed it was Athena,
Hope of Soldiers. Cries came from the suitors,
and Ageláos, Damástor's son, called out:                  215

"Mentor, don't let Odysseus lead you astray
to fight against us on his side.
Think twice: we are resolved—and we will do it—
after we kill them, father and son,
you too will have your throat slit for your pains        220
if you make trouble for us here. It means your life.
Your life—and cutting throats will not be all.
Whatever wealth you have, at home, or elsewhere,
we'll mingle with Odysseus' wealth. Your sons
will be turned out, your wife and daughters              225
banished from the town of Ithaka."

Athena's anger grew like a storm wind as he spoke
until she flashed out at Odysseus:

                              "Ah, what a falling off!
Where is your valor, where is the iron hand

that fought at Troy for Helen, pearl of kings,                    230
no respite and nine years of war? How many foes
your hand brought down in bloody play of spears?
What stratagem but yours took Priam's town?
How is it now that on your own door sill,
before the harriers of your wife, you curse your luck          235
not to be stronger?
                    Come here, cousin, stand by me,
and you'll see action! In the enemies' teeth
learn how Mentor, son of Álkimos,
repays fair dealing!"


                    For all her fighting words
she gave no overpowering aid—not yet;                          240
father and son must prove their mettle still.
Into the smoky air under the roof
the goddess merely darted to perch on a blackened beam—
no figure to be seen now but a swallow.


Command of the suitors had fallen to Agaláos.                   245
With him were Eurýnomos, Amphímedon,
Demoptólemos, Peisándros, Pólybos,
the best of the lot who stood to fight for their lives
after the streaking arrows downed the rest.
Ageláos rallied them with his plan of battle:                   250


"Friends, our killer has come to the end of his rope,
and much good Mentor did him, that blowhard, dropping in.
Look, only four are left to fight, in the light there at the door.
No scattering of shots, men, no throwing away good spears;
we six will aim a volley at Odysseus alone,                      255
and may Zeus grant us the glory of a hit.
If he goes down, the others are no problem."


At his command, then, "Ho!" they all let fly
as one man. But Athena spoiled their shots.
One hit the doorpost of the hall, another                       260
stuck in the door's thick timbering, still others
rang on the stone wall, shivering hafts of ash.
Seeing his men unscathed, royal Odysseus
gave the word for action.

                    "Now I say, friends,
the time is overdue to let them have it.                         265

Battlespoil they want from our dead bodies
to add to all they plundered here before."

Taking aim over the steadied lanceheads
they all let fly together. Odysseus killed
Demoptólemos; Telémakhos                                            270
killed Eurýadês; the swineherd, Élatos;
and Peisándros went down before the cowherd.
As these lay dying, biting the central floor,
their friends gave way and broke for the inner wall.
The four attackers followed up with a rush                          275
to take spears from the fallen men.

                              Re-forming,
the suitors threw again with all their strength,
but Athena turned their shots, or all but two.
One hit a doorpost in the hall, another
stuck in the door's thick timbering, still others               280
rang on the stone wall, shivering hafts of ash.
Amphímedon's point bloodied Telémakhos'
wrist, a superficial wound, and Ktésippos'
long spear passing over Eumaios' shield
grazed his shoulder, hurtled on and fell.                          285
No matter: with Odysseus the great soldier
the wounded threw again. And Odysseus raider of cities
struck Eurýdamas down. Telémakhos
hit Amphímedon, and the swineherd's shot
killed Pólybos. But Ktésippos, who had last evening thrown    290
a cow's hoof at Odysseus, got the cowherd's heavy cast
full in the chest—and dying heard him say:

"You arrogant joking bastard!
Clown, will you, like a fool, and parade your wit?
Leave jesting to the gods who do it better.                        295
This will repay your cow's-foot courtesy
to a great wanderer come home."

                              The master
of the black herds had answered Ktésippos.
Odysseus, lunging at close quarters, put a spear
through Ageláos, Damastor's son. Telémakhos                     300
hit Leókritos from behind and pierced him,
kidney to diaphragm. Speared off his feet,
he fell face downward on the ground.

At this moment that unmanning thunder cloud,
the aegis,[8] Athena's shield,                                    305
took form aloft in the great hall.
                           And the suitors mad with fear
at her great sign stampeded like stung cattle by a river
when the dread shimmering gadfly strikes in summer,
in the flowering season, in the long-drawn days.
After them the attackers wheeled, as terrible as falcons      310
from eyries in the mountains veering over and diving down
with talons wide unsheathed on flights of birds,
who cower down the sky in chutes and bursts along the
     valley—
but the pouncing falcons grip their prey, no frantic wing
     avails,
and farmers love to watch those beakèd hunters.              315
So these now fell upon the suitors in that hall,
turning, turning to strike and strike again,
while torn men moaned at death, and blood ran smoking
over the whole floor.
                           Now there was one
who turned and threw himself at Odysseus' knees—             320
Leódês, begging for his life:

                    "Mercy,
mercy on a suppliant, Odysseus!
Never by word or act of mine, I swear,
was any woman troubled here. I told the rest
to put an end to it. They would not listen,               325
would not keep their hands from brutishness,
and now they are all dying like dogs for it.
I had no part in what they did: my part
was visionary—reading the smoke of sacrifice.
Scruples go unrewarded if I die."                         330

The shrewd fighter frowned over him and said:

"You were diviner to this crowd? How often
you must have prayed my sweet day of return
would never come, or not for years!—and prayed
to have my dear wife, and beget children on her.         335
No plea like yours could save you
from this hard bed of death. Death it shall be!"

8. A magical shield (or breastplate) used by Athena and Zeus; it created a panic when displayed.

He picked up Ageláos' broadsword
from where it lay, flung by the slain man,
and gave Leódês' neck a lopping blow                          340
so that his head went down to mouth in dust.

One more who had avoided furious death
was the son of Terpis, Phêmios, the minstrel,
singer by compulsion to the suitors.
He stood now with his harp, holy and clear,                  345
in the wall's recess, under the window, wondering
if he should flee that way to the courtyard altar,
sanctuary of Zeus, the Enclosure God.[9]
Thighbones in hundreds had been offered there
by Laërtês and Odysseus. No, he thought;                     350
the more direct way would be best—to go
humbly to his lord. But first to save
his murmuring instrument he laid it down
carefully between the winebowl and a chair,
then he betook himself to Lord Odysseus,                     355
clung hard to his knees, and said:

                              "Mercy,
mercy on a suppliant, Odysseus!
My gift is song for men and for the gods undying.
My death will be remorse for you hereafter.
No one taught me: deep in my mind a god                      360
shaped all the various ways of life in song.
And I am fit to make verse in your company
as in the god's. Put aside lust for blood.
Your own dear son Telémakhos can tell you,
never by my own will or for love                             365
did I feast here or sing amid the suitors.
They were too strong, too many; they compelled me."

Telémakhos in the elation of battle
heard him. He at once called to his father:

"Wait: that one is innocent: don't hurt him.                 370
And we should let our herald live—Medôn;
he cared for me from boyhood. Where is *he*?
Has he been killed already by Philoítios
or by the swineherd? Else he got an arrow
in that first gale of bowshots down the room."               375

9. Zeus Herkeios, guardian of the inner space of the home.

Now this came to the ears of prudent Medôn
under the chair where he had gone to earth,
pulling a new-flayed bull's hide over him.
Quiet he lay while blinding death passed by.
Now heaving out from under                                    380
he scrambled for Telémakhos' knees and said:

"Here I am, dear prince; but rest your spear!
Tell your great father not to see in me
a suitor for the sword's edge—one of those
who laughed at you and ruined his property!"        385

The lord of all the tricks of war surveyed
this fugitive and smiled. He said:

"Courage: my son has dug you out and saved you.
Take it to heart, and pass the word along:
fair dealing brings more profit in the end.           390
Now leave this room. Go and sit down outdoors
where there's no carnage, in the court,
you and the poet with his many voices,
while I attend to certain chores inside."

At this the two men stirred and picked their way     395
to the door and out, and sat down at the altar,
looking around with wincing eyes
as though the sword's edge hovered still.
And Odysseus looked around him, narrow-eyed,
for any others who had lain hidden                    400
while death's black fury passed.
                              In blood and dust
he saw that crowd all fallen, many and many slain.

Think of a catch that fishermen haul in to a halfmoon bay
in a fine-meshed net from the white-caps of the sea:
how all are poured out on the sand, in throes for the salt sea,   405
twitching their cold lives away in Hêlios' fiery air:
so lay the suitors heaped on one another.

Odysseus at length said to his son:

"Go tell old Nurse I'll have a word with her.
What's to be done now weighs on my mind."            410

Telémakhos knocked at the women's door and called:

"Eurýkleia, come out here! Move, old woman.
You kept your eye on all our servant girls.
Jump, my father is here and wants to see you."

His call brought no reply, only the doors                    415
were opened, and she came. Telémakhos
led her forward. In the shadowy hall
full of dead men she found his father
spattered and caked with blood like a mountain lion
when he has gorged upon an ox, his kill—                    420
with hot blood glistening over his whole chest,
smeared on his jaws, baleful and terrifying—
even so encrimsoned was Odysseus
up to his thighs and armpits. As she gazed
from all the corpses to the bloody man                    425
she raised her head to cry over his triumph,
but felt his grip upon her, checking her.
Said the great soldier then:

                    "Rejoice
inwardly. No crowing aloud, old woman.
To glory over slain men is no piety.                    430
Destiny and the gods' will vanquished these,
and their own hardness. They respected no one,
good or bad, who came their way.
For this, and folly, a bad end befell them.
Your part is now to tell me of the women,                    435
those who dishonored me, and the innocent."

His own old nurse Eurýkleia said:

                    "I will, then.
Child, you know you'll have the truth from me.
Fifty all told they are, your female slaves,
trained by your lady and myself in service,                    440
wool carding and the rest of it, and taught
to be submissive. Twelve went bad,
flouting me, flouting Penélopê, too.
Telémakhos being barely grown, his mother
would never let him rule the serving women—                    445
but you must let me go to her lighted rooms
and tell her. Some god sent her a drift of sleep."

But in reply the great tactician said:

"Not yet. Do not awake her. Tell those women

who were the suitors' harlots to come here." 450

She went back on this mission through his hall.
Then he called Telémakhos to his side
and the two herdsmen. Sharply Odysseus said:

"These dead must be disposed of first of all.
Direct the women. Tables and chairs will be 455
scrubbed with sponges, rinsed and rinsed again.
When our great room is fresh and put in order,
take them outside, these women,
between the roundhouse and the palisade,
and hack them with your swordblades till you cut 460
the life out of them, and every thought of sweet
Aphrodîtê under the rutting suitors,
when they lay down in secret."

                      As he spoke
here came the women in a bunch, all wailing,
soft tears on their cheeks. They fell to work 465
to lug the corpses out into the courtyard
under the gateway, propping one
against another as Odysseus ordered,
for he himself stood over them. In fear
these women bore the cold weight of the dead. 470
The next thing was to scrub off chairs and tables
and rinse them down. Telémakhos and the herdsman
scraped the packed earth floor with hoes, but made
the women carry out all blood and mire.
When the great room was cleaned up once again, 475
at swordpoint they forced them out, between
the roundhouse and the palisade, pell-mell
to huddle in that dead end without exit.
Telémakhos, who knew his mind, said curtly:

"I would not give the clean death of a beast[1] 480
to trulls who made a mockery of my mother
and of me too—you sluts, who lay with suitors."

He tied one end of a hawser to a pillar
and passed the other about the roundhouse top,
taking the slack up, so that no one's toes 485
could touch the ground. They would be hung like doves

---

1. I.e., by sword or spear. Hanging was considered an ignominious way to die.

or larks in springès triggered in a thicket,
where the birds think to rest—a cruel nesting.
So now in turn each woman thrust her head
into a noose and swung, yanked high in air,                    490
to perish there most piteously.
Their feet danced for a little, but not long.

From storeroom to the court they brought Melánthios,
chopped with swords to cut his nose and ears off,
pulled off his genitals to feed the dogs                       495
and raging hacked his hands and feet away.

As their own hands and feet called for a washing,
they went indoors to Odysseus again.
Their work was done. He told Eurýkleia:

                              "Bring me
brimstone and a brazier—medicinal                              500
fumes to purify my hall. Then tell
Penélopê to come, and bring her maids.
All servants round the house must be called in."

His own old nurse Eurýkleia replied:

"Aye, surely that is well said, child. But let me                505
find you a good clean shirt and cloak and dress you.
You must not wrap your shoulders' breadth again
in rags in your own hall. That would be shameful."

Odysseus answered:

                              "Let me have the fire.
The first thing is to purify this place."                       510

With no more chat Eurýkleia obeyed
and fetched out fire and brimstone. Cleansing fumes
he sent through court and hall and storage chamber.
Then the old woman hurried off again
to the women's quarters to announce her news,                   515
and all the servants came now, bearing torches
in twilight, crowding to embrace Odysseus,
taking his hands to kiss, his head and shoulders,
while he stood there, nodding to every one,
and overcome by longing and by tears.                           520

## Book XXIII

### THE TRUNK OF THE OLIVE TREE

The old nurse went upstairs exulting,
with knees toiling, and patter of slapping feet,
to tell the mistress of her lord's return,
and cried out by the lady's pillow:

                              "Wake,
wake up, dear child! Penélopê, come down,                          5
see with your own eyes what all these years you longed for!
Odysseus is here! Oh, in the end, he came!
And he has killed your suitors, killed them all
who made his house a bordel and ate his cattle
and raised their hands against his son!"

                         Penélopê said:                          10

"Dear nurse . . . the gods have touched you.
They can put chaos into the clearest head
or bring a lunatic down to earth. Good sense
you always had. They've touched you. What is this
mockery you wake me up to tell me,                               15
breaking in on my sweet spell of sleep?
I had not dozed away so tranquilly
since my lord went to war, on that ill wind
to Ilion.

              Oh, leave me! Back down stairs!
If any other of my women came in babbling                        20
things like these to startle me, I'd see her
flogged out of the house! Your old age spares you that."

Eurýkleia said:

"Would I play such a trick on you, dear child?
It is true, true, as I tell you, he has come!                   25
That stranger they were baiting was Odysseus.
Telémakhos knew it days ago—
cool head, never to give his father away,
till he paid off those swollen dogs!"

The lady in her heart's joy now sprang up                       30
with sudden dazzling tears, and hugged the old one,
crying out:

        "But try to make it clear!
If he came home in secret, as you say,
could he engage them singlehanded? How?
They were all down there, still in the same crowd."          35


To this Eurýkleia said:


                "I did not see it,
I knew nothing; only I heard the groans
of men dying. We sat still in the inner rooms
holding our breath, and marvelling, shut in,
until Telémakhos came to the door and called me—          40
your own dear son, sent this time by his father!
So I went out, and found Odysseus
erect, with dead men littering the floor
this way and that. If you had only seen him!
It would have made your heart glow hot!—a lion          45
splashed with mire and blood.
                        But now the cold
corpses are all gathered at the gate,
and he has cleansed his hall with fire and brimstone,
a great blaze. Then he sent me here to you.
Come with me: you may both embark this time          50
for happiness together, after pain,
after long years. Here is your prayer, your passion,
granted: your own lord lives, he is at home,
he found you safe, he found his son. The suitors
abused his house, but he has brought them down."          55


The attentive lady said:


                "Do not lose yourself
in this rejoicing: wait: you know
how splendid that return would be for us,
how dear to me, dear to his son and mine;
but no, it is not possible, your notion          60
must be wrong.
            Some god has killed the suitors,
a god, sick of their arrogance and brutal
malice—for they honored no one living,
good or bad, who ever came their way.
Blind young fools, they've tasted death for it.          65
But the true person of Odysseus?
He lost his home, he died far from Akhaia."

The old nurse sighed:

>                        "How queer, the way you talk!
> Here he is, large as life, by his own fire,
> and you deny he ever will get home!                                    70
> Child, you always were mistrustful!
> But there is one sure mark that I can tell you:
> that scar left by the boar's tusk long ago.
> I recognized it when I bathed his feet
> and would have told you, but he stopped my mouth,                      75
> forbade me, in his craftiness.
>                        Come down,
> I stake my life on it, he's here!
> Let me die in agony if I lie!"

>                        Penélopê said:

> "Nurse dear, though you have your wits about you,
> still it is hard not to be taken in                                    80
> by the immortals. Let us join my son, though,
> and see the dead and that strange one who killed them."

She turned to descend the stair, her heart
in tumult. Had she better keep her distance
and question him, her husband? Should she run                           85
up to him, take his hands, kiss him now?
Crossing the door sill she sat down at once
in firelight, against the nearest wall,
across the room from the lord Odysseus.
                        There
leaning against a pillar, sat the man                                   90
and never lifted up his eyes, but only waited
for what his wife would say when she had seen him.
And she, for a long time, sat deathly still
in wonderment—for sometimes as she gazed
she found him—yes, clearly—like her husband,                           95
but sometimes blood and rags were all she saw.
Telémakhos' voice came to her ears:

>                        "Mother,
> cruel mother, do you feel nothing,
> drawing yourself apart this way from Father?
> Will you not sit with him and talk and question him?                   100
> What other woman could remain so cold?
> Who shuns her lord, and he come back to her

from wars and wandering, after twenty years?
Your heart is hard as flint and never changes!"

Penélopê answered:

                "I am stunned, child.                105
I cannot speak to him. I cannot question him.
I cannot keep my eyes upon his face.
If really he is Odysseus, truly home,
beyond all doubt we two shall know each other
better than you or anyone. There are             110
secret signs we know, we two."

                           A smile
came now to the lips of the patient hero, Odysseus,
who turned to Telémakhos and said:

"Peace: let your mother test me at her leisure.
Before long she will see and know me best.         115
These tatters, dirt—all that I'm caked with now—
make her look hard at me and doubt me still.
As to this massacre, we must see the end.
Whoever kills one citizen, you know,
and has no force of armed men at his back,       120
had better take himself abroad by night
and leave his kin. Well, we cut down the flower of Ithaka,
the mainstay of the town. Consider that."

Telémakhos replied respectfully:

                    "Dear Father,
enough that you yourself study the danger,      125
foresighted in combat as you are,
they say you have no rival.
                      We three stand
ready to follow you and fight. I say
for what our strength avails, we have the courage."

And the great tactician, Odysseus, answered:

                      "Good.      130
Here is our best maneuver, as I see it:
bathe, you three, and put fresh clothing on,
order the women to adorn themselves,

and let our admirable harper choose a tune
for dancing, some lighthearted air, and strum it.          135
Anyone going by, or any neighbor,
will think it is a wedding feast he hears.
These deaths must not be cried about the town
till we can slip away to our own woods. We'll see
what weapon, then, Zeus puts into our hands."              140

They listened attentively, and did his bidding,
bathed and dressed afresh; and all the maids
adorned themselves. Then Phêmios the harper
took his polished shell and plucked the strings,
moving the company to desire                                145
for singing, for the sway and beat of dancing,
until they made the manor hall resound
with gaiety of men and grace of women.
Anyone passing on the road would say:

"Married at last, I see—the queen so many courted.        150
Sly, cattish wife! She would not keep—not she!—
the lord's estate until he came."

                    So travellers'
thoughts might run—but no one guessed the truth.
Greathearted Odysseus, home at last,
was being bathed now by Eurýnomê                           155
and rubbed with golden oil, and clothed again
in a fresh tunic and a cloak. Athena
lent him beauty, head to foot. She made him
taller, and massive, too, with crisping hair
in curls like petals of wild hyacinth                      160
but all red-golden. Think of gold infused
on silver by a craftsman, whose fine art
Hephaistos taught him, or Athena: one
whose work moves to delight: just so she lavished
beauty over Odysseus' head and shoulders.                  165
He sat then in the same chair by the pillar,
facing his silent wife, and said:

                    "Strange woman,
the immortals of Olympos made you hard,
harder than any. Who else in the world
would keep aloof as you do from her husband                170
if he returned to her from years of trouble,
cast on his own land in the twentieth year?

Nurse, make up a bed for me to sleep on.
Her heart is iron in her breast."

                              Penélopê
spoke to Odysseus now. She said:

                              "Strange man,                    175
if man you are . . . This is no pride on my part
nor scorn for you—not even wonder, merely.
I know so well how you—how he—appeared
boarding the ship for Troy. But all the same . . .

Make up his bed for him, Eurýkleia.                            180
Place it outside the bedchamber my lord
built with his own hands. Pile the big bed
with fleeces, rugs, and sheets of purest linen."

With this she tried him to the breaking point,
and he turned on her in a flash raging:                        185

"Woman, by heaven you've stung me now!
Who dared to move my bed?
No builder had the skill for that—unless
a god came down to turn the trick. No mortal
in his best days could budge it with a crowbar.                190
There is our pact and pledge, our secret sign,
built into that bed—my handiwork
and no one else's!
                    An old trunk of olive
grew like a pillar on the building plot,
and I laid out our bedroom round that tree,                    195
lined up the stone walls, built the walls and roof,
gave it a doorway and smooth-fitting doors.
Then I lopped off the silvery leaves and branches,
hewed and shaped that stump from the roots up
into a bedpost, drilled it, let it serve                       200
as model for the rest. I planed them all,
inlaid them all with silver, gold and ivory,
and stretched a bed between—a pliant web
of oxhide thongs dyed crimson.
                              There's our sign!
I know no more. Could someone's else's hand                    205
have sawn that trunk and dragged the frame away?"

Their secret! as she heard it told, her knees
grew tremulous and weak, her heart failed her.

With eyes brimming tears she ran to him,
throwing her arms around his neck, and kissed him,                    210
murmuring:

"Do not rage at me, Odysseus!
No one ever matched your caution! Think
what difficulty the gods gave: they denied us
life together in our prime and flowering years,
kept us from crossing into age together.                              215
Forgive me, don't be angry. I could not
welcome you with love on sight! I armed myself
long ago against the frauds of men,
impostors who might come—and all those many
whose underhanded ways bring evil on!                                 220
Helen of Argos, daughter of Zeus and Leda,
would she have joined the stranger, lain with him,
if she had known her destiny? known the Akhaians
in arms would bring her back to her own country?
Surely a goddess moved her to adultery,                               225
her blood unchilled by war and evil coming,
the years, the desolation; ours, too.
But here and now, what sign could be so clear
as this of our own bed?
No other man has ever laid eyes on it—                                230
only my own slave, Aktoris, that my father
sent with me as a gift—she kept our door.
You make my stiff heart know that I am yours."

Now from his breast into his eyes the ache
of longing mounted, and he wept at last,                              235
his dear wife, clear and faithful, in his arms,
longed for
          as the sunwarmed earth is longed for by a swimmer
spent in rough water where his ship went down
under Poseidon's blows, gale winds and tons of sea.
Few men can keep alive through a big surf                             240
to crawl, clotted with brine, on kindly beaches
in joy, in joy, knowing the abyss behind:
and so she too rejoiced, her gaze upon her husband,
her white arms round him pressed as though forever.
The rose Dawn might have found them weeping still                     245
had not grey-eyed Athena slowed the night
when night was most profound, and held the Dawn
under the Ocean of the East. That glossy team,
Firebright and Daybright, the Dawn's horses
that drew her heavenward for men—Athena                               250

stayed their harnessing.
                    Then said Odysseus:

"My dear, we have not won through to the end.
One trial—I do not know how long—is left for me
to see fulfilled. Teirêsias' ghost forewarned me
the night I stood upon the shore of Death, asking                    255
about my friends' homecoming and my own.

But now the hour grows late, it is bed time,
rest will be sweet for us: let us lie down."

To this Penélopê replied:

                    "That bed,
that rest is yours whenever desire moves you,                    260
now the kind powers have brought you home at last.
But as your thought has dwelt upon it, tell me:
what is the trial you face? I must know soon;
what does it matter if I learn tonight?"

The teller of many stories said:

                              "My strange one,                    265
must you again, and even now,
urge me to talk? Here is a plodding tale;
no charm in it, no relish in the telling.
Teirêsias told me I must take an oar
and trudge the mainland, going from town to town,                    270
until I discover men who have never known
the salt blue sea, nor flavor of salt meat—
strangers to painted prows, to watercraft
and oars like wings, dipping across the water.
The moment of revelation he foretold                    275
was this, for you may share the prophecy:
some traveller falling in with me will say:
'A winnowing fan, that on your shoulder, sir?'
There I must plant my oar, on the very spot,
with burnt offerings to Poseidon of the Waters:                    280
a ram, a bull, a great buck boar. Thereafter
when I come home again, I am to slay
full hekatombs to the gods who own broad heaven,
one by one.
              Then death will drift upon me
from seaward, mild as air, mild as your hand,                    285
in my well-tended weariness of age,

contented folk around me on our island.
He said all this must come."

                    Penélopê said:
"If by the gods' grace age at least is kind,
we have that promise—trials will end in peace."                    290

So he confided in her, and she answered.
Meanwhile Eurýnomê and the nurse together
laid soft coverlets on the master's bed,
working in haste by torchlight. Eurýkleia
retired to her quarters for the night,                              295
and then Eurýnomê, as maid-in-waiting,
lighted her lord and lady to their chamber
with bright brands.

                    She vanished.
                                So they came
into that bed so steadfast, loved of old,
opening glad arms to one another.[2]                                300
Telémakhos by now had hushed the dancing,
hushed the women. In the darkened hall
he and the cowherd and the swineherd slept.

The royal pair mingled in love again
and afterward lay revelling in stories:                             305
hers of the siege her beauty stood at home
from arrogant suitors, crowding on her sight,
and how they fed their courtship on his cattle,
oxen and fat sheep, and drank up rivers
of wine out of the vats.

                    Odysseus told                                    310
of what hard blows he had dealt out to others
and of what blows he had taken—all that story.
She could not close her eyes till all was told.

His raid on the Kikonês, first of all,
then how he visited the Lotos Eaters,                               315
and what the Kyklops did, and how those shipmates,
pitilessly devoured, were avenged.
Then of his touching Aiolos's isle

---

2. Two great Alexandrian critics said that this line was the "end" of the Odyssey (though one of the words they are said to have used could mean simply "culmination"). Modern critics are divided; some find the rest of the poem banal, unartistic, full of linguistic anomalies, and so on. But if the poem stops here we are left in suspense about many important themes that have been developed and demand a sequel—the question of reprisals for the slaughter in the hall, to mention only one.

and how that king refitted him for sailing
to Ithaka; all vain: gales blew him back                    320
groaning over the fishcold sea. Then how
he reached the Laistrygonians' distant bay
and how they smashed his ships and his companions.
Kirkê, then: of her deceits and magic,
then of his voyage to the wide underworld                    325
of dark, the house of Death, and questioning
Teirêsias, Theban spirit.
                                    Dead companions,
many, he saw there, and his mother, too.
Of this he told his wife, and told how later
he heard the choir of maddening Seirênês,                    330
coasted the Wandering Rocks, Kharybdis' pool
and the fiend Skylla who takes toll of men.
Then how his shipmates killed Lord Hêlios' cattle
and how Zeus thundering in towering heaven
split their fast ship with his fuming bolt,                    335
so all hands perished.
                            He alone survived,
cast away on Kalypso's isle, Ogýgia.
He told, then, how that nymph detained him there
in her smooth caves, craving him for her husband,
and how in her devoted lust she swore                    340
he should not die nor grow old, all his days,
but he held out against her.
                                Last of all
what sea-toil brought him to the Phaiákians;
their welcome; how they took him to their hearts
and gave him passage to his own dear island                    345
with gifts of garments, gold and bronze . . .
                                        Remembering,
he drowsed over the story's end. Sweet sleep
relaxed his limbs and his care-burdened breast.

Other affairs were in Athena's keeping.
Waiting until Odysseus had his pleasure                    350
of love and sleep, the grey-eyed one bestirred
the fresh Dawn from her bed of paling Ocean
to bring up daylight to her golden chair,
and from his fleecy bed Odysseus
arose. He said to Penélopê:

                            "My lady,                    355
what ordeals have we not endured! Here, waiting

you had your grief, while my return dragged out—
my hard adventures, pitting myself against
the gods' will, and Zeus, who pinned me down
far from home. But now our life resumes:                    360
we've come together to our longed-for bed.
Take care of what is left me in our house;
as to the flocks that pack of wolves laid waste
they'll be replenished: scores I'll get on raids
and other scores our island friends will give me            365
till all the folds are full again.
                              This day
I'm off up country to the orchards. I must see
my noble father, for he missed me sorely.
And here is my command for you—a strict one,
though you may need none, clever as you are.                 370
Word will get about as the sun goes higher
of how I killed those lads. Go to your rooms
on the upper floor, and take your women. Stay there
with never a glance outside or a word to anyone."
Fitting cuirass and swordbelt to his shoulders,            375
he woke his herdsmen, woke Telémakhos,
ordering all in arms. They dressed quickly,
and all in war gear sallied from the gate,
led by Odysseus.
                    Now it was broad day
but these three men Athena hid in darkness,                 380
going before them swiftly from the town.


### Book XXIV

#### WARRIORS, FAREWELL

Meanwhile the suitors' ghosts were called away
by Hermês of Kyllênê,[3] bearing the golden wand
with which he charms the eyes of men or wakens
whom he wills.
                    He waved them on, all squeaking
as bats will in a cavern's underworld,                      5
all flitting, flitting criss-cross in the dark
if one falls and the rock-hung chain is broken.
So with faint cries the shades trailed after Hermês,
pure Deliverer.
                    He led them down dank ways,
over grey Ocean tides, the Snowy Rock,                      10

3. Hermês was born on Mount Kyllênê in Arcadia.

past shores of Dream and narrows of the sunset,
in swift flight to where the Dead inhabit
wastes of asphodel at the world's end.

Crossing the plain they met Akhilleus' ghost,
Patróklos and Antílokhos, then Aias, 15
noblest of Danaans after Akhilleus
in strength and beauty. Here the newly dead
drifted together, whispering. Then came
the soul of Agamémnon, son of Atreus,
in black pain forever, surrounded by men-at-arms 20
who perished with him in Aigísthos' hall.

Akhilleus greeted him:

"My lord Atreidês,
we held that Zeus who loves the play of lightning
would give you length of glory, you were king
over so great a host of soldiery 25
before Troy, where we suffered, we Akhaians.
But in the morning of your life
you met that doom that no man born avoids.
It should have found you in your day of victory,
marshal of the army, in Troy country: 30
then all Akhaia would have heaped your tomb
and saved your honor for your son. Instead
piteous death awaited you at home."

And Atreus' son replied:

"Fortunate hero,
son of Pêleus, godlike and glorious, 35
at Troy you died, across the sea from Argos,
and round you Trojan and Akhaian peers
fought for your corpse and died. A dustcloud wrought
by a whirlwind hid the greatness of you slain,
minding no more the mastery of horses. 40
All that day we might have toiled in battle
had not a storm from Zeus broken it off.
We carried you out of the field of war
down to the ships and bathed your comely body
with warm water and scented oil. We laid you 45
upon your long bed, and our officers
wept hot tears like rain and cropped their hair.
Then hearing of it in the sea, your mother, Thetis,
came with nereids of the grey wave crying
unearthly lamentation over the water, 50

and trembling gripped the Akhaians to the bone.
They would have boarded ship that night and fled
except for one man's wisdom—venerable
Nestor, proven counselor in the past.
He stood and spoke to allay their fear: 'Hold fast,      55
sons of the Akhaians, lads of Argos.
His mother it must be, with nymphs her sisters,
come from the sea to mourn her son in death.'

Veteran hearts at this contained their dread
while at your side the daughters of the ancient      60
seagod wailed and wrapped ambrosial shrouding
around you.
       Then we heard the Muses sing
a threnody in nine immortal voices.
No Argive there but wept, such keening rose
from that one Muse who led the song.
                   Now seven      65
days and ten, seven nights and ten, we mourned you,
we mortal men, with nymphs who know no death,
before we gave you to the flame, slaughtering
longhorned steers and fat sheep on your pyre.

Dressed by the nereids and embalmed with honey,      70
honey and unguent in the seething blaze,
you turned to ash. And past the pyre Akhaia's
captains paraded in review, in arms,
clattering chariot teams and infantry.
Like a forest fire the flame roared on, and burned      75
your flesh away. Next day at dawn, Akhilleus,
we picked your pale bones from the char to keep
in wine and oil. A golden amphora
your mother gave for this—Hephaistos' work,
a gift from Dionysos.[4] In that vase,      80
Akhilleus, hero, lie your pale bones mixed
with mild Patróklos' bones, who died before you,
and nearby lie the bones of Antílokhos,
the one you cared for most of all companions
after Patróklos.
       We of the Old Army,      85
we who were spearmen, heaped a tomb for these
upon a foreland over Hellê's waters,[5]
to be a mark against the sky for voyagers

---

4. A god of the countryside especially associated with wine. Rarely mentioned in Homer, he later presides, at the Athenian festivals, over tragedy and comedy.     5. I.e., the Hellespont, the strait separating Asia Minor from Europe, visible from Troy.

in this generation and those to come.
Your mother sought from the gods magnificent trophies        90
and set them down midfield for our champions. Often
at funeral games after the death of kings
when you yourself contended, you've seen athletes
cinch their belts when trophies went on view.
But these things would have made you stare—the treasures    95
Thetis on her silver-slippered feet
brought to your games—for the gods held you dear.
You perished, but your name will never die.
It lives to keep all men in mind of honor
forever, Akhilleus.

            As for myself, what joy                100
is this, to have brought off the war? Foul death
Zeus held in store for me at my coming home;
Aigísthos and my vixen cut me down."


While they conversed, the Wayfinder came near,
leading the shades of suitors overthrown                     105
by Lord Odysseus. The two souls of heroes
advanced together, scrutinizing these.
Then Agamémnon recognized Amphímedon,
son of Meláneus—friends of his on Ithaka—
and called out to him:


            "Amphímedon,                           110
what ruin brought you into this undergloom?
All in a body, picked men, and so young?
One could not better choose the kingdom's pride.
Were you at sea, aboard ship, and Poseidon
blew up a dire wind and foundering waves,                    115
or cattle-raiding, were you, on the mainland,
or in a fight for some stronghold, or women,
when the foe hit you to your mortal hurt?
Tell me, answer my question. Guest and friend
I say I am of yours—or do you not remember                   120
I visited your family there? I came
with Prince Meneláos, urging Odysseus
to join us in the great sea raid on Troy.
One solid month we beat our way, breasting
south sea and west, resolved to bring him round,             125
the wily raider of cities."


            The new shade said:
"O glory of commanders, Agamémnon,
all that you bring to mind I remember well.

As for the sudden manner of our death
I'll tell you of it clearly, first to last.                                    130
After Odysseus had been gone for years
we were all suitors of his queen. She never
quite refused, nor went through with a marriage,
hating it, ever bent on our defeat.
Here is one of her tricks: she placed her loom,                                135
her big loom, out for weaving in her hall,
and the fine warp of some vast fabric on it.
We were attending her, and she said to us:
'Young men, my suitors, now my lord is dead,
let me finish my weaving before I marry,                                       140
or else my thread will have been spun in vain.
This is a shroud I weave for Lord Laërtês
when cold Death comes to lay him on his bier.
The country wives would hold me in dishonor
if he, with all his fortune, lay unshrouded.'                                   145
We had men's hearts; she touched them; we agreed.
So every day she wove on the great loom—
but every night by torchlight she unwove it,
and so for three years she deceived the Akhaians.
But when the seasons brought the fourth around,                                150
as long months waned, and the slow days were spent,
one of her maids, who knew the secret, told us.
We found her unraveling the splendid shroud,
and then she had to finish, willy nilly—
finish, and show the big loom woven tight                                      155
from beam to beam with cloth. She washed the shrouding
clean as sun or moonlight.
                                       Then, heaven knows
from what quarter of the world, fatality
brought in Odysseus to the swineherd's wood
far up the island. There his son went too                                      160
when the black ship put him ashore from Pylos.
The two together planned our death-trap. Down
they came to the famous town—Telémakhos
long in advance: we had to wait for Odysseus.
The swineherd led him to the manor later                                       165
in rags like a foul beggar, old and broken,
propped on a stick. These tatters that he wore
hid him so well that none of us could know him
when he turned up, not even the older men.
We jeered at him, took potshots at him, cursed him.                            170
Daylight and evening in his own great hall
he bore it, patient as a stone. That night

the mind of Zeus beyond the stormcloud stirred him
with Telémakhos at hand to shift his arms
from mégaron to storage room and lock it.                      175
Then he assigned his wife her part: next day
she brought his bow and iron axeheads out
to make a contest. Contest there was none;
that move doomed us to slaughter. Not a man
could bend the stiff bow to his will or string it,             180
until it reached Odysseus. We shouted,
'Keep the royal bow from the beggar's hands
no matter how he begs!' Only Telémakhos
would not be denied.
                    So the great soldier
took his bow and bent it for the bowstring                     185
effortlessly. He drilled the axeheads clean,
sprang, and decanted arrows on the door sill,
glared, and drew again. This time he killed
Antínoös.
              There facing us he crouched
and shot his bolts of groaning at us, brought us               190
down like sheep. Then some god, his familiar,
went into action with him round the hall,
after us in a massacre. Men lay groaning,
mortally wounded, and the floor smoked with blood.

That was the way our death came, Agamémnon.                    195
Now in Odysseus' hall untended still
our bodies lie, unknown to friends or kinsmen
who should have laid us out and washed our wounds
free of the clotted blood, and mourned our passing.
So much is due the dead."
                          But Agamémnon's                      200
tall shade when he heard this cried aloud:

"O fortunate Odysseus, master mariner
and soldier, blessed son of old Laërtês!
The girl you brought home made a valiant wife!
True to her husband's honor and her own,                       205
Penélopê, Ikários' faithful daughter!
The very gods themselves will sing her story
for men on earth—mistress for her own heart,
Penélopê!
Tyndáreus' daughter waited, too—how differently!              210
Klytaimnéstra, the adulteress,
waited to stab her lord and king. That song

will be forever hateful. A bad name
she gave to womankind, even the best."

These were the things they said to one another                    215
under the rim of earth where Death is lord.

Leaving the town, Odysseus and his men
that morning reached Laërtês garden lands,
long since won by his toil from wilderness—
his homestead, and the row of huts around it                    220
where fieldhands rested, ate and slept. Indoors
he had an old slave woman, a Sikel, keeping
house for him in his secluded age.

Odysseus here took leave of his companions.

"Go make yourselves at home inside," he said.                    225
"Roast the best porker and prepare a meal.
I'll go to try my father. Will he know me?
Can he imagine it, after twenty years?"

He handed spear and shield to the two herdsmen,
and in they went, Telémakhos too. Alone                    230
Odysseus walked the orchard rows and vines.
He found no trace of Dólios and his sons
nor the other slaves—all being gone that day
to clear a distant field, and drag the stones
for a boundary wall.
                        But on a well-banked plot                    235
Odysseus found his father in solitude
spading the earth around a young fruit tree.

He wore a tunic, patched and soiled, and leggings—
oxhide patches, bound below his knees
against the brambles; gauntlets on his hands                    240
and on his head a goatskin cowl of sorrow.
This was the figure Prince Odysseus found—
wasted by years, racked, bowed under grief.
The son paused by a tall pear tree and wept,
then inwardly debated: should he run                    245
forward and kiss his father, and pour out
his tale of war, adventure, and return,
or should he first interrogate him, test him?
Better that way, he thought—
first draw him out with sharp words, trouble him.                    250

His mind made up, he walked ahead. Laërtês
went on digging, head down, by the sapling,
stamping the spade in. At his elbow then
his son spoke out:
                    "Old man, the orchard keeper
you work for is no townsman. A good eye                       255
for growing things he has; there's not a nurseling,
fig tree, vine stock, olive tree or pear tree
or garden bed uncared for on this farm.
But I might add—don't take offense—your own
appearance could be tidier. Old age                           260
yes—but why the squalor, and rags to boot?
It would not be for sloth, now, that your master
leaves you in this condition; neither at all
because there's any baseness in your self.
No, by your features, by the frame you have,                  265
a man might call you kingly,
one who should bathe warm, sup well, and rest easy
in age's privilege. But tell me:
who are your masters? whose fruit trees are these
you tend here? Tell me if it's true this island              270
is Ithaka, as that fellow I fell in with
told me on the road just now? He had
a peg loose, that one: couldn't say a word
or listen when I asked about my friend,
my Ithakan friend. I asked if he were alive                   275
or gone long since into the underworld.
I can describe him if you care to hear it:
I entertained the man in my own land
when he turned up there on a journey; never
had I a guest more welcome in my house.                       280
He claimed his stock was Ithakan: Laërtês
Arkeísiadês, he said his father was.
I took him home treated him well, grew fond of him—
though we had many guests—and gave him
gifts in keeping with his quality: seven                      285
bars of measured gold, a silver winebowl
filigreed with flowers, twelve light cloaks,
twelve rugs, robes and tunics—not to mention
his own choice of women trained in service,
the four well-favored ones he wished to take."                290

His father's eyes had filled with tears. He said:

"You've come to that man's island, right enough,

but dangerous men and fools hold power now.
You gave your gifts in vain. If you could find him
here in Ithaka alive, he'd make                                    295
return of gifts and hospitality,
as custom is, when someone has been generous.
But tell me accurately—how many years
have now gone by since that man was your guest?
your guest, my son—if he indeed existed—                           300
born to ill fortune as he was. Ah, far
from those who loved him, far from his native land,
in some sea-dingle fish have picked his bones,
or else he made the vultures and wild beasts
a trove ashore! His mother at his bier                             305
never bewailed him, nor did I, his father,
nor did his admirable wife, Penélopê,
who should have closed her husband's eyes in death
and cried aloud upon him as he lay.
So much is due the dead.

                    But speak out, tell me further:      310
who are you, of what city and family?
where have you moored the ship that brought you here,
where is your admirable crew? Are you a peddler
put ashore by the foreign ship you came on?"

Again Odysseus had a fable ready.                                  315

"Yes," he said, "I can tell you all those things.
I come from Rover's Passage where my home is,
and I'm King Allwoes' only son. My name
is Quarrelman.
             Heaven's power in the westwind
drove me this way from Sikania,[6]                                 320
off my course. My ship lies in a barren
cove beyond the town there. As for Odysseus,
now is the fifth year since he put to sea
and left my homeland—bound for death, you say.
Yet landbirds flying from starboard crossed his bow—              325
a lucky augury. So we parted joyously,
in hope of friendly days and gifts to come."

A cloud of pain had fallen on Laërtês.
Scooping up handfuls of the sunburnt dust
he sifted it over his grey head, and groaned,                      330

---

6. Another name for Sicily.

and the groan went to the son's heart. A twinge
prickling up through his nostrils warned Odysseus
he could not watch this any longer.
He leaped and threw his arms around his father,
kissed him, and said:

> "Oh, Father, I am he!                335
Twenty years gone, and here I've come again
to my own land!

> Hold back your tears! No grieving!
I bring good news—though still we cannot rest.
I killed the suitors to the last man!
Outrage and injury have been avenged!"                340
Laërtês turned and found his voice to murmur:

"If you are Odysseus, my son, come back,
give me some proof, a sign to make me sure."

His son replied:

> "The scar then, first of all.
Look, here the wild boar's flashing tusk                345
wounded me on Parnassos; do you see it?
You and my mother made me go, that time,
to visit Lord Autólykos, her father,
for gifts he promised years before on Ithaka.
Again—more proof—let's say the trees you gave me                350
on this revetted plot of orchard once.
I was a small boy at your heels, wheedling
amid the young trees, while you named each one.
You gave me thirteen pear, ten apple trees,
and forty fig trees. Fifty rows of vines                355
were promised too, each one to bear in turn.
Bunches of every hue would hang there ripening,
weighed down by the god of summer days."

The old man's knees failed him, his heart grew faint,
recalling all that Odysseus calmly told.                360
He clutched his son. Odysseus held him swooning
until he got his breath back and his spirit
and spoke again:

> "Zeus, Father! Gods above!—
you still hold pure Olympos, if the suitors
paid for their crimes indeed, and paid in blood!                365
But now the fear is in me that all Ithaka

will be upon us. They'll send messengers
to stir up every city of the islands."

Odysseus the great tactician answered:

"Courage, and leave the worrying to me.                          370
We'll turn back to your homestead by the orchard.
I sent the cowherd, swineherd, and Telémakhos
ahead to make our noonday meal."

                               Conversing
in this vein they went home, the two together,
into the stone farmhouse. There Telémakhos                          375
and the two herdsmen were already carving
roast young pork, and mixing amber wine.
During these preparations the Sikel woman
bathed Laërtês and anointed him,
and dressed him in a new cloak. Then Athena,                          380
standing by, filled out his limbs again,
gave girth and stature to the old field captain
fresh from the bathing place. His son looked on
in wonder at the godlike bloom upon him,
and called out happily:

                      "Oh, Father,                          385
surely one of the gods who are young forever
has made you magnificent before my eyes!"

Clearheaded Laërtês faced him, saying:

"By Father Zeus, Athena and Apollo,
I wish I could be now as once I was,                          390
commander of Kephallenians, when I took
the walled town, Nérikos,[7] on the promontory!
Would god I had been young again last night
with armor on me, standing in our hall
to fight the suitors at your side! How many                          395
knees I could have crumpled, to your joy!"

While son and father spoke, cowherd and swineherd
attended, waiting, for the meal was ready.
Soon they were all seated, and their hands
picked up the meat and bread.

---

7. On the mainland; its exact location is unknown.

                        But now old Dólios                    400
appeared in the bright doorway with his sons,
work-stained from the field. Laërtês' housekeeper,
who reared the boys and tended Dólios
in his bent age, had gone to fetch them in.
When it came over them who the stranger was                    405
they halted in astonishment. Odysseus
hit an easy tone with them. Said he:

"Sit down and help yourselves. Shake off your wonder.
Here we've been waiting for you all this time,
and our mouths watering for good roast pig!"                    410

But Dólios came forward, arms outstretched,
and kissed Odysseus' hand at the wrist bone,
crying out:

        "Dear master, you returned!
You came to us again! How we had missed you!
We thought you lost. The gods themselves have brought you!    415
Welcome, welcome; health and blessings on you!
And tell me, now, just one thing more: Penélopê,
does she know yet that you are on the island?
or should we send a messenger?"

Odysseus gruffly said,

                "Old man, she knows.                    420
Is it for you to think of her?"

                So Dólios
quietly took a smooth bench at the table
and in their turn his sons welcomed Odysseus,
kissing his hands; then each went to his chair
beside his father. Thus our friends                    425
were occupied in Laërtês house at noon.

Meanwhile to the four quarters of the town
the news ran: bloody death had caught the suitors;
and men and women in a murmuring crowd
gathered before Odysseus' hall. They gave                    430
burial to the piteous dead, or bore
the bodies of young men from other islands
down to the port, thence to be ferried home.

Then all the men went grieving to assembly
and being seated, rank by rank, grew still,                         435
as old Eupeithês rose to address them. Pain
lay in him like a brand for Antínoös,
the first man that Odysseus brought down,
and tears flowed for his son as he began:

"Heroic feats that fellow did for us                                440
Akhaians, friends! Good spearmen by the shipload
he led to war and lost—lost ships and men,
and once ashore again killed these, who were
the islands' pride.
                    Up with you! After him!—
before he can take flight to Pylos town                             445
or hide at Elis, under Epeian law!
We'd be disgraced forever! Mocked for generations
if we cannot avenge our sons' blood, and our brothers!
Life would turn to ashes—at least for me;
rather be dead and join the dead!
                                  I say                              450
we ought to follow now, or they'll gain time
and make the crossing."

                    His appeal, his tears,
moved all the gentry listening there;
but now they saw the crier and the minstrel
come from Odysseus' hall, where they had slept.                     455
The two men stood before the curious crowd,
and Medôn said:

                    "Now hear me, men of Ithaka.
When these hard deeds were done by Lord Odysseus
the immortal gods were not far off. I saw
with my own eyes someone divine who fought                          460
beside him, in the shape and dress of Mentor;
it was a god who shone before Odysseus,
a god who swept the suitors down the hall
dying in droves."

                    At this pale fear assailed them,
and next they heard again the old forecaster,                       465
Halithérsês Mastóridês. Alone
he saw the field of time, past and to come.
In his anxiety for them he said:

"Ithakans, now listen to what I say.
Friends, by your own fault these deaths came to pass.          470
You would not heed me nor the captain, Mentor;
would not put down the riot of your sons.
Heroic feats they did!—all wantonly
raiding a great man's flocks, dishonoring
his queen, because they thought he'd come no more.          475
Let matters rest; do as I urge; no chase,
or he who wants a bloody end will find it."

The greater number stood up shouting "Aye!"
But many held fast, sitting all together
in no mind to agree with him. Eupeithês          480
had won them to his side. They ran for arms,
clapped on their bronze, and mustered
under Eupeithês at the town gate
for his mad foray.
                    Vengeance would be his,
he thought, for his son's murder; but that day          485
held bloody death for him and no return.

At this point, querying Zeus, Athena said:

"O Father of us all and king of kings,
enlighten me. What is your secret will?
War and battle, worse and more of it,          490
or can you not impose a pact on both?"

The summoner of cloud replied:

                    "My child,
why this formality of inquiry?
Did you not plan that action by yourself—
see to it that Odysseus, on his homecoming,          495
should have their blood?
                    Conclude it as you will.
There is one proper way, if I may say so:
Odysseus' honor being satisfied,
let him be king by a sworn pact forever,
and we, for our part, will blot out the memory          500
of sons and brothers slain. As in the old time
let men of Ithaka henceforth be friends;
prosperity enough, and peace attend them."

Athena needed no command, but down
in one spring she descended from Olympos          505

just as the company of Odysseus finished
wheat crust and honeyed wine, and heard him say:

"Go out, someone, and see if they are coming."

One of the boys went to the door as ordered
and saw the townsmen in the lane. He turned                    510
swiftly to Odysseus.

                    "Here they come,"
he said, "best arm ourselves, and quickly."

All up at once, the men took helm and shield—
four fighting men, counting Odysseus,
with Dólios' half dozen sons. Laërtês                    515
armed as well, and so did Dólios—
greybeards, they could be fighters in a pinch.
Fitting their plated helmets on their heads
they sallied out, Odysseus in the lead.

Now from the air Athena, Zeus's daughter,                    520
appeared in Mentor's guise, with Mentor's voice,
making Odysseus' heart grow light. He said
to put cheer in his son:

                    "Telémakhos,
you are going into battle against pikemen
where hearts of men are tried. I count on you                    525
to bring no shame upon your forefathers.
In fighting power we have excelled this lot
in every generation."

                    Said his son:

"If you are curious, Father, watch and see
the stuff that's in me. No more talk of shame."                    530

And old Laërtês cried aloud:

"Ah, what a day for me, dear gods!
to see my son and grandson vie in courage!"

Athena halted near him, and her eyes
shone like the sea. She said:

                    "Arkeísiadês,                    535
dearest of all my old brothers-in-arms,

invoke the grey-eyed one and Zeus her father,
heft your spear and make your throw."

Power flowed into him from Pallas Athena,
whom he invoked as Zeus's virgin child,                        540
and he let fly his heavy spear.
                                        It struck
Eupeithês on the cheek plate of his helmet,
and undeflected the bronze head punched through.
He toppled, and his armor clanged upon him.
Odysseus and his son now furiously                             545
closed, laying on with broadswords, hand to hand,
and pikes: they would have cut the enemy down
to the last man, leaving not one survivor,
had not Athena raised a shout
that stopped all fighters in their tracks.


                                        "Now hold!"          550
she cried, "Break off this bitter skirmish;
end your bloodshed, Ithakans, and make peace."

Their faces paled with dread before Athena,
and swords dropped from their hands unnerved, to lie
strewing the ground, at the great voice of the goddess.       555
Those from the town turned fleeing for their lives.
But with a cry to freeze their hearts
and ruffling like an eagle on the pounce,
the lord Odysseus reared himself to follow—
at which the son of Kronos dropped a thunderbolt              560
smoking at his daughter's feet.
                                        Athena
cast a grey glance at her friend and said:

"Son of Laërtês and the gods of old,
Odysseus, master of land ways and sea ways,
command yourself. Call off this battle now,                   565
or Zeus who views the wide world may be angry."

He yielded to her, and his heart was glad.
Both parties later swore to terms of peace
set by their arbiter, Athena, daughter
of Zeus who bears the stormcloud as a shield—                 570
though still she kept the form and voice of Mentor.

# AESCHYLUS
## 524?–456 B.C.

The earliest documents in the history of the Western theater are the seven plays of Aeschylus which have come down to us through the more than two thousand years since his death. When he produced his first play in the opening years of the fifth century B.C., the performance that we know as drama was still less than half a century old; it was still open to innovation and Aeschylus, in fact, made such significant contributions to its development that he has been called "the creator of tragedy."

The origins of the theatrical contests in Athens are obscure; they were a puzzle even for Aristotle who in the fourth century B.C. wrote a famous treatise on tragedy. All that we know for certain is that the drama began as a religious celebration which took the form of song and dance.

Such ceremonies are of course to be found in the communal life of many early cultures but it was in Athens, and in Athens alone, that the ceremony gave rise to what we know as tragedy and comedy and produced dramatic masterpieces which are still admired, read, and performed.

At some time in the late sixth century B.C. the Athenians converted what seems to have been a rural celebration of Dionysus, a vegetation deity especially associated with the vine, into an annual city festival at which dancing choruses, competing for prizes, sang hymns of praise to the god. It was from this choral performance that tragedy and comedy developed; some unknown innovator (his name was probably Thespis) combined the choral song with the speech of a masked actor, who, playing a god or hero, engaged the chorus in dialogue. It was Aeschylus who added a second actor and so created the possibility of conflict and the prototype of the drama as we know it.

After the defeat of the Persian invaders (480–479 B.C.), as Athens with its fleets and empire moved toward supremacy in the Greek world, this spring festival became a splendid occasion; the Dionysia, as it was now called, lasted for four days, during which public business (except in emergencies) was suspended and prisoners released on bail for the duration of the festival. In an open-air theater which could seat 14,000 spectators, tragic and comic poets competed for the prizes offered by the city. Three poets in each genre had been selected by the magistrates for the year; after an opening day devoted to the traditional choral hymns, a tragic poet with three plays and a comic poet with one provided the program for each of the three remaining days.

The three tragedies could deal with quite separate stories or, as in the case of Aeschylus' *Oresteia*, with the successive stages of one extended action. By the time this trilogy was produced (458 B.C.) the number of actors had been raised to three; the spoken part of the performance became steadily more important. In the *Oresteia* an equilibrium between the two elements of the performance has been established; the actors, with their speeches, create the dramatic situation and its movement, the plot; the chorus, while contributing to dramatic suspense and illusion, ranges free of the immediate situation in its odes, which extend and amplify the significance of the action.

In 458 B.C. Aeschylus was at the end of a great career; he was to die, two years later, in the Greek city of Gela, in Sicily. He had begun his career as a dramatist before the Persian Wars, in the first days of the new Athenian democracy. He fought against the Persians at Marathon (where his brother was killed) and almost certainly also in the great sea fight at Salamis in 480 (his play, the *Persians*, produced in 472 B.C., contains what sounds like an eyewitness account of that battle). Only seven of his plays survive (we know that he produced 90); besides the *Persians* and the three plays of the *Oresteia*, we have the text of *Suppliants* (sometime in the 460s) and a famous and influential play, the *Prometheus Bound* (date unknown).

The *Oresteia* is a trilogy: the first play, *Agamemnon*, was followed at its performance by two more plays, the *Libation Bearers* and the *Eumenides*, which carried on its story and its theme to a conclusion. The theme of the trilogy is justice; and its story, like that of almost all Greek tragedies, is a legend which was already well-known to the audience that saw the first performance of the play. This particular legend, the story of the house of Atreus, was rich in dramatic potential, for it deals with a series of retributive murders which stained the hands of three generations of a royal family, and it has also a larger, a social and historical significance, of which Aeschylus took full advantage. The legend preserves the memory of an important historical process through which the Greeks had passed, the transition from tribal institutions of justice to communal justice, from a tradition which demanded that a murdered man's next of kin avenge his death, to a system requiring settlement of the private quarrel by the court of law, the typical institution of the city-state which replaced the primitive tribe. When Agamemnon returns victorious from Troy, he is killed by his wife, Clytemnestra, and her lover, Aegisthus, who is Agamemnon's cousin. Clytemnestra kills her husband to avenge her daughter Iphigenia, whom Agamemnon sacrificed to the goddess Artemis when he had to choose between his daughter's life and his ambition to conquer Troy. Aegisthus avenges the crime of a previous generation, the hideous murder of his brothers by Agamemnon's father, Atreus. The killing of Agamemnon is, by the standards of the old system, justice; but it is the nature of this justice that the process can never be arrested, that one act of violence must give rise to another. Agamemnon's murder must be avenged too, as it is in the second play of the trilogy by Orestes, his son, who kills both Aegisthus and his own mother, Clytemnestra. Orestes has acted justly according to the code of tribal society based on blood relationship, but in doing so he has violated the most sacred blood relationship of all, the bond between mother and son. The old system of justice has produced an insoluble dilemma.

At the end of the *Libation Bearers*, Orestes sees a vision of the Furies; they are serpent-haired female hunters, the avengers of blood. Agamemnon had a son to avenge him but for Clytemnestra there was no one to exact payment. This task is taken up by the Furies, who are the guardians of the ancient tribal sanctities; they enforce the old dispensation when no earthly agent is at hand to do so. Female themselves, they assert the claim of the mother against the son who killed her to avenge his father. At the end of the second play they are only a vision in Orestes' mind—"You can't see them," he says to the chorus. "*I* can; they drive me on. I must move on." But in the final play we see them too; they are the chorus, and they have pursued Orestes to the great shrine of Apollo at Delphi where he has come to seek refuge.

Apollo can save him from immediate destruction at the Furies' hands but he cannot resolve the dilemma; Orestes must go to Athens, where Athena, the patron goddess of the city, will set up the first court of law to try his case. At Athens, before the ancient court of the Areopagus, the Furies argue eloquently but Apollo himself arrives to testify that he ordered Orestes to act. Athena instructs the judges in Orestes' favor and Orestes, acquitted, goes home to Argos. The Furies threaten to turn their dreadful wrath against Athens itself but the goddess persuades them to accept a home deep in Athenian earth, to act as protectors of the court and of the land.

More important than the arguments employed in the trial and the decision reached by the judges is the fact of the court's establishment. This is the end of an old era and the beginning of a new. The existence of the court is a guarantee that the tragic series of events which drove Orestes to the murder of his mother will never be repeated. The system of communal justice, which allows consideration of circumstance and motive, and which punishes impersonally, has at last replaced the inconclusive anarchy of individual revenge.

But the play is concerned with much more than the history of human institutions, with more even than the general problem of violence between man and man for which the particular instances of the trilogy stand. It is also a religious statement. The whole sequence of events, stretching over many generations, is presented as the working out of the will of Zeus. The tragic action of the *Iliad* was also the expression of the will of Zeus (though it is characteristic of Homer that Achilles was at least equally responsible), but for Aeschylus the will of Zeus means something new. In this trilogy the working out of Zeus' will proceeds intricately through three generations of bloodshed to the creation of a human institution which will prevent any repetition of the cycle of murder that produced it. Agamemnon dies, and Clytemnestra dies in her turn, and Orestes is hounded over land and sea to his trial, but out of all this suffering comes an important advance in human understanding and civilization. The chorus of the *Agamemnon*, celebrating the power of Zeus, tells us that he

> . . . has led us on to know,
> that Helmsman lays it down as law
> that we must suffer, suffer into truth.

From the suffering comes knowledge of the truth, whereas in the *Iliad* nothing at all comes out of the suffering, except the certainty of more. "Far from the land of my fathers," says Achilles to Priam, "I sit here in Troy, and bring nothing but sorrow to you and your children"; but his last words to Priam are a reminder that this interval of sympathy is only temporary. After Hector's burial the war will go on as before. This is Zeus' will; Homer does not attempt to explain it. But the Aeschylean trilogy is nothing less than an attempt to justify the ways of God to man; the suffering is shown to us as the fulfillment of a purpose we can understand, a purpose beneficent to man.

The full scope of Zeus' will is apparent only to the audience, which follows the pattern of its execution through the three plays of the trilogy; as in the Book of Job, the characters who act and suffer are in the dark. They claim a knowledge of Zeus' will and boast that their actions are its fulfillment (it is in these terms that Agamemnon speaks of the sack of Troy, and Clytemnestra of Agamemnon's murder), and they are, of course, in one sense, right. But their knowledge is limited; Agamemnon does not realize that Zeus' will includes his death at the hands of Clytemnestra, nor Clytemnestra that it demands her death at the hands of her son. The chorus has, at times, a deeper understanding; in its opening ode it announces the law of Zeus, that men must learn by suffering, and at the end it recognizes the responsibility of Zeus in the death of Agamemnon—"all through the will of Zeus, the cause of all, the one who works it all." But the chorus cannot interpret the event in any way it can accept, for it can see no further than the immediate present; its knowledge of Zeus' law is an abstraction which it cannot relate to the terrible fact.

In this murky atmosphere (made all the more terrible by the beacon fire of the opening lines, which brings not light, but deeper darkness), one human being sees clear; she possesses the concrete vision of the future which complements the chorus' abstract knowledge of the law. This is the prophet Cassandra, Priam's daughter, brought from Troy as Agamemnon's share of the spoils. She has been given the power of true prophecy by the god Apollo, but the gift is nullified by the condition that her prophecies will never be believed. Like the Hebrew prophets, she sees reality—past, present, and future—so clearly that she is cut off from ordinary human beings by the clarity of her vision and the terrible burden of her knowledge; like them she expresses herself in poetic figures, and like them she is rejected by her hearers. To the everyday world, represented by the chorus, she appears to be mad, the fate of prophets in all ages; and it is only as she goes into the palace to the death she foresees that the old men of the chorus begin to accept, fearfully and hesitantly, the truth which she has been telling them.

The great scene in which she mouths her hysterical prophecies at them delays the action for which everything has been prepared—the death of Agamemnon. Before we hear his famous cry off stage, Cassandra presents us with a mysterious vision in which she combines cause, effect, and result: the murders which have led to this terrible moment, the death of Agamemnon (which will not take place until she leaves the stage), and the murders which will follow. We do not see Agamemnon's death—we see much more. The past, present, and future of Clytemnestra's action and Agamemnon's suffering are fused into a timeless unity in Cassandra's great lines, an unearthly unity which is dissolved only when Agamemnon, in the real world of time and space, screams in mortal agony.

The tremendous statement of the trilogy is made in a style which for magnificence and richness of suggestion can be compared only with the style of Shakespeare at the height of his poetic power, the Shakespeare of *King Lear* and *Antony and Cleopatra*. The language of the *Oresteia* is an Oriental carpet of imagery in which combinations of metaphor, which at first seem bombastic in their violence, take their place in the ordered pattern of the poem as a whole. An image, once introduced, recurs, and reappears again, to run its course verbally and visually through the whole length of the trilogy, richer in meaning with each fresh appearance. In the second choral ode, for example, the chorus, welcoming the news of Agamemnon's victory at Troy, sings of the net which Zeus and Night threw over the city, trapping the inhabitants like animals. The net is here an image of Zeus' justice, a retributive justice, since Troy is paying for the crime of taking Helen, and the image identifies Zeus' justice with Agamemnon's action in sacking the city. This image occurs again, with a different emphasis, in the hypocritical speech of welcome which Clytemnestra makes to her husband on his return. She tells how she feared for his safety at Troy, how she trembled at the rumors of his death:

> and the rumors spread and fester,
> a runner comes with something dreadful,
> close on his heels the next and his news worse,
> and they shout it out and the whole house can hear;
> and wounds—if he took one wound for each report
> to penetrate these walls, he's gashed like a dragnet. . . .

This vision of Agamemnon dead she speaks of as her fear, but we know that it represents her deepest desire, and more, the purpose which she is now preparing to execute. When, later, she stands in triumph over her husband's corpse, she uses the same image to describe the robe which she threw over his limbs to blind and baffle him before she stabbed him—"Inextricable like a net for fishes/I cast about him a vicious wealth of raiment"—and this time the image materializes into an object visible on stage. We can see the net, the gashed robe still folded round Agamemnon's body. We shall see it again, for in the second play Orestes, standing over his mother's body as she now stands over his father's, will display the robe before us, with its holes and bloodstains, as a justification for what he has just done. Elsewhere in the *Agamemnon* the chorus compares Cassandra to a wild animal caught in the net, and later Aegisthus exults to see Agamemnon's body lying "in the nets of Justice." For each speaker the image has a different meaning, but not one realizes the terrible sense in which it applies to them all. They are all caught in the net, the system of justice by vengeance which only binds tighter the more its captives struggle to free themselves. Clytemnestra attempts to escape, to arrest the process of the chain of murders and the working out of the will of Zeus. "But I will swear a pact with the spirit born within us," she says, but Agamemnon's body and the net she threw over him are there on the stage to remind us that her appeal will not be heard; one more generation must act and suffer before the net will vanish, never to be seen again.

Richmond Lattimore, *Aeschylus, Oresteia* (1953), contains a valuable introduction aimed at the general reader. Gilbert Murray, *Aeschylus, Creator of Tragedy* (1940), discusses the theme of the *Oresteia*.

# The Oresteia[1]

## Agamemnon

### Characters

| | |
|---|---|
| WATCHMAN | AEGISTHUS |
| CLYTAEMNESTRA | CHORUS, the Old Men of Argos |
| HERALD | and their Leader |
| AGAMEMNON | Attendants of Clytaemnestra and |
| CASSANDRA | of Agamemnon, bodyguard |
| | of Aegisthus |

[TIME AND SCENE: *A night in the tenth and final autumn of the Trojan war. The house of Atreus in Argos. Before it, an altar stands unlit; a watchman on the high roofs fights to stay awake.*]

WATCHMAN: Dear gods, set me free from all the pain,
  the long watch I keep, one whole year awake . . .
  propped on my arms, crouched on the roofs of Atreus
  like a dog.
      I know the stars by heart,
  the armies of the night, and there in the lead           5
  the ones that bring us snow or the crops of summer,
  bring us all we have—
  our great blazing kings of the sky,
  I know them, when they rise and when they fall . . .
  and now I watch for the light, the signal-fire[2]       10
  breaking out of Troy, shouting Troy is taken.
  So she commands, full of her high hopes.
  That woman[3]—she maneuvers like a man.

And when I keep to my bed, soaked in dew,
  and the thoughts go groping through the night       15
  and the good dreams that used to guard my sleep . . .
  not here, it's the old comrade, terror, at my neck.
  I mustn't sleep, no—

    [*Shaking himself awake.*]

              Look alive, sentry.
And I try to pick out tunes, I hum a little,       20
  a good cure for sleep, and the tears start,

1. Translated by Robert Fagles.   2. The fire the watchman waits to see is the bonfire nearest to Argos, the last in a chain extending all the way to Troy, each one visible, when fired at night, from the next.   3. Clytaemnestra.

I cry for the hard times come to the house,
no longer run like the great place of old.

Oh for a blessed end to all our pain,
some godsend burning through the dark—

[*Light appears slowly in the east; he struggles to his feet and scans it.*]

                           I salute you!
You dawn of the darkness, you turn night to day—        25
I see the light at last.
They'll be dancing in the streets of Argos[4]
thanks to you, thanks to this new stroke of—
                           Aieeeeee!
There's your signal clear and true, my queen!
Rise up from bed—hurry, lift a cry of triumph        30
through the house, praise the gods for the beacon,
if they've taken Troy . . .
                  But there it burns,
fire all the way. I'm for the morning dances.
Master's luck is mine. A throw of the torch
has brought us triple-sixes[5]—we have won!
My move now—                          35

[*Beginning to dance, then breaking off, lost in thought.*]

            Just bring him home. My king,
I'll take your loving hand in mine and then . . .
the rest is silence. The ox is on my tongue.[6]
Aye, but the house and these old stones,
give them a voice and what a tale they'd tell.        40
And so would I, gladly . . .
I speak to those who know; to those who don't
my mind's a blank. I never say a word.

[*He climbs down from the roof and disappears into the palace through a side entrance.* A CHORUS, *the old men of Argos who*

---

4. In Homer Agamemnon, son of Atreus, is King of Mycenae. Later Greek poets, however, referred to his kingdom as Argos or Mycenae, perhaps because the Achaeans in Homer are sometimes called Argives. In 463 B.C., just five years before the production of the play, Argos had defeated Mycenae in battle and put an end to the city, displacing the inhabitants or selling them into slavery. Soon after, Argos and Athens entered into an alliance, aimed, of course, at Sparta. Since in the last play of the trilogy this alliance will be alluded to, it is important for Aeschylus to establish the un-Homeric location of the action right at the beginning.    5. The highest throw in the ancient Greek dice game.    6. A proverbial phrase for enforced silence.

*have not learned the news of victory, enters and marches round
the altar.*]

CHORUS: Ten years gone, ten to the day
    our great avenger went for Priam—               45
        Menelaus and lord Agamemnon,[7]
two kings with the power of Zeus,
the twin throne, twin sceptre,
Atreus' sturdy yoke of sons
launched Greece in a thousand ships,            50
armadas cutting loose from the land,
armies massed for the cause, the rescue—

[*From within the palace* CLYTAEMNESTRA *raises a cry of* triumph.]

the heart within them screamed for all-out war!
Like vultures robbed of their young,
    the agony sends them frenzied,             55
soaring high from the nest, round and
round they wheel, they row their wings,
stroke upon churning thrashing stroke,
but all the labor, the bed of pain,
    the young are lost forever.              60
Yet someone hears on high—Apollo,
Pan, or Zeus[8]—the piercing wail
these guests of heaven raise,
and drives at the outlaws, late
but true to revenge, a stabbing Fury![9]        65

[CLYTAEMNESTRA *appears at the doors and pauses with her
entourage.*[1]]

So towering Zeus the god of guests[2]
drives Atreus' sons at Paris,
all for a woman manned by many
the generations wrestle, knees

7. Sons of Atreus, kings of Argos, commanders of the Greek expedition against Troy. *Priam:* King of Troy. His son Paris abducted (or seduced) Menelaus' wife, Helen.   8. Pan as a god of the wild places; Zeus because eagles and vultures were symbolic of his power; Apollo perhaps as a prophetic god: the movements of birds are regarded as prophetic signs.   9. The Greek word is *Erinyes.* This is the first mention of these avenging spirits who will actually appear on stage as the chorus of the final play.   1. There are no stage directions on the manuscript copies of the plays which have come down to us. Here the translator has the queen enter so that she will be visible on stage when the chorus addresses her by name in 94. Other scholars, pointing out that in Greek tragedy characters who are off stage are often addressed, disagree, and bring Clytaemnestra on stage only at 256.   2. Zeus was thought to be particularly interested in punishing those who violated the code of hospitality. Paris, a guest in Menelaus' house, had run away with his wife, Helen.

grinding the dust, the manhood drains,                                70
the spear snaps in the first blood rites
   that marry Greece and Troy.
And now it goes as it goes
and where it ends is Fate.
And neither by singeing flesh                                          75
nor tipping cups of wine[3]
nor shedding burning tears can you
enchant away the rigid Fury.

   [CLYTAEMNESTRA *lights the altarfires.*]

We are the old, dishonoured ones,[4]
the broken husks of men.                                               80
Even then they cast us off,
the rescue mission left us here
to prop a child's strength upon a stick.
What if the new sap rises in his chest?
He has no soldiery in him,                                             85
   no more than we,
and we are aged past aging,
gloss of the leaf shriveled,
three legs[5] at a time we falter on.
Old men are children once again,                                       90
   a dream that sways and wavers
into the hard light of day.
              But you,
daughter of Leda, queen Clytaemnestra,
what now, what news, what message
drives you through the citadel                                         95
   burning victims?[6] Look,
the city gods, the gods of Olympus,
gods of the earth and public markets—
all the altars blazing with your gifts!
   Argos blazes! Torches                                   100
race the sunrise up her skies—
drugged by the lulling holy oils,
   unadulterated,
run from the dark vaults of kings.
   Tell us the news!                                        105
What you can, what is right—

---

3. Neither by burnt sacrifice nor by pouring libations.    4. The general sense of the passage is
that only two classes of the male population are left in Argos, those who are too young to fight
and those who, like the chorus, are too old.    5. Because they walk with a stick to support
them.    6. Clytemnestra is sacrificing in thanksgiving for the news of Troy's fall; the chorus does
not know that the news has come via the signalfires.

Heal us, soothe our fears!
Now the darkness comes to the fore,
now the hope glows through your victims,
beating back this raw, relentless anguish                         110
      gnawing at the heart.


[CLYTAEMNESTRA *ignores them and pursues her rituals; they
assemble for the opening chorus.*]


O but I still have power to sound the god's command at the
      roads
that launched the kings. The gods breathe power through
      my song,
      my fighting strength, Persuasion grows with the years—
I sing how the flight of fury hurled the twin command,            115
            one will that hurled young Greece
and winged the spear of vengeance straight for Troy!
The kings of birds[7] to kings of the beaking prows, one black,
      one with a blaze of silver
            skimmed the palace spearhand right                    120
                  and swooping lower, all could see,
                        plunged their claws in a hare, a mother
      bursting with unborn young—the babies spilling,
quick spurts of blood—cut off the race just dashing into life!
Cry, cry for death, but good win out in glory in the end.         125
But the loyal seer[8] of the armies studied Atreus' sons,
two sons with warring hearts—he saw two eagle-kings
      devour the hare and spoke the things to come,[9]
"Years pass, and the long hunt nets the city of Priam,
            the flocks beyond the walls,                          130
a kingdom's life and soul—Fate stamps them out.
      Just let no curse of the gods lour on us first,
            shatter our giant armor
                  forged to strangle Troy. I see
                        pure Artemis bristle in pity[1]—          135
                              yes, the flying hounds[2] of the Father
                  slaughter for armies . . . their own victim . . a woman

---

7. Eagles. The chorus proceeds to describe the omen which accompanied the departure of the
army for Troy ten years before. Two eagles seized and tore a pregnant hare; this was interpreted
by the prophet Calchas as meaning that the two kings would destroy the city of Troy, thus killing
not only the living Trojans but the Trojan generations yet unborn.   8. Calchas.   9. The seer
identified the two eagles as symbolic of the two kings, their action as a symbolic prophecy of the
destruction of Troy.   1. Artemis, a virgin goddess, patron of hunting and the protectress of wild
life, she is angry that the eagles have destroyed a pregnant animal. The prophet fears that she may
turn her wrath against the kings whom the eagles represent.   2. The eagles.

trembling young, all born to die—She[3] loathes the eagles' feast!"
Cry, cry for death, but good win out in glory in the end.

"Artemis, lovely Artemis, so kind                                140
to the ravening lion's tender, helpless cubs,
the suckling young of beasts that stalk the wilds—
    bring this sign for all its fortune,
        all its brutal torment home to birth![4]
I beg you, Healing Apollo, soothe her before              145
her crosswinds hold us down and moor the ships too long,[5]
pressing us on to another victim . . .
    nothing sacred, no
        no feast to be eaten[6]
            the architect of vengeance                       150

[*Turning to the palace.*]

    growing strong in the house
    with no fear of the husband
here she waits
the terror raging back and back in the future

    the stealth, the law of the hearth, the mother—          155
        Memory womb of Fury child-avenging Fury!"
So as the eagles wheeled at the crossroads,
Calchas clashed out the great good blessings mixed with doom
    for the halls of kings, and singing with our fate
we cry, cry for death, but good win out in glory in the end.   160
Zeus, great nameless all in all,
if that name will gain his favor,[7]
    I will call him Zeus.
I have no words to do him justice,
weighing all in the balance,                                  165
    all I have is Zeus, Zeus—
lift this weight, this torment from my spirit,
    cast it once for all.

3. Artemis. A *woman trembling young*: Just as the eagles kill the hare, the kings will kill
Agamemnon's daughter Iphigenia. The Greek text refers only to the hare but the translator
has made the allusion clear.    4. Calchas prays that in spite of its bad aspects, the omen will be
truly prophetic, i.e., that the Achaeans will capture Troy. He goes on to anticipate and try to avert
some of the evils it portends.    5. He foresees the future. Artemis will send unfavorable winds
to prevent the sailing of the Greek expedition from Aulis, the port of embarkation. She will
demand the sacrifice of Agamemnon's daughter Iphigenia as the price of the fleet's release.
6. At an ordinary sacrifice the celebrants gave the gods their due portion and then feasted on the
animal's flesh. The word "sacrifice" comes to have the connotation of "feast." There will be no
feast at this sacrifice, since the victim will be a human being. The ominous phrase reminds us of
a feast of human flesh which has already taken place, Thyestes' feasting on his own children.
7. It was important, in prayer, to address the divinity by his or her right name: here the chorus
uses an inclusive formula—they call on Zeus by whatever name pleases him.

He who was so mighty once,[8]
storming for the wars of heaven, 170
   he has had his day.
And then his son[9] who came to power
   met his match in the third fall
   and he is gone. Zeus, Zeus—
raise your cries and sing him Zeus the Victor! 175
   You will reach the truth:

Zeus has led us on to know,
the Helmsman lays it down as law
that we must suffer, suffer into truth.
We cannot sleep, and drop by drop at the heart 180
the pain of pain remembered comes again,
and we resist, but ripeness comes as well
From the gods enthroned on the awesome rowing-bench[1]
   there comes a violent love.

So it was that day the king, 185
the steersman at the helm of Greece,
would never blame a word the prophet said—
swept away by the wrenching winds of fortune
he conspired! Weatherbound we could not sail,
our stores exhausted, fighting strength hard-pressed, 190
and the squadrons rode in the shallows off Chalkis[2]
   where the riptide crashes, drags,
and winds from the north pinned down our hulls at Aulis,
port of anguish . . . head winds starving,
sheets and the cables snapped 195
   and the men's minds strayed,
     the pride, the bloom of Greece
   was raked as time ground on,
ground down, and then the cure for the storm
and it was harsher—Calchas cried, 200
"My captains, Artemis must have blood!"—
   so harsh the sons of Atreus
     dashed their sceptres on the rocks,
   could not hold back the tears,

8. Uranus, father of Cronos, grandfather of Zeus, the first lord of heaven. This whole passage refers to a primitive legend which told how Uranus was violently supplanted by his son, Cronos, who was in his turn overthrown by his son, Zeus. This legend is made to bear new meaning by Aeschylus, for he suggests that it is not a meaningless series of acts of violence, but a progression to the rule of Zeus, who stands for order and justice. Thus the law of human life which Zeus proclaims and administers, that wisdom comes through suffering, has its counterpart in the history of the establishment of the divine rule. 9. Cronos. 1. The bench of the ship where the helmsman sat. 2. The unruly water of the narrows between Aulis on the mainland and Chalkis on the island of Euboea.

and I still can hear the older warlord saying,                    205
"Obey, obey, or a heavy doom will crush me!—
Oh but doom *will* crush me
   once I rend my child,
      the glory of my house—
  a father's hands are stained,                          210
blood of a young girl streaks the altar.
Pain both ways and what is worse?
Desert the fleets, fail the alliance?
  No, but stop the winds with a virgin's blood,
    feed their lust, their fury?—feed their fury!—     215
  Law is law!—
      Let all go well."


And once he slipped his neck in the strap of Fate,
his spirit veering black, impure, unholy,
once he turned he stopped at nothing,
    seized with the frenzy                             220
      blinding driving to outrage—
wretched frenzy, cause of all our grief!
Yes, he had the heart
    to sacrifice his daughter,
  to bless the war that avenged a woman's loss,               225
    a bridal rite that sped the men-of-war.
"My father, father!"—she might pray to the winds;
no innocence moves her judges mad for war.
Her father called his henchmen on,
    on with a prayer,                                 230
      "Hoist her over the altar
like a yearling, give it all your strength!
She's fainting—lift her,
  sweep her robes around her,
but slip this strap in her gentle curving lips . . .              235
  here, gag her hard, a sound will curse the house"—


and the bridle chokes her voice . . . her saffron robes
pouring over the sand
         her glance like arrows showering
wounding every murderer through with pity
  clear as a picture, live,                                 240
she strains to call their names . . .
I remember often the days with father's guests
when over the feast her voice unbroken,
  pure as the hymn her loving father

bearing third libations,[3] sang to Saving Zeus— 245
transfixed with joy, Atreus' offspring
   throbbing out their love.

What comes next? I cannot see it, cannot say.
The strong techniques of Calchas do their work.[4]
But Justice turns the balance scales, 250
   sees that we suffer
and we suffer and we learn.
And we will know the future when it comes.
Greet it too early, weep too soon.
   It all comes clear in the light of day. 255
Let all go well today, well as she could want,

    [*Turning to* CLYTAEMNESTRA.]

our midnight watch, our lone defender,
   single-minded queen.
LEADER:                We've come,
   Clytaemnestra. We respect your power.
   Right it is to honor the warlord's woman 260
   once he leaves the throne.
                  But why these fires?
Good news, or more good hopes? We're loyal,
we want to hear, but never blame your silence.
CLYTAEMNESTRA: Let the new day shine—as the proverb says—
   glorious from the womb of Mother Night. 265

    [*Lost in prayer, then turning to the* CHORUS.]

You will hear a joy beyond your hopes.
Priam's citadel—the Greeks have taken Troy!
LEADER: No, what do you mean? I can't believe it.
CLYTAEMNESTRA: Troy is ours. Is that clear enough?
LEADER:                       The joy of it,
   stealing over me, calling up my tears— 270
CLYTAEMNESTRA: Yes, your eyes expose your loyal hearts.
LEADER: And you have proof?
CLYTAEMNESTRA:           I do,
   I must. Unless the god is lying.

---

3. At the banquet three libations (offerings of wine) were poured, the third and last to Zeus the Savior. The last libation was accompanied by a hymn of praise.   4. This seems to refer to the sacrifice of Iphigenia. Some scholars take the Greek words to refer to the fulfillment of Calchas' prophecies.

LEADER:                     That,
or a phantom spirit sends you into raptures.
CLYTAEMNESTRA: No one takes me in with visions—senseless
   dreams.                                         275
LEADER: Or giddy rumor, you haven't indulged yourself—
CLYTAEMNESTRA: You treat me like a child, you mock me?
LEADER: Then when did they storm the city?
CLYTAEMNESTRA: Last night, I say, the mother of this morning.
LEADER: And who on earth could run the news so fast?       280
CLYTAEMNESTRA The god of fire—rushing fire from Ida![5]
   And beacon to beacon rushed it on to me,
   my couriers riding home the torch.
                              From Troy
   to the bare rock of Lemnos, Hermes' Spur,
   and the Escort winged the great light west          285
   to the Saving Father's face, Mount Athos hurled it
   third in the chain and leaping Oceana's back
   the blaze went dancing on to ecstasy—pitch-pine
   streaming gold like a new-born sun—and brought
   the word in flame to Mount Makistos' brow.        290
   No time to waste, straining, fighting sleep,
   that lookout heaved a torch glowing over
   the murderous straits of Euripos to reach
   Messapion's watchmen craning for the signal.
   Fire for word of fire! tense with the heather      295
   withered gray, they stack it, set it ablaze—
   the hot force of the beacon never flags,
   it springs the Plain of Asôpos, rears

---

5. The mountain range near Troy. The names which follow in this speech designate the places where beacon fires flashed the message of Troy's fall to Argos. The chain extends from Ida to Hermes' cliff on the island of Lemnos (off the coast of Asia Minor), to Mount Athos (which is situated on a rocky peninsula in north Greece), to Mount Makistos on the island of Euboea (off the coast of central Greece), to Messapion, a mountain of the mainland, to Kithairon, a mountain near Thebes, across Lake Gorgopis (the Gorgon's Eye) to Mount Aegiplanctus (the wild goat's range) on the Isthmus of Corinth, across the sea (the Saronic Gulf) to Mount Arachnaeus (Spider—Black Widow Mountain) in Argive territory. This fire is the one seen by the watchman at the beginning of the play. The speech has often been criticized as discursive, but it has great poetic importance. The image of the light which will dispel the darkness, first introduced by the watchman, is one of the dominant images of the trilogy, and is here developed with magnificent ambiguous effect. For the watchman the light means the safe return of Agamemnon and the restoration of order in the house; for Clytemnestra it means the return of Agamemnon to his death at her hands. Each swift jump of the racing light is one step nearer home and death for Agamemnon. The light the watchman longs for brings only greater darkness, but eventually it brings darkness for Clytemnestra too. The final emergence of the true light comes in the glare of the torchlight procession which ends the last play of the trilogy, a procession which symbolizes perfect reconciliation on both the human and the divine levels, and the working out of the will of Zeus in the substitution of justice for vengeance. The conception of the beacons as a chain of descendants (compare "the true son of the burning flanks of Ida," l. 311) is also important; the fire at Argos which announces Agamemnon's imminent death is a direct descendant of the fire on Ida which announces the sack of Troy and Agamemnon's sacrilegious conduct there. The metaphor thus reminds us of the sequence of crimes from generation to generation which is the history of the house of Pelops.

like a harvest moon to hit Kithairon's crest
and drives new men to drive the fire on. 300
That relay pants for the far-flung torch,
they swell its strength outstripping my commands
and the light inflames the marsh, the Gorgon's Eye,
it strikes the peak where the wild goats range—
my laws, my fire whips that camp! 305
They spare nothing, eager to build its heat,
and a huge beard of flame overcomes the headland
beetling down the Saronic Gulf, and flaring south
it brings the dawn to the Black Widow's face—
the watch that looms above your heads—and now 310
the true son of the burning flanks of Ida
crashes on the roofs of Atreus' sons!
And I ordained it all.
Torch to torch, running for their lives,
one long succession racing home my fire. 315
        One,
first in the laps and last,[6] wins out in triumph.
There you have my proof, *my* burning sign, I tell you—
the power my lord passed on from Troy to me!
LEADER: We'll thank the gods, my lady—first this story,
let me lose myself in the wonder of it all! 320
Tell it start to finish, tell us all.
CLYTAEMNESTRA: The city's ours—in our hands this very day!
I can hear the cries in crossfire rock the walls.
Pour oil and wine in the same bowl,
what have you, friendship? A struggle to the end. 325
So with the victors and the victims—outcries,
you can hear them clashing like their fates.

They are kneeling by the bodies of the dead,
embracing men and brothers, infants over
the aged loins that gave them life, and sobbing, 330
as the yoke constricts their last free breath,
for every dear one lost.
       And the others,
there, plunging breakneck through the night—
to breakfast on the last remains of Troy. 335
Not by rank but chance, by the lots they drew,
they lodge in the houses captured by the spear,
settling in so soon, released from the open sky,
the frost and dew. Lucky men, off guard at last,

6. The chain of beacons is compared to a relay race in which the runners carry torches: the last runner (who runs the final lap) comes in first to win.

they sleep away their first good night in years.                    340
If only they are revering the city's gods,
the shrines of the gods who love the conquered land,
no plunderer will be plundered in return.
Just let no lust, no mad desire[7] seize the armies
to ravish what they must not touch—                                  345
overwhelmed by all they've won!
               The run for home
and safety waits, the swerve at the post,[8]
the final lap of the gruelling two-lap race.
And even if the men come back with no offence
to the gods, the avenging dead may never rest—                       350
Oh let no new disaster strike! And here
you have it, what a woman has to say.
Let the best win out, clear to see.
A small desire but all that I could want.
LEADER: Spoken like a man, my lady, loyal,                           355
    full of self-command. I've heard your sign
    and now your vision.

       [*Reaching towards her as she turns and re-enters the palace.*]

              Now to praise the gods.
  The joy is worth the labor.
CHORUS: O Zeus my king and Night, dear Night,[9]
    queen of the house who covers us with glories,[1]              360
    you slung your net on the towers of Troy,
    neither young nor strong could leap
    the giant dredge net of slavery,
       all-embracing ruin.
    I adore you, iron Zeus of the guests                           365
    and your revenge—you drew your longbow
    year by year to a taut full draw
    till one bolt, not falling short
    or arching over the stars,
       could split the mark of Paris!                              370

  The sky stroke of god!—it is all Troy's to tell,
  but even I can trace it to its cause:
  god does as god decrees.

7. Clytaemnestra, who intends to murder Agamemnon on his return, hopes of course for the
opposite of what she here prays for. The audience was familiar with the traditional account,
according to which Agamemnon and his army failed signally to respect the gods and temples of
Troy.    8. Greek runners turned at the post and came back on a parallel track.    9. Troy fell
to a night attack.    1. An obscure expression in the original; the "glories" must be the moon and
stars.

And still some say
that heaven would never stoop to punish men 375
who trample the lovely grace of things[2]
untouchable. How wrong they are!
    A curse burns bright on crime—[3]
        full-blown, the father's crimes will blossom,
            burst into the son's. 380
Let there be less suffering . . .
give us the sense to live on what we need.

                    Bastions of wealth
                    are no defence for the man
                    who treads the grand altar of Justice 385
                        down and out of sight.

Persuasion, maddening child of Ruin
overpowers him—Ruin plans it all.
And the wound will smolder on,
    there is no cure, 390
a terrible brilliance kindles on the night.
He is bad bronze scraped on a touchstone:
put to the test, the man goes black.[4]
    Like the boy who chases
        a bird on the wing, brands his city, 395
            brings it down and prays,
but the gods are deaf
to the one who turns to crime, they tear him down.

                    So Paris learned:
                    he came to Atreus' house 400
                    and shamed the tables spread for guests,
                        he stole away the queen.

And she left her land *chaos*, clanging shields,
companions tramping, bronze prows, men in bronze,
    and she came to Troy with a dowry, death, 405
strode through the gates
        defiant in every stride,
as prophets of the house[5] looked on and wept,

---

2. The language throughout this passage is significantly general. The chorus refers to Paris but everything it says is equally applicable to Agamemnon, who sacrificed his daughter for his ambitions.    3. The original Greek is corrupt (i.e., has been garbled in the hand-written tradition) but seems to proclaim the doctrine that the sins of the fathers are visited on the children. So Paris (and Agamemnon) pay for the misdeeds of their ancestors (as well as their own).    4. Inferior bronze, adulterated with lead, turns black with use.    5. The house of Menelaus.

"Oh the halls and the lords of war,
   the bed and the fresh prints of love.            410
I *see* him, unavenging, unavenged,
the stun of his desolation is so clear—
   he longs for the one who lies across the sea
until her phantom seems to sway the house.

          Her curving images,           415
          her beauty hurts her lord,
          the eyes starve and the touch
            of love is gone,

"and radiant dreams are passing in the night,
the memories throb with sorrow, joy with pain . . .    420
   it is pain to dream and see desires
slip through the arms,
      a vision lost for ever
winging down the moving drifts of sleep."
So he grieves at the royal hearth         425
   yet others' grief is worse, far worse.
All through Greece for those who flocked to war
they are holding back the anguish now,
   you can feel it rising now in every house;
I tell you there is much to tear the heart.      430

          They knew the men they sent,
          but now in place of men
          ashes and urns come back
           to every hearth.[6]

War, War, the great gold-broker[7] of corpses    435
holds the balance of the battle on his spear!
Home from the pyres he sends them,
   home from Troy to the loved ones,
heavy with tears, the urns brimmed full,
   the heroes return in gold-dust,      440
dear, light ash for men; and they weep,
they praise them, "He had skill in the swordplay,"
   "He went down so tall in the onslaught,"
"All for another's woman." So they mutter
in secret and the rancor steals      445
   towards our staunch defenders, Atreus' sons.

---

6. This strikes a contemporary note. In Homer the fallen Achaeans are buried at Troy: it was in the Athens of Aeschylus that the dead were cremated on the battlefield and their ashes brought home for burial.    7. The war god is a broker who gives, in exchange for bodies, gold dust (the word used for "bodies" could mean living bodies or corpses); the "dust" he gives is of course the ashes of the warrior.

And there they ring the walls, the young,
the lithe, the handsome hold the graves
they won in Troy; the enemy earth
    rides over those who conquered.                    450

The people's voice is heavy with hatred,
now the curses of the people must be paid,
and now I wait, I listen . . .
    there—there is something breathing
under the night's shroud. God takes aim                         455
    at the ones who murder many;
the swarthy Furies stalk the man
gone rich beyond all rights—with a twist
    of fortune grind him down, dissolve him
into the blurring dead—there is no help.                        460
The reach for power can recoil,
the bolt of god can strike you at a glance.

    Make me rich with no man's envy,
    neither a raider of cities,[8] no,
    nor slave come face to face with life          465
      overpowered by another.

[*Speaking singly.*]

—Fire comes and the news is good,
    it races through the streets
but is it true? Who knows?
    Or just another lie from heaven?                     470

—Show us the man so childish, wonderstruck,
    he's fired up with the first torch,
then when the message shifts
he's sick at heart.
            —Just like a woman
to fill with thanks before the truth is clear.                  475

—So gullible. Their stories spread like wildfire,
    they fly fast and die faster;
rumors voiced by women come to nothing.
LEADER: Soon we'll know her fires for what they are,
her relay race of torches hand-to-hand—                         480

3. Later we will see Agamemnon come on stage with the spoils of Troy and Cassandra, his Trojan
captive. The chorus, which started out to sing a hymn of praise for the fall of Troy (l. 357) ends
in fear and despondency. They now question the truth of Clytaemnestra's announcement: perhaps
Troy has not fallen after all (l. 469).

know if they're real or just a dream,
the hope of a morning here to take our senses.
I see a herald running from the beach
and a victor's spray of olive shades his eyes
and the dust he kicks, twin to the mud of Troy,                    485
shows he has a voice—no kindling timber
on the cliffs, no signal-fires for him.
He can shout the news and give us joy,    or else . . . please, not
that.
      Bring it on,
good fuel to build the first god fires.                            490
And if anyone calls down the worst on Argos
let him reap the rotten harvest of his mind.

[*The* HERALD *rushes in and kneels on the ground.*]

HERALD: Good Greek earth, the soil of my fathers!
   Ten years out, and a morning brings me back.
   All hopes snapped but one—I'm home at last                      495
   Never dreamed I'd die in Greece, assigned
   the narrow plot I love the best.
                              And now
   I salute the land, the light of the sun,
   our high lord Zeus and the king of Pytho[9]—
   no more arrows, master, raining on our heads![1]               500
   At Scamander's banks we took our share,
   your longbow brought us down like plague.
   Now come, deliver us, heal us—lord Apollo!
   Gods of the market, here, take my salute.
   And you, my Hermes, Escort,                                     505
   loving Herald, the herald's shield and prayer![2]—
   And the shining dead[3] of the land who launched the armies,
   warm us home . . . we're all the spear has left.
   You halls of the kings, you roofs I cherish,
   sacred seats—you gods that catch the sun,                       510
   if your glances ever shone on him in the old days,
   greet him well—so many years are lost.
   He comes, he brings us light in the darkness,
   free for every comrade, Agamemnon lord of men.

   Give him the royal welcome he deserves!                         515
   He hoisted the pickaxe of Zeus who brings revenge,

9. Apollo.   1. Cf. the opening scene of the *Iliad*, Book I where Apollo punishes the Greeks
with his arrows (a metaphor for plague).   2. Hermes, the gods' messenger, was the patron deity
of heralds.   3. The heroes of past time, buried in the soil of Argos and worshipped.

he dug Troy down, he worked her soil down,
the shrines of her gods and the high altars, gone!—
and the seed of her wide earth he ground to bits.
That's the yoke he claps on Troy. The king,                    520
the son of Atreus comes. The man is blest,
the one man alive to merit such rewards.


Neither Paris nor Troy, partners to the end,
can say their work outweighs their wages now.
Convicted of rapine, stripped of all his spoils,                    525
and his father's house and the land that gave it life—
he's scythed them to the roots. The sons of Priam
pay the price twice over.

LEADER:                              Welcome home
    from the wars, herald, long live your joy.
HERALD:                                        *Our* joy—
    now I could die gladly. Say the word, dear gods.                    530
LEADER: Longing for your country left you raw?
HERALD: The tears fill my eyes, for joy.
LEADER:                                    You too,
    down the sweet disease that kills a man
    with kindness . . .
HERALD:            Go on, I don't see what you—
LEADER:                                        Love
    for the ones who love you—that's what took you.
HERALD:                                        You mean     535
    the land and the armies hungered for each other?
LEADER: There were times I thought I'd faint with longing.
HERALD: So anxious for the armies, why?
LEADER:                                    For years now,
    only my silence kept me free from harm.
HERALD:                                    What,
    with the kings gone did someone threaten you?
LEADER:                                    So much . . .     540
    now as you say,[4] it would be good to die.
HERALD: True, we *have* done well.
    Think back in the years and what have you?
    A few runs of luck, a lot that's bad.
    Who but a god can go through life unmarked?                    545
    A long, hard pull we had, if I would tell it all.
    The iron rations, penned in the gangways

---

4. Throughout this dialogue the chorus has been nerving itself to warn the herald that there may
be danger for Agamemnon at home; at this point its nerve fails, and it abandons the attempt.

hock by jowl like sheep. Whatever miseries
break a man, our quota, every sun-starved day.

Then on the beaches it was worse. Dug in                        550
under the enemy ramparts—deadly going.
Out of the sky, out of the marshy flats
the dews soaked us, turned the ruts we fought from
into gullies, made our gear, our scalps
crawl with lice.
                    And talk of the cold,                        555
the sleet to freeze the gulls, and the big snows
come avalanching down from Ida. Oh but the heat,
the sea and the windless noons, the swells asleep,
dropped to a dead calm . . .

But why weep now?                                                560
It's over for us, over for them.
The dead can rest and never rise gain;
no need to call their muster. We're alive,
do we have to go on raking up old wounds?
Good-bye to all that. Glad I am to say it.                       565

For us, the remains of the Greek contingents,
the good wins out, no pain can tip the scales,
not now. So shout this boast to the bright sun—
fitting it is—wing it over the seas and rolling earth:

"Once when an Argive expedition captured Troy                    570
they hauled these spoils back to the gods of Greece,
they bolted them high across the temple doors,
the glory of the past!"

                    And hearing that,
men will applaud our city and our chiefs,
and Zeus will have the hero's share of fame—                    575
he did the work.
                    That's all I have to say.
LEADER: I'm convinced, glad that I was wrong.
    Never too old to learn; it keeps me young.

    [CLYTAEMNESTRA *enters with her women.*]

First the house and the queen, it's their affair,
but I can taste the riches.

CLYTAEMNESTRA:                    I cried out long ago!—[5]            580
for joy, when the first herald came burning
through the night and told the city's fall.
And there were some who smiled and said,
"A few fires persuade you Troy's in ashes.
Women, women, elated over nothing."                                  585

You made me seem deranged.
For all that I sacrificed—a woman's way,
you'll say—station to station on the walls
we lifted cries of triumph that resounded
in the temples of the gods. We lulled and blessed        590
the fires with myrrh and they consumed our victims.

        [*Turning to the* HERALD.]

But enough. Why prolong the story?
From the king himself I'll gather all I need.
Now for the best way to welcome home
my lord, my good lord . . .No time to lose!                          595
What dawn can feast a woman's eyes like this?
I can see the light, the husband plucked from war
by the Saving God and open wide the gates.

Tell him that, and have him come with speed,
the people's darling—how they long for him.                          600
And for his wife,
may he return and find her true at hall,
just as the day he left her, faithful to the last.
A watchdog gentle to him alone,

        [*Glancing towards the palace.*]

                                    savage
to those who cross his path. I have not changed.                     605
The strains of time can never break our seal.
In love with a new lord, in ill repute I am
as practised as I am in dyeing bronze.[6]

That is my boast, teeming with the truth.
I am proud, a woman of my nobility—                                  610
I'd hurl it from the roofs!

5. As the Watchman had told her to (l. 30).    6. She is no more capable of adultery, she claims,
than she is of dyeing bronze. But she will later kill Agamemnon with a bronze weapon.

[*She turns sharply, enters the palace.*]

LEADER: She speaks well, but it takes no seer to know
    she only says what's right.

[*The* HERALD *attempts to leave; the leader takes him by the arm.*]

                Wait, one thing.
Menelaus, is he home too, safe with the men?[7]           615
The power of the land—dear king.
HERALD: I doubt that lies will help my friends,
    in the lean months to come.
LEADER: Help us somehow, tell the truth as well.
    But when the two conflict it's hard to hide—
    out with it.
HERALD:        He's lost, gone from the fleets![8]          620
    He and his ship, it's true.
LEADER:                After you watched him
    pulled away from Troy? Or did some storm
    attack you all and tear him off the line?
HERALD:                  There,
    like a marksman, the whole disaster cut to a word.
LEADER: How do the escorts give him out—dead or alive?     625
HERALD: No clear report. No one knows . . .
    only the wheeling sun that heats the earth of life.
LEADER: But then the storm—how did it reach the ships?
    How did it end? Were the angry gods on hand?
HERALD: This blessed day, ruin it with *them*?          630
    Better to keep their trophies far apart.

When a runner comes, his face in tears,
saddled with what his city dreaded most,[9]
the armies routed, two wounds in one,
one to the city, one to hearth and home . . .         635
our best men, droves of them, victims
herded from every house by the two-barb whip
that Ares[1] likes to crack,
                that charioteer
who packs destruction shaft by shaft,

---

7. The relevance of this question and the following speeches lies in the fact that Menelaus' absence makes Agamemnon's murder easier (his presence might have made it impossible), and in the fact that Menelaus is bringing Helen home; the choral ode which follows shows how much the chorus is obsessed with Helen's guilt—so much that it fails to recognize the true responsibility for the war and the imminence of disaster.   8. For what happened to Menelaus see his account in *Odyssey*, Book IV.   9. The Herald creates a vivid picture of a messenger bringing news of disaster to his city—a role he wishes to avoid.   1. The war god.

careering on with his brace of bloody mares— 640
When he comes in, I tell you, dragging that much pain, wail your
battle-hymn to the Furies, and high time!
But when he brings salvation home to a city
singing out her heart—
how can I mix the good with so much bad 645
and blurt out this?
        "Storms swept the Greeks,
and not without the anger of the gods!"

Those enemies for ages, fire[2] and water,
sealed a pact and showed it to the world—
they crushed our wretched squadrons.
               Night looming, 650
breakers lunging in for the kill
and the black gales come brawling out of the north—
ships ramming, prow into hooking prow, gored
by the rush-and-buck of hurricane pounding rain
by the cloudburst—
        ships stampeding into the darkness, 655
lashed and spun by the savage shepherd's hand![3]

But when the sun comes up to light the skies
I see the Aegean heaving into a great bloom
of corpses . . . Greeks, the pick of a generation
scattered through the wrecks and broken spars. 660

But not us, not our ship, our hull untouched.
Someone stole us away or begged us off.
No mortal—a god, death grip on the tiller,
or lady luck herself, perched on the helm,
she pulled us through, she saved us. Aye, 665
we'll never battle the heavy surf at anchor,
never shipwreck up some rocky coast.

But once we cleared that sea-hell, not even
trusting luck in the cold light of day,
we battened on our troubles, they were fresh— 670
the armada punished, bludgeoned into nothing.
And now if one of them still has the breath
he's saying *we* are lost. Why not?
We say the same of him. Well,
here's to the best.

2. I.e., lightning.    3. The ships were scattered like sheep dispersed by a cruel shepherd.

              And Menelaus?                                   675
Look to it, he's come back, and yet . . .
if a shaft of the sun can track him down,
alive, and his eyes full of the old fire—
thanks to the strategies of Zeus, Zeus
would never tear the house out by the roots—          680
then there's hope our man will make it home.

You've heard it all. Now you have the truth.

   [*Rushing out.*]

CHORUS: Who—what power named the name[4] that drove your fate?—
   what hidden brain could divine your future
   steer that word to the mark,                           685
   to the bride of spears,
         the whirlpool churning armies,
               Oh for all the world a Helen!
   Hell at the prows, hell at the gates
   hell on the men-of-war,                                690
   from her lair's sheer veils she drifted
         launched by the giant western wind,
               and the long tall waves of men in armor,[5]
   huntsmen trailing the oar-blades' dying spoor
   slipped into her moorings,                             695
         Simois'[6] mouth that chokes with foliage,
               bayed for bloody strife,
   for Troy's Blood Wedding Day—she drives her word,
   her burning will to the birth, the Fury
   late but true to the course,                           700
   to the tables shamed
         and Zeus who guards the hearth—[7]
               the Fury makes the Trojans pay!
   Shouting their hymns, hymns for the bride
   hymns for the kinsmen doomed                           705
   to the wedding march of Fate.
         Troy changed her tune in her late age,
               and I think I hear the dirges mourning
   "Paris, born and groomed for the bed of Fate!"
   They mourn with their life breath,                     710
         they sing their last, the sons of Priam
               born for bloody slaughter.

4. Helen. The name contains a Greek root *hele*—which means "destroy."   5. The Achaean
army which came after her, like huntsmen.   6. One of the rivers of Troy.   7. Zeus in his
capacity as protector of host and guest.

So a man once reared
a lion cub at hall, snatched
from the breast, still craving milk 715
    in the first flush of life.
A captivating pet for the young,
and the old men adored it, pampered it
    in their arms, day in, day out,
like an infant just born. 720
Its eyes on fire, little beggar,
fawning for its belly, slave to food.

    But it came of age
and the parent strain broke out
and it paid its breeders back. 725
    Grateful it was, it went
through the flock to prepare a feast,
an illicit orgy—the house swam with blood,
    none could resist that agony—
        massacre vast and raw! 730
From god there came a priest of ruin,
adopted by the house to lend it warmth.
And the first sensation Helen brought to Troy . . .
call it a spirit
    shimmer of winds dying 735
        glory light as gold
    shaft of the eyes dissolving, open bloom
    that wounds the heart with love.
But veering wild in mid-flight
she whirled her wedding on to a stabbing end, 740
slashed at the sons of Priam—heartmate, friend to the death,
        sped by Zeus who speeds the guest,
a bride of tears, a Fury.

There's an ancient saying,[8] old as man himself:
men's prosperity 745
        never will die childless,
            once full-grown it breeds.
        Sprung from the great good fortune in the race
        comes bloom on bloom of pain—
insatiable wealth! But not I, 750

8. These lines state the traditional Greek view that immoderate good fortune (or excellence of any kind beyond the average) is itself the cause of disaster. In the lines which follow, the chorus rejects this view and states that only an act of evil produces evil consequences. It later admits by implication (ll. 739 ff.) that those who are less prosperous are less likely to commit such an act.

I alone say this. Only the reckless act
can breed impiety, multiplying crime on crime,
    while the house kept straight and just
is blessed with radiant children.

    But ancient Violence longs to breed,           755
        new Violence comes
    when its fatal hour comes, the demon comes
    to take her toll—no war, no force, no prayer
        can hinder the midnight Fury stamped
    with parent Fury moving through the house.      760

    But Justice shines in sooty hovels,[9]
        loves the decent life.
    From proud halls crusted with gilt by filthy hands
        she turns her eyes to find the pure in spirit—
    spurning the wealth stamped counterfeit with praise,    765

[AGAMEMNON *enters in his chariot, his plunder borne before
him by his entourage; behind him, half hidden, stands* CASSAN-
DRA. *The old men press towards him.*]

Come, my king, the scourge of Troy,
    the true son of Atreus—
How to salute you, how to praise you
neither too high nor low, but hit          770
the note of praise that suits the hour?
So many prize some brave display,
they prefer some flaunt of honor
    once they break the bounds.[1]
When a man fails they share his grief,      775
but the pain can never cut them to the quick.
When a man succeeds they share his glory,
torturing their faces into smiles.
But the good shepherd knows his flock.
When the eyes seem to brim with love      780
    and it is only unction,
he will know, better than we can know.
That day you marshalled the armies
all for Helen—no hiding it now—
I drew you in my mind in black;      785
you seemed a menace at the helm,

9. The homes of the poor.   1. The chorus tries to warn Agamemnon against flatterers and
dissemblers, but he misses their drift.

sending men to the grave
to bring her home, that hell on earth.
But now from the depths of trust and love
I say Well fought, well won—                                                790
    the end is worth the labor!

                              Search, my kin, and learn at last
who stayed at home and kept their faith
    and who betrayed the city.

AGAMEMNON:                          First,
    with justice I salute my Argos and my gods,                        795
    my accomplices who brought me home and won
    my rights from Priam's Troy—the just gods.
No need to hear our pleas. Once for all
they consigned their lots to the urn of blood,[2]
they pitched on death for men, annihilation                          800
for the city. Hope's hand, hovering
over the urn of mercy, left it empty.
Look for the smoke—it is the city's seamark,
building even now.
                    The storms of ruin live!
Her last dying breath, rising up from the ashes                      805
sends us gales of incense rich in gold.

For that we must thank the gods with a sacrifice
our sons will long remember. For their mad outrage
of a queen we raped their city—we were right.
The beast of Argos, foals of the wild mare,[3]                        810
thousands massed in armor rose on the night
the Pleiades went down,[4] and crashing through
their walls our bloody lion lapped its fill,
gorging on the blood of kings.
                              Our thanks to the gods,
long drawn out, but it is just the prelude.                          815

[CLYTAEMNESTRA *approaches with her women; they are carrying
dark red tapestries.* AGAMEMNON *turns to the leader.*]

And your concern, old man, is on my mind.
I hear you and agree, I will support you.
How rare, men with the character to praise
a friend's success without a trace of envy,
poison to the heart—it deals a double blow.                          820

2. In an Athenian law court there were two urns, one for acquittal, one for condemnation, into
which the jurors dropped their pebbles. (The audience will see them on stage in the final play of
the trilogy.)    3. The wooden horse, the stratagem with which the Greeks captured the city.
4. The setting of the constellation called the Pleiades, late in the fall.

Your own losses weigh you down but then,
look at your neighbor's fortune and you weep.
Well I know. I understand society,
the fawning mirror of the proud.
                              My comrades . . .
they're shadows, I tell you, ghosts of men                    825
who swore they'd die for me. Only Odysseus:
I dragged that man to the wars[5] but once in harness
he was a trace-horse, he gave his all for me.
Dead or alive, no matter, I can praise him.

And now this cause involving men and gods.             830
We must summon the city for a trial,
found a national tribunal. Whatever's healthy,
shore it up with law and help it flourish.
Wherever something calls for drastic cures
we make our noblest effort: amputate or wield         835
the healing iron, burn the cancer at the roots.

Now I go to my father's house—
I give the gods my right hand, my first salute.
The ones who sent me forth have brought me home.

[*He starts down from the chariot, looks at* CLYTAEMNESTRA, *stops,
and offers up a prayer.*]

Victory, you have sped my way before,                 840
now speed me to the last.

[CLYTAEMNESTRA *turns from the king to the* CHORUS.]

CLYTAEMNESTRA:                    Old nobility of Argos
gathered here, I am not ashamed to tell you
how I love the man. I am older,
and the fear dies away . . . I am human.
Nothing I say was learned from others.                845
This is my life, my ordeal, long as the siege
he laid at Troy and more demanding.
                              First,
when a woman sits at home and the man is gone,
the loneliness is terrible,
unconscionable . . .                                  850

5. Feigning madness in order to escape going to Troy, Odysseus was tricked into demonstrating
his sanity. Agamemnon's remark shows that the truth is far from his mind; he has no thought that
his danger comes from a woman.

and the rumors spread and fester,
a runner comes with something dreadful,
close on his heels the next and his news worse,
and they shout it out and the whole house can hear;
and wounds—if he took one wound for each report          855
to penetrate these walls, he's gashed like a dragnet,
more, if he had only died . . .
for each death that swelled his record, he could boast
like a triple-bodied Geryon[6] risen from the grave,
"Three shrouds I dug from the earth, one for every body      860
that went down!"
                    The rumors broke like fever,
broke and then rose higher. There were times
they cut me down and eased my throat from the noose.
I wavered between the living and the dead.

    [*Turning to* AGAMEMNON.]

                                    And so
our child is gone, not standing by our side,                865
the bond of our dearest pledges, mine and yours;
by all rights our child should be here . . .
Orestes. You seem startled.
You needn't be. Our loyal brother-in-arms
will take good care of him, Strophios[7] the Phocian.        870
He warned from the start we count two griefs in one.
You risk all on the wars—and what if the people
rise up howling for the king, and anarchy
should dash our plans?
                        Men, it is their nature,
trampling on the fighter once he's down.                    875
Our child is gone. That is my self-defence
and it is true.
                    For me, the tears that welled
like springs are day. I have no tears to spare.
I'd watch till late at night, my eyes still burn,
I sobbed by the torch I lit for you alone.                  880

    [*Glancing towards the palace.*]

I never let it die . . . but in my dreams
the high thin wail of a gnat would rouse me,

---

6. A monster (eventually killed by Heracles) who had three bodies and three heads.  7. King of Phocis, a mountainous region near Delphi. His son, Pylades, accompanies Orestes when he returns to avenge Agamemnon's death.

piercing like a trumpet—I could see you
suffer more than all
the hours that slept with me could ever bear.                    885

I endured it all. And now, free of grief,
I would salute that man the watchdog of the fold,
the mainroyal,[8] saving stay of the vessel,
rooted oak that thrusts the roof sky-high,
the father's one true heir.                                      890
Land at dawn to the shipwrecked past all hope,
light of the morning burning off the night of storm,
the cold clear spring to the parched horseman—
O the ecstasy, to flee the yoke of Fate!
It is right to use the titles he deserves.                       895
Let envy keep her distance. We have suffered
long enough.

    [*Reaching towards* AGAMEMNON.]

           Come to me now, my dearest,
down from the car of war, but never set the foot
that stamped out Troy on earth again, my great one.

Women, why delay? You have your orders.                          900
Pave his way with tapestries.[9]

    [*They begin to spread the crimson tapestries between the king
and the palace doors.*]

           Quickly.
Let the red stream flow and bear him home
to the home he never hoped to see—Justice,
lead him in!
           Leave all the rest to me.
The spirit within me never yields to sleep.                      905
We will set things right, with the god's help.
We will do whatever Fate requires.

AGAMEMNON:                              There
    is Leda's daughter,[1] the keeper of my house.

---

8. Upper section of the mainmast.    9. To walk on those tapestries, wall hangings dyed with
the expensive crimson, would be an act of extravagant pride. Pride is the keynote of Agamemnon's
character, and it suits Clytaemnestra's sense of fitness that he should go into his death in godlike
state, "trampling royal crimson," the color of blood.    1. Clytaemnestra and Helen are both
daughters of Leda.

And the speech to suit my absence, much too long.
But the praise that does us justice,                                910
let it come from others, then we prize it.
                                        This—
you treat me like a woman. Groveling, gaping up at me—
what am I, some barbarian[2] peacocking out of Asia?
Never cross my path with robes and draw the lightning.
Never—only the gods deserve the pomps of honor              915
and the stiff brocades of fame. To walk on them . . .
I am human, and it makes my pulses stir
with dread.
                    Give me the tributes of a man
and not a god, a little earth to walk on,
not this gorgeous work.                                             920
There is no need to sound my reputation.
I have a sense of right and wrong, what's more—
heaven's proudest gift. Call no man blest
until he ends his life in peace, fulfilled.
If I can live by what I say, I have no fear.                        925

CLYTAEMNESTRA: One thing more. Be true to your ideals and tell
     me—
AGAMEMNON: True to my ideals? Once I violate them I am lost.
CLYTAEMNESTRA: Would you have sworn this act to god in a time of
     terror?
AGAMEMNON: Yes, if a prophet called for a last, drastic rite.
CLYTAEMNESTRA: But Priam—can you see him if he had your
     success?                                                      930
AGAMEMNON: Striding on the tapestries of God, I see him now.
CLYTAEMNESTRA: And *you* fear the reproach of common men?
AGAMEMNON: The voice of the people—aye, they have enormous
     power.
CLYTAEMNESTRA: Perhaps, but where's the glory without a little gall?
AGAMEMNON: And where's the woman in all this lust of glory?       935
CLYTAEMNESTRA: But the great victor—it becomes him to give way.
AGAMEMNON: Victory in this . . . war of ours, it means so much to
     you?
CLYTAEMNESTRA: O give way! The power is yours if you surrender all
     of your own free will to me.
AGAMEMNON:                        Enough.
     If you are so determined—                                     940

[*Turning to the women, pointing to his boots.*]

2. Foreigner, especially Asiatic. Aeschylus is thinking of the pomp and servility of the contemporary Persian court.

Let someone help me off with these at last.
Old slaves, they've stood me well.
                                        Hurry,
and while I tread his splendors dyed red in the sea,[3]
may no god watch and strike me down with envy
from on high. I feel such shame—                              945
to tread the life of the house, a kingdom's worth
of silver in the weaving.

[*He steps down from the chariot to the tapestries and reveals*
CASSANDRA, *dressed in the sacred regalia, the fillets, robes and*
*sceptre of Apollo.*]

                              Done is done.
Escort this stranger[4] in, be gentle.
Conquer with compassion. Then the gods
shine down upon you, gently. No one chooses                  950
the yoke of slavery, not of one's free will—
and she least of all. The gift of the armies,
flower and pride of all the wealth we won,
she follows me from Troy.
                              And now,
since you have brought me down with your insistence,         955
just this once I enter my father's house,
trampling royal crimson as I go.

[*He takes his first steps and pauses.*]

CLYTAEMNESTRA:                        There is the sea
and who will drain it dry? Precious as silver,
inexhaustible, ever-new, it breeds the more we reap it—
tides on tides of crimson dye our robes blood-red.          960
Our lives are based on wealth, my king,
the gods have seen to that.
Destitution, our house has never heard the word.
I would have sworn to tread on legacies of robes,
at one command from an oracle, deplete the house—           965
suffer the worst to bring that dear life back!

[*Encouraged,* AGAMEMNON *strides to the entrance.*]

---

3. The dye was made from shellfish.    4. Cassandra, daughter of Priam, Agamemnon's share
of the human booty of the sack of Troy. She was loved by Apollo and by him given the gift of
prophecy; but when she refused her love to the god he added to his gift the proviso that her
prophecies, though true, should never be believed until it was too late.

When the root lives on, the new leaves come back,
spreading a dense shroud of shade across the house
to thwart the Dog Star's fury.[5] So you return
to the father's hearth, you bring us warmth in winter                970
like the sun—
           And you are Zeus when Zeus
tramples the bitter virgin grape for new wine
and the welcome chill steals through the halls, at last
the master moves among the shadows of his house, fulfilled.

> [AGAMEMNON *goes over the threshold; the women gather up the*
> *tapestries while* CLYTAEMNESTRA *prays.*]

Zeus, Zeus, master of all fulfillment, now fulfil our prayers—    975
speed our rites to their fulfillment once for all!

> [*She enters the palace, the doors close, the old men huddle in*
> *terror.*]

CHORUS: Why, why does it rock me, never stops,
   this terror beating down my heart,
      this seer that sees it all—
   it beats its wings, uncalled unpaid                              980
   thrust on the lungs
   the mercenary song beats on and on
   singing a prophet's strain—
      and I can't throw it off
   like dreams that make no sense,                                  985
   and the strength drains
   that filled the mind with trust,
   and the years drift by and the driven sand
      has buried the mooring lines
   that churned when the armored squadrons cut for Troy . . .      990
   and now I believe it, I can prove he's home,
      my own clear eyes for witness—
                     *Agamemnon!*
   Still it's chanting, beating deep so deep in the heart
   this dirge of the Furies, oh dear god,
   not fit for the lyre,[6] its own master                         995
      it kills our spirit
   kills our hopes

---

5. The appearance of Sirius, the Dog Star, in the summer sky, marked the beginning of the hot season.    6. The lyre was played on joyful occasions (hence "lyric" poetry): the Furies' song is a dirge.

and it's real, true, no fantasy—
  stark terror whirls the brain
    and the end is coming        1000
      Justice comes to birth—
I pray my fears prove false and fall
and die and never come to birth!
Even exultant health, well we know,
  exceeds its limits,[7] comes so near disease    1005
it can breach the wall between them.

Even a man's fate, held true on course,
  in a blinding flash rams some hidden reef;
but if caution only casts the pick of the cargo—[8]
one well-balanced cast—          1010
the house will not go down, not outright;
laboring under its wealth of grief
the ship of state rides on.

Yes, and the great green bounty of god,
sown in the furrows year by year and reaped each fall   1015
can end the plague of famine.

But a man's life-blood
  is dark and mortal.
Once it wets the earth
what song can sing it back?         1020
Not even the master-healer[9]
  who brought the dead to life—
Zeus stopped the man before he did more harm.

Oh, if only the gods had never forged
  the chain that curbs our excess,       1025
    one man's fate curbing the next man's fate,
my heart would outrace my song, I'd pour out all I feel—
    but no, I choke with anguish,
      mutter through the nights.
Never to ravel out a hope in time       1030
and the brain is swarming, burning—

  [CLYTAEMNESTRA *emerges from the palace and goes to* CASSAN-
  DRA, *impassive in the chariot.*]

7. Excess, even in blessings like health, is always dangerous. The chorus fears that Agamemnon's triumphant success may threaten his safety.  8. These lines refer to a traditional Greek belief that the fortunate man could avert the envy of heaven by deliberately getting rid of some precious possession.  9. Asklepius, the great physician who was so skilled that he finally succeeded in restoring a dead man to life. Zeus struck him with a thunderbolt for going too far.

CLYTAEMNESTRA: Won't you come inside? I mean you, Cassandra.
    Zeus in all his mercy wants you to share
    some victory libations with the house.
    The slaves are flocking. Come, lead them                    1035
    up to the altar of the god who guards
    our dearest treasures.
                Down from the chariot,
    this is no time for pride. Why even Heracles,[1]
    he had to endure the bitter bread of slaves.                 1040
    But if the yoke descends on you, be grateful
    for a master born and reared in ancient wealth.
    Those who reap a harvest past their hopes
    are merciless to their slaves.
                    From us
    you will receive what custom says is right.                  1045

    [CASSANDRA *remains impassive.*]

LEADER: It's *you* she is speaking to, it's all too clear.
    You're caught in the nets of doom—obey
    if you can obey, unless you cannot bear to.
CLYTAEMNESTRA: Unless she's like a swallow, possessed
    of her own barbaric song,[2] strange, dark.                 1050
    I speak directly as I can—she must obey.
LEADER: Go with her. Make the best of it, she's right.
    Step down from the seat, obey her.
CLYTAEMNESTRA:              Do it *now*—
    I have no time to spend outside. Already
    the victims crowd the hearth, the Navelstone,[3]             1055
    to bless this day of joy I never hoped to see!—
    our victims waiting for the fire and the knife,
    and you,
    if you want to taste our mystic rites, come now.
    If my words can't reach you—

    [*Turning to the* LEADER.]

                      Give her a sign,                1060
    one of her exotic handsigns.
LEADER:                  I think
    the stranger needs an interpreter, someone clear.
    She's like a wild creature, fresh caught.

1. The Greek hero, famous for his twelve labors which rid the earth of monsters, was at one time forced to be the slave to Omphale, an Eastern queen.   2. The comparison of foreign speech to the twittering of a swallow was a Greek commonplace.   3. The hearth, which was the religious center of the home, with an altar of Zeus Herkeios, guardian of the enclosed space.

CLYTAEMNESTRA:                      She's mad,
    her evil genius murmuring in her ears.
    She comes from a *city* fresh caught.              1065
    She must learn to take the cutting bridle
    before she foams her spirit off in blood—
    and that's the last I waste on her contempt!

    [*Wheeling, re-entering the palace. The* LEADER *turns to* CAS-
    SANDRA, *who remains transfixed.*]

LEADER: Not I, I pity her. I will be gentle.
    Come, poor thing. Leave the empty chariot—       1070
    Of your own free will try on the yoke of Fate.
CASSANDRA: Aieeeeee! Earth—Mother—
        Curse of the Earth—Apollo Apollo!
LEADER: Why cry to Apollo?
    He's not the god to call with sounds of mourning.
CASSANDRA: Aieeeeee! Earth—Mother—          1075
    Rape of the Earth—Apollo Apollo!
LEADER: Again, it's a bad omen.
    She cries for the god who wants no part of grief.[4]

    [CASSANDRA *steps from the chariot, looks slowly towards the
    rooftops of the palace.*]

CASSANDRA: God of the long road,
      Apollo *Apollo* my destroyer—
    you destroy me once, destroy me twice—[5]       1080
LEADER: She's about to sense her own ordeal, I think.
    Slave that she is, the god lives on inside her.
CASSANDRA: God of the iron marches,
      Apollo *Apollo* my destroyer—
    where, where have you led[6] me now? what house—     1085
LEADER: The house of Atreus and his sons. Really—
    don't you know? It's true, see for yourself.
CASSANDRA: No . . . the house that hates god,
      an echoing womb of guilt, kinsmen
        torturing kinsmen, severed heads,      1090
    slaughterhouse of heroes, soil streaming blood—
LEADER: A keen hound, this stranger.

4. Apollo, and the Olympian gods in general, were not invoked in mourning or lamentation.
5. The name Apollo suggests the Greek word (*apollumi*) for "destroy." He "destroyed" her the first time when, as she tells later, he gave her the gift of true prophecy that no one would believe. *God of the long road:* Apollo Agyieus; this statue, a conical pillar, was set up outside the door of the house; no doubt there was one on stage.   6. The Greek word for led (a form of the verb *ago*) suggests the god's title Agyieus.

'Trailing murder, and murder she will find.
CASSANDRA: See, my witnesses—
    I trust to them, to the babies                                        1095
        wailing, skewered on the sword,
  their flesh charred, the father gorging on their parts—[7]
LEADER: We'd heard your fame as a seer,
  but no one looks for seers in Argos.
CASSANDRA: Oh no, what horror, what new plot,                                        1100
  new agony this?—[8]
  it's growing, massing, deep in the house,
      a plot, a monstrous—*thing*
        to crush the loved ones, no,
    there is no cure, and rescue's far away[9] and—                                        1105
LEADER: I can't read these signs; I knew the first,
  the city rings with them.
CASSANDRA: You, you godforsaken—you'd do *this?*
  The lord of your bed,
  you bathe him . . . his body glistens, then—                                        1110
      how to tell the climax?—
        comes so quickly, see.
    hand over hand shoots out, hauling ropes—
                        then lunge!
LEADER: Still lost. Her riddles, her dark words of god—
  I'm groping, helpless.
CASSANDRA:            No no, look *there!*—                                        1115
  what's that? some net flung out of hell—
    No, *she* is the snare,
  the bedmate, deathmate, murder's strong right arm!
    Let the insatiate discord in the race
  rear up and shriek "Avenge the victim—stone them dead!"                                        1120
LEADER: What Fury is this? Why rouse it, lift its wailing
  through the house? I hear you and lose hope.
CHORUS: Drop by drop at the heart, the gold of life ebbs out.
    We are the old soldiers . . . wounds will come
  with the crushing sunset of our lives.                                        1125
  Death is close, and quick.
CASSANDRA:            Look out! *look out!*—
  Ai, drag the great bull from the mate!—
    a thrash of robes, she traps him—
  writhing—
      black horn glints, twists—
               *she gores him through!*
    And now he buckles, look, the bath swirls red—                                        1130

---

7. The feast of Thyestes.    8. Cassandra foresees Clytaemnestra's murder of Agamemnon.
9. A reference to Menelaus (distant in space) and Orestes (distant in time).

There's stealth and murder in the cauldron, do you hear?
LEADER: I'm no judge, I've little skill with the oracles,
   but even I know danger when I hear it.
CHORUS: What good are the oracles to men? Words, more words,
      and the hurt comes on us, endless words          1135
   and a seer's techniques have brought us
   terror and the truth.
CASSANDRA: The agony—O I am breaking!—Fate's so hard,
      and the pain that floods my voice is mine alone.
   Why have you brought me here, tormented as I am?     1140
   Why, unless to die with him, why else?
LEADER AND CHORUS: Mad with the rapture—god speeds you on
      to the song, the deathsong,
   like the nightingale that broods on sorrow,[1]
      mourns her son, her son,                          1145
   her life inspired with grief for him,
   she lilts and shrills, dark bird that lives for night.
CASSANDRA: The nightingale—O for a song, a fate like hers!
      The gods gave her a life of ease, swathed her in wings,
   no tears, no wailing. The knife waits for me.        1150
   They'll splay me on the iron's double edge.
LEADER AND CHORUS: Why—what god hurls you on, stroke on stroke
      to the long dying fall?
   Why the horror clashing through your music,
      terror struck to song?—                           1155
   why the anguish, the wild dance?
   Where do your words of good and grief begin?
CASSANDRA: Ai, the wedding, wedding of Paris,
   death to the loved ones. Oh Scamander,[2]
   you nursed my father . . . once at your banks        1160
      I nursed and grew, and now at the banks
   of Acheron,[3] the stream that carries sorrow,
   it seems I'll chant my prophecies too soon.
LEADER AND CHORUS: What are you saying? Wait, it's clear,
, a child could see the truth, it wounds within,        1165
      like a bloody fang it tears—
   I hear your destiny—breaking sobs,
      cries that stab the ears,
CASSANDRA: Oh the grief, the grief of the city
   ripped to oblivion. Oh the victims,                  1170
   the flocks my father burned at the wall

---

1. Philomela was raped by Tereus, the husband of her sister Procne. The two sisters avenged themselves by killing Tereus' son, Itys, and serving up his flesh to Tereus to eat. Procne was changed into a nightingale mourning for Itys (the name is an imitation of the sound of the nightingale's song).  2. A Trojan river.  3. One of the rivers of the underworld.

rich herds in flames . . . no cure for the doom
that took the city after all, and I,
her last ember, I go down with her.

LEADER AND CHORUS: You cannot stop, your song goes on—    1175
   some spirit drops from the heights and treads you down
      and the brutal strain grows—
   your death-throes come and come and
      I cannot see the end!

CASSANDRA: Then off with the veils that hid the fresh young
    bride—[4]
                                        1180
we will see the truth.
Flare up once more, my oracle! Clear and sharp
as the wind that blows towards the rising sun,
I can feel a deeper swell now, gathering head
to break at last and bring the dawn of grief.    1185
No more riddles. I will teach you.
Come, bear witness, run and hunt with me.
We trail the old barbaric works of slaughter.

These roofs—look up—there is a dancing troupe
that never leaves. And they have their harmony    1190
but it is harsh, their words are harsh, they drink
beyond the limit. Flushed on the blood of men
their spirit grows and none can turn away
their revel breeding in the veins—the Furies!
They cling to the house for life. They sing,    1195
sing of the frenzy that began it all,
strain rising on strain, showering curses
on the man who tramples on his brother's bed.[5]

There. Have I hit the mark or not? Am I a fraud,
a fortune-teller babbling lies from door to door?    1200
Swear how well I know the ancient crimes
that live within this house.

LEADER:                 And if I did?
Would an oath bind the wounds and heal us?
But you amaze me. Bred across the sea,
your language strange, and still you sense the truth    1205
as if you had been here.

CASSANDRA:             Apollo the Prophet
introduced me to his gift.

LEADER: A *god*—and moved with love?

---

4. At this point, as the meter indicates, Cassandra changes from lyric song, the medium of emotion, to spoken iambic lines, the medium of rational discourse.   5. Thyestes, who seduced the wife of his brother, Atreus.

CASSANDRA: I was ashamed to tell this once,
  but now . . .
LEADER:          We spoil ourselves with scruples,          1210
  long as things go well.
CASSANDRA:          He came like a wrestler,
  magnificent, took me down and breathed his fire
  through me and—
LEADER:              You bore him a child?
CASSANDRA:                          I yielded,
  then at the climax I recoiled—I deceived Apollo!
LEADER: But the god's skills—they seized you even then?          1215
CASSANDRA: Even then I told my people all the grief to come.
LEADER: And Apollo's anger never touched you?—is it possible?
CASSANDRA: Once I betrayed him I could never be believed.
LEADER: We believe you. Your visions seem so true.
CASSANDRA:                          Aieeeee!—
  the pain, the terror! the birth-pang of the seer          1220
  who tells the truth—
                it whirls me, oh,
  the storm comes again, the crashing chords!
  Look, you see them nestling at the threshold?
  Young, young in the darkness like a dream,
  like children really, yes, and their loved ones          1225
  brought them down . . .
                their hands, they fill their hands
  with their own flesh, they are serving it like food,
  holding out their entrails . . . now it's clear,
  I can see the armfuls of compassion, see the father
  reach to taste and—
                For so much suffering,          1230
  I tell you, someone plots revenge.
  A lion who lacks a lion's heart,[6]
  he sprawled at home in the royal lair
  and set a trap for the lord on his return.
  My lord . . . I must wear his yoke, I am his slave.          1235
  The lord of the men-of-war, he obliterated Troy—
  he is so blind, so lost to that detestable hellhound
  who pricks her ears and fawns and her tongue draws out
  her glittering words of welcome—
                No, he cannot see
  the stroke that Fury's hiding, stealth, and murder.          1240
  What outrage—the woman kills the man!
                What to call

6. Aegisthus.

that . . . monster of Greece, and bring my quarry down?
Viper coiling back and forth?
                              Some sea-witch?—
Scylla[7] crouched in her rocky nest—nightmare of sailors?
Raging mother of death, storming deathless war against          1245
the ones she loves!
                    And how she howled in triumph,
boundless outrage. Just as the tide of battle
broke her way, she seems to rejoice that he
is safe at home from war, saved for her.
Believe me if you will. What will it matter                      1250
if you won't? It comes when it comes,
and soon you'll see it face to face
and say the seer was all too true.
You will be moved with pity.
LEADER:                        Thyestes' feast,
  the children's flesh—that I know,                              1255
  and the fear shudders through me. It's true,
  real, no dark signs about it. I hear the rest
  but it throws me off the scent.
CASSANDRA:                      Agamemnon.
  You will see him dead.
LEADER:                    Peace, poor girl!
  Put those words to sleep.
CASSANDRA:                  No use,                              1260
  the Healer[8] has no hand in this affair.
LEADER: Not if it's true—but god forbid it is!
CASSANDRA: You pray, and they close in to kill!
LEADER: What man prepares this, this dreadful—
CASSANDRA:                                  Man?
  You *are* lost, to every word I've said.
LEADER:                                Yes—                      1265
  I don't see who can bring the evil off.
CASSANDRA: And yet I know my Greek, too well.
LEADER: So does the Delphic oracle,[9]
  but he's hard to understand.
CASSANDRA:                      His *fire!*—
  sears me, sweeps me again—the torture!                         1270
  Apollo Lord of the Light, you burn,
  you blind me—
                Agony!
                      She is the lioness,
  she rears on her hind legs, she beds with the wolf
  when her lion king goes ranging—

---

7. A man-eating sea monster; see *Odyssey* XII.   8. Apollo.   9. Its replies were celebrated for their obscurity and ambiguity.

                                  she will kill me—
Ai, the torture!
                       She is mixing her drugs,                                   1275
adding a measure more of hate for me.
She gloats as she whets the sword for him.
He brought me home and we will pay in carnage.

Why mock yourself with these—trappings, the rod,
the god's wreath, his yoke around my throat?                          1280
Before I die I'll tread you—

   *[Ripping off her regalia, stamping it into the ground.]*

                        down, out,
die die die!
Now you're down. I've paid you back.
Look for another victim—I am free at last—
make her rich in all your curse and doom.

   *[Staggering backwards as if wrestling with a spirit tearing at her robes.]*

                                See,                  1285
Apollo himself, his fiery hands—I feel him again,
he's stripping off my robes, the Seer's robes!
And after he looked down and saw me mocked,
even in these, his glories, mortified by friends
I loved, and they hated me, they were so blind                       1290
to their own demise—
                        I went from door to door,
I was wild with the god, I heard them call me
"Beggar! Wretch! Starve for bread in hell!"

And I endured it all, and now he will
extort me as his due. A seer for the Seer.                           1295
He brings me here to die like this,
not to serve at my father's altar. No,
the block is waiting. The cleaver steams
with my life blood, the first blood drawn
for the king's last rites.

  *[Regaining her composure and moving to the altar.]*

                      We will die,                           1300
but not without some honor from the gods.

There will come another to avenge us,[1]
born to kill his mother, born
his father's champion. A wanderer, a fugitive
driven off his native land, he will come home                    1305
to cope the stones of hate that menace all he loves.
The gods have sworn a monumental oath: as his father lies
upon the ground he draws him home with power like a prayer.

Then why so pitiful, why so many tears?
I have seen my city faring as she fared,                        1310
and those who took her, judged by the gods,
faring as they fare. I must be brave.
It is my turn to die.

    [*Approaching the doors.*]

I address you as the Gates of Death.
I pray it comes with one clear stroke,                          1315
no convulsions, the pulses ebbing out
in gentle death. I'll close my eyes and sleep.
LEADER: So much pain, poor girl, and so much truth,
    you've told so much. But if you *see* it coming,
    clearly—how can you go to your own death,              1320
    like a beast to the altar driven on by god,
    and hold your head so high?
CASSANDRA:               No escape, my friends,
    not now.
LEADER:    But the last hour should be savored.
CASSANDRA: My time has come. Little to gain from flight.
LEADER: You're brave, believe me, full of gallant heart.       1325
CASSANDRA: Only the wretched go with praise like that.
LEADER: But to go nobly lends a man some grace.
CASSANDRA: My noble father—you and your noble children.

    [*She nears the threshold and recoils, groaning in revulsion.*]

LEADER: What now? what terror flings you back?
    Why? Unless some horror in the brain—
CASSANDRA:                  Murder.         1330
    The house breathes with murder—bloody shambles[2]!
LEADER: No, no, only the victims at the hearth.
CASSANDRA: I know that odor. I smell the open grave.

---

1. Orestes.    2. A slaughterhouse.

LEADER: But the Syrian myrrh,[3] it fills the halls with splendor,
 can't you sense it?
CASSANDRA:    Well, I must go in now,     1335
 mourning Agamemnon's death and mine.
 Enough of life!

  [*Approaching the doors again and crying out.*]

     Friends—I cried out,
not from fear like a bird fresh caught,
but that you will testify to *how* I died.
When the queen, woman for woman, dies for me,   1340
and a man falls for the man who married grief.
That's all I ask, my friends. A stranger's gift
for one about to die.
LEADER:     Poor creature, you
 and the end you see so clearly. I pity you.
CASSANDRA: I'd like a few words more, a kind of dirge,  1345
 it is my own. I pray to the sun,
 the last light I'll see,
 that when the avengers cut the assassins down
 they will avenge me too, a slave who died,
 an easy conquest.
     Oh men, your destiny.     1350
When all is well a shadow can overturn it.
When trouble comes a stroke of the wet sponge,
and the picture's blotted out. And that,
I think that breaks the heart.

  [*She goes through the doors.*]

CHORUS: But the lust for power never dies—    1355
 men cannot have enough.
 No one will lift a hand to send it
 from his door, to give it warning,
 "Power, never come again!"
 Take this man: the gods in glory      1360
 gave him Priam's city to plunder,
 brought him home in splendor like a god.
 But now if he must pay for the blood
  his fathers shed, and die for the deaths
 he brought to pass, and bring more death   1365
 to avenge his dying, show us one

---

3. Incense burned at the sacrifice. Another interpretation of this line runs: "What you speak of [i.e., the smell of the open grave] is no Syrian incense, giving splendor to the palace."

who boasts himself born free
of the raging angel, once he hears—

[*Cries break out within the palace.*]

AGAMEMNON:                               Aagh!
   Struck deep—the death-blow, deep—
LEADER:                              Quiet. Cries,
   but who? Someone's stabbed—
AGAMEMNON:

                                 Aaagh, again . . .        1370
   second blow—struck home.
LEADER:                         The work is done,
   you can feel it. The king, and the great cries—
   Close ranks now, find the right way out.

   [*But the old men scatter, each speaks singly.*]

CHORUS:—I say send out heralds, muster the guard,
   they'll save the house.
                         —And I say rush in now,        1375
   catch them red-handed—butchery running on their blades.

—Right with you, do something—now or never!

—Look at them, beating the drum for insurrection.

                                        —Yes,
   we're wasting time. They rape the name of caution,
   their hands will never sleep.

                         —Not a plan in sight.          1380
   Let men of action do the planning, too.

—I'm helpless. Who can raise the dead with words?

—What, drag out our lives? bow down to the tyrants,
   the ruin of the house?

                    —Never, better to die
   on your feet than live on your knees.

                         —Wait,                          1385
   do we take the cries for signs, prophesy like seers
   and give him up for dead?

          —No more suspicions,
not another word till we have proof.

          —Confusion
on all sides—one thing to do. See how it stands
with Agamemnon, once and for all we'll see—          1390

[*He rushes at the doors. They open and reveal a silver cauldron
that holds the body of* AGAMEMNON *shrouded in bloody robes,
with the body of* CASSANDRA *to his left and* CLYTAEMNESTRA
*standing to his right, sword in hand. She strides towards the
chorus.*]

CLYTAEMNESTRA: Words endless words I've said to serve the moment—
    now it makes me proud to tell the truth.
    How else to prepare a death for deadly men
    who seem to love you? How to rig the nets
    of pain so high no man can overleap them?          1395
    I brooded on this trial, this ancient blood feud
    year by year. At last my hour came.
    Here I stand and here I struck
    and here my work is done.
    I did it all. I don't deny it, no.          1400
    He had no way to flee or fight his destiny—

[*Unwinding the robes from* AGAMEMNON'S *body, spreading them
before the altar where the old men cluster around them, unified
as a chrous once again.*]

    our never-ending, all embracing net, I cast it
    wide for the royal haul, I coil him round and round
    in the wealth, the robes of doom, and then I strike him
    once, twice, and at each stroke he cries in agony—          1405
    he buckles at the knees and crashes here!
    And when he's down I add the third, last blow,
    to the Zeus who saves the dead beneath the ground
    I send that third blow[4] home in homage like a prayer.

    So he goes down, and the life is bursting out of him—          1410
    great sprays of blood, and the murderous shower
    wounds me, dyes me black and I, I revel
    like the Earth when the spring rains come down,

4. Like the third libation to Zeus above.

the blessed gifts of god, and the new green spear
splits the sheath and rips to birth in glory!                        1415

So it stands, elders of Argos gathered here.
Rejoice if you can rejoice—I glory.
And if I'd pour upon his body the libation
it deserves, what wine could match my words?
It is right and more than right. He flooded                          1420
the vessel of our proud house with misery,
with the vintage of the curse and now
he drains the dregs. My lord is home at last.
LEADER: You appall me, you, your brazen words—
exulting over your fallen king.
CLYTAEMNESTRA:                        And you,                        1425
you try me like some desperate woman.
My heart is steel, well you know. Praise me,
blame me as you choose. It's all one.
Here is Agamemnon, my husband made a corpse
by this right hand—a masterpiece of Justice.                         1430
Done is done.
CHORUS:          Woman!—what poison cropped from the soil
or strained from the heaving sea, what nursed you,
drove you insane? You brave the curse of Greece.
    You have cut away and flung away and now
the people cast you off to exile,                                    1435
broken with our hate.
CLYTAEMNESTRA:          And now you sentence me?—
you banish *me* from the city, curses breathing
down my neck? But *he*—
name one charge you brought against him then.
He thought no more of it than killing a beast,                       1440
and his flocks were rich, teeming in their fleece,
but he sacrificed his own child, our daughter,
the agony I labored into love,
to charm away the savage winds of Thrace.[5]
Didn't the law demand you banish him?—                               1445
hunt him from the land for all his guilt?
But now you witness what I've done
and you are ruthless judges.
                              Threaten away!
I'll meet you blow for blow. And if I fall
the throne is yours. If god decrees the reverse,                     1450

5. I.e., words from the North (at Aulis).

late as it is, old men, you'll learn your place.
CHORUS: Mad with ambition,
     shrilling pride!—some Fury
crazed with the carnage rages through your brain—
    I can see the flecks of blood inflame your eyes!       1455
But vengeance comes—you'll lose your loved ones,
stroke for painful stroke.
CLYTAEMNESTRA: Then learn this, too, the power of my oaths.
By the child's Rights I brought to birth,
by Ruin, by Fury—the three gods to whom       1460
I sacrificed this man—I swear my hopes
will never walk the halls of fear so long
as Aegisthus lights the fire on my hearth.
Loyal to me as always, no small shield
to buttress my defiance.
                    Here he lies.       1465
He brutalized me. The darling of all
the golden girls[6] who spread the gates of Troy.
And here his spear-prize . . . what wonders she beheld!—
the seer of Apollo shared my husband's bed,
his faithful mate who knelt at the rowing-benches,       1470
worked by every hand.
              They have their rewards.
He as you know. And she, the swan of the gods
who lived to sing her latest, dying song—
his lover lies beside him.
She brings a fresh, voluptuous relish to my bed!       1475
CHORUS: Oh quickly, let me die—
no bed of labor, no, no wasting illness . . .
bear me off in the sleep that never ends,
    now that he has fallen,
now that our dearest shield lies battered—       1480
    Woman made him suffer,
      woman struck him down.

        Helen the wild, maddening Helen,
        one for the many, the thousand lives
        you murdered under Troy, now you are crowned
        with this consummate wreath, the blood       1485
        that lives in memory, glistens age to age.
        Once in the halls she walked and she was war,
        angel of war, angel of agony, lighting men to death.

6. In Greek *Chryseidon*, which recalls the girl in the first book of the *Iliad*, Chryseis, whom Agamemnon said he preferred to Clytaemnestra (*Iliad*, l. 113).

CLYTAEMNESTRA: Pray no more for death, broken 1490
  as you are. And never turn
    your wrath on her, call her
  the scourge of men, the one alone
  who destroyed a myriad Greek lives—
  Helen the grief that never heals. 1495
CHORUS: The *spirit!*—you who tread
  the house and the twinborn sons of Tantalus—[7]
  *you* empower the sisters, Fury's twins
    whose power tears the heart!
  Perched on the corpse your carrion raven 1500
    glories in her hymn,
      her screaming hymn of pride.
CLYTAEMNESTRA: Now you set your judgment straight,
  you summon *him!* Three generations
    feed the spirit in the race. 1505
  Deep in the veins he feeds our bloodlust—
  aye, before the old wound dies
  it ripens in another flow of blood.
CHORUS: The great curse of the house, the spirit,
    dead weight wrath—and you can praise it! 1510
  Praise the insatiate doom that feeds
  relentless on our future and our sons.
  Oh all through the will of Zeus,
  the cause of all, the one who works it all.
    What comes to birth that is not Zeus? 1515
  Our lives are pain, what part not come from god?

      Oh, my king, my captain,
      how to salute you, how to mourn you?
      What can I say with all my warmth and love?
      Here in the black widow's web you lie, 1520
      gasping out your life
      in a sacrilegious death, dear god,
      reduced to a slave's bed,
      my king of men, yoked by stealth and Fate,
      by the wife's hand that thrust the two-edged sword. 1525

CLYTAEMNESTRA: You claim the work is mine, call me
  Agamemnon's wife—you are so wrong.
  Fleshed in the wife of this dead man,
    the spirit lives within me,
  our savage ancient spirit of revenge. 1530

---

7. Father of Pelops, grandfather of Atreus. "Sons" here must mean 'descendants,' i.e., Agamemnon and Menelaus.

In return for Atreus' brutal feast
he kills his perfect son—for every
murdered child, a crowning sacrifice.
CHORUS: And *you*, innocent of his murder?
> And who could swear to that? and how? . . .               1535
and still an avenger could arise,
bred by the fathers' crimes, and lend a hand.
He wades in the blood of brothers,
stream on mounting stream—black war erupts
> and where he strides revenge will stride,                 1540
clots will mass for the young who were devoured.


> Oh my king, my captain,
> how to salute you, how to mourn you?
> What can I say with all my warmth and love?
> Here in the black widow's web you lie,                    1545
> gasping out your life
> in a sacrilegious death, dear god,
> reduced to a slave's bed,
> my king of men, yoked by stealth and Fate,
> by the wife's hand that trust the two-edged sword.        1550


CLYTAEMNESTRA: No slave's death, I think—
no stealthier than the death he dealt
our house and the offspring of our loins,
> Iphigeneia, girl of tears.
Act for act, wound for wound!                               1555
Never exult in Hades, swordsman,
here you are repaid. By the sword
you did your work and by the sword you die.
CHORUS: The mind reels—where to turn?
> All plans dashed, all hope! I cannot think . . .          1560
the roofs are toppling, I dread the drumbeat thunder
the heavy rains of blood will crush the house
the first light rains are over—
Justice brings new acts of agony, yes,
on new grindstones Fate is grinding sharp the sword of Justice. 1565
Earth, dear Earth,
if only you'd drawn me under
long before I saw him huddled
in the beaten silver bath.
Who will bury him, lift his dirge?                          1570


[*Turning to* CLYTAEMNESTRA.]

You, can you dare *this?*
To kill your lord with your own hand
then mourn his soul with tributes, terrible tributes—
do his enormous works a great dishonor.
This god-like man, this hero. Who at the grave          1575
will sing his praises, pour the wine of tears?
Who will labour there with truth of heart?

CLYTAEMNESTRA: This is no concern of yours.
   The hand that bore and cut him down
will hand him down to Mother Earth.                      1580
This house will never mourn for him.
    Only our daughter Iphigeneia,
by all rights, will rush to meet him
first at the churning straits,[8]
the ferry over tears—                                    1585
she'll fling her arms around her father,
pierce him with her love.

CHORUS: Each charge meets counter-charge.
   None can judge between them. Justice.
The plunderer plunderd, the killer pays the price.       1590
The truth still holds while Zeus still holds the throne:
the one who acts must suffer—
that is law. Who can tear from the veins
the bad seed, the curse? The race is welded to its ruin.

CLYTAEMNESTRA: At last you see the future and the truth! 1595
   But I will swear a pact with the spirit
born within us. I embrace his works,
cruel as they are but done at last,
   if he will leave our house
in the future, bleed another line                        1600
with kinsmen murdering kinsmen.
Whatever he may ask. A few things
are all I need, once I have purged
our fury to destroy each other—
   purged it from our halls.

[AEGISTHUS *has emerged from the palace with his bodyguard and
stands triumphant over the body of* AGAMEMNON.]

AEGISTHUS:            O what a brilliant day      1605
   it is for vengeance! Now I can say once more
there are gods in heaven avenging men,
blazing down on all the crimes of earth.

---

8. The river of the lower world over which the dead were ferried.

Now at last I see this man brought down
in the Furies' tangling robes. It feasts my eyes—                    1610
he pays for the plot his father's hand contrived.

Atreus, this man's father, was king of Argos.
My father, Thyestes—let me make this clear—
Atreus' brother challenged him for the crown,
and Atreus drove him out of house and home                           1615
then lured him back, and home Thyestes came,
poor man, a suppliant to his own hearth,
to pray that Fate might save him.
                                        So it did.
There was no dying, no staining our native ground
with *his* blood. Thyestes was the guest,                            1620
and this man's godless father—

[*Pointing to* AGAMEMNON.]

the zeal of the host outstripping a brother's love,
made my father a feast that seemed a feast for gods,
a love feast of his children's flesh.
                                        He cuts
the extremities, feet and delicate hands                             1625
into small pieces, scatters them over the dish
and serves it to Thyestes throned on high.
He picks at the flesh he cannot recognize,
the soul of innocence eating the food of ruin—
look,

[*Pointing to the bodies at his feet.*]

            that feeds upon the house! And then,                     1630
when he sees the monstrous thing he's done, he shrieks,
he reels back head first and vomits up that butchery,
tramples the feast—brings down the curse of Justice:
"Crash to ruin, all the race of Peleisthenes,[9] crash down!"

So you see him, down. And I, the weaver of Justice,                  1635
plotted out the kill. Atreus drove us into exile,
my struggling father and I, a babe-in-arms,
his last son, but I became a man
and Justice brought me home. I was abroad
but I reached out and seized my man,                                 1640

9. A name sometimes inserted into the genealogy of the house of Tantalus.

link by link I clamped the fatal scheme
together. Now I could die gladly, even I—
now I see this monster in the nets of Justice.
LEADER: Aegisthus, you revel in pain—you sicken me.           1645
You say you killed the king in cold blood,
single-handed planned his pitiful death?
I say there's no escape. In the hour of judgment,
trust to this, your head will meet the people's
rocks and curses.
AEGISTHUS:          You say! you slaves at the oars—
while the master of the benches cracks the whip?
You'll learn, in your late age, how much it hurts
to teach old bones their place. We have techniques—
chains and the pangs of hunger,
two effective teachers, excellent healers.
They can even cure old men of pride and gall.              1655
Look—can't you see? The more you kick
against the pricks, the more you suffer.
LEADER: You, pathetic—
the king had just returned from battle.
You waited out the war and fouled his lair,                1660
you planned my great commander's fall.
AEGISTHUS:                          Talk on—
you'll scream for every word, my little Orpheus.[1]
We'll see if the world comes dancing to your song,
your absurd barking—snarl your breath away!
I'll make you dance, I'll bring you all to heel.           1665
LEADER: *You* rule Argos? You who schemed his death
but cringed to cut him down with your own hand?
AEGISTHUS: The treachery was the woman's work, clearly.
I was a marked man, his enemy for ages.
But I will use his riches, stop at nothing                 1670
to civilize his people. All but the rebel:
him I'll yoke and break—
no cornfed colt, running free in the traces.
Hunger, ruthless mate of the dark torture-chamber,
trains her eyes upon him till he drops!                    1675
LEADER: Coward, why not kill the man yourself?
Why did the woman, the corruption of Greece
and the gods of Greece, have to bring him down?
*Orestes*—If he still sees the light of day,
bring him home, good Fates, home to kill                   1680
this pair at last. Our champion in slaughter!

---

1. A mythical singer who charmed all nature with his music.

AEGISTHUS: Bent on insolence? Well, you'll learn, quickly.
  At them, men—you have your work at hand!

  [*His men drew swords; the old men take up their sticks.*]

LEADER: At them, fist at the hilt, to the last man—
AEGISTHUS: Fist at the hilt, I'm not afraid to die.                     1685
LEADER: It's death you want and death you'll have—
  we'll make that word your last.

  [CLYTAEMNESTRA *moves between them, restraining* AEGISTHUS.]

CLYTAEMNESTRA:                          No more, my dearest,
  no more grief. We have too much to reap
  right here, our mighty harvest of despair.
  Our lives are based on pain. No bloodshed now.                        1690

  Fathers of Argos, turn for home before you act
  and suffer for it. What we did was destiny.
  If we could end the suffering, how we would rejoice.
  The spirit's brutal hoof has struck our heart.
  And that is what a woman has to say.                                  1695
  Can you accept the truth?

  [CLYTAEMNESTRA *turns to leave.*]

AEGISTHUS:                          But these . . . mouths
  that bloom in filth—spitting insults in my teeth.
  You tempt your fates, you insubordinate dogs—
  to hurl abuse at me, your master!
LEADER:                          No Greek
  worth his salt would grovel at your feet.                            1700
AEGISTHUS: I—I'll stalk you all your days!
LEADER: Not if the spirit brings Orestes home.
AEGISTHUS: Exiles feed on hope—well I know.
LEADER:                                        More,
  gorge yourself to bursting—soil justice, while you can.
AEGISTHUS: I promise you, you'll pay, old fools—in good time,
    too!                                                               1705
LEADER: Strut on your own dunghill, you cock beside your mate.
CLYTAEMNESTRA: Let them howl—they're impotent. You and I have
    power now.
  We will set the house in order once for all.

  [*They enter the palace; the great doors close behind them; the
  old men disband and wander off.*]

## The Libation Bearers

### Characters

ORESTES, *son of Agamemnon and Clytaemnestra*
PYLADES, *his companion*
ELECTRA, *his sister*
CHORUS *of Slavewomen and their Leader*
CLYTAEMNESTRA
CILISSA, *Orestes' old nurse*
AEGISTHUS
*A servant of Aegisthus*
*Attendants of Orestes, bodyguard of Aegisthus*

[TIME AND SCENE: *Several years have passed since Agamemnon's death. At Argos, before the tomb of the kin and his fathers, stands an altar; behind it looms the house of Atreus.*
ORESTES *and* PYLADES *enter, dressed as travelers.* ORESTES *kneels and prays.*[1]]

ORESTES: Hermes, lord of the dead, look down and guard
the fathers' power. Be my savior, I beg you,
Be my comrade now.
                                    I have come home
to my own soil, an exile home at last.
Here at the mounded grave I call my father,                    5
Hear me—I am crying out to you . . .

[*He cuts two locks of hair and lays them on the grave.*]

There is a lock for Inachos[2] who nursed me
into manhood, there is one for death.

I was not here to mourn you when you died,
my father, never gave the last salute                          10
when they bore your corpse away.

[ELECTRA *and a chorus of slave-women enter in procession. They are dressed in black and bear libations, moving towards* ORESTES *at the grave.*]

---

1. The beginning of the play (perhaps as many as thirty lines) is missing in our manuscripts. Nine lines have been assembled from other ancient authors who quoted them.    2. The river of Thebes. Greek youths, on coming to manhood, offered a lock of their hair to the river of their country as thanks for the nurture it had helped to provide. And locks of hair were offered on the graves of the dead.

What's this?
Look, a company moving towards us. Women,
robed in black . . . so clear in the early light.

I wonder what they mean, what turn of fate?—
some new wound to the house?                                    15
Or perhaps they come to honor you, my father,
bearing cups[3] to soothe and still the dead.
That's right, it must be . . .
Electra, I think I see *her* coming, there,
my own sister, worn, radiant in her grief—                      20
Dear god, let me avenge my father's murder—
fight beside me now with all your might!

Out of their way, Pylades.[4] I must know
what they mean, these women turning towards us,
what their prayers call forth.                                  25

[*They withdraw behind the tomb.*]

CHORUS: Rushed from the house we come
       escorting cups for the dead,
    in step with the hands' hard beat,
       our cheeks glistening,
    flushed where the nails have raked new furrows running blood;[5] 30
    and life beats on, and through it all
    we nurse our lives with tears,
    to the sound of ripping linen beat our robes in sorrow,
       close to the breast the beats throb
    and laughter's gone and fortune throbs and throbs.          35
    Aie!—bristling Terror struck—
       Terror the seer of the house,
    the nightmare ringing clear
       breathed its wrath in sleep,
    in the midnight watch a cry!—the voice of Terror            40
    deep in the house, bursting down
    on the women's darkened chambers, yes,
    and the old ones, skilled at dreams, swore oaths to god
       and called,
    "The proud dead stir under earth,
    they rage against the ones who took their lives."           45

---

3. Libations, drink offerings to pour on the grave.   4. Son of Strophios, who was Orestes'
host in his kingdom of Phocis.   5. This and the following lines list the semiritual actions of
mourning for the dead: scratching the cheek, beating the head and breast, ripping clothes.

But the gifts,[6] the empty gifts
    she hopes will ward them off—
good Mother Earth!—that godless woman sends me here . . .
    I dread to say her prayer.
What can redeem the blood that wets the soil?          50
Oh for the hearthfire banked with grief,
    the rampart's down, a fine house down—
dark, dark, and the sun, the life is curst,
    and mist enshrouds the halls
        where the lords of war went down.        55

And the ancient pride no war,
    no storm, no force could tame,
ringing in all men's ears, in all men's hearts is gone.
    They are afraid. Success,
    they bow to success, more god than god himself.    60
    But justice waits and turns the scales:
      a sudden blow for some at dawn,
    for some in the no man's land of dusk
      her torments grow with time,
        and the lethal night takes others.    65

And the blood that Mother Earth consumes
clots hard, it won't seep through, it breds revenge
    and frenzy goes through the guilty,
seething like infection, swarming through the brain.
For the one who treads a virgin's bed        70
there is no cure. All the streams of the world,
    all channels run into one
to cleanse a man's red hands will swell the bloody tide.[7]

And I . . . Fate and the gods brought down their yoke,
they ringed our city, out of our fathers' halls        75
    they led us here as slaves.[8]
And the will breaks, we kneel at their command—
    our masters right or wrong!
      And we beat the tearing hatred down,
      behind our veils we weep for her,        80

    [*Turning to* ELECTRA.]

6. Clytaemnestra's nightmare is interpreted by the "old ones, skilled at dreams": the dead are angry with their killers. The gifts are the libations poured on the grave to appease the wrathful dead. They were a mixture of honey, oil, wine, milk, and water.    7. Bloodguilt can no more be washed away than virginity restored.    8. The chorus consists of women enslaved when their city was captured. It is not so stated in the text but they are probably Trojan captives brought home by Agamemnon.

her senseless fate.
Sorrow turns the secret heart to ice.

ELECTRA:                       Dear women,
  you keep the house in order, best you can;
  and now you've come to the grave to say a prayer
  with me, my escorts. I'll need your help with this.       85
  What to say when I pour the cup of sorrow?

   [*Lifting her libation cup.*]

  What kindness, what prayer can touch my father?
  Shall I say I ring him love for love, a woman's
  love for husband? My mother, love from her?
  I've no taste for that, no words to say           90
  as I run the honeyed oil on father's tomb.

  Or try the salute we often use at graves?
  "A wreath for a wreath. Now bring the givers
  gifts to match" . . . no, give them pain for pain.
  Or silent, dishonored, just as father died,       95
  empty it out for the soil to drink and then
  retrace my steps, like a slave sent out with scourings
  left from the purging of the halls, and throw
  the cup behind me, looking straight ahead.[9]
  Help me decide, my friends. Join me here.      100
  We nurse a common hatred in the house.
  Don't hide your feelings—no, fear no one.
  Destiny waits us all,

   [*Looking towards the tomb.*]

                 born free,
  or slaves who labor under another's hand.
  Speak to me, please. Perhaps you've had      105
  a glimpse of something better.

LEADER:                  I revere
  your father's death-mound like an altar.
  I'll say a word, now that you ask,
  that comes from deep within me.

ELECTRA:                Speak on,
  with everything you feel for father's grave.      110

LEADER: Say a blessing as you pour, for those who love you.

ELECTRA: And of the loved ones, whom to call my friends?

---

9. After throwing away refuse, an ancient Greek returned without looking back, as if afraid
that the action might have provoked some hostile powers.

LEADER: First yourself, then all who hate Aegisthus.
ELECTRA: I and you. I can say a prayer for us
   and then for—
LEADER:        You know, try to say it.            115
ELECTRA: There is someone else to rally to our side?
LEADER: Remember Orestes, even abroad and gone.
ELECTRA: Well said, the best advice I've had.
LEADER: Now for the murderers. Remember them and—
ELECTRA:                             What?
   I'm so unseasoned, teach me what to say.        120
LEADER: Let some god or man come down upon them.
ELECTRA: Judge or avenger, which?
LEADER: Just say "the one who murders in return!"
ELECTRA: How can I ask the gods for that
   and keep my conscience clear?
LEADER:            How not,[1]        125
   and pay the enemy back in kind?

    [ELECTRA *kneels at the grave in prayer.*]

ELECTRA:                   —Herald king
   of the world above and the quiet world below,
   lord of the dead, my Hermes, help me now.
   Tell the spirits underground to hear my prayers,
   and the high watch hovering over father's roofs,        130
   and have her listen too, the Earth herself
   who brings all things to life and makes them strong,
   then gathers in the rising tide once more.

   And I will tip libations to the dead.
   I call out to my father. Pity me,        135
   dear Orestes too.
   Rekindle the light that saves our house!
   We're auctioned off, drift like vagrants now.
   Mother has pawned us for a husband, Aegisthus,
   her partner in her murdering.
                    I go like a slave,        140
   and Orestes driven from his estates while they,
   they roll in the fruits of all your labors,
   magnificent and sleek. O bring Orestes home,
   with a happy twist of fate, my father. Hear me,
   make me far more self-possessed than mother,        145
   make this hand more pure.

---

1. Common Greek morality saw nothing wrong in individual vengeance. But it will lead, in this play, to a son's murder of a mother, and in the last play be superseded by communal justice.

These prayers for us. For our enemies I say,
Raise up your avenger, into the light, my father—
kill the killers in return, with justice!
So in the midst of prayers for good I place          150
this curse for them.
                          Bring up your blessings,
up into the air, led by the gods and Earth
and all the rights that bring us triumph.

[*Pouring libations on the tomb and turning to the women.*]

These are my prayers. Over them I pour libations.
Yours to adorn them with laments, to make them bloom,          155
so custom says—sing out and praise the dead.
CHORUS: Let the tears fall, ring out and die,
    die with the warlord at this bank,
this bulwark of the good, defence against the bad,
    the guilt, the curse we ward away          160
with prayer and all we pour. Hear me, majesty, hear me,
    lord of glory, from the darkness of your heart.
                                    Ohhhhhh!—

Dear god, let him come! Some man
with a strong spear, born to free the house,
    with the torsion bow of Scythia[2] bent for slaughter,          165
splattering shafts like a god of war—sword in fist
    for the slash-and-hack of battle!

[ELECTRA *remains at the grave, staring at the ground.*]

ELECTRA:                                    Father,
    you have it now, the earth has drunk your wine.
    Wait, friends, here's news. Come share it.
LEADER:                                    Speak on,
    my heart's a dance of fear.
ELECTRA:                          A lock of hair,          170
    here on the grave . . .
LEADER:                    Whose? A man's?
    A growing girl's?
ELECTRA:            And it has the marks,
    and anyone would think—
LEADER:                    What?
    We're old. You're young, now you teach us.
ELECTRA: No one could have cut this lock but I and—          175

2. The Scythians, who lived far to the north and east of Greece, were famous archers.

LEADER: Callous they are, the ones who ought to shear
   the hair and mourn.
ELECTRA:             Look at the texture, just like—
LEADER: Whose? I want to know.
ELECTRA:                Like mine, identical,
   can't you see?
LEADER:        Orestes . . . he brought a gift
   in secret?
ELECTRA: It's *his*—I can see his curls.            180
LEADER: And how could he risk the journey here?
ELECTRA: He sent it, true, a lock to honor father.
LEADER: All the more cause for tears. You mean
   he'll never set foot on native ground again.
ELECTRA:                      Yes!
   It's sweeping over me too—anguish like a breaker—    185
   a sword ripping through my heart!
   Tears come like the winter rains that flood the gates—
   can't hold them back, when I see this lock of hair.

How could I think another Greek[3] could play
the prince with this?
              *She'd* never cut it,       190
the murderess, my mother. She insults the name,
she and her godless spirit preying on her children.

But how, how can I come right out and say it *is*
the glory of the dearest man I know—Orestes?
Stop, I'm fawning on hope.
                Oh, if only       195
it had a herald's voice, kind and human—
I'm so shaken, torn—and told me clearly
to throw it away, they severed it from a head
that I detest. Or it could sorrow with me
like a brother, aye,       200
this splendor come to honor father's grave.
We call on the gods, and the gods well know
what storms torment us, sailors whirled to nothing.
But if we are to live and reach the haven,
one small seed could grow a mighty tree—       205
Look, tracks.
          A new sign to tell us more.
Footmarks . . . pairs of them, like mine.
Two outlines, two prints, his own, and there,
a fellow traveler's.

---

3. Only a close relative would have done it.

[*Putting her foot into* ORESTES' *print.*]

The heel, the curve of the arch
like twins.[4]

[*While* ORESTES *emerges from behind the grave, she follows
cautiously in his steps until they come together.*]

Step by step, my step in his . . .
                        we meet—      210
Oh the pain, like pangs of labor—this is madness!
ORESTES: Pray for the future. Tell the gods they've brought
    your prayers to birth, and pray that we succeed.

[ELECTRA *draws back, struggling for composure.*]

ELECTRA: The gods—why now? What have I ever won from them?
ORESTES: The sight you prayed to see for many years.      215
ELECTRA: And you know the one I call?
ORESTES:                            I know Orestes,
    know he moves you deeply.
ELECTRA:                     Yes,
    but now what's come to fill my prayers?
ORESTES: Here I am. Look no further.
    No one loves you more than I.
ELECTRA:                     No,      220
    it's a trap, stranger . . . a net you tie around me?
ORESTES: Then I tie myself as well.
ELECTRA:                     But the pain,
    you're laughing at all—
ORESTES:                Your pain is mine.
    If I laugh at yours, I only laugh at mine.
ELECTRA: *Orestes*—
    can I call you?—are you really—      225
ORESTES:                    I am!
    Open your eyes. So slow to learn.
    You saw the lock of hair I cut in mourning.
    You scanned my tracks, you could see my marks,
    your breath leapt, you all but saw me in the flesh—      230
    *Look*—

[*Holding the lock to his temple, then to* ELECTRA'S.]

4. Since Greeks wore open sandals they were much more conscious than we are of the shape of each others' feet. Cf. *Odyssey*, IV. 156, where Menelaus sees a resemblance between the feet of Telemachus and Odysseus.

put it where I cut it.
It's your brother's. Try, it matches yours.

[*Removing a strip of weaving from his clothing.*]

Work of your own hand, you tamped the loom,
look, there are wild creatures in the weaving.

[*She kneels beside him, weeping; he lifts her to her feet and they embrace.*]

No, no, control yourself—don't lose yourself in joy!          235
Our loved ones, well I know, would slit our throats.
LEADER: Dearest, the darling of your father's house,
    hope of the seed we nursed with tears—you save us.
    Trust to your power, win your father's house once more!
ELECTRA: You light to my eyes, four loves in one!          240
    I have to call you father, it is fate;
    and I turn to you the love I gave my mother—
    I despise her, she deserves it, yes,
    and the love I gave my sister, sacrificed
    on the cruel sword, I turn to you.          245
    You were my faith, my brother—
    you alone restore my self-respect.

    [*Praying.*]

Power and Justice, Saving Zeus, Third Zeus,[5]
almighty all in all, be with us now.
ORESTES: Zeus, Zeus, watch over all we do,          250
    fledglings reft of the noble eagle father.
    He died in the coils, the viper's dark embrace.
    We are his orphans worn down with hunger,
    weak, too young to haul the father's quarry
    home to shelter.
                    Look down on us!          255
    I and Electra, too, I tell you, children
    robbed of our father, both of us bound
    in exile from our house.
                    And what a father—
    a priest at sacrifice, he showered you
    with honors. Put an end to his nestlings now          260

5. Zeus is called on when the third libation is poured at the feast (see *Agamemnon*, l. 245, and note): Zeus was third in the succession of the rulers of the gods (see *Agamemnon*, l. 169 note).

and who will serve you banquets rich as his?
Destroy the eagle's brood, you can never
send a sign that wins all men's belief.
Rot the stock of a proud dynastic tree—
it can never shore your altar steaming                                265
with the oxen in the mornings. Tend us—
we seem in ruins now, I know. Up from nothing
rear a house to greatness.
LEADER:                            Softly, children,
white hopes of your father's hearth. Someone
might hear you, children, charmed with his own voice         270
blurt all this out to the masters. Oh, just once
to see them— live bones crackling in the fire
spitting pitch!
ORESTES:                Apollo will never fail me, no,
his tremendous power, his oracle charges me
to see this trial through.
                                I can still hear the god—         275
a high voice ringing with winters of disaster,
piercing the heart within me, warm and strong,
unless I hunt my father's murderers, cut them down
in their own style—they destroyed my birthright.
"Gore them like a bull!" he called, "or pay their debt         280
with your own life, one long career of grief."

He revealed so much about us,
told how the dead take root beneath the soil,
they grow with hate and plague the lives of men.
He told of the leprous boils that ride the flesh,[6]             285
their wild teeth gnawing the mother tissue, aye,
and a white scurf spreads like cancer over these,
and worse, he told how assaults of Furies spring
to life on the father's blood . . .
                                You can *see* them—
the eyes burning, grim brows working over you in the dark—   290
the dark sword of the dead!—your murdered kinsmen
pleading for revenge. And the madness haunts
the midnight watch, the empty terror shakes you,
harries, drives you on—an exile from your city—
a brazen whip will mutilate your back.                          295

For such as us, no share in the wine-bowl
no libations poured in love. You never see

6. This list of the loathsome afflictions which await the man who fails to avenge his murdered
father moves from disease to social ostracism; the man who fails in his duty dies cut off from
society and the gods.

your father's wrath but it pulls you from the altars.
There is no refuge, none to take you in.
A pariah, reviled, at long last you die,                    300
withered in the grip of all this dying.
Such oracles are persuasive, don't you think?
And even if I am not convinced,
the rough work of the world is still to do.
So many yearnings meet and urge me on.                      305
The god's commands. Mounting sorrow for father.
Besides, the lack of patrimony presses hard;
and my compatriots, the glory of men
who toppled Troy with nerves of singing steel,
go at the beck and call of a brace of women.                310
Womanhearted he is[7]—if not, we'll soon see.

[*The leader lights the altar fires.* ORESTES, ELECTRA, *and the
chorus gather for the invocation at the grave.*]

CHORUS: Powers of destiny, mighty queens of Fate!—
    by the will of Zeus your will be done,
    press on to the end now,
        Justice turns the wheel.                            315
    "Word for word, curse for curse
    be born now," Justice thunders,
        hungry for retribution,
    "stroke for bloody stroke be paid.
        The one who acts must suffer."                       320
    Three generations strong the word resounds.
ORESTES: Dear father, father of dread,
    what can I do or say to reach you now?
        What breath can reach from here
    to the bank where you lie moored at anchor?             325
    What light can match your darkness? None,
    but there is a kind of grace that comes
        when the tears revive a proud old house
    and Atreus' sons, the warlords lost and gone.
LEADER: The ruthless jaws of the fire,                       330
    my child, can never tame the dead,
        his rage inflames his sons.
    Men die and the voices rise, they light the guilty, true—
    cries raised for the fathers, clear and just,
        will hunt their killers harried to the end.          335
ELECTRA: Then hear me now, my father,
    it is my turn, my tears are welling now,

---

7. I.e. Aegisthus is a coward; Argos is ruled by a "brace of women."

as child by child we come
to the tomb and raise the dirge, my father.
Your grave receives a girl in prayer                                    340
and a man in flight, and we are one,
   and the pain is equal, whose is worse?
And who outwrestles death—what third last fall?[8]
CHORUS: But still some god, if he desires,
   may work our strains to a song of joy,                               345
from the dirges chanted over the grave
   may lift a hymn in the kings' halls
and warm the loving cup you stir this morning.
ORESTES:[9] If only at Troy
   a Lycian[1] cut you down, my father—                                 350
gone, with an aura left at home behind you,
   children to go their ways
and the eyes look on them bright with awe,
and the tomb you win on headlands seas away
   would buoy up the house . . .                                        355
LEADER: And loved by the men you loved
   who died in glory, there you'd rule
      beneath the earth—lord, prince,
stern aide to the giant kings who judge the shadows there.
You were a king of kings when you drew breath;                          360
   the mace you held could make men kneel or die.
ELECTRA: No, not under Troy!—
not dead and gone with them, my father,
hordes pierced by the spear Scamander washes down.
   Sooner the killers die                                               365
as they killed you—at the hands of friends,
and the news of death would come from far away,
   we'd never know this grief.
CHORUS: You are dreaming, children,
   dreams dearer than gold, more blest                                  370
than the Blest beyond the North Wind's raging.[2]
   Dreams are easy, oh,
but the double lash is striking home.
Now our comrades group underground.
Our masters' reeking hands are doomed—                                  375
   the children take the day!
ORESTES: That thrills his ear,
      that arrow lands!

8. There were three falls in a Greek wrestling match.   9. Compare this and the next stanza
with the speech of Achilles in Hades (*Odyssey* XXIV. 22).   1. Allies of the Trojans; their kings
were the famous warriors Glaukos and Sarpedon.   2. The land of the Hyperboreans, a legendary race of worshippers of Apollo who lived a paradisal life in the far North.

Zeus, Zeus, force up from the earth
destruction, late but true to the mark,                    380
to the reckless heart, the killing hand—
    for parents of revenge revenge be done.
LEADER: And the ripping cries of triumph mine
to sing when the man is stabbed,
        the woman dies—[3]                                  385
    why, why hide what's deep inside me,
        black wings beating, storming the spirit's prow—
            hurricane, slashing hatred!
ELECTRA: Both fists at once
    come down, come down—
        Zeus, crush their skulls! Kill! kill!                390
Now give the land some faith, I beg you,
from these ancient wrongs bring forth our rights.
    Hear me, Earth, and all you lords of death.
CHORUS: It is the law: when the blood of slaughter
    wets the ground it wants more blood.                    395
        Slaughter cries for the Fury
of those long dead to bring destruction
on destruction churning in its wake!
ORESTES: Sweet Earth, how long?—great lords of death, look on,
    you mighty curses of the dead. Look on                  400
the last of Atreus' children, here, the remnant
    helpless, cast from home . . . god, where to turn?
LEADER: And again my pulses race and leap,
    I can feel your sobs, and hope
            becomes despair                                 405
        and the heart goes dark to hear you—
    then the anguish ebbs, I see you stronger,
        hope and the light come on me.
ELECTRA: What hope?—what force to summon, what can help?
    What but the pain we suffer, bred by her?               410
So let her fawn. She can never soothe her young wolves—
    Mother dear, you bred our wolves' raw fury.
LEADER AND CHORUS: I beat and beat the dirge like a Persian mourner,[4]
    hands clenched tight and the blows are coming thick and fast,
        you can see the hands shoot out,                    415
            now hand over hand and down—the head pulsates,
                blood at the temples pounding to explode!
ELECTRA: Reckless, brutal mother—oh dear god!—
        the brutal, cruel cortège,
    the warlord stripped of his honor guard                 420

3. For the first time, the killing of Clytaemnestra is mentioned.    4. Oriental mourning was
thought to be even more wild and extravagant than Greek.

and stripped of mourning rites—
you dared entomb your lord unwept, unsung.
ORESTES: Shamed for all the world, you mean—
dear god, my father degraded so!
Oh she'll pay, 425
she'll pay, by the gods and these bare hands—
just let me take her life and *die!*[5]
LEADER AND CHORUS: Shamed? *Butchered*, I tell you—hands lopped,
strung to shackle his neck and arms!
So she worked, 430
she buried him, made your life a hell.
Your father mutilated[6]—do you hear?
ELECTRA: You tell him of father's death, but I was an outcast,
worthless, leashed like a vicious dog in a dark cell.
I wept—laughter died that day . . . 435
I wept, pouring out the tears behind my veils.
Hear *that*, my brother, carve it on your heart!
LEADER AND CHORUS: Let it ring in your ears
but let your heart stand firm.
The outrage stands as it stands, 440
you burn to know the end,
but first be strong, be steel, then down and fight.
ORESTES: I am calling you, my father—be with all you love!
ELECTRA: I am with you, calling through my tears.
LEADER AND CHORUS: We band together now, the call resounds— 445
hear us now, come back into the light.
Be with us, battle all you hate.
ORESTES: Now force *clash* with force—right with right!
ELECTRA: Dear gods, be just—win back our rights.
LEADER AND CHORUS: The flesh crawls to hear them pray. 450
the hour of doom has waited long . . .
pray for it once, and oh my god, it comes.
CHORUS: Oh, the torment bred in the race,
the grinding scream of death
and the stroke that hits the vein, 455
the haemorrhage none can staunch, the grief,
the curse no man can bear.

But there is a cure in the house
and not outside it, no,
not from others but from *them*, 460

---

5. This is not, as might appear from the translation, an expression of despair. The Greek phrase is an example of a fairly common formula which has the force: "I'd be willing to *die*, if I could only . . ." 6. This practice was supposed to prevent the dead man from rising from the grave to haunt his murderer.

their bloody strife. We sing to you,
dark gods beneath the earth.

Now hear, you blissful powers underground—
    answer the call, send help.
Bless the children, give them triumph now.                              465

[*They withdraw, while* ELECTRA *and* ORESTES *come to the altar.*]

ORESTES: Father, king, no royal death you died—
    give me the power now to rule our house.
ELECTRA: I need you too, my father.
    Help me kill her lover, then go free.
ORESTES: Then men will extend the sacred feast to you.          470
    Or else, when the steam and the rich savor burn
    for Mother Earth, you will starve for honor.
ELECTRA: And I will pour my birthright out to you—
    the wine of the fathers' house, my bridal wine,
    and first of all the shrines revere your tomb.                      475
ORESTES: O Earth, bring father up to watch me fight.
ELECTRA: O Persephone,[7] give us power—lovely, gorgeous power!
ORESTES: Remember the bath—they stripped away your life, my father.
ELECTRA: Remember the all-embracing net—they made it first for
    you.
ORESTES: Chained like a beast—chains of hate, not bronze, my
    father!                                                             480
ELECTRA: Shamed in the schemes, the hoods they slung around you!
ORESTES: Does our taunting wake you, oh my father?
ELECTRA: Do you lift your beloved head?
ORESTES: Send us justice, fight for all you love,
    or help us pin them grip for grip. They threw you—                 485
    don't you long to throw them down in turn?
ELECTRA: One last cry, father. Look at your nestlings
    stationed at your tomb—pity
    your son and daughter. We are all you have.
ORESTES: Never blot out the seed of Pelops here.                       490
    Then in the face of death you cannot die.

[*The* LEADER *comes forward again.*]

LEADER: The voices of children—salvation to the dead!
    Corks to the net, they rescue the linen meshes
    from the depths. This line will never drown!

7. Queen of the underworld.

ELECTRA: Hear us—the long wail we raise is all for you!                    495
    Honor our call and you will save yourself.
LEADER: And a fine thing it is to lengthen out the dirge;
    you adore a grave and fate they never mourned.
    But now for action—now you're set on action,
    put your stars to proof.
ORESTES:              So we will.                      500
    One thing first, I think it's on the track.
    Why did she send libations? What possessed her,
    so late, so salve a wound past healing?
    To the unforgiving dead she sends this sop,
    this . . . who am I to appreciate her gifts?                 505
    They fall so short of all her failings. True,
    "pour out your all to atone an act of blood,
    you work for nothing." So the saying goes.
    I'm ready. Tell me what you know.
LEADER:             I know, my boy,
    I was there. She had bad dreams. Some terror                 510
    came groping through the night, it shook her,
    and she sent these cups, unholy woman.
ORESTES: And you know the dream, you can tell it clearly?
LEADER: She dreamed she bore a snake, said so herself and . . .
ORESTES: Come to the point—where does the story end?              515
LEADER: . . . she swaddled it like a baby, laid it to rest.
ORESTES: And food, what did the little monster want?
LEADER: She gave it her breast to suck—she was dreaming.
ORESTES: And didn't it tear her nipple, the brute inhuman—
LEADER: Blood curdled the milk with each sharp tug . . .          520
ORESTES: No empty dream. The vision of a man.
LEADER: . . . and she woke with a scream, appalled,
    and rows of torches, burning out of the blind dark,
    flared across the halls to soothe the queen,
    and then she sent the libations for the dead,               525
    an easy cure she hopes will cut the pain.
ORESTES:               No,
    I pray to the Earth and father's grave to bring
    that dream to life in me. I'll play the seer—
    it all fits together, watch!
    If the serpent came from the same place as I,                530
    and slept in the bands that swaddled me, and its jaws
    spread wide for the breast that nursed me into life
    and clots stained the milk, mother's milk,
    and she cried in fear and agony—so be it.
    As she bred this sign, this violent prodigy                 535
    so she dies by violence. I turn serpent,

I kill her. So the vision says.
LEADER: You are the seer for me, I like your reading.
 Let it come! But now rehearse your friends.
 Say do this, or don't do that—                                          540
ORESTES: The plan is simple. My sister goes inside.
 And I'd have her keep the bond with me a secret.
 They killed an honored man by cunning, so
 they die by cunning, caught in the same noose.
 So he commands,                                                          545
 Apollo the Seer who's never lied before.

And I like a stranger, equipped for all events,
go to the outer gates with this man here,
Pylades, a friend, the house's friend-in-arms.
And we both will speak Parnassian, both try                               550
for the native tones of Delphi.[8]

                        Now, say none
at the doors will give us a royal welcome
(after all the house is ridden by a curse),
well then we wait . . . till a passer-by will stop
and puzzle and make insinuations at the house,                           555
"Aegisthus shuts his door on the man who needs him.
Why, I wonder—does he know? Is he home?"

But once through the gates, across the threshold,
once I find that man on *my* father's throne,
or returning late to meet me face to face,
and his eyes shift and fall—                                              560
                        I promise you,
before he can ask me, "Stranger, who are you?"—
I drop him dead, a thrust of the sword, and twist!
Our Fury never wants for blood. *His* she drinks unmixed,
our third libation poured to Saving Zeus.                                 565

  [*Turning to* ELECTRA.]

Keep a close watch inside, dear, be careful.
We must work together step by step.

  [*To the chorus.*]

---

8. Delphi is on the slopes of Mount Parnassus: the inhabitants of the area spoke a dialect which differed from that of Argos (and Athens). Of course, the actors playing Orestes and Pylades do not, in fact, switch to Parnassian dialect.

                                            And you,
better hold your tongues, religiously.
Silence, friends, or speak when it will help.

  [*Looking towards* PYLADES *and the death-mound and beyond.*]

For the rest, watch over me, I need you—                              570
guide my sword through struggle, guide me home!

  [*As* ORESTES, PYLADES, *and* ELECTRA *leave, the women reassem-
  ble for the chorus.*]

CHORUS: Marvels, the Earth breeds many marvels,
            terrible marvels overwhelm us.
      The heaving arms of the sea embrace and swarm
with savage life. And high in the no man's land of night        575
      torches[9] hang like swords. The hawk on the wing,
            the beast astride the fields
      can tell of the whirlwind's fury roaring strong.

      Oh but a man's high daring spirit,
            who can account for that? Or woman's                580
      desperate passion daring past all bounds?
      She couples with every form of ruin known to mortals.
      Woman, frenzied, driven wild with lust,
            twists the dark, warm harness
      of wedded love—tortures man and beast!                    585

      Well you know you with a sense of truth
            recall Althaia,[1]
      the heartless mother
      who killed her son,
      ai! what a scheme she had—                                 590
            she rushed his destiny,
            lit the bloody torch
      preserved from the day he left her loins with a cry—
            the life of the torch paced his,
      burning on till Fate burned out his life.                  595

      There is one more in the tales of hate:
            remember Scylla,[2]

_____

9. Comets, meteors, etc.    1. Mother of the hero Meleager. At his birth she was given a prophecy that his life would be no longer than that of a piece of wood then burning on the fire. She
extinguished it and hid it away. But when, now a young man, Meleager killed her brother in a
quarrel, she took it and threw it back on the fire, thus ending her son's life.    2. Daughter of
Nisos, King of Megara, who had a purple lock of hair which made it impossible for him to die.
When Megara was besieged by Minos, King of Crete, Scylla, bribed with a golden necklace, cut

the girl of slaughter
seduced by foes
to take her father's life.                                        600
    The gift of Minos,
      a choker forged in gold
turned her head and Nisos' immortal lock she cut
     as he slept away his breath . . .
ruthless bitch, now Hermes takes her down.                        605
Now that I call to mind old wounds that never heal—
    Stop, it's time for the wedded love-in-hate,[3]
for the curse of the halls,
    the woman's brazen cunning
      bent on her lord in arms,                    610
   her warlord's power—
      Do you respect such things?
I prize the hearthstone warmed by faith,
a woman's temper nothing bends to outrage.


First at the head of legendary crime stands Lemnos.[4]
    People shudder and moan, and can't forget—          615
each new horror that comes
    we call the hells of Lemnos.
      Loathed by the gods for guilt,
cast off by men, disgraced, their line dies out.
Who could respect what god detests?                               620
What of these tales have I not picked with justice?


      The sword's at the lungs!—it stabs deep,
      the edge cuts through and through
      and Justice drives it—Outrage still lives on,
      not trodden to pieces underfoot, not yet,          625
      though the laws lie trampled down,
      the majesty of Zeus.


      The anvil of Justice stands fast
      and Fate beats out her sword.
      Tempered for glory, a child will wipe clean        630
      the inveterate stain of blood shed long ago—
      Fury brings him home at last,
      the brooding mother Fury!

off her father's lock of hair. He died, and Scylla was changed into the sea monster of the
*Odyssey.*   **3.** This stanza refers to Clytaemnestra.   **4.** An island off the coast of Asia Minor.
The men of Lemnos brought back slave women from a war in neighboring Thrace: their wives,
angry and jealous because of their husbands' affection for these women, massacred all the men
on the island.

[*The women leave.* ORESTES *and* PYLADES *approach the house of Atreus.*]

ORESTES:                    Slave, the slave!—
  where is he? Hear me pounding the gates?
  Is there a man inside the house?                              635
  For the third time, come out of the halls!
  If Aegisthus has them welcome friendly guests.

  [*A voice from inside.*]

PORTER: All right, I hear you . . .
  Where do you come from, stranger? Who are you?
ORESTES: Announce me to the masters of the house.            640
  I've come for them, I bring them news.
                              Hurry,
  the chariot of the night is rushing on the dark!
  The hour falls, the traveler casts his anchor
  in an inn where every stranger feels at home.
                              Come out!
  Whoever rules the house. The woman in charge.             645
  No, the man, better that way.
  No scruples then. Say what you mean,
  man to man launch in and prove your point,
  make it clear, strong.

  [CLYTAEMNESTRA *emerges from the palace, attended by* ELEC-
  TRA.]

CLYTAEMNESTRA:            Strangers, please,
  tell me what you would like and it is yours.               650
  We've all you might expect in a house like ours.
  We have warm baths and beds to charm away your pains
  and the eyes of Justice look on all we do.
  But if you come for higher things, affairs
  that touch the state, that is the men's concern           655
  and I will stir them on.
ORESTES:              I am a stranger,
  from Daulis, close to Delphi, I'd just set out,
  packing my own burden bound for Argos
  (here I'd put my burden down and rest),
  when I met a perfect stranger, out of the blue,           660
  who asks about my way and tells me his.
                              Strophios,
  a Phocian, so I gathered in conversation.

"Well, my friend," he says, "out for Argos
in any case? Remember to tell the parents
he is dead, Orestes . . .

                promise me please      665
(it's only right), it will not slip your mind.
Then whatever his people want, to bring him home
or bury him here, an alien, all outcast here
forever, won't you ferry back their wishes?
As it is, a bronze urn is armor to his embers      670
The man's been mourned so well . . ."

                        I only tell you
what I heard. And am I speaking now
with guardians, kinsmen who will care?
It's hard to say. But a parent ought to know.

CLYTAEMNESTRA:                I, I—
your words, you storm us, raze us to the roots,      675
you curse of the house so hard to wrestle down!
How you range—targets at peace, miles away,
and a shaft from your lookout brings them down.
You strip me bare of all I love, destroy me,
now—Orestes.                        680
And he was trained so well, we'd been so careful,
kept his footsteps clear of the quicksand of death.
Just now, the hope of the halls, the surgeon to cure
our Furies' lovely revel—he seemed so close,
he's written off the rolls.

ORESTES:           If only I were . . .      685
my friends, with hosts as fortunate as you
if only I *could* be known for better news
and welcomed like a brother. The tie between
the host and stranger, what is kinder?
But what an impiety, so it seemed to me,      690
not to bring this to a head for loved ones.
I was bound by honor, bound by the rights
of hospitality.

CLYTAEMNESTRA: Nothing has changed.
For all that you receive what you deserve,
as welcome in these halls as one of us.      695
Wouldn't another bear the message just as well?
But you must be worn from the long day's journey—
time for your rewards.

    [*To* ELECTRA.]

          Escort him in,

where the men who come are made to feel at home.
He and his retinue, and fellow travelers.                              700
Let them taste the bounty of our house.
Do it, as if you depended on his welfare.

And we will rouse the powers in the house
and share the news. We never lack for loved ones,
we will probe this turn of fortune every way.                          705

[ELECTRA *leads* ORESTES, PYLADES, *and their retinue into the
halls;* CLYTAEMNESTRA *follows, while the chorus reassembles.*]

LEADER: Oh dear friends who serve the house,
    when can we speak out, when
can the vigor of our voices serve Orestes?
CHORUS: Queen of the Earth, rich mounded Earth,
    breasting over the lord of ships,                                  710
    the king's corpse at rest,
    hear us now, now help us,
        now the time is ripe—
    Down to the pit Persuasion goes
    with all her cunning. Hermes of Death,                             715
    the great shade patrols the ring
    to guide the struggles, drive the tearing sword.
LEADER: And I think our new friend is at his mischief.
    Look, Orestes' nurse in tears.

    [*Enter* CILISSA.[5]]

Where now, old-timer, padding along the gates?                         720
With pain a volunteer to go your way.
NURSE:                            "Aegisthus,"
    your mistress calling, "hurry and meet your guests.
There's news. It's clearer man to man, you'll see."

And she looks at the maids and pulls that long face
and down deep her eyes are laughing over the work                      725
that's done. Well and good for her. For the house
it's the curse all over—the strangers make that plain.
But let *him* hear, he'll revel once he knows.
                        Oh god,
the life is hard. The old griefs, the memories
mixing, cups of pain, so much pain in the halls,                       730

5. The nurse's name means simply "a woman from Cilicia" (in Asia Minor): she is a slave.

the house of Atreus . . . I suffered, the heart within me
always breaking, oh, but I never shouldered
misery like this. So many blows, good slave,
I took my blows.

            Now dear Orestes—
the sweetest, dearest plague of all our lives!                    735
Red from your mother's womb I took you, reared you . . .
nights, the endless nights I paced, your wailing
kept me moving—led me a life of labor,
all for what?

            And such care I gave it . . .
baby can't think for itself, poor creature.                    740
You have to nurse it, don't you? Read its mind,
little devil's got no words, it's still swaddled.
Maybe it wants a bite or a sip of something,
or its bladder pinches—a baby's soft insides
have a will of their own. I had to be a prophet.                    745
Oh I tried, and missed, believe you me, I missed,
and I'd scrub its pretty things until they sparkled.
Washerwoman and wet-nurse shared the shop.
A jack of two trades, that's me,
and an old hand at both . . .

                and so I nursed Orestes,                    750
yes, from his father's arms I took him once,
and now they say he's dead,
I've suffered it all, and now I'll fetch that man,
the ruination of the house—give him the news,
he'll relish every word.
LEADER:                        She tells him to come,                    755
  but how, prepared?
NURSE:                        Prepared, how else?
  I don't see . . .
LEADER:                      With his men, I mean, or all alone?
NURSE: Oh, she says to bring his bodyguard, his cut-throats.
LEADER: No, not now, not if you hate our master—
  tell him to come alone.                    760
  Nothing for him to fear then, when he hears.
  Have him come quickly, too, rejoicing all the way!
  The teller sets the crooked message straight.
NURSE:                            What,
  you're *glad* for the news that's come?
LEADER:                        Why not,
  if Zeus will turn the evil wind to good?                    765
NURSE: But how? Orestes, the hope of the house is gone.
LEADER: Not yet. It's a poor seer who'd say so.

---

NURSE: What are you saying?—something I don't know?

And lend a hand and scheme
for the rights, my Hermes,[8] help us,
sail the action on with all your breath.
    Reveal what's hidden, please,          805
    or say a baffling word
in the night and blind men's eyes—
when the morning comes your word is just as dark.

Soon, at last, in the dawn that frees the house,
    we sea-widows wed to the winds         810
        will beat our mourning looms of song
           and sing, "Our ship's come in!
        Mine, mine is the wealth that swells her holds—
those I love are home and free of death."

But you, when your turn in the action comes, be strong.    815
    When she cries "Son!" cry out "My *father's* son!"
        Go through with the murder—innocent at last.

Raise up the heart of Perseus[9] in your breast!
    And for all you love under earth
        and all above its rim, now scarf your eyes    820
           against the Gorgon's fury—
    In, go in for the slaughter now!

[*Enter* AEGISTHUS, *alone.*]

The butcher comes. Wipe out death with death.
AEGISTHUS: Coming, coming. Yes, I have my summons.
There's news, I gather, travelers here to tell it.    825
No joy in the telling, though—Orestes dead.
Saddle the house with a bloody thing like that
and it might just collapse. It's still raw
from the last murders, galled and raw.
But how to take the story, for living truth?    830
Or work of a woman's panic, gossip starting up
in the night to flicker out and die?

[*Turning to the* LEADER.]

                        Do you know?
Tell me, clear my mind.

---

8. In his capacity of god of the marketplace and of thieves: he is the appropriate divinity to steer the murder plan which is based on deceit.    9. The hero who killed the Gorgon, Medusa. Anyone who looked at her face was turned to stone; Perseus used a shield given him by Athena as a mirror.

LEADER:                          We've heard a little.
But get it from the strangers, go inside.
Messengers have no power. Nothing like                        835
a face-to-face encounter with the source.
AEGISTHUS: —Must see him, test the messenger. Where was he
when the boy died, standing on the spot?
Or is he dazed with rumor, mouthing hearsay?
No, he'll never trap me open-eyed!                            840

[*Striding through the doors.*]

CHORUS: Zeus, Zeus, what can I say?—
how to begin this prayer, call down
    the gods for help? what words
can reach the depth of all I feel?
Now they swing to the work,                                   845
the red edge of the cleaver
hacks at flesh and men go down.
Agamemnon's house goes down—
    all-out disaster now,
or a son ignites the torch of freedom,                        850
wins the throne, the citadel,
    the fathers' realms of god.
The last man on the bench, a challenger
must come to grips with two. Up,
like a young god, Orestes, wrestle—                           855
    let it be to win.

[*A scream inside the palace.*]

—Listen!
    —What's happening?
        —The house,
what have they done to the house?
LEADER:                          Back,
till the work is over! Stand back—
they'll count us clean of the dreadful business.              860

[*The women scatter; a wounded* SERVANT *of* AEGISTHUS *enters.*]

Look, the die is cast, the battle's done.
SERVANT:                                      Ai,
Ai, all over, master's dead—Aie,
a third, last salute. Aegisthus is no more.

[*Rushing at a side door, struggling to work it open.*]

Open up, wrench the bolts on the women's doors.
Faster! A strong young arm it takes,                                865
but not to save him now, he's finished.
What's the use?
                    Look—wake up!
                                        No good,
I call to the deaf, to sleepers . . . a waste of breath.
Where are you, Clytaemnestra? What are you doing?
LEADER: Her head is ripe for lopping on the block.               870
    She's next, and justice wields the axe.

    [*The door opens, and* CLYTAEMNESTRA *comes forth.*]

CLYTAEMNESTRA:                          What now?
    Why this shouting up and down the halls?
SERVANT: The dead are killing the living, I tell you!
CLYTAEMNESTRA: Ah, a riddle. I do well at riddles.
    By cunning we die, precisely as we killed.                   875
    Hand me the man-axe, someone, hurry!

    [*The* SERVANT *dashes out.*]

Now we will see. Win all or lose all,
we have come to this—the crisis of our lives.

    [*The main doors open;* ORESTES, *sword in hand, is standing
    over the body of* AEGISTHUS, *with* PYLADES *close behind him.*]

ORESTES: It's you I want. This one's had enough.
CLYTAEMNESTRA: Gone, my violent one—Aegisthus, very dear.       880
ORESTES: You love your man? Then lie in the same grave.
    You can never be unfaithful to the dead.

    [*Pulling her towards* AEGISTHUS' *body.*]

CLYTAEMNESTRA: Wait, son—no feeling for this, my child?
    The breast you held, drowsing away the hours,
    soft gums tugging the milk that made you grow?               885

    [ORESTES *turns to* PYLADES.]

ORESTES: What will I do, Pylades?—I dread to kill my mother!
PYLADES: What of the future? What of the Prophet God Apollo,

the Delphic voice, the faith and oaths we swear?
Make all mankind your enemy, not the gods.
ORESTES: O you win me over—good advice.

[*Wheeling on* CLYTAEMNESTRA, *thrusting her towards* AEGIS-
THUS.]

This way—    890

I want to butcher you—right across his body!
In life you thought he dwarfed my father—*Die!*—
go down with him forever!
You love this man,
the man you should have loved you hated.
CLYTAEMNESTRA: I gave you life. Let me die with you.   895
ORESTES: What—kill my father, then you'd live with me?
CLYTAEMNESTRA: Destiny had a hand in that, my child.
ORESTES: This too: destiny is handing you your death.
CLYTAEMNESTRA: You have no fear of a mother's curse, my son?
ORESTES: Mother? You flung me to a life of pain.   900
CLYTAEMNESTRA: Never flung you, placed you in a comrade's house.
ORESTES: —Disgraced me, sold me, a freeborn father's son.
CLYTAEMNESTRA: Oh? then name the price I took for you.
ORESTES: I am ashamed to mention it[1] in public.
CLYTAEMNESTRA: Please, and tell your father's failings, too.   905
ORESTES: Never judge him—he suffered, you sat here at home.
CLYTAEMNESTRA: It hurts women, being kept from men, my son.
ORESTES: Perhaps . . . but the man slaves to keep them safe at home.
CLYTAEMNESTRA: —I see murder in your eyes, my child—mother's
murder!
ORESTES: You are the murderer, not I—and you will kill yourself. 910
CLYTAEMNESTRA: Watch out—the hounds of a mother's curse will
hunt you down.
ORESTES: But how to escape a father's if I fail?
CLYTAEMNESTRA: I must be spilling live tears on a tomb of stone.[2]
ORESTES: Yes, my father's destiny—it decrees your death.
CLYTAEMNESTRA: Ai—you are the snake I bore[3]—I gave you life!
ORESTES: *Yes!*   915
That was the great seer, that terror in your dreams.
You killed and it was outrage—suffer outrage now.

[*He draws her over the threshold; the doors close behind them,
and the chorus gathers at the altar.*]

---

1. He means, of course, her adulterous liaison with Aegisthus.   2. This echoes a proverbial
expression for futile action—"pleading with a tomb."   3. Clytaemnestra remembers her dream
(ll. 514 ff.)

LEADER: I even mourn the victims' double fates.
But Orestes fought, he reached the summit
of bloodshed here—we'd rather have it so.                          920
The bright eye of the halls must never die.
CHORUS: Justice came at last to the sons of Priam,
late but crushing vengeance, yes,
but to Agamemnon's house returned
the double lion,[4]                                                925
the double onslaught
drove to the hilt—the exile sped by god,
by Delphi's just command that drove him home.

Lift the cry of triumph O! the master's house
wins free of grief, free of the ones                               930
who bled its wealth, the couple stained with murder,
free of Fate's rough path.
*He* came back with a lust for secret combat,
stealthy, cunning vengeance, yes,
but his hand was steered in open fight                             935
by god's true daughter,
Right, Right we call her,
we and our mortal voices aiming well—
she breathes her fury, shatters all she hates.

Lift the cry of triumph O! the master's house                      940
wins free of grief, free of the ones
who bled its wealth, the couple stained with murder,
free of Fate's rough path.

Apollo wills it so!—
Apollo, clear from the Earth's deep cleft                          945
his voice came shrill, "Now stealth will master stealth!"
And the pure god came down and healed our ancient wounds,
the heavens come, somehow, to lift our yoke of grief—
Now to praise the heavens' just command.

Look, the light is breaking!                                       950
The huge chain that curbed the halls gives way.
Rise up, proud house, long, too long
your walls lay fallen, strewn along the earth.

Time brings all to birth—
soon Time will stride through the gates with blessings,            955

---

4. Orestes and Pylades.

once the hearth burns off corruption, once
the house drives off the Furies. Look, the dice of Fate
   fall well for all to see. We sing how fortune smiles—
      the aliens in the house are routed out at last!

   Look, the light is breaking!                               960
The huge chain that curbed the halls gives way.
   Rise up, proud house, long, too long
your walls lay fallen, strewn along the earth.

[*The doors open. Torches light* PYLADES *and* ORESTES, *sword in
hand, standing over the bodies of* CLYTAEMNESTRA *and* AEGIS-
THUS, *as* CLYTAEMNESTRA *stood over the bodies of* AGAMEMNON
*and* CASSANDRA.]

ORESTES: Behold the double tyranny of our land!
   They killed my father, stormed my fathers' house.         965
   They had their power when they held the throne.
   Great lovers still, as you may read their fate.
   True to their oath, hand in hand they swore
   to kill my father, hand in hand to die.
   Now they keep their word.

[*Unwinding from the bodies on the bier the robes that* entangled AGAMEMNON, *he displays them, as* CLYTAEMNESTRA *had
displayed them, to the chorus at the altar.*]

                        Look once more on this,             970
you who gather here to attend our crimes—
the master-plot that bound my wretched father,
shackled his ankles, manacled his hands.
Spread it out! Stand in a ring around it,
a grand shroud for a man.

                        Here, unfurl it                      975
so the Father—no, not mine but the One
who watches over all, the Sun can behold
my mother's godless work. So he may come,
my witness when the day of judgment comes,
that I pursued this bloody death with justice,              980
mother's death.
                        Aegisthus, why mention him?
The adulterer dies. An old custom, justice.[5]
But she who plotted this horror against her husband,

---

5. An Athenian had the right to kill a man taken in adultery with his wife.

she carried his children, growing in her womb
and she—I loved her once                                    985
and now I loathe, I have to loathe—
                              what is she?

[*Kneeling by the body of his mother.*]

Some moray eel, some viper born to rot her mate
with a single touch, no fang to strike him,
just the wrong, the reckless fury in her heart!

[*Glancing back and forth from* CLYTAEMNESTRA *to the robes.*]

This—how can I dignify this . . . snare for a beast?—          990
sheath for a corpse's feet?
                              This winding-sheet,
this tent for the bath of death!
                              No, a hunting net,
a coiling—what to call—?
                              Foot-trap—
woven of robes . . .
why, this is perfect gear for the highwayman                    995
who entices guests and robs them blind and plies
the trade of thieves. With a sweet lure like this
he'd hoist a hundred lives and warm his heart.

Live with such a woman, marry *her*? Sooner
the gods destroy me—die without an heir!                        1000
CHORUS: Oh the dreadful work . . .
     Death calls and she is gone.
        But oh, for you, the survivor,
     suffering is just about to bloom.
ORESTES: Did she do the work or not?—Here, come close—          1005
     This shroud's my witness, dyed with Aegisthus' blade—
     Look, the blood ran here, conspired with time to blot
     the swirling dyes, the handsome old brocade.

     [*Clutching* AGAMEMNON'S *robes, burying his face in them and
     weeping.*]

Now I can praise you, now I am here to mourn.
You were my father's death, great robe, I hail you!             1010
Even if I must suffer the work and the agony
and all the race of man—
                              I embrace you . . . you,

my victory, are my guilt, my curse, and still—
CHORUS: No man can go through life
and reach the end unharmed.                                              1015
    Aye, trouble is now,
and trouble still to come.
ORESTES:                                    But *still*,
   that you may know—
            I see no end in sight,
I am a charioteer—the reins are flying, look,
the mares plunge off the track—
               my bolting heart,                   1020
it beats me down and terror beats the drum,
my dance-and-singing master pitched to fury—
And still, while I still have some self-control,
I say to my friends in public: I killed my mother,
not with a little justice. She was stained                               1025
with father's murder, she was cursed by god.
And the magic spells that fired up my daring?
One comes first. The Seer of Delphi who declared,
"Go through with this and you go free of guilt.
Fail and—"
         I can't repeat the punishment.                           1030
What bow could hit the crest of so much pain?

[PYLADES *gives* ORESTES *a branch of olive and invests him in the
robes of* APOLLO, *the wreath and insignia of suppliants to* DEL-
PHI.]

Now look on me, armed with the branch and wreath,
a suppliant bound for the Navelstone of Earth,
Apollo's sacred heights
where they say the fire of heaven[6] can never die.                      1035

[*Looking at his hand that still retains the sword.*]

I must escape this blood . . . it is my own.
—Must turn toward his hearth,
none but this, the Prophet God decreed.

I ask you, Argos and all my generations,
remember how these brutal things were done.                              1040
Be my witness to Menelaus when he comes.

6. A sacred fire was permanently maintained at Delphi: from it other fires, which had gone out
through natural calamities or the sack of a city, could be renewed. *Navelstone*: Delphi claimed to
be the center of the Earth: in the temple was a stone called the "navel."

And now I go, an outcast driven off the land,
in life, in death, I leave behind a name for—
LEADER: But you've done well. Don't burden yourself
    with bad omens, lash yourself with guilt.          1045
    You've set us free, the whole city of Argos,
    lopped the heads of these two serpents once for all.

[*Staring at the women and beyond,* ORESTES *screams in terror.*]

ORESTES: No, no! Women—look—like Gorgons,
    shrouded in black, their heads wreathed,
    swarming serpents!
                    —Cannot stay, I must move on.          1050
LEADER: What dreams can whirl you so? You of all men,
    you have your father's love. Steady, nothing
    to fear with all you've won.
ORESTES:                    No dreams, these torments,
    not to me, they're clear, real—the hounds
    of mother's hate.
LEADER:              The blood's still wet on your hands.          1055
    It puts a kind of frenzy in you . . .
ORESTES:                    *God Apollo!*
    Here they come, thick and fast,
    their eyes dripping hate—
LEADER:                    One thing
    will purge you. Apollo's touch will set you free
    from all your . . . torments.
ORESTES:                    You can't see them          1060
    I can, they drive me on! I must move on—

[*He rushes out;* PYLADES *follows close behind.*]

LEADER: Farewell then. God look down on you with kindness,
    guard you, grant you fortune.
CHORUS: Here once more, for the third time,
    the tempest in the race has struck          1065
    the house of kings and run its course.
        First the children eaten,
    the cause of all our pain, the curse.
    And next the kingly man's ordeal,
    the bath where the proud commander,          1070
    lord of Achaea's armies lost his life.
    And now a third has come, but who?
        A third like Saving Zeus?
    Or should we call him death?

Where will it end?—                                        1075
where will it sink to sleep and rest,
   this murderous hate, this Fury?


### The Eumenides
### Characters

THE PYTHIA, *the priestess of Apollo*
APOLLO
HERMES
ORESTES
THE GHOST *of Clytaemnestra*
CHORUS OF FURIES *and their Leader*
ATHENA
Escorting CHORUS *of Athenian women*
*Men of the jury, herald, citizens*


[TIME AND SCENE: *The* FURIES *have pursued* ORESTES *to the temple
of* APOLLO *at Delphi. It is morning. The priestess of the god appears
at the great doors and offers up her prayer.*]


PYTHIA: First of the gods I honor in my prayer is Mother Earth,
   the first of the gods to prophesy,[1] and next I praise
   Tradition, second to hold her Mother's mantic seat,
   so legend says, and third by the lots of destiny,
   by Tradition's free will—no force to bear her down—     5
   another Titan, child of the Earth, took her seat
   and Phoebe passed it on as a birthday gift to Phoebus,
   Phoebus a name for clear pure light derived from hers.
   Leaving the marsh and razorback of Delos,[2] landing
   at Pallas' headlands[3] flocked by ships, here he came    10
   to make his home Parnassus and the heights.[4]
   And an escort filled with reverence brought him on,
   the highway-builders, sons of the god of fire[5] who tamed
   the savage country, civilized the wilds—on he marched
   and the people lined his way to cover him with praise,    15
   led by Delphos lord, helm of the land, and Zeus
   inspired his mind with the prophet's skill, with godhead,

---

1. The Pythia (the priestess of Apollo's oracle) traces the peaceful succession of powers which
controlled the great prophetic site of Delphi. First Mother Earth, then Tradition (*Themis* in the
Greek), then Phoebe, grandmother of Apollo, who handed it over to him as a birthday gift. This
is a succession myth which stresses orderly, peaceful succession: in other versions Apollo fights
and kills a great serpent, Pytho, to gain possession.   2. The small rocky island in the Cyclades,
where Apollo was born.   3. I.e., the coast of Attica.   4. The oracular site is situated on the
lower slopes of the Parnassus mountain range (2,457 meters at its summit).   5. Athenians,
whose legendary ancestor Erechthonios was a son of Hephaestus, the smith-god.

made him fourth in the dynasty of seers to mount this throne,
but it is Zeus that Apollo speaks for, Father Zeus.
These I honor in the prelude of my prayers—these gods. 20
But Athena at the Forefront of the Temple[6] crowns our legends.
I revere the nymphs who keep the Corycian rock's deep hollows,[7]
loving haunt of birds where the spirits drift and hover.
And Great Dionysus[8] rules the land. I never forget that day
he marshalled his wild women in arms—he was all god, 25
he ripped Pentheus[9] down like a hare in the nets of doom.
And the rushing springs of Pleistos,[1] Poseidon's force I call,
and the king of the sky, the king of all fulfillment, Zeus.
Now the prophet goes to take her seat. God speed me—
grant me a vision greater than all my embarkations past! 30

[*Turning to the audience.*]

Where are the Greeks among you? Draw your lots and enter.
It is the custom here. I will tell the future
only as the god will lead the way.

[*She goes through the doors and reappears in a moment, shaken,
thrown to her knees by some terrific force.*]

Terrors—
terrors to tell, terrors all can see!—
they send me reeling back from Apollo's house. 35
The strength drains, it's very hard to stand,
crawling on all fours, no spring in the legs . . .
an old woman, gripped by fear, is nothing,
a child, nothing more.

[*Struggling to her feet, trying to compose herself.*]

I'm on my way to the vault, 40
it's green with wreaths, and there at the Navelstone[2]
I see a man—an abomination to god—
he holds the seat where suppliants sit for purging;
his hands dripping blood, and his sword just drawn,

6. *Pronaia*, the title of a temple of Athena situated at the entrance to the sacred precinct. 7. A capacious cave high above the site of Delphi, sacred to Pan and the nymphs. 8. This god, giver of wine and ecstasy, was thought to inhabit Delphi in the winter months, when Apollo left for the land of the Hyperboreans (the happy people who lived, as their name indicates, beyond the North wind). Dionysiac festivals at which women danced on the hills at night were held at Delphi in historical times. 9. A King of Thebes who resisted the establishment of Dionysiac rites in his domains. 1. The river (dry in summer) in the bottom of the deep gorge below Delphi. 2. A sacred stone which was supposed to mark the navel, i.e., the center of the earth.

and he holds a branch (it must have topped an olive)			45
wreathed with a fine tuft of wool,³ all piety,
fleece gleaming white. So far it's clear, I tell you.
But there in a ring around the man, an amazing company—
women, sleeping, nestling against the benches. . .
women? No,									50
Gorgons I'd call them; but then with Gorgons
you'd see the grim, inhuman . . .
						I saw a picture
years ago, the creatures tearing the feast
away from Phineus—⁴
						*These* have no wings,
I looked. But black they are, and so repulsive.			55
Their heavy, rasping breathing makes me cringe.
And their eyes ooze a discharge, sickening,
and what they wear⁵—to flaunt *that* at the gods,
the idols, sacrilege! even in the homes of men.
The tribe that produced that brood I never saw,			60
or a plot of ground to boast it nursed their kind
without some tears, some pain for all its labor.

Now for the outcome. This is his concern,
Apollo the master of this house, the mighty power.
Healer, prophet, diviner of signs, he purges			65
the halls of others—He must purge his own.

[*She leaves. The doors of the temple open and reveal* APOLLO
*rising over* ORESTES; *he kneels in prayer at the Navelstone, sur-*
*rounded by the* FURIES *who are sleeping.* HERMES *waits in the*
background.]

APOLLO: No, I will never fail you, through to the end
your guardian standing by your side or worlds away!
I will show no mercy to your enemies! Now
look at these—

[*Pointing to the* FURIES.]

						these obscenities!—I've caught them,		70
beaten them down with sleep.

---

**3.** Suppliants usually carried a branch of olive, hung with small woolen wreaths.	**4.** Whenever
he spread the table for a meal, the food was carried off by loathsome creatures—half bird, half
woman—called Harpies. The Pythia first thinks the Erinyes are Gorgons, but then rejects that
theory (we are not told why); her next guess, Harpies, has to be abandoned because the Erinyes
have no wings.	**5.** Long black robes.

They disgust me.
These gray, ancient children never touched
by god, man, or beast—the eternal virgins.
Born for destruction only, the dark pit,
they range the bowels of Earth, the world of death,            75
loathed by men and the gods who hold Olympus.

Nevertheless keep racing on and never yield.
Deep in the endless heartland they will drive you,
striding horizons, feet pounding the earth for ever,
on, on over seas and cities swept by tides!                    80
Never surrender, never brood on the labor.
And once you reach the citadel of Pallas,[6] kneel
and embrace her ancient idol in your arms and there,
with judges of your case, with a magic spell—
with words—we will devise the master-stroke                    85
that sets you free from torment once for all.
I persuaded you to take your mother's life.
ORESTES: Lord Apollo, you know the rules of justice,
know them well. Now learn compassion, too.
No one doubts your power to do great things.                   90
APOLLO: Remember that. No fear will overcome you.

[*Summoning* HERMES *from the shadows.*]

You, my brother, blood of our common Father,
Hermes, guard him well. Live up to your name,
good Escort. Shepherd him well, he is my suppliant,
and outlaws have their rights that Zeus reveres.               95
Lead him back to the world of men with all good speed.

[APOLLO *withdraws to his inner sanctuary;* ORESTES *leaves with*
HERMES *in the lead. The* GHOST OF CLYTAEMNESTRA *appears at
the Navelstone, hovering over the* FURIES *as they sleep.*]

THE GHOST OF CLYTAEMNESTRA:[7] You—how can you *sleep?*
Awake, awake—what use are sleepers now?
I go stripped of honor, thanks to you,
alone among the dead. And for those I killed                   100
the charges of the dead will never cease, never—
I wander in disgrace, I feel the guilt, I tell you,
withering guilt from all the outraged dead!

6. Athens, city of Pallas (Athena). *Ancient idol:* In a temple on the Acropolis at Athens there was
an ancient wooden statue of Athena.    7. She is not really a ghost. She tells us later what she is:
a dream in the head of the Furies. (l. 121).

But I suffered too, terribly, from dear ones,
and none of my spirits rages to avenge me.                          105
I was slaughtered by his matricidal hand.
See these gashes—

   [*Seizing one of the* FURIES *weak with sleep.*]

                 Carve them in your heart!
The sleeping rain has eyes that give us light;
we can never see our destiny by day.

And after all my libations . . . how you lapped                     110
the honey, the sober offerings poured to soothe you,
awesome midnight feasts[8] I burned at the hearthfire,
your dread hour never shared with gods.
All those rites, I see them trampled down.
And he springs free like a fawn, one light leap                     115
at that—he's through the thick of your nets,
he breaks away!
Mocking laughter twists across his face.
Hear me, I am pleading for my life.
Awake, my Furies, goddesses of the Earth!                           120
A dream is calling—Clytaemnestra calls you now.

   [*The* FURIES *mutter in their sleep.*]

Mutter on. Your man is gone, fled far away.
My son has friends to defend him, not like mine.

   [*They mutter again.*]

You sleep too much, no pity for my ordeal.
Orestes murdered his mother—he is gone.                             125

   [*They begin to moan.*]

Moaning, sleeping—onto your feet, quickly.
What is your work? What but causing pain?
Sleep and toil, the two strong conspirators,
they sap the mother dragon's deadly fury—

   [*The* FURIES *utter a sharp moan and moan again, but they are
still asleep.*]

---

8. Offerings to the Erinyes were made only at night. *Sober offerings*: No wine was included in offerings to them.

FURIES: Get him, get him, get him, get him—     130
  there he goes.
THE GHOST OF CLYTAEMNESTRA: The prey you hunt is just a dream—
  like hounds mad for the sport you bay him on,
  you never leave the kill.
                  But what are you *doing?*
  Up! don't yield to the labor, limp with sleep.
  Never forget my anguish.     135
  Let my charges hurt you, they are just;
  deep in the righteous heart they prod like spurs.

  You, blast him on with your gory breath,
  the fire of your vitals—wither him, after him,
  one last foray—waste him, burn him out!

    [*She vanishes. The lead* FURY *urges on the pack.*]

LEADER:                       Wake up!   140
  I rouse you, you rouse her. Still asleep?
  Onto your feet, kick off your stupor.
  See if this prelude has some grain of truth.

    [*The* FURIES *circle, pursuing the scent with hunting calls, and
    cry out singly when they find* ORESTES *gone.*]

FURIES: —Aieeeeee—no, no, *no*, they do us wrong, dear sisters.

  —The miles of pain, the pain I suffer . . .     145
  and all for nothing, all for pain, more pain,
    the anguish, oh, the grief too much to bear.

  —The quarry's slipped from the nets, our quarry lost and gone.

    —Sleep defeats me . . . I have lost the prey.

  —You—child of Zeus[9]—*you*, a common thief!   150

  —Young god, you have ridden down the powers
  proud with age. You worship the suppliant,
    the godless man who tears his parent's heart—

  —The matricide, you steal him away, and you a god!
    —Guilt both ways, and who can call it justice?   155

9. Apollo.

—Not I: her charges stalk my dreams,
Yes, the charioteer rides hard,
   her spurs digging the vitals,
  under the heart, under the heaving breast—

—I can feel the executioner's lash, it's searing         160
  deeper, sharper, the knives of burning ice—

—Such is your triumph, you young gods,
  world dominion past all rights.
   Your throne is streaming blood,
  blood at the foot, blood at the crowning head—      165

—I can see the Navelstone of the Earth, it's bleeding,
  bristling corruption, oh, the guilt it has to bear—

Stains on the hearth! The Prophet stains the vault,
  he cries it on, drives on the crime himself.
   Breaking the god's first law, he rates men first,      170
    destroys the old dominions of the Fates.

He wounds me too, yet *him* he'll never free,
  plunging under the earth, no freedom then:
   curst as he comes for purging, at his neck
    he feels new murder springing from his blood.     175

[APOLLO *strides from his sanctuary in full armor, brandishing his bow and driving back the* FURIES.]

APOLLO: Out, I tell you, out of these halls—fast!—
set the Prophet's chamber free!

[*Seizing one of the* FURIES, *shaking an arrow across her face.*]

                Or take
the flash and stab of this, this flying viper
whipped from the golden cord that strings my bow!

Heave in torment, black froth erupting from your lungs,   180
vomit the clots of all the murders you have drained.
But never touch my halls, you have no right.
Go where heads are severed,[1] eyes gouged out,

---

1. The methods of torture and execution listed by Apollo are what the Greeks saw as typically Eastern and, indeed, castration and impalement (188) were Persian, not Greek, customs. But

where Justice and bloody slaughter are the same . . .
castrations, wasted seed, young men's glories butchered,          185
extremities maimed, and huge stones at the chest,
and the victims wail for pity—
spikes inching up the spine, torsos stuck on spikes.

[*The* FURIES *close in on him.*]

So, you hear your love feast, yearn to have it all?
You revolt the gods. Your look,                                   190
your whole regalia gives you away—your kind
should infest a lion's cavern reeking blood.
But never rub your filth on the Prophet's shrine.
Out, you flock without a herdsman—out!
No god will ever shepherd you with love.                          195
LEADER: Lord Apollo, now it is your turn to listen.
    You are no mere accomplice in this crime.
    You did it all, and all the guilt is yours.
APOLLO: No, how? Enlarge on that, and only that.
LEADER: You commanded the guest to kill his mother.              200
APOLLO: —Commanded him to avenge his father, what of it?
LEADER: And then you dared embrace him, fresh from bloodshed.
APOLLO: Yes, I ordered him on, to my house, for purging.[2]
LEADER: And we sped him on, and you revile us?
APOLLO: Indeed, you are not fit to approach this house.          205
LEADER: And yet we have our mission and our—
APOLLO: Authority—you? Sound out your splendid power.
LEADER: Matricides: we drive them from their houses.
APOLLO: And what of the wife who strikes her husband down?
LEADER: That murder would not destroy one's flesh and blood.[3]  210
APOLLO: Why, you'd disgrace—obliterate the bonds of Zeus
    and Hera queen of brides! And the queen of love[4]
    you'd throw to the winds at a word, disgrace love,
    the source of mankind's nearest, dearest ties.
    Marriage of man and wife is Fate itself,                      215
    stronger than oaths, and Justice guards its life.

Apollo's dismissal of the Erinyes as non-Greek has no basis in fact: the Erinyes are not only Greek but much older than he is.    **2.** For ritual purification.    **3.** Crimes of blood relations against each other are the most heinous kind. But husband and wife are, and must be, of different blood. The Furies would have pursued Orestes if he had not avenged his father, and they pursue him now because he killed his mother, but the killing of a husband by a wife seems to them a lesser crime. They think and feel in tribal terms, those of a society which has not yet developed the city-state, the *polis,* in which the institution of marriage (which Apollo champions in his reply, 215ff.) was the guarantee of the legitimacy of male heirs for the transmittal of property from generation to generation.    **4.** Aphrodite. *Hera:* The marriage of Zeus and Hera was the divine model of earthly marriages and Hera was the goddess who presided over marriage ceremonies.

But if one destroys the other and you relent—
no revenge, not a glance in anger—then
I say your manhunt of Orestes is unjust.
Some things stir your rage, I see. Others,         220
atrocious crimes, lull your will to act.
                       Pallas
will oversee this trial. She is one of us.
LEADER: I will never let that man go free, never.
APOLLO: Hound him then, and multiply your pains.
LEADER: Never try to cut my power with your logic.     225
APOLLO: I'd never touch it, not as a gift—your power.
LEADER:                              Of course,
great as you are, they say, throned on high with Zeus.
But blood of the mother draws me on—must hunt
the man for Justice. Now I'm on his trail!

    [*Rushing out, with the* FURIES *in full cry.*]

APOLLO: And I will defend my suppliant and save him.     230
A terror to gods and men, the outcast's anger,
once I fail him, all of my own free will.

    [APOLLO *leaves. The scene changes to the Acropolis in Athens.*
    *Escorted by* HERMES, ORESTES *enters and kneels, exhausted, before*
    *the ancient shrine and idol of* ATHENA.]

ORESTES:                         Queen Athena,
under Apollo's orders I have come.
Receive me kindly. Curst and an outcast,
no suppliant for purging . . . my hands are clean.[5]     235
My murderous edge is blunted now, worn down at last
on the outland homesteads, beaten paths of men.
On and out over seas and dry frontiers,
I kept alive the Prophet's strong commands.
Struggling towards your house, your idol—

    [*Taking the knees of* ATHENA's *idol in his arms.*]

                           Goddess,     240
here I keep my watch,
I await the consummation of my trial.

---

5. Orestes has been given ritual purification by Apollo but he also claims that the blood guilt is now "worn down" by his travels and contacts with men (Cf. ll. 280–285).

[*The* FURIES *enter in pursuit but cannot find* ORESTES *who is entwined around* ATHENA's *idol. The* LEADER *sees the* footprints.]

LEADER:                                    At last!
  The clear trail of the man. After it, silent
  but it tracks his guilt to light. He's wounded—[6]
  go for the fawn, my hounds, the splash of blood,                245
  hunt him, rake him down.
                          Oh, the labor,
  the man-killing labor. My lungs are bursting . . .
  over the wide rolling earth we've ranged in flock,
  hurdling the waves in wingless flight and now we come,
  all hot pursuit, outracing ships astern—and now           250
  he's here, somewhere, cowering like a hare . . .
  the reek of human blood—it's laughter to my heart!

  [*Inciting a pair of* FURIES.]

  Look, look again, you two,
  scour the ground before he escapes—one dodge
  and the matricide slips free.

  [*Seeing* ORESTES, *one by one they press around him and* ATHENA's *idol.*]

FURIES:                        —There he is!                    255
  Clutching the knees of power[7] once again,
      twined in the deathless goddess' idol, look,
  he wants to go on trial for his crimes.
                              —Never . . .
      the mother's blood that wets the ground,
      you can never bring it back, dear god,                    260
  the Earth drinks, and the running life is gone.
                                  —No,
  you'll give me blood for blood, you must!
      Out of your living marrow I will drain
      my red libation, out of your veins I suck my good,
      my raw, brutal cups—
                          —Wither you alive,                    265
      drag you down and there you pay, agony
  for mother-killing agony!

6. The Furies track him down by scent of the blood he shed, as if he were a wounded animal leaving a trace behind him.    7. Orestes is clinging to the statue of the goddess Pallas Athena.

    —And there you will see them all.
Every mortal who outraged god or guest or loving parent:
each receives the pain his pains exact.

—A mighty god is Hades. There        270
at the last reckoning underneath the earth
 he scans all, he squares all men's accounts
and graves them on the tablets of his mind.

  [ORESTES *remains impassive.*]

ORESTES: I have suffered into truth. Well I know
 the countless arts of purging, where to speak,   275
 where silence is the rule. In this ordeal
 a compelling master urges me to speak.

  [*Looking at his hands.*]

The blood sleeps, it is fading on my hands
the stain of mother's murder washing clean.
It was still fresh at the god's hearth. Apollo    280
killed the swine and the purges drove it off.
Mine is a long story
if I'd start with the many hosts I met,
I lived with, and I left them all unharmed.
Time refines all things that age with time.    285

And now with pure, reverent lips I call
the queen of the land. Athena, help me!
Come without your spear—without a battle
you will win myself, my land, the Argive people[8]
true and just, your friends-in-arms for ever.   290
Where are you now? The scorching wilds of Libya,[9]
bathed by the Triton pool where you were born?
Robes shrouding your feet
or shod and on the march to aid allies?
Or striding the Giants' Plain,[1] marshal of armies,  295
hero scanning, flashing through the ranks?
           Come—

8. This is the first clear reference to the alliance which Athens had concluded with Argos in 459 B.C., the year before the production of the trilogy. 9. One of Athena's titles, Tritogeneia, was thought to derive from Lake Tritonis, in Libya, where some said she was born. There may be a contemporary allusion here; Athens was backing, with ships and troops, a Libyan ruler, Inaros, who was fighting the Persian rulers of Egypt. 1. Athena, a warrior-goddess, took a prominent part in the battle between the gods and the giants, in which Zeus and the Olympians won a decisive victory.

you can hear me from afar, you are a god
Set me free from this!
LEADER:                    Never—neither
Apollo's nor Athena's strength can save you.
Down you go, abandoned,                                             300
searching your soul for joy but joy is gone.
Bled white, gnawed by demons, a husk, a wraith—

[*She breaks off, waiting for reply, but* ORESTES *prays in silence.*]

No reply? you spit my challenge back?
You'll feast me alive, my fatted calf,
not cut on the altar first. Now hear my spell,                     305
the chains of song I sing to bind you tight.
FURIES:                    Come, Furies, dance!—
link arms for the dancing hand-to-hand,
now we long to reveal our art,
our terror, now to declare our right
    to steer the lives of men,                                     310
we all conspire, we dance! we are
the just and upright, we maintain.
Hold out your hands, if they are clean
    no fury of ours will stalk you,
you will go through life unscathed.                                315
But show us the guilty—one like this
    who hides his reeking hands,
and up from the outraged dead we rise,
witness bound to avenge their blood
we rise in flames against him to the end!                          320

Mother who bore me,
    O dear Mother Night,
to avenge the blinded dead
and those who see by day,
    now hear me! The whelp Apollo                                  325
spurns my rights, he tears this trembling victim
        from my grasp—the one to bleed,
    to atone away the mother-blood at last.

    Over the victim's burning head
this chant this frenzy striking frenzy                             330
    lightning crazing the mind
        this hymn of Fury

chaining the senses, ripping cross the lyre,[2]
    withering lives of men!
This, this is our right,
   spun for us by the Fates,                                      335
the ones who bind the world,
and none can shake our hold.
   Show us the mortals overcome,
insane to murder kin—we track them down
   till they go beneath the earth,                                340
and the dead find little freedom in the end.


      Over the victim's burning head
this chant this frenzy striking frenzy
     lightning crazing the mind
        this hymn of Fury                                   345
   chaining the senses, ripping cross the lyre,
     withering lives of men!


Even at birth, I say, our rights were so ordained.
   The deathless gods must keep their hands far off—
no god may share our cups, our solemn feasts.                        350
We want no part of their pious white robes—
   the Fates who gave us power made us free.


   Mine is the overthow of houses, yes,
   when warlust reared like a tame beast
     seizes near and dear—                                        355
       down on the man we swoop, aie!
        for all his power black him out!—
for the blood still fresh from slaughter on his hands.


So now, striving to wrench our mandate from the gods,
   we make ourselves exempt from their control,                    360
we brook no trial—no god can be our judge.


   [*Reaching towards* ORESTES.]


His breed, worthy of loathing, streaked with blood,
   Zeus slights, unworthy his contempt.


   Mine is the overthrow of houses, yes,
   when warlust reared like a tame beast                           365
     seizes near and dear—

---

2. Not accompanied by the lyre, an instrument associated with joyous occasions.

down on the man we sweep, aie!
   for all his power black him out!—
for the blood still fresh from slaughter on his hands.

And all men's dreams of grandeur                370
   tempting the heavens,
all melt down, under earth their pride goes down—
   lost in our onslaught, black robes swarming,
     Furies throbbing, dancing out our rage.

Yes! leaping down from the heights,                375
dead weight in the crashing footfall
   down we hurl on the runner
     breakneck for the finish—
cut him down, our fury stamps him down!

Down he goes, sensing nothing,                380
   blind with defilement . . .
darkness hovers over the man, dark guilt,
   and a dense pall overhangs his house,
     legend tells the story through her tears.

Yes! leaping down from the heights,                385
   dead weight in the crashing footfall
   down we hurl on the runner
     breakneck for the finish—
cut him down, our fury stamps him down!
     So the center holds.                390
   We are the skilled, the masterful,
    we the great fulfillers,
  memories of grief, we awesome spirits
    stern, unappeasable to man,
disgraced, degraded, drive our powers through;                395
banished far from god to a sunless, torchlit dusk,
   we drive men through their rugged passage,
    blinded dead and those who see by day.

     Then where is the man
not stirred with awe, not gripped by fear                400
   to hear us tell the law that
Fate ordains, the gods concede the Furies,
   absolute till the end of time?
  And so it holds, our ancient power still holds.
We are not without our pride, though beneath the earth                405

our strict battalions form their lines,
grouping through the mist and sun-starved night.

[*Enter* ATHENA, *armed for combat with her aegis and her spear.*]

ATHENA: From another world I heard a call for help.
I was on the Scamander's banks, just claiming Troy.
The Achaean warlords chose the hero's share                410
of what their spear had won—they decreed that land,
root and branch all mine, for all time to be,
for Theseus' sons[3] a rare, matchless gift.

Home from the wars I come, my pace unflagging,
wingless, flown on the whirring, breasting cape[4]           415
that yokes my racing spirit in her prime.

[*Unfurling the aegis, seeing* ORESTES *and the* FURIES *at her* shrine.]

And I see some new companions on the land.
Not fear, a sense of wonder fills my eyes.

Who are you? I address you all as one:
you, the stranger seated at my idol,                         420
and you, like no one born of the sown seed,
no goddess watched by the gods, no mortal either,
not to judge by your look at least, your features . . .
Wait, I call my neighbors into question.
They've done nothing wrong. It offends the rights,           425
it violates tradition.
LEADER:                         You will learn it all,
young daughter of Zeus, cut to a few words.
We are the everlasting children of the Night.
Deep in the halls of Earth they call us Curses.
ATHENA: Now I know your birth, your rightful name—           430
LEADER: But not our powers, and you will learn them quickly.
ATHENA: I can accept the facts, just tell them clearly.
LEADER: Destroyers of life: we drive them from their houses.

---

3. Homer does not mention it, but in later Athenian tradition, the two sons of Theseus, the
national hero who unified the whole of Attica under Athens, fought at Troy. This reference to
Athenian participation in the war may be another reference to contemporary reality; Athenians
had won a foothold in the Troad, the region around Troy, under the tyrant Pisistratus at the end
of the sixth century and in Aeschylus' day cities in and near the Troad, along the vital route for
grain of the Black Sea area, were part of the Athenian empire. But there is another reason for
introducing the subject of the Trojan war. In the *Agamemnon* the audience is given an almost
unrelievedly critical view of the war. But now Orestes is to be tried and acquitted; Agamemnon's
good name restored. The war has now to be presented in a favorable light. Cf. also ll. 469 ff.
4. The *aegis*, a cloak worn by Athena: it has the face of the Gorgon Medusa on it. Here Athena
uses it to fly; at other times it is used as a shield to produce terror as in *Odyssey*, XXII.

ATHENA: And the murderer's flight, where does it all end?

LEADER: Where there is no joy, the word is never used.                      435

ATHENA: Such flight for him? You shriek him on to that?

LEADER:                                                    Yes,
he murdered his mother—called that murder just.

ATHENA: And nothing forced him on, no fear of someone's anger?

LEADER: What spur would force a man to kill his mother?

ATHENA: Two sides are here, and only half is heard.                      440

LEADER: But the oath—he will neither take the oath nor give it,
no, his will is set.

ATHENA:                      And you are set
on the name of justice rather than the act.

LEADER: How? Teach us. You have a genius for refinements.

ATHENA: Injustice, I mean, should never triumph thanks to
oaths.                                                                      445

LEADER: Then examine him yourself, judge him fairly.

ATHENA: You would turn over responsibility to me,
to reach the final verdict?

LEADER:                              Certainly.
We respect you. You show us respect.

[ATHENA *turns to* ORESTES.]

ATHENA: Your turn, stranger. What do you say to this?                      450
Tell us your land, your birth, your fortunes.
Then defend yourself against their charge,
if trust in your rights has brought you here to guard
my hearth and idol, a suppliant for purging
like Ixion,[5] sacred. Speak to all this clearly,                      455
speak to me.

ORESTES:        Queen Athena, first,
the misgiving in your final words is strong.
Let me remove it. I haven't come for purging.
Look, not a stain on the hands that touch your idol.
I have proof for all I say, and it is strong.                      460

The law condemns the man of the violent hand
to silence, till a master trained at purging
slits the throat of a young suckling victim,
blood absolves his blood. Long ago
at the halls of others I was fully cleansed                      465
in the cleansing springs, the blood of many victims.
Threat of pollution—sweep it from your mind.
Now for my birth. You will know at once.

5. The Greek Cain, the first murderer. He killed his father-in-law; coming to Zeus as a suppliant, he was purified by the great god himself.

I am from Argos. My father, well you ask,
was Agamemnon, sea-lord of the men-of-war,                    470
your partisan when you made the city Troy
a city of the dead.
               What an ignoble death he died
when he came home—Ai! my blackhearted mother
cut him down, enveloped him in her handsome net—
it still attests his murder in the bath.                      475
But I came back, my years of exile weathered—
killed the one who bore me, I won't deny it,
killed her in revenge. I loved my father,
fiercely.
        And Apollo shares the guilt—
he spurred me on, he warned of the pains I'd feel            480
unless I acted, brought the guilty down.
But were we just or not? Judge us now.
My fate is in your hands. Stand or fall
I shall accept your verdict.
ATHENA:              Too large a matter,
some may think, for mortal men to judge.                      485
But by all rights not even I should decide
a case of murder—murder whets the passions.
Above all, the rites have tamed your wildness.
A suppliant, cleansed, you bring my house no harm.
If you are innocent, I'd adopt you for my city.              490

[*Turning to the* FURIES.]

But they have their destiny too, hard to dismiss,
and if they fail to win their day in court—
how it will spread, the venom of their pride,
plague everlasting blights our land, our future . . .
So it stands. A crisis either way.                            495

[*Looking back and forth from* ORESTES *to the* FURIES.]

Embrace the one? expel the other? It defeats me.

But since the matter comes to rest on us,
I will appoint the judges of manslaughter,
swear them in, and found a tribunal here
for all time to come.[6]

6. The Areopagus, which in Aeschylus' lifetime was the court which tried homicide cases.

[*To* ORESTES *and the* FURIES.]

My contestants,                                          500
summon your trusted witnesses and proofs,
your defenders under oath to help your cause.
And I will pick the finest men of Athens,
return and decide the issue fairly, truly—
bound to our oaths, our spirits bent on justice.          505

[ATHENA *leaves. The* FURIES *form their chorus.*]

FURIES: Here, now, is the overthrow
of every binding law[7]—once his appeal,
    his outrage wins the day,
his matricide! One act links all mankind,
hand to desperate hand in bloody license.                 510
    Over and over deathstrokes
        dealt by children wait their parents,
    mortal generations still unborn.

    We are the Furies still, yes
but now our rage that patrolled the crimes of men,        515
    that stalked their rage dissolves—
we loose a lethal tide to sweep the world!
Man to man foresees his neighbor's torments,
    groping to cure his own—
        poor wretch, there is no cure, no use,            520
    the drugs that ease him speed the next attack.
    Now when the sudden blows come down,
let no one sound the call that once brought help,
"Justice, hear me—Furies throned in power!"
    Oh I can hear the father now                           525
    or the mother sob with pain
        at the pain's onset . . . hopeless now,
    the house of Justice falls.

    There is a time when terror helps,
the watch man must stand guard upon the heart.            530
It helps, at times, to suffer into truth.
    Is there a man who knows no fear
    in the brightness of his heart,

7. The Furies argue that the acquittal of Orestes will be a precedent for universal crime. Furthermore, they will no longer, in that case, continue to see that vengeance is exacted; appeals to the
Furies for justice will be disregarded (523 ff.).

or a man's city, both are one,
that still reveres the rights?                                      535

    Neither the life of anarchy
    nor the life enslaved by tyrants, no,
        worship neither.
Strike the balance all in all and god will give you power;
    the laws of god may veer from north to south—          540
        we Furies plead for Measure.
    Violence is Impiety's child, true to its roots,
but the spirit's great good health breeds all we love
        and all our prayers call down,
           prosperity and peace.                        545

    All in all I tell you people,
    bow before the altar of the rights,
        revere it well.
Never trample it underfoot, your eyes set on spoils;
    revenge will hunt the godless day and night—          550
        the destined end awaits.
    So honor your parents first with reverence, I say,
    and the stranger guest you welcome to your house,
        turn to attend his needs,
        respect his sacred rights.                      555
    All of your own free will, all uncompelled,
    be just and you will never want for joy,
you and your kind can never be uprooted from the earth.
    But the reckless one—I warn the marauder
    dragging plunder, chaotic, rich beyond all rights:    560
        he'll strike his sails,
        harried at long last,
stunned when the squalls of torment break his spars to bits.

He cries to the deaf, he wrestles walls of sea
sheer whirlpools down, down, with the gods' laughter        565
breaking over the man's hot heart—they see him flailing, crushed.
    The one who boasted never to shipwreck
    now will never clear the cape and steer for home,
        who lived for wealth,
        golden his life long,                          570
rams on the reef of law and drowns unwept, unseen.

[*The scene has shifted to the Areopagus, the tribunal on the Crag of Ares.*[8] ATHENA *enters in procession with herald and ten* CITIZENS *she has chosen to be judges.*]

---

8. A literal translation of the word Areopagus.

ATHENA: Call for order, herald, marshal our good people.
    Lift the Etruscan battle-trumpet,[9]
    strain it to full pitch with human breath,
    crash out a stabbing blast along the ranks.                    575

> [*The trumpet sounds. The judges take up positions between the
> audience and the actors.* ATHENA *separates the* FURIES *and*
> ORESTES, *directing him to the Stone of Outrage and the leader
> to the Stone of Unmercifulness,*[1] *where the* FURIES *form their
> chorus. Then* ATHENA *takes her stand between two urns that
> will receive the ballots.*]

And while this court of judgment fills, my city,
    silence will be best. So that you can learn
    my everlasting laws. And you too,

> [*To* ORESTES *and the* FURIES.]

that our verdict may be well observed by all.

> [APOLLO *enters suddenly and looms behind* ORESTES.]

Lord Apollo—rule it over your own sphere!                        580
    What part have you in this? Tell us.[2]
APOLLO:                                I come
    as a witness. This man, according to custom,
    this suppliant sought out my house and hearth.
    I am the one who purged his bloody hands.
    His champion too, I share responsibility                       585
    for his mother's execution.
                                Bring on the trial.
    You know the rules, now turn them into justice.

> [ATHENA *turns to the* FURIES.]

ATHENA: The trial begins! Yours is the first word—
    the prosecution opens. Start to finish,
    set the facts before us, make them clear.                      590
LEADER: Numerous as we are, we will be brief.

> [*To* ORESTES.]

---

9. The Etruscans, a people living in central Italy, were supposed to have invented the trumpet.
1. Though Aeschylus does not mention them, we know that there were two stone bases on the
Areopagus where prosecutor and defendant took their places for the trial; naturally the Stone of
Unmercifulness was reserved for the prosecutor.    2. The manuscripts assign ll. 580–581 to the
leader of the chorus; the peremptory tone certainly sounds more suitable to the Furies than to
Athena.

Answer count for count, charge for charge.
First, tell us, did you kill your mother?
ORESTES: I killed her. There's no denying that.
LEADER: Three falls[3] in the match. One is ours already.          595
ORESTES: You exult before your man is on his back.
LEADER: But *how* did you kill her? You must tell us that.
ORESTES: I will. I drew my sword—more, I cut her throat.
LEADER: And who persuaded you? who led you on?
ORESTES: This god and his command.

    [*Indicating* APOLLO.]

                        He bears me witness.          600
LEADER: The Seer? He drove you on to matricide?
ORESTES:                          Yes,
   and to this hour I have no regrets.
LEADER:                          If the verdict
   brings you down, you'll change your story quickly.
ORESTES: I have my trust; my father will help me from the grave.
LEADER: Trust to corpses now! You made your mother one.          605
ORESTES: I do. She had two counts against her, deadly crimes.
LEADER: How? Explain that to your judges.
ORESTES: She killed her husband—killed my father too.
LEADER: But murder set her free, and you live on for trial.
ORESTES: She lived on. You never drove *her* into exile—why?          610
LEADER: The blood of the man she killed was not her own.
ORESTES: And I? Does mother's blood run in my veins?
LEADER: How could she breed you in her body, murderer?
   Disclaim your mother's blood? She gave you life.

    [ORESTES *turns to* APOLLO.]

ORESTES: Bear me witness—show me the way, Apollo!          615
   Did I strike her down with justice?
   Strike I did, I don't deny it, no.
   But how does our bloody work impress you now?—
   Just or not? Decide.
   I must make my case to them.

    [*looking to the judges.*]

   APOLLO:                          Just,          620
    I say, to you and your high court, Athena.
    Seer that I am, I never lie. Not once

---

3. There were three falls in a Greek wrestling match.

from the Prophet's thrones have I declared
a word that bears on man, woman or city
that Zeus did not command, the Olympian Father.                    625
This is *his* justice—omnipotent, I warn you.
Bend to the will of Zeus. No oath can match
the power of the Father.

LEADER:                           Zeus, you say,[4]
gave that command to your oracle? He charged
Orestes here to avenge his father's death                          630
and spurn hs mother's rights?

APOLLO:                         —Not the same
for a noble man to die, covered with praise,
his scepter the gift of god—murdererd, at that,
by a woman's hand, no arrows whipping in
from a distance as an Amazon would fight.[5]                       635
But as you will hear, Athena, and your people
poised to cast their lots and judge the case.

Home from the long campaign he came, more won
than lost on balance, home to her loyal, waiting arms,
the welcome bath . . .
                        he was just emerging at the edge,          640
and there she pitched her tent, her circling shroud—
she shackled her man in robes,
in her gorgeous never-ending web she chopped him down!

Such was the outrage of his death, I tell you,
the lord of the squadrons, that magnificent man.                   645
*Her* I draw to the life to lash your people,
marshalled to reach a verdict.

LEADER:                           Zeus, you say,
sets more store by a father's death? He shackled
his own father, Kronos proud with age.
Doesn't that contradict you?                                       650

[*To the judges.*]

Mark it well. I call you all to witness.

APOLLO:[6] You grotesque, loathsome—the gods detest you!
Zeus can break chains, we've cures for that,

---

4. The chorus wants Apollo to state clearly that Zeus gave him the specific instructions for Orestes to kill his father. When they have that assurance, they will face Apollo with a flagrant contradiction of his claim that Zeus is the champion of the father's rights (647–651).   5. The Amazons were a mythical tribe of female warriors, skilled archers, who were thought to have lived in Asia Minor on the Black Sea and to have once invaded Attica.   6. Apollo walks into the trap. Zeus only bound Kronos, he did not kill him, says Apollo. But Orestes did kill his mother.

countless ingenious ways to set us free.
But once the dust drinks down a man's blood,                    655
he is gone, once for all. No rising back,
no spell sung over the grave can sing him back—
not even Father can. Though all things else
he can overturn and never strain for breath.

LEADER:                                    So
you'd force this man's acquittal? Behold, Justice!              660

[*Exhibiting* APOLLO *and* ORESTES.]

Can a son spill his mother's blood on the ground,
then settle into his father's halls in Argos?
Where are the public altars he can use?
Can the kinsmen's holy water touch his hands?

APOLLO: Here is the truth, I tell you—see how right I am.       665
The woman you call the mother of the child[7]
is not the parent, just a nurse to the seed,
the new-sown seed that grows and swells inside her.
The *man* is the source of life—the one who mounts.
She, like a stranger for a stranger, keeps                      670
the shoot alive unless god hurts the roots.
I give you proof that all I say is true.
The father can father forth without a mother.
Here she stands, our living witness. Look—

[*Exhibiting* ATHENA.]

Child sprung full-blown from Olympian Zeus,                     675
never bred in the darkness of the womb
but such a stock no goddess could conceive!
And I, Pallas, with all my strong techniques
will rear your host and battlements to glory.
So I dispatched this suppliant to your hearth                   680
that he might be your trusted friend[8] for ever,
that you might win a new ally, dear goddess.
He and his generations arm-in-arm with yours,
your bonds stand firm for all posterity—

ATHENA:                                 Now
have we heard enough? May I have them cast                      685
their honest lots as conscience may decide?

---

7. This doctrine, that the woman is not really a parent of the child but merely a sort of receptacle and nurse, appears elsewhere in Greek literature also; it was a comforting formula for a society which, like the goddess Athena (752), honored the male. Apollo appeals for confirmation to the birth of the goddess herself; she had no mother but was born from the head of Zeus.   8. Another reference to the Athenian alliance with Argos.

LEADER: For us, we have shot our arrows, every one.
  I wait to hear how this ordeal will end.
ATHENA:                       Of course.
  And what can I do to merit your respect?
APOLLO: You have heard what you have heard.      690

   [*To the judges.*]

  Cast your lots, my friends,
  strict to the oath that you have sworn.
ATHENA:                   And now
  if you would hear my law, you men of Greece,
  you who will judge the first trial of bloodshed.

  Now and forever more, for Aegeus' people[9]     695
  this will be the court where judges reign.
  This is the Crag of Ares, where the Amazons
  pitched their tents when they came marching down
  on Theseus, full tilt in their fury, erecting
  a new city to overarch his city, towers thrust     700
  against his towers—they sacrificed to Ares,
  named this rock from that day onward Ares' Crag.

  Here from the heights, terror and reverence,
  my people's kindred powers
  will hold them from injustice through the day     705
  and through the mild night. Never pollute
  our law with innovations. No, my citizens,
  foul a clear well and you will suffer thirst.

  Neither anarchy nor tyranny,[1] my people.
  Worship the Mean, I urge you,     710
  shore it up with reverence and never
  banish terror from the gates, not outright.
  Where is the righteous man who knows no fear?
  The stronger your fear, your reverence for the just,
  the stronger your country's wall and city's safety,     715
  stronger by far than all men else possess
  in Scythia's rugged steppes[2] or Pelops' level plain.
  Untouched by lust for spoil, this court of law

9. The Athenians; Aegeus was the father of Theseus.    1. Athena repeats the advice and even
the words of the Furies (536 ff).    2. In S. Russia; *Pelops' level plain* is the Peloponnese—central
Greece. The expression may signify just geographical expanse but there is possibly also an appropriateness in the choice of the two locations; the Scythians were famous for their good laws and
the Peloponnese was the territory of Sparta, famous for its stable constitution.

majestic, swift to fury, rising above you
as you sleep, our night watch always wakeful,                    720
guardian of our land—I found it here and now.
So I urge you, Athens. I have drawn this out
to rouse you to your future. You must rise,
each man must cast his lot and judge the case,
reverent to his oath. Now I have finished.                       725

[*The judges come forward, pass between the urns and cast their
lots.*]

LEADER: Beware. Our united force can break your land.
   Never wound our pride, I tell you, never.
APOLLO: The oracles, not mine alone but Zeus', too—
   dread them, I warn you, never spoil their fruit.              730

[*The* LEADER *turns to* APOLLO.]

LEADER: You dabble in works of blood beyond your depth.
   Oracles, your oracles will be stained forever.
APOLLO: Oh, so the Father's judgment faltered when Ixion,
   the first man-slayer, came to him for purging?
LEADER: Talk on, talk on. But if I lose this trial
   I will return in force to crush the land.                     735
APOLLO: Never—among the gods, young and old,
   you go disgraced. I will triumph over you!
LEADER: Just as you triumphed in the house of Pheres,[3]
   luring the Fates to set men free from death.
APOLLO: What?—is it a crime to help the pious man,               740
   above all, when his hour of need has come?
LEADER: You brought them down, the oldest realms of order,
   seduced the ancient goddesses with wine.
APOLLO: *You* will fail this trial—in just a moment
   sprew your venom and never harm your enemies.                 745
LEADER: You'd ride me down, young god, for all my years?
   Well here I stand, waiting to learn the verdict.
   Torn with doubt . . . . to rage against the city or—
ATHENA: My work is here, to render the final judgment.
   Orestes,

[*Raising her arm, her hand clenched as if holding a ballot-stone.*]

3. Father of Admetus, king of Thessaly. Apollo repaid kindness shown him by Admetus by persuading the fates to let Admetus avoid an early death if he could find someone willing to die in
his stead. (His wife Alcestis was willing; this is the subject of Euripides' famous play *Alcestis*.)
According to the Furies (743) Apollo got the Fates drunk.

I will cast my lot for you.                                    750
No mother gave me birth.
I honor the male, in all things but marriage.
Yes, with all my heart I am my Father's child.
I cannot set more store by the woman's death—
she killed her husband, guardian of their house.    755
Even if the vote is equal, Orestes wins.[4]

Shake the lots from the urns. Quickly,
you of the jury charge to make the count.

[*Judges come forward, empty the urns, and count the ballot-stones.*]

ORESTES: O God of the Light, Apollo, how will the verdict go?
LEADER: O Night, dark mother, are you watching now?    760
ORESTES: Now for the goal—the noose, or the new day!
LEADER: Now we go down, or forge ahead in power.
APOLLO: Shake out the lots and count them fairly, friends.
  Honor Justice. An error in judgment now
  can mean disaster. The cast of a single lot    765
  restores a house to greatness.

[*Receiving the judges' count,* ATHENA *lifts her arm once more.*]

ATHENA:               The man goes free,
  cleared of the charge of blood. The lots are equal.
ORESTES: O Pallas Athena—you, you save my house!
  I was shorn of the fatherland but you
  reclaim it for me. Now any Greek will say,    770
  "He lives again, the man of Argos lives
  on his fathers' great estates. Thanks to Pallas,
  Apollo, and Zeus, the lord of all fulfillment,
  Third, Saving Zeus." He respected father's death,
  looked down on mother's advocates—

[*Indicating the* FURIES.]

                        he saved me.    775
And now I journey home. But first I swear
to you, your land and assembled host, I swear
by the future years that bring their growing yield

---

4. So, in Athenian courts, a split jury meant acquittal. Athena announces that if the votes are equal, she will give a casting vote for acquittal. (At the real court of the Areopagus, if the votes were equal, the defendant was declared acquitted by "the vote of Athena.")

that no man, no helmsman of Argos wars on Athens,
spears in the vanguard moving out for conquest.                    780
We ourselves, even if we must rise up from the grave,[5]
will deal with those who break the oath I take—
baffle them with disasters, curse their marches,
send them hawks on the left[6] at every crossing—
make their pains recoil upon their heads.                          785
But all who keep our oath, who uphold your rights
and citadel for ever, comrades spear to spear,
we bless with all the kindness of our heart.

Now farewell, you and the people of your city.
Good wrestling—a grip no foe can break.                            790
A saving hope, a spear to ring you triumph!

[*Exit* ORESTES, *followed by* APOLLO. *The* FURIES *reel in wild
confusion around* ATHENA.]

FURIES: You, you younger gods!—you have ridden down
    the ancient laws, wrenched them from my grasp—
  and I, robbed of my birthright, suffering, great with wrath,
    I loose my poison over the soil, aieee!—                       795
poison to match my grief comes pouring out my heart,
        cursing the land to burn it sterile and now
rising up from its roots a cancer blasting leaf and child,
        now for Justice, Justice!—cross the face of the earth
the bloody tide comes hurling, all mankind destroyed.              800
. . . Moaning, only moaning? What will I do?
    The mockery of it, Oh unbearable,
mortified by Athens,
we the daughters of Night,
our power stripped, cast down.
ATHENA:                        Yield to me.                         805
    No more heavy spirits. You were not defeated—
the vote was tied, a verdict fairly reached
with no disgrace to you, no, Zeus brought
luminous proof before us. He who spoke
god's oracle, he bore witness that Orestes                         810
did the work but should not suffer harm.

And now you'd vent your anger, hurt the land?
Consider a moment. Calm yourself. Never
render us barren, raining your potent showers

5. Orestes will be a "hero" in the Greek sense: a protecting spirit for the land.   6. Birds seen
on the left were a portent of a evil to come.

down like spears, consuming every seed.                          815
By all my rights I promise you your seat
in the depths of earth, yours by all rights—
stationed at hearths equipped with glistening thrones,
covered with praise! My people will revere you.

FURIES: You, you younger gods! you have ridden down            820
        the ancient laws, wrenched them from my grasp—
and I, robbed of my birthright, suffering, great with wrath,
        I loose my poison over the soil, aieee!—
poison to match my grief comes pouring out my heart,
        cursing the land to burn it sterile and now           825
rising up from its roots a cancer blasting leaf and child,
        now for Justice, Justice!—cross the face of the earth
the bloody tide comes hurling, all mankind destroyed.
. . . Moaning, only moaning? What will I do?
        The mockery of it, Oh unbearable,                     830
mortified by Athens,
we the daughters of Night,
our power stripped, cast down.
ATHENA:                  You have your power,
        you are goddesses—but not to turn
on the world of men and ravage it past cure.                  835
I put my trust in Zeus and . . . must I add this?
I am the only god who knows the keys
to the armory where his lightning-bolt is sealed.
No need of that, not here.
        Let me persuade you.
The lethal spell of your voice, never cast it                 840
down on the land and blight its harvest home.
Lull asleep that salt black wave of anger—
awesome, proud with reverence, live with me.
The land is rich, and more, when its first fruits,
offered for heirs and the marriage rites,[7] are yours      845
to hold forever, you will praise my words.
FURIES: But for me to suffer such disgrace . . . I,
        the proud heart of the past, driven under the earth,
condemned, like so much filth,
        and the fury in me breathing hatred—                  850
O good Earth,
        what is this stealing under the breast,
what agony racks the spirit? . . . Night, dear Mother Night!
All's lost, our ancient powers torn away by their cunning,

---

7. The Erinyes, as spirits of the earth, did in fact receive in Athens offerings for children born
and marriages made.

ruthless hands, the gods so hard to wrestle down                    855
  obliterate us all.
ATHENA:          I will bear with your anger.
  You are older. The years have taught you more,
  much more than I can know. But Zeus, I think,
  gave me some insight, too, that has its merits.
  If you leave for an alien land and alien people,              860
  you will come to love this land, I promise you.
  As time flows on, the honors flow through all
  my citizens, and you, throned in honor
  before the house of Erechtheus,[8] will harvest
  more from men and women moving in solemn file                 865
  than you can win throughout the mortal world.

  Here in our homeland never cast the stones
  that whet our bloodlust. Never waste our youth,
  inflaming them with the burning wine of strife.
  Never pluck the heart of the battle cock                      870
  and plant it in our people—intestine war
seething against themselves. Let our wars
  rage on abroad,[9] with all their force, to satisfy
  our powerful lust for fame. But as for the bird
  that fights at home—my curse on civil war.                    875

  This is the life I offer, it is yours to take.
  Do great things, feel greatness, greatly honored.
  Share this country cherished by the gods.
FURIES: But for me to suffer such disgrace . . . I,
  the proud heart of the past, driven under the earth,          880
  condemned, like so much filth,
     and the fury in me breathing hatred—
  O good Earth,
     what is this stealing under the breast,
  what agony racks the spirit? . . . Night, dear Mother Night!   885
  All's lost, our ancient powers torn away by their cunning,
  ruthless hands, the gods so hard to wrestle down
  obliterate us all.
ATHENA:         No, I will never tire
  of telling you your gifts. So that you,
  the older gods, can never say that I,                          890
  a young god and the mortals of my city
  drove you outcast, outlawed from the land.

8. The old shrine of Erechtheus on the Acropolis had been destroyed by the Persians in 480 B.C.;
in 421 B.C. the Athenians began the construction of the new Erechtheum, which, much damaged, still stands.    9. Athens was at this time at war with Sparta and her forces may still have
been engaged in Egypt.

But if you have any reverence for Persuasion,
the majesty of Persuasion,
the spell of my voice that would appease your fury—     895
Oh please stay . . .
                    and if you refuse to stay,
it would be wrong, unjust to afflict this city
with wrath, hatred, populations routed. Look,
it is all yours, a royal share of our land—
justly entitled, glorified for ever.

LEADER:                          Queen Athena,     900
where is the home you say is mine to hold?

ATHENA: Where all the pain and anguish end. Accept it.

LEADER: And if I do, what honor waits for me?

ATHENA: No house can thrive without you.

LEADER:                              You would do that,
grant me that much power?

ATHENA:                    Whoever reveres us—     905
we will raise the fortunes of their lives.

LEADER: And you will pledge me that, for all time to come?

ATHENA: Yes—I must never promise things I cannot do.

LEADER: Your magic is working . . . I can feel the hate,
the fury slip away.

ATHENA:              At last! And now take root     910
in the land and win yourself new friends.

LEADER:                              A spell—
what spell to sing? to bind the land for ever? Tell us.

ATHENA: Nothing that strikes a note of brutal conquest. Only peace—
blessings, rising up from the earth and the heaving sea,
and down the vaulting sky let the wind-gods breathe     915
a wash of sunlight streaming through the land,
and the yield of soil and grazing cattle flood
our city's life with power and never flag
with time. Make the seed of men live on,
the more they worship you the more they thrive.     920
I love them as a gardener loves his plants,
these upright men, this breed fought free of grief.
All that is yours to give.
                    And I,
in the trials of war where fighters burn for fame,
will never endure the overthrow of Athens—     925
all will praise her, victor city, pride of man.


[*The* FURIES *assemble, dancing around* ATHENA, *who becomes
their leader.*]

FURIES:                        I will embrace
                    one home with you, Athena,
                        never fail the city
                you and Zeus almighty, you and Ares                    930
                hold as the fortress of the gods, the shield
            of the high Greek altars, glory of the powers.
                        like a prophet's warm and kind,
                        that the rare good things of life              935
                            come rising crest on crest,
                    sprung from the rich black earth and
                gleaming with the bursting flash of sun.

ATHENA: These blessings I bestow on you, my people, gladly.
        I enthrone these strong, implacable spirits here              940
        and root them in our soil.

                            Theirs,
                theirs to rule the lives of men,
                    it is their fated power.
        But he who has never felt their weight,
        or known the blows of life and how they fall,                 945
        the crimes of his fathers hale him toward their bar,
        and there for all his boasts—destruction,
                silent, majestic in anger,
        crushes him to dust.

FURIES:

                            Yes and I ban
                the winds that rock the olive—                        950
                    hear my love, my blessing—
            thwart their scorching heat that blinds the buds,
                hold from our shores the killing icy gales,
        and I ban the blight that creeps on fruit and withers—
                God of creation, Pan, make flocks increase            955
                    and the ewes drop fine twin lambs
                        when the hour of labor falls.
                    And silver,[1] child of Earth,
                        secret treasure of Hermes,
            come to light and praise the gifts of god.

ATHENA: Blessings—now do you hear, you guards of Athens,              960
        all that she will do?
        Fury the mighty queen, the dread
        of the deathless gods and those beneath the earth,
        deals with mortals clearly, once for all.                     965

---

1. At Laurion, in SE Attica, silver had been mined for many years when, sometime before 480 B.C., rich new veins were discovered. The Athenians used the money to build the fleet which fought at Salamis.

She delivers songs to some, to others
   a blinding life of tears—
Fury works her will.

FURIES:
               And the lightning stroke
      that cuts men down before their prime, I curse,
       but the lovely girl who finds a mate's embrace,      970
the deep joy of wedded life—O grant that gift, that prize,
    you gods of wedlock, grant it, goddesses of Fate!
        Sisters born of the Night our mother,
            spirits steering law,
          sharing at all our hearths,      975
         at all times bearing down
        to make our lives more just,
      all realms exalt you highest of the gods.

ATHENA: Behold, my land, what blessings Fury kindly,
   gladly brings to pass—      980
I am in my glory! Yes, I love Persuasion;
she watched my words, she met their wild refusals.
Thanks to Zeus of the Councils who can turn
dispute to peace—he won the day.

[*To the* FURIES.]

Thanks to our duel for blessings;      985
we win through it all.

FURIES:
             And the brutal stife,
       the civil war devouring men, I pray
      that it never rages through our city, no
that the good Greek soil never drinks the blood of Greeks,
      shed in an orgy of reprisal life for life—      990
        that Fury like a beast will never
          rampage through the land.
       Give joy in return for joy,
         one common will for love,
        and hate with one strong heart:      995
     such union heals a thousand ills of man.

ATHENA: Do you *hear* how Fury sounds her blessings forth,
   how Fury finds the way?
Shining out of the terror of their faces
I can see great gains for you, my people.      1000
Hold them kindly, kind as they are to you.
Exalt them always, you exalt you land,

your city straight and just—
  its light goes through the world.

FURIES:
                         Rejoice,
                 rejoice in destined wealth,                    1005
                 rejoice, Athena's people—
                 poised by the side of Zeus,
           loved by the loving virgin girl,
                 achieve humanity at last,
                 nestling under Pallas' wings                   1010
           and blessed with Father's love.

ATHENA: You too rejoice! and I must lead the way
  to your chambers by the holy light of these,
           your escorts bearing fire.

[*Enter* ATHENA*'s entourage of women, bearing offerings and victims and torches still unlit.*]

Come, and speed beneath the earth                               1015
  by our awesome sacrifices,
keep destruction from the borders,
bring prosperity home to Athens,
triumph sailing in its wake.
                         And you,
my people born of the Rock King,[2]                             1020
lead on our guests for life, my city—
May they treat you with compassion,
compassionate as you will be to them.

FURIES:
                 Rejoice!—
           rejoice—the joy resounds—
           all those who dwell in Athens,                       1025
                 spirits and mortals, come,
                 govern Athena's city well,
           revere us well, we are your guests;
           you will learn to praise your Furies,
           you will praise the fortunes of your lives.          1030

ATHENA: My thanks! And I will speed your prayers, your blessings—
  lit by the torches breaking into flame
  I send you home, home to the core of Earth,
  escorted by these friends who guard my idol
  duty-bound.

2. A legendary ancestor, Cranaos, whose name means "rocky." The soil of Attica is not rich.

[ATHENA's *entourage comes forward, bearing crimson robes.*]

Bright eye of the land of Theseus,                1035
come forth, my splendid troupe. Girls and mothers,
trains of aged women grave in movement,
dress our Furies now in blood-red robes.[3]
Praise them—let the torch move on!
So the love this family bears towards our land      1040
will bloom in human strength from age to age.

[*The women invest the* FURIES *and sing the final chorus. Torches blaze; a procession forms, including the actors and the judges and the audience.* ATHENA *leads them from the theater and escorts them through the city.*]

THE WOMEN OF THE CITY: On, on, good spirits born for glory,
Daughters of Night, her children always young,
        now under loyal escort—
Blessings, people of Athens, sing your blessings out.      1045

Deep, deep in the first dark vaults of Earth,
sped by the praise and victims we will bring,
        reverence will attend you—
Blessings now, all people, sing your blessings out.

You great good Furies, bless the land with kindly hearts,    1050
you Awesome Spirits,[4] come—exult in the blazing torch,
        exultant in our fires, journey on.
Cry, cry in triumph, carry on the dancing on and on!
This peace between Athena's people and their guests
must never end. All-seeing Zeus and Fate embrace,       1055
        down they come to urge our union on—
Cry, cry, in triumph, carry on the dancing on and on!

---

# SOPHOCLES
## 496–406 B.C.

Aeschylus belonged to the generation which fought at Marathon; his manhood and his old age were passed in the heroic period of the Persian defeat

3. At the Great Panathenea, the principal festival of Athens, resident aliens as well as full citizens took part in the procession to the Acropolis. The resident aliens, *metics* as they were called, wore crimson cloaks on this occasion. The Furies are thus given residential status in Attic soil.
4. *Semnai* in Greek, a favorable formula for the Furies, like *Eumenides* (Kindly Ones), the title of the play.

on Greek soil and the war which Athens fought to liberate her kinsmen in the islands of the Aegean and on the Asiatic coast. Sophocles, his younger contemporary, lived to see an Athens which had advanced in power and prosperity far beyond the city that Aeschylus knew. The league of free Greek cities against Persia which Athens had led to victory in the Aegean had become an empire, in which Athens taxed and coerced the subject cities that had once been her free allies. Sophocles, born around 496 B.C., played his part, a prominent one, in the city's affairs. In 443 B.C. he served as one of the treasurers of the imperial league and, with Pericles, as one of the ten generals elected for the war against the island of Samos which tried to secede from the Athenian league a few years later. When the Athenian expedition to Sicily ended in disaster, Sophocles was appointed to a special committee set up in 411 B.C. to deal with the emergency. He died in 406, two years before Athens surrendered to Sparta.

His career as a brilliantly successful dramatist began in 468; in that year he won first prize at the Dionysia, competing against Aeschylus. Over the next sixty-two years he produced over a hundred and twenty plays; he won first prize no less than twenty-four times and when he was not first, came in second, never third.

Aeschylus had been actor as well as playwright and director but Sophocles, early in his career, gave up acting. It was he who added a third actor to the team; the early Aeschylean plays (*Persians, Seven Against Thebes*, and *Suppliants*) can be played by two actors (who of course can change masks to extend the range of *dramatis personae*). In the *Oresteia*, Aeschylus has taken advantage of the Sophoclean third actor; this makes possible the role of Cassandra, the one three-line speech of Pylades in *Libation Bearers*, and the trial scene in *Eumenides*. But Sophocles used his third actor to create complex triangular scenes like the dialogue between Oedipus and the Corinthian messenger, which reveals to a listening Jocasta the ghastly truth which Oedipus will not discover until the next scene.

We have only seven of his plays and not many of them can be accurately dated. The *Ajax* (which deals with the suicide of the hero whose shade turns silently away from Odysseus in the *Odyssey*) and the *Trachiniae* (the story of the death of Heracles) are both generally thought to be early productions. *Antigone* is fairly securely fixed in the late 440s and *Oedipus the King* was probably staged during the early years of the Peloponnesian War, which began in 431 B.C. For *Electra* we have no date but it is probably later than *Oedipus the King*. *Philoctetes*, a tale of the Trojan War, was staged in 409 B.C. and *Oedipus at Colonus*, which presents Oedipus' strangely triumphant death on Athenian soil, was produced after Sophocles' death.

Most of these plays date from the last half of the fifth century; they were written in and for an Athens that, since the days of Aeschylus, had undergone an intellectual revolution. It was in a time of critical re-evaluation of accepted standards and traditions (see pp. 6–9) that Sophocles, in the early years of the Peloponnesian war (431–404 B.C.), produced his masterpiece, *Oedipus the King*, and the problems of the time are reflected in the play.

## OEDIPUS THE KING

This tragedy, which deals with a man of high principles and probing intelligence who follows the prompting of that intelligence to the final consequence of true self-knowledge, which makes him put out his eyes, was as full of significance for Sophocles' contemporaries as it is for us. Unlike a modern dramatist, Sophocles used for his tragedy a story well known to the audience and as old as their own history, a legend told by father to son, handed down from generation to generation because of its implicit wealth of meaning, learned in childhood and rooted deep in the consciousness of every member of the community. Such a story the Greeks called a *myth*, and the use of it presented Sophocles, as it did Aeschylus in his trilogy, with material which, apart from its great inherent dramatic potential, already possessed the significance and authority which the modern dramatist must create for himself. It had the authority of history, for the history of ages which leave no records is myth—that is to say, the significant event of the past, stripped of irrelevancies and imaginatively shaped by the oral tradition. It had a religious authority, for the Oedipus story, like the story of the house of Atreus, is concerned with the relation between man and god. Lastly, and this is especially true of the Oedipus myth, it had the power, because of its subject matter, to arouse the irrational hopes and fears which lie deep and secret in the human consciousness.

The use of the familiar myth enabled the dramatist to draw on all its wealth of unformulated meaning, but it did not prevent him from striking a contemporary note. Oedipus, in Sophocles' play, is at one and the same time the mysterious figure of the past who broke the most fundamental human taboos and a typical fifth-century Athenian. His character contains all the virtues for which the Athenians were famous and the vices for which they were notorious. The best commentary on Oedipus' character is the speech which Thucydides, the contemporary historian of the Peloponnesian War, attributed to a Corinthian spokesman at Sparta: it is a hostile but admiring assessment of the Athenian genius. "Athenians . . . [are] equally quick in the conception and in the execution of every new plan"—so Oedipus has already sent to Delphi when the priest advises him to do so, and has already sent for Tiresias when the chorus suggests this course of action. "They are bold beyond their strength; they run risks which prudence would condemn"—as Oedipus risked his life to answer the riddle of the Sphinx and later, in spite of the oracle about his marriage, accepted the hand of the queen. "In the midst of misfortune they are full of hope"—so Oedipus, when he is told that he is not the son of Polybus and Merope, and Jocasta has already realized whose son he is, claims that he is the "child of Fortune." "When they do not carry out an intention which they have formed, they seem to have sustained a personal bereavement"—so Oedipus, shamed by Jocasta and the chorus into sparing Creon's life, yields sullenly and petulantly.

The Athenian devotion to the city, which received the main emphasis in Pericles' praise of Athens, is strong in Oedipus; his answer to the priest at the beginning of the play shows that he is a conscientious and patriotic ruler. His sudden unreasoning rage is the characteristic fault of Athenian democracy, which in 406 B.C., to give only one instance, condemned and executed the generals who had failed, in the stress of weather and battle, to pick up the drowned bodies of their own men killed in the naval engagement at Arginusae. Oedipus is like the fifth-century Athenian most of all in his confidence in the human intelligence, especially his own. This confidence takes him in the play through the whole cycle of the critical, rationalist movement of the century, from the piety and orthodoxy he displays in the opening scene, through his taunts at oracles when he hears that Polybus is dead, to the despairing courage with which he accepts the consequences when he sees the abyss opening at his feet. "Ah master, do I *have* to speak?" asks the herdsman from whom he is dragging the truth. "You have to," Oedipus replies. "And I *have* to hear." And hear he does. He learns that the oracle he had first fought against and then laughed at has been fulfilled; that every step his intelligence prompted was one step nearer to disaster; that his knowledge was ignorance, his clear vision blindness. Faced with the reality that his determined probing finally reveals, he puts out his eyes.

The relation of Oedipus' character to the development of the action is the basis of the most famous attempt to define the nature of the tragic process, Aristotle's theory that pity and terror are aroused most effectively by the spectacle of a man who is "not pre-eminent in virtue and justice, and yet on the other hand does not fall into misfortune through vice or depravity, but falls because of some mistake, one among the number of the highly renowned and prosperous, such as Oedipus." Other references by Aristotle to this play make it clear that this influential critical canon is based particularly on Sophocles' masterpiece and the canon has been universally applied to the play. But the great influence (and validity) of the Aristotelian theory should not be allowed to obscure the fact that Sophocles' *Oedipus the King* is more highly organized and economical than Aristotle implies. The fact that the critics have differed about the nature of Oedipus' mistake or frailty (his errors are many and his frailties include anger, impiety, and self-confidence) is a clue to the real situation. Oedipus falls not through "some vicious mole of nature" or some "particular fault" (to use Hamlet's terms), but because he is the man he is, because of all aspects of his character, good and bad alike; and the development of the action right through to the catastrophe shows us every aspect of his character at work in the process of self-revelation and self-destruction. His first decision in the play, to hear Creon's message from Delphi in public rather than, as Creon suggests, in private, is evidence of his kingly solicitude for his people and his trust in them, but it makes certain the full publication of the truth. His impetuous proclamation of a curse on the murderer of Laius, an unnecessary step prompted by his civic zeal, makes his final situation worse than it need have been. His anger at Tiresias forces a revelation which drives him on to accuse Creon; this in turn provokes Jocasta's revelations. And throughout the play his confidence in the efficacy of his own action, his hopefulness as the situation darkens, and his passion for discovering the truth, guide the steps of the investigation which is to reveal the detective as the criminal. All aspects of his character, good and bad alike, are equally involved; it is no frailty or error that leads him to the terrible truth, but his total personality.

The character of Oedipus as revealed in the play does something more than explain the present action, it also explains his past. In Oedipus' speeches and actions on stage we can see the man who, given the circumstances in which Oedipus was involved, would inevitably do just what Oedipus has done. Each action on stage shows us the mood in which he committed some action in the past; his angry death sentence on Creon reveals the man who killed Laius because of an insult on the highway; his impulsive proclamation of total excommunication for the unknown murderer shows us the man who, without forethought, accepted the hand of Jocasta; his intelligent, persistent search for the truth shows us the brain and the courage which solved the riddle of the Sphinx. The revelation of his character in the play is at once a re-creation of his past and an interpretation of the oracle which predicted his future.

This organization of the material is what makes it possible for us to accept the story as tragedy at all, for it emphasizes Oedipus' independence of the oracle. When we first see Oedipus, he has already committed the actions for which he is to suffer, actions prophesied, before his birth, by Apollo. But the dramatist's emphasis on Oedipus' character suggests that although Apollo has predicted what Oedipus will do, he does not determine it; Oedipus determines his own conduct, by being the man he is. Milton's explanation of a similar situation, Adam's fall and God's foreknowledge of it, may be applied to Oedipus; foreknowledge had no influence on his fault. The relationship between Apollo's prophecy and Oedipus' actions is not that of cause and effect. It is the relationship of two independent entities which are equated.

This correspondence between his character and his fate removes the obstacle to our full acceptance of the play which an external fate governing his action would set up. Nevertheless, we feel that he suffers more than he deserves. He has served as an example of the inadequacy of the human intellect and a warning that there is a power in the universe which humanity cannot control, nor even fully understand, but Oedipus the man still has our sympathy. Sophocles felt this too, and in a later play, his last, the *Oedipus at Colonus*, he dealt with the reward which finally balanced Oedipus' suffering. In *Oedipus the King* itself there is a foreshadowing of this final development; the last scene shows us a man already beginning to recover from the shock of the catastrophe and reasserting a natural superiority.

"I am going—you know on what condition?" he says to Creon when ordered back into the house, and a few lines later Creon has to say bluntly to him: "Still the king, the master of all things? No more; here your power ends." This renewed imperiousness is the first expression of a feeling on his part that he is not entirely guilty, a beginning of the reconstitution of the magnificent man of the opening scenes; it reaches its fulfillment in the final Oedipus play, the *Oedipus at Colonus*, in which he is a titanic figure, confident of his innocence and more masterful than he has ever been.

## Antigone

Though the *Antigone* was almost certainly produced before *Oedipus the King*, it deals with mythological events which, in the story, come after the exposure of Oedipus' identity and his self-blinding. Creon eventually expelled Oedipus from Thebes, to wander as a blind beggar, accompanied only by his daughter Antigone. His sons, Eteocles and Polynices, raised no hand to help him; when he died at Colonus, near Athens, Antigone returned to Thebes. Eteocles and Polynices, who had agreed to rule jointly, soon quarreled; they fought each other for the throne of Thebes. Eteocles expelled his brother, who recruited supporters in Argos; seven champions attacked the seven gates of Thebes. The assault was beaten off; but Polynices and Eteocles killed each other in the battle. The rule of Thebes fell to Creon. His first decision is to forbid burial to the corpse of Polynices, the traitor who brought foreign troops against his own city. Antigone disobeys the decree by scattering dust on the body; captured and brought before Creon, she defies him in the name of the eternal unwritten laws. In the struggle between them it is the king who in the end surrenders; he buries the body of Polynices and orders Antigone's release. But she has already killed herself in her underground prison, thus bringing about the two deaths which crush her enemy, the suicides of his son Haemon and of his wife Eurydice.

Antigone, as a heroine of the resistance to tyrannical power, has deservedly become one of the Western world's great symbolic figures; she is clearly presented, in her famous speech, as a champion of a higher morality against the overriding claims of state necessity, which the Sophist intellectuals of Sophocles' time had begun to formulate in philosophical terms. But Creon, too, is given his due; he is not a mere tyrant of melodrama but a ruler whose action stems from political and religious attitudes which were probably shared by many of the audience. Antigone and Creon clash not only as individuals, shaped with all Sophocles' dramatic genius (the ancient anonymous biography of Sophocles says truly that he could "match the moment with the action so as to create a whole character out of half a line or even a single word"), but also as representatives of two irreconcilable social and religious positions.

Antigone's chief loyalty is clearly to the family. She makes no distinction between the brothers though one was a patriot and the other a traitor, and when her sister Ismene refuses to help her defy the state to bury a brother she harshly disowns her. The denial of burial to Polynices strikes directly at her family loyalty, for it was the immemorial privilege and duty of the women of the house to mourn the dead man in unrestrained sorrow, sing his praises, wash his body, and consign him to the earth. Creon, on the other hand, sees loyalty to the state as the only valid criterion, and in his opening speech expressly repudiates one who "places a friend above the good of his own country" (the Greek word translated "friend" also means "relative"). This inaugural address of Creon repeats many concepts and even phrases that are to be found in the speeches of the democratic leader Pericles; and in fact, there was an ancient antagonism between the new democratic institutions which stressed the equal rights and obligations of all citizens and the old powerful families which through their wide influence had acted as separate factions in the body politic. The nature of Creon's assertion of state against family, refusal of burial to a corpse, is repellent, but the principle behind it was one most Athenians would have accepted as valid.

These opposing social viewpoints have their corresponding religious sanctions. For Antigone, the gods, especially the gods below, demand equality for all the dead, the common inalienable right of burial. But Creon's gods are the gods who protect the city; how, he asks, could those gods have any feeling for Polynices, a traitor who raised and led a foreign army against the city they protect and which contains their temples? Here again, there must have been many in the audience who saw merit in this argument.

But as the action develops, whatever validity Creon's initial position may have had is destroyed, and by Creon himself. For like all holders of absolute power, he proceeds, when challenged, to equate loyalty to the community with loyalty to himself—"the city *is* the king's—that's the law!" he tells his son Haemon. And in the end the prophet Tiresias tells him plainly that Antigone was right—the gods are on her side. He swallows his pride and surrenders, but too late. Antigone's suicide brings him to disaster in that institution, the family, which he subordinated to reasons of state; his son spits in his face before killing himself, and his wife dies cursing him as the murderer of his son.

Creon is punished, but Antigone is dead. As the play ends, the chorus points a moral: the "mighty blows of fate . . . at long last . . . will teach us wisdom." But the price of wisdom is high: the *Antigone*, like so many of the Shakespearean tragedies, leaves us with a poignant sense of loss.

C. H. Whitman, *Sophocles, A Study in Heroic Humanism* (1951), is a brilliant study, which explores an approach very different from that proposed here. S. M. Adams, *Sophocles the Playwright* (1957), pays particular attention to dramatic technique. B. M. W. Knox, *Oedipus at Thebes* (1957), is a detailed examination of the play in the context of its age; Knox's *The Heroic Temper* (1964) concentrates on the characters of Oedipus, Antigone, Electra, and Philoctetes. Sophocles, *The Three Theban Plays*, translated by R. Fagles, introductions and notes by B. Knox (1982), contains substantial introductions to *Oedipus the King* and *Antigone*.

# Oedipus the King[1]

## Characters

OEDIPUS, *king of Thebes*
A PRIEST *of Zeus*
CREON, *brother of Jocasta*
A CHORUS *of Theban citizens and their Leader*
TIRESIAS, *a blind prophet*
JOCASTA, *the queen, wife of Oedipus*
A MESSENGER *from Corinth*
A SHEPHERD
A MESSENGER *from inside the palace*
ANTIGONE, ISMENE, *daughters of Oedipus and Jocasta*
GUARDS *and attendants*
PRIESTS *of Thebes*

1. Translated by Robert Fagles.

[TIME AND SCENE: *The royal house of Thebes. Double doors
dominate the facade; a stone altar stands at the center of the
stage.*

    *Many years have passed since* OEDIPUS *solved the riddle of
the Sphinx and ascended the throne of Thebes, and now a plague has struck the city. A procession of priests enters; suppliants, broken and despondent, they carry branches wound in
wool and lay them on the altar.*

    *The doors open. Guards assemble.* OEDIPUS *comes forward,
majestic but for a telltale limp, and slowly views the condition
of his people.*]

OEDIPUS: Oh my children, the new blood of ancient Thebes,
    why are you here? Huddling at my altar,
    praying before me, your branches wound in wool.[2]
    Our city reeks with the smoke of burning incense,
    rings with cries for the Healer[3] and wailing for the dead.     5
    I thought it wrong, my children, to hear the truth
    from others, messengers. Here I am myself—
    you all know me, the world knows my fame:
    I am Oedipus.

      [*Helping a Priest to his feet.*]

                  Speak up, old man. Your years,
    your dignity—you should speak for the others.     10
    Why here and kneeling, what preys upon you so?
    Some sudden fear? some strong desire?
    You can trust me. I am ready to help,
    I'll do anything. I would be blind to misery
    not to pity my people kneeling at my feet.     15
PRIEST: Oh Oedipus, king of the land, our greatest power!
    You see us before you now, men of all ages
    clinging to your altars. Here are boys,
    still too weak to fly from the nest,
    and here the old, bowed down with the years,     20
    the holy ones—a priest of Zeus myself—and here
    the picked, unmarried men, the young hope of Thebes.
    And all the rest, your great family gathers now,
    branches wreathed, massing in the squares,
    kneeling before the two temples of queen Athena     25
    or the river-shrine where the embers glow and die

---

2. The insignia of suppliants, laid on the altar and left there until the suppliant's request was
granted. At the end of the scene, when Oedipus promises action, he will tell them to take the
branches away.   **3.** A title of Apollo.

and Apollo sees the future in the ashes.[4]
                                    Our city—
look around you, see with your own eyes—
our ship pitches wildly, cannot lift her head
from the depths, the red waves of death . . .                    30
Thebes is dying. A blight on the fresh crops
and the rich pastures, cattle sicken and die,
and the women die in labor, children stillborn,
and the plague, the fiery god of fever hurls down
on the city, his lightning slashing through us—              35
raging plague in all its vengeance, devastating
the house of Cadmus![5] And black Death luxuriates
in the raw, wailing miseries of Thebes.
Now we pray to you. You cannot equal the gods,
your children know that, bending at your altar.              40
But we do rate you first of men,
both in the common crises of our lives
and face-to-face encounters with the gods.
You freed us from the Sphinx,[6] you came to Thebes
and cut us loose from the bloody tribute[7] we had paid        45
that harsh, brutal singer. We taught you nothing,
no skill, no extra knowledge, still you triumphed.
A god was with you, so they say, and we believe it—
you lifted up our lives.
                          So now again,
Oedipus, king, we bend to you, your power—                   50
we implore you, all of us on our knees:
find us strength, rescue! Perhaps you've heard
the voice of a god or something from other men,
Oedipus . . . what do you know?
The man of experience—you see it every day—                  55
his plans will work in a crisis, his first of all.

Act now—we beg you, best of men, raise up our city!
Act, defend yourself, your former glory!
Your country calls you savior now
for your zeal, your action years ago.                        60
Never let us remember of your reign:
you helped us stand, only to fall once more.
Oh raise up our city, set us on our feet.

4. At a temple of Apollo in Thebes the priests foretold the future according to patterns they saw in the ashes of the burned flesh of sacrificial victims.    5. Mythical founder of Thebes and its first king.    6. The winged female monster which terrorized the city of Thebes until her riddle was finally answered by Oedipus. The riddle was: "What is it that walks on four feet and two feet and three feet and has only one voice; when it walks on most feet, it is weakest?" Oedipus' answer was Man. (He has four feet as a child crawling on "all fours," and three feet in old age when he walks with the aid of a stick.)    7. Many young men of Thebes had tried to answer the riddle, failed, and been killed.

The omens were good that day you brought us joy—
be the same man today!                                                    65
Rule our land, you know you have the power,
but rule a land of the living, not a wasteland.
Ship and towered city are nothing, stripped of men
alive within it, living all as one.

OEDIPUS:                                    My children,
I pity you. I see—how could I fail to see                                 70
what longings bring you here? Well I know
you are sick to death, all of you,
but sick as you are, not one is sick as I.
Your pain strikes each of you alone, each
in the confines of himself, no other. But my spirit                       75
grieves for the city, for myself and all of you.
I wasn't asleep, dreaming. You haven't wakened me—
I've wept through the nights, you must know that,
groping, laboring over many paths of thought.
After a painful search I found one cure:                                  80
I acted at once. I sent Creon,
my wife's own brother, to Delphi⁸—
Apollo the Prophet's oracle—to learn
what I might do or say to save our city.

Today's the day. When I count the days gone by                           85
it torments me . . . what is he doing?
Strange, he's late, he's gone too long.
But once he returns, then, then I'll be a traitor
if I do not do all the god makes clear.

PRIEST: Timely words. The men over there                                  90
are signaling—Creon's just arriving.

　　　[*Sighting* CREON, *then turning to the altar.*]

OEDIPUS:                                    Lord Apollo,
let him come with a lucky word of rescue,
shining like his eyes!

PRIEST: Welcome news, I think—he's crowned, look,
and the laurel wreath is bright with berries.⁹                           95

OEDIPUS: We'll soon see. He's close enough to hear—

　　　[*Enter* CREON *from the side; his face is shaded with a wreath.*]

---

8. The oracular shrine of Apollo at Delphi, below Mount Parnassus in central Greece.　　9. Creon
is wearing a crown of laurel as a sign that he brings good news.

Creon, prince, my kinsman, what do you bring us?
What message from the god?

CREON: Good news.
I tell you even the hardest things to bear,
if they should turn out well, all would be well.                                     100

OEDIPUS: Of course, but what were the god's *words?* There's no hope
and nothing to fear in what you've said so far.

CREON: If you want my report in the presence of these people,

[*Pointing to the priests while drawing* OEDIPUS *toward the palace.*]

I'm ready now, or we might go inside.

OEDIPUS: Speak out,
speak to us all. I grieve for these, my people,                                     105
far more than I fear for my own life.

CREON: Very well,
I will tell you what I heard from the god.
Apollo commands us—he was quite clear—
"Drive the corruption from the land,
don't harbor it any longer, past all cure,                                          110
don't nurse it in your soil—root it out!"

OEDIPUS: How can we cleanse ourselves—what rites?
What's the source of the trouble?

CREON: Banish the man, or pay back blood with blood.
Murder sets the plague-storm on the city.

OEDIPUS: Whose murder?                                                              115
Whose fate does Apollo bring to light?

CREON: Our leader,
my lord, was once a man named Laius,
before you came and put us straight on course.

OEDIPUS: I know—
or so I've heard. I never saw the man myself.

CREON: Well, he was killed, and Apollo commands us now—                             120
he could not be more clear,
"Pay the killers back—whoever is responsible."

OEDIPUS: Where on earth are they? Where to find it now,
the trail of the ancient guilt so hard to trace?

CREON: "Here in Thebes," he said.                                                   125
Whatever is sought for can be caught, you know,
whatever is neglected slips away.

OEDIPUS: But where,
in the palace, the fields or foreign soil,
where did Laius meet his bloody death?

CREON: He went to consult an oracle, Apollo said,                    130
   and he set out and never came home again.

OEDIPUS: No messenger, no fellow-traveler saw what happened?
   Someone to cross-examine?

CREON:                                    No,
   they were all killed but one. He escaped,
   terrified, he could tell us nothing clearly,                    135
   nothing of what he saw—just one thing.

OEDIPUS:                                    What's that?
   one thing could hold the key to it all,
   a small beginning give us grounds for hope.

CREON: He said thieves attacked them—a whole band,
   not single-handed, cut King Laius down.

OEDIPUS:                                    A thief,                    140
   so daring, so wild, he'd kill a king? Impossible,
   unless conspirators paid him off in Thebes.

CREON: We suspected as much. But with Laius dead
   no leader appeared to help us in our troubles.

OEDIPUS: Trouble? Your *king* was murdered—royal blood!                    145
   What stopped you from tracking down the killer
   then and there?

CREON:                        The singing, riddling Sphinx.
   She . . . persuaded us to let the mystery go
   and concentrate on what lay at our feet.

OEDIPUS:                                    No,
   I'll start again—I'll bring it all to light myself!                    150
   Apollo is right, and so are you, Creon,
   to turn our attention back to the murdered man.
   Now you have *me* to fight for you, you'll see:
   I am the land's avenger by all rights,
   and Apollo's champion too.                    155
   But not to assist some distant kinsman, no,
   for my own sake I'll rid us of this corruption.
   Whoever killed the king may decide to kill me too,
   with the same violent hand—by avenging Laius
   I defend myself.

   [*To the priests.*]

                Quickly, my children.                    160
  Up from the steps, take up your branches now.

   [*To the guards.*]

One of you summon the city[1] here before us,
tell them I'll do everything. God help us,
we will see our triumph—or our fall.

[OEDIPUS *and* CREON *enter the palace, followed by the guards.*]

PRIEST: Rise, my sons. The kindness we came for            165
Oedipus volunteers himself.
Apollo has sent his word, his oracle—
Come down, Apollo, save us, stop the plague.

[*The priests rise, remove their branches and exit to the side.*]
[*Enter a* CHORUS, *the citizens of Thebes, who have not heard
the news that* CREON *brings. They march around the altar,
chanting.*]

CHORUS:                                        Zeus!
Great welcome voice of Zeus,[2] what do you bring?
What word from the gold vaults of Delphi                    170
comes to brilliant Thebes? Racked with terror—
        terror shakes my heart
and I cry your wild cries, Apollo, Healer of Delos[3]
I worship you in dread . . . what now, what is your price?
some new sacrifice? some ancient rite from the past        175
come round again each spring?—
        what will you bring to birth?
Tell me, child of golden Hope
    warm voice that never dies!

You are the first I call, daughter of Zeus                  180
deathless Athena—I call your sister Artemis,[4]
heart of the market place enthroned in glory,
        guardian of our earth—
I call Apollo, Archer astride the thunderheads of heaven—
O triple shield against death, shine before me now!         185
If ever, once in the past, you stopped some ruin
launched against our walls
        you hurled the flame of pain
far, far from Thebes—you gods
    come now, come down once more!

1. Represented by the chorus which comes on to the circular dancing floor immediately after this
scene.   2. Apollo was his son, and spoke for him.   3. Apollo was born on the sacred island
of Delos.   4. Sister of Apollo: a goddess associated with hunting, and also a protector of women
in childbirth.

                                                     No, no                        190
the miseries numberless, grief on grief, no end—
too much to bear, we are all dying
O my people . . .
    Thebes like a great army dying
and there is no sword of thought to save us, no             195
and the fruits of our famous earth, they will not ripen
no and the women cannot scream their pangs to birth—
screams for the Healer, children dead in the womb
          and life on life goes down
                you can watch them go                       200
    like seabirds winging west, outracing the day's fire
down the horizon, irresistibly
          streaking on to the shores of Evening
                                                Death
so many deaths, numberless deaths on deaths, no end—
Thebes is dying, look, her children                         205
stripped of pity . . .
    generations strewn on the ground
unburied, unwept, the dead spreading death
and the young wives and gray-haired mothers with them
cling to the altars, trailing in from all over the city—    210
Thebes, city of death, one long cortege
          and the suffering rises
                wails for mercy rise
    and the wild hymn for the Healer blazes out
clashing with our sobs our cries of mourning—               215
    O golden daughter of god,[5] send rescue
    radiant as the kindness in your eyes!
Drive him back!—the fever, the god of death
          that raging god of war[6]
not armored in bronze, not shielded now, he burns me,       220
battle cries in the onslaught burning on—
O rout him from our borders!
Sail him, blast him out to the Sea-queen's chamber
          the black Atlantic gulfs
    or the northern harbor, death to all                    225
where the Thracian surf[7] comes crashing.
Now what the night spares he comes by day and kills—
the god of death.

---

5. Athena, daughter of Zeus.      6. The plague is identified with Ares, the war-god, though he comes now without armor and shield. Ares is not elsewhere connected with plague; this passage may be an allusion to the early years of the Peloponnesian War, when Spartan troops threatened the city from outside and the plague raged inside the walls.      7. Ares was thought to be at home among the savages of Thrace, to the northeast of Greece proper.

O lord of the stormcloud,
you who twirl the lightning, Zeus, Father,
thunder Death to nothing!                                          230

Apollo, lord of the light, I beg you—
    whip your longbow's golden cord
showering arrows on our enemies—shafts of power
champions strong before us rushing on!

Artemis, Huntress,                                                 235
torches flaring over the eastern ridges—
        ride Death down in pain!

God of the headdress gleaming gold, I cry to you—
your name and ours are, Dionysus—
    come with your face a flame with wine                          240
        your raving women's[8] cries
    your army on the march! Come with the lightning
come with torches blazing, eyes ablaze with glory!
Burn that god of death that all gods hate!

[OEDIPUS *enters from the palace to address the* CHORUS, *as if
addressing the entire city of Thebes.*]

OEDIPUS: You pray to the gods? Let me grant your prayers.          245
    Come, listen to me—do what the plague demands:
    you'll find relief and lift your head from the depths.

    I will speak out now as a stranger to the story,
    a stranger to the crime. If I'd been present then,
    there would have been no mystery, no long hunt                 250
    without a clue in hand. So now, counted
    a native Theban years after the murder,
    to all of Thebes I made this proclamation:
    if any one of you knows who murdered Laius,
    the son of Labdacus, I order him to reveal                     255
    the whole truth to me. Nothing to fear,
    even if he must denounce himself,
    let him speak up
    and so escape the brunt of the charge—
    he will suffer no unbearable punishment,                       260
    nothing worse than exile, totally unharmed.

---

8. The Bacchanals, nymphs or human female votaries of the god Dionysus (Bacchus) who celebrated him with wild dancing rites.

[OEDIPUS *pauses, waiting for a reply.*]

Next,
if anyone knows the murderer is a stranger,
a man from alien soil, come, speak up.
I will give him a handsome reward, and lay up
gratitude in my heart for him besides.                265

[*Silence again, no reply.*]

But if you keep silent, if anyone panicking,
trying to shield himself or friend or kin,
rejects my offer, then hear what I will do.
I order you, every citizen of the state
where I hold throne and power: banish this man—        270
whoever he may be—never shelter him, never
speak a word to him, never make him partner
to your prayers, your victims burned to the gods.
Never let the holy water touch his hands
Drive him out, each of you, from every home.            275
*He* is the plague, the heart of our corruption,
as Apollo's oracle has just revealed to me.
So I honor my obligations:
I fight for the god and for the murdered man.

Now my curse on the murderer. Whoever he is,          280
a lone man unknown in his crime
or one among many, let that man drag out
his life in agony, step by painful step—
I curse myself as well . . . if by any chance
he proves to be an intimate of our house,              285
here at my hearth, with my full knowledge,
may the curse I just called down on him strike me!
These are your orders: perform them to the last.
I command you, for my sake, for Apollo's, for this country
blasted root and branch by the angry heavens.          290
Even if god had never urged you on to act,
how could you leave the crime uncleansed so long?
A man so noble—your king, brought down in blood—
you should have searched. But I am the king now,
I hold the throne that he held then, possess his bed   295
and a wife who shares our seed . . . why, our seed
might be the same, children born of the same mother
might have created blood-bonds between us

if his hope of offspring hadn't met disaster—
but fate swooped at his head and cut him short.                    300
So I will fight for him as if he were my father,
stop at nothing, search the world
to lay my hands on the man who shed his blood,
the son of Labdacus descended of Polydorus,
Cadmus of old and Agenor, founder of the line:                    305
their power and mine are one.
                    Oh dear gods,
my curse on those who disobey these orders!
Let no crops grow out of the earth for them—
shrivel their women, kill their sons,
burn them to nothing in this plague                                310
that hits us now, or something even worse.
But you, loyal men of Thebes who approve my actions,
may our champion, Justice, may all the gods
be with us, fight beside us to the end!

LEADER: In the grip of your curse, my king, I swear                315
    I'm not the murderer, I cannot point him out.
    As for the search, Apollo pressed it on us—
    he should name the killer.
OEDIPUS:                    Quite right,
    but to force the gods to act against their will—
    no man has the power.
LEADER:                    Then if I might mention            320
    the next best thing . . .
OEDIPUS:                    The third best too—
    don't hold back, say it.
LEADER:                    I still believe . . .
    Lord Tiresias[9] sees with the eyes of Lord Apollo.
    Anyone searching for the truth, my king,
    might learn it from the prophet, clear as day.                325
OEDIPUS: I've not been slow with that. On Creon's cue
    I sent the escorts, twice, within the hour.
    I'm surprised he isn't here.
LEADER:                    We need him—
    without him we have nothing but old, useless rumors.
OEDIPUS: Which rumors? I'll search out every word.             330
LEADER: Laius was killed, they say, by certain travelers.
OEDIPUS: I know—but no one can find the murderer.
LEADER: If the man has a trace of fear in him
    he won't stay silent long,
    not with your curses ringing in his ears.                     335

9. The blind prophet of Thebes (whose ghost Odysseus goes to consult in Hades in *Odyssey* XI).

OEDIPUS: He didn't flinch at murder,
   he'll never flinch at words.

   [*Enter* TIRESIAS, *the blind prophet, led by a boy with escorts in
   attendance. He remains at a distance.*]

LEADER: Here is the one who will convict him, look,
   they bring him on at last, the seer, the man of god.
   The truth lives inside him, him alone.
OEDIPUS:                              O Tiresias,                    340
   master of all the mysteries of our life,
   all you teach and all you dare not tell,
   signs in the heavens, signs that walk the earth!
   Blind as you are, you can feel all the more
   what sickness haunts our city. You, my lord,                     345
   are the one shield, the one savior we can find.

   We asked Apollo—perhaps the messengers
   haven't told you—he sent his answer back:
   "Relief from the plague can only come one way.
   Uncover the murderers of Laius,                                  350
   put them to death or drive them into exile."
   So I beg you, grudge us nothing now, no voice,
   no message plucked from the birds, the embers
   or the other mantic ways within your grasp.
   Rescue yourself, your city, rescue me—                           355
   rescue everything infected by the dead.
   We are in your hands. For a man to help others
   with all his gifts and native strength:
   that is the noblest work.
TIRESIAS:                         How terrible—to see the truth
   when the truth is only pain to him who sees!                     360
   I knew it well, but I put it from my mind,
   else I never would have come.
OEDIPUS: What's this? Why so grim, so dire?
TIRESIAS: Just send me home. You bear your burdens,
   I'll bear mine. It's better that way,                            365
   please believe me.
OEDIPUS:                  Strange response . . . unlawful,
   unfriendly too to the state that bred and reared you—
   you withhold the word of god.
TIRESIAS:                           I fail to see
   that your own words are so well-timed.
   I'd rather not have the same thing said of me . . .             370
OEDIPUS: For the love of god, don't turn away,

not if you know something. We beg you,
all of us on our knees.
TIRESIAS:                    None of you knows—
and I will never reveal my dreadful secrets,
not to say your own.                                                            375
OEDIPUS: What? You know and you won't tell?
You're bent on betraying us, destroying Thebes?
TIRESIAS: I'd rather not cause pain for you or me.
So why this . . . useless interrogation?
You'll get nothing from me.
OEDIPUS:                    Nothing! You,                                         380
you scum of the earth, you'd enrage a heart of stone!
You won't talk? Nothing moves you?
Out with it, once and for all!
TIRESIAS: You criticize my temper . . . unaware
of the one[1] *you* live with, you revile me.                                    385
OEDIPUS: Who could restrain his anger hearing you?
What outrage—you spurn the city!
TIRESIAS: What will come will come.
Even if I shroud it all in silence.
OEDIPUS: What will come? You're bound to *tell* me that.                          390
TIRESIAS: I'll say no more. Do as you like, build your anger
to whatever pitch you please, rage your worst—
OEDIPUS: Oh I'll let loose, I have such fury in me—
now I see it all. You helped hatch the plot,
you did the work, yes, short of killing him                                      395
with your own hands—and given eyes I'd say
you did the killing single-handed!
TIRESIAS:                    Is that so!
I charge you, then, submit to that decree
you just laid down: from this day onward
speak to no one, not these citizens, not myself.                                 400
*You* are the curse, the corruption of the land!
OEDIPUS: You, shameless—
aren't you appalled to start up such a story?
You think you can get away with this?
TIRESIAS:                    I have already.
The truth with all its power lives inside me.                                    405
OEDIPUS: Who primed you for this? Not your prophet's trade.
TIRESIAS: You did, you forced me, twisted it out of me.
OEDIPUS: What? Say it again—I'll understand it better.
TIRESIAS: Didn't you understand, just now?
Or are you tempting me to talk?                                                  410

1. In the Greek the veiled reference to Jocasta is more forceful, since the word translated "the one" has a feminine ending (agreeing with the feminine noun *orgê*—"temper").

OEDIPUS: No, I can't say I grasped your meaning.
    Out with it, again!
TIRESIAS: I say you are the murderer you hunt.
OEDIPUS: That obscenity, twice—by god, you'll pay.
TIRESIAS: Shall I say more, so you can really rage?                    415
OEDIPUS: Much as you want. Your words are nothing—
    futile.
TIRESIAS: You cannot imagine . . . I tell you,
    you and your loved ones live together in infamy,
    you cannot see how far you've gone in guilt.
OEDIPUS: You think you can keep this up and never suffer?              420
TIRESIAS: Indeed, if the truth has any power.
OEDIPUS:                                            It does
    but not for you, old man. You've lost your power,
    stone-blind, stone-deaf—senses, eyes blind as stone!
TIRESIAS: I pity you, flinging at me the very insults
    each man here will fling at you so soon.
OEDIPUS:                                            Blind,                425
    lost in the night, endless night that cursed you!
    You can't hurt me or anyone else who sees the light—
    you can never touch me.
TIRESIAS:                     True, it is not your fate
    to fall at my hands. Apollo is quite enough,
    and he will take some pains to work this out.                       430
OEDIPUS: Creon! Is this conspiracy his or yours?
TIRESIAS: Creon is not your downfall, no, you are your own.
OEDIPUS:                                                    O power—
    wealth and empire, skill outstripping skill
    in the heady rivalries of life,
    what envy lurks inside you! Just for this,                          435
    the crown the city gave me—I never sought it,
    they laid it in my hands—for this alone, Creon,
    the soul of trust, my loyal friend from the start
    steals against me . . . so hungry to overthrow me
    he sets this wizard on me, this scheming quack,                     440
    this fortune-teller peddling lies, eyes peeled
    for his own profit—seer blind in his craft!

    Come here, you pious fraud. Tell me,
    when did you ever prove yourself a prophet?
    When the Sphinx, that chanting Fury kept her deathwatch here,
    why silent then, not a word to set our people free?
    There was a riddle, not for some passer-by to solve—
    it cried out for a prophet. Where were you?
    Did you rise to the crisis? Not a word,

you and your birds, your gods—nothing. 450
No, but I came by, Oedipus the ignorant,
*I* stopped the Sphinx! With no help from the birds,
the flight of my own intelligence hit the mark.

And this is the man you'd try to overthrow?
You think you'll stand by Creon when he's king? 455
You and the great mastermind—
you'll pay in tears, I promise you, for this,
this witch-hunt. If you didn't look so senile
the lash would teach you what your scheming means!
LEADER: I would suggest his words were spoken in anger, 460
Oedipus . . . yours too, and it isn't what we need.
The best solution to the oracle, the riddle
posed by god—we should look for that.
TIRESIAS: You are the king no doubt, but in one respect,
at least, I am your equal: the right to reply. 465
I claim that privilege too.
I am not your slave. I serve Apollo.
I don't need Creon to speak for me in public.
                                        So,
you mock my blindness? Let me tell you this.
You with your precious eyes, 470
you're blind to the corruption of your life,
to the house you live in, those you live with—
who *are* your parents? Do you know? All unknowing
you are the scourge of your own flesh and blood,
the dead below the earth and the living here above, 475
and the double lash of your mother and your father's curse
will whip you from this land one day, their footfall
treading you down in terror, darkness shrouding
your eyes that now can see the light!
          Soon, soon
you'll scream aloud—what haven won't reverberate? 480
What rock of Cithaeron[2] won't scream back in echo?
That day you learn the truth about your marriage,
the wedding-march that sang you into your halls,
the lusty voyage home to the fatal harbor!
And a crowd of other horrors you'd never dream 485
will level you with yourself and all your children.

There. Now smear us with insults—Creon, myself,
and every word I've said. No man will ever

---

2. The mountain range near Thebes, on which Oedipus was left to die when an infant.

be rooted from the earth as brutally as you.

OEDIPUS: Enough! Such filth from him? Insufferable—    490
what, still alive? Get out—
faster, back where you came from—vanish!

TIRESIAS: I would never have come if you hadn't called me here.

OEDIPUS: If I thought you would blurt out such absurdities,
you'd have died waiting before I'd had you summoned.    495

TIRESIAS: Absurd, am I! To you, not to your parents:
the ones who bore you found me sane enough.

OEDIPUS: Parents—who? Wait . . . who is my father?

TIRESIAS: This day will bring your birth and your destruction.

OEDIPUS: Riddles—all you can say are riddles, murk and
darkness.    500

TIRESIAS: Ah, but aren't you the best man alive at solving riddles?

OEDIPUS: Mock me for that, go on, and you'll reveal my greatness.

TIRESIAS: Your great good fortune, true, it was your ruin.

OEDIPUS: Not if I saved the city—what do I care?

TIRESIAS: Well then, I'll be going.

[*To his attendant.*]

Take me home, boy.    505

OEDIPUS: Yes, take him away. You're a nuisance here.
Out of the way, the irritation's gone.

[*Turning his back on* TIRESIAS, *moving toward the palace.*[3]]

TIRESIAS:                               I will go,
once I have said what I came here to say.
I'll never shrink from the anger in your eyes—
you can't destroy me. Listen to me closely:    510
the man you've sought so long, proclaiming,
cursing up and down, the murderer of Laius—
he is here. A stranger,
you may think, who lives among you,
he soon will be revealed a native Theban    515
but he will take no joy in the revelation.
Blind who now has eyes, beggar who now is rich,
he will grope his way toward a foreign soil,
a stick tapping before him step by step.
    [OEDIPUS *enters the palace.*]
Revealed at last, brother and father both    520

---

3. There are no stage directions in our texts. It is suggested here that Oedipus moves off stage and does not hear the critical section of Tiresias' speech (520 ff) which he could hardly fail to connect with the prophecy made to him by Apollo many years ago.

to the children he embraces, to his mother
son and husband both—he sowed the loins
his father sowed, he spilled his father's blood!

Go in and reflect on that, solve that.
And if you find I've lied                                            525
from this day onward call the prophet blind.

[TIRESIAS *and the boy exit to the side.*]

CHORUS:                                              Who—
  who is the man the voice of god enounces
  resounding out of the rocky gorge of Delphi?
     The horror too dark to tell,
  whose ruthless bloody hands have done the work?        530
  His time has come to fly
     to outrace the stallions of the storm
       his feet a streak of speed—
  Cased in armor, Apollo son of the Father
  lunges on him, lightning-bolts afire!                     535
  And the grim unerring Furies[4]
     closing for the kill.
     Look,
  the word of god has just come blazing
  flashing off Parnassus'[5] snowy heights!
     That man who left no trace—                        540
  after him, hunt him down with all our strength!
  Now under bristling timber
     up through rocks and caves he stalks
      like the wild mountain bull—
  cut off from men, each step an agony, frenzied, racing blind   545
  but he cannot outrace the dread voices of Delphi
  ringing out of the heart of Earth,
    the dark wings beating around him shrieking doom
      the doom that never dies, the terror—
  The skilled prophet scans the birds and shatters me with terror!
  I can't accept him, can't deny him, don't know what to say,
  I'm lost, and the wings of dark foreboding beating—
  I cannot see what's come, what's still to come . . .
  and what could breed a blood feud between
    Laius' house and the son of Polybus?[6]                    555
  I know of nothing, not in the past and not now,

4. Avenging spirits who pursued a murderer when no earthly avenger was at hand.    5. A mountain range in central Greece. The great oracular shrine of Apollo at Delphi was on its lower slopes.
6. King of Corinth and, so far as anyone except Tiresias knows, the father of Oedipus.

no charge to bring against our king, no cause
to attack his fame that rings throughout Thebes—
    not without proof—not for the ghost of Laius,
    not to avenge a murder gone without a trace.                    560

Zeus and Apollo know, they know, the great masters
    of all the dark and depth of human life.
But whether a mere man can know the truth,
whether a seer can fathom more than I—
there is no test, no certain proof                                 565
    though matching skill for skill
a man can outstrip a rival. No, not till I see
these charges proved will I side with his accusers.
We saw him then, when the she-hawk[7] swept against him,
saw with our own eyes his skill, his brilliant triumph—            570
    there was the test—he was the joy of Thebes!
    Never will I convict my king, never in my heart.

[*Enter* CREON *from the side.*]

CREON: My fellow-citizens, I hear King Oedipus
    levels terrible charges at me. I had to come.
    I resent it deeply. If, in the present crisis                  575
    he thinks he suffers any abuse from me,
    anything I've done or said that offers him
    the slightest injury, why, I've no desire
    to linger out this life, my reputation in ruins.
    The damage I'd face from such an accusation                    580
    is nothing simple. No, there's nothing worse:
    branded a traitor in the city, a traitor
    to all of you and my good friends.
LEADER:                            True,
    but a slur might have been forced out of him,
    by anger perhaps, not any firm conviction.                     585
CREON: The charge was made in public, wasn't it?
    I put the prophet up to spreading lies?
LEADER: Such things were said . . .
    I don't know with what intent, if any.
CREON: Was his glance steady, his mind right                       590
    when the charge was brought against me?
LEADER: I really couldn't say. I never look
    to judge the ones in power.

[*The doors open.* OEDIPUS *enters.*]

7. The Sphinx.

                        Wait,
here's Oedipus now.
OEDIPUS:                    You—here? You have the gall
  to show your face before the palace gates?                         595
  You, plotting to kill me, kill the king—
  I see it all, the marauding thief himself
  scheming to steal my crown and power!
                                        Tell me,
  in god's name, what did you take me for,
  coward or fool, when you spun out your plot?                        600
  Your treachery—you think I'd never detect it
  creeping against me in the dark? Or sensing it,
  not defend myself? Aren't you the fool,
  you and your high adventure. Lacking numbers,
  powerful friends, out for the big game of empire—                   605
  you need riches, armies to bring that quarry down!
CREON: Are you quite finished? It's your turn to listen
  for just as long as you've . . . instructed me.
  Hear me out, then judge me on the facts.
OEDIPUS: You've a wicked way with words, Creon,                       610
  but I'll be slow to learn—from you.
  I find you a menace, a great burden to me.
CREON: Just one thing, hear me out in this.
OEDIPUS:                                    Just one thing,
  don't tell *me* you're not the enemy, the traitor.
CREON: Look, if you think crude, mindless stubbornness                615
  such a gift, you've lost your sense of balance.
OEDIPUS: If you think you can abuse a kinsman,
  then escape the penalty, you're insane.
CREON: Fair enough, I grant you. But this injury
  you say I've done you, what is it?                                  620
OEDIPUS: Did you induce me, yes or no,
  to send for that sanctimonious prophet?
CREON: I did. And I'd do the same again.
OEDIPUS: All right then, tell me, how long is it now
  since Laius . . .
CREON:             Laius—what did *he* do?
OEDIPUS:                                    Vanished,                  625
  swept from sight, murdered in his tracks.
CREON: The count of the years would run you far back . . .
OEDIPUS: And that far back, was the prophet at his trade?
CREON: Skilled as he is today, and just as honored.
OEDIPUS: Did he ever refer to me then, at that time?
CREON:                                              No,                630
  never, at least, when I was in his presence.
OEDIPUS: But you did investigate the murder, didn't you?

CREON: We did our best, of course, discovered nothing.

OEDIPUS: But the great seer never accused me then—why not?

CREON: I don't know. And when I don't, I keep quiet.                    635

OEDIPUS: You do know this, you'd tell it too—
    if you had a shred of decency.

CREON:                         What?
    If I know, I won't hold back.

OEDIPUS:                    Simply this:
    if the two of you had never put heads together,
    we would never have heard about *my* killing Laius.                  640

CREON: If that's what he says . . . well, you know best.
    But now I have a right to learn from you
    as you just learned from me.

OEDIPUS:                    Learn your fill,
    you never will convict me of the murder.

CREON: Tell me, you're married to my sister, aren't you?                 645

OEDIPUS: A genuine discovery—there's no denying that.

CREON: And you rule the land with her, with equal power?

OEDIPUS: She receives from me whatever she desires.

CREON: And I am the third, all of us are equals?

OEDIPUS: Yes, and it's there you show your stripes—                      650
    you betray a kinsman.

CREON:                    Not at all.
    Not if you see things calmly, rationally,
    as I do. Look at it this way first:
    who in his right mind would rather rule
    and live in anxiety than sleep in peace?                             655
    Particularly if he enjoys the same authority.
    Not I, I'm not the man to yearn for kingship,
    not with a king's power in my hands. Who would?
    No one with any sense of self-control.
    Now, as it is, you offer me all I need,                              660
    not a fear in the world. But if I wore the crown . . .
    there'd be many painful duties to perform,
    hardly to my taste.
                        How could kingship
    please me more than influence, power
    without a qualm? I'm not that deluded yet,                           665
    to reach for anything but privilege outright,
    profit free and clear.
    Now all men sing my praises, all salute me,
    now all who request your favors curry mine.
    I am their best hope: success rests in me.                           670
    Why give up that, I ask you, and borrow trouble?
    A man of sense, someone who sees things clearly

would never resort to treason.
No, I've no lust for conspiracy in me,
nor could I ever suffer one who does.                         675

Do you want proof? Go to Delphi yourself,
examine the oracle and see if I've reported
the message word-for-word. This too:
if you detect that I and the clairvoyant
have plotted anything in common, arrest me,                   680
execute me. Not on the strength of one vote,
two in this case, mine as well as yours.
But don't convict me on sheer unverified surmise.
How wrong it is to take the good for bad,
purely at random, or take the bad for good.                   685
But reject a friend, a kinsman? I would as soon
tear out the life within us, priceless life itself.
You'll learn this well, without fail, in time.
Time alone can bring the just man to light—
the criminal you can spot in one short day.                   690

LEADER:                                    Good advice,
    my lord, for anyone who wants to avoid disaster.
    Those who jump to conclusions may go wrong.

OEDIPUS: When my enemy moves against me quickly
    plots in secret, I move quickly too, I must,
    I plot and pay him back. Relax my guard a moment,          695
    waiting his next move—he wins his objective,
    I lose mine.

CREON:           What do you want?
    You want me banished?

OEDIPUS:                      No, I want you dead.

CREON: Just to show how ugly a grudge can . . .

OEDIPUS:                                     So,
    still stubborn? you don't think I'm serious?               700

CREON: I think you're insane.

OEDIPUS:                      Quite sane—in my behalf.

CREON: Not just as much in mine?

OEDIPUS:                          You—my mortal enemy?

CREON: What if you're wholly wrong?

OEDIPUS:                              No matter—I must rule.

CREON: Not if you rule unjustly.

OEDIPUS:                         Hear him, Thebes, my city!

CREON: My city too, not yours alone!                          705

LEADER: Please, my lords.

    [Enter JOCASTA from the palace.]

Look, Jocasta's coming,
and just in time too. With her help
you must put this fighting of yours to rest.
JOCASTA: Have you no sense? Poor misguided men,
such shouting—why this public outburst?                    710
Aren't you ashamed, with the land so sick,
to stir up private quarrels?

[*To* OEDIPUS.]

Into the palace now. And Creon, you go home.
Why make such a furor over nothing?
CREON: My sister, it's dreadful . . . Oedipus, your husband,      715
he's bent on a choice of punishments for me,
banishment from the fatherland or death.
OEDIPUS: Precisely. I caught him in the act, Jocasta,
plotting, about to stab me in the back.
CREON: Never—curse me, let me die and be damned               720
if I've done you any wrong you charge me with.
JOCASTA: Oh god, believe it, Oedipus,
honor the solemn oath he swears to heaven.
Do it for me, for the sake of all your people.

[*The* CHORUS *begins to chant.*]

CHORUS: Believe it, be sensible                               725
    give way, my king, I beg you!
OEDIPUS: What do you want from me, concessions?
CHORUS: Respect him—he's been no fool in the past
    and now he's strong with the oath he swears to god.
OEDIPUS: You know what you're asking?
CHORUS:                               I do.
OEDIPUS:                                   Then out with it!    730
CHORUS: The man's your friend, your kin, he's under oath—
    don't cast him out, disgraced
    branded with guilt on the strength of hearsay only.
OEDIPUS: Know full well, if that is what you want
    you want me dead or banished from the land.               735
CHORUS:                                        Never—
    no, by the blazing Sun, first god of the heavens!
        Stripped of the gods, stripped of loved ones,
    let me die by inches if that ever crossed my mind.
    But the heart inside me sickens, dies as the land dies
    and now on top of the old griefs you pile this,           740
    your fury—both of you!

OEDIPUS:                    Then let him go,
  even if it does lead to my ruin, my death
  or my disgrace, driven from Thebes for life.
  It's you, not him I pity—your words move me.
  He, wherever he goes, my hate goes with him.                 745
CREON: Look at you, sullen in yielding, brutal in your rage—
  you'll go too far. It's perfect justice:
  natures like yours are hardest on themselves.
OEDIPUS: Then leave me alone—get out!
CREON:                              I'm going.
  You're wrong, so wrong. These men know I'm right.            750

  [*Exit to the side. The* CHORUS *turns to* JOCASTA.]

CHORUS: Why do you hesitate, my lady
  why not help him in?
JOCASTA: Tell me what's happened first.
CHORUS: Loose, ignorant talk started dark suspicions
  and a sense of injustice cut deeply too.                     755
JOCASTA: On both sides?
CHORUS:                    Oh yes.
JOCASTA:                              What did they say?
CHORUS: Enough, please, enough! The land's so racked already
  or so it seems to me . . .
  End the trouble here, just where they left it.
OEDIPUS: You see what comes of your good intentions now?        760
  And all because you tried to blunt my anger.
CHORUS:                                        My king,
  I've said it once, I'll say it time and again—
    I'd be insane, you know it,
  senseless, ever to turn my back on you.
  You who set our beloved land—storm-tossed, shattered—        765
  straight on course. Now again, good helmsman,
  steer us through the storm!

  [*The* CHORUS *draws away, leaving* OEDIPUS *and* JOCASTA *side by
  side.*]

JOCASTA:                              For the love of god,
  Oedipus, tell me too, what is it?
  Why this rage? You're so unbending.
OEDIPUS: I will tell you. I respect you, Jocasta,               770
  much more than these men here . . .

  [*Glancing at the* CHORUS.]

Creon's to blame, Creon schemes against me.
JOCASTA: Tell me clearly, how did the quarrel start?
OEDIPUS: He says *I* murdered Laius—I am guilty.
JOCASTA: How does he know? Some secret knowledge          775
    or simple hearsay?
OEDIPUS:                    Oh, he sent his prophet in
    to do his dirty work. You know Creon,
    Creon keeps his own lips clean.
JOCASTA:                              A prophet?
    Well then, free yourself of every charge!
    Listen to me and learn some peace of mind:          780
    no skill in the world,
    nothing human can penetrate the future.
    Here is proof, quick and to the point.

    An oracle came to Laius one fine day
    (I won't say from Apollo himself                     785
    but his underlings, his priests) and it declared
    that doom would strike him down at the hands of a son,
    our son, to be born of our own flesh and blood. But Laius,
    so the report goes at least, was killed by strangers,
    thieves, at a place where three roads meet . . . my son—   790
    he wasn't three days old and the boy's father
    fastened his ankles, had a henchman fling him away
    on a barren, trackless mountain.
                          There, you see?
    Apollo brought neither thing to pass. My baby
    no more murdered his father than Laius suffered—     795
    his wildest fear—death at his own son's hands.
    That's how the seers and all their revelations
    mapped out the future. Brush them from your mind.
    Whatever the god needs and seeks
    he'll bring to light himself, with ease.             800
OEDIPUS:                              Strange,
    hearing you just now . . . my mind wandered,
    my thoughts racing back and forth.
JOCASTA: What do you mean? Why so anxious, startled?
OEDIPUS: I thought I heard you say that Laius
    was cut down at a place where three roads meet.      805
JOCASTA: That was the story. It hasn't died out yet.
OEDIPUS: Where did this thing happen? Be precise.
JOCASTA: A place called Phocis, where two branching roads,
    one from Daulia, one from Delphi,
    come together—a crossroads.                          810
OEDIPUS: When? How long ago?

JOCASTA: The heralds no sooner reported Laius dead
   than you appeared and they hailed you king of Thebes.
OEDIPUS: My god, my god—what have you planned to do to me?
JOCASTA: What, Oedipus? What haunts you so?
OEDIPUS:                                    Not yet.          815
   Laius—how did he look? Describe him.
   Had he reached his prime?
JOCASTA:                      He was swarthy,
   and the gray had just begun to streak his temples,
   and his build . . . wasn't far from yours.
OEDIPUS:                              Oh no no,
   I think I've just called down a dreadful curse          820
   upon myself—I simply didn't know!
JOCASTA: What are you saying? I shudder to look at you.
OEDIPUS: I have a terrible fear the blind seer can see.
   I'll know in a moment. One thing more—
JOCASTA:                              Anything,
   afraid as I am—ask, I'll answer, all I can.          825
OEDIPUS: Did he go with a light or heavy escort,
   several men-at-arms, like a lord, a king?
JOCASTA: There were five in the party, a herald among them,
   and a single wagon carrying Laius.
OEDIPUS:                         Ai—
   now I can see it all, clear as day.          830
   Who told you all this at the time, Jocasta?
JOCASTA: A servant who reached home, the lone survivor.
OEDIPUS: So, could he still be in the palace—even now?
JOCASTA: No indeed. Soon as he returned from the scene
   and saw you on the throne with Laius dead and gone,          835
   he knelt and clutched my hand, pleading with me
   to send him into the hinterlands, to pasture,
   far as possible, out of sight of Thebes.
   I sent him away. Slave though he was,
   he'd earned that favor—and much more.          840
OEDIPUS: Can we bring him back, quickly?
JOCASTA: Easily. Why do you want him so?
OEDIPUS:                         I'm afraid,
   Jocasta, I have said too much already.
   That man—I've got to see him.
JOCASTA:                         Then he'll come.
   But even I have a right, I'd like to think,          845
   to know what's torturing you, my lord.
OEDIPUS: And so you shall—I can hold nothing back from you,
   now I've reached this pitch of dark foreboding.
   Who means more to me than you? Tell me,

whom would I turn toward but you                                    850
as I go through all this?

My father was Polybus, king of Corinth.
My mother, a Dorian, Merope. And I was held
the prince of the realm among the people there,
till something struck me out of nowhere,                            855
something strange . . . worth remarking perhaps,
hardly worth the anxiety I gave it.
Some man at a banquet who had drunk too much
shouted out—he was far gone, mind you—
that I am not my father's son. Fighting words!                      860
I barely restrained myself that day
but early the next I went to mother and father,
questioned them closely, and they were enraged
at the accusation and the fool who let it fly.
So as for my parents I was satisfied,                               865
but still this thing kept gnawing at me,
the slander spread—I had to make my move.

                                              And so,
unknown to mother and father I set out for Delphi,
and the god Apollo spurned me, sent me away
denied the facts I came for,                                        870
but first he flashed before my eyes a future
great with pain, terror, disaster—I can hear him cry,
"You are fated to couple with your mother, you will bring
a breed of children into the light no man can bear to see—
you will kill your father, the one who gave you life!"              875
I heard all that and ran. I abandoned Corinth,
from that day on I gauged its landfall only
by the stars, running, always running
toward some place where I would never see
the shame of all those oracles come true.                           880
And as I fled I reached that very spot
where the great king, you say, met his death.
Now, Jocasta, I will tell you all.
Making my way toward this triple crossroad
I began to see a herald, then a brace of colts                      885
drawing a wagon, and mounted on the bench . . . a man,
just as you've described him, coming face-to-face,
and the one in the lead and the old man himself
were about to thrust me off the road—brute force—
and the one shouldering me aside, the driver,                       890
I strike him in anger!—and the old man, watching me
coming up along his wheels—he brings down

his prod, two prongs straight at my head!
I paid him back with interest!
Short work, my god—with one blow of the staff                    895
in this right hand I knock him out of his high seat,
roll him out of the wagon, sprawling headlong—
I killed them all—every mother's son!

Oh, but if there is any blood-tie
between Laius and this stranger . . .                    900
what man alive more miserable than I?
More hated by the gods? *I* am the man
no alien, no citizen welcomes to his house,
law forbids it—not a word to me in public,
driven out of every hearth and home.                    905
And all these curses I—no one but I
brought down these piling curses on myself!
And you, his wife, I've touched your body with these,
the hands that killed your husband cover you with blood.

Wasn't I born for torment? Look me in the eyes!                    910
I am abomination—heart and soul!
I must be exiled, and even in exile
never see my parents, never set foot
on native ground again. Else I am doomed
to couple with my mother and cut my father down . . .                    915
Polybus who reared me, gave me life.
                         But why, why?
Wouldn't a man of judgment say—and wouldn't he be right—
some savage power has brought this down upon my head?

Oh no, not that, you pure and awesome gods,
never let me see that day! Let me slip                    920
from the world of man, vanish without a trace
before I see myself stained with such corruption,
stained to the heart.
LEADER: My lord, you fill our hearts with fear.
     But at least until you question the witness,                    925
     do take hope.
OEDIPUS:          Exactly. He is my last hope—
     I am waiting for the shepherd. He is crucial.
JOCASTA: And once he appears, what then? Why so urgent?
OEDIPUS: I will tell you. If it turns out that his story
     matches yours, I've escaped the worst.                    930
JOCASTA: What did I say? What struck you so?
OEDIPUS:                         You said *thieves*—

he told you a whole band of them murdered Laius.
So, if he still holds to the same number,
I cannot be the killer. One can't equal many.
But if he refers to one man, one alone,                        935
clearly the scales come down on me:
I am guilty.

JOCASTA:              Impossible. Trust me,
I told you precisely what he said,
and he can't retract it now;
the whole city heard it, not just I.                            940
And even if he should vary his first report
by one man more or less, still, my lord,
he could never make the murder of Laius
truly fit the prophecy. Apollo was explicit:
my son was doomed to kill my husband . . . my son,             945
poor defenseless thing, he never had a chance
to kill his father. They destroyed him first.

So much for prophecy. It's neither here nor there.
From this day on, I wouldn't look right or left.

OEDIPUS: True, true. Still, that shepherd,                      950
someone fetch him—now!

JOCASTA: I'll send at once. But do let's go inside.
I'd never displease you, least of all in this.

        [OEDIPUS *and* JOCASTA *enter the palace.*]

CHORUS: Destiny guide me always
Destiny find me filled with reverence                           955
      pure in word and deed.
Great laws tower above us, reared on high
born for the brilliant vault of heaven—
      Olympian Sky their only father,
nothing mortal, no man gave them birth,                         960
their memory deathless, never lost in sleep:
within them lives a mighty god, the god does not
      grow old.

Pride breeds the tyrant
violent pride, gorging, crammed to bursting
      with all that is overripe and rich with ruin—             965
clawing up to the heights, headlong pride
crashes down the abyss—sheer doom!
      No footing helps, all foothold lost and gone.
But the healthy strife that makes the city strong—

I pray that god will never end that wrestling:                    970
god, my champion, I will never let you go.
But if any man comes striding, high and mighty
    in all he says and does,
no fear of justice, no reverence
for the temples of the gods—                                      975
    let a rough doom tear him down,
repay his pride, breakneck, ruinous pride!
If he cannot reap his profits fairly
    cannot restrain himself from outrage—
mad, laying hands on the holy things untouchable!                 980

        Can such a man, so desperate, still boast
        he can save his life from the flashing bolts of god?
            If all such violence goes with honor now
                why join the sacred dance?

Never again will I go reverent to Delphi,                         985
    the inviolate heart of Earth
or Apollo's ancient oracle at Abae
or Olympia[8] of the fires—
    unless these prophecies all come true
for all mankind to point toward in wonder.                        990
King of kings, if you deserve your titles
    Zeus, remember, never forget!
    You and your deathless, everlasting reign.

        They are dying, the old oracles sent to Laius,
        now our masters strike them off the rolls.                995
            Nowhere Apollo's golden glory now—
                the gods, the gods go down.

    [*Enter* JOCASTA *from the palace, carrying a suppliant's branch
    wound in wool.*]

JOCASTA: Lords of the realm,[9] it occurred to me,
    just now, to visit the temples of the gods,
    so I have my branch in hand and incense too.                  1000

    Oedipus is beside himself. Racked with anguish,
    no longer a man of sense, he won't admit
    the latest prophecies are hollow as the old—
    he's at the mercy of every passing voice

---

8. Abae was a city in central Greece, and Olympia a site in the western Peloponnese, where there
were important oracles of Apollo and Zeus, respectively.    9. She is addressing the chorus.

if the voice tells of terror.                                              1005
I urge him gently, nothing seems to help,
so I turn to you, Apollo, you are nearest.

[*Placing her branch on the altar, while an old herdsman enters
from the side, not the one just summoned by the King but an
unexpected* MESSENGER *from Corinth.*]

I come with prayers and offerings . . . I beg you,
cleanse us, set us free of defilement!
Look at us, passengers in the grip of fear,                                1010
watching the pilot of the vessel go to pieces.

[*Approaching* JOCASTA *and the* CHORUS.]

MESSENGER: Strangers, please, I wonder if you could lead us
    to the palace of the king . . . I think it's Oedipus.
    Better, the man himself—you know where he is?
LEADER: This is his palace, stranger. He's inside.                         1015
    But here is his queen, his wife and mother
    of his children.
MESSENGER:          Blessings on you, noble queen,
    queen of Oedipus crowned with all your family—
    blessings on you always!
JOCASTA: And the same to you, stranger, you deserve it . . .               1020
    such a greeting. But what have you come for?
    Have you brought us news?
MESSENGER:                        Wonderful news—
    for the house, my lady, for your husband too.
JOCASTA: Really, what? Who sent you?
MESSENGER:                                  Corinth.
    I'll give you the message in a moment.                                 1025
    You'll be glad of it—how could you help it?—
    though it costs a little sorrow in the bargain.
JOCASTA: What can it be, with such a double edge?
MESSENGER: The people there, they want to make your Oedipus
    king of Corinth, so they're saying now.                                1030
JOCASTA: Why? Isn't old Polybus still in power?
MESSENGER: No more. Death has got him in the tomb.
JOCASTA: What are you saying? Polybus, dead?—dead?
MESSENGER:                                              If not,
    if I'm not telling the truth, strike me dead too.

[*To a servant.*]

JOCASTA: Quickly, go to your master, tell him this!          1035
    You prophecies of the gods, where are you now?
    This is the man that Oedipus feared for years,
    he fled him, not to kill him—and now he's dead,
    quite by chance, a normal, natural death,
    not murdered by his son.                                 1040

        [*Emerging from the palace.*]

OEDIPUS:                          Dearest,
    what now? Why call me from the palace?

        [*Bringing the* MESSENGER *closer.*]

JOCASTA: Listen to *him*, see for yourself what all
    those awful prophecies of god have come to.
OEDIPUS: And who is he? What can he have for me?
JOCASTA: He's from Corinth, he's come to tell you            1045
    your father is no more—Polybus—he's dead!

        [*Wheeling on the* MESSENGER.]

OEDIPUS: What? Let me have it from your lips.
MESSENGER:                                    Well,
    if that's what you want first, then here it is:
    make no mistake, Polybus is dead and gone.
OEDIPUS: How—murder? sickness?—what? what killed him?       1050
MESSENGER: A light tip of the scales can put old bones to rest.
OEDIPUS: Sickness then—poor man, it wore him down.
MESSENGER:                                    That,
    and the long count of years he's measured out.
OEDIPUS:                              So!
    Jocasta, why, why look to the Prophet's hearth,
    the fires of the future? Why scan the birds              1055
    that scream above our heads? They winged me on
    to the murder of my father, did they? That was my doom?
    Well look, he's dead and buried, hidden under the earth,
    and here I am in Thebes, I never put hand to sword—
    unless some longing for me wasted him away,              1060
    then in a sense you'd say I caused his death.
    But now, all those prophecies I feared—Polybus
    packs them off to sleep with him in hell!
    They're nothing, worthless.
JOCASTA:                          There.

Didn't I tell you from the start? 1065
OEDIPUS: So you did. I was lost in fear.
JOCASTA: No more, sweep it from your mind forever.
OEDIPUS: But my mother's bed, surely I must fear—
JOCASTA: Fear?
What should a man fear? It's all chance,
chance rules our lives. Not a man on earth 1070
can see a day ahead, groping through the dark.
Better to live at random, best we can.
And as for this marriage with your mother—
have no fear. Many a man before you,
in his dreams, has shared his mother's bed. 1075
Take such things for shadows, nothing at all—
Live, Oedipus,
as if there's no tomorrow!
OEDIPUS: Brave words,
and you'd persuade me if mother weren't alive.
But mother lives, so for all your reassurances 1080
I live in fear, I must.
JOCASTA: But your father's death,
that, at least, is a great blessing, joy to the eyes!
OEDIPUS: Great, I know . . . but I fear *her*—she's still alive.
MESSENGER: Wait, who is this woman, makes you so afraid?
OEDIPUS: Merope, old man. The wife of Polybus. 1085
MESSENGER: The queen? What's there to fear in her?
OEDIPUS: A dreadful prophecy, stranger, sent by the gods.
MESSENGER: Tell me, could you? Unless it's forbidden
other ears to hear.
OEDIPUS: Not at all.
Apollo told me once—it is my fate— 1090
I must make love with my own mother,
shed my father's blood with my own hands.
So for years I've given Corinth a wide berth,
and it's been my good fortune too. But still,
to see one's parents and look into their eyes 1095
is the greatest joy I know.
MESSENGER: You're afraid of that?
That kept you out of Corinth?
OEDIPUS: My *father*, old man—
so I wouldn't kill my father.
MESSENGER: So that's it.
Well then, seeing I came with such good will, my king,
why don't I rid you of that old worry now? 1100
OEDIPUS: What a rich reward you'd have for that!
MESSENGER: What do you think I came for, majesty?

So you'd come home and I'd be better off.

OEDIPUS: Never, I will never go near my parents.

MESSENGER: My boy, it's clear, you don't know what you're
    doing.                                                                       1105

OEDIPUS: What do you mean, old man? For god's sake, explain.

MESSENGER: If you ran from *them*, always dodging home . . .

OEDIPUS: Always, terrified Apollo's oracle might come true—

MESSENGER: And you'd be covered with guilt, from both your par-
    ents.

OEDIPUS: That's right, old man, that fear is always with me.        1110

MESSENGER: Don't you know? You've really nothing to fear.

OEDIPUS: But why? If I'm their son—Merope, Polybus?

MESSENGER: Polybus was nothing to you, that's why, not in blood.

OEDIPUS: What are you saying—Polybus was not my father?

MESSENGER: No more than I am. He and I are equals.        1115

OEDIPUS:                                           My father—
    how can my father equal nothing? You're nothing to me!

MESSENGER: Neither was he, no more your father than I am.

OEDIPUS: Then why did he call me his son?

MESSENGER:                               You were a gift,
    years ago—know for a fact he took you
    from my hands.

OEDIPUS:                No, from another's hands?        1120
    Then how could he love me so? He loved me, deeply . . .

MESSENGER: True, and his early years without a child
    made him love you all the more.

OEDIPUS:                      And you, did you . . .
    buy me? find me by accident?

MESSENGER:                  I stumbléd on you,
    down the woody flanks of Mount Cithaeron.

OEDIPUS:                    So close,        1125
    what were you doing here, just passing through?

MESSENGER: Watching over my flocks, grazing them on the slopes.

OEDIPUS: A herdsman, were you? A vagabond, scraping for wages?

MESSENGER: Your savior too, my son, in your worst hour.

OEDIPUS:                        Oh—
    when you picked me up, was I in pain? What exactly?        1130

MESSENGER: Your ankles . . . they tell the story. Look at them.

OEDIPUS: Why remind me of that, that old affliction?

MESSENGER: Your ankles were pinned together. I set you free.

OEDIPUS: That dreadful mark—I've had it from the cradle.

MESSENGER: And you got your name[1] from that misfortune too,        1135
    the name's still with you.

1. In Greek the name *Oidipous* suggests "swollen foot."

OEDIPUS:                    Dear god, who did it?—
   mother? father? Tell me.
MESSENGER:                 I don't know.
   The one who gave you to me, he'd know more.
OEDIPUS: What? You took me from someone else?
   You didn't find me yourself?
MESSENGER:                 No sir,                          1140
   another shepherd passed you on to me.
OEDIPUS: Who? Do you know? Describe him.
MESSENGER: He called himself a servant of . . .
   if I remember rightly—Laius.

   [JOCASTA *turns sharply.*]

OEDIPUS: The king of the land who ruled here long ago?      1145
MESSENGER: That's the one. That herdsman was *his* man.
OEDIPUS: Is he still alive? Can I see him?
MESSENGER: They'd know best, the people of these parts.

   [OEDIPUS *and the* MESSENGER *turn to the* CHORUS.]

OEDIPUS: Does anyone know that herdsman,
   the one he mentioned? Anyone seen him                    1150
   in the fields, here in the city? Out with it!
   The time has come to reveal this once for all.
LEADER: I think he's the very shepherd you wanted to see,
   a moment ago. But the queen, Jocasta,
   she's the one to say.
OEDIPUS:                 Jocasta,                          1155
   you remember the man we just sent for?
   Is *that* the one he means?
JOCASTA:                 That man . . .
   why ask? Old shepherd, talk, empty nonsense,
   don't give it another thought, don't even think—
OEDIPUS: What—give up now, with a clue like this?          1160
   Fail to solve the mystery of my birth?
   Not for all the world!
JOCASTA:                 Stop—in the name of god,
   if you love your own life, call off this search!
   My suffering is enough.
OEDIPUS:                 Courage!
   Even if my mother turns out to be a slave,               1165
   and I a slave, three generations back,
   *you* would not seem common.
JOCASTA:                 Oh no,

listen to me, I beg you, don't do this.
OEDIPUS: Listen to you? No more. I must know it all,
     must see the truth at last.
JOCASTA:                      No, please—                          1170
     for your sake—I want the best for you!
OEDIPUS: Your best is more than I can bear.
JOCASTA:                              You're doomed—
     may you never fathom who you are!

     [*To a servant.*]

OEDIPUS: Hurry, fetch me the herdsman, now!
     Leave her to glory in her royal birth.                        1175
JOCASTA: Aieeeeee—
                    man of agony—
     that is the only name I have for you,
     that, no other—ever, ever, ever!

     [*Flinging through the palace doors. A long, tense silence fol-
     lows.*]

LEADER: Where's she gone, Oedipus?
     Rushing off, such wild grief . . .                            1180
     I'm afraid that from this silence
     something monstrous may come bursting forth.
OEDIPUS: Let it burst! Whatever will, whatever must!
     I must know my birth, no matter how common
     it may be—I must see my origins face-to-face.                 1185
     She perhaps, she with her woman's pride
     may well be mortified by my birth,
     but I, I count myself the son of Chance,
     the great goddess, giver of all good things—
     I'll never see myself disgraced. She is my mother!            1190
     And the moons have marked me out, my blood-brothers,
     one moon on the wane, the next moon great with power.
     That is my blood, my nature—I will never betray it,
     never fail to search and learn my birth!
CHORUS: Yes—if I am a true prophet                                 1195
          if I can grasp the truth,
       by the boundless skies of Olympus,
     at the full moon of tomorrow, Mount Cithaeron
     you will know how Oedipus glories in you—
     you, his birthplace, nurse, his mountain-mother!              1200
     And we will sing you, dancing out your praise—
     you lift our monarch's heart!

Apollo, Apollo, god of the wild cry
   may our dancing please you!
                              Oedipus—
      son, dear child, who bore you?                          1205
Who of the nymphs who seem to live forever[2]
mated with Pan,[3] the mountain-striding Father?
Who was your mother? who, some bride of Apollo
the god who loves the pastures spreading toward the sun?
      Or was it Hermes, king of the lightning ridges?          1210
Or Dionysus,[4] lord of frenzy, lord of the barren peaks—
did he seize you in his hands, dearest of all his lucky finds?—
      found by the nymphs, their warm eyes dancing, gift
to the lord who loves them dancing out his joy!

[OEDIPUS *strains to see a figure coming from the distance.
Attended by palace guards, an old* SHEPHERD *enters slowly,
reluctant to approach the king.*]

OEDIPUS: I never met the man, my friends . . . still,          1215
   if I had to guess, I'd say that's the shepherd,
   the very one we've looked for all along.
   Brothers in old age, two of a kind,
   he and our guest here. At any rate
   the ones who bring him in are my own men,                   1220
   I recognize them.

[*Turning to the* LEADER.]

                     But you know more than I,
   you should, you've seen the man before.
LEADER: I know him, definitely. One of Laius' men,
   a trusty shepherd, if there ever was one.
OEDIPUS: You, I ask you first, stranger,                       1225
   you from Corinth—is this the one you mean?
MESSENGER: You're looking at him. He's your man.

[*To the* SHEPHERD.]

OEDIPUS: You, old man, come over here—
   look at me. Answer all my questions.
   Did you ever serve King Laius?
SHEPHERD:                              So I did . . .           1230

2. Nymphs were not immortal, like the gods, but lived much longer than mortals.    3. A woodland god; patron of shepherds and flocks.    4. Dionysus like Pan and Hermes haunted the wild
country, woods and mountains. Hermes was born on Mount Kyllene in Arcadia.

a slave, not bought on the block though,
   born and reared in the palace.
OEDIPUS: Your duties, your kind of work?
SHEPHERD: Herding the flocks, the better part of my life.
OEDIPUS: Where, mostly? Where did you do your grazing?    1235
SHEPHERD:                                              Well,
   Cithaeron sometimes, or the foothills round about.
OEDIPUS: This man—you know him? ever see him there?

   [*Confused, glancing from the* MESSENGER *to the King.*]

SHEPHERD: Doing what?—what man do you mean?

   [*Pointing to the* MESSENGER.]

OEDIPUS: This one here—ever have dealings with him?
SHEPHERD: Not so I could say, but give me a chance,    1240
   my memory's bad . . .
MESSENGER: No wonder he doesn't know me, master.
   But let me refresh his memory for him.
   I'm sure he recalls old times we had
   on the slopes of Mount Cithaeron;    1245
   he and I, grazing our flocks, he with two
   and I with one—we both struck up together,
   three whole seasons, six months at a stretch
   from spring to the rising of Arcturus in the fall,[5]
   then with winter coming on I'd drive my herds    1250
   to my own pens, and back he'd go with his
   to Laius' folds.

   [*To the* SHEPHERD.]

                    Now that's how it was,
   wasn't it—yes or no?
SHEPHERD:                    Yes, I suppose . . .
   it's all so long ago.
MESSENGER:              Come, tell me,
   you gave me a child back then, a boy, remember?    1255
   A little fellow to rear, my very own.
SHEPHERD: What? Why rake up that again?
MESSENGER: Look, here he is, my fine old friend—
   the same man who was just a baby then.
SHEPHERD: Damn you, shut your mouth—quiet!    1260

---

5. Arcturus is the principal star in the constellation Bootes. Its "rising" (i.e., its reappearance in the night sky just before dawn in September) signaled the end of summer.

OEDIPUS: Don't lash out at him, old man—
  you need lashing more than he does.
SHEPHERD:                                    Why,
  master, majesty—what have I done wrong?
OEDIPUS: You won't answer his question about the boy.
SHEPHERD: He's talking nonsense, wasting his breath.                 1265
OEDIPUS: So, you won't talk willingly—
  then you'll talk with pain.

  [*The guards seize the* SHEPHERD.]

SHEPHERD: No, dear god, don't torture an old man!
OEDIPUS: Twist his arms back, quickly!
SHEPHERD:                              God help us, why?—
  what more do you need to know?                                     1270
OEDIPUS: Did you give him that child? He's asking.
SHEPHERD: I did . . . I wish to god I'd died that day.
OEDIPUS: You've got your wish if you don't tell the truth.
SHEPHERD: The more I tell, the worse the death I'll die.
OEDIPUS: Our friend here wants to stretch things out, does he?     1275

  [*Motioning to his men for torture.*]

SHEPHERD: No, no, I gave it to him—I just said so.
OEDIPUS: Where did you get it? Your house? Someone else's?
HEPHERD: It wasn't mine, no, I got it from . . . someone.
OEDIPUS: Which one of them?

  [*Looking at the citizens.*]

                              Whose house?
SHEPHERD:                                   No—
  god's sake, master, no more questions!                            1280
OEDIPUS: You're a dead man if I have to ask again.
SHEPHERD: Then—the child came from the house . . .
  of Laius.
OEDIPUS: A slave? or born of his own blood?
SHEPHERD:                                    Oh no,
  I'm right at the edge, the horrible truth—I've got to say it!
OEDIPUS: And I'm at the edge of hearing horrors, yes, but I must
  hear!                                                             1285
SHEPHERD: All right! His son, they said it was—his son!
  But the one inside, your wife,
    she'd tell it best.

OEDIPUS: My wife—
    *she* gave it to you?                1290
SHEPHERD: Yes, yes, my king.
OEDIPUS: Why, what for?
SHEPHERD: To kill it.
OEDIPUS: Her own child,
    how could she?                1295
SHEPHERD: She was afraid—
    frightening prophecies.
OEDIPUS: What?
SHEPHERD: They said—
    he'd kill his parents.
OEDIPUS: But you gave him to this old man—why?                1300
SHEPHERD: I pitied the little baby, master,
    hoped he'd take off to his own country,
    far away, but he saved him for this, this fate.
    If you are the man he says you are, believe me,
    you were born for pain.                1305
OEDIPUS:              O god—
    all come true, all burst to light!
    O light—now let me look my last on you!
    I stand revealed at last—
    cursed in my birth, cursed in marriage,
    cursed in the lives I cut down with these hands!                1310

[*Rushing through the doors with a great cry. The Corinthian*
MESSENGER, *the* SHEPHERD *and attendants exit slowly to the* side.]

CHORUS: O the generations of men
    the dying generations—adding the total
    of all your lives I find they come to nothing . . .
        does there exist, is there a man on earth
    who seizes more joy than just a dream, a vision?                1315
    And the vision no sooner dawns than dies
    blazing into oblivion.

    You are my great example, you, your life
    your destiny, Oedipus, man of misery—
    I count no man blest.
              You outranged all men!                1320
      Bending your bow to the breaking-point
    you captured priceless glory, O dear god,
    and the Sphinx came crashing down,
        the virgin, claws hooked

like a bird of omen singing, shrieking death—                              1325
like a fortress reared in the face of death
you rose and saved our land.

From that day on we called you king
we crowned you with honors, Oedipus, towering over all—
mighty king of the seven gates of Thebes.                                  1330
But now to hear your story—is there a man more agonized?
More wed to pain and frenzy? Not a man on earth,
the joy of your life ground down to nothing
O Oedipus, name for the ages—
    one and the same wide harbor served you                1335
        son and father both
son and father came to rest in the same bridal chamber.
How, how could the furrows your father plowed
bear you, your agony, harrowing on
in silence O so long?

               But now for all your power     1340
Time, all-seeing Time has dragged you to the light,
judged your marriage monstrous from the start—
the son and the father tangling, both one—
O child of Laius, would to god
    I'd never seen you, never never!                        1345
    Now I weep like a man who wails the dead
and the dirge comes pouring forth with all my heart!
I tell you the truth, you gave me life
my breath leapt up in you
and now you bring down night upon my eyes.                                 1350

    [*Enter a* MESSNGER *from the palace.*]

MESSENGER: Men of Thebes, always first in honor,
    what horrors you will hear, what you will see,
    what a heavy weight of sorrow you will shoulder . . .
    if you are true to your birth, if you still have
    some feeling for the royal house of Thebes.                         1355
    I tell you neither the waters of the Danube
    nor the Nile[6] can wash this palace clean.
    Such things it hides, it soon will bring to light—
    terrible things, and none done blindly now,
    all done with a will. The pains                                   1360
    we inflict upon ourselves hurt most of all.

---

6. The Greek says Phasis—a river in Asia Minor. The translator has substituted a big river more familiar to modern readers.

LEADER: God knows we have pains enough already.
    What can you add to them?
MESSENGER: The queen is dead.
LEADER:                    Poor lady—how?
MESSENGER: By her own hand. But you are spared the worst,    1365
    you never had to watch . . . I saw it all,
    and with all the memory that's in me
    you will learn what that poor woman suffered.

Once she'd broken in through the gates,
dashing past us, frantic, whipped to fury,    1370
ripping her hair out with both hands—
straight to her rooms she rushed, flinging herself
across the bridal-bed, doors slamming behind her—
once inside, she wailed for Laius, dead so long,
remembering how she bore his child long ago    1375
the life that rose up to destroy him, leaving
its mother to mother living creatures
with the very son she'd borne.
Oh how she wept, mourning the marriage-bed
where she let loose that double brood—monsters—    1380
husband by her husband, children by her child.
                              And then—
but how she died is more than I can say. Suddenly
Oedipus burst in, screaming, he stunned us so
we couldn't watch her agony to the end,
our eyes were fixed on him. Circling    1385
like a maddened beast, stalking, here, there,
crying out to us—
                Give him a sword![7] His wife,
no wife, his mother, where can he find the mother earth
that cropped two crops at once, himself and all his children?
He was raging—one of the dark powers pointing the way,    1390
none of us mortals crowding around him, no,
with a great shattering cry—someone, something leading him on—
he hurled at the twin doors and bending the bolts back
out of their sockets, crashed through the chamber.
And there we saw the woman hanging by the neck,    1395
cradled high in a woven noose, spinning,
swinging back and forth. And when he saw her,
giving a low, wrenching sob that broke our hearts,
slipping the halter from her throat, he eased her down,
in a slow embrace he laid her down, poor thing . . .    1400
then, what came next, what horror we beheld!

---

7. Presumably so that he could kill himself.

He rips off her brooches, the long gold pins
holding her robes—and lifting them high,
looking sraight up into the points,
he digs them down the sockets of his eyes, crying, "You,          1405
you'll see no more the pain I suffered, all the pain I caused!
Too long you looked on the ones you never should have seen,
blind to the ones you longed to see, to know! Blind
from this hour on! Blind in the darkness—blind!"
His voice like a dirge, rising, over and over          1410
raising the pins, raking them down his eyes.
And at each stroke blood spurts from the roots,
splashing his beard, a swirl of it, nerves and clots—
black hail of blood pulsing, gushing down.

These are the griefs that burst upon them both,          1415
coupling man and woman. The joy they had so lately,
the fortune of their old ancestral house
was deep joy indeed. Now, in this one day,
wailing, madness and doom, death, disgrace,
all the griefs in the world that you can name,          1420
all are theirs forever.

LEADER:                          Oh poor man, the misery—
has he any rest from pain now?

          [*A voice within, in torment.*]

MESSENGER:                          He's shouting,
"Loose the bolts, someone, show me to all of Thebes!
My father's murderer, my mother's—"
No, I can't repeat it, it's unholy.          1425
Now he'll tear himself from his native earth,
not linger, curse the house with his own curse.
But he needs strength, and a guide to lead him on.
This is sickness more than he can bear.

          [*The palace doors open.*]

                          Look,
he'll show you himself. The great doors are opening—          1430
you are about to see a sight, a horror
even his mortal enemy would pity.

          [*Enter* OEDIPUS, *blinded, led by a boy. He stands at the palace
          steps, as if surveying his people once again.*]

CHORUS:                              O the terror—
  the suffering, for all the world to see,
  the worst terror that ever met my eyes.
  What madness swept over you? What god,                         1435
  what dark power leapt beyond all bounds,
  beyond belief, to crush your wretched life?—
  godforsaken, cursed by the gods!
  I pity you but I can't bear to look.
  I've much to ask, so much to learn,                            1440
  so much fascinates my eyes,
  but you . . . I shudder at the sight.
OEDIPUS:                              Oh, Ohh—
  the agony! I am agony—
  where am I going? where on earth?
      where does all this agony hurl me?                         1445
  where's my voice?—
      winging, swept away on a dark tide—
  My destiny, my dark power, what a leap you made!
CHORUS: To the depths of terror, too dark to hear, to see.
OEDIPUS: Dark, horror of darkness                                1450
  my darkness, drowning, swirling around me
  Crashing wave on wave—unspeakable, irresistible
      headwind, fatal harbor! Oh again,
  the misery, all at once, over and over
      the stabbing daggers, stab of memory                       1455
  raking me insane.
CHORUS:                  No wonder you suffer
  twice over, the pain of your wounds,
  the lasting grief of pain.
OEDIPUS:                      Dear friend, still here?
  Standing by me, still with a care for me,
      the blind man? Such compassion,                            1460
      loyal to the last. Oh it's you,
  I know you're here, dark as it is
  I'd know you anywhere, your voice—
  it's yours, clearly yours.
CHORUS:                      Dreadful, what you've done . . .
  how could you bear it, gouging out your eyes?                  1465
  What superhuman power drove you on?
OEDIPUS: Apollo, friends, Apollo—
  he ordained my agonies—these, my pains on pains!
      But the hand that struck my eyes was mine,
  mine alone—no one else—                                        1470
      I did it all myself!

What good were eyes to me?
Nothing I could see could bring me joy.
CHORUS: No, no, exactly as you say.
OEDIPUS:                              What can I ever see?
    What love, what call of the heart                          1475
can touch my ears with joy? Nothing, friends.
        Take me away, far, far from Thebes,
        quickly, cast me away, my friends—
    this great murderous ruin, this man cursed to heaven,
        the man the deathless gods hate most of all!      1480
CHORUS: Pitiful, you suffer so, you understand so much . . .
    I wish you'd never known.
OEDIPUS:                          Die, die—
    whoever he was that day in the wilds
  who cut my ankles free of the ruthless pins,
        he pulled me clear of death, he saved my life      1485
    for this, this kindness—
            Curse him, kill him!
    If I'd died then, I'd never have dragged myself,
    my loved ones through such hell.
CHORUS: Oh if only . . . would to god.
OEDIPUS:                          I'd never have come to this,
        my father's murderer—never been branded
    mother's husband, all men see me now! Now,
        loathed by the gods, son of the mother I defiled
        coupling in my father's bed, spawning lives in the loins
    that spawned my wretched life. What grief can crown this grief?
        It's mine alone, my destiny—I am Oedipus!
CHORUS: How can I say you've chosen for the best?
    Better to die than be alive and blind.
OEDIPUS: What I did was best—don't lecture me,
    no more advice. I, with *my* eyes,                          1500
    how could I look my father in the eyes
    when I go down to death? Or mother, so abused . . .
    I have done such things to the two of them,
    crimes too huge for hanging.
                        Worse yet,
    the sight of my children, born as they were born,      1505
    how could I long to look into their eyes?
    No, not with these eyes of mine, never.
    Not this city either, her high towers,
    the sacred glittering images of her gods—
    I am misery! I, her best son, reared                          1510
    as no other son of Thebes was ever reared,

I've stripped myself I gave the command myself.
All men must cast away the great blasphemer,
the curse now brought to light by the gods,
the son of Laius—I, my father's son!                          1515

Now I've exposed my guilt, horrendous guilt,
could I train a level glance on you, my countrymen?
Impossible! No, if I could just block off my ears,
the springs of hearing, I would stop at nothing—
I'd wall up my loathsome body like a prison,                  1520
blind to the sound of life, not just the sight.
Oblivion—what a blessing . . .
for the mind to dwell a world away from pain.

O Cithaeron, why did you give me shelter?
Why didn't you take me, crush my life out on the spot?        1525
I'd never have revealed my birth to all mankind.

O Polybus, Corinth, the old house of my fathers,
so I believed—what a handsome prince you raised
under the skin, what sickness to the core.
Look at me! Born of outrage, outrage to the core.             1530
O triple roads—it all comes back, the secret,
dark ravine, and the oaks closing in
where the three roads join . . .
You drank my father's blood, my own blood
spilled by my own hands—you still remember me?               1535
What things you saw me do? Then I came here
and did them all once more!
                          Marriages! O marriage,
you gave me birth, and once you brought me into the world
you brought my sperm rising back, springing to light
fathers, brothers, sons—one murderous breed—                 1540
brides, wives, mothers. The blackest things
a man can do, I have done them all!
                          No more—
it's wrong to name what's wrong to do. Quickly,
for the love of god, hide me somewhere,
kill me, hurl me into the sea                                  1545
where you can never look on me again.

[*Beckoning to the* CHORUS *as they shrink away.*]

                          Closer,

it's all right. Touch the man of grief.
Do. Don't be afraid. My troubles are mine
and I am the only man alive who can sustain them.

[*Enter* CREON *from the palace, attended by palace guards.*]

LEADER: Put your requests to Creon. Here he is,                     1550
 just when we need him. He'll have a plan, he'll act.
 Now that he's the sole defense of the country
 in your place.
OEDIPUS:          Oh no, what can I say to him?
 How can I ever hope to win his trust?
 I wronged him so, just now, in every way.                         1555
 You must see that—I was so wrong, so wrong.
CREON: I haven't come to mock you, Oedipus,
 or to criticize your former failings.

 [*Turning to the guards.*]

                                        You there,
 have you lost all respect for human feelings?
 At least revere the Sun, the holy fire                            1560
 that keeps us all alive. Never expose a thing
 of guilt and holy dread so great it appalls
 the earth, the rain from heaven, the light of day!
 Get him into the halls—quickly as you can.
 Piety demands no less. Kindred alone                              1565
 should see a kinsman's shame. This is obscene.
OEDIPUS: Please, in god's name . . . you wipe my fears away,
 coming so generously to me, the worst of men.
 Do one thing more, for your sake, not mine.
CREON: What do you want? Why so insistent?                        1570
OEDIPUS: Drive me out of the land at once, far from sight,
 where I can never hear a human voice.
CREON: I'd have done that already, I promise you.
 First I wanted the god to clarify my duties.
OEDIPUS: The god? His command was clear, every word:             1575
 death for the father-killer, the curse—
 he said destroy me!
CREON: So he did. Still, in such a crisis
 it's better to ask precisely what to do.
OEDIPUS:                          So miserable—
 you'd consult the god about a man like me?                       1580
CREON: By all means. And this time, I assume,
 even you will obey the god's decrees.

OEDIPUS:                          I will,
I will. And you, I command you—I beg you . . .
the woman inside, bury her as you see fit.
It's the only decent thing,                                    1585
to give your own the last rites. As for me,
never condemn the city of my fathers
to house my body, not while I'm alive, no,
let me live on the mountains, on Cithaeron,
my favorite haunt, I have made it famous.                      1590
Mother and father marked out that rock
to be my everlasting tomb—buried alive.
Let me die there, where they tried to kill me.

Oh but this I know: no sickness can destroy me,
nothing can. I would never have been saved                     1595
from death—I have been saved
for something great and terrible, something strange.
Well let my destiny come and take me on its way!
About my children, Creon, the boys at least,
don't burden yourself. They're men,                            1600
wherever they go, they'll find the means to live.
But my two daughters, my poor helpless girls,
clustering at our table, never without me
hovering near them . . . whatever I touched,
they always had their share. Take care of them,                1605
I beg you. Wait, better—permit me, would you?
Just to touch them with my hands and take
our fill of tears. Please . . . my king.
Grant it, with all your noble heart.
If I could hold them, just once, I'd think                     1610
I had them with me, like the early days
when I could see their eyes.

[ANTIGONE and ISMENE, two small childen, are led in from the
palace by a nurse.]

                          What's that
O god! Do I really hear you sobbing?—
my two children. Creon, you've pitied me?
Sent me my darling girls, my own flesh and blood!              1615
Am I right?
CREON:          Yes, it's my doing.
I know the joy they gave you all these years,
the joy you must feel now.
OEDIPUS:                          Bless you, Creon!

May god watch over you for this kindness,
better than he ever guarded me.

                              Children, where are you?    1620
Here, come quickly—

    [*Groping for* ANTIGONE *and* ISMENE, *who approach their father
    cautiously, then embrace him.*]

                    Come to these hands of mine,
your brother's hands, your own father's hands
that served his once bright eyes so well—
that made them blind. Seeing nothing, children,
knowing nothing, I became your father,                    1625
I fathered you in the soil that gave me life.

How I weep for you—I cannot see you now . . .
just thinking of all your days to come, the bitterness,
the life that rough mankind will thrust upon you.
Where are the public gatherings you can join,             1630
the banquets of the clans? Home you'll come,
in tears, cut off from the sight of it all,
the brilliant rites unfinished.
And when you reach perfection, ripe for marriage,
who will he be, my dear ones? Risking all                 1635
to shoulder the curse that weighs down my parents,
yes and you too—that wounds us all together.
What more misery could you want?
Your father killed his father, sowed his mother,
one, one and the selfsame womb sprang you—               1640
he cropped the very roots of his existence.

Such disgrace, and you must bear it all!
Who will marry you then? Not a man on earth.
Your doom is clear: you'll wither away to nothing,
single, without a child.

    [*Turning to* CREON.]

                    Oh Creon,                              1645
you are the only father they have now . . .
we who brought them into the world
are gone, both gone at a stroke—
Don't let them go begging, abandoned,
women without men. Your own flesh and blood!              1650

Never bring them down to the level of my pains.
Pity them. Look at them, so young, so vulnerable,
shorn of everything—you're their only hope.
Promise me, noble Creon, touch my hand!

[*Reaching toward* CREON, *who draws back.*]

You, little ones, if you were old enough                    1655
to understand, there is much I'd tell you.
Now, as it is, I'd have you say a prayer.
Pray for life, my children,
live where you are free to grow and season.
Pray god you find a better life than mine,                 1660
the father who begot you.
CREON:                        Enough.
    You've wept enough. Into the palace now.
OEDIPUS: I must, but I find it very hard.
CREON: Time is the great healer, you will see.
OEDIPUS: I am going—you know on what condition?            1665
CREON: Tell me. I'm listening.
OEDIPUS: Drive me out of Thebes, in exile.
CREON: Not I. Only the gods can give you that.
OEDIPUS: Surely the gods hate me so much—
CREON: You'll get your wish at once.
OEDIPUS:                          You consent?            1670
CREON: I try to say what I mean; it's my habit.
OEDIPUS: Then take me away. It's time.
CREON: Come along, let go of the children.
OEDIPUS:                          No—
    don't take them away from me, not now! No no no!

[*Clutching his daughters as the guards wrench them loose and
take them through the palace doors.*]

CREON: Still the king, the master of all things?          1675
    No more: here your power ends.
    None of your power follows you through life.

[*Exit* OEDIPUS *and* CREON *to the palace. The* CHORUS *comes forward to address the audience directly.*]
CHORUS: People of Thebes, my countrymen, look on Oedipus.
    He solved the famous riddle with his brilliance,
    he rose to power, a man beyond all power.            1680
    Who could behold his greatness without envy?

Now what a black sea of terror has overwhelmed him.
Now as we keep our watch and wait the final day,
count no man happy till he dies, free of pain at last.


[*Exit in procession.*]




# Antigone[1]

### *Characters*

ANTIGONE, *daughter of Oedipus and Jocasta*
ISMENE, *sister of Antigone*
A CHORUS, *of old Theban citizens and their* LEADER
CREON, *king of Thebes, uncle of Antigone and Ismene*
A SENTRY
HAEMON, *son of Creon and Eurydice*
TIRESIAS, *a blind prophet*
A MESSENGER
EURYDICE, *wife of Creon*
*Guards, attendants, and a boy*

[TIME AND SCENE: *The royal house of Thebes. It is still night,
and the invading armies of Argos have just been driven from
the city. Fighting on opposite sides, the sons of Oedipus, Eteocles and Polynices, have killed each other in combat. Their
uncle,* CREON, *is now king of Thebes.*

*Enter* ANTIGONE, *slipping through the central doors of the
palace. She motions to her sister,* ISMENE, *who follows her cautiously toward an altar at the center of the stage.*]

ANTIGONE: My own flesh and blood—dear sister, dear Ismene,
how many griefs our father Oedipus handed down!
Do you know one, I ask you, one grief
that Zeus will not perfect for the two of us
while we still live and breathe? There's nothing,              5
no pain—our lives are pain—no private shame,
no public disgrace, nothing I haven't seen
in your griefs and mine. And now this:
an emergency decree, they say, the Commander[2]
has just now declared for all of Thebes.                    10
What, haven't you heard? Don't you see?

1. Translated by Robert Fagles.     2. Creon. In the original he is given a military title; Antigone
will not refer to him as king.

The doom reserved for enemies
marches on the ones we love the most.
ISMENE: Not I, I haven't heard a word, Antigone.
  Nothing of loved ones,                          15
  no joy or pain has come my way, not since
  the two of us were robbed of our two brothers,
  both gone in a day, a double blow—
  not since the armies of Argos vanished,
  just this very night. I know nothing more,         20
  whether our luck's improved or ruin's still to come.
ANTIGONE: I thought so. That's why I brought you out here,
  past the gates, so you could hear in private.
ISMENE: What's the matter? Trouble, clearly . . .
  you sound so dark, so grim.                       25
ANTIGONE: Why not? Our own brothers' burial!
  Hasn't Creon graced one with all the rites,
  disgraced the other? Eteocles, they say,
  has been given full military honors,
  rightly so—Creon has laid him in the earth        30
  and he goes with glory down among the dead.
  But the body of Polynices, who died miserably—
  why, a citywide proclamation, rumor has it,
  forbids anyone to bury him, even mourn him.
  He's to be left unwept, unburied, a lovely treasure    35
  for birds that scan the field and feast to their heart's content.

  Such, I hear, is the martial law our good Creon
  lays down for you and me—yes, me, I tell you—
  and he's coming here to alert the uninformed
  in no uncertain terms,                       40
  and he won't treat the matter lightly. Whoever
  disobeys in the least will die, his doom is sealed:
  stoning to death inside the city walls!

  There you have it. You'll soon show what you are,
  worth your breeding, Ismene, or a coward—       45
  for all your royal blood.
ISMENE: My poor sister, if things have come to this,
  who am I to make or mend them, tell me,
  what good am I to you?
ANTIGONE:                Decide.
  Will you share the labor, share the work?       0
ISMENE: What work, what's the risk? What do you mean?

    [*Raising her hands.*]

ANTIGONE: Will you lift up his body with these bare hands
   and lower it with me?
ISMENE:             What? You'd bury him—
   when a law forbids the city?
ANTIGONE:           Yes!
   He is my brother and—deny it as you will—            55
   your brother too.
   No one will ever convict me for a traitor.
ISMENE: So desperate, and Creon has expressly—
ANTIGONE:                No,
   he has no right to keep me from my own.
ISMENE: Oh my sister, think—                60
   think how our own father died, hated,[3]
   his reputation in ruins, driven on
   by the crimes he brought to light himself
   to gouge out his eyes with his own hands—
   then mother . . . his mother and wife, both in one,     65
   mutilating her life in the twisted noose—
   and last, our two brothers dead in a single day,
   both shedding their own blood, poor suffering boys,
   battling out their common destiny hand-to-hand.

   Now look at the two of us left so alone . . .        70
   think what a death we'll die, the worst of all
   if we violate the laws and override
   the fixed decree of the throne, its power—
   we must be sensible. Remember we are women,
   we're not born to contend with men. Then too,     75
   we're underlings, ruled by much stronger hands,
   so we must submit in this, and things still worse.

   I, for one, I'll beg the dead to forgive me—
   I'm forced, I have no choice—I must obey
   the ones who stand in power. Why rush to extremes?    80
   It's madness, madness.
ANTIGONE:            I won't insist,
   no, even if you should have a change of heart,
   I'd never welcome you in the labor, not with me.
   So, do as you like, whatever suits you best—
   I will bury him myself.                85
   And even if I die in the act, that death will be a glory.
   I will lie with the one I love and loved by him—
   an outrage sacred to the gods! I have longer

3. This play was written before *Oedipus the King* and *Oedipus at Colonus*, which give us a different picture of Oedipus' end.

to please the dead than please the living here:
in the kingdom down below I'll lie forever.                    90
Do as you like, dishonor the laws
the gods hold in honor.
ISMENE:                    I'd do them no dishonor . . .
but defy the city? I have no strength for that.
ANTIGONE: You have your excuses. I am on my way,
I'll raise a mound for him, for my dear brother.              95
ISMENE: Oh Antigone, you're so rash—I'm so afraid for you!
ANTIGONE: Don't fear for me. Set your own life in order.
ISMENE: Then don't, at least, blurt this out to anyone.
Keep it a secret. I'll join you in that, I promise.
ANTIGONE: Dear god, shout it from the rooftops. I'll hate you    100
all the more for silence—tell the world!
ISMENE: So fiery—and it ought to chill your heart.
ANTIGONE: I know I please where I must please the most.
ISMENE: Yes, if you can, but you're in love with impossibility.
ANTIGONE: Very well then, once my strength gives out          105
I will be done at last.
ISMENE:                         You're wrong from the start,
you're off on a hopeless quest.
ANTIGONE: if you say so you will make me hate you,
and the hatred of the dead, by all rights,
will haunt you night and day.                                 110
But leave me to my own absurdity, leave me
to suffer this—dreadful thing. I will suffer
nothing as great as death without glory.

    [*Exit to the side.*]

ISMENE: Then go if you must, but rest assured,
wild, irrational as you are, my sister,                       115
you are truly dear to the ones who love you.

    [*Withdrawing to the palace.*]
    [*Enter a* CHORUS, *the old citizens of Thebes chanting as the sun
    begins to rise.*]

CHORUS:[4] Glory!—great beam of the sun, brightest of all
that ever rose on the seven gates of Thebes,
    you burn through night at last!
        Great eye of the golden day,                          120
    mounting the Dirce's[5] banks you throw him back—

4. The chorus of old men celebrates the victory won over the Argive forces and Polynices.
5. A river of the Theban plain.

the enemy out of Argos, the white shield,[6] the man of bronze—
he's flying headlong now
　　　the bridle of fate stampeding him with pain!

　　　　　And he had driven against our borders,　　　　　　125
　　　　　launched by the waring claims of Polynices—
　　　　　like an eagle screaming, winging havoc
　　　　　　　over the land, wings of armor
　　　　　shielded white as snow,
　　　　　a huge army massing,　　　　　　　　　　　　130
　　　　　crested helmets bristling for assault.

He hovered above our roofs, his vast maw gaping
closing down around our seven gates,
　　　his spears thirsting for the kill
　　　　　but now he's gone, look,　　　　　　　　　　135
before he could glut his jaws with Theban blood
or the god of fire put our crown of towers to the torch.
He grappled the Dragon[7] none can master—Thebes—
　　　the clang of our arms like thunder at his back!

　　　　　Zeus hates with a vengeance all bravado,　　　140
　　　　　the mighty boasts of men. He watched them
　　　　　coming on in a rising flood, the pride
　　　　　of their golden armor ringing shrill—
　　　　　and brandishing his lightning
　　　　　blasted the fighter just at the goal,[8]　　　　145
　　　　　rushing to shout his triumph from our walls.

Down from the heights he crashed, pounding down on the earth!
And moment ago, blazing torch in hand—
　　　mad for attack, ecstatic
he breathed his rage, the storm　　　　　　　　　　150
　　　of his fury hurling at our heads!
But now his high hopes have laid him low
and down the enemy ranks the iron god of war
　　　deals his rewards, his stunning blows—Ares[9]
　　　rapture of battle, our right arm in the crisis.　　　155

　　　　　Seven captains marshaled at seven gates
　　　　　seven against their equals, gave

---

6. The Argive soldiers' shields were painted white.　　7. According to legend, the Thebans sprang from the dragon's teeth sown by Cadmus.　　8. Capaneus, the most violent of the Seven against Thebes. He had almost scaled the wall when the lightning of Zeus threw him down.　　9. Not only the god of war but also one of the patron deities of Thebes.

their brazen trophies[1] up to Zeus
god of the breaking rout of battle,
all but two: those blood brothers,                              160
one father, one mother—matched in rage,
spears matched for the twin conquest—
clashed and won the common prize of death.

But now for Victory! glorious in the morning,
joy in her eyes to meet our joy                                 165
   she is winging[2] down to Thebes,
our fleets of chariots wheeling in her wake—
   Now let us win oblivion from the wars,
thronging the temples of the gods
in singing, dancing choirs through the night!                   170
    Lord Dionysus,[3] god of the dance
    that shakes the land of Thebes, now lead the way!

[*Enter* CREON *from the palace, attended by his guard.*]

But look, the king of the realm is coming,
Creon, the new man for the new day,
whatever the gods are sending now . . .                         175
what new plan will he launch?
Why this, this special session?
Why this sudden call to the old men
summoned at one command?

CREON: My countrymen,
the ship of state is safe. The gods who rocked her,             180
after a long, merciless pounding in the storm,
have righted her once more.
               Out of the whole city
I have called you here alone. Well I know,
first, your undeviating respect
for the throne and royal power of King Laius.                   185
Next, while Oedipus steered the land of Thebes,
and even after he died, your loyalty was unshakable
you still stood by their children. Now then,
since the two sons are dead—two blows of fate
in the same day, cut down by each other's hands,               190
both killers, both brothers stained with blood—

---

1. The vietors in Greek battle set up a trophy consisting of the armor of one of the enemy dead, fixed to a post and set up at the place where the enemy turned to run away.　2. Victory is portrayed in Greek painting and sculpture as a winged young woman.　3. A god of revel, but also a god born to Zeus and a Theban princess, Semele.

as I am next in kin to the dead,
I now possess the throne and all its powers.

Of course you cannot know a man completely,
his character, his principles, sense of judgment,                    195
not till he's shown his colors, ruling the people,
making laws. Experience, there's the test.
As I see it, whoever assumes the task,
the awesome task of setting the city's course,
and refuses to adopt the soundest policies                           200
but fearing someone, keeps his lips locked tight,
he's utterly worthless. So I rate him now,
I always have. And whoever places a friend
above the good of his own country, he is nothing:
I have no use for him. Zeus my witness,                              205
Zeus who sees all things, always—
I could never stand by silent, watching destruction
march against our city, putting safety to rout,
nor could I ever make that man a friend of mine
who menaces our country. Remember this:                              210
our country *is* our safety.
Only while she voyages true on course
can we establish friendships, truer than blood itself.
Such are my standards. They make our city great.

Closely akin to them I have proclaimed,                              215
just now, the following decree to our people
concerning the two sons of Oedipus.
Eteocles, who died fighting for Thebes,
excelling all in arms: he shall be buried,
crowned with a hero's honors, the cups we pour[4]                    220
to soak the earth and reach the famous dead.

But as for his blood brother, Polynices,
who returned from exile, home to his father-city
and the gods of his race, consumed with one desire—
to burn them roof to roots—who thirsted to drink                     225
his kinsmen's blood and sell the rest to slavery:
that man—a proclamation has forbidden the city
to dignify him with burial, mourn him at all.
No, he must be left unburied, his corpse
carrion for the birds and dogs to tear,                              230
an obscenity for the citizens to behold!

---

**4.** Libations (liquid offerings—wine, honey, etc.) poured on the grave.

These are my principles. Never at my hands
will the traitor be honored above the patriot.
But whoever proves his loyalty to the state—
I'll prize that man in death as well as life.                              235
LEADER: If this is your pleasure, Creon, treating
  our city's enemy and our friend this way . . .
  The power is yours, I suppose, to enforce it
  with the laws, both for the dead and all of us,
  the living.
CREON:          Follow my orders closely then,
  be on your guard.
LEADER:              We're too old.
  Lay that burden on younger shoulders.
CREON:                                No, no,
  I don't mean the body—I've posted guards already.
LEADER: What command for us then? What other service?
CREON: See that you never side with those who break my orders.  245
LEADER: Never. Only a fool could be in love with death.
CREON: Death is the price—you're right. But all too often
  the mere hope of money has ruined many men.

  [A SENTRY enters from the side.]

SENTRY:                                    My lord,
  I can't say I'm winded from running, or set out
  with any spring in my legs either—no sir,                                250
  I was lost in thought, and it made me stop, often,
  dead in my track, heeling, turning back,
  and all the time a voice inside me muttering,
  "Idiot, why? You're going straight to your death."
  Then muttering, "Stopped again, poor fool?                              255
  If somebody gets the news to Creon first,
  what's to save your neck?"
                          And so,
  mulling it over, on I trudge, dragging my feet,
  you can make a short road take forever . . .
  but at last, look, common sense won out,                                260
  I'm here, and I'm all yours,
  and even though I come empty-handed
  I'll tell my story just the same, because
  I've come with a good grip on one hope,
  what will come will come, whatever fate—                                265
CREON: Come to the point!
  What's wrong—why so afraid?
SENTRY: First, myself, I've got to tell you,

I didn't do it, didn't see who did—
    Be fair, don't take it out on me.                                    270
CREON: You're playing it safe, soldier,
    barricading yourself from any trouble.
    It's obvious, you've something strange to tell.
SENTRY: Dangerous too, and danger makes you delay
    for all you're worth.                                                275
CREON: Out with it—then dismiss!
SENTRY: All right, here it comes. The body—
    someone's just buried it, then run off . . .
    sprinkled some dry dust on the flesh,[5]
    given it proper rites.
CREON:                        What?                                      280
    What man alive would dare—
SENTRY:                              I've no idea, I swear it.
    There was no mark of a spade, no pickaxe there,
    no earth turned up, the ground packed hard and dry,
    unbroken, no tracks, no wheelruts, nothing,
    the workman left no trace. Just at sunup                             285
    the first watch of the day points it out—
    it was a wonder! We were stunned . . .
    a terrific burden too, for all of us, listen:
    you can't see the corpse, not that it's buried,
    really, just a light cover of road-dust on it,                       290
    as if someone meant to lay the dead to rest
    and keep from getting cursed.
    Not a sign in sight that dogs or wild beasts
    had worried the body, even torn the skin.
    But what came next! Rough talk flew thick and fast,                  295
    guard grilling guard—we'd have come to blows
    at last, nothing to stop it; each man for himself
    and each the culprit, no one caught red-handed,
    all of us pleading ignorance, dodging the charges,
    ready to take up red-hot iron in our fists,                          300
    go through fire,[6] swear oaths to the gods—
    "I didn't do it, I had no hand in it either,
    not in the plotting, not the work itself!"

    Finally, after all this wrangling came to nothing,
    one man spoke out and made us stare at the ground,                   305
    hanging our heads in fear. No way to counter him,
    no way to take his advice and come through

---

5. A symbolic burial, all Antigone could do alone, without Ismene's help.   6. Both traditional assertions of truthfulness, derived perhaps from some primitive ritual of ordeal—only the liar would get burned.

safe and sound. Here's what he said:
"Look, we've got to report the facts to Creon,
we can't keep this hidden." Well, that won out,                310
and the lot fell to me, condemned me,
unlucky as ever, I got the prize. So here I am,
against my will and yours too, well I know—
no one wants the man who brings bad news.
LEADER:                                                My king,
ever since he began I've been debating in my mind,           315
could this possibly be the work of the gods?
CREON:                                          Stop—
before you make me choke wth anger—the gods!
You, you're senile, must you be insane?
You say—why it's intolerable—say the gods
could have the slightest concern for the corpse?            320
Tell me, was it for meritorious service
they proceeded to bury him, prized him so? The hero
who came to burn their temples ringed with pillars,
their golden treasures—scorch their hallowed earth
and fling their laws to the winds.                          325
Exactly when did you last see the gods
celebrating traitors? Inconceivable!


No, from the first there were certain citizens
who could hardly stand the spirit of my regime,
grumbling against me in the dark, heads together,           330
tossing wildly, never keeping their neck beneath
the yoke, loyally submitting to their king.
These are the instigators, I'm convinced—
they've perverted my own guard, bribed them
to do their work.
                    Money! Nothing worse                    335
in our lives, so current, rampant, so corrupting.
Money—you demolish cities, rot men from their homes,
you train and twist good minds and set them on
to the most atrocious schemes. No limit,
you make them adept at every kind of outrage,               340
every godless crime—money!
                              Everyone—
the whole crew bribed to commit this crime,
they've made one thing sure at least:
sooner or later they will pay the price.


    [*Wheeling on the* SENTRY.]

                                        You—
I swear to Zeus as I still believe in Zeus,                          345
if you don't find the man who buried that corpse,
the very man, and produce him before my eyes,
simple death won't be enough for you,
not till we string you up alive
and wring the immorality out of you.                                 350
Then you can steal the rest of your days,
better informed about where to make a killing.
You'll have learned, at last, it doesn't pay
to itch for rewards from every hand that beckons.
Filthy profits wreck most men, you'll see—                           355
they'll never save your life.
SENTRY:                            Please,
    may I say a word or two, or just turn and go?
CREON: Can't you tell? Everything you say offends me.
SENTRY: Where does it hurt you, in the ears or in the heart?
CREON: And who are you to pinpoint my displeasure?                   360
SENTRY: The culprit grates on your feelings,
    I just annoy your ears.
CREON:                        Still talking?
    You talk too much! a born nuisance—
SENTRY:                                    Maybe so,
    but I never did this thing, so help me!
CREON:                                    Yes you did—
    what's more, you squandered your life for silver!                365
SENTRY: Oh it's terrible when the one who does the judging
    judges things all wrong.
CREON:                        Well now,
    you just be clever about your judgments—
    if you fail to produce the criminals for me,
    you'll swear your dirty money brought you pain.                  370

        [Turning sharply, reentering the palace.]

SENTRY: I hope he's found. Best thing by far.
    But caught or not, that's in the lap of fortune:
    I'll never come back, you've seen the last of me.
    I'm saved, even now, and I never thought,
    I never hoped—                                                  375
    dear gods, I owe you all my thanks!

        [Rushing out.]

CHORUS:                        Numberless wonders
    terrible wonders walk the world but none the match for man—

that great wonder crossing the heaving gray sea,
      driven on by the blasts of winter
on through breakers crashing left and right,                    380
   holds his steady course
and the oldest of the gods he wears away—
the Earth, the immortal, the inexhaustible—
as his powers go back and forth, year in, year out
with the breed of stallions[7] turning up the furrows.          385

And the blithe, lightheaded race of birds he snares,
the tribes of savage beasts, the life that swarms the depths—
      with one fling of his nets
woven and coiled tight, he takes them all,
   man the skilled, the brilliant!                              390
He conquers all, taming with his techniques
the prey that roams the cliffs and wild lairs,
training the stallion, clamping the yoke across
   his shaggy neck, and the tireless mountain bull.
And speech and thought, quick as the wind                      395
and the mood and mind for law that rules the city—
   all these he has taught himself
and shelter from the arrows of the frost
when there's rough lodging under the cold clear sky
and the shafts of lashing rain—                                400
   ready, resourceful man!
      Never without resources
never an impasse as he marches on the future—
only death, from Death alone he will find no rescue
but from desperate plagues he has plotted his escapes.         405

Man the master, ingenious past all measure
past all dreams, the skills within his grasp—
   he forges on, now to destruction
now again to greatness. When he weaves in
the laws of the land, and the justice of the gods              410
that binds his oaths together
      he and his city rise high—
         but the city casts out
that man who weds himself to inhumanity
thanks to reckless daring. Never share my hearth               415
never think my thoughts, whoever does such things.

   [*Enter* ANTIGONE *from the side, accompanied by the* SENTRY.]

7. Mules, the working animal of a Greek farmer.

Here is a dark sign from the gods—
what to make of this? I know her,
how can I deny it? That young girl's Antigone!
Wretched, child of a wretched father,                               420
Oedipus. Look, is it possible?
They bring you in like a prisoner—
why? did you break the king's laws?
Did they take you in some act of mad defiance?
SENTRY: She's the one, she did it single-handed—                    425
   we caught her burying the body. Where's Creon?

   [*Enter* CREON *from the palace.*]

LEADER: Back again, just in time when you need him.
CREON: In time for what? What is it?
SENTRY:                              My king,
   there's nothing you can swear you'll never do—
   second thoughts make liars of us all.                            430
   I could have sworn I wouldn't hurry back
   (what with your threats, the buffeting I just took),
   but a stroke of luck beyond our wildest hopes,
   what a joy, there's nothing like it. So,
   back I've come, breaking my oath, who cares?                     435
   I'm bringing in our prisoner—this young girl—
   we took her giving the dead the last rites.
   But no casting lots this time; this is *my* luck,
   my prize, no one else's.
                              Now, my lord,
   here she is. Take her, question her,                             440
   cross-examine her to your heart's content.
   But set me free, it's only right—
   I'm rid of this dreadful business once for all.
CREON: Prisoner! Her? You took her—where, doing what?
SENTRY: Burying the man. That's the whole story.
CREON:                                          What?       445
   You mean what you say, you're telling me the truth?
SENTRY: She's the one. With my own eyes I saw her
   bury the body, just what you've forbidden.
   There. Is that plain and clear?
CREON: What did you see? Did you catch her in the act?            450
SENTRY: Here's what happened. We went back to our post,
   those threats of yours breathing down our necks—
   we brushed the corpse clean of the dust that covered it,
   stripped it bare . . . it was slimy, going soft,
   and we took to high ground, backs to the wind                   455

so the stink of him couldn't hit us;
jostling, baiting each other to keep awake,
shouting back and forth—no napping on the job,
not this time. And so the hours dragged by
until the sun stood dead above our heads,                    460
a huge white ball in the noon sky, beating,
blazing down, and then it happened—
suddenly, a whirlwind!
Twisting a great dust-storm up from the earth,
a black plague of the heavens, filling the plain,           465
ripping the leaves off every tree in sight,
choking the air and sky. We squinted hard
and took our whipping from the gods.

And after the storm passed—it seemed endless—
there, we saw the girl!                                      470
And she cried out a sharp, piercing cry,
like a bird come back to an empty nest,
peering into its bed, and all the babies gone . . .
Just so, when she sees the corpse bare
she bursts into a long, shattering wail                     475
and calls down withering curses on the heads
of all who did the work. And she scoops up dry dust,
handfuls, quickly, and lifting a fine bronze urn,
lifting it high and pouring, she crowns the dead
with three full libations.
                              Soon as we saw                 480
we rushed her, closed on the kill like hunters,
and she, she didn't flinch. We interrogated her,
charging her with offenses past and present—
she stood up to it all, denied nothing. I tell you,
it made me ache and laugh in the same breath.               485
It's pure joy to escape the worst yourself,
it hurts a man to bring down his friends.
But all that, I'm afraid, means less to me
than my own skin. That's the way I'm made.

       [*Wheeling on* ANTIGONE.]

CREON:                                      You,
    with your eyes fixed on the ground—speak up.             490
    Do you deny you did this, yes or no?
ANTIGONE: I did it. I don't deny a thing.

       [*To the* SENTRY.]

CREON: You, get out, wherever you please—
   you're clear of a very heavy charge.

   [*He leaves;* CREON *turns back to* ANTIGONE.]

   You, tell me briefly, no long speeches—                              495
   were you aware a decree had forbidden this?
ANTIGONE: Well aware. How could I avoid it? It was public.
CREON: And still you had the gall to break this law?
ANTIGONE: Of course I did. It wasn't Zeus, not in the least,
   who made this proclamation—not to me.                               500
   Nor did that Justice, dwelling with the gods
   beneath the earth, ordain such laws for men.
   Nor did I think your edict had such force
   that you, a mere mortal, could override the gods,
   the great unwritten, unshakable traditions.                         505
   They are alive, not just today or yesterday:
   they live forever, from the first of time,
   and no one knows when they first saw the light.

   These laws—I was not about to break them,
   not out of fear of some man's wounded pride,                        510
   and face the retribution of the gods.
   Die I must, I've known it all my life—
   how could I keep from knowing?—even without
   your death-sentence ringing in my ears.
   And if I am to die before my time                                   515
   I consider that a gain. Who on earth
   alive in the midst of so much grief as I,
   could fail to find his death a rich reward?
   So for me, at least, to meet this doom of yours
   is precious little pain. But if I had allowed                       520
   my own mother's son to rot, an unburied corpse—
   that would have been an agony! This is nothing.
   And if my present actions strike you as foolish,
   let's just say I've been accused of folly
   by a fool.
LEADER:      Like father like daughter,                                525
   passionate, wild . . .
   she hasn't learned to bend before adversity.
CREON: No? Believe me, the stiffest stubborn wills
   fall the hardest; the toughest iron,
   tempered strong in the white-hot fire,                              530
   you'll see it crack and shatter first of all.
   And I've known spirited horses you can break

with a light bit—proud, rebellious horses.
There's no room for pride, not in a slave,
not with the lord and master standing by.                535

This girl was an old hand at insolence
when she overrode the edicts we made public.
But once she'd done it—the insolence,
twice over—to glory in it, laughing,
mocking us to our face with what she'd done.              540
I am not the man, not now: she is the man
if this victory goes to her and she goes free.

Never! Sister's child or closer in blood
than all my family clustered at my altar
worshipping Guardian Zeus—she'll never escape,           545
she and her blood sister, the most barbaric death.
Yes, I accuse her sister of an equal part
in scheming this, this burial.

    [*To his attendants.*]

                       Bring her here!
I just saw her inside, hysterical, gone to pieces.
It never fails: the mind convicts itself                 550
in advance, when scoundrels are up to no good,
plotting in the dark. Oh but I hate it more
when a traitor, caught red-handed,
  tries to glorify his crimes.
ANTIGONE: Creon, what more do you want                    555
  than my arrest and execution?
CREON: Nothing. Then I have it all.
ANTIGONE: Then why delay? Your moralizing repels me,
  every word you say—pray god it always will.
  So naturally all I say repels you too.

                          Enough.      560
Give me glory! What greater glory could I win
than to give my own brother decent burial?
These citizens here would all agree,

    [*To the* CHORUS.]

they'd praise me too
if their lips weren't locked in fear.                     565

    [*Pointing to* CREON.]

Lucky tyrants—the perquisites of power!
Ruthless power to do and say whatever pleases *them*.
CREON: You alone, of all the people in Thebes,
see things that way.
ANTIGONE:　　　　　They see it just that way
but defer to you and keep their tongues in leash.　570
CREON: And you, aren't you ashamed to differ so from them?
So disloyal!
ANTIGONE: Not ashamed for a moment,
not to honor my brother, my own flesh and blood.
CREON: Wasn't Eteocles a brother too—cut down, facing him?
ANTIGONE: Brother, yes, by the same mother, the same father.　575
CREON: Then how can you render his enemy such honors,
such impietes in his eyes?
ANTIGONE: He'll never testify to that,
Eteocles dead and buried.
CREON:　　　　　He will—
if you honor the traitor just as much as him.　580
ANTIGONE: But it was his brother, not some slave that died—
CREON: Ravaging our country!—
but Eteocles died fighting in our behalf.
ANTIGONE: No matter—Death longs for the same rites for all.
CREON: Never the same for the patriot and the traitor.　585
ANTIGONE: Who, Creon, who on earth can say the ones below
don't find this pure and uncorrupt?
CREON: Never. Once an enemy, never a friend,
not even after death.
ANTIGONE: I was born to join in love, not hate—　590
that is my nature.
CREON:　　　　Go down below and love,
if love you must—love the dead! while I'm alive,
no woman is going to lord it over me.

[*Enter* ISMENE *from the palace, under guard.*]

CHORUS:　　　　　　　　Look,
Ismene's coming, weeping a sister's tears,
loving sister, under a cloud . . .　595
her face is flushed, her cheeks streaming.
Sorrow puts her lovely radiance in the dark.
CREON:　　　　　　　　　　You—
in my own house you viper, slinking undetected,
sucking my life-blood! I never knew
I was breeding twin disasters, the two of you　600
rising up against my throne. Come, tell me,

will you confess your part in the crime or not?
  Answer me. Swear to me.
ISMENE:                          I did it, yes—
  if only she consents—I share the guilt,
  the consequences too.
ANTIGONE:                   No,                                   605
  Justice will never suffer that—not you,
  you were unwilling. I never bought you in.
ISMENE: But now you face such dangers . . . I'm not ashamed
  to sail through trouble with you,
  make your troubles mine.
ANTIGONE:                    Who did the work?              610
  Let the dead and the god of death bear witness!
  I have no love for a friend who loves in words alone.
ISMENE: Oh no, my sister, don't reject me, please,
  let me die beside you, consecrating
  the dead together.
ANTIGONE:               Never share my dying,                615
  don't lay claim to what you never touched.
  My death will be enough.
ISMENE: What do I care for life, cut off from you?
ANTIGONE: Ask Creon. Your concern is all for him.
ISMENE: Why abuse me so? It doesn't help you now.
ANTIGONE:                                    You're right—  620
  if I mock you, I get no pleasure from it,
  only pain.
ISMENE:      Tell me, dear one,
  what can I do to help you, even now?
ANTIGONE: Save yourself. I don't grudge you your survival.
ISMENE: Oh no, no, denied my portion in your death?       625
ANTIGONE: You chose to live, I chose to die.
ISMENE:                                Not, at least,
  without every kind of caution I could voice.
ANTIGONE: Your wisdom appealed to one world—mine, another.
ISMENE: But look, we're both guilty, both condemned to death.
ATIGONE: Courage! Live your life. I gave myself to death,    630
  long ago, so I might serve the dead.
CREON: They're both mad, I tell you, the two of them.
  One's just shown it, the other's been that way
  since she was born.
ISMENE:               True, my king,
  the sense we were born with cannot last forever . . .        635
  commit cruelty on a person long enough
  and the mind begins to go.
CREON:                      Yours did,

when you chose to commit your crimes with her.
ISMENE: How can I live alone, without her?
CREON:                                        Her?
   Don't even mention her—she no longer exists.                    640
ISMENE: What? You'd kill your own son's bride?
CREON:                                        Absolutely:
   there are other fields for him to plow.
ISMENE:                                   Perhaps,
   but never as true, as close a bond as theirs.
CREON: A worthless woman for my son? It repels me.
ISMENE: Dearest Haemon, your father wrongs you so!                 645
CREON: Enough, enough—you and your talk of marriage!
ISMENE: Creon—you're really going to rob your son of Antigone?
CREON: Death will do it for me—break their marriage off.
LEADER: So, it's settled then? Antigone must die?
CREON: Settled, yes—we both know that.                            650

   [*To the guards.*]

Stop wasting time. Take them in.
From now on they'll act like women.
Tie them up, no more running loose;
even the bravest will cut and run,
once they see Death coming for their lives.                        655

   [*The guards escort* ANTIGONE *and* ISMENE *into the palace.* CREON
   *remains while the old citizens form their* CHORUS.]

CHORUS: Blest, they are the truly blest who all their lives
      have never tasted devastation. For others, once
      the gods have rocked a house to its foundations
         the ruin will never cease, cresting on and on
   from one generation on throughout the race—                     660
   like a great mounting tide
   driven on by savage northern gales,
         surging over the dead black depths
   rolling up from the bottom dark heaves of sand
   and the headlands, taking the storm's onslaught full-force,     665
   roar, and the low moaning
                              echoes on and on
                                         and now
   as in ancient times I see the sorrows of the house,
   the living heirs of the old ancestral kings,
   piling on the sorrows of the dead

and one generation cannot free the next—                    670
some god will bring them crashing down,
the race finds no release.
And now the light, the hope
          springing up from the late last root
in the house of Oedipus, that hope's cut down in turn            675
by the long, bloody knife swung by the gods of death
by a senseless word
                    by fury at the heart.
                                        Zeus,
yours is the power, Zeus, what man on earth
can override it, who can hold it back?
Power that neither Sleep, the all-ensnaring                    680
     no, nor the tireless months of heaven
can ever overmaster—young through all time,
mighty lord of power, you hold fast
     the dazzling crystal mansions of Olympus.
And throughout the future, late and soon                    685
as through the past, your law prevails:
no towering form of greatness
          enters into the lives of mortals
               free and clear of ruin.
                         True,
our dreams, our high hopes voyaging far and wide              690
bring sheer delight to many, to many others
     delusion, blithe, mindless lusts
and the fraud steals on one slowly . . . unaware
till he trips and puts his foot into the fire.
     He was a wise old man who coined                    695
the famous saying: "Sooner or later
foul is fair, fair is foul
to the man the gods will ruin"—
     He goes his way for a moment only
          free of blinding ruin.                              700

[*Enter* HAEMON *from the palace.*]

     Here's Haemon now, the last of all your sons.
     Does he come in tears for his bride,
     his doomed bride, Antigone—
     bitter at being cheated of their marriage?
CREON: We'll soon know, better than seer could tell us.          705

[*Turning to* HAEMON.]

Son, you've heard the final verdict on your bride?
Are you coming now, raving against your father?
Or do you love me, no matter what I do?
HAEMON: Father, I'm your *son* . . . you in your wisdom
set my bearings for me—I obey you.                                710
No marriage could ever mean more to me than you,
whatever good direction you may offer.
CREON:                                              Fine, Haemon.
That's how you ought to feel within your heart,
subordinate to your father's will in every way.
That's what a man prays for: to produce good sons—      715
a household full of them, dutiful and attentive,
so they can pay his enemy back with interest
and match the respect their father shows his friend.
But the man who rears a brood of useless children,
what has he brought into the world, I ask you?             720
Nothing but trouble for himself, and mockery
from his enemies laughing in his face.
                                        Oh Haemon,
never lose your sense of judgment over a woman.
The warmth, the rush of pleasure, it all goes cold
in your arms, I warn you . . . a worthless woman         725
in your house, a misery in your bed.
What wound cuts deeper than a loved one
turned against you? Spit her out,
like a mortal enemy—let the girl go.
Let her find a husband down among the dead.               730
Imagine it: I caught her in naked rebellion,
the traitor, the only one in the whole city.
I'm not about to prove myself a liar,
not to my people, no, I'm going to kill her!
That's right—so let her cry for mercy, sing her hymns    735
to Zeus who defends all bonds of kindred blood.
Why, if I bring up my own kin to be rebels,
think what I'd suffer from the world at large.
Show me the man who rules his household well:
I'll show you someone fit to rule the state.             740
That good man, my son,
I have every confidence he and he alone
can give commands and take them too. Staunch
in the storm of spears he'll stand his ground,
a loyal, unflinching comrade at your side.               745

But whoever steps out of line, violates the laws
or presumes to hand out orders to his superiors,

he'll win no praise from me. But that man
the city places in authority, his orders
must be obeyed, large and small,                                    750
right and wrong.
        Anarchy—
show me a greater crime in all the earth!
She, she destroys cities, rips up houses,
breaks the ranks of spearmen into headlong rout.
But the ones who last it out, the great mass of them          755
owe their lives to discipline. Therefore
we must defend the men who live by law,
never let some woman triumph over us.
Better to fall from power, if fall we must,
at the hands of a man—never be rated                            760
inferior to a woman, never.
LEADER:               To us,
unless old age has robbed us of our wits,
you seem to say what you have to say with sense.
HAEMON: Father, only the gods endow a man with reason,
the finest of all their gifts, a treasure.                          765
Far be it from me—I haven't the skill,
and certainly no desire, to tell you when,
if ever, you make a slip in speech . . . though
someone else might have a good suggestion.

Of course it's not for you,                                          770
in the normal run of things, to watch
whatever men say or do, or find to criticize.
The man in the street, you know, dreads your glance,
he'd never say anything displeasing to your face.
But it's for me to catch the murmurs in the dark,              775
the way the city mourns for this young girl.
"No woman," they say, "ever deserved death less,
and such a brutal death for such a glorious action.
She, with her own dear brother lying in his blood—
she couldn't bear to leave him dead, unburied,               780
food for the wild dogs or wheeling vultures.
Death? She deserves a glowing crown of gold!"
So they say, and the rumor spreads in secret,
darkly . . .
        I rejoice to your success, father—
nothing more precious to me in the world.                      785
What medal of honor brighter to his children
than a father's glowing glory? Or a child's
to his proud father? Now don't, please,

be quite so single-minded, self-involved,
or assume the world is wrong and you are right.                  790
Whoever thinks that he alone possesses intelligence,
the gift of eloquence, he and no one else,
and character too . . . such men, I tell you,
spread them open—you will find them empty.

                          No,

it's no disgrace for a man, even a wise man,                     795
to learn many things and not to be too rigid.
You've seen trees by a raging winter torrent,
how many sway with the flood and salvage every twig,
but not the stubborn—they're ripped out, roots and all.
Bend or break. The same when a man is sailing:                   800
haul your sheets too taut, never give an inch,
you'll capsize, and go the rest of the voyage
keel up and the rowing-benches under.

Oh give way. Relax your anger—change!
I'm young, I know, but let me offer this:                        805
it would be best by far, I admit,
if a man were born infallible, right by nature.
If not—and things don't often go that way,
it's best to learn from those with good advice.

LEADER: You'd do well, my lord, if he's speaking to the point,  810
to learn from him,

    [*Turning to* HAEMON.]

                and you, my boy, from him.
You both are talking sense.

CREON:             So,
men our age, we're to be lectured, are we?—
schooled by a boy his age?

HAEMON: Only in what is right. But if I seem young,             815
look less to my years and more to what I do.

CREON: Do? Is admiring rebels an achievement?

HAEMON: I'd never suggest that you admire treason.

CREON:                          Oh?—
isn't that just the sickness that's attacked her?

HAEMON: The whole city of Thebes denies it, to a man.          820

CREON: And is Thebes about to tell me how to rule?

HAEMON: Now, you see? Who's talking like a child?

CREON: Am I to rule this land for others—or myself?

HAEMON: It's no city at all, owned by one man alone.

CREON: What? The city *is* the king's—that's the law!          825

HAEMON: What a splendid king you'd make of a desert island—
   you and you alone.

   [*To the* CHORUS.]

CREON:                       This boy, I do believe,
   is fighting on her side, the woman's side.
HAEMON: If you are a woman, yes—
   my concern is all for you.                                    830
CREON: Why, you degenerate—bandying accusations,
   threatening me with justice, your own father!
HAEMON: I see my father offending justice—wrong.
CREON:                                    Wrong?
   To protect my royal rights?
HAEMON:                       Protect your rights?
   When you trample down the honors of the gods?                 835
CREON: You, you soul of corruption, rotten through—
   woman's accomplice!
HAEMON:                  That may be,
   but you'll never find me accomplice to a criminal.
CREON: That's what *she* is,
   and every word you say is a blatant appeal for her—           840
HAEMON: And you, and me, and the gods beneath the earth.
CREON: You will never marry her, not while she's alive.
HAEMON: Then she'll die . . . but her death will kill another.
CREON: What, brazen threats? You go too far!
HAEMON:                                    What threat?
   Combating your empty, mindless judgments with a word?         845
CREON: You'll suffer for your sermons, you and your empty wisdom!
HAEMON: If you weren't my father, I'd say you were insane.
CREON: Don't flatter me with Father—you woman's slave!
HAEMON: You really expect to fling abuse at me
   and not receive the same?
CREON:                        Is that so!                        850
   Now, by heaven, I promise you, you'll pay—
   taunting, insulting me! Bring her out,
   that hateful—she'll die now, here,
   in front of his eyes, beside her groom!
HAEMON: No, no, she will never die beside me—                    855
   don't delude yourself. And you will never
   see me, never set eyes on my face again.
   Rage your heart out, rage with friends
   who can stand the sight of you.

   [*Rushing out.*]

LEADER: Gone, my king, in a burst of anger.                                860
    A temper young as his . . . hurt him once,
    he may do something violent.
CREON:                   Let him do—
    dream up something desperate, past all human limit!
    Good riddance. Rest assured,
    he'll never save those two young girls from death.            865
LEADER: Both of them, you really intend to kill them both?
CREON: No, not her, the one whose hands are clean—
    you're quite right.
LEADER:           But Antigone—
    what sort of death do you have in mind for her?
CREON: I'll take her down some wild, desolate path                         870
    never trod by men, and wall her up alive[8]
    in a rocky vault, and set out short rations,[9]
    just the measure piety demands
    to keep the entire city free of defilement.
    There let her pray to the one god she worships:                   875
    Death—who knows?—may just reprieve her from death.
    Or she may learn at last, better late than never,
    what a waste of breath it is to worship Death.

    [*Exit to the palace.*]

CHORUS: Love, never conquered in battle
    Love the plunderer laying waste the rich!                        880
    Love standing the night-watch
        guarding a girl's soft cheek,
    you range the seas, the shepherds' steadings off in the wilds—
    not even the deathless gods can flee your onset,
    nothing human born for a day—                                     885
    whoever feels your grip is driven mad.
                 Love!—
    you wrench the minds of the righteous into outrage,
    swerve them to their ruin—you have ignited this,
    this kindred strife, father and son at war
        and Love alone the victor—                                   890
    warm glance of the bride triumphant, burning with desire!
    Throned in power, side-by-side with the mighty laws!
    Irresistible Aphrodite,[1] never conquered—
    Love, you mock us for your sport.

8. The penalty originally proclaimed was death by stoning. But this demands the participation of the citizens and it may be that Creon, after listening to Haemon's remarks, is not as sure as he once was of popular support.  9. The penalty proposed by Creon seems to be imprisonment in a tomb with a certain ration of food. Since Antigone would die of starvation but not actually by anyone's hand, Creon seems to think that the city will not be "defiled," i.e., incur blood guilt.
1. Goddess of sexual love.

[ANTIGONE *is brought from the palace under guard.*]

> But now, even I'd rebel against the king,                          895
> I'd break all bounds when I see this—
> I fill with tears, I cannot hold them back,
> not any more . . . I see Antigone make her way
> to the bridal vault where all are laid to rest.

ANTIGONE: Look at me, men of my fatherland,                           900
>     setting out on the last road
> looking into the last light of day
> the last I'll ever see . . .
> the god of death who puts us all to bed
> takes me down to the banks of Acheron[2] alive—                     905
>     denied my part in the wedding-songs,
> no wedding-song in the dusk has crowned my marriage—
> I go to wed the lord of the dark waters.

CHORUS:
> Not crowned with glory,[3] or with a dirge,
> you leave for the deep pit of the dead.                             910
> No withering illness laid you low,
> no strokes of the sword—a law to yourself,
> alone, no mortal like you, ever, you go down
> to the halls of Death alive and breathing.

ANTIGONE: But think of Niobe[4]—well I know her story—                915
>     think what a living death she died,
> Tantalus' daughter, stranger queen from the east:
> there on the mountain heights, growing stone
> binding as ivy, slowly walled her round
> and the rains will never cease, the legends say                     920
> the snows will never leave her . . .
>     wasting away, under her brows the tears
> showering down her breasting ridge and slopes—
> a rocky death like hers puts me to sleep.

CHORUS:
> But she was a god, born of gods,                                    925
> and we are only mortals born to die.

---

2. A river of the world of the dead.    3. The usual version of this line is: "crowned with glory. . . ." The Greek word *oukoun* can be negative or positive, depending on the accent, which determines the pronunciation; since these written accents were not yet in use in Sophocles' time, no one will ever know for sure which meaning he intended. The present version is based on the belief that the chorus is expressing pity for Antigone's ignominious and abnormal death; she has no funeral at which her fame and praise are recited, she will not die by either of the usual causes— violence or disease—but by a living death. It is, as they say, her own choice: she is "a law to [herself]" (912).    4. A Phrygian princess married to Amphion, king of Thebes. She boasted that she had borne more children than Leto, mother of Apollo and Artemis; these two killed her children. She returned to Phrygia where she was turned into a rock on Mount Sipylus; the melting of the snow on the mountain caused "tears" to flow down the rock formation which resembled a woman's face.

And yet, of course, it's a great thing
for a dying girl to hear, even to hear
she shares a destiny equal to the gods,
during life and later, once she's dead.

ANTIGONE:                                    O you mock me!          930
  Why, in the name of all my fathers' gods
  why can't you wait till I am gone—
    must you abuse me to my face?
  O my city, all your fine rich sons!
  And you, you springs of the Dirce,                               935
  holy grove of Thebes where the chariots gather,
    you at least, you'll bear me witness, look,
  unmourned by friend and forced by such crude laws
  I go to my rockbound prison, strange new tomb—
    always a stranger, O dear god,                                 940
    I have no home on earth and none below,
      not with the living, not with the breathless dead.

CHORUS: You went too far, the last limits of daring—
  smashing against the high throne of Justice!
    Your life's in ruins, child—I wonder . . .                     945
  do you pay for your father's terrible ordeal?

ANTIGONE: There—at last you've touched it, the worst pain
  the worst anguish! Raking up the grief for father
    three times over, for all the doom
  that's struck us down, the brilliant house of Laius.             950
  O mother, your marriage-bed
  the coiling horrors, the coupling there—
    you with your own son, my father—doomstruck mother!
  Such, such were my parents, and I their wretched child.
  I go to them now, cursed, unwed, to share their home—            955
    I am a stranger! O dear brother, doomed
    in your marriage—your marriage murders mine,[5]
      your dying drags me down to death alive!

  [*Enter Creon.*]

CHORUS: Reverence asks some reverence in return—
  but attacks on power never go unchecked,                         960
    not by the man who holds the reins of power.
  Your own blind will, your passion has destroyed you.

ANTIGONE: No one to weep for me, my friends,
  no wedding-song—they take me away
  in all my pain . . . the road lies open, waiting.                965

5. Polynices had married the daughter of Adrastus of Argos, to seal the alliance which enabled
him to march against Thebes.

Never again, the law forids me to see
the sacred eye of day. I am agony!
No tears for the destiny that's mine,
no loved one mourns my death.
CREON:                            Can't you see?
If a man could wail his own dirge *before* he dies,                    970
he'd never finish.

[*To the guards.*]

                    Take her away, quickly!
Wall her up in the tomb, you have your orders.
Abandon her there, alone, and let her choose—
death or a buried life with a good roof for shelter.
As for myself, my hands are clean. This young girl—                    975
dead or alive, she will be stripped of her rights,
her stranger's rights,[6] here in the world above.
ANTIGONE: O tomb, my bridal-bed—my house, my prison
cut in the hollow rock, my everlasting watch!
I'll soon be there, soon embrace my own,                    980
the great growing family of our dead
Persephone[7] has received among her ghosts.
                                                I,
the last of them all, the most reviled by far,
go down before my destined time's run out.
But still I go, cherishing one good hope:                    985
my arrival may be dear to father,
dear to you, my mother,
dear to you, my loving brother, Eteocles—
When you died I washed you with my hands,
I dressed you all, I poured the sacred cups                    990
across your tombs. But now, Polynices,
because I laid your body out as well,
this, this is my reward. Nevertheless
I honored you—the decent will admit it—
well and wisely too.
                    Never, I tell you,                    995
if I had been the mother of children
or if my husband died, exposed and rotting—
I'd never have taken this ordeal upon myself,
never defied our people's will. What law,
you ask, do I satisfy with what I say?                    1000

6. The Greek words suggest that he sees her not as a citizen but as a resident alien; by her action
she has forfeited citizenship. But now she will be deprived even of that inferior status.    7. Queen
of the underworld.

A husband dead, there might have been another.
A child by another too, if I had lost the first.
But mother and father both lost in the halls of Death,
no brother could ever spring to light again.[8]
For this law alone I held you first in honor.                    1005
For this, Creon, the king, judges me a criminal
guilty of dreadful outrage, my dear brother!
And now he leads me off, a captive in his hands,
with no part in the bridal-song, the bridal-bed,
denied all joy of marriage, raising childen—                    1010
deserted so by loved ones, struck by fate,
I descend alive to the caverns of the dead.

What law of the mighty gods have I transgressed?
Why look to the heavens any more, tormented as I am?
Whom to call, what comrades now? Just think,                    1015
my reverence only brands me for irreverence!
Very well: if this is the pleasure of the gods,
once I suffer I will know that I was wrong.
But if these men are wrong, let them suffer
nothing worse than they mete out to me—                    1020
these masters of injustice!
LEADER: Still the same rough winds, the wild passion
raging through the girl.

   [*To the guards.*]

CREON:               Take her away.
   You're wasting time—you'll pay for it too.
ANTIGONE: Oh god, the voice of death. Its come, it's here.                    1025
CREON: True. Not a word of hope—your doom is sealed.
ANTIGONE: Land of Thebes, city of all my fathers—
   O you gods, the first gods of the race![9]
   They drag me away, now, no more delay.
   Look on me, you noble sons of Thebes—                    1030
   the last of a great line of kings,
   I alone, see what I suffer now

---

8. This strange justification for her action (ll. 995ff) has been considered unacceptable by many critics and they have suspected that it was an interpolation by some later producer of the play. But Aristotle quotes it in the next century and appears to have no doubt of its authenticity. If genuine, it does mean that Antigone momentarily abandons the laws she championed against Creon—that all men had a right to burial—and sees her motive as exclusive devotion to her dead brother. For someone facing the prospect of a slow and hideous death such a self-examination and realization is not impossible. And it makes no difference to the courage and tenacity of her defiance of state power.    9. The Theban royal house traced its ancestry through Harmonia, wife of Cadmus, to Aphrodite and Ares, her parents. Cadmus' daughter Semele was the mother, by Zeus, of the god Dionysus.

at the hands of what breed of men—
all for reverence, my reverence for the gods!

[*She leaves under guard: the* CHORUS *gathers.*]

CHORUS: Danaë, Danaë[1]—                                    1035
    even she endured a fate like yours,
        in all her lovely strength she traded
    the light of day for the bolted brazen vault—
    buried within her tomb, her bridal-chamber,
    wed to the yoke and broken.                            1040
        But she was of glorious birth
            my child, my child
    and treasured the seed of Zeus within her womb,
    the cloudburst streaming gold!
            The power of fate is a wonder,                 1045
            dark, terrible wonder—
            neither wealth nor armies
            towered walls nor ships
            black hulls lashed by the salt
            can save us from that force.                   1050

The yoke tamed him too
    young Lycurgus[2] flaming in anger
king of Edonia, all for his mad taunts
Dionysus clamped him down, encased
in the chain-mail of rock                                  1055
    and there his rage
        his terrible flowering rage burst—
sobbing, dying away ... at last that madman
came to know his god—
            the power he mocked, the power              1060
            he taunted in all his frenzy
            trying to stamp out
            the women strong with the god—
            the torch, the raving sacred cries—
            enraging the Muses who adore the flute.      1065
And far north[3] where the Black-Rocks

1. Daughter of Acrisius, king of Argos. It was prophesied that he would be killed by his daughter's son; so he shut her up in a bronze tower. But Zeus came to her in the form of a golden rainshower and she bore a son, Perseus, who did in the end kill his grandfather.    2. The Thracian (Edonian) king. He opposed the introduction of Dionysiac religion into his kingdom and was imprisoned by the god.    3. The whole story is difficult to follow and its application to the case of Antigone obscure. Cleopatra, the daughter of the Athenian princess Orithyia, whom Boreas the North Wind carried off to his home in Thrace, was maried to Phineus, the Thracian king, and bore him two sons. He tired of her, abandoned her, and married Eidothea, "a King's new queen" (l. 1073), who put out the eyes of the two sons of Cleopatra. Ares, the god of war, associated with Thrace, watched the savage act.

cut the sea in half
and murderous straits
split the coast of Thrace
    a forbidding city stands                                    1070
where once, hard by the walls
the savage Ares thrilled to watch
a king's new queen, a Fury rearing in rage
    against his two royal sons—
        her bloody hands, her dagger-shuttle        1075
stabbing out their eyes—cursed, blinding wounds—
their eyes blind sockets screaming for revenge!

They wailed in agony cries echoing cries
    the princes doomed at birth . . .
and their mother doomed to chains,                                 1080
walled up in a tomb of stone—[4]
    but she traced her own birth back
to a proud Athenian line and the high gods
and off in caverns half the world away,
born of the wild North Wind                                        1085
    she sprang on her father's gales,
        racing stallions up the leaping cliffs—
child of the heavens. But even on her the Fates
the gray everlasting Fates rode hard
my child, my child.

[*Enter* TIRESIAS, *a blind prophet, led by a boy.*]

TIRESIAS:               Lord of Thebes,                 1090
  I and the boy have come togther,
  hand in hand. Two see with the eyes of one . . .
  so the blind must go, with a guide to lead the way.
CREON: What is it, old Tiresias? What news now?
TIRESIAS: I will teach you. And you obey the seer.
CREON:                              I will,           1095
  I've never wavered from your advice before.
TIRESIAS: And so you kept the city straight on course.
CREON: I owe you a great deal, I swear to that.
TIRESIAS: Then reflect, my son: you are poised,
  once more, on the razor-edge of fate.                          1100
CREON: What is it? I shudder to hear you.

---

4. Lines 1080–1081 have no equivalent in the Greek text. They represent a belief that Sophocles' audience knew a version of the legend in which Cleopatra was imprisoned in a stone tomb (which is found in a later source). This would give a point of comparison to Antigone (like the mention of prison in the strophes dealing with Danaë and Lycurgus).

TIRESIAS:                                   You will learn
   when you listen to the warnings of my craft.
   As I sat on the ancient seat of augury,[5]
   in the sanctuary where every bird I know
   will hover at my hands—suddenly I hear it,         1105
   a strange voice in the wingbeats, unintelligible,
   barbaric, a mad scream! Talons flashing, ripping,
   they were killing each other—that much I knew—
   the murderous fury whirring in those wings
   made that much clear!
                         I was afraid,         1110
   I turned quickly, tasted the burnt-sacrifice,
   ignited the altar at all points—but no fire,
   the god in the fire never blazed.
   Not from those offerings . . . over the embers
   slid a heavy ooze from the long thighbones,         1115
   smoking, sputtering out, and the bladder
   puffed and burst—spraying gall into the air—
   and the fat wrapping the bones slithered off
   and left them glistening white. No fire!
   The rites failed that might have blazed the future     1120
   with a sign. So I learned from the boy here:
   he is my guide, as I am guide to others.
                        And it's you—
   your high resolve that sets this plague on Thebes.
   The public altars and sacred hearths are fouled,
   one and all, by the birds and dogs with carrion       1125
   torn from the corpse, the doomstruck son of Oedipus!
   and so the gods are deaf to our prayers, they spurn
   the offerings in our hands, the flame of holy flesh.
   No birds cry out an omen clear and true—
   they're gorged with the murdered victim's blood and fat.   1130
   Take these things to heart, my son, I warn you.
   All men make mistakes, it is only human.
   But once the wrong is done, a man
   can turn his back on folly, misfortune too,
   if he tries to make amends, however low he's fallen,    1135
   and stops his bullnecked ways. Stubbornness
   brands you for stupidity—pride is a crime.
   No, yield to the dead!
   Never stab the fighter when he's down.
   Where's the glory, killing the dead twice over?        1140

---

5. A place where the birds gathered, and Tiresias watched for omens.

I mean you well. I give you sound advice.
It's best to learn from a good adviser
when he speaks for your own good:
it's pure gain.
CREON:                  Old man—all of you! So,
you shoot your arrows at my head like archers at the target—    1145
I even have *him* loosed on me, this fortune-teller.
Oh his ilk has tried to sell me short
and ship me off for years. Well,
drive your bargains, traffic—much as you like—
in the gold of India, silver-gold of Sardis.[6]                      1150
You'll never bury that body in the grave,
not even if Zeus' eagles rip the corpse
and wing their rotten pickings off to the throne of god!
Never, not even in fear of such defilement
will I tolerate his burial, that traitor.                          1155
Well I know, we can't defile the gods—
no mortal has the power.
                              No,
reverend old Tiresias, all men fall,
it's only human, but the wisest fall obscenely
when they glorify obscene advice with rhetoric—                    1160
all for their own gain.
TIRESIAS: Oh god, is there a man alive
who knows, who actually believes . . .
CREON:                              What now?
What earth-shattering truth are you about to utter?
TIRESIAS: . . . just how much a sense of judgment, wisdom,         1165
is the greatest gift we have?
CREON:                          Just as much, I'd say,
as a twisted mind is the worst affliction known.
TIRESIAS: You are the one who's sick, Creon, sick to death.
CREON: I am in no mood to trade insults with a seer.
TIRESIAS: You have already, calling my prophecies a lie.
CREON:                                      Why not?  1170
You and the whole breed of seers are mad for money!
TIRESIAS: And the whole race of tyrants lusts for filthy gain.
CREON: This slander of yours—
are you aware you're speaking to the king?
TIRESIAS: Well aware. Who helped you save the city?
CREON:                                      You—      1175
you have your skills, old seer, but you lust for injustice!
TIRESIAS: You will drive me to utter the dreadful secret in my heart.

---

6. In Asia Minor. Electrum, a mixture of gold and silver, was found in a nearby river.

CREON: Spit it out! Just don't speak it out for profit.
TIRESIAS: Profit? No, not a bit of profit, not for you.
CREON: Know full well, you'll never buy off my resolve.  1180
TIRESIAS: Then know this too, learn this by heart!
  The chariot of the sun will not race through
  so many circuits more, before you have surrendered
  one born of your own loins, your own flesh and blood,
  a corpse for corpses given in return, since you have thrust  1185
  to the world below a child sprung for the world above,
  ruthlessly lodged a living soul within the grave—
  then you've robbed the gods below the earth,
  keeping a dead body here in the bright air,
  unburied, unsung, unhallowed by the rites.  1190

  You, you have no business with the dead,
  nor do the gods above—this is violence
  you have forced upon the heavens.
  And so the avengers, the dark destroyers late
  but true to the mark, now lie in wait for you,  1195
  the Furies sent by the gods and the god of death
  to strike you down with the pains that you perfected!

  There. Reflect on that, tell me I've been bribed.
  The day comes soon, no long test of time, not now,
  when the mourning cries for men and women break  1200
  throughout your halls. Great hatred rises against you—
  cities in tumult, all whose mutilated sons
  the dogs have graced with burial, or the wild beasts
  or a wheeling crow that wings the ungodly stench of carrion
  back to each city, each warrior's hearth and home.  1205

  These arrows for your heart! Since you've raked me
  I loose them like an archer in my anger,
  arrows deadly true. You'll never escape
  their burning, searing force.

  [*Motioning to his escort.*]

  Come, boy, take me home.  1210
  So he can vent his rage on younger men,
  and learn to keep a gentler tongue in his head
  and better sense than what he carries now.

  [*Exit to the side.*]

LEADER: The old man's gone, my king—
  terrible prophecies. Well I know,                                    1215
  since the hair on this old head went gray,
  he's never lied to Thebes.
CREON: I know it myself—I'm shaken, torn.
  It's a dreadful thing to yield . . . but resist now?
  Lay my pride bare to the blows of ruin?                             1220
  That's dreadful too.
LEADER:                    But good advice,
  Creon, take it now, you must.
CREON: What should I do? Tell me .   . I'll obey.
LEADER: Go! Free the girl from the rocky vault
  and raise a mound for the body you exposed.                         1225
CREON: That's your advice? You think I should give in?
LEADER: Yes, my king, quickly. Disasters sent by the gods
  cut short our follies in a flash.
CREON:                          Oh it's hard,
  giving up the heart's desire . . . but I will do it—
  no more fighting a losing battle with necessity.                    1230
LEADER: Do it now, go, don't leave it to others.
CREON: Now—I'm on my way! Come, each of you,
  take up axes, make for the high ground,
  over there, quickly! I and my better judgment
  have come round to this—I shackled her,                             1235
  I'll set her free myself. I am afraid . . .
  it's best to keep the established laws
  to the very day we die.

  [*Rushing out, followed by his entourage. The* CHORUS *clusters
  around the altar.*]

CHORUS: God of a hundred names!
                              Great Dionysus—
      Son and glory of Semele! Pride of Thebes—                       1240
  Child of Zeus whose thunder rocks the clouds—
  Lord of the famous lands of evening—
  King of the Mysteries!
                          King of Eleusis,[7] Demeter's plain
  her breasting hills that welcome in the world—
  Great Dionysus!
                      Bacchus, living in Thebes                       1245
  the mother-city of all your frenzied women—
                                          Bacchus

7. Near Athens, the site of the mysteries, the worship of Demeter, the grain and harvest goddess.
Dionysus (Bacchus) was among the divinities worshipped by the initiates.

living along the Ismenus'[8] rippling waters
standing over the field sown with the Dragon's teeth!

You—we have seen you through the flaring smoky fires,
    your torches blazing over the twin peaks[9]
where nymphs of the hallowed cave climb onward
        fired with you, your sacred rage—
we have seen you at Castalia's running spring
and down from the heights of Nysa[1] crowned with ivy
the greening shore rioting vines and grapes
    down you come in your storm of wild women
        ecstatic, mystic cries—
                        Dionysus—
down to watch and ward the roads of Thebes!
First of all cities, Thebes you honor first
you and your mother, bride of the lightning—
come, Dionysus! now your people lie
in the iron grip of plague,
come in your racing, healing stride
        down Parnassus's slopes
or across the moaning straits.
                        Lord of the dancing—
dance, dance the constellations breathing fire!
Great master of the voices of the night!
Child of Zeus, God's offspring, come, come forth!
Lord, king, dance with your nymphs, swirling, raving
arm-in-arm in frenzy through the night
    they dance you, Iacchus[2]—
                        Dance, Dionysus
giver of all good things!

[*Enter a* MESSENGER *from the side.*]

MESSENGER:                 Neighbors,
    friends of the house of Cadmus and the kings,
    there's not a thing in this mortal life of ours
    I'd praise or blame as settled once for all.
    Fortune lifts and Fortune fells the lucky
    and unlucky every day. No prophet on earth
    can tell a man his fate. Take Creon:
    there was a man to rouse your envy once,

1250

1255

1260

1265

1270

1275

8. A river at Thebes.  9. The two cliffs above Delphi, where Dionysus was thought to reside in the winter months.  1. A mountain associated with Dionysiac worship; there is more than one mountain so named but the reference here is probably to the one on the island of Euboea, off the Attic coast.  2. Dionysus.

as I see it. He saved the realm from enemies,                    1280
taking power, he alone, the lord of the fatherland,
he set us true on course—he flourished like a tree
with the noble line of sons he bred and reared . . .
and now it's lost, all gone.
                          Believe me,
when a man has squandered his true joys,                        1285
he's good as dead, I tell you, a living corpse.
Pile up riches in your house, as much as you like—
live like a king with a huge show of pomp,
but if real delight is missing from the lot,
I wouldn't give you a wisp of smoke for it,                      1290
not compared with joy.

LEADER:                         What now?
    What new grief do you bring the house of kings?

MESSENGER: Dead, dead—and the living are guilty of their death!

LEADER: Who's the murderer? Who is dead? Tell us.

MESSENGER: Haemon's gone, his blood spilled by the very
    hand—                                                        1295

LEADER: His father's or his own?

MESSENGER:                         His own . . .
    raging mad with his father for the death—

LEADER:                              Oh great seer,
    you saw it all, you brought your word to birth!

MESSENGER: Those are the facts. Deal with them as you will.


        [*As he turns to go,* EURYDICE *enters from the palace.*]


LEADER: Look, Eurydice. Poor woman, Creon's wife,              1300
    so close at hand. By chance perhaps,
    unless she's heard the news about her son.

EURYDICE:                              My countrymen,
    all of you—I caught the sound of your words
    as I was leaving to do my part,
    to appeal to queen Athena with my prayers.                  1305
    I was just loosing the bolts, opening the doors,
    when a voice filled with sorrow, family sorrow,
    struck my ears, and I fell back, terrified,
    into the women's arms—everything went black.
    Tell me the news, again, whatever it is . . .               1310
    sorrow and I are hardly strangers.
    I can bear the worst.

MESSENGER:                    I—dear lady,
    I'll speak as an eye-witness. I was there.
    And I won't pass over one word of the truth.

Why should I try to soothe you with a story,                                      1315
only to prove a liar in a moment?
Truth is always best.
                So,
I escorted your lord, I guided him
to the edge of the plain where the body lay,
Polynices, torn by the dogs and still unmourned.                                  1320
And saying a prayer to Hecate of the Crossroads,
Pluto[3] too, to hold their anger and be kind,
we washed the dead in a bath of holy water
and plucking some fresh branches, gathering . . .
what was left of him, we burned them all together                                 1325
and raised a high mound of native earth, and then
we turned and made for that rocky vault of hers,
the hollow, empty bed of the bride of Death.
And far off one of us heard a voice,
a long wail rising, echoing                                                       1330
out of that unhallowed wedding-chamber,
he ran to alert the master and Creon pressed on,
closer—the strange, inscrutable cry came sharper,
throbbing around him now, and he let loose
a cry of his own, enough to wrench the heart,                                     1335
"Oh god, am I the prophet now? going down
the darkest road I've ever gone? My son—
it's *his* dear voice, he greets me! Go, men,
closer, quickly! Go through the gap,
the rocks are dragged back—                                                       1340
right to the tomb's very mouth—and look,
see if it's Haemon's voice I think I hear,
or the gods have robbed me of my senses."

The king was shattered. We took his orders,
went and searched, and there in the deepest,                                      1345
dark recesses of the tomb we found her . . .
hanged by the neck in a fine linen noose,
strangled in her veils—and the boy,
his arms flung around her waist,
clinging to her, wailing for his bride,                                           1350
dead and down below, for his father's crimes
and the bed of his marriage blighted by misfortune.
When Creon saw him, he gave a deep sob,
he ran in, shouting, crying out to him,
"Oh my child—what have you done? what seized you,                                 1355

3. Divinities of the underworld. Pluto is another name of Hades; Hecate a goddess associated with
darkness and burial grounds. Offerings to her were left at crossroads.

what insanity? what disaster drove you mad?
Come out, my son! I beg you on my knees!"
But the boy gave him a wild burning glance,
spat in his face, not a word in reply,
he drew his sword—his father rushed out,                         1360
running as Haemon lunged and missed!—
and then, doomed, desperate with himself,
suddenly leaning his full weight on the blade,
he buried it in his body, halfway to the hilt.
And still in his senses, pouring his arms around her,            1365
he embraced the girl and breathing hard,
released a quick rush of blood,
bright red on her cheek glistening white.
And there he lies, body enfolding body . . .
he has won his bride at last, poor boy,                          1370
not here but in the houses of the dead.

Creon shows the world that of all the ills
afflicting men the worst is lack of judgment.

[EURYDICE *turns and reenters the palace.*]

LEADER: What do you make of that? The lady's gone,
    without a word, good or bad.
MESSENGER:                         I'm alarmed too               1375
    but here's my hope—faced with her son's death
    she finds it unbecoming to mourn in public.
    Inside, under her roof, she'll set her women
    to the task and wail the sorrow of the house.
    She's too discreet. She won't do something rash.             1380
LEADER: I'm not so sure. To me, at least,
    a long heavy silence promises danger,
    just as much as a lot of empty outcries.
MESSENGER: We'll see if she's holding something back,
    hiding some passion in her heart.                            1385
    I'm going in. You may be right—who knows?
    Even too much silence has its dangers.

[*Exit to the palace. Enter* CREON *from the side, escorted by
attendants carrying* HAEMON*'s body on a bier.*]

LEADER: The king himself! Coming toward us,
    look, holding the boy's head in his hands.
    Clear, damning proof, if it's right to say so—                1390
    proof of his own madness, no one else's,

no, his own blind wrongs.
CREON:                              Ohhh,
  so senseless, so insane . . . my crimes,
  my stubborn deadly—
  Look at us, the killer, the killed,                          1395
  father and son, the same blood—the misery!
  My plans, my mad fanatic heart,
  my son, cut off so young!
  Ai dead, lost to the world,
  not through your stupidity, no, my own.
LEADER:                                    Too late,      1400
  too late, you see what justice means.
CREON:                        Oh I've learned
  through blood and tears! Then, it was then,
  when the god came down and struck me—a great weight
  shattering, driving me down that wild savage path,
  ruining, trampling down my joy. Oh the agony,             1405
    the heartbreaking agonies of our lives.

  [*Enter the* MESSENGER *from the palace.*]

MESSENGER:                              Master,
  what a hoard of grief you have, and you'll have more.
  The grief that lies to hand you've brought yourself—

  [*Pointing to* HAEMON's *body.*]

  the rest, in the house, you'll see it all too soon.
CREON: What now? What's worse than this?
MESSENGER:                          The queen is dead.    1410
  The mother of this dead boy . . . mother to the end—
  poor thing, her wounds are fresh.
CREON:                          No, no,
  harbor of Death, so choked, so hard to cleanse!—
  why me? why are you killing me?
  Herald of pain, more words, more grief?                    1415
  I died once, you kill me again and again!
  What's the report, boy . . . some news for me?
  My wife dead? O dear god!
  Slaughter heaped on slaughter?

  [*The doors open; the body of* EURYDICE *is brought out on her
  bier.*]

MESSENGER:                  See for yourself:
  now they bring her body from the palace.
CREON:                                Oh no,         1420

another, a second loss to break the heart.
What next, what fate still waits for me?
I just held my son in my arms and now,
look, a new corpse rising before my eyes—
    wretched, helpless mother—O my son! 1425
MESSENGER: She stabbed herself at the altar,
    then her eyes went dark, after she'd raised
    a cry for the noble fate of Megareus,[4] the hero
    killed in the first assault, then for Haemon,
    then with her dying breath she called down 1430
    torments on your head—you killed her sons.
CREON:                                Oh the dread,
    I shudder with dread! Why not kill me too?—
    run me through with a good sharp sword?
    Oh god, the misery, anguish—
    I, I'm churning with it, going under. 1435
MESSENGER: Yes, and the dead, the woman lying there,
    piles the guilt of all their deaths on you.
CREON: How did she end her life, what bloody stroke?
MESSENER: She drove home to the heart with her own hand,
    once she learned her son was dead . . . that agony. 1440
CREON: And the guilt is all mine—
    can never be fixed on another man,
    no escape for me. I killed you,
    I, god help me, I admit it all!

    [*To his attendants.*]

Take me away, quickly, out of sight. 1445
    I don't even exist—I'm no one. Nothing.
LEADER: Good advice, if there's any good in suffering.
    Quickest is best when troubles block the way.

    [*Kneeling in prayer.*]

CREON: Come, let it come—that best of fates for me
    that brings the final day, best fate of all. 1450
    Oh quickly, now—
    so I never have to see another sunrise.
LEADER: That will come when it comes;
    we must deal with all that lies before us.
    The future rests with the ones who tend the future. 1455
CREON: That prayer—I poured my heart into that prayer!

---

4. Another son of Creon and Eurydice; he was killed during the siege of the city.

LEADER: No more prayers now. For mortal men
   there is no escape from the doom we must endure.
CREON: Take me away, I beg you, out of sight.
   A rash, indiscriminate fool!                       1460
   I murdered you, my son, against my will—
   you too, my wife . . .
                   Wailing wreck of a man,
  whom to look to? where to lean for support?

    [*Desperately turning from* HAEMON *to* EURYDICE *on their biers.*]

  Whatever I touch goes wrong—once more
  a crushing fate's come down upon my head!             1465

    [*The* MESSENGER *and attendants lead* CREON *into the palace.*]

CHORUS: Wisdom is by far the greatest part of joy,
   and reverence toward the gods must be safeguarded.
   The mighty words of the proud are paid in full
   with mighty blows of fate, and at long last
   those blows will teach us wisdom.                 1470

    [*The old citizens exit to the side.*]

---

# EURIPIDES
## 480–406 B.C.

Euripides' *Medea*, produced in 431 B.C., the year that brought the beginning
of the Peloponnesian War, appeared earlier than the *Oedipus the King* of
Sophocles, but it has a bitterness that is more in keeping with the spirit of
a later age. If the *Oedipus* is, in one sense, a warning to a generation which
has embarked on an intellectual revolution, the *Medea* is the ironic expression of the disillusion that comes after the ship-wreck. In this play we are
conscious for the first time of an attitude characteristic of modern literature,
the artist's feeling of separation from his audience, the isolation of the poet.
"Often previously," says Medea to the king,

> Through being considered clever
>    I have suffered much. . . .
> If you put new ideas before the eyes
>    of fools
> They'll think you foolish and
>    worthless into the bargain;

                    And if you are thought superior to
                       those who have
                    Some reputation for learning, you
                       will become hated.

The common background of audience and poet is disappearing, the old
certainties are being undermined, the city divided. Euripides is the first Greek
poet to suffer the fate of so many of the great modern writers: rejected by
most of his contemporaries (he rarely won first prize and was the favorite
target for the scurrilous humor of the comic poets), he was universally admired
and revered by the Greeks of the centuries that followed his death (406 B.C.).

It is significant that what little biographical information we have for Euripides makes no mention of military service or political office; unlike Aeschylus, who fought in the ranks at Marathon, and Sophocles, who took an
active part in public affairs from youth to advanced old age, Euripides seems
to have lived a private, an intellectual life. Younger than Sophocles (though
they died in the same year), he was more receptive to the critical theories
and the rhetorical techniques offered by the Sophist teachers; his plays often
subject received ideas to fundamental questioning, expressed in vivid dramatic debate. His *Medea* is typical of his iconoclastic approach; his choice
of subject and of central characters is in itself a challenge to established
canons. He still dramatizes myth, but the myth he chooses is exotic and
disturbing, and the protagonist is not a man but a woman. Medea is both
woman and foreigner; that is to say, in terms of the audience's prejudice and
practice she is a representative of the two free-born groups in Athenian society which had almost no rights at all (though the male foreign resident had
more rights than the native woman). The tragic hero is no longer a king,
"one who is highly renowned and prosperous such as Oedipus," but a woman,
who, because she finds no redress for her wrongs in society, is driven by her
passion to violate that society's most sacred laws in a rebellion against its
typical representative, Jason, her husband. She is not just a woman and a
foreigner; she is also a person of great intellectual power. Compared to her
the credulous king and her complacent husband are children, and once her
mind is made up, she moves them like pawns to their proper places in her
barbaric game. The myth is used for new purposes, to shock the members
of the audience, attack their deepest prejudices, and shake them out of their
complacent pride in the superiority of Greek masculinity.

But the play is more than a feminist melodrama. Before it is over, our
sympathies have come full circle; the contempt with which we regard the
Jason of the opening scenes turns to pity as we feel the measure of his loss
and the ferocity of Medea's revenge. Medea's passion has carried her too far;
the death of Creon and his daughter we might have accepted, but the murder of the children is too much. It was, of course, meant to be. Euripides'
theme, like Homer's, is violence, but this is the unspeakable violence of the
oppressed, which is greater than the violence of the oppressor and which,
because it has been long pent up, cannot be controlled.

In this, as in the other plays, the gods have their place. In the *Oresteia*
the will of Zeus is manifested in every action and implied in every word; in
*Oedipus the King* the gods bide their time and watch Oedipus fulfill the

truth of their prophecy, but in *Medea*, the divine will, which is revealed at
the end, is enigmatic and, far from bringing harmony, concludes the play
with a terrifying discord. All through *Medea* the human beings involved call
on the gods; two especially are singled out for attention, Earth and Sun. It
is by these two gods that Medea makes Aegeus swear to give her refuge in
Athens, the chorus invokes them to prevent Medea's violence against her
sons, and Jason wonders how Medea can look upon earth and sun after she
has killed her own children. These emphatic appeals clearly raise the question of the attitude of the gods, and the answer to the question is a shock.
We are not told what Earth does, but Sun sends the magic chariot on which
Medea makes her escape. His reason, too, is stated; it is not any concern for
justice, but the fact that Medea is his granddaughter. Euripides is here using
the letter of the myth for his own purposes. This jarring detail emphasizes
the significance of the whole. The play creates a world in which there is no
relation whatsoever between the powers which rule the universe and the
fundamental laws of human morality. It dramatizes disorder, not just the
disorder of the family of Jason and Medea, but the disorder of the universe
as a whole. It is the nightmare in which the dream of the fifth century was
to end, the senseless fury and degradation of permanent violence. "Flow
backward to your sources, sacred rivers," the chorus sings, "And let the
world's great order be reversed."

   G. M. A. Grube, *The Drama of Euripides* (1941), deals with the whole
range of Euripidean drama and includes biographical and historical background. *Euripides, A Collection of Critical Essays*, edited by E. Segal (1968),
contains perceptive analysis of *Medea*. B. M. W. Knox, "The *Medea* of
Euripides," and P. E. Easterling, "The Infanticide in Euripides' *Medea*,"
both in *Yale Classical Studies* 24 (1977), will be helpful to students.

# Medea[1]

## Characters

| | |
|---|---|
| MEDEA, *princess of Colchis and wife of Jason* | KREON, *king of Corinth* |
| | AIGEUS, *king of Athens* |
| JASON, *son of Aeson, king of Iolcos* | NURSE *to Medea* |
| | TUTOR *to Medea's children* |
| TWO CHILDREN *of Medea and Jason* | MESSENGER |
| | CHORUS OF CORINTHIAN WOMEN |

SCENE—*In front of Medea's house in Corinth. Enter from the house
Medea's* NURSE.

NURSE. How I wish the Argo[2] never had reached the land
   Of Colchis, skimming through the blue Symplegades,[3]

---

1. Translated by Rex Warner.    2. The ship in which Jason and his companions sailed on the
quest for the Golden Fleece.    3. Clashing rocks, which crushed ships endeavoring to pass between
them. They were supposed to be located at the Hellespont, the passage between the Mediterranean
and the Black sea.

Nor ever had fallen in the glades of Pelion[4]
The smitten fir-tree to furnish oars for the hands
Of heroes who in Pelias' name attempted                                5
The Golden Fleece![5] For then my mistress Medea
Would not have sailed for the towers of the land of Iolcos,
Her heart on fire with passionate love for Jason;
Nor would she have persuaded the daughers of Pelias
To kill their father,[6] and now be living here                       10
In Corinth with her husband and children. She gave
Pleasure to the people of her land of exile,
And she herself helped Jason in every way.
This is indeed the greatest salvation of all,—
For the wife not to stand apart from the husband.                      15
But now there's hatred everywhere. Love is diseased.
For, deserting his own children and my mistress,
Jason has taken a royal wife to his bed,
The daughter of the ruler of this land, Kreon.
And poor Medea is slighted, and cries aloud on the                     20
Vows they made to each other, the right hands clasped
In eternal promise. She calls upon the gods to witness
What sort of return Jason has made to her love.
She lies without food and gives herself up to suffering,
Wasting away every moment of the day in tears.                         25
So it has gone since she knew herself slighted by him.
Not stirring an eye, not moving her face from the ground,
No more than either a rock or surging sea water
She listens when she is given friendly advice.
Except that sometimes she twists back her white neck and               30
Moans to herself, calling out on her father's name,
And her land, and her home betrayed[7] when she came away with
A man who now is determined to dishonor her.
Poor creature, she has discovered by her sufferings
What it means to one not to have lost one's own country.               35
She has turned from the children and does not like to see them.
I am afraid she may think of some dreadful thing,
For her heart is violent. She will never put up with
The treatment she is getting. I know and fear her

---

4. A mountain in the north of Greece near Iolcos, the place from which Jason sailed.    5. Pelias seized the kingdom of Iolcos, expelling Aeson, Jason's father. When Jason came to claim his rights, Pelias sent him to get the Golden Fleece.    6. After Jason returned to Iolcos with the Fleece and Medea, Pelias' daughters were persuaded by Medea, who had a reputation as a sorceress, to cut Pelias up and boil the pieces, in order to restore him to youth. The experiment was, of course, unsuccessful, but the son of Pelias expelled Jason and Medea from the kingdom, and they took refuge in Corinth on the isthmus between the Peloponnese and Attica. In Euripides' time it was a wealthy trading city, a commercial rival of Athens.    7. Medea, daughter of the king of Colchis, fell in love with Jason and helped him to take the Golden Fleece away from her own country.

Lest she may sharpen a sword and thrust to the heart,        40
Stealing into the palace where the bed is made,
Or even kill the king and the new-wedded groom,
And thus bring a greater misfortune on herself.
She's a strange woman. I know it won't be easy
To make an enemy of her and come off best.                   45
But here the children come. They have finished playing.
They have no thought at all of their mother's trouble.
Indeed it is not usual for the young to grieve.

> [*Enter from the right the slave who is the* TUTOR *to Medea's two
> small children. The* CHILDREN *follow him.*]

TUTOR. You old retainer of my mistress's household,
Why are you standing here all alone in front of the          50
Gates and moaning to yourself over your misfortune?
Medea could not wish you to leave her alone.
NURSE. Old man, and guardian of the children of Jason,
If one is a good servant, it's a terrible thing
When one's master's luck is out; it goes to one's heart.     55
So I myself have got into such a state of grief
That a longing stole over me to come outside here
And tell the earth and air of my mistress's sorrows.
TUTOR. Has the poor lady not yet given up her crying?
NURSE. Given up? She's at the start, not halfway through her
tears.                                                        60
TUTOR. Poor fool,—if I may call my mistress such a name,—
How ignorant she is of trouble more to come.
NURSE. What do you mean, old man? You needn't fear to speak.
TUTOR. Nothing. I take back the words which I used just now.
NURSE. Don't, by your beard, hide this from me, your fellow-
servant.                                                     65
If need be, I'll keep quiet about what you tell me.
TUTOR. I heard a person saying, while I myself seemed
Not to be paying attention, when I was at the place
Where the old draught-players[8] sit, by the holy fountain,
That Kreon, ruler of the land, intends to drive              70
These children and their mother in exile from Corinth.
But whether what he said is really true or not
I do not know. I pray that it may not be true.
NURSE. And will Jason put up with it that his children
Should suffer so, though he's no friend to their mother?     75
TUTOR. Old ties give place to new ones. As for Jason, he
No longer has a feeling for this house of ours.
NURSE. It's black indeed for us, when we add new to old

---

8. Checker-players.

Sorrows before even the present sky has cleared.

TUTOR. But you be silent, and keep all this to yourself.                    80
It is not the right time to tell our mistress of it.

NURSE. Do you hear, children, what a father he is to you?
I wish he were dead,—but no, he is still my master.
Yet certainly he has proved unkind to his dear ones.

TUTOR. What's strange in that? Have you only just discovered    85
That everyone loves himself more than his neighbor?
Some have good reason, others get something out of it.
So Jason neglects his children for the new bride.

NURSE. Go indoors, children. That will be the best thing.
And you, keep them to themselves as much as possible.       90
Don't bring them near their mother in her angry mood.
For I've seen her already blazing her eyes at them
As though she meant some mischief and I am sure that
She'll not stop raging until she has struck at someone.
May it be an enemy and not a friend she hurts!              95

[MEDEA *is heard inside the house.*]

MEDEA. Ah, wretch! Ah, lost in my sufferings,
I wish, I wish I might die.

NURSE. What did I say, dear children? Your mother
Frets her heart and frets it to anger.
Run away quickly into the house,                           100
And keep well out of her sight.
Don't go anywhere near, but be careful
Of the wildness and bitter nature
Of that proud mind.
Go now! Run quickly indoors.                               105
It is clear that she soon will put lightning
In that cloud of her cries that is rising
With a passion increasing. Oh, what will she do,
Proud-hearted and not to be checked on her course,
A soul bitten into with wrong?                             110

[*The* TUTOR *takes the children into the house.*]

MEDEA. Ah, I have suffered
What should be wept for bitterly. I hate you,
Children of a hateful mother. I curse you
And your father. Let the whole house crash.

NURSE. Ah, I pity you, you poor creature.                  115
How can your children share in their father's
Wickedness? Why do you hate them? Oh children,
How much I fear that something may happen!
Great people's tempers are terrible, always
Having their own way, seldom checked,                      120
Dangerous they shift from mood to mood.

How much better to have been accustomed
To live on equal terms with one's neighbours.
I would like to be safe and grow old in a
Humble way. What is moderate sounds best,                    125
Also in practice *is* best for everyone.
Greatness brings no profit to people.
God indeed, when in anger, brings
Greater ruin to great men's houses.

> [*Enter, on the right, a* CHORUS OF CORINTHIAN WOMEN. *They
> have come to enquire about* MEDEA *and to attempt to console
> her.*]

CHORUS. I heard the voice, I heard the cry                    130
   Of Colchis' wretched daughter.
   Tell me, mother, is she not yet
   At rest? Within the double gates
   Of the court I heard her cry. I am sorry
   For the sorrow of this home. O, say, what has happened?    135
NURSE. There is no home. It's over and done with.
   Her husband holds fast to his royal wedding,
   While she, my mistress, cries out her eyes
   There in her room, and takes no warmth from
   Any word of any friend.                                   140
MEDEA. Oh, I wish
   That lightning from heaven would split my head open.
   Oh, what use have I now for life?
   I would find my release in death
   And leave hateful existence behind me.                    145
CHOR. O God and Earth and Heaven!
   Did you hear what a cry was that
   Which the sad wife sings?
   Poor foolish one, why should you long
   For that appalling rest?                                  150
   The final end of death comes fast.
   No need to pray for that.
   Suppose your man gives honor
   To another woman's bed.
   It often happens. Don't be hurt.                          155
   God will be your friend in this.
   You must not waste away
   Grieving too much for him who shared your bed.
MEDEA. Great Themis, lady Artemis,[9] behold
   The things I suffer, though I made him promise,           160
   My hateful husband. I pray that I may see him,

---

9. The protector of women in pain and distress. *Themis*: justice.

Him and his bride and all their palace shattered
For the wrong they dare to do me without cause.
Oh, my father! Oh, my country! In what dishonor
I left you, killing my own brother for it.[1]                              165
NURSE. Do you hear what she says, and how she cries
  On Themis, the goddess of Promises, and on Zeus,
  Whom we believe to be the Keeper of Oaths?
  Of this I am sure, that no small thing
  Will appease my mistress's anger.                                  170
CHOR. Will she come into our presence?
  Will she listen when we are speaking
  To the words we say?
  I wish she might relax her rage
  And temper of her heart.                                          175
  My willingness to help will never
  Be wanting to my friends.
  But go inside and bring her
  Out of the house to us,
  And speak kindly to her: hurry,                                    180
  Before she wrongs her own.
  This passion of hers moves to something great.
NURSE. I will, but I doubt if I'll manage
  To win my mistress over.
  But still I'll attempt it to please you.                          185
  Such a look she will flash on her servants
  If any comes near with a message,
  Like a lioness guarding her cubs.
  It is right, I think, to consider
  Both stupid and lacking in foresight                               190
  Those poets of old who wrote songs
  For revels and dinners and banquets,
  Pleasant sounds for men living at ease;
  But none of them all has discovered
  How to put an end with their singing                               195
  Or musical instruments grief,
  Bitter grief, from which death and disaster
  Cheat the hopes of a house. Yet how good
  If music could cure men of this! But why raise
  To no purpose the voice at a banquet? For *there* is               200
  Already abundance of pleasure for men
  With a joy of its own.
     [*The* NURSE *goes into the house.*]
CHOR. I heard a shriek that is laden with sorrow.

---

1. Medea killed him to delay the pursuit when she escaped with Jason.

Shrilling out her hard grief she cries out
Upon him who betrayed both her bed and her marriage.                    205
Wronged, she calls on the gods,
On the justice of Zeus, the oath sworn,
Which brought her away
To the opposite shore of the Greeks
Through the gloomy salt straits to the gateway                    210
Of the salty unlimited sea.

[MEDEA, *attended by servants, comes out of the house.*]

MEDEA. Women of Corinth, I have come outside to you
    Lest you should be indignant with me; for I know
    That many people are overproud, some when alone,
    And others when in company. And those who live                    215
    Quietly, as I do, get a bad reputation.
    For a just judgment is not evident in the eyes
    When a man at first sight hates another, before
    Learning his character, being in no way injured;
    And a foreigner especially must adapt himself.[2]                    220
    I'd not approve of even a fellow-countryman
    Who by pride and want of manners offends his neighbors.
    But on me this thing has fallen so unexpectedly,
    It has broken my heart. I am finished. I let go
    All my life's joy. My friends, I only want to die.                    225
    It was everything to me to think well of one man,
    And he, my own husband, has turned out wholly vile.
    Of all things which are living and can form a judgment
    We women are the most unfortunate creatures.[3]
    Firstly, with an excess of wealth it is required                    230
    For us to buy a husband and take for our bodies
    A master; for not to take one is even worse.
    And now the question is serious whether we take
    A good or bad one; for there is no easy escape
    For a woman, nor can she say no to her marriage.                    235
    She arrives among new modes of behavior and manners,
    And needs prophetic power, unless she has learnt at home,
    How best to manage him who shares the bed with her.
    And if we work out all this well and carefully,
    And the husband lives with us and lightly bears his yoke,                    240
    Then life is enviable. If not, I'd rather die.
    A man, when he's tired of the company in his home,
    Goes out of the house and puts an end to his boredom

---

2. Foreign residents were encouraged to come to Athens, but were rarely admitted to the rights of full citizenship, which was a jealously guarded privilege.　3. Athenian rights and institutions were made for men; the women had few privileges and almost no legal rights. The following two lines refer to the dowry which had to be provided for the bride.

And turns to a friend or companion of his own age.
But we are forced to keep our eyes on one alone.     245
What they say of us is that we have a peaceful time
Living at home, while they do the fighting in war.
How wrong they are! I would very much rather stand
Three times in the front of battle than bear one child.
Yet what applies to me does not apply to you.     250
You have a country. Your family home is here.
You enjoy life and the company of your friends.
But I am deserted, a refugee, thought nothing of
By my husband,—something he won in a foreign land.
I have no mother or brother, nor any relation     255
With whom I can take refuge in this sea of woe.
This much then is the service I would beg from you:
If I can find the means or devise any scheme
To pay my husband back for what he has done to me,—
Him and his father-in-law and the girl who married him,—     260
Just to keep silent. For in other ways a woman
Is full of fear, defenseless, dreads the sight of cold
Steel; but, when once she is wronged in the matter of love,
No other soul can hold so many thoughts of blood.

CHOR. This I will promise. You are in the right, Medea,     265
    In paying your husband back. I am not surprised at you
    For being sad. But look! I see our king Kreon
    Approaching. He will tell us of some new plan.
        [*Enter, from the right,* KREON, *with attendants.*]

KREON. You, with that angry look, so set against your husband,
    Medea, I order you to leave my territories     270
    An exile, and take along with you your two children,
    And not to waste time doing it. It is my decree,
    And I will see it done. I will not return home
    Until you are cast from the boundaries of my land.

MEDEA. Oh, this is the end for me. I am utterly lost.     275
    Now I am in the full force of the storm of hate
    And have no harbor from ruin to reach easily.
    Yet still, in spite of it all, I'll ask the question:
    What is your reason, Kreon, for banishing me?

KREON. I am afraid of you,—why should I dissemble it?—     280
    Afraid that you may injure my daughter mortally.
    Many things accumulate to support my feeling.
    You are a clever woman, versed in evil arts,
    And are angry at having lost your husband's love.
    I hear that you are threatening, so they tell me,     285
    To do something against my daughter and Jason
    And me, too. I shall take my precautions first.

I tell you, I prefer to earn your hatred now
Than to be soft-hearted and afterwards regret it.
MEDEA. This is not the first time, Kreon. Often previously 290
Through being considered clever I have suffered much.
A person of sense ought never to have his children
Brought up to be more clever than the average.
For, apart from cleverness bringing them no profit,
It will make them objects of envy and ill-will. 295
If you put new ideas before the eyes of fools
They'll think you foolish and worthless into the bargain;
And if you are thought superior to those who have
Some reputation for learning, you will become hated.
I have some knowledge myself of how this happens; 300
For being clever, I find that some will envy me,
Others object to me. Yet all my cleverness
Is not so much. Well, then, are you frightened, Kreon,
That I should harm you? There is no need. It is not
My way to transgress the authority of a king. 305
How have you injured me? You gave your daughter away
To the man you wanted. O, certainly I hate
My husband, but you, I think, have acted wisely;
Nor do I grudge it you that your affairs go well.
May the marriage be a lucky one! Only let me 310
Live in this land. For even though I have been wronged,
I will not raise my voice, but submit to my betters.
KREON. What you say sounds gentle enough. Still in my heart
I greatly dread that you are plotting some evil,
And therefore I trust you even less than before. 315
A sharp-tempered woman, or for that matter a man,
Is easier to deal with than the clever type
Who holds her tongue. No. You must go. No need for more
Speeches. The thing is fixed. By no manner of means
Shall you, an enemy of mine, stay in my country. 320
MEDEA. I beg you. By your knees, by your new-wedded girl.
KREON. Your words are wasted. You will never persuade me.
MEDEA. Will you drive me out, and give no heed to my prayers?
KREON. I will, for I love my family more than you.
MEDEA. O my country! How bitterly now I remember you! 325
KREON. I love my country too,—next after my children.
MEDEA. O what an evil to men is passionate love!
KREON. That would depend on the luck that goes along with it.
MEDEA. O God, do not forget who is the cause of this!
KREON. Go. It is no use. Spare me the pain of forcing you. 330
MEDEA. I'm spared no pain. I lack no pain to be spared me.
KREON. Then you'll be removed by force by one of my men.

MEDEA. No, Kreon, not that! But do listen, I beg you.

KREON. Woman, you seem to want to create a disturbance.

MEDEA. I *will* go into exile. *This* is not what I beg for.                    335

KREON. Why then this violence and clinging to my hand?

MEDEA. Allow me to remain here just for this one day,
    So I may consider where to live in my exile,
    And look for support for my children, since their father
    Chooses to make no kind of provision for them.                          340
    Have pity on them! You have children of your own.
    It is natural for you to look kindly on them.
    For myself I do not mind if I go into exile.
    It is the children being in trouble that I mind.

KREON. There is nothing tyrannical about my nature,                         345
    And by showing mercy I have often been the loser.
    Even now I know that I am making a mistake.
    All the same you shall have your will. But this I tell you,
    That if the light of heaven tomorrow shall see you,
    You and your children in the confines of my land,                       350
    You die. This word I have spoken is firmly fixed.
    But now, if you must stay, stay for this day alone.
    For in it you can do none of the things I fear.
        [*Exit* KREON *with his attendants.*]

CHOR. Oh, unfortunate one! Oh, cruel!
    Where will you turn? Who will help you?                                 355
    What house or what land to preserve you
    From ill can you find?
    Medea, a god has thrown suffering
    Upon you in waves of despair.

MEDEA. Things have gone badly every way. No doubt of that.                  360
    But not these things this far, and don't imagine so.
    There are still trials to come for the new-wedded pair,
    And for their relations pain that will mean something.
    Do you think that I would ever have fawned on that man
    Unless I had some end to gain or profit in it?                          365
    I would not even have spoken or touched him with my hands.
    But he has got to such a pitch of foolishness
    That, though he could have made nothing of all my plans
    By exiling me, he has given me this one day
    To stay here, and in this I will make dead bodies                       370
    Of three of my enemies,—father, the girl and my husband.
    I have many ways of death which I might suit to them,
    And do not know, friends, which one to take in hand;
    Whether to set fire underneath their bridal mansion,
    Or sharpen a sword and thrust it to the heart,                          375
    Stealing into the palace where the bed is made.

There is just one obstacle to this. If I am caught
Breaking into the house and scheming against it,
I shall die, and give my enemies cause for laughter.
It is best to go by the straight road, the one in which         380
I am most skilled, and make away with them by poison.
So be it then.
And now suppose them dead. What town will receive me?
What friend will offer me a refuge in his land,
Or the guarantee of his house and save my own life?         385
There is none. So I must wait a little time yet,
And if some sure defense should then appear for me,
In craft and silence I will set about this murder.
But if my fate should drive me on without help,
Even though death is certain, I will take the sword         390
Myself and kill, and steadfastly advance to crime.
It shall not be,—I swear it by her, my mistress,
Whom most I honor and have chosen as partner,
Hecate,[4] who dwells in the recesses of my hearth,—
That any man shall be glad to have injured me.         395
Bitter I will make their marriage for them and mournful,
Bitter the alliance and the driving me out of the land.
Ah, come, Medea, in your plotting and scheming
Leave nothing untried of all those things which you know.
Go forward to the dreadful act. The test has come         400
For resolution. You see how you are treated. Never
Shall you be mocked by Jason's Corinthian wedding,
Whose father was noble, whose grandfather Helios.[5]
You have the skill. What is more, you were born a woman,
And women, though most helpless in doing good deeds,         405
Are of every evil the cleverest of contrivers.

CHOR. Flow backward to your sources, sacred rivers,
    And let the world's great order be reversed.
    It is the thoughts of *men* that are deceitful,
    *Their* pledges that are loose.         410
    Story shall now turn my condition to a fair one,
    Women are paid their due.
    No more shall evil-sounding fame be theirs.

    Cease now, you muses of the ancient singers,
    To tell the tale of my unfaithfulness;         415
    For not on us did Phoebus,[6] lord of music,
    Bestow the lyre's divine
    Power, for otherwise I should have sung an answer

4. The patron of witchcraft, sometimes identified with Artemis. Medea has a statue and shrine of
Hecate in the house.   5. The sun, father of Medea's father, Aeëtes.   6. Apollo.

To the other sex. Long time
Has much to tell of us, and much of them.                    420

You sailed away from your father's home,
With a heart on fire you passed
The double rocks of the sea.
And now in a foreign country
You have lost your rest in a widowed bed,                    425
And are driven forth, a refugee
In dishonor from the land.

Good faith has gone, and no more remains
In great Greece a sense of shame.
It has flown away to the sky.                                430
No father's house for a haven
Is at hand for you now, and another queen
Of your bed has dispossessed you and
Is mistress of your home.
    [*Enter* JASON, *with attendants.*]
JASON. This is not the first occasion that I have noticed     435
    How hopeless it is to deal with a stubborn temper.
    For, with reasonable submission to our ruler's will,
    You might have lived in this land and kept your home.
    As it is you are going to be exiled for your loose speaking.
    Not that I mind myself. You are free to continue          440
    Telling everyone that Jason is a worthless man.
    But as to your talk about the king, consider
    Yourself most lucky that exile is your punishment.
    I, for my part, have always tried to calm down
    The anger of the king, and wished you to remain.          445
    But you will not give up your folly, continually
    Speaking ill of him, and so you are going to be banished.
    All the same, and in spite of your conduct, I'll not desert
    My friends, but have come to make some provision for you,
    So that you and the children may not be penniless         450
    Or in need of anything in exile. Certainly
    Exile brings many troubles with it. And even
    If you hate me, I cannot think badly of you.
MEDEA. O coward in every way,—that is what I call you,
    With bitterest reproach for your lack of manliness,       455
    You have come, you, my worst enemy, have come to me!
    It is not an example of over-confidence
    Or of boldness thus to look your friends in the face,
    Friends you have injured,—no, it is the worst of all
    Human diseases, shamelessness. But you did well           460

To come, for I can speak ill of you and lighten
My heart, and you will suffer while you are listening.
And first I will begin from what happened first.
I saved your life, and every Greek knows I saved it
Who was a ship-mate of yours aboard the Argo,                    465
When you were sent to control the bulls that breathed fire[7]
And yoke them, and when you would sow that deadly field.
Also that snake, who encircled with his many folds
The Golden Fleece and guarded it and never slept,
I killed, and so gave you the safety of the light.               470
And I myself betrayed my father and my home,
And came with you to Pelias' land of Iolcos.
And then, showing more willingness to help than wisdom,
I killed him, Pelias, with a most dreadful death
At his own daughters' hands, and took away your fear.            475
This is how I behaved to you, you wretched man,
And you forsook me, took another bride to bed
Though you had children; for, if that had not been,
You would have had an excuse for another wedding.
Faith in your word has gone. Indeed I cannot tell                480
Whether you think the gods whose names you swore by then
Have ceased to rule and that new standards are set up,
Since you must know you have broken your word to me.
O my right hand, and the knees which you often clasped
In supplication, how senselessly I am treated                    485
By this bad man, and how my hopes have missed their mark!
Come, I will share my thoughts as though you were a friend,—
You! Can I think that you would ever treat me well?
But I will do it, and these questions will make you
Appear the baser. Where am I to go? To my father's?              490
Him I betrayed and his land when I came with you.
To Pelias' wretched daughters? What a fine welcome
They would prepare for me who murdered their father!
For this is my position,—hated by my friends
At home, I have, in kindness to you, made enemies                495
Of others whom there was no need to have injured.
And how happy among Greek women you have made me
On your side for all this! A distinguished husband
I have,—for breaking promises. When in misery
I am cast out of the land and go into exile,                     500
Quite without friends and all alone with my children,

7. This and the following lines refer to ordeals through which Jason had to pass to win the Fleece, and in which Medea helped him. He had to yoke a team of firebreathing bulls, then sow a field which immediately sprouted armed warriors, then deal with the snake which guarded the Fleece.    8. Aphrodite, goddess of love.

That will be a fine shame for the new-wedded groom,
For his children to wander as beggars and she who saved him.
O God, you have given to mortals a sure method
Of telling the gold that is pure from the counterfeit;                    505
Why is there no mark engraved upon men's bodies,
by which we could know the true ones from the false ones?

CHOR. It is a strange form of anger, difficult to cure
When two friends turn upon each other in hatred.

JASON. As for me, it seems I must be no bad speaker.                       510
But, like a man who has a good grip of the tiller,
Reef up his sail, and so run away from under
This mouthing tempest, woman, of your bitter tongue.
Since you insist on building up your kindness to me,
My view is that Cypris[8] was alone responsible                           515
Of men and gods for the preserving of my life.
You are clever enough,—but really I need not enter
Into the story of how it was love's inescapable
Power that compelled you to keep my person safe.
On this I will not go into too much detail.                               520
In so far as you helped me, you did well enough.
But on this question of saving me, I can prove
You have certainly got from me more than you gave.
Firstly, instead of living among barbarians,
You inhabit a Greek land and understand our ways,                         525
How to live by law instead of the sweet will of force.
And all the Greeks considered you a clever woman.
You were honored for it; while, if you were living at
The ends of the earth, nobody would have heard of you.
For my part, rather than stores of gold in my house                       530
Or power to sing even sweeter songs than Orpheus,
I'd choose the fate that made me a distinguished man.
There is my reply to your story of my labors.
Remember it was you who started the argument.
Next for your attack on my wedding with the princess:                     535
Here I will prove that, first, it was a clever move,
Secondly, a wise one, and, finally, that I made it
In your best interests and the children's. Please keep calm.
When I arrived here from the land of Iolcos,
Involved, as I was, in every kind of difficulty,                          540
What luckier chance could I have come across than this,
An exile to marry the daughter of the king?
It was not,—the point that seems to upset you—that I
Grew tired of your bed and felt the need of a new bride;

---

8. Aphrodite, goddess of love.

Nor with any wish to outdo your number of children. 545
We have enough already. I am quite content.
But,—this was the main reason—that we might live well,
And not be short of anything. I know that all
A man's friends leave him stone-cold if he becomes poor.
Also that I might bring my children up worthily 550
Of my position, and, by producing more of them
To be brothers of yours, we would draw the families
Together and all be happy. You need no children.
And it pays me to do good to those I have now
By having others. Do you think this a bad plan? 555
You wouldn't if the love question hadn't upset you.
But you women have got into such a state of mind
That, if your life at night is good, you think you have
Everything; but, if in that quarter things go wrong,
You will consider your best and truest interests 560
Most hateful. It would have been better far for men
To have got their children in some other way, and women
Not to have existed. Then life would have been good.
CHOR. Jason, though you have made this speech of yours look well,
Still I think, even though others do not agree, 565
You have betrayed your wife and are acting badly.
MEDEA. Surely in many ways I hold different views
From others, for I think that the plausible speaker
Who is a villain deserves the greatest punishment.
Confident in his tongue's power to adorn evil, 570
He stops at nothing. Yet he is not really wise.
As in your case. There is no need to put on the airs
Of a clever speaker, for one word will lay you flat.
If you were not a coward, you would not have married
Behind my back, but discussed it with me first. 575
JASON. And you, no doubt, would have furthered the proposal,
If I had told you of it, you who even now
Are incapable of controlling your bitter temper.
MEDEA. It was not that. No, you thought it was not respectable
As you got on in years to have a foreign wife. 580
JASON. Make sure of this: it was not because of a woman
I made the royal alliance in which I now live,
But, as I said before, I wished to preserve you
And breed a royal progeny to be brothers
To the children I have now, a sure defense to us. 585
MEDEA. Let me have no happy fortune that brings pain with it,
Or prosperity which is upsetting to the mind!
JASON. Change your ideas of what you want, and show more sense.
Do not consider painful what is good for you,

Nor, when you are lucky, think yourself unfortunate.                    590
MEDEA. You can insult me. You have somewhere to turn to.
    But I shall go from this land into exile, friendless.
JASON. It was what you chose yourself. Don't blame others for it.
MEDEA. And how did I choose it? Did I betray my husband?
JASON. You called down wicked curses on the king's family.          595
MEDEA. A curse, that is what I am become to your house too.
JASON. I do not propose to go into all the rest of it;
    But, if you wish for the children or for yourself
    In exile to have some of my money to help you,
    Say so, for I am prepared to give with open hand,             600
    Or to provide you with introductions to my friends
    Who will treat you well. You are a fool if you do not
    Accept this. Cease your anger and you will profit.
MEDEA. I shall never accept the favors of friends of yours,
    Nor take a thing from you, so you need not offer it.            605
    There is no benefit in the gifts of a bad man.
JASON. Then, in any case, I call the gods to witness that
    I wish to help you and the children in every way,
    But you refuse what is good for you. Obstinately
    You push away your friends. You are sure to suffer for it.      610
MEDEA. Go! No doubt you hanker for your virginal bride,
    And are guilty of lingering too long out of her house.
    Enjoy your wedding. But perhaps,—with the help of God—
    You will make the kind of marriage that you will regret.
    [JASON *goes out with his attendants.*]
CHOR. When love is in excess                                         615
    It brings a man no honor
    Nor any worthiness.
    But if in moderation Cypris comes,
    There is no other power at all so gracious.
    O goddess, never on me let loose the unerring                  620
    Shaft of your bow in the poison of desire.

    Let my heart be wise.
    It is the gods' best gift.
    On me let mighty Cypris
    Inflict no wordy wars or restless anger                        625
    To urge my passion to a different love.
    But with discernment may she guide women's weddings,
    Honoring most what is peaceful in the bed.

    O country and home,
    Never, never may I be without you,                             630
    Living the hopeless life,

Hard to pass through and painful,
Most pitiable of all.
Let death first lay me low and death
Free me from this daylight.                                    635
There is no sorrow above
The loss of a native land.

I have seen it myself,
Do not tell of a secondhand story.
Neither city nor friend                                         640
Pitied you when you suffered
The worst of sufferings.
O let him die ungraced whose heart
Will not reward his friends,
Who cannot open an honest mind                                  645
No friend will he be of mine.
    [*Enter* AIGEUS, *king of Athens, an old friend of* MEDEA.]
AIGEUS. Medea, greeting! This is the best introduction
   Of which men know for conversation between friends.
MEDEA. Greeting to you too, Aigeus, son of King Pandion,
   Where have you come from to visit this country's soil?       650
AIGEUS. I have just left the ancient oracle of Phoebus.
MEDEA. And why did you go to earth's prophetic center?
AIGEUS. I went to inquire how children might be born to me.
MEDEA. Is it so? Your life still up to this point childless?
AIGEUS. Yes. By the fate of some power we have no children.     655
MEDEA. Have you a wife, or is there none to share your bed?
AIGEUS. There is. Yes, I am joined to my wife in marriage.
MEDEA. And what did Phoebus say to you about children?
AIGEUS. Words too wise for a mere man to guess their meaning.
MEDEA. Is it proper for me to be told the God's reply?          660
AIGEUS. It is. For sure what is needed is cleverness.
MEDEA. Then what was his message? Tell me, if I may hear.
AIGEUS. I am not to loosen the hanging foot of the wine-skin . . .⁹
MEDEA. Until you have done something, or reached some country?
AIGEUS. Until I return again to my hearth and house.            665
MEDEA. And for what purpose have you journeyed to this land?
AIGEUS. There is a man called Pittheus,¹ king of Troezen.
MEDEA. A son of Pelops, they say, a most righteous man.
AIGEUS. With him I wish to discuss the reply of the god.
MEDEA. Yes. He is wise and experienced in such matters.         670
AIGEUS. And to me also the dearest of all my spear-friends.²

9. This cryptic phrase probably means "not to have intercourse."   1. Aigeus' father-in-law.
*Troezen:* in the Peloponnese. Corinth was on the way from Delphi to Troezen.   2. Allies in
war, companions in fighting.   3. Athens, city of Pallas Athene.

MEDEA. Well, I hope you have good luck, and achieve your will.

AIGEUS. But why this downcast eye of yours, and this pale cheek?

MEDEA. O Aigeus, my husband has been the worst of all to me.

AIGEUS. What do you mean? Say clearly what has caused this
  grief. 675

MEDEA. Jason wrongs me, though I have never injured him.

AIGEUS. What has he done? Tell me about it in clearer words.

MEDEA. He has taken a wife to his house, supplanting me.

AIGEUS. Surely he would not dare to do a thing like that.

MEDEA. Be sure he has. Once dear, I now am slighted by him. 680

AIGEUS. Did he fall in love? Or is he tired of your love?

MEDEA. He was greatly in love, this traitor to his friends.

AIGEUS. Then let him go, if, as you say, he is so bad.

MEDEA. A passionate love,—for an alliance with the king.

AIGEUS. And who gave him his wife? Tell me the rest of it. 685

MEDEA. It was Kreon, he who rules this land of Corinth.

AIGEUS. Indeed, Medea, your grief was understandable.

MEDEA. I am ruined. And there is more to come: I am banished.

AIGEUS. Banished? By whom? Here you tell me of a new wrong.

MEDEA. Kreon drives me an exile from the land of Corinth. 690

AIGEUS. Does Jason consent? I cannot approve of this.

MEDEA. He pretends not to, but he will put up with it.
  Ah, Aigeus, I beg and beseech you, by your beard
  And by your knees I am making myself your suppliant,
  Have pity on me, have pity on your poor friend, 695
  And do not let me go into exile desolate,
  But receive me in your land and at your very hearth.
  So may your love, with God's help, lead to the bearing
  Of children, and so may you yourself die happy.
  You do not know what a chance you have come on here. 700
  I will end your childlessness, and I will make you able
  To beget children. The drugs I know can do this.

AIGEUS. For many reasons, woman, I am anxious to do
  This favor for you. First, for the sake of the gods,
  And then for the birth of children which you promise, 705
  For in that respect I am entirely at my wits' end.
  But this is my position: if you reach my land,
  I, being in my rights, will try to befriend you.
  But this much I must warn you of beforehand:
  I shall not agree to take you out of this country; 710
  But if you by yourself can reach my house, then you
  Shall stay there safely. To none will I give you up.
  But from this land you must make your escape yourself,
  For I do not wish to incur blame from my friends.

MEDEA. It shall be so. But, if I might have a pledge from you 715

For this, then I would have from you all I desire.

AIGEUS. Do you not trust me? What is it rankles with you?

MEDEA. I trust you, yes. But the house of Pelias hates me,
And so does Kreon. If you are bound by this oath,
When they try to drag me from your land, you will not          720
Abandon me; but if our pact is only words,
With no oath to the gods, you will be lightly armed,
Unable to resist their summons. I am weak,
While they have wealth to help them and a royal house.

AIGEUS. You show much foresight for such negotiations.          725
Well, if you will have it so, I will not refuse.
For, both on my side this will be the safest way
To have some excuse to put forward to your enemies,
And for you it is more certain. You may name the gods.

MEDEA. Swear by the plain of Earth, and Helios, father          730
Of my father, and name together all the gods. . . .

AIGEUS. That I will act or not act in what way? Speak.

MEDEA. That you yourself will never cast me from your land,
Nor, if any of my enemies should demand me,
Will you, in your life, willingly hand me over.               735

AIGEUS. I swear by the Earth, by the holy light of Helios,
By all the gods, I will abide by this you say.

MEDEA. Enough. And, if you fail, what shall happen to you?

AIGEUS. What comes to those who have no regard for heaven.

MEDEA. Go on your way. Farewell. For I am satisfied,           740
And I will reach your city as soon as I can,
Having done the deed I have to do and gained my end.
    [AIGEUS *goes out.*]

CHOR. May Hermes, god of travellers,
Escort you, Aigeus, to your home!
And may you have the things you wish                           745
So eagerly; for you
Appear to me to be a generous man.

MEDEA. God, and God's daughter, justice, and light of Helios!
Now, friends, has come the time of my triumph over
My enemies, and now my foot is on the road.                    750
Now I am confident they will pay the penalty.
For this man, Aigeus, has been like a harbor to me
In all my plans just where I was most distressed.
To him I can fasten the cable of my safety
When I have reached the town and fortress of Pallas.[3]        755
And now I shall tell to you the whole of my plan.
Listen to these words that are not spoken idly.

3. Athens, city of Pallas Athene.

I shall send one of my servants to find Jason
And request him to come once more into my sight.
And when he comes, the words I'll say will be soft ones.                760
I'll say that I agree with him, that I approve
The royal wedding he has made, betraying me.
I'll say it was profitable, an excellent idea.
But I shall beg that my children may remain here:
Not that I would leave in a country that hates me                          765
Children of mine to feel their enemies' insults,
But that by a trick I may kill the king's daughter.
For I will send the children with gifts in their hands
To carry to the bride, so as not to be banished,—
A finely woven dress and a golden diadem.                                   770
And if she takes them and wears them upon her skin
She and all who touch the girl will die in agony;
Such poison will I lay upon the gifts I send.
But there, however, I must leave that account paid.
I weep to think of what a deed I have to do                               775
Next after that; for I shall kill my own children.
My children, there is none who can give them safety.
And when I have ruined the whole of Jason's house,
I shall leave the land and flee from the murder of my
Dear children, and I shall have done a dreadful deed.                    780
For it is not bearable to be mocked by enemies.
So it must happen. What profit have I in life?
I have no land, no home, no refuge from my pain.
My mistake was made the time I left behind me
My father's house, and trusted the words of a Greek,                     785
Who, with heaven's help, will pay me the price for that.
For those children he had from me he will never
See alive again, nor will he on his new bride
Beget another child, for she is to be forced
To die a most terrible death by these my poisons.                         790
Let no one think me a weak one, feeble-spirited,
A stay-at-home, but rather just the opposite,
One who can hurt my enemies and help my friends;
For the lives of such persons are most remembered.
CHOR. Since you have shared the knowledge of your plan with
us,                                                                                           795
I both wish to help you and support the normal
Ways of mankind, and tell you not to do this thing.
MEDEA. I can do no other thing. It is understandable
For you to speak thus. You have not suffered as I have.
CHOR. But can you have the heart to kill your flesh and blood?        800
MEDEA. Yes, for this is the best way to wound my husband.

CHOR. And you too. Of women you will be most unhappy.
MEDEA. So it must be. No compromise is possible.
　　[*She turns to the* NURSE.]
　Go, you, at once, and tell Jason to come to me.
　You I employ on all affairs of greatest trust.　　　　　　805
　Say nothing of these decisions which I have made,
　If you love your mistress, if you were born a woman.
CHOR. From of old the children of Erechtheus[4] are
　Splendid, the sons of blessed gods. They dwell
　In Athens' holy and unconquered land,[5]　　　　　　　810
　Where famous Wisdom feeds them and they pass gaily
　Always through that most brilliant air where once, they say,
　That golden Harmony gave birth to the nine
　Pure Muses of Pieria.[6]

　And beside the sweet flow of Cephisos' stream,[7]　　　815
　Where Cypris sailed, they say, to draw the water,
　And mild soft breezes breathed along her path,
　And on her hair were flung the sweet-smelling garlands
　Of flowers of roses by the Lovers, the companions
　Of Wisdom, her escort, the helpers of men　　　　　　820
　In every kind of excellence.

　How then can these holy rivers
　Or this holy land love you,
　Or the city find you a home,
　You, who will kill your children,　　　　　　　　　825
　You, not pure with the rest?
　O think of the blow at your children
　And think of the blood that you shed.
　O, over and over I beg you,
　By your knees I beg you do not　　　　　　　　　　830
　Be the murderess of your babes!

　O where will you find the courage
　Or the skill of hand and heart,
　When you set yourself to attempt
　A deed so dreadful to do?　　　　　　　　　　　835
　How, when you look upon them,

---

4. An early king of Athens, a son of Hephaestus.　　5. It was the Athenians' boast that their descent from the original settlers was uninterrupted by an invasion. There is a topical reference here, for the play was produced in 431 B.C., in a time of imminent war.　　6. A fountain in Boeotia where the Muses were supposed to live. The sentence means that the fortunate balance ("Harmony") of the elements and the genius of the people produced the cultivation of the arts ("the nine pure Muses").　　7. Athenian river. Cypris, mentioned in the next line, is the goddess of love and therefore of the principle of fertility.

Can you tearlessly hold the decision
For murder? You will not be able,
When your children fall down and implore you,
You will not be able to dip                                           840
Steadfast your hand in their blood.

    *[Enter* JASON *with attendants.]*

JASON. I have come at your request. Indeed, although you are
    Bitter against me, this you shall have: I will listen
    To what new thing you want, woman, to get from me.
MEDEA. Jason, I beg you to be forgiving towards me                    845
    For what I said. It is natural for you to bear with
    My temper, since we have had much love together.
    I have talked with myself about this and I have
    Reproached myself. "Fool" I said, "why am I so mad?
    Why am I set against those who have planned wisely?   850
    Why make myself an enemy of the authorities
    And of my husband, who does the best thing for me
    By marrying royalty and having children who
    Will be as brothers to my own? What is wrong with me?
    Let me give up anger, for the gods are kind to me.   855
    Have I not children, and do I not know that we
    In exile from our country must be short of friends?"
    When I considered this I saw that I had shown
    Great lack of sense, and that my anger was foolish.
    Now I agree with you. I think that you are wise       860
    In having this other wife as well as me, and I
    Was mad. I should have helped you in these plans of yours,
    Have joined in the wedding, stood by the marriage bed,
    Have taken pleasure in attendance on your bride.
    But we women are what we are,—perhaps a little      865
    Worthless; and you men must not be like us in this,
    Nor be foolish in return when we are foolish.
    Now I give in, and admit that then I was wrong.
    I have come to a better understanding now.

    *[She turns towards the house.]*

Children, come here, my children, come outdoors to us!
Welcome your father with me, and say goodbye to him,
And with your mother, who just now was his enemy,
Join again in making friends with him who loves us.

    *[Enter the* CHILDREN, *attended by the* TUTOR.]*

We have made peace, and all our anger is over.
Take hold of his right hand,—O God, I am thinking            875
Of something which may happen in the secret future.
O children, will you just so, after a long life,
Hold out your loving arms at the grave? O children,

How ready to cry I am, how full of foreboding!
  I am ending at last this quarrel with your father,      880
  And, look, my soft eyes have suddenly filled with tears.
CHOR. And the pale tears have started also in my eyes.
  O may the trouble not grow worse than now it is!
JASON. I approve of what you say. And I cannot blame you
  Even for what you said before. It is natural      885
  For a woman to be wild with her husband when he
  Goes in for secret love. But now your mind has turned
  To better reasoning. In the end you have come to
  The right decision, like the clever woman you are.
  And of you, children, your father is taking care.      890
  He has made, with God's help, ample provision for you.
  For I think that a time will come when you will be
  The leading people in Corinth with your brothers.
  You must grow up. As to the future, your father
  And those of the gods who love him will deal with that.      895
  I want to see you, when you have become young men,
  Healthy and strong, better men than my enemies.
  Medea, why are your eyes all wet with pale tears?
  Why is your cheek so white and turned away from me?
  Are not these words of mine pleasing for you to hear?      900
MEDEA. It is nothing. I was thinking about these children.
JASON. You must be cheerful. I shall look after them well.
MEDEA. I will be. It is not that I distrust your words,
  But a woman is a frail thing, prone to crying.
JASON. But why then should you grieve so much for these
                              children?   905
MEDEA. I am their mother. When you prayed that they might live
  I felt unhappy to think that these things will be.
  But come, I have said something of the things I meant
  To say to you, and now I will tell you the rest.
  Since it is the king's will to banish me from here,—      910
  And for me too I know that this is the best thing,
  Not to be in your way by living here or in
  The king's way, since they think me ill-disposed to them,—
  I then am going into exile from this land;
  But do you, so that you may have the care of them,      915
  Beg Kreon that the children may not be banished.
JASON. I doubt if I'll succeed, but still I'll attempt it.
MEDEA. Then you must tell your wife to beg from her father
  That the children may be reprieved from banishment.
JASON. I will, and with her I shall certainly succeed.      920
MEDEA. If she is like the rest of us women, you will.
  And I too will take a hand with you in this business,

For I will send her some gifts which are far fairer,
I am sure of it, than those which now are in fashion,
A finely-woven dress and a golden diadem,                        925
And the children shall present them. Quick, let one of you
Servants bring here to me that beautiful dress.
    *[One of her attendants goes into the house.]*
She will be happy not in one way, but in a hundred,
Having so fine a man as you to share her bed,
And with this beautiful dress which Helios of old,               930
My father's father, bestowed on his descendants.
    *[Enter attendant carrying the poisoned dress and diadem.]*
There, children, take these wedding presents in your hands.
Take them to the royal princess, the happy bride,
And give them to her. She will not think little of them.

JASON. No, don't be foolish, and empty your hands of these.       935
    Do you think the palace is short of dresses to wear?
    Do you think there is no gold there? Keep them, don't give them
    Away. If my wife considers me of any value,
    She will think more of me than money, I am sure of it.

MEDEA. No, let me have my way. They say the gods themselves       940
    Are moved by gifts, and gold does more with men than words.
    Hers is the luck, her fortune that which god blesses;
    She is young and a princess; but for my children's reprieve
    I would give my very life, and not gold only.
    Go children, go together to that rich palace,                945
    Be suppliants to the new wife of your father,
    My lady, beg her not to let you be banished.
    And give her the dress,—for this is of great importance,
    That she should take the gift into her hand from yours.
    Go, quick as you can. And bring your mother good news         950
    By your success of those things which she longs to gain.
        *[JASON goes out with his attendants, followed by the TUTOR and
        the CHILDREN carrying the poisoned gifts.]*

CHOR. Now there is no hope left for the children's lives.
    Now there is none. They are walking already to murder.
    The bride, poor bride, will accept the curse of the gold,
    Will accept the bright diadem.                                955
    Around her yellow hair she will set that dress
    Of death with her own hands.
    The grace and the perfume and glow of the golden robe
    Will charm her to put them upon her and wear the wreath,
    And now her wedding will be with the dead below,             960
    Into such a trap she will fall,
    Poor thing, into such a fate of death and never
    Escape from under that curse.

You too, O wretched bridegroom, making your match with kings,
You do not see that you bring                                   965
Destruction on your children and on her,
Your wife, a fearful death.
Poor soul, what a fall is yours!


In your grief too I weep, mother of little children,
You who will murder your own,                                  970
In vengeance for the loss of married love
Which Jason has betrayed
As he lives with another wife.
    [*Enter the* TUTOR *with the* CHILDREN.]
TUTOR. Mistress, I tell you that these children are reprieved,
    And the royal bride has been pleased to take in her hands  975
    Your gifts. In that quarter the children are secure.
    But come,
    Why do you stand confused when you are fortunate?
    Why have you turned round with your cheek away from me?
    Are not these words of mine pleasing for you to hear?      980
MEDEA. Oh! I am lost!
TUTOR. That word is not in harmony with my tidings.
MEDEA. I am lost, I am lost!
TUTOR.                    Am I in ignorance telling you
    Of some disaster, and not the good news I thought?
MEDEA. You have told what you have told. I do not blame you.   985
TUTOR. Why then this downcast eye, and this weeping of tears?
MEDEA. Oh, I am forced to weep, old man. The gods and I,
    I in a kind of madness have contrived all this.
TUTOR. Courage! You too will be brought home by your children.
MEDEA. Ah, before that happens I shall bring others home.      990
TUTOR. Others before you have been parted from their children.
    Mortals must bear in resignation their ill luck.
MEDEA. That is what I shall do. But go inside the house,
    And do for the children your usual daily work.
    [*The* TUTOR *goes into the house.* MEDEA *turns to her* CHILDREN.]
O children, O my children, you have a city,                    995
You have a home, and you can leave me behind you,
And without your mother you may live there for ever.
But I am going in exile to another land
Before I have seen you happy and taken pleasure in you,
Before I have dressed your brides and made your marriage beds
And held up the torch at the ceremony of wedding.             1001
Oh, what a wretch I am in this my self-willed thought!
What was the purpose, children, for which I reared you?

For all my travail and wearing myself away?
They were sterile, those pains I had in the bearing of you.        1005
O surely once the hopes in you I had, poor me,
Were high ones: you would look after me in old age,
And when I died would deck me well with your own hands;
A thing which all would have done. O but now it is gone,
That lovely thought. For, once I am left without you,            1010
Sad will be the life I'll lead and sorrowful for me.
And you will never see your mother again with
Your dear eyes, gone to another mode of living.
Why, children, do you look upon me with your eyes?
Why do you smile so sweetly that last smile of all?              1015
Oh, Oh, what can I do? My spirit has gone from me,
Friends, when I saw that bright look in the children's eyes.
I cannot bear to do it. I renounce my plans
I had before. I'll take my children away from
This land. Why should I hurt their father with the pain          1020
They feel, and suffer twice as much of pain myself?
No, no, I will not do it. I renounce my plans.
Ah, what is wrong with me? Do I want to let go
My enemies unhurt and be laughed at for it?
I must face this thing. Oh, but what a weak woman               1025
Even to admit to my mind these soft arguments.
Children, go into the house. And he whom law forbids
To stand in attendance at my sacrifices,
Let him see to it. I shall not mar my handiwork.
Oh! Oh!                                                         1030
Do not, O my heart, you must not do these things!
Poor heart, let them go, have pity upon the children.
If they live with you in Athens they will cheer you.
No! By Hell's avenging furies it shall not be,—
This shall never be, that I should suffer my children           1035
To be the prey of my enemies' insolence.
Every way is it fixed. The bride will not escape.
No, the diadem is now upon her head, and she,
The royal princess, is dying in the dress, I know it.
But,—for it is the most dreadful of roads for me                1040
To tread, and them I shall send on a more dreadful still—
I wish to speak to the children.
    [*She calls the* CHILDREN *to her.*]
                                        Come, children, give
Me your hands, give your mother your hands to kiss them.
O the dear hands, and O how dear are these lips to me,          1045
And the generous eyes and the bearing of my children!
I wish you happiness, but not here in this world.

What is here your father took. O how good to hold you!
How delicate the skin, how sweet the breath of children!
Go, go! I am no longer able, no longer                                    1050
To look upon you. I am overcome by sorrow.
      [The CHILDREN *go into the house.*]
I know indeed what evil I intend to do,
But stronger than all my afterthoughts is my fury,
Fury that brings upon mortals the greatest evils.
      [*She goes out to the right, towards the royal palace.*]
CHOR. Often before                                                        1055
I have gone through more subtle reasons,
And have come upon questionings greater
Than a woman should strive to search out.
But we too have a goddess to help us
And accompany us into wisdom.                                             1060
Not all of us. Still you will find
Among many women a few,
And our sex is not without learning.
This I say, that those who have never
Had children, who know nothing of it,                                     1065
In happiness have the advantage
Over those who are parents.
The childless, who never discover
Whether children turn out as a good thing
Or as something to cause pain, are spared                                 1070
Many troubles in lacking this knowledge.
And those who have in their homes
The sweet presence of children, I see that their lives
Are all wasted away by their worries.
First they must think how to bring them up well and                       1075
How to leave them something to live on.
And then after this whether all their toil
Is for those who will turn out good or bad,
Is still an unanswered question.
And of one more trouble, the last of all,                                 1080
That is common to mortals I tell.
For suppose you have found them enough for their living,
Suppose that the children have grown into youth
And have turned out good, still, if God so wills it,
Death will away with your children's bodies,                              1085
And carry them off into Hades.
What is our profit, then, that for the sake of
Children the gods should pile upon mortals
After all else
This most terrible grief of all?                                          1090

[*Enter* MEDEA, *from the spectators' right.*]

MEDEA. Friends, I can tell you that for long I have waited
  For the event. I stare towards the place from where
  The news will come. And now, see one of Jason's servants
  Is on his way here, and that labored breath of his
  Shows he has tidings for us, and evil tidings.                    1095
    [*Enter, also from the right, the* MESSENGER.]

MESSENGER. Medea, you who have done such a dreadful thing,
  So outrageous, run for your life, take what you can,
  A ship to bear you hence or chariot on land.

MEDEA. And what is the reason deserves such flight as this?

MESS. She is dead, only just now, the royal princess,             1100
  And Kreon dead too, her father, by your poisons.

MEDEA. The finest words you have spoken. Now and hereafter
  I shall count you among my benefactors and friends.

MESS. What! Are you right in the mind? Are you not mad,
  Woman? The house of the king is outraged by you.                 1105
  Do you enjoy it? Not afraid of such doings?

MEDEA. To what you say I on my side have something too
  To say in answer. Do not be in a hurry, friend,
  But speak. How did they die? You will delight me twice
  As much again if you say they died in agony.                     1110

MESS. When those two children, born of you, had entered in,
  Their father with them, and passed into the bride's house,
  We were pleased, we slaves who were distressed by your wrongs.
  All through the house we were talking of but one thing,
  How you and your husband had made up your quarrel.               1115
  Some kissed the children's hands and some their yellow hair,
  And I myself was so full of my joy that I
  Followed the children into the women's quarters.
  Our mistress, whom we honor now instead of you,
  Before she noticed that your two children were there,            1120
  Was keeping her eye fixed eagerly on Jason.
  Afterwards however she covered up her eyes,
  Her cheek paled and she turned herself away from him,
  So disgusted was she at the children's coming there.
  But your husband tried to end the girl's bad temper,             1125
  And said "You must not look unkindly on your friends.
  Cease to be angry. Turn your head to me again.
  Have as your friends the same ones as your husband has.
  And take these gifts, and beg your father to reprieve
  These children from their exile. Do it for my sake."             1130
  She, when she saw the dress, could not restrain herself.
  She agreed with all her husband said, and before
  He and the children had gone far from the palace,

She took the gorgeous robe and dressed herself in it,
And put the golden crown around her curly locks,                    1135
And arranged the set of the hair in a shining mirror,
And smiled at the lifeless image of herself in it.
Then she rose from her chair and walked about the room,
With her gleaming feet stepping most soft and delicate,
All overjoyed with the present. Often and often                     1140
She would stretch her foot out straight and look along it.
But after that it was a fearful thing to see.
The color of her face changed, and she staggered back,
She ran, and her legs trembled, and she only just
Managed to reach a chair without falling flat down.                 1145
An aged woman servant who, I take it, thought
This was some seizure of Pan[8] or another god,
Cried out "God bless us," but that was before she saw
The white foam breaking through her lips and her rolling
The pupils of her eyes and her face all bloodless.                  1150
Then she raised a different cry from that "God bless us,"
A huge shriek, and the women ran, one to the king,
One to the newly wedded husband to tell him
What had happened to his bride; and with frequent sound
The whole of the palace rang as they went running.                  1155
One walking quickly round the course of a race-track
Would now have turned the bend and be close to the goal,
When she, poor girl, opened her shut and speechless eye,
And with a terrible groan she came to herself.
For a two-fold pain was moving up against her.                      1160
The wreath of gold that was resting around her head
Let forth a fearful stream of all-devouring fire,
And the finely-woven dress your children gave to her,
Was fastening on the unhappy girl's fine flesh.
She leapt up from the chair, and all on fire she ran,               1165
Shaking her hair now this way and now that, trying
To hurl the diadem away; but fixedly
The gold preserved its grip, and, when she shook her hair,
Then more and twice as fiercely the fire blazed out.
Till, beaten by her fate, she fell down to the ground,              1170
Hard to be recognised except by a parent.
Neither the setting of her eyes was plain to see,
Nor the shapeliness of her face. From the top of
Her head there oozed out blood and fire mixed together.
Like the drops on pine-bark, so the flesh from her bones            1175

8. As the god of wild nature he was supposed to be the source of the sudden, apparently causeless terror which solitude in wild surroundings may produce, and thence of all kinds of sudden madness. (Compare our word "panic.")

Dropped away, torn by the hidden fang of the poison.
It was a fearful sight; and terror held us all
From touching the corpse. We had learned from what had
                                                    happened.
But her wretched father, knowing nothing of the event,
Came suddenly to the house, and fell upon the corpse,          1180
And at once cried out and folded his arms about her,
And kissed her and spoke to her, saying, "O my poor child,
What heavenly power has so shamefully destroyed you?
And who has set me here like an ancient sepulchre,
Deprived of you? O let me die with you, my child!"             1185
And when he had made an end of his wailing and crying,
Then the old man wished to raise himself to his feet;
But, as the ivy clings to the twigs of the laurel,
So he stuck to the fine dress, and he struggled fearfully.
For he was trying to lift himself to his knee,                 1190
And she was pulling him down, and when he tugged hard
He would be ripping his aged flesh from his bones.
At last his life was quenched and the unhappy man
Gave up the ghost, no longer could hold up his head.
There they lie close, the daughter and the old father,         1195
Dead bodies, an event he prayed for in his tears.
As for your interests, I will say nothing of them,
For you will find your own escape from punishment.
Our human life I think and have thought a shadow,
And I do not fear to say that those who are held               1200
Wise amongst men and who search the reasons of things
Are those who bring the most sorrow on themselves.
For of mortals there is no one who is happy.
If wealth flows in upon one, one may be perhaps
Luckier than one's neighbor, but still not happy.              1205
        [Exit.]
CHOR. Heaven, it seems, on this day has fastened many
    Evils on Jason, and Jason has deserved them.
    Poor girl, the daughter of Kreon, how I pity you
    And your misfortunes, you who have gone quite away
    To the house of Hades because of marrying Jason.           1210
MEDEA. Women, my task is fixed: as quickly as I may
    To kill my children, and start away from this land,
    And not, by wasting time, to suffer my children
    To be slain by another hand less kindly to them.
    Force every way will have it they must die, and since      1215
    This must be so, then I, their mother, shall kill them.
    O arm yourself in steel, my heart! Do not hang back
    From doing this fearful and necessary wrong.

O come, my hand, poor wretched hand, and take the sword,
Take it, step forward to this bitter starting point,                1220
And do not be a coward, do not think of them,
How sweet they are, and how you are their mother. Just for
This one short day be forgetful of your children,
Afterwards weep; for even though you will kill them,
They were very dear,— O, I am an unhappy woman!                      1225
    *[With a cry she rushes into the house.]*
CHOR. O Earth, and the far shining
    Ray of the sun, look down, look down upon
    This poor lost woman, look, before she raises
    The hand of murder against her flesh and blood.
    Yours was the golden birth from which                            1230
    She sprang, and now I fear divine
    Blood may be shed by men.
    O heavenly light, hold back her hand,
    Check her, and drive from out the house
    The bloody Fury raised by fiends of Hell.                        1235

    Vain waste, your care of children;
    Was it in vain you bore the babes you loved,
    After you passed the inhospitable strait
    Between the dark blue rocks, Symplegades?
    O wretched one, how has it come,                                 1240
    This heavy anger on your heart,
    This cruel bloody mind?
    For God from mortals asks a stern
    Price for the stain of kindred blood
    In like disaster falling on their homes.                         1245
        *[A cry from one of the* CHILDREN *is heard.]*
CHOR. Do you hear the cry, do you hear the children's cry?
    O you hard heart, O woman fated for evil!
ONE OF THE CHILDREN. *[From within]* What can I do and how escape
    my mother's hands?
ONE OF THE CHILDREN. *[From within]* O my dear brother, I cannot
                                                              tell.
    We are lost.
CHOR. Shall I enter the house? O surely I should                     1250
    Defend the children from murder.
A CHILD. *[From within]* O help us, in God's name, for now we need
                                                        your help.
    Now, now we are close to it. We are trapped by the sword.
CHOR. O your heart must have been made of rock or steel,
    You who can kill                                                 1255
    With your own hand the fruit of your own womb.

Of one alone I have heard, one woman alone
Of those of old who laid her hands on her children,
Ino, sent mad by heaven when the wife of Zeus
Drove her out from her home and made her wander; 1260
And because of the wicked shedding of blood
Of her own children she threw
Herself, poor wretch, into the sea and stepped away
Over the sea-cliff to die with her two children.
What horror more can be? O women's love, 1265
So full of trouble,
How many evils have you caused already!

[*Enter* JASON, *with attendants.*]

JASON. You women, standing close in front of this dwelling,
Is she, Medea, she who did this dreadful deed,
Still in the house, or has she run away in flight? 1270
For she will have to hide herself beneath the earth,
Or raise herself on wings into the height of air,
If she wishes to escape the royal vengeance.
Does she imagine that, having killed our rulers,
She will herself escape uninjured from this house? 1275
But I am thinking not so much of her as for
The children,—her the king's friends will make to suffer
For what she did. So I have come to save the lives
Of my boys, in case the royal house should harm them
While taking vengeance for their mother's wicked deed. 1280
CHOR. O Jason, if you but knew how deeply you are
Involved in sorrow, you would not have spoken so.
JASON. What is it? That she is planning to kill me also?
CHOR. Your children are dead, and by their own mother's hand.
JASON. What! This is it? O woman, you have destroyed me. 1285
CHOR. You must make up your mind your children are no more.
JASON. Where did she kill them? Was it here or in the house?
CHOR. Open the gates and there you will see them murdered.
JASON. Quick as you can unlock the doors, men, and undo
The fastenings and let me see this double evil, 1290
My children dead and her,—O her I will repay.

[*His attendants rush to the door.* MEDEA *appears above the house in a chariot drawn by dragons. She has the dead bodies of the children with her.*]

MEDEA. Why do you batter these gates and try to unbar them,
Seeking the corpses and for me who did the deed?
You may cease your trouble, and, if you have need of me,
Speak, if you wish. You will never touch me with your hand, 1295
Such a chariot has Helios, my father's father,
Given me to defend me from my enemies.

JASON. You hateful thing, you woman most utterly loathed
   By the gods and me and by all the race of mankind,
   You who have had the heart to raise a sword against     1300
   Your children, you, their mother, and left me childless,—
   You have done this, and do you still look at the sun
   And at the earth, after these most fearful doings?
   I wish you dead. Now I see it plain, though at that time
   I did not, when I took you from your foreign home     1305
   And brought you to a Greek house, you, an evil thing,
   A traitress to your father and your native land.
   The gods hurled the avenging curse of yours on me.
   For your own brother you slew at your own hearthside,
   And then came aboard that beautiful ship, the Argo.     1310
   And that was your beginning. When you were married
   To me, your husband, and had borne children to me,
   For the sake of pleasure in the bed you killed them.
   There is no Greek woman who would have dared such deeds,
   Out of all those whom I passed over and chose you     1315
   To marry instead, a bitter destructive match,
   A monster not a woman, having a nature
   Wilder than that of Scylla[9] in the Tuscan sea.
   Ah! no, not if I had ten thousand words of shame
   Could I sting you. You are naturally so brazen.     1320
   Go, worker in evil, stained with your children's blood.
   For me remains to cry aloud upon my fate,
   Who will get no pleasure from my newly-wedded love,
   And the boys whom I begot and brought up, never
   Shall I speak to them alive. Oh, my life is over!     1325
MEDEA. Long would be the answer which I might have made to
   These words of yours, if Zeus the father did not know
   How I have treated you and what you did to me.
   No, it was not to be that you should scorn my love,
   And pleasantly live your life through, laughing at me;     1330
   Nor would the princess, nor he who offered the match,
   Kreon, drive me away without paying for it.
   So now you may call me a monster, if you wish,
   O Scylla housed in the caves of the Tuscan sea
   I too, as I had to, have taken hold of your heart.     1335
JASON. You feel the pain yourself. You share in my sorrow.
MEDEA. Yes, and my grief is gain when you cannot mock it.
JASON. O children, what a wicked mother she was to you!
MEDEA. They died from a disease they caught from their father.
JASON. I tell you it was not my hand that destroyed them.     1340

9. A monster located in the straits between Italy and Sicily, who snatched sailors off passing ships
and devoured them.

MEDEA. But it was your insolence, and your virgin wedding.

JASON. And just for the sake of that you chose to kill them.

MEDEA. Is love so small a pain, do you think, for a woman?

JASON. For a wise one, certainly. But you are wholly evil.

MEDEA. The children are dead. I say this to make you suffer.          1345

JASON. The children, I think, will bring down curses on you.

MEDEA. The gods know who was the author of this sorrow.

JASON. Yes, the gods know indeed, they know your loathsome heart.

MEDEA. Hate me. But I tire of your barking bitterness.

JASON. And I of yours. It is easier to leave you.                    1350

MEDEA. How then? What shall I do? I long to leave you too.

JASON. Give me the bodies to bury and to mourn them.

MEDEA. No, that I will not. I will bury them myself,
     Bearing them to Hera's temple on the promontory;
     So that no enemy may evilly treat them                          1355
     By tearing up their grave. In this land of Corinth
     I shall establish a holy feast and sacrifice[1]
     Each year for ever to atone for the blood guilt.
     And I myself go to the land of Erechtheus
     To dwell in Aigeus' house, the son of Pandion.                  1360
     While you, as is right, will die without distinction,
     Struck on the head by a piece of the Argo's timber,
     And you will have seen the bitter end of my love.

JASON. May a Fury for the children's sake destroy you,
     And justice, requitor of blood.                                 1365

MEDEA. What heavenly power lends an ear
     To a breaker of oaths, a deceiver?

JASON. O, I hate you, murderess of children.

MEDEA. Go to your palace. Bury your bride.

JASON. I go, with two children to mourn for.                         1370

MEDEA. Not yet do you feel it. Wait for the future.

JASON. Oh, children I loved!

MEDEA.                          I loved them, you did not.

JASON. You loved them, and killed them.

MEDEA.                                     To make you feel
                                              pain.                   1375

JASON. Oh, wretch that I am, how I long
     To kiss the dear lips of my children!

MEDEA. Now you would speak to them, now you would kiss them.
     Then you rejected them.

JASON.                          Let me, I beg you,                   1380
     Touch my boys' delicate flesh.

---

1. Some such ceremony was still performed at Corinth in Euripides' time.

MEDEA. I will not. Your words are all wasted.

JASON. O God, do you hear it, this persecution,
These my sufferings from this hateful
Woman, this monster, murderess of children?                    1385
Still what I can do that I will do:
I will lament and cry upon heaven,
Calling the gods to bear me witness
How you have killed my boys and prevent me from
Touching their bodies or giving them burial.                   1390
I wish I had never begot them to see them
Afterwards slaughtered by you.

CHOR. Zeus in Olympus is the overseer
Of many doings. Many things the gods
Achieve beyond our judgment. What we thought                   1395
Is not confirmed and what we thought not god
Contrives. And so it happens in this story.

---

# ARISTOPHANES
## 450?–385? B.C.

By the fifth century both tragedy and comedy were regularly produced at the winter festivals of the god Dionysus in Athens. Comedy, like tragedy, employed a chorus, that is to say, a group of dancers (who also sang) and actors, who wore masks; its tone was burlesque and parodic, though there was often a serious theme emphasized by the crude clowning and the free play of wit. The only comic poet of the fifth century whose work has survived is Aristophanes; in his thirteen extant comedies, produced over the years 425–388 B.C., the institutions and personalities of his time are caricatured and criticized in a brilliant combination of poetry and obscenity, of farce and wit, which has no parallel in European literature. It can be described only in terms of itself, by the adjective "Aristophanic."

He was born sometime in the middle of the fifth century and died in the next, around 385 B.C. The earliest of his plays to survive, *The Acharnians*, was produced in 425 B.C. and the bulk of his extant work dates from the years of the Peloponnesian War, 431–404 B.C. The war, in fact, is one of his comic targets; in *The Acharnians*, an Athenian citizen, fed up with the privations caused by the Spartan invasions which shut the Athenians inside their walls, makes a separate peace for himself and his family, defends his decision against an irate chorus of patriots (the Acharnians of the title), and proceeds to enjoy all the benefits of peace while his fellow citizens suffer as before. In the *Peace* (421 B.C.) another Athenian flies up to heaven on a gigantic dung-beetle (a parody of a Euripidean play in which a hero flew up on a winged horse); once arrived, he petitions Zeus to stop the war. Euripides

is another favorite target and was held up to ridicule in play after play; and
Socrates was the "hero" of a play, the *Clouds* (423 B.C.), which held him up
to ridicule as a sophistic charlatan. (Socrates refers to this play in his speech
in court, p. 817). In the *Birds* (414 B.C.) two Athenians, tired of the war and
taxes, go off to found a new city; they organize the birds, who cut off the
smoke of sacrifice which the gods live on, and force Zeus to surrender the
government of the universe to the birds. These plays are all excellent fooling;
they are also sexually and scatalogically explicit. But coarse humor and
exquisite wit combine with lyric poetry of a high quality and comic plots of
startling audacity to produce a mixture unlike anything that went before or
has come after it.

*Lysistrata*, which is outstanding among the Aristophanic comedies in its
coherence of structure and underlying seriousness of theme, was first produced in 411 B.C. In 413 the news of the total destruction of the Athenian
fleet in Sicily had reached Athens, and though heroic efforts to carry on the
war were under way, the confidence in victory with which Athens had begun
the war had gone forever. It is a recurring feature of Aristophanic comedy
that the comic hero upsets the *status quo*, to produce a series of extraordinary results which are exploited to the full for their comic potential. In this
play the Athenian women, who had no political rights, seize the Acropolis
and leave the men without women. At the same time similar revolutions
take place in all the Greek cities according to a coordinated plan. The men
are eventually "starved" into submission and the Spartans come to Athens
to end the war.

Aristophanes does not miss a trick in his exploitation of the possibilities
for ribald humor inherent in this situation, a female sex-strike against war;
Myrrhine's teasing game with her husband Cinesias, for example, is rare
fooling and the final appearance of the uncomfortably rigid Spartan ambassadors and their equally tense Athenian hosts is a visual and verbal climax
of astonishing brilliance. But underneath all the fooling real issues are pursued, and they come to the surface with telling effect in the argument between
Lysistrata and the magistrate who has been sent to suppress the revolt. Reversing
the words of Hector to Andromache, which had become proverbial, Lysistrata claims that "War shall be the concern of Women!"—it is too important
a matter to be left to men, for women are its real victims. And when asked
what the women will do, she explains that they will treat politics just as they
do wool in their household tasks: "when it's confused and snarled . . . draw
out a thread here and a thread there . . . we'll unsnarl this war. . . ."

We do not know how the Athenians welcomed the play. All we know is
that they were not impressed by its serious undertone; the war continued for
seven more exhausting years, until Athens' last fleet was defeated, the city
laid open to the enemy, the empire lost.

K. J. Dover, *Aristophanic Comedy* (1972), is a general survey of the years
and the whole range of Aristophanic comedy.

# Lysistrata[1]

## Characters in the Play[2]

LYSISTRATA ⎫
CALONICE ⎬ *Athenian women*
MYRRHINE ⎭
LAMPITO, *a Spartan woman*
LEADER *of the Chorus of Old Men*
CHORUS *of Old Men*
LEADER *of the Chorus of Old Women*
CHORUS *of Old Women*
ATHENIAN MAGISTRATE
THREE ATHENIAN WOMEN
CINESIAS, *an Athenian, husband of Myrrhine*
SPARTAN HERALD
SPARTAN AMBASSADORS
ATHENIAN AMBASSADORS
TWO ATHENIAN CITIZENS
CHORUS *of Athenians*
CHORUS *of Spartans*

SCENE: *In Athens, beneath the Acropolis. In the center of the stage is the Propylaea, or gate-way to the Acropolis; to one side is a small grotto, sacred to Pan. The Orchestra represents a slope leading up to the gate-way.*

*It is early in the morning.* LYSISTRATA *is pacing impatiently up and down.*

LYSISTRATA. If they'd been summoned to worship the God of Wine, or Pan, or to visit the Queen of Love, why, you couldn't have pushed your way through the streets for all the timbrels.[3] But now there's not a single woman here—except my neighbor; here she comes.

  [*Enter* CALONICE.]
Good day to you, Calonice.

CALONICE. And to you, Lysistrata. [*Noticing* LYSISTRATA'S *impatient air*] But what ails you? Don't scowl, my dear; it's not becoming to you to knit your brows like that.

LYSISTRATA. [*Sadly*] Ah, Calonice, my heart aches; I'm so annoyed at us women. For among men we have a reputation for sly trickery—

1. Translated by Charles T. Murphy. 2. As is usual in ancient comedy, the leading characters have significant names. *Lysistrata* is "She who disbands the armies"; Lampito is a celebrated Spartan name; *Cinesias*, although a real name in Athens, is chosen to suggest a Greek verb *kinein*, *to move*, then *to make love*, *to have intercourse*, and the name of his deme, *Paionidai*, suggests the verb *paiein*, which has about the same significance. 3. These instruments were used in most orgiastic cults, especially in the worship of Dionysus, the "God of Wine."

CALONICE. And rightly too, on my word!

LYSISTRATA. —but when they were told to meet here to consider a matter of no small importance, they lie abed and don't come.

CALONICE. Oh, they'll come all right, my dear. It's not easy for a woman to get out, you know. One is working on her husband, another is getting up the maid, another has to put the baby to bed, or wash and feed it.

LYSISTRATA. But after all, there are other matters more important than all that.

CALONICE. My dear Lysistrata, just what is this matter you've summoned us women to consider? What's up? Something big?

LYSISTRATA. Very big.

CALONICE. [Interested] Is it stout, too?

LYSISTRATA. [Smiling] Yes indeed—both big and stout.

CALONICE. What? And the women still haven't come?

LYSISTRATA. It's not what you suppose; they'd have come soon enough for that. But I've worked up something, and for many a sleepless night I've turned it this way and that.

CALONICE. [In mock disappointment] Oh, I guess it's pretty fine and slender, if you've turned it this way and that.

LYSISTRATA. So fine that the safety of the whole of Greece lies in us women.

CALONICE. In us women? It depends on a very slender reed then.

LYSISTRATA. Our country's fortunes are in our hands; and whether the Spartans shall perish—

CALONICE. Good! Let them perish, by all means.

LYSISTRATA. —and the Boeotians shall be completely annihilated.

CALONICE. Not completely! Please spare the eels.[4]

LYSISTRATA. As for Athens, I won't use any such unpleasant words. But you understand what I mean. But if the women will meet here—the Spartans, the Boeotians, and we Athenians—then all together we will save Greece.

CALONICE. But what could women do that's clever or distinguished? We just sit around all dolled up in silk robes, looking pretty in our sheer gowns and evening slippers.

LYSISTRATA. These are just the things I hope will save us: these silk robes, perfumes, evening slippers, rouge, and our chiffon blouses.

CALONICE. How so?

LYSISTRATA. So never a man alive will lift a spear against the foe—

CALONICE. I'll get a silk gown at once.

LYSISTRATA. —or take up his shield—

CALONICE. I'll put on my sheerest gown!

LYSISTRATA. —or sword.

4. A favorite Athenian delicacy from the Boeotian lakes, eels were then very rare in Athens because of the war.

CALONICE. I'll buy a pair of evening slippers.

LYSISTRATA. Well then, shouldn't the women have come?

CALONICE. Come? Why, they should have *flown* here.

LYSISTRATA. Well, my dear, just watch: they'll act in true Athenian fashion—everything too late! And now there's not a woman here from the shore or from Salamis.[5]

CALONICE. They're coming. I'm sure; at daybreak they were laying— to their oars to cross the straits.

LYSISTRATA. And those I expected would be the first to come—the women of Acharnae[6]—they haven't arrived.

CALONICE. Yet the wife of Theagenes[7] means to come: she consulted Hecate about it. [*Seeing a group of women approaching*] But look! Here come a few. And there are some more over here. Hurrah! Where do they come from?

LYSISTRATA. From Anagyra.[8]

CALONICE. Yes indeed! We've raised up quite a stink from Anagyra anyway.

[*Enter* MYRRHINE *in haste, followed by several other women.*]

MYRRHINE. [*Breathlessly*] Have we come in time, Lysistrata? What do you say? Why so quiet?

LYSISTRATA. I can't say much for you, Myrrhine, coming at this hour on such important business.

MYRRHINE. Why, I had trouble finding my girdle in the dark. But if it's so important, we're here now; tell us.

LYSISTRATA. No. Let's wait a little for the women from Boeotia and the Peloponnesus.

MYRRHINE. That's a much better suggestion. Look! Here comes Lampito now.

[*Enter* LAMPITO *with two other women.*]

LYSISTRATA. Greetings, my dear Spartan friend. How pretty you look, my dear. What a smooth complexion and well-developed figure! You could throttle an ox.

LAMPITO. Faith, yes, I think I could. I take exercises and kick my heels against my bum. [*She demonstrates with a few steps of the Spartan "bottom-kicking" dance.*]

LYSISTRATA. And what splendid breasts you have.

LAMPITO. La! You handle me like a prize steer.

LYSISTRATA. And who is this young lady with you?

LAMPITO. Faith, she's an Ambassadress from Boeotia.

LYSISTRATA. Oh yes, a Boeotian, and blooming like a garden too.

---

5. Just across the bay from Piraeus, the port of Athens.    6. A large village a few miles northwest of Athens.    7. A very superstitious Athenian (perhaps he was sitting in the audience) who never went out without consulting the shrine of Hecate at his doorstep.    8. A district south of Athens. It was also the name of a bad-smelling shrub and the phrase "to stir up the anagyra" was proverbially used to describe people who brought trouble on themselves by interfering.

CALONICE. [*Lifting up her skirt*] My word! How neatly her garden's weeded!

LYSISTRATA. And who is the other girl?

LAMPITO. Oh, she's a Corinthian swell.

MYRRHINE. [*After a rapid examination*] Yes indeed. She swells very nicely [*Pointing*] here and here.

LAMPITO. Who has gathered together this company of women?

LYSISTRATA. I have.

LAMPITO. Speak up, then. What do you want?

MYRRHINE. Yes, my dear, tell us what this important matter is.

LYSISTRATA. Very well, I'll tell you. But before I speak, let me ask you a little question.

MYRRHINE. Anything you like.

LYSISTRATA. [*Earnestly*] Tell me: don't you yearn for the fathers of your children, who are away at the wars? I know you all have husbands abroad.

CALONICE. Why, yes; mercy me! my husband's been away for five months in Thrace keeping guard on—Eucrates.[9]

MYRRHINE. And mine for seven whole months in Pylus.[1]

LAMPITO. And mine, as soon as ever he returns from the fray, readjusts his shield and flies out of the house again.

LYSISTRATA. And as for lovers, there's not even a ghost of one left. Since the Milesians revolted from us,[2] I've not even seen an eight-inch dingus to be a leather consolation for us widows. Are you willing, if I can find a way, to help me end the war?

MYRRHINE. Goodness, yes! I'd do it, even if I had to pawn my dress and—get drunk on the spot!

CALONICE. And I, even if I had to let myself be split in two like a flounder.

LAMPITO. I'd climb up Mt. Taygetus[3] if I could catch a glimpse of peace.

LYSISTRATA. I'll tell you, then, in plain and simple words. My friends, if we are going to force our men to make peace, we must do without—

MYRRHINE. Without what? Tell us.

LYSISTRATA. Will you do it?

MYRRHINE. We'll do it, if it kills us.

LYSISTRATA. Well, then we must do without sex altogether.

[*General consternation*] Why do you turn away? Where go you? Why turn so pale? Why those tears? Will you do it or not? What means this hesitation?

---

9. We have no details on this campaign in Thrace.    1. A point on the west coast of the Peloponnese held by an Athenian garrison.    2. The city of Miletus, an Athenian ally ever since the Persian war, had deserted the Athenian cause in the previous year. The objects Lysistrata speaks of were supposed to be manufactured there.    3. The mountain which towers over Sparta.

MYRRHINE. I won't do it! Let the war go on.

CALONICE. Nor I! Let the war go on.

LYSISTRATA. So, my little flounder? Didn't you say just now you'd split yourself in half?

CALONICE. Anything else you like. I'm willing, even if I have to walk through fire. Anything rather than sex. There's nothing like it, my dear.

LYSISTRATA. [*To* MYRRHINE] What about you?

MYRRHINE. [*Sullenly*] I'm willing to walk through fire, too.

LYSISTRATA. Oh vile and cursed breed! No wonder they make trage-dies about us: we're naught but "love-affairs and bassinets."[4] But you, my dear Spartan friend, if you alone are with me, our enter-prise might yet succeed. Will you vote with me?

LAMPITO. 'Tis cruel hard, by my faith, for a woman to sleep alone without her nooky; but for all that, we certainly do need peace.

LYSISTRATA. O my dearest friend! You're the only real woman here.

CALONICE. [*Wavering*] Well, if we do refrain from—[*Shuddering*] what you say (God forbid!), would that bring peace?

LYSISTRATA. My goodness, yes! If we sit at home all rouged and pow-dered, dressed in our sheerest gowns, and neatly depilated, our men will get excited and want to take us; but if you don't come to them and keep away, they'll soon make a truce.

LAMPITO. Aye; Menelaus caught sight of Helen's naked breast and dropped his sword, they say.

CALONICE. What if the men give us up?

LYSISTRATA. "Flay a skinned dog,"[5] as Pherecrates says.

CALONICE. Rubbish! These make-shifts are no good. But suppose they grab us and drag us into the bedroom?

LYSISTRATA. Hold on to the door.

CALONICE. And if they beat us?

LYSISTRATA. Give in with a bad grace. There's no pleasure in it for them when they have to use violence. And you must torment them in every possible way. They'll give up soon enough; a man gets no joy if he doesn't get along with his wife.

MYRRHINE. If this is your opinion, we agree.

LAMPITO. As for our own men, we can persuade them to make a just and fair peace; but what about the Athenian rabble? Who will persuade them not to start any more monkey-shines?

LYSISTRATA. Don't worry. We guarantee to convince them.

LAMPITO. Not while their ships are rigged so well and they have that mighty treasure in the temple of Athene.

LYSISTRATA. We've taken good care for that too: we shall seize the

---

4. In the *Tyro* of Sophocles, which had recently been produced, the heroine, who had borne twin sons to the god Poseidon, left them exposed in a bassinet.    5. A proverb for useless activity. *Pherecrates*: a fifth-century comic poet.

Acropolis today. The older women have orders to do this, and while we are making our arrangements, they are to pretend to make a sacrifice and occupy the Acropolis.

LAMPITO. All will be well then. That's a very fine idea.

LYSISTRATA. Let's ratify this, Lampito, with the most solemn oath.

LAMPITO. Tell us what oath we shall swear.

LYSISTRATA. Well said. Where's our Policewoman? [*To a Scythian slave*] What are you gaping at? Set a shield upside-down here in front of me, and give me the sacred meats.

CALONICE. Lysistrata, what sort of an oath are we to take?

LYSISTRATA. What oath? I'm going to slaughter a sheep over the shield, as they do in Aeschylus.[6]

CALONICE. Don't, Lysistrata! No oaths about peace over a shield.

LYSISTRATA. What shall the oath be, then?

CALONICE. How about getting a white horse somewhere and cutting out its entrails for the sacrifice?

LYSISTRATA. White horse indeed!

CALONICE. Well then, how shall we swear?

MYRRHINE. I'll tell you: let's place a large black bowl upside-down and then slaughter—a flask of Thasian wine.[7] And then let's swear—not to pour in a single drop of water.

LAMPITO. Lord! How I like that oath!

LYSISTRATA. Someone bring out a bowl and a flask.

[*A slave brings the utensils for the sacrifice.*]

CALONICE. Look, my friends! What a big jar! Here's a cup that 'twould give me joy to handle. [*She picks up the bowl.*]

LYSISTRATA. Set it down and put your hands on our victim.

[*As* CALONICE *places her hands on the flask*] O Lady of Persuasion and dear Loving Cup, graciously vouchsafe to receive this sacrifice from us women. [*She pours the wine into the bowl.*]

CALONICE. The blood has a good colour and spurts out nicely.

LAMPITO. Faith, it has a pleasant smell, too.

MYRRHINE. Oh, let me be the first to swear, ladies!

CALONICE. No, by our Lady! Not unless you're allotted the first turn.

LYSISTRATA. Place all your hands on the cup, and one of you repeat on behalf of all what I say. Then all will swear and ratify the oath.
*I will suffer no man, be he husband or lover,*

CALONICE. *I will suffer no man, be he husband or lover,*

LYSISTRATA. *To approach me all hot and horny.* [*As* CALONICE *hesitates*] Say it!

---

6. In Aeschylus' *Seven Against Thebes*, the enemy champions are described as swearing loyalty to each other and slaughtering a bull so that the blood flowed into the hollow of a shield.
7. Strong wine from the island of Thasos in the northern Aegean. In Athens the wife was in charge of the household supplies and it is a frequent Aristophanic joke to present her as addicted to the bottle.

CALONICE. [*Slowly and painfully*] To approach me all hot and horny.
   O Lysistrata, I feel so weak in the knees!

LYSISTRATA. *I will remain at home unmated,*

CALONICE. *I will remain at home unmated,*

LYSISTRATA. *Wearing my sheerest gown and carefully adorned,*

CALONICE. *Wearing my sheerest gown and carefully adorned,*

LYSISTRATA. *That my husband may burn with desire for me.*

CALONICE. *That my husband may burn with desire for me.*

LYSISTRATA. *And if he takes me by force against my will,*

CALONICE. *And if he takes me by force against my will,*

LYSISTRATA. *I shall do it badly and keep from moving.*

CALONICE. *I shall do it badly and keep from moving.*

LYSISTRATA. *I will not stretch my slippers toward the ceiling,*

CALONICE. *I will not stretch my slippers toward the ceiling,*

LYSISTRATA. *Nor will I take the posture of the lioness on the knife-
   handle.*

CALONICE. *Nor will I take the posture of the lioness on the knife-
   handle.*

LYSISTRATA. *If I keep this oath, may I be permitted to drink from this
   cup,*

CALONICE. *If I keep this oath, may I be permitted to drink from this
   cup,*

LYSISTRATA. *But if I break it, may the cup be filled with water.*

CALONICE. *But if I break it, may the cup be filled with water.*

LYSISTRATA. Do you all swear to this?

ALL. I do, so help me!

LYSISTRATA. Come then, I'll just consummate this offering.
      [*She takes a long drink from the cup.*]

CALONICE. [*Snatching the cup away*] Shares, my dear! Let's drink to
   our continued friendship.
      [*A shout is heard from off-stage.*]

LAMPITO. What's that shouting?

LYSISTRATA. That's what I was telling you: the women have just seized
   the Acropolis. Now, Lampito, go home and arrange matters in
   Sparta; and leave these two ladies here as hostages. We'll enter the
   Acropolis to join our friends and help them lock the gates.

CALONICE. Don't you suppose the men will come to attack us?

LYSISTRATA. Don't worry about them. Neither threats nor fire will
   suffice to open the gates, except on the terms we've stated.

CALONICE. I should say not! Else we'd belie our reputation as
   unmanageable pests.
      [LAMPITO *leaves the stage. The other women retire and enter
      the Acropolis through the Propylaea.*]
      [*Enter the* CHORUS OF OLD MEN, *carrying fire-pots and a load of
      heavy sticks.*]

**LEADER OF MEN.** Onward, Draces, step by step, though your shoulder's aching.

Cursèd logs of olive-wood, what a load you're making!

**FIRST SEMI-CHORUS OF OLD MEN.** [*Singing*]

Aye, many surprises await a man who lives to a ripe old age;

For who could suppose, Strymodorus my lad, that the women we've nourished (alas!),

Who sat at home to vex our days,

Would seize the holy image here

And occupy this sacred shrine,

With bolts and bars, with fell design,

To lock the Propylaea?

**LEADER OF MEN.** Come with speed, Philourgus, come! to the temple hast'ning.

There we'll heap these logs about in a circle round them,

And whoever has conspired, raising this rebellion,

Shall be roasted, scorched, and burnt, all without exception,

Doomed by one unanimous vote—but first the wife of Lycon.[8]

**SECOND SEMI-CHORUS.** [*Singing*]

No, no! by Demeter, while I'm alive, no woman shall mock at me.

Not even the Spartan Cleomenes,[9] our citadel first to seize,

Got off unscathed; for all his pride

And haughty Spartan arrogance,

He left his arms and sneaked away,

Stripped to his shirt, unkempt, unshav'd,

With six years' filth still on him.

**LEADER OF MEN.** I besieged that hero bold, sleeping at my station,

Marshalled at these holy gates sixteen deep against him.

Shall I not these cursèd pests punish for their daring,

Burning these Euripides-and-God-detested women?[1]

Aye! or else may Marathon overturn my trophy.[2]

**FIRST SEMI-CHORUS.** [*Singing*]

There remains of my road

Just this brow of the hill;

There I speed on my way.

8. The ancient commentaries tell us that she was called Rhodia and was not too careful about her reputation. 9. In 508 B.C., the Athenians expelled the tyrant Hippias and were about to install a democratic regime under the leadership of Cleisthenes when the oligarchic party appealed to Sparta for help. The Spartan king Cleomenes invaded Attica, seized the city, and began a purge of the democrats. A popular uprising, however, forced him into the Acropolis, where he was besieged; after two days he was allowed to withdraw with his troops and Cleisthenes began the reforms which established the democracy. 1. Euripides is always presented in Aristophanic comedy as a misogynist and hence hated by women in return. There does not seem to be any foundation for Aristophanes' view, though Euripides' realistic (if sympathetic) presentation of women may possibly have enraged Athenian society ladies. 2. If the chorus really fought at Marathon, they are very old men. The trophy was on a high mound which covered the Athenian dead and is still in place.

Drag the logs up the hill, though we're got no ass to help.
   (God! my shoulder's bruised and sore!)
   Onward still must we go
   Blow the fire! Don't let it go out
   Now we're near the end of our road.

ALL. [*Blowing on the fire-pots*]
   Whew! Whew! Drat the smoke!

SECOND SEMI-CHORUS. [*Singing*]
   Lord, what smoke rushing forth
   From the pot, like a dog
   Running mad, bites my eyes!
This must be Lemnos-fire.[3] What a sharp and stinging smoke!
   Rushing onward to the shrine
   Aid the gods. Once for all
   Show your mettle, Laches my boy!
   To the rescue hastening all!

ALL. [*Blowing on the fire-pots*] Whew! Whew! Drat the smoke!
   [*The chorus has now reached the edge of the Orchestra nearest
   the stage, in front of the Propylaea. They begin laying their logs
   and fire-pots on the ground.*]

LEADER OF MEN. Thank heaven, this fire is still alive. Now let's first
put down these logs here and place our torches in the pots to
catch; then let's make a rush for the gates with a battering-ram. If
the women don't unbar the gate at our summons, we'll have to
smoke them out.

   Let me put down my load. Ouch! That hurts! [*To the audience*]
Would any of the generals in Samos[4] like to lend a hand with this
log? [*Throwing down a log*] Well, *that* won't break my back any
more, at any rate. [*Turning to his fire-pot*] Your job, my little pot,
is to keep those coals alive and furnish me shortly with a red-hot
torch.

   O mistress Victory, be my ally and grant me to rout these audacious women in the Acropolis.

   [*While the men are busy with their logs and fires, the* CHORUS
   OF OLD WOMEN *enters, carrying pitchers of water.*]

LEADER OF WOMEN. What's this I see? Smoke and flames? Is that a
   fire ablazing?

Let's rush upon them. Hurry up! They'll find us women ready.

FIRST SEMI-CHORUS OF OLD WOMEN. [*Singing*]
   With wingèd foot onward I fly,
   Ere the flames consume Neodice;
   Lest Critylla be overwhelmed
  By a lawless, accurst herd of old men.

3. Lemnos is a volcanic island in the Aegean.   4. At this time, the headquarters of the Athenian fleet.

I shudder with fear. Am I too late to aid them?
At break of the day filled we our jars with water
Fresh from the spring, pushing our way straight through the crowds.
Oh, what a din!
Mid crockery crashing, jostled by slave-girls,
Sped we to save them, aiding our neighbors,
Bearing this water to put out the flames.

SECOND SEMI-CHORUS OF OLD WOMEN. [*Singing*]
Such news I've heard: doddering fools
Come with logs, like furnace-attendants,
Loaded down with three hundred pounds,
Breathing many a vain, blustering threat,
That all these abhorred sluts will be burnt to charcoal.
O goddess, I pray never may they be kindled;
Grant them to save Greece and our men; madness and war help
them to end.
With this as our purpose, golden-plumed Maiden,
Guardian of Athens, seized we thy precinct.
Be my ally, Warrior-maiden,
'Gainst these old men, bearing water with me.
[*The women have now reached their position in the Orchestra,
and their* LEADER *advances toward the* LEADER OF THE MEN.]

LEADER OF WOMEN. Hold on there! What's this, you utter scoundrels? No decent, God-fearing citizens would act like this.

LEADER OF MEN. Oho! Here's something unexpected: a swarm of women have come out to attack us.

LEADER OF WOMEN. What, do we frighten you? Surely you don't think we're too many for you. And yet there are ten thousand times more of us whom you haven't even seen.

LEADER OF MEN. What say, Phaedria?[5] Shall we let these women wag their tongues? Shan't we take our sticks and break them over their backs?

LEADER OF WOMEN. Let's set our pitchers on the ground; then if anyone lays a hand on us, they won't get in our way.

LEADER OF MEN. By God! If someone gave them two or three smacks on the jaw, like Bupalus,[6] they wouldn't talk so much!

LEADER OF WOMEN. Go on, hit me, somebody! Here's my jaw! But no other bitch will bite a piece out of you before me.

LEADER OF MEN. Silence! or I'll knock out your—senility!

LEADER OF WOMEN. Just lay one finger on Stratyllis, I dare you!

LEADER OF MEN. Suppose I dust you off with this fist? What will you do?

LEADER OF WOMEN. I'll tear the living guts out of you with my teeth.

5. A man's name; the remark is addressed to another member of the male chorus.    6. A sixth-century sculptor, the target of the poet Hipponax's satirical attracks.

LEADER OF MEN. No poet is more clever than Euripides: "There is no beast so shameless as a woman."

LEADER OF WOMEN. Let's pick up our jars of water, Rhodippe.

LEADER OF MEN. Why have you come here with water, you detestable slut?

LEADER OF WOMEN. And why have you come with fire, you funeral vault? To cremate yourself?

LEADER OF MEN. To light a fire and singe your friends.

LEADER OF WOMEN. And I've brought water to put out your fire.

LEADER OF MEN. What? You'll put out my fire?

LEADER OF WOMEN. Just try and see!

LEADER OF MEN. I wonder: shall I scorch you with this torch of mine?

LEADER OF WOMEN. If you've got any soap, I'll give you a bath.

LEADER OF MEN. Give *me* a bath, you stinking hag?

LEADER OF WOMEN. Yes—a bridal bath!

LEADER OF MEN. Just listen to her! What crust!

LEADER OF WOMEN. Well, I'm a free citizen.

LEADER OF MEN. I'll put an end to your bawling. [*The men pick up their torches.*]

LEADER OF WOMEN. You'll never do jury-duty[7] again. [*The women pick up their pitchers.*]

LEADER OF MEN. Singe her hair for her!

LEADER OF WOMEN. Do your duty, water! [*The women empty their pitchers on the men.*]

LEADER OF MEN. Ow! Ow! For heaven's sake!

LEADER OF WOMEN. Is it too hot?

LEADER OF MEN. What do you mean "hot"? Stop! What are you doing?

LEADER OF WOMEN. I'm watering you, so you'll be fresh and green.

LEADER OF MEN. But I'm all withered up with shaking.

LEADER OF WOMEN. Well, you've got a fire; why don't you dry yourself?

[*Enter an Athenian* MAGISTRATE, *accompanied by four Scythian policemen.*[8]]

MAGISTRATE. Have these wanton women flared up again with their timbrels and their continual worship of Sabazius?[9] Is this another Adonis-dirge[1] upon the roof-tops—which we heard not long ago in the Assembly? That confounded Demostratus was urging us to sail to Sicily, and the whirling women shouted, "Woe for Adonis!"

---

7. Paid attendance at the courts, the usual source of income for older Athenians.    8. The regular police of Athens. They carried bows and arrows.    9. The cult of the oriental deity Sabazius had been recently introduced in Athens. It was considered somewhat disorderly and immoral by religious conservatives.    1. The lament of the women for Adonis (Tammuz), another oriental cult. When the great expedition to Sicily set sail, the women were mourning the death of Adonis—a bad omen which proved all too true. Demostratus was one of the supporters of the expedition (the most prominent was Alcibiades) and he proposed to enroll heavy armed infantry from the island of Zacynthus, off the west coast of Greece, on the way to Sicily.

And then Demostratus said we'd best enroll the infantry from
Zacynthus, and a tipsy woman on the roof shrieked, "Beat your
breasts for Adonis!" And that vile and filthy lunatic forced his
measure through. Such license do our women take.

LEADER OF MEN. What if you heard of the insolence of these women
here? Besides their other violent acts, they threw water all over us,
and we have to shake out our clothes just as if we'd leaked in
them.

MAGISTRATE. And rightly, too, by God! For we ourselves lead the
women astray and teach them to play the wanton; from these roots
such notions blossom forth. A man goes into the jeweler's shop
and says, "About that necklace you made for my wife, goldsmith:
last night, while she was dancing, the fastening-bolt slipped out of
the hole. I have to sail over to Salamis today; if you're free, do
come around tonight and fit in a new bolt for her." Another goes
to the shoe-maker, a strapping young fellow with manly parts, and
says, "See here, cobbler, the sandal-strap chafes my wife's little—
toe; it's so tender. Come around during the siesta and stretch it a
little, so she'll be more comfortable." Now we see the results of
such treatment: here I'm a special Councillor and need money to
procure oars for the galleys; and I'm locked out of the Treasury by
these women.

But this is no time to stand around. Bring up crow-bars there!
I'll put an end to their insolence. [*To one of the policemen*] What
are you gaping at, you wretch? What are you staring at? Got an
eye out for a tavern, eh? Set your crow-bars here to the gates and
force them open. [*Retiring to safe distance*] I'll help from over
here.

[*The gates are thrown open and* LYSISTRATA *comes out followed
by several other women.*]

LYSISTRATA. Don't force the gates; I'm coming out of my own accord.
We don't need crow-bars here; what we need is good sound common-sense.

MAGISTRATE. Is that so, you strumpet? Where's my policeman? Officer, arrest her and tie her arms behind her back.

LYSISTRATA. By Artemis, if he lays a finger on me, he'll pay for it,
even if he is a public servant.

[*The policeman retires in terror.*]

MAGISTRATE. You there, are you afraid? Seize her round the waist—
and you, too. Tie her up, both of you!

FIRST WOMAN. [*As the second policeman approaches* LYSISTRATA] By
Pandrosus,[2] if you but touch her with your hand, I'll kick the
stuffings out of you.

2. A mythical Athenian princess.

[*The second policeman retires in terror.*]

MAGISTRATE. Just listen to that: "kick the stuffings out." Where's another policeman? Tie *her* up first, for her chatter.

SECOND WOMAN. By the Goddess of the Light, if you lay the tip of your finger on her, you'll soon need a doctor.

[*The third policeman retires in terror.*]

MAGISTRATE. What's this? Where's my policeman? Seize *her* too. I'll soon stop your sallies.

THIRD WOMAN. By the Goddess to Tauros,[3] if you go near her, I'll tear out your hair until it shrieks with pain.

[*The fourth policeman retires in terror.*]

MAGISTRATE. Oh, damn it all! I've run out of policemen. But women must never defeat us. Officers, let's charge them all together. Close up your ranks!

[*The policemen rally for a mass attack.*]

LYSISTRATA. By heaven, you'll soon find out that we have four companies of warrior-women, all fully equipped within!

MAGISTRATE. [*Advancing*] Twist their arms off, men!

LYSISTRATA. [*Shouting*] To the rescue, my valiant women!

O sellers-of-barley-green-stuffs-and-eggs,

O sellers-of-garlic, ye keepers-of-taverns, and vendors-of-bread,

Grapple! Smite! Smash!

Won't you heap filth on them? Give them a tongue-lashing!

[*The women beat off the policemen.*]

Halt! Withdraw! No looting on the field.

MAGISTRATE. Damn it! My police-force has put up a very poor show.

LYSISTRATA. What did you expect? Did you think you were attacking slaves? Didn't you know that women are filled with passion?

MAGISTRATE. Aye, passion enough—for a good strong drink!

LEADER OF MEN. O chief and leader of this land, why spend your words in vain?

Don't argue with these shameless beasts. You know not how we've fared:

A soapless bath they've given us; our clothes are soundly soaked.

LEADER OF WOMEN. Poor fool! You never should attack or strike a peaceful girl.

But if you do, your eyes must swell. For I am quite content

To sit unmoved, like modest maids, in peace and cause no pain;

But let a man stir up my hive, he'll find me like a wasp.

CHORUS OF MEN. [*Singing*]

O God, whatever shall we do with creatures like Womankind?

This can't be endured by any man alive. Question them!

---

3. Artemis.

Let us try to find out what this means.
To what end have they seized on this shrine,
   This steep and rugged, high and holy,
     Undefiled Acropolis?

LEADER OF MEN. Come, put your questions; don't give in, and probe her every statement.
For base and shameful it would be to leave this plot untested.

MAGISTRATE. Well then, first of all I wish to ask her this: for what purpose have you barred us from the Acropolis?

LYSISTRATA. To keep the treasure safe, so you won't make war on account of it.

MAGISTRATE. What? Do we make war on account of the treasure?

LYSISTRATA. Yes, and you cause all our other troubles for it, too. Peisander[4] and those greedy office-seekers keep things stirred up so they can find occasions to steal. Now let them do what they like: they'll never again make off with any of this money.

MAGISTRATE. What will you do?

LYSISTRATA. What a question! We'll administer it ourselves.

MAGISTRATE. *You* will administer the treasure?

LYSISTRATA. What's so strange in that? Don't we administer the household money for you?

MAGISTRATE. That's different.

LYSISTRATA. How is it different?

MAGISTRATE. We've got to make war with this money.

LYSISTRATA. But that's the very first thing: you mustn't make war.

MAGISTRATE. How else can we be saved?

LYSISTRATA. We'll save you.

MAGISTRATE. *You?*

LYSISTRATA. Yes, we!

MAGISTRATE. God forbid!

LYSISTRATA. We'll save you, whether you want it or not.

MAGISTRATE. Oh! This is terrible!

LYSISTRATA. You don't like it, but we're going to do it none the less.

MAGISTRATE. Good God! it's illegal!

LYSISTRATA. We *will* save you, my little man!

MAGISTRATE. Suppose I don't want you to?

LYSISTRATA. That's all the more reason.

MAGISTRATE. What business have you with war and peace?

LYSISTRATA. I'll explain.

MAGISTRATE. [*Shaking his fist*] Speak up, or you'll smart for it.

LYSISTRATA. Just listen, and try to keep your hands still.

MAGISTRATE. I can't. I'm so mad I can't stop them.

---

4. A leader of the war party.

FIRST WOMAN. Then you'll be the one to smart for it.

MAGISTRATE. Croak to yourself, old hag! [*To* LYSISTRATA] Now then, speak up.

LYSISTRATA. Very well. Formerly we endured the war for a good long time with our usual restraint, no matter what you men did. You wouldn't let us say "boo," although nothing you did suited us. But we watched you well, and though we stayed at home we'd often hear of some terribly stupid measure you'd proposed. Then, though grieving at heart, we'd smile sweetly and say, "What was passed in the Assembly today about writing on the treaty-stone?"[5] "What's that to you?" my husband would say. "Hold your tongue!" And I held my tongue.

FIRST WOMAN. But I wouldn't have—not I!

MAGISTRATE. You'd have been soundly smacked, if you hadn't kept still.

LYSISTRATA. So I kept still at home. Then we'd hear of some plan still worse than the first; we'd say, "Husband, how could you pass such a stupid proposal?" He'd scowl at me and say, "If you don't mind your spinning, your head will be sore for weeks. *War shall be the concern of Men.*"[6]

MAGISTRATE. And he was right, upon my word!

LYSISTRATA. Why right, you confounded fool, when your proposals were so stupid and we weren't allowed to make suggestions?

"There's not a *man* left in the country," says one. "No, not one," says another. Therefore all we women have decided in council to make a common effort to save Greece. How long should we have waited? Now, if you're willing to listen to our excellent proposals and keep silence for us in your turn, we still may save you.

MAGISTRATE. We men keep silence for you? That's terrible; I won't endure it!

LYSISTRATA. Silence!

MAGISTRATE. Silence for *you*, you wench, when you're wearing a snood? I'd rather die!

LYSISTRATA. Well, if that's all that bothers you—here! take my snood and tie it round your head. [*During the following words the women dress up the* MAGISTRATE *in women's garments.*] And *now* keep quiet! Here, take this spinning-basket, too, and card your wool with robes tucked up, munching on beans. *War shall be the concern of Women!*

LEADER OF WOMEN. Arise and leave your pitchers, girls; no time is this to falter.

We too must aid our loyal friends; our turn has come for action.

5. The text of a treaty was inscribed on a stone which was set up in a public place.
6. Hector to Andromache, *Iliad* VI, 492.

CHORUS OF WOMEN. [*Singing*]
I'll never tire of aiding them with song and dance; never may
Faintness keep my legs from moving to and fro endlessly.
    For I yearn to do all for my friends;
    They have charm, they have wit, they have grace,
        With courage, brains, and best of virtues—
            Patriotic sapience.
LEADER OF WOMEN. Come, child of manliest ancient dames, off-
spring of stinging nettles,
Advance with rage unsoftened; for fair breezes speed you onward.

LYSISTRATA. If only sweet Eros and the Cyprian Queen of Love shed
charm over our breasts and limbs and inspire our men with amo-
rous longing and priapic spasms, I think we may soon be called
Peacemakers among the Greeks.
MAGISTRATE. What will you do?
LYSISTRATA. First of all, we'll stop those fellows who run madly about
the Marketplace in arms.
FIRST WOMAN. Indeed we shall, by the Queen of Paphos.[7]
LYSISTRATA. For now they roam about the market, amid the pots and
greenstuffs, armed to the teeth like Corybantes.[8]
MAGISTRATE. That's what manly fellows ought to do!
LYSISTRATA. But it's so silly: a chap with a Gorgon-emblazoned shield
buying pickled herring.
FIRST WOMAN. Why, just the other day I saw one of those long-haired
dandies who command our cavalry ride up on horseback and pour
into his bronze helmet the egg-broth he'd bought from an old
dame. And there was a Thracian slinger too, shaking his lance
like Tereus;[9] he'd scared the life out of the poor fig-peddler and
was gulping down all her ripest fruit.
MAGISTRATE. How can you stop all the confusion in the various states
and bring them together?
LYSISTRATA. Very easily.
MAGISTRATE. Tell me how.
LYSISTRATA. Just like a ball of wool, when it's confused and snarled:
we take it thus, and draw out a thread here and a thread there with
our spindles; thus we'll unsnarl this war, if no one prevents us,
and draw together the various states with embassies here and
embassies there.
MAGISTRATE. Do you suppose you can stop this dreadful business
with balls of wool and spindles, you nit-wits?
LYSISTRATA. Why, if *you* had any wits, you'd manage all affairs of
state like our wool-working.

7. Aphrodite.    8. The armed priests of the goddess Cybele.    9. A mythical king of Thrace.
Thracian mercenaries had served in the Athenian ranks during the war.

MAGISTRATE. How so?

LYSISTRATA. First you ought to treat the city as we do when we wash
the dirt out of a fleece: stretch it out and pluck and thrash out of
the city all those prickly scoundrels; aye, and card out those who
conspire and stick together to gain office, pulling off their heads.
Then card the wool, all of it, into one fair basket of goodwill,
mingling in the aliens residing here, any loyal foreigners, and anyone who's in debt to the Treasury; and consider that all our colonies lie scattered round about like remnants; from all of these collect
the wool and gather it together here, wind up a great ball, and
then weave a good stout cloak for the democracy.

MAGISTRATE. Dreadful! Talking about thrashing and winding balls of
wool, when you haven't the slightest share in the war!

LYSISTRATA. Why, you dirty scoundrel, we bear more than twice as
much as you. First, we bear children and send off our sons as
soldiers.

MAGISTRATE. Hush! Let bygones be bygones!

LYSISTRATA. Then, when we ought to be happy and enjoy our youth,
we sleep alone because of your expeditions abroad. But never mind
us married women: I grieve most for the maids who grow old at
home unwed.

MAGISTRATE. Don't men grow old, too?

LYSISTRATA. For heaven's sake! That's not the same thing. When a
man comes home, no matter how grey he is, he soon finds a girl
to marry. But woman's bloom is short and fleeting; if she doesn't
grasp her chance, no man is willing to marry her and she sits at
home a prey to every fortune-teller.

MAGISTRATE. [Coarsely] But if a man can still get it up—

LYSISTRATA. See here, you: what's the matter? Aren't you dead yet?
There's plenty of room for you. Buy yourself a shroud and I'll bake
you a honey-cake.[1] [Handing him a copper coin for his passage
across the Styx] Here's your fare! Now get yourself a wreath.

   [During the following dialogue the women dress up the MAGIS-
   TRATE as a corpse.]

FIRST WOMAN. Here, take these fillets.

SECOND WOMAN. Here, take this wreath.

LYSISTRATA. What do you want? What's lacking? Get moving; off to
the ferry! Charon is calling you; don't keep him from sailing.

MAGISTRATE. Am I to endure these insults? By God! I'm going straight
to the magistrates to show them how I've been treated.

LYSISTRATA. Are you grumbling that you haven't been properly laid

---

1. The dead were provided with a honey cake to throw to Cerberus, the three-headed dog which
guarded the entry to the underworld. The copper coin was to pay the fare required by Charon,
the ferryman over the river Styx.

out? Well, the day after tomorrow we'll send around all the usual
offerings early in the morning.

[*The* MAGISTRATE *goes out still wearing his funeral decorations.*
LYSISTRATA *and the women retire into the Acropolis.*]

LEADER OF MEN. Wake, ye sons of freedom, wake! 'Tis no time for
sleeping. Up and at them, like a man! Let us strip for action.

[*The* CHORUS OF MEN *remove their outer cloaks.*]

CHORUS OF MEN. [*Singing*]
Surely there is something here greater than meets the eye;
For without a doubt I smell Hippias' tyranny.[2]
Dreadful fear assails me lest certain bands of Spartan men,
Meeting here with Cleisthenes,[3] have inspired through treachery
All these god-detested women secretly to seize
Athens' treasure in the temple, and to stop that pay
        Whence I live at my ease.

LEADER OF MEN. Now isn't it terrible for them to advise the state and
chatter about shields, being mere women?

And they think to reconcile us with the Spartans—men who
hold nothing sacred any more than hungry wolves. Surely this is
a web of deceit, my friends, to conceal an attempt at tyranny. But
they'll never lord it over me; I'll be on my guard and from now
on,

        "The blade I bear        A myrtle spray shall wear."

I'll occupy the market under arms and stand next to Aristogeiton.[4]

Thus I'll stand beside him. [*He strikes the pose of the famous
statue of the tyrannicides, with one arm raised.*] And here's my
chance to take this accurst old hag and—[*Striking the* LEADER OF
WOMEN] smack her on the jaw!

LEADER OF WOMEN. You'll go home in such a state your Ma won't
recognize you!

Ladies all, upon the ground let us place these garments.

[*The* CHORUS OF WOMEN *remove their outer garments.*]

CHORUS OF WOMEN. [*Singing*]
Citizens of Athens, hear useful words for the state.
Rightly; for it nurtured me in my youth royally.
As a child of seven years carried I the sacred box;[5]

2. The last tyrant of Athens, driven out in 510 B.C.    3. Not the great reformer who set up the
democracy, but a contemporary of Aristophanes, notorious for his effeminacy (and therefore suspect as a fellow-conspirator of the women).    4. One of the two heroes of the democracy who
assassinated Hipparchus, the brother of the tyrant Hippias. A drinking song which was frequently
heard at Athenian banquets ran: "In a branch of myrtle, I'll hide my sword, like Harmodius and
Aristogeiton, who killed the tyrant, and made Athens free."    5. This and the next four lines
describe the religious duties of a well-born Athenian girl. The sacred box contained religious
objects connected with the worship of Athena in the Erechtheum. The miller-maids ground flour

Then I was a Miller-maid, grinding at Athene's shrine;
Next I wore the saffron robe and played Brauronia's Bear;
And I walked as Basket-bearer, wearing chains of figs,
    As a sweet maiden fair.
LEADER OF WOMEN. Therefore, am I not bound to give good advice
to the city?

Don't take it ill that I was born a woman, if I contribute something better than our present troubles. I pay my share; for I contribute MEN. But you miserable old fools contribute nothing, and
after squandering our ancestral treasure, the fruit of the Persian
Wars, you make no contribution in return. And now, all on account
of you, we're facing ruin.

What, muttering, are you? If you annoy me, I'll take this hard,
rough slipper and—[*Striking the* LEADER OF MEN] smack you on
the jaw!

CHORUS OF MEN. [*Singing*]
This is outright insolence! Things go from bad to worse.
If you're men with any guts, prepare to meet the foe.
Let us strip our tunics off! We need the smell of male
Vigor. And we cannot fight all swaddled up in clothes.
    [*They strip off their tunics.*]
Come then, my comrades, on to the battle, ye who once to
    Leipsydrion[6] came;
Then ye were MEN. Now call back your youthful vigor.
        With light, wingèd footstep advance,
    Shaking old age from your frame.
LEADER OF MEN. If any of us give these wenches the slightest hold,
they'll stop at nothing: such is their cunning.

They will even build ships and sail against us, like Artemisia.[7]
Or if they turn to mounting, I count our Knights as done for: a
woman's such a tricky jockey when she gets astraddle, with a good
firm seat for trotting. Just look at those Amazons that Micon[8]
painted, fighting on horseback against men!

But we must throw them all in the pillory—[*Seizing and chok-
ing the* LEADER OF WOMEN] grabbing hold of yonder neck!
CHORUS OF WOMEN. [*Singing*]
'Ware my anger! Like a boar 'twill rush upon you men.

---

for sacred cakes. At Brauron in Attica, young girls who represented themselves as bears (the saffron
robe was a substitute for a more primitive bearskin) worshipped Artemis. In the Panathenaic
procession certain selected girls carried baskets on their heads.    6. The base of the. aristocratic
family of the Almaeonidae (the family of Pericles) in their first attempt to overthrow Hippias.
7. Queen of Halicarnassus in Asia Minor. She played a prominent part in Xerxes' invasion of
Greece and her ships fought at Salamis.    8. A painter who had lately decorated several public
buildings with frescos. The battles of the Greeks and Amazons were favorite subjects of sculptors
and painters all through the fifth century.

Soon you'll bawl aloud for help, you'll be so soundly trimmed!
Come, my friends, let's strip with speed, and lay aside these robes;
Catch the scent of women's rage. Attack with tooth and nail!
  [*They strip off their tunics.*]
Now then, come near me, you miserable man! you'll never eat
    garlic or black beans again.
And if you utter a single hard word, in rage I will "nurse" you as
    once
The beetle[9] requited her foe.

LEADER OF WOMEN. For you don't worry me; no, not so long as my
    Lampito lives and our Theban friend, the noble Ismenia.
  You can't do anything, not even if you pass a dozen—decrees!
  You miserable fool, all our neighbours hate you. Why, just the
  other day when I was holding a festival for Hecate, I invited as
  playmate from our neighbours the Boeotians a charming, well-
  bred Copaic—eel. But they refused to send me one on account of
  your decrees.
  And you'll never stop passing decrees until I grab your foot and—
  [*Tripping up the* LEADER OF MEN] toss you down and break your
  neck!

  [*Here an interval of five days is supposed to elapse.* LYSISTRATA
  *comes out from the Acropolis.*]

LEADER OF WOMEN. [*Dramatically*] Empress[1] of this great emprise
    and undertaking,
  Why come you forth, I pray, with frowning brow?

LYSISTRATA. Ah, these cursèd women! Their deeds and female notions
    make me pace up and down in utter despair.

LEADER OF WOMEN. Ah, what sayest thou?

LYSISTRATA. The truth, alas! the truth.

LEADER OF WOMEN. What dreadful tale hast thou to tell thy friends?

LYSISTRATA. 'Tis shame to speak, and not to speak is hard.

LEADER OF WOMEN. Hide not from me whatever woes we suffer.

LYSISTRATA. Well then, to put it briefly, we want—laying!

LEADER OF WOMEN. O Zeus, Zeus!

LYSISTRATA. Why call on Zeus? That's the way things are. I can no
    longer keep them away from the men, and they're all deserting. I
    caught one wriggling through a hole near the grotto of Pan, another
    sliding down a rope, another deserting her post; and yesterday I
    found one getting on a sparrow's back to fly off to Orsilochus,[2] and
    had to pull her back by the hair. They're digging up all sorts of
    excuses to get home. Look, here comes one of them now. [*A*

9. In a fable of Aesop the beetle revenges itself on the eagle by breaking its eggs.    1. The tone
of the following passage is mock-tragic.    2. The sparrow, Aphrodite's bird, pulled her chariot.
*Orsilochus* ran a house of ill-frame.

*woman comes hastily out of the Acropolis.*] Here you! Where are you off to in such a hurry?

FIRST WOMAN. I want to go home. My very best wool is being devoured by moths.

LYSISTRATA. Moths? Nonsense! Go back inside.

FIRST WOMAN. I'll come right back; I swear it. I just want to lay it out on the bed.

LYSISTRATA. Well, you won't lay it out, and you won't go home, either.

FIRST WOMAN. Shall I let my wool be ruined?

LYSISTRATA. If necessary, yes. [*Another woman comes out.*]

SECOND WOMAN. Oh dear! Oh dear! My precious flax! I left it at home all unpeeled.

LYSISTRATA. Here's another one, going home for her "flax." Come back here!

SECOND WOMAN. But I just want to work it up a little and then I'll be right back.

LYSISTRATA. No indeed! If you start this, all the other women will want to do the same. [*A third woman comes out.*]

THIRD WOMAN. O Eilithyia, goddess of travail, stop my labor till I come to a lawful spot![3]

LYSISTRATA. What's this nonsense?

THIRD WOMAN. I'm going to have a baby—right now!

LYSISTRATA. But you weren't even pregnant yesterday.

THIRD WOMAN. Well, I am today. O Lysistrata, do send me home to see a midwife, right away.

LYSISTRATA. What are you talking about? [*Putting her hand on her stomach*] What's this hard lump here?

THIRD WOMAN. A little boy.

LYSISTRATA. My goodness, what have you got there? It seems hollow; I'll just find out. [*Pulling aside her robe*] Why, you silly goose, you've got Athene's sacred helmet there. And you said you were having a baby!

THIRD WOMAN. Well, I *am* having one, I swear!

LYSISTRATA. Then what's this helmet for?

THIRD WOMAN. If the baby starts coming while I'm still in the Acropolis, I'll creep into this like a pigeon and give birth to it there.

LYSISTRATA. Stuff and nonsense! It's plain enough what you're up to. You just wait here for the christening of this—helmet.

THIRD WOMAN. But I can't sleep in the Acropolis since I saw the sacred snake.[4]

FIRST WOMAN. And I'm dying for lack of sleep: the hooting of the owls[5] keeps me awake.

3. The Acropolis was holy ground, and would be polluted by either birth or death.　4. A snake was kept in the Erechtheum.　5. The sacred bird of Athene.

LYSISTRATA. Enough of these shams, you wretched creatures. You
want your husbands, I suppose. Well, don't you think they want
us? I'm sure they're spending miserable nights. Hold out, my friends,
and endure for just a little while. There's an oracle that we shall
conquer, if we don't split up. [*Producing a roll of paper*] Here it
is.

FIRST WOMAN. Tell us what it says.

LYSISTRATA. Listen.

"When in the length of time the Swallows shall gather together,
Fleeing the Hoopoe's amorous flight and the Cockatoo shunning,
Then shall your woes be ended and Zeus who thunders in heaven
Set what's below on top—"

FIRST WOMAN. What? Are we going to be on top?

LYSISTRATA. "But if the Swallows rebel and flutter away from the
temple,
Never a bird in the world shall seem more wanton and worthless."

FIRST WOMAN. That's clear enough, upon my word!

LYSISTRATA. By all that's holy, let's not give up the struggle now.
Let's go back inside. It would be a shame, my dear friends, to
disobey the oracle.

[*The women all retire to the Acropolis again.*]

CHORUS OF MEN. [*Singing*]
    I have a tale to tell,
    Which I know full well.
        It was told me
        In the nursery.

    Once there was a likely lad,
        Melanion they name him;
    The thought of marriage made him mad,
        For which I cannot blame him.[6]

    So off he went to mountains fair;
        (No women to unbraid him!)
    A mighty hunter of the hare,
        He had a dog to aid him.

    He never came back home to see
        Detested women's faces.
    He showed a shrewd mentality.
        With him I'd fain change places!

6. The chorus of men here recasts a well-known myth for its own purposes. In the myth it was
Atalanta who avoided marriage, challenging her suitors to a foot race which she always won;
Melanion threw a golden apple in front of her; when she stopped to pick it up, she lost the race
to him.

ONE OF THE MEN. [*To one of the women*] Come here, old dame,
  give me a kiss.
WOMAN. You'll ne'er eat garlic, if you dare!
MAN. I want to kick you—just like this!
WOMAN. Oh, there's a leg with bushy hair!
MAN. Myronides and Phormio[7]
    Were hairy—and they thrashed the foe.

CHORUS OF WOMEN. [*Singing*]
            I have another tale,
            With which to assail
                Your contention
                'Bout Melanion.

            Once upon a time a man
                Named Timon[8] left our city,
            To live in some deserted land.
                (We thought him rather witty.)

            He dwelt alone amidst the thorn;
                In solitude he brooded.
            From some grim Fury he was born:
                Such hatred he exuded.

            He cursed you men, as scoundrels through
                And through, till life he ended.
            He couldn't stand the sight of YOU!
                But women he befriended.

WOMAN. [*To one of the men*] I'll smash your face in, if you like.
MAN. Oh no, please don't! You frighten me.
WOMAN. I'll lift my foot—and thus I'll strike.
MAN. Aha! Look there! What's that I see?
WOMAN. Whate'er you see, you cannot say
    That I'm not neatly trimmed today.
    [LYSISTRATA *appears on the wall of the Acropolis.*]
LYSISTRATA. Hello! Hello! Girls, come here quick!
    [*Several women appear beside her.*]
WOMAN. What is it? Why are you calling?
LYSISTRATA. I see a man coming: he's in a dreadful state. He's mad
    with passion. O Queen of Cyprus, Cythera, and Paphos, just keep
    on this way!
WOMAN. Where is the fellow?

7. Successful Athenian generals.    8. The famous misanthrope, the subject of Shakespeare's
play. There is no evidence that he "befriended" women; his hatred seems to have been directed
at the whole human race.

LYSISTRATA. There, beside the shrine of Demeter.

WOMAN. Oh yes, so he is. Who is he?

LYSISTRATA. Let's see. Do any of you know him?

MYRRHINE. Yes indeed. That's my husband, Cinesias.

LYSISTRATA. It's up to you, now: roast him, rack him, fool him, love him—and leave him! Do everything, except what our oath forbids.

MYRRHINE. Don't worry; I'll do it.

LYSISTRATA. I'll stay here to tease him and warm him up a bit. Off with you.

> [*The other women retire from the wall. Enter* CINESIAS *followed by a slave carrying a baby.* CINESIAS *is obviously in great pain and distress.*]

CINESIAS. [*Groaning*] Oh-h! Oh-h-h! This is killing me! O God, what tortures I'm suffering!

LYSISTRATA. [*From the wall*] Who's that within our lines?

CINESIAS. Me.

LYSISTRATA. A *man?*

CINESIAS. [*Pointing*] A *man*, indeed!

LYSISTRATA. Well, go away!

CINESIAS. Who are you to send me away?

LYSISTRATA. The captain of the guard.

CINESIAS. Oh, for heaven's sake, call out Myrrhine for me.

LYSISTRATA. Call Myrrhine? Nonsense! Who are you?

CINESIAS. Her husband, Cinesias of Paionidai.

LYSISTRATA. [*Appearing much impressed*] Oh, greetings, friend. Your name is not without honor here among us. Your wife is always talking about you, and whenever she takes an egg or an apple, she says, "Here's to my dear Cinesias!"

CINESIAS. [*Quivering with excitement*] Oh, ye gods in heaven!

LYSISTRATA. Indeed she does! And whenever our conversations turn to men, your wife immediately says, "All others are mere rubbish compared with Cinesias."

CINESIAS. [*Groaning*] Oh! Do call her for me.

LYSISTRATA. Why should I? What will you give me?

CINESIAS. Whatever you want. All I have is yours—and you see what I've got.

LYSISTRATA. Well then, I'll go down and call her. [*She descends.*]

CINESIAS. And hurry up! I've had no joy of life ever since she left home. When I go in the house, I feel awful: everything seems so empty and I can't enjoy my dinner. I'm in such a state all the time!

MYRRHINE. [*From behind the wall*] I *do* love him so. But he won't let me love him. No, no! Don't ask me to see him!

CINESIAS. O my darling, O Myrrhine honey, why do you do this to me? [MYRRHINE *appears on the wall.*] Come down here!

MYRRHINE. No, I won't come down.

CINESIAS. Won't you come, Myrrhine, when *I* call you?

MYRRHINE. No; you don't want me.

CINESIAS. *Don't want you?* I'm in agony!

MYRRHINE. I'm going now.

CINESIAS. Please don't! At least, listen to your baby. [*To the baby*] Here you, call your mamma! [*Pinching the baby*]

BABY. Ma-ma! Ma-ma! Ma-ma!

CINESIAS. [*To* MYRRHINE] What's the matter with you? Have you no pity for your child, who hasn't been washed or fed for five whole days?

MYRRHINE. Oh, poor child; your father pays no attention to you.

CINESIAS. Come down then, you heartless wretch, for the baby's sake.

MYRRHINE. Oh, what it is to be a mother! I've got to come down, I suppose. [*She leaves the wall and shortly reappears at the gate.*]

CINESIAS. [*To himself*] She seems much younger, and she has such a sweet look about her. Oh, the way she teases me! And her pretty, provoking ways make me burn with longing

MYRRHINE. [*Coming out of the gate and taking the baby*] O my sweet little angel. Naughty papa! Here, let Mummy kiss you, Mamma's little sweetheart! [*She fondles the baby lovingly.*]

CINESIAS. [*In despair*] You heartless creature, why do you do this? Why follow these other women and make both of us suffer so? [*He tries to embrace her.*]

MYRRHINE. Don't touch me!

CINESIAS. You're letting all our things at home go to wrack and ruin.

MYRRHINE. I don't care.

CINESIAS. You don't care that your wool is being plucked to pieces by the chickens?

MYRRHINE. Not in the least.

CINESIAS. And you haven't celebrated the rites of Aphrodite for ever so long. Won't you come home?

MYRRHINE. Not on your life, unless you men make a truce and stop the war.

CINESIAS. Well then, if that pleases you, we'll do it.

MYRRHINE. Well then, if that pleases *you*, I'll come home—afterwards! Right now I'm on oath not to.

CINESIAS. Then just lie down here with me for a moment.

MYRRHINE. No—[*In a teasing voice*] and yet, I won't say I don't love you.

CINESIAS. You love me? Oh, do lie down here, Myrrhine dear!

MYRRHINE. What, you silly fool! in front of the baby?

CINESIAS. [*Hastily thrusting the baby at the slave*] Of course not. Here—home! Take him, Manes! [*The slave goes off with the baby.*] See, the baby's out of the way. Now won't you lie down?

MYRRHINE. But where, my dear?

CINESIAS. Where? The grotto of Pan's a lovely spot.

MYRRHINE. How could I purify myself before returning to the shrine?

CINESIAS. Easily: just wash here in the Clepsydra.[9]

MYRRHINE. And then, shall I go back on my oath?

CINESIAS. On my head be it! Don't worry about the oath.

MYRRHINE. All right, then. Just let me bring out a bed.

CINESIAS. No, don't. The ground's all right.

MYRRHINE. Heavens, no! Bad as you are, I won't let you lie on the bare ground. [*She goes into the Acropolis.*]

CINESIAS. Why, she really loves me; it's plain to see.

MYRRHINE. [*Returning with a bed*] There! Now hurry up and lie down. I'll just slip off this dress. But—let's see: oh yes, I must fetch a mattress.

CINESIAS. Nonsense! No mattress for me.

MYRRHINE. Yes indeed! It's not nice on the bare springs.

CINESIAS. Give me a kiss.

MYRRHINE. [*Giving him a hasty kiss*] There! [*She goes.*]

CINESIAS. [*In mingled distress and delight*] Oh-h! Hurry back!

MYRRHINE. [*Returning with a mattress*] Here's the mattress; lie down on it. I'm taking my things off now—but—let's see: you have no pillow.

CINESIAS. I don't *want* a pillow!

MYRRHINE. But I do. [*She goes.*]

CINESIAS. Cheated again, just like Heracles and his dinner![1]

MYRRHINE. [*Returning with a pillow*] Here, lift your head. [*To herself, wondering how else to tease him*] Is that all?

CINESIAS. Surely that's all! Do come here, precious!

MYRRHINE. I'm taking off my girdle. But remember: don't go back on your promise about the truce.

CINESIAS. Hope to die, if I do.

MYRRHINE. You don't have a blanket.

CINESIAS. [*Shouting in exasperation*] I *don't want one!* I want to—

MYRRHINE. Sh-h! There, there, I'll be back in a minute. [*She goes.*]

CINESIAS. She'll be the death of me with these bed-clothes.

MYRRHINE. [*Returning with a blanket*] Here, get up.

CINESIAS. I've got *this* up!

MYRRHINE. Would you like some perfume?

CINESIAS. Good heavens, no! I won't have it!

MYRRHINE. Yes, you shall, whether you want it or not. [*She goes.*]

---

9. A spring on the Acropolis.     1. The point of this proverb seems to be that the hero is such a glutton that his hosts are never quick enough with their entertainment.

CINESIAS. O lord! Confound all perfumes anyway!

MYRRHINE. [*Returning with a flask*] Stretch out your hand and put some on.

CINESIAS. [*Suspiciously*] By God, I don't much like this perfume. It smells of shilly-shallying, and has no scent of the marriage-bed.

MYRRHINE. Oh dear! This is Rhodian perfume I've brought.

CINESIAS. It's quite all right dear. Never mind.

MYRRHINE. Don't be silly! [*She goes out with the flask.*]

CINESIAS. Damn the man who first concocted perfumes!

MYRRHINE. [*Returning with another flask*] Here, try this flask.

CINESIAS. I've got another one all ready for you. Come, you wretch, lie down and stop bringing me things.

MYRRHINE. All right; I'm taking off my shoes. But, my dear, see that you vote for peace.

CINESIAS. [*Absently*] I'll consider it. [MYRRHINE *runs away to the Acropolis.*] I'm ruined! The wretch has skinned me and run away! [*Chanting, in tragic style*] Alas! Alas! Deceived, deserted by this fairest of women, whom shall I—lay? Ah, my poor little child, how shall I nurture thee? Where's Cynalopex?[2] I needs must hire a nurse!

LEADER OF MEN. [*Chanting*] Ah, wretched man, in dreadful wise beguiled, bewrayed, thy soul is sore distressed. I pity thee, alas! alas! What soul, what loins, what liver could stand this strain? How firm and unyielding he stands, with naught to aid him of a morning.

CINESIAS. O lord! O Zeus! What tortures I endure!

LEADER OF MEN. This is the way she's treated you, that vile and cursèd wanton.

LEADER OF WOMEN. Nay, not vile and cursèd, but sweet and dear.

LEADER OF MEN. Sweet, you say? Nay, hateful, hateful!

CINESIAS. Hateful indeed! O Zeus, Zeus!
Seize her and snatch her away,
Like a handful of dust, in a mighty,
Fiery tempest! Whirl her aloft, then let her drop
Down to the earth, with a crash, as she falls—
On the point of this waiting
Thingummybob! [*He goes out.*]
   [*Enter a Spartan* HERALD, *in an obvious state of excitement, which he is doing his best to conceal.*]

HERALD. Where can I find the Senate or the Prytanes?[3] I've got an important message.
   [*The Athenian* MAGISTRATE *enters.*]

MAGISTRATE. Say there, are you a man or Priapus?[4]

2. A local brothel-keeper.  3. The permanent committee of the Council (Senate).  4. A god whose grossly phallic statue was set to guard orchards and gardens.

HERALD. [*In annoyance*] I'm a herald, you lout! I've come from Sparta
   about the truce.
MAGISTRATE. Is that a spear you've got under your cloak?
HERALD. No, of course not!
MAGISTRATE. Why do you twist and turn so? Why hold your cloak
   in front of you? Did you rupture yourself on the trip?
HERALD. By gum, the fellow's an old fool.
MAGISTRATE. [*Pointing*] Why, you dirty rascal, you're all excited.
HERALD. Not at all. Stop this tom-foolery.
MAGISTRATE. Well, what's that I see?
HERALD. A Spartan message-staff.[5]
MAGISTRATE. Oh, certainly! That's just the kind of message-staff I've
   got. But tell me the honest truth: How are things going in Sparta?
HERALD. All the land of Sparta is up in arms—and our allies are up,
   too. We need Pellene.[6]
MAGISTRATE. What brought this trouble on you? A sudden Panic?
HERALD. No, Lampito started it and then all the other women in
   Sparta with one account chased their husbands out of their beds.
MAGISTRATE. How do you feel?
HERALD. Terrible. We walk around the city bent over like men light-
   ing matches in a wind. For our women won't let us touch them
   until we all agree and make peace throughout Greece.
MAGISTRATE. This is a general conspiracy of the women; I see it now.
   Well, hurry back and tell the Spartans to send ambassadors here
   with full powers to arrange a truce. And I'll go tell the Council to
   choose ambassadors from here; I've got a little something here that
   will soon persuade them!
HERALD. I'll fly there; for you've made an excellent suggestion.
   [*The* HERALD *and the* MAGISTRATE *depart on opposite sides of
   the stage.*]
LEADER OF MEN. No beast or fire is harder than womankind to tame.
   Nor is the spotted leopard so devoid of shame.
LEADER OF WOMEN. Knowing this, you dare provoke us to attack?
   I'd be your steady friend, if you'd but take us back.
LEADER OF MEN. I'll never cease my hatred keen of womankind.
LEADER OF WOMEN. Just as you will. But now just let me help you
      find
   That cloak you threw aside. You look so silly there
   Without your clothes. Here, put it on and don't go bare.
LEADER OF MEN. That's very kind, and shows you're not entirely bad.
   But I threw off my things when I was good and mad.

5. An encoding device. The papyrus was wrapped round the staff on a spiral and the message
could be read only when the papyrus was wound round an exactly similar staff.    6. A city held
by the Athenians and claimed by the Spartans; also the name of a famous Athenian prostitute.

LEADER OF WOMEN. At last you seem a man, and won't be mocked, my lad.

If you'd been nice to me, I'd take this little gnat

That's in your eye and pluck it out for you, like that.

LEADER OF MEN. So that's what's bothered me and bit my eye so long!

Please dig it out for me. I own that I've been wrong.

LEADER OF WOMEN. I'll do so, though you've been a most ill-natured brat.

Ye gods! See here! A huge and monstrous little gnat!

LEADER OF MEN. Oh, how that helps! For it was digging wells in me.

And now it's out, my tears can roll down hard and free.

LEADER OF WOMEN. Here, let me wipe them off, although you're such a knave

And kiss me.

LEADER OF MEN. No!

LEADER OF WOMEN. Whate'er you say, a kiss I'll have. [*She kisses him.*]

LEADER OF MEN. Oh, confound these women! They've a coaxing way about them.

He was wise and never spoke a truer word, who said,

"We can't live with women, but we cannot live without them."

Now I'll make a truce with you. We'll fight no more: instead,

I will not injure you if you do me no wrong.

And now let's join our ranks and then begin a song.

COMBINED CHORUS. [*Singing*]

    Athenians, we're not prepared,

    To say a single ugly word

    About our fellow-citizens.

Quite the contrary: we desire but to say and to do

Naught but good. Quite enough are the ills now on hand.

    Men and women, be advised:

       If anyone requires

    Money—minae two or three—

       We've got what he desires.

    My purse is yours, on easy terms:

       When Peace shall reappear,

    Whate'er you've borrowed will be due.

       So speak up without fear.

    You needn't pay me back, you see,

    If you can get a cent from me!

We're about to entertain
    Some foreign gentlemen;
We've soup and tender, fresh-killed pork.
    Come round to dine at ten.

Come early; wash and dress with care,
    And bring the children, too.
Then step right in, no "by your leave."
    We'll be expecting you.

Walk in as if you owned the place.
You'll find the door—shut in your face!

[*Enter a group of Spartan Ambassadors; they are in the same desperate condition as the Herald in the previous scene.*]

LEADER OF CHORUS. Here come the envoys from Sparta, sprouting long beards and looking for all the world as if they were carrying pig-pens in front of them.

    Greetings, gentlemen of Sparta. Tell me, in what state have you come?

SPARTAN. Why waste words? You can plainly see what state we're come in!

LEADER OF CHORUS. Wow! You're in a pretty high-strung condition, and it seems to be getting worse.

SPARTAN. It's indescribable. Won't someone please arrange a peace for us—in any way you like.

LEADER OF CHORUS. Here come our own, native ambassadors, crouching like wrestlers and holding their clothes in front of them; this seems an athletic kind of malady.

[*Enter several Athenian Ambassadors.*]

ATHENIAN. Can anyone tell us where Lysistrata is? You see our condition.

LEADER OF CHORUS. Here's another case of the same complaint. Tell me, are the attacks worse in the morning?

ATHENIAN. No, we're always afflicted this way. If someone doesn't soon arrange this truce, you'd better not let me get my hands on—Cleisthenes!

LEADER OF CHORUS. If you're smart, you'll arrange your cloaks so none of the fellows who smashed the Hermae[7] can see you.

SPARTAN. Right you are; a very good suggestion.

ATHENIAN. Greetings, Spartan. We've suffered dreadful things.

---

7. Small statues of the god Hermes equipped with phalluses, which stood at the door of most Athenian houses. Just before the great expedition left for Sicily, rioters (probably oligarchic conspirators opposed to the expedition) smashed many of these statues.

SPARTAN. My dear fellow, we'd have suffered still worse if one of those fellows had seen us in this condition.

ATHENIAN. Well, gentlemen, we must get down to business. What's your errand here?

SPARTAN. We're ambassadors about peace.

ATHENIAN. Excellent; so are we. Only Lysistrata can arrange things for us; shall we summon her?

SPARTAN. Aye, and Lysistratus too, if you like.

LEADER OF CHORUS. No need to summon her, it seems. She's coming out of her own accord.

[Enter LYSISTRATA accompanied by a statue of a nude female figure, which represents Reconciliation.]

Hail, noblest of women; now must thou be
A judge shrewd and subtle, mild and severe,
Be sweet yet majestic: all manners employ.
The leaders of Hellas, caught by thy love-charms
Have come to thy judgment, their charges submitting.

LYSISTRATA. This is no difficult task, if one catch them still in amorous passion, before they've resorted to each other. But I'll soon find out. Where's Reconciliation? Go, first bring the Spartans here, and don't seize them rudely and violently, as our tactless husbands used to do, but as befits a woman, like an old, familiar friend; if they won't give you their hands, take them however you can. Then go fetch these Athenians here, taking hold of whatever they offer you. Now then, men of Sparta, stand here beside me, and you Athenians on the other side, and listen to my words.

I am a woman, it is true, but I have a mind; I'm not badly off in native wit, and by listening to my father and my elders, I've had a decent schooling.

Now I intend to give you a scolding which you both deserve. With one common font you worship at the same altars, just like brothers, at Olympia, at Thermopylae, at Delphi—how many more might I name, if time permitted;—and the Barbarians stand by waiting with their armies; yet you are destroying the men and towns of Greece.

ATHENIAN. Oh, this tension is killing me!

LYSISTRATA. And now, men of Sparta,—to turn to you—don't you remember how the Spartan Pericleidas came here once as a suppliant, and sitting at our altar, all pale with fear in his crimson cloak, begged us for an army?[8] For all Messene had attacked you and the god sent an earthquake too? Then Cimon went forth with

---

8. After a disastrous earthquake the Spartans were in great danger as a result of a rebellion of their serfs, the Helots. The Athenians under Cimon sent a large force of soldiers to help them (464 B.C.).

four thousand hoplites and saved all Lacedaemon. Such was the
aid you received from Athens, and now you lay waste the country
which once treated you so well.

ATHENIAN. [*Hotly*] They're in the wrong, Lysistrata, upon my word,
they are!

SPARTAN. [*Absently, looking at the statue of Reconciliation*] We're
in the wrong. What hips! How lovely they are!

LYSISTRATA. Don't think I'm going to let you Athenians off. Don't
you remember how the Spartans came in arms when you were
wearing the rough, sheepskin cloak of slaves and slew the host of
Thessalians, the comrades and allies of Hippias?[9] Fighting with
you on that day, alone of all the Greeks, they set you free and
instead of a sheepskin gave your folk a handsome robe to wear.

SPARTAN. [*Looking at* LYSISTRATA] I've never seen a more distinguished woman.

ATHENIAN. [*Looking at Reconciliation*] I've never seen a more voluptuous body!

LYSISTRATA. Why then, with these many noble deeds to think of, do
you fight each other? Why don't you stop this villainy? Why not
make peace? Tell me, what prevents it?

SPARTAN. [*Waving vaguely at Reconciliation*] We're willing, if you're
willing to give up your position on yonder flank.

LYSISTRATA. What position, my good man?

SPARTAN. Pylus; we've been panting for it for ever so long.

ATHENIAN. No, by God! You shan't have it!

LYSISTRATA. Let them have it, my friend.

ATHENIAN. Then, what shall we have to rouse things up?

LYSISTRATA. Ask for another place in exchange.

ATHENIAN. Well, let's see: first of all [*Pointing to various parts of
Reconciliation's anatomy*] give us Echinus[1] here, this Maliac Inlet
in back there, and these two Megarian legs.

SPARTAN. No, by heavens! You can't have *everything*, you crazy fool!

LYSISTRATA. Let it go. Don't fight over a pair of legs.

ATHENIAN [*Taking off his cloak*] I think I'll strip and do a little planting now.

SPARTAN. [*Following suit*] And I'll just do a little fertilizing, by gosh!

LYSISTRATA. Wait until the truce is concluded. Now if you've decided
on this course, hold a conference and discuss the matter with your
allies.

ATHENIAN. Allies? Don't be ridiculous! They're in the same state we

9. Hippias the tyrant had allowed exiled democrats to return to Attica but they had to stay
9. Hippias the tyrant had allowed exiled democrats to return to Attica but they had to stay outside
the city and wear sheepskins so that they could readily be identified. With the help of Spartan
soldiers the exiles and the people of Attica finally defeated the Thessalian troops of Hippias.
1. Like Pylus (on the "flank" of the Peloponnese), these names are all double-barrelled references
to territories in dispute in the war and salient portions of the anatomy of Reconciliation.

are. Won't all our allies want the same thing we do—to jump in
bed with their women?

SPARTAN. Ours will, I know.

ATHENIAN. Especially the Carystians,[2] by God!

LYSISTRATA. Very well. Now purify yourselves, that your wives may
feast and entertain you in the Acropolis; we've provisions by the
basketful. Exchange your oaths and pledges there, and then each
of you may take his wife and go home.

ATHENIAN. Let's go at once.

SPARTAN. Come on, where you will.

ATHENIAN. For God's sake, let's hurry!

[*They all go into the Acropolis.*]

CHORUS. [*Singing.*]
Whate'er I have of coverlets
    And robes of varied hue
And golden trinkets,—without stint
    I offer them to you.

Take what you will and bear it home,
    Your children to delight,
Or if your girl's a Basket-maid;
    Just choose whate'er's in sight.

There's naught within so well secured
    You cannot break the seal
And bear it off; just help yourselves;
    No hesitation feel.

But you'll see nothing, though you try,
Unless you've sharper eyes than I!

If anyone needs bread to feed
    A growing family,
I've lots of wheat and full-grown loaves;
    So just apply to me.

Let every poor man who desires
    Come round and bring a sack
To fetch the grain; my slave is there
    To load it on his back.

But don't come near my door, I say.
Beware the dog, and stay away!

2. The people of Carystus on the island of Euboea were supposed to be of pre-Hellenic stock and
therefore primitive and savage.

[*An* ATHENIAN *enters carrying a torch; he knocks at the gate.*]

ATHENIAN. Open the door! [*To the* CHORUS, *which is clustered around the gate*] Make way, won't you! What are you hanging around for? Want me to singe you with this torch? [*To himself*] No; it's a stale trick, I won't do it! [*To the audience*] Still, if I've got to do it to please *you*, I suppose I'll have to take the trouble.

[*A* SECOND ATHENIAN *comes out of the gate.*]

SECOND ATHENIAN. And I'll help you.

FIRST ATHENIAN. [*Waving his torch at the* CHORUS] Get out! Go bawl your heads off! Move on there, so the Spartans can leave in peace when the banquet's over.

[*They brandish their torches until the* CHORUS *leaves the Orchestra.*]

SECOND ATHENIAN. I've never seen such a pleasant banquet: the Spartans are charming fellows, indeed they are! And we Athenians are very witty in our cups.

FIRST ATHENIAN. Naturally: for when we're sober we're never at our best. If the Athenians would listen to me, we'd always get a little tipsy on our embassies. As things are now, we go to Sparta when we're sober and look around to stir up trouble. And then we don't hear what they say—and as for what they *don't* say, we have all sorts of suspicions. And then we bring back varying reports about the mission. But this time everything is pleasant; even if a man should sing the Telamon-song when he ought to sing "Cleitagoras,"[3] we'd praise him and swear it was excellent.

[*The two* CHORUSES *return, as a* CHORUS OF ATHENIANS *and a* CHORUS OF SPARTANS.]

Here they come back again. Go to the devil, you scoundrels!

SECOND ATHENIAN. Get out, I say! They're coming out from the feast.

[*Enter the Spartan and Athenian envoys, followed by* LYSISTRATA *and all the women.*]

SPARTAN. [*To one of his fellow-envoys*] My good fellow, take up your pipes; I want to do a fancy two-step and sing a jolly song for the Athenians.

ATHENIAN. Yes, do take your pipes, by all means. I'd love to see you dance.

SPARTAN. [*Singing and dancing with the* CHORUS OF SPARTANS]

    These youths inspire
To song and dance, O Memory;
Stir up my Muse, to tell how we
And Athens' men, in our galleys clashing

---

3. At an Athenian banquet each guest in turn, when the time came to sing, was supposed to cap the singer before him by choosing an appropriate drinking song.

At Artemisium,[4] 'gainst foemen dashing
   In godlike ire,
Conquered the Persian and set Greece free.

   Leonidas
Led on his valiant warriors
Whetting their teeth like angry boars.
Abundant foam on their lips was flow'ring,
A stream of sweat from their limbs was show'ring.
   The Persian was
Numberless as the sand on the shores.

O Huntress[5] who slayest the beasts in the glade,
O Virgin divine, hither come to our truce,
Unite us in bonds which all time will not loose.
Grant us to find in this treaty, we pray,
An unfailing source of true friendship today,
And all of our days, helping us to refrain
From weaseling tricks which bring war in their train.
   Then hither, come hither! O huntress maid.

LYSISTRATA. Come then, since all is fairly done, men of Sparta, lead
away your wives, and you, Athenians, take yours. Let every man
stand beside his wife, and every wife beside her man, and then, to
celebrate our fortune, let's dance. And in the future, let's take care
to avoid these misunderstandings.
CHORUS OF ATHENIANS. [*Singing and dancing*]
   Lead on the dances, your graces revealing.
   Call Artemis hither, call Artemis' twin,
   Leader of dances, Apollo the Healing,
   Kindly God—hither! let's summon him in!

     Nysian Bacchus call,
   Who with his Maenads, his eyes flashing fire,
     Dances, and last of all
   Zeus of the thunderbolt flaming, the Sire.
     And Hera in majesty,
     Queen of prosperity.

   Come, ye Powers who dwell above
   Unforgetting, our witnesses be
   Of Peace with bonds of harmonious love—

4. The indecisive naval battle which took place off the coast while Leonidas held the pass at
Thermopylae.   5. Artemis.

The Peace which Cypris has wrought for me.
    Alleluia! Io Paean!
    Leap in joy—hurrah! hurrah!
    'Tis victory—hurrah! hurrah!
    Euoi! Euoi! Euai! Euai!

LYSISTRATA. [*To the Spartans*] Come now, sing a new song to cap ours.
CHORUS OF SPARTANS. [*Singing and dancing*]
    Leaving Taygetus fair and renown'd,
    Muse of Laconia,[6] hither come:
    Amyclae's god in hymns resound,
    Athene of the Brazen Home,[7]
    And Castor and Pollux, Tyndareus' sons,
    Who sport where Eurotas[8] murmuring runs.

      On with the dance! Heia! Ho!
        All leaping along,
      Mantles a-swinging as we go!
        Of Sparta our song.
    There the holy chorus ever gladdens,
    There the beat of stamping feet,
    As our winsome fillies, lovely maidens,
    Dance, beside Eurotas' banks a-skipping,—
      Nimbly go to and fro
    Hast'ning, leaping feet in measures tripping,
    Like the Bacchae's revels, hair a-streaming.
    Leda's child, divine and mild,
    Leads the holy dance, her fair face beaming.
      On with the dance! as your hand
        Presses the hair
      Streaming away unconfined.
        Leap in the air
      Light as the deer; footsteps resound
      Aiding our dance, beating the ground.
    Praise Athene, Maid divine, unrivalled in her might,
    Dweller in the Brazen Home, unconquered in the fight.
    [*All go out singing and dancing.*]

---

6. The Spartan region. *Amyclae:* Part of Sparta.   7. The bronze-plated temple of Athena in Sparta.   8. The river of Sparta.

# PLATO

## 429–347 B.C.

Socrates himself (see pp. 8–9) wrote nothing; we know what we do about him mainly from the writings of his pupil Plato, a philosophical and literary genius of the first rank. It is very difficult to distinguish between what Socrates actually said and what Plato put into his mouth, but there is general agreement that the *Apology*, which Plato wrote as a representation of what Socrates said at his trial, is the clearest picture we have of the historical Socrates. He is on trial for impiety and "corrupting the youth." He deals with these charges, but he also takes the opportunity to present a defense and explanation of the mission to which his life has been devoted.

The *Apology* is a defiant speech; Socrates rides roughshod over legal forms and seems to neglect no opportunity of outraging his hearers. But this defiance is not stupidity (as he hints himself, he could, if he had wished, have made a speech to please the court), nor is it a deliberate courting of martyrdom. It is the only course possible for him in the circumstances if he is not to betray his life's work, for Socrates knows as well as his accusers that what the Athenians really want is to silence him without having to take his life. What Socrates is making clear is that there is no such easy way out; he will have no part of any compromise that would restrict his freedom of speech or undermine his moral position. The speech is a sample of what the Athenians will have to put up with if they allow him to live; he will continue to be the gadfly which stings the sluggish horse. He will go on persuading them not to be concerned for their persons or their property, but first and chiefly to care about the improvement of the soul. He has spent his life denying the validity of worldly standards, and he will not accept them now.

He was declared guilty, and condemned to death. Though influential friends offered means of escape (and there is reason to think the Athenians would have been glad to see him go) Socrates refused to disobey the laws: in any case he had already, in his court speech, rejected the possibility of living in some foreign city.

The sentence was duly carried out. And in Plato's account of the execution we can see the calmness and kindness of a man who has led a useful life and who is secure in his faith that, contrary to appearances, "no evil can happen to a good man, either in life or after death."

The form of the *Apology* is dramatic: Plato re-creates the personality of his beloved teacher by presenting him as speaking directly to the reader. In most of the many books which he wrote in the course of a long life (429–347 B.C.) he continued to feature Socrates as the principal speaker in philosophical dialogues which explored the ethical and political problems of the age: these dialogues (the *Republic* the most famous) were preserved in their entirety and have exerted an enormous influence on Western thought ever since. Plato also founded a philosophical school, the Academy, in 385 B.C., and it remained active as a center of philosophical training and research until it was suppressed by the Roman emperor Justinian in A.D. 529. Plato came from an aristocratic Athenian family and as a young man thought of a political career; the execution of Socrates by the courts of democratic Athens disgusted him with politics and prompted his famous remark that there was no hope for the cities until the rulers became philosophers or the philosophers rulers. His attempts, however, to influence real rulers, the tyrant Dionysius of Syracuse in Sicily and, later, his son, ended in failure.

A. E. Taylor, *Plato, The Man and His Work* (1927), is a detailed analysis of the whole corpus of Platonic dialogues. G. M. A. Grube, *Plato's Thought* (1935), studies six principal themes of Platonic philosophy. R. S. Brumbaugh, *Plato for the Modern Age* (1962), presents a general introduction with stress on the historical background and an emphasis on the scientific and mathematical aspects of Plato's thought.

# The Apology of Socrates[1]

How you, O Athenians, have been affected by my accusers, I cannot tell; but I know that they almost made me forget who I was—so persuasively did they speak; and yet they have hardly uttered a word of truth. But of the many falsehoods told by them, there was one which quite amazed me;—I mean when they said that you should be upon your guard and not allow yourselves to be deceived by the force of my eloquence. To say this, when they were certain to be detected as soon as I opened my lips and proved myself to be anything but a great speaker, did indeed appear to me most shameless—unless by the force of eloquence they mean the force of truth; for if such is their meaning, I admit that I am eloquent. But in how different a way from theirs! Well, as I was saying, they have scarcely spoken the truth at all; but from me you shall hear the whole truth: not, however, delivered after their manner in a set oration duly ornamented with words and phrases. No, by heaven! but I shall use the words and arguments which occur to me at the moment; for I am confident in the justice of my cause: at my time of life I ought not to be appearing before you, O men of Athens, in the character of a juvenile orator—let no one expect it of me. And I must beg of you to grant me a favour:—If I defend myself in my accustomed manner, and you hear me using the words which I have been in the habit of using in the agora,[2] at the tables of the money-changers, or anywhere else, I would ask you not to be surprised, and not to interrupt me on this account. For I am more than seventy years of age, and appearing now for the first time in a court of law, I am quite a stranger to the language of the place; and therefore I would have you regard me as if I were really a stranger, whom you would excuse if he spoke in his native tongue, and after the fashion of his country:—

1. Translated by Benjamin Jowett. "Apology" means "defense."     2. The market place.

Am I making an unfair request of you? Never mind the manner, which may or may not be good; but think only of the truth of my words, and give heed to that: let the speaker speak truly and the judge decide justly.

And first, I have to reply to the older charges[3] and to my first accusers, and then I will go on to the later ones. For of old I have had many accusers, who have accused me falsely to you during many years; and I am more afraid of them than of Anytus and his associates, who are dangerous, too, in their own way. But far more dangerous are the others, who began when you were children, and took possession of your minds with their falsehoods, telling of one Socrates, a wise man, who speculated about the heaven above, and searched into the earth beneath, and made the worse appear the better cause.[4] The disseminators of this tale are the accusers whom I dread; for their hearers are apt to fancy that such enquirers do not believe in the existence of the gods. And they are many, and their charges against me are of ancient date, and they were made by them in the days when you were more impressible than you are now—in childhood, or it may have been in youth—and the cause when heard went by default, for there was none to answer. And hardest of all, I do not know and cannot tell the names of my accusers; unless in the chance case of a Comic poet.[5] All who from envy and malice have persuaded you—some of them having first convinced themselves—all this class of men are most difficult to deal with; for I cannot have them up here, and cross-examine them, and therefore I must simply fight with shadows in my own defence, and argue when there is no one who answers. I will ask you then to assume with me, as I was saying, that my opponents are of two kinds; one recent, the other ancient: and I hope that you will see the propriety[6] of my answering the latter first, for these accusations you heard long before the others, and much oftener.

Well, then, I must make my defence, and endeavor to clear away in a short time, a slander which has lasted a long time. May I succeed, if to succeed be for my good and yours, or likely to avail me in my cause! The task is not an easy one; I quite understand the nature

3. Socrates had been the object of much criticism and satire for many years before the trial. He here disregards legal forms and announces that he will deal first with the prejudices that lie behind the formal charge that has been brought against him.    4. He was accused by some of his enemies of being a materialist philosopher who speculated about the physical nature of the universe, and by others of being one of the Sophists, professional teachers of rhetoric and other subjects, many of whom taught methods which were more effective than honest.    5. He is referring to the poet Aristophanes, whose play *The Clouds* (produced in 423 B.C.) is a broad satire on Socrates and his associates, and a good example of the prejudice Socrates is dealing with, for it presents him propounding fantastic theories about matter and religion, and teaching students how to avoid payment of debts.    6. He says this with his tongue in his cheek, for he is actually paying no attention to legal propriety. This becomes clearer below, where he goes so far as to paraphrase the actual terms of the indictment and put into the mouths of his accusers the prejudice he claims is the basis of their action.

of it. And so leaving the event with God, in obedience to the law I will now make my defence.

I will begin at the beginning, and ask what is the accusation which has given rise to the slander of me, and in fact has encouraged Meletus to prefer this charge against me. Well, what do the slanderers say? They shall be my prosecutors, and I will sum up their words in an affidavit: 'Socrates is an evil-doer, and a curious person, who searches into things under the earth, and in heaven, and he makes the worse appear the better cause; and he teaches the aforesaid doctrines to others.' Such is the nature of the accusation: it is just what you have yourselves seen in the comedy of Aristophanes, who has introduced a man whom he calls Socrates, going about and saying that he walks in air,[7] and talking a deal of nonsense concerning matters of which I do not pretend to know either much or little—not that I mean to speak disparagingly of any one who is a student of natural philosophy. I should be very sorry if Meletus could bring so grave a charge against me. But the simple truth is, O Athenians, that I have nothing to do with physical speculations. Very many of those here present are witnesses to the truth of this, and to them I appeal. Speak then, you who have heard me, and tell your neighbours whether any of you have ever known me hold forth in few words or in many upon such matters. . . . You hear their answer. And from what they say of this part of the charge you will be able to judge of the truth of the rest.

As little foundation is there for the report that I am a teacher, and take money;[8] this accusation has no more truth in it than the other. Although, if a man were really able to instruct mankind, to receive money for giving instruction would, in my opinion, be an honour to him. There is Gorgias of Leontium, and Prodicus of Ceos, and Hippias of Elis,[9] who go the round of the cities, and are able to persuade the young men to leave their own citizens by whom they might be taught for nothing, and come to them whom they not only pay, but are thankful if they may be allowed to pay them. There is at this time a Parian philosopher[1] residing in Athens, of whom I have heard; and I came to hear of him in this way:—I came across a man who has spent a world of money on the Sophists, Callias, the son of Hipponicus, and knowing that he had sons, I asked him: 'Callias,' I said, 'if your two sons were foals or calves, there would be no diffi-

---

7. In the comedy of Aristophanes Socrates first appears suspended in a basket, and when asked what he is doing replies, "I walk in air and contemplate the sun." He explains that only by suspending his intelligence can he investigate celestial matters.    8. Unlike Socrates, who beggared himself in the quest for truth, the professional teachers made great fortunes. The wealth of Protagoras, the first of the Sophists who demanded fees, was proverbial.    9. From Elis, in the Peloponnese; he claimed to be able to teach any and all subjects, including handicrafts. *Gorgias:* From Leontium in Sicily; he was famous as the originator of an antithetical, ornate prose style which had great influence. *Prodicus:* From Ceos, an island in the Aegean; he taught rhetoric and was well-known for his pioneering grammatical studies.    1. From Paros, a small island in the Aegean.

culty in finding some one to put over them; we should hire a trainer of horses, or a farmer probably, who would improve and perfect them in their own proper virtue and excellence; but as they are human beings, whom are you thinking of placing over them? Is there any one who understands human and political virtue? You must have thought about the matter, for you have sons; is there any one?' 'There is,' he said. 'Who is he?' said I; 'and of what country? and what does he charge?' 'Evenus the Parian,' he replied; 'he is the man, and his charge is five minae.'[2] Happy is Evenus, I said to myself; if he really has this wisdom, and teaches at such a moderate charge. Had I the same, I should have been very proud and conceited; but the truth is that I have no knowledge of the kind.

I dare say, Athenians, that some one among you will reply, 'Yes, Socrates, but what is the origin of these accusations which are brought against you; there must have been something strange which you have been doing? All these rumours and this talk about you would never have arisen if you had been like other men: tell us, then, what is the cause of them, for we should be sorry to judge hastily of you.' Now I regard this as a fair challenge, and I will endeavour to explain to you the reason why I am called wise and have such an evil fame. Please to attend then. And although some of you may think that I am joking, I declare that I will tell you the entire truth. Men of Athens, this reputation of mine has come of a certain sort of wisdom which I possess. If you ask me what kind of wisdom, I reply, wisdom such as may perhaps be attained by man, for to that extent I am inclined to believe that I am wise; whereas the persons of whom I was speaking have a superhuman wisdom, which I may fail to describe, because I have it not myself; and he who says that I have, speaks falsely, and is taking away my character. And here, O men of Athens, I must beg you not to interrupt me, even if I seem to say something extravagant. For the word which I will speak is not mine. I will refer you to a witness who is worthy of credit; that witness shall be the God of Delphi[3]—he will tell you about my wisdom, if I have any, and of what sort it is. You must have known Chaerephon; he was early a friend of mine, and also a friend of yours, for he shared in the recent exile of the people, and returned with you.[4] Well, Chaerephon, as you know, was very impetuous in all his doings, and he went to Delphi and boldly asked the oracle to tell him whether— as I was saying, I must beg you not to interrupt—he asked the oracle to tell him whether any one was wiser than I was, and the Pythian

2. A relatively moderate sum; Protagoras is said to have charged a hundred minae for a course of instruction.    3. The oracle of Apollo at Delphi.    4. One of Socrates' closest associates; he appears in Aristophanes' comedy. Chaerephon was an enthusiastic enough partisan of the democratic regime to have to go into exile in 404 B.C. when the Thirty Tyrants carried on an oligarchic reign of terror. The phrase "the recent exile of the people" refers to the exile into which all known champions of democracy were forced until the democracy was restored.

prophetess answered, that there was no man wiser. Chaerephon is
dead himself; but his brother, who is in court, will confirm the truth
of what I am saying.

Why do I mention this? Because I am going to explain to you why
I have such an evil name. When I heard the answer, I said to myself,
What can the god mean? and what is the interpretation of his riddle?
for I know that I have no wisdom, small or great. What then can he
mean when he says that I am the wisest of men? And yet he is a god,
and cannot lie; that would be against his nature. After long consideration, I thought of a method of trying the question. I reflected that
if I could only find a man wiser than myself, then I might go to the
god with a refutation in my hand. I should say to him, 'Here is a
man who is wiser than I am; but you said that I was the wisest.'
Accordingly I went to one who had the reputation of wisdom, and
observed him—his name I need not mention; he was a politician
whom I selected for examination—and the result was as follows: When
I began to talk with him, I could not help thinking that he was not
really wise, although he was thought wise by many, and still wiser
by himself; and thereupon I tried to explain to him that he thought
himself wise, but was not really wise; and the consequence was that
he hated me, and his enmity was shared by several who were present
and heard me. So I left him, saying to myself, as I went away: Well,
although I do not suppose that either of us knows anything really
beautiful and good, I am better off than he is,—for he knows nothing, and thinks that he knows; I neither know nor think that I know.
In this latter particular, then, I seem to have slightly the advantage
of him. Then I went to another who had still higher pretensions to
wisdom, and my conclusion was exactly the same. Whereupon I
made another enemy of him, and of many others besides him.

Then I went to one man after another, being not unconscious of
the enmity which I provoked, and I lamented and feared this: But
necessity was laid upon me,—the word of God, I thought, ought to
be considered first. And I said to myself, Go I must to all who appear
to know, and find out the meaning of the oracle. And I swear to you,
Athenians, by the dog I swear!5—for I must tell you the truth—the
result of my mission was just this: I found that the men most in
repute were all but the most foolish; and that others less esteemed
were really wiser and better. I will tell you the tale of my wanderings
and of the 'Herculean' labours, as I may call them, which I endured
only to find at last the oracle irrefutable. After the politicians, I went
to the poets; tragic, dithyrambic,6 and all sorts. And there, I said to
myself, you will be instantly detected; now you will find out that you
are more ignorant than they are. Accordingly, I took them some of

5. A euphemistic oath (compare, "by George").    6. The dithyramb was a short performance
by a chorus, produced, like tragedy, at state expense and at a public festival.

the most elaborate passages in their own writings, and asked what was the meaning of them—thinking that they would teach me something. Will you believe me? I am almost ashamed to confess the truth, but I must say that there is hardly a person present who would not have talked better about their poetry than they did themselves. Then I knew that not by wisdom do poets write poetry, but by a sort of genius and inspiration; they are like diviners or soothsayers who also say many fine things, but do not understand the meaning of them.[7] The poets appeared to me to be much in the same case; and I further observed that upon the strength of their poetry they believed themselves to be the wisest of men in other things in which they were not wise. So I departed, conceiving myself to be superior to them for the same reason that I was superior to the politicians.

At last I went to the artisans, for I was conscious that I knew nothing at all, as I may say, and I was sure that they knew many fine things; and here I was not mistaken, for they did know many things of which I was ignorant, and in this they certainly were wiser than I was. But I observed that even the good artisans fell into the same error as the poets;—because they were good workmen they thought that they also knew all sorts of high matters, and this defect in them overshadowed their wisdom; and therefore I asked myself on behalf of the oracle, whether I would like to be as I was, neither having their knowledge nor their ignorance, or like them in both; and I made answer to myself and to the oracle that I was better off as I was.

This inquisition has led to my having many enemies of the worst and most dangerous kind, and has given occasion also to many calumnies. And I am called wise, for my hearers always imagine that I myself possess the wisdom which I find wanting in others: but the truth is, O men of Athens, that God only is wise; and by his answer he intends to show that the wisdom of men is worth little or nothing; he is not speaking of Socrates, he is only using my name by way of illustration, as if he said, He, O men, is the wisest, who, like Socrates, knows that his wisdom is in truth worth nothing. And so I go about the world, obedient to the god, and search and make enquiry into the wisdom of any one, whether citizen or stranger, who appears to be wise; and if he is not wise, then in vindication of the oracle I show him that he is not wise; and my occupation quite absorbs me, and I have no time to give either to any public matter of interest or to any concern of my own, but I am in utter poverty by reason of my devotion to the god.

There is another thing:—young men of the richer classes, who have not much to do, come about me of their own accord; they like to hear the pretenders examined, and they often imitate me, and

---

7. For a fuller exposition of this famous theory of poetic inspiration see Plato's *Ion*.

proceed to examine others; there are plenty of persons, as they quickly discover, who think that they know something, but really know little or nothing; and then those who are examined by them instead of being angry with themselves are angry with me: This confounded Socrates, they say; this villainous misleader of youth!—and then if somebody asks them, Why, what evil does he practice or teach? they do not know, and cannot tell; but in order that they may not appear to be at a loss, they repeat the ready-made charges which are used against all philosophers about teaching things up in the clouds and under the earth, and having no gods, and making the worse appear the better cause; for they do not like to confess that their pretence of knowledge has been detected—which is the truth; and as they are numerous and ambitious and energetic, and are drawn up in battle array and have persuasive tongues, they have filled your ears with their loud and inveterate calumnies. And this is the reason why my three accusers, Meletus and Anytus and Lycon, have set upon me; Meletus, who has a quarrel with me on behalf of the poets; Anytus, on behalf of the craftsmen and politicians; Lycon, on behalf of the rhetoricians[8]: and as I said at the beginning, I cannot expect to get rid of such a mass of calumny all in a moment. And this, O men of Athens, is the truth and the whole truth; I have concealed nothing, I have dissembled nothing. And yet, I know that my plainness of speech makes them hate me, and what is their hatred but a proof that I am speaking the truth?—Hence has arisen the prejudice against me; and this is the reason of it, as you will find out either in this or in any future enquiry.

I have said enough in my defence against the first class of my accusers; I turn to the second class. They are headed by Meletus, that good man and true lover of his country, as he calls himself. Against these, too, I must try to make a defence:—Let their affidavit be read: it contains something of this kind: It says that Socrates is a doer of evil, who corrupts the youth; and who does not believe in the gods of the state, but has other new divinities of his own.[9] Such is the charge; and now let us examine the particular counts. He says that I am a doer of evil, and corrupt the youth; but I say, O men of Athens, that Meletus is a doer of evil, in that he pretends to be in earnest when he is only in jest, and is so eager to bring men to trial from a pretended zeal and interest about matters in which he really

8. The three accusers. Anytus was a prominent politician; the connection of Meletus with poetry and of Lycon with rhetoric is known only from this passage.    9. The precise meaning of the charge is not clear. As this translation indicates, the Greek words may mean "new divinities," with a reference to Socrates' famous inner voice, which from time to time warned him against action on which he had decided. Or the words may mean "practicing strange rites," though this charge is difficult to understand. In any case, the importance of the phrase is that it implies religious belief of some sort and can later be used against Meletus when he loses his head and accuses Socrates of atheism.

never had the smallest interest. And the truth of this I will endeavour to prove to you.

Come hither, Meletus, and let me ask a question of you.[1] You think a great deal about the improvement of youth?

Yes, I do.

Tell the judges, then, who is their improver; for you must know, as you have taken the pains to discover their corrupter, and are citing and accusing me before them. Speak, then, and tell the judges who their improver is.—Observe, Meletus, that you are silent, and have nothing to say. But is not this rather disgraceful, and a very considerable proof of what I was saying, that you have no interest in the matter? Speak up, friend, and tell us who their improver is.

The laws.

But that, my good sir, is not my meaning. I want to know who the person is, who, in the first place, knows the laws.

The judges,[2] Socrates, who are present in court.

What, do you mean to say, Meletus, that they are able to instruct and improve youth?

Certainly they are.

What, all of them, or some only and not others?

All of them.

By the goddess Here,[3] that is good news! There are plenty of improvers, then. And what do you say of the audience,—do they improve them?

Yes, they do.

And the senators?[4]

Yes, the senators improve them.

But perhaps the members of the assembly[5] corrupt them?— or do they too improve them?

They improve them.

Then every Athenian improves and elevates them; all with the exception of myself; and I alone am their corrupter? Is that what you affirm?

That is what I stoutly affirm.

I am very unfortunate if you are right. But suppose I ask you a question: How about horses?[6] Does one man do them harm and all

1. Socrates avails himself of his right to interrogate the accuser. He is, of course, a master in this type of examination, for he has spent his life in the practice of puncturing inflated pretensions and exposing logical contradictions in the arguments of his adversaries. He is here fulfilling his earlier promise to defend himself in the manner to which he has been accustomed and use the words which he has been in the habit of using in the agora (p. 816).    2. The jury. There was no judge in the Athenian law court. The Athenian jury was large; in this trial it probably consisted of five hundred citizens. In the following questions Socrates forces Meletus to extend the capacity to improve the youth to successively greater numbers, until it appears that the entire citizen body is a good influence and Socrates the only bad one. Meletus is caught in the trap of his own demagogic appeal.    3. Hera.    4. The members of the standing council of the assembly, five hundred in number.    5. The sovereign body in the Athenian constitution, theoretically an assembly of the whole citizen body.    6. This simple analogy is typical of the Socratic method; he is still defending himself in his accustomed manner.

the world good? Is not the exact opposite the truth? One man is able to do them good, or at least not many;—the trainer of horses, that is to say, does them good, and others who have to do with them rather injure them? Is not that true, Meletus, of horses, or any other animals? Most assuredly it is; whether you and Anytus say yes or no. Happy indeed would be the condition of youth if they had one corrupter only, and all the rest of the world were their improvers. But you, Meletus, have sufficiently shown that you never had a thought about the young: your carelessness is seen in your not caring about the very things which you bring against me.

And now, Meletus, I will ask you another question—by Zeus I will: Which is better, to live among bad citizens, or among good ones? Answer, friend, I say; the question is one which may be easily answered. Do not the good do their neighbours good, and the bad do them evil?

Certainly.

And is there any one who would rather be injured than benefited by those who live with him? Answer, my good friend, the law requires you to answer—does any one like to be injured?

Certainly not.

And when you accuse me of corrupting and deteriorating the youth, do you allege that I corrupt them intentionally or unintentionally?

Intentionally, I say.

But you have just admitted that the good do their neighbours good, and evil do them evil. Now, is that a truth which your superior wisdom has recognized thus early in life, and am I, at my age, in such darkness and ignorance as not to know that if a man with whom I have to live is corrupted by me, I am very likely to be harmed by him; and yet I corrupt him, and intentionally, too—so you say, although neither I nor any other human being is ever likely to be convinced by you. But either I do not corrupt them, or I corrupt them unintentionally; and on either view of the case you lie. If my offence is unintentional, the law has no cognizance of unintentional offences: you ought to have taken me privately, and warned and admonished me; for if I had been better advised, I should have left off doing what I only did unintentionally—no doubt I should; but you would have nothing to say to me and refused to teach me. And now you bring me up in this court, which is not a place of instruction, but of punishment.

It will be very clear to you, Athenians, as I was saying, that Meletus has no care at all, great or small, about the matter. But still I should like to know, Meletus, in what I am affirmed to corrupt the young. I suppose you mean, as I infer from your indictment, that I teach them not to acknowledge the gods which the state acknowledges, but some other new divinities or spiritual agencies in their stead. These are the lessons by which I corrupt the youth, as you say.

Yes, that I say emphatically.

Then, by the gods, Meletus, of whom we are speaking, tell me and the court, in somewhat plainer terms, what you mean! for I do not as yet understand whether you affirm that I teach other men to acknowledge some gods, and therefore that I do believe in gods, and am not an entire atheist—this you do not lay to my charge,—but only you say that they are not the same gods which the city recognizes—the charge is that they are different gods. Or, do you mean that I am an atheist simply, and a teacher of atheism?

I mean the latter—that you are a complete atheist.[7]

What an extraordinary statement! Why do you think so, Meletus? Do you mean that I do not believe in the godhead of the sun or moon, like other men?

I assure you, judges, that he does not: for he says that the sun is stone, and the moon earth.[8]

Friend Meletus, you think that you are accusing Anaxagoras: and you have but a bad opinion of the judges, if you fancy them illiterate to such a degree as not to know that these doctrines are found in the books of Anaxagoras the Clazomenian,[9] which are full of them. And so, forsooth, the youth are said to be taught them by Socrates, when there are not unfrequently exhibitions of them at the theatre[1] (price of admission one drachma at the most); and they might pay their money, and laugh at Socrates if he pretends to father these extraordinary views. And so, Meletus, you really think that I do not believe in any god?

I swear by Zeus that you believe absolutely in none at all.

Nobody will believe you, Meletus, and I am pretty sure that you do not believe yourself. I cannot help thinking, men of Athens, that Meletus is reckless and impudent, and that he has written this indictment in a spirit of mere wantonness and youthful bravado. Has he not compounded a riddle, thinking to try me? He said to himself:— I shall see whether the wise Socrates will discover my facetious contradiction, or whether I shall be able to deceive him and the rest of them. For he certainly does appear to me to contradict himself in

7. Meletus jumps at the most damaging charge, and falls into the trap.     8. Meletus falls back on the old prejudices which Socrates claims are the real indictment against him.     9. A fifth-century philosopher from Clazomenae in Asia Minor. He was an intimate friend of Pericles, but this did not save him from indictment for impiety. He was condemned, and forced to leave Athens. He is famous for his doctrine that matter was set in motion and ordered by Intelligence (Nous), which, however, did not create it. He also declared that the sun was a mass of red-hot metal larger than the Peloponnese, and that there were hills and ravines on the moon.     1. I.e., the doctrines of Anaxagoras are reflected in the works of the tragic poets; or the words may mean simply that Anaxagoras' book was on sale at the theater.

the indictment as much as if he said that Socrates is guilty of not believing in the gods, and yet of believing in them—but this is not like a person who is in earnest.

I should like you, O men of Athens, to join me in examining what I conceive to be his inconsistency; and do you, Meletus, answer. And I must remind the audience of my request that they would not make a disturbance[2] if I speak in my accustomed manner:

Did ever man, Meletus, believe in the existence of human things, and not of human beings? . . . I wish, men of Athens, that he would answer, and not be always trying to get up an interruption. Did ever any man believe in horsemanship, and not in horses? or in flute-playing, and not in flute-players? No, my friend; I will answer to you and to the court, as you refuse to answer for yourself. There is no man who ever did. But now please to answer the next question: Can a man believe in spiritual and divine agencies, and not in spirits or demigods?

He cannot.

How lucky I am to have extracted that answer, by the assistance of the court! But then you swear in the indictment that I teach and believe in divine or spiritual agencies (new or old, no matter for that); at any rate, I believe in spiritual agencies,—so you say and swear in the affidavit; and yet if I believe in divine beings, how can I help believing in spirits or demigods;—must I not? To be sure I must; and therefore I may assume that your silence gives consent. Now what are spirits or demigods? are they not either gods or the sons of gods?

Certainly they are.

But this is what I call the facetious riddle invented by you: the demigods or spirits are gods, and you say first that I do not believe in gods, and then again that I do believe in gods; that is, if I believe in demigods. For if the demigods are the illegitimate sons of gods, whether by the nymphs or by any other mothers, of whom they are said to be the sons—what human being will ever believe that there are no gods if they are the sons of gods? You might as well affirm the existence of mules, and deny that of horses and asses. Such nonsense, Meletus, could only have been intended by you to make trial of me. You have put this into the indictment because you had nothing real of which to accuse me. But no one who has a particle of understanding will ever be convinced by you that the same men can believe in divine and superhuman things, and yet not believe that there are gods and demigods and heroes.

I have said enough in answer to the charge of Meletus: any elaborate defence is unnecessary; but I know only too well how many are

---

2. The disturbance is presumably due to the frustration of the enemies of Socrates, who see him assuming complete control of the proceedings and turning them into a street-corner argument of the type in which he is invincible.

the enmities which I have incurred, and this is what will be my destruction if I am destroyed;—not Meletus, nor yet Anytus, but the envy and detraction of the world, which has been the death of many good men, and will probably be the death of many more; there is no danger of my being the last of them.

Some one will say: And are you not ashamed, Socrates, of a course of life which is likely to bring you to an untimely end? To him I may fairly answer: There you are mistaken: a man who is good for anything ought not to calculate the chance of living or dying; he ought only to consider whether in doing anything he is doing right or wrong— acting the part of a good man or of a bad. Whereas, upon your view, the heroes who fell at Troy were not good for much, and the son of Thetis[3] above all, who altogether despised danger in comparison with disgrace; and when he was so eager to slay Hector, his goddess mother said to him, that if he avenged his companion Patroclus, and slew Hector, he would die himself—'Fate,' she said, in these or the like words, 'waits for you next after Hector'; he, receiving this warning, utterly despised danger and death, and instead of fearing them, feared rather to live in dishonour, and not to avenge his friend. 'Let me die forthwith,' he replies, 'and be avenged of my enemy, rather than abide here by the beaked ships, a laughing-stock and a burden of the earth.' Had Achilles any thought of death and danger? For wherever a man's place is, whether the place which he has chosen or that in which he has been placed by a commander, there he ought to remain in hour of danger; he should not think of death or of anything but of disgrace. And this, O men of Athens, is a true saying.

Strange, indeed, would be my conduct, O men of Athens, if I who, when I was ordered by the generals whom you chose to command me at Potidaea and Amphipolis and Delium,[4] remained where they placed me, like any other man, facing death—if now, when, as I conceive and imagine, God orders me to fulfil the philosopher's mission of searching into myself and other men, I were to desert my post through fear of death, or any other fear; that would indeed be strange, and I might justly be arraigned in court for denying the existence of the gods, if I disobeyed the oracle because I was afraid of death, fancying that I was wise when I was not wise. For the fear of death is indeed the pretence of wisdom, and not real wisdom, being a pretence of knowing the unknown; and no one knows whether death, which men in their fear apprehend to be the greatest evil, may not be the greatest good. Is not this ignorance of a disgraceful sort, the ignorance which is the conceit that man knows what he

3. Achilles. See the *Iliad*, Book XVIII, ll. 94 ff.    4. Three of the battles in the Peloponnesian War in which Socrates had fought as an infantryman. The battle at Potidaea (in northern Greece) occurred in 432 B.C. (For a fuller account of Socrates' conduct there see Plato's *Symposium*.) The date of the battle at Amphipolis (in northern Greece) is uncertain. The battle at Delium (in central Greece) took place in 424 B.C.

does not know? And in this respect only I believe myself to differ from men in general, and may perhaps claim to be wiser than they are:—that whereas I know but little of the world below,[5] I do not suppose that I know: but I do know that injustice and disobedience to a better, whether God or man, is evil and dishonourable, and I will never fear or avoid a possible good rather than a certain evil. And therefore if you let me go now, and are not convinced by Anytus, who said that since I had been prosecuted I must be put to death (or if not that I ought never to have been prosecuted at all); and that if I escape now, your sons will all be utterly ruined by listening to my words—if you say to me, Socrates, this time we will not mind Anytus, and you shall be let off, but upon one condition, that you are not to enquire and speculate in this way any more, and that if you are caught doing so again you shall die:—if this was the condition on which you let me go, I should reply: Men of Athens, I honour and love you; but I shall obey God rather than you, and while I have life and strength I shall never cease from the practice and teaching of philosophy, exhorting any one whom I meet and saying to him after my manner: You, my friend,—a citizen of the great and mighty and wise city of Athens,—are you not ashamed of heaping up the greatest amount of money and honour and reputation, and caring so little about wisdom and truth and the greatest improvement of the soul, which you never regard or heed at all? And if the person with whom I am arguing, says: Yes, but I do care; then I do not leave him or let him go at once; but I proceed to interrogate and examine and cross-examine him, and if I think that he has no virtue in him, but only says that he has, I reproach him with undervaluing the greater, and overvaluing the less. And I shall repeat the same words to every one whom I meet, young and old, citizen and alien, but especially to the citizens, inasmuch as they are my brethren. For know that this is the command of God; and I believe that no greater good has ever happened in the state than my service to the God. For I do nothing but go about persuading you all, old and young alike, not to take thought for your persons or your properties, but first and chiefly to care about the greatest improvement of the soul. I tell you that virtue is not given by money, but that from virtue comes money and every other good of man, public as well as private. This is my teaching, and if this is the doctrine which corrupts the youth, I am a mischievous person. But if any one says that this is not my teaching, he is speaking an untruth. Wherefore, O men of Athens, I say to you, do as Anytus bids or not as Anytus bids, and either acquit me or not; but whichever you do, understand that I shall never alter my ways, not even if I have to die many times.

---

5. The next world. The dead were supposed to carry on a sort of existence below the earth.

Men of Athens, do not interrupt,[6] but hear me; there was an understanding between us that you should hear me to the end: I have something more to say, at which you may be inclined to cry out; but I believe that to hear me will be good for you, and therefore I beg that you will not cry out. I would have you know, that if you kill such an one as I am, you will injure yourselves more than you will injure me. Nothing will injure me, not Meletus nor yet Anytus—they cannot, for a bad man is not permitted to injure a better than himself. I do not deny that Anytus may, perhaps, kill him, or drive him into exile, or deprive him of civil rights; and he may imagine, and others may imagine, that he is inflicting a great injury upon him: but there I do not agree. For the evil of doing as he is doing—the evil of unjustly taking away the life of another—is greater far.

And now, Athenians, I am not going to argue for my own sake, as you may think, but for yours, that you may not sin against the God by condemning me, who am his gift to you. For if you kill me you will not easily find a successor to me, who, if I may use such a ludicrous figure of speech, am a sort of gadfly, given to the state by God; and the state is a great and noble steed who is tardy in his motions owing to his very size, and requires to be stirred into life. I am that gadfly which God has attached to the state, and all day long and in all places am always fastening upon you, arousing and persuading and reproaching you. You will not easily find another like me, and therefore I would advise you to spare me. I dare say that you may feel out of temper (like a person who is suddenly awakened from sleep), and you think that you might easily strike me dead as Anytus advises, and then you would sleep on for the remainder of your lives, unless God in his care of you sent you another gadfly. When I say that I am given to you by God, the proof of my mission is this:—if I had been like other men, I should not have neglected all my own concerns or patiently seen the neglect of them during all these years, and have been doing yours, coming to you individually like a father or elder brother, exhorting you to regard virtue; such conduct, I say, would be unlike human nature. If I had gained anything, or if my exhortations had been paid, there would have been some sense in my doing so; but now, as you will perceive, not even the impudence of my accusers dares to say that I have ever exacted or sought pay of any one; of that they have no witness. And I have a sufficient witness to the truth of what I say—my poverty.

Some one may wonder why I go about in private giving advice and busying myself with the concerns of others, but do not venture to come forward in public and advise the state. I will tell you why. You have heard me speak at sundry times and in divers places of an

6. The disturbance this time is presumably more general, for Socrates is defying the court and the people.

oracle or sign which comes to me, and is the divinity which Meletus ridicules in the indictment. This sign, which is a kind of voice, first began to come to me when I was a child; it always forbids but never commands me to do anything which I am going to do. This is what deters me from being a politician. And rightly, as I think. For I am certain, O men of Athens, that if I had engaged in politics, I should have perished long ago, and done no good either to you or to myself. And do not be offended at my telling you the truth: for the truth is, that no man who goes to war with you or any other multitude, honestly striving against the many lawless and unrighteous deeds which are done in a state, will save his life; he who will fight for the right, if he would live even for a brief space, must have a private station and not a public one.

I can give you convincing evidence of what I say, not words only, but what you value far more—actions. Let me relate to you a passage of my own life which will prove to you that I should never have yielded to injustice from any fear of death, and that 'as I should have refused to yield' I must have died at once. I will tell you a tale of the courts, not very interesting perhaps, but nevertheless true. The only office of state which I ever held, O men of Athens, was that of senator: the tribe Antiochis,[7] which is my tribe, had the presidency at the trial of the generals who had not taken up the bodies of the slain after the battle of Arginusae;[8] and you proposed to try them in a body, contrary to law, as you all thought afterwards; but at the time I was the only one of the Prytanes who was opposed to the illegality, and I gave my vote against you; and when the orators threatened to impeach and arrest me, and you called and shouted, I made up my mind that I would run the risk, having law and justice with me, rather than take part in your injustice because I feared imprisonment and death. This happened in the days of the democracy.[9] But when the oligarchy of the Thirty was in power,[1] they sent for me and four others into the rotunda, and bade us bring Leon the Salaminian

7. The Council of the Five Hundred consisted of fifty members of each of the ten tribes into which the population was divided. (Socrates' tribe, like the other nine, was named after a mythical hero, in this case Antiochus.) Each tribal delegation acted as a standing committee of the whole body for a part of the year. The members of this standing committee were called Prytanes. In acting as a member of the council Socrates was not "engaging in politics" but simply fulfilling his duty as a citizen when called upon.    8. An Athenian naval victory over Sparta, in 406 B.C. The Athenian commanders failed to pick up the bodies of a large number of Athenians whose ships had been destroyed. Whether they were prevented from doing so by the wind or simply neglected this duty in the excitement of victory is not known; in any case, the Athenian population suspected the worst and put all ten generals on trial, not in a court of law but before the assembly. The generals were tried not individually, but in a group, and condemned to death. The six who had returned to Athens were executed, among them a son of Pericles.    9. Socrates gives two instances of his political actions, one under the democracy and one under the Thirty Tyrants. In both cases, he was in opposition to the government.    1. In 404 B.C., with Spartan backing the Thirty Tyrants (as they were known to their enemies) ruled for eight months over a defeated Athens. Prominent among them was Critias, who had been one of the rich young men who listened eagerly to Socrates.

from Salamis,[2] as they wanted to put him to death. This was a specimen of the sort of commands which they were always giving with the view of implicating as many as possible in their crimes; and then I showed, not in word only but in deed, that, if I may be allowed to use such an expression, I cared not a straw for death, and that my great and only care was lest I should do an unrighteous or unholy thing. For the strong arm of that oppressive power did not frighten me into doing wrong; and when we came out of the rotunda the other four went to Salamis and fetched Leon, but I went quietly home. For which I might have lost my life, had not the power of the Thirty shortly afterwards come to an end. And many will witness to my words.

Now do you really imagine that I could have survived all these years, if I had led a public life, supposing that like a good man I had always maintained the right and had made justice, as I ought, the first thing? No indeed, men of Athens, neither I nor any other man. But I have been always the same in all my actions, public as well as private, and never have I yielded any base compliance to those who are slanderously termed my disciples, or to any other. Not that I have any regular disciples. But if any one likes to come and hear me while I am pursuing my mission, whether he be young or old, he is not excluded. Nor do I converse only with those who pay; but any one, whether he be rich or poor, may ask and answer me and listen to my words; and whether he turns out to be a bad man or a good one, neither result can be justly imputed to me; for I never taught or professed to teach him anything. And if any one says that he has ever learned or heard anything from me in private which all the world has not heard, let me tell you that he is lying.

But I shall be asked, Why do people delight in continually conversing with you? I have told you already, Athenians, the whole truth about this matter: they like to hear the cross-examination of the pretenders to wisdom; there is amusement in it. Now this duty of cross-examining other men has been imposed upon me by God; and has been signified to me by oracles, visions, and in every way in which the will of divine power was ever intimated to any one. This is true, O Athenians; or, if not true, would be soon refuted. If I am or have been corrupting the youth, those of them who are now grown up and become sensible that I gave them bad advice in the days of their youth should come forward as accusers, and take their revenge; or if they do not like to come themselves, some of their relatives, fathers, brothers, or other kinsmen, should say what evil their families have suffered at my hands. Now is their time. Many of them I

---

2. Athenian territory, an island off Piraeus, the port of Athens. *Rotunda:* The circular building in which the Prytanes held their meetings.

see in the court. There is Crito,[3] who is of the same age and of the same deme with myself, and there is Critobulus his son, whom I also see. Then again there is Lysanias of Sphettus, who is the father of Aeschines—he is present; and also there is Antiphon of Cephisus, who is the father of Epigenes; and there are the brothers of several who have associated with me. There is Nicostratus the son of Theos-dotides, and the brother of Theodotus (now Theodotus himself is dead, and therefore he, at any rate, will not seek to stop him); and there is Paralus the son of Demodocus, who had a brother Theages; and Adeimantus the son of Ariston, whose brother Plato[4] is present; and Aeantodorus, who is the brother of Apollodorus, whom I also see. I might mention a great many others, some of whom Meletus should have produced as witnesses in the course of his speech; and let him still produce them, if he has forgotten—I will make way for him. And let him say, if he has any testimony of the sort which he can produce. Nay, Athenians, the very opposite is the truth. For all these are ready to witness on behalf of the corrupter, of the injurer of their kindred, as Meletus and Anytus call me; not the corrupted youth only—there might have been a motive for that—but their uncorrupted elder relatives. Why should they too support me with their testimony? Why, indeed, except for the sake of truth and jus-tice, and because they know that I am speaking the truth, and that Meletus is a liar.

Well, Athenians, this and the like of this is all the defence which I have to offer. Yet a word more. Perhaps there may be some one who is offended at me, when he calls to mind how he himself on a similar, or even a less serious occasion, prayed and entreated the judges with many tears, and how he produced his children in court, which was a moving spectacle, together with a host of relations and friends;[5] whereas I, who am probably in danger of my life, will do none of these things. The contrast may occur to his mind, and he may be set against me, and vote in anger because he is displeased at me on this account. Now if there be such a person among you,— mind, I do not say that there is,—to him I may fairly reply: My friend, I am a man, and like other men, a creature of flesh and blood, and not 'of wood or stone,' as Homer says;[6] and I have a family, yes, and sons, O Athenians, three in number, one almost a man, and two others who are still young; and yet I will not bring any of them hither in order to petition you for an acquittal. And why not? Not from any self-assertion or want of respect for you. Whether

3. A friend of Socrates who later tried to persuade him to escape from prison. *Deme:* Precinct; the local unit of Athenian administration.    4. The writer of the *Apology.*    5. The accepted ending of the speech for the defense was an unrestrained appeal to the pity of the jury. Socrates' refusal to make it is another shock for the prejudices of the audience.    6. In the Odyssey, Book XIX, ll. 162–163, Penelope says to her husband Odysseus (who is disguised as a beggar), "Tell me of your family and where you come from. For you did not spring from an oak or a rock, as the old saying goes."

I am or am not afraid of death is another question, of which I will not now speak. But, having regard to public opinion, I feel that such conduct would be discreditable to myself, and to you, and to the whole state. One who has reached my years, and who has a name for wisdom, ought not to demean himself. Whether this opinion of me be deserved or not, at any rate the world has decided that Socrates is in some way superior to other men. And if those among you who are said to be superior in wisdom and courage, and any other virtue, demean themselves in this way, how shameful is their conduct! I have seen men of reputation, when they have been condemned, behaving in the strangest manner: they seemed to fancy that they were going to suffer something dreadful if they died, and that they could be immortal if you only allowed them to live; and I think that such are a dishonour to the state, and that any stranger coming in would have said of them that the most eminent men of Athens, to whom the Athenians themselves give honour and command, are no better than women. And I say that these things ought not to be done by those of us who have a reputation; and if they are done, you ought not to permit them; you ought rather to show that you are far more disposed to condemn the man who gets up a doleful scene and makes the city ridiculous, than him who holds his peace.

But, setting aside the question of public opinion, there seems to be something wrong in asking a favour of a judge, and thus procuring an acquittal, instead of informing and convincing him. For his duty is, not to make a present of justice, but to give judgment; and he has sworn that he will judge according to the laws, and not according to his own good pleasure; and we ought not to encourage you, nor should you allow yourself to be encouraged, in this habit of perjury—there can be no piety in that. Do not then require me to do what I consider dishonourable and impious and wrong, especially now, when I am being tried for impiety on the indictment of Meletus. For if, O men of Athens, by force of persuasion and entreaty I could overpower your oaths, then I should be teaching you to believe that there are no gods, and in defending should simply convict myself of the charge of not believing in them. But that is not so—far otherwise. For I do believe that there are gods, and in a sense higher than that in which any of my accusers believe in them. And to you and to God I commit my cause, to be determined by you as is best for you and me.[7]

7. The jury reaches a verdict of guilty. It appears from what Socrates says later that the jury was split, 280 for this verdict and 220 against it. The penalty is to be settled by the jury's choice between the penalty proposed by the prosecution and that offered by the defense. The jury itself cannot propose a penalty. Meletus demands death. Socrates must propose the lightest sentence he thinks he can get away with, but one heavy enough to satisfy the majority of the jury who voted him guilty. The prosecution probably expects him to propose exile from Athens, but Socrates surprises them.

There are many reasons why I am not grieved, O men of Athens, at the vote of condemnation. I expected it, and am only surprised that the votes are so nearly equal; for I had thought that the majority against me would have been far larger; but now, had thirty votes gone over to the other side, I should have been acquitted. And I may say, I think, that I have escaped Meletus. I may say more; for without the assistance of Anytus and Lycon, any one may see that he would not have had a fifth part of the votes,[8] as the law requires, in which case he would have incurred a fine of a thousand drachmae.

And so he proposes death as the penalty. And what shall I propose on my part, O men of Athens? Clearly that which is my due. And what is my due? What return shall be made to the man who has never had the wit to be idle during his whole life; but has been careless of what the many care for—wealth, and family interests, and military offices, and speaking in the assembly, and magistracies, and plots, and parties. Reflecting that I was really too honest a man to be a politician and live, I did not go where I could do no good to you or to myself; but where I could do the greatest good privately to every one of you, thither I went, and sought to persuade every man among you that he must look to himself, and seek virtue and wisdom before he looks to his private interests, and look to the state before he looks to the interests of the state; and that this should be the order which he observes in all his actions. What shall be done to such an one? Doubtless some good thing, O men of Athens, if he has his reward; and the good should be of a kind suitable to him. What would be a reward suitable to a poor man who is your benefactor, and who desires leisure that he may instruct you? There can be no reward so fitting as maintenance in the Prytaneum,[9] O men of Athens, a reward which he deserves far more than the citizen who has won the prize at Olympia in the horse or chariot race, whether the chariots were drawn by two horses or by many. For I am in want, and he has enough; and he only gives you the appearance of happiness, and I give you the reality. And if I am to estimate the penalty fairly, I should say that maintenance in the Prytaneum is the just return.

Perhaps you think that I am braving you in what I am saying now, as in what I said before about the tears and prayers. But this is not so. I speak rather because I am convinced that I never intentionally wronged any one, although I cannot convince you—the time has been too short; if there were a law at Athens, as there is in other cities, that a capital cause should not be decided in one day,[1] then I believe that I should have convinced you. But I cannot in a moment refute great slander; and, as I am convinced that I never wronged

8. Socrates jokingly divides the votes against him into three parts, one for each of his three accusers, and points out that Meletus' votes fall below the minimum necessary to justify the trial.    9. The place in which the Prytanes, as representatives of the city, entertained distinguished visitors and winners at the athletic contests at Olympia.    1. There was such a law in Sparta.

another, I will assuredly not wrong myself. I will not say of myself that I deserve any evil, or propose any penalty. Why should I? Because I am afraid of the penalty of death which Meletus proposes? When I do not know whether death is a good or an evil, why should I propose a penalty which would certainly be an evil? Shall I say imprisonment? And why should I live in prison, and be the slave of the magistrates of the year—of the Eleven?[2] Or shall the penalty be a fine, and imprisonment until the fine is paid? There is the same objection. I should have to lie in prison, for money I have none, and cannot pay. And if I say exile (and this may possibly be the penalty which you will affix), I must indeed be blinded by the love of life, if I am so irrational as to expect that when you, who are my own citizens, cannot endure my discourses and words, and have found them so grievous and odious that you will have no more of them, others are likely to endure me. No indeed, men of Athens, that is not very likely. And what a life should I lead, at my age, wandering from city to city, ever changing my place of exile, and always being driven out! For I am quite sure that wherever I go, there, as here, the young men will flock to me; and if I drive them away, their elders will drive me out at their request; and if I let them come, their fathers and friends will drive me out for their sakes.

Some one will say: Yes, Socrates, but cannot you hold your tongue, and then you may go into a foreign city, and no one will interfere with you? Now I have great difficulty in making you understand my answer to this. For if I tell you that to do as you say would be a disobedience to the God, and therefore that I cannot hold my tongue, you will not believe that I am serious; and if I say again that daily to discourse about virtue, and of those other things about which you hear me examining myself and others, is the greatest good of man, and that the unexamined life is not worth living, you are still less likely to believe me. Yet I say what is true, although a thing of which it is hard for me to persuade you. Also, I have never been accustomed to think that I deserve to suffer any harm. Had I money I might have estimated the offence at what I was able to pay, and not have been much the worse. But I have none, and therefore I must ask you to proportion the fine to my means. Well, perhaps I could afford a mina,[3] and therefore I propose that penalty: Plato, Crito, Critobulus, and Appollodorus, my friends here, bid me say thirty minae, and they will be the sureties. Let thirty minae be the penalty; for which sum they will be ample security to you.[4]

---

2. A committee which had charge of prisons and of public executions.     3. It is almost impossible to express the value of ancient money in modern terms. A mina was a considerable sum; in Aristotle's time (fourth century B.C.) one mina was recognized as a fair ransom for a prisoner of war.     4. The jury decides for death (according to a much later source, the vote this time was 300 to 200). The decision is not surprising in view of Socrates' intransigence. Socrates now makes a final statement to the court.

Not much time will be gained, O Athenians, in return for the evil name which you will get from the detractors of the city, who will say that you killed Socrates, a wise man; for they will call me wise, even although I am not wise, when they want to reproach you. If you had waited a little while, your desire would have been fulfilled in the course of nature. For I am far advanced in years, as you may perceive, and not far from death. I am speaking now not to all of you, but only to those who have condemned me to death. And I have another thing to say to them: You think that I was convicted because I had no words of the sort which would have procured my acquittal—I mean, if I had thought fit to leave nothing undone or unsaid. Not so; the deficiency which led to my conviction was not of words—certainly not. But I had not the boldness or impudence or inclination to address you as you would have liked me to do, weeping and wailing and lamenting, and saying and doing many things which you have been accustomed to hear from others, and which, as I maintain, are unworthy of me. I thought at the time that I ought not to do anything common or mean when in danger: nor do I now repent of the style of my defence; I would rather die having spoken after my manner, than speak in your manner and live. For neither in war nor yet at law ought I or any man to use every way of escaping death. Often in battle there can be no doubt that if a man will throw away his arms, and fall on his knees before his pursuers, he may escape death; and in other dangers there are other ways of escaping death, if a man is willing to say and do anything. The difficulty, my friends, is not to avoid death, but to avoid unrighteousness; for that runs faster than death. I am old and move slowly, and the slower runner has overtaken me, and my accusers are keen and quick, and the faster runner, who is unrighteousness, has overtaken them. And now I depart hence condemned by you to suffer the penalty of death,—they too go their ways condemned by the truth to suffer the penalty of villainy and wrong; and I must abide by my award—let them abide by theirs. I suppose that these things may be regarded as fated,—and I think that they are well.

And now, O men who have condemned me, I would fain prophesy to you; for I am about to die, and in the hour of death men are gifted with prophetic power.[5] And I prophesy to you who are my murderers, that immediately after my departure punishment far heavier than you have inflicted on me will surely await you. Me you have killed because you wanted to escape the accuser, and not to give an account of your lives. But that will not be as you suppose: far otherwise. For I say that there will be more accusers of you than there are now;[6] accusers whom hitherto I have restrained: and as they are

5. As the dying Hector foretells the death of Achilles; see the *Iliad*, Book XXII, 11. 355–360.
6. Socrates' prophecy was fulfilled, for all of the many different philosophical schools of the early fourth century claimed descent from Socrates and developed one or another aspect of his teachings.

younger they will be more inconsiderate with you, and you will be more offended at them. If you think that by killing men you can prevent some one from censuring your evil lives, you are mistaken; that is not a way of escape which is either possible or honourable; the easiest and the noblest way is not to be disabling others, but to be improving yourselves. This is the prophecy which I utter before my departure to the judges who have condemned me.

Friends, who would have acquitted me, I would like also to talk with you about the thing which has come to pass, while the magistrates are busy, and before I go to the place at which I must die. Stay then a little, for we may as well talk with one another while there is time. You are my friends, and I should like to show you the meaning of this event which has happened to me. O my judges—for you I may truly call judges—I should like to tell you of a wonderful circumstance. Hitherto the divine faculty of which the internal oracle is the source has constantly been in the habit of opposing me even about trifles, if I was going to make a slip or error in any matter; and now as you see there has come upon me that which may be thought, and is generally believed to be, the last and worst evil. But the oracle made no sign of opposition, either when I was leaving my house in the morning, or when I was on my way to the court, or while I was speaking, at anything which I was going to say; and yet I have often been stopped in the middle of a speech, but now in nothing I either said or did touching the matter in hand has the oracle opposed me. What do I take to be the explanation of this silence? I will tell you. It is an intimation that what has happened to me is a good, and that those of us who think that death is an evil are in error. For the customary sign would surely have opposed me had I been going to evil and not to good.

Let us reflect in another way, and we shall see that there is great reason to hope that death is a good; for one of two things—either death is a state of nothingness and utter unconsciousness, or, as men say, there is a change and migration of the soul from this world to another. Now if you suppose that there is no consciousness, but a sleep like the sleep of him who is undisturbed even by dreams, death will be an unspeakable gain. For if a person were to select the night in which his sleep was undisturbed even by dreams, and were to compare with this the other days and nights of his life, and then were to tell us how many days and nights he had passed in the course of his life better and more pleasantly than this one, I think that any man, I will not say a private man, but even the great king will not find many such days or nights, when compared with the others. Now if death be of such a nature, I say that to die is gain; for eternity is then only a single night. But if death is the journey to another place, and there, as men say, all the dead abide, what good, O my friends and judges, can be greater than this? If indeed when the pilgrim arrives in the world below, he is delivered from the professors of justice in this world, and finds the true judges who are said to give judgment there, Minos and Rhadamanthus and Aeacus and Triptolemus,[7] and other sons of God who were righteous in their own life, that pilgrimage will be worth making. What would not a man give if he might converse with Orpheus and Musaeus[8] and Hesiod and Homer? Nay, if this be true, let me die again and again. I myself, too, shall have a wonderful interest in there meeting and conversing with Palamedes, and Ajax the son of Telamon,[9] and any other ancient hero who has suffered death through an unjust judgment; and there will be no small pleasure, as I think, in comparing my own sufferings with theirs. Above all, I shall then be able to continue my search into true and false knowledge; as in this world, so also in the next and I shall find out who is wise, and who pretends to be wise, and is not. What would not a man give, O judges, to be able to examine the leader of the great Trojan expedition; or Odysseus or Sisyphus,[1] or numberless others, men and women too! What infinite delight would there be in conversing with them and asking them questions! In another world they do not put a man to death for asking questions: assuredly not. For besides being happier than we are, they will be immortal, if what is said is true.

Wherefore, O judges, be of good cheer about death, and know of a certainty, that no evil can happen to a good man, either in life or after death. He and his are not neglected by the gods; nor has my own approaching end happened by mere chance. But I see clearly that the time had arrived when it was better for me to die and be released from trouble; wherefore the oracle gave no sign. For which reason, also, I am not angry with my condemners, or with my accusers; they have done me no harm, although they did not mean to do me any good; and for this I may gently blame them.

Still I have a favour to ask of them. When my sons are grown up, I would ask you, O my friends, to punish them; and I would have you trouble them, as I have troubled you, if they seem to care about riches, or anything more than about virtue; or if they pretend to be something when they are really nothing,—then reprove them, as I have reproved you, for not caring about that for which they ought to care, and thinking that they are something when they are really

---

7. Minos appears as a judge of the dead in Homer's *Odyssey*, Book XI; Rhadamanthus and Aeacus, like Minos, were models of just judges in life and after death; Triptolemus, the mythical inventor of agriculture, is associated with judgment in the next world only in this passage. The first three are sons of Zeus.    8. Legendary poets and religious teachers. *Hesiod:* Early Greek poet (eighth century B.C.?) who wrote *The Works and Days*, a didactic poem containing precepts for the farmer.    9. Both victims of unjust trials. Palamedes, one of the Greek chieftains at Troy, was unjustly executed for treason on the false evidence of his enemy Odysseus, and Ajax committed suicide after the arms of the dead Achilles were adjudged to his enemy Odysseus as the bravest warrior on the Greek side.    1. Odysseus was the most cunning of the Greek chieftains at Troy, the hero of Homer's *Odyssey*; Sisyphus, was famous for his unscrupulousness and cunning. Each is presumably an example of the man who "pretends to be wise and is not."

nothing. And if you do this, both I and my sons will have received justice at your hands.

The hour of departure has arrived, and we go our ways—I to die, and you to live. Which is better God only knows.

# Phaedo[2]

## [The Death of Socrates]

[The narrator, Phaedo, who was present at the execution of Socrates, gives his friend Echecrates an account of Socrates' last hours. Many of his friends were with him on that day, among them Crito and two Theban philosophers, Simmias and Cebes. These two engaged him in an argument about the immortality of the soul, which Socrates succeeded in proving to their satisfaction. He concluded with an account of the next world, describing the place of reward for the virtuous and of punishment for the wicked. The opening words of the following selection are his conclusion of the argument.]

A man of sense ought not to say, nor will I be very confident, that the description which I have given of the soul and her mansions is exactly true. But I do say that, inasmuch as the soul is shown to be immortal, he may venture to think, not improperly or unworthily, that something of the kind is true. The venture is a glorious one, and he ought to comfort himself with words like these, which is the reason why I lengthen out the tale. Wherefore, I say, let a man be of good cheer about his soul, who having cast away the pleasures and ornaments of the body as alien to him and working harm rather than good, has sought after the pleasures of knowledge; and has arrayed the soul, not in some foreign attire, but in her own proper jewels, temperance, and justice, and courage, and nobility, and truth—in these adorned she is ready to go on her journey to the world below, when her hour comes. You, Simmias and Cebes, and all other men, will depart at some time or other. Me already, as a tragic poet would say, the voice of fate calls. Soon I must drink the poison;[3] and I think that I had better repair to the bath first, in order that the women may not have the trouble of washing my body after I am dead.

When he had done speaking, Crito said: And have you any commands for us, Socrates—anything to say about your children, or any other matter in which we can serve you?

Nothing particular, Crito, he replied: only, as I have always told you, take care of yourselves; that is a service which you may be ever rendering to me and mine and to all of us, whether you promise to do so or not. But if you have no thought for yourselves, and care not to walk according to the rule which I have prescribed for you, not

2. Translated by Benjamin Jowett.　　3. Hemlock. This was the regular method of execution at Athens. The action of the poison is described below.

now for the first time, however much you may profess or promise at the moment, it will be of no avail.

We will do our best, said Crito: And in what way shall we bury you?

In any way that you like; but you must get hold of me, and take care that I do not run away from you. Then he turned to us, and added with a smile:—I cannot make Crito believe that I am the same Socrates who have been talking and conducting the argument; he fancies that I am the other Socrates whom he will soon see, a dead body—and he asks, How shall he bury me? And though I have spoken many words in the endeavour to show that when I have drunk the poison I shall leave you and go to the joys of the blessed,—these words of mine, with which I was comforting you and myself, have had, as I perceive, no effect upon Crito. And therefore I want you to be surety for me to him now, as at the trial he was surety to the judges for me: but let the promise be of another sort; for he was surety for me to the judges that I would remain, and you must be my surety to him that I shall not remain, but go away and depart; and then he will suffer less at my death, and not be grieved when he sees my body being burned or buried. I would not have him sorrow at my hard lot, or say at the burial, Thus we lay out Socrates, or, Thus we follow him to the grave or bury him; for false words are not only evil in themselves, but they inflict the soul with evil. Be of good cheer then, my dear Crito, and say that you are burying my body only, and do with that whatever is usual, and what you think best.

When he had spoken these words, he arose and went into a chamber to bathe; Crito followed him and told us to wait. So we remained behind, talking and thinking of the subject of discourse, and also of the greatness of our sorrow; he was like a father of whom we were being bereaved, and we were about to pass the rest of our lives as orphans. When he had taken the bath his children were brought to him (he had two young sons and an elder one); and the women of his family also came, and he talked to them and gave them a few directions in the presence of Crito; then he dismissed them and returned to us.

Now the hour of sunset was near, for a good deal of time had passed while he was within. When he came out, he sat down with us again after his bath, but not much was said. Soon the jailer, who was the servant of the Eleven, entered and stood by him, saying:— To you, Socrates, whom I know to be the noblest and gentlest and best of all who ever came to this place, I will not impute the angry feeling of other men, who rage and swear at me, when, in obedience to the authorities, I bid them drink the poison—indeed, I am sure that you will not be angry with me; for others, as you are aware, and not I, are to blame. And so fare you well, and try to bear lightly what must needs be—you know my errand. Then bursting into tears he turned away and went out.

Socrates looked at him and said: I return your good wishes, and will do as you bid. Then turning to us, he said, How charming the man is: since I have been in prison he has always been coming to see me, and at times he would talk to me, and was as good to me as could be, and now see how generously he sorrows on my account. We must do as he says, Crito; and therefore let the cup be brought, if the poison is prepared: if not, let the attendant prepare some.

Yet, said Crito, the sun is still upon the hill-tops, and I know that many a one has taken the draught late, and after the announcement has been made to him, he has eaten and drunk, and enjoyed the society of his beloved: do not hurry—there is time enough.

Socrates said: Yes, Crito, and they of whom you speak are right in so acting, for they think that they will be gainers by the delay; but I am right in not following their example, for I do not think that I should gain anything by drinking the poison a little later; I should only be ridiculous in my own eyes for sparing and saving a life which is already forfeit. Please then to do as I say, and not to refuse me.

Crito made a sign to the servant, who was standing by; and he went out, and having been absent for some time, returned with the jailer carrying the cup of poison. Socrates said: You, my good friend, who are experienced in these matters, shall give me directions how I am to proceed. The man answered: You have only to walk about until your legs are heavy, and then to lie down, and the poison will act. At the same time he handed the cup to Socrates, who in the easiest and gentlest manner, without the least fear or change of colour or feature, looking at the man with all his eyes, Echecrates, as his manner was,[4] took the cup and said: What do you say about making a libation[5] out of this cup to any god? May I, or not? The man answered: We only prepare, Socrates, just so much as we deem enough. I understand, he said: but I may and must ask the gods to prosper my journey from this to the other world—even so— and so be it according to my prayer. Then raising the cup to his lips, quite readily and cheerfully he drank off the poison. And hitherto most of us had been able to control our sorrow; but now when we saw him drinking, and saw too that he had finished the draught, we could no longer forbear, and in spite of myself my own tears were flowing fast; so that I covered my face and wept, not for him, but at the thought of my own calamity in having to part from such a friend. Nor was I the first; for Crito, when he found himself unable to restrain his tears, had got up, and I followed; and at that moment, Apollodorus, who had been weeping all the time, broke out in a loud and passion-

---

4. Socrates was famous for his projecting eyes and his intent stare.    5. He asks if he may pour a little of it out in honor of the gods, as if it were wine.

ate cry which made cowards of us all. Socrates alone retained his calmness: What is this strange outcry? he said. I sent away the women mainly in order that they might not misbehave in this way, for I have been told that a man should die in peace. Be quiet then, and have patience. When we heard his words we were ashamed, and refrained our tears; and he walked about until, as he said, his legs began to fail, and then he lay on his back, according to directions, and the man who gave him the poison now and then looked at his feet and legs; and after a while he pressed his foot hard, and asked him if he could feel; and he said, No; and then his leg, and so upwards and upwards, and showed us that he was cold and stiff. And he felt them himself, and said: When the poison reaches the heart, that will be the end. He was beginning to grow cold about the groin, when he uncovered his face, for he had covered himself up, and said—they were his last words—he said: Crito, I owe a cock to Asclepius;[6] will you remember to pay the debt? The debt shall be paid, said Crito; is there anything else? There was no answer to this question; but in a minute or two a movement was heard, and the attendants uncovered him; his eyes were set, and Crito closed his eyes and mouth.

Such was the end, Echecrates, of our friend; concerning whom I may truly say, that of all men of his time whom I have known, he was the wisest and justest and best.

---

# ARISTOTLE
## 384–322 B.C.

One member of Plato's Academy, Aristotle (384–322 B.C.), was to become as celebrated and influential as his teacher.

He was not, like Plato, a native Athenian; he was born in the north of Greece, at Stagira, close to the kingdom of Macedonia, which was eventually to become the dominant power in the Greek world. Aristotle entered the Academy at the age of 17 but left it when Plato died (348). He carried on his researches (he was especially interested in zoology) at various places on the Aegean, served as tutor to the young Alexander, son of Philip II of Macedon, and returned to Athens in 355, to found his own philosophical school, the Lyceum. Here he established the world's first research library and at the Lyceum he and his pupils carried on research in zoology, botany, biology, physics, political science, ethics, logic, music, and mathematics. He left Athens when Alexander died in Babylon (323 B.C.) and the Athenians, for a while, were able to demonstrate their hatred of Macedon and everything connected with it; he died a year later.

The scope of his written work, philosophical and scientific, is immense; he is represented here by some excerpts from the *Poetics*, the first systematic work of literary criticism in our tradition.

---

6. A sacrifice to the god of healing, perhaps as a thank offering for the painlessness of his death.

*Aristotle's Poetics*, translated, with an introduction and notes by James Hulton (1982), is the best source for the student.

# Poetics[1]

. . . Thus, Tragedy is an imitation of an action that is serious, complete, and possessing magnitude; in embellished language, each kind of which is used separately in the different parts; in the mode of action and not narrated; and effecting through pity and fear [what we call] the *catharsis*[2] of such emotions. By "embellished language" I mean language having rhythm and melody, and by "separately in different parts" I mean that some parts of a play are carried on solely in metrical speech while others again are sung.

*The constituent parts of tragedy.* Since the imitation is carried out in the dramatic mode by the personages themselves, it necessarily follows, first, that the arrangement of Spectacle will be a part of tragedy, and next, that Melody and Language will be parts, since these are the media in which they effect the imitation. By "language" I mean precisely the composition of the verses, by "melody" only that which is perfectly obvious. And since tragedy is the imitation of an action and is enacted by men in action, these persons must necessarily possess certain qualities of Character and Thought, since these are the basis for our ascribing qualities to the actions themselves— character and thought are two natural causes of actions—and it is in their actions that men universally meet with success or failure. The imitation of the action is the Plot. By plot I here mean the combination of the events; Character is that in virtue of which we say that the personages are of such and such a quality; and Thought is present in everything in their utterances that aims to prove a point or that expresses an opinion. Necessarily, therefore, there are in tragedy as a whole, considered as a special form, six constituent elements, viz. Plot, Character, Language, Thought, Spectacle, and Melody. Of these elements, two [Language and Melody] are the *media* in which they effect the imitation, one [Spectacle] is the *manner*, and three [Plot, Character, Thought] are the *objects* they imitate; and besides these there are no other parts. So then they employ these six forms, not just some of them so to speak; for every drama has spectacle, character, plot, language, melody, and thought in the same sense,

1. Selected passages. Translated by James Hutton.    2. This is probably the most disputed passage in European literary criticism. There are two main schools of interpretation; they differ in their understanding of the metaphor implied in the word *katharsis*. Some critics take the word to mean "purification" implying a metaphor from the religious process of purification from guilt; the passions are "purified" by the tragic performance since the excitement of these passions by the performance weakens them and reduces them to just proportions in the individual. (This theory was supported by the German critic Lessing.) Others take the metaphor to be medical, reading the word as "purging" and interpreting the phrase to mean that the tragic performance excites the emotions only to allay them, thus ridding the spectator of the disquieting emotions from which he suffers in everyday life; tragedy thus has a therapeutic effect.

but the most important of them is the organization of the events [the plot].

*Plot and character.* For tragedy is not an imitation of men but of actions and of life. It is in action that happiness and unhappiness are found, and the end[3] we aim at is a kind of activity, not a quality; in accordance with their characters men are of such and such a quality, in accordance with their actions they are fortunate or the reverse. Consequently, it is not the purpose of presenting their characters that the agents engage in action, but rather it is for the sake of their actions that they take on the characters they have. Thus, what happens—that is, the plot—is the end for which a tragedy exists, and the end or purpose is the most important thing of all. What is more, without action there could not be a tragedy, but there could be without characterization. . . .

Now that the parts are established, let us next discuss what qualities the plot should have, since plot is the primary and most important part of tragedy. I have posited that tragedy is an imitation of an action that is a whole and complete in itself and of a certain magnitude—for a thing may be a whole, and yet have no magnitude to speak of. Now a thing is a whole if it has a beginning, a middle, and an end. A beginning is that which does not come necessarily after something else, but after which it is natural for another thing to exist or come to be. An end, on the contrary, is that which naturally comes after something else, either as its necessary sequel or as its usual [and hence probable] sequel, but itself has nothing after it. A middle is that which both comes after something else and has another thing following it. A well-constructed plot, therefore, will neither begin at some chance point nor end at some chance point, but will observe the principles here stated.

Contrary to what some people think, a plot is not ipso facto a unity if it revolves about one man. Many things, indeed an endless number of things, happen to any one man some of which do not go together to form a unity, and similarly among the actions one man performs there are many that do not go together to produce a single unified action. Those poets seem all to have erred, therefore, who have composed a *Heracleid*, a *Theseid*, and other such poems, it being their idea evidently that since Heracles was one man, their plot was bound to be unified. . . .

From what has already been said, it will be evident that the poet's function is not to report things that have happened, but rather to tell of such things as might happen, things that are possibilities by virtue of being in themselves inevitable or probable. Thus the difference between the historian and the poet is not that the historian employs

3. Purpose.

prose and the poet verse—the work of Herodotus[4] could be put into verse, and it would be no less a history with verses than without them; rather the difference is that the one tells of things that have been and the other of such things as might be. Poetry, therefore, is a more philosophical and a higher thing than history, in that poetry tends rather to express the universal, history rather the particular fact. A universal is: The sort of thing that (in the circumstances) a certain kind of person will say or do either probably or necessarily, which in fact is the universal that poetry aims for (with the addition of names for the persons); a particular, on the other hand is: What Alcibiades[5] did or had done to him. . . .

Among plots and actions of the simple type, the episodic form is the worst. I call episodic a plot in which the episodes follow one another in no probable or inevitable sequence. Plots of this kind are constructed by bad poets on their own account, and by good poets on account of the actors; since they are composing entries for a competitive exhibition, they stretch the plot beyond what it can bear and are often compelled, therefore, to dislocate the natural order. . . .

Some plots are simple, others complex; indeed the actions of which the plots are imitation are at once so differentiated to begin with. Assuming the action to be continuous and unified, as already defined, I call that action simple in which the change of fortune takes place without a reversal or recognition, and that action complex in which the change of fortune involves a recognition or a reversal or both. These events [recognitions and reversals] ought to be so rooted in the very structure of the plot that they follow from the preceding events as their inevitable or probable outcome; for there is a vast difference between following from and merely following after. . . .

Reversal (Peripety) is, as aforesaid, a change from one state of affairs to its exact opposite, and this, too, as I say, should be in conformance with probability or necessity. For example, in *Oedipus*, the messenger[6] comes to cheer Oedipus by relieving him of fear with regard to his mother, but by revealing his true identity, does just the opposite of this. . . .

Recognition, as the word itself indicates, is a change from ignorance to knowledge, leading either to friendship or to hostility on the part of those persons who are marked for good fortune or bad. The best form of recognition is that which is accompanied by a reversal, as in the example from *Oedipus*. . . .

Next in order after the points I have just dealt with, it would seem necessary to specify what one should aim at and what avoid in the construction of plots, and what it is that will produce the effect proper to tragedy.

Now since in the finest kind of tragedy the structure should be

---

**4.** The historian of the Persian wars, a contemporary of Sophocles.    **5.** A brilliant but unscrupulous Athenian statesman of the fifth century B.C.    **6.** The Corinthian herdsman.

complex and not simple, and since it should also be a representation of terrible and piteous events (that being the special mark of this type of imitation) in the first place, it is evident that good men ought not to be shown passing from prosperity to misfortune, for this does not inspire either pity or fear, but only revulsion; nor evil men rising from ill fortune to prosperity, for this is the most untragic plot of all—it lacks every requirement, in that it neither elicits human sympathy nor stirs pity or fear. And again, neither should an extremely wicked man be seen falling from prosperity into misfortune, for a plot so constructed might indeed call forth human sympathy, but would not excite pity or fear, since the first is felt for a person whose misfortune is undeserved and the second for someone like ourselves—pity for the man suffering undeservedly, fear for the man like ourselves—and hence neither pity nor fear would be aroused in this case. We are left with the man whose place is between these extremes. Such is the man who on the one hand is not pre-eminent in virtue and justice, and yet on the other hand does not fall into misfortune through vice or depravity, but falls because of some mistake;[7] one among the number of the highly renowned and prosperous, such as Oedipus and Thyestes and other famous men from families like theirs.

It follows that the plot which achieves excellence will necessarily be single in outcome and not, as some contend, double and will consist in a change of fortune, not from misfortune to prosperity, but the opposite from prosperity to misfortune, occasioned not by depravity, but by some great mistake on the part of one who is either such as I have described or better than this rather than worse. (What actually has taken place confirms this; for though at first the poets accepted whatever myths came to hand, today the finest tragedies are founded upon the stories of only a few houses, being concerned, for example, with Alcmeon, Oedipus, Orestes, Meleager, Thyestes, Telephus, and such others as have chanced to suffer terrible things or to do them.) So, then, tragedy having this construction is the finest kind of tragedy from an artistic point of view. And consequently, those persons fall into the same error who bring it as a charge against Euripides that this is what he does in his tragedies and that most of his plays have unhappy endings. For this is in fact the right procedure, as I have said; and the best proof is that on the stage and in the dramatic contests, plays of this kind seem the most tragic, provided they are successfully worked out, and Euripides, even if in everything else his management is faulty, seems at any rate the most tragic of the poets. . . .

In the characters and the plot construction alike, one must strive for that which is either necessary or probable, so that whatever a

---

7. The Greek word is *hamartia*. It has sometimes been translated as "flaw" (hence the expression "tragic flaw") and thought of as a moral defect, but comparison with Aristotle's use of the word in other contexts suggests strongly that he means by it "mistake" or "error" (of judgment).

character of any kind says or does may be the sort of thing such a character will inevitably or probably say or do and the events of the plot may follow one after another either inevitably or with probability. (Obviously, then, the denouement of the plot should arise from the plot itself and not be brought about "from the machine,"[8] as it is in *Medea* and in the embarkation scene in the *Iliad*.[9] The machine is to be used for matters lying outside the drama, either antecedents of the action which a human being cannot know, or things subsequent to the action that have to be prophesied and announced; for we accept it that the gods see everything. Within the events of the plot itself, however, there should be nothing unreasonable, or if there is, it should be kept outside the play proper, as is done in the *Oedipus* of Sophocles.) . . .

*The chorus in tragedy.* The chorus ought to be regarded as one of the actors, and as being part of the whole and integrated into performance, not in Euripides' way but in that of Sophocles. In the other poets, the choral songs have no more relevance to the plot than if they belonged to some other play. And so nowadays, following the practice introduced by Agathon,[1] the chorus merely sings interludes. But what difference is there between the singing of interludes and taking a speech or even an entire episode from one play and inserting it into another?

---

8. Literally the machine which was employed in the theater to show the gods flying in space. It has come to mean any implausible way of solving the complications of the plot. Medea escapes from Corinth "on the machine" in her magic chariot.    9. Aristotle refers to an incident in the second book of the *Iliad*; an attempt of the Greek rank and file to return home and abandon the siege is arrested by the intervention of Athena. (If it were a drama she would appear "on the machine.")    1. A younger contemporary of Euripides; most of his plays were produced in the fourth century B.C.

# VIRGIL

## 70–19 B.C.

Publius Virgilius Maro was born in 70 B.C. in the north of Italy. Very little is known about his life. The earliest work which is certainly his is the *Bucolics*, a collection of poems in the pastoral genre which have had enormous influence. These were followed by the *Georgics*, a didactic poem on farming, in four books, which many critics consider his finest work. The *Aeneid*, the Roman epic, was left unfinished at his early death in 19 B.C.

Like all the Latin poets, Virgil built on the solid foundations of his Greek predecessors. The story of Aeneas, the Trojan prince who came to Italy and whose descendants founded Rome, combines the themes of the *Odyssey* (the wanderer in search of home) and the *Iliad* (the hero in battle). Virgil borrows Homeric turns of phrase, similes, sentiments, whole incidents: his Aeneas, like Achilles, sacrifices prisoners to the shade of a friend and, like Odysseus, descends alive to the world of the dead. But unlike Achilles, Aeneas does not satisfy the great passion of his life, nor, like Odysseus, does he find a home in which to end his days in peace. The personal objectives of both of Homer's heroes are sacrificed by Aeneas for a greater objective. There is something greater than himself. His mission, imposed on him by the gods, is to found a city, from which, in the fullness of time, will spring the Roman state.

Homer presents us in the *Iliad* with the tragic pattern of the individual will, Achilles' wrath. But Aeneas is more than an individual. He is the prototype of the ideal Roman ruler; his qualities are the devotion to duty and the seriousness of purpose which were to give the Mediterranean world two centuries of ordered government. Aeneas' mission begins in disorder in the burning city of Troy, but he leaves it carrying his father on his shoulders and leading his little son by the hand. This famous picture emphasizes the fact that, unlike Achilles, he is securely set in a continuity of generations, the immortality of the family group, just as his mission to found a city, a home for the gods of Troy whose statues he carries with him, places him in a political and religious continuity. Achilles has no future. When he mentions his father and son, neither of whom he will see again, he emphasizes for us the loneliness of his short career; the brilliance of his life is that of a meteor which burns itself out to darkness. Odysseus has a father, wife, and son, and his heroic efforts are directed toward re-establishing himself in his proper context, that home in which he will be no longer man in a world of magic and terror, but man in an organized and continuous community. But he fights for himself. Aeneas, on the other hand, suffers and fights, not for himself but for the future; his own life is unhappy and his death miserable. Yet he can console himself with the glory of his sons to come, the pageant of Roman achievement which he is shown by his father in the world below and which he carries on his shield. Aeneas' future is Virgil's present; the consolidation of the Roman peace under Augustus is the reward of Aeneas' unhappy life of effort and suffering.

Summarized like this, the *Aeneid* sounds like propaganda, which, in one sense of the word, it is. What saves it from the besetting fault of even the best propaganda—the partial concealment of the truth—is the fact that Virgil maintains an independence of the power which he is celebrating and sees his hero in the round. He knows that the Roman ideal of devotion to duty has another side, the suppression of many aspects of the personality; that the man who wins and uses power must sacrifice much of himself, must live a life which, compared with that of Achilles or Odysseus, is constricted. In Virgil's poem Aeneas betrays the great passion of his life, his love for Dido, queen of Carthage. He does it reluctantly, but nevertheless he leaves her, and the full realization of what he has lost comes to him only when he meets her ghost in the world below. He weeps (as he did not at Carthage) and he pleads, in stronger terms than he did then, the overriding power which forced him to depart: "I left your land against my will, my queen." She leaves him without a word, her silence as impervious to pleas and tears as his at Carthage once, and he follows her weeping as she goes back to join her first love, her husband Sychaeus. He has sacrificed his love to something greater, but this does not insulate him from unhappiness. The limitations upon the dedicated man are emphasized by the contrasting figure of Dido, who follows her own impulse always, even in death. By her death, Virgil tells us expressly, she forestalls fate, breaks loose from the pattern in which Aeneas remains to the bitter end.

The angry reactions which this part of the poem has produced in many critics are the true measure of Virgil's success. Aeneas does act in such a way that he forfeits much of our sympathy, but this is surely exactly what Virgil intended. The Dido episode is not, as many critics have supposed, a flaw in the great design, a case of Virgil's sympathy outrunning his admiration for Aeneas; it is Virgil's emphatic statement of the sacrifice which the Roman ideal of duty demands. Aeneas' sacrifice is so great that few of us could make it ourselves, and none of us can contemplate it in another without a feeling of loss. It is an expression of the famous Virgilian sadness which informs every line of the *Aeneid* and which makes a poem that was in its historical context a command performance into the great epic which has dominated Western literature ever since.

W. A. Camps, *An Introduction to Virgil's Aeneid* (1969), is a short and simply written discussion of all aspects of the poem. *Virgil: A Collection of Critical Essays*, edited by Steele Commager (1966), contains essays by various hands, ten of them on the *Aeneid*.

---

# Virgil in Latin

Conticuere omnes intentique ora tenebant;
inde toro pater Aeneas sic orsus ab alto:
    Infandum, regina, iubes renouare dolorem,
Troianas ut opes et lamentabile regnum
eruerint Danai, quaeque ipse miserrima uidi

> et quorum pars magna fui. quis talia fando
> Myrmidonum Dolopomue aut duri miles Ulixi
> temperet a lacrimis? et iam nox umida caelo
> praecipitat suadentque cadentia sidera somnos.
> sed si tantus amor casus cognoscere nostros
> et breuiter Troiae supremum audire laborem,
> quamquam animus meminisse horret luctuque refugit,
> incipiam.

This is the beginning of Book II of the *Aeneid*; Aeneas, at the banquet in Carthage, tells the story of the fall of Troy. The long lines do not employ rhyme but they have a regular rhythmic pattern based not on stress, as in English verse, but on length of syllable, i.e., the time taken to pronounce it. Some vowels are naturally long and others naturally short; but a short vowel may be made long by position, i.e., if it is followed by two consonants it takes just as much time to pronounce as if it were naturally long. The line consists of six feet, either dactyl $-\cup\cup$ or spondee $--$. In the first four feet various combinations are employed, but the last two feet, except in cases where a special effect is sought, are always dactyl plus spondee.

This hexameter (six foot) line is capable of great variety, contained always in the formal pattern. Unfortunately, attempts to reproduce its disciplined variety in English stressed verse (Longfellow's "This is the forest primeval . . ." for example) have not proved successful and our translator has used a modern adaptation of the basic English line, the iambic pentameter of Shakespeare and Milton.

The subtle variation of the rhythm is not the only problem faced by the translator; he must also try to compensate for the loss of effects which depend on the flexibility of Latin word order. In English, syntactical relationship is determined by that order: "man bites dog" means the opposite of "dog bites man." In Latin, since the terminations of the nouns show who does what to whom, "man bites dog" is *vir mordet canem* and "dog bites man" *canis mordet virum*. Consequently the words can be arranged in any order with no change of meaning. *Virum canis mordet, canis virum mordet,* and any other combination of these three elements all mean the same thing: "dog bites man." But the word order is not without its force: it can indicate emphasis. Normal order—subject, object, verb (for the Latin verb tends towards the end of the sentence)—would be *canis virum mordet*. But putting *virum*, the object, first—*virum canis mordet*—would draw attention to the word: "it was a *man* the dog bit."

This is a simple example; much more complicated effects are available to a poet in extended sentences. Line 3 of the passage quoted above, for example—*Infandum, regina, iubes renovare dolorem*—uses the flexibility of word order not only for emphasis but also to explore the possibilities of ambiguity and surprise offered by a highly inflected language. *Infandum*—"unspeakable, something that cannot be said"—is the first word and we do not know from its termination whether it is subject or object nor whether it is to be understood as a noun—"an unspeakable thing"—or an adjective for which a noun will be supplied later. *Regina* ("queen") could, according to its termination, be the subject of the sentence, but the context, Aeneas' reply to the Queen's request for his story, suggests strongly that it is a form of address: "Unspeakable, oh Queen. . . ." The subject comes with the next word, the verb *iubes;* its termination shows that this is the second person, the "you" form—"you command." She has commanded something unspeakable; is the reader being prepared for a refusal on the part of Aeneas to tell his story? *Renovare* defines the Queen's order—"to renew"—and *dolorem* tells us what he is to renew—"sorrow." And the termination of this word suggests that the first word of the line *infandum,* is in fact an adjective defining *dolorem.* The line, at this last word, re-forms itself into an unexpected pattern: "Unspeakable, oh Queen, is the sorrow you command me to renew." The line is enclosed between the two most important words in Aeneas' statement, *infandum* and *dolorem;* its last word imposes upon us a slight change in our understanding of its first and so redirects attention to that solemn opening word of Aeneas' evocation of the fall of Troy, three long syllables heavy with grief for the lost splendor of a city that is now ash and rubble.

# The Aeneid[1]

## Book I

I sing of warfare and a man at war.[2]
From the sea-coast of Troy in early days
He came to Italy by destiny,
To our Lavinian western shore,[3]
A fugitive, this captain, buffeted          5
Cruelly on land as on the sea
By blows from powers of the air—behind them
Baleful Juno[4] in her sleepless rage.
And cruel losses were his lot in war,
Till he could found a city and bring home          10
His gods to Latium,[5] land of the Latin race,
The Alban lords,[6] and the high walls of Rome.
Tell me the causes now, O Muse, how galled
In her divine pride, and how sore at heart
From her old wound, the queen of gods compelled him—          15

---

1. Abridged. Translated by Robert Fitzgerald.     2. Aeneas, one of the Trojan champions in the fight for Troy, son of Aphrodite (Venus) and Anchises, a member of the royal house of Troy. Aeneas survived the fall of the city and set off in search of another home. After years of wandering he settled in Italy, and from his line sprang, in the fullness of time, the founders of Rome. 3. The west coast of Italy in the vicinity of Rome, named after the nearby city of Lavinium. Lavinia is the name of the Italian princess whom Aeneas is eventually to marry.     4. The Latin equivalent of Hera, wife of the ruler of the gods. As in the *Iliad,* she is a bitter enemy of the Trojans.     5. The coastal plain on which Rome is situated.     6. The city of Alba Longa was to be founded by Aeneas' son Ascanius, and from it were to come Romulus and Remus, the builders of Rome.

A man apart, devoted to his mission—
To undergo so many perilous days
And enter on so many trials. Can anger
Black as this prey on the minds of heaven?
Tyrian[7] settlers in that ancient time                                    20
Held Carthage,[8] on the far shore of the sea,
Set against Italy and Tiber's[9] mouth,
A rich new town, warlike and trained for war.
And Juno, we are told, cared more for Carthage
Than for any walled city of the earth,                                    25
More than for Samos,[1] even. There her armor
And chariot were kept, and, fate permitting,
Carthage would be the ruler of the world.
So she intended, and so nursed that power.
But she had heard long since                                              30
That generations born of Trojan blood
Would one day overthrow her Tyrian walls,
And from that blood a race would come in time
With ample kingdoms, arrogant in war,
For Libya's ruin: so the Parcae[2] spun.                                   35
In fear of this, and holding in memory
The old war she had carried on at Troy
For Argos'[3] sake (the origins of that anger,
That suffering, still rankled: deep within her,
Hidden away, the judgment Paris gave,[4]                                   40
Snubbing her loveliness; the race she hated;
The honors given ravished Ganymede),
Saturnian Juno,[5] burning for it all,
Buffeted on the waste of sea those Trojans
Left by the Greeks and pitiless Achilles,                                  45
Keeping them far from Latium. For years
They wandered as their destiny drove them on
From one sea to the next: so hard and huge
A task it was to found the Roman people.

---

7. From Tyre, the principal city of the Phoenicians, a seafaring people, located on the coast of
Palestine.     8. On the coast of North Africa, opposite Sicily. Originally a Tyrian colony, it
became a rich commercial center, controlling traffic in the Western Mediterranean. In the third
and second centuries B.C. Carthage fought a series of bitter wars against Rome for the domination
of the area. Carthage was captured and destroyed by the Romans in 146 B.C.     9. The river that
flows through Rome.     1. A large island off the coast of Asia Minor, famous for its cult of Hera
(Juno).     2. The Fates, who were imagined as female divinities, who spun human destinies.
*Libya:* An inclusive name for the North African coast.     3. Home city of the Achaean Kings
Agamemnon and Menelaus; Menelaus' wife Helen ran off to Troy with Paris and the Achaeans
laid siege to Troy. The goddess Hera (Juno) supported the Achaean side.     4. Paris, son to King
Priam of Troy, was chosen to judge which was the most beautiful goddess—Hera, Aphrodite, or
Athena. All three attempted to bribe him, but Aphrodite's promise, the love of Helen, prevailed
and he awarded her the prize.     5. Juno's father was Saturn (Greek Kronos). *Ganymede:* A
beautiful Trojan boy taken up into heaven by Jupiter.

## [AENEAS ARRIVES IN CARTHAGE]

[The story opens with a storm, provoked by Juno's agency, which
scatters Aeneas' fleet off Sicily and separates him from his companions. He lands on the African coast near Carthage. Setting out with
his friend Achates to explore the country, he meets his mother, Venus
(Aphrodite), who tells him that the rest of his ships are safe and
directs him to the city just founded by Dido, the queen of Carthage.
Venus surrounds Aeneas and Achates with a cloud so that they can
see without being seen.]

                       Meanwhile
The two men pressed on where the pathway led,
Soon climbing a long ridge that gave a view
Down over the city and facing towers.
Aeneas found, where lately huts had been,                          5
Marvelous buildings, gateways, cobbled ways,
And din of wagons. There the Tyrians
Were hard at work: laying courses for walls,
Rolling up stones to build the citadel,
While others picked out building sites and plowed                  10
A boundary furrow. Laws were being enacted,
Magistrates and a sacred senate chosen.
Here men were dredging harbors, there they laid
The deep foundation of a theater,
And quarried massive pillars to enhance                            15
The future stage—as bees in early summer
In sunlight in the flowering fields
Hum at their work, and bring along the young
Full-grown to beehood; as they cram their combs
With honey, brimming all the cells with nectar,                    20
Or take newcomers' plunder, or like troops
Alerted, drive away the lazy drones,
And labor thrives and sweet thyme scents the honey.
Aeneas said: "How fortunate these are
Whose city walls are rising here and now!"                         25

He looked up at the roofs, for he had entered,
Swathed in cloud—strange to relate—among them,
Mingling with men, yet visible to none.
In mid-town stood a grove that cast sweet shade
Where the Phoenicians, shaken by wind and sea,                     30
Had first dug up that symbol Juno showed them,
A proud warhorse's head: this meant for Carthage
Prowess in war and ease[6] of life through ages.
Here being built by the Sidonian[7] queen

---

6. Because they would have a land fertile enough to support horses.　　7. From Sidon, another
city of the Phoenicians.

Was a great temple planned in Juno's honor,                35
Rich in offerings and the godhead there.
Steps led up to a sill of bronze, with brazen
Lintel, and bronze doors on groaning pins.
Here in this grove new things that met his eyes
Calmed Aeneas' fear for the first time.                    40
Here for the first time he took heart to hope
For safety, and to trust his destiny more
Even in affliction. It was while he walked
From one to another wall of the great temple
And waited for the queen, staring amazed                   45
At Carthaginian promise, at the handiwork
Of artificers and the toil they spent upon it:
He found before his eyes the Trojan battles
In the old war, now known throughout the world—
The great Atridae, Priam, and Achilles,[8]                 50
Fierce in his rage at both sides. Here Aeneas
Halted, and tears came.
                        "What spot on earth,"
He said, "what region of the earth, Achatës,
Is not full of the story of our sorrow?
Look, here is Priam. Even so far away                      55
Great valor has due honor; they weep here
For how the world goes, and our life that passes
Touches their hearts. Throw off your fear. This fame
Insures some kind of refuge."
                        He broke off
To feast his eyes and mind on a mere image,               60
Sighing often, cheeks grown wet with tears,
To see again how, fighting around Troy,
The Greeks broke here, and ran before the Trojans,
And there the Phrygians[9] ran, as plumed Achilles
Harried them in his warcar. Nearby, then,                  65
He recognized the snowy canvas tents
Of Rhesus,[1] and more tears came: these, betrayed
In first sleep, Diomedes devastated,
Swording many, till he reeked with blood,
Then turned the mettlesome horses toward the beachhead    70
Before they tasted Trojan grass or drank
At Xanthus ford.

---

8. The greatest warrior on the Achaean side; he quarreled with Agamemnon (hence "rage at both sides"). *Atridae*: Sons of Atreus: Agamemnon and Menelaus.    9. Trojans.    1. King of Thrace, who came to the help of Troy just before the end of the war. An oracle proclaimed that if his horses ate Trojan grass and drank the water of the river Xanthus, Troy would not fall. Odysseus and Diomedes went into the Trojan lines at night, killed the king, and stole the horses.

                    And on another panel
Troilus,[2] without his armor, luckless boy,
No match for his antagonist, Achilles,
Appeared pulled onward by his team: he clung          75
To his warcar, though fallen backward, hanging
On to the reins still, head dragged on the ground,
His javelin scribbling S's in the dust.
Meanwhile to hostile Pallas'[3] shrine
The Trojan women walked with hair unbound,            80
Bearing the robe of offering, in sorrow,
Entreating her, beating their breasts. But she,
Her face averted, would not raise her eyes.
And there was Hector, dragged around Troy walls
Three times, and there for gold Achilles sold him,    85
Bloodless and lifeless. Now indeed Aeneas
Heaved a mighty sigh from deep within him,
Seeing the spoils, the chariot, and the corpse
Of his great friend, and Priam, all unarmed,
Stretching his hands out.
                          He himself he saw            90
In combat with the first of the Achaeans,
And saw the ranks of Dawn, black Memnon's[4] arms;
Then, leading the battalion of Amazons
With half-moon shields, he saw Penthesilëa[5]
Fiery amid her host, buckling a golden                 95
Girdle beneath her bare and arrogant breast,
A girl who dared fight men, a warrior queen.
Now, while these wonders were being surveyed
By Aeneas of Dardania,[6] while he stood
Enthralled, devouring all in one long gaze,            100
The queen paced toward the temple in her beauty,
Dido, with a throng of men behind.


As on Eurotas bank or Cynthus[7] ridge
Diana trains her dancers, and behind her
On every hand the mountain nymphs appear,             105
A myriad converging; with her quiver
Slung on her shoulders, in her stride she seems
The tallest, taller by a head than any,
And joy pervades Latona's[8] quiet heart:
So Dido seemed, in such delight she moved             110

2. A young son of Priam, killed by Achilles.    3. Athena (cf. *Iliad*, VI. 297 ff.).    4. King of
the Aethiopians, who fought on the Trojan side. *Achaeans:* Greeks.    5. Queen of the Amazons, killed by Achilles.    6. Another name for the kingdom of Troy.    7. A mountain on the
island of Delos, birthplace of Diana (Artemis), virgin goddess of the hunt. *Eurotas:* A river near
Sparta where Artemis was worshipped.    8. Leto, mother of Diana.

Amid her people, cheering on the toil
Of a kingdom in the making. At the door
Of the goddess' shrine, under the temple dome,
All hedged about with guards on her high throne,
She took her seat. Then she began to give them                      115
Judgments and rulings, to apportion work
With fairness, or assign some tasks by lot,
When suddenly Aeneas saw approaching,
Accompanied by a crowd, Antheus and Sergestus
And brave Cloanthus,[9] with a few companions,                      120
Whom the black hurricane had driven far
Over the sea and brought to other coasts.
He was astounded, and Achatës too
Felt thrilled by joy and fear: both of them longed
To take their friends' hands, but uncertainty                      125
Hampered them. So, in their cloudy mantle,
They hid their eagerness, waiting to learn
What luck these men had had, where on the coast
They left their ships, and why they came. It seemed
Spokesmen for all the ships were now arriving,                      130
Entering the hall, calling for leave to speak.
When all were in, and full permission given
To make their plea before the queen, their eldest,
Ilioneus, with composure said:
                    "Your majesty,
Granted by great Jupiter freedom to found                      135
Your new town here and govern fighting tribes
With justice—we poor Trojans, worn by winds
On every sea, entreat you: keep away
Calamity of fire from our ships!
Let a godfearing people live, and look
More closely at our troubles. Not to ravage                      140
Libyan hearths or turn with plunder seaward
Have we come; that force and that audacity
Are not for beaten men.
                    There is a country
Called by the Greeks Hesperia,[1] very old,
Potent in warfare and in wealth of earth;                      145
Oenotrians[2] farmed it; younger settlers now,
The tale goes, call it by their chief's[3] name, Italy.
We laid our course for this.
But stormy Orion[4] and a high sea rising

---

9. Ship captains of Aeneas' fleet from whom he had been separated in the storm.   1. Italy,
literally "the western country."   2. The original inhabitants of Italy.   3. Italus.   4. The
setting of this constellation in November signaled the onset of stormy weather at sea.

Deflected us on shoals and drove us far,                    150
With winds against us, into whelming waters,
Unchanneled reefs. We kept afloat, we few,
To reach your coast. What race of men is this?
What primitive state could sanction this behavior?
Even on beaches we are denied a landing,                    155
Harried by outcry and attack, forbidden
To set foot on the outskirts of your country.
If you care nothing for humanity
And merely mortal arms, respect the gods
Who are mindful of good actions and of evil!                    160

We had a king, Aeneas—none more just,
More zealous, greater in warfare and in arms.
If fate preserves him, if he does not yet
Lie spent amid the insensible shades but still
Takes nourishment of air, we need fear nothing;                    165
Neither need you repent of being first
In courtesy, to outdo us. Sicily too
Has towns and plowlands and a famous king
Of Trojan blood, Acestës. [5] May we be
Permitted here to beach our damaged ships,                    170
Hew timbers in your forest, cut new oars,
And either sail again for Latium, happily,
If we recover shipmates and our king,
Or else, if that security is lost,
If Libyan waters hold you, Lord Aeneas,                    175
Best of Trojans, hope of Iulus[6] gone,
We may at least cross over to Sicily
From which we came, to homesteads ready there,
And take Acestës for our king."
                              Ilioneus
Finished, and all the sons of Dardanus[7]                    180
Murmured assent. Dido with eyes downcast
Replied in a brief speech:
                    "Cast off your fear,
You Teucrians,[8] put anxiety aside.
Severe conditions and the kingdom's youth
Constrain me to these measures, to protect                    185
Our long frontiers with guards.
                    Who has not heard
Of the people of Aeneas, of Troy city,

5. A Sicilian king. His mother was a Trojan and he had offered Aeneas and his men a home in his dominions.    6. Ascanius, Aeneas' son.    7. Ancestor of the Trojans.    8. Another name for Trojans.

Her valors and her heroes, and the fires
Of the great war? We are not so oblivious,
We Phoenicians. The sun yokes his team                         190
Within our range[9] at Carthage. Whether you choose
Hesperia Magna and the land of Saturn
Or Eryx[1] in the west and King Acestës,
I shall dispatch you safely with an escort,
Provisioned from my stores. Or would you care                  195
To join us in this realm on equal terms?
The city I build is yours; haul up your ships;
Trojan and Tyrian will be all one to me.
If only he were here, your king himself,
Caught by the same easterly, Aeneas!                           200
Indeed, let me send out trustworthy men
Along the coast, with orders to comb it all
From one end of Libya to the other,
In case the sea cast the man up and now
He wanders lost, in town or wilderness."                       205

Elated at Dido's words, both staunch Achatës
And father Aeneas had by this time longed
To break out of the cloud. Achatës spoke
With urgency:
              "My lord, born to the goddess,
What do you feel, what is your judgment now?                   210
You see all safe, our ships and friends recovered.
One is lost;[2] we saw that one go down
Ourselves, amid the waves. Everything else
Bears out your mother's own account of it."

He barely finished when the cloud around them                  215
Parted suddenly and thinned away
Into transparent air. Princely Aeneas
Stood and shone in the bright light, head and shoulders
Noble as a god's. For she who bore him[3]
Breathed upon him beauty of hair and bloom                     220
Of youth and kindled brilliance in his eyes,
As an artist's hand gives style to ivory,
Or sets pure silver, or white stone of Paros,[4]
In framing yellow gold. Then to the queen

9. This sentence seems to mean: "we are not outside the circuit of the sun, we are part of the civilized world and hear the news."    1. On the West coast of Sicily. *Hesperia Magna:* 'Great' Westland, i.e., Italy as opposed to Sicily. *Land of Saturn:* An old legend connected Italy with Saturn (Cronos), the father of Jupiter (Zeus). The "age of Saturn" was the Golden Age.    2. One ship, captained by Orontes, was sunk in the storm in sight of Aeneas.    3. Venus (Aphrodite).
4. The marble of the island of Paros was famous.

He spoke as suddenly as, to them all,                      225
He had just appeared:
                    "Before your eyes I stand,
Aeneas the Trojan, that same one you look for,
Saved from the sea off Libya.
                              You alone,
Moved by the untold ordeals of old Troy,
Seeing us few whom the Greeks left alive,                  230
Worn out by faring ill on land and sea,
Needy of everything—you'd give these few
A home and city, allied with yourselves.
Fit thanks for this are not within our power,
Not to be had from Trojans anywhere                        235
Dispersed in the great world.
                              May the gods—
And surely there are powers that care for goodness,
Surely somewhere justice counts—may they
And your own consciousness of acting well
Reward you as they should. What age so happy              240
Brought you to birth? How splendid were your parents
To have conceived a being like yourself!
So long as brooks flow seaward, and the shadows
Play over mountain slopes, and highest heaven
Feeds the stars, your name and your distinction           245
Go with me, whatever lands may call me."

With this he gave his right hand to his friend
Ilioneus, greeting Serestus with his left,
Then took the hands of those brave men, Cloanthus,
Gyas, and the rest.
                    Sidonian Dido                          250
Stood in astonishment, first at the sight
Of such a captain, then at his misfortune,
Presently saying:
                    "Born of an immortal
Mother though you are, what adverse destiny
Dogs you through these many kinds of dangers?             255
What rough power brings you from sea to land
In savage places? Are you truly he,
Aeneas, whom kind Venus bore
To the Dardanian, the young Anchisës,
Near to the stream of Phrygian[5] Simoïs?                  260
I remember the Greek, Teucer,[6] came to Sidon,

5. Trojan.    6. A Greek warrior who fought at Troy and afterward was exiled from his home.
He founded a city on the island of Cyprus. (Not to be confused with the Trojan king, Teucer.)

Exiled, and in search of a new kingdom.
Belus, my father, helped him. In those days
Belus campaigned with fire and sword on Cyprus
And won that island's wealth. Since then, the fall          265
Of Troy, your name, and the Pelasgian[7] kings
Have been familiar to me. Teucer, your enemy,
Spoke often with admiration of the Teucrians[8]
And traced his own descent from Teucrian stock.
Come, then, soldiers, be our guests. My life              270
Was one of hardship and forced wandering
Like your own, till in this land at length
Fortune would have me rest. Through pain I've learned
To comfort suffering men."
                                        She led Aeneas
Into the royal house, but not before                      275
Declaring a festal day in the gods' temples.
As for the ships' companies, she sent
Twenty bulls to the shore, a hundred swine,
Huge ones, with bristling backs, and fatted lambs,
A hundred of them, and their mother ewes—                 280
All gifts for happy feasting on that day.

Now the queen's household made her great hall glow
As they prepared a banquet in the kitchens.
Embroidered table cloths, proud crimson-dyed,
Were spread, and set with massive silver plate,           285
Or gold, engraved with brave deeds of her fathers,
A sequence carried down through many captains
In a long line from the founding of the race.

[At the banquet which Dido gives for Aeneas, he relates, at her
request, the story of the fall of Troy.]

## Book II

### [THE FALL OF TROY]

The room fell silent, and all eyes were on him,
As Father Aeneas from his high couch began:

"Sorrow too deep to tell, your majesty,
You order me to feel and tell once more:
How the Danaans[9] leveled in the dust                     5
The splendor of our mourned-forever kingdom—
Heartbreaking things I saw with my own eyes

7. Greek.    8. Trojans.    9. Greeks.

And was myself a part of. Who could tell them,
Even a Myrmidon or Dolopian[1]
Or ruffian of Ulysses, without tears?                               10
Now, too, the night is well along, with dewfall
Out of heaven, and setting stars weigh down
Our heads toward sleep. But if so great desire
Moves you to hear the tale of our disasters,
Briefly recalled, the final throes of Troy,                         15
However I may shudder at the memory
And shrink again in grief, let me begin.

Knowing their strength broken in warfare, turned
Back by the fates, and years—so many years—
Already slipped away, the Danaan captains                           20
By the divine handicraft of Pallas built
A horse of timber, tall as a hill,
And sheathed its ribs with planking of cut pine.
This they gave out to be an offering
For a safe return by sea, and the word went round.                  25
But on the sly they shut inside a company
Chosen from their picked soldiery by lot,
Crowding the vaulted caverns in the dark—
The horse's belly—with men fully armed.

Offshore there's a long island, Tenedos,                            30
Famous and rich while Priam's kingdom lasted,
A treacherous anchorage now, and nothing more.
They crossed to this and hid their ships behind it
On the bare shore beyond. We thought they'd gone,
Sailing home to Mycenae before the wind,                            35
So Teucer's town is freed of her long anguish,
Gates thrown wide! And out we go in joy
To see the Dorian[2] campsites, all deserted,
The beach they left behind. Here the Dolopians
Pitched their tents, here cruel Achilles lodged,                    40
There lay the ships, and there, formed up in ranks,
They came inland to fight us. Of our men
One group stood marveling, gaping up to see
The dire gift of the cold unbedded goddess,[3]
The sheer mass of the horse.

                       Thymoetes shouts                45
It should be hauled inside the walls and moored
High on the citadel—whether by treason

---

1. Soldiers of Achilles. *Ulysses:* Odysseus.    2. Another name for the Greeks.    3. Athena
(Minerva) was a virgin goddess.

Or just because Troy's fate went that way now.
Capys opposed him; so did the wiser heads:
'Into the sea with it,' they said, 'or burn it,                    50
Build up a bonfire under it,
This trick of the Greeks, a gift no one can trust,
Or cut it open, search the hollow belly!'

Contrary notions pulled the crowd apart.
Next thing we knew, in front of everyone,                          55
Laocoön with a great company
Came furiously running from the Height,[4]
And still far off cried out: 'O my poor people,
Men of Troy, what madness has come over you?
Can you believe the enemy truly gone?                              60
A gift from the Danaans, and no ruse?
Is that Ulysses' way, as you have known him?
Achaeans must be hiding in this timber,
Or it was built to butt against our walls,
Peer over them into our houses, pelt                               65
The city from the sky. Some crookedness
Is in this thing. Have no faith in the horse!
Whatever it is, even when Greeks bring gifts
I fear them, gifts and all.'
                              He broke off then
And rifled his big spear with all his might                        70
Against the horse's flank, the curve of belly.
It stuck there trembling, and the rounded hull
Reverberated groaning at the blow.
If the gods' will had not been sinister,
If our own minds had not been crazed,                              75
He would have made us foul that Argive den
With bloody steel, and Troy would stand today—
O citadel of Priam, towering still!

But now look: hillmen, shepherds of Dardania,
Raising a shout, dragged in before the king                        80
An unknown fellow with hands tied behind—
This all as he himself had planned,
Volunteering, letting them come across him,
So he could open Troy to the Achaeans.
Sure of himself this man was, braced for it                        85
Either way, to work his trick or die.
From every quarter Trojans run to see him,

4. The citadel, the acropolis.

Ring the prisoner round, and make a game
Of jeering at him. Be instructed now
In Greek deceptive arts: one barefaced deed                    80
Can tell you of them all.
As the man stood there, shaken and defenceless,
Looking around at ranks of Phrygians,
'Oh god,' he said, 'what land on earth, what seas
Can take me in? What's left me in the end,                     95
Outcast that I am from the Danaans,
Now the Dardanians will have my blood?

The whimpering speech brought us up short; we felt
A twinge for him. Let him speak up, we said,
Tell us where he was born, what news he brought,               100
What he could hope for as a prisoner.
Taking his time, slow to discard his fright,
He said:
            'I'll tell you the whole truth, my lord,
No matter what may come of it. Argive
I am by birth, and will not say I'm not.                       105
That first of all: Fortune has made a derelict
Of Sinon, but the bitch
Won't make an empty liar of him, too.
Report of Palamedes⁵ may have reached you,
Scion of Belus' line, a famous man                             110
Who gave commands against the war. For this,
On a trumped-up charge, on perjured testimony,
The Greeks put him to death—but now they mourn him,
Now he has lost the light. Being kin to him,
In my first years I joined him as companion,                   115
Sent by my poor old father on this campaign,
And while he held high rank and influence
In royal councils, we did well, with honor.
Then by the guile and envy of Ulysses—
Nothing unheard of there!—he left this world,                  120
And I lived on, but under a cloud, in sorrow,
Raging for my blameless friend's downfall.
Demented, too, I could not hold my peace
But said if I had luck, if I won through
Again to Argos, I'd avenge him there.                          125
And I roused hatred with my talk; I fell
Afoul now of that man. From that time on,

---

5. A Greek warrior who advised Agamemnon to abandon the war against Troy; his downfall was
engineered by Ulysses (Odysseus), who planted forged proofs of dealings with the enemy in his
tent.

Day in, day out, Ulysses
Found new ways to bait and terrify me,
Putting out shady rumors among the troops,                     130
Looking for weapons he could use against me.
He could not rest till Calchas[6] served his turn—
But why go on? The tale's unwelcome, useless,
If Achaeans are all one,
And it's enough I'm called Achaean, then               135
Exact the punishment, long overdue;
The Ithacan[7] desires it; the Atridae
Would pay well for it.'
     Burning with curiosity,
We questioned him, called on him to explain—
Unable to conceive such a performance,                   140
The art of the Pelasgian. He went on,
Atremble, as though he feared us:
      'Many times
The Danaans wished to organize retreat,
To leave Troy and the long war, tired out.
If only they had done it! Heavy weather                  145
At sea closed down on them, for a fresh gale
From the Southwest would keep them from embarking,
Most of all after this figure here,
This horse they put together with maple beams,
Reached its full height. Then wind and thunderstorms     150
Rumbled in heaven. So in our quandary
We sent Eurypylus to Phoebus'[8] oracle,
And he brought back this grim reply:

'Blood and a virgin slain[9]
You gave to appease the winds, for your first voyage     155
Troyward, O Danaans. Blood again
And Argive blood, one life, wins your return.'

When this got round among the soldiers, gloom
Came over them, and a cold chill that ran
To the very marrow. Who had death in store?             160
Whom did Apollo call for? Now the man
Of Ithaca haled Calchas out among us
In tumult, calling on the seer to tell
The true will of the gods. Ah, there were many
Able to divine the crookedness                           165
And cruelty afoot for me, but they

6. The prophet of the Greek army.  7. Ulysses.  8. Apollo. *Eurypylus:* A minor Greek chieftain.  9. Iphigenia, Agamemnon's daughter.

Looked on in silence. For ten days the seer
Kept still, kept under cover, would not speak
Of anyone, or name a man for death,
Till driven to it at last by Ulysses' cries—                    170
By prearrangement—he broke silence, barely
Enough to designate me for the altar.
Every last man agreed. The torments each
Had feared for himself, now shifted to another,
All could endure. And the infamous day came,                    175
The ritual, the salted meal,[1] the fillets . . .
I broke free, I confess it, broke my chains,
Hid myself all night in a muddy marsh,
Concealed by reeds, waiting for them to sail
If they were going to.
                    Now no hope is left me                      180
Of seeing my home country ever again,
My sweet children, my father, missed for years.
Perhaps the army will demand they pay
For my escape, my crime here, and their death,
Poor things, will be my punishment. Ah, sir,                    185
I beg you by the gods above, the powers
In whom truth lives, and by what faith remains
Uncontaminated to men, take pity
On pain so great and so unmerited!'

For tears we gave him life, and pity, too.                      190
Priam himself ordered the gyves removed
And the tight chain between. In kindness then
He said to him:
                    'Whoever you may be,
The Greeks are gone; forget them from now on;
You shall be ours. And answer me these questions:              195
Who put this huge thing up, this horse?
Who designed it? What do they want with it?
Is it religious or a means of war?'

These were his questions. Then the captive, trained
In trickery, in the stagecraft of Achaea,                       200
Lifted his hands unfettered to the stars.
'Eternal fires of heaven,' he began,
'Powers inviolable, I swear by thee,
As by the altars and blaspheming swords
I got away from, and the gods' white bands[2]                   205

1. The paraphernalia of animal sacrifice. *Fillets* are tufts of wool attached to the victim.
2. Fillets.

I wore as one chosen for sacrifice,
This is justice, I am justified
In dropping all allegiance to the Greeks—
As I had cause to hate them; I may bring
Into the open what they would keep dark.                    210
No laws of my own country bind me now.
Only be sure you keep your promises
And keep faith, Troy, as you are kept from harm
If what I say proves true, if what I give
Is great and valuable.
              The whole hope                                215
Of the Danaans, and their confidence
In the war they started, rested all along
In help from Pallas. Then the night came
When Diomedes and that criminal,
Ulysses, dared to raid her holy shrine.                     220
They killed the guards on the high citadel
And ripped away the statue, the Palladium,[3]
Desecrating with bloody hands the virginal
Chaplets of the goddess. After that,
Danaan hopes waned and were undermined,                     225
Ebbing away, their strength in battle broken,
The goddess now against them. This she made
Evident to them all with signs and portents.
Just as they set her statue up in camp,
The eyes, cast upward, glowed with crackling flames,        230
And salty sweat ran down the body. Then—
I say it in awe—three times, up from the ground,
The apparition of the goddess rose
In a lightning flash, with shield and spear atremble.
Calchas divined at once that the sea crossing               235
Must be attempted in retreat—that Pergamum[4]
Cannot be torn apart by Argive swords
Unless at Argos first they beg new omens,
Carrying homeward the divine power
Brought overseas in ships. Now they are gone                240
Before the wind to the fatherland, Mycenae,
Gone to enlist new troops and gods. They'll cross
The water again and be here, unforeseen.
So Calchas read the portents. Warned by him,
They set this figure up in reparation                       245
For the Palladium stolen, to appease
The offended power and expiate the crime.

3. A statue of Pallas, kept in her shrine at Troy. There was an oracle which stated that Troy could
not be captured as long as it remained in place.    4. The name of the citadel of Troy.

Enormous, though, he made them build the thing
With timber braces, towering to the sky,
Too big for the gates, not to be hauled inside                    250
And give the people back their ancient guardian.
If any hand here violates this gift
To great Minerva, then extinction waits,
Not for one only—would god it were so—
But for the realm of Priam and all Phrygians.                     255
If this proud offering, drawn by your hands,
Should mount into your city, then so far
As the walls of Pelops' town[5] the tide of Asia
Surges in war: that doom awaits our children.'

This fraud of Sinon, his accomplished lying,                      260
Won us over; a tall tale and fake tears
Had captured us, whom neither Diomedes
Nor Larisaean Achilles[6] overpowered,
Nor ten long years, nor all their thousand ships.

And now another sign, more fearful still,                         265
Broke on our blind miserable people,
Filling us all with dread. Laocoön,
Acting as Neptune's[7] priest that day by lot,
Was on the point of putting to the knife
A massive bull before the appointed altar,                        270
When ah—look there!
From Tenedos, on the calm sea, twin snakes—
I shiver to recall it—endlessly
Coiling, uncoiling, swam abreast for shore,
Their underbellies showing as their crests                        275
Reared red as blood above the swell; behind
They glided with great undulating backs.
Now came the sound of thrashed seawater foaming;
Now they were on dry land, and we could see
Their burning eyes, fiery and suffused with blood,                280
Their tongues a-flicker out of hissing maws.
We scattered, pale with fright. But straight ahead
They slid until they reached Laocoön.
Each snake enveloped one of his two boys,
Twining about and feeding on the body.                            285
Next they ensnared the man as he ran up
With weapons: coils like cables looped and bound him
Twice round the middle; twice about his throat

5. Argos. Pelops was the father of Atreus.    6. So called after Larissa, a town in his homeland
of Thessaly.    7. Poseidon.

They whipped their back-scales, and their heads towered,
While with both hands he fought to break the knots,                          290
Drenched in slime, his head-bands black with venom,
Sending to heaven his appalling cries
Like a slashed bull escaping from an altar,
The fumbled axe shrugged off. The pair of snakes
Now flowed away and made for the highest shrines,                            295
The citadel of pitiless Minerva,
Where coiling they took cover at her feet
Under the rondure of her shield. New terrors
Ran in the shaken crowd: the word went round
Laocoön had paid, and rightfully,                                            300
For profanation of the sacred hulk
With his offending spear hurled at its flank.

'The offering must be hauled to its true home,'
They clamored. 'Votive prayers to the goddess
Must be said there!'
                    So we breached the walls                                305
And laid the city open. Everyone
Pitched in to get the figure underpinned
With rollers, hempen lines around the neck.
Deadly, pregnant with enemies, the horse
Crawled upward to the breach. And boys and girls                            310
Sang hymns around the towrope as for joy
They touched it. Rolling on, it cast a shadow
Over the city's heart. O Fatherland,
O Ilium, home of gods! Defensive wall
Renowned in war for Dardanus's people!                                       315
There on the very threshold of the breach
It jarred to a halt four times, four times the arms
In the belly thrown together made a sound—
Yet on we strove unmindful, deaf and blind,
To place the monster on our blessed height.                                  320
Then, even then, Cassandra's[8] lips unsealed
The doom to come: lips by a god's command
Never believed or heeded by the Trojans.
So pitiably we, for whom that day
Would be the last, made all our temples green                                325
With leafy festal boughs throughout the city.

As heaven turned, Night from the Ocean stream
Came on, profound in gloom on earth and sky

---

8. A prophetess, daughter of Priam, King of Troy. She foretold the future correctly, but no one
believed what she said (cf. Aeschylus, *Agamemnon*, 11. 1206 ff).

And Myrmidons in hiding. In their homes
The Teucrians lay silent, wearied out,                    330
And sleep enfolded them. The Argive fleet,
Drawn up in line abreast, left Tenedos
Through the aloof moon's friendly stillnesses
And made for the familiar shore. Flame signals
Shone from the command ship. Sinon, favored      335
By what the gods unjustly had decreed,
Stole out to tap the pine walls and set free
The Danaans in the belly. Opened wide,
The horse emitted men; gladly they dropped
Out of the cavern, captains first, Thessandrus,      340
Sthenelus and the man of iron, Ulysses;
Hand over hand upon the rope, Acamas, Thoas,
Neoptolemus[9] and Prince Machaon,
Menelaus and then the master builder,
Epeos, who designed the horse decoy.                    345
Into the darkened city, buried deep
In sleep and wine, they made their way,
Cut the few sentries down,
Let in their fellow soldiers at the gate,
And joined their combat companies as planned.      350

That time of night it was when the first sleep,
Gift of the gods, begins for ill mankind,
Arriving gradually, delicious rest.
In sleep, in dream, Hector appeared to me,
Gaunt with sorrow, streaming tears, all torn—        355
As by the violent car on his death day—
And black with bloody dust,
His puffed-out feet cut by the rawhide thongs.
Ah god, the look of him! How changed
From that proud Hector who returned to Troy        360
Wearing Achilles' armor,[1] or that one
Who pitched the torches on Danaan ships;
His beard all filth, his hair matted with blood,
Showing the wounds, the many wounds, received
Outside his father's city walls. I seemed              365
Myself to weep and call upon the man
In grieving speech, brought from the depth of me:

'Light of Dardania, best hope of Troy,
What kept you from us for so long, and where?

9. Son of Achilles.    1. He stripped it from the corpse of Patroclus, Achilles' close friend, whom
Hector killed in battle. Achilles revenged Patroclus by killing Hector.

From what far place, O Hector, have you come,                    370
Long, long awaited? After so many deaths
Of friends and brothers, after a world of pain
For all our folk and all our town, at last,
Boneweary, we behold you! What has happened
To ravage your serene face? Why these wounds?'               375

He wasted no reply on my poor questions
But heaved a great sigh from his chest and said:
'Ai! Give up and go, child of the goddess,
Save yourself, out of these flames. The enemy
Holds the city walls, and from her height                          380
Troy falls in ruin. Fatherland and Priam
Have their due; if by one hand our towers
Could be defended, by this hand, my own,
They would have been. Her holy things, her gods
Of hearth and household[2] Troy commends to you.            385
Accept them as companions of your days;
Go find for them the great walls that one day
You'll dedicate, when you have roamed the sea.'

As he said this, he brought out from the sanctuary
Chaplets and Vesta, Lady of the Hearth,                            390
With her eternal fire.[3]
                              While I dreamed,
The turmoil rose, with anguish, in the city.
More and more, although Anchises'[4] house
Lay in seclusion, muffled among trees,
The din at the grim onset grew; and now                           395
I shook off sleep, I climbed to the roof top
To cup my ears and listen. And the sound
Was like the sound a grassfire makes in grain,
Whipped by a Southwind, or a torrent foaming
Out of a mountainside to strew in ruin                            400
Fields, happy crops, the yield of plowing teams,
Or woodlands borne off in the flood; in wonder
The shepherd listens on a rocky peak.
I knew then what our trust had won for us,
Knew the Danaan fraud: Deïphobus'[5]                              405
Great house in flames, already caving in
Under the overpowering god of fire;
Ucalegon's already caught nearby;

---

2. The Romans kept images of household gods, the Penates, in a shrine in the home. The custom is here transferred, unhistorically, to Troy.   3. Vesta was the goddess of the hearth and fire, which, in the temple, was never allowed to go out.   4. Aeneas' father.   5. A son of Priam.

The glare lighting the straits beyond Sigeum;[6]
The cries of men, the wild calls of the trumpets.                    410

To arm was my first maddened impulse—not
That anyone had a fighting chance in arms;
Only I burned to gather up some force
For combat, and to man some high redoubt.
So fury drove me, and it came to me                                  415
That meeting death was beautiful in arms.
Then here, eluding the Achaean spears,
Came Panthus, Orthrys' son, priest of Apollo,
Carrying holy things, our conquered gods,
And pulling a small grandchild along: he ran                         420
Despairing to my doorway.
                        'Where's the crux,
Panthus,' I said. 'What strongpoint shall we hold?'

Before I could say more, he groaned and answered:
'The last day for Dardania has come,
The hour not to be fought off any longer.                            425
Trojans we have been; Ilium has been;
The glory of the Teucrians is no more;
Black Jupiter has passed it on to Argos.
Greeks are the masters in our burning city.
Tall as a cliff, set in the heart of town,                           430
Their horse pours out armed men. The conqueror,
Gloating Sinon, brews new conflagrations.
Troops hold the gates—as many thousand men
As ever came from great Mycenae; others
Block the lanes with crossed spears; glittering                      435
In a combat line, swordblades are drawn for slaughter.
Even the first guards at the gates can barely
Offer battle, or blindly make a stand.'

Impelled by these words, by the powers of heaven,
Into the flames I go, into the fight,                                440
Where the harsh Fury, and the din and shouting,
Skyward rising, calls. Crossing my path
In moonlight, five fell in with me, companions:
Ripheus, and Epytus, a great soldier,
Hypanis, Dymas, cleaving to my side                                  445
With young Coroebus, Mygdon's son. It happened
That in those very days this man had come

6. A promontory overlooking the straits which connect the Aegean with the Black Sea.

To Troy, aflame with passion for Cassandra,
Bringing to Priam and the Phrygians
A son-in-law's right hand. Unlucky one,                          450
To have been deaf to what his bride foretold!
Now when I saw them grouped, on edge for battle,
I took it all in and said briefly,
                              'Soldiers,
Brave as you are to no end, if you crave
To face the last fight with me, and no doubt of it,            455
How matters stand for us each one can see.
The gods by whom this kingdom stood are gone,
Gone from the shrines and altars. You defend
A city lost in flames. Come, let us die,
We'll make a rush into the thick of it.                          460
The conquered have one safety: hope for none.'

The desperate odds doubled their fighting spirit:
From that time on, like predatory wolves
In fog and darkness, when a savage hunger
Drives them blindly on, and cubs in lairs                        465
Lie waiting with dry famished jaws—just so
Through arrow flights and enemies we ran
Toward our sure death, straight for the city's heart,
Cavernous black night over and around us.
Who can describe the havoc of that night                         470
Or tell the deaths, or tally wounds with tears?
The ancient city falls, after dominion
Many long years. In windrows on the streets,
In homes, on solemn porches of the gods,
Dead bodies lie. And not alone the Trojans                       475
Pay the price with their heart's blood; at times
Manhood returns to fire even the conquered
And Danaan conquerors fall. Grief everywhere,
Everywhere terror, and all shapes of death.

Androgeos was the first to cross our path                        480
Leading a crowd of Greeks; he took for granted
That we were friends, and hailed us cheerfully:

'Men, get a move on! Are you made of lead
To be so late and slow? The rest are busy
Carrying plunder from the fires and towers.                      485
Are you just landed from the ships?'
                              His words
Were barely out, and no reply forthcoming

Credible to him, when he knew himself
Fallen among enemies. Thunderstruck,
He halted, foot and voice, and then recoiled                490
Like one who steps down on a lurking snake
In a briar patch and jerks back, terrified,
As the angry thing rears up, all puffed and blue.
So backward went Androgeos in panic.
We were all over them in a moment, cut                495
And thrust, and as they fought on unknown ground,
Startled, unnerved, we killed them everywhere.
So Fortune filled our sails at first. Coroebus,
Elated at our feat and his own courage,
Said:
     'Friends, come follow Fortune. She has shown        500
The way to safety, shown she's on our side.
We'll take their shields and put on their insignia!
Trickery, bravery: who asks, in war?
The enemy will arm us.'
          He put on
The plumed helm of Androgeos, took the shield        505
With blazon and the Greek sword to his side.
Ripheus, Dymas—all were pleased to do it,
Making the still fresh trophies our equipment.
Then we went on, passing among the Greeks,
Protected by our own gods now no longer;                510
Many a combat, hand to hand, we fought
In the black night, and many a Greek we sent
To Orcus.[7] There were some who turned and ran
Back to the ships and shore; some shamefully
Clambered again into the horse, to hide                515
In the familiar paunch.
           When gods are contrary
They stand by no one. Here before us came
Cassandra, Priam's virgin daughter, dragged
By her long hair out of Minerva's shrine,
Lifting her brilliant eyes in vain to heaven—        520
Her eyes alone, as her white hands were bound.
Coroebus, infuriated, could not bear it,
But plunged into the midst to find his death.
We all went after him, our swords at play,
But here, here first, from the temple gable's height,        525
We met a hail of missiles from our friends,
Pitiful execution, by their error,

7. The abode of the dead.

Who thought us Greek from our Greek plumes and shields.
Then with a groan of anger, seeing the virgin
Wrested from them, Danaans from all sides                                    530
Rallied and attacked us: fiery Ajax,[8]
Atreus' sons, Dolopians in a mass—
As, when a cyclone breaks, conflicting winds
Will come together, Westwind, Southwind, Eastwind
Riding high out of the Dawnland; forests                                     535
Bend and roar, and raging all in spume
Nereus[9] with his trident churns the deep.
Then some whom we had taken by surprise
Under cover of night throughout the city
And driven off, came back again: they knew                                   540
Our shields and arms for liars now, our speech
Alien to their own. They overwhelmed us.
Coroebus fell at the warrior goddess' altar,
Killed by Peneleus; and Ripheus fell,
A man uniquely just among the Trojans,                                       545
The soul of equity; but the gods would have it
Differently. Hypanis, Dymas died,
Shot down by friends; nor did your piety,
Panthus, nor Apollo's fillets shield you
As you went down.
         Ashes of Ilium!                                      550
Flames that consumed my people! Here I swear
That in your downfall I did not avoid
One weapon, one exchange with the Danaans,
And if it had been fated, my own hand
Had earned my death. But we were torn away                                   555
From that place—Iphitus and Pelias too,
One slow with age, one wounded by Ulysses,
Called by a clamor at the hall of Priam.
Truly we found here a prodigious fight,
As though there were none elsewhere, not a death                             560
In the whole city: Mars[1] gone berserk, Danaans
In a rush to scale the roof; the gate besieged
By a tortoise shell of overlapping shields.[2]
Ladders clung to the wall, and men strove upward
Before the very doorposts, on the rungs,                                     565
Left hand putting the shield up, and the right

8. Not the great Ajax, son of Telamon (who had killed himself before Troy fell—see *Odyssey*, Book XI), but the lesser Ajax, son of Oileus. His rape of Cassandra after dragging her away from Athena's temple was eventually punished: he was drowned on his way home. 9. An old sea-god, father of the sea-nymphs, the Nereids. 1. The Roman war-god (Ares). 2. Roman soldiers, when attacking a walled position, shielded their heads from missiles from above by a roof of interlocking shields—like the plates of a tortoise shell.

Reaching for the cornice. The defenders
Wrenched out upperworks and rooftiles: these
For missiles, as they saw the end, preparing
To fight back even on the edge of death.                    570
And gilded beams, ancestral ornaments,
They rolled down on the heads below. In hall
Others with swords drawn held the entrance way,
Packed there, waiting. Now we plucked up heart
To help the royal house, to give our men                    575
A respite, and to add our strength to theirs,
Though all were beaten. And we had for entrance
A rear door, secret, giving on a passage
Between the palace halls; in other days
Andromachë, poor lady, often used it,                    580
Going alone to see her husband's parents
Or taking Astyanax[3] to his grandfather.
I climbed high on the roof, where hopeless men
Were picking up and throwing futile missiles.
Here was a tower like a promontory                    585
Rising toward the stars above the roof:
All Troy, the Danaan ships, the Achaean camp,
Were visible from this. Now close beside it
With crowbars, where the flooring made loose joints,
We pried it from its bed and pushed it over.                    590
Down with a rending crash in sudden ruin
Wide over the Danaan lines it fell;
But fresh troops moved up, and the rain of stones
With every kind of missile never ceased.

Just at the outer doors of the vestibule                    595
Sprang Pyrrhus[4] all in bronze and glittering,
As a serpent, hidden swollen underground
By a cold winter, writhes into the light,
On vile grass fed, his old skin cast away,
Renewed and glossy, rolling slippery coils,                    600
With lifted underbelly rearing sunward
And triple tongue a-flicker. Close beside him
Giant Periphas and Automedon,
His armor-bearer, once Achilles' driver,
Besieged the place with all the young of Scyros,[5]                    605
Hurling their torches at the palace roof.
Pyrrhus shouldering forward with an axe
Broke down the stony threshold, forced apart

3. Son of Hector and Andromache.    4. Another name of Neoptolemus, the son of Achilles.
5. Island in the North Aegean where Neoptolemus grew up.

Hinges and brazen door-jambs, and chopped through
One panel of the door, splitting the oak,                          610
To make a window, a great breach. And there
Before their eyes the inner halls lay open,
The courts of Priam and the ancient kings,
With men-at-arms ranked in the vestibule.
From the interior came sounds of weeping,                          615
Pitiful commotion, wails of women
High-pitched, rising in the formal chambers
To ring against the silent golden stars;
And, through the palace, mothers wild with fright
Ran to and fro or clung to doors and kissed them.                  620
Pyrrhus with his father's brawn stormed on,
No bolts or bars or men availed to stop him:
Under his battering the double doors
Were torn out of their sockets and fell inward.
Sheer force cleared the way: the Greeks broke through              625
Into the vestibule, cut down the guards,
And made the wide hall seethe with men-at-arms—
A tumult greater than when dykes are burst
And a foaming river, swirling out in flood,
Whelms every parapet and races on                                  630
Through fields and over all the lowland plains,
Bearing off pens and cattle. I myself
Saw Neoptolemus furious with blood
In the entrance way, and saw the two Atridae;
Hecuba[6] I saw, and her hundred daughters,                        635
Priam before the altars, with his blood
Drenching the fires that he himself had blessed.
Those fifty bridal chambers, hope of a line
So flourishing; those doorways high and proud,
Adorned with takings of barbaric gold,                             640
Were all brought low: fire had them, or the Greeks.

What was the fate of Priam, you may ask.
Seeing his city captive, seeing his own
Royal portals rent apart, his enemies
In the inner rooms, the old man uselessly                          645
Put on his shoulders, shaking with old age,
Armor unused for years, belted a sword on,
And made for the massed enemy to die.
Under the open sky in a central court
Stood a big altar; near it, a laurel tree                          650

6. Wife of Priam and mother of Hector.

Of great age, leaning over, in deep shade
Embowered the Penatës.[7] At this altar
Hecuba and her daughters, like white doves
Blown down in a black storm, clung together,
Enfolding holy images in their arms.                        655
Now, seeing Priam in a young man's gear,
She called out:

   'My poor husband, what mad thought
Drove you to buckle on these weapons?
Where are you trying to go? The time is past
For help like this, for this kind of defending,              660
Even if my own Hector could be here.
Come to me now: the altar will protect us,
Or else you'll die with us.'

      She drew him close,
Heavy with years, and made a place for him
To rest on the consecrated stone.

        Now see                   665
Politës, one of Priam's sons, escaped
From Pyrrhus' butchery and on the run
Through enemies and spears, down colonnades,
Through empty courtyards, wounded. Close behind
Comes Pyrrhus burning for the death-stroke: has him,           670
Catches him now, and lunges with the spear.
The boy has reached his parents, and before them
Goes down, pouring out his life with blood.
Now Priam, in the very midst of death,
Would neither hold his peace nor spare his anger.              675

'For what you've done, for what you've dared,' he said,
'If there is care in heaven for atrocity,
May the gods render fitting thanks, reward you
As you deserve. You forced me to look on
At the destruction of my son: defiled                         680
A father's eyes with death. That great Achilles
You claim to be the son of—and you lie—
Was not like you to Priam, his enemy;
To me who threw myself upon his mercy
He showed compunction, gave me back for burial                685
The bloodless corpse of Hector, and returned me
To my own realm.'

     The old man threw his spear
With feeble impact; blocked by the ringing bronze,

---

7. The (Roman) gods of the household.

It hung there harmless from the jutting boss.
Then Pyrrhus answered:

                     'You'll report the news         690
To Pelidës,[8] my father; don't forget
My sad behavior, the degeneracy
Of Neoptolemus. Now die.'

                With this,
To the altar step itself he dragged him trembling,
Slipping in the pooled blood of his son,         695
And took him by the hair with his left hand.
The sword flashed in his right; up to the hilt
He thrust it in his body.

             That was the end
Of Priam's age, the doom that took him off,
With Troy in flames before his eyes, his towers    700
Headlong fallen—he that in other days
Had ruled in pride so many lands and peoples,
The power of Asia.

          On the distant shore
The vast trunk headless lies without a name.

For the first time that night, inhuman shuddering    705
Took me, head to foot. I stood unmanned,
And my dear father's image came to mind
As our king, just his age, mortally wounded,
Gasped his life away before my eyes.
Creusa[9] came to mind, too, left alone;        710
The house plundered; danger to little Iulus.
I looked around to take stock of my men,
But all had left me, utterly played out,
Giving their beaten bodies to the fire
Or plunging from the roof.

           It came to this,    715
That I stood there alone. And then I saw
Lurking beyond the doorsill of the Vesta,
In hiding, silent, in that place reserved,
The daughter of Tyndareus.[1] Glare of fires
Lighted my steps this way and that, my eyes    720
Glancing over the whole scene, everywhere.
That woman, terrified of the Trojans' hate
For the city overthrown, terrified too
Of Danaan vengeance, her abandoned husband's
Anger after years—Helen, that Fury        725
Both to her own homeland and Troy, had gone

---

8. Achilles, son of Peleus.    9. Aeneas' wife. *Iulus*: his son, also known as Ascanius.    1. Helen.

To earth, a hated thing,'before the altars.
Now fires blazed up in my own spirit—
A passion to avenge my fallen town
And punish Helen's whorishness.
                                        'Shall this one                    730
Look untouched on Sparta and Mycenae
After her triumph, going like a queen,
And see her home and husband, kin and children,
With Trojan girls for escort, Phrygian slaves?
Must Priam perish by the sword for this?                                  735
Troy burn, for this? Dardania's littoral
Be soaked in blood, so many times, for this?
Not by my leave. I know
No glory comes of punishing a woman,
The feat can bring no honor. Still, I'll be                               740
Approved for snuffing out a monstrous life,
For a just sentence carried out. My heart
Will teem with joy in this avenging fire,
And the ashes of my kin will be appeased.'


So ran my thoughts. I turned wildly upon her,                            745
But at that moment, clear, before my eyes—
Never before so clear—in a pure light
Stepping before me, radiant through the night,
My loving mother[2] came: immortal, tall,
And lovely as the lords of heaven know her.                              750
Catching me by the hand, she held me back,
Then with her rose-red mouth reproved me:
                                                    'Son,
Why let such suffering goad you on to fury
Past control? Where is your thoughtfulness
For me, for us? Will you not first revisit                                755
The place you left your father, worn and old,
Or find out if your wife, Creusa, lives,
And the young boy, Ascanius—all these
Cut off by Greek troops foraging everywhere?
Had I not cared for them, fire would by now                               760
Have taken them, their blood glutted the sword.
You must not hold the woman of Laconia,[3]
That hated face, the cause of this, nor Paris.
The harsh will of the gods it is, the gods,
That overthrows the splendor of this place                                765
And brings Troy from her height into the dust.

2. Venus (Aphrodite).    3. Sparta; she means Helen.

Look over there: I'll tear away the cloud
That curtains you, and films your mortal sight,
The fog around you.—Have no fear of doing
Your mother's will, or balk at obeying her.—          770
Look: where you see high masonry thrown down,
Stone torn from stone, with billowing smoke and dust,
Neptune is shaking from their beds the walls
That his great trident pried up, undermining,
Toppling the whole city down. And look:              775
Juno in all her savagery holds
The Scaean Gates,[4] and raging in steel armor
Calls her allied army from the ships.
Up on the citadel—turn, look—Pallas Tritonia[5]
Couched in a stormcloud, lightening, with her Gorgon![6]   780
The Father himself empowers the Danaans,
Urges assaulting gods on the defenders.
Away, child; put an end to toiling so.
I shall be near, to see you safely home.'

She hid herself in the deep gloom of night,            785
And now the dire forms appeared to me
Of great immortals, enemies of Troy.
I knew the end then: Ilium was going down
In fire, the Troy of Neptune[7] going down,
As in high mountains when the countrymen           790
Have notched an ancient ash, then make their axes
Ring with might and main, chopping away
To fell the tree—ever on the point of falling,
Shaken through all its foliage, and the treetop
Nodding; bit by bit the strokes prevail             795
Until it gives a final groan at last
And crashes down in ruin from the height.

Now I descended where the goddess guided,
Clear of the flames, and clear of enemies,
For both retired; so gained my father's door,       800
My ancient home. I looked for him at once,
My first wish being to help him to the mountains;
But with Troy gone he set his face against it,
Not to prolong his life, or suffer exile.

---

4. One of the principal entrances to Troy.      5. Athena (Minerva). The significance of the adjective Tritonia is not known; perhaps a reference to her birthplace, Lake Tritonis, in North Africa. (But the birthplace legend may have been invented to explain the title )      6. Monster whose appearance turned men to stone. Athena had a Gorgon face on her shield.      7. Although Neptune (Poseidon) is now one of the powers hostile to Troy, he helped to build it.

'The rest of you, all in your prime,' he said,                    805
'Make your escape; you are still hale and strong.
If heaven's lords had wished me a longer span
They would have saved this home for me. I call it
More than enough that once before I saw
My city taken and wrecked,[8] and went on living.          810
Here is my death bed, here. Take leave of me.
Depart now. I'll find death with my sword arm.
The enemy will oblige; they'll come for spoils.
Burial can be dispensed with. All these years
I've lingered in my impotence,[9] at odds                    815
With heaven, since the Father of gods and men
Breathed high winds of thunderbolt upon me
And touched me with his fire.'
                                        He spoke on
In the same vein, inflexible. The rest of us,
Creusa and Ascanius and the servants,                      820
Begged him in tears not to pull down with him
Our lives as well, adding his own dead weight
To the fates' pressure. But he would not budge,
He held to his resolve and to his chair.
I felt swept off again to fight, in misery                       825
Longing for death. What choices now were open,
What chance had I?
                        'Did you suppose, my father,
That I could tear myself away and leave you?
Unthinkable; how could a father say it?
Now if it please the powers above that nothing        830
Stand of this great city; if your heart
Is set on adding your own death and ours
To that of Troy, the door's wide open for it:
Pyrrhus will be here, splashed with Priam's blood;
He kills the son before his father's eyes,                     835
The father at the altars.
                                My dear mother,
Was it for this, through spears and fire, you brought me,
To see the enemy deep in my house,
To see my son, Ascanius, my father,
And near them both, Creusa,                                  840
Butchered in one another's blood? My gear,
Men, bring my gear. The last light calls the conquered.
Give me back to the Greeks. Let me take up

8. Troy had been captured and sacked once before, by the hero Heracles.    9. Anchises was punished by Jupiter (Zeus) for being the lover of Venus (Aphrodite), the mother of his son Aeneas. Anchises was struck by a thunderbolt and crippled.

The combat once again. We shall not all
Die this day unavenged.'
                              I buckled on                               845
Swordbelt and blade and slid my left forearm
Into the shield-strap, turning to go out,
But at the door Creusa hugged my knees,
Then held up little Iulus to his father.

'If you are going out to die, take us                                    850
To face the whole thing with you. If experience
Leads you to put some hope in weaponry
Such as you now take, guard your own house here.
When you have gone, to whom is Iulus left?
Your father? Wife?—one called that long ago.'                           855

She went on, and her wailing filled the house,
But then a sudden portent came, a marvel:
Amid his parents' hands and their sad faces
A point on Iulus' head seemed to cast light,
A tongue of flame that touched but did not burn him,                     860
Licking his fine hair, playing round his temples.
We, in panic, beat at the flaming hair
And put the sacred fire out with water;
Father Anchises lifted his eyes to heaven
And lifted up his hands, his voice, in joy:                              865

'Omnipotent Jupiter, if prayers affect you,
Look down upon us, that is all I ask,
If by devotion to the gods we earn it,
Grant us a new sign, and confirm this portent!'
The old man barely finished when it thundered                           870
A loud crack on the left. Out of the sky
Through depths of night a star fell trailing flame
And glided on, turning the night to day.
We watched it pass above the roof and go
To hide its glare, its trace, in Ida's[1] wood;                         875
But still, behind, the luminous furrow shone
And wide zones fumed with sulphur.
                              Now indeed
My father, overcome, addressed the gods,
And rose in worship of the blessed star.

'Now, now, no more delay. I'll follow you.                              880
Where you conduct me, there I'll be.

1. The mountain range near Troy.

                                    Gods of my fathers,
Preserve this house, preserve my grandson. Yours
This portent was. Troy's life is in your power.
I yield. I go as your companion, son.'
Then he was still. We heard the blazing town                    885
Crackle more loudly, felt the scorching heat.


'Then come, dear father. Arms around my neck:
I'll take you on my shoulders, no great weight.
Whatever happens, both will face one danger,
Find one safety. Iulus will come with me,                       890
My wife at a good interval behind.
Servants, give our attention to what I say.
At the gate inland there's a funeral mound
And an old shrine of Ceres the Bereft;[2]
Near it an ancient cypress, kept alive                          895
For many years by our fathers' piety.
By various routes we'll come to that one place.
Father, carry our hearthgods, our Penatës.
It would be wrong for me to handle them—
Just come from such hard fighting, bloody work—                 900
Until I wash myself in running water.'


When I had said this, over my breadth of shoulder
And bent neck, I spread out a lion skin
For tawny cloak and stooped to take his weight.
Then little Iulus put his hand in mine                          905
And came with shorter steps beside his father.
My wife fell in behind. Through shadowed places
On we went, and I, lately unmoved
By any spears thrown, any squads of Greeks,
Felt terror now at every eddy of wind,                          910
Alarm at every sound, alert and worried
Alike for my companion and my burden.
I had got near the gate, and now I thought
We had made it all the way, when suddenly
A noise of running feet came near at hand,                      915
And peering through the gloom ahead, my father
Cried out:
              'Run, boy; here they come; I see
Flame light on shields, bronze shining.'
                                          I took fright,
And some unfriendly power, I know not what,

2. Ceres (Demeter) mourning the loss of her daughter Proserpina (Persephone).

Stole all my addled wits—for as I turned                      920
Aside from the known way, entering a maze
Of pathless places on the run—
                                    Alas,
Creusa, taken from us by grim fate, did she
Linger, or stray, or sink in weariness?
There is no telling. Never would she be                       925
Restored to us. Never did I look back
Or think to look for her, lost as she was,
Until we reached the funeral mound and shrine
Of venerable Ceres. Here at last
All came together, but she was not there;                     930
She alone failed her friends, her child, her husband.
Out of my mind, whom did I not accuse,
What man or god? What crueller loss had I
Beheld, that night the city fell? Ascanius,
My father, and the Teucrian Penates,                          935
I left in my friends' charge, and hid them well
In a hollow valley.
                        I turned back alone
Into the city, cinching my bright harness.
Nothing for it but to run the risks
Again, go back again, comb all of Troy,
And put my life in danger as before:                          940
First by the town wall, then the gate, all gloom,
Through which I had come out—and so on backward,
Tracing my own footsteps through the night;
And everywhere my heart misgave me: even
Stillness had its terror. Then to our house,                  945
Thinking she might, just might, have wandered there.
Danaans had got in and filled the place,
And at that instant fire they had set,
Consuming it, went roofward in a blast;
Flames leaped and seethed in heat to the night sky.           950
I pressed on, to see Priam's hall and tower.
In the bare colonnades of Juno's shrine
Two chosen guards, Phoenix and hard Ulysses,
Kept watch over the plunder. Piled up here
Were treasures of old Troy from every quarter,                955
Torn out of burning temples: altar tables,
Robes, and golden bowls. Drawn up around them,
Boys and frightened mothers stood in line.
I even dared to call out in the night;
I filled the streets with calling; in my grief                960
Time after time I groaned and called Creusa,

Frantic, in endless quest from door to door.
Then to my vision her sad wraith appeared—
Creusa's ghost, larger than life, before me.
Chilled to the marrow, I could feel the hair                    965
On my head rise, the voice clot in my throat;
But she spoke out to ease me of my fear:

'What's to be gained by giving way to grief
So madly, my sweet husband? Nothing here
Has come to pass except as heaven willed.                    970
You may not take Creusa with you now;
It was not so ordained, nor does the lord
Of high Olympus give you leave. For you
Long exile waits, and long sea miles to plough.
You shall make landfall on Hesperia                    975
Where Lydian Tiber[3] flows, with gentle pace,
Between rich farmlands, and the years will bear
Glad peace, a kingdom, and a queen for you.
Dismiss these tears for your beloved Creusa.
I shall not see the proud homelands of Myrmidons                    980
Or of Dolopians, or go to serve
Greek ladies, Dardan lady that I am
And daughter-in-law of Venus the divine.
No: the great mother of the gods[4] detains me
Here on these shores. Farewell now; cherish still                    985
Your son and mine.'
                    With this she left me weeping,
Wishing that I could say so many things,
And faded on the tenuous air. Three times
I tried to put my arms around her neck,
Three times enfolded nothing, as the wraith                    990
Slipped through my fingers, bodiless as wind,
Or like a flitting dream.
                    So in the end
As night waned I rejoined my company.
And there to my astonishment I found
New refugees in a great crowd: men and women                    995
Gathered for exile, young—pitiful people
Coming from every quarter, minds made up,
With their belongings, for whatever lands
I'd lead them to by sea.
                    The morning star

3. The Tiber River was the center of many Etruscan settlements and the Etruscans were supposed
to be immigrants from Lydia, in Asia Minor.      4. Cybele, an Asiatic mother-goddess worshipped (according to Virgil) at Troy.

Now rose on Ida's ridges, bringing day.                        1000
Greeks had secured the city gates. No help
Or hope of help existed.
So I resigned myself, picked up my father,
And turned my face toward the mountain range."

[Aeneas goes on to tell the story of his wanderings in search of a new
home. By the end of the evening, Dido, already falling in love with
him before the banquet (through the intervention of Venus and Juno,
who both promote the affair, each for different reasons), now feels
the full force of her passion for Aeneas.]

### Book IV

#### [AENEAS ABANDONS DIDO]

The queen, for her part, all that evening ached
With longing that her heart's blood fed, a wound
Or inward fire eating her away.
The manhood of the man, his pride of birth,
Came home to her time and again; his looks,                    5
His words remained with her to haunt her mind,
And desire for him gave her no rest.
                                   When Dawn
Swept earth with Phoebus' torch and burned away
Night-gloom and damp, this queen, far gone and ill,
Confided to the sister of her heart:
"My sister Anna, quandaries and dreams                         10
Have come to frighten me—such dreams!
                              Think what a stranger

Yesterday found lodging in our house:
How princely, how courageous, what a soldier.
I can believe him in the line of gods,
And this is no delusion. Tell-tale fear                        15
Betrays inferior souls. What scenes of war
Fought to the bitter end he pictured for us!
What buffetings awaited him at sea!
Had I not set my face against remarriage
After my first love died[5] and failed me, left me             20
Barren and bereaved—and sick to death
At the mere thought of torch and bridal bed—
I could perhaps give way in this one case
To frailty. I shall say it: since that time
Sychaeus, my poor husband, met his fate,                       25

5. Her first husband, Sychaeus, was murdered by Pygmalion, king of Tyre, Dido's brother. Her
husband's ghost warned her in a dream to leave Tyre and seek a new home.

And blood my brother shed stained our hearth gods,
This man alone has wrought upon me so
And moved my soul to yield. I recognize
The signs of the old flame, of old desire.
But O chaste life, before I break your laws,                    30
I pray that Earth may open, gape for me
Down to its depth, or the omnipotent
With one stroke blast me to the shades, pale shades
Of Erebus[6] and the deep world of night!
That man who took me to himself in youth                    35
Has taken all my love; may that man keep it,
Hold it forever with him in the tomb."

At this she wept and wet her breast with tears.
But Anna answered:
                        "Dearer to your sister
Than daylight is, will you wear out your life,                    40
Young as you are, in solitary mourning,
Never to know sweet children, or the crown
Of joy that Venus brings? Do you believe
This matters to the dust, to ghosts in tombs?
Granted no suitors up to now have moved you,                    45
Neither in Libya nor before, in Tyre—
Iarbas[7] you rejected, and the others,
Chieftains bred by the land of Africa
Their triumphs have enriched—will you contend
Even against a welcome love? Have you                    50
Considered in whose lands you settled here?
On one frontier the Gaetulans,[8] their cities,
People invincible in war—with wild
Numidian[9] horsemen, and the offshore banks,
The Syrtës; on the other, desert sands,                    55
Bone-dry, where fierce Barcaean nomads[1] range.
Or need I speak of future wars brought on
From Tyre, and the menace of your brother?[2]
Surely by dispensation of the gods
And backed by Juno's will, the ships from Ilium                    60
Held their course this way on the wind.
                                Sister,
What a great city you'll see rising here,
And what a kingdom, from this royal match!
With Trojan soldiers as companions in arms

6. The lower depths of Hades.    7. The most prominent of Dido's African suitors.    8. A savage African people living southwest of Carthage.    9. The most powerful of the local tribes. Syrtes: on the coast to the west.    1. To the East.    2. Pygmalion, King of Tyre, who had murdered Dido's husband.

By what exploits will Punic[3] glory grow!                                    65
Only ask the indulgence of the gods,
Win them with offerings, give your guests ease,
And contrive reasons for delay, while winter
Gales rage, drenched Orion storms at sea,
And their ships, damaged still, face iron skies."                              70

This counsel fanned the flame, already kindled,
Giving her hesitant sister hope, and set her
Free of scruple. Visiting the shrines
They begged for grace at every altar first,
Then put choice rams and ewes to ritual death                                  75
For Ceres Giver of Laws,[4] Father Lyaeus,
Phoebus, and for Juno most of all
Who has the bonds of marriage in her keeping.
Dido herself, splendidly beautiful,
Holding a shallow cup, tips out the wine                                       80
On a white shining heifer, between the horns,
Or gravely in the shadow of the gods
Approaches opulent altars. Through the day
She brings new gifts, and when the breasts are opened
Pores over organs,[5] living still, for signs.                                 85
Alas, what darkened minds have soothsayers!
What good are shrines and vows to maddened lovers?
The inward fire eats the soft marrow away,
And the internal wound bleeds on in silence.

Unlucky Dido, burning, in her madness                                          90
Roamed through all the city, like a doe
Hit by an arrow shot from far away
By a shepherd hunting in the Cretan woods—
Hit by surprise, nor could the hunter see
His flying steel had fixed itself in her;                                      95
But though she runs for life through copse and glade
The fatal shaft clings to her side.
                         Now Dido
Took Aeneas with her among her buildings,
Showed her Sidonian[6] wealth, her walls prepared,
And tried to speak, but in mid-speech grew still.                              100

3. Carthaginian.   4. Ceres (Demeter) the goddess who guarantees the growth of crops, Lyaeus
(Dionysus-Bacchus) the wine god, and Phoebus (Apollo) are selected as deities especially connected with the founding of cities; one of Apollo's titles is "Founder," and Ceres and Dionysus
(Bacchus) control the essential crops which will enable the colonists to live. Dido prays to these
gods at the moment when she is about to abandon her responsibilities as founder of a city; a
similar irony is present in her prayer to Juno, whose "business" is the marriage-bond, at the
moment when she is about to break her long fidelity to the memory of Sychaeus.   5. An Etruscan and Roman practice was to inspect the entrails of the sacrificial victim and interpret irregular
or unusual features as signs of what the future held in store.   6. Sidon is the Phoenician city
from which Dido fled, to found Carthage.

When the day waned she wanted to repeat
The banquet as before, to hear once more
In her wild need the throes of Ilium,
And once more hung on the narrator's words.
Afterward, when all the guests were gone,                    105
And the dim moon in turn had quenched her light,
And setting stars weighed weariness to sleep,
Alone she mourned in the great empty hall
And pressed her body on the couch he left:
She heard him still, though absent—heard and saw him.        110
Or she would hold Ascanius in her lap,
Enthralled by him, the image of his father,
As though by this ruse to appease a love
Beyond all telling.
                    Towers, half-built, rose
No farther; men no longer trained in arms                    115
Or toiled to make harbors and battlements
Impregnable. Projects were broken off,
Laid over, and the menacing huge walls
With cranes unmoving stood against the sky.

[Juno proposes to Venus that Dido and Aeneas be married, which
would guarantee the unity of Carthage and Troy and peace between
Juno and Venus. Her aim is of course to ensure that the imperial
destiny reserved for Rome be transferred to Carthage. Venus, confident of the future, which has been explained to her by Jupiter, consents to the scheme. Dido organizes a hunt, which is broken up by
a storm, and Dido and Aeneas take shelter in a cave, where their
love is consummated. There is no formal marriage, but Dido henceforth feels justified in assuming the dignity and rights of a wife. Their
love is rumored abroad, and when the African prince Iarbas hears of
it, he appeals to Jupiter for satisfaction.]

                    Pleas like this                         120
From the man clinging to his altars reached
The ears of the Almighty. Now he turned
His eyes upon the queen's town and the lovers
Careless of their good name; then spoke to Mercury,[7]
Assigning him a mission:
                    "Son, bestir yourself,                 125
Call up the Zephyrs,[8] take to your wings and glide.
Approach the Dardan captain where he tarries
Rapt in Tyrian Carthage, losing sight
Of future towns the fates ordain. Correct him,

---

7. The Latin equivalent of the Greek Hermes, the divine messenger.    8. The west winds.

Carry my speech to him on the running winds:                    130
No son like this did his enchanting mother
Promise to us, nor such did she deliver
Twice from peril at the hands of Greeks.
He was to be the ruler of Italy,
Potential empire, armorer of war;                               135
To father men from Teucer's[9] noble blood
And bring the whole world under law's dominion.
If glories to be won by deeds like these
Cannot arouse him, if he will not strive
For his own honor, does he begrudge his son,                    140
Ascanius, the high strongholds of Rome?
What has he in mind? What hope, to make him stay
Amid a hostile race, and lose from view
Ausonian[1] progeny, Lavinian lands?
The man should sail: that is the whole point.                   145
Let this be what you tell him, as from me."

He finished and fell silent. Mercury
Made ready to obey the great command
Of his great father, and he first tied on
The golden sandals, winged, that high in air                    150
Transport him over seas or over land
Abreast of gale winds; then he took the wand
With which he summons pale souls out of Orcus
And ushers others to the undergloom,
Lulls men to slumber or awakens them,                           155
And opens dead men's eyes. This wand in hand,
He can drive winds before him, swimming down
Along the stormcloud. Now aloft, he saw
The craggy flanks and crown of patient Atlas,[2]
Giant Atlas, balancing the sky                                  160
Upon his peak—his pine-forested head
In vapor cowled, beaten by wind and rain.
Snow lay upon his shoulders, rills cascaded
Down his ancient chin and beard a-bristle,
Caked with ice. Here Mercury of Cyllenë[3]                      165
Hovered first on even wings, then down
He plummeted to sea-level and flew on
Like a low-flying gull that skims the shallows
And rocky coasts where fish ply close inshore.

9. First of the Trojan Kings.     1. Italian.     2. A high mountain range in western North Africa.
Virgil is referring, by the personification of the mountain, to the legend that the Titan Atlas was
punished for his part in the revolt against Zeus (Jupiter) by being made to hold up the sky on his
shoulders.     3. A mountain in Arcadia, birthplace of Hermes-Mercury.

So, like a gull between the earth and sky,                    170
The progeny of Cyllenë, on the wing
From his maternal grandsire, split the winds
To the sand bars of Libya.
                              Alighting tiptoe
On the first hutments, there he found Aeneas
Laying foundations for new towers and homes.                  175
He noted well the swordhilt the man wore,
Adorned with yellow jasper; and the cloak
Aglow with Tyrian dye upon his shoulders—
Gifts of the wealthy queen, who had inwoven
Gold thread in the fabric. Mercury                            180
Took him to task at once:
                              "Is it for you
To lay the stones for Carthage's high walls,
Tame husband that you are, and build their city?
Oblivious of your own world, your own kingdom!
From bright Olympus he that rules the gods                    185
And turns the earth and heaven by his power—
He and no other sent me to you, told me
To bring this message on the running winds:
What have you in mind? What hope, wasting your days
In Libya? If future history's glories                         190
Do not affect you, if you will not strive
For your own honor, think of Ascanius,
Think of the expectations of your heir,
Iulus, to whom the Italian realm, the land
Of Rome, are due."
                              And Mercury, as he spoke,        195
Departed from the visual field of mortals
To a great distance, ebbed in subtle air.
Amazed, and shocked to the bottom of his soul
By what his eyes had seen, Aeneas felt
His hackles rise, his voice choke in his throat.              200
As the sharp admonition and command
From heaven had shaken him awake, he now
Burned only to be gone, to leave that land
Of the sweet life behind. What can he do? How tell
The impassioned queen and hope to win her over?               205
What opening shall he choose? This way and that
He let his mind dart, testing alternatives,
Running through every one. And as he pondered
This seemed the better tactic: he called in
Mnestheus, Sergestus and stalwart Serestus,                   210
Telling them:

"Get the fleet ready for sea,
But quietly, and collect the men on shore.
Lay in ship stores and gear."
                          As to the cause
For a change of plan, they were to keep it secret,
Seeing the excellent Dido had no notion,                          215
No warning that such love could be cut short;
He would himself look for the right occasion,
The easiest time to speak, the way to do it.
The Trojans to a man gladly obeyed.

The queen, for her part, felt some plot afoot                     220
Quite soon—for who deceives a woman in love?
She caught wind of a change, being in fear
Of what had seemed her safety. Evil Rumor,[4]
Shameless as before, brought word to her
In her distracted state of ships being rigged                     225
In trim for sailing. Furious, at her wits' end,
She traversed the whole city, all aflame
With rage, like a Bacchantë[5] driven wild
By emblems shaken, when the mountain revels
Of the odd year possess her, when the cry                         230
Of Bacchus rises and Cithaeron[6] calls
All through the shouting night. Thus it turned out
She was the first to speak and charge Aeneas:

"You even hoped to keep me in the dark
As to this outrage, did you, two-faced man,                       235
And slip away in silence? Can our love
Not hold you, can the pledge we gave not hold you,
Can Dido not, now sure to die in pain?
Even in winter weather must you toil
With ships, and fret to launch against high winds                 240
For the open sea? Oh, heartless!
                          Tell me now,
If you were not in search of alien lands
And new strange homes, if ancient Troy remained,
Would ships put out for Troy on these big seas?
Do you go to get away from me? I beg you,                         245
By these tears, by your own right hand,[7] since I
Have left my wretched self nothing but that—

4. Earlier, Rumor (personified as a semi-divine being) had spread the report of Dido's "marriage" which had incited Iarbas to make his indignant prayer to Jupiter.   5. A female devotee of the god Dionysus (Bacchus), in an ecstatic trance at the Dionysian festival, held every other year.   6. Mountain near Thebes, sacred to Dionysus.   7. The handclasp with which he pledged his love and which Dido takes as an earnest of marriage.

Yes, by the marriage that we entered on,
If ever I did well and you were grateful
Or found some sweetness in a gift from me,                    250
Have pity now on a declining house!
Put this plan by, I beg you, if a prayer
Is not yet out of place.
Because of you, Libyans and nomad kings
Detest me, my own Tyrians are hostile;                    255
Because of you, I lost my integrity
And that admired name by which alone
I made my way once toward the stars.
                              To whom
Do you abandon me, a dying woman,
Guest that you are—the only name now left                    260
From that of husband? Why do I live on?
Shall I, until my brother Pygmalion comes
To pull my walls down? Or the Gaetulan
Iarbas leads me captive? If at least
There were a child by you for me to care for,                    265
A little one to play in my courtyard
And give me back Aeneas, in spite of all,
I should not feel so utterly defeated,
Utterly bereft."
                    She ended there.
The man by Jove's command held fast his eyes                    270
And fought down the emotion in his heart.
At length he answered:
                         "As for myself, be sure
I never shall deny all you can say,
Your majesty, of what you meant to me.
Never will the memory of Elissa[8]                    275
Stale for me, while I can still remember
My own life, and the spirit rules my body.
As to the event, a few words. Do not think
I meant to be deceitful and slip away.
I never held the torches of a bridegroom,                    280
Never entered upon the pact of marriage.
If Fate permitted me to spend my days
By my own lights, and make the best of things
According to my wishes, first of all
I should look after Troy and the loved relics                    285
Left me of my people. Priam's great hall
Should stand again; I should have restored the tower

8. Another name of Dido.

Of Pergamum for Trojans in defeat.
But now it is the rich Italian land
Apollo tells me I must make for: Italy,                                    290
Named by his oracles. There is my love;
There is my country. If, as a Phoenician,
You are so given to the charms of Carthage,
Libyan city that it is, then tell me,
Why begrudge the Teucrian new lands                                        295
For homesteads in Ausonia? Are we not
Entitled, too, to look for realms abroad?
Night never veils the earth in damp and darkness,
Fiery stars never ascend the east,
But in my dreams my father's troubled ghost[9]                             300
Admonishes and frightens me. Then, too,
Each night thoughts come of young Ascanius,
My dear boy wronged, defrauded of his kingdom,
Hesperian lands of destiny. And now
The gods' interpreter, sent by Jove himself—                               305
I swear it by your head and mine—has brought
Commands down through the racing winds! I say
With my own eyes in full daylight I saw him
Entering the building! With my very ears
I drank his message in! So please, no more                                 310
Of these appeals that set us both afire.
I sail for Italy not of my own free will."

During all this she had been watching him
With face averted, looking him up and down
In silence, and she burst out raging now:                                  315

"No goddess was your mother. Dardanus
Was not the founder of your family.
Liar and cheat! Some rough Caucasian[1] cliff
Begot you on flint. Hyrcanian tigresses
Tendered their teats to you. Why should I palter?                          320
Why still hold back for more indignity?
Sigh, did he, while I wept? Or look at me?
Or yield a tear, or pity her who loved him?
What shall I say first, with so much to say?
The time is past when either supreme Juno                                  325
Or the Saturnian father[2] viewed these things
With justice. Faith can never be secure.

9. Anchises had died in Sicily just before Aeneas, leaving for Italy, was blown by the storm winds to Carthage.    1. The Caucasus is a mountain range near the Caspian Sea. It had connotations of outlandishness and of cruelty. *Hyrcanian*: From the same general areas as the Caucasus. 2. Jupiter (son of Saturn).

I took the man in, thrown up on this coast
In dire need, and in my madness then
Contrived a place for him in my domain,                    330
Rescued his lost fleet, saved his shipmates' lives.
Oh, I am swept away burning by furies!
Now the prophet Apollo, now his oracles,
Now the gods' interpreter, if you please,
Sent down by Jove[3] himself, brings through the air       335
His formidable commands! What fit employment
For heaven's high powers! What anxieties
To plague serene immortals![4] I shall not
Detain you or dispute your story. Go,
Go after Italy on the sailing winds,                       340
Look for your kingdom, cross the deepsea swell!
If divine justice counts for anything,
I hope and pray that on some grinding reef
Midway at sea you'll drink your punishment
And call and call on Dido's name!                          345
From far away I shall come after you
With my black fires, and when cold death has parted
Body from soul I shall be everywhere
A shade to haunt you! You will pay for this,
Unconscionable! I shall hear! The news will reach me       350
Even among the lowest of the dead!"

At this abruptly she broke off and ran
In sickness from his sight and the light of day,
Leaving him at a loss, alarmed, and mute
With all he meant to say. The maids in waiting             355
Caught her as she swooned and carried her
To bed in her marble chamber.
                          Duty-bound,
Aeneas, though he struggled with desire
To calm and comfort her in all her pain,
To speak to her and turn her mind from grief,              360
And though he sighed his heart out, shaken still
With love of her, yet took the course heaven gave him
And went back to the fleet. Then with a will
The Teucrians fell to work and launched ships
Along the whole shore: slick with tar each hull           365
Took to the water. Eager to get away,
The sailors brought oar-boughs out of the woods
With leaves still on, and oaken logs unhewn.

3. Jupiter.    4. Dido is referring to the Epicurean idea that the gods are unaffected by human
events.

Now you could see them issuing from the town
To the water's edge in streams, as when, aware                    370
Of winter, ants will pillage a mound of spelt
To store it in their granary; over fields
The black battalion moves, and through the grass
On a narrow trail they carry off the spoil;
Some put their shoulders to the enormous weight                   375
Of a trundled grain, while some pull stragglers in
And castigate delay; their to-and-fro
Of labor makes the whole track come alive.
At that sight, what were your emotions, Dido?
Sighing how deeply, looking out and down                          380
From your high tower on the seething shore
Where all the harbor filled before your eyes
With bustle and shouts! Unconscionable Love,
To what extremes will you not drive our hearts!
She now felt driven to weep again, again                          385
To move him, if she could, by supplication,
Humbling her pride before her love— to leave
Nothing untried, not to die needlessly.

"Anna, you see the arc of waterfront
All in commotion: they come crowding in                           390
From everywhere. Spread canvas calls for wind,
The happy crews have garlanded the sterns.
If I could brace myself for this great sorrow,
Sister, I can endure it, too. One favor,
Even so, you may perform for me.                                  395
Since that deserter chose you for his friend
And trusted you, even with private thoughts,
Since you alone know when he may be reached,
Go, intercede with our proud enemy.
Remind him that I took no oath at Aulis[5]                        400
With Danaans to destroy the Trojan race;
I sent no ship to Pergamum. Never did I
Profane his father Anchises' dust and shade.
Why will he not allow my prayers to fall
On his unpitying ears? Where is he racing?                        405
Let him bestow one last gift on his mistress:
This, to await fair winds and easier flight.
Now I no longer plead the bond he broke
Of our old marriage, nor do I ask that he
Should live without his dear love, Latium,                        410

5. The harbor from which the Greek fleet left for Troy.

Or yield his kingdom. Time is all I beg,
Mere time, a respite and a breathing space
For madness to subside in, while my fortune
Teaches me how to take defeat and grieve.
Pity your sister. This is the end, this favor—                    415
To be repaid with interest when I die."

She pleaded in such terms, and such, in tears,
Her sorrowing sister brought him, time and again.
But no tears moved him, no one's voice would he
Attend to tractably. The fates opposed it;                        420
God's will blocked the man's once kindly ears.
And just as when the north winds from the Alps
This way and that contend among themselves
To tear away an oaktree hale with age,
The wind and tree cry, and the buffeted trunk                     425
Showers high foliage to earth, but holds
On bedrock, for the roots go down as far
Into the underworld as cresting boughs
Go up in heaven's air: just so this captain,
Buffeted by a gale of pleas                                       430
This way and that way, dinned all day long,
Felt their moving power in his great heart,
And yet his will stood fast; tears fell in vain.

On Dido in her desolation now
Terror grew at her fate. She prayed for death,                    435
Being heartsick at the mere sight of heaven.
That she more surely would perform the act
And leave the daylight, now she saw before her
A thing one shudders to recall: on altars
Fuming with incense where she placed her gifts,                   440
The holy water blackened, the spilt wine
Turned into blood and mire. Of this she spoke
To no one, not to her sister even. Then, too,
Within the palace was a marble shrine
Devoted to her onetime lord, a place                              445
She held in wondrous honor, all festooned
With snowy fleeces and green festive boughs.
From this she now thought voices could be heard
And words could be made out, her husband's words,
Calling her, when midnight hushed the earth;                      450
And lonely on the rooftops the night owl
Seemed to lament, in melancholy notes,
Prolonged to a doleful cry. And then, besides,

The riddling words of seers in ancient days,
Foreboding sayings, made her thrill with fear.                    455
In nightmare, fevered, she was hunted down
By pitiless Aeneas, and she seemed
Deserted always, uncompanioned always,
On a long journey, looking for her Tyrians
In desolate landscapes
                       as Pentheus[6] gone mad           460
Sees the oncoming Eumenidës and sees
A double sun and double Thebes appear,
Or as when, hounded on the stage, Orestës[7]
Runs from a mother armed with burning brands,
With serpents hellish black,                                       465
And in the doorway squat the Avenging Ones.

So broken in mind by suffering, Dido caught
Her fatal madness and resolved to die.
She pondered time and means, then visiting
Her mournful sister, covered up her plan                          470
With a calm look, a clear and hopeful brow.

"Sister, be glad for me! I've found a way
To bring him back or free me of desire.
Near to the Ocean boundary, near sundown,
The Aethiops' farthest territory lies,                            475
Where giant Atlas turns the sphere of heaven
Studded with burning stars. From there
A priestess of Massylian[8] stock has come;
She had been pointed out to me: custodian
Of that shrine named for daughters of the west,                   480
Hesperidës;[9] and it is she who fed
The dragon, guarding well the holy boughs
With honey dripping slow and drowsy poppy.
Chanting her spells she undertakes to free
What hearts she wills, but to inflict on others                   485
Duress of sad desires; to arrest
The flow of rivers, make the stars move backward,

6. King of Thebes. He persecuted the worshippers of the new god Dionysus and imprisoned the god himself. He was later mocked by the god, who inspired him with the Dionysiac spirit (and perhaps with wine) so that he saw double. In this state he was led off to his death on Cithaeron. These events are dramatized in Euripides' play *The Bacchanals (Bacchae)* but the Eumenides (Furies) are not mentioned there. Perhaps Virgil is using them simply as a symbol for madness. 7. Another reference to Greek tragedy. In the *Choephoroe* (The Libation Bearers) of Aeschylus, Orestes kills his mother Clytemnestra, and is pursued by the Furies. In other tragic contexts he is represented as pursued by the ghost of his mother. 8. From the African tribe. 9. The daughters of Hesperus, in the west, who lived in a garden which contained golden apples, guarded by a dragon.

Call up the spirits of deep Night. You'll see
Earth shift and rumble underfoot and ash trees
Walk down mountainsides. Dearest, I swear                      490
Before the gods and by your own sweet self,
It is against my will that I resort
For weaponry to magic powers. In secret
Build up a pyre in the inner court
Under the open sky, and place upon it                          495
The arms that faithless man left in my chamber,
All his clothing, and the marriage bed
On which I came to grief—solace for me
To annihilate all vestige of the man,
Vile as he is: my priestess shows me this."                    500

While she was speaking, cheek and brow grew pale.
But Anna could not think her sister cloaked
A suicide in these unheard-of rites;
She failed to see how great her madness was
And feared no consequence more grave                           505
Than at Sychaeus' death. So, as commanded,
She made the preparations. For her part,
The queen, seeing the pyre in her inmost court
Erected huge with pitch-pine and sawn ilex,
Hung all the place under the sky with wreaths                  510
And crowned it with funereal cypress boughs.
On the pyre's top she put a sword he left
With clothing, and an effigy on a couch,
Her mind fixed now ahead on what would come.
Around the pyre stood altars, and the priestess,              515
Hair unbound, called in a voice of thunder
Upon three hundred gods, on Erebus,[1]
On Chaos, and on triple Hecatë,
Three-faced Diana. Then she sprinkled drops
Purportedly from the fountain of Avernus.[2]                  520
Rare herbs were brought out, reaped at the new moon
By scythes of bronze, and juicy with a milk
Of dusky venom; then the rare love-charm
Or caul torn from the brow of a birthing foal
And snatched away before the mother found it.                  525
Dido herself with consecrated grain
In her pure hands, as she went near the altars,

1. The lowest depth of the underworld. *Chaos:* Greek personification of the disorder which preceded the creation of the universe. *Hecatë:* Title of Diana as goddess of sorcery; she is Hecatë, the moon, and Diana the virgin huntress.    2. A lake in southern Italy which was supposed to be the entrance to the lower world.

Freed one foot from sandal straps, let fall
Her dress ungirdled, and, now sworn to death,
Called on the gods and stars that knew her fate.                530
She prayed then to whatever power may care
In comprehending justice for the grief
Of lovers bound unequally by love.

The night had come, and weary in every land
Men's bodies took the boon of peaceful sleep.                535
The woods and the wild seas had quieted
At that hour when the stars are in mid-course
And every field is still; cattle and birds
With vivid wings that haunt the limpid lakes
Or nest in thickets in the country places                540
All were asleep under the silent night.
Not, though, the agonized Phoenician queen:
She never slackened into sleep and never
Allowed the tranquil night to rest
Upon her eyelids or within her heart.                545
Her pain redoubled; love came on again,
Devouring her, and on her bed she tossed
In a great surge of anger.
                         So awake,
She pressed these questions, musing to herself:

"Look now, what can I do? Turn once again                550
To the old suitors, only to be laughed at—
Begging a marriage with Numidians
Whom I disdained so often? Then what? Trail
The Ilian ships and follow like a slave
Commands of Trojans? Seeing them so agreeable,                555
In view of past assistance and relief,
So thoughtful their unshaken gratitude?
Suppose I wished it, who permits or takes
Aboard their proud ships one they so dislike?
Poor lost soul, do you not yet grasp or feel                560
The treachery of the line of Laömedon?[3]
What then? Am I to go alone, companion
Of the exultant sailors in their flight?
Or shall I set out in their wake, with Tyrians,
With all my crew close at my side, and send                565
The men I barely tore away from Tyre
To sea again, making them hoist their sails

3. A king of Troy who twice broke his promise, once to Heracles and once to Apollo and Poseidon.

To more sea-winds? No: die as you deserve,
Give pain quietus with a steel blade.
                                   Sister,
You are the one who gave way to my tears                    570
In the beginning, burdened a mad queen
With sufferings, and thrust me on my enemy.
It was not given me to lead my life
Without new passion, innocently, the way
Wild creatures live, and not to touch these depths.          575
The vow I took to the ashes of Sychaeus
Was not kept."
                   So she broke out afresh
In bitter mourning. On his high stern deck
Aeneas, now quite certain of departure,
Everything ready, took the boon of sleep.                    580
In dream the figure of the god returned
With looks reproachful as before: he seemed
Again to warn him, being like Mercury
In every way, in voice, in golden hair,
And in the bloom of youth.
                             "Son of the goddess,             585
Sleep away this crisis, can you still?
Do you not see the dangers growing round you,
Madman, from now on? Can you not hear
The offshore westwind blow? The woman hatches
Plots and drastic actions in her heart,                      590
Resolved on death now, whipping herself on
To heights of anger. Will you not be gone
In flight, while flight is still within your power?
Soon you will see the offing boil with ships
And glare with torches; soon again                           595
The waterfront will be alive with fires,
If Dawn comes while you linger in this country.
Ha! Come, break the spell! Woman's a thing
Forever fitful and forever changing."

At this he merged into the darkness. Then                    600
As the abrupt phantom filled him with fear,
Aeneas broke from sleep and roused his crewmen:
"Up, turn out now! Oarsmen, take your thwarts!
Shake out sail! Look here, for the second time
A god from heaven's high air is goading me                   605
To hasten our break away, to cut the cables.
Holy one, whatever god you are,
We go with you, we act on your command

Most happily! Be near, graciously help us,
Make the stars in heaven propitious ones!"                             610

He pulled his sword aflash out of its sheath
And struck at the stern hawser. All the men
Were gripped by his excitement to be gone,
And hauled and hustled. Ships cast off their moorings,
And an array of hulls hid inshore water                                615
As oarsmen churned up foam and swept to sea.

Soon early Dawn, quitting the saffron bed
Of old Tithonus,[4] cast new light on earth,
And as air grew transparent, from her tower
The queen caught sight of ships on the seaward reach                   620
With sails full and the wind astern. She knew
The waterfront now empty, bare of oarsmen.
Beating her lovely breast three times, four times,
And tearing her golden hair,
                              "O Jupiter,"
She said, "will this man go, will he have mocked                       625
My kingdom, stranger that he was and is?
Will they not snatch up arms and follow him
From every quarter of the town? and dockhands
Tear out ships from moorings? On! Be quick
With torches! Give out arms! Unship the oars!                          630
What am I saying? Where am I? What madness
Takes me out of myself? Dido, poor soul,
Your evil doing has come home to you.
Then was the right time, when you offered him
A royal scepter. See the good faith and honor                          635
Of one they say bears with him everywhere
The hearthgods of his country! One who bore
His father, spent with age, upon his shoulders!
Could I not then have torn him limb from limb
And flung the pieces on the sea? His company,                          640
Even Ascanius could I not have minced
And served up to his father at a feast?
The luck of battle might have been in doubt—
So let it have been! Whom had I to fear,
Being sure to die? I could have carried torches                        645
Into his camp, filled passage ways with flame,
Annihilated father and son and followers
And given my own life on top of all!

4. Human consort of Eos-Aurora, the dawn-goddess. He is "old" because although she made him immortal when she took him to her bed, she forgot to obtain for him the gift of eternal youth.

O Sun, scanning with flame all works of earth,
And thou, O Juno, witness and go-between 650
Of my long miseries; and Hecatë,
Screeched for at night at crossroads in the cities;
And thou, avenging Furies, and all gods
On whom Elissa dying may call: take notice,
Overshadow this hell with your high power, 655
As I deserve, and hear my prayer!
If by necessity that impious wretch
Must find his haven and come safe to land,
If so Jove's destinies require, and this,
His end in view, must stand, yet all the same 660
When hard beset in war by a brave people,
Forced to go outside his boundaries
And torn from Iulus, let him beg assistance,
Let him see the unmerited deaths of those
Around and with him, and accepting peace 665
On unjust terms, let him not, even so,
Enjoy his kingdom or the life he longs for,
But fall in battle before his time and lie
Unburied on the sand![5] This I implore,
This is my last cry, as my last blood flows. 670
Then, O my Tyrians, besiege with hate
His progeny and all his race to come:
Make this your offering to my dust. No love,
No pact must be between our peoples;[6] No,
But rise up from my bones, avenging spirit![7] 675
Harry with fire and sword the Dardan countrymen
Now, or hereafter, at whatever time
The strength will be afforded. Coast with coast
In conflict, I implore, and sea with sea,
And arms with arms: may they contend in war, 680
Themselves and all the children of their children!"

Now she took thought of one way or another,
At the first chance, to end her hated life,
And briefly spoke to Barcë, who had been

5. This prophecy of Dido's, expressed in the form of a wish, is destined to come true. Aeneas meets resistance in Italy; at one point in the war he has to leave Ascanius behind and go to beg aid from an Italian king, Evander. The final peace is made on condition that the name of his people be changed from "Trojans" to "Latins"; and he is eventually drowned in an Italian river. Aeneas' reward for all his struggles is to come not during his life, but in the glory of the generations which succeed him.  6. In fact, the Romans and Carthaginians fought three separate wars (called Punic Wars from the Roman word for the Carthaginians). Rome won them all (though she almost lost the second one): after the third, the city of Carthage was razed to the ground. 7. Dido foresees the harrying of Italy by the Carthaginian general Hannibal, who in the third century B.C. invaded Italy, defeating the Romans in battle after battle, but failed to capture Rome.

Sychaeus' nurse; her own an urn of ash                685
Long held in her ancient fatherland.
                                      "Dear nurse,
Tell Sister Anna to come here, and have her
Quickly bedew herself with running water
Before she brings out victims for atonement.
Let her come that way. And you, too, put on       690
Pure wool around your brows. I have a mind
To carry out that rite to Stygian Jove[8]
That I have readied here, and put an end
To my distress, committing to the flames
The pyre of that miserable Dardan."              695

At this with an old woman's eagerness
Barcë hurried away. And Dido's heart
Beat wildly at the enormous thing afoot.
She rolled her bloodshot eyes, her quivering cheeks
Were flecked with red as her sick pallor grew      700
Before her coming death. Into the court
She burst her way, then at her passion's height
She climbed the pyre and bared the Dardan sword—
A gift desired once, for no such need.
Her eyes now on the Trojan clothing there        705
And the familiar bed, she paused a little,
Weeping a little, mindful, then lay down
And spoke her last words:
                       "Remnants dear to me
While god and fate allowed it, take this breath
And give me respite from these agonies.         710
I lived my life out to the very end
And passed the stages Fortune had appointed.
Now my tall shade goes to the under world.
I built a famous town, saw my great walls,
Avenged my husband, made my hostile brother   715
Pay for his crime. Happy, alas, too happy,
If only the Dardanian keels had never
Beached on our coast." And here she kissed the bed.
"I die unavenged," she said, "but let me die.
This way, this way,[9] a blessed relief to go      720
Into the undergloom. Let the cold Trojan,
Far at sea, drink in this conflagration
And take with him the omen of my death!"

---

8. Jove (Jupiter) as lord of the Underworld, where flowed the river Styx.   9. In Latin *sic, sic*—
the repetition represents the two thrusts of the sword.

Amid these words her household people saw her
Crumpled over the steel blade, and the blade                    725
Aflush with red blood, drenched her hands. A scream
Pierced the high chambers. Now through the shocked city
Rumor went rioting, as wails and sobs
With women's outcry echoed in the palace
And heaven's high air gave back the beating din,               730
As though all Carthage or old Tyre fell
To storming enemies,[1] and, out of hand,
Flames billowed on the roofs of men and gods.
Her sister heard the trembling, faint with terror,
Lacerating her face, beating her breast,                        735
Ran through the crowd to call the dying queen:

"It came to this, then, sister? You deceived me?
The pyre meant this, altars and fires meant this?
What shall I mourn first, being abandoned? Did you
Scorn your sister's company in death?                           740
You should have called me out to the same fate!
The same blade's edge and hurt, at the same hour,
Should have taken us off. With my own hands
Had I to build this pyre, and had I to call
Upon our country's gods, that in the end                       745
With you placed on it there, O heartless one,
I should be absent? You have put to death
Yourself and me, the people and the fathers
Bred in Sidon, and your own new city.
Give me fresh water, let me bathe her wound                    750
And catch upon my lips any last breath
Hovering over hers."
                          Now she had climbed
The topmost steps and took her dying sister
Into her arms to cherish, with a sob,
Using her dress to stanch the dark blood flow.                 755
But Dido trying to lift her heavy eyes
Fainted again. Her chest-wound whistled air.
Three times she struggled up on one elbow
And each time fell back on the bed. Her gaze
Went wavering as she looked for heaven's light                 760
And groaned at finding it. Almighty Juno,
Filled with pity for this long ordeal
And difficult passage, now sent Iris[2] down

1. These lines prefigure the capture and destruction of Carthage in the Third Punic War (146 B.C.).    2. As in Homer, a divine messenger. Sometimes identified with the rainbow (hence "humid Iris" l. 771 below).

Out of Olympus to set free
The wrestling spirit from the body's hold.                                            765
For since she died, not at her fated span
Nor as she merited, but before her time
Enflamed and driven mad, Proserpina[3]
Had not yet plucked from her the golden hair,
Delivering her to Orcus of the Styx.                                                  770
So humid Iris through bright heaven flew
On saffron-yellow wings, and in her train
A thousand hues shimmered before the sun.
At Dido's head she came to rest.
                                        "This token
Sacred to Dis[4] I bear away as bidden                                                775
And free you from your body."
                                        Saying this,
She cut a lock of hair. Along with it
Her body's warmth fell into dissolution,
And out into the winds her life withdrew.

[After his hurried departure from Carthage, Aeneas goes to Sicily, to the kingdom of his friend Acestes. There he organizes funeral games in honor of his father, Anchises (who had died in Sicily on their first visit there), and leaves behind those of his following who are unwilling to go on to the uncertainty of a settlement in Italy. Once on Italian soil, Aeneas, obeying instructions from his dead father who had appeared to him in a dream, consults the Sibyl, who guides him down to the world of the dead. There he is to see his father and the vision of his race, which is to be his only reward, for he will die before his people are settled in their new home.]

## Book VI

### [AENEAS IN THE UNDERWORLD]

Gods who rule the ghosts; all silent shades;
And Chaos and infernal Fiery Stream,[5]
And regions of wide night without a sound,
May it be right to tell what I have heard,
May it be right, and fitting, by your will,                                          5
That I describe the deep world sunk in darkness
Under the earth.

---

3. The queen of the underworld. Before an animal was sacrificed, some hair was cut from the forehead: before a human being died, Proserpina (Persephone) was thought to cut a lock of hair as an offering to Dis, the god of the underworld. Since Dido by her suicide has anticipated her fated day, Proserpina cannot cut the lock; Juno sends Iris to do it.   4. Roman name for Greek Hades, god of the underworld.   5. A translation of *Phlegethon*, the name of one of the Underworld rivers.

Now dim to one another
In desolate night they[6] walked on through the gloom,
Through Dis's homes all void, and empty realms,
As one goes through a wood by a faint moon's 10
Treacherous light, when Jupiter veils the sky
And black night blots the colors of the world.
Before the entrance, in the jaws of Orcus,
Grief and avenging Cares have made their beds,
And pale Diseases and sad Age are there, 15
And Dread, and Hunger that sways men to crime,
And sordid Want—in shapes to affright the eyes—
And Death and Toil and Death's own brother, Sleep,
And the mind's evil joys; on the door sill
Death-bringing War, and iron cubicles 20
Of the Eumenidës, and raving Discord,
Viperish hair bound up in gory bands.
In the courtyard a shadowy giant elm
Spreads ancient boughs, her ancient arms where dreams,
False dreams, the old tale goes, beneath each leaf 25
Cling and are numberless. There, too,
About the doorway forms of monsters crowd—
Centaurs,[7] twiformed Scyllas, hundred-armed
Briareus, and the Lernaean hydra[8]
Hissing horribly, and the Chimaera 30
Breathing dangerous flames, and Gorgons, Harpies,[9]
Huge Geryon,[1] triple-bodied ghost.
Here, swept by sudden fear, drawing his sword,
Aeneas stood on guard with naked edge
Against them as they came. If his companion, 35
Knowing the truth, had not admonished him
How faint these lives were—empty images
Hovering bodiless—he had attacked
And cut his way through phantoms, empty air.

The path goes on from that place to the waves 40
Of Tartarus's Acheron.[2] Thick with mud,
A whirlpool out of a vast abyss
Boils up and belches all the silt it carries

6. Aeneas and the Sibyl.    7. Mythical creatures, half man, half horse—a byword for violence.
*Scyllas:* Many-headed monsters. *Briareus* had fifty heads.    8. Many-headed serpent killed by
Heracles. Each time one head was cut off, two new ones grew in its place. *Chimaera:* One-third
lion, one-third goat, one-third snake.    9. Not, here, the creatures which carried off the food of
Phineus' table but spirits of the storm wind which carry souls off to Hades. *Gorgons:* Monsters
whose look could turn people to stone.    1. A giant with three bodies: an opponent of
Heracles.    2. One of the rivers of the underworld. *Tartarus:* The lower depths of the underworld.

Into Cocytus.[3] Here the ferryman,
A figure of fright, keeper of waters and streams,                    45
Is Charon,[4] foul and terrible, his beard
Grown wild and hoar, his staring eyes all flame,
His sordid cloak hung from a shoulder knot.
Alone he poles his craft and trims the sails
And in his rusty hull ferries the dead,                              50
Old now—but old age in the gods is green.

Here a whole crowd came streaming to the banks,
Mothers and men, the forms with all life spent
Of heroes great in valor, boys and girls
Unmarried, and young sons laid on the pyre                          55
Before their parents' eyes—as many souls
As leaves that yield their hold on boughs and fall
Through forests in the early frost of autumn,
Or as migrating birds from the open sea
That darken heaven when the cold season comes                       60
And drives them overseas to sunlit lands.
There all stood begging to be first across
And reached out longing hands to the far shore.

But the grim boatman now took these aboard,
Now those, waving the rest back from the strand.                    65
In wonder at this and touched by the commotion,
Aeneas said:
            "Tell me, Sister, what this means,
The crowd at the stream. Where are the souls bound?
How are they tested, so that these turn back,
While those take oars to cross the dead-black water?"               70

Briefly the ancient priestess answered him:

"Cocytus is the deep pool that you see,
The swamp of Styx beyond, infernal power
By which the gods take oath and fear to break it.
All in the nearby crowd you notice here                             75
Are pauper souls of the unburied.
Charon's the boatman. Those the water bears
Are souls of buried men. He may not take them
Shore to dread shore on the hoarse currents there
Until their bones rest in the grave, or till                        80

3. Another infernal river. The name suggests in Greek, "mourning," "lamentation."   4. The
ferryman who took the souls across the river. He is a god, and very old, but age in gods does not
affect their vitality or strength ("old age in the gods is green").

They flutter and roam this side a hundred years;
They may have passage then, and may return
To cross the deeps they long for."

                        Anchises' son
Had halted, pondering on so much, and stood
In pity for the souls' hard lot. Among them          85
He saw two sad ones of unhonored death,
Leucaspis and the Lycian fleet's commander,
Orontës,[5] who had sailed the windy sea
From Troy together, till the Southern gale
Had swamped and whirled them down, both ship and men.    90
Of a sudden he saw his helmsman, Palinurus,
Going by, who but a few nights before
On course from Libya, as he watched the stars,
Had been pitched overboard astern. As soon
As he made sure of the disconsolate one          95
In all the gloom, Aeneas called:

                      "Which god
Took you away from us and put you under,
Palinurus? Tell me. In this one prophecy
Apollo, who had never played me false,
Falsely foretold you'd be unharmed at sea        100
And would arrive at the Ausonian coast.
Is the promise kept?"

                But the shade said:

                          "Phoebus' caldron[6]
Told you no lie, my captain, and no god
Drowned me at sea. The helm that I hung on to,
Duty bound to keep our ship on course,        105
By some great shock chanced to be torn away,
And I went with it overboard. I swear
By the rough sea, I feared less for myself
Than for your ship: with rudder gone and steersman
Knocked overboard, it might well come to grief        110
In big seas running. Three nights, heavy weather
Out of the South on the vast water tossed me.
On the fourth dawn, I sighted Italy
Dimly ahead, as a wave-crest lifted me.
By turns I swam and rested, swam again        115
And got my footing on the beach, but savages
Attacked me as I clutched at a cliff-top,
Weighted down by my wet clothes. Poor fools,

---

5. Trojans lost at sea in the storm which took Aeneas to Carthage.    6. The Pythia, priestess of
Apollo at Delphi, delivered the god's prophecies seated on a tripod, a three-legged shallow caldron.

They took me for a prize and ran me through.
Surf has me now, and sea winds, washing me                    120
Close inshore.
          By heaven's happy light
And the sweet air, I beg you, by your father,
And by your hopes of Iulus' rising star,
Deliver me from this captivity,
Unconquered friend! Throw earth on me—you can—      125
Put in to Velia[7] port! Or if there be
Some way to do it, if your goddess mother
Shows a way—and I feel sure you pass
These streams and Stygian marsh by heaven's will—
Give this poor soul your hand, take me across,                130
Let me at least in death find quiet haven."
When he had made his plea, the Sibyl said:
"From what source comes this craving, Palinurus?
Would you though still unburied see the Styx
And the grim river of the Eumenidës,                         135
Or even the river bank, without a summons?
Abandon hope by prayer to make the gods
Change their decrees. Hold fast to what I say
To comfort your hard lot: neighboring folk
In cities up and down the coast will be                      140
Induced by portents to appease your bones,
Building a tomb and making offerings there
On a cape forever named for Palinurus."


The Sibyl's words relieved him, and the pain
Was for a while dispelled from his sad heart,               145
Pleased at the place-name. So the two walked on
Down to the stream. Now from the Stygian water
The boatman, seeing them in the silent wood
And headed for the bank, cried out to them
A rough uncalled-for challenge:
                              "Who are you                   150
In armor, visiting our rivers? Speak
From where you are, stop there, say why you come.
This is the region of the Shades, and Sleep,
And drowsy Night. It breaks eternal law
For the Stygian craft to carry living bodies.               155
Never did I rejoice, I tell you, letting
Alcidës[8] cross, or Theseus and Pirithous,

7. South of the Bay of Naples, near Cape Palinuro (which is still named after Aeneas' pilot).
8. Heracles. One of his labors was to bring Cerberus, the watchdog of Hades, up from the lower
world. *Theseus . . . Pirithoüs*: They came to kidnap Proserpina (Persephone): they failed and were
imprisoned but Heracles rescued Theseus.

Demigods by paternity though they were,
Invincible in power. One forced in chains
From the king's own seat the watchdog of the dead          160
And dragged him away trembling. The other two
Were bent on carrying our lady off
From Dis's chamber."
                        This the prophetess
And servant of Amphrysian Apollo[9]
Briefly answered:
                        "Here are no such plots,          165
So fret no more. These weapons threaten nothing.
Let the great watchdog at the door howl on
Forever terrifying the bloodless shades.
Let chaste Proserpina remain at home
In her uncle's house. The man of Troy, Aeneas,           170
Remarkable for loyalty, great in arms,
Goes through the deepest shades of Erebus
To see his father.
                        If the very image
Of so much goodness moves you not at all,
Here is a bough"[1]—at this she showed the bough         175
That had been hidden, held beneath her dress—
"You'll recognize it."
                        Then his heart, puffed up
With rage, subsided. They had no more words.
His eyes fixed on the ancient gift, the bough,
The destined gift, so long unseen, now seen,             180
He turned his dusky craft and made for shore.
There from the long thwarts where they sat he cleared
The other souls and made the gangway wide,
Letting the massive man step in the bilge.
The leaky coracle groaned at the weight                  185
And took a flood of swampy water in.
At length, on the other side, he put ashore
The prophetess and hero in the mire,
A formless ooze amid the grey-green sedge.
Great Cerberus barking with his triple throat            190
Makes all that shoreline ring, as he lies huge
In a facing cave. Seeing his neck begin
To come alive with snakes, the prophetess
Tossed him a lump of honey and drugged meal
To make him drowse. Three ravenous gullets gaped         195

9. An elaborate learned allusion. Apollo had once served as herdsman to King Admetus on the
banks of the river Amphrysus in Thessaly.    1. The golden bough which Aeneas had been ordered
to take as tribute to Proserpina.

And he snapped up the sop. Then his great bulk
Subsided and lay down through all the cave.
Now seeing the watchdog deep in sleep, Aeneas
Took the opening: swiftly he turned away
From the river over which no soul returns.                                    200

Now voices crying loud were heard at once—
The souls of infants wailing. At the door
Of the sweet life they were to have no part in,
Torn from the breast, a black day took them off
And drowned them all in bitter death. Near these                              205
Were souls falsely accused, condemned to die.
But now without a judge, or jurymen,
Had these souls got their places: Minos[2] reigned
As the presiding judge, moving the urn,
And called a jury of the silent ones                                          210
To learn of lives and accusations. Next
Were those sad souls, benighted, who contrived
Their own destruction, and as they hated daylight,
Cast their lives away. How they would wish
In the upper air now to endure the pain                                       215
Of poverty and toil! But iron law
Stands in the way, since the drear hateful swamp
Has pinned them down here, and the Styx that winds
Nine times around exerts imprisoning power.
Not far away, spreading on every side,                                        220
The Fields of Mourning came in view, so called
Since here are those whom pitiless love consumed
With cruel wasting, hidden on paths apart
By myrtle woodland growing overhead.
In death itself, pain will not let them be.                                   225
He saw here Phaedra, Procris, Eriphylë[3]
Sadly showing the wounds her hard son gave;
Evadnë and Pasiphaë, at whose side
Laodamia[4] walked, and Caeneus,[5]

2. King of Crete, now judge of the dead. *The urn:* The magistrate of a Roman court decided the
order in which cases were to be heard by drawing lots from an urn. *Silent ones:* The dead.
3. She betrayed her husband for gold and was killed by her own son. *Phaedra:* Wife of Theseus,
king of Athens, who fell in love with Hippolytus, her husband's son by another woman; the result
was her death by suicide and Hippolytus' death through his father's curse. *Procris:* Killed by her
husband in an accident which was brought about by her own jealousy.    4. She begged to be
allowed to talk with her dead husband; the request was granted by the gods and when his time
came to return, she went back with him to the land of the dead. *Evadnë:* Threw herself on the
pyre of her husband, who was killed by Zeus for impiety. *Pasiphaë:* Wife of Minos of Crete, she
conceived a monstrous love for a bull, and gave birth to the Minotaur.    5. Virgil's words in the
original are ambiguous (perhaps to reflect the ambiguity of the sex of Caeneus). The usual explanation of the passage is that Caenis (a woman) was changed by Poseidon into a man (Caeneus)
but returned to her original sex after death. Since the name occurs here in a catalogue of women,
this seems the most likely explanation.

A young man once, a woman now, and turned                                    230
Again by fate into the older form.
Among them, with her fatal wound still fresh,
Phoenician Dido wandered the deep wood.
The Trojan captain paused nearby and knew
Her dim form in the dark, as one who sees,                                   235
Early in the month, or thinks to have seen, the moon
Rising through cloud, all dim. He wept and spoke
Tenderly to her:
                    "Dido, so forlorn,
The story then that came to me was true,
That you were out of life, had met your end                                  240
By your own hand. Was I, was I the cause?
I swear by heaven's stars, by the high gods,
By any certainty below the earth,
I left your land against my will, my queen.
The gods' commands drove me to do their will,                                245
As now they drive me through this world of shades,
These mouldy waste lands and these depths of night.
And I could not believe that I would hurt you
So terribly by going. Wait a little.
Do not leave my sight.                                                       250
Am I someone to flee from? The last word
Destiny lets me say to you is this."

Aeneas with such pleas tried to placate
The burning soul, savagely glaring back,
And tears came to his eyes. But she had turned                               255
With gaze fixed on the ground as he spoke on,
Her face no more affected than if she were
Immobile granite or Marpesian[6] stone.
At length she flung away from him and fled,
His enemy still, into the shadowy grove                                      260
Where he whose bride she once had been, Sychaeus,
Joined in her sorrows and returned her love.
Aeneas still gazed after her in tears,
Shaken by her ill fate and pitying her.

[After being shown a pageant of the great Romans who will make
Rome mistress of the world, Aeneas returns to the upper air and
begins his settlement in Italy. He is offered the hand of the princess
Lavinia by her father Latinus, but this provokes a war against the
Trojans, led by King Turnus of Laurentum, in the course of which
Aeneas is wounded and stops by a stream to rest. At this point his

6. Marpessa was a marble quarry on the island of Paros.

mother, Venus, comes to him with the armor made for him by Vulcan (Hephaestus), her husband; on the shield is carved a representation of the future glories of Rome.]

## Book VIII

### [THE SHIELD OF AENEAS]

Venus the gleaming goddess,
Bearing her gifts, came down amid high clouds
And far away still, in a vale apart,
Sighted her son beside the ice-cold stream.
Then making her appearance as she willed                    5
She said to him:
         "Here are the gifts I promised,
Forged to perfection by my husband's craft,
So that you need not hesitate to challenge
Arrogant Laurentines or savage Turnus,
However soon, in battle."
             As she spoke                    10
Cytherëa[7] swept to her son's embrace
And placed the shining arms before his eyes
Under an oak tree. Now the man in joy
At a goddess' gifts, at being so greatly honored,
Could not be satisfied, but scanned each piece              15
In wonder and turned over in his hands
The helmet with its terrifying plumes
And gushing flames, the sword-blade edged with fate,
The cuirass of hard bronze, blood-red and huge—
Like a dark cloud burning with sunset light                 20
That sends a glow for miles—the polished greaves[8]
Of gold and silver alloy, the great spear,
And finally the fabric of the shield
Beyond description.
         There the Lord of Fire,
Knowing the prophets, knowing the age to come,             25
Had wrought the future story of Italy,
The triumphs of the Romans: there one found
The generations of Ascanius' heirs,
The wars they fought, each one. Vulcan[9] had made
The mother wolf,[1] lying in Mars' green grotto;            30

7. A title of Venus, who was born from the sea-foam off the Greek island of Cythera.    8. Leg pieces.    9. Hephaestus, the "Lord of Fire."    1. The twins who were to build Rome, Romulus and Remus, sons of Mars the war-god, were cast out into the woods, and there suckled by a she-wolf.

Made the twin boys at play about her teats,
Nursing the mother without fear, while she
Bent round her smooth neck fondling them in turn
And shaped their bodies with her tongue.
                                                    Nearby,
Rome had been added by the artisan,                                    35
And Sabine women[2] roughly carried off
Out of the audience at the Circus games;
Then suddenly a new war coming on
To pit the sons of Romulus against
Old Tatius[3] and his austere town of Curës.                           40
Later the same kings, warfare laid aside,
In arms before Jove's altar stood and held
Libation dishes as they made a pact
With offering of wine. Not far from this
Two four-horse war-cars, whipped on, back to back,                     45
Had torn Mettus[4] apart (still, man of Alba,
You should have kept your word) and Roman Tullus
Dragged the liar's rags of flesh away
Through woods where brambles dripped a bloody dew.
There, too, Porsenna[5] stood, ordering Rome                           50
To take the exiled Tarquin back, then bringing
The whole city under massive siege.
There for their liberty Aeneas' sons
Threw themselves forward on the enemy spears.
You might have seen Porsenna imaged there                              55
To the life, a menacing man, a man in anger
At Roman daring: Cocles[6] who downed the bridge,
Cloelia who broke her bonds and swam the river.

On the shield's upper quarter Manlius,[7]
Guard of the Tarpeian Rock, stood fast                                 60
Before the temple and held the Capitol,
Where Romulus' house[8] was newly thatched and rough.
Here fluttering through gilded porticos

2. The newly founded city of Rome consisted almost entirely of men; the Romans decided to steal the wives of their neighbors, the Sabines. They invited them to an athletic festival and at a given signal, every Roman carried off a Sabine bride. The war which followed ended in the amalgamation of the Roman and Sabine peoples.   3. A Sabine king.   4. Of Alba. He broke an agreement made during the early wars of Rome and was punished by being torn apart by two chariots moving in opposite directions. *Tullus:* The Roman king who punished Mettus.   5. The Etruscan king who attempted to restore the last of the Roman kings, Tarquin, to the throne from which he had been expelled.   6. Horatius Cocles, who with two companions defended the bridge across the Tiber to give the Romans time to destroy it. *Cloelia:* A Roman hostage held by Porsenna.   7. Consul in 392 B.C.; he was in charge of the citadel ("Tarpeian Rock") at a time when the Gauls from the north held all the rest of the city. They made a night attack on the citadel, but Manlius, awakened by the cackling of the sacred geese, beat it off, and saved Rome.   8. In Virgil's time there was still preserved at Rome a rustic building which was supposed to have been the dwelling place of Romulus.

At night, the silvery goose warned of the Gauls
Approaching: under cover of the darkness                    65
Gauls amid the bushes had crept near
And now lay hold upon the citadel.
Golden locks they had and golden dress,
Glimmering with striped cloaks, their milky necks
Entwined with gold. They hefted Alpine spears,             70
Two each, and had long body shields for cover.
Vulcan had fashioned naked Luperci
And Salii[9] leaping there with woolen caps
And fallen-from-heaven shields, and put chaste ladies
Riding in cushioned carriages through Rome                 75
With sacred images. At a distance then
He pictured the deep hell of Tartarus,
Dis's high gate, crime's punishments, and, yes,
You, Catiline,[1] on a precarious cliff
Hanging and trembling at the Furies' glare.                80
Then, far away from this, were virtuous souls
And Cato[2] giving laws to them. Mid-shield,
The pictured sea flowed surging, all of gold,
As whitecaps foamed on the blue waves, and dolphins
Shining in silver round and round the scene                85
Propelled themselves with flukes and cut through billows.
Vivid in the center were the bronze-beaked
Ships and the fight at sea off Actium.[3]
Here you could see Leucata all alive
With ships maneuvering, sea glowing gold,                   90
Augustus Caesar leading into battle
Italians, with both senators and people,
Household gods and great gods: there he stood
High on the stern, and from his blessed brow
Twin flames gushed upward, while his crest revealed        95
His father's star. Apart from him, Agrippa,[4]
Favored by winds and gods, led ships in column,
A towering figure, wearing on his brows

9. The twelve priests of Mars, who danced in his honor carrying shields which had fallen from heaven. *Luperci*: Priests of Lupercus, a Roman god corresponding to the Greek Pan.    1. Leader of a conspiracy to overthrow the republic which was halted mainly through the efforts of Cicero, consul in 63 B.C. Catiline is the type of discord, representing the civil war which almost destroyed the Roman state, and to which Augustus later put an end.    2. The noblest of the republicans who had fought Julius Caesar; he stood for honesty and the seriousness which the Romans most admired. He committed suicide in 47 B.C. after Caesar's victory in Africa. Before taking his life he read through Plato's *Phaedo*, a dialogue concerned with the immortality of the soul, which ends with an account of the death of Socrates.    3. On the west coast of Greece. The naval battle fought here in 31 B.C. was the decisive engagement of the civil war. Augustus, the master of the western half of the empire, defeated Antony, who held the eastern half and was supported by Cleopatra, queen of Egypt. *Leucata*: A promontory near Actium; there was a temple of Apollo on it.    4. Augustus' admiral at Actium.

The coronet adorned with warships' beaks,
Highest distinction for command at sea.                                100
Then came Antonius with barbaric wealth
And a diversity of arms, victorious
From races of the Dawnlands and Red Sea,
Leading the power of the East, of Egypt,
Even of distant Bactra[5] of the steppes.                              105
And in his wake the Egyptian consort came
So shamefully. The ships all kept together
Racing ahead, the water torn by oar-strokes,
Torn by the triple beaks, in spume and foam.
All made for the open sea. You might believe                           110
The Cyclades[6] uprooted were afloat
Or mountains running against mountain heights
When seamen in those hulks pressed the attack
Upon the other turreted ships. They hurled
Broadsides of burning flax on flying steel,                            115
And fresh blood reddened Neptune's fields. The queen
Amidst the battle called her flotilla on
With a sistrum's[7] beat, a frenzy out of Egypt,
Never turning her head as yet to see
Twin snakes of death behind, while monster forms                       120
Of gods of every race, and the dog-god
Anubis[8] barking, held their weapons up
Against our Neptune, Venus, and Minerva.
Mars, engraved in steel, raged in the fight
As from high air the dire Furies came                                  125
With Discord, taking joy in a torn robe,
And on her heels, with bloody scourge, Bellona.[9]

Overlooking it all, Actian Apollo[1]
Began to pull his bow. Wild at this sight,
All Egypt, Indians, Arabians, all                                      130
Sabaeans[2] put about in flight, and she,
The queen, appeared crying for winds to shift
Just as she hauled up sail and slackened sheets.
The Lord of Fire had portrayed her there,
Amid the slaughter, pallid with death to come,                        135
Then borne by waves and wind from the northwest,
While the great length of mourning Nile awaited her
With open bays, calling the conquered home

5. On the borders of India.    6. The islands of the southern Aegean Sea.    7. An Oriental
rattle, used in the worship of Isis.    8. The Egyptian death-god, depicted with the head of a
jackal.    9. A Roman war-goddess.    1. So called because of his temple at Actium; the temple
(and its cult statue) overlooked the sea battle.    2. Arabs from the Yemen.

To his blue bosom and his hidden streams.
But Caesar then in triple triumph[3] rode                           140
Within the walls of Rome, making immortal
Offerings to the gods of Italy—
Three hundred princely shrines throughout the city.
There were the streets, humming with festal joy
And games and cheers, an altar to every shrine,                    145
To every one a mothers' choir, and bullocks
Knifed before the altars strewed the ground.
The man himself, enthroned before the snow-white
Threshold of sunny Phoebus, viewed the gifts
The nations of the earth made, and he fitted them                  150
To the tall portals. Conquered races passed
In long procession, varied in languages
As in their dress and arms. Here Mulciber,[4]
Divine smith, had portrayed the Nomad tribes
And Afri with ungirdled flowing robes,                             155
Here Leleges and Carians,[5] and here
Gelonians with quivers. Here Euphrates,
Milder in his floods now, there Morini,[6]
Northernmost of men; here bull-horned Rhine,
And there the still unconquered Scythian Dahae;                    160
Here, vexed at being bridged, the rough Araxes.[7]
All these images on Vulcan's shield,
His mother's gift, were wonders to Aeneas.
Knowing nothing of the events themselves,
He felt joy in their pictures, taking up                           165
Upon his shoulder all the destined acts
And fame of his descendants.

[In the course of the desperate battles which follow, the young
Pallas, entrusted to Aeneas' care by his father, is killed by the Italian
champion Turnus, who takes and wears the belt of Pallas as the spoil
of victory. The fortunes of the war later change in favor of the Trojans, and Aeneas kills the Etruscan King Mezentius, Turnus' ally.
Eventually, as the Italians prepare to accept the generous peace terms
offered by Aeneas, Turnus forestalls them by accepting Aeneas' challenge to single combat to decide the issue. But this solution is frustrated by the intervention of Juno, who foresees Aeneas' victory. She
prompts Turnus' sister, the river nymph Juturna, to intervene in an
attempt to save Turnus' life. Juturna stirs up the Italians who are

3. In 29 B.C. Augustus celebrated a triple triumph for victories in Dalmatia, at Actium, and at
Alexandria.    4. Another name of Vulcan.    5. Peoples of Asia Minor. *Gelonians*: From Scythia (in the Balkans).    6. A Belgian tribe.    7. A turbulent river in Armenia. Augustus built a
new bridge over it.

watching the champions prepare for the duel; the truce is broken,
and in the subsequent fighting Aeneas is wounded by an arrow. Healed
by Venus, he returns to the fight, and the Italians are driven back.
Turnus finally faces his adversary. His sword breaks on the armor
forged by Vulcan, and he runs from Aeneas; he is saved by Juturna,
who, assuming the shape of his charioteer, hands him a fresh sword.
At this point Jupiter intervenes to stop the vain attempts of Juno and
Juturna to save Turnus.]

## Book XII

### [THE DEATH OF TURNUS]

Omnipotent Olympus' king meanwhile
Had words for Juno, as she watched the combat
Out of a golden cloud. He said:
                              "My consort,
What will the end be? What is left for you?
You yourself know, and say you know, Aeneas                         5
Born for heaven, tutelary of this land,
By fate to be translated to the stars.[8]
What do you plan? What are you hoping for,
Keeping your seat apart in the cold clouds?
Fitting, was it, that a mortal archer                              10
Wound an immortal? That a blade let slip
Should be restored to Turnus, and new force
Accrue to a beaten man? Without your help
What could Juturna do? Come now, at last
Have done, and heed our pleading, and give way.                    15
Let yourself no longer be consumed
Without relief by all that inward burning;
Let care and trouble not forever come to me
From your sweet lips. The finish is at hand.
You had the power to harry men of Troy                             20
By land and sea, to light the fires of war
Beyond belief, to scar a family
With mourning before marriage.[9] I forbid
Your going further."
                        So spoke Jupiter,
And with a downcast look Juno replied:                             25

"Because I know that is your will indeed,
Great Jupiter, I left the earth below,

8. Aeneas is destined for immortality: after his death, he will be worshipped as a local god.
9. A reference not only to the Italian losses but also to the suicide of Amata, wife of King Latinus,
who hanged herself when the Trojans assaulted the city just before the duel between Aeneas and
Turnus began.

Though sore at heart, and left the side of Turnus.
Were it not so, you would not see me here
Suffering all that passes, here alone,                             30
Resting on air. I should be armed in flames
At the very battle-line, dragging the Trojans
Into a deadly action. I persuaded
Juturna—I confess—to help her brother
In his hard lot, and I approved her daring                         35
Greater difficulties to save his life,
But not that she should fight with bow and arrow.
This I swear by Styx' great fountainhead
Inexorable, which high gods hold in awe.
I yield now and for all my hatred leave                            40
This battlefield. But one thing not retained
By fate I beg for Latium, for the future
Greatness of your kin: when presently
They crown peace with a happy wedding day—
So let it be—and merge their laws and treaties,                    45
Never command the land's own Latin folk
To change their old name, to become new Trojans,
Known as Teucrians; never make them alter
Dialect or dress. Let Latium be.
Let there be Alban kings for generations,                          50
And let Italian valor be the strength
Of Rome in after times. Once and for all
Troy fell, and with her name let her lie fallen."

The author of men and of the world replied
With a half-smile:
                    "Sister of Jupiter[1]                          55
Indeed you are, and Saturn's other child,
To feel such anger, stormy in your breast.
But come, no need; put down this fit of rage.
I grant your wish, I yield, I am won over
Willingly. Ausonian folk will keep                                 60
Their fathers' language and their way of life,
And, that being so, their name. The Teucrians
Will mingle and be submerged, incorporated.
Rituals and observances of theirs
I'll add, but make them Latin, one in speech.                      65
The race to come, mixed with Ausonian blood,
Will outdo men and gods in its devotion,

---

1. Jupiter and Juno, like their prototypes Zeus and Hera, are brother and sister as well as husband and wife.

You shall see—and no nation on earth
Will honor and worship you so faithfully."

To all this Juno nodded in assent                              70
And, gladdened by his promise, changed her mind.
Then she withdrew from sky and cloud.
                                That done,
The Father set about a second plan—
To take Juturna from her warring brother.
Stories are told of twin fiends, called the Dirae,[2]          75
Whom, with Hell's Megaera, deep Night bore
In one birth. She entwined their heads with coils
Of snakes and gave them wings to race the wind.
Before Jove's throne, a step from the cruel king,
These twins attend him and give piercing fear                  80
To ill mankind, when he who rules the gods
Deals out appalling death and pestilence,
Or war to terrify our wicked cities.
Jove now dispatched one of these, swift from heaven,
Bidding her be an omen to Juturna.                             85
Down she flew, in a whirlwind borne to earth,
Just like an arrow driven through a cloud
From a taut string, an arrow armed with gall
Of deadly poison, shot by a Parthian—[3]
A Parthian or a Cretan—for a wound                             90
Immedicable; whizzing unforeseen
It goes through racing shadows: so the spawn
Of Night went diving downward to the earth.

On seeing Trojan troops drawn up in face
Of Turnus' army, she took on at once                           95
The shape of that small bird[4] that perches late
At night on tombs or desolate roof-tops
And troubles darkness with a gruesome song.
Shrunk to that form, the fiend in Turnus' face
Went screeching, flitting, flitting to and fro                 100
And beating with her wings against his shield.
Unstrung by numbness, faint and strange, he felt
His hackles rise, his voice choke in his throat.
As for Juturna, when she knew the wings,
The shriek to be the fiend's, she tore her hair,              105

2. Lit. "dreadful ones" (the termination shows they are female, like the Erinyes). One of them is
called Megaera.    3. Parthia was the most dangerous neighbor of the Roman Empire in the east.
Parthian mounted archers were famous, as were Cretan archers.    4. The owl.

Despairing, then she fell upon her cheeks
With nails, upon her breast with clenched hands.

"Turnus, how can your sister help you now?
What action is still open to me, soldierly
Though I have been? Can I by any skill                          110
Hold daylight for you? Can I meet and turn
This deathliness away? Now I withdraw,
Now leave this war. Indecent birds, I fear you;
Spare me your terror. Whip-lash of your wings
I recognize, that ghastly sound, and guess                      115
Great-hearted Jupiter's high cruel commands.
Returns for my virginity,[5] are they?
He gave me life eternal—to what end?
Why has mortality been taken from me?
Now beyond question I could put a term                          120
To all my pain, and go with my poor brother
Into the darkness, his companion there.
Never to die? Will any brook of mine
Without you, brother, still be sweet to me?
If only earth's abyss were wide enough                          125
To take me downward, goddess though I am,
To join the shades below!"
                         So she lamented,
Then with a long sigh, covering up her head
In her grey mantle, sank to the river's depth.

Aeneas moved against his enemy                                  130
And shook his heavy pine-tree spear. He called
From his hot heart:
                    "Rearmed now, why so slow?
Why, even now, fall back? The contest here
Is not a race, but fighting to the death
With spear and sword. Take on all shapes there are,            135
Summon up all your nerve and skill, choose any
Footing, fly among the stars, or hide
In caverned earth—"
                     The other shook his head,
Saying:
        "I do not fear your taunting fury,
Arrogant prince. It is the gods I fear                          140
And Jove my enemy."
                     He said no more,

---

5. Jupiter had been the lover of Juturna and had rewarded her with immortality.

But looked around him. Then he saw a stone,
Enormous, ancient, set up there to prevent
Landowners' quarrels. Even a dozen picked men
Such as the earth produces in our day                          145
Could barely lift and shoulder it. He swooped
And wrenched it free, in one hand, then rose up
To his heroic height, ran a few steps,
And tried to hurl the stone against his foe—
But as he bent and as he ran                                   150
And as he hefted and propelled the weight
He did not know himself. His knees gave way,
His blood ran cold and froze. The stone itself,
Tumbling through space, fell short and had no impact.

Just as in dreams when the night-swoon of sleep               155
Weighs on our eyes, it seems we try in vain
To keep on running, try with all our might,
But in the midst of effort faint and fail;
Our tongue is powerless, familiar strength
Will not hold up our body, not a sound                         160
Or word will come: just so with Turnus now:
However bravely he made shift to fight
The immortal fiend blocked and frustrated him.
Flurrying images passed through his mind.
He gazed at the Tutulians,[6] and beyond them,                165
Gazed at the city, hesitant, in dread.
He trembled now before the poised spear-shaft
And saw no way to escape; he had no force
With which to close, or reach his foe, no chariot
And no sign of the charioteer, his sister.                     170
At a dead loss he stood. Aeneas made
His deadly spear flash in the sun and aimed it,
Narrowing his eyes for a lucky hit.
Then, distant still, he put his body's might
Into the cast. Never a stone that soared                       175
From a wall-battering catapult went humming
Loud as this, nor with so great a crack
Burst ever a bolt of lightning. It flew on
Like a black whirlwind bringing devastation,
Pierced with a crash the rim of sevenfold shield,             180
Cleared the cuirass' edge, and passed clean through
The middle of Turnus' thigh. Force of the blow
Brought the huge man to earth, his knees buckling,

6. The Italian troops watching the combat between Turnus and Aeneas.

And a groan swept the Rutulians as they rose,
A groan heard echoing on all sides from all                    185
The mountain range, and echoed by the forests.
The man brought down, brought low, lifted his eyes
And held his right hand out to make his plea:

"Clearly I earned this, and I ask no quarter.
Make the most of your good fortune here.                       190
If you can feel a father's grief—and you, too,
Had such a father in Anchises—then
Let me bespeak your mercy for old age
In Daunus,[7] and return me, or my body,
Stripped, if you will, of life, to my own kin.                 195
You have defeated me. The Ausonians
Have seen me in defeat, spreading my hands.
Lavinia is your bride. But go no further
Out of hatred."
                    Fierce under arms, Aeneas
Looked to and fro, and towered, and stayed his hand            200
Upon the sword-hilt. Moment by moment now
What Turnus said began to bring him round
From indecision. Then to his glance appeared
The accurst swordbelt surmounting Turnus' shoulder,
Shining with its familiar studs—the strap                      205
Young Pallas wore when Turnus wounded him
And left him dead upon the field; now Turnus
Bore that enemy token on his shoulder—
Enemy still. For when the sight came home to him,
Aeneas raged at the relic of his anguish                       210
Worn by this man as trophy. Blazing up
And terrible in his anger, he called out:

"You in your plunder, torn from one of mine,
Shall I be robbed of you? This wound will come
From Pallas: Pallas makes this offering                        215
And from your criminal blood exacts his due."

He sank his blade in fury in Turnus' chest.
Then all the body slackened in death's chill,
And with a groan for that indignity
His spirit fled into the gloom below.

7. Father of Turnus.

# OVID

## 43 B.C.–A.D. 17

Virgil had grown to manhood in the years of civil war, when no man's property, nor even his life, was safe. He knew all too well the horrors that would inevitably recur if Augustus' attempt to establish stable government should fail; like all his generation, he knew how precarious the newfound peace was and felt himself deeply engaged in the Augustan program. But a new generation of poets, who had not known the time of troubles, took all that had been achieved for granted, and turned to new themes. The most brilliant of them, Ovid, was a boy of eleven when Octavius defeated Anthony at Actium; the early years of his manhood, far from being dominated by fear of chaos come again, were marked by rapid literary and social success in the brilliant society of a capital intent on enjoying the peace and prosperity which had been restored with so much effort.

Ovid was a versifier of genius; "whatever I tried to say," he wrote, "came out in verse," and Pope adapted the line for his own case: "I lisped in numbers for the numbers came." Elegance, wit, and precision remained the hallmarks of Ovid's poetry throughout his long and productive career; though his themes are often frivolous, the technical perfection of the medium carries the dazzled reader along. The *Amores*, unabashed chronicles of a Roman Don Juan, was his first publication: it was soon followed by the *Art of Love*, a handbook of seduction (originally circulated as Books I and II, for men— Book III, for women, was added by popular request).

In A.D. 8 Ovid was banished by imperial decree to the town of Tomi, in what is now Rumania: it was outside the frontiers of the empire. He remained there until his death in A.D. 17, sending back to Rome poetic epistles, the *Sorrows*, which asked for pardon but to no effect. The reason for his banishment is not known: involvement in some scandal concerning Augustus' daughter Julia is a possibility, but the cynical love poetry may have been a contributing factor. Augustus was trying hard, by propaganda and legislation, to revive old Roman standards of morality and Ovid's *Art of Love* was not exactly helpful. His most influential work, the *Metamorphoses*, is a treasure house of Greek and Roman mythological stories brilliantly combined in a long narrative and retold with such wit, charm, and surpassing beauty that poets ever since, Chaucer, Shakespeare, and Milton among them, have used it as a source.

It consists of fifteen books; beginning with the creation of the world, the transformation of matter into living bodies, Ovid regales his readers with tales of human beings changed into animals, flowers, trees, proceeding through Greek myth to stories of early Rome and so to his own day—the ascension of the murdered Julius Caesar to the heavens in the form of a star and the divine promise that Augustus too, on some day far in the future, will become a god. Our selection contains one of the best known episodes, Apollo and Daphne from Book I, and from Book XV, the long discourse of the philos-

opher Pythagoras who preaches the doctrine of impermanence, of unceasing
change.

H. Fraenkel, *Ovid: A Poet Between Two Worlds* (1945), looks at Ovid as
a poet in a historical context. G. K. Galinsky, *Ovid's Metamorphoses: An
Introduction to the Basic Aspects* (1975), is a useful guide.

# Metamorphoses[1]

My intention is to tell of bodies changed
To different forms; the gods, who made the changes,
Will help me—or I hope so—with a poem
That runs from the world's beginning to our own days.[2]

## THE CREATION

Before the ocean was, or earth, or heaven,                              5
Nature was all alike, a shapelessness,
Chaos, so-called, all rude and lumpy matter,
Nothing but bulk, inert, in whose confusion
Discordant atoms warred: there was no sun
To light the universe; there was no moon                                10
With slender silver crescents filling slowly;
No earth hung balanced in surrounding air;
No sea reached far along the fringe of shore.
Land, to be sure, there was, and air, and ocean,
But land on which no man could stand, and water                         15
No man could swim in, air no could breathe,
Air without light, substance forever changing,
Forever at war: within a single body
Heat fought with cold, wet fought with dry, the hard
Fought with the soft, things having weight contended                    20
With weightless things.
            Till God, or kindlier Nature,
Settled all argûment, and separated
Heaven from earth, water from land, our air
From the high stratosphere, a liberation
So things evolved, and out of blind confusion                           25
Found each its place, bound in eternal order.
The force of fire, that weightless element,
Leaped up and claimed the highest place[3] in heaven;
Below it, air; and under them the earth

1. A selection. Translated by Rolfe Humphries.    2. In fact the last metamorphosis in the poem
is that of the soul of the murdered dictator, Julius Caesar, which is turned into a star. Caesar was
murdered in 44 B.C.; Ovid was born in the next year, 43 B.C.    3. The upper atmosphere, the
*aether* as the Greeks called it, was thought of as a fiery element.

Sank with its grosser portions; and the water,                    30
Lowest of all, held up, held in, the land.


Whatever god it was, who out of chaos
Brought order to the universe, and gave it
Division, subdivision, he molded earth,
In the beginning, into a great globe,                    35
Even on every side, and bade the waters
To spread and rise, under the rushing winds,
Surrounding earth; he added ponds and marshes,
He banked the river-channels, and the waters
Feed earth or run to sea, and that great flood                    40
Washes on shores, not banks. He made the plains
Spread wide, the valleys settle, and the forest
Be dressed in leaves; he made the rocky mountains
Rise to full height, and as the vault of Heaven
Has two zones,[4] left and right, and one between them                    45
Hotter than these, the Lord of all Creation
Marked on the earth the same design and pattern.
The torrid zone too hot for men to live in,
The north and south too cold, but in the middle
Varying climate, temperature and season.                    50
Above all things the air, lighter than earth,
Lighter than water, heavier than fire,
Towers and spreads; there mist and cloud assemble,
And fearful thunder and lightning and cold winds,
But these, by the Creator's order, held                    55
No general dominion; even as it is,
These brothers brawl and quarrel; though each one
Has his own quarter, still, they come near tearing
The universe apart. Eurus is monarch
Of the lands of dawn,[5] the realms of Araby,                    60
The Persian ridges under the rays of morning.
Zephyrus holds the west that glows at sunset,
Boreas, who makes men shiver, holds the north,
Warm Auster governs in the misty southland,
And over them all presides the weightless ether,                    65
Pure without taint of earth.
                              These boundaries given,
Behold, the stars, long hidden under darkness,
Broke through and shone, all over the spangled heaven,
Their home forever, and the gods lived there,

---

**4.** I.e., two zones to the "right" (the north) and two to the "left" (the south).    **5.** I.e., the sunrise, the east. *Eurus:* The east wind.

And shining fish were given the waves for dwelling                    70
And beasts the earth, and birds the moving air.

But something else was needed, a finer being,
More capable of mind, a sage, a ruler,
So Man was born, it may be, in God's image,
Or Earth, perhaps, so newly separated                                 75
From the old fire of Heaven, still retained
Some seed of the celestial force which fashioned
Gods out of living clay and running water.
All other animals look downward; Man,
Alone, erect, can raise his face toward Heaven.                       80

## THE FOUR AGES[6]

The Golden Age was first, a time that cherished
Of its own will, justice and right; no law,
No punishment, was called for; fearfulness
Was quite unknown, and the bronze tablets held
No legal threatening; no suppliant throng                             85
Studied a judge's face; there were no judges,
There did not need to be. Trees had not yet
Been cut and hollowed, to visit other shores.
Men were content at home, and had no towns
With moats and walls around them; and no trumpets                     90
Blared out alarums; things like swords and helmets
Had not been heard of. No one needed soldiers.
People were unaggressive, and unanxious;
The years went by in peace. And Earth, untroubled,
Unharried by hoe or plowshare, brought forth all                      95
That men had need for, and those men were happy,
Gathering berries from the mountain sides,
Cherries, or blackcaps, and the edible acorns.
Spring was forever, with a west wind blowing
Softly across the flowers no man had planted,                         100
And Earth, unplowed, brought forth rich grain; the field,
Unfallowed, whitened with wheat, and there were rivers
Of milk, and rivers of honey, and golden nectar
Dripped from the dark-green oak-trees.
                                                    After Saturn[7]
Was driven to the shadowy land of death,                              105
And the world was under Jove, the Age of Silver

6. In this myth of the four ages Ovid is following the account of the archaic Greek poet Hesiod (who, however, counted five ages; he interposed the age of the heroes, the wars of Thebes and Troy, between the Bronze and Iron ages).    7. Father of Jove (Jupiter), who, like his counterpart Zeus, overthrew his father's regime.

Came in, lower than gold, better than bronze.
Jove made the springtime shorter, added winter,
Summer, and autumn, the seasons as we know them.
That was the first time when the burnt air glowed          110
White-hot, or icicles hung down in winter.
And men built houses for themselves; the caverns,
The woodland thickets, and the bark-bound shelters
No longer served; and the seeds of grain were planted
In the long furrows, and the oxen struggled              115
Groaning and laboring under the heavy yoke.

Then came the Age of Bronze, and dispositions
Took on aggressive instincts, quick to arm,
Yet not entirely evil. And last of all
The Iron Age succeeded, whose base vein                   120
Let loose all evil: modesty and truth
And righteousness fled earth, and in their place
Came trickery and slyness, plotting, swindling,
Violence and the damned desire of having.
Men spread their sails to winds unknown to sailors,       125
The pines came down their mountain-sides, to revel
And leap in the deep waters,[8] and the ground,
Free, once, to everyone, like air and sunshine,
Was stepped off by surveyors. The rich earth,
Good giver of all the bounty of the harvest,              130
Was asked for more; they dug into her vitals,
Pried out the wealth a kinder lord had hidden
In Stygian shadow,[9] all that precious metal,
The root of evil. They found the guilt of iron,
And gold, more guilty still. And War came forth           135
That uses both to fight with; bloody hands
Brandished the clashing weapons. Men lived on plunder.
Guest was not safe from host, nor brother from brother,
A man would kill his wife, a wife her husband,
Stepmothers, dire and dreadful, stirred their brews       140
With poisonous aconite, and sons would hustle
Fathers to death, and Piety lay vanquished,
And the maiden Justice, last of all immortals,
Fled from the bloody earth.
                    Heaven was no safer.
Giants attacked the very throne of Heaven,                145
Piled Pelion on Ossa,[1] mountain on mountain
Up to the very stars. Jove struck them down

---

8. I.e., after they were made into ships.     9. The Styx is one of the rivers of the underworld.
1. Two mountains in central Greece, south of Olympus.

With thunderbolts, and the bulk of those huge bodies
Lay on the earth, and bled, and Mother Earth,
Made pregnant by that blood, brought forth new bodies,          150
And gave them, to recall her older offspring,
The forms of men. And this new stock was also
Contemptuous of gods, and murder-hungry
And violent. You would know they were sons of blood.


### JOVE'S INTERVENTION

And Jove was witness from his lofty throne                       155
Of all this evil, and groaned as he remembered
The wicked revels of Lycaon's[2] table,
The latest guilt, a story still unknown
To the high gods. In awful indignation
He summoned them to council. No one dawdled.                     160
Easily seen when the night skies are clear,
The Milky Way shines white. Along this road
The gods move toward the palace of the Thunderer,
His royal halls, and, right and left, the dwellings
Of other gods are open, and guests come thronging.              165
The lesser gods live in a meaner section,
An area not reserved, as this one is,
For the illustrious Great Wheels of Heaven.
(Their Palatine Hill,[3] if I might call it so.)

They took their places in the marble chamber                     170
Where high above them all their king was seated,
Holding his ivory sceptre, shaking out
Thrice, and again, his awful locks, the sign
That made the earth and stars and ocean tremble,
And then he spoke, in outrage: "I was troubled                   175
Less for the sovereignty of all the world
In that old time when the snake-footed giants
Laid each his hundred hands on captive Heaven.
Monstrous they were, and hostile, but their warfare
Sprung from one source, one body. Now, wherever                  180
The sea-gods roar around the earth, a race
Must be destroyed, the race of men. I swear it!
I swear by all the Stygian rivers gliding
Under the world, I have tried all other measures.
The knife must cut the cancer out, infection                     185
Averted while it can be, from our numbers.
Those demigods, those rustic presences,

2. King of Arcadia, in the Peloponnese.    3. The hill of Rome where the emperor Augustus
lived.

Nymphs, fauns, and satyrs, wood and mountain dwellers,
We have not yet honored with a place in Heaven,
But they should have some decent place to dwell in,    190
In peace and safety. Safety? Do you reckon
They will be safe, when I, who wield the thunder,
Who rule you all as subjects, am subjected
To the plottings of the barbarous Lycaon?"

They burned, they trembled. Who was this Lycaon,    195
Guilty of such rank infamy? They shuddered
In horror, with a fear of sudden ruin,
As the whole world did later, when assassins
Struck Julius Caesar down, and Prince Augustus
Found satisfaction in the great devotion    200
That cried for vengeance, even as Jove took pleasure,
Then, in the gods' response. By word and gesture
He calmed them down, awed them again to silence,
And spoke once more:

### THE STORY OF LYCAON

       "He has indeed been punished.
On that score have no worry. But what he did,    205
And how he paid, are things that I must tell you.
I had heard the age was desperately wicked,
I had heard, or so I hoped, a lie, a falsehood,
So I came down, as man, from high Olympus,
Wandered about the world. It would take too long    210
To tell you how widespread was all that evil.
All I had heard was grievous understatement!
I had crossed Maenala, a country bristling
With dens of animals, and crossed Cyllene,
And cold Lycaeus' pine woods.[4] Then I came    215
At evening, with the shadows growing longer,
To an Arcadian palace, where the tyrant
Was anything but royal in his welcome.
I gave a sign that a god had come, and people
Began to worship, and Lycaon mocked them,    220
Laughed at their prayers, and said: 'Watch me find out
Whether this fellow is a god or mortal,
I can tell quickly, and no doubt about it.'
He planned, that night, to kill me while I slumbered;
That was his way to test the truth. Moreover,    225
And not content with that, he took hostage,

4. Maenala, Cyllene, and Lycaeus are mountains in Arcadia.

One sent by the Molossians,[5] cut his throat,
Boiled pieces of his flesh, still warm with life,
Broiled others, and set them before me on the table.
That was enough. I struck, and the bolt of lightning          230
Blasted the household of that guilty monarch.
He fled in terror, reached the silent fields,
And howled,[6] and tried to speak. No use at all!
Foam dripped from his mouth; bloodthirsty still, he turned
Against the sheep, delighting still in slaughter,             235
And his arms were legs, and his robes were shaggy hair,
Yet he is still Lycaon, the same grayness,
The same fierce face, the same red eyes, a picture
Of bestial savagery. One house has fallen,
But more than one deserves to. Fury reigns                    240
Over all the fields of Earth. They are sworn to evil,
Believe it. Let them pay for it, and quickly!
So stands my purpose."
                              Part of them approved
With words and added fuel to his anger,
And part approved with silence, and yet all                   245
Were grieving at the loss of humankind,
Were asking what the world would be, bereft
Of mortals: who would bring their altars incense?
Would earth be given the beasts, to spoil and ravage?
Jove told them not to worry; he would give them               250
Another race, unlike the first, created
Out of a miracle; he would see to it.

He was about to hurl his thunderbolts
At the whole world, but halted, fearing Heaven
Would burn from fire so vast, and pole to pole                255
Break out in flame and smoke, and he remembered
The fates had said that some day land and ocean,
The vault of Heaven, the whole world's mighty fortress,
Besieged by fire, would perish. He put aside
The bolts made in Cyclopean[7] workshops; better,             260
He thought, to drown the world by flooding water.

### THE FLOOD

So, in the cave of Aeolus,[8] he prisoned
The North-wind, and the West-wind, and such others

5. A tribe located in Epirus, the northernmost extremity of Greece.    6. The beginning of the
first metamorphosis—Lycaon (the first part of whose name is the Greek for "wolf") becomes a
wolf.    7. Made by the Cyclopes, one-eyed giants like Polyphemus in the *Odyssey* (Book IX).
But unlike Polyphemus and his pastoral relatives, these Cyclopes are metalworkers who forge the
thunderbolts of Jupiter (Zeus).    8. King of the winds (cf. *Odyssey* Book X).

As ever banish cloud, and he turned loose
The South-wind, and the South-wind came out streaming     265
With dripping wings, and pitch-black darkness veiling
His terrible countenance. His beard is heavy
With rain-cloud, and his hoary locks a torrent,
Mists are his chaplet, and his wings and garments
Run with the rain. His broad hands squeeze together     270
Low-hanging clouds, and crash and rumble follow
Before the cloudburst, and the rainbow, Iris,
Draws water from the teeming earth, and feeds it
Into the clouds again. The crops are ruined,
The farmers' prayers all wasted, all the labor     275
Of a long year, comes to nothing.

                     And Jove's anger,
Unbounded by his own domain, was given
Help by his dark-blue brother. Neptune[9] called
His rivers all, and told them, very briefly,
To loose their violence, open their houses,     280
Pour over embankments, let the river horses
Run wild as ever they would. And they obeyed him.
His trident struck the shuddering earth; it opened
Way for the rush of waters. The leaping rivers
Flood over the great plains. Not only orchards     285
Are swept away, not only grain and cattle,
Not only men and houses, but altars, temples,
And shrines with holy fires. If any building
Stands firm, the waves keep rising over its roof-top,
Its towers are under water, and land and ocean     290
Are all alike, and everything is ocean,
An ocean with no shore-line.

                  Some poor fellow
Seizes a hill-top; another, in a dinghy,
Rows where he used to plough, and one goes sailing
Over his fields of grain or over the chimney     295
Of what was once his cottage. Someone catches
Fish in the top of an elmtree, or an anchor
Drags in green meadow-land, or the curved keel brushes
Grape-arbors under water. Ugly sea-cows
Float where the slender she-goats used to nibble     300
The tender grass, and the Nereids[1] come swimming
With curious wonder, looking, under water,
At houses, cities, parks, and groves. The dolphins
Invade the woods and brush against the oak-trees;

9. (Poseidon) the sea god.    1. Sea-nymphs.

The wolf swims with the lamb; lion and tiger                    305
Are borne along together; the wild boar
Finds all his strength is useless, and the deer
Cannot outspeed that torrent; wandering birds
Look long, in vain, for landing-place, and tumble,
Exhausted, into the sea. The deep's great license            310
Has buried all the hills and new waves thunder
Against the mountain-tops. The flood has taken
All things, or nearly all, and those whom water,
By chance, has spared, starvation slowly conquers.

### DEUCALION AND PYRRHA

Phocis, a fertile land, while there was land,                   315
Marked off Oetean from Boeotian[2] fields.
It was ocean now, a plain of sudden waters.
There Mount Parnassus lifts its twin peaks skyward,
High, steep, cloud-piercing. And Deucalion came there
Rowing his wife. There was no other land,                       320
The sea had drowned it all. And here they worshipped
First the Corycian nymphs[3] and native powers,
Then Themis, oracle and fate-revealer.
There was no better man than this Deucalion,
No one more fond of right; there was no woman               325
More scrupulously reverent than Pyrrha.
So, when Jove saw the world was one great ocean,
Only one woman left of all those thousands,
And only one man left of all those thousands,
Both innocent and worshipful, he parted                          330
The clouds, turned loose the North-wind, swept them off,
Showed earth to heaven again, and sky to land,
And the sea's anger dwindled, and King Neptune
Put down his trident, calmed the waves, and Triton,
Summoned from far down under, with his shoulders            335
Barnacle-strewn, loomed up above the waters,
The blue-green sea-god, whose resounding horn
Is heard from shore to shore. Wet-bearded, Triton
Set lip to that great shell, as Neptune ordered,
Sounding retreat, and all the lands and waters             340
Heard and obeyed. The sea has shores; the rivers,
Still running high, have channels; the floods dwindle,

---

2. On the Theban plain. *Phocis*: A district in central Greece, north of the Gulf of Corinth.
*Oetean*: Mt. Oeta is in southern Thessaly.    3. The Corycian cave is high above Delphi, on the
upper slopes of Parnassus. *Themis*: "Tradition" in Greek, one of the predecessors of Apollo at
Delphi.

Hill-tops are seen again; the trees, long buried,
Rise with their leaves still muddy. The world returns.

Deucalion saw that world, all desolation,                              345
All emptiness, all silence, and his tears
Rose as he spoke to Pyrrha: "O my wife,
The only woman, now, on all this earth,
My consort and my cousin and my partner
In these immediate dangers, look! Of all the lands                     350
To East or West, we two, we two alone,
Are all the population. Ocean holds
Everything else; our foothold, our assurance,
Are small as they can be, the clouds still frightful.
Poor woman—well, we are not all alone—                                 355
Suppose you had been, how would you bear your fear?
Who would console your grief? My wife, believe me,
Had the sea taken you, I would have followed.
If only I had the power, I would restore
The nations as my father[4] did, bring clay                            360
To life with breathing. As it is, we two
Are all the human race, so Heaven has willed it,
Samples of men, mere specimens."
                                    They wept,
and prayed together, and having wept and prayed,
Resolved to make petition to the goddess                               365
To seek her aid through oracles. Together
They went to the river-water, the stream Cephisus,
Still far from clear, but flowing down its channel,
And they took river-water, sprinkled foreheads,
Sprinkled their garments, and they turned their steps                  370
To the temple of the goddess, where the altars
Stood with the fires gone dead, and ugly moss
Stained pediment and column. At the stairs
They both fell prone, kissed the chill stone in prayer:
"If the gods' anger ever listens                                       375
To righteous prayers, O Themis, we implore you,
Tell us by what device our wreck and ruin
May be repaired. Bring aid, most gentle goddess,
To sunken circumstance."
                         And Themis heard them,
And gave this oracle: "Go from the temple,                             380
Cover your heads, loosen your robes, and throw
Your mother's bones behind you!" Dumb, they stood

---

4. Prometheus. A Greek legend credited him with making the first human beings out of clay.

In blank amazement, a long silence, broken
By Pyrrha, finally: she would not do it!
With trembling lips she prays whatever pardon       385
Her disobedience might merit, but this outrage
She dare not risk, insult her mother's spirit
By throwing her bones around. In utter darkness
They voice the cryptic saying over and over,
What can it mean? They wonder. At last Deucalion       390
Finds the way out: "I might be wrong, but surely
The holy oracles would never counsel
A guilty act. The earth is our great mother,
And I suppose those bones the goddess mentions
Are the stones of earth; the order means to throw them,       395
The stones, behind us."
                              She was still uncertain,
And he by no means sure, and both distrustful
Of that command from Heaven; but what damage,
What harm, would there be in trying? They descended,
Covered their heads, loosened their garments, threw       400
The stones behind them as the goddess ordered.
The stones—who would believe it, had we not
The unimpeachable witness of Tradition?—
Began to lose their hardness, to soften, slowly,
To take on form, to grow in size, a little,       405
Become less rough, to look like human beings,
Or anyway as much like human beings
As statues do, when the sculptor is only starting,
Images half blocked out. The earthy portion,
Damp with some moisture, turned to flesh, the solid       410
Was bone, the veins were as they always had been.
The stones the man had thrown turned into men,
The stones the woman threw turned into women,
Such being the will of God. Hence we derive
The hardness that we have, and our endurance       415
Gives proof of what we have come from.
                                        Other forms
Of life came into being, generated
Out of the earth: the sun burnt off the dampness,
Heat made the slimy marshes swell; as seed
Swells in a mother's womb to shape and substance,       420
So new forms came to life. When the Nile river
Floods and recedes and the mud is warmed by sunshine,
Men, turning over the earth, find living things,
And some not living, but nearly so, imperfect,

On the verge of life,[5] and often the same substance          425
Is part alive, part only clay. When moisture
Unites with heat, life is conceived; all things
Come from this union. Fire may fight with water,
But heat and moisture generate all things,
Their discord being productive. So when earth,          430
After that flood, still muddy, took the heat,
Felt the warm fire of sunlight, she conceived,
Brought forth, after their fashion, all the creatures,
Some old, some strange and monstrous.

                              One, for instance,
She bore unwanted, a gigantic serpent,[6]          435
Python by name, whom the new people dreaded,
A huge bulk on the mountain-side. Apollo,
God of the glittering bow, took a long time
To bring him down, with arrow after arrow
He had never used before except in hunting          440
Deer and the skipping goats. Out of the quiver
Sped arrows by the thousand, till the monster,
Dying, poured poisonous blood on those black wounds.
In memory of this, the sacred games,
Called Pythian, was established, and Apollo          445
Ordained for all young winners in the races,
On foot or chariot, for victorious fighters,
The crown of oak. That was before the laurel,
That was before Apollo wreathed his forehead
With garlands from that tree, or any other.          450

### APOLLO AND DAPHNE

Now the first girl Apollo loved was Daphne,
Whose father was the river-god Peneus,[7]
And this was no blind chance, but Cupid's malice.
Apollo, with pride and glory still upon him
Over the Python slain, saw Cupid bending          455
His tight-strung little bow. "O silly youngster,"
He said, "What are you doing with such weapons?

5. This strange doctrine, the automatic generation of living species in warm river mud, stems from Greek philosophical speculation about the origins of life.    6. Pytho. The following lines are a good example of Ovid's witty and skilful transitions from one story to another: he will vary them like a virtuoso in the course of the fifteen books. From the spontaneous birth of animals in the Nile mud he singles out one, Pytho, killed by Apollo, who instituted games in commemoration of the feat and decreed for the winner a crown of oak. As everyone of his readers knew, the crown at the Pythian games was of laurel. But, says Ovid, the laurel did not then exist and this launches him on the story of its origin, the transformation of Daphne (the name means "laurel").    7. The main river of Thessaly.

Those are for grown-ups! The bow is for my shoulders;
I never fail in wounding beast or mortal,
And not so long ago I slew the Python                                    460
With countless darts; his bloated body covered
Acre on endless acre, and I slew him!
The torch, my boy, is enough for you to play with,
To get the love-fires burning. Do not meddle
With honors that are mine!" And Cupid answered:                          465
"Your bow shoots everything, Apollo—maybe—
But mine will fix you! You are far above
All creatures living, and by just that distance
Your glory less than mine." He shook his wings,
Soared high, came down to the shadows of Parnassus,                      470
Drew from his quiver different kinds of arrows,
One causing love, golden and sharp and gleaming,
The other blunt, and tipped with lead, and serving
To drive all love away, and this blunt arrow
He used on Daphne, but he fired the other,                               475
The sharp and golden shaft, piercing Apollo
Through bones, through marrow, and at once he loved
And she at once fled from the name of lover,
Rejoicing in the woodland hiding places
And spoils of beasts which she had taken captive,                       480
A rival of Diana, virgin goddess.[8]
She had many suitors, but she scorned them all;
Wanting no part of any man, she travelled
The pathless groves, and had no care whatever
For husband, love, or marriage. Her father often                        485
Said, "Daughter, give me a son-in-law!" and "Daughter,
Give me some grandsons!" But the marriage torches
Were something hateful, criminal, to Daphne,
So she would blush, and put her arms around him,
And coax him: "Let me be a virgin always;                               490
Diana's father said she might. Dear father!
Dear father—please!" He yielded, but her beauty
Kept arguing against her prayer. Apollo
Loves at first sight; he wants to marry Daphne,
He hopes for what he wants—all wishful thinking!—                       495
Is fooled by his own oracles. As stubble
Burns when the grain is harvested, as hedges
Catch fire from torches that a passer-by
Has brought too near, or left behind in the morning,
So the god burned, with all his heart, and burning                      500

8. Or Artemis, a hunting goddess, daughter of Jupiter (Zeus).

Nourished that futile love of his by hoping.
He sees the long hair hanging down her neck
Uncared for, says, "But what if it were combed?"
He gazes at her eyes—they shine like stars!
He gazes at her lips, and knows that gazing          505
Is not enough. He marvels at her fingers,
Her hands, her wrists, her arms, bare to the shoulder,
And what he does not see he thinks is better.
But still she flees him, swifter than the wind,
And when he calls she does not even listen:          510
"Don't run away, dear nymph! Daughter of Peneus,
Don't run away! I am no enemy,
Only your follower: don't run away!
The lamb flees from the wolf, the deer the lion,
The dove, on trembling wing, flees from the eagle.   515
All creatures flee their foes. But I, who follow,
Am not a foe at all. Love makes me follow,
Unhappy fellow that I am, and fearful
You may fall down, perhaps, or have the briars
Make scratches on those lovely legs, unworthy        520
To be hurt so, and I would be the reason.
The ground is rough here. Run a little slower,
And I will run, I promise, a little slower.
Or wait a minute: be a little curious
Just who it is you charm. I am no shepherd,          525
No mountain-dweller, I am not a ploughboy,
Uncouth and stinking of cattle. You foolish girl,
You don't know who it is you run away from,
That must be why you run. I am lord of Delphi
And Tenedos and Claros and Patara.[9]                530
Jove is my father. I am the revealer
Of present, past and future; through my power
The lyre and song make harmony; my arrow
Is sure in aim—there is only one arrow surer,
The one that wounds my heart. The power of healing   535
Is my discovery; I am called the Healer
Through all the world: all herbs are subject to me.
Alas for me, love is incurable
With any herb; the arts which cure the others
Do me, their lord, no good!"
                              He would have said   540
Much more than this, but Daphne, frightened, left him
With many words unsaid, and she was lovely

9. All famous oracular shrines of Apollo.

Even in flight, her limbs bare in the wind,
Her garments fluttering, and her soft hair streaming,
More beautiful than ever. But Apollo,                          545
Too young a god to waste his time in coaxing,
Came following fast. When a hound starts a rabbit
In an open field, one runs for game, one safety,
He has her, or thinks he has, and she is doubtful
Whether she's caught or not, so close the margin,             550
So ran the god and girl, one swift in hope,
The other in terror, but he ran more swiftly,
Borne on the wings of love, gave her no rest,
Shadowed her shoulder, breathed on her streaming hair.
Her strength was gone, worn out by the long effort           555
Of the long flight; she was deathly pale, and seeing
The river of her father, cried "O help me,
If there is any power in the rivers,
Change and destroy the body which has given
Too much delight!" And hardly had she finished,              560
When her limbs grew numb and heavy, her soft breasts
Were closed with delicate bark, her hair was leaves,
Her arms were branches, and her speedy feet
Rooted and held, and her head became a tree top,
Everything gone except her grace, her shining.               565
Apollo loved her still. He placed his hand
Where he had hoped and felt the heart still beating
Under the bark; and he embraced the branches
As if they still were limbs, and kissed the wood,
And the wood shrank from his kisses, and the god             570
Exclaimed: "Since you can never be my bride,
My tree at least you shall be! Let the laurel
Adorn, henceforth, my hair, my lyre, my quiver:
Let Roman victors, in the long procession,
Wear laurel wreaths for triumph and ovation.                 575
Beside Augustus' portals let the laurel
Guard and watch over the oak, and as my head
Is always youthful, let the laurel always
Be green and shining!" He said no more. The laurel,
Stirring, seemed to consent, to be saying *Yes*.            580

There is a grove in Thessaly, surrounded
By woodlands with steep slopes; men call it Tempe.
Through this the Peneus River's foamy waters
Rise below Pindus mountain. The cascades
Drive a fine smoky mist along the tree tops,                 585
Frail clouds, or so it seems, and the roar of the water

Carries beyond the neighborhood. Here dwells
The mighty god himself,[1] his holy of holies
Is under a hanging rock; it is here he gives
Laws to the nymphs, laws to the very water.                    590
And here came first the streams of his own country
Not knowing what to offer, consolation
Or something like rejoicing: crowned with poplars
Sperchios came, and restless Enipeus,
Old Apidanus, Aeas, and Amphrysos[2]                           595
The easy-going. And all the other rivers
That take their weary waters into oceans
All over the world, came there, and only one
Was absent, Inachus,[3] hiding in his cavern,
Salting his stream with tears, oh, most unhappy,               600
Mourning a daughter lost. Her name was Io,
Who might, for all he knew, be dead or living,
But since he can not find her anywhere
He thinks she must be nowhere, and his sorrow
Fears for the worst.

### JOVE AND IO

                        Jove had seen Io coming
From the river of her father, and had spoken:                  605
"O maiden, worthy of the love of Jove,
And sure to make some lover happy in bed,
Come to the shade of these deep woods" (he showed them)
"Come to the shade, the sun is hot and burning,
No beasts will hurt you there, I will go with you,             610
If a god is at your side, you will walk safely
In the very deepest woods. I am a god,
And no plebeian godling, either, but the holder
Of Heaven's scepter, hurler of the thunder.
Oh, do not flee me!" She had fled already                      615
Leaving Lyrcea's plains, and Lerna's[4] meadows,
When the god hid the lands in murk and darkness
And stayed her flight, and took her.
                              Meanwhile Juno
Looked down on Argos: what could those clouds be doing         620
In the bright light of day? They were not mists
Rising from rivers or damp ground. She wondered,
Took a quick look around to see her husband,
Or see where he might be—she knew his cheating!

1. The river Peneus.    2. Thessalain rivers.    3. A river near Argos.    4. A marsh in the
territory of Argos.

So when she did not find him in the heaven,
She said, "I am either wrong, or being wronged,"                    625
Came gliding down from Heaven, stood on earth,
Broke up the clouds. But Jove, ahead of time,
Could tell that she was coming; he changed Io
Into a heifer, white and shining, lovely
Even in altered form, and even Juno                                630
Looked on, though hating to, with admiration,
And asked whom she belonged to, from what pasture,
As if she did not know! And Jove, the liar,
To put a stop to questions, said she had sprung
Out of the earth, full-grown. Then Juno asked him,                 635
"Could I have her, as a present?" What could he do?
To give his love away was surely cruel,
To keep her most suspicious. Shame on one side
Says *Give her up!* and love says *Don't!* and shame
Might have been beaten by love's argument,                         640
But then, if he refused his wife the heifer,
So slight a present—if he should refuse it,
Juno might think perhaps it was no heifer!

Her rival thus disposed of, still the goddess
Did not at once abandon all suspicion.                             645
Afraid of Jove, and worried over his cheating,
She turned her over to the keeping of Argus
Who had a hundred eyes; two at a time,
No more than two, would ever close in slumber,
The rest kept watch. No matter how he stood,                       650
Which way he turned, he always looked at Io,
Always had Io in sight. He let her graze
By daylight, but at sundown locked her in,
Hobbled and haltered. She would feed on leaves
And bitter grasses, and her couch, poor creature,                  655
Was ground, not always grassy, and the water
She drank was muddy, often. When she wanted
To reach toward Argus her imploring arms,
She had no arms to reach with; when she tried
To plead, she only lowed, and her own voice                        660
Filled her with terror. When she came to the river,
Her father's, where she used to play, and saw,
Reflected in the stream, her jaws and horns,
She fled in panic. None of her sisters knew her,
And Inachus, her father, did not know her,                         665
But following them, she let them pet and praise her.
Old Inachus pulled grass and gave it to her,

And she licked his hand and tried to give it kisses,
Could not restrain her tears. If she could talk,
She would ask for help, and tell her name and sorrow,                    670
But as it was, all she could do was furrow
The dust with one forefoot, and make an I,
And then an O beside it, spelling her name,
Telling the story of her changed condition.
Her father knew her, cried, "Alas for me!"                    675
Clung to her horns and snowy neck, poor heifer,
Crying, "Alas for me! I have sought you, daughter,
All over the world, and now that I have found you,
I have found a greater grief. You do not answer,
And what you think is sighing comes out mooing!                    680
And all the while I, in my ignorance, counted
On marriage for you, wanting, first, a son,
Then, later, grandsons; now your mate must be
Selected from some herd, your son a bullock.
Not even death can end my heavy sorrow.                    685
It hurts to be a god; the door of death,
Shut in my face, prolongs my grief forever."
And both of them were weeping, but their guardian,
Argus the star-eyed, drove her from her father
To different pasture-land, and sat there, watching,                    690
Perched on a mountain-top above the valley.
Jove could not bear her sorrows any longer;
He called his son, born of the shining Pleiad,[5]
Told him *Kill Argus!* And Mercury came flying
On winged sandals, wearing the magic helmet,                    695
Bearing the sleep-producing wand, and lighted
On earth, and put aside the wings and helmet
Keeping the wand. With this he plays the shepherd
Across the pathless countryside, a driver
Of goats, collected somewhere, and he goes                    700
Playing a little tune on a pipe of reeds,
And this new sound is wonderful to Argus.
"Whoever you are, come here and sit beside me,"
He says, "This rock is in the shade; the grass
Is nowhere any better." And Mercury joins him,                    705
Whiling the time away with conversation
And soothing little melodies, and Argus
Has a hard fight with drowsiness; his eyes,
Some of them, close, but some of them stay open.
To keep himself awake by listening,                    710

---

5. Maia, daughter of Atlas. She and her six sisters became stars, the Pleiades.

He asks about the pipe of reeds, how was it
This new invention came about?
                                    The god
Began the story: "On the mountain slopes
Of cool Arcadia, a woodland nymph
Once lived, with many suitors, and her name          715
Was Syrinx.[6] More than once the satyrs chased her,
And so did other gods of field or woodland,
But always she escaped them, virgin always
As she aspired to be, one like Diana,
Like her in dress and calling, though her bow        720
Was made of horn, not gold, but even so,
She might, sometimes, be taken for the goddess.
Pan,[7] with a wreath of pine around his temples,
Once saw her coming back from Mount Lycaeus,[8]
And said" and Mercury broke off the story            725
And then went on to tell what Pan had told her,
How she said *No*, and fled, through pathless places,
Until she came to Ladon's river, flowing
Peaceful along the sandy banks, whose water
Halted her flight, and she implored her sisters[9]    730
To change her form, and so, when Pan had caught her
And thought he held a nymph, it was only reeds
That yielded in his arms, and while he sighed,
The soft air stirring in the reeds made also
The echo of a sigh. Touched by this marvel,          735
Charmed by the sweetness of the tone, he murmured
*This much I have!* and took the reeds, and bound them
With wax, a tall and shorter one together,
And called them Syrinx, still.
                                    And Mercury
Might have told more, but all the eyes of Argus,      740
He saw, had closed, and he made the slumber deeper
With movements of the wand, and then he struck
The nodding head just where it joins the shoulder,
Severed it with the curving blade, and sent it
Bloody and rolling over the rocks. So Argus          745
Lay low, and all the light in all those eyes
Went out forever, a hundred eyes, one darkness.
And Juno took the eyes and fastened them

---

6. The name means "shepherd's pipe." It is made of reeds. *Satyrs:* Woodland creatures, half
animal, half man, bald, bearded, and highly sexed.    7. A god of the wild mountain pastures
and woods.    8. An Arcadian mountain, sacred to Pan.    9. The water-nymphs of the river
Ladon.

On the feathers of a bird of hers, the peacock,
So that the peacock's tail is spread with jewels,                    750
And Juno, very angry, sent a fury
To harass Io, to drive her mad with terror,
In flight all over the world. At last a river
Halted her flight, the Nile, and when she came there
She knelt beside the stream, lifted her head,                    755
The only gesture she could make of praying,
And seemed, with groans and tears and mournful lowing,
To voice complaint to Jove, to end her sorrows,
And he was moved to pity; embracing Juno
He begged her: "End this punishment; hereafter                    760
Io, I swear, will never cause you anguish,"
And what he swore he called the Styx to witness.
And Juno was appeased. Io became
What once she was, again; the bristles vanish,
The horns are gone, the great round eyes grow smaller,                    765
The gaping jaws are narrower, the shoulders
Return, she has hands again, and toes and fingers,
The only sign of the heifer is the whiteness.
She stands erect, a nymph again, still fearful
That speech may still be mooing, but she tries                    770
And little by little gains back the use of language.
Now people, robed in linen, pay her homage,
A very goddess, and a son is born,
Named Epaphus, the seed of Jove; his temples
Are found beside his mother's in many cities.[1]                    775


## Book XV

[By the beginning of Book XV, Ovid has pursued the theme of
metamorphosis through all the cycles of Greek mythology and has
turned to the legends of early Rome. After Rome's founder and first
king, Romulus the warrior, came Numa, the peaceful giver of laws
and religious rites. Ovid has him journey to Croton in Southern Italy
to listen to the teachings of the Greek philosopher Pythagoras. The
teachings of Pythagoras, in Ovid at any rate, are an exposition of the
theme of metamorphosis from a philosophical and religious stand-
point, a striking contrast to the witty and generally amatory treatment
of the subject so far.]

1. The next line runs: "His boon companion was young Phaethon . . ." It is Ovid's transition to
the next extended narrative, that of Phaethon and the chariot of the sun, which occupies the next
400 lines or so.

## THE TEACHINGS OF PYTHAGORAS

There was a man here, Samian born,[2] but he
Had fled from Samos, for he hated tyrants
And chose, instead, an exile's lot. His thought
Reached far aloft, to the great gods in Heaven,
And his imagination looked on visions                                    5
Beyond his mortal sight. All things he studied
With watchful eager mind, and he brought home
What he had learned and sat among the people
Teaching them what was worthy, and they listened
In silence, wondering at the revelations                                10
How the great world began, the primal cause,
The nature of things, what God is, whence the snows
Come down, where lightning breaks from, whether wind
Or Jove speaks in the thunder from the clouds,
The cause of earthquakes, by what law the stars                         15
Wheel in their courses, all the secrets hidden
From man's imperfect knowledge. He was first
To say that animal food should not be eaten,
And learnèd as he was, men did not always
Believe him when he preached "Forbear, O mortals,                       20
To spoil your bodies with such impious food!
There is corn for you, apples, whose weight bears down
The bending branches; there are grapes that swell
On the green vines, and pleasant herbs, and greens
Made mellow and soft with cooking; there is milk                        25
And clover-honey. Earth is generous
With her provision, and her sustenance
Is very kind; she offers, for your tables,
Food that requires no bloodshed and no slaughter.
Meat is for beasts to feed on, yet not all                              30
Are carnivores, for horses, sheep, and cattle
Subsist on grass, but those whose disposition
Is fierce and cruel, tigers, raging lions,
And bears and wolves delight in bloody feasting.
Oh, what a wicked thing it is for flesh                                 35
To be the tomb of flesh, for the body's craving
To fatten on the body of another,
For one live creature to continue living

---

2. The historical Pythagoras (sixth century B.C.) was born in Samos, a Greek island off the coast
of Asia Minor, but emigrated to Croton in southern Italy. He founded a philosophical school
which seems to have been more like a religious brotherhood; the Pythagoreans were vegetarians;
they believed in the transmigration of souls from men to animals and vice versa. Consequently,
they were opposed to animal sacrifice. They were noted also for their skill as mathematicians
(Pythagoras' theorem).

Through one live creature's death. In all the richness
That Earth, the best of mothers, tenders to us,                    40
Does nothing please except to chew and mangle
The flesh of slaughtered animals? The Cyclops
Could do no worse! Must you destroy another
To satiate your greedy-gutted cravings?
There was a time, the Golden Age, we call it,                      45
Happy in fruits and herbs, when no men tainted
Their lips with blood, and birds went flying safely
Through air, and in the fields the rabbits wandered
Unfrightened, and no little fish was ever
Hooked by its own credulity: all things                           50
Were free from treachery and fear and cunning,
And all was peaceful. But some innovator,
A good-for-nothing, whoever he was, decided,
In envy, that what lions ate was better,
Stuffed meat into his belly like a furnace,                       55
And paved the way for crime. It may have been
That steel was warmed and dyed with blood through killing
Dangerous beasts, and that could be forgiven
On grounds of self-defense; to kill wild beasts
Is lawful, but they never should be eaten.                        60

One crime leads to another: first the swine
Were slaughtered, since they rooted up the seeds
And spoiled the season's crop; then goats were punished
On vengeful altars for nibbling at the grape-vines.
These both deserved their fate, but the poor sheep,               65
What had they ever done, born for man's service,
But bring us milk, so sweet to drink, and clothe us
With their soft wool, who give us more while living
Than ever they could in death? And what had oxen,
Incapable of fraud or trick or cunning,                           70
Simple and harmless, born to a life of labor,
What had they ever done? None but an ingrate,
Unworthy of the gift of grain, could ever
Take off the weight of the yoke, and with the axe
Strike at the neck that bore it, kill his fellow                  75
Who helped him break the soil and raise the harvest.
It is bad enough to do these things; we make
The gods our partners in the abomination,
Saying they love the blood of bulls in Heaven.
So there he stands, the victim at the altars,                     80
Without a blemish, perfect (and his beauty
Proves his own doom), in sacrificial garlands,

Horns tipped with gold, and hears the priest intoning:
Not knowing what he means, watches the barley
Sprinkled between his horns, the very barley                    85
He helped make grow, and then is struck
And with his blood he stains the knife whose flashing
He may have seen reflected in clear water.
Then they tear out his entrails, peer, examine,
Search for the will of Heaven, seeking omens.                   90
And then, so great man's appetite for food
Forbidden, then, O human race, you feed,
You feast, upon your kill. Do not do this,
I pray you, but remember: when you taste
The flesh of slaughtered cattle, you are eating                 95
Your fellow-workers.
                    "Now, since the god inspires me,
I follow where he leads, to open Delphi,
The very heavens, bring you revelation
Of mysteries, great matters never traced
By any mind before, and matters lost                            100
Or hidden and forgotten, these I sing.
There is no greater wonder than to range
The starry heights, to leave the earth's dull regions,
To ride the clouds, to stand on Atlas' shoulders,
And see, far off, far down, the little figures                  105
Wandering here and there, devoid of reason,
Anxious, in fear of death, and so advise them,
And so make fate an open book.
                    "O mortals,
Dumb in cold fear of death, why do you tremble
At Stygian rivers, shadows, empty names,                        110
The lying stock of poets, and the terrors
Of a false world? I tell you that your bodies
Can never suffer evil, whether fire
Consumes them, or the waste of time. Our souls
Are deathless; always, when they leave our bodies,              115
They find new dwelling-places. I myself,
I well remember, in the Trojan War
Was Panthous' son, Euphorbus, and my breast
Once knew the heavy spear of Menelaus.[3]
Not long ago, in Argos, Abas'[4] city,                          120
In Juno's temple, I saw the shield I carried
On my left arm. All things are always changing,
But nothing dies. The spirit comes and goes,

3. This claim is found in early, reliable sources.    4. A mythical king of Argos.

Is housed wherever it wills, shifts residence
From beasts to men, from men to beasts, but always          125
It keeps on living. As the pliant wax
Is stamped with new designs, and is no longer
What once it was, but changes form, and still
Is pliant wax, so do I teach that spirit
Is evermore the same, though passing always               130
To ever-changing bodies. So I warn you,
Lest appetite murder brotherhood, I warn you
By all the priesthood in me, do not exile
What may be kindred souls by evil slaughter.
Blood should not nourish blood.

                      "Full sail, I voyage          135
Over the boundless ocean, and I tell you
Nothing is permanent in all the world.
All things are fluent; every image forms,
Wandering through change. Time is itself a river
In constant movement, and the hours flow by               140
Like water, wave on wave, pursued, pursuing,
Forever fugitive, forever new.
That which has been, is not; that which was not,
Begins to be; motion and moment always
In process of renewal. Look, the night,                   145
Worn out, aims toward the brightness, and sun's glory
Succeeds the dark. The color of the sky
Is different at midnight, when tired things
Lie all at rest, from what it is at morning
When Lucifer rides his snowy horse, before               150
Aurora paints the sky for Phoebus'[5] coming.
The shield of the god reddens at early morning,
Reddens at evening, but is white at noonday
In purer air, farther from earth's contagion.
And the Moon-goddess changes in the nighttime,           155
Lesser today than yesterday, if waning,
Greater tomorrow than today, when crescent.

Notice the year's four seasons: they resemble
Our lives. Spring is a nursling, a young child,
Tender and young, and the grass shines and buds          160
Swell with new life, not yet full-grown nor hardy,
But promising much to husbandmen, with blossom
Bright in the fertile fields. And then comes summer
When the year is a strong young man, no better time

5. The sun. *Lucifer:* The morning star.

Than this, no richer, no more passionate vigor.                     165
Then comes the prime of Autumn, a little sober,
But ripe and mellow, moderate of mood,
Halfway from youth to age, with just a showing
Of gray around the temples. And then Winter,
Tottering, shivering, bald or gray, and agèd.                       170

Our bodies also change. What we have been,
What we now are, we shall not be tomorrow.
There was a time when we were only seed,
Only the hope of men, housed in the womb,
Where Nature shaped us, brought us forth, exposed us           175
To the void air, and there in light we lay,
Feeble and infant, and were quadrupeds
Before too long, and after a little wobbled
And pulled ourselves upright, holding a chair,
The side of the crib, and strength grew into us,                180
And swiftness; youth and middle age went swiftly
Down the long hill toward age, and all our vigor
Came to decline, so Milon, the old wrestler,
Weeps when he sees his arms whose bulging muscles
Were once like Hercules', and Helen weeps              185
To see her wrinkles in the looking glass:
Could this old woman ever have been ravished,
Taken twice over?[6] Time devours all things
With envious Age, together. The slow gnawing
Consumes all things, and very, very slowly.                      190

Not even the so-called elements are constant.
Listen, and I will tell you of their changes.
There are four of them, and two, the earth and water,
Are heavy, and their own weight bears them downward,
And two, the air and fire (and fire is purer                     195
Even than air) are light, rise upward
If nothing holds them down. These elements
Are separate in space, yet all things come
From them and into them, and they can change
Into each other. Earth can be dissolved              200
To flowing water, water can thin to air,
And air can thin to fire, and fire can thicken
To air again, and air condense to water,
And water be compressed to solid earth.
Nothing remains the same: the great renewer,         205

6. Once by Theseus, then by Paris.

Nature, makes form from form, and, oh, believe me
That nothing ever dies. What we call birth
Is the beginning of a difference,
No more than that, and death is only ceasing
Of what had been before. The parts may vary,                    210
Shifting from here to there, hither and yon,
And back again, but the great sum is constant.


Nothing, I am convinced, can be the same
Forever. There was once an Age of Gold,
Later, an Age of Iron. Every place                              215
Submits to Fortune's wheel. I have seen oceans
That once were solid land, and I have seen
Lands made from ocean. Often sea-shells lie
Far from the beach, and men have found old anchors
On mountain-tops. Plateaus have turned to valleys,             220
Hills washed away, marshes become dry desert,
Deserts made pools. Here Nature brings forth fountains,
There shuts them in; when the earth quakes, new rivers
Are born and old ones sink and dry and vanish.
Lycus,[7] for instance, swallowed by the earth                 225
Emerges far away, a different stream,
And Erasinus disappears, goes under
The ground, and comes to light again in Argos,
And Mysus, so the story goes, was tired
Of his old source and banks and went elsewhere                 230
And now is called Caicus. The Anigrus[8]
Was good to drink from once, but now rolls down
A flood that you had better leave alone,
Unless the poets lie, because the Centaurs
Used it to wash their wounds from Hercules' arrows.[9]         235
And Hypanis, rising from Scythian mountains,
Once fresh and sweet to the taste, is salty and brackish.


Antissa, Pharos, Tyre,[1] all inland cities,
Were islands once, Leucas and Zancle[2] mainland,
And Helice and Buris,[3] should you seek them,                 240
Those old Achaian cities, you would find them
Under the waves, and mariners can show you

---

7. A river of Asia Minor, as is Mysus, below.    8. A river of Elis, in the western Peloponnese.
9. They were poison-tipped. *Hypanis:* A river in Scythia, running into the Black Sea.    1. A
Phoenician trading city on the coast of Lebanon. *Antissa.* On the island of Lesbos. *Pharos:* Peninsula connected to the mainland of Alexandria in Egypt.    2. Off the coast of Sicily. *Leucas:* A
large island off the west coast of Greece.    3. Coastal cities in Achaea, which disappeared into
the sea in 373 B.C.

The sloping ramps, the buried walls. Near Troezen[4]
Stands a high treeless hill, a level plain
Until the violent winds, penned underground,                    245
Stifled in gloomy caverns, struggled long
For freer air to breathe, since that black prison
Had never a chink, made the ground swell to bursting,
The way one blows a bladder or a goatskin,
And where that blister or that bubble grew                      250
Out of the ground, the lump remained and hardened
With time, and now it seems a rounded hill-top.


Example on example! I could cite you
So many more that I have seen or heard of.
Just a few more. The element of water                           255
Gives and receives strange forms. At midday Ammon[5]
Is cold, but warm in the morning and the evening.
The Athamanians[6] set wood on fire
By pouring water on it in the dark of the moon,
And the Ciconian[7] people have a river                         260
They never drink, for they would turn to marble.
Crathis and Sybaris,[8] in our own country,
Turn hair the color of platinum or gold,
And there are other streams, more marvelous even,
Whose waters affect the mind as well as body.                   265
You have heard about Salmacis;[9] there are lakes
In Ethiopia where a swallow of the water
Will drive you raving mad or hold you rigid
In catatonic lethargy. No man
Who likes his wine should ever drink from Clytor[1]             270
Or he would hate it; something in that water,
It may be, counteracts the heat of wine,
Or possibly, and so the natives tell us,
Melampus,[2] when he cured the maddened daughters
Of Proetus by his herbs and magic singing,                      275
Threw in that spring mind-clearing hellebore,[3]
So that a hatred of wine stays in those waters.
Lyncestis[4] river is just the opposite;

4. In the Peloponnese, across from Attica. The mountain on the peninsula of Methana, north of
Troezen, is made of volcanic rock.    5. The spring at the site of the oracle of Ammon, in
Libya.    6. A people of northwestern Greece. This miraculously hot spring was supposed to have
been at Dodona, an oracular shrine in that region.    7. A Thracian tribe.    8. Rivers in southern Italy.    9. In Book IV, Ovid had already explained that bathing in the spring of Salmacis (in
Caria, a district of Asia Minor) made men soft and weak.    1. In Arcadia.    2. A prophet, who
cured the daughters of Proetus, King of Argos. They had been driven mad in punishment for their
pride; the madness, inflicted by Juno, made them imagine they were cows.    3. A drug made
from herbs, which was supposed to restore sanity.    4. The Lyncestae were a tribe in Macedonia.

Whoever drinks too freely there will stagger
As if he had taken undiluted wine.                                    280
At Pheneus, in Arcadia, there are springs
Harmless by day, injurious in the nighttime.
As lakes and rivers vary in their virtues,
So lands can change. The little island Delos
Once floated on the waters, but now stands firm,                      285
And Jason's Argo, as you well remember,
Dreaded the Clashing Rocks,[5] the high-flung spray,
Immovable now, contemptuous of the winds.
Etna,[6] whose furnaces glow hot with sulphur,
Will not be fiery always in the future,                               290
And was not always fiery in the past.
The earth has something animal about it,
Living almost, with many lungs to breathe through,
Sending out flames, but the passages of breathing
Are changeable; some caverns may be closed                            295
And new ones open whence the fire can issue.
Deep caves compress the violent winds, which drive
Rock against rock, imprisoning the matter
That holds the seeds of flame, and this bursts blazing
Ignited by the friction, and the caves                                300
Cool when the winds are spent. The tars and pitches,
The yellow sulphur with invisible burning,
Are no eternal fuel, so volcanoes,
Starved of their nourishment, devour no longer,
Abandon fire, as they have been abandoned.                            305

Far to the north, somewhere around Pallene,[7]
The story goes, there is a lake where men
Who plunge nine times into the chilly waters
Come out with downy feathers over their bodies.
This I do not believe, nor that the women                             310
Of Scythia sprinkle their bodies with magic juices
For the same purpose and effect.
                              "However,
There are stranger things that have been tried and tested
And these we must believe. You have seen dead bodies,
Rotten from time or heat, breed smaller creatures.                    315
Bury the carcasses of slaughtered bullocks,
Chosen for sacrifice (all men know this),
And from the putrid entrails will come flying

---

5. Two rocks in the Black Sea which crushed any ship that came between them; after the Argo
passed through them successfully, they remained fixed in place forever.    6. The volcano (still
active) in northeast Sicily.    7. A peninsula in Macedonia.

The flower-culling bees,[8] whose actions prove
Their parenthood, for they are fond of meadows,        320
Are fond of toil, and work with hopeful spirit.
The horse, being warlike, after he is buried
Produces hornets. Cut a sea-crab's claws,
Bury the rest of the body, and a scorpion
Comes from the ground. And worms that weave cocoons    325
White on the leaves of the trees, as country people
Know well, turn into moths with death's-head marking.
The mud holds seeds that generate green frogs,
Legless at first, but the legs grown, to swim with,
And take long jumps with, later. And a bear-cub,       330
New-born, is not a bear at all, but only
A lump, hardly alive, whose mother gives it
A licking into shape, herself as model.
The larvae of the honey-bearing bees,
Safe in hexagonal waxen cells, are nothing             335
But wormlike bodies; feet and wings come later.
Who would believe that from an egg would come
Such different wonders as Juno's bird, the peacock,
Jove's eagle, Venus' dove, and all the fliers?
Some people think that when the human spine            340
Has rotted in the narrow tomb, the marrow
Is changed into a serpent.
                        "All these things
Have their beginning in some other creature,
But there is one bird which renews itself
Out of itself. The Assyrians call it the phoenix.      345
It does not live on seeds nor the green grasses,
But on the gum of frankincense and juices
Of cardamon. It lives five centuries,
As you may know, and then it builds itself
A nest in the highest branches of a palm-tree,         350
Using its talons and clean beak to cover
This nest with cassia and spikes of spikenard,
And cinnamon and yellow myrrh, and there
It dies among the fragrance, and from the body
A tiny phoenix springs to birth, whose years           355
Will be as long. The fledgling, gaining strength
To carry burdens, lifts the heavy nest,
His cradle and the old one's tomb, and bears it
Through the thin air to the city of the Sun
And lays it as an offering at the doors                360

---

8. Compare the riddle Sampson put to the Philistines, *Judges* XIV: 5–18.

Of the Sun-god's holy temple.
                              "Wonders, wonders!
The same hyena can be male or female,
To take or give the seed of life, at pleasure,
And the chameleon, a little creature
Whose food is wind and air, takes on the color          365
Of anything it rests on. India, conquered,
Gave Bacchus,[9] tendril-crowned, the tawny lynxes
Whose urine, when it met the air, was hardened
Becoming stone; so coral also hardens
At the first touch of air, while under water             370
It sways, a pliant weed.
                         "The day will end,
The Sun-god plunge tired horses in the ocean
Before I have the time I need to tell you
All of the things that take new forms. We see
The eras change, nations grow strong, or weaken,        375
Like Troy, magnificent in men and riches,
For ten years lavish with her blood, and now
Displaying only ruins and for wealth
The old ancestral tombs. Sparta, Mycenae,
Athens, and Thebes, all flourished once, and now        380
What are they more than names? I hear that Rome
Is rising, out of Trojan blood, established
On strong and deep foundations, where the Tiber
Comes from the Apennines.[1] Rome's form is changing
Growing to greatness, and she will be, some day,        385
Head of the boundless world; so we are told
By oracles and seers. I can remember
When Troy was tottering ruinward, a prophet,
Helenus, son of Priam, told Aeneas
In consolation for his doubts and weeping               390
'O son of Venus, if you bear in mind
My prophecies, Troy shall not wholly perish
While you are living: fire and sword will give you
Safe passage through them; you will carry on
Troy's relics, till a land, more friendly to you        395
Than your own native soil, will give asylum.
I see the destined city for the Trojans
And their sons' sons, none greater in all the ages,
Past, present, or to come. Through long, long eras
Her famous men will bring her power, but one,           400

9. The god Dionysus with his army of maenads and satyrs conquered the Indians.    1. The
mountainous spine of the Italian peninsula. *Tiber:* The river that flows through Rome.

Sprung from Iulus' blood,[2] will make her empress
Of the whole world, and after earth has used him
The heavens will enjoy him, Heaven will be
His destination.' What Helenus told Aeneas,
I have told you, I remember, and I am happy                          405
That for our kin[3] new walls, at last, are rising,
That the Greek victory was to such good purpose.


We must not wander far and wide, forgetting
The goal of our discourse. Remember this:
The heavens and all below them, earth and her creatures,       410
All change, and we, part of creation, also
Must suffer change. We are not bodies only,
But wingèd spirits, with the power to enter
Animal forms, house in the bodies of cattle.
Therefore, we should respect those dwelling-places             415
Which may have given shelter to the spirit
Of fathers, brothers, cousins, human beings
At least, and we should never do them damage,
Not stuff ourselves like the cannibal Thyestes.[4]
An evil habit, impious preparation,                            420
Wicked as human bloodshed, to draw the knife
Across the throat of the calf, and hear its anguish
Cry to deaf ears! And who could slay
The little goat whose cry is like a baby's,
Or eat a bird he has himself just fed?                         425
One might as well do murder; he is only
The shortest step away. Let the bull plow
And let him owe his death to length of days;
Let the sheep give you armor for rough weather,
The she-goats bring full udders to the milking.                430
Have done with nets and traps and snares and springes,
Bird-lime and forest-beaters, lines and fish-hooks.
Kill, if you must, the beasts that do you harm,
But, even so, let killing be enough;
Let appetite refrain from flesh, take only                     435
A gentler nourishment."

---

2. Augustus.   3. Pythagoras, who was in a former incarnation Euphorbus (cf. 1. 118) speaks
here as a Trojan.   4. His brother Atreus tricked him into eating the flesh of his own children.
(Cf. Aeschylus, *Agamemnon*).

# THE NEW TESTAMENT

In the last years of Augustus' life, in the Roman province of Judea, there was born to Joseph, a carpenter of Nazareth, and his wife, Mary, a son who was in the tradition of the Hebrew prophets but was also the bearer of a message that was to transform the world. His life on earth was short; it ended in the agony of crucifixion at about His thirty-third year. This event is a point of intersection of the three main lines of development of the ancient world—Hebrew, Greek, and Latin—for this Hebrew prophet was executed by a Roman governor, and His life and teachings were written down in the Greek language. These documents, which eventually, with some additions, constituted what we now know as the New Testament, circulated in the Greek-speaking half of the Roman Empire and later, in a Latin translation, in the West. They became the sacred texts of a church which, at first persecuted by and then triumphantly associated with Roman imperial power, outlasted the destruction of the empire and ruled over a spiritual kingdom which still exists.

The teaching of Christ was revolutionary not only in terms of Greek and Roman feeling but also in terms of the Hebrew religious tradition. The Hebrew idea of a personal God who is yet not anthropomorphic, who is omnipotent, omniscient, and infinitely just, was now broadened to include among His attributes an infinite mercy which tempered the justice. Greek and Roman religion was outward and visible, the formal practice of ritual acts in a social context; Christianity was inward and spiritual, the important relationship was that between the individual soul and God. All human beings were on an equal plane in the eyes of their Creator. This idea ran counter to the theory and practice of an institution basic to the economy of the ancient world, slavery. Like the earlier Hebrew prophets, Christ was rejected by His own people, as prophets have always been, and His death on the cross and His resurrection provided His followers and the future converts with an unforgettable symbol of a new dispensation, the son of God in human form suffering to atone for the sins of humanity, the supreme expression of divine mercy. This conception is the basis of the teaching of Paul, the apostle to the gentiles, who in the middle years of the first century A.D. changed Christianity from a Jewish sect to a world-wide movement with flourishing churches all over Asia Minor and Greece, and even in Rome. The burden of his teaching was the frailty and corruption of this life and world, and the certainty of resurrection. "For this corruptible must put on incorruption, and this mortal must put on immortality." To those who had accepted this vision the secular materialism that was the dominant view in the new era of peace and progress guaranteed by the stabilization of Roman rule was no longer tenable.

Recommended reading is Bruce M. Metzgar, *The New Testament, Its Background, Growth, and Content* (1965).

# The New Testament[1]

## [The Birth and Youth of Jesus][2]

2. And it came to pass in those days, that there went out a decree from Cæsar Augustus, that all the world[3] should be taxed. (And this taxing was first made when Cyrenius was governor of Syria.) And all went to be taxed, every one into his own city. And Joseph also went up from Galilee, out of the city of Nazareth, into Judæa, unto the city of David, which is called Bethlehem; (because he was of the house and lineage of David:) to be taxed with Mary his espoused wife, being great with child. And so it was, that, while they were there, the days were accomplished that she should be delivered. And she brought forth her firstborn son, and wrapped him in swaddling clothes, and laid him in a manger; because there was no room for them in the inn. And there were in the same country shepherds abiding in the field, keeping watch over their flock by night. And, lo, the angel of the Lord came upon them, and the glory of the Lord shone round about them: and they were sore afraid. And the angel said unto them, Fear not: for, behold, I bring you good tidings of great joy, which shall be to all people. For unto you is born this day in the city of David a Saviour, which is Christ[4] the Lord. And this shall be a sign unto you; ye shall find the babe wrapped in swaddling clothes, lying in a manger. And suddenly there was with the angel a multitude of the heavenly host praising God, and saying, Glory to God in the highest, and on earth peace, good will toward men. And it came to pass, as the angels were gone away from them into heaven, the shepherds said one to another, Let us now go even unto Bethlehem, and see this thing which is come to pass, which the Lord hath made known unto us. And they came with haste, and found Mary, and Joseph, and the babe lying in a manger. And when they had seen it, they made known abroad the saying which was told them concerning this child. And all they that heard it wondered at those things which were told them by the shepherds. But Mary kept all these things, and pondered them in her heart. And the shepherds returned, glorifying and praising God for all the things that they had heard and seen, as it was told unto them. And when eight days were accomplished for the circumcising of the child, his name was called JESUS,[5] which was so named of the angel[6] before he was conceived in the womb. And when the days of her purification according to the law of Moses were accomplished,[7] they brought him to Jerusalem, to present him to the Lord; (as it is written in the law of the

1. The text of these selections is that of the King James, or Authorized, Version.  2. Luke 2:1–52.  3. The Roman Empire.  4. A Greek word meaning "anointed," used of kings, priests, and the Deliverer promised by the Prophets.  5. A form of the name Joshua, which means "he shall save."  6. In the Annunciation to Mary. (Luke 1:31.)  7. For the law here referred to, see Leviticus 12.

Lord, Every male that openeth the womb[8] shall be called holy to the Lord;) and to offer a sacrifice according to that which is said in the law of the Lord, A pair of turtledoves, or two young pigeons. And, behold, there was a man in Jerusalem, whose name was Simeon; and the same man was just and devout, waiting for the consolation of Israel: and the Holy Ghost was upon him. And it was revealed unto him by the Holy Ghost, that he should not see death, before he had seen the Lord's Christ. And he came by the Spirit into the temple: and when the parents brought in the child Jesus, to do for him after the custom of the law, then took he him up in his arms, and blessed God, and said, Lord, now lettest thou thy servant depart in peace, according to thy word: for mine eyes have seen thy salvation, which thou hast prepared before the face of all people; a light to lighten the Gentiles,[9] and the glory of thy people Israel. And Joseph and his mother marvelled at those things which were spoken of him. And Simeon blessed them, and said unto Mary his mother, Behold, this child is set for the fall and rising again[1] of many in Israel; and for a sign which shall be spoken against; (yea, a sword shall pierce through thy own soul also,) that the thoughts of many hearts may be revealed. And there was one Anna, a prophetess, the daughter of Phanuel, of the tribe of Aser: she was of a great age, and had lived with an husband seven years from her virginity; and she was a widow of about fourscore and four years, which departed not from the temple, but served God with fastings and prayers night and day. And she coming in that instant gave thanks likewise unto the Lord, and spoke of him to all them that looked for redemption in Jerusalem. And when they had performed all things according to the law of the Lord, they returned into Galilee, to their own city Nazareth. And the child grew, and waxed strong in spirit, filled with wisdom: and the grace of God was upon him. Now his parents went to Jerusalem every year at the feast of the passover. And when he was twelve years old, they went up to Jerusalem after the custom of the feast. And when they had fulfilled the days, as they returned, the child Jesus tarried behind in Jerusalem; and Joseph and his mother knew not of it. But they, supposing him to have been in the company, went a day's journey; and they sought him among their kinsfolk and acquaintance. And when they found him not, they turned back again to Jerusalem, seeking him. And it came to pass that after three days they found him in the temple, sitting in the midst of the doctors,[2] both hearing them, and asking them questions. And all that heard him were astonished at his understanding and answers. And when they saw him, they were amazed: and his mother said unto him, Son, why

8. First-born son, regarded as belonging to God. See Exodus 13:2.    9. Non-Jews.    1. The Greek word is the one always used of the resurrection of the dead.    2. Teachers, rabbis.

hast thou thus dealt with us? behold, thy father and I have sought thee sorrowing. And he said unto them, How is it that ye sought me? wist ye not that I must be about my Father's business? And they understood not the saying which he spake unto them. And he went down with them, and came to Nazareth, and was subject unto them: but his mother kept all these sayings in her heart. And Jesus increased in wisdom and stature, and in favour with God and man.

### [The Teaching of Jesus: The Sermon on the Mount[3]]

5. And seeing the multitudes, he went up into a mountain: and when he was set, his disciples came unto him: and he opened his mouth, and taught them, saying, Blessed are the poor in spirit: for theirs is the kingdom of heaven. Blessed are they that mourn: for they shall be comforted. Blessed are the meek: for they shall inherit the earth. Blessed are they which do hunger and thirst after righteousness: for they shall be filled. Blessed are the merciful: for they shall obtain mercy. Blessed are the pure in heart: for they shall see God. Blessed are the peacemakers: for they shall be called the children of God. Blessed are they which are persecuted for righteousness' sake: for theirs is the kingdom of heaven. Blessed are ye, when men shall revile you, and persecute you, and shall say all manner of evil against you falsely, for my sake. Rejoice, and be exceeding glad: for great is your reward in heaven: for so persecuted they the prophets which were before you.

Ye are the salt of the earth: but if the salt have lost his savour, wherewith shall it be salted?[4] it is thenceforth good for nothing, but to be cast out, and to be trodden under foot of men. Ye are the light of the world. A city that is set on a hill cannot be hid. Neither do men light a candle, and put it under a bushel,[5] but on a candlestick; and it giveth light unto all that are in the house. Let your light so shine before men, that they may see your good works, and glorify your Father which is in heaven.

Think not that I am come to destroy the law, or the prophets: I am not come to destroy, but to fulfil. For verily I say unto you, Till heaven and earth pass, one jot or one tittle shall in no wise pass from the law, till all be fulfilled. Whosoever therefore shall break one of these least commandments, and shall teach men so, he shall be called the least in the kingdom of heaven: but whosoever shall do and teach them, the same shall be called great in the kingdom of heaven. For I say unto you, That except your righteousness shall exceed the righteousness of the scribes and Pharisees,[6] ye shall in no case enter into the kingdom of heaven.

3. Matthew 5:1–7:29.    4. How can it regain its savor?    5. A household vessel with the capacity of a bushel.    6. A sect which insisted on strict observance of the Mosaic law. *Scribes:* The official interpreters of the Sacred Scriptures.

Ye have heard that it was said by them of old time, Thou shalt not kill; and whosoever shall kill shall be in danger of the judgment: but I say unto you, That whosoever is angry with his brother without a cause shall be in danger of the judgment: and whosoever shall say to his brother, Raca,[7] shall be in danger of the council: but whosoever shall say, Thou fool, shall be in danger of hell fire.[8] Therefore if thou bring thy gift to the altar, and there rememberest that thy brother hath ought against thee; leave there thy gift before the altar, and go thy way; first be reconciled to thy brother, and then come and offer thy gift. Agree with thine adversary quickly, whiles thou art in the way with him; lest at any time the adversary deliver thee to the judge, and the judge deliver thee to the officer, and thou be cast into prison. Verily I say unto thee, Thou shalt by no means come out thence, till thou hast paid the uttermost farthing.

Ye have heard that it was said by them of old time, Thou shalt not commit adultery: but I say unto you, That whosoever looketh on a woman to lust after her hath committed adultery with her already in his heart. And if thy right eye offend thee, pluck it out, and cast it from thee: for it is profitable for thee that one of thy members should perish, and not that thy whole body should be cast into hell. And if thy right hand offend thee, cut it off, and cast it from thee: for it is profitable for thee that one of thy members should perish, and not that thy whole body should be cast into hell. It hath been said, Whosoever shall put away his wife, let him give her a writing of divorcement: but I say unto you, That whosoever shall put away his wife, saving for the cause of fornication, causeth her to commit adultery: and whosoever shall marry her that is divorced committeth adultery.

Again, ye have heard that it hath been said by them of old time, Thou shalt not forswear thyself, but shalt perform unto the Lord thine oaths: but I say unto you, Swear not at all; neither by heaven; for it is God's throne: nor by the earth; for it is his footstool: neither by Jerusalem; for it is the city of the great King. Neither shalt thou swear by thy head, because thou canst not make one hair white or black. But let your communication be, Yea, yea; Nay, nay: for whatsoever is more than these cometh of evil.

Ye have heard that it hath been said, An eye for an eye, and a tooth for a tooth: but I say unto you, That ye resist not evil: but whosoever shall smite thee on thy right cheek, turn to him the other

7. The word means "empty." 8. The reference is to Jewish legal institutions. The penalties which might be inflicted for murder (see the opening sentence of this paragraph) were death by the sword (a sentence of a local court, "the judgment"), death by stoning (the sentence of a higher court, "the council"), and lastly the burning of the criminal's body in the place where refuse was thrown, Gehenna, which is hence used as a name for hell. Jesus compares the different degrees of punishment (administered by God) for the new sins which he here lists to the degrees of punishment recognized by Jewish law.

also. And if any man will sue thee at the law, and take away thy coat, let him have thy cloak also. And whosoever shall compel thee to go a mile, go with him twain. Give to him that asketh thee, and from him that would borrow of thee turn not thou away.

Ye have heard that it hath been said, Thou shalt love thy neighbour, and hate thine enemy. But I say unto you, Love your enemies, bless them that curse you, do good to them that hate you, and pray for them which despitefully use you, and persecute you; that ye may be the children of your Father which is in heaven: for he maketh his sun to rise on the evil and on the good, and sendeth rain on the just and on the unjust. For if ye love them which love you, what reward have ye? do not even the publicans[9] the same? And if ye salute your brethren only, what do ye more than others? do not even the publicans so? Be ye therefore perfect, even as your Father which is in heaven is perfect.

6. Take heed that ye do not your alms before men, to be seen of them: otherwise ye have no reward of your Father which is in heaven. Therefore when thou doest thine alms, do not sound a trumpet before thee, as the hypocrites do in the synagogues and in the streets, that they may have glory of men. Verily I say unto you, They have their reward. But when thou doest alms, let not thy left hand know what thy right hand doeth: that thine alms may be in secret: and thy Father which seeth in secret himself shall reward thee openly.

And when thou prayest, thou shalt not be as the hypocrites are: for they love to pray standing in the synagogues and in the corners of the streets, that they may be seen of men. Verily I say unto you, They have their reward. But thou, when thou prayest, enter into thy closet, and when thou hast shut thy door, pray to thy Father which is in secret; and thy Father which seeth in secret shall reward thee openly. But when ye pray, use not vain repetitions, as the heathen do; for they think that they shall be heard for their much speaking. Be not ye therefore like unto them: for your Father knoweth what things ye have need of, before ye ask him. After this manner therefore pray ye: Our Father which art in heaven, Hallowed be thy name. Thy kingdom come. Thy will be done in earth, as it is in heaven. Give us this day our daily bread. And forgive us our debts, as we forgive our debtors. And lead us not into temptation, but deliver us from evil: For thine is the kingdom, and the power, and the glory, for ever. Amen. For if ye forgive men their trespasses, your heavenly Father will also forgive you: but if ye forgive not men their trespasses, neither will your Father forgive your trespasses.

Moreover when ye fast, be not, as the hypocrites, of a sad counte-

9. The men who collected the taxes for the Roman tax-farming corporations; they were, naturally, universally despised and hated.

nance: for they disfigure their faces, that they may appear unto men to fast. Verily I say unto you, They have their reward. But thou, when thou fastest, anoint thine head, and wash thy face; that thou appear not unto men to fast, but unto thy Father which is in secret: and thy Father, which seeth in secret shall reward thee openly.

Lay not up for yourselves treasures upon earth, where moth and rust doth corrupt, and where thieves break through and steal: but lay up for yourselves treasures in heaven, where neither moth nor rust doth corrupt, and where thieves do not break through nor steal: for where your treasure is, there will your heart be also. The light of the body is the eye: if therefore thine eye be single,[1] thy whole body shall be full of light. But if thine eye be evil, thy whole body shall be full of darkness. If therefore the light that is in thee be darkness, how great is that darkness!

No man can serve two masters: for either he will hate the one, and love the other; or else he will hold to the one, and despise the other. Ye cannot serve God and Mammon. Therefore I say unto you, Take no thought for your life, what ye shall eat, or what ye shall drink; nor yet for your body, what ye shall put on. Is not the life more than meat, and the body than raiment? Behold the fowls of the air: for they sow not, neither do they reap, nor gather into barns; yet your heavenly Father feedeth them. Are ye not much better than they? Which of you by taking thought can add one cubit unto his stature? And why take ye thought for raiment? Consider the lilies of the field, how they grow; they toil not, neither do they spin: and yet I say unto you that even Solomon in all his glory was not arrayed like one of these. Wherefore, if God so clothe the grass of the field, which to-day is, and to-morrow is cast into the oven, shall he not much more clothe you, O ye of little faith? Therefore take no thought, saying, What shall we eat? or, What shall we drink? or, Wherewithal shall we be clothed? (For after all these things do the Gentiles seek:) for your heavenly Father knoweth that ye have need of all these things. But seek ye first the kingdom of God, and his righteousness; and all these things shall be added unto you. Take therefore no thought for the morrow: for the morrow shall take thought for the things of itself. Sufficient unto the day is the evil thereof.

7. Judge not, that ye be not judged. For with what judgment ye judged, ye shall be judged: and with what measure ye mete, it shall be measured to you again. And why beholdest thou the mote that is in thy brother's eye, but considerest not the beam that is in thine own eye? Or how wilt thou say to thy brother, Let me pull out the mote out of thine eye; and, behold, a beam is in thine own eye?

1. Clear.

Thou hypocrite, first cast out the beam out of thine own eye; and then shalt thou see clearly to cast out the mote out of thy brother's eye.

Give not that which is holy unto the dogs, neither cast ye your pearls before swine, lest they trample them under their feet, and turn again and rend you.

Ask, and it shall be given you; seek, and ye shall find; knock, and it shall be opened unto you: for every one that asketh receiveth; and he that seeketh findeth; and to him that knocketh it shall be opened. Or what man is there of you, whom if his son ask bread, will he give him a stone? Or if he ask a fish, will he give him a serpent? If ye then, being evil, know how to give good gifts unto your children, how much more shall your Father which is in heaven give good things to them that ask him? Therefore all things whatsoever ye would that men should do to you, do ye even so to them: for this is the law and the prophets.

Enter ye in at the strait gate: for wide is the gate, and broad is the way, that leadeth to destruction, and many there be which go in thereat: because strait is the gate, and narrow is the way, which leadeth unto life, and few there be that find it.

Beware of false prophets, which come to you in sheep's clothing, but inwardly they are ravening wolves. Ye shall know them by their fruits. Do men gather grapes of thorns, or figs of thistles? Even so every good tree bringeth forth good fruit; but a corrupt tree bringeth forth evil fruit. A good tree cannot bring forth evil fruit, neither can a corrupt tree bring forth good fruit. Every tree that bringeth not forth good fruit is hewn down, and cast into the fire. Wherefore by their fruits ye shall know them.

Not every one that saith unto me, Lord, Lord, shall enter into the kingdom of heaven; but he that doeth the will of my Father which is in heaven. Many will say to me in that day, Lord, Lord, have we not prophesied in thy name? and in thy name have cast out devils? and in thy name done many wonderful works? And then will I profess unto them, I never knew you: depart from me, ye that work iniquity.

Therefore whosoever heareth these sayings of mine, and doeth them, I will liken him unto a wise man, which built his house upon a rock: and the rain descended, and the floods came and the winds blew, and beat upon that house; and it fell not: for it was founded upon a rock. And every one that heareth these sayings of mine, and doeth them not, shall be likened unto a foolish man, which built his house upon the sand: and the rain descended, and the floods came, and the winds blew, and beat upon that house; and it fell: and great was the fall of it. And it came to pass, when Jesus had ended these sayings, the people were astonished at his doctrine: for he taught them as one having authority, and not as the scribes.

## [PARABLES OF JESUS][2]

15. Then drew near unto him all the publicans and sinners for to hear him. And the Pharisees and scribes murmured, saying, This man receiveth sinners, and eateth with them.

And he spoke this parable unto them, saying, What man of you, having a hundred sheep, if he lose one of them, doth not leave the ninety and nine in the wilderness, and go after that which is lost, until he find it? And when he hath found it, he layeth it on his shoulders, rejoicing. And when he cometh home, he calleth together his friends and neighbours, saying unto them, Rejoice with me; for I have found my sheep which was lost. I say unto you that likewise joy shall be in heaven over one sinner that repenteth, more than over ninety and nine just persons, which need no repentance.

Either what woman having ten pieces of silver, if she lose one piece, doth not light a candle, and sweep the house, and seek diligently till she find it? And when she hath found it, she calleth her friends and her neighbours together, saying, Rejoice with me; for I have found the piece which I had lost. Likewise, I say unto you, there is joy in the presence of the angels of God over one sinner that repenteth.

And he said, A certain man had two sons: and the younger of them said to his father, Father, give me the portion of goods that falleth to me. And he divided unto them his living. And not many days after the younger son gathered all together, and took his journey into a far country, and there wasted his substance with riotous living. And when he had spent all, there arose a mighty famine in that land; and he began to be in want. And he went and joined himself to a citizen of that country; and he sent him into his fields to feed swine. And he would fain have filled his belly with the husks that the swine did eat: and no man gave unto him. And when he came to himself, he said, How many hired servants of my father's have bread enough and to spare, and I perish with hunger! I will arise and go to my father, and will say unto him, Father, I have sinned against heaven, and before thee, and am no more worthy to be called thy son: make me as one of thy hired servants. And he arose, and came to his father. But when he was yet a great way off, his father saw him, and had compassion, and ran, and fell on his neck, and kissed him. And the son said unto him, Father, I have sinned against heaven, and in thy sight, and am no more worthy to be called thy son. But the father

2. Luke 15:1–32.

said to his servants, Bring forth the best robe, and put it on him; and put a ring on his hand, and shoes on his feet: and bring hither the fatted calf, and kill it; and let us eat, and be merry: for this my son was dead, and is alive again; he was lost, and is found. And they began to be merry. Now his elder son was in the field: and as he came and drew nigh to the house, he heard musick and dancing. And he called one of the servants, and asked what these things meant. And he said unto him, Thy brother is come; and thy father hath killed the fatted calf, because he hath received him safe and sound. And he was angry, and would not go in: therefore came his father out, and intreated him. And he answering said to his father, Lo, these many years do I serve thee, neither transgressed I at any time thy commandment: and yet thou never gavest me a kid, that I might make merry with my friends: but as soon as this thy son was come, which hath devoured thy living with harlots, thou hast killed for him the fatted calf. And he said unto him, Son, thou art ever with me, and all that I have is thine. It was meet that we should make merry, and be glad: for this thy brother was dead, and is alive again; and was lost, and is found.

## [THE BETRAYAL OF JESUS][3]

26. . . . Then one of the twelve, called Judas Iscariot, went unto the chief priests, and said unto them, What will ye give me, and I will deliver him unto you? And they covenanted with him for thirty pieces of silver. And from that time he sought opportunity to betray him.

Now the first day of the feast of unleavened bread[4] the disciples came to Jesus, saying unto him, Where wilt thou that we prepare for thee to eat the passover? And he said, Go into the city to such a man, and say unto him, The Master saith, My time is at hand; I will keep the passover at thy house with my disciples. And the disciples did as Jesus had appointed them; and they made ready the passover. Now when the even was come, he sat down with the twelve. And as they did eat, he said, Verily I say unto you, that one of you shall betray me. And they were exceeding sorrowful, and began every one of them to say unto him, Lord, is it I? And he answered and said, He that dippeth his hand with me in the dish, the same shall betray me. The Son of man goeth as it is written of him: but woe unto that man by whom the Son of man is betrayed! it had been good for that man if he had not been born. Then Judas, which betrayed him, answered and said, Master, is it I? He said unto him, Thou hast said.

And as they were eating, Jesus took bread, and blessed it, and brake it, and gave it to the disciples, and said, Take, eat; this is my

3. Matthew 26:14–75.    4. Held in remembrance of the delivery of the Jews from captivity in Egypt. See Exodus 12.

body. And he took the cup, and gave thanks, and gave it to them, saying, Drink ye all of it; for this is my blood of the new testament,[5] which is shed for many for the remission of sins. But I say unto you, I will not drink henceforth of this fruit of the vine, until that day when I drink it new with you in my Father's kingdom. And when they had sung an hymn, they went out into the mount of Olives. Then saith Jesus unto them, All ye shall be offended[6] because of me this night: for it is written,[7] I will smite the shepherd, and the sheep of the flock shall be scattered abroad. But after I am risen again, I will go before you into Galilee. Peter answered and said unto him, Though all men shall be offended because of thee, yet will I never be offended. Jesus said unto him, Verily I say unto thee, That this night, before the cock crow, thou shalt deny me thrice. Peter said unto him, Though I should die with thee, yet will I not deny thee. Likewise also said all the disciples.

Then cometh Jesus with them unto a place called Gethsemane, and saith unto the disciples, Sit ye here, while I go and pray yonder. And he took with him Peter and the two sons of Zebedee,[8] and began to be sorrowful and very heavy. Then saith he unto them, My soul is exceeding sorrowful, even unto death: tarry ye here, and watch with me.[9] And he went a little farther, and fell on his face, and prayed, saying, O my Father, if it be possible, let this cup pass from me: nevertheless, not as I will, but as thou wilt. And he cometh unto the disciples, and findeth them asleep, and saith unto Peter, What, could ye not watch with me one hour? Watch and pray, that ye enter not into temptation: the spirit indeed is willing, but the flesh is weak. He went away again the second time, and prayed, saying, O my Father, if this cup may not pass away from me, except I drink it, thy will be done. And he came and found them asleep again: for their eyes were heavy. And he left them, and went away again, and prayed the third time, saying the same words. Then cometh he to his disciples, and saith unto them, Sleep on now, and take your rest: behold, the hour is at hand, and the Son of man is betrayed into the hands of sinners. Rise, let us be going: behold, he is at hand that doth betray me.

And while he yet spake, lo, Judas, one of the twelve, came, and with him a great multitude with swords and staves, from the chief priests and elders of the people. Now he that betrayed him gave them a sign, saying, Whomsoever I shall kiss, that same is he: hold him fast. And forthwith he came to Jesus and said, Hail, master; and kissed him. And Jesus said unto him, Friend, wherefore art thou

5. I.e., of the new covenant, or agreement. Jesus compares himself to the lamb that was killed at the Passover as a sign of the covenant between God and the Jews.    6. The Greek means literally, "you will be made to stumble."    7. See Zechariah 13:7.    8. James and John.    9. Stay awake.

come? Then came they and laid hands on Jesus, and took him. And behold, one of them which were with Jesus[1] stretched out his hand, and drew his sword, and struck a servant of the high priest's, and smote off his ear. Then said Jesus unto him, Put up again thy sword into his place: for all they that take the sword shall perish with the sword. Thinkest thou that I cannot now pray to my Father, and he shall presently give me more than twelve legions of angels?[2] But how then shall the scriptures be fulfilled, that thus it must be? In that same hour said Jesus to the multitudes, Are ye come out as against a thief with swords and staves for to take me? I sat daily with you teaching in the temple, and ye laid no hold on me. But all this was done that the scriptures of the prophets might be fulfilled. Then all the disciples forsook him, and fled.

And they that had laid hold on Jesus led him away to Caiaphas the high priest, where the scribes and the elders were assembled. But Peter followed him afar off unto the high priest's palace, and went in, and sat with the servants, to see the end. Now the chief priests, and elders, and all the council, sought false witness against Jesus, to put him to death; but found none: yea, though many false witnesses came, yet found they none. At the last came two false witnesses, and said, This fellow said, I am able to destroy the temple of God, and to build it in three days. And the high priest arose, and said unto him, Answerest thou nothing? What is it which these witness against thee? But Jesus held his peace. And the high priest answered and said unto him, I adjure thee by the living God, that thou tell us whether thou be the Christ, the Son of God. Jesus saith unto him, Thou hast said: nevertheless I say unto you, Hereafter shall ye see the Son of man sitting on the right hand of power, and coming in the clouds of heaven. Then the high priest rent his clothes, saying, He hath spoken blasphemy; what further need have we of witnesses? behold, now ye have heard his blasphemy. What think ye? They answered and said, He is guilty of death.[3] Then did they spit in his face, and buffeted him; and others smote him with the palms of their hands, saying, Prophesy unto us, thou Christ, Who is he that smote thee?

Now Peter sat without in the palace: and a damsel came unto him, saying, Thou also wast with Jesus of Galilee. But he denied before them all, saying, I know not what thou sayest. And when he was gone out into the porch, another maid saw him and said unto them that were there, This fellow was also with Jesus of Nazareth. And again he denied with an oath, I do not know the man. And after a while came unto him they that stood by, and said to Peter, Surely

1. This was Peter.  2. The legion was a Roman military formation; its full complement was six thousand men.  3. Liable to the death penalty.

thou also art one of them; for thy speech bewrayeth thee.[4] Then
began he to curse and to swear, saying, I know not the man. And
immediately the cock crew. And Peter remembered the word of Jesus,
which said unto him, Before the cock crow thou shalt deny me thrice.
And he went out, and wept bitterly.

### [THE TRIAL AND CRUCIFIXION OF JESUS][5]

27. When the morning was come, all the chief priests and elders
of the people took counsel against Jesus to put him to death: and
when they had bound him, they led him away, and delivered him
to Pontius Pilate the governor.[6]

Then Judas, which had betrayed him, when he saw that he was
condemned, repented himself, and brought again the thirty pieces
of silver to the chief priests and elders, saying, I have sinned in that
I have betrayed the innocent blood. And they said, What is that to
us? see thou to that. And he cast down the pieces of silver in the
temple, and departed, and went and hanged himself. And the chief
priests took the silver pieces, and said, It is not lawful for to put them
into the treasury, because it is the price of blood. And they took
counsel, and bought with them the potter's field,[7] to bury strangers
in. Wherefore that field was called, The field of blood, unto this
day. Then was fulfilled that which was spoken by Jeremy the prophet,[8]
saying, And they took the thirty pieces of silver, the price of him that
was valued, whom they of the children of Israel did value; and gave
them for the potter's field, as the Lord appointed me. And Jesus
stood before the governor: and the governor asked him, saying, Art
thou the King of the Jews? And Jesus said unto him, Thou sayest.

And when he was accused of the chief priests and elders, he
answered nothing. Then said Pilate unto him, Hearest thou not how
many things they witness against thee? And he answered him to never
a word; insomuch that the governor marvelled greatly. Now at that
feast the governor was wont to release unto the people a prisoner,
whom they would. And they had then a notable prisoner, called
Barabbas.[9] Therefore when they were gathered together, Pilate said
unto them, Whom will ye that I release unto you? Barabbas, or Jesus
which is called Christ? For he knew that for envy they had delivered
him.[1]

When he was set down on the judgment seat, his wife sent unto

---

**4.** Betrays. Peter's speech revealed his Galilean origin.     **5.** Matthew 27:1–66.     **6.** His official title was procurator of the province of Judea. The Roman policy was to allow the Jews as
much independence as possible (especially in religious matters), but only the Roman authorities
could impose a death sentence.     **7.** A field which had been dug for potter's clay, and was
consequently not worth very much as land.     **8.** Jeremiah. The prophecy here quoted is a version of Zechariah 11:13.     **9.** Under sentence of death for sedition and murder.     **1.** I.e., to
the Roman authorities.

him, saying, Have thou nothing to do with that just man: for I have suffered many things this day in a dream because of him. But the chief priests and elders persuaded the multitude that they should ask Barabbas, and destroy Jesus. The governor answered and said unto them, Whether of the twain will ye that I release unto you? They said, Barabbas. Pilate saith unto them, What shall I do then with Jesus which is called Christ? They all say unto him, Let him be crucified.[2] And the governor said, Why, what evil hath he done? But they cried out the more, saying, Let him be crucified.

When Pilate saw that he could prevail nothing, but that rather a tumult was made, he took water, and washed his hands before the multitude, saying, I am innocent of the blood of this just person: see ye to it. Then answered all the people, and said, His blood be on us, and on our children.

Then released he Barabbas unto them: and when he had scourged[3] Jesus, he delivered him to be crucified. Then the soldiers of the governor took Jesus into the common hall, and gathered unto him the whole band of soldiers. And they stripped him, and put on him a scarlet robe.

And when they had platted a crown of thorns, they put it upon his head, and a reed[4] in his right hand: and they bowed the knee before him, and mocked him, saying, Hail, King of the Jews! And they spit upon him, and took the reed, and smote him on the head. And after that they had mocked him, they took the robe off from him, and put his own raiment on him, and led him away to crucify him. And as they came out, they found a man of Cyrene,[5] Simon by name: him they compelled to bear his cross. And when they were come unto a place called Golgotha, that is to say, a place of a skull,

They gave him vinegar to drink mingled with gall:[6] and when he had tasted thereof, he would not drink. And they crucified him, and parted his garments, casting lots: that it might be fulfilled which was spoken by the prophet, They parted my garments among them, and upon my vesture did they cast lots.[7] And sitting down they watched him there; and set up over his head his accusation written, THIS IS JESUS THE KING OF THE JEWS. Then were there two thieves crucified with him, one on the right hand, and another on the left.

And they that passed by reviled him, wagging their heads, and saying, Thou that destroyest the temple, and buildest it in three days, save thyself. If thou be the Son of God, come down from the cross. Likewise also the chief priests mocking him, with the scribes and elders, said, He saved others; himself he cannot save. If he be the

2. The regular Roman punishment for sedition.　3. Whipped, a routine part of the punishment.　4. To represent the king's scepter.　5. On the coast of North Africa.　6. The Greek word translated "vinegar" describes a sour wine which was the regular drink of the Roman soldiery. The addition of bitter gall is further mockery.　7. *That it might . . . cast lots:* It is generally agreed that this is a late addition to the text.

King of Israel, let him now come down from the cross, and we will believe him. He trusted in God; let him deliver him now, if he will have him: for he said, I am the Son of God. The thieves also, which were crucified with him, cast the same in his teeth. Now from the sixth hour there was darkness over all the land unto the ninth hour. And about the ninth hour Jesus cried with a loud voice, saying, Eli, Eli, lama sabachthani? that is to say, My God, my God, why hast thou forsaken me?[8] Some of them that stood there, when they heard that, said, This man calleth for Elias.[9] And straightway one of them ran, and took a sponge, and filled it with vinegar, and put it on a reed, and gave him to drink. The rest said, Let be, let us see whether Elias will come to save him.

Jesus, when he had cried again with a loud voice, yielded up the ghost. And, behold, the veil of the temple[1] was rent in twain from the top to the bottom; and the earth did quake, and the rocks rent; and the graves were opened; and many bodies of the saints which slept arose, and came out of the graves after his resurrection, and went into the holy city, and appeared unto many. Now when the centurion,[2] and they that were with him, watching Jesus, saw the earthquake, and those things that were done, they feared greatly, saying, Truly this was the Son of God. And many women were there beholding afar off, which followed Jesus from Galilee, ministering unto him: among which was Mary Magdalene, and Mary the mother of James and Joses, and the mother of Zebedee's children. When the even was come, there came a rich man of Arimathæa, named Joseph, who also himself was Jesus' disciple. He went to Pilate, and begged the body of Jesus. Then Pilate commanded the body to be delivered. And when Joseph had taken the body, he wrapped it in clean linen cloth, and laid it in his own new tomb, which he had hewn out in the rock: and he rolled a great stone to the door of the sepulchre, and departed. And there was Mary Magdalene, and the other Mary, sitting over against the sepulchre.

Now the next day, that followed the day of the preparation, the chief priests and Pharisees came together unto Pilate, saying, Sir, we remember that that deceiver said, while he was yet alive, After three days I will rise again. Command therefore that the sepulchre be made sure[3] until the third day, lest his disciples come by night, and steal him away, and say unto the people, He is risen from the dead: so the last error shall be worse than the first. Pilate said unto them, Ye have a watch:[4] go your way, make it as sure as ye can. So they went, and made the sepulchre sure, sealing the stone, and setting a watch.

8. The opening words of Psalm 22. The actual words of Jesus, "Eli, Eli, lama sabachthani?" are Aramaic, the spoken Hebrew of the period.    9. The prophet Elijah.    1. The curtain which screened off the holy of holies.    2. The Roman officer in charge of the execution. 3. Guarded.    4. Police force.

## [THE RESURRECTION][5]

28. In the end of the sabbath, as it began to dawn toward the first day of the week, came Mary Magdalene and the other Mary to see the sepulchre. And, behold, there was a great earthquake: for the angel of the Lord descended from heaven, and came and rolled back the stone from the door, and sat upon it. His countenance was like lightning, and his raiment white as snow: and for fear of him the keepers did shake, and became as dead men. And the angel answered and said unto the women, Fear not ye: for I know that ye seek Jesus, which was crucified. He is not here: for he is risen, as he said. Come, see the place where the Lord lay. And go quickly, and tell his disciples that he is risen from the dead; and, behold, he goeth before you into Galilee; there shall ye see him: lo, I have told you. And they departed quickly from the sepulchre with fear and great joy; and did run to bring his disciples word.

And as they went to tell his disciples, behold, Jesus met them, saying, All hail! And they came and held him by the feet, and worshipped him. Then said Jesus unto them, Be not afraid: go tell my brethren that they go into Galilee, and there shall they see me.

Now when they were going, behold, some of the watch came into the city, and shewed unto the chief priests all the things that were done. And when they were assembled with the elders, and had taken counsel, they gave large money unto the soldiers, saying, Say ye, His disciples came by night, and stole him away while we slept. And if this come to the governor's ears, we will persuade him, and secure you. So they took the money, and did as they were taught: and this saying is commonly reported among the Jews until this day.

Then the eleven disciples went away into Galilee, into a mountain where Jesus had appointed them. And when they saw him, they worshipped him: but some doubted. And Jesus came and spake unto them, saying, All power is given unto me in heaven and in earth.

Go ye therefore, and teach all nations, baptizing them in the name of the Father, and of the Son, and of the Holy Ghost: teaching them to observe all things whatsoever I have commanded you: and, lo, I am with you always, even unto the end of the world. Amen.

---

# PETRONIUS

## died A.D. 65

It is not certain that Titus Petronius (Arbiter) was the author of the *Satyricon*, but he is the best candidate. A friend of Nero's, he committed suicide

5. Matthew 28:1–20.

at the imperial order after becoming involved in the Pisonian conspiracy against the emperor in A.D. 65. A brilliant account of Petronius' character and death is given by Tacitus in the eighteenth and nineteenth chapters of Book XVI of the *Annals*.

It is in the satiric masterpiece of this Roman aristocrat that the pragmatic, materialistic attitude Christianity was to supplant is most clearly displayed. It was probably written during the principate of Nero (A.D. 54–68), a period in which the material benefits and the spiritual weakness of the new order had already become apparent. The *Satyricon* itself has survived only in fragments; we know nothing certain about the scope of the work as a whole, but from the fragments it is clear that this book is the work of a satiric genius, perhaps the most original genius of Latin literature.

"Dinner with Trimalchio," one of the longer fragments, selections from which are included here, shows us a tradesman's world. The narrator, a student of literature, and his cronies may have an aristocratic disdain for the businessmen at whose tables they eat, but they know that Trimalchio and his kind have inherited the earth. Trimalchio began life as a foreign slave, but he is now a multimillionaire. The representative of culture, Agamemnon the teacher, drinks his wine and praises his fatuous remarks; he is content to be the court jester, the butt of Trimalchio's witticisms. Trimalchio knows no god but Mercury, the patron of business operations, but the gold bracelet, a percentage of his income which he has dedicated to Mercury, he wears on his own arm. He identifies himself with the god, and worships himself, the living embodiment of the power of money. The conversation at his table is a sardonic revelation of the temper of a whole civilization. Written in brilliantly humorous and colloquial style it exposes mercilessly a blindness to spiritual values of any kind, a distrust of the intellect, and a ferocious preoccupation with the art of cheating one's neighbor. The point is made more effective by the conscious evocation of the epic tradition throughout the work. The names alone of the teacher, Agamemnon, and his assistant in instruction, Menelaus; the wall paintings which show "the Iliad and the Odyssey and the gladiator's show given by Laenas"; Trimalchio's exhibition of monstrous ignorance of Homer (which nobody dares to correct); the Nestorian tone of Ganymedes, who regrets the old days when men were men (he is talking of the time when Safinius forced the bakers to lower the price of bread)—one touch after another reminds us that these figures are the final product of a tradition that began with Achilles and Odysseus.

The satire is witty, but it is nonetheless profound. All of them live for the moment, in material enjoyment, but they know that it cannot last. "Let us remember the living" is their watchword, but they cannot forget the dead. And as the banquet goes on, the thought of death, suppressed beneath the debased Epicureanism of Trimalchio and his associates, emerges slowly to the surface of their consciousness and comes to dominate it completely. The last arrival at the banquet is Habinnas the undertaker, and his coming coincides with the last stage of Trimalchio's drunkenness, the maudlin exhibition of his funeral clothes and the description of his tomb. "I would that I were dead," says the Sibyl in the story Trimalchio tells early in the evening; at its end he himself acts out his own funeral, complete with ointment, robes, wine, and trumpet players. The fact of death, the one fact which the practical materialism of Trimalchio and his circle can neither deny nor assimilate, asserts itself triumphantly as the supreme fact in the emptiness of Trimalchio's mind.

The introduction to *Petronius. The Satyricon*, translated by J. P. Sullivan (1977), will be helpful to the student.

## Dinner with Trimalchio[1]

[The narrator, Encolpius, is a penniless vagabond who is a student of rhetoric under a master named Agamemnon. His close associates are Ascyltus, a fellow student, and Giton, a handsome boy who has no particular occupation. After some disreputable and very tiring adventures they are invited, as pupils of Agamemnon, to a banquet. The scene of the story is an unidentified city in southern Italy, the time probably about A.D. 50.]

The next day but one finally arrived. But we were so knocked about that we wanted to run rather than rest. We were mournfully discussing how to avoid the approaching storm,[2] when one of Agamemnon's slaves broke in on our frantic debate.

"Here," said he, "don't you know who's your host today? It's Trimalchio—he's terribly elegant. . . . He has a clock[3] in the dining-room and a trumpeter[4] all dressed up to tell him how much longer he's got to live."

This made us forget all our troubles. We dressed carefully and told Giton, who was very kindly acting as our servant, to attend us at the baths.[5]

We did not take our clothes off but began wandering around, or rather exchanging jokes while circulating among the little groups. Suddenly we saw a bald old man in a reddish shirt, playing ball with some long-haired boys. It was not so much the boys that made us watch, although they alone were worth the trouble, but the old gentleman himself. He was taking his exercise in slippers and throwing a green ball around. But he didn't pick it up if it touched the ground; instead there was a slave holding a bagful, and he supplied them to the players. We noticed other novelties. Two eunuchs stood around at different points: one of them carried a silver chamber pot, the other counted the balls, not those flying from hand to hand according to the rules, but those that fell to the ground. We were still admiring these elegant arrangements when Menelaus[6] hurried up to us.

1. Translated by J. P. Sullivan.    2. A repetition of the unsavory incidents they have just experienced.    3. At this period a rare and expensive article. *Trimalchio:* The name suggests "triply blessed" or "triply powerful."    4. To sound off every hour on the hour.    5. A public institution. They were magnificent buildings, containing not only baths of many types and temperatures, but places for conversation and games and even libraries.    6. Appropriately enough, Agamemnon's assistant in instruction.

"This is the man you'll be dining with," he said. "In fact, you are now watching the beginning of the dinner."

No sooner had Menelaus spoken than Trimalchio snapped his fingers. At the signal the eunuch brought up the chamber pot for him, while he went on playing. With the weight off his bladder, he demanded water for his hands, splashed a few drops on his fingers and wiped them on a boy's head.

It would take too long to pick out isolated incidents. Anyway, we entered the baths where we began sweating at once and we went immediately into the cold water. Trimalchio had been smothered in perfume and was already being rubbed down, not with linen towels, but with bath-robes of the finest wool. As this was going on, three masseurs sat drinking Falernian[7] in front of him. Through quarreling they spilled most of it and Trimalchio said they were drinking his health.[8] Wrapped in thick scarlet felt he was put into a litter. Four couriers with lots of medals went in front, as well as a go-cart in which his favourite boy was riding—a wizened, bleary-eyed youngster, uglier than his master. As he was carried off, a musician with a tiny set of pipes took his place by Trimalchio's head and whispered a tune in his ear the whole way.

We followed on, choking with amazement by now, and arrived at the door with Agamemnon at our side. On the doorpost a notice was fastened which read:

ANY SLAVE LEAVING THE HOUSE WITHOUT HIS MASTER'S
PERMISSION WILL RECEIVE ONE HUNDRED LASHES

Just at the entrance stood the hall-porter, dressed in a green uniform with a belt of cherry red. He was shelling peas into a silver basin. Over the doorway hung—of all things—a golden cage from which a spotted magpie greeted visitors.

As I was gaping at all this, I almost fell over backwards and broke a leg. There on the left as one entered, not far from the porter's cubbyhole, was a huge dog with a chain round its neck. It was painted on the wall and over it, in big capitals, was written:

BEWARE OF THE DOG

My colleagues laughed at me, but when I got my breath back I went to examine the whole wall. There was a mural of a slave market, price tags and all. Then Trimalchio himself, holding a wand of Mercury and being led into Rome by Minerva.[9] After this a picture of how he learned accounting and, finally how he became a steward. The painstaking artist had drawn it all in great detail with descriptions underneath. Just where the colonnade ended Mercury hauled

7. A famous wine from Campania south of Rome.     8. He claims they are pouring a libation.
9. Athena, patron goddess of arts and skills. *Mercury* (Hermes): As a trickster, the patron god of thieves and businessmen.

him up by the chin and rushed him to a high platform. . . .

I began asking the porter what were the pictures they had in the middle.

"The *Iliad*, and *Odyssey*, and the gladiatorial show given by Laenas," he told me.

Time did not allow us to look at many things there . . . by now we had reached the dining-room. . . .

Finally we took our places. Boys from Alexandria poured iced water over our hands. Others followed them and attended to our feet, removing any hangnails with great skill. But they were not quiet even during this troublesome operation: they sang away at their work. I wanted to find out if the whole staff were singers, so I asked for a drink. In a flash a boy was there, singing in a shrill voice while he attended to me—and anyone else who was asked to bring something did the same. It was more like a musical comedy than a respectable dinner party.

Some extremely elegant hors d'oeuvre were served at this point—by now everyone had taken his place with the exception of Trimalchio, for whom, strangely enough, the place at the top was reserved. The dishes for the first course included an ass of Corinthian bronze with two panniers, white olives on one side and black on the other. Over the ass were two pieces of plate, with Trimalchio's name and the weight of the silver inscribed on the rims. There were some small iron frames shaped like bridges supporting dormice sprinkled with honey and poppy seed. There were steaming hot sausages too, on a silver gridiron with damsons and pomegranate seeds underneath.

We were in the middle of these elegant dishes when Trimalchio himself was carried in to the sound of music and set down on a pile of tightly stuffed cushions. The sight of him drew an astonished laugh from the guests. His cropped head stuck out from a scarlet coat; his neck was well muffled up and he had put round it a napkin with a broad purple stripe and tassels dangling here and there. On the little finger of his left hand he wore a heavy gilt ring and a smaller one on the last joint of the next finger. This I thought was solid gold, but actually it was studded with little iron stars. And to show off even more of his jewellery, he had his right arm bare and set off by a gold armlet and an ivory circlet fastened with a gleaming metal plate.

After picking his teeth with a silver toothpick, he began: "My friends, I wasn't keen to come into the dining room yet. But if I stayed away any more, I would have kept you back, so I've deprived myself of all my little pleasures for you. However, you'll allow me to finish my game."

A boy was at his heels with a board of terebinth wood[1] with glass

---

1. A very hard wood which takes a high polish and is very expensive (like everything Trimalchio has).

squares, and I noticed the very last word in luxury—instead of white and black pieces he had gold and silver coins. While he was swearing away like a trooper over his game and we were still on the hors d'oeuvre, a tray was brought in with a basket on it. There sat a wooden hen, its wings spread round it the way hens are when they are broody. Two slaves hurried up and as the orchestra played a tune they began searching through the straw and dug out peahens' eggs, which they distributed to the guests.

Trimalchio turned to look at this little scene and said: "My friends, I gave orders for that bird to sit on some peahens' eggs. I hope to goodness they are not starting to hatch. However, let's try them and see if they are still soft."

We took up our spoons (weighing at least half a pound each) and cracked the eggs, which were made of rich pastry. To tell the truth, I nearly threw away my share, as the chicken seemed already formed. But I heard a guest who was an old hand say: "There should be something good here." So I searched the shell with my fingers and found the plumpest little figpecker, all covered with yolk and seasoned with pepper.

At this point Trimalchio became tired of his game and demanded that all the previous dishes be brought to him. He gave permission in a loud voice for any of us to have another glass of mead if we wanted it. Suddenly there was a crash from the orchestra and a troop of waiters—still singing—snatched away the hors d'oeuvre. However in the confusion one of the side-dishes happened to fall and a slave picked it up from the floor. Trimalchio noticed this, had the boy's ears boxed and told him to throw it down again. A cleaner came in with a broom and began to sweep up the silver plate along with the rest of the rubbish. Two long-haired Ethiopians followed him, carrying small skin bottles like those they use for scattering sand in the circus, and they poured wine over our hands—no one ever offered us water.

Our host was complimented on these elegant arrangements. "You've got to fight fair," he replied. "That is why I gave orders for each guest to have his own table. At the same time these smelly slaves won't crowd so."

Carefully sealed wine bottles were immediately brought, their necks labelled:

FALERNIAN

CONSUL OPIMIUS

ONE HUNDRED YEARS OLD[2]

While we were examining the labels, Trimalchio clapped his hands and said with a sigh:

2. The wine was labeled with the name of the man who was consul in the year it was bottled. Opimius was consul in 121 B.C. Since it was in this year that the custom of dating the wine by

"Wine has a longer life than us poor folks. So let's wet our whistles. Wine is life. I'm giving you real Opimian. I didn't put out such good stuff yesterday, though the company was much better class."

   Naturally we drank and missed no opportunity of admiring his elegant hospitality. In the middle of this a slave brought in a silver skeleton, put together in such a way that its joints and backbone could be pulled out and twisted in all directions. After he had flung it about on the table once or twice, its flexible joints falling into various postures, Trimalchio recited:

> "Man's life alas! is but a span,
> So let us live it while we can,
> We'll be like this when dead."

After our applause the next course was brought in. Actually it was not as grand as we expected, but it was so novel that everyone stared. It was a deep circular tray with the twelve signs of the Zodiac arranged round the edge. . . .

   After this course Trimalchio got up and went to the toilet. Free of his domineering presence, we began to strike up a general conversation. Dama[3] started off by calling for bigger glasses.

   "The day's nothin'," he said, "It's night 'fore y'can turn around. So the best thing's get out of bed and go straight to dinner. Lovely cold weather we've had too. M'bath hardly thawed me out. Still, a hot drink's as good as an overcoat. I've been throwin' it back neat, and I'm pretty tight—the wine's gone to m'head."

   This started Seleucus off.

   "Me now," he said, "I don't have a bath every day. It's like gettin' rubbed with fuller's[4] earth, havin' a bath. The water bites into you, and as the days go by, your heart turns to water. But when I've knocked back a hot glass of wine and honey, kiss-my-arse I say to the cold weather. Mind you, I couldn't have a bath—I was at a funeral today. Poor old Chrysanthus has just given up the ghost—nice man he was! It was only the other day he stopped me in the street. I still seem to hear his voice. Dear, dear! We're just so many walking bags of wind. We're worse than flies—at least flies have got some strength in them, but we're no more than empty bubbles.

   "And what would he have been like if he hadn't been on a diet? For five days he didn't take a drop of water or a crumb of bread into his mouth. But he's gone to join the majority. The doctors finished him—well, hard luck, more like. After all, a doctor is just to put your mind at rest. Still, he got a good sendoff—he had a bier and all

the consul's name began, Trimalchio's wine was the oldest possible. If genuine, it would have been undrinkable.     3. One of Trimalchio's friends. Like those of Seleucus and Phileros who join the conversation later, his name is Greek.     4. *Fuller:* A cleaner (of woollen cloaks). They used very strong solvents.

beautifully draped. His mourners—several of his slaves were left their freedom—did him proud, even though his widow was a bit mean with her tears. Suppose now he hadn't been so good to her! But women as a sex are real vultures. It's no good doing them a favour, you might as well throw it down a well. An old passion is just an ulcer."

He was being a bore and Phileros said loudly:

"Let's think of the living. He's got what he deserved. He lived an honest life and he died an honest death. What has he got to complain about? He started out in life with just a penny and he was ready to pick up less than that from a muck-heap, if he had to use his teeth. He went up in the world. He got bigger and bigger till he got where you see, like a honeycomb. I honestly think he left a solid hundred thousand and he had the lot in hard cash. But I'll be honest about it—seeing I'm a bit of a cynic—he had a foul mouth and too much lip. He wasn't a man, he was just murder.

"Now his brother was a fine man, a real friend to his friends, always ready with a helping hand or a decent meal.

"Chrysanthus had bad luck at first, but the first vintage set him on his feet. He fixed his own price when he sold the wine. And what properly kept his head above water was a legacy he came in for, when he pocketed more than was left to him. And the blockhead, when he had a quarrel with his brother, cut him out of his will in favour of some sod we've never heard of. You're leaving a lot behind when you leave your own flesh and blood. But he took advice from his slaves and they really fixed him. It's never right to believe all you're told, especially for a business man. But it's true he enjoyed himself while he lived. You got it, you keep it. He was certainly Fortune's favourite—lead turned to gold in his hand. Mind you, it's easy when everything runs smoothly.

"And how old do you think he was? Seventy or more! But he was hard as nails and carried his age well. His hair was black as a raven's wing. I knew the man for ages and ages and he was still an old lecher. I honestly don't think he left the dog alone. What's more, he liked little boys—he could turn his hand to anything. Well, I don't blame him—after all, he couldn't take anything else with him."

This was Phileros, then Ganymedes said:

"You're all talking about things that don't concern heaven or earth. Meanwhile, no one gives a damn the way we're hit by the corn situation. Honest to God, I couldn't get hold of a mouthful of bread today. And look how there's still no rain. It's been absolute starvation for a whole year now. To hell with the food officers! They're in with the bakers—'You be nice to me and I'll be nice to you.' So the little man suffers, while those grinders of the poor never stop celebrating. Oh, if only we still had the sort of men I found here when I first arrived from Asia. Like lions they were. That was the life! Come one, come all! If white flour was inferior to the very finest, they'd thrash those bogeymen till they thought God Almighty was after them.

"I remember Safinius—he used to live by the old arch then; I was a boy at the time. He wasn't a man, he was all pepper. He used to scorch the ground wherever he went. But he was dead straight—don't let him down and he wouldn't let you down. You'd be ready to play *morra*[5] with him in the dark. But on the city council, how he used to wade into some of them—no beating about the bush, straight from the shoulder! And when he was in court, his voice got louder and louder like a trumpet. He never sweated or spat—I think there was a touch of the old acid about him. And very affable he was when you met him, calling everyone by name just like one of us. Naturally at the time corn was dirt cheap. You could buy a penny loaf that two of you couldn't get through. Today—I've seen bigger bull's-eyes.

"Ah me! It's getting worse every day. This place is going down like a calf's tail. But why do we have a third-rate food officer who wouldn't lose a penny to save our lives? He sits at home laughing and rakes in more money a day than anyone else's whole fortune. I happen to know he's just made a thousand in gold. But if we had any balls at all, he wouldn't be feeling so pleased with himself. People today are lions at home and foxes outside.

"Take me, I've already sold the rags off my back for food and if this shortage continues, I'll be selling my bit of a house. What's going to happen to this place if neither god nor man will help us? As I hope to go home tonight, I'm sure all this is heaven's doing.

"Nobody believes in heaven, see, nobody fasts, nobody gives a damn for the Almighty. No, people only bow their heads to count their money. In the old days high-class ladies used to climb up the hill barefoot, their hair loose and their hearts pure, and ask God for rain. And he'd send it down in bucketfuls right away—it was then or never—and everyone went home like drowned rats. Since we've given up religion the gods nowadays keep their feet well wrapped up. The fields just lie . . . ."

"Please, please," broke in Echion the rag merchant, "be a bit more cheerful. 'First it's one thing, then another,' as the yokel said when he lost his spotted pig. What we haven't got today, we'll have tomorrow. That's the way life goes. Believe me, you couldn't name a better country, if it had the people. As things are, I admit, it's having a hard time, but it isn't the only place. We mustn't be soft. The sky don't get no nearer wherever you are. If you were some-

5. A game (still played in southern Italy) which requires the players to match the number of fingers held out by the opponent.

where else, you'd be talking about the pigs walking round ready roasted back here.

"And another thing, we'll be having a holiday with a three-day show that's the best ever—and not just a hack troupe of gladiators but freedmen for the most part. My old friend Titus has a big heart and a hot head. Maybe this, maybe that, but something at all events. I'm a close friend of his and he does nothing by halves. He'll give us cold steel, no quarter and the slaughterhouse right in the middle where all the stands can see it. And he's got the wherewithal—he was left thirty million when his poor father died. Even if he spent four hundred thousand, his pocket won't feel it and he'll go down in history. He's got some big brutes already, and a woman who fights in a chariot and Glyco's steward,[6] who was caught having fun with his mistress. You'll see quite a quarrel in the crowd between jealous husbands and romantic lovers. But that half-pint Glyco threw his steward to the lions, which is just giving himself away. How is it the servant's fault when he's forced into it? It's that old pisspot who really deserves to be tossed by a bull. But if you can't beat the ass you beat the saddle. But how did Glyco imagine the poisonous daughter of Hermogenes[7] would ever turn out well? The old man could cut the claws off a flying kite, and a snake don't hatch old rope. Glyco— well, Glyco's got his. He's branded for as long as he lives and only the grave will get rid of it. But everyone pays for their mistakes.

"But I can almost smell the dinner Mammaea is going to give us[8]—two denarii apiece for me and the family. If he really does it, he'll make off with all Norbanus's votes, I tell you he'll win at a canter. After all, what good has Nobanus done us? He put on some half-pint gladiators, so done in already that they'd have dropped if you blew at them. I've seen animal-killers[9] fight better. As for the horsemen killed, he got them off a lamp[1]—they ran round like cocks in a backyard. One was just a carthorse, the other couldn't stand up, and the reserve was just one corpse instead of another—he was prac- tically hamstrung. One boy did have a bit of spirit—he was in Thra- cian armour,[2] and even he didn't show any initiative. In fact, they were all flogged afterwards, there were so many shouts of 'Give 'em what for!' from the crowd. Pure yellow, that's all. 'Well, I've put on a show for you,' he says. 'And I'm clapping you,' says I. 'Reckon it up—I'm giving more than I got. So we're quits.'

"Hey, Agamemnon! I suppose you're saying 'What is that bore

6. A household slave. His master was permitted by law to punish him by forcing him to fight wild beasts in the arena.    7. Presumably the father of Glyco's wife.    8. A public banquet, given by Mammaea as part of his electoral compaign. His rival Norbanus has been giving gladiatorial shows.    9. Professional fighters of wild animals, considered inferior to gladiators.    1. They were as small as the horsemen depicted on a lamp.    2. Light armor, such as that worn by soldiers from Thrace, a savage country northeast of Greece.

going on and on about?' It's because a good talker like you don't talk. You're a cut above us, and so you laugh at what us poor people say. We all know you're off your head with all that reading. But never mind! Some day I'll get you to come down to my place in the country and have a look at our little cottage. We'll find something to eat—a chicken, some eggs. It'll be nice, even though the unreliable weather this year has made off with everything. Anyway, we'll find enough to fill our bellies.

"And my kid is growing up to be a pupil of yours. He can divide by four already. If God spares him, you'll have him ready to do anything for you. In his spare time, he won't take his head out of his exercise book. He's clever and there's good stuff in him, even if he is crazy about birds. Only yesterday I killed his three goldfinches and told him a weasel ate them. But he's found some other silly hobbies, and he's having a fine time painting. Still, he's already well ahead with his Greek, and he's starting to take to his Latin, though his tutor is too pleased with himself and unreliable—he just comes and goes. He knows his stuff but doesn't want to work. There is another one as well, not so clever but he is conscientious—he teaches the boy more than he knows himself. In fact, he makes a habit of coming around on holidays, and whatever you give him, he's happy.

"Anyway, I've just bought the boy some law books, as I want him to pick up some legal training for home use. There's a living in that sort of thing. He's done enough dabbling in poetry and such like. If he objects, I've decided he'll learn a trade—barber, auctioneer, or at least a barrister—something he can't lose till he dies. Well, yesterday I gave it to him straight: 'Believe me, my lad, any studying you do will be for your own good. You see Phileros the solicitor—if he hadn't studied, he'd be starving today. It's not so long since he was humping round loads on his back. Now he can even look Norbanus in the face. An education is an investment, and a proper profession never goes dead on you.' "

This was the sort of conversation flying round when Trimalchio came in, dabbed his forehead and washed his hands in perfume. There was a short pause, then he said:

"Excuse me, dear people, my inside has not been answering the call for several days now. The doctors are puzzled. But some pomegranate rind and resin in vinegar has done me good. But I hope now it will be back on its good behaviour. Otherwise my stomach rumbles like a bull. So if any of you wants to go out, there's no need for him to be embarrassed. None of us was born solid. I think there's nothing so tormenting as holding yourself in. This is the one thing even God Almighty can't object to. Yes, laugh, Fortunata,[3] but you

---

3. Trimalchio's wife.

generally keep me up all night with this sort of thing.

"Anyway, I don't object to people doing what suits them even in the middle of dinner—and the doctors forbid you to hold yourself in. Even if it's a longer business, everything is there just outside—water, bowls, and all the other little comforts. Believe me, if the wind goes to your brain it starts flooding your whole body too. I've known a lot of people die from this because they wouldn't be honest with themselves."

We thanked him for being so generous and considerate and promptly proceeded to bury our amusement in our glasses. Up to this point we'd not realized we were only in mid-stream, as you might say.

The orchestra played, the tables were cleared, and then three white pigs were brought into the dining-room, all decked out in muzzles and bells. The first, the master of ceremonies announced, was two years old, the second three, and the third six. I was under the impression that some acrobats were on their way in and the pigs were going to do some tricks, the way they do in street shows. But Trimalchio dispelled this impression by asking:

"Which of these would you like for the next course? Any clodhopper can do you a barnyard cock or a stew and trifles like that, but my cooks are used to boiling whole calves."

He immediately sent for the chef and without waiting for us to choose he told him to kill the oldest pig.

He then said to the man in a loud voice:

"Which division are you from?"

When he replied he was from number forty, Trimalchio asked:

"Were you bought or were you born here?"

"Neither," said the chef, "I was left to you in Pansa's will."

"Well, then," said Trimalchio, "see you serve it up carefully—otherwise I'll have you thrown into the messenger's division."

So the chef, duly reminded of his master's magnificence, went back to his kitchen, the next course leading the way.

Trimalchio looked around at us with a gentle smile: "If you don't like the wine, I'll have it changed. It is up to you to do it justice. I don't buy it, thank heaven. In fact, whatever wine really tickles your palate this evening, it comes from an estate of mine which as yet I haven't seen. It's said to join my estates at Tarracina and Tarentum. What I'd like to do now is add Sicily to my little bit of land, so that when I want to go to Africa, I could sail there without leaving my own property.

"But tell me, Agamemnon, what was your debate about today? Even though I don't go in for the law, still I've picked up enough education for home consumption. And don't you think I turn my nose up at studying, because I have two libraries, one Greek, one Latin. So tell us, just as a favour, what was the topic of your debate?"

Agamemnon was just beginning, "A poor man and a rich man were enemies . . ." when Trimalchio said: "What's a poor man?" "Oh, witty!" said Agamemnon, and then told us about some fictitious case or other. Like lightning Trimalchio said: "If this happened, it's not a fictitious case—if it didn't happen, then it's nothing at all."

We greeted this witticism and several more like it with the greatest enthusiasm.

"Tell me, my dear Agamemnon," continued Trimalchio, "do you remember the twelve labours of Hercules and the story of Ulysses—how the Cyclops tore out his thumb with a pair of pincers.[4] I used to read about them in Homer, when I was a boy. In fact, I actually saw the Sibyl at Cumae with my own eyes dangling in a bottle, and when the children asked her in Greek: 'What do you want, Sibyl?' she used to answer: 'I want to die.' "

[Presents for the guests are distributed with a slave announcing the nature of each gift and making in each case an atrocious pun on the name of the guest.]

We laughed for ages. There were hundreds of things like this but they've slipped my mind now.

Ascyltus, with his usual lack of restraint, found everything extremely funny, lifting up his hands and laughing till the tears came. Eventually one of Trimalchio's freedman[5] friends flared up at him—the one sitting above me, in fact.

"You with the sheep's eyes," he said, "what's so funny? Isn't our host elegant enough for you? You're better off, I suppose, and used to a bigger dinner. Holy guardian here preserve me! If I was sitting by him, I'd make him bleat! A fine pippin he is to be laughing at other people! Some fly-by-night from god knows where—not worth his own piss. In fact, if I pissed round him, he wouldn't know where to turn.

"By god, it takes a lot to make me boil, but if you're too soft, worms like this only come to the top. Look at him laughing! What's he got to laugh at? Did his father pay cash for him? You're a Roman knight,[6] are you? Well, my father was a king.

" '*Why are you only a freedman?*' did you say? Because I went into service voluntarily. I wanted to be a Roman citizen, not a subject with taxes to pay. And today, I hope no one can laugh at the way I live. I'm a man among men, and I walk with my head up. I don't owe anybody a penny—there's never been a court-order out for me. No one's said '*Pay up!*' to me in the street.

**4.** Trimalchio refers to Odysseus' adventures in the cave of the Cyclops (*Odyssey*, Book IX). In spite of what he goes on to say, he has obviously not read Homer.     **5.** A former slave who had bought his freedom.     **6.** A Roman class including all who had property above a certain amount.

"I've bought a bit of land and some tiny pieces of plate. I've twenty bellies to feed, as well as a dog. I bought my old woman's freedom so nobody could wipe his dirty hands on *her* hair. Four thousand I paid for myself. I was elected to the Augustan College[7] and it cost me nothing. I hope when I die I won't have to blush in my coffin.

"But you now, you're such a busybody you don't look behind you. You see a louse on somebody else, but not the fleas on your own back. You're the only one who finds us funny. Look at the professor now—he's an older man than you and we get along with him. But you're still wet from your mother's milk and not up to your ABC yet. Just a crackpot—you're like a piece of wash-leather in soak, softer but no better! You're grander than us—well, have two dinners and two suppers! I'd rather have my good name than any amount of money. When all's said and done, who's ever asked me for money twice? For forty years I slaved but nobody ever knew if I was a slave or a free man. I came to this colony when I was a lad with long hair—the town-hall hadn't been built then. But I worked hard to please my master—there was a real gentleman, with more in his little finger-nail than there is in your whole body. And I had people in the house who tried to trip me up one way or another, but still—thanks be to his guardian spirit!—I kept my head above water. That's real success: being born free is as easy as all get-out. Now what are you gawping at, like a goat in a vetch field?"

At this remark, Giton, who was waiting on me, could not suppress his laughter and let out a filthy guffaw, which did not pass unnoticed by Ascyltus's opponent. He turned his abuse on the boy.

"So!" he said, "you're amused too, are you, you curly-headed onion? A merry Saturnalia[8] to you! Is it December, I'd like to know? When did *you* pay your liberation tax?[9] Look, he doesn't know what to do, the gallow's bird, the crow's meat.

"God's curse on you, and your master too, for not keeping you under control! As sure as I get my bellyful, it's only because of Trimalchio that I don't take it out of you here and now. He's a freedman like myself. We're doing all right, but those good-for-nothings, well—. It's easy to see, like master, like man. I can hardly hold myself back, and I'm not naturally hot-headed—but once I start, I don't give a penny for my own mother.

"All right! I'll see you when we get outside, you rat, you excrescence. I'll knock your master in the dirt before I'm an inch taller or shorter. And I won't let you off either, by heaven, even if you scream down God Almighty. Your cheap curls and your no-good master won't be much use to you then—I'll see to that. I'll get my teeth into

---

7. The state religion was the worship of Augustus, the emperor. The office of priest might be sold or conferred.     8. A December festival in honor of an ancient Italian deity at which the normal order of everyday life was reversed and the slaves and children made fun of their masters.
9. The freed slave had to pay 5 per cent of his value to the treasury.

you, all right. Either I'm much mistaken about myself or you won't
be laughing at us behind your golden beard. Athena's curse on you
and the man who first made you such a forward brat.

"I didn't learn no geometry or criticism and such silly rubbish, but
I can read the letters on a notice board and I can do my percentages
in metal, weights, and money. In fact, if you like, we'll have a bet.
Come on, here's my cash. Now you'll see how your father wasted
his money, even though you do know how to make a speech.

"Try this:

> Something we all have.
> Long I come, broad I come. What am I?

"I'll give you it: something we all have that runs and doesn't move
from its place: something we all have that grows and gets smaller.[1]

"You're running round in circles, you've had enough, like the
mouse in the pisspot. So either keep quiet or keep out of the way of
your betters, they don't even know you're alive—unless you think I
care about your box-wood rings that you swiped from your girl friend!
Lord make me lucky! Let's go into town and borrow some money.
You'll soon see they trust this iron one.

"Pah! a drownded fox makes a nice sight, I must say. As I hope to
make my pile and die so famous that people swear by my dead body,
I'll hound you to death. And he's a nice thing too—the one who
taught you all these tricks—a muttonhead, not a master. We learned
different. Our teacher used to say: 'Are your things in order? Go
straight home. No looking around. And be polite to your elders.'
Nowadays it's all an absolute muck-heap. They turn out nobody
worth a penny. I'm like you see me and I thank God for the way I
was learnt." . . .

In the middle of all this, a lictor[2] knocked at the double doors and
a drunken guest entered wearing white, followed by a large crowd of
people. I was terrified by this lordly apparition and thought it was
the chief magistrate arriving. So I tried to rise and get my bare feet
on the floor. Agamemnon laughed at this panic and said:

"Get hold of yourself, you silly fool. This is Habinnas—Augustan
College and monumental mason."

Relieved by this information I resumed my position and watched
Habinnas' entry with huge admiration. Being already drunk, he had
his hands on his wife's shoulders; loaded with several garlands, oil
pouring down his forehead and into his eyes, he settled himself into
the place of honour and immediately demanded some wine and hot

1. There is no agreement about the correct answer to these riddles. Suggested answers are, to the
first, the foot; the second, the eye; the third, the hair.   2. A magistrate's attendant.

water. Trimalchio, delighted by these high spirits, demanded a larger cup for himself and asked how he had enjoyed it all.

"The only thing we missed," replied Habinnas, "was yourself— the apple of my eye was here. Still, it was damn good. Scissa was giving a ninth-day dinner[3] in honour of a poor slave of hers she'd freed on his death-bed. And I think she'll have a pretty penny to pay in liberation tax because they reckon he was worth fifty thousand. Still, it was pleasant enough, even if we did have to pour half our drinks over his wretched bones."

"Well," said Trimalchio, "what did you have for dinner?"

"I'll tell you if I can—I've such a good memory that I often forget my own name. For the first course we had a pig crowned with sausages and served with blood-puddings and very nicely done giblets, and of course beetroot and pure wholemeal bread—which I prefer to white myself: it's very strengthening and I don't regret it when I do my business. The next course was cold tart and a concoction of first-class Spanish wine poured over hot honey. I didn't eat anything at all of the actual tart, but I dived right into the honey. Scattered round were chickpeas, lupines, a choice of nuts and an apple apiece— though I took two. And look, I've got them tied up in a napkin, because if I don't take something in the way of a present to my youngster, I'll have a row on my hands.

"Oh, yes, my good lady reminds me. We had a hunk of bearmeat set before us, which Scintilla was foolish enough to try, and she practically spewed up her guts; but I ate more than a pound of it, as it tasted like real wild-boar. And I say if bears can eat us poor people, it's all the more reason why us poor people should eat bears.

"To finish up with, we had some cheese basted with new wine, snails all round, chitterlings, plates of liver, eggs in pastry hoods, turnips, mustard, and some filthy concoction—good riddance to that. There were pickled cumin seeds too, passed round in a bowl and some people were that bad-mannered they took three handfuls. You see, we sent the ham away.

"But tell me something, Gaius, now I ask—why isn't Fortunata at the table?"

"You know her," replied Trimalchio, "unless she's put the silver away and shared out the left-overs among the slaves, she won't put a drop of water to her mouth."

"All the same," retorted Habinnas, "unless she sits down, I'm shagging off."

And he was starting to get up, when at a given signal all the servants shouted "*Fortunata*" four or five times. So in she came with her skirt tucked up under a yellow sash to show her cerise petticoat

---

3. On the last day of the mourning period.

underneath, as well as her twisted anklets and gold-embroidered slippers. Wiping her hands on a handkerchief which she carried round her neck, she took her place on the couch where Habbinas' wife was reclining. She kissed her. "Is it really you?" she said, clapping her hands together.

It soon got to the point where Fortunata took the bracelets from her great fat arms and showed them to the admiring Scintilla. In the end she even undid her anklets and her gold hair net, which she said was pure gold. Trimalchio noticed this and had it all brought to him and commented:

"A woman's chains, you see. This is the way us poor fools get robbed. She must have six and a half pounds on her. Still, I've got a bracelet myself, made up from one-tenth per cent to Mercury[4]—and it weighs not an ounce less than ten pounds."

Finally, for fear he looked like a liar, he even had some scales brought in and had them passed round to test the weight.

Scintilla was no better. From round her neck she took a little gold locket, which she called her "lucky box." From it she extracted two earrings and in her turn gave them to Fortunata to look at.

"A present from my good husband," she said, "and no one has a finer set."

"Hey!" said Habinnas, "you cleaned me out to buy you a glass bean. Honestly, if I had a daughter, I'd cut her little ears off. If there weren't any women, everything would be dirt cheap. As it is, we've got to drink cold water and piss it out hot."

Meanwhile, the women giggled tipsily between themselves and kissed each other drunkenly, one crying up her merits as a housewife, the other crying about her husband's demerits and boy friends. While they had their heads together like this, Habinnas rose stealthily and taking Fortunata's feet, flung them up over the couch.

"Oh, oh!" she shrieked, as her underskirt wandered up over her knees. So she settled herself in Scintilla's lap and hid her disgusting red face in her handkerchief.

Then came an interval, after which Trimalchio called for dessert. . . .

Fortunata was now wanting to dance, and Scintilla was doing more clapping than talking, when Trimalchio said:

"Philargyrus—even though you are such a terrible fan of the Greens[5]—you have my permission to join us. And tell your dear Menophila to sit down as well."

Need I say more? We were almost thrown out of our places, so completely did the household fill the dining-room. I even noticed that the chef was actually given a place above me, and he was reek-

---

4. Trimalchio sets aside a percentage of his profits to offer to his patron deity.   5. One of the teams in the chariot races.

ing of pickles and sauce. And he wasn't satisfied with just having a place, but he had to start straight off on an imitation of the tragedian Ephesus, and then challenge his master to bet against the Greens winning at the next races.

Trimalchio became expansive after this argument.

"My dear people," he said, "slaves are human beings too. They drink the same milk as anybody else, even though luck's been agin 'em. Still, if nothing happens to me, they'll have their taste of freedom soon. In fact, I'm setting them all free in my will. I'm giving Philargyrus a farm, what's more, and the woman he lives with. As for Cario, I'm leaving him a block of flats, his five per cent manumission tax, and a bed with all the trimmings. I'm making Fortunata my heir, and I want all my friends to look after her.

"The reason I'm telling everyone all this is so my household will love me now as much as if I was dead."

Everyone began thanking his lordship for his kindness, when he became very serious and had a copy of his will brought in. Amid the sobs of his household he read out the whole thing from beginning to end.

Then looking at Habinnas, he said:

"What have you to say, my dear old friend? Are you building my monument the way I told you? I particularly want you to keep a place at the foot of my statue and put a picture of my pup there, as well as paintings of wreaths, scent-bottles, and all the contests of Petraites,[6] and thanks to you I'll be able to live on after I'm dead. And another thing! See that it's a hundred feet facing the road and two hundred back into the field. I want all the various sorts of fruit round my ashes and lots and lots of vines. After all, it's a big mistake to have nice houses just for when you're alive and not worry about the one we have to live in for much longer. And that's why I want this written up before anything else:

### THIS MONUMENT DOES NOT GO TO THE HEIR

"But I'll make sure in my will that I don't get done down once I'm dead. I'll put one of my freedmen in charge of my tomb to look after it and not let people run up and shit on my monument. I'd like you to put some ships there too, sailing under full canvas, and me sitting on a high platform in my robes of office, wearing five gold rings and pouring out a bagful of money for the people. You know I gave them all a dinner and two denarii apiece. Let's have in a banqueting hall as well, if you think it's a good idea, and show the whole town having a good time. Put up a statue of Fortunata on my right, holding a dove, and have her leading her little dog tied to her belt—and this

---

6. A popular gladiator.

dear little chap as well, and great big wine jars sealed up so the wine won't spill. And perhaps you could carve me a broken wine jar and boy crying over it. A clock in the middle, so that anybody who looks at the time, like it or not, has got to read my name. As for the inscription now, take a good look and see if this seems suitable enough:

HERE SLEEPS

GAIUS POMPEIUS TRIMALCHIO

MAECENATIANUS

ELECTED TO THE AUGUSTAN COLLEGE IN HIS ABSENCE

HE COULD HAVE BEEN ON EVERY BOARD IN ROME

BUT HE REFUSED

GOD-FEARING BRAVE AND TRUE

A SELF-MADE MAN

HE LEFT AN ESTATE OF 30,000,000

AND HE NEVER HEARD A PHILOSOPHER

FAREWELL

AND YOU FARE WELL, TRIMALCHIO."

[After a visit to the baths, where Encolpius and his friends made an unsuccessful attempt to escape, the dinner is resumed.]

After this dish Trimalchio looked at the servants and said:

"Why haven't you had dinner yet? Off you go and let some others come on duty."

Up came another squad and as the first set called out: "Good night, Gaius!" the new arrivals shouted: "Good evening, Gaius!"

This led to the first incident that damped the general high spirits. Not a bad-looking boy entered with the newcomers and Trimalchio jumped at him and began kissing him at some length. Fortunata, asserting her just and legal rights, began hurling insults at Trimalchio, calling him a low scum and a disgrace, who couldn't control his beastly desires. "You dirty dog!" she finally added.

Trimalchio took offence at this abuse and flung his glass into Fortunata's face. She screamed as though she'd lost an eye and put her trembling hands across her face. Scintilla was terrified too and hugged the quaking woman to her breast. An obliging slave pressed a little jug of cold water to her cheek, while Fortunata rested her head on it and began weeping. Trimalchio just said:

"Well, well, forgotten her chorus days, has she? She doesn't remember, but she was bought and sold, and I took her away from it all and made her as good as the next. Yet she puffs herself up like a frog and doesn't even spit for luck. Just a great hunk, not a woman. But those as are born over a shop don't dream of a house. May I never have a day's good luck again, if I don't teach that Cassandra in clogs some manners!

"There was I, not worth twopence, and I could have had ten million. And you know I'm not lying about it. Agatho, who ran a perfume shop for the lady next door, he took me on one side and said: 'You don't want to let your family die out, you know!' But me, trying to do the right thing and not wanting to look changeable, I cut my own throat.

"All right! I'll make you want to dig me up with your bare nails. Just so you'll know on the spot what you've done for yourself—Habinnas! I don't want you to put her statue on my tomb, so at least when I'm dead I won't have any more squabbles. And another thing! just to show I can get my own back—when I'm dead I don't want her to kiss me."

After this thunderbolt, Habinnas began asking him to calm down: "None of us are without faults," he said, "we're not gods, we're human!" Scintilla said the same, calling him Gaius, and she began asking him, in the name of his guardian spirit, to give in.

Trimalchio held back his tears no longer. "I ask you, Habinnas," he said, "as you hope to enjoy your bit of savings—if I did anything wrong, spit in my face. I kissed this very careful little fellow, not for his pretty face, but because he's careful with money—he says his ten times table, he reads a book at sight, he's got himself some Thracian kit out of his daily allowance, and he's bought himself an easy chair and two cups out of his own pocket. Doesn't he deserve to be the apple of my eye? But Fortunata won't have it.

"Is that the way you feel, high heels? I'll give you a piece of advice: don't let your good luck turn your head, you kite, and don't make me show my teeth, my little darling—otherwise you'll feel my temper. You know me: once I've decided on something, it's fixed with a twelve-inch nail.

"But to come back to earth—I want you to enjoy yourselves, my dear people. After all, I was once like you are, but being the right sort, I got where I am. It's the old headpiece that makes a man, the rest is all rubbish. 'Buy right—sell right!'—that's me! Different people will give you a different line. I'm just on top of the world, I'm that lucky.

"But you, you snoring thing, are you still moaning? I'll give you something to moan about in a minute.

"However, as I'd started to say, it was my shrewd way with money that got me to my present position. I came from Asia as big as this candlestick. In fact, every day I used to measure myself against it, and to get some whiskers round my beak quicker, I used to oil my lips from the lamp. Still, for fourteen years I was the old boy's fancy. And there's nothing wrong if the boss wants it. But I did all right by the old girl too. You know what I mean—I don't say anything because I'm not the boasting sort.

"Well, as heaven will have it, I became boss in the house, and the old boy, you see, couldn't think of anything but me. That's about it—he made me co-heir with the Emperor[7] and I got a senator's fortune. But nobody gets enough, never. I wanted to go into business. Not to make a long story of it, I built five ships, I loaded them with wine—it was absolute gold at the time—and I sent them to Rome. You'd have thought I ordered it—every single ship was wrecked. That's fact, not fable! In one single day Neptune swallowed up thirty million. Do you think I gave up? This loss honestly wasn't more than a flea-bite to me—it was as if nothing had happened. I built more boats, bigger and better and luckier, so nobody could say I wasn't a man of courage. You know, the greater the ship, the greater the confidence. I loaded them again—with wine, bacon, beans, perfumes and slaves. At this point Fortunata did the decent thing, because she sold off all her gold trinkets, all her clothes, and put ten thousand in gold pieces in my hand. This was the yeast my fortune needed to rise. What heaven wants, soon happens. In one voyage I carved out a round ten million. I immediately bought back all my old master's estates. I built a house, I invested in slaves, and I bought up the horse trade. Whatever I touched grew like a honeycomb. Once I had more than the whole country, then down tools! I retired from business and began advancing loans through freedmen.

"Actually I was tired of trading on my own account, but it was an astrologer who convinced me. He happened to come to our colony, a sort of Greek, Serapa by name, and he could have told heaven itself what to do. He even told me things I'd forgotten. He went through everything for me from A to Z. He knew me inside out—the only thing he didn't tell me was what I ate for dinner the day before. You'd have thought he'd never left my side.

"Wasn't there that thing, Habinnas?—I think you were there: 'You got your lady wife out of those *certain circumstances*. You are not lucky in your friends. Nobody thanks you enough for your trouble. You have large estates. You are nursing a viper in your bosom.'

"And he said—though I shouldn't tell you—I have thirty years, four months, two days to live. What's more, I shall soon receive a legacy. My horoscope tells me this. If I'm allowed to join my estates to Apulia,[8] I'll have lived enough.

"Meantime, under the protection of Mercury, I built this house. As you know, it was still a shack, now it's a shrine. It has four dining-rooms, twenty bedrooms, two marble colonnades, a row of box-rooms up above, a bedroom where I sleep myself, a nest for this viper, and a really good lodge for the porter. The guest apartment

---

7. An honor which Trimalchio shared with many others, for it was customary (as a prudent measure, to avoid confiscation on some pretext or other) to include a bequest to the emperor in one's will.    8. The southeastern extremity of Italy.

takes a hundred guests. In fact, when Scaurus[9] came here, he didn't want to stay anywhere else, even though he's got his father's guest house down by the sea. And there are a lot of other things I'll show you in a second.

"Believe me: have a penny, and you're worth a penny. You got something, you'll be thought something. Like your old friend—first a frog, now a king.

"Meantime, Stichus, bring out the shroud and the things I want to be buried in. Bring some cosmetic cream too, and a sample from that jar of wine I want my bones washed in."

Stichus did not delay over it, but brought his white shroud and his formal dress into the dining-room . . . Trimalchio told us to examine them and see if they were made of good wool. Then he said with a smile:

"Now you, Stichus, see no mice or moths get at those—otherwise I'll burn you alive. I want to be buried in style, so the whole town will pray for my rest."

He opened a bottle of nard on the spot, rubbed some on all of us and said:

"I hope this'll be as nice when I'm dead as when I'm alive." The wine he had poured into a big decanter and he said:

"I want you to think you've been invited to my wake."

The thing was becoming absolutely sickening, when Trimalchio, showing the effects of his disgusting drunkenness, had a fresh entertainment brought into the dining-room, some cornet players. Propped up on a lot of cushions, he stretched out along the edge of the couch and said: "Pretend I'm dead and say something nice."

The cornet players struck up a dead march. One man in particular, the slave of his undertaker (who was the most respectable person present) blew so loudly that he roused the neighbourhood. As a result, the fire brigade, thinking Trimalchio's house was on fire, suddenly broke down the front door and began kicking up their own sort of din with their water and axes.

Seizing this perfect chance, we gave Agamemnon the slip and escaped as rapidly as if there really were a fire.

---

# ST. AUGUSTINE

## A.D. 354–430

Aurelius Augustinus was born in 354 A.D. at Tagaste, in North Africa. He was baptized as a Christian in 387 A.D. and ordained bishop of Hippo, in

9. Unknown. The name is aristocratic but our translator suggests Trimalchio may be referring to a well-known manufacturer of fish sauce from Pompeii.

North Africa, in 395 A.D. When he died there in 430 A.D., the city was besieged by Gothic invaders. Besides the *Confessions* (begun in 397 A.D.) he wrote *The City of God* (finished in 426 A.D.) and many polemical works against schismatics and heretics.

He was born into a world which no longer enjoyed the "Roman peace." Invading barbarians had pierced the empire's defenses and were increasing their pressure every year. The economic basis of the empire was cracking under the strain of the enormous taxation needed to support the army; the land was exhausted. The empire was Christian, but the Church was split, beset by heresies and organized heretical sects. The empire was about to go down to destruction, and there was every prospect that the Church would go down with it.

Augustine, one of the men responsible for the consolidation of the Church in the West, especially for the systematization of its doctrine and policy, was not converted to Christianity until he had reached middle life. "Late have I loved Thee, O Beauty so ancient and so new," he says in his *Confessions*, written long after his conversion. The lateness of his conversion and his regret for his wasted youth were among the sources of the energy which drove him to assume the intellectual leadership of the Western Church and to guarantee, by combating heresy on the one hand and laying new ideological foundations for Christianity on the other, the Church's survival through the dark centuries to come. Augustine had been brought up in the literary and philosophical tradition of the classical world, and it is partly because of his assimilation of classical literature and method to Christian training and teaching that the literature of the ancient world survived at all when Roman power collapsed in a welter of bloodshed and destruction which lasted for generations.

In his *Confessions* he set down, for the benefit of others, the story of his early life and his conversion to Christianity. This is, as far as we know, the first authentic ancient autobiography, and that fact itself is a significant expression of the Christian spirit, which proclaims the value of the individual soul and the importance of its relation with God. Throughout the *Confessions* Augustine talks directly to God, in humility, yet conscious that God is concerned for him personally. At the same time he comes to an understanding of his own feelings and development as a human being which marks his *Confessions* as one of the great literary documents of the Western world. His description of his childhood is the only detailed account of the childhood of a great man which antiquity has left us, and his accurate observation and keen perception are informed by the Hebrew and Christian idea of the sense of sin. "So small a boy and so great a sinner"—from the beginning of his narrative to the end Augustine sees man not as the Greek at his most optimistic tended to see him, the center and potential master of the universe, but as a child, wandering in ignorance, capable of reclamation only through the divine mercy which waits eternally for him to turn to it.

In Augustine are combined the intellectual tradition of the ancient world at its best and the religious feeling which was characteristic of the Middle Ages. The transition from the old world to the new can be seen in his pages; his analytical intellect pursues its Odyssey through strange and scattered islands—the mysticism of the Manichees, the skepticism of the Academic philosophers, the fatalism of the astrologers—until he finds his home in the Church, to which he was to render such great service. His account of his conversion in the garden at Milan records the true moment of transition from the ancient to the medieval world. The innumerable defeats and victories, the burning towns and ravaged farms, the bloodshed, dates, and statistics of the end of an era are all illuminated and ordered by this moment in the history of the human spirit. Here is the point of change itself.

For criticism and biography, see P. Brown, *Augustine of Hippo* (1967), an authoritative and engrossing account of his whole career.

# Confessions[1]

## [Childhood]

### Book I

What have I to say to Thee, God, save that I know not where I came from, when I came into this life-in-death—or should I call it death-in-life? I do not know. I only know that the gifts Your mercy had provided sustained me from the first moment: not that I remember it but so I have heard from the parents of my flesh, the father from whom, and the mother in whom, You fashioned me in time.

Thus for my sustenance and my delight I had woman's milk: yet it was not my mother or my nurses who stored their breasts for me: it was Yourself, using them to give me the food of my infancy, according to Your ordinance and the riches set by You at every level of creation. It was by Your gift that I desired what You gave and no more, by Your gift that those who suckled me willed to give me what You had given them: for it was by the love implanted in them by You that they gave so willingly that milk which by Your gift flowed in the breasts. It was a good for them that I received good from them, though I received it not *from* them but only through them: since all good things are from You, O God, and *from God is all my health*.[2] But this I have learnt since: You have made it abundantly clear by all that I have seen You give, within me and about me. For at that time I knew how to suck, to lie quiet when I was content, to cry when I was in pain: and that was all I knew.

Later I added smiling to the things I could do, first in sleep, then awake. This again I have on the word of others, for naturally I do not remember; in any event, I believe it, for I have seen other infants do the same. And gradually I began to notice where I was, and the will grew in me to make my wants known to those who might satisfy them; but I could not, for my wants were within me and those others

1. Abridged. Translated by F. J. Sheed.    2. Throughout the *Confessions*, Augustine quotes liberally from the Bible; this citation, set off like the others in italics, has no special significance, but where a quotation alludes to a passage which bears more directly on Augustine's situation, it is glossed.

were outside: nor had they any faculty enabling them to enter into my mind. So I would fling my arms and legs about and utter sounds, making the few gestures in my power—these being as apt to express my wishes as I could make them: but they were not very apt. And when I did not get what I wanted, either because my wishes were not clear or the things not good for me, I was in a rage—with my parents as though I had a right to their submission, with free human beings as though they had been bound to serve me; and I took my revenge in screams. That infants are like this, I have learnt from watching other infants; and that I was like it myself I have learnt more clearly from these other infants, who did not know me, than from my nurses who did.

\* \* \*

From infancy I came to boyhood, or rather it came to me, taking the place of infancy. Yet infancy did not go: for where was it to go to? Simply it was no longer there. For now I was not an infant, without speech, but a boy, speaking. This I remember; and I have since discovered by observation how I learned to speak. I did not learn by elders teaching me words in any systematic way, as I was soon after taught to read and write. But of my own motion, using the mind which You, my God, gave me, I strove with cries and various sounds and much moving of my limbs to utter the feelings of my heart—all this in order to get my own way. Now I did not always manage to express the right meanings to the right people. So I began to reflect [I observed that] my elders would make some particular sound, and as they made it would point at or move towards some particular thing: and from this I came to realize that the thing was called by the sound they made when they wished to draw my attention to it. That they intended this was clear from the motions of their body, by a kind of natural language common to all races which consists in facial expressions, glances of the eye, gestures, and the tones by which the voice expresses the mind's state—for example whether things are to be sought, kept, thrown away, or avoided. So, as I heard the same words again and again properly used in different phrases, I came gradually to grasp what things they signified; and forcing my mouth to the same sounds, I began to use them to express my own wishes. Thus I learnt to convey what I meant to those about me; and so took another long step along the stormy way of human life in society, while I was still subject to the authority of my parents and at the beck and call of my elders.

O God, my God, what emptiness and mockeries did I now experience: for it was impressed upon me as right and proper in a boy to obey those who taught me, that I might get on in the world and excel in the handling of words[3] to gain honor among men and deceitful riches. I, poor wretch, could not see the use of the things I was sent to school to learn; but if I proved idle in learning, I was soundly beaten. For this procedure seemed wise to our ancestors: and many, passing the same way in days past, had built a sorrowful road by which we too must go, with multiplication of grief and toil upon the sons of Adam.

Yet, Lord, I observed men praying to You: and I learnt to do likewise, thinking of You (to the best of my understanding) as some great being who, though unseen, could hear and help me. As a boy I fell into the way of calling upon You, my Help and my Refuge; and in those prayers I broke the strings of my tongue—praying to You, small as I was but with no small energy, that I might not be beaten at school. And when You did not hear me (*not as giving me over to folly*),[4] my elders and even my parents, who certainly wished me no harm, treated my stripes as a huge joke, which they were very far from being to me. Surely, Lord, there is no one so steeled in mind or cleaving to You so close—or even so insensitive, for that might have the same effect—as to make light of the racks and hooks and other torture instruments[5] (from which in all lands men pray so fervently to be saved) while truly loving those who are in such bitter fear of them. Yet my parents seemed to be amused at the torments inflicted upon me as a boy by my masters, though I was no less afraid of my punishments or zealous in my prayers to You for deliverance. But in spite of my terrors I still did wrong, by writing or reading or studying less than my set tasks. It was not, Lord, that I lacked mind or memory, for You had given me as much of these as my age required; but the one thing I revelled in was play; and for this I was punished by men who after all were doing exactly the same things themselves. But the idling of men is called business; the idling of boys, though exactly like, is punished by those same men: and no one pities either boys or men. Perhaps an unbiased observer would hold that I was rightly punished as a boy for playing with a ball: because this hindered my progress in studies—studies which would give me the opportunity as a man to play at things more degraded. And what difference was there between me and the master who flogged me? For if on some trifling point he had the worst of the argument with some fellow-master, he was more torn with angry vanity than I when I was beaten in a game of ball.

\*        \*        \*

3. The study of rhetoric, which was the passport of eminence in public life.    4. Augustine recognizes the necessity of this rigorous training; that he never forgot its harshness is clear from his remark in the *City of God*, Book XXI, Section 14: "If a choice were given him between suffering death and living his early years over again, who would not shudder and choose death?" 5. The instruments of public execution.

But to continue with my boyhood, which was in less peril of sin than
my adolescence. I disliked learning and hated to be forced to it. But
I *was* forced to it, so that good was done to me though it was not my
doing. Short of being driven to it, I certainly would not have learned.
But no one does well against his will, even if the thing he does is a
good thing to do. Nor did those who forced me do well: it was by
You, O God, that well was done. Those others had no deeper vision
of the use to which I might put all they forced me to learn, but to
sate the insatiable desire of man for wealth that is but penury and
glory that is but shame. But You, Lord, *by Whom the very hairs of
our head are numbered,*[6] used for my good the error of those who
urged me to study; but my own error, in that I had no will to learn,
you used for my punishment—a punishment richly deserved by one
so small a boy and so great a sinner. Thus, You brought good for me
out of those who did ill, and justly punished me for the ill I did
myself. So You have ordained and so it is: that every disorder of the
soul is its own punishment.

To this day I do not quite see why I so hated the Greek tongue[7]
that I was made to learn as a small boy. For I really liked Latin—not
the rudiments that we got from our first teachers but the literature
that we came to be taught later. For the rudiments—reading and
writing and figuring—I found as hard and hateful as Greek. Yet this
too could come only from sin and the vanity of life, because *I was
flesh, and a wind that goes away and returns not.* For those first
lessons were the surer. I acquired the power I still have to read what
I find written and to write what I want to express; whereas in the
studies that came later I was forced to memorize the wanderings of
Aeneas[8]—whoever *he* was—while forgetting my own wanderings; and
to weep for the death of Dido who killed herself for love,[9] while
bearing dry-eyed my own pitiful state, in that among these studies I
was becoming dead to You, O God, my life.

Nothing could be more pitiful than a pitiable creature who does
not see to pity himself, and weeps for the death that Dido suffered
through love of Aeneas and not for the death he suffers himself through
not loving You, O God, Light of my heart, Bread of my soul, Power
wedded to my mind and the depths of my thought. I did not love
You and I went away from You in fornication:[1] and all around me
in my fornication echoed applauding cries "Well done! Well done!"
*For the friendship of this world is fornication against Thee*: and the
world cries "Well done" so loudly that one is ashamed of unmanli-

<hr>

6. Who knows and attends to the smallest detail of each life. [Matthew 10:30.]    7. Important
not only for gaining knowledge of Greek literature but also because it was the official language of
the Eastern half of the Roman Empire. Augustine never really mastered Greek, though his remark
elsewhere, that he had acquired so little Greek that it amounted to practically none, is
overmodest.    8. Virgil's *Aeneid*, Book III.    9. *Aeneid*, Book IV.    1. Metaphorically in this
instance.

ness not to do it. And for this I did not grieve; but I grieved for Dido, slain as she sought by the sword an end to her woe, while I too followed after the lowest of Your creatures, forsaking You, earth going unto earth. And if I were kept from reading, I grieved at not reading the tales that caused me such grief. This sort of folly is held nobler and richer than the studies by which we learn to read and write!

But now let my God cry aloud in my soul, and let Your truth assure me that it is not so: the earlier study is the better. I would more willingly forget the wanderings of Aeneas and all such things than how to write and read. Over the entrance of these grammar schools hangs a curtain:[2] but this should be seen not as lending honor to the mysteries, but as a cloak to the errors taught within. Let not those masters—who have now lost their terrors for me—cry out against me, because I confess to You, my God, the desire of my soul, and find soul's rest in blaming my evil ways that I may love Your holy ways. Let not the buyers or sellers of book-learning cry out against me. If I ask them whether it is true, as the poet says, that Aeneas ever went to Carthage, the more ignorant will have to answer that they do not know, the more scholarly that he certainly did not. But if I ask with what letters the name Aeneas is spelt, all whose schooling has gone so far will answer correctly, according to the convention men have agreed upon for the use of letters. Or again, were I to ask which loss would be more damaging to human life—the loss from men's memory of reading and writing or the loss of these poetic imaginings—there can be no question what anyone would answer who had not lost his own memory. Therefore as a boy I did wrong in liking the empty studies more than the useful—or rather in loving the empty and hating the useful. For one and one make two, two and two make four, I found a loathsome refrain; but such empty unrealities as the Wooden Horse with its armed men, and Troy on fire, and Creusa's Ghost, were sheer delight.[3]

Give me leave, O my God, to speak of my mind, Your gift, and of the follies in which I wasted it. It chanced that a task was set me, a task which I did not like but had to do. There was the promise of glory if I won, the fear of ignominy, and a flogging as well, if I lost. It was to declaim the words uttered by Juno in her rage and grief when she could not keep the Trojan prince from coming to Italy.[4] I had learnt that Juno had never said these words, but we were compelled to err in the footsteps of the poet who had invented them: and it was our duty to paraphrase in prose what he had said in verse. In

2. School was often held in a building open on one side and curtained off from the street. 3. *Aeneid*, Book II.    4. Augustine was assigned the task of delivering a prose paraphrase of Juno's angry speech in the *Aeneid*, Book I. (She complains that her enemies, the Trojans under Aeneas, are on their way to their destined goal in Italy in spite of her resolution to prevent them.) Rhetorical exercises such as this were common in the schools, since they served the double purpose of teaching literature and rhetorical composition at the same time.

this exercise that boy won most applause in whom the passions of grief and rage were expressed most powerfully and in the language most adequate to the majesty of the personage represented.

What could all this mean to me, O My true Life, My God? Why was there more applause for the performance I gave than for so many classmates of my own age? Was not the whole business so much smoke and wind? Surely some other matter could have been found to exercise mind and tongue. Thy praises, Lord, might have upheld the fresh young shoot of my heart, so that it might not have been whirled away by empty trifles, defiled, a prey to the spirits of the air. For there is more than one way of sacrificing to the fallen angels.

\*     \*     \*

## [The Pear Tree]

### Book II

I propose now to set down my past wickedness and the carnal corruptions of my soul, not for love of them but that I may love Thee, O my God. I do it for love of Thy love, passing again in the bitterness of remembrance over my most evil ways that Thou mayest thereby grow ever lovelier to me, O Loveliness that dost not deceive, Loveliness happy and abiding: and I collect my self out of that broken state in which my very being was torn asunder because I was turned away from Thee, the One, and wasted myself upon the many.

Arrived now at adolescence I burned for all the satisfactions of hell, and I sank to the animal in a succession of dark lusts: *my beauty consumed away*, and I stank in Thine eyes, yet was pleasing in my own and anxious to please the eyes of men.

My one delight was to love and to be loved. But in this I did not keep the measure of mind to mind, which is the luminous line of friendship; but from the muddy concupiscence of the flesh and the hot imagination of puberty mists steamed up to becloud and darken my heart so that I could not distinguish the white light of love from the fog of lust. Both love and lust boiled within me, and swept my youthful immaturity over the precipice of evil desires to leave me half drowned in a whirlpool of abominable sins. Your wrath had grown mighty against me and I knew it not. I had grown deaf from the clanking of the chain of my mortality, the punishment for the pride of my soul: and I departed further from You, and You left me to myself: and I was tossed about and wasted and poured out and boiling over in my fornications: and You were silent, O my late-won Joy. You were silent, and I, arrogant and depressed, weary and restless, wandered further and further from You into more and more sins which could bear no fruit save sorrows.

\*     \*     \*

Where then was I, and how far from the delights of Your house, in that sixteenth year of my life in this world, when the madness of lust—needing no licence from human shamelessness, receiving no licence from Your laws—took complete control of me, and I surrendered wholly to it? My family took no care to save me from this moral destruction by marriage: their only concern was that I should learn to make as fine and persuasive speeches as possible.

*    *    *

Your law, O Lord, punishes theft; and this law is so written in the hearts of men that not even the breaking of it blots it out: for no thief bears calmly being stolen from—not even if he is rich and the other steals through want. Yet I chose to steal, and not because want drove me to it—unless a want of justice and contempt for it and an excess for iniquity. For I stole things which I already had in plenty and of better quality. Nor had I any desire to enjoy the things I stole, but only the stealing of them and the sin. There was a pear tree near our vineyard, heavy with fruit, but fruit that was not particularly tempting either to look at or to taste. A group of young blackguards, and I among them, went out to knock down the pears and carry them off late one night, for it was our bad habit to carry on our games in the streets till very late. We carried off an immense load of pears, not to eat—for we barely tasted them before throwing them to the hogs. Our only pleasure in doing it was that it was forbidden. Such was my heart, O God, such was my heart: yet in the depth of the abyss You had pity on it. Let that heart now tell You what it sought when I was thus evil for no object, having no cause for wrongdoing save my wrongness. The malice of the act was base and I loved it—that is to say I loved my own undoing, I loved the evil in me—not the thing for which I did the evil, simply the evil: my soul was depraved, and hurled itself down from security in You into utter destruction, seeking no profit from wickedness but only to be wicked.

*    *    *

[Student at Carthage]

## Book III

I came to Carthage[5] where a cauldron of illicit loves leapt and boiled about me. I was not yet in love, but I was in love with love, and from the very depth of my need hated myself for not more keenly feeling the need. I sought some object to love, since I was thus in love with loving; and I hated security and a life with no snares for my feet. For within I was hungry, all for the want of that spiritual

5. The capital city of the province, where Augustine went to study rhetoric.

food which is Thyself, my God; yet [though I was hungry for want of it] I did not hunger for it: I had no desire whatever for incorruptible food, not because I had it in abundance but the emptier I was, the more I hated the thought of it. Because of all this my soul was sick, and broke out in sores, whose itch I agonized to scratch with the rub of carnal things—carnal, yet if there were no soul in them, they would not be objects of love. My longing then was to love and to be loved, but most when I obtained the enjoyment of the body of the person who loved me.

Thus I polluted the stream of friendship with the filth of unclean desire and sullied its limpidity with the hell of lust. And vile and unclean as I was, so great was my vanity that I was bent upon passing for clean and courtly. And I did fall in love, simply from wanting to. O my God, my Mercy, with how much bitterness didst Thou in Thy goodness sprinkle the delights of that time! I was loved, and our love came to the bond of consummation: I wore my chains with bliss but with torment too, for I was scourged with the red hot rods of jealousy, with suspicions and fears and tempers and quarrels.

I developed a passion for stage plays, with the mirror they held up to my own miseries and the fuel they poured on my flame. How is it that a man wants to be made sad by the sight of tragic sufferings that he could not bear in his own person? Yet the spectator does want to feel sorrow, and it is actually his feeling of sorrow that he enjoys. Surely this is the most wretched lunacy? For the more a man feels such sufferings in himself, the more he is moved by the sight of them on the stage. Now when a man suffers himself, it is called misery; when he suffers in the suffering of another, it is called pity. But how can the unreal sufferings of the stage possibly move pity? The spectator is not moved to aid the sufferer but merely to be sorry for him; and the more the author of these fictions makes the audience grieve, the better they like him. If the tragic sorrows of the characters—whether historical or entirely fictitious—be so poorly represented that the spectator is not moved to tears, he leaves the theatre unsatisfied and full of complaints; if he *is* moved to tears, he stays to the end, fascinated and revelling in it.

\*          \*          \*

Those of my occupations at that time which were held as reputable[6] were directed towards the study of the law, in which I meant to excel—and the less honest I was, the more famous I should be. The very limit of human blindness is to glory in being blind. By this time I was a leader in the School of Rhetoric and I enjoyed this high station and was arrogant and swollen with importance: though You

6. I.e. his rhetorical studies.

know, O Lord, that I was far quieter in my behavior and had no share in the riotousness of the *eversores*—the Overturners[7]—for this blackguardly diabolical name they wore as the very badge of sophistication. Yet I was much in their company and much ashamed of the sense of shame that kept me from being like them. I was with them and I did for the most part enjoy their companionshhip, though I abominated the acts that were their specialty—as when they made a butt of some hapless newcomer, assailing him with really cruel mockery for no reason whatever, save the malicious pleasure they got from it. There was something very like the action of devils in their behavior. They were rightly called Overturners, since they had themselves been first overturned and perverted, tricked by those same devils who were secretly mocking them in the very acts by which they amused themselves in mocking and making fools of others.

With these men as companions of my immaturity, I was studying the books of eloquence; for in eloquence it was my ambition to shine, all from a damnable vaingloriousness and for the satisfaction of human vanity. Following the normal order of study I had come to a book of one Cicero, whose tongue[8] practically everyone admires, though not his heart. That particular book is called *Hortensius*[9] and contains an exhortation to philosophy. Quite definitely it changed the direction of my mind, altered my prayers to You, O Lord, and gave me a new purpose and ambition. Suddenly all the vanity I had hoped in I saw as worthless, and with an incredible intensity of desire I longed after immortal wisdom. I had begun that journey upwards by which I was to return to You. My father was now dead two years; I was eighteen and was receiving money from my mother for the continuance of my study of eloquence. But I used that book not for the sharpening of my tongue; what won me in it was what it said, not the excellence of its phrasing.

*     *     *

So I resolved to make some study of the Sacred Scriptures and find what kind of books they were. But what I came upon was something not grasped by the proud, not revealed either to children, something utterly humble in the hearing but sublime in the doing, and shrouded deep in mystery. And I was not of the nature to enter into it or bend my neck to follow it. When I first read those Scriptures, I did not feel in the least what I have just said; they seemed to me unworthy to be compared with the majesty of Cicero. My conceit was repelled by their simplicity, and I had not the mind to penetrate into their

7. A group of students who prided themselves on their wild actions and indiscipline; *eversores* is the Latin word that means "Overturners."   8. Style.   9. Only fragments of this dialogue remain. In it Cicero replies to an opponent of philosophy with an impassioned defense of the intellectual life.

depths. They were indeed of a nature to grow in Your little ones.[1] But I could not bear to be a little one; I was only swollen with pride, but to myself I seemed a very big man.

*　　*　　*

## [Worldly Ambitions]

### Book VI

By this time my mother had come to me, following me over sea and land with the courage of piety and relying upon You in all perils. For they were in danger from a storm, and she reassured even the sailors—by whom travelers newly ventured upon the deep are ordinarily reassured—promising them safe arrival because thus You had promised her in a vision. She found me in a perilous state through my deep despair of ever discovering the truth. But even when I told her that if I was not yet a Catholic Christian, I was no longer a Manichean,[2] she was not greatly exultant as at some unlooked-for good news, because she had already received assurance upon that part of my misery; she bewailed me as one dead certainly, but certainly to be raised again by You, offering me in her mind as one stretched out dead, that You might say to the widow's son: "*Young man, I say to thee arise*":[3] and he should sit up and begin to speak and You should give him to his mother.

*　　*　　*

Nor did I then groan in prayer for Your help. My mind was intent upon inquiry and unquiet for argumentation. I regarded Ambrose[4] as a lucky man by worldly standards to be held in honor by such important people: only his celibacy seemed to me a heavy burden. I had no means of guessing, and no experience of my own to learn from, what hope he bore within him, what struggles he might have against the temptations that went with his high place, what was his consolation in adversity, and on what joys of Your bread the hidden mouth of his heart fed. Nor did he know how I was inflamed nor the depth of my peril. I could not ask of him what I wished as I wished, for I was kept from any face to face conversation with him by the throng of men with their own troubles, whose infirmities he served.

1. Refers not only to the rhetorical simplicity of Jesus' teachings but his interest in teaching children, "for to such belongs the kingdom of heaven." [Matthew 19:14.]  2. Augustine had for nine years been a member of this religious sect, which followed the teaching of the Babylonian mystic Mani (216–77). The Manicheans believed that the world was a battleground for the forces of good and evil: redemption in a future life would come to the Elect, who renounced worldly occupations and possessions and practiced a severe asceticism (including abstention from meat). Augustine's mother, Monica, was a Christian, and lamented her son's Manichean beliefs. 3. Luke 7:14, recounting one of Christ's miracles.  4. The leading personality among the Christians of the West. Not many years after this he defied the power of the emperor Theodosius, and forced him to beg for God's pardon in the church at Milan for having put the inhabitants of Thessalonica to the sword.

The very little time he was not with these he was refreshing either his body with necessary food or his mind with reading. When he read, his eyes traveled across the page and his heart sought into the sense, but voice and tongue were silent. No one was forbidden to approach him nor was it his custom to require that visitors should be announced: but when we came into him we often saw him reading and always to himself; and after we had sat long in silence, unwilling to interrupt a work on which he was so intent, we would depart again. We guessed that in the small time he could find for the refreshment of his mind, he would wish to be free from the distraction of other men's affairs and not called away from what he was doing. Perhaps he was on his guard lest [if he read aloud] someone listening should be troubled and want an explanation if the author he was reading expressed some idea over-obscurely, and it might be necessary to expound or discuss some of the more difficult questions. And if he had to spend time on this, he would get through less reading than he wished. Or it may be that his real reason for reading to himself was to preserve his voice, which did in fact readily grow tired. But whatever his reason for doing it, that man certainly had a good reason.

✻    ✻    ✻

I was all hot for honors, money, marriage: and You made mock of my hotness. In my pursuit of these, I suffered most bitter disappointments, but in this You were good to me since I was thus prevented from taking delight in anything not Yourself. Look now into my heart, Lord, by whose will I remember all this and confess it to You. Let my soul cleave to You now that You have freed it from the tenacious hold of death. At that time my soul was in misery, and You pricked the soreness of its wound, that leaving all things it might turn to You, who are over all and without whom all would return to nothing, that it might turn to You and be healed. I was in utter misery and there was one day especially on which You acted to bring home to me the realization of my misery. I was preparing an oration in praise of the Emperor[5] in which I was to utter any number of lies to win the applause of people who knew they were lies. My heart was much wrought upon by the shame of this and inflamed with the fever of the thoughts that consumed it. I was passing along a certain street in Milan when I noticed a beggar. He was jesting and laughing and I imagine more than a little drunk. I fell into gloom and spoke to the friends who were with me about the endless sorrows that our own insanity brings us: for here was I striving away, dragging the load of my unhappiness under the spurring of my desires, and mak-

---

5. Probably the young Valentinian, whose court was at Milan.

ing it worse by dragging it: and with all our striving, our one aim was to arrive at some sort of happiness without care: the beggar had reached the same goal before us, and we might quite well never reach it at all. The very thing that he had attained by means of a few pennies begged from passers-by—namely the pleasure of a temporary happiness—I was plotting for with so many a weary twist and turn.

Certainly his joy was no true joy; but the joy I sought in my ambition was emptier still. In any event he was cheerful and I worried, he had no cares and I nothing but cares. Now if anyone had asked me whether I would rather be cheerful or fearful, I would answer: "Cheerful"; but if he had gone on to ask whether I would rather be like that beggar or as I actually was, I would certainly have chosen my own state though so troubled and anxious. Now this was surely absurd. It could not be for any true reason. I ought not to have preferred my own state rather than his merely because I was the more learned, since I got no joy from my learning, but sought only to please men by it—not even to teach them, only to please them. Therefore did You break my bones with the rod of Your discipline.

*   *   *

Great effort was made to get me married. I proposed, the girl was promised me. My mother played a great part in the matter for she wanted to have me married and then cleansed with the saving waters of baptism,[6] rejoicing to see me grow every day more fitted for baptism and feeling that her prayers and Your promises were to be fulfilled in my faith. By my request and her own desire she begged You daily with the uttermost intensity of her heart to show her in a vision something of my future marriage, but You would never do it. She did indeed see certain vain fantasies, under the pressure of her mind's preoccupation with the matter; and she told them to me, not, however, with the confidence she always had when You had shown things to her, but as if she set small store by them; for she said that there was a certain unanalyzable savor, not to be expressed in words, by which she could distinguish between what You revealed and the dreams of her own spirit. Still she pushed on with the matter of my marriage, and the girl was asked for. She was still two years short of the age for marriage[7] but I liked her and agreed to wait.

There was a group of us friends who had much serious discussion together, concerning the cares and troubles of human life which we found so hard to endure. We had almost decided to seek a life of peace, away from the throng of men. This peace we hoped to attain by putting together whatever we could manage to get, and making one common household for all of us: so that in the clear trust of

6. He could not be baptized while living in sin with his mistress, a liaison that resulted in the birth of a son, Adeodatus, who later accompanied Augustine to Italy.    7. The legal age was twelve years. Augustus was in his early thirties.

friendship, things should not belong to this or that individual, but one thing should be made of all our possessions, and belong wholly to each one of us, and everybody own everything. It seemed that there might be perhaps ten men in this fellowship. Among us there were some very rich men, especially Romanianus, our fellow towns-man, who had been a close friend of mine from childhood and had been brought to the court in Milan by the press of some very urgent business. He was strongest of all for the idea and he had considerable influence in persuasion because his wealth was much greater than anyone else's. We agreed that two officers should be chosen every year to handle the details of our life together, leaving the rest undisturbed. But then we began to wonder whether our wives would agree, for some of us already had wives and I meant to have one. So the whole plan, which we had built up so neatly, fell to pieces in our hands and was simply dropped. We returned to our old sighing and groaning and treading of this world's broad and beaten ways:[8] for many thoughts were in our hearts, but *Thy counsel standeth forever.* And out of Thy counsel didst Thou deride ours and didst prepare Thine own things for us, meaning to *give us meat in due season and to open Thy hands and fill our souls with Thy blessing.*

Meanwhile my sins were multiplied. She with whom I had lived so long was torn from my side as a hindrance to my forthcoming marriage. My heart which had held her very dear was broken and wounded and shed blood. She went back to Africa, swearing that she would never know another man, and left with me the natural son I had had of her. But I in my unhappiness could not, for all my manhood, imitate her resolve. I was unable to bear the delay of two years which must pass before I was to get the girl I had asked for in marriage. In fact it was not really marriage that I wanted. I was simply a slave to lust. So I took another woman, not of course as a wife; and thus my soul's disease was nourished and kept alive as vigorously as ever, indeed worse than ever, that it might reach the realm of matrimony in the company of its ancient habit. Nor was the wound healed that had been made by the cutting off of my former mistress. For there was first burning and bitter grief; and after that it festered, and as the pain grew duller it only grew more hopeless.

\*     \*     \*

## [Conversion]

## Book VIII

\*     \*     \*

Thus I was sick at heart and in torment, accusing myself with a new intensity of bitterness, twisting and turning in my chain in the hope

8. Cf. Matthew 7:13: "Broad is the way that leadeth to destruction," that is, to damnation.

that it might be utterly broken, for what held me was so small a thing! But it still held me. And You stood in the secret places of my soul, O Lord, in the harshness of Your mercy redoubling the scourges of fear and shame lest I should give way again and that small slight tie which remained should not be broken but should grow again to full strength and bind me closer even than before. For I kept saying within myself: "Let it be now, let it be now," and by the mere words I had begun to move toward the resolution. I almost made it, yet I did not quite make it. But I did not fall back into my original state, but as it were stood near to get my breath. And I tried again and I was almost there, and now I could all but touch it and hold it: yet I was not quite there, I did not touch it or hold it. I still shrank from dying unto death and living unto life. The lower condition which had grown habitual was more powerful than the better condition which I had not tried. The nearer the point of time came in which I was to become different, the more it struck me with horror; but it did not force me utterly back nor turn me utterly away, but held me there between the two.

Those trifles of all trifles, and vanities of vanities, my one-time mistresses, held me back, plucking at my garment of flesh and murmuring softly: "Are you sending us away?" And "From this moment shall we not be with you, now or forever?" And "From this moment shall this or that not be allowed you, now or forever?" What were they suggesting to me in the phrase I have written "this or that," what were they suggesting to me, O my God? Do you in your mercy keep from the soul of Your servant the vileness and uncleanness they were suggesting. And now I began to hear them not half so loud; they no longer stood against me face to face, but were softly muttering behind my back and, as I tried to depart, plucking stealthily at me to make me look behind. Yet even that was enough, so hesitating was I, to keep me from snatching myself free, from shaking them off and leaping upwards on the way I was called: for the strong force of habit said to me: "Do you think you can live without them?"

But by this time its voice was growing fainter. In the direction toward which I had turned my face and was quivering in fear of going, I could see the austere beauty of Continence, serene and indeed joyous but not evilly, honorably soliciting me to come to her and not linger, stretching forth loving hands to receive and embrace me, hands full of multitudes of good examples. With her I saw such hosts of young men and maidens, a multitude of youth and of every age, gray widows and women grown old in virginity, and in them all Continence herself, not barren but the fruitful mother of children, her joys, by You, Lord, her Spouse. And she smiled upon me and her smile gave courage as if she were saying: "Can you not do what these men have done, what these women have done? Or could men or women have done such in themselves, and not in the Lord their God? The Lord their God gave me to them. Why do you stand upon yourself and so not stand at all? Cast yourself upon Him and be not afraid; He will not draw away and let you fall. Cast yourself without fear, He will receive you and heal you."

Yet I was still ashamed, for I could still hear the murmuring of those vanities, and I still hung hesitant. And again it was as if she said: "Stop your ears against your unclean members, that they may be mortified. They tell you of delights, but not of such delights as the law of the Lord your God tells." This was the controversy raging in my heart, a controversy about myself against myself. And Alypius[9] stayed by my side and awaited in silence the issue of such agitation as he had never seen in me.

When my most searching scrutiny had drawn up all my vileness from the secret depths of my soul and heaped it in my heart's sight, a mighty storm arose in me, bringing a mighty rain of tears. That I might give way to my tears and lamentations, I rose from Alypius: for it struck me that solitude was more suited to the business of weeping. I went far enough from him to prevent his presence from being an embarrassment to me. So I felt, and he realized it. I suppose I had said something and the sound of my voice was heavy with tears. I arose, but he remained where we had been sitting, still in utter amazement. I flung myself down somehow under a certain fig tree and no longer tried to check my tears, which poured forth from my eyes in a flood, *an acceptable sacrifice to Thee.* And much I said not in these words but to this effect: "*And Thou, O Lord, how long? How long, Lord; wilt Thou be angry forever? Remember not our former iniquities.*"[1] For I felt that I was still bound by them. And I continued my miserable complaining: "How long, how long shall I go on saying tomorrow and again tomorrow? Why not now, why not have an end to my uncleanness this very hour?"

Such things I said, weeping in the most bitter sorrow of my heart. And suddenly I heard a voice from some nearby house, a boy's voice or a girl's voice, I do not know: but it was a sort of singsong, repeated again and again. "Take and read, take and read." I ceased weeping and immediately began to search my mind most carefully as to whether children were accustomed to chant these words in any kind of game, and I could not remember that I had ever heard any such thing. Damming back the flood of my tears I arose, interpreting the incident as quite certainly a divine command to open my book of Scripture and read the passage at which I should open. For it was part of

---

9. A student of Augustine's at Carthage; he had joined the Manichees with Augustine, followed him to Rome and Milan, and now shared his desires and doubts. Alypius finally became a bishop in North Africa.     1. The quotation is from Psalm 79; Augustine compares his spiritual despair with that of captive and subjected Israel.

what I had been told about Anthony,[2] that from the Gospel which he happened to be reading he had felt that he was being admonished as though what he read was spoken directly to himself: *Go, sell what thou hast and give to the poor and thou shalt have treasure in heaven; and come follow Me.*[3] By this experience he had been in that instant converted to You. So I was moved to return to the place where Alypius was sitting, for I had put down the Apostle's[4] book there when I arose. I snatched it up, opened it and in silence read the passage upon which my eyes first fell: *Not in rioting and drunkenness, not in chambering and impurities, not in contention and envy, but put ye on the Lord Jesus Christ and make not provision for the flesh in its concupiscences.* [Romans xiii, 13.] I had no wish to read further, and no need. For in that instant, with the very ending of the sentence, it was as though a light of utter confidence shone in all my heart, and all the darkness of uncertainty vanished away. Then leaving my finger in the place or marking it by some other sign, I closed the book and in complete calm told the whole thing to Alypius and he similarly told me what had been going on in himself, of which I knew nothing. He asked to see what I had read. I showed him, and he looked further than I had read. I had not known what followed. And this is what followed: *"Now him that is weak in faith, take unto you."* He applied this to himself and told me so. And he was confirmed by this message, and with no troubled wavering gave himself to God's goodwill and purpose—a purpose indeed most suited to his character, for in these matters he had been immeasurably better than I.

Then we went in to my mother and told her, to her great joy. We related how it had come about: she was filled with triumphant exultation, and praised You who are mighty beyond what we ask or conceive: for she saw that You had given her more than with all her pitiful weeping she had ever asked. For You converted me to Yourself so that I no longer sought a wife nor any of this world's promises, but stood upon that same rule of faith in which You had shown me to her so many years before.[5] Thus You changed her mourning into joy, a joy far richer than she had thought to wish, a joy much dearer and purer than she had thought to find in grandchildren of my flesh.

## [Death of His Mother]

### Book IX

\*　　\*　　\*

And I thought it would be good in Your sight if I did not dramatically snatch my tongue's service from the speech-market but quietly with-

---

**2.** The Egyptian saint whose abstinence and self-control are still proverbial; he was one of the founders of the system of monastic life. **3.** *Luke* 18:22. **4.** Paul. **5.** At Carthage, when Augustine was still a Manichee, Monica had dreamed that she was standing on a wooden ruler weeping for her son, and then saw that he was standing on the same ruler as herself.

drew; but that in any event withdraw I must, so that youths—not students of Your law or Your peace but of lying follies and the conflicts of the law—should no longer buy at my mouth the tools of their madness. Fortunately it happened that there were only a few days left before the Vintage Vacation,[6] and I decided to endure them so that I might leave with due deliberation, seeing that I had been redeemed by You and was not going to put myself up for sale again. Our purpose therefore was known to You, but not to men other than our own friends. We had agreed among ourselves not to spread the news abroad at all, although, in our ascent from *the valley of tears and our singing of the song of degrees*, You had given us *sharp arrows* and *burning coals* against *cunning tongues* that might argue against us with pretended care for our interest, might destroy us saying that they loved us: as men consume food saying that they love it.

*       *       *

Furthermore that very summer, under the too heavy labor of teaching, my lungs had begun to give way and I breathed with difficulty,[7] the pain in my breast showed that they were affected and they no longer let me talk with any strength for too long at a time. At first this had disturbed me, because it made it practically a matter of necessity that I should lay down the burden of teaching, or at least give it up for the time if I was to be cured and grow well again. But when the full purpose of giving myself leisure to meditate on how You are the Lord arose in me and became a settled resolve—as you know, O my God—I actually found myself glad to have this perfectly truthful excuse to offer parents who might be offended and for their children's sake would never willingly have let me give up teaching. So I was full of joy, and I put up with the space of time that still had to run—I fancy it was about twenty days. But to bear the time took considerable fortitude. Desire for money, which formerly had helped me to bear the heavy labor of teaching, was quite gone; so that I should have [had nothing to help me bear it and so] found it altogether crushing if patience had not taken the place of covetousness. Some of Your servants, my brethren, may think that I sinned in this, since having enrolled with all my heart in Your service, I allowed myself to sit for so much as an hour in the chair of untruthfulness. It may be so. But, most merciful Lord, have You not pardoned and remitted this sin, along with others most horrible and deadly, in the holy water of baptism?

*       *       *

And now the day was come on which I was to be set free from the teaching of Rhetoric in fact, as I was already free in mind. And so it

6. This grape-harvesting and wine-making holiday lasted from the end of August to the middle of October.    7. Since he not only lectured but also read aloud, as is suggested by his comments on Ambrose's silent reading (Book VI).

came about. You delivered my tongue as You had already delivered
my heart, and I rejoiced and praised You, and so went off with my
friends to the country-house.[8] The amount of writing I did there—
the writing was now in your service but during this breathing-space
still smacked of the school of pride—my books[9] exist to witness, with
the record they give of discussions either with my friends there present or with Yourself when I was alone with You; and there are my
letters to show what correspondence I had with Nebridius[1] while he
was away.

                                *        *        *

When the Vintage Vacation was over I gave the people of Milan
notice that they must find someone else to sell the art of words to
their students, because I had chosen to serve You, and because owing
to my difficulty in breathing and the pain in my lungs I could not
continue my teaching. And in a letter I told Your bishop, the holy
Ambrose, of my past errors and my present purpose, that he might
advise me which of Your Scriptures I should especially read to prepare me and make me more fit to receive so great a grace. He told
me to read Isaias the prophet, I imagine because he more clearly
foretells the gospel and the calling of the gentiles[2] than the other Old
Testament writers; but I did not understand the first part of this book,
and thinking that it would be all of the same kind, put it aside meaning to return to it when I should be more practised in the Lord's way
of speech.

When the time had come to give in my name for baptism, we left
the country and returned to Milan. Alypius had decided to be born
again in You at the same time, for he was already endowed with the
humility that Your sacraments require, and had brought his body so
powerfully under control that he could tread the icy soil of Italy with
bare feet, which required unusual fortitude. We also took with us
the boy Adeodatus, carnally begotten by me in my sin. You had
made him well. He was barely fifteen, yet he was more intelligent
than many a grave and learned man. In this I am but acknowledging
to You Your own gifts, O Lord my God, Creator of all and powerful
to reshape our shapelessness: for I had no part in that boy but the
sin. That he had been brought up by us in Your way was because
You had inspired us, no other. I do but acknowledge to You Your

8. At Cassiciacum, in the country, placed at his disposal by a friend.    9. While at Cassiciacum, Augustine wrote a book attacking the Academic philosophers, a book on the happy life, and
another entitled De ordine, a treatise on divine providence.    1. Nebridius came from Carthage
to Milan with Augustine, shared his spiritual pilgrimage through the pagan philosophies and
Manichean doctrines to become a Christian, and returned to Africa where he died. Augustine's
letters to Nebridius are still extant.    2. The appeal of Christ's apostles to peoples outside the
Hebrew nation: "I am sought of them that asked not for me: I am found of them that sought me
not." [Isaiah 65.1 ff.]

own gifts. There is a book of mine called *De Magistro:*[3] it is a dialogue between him and me. You know, O God, that all the ideas which are put into the mouth of the other party to the dialogue were truly his, though he was but sixteen. I had experience of many other remarkable qualities in him. His great intelligence filled me with a kind of awe: and who but You could be the maker of things so wonderful? But You took him early from this earth, and I think of him utterly without anxiety, for there is nothing in his boyhood or youth or anywhere in him to cause me to fear. We took him along with us, the same age as ourselves in Your grace, to be brought up in Your discipline: and we were baptized, and all anxiety as to our past life fled away. The days were not long enough as I meditated, and found wonderful delight in meditating, upon the depth of Your design for the salvation of the human race. I wept at the beauty of Your hymns and canticles, and was powerfully moved at the sweet sound of Your Church's singing. Those sounds flowed into my ears, and the truth streamed into my heart: so that my feeling of devotion overflowed, and the tears ran from my eyes, and I was happy in them.

It was only a little while before that the church of Milan had begun to practice this kind of consolation and exultation, to the great joy of the brethen singing together with heart and voice. For it was only about a year, or not much more, since Justina, the mother of the boy emperor Valentinian, was persecuting Your servant Ambrose in the interests of her own heresy: for she had been seduced by the Arians.[4] The devoted people had stayed day and night in the church, ready to die with their bishop, Your servant. And my mother, Your handmaid, bearing a great part of the trouble and vigil, had lived in prayer. I also, though still not warmed by the fire of Your Spirit, was stirred to excitement by the disturbed and wrought-up state of the city. It was at this time that the practice was instituted of singing hymns and psalms after the manner of the Eastern churches,[5] to keep the people from being altogether worn out with anxiety and want of sleep. The custom has been retained from that day to this, and has been imitated by many, indeed in almost all congregations throughout the world.

At this time You revealed to Your bishop Ambrose in a vision the

---

3. *The Teacher,* written at Tagaste in Africa two years after Augustine's baptism and shortly after his return from Italy. The subject is teaching and the thesis that only God is the cause for man's acquisition of learning and truth.     4. Members of a heretical sect who followed the doctrine of Arius (A.D. 250?–336) that the Son had not existed from all eternity and was therefore inferior to the Father. At the Council of Nicaea (A.D. 325) Arius and his followers were declared heretical, but the Arian heresy remained a serious problem for the Church for many years. Justina demanded that Ambrose allow the Arians to hold public services inside the walls of Milan.     5. The Greek-speaking churches of the Eastern half of the empire. They split off from the Catholic Church in the ninth century.

place where the bodies of the martyrs Protasius and Gervasius[6] lay hid, which You had for so many years kept incorrupt in the treasury of Your secret knowledge that You might bring them forth at the proper moment to check a woman's fury—the woman being the ruler of the Empire![7] For when they were discovered and dug up and with due honor brought to Ambrose's basilica, not only were people cured who had been tormented by evil spirits—and the devils themselves forced to confess it—but also there was a man, a citizen well known to the city, who had been blind for many years: he asked what was the cause of the tumultuous joy of the people, and when he heard, he sprang up and asked his guide to lead him into the place. When he arrived there he asked to be allowed to touch with his handkerchief the place on which lay the saints, whose death is precious in Your sight. He did so, put the handkerchief to his eyes, and immediately they were opened. The news spread abroad, Your praises glowed and shone, and if the mind of that angry woman was not brought to the sanity of belief, it was at least brought back from the madness of persecution. Thanks be to my God! From what and towards what have You led my memory, that it should confess to You these great things which I had altogether forgotten? Yet even then, *when the odor of Thy ointments was so sweet smelling,* I did *not run after Thee*: and for this I wept all the more now when I heard Your hymns and canticles, as one who had then sighed for You and now breathed in You, breathed so far as the air allows in this our house of grass.[8]

You, Lord, who make men of one mind to dwell in one house brought to our company a young man of our own town, Evodius. He had held office in the civil service, had been converted and baptized before us, had resigned from the state's service, and given himself to Yours. We kept together, meaning to live together in our devout purpose. We thought deeply as to the place in which we might serve You most usefully. As a result we started back for Africa. And when we had come as far as Ostia[9] on the Tiber, my mother died. I pass over many things, for I must make haste. Do You, O my God, accept my confessions and my gratitude for countless things of which I say nothing. But I will not omit anything my mind brings forth concerning her, Your servant, who brought me forth—brought me forth in the flesh to this temporal light, and in her heart to light eternal. Not of her gifts do I speak but of Your gifts in her. For she did not bring herself into the world or educate herself in the world: it was You who created her, nor did her father or mother know what kind of being was to come forth from them. It was the scepter of

6. Two beheaded skeletons discovered by St. Ambrose at Milan were identified as the relics of these saints: nothing certain is known about them but they were said to have been martyred in the second century A.D.    7. Justina.    8. "All flesh is grass. . . . The grass withers, the flower fades, but the word of our God will stand forever." [Isaiah 40:6–8.]    9. A port on the southwest coast of Italy; it was the port of Rome and the point of departure for Africa.

Your Christ, the discipline of your Only-Begotten, that brought her up in holy fear, in a Catholic family which was a worthy member of Your church. Yet it was not the devotion of her mother in her upbringing that she talked most of, but of a certain aged servant, who had indeed carried my mother's father on her back when he was a baby, as little ones are accustomed to be carried on the backs of older girls. Because of this, because also of her age and her admirable character, she was very much respected by her master and mistress in their Christian household. As a result she was given charge of her master's daughters. This charge she fulfilled most conscientiously, checking them sharply when necessary with holy severity and teaching them soberly and prudently. Thus, except at the times when they ate—and that most temperately—at their parents' table, she would not let them even drink water, no matter how tormenting their thirst. By this she prevented the forming of a bad habit, and she used to remark very sensibly: "Now you drink water because you are not allowed to have wine: but when you are married, and thus mistresses of food-stores and wine-cellars, you will despise water, but the habit of drinking will still remain." By this kind of teaching and the authority of her commands she moderated the greediness that goes with childhood and brought the little girls' thirst to such a control that they no longer wanted what they ought not to have.

Yet, as Your servant told me, her son, there did steal upon my mother an inclination to wine. For when, in the usual way, she was sent by her parents, as a well-behaved child, to draw wine from the barrel, she would dip the cup in, but before pouring the wine from the cup into the flagon, she would sip a little with the very tip of her lips, only a little because she did not yet like the taste sufficiently to take more. Indeed she did it not out of any craving for wine, but rather from the excess of childhood's high spirits, which tend to boil over in absurdities, and are usually kept in check by the authority of elders. And so, adding to that daily drop a little more from day to day—for he that despises small things, falls little by little—she fell into the habit, so that she would drink off greedily cups almost full of wine. Where then was that wise old woman with her forceful prohibitions? Could anything avail against the evil in us, unless Your healing, O Lord, watched over us? When our father and mother and nurses are absent, You are present, who created us, who call us, who can use those placed over us for some good unto the salvation of our souls. What did You do then, O my God? How did You cure her, and bring her to health? From another soul you drew a harsh and cutting sarcasm, as though bringing forth a surgeon's knife from Your secret store, and with one blow amputated that sore place. A maidservant with whom she was accustomed to go to the cellar, one day fell into a quarrel with her small mistress when no one else chanced to be about, and hurled at her the most biting insult possible, calling her a drunkard. My mother was pierced to the quick, saw her fault in its true wickedness, and instantly condemned it and gave it up. Just as the flattery of a friend can pervert, so the insult of an enemy can sometimes correct. Nor do You, O God, reward men according to what You do by means of them, but according to what they themselves intended. For the girl being in a temper wanted to enrage her young mistress, not to amend her, for she did it when no one else was there, either because the time and place happened to be thus when the quarrel arose, or because she was afraid that elders[1] would be angry because she had not told it sooner. But You, O Lord, Ruler of heavenly things and earthly, who turn to Your own purposes the very depths of rivers as they run and order the turbulence of the flow of time, did by the folly of one mind bring sanity to another; thus reminding us not to attribute it to our own power if another is amended by our word, even if we meant to amend him.

My mother, then, was modestly and soberly brought up, being rather made obedient to her parents by You than to You by her parents. When she reached the age for marriage, and was bestowed upon a husband, she served him as her lord. She used all her effort to win him to You, preaching You to him by her character, by which You made her beautiful to her husband, respected and loved by him and admirable in his sight. For she bore his acts of unfaithfulness quietly, and never had any jealous scene with her husband about them. She awaited Your mercy upon him, that he might grow chaste through faith in You. And as a matter of fact, though generous beyond measure, he had a very hot temper. But she knew that a woman must not resist a husband in anger, by deed or even by word. Only, when she saw him calm again and quiet, she would take the opportunity to give him an explanation of her actions, if it happened that he had been roused to anger unreasonably. The result was that whereas many matrons with much milder husbands carried the marks of blows to disfigure their faces, and would all get together to complain of the way their husbands behaved, my mother—talking lightly but meaning it seriously—advised them against their tongues: saying that from the day they heard the matrimonial contract read to them they should regard it as an instrument by which they became servants; and from that time they should be mindful of their condition and not set themselves up against their masters. And they often expressed amazement—for they knew how violent a husband she had to live with—that it had never been heard, and there was no mark to show, that Patricius[2] had beaten his wife or that there had been any family

1. Leaders of the church.    2. Augustine's father.

quarrel between them for so much as a single day. And when her
friends asked her the reason, she taught them her rule, which was as
I have just said. Those who followed it, found it good and thanked
her; those who did not, went on being bullied and beaten.

Her mother-in-law began by being angry with her because of the
whispers of malicious servants. But my mother won her completely
by the respect she showed, and her unfailing patience and mildness.
She ended by going to her son, telling him of the tales the servants
had bandied about to the destruction of peace in the family between
herself and her daughter-in-law, and asking him to punish them for
it. So he, out of obedience to his mother and in the interests of order
in the household and peace among his womenfolk, had the servants
beaten whose names he had been given, as she had asked when
giving them. To which she added the promise that anyone must
expect a similar reward from her own hands who should think to
please her by speaking ill of her daughter-in-law. And as no one had
the courage to do so, they lived together with the most notable degree
of kindness and harmony.

This great gift also, O my God, my Mercy, You gave to Your
good servant, in whose womb You created me, that she showed herself, wherever possible, a peacemaker between people quarreling and
minds at discord. For swelling and undigested discord often belches
forth bitter words when in the venom of intimate conversation with
a present friend hatred at its rawest is breathed out upon an absent
enemy. But when my mother heard bitter things said by each of the
other, she never said anything to either about the other save what
would help to reconcile them. This might seem a small virtue, if I
had not had the sorrow of seeing for myself so many people who—
as if by some horrible widespreading infection of sin—not only tell
angry people the things their enemies said in anger, but even add
things that were never said at all. Whereas, on the contrary, ordinary
humanity would seem to require not merely that we refrain from
exciting or increasing wrath among men by evil speaking, but that
we study to extinguish wrath by kind speaking. Such a one was she:
and You were the master who taught her most secretly in the school
of her heart.

The upshot was that toward the very end of his life she won her
husband to You; and once he was a Christian she no longer had to
complain of the things she had had to bear with before he was a
Christian. Further, she was a servant of Your servants. Such of them
as knew her praised and honored and loved You, O God, in her; for
they felt Your presence in her heart, showing itself in the fruit of her
holy conversation. She had been *the wife of one husband, had requited
her parents, had governed her house* piously, *was well reported of for*

*good works. She had brought up her children,*[3] being in labor of them as often as she saw them swerving away from You. Finally of all of us Your servants, O Lord—since by Your gift You suffer us to speak—who before her death were living together[4] after receiving the grace of baptism, she took as much care as if she had been the mother of us all, and served us as if she had been the daughter of us all.

When the day was approaching on which she was to depart this life—a day that You knew though we did not—it came about, as I believe by Your secret arrangement, that she and I stood alone leaning in a window, which looked inwards to the garden within the house where we were staying, at Ostia on the Tiber; for there we were away from everybody, resting for the sea voyage from the weariness of our long journey by land. There we talked together, she and I alone, in deep joy; and *forgetting the things that were behind and looking forward to those that were before,* we were discussing in the presence of Truth, which You are, what the eternal life of the saints could be like, *which eye has not seen nor ear heard, nor has it entered into the heart of man.* But with the mouth of our heart we panted for the high waters of Your fountain, the fountain of the life which is with You: that being sprinkled from that fountain according to our capacity, we might in some sense meditate upon so great a matter.

And our conversation had brought us to this point, that any pleasure whatsoever of the bodily senses, in any brightness whatsoever of corporeal light, seemed to us not worthy of comparison with the pleasure of that eternal Light, not worthy even of mention. Rising as our love flamed upward towards that Selfsame,[5] we passed in review the various levels of bodily things, up to the heavens themselves, whence sun and moon and stars shine upon this earth. And higher still we soared, thinking in our minds and speaking and marveling at Your works: and so we came to our own souls, and went beyond them to come at last to that region of richness unending, where You feed Israel forever with the food of truth: and there life is that Wisdom by which all things are made, both the things that have been and the things that are yet to be. But this Wisdom itself is not made: it is as it has ever been, and so it shall be forever: indeed "has ever been" and "shall be forever" have no place in it, but it simply is, for it is eternal: whereas "to have been" and "to be going to be" are not eternal. And while we were thus talking of His Wisdom and panting for it, with all the effort of our heart we did for one instant attain to touch it; then sighing, and leaving the first fruits of our spirit bound to it, we returned to the sound of our own tongue, in which a word has both beginning and ending. For what is like to your Word, Our

---

3. Augustine is quoting Paul's description of the duties of a widow. [I Timothy 5.]   4. Augustine and his fellow converts.   5. Reality, the divine principle. This ecstasy of Augustine and Monica is throughout described in philosophical terms, in which God is Wisdom.

Lord, who abides in Himself forever, yet grows not old and makes all things new!

So we said: If to any man the tumult of the flesh grew silent, silent the images of earth and sea and air: and if the heavens grew silent, and the very soul grew silent to herself and by not thinking of self mounted beyond self: if all dreams and imagined visions grew silent, and every tongue and every sign and whatsoever is transient—for indeed if any man could hear them, he should hear them saying with one voice: We did not make ourselves, but He made us who abides forever: but if, having uttered this and so set us to listening to Him who made them, they all grew silent, and in their silence He alone spoke to us, not by them but by Himself: so that we should hear His word, not by any tongue of flesh nor the voice of an angel nor the sound of thunder nor in the darkness of a parable,[6] but that we should hear Himself whom in all these things we love, should hear Himself and not them: just as we two had but now reached forth and in a flash of the mind attained to touch the eternal Wisdom which abides over all: and if this could continue, and all other visions so different be quite taken away, and this one should so ravish and absorb and wrap the beholder in inward joys that his life should eternally be such as that one moment of understanding for which we had been sighing—would not this be: *Enter Thou into the joy of Thy Lord?* But when shall it be? Shall it be when *we shall all rise again* and *shall not all be changed?*[7]

Such thoughts I uttered, though not in that order or in those actual words; but You know, O Lord, that on that day when we talked of these things the world with all its delights seemed cheap to us in comparison with what we talked of. And my mother said: "Son, for my own part I no longer find joy in anything in this world. What I am still to do here and why I am here I know not, now that I no longer hope for anything from this world. One thing there was, for which I desired to remain still a little longer in this life, that I should see you a Catholic Christian before I died. This God has granted me in superabundance, in that I now see you His servant to the contempt of all worldly happiness. What then am I doing here?"

What answer I made, I do not clearly remember; within five days or not much longer she fell into a fever. And in her sickness, she one day fainted away and for the moment lost consciousness. We ran to her but she quickly returned to consciousness, and seeing my brother and me standing by her she said as one wondering: "Where was I?" Then looking closely upon us as we stood wordless in our

6. Alludes to Luke 8:10: "To you [the disciples of Jesus] it has been given to know the secrets of the kingdom of God; but for others they are in parables, so that seeing they may not see, and hearing they may not understand."    7. Refers to the Last Judgment, when "the trumpet shall sound, and the dead shall be raised incorruptible, and we shall be changed." [I Corinthians 15:52.]

grief, she said: "Here you will bury your mother." I stayed silent and checked my weeping. But my brother said something to the effect that he would be happier if she were to die in her own land and not in a strange country. But as she heard this she looked at him anxiously, restraining him with her eye because he savored of earthly things, and then she looked at me and said: "See the way he talks." And then she said to us both: "Lay this body wherever it may be. Let no care of it disturb you: this only I ask of you that you should remember me at the altar of the Lord wherever you may be." And when she had uttered this wish in such words as she could manage, she fell silent as her sickness took hold of her more strongly.

But as I considered Your gifts, O unseen God, which You send into the hearts of Your faithful to the springing up of such wonderful fruits, I was glad and gave thanks to You, remembering what I had previously known of the care as to her burial which had always troubled her: for she had arranged to be buried by the body of her husband. Because they had lived together in such harmony, she had wished—so little is the human mind capable of rising to the divine—that it should be granted her, as an addition to her happiness and as something to be spoken of among men, that after her pilgrimage beyond the sea the earthly part of man and wife should lie together under the same earth. Just when this vain desire had begun to vanish from her heart through the fullness of Your goodness, I did not know; but I was pleased and surprised that it had now so clearly vanished: though indeed in the conversation we had had together at the window, when she said: "What am I still doing here?" there had appeared no desire to die in her own land. Further I heard afterwards that in the time we were at Ostia, she had talked one day to some of my friends, as a mother talking to her children, of the contempt of this life and of the attraction of death. I was not there at the time. They marveled at such courage in a woman—but it was You who had given it to her—and asked if she was not afraid to leave her body so far from her own city. But she said: "Nothing is far from God, and I have no fear that He will not know at the end of the world from what place He is to raise me up." And so on the ninth day of her illness, in the fifty-sixth year of her life and the thirty-third of mine, that devout and holy soul was released from the body.

I closed her eyes; and an immeasurable sorrow flowed into my heart and would have overflowed in tears. But my eyes under the mind's strong constraint held back their flow and I stood dry-eyed. In that struggle it went very ill with me. As she breathed her last, the child Adeodatus broke out into lamentation and we all checked him and brought him to silence. But in this very fact the childish element in me, which was breaking out into tears, was checked and brought to silence by the manlier voice of my mind. For we felt that it was not fitting that her funeral should be solemnized with moaning and weeping and lamentation, for so it is normal to weep when death is seen as sheer misery or as complete extinction. But she had not died miserably, nor did she wholly die. Of the one thing we were sure by reason of her character, of the other by the reality of our faith.

What then was it that grieved my heart so deeply? Only the newness of the wound, in finding the custom I had so loved of living with her suddenly snapped short. It was a joy to me to have this one testimony from her: when her illness was close to its end, meeting with expressions of endearment such services as I rendered, she called me a dutiful loving son, and said in the great affection of her love that she had never heard from my mouth any harsh or reproachful word addressed to herself. But what possible comparison was there, O my God who made us, between the honor I showed her and the service she had rendered me?

Because I had now lost the great comfort of her, my soul was wounded and my very life torn asunder, for it had been one life made of hers and mine together. When the boy had been quieted and ceased weeping, Evodius took up the psalter and began to chant— with the whole house making the responses—the psalm *Mercy and judgment I will sing to Thee, O Lord.*[8] And when they heard what was being done, many of the brethren and religious women came to us; those whose office it was were making arrangement for the burial, while, in another part of the house where it could properly be done I discoursed, with friends who did not wish to leave me by myself, upon matters suitable for that time. Thus I used truth as a kind of fomentation[9] to bring relief to my torment, a torment known to You, but not known to those others: so that listening closely to me they thought that I lacked all feeling of grief. But in Your ears, where none of them could hear, I accused the emotion in me as weakness; and I held in the flood of my grief. It was for the moment a little diminished, but returned with fresh violence, not with any pouring of tears or change of countenance: but I knew what I was crushing down in my heart. I was very much ashamed that these human emotions could have such power over me—though it belongs to the due order and the lot of our earthly condition that they should come to us—and I felt a new grief at my grief and so was afflicted with a twofold sorrow.

When the body was taken to burial, I went and returned without tears. During the prayers which we poured forth to you when the sacrifice of our redemption[1] was offered for her—while the body, as the custom there is, lay by the grave before it was actually buried— during those prayers I did not weep. Yet all that day I was heavy with

8. The opening words of Psalm 101.    9. Soothing dressing for a wound.    1. Perhaps a communion service.

grief within and in the trouble of my mind I begged of You in my
own fashion to heal my pain; but You would not—I imagine because
You meant to impress upon my memory by this proof how strongly
the bond of habit holds the mind even when it no longer feeds upon
deception. The idea came to me to go and bathe, for I had heard
that the bath—which the Greeks call βαλανειον— is so called because
it drives anxiety from the mind.[2] And this also I acknowledge to Your
mercy, O Father of orphans, that I bathed and was the same man
after as before. The bitterness of grief had not sweated out of my
heart. Then I fell asleep, and woke again to find my grief not a little
relieved. And as I was in bed and no one about, I said over those
true verses that Your servant Ambrose wrote of You:

> Deus creator omnium
> polique rector vestiens
> diem decoro lumine,
> noctem sopora gratia,
>
> artus solutos ut quies
> reddat laboris usui
> mentesque fessas allevet
> luctusque solvat anxios.[3]

And then little by little I began to recover my former feeling about
Your handmaid, remembering how loving and devout was her conversation with You, how pleasant and considerate her conversation
with me, of which I was thus suddenly deprived. And I found solace
in weeping in Your sight both about her and for her, about myself
and for myself. I no longer tried to check my tears, but let them flow
as they would, making them a pillow for my heart: and it rested upon
them, for it was Your ears that heard my weeping, and not the ears
of a man, who would have misunderstood my tears and despised
them. But now, O Lord, I confess it to You in writing, let him read
it who will and interpret it as he will: and if he sees it as sin that for
so small a portion of an hour I wept for my mother, now dead and
departed from my sight, who had wept so many years for me that I
should live ever in Your sight—let him not scorn me but rather, if
he is a man of great charity, let him weep for my sins to You, the
Father of all the brethren of Your Christ.

Now that my heart is healed of that wound, in which there was
perhaps too much of earthly affection, I pour forth to You, O our
God, tears of a very different sort for Your handmaid—tears that flow

---

2. Augustine evidently derives balaneion, the Greek word for "bath," from the words *ballo* and
*ania*, which mean "cast away" and "sorrow" respectively.    3. "God, the creator of all things
and ruler of the heavens, / you who clothe the day with the glory of light / and the night with the
gift of sleep, / so that rest may relax the limbs / and restore them for the day's work, / relieve the
fatigue of the mind / and dispel anxiety and grief."

from a spirit shaken by the thought of the perils there are for every soul that dies in Adam.[4] For though she had been made alive in Christ, and while still in the body had so lived that Your name was glorified in her faith and her character, yet I dare not say that from the moment of her regeneration in baptism no word issued from her mouth contrary to Your Command. Your Son, who is Truth, has said: *Whosoever shall say to his brother, Thou fool, shall be in danger of hell fire;*[5] and it would go ill with the most praiseworthy life lived by men, if You were to examine it with Your mercy laid aside! But because You do not enquire too fiercely into our sins, we have hope and confidence of a place with You. Yet if a man reckons up before You the merits he truly has, what is he reckoning except Your own gifts? If only men would know themselves to be but men, so that he that glories would glory in the Lord!

Thus, my Glory and my Life, God of my heart, leaving aside for this time her good deeds, for which I give thanks to Thee in joy, I now pray to Thee for my mother's sins. Grant my prayer through the true Medicine of our wounds,[6] who hung upon the cross and who now sitting at Thy right hand makes intercession for us. I know that she dealt mercifully, and from her heart forgave those who trespassed against her: do Thou also forgive such trespasses as she may have been guilty of in all the years since her baptism, forgive them, Lord, forgive them, I beseech Thee: enter not into judgment with her. Let Thy mercy be exalted above Thy justice for Thy words are true and Thou hast promised that the merciful shall obtain mercy. That they should be merciful is Thy gift who *hast mercy on whom Thou wilt, and wilt have compassion on whom Thou wilt.*

And I believe that Thou hast already done what I am now asking; but be not offended, Lord, at the things my mouth would utter. For on that day when her death was so close, she was not concerned that her body should be sumptuously wrapped or embalmed with spices, nor with any thought of choosing a monument or even for burial in her own country. Of such things she gave us no command, but only desired to be remembered at Thy altar, which she had served without ever missing so much as a day, on which she knew that the holy Victim was offered; *by whom the handwriting is blotted out of the decree that was contrary to us,*[7] by which offering too the enemy was overcome who, reckoning our sins and seeking what may be laid to our charge, found nothing in Him, in whom we are conquerors. Who shall restore to Him his innocent blood? Who shall give Him

---

4. That is, with the curse of Adam not nullified through baptism in Jesus Christ and conformity with his teachings.    5. From Jesus' Sermon on the Mount. He is preaching a more severe moral code than the traditional one that whoever kills shall be liable to judgment.    6. I.e., Jesus Christ.    7. Alludes to Christ's redemption of humanity from the curse of Adam through the Crucifixion.

back the price by which He purchased us and so take us from Him? To this sacrament of our redemption Thy handmaid had bound her soul by the bond of faith. Let none wrest her from Thy protection; let neither the lion nor the dragon[8] bar her way by force or craft. For she will not answer that she owes nothing, lest she should be contradicted and confuted by that cunning accuser: but she will answer that her debts have been remitted by Him, to whom no one can hand back the price which He paid for us, though He owed it not.

So let her rest in peace, together with her husband, for she had no other before nor after him, but served him, in patience bringing forth fruit for Thee, and winning him likewise for Thee. And inspire, O my Lord my God, inspire Thy servants my brethren, Thy sons my masters, whom I serve with heart and voice and pen, that as many of them as read this may remember at Thy altar Thy servant Monica, with Patricius, her husband, by whose bodies Thou didst bring me into this life, though how I know not.[9] May they with loving mind remember these who were my parents in this transitory light, my brethren who serve Thee as our Father in our Catholic mother, and those who are to be fellow citizens with me in the eternal Jerusalem,[1] which Thy people sigh for in their pilgrimage from birth until they come there: so that what my mother at her end asked of me may be fulfilled more richly in the prayers of so many gained for her by my Confessions than by my prayers alone.

*          *          *

8. Psalm 91.13 invokes God's protection of the godly: "Thou shalt tread upon the lion and the adder; the young lion and the dragon shalt thou trample under feet."    9. I.e., Augustine does not understand the seemingly miraculous process by which the fetus grows in the womb.
1. Heaven.

# Masterpieces of the
# Middle Ages

The period of the Middle Ages—approximately A.D. 500–1500—encompasses a thousand years of European history distinguished by the unique fusion of a Heroic-Age society with Greco-Roman culture and Christian religion. The era is fairly well marked off by the emergence and disappearance of certain massive forces. It begins with the collapse of the Roman Empire in Western Europe, a development coincident with and partly occasioned by the settlement of Germanic peoples within the territory of the empire. It ends with the discovery of the Western Hemisphere, the invention of the printing press, the consolidation of strong national states, the break in religious unity brought about by the Protestant Reformation, and the renewal—after a lapse of nearly a thousand years—of direct contact with Greek art, thought, and literature. The medieval centuries created, or at least refashioned, and bequeathed to us such institutional patterns as the Christian church; the monarchical state; the town and village; the traditional European social order—the "lords spiritual," the "lords temporal," with the hierarchy of nobility and gentry ranging from duke to knight, and the third, or bourgeois, estate; the university; the system and logical method of Scholastic philosophy; Romanesque and Gothic architecture; and a rich variety of literary forms.

The literature of the earlier Middle Ages reflects directly and clearly the life and civilization of a Heroic Age. The dominant figure is the fighting king or chieftain; the favorite pursuit is war; the characteristic goals are power, wealth, and glory; and the primary virtues, accordingly, are valor and loyalty. The literary pattern is based on actuality, of which it presents a kind of idealization. In early Germanic and Celtic society the king ruled a small, essentially tribal nation; he and his companions in battle constituted a formal or informal noble class controlling the life of the people. The poems of such a society naturally tell chiefly of the fights of great champions, though also of the druids or other counselors who advised them and of the minstrels who entertained them. The proportions and the emphasis are much the same in the literature of the Irish, the Scandinavians, the French of the twelfth century, the Germans of the thirteenth. The hero of the *Song of Roland*, a twelfth-century French work, combines the fighting chieftain, serving his king, with the devout Crusader; and Archbishop Turpin is both spiritual adviser and fighting champion.

In the literature of the fourteenth century, the warrior plays a smaller role and is assimilated to the more extensive pattern of later medieval civilization. Thus in Dante's Heaven only one of the nine celestial spheres—Mars—

is occupied by great men-at-arms, all devout Christians, of course. Chaucer's Knight and Squire are only two among twenty-nine pilgrims on their way to Canterbury. The Knight is devoted to truth and honor, generosity, and courteous conduct, while his son, along with other virtues appropriate to a young soldier, possesses those of a courtly lover. The fighting champion of the Heroic Age has become the "officer and gentleman" of the modern world.

This gradual assimilation of the Celtic and Germanic hero to a civilization in which Christianity ordered the Greco-Roman culture to new ends was made possible by the religious unity and authority of Western Europe. The medieval millennium was indeed an age of faith, though it was far from being an age of religious passivity or inertia. The first half of the period was occupied in winning the new peoples of Europe to Christianity. When this had been accomplished, the Crusades began—a series of holy wars intended to rescue Palestine from pagan occupation and, in general, to defeat and either destroy or convert the pagans, chiefly Mohammedans. But the Greek and Arabic learning and philosophy which these non-Christian people introduced into Europe in the twelfth and thirteenth centuries demanded an intellectual alertness. The sharpness of the Crusader's sword had to be matched by the acumen of the Scholastic philosopher; one of the chief works of St. Thomas Aquinas is a summation of principles in defense of Christianity "against the pagans" (his *summa contra Gentiles*). Medieval Christianity could never afford to take itself for granted. For the first four centuries after Christ the new religion was aggressively on the defensive; thereafter it had to be actively on the offensive in both the practical and the ideological spheres. Nevertheless, in Western Europe itself the combination of theological unity and ecclesiastical authority was a phenomenon unmatched either before or after the Middle Ages. The Roman Empire had provided political unity, law, and order, to assure the success of secular pursuits. Beyond that, it had left moral and spiritual problems to be handled by the individual, singly or in voluntary or ethnic groups. In medieval Europe political disunity was at something like a maximum; but under the leadership and direction of the Church there was achieved a remarkable unanimity of spiritual, moral, and intellectual attitudes and ideals.

The community of European culture in this period was such that the productions of individual countries look like regional manifestations of a central nuclear force. Generally speaking, students and scholars moved freely from land to land; monks, abbots, and bishops might be sent from the country of their birth to serve or preside in distant places; artists and poets wandered widely either in the train of or in search of patrons. Besides his native tongue, the educated man might be expected to speak and write the common "standard" language of Europe—Latin. In an age when the political state was relatively weak, a man's strongest loyalties were to an individual, a feudal lord, for example; to a code, such as the code of chivalry; to an order—of monks or friars or knights; or simply to the Church itself, if, like so many medieval men of intellectual interests, he was a cleric of some sort.

These ties—except for the feudal, and sometimes including that also— were *international* in nature. In such a cultural atmosphere the themes and subjects and techniques of art and literature circulated freely throughout

Europe. The *Gothic* architecture of a building is a more central aspect of it than the fact that it was designed and built by an English, a French, a German, or an Italian school of builders. Christianity itself furnished a common subject matter for painters, sculptors, and countless others skilled in the graphic and plastic arts; the biblical stories and scenes had the same meaning in every country. The stories of Charlemagne, Roland, and Arthur, of Aeneas, of Troy and Thebes, were European literary property. They were handled and rehandled, copied, translated, adapted, expanded, condensed, and in general appropriated by innumerable authors, writing in various languages, with no thought of property rights or misgivings about plagiarism. There were no copyright regulations and no author's royalties to motivate insistence on individuality of authorship; there was comparatively little concern about the identity of the artist. Many medieval poems and tales are anonymous, including some of the greatest.

The submergence of the artist in his work is accounted for in part, at least, by the medieval system of human values. The dominant hierarchy of values—we have seen that it did not dominate universally, especially in the literature of northern Europe—was based on the Christian view of man. Man, in this conception, is a creature of God, toward whom he is inevitably oriented but from whom he is separated by the world in which he must live his earthly, mortal life. Human civilization under Christian direction may be regarded as ideally designed—even if not actually so functioning—to assist man on his way to union with God. This is the criterion for the ultimate appraisal of all the institutions of society and all the patterns of culture. Hence derive the scale, the order, the hierarchical categories of medieval life and thought. Since the spiritual side of man transcends the material, the saint becomes the ideal. The saint is one whose life is most fully subdued, assimilated, and ordered to the spiritual. On earth he may be a hermit, like Cuthbert; a reformer of monasteries, like Bernard; a philosopher and a theologian, like Aquinas; a king, like Louis IX of France; or a humble man in private life. Since communion with God—the essential aspect of bliss in heaven—is an experience of the soul, the contemplative life, which prepares for the mystical communion, is superior to any form of the active life. Hence the monk—by virtue of his vocation—has an advantage over the secular priest, just as the priest is, other things being equal, in a position spiritually more desirable than that of the layman. As a whole, medieval literature is a study in human life judged according to this scale of values. The scale is represented clearly in Dante's *Divine Comedy*. Secular-value patterns are assimilated to it, for instance in the *Song of Roland;* or it may be taken for granted without much emphasis, as in Chaucer's works. But it is always there, whether below or above the surface. For the modern reader it supplies a focus for the adequate reading and understanding of most of the literature of the Middle Ages.

Robert S. Hoyt, *Europe in the Middle Ages* (1957), is a good historical survey. For a view of medieval thought and culture as a whole, the standard older work is H. O. Taylor, *The Mediaeval Mind*, 2 vols., 4th ed. (1925). A more recent book is F. B. Artz, *The Mind of the Middle Ages*, 2d ed. (1954).

# THE WANDERER

This anonymous poem of the eighth or ninth century A.D. offers us a vivid reflection not only of Old English but of Germanic life generally in its time and long before. The opening and the closing lines provide a framework of devout Christian faith for the soliloquy or dramatic monologue spoken by the "wanderer," or solitary or lonely man. The speaker has been the liege-man of a beloved, generous chieftain, a lord who has long given him both affection and a home. Now that his lord is dead, he must go in search of another. Meanwhile he gives utterance in soliloquy to the deep emotions which his stoic code—the British stiff upper lip—forbids him to disclose to other men. The geography of the poem is that of the British islands and northern coasts, the landscape rather a seascape, with its rough winds and wild seabirds. The wanderer feels keenly the contrast between these wintry scenes and the happiness and warmth of his lost lord's hall. He is thus led to a pessimistic view of the course of the world and the lot of the people in it; like many poets before and since, he sorrowfully asks, "Where have the good friends and good things gone?" The poet's concluding reliance on "the heavenly Father, our Fortress and Strength" is the typical attitude of the medieval Christian. But the poem has a convincing reality not dependent on religious faith.

Our translator (like Auden in his rendering of the Icelandic *Song of The Seeress*) uses an alliterative pattern broadly similar to that of the Old English original. Thus each line of verse contains two or more stressed syllables with the same sound; for example, "Oft the Wanderer, weary of exile" shows alliteration with the consonant *w*. Further, any vowel or diphthong may alliterate with any other, as in "Earneth no help. Eager for honor."

For historical background and English life in the Old English period (c. 500–1100), Dorothy Whitelock, *The Beginnings of English Society* (1952), is excellent and highly readable. For Old English literature in general, see S. B. Greenfield, *A Critical History of Old English Literature* (1965), and C. L. Wrenn, *A Study of Old English Literature* (1966).

## The Wanderer[1]

Oft to the Wanderer, weary of exile,
Cometh God's pity, compassionate love,
Though woefully toiling on wintry seas
With churning oar in the icy wave,
Homeless and helpless he fled from Fate.          5
Thus saith the Wanderer mindful of misery,
Grievous disasters, and death of kin:
"Oft when the day broke, oft at the dawning,
Lonely and wretched I wailed my woe.

1. Translated by Charles W. Kennedy.

No man is living, no comrade left,                          10
To whom I dare fully unlock my heart.
I have learned truly the mark of a man
Is keeping his counsel and locking his lips,
Let him think what he will! For, woe of heart
Withstandeth not Fate; a failing spirit                     15
Earneth no help. Men eager for honor
Bury their sorrow deep in the breast.
So have I also, often, in wretchedness
Fettered my feelings, far from my kin,
Homeless and hapless, since days of old,                    20
When the dark earth covered my dear lord's face,
And I sailed away with sorrowful heart,
Over wintry seas, seeking a gold-lord,
If far or near lived one to befriend me
With gift in the mead-hall[2] and comfort for grief.        25
Who bears it, knows what a bitter companion,
Shoulder to shoulder, sorrow can be,
When friends are no more. His fortune is exile,
Not gifts of fine gold; a heart that is frozen,
Earth's winsomeness dead. And he dreams of the hallmen,     30
The dealing of treasure, the days of his youth,
When his lord bade welcome to wassail and feast.
But gone is that gladness, and never again
Shall come the loved counsel of comrade and king.
Even in slumber his sorrow assaileth,                       35
And, dreaming, he claspeth his dear lord again,
Head on knee, hand on knee, loyally laying,
Pledging his liege as in days long past.
Then from his slumber he starts lonely-hearted,
Beholding gray stretches of tossing sea,                    40
Sea-birds bathing, with wings outspread,
While hail-storms darken, and driving snow.
Bitterer then is the bane of his wretchedness,
The longing for loved one: his grief is renewed.
The forms of his kinsmen take shape in the silence;         45
In rapture he greets them; in gladness he scans
Old comrades remembered. But they melt into air
With no word of greeting to gladden his heart.
Then again surges his sorrow upon him;
And grimly he spurs on his weary soul                       50
Once more to the toil of the tossing sea.
No wonder therefore, in all the world,

2. The large public room where a king or chieftain dispensed food and drink to the warriors who served him. Mead is a fermented beverage with a honey base.

If a shadow darkens upon my spirit
When I reflect on the fates of men—
How one by one proud warriors vanish                              55
From the halls that knew them, and day by day
All this earth ages and droops unto death.
No man may know wisdom till many a winter
Has been his portion. A wise man is patient,
Not swift to anger, nor hasty of speech,                         60
Neither too weak, nor too reckless, in war,
Neither fearful nor fain, nor too wishful of wealth,
Nor too eager in vow—ere he know the event.
A brave man must bide when he speaketh his boast
Until he know surely the goal of his spirit.                     65
A wise man will ponder how dread is that doom
When all this world's wealth shall be scattered and
     waste—
As now, over all, through the regions of earth,
Walls stand rime-covered and swept by the winds.
The battlements crumble, the wine-halls decay;                   70
Joyless and silent the heroes are sleeping
Where the proud host fell by the wall they defended.
Some battle launched on their long, last journey;
One a bird bore o'er the billowing sea;
One the gray wolf slew; one a grieving earl                      75
Sadly gave to the grave's embrace.
The Warden of men hath wasted this world
Till the sound of music and revel is stilled,
And these giant-built structures stand empty of life.
He who shall muse on these mouldering ruins,                     80
And deeply ponder this darkling life,
Must brood on old legends of battle and bloodshed,
And heavy the mood that troubles his heart:
Where now is the warrior? Where is the war-horse?
Bestowal of treasure, and sharing of feast?                      85
Alas! the bright ale-cup, the byrny-clad[3] warrior,
The prince in his splendor—those days are long sped
In the night of the past, as if they never had been!'
And now remains only, for warriors' memorial,
A wall wondrous high with serpent shapes carved.                 90
Storms of ash-spears have smitten the earls,
Carnage of weapon, and conquering Fate.
Storms now batter these ramparts of stone;
Blowing snow and the blast of winter

---

3. Wearing a coat of iron mail.

Enfold the earth; night-shadows fall                              95
Darkly lowering, from the north driving
Raging hail in wrath upon men.
Wretchedness fills the realm of earth,
And Fate's decrees transform the world.
Here wealth is fleeting, friends are fleeting,              100
Man is fleeting, maid is fleeting;
All the foundation of earth shall fail!"
Thus spake the sage in solitude pondering.
Good man is he who guardeth his faith.
He must never too quickly unburden his breast              105
Of its sorrow, but eagerly strive for redress;
And happy the man who seeketh for mercy
From his heavenly Father, our Fortress and Strength.

---

# THE STORY OF DEIRDRE

Like the Greeks, the Germanic and Celtic peoples had a Heroic Age. For some centuries after about 1000 B.C., the Celts were the dominant people in Europe north of the Mediterranean and south of Scandinavia; their settlements extended from western Asia (Galatia) to Ireland. In medieval and modern times they are represented by the ethnic groups and languages known as Irish, Scottish Gaelic, Manx, Welsh, Cornish, and Breton. As with the epics of Homer, the early Irish literature reflects the civilization and culture of *their* Heroic Age, from approximately the second century B.C. to the fourth century A.D. It was an era of kings not of all Ireland but of each of the four or five provinces, such as Ulaid [OO-lid] (modern Ulster) and Connachta [CON-NAK-ta] (modern Connaught, in the west); below these were the kings of the many small tribal nations. There were no cities; the political and social capital was the king's court, a compound of wooden buildings dominated by a large hall or room in which the ruler sat in state (more or less), surrounded by liegemen who, along with the women, slept on beds or on the floor at night. Warriors traveled and fought in two-wheeled chariots drawn by a pair of horses and driven by a charioteer. In this preliterate time learning was the prerogative of the druids, a quasi-professional, perhaps quasi-priestly class who transmitted knowledge orally from one generation to the next. According to the early literature, the kings often looked to them for advice, and they were believed to have the gift of prophecy.

Attached to the royal court there was also apt to be a more or less official story-teller (*scelaige*, [skay-lig-eh] in Irish), who entertained the company with traditional tales (*scela*) [skay-lah] of great men and women and their notable deeds. There was a hierarchy of competence among these professional entertainers; a person holding the highest rank, that of *ollave* [ol-lav], was expected, according to one account, to have a repertory of 350 stories. Probably he called on his memory of outlines of the plots, while depending on his creative imagination for narrative detail. This may account for the brevity of some of the early texts, such as *The Story of Deirdre*. The ordinary use of writing—as distinct from Ogham inscriptions using notches scratched originally on stone or wood or horn—came in with the conversion to Christianity, beginning in the fifth century. The oldest texts of the tales of the Ulster Cycle, as they are called, were written in the eighth and ninth centuries (the extant manuscripts date from the twelfth century and later). The writers—and copiers—were, of course, Christian; this, along with the time interval, explains the paucity of information in the stories about the religion of the Irish before the conversion. Besides, the principal characters may originally have been figures of regeneration or fertility myths, and thus gods, or supernatural beings, who in later, Christian tradition became human. This is doubtless why the heroes and heroines are so often supermen and "bionic" women. What would be miracles wrought by saints in Christian legend are reported as powers of magic attributed to superhuman heroes. We can recognize this in the prowess of Noisiu [Noy-shu] and his two brothers in the Deirdre story—together, "they could hold off the entire province of Ulaid," and they were as swift as hunting dogs. And the strength and skills of Cuchulainn [Cu-húl-in] the central figure of the *Cattle Raid of Cooley*, greatest and longest work of the Ulster cycle, are nearly always possible only for a Superman. But his character and personality, like those of Deirdre and Noisiu, are fully and attractively human.

The traditional Irish title of our story was *The Exile of the Sons of Uisliu* [Wees-li-u], in allusion to their flight from the court of Conchobur (Conco-vor] and subsequent sojourn and travel in Scotland and elsewhere. The prose narrative is brief and bare, yet extraordinarily vivid and moving. The poems in clear images bring before us the (partly) happy life of the exiles as they camp in the open forest, and thus vary the deep mood of fatalistic prophecy at the beginning of the story and, later, the unalloyed pathos of Deirdre's grief for the slain Noisiu. Deirdre and Noisiu are as star-crossed lovers as ever were Juliet and Romeo. Their love, indeed, does not begin in the manner of courtly romance; instead, Noisiu must choose between disobedience to Conchobur and the disgrace which will fall upon him if he refuses Deirdre's challenge. But, once the choice is made, the commitment and the devotion of the pair are total and unswerving; and, like Shakespeare's Juliet, Deirdre is the stronger and the more articulate character.

Deirdre has been called the Irish Helen, in allusion to the wife of the Argive king Menelaos, whose abduction by the prince Paris led to the Trojan War. The fatal beauty of one woman caused the destruction of Troy; that of the other woman caused the burning of Emuin Machae [Ev-in Mah-ka], King Conchobur's capital. For more than a millennium Deirdre has haunted the memory and imagination of Irish poets. If Helen's face launched a thousand ships, Deirdre's story inspired a multitude of writers. Among the works of modern Anglo-Irish authors are Synge's *Deirdre of the Sorrows*, a three-act play first produced in 1910 at the Abbey Theatre in Dublin, shorter dramas by Yeats and AE (George William Russell), and a novelistic treatment by James Stephens.

Our ancient narrative begins with the birth of Deirdre at the court of Conchobur, king of the Ulaid, as the people of Ulster were then called. The scene may remind us of situations in Homer; for instance, the company surrounding King Alcinous when Odysseus is invited to tell his story were also eating and drinking. The Greek minstrel has his counterpart in the Irish storyteller; the setting, simpler and cruder than that in Phaeacia, has more ominous elements of wonder and awe. By marvel and by prophecy alike Deirdre is destined for no ordinary life. As in Greek epic and tragedy, the portrayal of major figures may vary from story to story. Creon in *Oedipus the King* is a patient, benign person, unlike the rigid ruler of *Antigone*. In most Irish narratives Conchubur is favorably shown as a beneficent king of the Ulaid and protector of the great Cuchulainn, his nephew. But in the Deirdre story he is the relentless and unscrupulous enemy of the lovers. After promising them a safe return to his court, he plots the assassination of Noisiu and his brothers. They had sworn to eat no food after landing in Ireland until they reached Conchubur's capital. Hence Conchubur first detaches Fergus, the principal "guarantor" on whom Noisiu and Deirdre rely for their safety, from the party of returning travelers. To do this he makes use of a peculiar Irish custom, known as the *geis* [gaysh]—a kind of tabu to which a person might be subject. Now Fergus has a *geis* which requires him never to refuse an invitation to food or drink. He is thus obliged to remain behind while Noisiu and most of the entourage go on—and fall into the power of Conchubur. Later, Fergus will take spectacular revenge; but by then, of course, the sons of Uisliu have been slain and Deirdre made a helpless captive of the king.

An excellent translation of the *Cattle Raid of Cooley* is available in Thomas Kinsella, *The Táin*, translated from the Irish Epic *Táin Bó Cúailnge* [Tawn Bo Koo-ling-e] (1970). Several shorter tales of the Ulster cycle are admirably translated in Jeffrey Gantz, *Early Irish Myths and Sagas* (1981). Kenneth H. Jackson, *The Oldest Irish Tradition: A Window on the Iron Age* (1964), is the best brief account of Heroic Age civilization and literature in Ireland, (55 pp.). Proinsias Mac Cana, *Celtic Mythology* (1970), is clear, brief, and handsomely illustrated.

# The Story of Deirdre[1]

The Ulaid were drinking at the house of Fedilmid[2] son of Dall, Conchubur's storyteller, and Fedilmid's wife was standing over them and serving, even though she was with child. Drinking horns and portions of food went round, and the house was filled with drunken shouting. When it came time to sleep, Fedilmid's wife rose to go to her bed, but as she crossed the house the child in her womb screamed so that it was heard throughout the court. At that scream the men all rose, and they were standing chin to chin, but Senchae[3] son of Ailill quieted them, saying 'Do not disturb each other! Let the woman be brought to us that we might learn what caused that noise.' So the woman was brought to them, and her husband asked her:

---

1. Translated by Jeffrey Gantz.    2. [Fay-dil-mid].    3. [Shen-kay]: A wise counselor at the court of King Conchubur. *Ailill* [Al-il]: This is not the same man as Ailill, king of Connachta.

What is this violent noise that resounds,
   that rages in your roaring womb?
The outcry between your two sides—mighty its sound—
crushes the ears of those who hear it.
My heart is terribly wounded:
   a great fear has seized it.

Then Fedilmid's wife spoke to Cathub,[4] for he was a wise man:

Listen to Cathub, fair of face,
a handsome prince, great and powerful his crown,
   exalted by his druid wisdom.
I myself do not have the white[5] words
through which my husband might obtain
   an answer to his question,
for, though it cried out in the cradle of my body,
no woman knows
   what her womb bears.

And Cathub replied:

In the cradle of your womb there cried out
a woman with twisted yellow hair
   and beautiful grey green eyes.
Foxglove her purple pink cheeks,
the colour of snow her flawless teeth,
   brilliant her Parthian-red[6] lips.
A woman over whom there will be great slaughter
among the chariot-warriors of Ulaid.
There screams in your roaring womb
a tall, beautiful, long-haired woman
   whom champions will contest,
   whom high kings will woo;
and to the west of Conchubur's province
there will be a rich harvest of fighting men.
Parthian-red lips will frame
   those flawless teeth;
high queens will envy her
   her matchless, faultless form.

Then Cathub placed his hand on the woman's womb, and the child murmured, and he said 'Indeed, it is a girl, and her name will be Derdriu,[7] and there will be trouble on her account.' After the girl had been born, Cathub said:

Though you may have fame and beauty,
   Derdriu, you will destroy much;
Ulaid will suffer on your account,
   fair daughter of Fedilmid.

4. A seer or druid endowed with the gift of prophecy.    5. I.e., true, wise.    6. A deep, rich color, traditionally associated with the Eastern country of Parthia.    7. [Der-dri-oo]: The nominative case form of the name in Irish.

And after that there will be still more deaths
because of you, woman like a flame.
In your lifetime—hear this—
the three sons of Uisliu will be exiled.

In your lifetime a violent deed
will be done at Emuin;
repented thereafter will be the treachery
that violated the guarantee of mighty Fergus.

Because of you, woman of fate,
Fergus will be exiled from Ulaid,
and—a deed that will cause much weeping—
Conchubur's son Fiachnae[8] will be slain.

Because of you, woman of fate,
Gerrce[9] son of Illadán will be slain,
and—a crime no less awful—
Éogan[1] son of Durthacht will be destroyed.

You will do a frightful fierce deed[2]
out of anger at Ulaid's high king;
your grave will be everywhere[3]—
yours will be a famous tale, Derdriu.

'Let the child be slain!' said the young warriors. 'No,' said Conchubur, 'I will take her away tomorrow, and I will rear her as I see fit, and she will be my companion.' And none of the Ulaid dared oppose him. Derdriu was reared by Conchubur until she was by far the most beautiful woman in Ériu.[4] She was reared in a court apart, lest any of the Ulaid see her before she was to sleep with Conchubur, and no one was allowed into that court save her foster-father and her foster-mother[5] and a woman named Lebarcham who was a satirist[6] and could not be barred.

One day, in winter, Derdriu's foster-father was outside, in the snow, flaying a weaned calf for her. Derdriu saw a raven drinking the blood on the snow, and she said to Lebarcham 'I could love a man with those three colours: hair like a raven, cheeks like blood and body like snow.' 'Then luck and good fortune are with you,' answered Lebarcham, 'for such a man is not far off. In fact, he is quite near: Noísiu son of Uisliu.' Derdriu replied 'I will be ill, then, until I see him.'[7]

8. [Fee-ak-nay]: He will be killed in revenge for the treacherous attack on Noísiu, as the narrative tells.    9. [Ger-kay]: Nothing further is told of him. *Illadán:* [Il-lah-don]    1. [Yóg-an]. *Durthacht* [Door-thakt]: Éogan will be the actual slayer of Noísiu. The narrative does not tell us how Éogan met death.    2. Perhaps a reference to Deirdre's violent suicide.    3. Many places in Ireland will claim to be Deirdre's grave—an indication of her fame.    4. [A-ri-oo]: The usual name of Ireland in the Irish language.    5. Children of the higher classes were often brought up by foster parents; here the names are not given.    6. Satirists—often female—were a prominent feature of early Irish society and literature. It was believed that their invectives could inflict physical injury (through the magical power of words). *Lebarcham:* [Lay-vor-kam].    7. Besides love at first sight, familiar elsewhere in the world, love *before* first sight is frequent in early Irish literature—inspired, as here, by report.

It happened one day that Noísiu was standing alone on the rampart of the stronghold of Emuin, and he was singing. The singing of
the sons of Uisliu was very melodious: every cow that heard it gave
two thirds more milk, and every man who heard it grew peaceful and
sated with music. The sons of Uisliu were also good fighters: when
they stood back to back, they could hold off the entire province of
Ulaid. Moreover, they were as swift as hunting hounds and could
overtake and kill wild animals.

When Noísiu was outside alone, then, Derdriu stole out to him
and made as if to go past, and he did not recognize her. 'A fine
heifer[8] that that is going by,' he said. 'The heifers are bound to be
fine where there are no bulls,' she answered. 'You have the bull of
the province: the king of Ulaid,' Noísiu said. 'Between the two of
you, I would choose a young bull like yourself,' Derdriu replied.
'No! There is Cathub's prophecy,' said Noísiu. 'Are you rejecting
me, then?' she asked. 'I am, indeed,' he answered. At that, Derdriu
leapt at him and seized him by the ears, saying 'Two ears of shame
and mockery these unless you take me with you!' 'Away from me,
woman!' Noísiu said. 'Too late!'[9] answered Derdriu.

With that, Noísiu began to sing.[1] When the Ulaid heard his singing they rose up against each other, but the other sons of Uisliu[2]
went out to restrain their brother. 'What are you doing?' they asked.
'The Ulaid will be coming to blows on your account.' Then Noísiu
told his brothers what had happened. 'Evil will come of this,' they
said. 'Even so, you will not be disgraced while we are alive. We will
all take her to another land—there is not in Ériu a king who will
turn us away.' That was their advice. They departed that night: three
fifties of warriors and three fifties of women and three fifties of hounds
and three fifties of servants and Derdriu mingled in with them.

For a long time, the brothers found protection with kings throughout Ériu, though through his snares and treacheries Conchubur often
attempted to destroy them, from Ess Rúaid[3] to the south-west and
then back north-east to Bend Étair. Finally, the Ulaid drove them
out of Ériu and into Albu;[4] there, they settled in the wilderness, and,
when the game of the mountains ran out, they helped themselves to
cattle. One day, the men of Albu gathered to destroy them, so they
went to the king of Albu, and he took them into his entourage; they
became mercenaries and erected their dwellings on the green. Because

8. No disrespect is intended; rather, admiration. Cattle were a principal form of wealth in the
Irish Heroic Age. And one might compare our use of "lamb" or "chick" or "fox" to refer to an
attractive young person.     9. The challenge ("two ears of shame and mockery") has already been
uttered (and is irreversible).     1. The reticent author does not say whether in exultation or dismay; at any rate, the Ulaid are apparently upset by the loudness of the song.     2. Aindle [End-
lay] and Arddán [Ard-dahn]; their names are given in a stanza below.     3. [Es-roo-a]: The modern Asseroe, in the county Donegal. Bend Étair [A-tare]: the Hill of Howth, in Dublin Bay.
4. Probably Scotland.

of Derdriu, they built their houses so that no one could see her, for they feared there might be killing on her account.

Early one morning, however, the king's steward went out round the house of Derdriu and Noísiu, and he saw the lovers sleeping. At once, he went and awakened the king, saying 'Until now, we have not found a woman worthy of you. But there is with Noísiu son of Uisliu a woman worthy of the king of the western world. Let Noísiu be slain that the woman might sleep with you.' 'No,' replied the king, 'but go to her each day in secret and woo her for me.'

The steward did that, but everything he said to Derdriu she told Noísiu the same night. Since nothing could be got from her, the sons of Uisliu were sent into battles and hazards and dangerous situations that they might be killed, but they were so hardy that every attempt failed. So the men of Albu gathered to kill them; they told Derdriu, and she told Noísiu, saying 'Depart! Unless you leave tonight, you will be slain tomorrow.' That night, Derdriu and the sons of Uisliu departed and went to an island in the sea.

This news reached the Ulaid, and they said to Conchubur 'A pity that the sons of Uisliu should die in a strange land because of a bad woman. Better that you should be lenient and not slay them—let them return and take them in.' 'Let them come, then,' said Conchubur, 'or let guarantors[5] be sent to them.' That message was taken to Noísiu and his brothers, and they replied 'A welcome message that. We will come; we ask for Fergus as a guarantor, and Dubthach,[6] and Conchubur's son Cormac.'

So these men went to Albu and accompanied Derdriu and the sons of Uisliu back to Ériu. On Conchubur's orders, however, the Ulaid all strove to invite Fergus to feasts[7] and banquets, for the sons of Uisliu had sworn that the first food they touched in Ériu would be Conchubur's. Thus, Fergus and Dubthach remained behind, while Fergus's son Fíachu[8] went on with Derdriu and the sons of Uisliu until they reached the green of Emuin Machae. Meanwhile, Éogan son of Durthacht, the king of Fernmag,[9] had made up with Conchubur—the two had long been at odds—and had been charged to kill the sons of Uisliu, who would be kept from Conchubur by the king of Ulaid's mercenaries.

The sons of Uisliu were waiting in the centre of the green; the women of Emuin were sitting along the ramparts; Éogan was crossing the green with his troops. Fíachu came up to join Noísiu. Éogan, however, greeted Noísiu with the point of his spear and broke his back. At that, Fíachu put his arms round Noísiu and pulled him down and covered him, so that thereafter Noísiu was struck from

5. Men who would pledge themselves to assure the safety of Noísiu and the rest of the exiles. The guarantors are named a few lines below.   6. [Doov-thak].   7. Conchubur's strategy is explained in the *Introduction*, above.   8. [Fee-ah-koo].   9. [Fern-moy].

above through the son of Fergus. The sons of Uisliu were then hunted
from one end of the green to the other, and no one escaped save by
point of spear and edge of sword. Derdriu was taken to stand beside
Conchubur, her hands tied behind her.

This news reached Fergus and Dubthach and Cormac, and at
once they went to Emuin and performed great deeds. Dubthach killed
Conchubur's son Mane[1] and dispatched Fíachnae, the son of Conchubur's daughter Fedelm,[2] with a single blow; Fergus killed
Traigthrén[3] son of Traiglethan and his brother. Conchubur was outraged, and a battle ensued: in one day, three hundred Ulaid fell, and
Dubthach slew the young women of the province, and Fergus fired
Emuin. Afterwards, Fergus and Dubthach and Cormac and their
followers went to Connachta, for they knew that Ailill and Medb[4]
would maintain them, though Connachta was no refuge of love for
men from Ulaid. Three thousand was the number of the exiles, and,
for sixteen years, these people saw that there was weeping and trembling in Ulaid every night.

Derdriu spent the year following Noísiu's death with Conchubur,
and, during that time, she neither laughed nor smiled, nor did she
ever have her fill of food or sleep. She never lifted her head from her
knee, and, whenever musicians were brought to her, she recited this
poem:

> Fair to you the ardent warriors
> who march into Emuin after an expedition;
> more nobly did they march to their
> dwelling,
> the three very heroic sons of Uisliu.
>
> Noísiu with fine hazel mead
> (I would wash him by the fire),
> Arddán with a stag or fine pig,
> Tall Aindle with a load on his back.
>
> Sweet to you the fine mead
> that battle-glorious Conchubur drinks;
> but often I had before me, across the ocean,
> food that was sweeter.
>
> When modest Noísiu spread out
> the cooking hearth on the wild forest floor,
> sweeter than any honeyed food
> was what the son of Uisliu prepared.
>
> Melodious always to you
> your pipers and trumpeters;

1. [Mah-nay].    2. [Fay-delm].    3. [Trayg-thrayn]. *Traiglethan* [Trayg-leth-an].    4. [Mayv].
Ailill and Medb were the king and queen of the province of Connachta.

yet today I tell you
I have heard music that was sweeter.

Melodious to Conchubur, your king,
his pipers and trumpeters;
sweeter to me—fame of hosts—
the singing of the sons of Uisliu.

A wave the sound of Noísiu's voice—
his singing was always sweet;
Arddán's baritone was good,
and Aindle's tenor from his hunting lodge.

Noísiu's grave has now been made,
and the accompaniment was mournful.
For him I poured out—hero of heroes—
the deadly drink that killed him. [5]

Dear his short shining hair, .
a handsome man, even very beautiful;
sad that I cannot await him today,
cannot expect the son of Uisliu.

Dear his desire, right and proper,
dear this modest noble warrior;
after his going to the forest's edge,
dear his company in the early morning.

Dear the grey eyes that women loved;
fierce they were to foes.
After a circuit of the forest—a noble union—
dear his tenor through the great dark wood.

I do not sleep now,
nor do I brighten my nails:
there is no joy for me
since the son of Tindell[6] will not come.

I do not sleep
but lie awake half the night;
my thoughts flee from these hosts,
I neither eat nor smile.

I have today no cause for joy
in the assembly of Emuin—throng of
chieftains—
no peace, no delight, no comfort,
no great house, no fine adornments.

And when Conchubur tried to comfort her, she would recite this poem to him:

5. A figurative expression—she was the cause of his death.   6. The mother of Noisiu and his brothers.

Conchubur, be quiet!
You have brought me grief upon sorrow;
as long as I live, surely,
your love will be of no concern to me.

You have taken from me—a great crime—
the one I thought most beautiful on earth,
the one I loved most.
I will not see him again until I die.

His absence is my despair,
the absence of the son of Uisliu.
A jet black cairn over his white body
once so well known among men.

Brighter than a river meadow his glistening
cheeks,
red his lips, beetle-black his brows;
the noble colour of snow
his shining, pearly teeth.

Well known his bright garb
among the warriors of Albu;
fair and brilliant his mantle—a noble
union—
with its fringe of red gold.

A true treasure his satin tunic
with its hundred gems—a gentle number—
and for decoration, clear and shining,
fifty ounces of white gold.

A gold-hilted sword in his hand,
two steely spears with javelin points;
a shield with a rim of yellow gold
and a boss of silver.

Fair Fergus betrayed us[7]
after bringing us across the great sea;
he sold his honour for beer,
his great deeds are no more.

Although the Ulaid might gather
about Conchubur upon the plain,
I would forsake them all, openly,
for the company of Noísiu son of Uisliu.

Break no more my heart today—
I will reach my early grave soon enough.
Sorrow is stronger than the sea
if you are wise, Conchubur.

7. Deirdre may have been unaware of the dilemma in which Fergus was caught; see the *Introduction*.

'What do you hate most that you see?' asked Conchubur. 'Yourself, surely, and Éogan son of Durthacht,' she replied. 'Then you will spend a year with Éogan,' Conchubur said. He took her to Éogan. The following day they went to a fair at Emuin Machae, Derdriu standing behind Éogan in his chariot. She had sworn that she would never see her two companions together in the same place. 'Well, Derdriu,' said Conchubur, 'it is the eye of a ewe between two rams you make between myself and Éogan.' There was a great boulder before Derdriu. She let her head be driven against it, and the boulder made fragments of her head, and she died.

---

# THE SONG OF THE SEERESS

People originally from the Scandinavian countries played an important part in the history of northwestern Europe between the eighth and the eleventh centuries A.D. These Danes, Norwegians, and Swedes form a northern group of the Germanic branch of the Indo-European–speaking nations. First as raiders and then as permanent settlers, they occupied the coasts of Ireland, most of England except the southwest, and the peninsula of France hence called Normandy. In the late ninth century they—chiefly the Norwegians—settled Iceland, which continued as an independent country until near the middle of the thirteenth century. Like the Celts, these Norsemen had a rich "oral literature"; for them also the ordinary use of writing began with the conversion to Christianity in the eleventh century. What is notable about them, among the Germanic nations, is the transmission or composition of an abundant pagan mythology. The English, the Germans, and the Dutch in later times kept little of their pre-Christian religious heritage except the names of four of the days of the week. Thus Tuesday preserves the memory of Tiu (Norse Tyr); Wednesday is the day of Woden (Norse Odin); Thursday belongs to Thor; and Friday is the day of the goddess of love and fertility, Freya. But the Norse, and especially the Icelanders, have left us some twenty or twenty-five narrative poems about the gods and the earliest Germanic heroes. In these we hear of Thor's fights against the Giants and the Midgard Serpent, a dragon who lives in the ocean surrounding all the lands; of Odin's contests with elves and his numerous adventures in pursuit of hidden knowledge; and of his dealings with Brunhild, Sigurd (the German Siegfried), Sigmund, and others. From this as ultimate source come the figures and part of the plot framework of Wagner's operatic sequence the *Ring of the Nibelung*. The English and the Germans retained a vivid memory of the demigod Wayland, the marvelous smith; but to understand the allusions to him in their traditions we must turn to the Norse *Völundarkvitha* for the full story.

Although *The Song of the Seeress* incorporates or builds on many of the myths of the gods, it is well-nigh unique. It is cast in the form of a dialogue between Odin and Heidi, the seeress; he has called her from the dead to answer his questions. In this way the poet presents a vision of the universe: in the beginning, nothing but a primordial giant and empty space, "a yawning gap"; then the shaping of a world order from the body of the giant; then the emergence of the divine figures and the appearance of men and women; the continual confrontation of the gods and the monsters who seek to reduce the cosmos to chaos; and the Armageddon-like end in reciprocal destruction—and a final vision of benevolence and order restored. The poet is often concise and allusive; he was speaking to an audience familiar with the myths beyond our knowledge; we cannot always be sure that we are reading him aright. The *Song* was probably composed near the end of the pagan period (Iceland accepted Christianity in the year 1000); the last section apparently shows influence from Christian ideas about "a new heaven and earth." It is impossible to say how many of the myths in the *Song* and in the other poems of this group (the *Elder Edda*) were a common Germanic heritage and how many were known only among the Scandinavians, or some of them. In any case, our own "nuclear" age should not find it difficult to understand the pervading conception of the *Song*: civilization and life itself are constantly threatened by evil powers; the gods meanwhile carry on a cold war to keep them at bay for as long as possible. Many readers will find the portrayal of this struggle not unlike that in J. R. R. Tolkien's *The Lord of the Rings*. To some degree, indeed, the modern author has borrowed the mood and tone of the poem, as well as some proper names; strophe 15 has a number of names used or adapted by Tolkien. And the translators' dedication acknowledges *their* relationship—"For J. R. R. Tolkien."

In his translation the poet W. H. Auden uses a verse form similar to the Norse original. Each line or verse contains at least two, sometimes three alliterating, stressed syllables; thus, in the first line of the poem:
    "Heidi men call me when their homes I visit,"
"Heidi" and "homes" alliterate, that is, begin with the same sound, the consonant *h*. The fourth line has three alliterating syllables:
    "To wicked women welcome always."
Further, any vowel or diphthong may alliterate with any other; thus in line 11,
    "Odin, I know where your eye is concealed,"
the required alliteration is provided by "Odin" and "eye," while "I" may offer a third syllable if it is stressed in reading.

Translations of the poems in the *Elder Edda* (besides Taylor and Auden): Henry Adams Bellows, *The Poetic Edda* (1923; and later printings), and L. M. Hollander, *The Poetic Edda* (1962). For the background see E. O. G. Turville-Petre, *Myth and Religion of the North* (1964), as well as his *Origins of Icelandic Literature* (1953).

# Song of the Seeress[1]

Heidi men call me when their homes I visit,                    1
A far-seeing witch, wise in talismans,

---

1. Translated by Paul B. Taylor and W. H. Auden.

Caster of spells, cunning in magic,
To wicked women welcome[2] always.

Arm-rings and necklaces, Odin, you gave me                    2
To learn my lore, to learn my magic:
Wider and wider through all worlds[3] I see.

Outside I sat by myself when you came,                    3
Terror of the Gods, and gazed in my eyes.
What do you ask of me? Why tempt me?
Odin, I know where your eye is concealed,[4]
Hidden away in the Well of Mimir:
Mimir each morning his mead drinks
From Valfather's Pledge. *Well, would you know
    more?*[5]

Of Heimdal,[6] too, and his horn I know,                    4
Hidden under the holy tree;
Down on it pours a precious stream
From Valfather's Pledge. *Well, would you know
    more?*

Silence I ask of the Sacred Folk,[7]                    5
Silence of the kith and kin of Heimdal:
At your will, Valfather, I shall well relate
The old songs of men I remember best.

I tell of giants from times forgotten,                    6
Those who fed me in former days:
Nine Worlds I can reckon, nine roots of the Tree,
The wonderful Ash, way under the ground.

When Ymir[8] lived long ago                    7
Was no sand or sea, no surging waves,
Nowhere was there earth nor heaven above,
But a grinning gap and grass nowhere.

2. Witches and seeresses had a bad reputation generally in Scandinavia—despite their recognized knowledge.    3. The divisions of the universe in which, severally, lived gods, elves, dwarfs, etc.    4. At some time in the past Odin had given Mimir one of his eyes in return for secret knowledge (hence Odin is regularly represented with one eye). As the poem says, Mimir (a supernatural being) used the eye as a drinking cup. *Valfather*: An epithet of Odin—"Father (i.e., ruler or protector) of the slain."    5. This query, repeated several times in the poem, dramatizes the tension between the seeress and Odin. Although she boasts of her knowledge, she would like to be released as soon as possible.    6. Watchman of the gods, whose horn can summon or warn. *The holy tree*: The World-Ash; see strophe 6 below.    7. The assembly of gods who, apparently, will hear her along with Odin.    8. The primeval giant from whom the universe was shaped.

The Sons of Bur[9] then built up the lands,                                   8
Molded in magnificence Middle Earth:[1]
Sun stared from the south on the stones of their hall,
From the ground there sprouted green leeks.

Sun turned from the south, Sister of Moon,                                    9
Her right arm rested on the rim of Heaven;
She had no inkling where her hall was,
Nor Moon a notion of what might he had,
The planets knew not where their places were.[2]

The High Gods gathered in council                                            10
In their Hall of Judgment, all the rulers:
To Night and to Nightfall their names gave,
The Morning they named and the Mid-Day,
Mid-Winter, Mid-Summer, for the assigning of years.

At Idavale the Aesir[3] met:                                                 11
Temple and altar they timbered and raised,
Set up a forge to smithy treasures,
Tongs they fashioned and tools wrought;

Played chess[4] in the court and cheerful were;                             12
Gold they lacked not, the gleaming metal.
Then came Three, the Thurse Maidens,[5]
Rejoicing in their strength, from Gianthome.

The High Gods gathered in council                                           13
In their Hall of Judgment: Who of the dwarfs
Should mold man by mastercraft
From Brimir's blood and Bláin's limbs?[6]

Mótsognir was their mighty ruler,                                           14
Greatest of dwarfs, and Durin after him:
The dwarfs did as Durin directed,
Many man-forms made from the earth.

---

9. Odin and his brothers Ve and Vili.     1. In the newly ordered world, Asgard, the realm of
the gods, was at the center; next was the earth; farthest out was Utgard, including the realms of
the giants and other creatures. Earth was in the middle, hence Middle Earth. A similar arrangement in the Tolkien books.     2. At first the sun, moon, and planets had no regular orbits; the
gods ordained the regularity we know, and hence the boundaries of day and night, the seasons,
etc., as the following strophe sets forth.     3. Aesir is a plural noun; it designates the principal
family of the gods. *Idavale*: We are never told where this was, perhaps in the general realm of
Asgard.     4. More likely a game such as backgammon.     5. Giantesses; but they appear out of
place at this point in the poem.     6. These may be other names for the primeval giant Ymir or,
possibly, intermediate members of the Giant family. The "man" of strophe 13 would seem actually
to refer to the dwarfs, which were of human shape. At any rate, the following passage is concerned
with dwarfs, not men and women.

Nýi and Nídi, Nordri, Sudri, 15
Austri and Vestri, Althjóf, Dvalin,
Bívor, Bávor, Bömbur, Nóri,
An and Ánar, Óinn, Mjödvitnir,
Veig and Gandálf, Vindálf, Thorin,
Thrór and Thráin, Thekkur, Littur,
Vitur, Nyr and Nýrádur,
Fíli, Kíli, Fundin, Náli,
Hefti, Víli, Hanar, Svíur,
Billing, Brúni, Bíldur, and Buri,
Frár, Hornbori, Fraegur, Lóni,
Aurvangur, Jari, Eikinskjaldi:
(All Durin's folk I have duly named.)

I must tell of the dwarves in Dvalin's[7] host; 16
Like lions they were in Lokar's time:
In Juravale's marsh they made their dwelling,
From their stone hall set out on journeys.

There was Draupnir and Dólgthrasir, 17
Hár, Haugspori, Hlévangur, Glói,
Dori, Ori, Dufur, Andvari,
Skirfir, Virfir, Skáfidur, Ái,
Álf and Yngvi, Eikinskjaldi,
Fjalar and Frosti, Finn and Ginnar:
Men will remember while men live
The long line of Lofar's forebears.

Then from the host Three[8] came, 18
Great, merciful, from the god's home:
*Ash* and *Elm* on earth they found,
Faint, feeble, with no fate assigned them.

Breath they had not, nor blood nor senses, 19
Nor language possessed, nor life-hue:
Odin gave them breath, Haenir senses,
Blood and life-hue Lodur gave.

I know an ash-tree, named Yggdrasil:[9] 20
Sparkling showers are shed on its leaves
That drip dew into the dales below.

---

7. A chief of dwarfs, as probably were also Lokar and Lofar. *Juravale:* Not identified. 8. The gods Odin, Haenir, and Lodur, as explained below. *Ash and Elm:* The first man and woman. 9. The name of the tree; literally, the "steed of Ygg," another name of Odin. Odin hanged himself on the tree in order to gain secret knowledge.

By Urd's Well it waves evergreen,
Stands over that still pool,
Near it a bower whence now there come
The Fate Maidens, first Urd.
Skuld second, scorer of runes,[1]
Then Verdandi, third of the Norms:
The laws that determine the lives of men
They fixed forever and their fate sealed.

The first war in the world I well remember,                    21
When Gullveg[2] was spitted on spear points
And burned in the hall of the High God:
Thrice burned, thrice reborn
Often laid low, she lives yet.
The gods hastened to their Hall of Judgment,                    22
Sat in council to decide whether
To endure great loss in loud strife
Or let both command men's worship.

At the host Odin hurled his spear                    23
In the first world-battle; broken was the plankwall
Of the god's fortress: the fierce Vanes
Caused war to occur in the fields.

The gods hastened to their Hall of Judgment,                    24
Sat in council to discover who
Had tainted all the air with corruption
And Odin's Maid offered to the giants.[3]

One Thor felled[4] in his fierce rage;                    25
Seldom he sits when of such he hears:
Oaths were broken, binding vows,
Solemn agreements sworn between them.

Valkyries[5] I saw, coming from afar,                    26
Eagerly riding to aid the Goths;

1. She used the runic alphabet to inscribe prophecies (on wood or stone). *Urd*: That which has come about—the Past; *Skuld*: That which is destined—the Future; *Verdandi*: That which is becoming—the Present. *Norns*: Fates.    2. The mysterious Gullveg was somehow connected, apparently, with the conflict between two families of gods, the Aesir and the Vanes (Frey and Freya, god and goddess of love and fertility). The myth probably reflects first war, then reconciliation between peoples who had different deities.    3. This was Loki, a clever but (usually) malevolent figure who often sits with the gods but is actually an ally of the giants and monsters. He contracted with the giants to give them Freya ("Odin's Maid")—and the sun and moon—in payment for building the citadel Asgard, and the gods were committed to the bargain.    4. Thor slew one of the giants. *Oaths were broken*: When the gods finally realized the enormity of the bargain they broke the contract.    5. Literally, "choosers of the slain" in battles, in obedience to Odin, their father. (One of the operas in Wagner's *Ring* is *The Valkyries*.) *Goths*: I.e., men.

Skuld bore one shield, Skögul another,
Gunn, Hild, Göngul and Spearskögul:
Duly have I named the Daughters of Odin,
The valiant riders, the Valkyries.

Baldur I saw, the bleeding god,                              27
His fate still hidden, Odin's son:
Tall on the plain a plant grew,
A slender marvel, the mistletoe.

From that fair shrub, shot by Hödur,                        28
Flew the fatal dart that felled the God,[6]
But Baldur's Brother was born soon after:
Though one night old, Odin's Son
Took a vow to avenge that death.

His hands he washed not nor his hair combed                 29
Till Baldur's Bane[7] was borne to the pyre:
Deadly the bow drawn by Vali,
The strong string of stretched gut,
But Frigg[8] wept in Fensalir
For the woe of Valhalla. *Well, would you know
    more?*

I see one in bonds by the boiling springs;[9]               30
Like Loki he looks, loathsome to view:
There Sigyn sits, sad by her husband,
In woe by her man. *Well, would you know more?*

From the east through Venom Valley runs                     31
Over jagged rocks the River Gruesome.

North, in Darkdale, stands the dwelling place               32
Of Sindri's kin,[1] covered with gold;
A hall also in Everfrost,
The banquet hall of Brimir the Giant.

A third I see, that no sunlight reaches,                    33
On Dead Man's Shore: the doors face northward,
Through its smoke vent venom drips,
Serpent skins enskein that hall.

6. Loki induced the blind god Hödur to cast a spear made of mistletoe at Baldur, who was invulnerable to any other material.    7. Baldur's slayer, Hödur, was slain in turn by Vali, a son of Odin. The line refers to cremation on a funeral pyre.    8. The wife of Odin and mother of Baldur; Fensalir is the name of her dwelling. *Valhalla*: Odin's great hall.    9. Loki has been captured by the gods and placed in bonds. Sigyn is Loki's wife.    1. The dwarves.

Men wade there,[2] tormented by the stream,                                          34
Vile murderers, men forsworn,
And artful seducers of other men's wives:
Nidhógg[3] sucks blood from the bodies of the dead,
The Wolf rends them. *Well, would you know more?*
In the east dwells a crone,[4] in Ironwood:                                          35
The brood of Fenris are bred there,
Wolf-monsters, one of whom
Eventually shall devour the sun.

The giant's Watchman, joyful Eggthur,                                               36
Sits on his howe and harps well:
The red cock,[5] called All-Knower
Boldly crows from Birdwood.

Goldencomb to the Gods crows,                                                       37
Who wakes the warriors in Valhalla:
A soot-red hen also calls
From Hel's Hall, deep under the ground.

Loud howls Garm before Gnipahellir,[6]                                              38
Bursting his fetters, Fenris runs:
Further in the future, afar I behold
The Twilight of the gods[7] who gave victory.

Brother shall strike brother and both fall,                                         39
Sisters' sons slay each other,
Evil be on earth, an Age of Whoredom,
Of sharp sword-play and shields' clashing,
A Wind-Age, a Wolf-Age, till the world ruins:
No man to another shall mercy show.

The waters are troubled, the waves surge up:                                        40
Announcing now the knell of Fate,
Heimdal winds his horn aloft,[8]
On Hel's Road all men tremble.

---

2. The river is in Hel, a cold, dark area, the abode of the dead, where crimes committed in life are punished.    3. A dragon; he also gnaws at the roots of the World-Ash. *The Wolf:* It is uncertain whether this is one of the family of Fenris (strophe 35) or another wolf.    4. The mother of two wolves; one, Skoll, will swallow the sun at the end of the world-order; the other, Hati, will swallow the moon. *Ironwood* and *Birdwood* are not precisely located by the poet.    5. The red cock in the Giants' realm, Goldencomb in Valhalla, the hall of Odin, and the "red hen" in Hel form a series. *Howe:* A mound or low hill.    6. The entrance to Hel, guarded by the monstrous dog Garm.    7. "Twilight" corresponds to the term used in Wagner's opera *Götterdämmerung,* but the Norse term almost certainly means "the destruction of the gods."    8. As a warning signal that the monsters are approaching Asgard, the capital of the gods.

Yggdrasil trembles, the towering Ash                    41
Groans in woe; the Wolf is loose:
Odin speaks with the head of Mimir
Before he is swallowed by Surt's kin.[9]

From the east drives Hrym,[1] lifts up his shield,                    42
The squamous serpent squirms with rage,
The Great Worm with the waves contending,
The pale-beaked eagle pecks at the dead,
Shouting for joy: the ship Naglfar[2]

Sails out from the east, at its helm Loki,                    43
With the children of darkness, the doom-bringers,
Offspring of monsters, allies of the Wolf,
All who Byleist's Brother[3] follow.

What of the gods? What of the elves?                    44
Gianthome groans, the gods are in council,
The dwarves grieve before their door of stone,
Masters of walls. *Well, would you know more?*

Surt with the bane-of-branches[4] comes                    45
From the south, on his sword the sun of the Valgods,
Crags topple, the crone falls headlong,
Men tread Hel's Road, the Heavens split open.

A further woe falls upon Hiln[5]                    46
As Odin comes forth to fight the Wolf;
The killer of Beli[6] battles with Surt:
Now shall fall Frigg's beloved.

Now valiant comes Valfather's Son,                    47
Vidar, to vie with Valdyr[7] in battle,
Plunges his sword into the Son of Hvedrung,
Avenging his father with a fell thrust.
Now the Son of Hlödyn and Odin[8] comes                    48

9. Fenris, the wolf who will finally swallow Odin. Surt was a giant whose weapon was fire (hence the name—Surtsey, Surt's island—given to the island formed by the volcanic eruption off the south coast of Iceland in 1963).    1. The leader of the Giants in the final assault. *The squamous serpent . . . the Great Worm*: Both terms refer to the Midgard serpent or dragon who lies in the ocean.    2. A ship made of dead men's fingernails.    3. Loki.    4. An epithet of fire, which destroys the limbs of trees. *Sun of the Valgods*: More literally, the sun is reflected from the sword of the Battle-gods. *The Crone*: The mother of two wolves who will swallow the sun and moon.    5. Another name of Frigg, wife of Odin.    6. The god Frey; Beli was a giant. *Frigg's beloved*: Her husband, Odin.    7. The wolf Fenris, who is also the "Son of Hvethrung."    8. Thor, who destroys the Midgard Serpent but is himself mortally injured by the poison of the Serpent. The Icelandic text is not clear, but Fenris must be incorrect here, for he has already been slain.

To fight with Fenris; fiercest of warriors,
He mauls in his rage all Middle Earth;
Men in fear all flee their homesteads;
Nine paces back steps Bur's Son,[9]
Retreats from the Worm, of taunts unafraid.

Now death is the portion of doomed men,                              49
Red with blood the buildings of gods,
The sun turns black in the summer after,
Winds whine. *Well, would you know more?*

Earth sinks in the sea, the sun turns black,                         50
Cast down from Heaven are the hot stars,
Fumes reek, into flames burst,
The sky itself is scorched with fire.

I see Earth rising a second time                                     51
Out of the foam, fair and green;
Down from the fells, fish to capture,
Wings the eagle; waters flow.

At Idavale the Aesir meet:                                           52
They remember the Worm of Middle Earth,
Ponder again the Great Twilight
And the ancient runes of the High God.

Boards shall be found of a beauty to wonder at,                      53
Boards of gold in the grass long after,
The chess boards they owned in the olden days.

Unsown acres shall harvests bear,                                    54
Evil be abolished, Baldur return
And Hropt's[1] Hall with Hödur rebuild,
Wise gods. *Well, would you know more?*

Haenir shall wield the wand of prophecy,                             55
The sons of two brothers[2] set up their dwelling
In wide Windhome. *Well, would you know more?*

Fairer than sunlight, I see a hall,                                  56
A hall thatched with gold in Gimlé:[3]
Kind lords shall live there in delight for ever.

---

9. Thor.   1. Hropt was another name for Odin.   2. Perhaps the sons of Ve and Vili, brothers of Odin.   3. Apparently "meadow of gems"—a name for a kind of earthly paradise.

Now rides the Strong One[4] to Rainbow Door,                    57
Powerful from heaven, the All-Ruler:
From the depths below a drake comes flying,
The Dark Dragon[5] from Darkfell,
Bears on his pinions the bodies of men,
Soars overhead. I sink now.[6]

---

# THORSTEIN THE STAFF-STRUCK

Medieval Iceland produced not only a unique and highly interesting body
of poetry but also some of the best prose narratives in European literature.
Some of these, like the *Saga of the Volsungs*, deal with figures of early
Germanic tradition. But some thirty or forty, called sagas of Icelanders, are
about men and women who lived in Iceland (and often in Norway in their
youth) from the late ninth to the early eleventh centuries. Written mostly in
the thirteenth century, they may remind us a bit of the historical novels of
a later time. But in the historical novel, usually, the major characters are
fictional, products of the author's invention, while those well known to history serve as framework or background. In the Icelandic saga the converse is
true: the principal figures were actual people attested by documents and
other evidence, as were also most of the events and acts attributed to them.
Oral tradition bridged the interval between the tenth century and the thirteenth. Thus the author of an extant saga was free to shape characterization,
motivation, mood, and tone as he saw fit. It is now believed that the milieu
of thirteenth-century Iceland may have influenced features of some of these
narratives. A few may have been entirely fictional, except for the use of the
names of actual persons. Like the Eddic poems, the sagas are nearly always
anonymous. Some of the most notable are of novel length, like the *Saga of
the Laxdalers* or the Grettir saga, or the *Saga of Burnt Njal*, greatest of all.

As must be evident, the story of Thorstein the Staff-Struck is very short;
in fact, it was not called a saga but a *tháttr*, literally, a "thread." Nevethe-
less, it shows the characteristic features of a family saga. Although the action
is "strong," to use a modern term—people kill and get killed—violence is
not included for its own sake; instead, it interests the narrator chiefly as an
expression of personality and character. The incidents of the story are conducted in such a way as to distinguish sharply nearly all of the participants;
these are all members of one or the other of two families or households who
live in northeast Iceland. The "fierce," now aged but still irascible Thorarin
is contrasted with his husky and confident but even-tempered son Thorstein;
only when the insolent Thord wilfully insults him does Thorstein take action.
In prosecuting Thorstein for manslaughter, Bjarni, Thord's employer and

4. Apparently a benevolent deity, but the name is uncertain. The Rainbow Door is probably the
earth; in Norse mythology the rainbow was a bridge reaching from heaven to earth.    5. Neither
his identity nor his role is clear.    6. The seeress ends her discourse; she will now return to the
realm of the dead.

also the district chieftain, fullfils a more or less automatic obligation. However, when Thorstein ignores the sentence of exile, Bjarni (whose responsibility it was to attack Thorstein) takes no action. We learn that he is unwilling
to deprive the infirm, nearly blind Thorarin of his son's support. Nevertheless, when Bjarni overhears the malicious gossip of Thorhall and Thorvald,
he sends them out with instructions to kill Thorstein. We are not told what
he expected would happen, but when he learns that Thorstein has slain the
two brothers, once again he does nothing; when his wife Rannveig goads
him, he remarks that "Thorstein has never killed anyone without a good
reason." All the same, when she tells him of the taunts in circulation about
him, he decides that he cannot avoid a confrontation with Thorstein.

Although the circumstances are different, Bjarni's motive in his (reluctant) challenge of Thorstein is the same as the latter's when he (at last)
challenges Thord. Each man considers the respect of the community essential to his self-respect; hence they act as the code required regardless of their
personal inclination or of the intrinsic merits of the case. The thirteenth-
century Christian author faithfully presents this pre-Christian pattern; the
ethical dilemma, unacknowledged by the protagonists, is implicit in the
narration. Hence in the final encounter Bjarni and Thorstein carry out the
*form* of conduct which tradition made obligatory, while the *manner* in which
they do so insures a morally satisfactory result.

Readers will enjoy this succinct narrative best if they ask themselves such
questions—among others—as, What purposes are served by the dialogue?
What is Thorarin's motive for each of his acts? How does the author make
use of the two female characters?

A concise general account of the family sagas is Peter Hallberg, translated
by Paul Schach, *The Icelandic Saga* (1962). A critical study of structure and
organization, with plot summaries, is Theodore M. Anderson, *The Icelandic
Family Saga* (1967). Admirable translations of several of the principal sagas
are available in the Penguin paperback series.

## Thorstein the Staff-Struck[1]

There was a man called Thorarin who lived at Sunnudale; he was
old and nearly blind. He had been a fierce viking in his younger
years, and even in his old age he was very hard to deal with. He had
an only son, Thorstein, who was a tall man, powerful but even-
tempered; he worked so hard on his father's farm that three other
men could hardly have done any better. Thorarin had little money,
but a good many weapons. He and his son owned some breeding
horses and that was their main source of income, for the young colts
they sold never failed in spirit or strength.

Bjarni of Hof[2] had a servant called Thord who looked after his
riding horses and was considered very good at the job. Thord was an
arrogant man and would never let anyone forget the fact that he was

1. Translated, with footnotes, by Hermann Pálsson.　2. Bjarni of Hof was the local chieftain,
and the wealthiest and most powerful farmer in the district.

in the service of a chieftain. But this didn't make him a better man and added nothing to his popularity. Bjarni also had two brothers working for him who were called Thorhall and Thorvald, both great scandalmongers about any gossip they heard in the district.

Thorstein and Thord arranged a horse-fight for their young stallions.[3] During the fight, Thord's horse started giving way, and when Thord realized he was losing, he struck Thorstein's horse a hard blow on the jaw. Thorstein saw this and hit back with an even heavier blow at Thord's horse, forcing it to back away. This got the spectators shouting with excitement. Then Thord aimed a blow at Thornstein with his horse-goad, hitting him so hard on the eye-brow that the skin broke and the lid fell hanging down over the eye. Thorstein tore a piece off his shirt and bandaged his head. He said nothing about what had happened, apart from asking people to keep this from his father. That should have been the end of the incident, but Thorvald and Thorhall kept jeering at Thorstein and gave him the nickname Staff-Struck.

One morning that winter just before Christmas, when the women at Sunnudale were getting up for their work, Thorstein went out to feed the cattle. He soon came back and lay down on a bench. His father, old Thorarin, came into the room and asked who was lying there. Thorstein told him.

'Why are you up so early, son?' said Thorarin.

Thorstein answered, 'It seems to me there aren't many men about to share the work with me.'

'Have you got a head-ache, son?' said Thorarin.

'Not that I've noticed,' said Thorstein.

'What can you tell me about the horse-fight last summer, son?' said Thorarin. 'Weren't you beaten senseless like a dog?'

'It's no credit to me if you call it a deliberate blow, not an accident,' said Thorstein.

Thorarin said, 'I'd never have thought I could have a coward for a son.'

'Father,' said Thorstein, 'Don't say anything now that you'll live to regret later.'

'I'm not going to say as much as I've a mind to,' said Thorarin.

Thorstein got to his feet, seized his weapons and set off. He came to the stable where Thord was grooming Bjarni's horses, and when he saw Thord he said, 'I'd like to know, friend Thord, whether it was accidental when you hit me in the horse-fight last summer, or deliberate. If it was deliberate, you'll be willing to pay me compensation.'

'If only you were double-tongued,' said Thord, 'then you could

3. Horse-fights used to be a favourite sport in Iceland. Two stallions were pitted against one another, and behind each of them there was a man equipped with a goad to prod them on. At these horse fights tempers would often run high.

easily speak with two voices and call the blow accidental with one and deliberate with the other. That's all the compensation you're getting from me.'

'In that case don't expect me to make this claim a second time,' said Thorstein.

With that he rushed at Thord and dealt him his death-blow. Then he went up to the house at Hof where he saw a woman standing outside the door. 'Tell Bjarni that a bull has gored Thord, his horse-boy,' he said to her, 'and also that Thord will be waiting for him at the stable.'

'Go back home, man,' she said. 'I'll tell Bjarni in my own good time.'

Thorstein went back home, and the woman carried on with her work.

After Bjarni had got up that morning and was sitting at table, he asked where Thord could be, and was told he had gone to see to the horses.

'I'd have thought he'd be back by now, unless something has happened to him,' said Bjarni.

The woman Thorstein had spoken to broke in. 'It's true what we women are often told, we're not very clever. Thorstein the Staff-Struck came here this morning and he said Thord had been gored by a bull and couldn't look after himself. I didn't want to wake you, and then I forgot all about it.'

Bjarni left the table, went over to the stable and found Thord lying there, dead. Bjarni had him buried, then brought a court action against Thorstein and had him sentenced to outlawry for manslaughter. But Thorstein stayed on at Sunnudale and worked for his father, and Bjarni did nothing more about it.

One day in the autumn when the men of Hof were busy singeing sheep's heads[4], Bjarni lay down on top of the kitchen wall to listen to their talk. Now the brothers Thorhall and Thorvald started gossiping; 'It never occurred to us when we came to live here with Killer-Bjarni[5] that we'd be singeing lambs' heads while his outlaw Thorstein is singeing the heads of wethers. It would have been better for Bjarni to have been more lenient with his kinsmen at Bodvarsdale and not to let his outlaw at Sunnudale act just like his own equal. But "A wounded coward lies low," and it's not likely that he'll ever wipe away this stain on his honour.'

One of the men said, 'Those words were better left unsaid, the trolls must have twisted your tongue. I think Bjarni simply isn't pre-

4. In Iceland, as in some other sheep-raising countries, sheep's heads were (and still are) considered a great delicacy. The heads are singed over a fire to remove all traces of wool before they are cleaned and cooked.    5. The name Killer-Bjarni is an allusion to the fact that Bjarni fought and killed some of his own kinsmen in the battle of Bodvarsdale which is mentioned in the following sentence.

pared to take the only breadwinner at Sunnudale away from Thorstein's blind father and other dependents there. I'll be more than surprised if you singe many more lambs' heads here, or tattle on much longer about the fight at Bodvarsdale.'

Then they went inside to have their meal, and after that to bed. Bjarni gave no sign that he had heard anything of what had been said. But early next morning he roused Thorhall and Thorvald and told them to ride over to Sunnudale and bring him Thorstein's severed head before mid-morning. 'I think you're more likely than anyone else to wipe away that stain from my honour, since I haven't the courage to do it for myself,' he said.

The brothers realized they had said too much, but they set off and went over to Sunnudale. Thorstein was standing in the doorway, sharpening a short sword. He asked them where they were going, and they told him they were looking for some horses. Thorstein said they didn't have very far to go. 'The horses are down by the fence.'

Thorstein came outside, and as they were walking together across the meadow, Thorvald raised his axe and rushed at him. But Thorstein pushed him back so hard that he fell, then ran him through with the short sword. Thorhall tried to attack Thorstein and went the same way as his brother. Thorstein tied them to their saddles, fixed the reins to the horses' manes, and drove them off.

The horses went back to Hof. Some of the servants there were out of doors and went inside to tell Bjarni that Thorvald and Thorhall had come back and their journey hadn't been wasted. Bjarni went outside and saw what had happened. He said nothing and had the two men buried. Then everything was quiet till after Christmas.

One evening after Bjarni and his wife Rannveig had gone to bed, she said to him, 'What do you think everyone in the district is talking about these days?'

'I couldn't say,' said Bjarni. 'In my opinion most people talk a lot of rubbish.'

'This is what people are mainly talking about now,' she continued: 'They're wondering how far Thorstein the Staff-Struck can go before you bother to take revenge. He's killed three of your servants, and your supporters are beginning to doubt whether you can protect them, seeing that you've failed to avenge this. You often take action when you shouldn't and hold back when you should.'

'It's the same old story,' said Bjarni, 'no one seems willing to learn from another man's lesson. Thorstein has never killed anyone without a good reason—but still, I'll think about your suggestion.'

With that they dropped the subject and slept through the night. In the morning Rannveig woke up as Bjarni was taking down his sword and shield. She asked him where he was going.

'The time has come for me to settle that matter of honour between

Thorstein of Sunnudale and myself,' he said.

'How many men are you taking with you?' she asked.

'I'm not taking a whole army to attack Thorstein,' he said. 'I'm going alone.'

'You mustn't do that,' she said, 'risking your life against the weapons of that killer.'

'You're a typical woman,' said Bjarni, 'arguing against the very thing you were urging just a few hours ago! There's a limit to my patience, I can only stand so much taunting from you and others. And once my mind's made up, there's no point in trying to hold me back.'

Bjarni went over to Sunnudale. He saw Thorstein standing in the doorway, and they exchanged some words.

'You'll fight me in single combat,' said Bjarni, 'on that hillock over there in the home-meadow.'

'I'm in no way good enough to fight you,' said Thorstein. 'I give you my promise to leave the country with the first ship that sails abroad. I know a generous man like you will provide my father with labour to run the farm if I go away.'

'You can't talk yourself out of this now,' said Bjarni.

'You'll surely let me go and see my father first,' said Thorstein.

'Certainly,' said Bjarni.

Thorstein went inside and told his father that Bjarni had come and challenged him to a duel.

The old man said, 'Anybody who offends a more powerful man in his own district can hardly expect to wear out many more new shirts. In my opinion your offences are so serious, I can't find any excuse for you. So you'd better take your weapons and defend yourself the best you can. In my younger days I'd never have given way before someone like Bjarni, great fighting-man though he may be. I'd much rather lose you than have a coward for a son.'

Thorstein went outside and walked with Bjarni up the hillock. They started fighting with determination and destroyed each other's shield. When they had been fighting for a long time, Bjarni said to Thorstein, 'I'm getting very thirsty now, I'm not so used to hard work as you are.'

'Go down to the stream then and drink,' said Thorstein.

Bjarni did so, and laid the sword down beside him. Thorstein picked it up, examined it and said, 'You can't have been using this sword at Bodvarsdale.'

Bjarni said nothing, and they went back to the hillock. After they'd been fighting for a time, it became obvious to Bjarni that Thorstein was a highly skilled fighter, and the outcome seemed less certain than he'd expected.

'Everything seems to go wrong for me today,' he said. 'Now my shoe-thong's loose.'

'Tie it up then,' said Thorstein.

When Bjarni bent down to tie it, Thorstein went into the house and brought back two shields and a sword. He joined Bjarni on the hillock and said, 'Here's a sword and shield my father sends you. The sword shouldn't get so easily blunted as the one you've been using. And I don't want to stand here any longer with no shield to protect me against your blows. I'd very much like us to stop this game now, for I'm afraid your good luck will prove stronger than my bad luck. Every man wants to save his life, and I would too, if I could.'

'There's no point in your trying to talk yourself out of this,' said Bjarni. 'The fight must go on.'

'I wouldn't like to be the first to strike,' said Thorstein.

Then Bjarni struck at Thorstein, destroying his shield, and Thorstein hacked down Bjarni's shield in return.

'That was a blow,' said Bjarni.

Thorstein replied, 'Yours wasn't any lighter.'

Bjarni said, 'Your sword seems to be biting much better now than it was earlier.'

'I want to save myself from the foulest of luck if I possibly can,' said Thorstein. 'It scares me to have to fight you, so I want you yourself to settle the matter between us.'

It was Bjarni's turn to strike. Both men had lost their shields. Bjarni said, 'It would be a great mistake in one stroke both to throw away good fortune and do wrong. In my opinion I'd be fully paid for my three servants if you took their place and served me faithfully.'

Thorstein said, 'I've had plenty of opportunity today to take advantage of you, if my bad luck had been stronger than your good luck. I'll never deceive you.'

'Now I can see what a remarkable man you must be,' said Bjarni. 'You'll allow me to go inside to see your father and tell him about this in my own words?'

'You can go if you want as far as I'm concerned,' said Thorstein, 'but be on your guard.'

Bjarni went up to the bed-closet where Old Thorarin was lying. Thorarin asked who was there, and Bjarni told him.

'What's your news, friend Bjarni?' said Thorarin.

'The killing of Thorstein, your son,' said Bjarni.

'Did he put up any defence at all?' asked Thorarin.

'I don't think there's ever been a better fighter than your son, Thorarin,' said Bjarni.

'It's no wonder your opponents at Bodvarsdale found you so hard to deal with,' said Thorarin, 'seeing that you've overcome my son.'

Bjarni said, 'I want to invite you to come over to Hof and take the seat of honour there for the rest of your life. I'll be just like a son to you.'

'I'm in the same position now as any other pauper,' said Thorarin. 'Only a fool accepts a promise gladly, and promises of chieftains like yourself aren't usually honoured for more than a month after the event, while you're trying to console us. After that we're treated as ordinary paupers, though our grief doesn't grow any the less for that. Still, anyone who shakes hands on a bargain with a man of your character should be satisfied, in spite of other men's lessons. So I'd like to shake hands with you, and you'd better come into the bed-closet to me. Come closer now, for I'm an old man and trembling on my feet because of ill-health and old age. And I must admit, the loss of my son has upset me a bit.'

Bjarni went into the bed-closet and shook Thorarin by the hand. Then he realized the old man was groping for a short sword with the idea of thrusting it at him. Bjarni pulled back his hand and said, 'You merciless old rascal! I can promise you now you'll get what you deserve. Your son Thorstein is alive and well, and he'll come with me over to Hof, but you'll be given slaves to run the farm for you, and never suffer any want for the rest of your life.'

Thorstein went with Bjarni over to Hof, and stayed in his service for the rest of his life. He was considered a man of great courage and integrity. Bjarni kept his standing and became better-liked and more self-controlled the older he grew. He was a very trustworthy man. In the last years of his life he became a devout Christian and went to Rome on pilgrimage. He died on that journey, and is buried at a town called Sutri,[6] just north of Rome.[7]

---

# THE SONG OF ROLAND

With some literal inaccuracy, but with substantial truth, it has been said that French literature begins with the *Song of Roland*. Certainly it is the first great narrative poem in that language. Of unknown authorship and date, it was apparently composed in the decade or decades after the year 1100. Imbued with the spirit of the First Crusade, it seems to reproduce some details of the campaigns and expeditions to capture and hold the Holy Land for Christendom. The story it tells was developed from a historical incident in the career of Charlemagne (Charles the Great). As the Emperor was returning from a

6. The MSS have Vateri which is probably a scribal error. The town Sutri is mentioned elsewhere in early Icelandic records.    7. The story concludes with a long account of Bjarni's descendants, extending into the thirteenth century. [Editor's note.]

successful war in northern Spain, the Gascons attacked his baggage train
and rearguard in the mountain passes of the Pyrenees. The rearguard perished, including Roland, the prefect of the Breton March. These events
occurred in the year 778. Our poet of the twelfth century has transformed
them—somewhat as Geoffrey of Monmouth, Chrétien de Troyes, and Malory
transformed incidents involving the probably also historical Arthur, his exploits,
and the deeds of his warriors. The Charles of the *Roland*, a magnificent
figure, is white-haired and venerable, and not without a touch of the miraculous: though still valiant in fight, he is reputed among the enemy to be two
hundred years old, or more. He is served especially by a choice band of
leaders, the twelve peers, of whom the chief is Roland, his nephew—a relationship that in Heroic narrative intensifies either loyalty or disloyalty. The
enemy, too, has been changed. Not a few border Gascons or Basques, but
enormous Saracen armies fight against Roland and the Emperor. Thus we
have a holy war; all the motives of a Crusade are invoked in this struggle of
Christians against Mohammedans. Keeping the Emperor as the central
*background* figure, the poet has concentrated his efforts on Roland as the
hero, the central *foreground* character. Close beside him stand Oliver, the
wise and faithful friend, and Ganelon, whose hatred of Roland leads him to
treason against Charles.

The world of the poem is an idealization of feudal society in the early
twelfth century. This society was headed by proud barons—a hereditary
nobility—whose independent spirit found liberal scope in valiant action,
fierce devotion, and bitter personal antagonism. A man was esteemed for his
prowess in battle, for his loyalty to his king or other feudal chief, and for his
wisdom, as the portrait of Oliver reminds us. The action of the poem is
infused with a warm glow of patriotic feeling—not the flag-waving variety,
but a cherishing love of the homeland, "sweet France." It might be called
regional rather than political patriotism, for in a feudal regime a man's binding obligations are to his lord rather than to the country as a whole. Yet the
larger issue enters, in a special way: in the second half of the poem, Ganelon
is finally condemned and punished because in compassing the destruction
of Roland he has injured the king and the French nation; the poet denies
Ganelon's claim that these are separable things.

The present volume includes only the first half of the poem, but this
portion has a satisfactory completeness. We see the anger of Ganelon at
Roland, out of which grows his treachery and the attack of the Saracens; the
valor of Roland, and the rest, in battle; and their heroic death. The second
half of the poem relates the vengeance taken by Charles against the Saracens—in two separate battles—and the trial and execution of Ganelon.
Although the *Song of Roland* was the work, and probably the *written* work,
of a well-educated man, during the period immediately following its composition it was sung or chanted. It is divided into strophes averaging fourteen
lines, each of ten (or eleven) syllables.

It is easy to see why modern French readers and critics assign the *Roland*
a high place in their national literature. Inherent in its structure and texture
are the qualities especially esteemed in the French literary tradition—clarity
of focus, lucidity in exposition and narration, definite design, and mastery
of technical detail. In the poem as a whole—even in our abridgment of a

part—scale and proportion are evident. The succession of quarrels, treachery, and battles is only the raw material out of which the poet has built a
highly wrought work of art. The emphasis on action—on what Roland,
Ganelon, and Oliver do and say—has been recognized since Aristotle as the
right method for a poet. But mere action is the formula of the adventure
story. The great-literature standard requires that the action have significance. This significance the author of the *Roland* has provided in rich and
ordered variety. The acts of the hero, of his friend, and of his foe are presented as part of the total character of each; they grow out of the whole man,
including his temperament and personality. But they are also presented against
an ethical and social background. Every act, every decision, bears a relation
to the feudal code of conduct, of right and wrong, and hence is an indication
of human good or evil. Courage rather than cowardice, loyalty rather than
treachery, judgment rather than folly—a belief in these criteria is implicit
or explicit in the presentation of each action. And they apply to the outermost frame within which the poet has placed the specific events of the narrative—the contest between Christianity and paganism. For to the author
and his audience the Christian cause is just, the Saracen, unjust. Roland,
fighting for the crusading Emperor, is *right*; Ganelon, aiding the heathen
enemy against his brother-in-arms, is doubly *wrong*.

The man who brings about the death of Roland and twenty thousand
Franks is no mean and petty villain. The husband of the Emperor's sister
and the stepfather of Roland, he holds a very high place in Charles's council. Nor does he lack the ability or the personality to sustain this position.
He has no hesitation in speaking against Roland in the first discussion of the
Saracen proposals; his nomination as envoy to King Marsile is readily accepted
by Charles; and his success in his treachery is a brilliant feat. For in order to
accomplish it he must first provoke the now peacefully inclined Marsile to
wrath and then turn this anger against Roland. To this end he takes a calculated risk for the sake of a calculated—but far from guaranteed—result.
Insulting Marsile deliberately, in the name of the Emperor, he makes himself the first target of the Saracen king's fury and definitely endangers his
own life. Luckily for him, the king's hand is stayed; and the Saracen nobles
applaud Ganelon's magnificent courage. The rest is comparatively easy—
though everything now depends on Ganelon's success in getting Roland
placed in command of the rear guard. That he succeeds is the more credible
because it was Roland who previously nominated Ganelon for the embassy:
Roland and Charles may be expected to act, as in fact they do, on the
principle that turn about is fair play.

To the twelfth-century poet and his audience of proud knights the question of motive in Ganelon's hatred of Roland doubtless presented little difficulty. Indeed, if Ganelon had not resorted to treason, a tenable defense of
his attitude could be established. For it may well be that he is honestly
opposed to the policy of relentless war against the Saracens. His speech at
the first council, urging acceptance of Marsile's proposals, wins the support
of the wise counselor Naimes, and carries the day. An advocate of peace
would obviously regard the uncompromising spokesman of the war party—
Roland—as his opponent. Later, talking with the Saracen envoy Blancan-

drin, Ganelon plausibly represents Roland as the chief obstacle to pacific relations between the two peoples. To be sure, Ganelon is now plotting against Roland; but that should not blind us to the possibility that he honestly differs with Roland about this question of the Emperor's foreign policy. When we have said this, and when we have recognized the faults in Roland's personality that might normally vex another powerful, but less powerful, courtier, we have said all that can be said in defense of Ganelon. His acts put him quite beyond the possibility of moral justification. But justifying him is one thing; understanding him is quite another, and this the author has enabled us to do.

In Roland the poet has created one of the great heroes of European literature. Like Achilles, Aeneas, and Hamlet, he is the embodiment of a definite ideal of humanity. The ideal that Roland incarnates is that of feudal chivalry. Roland exhibits in superlative degree the traits and attitudes which feudal society and institutions sought to produce in a whole class. He is a supremely valiant fighter, a completely faithful vassal, and a warmly affectionate friend; and, since his creator lived in the early twelfth century, his fervent Christianity bears the Crusader's stamp. His words to his friend Oliver before the battle epitomize his vocation as he sees it:

> A man must bear some hardships for his lord,
> stand everything, the great heat, the great cold,
> lose the hide and hair on him for his good lord.
> Now let each man make sure to strike hard here:
> let them not sing a bad song about us!
> Pagans are wrong and Christians are right!
> They'll make no bad example of me this day!

This is the code of a man of action, of one to whom action appears as duty. Neither here nor elsewhere in the poem is Roland touched by any sense of the "doubtful doom of human kind" that haunts Aeneas. Nor has he ever dreamt of most of the things in Hamlet's philosophy. In assurance and self-reliance he is much closer to Achilles, except that Achilles fought essentially for himself—certainly not for Agamemnon! In Roland the man is wholly assimilated to the vassal. The ceiling above him is lower, the pattern he follows is more limited, than those of Achilles, Aeneas, and Hamlet; yet within his pattern Roland achieves perfection, as they do in theirs.

Roland's feats in battle require no analysis; they are bright and glorious; they outshine the great deeds of his noble comrades. This superiority is no more than the poet has led us to expect. It is the hero's weakness—weakness counterpoised to his greatness—that gives the poem depth and produces the tension that commands our interest. Roland's defect has been called the excess of his special virtue—confidence, courage, bravery; if assurance outstrips prudence, then bravery becomes recklessness, which can bring disaster upon the hero and those for whom he is responsible. The author carefully shows us that Roland has no habit or instinct of caution to match his mar-

velous courage. Charles notes the vindictive manner in which Ganelon proposes Roland for the rear guard, and though at a loss to divine its meaning,
is moved to assign half his entire army to Roland. But Roland either has not
noticed the gleam of triumph in Ganelon's eye, or, if he has, loftily disregards it and firmly refuses to take more than twenty thousand men, a relatively small force.

So far Roland has done nothing definitely wrong, though he has revealed
a certain lack of perception and of intuitive prudence. But he does do wrong
when, surprised by an army of a hundred thousand Saracens, he refuses to
blow the horn that would summon Charles to the rescue. The error is
emphasized by the repetition in Oliver's effort to persuade him, and the
relationship between Roland's refusal and his rashness of character is made
apparent both through his answers and through the contrast with Oliver.
Roland fears that asking for help would make him look foolish among the
Franks—instead, he will slay the foe himself; he will not leave his kin at
home open to reproach because of him; if, as Oliver says, the rearguard is
hopelessly outnumbered, then death is better than disgrace. Actually, Roland
is confident of victory despite the odds. His judgment is not equal to his
daring. As the poet sums it up, "Roland is fierce and Oliver wise."

Hence catastrophe ensues. But it is catastrophe redeemed by glorious her-
oism, as well as self-sacrificing penitence. When, despite tremendous exploits
by the Franks, especially by Roland, all but a handful of the rearguard have
been slain, Roland wishes to sound the horn to let the Emperor know what
has happened. But now Oliver dissents on the ground of honor: Roland had
refused to summon Charles to a rescue, and it would be shameful to summon him only to witness a disaster. The repetitions in this scene balance
those of the earlier one. Though the question is decided by Archbishop
Turpin, the argument has embittered Oliver against Roland. Hence it is that
when, blinded by his own blood, Oliver later strikes Roland, his comrade
has to ask whether the blow was intentional. Roland's humility here is a part
of his penitence, a penitence never put into words but sublimely revealed in
deeds. Exhausted by battle as he is, his superhuman and repeated blasts on
the horn burst his temples. The angels and archangels who receive his soul
in Paradise are functional symbols of his final triumph in defeat. The poet
does not remit the penalty of Roland's error, which is paid by his death. But
his victory combines an epic with a tragic conclusion; atonement and
redemption, not merely death, is the end, as it is in another profoundly
Christian poem of action, Milton's *Samson Agonistes*.

The best summary in English of information about the origin and nature
of the poem is contained in the introduction to the edition by T. A. Jenkins,
*La Chanson de Roland* (1924). For discussion against the background of the
*chanson de geste* in general, see Urban Tigner Holmes, *A History of Old
French Literature* (1938). P. le Gentil, *The "Chanson de Roland"* (1969),
provides technical information in the first half and a more general commentary in the second. J. J. Duggan, *The Song of Roland*, makes the strongest
case for it as the work of an oral poet.

# The Song of Roland[1]

### 1.

CHARLES THE KING, our Emperor, the Great,
has been in Spain for seven full years,
has conquered the high land down to the sea.
There is no castle that stands against him now,
no wall, no citadel left to break down—
except Saragossa, high on a mountain.[2]
King Marsilion holds it, who does not love God,
who serves Mahumet and prays to Apollin.[3]
He cannot save himself: his ruin will find him there. AOI.[4]

### 2.

King Marsilion was in Saragossa.
He has gone forth into a grove, beneath its shade,
and he lies down on a block of blue marble,
twenty thousand men, and more, all around him.
He calls aloud to his dukes and his counts:
"Listen, my lords, to the troubles we have.
The Emperor Charles of the sweet land of France
has come into this country to destroy us.
I have no army able to give him battle,
I do not have the force to break his force.
Now act like my wise men: give me counsel,
save me, save me from death, save me from shame!"
No pagan there has one word to say to him
except Blancandrin, of the castle of Valfunde.

### 3.

One of the wisest pagans was Blancandrin,
brave and loyal, a great mounted warrior,
a useful man, the man to aid his lord;
said to the King: "Do not give way to panic.
Do this: send Charles, that wild, terrible man,
tokens of loyal service and great friendship:
you will give him bears and lions and dogs,
seven hundred camels, a thousand molted hawks,

*(line numbers: 5, 10, 15, 20, 25, 30)*

---

1. Abridged. Translated, with footnotes, by Frederick Goldin. Additional notes provided by the editor.    2. Saragossa, in northeastern Spain, is not actually on a mountain top. The poet's geography is not always accurate.    3. The Greek god Apollo; but the poet is mistaken, for these people worship only one god, Allah. *Mahumet:* A variation of Muhammed, the founder of the Islamic religion.    4. These three mysterious letters appear at certain moments throughout the text, 180 times in all. No one has ever adequately explained them, though every reader feels their effect.

four hundred mules weighed down with gold and silver,
and fifty carts, to cart it all away:
he'll have good wages for his men who fight for pay.
Say he's made war long enough in this land:                    35
let him go home, to France, to Aix,[5] at last—
come Michaelmas you will follow him there,
say you will take their faith, become a Christian,
and be his man with honor, with all you have.
If he wants hostages, why, you'll send them,                   40
ten, or twenty, to give him security.
Let us send him the sons our wives have borne.
I'll send my son with all the others named to die.
It is better that they should lose their heads[6]
than that we, Lord, should lose our dignity                    45
and our honors—and be turned into beggars!" AOI.

4.

Said Blancandrin: "By this right hand of mine
and by this beard that flutters on my chest,
you will soon see the French army disband,
the Franks will go to their own land, to France.             50
When each of them is in his dearest home,
King Charles will be in Aix, in his chapel.
At Michaelmas he will hold a great feast—
that day will come, and then our time runs out,
he'll hear no news, he'll get no word from us.              55
This King is wild, the heart in him is cruel:
he'll take the heads of the hostages we gave.
It is better, Lord, that they lose their heads
than that we lose our bright, our beautiful Spain—
and nothing more for us but misery and pain!"               60
The pagans say: "It may be as he says."

5.

King Marsilion brought his counsel to end,
then he summoned Clarin of Balaguét,
Estramarin and Eudropin, his peer,
And Priamun, Guarlan, that bearded one,                      65
and Machiner and his uncle Maheu,
and Joüner, Malbien from over-sea,
and Blancandrin, to tell what was proposed.

5. Aachen (Aix-la-Chapelle), capital of Charlemagne's empire. *Michaelmas*: The feast of Saint
Michael, September 29.   6. The speaker expects that the hostages will be killed by the French
when the deception becomes clear. Sometime before, hostages sent by the French had been
similarly slain; see 11. 207–09 below.

From the worst of criminals he called these ten.
"Barons, my lords, you're to go to Charlemagne;                     70
he's at the siege of Cordres,[7] the citadel.
Olive branches are to be in your hands—
that signifies peace and humility.
If you've the skill to get me an agreement,
I will give you a mass of gold and silver                           75
and lands and fiefs, as much as you could want."
Say the pagans: "We'll benefit from this!" AOI.

### 6.

Marsilion brought his council to an end,
said to his men: "Lords, you will go on now,
and remember: olive branches in your hands;                         80
and in my name tell Charlemagne the King
for his god's sake to have pity on me—
he will not see a month from this day pass
before I come with a thousand faithful;
say I will take that Christian religion                             85
and be his man in love and loyalty.
If he wants hostages, why, he'll have them."
Said Blancandrin: "Now you will get good terms." AOI.

### 7.

King Marsilion had ten white mules led out,
sent to him once by the King of Suatilie,[8]                        90
with golden bits and saddles wrought with silver.
The men are mounted, the men who brought the message,
and in their hands they carry olive branches.
They came to Charles, who has France in his keeping.
He cannot prevent it: they will fool him. AOI.                      95

### 8.

The Emperor is secure and jubilant:
he has taken Cordres, broken the walls,
knocked down the towers with his catapults.
And what tremendous spoils his knights have won—
gold and silver, precious arms, equipment.                          100
In the city not one pagan remained
who is not killed or turned into a Christian.
The Emperor is in an ample grove,
Roland and Oliver are with him there,
Samson the Duke and Anséis the fierce,                              105

7. Córdoba, in southern Spain.    8. A subordinate king, owing allegiance to Marsilion.

Geoffrey d'Anjou, the King's own standard-bearer;
and Gerin and Gerer, these two together always,
and the others, the simple knights, in force:
fifteen thousand from the sweet land of France.
The warriors sit on bright brocaded silk;                                110
they are playing at tables to pass the time,
the old and the wisest men sitting at chess,
the young light-footed men fencing with swords.
Beneath a pine, beside a wild sweet-briar,
there was a throne, every inch of pure gold.                              115
There sits the King, who rules over sweet France.
His beard is white, his hair flowering white.
That lordly body! the proud fierce look of him!—
If someone should come here asking for him,
     there'd be no need to point out the King of France.
The messengers dismounted, and on their feet                              120
they greeted him in all love and good faith.

          9.

Blancandrin spoke, he was the first to speak,
said to the King: "Greetings, and God save you,
that glorious God whom we all must adore.
Here is the word of the great king Marsilion:                             125
he has looked into this law of salvation,
wants to give you a great part of his wealth,
bears and lions and hunting dogs on chains,
seven hundred camels, a thousand molted hawks,
four hundred mules packed tight with gold and silver,                     130
and fifty carts, to cart it all away;
and there will be so many fine gold bezants,[9]
you'll have good wages for the men in your pay.
You have stayed long—long enough!—in this land,
it is time to go home, to France, to Aix.                                 135
My master swears he will follow you there."
The Emperor holds out his hands toward God,
bows down his head, begins to meditate. AOI.

          10.

The Emperor held his head bowed down;
never was he too hasty with his words:                                    140
his custom is to speak in his good time.
When his head rises, how fierce the look of him;
he said to them: "You have spoken quite well.

---

9. Gold coins; the name is derived from Byzantium.

King Marsilion is my great enemy.
Now all these words that you have spoken here—       145
how far can I trust them? How can I be sure?"
The Saracen: "He wants to give you hostages.
How many will you want? ten? fifteen? twenty?
I'll put my son with the others named to die.[1]
You will get some, I think, still better born.       150
When you are at home in your high royal palace,
at the great feast of Saint Michael-in-Peril,[2]
the lord who nurtures me will follow you,
and in those baths[3]—the baths God made for you—
my lord will come and want to be made Christian."       155
King Charles replies: "He may yet save his soul." AOI.

### 11.

Late in the day it was fair, the sun was bright.
Charles has them put the ten mules into stables.
The King commands a tent pitched in the broad grove,
and there he has the ten messengers lodged;       160
twelve serving men took splendid care of them.
There they remained that night till the bright day.
The Emperor rose early in the morning,
the King of France, and heard the mass and matins.
And then the King went forth beneath a pine,       165
calls for his barons to complete his council:
he will proceed only with the men of France. AOI.

### 12.

The Emperor goes forth beneath a pine,
calls for his barons to complete his council:
Ogier the Duke, and Archbishop Turpin,       170
Richard the Old, and his nephew Henri;
from Gascony, the brave Count Acelin,
Thibaut of Reims, and his cousin Milun;
and Gerer and Gerin, they were both there,
and there was Count Roland, he came with them,       175
and Oliver, the valiant and well-born;
a thousand Franks of France, and more, were there.
Ganelon came, who committed the treason.[4]
Now here begins the council that went wrong. AOI.

---

1. That is, if the promise is broken. *Saracen:* The usual term for the enemy.   2. The epithet
"in peril of the sea" was applied to the famous sanctuary of Saint Michael on the Normandy coast
because it could only be reached on foot at low tide, and pilgrims were endangered by the incom-
ing tide; eventually the phrase was applied to the saint himself.   3. Famous healing springs at
Aix.   4. The poet anticipates the treason that Ganelon will commit. The next line represents a
similar anticipation: the plan adopted at the council will prove to be a mistake.

13.

"Barons, my lords," said Charles the Emperor,                    180
"King Marsilion has sent me messengers,
wants to give me a great mass of his wealth,
bears and lions and hunting dogs on chains,
seven hundred camels, a thousand molting hawks,
four hundred mules packed with gold of Araby,         185
and with all that, more than fifty great carts;
but also asks that I go back to France:
he'll follow me to Aix, my residence,
and take our faith, the one redeeming faith,
become a Christian, hold his march[5] lands from me.   190
But what lies in his heart? I do not know."
And the French say: "We must be on our guard!" AOI.

14.

The Emperor has told them what was proposed.
Roland the Count will never assent to that,
gets to his feet, comes forth to speak against it;    195
says to the King: "Trust Marsilion—and suffer!
We came to Spain seven long years ago,
I won Noples for you, I won Commibles,
I took Valterne and all the land of Pine,
and Balaguer and Tudela and Seville.                  200
And then this king, Marsilion, played the traitor:
he sent you men, fifteen of his pagans—
and sure enough, each held an olive branch;
and they recited just these same words to you.
You took counsel with all your men of France;        205
they counseled you to a bit of madness:
you sent two Counts across to the Pagans,
one was Basan, the other was Basile.
On the hills below Haltille, he took their heads.
They were your men. Fight the war you came to fight!  210
Lead the army you summoned on to Saragossa!
Lay siege to it all the rest of your life!
Avenge the men that this criminal murdered!" AOI.

15.

The Emperor held his head bowed down with this,
and stroked his beard, and smoothed his mustache down,   215
and speaks no word, good or bad, to his nephew.
The French keep still, all except Ganelon:

5. A frontier province or territory.

he gets to his feet and, come before King Charles,
how fierce he is as he begins his speech;
said to the King: "Believe a fool—me or                    220
another—and suffer! Protect your interest!
When Marsilion the King sends you his word
that he will join his hands[6] and be your man,
and hold all Spain as a gift from your hands
and then receive the faith that we uphold—                    225
whoever urges that we refuse this peace,
that man does not care, Lord, what death we die.
That wild man's counsel must not win the day here—
let us leave fools, let us hold with wise men!" AOI.

#### 16.

And after that there came Naimon the Duke—                    230
no greater vassal in that court than Naimon—
said to the King: "You've heard it clearly now,
Count Ganelon has given you your answer:
let it be heeded, there is wisdom in it.
King Marsilion is beaten in this war,                    235
you have taken every one of his castles,
broken his walls with your catapults,
burnt his cities and defeated his men.
Now when he sends to ask you to have mercy,
it would be a sin to do still more to him.                    240
Since he'll give you hostages as guarantee,
this great war must not go on, it is not right."
And the French say: "The Duke has spoken well." AOI.

#### 17.

"Barons, my lords, whom shall we send down there,
to Saragossa, to King Marsilion?"                    245
Naimon replies, "I'll go, if you grant it!
At once, my lord! give me the glove and the staff."[7]
The King replies: "You're a man of great wisdom:
now by my beard, now by this mustache of mine,
*you* will not go so far from me this year; or ever.                    250
Go take your seat when no one calls on you."

#### 18.

"Barons, my lords, whom can we send down there,
to this Saracen who holds Saragossa?"
Roland replies: "I can go there! No trouble!"

6. Part of the gesture of homage; the lord enclosed the joined hands of his vassal with his own hands.    7. Symbols of his commission from the Emperor Charles.

"No, no, not you!" said Oliver the Count,                                255
"that heart in you is wild, spoils for a fight,
how I would worry—you'd fight with them, I know.
Now I myself could go, if the King wishes."
The King replies: "Be still, the two of you!
Not you, not he—neither will set foot there.                             260
Now by this beard, as sure as you see white,
let no man here name one of the Twelve Peers!"
The French keep still, see how he silenced them.


     19.
Turpin of Reims has come forth from the ranks,
said to the King: "Let your Franks have a rest.                          265
You have been in this land for seven years,
the many pains, the struggles they've endured!
I'm the one, Lord, give me the glove and the staff,
and I'll go down to this Saracen of Spain
and then I'll see what kind of man we have."                             270
The Emperor replies to him in anger:
"Now you go back and sit on that white silk
and say no more unless I command it!" AOI.


     20.
"My noble knights," said the Emperor Charles,
"choose me one man: a baron from my march,                               275
to bring my message to King Marsilion."[8]
And Roland said: "Ganelon, my stepfather."
The French respond: "Why, that's the very man!
pass this man by and you won't send a wiser."
And hearing this Count Ganelon began to choke,                           280
pulls from his neck the great furs of marten
and stands there now, in his silken tunic,
eyes full of lights, the look on him of fury,
he has the body, the great chest of a lord;
stood there so fair, all his peers gazed on him;                        285
said to Roland: "Madman, what makes you rave?
Every man knows I am your stepfather,
yet you named me to go to Marsilion.
Now if God grants that I come back from there,
you will have trouble: I'll start a feud with you,                       290
it will go on till the end of your life."
Roland replies: "What wild words—all that blustering!
Every man knows that threats don't worry me.

8. Charlemagne wants them to choose a baron from an outlying region and not one of the Twelve
Peers, the circle of his dearest men.

But we need a wise man to bring the message:
if the King wills, I'll gladly go in your place."                                295

### 21.

Ganelon answers: "You will not go for me. AOI.
You're not my man, and I am not your lord.
Charles commands me to perform this service:
I'll go to Marsilion in Saragossa.
And I tell you, I'll play a few wild tricks                                       300
before I cool the anger in me now."
When he heard that, Roland began to laugh. AOI.

### 22.

Ganelon sees: *Roland laughing at him!*
and feels such pain he almost bursts with rage,
needs little more to go out of his mind;                                          305
says to the Count: "I have no love for you,
you *made* this choice fall on me, and that was wrong.
Just Emperor, here I am, before you.
I have one will: to fulfill your command."

### 23.

"I know now I must go to Saragossa. AOI.                                           310
Any man who goes there cannot return.
And there is this: I am your sister's husband,
have a son by her, the finest boy there can be,
Baldewin," says he, "who will be a good man.
To him I leave my honors, fiefs, and lands.                                        315
Protect my son: these eyes will never see him."
Charles answers him: "That tender heart of yours!
You have to go, I have commanded it."

### 24.

And the King said: "Ganelon, come forward, AOI.
come and receive the staff and the glove.                                         320
You have heard it: the Franks have chosen you."
Said Ganelon: "Lord, it's Roland who did this.
In all my days I'll have no love for him,
or Oliver, because he's his companion,
or the Twelve Peers, because they love him so.                                    325
I defy them, here in your presence, Lord."
And the King said: "What hate there is in you!
You will go there, for I command you to."
"I can go there, but I'll have no protector. AOI.
Basile had none, nor did Basan his brother."                                      330

25.

The Emperor offers him his right glove.
But Ganelon would have liked not to be there.
When he had to take it, it fell to the ground.
"God!" say the French, "What's that going to mean?
What disaster will this message bring us!"                           335
Said Ganelon: "Lords, you'll be hearing news."

26.

Said Ganelon: "Lord, give me leave to go,
since go I must, there's no reason to linger."
And the King said: "In Jesus' name and mine,"
absolved him and blessed him with his right hand.          340
Then he gave him the letter and the staff.

27.

Count Ganelon goes away to his camp.
He chooses, with great care, his battle-gear,
picks the most precious arms that he can find.
The spurs he fastened on were golden spurs;                   345
he girds his sword, Murgleis, upon his side;
he has mounted Tachebrun, his battle horse,
his uncle, Guinemer, held the stirrup.
And there you would have seen brave men in tears,
his men, who say: "Baron, what bad luck for you!           350
All your long years in the court of the King,
always proclaimed a great and noble vassal!
Whoever it was doomed you to go down there—
Charlemagne himself will not protect that man.
Roland the Count should not have thought of this—        355
and you the living issue of a mighty line!"
And then they say: "Lord, take us there with you!"
Ganelon answers: "May the Lord God forbid!
It is better that I alone should die
than so many good men and noble knights.
You will be going back, Lords, to sweet France:              360
go to my wife and greet her in my name,
and Pinabel, my dear friend and peer,
and Baldewin, my son, whom you all know:
give him your aid, and hold him as your lord."
And he starts down the road; he is on his way. AOI.        365

28.

Ganelon rides to a tall olive tree,
there he has joined the pagan messengers.

And here is Blancandrin, who slows down for him:
and what great art they speak to one another.
Said Blancandrin: "An amazing man, Charles! 370
conquered Apulia, conquered all of Calabria,
crossed the salt sea on his way into England,
won its tribute,[9] got Peter's pence for Rome:
what does he want from us here in our march?"
Ganelon answers: "That is the heart in him. 375
There'll never be a man the like of him." AOI.

### 29.

Said Blancandrin: "The Franks are a great people.
Now what great harm all those dukes and counts do
to their own lord when they give him such counsel:
they torment him, they'll destroy him, and others." 380
Ganelon answers: "Well, now, I know no such man
except Roland, who'll suffer for it yet.
One day the Emperor was sitting in the shade:
his nephew came, still wearing his hauberk,
he had gone plundering near Carcassonne; 385
and in his hand he held a bright red apple:
'Dear Lord, here, take,' said Roland to his uncle;
'I offer you the crowns of all earth's kings.'
Yes, Lord, that pride of his will destroy him,
for every day he goes riding at death. 390
And *should* someone kill him, we would have peace." AOI.

### 30.

Said Blancandrin: "A wild man, this Roland!
wants to make every nation beg for his mercy
and claims a right to every land on earth!
But what men support him, if that is his aim?" 395
Ganelon answers: "Why, Lord, the men of France.
They love him so, they will never fail him.
He gives them gifts, masses of gold and silver,
mules, battle horses, brocaded silks, supplies.
And it is all as the Emperor desires: 400
he'll win the lands from here to the Orient." AOI.

### 31.

Ganelon and Blancandrin rode on until
each pledged his faith to the other and swore

9. Although begun perhaps as early as the eighth century, it was not due to any effort of Charlemagne, who did not in fact visit England. Peter's pence: A tribute of one penny per house "for the use of Saint Peter," that is, for the Pope in Rome.

they'd find a way to have Count Roland killed.
They rode along the paths and ways until,                          405
in Saragossa, they dismount beneath a yew.
There was a throne in the shade of a pine,
covered with silk from Alexandria.
There sat the king who held the land of Spain,
and around him twenty thousand Saracens.                           410
There is no man who speaks or breathes a word,
poised for the news that all would like to hear.
Now here they are: Ganelon and Blancandrin.

### 32.

Blancandrin came before Marsilion,
his hand around the fist of Ganelon,                               415
said to the King: "May Mahumet save you,
and Apollin, whose sacred laws we keep!
We delivered your message to Charlemagne:
when we finished, he raised up both his hands
and praised his god. He made no other answer.                     420
Here he sends you one of his noble barons,
a man of France, and very powerful.
You'll learn from him whether or not you'll have peace."
"Let him speak, we shall hear him," Marsilion answers. AOI.

### 33.

But Ganelon had it all well thought out.                          425
With what great art he commences his speech,
a man who knows his way about these things;
·said to the King: "May the Lord God save you,
that glorious God, whom we must all adore.
Here is the word of Charlemagne the King:                         430
you are to take the holy Christian faith;
he will give you one half of Spain in fief.
If you refuse, if you reject this peace,
you will be taken by force, put into chains,
and then led forth to the King's seat at Aix;                     435
you will be tried; you will be put to death:
you will die there, in shame, vilely, degraded."
King Marsilion, hearing this, was much shaken.
In his hand was a spear, with golden feathers.
He would have struck, had they not held him back. AOI.          440

### 34.

Marsilion the King—his color changed!
He shook his spear, waved the shaft to and fro.

When he saw that, Ganelon laid hand to sword,
he drew it out two fingers from its sheath;
and spoke to it: "How beautiful and bright!                    445
How long did I bear you in the King's court
before I died! The Emperor will not say
I died alone in that foreign country:
they'll buy you first, with the best men they have!"
The pagans say: "Let us break up this quarrel!"                    450


   35.
The pagan chiefs pleaded with Marsilion
till he sat down once again on his throne.
The Caliph[1] spoke: "You did us harm just now,
served us badly, trying to strike this Frenchman.
You should have listened, you should have heard him out."                    455
Said Ganelon: "Lord, I must endure it.
I shall not fail, for all the gold God made,
for all the wealth there may be in this land,
to tell him, as long as I have breath, all
that Charlemagne—that great and mighty King!—                    460
has sent through me to his mortal enemy."
He is buckled in a great cloak of sable,
covered with silk from Alexandria:
he throws it down. Blancandrin picks it up.
But his great sword he will never throw down!                    465
In his right fist he grasps its golden pommel.
Say the pagans: "That's a great man! A noble!" AOI.


   36.
Now Ganelon drew closer to the King
and said to him: "You are wrong to get angry,
for Charles, who rules all France, sends you this word:                    470
you are to take the Christian people's faith;
he will give you one half of Spain in fief,
the other half goes to his nephew: Roland—
quite a partner you will be getting there!
If you refuse, if you reject this peace,                    475
he will come and lay siege to Saragossa;
you will be taken by force, put into chains,
and brought straight on to Aix, the capital.
No saddle horse, no war horse for you then,
no he-mule, no she-mule for you to ride:                    480
you will be thrown on some miserable dray;

---

1. A high official of King Marsilion.

you will be tried, and you will lose your head.
Our Emperor sends you this letter."
He put the letter in the pagan's right fist.

### 37.

Marsilion turned white; he was enraged;                    485
he breaks the seal, he's knocked away the wax,
runs through the letter, sees what is written there:
"Charles sends me word, this king who rules in France:
I'm to think of his anger and his grief—
he means Basan and his brother Basile,                     490
I took their heads in the hills below Haltille;
if I want to redeem the life of my body,
I must send him my uncle: the Algalife.[2]
And otherwise he'll have no love for me."
Then his son came and spoke to Marsilion,                  495
said to the King: 'Ganelon has spoken madness.
He crossed the line, he has no right to live.
Give him to me, I will do justice on him."
When he heard that, Ganelon brandished his sword;
he runs to the pine, set his back against the trunk.       500

### 38.

King Marsilion went forth into the orchard,
he takes with him the greatest of his men;
Blancandrin came, that gray-haired counselor,
and Jurfaleu, Marsilion's son and heir,
the Algalife, uncle and faithful friend.                   505
Said Blancandrin: "Lord, call the Frenchman back.
He swore to me to keep faith with our cause."
And the King said: "Go, bring him back here, then."
He took Ganelon's right hand by the fingers,
leads him into the orchard before the King.                510
And there they plotted that criminal treason. AOI.

### 39.

Said Marsilion: "My dear Lord Ganelon,
that was foolish, what I just did to you,
I showed my anger, even tried to strike you.
Here's a pledge of good faith, these sable furs,           515
the gold alone worth over five hundred pounds:
I'll make it all up before tomorrow night."

2. The Caliph.

Ganelon answers: "I will not refuse it.
May it please God to reward you for it." AOI.


40.
Said Marsilion: "I tell you, Ganelon,                              520
I have a great desire to love you dearly.
I want to hear you speak of Charlemagne.
He is so old, he's used up all his time—
from what I hear, he is past two hundred!
He has pushed his old body through so many lands,               525
taken so many blows on his buckled shield,
made beggars of so many mighty kings:
when will he lose the heart for making war?"
Ganelon answers: "Charles is not one to lose heart.
No man sees him, no man learns to know him                      530
who does not say: the Emperor is great.
I do not know how to praise him so highly
that his great merit would not surpass my praise.
Who could recount his glory and his valor?
God put the light in him of such lordliness,                    535
he would choose death before he failed his barons."


41.
Said the pagan: "I have reason to marvel
at Charlemagne, a man so old and gray—
he's two hundred years old, I hear, and more;
he has tortured his body through so many lands,                 540
and borne so many blows from lance and spear,
made beggars of so many mighty kings:
when will he lose the heart for making war?"
"Never," said Ganelon, "while his nephew lives,
he's a fighter, there's no vassal like him                      545
        under the vault of heaven. And he has friends.
There's Oliver, a good man, his companion.
And the Twelve Peers, whom Charles holds very dear,
form the vanguard, with twenty thousand knights.
Charles is secure, he fears no man on earth." AOI.


42.
Said the pagan: "Truly, how I must marvel                       550
at Charlemagne, who is so gray and white—
over two hundred years, from what I hear;
gone through so many lands a conqueror,
and borne so many blows from strong sharp spears,

killed and conquered so many mighty kings:     555
when will he lose the heart for making war?"
"Never," said Ganelon, "while one man lives: Roland!
no man like him from here to the Orient!
There's his companion, Oliver, a brave man.
And the Twelve Peers, whom Charles holds very dear,     560
form the vanguard, with twenty thousand Franks.
Charles is secure, he fears no man alive." AOI.

      43.
"Dear Lord Ganelon," said Marsilion the King,
"I have my army, you won't find one more handsome:
I can muster four hundred thousand knights!     565
With this host, now, can I fight Charles and the French?"
Ganelon answers: "No, no, don't try that now,
you'd take a loss: thousands of your pagans!
Forget such foolishness, listen to wisdom:
send the Emperor so many gifts     570
there'll be no Frenchman there who does not marvel.
For twenty hostages—those you'll be sending—
he will go home: home again to sweet France!
And he will leave his rear-guard behind him.
There will be Roland, I do believe, his nephew,     575
and Oliver, brave man, born to the court.
These Counts are dead, if anyone trusts me.
Then Charles will see that great pride of his go down,
he'll have no heart to make war on you again." AOI.

      44.
"Dear Lord Ganelon," said Marsilion the King,     580
"What must I do to kill Roland the Count?"
Ganelon answers: "Now I can tell you that.
The King will be at Cize,[3] in the great passes,
he will have placed his rear-guard at his back:
there'll be his nephew, Count Roland, that great man,     585
and Oliver, in whom he puts such faith,
and twenty thousand Franks in their company.
Now send one hundred thousand of your pagans
against the French—let them give the first battle.
The French army will be hit hard and shaken.     590
I must tell you: your men will be martyred.
Give them a second battle, then, like the first.
One will get him, Roland will not escape.

3. The pass through the Pyrenees.

Then you'll have done a deed, a noble deed,
and no more war for the rest of your life!" AOI.                    595

    45.
"If someone can bring about the death of Roland,
then Charles would lose the right arm of his body,
that marvelous army would disappear—
never again could Charles gather such forces.
Then peace at last for the Land of Fathers!"[4]                    600
When Marsilion heard that, he kissed his neck.
Then he begins to open up his treasures. AOI.

    46.
Marsilion said, "Why talk. . . .
No plan has any worth which one. . . .[5]
Now swear to me that you will betray Roland."                    605
Ganelon answers: "Let it be as you wish."
On the relics in his great sword Murgleis
he swore treason and became a criminal. AOI.

    47.
There stood a throne made all of ivory.
Marsilion commands them bring forth a book:                    610
it was the law of Mahum and Tervagant.[6]
This is the vow sworn by the Saracen of Spain:
if he shall find Roland in the rear-guard,
he shall fight him, all his men shall fight him,
and once he finds Roland, Roland will die.                    615
Says Ganelon: "May it be as you will." AOI.

    48.
And now there came a pagan, Valdabrun,
he was the man who raised Marsilion.
And, all bright smiles, he said to Ganelon:
"You take my sword, there's no man has one better:                    620
a thousand coins, and more, are in the hilt.
It is a gift, dear lord, made in friendship,
only help us to Roland, that great baron,
let us find him standing in the rear-guard."
"It shall be done," replies Count Ganelon.                    625
And then they kissed, on the face, on the chin.

---

4. *Tere Major*, in the text, can mean either "the great land," or "the land of fathers, ancestors."
It always refers to France.    5. Parts of lines 603–604 are unintelligible in the manuscript.
6. A fictitious deity whom the poet mistakenly says the Saracens worshipped.

49.

And there came then a pagan, Climborin,
and, all bright smiles, he said to Ganelon:
"You take my helmet, I never saw one better,
only help us to Roland, lord of the march,                    630
show us the way to put Roland to shame."
"It shall be done," replied Count Ganelon.
And then they kissed, on the face, on the mouth. AOI.

50.

And then there came the Queen, Bramimunde;
said to the Count: "Lord, I love you well,                    635
for my lord and all his men esteem you so.
I wish to send your wife two necklaces,
they are all gold, jacinths, and amethysts,
they are worth more than all the wealth of Rome.
Your Emperor has never seen their like."                      640
He has taken them, thrusts them into his boot. AOI.

51.

The King calls for Malduit, his treasurer:
"The gifts for Charles—is everything prepared?"
And he replies: "Yes, Lord, and well prepared:
seven hundred camels, packed with gold and silver,           645
and twenty hostages, the noblest under heaven." AOI.

52.

Marsilion took Ganelon by the shoulder
and said to him: "You're a brave man, a wise man.
Now by that faith you think will save your soul,
take care you do not turn your heart from us.                 650
I will give you a great mass of my wealth,
ten mules weighed down with fine Arabian gold;
and come each year, I'll do the same again.
Now you take these, the keys to this vast city:
present King Charles with all of its great treasure;          655
then get me Roland picked for the rear-guard.
Let me find him in some defile or pass,
I will fight him, a battle to the death."
Ganelon answers: "It's high time that I go."
Now he is mounted, and he is on his way. AOI.               660

53.

The Emperor moves homeward, he's drawing near.
Now he has reached the city of Valterne:
Roland had stormed it, destroyed it, and it stood

from that day forth a hundred years laid waste.
Charles is waiting for news of Ganelon                        665
and the tribute from Spain, from that great land.
In the morning, at dawn, with the first light,
Count Ganelon came to the Christian camp. AOI.

54.
The Emperor rose early in the morning,
the King of France, and has heard mass and matins.       670
On the green grass he stood before his tent.
Roland was there, and Oliver, brave man,
Naimon the Duke, and many other knights.
Ganelon came, the traitor, the foresworn.
With what great cunning he commences his speech;        675
said to the King: "May the Lord God save you!
Here I bring you the keys to Saragossa.
And I bring you great treasure from that city,
and twenty hostages, have them well guarded.
And good King Marsilion sends you this word:             680
Do not blame him concerning the Algalife:
I saw it all myself, with my own eyes:
four hundred thousand men, and all in arms,
their hauberks on, some with their helms laced on,
swords on their belts, the hilts enameled gold,
who went with him to the edge of the sea.                685
They are in flight: it is the Christian faith—
they do not want it, they will not keep its law.
They had not sailed four full leagues out to sea
when a high wind, a tempest swept them up.
They were all drowned; you will never see them;         690
if he were still alive, I'd have brought him.
As for the pagan King, Lord, believe this:
before you see one month from this day pass,
he'll follow you to the Kingdom of France
and take the faith—he will take your faith, Lord,       695
and join his hands and become your vassal.
He will hold Spain as a fief from your hand."
Then the King said: "May God be thanked for this.
You have done well, you will be well rewarded."
Throughout the host they sound a thousand trumpets.     700
The French break camp, strap their gear on their pack-horses.
They take the road to the sweet land of France. AOI.

55.
King Charlemagne laid waste the land of Spain,
stormed its castles, ravaged its citadels.

The King declares his war is at an end.                                    705
The Emperor rides toward the land of sweet France.
Roland the Count affixed the gonfanon,[7]
raised it toward heaven on the height of a hill;
the men of France make camp across that country.
Pagans are riding up through these great valleys,                          710
their hauberks on, their tunics of double mail,
their helms laced on, their swords fixed on their belts,
shields on their necks, lances trimmed with their banners.
In a forest high in the hills they gathered:
four hundred thousand men waiting for dawn.                                 715
God, the pity of it! the French do not know! AOI.

     56.
The day goes by; now the darkness of night.
Charlemagne sleeps, the mighty Emperor.
He dreamt he was at Cize, in the great passes,
and in his fists held his great ashen lance.                               720
Count Ganelon tore it away from him
and brandished it, shook it with such fury
the splinters of the shaft fly up toward heaven.
Charlemagne sleeps, his dream does not wake him.

     57.
And after that he dreamed another vision:                                  725
he was in France, in his chapel at Aix,
a cruel wild boar was biting his right arm;
saw coming at him—from the Ardennes—a leopard,
it attacked him, fell wildly on his body.
And a swift hound running down from the hall                               730
came galloping, bounding over to Charles,
tore the right ear off that first beast, the boar,
turns, in fury, to fight against the leopard.
And the French say: It is a mighty battle,
but cannot tell which one of them will win.                                735
Charlemagne sleeps, his dream does not wake him. AOI.

     58.
The day goes by, and the bright dawn arises.
Throughout that host. . . .[8]
The Emperor rides forth with such fierce pride.
"Barons, my lords," said the Emperor Charles,                              740
"look at those passes, at those narrow defiles—

---

7. Pennant.     8. Second hemistich unintelligible in the manuscript.

pick me a man to command the rear-guard."
Ganelon answers: "Roland, here, my stepson.
You have no baron as great and brave as Roland."
When he hears that, the King stares at him in fury;                745
and said to him: "You are the living devil,
a mad dog—the murderous rage in you!
And who will precede me, in the vanguard?"
Ganelon answers, "Why, Ogier of Denmark,
you have no baron who could lead it so well."                    750

### 59.

Roland the Count, when he heard himself named,
knew what to say, and spoke as a knight must speak:
"Lord Stepfather, I have to cherish you!
You have had the rear-guard assigned to me.
Charles will not lose, this great King who rules France,          755
I swear it now, one palfrey, one war horse—
        while I'm alive and know what's happening—
one he-mule, one she-mule that he might ride,
Charles will not lose one sumpter, not one pack horse
that has not first been bought and paid for with swords."
Ganelon answers: "You speak the truth, I know." AOI.              760

### 60.

When Roland hears he will lead the rear-guard,
he spoke in great fury to his stepfather:
"Hah! you nobody, you base-born little fellow,
and did you think the glove would fall from my hands
as the staff fell from yours before King Charles?"[9] AOI.        765

### 61.

"Just Emperor," said Roland, that great man,
"give me the bow that you hold in your hand.
And no man here, I think, will say in reproach
I let it drop, as Ganelon let the staff drop
from his right hand, when he should have taken it."              770
The Emperor bowed down his head with this,
he pulled his beard, he twisted his mustache,
cannot hold back, tears fill his eyes, he weeps.

### 62.

And after that there came Naimon the Duke,
no greater vassal in the court than Naimon,                      775

9. Ganelon had let fall a glove, not a staff (line 333). For this and other less objective reasons, some editors have questioned the authenticity of this *laisse*. In the following *laisse*, at line 769, a reviser tried to make the text more consistent by adding the reference to the staff.

said to the King: "You've heard it clearly now:
it is Count Roland. How furious he is.
He is the one to whom the rear-guard falls,
no baron here can ever change that now.
Give him the bow that you have stretched and bent,          780
and then find him good men to stand with him."
The King gives him the bow; Roland has it now.

        63.
The Emperor calls forth Roland the Count:
"My lord, my dear nephew, of course you know
I will give you half my men, they are yours.          785
Let them serve you, it is your salvation."
"None of that!" said the Count. "May God strike me
if I discredit the history of my line.
I'll keep twenty thousand Franks—they are good men.
Go your way through the passes, you will be safe.          790
You must not fear any man while I live."

        64.
Roland the Count mounted his battle horse. AOI.
Oliver came to him, his companion.
And Gerin came, and the brave Count Gerer,
and Aton came, and there came Berenger,          795
And Astor came, and Anseïs, fierce and proud,
and the old man Gerard of Roussillon,
and Gaifier, that great and mighty duke.
Said the Archbishop: "I'm going, by my head!"
"And I with you," said Gautier the Count,          800
"I am Count Roland's man and must not fail him."
And together they choose twenty thousand men. AOI.

        65.
Roland the Count summons Gautier de l'Hum:
"Now take a thousand Franks from our land, France,
and occupy those passes and the heights there.          805
The Emperor must not lose a single man." AOI.
Gautier replies: "Lord, I'll fight well for you."
And with a thousand French of France, their land,
Gautier rides out to the hills and defiles;
will not come down, for all the bad news, again,          810
till seven hundred swords have been drawn out.
King Almaris of the Kingdom of Belferne
gave them battle that day, and it was bitter.

66.

High are the hills, the valleys tenebrous,
the cliffs are dark, the defiles mysterious.                    815
That day, and with much pain, the French passed through.
For fifteen leagues around one heard their clamor.
When they reach Tere Majur, the Land of Fathers,
they beheld Gascony, their lord's domain.
Then they remembered: their fiefs, their realms, their honors,    820
remembered their young girls, their gentle wives:
not one who does not weep for what he feels.
Beyond these others King Charles is in bad straits:
his nephew left in the defiles of Spain!
feels the pity of it; tears break through. AOI.                    825

67.

And the Twelve Peers are left behind in Spain,
and twenty thousand Franks are left with them.
They have no fear, they have no dread of death.
The Emperor is going home to France.
Beneath his cloak, his face shows all he feels.                    830
Naimon the Duke is riding beside him;
and he said to the King: "What is this grief?"
And Charles replies: "Whoever asks me, wrongs me.
I feel such pain, I cannot keep from wailing.
France will be destroyed by Ganelon.                               835
Last night I saw a vision brought by angels:
the one who named my nephew for the rear-guard
shattered the lance between my fists to pieces.
I have left him in a march among strangers.
If I lose him, God! I won't find his like." AOI.                   840

68.

King Charles the Great cannot keep from weeping.
A hundred thousand Franks feel pity for him;
and for Roland, an amazing fear.
Ganelon the criminal has betrayed him;
got gifts for it from the pagan king,                              845
gold and silver, cloths of silk, gold brocade,
mules and horses and camels and lions.
Marsilion sends for the barons of Spain,
counts and viscounts and dukes and almaçurs,
and the emirs,[1] and the sons of great lords:                    850

1. *Almaçurs . . . emirs:* Lords of high rank.

four hundred thousand assembled in three days.
In Saragossa he has them beat the drums,
they raise Mahumet upon the highest tower:
no pagan now who does not worship him
and adore him. Then they ride, racing each other,　855
search through the land, the valleys, the mountains;
and then they saw the banners of the French.
The rear-guard of the Twelve Companions
will not fail now, they'll give the pagans battle.


69.

Marsilion's nephew has come forward　　　　　860
riding a mule that he goads with a stick;
said—a warrior's laugh on him—to his uncle:
"Dear Lord and King, how long I have served you,
and all the troubles, the pains I have endured,
so many battles fought and won on the field　865
Give me a fief, the first blow at Roland.
I will kill him, here's the spear I'll do it with.
If Mahumet will only stand by me,
I will set free every strip of land in Spain,
from the passes of Aspre to Durestant.　　　870
Charles will be weary, his Franks will give it up:
and no more war for the rest of your life!"
King Marsilion gave him his glove, as sign. AOI.


70.

The King's nephew holds the glove in his fist,
speaks these proud words to Marsilion his uncle:　875
"You've given me, dear Lord, King, a great gift!
Choose me twelve men, twelve of your noble barons,
and I will fight against the Twelve Companions."
And Falsaron was the first to respond—
he was the brother of King Marsilion:　　　880
"Dear Lord, Nephew, it's you and I together!
We'll fight, that's sure! We'll battle the rear-guard
of Charlemagne's grand army! We are the ones!
We have been chosen. We'll kill them all! It is fated." AOI.


71.

And now again: there comes King Corsablis,　885
a Berber, a bad man, a man of cunning;
and now he spoke as a brave vassal speaks:
for all God's gold he would not be a coward.
Now rushing up: Malprimis de Brigal,

faster on his two feet than any horse;                              890
and cries great-voiced before Marsilion:
"I'm on my way to Rencesvals to fight!
Let me find Roland, I won't stop till I kill him!"

[Lines 894–993 continue the rollcall of volunteers.]

        79.
They arm themselves in Saracen hauberks,
all but a few are lined with triple mail;                           995
they lace on their good helms of Saragossa,
gird on their swords, the steel forged in Vienne;
they have rich shields, spears of Valencia,
and gonfanons of white and blue and red.
They leave the mules and riding horses now,                        1000
mount their war horses and ride in close array.
The day was fair, the sun was shining bright,
all their armor was aflame with the light;
a thousand trumpets blow: that was to make it finer.
That made a great noise, and the men of France heard.              1005
Said Oliver: "Companion, I believe
we may yet have a battle with the pagans."
Roland replies: "Now may God grant us that.
We know our duty: to stand here for our King.
A man must bear some hardships for his lord,                       1010
stand everything, the great heat, the great cold,
lose the hide and hair on him for his good lord.
Now let each man make sure to strike hard here:
let them not sing a bad song about us!
Pagans are wrong and Christians are right!                         1015
They'll make no bad example of me this day!" AOI.

        80.
Oliver climbs to the top of a hill,
looks to his right, across a grassy vale,
sees the pagan army on its way there;
and called down to Roland, his companion:                          1020
"That way, toward Spain: the uproar I see coming!
All their hauberks, all blazing, helmets like flames!
It will be a bitter thing for our French.
Ganelon knew, that criminal, that traitor,
when he marked us out before the Emperor."                         1025
"Be still, Oliver," Roland the Count replies.
"He is my stepfather—my stepfather.
        I won't have you speak one word against him."

### 81.

Oliver has gone up upon a hill,
sees clearly now: the kingdom of Spain,
and the Saracens assembled in such numbers:          1030
helmets blazing, bedecked with gems in gold,
those shields of theirs, those hauberks sewn with brass,
and all their spears, the gonfanons affixed;
cannot begin to count their battle corps,
there are too many, he cannot take their number.          1035
And he is deeply troubled by what he sees.
He made his way quickly down from the hill,
came to the French, told them all he had seen.

### 82.

Said Oliver: "I saw the Saracens,
no man on earth ever saw more of them—          1040
one hundred thousand, with their shields, up in front,
helmets laced on, hauberks blazing on them,
the shafts straight up, the iron heads like flames—
you'll get a battle, nothing like it before.
My lords, my French, may God give you the strength.          1045
Hold your ground now! Let them not defeat us!"
And the French say: "God hate the man who runs!
We may die here, but no man will fail you." AOI.

### 83.

Said Oliver: "The pagan force is great;
from what I see, our French here are too few.          1050
Roland, my companion, sound your horn then,
Charles will hear it, the army will come back."
Roland replies: "I'd be a fool to do it.
I would lose my good name all through sweet France.
I will strike now, I'll strike with Durendal,          1055
the blade will be bloody to the gold from striking!
These pagan traitors came to these passes doomed!
I promise you, they are marked men, they'll die." AOI.

### 84.

"Roland, Companion, now sound the olifant,[2]
Charles will hear it, he will bring the army back,          1060
the King will come with all his barons to help us."
Roland replies: "May it never please God

---

2. The word (which is a form of "elephant") means (a) "ivory," (b) "a horn made of ivory," and
is used specifically, almost as a proper name, to denote Roland's horn, made of an elephant's·
tusk, and adorned with gold and jewels about the rim.

that my kind should be shamed because of me,
or that sweet France should fall into disgrace.
Never! Never! I'll strike with Durendal,                                    1065
I'll strike with this good sword strapped to my side,
you'll see this blade running its whole length with blood.
These pagan traitors have gathered here to die.
I promise you, they are all bound for death." AOI.

### 85.

"Roland, Companion, sound your olifant now,                                 1070
Charles will hear it, marching through those passes.
I promise you, the Franks will come at once."
Roland replies: "May it never please God
that any man alive should come to say
that pagans—pagans!—once made me sound this horn:                           1075
no kin of mine will ever bear that shame.
Once I enter this great battle coming
and strike my thousand seven hundred blows,
you'll see the bloody steel of Durendal.
These French are good—they will strike like brave men.                      1080
Nothing can save the men of Spain from death."

### 86.

Said Oliver: "I see no blame in it—
I watched the Saracens coming from Spain,
the valleys and mountains covered with them,
every hillside and every plain all covered,                                 1085
hosts and hosts everywhere of those strange men—
and here we have a little company."
Roland replies: "That whets my appetite.
May it not please God and his angels and saints
to let France lose its glory because of me—                                 1090
let me not end in shame, let me die first.
The Emperor loves us when we fight well."

### 87.

Roland is good, and Oliver is wise,
both these vassals men of amazing courage:
once they are armed and mounted on their horses,                            1095
they will not run, though they die for it, from battle.
Good men, these Counts, and their words full of spirit.
Traitor pagans are riding up in fury.
Said Oliver: "Roland, look—the first ones,
on top of us—and Charles is far away.                                       1100
You did not think it right to sound your olifant:

if the King were here, we'd come out without losses.
Now look up there, toward the passes of Aspre—
you can see the rear-guard: it will suffer.
No man in that detail will be in another."          1105
Roland replies: "Don't speak such foolishness—
shame on the heart gone coward in the chest.
We'll hold our ground, we'll stand firm—we're the ones!
We'll fight with spears, we'll fight them hand to hand!" AOI.

### 88.

When Roland sees that there will be a battle,          1110
it makes him fiercer than a lion or leopard;
shouts to the French, calls out to Oliver:
"Lord, companion: friend, do not say such things.
The Emperor, who left us these good French,
had set apart these twenty thousand men:          1115
he knew there was no coward in their ranks.
A man must meet great troubles for his lord,
stand up to the great heat and the great cold,
give up some flesh and blood—it is his duty.
Strike with the lance, I'll strike with Durendal—          1120
it was the King who gave me this good sword!
If I die here, the man who gets it can say:
it was a noble's, a vassal's, a good man's sword."

### 89.

And now there comes the Archbishop Turpin.
He spurs his horse, goes up into a mountain,          1125
summons the French; and he preached them a sermon:
"Barons, my lords, Charles left us in this place.
We know our duty: to die like good men for our King.
Fight to defend the holy Christian faith.
Now you will have a battle, you know it now,          1130
you see the Saracens with your own eyes.
Confess your sins, pray to the Lord for mercy.
I will absolve you all, to save your souls.
If you die here, you will stand up holy martyrs,
you will have seats in highest Paradise."          1135
The French dismount, cast themselves on the ground;
the Archbishop blesses them in God's name.
He commands them to do one penance: strike.

### 90.

The French arise, stand on their feet again;
they are absolved, released from all their sins:          1140

the Archbishop has blessed them in God's name.
Now they are mounted on their swift battle horses,
bearing their arms like faithful warriors;
and every man stands ready for the battle.
Roland the Count calls out to Oliver:                                    1145
"Lord, Companion, you knew it, you were right,
Ganelon watched for his chance to betray us,
got gold for it, got goods for it, and money.
The Emperor will have to avenge us now.
King Marsilion made a bargain for our lives,                             1150
but still must pay, and that must be with swords." AOI.


    91.
Roland went forth into the Spanish passes
on Veillantif, his good swift-running horse.
He bears his arms—how they become this man!—
grips his lance now, hefting it, working it,                             1155
now swings the iron point up toward the sky,
the gonfanon all white laced on above—
the golden streamers beat down upon his hands:
a noble's body, the face aglow and smiling.
Close behind him his good companion follows;                            1160
the men of France hail him: their protector!
He looks wildly toward the Saracens,
and humbly and gently to the men of France;
and spoke a word to them, in all courtesy:
"Barons, my lords, easy now, keep at a walk.                            1165
These pagans are searching for martyrdom.
We'll get good spoils before this day is over,
no king of France ever got such treasure!"
And with these words, the hosts are at each other. AOI.


    92.
Said Oliver: "I will waste no more words.                                1170
You did not think it right to sound your olifant,
there'll be no Charles coming to your aid now.
He knows nothing, brave man, he's done no wrong;
those men down there—they have no blame in this.
Well, then, ride now, and ride with all your might!                     1175
Lords, you brave men, stand your ground, hold the field!
Make up your minds, I beg you in God's name,
to strike some blows, take them and give them back!
Here we must not forget Charlemagne's war cry."
And with that word the men of France cried out.                         1180

A man who heard that shout: Munjoie! Munjoie![3]
would always remember what manhood is.
Then they ride, God! Look at their pride and spirit!
and they spur hard, to ride with all their speed,
come on to strike—what else would these men do?          1185
The Saracens kept coming, never fearing them.
Franks and pagans, here they are, at each other.

### 93.

Marsilion's nephew is named Aëlroth.
He rides in front, at the head of the army,
comes on shouting insults against our French:          1190
"French criminals, today you fight our men.
One man should have saved you: he betrayed you.
A fool, your King, to leave you in these passes.
This is the day sweet France will lose its name,
and Charlemagne the right arm of his body."          1195
When he hears that—God!—Roland is outraged!
He spurs his horse, gives Veillantif its head.
The Count comes on to strike with all his might,
smashes his shield, breaks his hauberk apart,
and drives: rips through his chest, shatters the bones,          1200
knocks the whole backbone out of his back,
casts out the soul of Aëlroth with his lance;
which he thrusts deep, makes the whole body shake,
throws him down dead, lance straight out,[4] from his horse;
he has broken his neck; broken it in two.          1205
There is something, he says, he must tell him:
"Clown! Nobody! Now you know Charles is no fool,
he never was the man to love treason.
It took his valor to leave us in these passes!
France will not lose its name, sweet France! today.          1210
Brave men of France, strike hard! The first blow is ours!
We're in the right, and these swine in the wrong!" AOI.

### 94.

A duke is there whose name is Falsaron,
he was the brother of King Marsilion,
held the wild land of Dathan and Abiram;[5]          1215

---

3. A mountjoy (montjoie) was (according to Littré) a mound or cairn of stones set up to mark the site of a victory. The old French war cry, "Montjoie St.-Denis!" or, briefly, "Montjoie!" derived from the cairn set up at St.-Denis on the site of the saint's martyrdom (his spiritual victory). Others derive "Montjoie" from the Hill of Rama, called "Mons Gaudii," from which pilgrims obtained their first view of Jerusalem.    4. The lance is held, not thrown, and used to knock the enemy from his horse. To throw one's weapons is savage and ignoble. Note *laisses* 154 and 160, and the outlandish names of the things the pagans throw at Roland, Gautier, and Turpin.    5. See Numbers, 16:1–35.

under heaven, no criminal more vile;
a tremendous forehead between his eyes—
a good half-foot long, if you had measured it.
His pain is bitter to see his nephew dead;
rides out alone, baits the foe with his body,                    1220
and riding shouts the war cry of the pagans,
full of hate and insults against the French:
"This is the day sweet France will lose its honor!"
Oliver hears, and it fills him with fury,
digs with his golden spurs into his horse,                    1225
comes on to strike the blow a baron strikes,
smashes his shield, breaks his hauberk apart,
thrusts into him the long streamers of his gonfalon,
knocks him down, dead, lance straight out, from the saddle;
looks to the ground and sees the swine stretched out,                    1230
and spoke these words—proud words, terrible words:
"You nobody, what are your threats to me!
Men of France, strike! Strike and we will beat them!"
Munjoie! he shouts—the war cry of King Charles. AOI.

> 95.

A king is there whose name is Corsablis,                    1235
a Berber, come from that far country.
He spoke these words to all his Saracens:
"Now here's one battle we'll have no trouble with,
look at that little troop of Frenchmen there,
a few odd men—they're not worth noticing!                    1240
King Charles won't save a single one of them.
Their day has come, they must all die today."
And Archbishop Turpin heard every word:
no man on earth he wants so much to hate!
digs with spurs of fine gold into his horse,                    1245
comes on to strike with all his awful might;
smashed through his shield, burst the rings of his hauberk,
sent his great lance into the body's center,
drove it in deep, he made the dead man shake,
knocked him down, dead, lance straight out, on the road;                    1250
looks to the ground and sees the swine stretched out;
there is something, he says, he must tell him:
"You pagan! You nobody! You told lies there:
King Charles my lord is our safeguard forever!
Our men of France have no heart for running.                    1255
As for your companions—we'll nail them to the ground;
and then you must all die the second death.[6]

6. The death of the soul, eternal damnation. See Revelation, 20:11–15; 21:8.

At them, you French! No man forget what he is!
Thanks be to God, now the first blow is ours";
and shouts Munjoie! Munjoie! to hold the field.          1260

[Lines 1261–1347 narrate a series of single combats, many of them
     quite similar.]

        111.
The French have fought with all their hearts and strength,
pagans are dead by the thousands, in droves:
of one hundred thousand, not two are saved.          1440
Said the Archbishop: "Our men! What valiant fighters!
No king under heaven could have better.
It is written in the Gesta Francorum:[7]
our Emperor's vassals were all good men."
They walk over the field to seek their dead,          1445
they weep, tears fill their eyes, in grief and pity
for their kindred, with love, with all their hearts.
Marsilion the King, with all his men
     in that great host, rises up before them. AOI.

        112.
King Marsilion comes along a valley
with all his men, the great host he assembled:          1450
twenty divisions, formed and numbered by the King,
helmets ablaze with gems beset in gold,
and those bright shields, those hauberks sewn with brass.
Seven thousand clarions sound the pursuit,
and the great noise resounds across that country.          1455
Said Roland then: "Oliver, Companion, Brother,
that traitor Ganelon has sworn our deaths:
it is treason, it cannot stay hidden,
the Emperor will take his terrible revenge.
We have this battle now, it will be bitter,          1460
no man has ever seen the like of it.
I will fight here with Durendal, this sword,
and you, my companion, with Halteclere—
we've fought with them before, in many lands!
how many battles have we won with these two!          1465
Let no one sing a bad song of our swords." AOI.

        113.
When the French see the pagans so numerous,
the fields swarming with them on every side,

7. "The deeds of the French." The reference is to a Latin account of these events; it has not
survived.

they call the names of Oliver, and Roland,
and the Twelve Peers: protect them, be their warranter.      1470
The Archbishop told them how he saw things:
"Barons, my lords, do not think shameful thoughts,
do not, I beg you all in God's name, run.
Let no brave man sing shameful songs of us:
let us all die here fighting: that is far better.            1475
We are promised: we shall soon find our deaths,
after today we won't be living here.
But here's one thing, and I am your witness:
Holy Paradise lies open to you,
you will take seats among the Innocents."[8]               1480
And with these words the Franks are filled with joy,
there is no man who does not shout Munjoie! AOI.

        114.

A Saracen was there of Saragossa,
half that city was in this pagan's keeping,
this Climborin, who fled before no man,                     1485
who took the word of Ganelon the Count,
kissed in friendship the mouth that spoke that word,
gave him a gift: his helmet and its carbuncle.
Now he will shame, says he, the Land of Fathers,
he will tear off the crown of the Emperor;                  1490
sits on the horse that he calls Barbamusche,
swifter than the sparrowhawk, than the swallow;
digs in his spurs, gives that war horse its head,
comes on to strike Engeler of Gascony,
whose shield and fine hauberk cannot save him;             1495
gets the head of his spear into his body,
drives it in deep, gets all the iron through,
throws him back, dead, lance straight out, on the field.
And then he cries: "It's good to kill these swine!
At them, Pagans! At them and break their ranks!"           1500
"God!" say the French, "the loss of that good man!" AOI.

        115.

Roland the Count calls out to Oliver:
"Lord, Companion, there is Engeler dead,
we never had a braver man on horse."
The Count replies: "God let me avenge him";                1505
and digs with golden spurs into his horse,
grips—the steel running with blood—Halteclere,
comes on to strike with all his mighty power:

8. The infants slain by King Herod; see *Matthew* 2:13–18.

the blow comes flashing down; the pagan falls.
Devils take away the soul of Climborin.                          1510
And then he killed Alphaïen the duke,
cut off the head of Escababi,
struck from their horses seven great Arrabites:
they'll be no use for fighting any more!
And Roland said: "My companion is enraged!                       1515
Why, he compares with me! he earns his praise!
Fighting like that makes us dearer to Charles";
lifts up his voice and shouts. "Strike! you are warriors!" AOI.

[Lines 1519–1627 narrate another series of single combats.]

125.

Marsilion sees his people's martyrdom.
He commands them: sound his horns and trumpets;
and he rides now with the great host he has gathered.            1630
At their head rides the Saracen Abisme:
no worse criminal rides in that company,
stained with the marks of his crimes and great treasons,
lacking the faith in God, Saint Mary's son.
And he is black, as black as melted pitch,                       1635
a man who loves murder and treason more
than all the gold of rich Galicia,
no living man ever saw him play or laugh;
a great fighter, a wild man, mad with pride,
and therefore dear to that criminal king;                        1640
holds high his dragon,[9] where all his people gather.
The Archbishop will never love that man,
no sooner saw than wanted to strike him;
considered quietly, said to himself:
"That Saracen—a heretic, I'll wager.                             1645
Now let me die if I do not kill him—
I never loved cowards or cowards' ways." AOI.

126.

Turpin the Archbishop begins the battle.
He rides the horse that he took from Grossaille,
who was a king this priest once killed in Denmark.              1650
Now this war horse is quick and spirited,
his hooves high-arched, the quick legs long and flat,
short in the thigh, wide in the rump, long in the flanks,
and the backbone so high, a battle horse!
and that white tail, the yellow mane on him,                    1655
the little ears on him, the tawny head!

9. Banner.

No beast on earth could ever run with him.
The Archbishop—that valiant man!—spurs hard,
he will attack Abisme, he will not falter,
strikes on his shield, a miraculous blow:                                1660
a shield of stones, of amethysts, topazes,
esterminals,[1] carbuncles all on fire—
a gift from a devil, in Val Metas,
sent on to him by the Amiral Galafre.
There Turpin strikes, he does not treat it gently—                       1665
after that blow, I'd not give one cent for it;
cut through his body, from one side to the other,
and casts him down dead in a barren place.
And the French say: "A fighter, that Archbishop!
Look at him there, saving souls with that crozier!"                      1670

    127.

Roland the Count calls out to Oliver:
"Lord, Companion, now you have to agree
the Archbishop is a good man on horse,
there's none better on earth or under heaven,
he knows his way with a lance and a spear."                              1675
The Count replies: "Right! Let us help him then."
And with these words the Franks began anew,
the blows strike hard, and the fighting is bitter;
there is a painful loss of Christian men.
To have seen them, Roland and Oliver,                                    1680
these fighting men, striking down with their swords,
the Archbishop with them, striking with his lance!
One can recount the number these three killed:
it is written—in charters, in documents;
the Geste tells it: it was more than four thousand.                      1685
Through four assaults all went well with our men;
then comes the fifth, and that one crushes them.
They are all killed, all these warriors of France,
all but sixty, whom the Lord God has spared:
they will die too, but first sell themselves dear. AOI.                  1690

    128.

Count Roland sees the great loss of his men,
calls on his companion, in God's name, what would you do?
All these good men you see stretched on the ground.
We can mourn for sweet France, fair land of France!                      1695
a desert now, stripped of such great vassals.
Oh King, and friend, if only you were here!
Oliver, Brother, how shall we manage it?

1. Precious ornaments.

What shall we do to get word to the King?"
Said Oliver: "I don't see any way.                                     1700
I would rather die now than hear us shamed." AOI.


     129.
And Roland said: "I'll sound the olifant,
Charles will hear it, drawing through the passes,
I promise you, the Franks will return at once."
Said Oliver: "That would be a great disgrace,                          1705
a dishonor and reproach to all your kin,
the shame of it would last them all their lives.
When I urged it, you would not hear of it;
you will not do it now with my consent.
It is not acting bravely to sound it now—                              1710
look at your arms, they are covered with blood."
The Count replies: "I've fought here like a lord."[9] AOI.


     130.
And Roland says: "We are in a rough battle.
I'll sound the olifant, Charles will hear it."
Said Oliver: "No good vassal would do it.                              1715
When I urged it, friend, you did not think it right.
If Charles were here, we'd come out with no losses.
Those men down there—no blame can fall on them."
Oliver said: "Now by this beard of mine,
If I can see my noble sister, Aude,                                    1720
once more, you will never lie in her arms!"[1] AOI.


     131.
And Roland said: "Why are you angry at me?"
Oliver answers: "Companion, it is your doing.
I will tell you what makes a vassal good:
     it is judgment, it is never madness;
restraint is worth more than the raw nerve of a fool.                  1725
Frenchmen are dead because of your wildness.
And what service will Charles ever have from us?
If you had trusted me, my lord would be here,
we would have fought this battle through to the end,
Marsilion would be dead, or our prisoner.                              1730
Roland, your prowess—had we never seen it!
     And now, dear friend, we've seen the last of it.

---

9. Some have found lines 1710–12 difficult. Oliver means: We have fought this far—look at the
enemy's blood on your arms: It is too late, it would be a disgrace to summon help when there is
no longer any chance of being saved. And Roland thinks that that is the one time when it is not a
disgrace.    1. Aude had been betrothed to Roland.

No more aid from us now for Charlemagne,
a man without equal till Judgment Day,
you will die here, and your death will shame France.
We kept faith, you and I, we were companions;          1735
    and everything we were will end today.
We part before evening, and it will be hard." AOI.

132.
Turpin the Archbishop hears their bitter words,
digs hard into his horse with golden spurs
and rides to them; begins to set them right:
"You, Lord Roland, and you, Lord Oliver,          1740
I beg you in God's name do not quarrel.
To sound the horn could not help us now, true,
but still it is far better that you do it:
let the King come, he can avenge us then—
these men of Spain must not go home exulting!          1745
Our French will come, they'll get down on their feet,
and find us here—we'll be dead, cut to pieces.
They will lift us into coffins on the backs of mules,
and weep for us, in rage and pain and grief,
and bury us in the courts of churches;          1750
and we will not be eaten by wolves or pigs or dogs."
Roland replies, "Lord, you have spoken well." AOI.

133.
Roland has put the olifant to his mouth,
he sets it well, sounds it with all his strength.
The hills are high, and that voice ranges far,          1755
they heard it echo thirty great leagues away.
King Charles heard it, and all his faithful men.
And the King says: "Our men are in a battle."
And Ganelon disputed him and said:
"Had someone else said that, I'd call him liar!" AOI.          1760

134.
And now the mighty effort of Roland the Count:
he sounds his olifant; his pain is great,
and from his mouth the bright blood comes leaping out,
and the temple bursts in his forehead.
That horn, in Roland's hands, has a mighty voice:          1765
King Charles hears it drawing through the passes.
Naimon heard it, the Franks listen to it.
And the King said: "I hear Count Roland's horn;
he'd never sound it unless he had a battle."

Says Ganelon: "Now no more talk of battles!                    1770
You are old now, your hair is white as snow,
the things you say make you sound like a child.
You know Roland and that wild pride of his—
what a wonder God has suffered it so long!
Remember? he took Noples without your command:                 1775
the Saracens rode out, to break the siege;
they fought with him, the great vassal Roland.
Afterwards he used the streams to wash the blood
from the meadows: so that nothing would show.
He blasts his horn all day to catch a rabbit,                  1780
he's strutting now before his peers and bragging—
who under heaven would dare meet him on the field?
So now: ride on! Why do you keep on stopping?
The Land of Fathers lies far ahead of us." AOI.

135.
The blood leaping from Count Roland's mouth,                    1785
the temple broken with effort in his forehead,
he sounds his horn in great travail and pain.
King Charles heard it, and his French listen hard.
And the King said: "That horn has a long breath!"
Naimon answers: "It is a baron's breath.                       1790
There is a battle there, I know there is.
*He* betrayed him! and now asks you to fail him!
Put on your armor! Lord, shout your battle cry,
and save the noble barons of your house!
You hear Roland's call. He is in trouble."                     1795

136.
The Emperor commanded the horns to sound,
the French dismount, and they put on their armor:
their hauberks, their helmets, their gold-dressed swords,
their handsome shields; and take up their great lances,
the gonfalons of white and red and blue.                       1800
The barons of that host mount their war horses
and spur them hard the whole length of the pass;
and every man of them says to the other:
"If only we find Roland before he's killed,
we'll stand with him, and then we'll do some fighting!"        1805
What does it matter what they say? They are too late.

137.
It is the end of day, and full of light,
arms and armor are ablaze in the sun,

and fire flashes from hauberks and helmets,
and from those shields, painted fair with flowers,                    1810
and from those lances, those gold-dressed gonfanons.
The Emperor rides on in rage and sorrow,
the men of France indignant and full of grief.
There is no man of them who does not weep,
they are in fear for the life of Roland.                    1815
The King commands: seize Ganelon the Count!
and gave him over to the cooks of his house;
summons the master cook, their chief, Besgun:
"Guard him for me like the traitor he is:
he has betrayed the barons of my house."                    1820
Besgun takes him, sets his kitchen comrades,
a hundred men, the best, the worst, on him;
and they tear out his beard and his mustache,
each one strikes him four good blows with his fist;
and they lay into him with cudgels and sticks,                    1825
put an iron collar around his neck
and chain him up, as they would chain a bear;
dumped him, in dishonor, on a packhorse,
and guard him well till they give him back to Charles.

        138.
High are the hills, and tenebrous, and vast, AOI.                    1830
the valleys deep, the raging waters swift;
to the rear, to the front, the trumpets sound:
they answer the lone voice of the olifant.
The Emperor rides on, rides on in fury,
the men of France in grief and indignation.                    1835
There is no man who does not weep and wail,
and they pray God: protect the life of Roland
till they come, one great host, into the field
and fight at Roland's side like true men all.
What does it matter what they pray? It does no good.                    1840
They are too late, they cannot come in time. AOI.

        139.
King Charles the Great rides on, a man in wrath,
his great white beard spread out upon his hauberk.[2]
All the barons of France ride spurring hard,
there is no man who does not wail, furious                    1845
not to be with Roland, the captain count,
who stands and fights the Saracens of Spain,

---

2. The beard spread out upon the hauberk is a gesture of defiance toward the enemy.

so set upon, I cannot think his soul abides.
God! those sixty men who stand with him, what men!
No king, no captain ever stood with better. AOI.          1850


        140.
Roland looks up on the mountains and slopes,
sees the French dead, so many good men fallen,
and weeps for them, as a great warrior weeps:
"Barons, my lords, may God give you his grace,
may he grant Paradise to all your souls,          1855
make them lie down among the holy flowers.
I never saw better vassals than you.
All the years you've served me, and all the times,
the mighty lands you conquered for Charles our King!
The Emperor raised you for this terrible hour!          1860
Land of France, how sweet you are, native land,
laid waste this day, ravaged, made a desert.
Barons of France, I see you die for me,
and I, your lord—I cannot protect you.
May God come to your aid, that God who never failed.          1865
Oliver, brother, now I will not fail *you*.
I will die here—of grief, if no man kills me.
Lord, Companion, let us return and fight."


        141.
Roland returned to his place on the field,
strikes—a brave man keeping faith—with Durendal,          1870
struck through Faldrun de Pui, cut him to pieces,
and twenty-four of the men they valued most;
no man will ever want his vengeance more!
As when the deer turns tail before the dogs,
so the pagans flee before Roland the Count.          1875
Said the Archbishop: "You! Roland! What a fighter!
Now that's what every knight must have in him
who carries arms and rides on a fine horse:
he must be strong, a savage, when he's in battle;
for otherwise, what's he worth? Not four cents!          1880
Let that four-cent man be a monk in some minster,
and he can pray all day long for our sins."
Roland replies: "Attack, do not spare them!"
And with that word the Franks began again.
There was a heavy loss of Christian men.          1885


        142.
When a man knows there'll be no prisoners,
what will that man not do to defend himself!

And so the Franks fight with the fury of lions.
Now Marsilion, the image of a baron,
mounted on that war horse he calls Gaignun, 1890
digs in his spurs, comes on to strike Bevon,
who was the lord of Beaune and of Dijon;
smashes his shield, rips apart his hauberk,
knocks him down, dead, no need to wound him more.
And then he killed Yvorie and Yvon, 1895
and more: he killed Gerard of Rousillon.
Roland the Count is not far away now,
said to the pagan: "The Lord God's curse on you!
You kill my companions, how you wrong me!
You'll feel the pain of it before we part, 1900
you will learn my sword's name by heart today";
comes on to strike—the image of a baron.
He has cut off Marsilion's right fist;
now takes the head of Jurfaleu the blond—
the head of Jurfaleu! Marsilion's son. 1905
The pagans cry: "Help, Mahumet! Help us!
Vengeance, our gods, on Charles! the man who set
these criminals on us in our own land,
they will not quit the field, they'll stand and die!"
And one said to the other: "Let us run then." 1910
And with that word, some hundred thousand flee.
Now try to call them back: they won't return. AOI.

    143.
What does it matter? If Marsilion has fled,
his uncle has remained: the Algalife,[3]
who holds Carthage, Alfrere, and Garmalie, 1915
and Ethiopia: a land accursed;
holds its immense black race under his power,
the huge noses, the enormous ears on them;
and they number more than fifty thousand.
These are the men who come riding in fury, 1920
and now they shout that pagan battle cry.
And Roland said: "Here comes our martyrdom;
I see it now: we have not long to live.
But let the world call any man a traitor
    who does not make them pay before he dies!
My lords, attack! Use those bright shining swords! 1925
Fight a good fight for your deaths and your lives,
let no shame touch sweet France because of us!
When Charles my lord comes to this battlefield

3. The Caliph, Marsilion's uncle, whom Ganelon lied about to Charlemagne. See lines 680–91
(also lines 453, 493, 505).

and sees how well we punished these Saracens,
finds fifteen of their dead for one of ours,                          1930
I'll tell you what he will do: he will bless us." AOI.

### 144.

When Roland sees that unbelieving race,
those hordes and hordes blacker than blackest ink—
no shred of white on them except their teeth—
then said the Count: "I see it clearly now,                          1935
we die today: it is there before us.
Men of France, strike! I will start it once more."
Said Oliver: "God curse the slowest man."
And with that word, the French strike into battle.

### 145.

The Saracens, when they saw these few French,                        1940
looked at each other, took courage, and presumed,
telling themselves: "The Emperor is wrong!"
The Algalife rides a great sorrel horse,
digs into it with his spurs of fine gold,
strikes Oliver, from behind, in the back,                            1945
shattered the white hauberk upon his flesh,
drove his spear through the middle of his chest;
and speaks to him: "Now you feel you've been struck!
Your great Charles doomed you when he left you in this pass.
That man wronged us, he must not boast of it.                        1950
I've avenged all our dead in you alone!"

### 146.

Oliver feels: he has been struck to death;
grips Halteclere, that steel blade shining, strikes
on the gold-dressed pointed helm of the Algalife,
sends jewels and flowers crackling down to the earth,                1955
into the head, into the little teeth;
draws up his flashing sword, casts him down, dead,
and then he says: "Pagan, a curse on you!
If only I could say Charles has lost nothing—
but no woman, no lady you ever knew                                  1960
will hear you boast, in the land you came from,
that you could take one thing worth a cent from me,
or do me harm, or do any man harm";
then cries out to Roland to come to his aid. AOI.

### 147.

Oliver feels he is wounded to death,                                 1965
will never have his fill of vengeance, strikes,

as a baron strikes, where they are thickest,
cuts through their lances, cuts through those buckled shields,
through feet, through fists, through saddles, and through flanks.
Had you seen him, cutting the pagans limb          1970
from limb, casting one corpse down on another,
you would remember a brave man keeping faith.
Never would he forget Charles' battle-cry,
Munjoie! he shouts, that mighty voice ringing;
calls to Roland, to his friend and his peer:          1975
"Lord, Companion, come stand beside me now.
We must part from each other in pain today." AOI.

###### 148.
Roland looks hard into Oliver's face,
it is ashen, all its color is gone,
the bright red blood streams down upon his body,          1980
Oliver's blood spattering on the earth.
"God!" said the Count, "I don't know what to do,
Lord, Companion, your fight is finished now.
There'll never be a man the like of you.
Sweet land of France, today you will be stripped          1985
of good vassals, laid low, a fallen land!
The Emperor will suffer the great loss";
faints with that word, mounted upon his horse. AOI.

###### 149.
Here is Roland, lords, fainted on his horse,
and Oliver the Count, wounded to death:          1990
he has lost so much blood, his eyes are darkened—
he cannot see, near or far, well enough
to recognize a friend or enemy:
struck when he came upon his companion,
strikes on his helm, adorned with gems in gold,          1995
cuts down straight through, from the point to the nasal,[4]
but never harmed him, he never touched his head.
Under this blow, Count Roland looked at him;
and gently, softly now, he asks of him:
"Lord, Companion, do you mean to do this?          2000
It is Roland, who always loved you greatly.
You never declared that we were enemies."
Said Oliver: "Now I hear it is you—
I don't see you, may the Lord God see you.
Was it you that I struck? Forgive me then."          2005
Roland replies: "I am not harmed, not harmed,

---

4. The nosepiece protruding down from the cone-shaped helmet.

I forgive you, Friend, here and before God."
And with that word, each bowed to the other.
And this is the love, lords, in which they parted.


150.

Oliver feels: death pressing hard on him;                        2010
his two eyes turn, roll up into his head,
all hearing is lost now, all sight is gone;
gets down on foot, stretches out on the ground,
cries out now and again: *mea culpa!*[5]
his two hands joined, raised aloft toward heaven,              2015
he prays to God: grant him His Paradise;
and blesses Charles, and the sweet land of France,
his companion, Roland, above all men.
The heart fails him, his helmet falls away,
the great body settles upon the earth.                          2020
The Count is dead, he stands with us no longer.
Roland, brave man, weeps for him, mourns for him,
you will not hear a man of greater sorrow.


151.

Roland the Count, when he sees his friend dead,
lying stretched out, his face against the earth,                2025
softly, gently, begins to speak the regret:[6]
"Lord, Companion, you were brave and died for it.
We have stood side by side through days and years,
you never caused me harm, I never wronged you;
when you are dead, to be alive pains me."                       2030
And with that word the lord of marches faints
upon his horse, which he calls Veillantif.
He is held firm by his spurs of fine gold,
whichever way he leans, he cannot fall.


152.

Before Roland could recover his senses                          2035
and come out of his faint, and be aware,
a great disaster had come forth before him:
the French are dead, he has lost every man
except the Archbishop, and Gautier de l'Hum,
who has come back, down from that high mountain:                2040
he has fought well, he fought those men of Spain.
His men are dead, the pagans finished them;

5. "My guilt." A formula used in the confession of one's sins.    6. What follows is a formal and
customary lament for the dead.

flees now down to these valleys, he has no choice,
and calls on Count Roland to come to his aid:
"My noble Count, my brave lord, where are you?                2045
I never feared whenever you were there.
It is Walter: I conquered Maëlgut,
my uncle is Droün, old and gray: your Walter
and always dear to you for the way I fought;
and I have fought this time: my lance is shattered,          2050
my good shield pierced, my hauberk's meshes broken;
and I am wounded, a lance struck through my body.
I will die soon, but I sold myself dear."
And with that word, Count Roland has heard him,
he spurs his horse, rides spurring to his man. AOI.          2055


      153.
Roland in pain, maddened with grief and rage:
rushes where they are thickest and strikes again,
strikes twenty men of Spain, strikes twenty dead,
and Walter six, and the Archbishop five.
The pagans say: "Look at those criminals!                    2060
Now take care, Lords, they don't get out alive,
only a traitor will not attack them now!
Only a coward will let them save their skins!"
And then they raise their hue and cry once more,
rush in on them, once more, from every side. AOI.            2065


      154.
Count Roland was always a noble warrior,
Gautier de l'Hum is a fine mounted man,
the Archbishop, a good man tried and proved:
not one of them will ever leave the others;
strike, where they are thickest, at the pagans.             2070
A thousand Saracens get down on foot,
and forty thousand more are on their mounts:
and I tell you, not one will dare come close,
they throw, and from afar, lances and spears,
wigars and darts, mizraks, javelins, pikes.                 2075
With the first blows they killed Gautier de l'Hum
and struck Turpin of Reims, pierced through his shield,
broke the helmet on him, wounded his head;
ripped his hauberk, shattered its rings of mail,
and pierced him with four spears in his body,               2080
the war horse killed under him; and now there comes
great pain and rage when the Archbishop falls. AOI.

155.

Turpin of Reims, when he feels he is unhorsed,
struck to the earth with four spears in his body,
quickly, brave man, leaps to his feet again;                    2085
his eyes find Roland now, he runs to him
and says one word: "See! I'm not finished yet!
What good vassal ever gives up alive!";
and draws Almace, his sword, that shining steel!
and strikes, where they are thickest, a thousand blows, and      2090
    more.
Later, Charles said: Turpin had spared no one;
he found four hundred men prostrate around him,
some of them wounded, some pierced from front to back,
some with their heads hacked off. So says the Geste,
and so says one who was there, on that field,                    2095
the baron Saint Gilles,[3] for whom God performs miracles,
who made the charter setting forth these great things
        in the Church of Laon. Now any man
who does not know this much understands nothing.

156.

Roland the Count fights well and with great skill,
but he is hot, his body soaked with sweat;                       2100
has a great wound in his head, and much pain,
his temple broken because he blew the horn.
But he must know whether King Charles will come;
draws out the olifant, sounds it, so feebly.
The Emperor drew to a halt, listened.                            2105
"Seigneurs," he said, "it goes badly for us—
My nephew Roland falls from our ranks today.
I hear it in the horn's voice: he hasn't long.
Let every man who wants to be with Roland
ride fast! Sound trumpets! Every trumpet in this host!"          2110
Sixty thousand, on these words, sound, so high
the mountains sound, and the valleys resound.
The pagans hear: it is no joke to them;
cry to each other: "We're getting Charles on us!"

157.

The pagans say: "The Emperor is coming, AOI.                     2115
listen to their trumpets—it is the French!
If Charles comes back, it's all over for us,
if Roland lives, this war begins again

3. Saint Gilles of Provence: These lines explain how the story of Rencesvals could be told after
all who had fought there died.

and we have lost our land, we have lost Spain."
Some four hundred, helmets laced on, assemble,                    2120
some of the best, as they think, on that field.
They storm Roland, in one fierce, bitter attack.
And now Count Roland has some work on his hands. AOI.

### 158.

Roland the Count, when he sees them coming,
how strong and fierce and alert he becomes!                       2125
He will not yield to them, not while he lives.
He rides the horse they call Veillantif, spurs,
digs into it with his spurs of fine gold,
and rushes at them all where they are thickest,
the Archbishop—that Turpin!—at his side.                         2130
Said one man to the other: "Go at it, friend.
The horns we heard were the horns of the French,
King Charles is coming back with all his strength."[4]

### 159.

Roland the Count never loved a coward,
a blusterer, an evil-natured man,                                 2135
a man on horse who was not a good vassal.
And now he called to Archbishop Turpin:
"You are on foot, Lord, and here I am mounted,
and so, here I take my stand: for love of you.
We'll take whatever comes, the good and bad,                     2140
together, Lord: no one can make me leave you.
They will learn our swords' names today in battle,
the name of Almace, the name of Durendal!"
Said the Archbishop: "Let us strike or be shamed!
Charles is returning, and he brings our revenge."                2145

### 160.

Say the pagans: "We were all born unlucky!
The evil day that dawned for us today!
We have lost our lords and peers, and now comes Charles—
that Charlemagne!—with his great host. Those trumpets!
that shrill sound on us—the trumpets of the French!              2150
And the loud roar of that Munjoie! This Roland
is a wild man, he is too great a fighter—
What man of flesh and blood can ever hope
to bring him down? Let us cast at him, and leave him there."
And so they did: arrows, wigars, darts,                          2155

---

4. Lines 2131–33 could be spoken either by Roland and the Archbishop or by the pagans.

lances and spears, javelots dressed with feathers;
struck Roland's shield, pierced it, broke it to pieces,
ripped his hauberk, shattered its rings of mail,
but never touched his body, never his flesh.
They wounded Veillantif in thirty places,          2160
struck him dead, from afar, under the Count.
The pagans flee, they leave the field to him.
Roland the Count stood alone, on his feet. AOI.

### 161.

The pagans flee, in bitterness and rage,
strain every nerve running headlong toward Spain,          2165
and Count Roland has no way to chase them,
he has lost Veillantif, his battle horse;
he has no choice, left alone there on foot.
He went to the aid of Archbishop Turpin,
unlaced the gold-dressed helmet, raised it from his head,          2170
lifted away his bright, light coat of mail,
cut his under tunic into some lengths,
stilled his great wounds with thrusting on the strips;
then held him in his arms, against his chest,
and laid him down, gently, on the green grass;          2175
and softly now Roland entreated him:
"My noble lord, I beg you, give me leave:
our companions, whom we have loved so dearly,
are all dead now, we must not abandon them.
I want to look for them, know them once more,          2180
and set them in ranks, side by side, before you."
Said the Archbishop: "Go then, go and come back.
The field is ours, thanks be to God, yours and mine."

### 162.

So Roland leaves him, walks the field all alone,
seeks in the valleys, and seeks in the mountains.          2185
He found Gerin, and Gerer his companion,
and then he found Berenger and Otun,
Anseïs and Sansun, and on that field
he found Gerard the old of Roussillon;
and caried them, brave man, all, one by one,          2190
came back to the Archbishop with these French dead,
and set them down in ranks before his knees.
The Archbishop cannot keep from weeping,
raises his hand and makes his bendiction;
and said: "Lords, Lords, it was your terrible hour.          2195
May the Glorious God set all your souls
among the holy flowers of Paradise!

Here is my own death, Lords, pressing on me,
I shall not see our mighty Emperor."

### 163.
And Roland leaves, seeks in the field again;                    2200
he has found Oliver, his companion,
held him tight in his arms against his chest;
came back to the Archbishop, laid Oliver
down on a shield among the other dead.
The Archbishop absolved him, signed him with the Cross.         2205
And pity now and rage and grief increase;
and Roland says: "Oliver, dear companion,
you were the son of the great duke Renier,
who held the march of the vale of Runers.
Lord, for shattering lances, for breaking shields,             2210
for making men great with presumption weak with fright,
for giving life and counsel to good men,
for striking fear in that unbelieving race,
no warrior on earth surpasses you."

### 164.
Roland the Count, when he sees his peers dead,                  2215
and Oliver, whom he had good cause to love,
felt such grief and pity, he begins to weep;
and his face lost its color with what he felt:
a pain so great he cannot keep on standing,
he has no choice, falls fainting to the ground.                 2220
Said the Archbishop: "Baron, what grief for you."

### 165.
The Archbishop, when he saw Roland faint,
felt such pain then as he had never felt;
stretched out his hand and grasped the olifant.
At Rencesvals there is a running stream:                        2225
he will go there and fetch some water for Roland;
and turns that way, with small steps, staggering;
he is too weak, he cannot go ahead,
he has no strength: all the blood he has lost.
In less time than a man takes to cross a little field          2230
that great heart fails, he falls forward, falls down;
and Turpin's death comes crushing down on him.

### 166.
Roland the Count recovers from his faint,
gets to his feet, but stands with pain and grief;
looks down the valley, looks up the mountain, sees:            2235

on the green grass, beyond his companions,
that great and noble man down on the ground,
the Archbishop, whom God sent in His name;
who confesses his sins, lifts up his eyes,
holds up his hands joined together to heaven,                    2240
and prays to God: grant him that Paradise.
Turpin is dead, King Charles' good warrior.
In great battles, in beautiful sermons
he was ever a champion against the pagans.
Now God grant Turpin's soul His holy blessing. AOI.             2245

### 167.

Roland the Count sees the Archbishop down,
sees the bowels fallen out of his body,
and the brain boiling down from his forehead.
Turpin has crossed his hands upon his chest
beneath the collarbone, those fine white hands.                  2250
Roland speaks the lament, after the custom
followed in his land: aloud, with all his heart:
"My noble lord, you great and well-born warrior,
I commend you today to the God of Glory,
whom none will ever serve with a sweeter will.
Since the Apostles no prophet the like of you[5]                 2255
arose to keep the faith and draw men to it.
May your soul know no suffering or want,
and behold the gate open to Paradise."

### 168.

Now Roland feels that death is very near.
His brain comes spilling out through his two ears;               2260
prays to God for his peers: let them be called;
and for himself, to the angel Gabriel;
took the olifant: there must be no reproach!
took Durendal his sword in his other hand,
and farther than a crossbow's farthest shot                      2265
he walks toward Spain, into a fallow land,
and climbs a hill: there beneath two fine trees
stand four great blocks of stone, all are of marble;
and he fell back, to earth, on the green grass,
has fainted there, for death is very near.                       2270

### 169.

High are the hills, and high, high are the trees;
there stand four blocks of stone, gleaming of marble.

---

5. Compare Deuteronomy, 34:10, on the death of Moses.

Count Roland falls fainting on the green grass,
and is watched, all this time, by a Saracen:
who has feigned death and lies now with the others,                    2275
has smeared blood on his face and on his body;
and quickly now gets to his feet and runs—
a handsome man, strong, brave, and so crazed with pride
that he does something mad and dies for it:
laid hands on Roland, and on the arms of Roland,                    2280
and cried: "Conquered! Charles's nephew conquered!
I'll carry this sword home to Arabia!"
As he draws it, the Count begins to come round.


        170.
Now Roland feels: *someone taking his sword!*
opened his eyes, and had one word for him:                    2285
"I don't know you, you aren't one of ours";
grasps that olifant that he will never lose,
strikes on the helm beset with gems in gold,
shatters the steel, and the head, and the bones,
sent his two eyes flying out of his head,                    2290
dumped him over stretched out at his feet dead;
and said: "You nobody! how could you dare
lay hands on me—rightly or wrongly: how?
Who'll hear of this and not call you a fool?
Ah! the bell-mouth of the olifant is smashed,                    2295
the crystal and the gold fallen away."


        171.
Now Roland the Count feels: his sight is gone;
gets on his feet, draws on his final strength,
the color on his face lost now for good.
Before him stands a rock; and on that dark rock                    2300
in rage and bitterness he strikes ten blows:
the steel blade grates, it will not break, it stands unmarked.
"Ah!" said the Count, "Blessed Mary, your help!
Ah Durendal, good sword, your unlucky day,
for I am lost and cannot keep you in my care.                    2305
The battles I have won, fighting with you,
the mighty lands that holding you I conquered,
that Charles rules now, our King, whose beard is white!
Now you fall to another: it must not be
a man who'd run before another man!
For a long while a good vassal held you:                    2310
there'll never be the like in France's holy land."

### 172.

Roland strikes down on that rock of Cerritania:
the steel blade grates, will not break, stands unmarked.
Now when he sees he can never break that sword,
Roland speaks the lament, in his own presence:                    2315
"Ah Durendal, how beautiful and bright!
so full of light, all on fire in the sun!
King Charles was in the vales of Moriane
when God sent his angel and commanded him,
from heaven, to give you to a captain count.                      2320
That great and noble King girded it on me.
And with this sword I won Anjou and Brittany,
I won Poitou, I won Le Maine for Charles,
and Normandy, that land where men are free,
I won Provence and Aquitaine with this,                           2325
and Lombardy, and every field of Romagna,
I won Bavaria, and all of Flanders,
all of Poland, and Bulgaria, for Charles,
Constantinople, which pledged him loyalty,
and Saxony, where he does as he wills;                            2330
and with this sword I won Scotland and Ireland,
and England, his chamber, his own domain—
the lands, the nations I conquered with this sword,
for Charles, who rules them now, whose beard is white!
Now, for this sword, I am pained with grief and rage:             2335
Let it not fall to pagans! Let me die first!
Our Father God, save France from that dishonor."

### 173.

Roland the Count strikes down on a dark rock,
and the rock breaks, breaks more than I can tell,
and the blade grates, but Durendal will not break,               2340
the sword leaped up, rebounded toward the sky.
The Count, when he sees that sword will not be broken,
softly, in his own presence, speaks the lament:
"Ah Durendal, beautiful, and most sacred,
the holy relics in this golden pommel!                            2345
Saint Peter's tooth and blood of Saint Basile,
a lock of hair of my lord Saint Denis,
and a fragment of blessed Mary's robe:
your power must not fall to the pagans,
you must be served by Christian warriors.                         2350
May no coward ever come to hold you!
It was with you I conquered those great lands

that Charles has in his keeping, whose beard is white,
the Emperor's lands, that make him rich and strong."

### 174.

Now Roland feels: death coming over him,                2355
death descending from his temples to his heart.
He came running underneath a pine tree
and there stretched out, face down, on the green grass,
lays beneath him his sword and the olifant.
He turned his head toward the Saracen hosts,            2360
and this is why: with all his heart he wants
King Charles the Great and all his men to say,
he died, that noble Count, a conqueror;
makes confession, beats his breast often, so feebly,
offers his glove, for all his sins, to God. AOI.         2365

### 175.

Now Roland feels that his time has run out;
he lies on a steep hill, his face toward Spain;
and with one of his hands he beat his breast:
"Almighty God, *mea culpa* in thy sight,[1]
forgive my sins, both the great and the small,          2370
sins I committed from the hour I was born
until this day, in which I lie struck down."
And then he held his right glove out to God.
Angels descend from heaven and stand by him. AOI.

### 176.

Count Roland lay stretched out beneath a pine;          2375
he turned his face toward the land of Spain,
began to remember many things now:
how many lands, brave man, he had conquered;
and he remembered: sweet France, the men of his line,
remembered Charles, his lord, who fostered him:         2380
cannot keep, remembering, from weeping, sighing;
but would not be unmindful of himself:
he confesses his sins, prays God for mercy:
"Loyal Father, you who never failed us,
who resurrected Saint Lazarus from the dead,            2385
and saved your servant Daniel from the lions:[2]
now save the soul of me from every peril
for the sins I committed while I still lived."

1. See Psalm 51:4.    2. See Daniel, 6:12–23. For the raising of Lazarus, see the Gospel of
St. John, 11:1–44.

Then he held out his right glove to his Lord:
Saint Gabriel took the glove from his hand.                                    2390
He held his head bowed down upon his arm,
he is gone, his two hands joined, to his end.
Then God sent him his angel Cherubin[3]
and Saint Michael, angel of the sea's Peril;
and with these two there came Saint Gabriel:                                   2395
they bear Count Roland's soul to Paradise.

*       *       *

---

# MARIE DE FRANCE

So far as we know, the first woman to write poetry in French was Marie de
France, who lived in the last third of the twelfth century. As often with
medieval authors, the name does not identify her with any specific historical
figure; but it indicates that she was a French native. Her works show that
she was associated in some way with the court of King Henry II of England,
husband of the famous Queen Eleanor of Aquitaine. Marie was probably
familiar with English as well as Latin and French. A versatile writer, she
produced works in three varieties of literature: fables, visions of purgatory,
and *lais*. She may or may not have been the first author of Breton *lais* and
thus have given a designation to the genre. These were comparatively short
narratives based in varying degrees on a story or song circulated by traveling
entertainers (*jongleurs*) from the northwestern province of France known as
Brittany. These were presumably in Breton, originally the Celtic language
of Brittany, but none have come down to us. For French and English poets,
a Breton *lai* was a narrative of moderate length recounting an event remarkable in some way, often associated with the magical or miraculous; most
often, the "adventure" involves what we should call romantic love. Thus
*Eliduc*, the longest of Marie's dozen *lais*, has been called a story of a man
with two wives. In that respect it recalls the better-known story of Tristan
and the two Isoldes. As Marie rightly says, her tale centers on the two women;
it's a pity that her change of the title to *Guildelüec and Guilliadun* has not
prevailed in literary history.

Our poem, in 1,184 eight-syllable rhyming lines, tells a fairly complicated story in a simple, straightforward way. Setting and background, royal
courts, and warfare provide a light framework and milieu; focus and concentration are on the diverse emotions of the protagonists and the conflicts of
loyalties that arise among them. As in medieval romance generally, love is
treated sympathetically, but Marie has her own way when it comes to getting
her lovers into and out of their difficulties. She spends more effort on the
sudden rapture of the princess Guilliadun over the foreign knight Eliduc,
her introspection, her confidences and planning with the page, etc., than

---

3. The poet seems to have regarded this as the name of a single angel.

on the response of the knight. Contrary to the situation in many romances, they do not become physical lovers; the princess hopes for marriage; Eliduc does not tell her that he already has a wife. That disclosure comes only when a sailor accuses her of wickedly seeking another woman's husband and hence of responsibility for the storm which threatens the lives of all on board; the shock all but—and apparently—kills her. The management of overall plot is admirable here. No less remarkable is the understanding and selflessness shown by Guildelüec, who amiably takes vows as a nun—thereby renouncing her rights as a wife. Thus the lovers are able to marry, and Marie accords them many years of happiness together. Finally, they in their turn renounce the world and end their lives respectively in monastery and convent. Thus, by a skillfully devised plot and careful—if slightly improbable—characterization, the author reconciles the claims of love with those of traditional morality and the Christian religion.

## Eliduc[1]

I am going to give you the full story of a very old Celtic tale, at least as I've been able to understand the truth of it.

In Brittany there was once a knight called Eliduc. He was a model of his type, one of the bravest men in the country, and he had a wife of excellent and influential family, as finely bred as she was faithful to him. They lived happily for several years, since it was a marriage of truth and love. But then a war broke out and he went away to join the fighting. There he fell in love with a girl, a ravishingly pretty princess called Guilliadun. The Celtic name of the wife who stayed at home was Guildelüec, and so the story is called *Guildelüec and Guilliadun* after their names. Its original title was *Eliduc*, but it was changed because it's really about the two women. Now I'll tell you exactly how it all happened.

Eliduc's overlord was the king of Brittany, who was very fond of the knight and looked after his interests. Eliduc served him faithfully—whenever the king had to go abroad, Eliduc was left in charge of his territories, and kept them safe by his military skills. He got many favors in return. He was allowed to hunt in the royal forests. No gamekeeper, even the most resolute, dared stand in his way or complain about him. But other people's envy of his good luck did its usual work. He was slandered and traduced, and brought into bad relations with the king. Finally he was dismissed from the court without any reason. Left in the dark, Eliduc repeatedly asked to be allowed to defend himself before the king—the slanders were lies, he had served the king well, and happily so. But no answer came from the court. Convinced he would never get a hearing, Eliduc decided to go into exile. So he went home and called together all his friends.

1. Translated by John Fowles. The punctuation ". . ." does not indicate omissions from this text.

He told them how things lay with the king, of the anger toward him. Eliduc had done the best he could and there was no justice in the royal resentment. When the plowman gets the rough edge of his master's tongue, the peasants have a proverb: *Never trust a great man's love.* If someone in Eliduc's position is sensible, he puts more trust in the love of his neighbors. So now he says[2] he's sick of Brittany, he'll cross the sea to England and amuse himself there for awhile. He'll leave his wife at home; have his servants take care of her, along with his friends.

Once it was made, he kept to this decision. He fitted himself—and the ten horsemen he took with him—out handsomely for the journey. His friends were very sad to see him go, and as for his wife . . . she accompanied him for the first part of the journey, in tears that she was losing him. But he swore solemnly that he would stay true to her. Then he says good-bye and rides straight on to the sea. There he takes ship, crosses successfully and arrives at the port of Totnes.[3]

There were several kings in that part of England, and they were at war. Toward Exeter in this country there lived a very powerful old man. He had no male heir, simply an unmarried daughter. This explained the present war: because he had refused her hand to an equal from another dynasty, the other king was putting all his land to the sack. He had trapped the old king in one of his fortified cities.[4] No one there had the courage to go out and join combat, general or single, with the invader. Eliduc heard about all this and decided that since there was war he would stay in those parts instead of going on. He wanted to help the besieged king, who was getting into worse and worse trouble and faced with ruin and disaster. He would hire himself out as a mercenary.[5]

He sent messengers to the king, explaining in a letter that he had left his own country and had come to help him; but he was at the king's disposal and if he didn't want Eliduc's services, then Eliduc asked only for safe-conduct through his lands, so that he could go and offer his fighting abilities somewhere else. When the king saw the messengers, he was delighted and welcomed them warmly. He summoned the castle commander and ordered that an escort be provided immediately for Eliduc and that he should be brought to him.

2. The shifts to the narrative present (like those into dialogue) are all in the original. [Translator's note.]   3. On the southern coast of England.   4. The text says "in a castle," but it seems clear that Exeter, then a walled city, is meant. Marie would have known of its importance in West Saxon times and of William the Conqueror's siege of 1068. [Translator's note.]   5. . . . *en soudees remaneir.* The knight *soudoyer* has to be understood (at least in romance) in a far more honorable, and honordriven, sense than in the contemporary or even the Renaissance use of "mercenary." Perhaps the Japanese samurai is the best equivalent. [Translator's note.] Similarly, the Knight of Chaucer's *Canterbury Tales* was an honorable mercenary; see the *General Prologue,* ll. 46–65.

Then the king had lodgings arranged. All that was necessary for a month's stay was also provided.

The escort were armed and horsed and sent to fetch Eliduc. He was received with great honor, having made the journey without trouble. His lodging was with a rich townsman, a decent and well-mannered man who gave up his tapestry-hung best room to the knight. Eliduc had a good meal prepared and invited to it all the other anxious knights[6] who were quartered in the city. He forbade his own men, even the most grabbing, to accept any gift or wages for the first forty days.

On his third day at Exeter the cry ran through the city that the enemy had arrived and were all over the surrounding countryside—and already preparing an attack on the city gates. Eliduc heard the uproar from the panicking townspeople and immediately donned armor. His companions did the same. There were fourteen other knights capable of fighting in the town, the rest being wounded, or captured. Seeing Eliduc mount his horse, they go to their lodgings and put on their own armor as well. They won't wait to be called, they'll go out of the gates with him.

"We'll ride with you, sir," they now say. "And whatever you do, we'll do the same."

Eliduc answers. "My thanks. Is there anyone here who knows an ambush place? A defile? Somewhere where we might catch them hopping? If we wait here, we'll get a good fight. But we have no advantage. Has anyone a better plan?"

"There's a narrow cart road, sir. Beside that wood by the flax field over there. When they've got enough loot, they'll return by it. They ride back carelessly from such work, as a rule. Like that they're asking for a quick death."

It could be over in a flash; and much damage done.

"My friends," said Eliduc, "one thing for certain. Nothing venture, even when things look hopeless, then nothing gain—either in war or reputation. You're all the king's men, you owe him complete loyalty. So follow me. Wherever I go, and do as I do. I promise you there won't be setbacks if I can help it. We may not get any loot. But we'll never be forgotten if we beat the enemy today."

His confidence spread to the other knights and they led him to the wood. There they hid by the road and waited for the enemy to return from their raid. Eliduc had planned everything, showed them how they should charge at the gallop and what to cry. When the enemy reached the narrow place, Eliduc shouted the battle challenge, then cried to his friends to fight well. They struck hard, and gave no

6. Anxious because of their precarious or uncertain status.

quarter. Taken by surprise, the enemy were soon broken and put to flight. The engagement was brief. They captured the officer in command and many other knights, whom they entrust to their squires. Eliduc's side had had twenty-five men, and they took thirty of the enemy. They also took a great deal of armor, and a quantity of other valuable things. Now they return triumphantly to the city, full of this splendid victory. The king was there on a tower, desperately anxious for his men. He complained bitterly, having convinced himself that Eliduc was a traitor and had lost him all his knights.

They come in a crowd, some laden, others bound—many more on the return than at the going out, which was why the king was misled and stayed in doubt and suspense. He orders the city gates closed and the people up on the walls, bows and other weapons at the ready. But they have no need of them. Eliduc's party had sent a squire galloping on ahead to explain what had happened. The man told the king about the Breton mercenary, how he had driven the enemy away, how well he had conducted himself. There was never a better handler of arms on horseback. He had personally captured the enemy commander and taken twenty-nine prisoners, besides wounding and killing many others.

When the king hears the good news, he's beside himself with joy. He came down from the tower and went to meet Eliduc; then thanked him for all he had done and gave him all the prisoners for ransoming. Eliduc shared out the armor among the other knights, keeping no more for his own men than three horses that had been allocated to them. He distributed everything else, even his own rightful part as well, among the prisoners and the other people.

After this exploit the king made Eliduc his favorite. He retained him and his companions for a whole year and Eliduc gave his oath of faithful service. He then became the protector of the king's lands.

The king's young daughter heard all about Eliduc and his splendid actions—how good-looking he was, such a proud knight, how civilized and openhanded. She sent one of her personal pages to request, to *beg* Eliduc to come and amuse her. They must talk, get to know each other, and she would be very hurt if he didn't come. Eliduc replies: of course he'll come, he looks forward very much to meeting her. He got on his horse; and taking a servant with him, he goes to chat with the girl. When he's at the door of her room, he sends the page ahead. He doesn't barge in, but waits a little, till the page comes back. Then with gentle expression, sincere face and perfect good manners he addressed the young lady formally and thanked her for having invited him to visit her. Guilliadun was very pretty, and she took him by the hand and led him to a couch, where they sat and talked of this and that. She kept stealing looks at him . . . his face, his body, his every expression . . . and said to herself how attractive he was, how close to her ideal man. Love fires his arrow, she falls headlong in love. She goes pale, she sighs, but she can't declare herself, in case he despises her for it.

Eliduc stayed a long time, but in the end took his leave and went away. Guilliadun was very unwilling to let him go, but there it was. He returned to his lodgings, unsmiling and very thoughtful. The girl alarmed him, since she was the king's daughter and he the king's servant. She had seemed so shy, yet subtly accused him of something. He feels badly done by[7]—to have been so long in the country, yet not to have seen her once till now. Yet when he said that to himself, he felt ashamed. He remembered his wife, and how he had promised to behave as a husband should.

Now she had met him, the girl wanted to make Eliduc her lover. She had never liked a man more—if only she can, if only he'll agree. All night she was awake thinking of him, and had neither rest nor sleep. The next morning she got up at dawn and went to a window and called down to her page. Then she revealed everything to him.

"Dear God," she says, "I'm in such a state, I've fallen into such a trap. I love the new mercenary. Eliduc. Who's fought so brilliantly. I haven't slept a wink all night, my eyes just wouldn't shut. If he's really in love with me, if he'll only show he's serious, I'll do anything he likes. And there's so much to hope for—he could be king here one day. I'm mad about him. He's so intelligent, so easy-mannered. If he doesn't love me, I'll die of despair."

When he'd heard all she had to say, the young page gave her good advice: no need to give up hope so soon.

"My lady, if you're in love with him, then let him know it. Send him a belt or a ribbon—or a ring. To see if it pleases him. If he's happy to accept the gift, looks glad to heard from you, then you're in. He loves you. And show me an emperor who wouldn't dance for joy if he knew you fancied him."

The girl mulled over this advice.

"But how shall I know just by a gift whether he really wants me? You don't realize. A gentleman has to accept, whether he likes the sender or not. One has to take such things with good grace. I should loathe it if he made fun of me. But perhaps you could learn something from his expression. So get ready. Quickly. And go."

"I am ready."

"Take him this gold ring. And here, give him my belt. And be very warm when you greet him for me."

The page turned away, leaving her in such a state that she very nearly calls him back. Nevertheless she lets him go—and then begins to rave to herself.

---

7. The Old French is less specific: it is too bad it turned out they hadn't met.

"Oh God, I've fallen in love with a foreigner! I don't even know if he's of good family. Whether he won't suddenly disappear. I shall be left in despair. I'm insane to have made it all so obvious. I'd never even spoken with him before yesterday, and now I'm throwing myself at him. I think he'll just despise me. No he won't, if he's nice he'll like me for it. It's all in the lap of the gods now. If he doesn't care for me at all, I shall feel such a fool. I'll never be happy again, as long as I live."

Meanwhile, as she agonized on like that, the page rode fast on his way. He found Eliduc and gave him in private the kind of greetings the girl had asked. Then he handed him the little ring and the belt. The knight had thanked him, then put the ring on his finger and fastened the belt[8] around his waist. But he said nothing else to the page, asked him nothing—except that he offered him his own ring and belt in return. But the page didn't accept them and went away back to his young mistress. He found her in her room; then passed on Eliduc's return of greetings and thanks.

"For pity's sake, don't hide the truth. Does he really love me?"

"I think so. He wouldn't deceive you. In my opinion he's playing polite and being shrewd—he knows how to hide his feelings. I said hallo to him for you and gave him the presents. He put the belt on himself, and was rather careful to get it right. Then the ring on his finger. I didn't say anything else to him. Or he to me."

"But did he realize what it meant? Because if he didn't, I'm lost!"

"I honestly don't know. But if you must have my solemn opinion, then, well, since he didn't turn up his nose at what you sent, he doesn't exactly . . . hate you?"

"Stop teasing me, you cheeky boy! I'm perfectly well aware he doesn't hate me. How could I ever hurt him? Except by loving him so much. But if he does, he deserves to die. Until I've spoken with him myself, I won't have anything to do with him. Either through you or anyone else. I'll show him myself how wanting him tears me apart. But if only I knew how long he was staying here!"

"Lady, the king has him under contract for a year. That ought to be time enough to show him how you feel?"

When she heard Eliduc wasn't going away, Guilliadun was in ecstasy: how wonderful that he must stay! What she didn't know was the torment Eliduc had been in from the moment he set eyes on her. Fear had dealt him a cruel hand—that promise to his wife when he left home, that he'd never look at another woman. Now his heart was in a vise. He wanted to stay faithful. But nothing could hide the fact that he had hopelessly fallen for Guilliadun and her prettiness. To see her again and talk with her, kiss her and hold her in his arms

---

8. The fashionable belt of the Middle Ages had links, with a hook at one end. It was fastened with a free end left hanging at the side.

. . . yet he could never show her this longing, which would disgrace him—on the one hand for breaking his promise to his wife, on the other because of his relationship with the king. He was torn in two; then mounted his horse, and havered no more. He calls his friends to him, then goes to the castle to speak to the king. If it can be managed, he will see the girl—and that is why he hurries so.

The king has just risen from table and gone to his daughter's rooms, and now he's begun to play chess with a knight from overseas. On the other side of the chessboard, his daughter had to show the moves. Eliduc came forward. The king greeted him kindly and made Eliduc sit beside him. He spoke to his daughter.

"My dear, you must get to know this gentleman. And pay him every honor. There's no finer knight in the country."

The girl was delighted to hear this command from her father. She stands up, invites Eliduc to sit with her well away from the others. Both are struck dumb with love. She dared not explain herself to him, and he was afraid to speak as well . . . except to thank her for the presents she had sent him: he had never liked a present so much. She tells him she is pleased that he is pleased. Then suddenly why she sent him the ring, and her belt as well—that her body was his, she couldn't resist, she loved him to madness, she gave herself to his every wish. If she couldn't have him, he knew, he must know it was true, no other man would ever have her.

Now it was Eliduc's turn.

"Princess, I'm so happy that you love me. All joy. That you should like me so much—how could I feel otherwise? I shan't ever forget it. You know I'm promised to your father for a year, under oath that I shan't leave till the war's ended. Then I shall go home. Provided you'll let me. I don't want to stay here."

"Eliduc, I'm so grateful for your frankness. You're so honest, you know such a lot. Long before you go you'll have decided what to do with me. I love you, I trust you more than anything else in the world."

They knew now that they were sure of each other; and on that occasion no more was said.

Eliduc goes back to his lodgings, enchanted at how well things have turned out. He can talk as often as he likes with Guilliadun, they're wildly in love.

He now occupied himself so well with the war that he captured the enemy king, and liberated the old king's country. His military reputation grew, as did that of his ingenuity and public generosity. On this side of his life everything went very well.

But during this same time the king of Brittany had sent three messengers over the sea to find Eliduc. Things at home were in a very bad way, and getting worse. All his strong points were under siege, his lands being put to the sword. With increasing bitterness, the king regretted having driven Eliduc away. His judgment had been distorted by the malicious advice he had listened to. Already he had thrown the treacherous clique who had blackened Eliduc and intrigued against him into permanent exile. Now, in his hour of great need, he commanded, he summoned, he begged Eliduc—in the name of the trust that had existed between them ever since the knight first paid homage to him—to come and save the situation. He was in the direst straits.

Eliduc read this news. It distressed him deeply. He thought of Guilliadun. He loved her now to the anguished depths of his being, and she felt the same for him. But there had been no madness between them—nothing improper, theirs was no casual affair. Caressing and talking, giving each other lovely presents—the passionate feeling between them hadn't gone beyond that. She kept it so on purpose, because of what she hoped. She thought he'd be entirely hers, and hers alone, if she played her cards right.

She did not know there was a wife.

"Alas," thinks Eliduc to himself, "I've gone astray. I've stayed too long here. It was cursed, the day I first set eyes on this country. I've fallen head over heels in love. And she with me. If I have to say farewell to her now, one of us will die. Perhaps both. And yet I must go, the king of Brittany's letter commands it, and there's my promise to him. To say nothing of the one I swore my wife. I must pull myself together. I can't stay any longer, I have no alternative. If I were to marry Guilliadun, the Church would never stand for it. In all ways it's a mess. And oh God, to think of never seeing her again! I must be open with her, whatever the cost. I'll do whatever she wants, whichever way she sees it. Her father has got a decent peace, no one wants war with him anymore. I'll plead the king of Brittany's need and ask for permission to leave before the day's out. It was what was agreed—I'd go to him as soon as we had peace here. I'll see Guilliadun and explain the whole business. Then she can tell me what she wants, and I'll do my best to make it come true."

Without further delay, Eliduc went to the king to seek leave. He explained the situation in Brittany and showed him the letter the king there had sent him—the cry for help. The old king reads the command and realizes he will lose Eliduc. He is very upset and worried. He offered him a share of his possessions, a third of his heritage, his treasury—if he'll only stay, he'll do so much for him that Eliduc will be eternally grateful.

But Eliduc stayed firm.

"At this juncture, since my king's in danger and he's taken such trouble to find me, I must go to his assistance. Nothing would make me stop here. But if you ever need my services again, I'll willingly return—and bring plenty of other knights with me."

At that the king thanked him and gave him leave to go without further argument. He puts all his household possessions at Eliduc's disposal—gold and silver, hounds and horses and beautiful silk. Eliduc took no more than he needed. Then he politely told the king that he would like very much to speak with his daughter, if it were allowed.

"Consent is a pleasure," said the king.

Eliduc sends a young lady ahead to open the door of Guilliadun's room. Then he goes in to speak with her. When she saw him, she cried out his name and passionately clung to him. Then they discussed his problem, and he explained briefly the necessity for his journey. But when he had made it all clear, and yet pointedly still not asked for her permission to leave, for his freedom, she nearly fainted with the shock. Her face went white. When Eliduc sees the agony she is in, he begins to go mad. He keeps kissing her mouth and begins to cry in sympathy. At last he takes her in his arms and holds her until she recovers.

"You sweetest thing, oh God, listen—you're life and death to me, you're my whole existence. That's why I've come. So that we can talk about it, and trust each other. I must go home. I've got your father's permission. But I'll do whatever you want. Whatever may happen to me."

"Then take me with you, if you don't want to stay! If you don't, I'll kill myself. Nothing good or happy will ever happen to me again."

Gently Eliduc tells her how much he loves her; how beautiful she is. "But I've solemnly sworn to obey your father. If I take you away with me I'll be breaking my oath to him before its term is over. I swear, I promise you with all my heart that if you'll let me leave you now for a while, but name a day on which I must come back, then nothing on earth will stop me doing so—as long as I'm alive and in good health. My life's entirely in your hands."

She loved him so much. So she gave him a final date, a day by which he must return and take her away. They parted in tears and misery, exchanging their gold rings and tenderly kissing each other.

Eliduc rode to the sea. The wind was good and the crossing quick. When he gets home, the king of Brittany is overjoyed, and so are Eliduc's relations and friends and everyone else—and especially his wife, who remained as attractive and worthy of him as ever. But all the time Eliduc stayed turned in on himself, because of the shock of his love affair in England. Nothing he saw gave him any pleasure, he wouldn't smile—he'll never be happy till he sees Guilliadun again. His wife was very depressed by his secretive behavior, since she had no idea what caused it. She felt sorry for herself; kept asking if he hadn t heard from someone that she'd misbehaved while he was abroad. She'll willingly defend herself before the world, whenever he wants.

"My lady, no one's accused you of anything bad. But I've solemnly sworn to the king in the country where I've been that I shall return to him. He has great need of me. I told him I'd be on my way within a week, as soon as the king of Brittany had peace. I've got a huge task ahead of me before I can return. I can't take pleasure in anything at all until I've got back there. I *will* not break promises."

And that was all he told his wife. He went to join the king of Brittany and helped him greatly. The king adopted his strategy and saved his kingdom. But when the date approached that Guilliadun had named, Eliduc intervened to make peace. He agreed to all the terms the enemy wanted,[9] then he got ready to travel and picked his companions—two nephews he was fond of and one of his pages, a boy who had known what was going on and had carried messages between Eliduc and Guilliadun. Besides them, only his squires; he didn't want anyone else. He made these companions swear to keep the secret.

He waits no longer, puts to sea and soon arrives in Totnes. At last he was back where he was so longed for. Eliduc was very cunning. He found an inn well away from the harbor, since he was very anxious not to be seen . . . traced and recognized. He got his page ready and sent him to Guilliadun to tell her he had returned and kept strictly to his promise. By night, when darkness had fallen, she must slip out of the city; the page would escort her and Eliduc come to meet her. The boy changed into a disguise and went all the way on foot straight to Exeter. He cleverly found a way to get into her private apartments; then greeted the princess and told her her lover had come back. He found her sad and hopeless, but when she hears the news she breaks down and begins to cry, then kisses and kisses the page. He told her she must leave with him that evening; and they spent the whole day planning their escape in every detail.

When night had come, they stole cautiously out of the city alone together. They were terrified someone might see them. She wore a silk dress delicately embroidered in gold and a short cloak.

About a bowshot from the city gate there was a copse enclosed in a fine garden. Eliduc, who had come to fetch her, waited under the hedge. The page led her to the place. Eliduc sprang down from his horse and kissed her: such joy to meet again. He helped her onto a horse, then mounted his own and took her bridle. They rode quickly away, back to the port of Totnes, and boarded the ship at once: no other passengers but Eliduc's men and his beloved Guilliadun. They had favorable winds and settled weather, but when they came near

*9. The Old French says that he reconciled the enemy (to the king).

the coast of Brittany they ran into a storm. A contrary wind drove them out away from the harbor. Then the mast split and broke, and they lost all the sails. They prayed in despair—to God, to St. Nicholas and St. Clement—to Our Lady, that she might invoke Christ's protection for them, save them from drowning and bring them to land. Backward and forward they were driven along the coast, the storm raging around them. One of the sailors began to shout.

"What are we doing? My lord, it's the girl you've brought aboard who's going to drown us all. We'll never reach land. You have a proper wife at home. But now you want another woman. It's against God and the law. Against all decency and religion. So let's throw her in the sea, and save our skins."

Eliduc hears what the man cries, and nearly goes berserk.

"You son of a whore, you fiend, you rat—shut your mouth! If she goes into the sea, I'll make you pay for it!"

He held Guilliadun in his arms, gave her what comfort he could. She was seasick, and riven by what she'd just heard: that her lover had a wife at home. She fainted and fell to the deck, deathly pale; and stayed like that, without breath or sign of consciousness. Eliduc knew she was only there because of him, and sincerely thought she was dead. He was in agony. He stood up and rushed at the sailor and struck him down with an oar. The man collapsed to the deck and Eliduc kicked the body over the side, where the waves took it away. As soon as he had done that, he went to the helm. There he steered and held the ship so well that they came to the harbor and land. When they were safely in, he cast anchor and had the gangway let down. Still Guilliadun lay unconscious, her only appearance that of death. Eliduc wept without stop—if he had had his way, he would have been dead with her. He asked his companions their advice, where he could carry her. He refused to leave her side until she was buried with every honor and full ritual, and laid to rest in holy ground. She was a king's daughter, it was her due. But his men were at a loss and could suggest nothing. Eliduc began to think for himself. His own house was not far from the sea, not a day's ride away. There was a forest around it, some thirty miles across. A saintly hermit had lived there for forty years and had a chapel. Eliduc had often spoken with him.

I'll take her there, Eliduc said to himself, I'll bury her in his chapel. Then bestow land and found an abbey or a monastery. Nuns or canons, who can pray for her every day, may God have mercy on her soul.

He had horses brought and ordered everyone to mount, then made them promise they would never betray him. He carried Guilliadun's body in front of him, on his own horse. They took the most direct road and soon entered the forest. At last they came to the chapel, and called and knocked. But no voice answered and the door stayed closed. Eliduc made one of his men climb in and open it. They found a fresh tomb: the pure and saintly hermit had died that previous week. They stood there sad and dismayed. The men wanted to prepare the grave in which Eliduc must leave Guilliadun forever, but he made them withdraw outside the chapel.

"This isn't right. I need advice first from the experts on how I can glorify this place with an abbey or a convent. For now we'll lay Guilliadun before the altar and leave her in God's care."

He had bedding brought and they quickly made a resting place for the girl; then laid her there, and left her for dead. But when Eliduc came to leave the chapel, he thought he would die of pain. He kissed her eyes, her face.

"Darling heart, may it please God I'll never bear arms again or live in the outer world. I damn the day you ever saw me. Dear gentle thing, why did you come with me? Not even a queen could have loved me more trustingly. More deeply. My heart breaks for you. On the day I bury you, I'll enter a monastery. Then come here every day and weep all my desolation out on your tomb."

Abruptly then he turned from the girl's body and closed the chapel door.

He had sent a messenger on ahead to tell his wife he was coming, but tired and worn. Full of happiness at the news, she dressed to meet him; and welcomed him back affectionately. But she had little joy of it. Eliduc gave her not a single smile or a kind word. No one dared to ask why. He stayed like that for a couple of days—each early morning, having heard mass, he took the road to the forest and the chapel where Guilliadun lay . . . still unconscious, without breathing, no sign of life. Yet something greatly puzzled him: she had hardly lost color, her skin stayed pink and white, only very faintly pale. In profound despair, Eliduc wept and prayed for her soul. Then having done that, he returned home.

The following day, when he came out of the church after mass, there was a spy—a young servant his wife had promised horses and arms to if he could follow at a distance and see which way his master went. The lad did as she ordered. He rides into the forest after Eliduc without being seen. He watched well, saw how Eliduc went into the chapel, and heard the state he was in. As soon as Eliduc came out, the servant went home and told his mistress everything—all the sounds of anguish her husband had made inside the chapel. From being resentful, she now felt touched.

"We'll go there as soon as possible and search the place. Your master must be off soon to court, to confer with the king. The hermit died some time ago. I know Eludic was very fond of him, but that wouldn't make him behave like this. Not show such grief."

Thus for the time being she left the mystery.

That very same afternoon Eliduc set off to speak with the king of Brittany. His wife took the servant with her and he led her to the hermitage chapel. As soon as she went in she saw the bed and the girl lying on it, as fresh as a first rose. She pulled back the covering and revealed the slender body, the slim arms, the white hands with their long and delicately smooth-skinned fingers. She knew the truth at once—why Eliduc had his tragic face. She called the servant forward and showed him the miraculous corpse.

"Do you see this girl? She's as lovely as a jewel. She's my husband's mistress. That's why he's so miserable. Somehow it doesn't shock me. So pretty . . . to have died so young. I feel only pity for her. And I still love him. It's a tragedy for us all."

She began to cry, in sympathy for Guilliadun. But as she sat by the deathbed with tears in her eyes a weasel darts out from beneath the altar. The servant struck at it with a stick to stop it running over the corpse. He killed it, then threw the small body into the middle of the chancel floor. It had not been there long when its mate appeared and saw where it lay. The living animal ran around the dead one's head and touched it several times with a foot. But when this failed, it seemed distressed. Suddenly it ran out of the chapel into the forest grass. There it picked a deep red flower with its teeth, then carried it quickly back and placed it in the mouth of the weasel the servant had killed. Instantly the animal came back to life. The wife had watched all this, and now she cried out to the servant.

"Catch it! Throw, boy! Don't let it escape!"

He hurled his stick and hit the weasel. The blossom fell from between its teeth. Eliduc's wife went and picked it up, then returned and placed the exquisite red flower in Guilliadun's mouth. For a second or two nothing happened, but then the girl stirred, sighed, and opened her eyes.[1]

"Good lord," she murmured, "how long I've slept!"

When the wife heard her speak, she thanked heaven. Then she asked Guilliadun who she was.

"My lady, I'm British born, the daughter of a king there. I fell hopelessly in love with a knight, a brave mercenary called Eliduc. He eloped with me. But he was wicked, he deceived me. He had a wife all the time. He never told me, never gave me the least hint. When I heard the truth, I fainted with the agony of it. Now he's brutally left me helpless here in a foreign country. He tricked me, I don't know what will become of me. Women are mad to trust in men."

"My dear," said the lady, "he's been quite inconsolable. I can assure you of that. He thinks you're dead, he's been mad with grief.

---

1. Abundant parallels from folklore represent an animal as having the gift of immortality—or being able to restore life after apparent death.

He's come here to look at you every day. But obviously you've always been unconscious. I'm his real wife, and I'm deeply sorry for him. He was so unhappy . . . I wanted to find out where he was disappearing to, so I had him followed, and that's how I found you. And now I'm glad you're alive after all. I'm going to take you away with me. And give you back to him. I'll tell the world he's not to blame for anything. Then I shall take the veil."

She spoke so comfortingly that Guilliadun went home with her. The wife made the servant get ready and sent him after Eliduc. He rode hard and soon came up with him. The lad greeted Eliduc respectfully, then tells him the whole story. Eliduc leaps on a horse, without waiting for his friends. That same night he was home, and found Guilliadun restored to life. He gently thanks his wife, he's in his seventh heaven, he's never known such happiness. He can't stop kissing Guilliadun; and she keeps kissing him shyly back. They can't hide their joy at being reunited. When Eliduc's wife saw how things stood, she told her husband her plans. She asked his formal permission for a separation, she wished to become a nun and serve God. He must give her some of his land and she would found an abbey on it. And then he must marry the girl he loved so much, since it was neither decent nor proper, besides being against the law, to live with two wives. Eliduc did not try to argue with her; he'll do exactly as she wants and give her the land.

In the same woodlands near the castle that held the hermitage chapel he had a church built, and all the other offices of a nunnery. Then he settled a great deal of property and other possessions on it. When everything was ready, his wife took the veil, along with thirty other nuns. Thus she established her order and her new way of life.

Eliduc married Guilliadun. The wedding was celebrated with great pomp and circumstance, and for a long time they lived happily together in a perfect harmony of love. They gave a great deal away and performed many good deeds, so much so that in the end they also turned religious. After great deliberation and forethought, Eliduc had a church built on the other side of his castle and endowed it with all his money and the greater part of his estate. He appointed servants and other religious people to look after the order and its buildings. When all was ready, he delays no more: he surrenders himself with his servants to omnipotent God. And Guilliadun, whom he loved so much, he sent to join his first wife. Guildelüec received her as if she were her own sister and did her great honor, teaching her how to serve God and live the religious life of the order. They prayed for the salvation of Eliduc's soul, and in his turn he prayed for both of them. He found out by messengers how they were, how they comforted each other. All three tried in their own ways to love God with true faith; and in the end, by the mercy of God in whom all truth reposes, each died a peaceful death.

The noble Celts composed this story long ago to enshrine the strange adventure of these three. May it never be forgotten!

---

# DANTE ALIGHIERI
## 1265–1321

The greatest poem of the Middle Ages, called by its author a comedy and designated by later centuries *The Divine Comedy (La divina commedia)*, was written in the early fourteenth century. The poet, Dante Alighieri, was born in late May 1265, in Florence, Italy. In 1291 he married Gemma Donati, by whom he had two sons and one or two daughters. In 1295 he was a member of the "people's council" of Florence, and in 1300 served for two months, the usual term, as one of the six priors, or magistrates, of Florence. In 1302 the Blacks, opponents of the Whites (a political group with which Dante was affiliated), seized power in Florence, and he, with other White leaders, was exiled. Dante had gone to Rome on a mission to Pope Boniface in 1301, and as the decree of banishment was soon coupled with a condemnation to execution by fire (on false charges of corruption in office), he never returned to his native city. The last twenty years of his life, from 1301 to 1321, were spent in exile in various parts of Italy and possibly elsewhere. He died at Ravenna in September 1321.

*The New Life* was probably written about 1292. It consists of sonnets and odes with a prose account and running commentary by the poet; the poems were mostly inspired by Beatrice. *The Banquet*, of uncertain date, unfinished, is a work of encyclopedic scope in the form of a prose commentary on a series of the poet's odes *(canzoni)*. *On the Vernacular Language*, in Latin prose, of uncertain date, unfinished, is an essay on language and poetry, especially on the dialects of Italy and Provence; it is of great linguistic and literary interest. *On Single Government*, in Latin prose, of uncertain date, presents a closely reasoned defense of world government, together with an attempt to demonstrate the independent status of the Holy Roman Empire and the Papacy.

*The Divine Comedy*, date of beginning uncertain, was apparently finished shortly before Dante's death in 1321. The poem is in many ways both the supreme and the centrally representative expression of medieval man in imaginative literature. But to appreciate the poem adequately in this light a reader must know it in its entirety, since it is an organic whole designed with the utmost symmetry. The present volume contains the entire *Inferno* and several cantos from the other two divisions. It will be best to look rapidly at the general plan and then concentrate on the part included in this book.

The three great divisions of the poem, *Hell (Inferno)*, *Purgatory (Purgatorio)*, and *Paradise (Paradiso)*, are of identical length; each of the last two has thirty-three cantos, and the first, the *Inferno*, has thirty-four; but the opening canto is a prologue to the entire poem. The total, one hundred, is the square of ten, regarded in the thought of the time as a perfect number. The three divisions correspond in number to the Trinity. Nine, the square

of three, figures centrally in the interior structure of each of the three divisions. In Hell, the lost souls are arranged in three main groups, and occupy
nine circles. Most of the circles are themselves subdivided. Hell itself is a
funnel-shaped opening in the earth extending from the surface to the center.
Dante's journey thus takes him steadily downward through the nine concentric circles. The progression is from the least to the greatest types of evil; all
the souls are irrevocably condemned, but all are not intrinsically equal in
the degree or nature of their sinfulness. Thus, as we follow Dante in his
descent, we find first an ante-Hell, the abode of those who refused to choose
between right and wrong; then the boundary river, Acheron; then a circle
for virtuous pagans who knew not Christ; and then a series of circles occupied by those guilty of sins of self-indulgence, or Incontinence, of all kinds.
These include the illicit lovers, the gluttons, the hoarders and spendthrifts,
and those of violent or sullen disposition. Comparable classes and subclasses
are found within the other two main groups of sinners, those guilty respectively of Violence and of Fraud, the latter including treachery and treason.
At the bottom is the fallen angel, Satan, or Lucifer.

Purgatory is situated on a lofty mountain rising on an island in the sea. It
is divided into the ante-Purgatory, which is the lower half of the mountain;
Purgatory proper, just above; and the Earthly Paradise, or Garden of Eden,
at the summit. Purgatory proper is arranged in a series of seven ledges encircling the mountain, each devoted to the purification of souls from particular
kinds of sinful disposition—Pride, Envy, Anger, Sloth, Avarice, Gluttony,
and Illicit Love. These seven divisions, plus the ante-Purgatory and the Earthly
Paradise, make a total of nine.

The *Paradise* takes us, in ascending order, through the circles of the seven
planets of medieval astronomy, the moon, Mercury, Venus, the sun, Mars,
Jupiter, and Saturn; then through the circles of the fixed stars and the *primum mobile*, or outermost circle, which moves the others; and finally to the
Empyrean, or Heaven itself, the abode of God, the angels, and the redeemed
souls. Again we have nine circles, besides the Empyrean, inclusion of which
would give a total of ten. Such is the vast design and scope of *The Divine
Comedy* as a whole.

### INFERNO

The poem itself begins with action, not outline; explanations come along in
suitable places; they are part of the traveler's experience. We shall do well to
follow the hint. The incidents recounted in Canto I of the *Inferno* are concrete and definite; their literal meaning is perfectly plain. As critics have
often said, Dante is a highly visual poet; he gives us clear pictures or images.
Beginning with a man lost in a wood, hindered by three beasts from escape
by his own effort, the canto might well be the start of a tale of unusual but
quite earthly adventures. But when the stranger Dante meets identifies himself as the shade of the poet Virgil and offers to conduct him through realms
which, though not named, can only be Hell and Purgatory, we realize that
there is a meaning beyond the one which appears on the surface. We recognize that the wood, the mountain, the sun, and the three beasts, though
casually introduced, are not casual features of the scene. They represent
something other than themselves; they are symbols. In the light of the entire

poem, it is usually possible to tell what these other things are, and in this volume the headnotes and footnotes identify them. Occasionally, however, there is doubt. What do the three beasts stand for? A lack of certainty is not a serious disadvantage to readers; they should regard it as a challenge to reach a correct decision for themselves. Indeed, if they go on to read the entire poem, they may arrive at an identification that seems sounder and more consistent with the work as a whole than those proposed. Meanwhile, there is no ambiguity about the animals themselves; they are the satisfying and specific images of poetry.

The simple style of this first canto may surprise readers who have been told that *The Divine Comedy* is one of the five or six great poems of European literature, especially if they assume that it will sound like an epic. For Dante begins with neither the splendor of Homer nor the stateliness of Virgil nor the grandeur of Milton. Indeed, except for the use of verse, Canto I seems more like a narrative by Defoe or Swift, particularly at the outset. It is quiet, factual, economical; it convinces us by its air of serious simplicity. Dante called the poem a comedy, in accordance with the use of the term in his day, not only because it began in misery and ended in happiness, but also because in that literary form a sustained loftiness of style was not requisite. In other words, he is free to use the whole range of style, from the humblest, including the colloquial and the humorous, to the highest. There is, indeed, a great variety of tone in the poem. Yet readers will doubtless eventually agree that Dante strikes the right note *for him* at the beginning. Variation will result chiefly from change in intensity, achieved by differing degrees of concentration and repetition—rather than from a shift to the "grand style." This unpretentious manner is, we see, most suitable to a prolonged work of serious fiction in which the author is the central character. For *The Divine Comedy* is not primarily a Cook's tour of the world of the dead; it is an account of the effect of such a journey on the man who takes it—Dante. It is a record of his moral and spiritual experience of illumination, regeneration, and beatitude. We are interested partly because of the unique and individual character of the traveler—Dante as the man he was, the man revealed in the poem—and partly because the experience of the author is imaginatively available and meaningful to all of us.

In Canto IV we come to the first of the nine concentric circles of Hell. Here are the noble heroes, wise philosophers, and inspired poets of the ancient—and medieval—pagan world. They are excluded from Heaven because they knew nothing of Christ and his religion. This fate may seem harsh to us, but the orthodox view recognized only one gate to Heaven. These spirits suffer no punishment, Virgil (who is one of them) tells Dante, only "without hope, we live on in desire." Here Dante's fervent pity and sympathy at once nourish and mirror the reader's; but there is no rebellion against God's decree. Further explanation, and thereby justification, in Dante's view, will come as the poem progresses toward its goal.

With Canto V we reach the second circle, the first of those containing souls guilty of active sin unrepented at the time of death, and hence suffering a penalty in Hell. Here, therefore, is found the contemptuous and monstrous judge Minos, another figure taken from classical myth and freely adapted to Dante's purposes. The souls assigned to the second circle are those guilty of unlawful love. The poet's method here, as throughout the journey, is first to point out a number of prominent figures who would be familiar to his fourteenth-century readers, and then to concentrate attention on a very few, one or two in each circle, telling more about them and eliciting his own story from each. In general, Dante lets the place and condition in which the sinners are found serve as a minimum essential of information. For the penalties in the various circles are of many different kinds. Their fundamental characteristic is appropriateness to the particular sin; this is one of the principal differences between the punishments in Dante's Hell and the miscellaneous and arbitrary horrors of many accounts of the place. In Dante the penalties symbolize the sin. Thus the illicit lovers of the second circle are continually blown about by storm winds, for their sin consisted in the surrender of reason to lawless passions.

Here we find Paolo and Francesca, the best-known figures of the entire *Divine Comedy*. Like all the human beings presented in the poem, they actually existed. They lived in Italy about the time of Dante's childhood and early youth, and were slain by Francesca's husband, a brother of Paolo. Dante's method, it is hence clear, is not to build up an allegorical cast of personified abstractions. Instead of, say, Passion and Rebellion, he portrays Paolo and Francesca. They represent, or symbolize, sinful love by example. They show how an intrinsically noble emotion, love, if contrary to God's law, can bring two essentially fine persons to damnation and spiritual ruin. The tenderness and the sympathy with which the story is told are famous. But its pathos, and Dante's personal response of overwhelming pity, should not blind us to the *justice* of the penalty. The poet who describes himself as fainting at the end of Francesca's recital is the same man who consigned her to Hell. His purpose is partly to portray the attractiveness of sin, an especially congenial theme when *this* is the sin involved—both for Dante and for most readers. But although Dante allows the lovers the bitter sweetness of inseparability in Hell, the modern "romantic" idea that union anywhere is sufficient happiness for lovers does not even occur to him. Paolo and Francesca indeed have their love; but they have lost God and thus corrupted their personalities—their inmost selves—from order into anarchy; they are the reverse of happy. In a sense, they have what they wanted, they continue in the lawless condition which they chose on earth. But that condition, seen from the point of view of eternity, is not bliss; it is, in effect, Hell.

In Canto X we are among the heretics in their flaming tomb in the sixth circle. Situated within the walled city of Dis—the capital, as it were, of Hell—this circle is a kind of border between the upper Hell (devoted to punishments for Incontinence) and the lower (concerned with Violence and Fraud). Here Dante portrays the proud aristocrat Farinata and his associate, the elder Cavalcante, father of Dante's closest friend. Their crime is heresy, a flagrant aspect of intellectual pride. But there is a nobility in Farinata's pride; Dante, like the reader, admires the splendid self-sufficiency of a man who, in this situation, can seem "to hold all Hell in disrespect." And the essence of the aristocratic nature is distilled in his address to Dante as "the great soul stared almost contemptuously, / before he asked: 'Of what line do you come?' " and in his abrupt resumption of the conversation interrupted by Cavalcante. Alongside the haughtiness of Farinata, Dante sets the pathetic—and mistaken—grief of Cavalcante for his son; each portrait gains in effect by the extreme contrast.

Canto XIII shows us one group of those guilty of Violence; for the suicides have been violent against themselves. Here they are turned into monstrous trees, their misery finding expression when a bough is plucked. In the eyes of the Church, suicide was murder, in no way diminished by the fact that the slayer and the victim were the same. By representing in Pier delle Vigne a man who had every human motive to end his life, Dante achieves the deepest pathos and evokes our shuddering pity. As Francesca displays in her dramatic monologue the charm and the potential weakness of her character, as Farinata's manner of speech portrays his nature, so Pier delle Vigne by his exact and legal-sounding language lets us see the careful, methodical counselor whose sense of logic and sense of justice were so outraged that he saw no point in enduring life any longer. His judgment is still unimpaired; he does not reproach his king, only the jealous courtiers who misled him. The Wood of the Suicides is one of the greatest—among many admirable— examples of landscape in Hell assimilated to theme and situation.

Canto XV describes the meeting of Dante and his venerable teacher and adviser, the scholar Brunetto Latini. We are in another ring of the seventh circle, among more of those who have sinned through Violence. The impact of this scene results from the contrast between the dignity of the man and the indignity of his condition in hell, and by the tact with which both he and Dante ignore it for the moment. Brunetto, with the others guilty of homosexual vice, must move continually along a sandy desert under a shower of fiery flakes. Dante accords him the utmost respect and expresses his gratitude in the warmest terms; and something like their earthly relationship of teacher and pupil is re-enacted, for Brunetto is keenly interested in Dante's prospects in life. In the final image of Brunetto running, not like the loser, but like the winner of a race, Dante extracts dignity and victory out of indignity itself.

The presence of people like those we have been reviewing will remind the reader that Hell is not reserved exclusively for arrant ruffians, hoodlums, and scoundrels. They are there, of course; but so are many "nice," many charming, and some noble and great, men and women. These are in Hell because they preferred something else—no matter what—to God; at the moment of death they were therefore in rebellion against Him. God and Heaven would not be congenial to them, *as they are and as He is;* and there is no acceptable repentance after death. Hence they go on unchanged—only now experiencing the harsher aspects of the sin in which they chose to live.

In Canto XVII the travelers are carried on the back of the flying monster Geryon down the deep descent from the seventh to the eighth circle. With the face of a just man and the body of a serpent, Geryon symbolizes Fraud. He is one of the most exciting figures in Hell. In an age before ferris wheels and airplanes, he gives our poets a ride that anticipates some of the terrifying thrill which a young child may feel in an airplane journey. The eighth circle is subdivided into ten chasms or trenches (Malebolge), each with its own kind of sinners: seducers and panders; flatterers; simoniacs (buyers and sellers of appointments in the Church); sorcerers; grafters; hypocrites; thieves; evil counselors; trouble-makers; forgers, and impostors.

Most readers will agree that the punishments here fit the crimes; indeed, reflection will usually intensify this conviction. It is a long catalogue of iniquity; much, but not all, is sordid. Dante has avoided monotony not only by the vividness and intensity of the separate scenes but also by their ingenious variety and by the frequent changes of pace in the narrative. The satirical situation and fierce denunciation of the simoniacs is followed by the quiet horror of the sorcerers with twisted necks. The hilarious episode of the grafters precedes the encounter with the solemn, slow-walking hypocrites; and these are succeeded by the macabre serpent-transformations of the thieves. Nevertheless, our steadily deepening descent in hell gradually produces a sense of oppressiveness. This is appropriate and deliberate; it is a part of Dante's total design. But he recognizes the need of momentary relief, a breath of fresh air, a reminder of the world above. These he provides, for example, in the long simile describing the shipyard in Venice (the opening of Canto XXI) or the picture of the peasant and his two sallies outside on a winter morning (the opening of Canto XXIV).

The episode of the grafters (Cantos XXI and XXII) probably has biographical relevance for Dante. During his absence from Florence on business of state, the opposing political party seized power and sentenced Dante to death if he should return to Florence. The quite unfounded charge against him was misappropriation of public funds. In these cantos Dante cuts a ludicrous figure: fearful, cowering, in constant danger from the demons. He escapes their clutches, first by a distraction and then by belated vigilance. The whole sequence affords an oblique and amusing view of an actual episode. It is worth noting also that here, and here only, in the poem, we find ourselves in the kind of hell known in popular lore and anecdote, with winged devils playing rough jokes on their human prey. Scenes, style, and language alike here show one extreme of the range of the poem—the "low" comic. Dante very unobtrusively indicates his awareness of this by the contrasting allusions found in Canto XX, line 113 and Canto XXI, line 2.

Cantos XXVI and XXVII take us among the wicked counselors, who occupy the eighth chasm, or subdivision, of the eighth circle. Appearing at a distance like fireflies in a summer valley, these souls are wrapped in individual, or occasionally twin, flames. Fire is a fit punishment for those who used the flame of intellect to accomplish evil. When the two poets approach more closely, Virgil identifies one flame as that of Ulysses (Odysseus) and Diomede, who burn together. Among the deceptions devised by Ulysses was the wooden horse, which made possible the capture of Troy. It will strike the reader as strange that a man should suffer for his powers as a military tactician. But the Greeks were enemies of the Trojans, whom the Romans and later most of the nations of Western Europe regarded as their ancestors. Ulysses was on the wrong side, and was responsible for his deeds; but Dante mingles with his condemnation an admiration of the man's mental powers. Ulysses remains aloof; he does not converse with Dante, like most of the souls we have met. Instead, as Dorothy Sayers puts it in the notes to her translation of the poem, Virgil conjures the flame into monologue. Thus we are told how Ulysses determined not to return home after the Trojan War but to explore the western ocean instead. In this narrative, apparently invented by Dante, Ulysses becomes the type of the adventuring and searching spirit of man; the voyage is an act of the mind and soul as well as the body. When he has sailed within sight of a mountainous island, his ship is wrecked by a storm and he perishes. Since, as other parts of the poem indicate, this is the island of Purgatory, the episode clearly has symbolic significance. On this island is the Earthly Paradise, or Garden of Eden, lost to man by the sin of Adam. Man, unassisted by divine grace—pagan man, represented by Ulysses—cannot regain it by his own intelligence, although the effort toward that end is noble in itself.

The other evil counselor, Guido da Montefeltro, talks fluently in Canto XXVII; he shows a quite earthly eagerness for news, crafty, garrulous old intriguer that he is. It is a neat irony that, in spite of his deserved reputation for cleverness, Dante shows him twice deceived: first on earth, as he himself relates, and now in Hell—he does not want his story known and is convinced that Dante will never return to earth to tell it. He sketches in detail, with recollective acidity, the steps by which the pope led him, an aging and reformed man, to return for a moment to his old ways. He even includes the contest of St. Francis and the devil for his soul at his death, along with the devil's bitter witticism: you didn't think I was a logician, perhaps!

In Cantos XXXII and XXXIII we have reached the ninth and last circle, where the traitors are immersed in ice that symbolizes their unfeeling hearts. At the end of one canto we are shown the horror of Ugolino gnawing the skull of his enemy Ruggieri, both partly fastened in the ice. Dante does not concentrate on the acts which have put either man in Hell. Instead he lets Ugolino tell us, in the next canto, why his hatred of Ruggieri is so implacable. The fearful pathos, the power, and at the same time the restraint and compression of this narrative make it one of the finest episodes in the poem.

The last canto, Canto XXXIV, shows us the enormous shape of the fallen angel, Satan, fixed at the bottom of Hell, where the motion of his wings freezes the ice in which we have found the traitors immersed. In one of his three mouths he holds Judas Iscariot, who betrayed Christ; in the other two are Brutus and Cassius, who plotted the assassination of Julius Caesar. Dante did not regard them, as we generally do today, as perhaps misguided patriots; to him they were the destroyers of a providentially ordained ruler. Readers who remember Milton's *Paradise Lost* may be surprised at the absence of any interior presentation of Satan. One critic regrets that his suffering is not shown as different from that of the other inhabitants of Hell. But the fact is that his suffering is not presented at all; he is not a person, to Dante, but an object, a part of the machinery and geography of Hell. For *The Divine Comedy* is occupied exclusively with human sin, human redemption, and human beatitude.

### PURGATORY

At the beginning of the *Purgatory*, Dante and Virgil have once more reached the surface of the earth and can look up and see the sky and the stars. Their long climb from the bottom of Hell, where they left Satan, has brought them out on the shore of the mountain-island of Purgatory. The scene and the situation are presented by Dante with a bold and happy use of imaginative symbols. Guided by Reason in the person of Virgil, Dante, a man still in the earthly life, has looked closely at sin and evil—in Hell—and turned away from them, and is now in search of the means of self-correction and purification. He arrives on the island shore, just before dawn, to find the reverend figure of Cato acting as guardian of the mountain. The austerely glorious figure of Cato, his face illumined by rays from stars representing the pagan virtues of Prudence, Temperance, Fortitude, and Justice, embodies the highest moral and ethical ideal available to man without divine revelation, pre- or post-Christian. Dante meets him, appropriately, before dawn—before the sun of God's illumination has risen. These elements in the situation, together with the reference to his sojourn with Marcia, his wife, in the circle of virtuous pagans in Hell, make Cato a remarkable transition or border symbol, standing both between Hell and Purgatory and between Greco-Roman philosophy and ethics and the dispensation of the Old and New Testaments.

These opening cantos admirably set quite a new tone in the second great division of the poem. They show us joy and brightness, cheer and hope, contrasting totally with the darkness and misery of Hell. They show us an angel arriving with a cargo of souls, all joyfully singing. They accustom us to a different set of attitudes, a different kind of people, and especially, they portray the naïveté, the almost childlike lack of intellectual and moral sophistication, the need of orientation, which characterize the penitent soul at this point in its progress to perfection. As yet uninstructed and spiritually immature, it looks back, seeking to carry on the harmless but no longer suitable delights of earthly life. Dante—and Virgil—share this simplicity to the full.

Cantos III–XVIII, not included in this book, take the reader along the slopes of the lower half of the mountain—the ante-Purgatory, where some of the souls must wait for varying periods of time (and for different reasons) before entering Purgatory itself—and through four of the seven terraces, those devoted to purgation from Pride, Envy, Anger, and Sloth. In Canto XIX we go on to the fifth of the ledges encircling the mountain, that in which the souls are purified of Avarice. There we meet Pope Adrian, one of Dante's most vivid illustrations of the anguish of purification. Concisely he sketches for Dante the poignant story of his late conversion (to the reality of the Christian life), his repentance, and his present hard penance. Only when, after a life of self-seeking, he had attained the pinnacle of the papacy did disillusionment come—and spiritual discovery: "I saw no heart's rest there, nor ease from strife." Now he recognizes the equity of the reforming penalty:

> We would not raise our eyes to the shining spheres
> but kept them turned to mundane things: so Justice
> bends them to earth here in this place of tears.

Dante, on learning from Adrian's words that he was a pope, has knelt down in respect. But Adrian, perceiving this without lifting his eyes from the ground, peremptorily corrects Dante: there are no popes here. All the hierarchies and social orders of earth are annihilated in Purgatory—and, we may add, the hierarchy of Heaven is not that of earth. Having answered Dante's questions, Adrian bids him go on—he hinders the task of penitence. Finally, remembering that Dante had offered to carry news of him to those possibly dear to him on earth, which might lead to helpful prayers, the old man adds that he has only a niece there who, if not corrupted by the bad example of his family, could possibly help him. But for this soul, absorbed in his penance, the earth has receded far away, and Heaven is not yet attained; he is essentially alone with his suffering.

The remaining parts of the *Purgatory* included in this book, Cantos XXVII, XXX, and XXXI, add a dimension to Dante's role in the poem. He is, as has been said, the protagonist throughout; the journey and all its disclosures are carried out for his benefit. In Hell, to be sure, he could do little except look and learn; yet his emotional education through the revelation of perfected evil was a large and positive achievement. As a candidate for salvation, he has learned to abhor sin more completely in proportion as he has been shown its real nature; while, as a man of flesh and blood, he has felt alternate pity and hate for the sinners. Along the penitential ledges of Purgatory he has partially assimilated himself to the penitents; he has felt humility while among those purging themselves of Pride, and generosity among those seeking to root out Envy from their natures. On the seventh terrace, he has recognized an even closer kinship with those engaged in refining their love by fire. But now this same fire, it develops, is the boundary between Purgatory and the Earthly Paradise at the top of the mountain. To reach that goal, Dante must go through the fire. Remembering "human bodies / I once saw burned," he is overcome by a terrible fear. The encouraging words of the angel guardian of the ledge, the assurances of Virgil, who reminds him of perils safely passed— neither avail to move him until he is told that Beatrice is beyond the wall of flame. Then his resistance melts and he perseveres through the frightful but harmless fire. It is now nearly sunset, when all ascent ceases, but next morning Dante takes the few last steps to the Earthly Paradise. Here Virgil, who has guided him through Hell and Purgatory, gives him a farewell benediction. Dante, says Virgil, has explored evil in its final effects (Hell) and the means of correcting the human inclinations that produce it (in Purgatory). His regenerated will is now truly free, and he may fearlessly follow its direction. He no longer needs the guidance of a teacher of morality (Virgil) nor a political structure ("crown") nor an ecclesiastical institution ("mitre"). In short, he has regained the condition of man before the Fall.

These words apply to Dante in his role as a kind of Everyman, representing whoever has fully discerned the nature of evil and wholly freed himself from the impulses to sin. They apply to every soul when it completes the experience of Purgatory; if they did not, the soul would not be ready to go to Heaven, to enter the presence of God. But obviously they cannot apply, actually and practically, to any man still living on earth. That they were not meant as a literal description of Dante the Italian poet and political exile from Florence is clear enough from the events of Cantos XXX and XXXI. For if Dante has already perfected himself by penance, why should he now, in the scenes with Beatrice, repeat the painful experience of rebuke, confession, and satisfaction? It is this latter series of incidents that constitutes Dante's personal, individual experience of correction and purification.

In the midst of the celestial pageant that moves before Dante in the Earthly Paradise appears a lady whom he instantly recognizes as one who was the object of his idealizing love when she lived as a woman on earth. Turning excitedly to confide this to Virgil, he cannot find him anywhere, and is stricken with grief. Presently the Lady names herself as Beatrice—whom the reader will remember for two reasons: she sent Virgil to guide her endangered servant, Dante, through Hell and Purgatory; and to see her Dante forced himself to go through the barrier of fire. There is no cause to doubt that, like the other human beings in the poem, Beatrice is an actual person transformed by the shaping imagination of the poet. What she was to Dante in her earthly life he tells us in the *New Life (Vita nuova)*, written not long after her death in 1290. She was an incarnation of beauty and virtue; simply by existing, she engrossed the young Dante's ardent but remote devotion; her smile or greeting left him in trembling rapture. This was the full extent of the relationship between them. But the poems in the *New Life* are mostly inspired by the thought of her, whether on earth or in heaven. In short, she was a real woman who, even in this world, was an ideal for Dante, and after death became an even more glorious image of goodness and divine wisdom. The last section of the *New Life* records Dante's resolution to devote a great work to her, when he shall be qualified to achieve it; *The Divine Comedy* is that work. We have seen that he makes her the instigator of the imaginary journey through two realms of the life after death and the motive for his endurance of the fire. Now, as successor to Virgil, she comes to guide him herself through the heavenly paradise. In the same way that Virgil is Reason without ceasing to be Virgil, Beatrice fulfills the role of Divine Revelation without ceasing to be Beatrice.

It is in this dual character, part beloved woman and part the voice of divine wisdom, that Beatrice, in Canto XXXI, unsparingly rebukes Dante. He had loved her mortal beauty as an image of the immortal; when death destroyed it, his devotion ought thenceforth to have fixed itself on the immortal and indestructible virtue of which that beauty had been the image. Instead, he turned aside to the lure of material things. Dante accepts the reproach with the utmost contrition. It is quite probable that this episode is based on some actual lapse, in Dante's life, from his highest moral ideal. These passages, then, recount his own personal experience of purgation, the autobiographical analogue of the penitence and purification portrayed on the mountain as a whole.

### PARADISE

Like the invocations of *Paradise Lost*, that with which Dante begins the third division of his poem expresses his sense of the loftiness of the theme. Like Milton, he is venturing things unattempted hitherto in prose or rhyme. The three invocations of *The Divine Comedy* are incremental; the first (in Canto II of the *Hell*) is brief and unobtrusive, the second (in Canto I of the *Purgatory*) more extended, and the third (in Canto I of the *Paradise*) by its earnestness and solemnity indicates the epic stature, though not epic form, which he expects the poem to attain. The *Paradise* offers us an imagined experience of the entire celestial universe as it was charted by medieval astronomy. In that cosmology, the sun, the moon, and the rest, though immensely distant, had not retreated from the earth according to the scale established by modern knowledge. Dante's world is geocentric; the planetary circles, including those of the sun and moon, revolve about the earth, as does the circle of the stars—as does, in fact, everything except the "real" Heaven, or Empyrean, the abode of God and the saints and angels. The *Paradise* is the chronicle of an ascent from planet to planet, until finally Dante is in the Empyrean itself. In each planet a group of redeemed and perfected souls, come from their proper dwelling in the Empyrean, are present to converse with Dante and his guide, Beatrice. Their successive discussions set forth the essentials of Christian doctrine, along with the fundamental scientific concepts of the time; and they themselves exemplify various kinds and degrees of beatitude. For Dante—and the reader—the experience is educational, morally edifying, and spiritually preparatory for the vision with which the poem ends. In Canto III Dante learns of the hierarchy of souls in Heaven; not all are equal, indeed, no two are identical in bliss; yet each is completely satisfied, fulfilled, and happy—"in His will is our peace." Piccarda, the not wholly blameless nun who speaks these words, is among the souls encountered in the moon, the group of lowest rank in Heaven. From these we rise to higher and higher kinds of blessed souls, each rejoicing wholly in God in its predestined way and in accordance with its capacity.

When all the cycles of the cosmos have been traversed, we come, in Canto XXXI, to Heaven itself, the real home of the blessed. Here the souls are arranged in the form of a great white rose; God is at the center—an ineffable brightness—and the souls have the aspect of rows of petals. Here Beatrice, who has set forth the truths of Divine Revelation throughout the journey, goes back to her place in Heaven, and St. Bernard, the great mystic of the twelfth century, becomes Dante's guide, or rather sponsor. For what remains is that Dante should be vouchsafed a vision in which, for an instant, he may see God as He really is—in so far as his human capacity enables him to do so. The last canto, Canto XXXIII, opens with Bernard's prayer to the Virgin Mary for intercession in Dante's behalf. There is no religious lyric poetry of greater depth or simplicity or beauty than this prayer; its intimacy, tenderness, and humility are consummate.

To obtain, to endure, such a vision is just within the limit of Dante's powers. It transports him into an utterly different kind of being; it leaves him with the memory of an overpowering but indescribable experience. For of course no mystic can ever reveal the content of his vision; it does not belong to the order of reportable things. Dante can only tell us that he discerned with direct but momentary certitude the identity of God as inclusive of man and of universal love, and that he knew himself to be at that instant one with Him.

*The Divine Comedy* thus ends both quietly and climactically. For this union with God was the purpose of the entire long and arduous journey. This is the good which St. Thomas Aquinas, and Boethius before him, pointed out as the goal of man, as of the entire creation. But what the philosophers prove, Dante experiences, imaginatively. And we reach both center and summit of the medieval structure of human life in proportion as we can follow the record of that experience.

### DANTE IN ITALIAN

This book presents the *Inferno* complete, together with several cantos of the *Purgatorio* and *Paradiso*, in English translation. Our translator is the contemporary American poet John Ciardi. As with some other poems in the book, the reader may find it interesting to have a brief look at the Italian text, so here are the opening lines of the *Inferno* in the original language.

> Nel mezzo del cammin di nostra vita
> mi retrovai per una selva oscura
> ché la diritta via era smarrita.

> Ah, quanto a dir qual era è cosa dura
> esta selva selvaggia e aspra e forte
> che nel pensier rinova la paura!

> Tant'è amara che poco è più morte;
> ma per trattar del ben ch'io vi trovai,
> dirò dell'altre cose ch'i' v'ho scorte.

> Io non so ben ridir com'io v'entrai,
> tant'era pieno di sonno a quel punto
> che la verace via abbandonai.

The individual lines are metrically similar to most lines in Chaucer or Shakespeare; they regularly have five metrical feet, each consisting of an unstressed syllable followed by a stressed one, or vice versa, with the possibility of an additional unstressed syllable or two somewhere within the line. But the most notable metrical feature of the *Divine Comedy* is the pattern of rhymes, or the *terza rima*. Thus the lines form groups of three: *vita* in the first line above rhymes with the last two syllables of *smarrita* in the third line, while *oscura* in the second line rhymes with *dura* in the first line and *paura* in the third line of the next group. Thus the groups are independent units interlocked by the sequence of rhymes. This overall structure reminds the reader of the Christian Trinity: God the Father, Son, and Holy Spirit; it is one expression of the poet's religious devotion. In his translation Ciardi maintains the separation into groups of three lines: *astray* in the first line rhymes with *I say* in the third. But he does not keep the interlocking rhyme scheme: *myself* in line two of the first group does not rhyme with *drear* and *fear* in the second group. The sound structure of the Italian language makes Dante's rhyme patterns easier than this arrangement would be in an English poem. Attempts to reproduce it entirely have not been very successful in our language.

The best sources are T. S. Eliot, "Dante," most easily available in his *Selected Essays* (1932); George Santayana, "Dante," in *Three Philosophical Poets* (1910); and the introduction and notes by Dorothy Sayers to her translation of the *Inferno* (1949). See also her *Introductory Papers on Dante* (1954) and *Further Papers on Dante* (1957). Also helpful is Michele Barbi, *Life of Dante*, translated by Paul G. Ruggiers, 1954. Recent studies include R. Hollander, *Allegory in Dante's "Commedia"* (1969).

**Island of Purgatory**

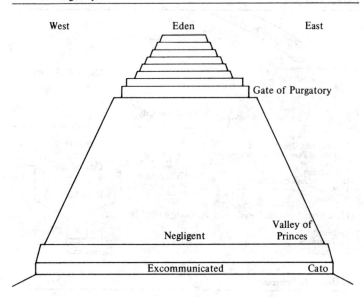

West                           Eden                          East

Gate of Purgatory

Negligent

Valley of
Princes

Excommunicated                                    Cato

**Eden and Purgatory**

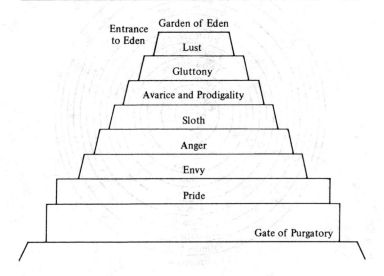

Entrance
to Eden          Garden of Eden

Lust

Gluttony

Avarice and Prodigality

Sloth

Anger

Envy

Pride

Gate of Purgatory

## The Slope of Hell

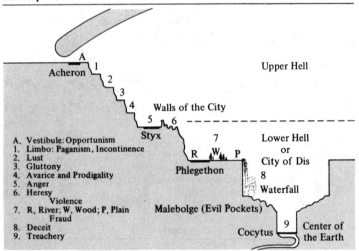

Upper Hell

A    1
Acheron
        2
          3
            4    Walls of the City
              5    6
            Styx        7    Lower Hell
A. Vestibule: Opportunism                    or
1. Limbo: Paganism, Incontinence    R  W  P   City of Dis
2. Lust                                      8
3. Gluttony                Phlegethon
4. Avarice and Prodigality                Waterfall
5. Anger
6. Heresy                Malebolge (Evil Pockets)
        Violence
7. R, River; W, Wood; P, Plain
        Fraud                          9   Center of
8. Deceit              Cocytus              the Earth
9. Treachery

## The Heavenly Spheres

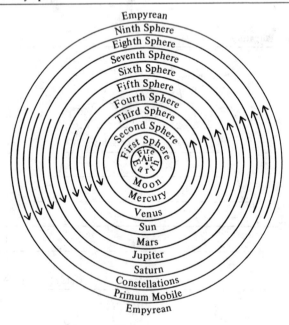

Empyrean
Ninth Sphere
Eighth Sphere
Seventh Sphere
Sixth Sphere
Fifth Sphere
Fourth Sphere
Third Sphere
Second Sphere
First Sphere
Fire
Air
Earth
Moon
Mercury
Venus
Sun
Mars
Jupiter
Saturn
Constellations
Primum Mobile
Empyrean

# The Divine Comedy[1]

## Inferno

### CANTO I

#### The Dark Wood of Error

Midway in his allotted threescore years and ten, Dante comes to himself with a start and realizes that he has strayed from the True Way into the Dark Wood of Error (Worldliness). As soon as he has realized his loss, Dante lifts his eyes and sees the first light of the sunrise (the Sun is the Symbol of Divine Illumination) lighting the shoulders of a little hill (The Mount of Joy). It is the Easter Season, the time of resurrection, and the sun is in its equinoctial rebirth. This juxtaposition of joyous symbols fills Dante with hope and he sets out at once to climb directly up the Mount of Joy, but almost immediately his way is blocked by the Three Beasts of Worldliness: The Leopard of Malice and Fraud, The Lion of Violence and Ambition, and The She-Wolf of Incontinence. These beasts, and especially the She-Wolf, drive him back despairing into the darkness of error. But just as all seems lost, a figure appears to him. It is the shade of Virgil, Dante's symbol of Human Reason.

Virgil explains that he has been sent to lead Dante from error. There can, however, be no direct ascent past the beasts: the man who would escape them must go a longer and harder way. First he must descend through Hell (The Recognition of Sin), then he must ascend through Purgatory (The Renunciation of Sin), and only then may he reach the pinnacle of joy and come to the Light of God. Virgil offers to guide Dante, but only as far as Human Reason can go. Another guide (Beatrice, symbol of Divine Love) must take over for the final ascent, for Human Reason is self-limited. Dante submits himself joyously to Virgil's guidance and they move off.

Midway in our life's journey,[2] I went astray
    from the straight road and woke to find myself
    alone in a dark wood. How shall I say
what wood that was! I never saw so drear,
    so rank, so arduous a wilderness!         5
    Its very memory gives a shape to fear.
Death could scarce be more bitter than that place!
    But since it came to good, I will recount
    all that I found revealed there by God's grace.
How I came to it I cannot rightly say,         10

---

1. The *Inferno* complete, with selections from the *Purgatorio* and *Paradiso*. Translated, with notes and commentary, by John Ciardi.    2. The Biblical life span is three-score years and ten. The action opens in Dante's thirty-fifth year, i.e., A.D. 1300.

so drugged and loose with sleep had I become
   when I first wandered there from the True Way.
But at the far end of that valley of evil
   whose maze had sapped my very heart with fear,
   I found myself before a little hill               15
and lifted up my eyes. Its shoulders glowed
   already with the sweet rays of that planet[3]
   whose virtue leads men straight on every road,
and the shining strengthened me against the fright
   whose agony had wracked the lake of my heart     20
   through all the terrors of that piteous night.
Just as a swimmer, who with his last breath
   flounders ashore from perilous seas, might turn
   to memorize the wide water of his death—
so did I turn, my soul still fugitive             25
   from death's surviving image, to stare down
   that pass that none had ever left alive.
And there I lay to rest from my heart's race
   till calm and breath returned to me. Then rose
   and pushed up that dead slope at such a pace     30
each footfall rose above the last.[4] And lo!
   almost at the beginning of the rise
   I faced a spotted Leopard, all tremor and flow
and gaudy pelt. And it would not pass, but stood
   so blocking my every turn that time and again    35
   I was on the verge of turning back to the wood.
This fell at the first widening of the dawn
   as the sun was climbing Aries with those stars
   that rode with him to light the new creation.[5]
Thus the holy hour and the sweet season     40
   of commemoration did much to arm my fear
   of that bright murderous beast with their good omen.
Yet not so much but what I shook with dread
   at sight of a great Lion that broke upon me
   raging with hunger, its enormous head     45

3. The sun. Ptolemaic astronomers considered it a planet. It is also symbolic of God as He who lights man's way.    4. The literal rendering would be: "So that the fixed foot was ever the lower." "Fixed" has often been translated "right" and an ingenious reasoning can support that reading, but a simpler explanation offers itself and seems more competent: Dante is saying that he climbed with such zeal and haste that every footfall carried him above the last despite the steepness of the climb. At a slow pace, on the other hand, the rear foot might be brought up only as far as the forward foot.    5. The medieval tradition had it that the sun was in Aries at the time of the Creation. The significance of the astronomical and religious conjunction is an important part of Dante's intended allegory. It is just before dawn of Good Friday A.D. 1300 when he awakens in the Dark Wood. Thus his new life begins under Aries, the sign of creation, at dawn (rebirth) and in the Easter season (resurrection). Moreover the moon is full and the sun is in the equinox, conditions that did not fall together on any Friday of 1300. Dante is obviously constructing poetically the perfect Easter as a symbol of his new awakening.

held high as if to strike a mortal terror
   into the very air. And down his track,
   a She-Wolf drove upon me, a starved horror
ravening and wasted beyond all belief.[6]
   She seemed a rack for avarice, gaunt and craving.      50
   Oh many the souls she has brought to endless grief!
She brought such heaviness upon my spirit
   at sight of her savagery and desperation,
   I died from every hope of that high summit.
And like a miser—eager in acquisition      55
   but desperate in self-reproach when Fortune's wheel
   turns to the hour of his loss—all tears and attrition
I wavered back; and still the beast pursued,
   forcing herself against me bit by bit
   till I slid back into the sunless wood.      60
And as I fell to my soul's ruin, a presence
   gathered before me on the discolored air,
   the figure of one who seemed hoarse from long silence.
At sight of him in that friendless waste I cried:
   "Have pity on me, whatever thing you are,      65
   whether shade or living man." And it replied:
"Not man, though man I once was, and my blood
   was Lombard, both my parents Mantuan.
   I was born, though late, *sub Julio*,[7] and bred
in Rome under Augustus in the noon      70
   of the false and lying gods. I was a poet
   and sang of old Anchises' noble son[8]
who came to Rome after the burning of Troy.
   But you—why do *you* return to these distresses
   instead of climbing that shining Mount of Joy      75
which is the seat and first cause of man's bliss?"
   "And are you then that Virgil and that fountain
   of purest speech?" My voice grew tremulous:
"Glory and light of poets! now may that zeal
   and love's apprenticeship that I poured out      80
   on your heroic verses serve me well!
For you are my true master and first author,
   the sole maker from whom I drew the breath
   of that sweet style whose measures have brought me honor.
See there, immortal sage, the beast I flee.      85

6. These three beasts undoubtedly are taken from *Jeremiah* v, 6. Many additional and incidental interpretations have been advanced for them, but the central interpretation must remain as noted. They foreshadow the three divisions of Hell (incontinence, violence, and fraud) which Virgil explains at length in Canto XI, 16–111. I am not at all sure but what the She-Wolf is better interpreted as Fraud and the Leopard as Incontinence. Good arguments can be offered either way.    7. *sub Julio*: In the reign of Julius Caesar.    8. Aeneas.

For my soul's salvation, I beg you, guard me from her,
    for she has struck a mortal tremor through me."
And he replied, seeing my soul in tears:

"He must go by another way who would escape
    this wilderness, for that mad beast that fleers                    90
before you there, suffers no man to pass.

    She tracks down all, kills all, and knows no glut,
    but, feeding, she grows hungrier than she was.
She mates with any beast, and will mate with more

    before the Greyhound[9] comes to hunt her down.                    95
    He will not feed on lands nor loot, but honor
and love and wisdom will make straight his way.

    He will rise between Feltro and Feltro, and in him
    shall be the resurrection and new day
of that sad Italy for which Nisus died,                                100

    and Turnus, and Euryalus, and the maid Camilla.[1]
    He shall hunt her through every nation of sick pride
till she is driven back forever to Hell

    whence Envy first released her on the world.
    Therefore, for your own good, I think it well                      105
you follow me and I will be your guide

    and lead you forth through an eternal place.
    There you shall see the ancient spirits tried
in endless pain, and hear their lamentation

    as each bemoans the second death[2] of souls.                      110
    Next you shall see upon a burning mountain
souls in fire and yet content in fire,

    knowing that whensoever it may be
    they yet will mount into the blessed choir.
To which, if it is still your wish to climb,                           115

    a worthier spirit shall be sent to guide you.
    With her shall I leave you, for the King of Time,
who reigns on high, forbids me to come there

    since, living, I rebelled against his law.[3]
He rules the waters and the land and air                               120
and there holds court, his city and his throne.

    Oh blessed are they he chooses!" And I to him:
    "Poet, by that God to you unknown,

9. Almost certainly refers to Can Grande della Scala (1290–1329), great Italian leader born in
Verona, which lies between the towns of Feltre and Montefeltro.     1. All were killed in the war
between the Trojans and the Latians when, according to legend, Aeneas led the survivors of Troy
into Italy. Nisus and Euryalus (*Aeneid* IX) were Trojan comrades-in-arms who died together.
Camilla (*Aeneid* XI) was the daughter of the Latian king and one of the warrior women. She was
killed in a horse charge against the Trojans after displaying great gallantry. Turnus (*Aeneid* XII)
was killed by Aeneas in a duel.     2. Damnation. "This is the second death, even the lake of
fire." (Revelation xx, 14)    3. Salvation is only through Christ in Dante's theology. Virgil lived
and died before the establishment of Christ's teachings in Rome, and cannot therefore enter
Heaven.

lead me this way. Beyond this present ill
   and worse to dread, lead me to Peter's gate[4]                    125
   and be my guide through the sad halls of Hell."
And he then: "Follow." And he moved ahead
in silence, and I followed where he led.

CANTO II

*The Descent*

   It is evening of the first day (Friday). Dante is following Virgil and
finds himself tired and despairing. How can he be worthy of such a
vision as Virgil has described? He hesitates and seems about to abandon his first purpose.

   To comfort him Virgil explains how Beatrice descended to him in
Limbo and told him of her concern for Dante. It is she, the symbol
of Divine Love, who sends Virgil to lead Dante from error. She has
come into Hell itself on this errand, for Dante cannot come to Divine
Love unaided; Reason must lead him. Moreover Beatrice has been
sent with the prayers of the Virgin Mary (Compassion), and of Saint
Lucia (Divine Light). Rachel (The Contemplative Life) also figures
in the heavenly scene which Virgil recounts.

   Virgil explains all this and reproaches Dante: how can he hesitate
longer when such heavenly powers are concerned for him, and Virgil himself has promised to lead him safely?

   Dante understands at once that such forces cannot fail him, and
his spirits rise in joyous anticipation.

The light was departing. The brown air drew down
   all the earth's creatures, calling them to rest
   from their day-roving, as I, one man alone,
prepared myself to face the double war
   of the journey and the pity, which memory                        5
   shall here set down, nor hesitate, nor err.
O Muses! O High Genius! Be my aid!
   O Memory, recorder of the vision,
   here shall your true nobility be displayed!
Thus I began: "Poet, you who must guide me,                           10
   before you trust me to that arduous passage,
   look to me and look through me—can I be worthy?
You sang how the father of Sylvius,[5] while still

4. The gate of Purgatory. (See *Purgatorio* IX, 76 ff.) The gate is guarded by an angel with a
gleaming sword. The angel is Peter's vicar (Peter, the first Pope, symbolized all Popes; i.e., Christ's
vicar on earth) and is entrusted with the two great keys. Some commentators argue that this is the
gate of Paradise, but Dante mentions no gate beyond this one in his ascent to Heaven. It should
be remembered, too, that those who pass the gate of Purgatory have effectively entered Heaven.
5. Aeneas. Lines 13–30 are a fair example of the way in which Dante absorbed pagan themes
into his Catholicism. According to Virgil, Aeneas is the son of mortal Anchises and of Venus.

in corruptible flesh won to that other world,
  crossing with mortal sense the immortal sill.         15
But if the Adversary of all Evil
  weighing his consequence and who and what
  should issue from him, treated him so well—
that cannot seem unfitting to thinking men,
  since he was chosen father of Mother Rome         20
  and of her Empire by God's will and token.
Both, to speak strictly, were founded and foreknown
  as the established Seat of Holiness
  for the successors of Great Peter's throne.
In that quest, which your verses celebrate,         25
  he learned those mysteries from which arose
  his victory and Rome's apostolate.
There later came the chosen vessel, Paul,
  bearing the confirmation of that Faith
  which is the one true door to life eternal.         30
But I—how should I dare? By whose permission?
  I am not Aeneas. I am not Paul.
  Who could believe me worthy of the vision?
How, then, may I presume to this high quest
  and not fear my own brashness? You are wise         35
  and will grasp what my poor words can but suggest."
As one who unwills what he wills, will stay
  strong purposes with feeble second thoughts
  until he spells all his first zeal away—
so I hung back and balked on that dim coast         40
  till thinking had worn out my enterprise,
  so stout at starting and so early lost.
"I understand from your words and the look in your eyes,"
  that shadow of magnificence answered me,
  "your soul is sunken in that cowardice         45
that bears down many men, turning their course
  and resolution by imagined perils,
  as his own shadow turns the frightened horse.
To free you of this dread I will tell you all
  of why I came to you and what I heard         50

Venus, in her son's interest, secures a prophecy and a promise from Jove to the effect that Aeneas
is to found a royal line that shall rule the world. After the burning of Troy, Aeneas is directed by
various signs to sail for the Latian lands (Italy) where his destiny awaits him. After many misadventures, he is compelled (like Dante) to descend to the underworld of the dead. There he finds
his father's shade, and there he is shown the shades of the great kings that are to stem from him.
(*Aeneid* VI, 921 ff.) Among them are Romulus, Julius Caesar, and Augustus Caesar. The full
glory of the Roman Empire is also foreshadowed to him. Dante, however, continues the Virgilian
theme and includes in the predestination not only the Roman Empire but the Holy Roman
Empire and its Church. Thus what Virgil presented as an arrangement of Jove, a concession to
the son of Venus, becomes part of the divine scheme of the Catholic God, and Aeneas is cast as
a direct forerunner of Peter and Paul.

when first I pitied you. I was a soul
among the souls of Limbo,[6] when a Lady
   so blessed and so beautiful, I prayed her
   to order and command my will, called to me.
Her eyes were kindled from the lamps of Heaven.     55
   Her voice reached through me, tender, sweet, and low.
   An angel's voice, a music of its own:
'O gracious Mantuan whose melodies
   live in earth's memory and shall live on
   till the last motion ceases in the skies,     60
my dearest friend, and fortune's foe, has strayed
   onto a friendless shore and stands beset
   by such distresses that he turns afraid
from the True Way, and news of him in Heaven
   rumors my dread he is already lost.     65
   I come, afraid that I am too-late risen.
Fly to him and with your high counsel, pity,
   and with whatever need be for his good
   and soul's salvation, help him, and solace me.
It is I, Beatrice, who send you to him.     70
   I come from the blessed height for which I yearn.
   Love called me here. When amid Seraphim
I stand again before my Lord, your praises
   shall sound in Heaven.' She paused, and I began:
   'O Lady of that only grace that raises     75
feeble mankind within its mortal cycle
   above all other works God's will has placed
   within the heaven of the smallest circle;[7]
so welcome is your command that to my sense,
   were it already fulfilled, it would yet seem tardy.     80
   I understand, and am all obedience.
But tell me how you dare to venture thus
   so far from the wide heaven of your joy
   to which your thoughts yearn back from this abyss.'
'Since what you ask,' she answered me, 'probes near     85
   the root of all, I will say briefly only
   how I have come through Hell's pit without fear.
Know then, O waiting and compassionate soul,

---

6. See Canto IV, lines 31–45, where Virgil explains his state in Hell.    7. The moon. "Heaven"
here is used in its astronomical sense. All within that circle is the earth. According to the Ptolemaic system the earth was the center of creation and was surrounded by nine heavenly spheres
(nine heavens) concentrically placed around it. The moon was the first of these, and therefore the
smallest. A cross section of this universe could be represented by drawing nine concentric circles
(at varying distances about the earth as a center). Going outward from the center these circles
would indicate, in order, the spheres of: The Moon, Mercury, Venus, The Sun, Mars, Jupiter,
Saturn, The Fixed Stars, and The Primum Mobile. Beyond the Primum Mobile lies the Empyrean.

that is to fear which has the power to harm,
and nothing else is fearful even in Hell.                    90
I am so made by God's all-seeing mercy
your anguish does not touch me, and the flame
of this great burning has no power upon me.
There is a Lady in Heaven so concerned
for him I send you to, that for her sake          95
the strict decree is broken. She has turned
and called Lucia[8] to her wish and mercy
saying: 'Thy faithful one is sorely pressed;
in his distresses I commend him to thee.'
Lucia, that soul of light and foe of all                     100
cruelty, rose and came to me at once
where I was sitting with the ancient Rachel,[9]
saying to me: 'Beatrice, true praise of God,
why dost thou not help him who loved thee so
that for thy sake he left the vulgar crowd?       105
Dost thou not hear his cries? Canst thou not see
the death he wrestles with beside that river
no ocean can surpass for rage and fury?'
No soul of earth was ever as rapt to seek
its good or flee its injury as I was—              110
when I had heard my sweet Lucia speak—
to descend from Heaven and my blessed seat
to you, laying my trust in that high speech
that honors you and all who honor it.'
She spoke and turned away to hide a tear           115
that, shining, urged me faster. So I came
and freed you from the beast that drove you there,
blocking the near way to the Heavenly Height.
    And now what ails you? Why do you lag? Why
this heartsick hesitation and pale fright          120
when three such blessed Ladies lean from Heaven
in their concern for you and my own pledge
of the great good that waits you has been given?"
As flowerlets drooped and puckered in the night
turn up to the returning sun and spread           125
their petals wide on his new warmth and light—
just so my wilted spirits rose again
and such a heat of zeal surged through my veins
that I was born anew. Thus I began:
"Blesséd be that Lady of infinite pity,            130
and blesséd be thy taxed and courteous spirit
that came so promptly on the word she gave thee.

8. Allegorically she represents Divine Light. Her name in Italian inevitably suggests "luce" (light), and she is the patron saint of eyesight.    9. Represents the Contemplative Life.

Thy words have moved my heart to its first purpose.
　My Guide! My Lord! My Master! Now lead on:
　one will shall serve the two of us in this."                    135
He turned when I had spoken, and at his back
I entered on that hard and perilous track.


CANTO III

*The Vestibule of Hell    The Opportunists*

　The Poets pass the Gate of Hell and are immediately assailed by
cries of anguish. Dante sees the first of the souls in torment. They
are The Opportunists, those souls who in life were neither for good
nor evil but only for themselves. Mixed with them are those outcasts
who took no sides in the Rebellion of the Angels. They are neither
in Hell nor out of it. Eternally unclassified, they race round and
round pursuing a wavering banner that runs forever before them
through the dirty air; and as they run they are pursued by swarms of
wasps and hornets, who sting them and produce a constant flow of
blood and putrid matter which trickles down the bodies of the sinners
and is feasted upon by loathsome worms and maggots who coat the
ground.
　The law of Dante's Hell is the law of symbolic retribution. As they
sinned so are they punished. They took no sides, therefore they are
given no place. As they pursued the ever-shifting illusion of their
own advantage, changing their courses with every changing wind, so
they pursue eternally an elusive, ever-shifting banner. As their sin
was a darkness, so they move in darkness. As their own guilty conscience pursued them, so they are pursued by swarms of wasps and
hornets. And as their actions were a moral filth, so they run eternally
through the filth of worms and maggots which they themselves feed.
　Dante recognizes several, among them Pope Celestine V, but
without delaying to speak to any of these souls, the Poets move on to
Acheron, the first of the rivers of Hell. Here the newly-arrived souls
of the damned gather and wait for monstrous Charon to ferry them
over to punishment. Charon recognizes Dante as a living man and
angrily refuses him passage. Virgil forces Charon to serve them, but
Dante swoons with terror, and does not reawaken until he is on the
other side.

I AM THE WAY INTO THE CITY OF WOE.
　I AM THE WAY TO A FORSAKEN PEOPLE.
　I AM THE WAY INTO ETERNAL SORROW.
SACRED JUSTICE MOVED MY ARCHITECT.
　I WAS RAISED HERE BY DIVINE OMNIPOTENCE,                    5
　PRIMORDIAL LOVE AND ULTIMATE INTELLECT.

ONLY THOSE ELEMENTS TIME CANNOT WEAR[1]
     WERE MADE BEFORE ME, AND BEYOND TIME I STAND.[2]
     ABANDON ALL HOPE YE WHO ENTER HERE.[3]
These mysteries I read cut into stone                              10
     above a gate. And turning I said: "Master,
     what is the meaning of this harsh inscription?"
And he then as initiate to novice:
     "Here must you put by all division of spirit
     and gather your soul against all cowardice.          15
This is the place I told you to expect.
     Here you shall pass among the fallen people,
     souls who have lost the good of intellect."
So saying, he put forth his hand to me,
     and with a gentle and encouraging smile              20
     he led me through the gate of mystery.
Here sighs and cries and wails coiled and recoiled
     on the starless air, spilling my soul to tears.
     A confusion of tongues and monstrous accents toiled
in pain and anger. Voices hoarse and shrill              25
     and sounds of blows, all intermingled, raised
     tumult and pandemonium that still
whirls on the air forever dirty with it
     as if a whirlwind sucked at sand. And I,
     holding my head in horror, cried: "Sweet Spirit,     30
what souls are these who run through this black haze?"
     And he to me: "These are the nearly soulless
     whose lives concluded neither blame nor praise.
They are mixed here with that despicable corps
     of angels who were neither for God nor Satan,        35
     but only for themselves. The High Creator
scourged them from Heaven for its perfect beauty,
     and Hell will not receive them since the wicked
     might feel some glory over them." And I:
"Master, what gnaws at them so hideously                 40
     their lamentation stuns the very air?"
     "They have no hope of death," he answered me,
"and in their blind and unattaining state
     their miserable lives have sunk so low
     that they must envy every other fate.                45
No word of them survives their living season.
     Mercy and Justice deny them even a name.

1. The Angels, the Empyrean, and the First Matter are the elements time cannot wear, for they
will last to all time. Man, however, in his mortal state, is not eternal. The Gate of Hell, therefore,
was created before man.    2. So odious is sin to God that there can be no end to its just
punishment.    3. The admonition, of course, is to the damned and not to those who come on
Heaven-sent errands.

Let us not speak of them: look, and pass on."
I saw a banner there upon the mist.
   Circling and circling, it seemed to scorn all pause.       50
   So it ran on, and still behind it pressed
a never-ending rout of souls in pain.
   I had not thought death had undone so many
   as passed before me in that mournful train.
And some I knew among them; last of all              55
   I recognized the shadow of that soul
   who, in his cowardice, made the Great Denial.[4]
At once I understood for certain: these
   were of that retrograde and faithless crew
   hateful to God and to His enemies.             60
These wretches never born and never dead
   ran naked in a swarm of wasps and hornets
   that goaded them the more the more they fled,
and made their faces stream with bloody gouts
   of pus and tears that dribbled to their feet       65
   to be swallowed there by loathsome worms and maggots.
Then looking onward I made out a throng
   assembled on the beach of a wide river,
   whereupon I turned to him: "Master, I long
to know what souls these are, and what strange usage   70
   makes them as eager to cross as they seem to be
   in this infected light." At which the Sage:
"All this shall be made known to you when we stand
   on the joyless beach of Acheron." And I
   cast down my eyes, sensing a reprimand       75
in what he said, and so walked at his side
   in silence and ashamed until we came
   through the dead cavern to that sunless tide.
There, steering toward us in an ancient ferry
   came an old man[5] with a white bush of hair,      80
   bellowing: "Woe to you depraved souls! Bury
here and forever all hope of Paradise:
   I come to lead you to the other shore,
   into eternal dark, into fire and ice.

---

4. This is almost certainly intended to be Celestine V, who became Pope in 1294. He was a man of saintly life, but allowed himself to be convinced by a priest named Benedetto that his soul was in danger since no man could live in the world without being damned. In fear for his soul he withdrew from all worldly affairs and renounced the papacy. Benedetto promptly assumed the mantle himself and became Boniface VIII, a Pope who became for Dante a symbol of all the worst corruptions of the church. Dante also blamed Boniface and his intrigues for many of the evils that befell Florence. We shall learn in Canto XIX that the fires of Hell are waiting for Boniface in the pit of the Simoniacs, and we shall be given further evidence of his corruption in Canto XXVII. Celestine's great guilt is that his cowardice (in selfish terror for his own welfare) served as the door through which so much evil entered the church.    5. Charon. He is the ferryman of dead souls across the Acheron in all classical mythology.

And you who are living yet, I say begone      85
     from these who are dead." But when he saw me stand
     against his violence he began again:
"By other windings and by other steerage
     shall you cross to that other shore. Not here! Not here!
     A lighter craft than mine must give you passage."[6]      90
And my Guide to him: "Charon, bite back your spleen:
     this has been willed where what is willed must be,
     and is not yours to ask what it may mean."
The steersman of that marsh of ruined souls,
     who wore a wheel of flame around each eye,      95
     stifled the rage that shook his woolly jowls.
But those unmanned and naked spirits there
     turned pale with fear and their teeth began to chatter
     at sound of his crude bellow. In despair
they blasphemed God,[7] their parents, their time on earth,      100
     the race of Adam, and the day and the hour
     and the place and the seed and the womb that gave them birth.
But all together they drew to that grim shore
     where all must come who lose the fear of God.
     Weeping and cursing they come for evermore,      105
and demon Charon with eyes like burning coals
     herds them in, and with a whistling oar
     flails on the stragglers to his wake of souls.
As leaves in autumn loosen and stream down
     until the branch stands bare above its tatters      110
     spread on the rustling ground, so one by one
the evil seed of Adam in its Fall
     cast themselves, at his signal, from the shore
     and streamed away like birds who hear their call.
So they are gone over that shadowy water,      115
     and always before they reach the other shore
     a new noise stirs on this, and new throngs gather.
"My son," the courteous Master said to me,
     "all who die in the shadow of God's wrath
     converge to this from every clime and country.      120
And all pass over eagerly, for here
     Divine Justice transforms and spurs them so
     their dread turns wish: they yearn for what they fear.[8]
No soul in Grace comes ever to this crossing;

6. Charon recognizes Dante not only as a living man but as a soul in grace, and knows, therefore, that the Infernal Ferry was not intended for him. He is probably referring to the fact that souls destined for Purgatory and Heaven assemble not at his ferry point, but on the banks of the Tiber, from which they are transported by an Angel. 7. The souls of the damned are not permitted to repent, for repentance is a divine grace. 8. Hell (allegorically Sin) is what the souls of the damned really wish for. Hell is their actual and deliberate choice, for divine grace is denied to none who wish for it in their hearts. The damned must, in fact, deliberately harden their hearts to God in order to become damned. Christ's grace is sufficient to save all who wish for it.

therefore if Charon rages at your presence                    125
    you will understand the reason for his cursing."
When he had spoken, all the twilight country
    shook so violently, the terror of it
    bathes me with sweat even in memory:
the tear-soaked ground gave out a sigh of wind              130
    that spewed itself in flame on a red sky,
    and all my shuttered senses left me. Blind,
like one whom sleep comes over in a swoon,
I stumbled into darkness and went down.[9]

CANTO IV

*Circle One: Limbo    The Virtuous Pagans*

Dante wakes to find himself across Acheron. The Poets are now
on the brink of Hell itself, which Dante conceives as a great funnel-
shaped cave lying below the northern hemisphere with its bottom
point at the earth's center. Around this great circular depression runs
a series of ledges, each of which Dante calls a Circle. Each circle is
assigned to the punishment of one category of sin.

As soon as Dante's strength returns, the Poets begin to cross the
First Circle. Here they find the Virtuous Pagans. They were born
without the light of Christ's revelation, and, therefore, they cannot
come into the light of God, but they are not tormented. Their only
pain is that they have no hope.

Ahead of them Dante sights a great dome of light, and a voice
trumpets through the darkness welcoming Virgil back, for this is his
eternal place in Hell. Immediately the great Poets of all time appear—
Homer, Horace, Ovid, and Lucan. They greet Virgil, and they make
Dante a sixth in their company.

With them Dante enters the Citadel of Human Reason and sees
before his eyes the Master Souls of Pagan Antiquity gathered on a
green, and illuminated by the radiance of Human Reason. This is
the highest state man can achieve without God, and the glory of it
dazzles Dante, but he knows also that it is nothing compared to the
glory of God.

A monstrous clap of thunder broke apart
    the swoon that stuffed my head; like one awakened
    by violent hands, I leaped up with a start.

9. This device (repeated at the end of Canto V) serves a double purpose. The first is technical:
Dante uses it to cover a transition. We are never told how he crossed Acheron, for that would
involve certain narrative matters he can better deal with when he crosses Styx in Canto VII. The
second is to provide a point of departure for a theme that is carried through the entire descent: the
theme of Dante's emotional reaction to Hell. These two swoons early in the descent show him
most susceptible to the grief about him. As he descends, pity leaves him, and he even goes so far
as to add to the torments of one sinner. The allegory is clear: we must harden ourselves against
every sympathy for sin.

And having risen; rested and renewed,
   I studied out the landmarks of the gloom                5
   to find my bearings there as best I could.
And I found I stood on the very brink of the valley
   called the Dolorous Abyss, the desolate chasm
   where rolls the thunder of Hell's eternal cry,
so depthless-deep and nebulous and dim                10
   that stare as I might into its frightful pit
   it gave me back no feature and no bottom.
Death-pale,[1] the Poet spoke: "Now let us go
   into the blind world waiting here below us.
   I will lead the way and you shall follow."             15
And I, sick with alarm at his new pallor,
   cried out, "How can I go this way when you
   who are my strength in doubt turn pale with terror?"
And he: "The pain of these below us here,
   drains the color from my face for pity,              20
   and leaves this pallor you mistake for fear.
Now let us go, for a long road awaits us."
   So he entered and so he led me in
   to the first circle and ledge of the abyss.
No tortured wailing rose to greet us here           25
   but sounds of sighing rose from every side,
   sending a tremor through the timeless air,
a grief breathed out of untormented sadness,
   the passive state of those who dwelled apart,
   men, women, children—a dim and endless congress.    30
And the Master said to me: "You do not question
   what souls these are that suffer here before you?
   I wish you to know before you travel on
that these were sinless. And still their merits fail,
   for they lacked Baptism's grace, which is the door    35
   of the true faith *you* were born to. Their birth fell
before the age of the Christian mysteries,
   and so they did not worship God's Trinity
   in fullest duty. I am one of these.
For such defects are we lost, though spared the fire    40
   and suffering Hell in one affliction only:
   that without hope we live on in desire."
I thought how many worthy souls there were
   suspended in that Limbo, and a weight
   closed on my heart for what the noblest suffer.    45

---

1. Virgil is most likely affected here by the return to his own place in Hell. "The pain of these below" then (line 19) would be the pain of his own group in Limbo (the Virtuous Pagans) rather than the total of Hell's suffering.

"Instruct me, Master and most noble Sir,"
   I prayed him then, "better to understand
   the perfect creed that conquers every error:
has any, by his own or another's merit,
   gone ever from this place to blessedness?"           50
   He sensed my inner question and answered it:
"I was still new to this estate of tears
   when a Mighty One[2] descended here among us,
   crowned with the sign of His victorious years.
He took from us the shade of our first parent,        55
   of Abel, his pure son, of ancient Noah,
   of Moses, the bringer of law, the obedient.
Father Abraham, David the King,
   Israel with his father and his children,
   Rachel, the holy vessel of His blessing,         60
and many more He chose for elevation
   among the elect. And before these, you must know,
   no human soul had ever won salvation."
We had not paused as he spoke, but held our road
   and passed meanwhile beyond a press of souls      65
   crowded about like trees in a thick wood.
And we had not traveled far from where I woke
   when I made out a radiance before us
   that struck away a hemisphere of dark.
We were still some distance back in the long night,    70
   yet near enough that I half-saw, half-sensed,
   what quality of souls lived in that light.
"O ornament of wisdom and of art,
   what souls are these whose merit lights their way
   even in Hell. What joy sets them apart?"        75
And he to me: "The signature of honor
   they left on earth is recognized in Heaven
   and wins them ease in Hell out of God's favor."
And as he spoke a voice rang on the air:
   "Honor the Prince of Poets; the soul and glory    80
   that went from us returns. He is here! He is here!"
The cry ceased and the echo passed from hearing;
   I saw four mighty presences come toward us
   with neither joy nor sorrow in their bearing.
"Note well," my Master said as they came on,     85
   "that soul that leads the rest with sword in hand

2. Christ. His name is never directly uttered in Hell. *Descended here*: The legend of the Harrowing of Hell is apocryphal. It is based on I Peter iii, 19: "He went and preached unto the spirits in prison." The legend is that Christ in the glory of His resurrection descended into Limbo and took with Him to Heaven the first human souls to be saved. The event would, accordingly, have occurred in A.D. 33 or 34. Virgil died in 19 B.C.

as if he were their captain and champion.
It is Homer, singing master of the earth.
    Next after him is Horace, the satirist,
    Ovid is third, and Lucan is the fourth.                    90
Since all of these have part in the high name
    the voice proclaimed, calling me Prince of Poets,
    the honor that they do me honors them."
So I saw gathered at the edge of light
    the masters of that highest school whose song              95
    outsoars all others like an eagle's flight.
And after they had talked together a while,
    they turned and welcomed me most graciously,
    at which I saw my approving Master smile.
And they honored me far beyond courtesy,                       100
    for they included me in their own number,
    making me sixth in that high company.
So we moved toward the light, and as we passed
    we spoke of things as well omitted here
    as it was sweet to touch on there. At last                 105
we reached the base of a great Citadel
    circled by seven towering battlements
    and by a sweet brook flowing round them all.[3]
This we passed over as if it were firm ground.[4]
    Through seven gates I entered with those sages             110
    and came to a green meadow blooming round.
There with a solemn and majestic poise
    stood many people gathered in the light,
    speaking infrequently and with muted voice.
Past that enameled green we six withdrew                       115
    into a luminous and open height
    from which each soul among them stood in view.
And there directly before me on the green

3. The most likely allegory is that the Citadel represents philosophy (that is, human reason without the light of God) surrounded by seven walls which represent the seven liberal arts, or the seven sciences, or the seven virtues. Note that Human Reason makes a light of its own, but that it is a light in darkness and forever separated from the glory of God's light. The *sweet brook flowing* round them all has been interpreted in many ways. Clearly fundamental, however, is the fact that it divides those in the Citadel (those who wish to know) from those in the outer darkness.
4. Since Dante still has his body, and since all others in Hell are incorporeal shades, there is a recurring narrative problem in the *Inferno* (and through the rest of the *Commedia*): how does flesh act in contact with spirit? In the *Purgatorio* Dante attempts to embrace the spirit of Casella and his arms pass through him as if he were empty air. In the Third Circle, below (Canto VI, 34–36), Dante steps on some of the spirits lying in the slush and his foot passes right through them. (The original lines offer several possible readings of which I have preferred this one.) And at other times Virgil, also a spirit, picks Dante up and carries him bodily. It is clear, too, that Dante means the spirits of Hell to be weightless. When Virgil steps into Phlegyas' bark (Canto VIII) it does not settle into the water, but it does when Dante's living body steps aboard. There is no narrative reason why Dante should not sink into the waters of this stream and Dante follows no fixed rule in dealing with such phenomena, often suiting the physical action to the allegorical need. Here, the moat probably symbolizes some requirement (The Will to Know) which he and the other poets meet without difficulty.

the master souls of time were shown to me.
  I glory in the glory I have seen!⁵                                    120
Electra stood in a great company
  among whom I saw Hector and Aeneas
  and Caesar in armor with his falcon's eye.
I saw Camilla, and the Queen Amazon
  across the field. I saw the Latian King                              125
  seated there with his daughter by his throne.
And the good Brutus who overthrew the Tarquin:
  Lucrezia, Julia, Marcia, and Cornelia;
  and, by himself apart, the Saladin.
And raising my eyes a little I saw on high                             130
  Aristotle, the master of those who know,
  ringed by the great souls of philosophy.
All wait upon him for their honor and his.
  I saw Socrates and Plato at his side
  before all others there. Democritus                                  135
who ascribes the world to chance, Diogenes,
  and with him there Thales, Anaxagoras,
  Zeno, Heraclitus, Empedocles.
And I saw the wise collector and analyst—
  Dioscorides I mean. I saw Orpheus there,                             140
  Tully, Linus, Seneca the moralist,
Euclid the geometer, and Ptolemy,
  Hippocrates, Galen, Avicenna,
  and Averrhoës of the Great Commentary.
I cannot count so much nobility;                                       145
  my longer theme pursues me so that often
  the word falls short of the reality.
The company of six is reduced by four.
  My Master leads me by another road
  out of that serenity to the roar                                     150

---

5. The inhabitants of the citadel fall into three main groups: 1. *The heroes and heroines:* All of
these it must be noted were associated with the Trojans and their Roman descendants. The Electra
Dante mentions here is not the sister of Orestes (see Euripides' *Electra*) but the daughter of Atlas
and the mother of Dardanus, the founder of Troy. 2. *The philosophers:* Most of this group is made
up of philosophers whose teachings were, at least in part, acceptable to church scholarship.
Democritus, however, "who ascribed the world to chance," would clearly be an exception. The
group is best interpreted, therefore, as representing the highest achievements of Human Reason
unaided by Divine Love. *Plato and Aristotle:* Through a considerable part of the Middle Ages
Plato was held to be the fountainhead of all scholarship, but in Dante's time practically all learning was based on Aristotelian theory as interpreted through the many commentaries. *Linus:* the
Italian is "Lino" and for it some commentators read "Livio" (Livy). 3. *The naturalists:* They are
less well known today. In Dante's time their place in scholarship more or less corresponded to the
role of the theoretician and historian of science in our universities. *Avicenna* (his major work was
in the eleventh century) and *Avverhoës* (twelfth century) were Arabian philosophers and physicians
especially famous in Dante's time for their commentaries on Aristotle. *Great Commentary:* has
the force of a title, i.e., The Great Commentary as distinguished from many lesser commentaries.
*The Saladin:* This is the famous Saladin who was defeated by Richard the Lion-Heart, and
whose great qualities as a ruler became a legend in medieval Europe.

and trembling air of Hell. I pass from light
into the kingdom of eternal night.

CANTO V

*Circle Two     The Carnal*

The Poets leave Limbo and enter the Second Circle. Here begin
the torments of Hell proper, and here, blocking the way, sits Minos,
the dread and semi-bestial judge of the damned who assigns to each
soul its eternal torment. He orders the Poets back; but Virgil silences
him as he earlier silenced Charon, and the Poets move on.

They find themselves on a dark ledge swept by a great whirlwind,
which spins within it the souls of the Carnal, those who betrayed
reason to their appetites. Their sin was to abandon themselves to the
tempest of their passions: so they are swept forever in the tempest of
Hell, forever denied the light of reason and of God. Virgil identifies
many among them. Semiramis is there, and Dido, Cleopatra, Helen,
Achilles, Paris, and Tristan. Dante sees Paolo and Francesca swept
together, and in the name of love he calls to them to tell their sad
story. They pause from their eternal flight to come to him, and Francesca tells their history while Paolo weeps at her side. Dante is so
stricken by compassion at their tragic tale that he swoons once again.

So we went down to the second ledge alone;
    a smaller circle[6] of so much greater pain
    the voice of the damned rose in a bestial moan.
There Minos[7] sits, grinning, grotesque, and hale.
    He examines each lost soul as it arrives                              5
    and delivers his verdict with his coiling tail.
That is to say, when the ill-fated soul
    appears before him it confesses all,
    and that grim sorter of the dark and foul
decides which place in Hell shall be its end,                            10
    then wraps his twitching tail about himself
    one coil for each degree it must descend.
The soul descends and others take its place:
    each crowds in its turn to judgment, each confesses,
    each hears its doom and falls away through space.                    15
"O you who come into this camp of woe,"

6. The pit of Hell tapers like a funnel. The circles of ledges accordingly grow smaller as they
descend.     7. The son of Europa and of Zeus who descended to her in the form of a bull. Minos
became a mythological king of Crete, so famous for his wisdom and justice that after death his
soul was made judge of the dead. Virgil presents him fulfilling the same office at Aeneas' descent
to the underworld. Dante, however, transforms him into an irate and hideous monster with a tail.
The transformation may have been suggested by the form Zeus assumed for the rape of Europa—
the monster is certainly bullish enough here—but the obvious purpose of the brutalization is to
present a figure symbolic of the guilty conscience of the wretches who come before it to make
their confessions.

cried Minos when he saw me turn away
  without awaiting his judgment, "watch where you go
once you have entered here, and to whom you turn!
  Do not be misled by that wide and easy passage!"          20
  And my Guide to him: "That is not your concern;
it is his fate to enter every door.
  This has been willed where what is willed must be,
  and is not yours to question. Say no more."
Now the choir of anguish, like a wound,                     25
  strikes through the tortured air. Now I have come
  to Hell's full lamentation, sound beyond sound.
I came to a place stripped bare of every light
  and roaring on the naked dark like seas
  wracked by a war of winds. Their hellish flight          30
of storm and counterstorm through time foregone,
  sweeps the souls of the damned before its charge.
  Whirling and battering it drives them on,
and when they pass the ruined gap of Hell[8]
  through which we had come, their shrieks begin anew.     35
  There they blaspheme the power of God eternal.
And this, I learned, was the never ending flight
  of those who sinned in the flesh, the carnal and lusty
  who betrayed reason to their appetite.
As the wings of wintering starlings bear them on           40
  in their great wheeling flights, just so the blast
  wherries these evil souls through time foregone.
Here, there, up, down, they whirl and, whirling, strain
  with never a hope of hope to comfort them,
  not of release, but even of less pain.                   45
As cranes go over sounding their harsh cry,
  leaving the long streak of their flight in air,
  so come these spirits, wailing as they fly.
And watching their shadows lashed by wind, I cried:
  "Master, what souls are these the very air               50
  lashes with its black whips from side to side?"
"The first of these whose history you would know,"
  he answered me, "was Empress of many tongues.[9]
  Mad sensuality corrupted her so
that to hide the guilt of her debauchery                    55
  she licensed all depravity alike,

---

8. See note to Canto II, 53. At the time of the Harrowing of Hell a great earthquake shook the
underworld shattering rocks and cliffs. Ruins resulting from the same shock are noted in Canto
XII, 34, and Canto XXI, 112 ff. At the beginning of Canto XXIV, the Poets leave the *bolgia* of
the Hypocrites by climbing the ruined slabs of a bridge that was shattered by this earthquake.
9. Semiramis, a legendary queen of Assyria who assumed full power at the death of her husband,
Ninus.

and lust and law were one in her decree.
She is Semiramis of whom the tale is told
   how she married Ninus and succeeded him
   to the throne of that wide land the Sultans hold.          60
The other is Dido;[1] faithless to the ashes
   of Sichaeus, she killed herself for love.
   The next whom the eternal tempest lashes
is sense-drugged Cleopatra. See Helen there,
   from whom such ill arose. And great Achilles,[2]
   who fought at last with love in the house of prayer.
And Paris. And Tristan." As they whirled above
   he pointed out more than a thousand shades
   of those torn from the mortal life by love.
I stood there while my Teacher one by one          70
   named the great knights and ladies of dim time;
   and I was swept by pity and confusion.
At last I spoke: "Poet, I should be glad
   to speak a word with those two swept together
   so lightly on the wind and still so sad."[3]          75
And he to me: "Watch them. When next they pass,
   call to them in the name of love that drives
   and damns them here. In that name they will pause."
Thus, as soon as the wind in its wild course
   brought them around, I called: "O wearied souls!      80
   if none forbid it, pause and speak to us."
As mating doves that love calls to their nest
   glide through the air with motionless raised wings,
   borne by the sweet desire that fills each breast—
Just so those spirits turned on the torn sky          85
   from the band where Dido whirls across the air;
   such was the power of pity in my cry.
"O living creature, gracious, kind, and good,

1. Queen and founder of Carthage. She had vowed to remain faithful to her husband, Sichaeus, but she fell in love with Aeneas. When Aeneas abandoned her she stabbed herself on a funeral pyre she had had prepared.
   According to Dante's own system of punishments, she should be in the Seventh Circle (Canto XIII) with the suicides. The only clue Dante gives to the tempering of her punishment is his statement that "she killed herself for love." Dante always seems readiest to forgive in that name.
2. He is placed among this company because of his passion for Polyxena, the daughter of Priam. For love of her, he agreed to desert the Greeks and to join the Trojans, but when he went to the temple for the wedding (according to the legend Dante has followed) he was killed by Paris.
3. Paolo and Francesca. In 1275 Giovanni Malatesta of Rimini, called Giovanni the Lame, a somewhat deformed but brave and powerful warrior, made a political marriage with Francesca, daughter of Guido da Polenta of Ravenna. Francesca came to Rimini and there an amour grew between her and Giovanni's younger brother Paolo. Despite the fact that Paolo had married in 1269 and had become the father of two daughters by 1275, his affair with Francesca continued for many years. It was sometime between 1283 and 1286 that Giovanni surprised them in Francesca's bedroom and killed both of them. Around these facts the legend has grown that Paolo was sent by Giovanni as his proxy to the marriage, that Francesca thought he was her real bridegroom and accordingly gave him her heart irrevocably at first sight. The legend obviously increases the pathos, but nothing in Dante gives it support.

going this pilgrimage through the sick night,
visiting us who stained the earth with blood,                    90
were the King of Time our friend, we would pray His peace
    on you who have pitied us. As long as the wind
    will let us pause, ask of us what you please.
The town where I was born lies by the shore
    where the Po descends into its ocean rest                     95
    with its attendant streams in one long murmur.
Love, which in gentlest hearts will soonest bloom
    seized my lover with passion for that sweet body
    from which I was torn unshriven to my doom.
Love, which permits no loved one not to love,                    100
    took me so strongly with delight in him
    that we are one in Hell, as we were above.[4]
Love led us to one death. In the depths of Hell
    Caïna waits for him[5] who took our lives."
    This was the piteous tale they stopped to tell.              105
And when I had heard those world-offended lovers
    I bowed my head. At last the Poet spoke:
    "What painful thoughts are these your lowered brow covers?"
When at length I answered, I began: "Alas!
    What sweetest thoughts, what green and young desire           110
    led these two lovers to this sorry pass."
Then turning to those spirits once again,
    I said: "Francesca, what you suffer here
    melts me to tears of pity and of pain.
But tell me: in the time of your sweet sighs                     115
    by what appearances found love the way
    to lure you to his perilous paradise?"
And she: "The double grief of a lost bliss
    is to recall its happy hour in pain.
    Your Guide and Teacher knows the truth of this.              120
But if there is indeed a soul in Hell
    to ask of the beginning of our love
    out of his pity, I will weep and tell:
On a day for dalliance we read the rhyme
    of Lancelot,[6] how love had mastered him.                   125

---

4. At many points of the *Inferno* Dante makes clear the principle that the souls of the damned
are locked so blindly into their own guilt that none can feel sympathy for another, or find any
pleasure in the presence of another. The temptation of many readers is to interpret this line
romantically: i.e., that the love of Paolo and Francesca survives Hell itself. The more Dantean
interpretation, however, is that they add to one another's anguish (a) as mutual reminders of their
sin, and (b) as insubstantial shades of the bodies for which they once felt such great passion.
5. Giovanni Malatesta was still alive at the writing. His fate is already decided, however, and
upon his death, his soul will fall to Caïna, the first ring of the last circle (Canto XXXII), where lie
those who performed arts of treachery against their kin.   6. The story exists in many forms. The
details Dante makes use of are from an Old French version.

We were alone with innocence and dim time.[7]
Pause after pause that high old story drew
  our eyes together while we blushed and paled;
  but it was one soft passage overthrew
our caution and our hearts. For when we read          130
  how her fond smile was kissed by such a lover,
  he who is one with me alive and dead
breathed on my lips the tremor of his kiss.
  That book, and he who wrote it, was a pander.[8]
  That day we read no further." As she said this,     135
the other spirit, who stood by her, wept
  so piteously, I felt my senses reel
  and faint away with anguish. I was swept
by such a swoon as death is, and I fell,
as a corpse might fall, to the dead floor of Hell.    140

### CANTO VI

*Circle Three    The Gluttons*

Dante recovers from his swoon and finds himself in the Third
Circle. A great storm of putrefaction falls incessantly, a mixture of
stinking snow and freezing rain, which forms into a vile slush underfoot. Everything about this Circle suggests a gigantic garbage dump.
The souls of the damned lie in the icy paste, swollen and obscene,
and Cerberus, the ravenous three-headed dog of Hell, stands guard
over them, ripping and tearing them with his claws and teeth.

These are the Gluttons. In life they made no higher use of the
gifts of God than to wallow in food and drink, producers of nothing
but garbage and offal. Here they lie through all eternity, themselves
like garbage, half-buried in fetid slush, while Cerberus slavers over
them as they in life slavered over their food.

As the Poets pass, one of the speakers sits up and addresses Dante.
He is Ciacco, The Hog, a citizen of Dante's own Florence. He recognizes Dante and asks eagerly for news of what is happening there.
With the foreknowledge of the damned, Ciacco then utters the first
of the political prophecies that are to become a recurring theme of
the Inferno. The poets then move on toward the next Circle, at the
edge of which they encounter the monster Plutus.

My senses had reeled from me out of pity
  for the sorrow of those kinsmen and lost lovers.

---

7. The original simply reads "We were alone, suspecting nothing." "Dim time" is rhyme-forced,
but not wholly outside the legitimate implications of the original, I hope. The old courtly romance
may well be thought of as happening in the dim ancient days. The apology, of course, comes
after the fact: one does the possible then argues for justification, and there probably is none.
8. "Galeotto," the Italian word for "pander," is also the Italian rendering of the name of Galle-
hault, who in the French Romance Dante refers to here, urged Lancelot and Guinevere on to
love.

Now they return, and waking gradually,
I see new torments and new souls in pain
   about me everywhere. Wherever I turn 5
   away from grief I turn to grief again.
I am in the Third Circle of the torments.
   Here to all time with neither pause nor change
   the frozen rain of Hell descends in torrents.
Huge hailstones, dirty water, and black snow 10
   pour from the dismal air to putrefy
   the putrid slush that waits for them below.
Here monstrous Cerberus,[9] the ravening beast,
   howls through his triple throats like a mad dog
   over the spirits sunk in that foul paste. 15
His eyes are red, his beard is greased with phlegm,
   his belly is swollen, and his hands are claws
   to rip the wretches and flay and mangle them.
And they, too, howl like dogs in the freezing storm,
   turning and turning from it as if they thought 20
   one naked side could keep the other warm.
When Cerberus discovered us in that swill
   his dragon-jaws yawed wide, his lips drew back
   in a grin of fangs. No limb of him was still.
My Guide bent down and seized in either fist 25
   a clod of the stinking dirt that festered there
   and flung them down the gullet of the beast.
As a hungry cur will set the echoes raving
   and then fall still when he is thrown a bone,
   all of his clamor being in his craving, 30
so the three ugly heads of Cerberus,
   whose yowling at those wretches deafened them,
   choked on their putrid sops and stopped their fuss.
We made our way across the sodden mess
   of souls the rain beat down, and when our steps 35
   fell on a body, they sank through emptiness.
All those illusions of being seemed to lie
   drowned in the slush; until one wraith among them
   sat up abruptly and called as I passed by:
"O you who are led this journey through the shade 40
   of Hell's abyss, do you recall this face?
   You had been made before I was unmade."[1]

9. In classical mythology Cerberus appears as a three-headed dog. His master was Pluto, king of the Underworld. Cerberus was placed at the Gate of the Underworld to allow all to enter, but none to escape. His three heads and his ravenous disposition make him an apt symbol of gluttony. *Like a mad dog:* Dante seems clearly to have visualized him as a half-human monster. The beard (line 16) suggests that at least one of his three heads is human, and many illuminated manuscripts so represent him.   1. That is, "you were born before I died." The further implication is that they must have seen one another in Florence, a city one can still walk across in twenty minutes, and around in a very few hours. Dante certainly would have known everyone in Florence.

And I: "Perhaps the pain you suffer here
    distorts your image from my recollection.
    I do not know you as you now appear."           45
And he to me: "Your own city, so rife
    with hatred that the bitter cup flows over
    was mine too in that other, clearer life.
Your citizens nicknamed me Ciacco, The Hog:
    gluttony was my offense, and for it          50
    I lie here rotting like a swollen log.
Nor am I lost in this alone; all these
    you see about you in this painful death
    have wallowed in the same indecencies."
I answered him: "Ciacco, your agony          55
    weighs on my heart and calls my soul to tears;
    But tell me, if you can, what is to be
for the citizens of that divided state,
    and whether there are honest men among them,
    and for what reasons we are torn by hate."          60
And he then: "After many words given and taken
    it shall come to blood; White shall rise over Black
    and rout the dark lord's force, battered and shaken.
Then it shall come to pass within three suns
    that the fallen shall arise, and by the power          65
    of one now gripped by many hesitations
Black shall ride on White for many years,
    loading it down with burdens and oppressions
    and humbling of proud names and helpless tears.
Two are honest, but none will heed them. There,     70
    pride, avarice, and envy are the tongues
    men know and heed, a Babel of despair."[2]
Here he broke off his mournful prophecy.
    And I to him: "Still let me urge you on
    to speak a little further and instruct me:          75
Farinata and Tegghiaio, men of good blood,

2. This is the first of the political prophecies that are to become a recurring theme of the *Inferno*.
(It is the second if we include the political symbolism of the Greyhound in Canto I.) Dante is, of
course, writing after these events have all taken place. At Easter time of 1300, however, the events
were in the future.
    The Whites and the Blacks of Ciacco's prophecy should not be confused with the Guelphs and
the Ghibellines. The internal strife between the Guelphs and the Ghibellines ended with the total
defeat of the Ghibellines. By the end of the 13th century that strife had passed. But very shortly a
new feud began in Florence between White Guelphs and Black Guelphs. A rather gruesome
murder perpetrated by Focaccio de' Cancellieri became the cause of new strife between two branches
of the Cancellieri family. On May 1 of 1300 the White Guelphs (Dante's party) drove the Black
Guelphs from Florence in bloody fighting. Two years later, however ("within three suns"), the
Blacks, aided by Dante's detested Boniface VIII, returned and expelled most of the prominent
Whites, among them Dante; for he had been a member of the Priorate (City Council) that issued
a decree banishing the leaders of both sides. This was the beginning of Dante's long exile from
Florence.

Jacopo Rusticucci, Arrigo, Mosca,[3]
and the others who set their hearts on doing good—
where are they now whose high deeds might be-gem
   the crown of kings? I long to know their fate.                          80
   Does Heaven soothe or Hell envenom them?"
And he: "They lie below in a blacker lair.
   A heavier guilt draws them to greater pain.
   If you descend so far you may see them there.
But when you move again among the living,                                           85
   oh speak my name to the memory of men![4]
   Having answered all, I say no more." And giving
his head a shake, he looked up at my face
   cross-eyed, then bowed his head and fell away
   among the other blind souls of that place.                                90
And my Guide to me: "He will not wake again
   until the angel trumpet sounds the day
   on which the host shall come to judge all men.
Then shall each soul before the seat of Mercy
   return to its sad grave and flesh and form                                 95
   to hear the edict of Eternity."
So we picked our slow way among the shades
   and the filthy rain, speaking of life to come.
   "Master," I said, "when the great clarion fades
into the voice of thundering Omniscience,                                           100
   what of these agonies? Will they be the same,
   or more, or less, after the final sentence?"
And he to me: "Look to your science[5] again
   where it is written: the more a thing is perfect
   the more it feels of pleasure and of pain.                                  105
As for these souls, though they can never soar
   to true perfection, still in the new time
   they will be nearer it than they were before."
And so we walked the rim of the great ledge
   speaking of pain and joy, and of much more                                  110
   that I will not repeat, and reached the edge
where the descent begins. There, suddenly,
   we came on Plutus, the great enemy.

---

**3.** Farinata will appear in Canto X among the Heretics: Tegghiaio and Jacopo Rusticucci, in Canto XVI with the homosexuals, Mosca in Canto XXVIII with the sowers of discord. Arrigo does not appear again and he has not been positively identified. Dante probably refers here to Arrigo (or Oderigo) dei Fifanti, one of those who took part in the murder of Buondelmonte (Canto XXVIII, line 106, note).   **4.** Excepting those shades in the lowest depths of Hell whose sins are so shameful that they wish only to be forgotten, all of the damned are eager to be remembered on earth. The concept of the family name and of its survival in the memories of men were matters of first importance among Italians of Dante's time, and expressions of essentially the same attitude are common in Italy today.   **5.** "Science" to the man of Dante's time meant specifically "the writings of Aristotle and the commentaries upon them."

CANTO VII

*Circle Four    The Hoarders and the Wasters*
*Circle Five    The Wrathful and the Sullen*

Plutus menaces the Poets, but once more Virgil shows himself more powerful than the rages of Hell's monsters. The Poets enter the Fourth Circle and find what seems to be a war in progress.

The sinners are divided into two raging mobs, each soul among them straining madly at a great boulder-like weight. The two mobs meet, clashing their weights against one another, after which they separate, pushing the great weights apart, and begin over again.

One mob is made up of the Hoarders, the other of the Wasters. In life, they lacked all moderation in regulating their expenses; they destroyed the light of God within themselves by thinking of nothing but money. Thus in death, their souls are encumbered by dead weights (mundanity) and one excess serves to punish the other. Their souls, moreover, have become so dimmed and awry in their fruitless rages that there is no hope of recognizing any among them.

The Poets pass on while Virgil explains the function of Dame Fortune in the Divine Scheme. As he finishes (it is past midnight now of Good Friday) they reach the inner edge of the ledge and come to a Black Spring which bubbles murkily over the rocks to form the Marsh of Styx, which is the Fifth Circle, the last station of the Upper Hell.

Across the marsh they see countless souls attacking one another in the foul slime. These are the Wrathful and the symbolism of their punishment is obvious. Virgil also points out to Dante certain bubbles rising from the slime and informs him that below that mud lie entombed the souls of the Sullen. In life they refused to welcome the sweet light of the Sun (Divine Illumination) and in death they are buried forever below the stinking waters of the Styx, gargling the words of an endless chant in a grotesque parody of singing a hymn.

"Papa Satán, Papa Satán, aleppy,"[6]
    Plutus[7] clucked and stuttered in his rage;
    and my all-knowing Guide, to comfort me:

6. Virgil, the all-knowing, may understand these words, but no one familiar with merely human languages has deciphered them. In Canto XXXI the monster Nimrod utters a similar meaningless jargon, and Virgil there cites it as evidence of the dimness of his mind. Gibberish is certainly a characteristic appropriate to monsters, and since Dante takes pains to make the reference to Satan apparent in the gibberish, it is obviously infernal and debased, and that is almost certainly all he intended.

    The word "papa" as used here probably means "Pope" rather than "father." "Il papa santo" is the Pope. "Papa Satán" would be his opposite number. In the original the last word is "aleppe." On the assumption that jargon translates jargon I have twisted it a bit to rhyme with "me."    7. In Greek mythology, Plutus was the God of Wealth. Many commentators suggest that Dante confused him with Pluto, the son of Saturn and God of the Underworld. But in that case, Plutus would be identical with Lucifer himself and would require a central place in Hell, whereas the classical function of Plutus as God of Material Wealth makes him the ideal overseer of the miserly and the prodigal.

"Do not be startled, for no power of his,
   however he may lord it over the damned,                    5
   may hinder your descent through this abyss."
And turning to that carnival of bloat
   cried: "Peace, you wolf of Hell. Choke back your bile
   and let its venom blister your own throat.
Our passage through this pit is willed on high                10
   by that same Throne that loosed the angel wrath
   of Michael on ambition and mutiny."
As puffed out sails fall when the mast gives way
   and flutter to a self-convulsing heap—
   so collapsed Plutus into that dead clay.                   15
Thus we descended the dark scarp of Hell
   to which all the evil of the Universe
   comes home at last, into the Fourth Great Circle
and ledge of the abyss. O Holy Justice,
   who could relate the agonies I saw!                        20
   What guilt is man that he can come to this?
Just as the surge Charybdis[8] hurls to sea
   crashes and breaks upon its countersurge,
   so these shades dance and crash eternally.
Here, too, I saw a nation of lost souls,                      25
   far more than were above: they strained their chests
   against enormous weights, and with mad howls
rolled them at one another. Then in haste
   they rolled them back, one party shouting out:
   "Why do you hoard?" and the other: "Why do you waste?"     30
So back around that ring they puff and blow,
   each faction to its course, until they reach
   opposite sides, and screaming as they go
the madmen turn and start their weights again
   to crash against the maniacs. And I,                       35
   watching, felt my heart contract with pain.
"Master," I said, "what people can these be?
   And all those tonsured ones there on our left—
   is it possible they all were of the clergy?"
And he: "In the first life beneath the sun                    40
   they were so skewed and squinteyed in their minds
   their misering or extravagance mocked all reason.
The voice of each clamors its own excess
   when lust meets lust at the two points of the circle
   where opposite guilts meet in their wretchedness.          45
These tonsured wraiths of greed were priests indeed,
   the popes and cardinals, for it is in these

8. A famous whirlpool in the Straits of Sicily.

the weed of avarice sows its rankest seed."
And I to him: "Master, among this crew
   surely I should be able to make out                                  50
   the fallen image of some soul I knew."
And he to me: "This is a lost ambition.
   In their sordid lives they labored to be blind,
   and now their souls have dimmed past recognition.
All their eternity is to butt and bray:                                          55
   one crew will stand tight-fisted, the other stripped
   of its very hair at the bar of Judgment Day.
Hoarding and squandering wasted all their light
   and brought them screaming to this brawl of wraiths.
   You need no words of mine to grasp their plight.                       60
Now may you see the fleeting vanity
   of the goods of Fortune for which men tear down
   all that they are, to build a mockery.
Not all the gold that is or ever was
   under the sky could buy for one of these                              65
   exhausted souls the fraction of a pause."
"Master," I said, "tell me—now that you touch
   on this Dame Fortune[9]—what *is* she, that she holds
   the good things of the world within her clutch?"
And he to me: "O credulous mankind,                                              70
   is there one error that has wooed and lost you?
   Now listen, and strike error from your mind:
That king whose perfect wisdom transcends all,
   made the heavens and posted angels on them
   to guide the eternal light that it might fall                         75
from every sphere to every sphere the same.
   He made earth's splendors by a like decree
   and posted as their minister this high Dame,
the Lady of Permutations. All earth's gear
   she changes from nation to nation, from house to house,                80
   in changeless change through every turning year.
No mortal power may stay her spinning wheel.
   The nations rise and fall by her decree.
   None may foresee where she will set her heel:[1]
she passes, and things pass. Man's mortal reason                                 85
   cannot encompass her. She rules her sphere
   as the other gods[2] rule theirs. Season by season

---

9. A central figure in medieval mythology. She is almost invariably represented as a female figure holding an ever-revolving wheel symbolic of Chance. Dante incorporates her into his scheme of the Universe, ranking her among the angels, and giving her a special office in the service of the Catholic God.  1. A literal translation of the original would be "She is hidden like a snake in the grass." To avoid the comic overtone of that figure in English, I have substituted another figure which I believe expresses Dante's intent without destroying his tone.  2. Dante can only mean here "the other angels and ministers of God."

her changes change her changes endlessly,
    and those whose turn has come press on her so,
    she must be swift by hard necessity.                90
And this is she so railed at and reviled
    that even her debtors in the joys of time
    blaspheme her name. Their oaths are bitter and wild,
but she in her beatitude does not hear.
    Among the Primal Beings of God's joy           95
    she breathes her blessedness and wheels her sphere.
But the stars that marked our starting fall away.[3]
    We must go deeper into greater pain,
    for it is not permitted that we stay."
And crossing over to the chasm's edge           100
    we came to a spring[4] that boiled and overflowed
    through a great crevice worn into the ledge.
By that foul water, black from its very source,
    we found a nightmare path among the rocks
    and followed the dark stream along its course.       105
Beyond its rocky race and wild descent
    the river floods and forms a marsh called Styx,[5]
    a dreary swampland, vaporous and malignant.
And I, intent on all our passage touched,
    made out a swarm of spirits in that bog       110
    savage with anger, naked, slime-besmutched.
They thumped at one another in that slime
    with hands and feet, and they butted, and they bit
    as if each would tear the other limb from limb.
And my kind Sage: "My son, behold the souls      115
    of those who lived in wrath. And do you see
    the broken surfaces of those water-holes
on every hand, boiling as if in pain?
    There are souls beneath that water. Fixed in slime
    they speak their piece, end it, and start again:    120
'Sullen were we in the air made sweet by the Sun;
    in the glory of his shining our hearts poured
    a bitter smoke. Sullen were we begun;
sullen we lie forever in this ditch.'
    This litany they gargle in their throats      125

---

3. It is now past midnight of Good Friday.    4. All the waters of Hell derive from one source
(see Canto XIV, lines 12 following). This black spring must therefore be the waters of Acheron
boiling out of some subterranean passage.    5. The river Styx figures variously in classic mythology, but usually (and in later myths always) as a river of the Underworld. Dante, to heighten
his symbolism, makes it a filthy marsh. This marsh marks the first great division of Hell. Between Acheron and Styx are punished the sins of Incontinence (the Sins of the She-Wolf). This
is the Upper Hell. Beyond Styx rise the flaming walls of the infernal city of Dis, within which
are punished Violence and Fraud (the sins of the Lion, and the Sins of the Leopard).

as if they sang, but lacked the words and pitch."
Then circling on along that filthy wallow,
  we picked our way between the bank and fen,
  keeping our eyes on those foul souls that swallow
the slime of Hell. And so at last we came                    130
to foot of a Great Tower that has no name.[6]

### CANTO VIII

*Circle Five: Styx    The Wrathful, Phlegyas*
*Circle Six: Dis    The Fallen Angels*

The Poets stand at the edge of the swamp, and a mysterious signal
flames from the great tower. It is answered from the darkness of the
other side, and almost immediately the Poets see Phlegyas, the Boatman of Styx, racing toward them across the water, fast as a flying
arrow. He comes avidly, thinking to find new souls for torment, and
he howls with rage when he discovers the Poets. Once again, however, Virgil conquers wrath with a word and Phlegyas reluctantly
gives them passage.

As they are crossing, a muddy soul rises before them. It is Filippo
Argenti, one of the Wrathful. Dante recognizes him despite the filth
with which he is covered, and he berates him soundly, even wishing
to see him tormented further. Virgil approves Dante's disdain and,
as if in answer to Dante's wrath, Argenti is suddenly set upon by all
the other sinners present, who fall upon him and rip him to pieces.

The boat meanwhile has sped on, and before Argenti's screams
have died away, Dante sees the flaming red towers of Dis, the Capital of Hell. The great walls of the iron city block the way to the
Lower Hell. Properly speaking, all the rest of Hell lies within the city
walls, which separate the Upper and the Lower Hell.

Phlegyas deposits them at a great Iron Gate which they find to be
guarded by the Rebellious Angels. These creatures of Ultimate Evil,
rebels against God Himself, refuse to let the Poets pass. Even Virgil
is powerless against them, for Human Reason by itself cannot cope
with the essence of Evil. Only Divine Aid can bring hope. Virgil
accordingly sends up a prayer for assistance and waits anxiously for a
Heavenly Messenger to appear.

Returning to my theme,[7] I say we came
  to the foot of a Great Tower; but long before

---

6. No special significance need be attributed to the Tower. It serves as a signaling point for calling
the ferryman from Dis.    7. There is evidence that Dante stopped writing for a longer or shorter
period between the seventh and eighth Cantos. None of the evidence is conclusive but it is quite
clear that the plan of the *Inferno* changes from here on. Up to this point the Circles have been
described in one canto apiece. If this was Dante's original plan, Hell would have been concluded
in five more Cantos, since there are only Nine Circles in all. But in the later journey the Eighth
Circle alone occupies thirteen Cantos. Dante's phrase may be simply transitional, but it certainly
marks a change in the plan of the poem.

we reached it through the marsh, two horns of flame
flared from the summit, one from either side,
   and then, far off, so far we scarce could see it     5
   across the mist, another flame replied.
I turned to that sea of all intelligence
   saying: "What is this signal and counter-signal?
   Who is it speaks with fire across this distance?"
And he then: "Look across the filthy slew:     10
   you may already see the one they summon,
   if the swamp vapors do not hide him from you."
No twanging bowspring ever shot an arrow
   that bored the air it rode dead to the mark
   more swiftly than the flying skiff whose prow     15
shot toward us over the polluted channel
   with a single steersman at the helm who called:
   "So, do I have you at last, you whelp of Hell?"
"Phlegyas, Phlegyas,"[8] said my Lord and Guide,
   "this time you waste your breath: you have us only     20
   for the time it takes to cross to the other side."
Phlegyas, the madman, blew his rage among
   those muddy marshes like a cheat deceived,
   or like a fool at some imagined wrong.
My Guide, whom all the fiend's noise could not nettle,     25
   boarded the skiff, motioning me to follow:
   and not till I stepped aboard did it seem to settle[9]
into the water. At once we left the shore,
   that ancient hull riding more heavily
   than it had ridden in all of time before     30
And as we ran on that dead swamp, the slime
   rose before me, and from it a voice cried:
   "Who are you that come here before your time?"
And I replied: "If I come, I do not remain.
   But you, who are *you*, so fallen and so foul?"     35
   And he: "I am one who weeps." And I then:
"May you weep and wail to all eternity,
   for I know you, hell-dog, filthy as you are."[1]
     Then he stretched both hands to the boat, but warily

8. Mythological King of Boeotia. He was the son of Ares (Mars) by a human mother. Angry at Apollo, who had seduced his daughter (Aesculapius was born of this union), he set fire to Apollo's temple at Delphi. For this offense, the God killed him and threw his soul into Hades under sentence of eternal torment. Dante's choice of a ferryman is especially apt. Phlegyas is the link between the Wrathful (to whom his paternity relates him) and the Rebellious Angels who menaced God (as he menaced Apollo).    9. Because of his living weight.    1. Filippo Argenti was one of the Adimari family, who were bitter political enemies of Dante. Dante's savagery toward him was probably intended in part as an insult to the family. He pays them off again in the Paradiso when he has Cacciaguida call them "The insolent gang that makes itself a dragon to chase those who run away, but is sweet as a lamb to any who show their teeth—or their purse."

the Master shoved him back, crying, "Down! Down!                40
   with the other dogs!" Then he embraced me saying:
   "Indignant spirit, I kiss you as you frown.
Blessed be she who bore you.[2] In world and time
   this one was haughtier yet. Not one unbending
   graces his memory. Here is his shadow in slime.                45
How many living now, chancellors of wrath,
   shall come to lie here in this pigmire,
   leaving a curse to be their aftermath!"
And I: "Master, it would suit my whim
   to see the wretch scrubbed down into the swill                50
   before we leave this stinking sink and him."
And he to me: "Before the other side
   shows through the mist, you shall have all you ask.
   This is a wish that should be gratified."
And shortly after, I saw the loathsome spirit                55
   so mangled by a swarm of muddy wraiths
   that to this day I praise and thank God for it.
"After Filippo Argenti!" all cried together.
   The maddog Florentine wheeled at their cry
   and bit himself for rage. I saw them gather.                60
And there we left him. And I say no more.
   But such a wailing beat upon my ears,
   I strained my eyes ahead to the far shore.
"My son," the Master said, "the City called Dis[3]
   lies just ahead, the heavy citizens,                65
   the swarming crowds of Hell's metropolis."
And I then: "Master, I already see
   the glow of its red mosques,[4] as if they came
   hot from the forge to smolder in this valley."
And my all-knowing Guide: "They are eternal                70
   flues to eternal fire that rages in them
   and makes them glow across this lower Hell."
And as he spoke we entered the vast moat
   of the sepulchre. Its wall seemed made of iron
   and towered above us in our little boat.                75
We circled through what seemed an endless distance
   before the boatman ran his prow ashore

2. These were Luke's words to Christ. To have Virgil apply them to Dante after such violence seems shocking, even though the expression is reasonably common in Italian. But Dante does not use such devices lightly. The *Commedia*, it must be remembered, is a vision of the progress of man's soul toward perfection. In being contemptuous of Wrath, Dante is purging it from his soul. He is thereby growing nearer to perfection, and Virgil, who has said nothing in the past when Dante showed pity for other sinners (though Virgil will later take him to task for daring to pity those whom God has shut off from pity), welcomes this sign of relentless rejection. Only by a ruthless enmity toward evil may the soul be purified.    3. Pluto, King of the Underworld of ancient mythology, was sometimes called Dis. This, then, is his city, the metropolis of Satan. 4. To a European of Dante's time a mosque would seem the perversion of a church, the impious counterpart of the House of God, just as Satan is God's impious counterpart.

crying: "Out! Out! Get out! This is the entrance."
Above the gates more than a thousand shades
 of spirits purged from Heaven[5] for its glory    80
 cried angrily: "Who is it that invades
Death's Kingdom in his life?" My Lord and Guide
 advanced a step before me with a sign
 that he wished to speak to some of them aside.
They quieted somewhat, and one called, "Come,   85
 but come alone. And tell that other one,
 who thought to walk so blithely through death's kingdom,
he may go back along the same fool's way
 he came by. Let him try his living luck.
 You who are dead can come only to stay."    90
Reader, judge for yourself, how each black word
 fell on my ears to sink into my heart:
 I lost hope of returning to the world.
"O my beloved Master, my Guide in peril,
 who time and time again[6] have seen me safely   95
along this way, and turned the power of evil,
stand by me now," I cried, "in my heart's fright.
 And if the dead forbid our journey to them,
 let us go back together toward the light."
My Guide then, in the greatness of his spirit:   100
 "Take heart. Nothing can take our passage from us
 when such a power has given warrant for it.
Wait here and feed your soul while I am gone
 on comfort and good hope; I will not leave you
 to wander in this underworld alone."    105
So the sweet Guide and Father leaves[7] me here,
 and I stay on in doubt with yes and no
 dividing all my heart to hope and fear.
I could not hear my Lord's words, but the pack
 that gathered round him suddenly broke away   110
 howling and jostling and went pouring back,
slamming the towering gate hard in his face.
 That great Soul stood alone outside the wall.
 Then he came back; his pain showed in his pace.
His eyes were fixed upon the ground, his brow   115
 had sagged from its assurance. He sighed aloud:
 "Who has forbidden me the halls of sorrow?"
And to me he said: "You need not be cast down
 by my vexation, for whatever plot

5. The Rebellious Angels. We have already seen, on the other side of Acheron, the Angels who sinned by refusing to take sides. 6. A literal translation of the original would read "more than seven times." "Seven" is used here as an indeterminate number indicating simply "quite a number of times." Italian makes rather free use of such numbers. 7. Dante shifts tenses more freely than English readers are accustomed to.

these fiends may lay against us, we will go on.                              120
This insolence of theirs is nothing new:
    they showed it once at a less secret gate[8]
    that still stands open for all that they could do—
the same gate where you read the dead inscription;
    and through it at this moment a Great One[9] comes.          125
    Already he has passed it and moves down
ledge by dark ledge. He is one who needs no guide,
    and at his touch all gates must spring aside."

CANTO IX

*Circle Six    The Heretics*

At the Gate of Dis the Poets wait in dread. Virgil tries to hide his
anxiety from Dante, but both realize that without Divine Aid they
will surely be lost. To add to their terrors Three Infernal Furies,
symbols of Eternal Remorse, appear on a near-by tower, from which
they threaten the Poets and call for Medusa to come and change
them to stone. Virgil at once commands Dante to turn and shut his
eyes. To make doubly sure, Virgil himself places his hands over
Dante's eyes, for there is an Evil upon which man must not look if
he is to be saved.

But at the moment of greatest anxiety a storm shakes the dirty air
of Hell and the sinners in the marsh begin to scatter like frightened
Frogs. The Heavenly Messenger is approaching. He appears walking
majestically through Hell, looking neither to right nor to left. With
a touch he throws open the Gate of Dis while his words scatter the
Rebellious Angels. Then he returns as he came.

The Poets now enter the gate unopposed and find themselves in
the Sixth Circle. Here they find a countryside like a vast cemetery.
Tombs of every size stretch out before them, each with its lid lying
beside it, and each wrapped in flames. Cries of anguish sound endlessly from the entombed dead.

This is the torment of the Heretics of every cult. By Heretic, Dante
means specifically those who did violence to God by denying
immortality. Since they taught that the soul dies with the body, so
their punishment is an eternal grave in the fiery morgue of God's
wrath.

My face had paled to a mask of cowardice
    when I saw my Guide turn back. The sight of it

---

8. The Gate of Hell. According to an early medieval tradition, these demons gathered at the
outer gate to oppose the descent of Christ into Limbo at the time of the Harrowing of Hell, but
Christ broke the door open and it has remained so ever since. The service of the Mass for Holy
Saturday still sings *Hodie portas mortis et seras pariter Salvator noster disrupit*. (On this day our
Savour broke open the door of the dead and its lock as well.)    9. A Messenger of Heaven. He
is described in the next Canto.

the sooner brought the color back to his.
He stood apart like one who strains to hear
    what he cannot see, for the eye could not reach far       5
    across the vapors of that midnight air.
"Yet surely we were meant to pass these tombs,"
    he said aloud. "If not . . . so much was promised . . .
    Oh how time hangs and drags till our aid comes!"
I saw too well how the words with which he ended       10
    covered his start, and even perhaps I drew
    a worse conclusion from that than he intended.
"Tell me, Master, does anyone ever come
    from the first ledge,[1] whose only punishment
    is hope cut off, into this dreary bottom?"       15
I put this question to him, still in fear
    of what his broken speech might mean; and he:
    "Rarely do any of us enter here.
Once before, it is true, I crossed through Hell
    conjured by cruel Erichtho[2] who recalled       20
    the spirits to their bodies. Her dark spell
forced me, newly stripped of my mortal part,
    to enter through this gate and summon out
    a spirit from Judaïca.[3] Take heart,
That is the last depth and the darkest lair       25
    and the farthest from Heaven which encircles all,
    and at that time I came back even from there.
The marsh from which the stinking gasses bubble
    lies all about this capital of sorrow
    whose gates we may not pass now without trouble."       30
All this and more he expounded; but the rest
    was lost on me, for suddenly my attention
    was drawn to the turret with the fiery crest
where all at once three hellish and inhuman
    Furies[4] sprang to view, bloodstained and wild. .       35
    Their limbs and gestures hinted they were women.
Belts of greenest hydras wound and wound
    about their waists, and snakes and horned serpents
    grew from their heads like matted hair and bound
their horrid brows. My Master, who well knew       40
    the handmaids of the Queen of Woe,[5] cried: "Look:

---

1. Limbo.  2. A sorceress drawn from Lucan (*Pharsalia* VI, 508ff).  3. Judaïca (or Judecca) is the final pit of Hell. Erichtho called up the spirit in order to foretell the outcome of the campaign between Pompey and Caesar. There is no trace of the legend in which Virgil is chosen for the descent; Virgil, in fact, was still alive at the time of the battle of Pharsalia.  4. Or Erinyes. In classical mythology they were especially malignant spirits who pursued and tormented those who had violated fundamental taboos (desecration of temples, murder of kin, etc.). They are apt symbols of the guilty conscience of the damned.  5. Proserpine (or Hecate) was the wife of Pluto, and therefore Queen of the Underworld.

the terrible Erinyes of Hecate's crew.
That is Megaera to the left of the tower.
   Alecto is the one who raves on the right.
   Tisiphone stands between." And he said no more.    45
With their palms they beat their brows, with their nails they clawed
   their bleeding breasts. And such mad wails broke from them
   that I drew close to the Poet, overawed.
And all together screamed, looking down at me:
   "Call Medusa that we may change him to stone!    50
   Too lightly we let Theseus go free."[6]
"Turn your back and keep your eyes shut tight;
   for should the Gorgon come and you look at her,
   never again would you return to the light."
This was my Guide's command. And he turned me about    55
   himself, and would not trust my hands alone,
   but, with his placed on mine, held my eyes shut.
Men of sound intellect and probity,
   weigh with good understanding what lies hidden
   behind the veil of my strange allegory![7]    60
Suddenly there broke on the dirty swell
   of the dark marsh a squall of terrible sound
   that sent a tremor through both shores of Hell;
a sound as if two continents of air,
   one frigid and one scorching, clashed head on    65
   in a war of winds that stripped the forests bare,
ripped off whole boughs and blew them helter skelter
   along the range of dust it raised before it
   making the beasts and shepherds run for shelter.
The Master freed my eyes. "Now turn," he said,    70
   "and fix your nerve of vision on the foam
   there where the smoke is thickest and most acrid."
As frogs before the snake that hunts them down
   churn up their pond in flight, until the last
   squats on the bottom as if turned to stone—    75
so I saw more than a thousand ruined souls
   scatter away from one who crossed dry-shod
   the Stygian marsh into Hell's burning bowels.
With his left hand he fanned away the dreary

6. Theseus and Pirithous tried to kidnap Hecate. Pirithous was killed in the attempt and Theseus was punished by being chained to a great rock. He was later set free by Hercules, who descended to his rescue in defiance of all the powers of Hell. The meaning of the Furies' cry is that Dante must be made an example of. Had they punished Theseus properly, men would have acquired more respect for their powers and would not still be attempting to invade the Underworld. The Gorgon. She turned to stone whoever looked at her.   7. Most commentators take this to mean the allegory of the Three Furies, but the lines apply as aptly to the allegory that follows. Dante probably meant both. Almost certainly, too, "my strange allegory" refers to the whole Commedia.

vapors of that sink as he approached; 80
and only of that annoyance did he seem weary.
Clearly he was a Messenger from God's Throne,
and I turned to my Guide; but he made me a sign
that I should keep my silence and bow down.
Ah, what scorn breathed from that Angel-presence! 85
He reached the gate of Dis and with a wand
he waved it open, for there was no resistance.
"Outcasts of Heaven, you twice-loathsome crew,"
he cried upon that terrible sill of Hell,
"how does this insolence still live in you? 90
Why do you set yourselves against that Throne
whose Will none can deny, and which, times past,
has added to your pain for each rebellion?
Why do you butt against Fate's ordinance?
Your Cerberus, if you recall, still wears 95
his throat and chin peeled for such arrogance."[8]
Then he turned back through the same filthy tide
by which he had come. He did not speak to us,
but went his way like one preoccupied
by other presences than those before him. 100
And we moved toward the city, fearing nothing
after his holy words. Straight through the dim
and open gate we entered unopposed.
And I, eager to learn what new estate
of Hell those burning fortress walls enclosed, 105
began to look about the very moment
we were inside, and I saw on every hand
a countryside of sorrow and new torment.
As at Arles where the Rhone sinks into stagnant marshes,
as at Pola[9] by the Quarnaro Gulf, whose waters 110
close Italy and wash her farthest reaches,
the uneven tombs cover the even plain—
such fields I saw here, spread in all directions,
except that here the tombs were chests of pain:
for, in a ring around each tomb, great fires 115
raised every wall to a red heat. No smith
works hotter iron in his forge. The biers
stood with their lids upraised, and from their pits
an anguished moaning rose on the dead air
from the desolation of tormented spirits. 120

8. When Cerberus opposed the fated entrance of Hercules into Hell, Hercules threw a chain about his neck and dragged him to the upperworld. Cerberus' throat, according to Dante, is still peeled raw from it.  9. *Arles . . . Pola:* Situated as indicated on the Rhone and the Quarnaro Gulf respectively, these cities were the sites of great cemeteries dating back to the time of Rome. The Quarnaro Gulf is the body of water on which Fiume is situated.

And I: "Master, what shades are these who lie
  buried in these chests and fill the air
  with such a painful and unending cry?"
"These are the arch-heretics of all cults,
  with all their followers," he replied. "Far more                    125
  than you would think lie stuffed into these vaults.
Like lies with like in every heresy,
  and the monuments are fired, some more, some less;
  to each depravity its own degree."
He turned then, and I followed through that night                    130
  between the wall and the torments, bearing right. [1]

CANTO X

*Circle Six   The Heretics*

As the Poets pass on, one of the damned hears Dante speaking,
recognizes him as a Tuscan, and calls to him from one of the fiery
tombs. A moment later he appears. He is Farinata degli Uberti, a
great war-chief of the Tuscan Ghibellines. The majesty and power
of his bearing seem to diminish Hell itself. He asks Dante's lineage
and recognizes him as an enemy. They begin to talk politics, but are
interrupted by another shade, who rises from the same tomb.

This one is Cavalcante dei Cavalcanti, father of Guido Cavalcanti, a contemporary poet. If it is genius that leads Dante on his
great journey, the shade asks, why is Guido not with him? Can Dante
presume to a greater genius than Guido's? Dante replies that he comes
this way only with the aid of powers Guido has not sought. His reply
is a classic example of many-leveled symbolism as well as an overt
criticism of a rival poet. The senior Cavalcanti mistakenly infers from
Dante's reply that Guido is dead, and swoons back into the flames.

Farinata, who has not deigned to notice his fellow-sinner, continues from the exact point at which he had been interrupted. It is as if
he refuses to recognize the flames in which he is shrouded. He proceeds to prophesy Dante's banishment from Florence, he defends his
part in Florentine politics, and then, in answer to Dante's question,
he explains how it is that the damned can foresee the future but have
no knowledge of the present. He then names others who share his
tomb, and Dante takes his leave with considerable respect for his
great enemy, pausing only long enough to leave word for Cavalcanti
that Guido is still alive.

We go by a secret path along the rim
  of the dark city, between the wall and the torments.

1. Through all of Hell the Poets bear left in their descent with only two exceptions, the first in
their approach to the Heretics, the second in their approach to Geryon, the monster of fraud (see
note XVII, 4 below). Note that both these exceptions occur at a major division of the *Inferno*.
There is no satisfactory explanation of Dante's allegorical intent in making these exceptions.

My Master leads me and I follow him.
"Supreme Virtue, who through this impious land
    wheel me at will down these dark gyres," I said,                    5
    "speak to me, for I wish to understand.
Tell me, Master, is it permitted to see
    the souls within these tombs? The lids are raised,
    and no one stands on guard." And he to me:
"All shall be sealed forever on the day                                 10
    these souls return here from Jehosaphat[2]
    with the bodies they have given once to clay.
In this dark corner of the morgue of wrath
    lie Epicurus[3] and his followers,
    who make the soul share in the body's death.                        15
And here you shall be granted presently
    not only your spoken wish, but that other as well,[4]
    which you had thought perhaps to hide from me."
And I: "Except to speak my thoughts in few
    and modest words, as I learned from your example,                   20
    dear Guide, I do not hide my heart from you."
"O Tuscan, who go living through this place
    speaking so decorously,[5] may it please you pause
    a moment on your way, for by the grace
of that high speech in which I hear your birth,                         25
    I know you for a son of that noble city
    which perhaps I vexed too much in my time on earth."
These words broke without warning from inside
    one of the burning arks. Caught by surprise,
    I turned in fear and drew close to my Guide.                        30
And he: "Turn around. What are you doing? Look there:
    it is Farinata[6] rising from the flames.

---

2. A valley outside Jerusalem. The popular belief that it would serve as the scene of the Last Judgment was based on *Joel* iii, 2, 12. 3. The Greek philosopher. The central aim of his philosophy was to achieve happiness, which he defined as the absence of pain. For Dante this doctrine meant the denial of the Eternal life, since the whole aim of the Epicurean was temporal happiness. 4. "All knowing" Virgil is frequently presented as being able to read Dante's mind. The "other wish" is almost certainly Dante's desire to speak to someone from Florence with whom he could discuss politics. Many prominent Florentines were Epicureans. 5. Florence lies in the province of Tuscany. Italian, to an extent unknown in America, is a language of dialects, all of them readily identifiable even when they are not well understood by the hearer. Dante's native Tuscan has become the main source of modern official Italian. Two very common sayings still current in Italy are: "*Lingua toscana, lingua di Dio*" (the Tuscan tongue is the language of God) and—to express the perfection of Italian speech—"*Lingua toscana in bocca romana* (the Tuscan tongue in a Roman mouth). 6. Farinata degli Uberti was head of the ancient noble house of the Uberti. He became leader of the Ghibellines of Florence in 1239, and played a large part in expelling the Guelphs in 1248. The Guelphs returned in 1251, but Farinata remained. His arrogant desire to rule singlehanded led to difficulties, however, and he was expelled in 1258. With the aid of the Manfredi of Siena, he gathered a large force and defeated the Guelphs at Montaperti on the River Arbia in 1260. Re-entering Florence in triumph, he again expelled the Guelphs, but at the Diet of Empoli, held by the victors after the battle of Montaperti, he alone rose in open counsel to resist the general sentiment that Florence should be razed. He died in Florence in 1264. In 1266 the Guelphs once more returned and crushed forever the power of the Uberti,

From the waist up his shade will be made clear."
My eyes were fixed on him already. Erect,
 he rose above the flame, great chest, great brow;   35
 he seemed to hold all Hell in disrespect.
My Guide's prompt hands urged me among the dim
 and smoking sepulchres to that great figure,
 and he said to me: "Mind how you speak to him."
And when I stood alone at the foot of the tomb,   40
 the great soul stared almost contemptuously,
 before he asked: "Of what line do you come?"
Because I wished to obey, I did not hide
 anything from him: whereupon, as he listened,
 he raised his brows a little, then replied:   45
"Bitter enemies, were they to me,
 to my fathers, and to my party, so that twice
 I sent them scattering from high Italy."
"If they were scattered, still from every part
 they formed again and returned both times," I answered,   50
 "but yours have not yet wholly learned that art."
At this another shade[7] rose gradually,
 visible to the chin. It had raised itself,
 I think, upon its knees, and it looked around me
as if it expected to find through that black air   55
 that blew about me, another traveler.
 And weeping when it found no other there,
turned back. "And if," it cried, "you travel through
 this dungeon of the blind by power of genius,
 where is my son? why is he not with you?"   60
And I to him: "Not by myself[8] am I borne
 this terrible way. I am led by him who waits there,
 and whom perhaps your Guido held in scorn."
For by his words and the manner of his torment
 I knew his name already, and could, therefore,   65
 answer both what he asked and what he meant.
Instantly he rose to his full height:
 "He *held?* What is it you say? Is he dead, then?
 Do his eyes no longer fill with that sweet light?"
And when he saw that I delayed a bit   70
 in answering his question, he fell backwards
 into the flame, and rose no more from it.

---

destroying their palaces and issuing special decrees against persons of the Uberti line. In 1283 a decree of heresy was published against Farinata. 7. Cavalcante dei Cavalcanti was a famous Epicurean ("like lies with like"). He was the father of Guido Cavalcanti, a poet and friend of Dante. Guido was also Farinata's son-in-law. 8. Cavalcanti assumes that the resources of human genius are all that are necessary for such a journey. (It is an assumption that well fits his character as an Epicurean.) Dante replies as a man of religion that other aid is necessary.

But that majestic spirit at whose call
   I had first paused there, did not change expression,
   nor so much as turn his face to watch him fall.         75
"And if," going on from his last words, he said,
   "men of my line have yet to learn that art,
   that burns me deeper than this flaming bed.
But the face of her who reigns in Hell[9] shall not
   be fifty times rekindled in its course         80
   before you learn what griefs attend that art.
And as you hope to find the world again,
   tell me: why is that populace[1] so savage
   in the edicts they pronounce against my strain?"
And I to him: "The havoc and the carnage         85
   that dyed the Arbia red at Montaperti
   have caused these angry cries in our assemblage."
He sighed and shook his head. "I was not alone
   in that affair," he said, "not certainly
   would I have joined the rest without good reason.         90
But I *was* alone at that time when every other
   consented to the death of Florence; I
   alone with open face defended her."
"Ah, so may your soul sometime have rest,"
   I begged him, "solve the riddle that pursues me         95
   through this dark place and leaves my mind perplexed:
you seem to see in advance all time's intent,
   if I have heard and understood correctly;
   but you seem to lack all knowledge of the present."
"We see asquint, like those whose twisted sight         100
   can make out only the far-off," he said,
   "for the King of All still grants us that much light.
When things draw near, or happen, we perceive
   nothing of them. Except what others bring us
   we have no news of those who are alive.         105
So may you understand that all we know
   will be dead forever from that day and hour
   when the Portal of the Future is swung to."
Then, as if stricken by regret, I said:
   "Now, therefore, will you tell that fallen one         110
   who asked about his son, that he is not dead,
and that, if I did not reply more quickly,
   it was because my mind was occupied
   with this confusion you have solved for me."

9. Hecate or Proserpine. She is also the moon goddess. The sense of this prophecy, therefore, is that Dante will be exiled within fifty full moons. Dante was banished from Florence in 1302, well within the fifty months of the prophecy.   1. The Florentines.

And now my Guide was calling me. In haste,                        115
   therefore, I begged that mighty shade to name
   the others who lay with him in that chest.
And he: "More than a thousand cram this tomb.
   The second Frederick[2] is here, and the Cardinal
   of the Ubaldini.[3] Of the rest let us be dumb."          120
And he disappeared without more said, and I
   turned back and made my way to the ancient Poet,
   pondering the words of the dark prophecy.
He moved along, and then, when we had started,
   he turned and said to me, "What troubles you?            125
   Why do you look so vacant and downhearted?"
And I told him. And he replied: "Well may you bear
   those words in mind." Then, pausing, raised a finger:
   "Now pay attention to what I tell you here:
when finally you stand before the ray                             130
   of that Sweet Lady[4] whose bright eye sees all,
   from her you will learn the turnings of your way."
So saying, he bore left, turning his back
   on the flaming walls, and we passed deeper yet
   into the city of pain, along a track                      135
that plunged down like a scar into a sink
which sickened us already with its stink.


CANTO XI

*Circle Six     The Heretics*

    The Poets reach the inner edge of the Sixth Circle and find a great
jumble of rocks that had once been a cliff, but which has fallen into
rubble as the result of the great earthquake that shook Hell when
Christ died. Below them lies the Seventh Circle, and so fetid is the
air that arises from it that the Poets cower for shelter behind a great
tomb until their breaths can grow accustomed to the stench.
    Dante finds an inscription on the lid of the tomb labeling it as the
place in Hell of Pope Anastasius.
    Virgil takes advantage of the delay to outline in detail The Divi-
sion of the Lower Hell, a theological discourse based on *The Ethics*
and *The Physics* of Aristotle with subsequent medieval interpretations. Virgil explains also why it is that the Incontinent are not pun-

---

2. The Emperor Frederick II. In Canto XIII Dante has Pier delle Vigne speak of him as one
worthy of honor, but he was commonly reputed to be an Epicurean.    3. In the original Dante
refers to him simply as "il Cardinale." Ottaviano degli Ubaldini (born *circa* 1209, died 1273)
became a Cardinal in 1245, but his energies seem to have been directed exclusively to money and
political intrigue. When he was refused an important loan by the Ghibellines, he is reported by
many historians as having remarked: "I may say that if I have a soul, I have lost it in the cause of
the Ghibellines, and no one of them will help me now." The words "If I have a soul" would be
enough to make him guilty in Dante's eyes of the charge of heresy.    4. Beatrice.

ished within the walls of Dis, and rather ingeniously sets forth the
reasons why Usury is an act of Violence against Art, which is the
child of Nature and hence the Grandchild of God. (By "Art," Dante
means the arts and crafts by which man draws from nature, i.e.,
Industry.)

As he concludes he rises and urges Dante on. By means known
only to Virgil, he is aware of the motion of the stars and from them
he sees that it is about two hours before Sunrise of Holy Saturday.


We came to the edge of an enormous sink
    rimmed by a circle of great broken boulders.[5]
    Here we found ghastlier gangs. And here the stink
thrown up by the abyss so overpowered us
    that we drew back, cowering behind the wall              5
    of one of the great tombs; and standing thus,
I saw an inscription in the stone, and read:
    "I guard Anastasius, once Pope,
    he whom Photinus[6] led from the straight road."
"Before we travel on to that blind pit                  10
    we must delay until our sense grows used
    to its foul breath, and then we will not mind it,"
my Master said. And I then: "Let us find
    some compensation for the time of waiting."
And he: "You shall see I have just that in mind.       15
My son," he began, "there are below this wall
    three smaller circles,[7] each in its degree
    like those you are about to leave, and all
are crammed with God's accurst. Accordingly,
    that you may understand their sins at sight,         20
    I will explain how each is prisoned, and why.
Malice is the sin most hated by God.
    And the aim of malice is to injure others
    whether by fraud or violence. But since fraud
is the vice of which man alone is capable,           25
    God loathes it most. Therefore, the fraudulent
    are placed below, and their torment is more painful.
The first below are the violent. But as violence
    sins in three persons, so is that circle formed

5. These boulders were broken from the earthquake that shook Hell at the death of Christ.
6. Anastasius II was Pope from 496 to 498. This was the time of schism between the Eastern
(Greek) and Western (Roman) churches. Photinus, deacon of Thessalonica, was of the Greek
church and held to the Acacian heresy, which denied the divine paternity of Christ. Dante follows
the report that Anastasius gave communion to Photinus, thereby countenancing his heresy. Dante's
sources, however, had probably confused Anastasius II, the Pope, with Anastasius I, who was
Emperor from 491 to 518. It was the Emperor Anastasius who was persuaded by Photinus to
accept the Acacian heresy.    7. The Poets are now at the cliff that bounds the Sixth Circle.
Below them lies Circles Seven, Eight, and Nine. They are smaller in circumference, being closer
to the center, but they are all intricately subdivided, and will be treated at much greater length
than were the Circles of Upper Hell.

of three descending rounds of crueler torments.                    30
Against God, self, and neighbor is violence shown.
    Against their persons and their goods, I say,
    as you shall hear set forth with open reason.
Murder and mayhem are the violation
    of the person of one's neighbor: and of his goods;          35
    harassment, plunder, arson, and extortion.
Therefore, homicides, and those who strike
    in malice—destroyers and plunderers—all lie
    in that first round, and like suffers with like.
A man may lay violent hands upon his own                       40
    person and substance; so in that second round
    eternally in vain repentance moan
the suicides and all who gamble away
    and waste the good and substance of their lives
    and weep in that sweet time when they should be gay.         45
Violence may be offered the deity
    in the heart that blasphemes and refuses Him
    and scorns the gifts of Nature, her beauty and bounty.
Therefore, the smallest round brands with its mark
    both Sodom and Cahors,[8] and all who rail                   50
    at God and His commands in their hearts' dark.
Fraud, which is a canker to every conscience,
    may be practiced by a man on those who trust him,
    and on those who have reposed no confidence.
The latter mode seems only to deny                             55
    the bond of love which all men have from Nature;
    therefore within the second circle lie
simoniacs, sycophants, and hypocrites,
    falsifiers, thieves, and sorcerers,
    grafters, pimps, and all such filthy cheats.                 60
The former mode of fraud not only denies
    the bond of Nature, but the special trust
    added by bonds of friendship or blood-ties.
Hence, at the center point of all creation,[9]
    in the smallest circle, on which Dis is founded,             65
    the traitors lie in endless expiation."
"Master," I said, "the clarity of your mind
    impresses all you touch; I see quite clearly
    the orders of this dark pit of the blind.
But tell me: those who lie in the swamp's bowels,              70

8. Both these cities are used as symbols for the sins that are said to have flourished within them. Sodom (*Genesis* xix) is, of course, identified with unnatural sex practices. Cahors, a city in southern France, was notorious in the Middle Ages for its usurers.    9. In the Ptolemaic system the earth was the center of the Universe. In Dante's geography, the bottom of Hell is the center of the earth.

those the wind blows about, those the rain beats,
  and those who meet and clash with such mad howls[1]—
why are *they* not punished in the rust-red city[2]
  if God's wrath be upon them? and if it is not,
  why must they grieve through all eternity?"                    75
And he: "Why does your understanding stray
  so far from its own habit? or can it be
  your thoughts are turned along some other way?
Have you forgotten that your *Ethics*[3] states
  the three main dispositions of the soul                    80
  that lead to those offenses Heaven hates—
incontinence, malice, and bestiality?
  and how incontinence offends God least
  and earns least blame from Justice and Charity?
Now if you weigh this doctrine and recall                    85
  exactly who they are whose punishment
  lies in that upper Hell outside the wall,
you will understand at once why they are confined
  apart from these fierce wraiths, and why less anger
  beats down on them from the Eternal Mind."                    90
"O sun which clears all mists from troubled sight,
  such joy attends your rising that I feel
  as grateful to the dark as to the light.
Go back a little further," I said, "to where
  you spoke of usury as an offense                    95
  against God's goodness. How is that made clear?"
"Philosophy makes plain by many reasons,"
  he answered me, "to those who heed her teachings,
  how all of Nature,—her laws, her fruits, her seasons,—
springs from the Ultimate Intellect and Its art:                    100
  and if you read your *Physics*[4] with due care,
  you will note, not many pages from the start,
that Art strives after her by imitation,
  as the disciple imitates the master;
  Art, as it were, is the Grandchild of Creation.                    105
By this, recalling the Old Testament
  near the beginning of Genesis, you will see
  that in the will of Providence, man was meant
to labor and to prosper. But usurers,
  by seeking their increase in other ways,                    110
  scorn Nature in herself and her followers.
But come, for it is my wish now to go on:

---

1. These are, of course, the sinners of the Upper Hell.   2. Dis. All of Lower Hell is within the
city walls.   3. *The Ethics* of Aristotle.   4. *The Physics* of Aristotle.

the wheel turns and the Wain lies over Caurus,[5]
the Fish are quivering low on the horizon,
and there beyond us runs the road we go                              115
down the dark scarp into the depths below."


CANTO XII

*Circle Seven: Round One    The Violent Against Neighbors*

The Poets begin the descent of the fallen rock wall, having first to
evade the Minotaur, who menaces them. Virgil tricks him and the
Poets hurry by.

Below them they see the River of Blood, which marks the First
Round of the Seventh Circle as detailed in the previous Canto. Here
are punished the Violent Against Their Neighbors, great war-mak-
ers, cruel tyrants, highwaymen—all who shed the blood of their fellowmen. As they wallowed in blood during their lives, so they are
immersed in the boiling blood forever, each according to the degree
of his guilt, while fierce Centaurs patrol the banks, ready to shoot
with their arrows any sinner who raises himself out of the boiling
blood beyond the limits permitted him. Alexander the Great is here,
up to his lashes in the blood, and with him Attila, the Scourge of
God. They are immersed in the deepest part of the river, which
grows shallower as it circles to the other side of the ledge, then deep-
ens again.

The Poets are challenged by the Centaurs, but Virgil wins a safe
conduct from Chiron, their chief, who assigns Nessus to guide them
and to bear them across the shallows of the boiling blood. Nessus
carries them across at the point where it is only ankle deep and
immediately leaves them and returns to his patrol.


The scene that opened from the edge of the pit
    was mountainous, and such a desolation
    that every eye would shun the sight of it:
a ruin like the Slides of Mark[6] near Trent
    on the bank of the Adige, the result of an earthquake          5
    or of some massive fault in the escarpment—
for, from the point on the peak where the mountain split
    to the plain below, the rock is so badly shattered

5. The Wain is the constellation of the Great Bear. Caurus was the northwest wind in classical
mythology. Hence the constellation of the Great Bear now lies in the northwest. The Fish is the
constellation and zodiacal sign of Pisces. It is just appearing over the horizon. The next sign of
the zodiac is Aries. We know from Canto I that the sun is in Aries, and since the twelve signs of
the zodiac each cover two hours of the day, it must now be about two hours before dawn. It is,
therefore, approximately 4:00 A.M. of Holy Saturday. The stars are not visible in Hell, but throughout
the *Inferno* Virgil reads them by some special power which Dante does not explain.    6. *Li
Slavoni di Marco* are about two miles from Rovereto (between Verona and Trent) on the left bank
of the River Adige.

a man at the top might make a rough stair of it.[7]
Such was the passage down the steep, and there                    10
    at the very top, at the edge of the broken cleft,
    lay spread the Infamy of Crete,[8] the heir
of bestiality and the lecherous queen
    who hid in a wooden cow. And when he saw us,
    he gnawed his own flesh in a fit of spleen.                   15
And my Master mocked: "How you do pump your breath!
    Do you think, perhaps, it is the Duke of Athens,
    who in the world above served up your death?
Off with you, monster; this one does not come
    instructed by your sister, but of himself                     20
    to observe your punishment in the lost kingdom."
As a bull that breaks its chains just when the knife
    has struck its death-blow, cannot stand nor run
    but leaps from side to side with its last life—
so danced the Minotaur, and my shrewd Guide                       25
    cried out: "Run now! While he is blind with rage!
    Into the pass, quick, and get over the side!"
So we went down across the shale and slate
    of that ruined rock, which often slid and shifted
    under me at the touch of living weight.                       30
I moved on, deep in thought; and my Guide to me:
    "You are wondering perhaps about this ruin
    which is guarded by the beast upon whose fury
I played just now. I should tell you that when last
    I came this dark way to the depths of Hell,                   35
    this rock had not yet felt the ruinous blast.[9]
But certainly, if I am not mistaken,
    it was just before the coming of Him who took
    the souls from Limbo, that all Hell was shaken
so that I thought the universe felt love                          40
    and all its elements moved toward harmony,

7. I am defeated in all attempts to convey Dante's emphasis in any sort of a verse line. The sense of the original: "It might provide some sort of a way down for one who started at the top, but (by implication) would not be climbable from below."    8. This is the infamous Minotaur of classical mythology. His mother was Pasiphaë, wife of Minos, the King of Crete. She conceived an unnatural passion for a bull, and in order to mate with it, she crept into a wooden cow. From this union the Minotaur was born, half-man, half-beast. King Minos kept him in an ingenious labyrinth from which he could not escape. When Androgeos, the son of King Minos, was killed by the Athenians, Minos exacted an annual tribute of seven maidens and seven youths. These were annually turned into the labyrinth and there were devoured by the Minotaur. The monster was finally killed by Theseus, Duke of Athens. He was aided by Ariadne, daughter of Minos (and half-sister of the monster). She gave Theseus a ball of cord to unwind as he entered the labyrinth and a sword with which to kill the Minotaur.    9. According to *Matthew* xxvii, 51, an earthquake shook the earth at the moment of Christ's death. These stones, Dante lets us know, were broken off in that earthquake. We shall find other effects of the same shock in the Eighth Circle. It is worth noting also that both the Upper (See Canto V, 34) and the Lower Hell begin with evidences of this ruin. For details of Virgil's first descent see notes to Canto IX.

   whereby the world of matter, as some believe,
has often plunged to chaos.[1] It was then,
   that here and elsewhere in the pits of Hell,
   the ancient rock was stricken and broke open.                    45
But turn your eyes to the valley; there we shall find
   the river of boiling blood[2] in which are steeped
   all who struck down their fellow men." Oh blind!
Oh ignorant, self-seeking cupidity
   which spurs us so in the short mortal life                       50
   and steeps us so through all eternity!
I saw an arching fosse that was the bed
   of a winding river circling through the plain
   exactly as my Guide and Lord had said.
A file of Centaurs[3] galloped in the space                         55
   between the bank and the cliff, well armed with arrows,
   riding as once on earth they rode to the chase.
And seeing us descend, that straggling band
   halted, and three of them moved out toward us,
   their long bows and their shafts already in hand.                60
And one of them cried out while still below:
   "To what pain are you sent down that dark coast?
   Answer from where you stand, or I draw the bow!"
"Chiron[4] is standing there hard by your side;
   our answer will be to him. This wrath of yours                   65
   was always your own worst fate," my Guide replied.
And to me he said: "That is Nessus, who died in the wood
   for insulting Dejanira.[5] At his death
   he plotted his revenge in his own blood.
The one in the middle staring at his chest                          70
   is the mighty Chiron, he who nursed Achilles:
   the other is Pholus,[6] fiercer than all the rest.

---

1. The Greek philosopher, Empedocles, taught that the universe existed by the counter-balance
(discord or mutual repulsion) of its elements. Should the elemental matter feel harmony (love or
mutual attraction) all would fly together into chaos.    2. Phlegethon, the river that circles through
the First Round of the Seventh Circle, then sluices through the wood of the suicides (the Second
Round) and the burning sands (Third Round) to spew over the Great Cliff into the Eighth Circle,
and so, eventually, to the bottom of Hell (Cocytus).    3. Creatures of classical mythology, half-
horse, half-men. They were skilled and savage hunters, creatures of passion and violence. Like
the Minotaur, they are symbols of the bestial-human, and as such, they are fittingly chosen as the
tormentors of these sinners.    4. The son of Saturn and of the nymph Philira. He was the wisest
and most just of the Centaurs and reputedly was the teacher of Achilles and of other Greek heroes
to whom he imparted great skill in bearing arms, medicine, astronomy, music, and augury. Dante
places him far down in Hell with the others of his kind, but though he draws Chiron's coarseness,
he also grants him a kind of majestic understanding.    5. Nessus carried travelers across the
River Evenus for hire. He was hired to ferry Dejanira, the wife of Hercules, and tried to abduct
her, but Hercules killed him with a poisoned arrow. While Nessus was dying, he whispered to
Dejanira that a shirt stained with his poisoned blood would act as a love charm should Hercules'
affections stray. When Hercules fell in love with Iole, Dejanira sent him a shirt stained with the
Centaur's blood. The shirt poisoned Hercules and he died in agony.    6. A number of classical
poets mention Pholus but very little else is known of him.

They run by that stream in thousands, snapping their bows
   at any wraith who dares to raise himself
   out of the blood more than his guilt allows."         75
We drew near those swift beasts. In a thoughtful pause
   Chiron drew an arrow, and with its notch
   he pushed his great beard back along his jaws.
And when he had thus uncovered the huge pouches
   of his lips, he said to his fellows: "Have you noticed      80
   how the one who walks behind moves what he touches?
That is not how the dead go." My good Guide,
   already standing by the monstrous breast
   in which the two mixed natures joined, replied:
"It is true he lives; in his necessity         85
   I alone must lead him through this valley.
   Fate brings him here, not curiosity.
From singing Alleluia the sublime
   spirit[7] who sends me came. He is no bandit.
   Nor am I one who ever stooped to crime.      90
But in the name of the Power by which I go
   this sunken way across the floor of Hell,
   assign us one of your troop whom we may follow,
that he may guide us to the ford, and there
   carry across on his back the one I lead,      95
   for he is not a spirit to move through air."
Chiron turned his head on his right breast[8]
   and said to Nessus: "Go with them, and guide them,
   and turn back any others that would contest
their passage." So we moved beside our guide      100
   along the bank of the scalding purple river
   in which the shrieking wraiths were boiled and dyed.
Some stood up to their lashes in that torrent,
   and as we passed them the huge Centaur said:
   "These were the kings of bloodshed and despoilment.      105
Here they pay for their ferocity.
   Here is Alexander.[9] And Dionysius,
   who brought long years of grief to Sicily.
That brow you see with the hair as black as night
   is Azzolino;[1] and that beside him, the blonde,      110
   is Opizzo da Esti,[2] who had his mortal light

7. Beatrice.   8. The right is the side of virtue and honor. In Chiron it probably signifies his human side as opposed to his bestial side.   9. Alexander the Great. *Dionysius:* Dionysius I (died 367 B.C.) and his son, Dionysius II (died 343), were tyrants of Sicily. Both were infamous as prototypes of the bloodthirsty and exorbitant ruler. Dante may intend either or both.   1. Ezzelino da Romano, Count of Onora (1194–1259). The cruelest of the Ghibelline tyrants. In 1236 Frederick II appointed Ezzelino his vicar in Padua. Ezzelino became especially infamous for his bloody treatment of the Paduans, whom he slaughtered in great numbers.   2. Marquis of Ferrara (1264–1293). The account of his life is confused. One must accept Dante's facts as given.

blown out by his own stepson." I turned then
to speak to the Poet but he raised a hand:
"Let him be the teacher now, and I will listen."
Further on, the Centaur stopped beside                    115
a group of spirits steeped as far as the throat
in the race of boiling blood, and there our guide
pointed out a sinner who stood alone:
"That one before God's altar pierced a heart
still honored on the Thames."[3] And he passed on.        120
We came in sight of some who were allowed
to raise the head and all the chest from the river,
and I recognized many there. Thus, as we followed
along the stream of blood, its level fell
until it cooked no more than the feet of the damned.      125
And here we crossed the ford to deeper Hell.
"Just as you see the boiling stream grow shallow
along this side," the Centaur said to us
when we stood on the other bank, "I would have you know
that on the other, the bottom sinks anew                  130
more and more, until it comes again
full circle to the place where the tyrants stew.
It is there that Holy Justice spends its wrath
on Sextua[4] and Pyrrhus through eternity,
and on Attila,[5] who was a scourge on earth:             135
and everlastingly milks out the tears
of Rinier da Corento and Rinier Pazzo,[6]
those two assassins who for many years
stalked the highways, bloody and abhorred."
And with that he started back across the ford.            140

CANTO XIII

*Circle Seven: Round Two    The Violent Against Themselves*

Nessus carries the Poets across the river of boiling blood and leaves
them in the Second Round of the Seventh Circle, The Wood of the
Suicides. Here are punished those who destroyed their own lives and
those who destroyed their substance.

---

**3.** The sinner indicated is Guy de Montfort. His father, Simon de Montfort, was a leader of the
barons who rebelled against Henry III and was killed at the battle of Evesham (1265) by Prince
Edward (later Edward I). In 1271, Guy (then Vicar General of Tuscany) avenged his father's death
by murdering Henry's nephew (who was also named Henry). The crime was openly committed in
a church at Viterbo. The murdered Henry's heart was sealed in a casket and sent to London,
where it was accorded various honors.    **4.** Probably the younger son of Pompey the Great. His
piracy is mentioned in Lucan (*Pharsalia*, VI, 420–422). *Pyrrhus:* Pyrrhus, the son of Achilles,
was especially bloodthirsty at the sack of Troy. Pyrrhus, King of Epirus (319–372 B.C.), waged
relentless and bloody war against the Greeks and Romans. Either may be intended.    **5.** King of
the Huns from 433 to 453. He was called the Scourge of God.    **6.** Both were especially bloodthirsty robber-barons of the thirteenth century.

The souls of the Suicides are encased in thorny trees whose leaves are eaten by the odious Harpies, the overseers of these damned. When the Harpies feed upon them, damaging their leaves and limbs, the wound bleeds. Only as long as the blood flows are the souls of the trees able to speak. Thus, they who destroyed their own bodies are denied a human form; and just as the supreme expression of their lives was self-destruction, so they are permitted to speak only through that which tears and destroys them. Only through their own blood do they find voice. And to add one more dimension to the symbolism, it is the Harpies—defilers of all they touch—who give them their eternally recurring wounds.

The Poets pause before one tree and speak with the soul of Pier delle Vigne. In the same wood they see Jacomo da Sant' Andrea, and Lano da Siena, two famous Squanderers and Destroyers of Goods pursued by a pack of savage hounds. The hounds overtake Sant' Andrea, tear him to pieces and go off carrying his limbs in their teeth, a self-evident symbolic retribution for the violence with which these sinners destroyed their substance in the world. After this scene of horror, Dante speaks to an Unknown Florentine Suicide whose soul is inside the bush which was torn by the hound pack when it leaped upon Sant' Andrea.

Nessus had not yet reached the other shore
   when we moved on into a pathless wood
   that twisted upward from Hell's broken floor.
Its foliage was not verdant, but nearly black.
   The unhealthy branches, gnarled and warped and tangled,     5
   bore poison thorns instead of fruit. The track
of those wild beasts that shun the open spaces
   men till between Cecina and Corneto
   runs through no rougher nor more tangled places.[7]
Here nest the odious Harpies[8] of whom my Master     10
   wrote how they drove Aeneas and his companions
   from the Strophades with prophecies of disaster.
Their wings are wide, their feet clawed, their huge bellies
   covered with feathers, their necks and faces human.
   They croak eternally in the unnatural trees.     15
"Before going on, I would have you understand,"
   my Guide began, "we are in the second round

7. The reference here is to the Maremma district of Tuscany which lies between the mountains and the sea. The river Cecina is the northern boundary of this district; Corneto is on the river Marta, which forms the southern boundary. It is a wild district of marsh and forest.   8. These hideous birds with the faces of malign women were often associated with the Erinyes (Furies). Their original function in mythology was to snatch away the souls of men at the command of the Gods. Later, they were portrayed as defilers of food, and, by extension, of everything they touched. The islands of the Strophades were their legendary abode. Aeneas and his men landed there and fought with the Harpies, who drove them back and pronounced a prophecy of unbearable famine upon them.

and shall be till we reach the burning sand.[9]
Therefore look carefully and you will see
  things in this wood, which, if I told them to you                   20
  would shake the confidence you have placed in me."
I heard cries of lamentation rise and spill
  on every hand, but saw no souls in pain
  in all that waste; and, puzzled, I stood still.
I think perhaps he thought that I was thinking[1]                            25
  those cries rose from among the twisted roots
  through which the spirits of the damned were slinking
to hide from us. Therefore my Master said:
  "If you break off a twig, what you will learn
  will drive what you are thinking from your head."                      30
Puzzled, I raised my hand a bit an slowly
  broke off a branchlet from an enormous thorn:
  and the great trunk of it cried: "Why do you break me?"
And after blood had darkened all the bowl
  of the wound, it cried again: "Why do you tear me?                     35
  Is there no pity left in any soul?
Men we were, and now we are changed to sticks;
  well might your hand have been more merciful
  were we no more than souls of lice and ticks."
As a green branch with one end all aflame                                    40
  will hiss and sputter sap out of the other
  as the air escapes—so from that trunk there came
words and blood together, gout by gout.
  Startled, I dropped the branch that I was holding
  and stood transfixed by fear, half turned about                       45
to my Master, who replied: "O wounded soul,
  could he have believed before what he has seen
  in my verses only,[2] you would yet be whole,
for his hand would never have been raised against you.
  But knowing this truth could never be believed                        50
  till it was seen, I urged him on to do
what grieves me now; and I beg to know your name,
  that to make you some amends in the sweet world
  when he returns, he may refresh your fame."
And the trunk: "So sweet those words to me that I                            55

9. The Third Round of this Circle.     1. The original is *"Cred' io ch'ei credette ch'io credesse."*
This sort of word play was considered quite elegant by medieval rhetoricians and by the ornate
Sicilian School of poetry. Dante's style is based on a rejection of all such devices in favor of a
sparse and direct diction. The best explanation of this unusual instance seems to be that Dante is
anticipating his talk with Pier delle Vigne, a rhetorician who, as we shall see, delights in this sort
of locution.     2. The *Aeneid*, Book III, describes a similar bleeding plant. There, Aeneas pulls
at a myrtle growing on a Thracian hillside. It bleeds where he breaks it and a voice cries out of
the ground. It is the voice of Polydorus, son of Priam and friend of Aeneas. He had been treach-
erously murdered by the Thracian king.

cannot be still, and may it not annoy you
   if I seem somewhat lengthy in reply.
I am he who held both keys to Frederick's heart,[3]
   locking, unlocking with so deft a touch
   that scarce another soul had any part         60
in his most secret thoughts. Through every strife
   I was so faithful to my glorious office
   that for it I gave up both sleep and life.
That harlot, Envy, who on Caesar's[4] face
   keeps fixed forever her adulterous stare,
   the common plague and vice of court and palace,
inflamed all minds against me. These inflamed
   so inflamed him that all my happy honors
   were changed to mourning. Then, unjustly blamed,
my soul, in scorn, and thinking to be free         70
   of scorn in death, made me at last, though just,
   unjust to myself. By the new roots[5] of this tree
I swear to you that never in word or spirit
   did I break faith to my lord and emperor
   who was so worthy of honor in his merit.        75
If either of you return to the world, speak for me,
   to vindicate in the memory of men
   one who lies prostrate from the blows of Envy."
The Poet stood. Then turned. "Since he is silent,"
   he said to me, "do not you waste this hour,        80
   if you wish to ask about his life or torment."
And I replied: "Question him for my part,
   on whatever you think I would do well to hear;
   I could not, such compassion chokes my heart."
The Poet began again: "That this man may        85
   with all his heart do for you what your words
   entreat him to, imprisoned spirit, I pray,
tell us how the soul is bound and bent
   into these knots, and whether any ever
   frees itself from such imprisonment."        90
At that the trunk blew powerfully, and then

---

3. Pier delle Vigne 1190–1249. A famous and once-powerful minister of Emperor Frederick II.
He enjoyed Frederick's whole confidence until 1247 when he was accused of treachery and was
imprisoned and blinded. He committed suicide to escape further torture. (For Frederick see Canto
X.) Pier delle Vigne was famous for his eloquence and for his mastery of the ornate Provençal-
inspired Sicilian School of Italian Poetry, and Dante styles his speech accordingly. It is worth
noting, however, that the style changes abruptly in the middle of line 72. There, his courtly
preamble finished, delle Vigne speaks from the heart, simply and passionately. *Who held both
keys:* The phrasing unmistakably suggests the Papal keys; delle Vigne may be suggesting that he
was to Frederick as the Pope is to God.    **4.** Frederick II was of course Caesar of the Roman
Empire, but in this generalized context "Caesar" seems to be used as a generic term for any great
ruler, i.e., "The harlot, Envy, never turns her attention from those in power."    **5.** Pier delle
Vigne had only been in Hell fifty-one years, a short enough time on the scale of eternity.

the wind became a voice that spoke these words:
"Briefly is the answer given: when
out of the flesh from which it tore itself,
  the violent spirit comes to punishment,                    95
  Minos assigns it to the seventh shelf.
It falls into the wood, and landing there,
  wherever fortune flings it,[6] it strikes root,
  and there it sprouts, lusty as any tare,
shoots up a sapling, and becomes a tree.                     100
  The Harpies, feeding on its leaves then, give it
  pain and pain's outlet simultaneously.[7]
Like the rest, we shall go for our husks on Judgment Day,
  but not that we may wear them, for it is not just
  that a man be given what he throws away.                   105
Here shall we drag them and in this mournful glade
  our bodies will dangle to the end of time,
  each on the thorns of its tormented shade."
We waited by the trunk, but it said no more;
  and waiting, we were startled by a noise                   110
  that grew through all the wood. Just such a roar
and trembling as one feels when the boar and chase
  approach his stand, the beasts and branches crashing
  and clashing in the heat of the fierce race.
And there on the left, running so violently                  115
  they broke off every twig in the dark wood,
  two torn and naked wraiths went plunging by me.
The leader cried, "Come now, O Death! Come now!"
  And the other, seeing that he was outrun
  cried out: "Your legs were not so ready, Lano,[8]          120
in the jousts at the Toppo." And suddenly in his rush,
  perhaps because his breath was failing him,
  he hid himself inside a thorny bush
and cowered among its leaves. Then at his back,
  the wood leaped with black bitches, swift as greyhounds    25
  escaping from their leash, and all the pack
sprang on him; with their fangs they opened him
  and tore him savagely, and then withdrew,
  carrying his body with them, limb by limb.
Then, taking me by the hand across the wood,                 130

6. Just as the soul of the suicide refused to accept divine regulation of its mortal life span, so
eternal justice takes no special heed of where the soul falls.   7. Suicide also gives pain and its
outlet simultaneously.    8. Lano da Siena, a famous squanderer. He died at the ford of the river
Toppo near Arezzo in 1287 in a battle against the Aretines. Boccaccio writes that he deliberately
courted death having squandered all his great wealth and being unwilling to live on in poverty.
Thus his companion's jeer probably means: "You were not so ready to run then, Lano: why are
you running now?"

my Master led me toward the bush. Lamenting,
  all its fractures blew out words and blood:
"O Jacomo da Sant' Andrea!"[9] it said,
  "what have you gained in making me your screen?
  What part had I in the foul life you led?"           135
And when my Master had drawn up to it
  he said: "Who were you, who through all your wounds
  blow out your blood with your lament, sad spirit?"
And he to us: "You who have come to see
  how the outrageous mangling of these hounds      140
  has torn my boughs and stripped my leaves from me,
O heap them round my ruin! I was born
  in the city that tore down Mars and raised the Baptist.[1]
  On that account the God of War has sworn
her sorrow shall not end. And were it not         145
  that something of his image still survives
  on the bridge across the Arno, some have thought
those citizens who of their love and pain
  afterwards rebuilt it from the ashes
  left by Attila,[2] would have worked in vain.       150
I am one who has no tale to tell:
I made myself a gibbet of my own lintel."

CANTO XIV

*Circle Seven: Round Three   The Violent Against God, Nature,
and Art*

Dante, in pity, restores the torn leaves to the soul of his countryman and the Poets move on to the next round, a great Plain of
Burning Sand upon which there descends an eternal slow Rain of
Fire. Here, scorched by fire from above and below, are three classes
of sinners suffering differing degrees of exposure to the fire. The
Blasphemers (The Violent Against God) are stretched supine upon
the sand, the Sodomites (The Violent Against Nature) run in endless
circles, and the Usurers (The Violent Against Art, which is the
Grandchild of God) huddle on the sands.

---

9. A Paduan with an infamous lust for laying waste his own goods and those of his neighbors.
Arson was his favorite prank. On one occasion, to celebrate the arrival of certain noble guests, he
set fire to all the workers' huts and outbulidings of his estate. He was murdered in 1239, probably
by assassins hired by Ezzolino (for whom see Canto XII).    1. Florence. Mars was the first
patron of the city and when the Florentines were converted to Christianity they pulled down his
equestrian statue and built a church on the site of his temple. The statue of Mars was placed on a
tower beside the Arno. When Totila (see note to line 150) destroyed Florence the tower fell into
the Arno and the statue with it. Legend has it that Florence could never have been rebuilt had
not the mutilated statue been rescued. It was placed on the Ponte Vecchio but was carried away
in the flood of 1333.    2. Dante confuses Attila with Totila, King of the Ostrogoths (died 552).
He destroyed Florence in 542. Attila (d. 453), King of the Huns, destroyed many cities of northern
Italy, but not Florence.

The Poets find Capaneus stretched out on the sands, the chief sinner of that place. He is still blaspheming God. They continue along the edge of the Wood of the Suicides and come to a blood-red rill which flows boiling from the Wood and crosses the burning plain. Virgil explains the miraculous power of its waters and discourses on the Old Man of Crete and the origin of all the rivers of Hell.

The symbolism of the burning plain is obviously centered in sterility (the desert image) and wrath (the fire image). Blasphemy, sodomy, and usury are all unnatural and sterile actions: thus the unbearing desert is the eternity of these sinners; and thus the rain, which in nature should be fertile and cool, descends as fire. Capaneus, moreover, is subjected not to the wrath of nature (the sands below) and the wrath of God (the fire from above), but is tortured most by his own inner violence, which is the root of blasphemy.

Love of that land that was our common source
    moved me to tears; I gathered up the leaves
    and gave them back. He was already hoarse.
We came to the edge of the forest where one goes
    from the second round to the third, and there we saw     5
    what fearful arts the hand of Justice knows.
To make these new things wholly clear, I say
    we came to a plain whose soil repels all roots.
    The wood of misery rings it the same way
the wood itself is ringed by the red fosse.     10
    We paused at its edge: the ground was burning sand,
    just such a waste as Cato marched across.[3]
O endless wrath of God: how utterly
    thou shouldst become a terror to all men
    who read the frightful truths revealed to me!     15
Enormous herds of naked souls I saw,
    lamenting till their eyes were burned of tears;
    they seemed condemned by an unequal law,
for some were stretched supine upon the ground,
    some squatted with their arms about themselves,     20
    and others without pause roamed round and round.
Most numerous were those that roamed the plain.
    Far fewer were the souls stretched on the sand,
    but moved to louder cries by greater pain.
And over all that sand on which they lay     25
    or crouched or roamed, great flakes of flame fell slowly
    as snow falls in the Alps on a windless day.
Like those Alexander met in the hot regions
    of India, flames raining from the sky

3. In 47 B.C., Cato of Utica led an army across the Libyan desert. Lucan described the march in *Pharsalia* IX, 587 ff.

to fall still unextinguished on his legions:                          30
whereat he formed his ranks, and at their head
  set the example, trampling the hot ground
  for fear the tongues of fire might join and spread—[4]
just so in Hell descended the long rain
  upon the damned, kindling the sand like tinder                35
  under a flint and steel, doubling the pain.
In a never-ending fit upon those sands,
  the arms of the damned twitched all about their bodies,
  now here, now there, brushing away the brands.
"Poet," I said, "master of every dread                                 40
  we have encountered, other than those fiends
  who sallied from the last gate of the dead—
who is that wraith who lies along the rim
  and sets his face against the fire in scorn,
  so that the rain seems not to mellow him?"                     45
And he himself,[5] hearing what I had said
  to my Guide and Lord concerning him, replied:
  "What I was living, the same am I now, dead.
Though Jupiter wear out his sooty smith
  from whom on my last day he snatched in anger                  50
  the jagged thunderbolt he pierced me with;
though he wear out the others one by one
  who labor at the forge at Mongibello[6]
  crying again 'Help! Help! Help me, good Vulcan!'
as he did at Phlegra[7] and hurl down endlessly                        55
  with all the power of Heaven in his arm,
  small satisfaction would he win from me."
At this my Guide spoke with such vehemence
  as I had not heard from him in all of Hell:
  "O Capaneus, by your insolence                                 60
you are made to suffer as much fire inside
  as falls upon you. Only your own rage
  could be fit torment for your sullen pride."
Then he turned to me more gently. "That," he said,
  "was one of the Seven who laid siege to Thebes.                 65
  Living, he scorned God, and among the dead
he scorns Him yet. He thinks he may detest
  God's power too easily, but as I told him,

4. This incident of Alexander the Great's campaign in India is described in *De Meteoris* of Alber-
tus Magnus and was taken by him with considerable alteration from a letter reputedly sent to
Aristotle by Alexander.    5. Capaneus, one of the seven captains who warred on Thebes. As he
scaled the walls of Thebes, Capaneus defied Jove to protect them. Jove replied with a thunderbolt
that killed the blasphemer with his blasphemy still on his lips. (Statius, *Thebiad* x, 845 ff.)
6. Mt. Etna. Vulcan was believed to have his smithy inside the volcano.    7. At the battle of
Phlegra in Thessaly the Titans tried to storm Olympus. Jove drove them back with the help of the
thunderbolts Vulcan forged for him.

his slobber is a fit badge for his breast.
Now follow me; and mind for your own good　　　　70
　　you do not step upon the burning sand,
　　but keep well back along the edge of the wood."
We walked in silence then till we reached a rill
　　that gushes from the wood;[8] it ran so red
　　the memory sends a shudder through me still.　　　75
As from the Bulicame[9] springs the stream
　　the sinful women keep to their own use;
　　so down the sand the rill flowed out in steam.
The bed and both its banks were petrified,
　　as were its margins; thus I knew at once　　　80
　　our passage through the sand lay by its side.
"Among all other wonders I have shown you
　　since we came through the gate denied to none,
　　nothing your eyes have seen is equal to
the marvel of the rill by which we stand,　　　85
　　for it stifles all the flames above its course
　　as it flows out across the burning sand."
So spoke my Guide across the flickering light,
　　and I begged him to bestow on me the food
　　for which he had given me the appetite.　　　90
"In the middle of the sea, and gone to waste,
　　there lies a country known as Crete," he said,
　　"under whose king the ancient world was chaste.
Once Rhea[1] chose it as the secret crypt
　　and cradle of her son; and better to hide him,　　　95
　　her Corybantes raised a din when he wept.
An ancient giant[2] stands in the mountain's core.
　　He keeps his shoulder turned toward Damietta,

8. The rill, still blood-red and still boiling, is the overflow of Phlegethon which descends across
the Wood of the Suicides and the Burning Plain to plunge over the Great Cliff into the Eighth
Circle. It is clearly a water of marvels, for it not only petrifies the sands over which it flows, but
its clouds of steam quench all the flames above its course.　　9. A hot sulphur spring near Viterbo.
The choice is strikingly apt, for the waters of the Bulicame not only boil and steam but have a
distinctly reddish tint as a consequence of their mineral content. A part of the Bulicame flows out
through what was once a quarter reserved to prostitutes; and they were given special rights to the
water, since they were not permitted to use the public baths.　　1. Wife of Saturn (Cronos) and
mother of Jove (Zeus). It had been prophesied to Saturn that one of his own children would
dethrone him. To nullify the prophecy Saturn devoured each of his children at birth. On the
birth of Jove, Rhea duped Saturn by letting him bolt down a stone wrapped in baby clothes. After
this tribute to her husband's appetite she hid the infant on Mount Ida in Crete. There she posted
her Corybantes (or Bacchantes) as guards and instructed them to set up a great din whenever the
baby cried. Thus Saturn would not hear him. The Corybantic dances of the ancient Greeks were
based on the frenzied shouting and clashing of swords on shields with which the Corybantes
protected the infant Jove.　　2. This is the Old Man of Crete. The original of this figure occurs
in Daniel ii, 32–34, where it is told by Daniel as Nebuchadnezzar's dream. Dante follows the
details of the original closely but adds a few of his own and a totally different interpretation. In
Dante each metal represents one of the ages of man, each deteriorating from the Golden Age of
Innocence. The left foot, terminating the Age of Iron, is the Holy Roman Empire. The right foot,
of terra cotta, is the Roman Catholic Church, a more fragile base than the left, but the one upon

and looks toward Rome as if it were his mirror.
His head is made of gold; of silverwork                              100
    his breast and both his arms, of polished brass
    the rest of his great torso to the fork.
He is of chosen iron from there down,
    except that his right foot is terra cotta;
    it is this foot he rests more weight upon.                       105
Every part except the gold is split
    by a great fissure from which endless tears
    drip down and hollow out the mountain's pit.
Their course sinks to this pit from stone to stone,
    becoming Acheron, Phlegethon, and Styx.                          110
    Then by this narrow sluice they hurtle down
to the end of all descent, and disappear
    into Cocytus.[3] You shall see what sink that is
    with your own eyes. I pass it in silence here."
And I to him: "But if these waters flow                              115
    from the world above, why is this rill met only
    along this shelf?" And he to me: "You know
the place is round, and though you have come deep
    into the valley through the many circles,
    always bearing left along the steep,                             120
you have not traveled any circle through
    its total round; hence when new things appear
    from time to time, that hardly should surprise you."
And I: "Where shall we find Phlegethon's course?
    And Lethe's? One you omit, and of the other                      125
    you only say the tear-flood is its source.
"In all you ask of me you please me truly,"
    he answered, "but the red and boiling water
    should answer the first question you put to me
and you shall stand by Lethe, but far hence:                         130
    there, where the spirits go to wash themselves
    when their guilt has been removed by penitence."
And then he said: "Now it is time to quit
    this edge of shade: follow close after me
    along the rill, and do not stray from it;                        135
for the unburning margins form a lane,
and by them we may cross the burning plain."

which the greater weight descends. The tears of the woes of man are a Dantean detail: they flow
down the great fissure that defaces all but the Golden Age. Thus, starting in woe, they flow
through man's decline, into the hollow of the mountain and become the waters of all Hell.
Dante's other major addition is the site and position of the figure: equidistant from the three
continents, the Old Man stands at a sort of center of Time, his back turned to Damietta in Egypt
(here symbolizing the East, the past, the birth of religion) and fixes his gaze upon Rome (the
West, the future, the Catholic Church). It is certainly the most elaborately worked single symbol
in the *Inferno*.    3. The frozen lake that lies at the bottom of Hell. (See Cantos XXXII–XXXIV.)

CANTO XV

*Circle Seven: Round Three    The Violent Against Nature*

Protected by the marvelous powers of the boiling rill, the Poets
walk along its banks across the burning plain. The Wood of the
Suicides is behind them; the Great Cliff at whose foot lies the Eighth
Circle is before them.

They pass one of the roving bands of Sodomites. One of the sinners stops Dante, and with great difficulty the Poet recognizes him
under his baked features as Ser Brunetto Latino. This is a reunion
with a dearly-loved man and writer, one who had considerably influenced Dante's own development, and Dante addresses him with great
and sorrowful affection, paying him the highest tribute offered to any
sinner in the Inferno. Brunetto prophesies Dante's sufferings at the
hands of the Florentines, gives an account of the souls that move
with him through the fire, and finally, under Divine Compulsion,
races off across the plain.


We go by one of the stone margins now
   and the steam of the rivulet makes a shade above it,
   guarding the stream and banks from the flaming snow.
As the Flemings in the lowland between Bruges
   and Wissant, under constant threat of the sea,             5
   erect their great dikes to hold back the deluge;[4]
as the Paduans along the shores of the Brent
   build levees to protect their towns and castles
   lest Chiarentana drown in the spring torrent—
to the same plan, though not so wide nor high,[5]          10
   did the engineer, whoever he may have been,
   design the margin we were crossing by.
Already we were so far from the wood
   that even had I turned to look at it,
   I could not have made it out from where I stood,       15
when a company of shades came into sight
   walking beside the bank. They stared at us
   as men at evening by the new moon's light
stare at one another when they pass by
   on a dark road, pointing their eyebrows toward us   20
   as an old tailor squints at his needle's eye.
Stared at so closely by that ghostly crew,
   I was recognized by one who seized the hem
   of my skirt and said: "Wonder of wonders! You?"

**4.** Dante compares the banks of the rill of Phlegethon to the dikes built by the Flemings to hold
back the sea, and to those built by the Paduans to hold back the spring floods of the river Brent.
Chiarentana (Latin: Clarentana) was a Duchy of the Middle Ages. Its territory included the headwaters of the Brent (Brenta).    **5.** Their width is never precisely specified, but we shall see when
Dante walks along speaking to Ser Brunetto (line 40) that their height is about that of a man.

And I, when he stretched out his arm to me,                       25
   searched his baked features closely, till at last
   I traced his image from my memory
in spite of the burnt crust, and bending near
   to put my face closer to his, at last
   I answered: "Ser Brunetto, are *you* here?"[6]               30
"O my son! may it not displease you," he cried,
   "if Brunetto Latino leave his company
   and turn and walk a little by your side."
And I to him: "With all my soul I ask it.
   Or let us sit together, if it please him                   35
   who is my Guide and leads me through this pit."
"My son!" he said, "whoever of this train
   pauses a moment, must lie a hundred years
   forbidden to brush off the burning rain.
Therefore, go on; I will walk at your hem,[7]                      40
   and then rejoin my company, which goes
   mourning eternal loss in eternal flame."
I did not dare descend to his own level
   but kept my head inclined, as one who walks
   in reverence meditating good and evil.                     45
"What brings you here before your own last day?
   What fortune or what destiny?" he began.
   "And who is he that leads you this dark way?"
"Up there in the happy life I went astray
   in a valley," I replied, "before I had reached              50
   the fullness of my years. Only yesterday
at dawn I turned from it. This spirit showed
   himself to me as I was turning back,
   and guides me home again along this road."
And he: "Follow your star, for if in all                           55
   of the sweet life I saw one truth shine clearly,
   you cannot miss your glorious arrival.
And had I lived to do what I meant to do,
   I would have cheered and seconded your work,
   observing Heaven so well disposed toward you.                60
But that ungrateful and malignant stock

6. Born between 1210 and 1230, died 1294. A prominent Florentine Guelph who held, among many other posts, that of notary, whence the title *Ser* (sometimes *Sere*). He was not Dante's schoolmaster as many have supposed—he was much too busy and important a man for that. Dante's use of the word "master" is to indicate spiritual indebtedness to Brunetto and his works. It is worth noting that Dante addresses him in Italian as "voi" instead of using the less respectful "tu" form. Farinata is the only other sinner so addressed in the *Inferno*. Brunetto's two principal books, both of which Dante admires, were the prose *Livre dou Tresor* (*The Book of the Treasure*) and the poetic *Tesoretta* (*The Little Treasure*). Dante learned a number of his devices from the allegorical journey which forms the *Tesoretto*.   7. Dante is standing on the dike at approximately the level of Brunetto's head and he cannot descend because of the rain of fire and the burning sands.

that came down from Fiesole of old
and still smacks of the mountain and the rock,
for your good works will be your enemy.[8]
    And there is cause: the sweet fig is not meant          65
    to bear its fruit beside the bitter sorb-tree.[9]
Even the old adage calls them blind,[1]
    an envious, proud, and avaricious people:
    see that you root their customs from your mind.
It is written in your stars, and will come to pass,         70
    that your honours shall make both sides hunger for you:[2]
    but the goat shall never reach to crop that grass.
Let the beasts of Fiesole[3] devour their get
    like sows, but never let them touch the plant,
    if among their rankness any springs up yet,           75
in which is born again the holy seed
    of the Romans who remained among their rabble
    when Florence made a new nest for their greed."
"Ah, had I all my wish," I answered them,
    "you would not yet be banished from the world       80
    in which you were a radiance among men,
for that sweet image, gentle and paternal,
    you were to me in the world when hour by hour
    you taught me how man makes himself eternal,
lives in my mind, and now strikes to my heart;         85
    and while I live, the gratitude I owe it
    will speak to men out of my life and art.
What you have told me of my course, I write
    by another text I save to show a Lady[4]
    who will judge these matters, if I reach her height.     90
This much I would have you know: so long, I say,
    as nothing in my conscience troubles me
    I am prepared for Fortune, come what may.
Twice already in the eternal shade
    I have heard this prophecy;[5] but let Fortune turn     95

---

8. The ancient Etruscan city of Fiesole was situated on a hill about three miles north of the present site of Florence. According to legend, Fiesole had taken the side of Catiline in his war with Julius Caesar. Caesar destroyed the town and set up a new city called Florence on the Arno, peopling it with Romans and Fiesolans. The Romans were the aristocracy of the new city, but the Fiesolans were a majority. Dante ascribes the endless bloody conflicts of Florence largely to the internal strife between these two strains. His scorn of the Fiesolans is obvious in this passage. Dante proudly proclaimed his descent from the Roman strain.     9. A species of tart apple. 1. The source of this proverbial expression, "Blind as a Florentine," can no longer be traced with any assurance, though many incidents from Florentine history suggest possible sources. 2. Brunetto can scarcely mean that both sides will hunger to welcome the support of a man of Dante's distinction. Rather, that both sides will hunger to destroy him. (See also lines 94–95. Dante obviously accepts this as another dark prophecy.)     3. The Fiesolans themselves. 4. Beatrice.     5. The prophecies of Ciacco (Canto VI) and of Farinata (Canto X) are the other two places at which Dante's exile and suffering are foretold. Dante replies that come what may he will remain true to his purpose through all affliction; and Virgil turns to look proudly at his pupil uttering a proverb: *"Bene ascolta chi la nota,"* i.e., "Well heeded is well heard."

her wheel as she please, and the countryman his spade."
My guiding spirit paused at my last word
  and, turning right about, stood eye to eye
  to say to me: "Well heeded is well heard."
But I did not reply to him, going on                          100
  with Ser Brunetto to ask him who was with him
  in the hot sands, the best-born and best known.
And he to me: "Of some who share this walk
  it is good to know; of the rest let us say nothing,
  for the time would be too short for so much talk.           105
In brief, we all were clerks and men of worth,
  great men of letters, scholars of renown;
  all by the one same crime defiled on earth.
Priscian[6] moves there along the wearisome
  sad way, and Francesco d'Accorso,[7] and also there,        110
  if you had any longing for such scum,
you might have seen that one the Servant of Servants[8]
  sent from the Arno to the Bacchiglione
  where he left his unnatural organ[9] wrapped in cerements.
I would say more, but there across the sand                   115
  a new smoke rises and new people come,
  and I must run to be with my own band.
Remember my *Treasure*, in which I still live on:
  I ask no more." He turned then, and he seemed,
  across that plain, like one of those who run                120
for the green cloth at Verona;[1] and of those,
more like the one who wins, than those who lose.

## CANTO XVI

*Circle Seven: Round Three   The Violent Against Nature and Art*

The Poets arrive within hearing of the waterfall that plunges over
the Great Cliff into the Eighth Circle. The sound is still a distant
throbbing when three wraiths, recognizing Dante's Florentine dress,
detach themselves from their band and come running toward him.
They are Jacopo Rusticucci, Guido Guerra, and Tegghiaio Aldobrandi, all of them Florentines whose policies and personalities Dante

7. Florentine scholar. He served as a professor at Bologna and, from 1273 to 1280, at Oxford. He died in Bologna in 1294.    8. Dante's old enemy, Boniface VIII. *Survus servorum* is technically a correct papal title, but there is certainly a touch of irony in Dante's application of it in this context. In 1295 Boniface transferred Bishop Andrea de'Mozzi from the Bishopric of Florence (on the Arno) to that of Vicenza (on the Bacchiglione). The transference was reputedly brought about at the request of the Bishop's brother, Tommaso de' Mozzi of Florence, who wished to remove from his sight the spectacle of his brother's stupidity and unnatural vices.    9. The original, *mal protesi nervi*, contains an untranslatable word-play. *Nervi* may be taken as "the male organ" and *protesi* for "erected"; thus the organ aroused to passion for unnatural purposes (*mal*). Or *nervi* may be taken as "nerves" and *mal protesi* for "dissolute." Taken in context, the first rendering strikes me as more Dantean.    1. On the first Sunday of Lent all the young men of Verona ran a race for the prize of green cloth. The last runner in was given a live rooster and was required to carry it through the town.

admired. Rusticucci and Tegghiaio have already been mentioned in
a highly complimentary way in Dante's talk with Ciacco (Canto VI).

The sinners ask for news of Florence, and Dante replies with a
passionate lament for her present degradation. The three wraiths return
to their band and the Poets continue to the top of the falls. Here, at
Virgil's command, Dante removes a Cord from about his waist and
Virgil drops it over the edge of the abyss. As if in answer to a signal,
a great distorted shape comes swimming up through the dirty air of
the pit.


We could already hear the rumbling drive
    of the waterfall in its plunge to the next circle,
    a murmur like the throbbing of a hive,
when three shades turned together on the plain,
    breaking toward us from a company              5
    that went its way to torture in that rain.
They cried with one voice as they ran toward me:
    "Wait, oh wait, for by your dress you seem
    a voyager from our own tainted country."
Ah! what wounds I saw, some new, some old,          10
    branded upon their bodies! Even now
    the pain of it in memory turns me cold.
My Teacher heard their cries, and turning-to,
    stood face to face. "Do as they ask," he said,
    "for these are souls to whom respect is due;       15
and were it not for the darting flames that hem
    our narrow passage in, I should have said
    it were more fitting you ran after them."
We paused, and they began their ancient wail
    over again, and when they stood below us       20
    they formed themselves into a moving wheel.
As naked and anointed champions do
    in feeling out their grasp and their advantage
    before they close in for the thrust or blow—
so circling, each one stared up at my height,       25
    and as their feet moved left around the circle,
    their necks kept turning backward to the right.
"If the misery of this place, and our unkempt
    and scorched appearance," one of them began,
    "bring us and what we pray into contempt,      30
still may our earthly fame move you to tell
    who and what you are, who so securely
    set your live feet to the dead dusts of Hell.
This peeled and naked soul who runs before me
    around this wheel, was higher than you think     35

there in the world, in honor and degree.
Guido Guerra[2] was the name he bore,
  the good Gualdrada's[3] grandson. In his life
  he won great fame in counsel and in war.
The other who behind me treads this sand                    40
  was Tegghiaio Aldobrandi,[4] whose good counsels
  the world would have done well to understand.
And I who share their torment, in my life
  was Jacopo Rusticucci;[5] above all
  I owe my sorrows to a savage wife."                       45
I would have thrown myself to the plain below
  had I been sheltered from the falling fire;
  and I think my Teacher would have let me go.
But seeing I should be burned and cooked, my fear
  overcame the first impulse of my heart                    50
  to leap down and embrace them then and there.
"No contempt," I said, "but the compassion
  that seizes on my soul and memory
  at the thought of you tormented in this fashion—
it was grief that choked my speech when through the scorching   55
  air of this pit my Lord announced to me
  that such men as you are might be approaching.
I am of your own land, and I have always
  heard with affection and rehearsed with honor
  your name and the good deeds of your happier days.         60
Led by my Guide and his truth, I leave the gall
  and go for the sweet apples of delight.
  But first I must descend to the center of all."
"So may your soul and body long continue
  together on the way you go," he answered,                   65

2. Around 1220–1272. A valiant leader of the Guelphs (hence his name which signifies Guido of War) despite his Ghibelline origin as one of the counts of Guidi. It is a curious fact, considering the prominence of Guido, that Dante is the only writer to label him a sodomite.   3. The legend of "the good Gualdrada," Guido Guerra's grandmother, is a typical example of the medieval talent for embroidery. She was the daughter of Bellincione Berti de' Ravignana. The legend is that Emperor Otto IV saw her in church and, attracted by her beauty, asked who she was. Bellincione replied that she was the daughter of one whose soul would be made glad to have the Emperor salute her with a kiss. The young-lady-of-all-virtues, hearing her father's words, declared that no man might kiss her unless he were her husband. Otto was so impressed by the modesty and propriety of this remark that he married her to one of his noblemen and settled a large estate upon the couple. It was from this marriage that the counts Guidi de Modigliano (among them Guido Guerra) were said to descend. Unfortunately for the legend, Otto's first visit to Italy was in 1209, and surviving records show that Count Guido had already had two children by his wife Gualdrada as early as 1202.   4. Date of birth unknown. He died shortly before 1266. A valiant knight of the family degli Adimari of the Guelph nobles. With Guido Guerra he advised the Florentines not to move against the Sienese at the disastrous battle of Montaperti (See Farinata, Canto X), knowing that the Sienese had been heavily reinforced by mercenaries. It is probably these good counsels that "the world would have done well to understand." This is another case in which Dante is the only writer to bring the charge of sodomy.   5. Dates of birth and death unknown, but mention of him exists in Florentine records of 1235, 1236, 1254, and 1266. A rich and respected Florentine knight. Dante's account of his sin and of its cause is the only record and it remains unsupported: no details of his life are known.

"and the honor of your days shine after you—
tell me if courtesy and valor raise
    their banners in our city as of old,
    or has the glory faded from its days?
For Borsiere,[6] who is newly come among us                    70
    and yonder goes with our companions in pain,
    taunts us with such reports, and his words have stung us."
"O Florence! your sudden wealth and your upstart
    rabble, dissolute and overweening,
    already set you weeping in your heart!"                    75
I cried with face upraised, and on the sand
    those three sad spirits looked at one another
    like men who hear the truth and understand.
"If this be your manner of speaking, and if you can
    satisfy others with such ease and grace,"                  80
    they said as one, "we hail a happy man.
Therefore, if you win through this gloomy pass
    and climb again to see the heaven of stars;
    when it rejoices you to say 'I was',
speak of us to the living." They parted then,                  85
    breaking their turning wheel, and as they vanished
    over the plain, their legs seemed wings. "Amen"
could not have been pronounced between their start
    and their disappearance over the rim of sand.
    And then it pleased my Master to depart.                   90
A little way beyond we felt the quiver
    and roar of the cascade, so close that speech
    would have been drowned in thunder. As that river—[7]
the first one on the left of the Appennines
    to have a path of its own from Monte Veso                  95
    to the Adriatic Sea—which, as it twines
is called the Acquacheta from its source
    until it nears Forli, and then is known
    as the Montone in its further course—
resounds from the mountain in a single leap                   100
    there above San Benedetto dell'Alpe
    where a thousand falls might fit into the steep;
so down from a sheer bank, in one enormous

---

6. "Borsiere" in Italian means "pursemaker," and the legend has grown without verification or
likelihood that this was his origin. He was a courtier, a peacemaker, and an arranger of marriages.
Boccaccio speaks of him in highly honorable terms in the Eighth Tale of the First Day of the
*Decameron.*    7. The water course described by Dante and made up of the Acquacheta and the
Montone flows directly into the sea without draining into the Po. The placement of it as "first on
the left of the Appennines" has been shown by Casella to result from the peculiar orientation of
the maps of Dante's time. The "river" has its source and course along a line running almost
exactly northwest from Florence. San Benedetto dell' Alpe is a small monastery situated on that
line about twenty-five miles from Florence.

plunge, the tainted water roared so loud
   a little longer there would have deafened us.                          105
I had a cord bound round me like a belt[8]
   which I had once thought I might put to use
   to snare the leopard with the gaudy pelt.
When at my Guide's command I had unbound
   its loops from about my habit, I gathered it                          110
   and held it out to him all coiled and wound.
He bent far back to his right, and throwing it
   out from the edge, sent it in a long arc
   into the bottomless darkness of the pit.
"Now surely some unusual event,"                                         115
   I said to myself, "must follow this new signal
   upon which my good Guide is so intent."
Ah, how cautiously a man should breathe
   near those who see not only what we do,
   but have the sense which reads the mind beneath!                      120
He said to me: "You will soon see arise
   what I await, and what you wonder at;
   soon you will see the thing before your eyes."
To the truth which will seem falsehood every man
   who would not be called a liar while speaking fact                    125
   should learn to seal his lips as best he can.
But here I cannot be still: Reader, I swear
   by the lines of my Comedy—so may it live—
   that I saw swimming up through that foul air
a shape to astonish the most doughty soul,                               130
   a shape like one returning through the sea
   from working loose an anchor run afoul
of something on the bottom—so it rose,
its arms spread upward and its feet drawn close.

### CANTO XVII

*Circle Seven: Round Three   The Violent Against Art. Geryon*

   The monstrous shape lands on the brink and Virgil salutes it ironically. It is Geryon, the Monster of Fraud. Virgil announces that
they must fly down from the cliff on the back of this monster. While

8. As might be expected many ingenious explanations have been advanced to account for the
sudden appearance of this cord. It is frequently claimed, but without proof, that Dante had been
a minor friar of the Franciscans but had left without taking vows. The explanation continues that
he had clung to the habit of wearing the white cord of the Franciscans, which he now produces
with the information that he had once intended to use it to snare the Leopard. One invention is
probably as good as another. What seems obvious is that the narrative required some sort of device
for signaling the monster, and that to meet his narrative need, Dante suddenly invented the
business of the cord.

Virgil negotiates for their passage, Dante is sent to examine the Usurers
(The Violent Against Art).

These sinners sit in a crouch along the edge of the burning plain
that approaches the cliff. Each of them has a leather purse around
his neck, and each purse is blazoned with a coat of arms. Their eyes,
gushing with tears, are forever fixed on these purses. Dante recognizes none of these sinners, but their coats of arms are unmistakably
those of well-known Florentine families.

Having understood who they are and the reason for their present
condition, Dante cuts short his excursion and returns to find Virgil
mounted on the back of Geryon. Dante joins his Master and they fly
down from the great cliff.

Their flight carries them from the Hell of the Violent and the
Bestial (The Sins of the Lion) into the Hell of the Fraudulent and
Malicious (The Sins of the Leopard).

"Now see the sharp-tailed beast that mounts the brink.
    He passes mountains, breaks through walls and weapons.
    Behold the beast that makes the whole world stink."[9]
These were the words my Master spoke to me;
    then signaled the weird beast to come to ground                    5
    close to the sheer end of our rocky levee.
The filthy prototype of Fraud drew near
    and settled his head and breast upon the edge
    of the dark cliff, but let his tail hang clear.
His face was innocent of every guile,                                  10
    benign and just in feature and expression;
    and under it his body was half reptile.
His two great paws were hairy to the armpits;
    all his back and breast and both his flanks
    were figured with bright knots and subtle circlets:                15
never was such a tapestry of bloom
    woven on earth by Tartar or by Turk,[1]
    nor by Arachne[2] at her flowering loom.
As a ferry sometimes lies along the strand,
    part beached and part afloat; and as the beaver,[3]                20

9. Geryon, a mythical king of Spain represented as a giant with three heads and three bodies. He
was killed by Hercules, who coveted the king's cattle. A later tradition represents him as killing
and robbing strangers whom he lured into his realm. It is probably on this account that Dante
chose him as the prototype of fraud, though in a radically altered bodily form. Some of the details
of Dante's Geryon may be drawn from *Revelations* ix, 9–20, but most of them are almost certainly
his own invention: a monster with the general shape of a dragon but with the tail of a scorpion,
hairy arms, a gaudily-marked reptilian body, and the face of a just and honest man.    1. These
were the most skilled weavers of Dante's time.    2. She was so famous as a spinner and weaver
that she challenged Minerva to a weaving contest. There are various accounts of what happened
in the contest, but all of them end with the goddess so moved to anger that she changed Arachne
into a spider.    3. Dante's description of the beaver is probably drawn from some old bestiary or
natural history. It may be based on the medieval belief that the beaver fished by crouching on the
bank, scooping the fish out with its tail. *The guzzling Germans:* The heavy drinking of the Germans was proverbial in the Middle Ages and far back into antiquity.

up yonder in the guzzling Germans' land,
squats halfway up the bank when a fight is on—
    just so lay that most ravenous of beasts
    on the rim which bounds the burning sand with stone.
His tail twitched in the void beyond that lip,                    25
    thrashing, and twisting up the envenomed fork
    which, like a scorpion's stinger, armed the tip.
My Guide said: "It is time now we drew near
    that monster." And descending on the right[4]
    we moved ten paces outward to be clear                       30
of sand and flames. And when we were beside him,
    I saw upon the sand a bit beyond us
    some people crouching close beside the brim.[5]
The Master paused. "That you may take with you
    the full experience of this round," he said,                 35
    "go now and see the last state of that crew.
But let your talk be brief, and I will stay
    and reason with this beast till you return,
    that his strong back may serve us on our way."
So further yet along the outer edge                              40
    of the seventh circle I moved on alone.
    And came to the sad people of the ledge.
Their eyes burst with their grief; their smoking hands
    jerked about their bodies, warding off
    now the flames and now the burning sands.                    45
Dogs in summer bit by fleas and gadflies,
    jerking their snouts about, twitching their paws
    now here, now there, behave no otherwise.
I examined several faces there among
    that sooty throng, and I saw none I knew;                    50
    but I observed that from each neck there hung
an enormous purse, each marked with its own beast
    and its own colors like a coat of arms.
    On these their streaming eyes appeared to feast.
Looking about, I saw one purse display                          55
    azure on or, a kind of lion;[6] another,
    on a blood red field, a goose whiter than whey.[7]

---

4. The Poets had crossed on the right bank of the rill. In the course of Geryon's flight they will be carried to the other side of the falls, thus continuing their course to the left. It should be noted that inside the walls of Dis, approaching the second great division of Hell (as here the third) they also moved to the right. No satisfactory reason can be given for these exceptions.    5. The Usurers. Virgil explains in Canto XI why they sin against Art, which is the Grandchild of God. They are the third and final category of the Violent against God and His works.    6. The arms of the Gianfigliazzi of Florence were a lion azure on a field of gold. The sinner bearing this purse must be Catello di Rosso Gianfigliazzi, who set up as a usurer in France and was made a knight on his return to Florence.    7. A white goose on a red field was the arms of the noble Ghibelline family of the Ubriachi, or Ebriachi, of Florence. The wearer is probably Ciappo Ubriachi, a notorious usurer.

And one that bore a huge and swollen sow
  azure on field argent[8] said to me:
    "What are you doing in this pit of sorrow?                    60
Leave us alone! And since you have not yet died,
  I'll have you know my neighbor Vitaliano[9]
  has a place reserved for him here at my side.
A Paduan among Florentines, I sit here
  while hour by hour they nearly deafen me                        65
  shouting: 'Send us the sovereign cavalier
with the purse of the three goats!' "[1] He half arose,
  twisted his mouth, and darted out his tongue
  for all the world like an ox licking its nose.
And I, afraid that any longer stay                                70
  would anger him who had warned me to be brief,
  left those exhausted souls without delay.
Returned, I found my Guide already mounted
  upon the rump of that monstrosity.
    He said to me: "Now must you be undaunted:                    75
this beast must be our stairway to the pit:
  mount it in front, and I will ride between
  you and the tail, lest you be poisoned by it."
Like one so close to the quartanary chill[2]
  that his nails are already pale and his flesh trembles          80
  at the very sight of shade or a cool rill—
so did I tremble at each frightful word.
  But his scolding filled me with that shame that makes
  the servant brave in the presence of his lord.
I mounted the great shoulders of that freak                       85
  and tried to say "Now help me to hold on!"
  But my voice clicked in my throat and I could not speak.
But no sooner had I settled where he placed me
  than he, my stay, my comfort, and my courage
  in other perils, gathered and embraced me.                      90
Then he called out: "Now, Geryon, we are ready:
  bear well in mind that his is living weight
  and make your circles wide and your flight steady."
As a small ship slides from a beaching or its pier,

---

8. These are the arms of the Scrovegni of Padua. The bearer is probably Reginaldo Scrovegni.
9. Vitaliano di Iacopo Vitaliani, another Paduan.    1. Giovanni di Buiamonte was esteemed in
Florence as "the sovereign cavalier" and was chosen for many high offices. He was a usurer and
a gambler who lost great sums at play. Dante's intent is clearly to bewail the decay of standards
which permits Florence to honor so highly a man for whom Hell is waiting so dismally. Buiamonte was of the Becchi family whose arms were three black goats on a gold field. "Becchi" in
Italian is the plural form of the word for "goat."    2. Quartan fever is an ague that runs a four-
day cycle with symptoms roughly like those of malaria. At the approach of the chill, Dante intends
his figure to say, any thought of coolness strikes terror into the shivering victim.

backward, backward—so that monster slipped                    95
    back from the rim. And when he had drawn clear
he swung about, and stretching out his tail
    he worked it like an eel, and with his paws
    he gathered in the air, while I turned pale.
I think there was no greater fear the day                     100
    Phaeton[3] let loose the reins and burned the sky
    along the great scar of the Milky Way,
nor when Icarus, too close to the sun's track
    felt the wax melt, unfeathering his loins,
    and heard his father cry "Turn back! Turn back!"—[4]       105
than I felt when I found myself in air,
    afloat in space with nothing visible
    but the enormous beast that bore me there.
Slowly, slowly, he swims on through space,
    wheels and descends, but I can sense it only              110
    by the way the wind blows upward past my face.
Already on the right I heard the swell
    and thunder of the whirlpool. Looking down
    I leaned my head out and stared into Hell.
I trembled again at the prospect of dismounting              115
    and cowered in on myself, for I saw fires
    on every hand, and I heard a long lamenting.
And then I saw—till then I had but felt it—
    the course of our down-spiral to the horrors
    that rose to us from all sides of the pit.               120
As a flight-worn falcon sinks down wearily
    though neither bird nor lure has signalled it,[5]
    the falconer crying out: "What! spent already!"—
then turns and in a hundred spinning gyres
    sulks from her master's call, sullen and proud—          125
    so to that bottom lit by endless fires
the monster Geryon circled and fell,
    setting us down at the foot of the precipice
    of ragged rock on the eighth shelf of Hell.
And once freed of our weight, he shot from there             130
into the dark like an arrow into air.

3. Son of Apollo who drove the chariot of the sun. Phaeton begged his father for a chance to drive the chariot himself but he lost control of the horses and Zeus killed him with a thunderbolt for fear the whole earth would catch fire. The scar left in the sky by the runaway horses is marked by the Milky Way.    4. Daedalus, the father of Icarus, made wings for himself and his son and they flew into the sky, but Icarus, ignoring his father's commands, flew too close to the sun. The heat melted the wax with which the wings were fastened and Icarus fell into the Aegean and was drowned.    5. Falcons, when sent aloft, were trained to circle until sighting a bird, or until signaled back by the lure (a stuffed bird). Flight-weary, Dante's metaphoric falcon sinks bit by bit, rebelling against his training and sulking away from his master in wide slow circles.

CANTO XVIII

*Circle Eight (Malebolge)    The Fraudulent and Malicious*
*Bolgia One    The Panderers and Seducers*
*Bolgia Two    The Flatterers*

Dismounted from Geryon, the Poets find themselves in the Eighth
Circle, called Malebolge (The Evil Ditches). This is the upper half
of the Hell of the Fraudulent and Malicious. Malebolge is a great
circle of stone that slopes like an amphitheater. The slopes are divided
into ten concentric ditches; and within these ditches, each with his
own kind, are punished those guilty of Simple Fraud.

A series of stone dikes runs like spokes from the edge of the great
cliff face to the center of the place, and these serve as bridges.

The Poets bear left toward the first ditch, and Dante observes below
him and to his right the sinners of the first bolgia, The Panderers
and Seducers. These make two files, one along either bank of the
ditch, and are driven at an endless fast walk by horned demons who
hurry them along with great lashes. In life these sinners goaded others on to serve their own foul purposes; so in Hell are they driven in
their turn. The horned demons who drive them symbolize the sinners' own vicious natures, embodiments of their own guilty consciences. Dante may or may not have intended the horns of the
demons to symbolize cuckoldry and adultery.

The Poets see Venedico Caccianemico and Jason in the first pit,
and pass on to the second, where they find the souls of the Flatterers
sunk in excrement, the true equivalent of their false flatteries on
earth. They observe Alessio Interminelli and Thaïs, and pass on.

There is in Hell a vast and sloping ground
    called Malebolge,[6] a lost place of stone
    as black as the great cliff that seals it round.
Precisely in the center of that space
    there yawns a well extremely wide and deep.[7]                        5
    I shall discuss it in its proper place.
The border that remains between the well-pit
    and the great cliff forms an enormous circle,
    and ten descending troughs are cut in it,
offering a general prospect like the ground                              10
    that lies around one of those ancient castles
    whose walls are girded many times around
by concentric moats. And just as, from the portal,

6. *Bolgia* in Italian equals "ditch" or "pouch." That combination of meanings is not possible in
a single English word, but it is well to bear in mind that Dante intended both meanings: not only
a ditch of evil, but a pouch full of it, a filthy treasure of ill-gotten souls.    7. This is the final pit
of Hell, and in it are punished the Treacherous (those Guilty of Compound Fraud). Cantos
XXIX–XXXIV will deal with this part of Hell.

the castle's bridges run from moat to moat
   to the last bank; so from the great rock wall           15
across the embankments and the ditches, high
   and narrow cliffs run to the central well,
   which cuts and gathers them like radii.
Here, shaken from the back of Geryon,
   we found ourselves. My Guide kept to the left        20
   and I walked after him. So we moved on.
Below, on my right, and filling the first ditch
   along both banks, new souls in pain appeared,
   new torments, and new devils black as pitch.
All of these sinners were naked; on our side           25
   of the middle they walked toward us; on the other,
   in our direction, but with swifter stride.
Just so the Romans, because of the great throng
   in the year of the Jubilee, divide the bridge[8]
   in order that the crowds may pass along,          30
so that all face the Castle as they go
   on one side toward St. Peter's, while on the other,
   all move along facing toward Mount Giordano.
And everywhere along that hideous track
   I saw horned demons with enormous lashes        35
   move through those souls, scourging them on the back.
Ah, how the stragglers of that long rout stirred
   their legs quick-march at the first crack of the lash!
   Certainly no one waited a second, or third!
As we went on, one face in that procession        40
   caught my eye and I said: "That sinner there:
   It is certainly not the first time I've seen that one."
I stopped, therefore, to study him, and my Guide
   out of his kindness waited, and even allowed me
   to walk back a few steps at the sinner's side.        45
And that flayed spirit, seeing me turn around,
   thought to hide his face, but I called to him:
   "You there, that walk along with your eyes on the ground—
if those are not false features, then I know you
   as Venedico Caccianemico of Bologna:[9]        50
   what brings you here among this pretty crew?"
And he replied: "I speak unwillingly,
   but something in your living voice, in which
   I hear the world again, stirs and compels me.

8. Boniface VIII had proclaimed 1300 a Jubilee Year, and consequently throngs of pilgrims had come to Rome. Since the date of the vision is also 1300, the Roman throngs are moving back and forth across the Tiber via Ponte Castello Sant' Angelo at the very time Dante is watching the sinners in Hell.    9. To win the favor of the Marquis Obbizo da Este of Ferrara, Caccianemico acted as the procurer of his own sister Ghisola, called "la bella" or "Ghisolabella."

It was I who brought the fair Ghisola 'round                    55
   to serve the will and lust of the Marquis,
   however sordid that old tale may sound.
There are many more from Bologna who weep away
   eternity in this ditch; we fill it so
   there are not as many tongues that are taught to say    60
'sipa'[1] in all the land that lies between
   the Reno and the Saveno, as you must know
   from the many tales of our avarice and spleen."
And as he spoke, one of those lashes fell
   across his back, and a demon cried, "Move on,           65
   you pimp, there are no women here to sell."
Turning away then, I rejoined my Guide.
   We came in a few steps to a raised ridge
   that made a passage to the other side.
This we climbed easily, and turning right                       70
   along the jagged crest, we left behind
   the eternal circling of those souls in flight.
And when we reached the part at which the stone
   was tunneled for the passage of the scourged,
   my Guide said, "Stop a minute and look down             75
on these other misbegotten wraiths of sin.
   You have not seen their faces, for they moved
   in the same direction we were headed in."
So from that bridge we looked down on the throng
   that hurried toward us on the other side.                80
   Here, too, the whiplash hurried them along.
And the good Master, studying that train,
   said: "Look there, at that great soul that approaches
   and seems to shed no tears for all his pain—
what kingliness moves with him even in Hell!                    85
   It is Jason,[2] who by courage and good advice
   made off with the Colchian Ram. Later it fell
that he passed Lemnos, where the women of wrath,
   enraged by Venus' curse that drove their lovers
   out of their arms, put all their males to death.         90

---

1. Bolognese dialect for "sì," i.e., "yes." Bologna lies between the Savena and the Reno. This is a master taunt at Bologna as a city of panderers and seducers, for it clearly means that the Bolognese then living on earth were fewer in number than the Bolognese dead who had been assigned to this *bolgia*.    2. Leader of the Argonauts. He carried off the Colchian Ram (*i.e.*, The Golden Fleece). "The good advice" that helped him win the fleece was given by Medea, daughter of the King of Colchis, whom Jason took with him and later abandoned for Creusa ("Also for Medea is vengeance taken.") In the course of his very Grecian life, Jason had previously seduced Hypsipyle and deserted her to continue his voyage after the fleece. She was one of the women of Lemnos whom Aphrodite, because they no longer worshiped her, cursed with a foul smell which made them unbearable to their husbands and lovers. The women took their epic revenge by banding together to kill all their males, but Hypsipyle managed to save her father, King Thoas, by pretending to the women that she had already killed him.

There with his honeyed tongue and his dishonest
   lover's wiles, he gulled Hypsipyle,
   who, in the slaughter, had gulled all the rest.
And there he left her, pregnant and forsaken.
   Such guilt condemns him to such punishment;        95
   and also for Medea is vengenace taken.
All seducers march here to the whip.
   And let us say no more about this valley
   and those it closes in its stony grip."
We had already come to where the walk        100
   crosses the second bank, from which it lifts
   another arch, spanning from rock to rock.
Here we heard people whine in the next chasm,
   and knock and thump themselves with open palms,
   and blubber through their snouts as if in a spasm.        105
Steaming from that pit, a vapour rose
   over the banks, crusting them with a slime
   that sickened my eyes and hammered at my nose.
That chasm sinks so deep we could not sight
   its bottom anywhere until we climbed        110
   along the rock arch to its greatest height.
Once there, I peered down; and I saw long lines
   of people in a river of excrement
   that seemed the overflow of the world's latrines.
I saw among the felons of that pit        115
   one wraith who might or might not have been tonsured—
   one could not tell, he was so smeared with shit.
He bellowed: "You there, why do you stare at me
   more than at all the others in this stew?"
   And I to him: "Because if memory        120
serves me, I knew you when your hair was dry.
   You are Alessio Interminelli da Lucca.[3]
   That's why I pick you from this filthy fry."
And he then, beating himself on his clown's head:
   "Down to this have the flatteries I sold        125
   the living sunk me here among the dead."
And my Guide prompted then: "Lean forward a bit
   and look beyond him, there—do you see that one
   scratching herself with dungy nails, the strumpet
who fidgets to her feet, then to a crouch?        130
   It is the whore Thaïs[4] who told her lover

---

3. One of the noble family of the Interminelli or Interminei, a prominent White family of Lucca.
About all that is known of Alessio is the fact that he was still alive in 1295.    4. The flattery
uttered by Thaïs is put into her mouth by Terence in his *Eunuchus* (Act II, 1:1–2). Thaïs' lover
had sent her a slave, and later sent a servant to ask if she thanked him much. *Magnas vero agere
gratias Thais mihi?* The servant reported her as answering *Ingentes!* Cicero later commented on

when he sent to ask her, 'Do you thank me much?'
'Much? Nay, past all believing!' And with this
let us turn from the sight of this abyss."

CANTO XIX

*Circle Eight: Bolgia Three    The Simoniacs*

 Dante comes upon the Simoniacs (sellers of ecclesiastic favors and offices) and his heart overflows with the wrath he feels against those who corrupt the things of God. This *bolgia* is lined with round tube-like holes and the sinners are placed in them upside down with the soles of their feet ablaze. The heat of the blaze is proportioned to their guilt.

 The holes in which these sinners are placed are debased equivalents of the baptismal fonts common in the cities of Northern Italy and the sinners' confinement in them is temporary: as new sinners arrive, the souls drop through the bottom of their holes and disappear eternally into the crevices of the rock.

 As always, the punishment is a symbolic retribution. Just as the Simoniacs made a mock of holy office, so are they turned upside down in a mockery of the baptismal font. Just as they made a mockery of the holy water of baptism, so is their hellish baptism by fire, after which they are wholly immersed in the crevices below. The oily fire that licks at their soles may also suggest a travesty on the oil used in Extreme Unction (last rites for the dying).

 Virgil carries Dante down an almost sheer ledge and lets him speak to one who is the chief sinner of that place, Pope Nicholas III. Dante delivers himself of another stirring denunciation of those who have corrupted church office, and Virgil carries him back up the steep ledge toward the Fourth Bolgia.

O Simon Magus![5] O you wretched crew
  who follow him, pandering for silver and gold
  the things of God which should be wedded to
love and righteousness! O thieves for hire,
  now must the trump of judgment sound your doom          5
  here in the third fosse of the rim of fire!
We had already made our way across
  to the next grave, and to that part of the bridge[6]
  which hangs above the mid-point of the fosse.
O Sovereign Wisdom, how Thine art doth shine          10

the passage as an example of immoderate flattery, and Dante's conception of Thaïs probably springs from this source. (*De Amicitia*, 26.)    5. Simon the Samarian magician (see *Acts* viii, 9–24) from whom the word "Simony" derives. Upon his conversion to Christianity he offered to buy the power to administer the Holy Ghost and was severely rebuked by Peter.    6. The Center point, obviously the best observation point. *The next grave:* The next *bolgia*.

in Heaven, on Earth, and in the Evil World![7]
How justly doth Thy power judge and assign!
I saw along the walls and on the ground
   long rows of holes cut in the livid stone;
   all were cut to a size, and all were round.           15
They seemed to be exactly the same size
   as those in the font of my beautiful San Giovanni,
   built to protect the priests who come to baptize;[8]
(one of which, not so long since, I broke open
   to rescue a boy who was wedged and drowning in it.    20
   Be this enough to undeceive all men.)[9]
From every mouth a sinner's legs stuck out
   as far as the calf. The soles were all ablaze
   and the joints of the legs quivered and writhed about.
Withes and tethers would have snapped in their throes.    25
   As oiled things blaze upon the surface only,
   so did they burn from the heels to the points of their toes.
"Master," I said, "who is that one in the fire
   who writhes and quivers more than all the others?[1]
   From him the ruddy flames seem to leap higher."      30
And he to me: "If you wish me to carry you down
   along that lower bank, you may learn from him
   who he is, and the evil he has done."
And I: "What you will, I will. You are my lord
   and know I depart in nothing from your wish;      35
   and you know my mind beyond my spoken word."
We moved to the fourth ridge, and turning left
   my Guide descended by a jagged path
   into the strait and perforated cleft.
Thus the good Master bore me down the dim      40
   and rocky slope, and did not put me down
   till we reached the one whose legs did penance for him.
"Whoever you are, sad spirit," I began,
   "who lie here with your head below your heels
   and planted like a stake—speak if you can."      45
I stood like a friar who gives the sacrament
   to a hired assassin, who, fixed in the hole,

7. Hell.   8. It was the custom in Dante's time to baptize only on Holy Saturday and on Pen-
tecost. These occasions were naturally thronged, therefore, and to protect the priests a special font
was built in the Baptistry of San Giovanni with marble stands for the priests, who were thus
protected from both the crowds and the water in which they immersed those to be baptized. The
Baptistry is still standing, but the font is no longer in it. A similar font still exists, however, in the
Baptistry at Pisa.   9. In these lines Dante is replying to a charge of sacrilege that had been
rumored against him. One day a boy playing in the baptismal font became jammed in the marble
tube and could not be extricated. To save the boy from drowning, Dante took it upon himself to
smash the tube.   1. The fire is proportioned to the guilt of the sinner. These are obviously the
feet of the chief sinner of this *bolgia*. In a moment we shall discover that he is Pope Nicholas III.

recalls him, and delays his death a moment.[2]
"Are you there already, Boniface?[3] Are you there
    already?" he cried. "By several years the writ          50
    has lied. And all that gold, and all that care—
are you already sated with the treasure
    for which you dared to turn on the Sweet Lady
    and trick and pluck and bleed her at your pleasure?"
I stood like one caught in some raillery,          55
    not understanding what is said to him,
    lost for an answer to such mockery.
Then Virgil said. "Say to him: 'I am not he,
    I am not who you think.' " And I replied
    as my good Master had instructed me.          60
The sinner's feet jerked madly; then again
    his voice rose, this time choked with sighs and tears,
    and said at last: "What do you want of me then?
If to know who I am drives you so fearfully
    that you descend the bank to ask it, know          65
    that the Great Mantle[4] was once hung upon me.
And in truth I was a son of the She-Bear,[5]
    so sly and eager to push my whelps ahead,
    that I pursed wealth above, and myself here.[6]
Beneath my head are dragged all who have gone          70
    before me in buying and selling holy office;
    there they cower in fissures of the stone.
I too shall be plunged down when that great cheat
    for whom I took you comes here in his turn.
    Longer already have I baked my feet          75
and been planted upside-down, than he shall be
    before the west sends down a lawless Shepherd[7]
    of uglier deeds to cover him and me.
He will be a new Jason of the Maccabees;

---

2. Persons convicted of murdering for hire were sometimes executed by being buried alive upside down. If the friar were called back at the last moment, he should have to bend over the hole in which the man is fixed upside down awaiting the first shovelful of earth.   3. The speaker is Pope Nicholas III, Giovanni Gaetano degli Orsini, Pope from 1277–1280. His presence here is self-explanatory. He is awaiting the arrival of his successor, Boniface VIII, who will take his place in the stone tube and who will in turn be replaced by Clement V, a Pope even more corrupt than Boniface. With the foresight of the damned he had read the date of Boniface's death (1303) in the Book of Fate. Mistaking Dante for Boniface, he thinks his foresight has erred by three years, since it is now 1300.   4. Of the Papacy.   5. Nicholas' family name, degli Orsini, means in Italian "of the bear cubs."   6. A play on the second meaning of *bolgia* (i.e., "purse"). "Just as I put wealth in my purse when alive, so am I put in this foul purse now that I am dead."   7. Clement V, Pope from 1305 to 1314. He came from Gascony (the West) and was involved in many intrigues with the King of France. It was Clement V who moved the Papal See to Avignon where it remained until 1377. He is compared to Jason (see *Maccabees* iv, 7ff.) who bought an appointment as High Priest of the Jews from King Antiochus and thereupon introduced pagan and venal practices into the office in much the same way as Clement used his influence with Philip of France to secure and corrupt his high office. Clement will succeed Boniface in Hell because Boniface's successor, Benedictus XI (1303–1304), was a good and holy man.

and just as that king bent to his high priests' will,          80
so shall the French king do as this one please."
Maybe—I cannot say—I grew too brash
 at this point, for when he had finished speaking
 I said: "Indeed! Now tell me how much cash
our Lord required of Peter in guarantee          85
 before he put the keys into his keeping?
 Surely he asked nothing but 'Follow me!'
Nor did Peter, nor the others, ask silver or gold
 of Matthew when they chose him for the place
 the despicable and damned apostle sold.[8]          90
Therefore stay as you are; this hole well fits you—
 and keep a good guard on the ill-won wealth
 that once made you so bold toward Charles of Anjou.[9]
And were it not that I am still constrained
 by the reverence I owe to the Great Keys[1]          95
 you held in life, I should not have refrained
from using other words and sharper still;
 for this avarice of yours grieves all the world,
 tramples the virtuous, and exalts the evil.
Of such as you was the Evangelist's[2] vision          100
 when he saw She who Sits upon the Waters
 locked with the Kings of earth in fornication.
She was born with seven heads and ten enormous
 and shining horns strengthened and made her glad
 as long as love and virtue pleased her spouse.          105
Gold and silver are the gods you adore!
 In what are you different from the idolator,
 save that he worships one, and you a score?
Ah Constantine, what evil marked the hour—
 not of your conversion, but of the fee
 the first rich Father[3] took from you in dower!"          110

8. Upon the expulsion of Judas from the band of Apostles, Matthias was chosen in his place.
9. The seventh son of Louis VIII of France. Charles became King of Naples and of Sicily largely through the good offices of Pope Urban IV and later of Clement IV. Nicholas III withdrew the high favor his predecessors had shown Charles, but the exact nature and extent of his opposition are open to dispute. Dante probably believed, as did many of his contemporaries, that Nicholas instigated the massacre called the Sicilian Vespers, in which the Sicilians overthrew the rule of Charles and held a general slaughter of the French who had been their masters. The Sicilian Vespers, however, was a popular and spontaneous uprising, and it did not occur until Nicholas had been dead for two years.   1. Of the Papacy.   2. St. John the Evangelist. His vision of She who sits upon the waters is set forth in *Revelations* xvii. The Evangelist intended it as a vision of Pagan Rome, but Dante interprets it as a vision of the Roman Church in its simoniacal corruption. The seven heads are the seven sacraments; the ten horns, the ten commandments.
3. Silvester (Pope from 314 to 355). Before him the Popes possessed nothing, but when Constantine was converted and Catholicism became the official religion of the Empire, the church began to acquire wealth. Dante and the scholars of his time believed, according to a document called "The Donation of Constantine," that the Emperor had moved his Empire to the East in order to leave sovereignty of the West to the Church. The document was not shown to be a forgery until the fifteenth century.

And as I sang him this tune, he began to twitch
   and kick both feet out wildly, as if in rage
   or gnawed by conscience—little matter which.
And I think, indeed, it pleased my Guide: his look       115
   was all approval as he stood beside me
   intent upon each word of truth I spoke.
He approached, and with both arms he lifted me,
   and when he had gathered me against his breast,
   remounted the rocky path out of the valley,       120
nor did he tire of holding me clasped to him,
   until we reached the topmost point of the arch
   which crosses from the fourth to the fifth rim
of the pits of woe. Arrived upon the bridge,
   he tenderly set down the heavy burden       125
   he had been pleased to carry up that ledge
which would have been hard climbing for a goat.
Here I looked down on still another moat.

CANTO XX

*Circle Eight: Bolgia Four    The Fortune Tellers and Diviners*

Dante stands in the middle of the bridge over the Fourth Bolgia
and looks down at the souls of the Fortune Tellers and Diviners.
Here are the souls of all those who attempted by forbidden arts to
look into the future. Among these damned are: Amphiareus, Tiresias, Aruns, Manto, Eurypylus, Michael Scott, Guido Bonatti, and
Asdente.

Characteristically, the sin of these wretches is reversed upon them:
their punishment is to have their heads turned backwards on their
bodies and to be compelled to walk backwards through all eternity,
their eyes blinded with tears. Thus, those who sought to penetrate
the future cannot even see in front of themselves; they attempted to
move themselves forward in time, so must they go backwards through
all eternity; and as the arts of sorcery are a distortion of God's law, so
are their bodies distorted in Hell.

No more need be said of them: Dante names them, and passes on
to fill the Canto with a lengthy account of the founding of Virgil's
native city of Mantua.

Now must I sing new griefs, and my verses strain
   to form the matter of the Twentieth Canto
   of Canticle One,[4] the Canticle of Pain.
My vantage point[5] permitted a clear view

---

4. *The Inferno.* The other Canticles are, of course, *The Purgatorio* and *The Paradiso.*   5. Virgil,
it will be recalled, had set Dante down on the bridge across the Fourth Bolgia.

of the depths of the pit below: a desolation                          5
   bathed with the tears of its tormented crew,
who moved about the circle of the pit
   at' about the pace of a litany procession.[6]
   Silent and weeping, they wound round and round it.
And when I looked down from their faces,[7] I saw                     10
   that each of them was hideously distorted
   between the top of the chest and the lines of the jaw;
for the face was reversed on the neck, and they came on
   backwards, staring backwards at their loins,[8]
   for to look before them was forbidden. Someone,                    15
sometime, in the grip of a palsy may have been
   distorted so, but never to my knowledge;
   nor do I believe the like was ever seen.
Reader, so may God grant you to understand
   my poem and profit from it, ask yourself                           20
   how I could check my tears, when near at hand
I saw the image of our humanity
   distorted so that the tears that burst from their eyes
   ran down the cleft of their buttocks. Certainly
I wept. I leaned against the jagged face                              25
   of a rock and wept so that my Guide said: "Still?
   Still like the other fools? There is no place
for pity here. Who is more arrogant
   within his soul, who is more impious
   than one who dares to sorrow at God's judgment?                    30
Lift up your eyes, lift up your eyes and see
   him the earth swallowed before all the Thebans,
   at which they cried out: 'Whither do you flee,
Amphiareus?[9] Why do you leave the field?'
   And he fell headlong through the gaping earth                      35
   to the feet of Minos, where all sin must yield.
Observe how he has made a breast of his back.
   In life he wished to see too far before him,
   and now he must crab backwards round this track.
And see Tiresias,[1] who by his arts                                  40

6. The litanies are chanted not only in church (before the mass), but sometimes in procession,
the priest chanting the prayers and the marchers the response. As one might gather from the
context, the processions move very slowly.    7. A typically Dantean conception. Dante often
writes as if the eye pin-pointed on one feature of a figure seen at a distance. The pin-point must
then be deliberately shifted before the next feature can be observed. As far as I know, this stylistic
device is peculiar to Dante.    8. General usage seems to have lost sight of the fact that the first
meaning of "loin" is "that part of a human being or quadruped on either side of the spinal column
between the hipbone and the false ribs." (Webster.)    9. Another of the seven Captains who
fought against Thebes (v. Capaneus, Canto XIV). Statius (*Thebaid* VII, 690 ff. and VIII, 8 ff.)
tells how he foresaw his own death in this war, and attempted to run away from it, but was
swallowed in his flight by an earthquake. I have Romanized his name from "Amphiaraus."
1. A Theban diviner and magician. Ovid (*Metamorphoses* III) tells how he came on two twined
serpents, struck them apart with his stick, and was thereupon transformed into a woman. Seven
years later he came on two serpents similarly entwined, struck them apart, and was changed back.

succeeded in changing himself from man to woman,
    transforming all his limbs and all his parts;
later he had to strike the two twined serpents
    once again with his conjurer's wand before
    he could resume his manly lineaments.                          45
And there is Aruns,[2] his back to that one's belly,
    the same who in the mountains of the Luni
    tilled by the people of Carrara's valley,
made a white marble cave his den, and there
    with unobstructed view observed the sea                         50
    and the turning constellations year by year.
And she whose unbound hair flows back to hide
    her breasts—which you cannot see—and who also wears
    all of her hairy parts on that other side,
was Manto, who searched contries far and near,                      55
    then settled where I was born.[3] In that connection
    there is a story I would have you hear.
Tiresias was her sire. After his death,
    Thebes, the city of Bacchus, became enslaved,
    and for many years she roamed about the earth.                  60
High in sweet Italy, under the Alps that shut
    the Tyrolean gate of Germany, there lies
    a lake known as Benacus[4] roundabout.
Through endless falls, more than a thousand and one,
    Mount Appennine from Garda to Val Cammonica                     65
    is freshened by the waters that flow down
into the lake. At its center is a place
    where the Bishops of Brescia, Trentine, and Verona
    might all give benediction with equal grace.
Peschiera, the beautiful fortress, strong in war                    70
    against the Brescians and the Bergamese,
    sits at the lowest point along that shore.
There, the waters Benacus cannot hold
    within its bosom, spill and form a river
    that winds away through pastures green and gold.                75
But once the water gathers its full flow,
    it is called Mincius rather than Benacus
    from there to Governo, where it joins the Po.

---

2. An Etruscan soothsayer (see Lucan, *Pharsalia*, I, 580 ff.) He foretold the war between Pompey
and Julius Caesar, and also that it would end with Caesar's victory and Pompey's death. *Luni:*
Also *Luna.* An ancient Etruscan city. *Carrara's valley:* The Carrarese valley is famous for its
white (Carrara) marble.    3. Dante's version of the founding of Mantua is based on a reference
in the *Aeneid* X, 198–200.    4. The ancient name for the famous Lago di Garda, which lies a
short distance north of Mantua. The other places named in this passage lie around Lago di Garda.
On an island in the lake the three dioceses mentioned in line 68 conjoined. All three bishops,
therefore, had jurisdiction on the island.

Still near its source, it strikes a plain, and there
   it slows and spreads, forming an ancient marsh      80
   which in the summer heats pollutes the air.
The terrible virgin, passing there by chance,
   saw dry land at the center of the mire,
   untilled, devoid of all inhabitants.
There, shunning all communion with mankind,      85
   she settled with the ministers of her arts,
   and there she lived, and there she left behind
her vacant corpse. Later the scattered men
   who lived nearby assembled on that spot
   since it was well defended by the fen.      90
Over those whited bones they raised the city,
   and for her who had chosen the place before all others
   they named it—with no further augury—
Mantua. Far more people lived there once—
   before sheer madness prompted Casalodi      95
   to let Pinamonte play him for a dunce.[5]
Therefore, I charge you, should you ever hear
   other accounts of this, to let no falsehood
   confuse the truth which I have just made clear."
And I to him: "Master, within my soul      100
   your word is certainty, and any other
   would seem like the dead lumps of burned out coal.
But tell me of those people moving down
   to join the rest. Are any worth my noting?
   For my mind keeps coming back to that alone."      105
And he: "That one whose beard spreads like a fleece
   over his swarthy shoulders, was an augur
   in the days when so few males remained in Greece
that even the cradles were all but empty of sons.
   He chose the time for cutting the cable at Aulis,      110
   and Calchas joined him in those divinations.
He is Eurypylus.[6] I sing him somewhere
   in my High Tragedy; you will know the place
   who know the whole of it. The other there,
the one beside him with the skinny shanks      115

5. Albert, Count of Casalodi and Lord of Mantua, let himself be persuaded by Pinamonte de Buonaccorsi to banish the nobles from Mantua as a source of danger to his rule. Once the nobles had departed, Pinamonte headed a rebellion against the weakened lord and took over the city himself.    6. According to Greek custom an augur was summoned before each voyage to choose the exact propitious moment for departure (cutting the cables). Dante has Virgil imply that Eurypylus and Calchas were selected to choose the moment for Agamemnon's departure from Aulis to Troy. Actually, according to the *Aeneid*, Eurypylus was not at Aulis. The *Aeneid* (II, 110 ff.) tells how Eurypylus and Calchas were both consulted in choosing the moment for the departure from Troy. Dante seems to have confused the two incidents. *Even the cradles were all but empty of sons*: At the time of the Trojan Wars, Greece was said to be so empty of males that scarcely any were to be found even in the cradles.

was Michael Scott,[7] who mastered every trick
    of magic fraud, a prince of mountebanks.
See Guido Bonatti[8] there; and see Asdente,
    who now would be wishing he had stuck to his last,
    but repents too late, though he repents aplenty.          120
And see on every hand the wretched hags
    who left their spinning and sewing for soothsaying
    and casting of spells with herbs, and dolls, and rags.
But come: Cain with his bush of thorns[9] appears
    already on the wave below Seville,                        125
    above the boundary of the hemispheres;
and the moon was full already yesternight.
    as you must well remember from the wood,
    for it certainly did not harm you when its light
shone down upon your way before the dawn."                   130
And as he spoke to me, we traveled on.


### CANTO XXI

*Circle Eight: Bolgia Five    The Grafters*

The Poets move on, talking as they go, and arrive at the Fifth
Bolgia. Here the Grafters are sunk in boiling pitch and guarded by
Demons, who tear them to pieces with claws and grappling hooks if
they catch them above the surface of the pitch.

The sticky pitch is symbolic of the sticky fingers of the Grafters. It
serves also to hide them from sight, as their sinful dealings on earth
were hidden from men's eyes. The demons, too, suggest symbolic
possibilities, for they are armed with grappling hooks and are forever
ready to rend and tear all they can get their hands on.

The Poets watch a demon arrive with a grafting Senator of Lucca
and fling him into the pitch where the demons set upon him.

To protect Dante from their wrath, Virgil hides him behind some
jagged rocks and goes ahead alone to negotiate with the demons.
They set upon him like a pack of mastiffs, but Virgil secures a safe-
conduct from their leader, Malacoda. Thereupon Virgil calls Dante
from hiding, and they are about to set off when they discover that
the Bridge Across the Sixth Bolgia lies shattered. Malacoda tells them
there is another further on and sends a squad of demons to escort

7. An Irish scholar of the first half of the thirteenth century. His studies were largely in the occult.
Sir Walter Scott refers to him in *The Lay of the Last Minstrel.*    8. A thirteenth-century astrologer of Forli. He was court astrologer to Guido da Montefeltro (see Canto XXVII) advising him
in his wars. *Asdente:* A shoemaker of Parma who turned diviner and won wide fame for his
forecastings in the last half of the thirteenth century.    9. The Moon. Cain with a bush of thorns
was the medieval equivalent of our Man in the Moon. Dante seems to mean by "Seville" the
whole area of Spain and the Straits of Gibraltar (Pillars of Hercules), which were believed to be
the western limit of the world. The moon is setting (i.e., it appears on the western waves) on the
morning of Holy Saturday, 1300.

them. Their adventures with the demons continue through the next
Canto.

These two Cantos may conveniently be remembered as the Gargoyle Cantos. If the total *Commedia* is built like a cathedral (as so
many critics have suggested), it is here certainly that Dante attaches
his grotesqueries. At no other point in the *Commedia* does Dante
give such free rein to his coarsest style.

Thus talking of things which my Comedy does not care
    to sing, we passed from one arch to the next
    until we stood upon its summit. There
we checked our steps to study the next fosse
    and the next vain lamentations of Malebolge;      5
    awesomely dark and desolate it was.
As in the Venetian arsenal,[1] the winter through
    there boils the sticky pitch to caulk the seams
    of the sea-battered bottoms when no crew
can put to sea—instead of which, one starts      10
    to build its ship anew, one plugs the planks
    which have been sprung in many foreign parts;
some hammer at a mast, some at a rib;
    some make new oars, some braid and coil new lines;
    one patches up the mainsail, one the jib—      15
so, but by Art Divine and not by fire,
    a viscid pitch boiled in the fosse below
    and coated all the bank with gluey mire.
I saw the pitch; but I saw nothing in it
    except the enormous bubbles of its boiling,      20
    which swelled and sank, like breathing, through all the pit.
And as I stood and stared into that sink,
    my Master cried, "Take care!" and drew me back
    from my exposed position on the brink.
I turned like one who cannot wait to see      25
    the thing he dreads, and who, in sudden fright,
    runs while he looks, his curiosity
competing with his terror—and at my back
    I saw a figure that came running toward us
    across the ridge, a Demon huge and black.      30
Ah what a face he had, all hate and wildness!
    Galloping so, with his great wings outspread
    he seemed the embodiment of all bitterness.
Across each high-hunched shoulder he had thrown
    one haunch of a sinner, whom he held in place      35
    with a great talon round each ankle bone.

1. The arsenal was not only an arms manufactory but a great center of shipbuilding and
repairing.

"Blacktalons² of our bridge," he began to roar,
   "I bring you one of Santa Zita's³ Elders!
   Scrub him down while I go back for more:
I planted a harvest of them in that city:                40
   everyone there is a grafter except Bonturo.⁴
   There 'Yes' is 'No' and 'No' is 'Yes' for a fee."
Down the sinner plunged, and at once the Demon
   spun from the cliff; no mastiff ever sprang
   more eager from the leash to chase a felon.          45
Down plunged the sinner and sank to reappear
   with his backside arched and his face and both his feet
   glued to the pitch, almost as if in prayer.
But the Demons under the bridge, who guard that place
   and the sinners who are thrown to them, bawled out:     50
   "You're out of bounds here for the Sacred Face:⁵
this is no dip in the Serchio: take your look
   and then get down in the pitch. And stay below
   unless you want a taste of a grappling hook."
Then they raked him with more than a hundred hooks     55
   bellowing: "Here you dance below the covers.
   Graft all you can there: no one checks your books."
They dipped him down into that pitch exactly
   as a chef makes scullery boys dip meat in a boiler,
   holding it with their hooks from floating free.         60
And the Master said: "*You* had best not be seen⁶
   by these Fiends till I am ready. Crouch down here.
   One of these rocks will serve you as a screen.
And whatever violence you see done to me,
   you have no cause to fear. I know these matters:      65
   I have been through this once and come back safely."
With that, he walked on past the end of the bridge;
   and it wanted all his courage to look calm
   from the moment he arrived on the sixth ridge.
With that same storm and fury that arouses          70
   all the house when the hounds leap at a tramp

---

2. The original is Malebranche, i.e., "Evil Claws."    3. The patron saint of the city of Lucca. "One of Santa Zita's Elders" would therefore equal "One of Lucca's Senators" (i.e., Aldermen). Commentators have searched the records of Luccan Aldermen who died on Holy Saturday of 1300, and one Martino Bottaio has been suggested as the newcomer, but there is no evidence that Dante had a specific man in mind. More probably he meant simply to underscore the fact that Lucca was a city of grafters, just as Bologna was represented as a city of panderers and seducers. 4. Bonturo Dati, a politician of Lucca. The phrase is ironic: Bonturo was the most avid grafter of them all.    5. *Il volto santo* was an ancient wooden image of Christ venerated by the Luccanese. These ironies and the grotesqueness of the Elder's appearance mark the beginning of the gargoyle dance that swells and rolls through this Canto and the next. *Serchio*: A river near Lucca.    6. It is only in the passage through this Bolgia, out of the total journey, that Dante presents himself as being in physical danger. Since his dismissal from office and his exile from Florence (on pain of death if he return) was based on a false charge of grafting, the reference is pointedly autobiographical.

who suddenly falls to pleading where he pauses—
so rushed those Fiends from below, and all the pack
    pointed their gleaming pitchforks at my Guide.
    But he stood fast and cried to them: "Stand back!        75
Before those hooks and grapples make too free,
    send up one of your crew to hear me out,
    then ask yourselves if you still care to rip me."
All cried as one: "Let Malacoda[7] go."
    So the pack stood and one of them came forward,       80
    saying: "What good does he think *this* will do?"
"Do you think, Malacoda," my good Master said,
    "you would see me here, having arrived this far
    already, safe from you and every dread,
without Divine Will and propitious Fate?       85
    Let me pass on, for it is willed in Heaven
    that I must show another this dread state."
The Demon stood there on the flinty brim,
    so taken aback he let his pitchfork drop;
    then said to the others: "Take care not to harm him!"    90
"O you crouched like a cat," my Guide called to me,
    "among the jagged rock piles of the bridge,
    come down to me, for now you may come safely."
Hearing him, I hurried down the ledge;
    and the Demons all pressed forward when I appeared,    95
    so that I feared they might not keep their pledge.
So once I saw the Pisan infantry
    march out under truce from the fortress at Caprona,
    staring in fright at the ranks of the enemy.[8]
I pressed the whole of my body against my Guide,    100
    and not for an instant did I take my eyes
    from those black fiends who scowled on every side.
They swung their forks saying to one another:
    "Shall I give him a touch in the rump?" and answering:
    "Sure; give him a taste to pay him for his bother."    105
But the Demon who was talking to my Guide
    turned round and cried to him: "At ease there, Snatcher!"
    And then to us: "There's no road on this side:

7. The name equals "Bad Tail," or "Evil Tail." He is the captain of these grim and semi-military police. I have not translated his name as I have those of the other fiends, since I cannot see that it offers any real difficulty to an English reader.    8. A Tuscan army attacked the fortress of Caprona near Pisa in 1289 and after fierce fighting the Pisan defenders were promised a safe-conduct if they would surrender. Dante was probably serving with the Tuscans (the opening lines of the next Canto certainly suggest that he had seen military service). In some accounts it is reported that the Tuscans massacred the Pisans despite their promised safe-conduct—an ominous analogy if true. In any case the emerging Pisans would be sufficiently familiar with the treacheries of Italian politics to feel profoundly uneasy at being surrounded by their enemies under such conditions.

the arch lies all in pieces in the pit.
   If you *must* go on, follow along this ridge;         110
   there's another cliff to cross by just beyond it.[9]
In just five hours it will be, since the bridge fell,
   a thousand two hundred sixty-six years and a day;[1]
   that was the time the big quake shook all Hell.
I'll send a squad of my boys along that way         115
   to see if anyone's airing himself below:
   you can go with them: there will be no foul play.
Front and center here, Grizzly and Hellken,"
   he began to order them. "You too, Deaddog.
   Curlybeard, take charge of a squad of ten.         120
Take Grafter and Dragontooth along with you.
   Pigtusk, Catclaw, Cramper, and Crazyred.
   Keep a sharp lookout on the boiling glue
as you move along, and see that these gentlemen
   are not molested until they reach the crag         125
   where they can find a way across the den."
"In the name of heaven, Master," I cried, "what sort
   of guides are these? Let us go on alone
   if you know the way. Who can trust such an escort!
If you are as wary as you used to be         130
   you surely see them grind their teeth at us,
   and knot their beetle brows so threateningly."
And he: "I do not like this fear in you.
   Let them gnash and knot as they please; they menace only    135
   the sticky wretches simmering in that stew."
They turned along the left bank in a line;
   but before they started, all of them together
   had stuck their pointed tongues out as a sign
to their Captain that they wished permission to pass,
   and he had made a trumpet of his ass.         140

### CANTO XXII

*Circle Eight: Bolgia Five     The Grafters*

   The poets set off with their escorts of demons. Dante sees the
Grafters lying in the pitch like frogs in water with only their muzzles

9. Malacoda is lying, as the Poets will discover: all the bridges across the Sixth Bolgia have fallen as a result of the earthquake that shook Hell at the death of Christ.     1. Christ died on Good Friday of the year 34, and it is now Holy Saturday of the year 1300, five hours before the hour of his death. Many commentators (and Dante himself in the *Convivio*) place the hour of Christ's death at exactly noon. Accordingly, it would now be 7:00 A.M. of Holy Saturday—exactly eight minutes since the Poets left the bridge over the Fourth Bolgia (at moonset). In the gospels of Matthew, Mark, and Luke, however, the hour of Christ's death is precisely stated as 3:00 P.M. Dante would certainly be familiar with the Synoptic Gospels, and on that authority it would now be 10:00 A.M.

out. They disappear as soon as they sight the demons and only a
ripple on the surface betrays their presence.

One of the Grafters, An Unidentified Navarrese, ducks too late
and is seized by the demons who are about to claw him, but Curlybeard holds them back while Virgil questions him. The wretch speaks
of his fellow sinners, Friar Gomita and Michel Zanche, while the
uncontrollable demons rake him from time to time with their hooks.

The Navarrese offers to lure some of his fellow sufferers into the
hands of the demons, and when his plan is accepted he plunges into
the pitch and escapes. Hellken and Grizzly fly after him, but too
late. They start a brawl in mid-air and fall into the pitch themselves.
Curlybeard immediately organizes a rescue party and the Poets, fearing the bad temper of the frustrated demons, take advantage of the
confusion to slip away.

I have seen horsemen breaking camp. I have seen
   the beginning of the assault, the march and muster,
   and at times the retreat and riot. I have been
where chargers trampled your land, O Aretines![2]
   I have seen columns of foragers, shocks of tourney,          5
   and running of tilts.[3] I have seen the endless lines
march to bells,[4] drums, trumpets, from far and near.
   I have seen them march on signals from a castle.[5]
   I have seen them march with native and foreign gear.
But never yet have I seen horse or foot,                        10
   nor ship in range of land nor sight of star,
   take its direction from so low a toot.
We went with the ten Fiends—ah, savage crew!—
   but "In church with saints; with stewpots in the tavern,"
   as the old proverb wisely bids us do.                        15
All my attention was fixed upon the pitch:
   to observe the people who were boiling in it,
   and the customs and the punishments of that ditch.
As dolphins surface and begin to flip
   their arched backs from the sea, warning the sailors          20
   to fall-to and begin to secure ship—[6]
So now and then, some soul, to ease his pain.
   showed us a glimpse of his back above the pitch

2. The people of Arezzo. In 1289 the Guelphs of Florence and Lucca defeated the Ghibellines
of Arrezo at Campaldino. Dante was present with the Guelphs, though probably as an observer
and not as a warrior.    3. A tourney was contested by groups of knights in a field; a tilt by
individuals who tried to unhorse one another across a barrier.    4. The army of each town was
equipped with a chariot on which bells were mounted. Signals could be given by the bells and
special decorations made the chariot stand out in battle. It served therefore as a rallying point.
5. When troops were in sight of their castle their movements could be directed from the towers—
by banners in daytime and by fires at night, much as some naval signals are still given today.
6. It was a common belief that when dolphins began to leap around a ship they were warning the
sailors of an approaching storm.

and quick as lightning disappeared again.
And as, at the edge of a ditch, frogs squat about                    25
   hiding their feet and bodies in the water,
   leaving only their muzzles sticking out—
so stood the sinners in that dismal ditch;
   but as Curlybeard approached, only a ripple
   showed where they had ducked back into the pitch.                    30
I saw—the dread of it haunts me to this day—
   one linger a bit too long, as it sometimes happens
   one frog remains when another spurts away;
and Catclaw, who was nearest, ran a hook
   through the sinner's pitch hair and hauled him in.                    35
   He looked like an otter dripping from the brook.
I knew the names of all the Fiends by then;
   I had made a note of them at the first muster,
   and, marching, had listened and checked them over again.
"Hey, Crazyred," the crew of Demons cried                    40
   all together, "give him a taste of your claws.
   Dig him open a little. Off with his hide."
And I then: "Master, can you find out, please,
   the name and history of that luckless one
   who has fallen into the hands of his enemies?"                    45
My Guide approached that wraith from the hot tar
   and asked him whence he came. The wretch replied:
   "I was born and raised in the Kingdom of Navarre.
My mother placed me in service to a knight;
   for she had borne me to a squanderer                    50
   who killed himself when he ran through his birthright.
Then I became a domestic in the service
   of good King Thibault.[7] There I began to graft,
   and I account for it in this hot crevice."
And Pigtusk, who at the ends of his lower lip                    55
   shot forth two teeth more terrible than a boar's,
   made the wretch feel how one of them could rip.
The mouse had come among bad cats, but here
   Curlybeard locked arms around him crying:
   "While I've got hold of him the rest stand clear!"                    60
And turning his face to my Guide: "If you want to ask him
   anything else," he added, "ask away
   before the others tear him limb from limb."
And my Guide to the sinner; "I should like to know
   if among the other souls beneath the pitch                    65

7. Thibault II was King of Navarre, a realm that lay in what is now northern Spain.

are any Italians'?"[8] And the wretch: "Just now
I left a shade who came from parts near by.
  Would I were still in the pitch with him, for then
  these hooks would not be giving me cause to cry."
And suddenly Grafter bellowed in great heat:                    70
  "We've stood enough!" And he hooked the sinner's arm
  and, ranking it, ripped off a chunk of meat.
Then Dragontooth wanted to play, too, reaching down
  for a catch at the sinner's legs; but Curlybeard
  wheeled round and round with a terrifying frown,            75
and when the Fiends had somewhat given ground
  and calmed a little, my Guide, without delay,
  asked the wretch, who was staring at his wound:
"Who was the sinner from whom you say you made
  your evil-starred departure to come ashore                  80
  among these Fiends?" And the wretch: "It was the shade
of Friar Gomita of Gallura,[9] the crooked stem
  of every Fraud: when his master's enemies
  were in his hands, he won high praise from them.
He took their money without case or docket,                   85
  and let them go. He was in all his dealings
  no petty bursar, but a kingly pocket.
With him, his endless crony in the fosse,
  is Don Michel Zanche of Logodoro;[1]
  they babble about Sardinia wihout pause.                    90
But look! See that fiend grinning at your side!
  There is much more that I should like to tell you,
  but oh, I think he means to grate my hide!"
But their grim sergeant wheeled, sensing foul play,
  and turning on Cramper, who seemed set to strike,           95
  ordered: "Clear off, you buzzard. Clear off, I say!"
"If either of you would like to see and hear
  Tuscans or Lombards," the pale sinner said,
  "I can lure them out of hiding if you'll stand clear
and let me sit here at the edge of the ditch,                 100
  and get all these Blacktalons out of sight;

8. Dante uses the term *Latino* strictly speaking, a person from the area of ancient Latium, now (roughly) Lazio, the province in which Rome is located. It was against the Latians that Aeneas fought on coming to Italy. More generally, Dante uses the term for any southern Italian. Here, however, the usage seems precise, since the sinner refers to "points near by" and means Sardinia. Rome is the point in Italy closest to Sardinia.    9. In 1300 Sardinia was a Pisan possession, and was divided into four districts, of which Gallura was the northeast. Friar Gomita administered Gallura for his own considerable profit. He was hanged by the Pisan governor when he was found guilty of taking bribes to let prisoners escape.    1. He was made Vicar of Logodoro when the King of Sardinia went off to war. The King was captured and did not return. Michel maneuvered a divorce for the Queen and married her himself. About 1290 he was murdered by his son-in-law, Branca d'Oria (see Canto XXXIII).

for while they're here, no one will leave the pitch.
In exchange for myself, I can fish you up as pretty
   a mess of souls as you like. I have only to whistle
   the way we do when one of us gets free."          105
Deaddog raised his snout as he listened to him;
   then, shaking his head, said, "Listen to the grafter
   spinning his tricks so he can jump from the brim!"
And the sticky wretch, who was all treachery:
   "Oh I am more than tricky when there's a chance        110
   to see my friends in greater misery."
Hellken, against the will of all the crew,
   could hold no longer. "If you jump," he said
   to the scheming wretch, "I won't come after you
at a gallop, but like a hawk after a mouse.        115
   We'll clear the edge and hide behind the bank:
   let's see if you're trickster enough for all of us."
Reader, here is new game! The Fiends withdrew
   from the bank's edge, and Deaddog, who at first
   was most against it, led the savage crew.        120
The Navarrese chose his moment carefully:
   and planting both his feet against the ground,
   he leaped, and in an instant he was free.
The Fiends were stung with shame, and of the lot
   Hellken most, who had been the cause of it.        125
   He leaped out madly bellowing: "You're caught!"
but little good it did him; terror pressed
   harder than wings; the sinner dove from sight
   and the Fiend in full flight had to raise his breast.
A duck, when the falcon dives, will disappear        130
   exactly so, all in a flash, while he
   returns defeated and weary up the air.
Grizzly, in a rage at the sinner's flight,
   flew after Hellken, hoping the wraith would escape,
   so he might find an excuse to start a fight.        135
And as soon as the grafter sank below the pitch,
   Grizzly turned his talons against Hellken,
   locked with him claw to claw above the ditch.
But Hellken was sparrowhawk enough for two
   and clawed him well; and ripping one another,        140
   they plunged together into the hot stew.
The heat broke up the brawl immediately,
   but their wings were smeared with pitch and they could not rise.
   Curlybeard, upset as his company,
commanded four to fly to the other coast        145
   at once with all their grapples. At top speed

the Fiends divided, each one to his post.
Some on the near edge, some along the far,
   they stretched their hooks out to the clotted pair
   who were already cooked deep through the scar       150
of their first burn. And turning to one side
we slipped off, leaving them thus occupied.

CANTO XXIII

*Circle Eight: Bolgia Six   The Hypocrites*

    The Poets are pursued by the Fiends and escape them by sliding down the sloping bank of the next pit. They are now in the Sixth Bolgia. Here the Hypocrites, weighted down by great leaden robes, walk eternally round and round a narrow track. The robes are brilliantly gilded on the outside and are shaped like a monk's habit, for the hypocrite's outward appearance shines brightly and passes for holiness, but under that show lies the terrible weight of his deceit which the soul must bear through all eternity.

    The Poets talk to Two Jovial Friars and come upon Caiaphas, the chief sinner of that place. Caiaphas was the High Priest of the Jews who counseled the Pharisees to crucify Jesus in the name of public expedience. He is punished by being himself crucified to the floor of Hell by three great stakes, and in such a position that every passing sinner must walk upon him. Thus he must suffer upon his own body the weight of all the world's hypocrisy, as Christ suffered upon his body the pain of all the world's sins.

    The Jovial Friars tell Virgil how he may climb from the pit, and Virgil discovers that Malacoda lied to him about the bridges over the Sixth Bolgia.

Silent, apart, and unattended we went
   as Minor Friars go when they walk abroad,
   one following the other. The incident
recalled the fable of the Mouse and the Frog
   that Aesop tells.[2] For compared attentively     5
   point by point, "pig" is no closer to "hog"
than the one case to the other. And as one thought
   springs from another, so the comparison
   gave birth to a new concern, at which I caught

2. The fable was not by Aesop, but was attributed to him in Dante's time: A mouse comes to a body of water and wonders how to cross. A frog, thinking to drown the mouse, offers to ferry him, but the mouse is afraid he will fall off. The frog thereupon suggests that the mouse tie himself to one of the frog's feet. In this way they start across, but in the middle the frog dives from under the mouse, who struggles desperately to stay afloat while the frog tries to pull him under. A hawk sees the mouse struggling and swoops down and seizes him; but since the frog is tied to the mouse, it too is carried away, and so both of them are devoured. The mouse would be the Navarrese Grafter. The frog would be the two fiends, Grizzly and Hellken. By seeking to harm the Navarrese they came to grief themselves.

my breath in fear. This thought ran through my mind:          10
   "These Fiends, through us, have been made ridiculous,
   and have suffered insult and injury of a kind
to make them smart. Unless we take good care—
   now rage is added to their natural spleen—
   they will hunt us down as greyhounds hunt the hare."      15
Already I felt my scalp grow tight with fear.
   I was staring back in terror as I said:
   "Master, unless we find concealment here
and soon, I dread the rage of the Fiends: already
   they are yelping on our trail: I imagine them              20
   so vividly I can hear them now." And he:
"Were I a pane of leaded glass,³ I could not
   summon your outward look more instantly
   into myself, than I do your inner thought.
Your fears were mixed already with my own                     25
   with the same suggestion and the same dark look;
   so that of both I form one resolution:
the right bank may be sloping: in that case
   we may find some way down to the next pit
   and so escape from the imagined chase."                    30
He had not finished answering me thus
   when, not far off, their giant wings outspread,
   I saw the Fiends come charging after us.
Seizing me instantly in his arms, my Guide—
   like a mother wakened by a midnight noise                  35
   to find a wall of flame at her bedside
(who takes her child and runs, and more concerned
   for him than for herself, does not pause even
   to throw a wrap about her) raised me, turned,
and down the rugged bank from the high summit                 40
   flung himself down supine onto the slope
   which walls the upper side of the next pit.
Water that turns the great wheel of a land-mill
   never ran faster through the end of a sluice
   at the point nearest the paddles⁴—as down that hill       45
my Guide and Master bore me on his breast,
   as if I were not a companion, but a son.
   And the soles of his feet had hardly come to rest
on the bed of the depth below, when on the height
   we had just left, the Fiends beat their great wings.       50

3. A mirror. Mirrors were backed with lead in Dante's time.    4. The sharp drop of the sluice makes the water run faster at the point at which it hits the wheel. *Land-mill:* As distinguished from the floating mills common in Dante's time and up to the advent of the steam engine. These were built on rafts that were anchored in the swift-flowing rivers of Northern Italy.

But now they gave my Guide no cause for fright;
for the Providence that gave them the fifth pit
    to govern as the ministers of Its will,
    takes from their souls the power of leaving it,
About us now in the depth of the pit we found        55
    a painted people, weary and defeated.
    Slowly, in pain, they paced it round and round.
All wore great cloaks cut to as ample a size
    as those worn by the Benedictines of Cluny.[5]
    The enormous hoods were drawn over their eyes.    60
The outside is all dazzle, golden and fair;
    the inside, lead, so heavy that Frederick's capes,[6]
    compared to these, would seem as light as air.
O weary mantle for eternity!
    We turned to the left again along their course,    65
    listening to their moans of misery,
but they moved so slowly down that barren strip,
    tired by their burden, that our company
    was changed at every movement of the hip.
And walking thus, I said: "As we go on,    70
    may it please you to look about among these people
    for any whose name or history may be known."
And one who understood Tuscan cried to us there
    as we hurried past: "I pray you check your speed.
    you who run so fast through the sick air:    75
it may be I am one who will fit your case."
    And at his words my Master turned and said:
    "Wait now, then go with him at his own pace."
I waited there, and saw along that track
    two souls who seemed in haste to be with me;    80
    but the narrow way and their burden held them back.
When they had reached me down that narrow way
    they stared at me in silence and amazement,
    then turned to one another. I heard one say:
"This one seems, by the motion of his throat,    85
    to be alive; and if they are dead, how is it
    they are allowed to shed the leaden coat?"
And then to me "O Tuscan, come so far
    to the college of the sorry hypocrites,
    do not disdain to tell us who you are."    90
And I: "I was born and raised a Florentine

5. The habit of these monks was especially ample and elegant. St. Bernard once wrote ironically
to a nephew who had entered this monastery: "If length of sleeves and amplitude of hood made
for holiness, what could hold me back from following [your lead]."    6. Frederick II executed
persons found guilty of treason by fastening them into a sort of leaden shell. The doomed man
was then placed in a cauldron over a fire and the lead was melted around him.

on the green and lovely banks of Arno's waters,
    I go with the body that was always mine.
But who are *you*, who sighing as you go
    distill in floods of tears that drown your cheeks?      95
    What punishment is this that glitters so?"
"These burnished robes are of thick lead," said one,
    "and are hung on us like counterweights, so heavy
    that we, their weary fulcrums, creak and groan.
Jovial Friars[7] and Bolognese were we.      100
    We were chosen jointly by your Florentines
    to keep the peace,[8] and office usually
held by a single man; near the Gardingo[9]
    one still may see the sort of peace we kept.
    I was called Catalano, he, Loderingo."      105
I began: "O Friars, your evil . . ."—and then I saw
    a figure crucified upon the ground[1]
    by three great stakes, and I fell still in awe.
When he saw me there, he began to puff great sighs
    into his beard, convulsing all his body;      110
    and Friar Catalano, following my eyes,
said to me: "That one nailed across the road
    counselled the Pharisees that it was fitting
    one man be tortured for the public good.
Naked he lies fixed there, as you see,      115
    in the path of all who pass; there he must feel
    the weight of all through all eternity.
His father-in-law[2] and the others of the Council
    which was a seed of wrath to all the Jews,
    are similarly staked for the same evil."      120
Then I saw Virgil marvel[3] for a while
    over that soul so ignominiously
    stretched on the cross in Hell's eternal exile.

7. A nickname given to the military monks of the order of the Glorious Virgin Mary founded at Bologna in 1261. Their original aim was to serve as peacemakers, enforcers of order, and protectors of the weak, but their observance of their rules became so scandalously lax, and their management of worldly affairs so self-seeking, that the order was disbanded by Papal decree. 8. Catalano dei Malavolti (c. 1210–1285), a Guelph, and Loderingo degli Andolo (c. 1210–1293), a Ghibelline, were both Bolognese and, as brothers of the Jovial Friars, both had served as *podestà* (the chief officer charged with keeping the peace) of many cities for varying terms. In 1266 they were jointly appointed to the office of *podestà* of Florence on the theory that a bipartisan administration by men of God would bring peace to the city. Their tenure of office was marked by great violence, however; and they were forced to leave in a matter of months. Modern scholarship has established the fact that they served as instruments of Clement IV's policy in Florence, working at his orders to overthrow the Ghibellines under the guise of an impartial administration.      9. The site of the palace of the Ghibelline family degli Uberti. In the riots resulting from the maladministration of the two Jovial Friars, the Ghibellines were forced out of the city and the Uberti palace was razed.      1. Caiaphas. His words were: "It is expedient that one man shall die for the people and that the whole nation perish not." (*John* xi, 50).      2. Annas, father-in-law of Caiaphas, was the first before whom Jesus was led upon his arrest. (*John* xviii, 13). He had Jesus bound and delivered to Caiaphas.      3. Caiaphas had not been there on Virgil's first descent into Hell.

Then, turning, he asked the Friar: "If your law permit,
   can you tell us if somewhere along the right                   125
   there is some gap in the stone wall of the pit
through which we two may climb to the next brink
   without the need of summoning the Black Angels
   and forcing them to raise us from this sink?"
He: "Nearer than you hope, there is a bridge                  130
   that runs from the great circle of the scarp
   and crosses every ditch from ridge to ridge,
except that in this it is broken; but with care
   you can mount the ruins which lie along the slope
   and make a heap on the bottom." My Guide stood there   135
motionless for a while with a dark look.
   At last he said: "He[4] lied about this business,
   who spears the sinners yonder with his hook."
And the Friar: "Once at Bolgna I heard the wise
   discussing the Devil's sins; among them I heard          140
   that he is a liar and the father of lies."
When the sinner had finished speaking, I saw the face
   of my sweet Master darken a bit with anger:
   he set off at a great stride from that place,
and I turned from that weighted hypocrite               145
to follow in the prints of his dear feet.

### CANTO XXIV

*Circle Eight: Bolgia Seven    The Thieves*

The Poets climb the right bank laboriously, cross the bridge of the
Seventh Bolgia and descend the far bank to observe the Thieves.
They find the pit full of monstrous reptiles who curl themselves about
the sinners like living coils of rope, binding each sinner's hands behind
his back, and knotting themselves through the loins. Other reptiles
dart about the place, and the Poets see one of them fly through the
air and pierce the jugular vein of one sinner who immediately bursts
into flames until only ashes remain. From the ashes the sinner reforms
painfully.

These are Dante's first observations of the Thieves and will be
carried further in the next Canto, but the first allegorical retribution
is immediately apparent. Thievery is reptilian in its secrecy; therefore
it is punished by reptiles. The hands of the thieves are the agents of
their crimes; therefore they are bound forever. And as the thief destroys
his fellowmen by making their substance disappear, so is he painfully
destroyed and made to disappear, not once but over and over again.

4. Malacoda.

The sinner who has risen from his own ashes reluctantly identifies himself as Vanni Fucci. He tells his story, and to revenge himself for having been forced to reveal his identity he utters a dark prophecy against Dante.

In the turning season of the youthful year,
    when the sun is warming his rays beneath Aquarius[5]
    and the days and nights already begin to near
their perfect balance; the hoar-frost copies then
    the image of his white sister on the ground,        5
    but the first sun wipes away the work of his pen.[6]
The peasants who lack fodder then arise
    and look about and see the fields all white,
    and hear their lambs bleat; then they smite their thighs,[7]
go back into the house, walk here and there,        10
    pacing, fretting, wondering what to do,
    then come out doors again, and there, despair
falls from them when they see how the earth's face
    has changed in so little time, and they take their staffs
    and drive their lambs to feed—so in that place        15
when I saw my Guide and Master's eyebrows lower,
    my spirits fell and I was sorely vexed;
    and as quickly came the plaster to the sore:
for when he had reached the ruined bridge, he stood
    and turned on me that sweet and open look        20
    with which he had greeted me in the dark wood.
When he had paused and studied carefully
    the heap of stones, he seemed to reach some plan,
    for he turned and opened his arms and lifted me.
Like one who works and calculates ahead,        25
    and is always ready for what happens next—
    so, raising me above that dismal bed
to the top of one great slab of the fallen slate,
    he chose another saying: "Climb here, but first
    test it to see if it will hold your weight."        30
It was no climb for a lead-hung hypocrite:
    for scarcely we—he light and I assisted—
    could crawl handhold by handhold from the pit;
and were it not that the bank along this side
    was lower than the one down which we had slid,       35
    I at least—I will not speak for my Guide—
would have turned back. But as all of the vast rim

5. The zodiacal sign for the period from January 21 to February 21. The sun is moving north then to approach the vernal equinox (March 21), at which point the days and the nights are equal. The Italian spring comes early, and the first warm days would normally occur under Aquarius. 6. The hoar-frost looks like snow but melts away as soon as the sun strikes it. 7. A common Italian gesture of vexation, about equivalent to smiting the forehead with the palm of the hand.

of Malebolge leans toward the lowest well,
  so each succeeding valley and each brim
is lower than the last. We climbed the face                          40
  and arrived by great exertion to the point
  where the last rock had fallen from its place.
My lungs were pumping as if they could not stop;
  I thought I could not go on, and I sat exhausted
  the instant I had clambered to the top.                            45
"Up on your feet! This is no time to tire!"
  my Master cried. "The man who lies asleep
  will never waken fame, and his desire
and all his life drift past him like a dream,
  and the traces of his memory fade from time                       50
  like smoke in air, or ripples on a stream.
Now, therefore, rise. Control your breath, and call
  upon the strength of soul that wins all battles
  unless it sink in the gross body's fall.
There is a longer ladder yet to climb:                              55
  this much is not enough. If you understand me,
  show that you mean to profit from your time."
I rose and made my breath appear more steady
  than it really was, and I replied: "Lead on
  as it pleases you to go: I am strong and ready."                   60
We picked our way up the cliff, a painful climb,[8]
  for it was narrower, steeper, and more jagged
  than any we had crossed up to that time.
I moved along, talking to hide my faintness,
  when a voice that seemed unable to form words                     65
  rose from the depths of the next chasm's darkness.
I do not know what it said, though by then the Sage
  had led me to the top of the next arch;
  but the speaker seemed in a tremendous rage.
I was bending over the brim, but living eyes                        70
  could not plumb to the bottom of that dark;
  therefore I said, "Master, let me advise
that we cross over and climb down the wall:
  for just as I hear the voice without understanding,
  so I look down and make out nothing at all."                      75
"I make no other answer than the act,
  the Master said: "the only fit reply
  to a fit request is silence and the fact."
So we moved down the bridge to the stone pier
  that shores the end of the arch on the eighth bank,               80

---

8. The "top" Dante mentions in line 45 must obviously have been the top of the fallen stone that was once the bridge. There remains the difficult climb up the remainder of the cliff.

and there I saw the chasm's depths made clear;
and there great coils of serpents met my sight,
    so hideous a mass that even now
    the memory makes my blood run cold with fright.
Let Libya[9] boast no longer, for though its sands         85
    breed chelidrids, jaculi, and phareans,
    cenchriads, and two-headed amphisbands,
it never bred such a variety
    of vipers, no, not with all Ethiopia
    and all the lands that lie by the Red Sea.         90
Amid that swarm, naked and without hope,
    people ran terrified, not even dreaming
    of a hole to hide in, or of heliotrope.[1]
Their hands were bound behind by coils of serpents
    which thrust their heads and tails between the loins    95
    and bunched in front, a mass of knotted torments.
One of the damned came racing round a boulder,
    and as he passed us, a great snake shot up
    and bit him where the neck joins with the shoulder.
No mortal pen—however fast it flash         100
    over the page—could write down *o* or *i*
    as quickly as he flamed and fell in ash;
and when he was dissolved into a heap
    upon the ground, the dust rose of itself
    and immediately resumed its former shape.     105
Precisely so, philosophers declare,
    the Phoenix dies and then is born again
    when it approaches its five hundredth year.[2]
It lives on tears of balsam and of incense;
    in all its life it eats no herb or grain,     110
    and nard and precious myrrh sweeten its cerements.
And as a person fallen in a fit,
    possessed by a Demon or some other seizure
    that fetters him without his knowing it,
struggles up to his feet and blinks his eyes     115
    (still stupefied by the great agony
    he has just passed), and, looking round him, sighs—
such was the sinner when at last he rose.

---

9. *Libya . . . Ethiopia . . . lands that lie by the Red Sea:* The desert areas of the Mediterranean shores. Lucan's *Pharsalia* describes the assortment of monsters listed here by Dante. I have rendered their names from Latin to English jabberwocky to avoid problems of pronunciation. In Lucan *chelydri* make their trails smoke and burn, they are amphibious; *jaculi* fly through the air like darts piercing what they hit; *pharese* plow the ground with their tails; *cenchri* waver from side to side when they move; and *amphisboenae* have a head at each end.     1. Not the flower, but the bloodstone, a spotted chalcedony. It was believed to make the wearer invisible.     2. The fabulous Phoenix of Arabia was the only one of its kind in the world. Every five hundred years it built a nest of spices and incense which took fire from the heat of the sun and the beating of the Phoenix's wings. The Phoenix was thereupon cremated and was then re-born from its ashes.

O Power of God! How dreadful is Thy will
    which in its vengeance rains such fearful blows.    120
Then my Guide asked him who he was. And he
    answered reluctantly: "Not long ago
    I rained into this gullet from Tuscany.
I am Vanni Fucci,[3] the beast. A mule among men,
    I chose the bestial life above the human.    125
    Savage Pistoia was my fitting den."
And I to my Guide: "Detain him a bit longer
    and ask what crime it was that sent him here;
    I knew him as a man of blood and anger."[4]
The sinner, hearing me, seemed discomforted,    130
    but he turned and fixed his eyes upon my face
    with a look of dismal shame; at length he said:
"That you have found me out among the strife
    and misery of this place, grieves my heart more
    than did the day that cut me from my life.    135
But I am forced to answer truthfully:
    I am put down so low because it was I
    who stole the treasure from the Sacristy,
for which others once were blamed. But that you may
    find less to gloat about if you escape here,    140
    prick up your ears and listen to what I say:
First Pistoia is emptied of the Black,
    then Florence changes her party and her laws.
    From Valdimagra the God of War brings back
a fiery vapor wrapped in turbid air:    145
    then in a storm of battle at Piceno
    the vapor breaks apart the mist, and there
every White shall feel his wounds anew.
And I have told you this that it may grieve you."[5]    150

CANTO XXV

*Circle Eight: Bolgia Seven*    *The Thieves*

Vanni's rage mounts to the point where he hurls an ultimate
obscenity at God, and the serpents immediately swarm over him,

---

3. The bastard son of Fuccio de Lazzeri, a nobleman (Black) of Pistoia. In 1293 with two accomplices
he stole the treasure of San Jacopo in the Duomo of San Zeno. Others were accused, and one
man spent a year in jail on this charge before the guilty persons were discovered. Vanni Fucci
had escaped from Pistoia by then, but his accomplices were convicted.    4. Dante (the traveler
within the narrative rather than Dante the author) claims that he did not know Fucci was a thief,
but only that he was a man of blood and violence. He should therefore be punished in the Seventh
Circle.    5. In May of 1301 the Whites of Florence joined with the Whites of Pistoia to expel
the Pistoian Blacks and destroy their houses. The ejected Blacks fled to Florence and joined forces
with the Florentine Blacks. On November 1st of the same year, Charles of Valois took Florence
and helped the Blacks drive out the Whites. Piceno was the scene of a battle in which the Blacks
of Florence and Lucca combined in 1302 to capture Serravalle, a White strong point near Pistoia.

driving him off in great pain. The Centaur, Cacus, his back covered
with serpents and a fire-eating dragon, also gives chase to punish the
wretch.

Dante then meets Five Noble Thieves of Florence and sees the
further retribution visited upon the sinners. Some of the thieves appear
first in human form, others as reptiles. All but one of them suffer a
painful transformation before Dante's eyes. Agnello appears in human
form and is merged with Cianfa, who appears as a six-legged lizard.
Buoso appears as a man and changes form with Francesco, who first
appears as a tiny reptile. Only Puccio Sciancato remains unchanged,
though we are made to understand that his turn will come.

For endless and painful transformation is the final state of the
thieves. In life they took the substance of others, transforming it into
their own. So in Hell their very bodies are constantly being taken
from them, and they are left to steal back a human form from some
other sinner. Thus they waver constantly between man and reptile,
and no sinner knows what to call his own.

When he had finished, the thief—to his disgrace—
    raised his hands with both fists making figs,[6]
    and cried: "Here, God! I throw them in your face!"
Thereat the snakes became my friends, for one
    coiled itself about the wretch's neck                 5
    as if it were saying: "You shall not go on!"
and another tied his arms behind him again,
    knotting its head and tail between his loins
    so tight he could not move a finger in pain.
Pistoia! Pistoia! why have you not decreed              10
    to turn yourself to ashes and end your days,
    rather than spread the evil of your seed!
In all of Hell's corrupt and sunken halls
    I found no shade so arrogant toward God,
    not even him who fell from the Theban walls!        15
Without another word, he fled; and there
    I saw a furious Centaur race up, roaring:
    "Where is the insolent blasphemer? Where?"
I do not think as many serpents swarm
    in all the Maremma as he bore on his back        20
    from the haunch to the first sign of our human form.
Upon his shoulders, just behind his head
    a snorting dragon whose hot breath set fire
    to all it touched, lay with its wings outspread.

6. An obscene gesture made by closing the hand into a fist with the thumb protruding between
the first and second fingers. The fig is an ancient symbol for the vulva, and the protruding thumb
is an obvious phallic symbol. The gesture is still current in Italy and has lost none of its obscene
significance since Dante's time.

My Guide said: "That is Cacus.[7] Time and again    25
   in the shadow of Mount Aventine he made
   a lake of blood upon the Roman plain.
He does not go with his kin by the blood-red fosse
   because of the cunning fraud with which he stole
   the cattle of Hercules. And thus it was    30
his thieving stopped, for Hercules found his den
   and gave him perhaps a hundred blows with his club,
   and of them he did not feel the first ten."
Meanwhile, the Centaur passed along his way,
   and three wraiths came. Neither my Guide nor I    35
   knew they were there until we heard them say:
"You there—who are you?" There our talk fell still
   and we turned to stare at them. I did not know them,
   but by chance it happened, as it often will,
one named another. "Where is Cinfa?" he cried;    40
   "Why has he fallen back?" I placed a finger
   across my lips as a signal to my Guide.
Reader, should you doubt what next I tell,
   it will be no wonder, for though I saw it happen,
   I can scarce believe it possible, even in Hell.    45
For suddenly, as I watched, I saw a lizard
   come darting forward on six great taloned feet
   and fasten itself to a sinner from crotch to gizzard.
Its middle feet sank in the sweat and grime
   of the wretch's paunch, its forefeet clamped his arms,    50
   its teeth bit through both cheeks. At the same time
its hind feet fastened on the sinner's thighs:
   its tail thrust through his legs and closed its coil
   over his loins. I saw it with my own eyes!
No ivy ever grew about a tree    55
   as tightly as that monster wove itself
   limb by limb about the sinner's body;
they fused like hot wax, and their colors ran
   together until neither wretch nor monster
   appeared what he had been when he began:    60
just so, before the running edge of the heat
   on a burning page, a brown discoloration
   changes to black as the white dies from the sheet.
The other two cried out as they looked on:

7. The son of Vulcan. He lived in a cave at the foot of Mount Aventine, from which he raided the herds of the cattle of Hercules, which pastured on the Roman plain. Hercules clubbed him to death for his thievery, beating him in rage long after he was dead. Cacus is condemned to the lower pit for his greater crime, instead of guarding Phlegethon with his brother centaurs. Virgil, however, did not describe him as a Centaur (V. *Aeneid* VIII, 193–267). Dante's interpretation of him is probably based on the fact that Virgil referred to him as "half-human."

"Alas! Alas! Agnello, how you change!                     65
    Already you are neither two nor one!"
The two heads had already blurred and blended;
    now two new semblances appeared and faded,
    one face where neither face began nor ended.
From the four upper limbs of man and beast                70
    two arms were made, then members never seen
    grew from the thighs and legs, belly and breast.
Their former likenesses mottled and sank
    to something that was both of them and neither;
    and so transformed, it slowly left our bank.          75
As lizards at high noon of a hot day
    dart out from hedge to hedge, from shade to shade,
    and flash like lightning when they cross the way,
so toward the bowels of the other two,
    shot a small monster; livid, furious,                 80
    and black as a pepper corn. Its lunge bit through
that part[8] of one of them from which man receives
    his earliest nourishment; then it fell back
    and lay sprawled out in front of the two thieves.
Its victim stared at it but did not speak:                85
    indeed, he stood there like a post, and yawned
    as if lack of sleep, or a fever, had left him weak.
The reptile stared at him, he at the reptile;
    from the wound of one and from the other's mouth
    two smokes poured out and mingled, dark and vile.     90
Now let Lucan be still with his history
    of poor Sabellus and Nassidius,[9]
    and wait to hear what next appeared to me.
Of Cadmus and Arethusa be Ovid silent.
    I have no need to envy him those verses               95
    where he makes one a fountain, and one a serpent:
for he never transformed two beings face to face
    in such a way that both their natures yielded
    their elements each to each, as in this case.
Responding sympathetically to each other,                100
    the reptile cleft his tail into a fork,
    and the wounded sinner drew his feet together.
The sinner's legs and thighs began to join:
    they grew together so, that soon no trace
    of juncture could be seen from toe to loin.           105

8. The navel.   9. In *Pharsalia* (IX, 761 ff.) Lucan relates how Sabellus and Nassidius, two soldiers of the army Cato led across the Libyan desert, were bitten by monsters. Sabellus melted into a puddle and Nassidius swelled until he popped his coat of mail. In his *Metamorphoses*, Ovid wrote how Cadmus was changed into a serpent (IV, 562–603) and how Arethusa was changed into a fountain (V, 572–661).

Point by point the reptile's cloven tail
   grew to the form of what the sinner lost;
   one skin began to soften, one to scale.
The armpits swallowed the arms, and the short shank
   of the reptile's forefeet simultaneously                    110
   lengthened by as much as the man's arms shrank.
Its hind feet twisted round themselves and grew
   the member man conceals; meanwhile the wretch
   from his one member generated two.
The smoke swelled up about them all the while:                      115
   it tanned one skin and bleached the other; it stripped
   the hair from the man and grew it on the reptile.
While one fell to his belly, the other rose
   without once shifting the locked evil eyes
   below which they changed snouts as they changed pose.         120
The face of the standing one drew up and in
   toward the temples, and from the excess matter
   that gathered there, ears grew from the smooth skin;
while of the matter left below the eyes
   the excess became a nose, at the same time                    125
   forming the lips to an appropriate size.
Here the face of the prostrate felon slips,
   sharpens into a snout, and withdraws its ears
   as a snail pulls in its horns. Between its lips
the tongue, once formed for speech, thrusts out a fork;             130
   the forked tongue of the other heals and draws
   into his mouth. The smoke has done its work.
The soul that had become a beast went flitting
   and hissing over the stones, and after it
   the other walked along talking and spitting.                  135
Then turning his new shoulders, said to the one
   that still remained: "It is Buoso's turn to go
   crawling along this road as I have done."
Thus did the ballast of the seventh hold
   shift and reshift; and may the strangeness of it              140
   excuse my pen if the tale is strangely told.
And though all this confused me, they did not flee
   so cunningly but what I was aware
   that it was Puccio Sciancato alone of the three
that first appeared, who kept his old form still.                   145
The other was he for whom you weep, Gaville.[1]

---

1. Francesco dei Cavalcanti. He was killed by the people of Gaville (a village in the Valley of the Arno). His kinsmen rallied immediately to avenge his death, and many of the townsmen of Gaville were killed in the resulting feud.

CANTO XXVI

*Circle Eight: Bolgia Eight    The Evil Counselors*

Dante turns from the Thieves toward the Evil Counselors of the next Bolgia, and between the two he addresses a passionate lament to Florence prophesying the griefs that will befall her from these two sins. At the purported time of the Vision, it will be recalled, Dante was a Chief Magistrate of Florence and was forced into exile by men he had reason to consider both thieves and evil counselors. He seems prompted, in fact, to say much more on this score, but he restrains himself when he comes in sight of the sinners of the next Bolgia, for they are a moral symbolism, all men of gift who abused their genius, perverting it to wiles and stratagems. Seeing them in Hell he knows his must be another road: his way shall not be by deception.

So the Poets move on and Dante observes the Eighth Bolgia in detail. Here the Evil Counselors move about endlessly, hidden from view inside great flames. Their sin was to abuse the gifts of the Almighty, to steal his virtues for low purposes. And as they stole from God in their lives and worked by hidden ways, so are they stolen from sight and hidden in the great flames which are their own guilty consciences. And as, in most instances at least, they sinned by glibness of tongue, so are the flames made into a fiery travesty of tongues.

Among the others, the Poets see a great doubleheaded flame, and discover that Ulysses and Diomede are punished together within it. Virgil addresses the flame, and through its wavering tongue Ulysses narrates an unforgettable tale of his last voyage and death.

Joy to you, Florence, that your banners swell,
    beating their proud wings over land and sea.
    and that your name expands through all of Hell!
Among the thieves I found five who had been
    your citizens, to my shame; nor yet shall you                5
    mount to great honor peopling such a den!
But if the truth is dreamed of toward the morning,[2]
    you soon shall feel what Prato[3] and the others
    wish for you. And were that day of mourning
already come it would not be too soon.                            10
    So may it come, since it must! for it will weigh
    more heavily on me as I pass my noon.

2. A semi-proverbial expression. It was a common belief that those dreams that occur just before waking foretell the future. "Morning" here would equal both "the rude awakening" and the potential "dawn of a new day."    3. Not the neighboring town (which was on good terms with Florence) but Cardinal Niccolò da Prato, papal legate from Benedict XI to Florence. In 1304 he tried to reconcile the warring factions, but found that neither side would accept mediation. Since none would be blessed, he cursed all impartially and laid the city under an interdict (i.e., forbade the offering of the sacraments). Shortly after this rejection by the Church, a bridge collapsed in Florence, and later a great fire broke out. Both disasters cost many lives, and both were promptly attributed to the Papal curse.

We left that place. My Guide climbed stone by stone
   the natural stair by which we had descended
   and drew me after him. So we passed on,           15
and going our lonely way through that dead land
   among the crags and crevices of the cliff,
   the foot could make no way without the hand.
I mourned among those rocks, and I mourn again
   when memory returns to what I saw:             20
   and more than usually I curb the strain
of my genius, lest it stray from Virtue's course;
   so if some star, or a better thing, grant me merit,
   may I not find the gift cause for remorse.
As many fireflies as the peasant sees           25
   when he rests on a hill and looks into the valley
   (where he tills or gathers grapes or prunes his trees)
in that sweet season when the face of him
   who lights the world rides north, and at the hour
   when the fly yields to the gnat and the air grows dim—    30
such myriads of flames I saw shine through
   the gloom of the eighth abyss when I arrived
   at the rim from which its bed comes into view.
As he the bears avenged[4] so fearfully
   beheld Elijah's chariot depart—            35
   the horses rise toward heaven—but could not see
more than the flame, a cloudlet in the sky,
   once it had risen—so within the fosse
   only those flames, forever passing by
were visible, ahead, to right, to left;          40
   for though each steals a sinner's soul from view
   not one among them leaves a trace of the theft.
I stood on the bridge, and leaned out from the edge;
   so far, that but for a jut of rock I held to
   I should have been sent hurtling from the ledge    45
without being pushed. And seeing me so intent,
   my Guide said: "There are souls within those flames;
   each sinner swathes himself in his own torment."
"Master," I said, "your words make me more sure,
   but I had seen already that it was so          50
   and meant to ask what spirit must endure
the pains of that great flame which splits away
   in two great horns, as if it rose from the pyre

---

4. Elisha saw Elijah translated to Heaven in a fiery chariot. Later he was mocked by some children, who called out tauntingly that he should "Go up" as Elijah had. Elisha cursed the children
in the name of the Lord, and bears came suddenly upon the children and devoured them. (2
*Kings* ii, 11–24.)

where Eteocles and Polynices lay?"[5]
He answered me: "Forever round this path     55
   Ulysses and Diomede[6] move in such dress,
   united in pain as once they were in wrath;
there they lament the ambush of the Horse
   which was the door through which the noble seed
   of the Romans issued from its holy source;     60
there they mourn that for Achilles slain
   sweet Deidamia weeps even in death;
   there they recall the Palladium in their pain."
"Master," I cried, "I pray you and repray
   till my prayer becomes a thousand—if these souls     65
   can still speak from the fire, oh let me stay
until the flame draws near! Do not deny me:
   You see how fervently I long for it!"
And he to me: "Since what you ask is worthy,
it shall be. But be still and let me speak;     70
   for I know your mind already, and they perhaps
   might scorn your manner of speaking, since they were Greek."
And when the flame had come where time and place
   seemed fitting to my Guide, I heard him say
   these words to it: "O you two souls who pace     75
together in one flame!—if my days above
   won favor in your eyes, if I have earned
   however much or little of your love
in writing my High Verses, do not pass by,
   but let one of you[7] be pleased to tell where he,     80
   having disappeared from the known world, went to die."
As if it fought the wind, the greater prong
   of the ancient flame began to quiver and hum;
   then moving its tip as if it were the tongue
that spoke, gave out a voice above the roar.     85

5. Eteocles and Polynices, sons of Oedipus, succeeded jointly to the throne of Thebes, and came to an agreement whereby each one would rule separately for a year at a time. Eteocles ruled the first year and when he refused to surrender the throne at the appointed time, Polynices led the Seven against Thebes in a bloody war. In single combat the two brothers killed one another. Statius (*Thebaid* XII, 429 ff.) wrote that their mutual hatred was so great that when they were placed on the same funeral pyre the very flame of their burning drew apart in two great raging horns.    6. They suffer here for their joint guilt in counseling and carrying out many stratagems which Dante considered evil, though a narrator who was less passionately a partisan of the Trojans might have thought their actions justifiable methods of warfare. Their first sin was the stratagem of the Wooden Horse, as a result of which Troy fell and Aeneas went forth to found the Roman line. The second evil occurred at Scyros. There Ulysses discovered Achilles in female disguise, hidden by his mother, Thetis, so that he would not be taken off to the war. Deidamia was in love with Achilles and had borne him a son. When Ulysses persuaded her lover to sail for Troy, she died of grief. The third count is Ulysses' theft of the sacred statue of Pallas from the Palladium. Upon the statue, it was believed, depended the fate of Troy. Its theft, therefore, would result in Troy's downfall.    7. Ulysses. He is the figure in the larger horn of the flame (which symbolizes that his guilt, as leader, is greater than that of Diomede). His memorable account of his last voyage and death is purely Dante's invention.

"When I left Circe,"[8] it said, "who more than a year
    detained me near Gaëta long before
Aeneas came and gave the place that name,
    not fondness for my son, nor reverence
    for my aged father, nor Penelope's[9] claim                    90
to the joys of love, could drive out of my mind
    the lust to experience the far-flung world
    and the failings and felicities of mankind.
I put out on the high and open sea
    with a single ship and only those few souls                    95
    who stayed true when the rest deserted me.
As far as Morocco and as far as Spain
    I saw both shores;[1] and I saw Sardinia
    and the other islands of the open main.
I and my men were stiff and slow with age                          100
    when we sailed at last into the narrow pass[2]
    where, warning all men back from further voyage,
Hercules' Pillars rose upon our sight.
    Already I had left Ceuta on the left;
    Seville[3] now sank behind me on the right.                    105
'Shipmates,' I said, 'who through a hundred thousand
    perils have reached the West, do not deny
    to the brief remaining watch our senses stand
experience of the world beyond the sun.
    Greeks! You were not born to live like brutes,                 110
    but to press on toward manhood and recognition!'
With this brief exhortation I made my crew
    so eager for the voyage I could hardly
    have held them back from it when I was through;
and turning our stern toward morning, our bow toward night,        115
    we bore southwest out of the world of man;
    we made wings of our oars for our fool's flight.
That night we raised the other pole ahead
    with all its stars, and ours had so declined
    it did not rise out of its ocean bed.[4]                       120
Five times since we had dipped our bending oars
    beyond the world, the light beneath the moon
    had waxed and waned, when dead upon our course

---

8. She changed Ulysses' men to swine and kept him a prisoner, though with rather exceptional
accommodations. *Gaëta*: Southeastern Italian coastal town. According to Virgil (*Aeneid*, VII,
1 ff.) it was earlier named Caieta by Aeneas in honor of his aged nurse.    9. Ulysses' wife.
1. Of the Mediterranean.    2. The straits of Gilbraltar, formerly called the Pillars of Hercules.
They were presumed to be the Western limit beyond which no man could navigate.    3. In
Dante's time this was the name given to the general region of Spain. Having passed through the
Straits, the men are now in the Atlantic. *Ceuta*: In Africa, opposite Gibraltar.    4. They drove
south across the equator, observed the southern stars, and found that the North Star had sunk
below the horizon.

we sighted, dark in space, a peak so tall
    I doubted any man had seen the like.[5]                 125
Our cheers were hardly sounded, when a squall
broke hard upon our bow from the new land:
    three times it sucked the ship and the sea about
    as it pleased Another to order and command.
At the fourth, the poop rose and the bow went down     130
till the sea closed over us and the light was gone."

### CANTO XXVII

*Circle Eight: Bolgia Eight     The Evil Counselors*

    The double flame departs at a word from Virgil and behind it
appears another which contains the soul of Count Guido da Montefeltro, a Lord of Romagna. He had overheard Virgil speaking Italian, and the entire flame in which his soul is wrapped quivers with
his eagerness to hear recent news of his wartorn country. (As Farinata has already explained, the spirits of the damned have prophetic
powers, but lose all track of events as they approach.)

    Dante replies with a stately and tragic summary of how things
stand in the cities of Romagna. When he has finished, he asks
Guido for his story, and Guido recounts his life, and how Boniface
VIII persuaded him to sin.

When it had finished speaking, the great flame
    stood tall and shook no more. Now, as it left us
    with the sweet Poet's license, another[6] came
along that track and our attention turned
    to the new flame: a strange and muffled roar     5
    rose from the single tip to which it burned.
As the Sicilian bull[7]—that brazen spit
    which bellowed first (and properly enough)
    with the lament of him whose file had tuned it—
was made to bellow by its victim's cries     10
    in such a way, that though it was of brass,
    it seemed itself to howl and agonize:
so lacking any way through or around
    the fire that sealed them in, the mournful words
    were changed into its language. When they found     15

---

5. Purgatory. They sight it after five months of passage. According to Dante's geography, the Northern hemisphere is land and the Southern is all water except for the Mountain of Purgatory which rises above the surface at a point directly opposite Jerusalem.     6. Guido da Montefeltro (1223–1298). As head of the Ghibellines of Romagna, he was reputed the wisest and cunningest man in Italy.     7. In the sixth century B.C. Perillus of Athens constructed for Phalaris, Tyrant of Sicily, a metal bull to be used as an instrument of torture. When victims were placed inside it and roasted to death, their screams passed through certain tuned pipes and emerged as a burlesque bellowing of the bull. Phalaris accepted delivery and showed his gratitude by appointing the inventor the bull's first victim. Later Phalaris was overthrown, and he, too, took his turn inside the bull.

their way up the tip, imparting to it
   the same vibration given them in their passage
   over the tongue of the conealed sad spirit,
we heard it say: "O you at whom I aim
   my voice, and who were speaking Lombard, saying:      20
   'Go now, I ask no more,'[8] just as I came—
though I may come a bit late to my turn,
   may it not annoy you to pause and speak a while:
   you see it does not annoy me— and I burn.
If you have fallen only recently        25
   to this blind world from that sweet Italy
   where I acquired my guilt, I pray you, tell me:
is there peace or war in Romagna? for on earth
   I too was of those hills between Urbino
   and the fold from which the Tiber springs to birth."[9]    30
I was still staring at it from the dim
   edge of the pit when my Guide nudged me, saying:
   "This one is Italian; *you* speak to him."
My answer was framed already; without pause
   I spoke these words to it: "O hidden soul,      35
   your sad Romagna is not and never was
without war in her tyrants' raging blood;
   but none flared openly when I left just now.
   Ravenna's fortunes stand as they have stood
these many years: Polenta's eagles brood      40
   over her walls, and their pinions cover Cervia.[1]
   The city that so valiantly withstood
the French, and raised a mountain of their dead,
   feels the Green Claws again.[2] Still in Verrucchio
   the Aged Mastiff and his Pup, who shed      45
Montagna's blood, raven in their old ranges.[3]
   the cities of Lamone and Santerno
   are led by the white den's Lion, he who changes
his politics with the compass.[4] And as the city

---

8. These are the words with which Virgil dismisses Ulysses and Diomede, his "license."
9. Romagna is the district that runs south from the Po along the east side of the Apennines.
Urbino is due east of Florence and roughly south of Rimini. Between Urbino and Florence rise
the Coronaro Mountains which contain the headwaters of the Tiber.   1. In 1300 Ravenna was
ruled by Guido Vecchio da Polenta, father of Francesca da Rimini. His arms bore an eagle and
his domain included the small city of Cervia about twelve miles south of Revenna.   2. The city
is Forlì. In 1282 Guido da Montefeltro defended Forli from the French, but in 1300 it was under
the despotic rule of Sinibaldo degli Ordelaffi, whose arms were a green lion.   3. Verrucchio
was the castle of Malatesta and his son Malatestino, Lords of Rimini, whom Dante calls dogs for
their cruelty. Montagna de' Parcitati, the leader of Rimini's Ghibellines, was captured by Malatesta in 1295 and murdered in captivity by Malatestino.   4. Maginardo de' Pagani (died 1302)
ruled Faenza, on the River Lamone, and Imola, close by the River Santerno. His arms were a
blue lion on a white field (hence "the Lion from the white den"). He supported the Ghibellines
in the north, but the Guelphs in the south (Florence), changing his politics according to the
direction in which he was facing.

the Savio washes[5] lies between plain and mountain,                    50
    so it lives between freedom and tyranny.
Now, I beg you, let us know your name;
    do not be harder than one has been to you;
    so, too, you will preserve your earthly fame."
And when the flame had roared a while beneath                           55
    the ledge on which we stood, it swayed its tip
    to and fro, and then gave forth this breath:
"If I believed that my reply were made
    to one who could ever climb to the world again,
    this flame would shake no more. But since no shade      60
ever returned—if what I am told is true—
    from this blind world into the living light,
    without fear of dishonor I answer you.
I was a man of arms: then took the rope
    of the Franciscans, hoping to make amends:              65
    and surely I should have won to all my hope
but for the Great Priest[6]—may he rot in Hell!—
    who brought me back to all my earlier sins;
    and how and why it happened I wish to tell
in my own words: while I was still encased                  70
    in the pulp and bone my mother bore, my deeds
    were not of the lion but of the fox: I raced
through tangled ways; all wiles were mine from birth,
    and I won to such advantage with my arts
    that rumor of me reached the ends of the earth.         75
But when I saw before me all the signs
    of the time of life that cautions every man
    to lower his sail and gather in his lines,
that which had pleased me once, troubled my spirit,
    and penitent and confessed, I became a monk.            80
    Alas! What joy I might have had of it!
It was then the Prince of the New Pharisees[7] drew
    his sword and marched upon the Lateran—
    and not against the Saracen or the Jew,
for every man that stood against his hand                   85
    was a Christian soul: not one had warred on Acre,
    nor been a trader in the Sultan's land.[8]
It was he abused his sacred vows and mine:

---

5. Cesena. It ruled itself for a number of years, but was taken over by Malatestino in 1314. It lies between Forlì and Rimini.    6. Boniface VIII, so called as Pope.    7. Also Boniface. *Marched upon the Lateran:* Boniface had had a long-standing feud with the Colonna family. In 1297 the Colonna walled themselves in a castle twenty-five miles east of Rome at Penestrino (now called Palestrina) in the Lateran. On Guido's advice the Pope offered a fair-sounding amnesty which he had no intention of observing. When the Colonna accepted the terms and left the castle, the Pope destroyed it, leaving the Colonna without a refuge.    8. It was the Saracens who opposed the crusaders at Acre, the Jews who traded in the Sultan's land.

his Office and the Cord I wore, which once
    made those it girded leaner. As Constantine      90
sent for Silvestro to cure his leprosy,[9]
    seeking him out among Soracte's cells;
    so this one from his great throne sent for me
to cure the fever of pride that burned his blood.
    He demanded my advice, and I kept silent      95
    for his words seemed drunken to me. So it stood
until he said: "Your soul need fear no wound;
    I absolve your guilt beforehand; and now teach me
    how to smash Penestrino to the ground.
The Gates of Heaven, as you know, are mine      100
    to open and shut, for I hold the two Great Keys
    so easily let go by Celestine."[1]
His weighty arguments led me to fear
    silence was worse than sin. Therefore, I said:
    "Holy Father, since you clean me here      105
of the guilt into which I fall, let it be done:
    long promise and short observance[2] is the road
    that leads to the sure triumph of your throne."
Later, when I was dead, St. Francis came
    to claim my soul,[3] but one of the Black Angels      110
    said: 'Leave him. Do not wrong me. This one's name
went into my book the moment he resolved
    to give false counsel. Since then he has been mine,
    for who does not repent cannot be absolved;
nor can we admit the possibility      115
    of repenting a thing at the same time it is willed,
    for the two acts are contradictory.'
Miserable me! with what contrition
    I shuddered when he lifted me, saying: 'Perhaps
    you hadn't heard that I was a logician.'      120
He carried me to Minos: eight times round
    his scabby back the monster coiled his tail,
    then biting it in rage he pawed the ground
and cried: 'This one is for the thievish fire!'
    And, as you see, I am lost accordingly,      125
    grieving in heart as I go in this attire."
His story told, the flame began to toss

9. In the persecutions of the Christians by the Emperor Constantine, Pope Sylvester I took refuge in the caves of Mount Soracte near Rome. (It is now called Santo Oreste.) Later, according to legend, Constantine was stricken by leprosy and sent for Sylvester, who cured him and converted him to Christianity, in return for which the Emperor was believed to have made the famous "Donation of Constantine." (See Canto XIX.)    1. Celestine V under the persuasion of Boniface abdicated the Papacy. (See Canto III notes.)    2. This is the advice upon which Boniface acted in trapping the Colonna with his hypocritical amnesty.    3. To gather in the soul of one of his monks. *Black Angel:* A devil.

and writhe its horn. And so it left, and we
crossed over to the arch of the next fosse
where from the iron treasury of the Lord                    130
the fee of wrath is paid the Sowers of Discord.[4]

CANTO XXVIII

*Circle Eight: Bolgia Nine    The Sowers of Discord*

The Poets come to the edge of the Ninth Bolgia and look down at
a parade of hideously mutilated souls. These are the Sowers of Discord, and just as their sin was to rend asunder what God had meant
to be united, so are they hacked and torn through all eternity by a
great demon with a bloody sword. After each mutilation the souls
are compelled to drag their broken bodies around the pit and to return
to the demon, for in the course of the circuit their wounds knit in
time to be inflicted anew. Thus is the law of retribution observed,
each sinner suffering according to his degree.

Among them Dante distinguishes three classes with varying degrees
of guilt within each class. First come the Sowers of Religious Discord. Mahomet is chief among them, and appears first, cleft from
crotch to chin, with his internal organs dangling between his legs.
His son-in-law, Ali, drags on ahead of him, cleft from topknot to
chin. These reciprocal wounds symbolize Dante's judgment that,
between them, these two sum up the total schism between Christianity and Mohammedanism. The revolting details of Mahomet's condition clearly imply Dante's opinon of that doctrine. Mahomet issues
an ironic warning to another schismatic, Fra Dolcino.

Next come the Sowers of Political Discord, among them Pier da
Medicina, the Tribune Curio, and Mosca dei Lamberti, each mutilated according to the nature of his sin.

Last of all is Bertrand de Born, Sower of Discord Between Kinsmen. He separated father from son, and for that offense carries his
head separated from his body, holding it with one hand by the hair,
and swinging it as if it were a lantern to light his dark and endless
way. The image of Bertrand raising his head at arm's length in order
that it might speak more clearly to the Poets on the ridge is one of
the most memorable in the *Inferno*. For some reason that cannot be
ascertained, Dante makes these sinners quite eager to be remembered in the world, despite the fact that many who lie above them in
Hell were unwilling to be recognized.

Who could describe, even in words set free
    of metric and rhyme and a thousand times retold,

---

4. I have taken liberties with these lines in the hope of achieving a reasonably tonic final couplet.
The literal reading is: "In which the fee is paid to those who, sowing discord, acquire weight (of
guilt and pain)."

the blood and wounds that now were shown to me!
At grief so deep the tongue must wag in vain;
   the language of our sense and memory             5
   lacks the vocabulary of such pain.
If one could gather all those who have stood
   through all of time on Puglia's[5] fateful soil
   and wept for the red running of their blood
in the war of the Trojans;[6] and in that long war        10
   which left so vast a spoil of golden rings,
   as we find written in Livy, who does not err;[7]
along with those whose bodies felt the wet
   and gaping wounds of Robert Guiscard's lances;[8]
   with all the rest whose bones are gathered yet     15
at Ceperano where every last Pugliese
   turned traitor;[9] and with those from Tagliacozzo
   where Alardo won without weapons[1]—if all these
were gathered, and one showed his limbs run through,
   another his lopped off, that could not equal      20
   the mutilations of the ninth pit's crew.
A wine tun when a stave or cant-bar starts
   does not split open as wide as one I saw
   split from his chin to the mouth with which man farts.
Between his legs all of his red guts hung          25
   with the heart, the lungs, the liver, the gall bladder,
   and the shriveled sac that passes shit to the bung.
I stood and stared at him from the stone shelf;
   he noticed me and opening his own breast
   with both hands cried: "See how I rip myself!     30
See how Mahomet's mangled and split open!
   Ahead of me walks Ali[2] in his tears,
   his head cleft from the top-knot to the chin.

---

5. I have used the modern name but some of the events Dante narrates took place in the ancient province of Apulia. The southeastern area of Italy is the scene of all the fighting Dante mentions in the following passage. It is certainly a bloody total of slaughter that Dante calls upon to illustrate his scene.  6. The Romans (descended from the Trojans) fought the native Samnites in a long series of raids and skirmishes from 343–290 B.C.  7. The Punic Wars (264–146 B.C.). Livy writes that in the battle of Cannae (216 B.C.) so many Romans fell that Hannibal gathered three bushels of gold rings from the fingers of the dead and produced them before the Senate at Carthage.  8. Dante places Guiscard (1015–1085) in the *Paradiso* among the Warriors of God. He fought the Greeks and Saracens in their attempted invasion of Italy.  9. In 1266 the Pugliese under Manfred, King of Sicily, were charged with holding the pass at Ceperano against Charles of Anjou. The Pugliese, probably under Papal pressure, allowed the French free passage, and Charles went on to defeat Manfred at Benevento. Manfred himself was killed in that battle.
1. At Tagliacozzo (1268) in a continuation of the same strife, Charles of Anjou used a stratagem suggested to him by Alard de Valéry and defeated Conradin, nephew of Manfred. "Won without weapons" is certainly an overstatement: what Alardo suggested was a simple but effective conceal-ment of reserve troops. When Conradin seemed to have carried the day and was driving his foes before him, the reserve troops broke on his flank and rear, and defeated Conradin's out-positioned forces.  2. Ali succeeded Mahomet to the Caliphate, but not until three of the disciples had preceded him. Mahomet died in 632, and Ali did not assume the Caliphate until 656.

And all the other souls that bleed and mourn
   along this ditch were sowers of scandal and schism:     35
   as they tore others apart, so are they torn.
Behind us, warden of our mangled horde,
   the devil who butchers us and sends us marching
   waits to renew our wounds with his long sword
when we have made the circuit of the pit;     40
   for by the time we stand again before him
   all the wounds he gave us last have knit.
But who are you that gawk down from that sill—
   probably to put off your own descent
   to the pit you are sentenced to for your own evil?"     45
"Death has not come for him, guilt does not drive
   his soul to torment," my sweet Guide replied.
   "That he may experience all while yet alive
I, who am dead, must lead him through the drear
   and darkened halls of Hell, from round to round:     50
   and this is true as my own standing here."
More than a hundred wraiths who were marching under
   the sill on which we stood, paused at his words
   and stared at me, forgetting pain in wonder.
"And if you do indeed return to see     55
   the sun again, and soon, tell Fra Dolcino[3]
   unless he longs to come and march with me
he would do well to check his groceries
   before the winter drives him from the hills
   and gives the victory to the Novarese."     60
Mahomet, one foot raised, had paused to say
   these words to me. When he had finished speaking
   he stretched it out and down, and moved away.
Another—he had his throat slit, and his nose
   slashed off as far as the eyebrows, and a wound     65
   where one of his ears had been—standing with those
who stared at me in wonder from the pit,
   opened the grinning wound of his red gullet
   as if it were a mouth, and said through it:
"O soul unforfeited to misery     70
   and whom—unless I take you for another—
   I have seen above in our sweet Italy;
if ever again you see the gentle plain

---

3. In 1300 Fra Dolcino took over the reformist order called the Apostolic Brothers, who preached,
among other things, the community of property and of women. Clement V declared them heretical and ordered a crusade against them. The brotherhood retired with its women to an impregnable position in the hills between Novara and Vercelli, but their supplies gave out in the course
of a year-long siege, and they were finally starved out in March of 1307. Dolcino and Margaret
of Trent, his "Sister in Christ," were burned at the stake at Vercelli the following June.

that slopes down from Vercelli to Marcabò,[4]
remember Pier da Medicina in pain,                                    75
and announce this warning to the noblest two
    of Fano, Messers Guido and Angiolello:
    that unless our foresight sees what is not true
they shall be thrown from their ships into the sea
    and drown in the raging tides near La Cattolica        80
    to satisfy a tyrant's treachery.[5]
Neptune never saw so gross a crime
    in all the seas from Cyprus to Majorca,
    not even in pirate raids, nor the Argive time.[6]
The one-eyed traitor,[7] lord of the demesne                    85
    whose hill and streams one who walks here beside me
    will wish eternally he had never seen,
will call them to a parley, but behind
    sweet invitations he will work it so
    they need not pray against Focara's wind."                  90
And I to him: "If you would have me bear
    your name to time, show me the one who found
    the sight of that land so harsh, and let me hear
his story and his name." He touched the cheek            95
    of one nearby, forcing the jaws apart,
    and said: "This is the one; he cannot speak.
This outcast settled Caesar's doubts that day
    beside the Rubicon by telling him:
    'A man prepared is a man hurt by delay.' "
Ah, how wretched Curio[8] seemed to me                       100
    with a bloody stump in his throat in place of the tongue
    which once had dared to speak so recklessly!
And one among them with both arms hacked through
    cried out, raising his stumps on the foul air
    while the blood bedaubed his face: "Remember, too,     105
Mosca dei Lamberti,[9] alas, who said

4. Vercelli is the most western town in Lombardy. Marcabò stands near the mouth of the Po.
5. Malatestino da Rimini (see preceding Canto), in a move to annex the city of Fano, invited
Guido del Cassero and Angioletto da Carignano, leading citizens of Fano, to a conference at La
Cattolica, a point on the Adriatic midway between Fano and Rimini. At Malatestino's orders the
two were thrown overboard off Focara, a headland swept by such dangerous currents that approaching
sailors sued to offer prayers for a safe crossing.        6. The Greeks were raiders and pirates. *Cyprus
. . . Majorca*: These islands are at opposite ends of the Mediterranean.        7. Malatestino.
8. This is the Roman Tribune Curio, who was banished from Rome by Pompey and joined
Caesar's forces, advising him to cross the Rubicon, which was then the boundary between Gaul
and the Roman Republic. The crossing constituted invasion, and thus began the Roman Civil
War. The Rubicon flows near Rimini.        9. Dante had asked Ciacco (Canto VI) for news of
Mosca as a man of good works. Now he finds him, his merit canceled by his greater sin. Buondelmonte dei Buondelmonti had insulted the honor of the Amidei by breaking off his engagement
to a daughter of that line in favor of a girl of the Donati. When the Amidei met to discuss what
should be done, Mosca spoke for the death of Buondelmonts. The Amidei acted upon his advice
and from that murder sprang the bloody feud between the Guelphs and Ghibellines of Florence.

'A thing done has an end!' and with those words
planted the fields of war with Tuscan dead."
"And brought about the death of all your clan!"
I said, and he, stung by new pain on pain,                              110
ran off; and in his grief he seemed a madman.
I stayed to watch those broken instruments,
and I saw a thing so strange I should not dare
to mention it without more evidence
but that my own clear conscience strengthens me,                        115
that good companion that upholds a man
within the armor of his purity.
I saw it there; I seem to see it still—
a body without a head, that moved along
like all the others in that spew and spill.                             120
It held the severed head by its own hair,
swinging it like a lantern in its hand;
and the head looked at us and wept in its despair.
It made itself a lamp of its own head,
and they were two in one and one in two;                                125
how this can be, He knows who so commanded.
And when it stood directly under us
it raised the head at arm's length toward our bridge
the better to be heard, and swaying thus
it cried: "O living soul in this abyss,                                 130
see what a sentence has been passed upon me,
and search all Hell for one to equal this!
When you return to the world, remember me:
I am Bertrand de Born,[1] and it was I
who set the young king on to mutiny,                                    135
son against father, father against son
as Achitophel[2] set Absalom and David;
and since I parted those who should be one
in duty and in love, I bear my brain
divided from its source within this trunk;                              140
and walk here where my evil turns to pain,
an eye for an eye to all eternity:
thus is the law of Hell observed in me."

CANTO XXIX

*Circle Eight: Bolgia Ten    The Falsifiers (Class I, Alchemists)*

Dante lingers on the edge of the Ninth Bolgia expecting to see one
of his kinsmen, Geri del Bello, among the Sowers of Discord. Virgil,

1. (1140–1215), a great knight and master of the troubadours of Provence. He is said to have
instigated a quarrel between Henry II of England and his son Prince Henry, called "The Young
King" because he was crowned within his father's lifetime.    2. One of David's counselors, who
deserted him to assist the rebellious Absalom. (II *Samuel*, xv–xvii.)

however, hurries him on, since time is short, and as they cross the bridge over the Tenth Bolgia, Virgil explains that he had a glimpse of Geri among the crowd near the bridge and that he had been making threatening gestures at Dante.

The Poets now look into the last Bolgia of the Eighth Circle and see The Falsifiers. They are punished by afflictions of every sense: by darkness, stench, thirst, filth, loathsome diseases, and a shrieking din. Some of them, moreover, run ravening through the pit, tearing others to pieces. Just as in life they corrupted society by their falsifications, so in death these sinners are subjected to a sum of corruptions. In one sense they figure forth what society would be if all falsifiers succeeded—a place where the senses are an affliction (since falsification deceives the senses) rather than a guide, where even the body has no honesty, and where some lie prostrate while others run ravening to prey upon them.

Not all of these details are made clear until the next Canto, for Dante distinguishes four classes of Falsifiers, and in the present Canto we meet only the first class, The Alchemists, the Falsifiers of Things. Of this class are Griffolino D'arezzo and Capocchio, with both of whom Dante speaks.

The sight of that parade of broken dead
  had left my eyes so sotted with their tears
  I longed to stay and weep, but Virgil said:
"What are you waiting for? Why do you stare
  as if you could not tear your eyes away          5
  from the mutilated shadows passing there?
You did not act so in the other pits.
  Consider—if you mean perhaps to count them—
  this valley and its train of dismal spirits.
winds twenty-two miles round.[3] The moon already      10
  is under our feet;[4] the time we have is short,
  and there is much that you have yet to see."
"Had you known what I was seeking," I replied,
  "you might perhaps have given me permission
  to stay on longer." (As I spoke, my Guide      15
had started off already, and I in turn
  had moved along behind him; thus, I answered
  as we moved along the cliff.) "Within that cavern
upon whose brim I stood so long to stare,
  I think a spirit of my own blood mourns      20
  the guilt that sinners find so costly there."
And the Master then: "Hereafter let your mind
  turn its attention to more worthy matters

3. Another instance of "poetic" rather than "literal" detail. Dante's measurements cannot be made to fit together on any scale map.    4. If the moon, nearly at full, is under their feet, the sun must be overhead. It is therefore approximately noon of Holy Saturday.

and leave him to his fate among the blind;
for by the bridge and among that shapeless crew                        25
   I saw him point to you with threatening gestures,
   and I heard him called Geri del Bello.[5] You
were occupied at the time with that headless one
   who in his life was master of Altaforte,[6]
   and did not look that way; so he moved on."                  30
"O my sweet Guide," I answered. "his death came
   by violence and is not yet avenged
   by those who share his blood, and, thus, his shame.
For this he surely hates his kin, and, therefore,
   as I suppose, he would not speak to me;                      35
   and in that he makes me pity him the more."
We spoke of this until we reached the edge
   from which, had there been light, we could have seen
   the floor of the next pit. Out from that ledge
Malebolge's final cloister lay outspread,                              40
   and all of its lay brethren might have been
   in sight but for the murk; and from those dead
such shrieks and strangled agonies shrilled through me
   like shafts, but barbed with pity, that my hands
   flew to my ears. If all the misery                            45
that crams the hospitals of pestilence
   in Maremma, Valdichiano, and Sardinia[7]
   in the summer months when death sits like a presence
on the marsh air, were dumped into one trench—
   that might suggest their pain. And through the screams,         50
   putrid flesh spread up its sickening stench.
Still bearing left we passed from the long sill
   to the last bridge of Malebolge. There
   the reeking bottom was more visible.
There, High Justice, sacred ministress                                 55
   of the First Father, reigns eternally
   over the falsifiers in their distress.
I doubt it could have been such pain to bear
   the sight of the Aeginian people dying[8]
   that time when such malignance rode the air                    60
that every beast down to the smallest worm

---

5. A cousin of Dante's father. He became embroiled in a quarrel with the Sacchetti of Florence
and was murdered. At the time of the writing he had not been avenged by his kinsmen in accord
with the clan code of a life for a life.   6. Bertrand de Born was Lord of Hautefort.   7. Malarial
plague areas. Valdichiano and Maremma were swamp areas of eastern and western Tuscany.
8. Juno, incensed that the nymph Aegina let Jove possess her, set a plague upon the island that
bore her name. Every animal and every human died until only Aeacus, the son born to Aegina
of Jove, was left. He prayed to his father for aid and Jove repopulated the island by transforming
the ants at his son's feet into men. The Aeginians have since been called Myrmidons, from the
Greek word for ant. Ovid (*Metamorphoses* VII, 523–660).

shriveled and died (it was after that great plague
   that the Ancient People, as the poets affirm,
were reborn from the ants)—as it was to see
   the spirits lying heaped on one another          65
   in the dank bottom of that fetid valley.
One lay gasping on another's shoulder,
   one on another's belly; and some were crawling
   on hands and knees among the broken boulders.
Silent, slow step by step, we moved ahead           70
   looking at and listening to those souls
   too weak to raise themselves from their stone bed.
I saw two there like pans that are put
   one against the other to hold their warmth.
   They were covered with great scabs from head to foot.   75
No stable boy in a hurry to go home,[9]
   or for whom his master waits impatiently,
   ever scrubbed harder with his currycomb
than those two spirits of the stinking ditch
   scrubbed at themselves with their own bloody claws   80
   to ease the furious burning of the itch.
And as they scrubbed and clawed themselves, their nails
   drew down the scabs the way a knife scrapes bream
   or some other fish with even larger scales.
"O you," my Guide called out to one, "you there        85
   who rip your scabby mail as if your fingers
   were claws and pincers; tell us if this lair
counts any Italians among those who lurk
   in its dark depths; so may your busy nails
   eternally suffice you for your work."                  90
"We both are Italian whose unending loss
   you see before you," he replied in tears.
   "But who are you who come to question us?"
"I am a shade," my Guide and Master said,
   "who leads this living man from pit to pit            95
   to show him Hell as I have been commanded."
The sinners broke apart as he replied
   and turned convulsively to look at me,
   as others did who overheard my Guide.
My Master, then, ever concerned for me,                100
   turned and said: "Ask them whatever you wish."
   And I said to those two wraiths of misery:

9. The literal text would be confusing here. I have translated one possible interpretation of it as
offered by Giuseppe Vandelli. The original line is *"ne da colui che mal volentier vegghia"* ("nor
by one who unwillingly stays awake," or less literally, but with better force: "nor by one who fights
off sleep").

"So may the memory of your names and actions
    not die forever from the minds of men
    in that first world, but live for many suns,         105
tell me who you are and of what city;
    do not be shamed by your nauseous punishment
    into concealing your identity."
"I was a man of Arezzo,"[1] one replied,
    "and Albert of Siena had me burned;         110
    but I am not here for the deed for which I died.
It is true that jokingly I said to him once:
    'I know how to raise myself and fly through air';
    and he—with all the eagerness of a dunce—
wanted to learn. Because I could not make         115
    a Daedalus of him—for no other reason—
    he had his father burn me at the stake.
But Minos, the infallible, had me hurled
    here to the final bolgia of the ten
    for the alchemy I practiced in the world."         120
And I to the Poet: "Was there ever a race
    more vain than the Sienese? Even the French,
    compared to them, seem full of modest grace."
And the other leper answered mockingly:
    "Excepting Stricca, who by careful planning         125
    managed to live and spend so moderately;
and Niccolò, who in his time above
    was first of all the shoots in that rank garden
    to discover the costly uses of the clove;
and excepting the brilliant company of talents         130
    in which Caccia squandered his vineyards and his woods,
    and Abbagliato displayed his intelligence.[2]
But if you wish to know who joins your cry
    against the Sienese, study my face
    with care and let it make its own reply.         135
So you will see I am the suffering shadow
    of Capocchio,[3] who, by practicing alchemy,
    falsified the metals, and you must know,
unless my mortal recollection strays
how good an ape I was of Nature's ways."         140

1. Griffolino D'arezzo, an alchemist who extracted large sums of money from Alberto da Siena on the promise of teaching him to fly like Daedalus. When the Sienese oaf finally discovered he had been tricked, he had his "father," the Bishop of Siena, burn Griffolino as a sorcerer. Griffolino, however, is not punished for sorcery, but for falsification of silver and gold through alchemy. 2. *Stricca . . . Niccolò . . . Caccia . . . Abbagliato:* All of these Sienese noblemen were members of the Spendthrift Brigade and wasted their substance in competitions of riotous living. Lano (Canto XIII) was also of this company. Niccolò die Salimbeni discovered some recipe (details unknown) prepared with fabulously expensive spices. 3. Reputedly a Florentine friend of Dante's student days. For practicing alchemy he was burned at the stake at Siena in 1293.

CANTO XXX

*Circle Eight: Bolgia Ten    The Falsifiers (The Remaining Three*
*Classes: Evil Impersonators, Counterfeiters, False Witnesses)*

Just as Capocchio finishes speaking, two ravenous spirits come racing through the pit; and one of them, sinking his tusks into Capocchio's neck, drags him away like prey. Capocchio's companion, Griffolino, identifies the two as Gianni Schicchi and Myrrha, who run ravening through the pit through all eternity, snatching at other souls and rending them. These are the Evil Impersonators, Falsifiers of Persons. In life they seized upon the appearance of others, and in death they must run with never a pause, seizing upon the infernal apparition of these souls, while they in turn are preyed upon by their own furies.

Next the Poets encounter Master Adam, a sinner of the third class, a Falsifier of Money, i.e., a Counterfeiter. Like the alchemists, he is punished by a loathsome disease and he cannot move from where he lies, but his disease is compounded by other afflictions, including an eternity of unbearable thirst. Master Adam identifies two spirits lying beside him as Potiphar's Wife and Sinon the Greek, sinners of the fourth class, The False Witness, i.e., Falsifiers of Words.

Sinon, angered by Master Adam's identification of him, strikes him across the belly with the one arm he is able to move. Master Adam replies in kind, and Dante, fascinated by their continuing exchange of abuse, stands staring at them until Virgil turns on him in great anger, for "The wish to hear such baseness is degrading." Dante burns with shame, and Virgil immediately forgives him because of his great and genuine repentance.

At the time when Juno took her furious
    revenge for Semele, striking in rage
    again and again at the Theban royal house,[4]
King Athamas, by her contrivance, grew
    so mad, that seeing his wife out for an airing            5
    with his two sons, he cried to his retinue:
"Out with the nets there! Nets across the pass!
    for I will take this lioness and her cubs!"
    And spread his talons, mad and merciless,
and seizing his son Learchus, whirled him round           10
    and brained him on a rock; at which the mother
    leaped into the sea with her other son and drowned.
And when the Wheel of Fortune spun about

---

4. As in the case of the Aeginians, Jove begot a son (Bacchus) upon a mortal (Semele, daughter of the King Cadmus of Thebes); and Juno, who obviously could not cope with her husband's excursions directly, turned her fury upon the mortals in a number of godlike ways, among them inducing the madness of King Athamas (Semele's brother-in-law) which Ovid recounts in *Metamorphoses* IV, 512 ff.

to humble the all-daring Trojan's pride
   so that both king and kingdom were wiped out;      15
Hecuba[5]—mourning, wretched, and a slave—
   having seen Polyxena sacrificed,
   and Polydorus dead without a grave;
lost and alone, beside an alien sea,
   began to bark and growl like a dog      20
   in the mad seizure of her misery.
But never in Thebes nor Troy were Furies seen
   to strike at man or beast in such mad rage
   as two I saw, pale, naked, and unclean,
who suddenly came running toward us then,      25
   snapping their teeth as they ran, like hungry swine
   let out to feed after a night in the pen.
One of them sank his tusks so savagely
   into Capocchio's neck, that when he dragged him,
   the ditch's rocky bottom tore his belly.      30
And the Aretine,[6] left trembling by me, said:
   "That incubus, in life, was Gianni Schicchi;[7]
   here he runs rabid, mangling the other dead."
"So!" I answered, "and so may the other one
   not sink its teeth in you, be pleased to tell us      35
   what shade it is before it races on."
And he: "That ancient shade in time above
   was Myrrha,[8] vicious daughter of Cinyras
   who loved her father with more than rightful love.
She falsified another's form and came      40
   disguised to sin with him just as that other
   who runs with her, in order that he might claim
the fabulous lead-mare, lay under disguise
   on Buoso Donati's death bed and dictated
   a spurious testament to the notaries."      45
And when the rabid pair had passed from sight,
   I turned to observe the other misbegotten
   spirits that lay about to left and right.

---

5. Wife of King Priam. When Troy fell she was taken to Greece as a slave. En route she was forced to witness the sacrifice of her daughter and to look upon her son lying murdered and unburied. She went mad in her affliction and fell to howling like a dog. Ovid (*Metamorphoses* XIII, 568 ff.) describes her anguish but does not say she was changed into a dog. 6. Capocchio's companion, Griffolino. 7. Of the Cavalcanti of Florence. When Buoso di Donati (see Canto XXV) died, his son, Simone, persuaded Schicchi to impersonate the dead man and to dictate a will in Simone's favor. Buoso was removed from the death bed, Schicchi took his place in disguise, and the will was dictated to a notary as if Buoso were still alive. Schicchi took advantage of the occasion to make several bequests to himself, including one of a famous and highly-prized mare. 8. Moved by an incestuous passion for her father, the King of Cyprus, she disguised herself and slipped into his bed. After he had mated with her, the king discovered who she was and threatened to kill her but she ran away and was changed into a myrtle. Adonis was born from her trunk. (Ovid, *Metamorphoses* X, 298 ff.)

And there I saw another husk of sin,
   who, had his legs been trimmed away at the groin,      50
   would have looked for all the world like a mandolin.
The dropsy's heavy humors, which so bunch
   and spread the limbs, had disproportioned him
   till his face seemed much too small for his swollen paunch.
He strained his lips apart and thrust them forward      55
   the way a sick man, feverish with thirst,
   curls one lip toward the chin and the other upward.
"O you exempt from every punishment
   of this grim world (I know not why)," he cried,
   "look well upon the misery and debasement      60
of him who was Master Adam.[9] In my first
   life's time, I had enough to please me: here,
   I lack a drop of water for my thirst.
The rivulets that run from the green flanks
   of Casentino[1] to the Arno's flood,      65
   spreading their cool sweet moisture through their banks,
run constantly before me, and their plash
   and ripple in imagination dries me
   more than the disease that eats my flesh.
Inflexible Justice that has forked and spread      70
   my soul like hay, to search it the more closely,
   finds in the country where my guilt was bred
this increase of my grief; for there I learned,
   there in Romena, to stamp the Baptist's image[2]
   on alloyed gold—till I was bound and burned.      75
But could I see the soul of Guido here,
   or of Alessandro, or of their filthy brother,[3]
   I would not trade that sight for all the clear
cool flow of Branda's fountain.[4] One of the three—
   if those wild wraiths who run here are not lying—      80
   is here already.[5] But small good it does me
when my legs are useless! Were I light enough
   to move as much as an inch in a hundred years,
   long before this I would have started off
to cull him from the freaks that fill this fosse,      85
   although it winds on for eleven miles
   and is no less than half a mile across.

9. Of Brescia. Under the orders of the Counts Guidi of Romena, he counterfeited Florentine florins of twenty-one rather than twenty-four carat gold, and on such a scale that a currency crisis arose in Northern Italy. He was burned at the stake by the Florentines in 1281.   1. A mountainous district in which the Arno rises.   2. John the Baptist's. As patron of Florence, his image was stamped on the florins.   3. The Counts Guidi.   4. A spring near Romena. The famous fountain of Branda is in Siena, but Adam is speaking of his home country and must mean the spring.   5. Guido died before 1300.

Because of them I lie here in this pig-pen;
     it was they persuaded me to stamp the florins
     with three carats of alloy." And I then:             90
"Who are those wretched two sprawled alongside
     your right-hand borders, and who seem to smoke
     as a washed hand smokes in winter?" He replied:
"They were here when I first rained into this gully,
     and have not changed position since, nor may they,       95
     as I believe, to all eternity.
One is the liar who charged young Joseph wrongly:[6]
     the other, Sinon,[7] the false Greek from Troy.
     A burning fever makes them reek so strongly."
And one of the false pair, perhaps offended           100
     by the manner of Master Adam's presentation,
     punched him in the rigid and distended
belly—it thundered like a drum—and he
     retorted with an arm blow to the face
     that seemed delivered no whit less politely,       105
saying to him: "Although I cannot stir
     my swollen legs, I still have a free arm
     to use at times when nothing else will answer."
And the other wretch said: "It was not so free
     on your last walk to the stake, free as it was      110
     when you were coining." And he of the dropsy:
"That's true enough, but there was less truth in you
     when they questioned you at Troy." And Sinon then:
     "For every word I uttered that was not true
you uttered enough false coins to fill a bushel:      115
     I am put down here for a single crime,
     but you for more than any Fiend in Hell."[8]
"Think of the Horse," replied the swollen shade,
     "and may it torture you, perjurer, to recall
     that all the world knows the foul part you played."      120
"And to you the torture of the thirst that fries
     and cracks your tongue," said the Greek, "and of the water
     that swells your gut like a hedge before your eyes."
And the coiner: "So is your own mouth clogged
     with the filth that stuffs and sickens it as always;      125
     if I am parched while my paunch is waterlogged,
you have the fever and your cankered brain;
     and were you asked to lap Narcissus' mirror[9]

---

6. Potiphar's wife bore false witness against Joseph. (*Genesis* xxxix, 6–23.)     7. The Greek who glibly talked the Trojans into taking the Horse inside the city walls (*Aeneid* II, 57–194.) 8. Dante must reckon each false florin as a separate sin.     9. A pool of water. Ovid (*Metamorpheses* III, 407–510) tells how the young Narcissus fell in love with his own reflection in a pool. He remained bent over the reflection till he wasted away and was changed into a flower.

you would not wait to be invited again."
I was still standing, fixed upon those two                              130
  when the Master said to me: "Now keep on looking
  a little longer and I quarrel with you."
When I heard my Master raise his voice to me,
  I wheeled about with such a start of shame
  that I grow pale yet at the memory.                                   135
As one trapped in a nightmare that has caught
  his sleeping mind, wishes within the dream
  that it were all a dream, as if it were not—
such I became: my voice could not win through
  my shame to ask his pardon; while my shame                           140
  already won more pardon than I knew.
"Less shame," my Guide said, ever just and kind,
  "would wash away a greater fault than yours.
  Therefore, put back all sorrow from your mind;
and never forget that I am always by you                                145
  should it occur again, as we walk on,
  that we find ourselves where others of this crew
fall to such petty wrangling and upbraiding.
The wish to hear such baseness is degrading."

CANTO XXXI

*The Central Pit of Malebolge    The Giants*

  Dante's spirits rise again as the Poets approach the Central Pit, a
great well, at the bottom of which lies Cocytus, the Ninth and final
circle of Hell. Through the darkness Dante sees what appears to be
a city of great towers, but as he draws near he discovers that the great
shapes he has seen are the Giants and Titans who stand perpetual
guard inside the well-pit with the upper halves of their bodies rising
above the rim.
  Among the Giants, Virgil identifies Nimrod, builder of the Tower
of Babel; Ephialtes and Briareus, who warred against the Gods; and
Tityos and Typhon, who insulted Jupiter. Also here, but for no specific offense, is Antaeus, and his presence makes it clear that the
Giants are placed here less for their particular sins than for their
general natures.
  These are the sons of earth, embodiments of elemental forces
unbalanced by love, desire without restraint and without acknowledgment of moral and theological law. They are symbols of the earth-
trace that every devout man must clear from his soul, the unchecked
passions of the beast. Raised from the earth, they make the very gods
tremble. Now they are returned to the darkness of their origins,
guardians of earth's last depth.

At Virgil's persuasion, Antaeus takes the Poets in his huge palm
and lowers them gently to the final floor of Hell.

One and the same tongue had first wounded me
   so that the blood came rushing to my cheeks,
   and then supplied the soothing remedy.
Just so, as I have heard, the magic steel
   of the lance that was Achilles' and his father's         5
   could wound at a touch, and, at another, heal.[1]
We turned our backs on the valley and climbed from it
   to the top of the stony bank that walls it round,
   crossing in silence to the central pit.
Here it was less than night and less than day;         10
   my eyes could make out little through the gloom,
   but I heard the shrill note of a trumpet bray
louder than any thunder. As if by force,
   it drew my eyes; I stared into the gloom
   along the path of the sound back to its source.         15
After the bloody rout when Charlemagne
   had lost the band of Holy Knights, Roland[2]
   blew no more terribly for all his pain.
And as I stared through that obscurity,
   I saw what seemed a cluster of great towers,         20
   whereat I cried: "Master, what is this city?"
And he: "You are still too far back in the dark
   to make out clearly what you think you see;
   it is natural that you should miss the mark:
You will see clearly when you reach that place         25
   how much your eyes mislead you at a distance;
   I urge you, therefore, to increase your pace."
Then taking my hand in his, my Master said:
   "The better to prepare you for strange truth,
   let me explain those shapes you see ahead:         30
they are not towers but giants. They stand in the well
   from the navel down; and stationed round its bank
   they mount guard on the final pit of Hell."
Just as a man in a fog that starts to clear

---

1. Peleus, father of Achilles, left this magic lance to his son. (Ovid, *Metamorphoses* XIII, 171 ff.)
Sonneteers of Dante's time made frequent metaphoric use of this lance: just as the lance could
cure and then heal, so could the lady's look destroy with love and her kiss make whole.
2. Nephew of Charlemagne, hero of the French epic poem, the *Song of Roland*. He protected
the rear of Charlemagne's column on the return march through the Pyrenees from a war against
the Saracens. When he was attacked he was too proud to blow his horn as a signal for help, but
as he was dying he blew so prodigious a blast that it was heard by Charlemagne eight miles away.
*Band of Holy Knights*: The original is "*la santa gesta*," which may be interpreted as "the holy
undertaking." "*Gesta*," however, can also mean "a sworn band or fellowship of men at arms"
(such as the Knights of the Round Table), and since it was his Knights, rather than his undertaking, that Charlemagne lost, the second rendering seems more apt in context.

begins little by little to piece together
  the shapes the vapor crowded from the air—          35
so, when those shapes grew clearer as I drew
  across the darkness to the central brink,
  error fled from me; and my terror grew.
For just as at Montereggione[3] the great towers       40
  crown the encircling wall; so the grim giants
  whom Jove still threatens when the thunder roars
raised from the rim of stone about that well
  the upper halves of their bodies, which loomed up
  like turrets through the murky air of Hell.       45
I had drawn close enough to one already
  to make out the great arms along his sides,
  the face, the shoulders, the breast, and most of the belly.
Nature, when she destroyed the last exemplars
  on which she formed those beasts, surely did well      50
  to take such executioners from Mars.
And if she has not repented the creation
  of whales and elephants, the thinking man
  will see in that her justice and discretion:
for where the instrument of intelligence      55
  is added to brute power and evil will,
  mankind is powerless in its own defense.
His face, it seemed to me, was quite as high
  and wide as the bronze pine cone in St. Peter's[4]
  with the rest of him proportioned accordingly:      60
so that the bank, which made an apron for him
  from the waist down, still left so much exposed
  that three Frieslanders[5] standing on the rim,
one on another, could not have reached his hair;
  for to that point at which men's capes are buckled,      65
  thirty good hand-spans[6] of brute bulk rose clear.
"Rafel mahee amek zabi almit,"[7]
  began a bellowed chant from the brute mouth
  for which no sweeter psalmody was fit.
And my Guide in his direction: "Babbling fool,      70
  stick to your horn and vent yourself with it
  when rage or passion stir your stupid soul.
Feel there around your neck, you muddle-head,

---

3. A castle in Val d'Elsa near Siena built in 1213. Its walls had a circumference of more than
half a kilometer and were crowned by fourteen great towers, most of which are now destroyed.
4. Originally a part of a fountain. In Dante's time it stood in front of the Basilica of St. Peter. It
is now inside the Vatican. It stands about thirteen feet high (Scartazzini-Vandelli give the height
as four meters) but shows signs of mutilation that indicate it was once higher.   5. The men of
Friesland were reputed to be the tallest in Europe.   6. Dante uses the word "palma," which in
Italian signifies the spread of the open hand.   7. This line, as Virgil explains below, is Nimrod's
gibberish.

and find the cord; and there's the horn itself,
    there on your overgrown chest." To me he said:                    75
"His very babbling testifies the wrong
    he did on earth: he is Nimrod,[8] through whose evil
    mankind no longer speaks a common tongue.
Waste no words on him: it would be foolish.
    To him all speech is meaningless; as his own,                    80
    which no one understands, is simply gibberish."
We moved on, bearing left along the pit,
    and a crossbow-shot away we found the next one,
    an even huger and more savage spirit.
What master could have bound so gross a beast                        85
    I cannot say, but he had his right arm pinned
    behind his back, and the left across his breast
by an enormous chain that wound about him
    from the neck down, completing five great turns
    before it spiraled down below the rim.                           90
"This piece of arrogance," said my Guide to me,
    "dared try his strength against the power of Jove;
    for which he is rewarded as you see.
He is Ephialtes,[9] who made the great endeavour
    with the other giants who alarmed the Gods;                      95
    the arms he raised then, now are bound forever."
"Were it possible, I should like to take with me,"
    I said to him, "the memory of seeing
    the immeasurable Briareus."[1] And he:
"Nearer to hand, you may observe Antaeus[2]                         100
    who is able to speak to us, and is not bound.
    It is he will set us down in Cocytus,[3]
the bottom of all guilt. The other hulk
    stands far beyond our road. He too, is bound
    and looks like this one, but with a fiercer sulk."              105
No earthquake in the fury of its shock
    ever seized a tower more violently,

---

8. The first king of Babylon, supposed to have built the Tower of Babel, for which he is punished, in part, by the confusion of his own tongue and understanding. Nothing in the Biblical reference portrays him as one of the earth-giants.    9. Son of Neptune (the sea) and Iphimedia. With his brother, Otus, he warred against the Gods striving to pile Mt. Ossa on Mt. Olympus, and Mt. Pelion on Mt. Ossa. Apollo restored good order by killing the two brothers.    1. Another of the giants who rose against the Olympian Gods. Virgil speaks of him as having a hundred arms and fifty hands (*Aeneid* X, 565–568), but Dante has need only of his size, and of his sin, which he seems to view as a kind of revolt of the angels, just as the action of Ephialtes and Otus may be read as a pagan distortion of the Tower of Babel legend. He was the son of Uranus and Tellus. 2. The son of Neptune and Tellus (the earth). In battle, his strength grew every time he touched the earth, his mother. He was accordingly invincible until Hercules killed him by lifting him over his head and strangling him in mid-air. Lucan (*Pharsalia* IV, 595–660) describes Antaeus' great lion-hunting feat in the valley of Zama where, in a later era, Scipio defeated Hannibal. Antaeus did not join in the rebellion against the Gods and therefore he is not chained.    3. The final pit of Hell.

than Ephialtes, hearing, began to rock.
Then I dreaded death as never before;
  and I think I could have died for very fear 110
  had I not seen what manacles he wore.
We left the monster, and not far from him
  we reached Antaeus, who to his shoulders alone
  soared up a good five ells above the rim.
"O soul who once in Zama's fateful vale— 115
  where Scipio became the heir of glory
  when Hannibal and all his troops turned tail—
took more than a thousand lions for your prey;
  and in whose memory many still believe
  the sons of earth would yet have won the day 120
had you joined with them against High Olympus—
  do not disdain to do us a small service,
  but set us down where the cold grips Cocytus.
Would you have us go to Tityos or Typhon?[4]—
  this man can give you what is longed for here: 125
  therefore do not refuse him, but bend down.
For he can still make new your memory:
  he lives, and awaits long life, unless Grace call him
  before his time to his felicity."
Thus my Master to that Tower of Pride; 130
  and the giant without delay reached out the hands
  which Hercules had felt, and raised my Guide.
Virgil, when he felt himself so grasped,
  called to me: "Come, and I will hold you safe."
  And he took me in his arms and held me clasped. 135
The way the Carisenda[5] seems to one
  who looks up from the leaning side when clouds
  are going over it from that direction,
making the whole tower seem to topple—so
  Antaeus seemed to me in the fraught moment 140
  when I stood clinging, watching from below
as he bent down; while I with heart and soul
  wished we had gone some other way, but gently
  he set us down inside the final hole
whose ice holds Judas and Lucifer in its grip. 145
Then straightened like a mast above a ship.

4. Also sons of Tellus. They offended Jupiter, who had them hurled into the crater of Etna, below which the Lake Tartarus was supposed to lie.   5. A leaning tower of Bologna.

## CANTO XXXII

*Circle Nine: Cocytus    Compound Fraud*
*Round One: Caïna    The Treacherous to Kin*
*Round Two: Antenora    The Treacherous to Country*

At the bottom of the well Dante finds himself on a huge frozen
lake. This is Cocytus, the Ninth Circle, the fourth and last great
water of Hell, and here, fixed in the ice, each according to his guilt,
are punished sinners guilty of Treachery Against Those to Whom
They Were Bound by Special Ties. The ice is divided into four concentric rings marked only by the different positions of the damned
within the ice.

This is Dante's symbolic equivalent of the final guilt. The treacheries of these souls were denials of love (which is God) and of all
human warmth. Only the remorseless dead center of the ice will
serve to express their natures. As they denied God's love, so are they
furthest removed from the light and warmth of His Sun. As they
denied all human ties, so are they bound only by the unyielding ice.

The first round is Caïna, named for Cain. Here lie those who
were treacherous against blood ties. They have their necks and heads
out of the ice and are permitted to bow their heads—a double boon
since it allows them some protection from the freezing gale and,
further, allows their tears to fall without freezing their eyes shut.
Here Dante sees Alessandro and Napoleone degli Alberti, and he
speaks to Camicion, who identifies other sinners of this round.

The second round is Antenora, named for Antenor, the Trojan
who was believed to have betrayed his city to the Greeks. Here lie
those guilty of Treachery to Country. They, too, have their heads
above the ice, but they cannot bend their necks, which are gripped
by the ice. Here Dante accidentally kicks the head of Bocca Degli
Abbati and then proceeds to treat him with a savagery he had shown
to no other soul in Hell. Bocca names some of his fellow traitors,
and the Poets pass on to discover two heads frozen together in one
hole. One of them is gnawing the nape of the other's neck.

If I had rhymes as harsh and horrible
    as the hard fact of that final dismal hole
    which bears the weight of all the steeps of Hell,
I might more fully press the sap and substance
    from my conception; but since I must do            5
    without them, I begin with some reluctance.
For it is no easy undertaking, I say,
    to describe the bottom of the Universe;
    nor is it for tongues that only babble child's play.
But may those Ladies of the Heavenly Spring[6]         10

6. The Muses. They so inspired Amphion's hand upon the lyre that the music charmed blocks
of stone out of Mount Cithaeron, and the blocks formed themselves into the walls of Thebes.

who helped Amphion wall Thebes, assist my verse,
   that the word may be the mirror of the thing.
O most miscreant rabble, you who keep
   the stations of that place whose name is pain,
   better had you been born as goats or sheep!       15
We stood now in the dark pit of the well,
   far down the slope below the Giant's feet,
   and while I still stared up at the great wall,
I heard a voice cry: "Watch which way you turn:
   take care you do not trample on the heads       20
   of the forsworn and miserable brethren."
Whereat I turned and saw beneath my feet
   and stretching out ahead, a lake so frozen
   it seemed to be made of glass. So thick a sheet
never yet hid the Danube's winter course,       25
   nor, far away beneath the frigid sky,
   locked the Don up in its frozen source:
for were Tanbernick and the enormous peak
   of Pietrapana[7] to crash down on it,
   not even the edges would so much as creak.       30
The way frogs sit to croak, their muzzles leaning
   out of the water, at the time and season
   when the peasant woman dreams of her day's gleaning—[8]
Just so the livid dead are sealed in place
   up to the part at which they blushed for shame,      35
   and they beat their teeth like storks. Each holds his face
bowed toward the ice, each of them testifies
   to the cold with his chattering mouth, to his heart's grief
   with tears that flood forever from his eyes.
When I had stared about me, I looked down      40
   and at my feet I saw two clamped together
   so tightly that the hair of their heads had grown
together. "Who are you," I said, "who lie
   so tightly breast to breast?" They strained their necks,
   and when they had raised their heads as if to reply,     45
the tears their eyes had managed to contain
   up to that time gushed out, and the cold froze them
   between the lids, sealing them shut again
tighter than any clamp grips wood to wood,
   and mad with pain, they fell to butting heads     50
   like billy-goats in a sudden savage mood.
And a wraith who lay to one side and below,
   and who had lost both ears to frostbite, said,
   his head still bowed: "Why do you watch us so?

7. There is no agreement on the location of the mountain Dante called Tanbernick. Pietrapana, today known as *la Pania*, is in Tuscany.    8. The summer.

If you wish to know who they are[9] who share one doom,          55
   they owned the Bisenzio's valley with their father,
   whose name was Albert. They spring from one womb,
and you may search through all Caïna's crew
   without discovering in all this waste
   a squab more fit for the aspic than these two;          60
not him whose breast and shadow a single blow
   of the great lance of King Arthur pierced with light;[1]
   nor yet Focaccia[2] nor this one fastened so
into the ice that his head is all I see,
   and whom, if you are Tuscan, you know well—          65
   his name on the earth was Sassol Mascheroni.[3]
And I—to tell you all and so be through—
   was Camicion de' Pazzi.[4] I wait for Carlin
   beside whose guilt my sins will shine like virtue."
And leaving him,[5] I saw a thousand faces          70
   discolored so by cold, I shudder yet
   and always will when I think of those frozen places.
As we approached the center of all weight,
   where I went shivering in eternal shade,
   whether it was my will, or chance, or fate,          75
I cannot say, but as I trailed my Guide
   among those heads, my foot struck violently
   against the face of one.[6] Weeping, it cried:
"Why do you kick me? If you were not sent
   to wreak a further vengeance for Montaperti,          80
   why do you add this to my other torment?"
"Master," I said, "grant me a moment's pause
   to rid myself of a doubt concerning this one;
   then you may hurry me at your own pace."
The Master stopped at once, and through the volley          85
   of foul abuse the wretch poured out, I said:
   "Who are you who curse others so?" And he:

9. Alessandro and Napoleone, Counts of Mangona. Among other holdings, they inherited a
castle in the Val di Bisenzio. They seemed to have been at odds on all things and finally killed
one another in a squabble over their inheritance and their politics (Alessandro was a Guelph and
Napoleone a Ghibelline).   1. Modred, King Arthur's traitorous nephew. He tried to kill Arthur,
but the king struck him a single blow of his lance, and when it was withdrawn, a shaft of light
passed through the gaping wound and split the shadow of the falling traitor.   2. Of the Cancellieri of Pistoia. He murdered his cousin (among others) and may have been the principal cause of
a great feud that divided the Cancellieri, and split the Guelphs into the White and Black parties.
3. Of the Toschi of Florence. He was appointed guardian of one of his nephews and murdered
him to get the inheritance for himself.   4. Alberto Camicion de' Pazzi of Valdarno. He murdered a kinsman. *Carlin:* Carlino de' Pazzi, relative of Alberto. He was charged with defending
for the Whites the castle of Piantravigne in Valdarno but surrendered it for a bribe. He belongs
therefore in the next lower circle, Antenora, as a traitor to his country, and when he arrives there
his greater sin will make Alberto seem almost virtuous by comparison.   5. These words mark
the departure from Caïna to Antenora.   6. Bocca degli Abbati, a traitorous Florentine. At the
battle of Montaperti (cf. Farinata, Canto X) he hacked off the hand of the Florentine standard
bearer. The cavalry, lacking a standard around which it could rally, was soon routed.

"And who are *you* who go through the dead larder
   of Antenora kicking the cheeks of others
   so hard, that were you alive, you could not kick harder?"          90
"I *am* alive," I said, "and if you seek fame,
   it may be precious to you above all else
   that my notes on this descent include your name."
"Exactly the opposite is my wish and hope,"
   he answered. "Let me be; for it's little you know               95
   of how to flatter on this icy slope."
I grabbed the hair of his dog's-ruff and I said:
   "Either you tell me truly who you are,
   or you won't have a hair left on your head."
And he: "Not though you snatch me bald. I swear                    100
   I will not tell my name nor show my face.
   Not though you rip until my brain lies bare."
I had a good grip on his hair; already
   I had yanked out more than one fistful of it,
   while the wretch yelped, but kept his face turned from me;      105
when another said: "Bocca, what is it ails you?
   What the Hell's wrong?[7] Isn't it bad enough
   to hear you bang your jaws? Must you bark too?"
"Now filthy traitor, say no more!" I cried,
   "for to your shame, be sure I shall bear back                   110
   a true report of you." The wretch replied:
"Say anything you please but go away.
   And if you *do* get back, don't overlook
   that pretty one who had so much to say
just now. Here he laments the Frenchman's price.                  115
   'I saw Buoso da Duera,'[8] you can report,
   'where the bad salad is kept crisp on ice.'
And if you're asked who else was wintering here,
   Beccheria,[9] whose throat was slit by Florence,
   is there beside you. Gianni de' Soldanier[1]                    120
is further down, I think, with Ganelon,[2]

---

7. In the circumstances, a monstrous pun. The original is *"qual diavolo ti tocca?"* (what devil touches, or molests, you?) a standard colloquialism for "what's the matter with you?" A similar pun occurs in line 117 "kept crisp (cool) on ice. Colloquially *"stare fresco"* (to be or to remain cool) equals "to be left out in the cold," i.e., to be out of luck.     8. Of Cremona. In 1265 Charles of Anjou marched against Manfred and Naples (see Canto XIX), and Buoso da Duera was sent out in charge of a Ghibelline army to oppose the passage of one of Charles' armies, but accepted a bribe and let the French pass unopposed. The event took place near Parma.     9. Tesauro dei Beccheria of Pavia, Abbot of Vallombrosa and Papal Legate (of Alexander IV) in Tuscany. The Florentine Guelphs cut off his head in 1258 for plotting with the expelled Ghibellines. 1. A Florentine Ghibelline of ancient and noble family. In 1265, however, during the riots that occurred under the Two Jovial Friars, he deserted his party and became a leader of the commoners (Guelphs). In placing him in Antenora, Dante makes no distinction between turning on one's country and turning on one's political party, not at least if the end is simply for power.     2. It was Ganelon who betrayed Roland to the Saracens. (See Canto XXXI.)

and Tebaldello,[3] who opened the gates of Faenza
and let Bologna steal in with the dawn."
Leaving him then, I saw two souls together
in a single hole, and so pinched in by the ice                    125
that one head made a helmet for the other.
As a famished man chews crusts—so the one sinner
sank his teeth into the other's nape
at the base of the skull, gnawing his loathsome dinner.
Tydeus in his final raging hour                                   130
gnawed Menalippus' head[4] with no more fury
than this one gnawed at skull and dripping gore.
"You there," I said, "who show so odiously
your hatred for that other, tell me why
on this condition: that if in what you tell me                    135
you seem to have a reasonable complaint
against him you devour with such foul relish,
I, knowing who you are, and his soul's taint,
may speak your cause to living memory,                            140
God willing the power of speech be left to me."

## CANTO XXXIII

*Circle Nine: Cocytus    Compound Fraud*
*Round Two: Antenora    The Treacherous to Country*
*Round Three: Ptolomea    The Treacherous to Guests and Hosts*

In reply to Dante's exhortation, the sinner who is gnawing his
companion's head looks up, wipes his bloody mouth on his victim's
hair, and tells his harrowing story. He is Count Ugolino and the
wretch he gnaws is Archbishop Ruggieri. Both are in Antenora for
treason. In life they had once plotted together. Then Ruggieri betrayed
his fellow-plotter and caused his death, by starvation, along with his
four "sons." In the most pathetic and dramatic passage of the Inferno,
Ugolino details how their prison was sealed and how his "sons" dropped
dead before him one by one, weeping for food. His terrible tale serves
only to renew his grief and hatred, and he has hardly finished it
before he begins to gnaw Ruggieri again with renewed fury. In the
immutable Law of Hell, the killer-by-starvation becomes the food of
his victim.

The Poets leave Ugolino and enter Ptolomea, so named for the
Ptolomaeus of *Maccabees*, who murdered his father-in-law at a ban-

3. Tebaldello de' Zambrasi of Faenza. At dawn on November 13, 1280, he opened the city
gates and delivered Faenza to the Bolognese Guelphs in order to revenge himself on the
Chibelline family of the Lambertazzi who, in 1274, had fled from Bologna to take refuge in
Faenza.    4. Statius recounts in the *Thebaid* that Tydeus killed Menalippus in battle but fell
himself mortally wounded. As he lay dying he had Menalippus' head brought to him and fell to
gnawing it in his dying rage.

quet. Here are punished those who were Treacherous Against the Ties of Hospitality. They lie with only half their faces above the ice and their tears freeze in their eye sockets, sealing them with little crystal visors. Thus even the comfort of tears is denied them. Here Dante finds Friar Alberigo and Branca D'Oria, and discovers the terrible power of Ptolomea: so great is its sin that the souls of the guilty fall to its torments even before they die, leaving their bodies still on earth, inhabited by Demons.

The sinner raised his mouth from his grim repast
   and wiped it on the hair of the bloody head
   whose nape he had all but eaten away. At last
he began to speak: "You ask me to renew
   a grief so desperate that the very thought         5
   of speaking of it tears my heart in two.
But if my words may be a seed that bears
   the fruit of infamy for him I gnaw,
   I shall weep, but tell my story through my tears.
Who you may be, and by what powers you reach      10
   into this underworld, I cannot guess,
   but you seem to me a Florentine by your speech.
I was Count Ugolino,[5] I must explain;
   this reverend grace is the Archbishop Ruggieri:
   now I will tell you why I gnaw his brain.      15
That I, who trusted him, had to undergo
   imprisonment and death through his treachery,
   you will know already.[6] What you cannot know—
that is, the lingering inhumanity
   of the death I suffered—you shall hear in full:     20
   then judge for yourself if he has injured me.
A narrow window in that coop[7] of stone
   now called the Tower of Hunger for my sake
   (within which others yet must pace alone)
had shown me several waning moons already[8]     25
   between its bars, when I slept the evil sleep
   in which the veil of the future parted for me.
This beast[9] appeared as master of a hunt

5. Count of Donoratico and a member of the Guelph family della Gherardesca. He and his nephew, Nino de' Visconti, led the two Guelph factions of Pisa. In 1288 Ugolino intrigued with Archbishop Ruggieri degli Ubaldini, leader of the Ghibellines, to get rid of Visconti and to take over the command of all the Pisan Guelphs. The plan worked, but in the consequent weakening of the Guelphs, Ruggieri saw his chance and betrayed Ugolino, throwing him into prison with his sons and his grandsons. In the following year the prison was sealed up and they were left to starve to death.   6. News of Ugolino's imprisonment and death would certainly have reached Florence. *What you cannot know:* No living man could know what happened after Ugolino and his sons were sealed in the prison and abandoned.   7. Dante uses the word *muda*, in Italian signifying a stone tower in which falcons were kept in the dark to moult. From the time of Ugolino's death it became known as The Tower of Hunger.   8. Ugolino was jailed late in 1288. He was sealed in to starve early in 1289.   9. Ruggieri.

chasing the wolf and his whelps across the mountain
 that hides Lucca from Pisa.[1] Out in front 30
of the starved and shrewd and avid pack he had placed
 Gualandi and Sismondi and Lanfranchi[2]
 to point his prey. The father and sons had raced
a brief course only when they failed of breath
 and seemed to weaken; then I thought I saw 35
 their flanks ripped open by the hounds' fierce teeth.
Before the dawn, the dream still in my head,
 I woke and heard my sons,[3] who were there with me,
 cry from their troubled sleep, asking for bread.
You are cruelty itself if you can keep 40
 your tears back at the thought of what foreboding
 stirred in my heart; and if you do not weep,
at what are you used to weeping?—The hour when food
 used to be brought, drew near. They were now awake,
 and each was anxious from his dream's dark mood. 45
And from the base of that horrible tower I heard
 the sound of hammers nailing up the gates:
 I stared at my sons' faces without a word.
I did not weep: I had turned stone inside.
 They wept. 'What ails you, Father, you look so strange,' 50
 my little Anselm, youngest of them, cried.
But I did not speak a word nor shed a tear:
 not all that day nor all that endless night,
 until I saw another sun appear.
When a tiny ray leaked into that dark prison 55
 and I saw staring back from their four faces
 the terror and the wasting of my own,
I bit my hands in helpless grief. And they,
 thinking I chewed myself for hunger, rose
 suddenly together. I heard them say: 60
'Father, it would give us much less pain
 if you ate us: it was you who put upon us
 this sorry flesh; now strip it off again.'
I calmed myself to spare them. Ah! hard earth,
 why did you not yawn open? All that day 65
 and the next we sat in silence. On the fourth,
Gaddo, the eldest, fell before me and cried,
 stretched at my feet upon that prison floor:
 'Father, why don't you help me?' There he died.

1. These two cities would be in view of one another were it not for Monte San Giuliano.
2. Three Pisan nobles, Ghibellines and friends of the Archbishop. 3. Actually two of the boys
were grandsons and all were considerably older than one would gather from Dante's account.
Anselm, the younger grandson, was fifteen. The others were really young men and were certainly
old enough for guilt despite Dante's charge in line 90.

And just as you see me, I saw them fall                                    70
  one by one on the fifth day and the sixth.
  Then, already blind, I began to crawl
from body to body shaking them frantically.
  Two days I called their names, and they were dead.
  Then fasting overcame my grief and me."[4]                       75
His eyes narrowed to slits when he was done,
  and he seized the skull again between his teeth
  grinding it as a mastiff grinds a bone.
Ah, Pisa! foulest blemish on the land
  where "sì" sounds sweet and clear,[5] since those nearby you   80
  are slow to blast the ground on which you stand,
may Caprara and Gorgona[6] drift from place
  and dam the flooding Arno at its mouth
  until it drowns the last of your foul race!
For if to Ugolino falls the censure                                        85
  for having betrayed your castles,[7] you for your part
  should not have put his sons to such a torture:
you modern Thebes![8] those tender lives you spilt—
  Brigata, Uguccione, and the others
  I mentioned earlier—were too young for guilt!                   90
We passed on further,[9] where the frozen mine
  entombs another crew in greater pain;
  these wraiths are not bent over, but lie supine.
Their very weeping closes up their eyes;
  and the grief that finds no outlet for its tears               95
  turns inward to increase their agonies:
for the first tears that they shed knot instantly
  in their eye-sockets, and as they freeze they form
  a crystal visor above the cavity.
And despite the fact that standing in that place                           100
  I had become as numb as any callus,
  and all sensation had faded from my face,
somehow I felt a wind begin to blow,
  whereat I said: "Master, what stirs this wind?

---

4. I.e., he died. Some interpret the line to mean that Ugolino's hunger drove him to cannibalism. Ugolino's present occupation in Hell would certainly support that interpretation but the fact is that cannibalism is the one major sin Dante does not assign a place to in Hell. So monstrous would it have seemed to him that he must certainly have established a special punishment for it. Certainly he could hardly have relegated it to an ambiguity. Moreover, it would be a sin of bestiality rather than of fraud, and as such it would be punished in the Seventh Circle. 5. Italy. 6. These two islands near the mouth of the Arno were Pisan possessions in 1300. 7. In 1284, Ugolino gave up certain castles to Lucca and Florence. He was at war with Genoa at the time and it is quite likely that he ceded the castles to buy the neutrality of these two cities, for they were technically allied with Genoa. Dante, however, must certainly consider the action as treasonable, for otherwise Ugolino would be in Caïna for his treachery to Visconti. 8. Thebes, as a number of the foregoing notes will already have made clear, was the site of some of the most hideous crimes of antiquity. 9. Marks the passage into Ptolomea.

Is not all heat extinguished here below?"[1]                                    105
And the Master said to me: "Soon you will be
    where your own eyes will see the source and cause
    and give you their own answer to the mystery."
And one of those locked in that icy mall
    cried out to us as we passed: "O souls so cruel                            110
    that you are sent to the last post of all,
relieve me for a little from the pain
    of this hard veil; let my heart weep a while
    before the weeping freeze my eyes again."
And I to him: "If you would have my service,                                   115
    tell me your name; then if I do not help you
    may I descend to the last rim of the ice."[2]
"I am Friar Alberigo,"[3] he answered therefore,
    "the same who called for the fruits from the bad garden.
    Here I am given dates for figs full store."                                120
"What! Are you dead already?" I said to him.
    And he then: "How my body stands in the world
    I do not know. So privileged is this rim
of Ptolomea, that often souls fall to it
    before dark Atropos[4] has cut their thread.                               125
    And that you may more willingly free my spirit
of this glaze of frozen tears that shrouds my face,
    I will tell you this: when a soul betrays as I did,
    it falls from flesh, and a demon takes its place,
ruling the body till its time is spent.                                        130
    The ruined soul rains down into this cistern.
    So, I believe, there is still evident
in the world above, all that is fair and mortal
    of this black shade who winters here behind me.
    If you have only recently crossed the portal                              135
from that sweet world, you surely must have known
    his body: Branca D'Oria[5] is its name,
    and many years have passed since he rained down."
"I think you are trying to take me in," I said,
    "Ser Branca D'Oria is a living man;                                        140

1. Dante believed (rather accurately, by chance) that all winds resulted from "exhalations of heat." Cocytus, however, is conceived as wholly devoid of heat, a metaphysical absolute zero. The source of the wind, as we discover in the next Canto, is Satan himself.   2. Dante is not taking any chances; he has to go on to the last rim in any case. The sinner, however, believes him to be another damned soul and would interpret the oath quite otherwise than as Dante meant it.   3. Of the Manfredi of Faenza. He was another Jovial Friar. In 1284 his brother Manfred struck him in the course of an argument. Alberigo pretended to let it pass, but in 1285 he invited Manfred and his son to a banquet and had them murdered. The signal to the assassins was the words: "Bring in the fruit." Friar Alberigo's bad fruit," became a proverbial saying.   4. The Fate who cuts the thread of life.   5. A Genoese Ghibelline. His sin is identical in kind to that of Friar Alberigo. In 1275 he invited his father-in-law, Michel Zanche (see Canto XXII), to a banquest and had him and his companions cut to pieces. He was assisted in the butchery by his nephew.

he eats, he drinks, he fills his clothes and his bed."
"Michel Zanche had not yet reached the ditch
  of the Black Talons," the frozen wraith replied,
  "there where the sinners thicken in hot pitch,
when this one left his body to a devil,                            145
  as did his nephew and second in treachery,
  and plumbed like lead through space to this dead level.
But now reach out your hand, and let me cry."
  And I did not keep the promise I had made,
  for to be rude to him was courtesy.                        150
Ah, men of Genoa! souls of little worth,
  corrupted from all custom of righteousness,
  why have you not been driven from the earth?
For there beside the blackest soul of all
  Romagna's evil plain, lies one of yours                     155
  bathing his filthy soul in the eternal
glacier of Cocytus for his foul crime,
while he seems yet alive in world and time!

## CANTO XXXIV

*Ninth Circle: Cocytus  Compound Fraud*
*Round Four: Judecca  The Treacherous to Their Masters*
*The Center:  Satan*

"On march the banners of the King," Virgil begins as the Poets
face the last depth. He is quoting a medieval hymn, and to it he adds
the distortion and preversion of all that lies about him. "On march
the banners of the King—of Hell." And there before them, in an
infernal parody of Godhead, they see Satan in the distance, his great
wings beating like a windmill. It is their beating that is the source of
the icy wind of Cocytus, the exhalation of all evil.

All about him in the ice are strewn the sinners of the last round,
Judecca, named for Judas Iscariot. These are the Treacherous to
Their Masters. They lie completely sealed in the ice, twisted and
distorted into every conceivable posture. It is impossible to speak to
them, and the Poets move on to observe Satan.

He is fixed into the ice at the center to which flow all the rivers of
guilt; and as he beats his great wings as if to escape, their icy wind
only freezes him more surely into the polluted ice. In a grotesque
parody of the Trinity, he has three faces, each a different color, and
in each mouth he clamps a sinner whom he rips eternally with his
teeth. Judas Iscariot is in the central mouth: Brutus and Cassius in
the mouths on either side.

Having seen all, the Poets now climb through the center, grappling hand over hand down the hairy flank of Satan himself—a last

supremely symbolic action—and at last, when they have passed the
center of all gravity, they emerge from Hell. A long climb from the
earth's center to the Mount of Purgatory awaits them, and they push
on without rest, ascending along the sides of the river Lethe, till they
emerge once more to see the stars of Heaven, just before dawn on
Easter Sunday.

"On march the banners of the King of Hell,"[6]
   my Master said. "Toward us. Look straight ahead:
   can you make him out at the core of the frozen shell?"
Like a whirling windmill seen afar at twilight,
   or when a mist has risen from the ground—            5
   just such an engine rose upon my sight
stirring up such a wild and bitter wind
   I cowered for shelter at my Master's back,
   there being no other windbreak I could find.
I stood now where the souls of the last class            10
   (with fear my verses tell it) were covered wholly;
   they shone below the ice like straws in glass.
Some lie stretched out; others are fixed in place
   upright, some on their heads, some on their soles;
   another, like a bow, bends foot to face.            15
When we had gone so far across the ice
   that it pleased my Guide to show me the foul creature[7]
   which once had worn the grace of Paradise,
he made me stop, and, stepping aside, he said:
   "Now see the face of Dis! This is the place        20
   where you must arm your soul against all dread."
Do not ask, Reader, how my blood ran cold
   and my voice choked up with fear. I cannot write it:
   this is a terror that cannot be told.
I did not die, and yet I lost life's breath:          25
   imagine for youself what I became,
   deprived at once of both my life and death.
The Emperor of the Universe of Pain
   jutted his upper chest above the ice;
   and I am closer in size to the great mountain       30
the Titans make around the central pit,
   than they to his arms. Now, starting from this part,
   imagine the whole that corresponds to it!
If he was once as beautiful as now
   he is hideous, and still turned on his Maker,      35

6. *On march the banners of the King*: The hymn (*Vexilla regis prodeunt*) was written in the sixth
century by Venantius Fortunatus, Bishop of Poitiers. The original celebrates the Holy Cross, and
is part of the service for Good Friday to be sung at the moment of uncovering the cross.
7. Satan.

well may he be the source of every woe!
With what a sense of awe I saw his head
   towering above me! for it had three faces:
   one was in front, and it was fiery red;
the other two, as weirdly wonderful,             40
   merged with it from the middle of each shoulder
   to the point where all converged at the top of the skull;
the right was something between white and bile;
   the left was about the color that one finds
   on those who live along the banks of the Nile.       45
Under each head two wings rose terribly,
   their span proportioned to so gross a bird:
   I never saw such sails upon the sea.
They were not feathers—their texture and their form
   were like a bat's wings—and he beat them so       50
   that three winds blew from him in one great storm:
it is these winds that freeze all Cocytus.
   He wept from his six eyes, and down three chins
   the tears ran mixed with bloody froth and pus.[8]
In every mouth he worked a broken sinner        55
   between his rake-like teeth. Thus he kept three
   in eternal pain at his eternal dinner.
For the one in front the biting seemed to play
   no part at all compared to the ripping: at times
   the whole skin of his back was flayed away.       60
"That soul that suffers most," explained my Guide,
   "is Judas Iscariot, he who kicks his legs
   on the fiery chin and has his head inside.
Of the other two, who have their heads thrust forward,
   the one who dangles down from the black face     65
   is Brutus: note how he writhes without a word.
And there, with the huge and sinewy arms,[9] is the soul
   of Cassius.—But the night is coming on[1]
   and we must go, for we have seen the whole."
Then, as he bade, I clasped his neck, and he,      70
   watching for a moment when the wings
   were opened wide, reached over dexterously
and seized the shaggy coat of the king demon;
   then grappling matted hair and frozen crusts
   from one tuft to another, clambered down.     75
When we had reached the joint where the great thigh

---

8. The gore of the sinners he chews which is mixed with his slaver.   9. The Cassius who betrayed Caesar was more generally described in terms of Shakespeare's "lean and hungry look." Another Cassius is described by Cicero (*Catiline* III) as huge and sinewy. Dante probably confused the two.   1. It is now Saturday evening.

merges into the swelling of the haunch,
   my Guide and Master, straining terribly,
turned his head to where his feet had been
   and began to grip the hair as if he were climbing;     80
   so that I thought we moved toward Hell again.
"Hold fast!" my Guide said, and his breath came shrill[2]
   with labor and exhaustion. "There is no way
   but by such stairs to rise above such evil."
At last he climbed out through an opening     85
   in the central rock, and he seated me on the rim;
   then joined me with a nimble backward spring.
I looked up, thinking to see Lucifer
   as I had left him, and I saw instead
   his legs projecting high into the air.     90
Now let all those whose dull minds are still vexed
   by failure to understand what point it was
   I had passed through, judge if I was perplexed.
"Get up. Up on your feet," my Master said.
   "The sun already mounts to middle tierce,[3]     95
   and a long road and hard climbing lie ahead."
It was no hall of state we had found there,
   but a natural animal pit hollowed from rock
   with a broken floor and a close and sunless air.
"Before I tear myself from the Abyss,"     100
   I said when I had risen, "O my Master,
   explain to me my error in all this:
where is the ice? and Lucifer—how has he
   been turned from top to bottom: and how can the sun
   have gone from night to day so suddenly?"     105
And he to me: "You imagine you are still
   on the other side of the center where I grasped
   the shaggy flank of the Great Worm of Evil
which bores through the world—you *were* while I climbed down, 110
   but when I turned myself about, you passed
   the point to which all gravities are drawn.
You are under the other hemisphere where you stand;
   the sky above us is the half opposed
   to that which canopies the great dry land.
Under the mid-point of that other sky     115
   the Man who was born sinless and who lived
   beyond all blemish, came to suffer and die.

---

2. CF. Canto XXIII, 85, where the fact that Dante breathes indicates to the Hypocrites that he is alive. Virgil's breathing is certainly a contradiction.     3. In the canonical day tierce is the period from about six to nine A.M. Middle tierce, therefore, is seven-thirty. In going through the center point, they have gone from night to day. They have moved ahead twelve hours.

You have your feet upon a little sphere
   which forms the other face of the Judecca.
   There it is evening when it is morning here.      120
And this gross Fiend and Image of all Evil
   who made a stairway for us with his hide
   is pinched and prisoned in the ice-pack still.
On this side he plunged down from heaven's height,
   and the land that spread here once hid in the sea      125
   and fled North to our hemisphere for fright;
and it may be that moved by that same fear,
   the one peak[4] that still rises on this side
   fled upward leaving this great cavern here."
Down there, beginning at the further bound      130
   of Beelzebub's dim tomb, there is a space
   not known by sight, but only by the sound
of a little stream[5] descending through the hollow
   it has eroded from the massive stone
   in its endlessly entwining lazy flow."      135
My Guide and I crossed over and began
   to mount that little known and lightless road
   to ascend into the shining world again.
He first, I second, without thought of rest
   we climbed the dark until we reached the point      140
   where a round opening brought in sight the blest
and beauteous shining of the Heavenly Cars.
And we walked out once more beneath the Stars.[6]

## Purgatorio

### CANTO I

*Ante-Purgatory:*
*The Shore of the Island   Cato of Utica*

The Poets emerge from Hell just before dawn of Easter Sunday
(April 10, 1300), and Dante revels in the sight of the rediscovered
heavens. As he looks eagerly about at the stars, he sees nearby an old
man of impressive bearing. The ancient is Cato of Utica, guardian
of the shores of Purgatory. Cato challenges the Poets as fugitives
from Hell, but Virgil, after first instructing Dante to kneel in rever-

---

4. The Mount of Purgatory.   5. Lethe. In classical mythology, the river of forgetfulness, from
which souls drank before being born. In Dante's symbolism it flows down from Purgatory, where
it has washed away the memory of sin from the souls who are undergoing purification. That
memory it delivers to Hell, which draws all sin to itself.   6. Dante ends each of the three
divisions of the *Commedia* with this word. Every conclusion of the upward soul is toward the
stars, God's shining symbols of hope and virtue. It is just before dawn of Easter Sunday that the
Poets emerge.

ence, explains Dante's mission and Beatrice's command. Cato then
gives them instructions for proceeding.

The Poets have emerged at a point a short way up the slope of
Purgatory. It is essential, therefore, that they descend to the lowest
point and begin from there, an allegory of Humility. Cato, accordingly, orders Virgil to lead Dante to the shore, to wet his hands in
the dew of the new morning, and to wash the stains of Hell from
Dante's face and the film of Hell's vapors from Dante's eyes. Virgil
is then to bind about Dante's waist one of the pliant reeds (symbolizing Humility) that grow in the soft mud of the shore.

Having so commanded, Cato disappears. Dante arises in silence
and stands waiting, eager to begin. His look is all the communication that is necessary. Virgil leads him to the shore and performs all
that Cato has commanded, Dante's first purification is marked by a
miracle: when Virgil breaks off a reed, the stalk immediately regen-
erates a new reed, restoring itself exactly as it had been.

For better waters now the little bark
   of my indwelling powers raises her sails,
   and leaves behind that sea so cruel and dark.
Now shall I sing that second kingdom[7] given
   the soul of man wherein to purge its guilt                 5
   and so grow worthy to ascend to Heaven.
Yours am I, sacred Muses! To you I pray.
   Here let dead poetry[8] rise once more to life,
   and here let sweet Calliope[9] rise and play
some far accompaniment in that high strain                10
   whose power the wretched Pierides once felt
   so terribly they dared not hope again.
Sweet azure of the sapphire of the east
   was gathering on the serene horizon
   its pure and perfect radiance—a feast                15
to my glad eyes, reborn to their delight,
   as soon as I had passed from the dead air[1]
   which had oppressed my soul and dimmed my sight.
The planet whose sweet influence strengthens love[2]
   was making all the east laugh with her rays,          20
   veiling the Fishes, which she swam above.

7. Purgatory.   8. The verses that sang of Hell. Dante may equally have meant that poetry as
an art has long been surpassed by history as the medium for great subjects. Here poetry will return
to its classic state.   9. Muse of Epic Poetry. Dante exhorts Calliope to fill him with the strains
of the music she played in the defeat of the Pierides, the nine daughters of Pierius, King of
Thessaly. They presumed to challenge the Muses to a contest of song. After their defeat they were
changed into magpies for their presumption. Ovid (*Metamorphoses*, V, 294–340 and 662–678)
retells the myth in detail.   1. Of Hell.   2. Venus. Here, as morning star, Venus is described
as rising in Pisces, the Fishes, the zodiacal sign immediately preceding Aries. In Canto I of the
*Inferno* Dante has made it clear that the Sun is in Aries. Hence it is about to rise.

I turned then to my right and set my mind
  on the other pole, and there I saw four stars[3]
  unseen by mortals since the first mankind.[4]
The heavens seemed to revel in their light.             25
  O widowed Northern Hemisphere, bereft
  forever of the glory of that sight!
As I broke off my gazing, my eyes veered
  a little to the left, to the other pole[5]
  from which, by then, the Wain had disappeared.    30
I saw, nearby, an ancient man, alone.[6]
  His bearing filled me with such reverence,
  no father could ask more from his best son.
His beard was long and touched with strands of white,
  as was his hair, of which two tresses fell          35
  over his breast. Rays of the holy light
that fell from the four stars made his face glow
  with such a radiance that he looked to me
  as if he faced the sun. And standing so,
he moved his venerable plumes and said:        40
  "Who are you two who climb by the dark stream
  to escape the eternal prison of the dead?
Who led you? or what served you as a light
  in your dark flight from the eternal valley,
  which lies forever blind in darkest night?    45
Are the laws of the pit so broken? Or is new counsel
  published in Heaven that the damned may wander
  onto my rocks from the abyss of Hell?"
At that my Master laid his hands upon me,
  instructing me by word and touch and gesture    50

3. Modern readers are always tempted to identify these four stars as the Southern Cross, but it is almost certain that Dante did not know about that formation. In VIII, 89, Dante mentions three other stars as emphatically as he does these four and no one has been tempted to identify them on the star-chart. Both constellations are best taken as allegorical. The four stars represent the Four Cardinal Virtues: Prudence, Justice, Fortitude, and Temperance. Dante will encounter them again in the form of nymphs when he achieves the Earthly Paradise.    4. *The first mankind:* Adam and Eve. In Dante's geography, the Garden of Eden (the Earthly paradise) was at the top of the Mount of Purgatory, which was the only land in the Southern Hemisphere. All of what were called "the southern continents" were believed to lie north of the equator. When Adam and Eve were driven from the Garden, therefore, they were driven into the Northern Hemisphere, and no living soul since had been far enough south to see those stars. Ulysses and his men (*Inferno,* XXVII) had come within sight of the Mount of Purgatory, but Ulysses mentioned nothing of having seen these stars.    5. The North Pole. The Wain (Ursa Major, i.e., the Big Dipper) is below the horizon.    6. Marcus Porcious Cato, the younger, 95–46 B.C. In the name of freedom, Cato opposed the policies of both Caesar and Pompey, but because he saw Caesar as the greater evil joined forces with Pompey. After the defeat of his cause at the Battle of Thapsus, Cato killed himself with his own sword rather than lose his freedom. Virgil lauds him in the *Aeneid* as a symbol of perfect devotion to liberty, and all writers of Roman antiquity have given Cato a similar high place. Dante spends the highest praises on him both in *De Monarchia* and *Il Donvivio.* Why Cato should be so signally chosen by God as the special guardian of Purgatory has been much disputed. Cato may be taken as representative of supreme virtue short of godliness. He has accomplished everything but the purifying total surrender of his will to God. As such he serves as an apt transitional symbol, being the highest rung on the ladder of natural virtue, but the lowest on the ladder of those godly virtues to which Purgatory is the ascent.

to show my reverence in brow and knee,
then answered him: "I do not come this way
   of my own will or powers. A Heavenly Lady
   sent me to this man's aid in his dark day.
But since your will is to know more, my will     55
   cannot deny you; I will tell you truly
   why we have come and how. This man has still
to see his final hour, though in the burning
   of his own madness he had drawn so near it
   his time was perilously short for turning.     60
As I have told you, I was sent to show
   the way his soul must take for its salvation;
   and there is none but this by which I go.
I have shown him the guilty people. Now I mean
   to lead him through the spirits in your keeping,     65
   to show him those whose suffering makes them clean.
By what means I have led him to this strand
   to see and hear you, takes too long to tell:
   from Heaven is the power and the command.
Now may his coming please you, for he goes     70
   to win his freedom; and how dear that is
   the man who gives his life for it best knows.
You know it, who in that cause found death sweet
   in Utica where you put off that flesh
   which shall rise radiant at the Judgment Seat.     75
We do not break the Laws: this man lives yet,
   and I am of that Round not ruled by Minos,[7]
   with your own Marcia,[8] whose chaste eyes seem set
in endless prayers to you. O blessed breast
   to hold her yet your own! for love of her     80
   grant us permission to pursue our quest
across your seven kingdoms. When I go
   back to her side I shall bear thanks of you,
   if you will let me speak your name below."
"Marcia was so pleasing in my eyes     85
   there on the other side," he answered then
   "that all she asked, I did. Now that she lies
beyond the evil river, no word or prayer
   of hers may move me. Such was the Decree

---

7. The Judge of the Damned. The round in Hell not ruled by Minos is Limbo, the final resting place of the Virtuous Pagans. Minos (see *Inferno*, V) is stationed at the entrance to the second circle of Hell. The souls in Limbo (the first circle) have never had to pass before him to be judged.    8. The daughter of the consul Philippus and Cato's second wife, bearing his three children. In 56 B.C., in an unusual transaction approved by her father, Cato released her in order that she might marry his friend Hortensius. (Hence line 87: "that all she asked I did.") After the death of Hortensius, Cato took her back.

pronounced upon us when I rose from there.                        90
But if, as you have said, a Heavenly Dame
    orders your way, there is no need to flatter:
    you need but ask it of me in her name.
Go then, and lead this man, but first see to it
    you bind a smooth green reed about his waist       95
    and clean his face of all trace of the pit
For it would not be right that one with eyes
    still filmed by mist should go before the angel
    who guards the gate: he is from Paradise.
All round the wave-wracked shore-line, there below,   100
    reeds grow in the soft mud. Along that edge
    no foliate nor woody plant could grow,
for what lives in that buffeting must bend.
    Do not come back this way: the rising sun
    will light an easier way you may ascend."          105
With that he disappeared; and silently
    I rose and moved back till I faced my Guide,
    my eyes upon him, waiting. He said to me:
"Follow my steps and let us turn again:
    along this side there is a gentle slope            110
    that leads to the low boundaries of the plain."
The dawn, in triumph, made the day-breeze flee
    before its coming, so that from afar
    I recognized the trembling of the sea.
We strode across that lonely plain like men           115
    who seek the road they strayed from and who count
    the time lost till they find it once again.
When we had reached a place along the way
    where the cool morning breeze shielded the dew
    against the first heat of the gathering day,       120
with gentle graces my Sweet Master bent
    and laid both outspread palms upon the grass.
    Then I, being well aware of his intent,
lifted my tear-stained cheeks to him, and there
    he made me clean, revealing my true color          125
    under the residues of Hell's black air.
We moved on then to the deserted strand
    which never yet has seen upon its waters
    a man who found his way back to dry land.
There, as it pleased another, he girded me.           130
    Wonder of wonders! when he plucked a reed
    another took its place there instantly,
arising from the humble stalk he tore
so that it grew exactly as before.

CANTO II

*Ante-Purgatory:*
*The Shore of the Island    The Angel Boatman, Casella, Cato of*
  *Utica*

It is dawn. Dante, washed, and girded by the reed, is standing by
the shore when he sees a light approaching at enormous speed across
the sea. The light grows and becomes visible as The Angel Boatman
who ferries the souls of the elect from their gathering place at The
Mouth of the Tiber to the shore of Purgatory.

The newly arrived souls debark and, taking the Poets as familiars
of the place, ask directions. Virgil explains that he and Dante are
new arrivals but that they have come by the dark road through Hell.
The newly arrived souls see by his breathing that Dante is alive and
crowd about him. One of the new souls is Casella, a musician who
seems to have been a dear friend of Dante's. Dante tries three times
to clasp him to his bosom, but each time his arms pass through
empty air. Casella explains the function of the Angel Boatman and
then, at Dante's request, strikes up a song, one of Dante's own canzone that Casella had set to music. Instantly, Cato descends upon
the group, berating them, and they break like startled pigeons up the
slope toward the mountain.

The sun already burned at the horizon,
    while the high point of its meridian circle
    covered Jerusalem, and in opposition
equal Night revolved about the Ganges
    bearing the Scales that fall out of hand                          5
    as she grows longer with the season's changes:
thus, where I was, Aurora in her passage
    was losing the pale blushes from her cheeks
    which turned to orange with increasing age.[9]
We were still standing by the sea's new day                          10
    like travelers pondering the road ahead
    who send their souls on while their bones delay;
when low above the ocean's western rim,
    as Mars, at times, observed through the thick vapors
    that form before the dawn, burns red and slim;                    15
just so—so may I hope to see it again!—
    a light appeared, moving above the sea
    faster than any flight. A moment then
I turned my eyes to question my sweet Guide,
    and when I looked back to that unknown body                       20
    I found its mass and brightness magnified.

9. The bit of erudite affectation in which Dante indulges in lines 1–9 means simply, "It was
dawn."

Then from each side of it came into view
   an unknown something-white; and from beneath it,
   bit by bit, another whiteness grew.
We watched till the white objects at each side           25
   took shape as wings, and Virgil spoke no word.
   But when he saw what wings they were, he cried:
"Down on your knees! It is God's angel comes!
   Down! Fold your hands! From now on you shall see
   many such ministers in the high kingdoms.           30
See how he scorns man's tools: he needs no oars
   nor any other sail than his own wings
   to carry him between such distant shores.
See how his pinions tower upon the air,
   pointing to Heaven: they are eternal plumes      35
   and do not moult like feathers or human hair."
Then as that bird of heaven closed the distance
   between us, he grew brighter and yet brighter
   until I could no longer bear the radiance,
and bowed my head. He steered straight for the shore,    40
   his ship so light and swift it drew no water;
   it did not seem to sail so much as soar.
Astern stood the great pilot of the Lord,
   so fair his blessedness seemed written on him;
   and more than a hundred souls were seated forward,   45
singing as if they raised a single voice
   *in exitu Israel de Aegypto.*[1]
   Verse after verse they made the air rejoice.
The angel made the sign of the cross, and they
   cast themselves, at his signal, to the shore.[2]      50
   Then, swiftly as he had come, he went away.
The throng he left seemed not to understand
   what place it was, but stood and stared about
   like men who see the first of a new land.
The sun, who with an arrow in each ray          55
   had chased the Goat[3] out of the height of Heaven,
   on every hand was shooting forth the day,
when those new souls looked up to where my Guide
   and I stood, saying to us, "If you know it,
   show us the road that climbs the mountainside."   60
Virgil replied: "You think perhaps we two
   have had some long experience of this place,
   but we are also pilgrims, come before you
only by very little, though by a way

---

1. When Israel out of Egypt came. Psalm CXIII.  2. Note that this is exactly what Dante says of the sinners leaving Charon's ferry in *Inferno*, III, 113.  3. Capricorn.

so steep, so broken, and so tortuous                                    65
  the climb ahead of us will seem like play."
The throng of souls, observing by my breath
  I was still in the body I was born to,
  stared in amazement and grew pale as death.
As a crowd, eager for news, will all but smother                        70
  a messenger who bears the olive branch,[4]
  and not care how they trample one another—
so these, each one of them a soul elect,
  pushed close to stare at me, well-nigh forgetting
  the way to go to make their beauty perfect.                           75
One came forward to embrace me, and his face
  shone with such joyous love that, seeing it,
  I moved to greet him with a like embrace.
O solid seeming shadows! Three times there
  I clasped my hands behind him, and three times            80
  I drew them to my breast through empty air.
Amazed, I must have lost all color then,
  for he smiled tenderly and drew away,
  and I lunged forward as if to try again.
In a voice as gentle as a melody                                        85
  he bade me pause; and by his voice I knew him,
  and begged him stay a while and speak to me.
He answered: "As I loved you in the clay
  of my mortal body, so do I love you freed:
  therefore I pause. But what brings you this way?"         90
"Casella[5] mine, I go the way I do
  in the hope I may return here," I replied.
  "But why has so much time been taken from you?"
And he: "I am not wronged if he whose usage
  accepts the soul at his own time and pleasure             95
  has many times refused to give me passage:
his will moves in the image and perfection
  of a Just Will; indeed, for three months now
  he has taken all who asked,[6] without exception.
And so it was that in my turn I stood                                  100

4. In Dante's time couriers bore the olive branch to indicate not only peace but good news in
general.    5. *Casella:* Practically all that is known about Casella has been drawn from the text
itself. He seems to have died several months before Dante began his journey, hence early in 1300
or late in 1299. There is no explanation of his delay in reaching Purgatory (the time that has been
taken from him). Dante later meets several classes of sinners who must spend a certain period of
waiting before they can begin their purification. Clearly it is Dante's conception that the souls
bound for Purgatory do not always proceed instantly to their destination, but may be required to
expiate by a delay at their gathering point by the mouth of the Tiber (line 101). Casella was a
musician and is known to have set some of Dante's *canzone* to music. The song he strikes up (line
112) is such a *canzone*.    6. Boniface VIII decreed a Jubilee Year from Christmas 1299 to Christmas
1300. (*See Inferno,* XVIII, 28–33 and note.) His decree extended special indulgences even to the
dead. Hence the Angel's permissiveness.

upon that shore where Tiber's stream grows salt,
    and there was gathered to my present good.
It is back to the Tiber's mouth he has just flown,
    for there forever is the gathering place
    of all who do not sink to Acheron."           105
"If no new law has stripped you of your skill
    or of the memory of those songs of love
    that once could calm all passion from my will,"
I said to him, "Oh sound a verse once more
    to soothe my soul which, with its weight of flesh    110
    and the long journey, sinks distressed and sore."
"Love that speaks its reasons in my heart,"
    he sang then, and such grace flowed on the air
    that even now I hear that music start.
My Guide and I and all those souls of bliss         115
    stood tranced in song; when suddenly we heard
    the Noble Elder cry: "What's this! What's this!
Negligence! Loitering! O laggard crew
    run to the mountain and strip off the scurf
    that lets not God be manifest in you!"         120
Exactly as a flock of pigeons gleaning
    a field of stubble, pecking busily,
    forgetting all their primping and their preening,
will rise as one and scatter through the air,
    leaving their feast without another thought    125
    when they are taken by a sudden scare—
so that new band, all thought of pleasure gone,
    broke from the feast of music with a start
    and scattered for the mountainside like one
who leaps and does not look where he will land.    130
Nor were my Guide and I inclined to stand.

CANTO XIX

*The Fourth Cornice   The Slothful*
*Dante's Dream of Sirena*
*The Ascent   The Angel of Zeal*
*The Fifth Cornice   The Hoarders and Wasters (The Avaricious)*

    Just before morning (when the truth is dreamed) Dante dreams of
The Siren that lures the souls of men to incontinent worldliness.
Hideous in her true form, the Siren grows irresistible in men's eyes
as they look upon her. A Heavenly Lady races in upon the dream
and calls to Virgil who, thus summoned, strips the Siren, exposing
her filthy body. Such a stench rises from her, so exposed, that Dante

wakens shuddering, to find Virgil calling him to resume the journey.

The Angel of Zeal shows them the passage, and when his wings
have fanned the Poets, Dante casts off his depression and lethargy,
and rushes up the remaining length of the passage.

Arrived at The Fifth Cornice, Virgil inquires the way of one of
the souls of The Hoarders and Wasters, who lie motionless and outstretched, bound hand and foot, with their faces in the dust.

The soul of Pope Adrian V replies that, if they have incurred no
guilt by Hoarding or Wasting, they may pass on to the right. Dante
kneels in reverence to Adrian and is scolded for doing so. Adrian
then dismisses Dante in order to resume his purification. Adrian's
last request is that his niece, Alagia, be asked to pray for his soul.


At the hour when the heat of the day is overcome
   by Earth, or at times by Saturn, and can no longer
   temper the cold of the moon;[7] when on the dome
of the eastern sky the geomancers sight
   Fortuna Major[8] rising on a course                 5
   on which, and soon, it will be drowned in light;
there came to me in a dream a stuttering crone,
   squint-eyed, clubfooted, both her hands deformed,
   and her complexion like a whitewashed stone.
I stared at her; and just as the new sun                    10
   breathes life to night-chilled limbs, just so my look
   began to free her tongue, and one by one
drew straight all her deformities, and warmed
   her dead face, till it bloomed as love would wish it
   for its delight. When she was thus transformed,        15
her tongue thus loosened, she began to sing
   in such a voice that only with great pain
   could I have turned from her soliciting.
"I am," she sang, "Sirena.[9] I am she
   whose voice is honeyed with such sweet enticements     20
   it trances sailing men far out to sea.
I turned Ulysses from his wanderer's way[1]

7. An intricate passage based on the medieval belief that sunlight reflected from earth to the moon
produced warmth on the moon, whereas sunlight reflected from the moon to the earth produced
cold on the earth. *At the hour:* Before dawn. The accumulated heat of the day would have been
dissipated through the long night and could no longer temper the cold of the moon. *Overcome by
Earth:* The last heat of the day is overcome by the night-chilled earth. *Or at times by Saturn:* The
times would be those in which Saturn draws close to the horizon. Saturn was believed to be a cold
planet, as opposed to Mars, a hot planet.    8. A conjunction of the last stars of Aquarius and
the first of Pisces, supposed to signify great good fortune. In this season these stars would be rising
just before dawn, hence the sun is coming up behind them and their course will soon be drowned
in light.    9. The Sirens were mythological creatures, usually of great beauty, and with the
power of singing so entrancingly that they charmed the souls of men. They were usually presented
as luring sailors at sea to their destruction. Dante's Sirena is a Christian adaptation.    1. In the
Homeric version Ulysses escapes the Siren's blandishments by stuffing his ears with wax and
having himself lashed to the mast of his ship. Dante may, perhaps, be following another version
of the myth, but more probably he means to portray the Siren as a liar.

with my charmed song, and few indeed who taste
   how well I satisfy would think to stray."
Her mouth had not yet shut when at my side                                    25
   appeared a saintly lady,[2] poised and eager
   to heap confusion on the Siren's pride.
"O Virgil, Virgil! Who," she cried, "is this?"
   Roused by her indignation, Virgil came:
   his eyes did not once leave that soul of bliss.                      30
He seized the witch, and with one rip laid bare
   all of her front, her loins and her foul belly:
   I woke sick with the stench that rose from there.
I turned then, and my Virgil said to me:
   "I have called at least three times now. Rise and come              35
   and let us find your entrance." Willingly
I rose to my feet. Already the high day
   lit all the circles of the holy mountain.
   The sun was at our backs as we took our way.
I followed in his steps, my brow as drawn                                     40
   as is a man's so bowed with thought he bends
   like half an arch of a bridge. And moving on,
I heard the words: "Come. This is where you climb"[3]
   pronounced in such a soft and loving voice
   as is not heard here in our mortal time.                             45
With swanlike wings outspread, he who had spoken
   summoned us up between the walls of rock.
   He fanned us with his shining pinions then,
affirming over us as we went by
   *"blessed are they that mourn"*[4]—for they shall have             50
   their consolation given them on high.
"What ails you?" said my Guide. "What heavy mood
   makes you stare at the ground?" (We were by then
   above the point at which the Angel stood.)
And I: "An apparition clouds my spirit,                                       55
   a vision from a dream so strange and dreadful
   I cannot seem to leave off thinking of it."
"Did you see that ageless witch," he said, "for whom
   —and for no other—those above us weep?
   And did you see how men escape her doom?                             60
Let it teach your heels to scorn the earth, your eyes
   to turn to the high lure the Eternal King
   spins with his mighty spheres across the skies."
As falcons stare at their feet until they hear

2. She may be Beatrice, or she may be Provenient Grace, but any identification is speculative.
3. Spoken by the Angel of Zeal.    4. The Fourth Beatitude. "Blessed are they that mourn: for
they shall be comforted." (*Matthew*, iv, 5).

the wished-for call, then leap with wings outspread     65
   in eagerness for the meat that waits them there;
so did I move: filled with desire, I ran
   up the remaining length of the rock passage
   to the point at which the next great Round began.
When I stood on the fifth ledge and looked around,     70
   I saw a weeping people everywhere
   lying outstretched and face-down on the ground.
"My soul cleaves to the dust,"[5] I heard them cry
   over and over as we stood among them;
   and every word was swallowed by a sigh.     75
"O Chosen of God, spirits whose mournful rites
   both Hope and Justice make less hard to bear,
   show us the passage to the further heights."
"If you have not been sentenced to lie prone
   in the bitter dust, and seek the nearest way,     80
   keep the rim to your right as you go on."
So spoke the Poet, and so a voice replied
   from the ground in front of us. I took good note
   of what its way of speaking did not hide.[6]
I turned my eyes to Virgil then, and he     85
   gave me a happy sign of his permission
   to do what my eyes asked. Being thus free
to act according to my own intention,
   I moved ahead and stood above that soul
   whose speaking had attracted my attention,     90
saying: "O Soul in whom these tears prepare
   that without which no soul can turn to God,
   put off a while, I beg, your greater care,
to tell me who you were, why you lie prone,
   and if there is some way that I may serve you     95
   in the world I left while still in flesh and bone."
"Why Heaven makes us turn our backs shall be
   made known to you," the spirit said, "but first
   *scias quod ego fui successor Petri*.[7]
Between Sestri and Chiaveri, flowing on     100
   through a fair land, there is a pleasant river[8]
   from which the title of my line is drawn.
A single month, a month and some few days

---

5. Psalm CXIX.    6. The soul has said, "If you have not been sentenced to lie prone in the bitter dust." The implication is—and it is the first time the point has emerged clearly—that souls may pass through some of the Cornices without delay, if they are free of the taint of sin there punished.    7. "Know that I was Peter's successor." The speaker is Pope Adrian V. He died in 1276 after having been Pope for thirty-eight days.    8. The Lavagna. It flows between Sestri and Chiaveri, small coastal towns near Genoa. Adrian, born Ottobuono de' Fieschi, was the line of the Counts of Lavagna.

I came to know on my own weary body
  how heavily the Papal Mantle weighs         105
upon the wearer who would take good care
  to keep it from the mire; compared to that
  all other burdens are as light as air.
My conversion, alas, came late; for only when
  I had been chosen Pastor of Holy Rome         110
  did I see the falseness in the lives of men.
I saw no heart's rest there, nor ease from strife,
  nor any height the flesh-bound soul might climb,
  and so I came to love this other life.
My soul was lost to God until that moment,         115
  and wholly given over to avarice;
  such was my sin, such is my punishment.
The nature of avarice is here made plain
  in the nature of its penalty; there is not
  a harsher forfeit paid on the whole mountain.         120
We would not raise our eyes to the shining spheres
  but kept them turned to mundane things: so Justice
  bends them to earth here in this place of tears.
As Avarice, there, quenched all our souls' delight
  in the good without which all our works are lost,         125
  so, here, the hand of Justice clamps us tight.
Taken and bound here hand and foot, we lie
  outstretched and motionless; and here we stay
  at the just pleasure of the Father on High."
I had knelt to him. Now I spoke once more.         130
  That spirit sensed at once my voice was nearer
  and guessed my reverence. "Why do you lower
your knees into the dust?" he said to me.
  And I: "My conscience troubled me for standing
  in the presence of your rank and dignity."         135
"Straighten your legs, my brother! Rise from error!"
  he said. "I am, like you and all the others,
  a fellow servant of one Emperor.
It is written in holy scripture *Neque nubent;*[9]
  if ever you understood that sacred text,         140
  my reason for speaking will be evident.
Now go your way. I wish to be alone.
  Your presence here distracts me from the tears
  that make me ready. And to your last question:

---

9. . . . They neither marry [nor are given in marriage but are as the angels of God in heaven]"
(*Matthew*, xxii, 30). These were Christ's words when asked to which husband a remarried widow
would belong in Heaven. Adrian obviously extends the meaning to include the cancellation of all
earthly contracts, fealties, and honors.

I have a niece, Alagia,[1] still on earth.                        145
    If she can but avoid the bad example
    those of our line have set, her native worth
will lead her yet the way the blessed go.
And she alone remains to me below."

*       *       *


CANTO XXVII

*The Seventh Cornice    The Angel of Chastity*
*The Wall of Fire*
*The Earthly Paradise    The Angel Guardian*

A little before sunset of the third day on the Mountain the Poets
come to the further limit of the Seventh Cornice and are greeted by
The Angel of Chastity, who tells them they must pass through the
wall of fire. Dante recoils in terror, but Virgil persuades him to enter
in Beatrice's name.

They are guided through the fire by a chant they hear coming
from the other side. Emerging, they find it is sung by The Angel
Guardian of the Earthly Paradise, who stands in a light so brilliant
that Dante cannot see him.

The Angel hurries them toward the ascent, but night overtakes
them, and the Poets lie down to sleep, each on the step on which he
finds himself. (For Statius it will be the last sleep, since there is no
night in Heaven.) There, just before dawn, Dante has a prophetic
Dream of Leah and Rachel, which foreshadows the appearance, above,
of Matilda and Beatrice.

Day arrives; the Poets rise and race up the rest of the ascent until
they come in sight of The Earthly Paradise. Here Virgil Speaks His
Last Words, for the Poets have now come to the limit of Reason,
and Dante is now free to follow his every impulse, since all motion
of sin in him has been purged away.


As the day stands when the Sun begins to glow
    over the land where his Maker's blood was shed,
    and the scales of Libra ride above the Ebro,
while Ganges' waters steam in the noonday glare—[2]
    so it stood, the light being nearly faded,                     5
    when we met God's glad Angel[3] standing there
on the rocky ledge beyond the reach of the fire,

1. Daughter of Niccolò di Tedisio di Ugone de' Fieschi and wife of Moroello Malaspina, Marquis
of Giovagallo. Dante had been well received by Malaspina and knew and admired his wife for her
good works.    2. It is shortly before sunset of the third day on the Mountain. Dante's details
here are the reverse of those given at the opening of II, which see. *The land where his Maker's
blood was shed:* Jerusalem. *The Ebro:* For Spain.    3. The Angel of Chastity. He is standing on
the narrow rocky path outside the wall of fire.

and caroling *"Beati mundo corde"*[4]
   in a voice to which no mortal could aspire.
Then: "Blessèd ones, till by flame purified                    10
   no soul may pass this point. Enter the fire
   and heed the singing from the other side."
These were his words to us when we had come
   near as we could, and hearing them, I froze
   as motionless as one laid in his tomb.                    15
I lean forward over my clasped hands and stare
   into the fire, thinking of human bodies
   I once saw burned,[5] and once more see them there.
My kindly escorts heard me catch my breath
   and turned, and Virgil said: "Within that flame                    20
   there may be torment, but there is no death.
Think well, my son, what dark ways we have trod . . .
   I guided you unharmed on Geryon:[6]
   shall I do less now we are nearer God?
Believe this past all doubt: were you to stay                    25
   within that womb of flame a thousand years,
   it would not burn a single hair away.
And if you still doubt my sincerity,
   but reach the hem of your robe into the flame:
   your hands and eyes will be your guarantee.                    30
My son, my son, turn here with whole assurance.
   Put by your fears and enter to your peace."
   And I stood fixed, at war with my own conscience.
And seeing me still stubborn, rooted fast,
   he said, a little troubled: "Think, my son,                    35
   you shall see Beatrice when this wall is past."
As Pyramus, but one breath from the dead,
   opened his eyes when he heard Thisbe's name,[7]
   and looked at her, when the mulberry turned red—
just so my hard paralysis melted from me,                    40
   and I turned to my Leader at that name
   which wells forever in my memory;
at which he wagged his head, as at a child

---

4. "Blessed are the pure in heart [for they shall see God]." (*Matthew*, v, 8.)    5. Dante must mean as a witness at an execution. Burnings at the stake generally took place in public squares. They were a rather common spectacle. Dante's sentence of exile, it is relevant to note, decreed that he was to be burned if taken on Florentine territory.    6. *Geryon:* The Monster of Fraud. See *Inferno*, XVII.    7. Famous tragic lovers of Babylon. Ovid (*Metamorphoses*, IV, 55–166) tells their story. At a tryst by a mulberry (which in those days bore white fruit) Thisbe was frightened by a lion and ran off, dropping her veil. The lion, his jaws bloody from a recent kill, tore at the veil, staining it with blood. Pyramus, arriving later, saw the stained veil, concluded that Thisbe was dead, and stabbed himself. Thisbe, returning, found him and cried to him to open his eyes for his Thisbe. At that name Pyramus opened his eyes, looked at her, and died. Thisbe, invoking the tree to darken in their memory, thereupon stabbed herself. (*Cf.* Shakespeare's *Romeo and Juliet*.) The mulberry roots drank their blood and the fruit turned red ever after.

won over by an apple. Then he said:
    "Well, then, what are we waiting for?" and smiled.     45
He turned then and went first into the fire,
    requesting Statius, who for some time now
    had walked between us, to bring up the rear.
Once in the flame, I gladly would have cast
    my body into boiling glass to cool it     50
    against the measureless fury of the blast.
My gentle father, ever kind and wise,
    strengthened me in my dread with talk of Beatrice,
    saying: "I seem already to see her eyes."
From the other side, to guide us, rose a paean,     55
    and moving toward it, mindless of all else,
    we emerged at last where the ascent began.
There I beheld a light[8] that burned so brightly
    I had to look away; and from it rang:
    "*Venite benedicti patris mei.*"[9]     60
"Night falls," it added, "the sun sinks to rest;
    do not delay but hurry toward the height
    while the last brightness lingers in the west."
Straight up through the great rock-wall lay the way
    on such a line that, as I followed it,     65
    my body blocked the sun's last level ray.
We had only climbed the first few stairs as yet
    when I and my two sages saw my shadow[1]
    fade from me; and we knew the sun had set.
Before the vast sweep of the limned horizon     70
    could fade into one hue and night win all
    the immeasurable air to its dominion,
each made the step on which he stood his bed,
    for the nature of the Mount not only stopped us
    but killed our wish to climb, once day had fled.     75
As goats on a rocky hill will dance and leap,
    nimble and gay, till they find grass, and then,
    while they are grazing, grow as tame as sheep
at ease in the green shade when the sun is high
    and the shepherd stands by, leaning on his staff,     80
    and at his ease covers them with his eye—
and as the herdsman beds down on the ground,
    keeping his quiet night watch by his flock
    lest it be scattered by a wolf or hound;
just so we lay there, each on his stone block,     85

8. This is the Angel Guardian of the Earthly Paradise.   9. "Come ye blessèd of my Father."
(*Matthew*, xxv, 34.)   1. Virgil and Statius, of course, cast none.

I as the goat, they as my guardians,
  shut in on either side by walls of rock.
I could see little ahead—rock blocked the way—
  but through that little I saw the stars grow larger,
  brighter than mankind sees them. And as I lay,                90
staring and lost in thought, a sleep came on me—
  the sleep that oftentimes presents the fact
  before the event, a sleep of prophecy.
At the hour, I think, when Venus, first returning
  out of the east, shone down upon the mountain—[2]            95
  she who with fires of love comes ever-burning—
I dreamed I saw a maiden innocent
  and beautiful, who walked a sunny field
  gathering flowers, and caroling as she went:
"Say I am Leah if any ask my name,                             100
  and my white hands weave garlands wreath on wreath
  to please me when I stand before the frame
of my bright glass. For this my fingers play
  among these blooms. But my sweet sister Rachel[3]
  sits at her mirror motionless all day.                       105
To stare into her own eyes endlessly
  is all her joy, as mine is in my weaving.
  She looks, I do. Thus live we joyously."
Now eastward the new day rayed Heaven's dome
  (the sweeter to the returning wanderer                       110
  who wakes from each night's lodging nearer home),
and the shadows fled on every side as I
  stirred from my sleep and leaped upon my feet,
  seeing my Lords already standing by.
"This is the day your hungry soul shall be                     115
  fed on the golden apples men have sought
  on many different boughs so ardently."
These were the very words which, at the start,
  my Virgil spoke to me, and there have never
  been gifts as dear as these were to my heart.                120
Such waves of yearning to achieve the height
  swept through my soul, that at each step I took
  I felt my feathers growing for the flight.
When we had climbed the stairway to the rise
  of the topmost step, there with a father's love              125
  Virgil turned and fixed me with his eyes.

2. It is the hour before dawn, in which the truth is dreamed.    3. Leah and Rachel were,
respectively, the first- and second-born daughters of Laban and the first and second wives of Jacob.
Many authors before Dante had interpreted them as representing the Active and the Contemplative Life of the Soul. Leah's white hands (*le belle mani*) symbolize the Active Life, as Rachel's
eyes (lines 104–108) symbolize the Contemplative Life.

"My son," he said, "you now have seen the torment
  of the temporal and the eternal fires;
  here, now, is the limit of my discernment.
I have led you here by grace of mind and art;                    130
  now let your own good pleasure be your guide;
  you are past the steep ways, past the narrow part.
See there the sun that shines upon your brow,
  the sweet new grass, the flowers, the fruited vines
  which spring up without need of seed or plow.                  135
Until those eyes come gladdened which in pain
  moved me to come to you and lead your way,
  sit there at ease or wander through the plain.
Expect no more of me in word or deed:
  here your will is upright, free, and whole,                    140
  and you would be in error not to heed
whatever your own impulse prompts you to:
lord of yourself I crown and mitre you."[4]

*     *     *

CANTO XXX

*The Earthly Paradise    Beatrice*
*Virgil Vanishes*

The procession [of the Heavenly Pageant] halts and the Prophets
turn to the chariot and sing "Come, my bride, from Lebanon." They
are summoning Beatrice, who appears on the left side of the chariot,
half-hidden from view by showers of blossoms poured from above by
A Hundred Angels. Dante, stirred by the sight, turns to Virgil to
express his overflowing emotions, and discovers that Virgil Has Vanished.

Because he bursts into tears at losing Virgil Dante Is Reprimanded
by Beatrice. The Angel Choir overhead immediately breaks into a
Psalm of Compassion, but Beatrice, still severe, answers by detailing
Dante's offenses in not making proper use of his great gifts. It would
violate the ordering of the Divine Decree, she argues, to let Dante
drink the waters of Lethe, thereby washing all memory of sin from
his soul, before he had shed the tears of a real repentance.

When the Septentrion of the First Heaven,[5]
  which does not rise nor set, and which has never
  been veiled from sight by any mist but sin,

4. Crown as king of your physical self and mitre (as a bishop) as lord of your soul.   5. The
Septentrion is the seven stars of the Big Dipper. Here Dante means the seven candelabra [of the
Heavenly Pageant]. They are the Septentrion of the First Heaven (the empyrean) as distinct from
the seven stars of the dipper which occur lower down in the Sphere of the Fixed Stars.

and which made every soul in that high court
   know its true course (just as the lower Seven                     5
   direct the helmsman to his earthly port),
had stopped; the holy prophets,[6] who till then
   had walked between the Griffon and those lights,
   turned to the car like souls who cry "Amen."
And one among them[7] who seemed sent from Heaven              10
   clarioned: "*Veni, sponsa, de Libano,*"[8]
   three times, with all the others joining in.
As, at the last trump every saint shall rise
   out of the grave, ready with voice new-fleshed
   to carol *Alleluliah* to the skies;                            15
just so, above the chariot, at the voice
   of such an elder, rose a hundred Powers
   and Principals[9] of the Eternal Joys,
all saying together: "*Benedictus qui venis*";[1]
   then, scattering flowers about on every side:                  20
   "*Manibus o date lilia plenis.*"[2]
Time and again at daybreak I have seen
   the eastern sky glow with a wash of rose
   while all the rest hung limpid and serene,
and the Sun's face rise tempered from its rest                       25
   so veiled by vapors that the naked eye
   could look at it for minutes undistressed.
Exactly so, within a cloud of flowers
   that rose like fountains from the angels' hands
   and fell about the chariot in showers,                         30
a lady[3] came in view: an olive crown
   wreathed her immaculate veil, her cloak was green,
   the colors of live flame played on her gown.
My soul—such years had passed since last it saw[4]
   that lady and stood trembling in her presence,                 35
   stupefied by the power of holy awe—
now, by some power that shone from her above
   the reach and witness of my mortal eyes,
   felt the full mastery of enduring love.
The instant I was smitten by the force,                              40

6. The twenty-four elders who represent the books of the Old Testament. *Griffon:* A mythical figure with the fore parts of an eagle and the hind parts of a lion, here meant to represent the dual role of Christ as God and Man.    7. *The Song of Solomon.*    8. "Come [with me] from Lebanon, my spouse." *Song of Solomon,* iv. 8. This cry, re-echoed by choirs of angels, summons Beatrice.    9. Angels.    1. "Blessed is he who cometh." (*Matthew,* xxi, 9.)    2. "Oh, give lilies with full hands." These are the words of Anchises in honor of Marcellus. (*Aeneid,* VI, 883). Thus they are not only apt to the occasion but their choice is a sweetly conceived last literary compliment to Virgil before he vanishes.    3. Beatrice. She is dressed in the colors of Faith (white), Hope (green), and Caritas (red).    4. Beatrice died in 1290. Thus Dante has passed ten years without sight of her.

which had already once transfixed my soul
    before my boyhood years had run their course,
I turned left with the same assured belief
    that makes a child run to its mother's arms
    when it is frightened or has come to grief,                    45
to say to Virgil: "There is not within me
    one drop of blood unstirred. I recognize
    the tokens of the ancient flame." But he,
he had taken his light from us. He had gone.
    Virgil had gone. Virgil, the gentle Father                     50
    to whom I gave my soul for its salvation!
Not all that sight of Eden lost to view
    by our First Mother could hold back the tears
    that stained my cheeks so lately washed with dew.[5]
"Dante,[6] do not weep yet, though Virgil goes.                    55
    Do not weep yet, for soon another wound
    shall make you weep far hotter tears than those!"
As an admiral takes his place at stern or bow
    to observe the handling of his other ships
    and spur all hands to do their best—so now,                    60
on the chariot's left side, I saw appear
    when I turned at the sound of my own name
    (which, necessarily, is recorded here),
that lady who had been half-veiled from view
    by the flowers of the angel-revels. Now her eyes               65
fixed me across the stream, piercing me through.
And though the veil she still wore, held in place
    by the wreathed flowers of wise Minerva's leaves,[7]
    let me see only glimpses of her face,
her stern and regal bearing made me dread                          70
    her next words, for she spoke as one who saves
    the heaviest charge till all the rest are read.
"Look at me well. I am she. I am Beatrice.
    How dared you make your way to this high mountain?
    Did you not know that here man lives in bliss?"                75
I lowered my head and looked down at the stream.
    But when I saw myself reflected there,
    I fixed my eyes upon the grass for shame.
I shrank as a wayward child in his distress
    shrinks from his mother's sternness, for the taste             80
    of love grown wrathful is a bitterness.
She paused. At once the angel chorus sang
    the blessed psalm: "*In te, Domine, speravi.*"

5. By Virgil. I, 124.    6. This is the only point in the *Commedia* at which Dante mentions his
own name.    7. The olive crown.

As far as *"pedes meos"* their voices rang.[8]
As on the spine of Italy the snow                              85
    lies frozen hard among the living rafters[9]
    in winter when the northeast tempests blow;
then, melting if so much as a breath stir
    from the land of shadowless noon,[1] flows through itself
    like hot wax trickling down a lighted taper—             90
just so I froze, too cold for sighs or tears
    until I heard that choir whose notes are tuned
    to the eternal music of the spheres.
But when I heard the voice of their compassion
    plead for me more than if they had cried out:           95
    "Lady, why do you treat him in this fashion?";
the ice, which hard about my heart had pressed,
    turned into breath and water, and flowed out
    through eyes and throat in anguish from my breast.
Still standing at the chariot's left side,                     100
    she turned to those compassionate essences
    whose song had sought to move her, and replied:
"You keep your vigil in the Eternal Day
    where neither night nor sleep obscures from you
    a single step the world takes on its way;                105
but I must speak with greater care that he
    who weeps on that far bank may understand
    and feel a grief to match his guilt. Not only
by the workings of the spheres that bring each seed
    to its fit end according to the stars                    110
    that ride above it, but by gifts decreed
in the largesse of overflowing Grace,
    whose rain has such high vapors for its source
    our eyes cannot mount to their dwelling place;
this man, potentially was so endowed                          115
    from early youth that marvelous increase
    should have come forth from every good he sowed.
But richest soil the soonest will grow wild
    with bad seed and neglect. For a while I stayed him
    with glimpses of my face. Turning my mild                120
and youthful eyes into his very soul,
    I let him see their shining, and I led him
    by the straight way, his face to the right goal.
The instant I had come upon the sill

8. In mercy the angel chorus sings Psalm XXXI, 1–8, beginning "In thee, O Lord, do I put my trust" and continuing as far as "thou hast set my feet in a large room."    9. The trees. *The spine of Italy:* The Apennines.    1. *The land of shadowless noon:* Africa. In equatorial regions the noonday sun is at the zenith over each point twice a year. Its rays then fall straight down and objects cast no shadows.

of my second age,[2] and crossed and changed my life,                    125
he left me and let others shape his will.
When I rose from the flesh into the spirit,
  to greater beauty and to greater virtue,
  he found less pleasure in me and less merit.
He turned his steps aside from the True Way,                              130
  pursuing the false images of good
  that promise what they never wholly pay.
Not all the inspiration I won by prayer
  and brought to him in dreams and meditations
  could call him back, so little did he care.                             135
He fell so far from every hope of bliss
  that every means of saving him had failed
  except to let him see the damned. For this
I visited the portals of the dead
  and poured my tears and prayers before that spirit                      140
  by whom his steps have, up to now, been led.
The seal Almighty God's decree has placed
  on the rounds of His creation would be broken
  were he to come past Lethe and to taste
the water that wipes out the guilty years                                 145
without some scot of penitential tears!"[3]


## CANTO XXXI

### *The Earthly Paradise*    *Lethe; Beatrice, Matilda*

Beatrice continues her reprimand, forcing Dante to confess his
faults until he swoons with grief and pain at the thought of his sin.
He wakes to find himself in Lethe, held in the arms of Matilda, who
leads him to the other side of the stream and there immerses him
that he may drink the waters that wipe out all memory of sin.

Matilda then leads him to The Four Cardinal Virtues, who dance
about him and lead him before The Griffon where he may look into
The Eyes of Beatrice. In them Dante sees, in a First Beatific Vision,
the radiant reflection of the Griffon, who appears now in his human
and now in his godly nature.

The Three Theological Virtues now approach and beg that Dante
may behold The Smile of Beatrice. Beatrice removes her veil, and
in a Second Beatific Vision, Dante beholds the splendor of the unveiled
shining of Divine Love.

---

2. Beatrice's womanhood. When she had reached the full bloom of youth Dante turned from her
and wrote to his *donna gentile*. [The *donna gentile* (noble or gentle lady) is not identified by
name.] Allegorically, he turned from divine "sciences" to an overreliance upon philosophy (the
human "sciences"). For this sin he must suffer.    3. In passing Lethe and drinking its waters,
the soul loses all memory of guilt. This, therefore, is Dante's last opportunity to do penance.

"You, there, who stand upon the other side—"[4]
   (turning to me now, who had thought the edge
   of her discourse was sharp, the point) she cried
without pause in her flow of eloquence,
     "Speak up! Speak up! Is it true? To such a charge       5
     your own confession must give evidence."
I stood as if my spirit had turned numb:
   the organ of my speech moved, but my voice
   died in my throat before a word could come.
Briefly she paused, then cried impatiently:         10
   "What are you thinking? Speak up, for the waters[5]
   have yet to purge sin from your memory."
Confusion joined to terror forced a broken
   "yes" from my throat, so weak that only one
   who read my lips would know that I had spoken.      15
As an arbalest will snap when string and bow
   are drawn too tight by the bowman, and the bolt
   will strike the target a diminished blow—[6]
so did I shatter, strengthless and unstrung,
   under her charge, pouring out floods of tears,      20
   while my voice died in me on the way to my tongue.
And she: "Filled as you were with the desire
   I taught you for That Good beyond which nothing
   exists on earth to which man may aspire,
what yawning moats or what stretched chain-lengths[7] lay   25
   across your path to force you to abandon
   all hope of pressing further on your way?
What increase or allurement seemed to show
   in the brows of others that you walked before them
   as a lover walks below his lady's window?"      30
My breath dragged from me in a bitter sigh;
   I barely found a voice to answer with;
   my lips had trouble forming a reply.
In tears I said: "The things of the world's day,
   false pleasures and enticements, turned my steps     35
   as soon as you had ceased to light my way."
And she: "Had you been silent, or denied
   what you confess, your guilt would still be known
   to Him from Whom no guilt may hope to hide.
But here, before our court, when souls upbraid     40

4. Of Lethe. But also the other side of the immortal life, i.e., still living.    5. Of Lethe.
6. The figure is a bit confusing. Dante seems to say that the bolt (corresponding to an arrow) of a
crossbow strikes the target with less force when the bow snaps. He does not stop to consider that
the bolt may miss the target entirely. Nevertheless, the intent of his figure is clear enough.
7. These were, of course, defensive military measures. The moats guarded castles. The chains
were strung to block roads, bridges, and gates.

themselves for their own guilt in true remorse,
  the grindstone is turned back against the blade.[8]
In any case that you may know your crime
  truly and with true shame and so be stronger
  against the Siren's song another time,              45
control your tears and listen with your soul
  to learn how my departure from the flesh
  ought to have spurred you to the higher goal.
Nothing in Art or Nature could call forth
  such joy from you, as sight of that fair body       50
  which clothed me once and now sifts back to earth.
And if my dying turned that highest pleasure
  to very dust, what joy could still remain
  in mortal things for you to seek and treasure?
At the first blow you took from such vain things     55
  your every thought should have been raised to follow
  my flight above decay. Nor should your wings
have been weighed down by any joy below—
  love of a maid,[9] or any other fleeting
  and useless thing—to wait a second blow.        60
The fledgling waits a second shaft, a third;
  but nets[1] are spread and the arrow sped in vain
  in sight or hearing of the full-grown bird."
As a scolded child, tongue tied for shame, will stand
  and recognize his fault, and weep for it,        65
  bowing his head to a just reprimand,
so did I stand. And she said: "If to hear me
  grieves you, now raise your beard and let your eyes
  show you a greater cause for misery."[2]
The blast that blows from Libya's hot sand,       70
  or the Alpine gale, overcomes less resistance
  uprooting oaks than I, at her command,
overcame then in lifting up my face;
  for when she had referred to it as my "beard"
  I sensed too well the venom of her phrase.      75
When I had raised my eyes with so much pain,
  I saw those Primal Beings, now at rest,
  who had strewn blossoms round her thick as rain;
and with my tear-blurred and uncertain vision
  I saw Her turned to face that beast which is     80

8. Turning the grindstone away from the blade sharpens it. Turning it back against the blade
dulls it. Thus Beatrice is saying that when a soul openly confesses in true repentance what could
not in any case be hidden from God, the sword of Justice is blunted, i.e., no longer cuts as
deeply.    9. Dante mentions another maiden in some of his songs but in an indefinite way. No
specific reference can be attached to these words.    1. Sometimes used for trapping birds.
2. The sight of her accompanied by the guilty knowledge that he had turned away from so much
beauty and perfection.

one person in two natures without division.[3]
Even veiled and across the river from me
　　her face outshone its first-self[4] by as much
　　as she outshone all mortals formerly.
And the thorns of my repentance pricked me so                85
　　that all the use and substance of the world
　　I most had loved, now most appeared my foe.
Such guilty recognition gnawed my heart
　　I swooned for pain; and what I then became
　　she best knows who most gave me cause to smart.          90
When I returned to consciousness at last
　　I found the lady who had walked alone[5]
　　bent over me. "Hold fast!" she said, "Hold fast!"
She had drawn me into the stream up to my throat,
　　and pulling me behind her, she sped on                   95
　　over the water, light as any boat.
Nearing the sacred bank, I heard her say
　　in tones so sweet I cannot call them back,
　　much less describe them here: "*Asperges me.*"[6]
Then the sweet lady took my head between                    100
　　her open arms, and embracing me, she dipped me
　　and made me drink the waters that make clean.
Then raising me in my new purity
　　she led me to the dance of the Four Maidens;[7]
　　each raised an arm and so joined hands above me.         105
"Here we are nymphs; stars are we in the skies.
　　Ere Beatrice went to earth we were ordained
　　her handmaids. We will lead you to her eyes;
but that your own may see what joyous light
　　shines in them, yonder Three,[8] who see more deeply,   110
　　will sharpen and instruct your mortal sight."
Thus they sang, then led me to the Griffon.
　　Behind him, Beatrice waited. And when I stood
　　at the Griffon's breast, they said in unison:
"Look deep, look well, however your eyes may smart.         115
　　We have led you now before those emeralds[9]

3. The Griffon. He is the masque of Christ and represents His two aspects as man and God.
4. Her mortal self.     5. Matilda, who appears in Canto XXVIII, having been foreshadowed by
Leah in Dante's dream (XXVII)). She may be taken to symbolize the Active Life of the Soul.
6. *Asperges me hyssopo, et mundabor; lavabis me, et super nivem dealbabor.* ("Purge me with
hyssop, and I shall be clean; wash me, and I shall be whiter than snow.") *Psalms* li, 7. These are
the words the priest utters when he sprinkles holy water over the confessed sinner to absolve
him.     7. The Four Cardinal Virtues: Justice, Prudence, Fortitude, and Temperance. In their
present manifestation they are nymphs. In another manifestation they are the four stars Dante saw
above him when he arrived at the base of the mountain. (I, 23, note.)     8. The Theological
Virtues: Faith, Hope, and Charity (*i.e., Caritas*).     9. The eyes of Beatrice. Dante may have
intended to describe them as green (hazel) but more likely his choice of words here is meant only
to signify "jewel bright." Green is, of course, the color of Hope, and an allegorical significance
may be implied in that.

from which Love shot his arrows through your heart."
A thousand burning passions, every one
   hotter than any flame, held my eyes fixed
   to the lucent eyes she held fixed on the Griffon.     120
Like sunlight in a glass the twofold creature
   shone from the deep reflection of her eyes,
   now in the one, now in the other nature.
Judge, reader, if I found it passing strange
   to see the thing unaltered in itself     125
   yet in its image working change on change.
And while my soul in wonder and delight
   was savoring that food which in itself
   both satisfies and quickens appetite,[1]
the other Three, whose bearing made it clear     130
   they were of higher rank, came toward me dancing
   to the measure of their own angelic air.
"Turn, Beatrice, oh turn the eyes of grace,"
   was their refrain, "upon your faithful one
   who comes so far to look upon your face.     135
Grant us this favor of your grace: reveal
   your mouth to him, and let his eyes behold
   the Second Beauty,[2] which your veils conceal."
O splendor of the eternal living light!
   who that has drunk deep of Parnassus' waters,[3]     140
   or grown pale in the shadow of its height,
would not, still, feel his burdened genius fail
   attempting to describe in any tongue
   how you appeared when you put by your veil
in that free air open to heaven and earth     145
whose harmony is your shining shadowed forth!

        *     *     *

## Paradiso

### CANTO I

*The Earthly Paradise   The Invocation*
*Ascent to Heaven   The Sphere of Fire, The Music of the Spheres*

    Dante States his supreme theme as Paradise itself and invokes the
aid not only of the Muses but of Apollo.
    Dante and Beatrice are in The Earthly Paradise, the Sun is at the

1. "They that eat me shall yet be hungry, and they that drink me shall yet be thirsty." (*Ecclesiasticus*, xxiv, 21.)   2. The smile of Beatrice (Divine Love). Dante was led to the First Beauty by the Four Cardinal Virtues. Now the Three Theological Virtues, as higher beings, lead him to the second, and higher beauty, which is the joy of Divine Love in receiving the purified soul. 3. The fountain of Castalia. To drink from it is to receive poetic gifts. To grow pale in the shadow of Parnassus signifies to labor at mastering the art of poetry.

Vernal Equinox, it is noon at Purgatory and midnight at Jerusalem
when Dante sees Beatrice turn her eyes to stare straight into the sun
and reflexively imitates her gesture. At once it is as if a second sun
had been created, its light dazzling his senses, and Dante feels the
ineffable change of his mortal soul into Godliness.

These phenomena are more than his senses can grasp, and Beatrice must explain to him what he himself has not realized: that he
and Beatrice are soaring toward the height of Heaven at an incalcu-
lable speed.

Thus Dante climaxes the master metaphor in which purification
is equated to weightlessness. Having purged all dross from his soul
he mounts effortlessly, without even being aware of it at first, to his
natural goal in the Godhead. So they pass through The Sphere of
Fire, and so Dante first hears The Music of the Spheres.

The glory of Him who moves all things rays forth
   through all the universe, and is reflected
   from each thing in proportion to its worth.
I have been in that Heaven of His most light,
   and what I saw, those who descend from there      5
   lack both the knowledge and the power to write.
For as our intellect draws near its goal
   it opens to such depths of understanding
   as memory cannot plumb within the soul.
Nevertheless, whatever portion time      10
   still leaves me of the treasure of that kingdom
   shall now become the subject of my rhyme.
O good Apollo,[4] for this last task, I pray
   you make me such a vessel of your powers
   as you deem worthy to be crowned with bay.[5]      15
One peak of cleft Parnassus heretofore
   has served my need, now must I summon both[6]
   on entering the arena one time more.
Enter my breast, I pray you, and there breathe
   as high a strain as conquered Marsyas      20
   that time you drew his body from its sheath.[7]
O power divine, but lend to my high strain
   so much as will make clear even the shadow
   of that High Kingdom stamped upon my brain,

4. The God of Poetry, and the father of the Muses. Note, too, that Apollo is identified with the
Sun and that Dante has consistently used the Sun as a symbol for God.   5. The laurel wreath
awarded to poets and conquerors.   6. Parnassus has two peaks: Nisa, which was sacred to the
Muses; and Cyrrha, which was sacred to Apollo. Heretofore Nisa has been enough for Dante's
need, but for this last canticle he must summon aid from both peaks (i.e., from all the Muses and
from Apollo as well).   7. The satyr Marsyas challenged Apollo to a singing contest and was
defeated. Ovid (*Metamorphoses*, VI, 382–400) recounts in gory detail how Apollo thereupon
punished him by pulling him out of his skin leaving all the uncovered organs still functioning.

and you shall see me come to your dear grove[8]                    25
 to crown myself with those green leaves which you
 and my high theme shall make me worthy of.
So seldom are they gathered, Holy Sire,
 to crown an emperor's or a poet's triumph
 (oh fault and shame of mortal man's desire!)              30
that the glad Delphic god must surely find
 increase of joy in the Peneian frond[9]
 when any man thirsts for it in his mind.
Great flames are kindled where the small sparks fly.
 So after me, perhaps, a better voice                         35
 shall raise such prayers that Cyrrha[1] will reply.
The lamp of the world rises to mortal view
 from various stations, but that point which joins
 four circles with three crosses, it soars through
to a happier course in happier conjunction                         40
 wherein it warms and seals the wax of the world
 closer to its own nature and high function.[2]
That glad conjunction had made it evening here
 and morning there; the south was all alight,
 while darkness rode the northern hemisphere;               45
when I saw Beatrice had turned left to raise
 her eyes up to the sun; no eagle ever
 stared at its shining with so fixed a gaze.[3]
And as a ray descending from the sky
 gives rise to another, which climbs back again,             50
 as a pilgrim yearns for home; so through my eye
her action, like a ray into my mind,
 gave rise to mine: I stared into the sun
 so hard that here it would have left me blind;

---

8. In which grows the sacred laurel, or bay.    9. The laurel or bay, so called for Daphne, daughter of the river god Peneus. Cupid, to avenge a taunt, fired an arrow of love into Apollo and an arrow of aversion into Daphne. Fleeing from the inflamed Apollo, Daphne prayed to her father and was changed into a laurel tree. *The glad Delphic god:* Apollo.    1. Apollo's sacred peak, here taken for Apollo himself. If Apollo does not heed his prayer, Dante will at least show the way, and perhaps a better poet will come after him and have his prayer answered by Apollo, whereby Paradise will at last be well portrayed.    2. Short of pages of diagrams, there is no way of explaining Dante's astronomical figure in detail. A quick gloss must do: *The lamp:* The Sun. *Various stations:* various points on the celestial horizon from which the sun rises at various times of the year. *Four circles with three crosses:* The four circles here intended are: (1) the celestial horizon, (2) the celestial equator, (3) the ecliptic, and (4) equinoxial colure, the great circle drawn through both poles and the two equinoxial points. When the sun is in this position the time is sunrise of the vernal equinox and all four circles meet, each of the other three forming a cross with the celestial horizon. Astrologers took this to be a particularly auspicious conjunction. Its *happier course* (line 40) brings the brighter and longer days of summer. Its *happier conjunction* (line 40) with the stars of Aries bring it back to the sign of the first creation (see *Inferno,* I, 38–39, note). And certainly the fact that the diagram forms three crosses would weigh it with the good omens of both the cross and trinity. All would once more be in God's shaping hand. So the *wax of the world* (line 41) is warmed and sealed, in a first sense by the warmth of approaching summer, and in a clearly implicit spiritual sense by the favor of God's will upon His creation.    3. In the Middle Ages men believed that the eagle was able to stare directly into the sun.

but much is granted to our senses there,                    55
 in that garden made to be man's proper place,
 that is not granted us when we are here.
I had to look away soon, and yet not
 so soon but what I saw him spark and blaze
 like new-tapped iron when it pours white-hot.          60
And suddenly, as it appeared to me,
 day was added to day, as if He who can
 had added a new sun to Heaven's glory.
Beatrice stared at the eternal spheres
 entranced, unmoving; and I looked away                 65
 from the sun's height to fix my eyes on hers.
And as I looked, I felt begin within me
 what Glaucus felt eating the herb that made him
 a god among the others in the sea.[4]
How speak trans-human change to human sense?                70
 Let the example speak until God's grace
 grants the pure spirit the experience.
Whether I rose in only the last created
 part of my being,[5] O Love that rulest Heaven
 Thou knowest, by whose lamp I was translated.          75
When the Great Wheel that spins eternally
 in longing for Thee,[6] captured my attention
 by that harmony attuned and heard by Thee,
I saw ablaze with sun from side to side
 a reach of Heaven:[7] not all the rains and rivers     80
 of all of time could make a sea so wide.
That radiance and that new-heard melody
 fired me with such a yearning for their Cause
 as I had never felt before. And she
who saw my every thought as well as I,                      85
 saw my perplexity: before I asked
 my question she had started her reply.
Thus she began: "You dull your own perceptions
 with false imaginings and do not grasp
 what would be clear but for your preconceptions.       90
You think you are still on earth: the lightning's spear
 never fled downward from its natural place

---

4. The fisherman Glaucus, noting how his catch revived and leaped into the sea after being laid upon a certain herb, ate some of it and was transformed into a god (Ovid, *Metamorphoses*, XIII, 898–968).    5. The soul, which is created after the body. (See *Purgatorio*, XXV, 37–75.) O *Love that rulest Heaven*: God. *Whose lamp*: Beatrice as the reflector of God's love.    6. Dante says, literally: "The wheel that Thou, in being desired [i.e., loved] by it, makest eternal." The Great Wheel is the Primum Mobile, its motion deriving from the love of God. *That harmony*: The Music of the Spheres.    7. Dante believed that the earth's atmosphere extended as high as the Sphere of the Moon. Beyond the Moon is another atmosphere of fire. This sphere of fire was believed to cause lightning. (See also line 115, "the fire about the moon".)

as rapidly as you are rising there."
I grasped her brief and smiling words and shed
  my first perplexity, but found myself                    95
  entangled in another, and I said:
"My mind, already recovered from the surprise
  of the great marvel you have just explained,
  is now amazed anew: how can I rise
in my gross body through such aery substance?"            100
  She sighed in pity and turned as might a mother
  to a delirious child. "The elements
of all things," she began, "whatever their mode,
  observe an inner order. It is this form
  that makes the universe resemble God.                   105
In this the higher creatures see the hand
  of the Eternal Worth, which is the goal
  to which these norms conduce, being so planned.
All Being within this order, by the laws
  of its own nature is impelled to find                    110
  its proper station round its Primal Cause.
Thus every nature moves across the tide
  of the great sea of being to its own port,
  each with its given instinct as its guide.
This instinct draws the fire about the moon.              115
  It is the mover in the mortal heart.
  It draws the earth together and makes it one.
Not only the brute creatures, but all those
  possessed of intellect and love, this instinct
  drives to their mark as a bow shoots forth its arrows.   120
The Providence that makes all things hunger here
  satisfies forever with its light
  the heaven within which whirls the fastest sphere.[8]
And to it now, as to a place foretold,
  are we two soaring, driven by that bow                   125
  whose every arrow finds a mark of gold.
It is true that oftentimes the form of a thing
  does not respond to the intent of the art,
  the matter being deaf to summoning—
just so, the creature sometimes travels wide              130
  of this true course, for even when so driven
  it still retains the power to turn aside
(exactly as we may see the heavens' fire
  plunge from a cloud) and its first impulse may
  be twisted earthward by a false desire.                  135

8. The Primum Mobile.

You should not, as I see it, marvel more
    at your ascent than at a river's fall
    from a high mountain to the valley floor.
If you, free as you are of every dross,
    had settled and had come to rest below,                140
    that would indeed have been as marvelous[9]
as a still flame there in the mortal plain."
So saying, she turned her eyes to Heaven again.


                    *        *        *


                    CANTO III

*The First Sphere: The Moon    The Inconstant Piccarda, Constance*

    As Dante is about to speak to Beatrice he sees the dim traceries of
human faces and taking them to be reflections, he turns to see what
souls are being so reflected. Beatrice, as ever, explains that these
pallid images are the souls themselves. They are The Inconstant, the
souls of those who registered holy vows in Heaven, but who broke or
scanted them.
    Among them Piccarda Donati identifies herself, and then identi-
fies The Empress Constance. Both, according to Dante's beliefs, had
taken vows as nuns but were forced to break them in order to contract
a political marriage. Not all the souls about them need have failed
in the same vows, however. Any failure to fulfill a holy vow (of holy
orders, to go on a pilgrimage, to offer special services to God) might
place the soul in this lowest class of the blessed.
    Piccarda explains that every soul in Heaven rejoices in the entire
will of God and cannot wish for a higher place, for to do so would
be to come into conflict with the will of God. In the perfect harmony
of bliss, everywhere in Heaven is Paradise.


That sun that breathed love's fire into my youth[1]
    had thus resolved for me, feature by feature—
    proving, disproving—the sweet face of truth.
I, raising my eyes to her eyes to announce
    myself resolved of error, and well assured,                5
    was about to speak; but before I could pronounce
my first word, there appeared to me a vision.
    It seized and held me so that I forgot
    to offer her my thanks and my confession.
As in clear glass when it is polished bright,                10
    or in a still and limpid pool whose waters
    are not so deep that the bottom is lost from sight,

9. Because then it would be going against the order of the universe. What is purified must ascend
to God as inevitably as earthly waters must flow downhill.    1. Beatrice.

a footnote of our lineaments[2] will show,
   so pallid that our pupils could as soon
   make out a pearl upon a milk-white brow—[3]         15
so I saw many faces eager to speak,
   and fell to the error opposite the one
   that kindled love for a pool in the smitten Greek.[4]
And thinking the pale traces I saw there
   were reflected images, I turned around         20
   to face the source—but my eyes met empty air.
I turned around again like one beguiled,
   and took my line of sight from my sweet guide
   whose sacred eyes grew radiant as she smiled.
"Are you surprised that I smile at this childish act         25
   of reasoning?" she said, "since even now
   you dare not trust your sense of the true fact,
but turn, as usual, back to vacancy?
   These are true substances you see before you.
   They are assigned here for inconstancy         30
to holy vows. Greet them. Heed what they say,
   and so believe; for the True Light[5] that fills them
   permits no soul to wander from its ray."
So urged, I spoke to those pale spirits, turning
   to one who seemed most eager, and began         35
   like one whose mind goes almost blank with yearning.
"O well created soul, who in the sun
   of the eternal life drinks in the sweetness
   which, until tasted, is beyond conception;
great would be my joy would you confide         40
   to my eager mind your earthly name and fate."
   That soul with smiling eyes, at once replied:
"The love that fills us will no more permit
   hindrance to a just wish than does that Love[6]
   that wills all of Its court to be like It.         45
I was a virgin sister[7] there below,
   and if you search your memory with care,
   despite my greater beauty, you will know
I am Piccarda,[8] and I am placed here

---

2. The figure seems oddly out of context but its intent is clear: Dante is suggesting that the image is related to the face as a footnote is related to the text.   3. The brow would have to be death-pale as marble, but perhaps Dante intends these spirits to be chalky-white.   4. Narcissus. His error was in taking a reflection (his own) to be a real face. Dante's opposite error is in taking real faces to be reflections.   5. God.   6. God, as the essence of *Caritas.*   7. A nun. 8. Piccarda Donati was the daughter of Simone Donati (*Inferno,* XXV, 32) and sister of Forese (*Purgatorio,* XXIII, 48) and of the war-leader, Corso (*Purgatorio,* XXIV, 82ff.). Forese was Dante's friend. Dante was married to Gemma Donati, who also had a brother named Forese, but Piccarda's family was grander than Dante's in-laws. Piccarda was already a nun and living in her convent when her brother Corso, needing to establish a political alliance, forced her to marry Rossellino della Tossa of Florence. Various commentators report that Piccarda sickened and soon died as a consequence of having been so forced against her will and vows.

among these other souls of blessedness          50
  to find my blessedness in the slowest sphere.
Our wishes, which can have no wish to be
  but in the pleasure of the Holy Ghost,
  rejoice in being formed to His decree.
And this low-seeming post which we are given          55
  is ours because we broke, or, in some part,
  slighted the vows we offered up to Heaven."
And I then: "Something inexpressibly
  divine shines in your face, subliming you
  beyond your image in my memory:          60
therefore I found you difficult to place;
  but now, with the assistance of your words,
  I find the memory easier to retrace.[9]
But tell me, please: do you who are happy here
  have any wish to rise to higher station,          65
  to see more, or to make yourselves more dear?"[1]
She smiled, as did the spirits at her side;
  then, turning to me with such joy she seemed
  to burn with the first fire of love, replied:
"Brother, the power of love, which is our bliss,          70
  calms all our will. What we desire, we have.
  There is in us no other thirst than this.
Were we to wish for any higher sphere,
  then our desires would not be in accord
  with the high will of Him who wills us here;          75
and if love is our whole being, and if you weigh
  love's nature well, then you will see that discord
  can have no place among these circles. Nay,
the essence of this blessèd state of being
  is to hold all our will within His will,          80
  whereby our wills are one and all-agreeing.
And so the posts we stand from sill to sill
  throughout this realm, please all the realm as much
  as they please Him who wills us to His will.
In His will is our peace. It is that sea          85
  to which all moves, all that Itself creates
  and Nature bears through all Eternity."
Then was it clear to me that everywhere
  in Heaven is Paradise, though the Perfect Grace
  does not rain down alike on all souls there.          90
But as at times when we have had our fill

9. A desperate simplification of Dante's untranslatable "*m'è più latino*" (literally: "it is more Latin
to me"). Learned men of Dante's time used Latin naturally and gracefully. Thus to make a thing
"more Latin" was to facilitate it. An opposite form of a similar idiom is our still current "It's Greek
to me."    1. More dear to God.

of one food and still hunger for another,
  we put this by with gratitude, while still
asking for that—just so I begged to know,
  by word and sign, through what warp she had not        95
  entirely passed the shuttle[2] of her vow.
"The perfection of her life and her great worth
  enshrine a lady[3] hereabove," she said,
  "in whose rule some go cloaked and veiled on earth,
that till their death they may live day and night         100
  with that sweet Bridegroom[4] who accepts of love
  all vows it makes that add to His delight.[5]
As a girl, I fled the world to walk the way
  she walked, and closed myself into her habit,
  pledged to her sisterhood till my last day.        105
Then men came, men more used to hate than love.
  They tore me away by force from the sweet cloister.
  What my life then became is known above.
This other splendor who lets herself appear[6]
  here to my right to please you, shining full       110
  of every blessedness that lights this sphere,
understands in herself all that I say.
  She, too, was a nun. From her head as from mine
  the shadow of the veil was ripped away.
Against her will and all propriety        115
  she was forced back to the world. Yet even there
  her heart was ever veiled in sanctity.
She is the radiance of the Empress Constance,[7]
  who by the second blast of Swabia
  conceived and bore its third and final puissance."[8]    120
She finished, and at once began to sing
  *Ave Maria,* and singing, sank from view
  like a weight into deep water, plummeting
out of my sight, which followed while it could,

---

2. The vertical strings of a loom are the warp. Across them the shuttle draws the woof. Not to draw the shuttle entirely through is to leave the weaving unfinished, hence her vow unfulfilled. 3. Saint Clara of Assisi (1194–1253). Born Chiara Sciffi, she became a disciple of St. Francis and, under his influence, founded in 1212 an order of nuns. *Hereabove:* Higher in Heaven. Probably in the Empyrean, but Dante does not mention her again. 4. Christ. He is so called several times in the New Testament. 5. Only those vows that conform to His love are acceptable. A vow to perform a trivial or an evil action would have no standing. 6. Dante says, "who shows herself to you." Clearly, the souls in Paradise can make themselves visible or invisible at will (i.e., Heaven reveals itself of its own love). At the end of the conversation the whole company withdraws from sight. 7. (1154–1198). As the last of the line of Norman kings who took southern Italy in the eleventh century, she was Empress of the Two Sicilies (Sicily and Naples). She married the Emperor Henry VI in 1185 and became the mother of Frederick II. Dante follows a legend, for which there was no basis in fact, that she had become a nun and was forced to leave her convent to marry Henry. 8. The three blasts of Swabia are the three great princes whose origins were in Swabia (in Germany). Frederick Barbarossa was the first. His son, Henry VI, was the second. To Henry, Constance bore the third, Frederick II.

and then, having lost her, turned about once more 125
 to the target of its greater wish and good,
and wholly gave itself to the delight
 of the sweet vision of Beatrice. But she
 flashed so radiantly upon my sight
that I, at first, was blinded, and thus was slow 130
to ask of her what I most wished to know.

### CANTO XXXI

*The Empyrean The Mystic Rose, The Angel Host, Beatrice Leaves Dante, St. Bernard*

The Second Soldiery of the Church Triumphant is the Angel Host and Dante now receives a vision of them as a Swarm of Bees in eternal transit between God and the Rose.

Dante turns from that rapturous vision to speak to Beatrice and finds in her place a reverend elder. It is St. Bernard, who will serve as Dante's guide to the ultimate vision of God. Bernard shows Dante his Last Vision of Beatrice, who has resumed her throne among the blessed. Across the vastness of Paradise, Dante sends his soul's prayer of thanks to her. Beatrice Smiles down at Dante a last time, then turns her eyes forever to the Eternal Fountain of God.

Bernard, the most faithful of the worshippers of the Virgin, promises Dante the final vision of God through the Virgin's intercession. Accordingly, he instructs Dante to raise his eyes to her throne. Dante obeys and burns with bliss at the vision of her splendor.

Then, in the form of a white rose, the host
 of the sacred soldiery[9] appeared to me,
 all those whom Christ in his own blood espoused.
But the other host (who soar, singing and seeing
 His glory, who to will them to his love 5
 made them so many in such blissful being,
like a swarm of bees who in one motion dive

9. In XXX, 43, Beatrice promised that Dante would see both hosts of Paradise. The first host is of the sacred soldiery, those who were once mortal and who were redeemed by Christ. They are seated upon the thrones of the Mystic Rose in which are gathered eternally the essences of all those heavenly souls that manifested themselves to Dante in the various spheres below, moved by *caritas* to reveal themselves to Dante at the various levels of his developing understanding. How these souls could be eternally within the Rose while yet manifesting themselves to Dante in the various spheres is, of course, one of the mysteries to be grasped only by revelation. The essential point is that Dante becomes better able to see; the vision of Heaven unfolds to him ever more clearly and ever more profoundly. The second soldiery is of the angels who never left heaven. They soar above the Rose like Heavenly bees, in constant motion between the Rose and the radiance of God. Unlike earthly bees, however, it is from God, the mystical hive of grace, that they bring the sweetness to the flower, bearing back to God, of course, the bliss of the souls of Heaven. (See lines 16–18). The first host is more emphatically centered on the aspect of God as the Son; the second, on the aspect of God as the Father.

into the flowers, and in the next return
  the sweetness of their labors to the hive)
flew ceaselessly to the many-petaled rose          10
  and ceaselessly returned into that light
  in which their ceaseless love has its repose.
Like living flame their faces seemed to glow.[1]
  Their wings were gold. And all their bodies shone[2]
  more dazzling white than any earthly snow.         15
On entering the great flower they spread about them,
  from tier to tier, the ardor and the peace
  they had acquired in flying close to Him.
Nor did so great a multitude in flight
  between the white rose and what lies above it      20
  block in the least the glory of that light;
for throughout all the universe God's ray
  enters all things according to their merit,
  and nothing has the power to block its way.
This realm of ancient bliss shone, soul on soul,      25
  with new and ancient beings, and every eye
  and every love was fixed upon one goal.
O Threefold Light which, blazoned in one star,
  can so content their vision with your shining,
  look down upon us in the storm we are!        30
If the barbarians (coming from that zone
  above which Helice[3] travels every day
  wheeling in heaven with her belovèd son)
looking at Rome, were stupefied to see
  her works in those days when the Lateran[4]     35
  outshone all else built by humanity;
What did I feel on reaching such a goal
  from human to blest, from time to eternity,
  from Florence to a people just and whole—[5]
by what amazement was I overcome?        40
  Between my stupor and my new-found joy
  my bliss was to hear nothing and be dumb.
And as a pilgrim at the shrine of his vow
  stares, feels himself reborn, and thinks already

---

1. See the vision of God and Heaven in *Ezekiel*, I, 14 ff.    2. See the similar vision in *Daniel*, X, 4 ff.    3. The nymph Helice (I am afraid the reader will have to Anglicize her name as HEL-ces) attracted Zeus and was turned into a bear by jealous Hera. Zeus translated his nymph to heaven as Ursa Major, the constellation of the Great Bear which contains the Big Dipper. Arcas, her son by Zeus, was translated to Ursa Minor, within which he forms the Little Dipper. The two dippers, being near the pole, are always above the horizon in the northland, the zone from which the barbarians came.    4. Today a section of old Rome. Here Dante uses it to signify Rome in general.    5. This is Dante's last mention of Florence. Note that Florence has not improved but that on the universal scale it has become too insignificant for the sort of denunciation he once heaped upon it.

how he may later describe it[6]—just so now                              45
I stood and let my eyes go wandering out
    into that radiance from rank to rank,
    now up, now down, now sweeping round about.
I saw faces that compelled love's charity
    lit by Another's lamp and their own smiles,                          50
    and gestures graced by every dignity.
Without having fixed on any part, my eyes
    already had taken in and understood
    the form and general plan of Paradise:
and—my desire rekindled—I wheeled about                                  55
    to question my sweet lady on certain matters
    concerning which my mind was still in doubt.
One thing I expected; another greeted me:
    I thought to find Beatrice there; I found instead
    an elder[7] in the robes of those in glory.                          60
His eyes and cheeks were bathed in the holy glow
    of loving bliss; his gestures, pious grace.
    He seemed a tender father standing so.
"She—where is she?" I cried in sudden dread.
    "To lead you to the goal of all your wish                            65
    Beatrice called me from my place," he said;
"And if you raise your eyes you still may find her
    in the third circle down[8] from the highest rank
    upon the throne her merit has assigned her."
Without reply I looked up to that height                                 70
    and saw her draw an aureole round herself
    as she reflected the Eternal Light.
No mortal eye, though plunged to the last bounds
    of the deepest sea, has ever been so far
    from the topmost heaven to which the thunder sounds                  75
as I was then from Beatrice; but there
    the distance did not matter, for her image
    reached me unblurred by any atmosphere.
"O lady in whom my hope shall ever soar

6. It was a custom of the pious, as thanks for an answered prayer, to win forgiveness of sins,
or as a testimony of faith, to vow a journey to a stated shrine or temple. Such pilgrimages were
often dangerous. Travel was rare in the Middle Ages, and the pilgrim returned from far shrines
was much sought after for the hopefully miraculous, and in any case rare, news he brought back.
How could Dante, having traveled to the Infinite Summit, fail to think ahead to the way he would
speak his vision to mankind?     7. St. Bernard (1090–1153), the famous Abbot of Clairvaux, a
contemplative mystic and author. Under him the Cistercian Order (a branch of the Benedictines
with a stricter rule than the original order) flourished and spread. All Cistercian monasteries are
especially dedicated to the Virgin, and St. Bernard is particularly identified with her worship.
8. In the Mystic Rose, Mary sits in the topmost tier, Eve directly below her, Rachel (the Contemplative Life) below Eve. Beatrice sits to the right of Rachel. In Dante, of course, every mention
of three must suggest trinity, but the reader is left to decide for himself the significance of the
Mary-Eve-Rachel trinity.

and who for my salvation suffered even                          80
  to set your feet upon Hell's broken floor;[9]
through your power and your excellence alone
  have I recognized the goodness and the grace
  inherent in the things I have been shown.
You have led me from my bondage and set me free                 85
  by all those roads, by all those loving means
  that lay within your power and charity.
Grant me your magnificence that my soul,
  which you have healed, may please you when it slips
  the bonds of flesh and rises to its goal."                90
Such was my prayer, and she—far up a mountain,
  as it appeared to me—looked down and smiled.
  Then she turned back to the Eternal Fountain.
And the holy Elder said: "I have been sent
  by prayer and sacred love to help you reach                95
  the perfect consummation of your ascent.
Look round this garden, therefore, that you may
  by gazing at its radiance, be prepared
  to lift your eyes up to the Trinal Ray.
The Queen of Heaven, for whom in whole devotion                 100
  I burn with love, will grant us every grace
  because I am Bernard, her faithful one."
As a stranger afar—a Croat,[1] if you will—
  comes to see our Veronica,[2] and awed
  by its ancient fame, can never look his fill,                105
but says to himself as long as it is displayed:
  "My Lord, Jesus Christ, true God, and is this then
  the likeness of thy living flesh portrayed?"—
just so did I gaze on the living love
  of him who in this world, through contemplation,            110
  tasted the peace which ever dwells above.[3]
"Dear son of Grace," he said, "you cannot know
  this state of bliss while you yet keep your eyes
  fixed only on those things that lie below;
rather, let your eyes mount to the last round                   115
  where you shall see the Queen to whom this realm

9. As she did when she descended to Limbo (as, of course, a manifestation) to summon Virgil.
1. Probably used here in a generic sense to signify the native of any far-off Christian land, but Croatia, aside from lying at one of the outer limits of Christianity, was also known for the ardor of its religious belief.    2. From *vera icon*, the true image. Certainly the most famous relic in St. Peter's, the Veronica was the handkerchief of the faithful follower ever after known as St. Veronica. She gave it to Jesus to wipe the blood from his face on the road to Calvary, and what was believed to be the true likeness of Jesus was believed to have appeared on what was believed to be the cloth in what was believed to be His own blood.    3. According to legend, Bernard was rewarded for his holiness by being permitted a vision of Heaven's blessedness while he was yet on earth.

is subject and devoted, throned and crowned."
I looked up: by as much as the horizon
   to eastward in the glory of full dawn
   outshines the point at which the sun went down;[4]      120
by so much did one region on the height
   to which I raised my eyes out of the valley
   outshine the rays of every other light.
And as the sky is brightest in that region
   where we on earth expect to see the shaft      125
   of the chariot so badly steered by Phaeton,
while to one side and the other it grows dim—
   just so that peaceful oriflamme lit the center
   and faded equally along either rim.[5]
And in the center, great wings spread apart,      130
   more than a thousand festive angels shone,
   each one distinct in radiance and in art.[6]
I saw there, smiling at this song and sport,
   her whose beauty entered like a bliss
   into the eyes of all that sainted court.      135
And even could my speech match my conception,
   yet I would not dare make the least attempt
   to draw her delectation and perfection.
Bernard, seeing my eyes so fixed and burning
   with passion on his passion, turned his own      140
   up to that height with so much love and yearning
that the example of his ardor sent
   new fire through me, making my gaze more ardent.

## CANTO XXXII

*The Empyrean*   St. Bernard, The Virgin Mary, The Thrones of the
Blessed

His eyes fixed blissfully on the vision of the Virgin Mary, Bernard
recites the orders of the Mystic Rose, identifying the thrones of the
most blessed.

Mary's Throne is on the topmost tier of the Heavenly Stadium.
Directly across from it rises the Throne of John the Baptist. From

4. The comparison is not, as careless readers sometimes take it to be, between a dawn and a
sunset (whose brightnesses would be approximately equal) but between the eastern and western
horizons at dawn. Bright as Heaven is, Mary outshines it as the east outshines the west at
daybreak.   5. The shaft of the chariot of the Sun would project ahead of the horses. It would,
therefore, be the first point of light of the new dawn, that moment when light glows on the eastern
rim while the horizon to north and south is still dark. Thus Mary not only outshines all heaven
as the east at daybreak outshines the west, but even at the uppermost tier of the blessed, those
radiances at either side of her are dim by comparison.   6. Motion. No two angel beings are
exactly equal in their brightness, nor in the speed of their flight. These festive angels are, of
course, another manifestation of the Angel Hierarchy.

her throne to the central arena (The Yellow of the Rose) descends a
Line of Christian Saints. These two radii form a diameter that divides
the stadium. On one side are throned Those Who Believe in Christ
to Come; on the other, Those who Believed in Christ Descended.
The lower half of the Rose contains, on one side, the Pre-Christian
Children Saved by Love, and on the other, the Christian Children
saved by Baptism.

Through all these explanations, Bernard has kept his eyes fixed in
adoration upon the Virgin. Having finished his preliminary instruction of Dante, Bernard now calls on him to join in a Prayer to the
Virgin.

Still rapt in contemplation,[7] the sainted seer
  assumed the vacant office of instruction,
  beginning with these words I still can hear:
"The wound that Mary healed with balm so sweet
  was first dealt and then deepened by that being                5
  who sits in such great beauty at her feet.[8]
Below her, in the circle sanctified
  by the third rank of loves, Rachel is throned
  with Beatrice, as you see, there at her side.
Sarah[9] and Rebecca and Judith and she[1]                      10
  who was the great-grandmother of the singer
  who for his sins cried, 'Lord, have mercy on me!'—
as I go down the great ranks tier by tier,
  naming them for you in descending order,
  petal by petal, you shall see them clear.                      15
And down from the seventh, continuing from those
  in the first six tiers, a line of Hebrew women
  forms a part in the tresses of the rose.[2]
Arranged to form a wall thus, they divide
  all ranks according to the view of Christ                      20
  that marked the faith of those on either side.
On this side, where the flower is in full bloom[3]

7. Of the Virgin. His eyes have not left her. Nor do they turn again to Dante. *The vacant office
of instruction:* Formerly held by Beatrice. *I still can hear:* A rhyme-forced addition, not in Dante's
text.    8. Mary, Mother of God, sits in the uppermost tier. At her feet in the second tier sits
Eve, Mother of Man. *The wound:* Original sin. *Balm so sweet:* Jesus. *Dealt:* The first fault, Eve's
disobedience. *Deepened:* Her seduction of Adam, thus spreading sin to all mankind. *In such great
beauty:* Eve, having been created directly by God, was perfect in her beauty.    9. Wife of Abraham. *Hebrews,* XI, 11–14, cites her as the mother (by miraculous fertility in her old age) of the
Jews who foresaw Christ's coming and believed in him. *Rebecca:* Wife of Isaac. *Judith:* She killed
Holofernes and freed the Jews.    1. Ruth, great-grandmother of David ("that singer.") *Who for
his sins:* His lust for Bathsheba, wife of Uriah. In order to marry Bathsheba, David sent Uriah to
his death in the first line of battle. David's lament is in *Psalm L.*    2. As if the rose were a head
of hair and that vertical row of Hebrew women formed a part in it. In the next line the part
becomes a wall.    3. That half of the rose-stadium that holds the pre-Christian believers would
naturally be completely filled. On the other side there are thrones waiting for those who have yet
to win salvation through Christ Descended. Dante, in fact, is laboring to earn one of them for
himself. The Day of Judgment will be upon mankind when the last throne is filled, for Heaven
will then be complete.

to its last petal, are arranged all those
    whose faith was founded upon Christ to Come;
on that, where the half circles show the unblended        25
    gaps of empty seats, are seated those
    whose living faith was fixed on Christ Descended.
And as, on this side, the resplendent throne
    of Heaven's Lady, with the thrones below it,
    establishes the line of that division;                30
so, facing hers, does the throned blessedness
    of the Great John[4] who, ever holy, bore
    the desert, martyrdom, and Hell's distress;
and under him, forming that line are found
    Francis, Benedict, Augustine, and others            35
    descending to this center round by round.
Now marvel at all-foreseeing profundity:
    this garden shall be complete when the two aspects
    of the one faith have filled it equally.
And know that below that tier that cuts the two          40
    dividing walls at their centerpoint, no being
    has won his seat of glory by his own virtue,
but by another's, under strict condition;
    for all of these were spirits loosed from flesh
    before they had matured to true volition.[5]        45
You can yourself make out their infant graces:
    you need no more than listen to their treble
    and look attentively into their faces.
You do not speak now: many doubts confound you.[6]
    Therefore, to set you free I shall untie            50
    the cords in which your subtle thoughts have bound you.
Infinite order rules in this domain.
    Mere accidence can no more enter in
    than hunger can, or thirst, or grief, or pain.
All you see here is fixed by the decree                   55
    of the eternal law, and is so made
    that the ring goes on the finger perfectly.
These, it follows, who had so short a pause
    in the lower life are not ranked higher or lower
    among themselves without sufficient cause.          60

---

4. *The Great John:* The Baptist. He denounced Herod Antipos and was beheaded two years before
the Crucifixion. He had to wait in Limbo for two years, therefore, till Christ came for him at the
Resurrection.    5. The lower half of the rose-stadium contains the blessed infants, the souls of
those who died before they had achieved the true volition of reason and faith. Salvation is granted
them not directly through belief in Christ but through the faith and prayers of their parents,
relatives, and others of the faithful who interceded for them.    6. The infants are ranked in tiers
that indicate degrees of heavenly merit. But if they were saved through no merit of their own,
how can one be more worthy than the other? Such is Dante's doubt, which Bernard goes on to
set at rest by telling him, in essence, that God knows what He is doing.

The king in whom this realm abides unchanging
  in so much love and bliss that none dares will
  increase of joy, creating and arranging
the minds of all in the glad Paradise
  of His own sight, grants them degrees of grace         65
  as He sees fit. Here let the effect suffice.[7]
Holy Scripture clearly and expressly
  notes this effect upon those twins who fought
  while still within their mother.[8] So we see
how the Supreme light fittingly makes fair          70
  its aureole by granting them their graces
  according to the color of their hair.[9]
Thus through no merit of their works and days
  they are assigned their varying degrees
  by variance only in original grace.         75
In the first centuries of man's creation
  their innocence and the true faith of their parents
  was all they needed to achieve salvation.
When the first age of man had run its course,
  then circumcision was required of males,         80
  to give their innocent wings sufficient force.
But when the age of grace came to mankind
  then, unless perfectly baptized in Christ,
  such innocents went down among the blind.[1]
Look now on her who most resembles Christ,[2]       85
  for only the great glory of her shining
  can purify your eyes to look on Christ."
I saw such joy rain down upon that face—[3]
  borne to it by those blest Intelligences
  created thus to span those heights of space—       90
that through all else on the long road I trod
  nothing had held my soul so fixed in awe,
  nor shown me such resemblances to God.
The self-same Love that to her first descended[4]
  singing *"Ave Maria, gratia plena"*        95
  stood before her with its wings extended.
Thus rang the holy chant to Heaven's Queen

---

7. The cause is buried in God's mind. The effect must speak for itself.    8. Jacob and Esau. According to Genesis, XXV, 21 ff., they were at odds while still in their mother's womb. (Cf. the legend of Polyneices and Eteocles, twin sons of Oedipus and Jocasta.) Dante follows St. Paul (*Romans*, IX, 11–13) in interpreting the division between Jacob and Esau as a working of God's unfathomable will. "Even as it is written, Jacob I loved, but Esau I hated." Man can note the will of God in such matters ("the effect") but cannot plumb its causes.    9. For what may seem to be superficial reasons. Esau (*Genesis*, XXV, 25) was red-headed.    1. Among the souls of Hell. Such infants were assigned to Limbo.    2. The Virgin Mary.    3. Mary's.    4. The archangel Gabriel, the Angel of the Annunciation. Dante seems to conceive of Gabriel suspended in air before her, repeating the blissful chant of the Annunciation as he had first hymned it in Nazareth.

and all the blessed court joined in the song,
and singing, every face grew more serene.
"O holy Father, who endures for me                                    100
the loss of being far from the sweet place
where fate has raised your throne eternally,
who is that angel who with such desire
gazes into the eyes of our sweet Queen,
so rapt in love he seems to be afire?"                                105
Thus did I seek instruction from that Great One
who drew the beauty of his light from Mary
as the morning star draws beauty from the sun.
And he: "As much as angel or soul can know
of exultation, gallantry, and poise                                   110
there is in him; and we would have it so,
for it was he who brought the victory[5]
to Mary when the Son of God had willed
to bear the weight of human misery.
But let your eyes go where my words point out                         115
among this court, and note the mighty peers
of the empire of the just and the devout.
Those two whose bliss it is to sit so close
to the radiance of the Empress of All Joy
are the two eternal roots of this our rose:[6]                        120
The one just to the left of her blessedness
is the father whose unruly appetite
left man the taste for so much bitterness;
and on her right, that ancient one you see
is the father of Holy Church to whom Christ gave                      125
the twin keys to this flower of timeless beauty.
And that one who in his prophetic sight
foretold the evil days of the Sweet Bride
won by the spear and nails,[7] sits on his right.
While by the other father and first man                               130
sits the great leader to whom manna fell
to feed an ingrate and rebellious clan.[8]
Across the circle from Peter, behold Anna.[9]
She feels such bliss in looking at her daughter
she does not move her eyes to sing 'Hosanna!'                         135

5. (Dante says "the palm.") Of God's election, that she bear the promised Messiah.     6. Adam
and St. Peter. Adam as Father of Mankind, Peter as Father of the Church. Note that Peter has
the place of honor on the right.     7. St. John the Evangelist. His *Apocalypse* was received as the
prophetic book in which the entire history of the Church is foretold. He sits on Peter's right.
8. Moses.     9. Ste. Anna, Ste. Anne, mother of the Virgin. Her position directly across the
circle from Peter's puts her to the right of John the Baptist. *Does not move her eyes to sing 'Hos-*
*anna!'*: Like all the other heavenly beings, she constantly sings the praise of God. All others,
naturally enough, look up as they sing. She, however, is so filled with bliss by the sight of Mary
that she does not turn her eyes from her blessed daughter.

And opposite the father of us all
   sits Lucy,[1] who first urged your lady to you
   when you were blindly bent toward your own fall.
But the time allowed for this dream vision flies.
   As a tailor must cut the gown from what cloth is given,        140
   just so must we move on, turning our eyes
to the Primal Love, that as your powers advance
   with looking toward him, you may penetrate
   as deep as may be through His radiance.
But lest you should fall backward when you flare        145
   your mortal wings, intending to mount higher,
   remember grace must be acquired through prayer.
Therefore I will pray that blessed one[2]
   who has the power to aid you in your need.
   See that you follow me with such devotion        150
your heart adheres to every word I say."
And with those words the saint began to pray.

CANTO XXXIII

*The Empyrean    St. Bernard, Prayer to the Virgin, The Vision of
God*

St. Bernard offers a lofty Prayer to the Virgin, asking her to intercede
in Dante's behalf, and in answer Dante feels his soul swell with new
power and grow calm in rapture as his eyes are permitted the Direct
Vision of God.

There can be no measure of how long the vision endures. It passes,
and Dante is once more mortal and fallible. Raised by God's presence, he had looked into the Mystery and had begun to understand
its power and majesty. Returned to himself, there is no power in him
capable of speaking the truth of what he saw. Yet the impress of the
truth is stamped upon his soul, which he now knows will return to
be one with God's Love.

"Virgin Mother, daughter of thy son;
   humble beyond all creatures and more exalted;
   predestined turning point of God's intention;
thy merit so ennobled human nature
   that its divine Creator did not scorn        5
   to make Himself the creature of His creature.
The Love that was rekindled in Thy womb
   sends forth the warmth of the eternal peace
   within whose ray this flower has come to bloom.

1. See *Inferno*, II, 97–100. It was she who first sent Beatrice to rescue Dante from the Dark
Wood of Error. She sits opposite Adam. She would, accordingly, be to the left of John the
Baptist.   2. Mary.

Here, to us, thou art the noon and scope                10
  of Love revealed; and among mortal men,
  the living fountain of eternal hope.
Lady, thou art so near God's reckonings
  that who seeks grace and does not first seek thee
  would have his wish fly upward without wings.        15
Not only does thy sweet benignity
  flow out to all who beg, but oftentimes
  thy charity arrives before the plea.
In thee is pity, in thee munificence,
  in thee the tenderest heart, in thee unites          20
  all that creation knows of excellence!
Now comes this man who from the final pit
  of the universe up to this height has seen,
  one by one, the three lives of the spirit.
He prays to thee in fervent supplication              25
  for grace and strength, that he may raise his eyes
  to the all-healing final revelation.
And I, who never more desired to see
  the vision myself than I do that he may see It,
  add my own prayer, and pray that it may be          30
enough to move you to dispel the trace
  of every mortal shadow by thy prayers
  and let him see revealed the Sum of Grace.
I pray thee further, all-persuading Queen,
  keep whole the natural bent of his affections[3]     35
  and of his powers after his eyes have seen.
Protect him from the stirrings of man's clay;[4]
  see how Beatrice and the blessed host
  clasp reverent hands to join me as I pray."
The eyes[5] that God reveres and loves the best        40
  glowed on the speaker, making clear the joy
  with which true prayer is heard by the most blest.
Those eyes turned then to the Eternal Ray,
  through which, we must indeed believe, the eyes
  of others do not find such ready way.                45
And I, who neared the goal of all my nature,
  felt my soul, at the climax of its yearning,
  suddenly, as it ought, grow calm with rapture.
Bernard then, smiling sweetly, gestured to me
  to look up, but I had already become                 50

3. Bernard is asking Mary to protect Dante lest the intensity of the vision overpower his
faculties.     4. Protect him from the stirrings of base human impulse, especially from pride, for
Dante is about to receive a grace never before granted to any man and the thought of such glory
might well move a mere mortal to an hybris that would turn glory to sinfullness.     5. Of Mary.

within myself all he would have me be.[6]
Little by little as my vision grew
   it penetrated further through the aura
   of the high lamp which in Itself is true.[7]
What then I saw is more than tongue can say.          55
   Our human speech is dark before the vision.
   The ravished memory swoons and falls away.
As one who sees in dreams and wakes to find
   the emotional impression of his vision
   still powerful while its parts fade from his mind—      60
just such am I, having lost nearly all
   the vision itself, while in my heart I feel
   the sweetness of it yet distill and fall.
So, in the sun, the footprints fade from snow.
   On the wild wind that bore the tumbling leaves      65
   the Sybil's oracles were scattered so.[8]
O Light Supreme who doth Thyself withdraw
   so far above man's mortal understanding,
   lend me again some glimpse of what I saw;
make Thou my tongue so eloquent it may          70
   of all Thy glory speak a single clue
   to those who follow me in the world's day;
for by returning to my memory
   somewhat, and somewhat sounding in these verses,
   Thou shalt show man more of Thy victory.      75
So dazzling was the splendor of that Ray,
   that I must certainly have lost my senses
   had I, but for an instant, turned away.[9]
And so it was, as I recall, I could
   the better bear to look, until at last      80
   my vision made one with the Eternal Good.
Oh grace abounding that had made me fit
   to fix my eyes on the eternal light
   until my vision was consumed in it!
I saw within Its depth how It conceives      85

6. I.e., "But I had already fixed my entire attention upon the vision of God." But if so, how could Dante have seen Bernard's smile and gesture? Eager students like to believe they catch Dante in a contradiction here. Let them bear in mind that Dante is looking directly at God, as do the souls of Heaven, who thereby acquire—insofar as they are able to contain it—God's own knowledge. As a first stirring of that heavenly power, therefore, Dante is sharing God's knowledge of St. Bernard.   7. The light of God is the one light whose source is Itself. All others are a reflection of this.   8. The Cumean Sibyl (Virgil describes her in *Aeneid*, III, 441 ff.) wrote her oracles on leaves, one letter to a leaf, then sent her message scattering on the wind. Presumably, the truth was all contained in that strew, could one only gather all the leaves and put the letters in the right order.   9. How can a light be so dazzling that the beholder would swoon if he looked away for an instant? Would it not be, rather, in looking at, not away from, the overpowering vision that the viewer's senses would be overcome? So it would be on earth. But now Dante, with the help of all heaven's prayers, is in the presence of God and strengthened by all he sees. It is by being so strengthened that he can see yet more.

all things in a single volume bound by Love,
    of which the universe is the scattered leaves;
substance,[1] accident, and their relation
    so fused that all I say could do no more
    than yield a glimpse of that bright revelation.                    90
I think I saw the universal form
    that binds these things,[2] for as I speak these words
    I feel my joy swell and my spirits warm.
Twenty-five centuries since Neptune saw
    the Argo's keel have not moved all mankind,                        95
    recalling that adventure, to such awe
as I felt in an instant. My tranced being
    stared fixed and motionless upon that vision,
    ever more fervent to see in the act of seeing.
Experiencing that Radiance, the spirit                                 100
    is so indrawn it is impossible
    even to think of ever turning from It.
For the good which is the will's ultimate object
    is all subsumed in It; and, being removed,
    all is defective which in It is perfect.                           105
Now in my recollection of the rest
    I have less power to speak than any infant
    wetting its tongue yet at its mother's breast;
and not because that Living Radiance bore
    more than one semblance, for It is unchanging                      110
    and is forever as it was before;
rather, as I grew worthier to see,
    the more I looked, the more unchanging semblance
    appeared to change with every change in me.
Within the depthless deep and clear existence                         115
    of that abyss of light three circles shown—
    three in color, one in circumference:
the second from the first, rainbow from rainbow;
    the third, an exhalation of pure fire
    equally breathed forth by the other two.                          120
But oh how much my words miss my conception,
    which is itself so far from what I saw
    that to call it feeble would be rank deception!
O Light Eternal fixed in Itself alone,
    by Itself alone understood, which from Itself                     125
    loves and glows, self-knowing and self-known;
that second aureole which shone forth in Thee,
    conceived as a reflection of the first—

1. Matter, all that exists in itself. *Accident:* All that exists as a phase of matter.    2. Substance and accident.

or which appeared so to my scrutiny—
seemed in Itself of Its own coloration                                              130
   to be painted with man's image. I fixed my eyes
   on that alone in rapturous contemplation.
Like a geometer wholly dedicated
   to squaring the circle, but who cannot find,
   think as he may, the principle indicated—                              135
so did I study the supernal face.
   I yearned to know just how our image merges
   into that circle, and how it there finds place;
but mine were not the wings for such a flight.
   Yet, as I wished, the truth I wished for came                          140
   cleaving my mind in a great flash of light.
Here my powers rest from their high fantasy,
   but already I could feel my being turned—
   instinct and intellect balanced equally
as in a wheel whose motion nothing jars—                                            145
by the Love that moves the Sun and the other stars.

---

# GIOVANNI BOCCACCIO

## 1313–1375

The tales of Boccaccio's *Decameron* (completed about 1353) constitute the
greatest achievement of prose fiction in a vernacular language of southern
Europe during the medieval centuries. In his hundred stories the Italian
author presents a great variety of people and situations, aptly and often acutely
characterized, and abundant dialogue of varying liveliness and realism.

   Born in 1313 in Paris, Giovanni Boccaccio was the son of a Florentine
businessman and a Frenchwoman. He was apparently taken to Italy in
infancy, and in 1328 was sent to Naples to learn commerce in the office of
his father's partner; but after six years, bored with business, he turned to the
study of canon law. In 1336 Boccaccio saw Maria d'Aquino in a church at
Naples; she is represented as Fiammetta in several of his works, including
the *Decameron*. A romantic affair ended in Maria's desertion of her lover,
and finally in her death in the plague of 1348. In 1341 Boccaccio returned
to Florence. After 1351 he was greatly influenced by Petrarch, and turned
in his writing from Italian poetry and prose fiction to Latin works of a scholarly nature. He sheltered Leon Pilatus, inducing him to make the first translation of Homer from Greek. Unlike Petrarch, Boccaccio was devoted to the
study of Dante, of whom he wrote a biography; in 1373 he was appointed to
a Dante chair or lectureship in Florence. He died in 1375.

   Like Chaucer, who wrote his *Canterbury Tales* several decades later, Boccaccio provides a dramatic framework for his narrations. But his storytellers
are not miscellaneous pilgrims traveling to a famous shrine; they are seven

young ladies and three young gentlemen who have withdrawn from Florence to the countryside, to escape the Black Death, or plague, of 1348. They engage in gay banter and good-natured raillery; but, as they are all refined and cultivated young people with no occupational bias or ingrained prejudices, their relationships are polite rather than boisterous and lack the force and depth and vitality of those portrayed in *The Canterbury Tales*. They agree on a plan of storytelling—and adhere to it (with slight changes). Here there is no drunken miller, such as interrupts Chaucer's pilgrims, to upset the seemly orderliness acceptable to gentlefolk, for there are no other folk present. Each member of the company is to tell a tale each day; on some days a general topic is assigned, on others each narrator follows his own taste and judgment.

The story about Brother Alberto and his impersonation of the angel Gabriel, a bawdy tale of amorous intrigue and deception, exemplifies what most modern readers regard as typical of the *Decameron*. Like Chaucer's *Miller's Tale*, it presents a (moderately) clever person successfully deceiving a very foolish one, but eventually punished for his trickery. In the present story, the man is the trickster and the woman is the foolish dupe, but these roles are often reversed in other stories of the *Decameron*; indeed, Boccaccio digresses during the introduction to the fourth day to assert his devotion to women—the Muses, after all, were women—and, indeed, the women storytellers outnumber the men. He nonetheless knew that some women are foolish, just as he knew, though he was a devout Christian, that some priests and friars fall short of their vocation. Like other authors of his time, he saw nothing wrong in acknowledging these facts and turning them to artistic use.

If reduced to the bare essentials of its plot, this tale could be told far more briefly, as a mere anecdote, a joke. Indeed, it may well have been in circulation as an anecdote both before and after Boccaccio. But he gives it literary value by the way he handles it. He makes the reader see the successive scenes in vivid detail, he creates memorable and amusing characters, and he relates the incidents of the narrative closely to the personalities of those characters. Lisetta is not only credulous but also inordinately vain—her credulity derives from her vanity—and it is because of these qualities that she can be taken in by Brother Alberto's preposterous account of the angel's interest in her. The reader also notices the tacit perception of Lisetta's woman friend, who at once sees through the friar's scheme but, instead of disabusing her foolish friend, leads her on and then gleefully reveals the whole story to the outside world. And Alberto, though clever, is not as cautious as he should be. Otherwise, once warned, he would not have exposed himself to discovery and disgrace.

The story of Federigo and his falcon is told on a day devoted to accounts of love that turns out happily after difficulties on the way. It presents the courtly-love relationship—or one of the possible relationships—in a remarkable combination of realism and nobility. Federigo's conduct perfectly fulfills the code; he devotes himself completely to Monna Giovanna, and his failure to receive any return in no way disturbs the pattern of that devotion. He never repines or complains; his lady's married or widowed condition is all one to him; and, having spent his fortune in the futile effort to attract her, he lives with resignation on his tiny estate. But Federigo is genuinely

high-minded and noble; he has absorbed the ideals and not merely the etiquette of courtly love. His declaration, when Giovanna comes to call, that
he has gained and not lost by his service to her, might be politeness learned
out of a book—a romance, for example. But his sacrifice of the falcon to
provide her with a good meal is a splendid and magnificent folly that could
come only from an almost unbelievably generous heart. His grief at the
outcome is probably sharper than Giovanna's, despite the painful disappointment which it produces for her.

Giovanna's dignity and charm and sensitivity are as clear to us as they
evidently are to Federigo. Unwilling, whether as wife or widow, to have a
romance with Federigo, she does not encourage him. Yet she knows that he
loves her and that he has squandered his wealth on her account. We see her
distress at having to ask him for anything, let alone the falcon, his most
cherished possession. But when love for her young son, mortally ill, forces
her to it, she acts with grace and decorum. And with something more; for
she has discerned the nobleness of temper in Federigo through his consistently courteous behavior. It is that to which she appeals, not to any obligation of a courtly lover to please his lady. Later, when her brothers convince
her that she should remarry, she also shows both generosity and independence of character. She gives Federigo his reward by marrying him—and
seeing that his new fortune is not wasted! The happy ending is agreeable;
but the notable achievement of the story is the brief but complete and poignant depiction of the dilemmas faced by the two against a background of
preliminary characterization which gives their decision full significance.

Two good biographies are T. C. Chubb, *The Life of Giovanni Boccaccio*
(1930), and Edward Hutton, *Giovanni Boccaccio* (1910). Interesting and
sensitive criticism is to be found in Charles G. Osgood, *Boccaccio on Poetry*
(1930). John Addington Symonds, *Giovanni Boccaccio* (1895), has been
reissued (1968). A. D. Scaglione, *Nature and Love in the Middle Ages* (1963),
is a useful discussion of the *Decameron*. Twenty-one of the tales from the
*Decameron* will be found in Mark Musa and Peter E. Bondanella, *Giovanni
Boccaccio, The Decameron, A New Translation* (1977).

# The Decameron[1]

## *The Author's Introduction*

Thirteen hundred and forty-eight years had already passed after
the fruitful Incarnation of the Son of God when into the distinguished city of Florence, more noble than any other Italian city,
there came the deadly pestilence. It started in the East, either because
of the influence of heavenly bodies or because of God's just wrath as
a punishment to mortals for our wicked deeds, and it killed an infinite number of people. Without pause it spread from one place and
it stretched its miserable length over the West. And against this pes-

---

1. These selections translated by Mark Musa and Peter E. **Bondanella**.

tilence no human wisdom or foresight was of any avail; quantities of filth were removed from the city by officials charged with this task; the entry of any sick person into the city was prohibited; and many directives were issued concerning the maintenance of good health. Nor were the humble supplications, rendered not once but many times to God by pious people, through public processions or by other means, efficacious; for almost at the beginning of springtime of the year in question the plague began to show its sorrowful effects in an extraordinary manner. It did not act as it had done in the East, where bleeding from the nose was a manifest sign of inevitable death, but it began in both men and women with certain swellings either in the groin or under the armpits, some of which grew to the size of a normal apple and others to the size of an egg (more or less), and the people called them buboes. And from the two parts of the body already mentioned, within a brief space of time, the said deadly buboes began to spread indiscriminately over every part of the body; and after this, the symptoms of the illness changed to black or livid spots appearing on the arms and thighs, and on every part of the body, some large ones and sometimes many little ones scattered all around. And just as the buboes were originally, and still are, a very certain indication of impending death, in like manner these spots came to mean the same thing for whoever had them. Neither a doctor's advice nor the strength of medicine could do anything to cure this illness; on the contrary, either the nature of the illness was such that it afforded no cure, or else the doctors were so ignorant that they did not recognize its cause and, as a result, could not prescribe the proper remedy (in fact, the number of doctors, other than the well-trained, was increased by a large number of men and women who had never had any medical training); at any rate, few of the sick were ever cured, and almost all died after the third day of the appearance of the previously described symptoms (some sooner, others later), and most of them died without fever or any other side effects.

This pestilence was so powerful that it was communicated to the healthy by contact with the sick, the way a fire close to dry or oily things will set them aflame. And the evil of the plague went even further: not only did talking to or being around the sick bring infection and a common death, but also touching the clothes of the sick or anything touched or used by them seemed to communicate this very disease to the person involved. What I am about to say is incredible to hear, and if I and others had not witnessed it with our own eyes, I should not dare believe it (let alone write about it), no matter how trustworthy a person I might have heard it from. Let me say, then, that the power of the plague described here was of such virulence in spreading from one person to another that not only did it pass from one man to the next, but, what's more, it was often transmitted from the garments of a sick or dead man to animals that not only became contaminated by the disease, but also died within a brief period of time. My own eyes, as I said earlier, witnessed such a thing one day: when the rags of a poor man who died of this disease were thrown into the public street, two pigs came upon them, as they are wont to do, and first with their snouts and then with their teeth they took the rags and shook them around; and within a short time, after a number of convulsions, both pigs fell dead upon the ill-fated rags, as if they had been poisoned. From these and many similar or worse occurrences there came about such fear and such fantastic notions among those who remained alive that almost all of them took a very cruel attitude in the matter; that is, they completely avoided the sick and their possessions; and in so doing, each one believed that he was protecting his good health.

There were some people who thought that living moderately and avoiding all superfluity might help a great deal in resisting this disease, and so, they gathered in small groups and lived entirely apart from everyone else. They shut themselves up in those houses where there were no sick people and where one could live well by eating the most delicate of foods and drinking the finest of wines (doing so always in moderation), allowing no one to speak about or listen to anything said about the sick and the dead outside; these people lived, spending their time with music and other pleasures that they could arrange. Others thought the opposite: they believed that drinking too much, enjoying life, going about singing and celebrating, satisfying in every way the appetites as best one could, laughing, and making light of everything that happened was the best medicine for such a disease; so they practiced to the fullest what they believed by going from one tavern to another all day and night, drinking to excess; and often they would make merry in private homes, doing everything that pleased or amused them the most. This they were able to do easily, for everyone felt he was doomed to die and, as a result, abandoned his property, so that most of the houses had become common property, and any stranger who came upon them used them as if he were their rightful owner. In addition to this bestial behavior, they always managed to avoid the sick as best they could. And in this great affliction and misery of our city the revered authority of the laws, both divine and human, had fallen and almost completely disappeared, for, like other men, the ministers and executors of the laws were either dead or sick or so short of help that it was impossible for them to fulfill their duties; as a result, everybody was free to do as he pleased.

Many others adopted a middle course between the two attitudes just described: neither did they restrict their food or drink so much as the first group nor did they fall into such dissoluteness and drunkenness as the second; rather, they satisfied their appetites to a moderate degree. They did not shut themselves up, but went around carrying in their hands flowers, or sweet-smelling herbs, or various kinds of spices; and often they would put these things to their noses, believing that such smells were a wonderful means of purifying the brain, for all the air seemed infected with the stench of dead bodies, sickness, and medicines.

Others were of a crueler opinion (though it was, perhaps, a safer one): they maintained that there was no better medicine against the plague than to flee from it; and convinced of this reasoning, not caring about anything but themselves, men and women in great numbers abandoned their city, their houses, their farms, their relatives, and their possessions and sought other places, and they went at least as far away as the Florentine countryside—as if the wrath of God could not pursue them with this pestilence wherever they went but would only strike those it found within the walls of the city! Or perhaps they thought that Florence's last hour had come and that no one in the city would remain alive.

And not all those who adopted these diverse opinions died, nor did they all escape with their lives; on the contrary, many of those who thought this way were falling sick everywhere, and since they had given, when they were healthy, the bad example of avoiding the sick, they, in turn, were abandoned and left to languish away without care. The fact was that one citizen avoided another, that almost no one cared for his neighbor, and that relatives rarely or hardly ever visited each other—they stayed far apart. This disaster had struck such fear into the hearts of men and women that brother abandoned brother, uncle abandoned nephew, sister left brother, and very often wife abandoned husband, and—even worse, almost unbelievable—fathers and mothers neglected to tend and care for their children, as if they were not their own.

Thus, for the countless multitude of men and women who fell sick, there remained no support except the charity of their friends (and these were few) or the avarice of servants, who worked for inflated salaries and indecent periods of time and who, in spite of this, were few and far between; and those few were men or women of little wit (most of them not trained for such service) who did little else but hand different things to the sick when requested to do so or watch over them while they died, and in this service, they very often lost their own lives and their profits. And since the sick were abandoned by their neighbors, their parents, and their friends and there was a scarcity of servants, a practice that was almost unheard of before spread through the city: when a woman fell sick, no matter how attractive or beautiful or noble she might be, she did not mind having a manservant (whoever he might be, no matter how young or old he was), and she had no shame whatsoever in revealing any part of her body to him—the way she would have done to a woman—when the necessity of her sickness required her to do so. This practice was, perhaps, in the days that followed the pestilence, the cause of looser morals in the women who survived the plague. And so, many people died who, by chance, might have survived if they had been attended to. Between the lack of competent attendants, which the sick were unable to obtain, and the violence of the pestilence, there were so many, many people who died in the city both day and night that it was incredible just to hear this described, not to mention seeing it! Therefore, out of sheer necessity, there arose among those who remained alive customs which were contrary to the established practices of the time.

It was the custom, as it is again today, for the women, relatives, and neighbors to gather together in the house of a dead person and there to mourn with the women who had been dearest to him; on the other hand, in front of the deceased's home, his male relatives would gather together with his male neighbors and other citizens, and the clergy also came (many of them, or sometimes just a few) depending upon the social class of the dead man. Then, upon the shoulders of his equals, he was carried to the church chosen by him before death with the funeral pomp of candles and chants. With the fury of the pestilence increasing, this custom, for the most part, died out and other practices took its place. And so, not only did people die without having a number of women around them, but there were many who passed away without even having a single witness present, and very few were granted the piteous laments and bitter tears of their relatives; on the contrary, most relatives were somewhere else, laughing, joking, and amusing themselves; even the women learned this practice too well, having put aside, for the most part, their womanly compassion for their own safety. Very few were the dead whose bodies were accompanied to the church by more than ten or twelve of their neighbors, and these dead bodies were not even carried on the shoulders of honored and reputable citizens but rather by gravediggers from the lower classes that were called *becchini*. Working for pay, they would pick up the bier and hurry it off, not to the church the dead man had chosen before his death but, in most cases, to the church closest by, accompanied by four or six churchmen with just a few candles, and often none at all. With the help of these *becchini*, the churchmen would place the body as fast as they could in whatever unoccupied grave they could find, without going to the trouble of saying long or solemn burial services.

The plight of the lower class and, perhaps, a large part of the middle class, was even more pathetic: most of them stayed in their homes or neighborhoods either because of their poverty or their hopes for remaining safe, and every day they fell sick by the thousands; and not having servants or attendants of any kind, they almost always died. Many ended their lives in the public streets, during the day or at night, while many others who died in their homes were discovered dead by their neighbors only by the smell of their decomposing bodies. The city was full of corpses. The dead were usually given the same treatment by their neighbors, who were moved more by the fear that the decomposing corpses would contaminate them than by any charity they might have felt towards the deceased: either by themselves or with the assistance of porters (when they were available), they would drag the corpse out of the home and place it in front of the doorstep where, usually in the morning, quantities of dead bodies could be seen by any passerby; then, they were laid out on biers, or for lack of biers, on a plank. Nor did a bier carry only one corpse; sometimes it was used for two or three at a time. More than once, a single bier would serve for a wife and husband, two or three brothers, a father or son, or other relatives, all at the same time. And countless times it happened that two priests, each with a cross, would be on their way to bury someone, when porters carrying three or four biers would just follow along behind them; and where these priests thought they had just one dead man to bury, they had, in fact, six or eight and sometimes more. Moreover, the dead were honored with no tears or candles or funeral mourners but worse: things had reached such a point that the people who died were cared for as we care for goats today. Thus, it became quite obvious that what the wise had not been able to endure with patience through the few calamities of everyday life now became a matter of indifference to even the most simple-minded people as a result of this colossal misfortune.

So many corpses would arrive in front of a church every day and at every hour that the amount of holy ground for burials was certainly insufficient for the ancient custom of giving each body its individual place; when all the graves were full, huge trenches were dug in all of the cemeteries of the churches and into them the new arrivals were dumped by the hundreds; and they were packed in there with dirt, one on top of another, like a ship's cargo, until the trench was filled.

But instead of going over every detail of the past miseries which befell our city, let me say that the same unfriendly weather there did not, because of this, spare the surrounding countryside any evil; there, not to speak of the towns which, on a smaller scale, were like the city, in the scattered villages and in the fields the poor, miserable peasants and their families, without any medical assistance or aid of servants, died on the roads and in their fields and in their homes, as many by day as by night, and they died not like men but more like wild animals. Because of this they, like the city dwellers, became careless in their ways and did not look after their possessions or their businesses; furthermore, when they saw that death was upon them, completely neglecting the future fruits of their past labors, their livestock, their property, they did their best to consume what they already had at hand. So, it came about that oxen, donkeys, sheep, pigs, chickens and even dogs, man's most faithful companion, were driven from their homes into the fields, where the wheat was left not only unharvested but also unreaped, and they were allowed to roam where they wished; and many of these animals, almost as if they were rational beings, returned at night to their homes without any guidance from a shepherd, satiated after a good day's meal.

Leaving the countryside and returning to the city, what more can one say, except that so great was the cruelty of Heaven, and, perhaps, also that of man, that from March to July of the same year, between the fury of the pestiferous sickness and the fact that many of the sick were badly treated or abandoned in need because of the fear that the healthy had, more than one hundred thousand human beings are believed to have lost their lives for certain inside the walls of the city of Florence whereas, before the deadly plague, one would not have estimated that there were actually that many people dwelling in that city.

Oh, how many great palaces, beautiful homes, and noble dwellings, once filled with families, gentlemen, and ladies, were now emptied, down to the last servant! How many notable families, vast domains, and famous fortunes remained without legitimate heir! How many valiant men, beautiful women, and charming young men, who might have been pronounced very healthy by Galen, Hippocrates, and Aesculapius[2] (not to mention lesser physicians), dined in the morning with their relatives, companions, and friends and then in the evening took supper with their ancestors in the other world!

Reflecting upon so many miseries makes me very sad; therefore, since I wish to pass over as many as I can, let me say that as our city was in this condition, almost emptied of inhabitants, it happened (as I heard it later from a person worthy of trust) that one Tuesday morning in the venerable church of Santa Maria Novella there was hardly any congregation there to hear the holy services except for seven young women, all dressed in garments of mourning as the times demanded, each of whom was a friend, neighbor, or relative of the other, and none of whom had passed her twenty-eighth year, nor was any of them younger than eighteen; all were educated and of

---

2. Roman god of medicine and healing, often identified with Asclepius, Apollo's son, who was the Greek god of medicine. *Galen:* Greek anatomist and physician (A.D. 130?–201?). *Hippocrates:* Greek Physician (160?–377? B.C.), to whom the Hippocratic oath, administered to new physicians, is attributed.

noble birth and beautiful to look at, well-mannered and gracefully
modest. I would tell you their real names, if I did not have a good
reason for not doing so, which is this: I do not wish any of them to
be embarrassed in the future because of the things that they said to
each other and what they listened to—all of which I shall later recount.
Today the laws regarding pleasure are again strict, more so than at
that time (for the reasons mentioned above when they were very lax),
not only for women of their age but even for those who were older;
nor would I wish to give an opportunity to the envious, who are
always ready to attack every praiseworthy life, to diminish in any way
with their indecent talk the dignity of these worthy ladies. But, so
that you may understand clearly what each of them had to say, I
intend to call them by names which are either completely or in part
appropriate to their personalities. We shall call the first and the oldest Pampinea and the second Fiammetta, the third Filomena, and
the fourth Emilia, and we shall name the fifth Lauretta and the sixth
Neifile, and the last, not without reason, we shall call Elissa.[3] Not
by prior agreement, but purely by chance, they gathered together in
one part of the church and were seated almost in a circle, saying
their rosaries; after many sighs, they began to discuss among themselves various matters concerning the nature of the times, and after
a while, as the others fell silent, Pampinea began to speak in this
manner:

"My dear ladies, you have often heard, as I have, how a proper
use of one's reason does harm to no one. It is only natural for everyone born on this earth to aid, preserve, and defend his own life to
the best of his ability; this is a right so taken for granted that it has,
at times, permitted men to kill each other without blame in order to
defend their own lives. And if the laws dealing with the welfare of
every human being permit such a thing, how much more lawful,
and with no harm to anyone, is it for us, or anyone else, to take all
possible precautions to preserve our own lives! When I consider what
we have been doing this morning and in the past days and what we
have spoken about, I understand, and you must understand too, that
each one of us is afraid for her life; nor does this surprise me in the
least—rather I am greatly amazed that since each of us has the natural feelings of a woman, we do not find some remedy for ourselves
to cure what each one of us dreads. We live in the city, in my opinion, for no other reason than to bear witness to the number of dead
bodies that are carried to burial, or to listen whether the friars (whose
number has been reduced to almost nothing) chant their offices at
the prescribed hours, or to demonstrate to anyone who comes here
the quality and the quantity of our miseries by our garments of

3. Perhaps the reason is that like her namesake, the Carthaginian queen, who is better known as
Dido, Boccaccio's Elissa is dominated by a violent passion.

mourning. And if we leave the church, either we see dead or sick bodies being carried all about, or we see those who were once condemned to exile for their crimes by the authority of the public laws making sport of these laws, running about wildly through the city, because they know that the executors of these laws are either dead or dying; or we see the scum of our city, avid for our blood, who call themselves *becchini* and who ride about on horseback torturing us by deriding everything, making our losses more bitter with their disgusting songs. Nor do we hear anything but 'So-and-so is dead,' and 'So-and-so is dying'; and if there were anyone left to mourn, we should hear nothing but piteous laments everywhere. I do not know if what happens to me also happens to you in your homes, but when I go home I find no one there except my maid, and I become so afraid that my hair stands on end, and wherever I go or sit in my house, I seem to see the shadows of those who have passed away, not with the faces that I remember, but with horrible expressions that terrify me. For these reasons, I am uncomfortable here, outside, and in my home, and the more so since it appears that no one like ourselves, who is well off and who has some other place to go, has remained here except us. And if there are any who remain, according to what I hear and see, they do whatever their hearts desire, making no distinction between what is proper and what is not, whether they are alone or with others, by day or by night; and not only laymen but also those who are cloistered in convents have broken their vows of obedience and have given themselves over to carnal pleasures, for they have made themselves believe that these things are permissible for them and are improper for others, and thinking that they will escape with their lives in this fashion, they have become wanton and dissolute.

"If this is the case, and plainly it is, what are we doing here? What are we waiting for? What are we dreaming about? Why are we slower to protect our health than all the rest of the citizens? Do we hold ourselves less dear than all the others? Or do we believe that our own lives are tied by stronger chains to our bodies than those of others and, therefore, that we need not worry about anything which might have the power to harm them? We are mistaken and deceived, and we are mad if we believe it. We shall have clear proof of this if we just call to mind how many young men and ladies have been struck down by this cruel pestilence. I do not know if you agree with me, but I think that, in order not to fall prey, out of laziness or presumption, to what we might well avoid, it might be a good idea for all of us to leave this city, just as many others before us have done and are still doing. Let us avoid like death itself the ugly examples of others, and go to live in a more dignified fashion in our country houses (of which we all have several) and there let us take what enjoyment, what happiness, and what pleasure we can, without going beyond the rules of reason in any way. There we can hear the birds sing, and we can see the hills and the pastures turning green, the wheat fields moving like the sea, and a thousand kinds of trees; and we shall be able to see the heavens more clearly which, though they still may be cruel, nonetheless will not deny to us their eternal beauties, which are much more pleasing to look at than the empty walls of our city. Besides all this, there in the country the air is much fresher, and the necessities for living in such times as these are plentiful there, and there are just fewer troubles in general; though the peasants are dying there even as the townspeople here, the displeasure is the less in that there are fewer houses and inhabitants than in the city. Here on the other hand, if I judge correctly, we would not be abandoning any-one; on the contrary, we can honestly say it is we ourselves that have been abandoned, for our loved ones are either dead or have fled and have left us alone in such affliction as though we did not belong to them. No reproach, therefore, can come to us if we follow this course of action, whereas sorrow, worry, and perhaps even death can come if we do not follow this course. So, whenever you like, I think it would be well to take our servants, have all our necessary things sent after us, and go from one place one day to another the next, enjoying what happiness and merriment these times permit; let us live in this manner (unless we are overtaken first by death) until we see what ending Heaven has reserved for these horrible times. And remember that it is no more forbidden for us to go away virtuously than it is for most other women to remain here dishonorably."

When they had listened to what Pampinea had said, the other women not only praised her advice but were so anxious to follow it that they had already begun discussing among themselves the details, as if they were going to leave that very instant. But Filomena, who was most discerning, said:

"Ladies, regardless of how convincing Pampinea's arguments are, that is no reason to rush into things, as you seem to wish to do. Remember that we are all women, and any young girl can tell you that women do not know how to reason in a group when they are without the guidance of some man who knows how to control them. We are changeable, quarrelsome, suspicious, timid, and fearful, because of which I suspect that this company will soon break up without honor to any of us if we do not take a guide other than ourselves. We would do well to resolve this matter before we depart."

Then Elissa said:

"Men are truly the leaders of women, and without their guidance, our actions rarely end successfully. But how are we to find any men? We all know that the majority of our relatives are dead and those who remain alive are scattered here and there in various groups, not knowing where we are (they, too, are fleeing precisely what we seek to avoid), and since taking up with strangers would be unbecoming to us, we must, if we wish to leave for the sake of our health, find a means of arranging it so that while going for our own pleasure and repose, no trouble or scandal follow us."

While the ladies were discussing this, three young men came into the church, none of whom was less than twenty-five years of age. Neither the perversity of the times nor the loss of friends or parents, nor fear for their own lives had been able to cool, much less extinguish, the love those lovers bore in their hearts. One of them was called Panfilo, another Filostrato, and the last Dioneo, each one very charming and well-bred; and in those turbulent times they sought their greatest consolation in the sight of the ladies they loved, all three of whom happened to be among the seven ladies previously mentioned, while the others were close relatives of one or the other of the three men. No sooner had they sighted the ladies than they were seen by them, whereupon Pampinea smiled and said:

"See how Fortune favors our plans and has provided us with these discreet and virtuous young men, who would gladly be our guides and servants if we do not hesitate to accept them for such service."

Then Neifile's face blushed out of embarrassment, for she was one of those who was loved by one of the young men, and she said:

"Pampinea, for the love of God, be careful what you say! I realize very well that nothing but good can be said of any of them, and I believe that they are capable of doing much more than that task and, likewise, that their good and worthy company would be fitting not only for us but for ladies much more beautiful and attractive than we are, but it is quite obvious that some of them are in love with some of us who are here present, and I fear that if we take them with us, slander and disapproval will follow, through no fault of ours or of theirs."

Then Filomena said:

"That does not matter at all; as long as I live with dignity and have no remorse of conscience about anything, let anyone who wishes say what he likes to the contrary: God and Truth will take up arms in my defense. Now, if they were just prepared to come with us, as Pampinea says, we could truly say that Fortune was favorable to our departure."

When the others heard her speak in such a manner, the argument was ended, and they all agreed that the young men should be called over, told about their intentions, and asked if they would be so kind as to accompany the ladies on such a journey. Without further discussion, then, Pampinea, who was related to one of the men, rose to her feet and made her way to where they stood gazing at the ladies, and she greeted them with a cheerful expression, outlined their plan to them, and begged them, in everyone's name, to keep them company in the spirit of pure and brotherly affection.

At first the young men thought they were being mocked, but when they saw that the lady was speaking seriously, they gladly consented; and in order to start without delay and put the plan into action, before leaving the church they agreed upon what preparations must be made for their departure. And when everything had been arranged and word had been sent on to the place they intended to go, the following morning (that is, Wednesday) at the break of dawn the ladies with some of their servants and the three young men with three of their servants left the city and set out on their way; they had traveled no further than two short miles when they arrived at the first stop they had agreed upon.

The place was somewhere on a little mountain, at some distance away from our roads, full of various shrubs and plants with rich, green foliage—most pleasant to look at; at the top there was a country mansion with a beautiful large inner courtyard with open colonnades, halls, and bedrooms, all of them beautiful in themselves and decorated with cheerful and interesting paintings; it was surrounded by meadows and marvelous gardens, with wells of fresh water and cellars full of the most precious wines, the likes of which were more suitable for expert drinkers than for sober and dignified ladies. And the group discovered, to their delight, that the entire palace had been cleaned and the beds made in the bedchambers, and that fresh flowers and rushes had been strewn everywhere. Soon after they arrived and were resting, Dioneo, who was more attractive and wittier than either of the other young men, said:

"Ladies, more than our preparations, it was your intelligence that guided us here. I do not know what you intend to do with your thoughts, but I left mine inside the city walls when I passed through them in your company a little while ago; and so, you must either make up your minds to enjoy yourselves and laugh and sing with me (as much, let me say, as your dignity permits), or you must give me leave to return to my worries and to remain in our troubled city."

To this Pampinea, who had driven away her sad thoughts in the same way, replied happily:

"Dioneo, you speak very well: let us live happily, for after all it was unhappiness that made us flee the city. But when things are not organized they cannot long endure, and since I began the discussions which brought this fine company together, and since I desire the continuation of our happiness, I think it is necessary that we choose a leader from among us, whom we shall honor and obey as our superior and whose every thought shall be to keep us living happily. And in order that each one of us may feel the weight of this responsibility together with the pleasure of its authority, so that no one of us who has not experienced it can envy the others, let me say that both the weight and the honor should be granted to each one of us in turn for a day; the first will be chosen by election; the others that follow will be whomever he or she that will have the rule for that day chooses as the hour of vespers[4] approaches; this ruler, as long as his reign endures, will organize and arrange the place and the manner in which we will spend our time."

These words greatly pleased everyone, and they unanimously elected Pampinea queen for the first day; Filomena quickly ran to a laurel bush, whose leaves she had always heard were worthy of praise and bestowed great honor upon those crowned with them; she plucked several branches from it and wove them into a handsome garland of honor. And when it would be placed upon the head of any one of them, it was to be to all in the group a clear symbol of royal rule and authority over the rest of them for as long as their company stayed together.

After she had been chosen queen, Pampinea ordered everyone to refrain from talking; then, she sent for the four servants of the ladies and for those of the three young men, and as they stood before her in silence, she said:

"Since I must set the first example for you all in order that it may be bettered and thus allow our company to live in order and in plea-sure, and without any shame, and so that it may last as long as we wish, I first appoint Parmeno, Dioneo's servant, as my steward, and I commit to his care and management all our household and every-thing which pertains to the services of the dining hall. I wish Sirisco, the servant of Panfilo, to act as our buyer and treasurer and follow the orders of Parmeno. Tindaro, who is in the service of Filostrato, shall wait on Filostrato and Dioneo and Panfilo in their bedcham-bers when the other two are occupied with their other duties and cannot do so. Misia, my servant, and Licisca, Filomena's, will be occupied in the kitchen and will prepare those dishes which are ordered by Parmeno. Chimera, Lauretta's servant, and Stratilia, Fiammetta's servant, will take care of the bedchambers of the ladies and the cleaning of those places we use. And in general, we desire and command each of you, if you value our favor and good graces, to be sure—no matter where you go or come from, no matter what you hear or see—to bring us back nothing but pleasant news."

And when these orders, praised by all present, were delivered, Pampinea rose happily to her feet and said:

"Here there are gardens and meadows and many other pleasant places, which all of us can wander about in and enjoy as we like; but at the hour of tierce[5] let everyone be here so that we can eat in the cool of the morning."

4. Late afternoon; the sixth of the seven times of day set aside for prayer by canon law.    5. The third canonical hour, 9 A.M.

After the merry group had been given the new queen's permission, the young men, together with the beautiful ladies, set off slowly through a garden, discussing pleasant matters, making themselves beautiful garlands of various leaves and singing love songs. After the time granted them by the queen had elapsed, they returned home and found Parmeno busy carrying out the duties of his task; for as they entered a hall on the ground floor, they saw the tables set with the whitest of linens and with glasses that shone like silver and everything decorated with broom blossoms; then, they washed their hands and, at the queen's command, they all sat down in the places assigned them by Parmeno. The delicately cooked foods were brought in and very fine wines were served; the three servants in silence served the tables. Everyone was delighted to see everything so beautiful and well arranged, and they ate merrily and with pleasant conversation. Since all the ladies and young men knew how to dance (and some of them even knew how to play and sing very well), when the tables had been cleared, the queen ordered that instruments be brought, and on her command, Dioneo took a lute and Fiammetta a viola, and they began softly playing a dance tune. After the queen had sent the servants off to eat, she began to dance together with the other ladies and two of the young men; and when that was over, they all began to sing carefree and gay songs. In this manner they continued until the queen felt that it was time to retire; therefore, at the queen's request, the three young men went off to their chambers (which were separate from those of the ladies), where they found their beds prepared and the rooms as full of flowers as the halls; the ladies, too, discovered their chambers decorated in like fashion. Then they all undressed and fell asleep.

Not long after the hour of nones,[6] the queen arose and had the other ladies and young men awakened, stating that too much sleep in the daytime was harmful; then they went out onto a lawn of thick, green grass, where no ray of the sun could penetrate; and there, with a gentle breeze caressing them, they all sat in a circle upon the green grass, as was the wish of their queen. Then she spoke to them in this manner:

"As you see, the sun is high, the heat is great, and nothing can be heard except the cicadas in the olive groves; therefore, to wander about at this hour would be, indeed, foolish. Here it is cool and fresh and, as you see, there are games and chessboards with which all of you can amuse yourselves to your liking. But if you take my advice in this matter, I suggest we spend this hot part of the day not in playing games (a pastime which of necessity disturbs the player who loses without providing much pleasure either for his opponents or for those who watch) but rather in telling stories, for this way one

6. That is, they rested during the early afternoon taking a *siesta. Nones:* The fifth canonical hour, 3 P.M.

person, by telling a story, can provide amusement for the entire company. In the time it takes for the sun to set and the heat to become less oppressive, you will each have told a little story, and then we can go wherever we like to amuse ourselves; so, if what I say pleases you (and in this I am willing to follow your pleasure), then, let us do it; if not, then let everyone do as he pleases until the hour of vespers."

The entire group of men and women liked the idea of telling stories.

"Then," said the queen, "if this is your wish, for this first day I order each of you to tell a story about any subject he likes."

And turning to Panfilo, who sat on her right, she ordered him in a gracious manner to begin with one of his tales; whereupon, hearing her command, Panfilo, while everyone listened, began at once as follows:

### The Second Tale of the Fourth Day[7]

Gracious ladies, there was once in Imola a man of wicked and corrupt ways named Berto della Massa, whose evil deeds were so well known by the people of Imola that nobody there would believe him when he told the truth, not to mention when he lied. Realizing that his tricks would no longer work there, in desperation he moved to Venice, that receptacle of all forms of wickedness, thinking that he would adopt a different style of trickery there from what he had used anywhere else before. And almost as if his conscience were struck with remorse for his evil deeds committed in the past, he gave every sign of a man who had become truly humble and most religious; in fact, he went and turned himself into a minor friar, taking the name of Brother Alberto da Imola; and in this disguise he pretended to lead an ascetic life, praising repentance and abstinence, and never eating meat nor drinking wine unless they were of a quality good enough for him.

Never before had such a thief, pimp, forger, and murderer become so great a preacher without having abandoned these vices, even while he may have been practicing them in secret. And besides this, after he became a priest, whenever he celebrated the mass at the altar, in view of all the congregation, he would weep when it came to the Passion of Our Savior, for he was a man to whom tears cost very little when they were called for. And in short, between his sermons and his tears, he managed to beguile the Venetians to such an extent that he was almost always made the trustee and guardian of every

---

7. Told by Pampinea. On the fourth day, in Filostrato's reign, the friends were to tell love stories with unhappy endings.

will that was made, the keeper of many people's money, and confessor and advisor to the majority of men and women; and acting in this way, he changed from a wolf into a shepherd, and his reputation for sanctity in those parts was far greater than St. Francis's was in Assisi.

Now it happened that there was a foolish and silly young woman named Madonna Lisetta da Ca' Quirino (the wife of a great merchant who had gone with his galleys to Flanders) who, along with other ladies, went to be confessed by this holy friar. She was kneeling at his feet and, being a Venetian (and, as such, a gossip like all of them), she was asked by Brother Alberto halfway through her confession if she had a lover. To this question she crossly replied:

"What, my dear brother, don't you have eyes in your head? Do my charms appear to you to be like all those of other women? I could have even more lovers than I want, but my beauty is not to be enjoyed by just anyone. How many ladies do you know who possess such charms as mine, charms which would make me beautiful even in paradise?"

And then she kept on saying so many things about her beauty that it became boring to listen to her. Brother Alberto realized immediately that she was a simpleton, and since he thought she was just the right terrain for plowing, he fell passionately in love with her right then and there; but putting aside his flatteries for a more appropriate time, and reassuming his saintly manner, he began to reproach her and to tell her that her attitude was vainglorious and other such things; and so the lady told him that he was a beast and that he did not know one beauty from another; and because he did not want to upset her too much, Brother Alberto, after having confessed her, let her go off with the other women.

After a few days, he went with a trusted companion to Madonna Lisetta's home and taking her into a room where they could be seen by no one, he threw himself on his knees before her and said:

"My lady, I beg you in God's name to forgive me for speaking to you as I did last Sunday about your beauty, for I was so soundly punished the following night that I have not been able to get up until today."

"And who punished you in this way?" asked Lady Halfwit.

"I shall tell you," replied Brother Alberto. "As I was praying that night in my cell, as I always do, I suddenly saw a glowing light, and before I was able to turn around to see what it was, I saw a very beautiful young man with a large stick in his hand who took me by the collar, dragged me to my feet, and gave me so many blows that he broke practically everything in my body. I asked him why he had done this and he replied:

'Because yesterday you presumed to reproach the celestial beauty of Madonna Lisetta whom I love more than anything else except God.'

"And then I asked: 'Who are you?'

"He replied that he was the angel Gabriel.

" 'Oh My Lord,' I said, 'I beg you to forgive me.'

" 'I shall forgive you on one condition,' he said, 'that you go to her as soon as you are able and beg her forgiveness; and if she does not pardon you, I shall return here and beat you so soundly that you will be sorry for the rest of your life.' "

Lady Lighthead, who was as smart as salt is sweet, enjoyed hearing all these words and believed them all, and after a moment she said:

"I told you, Brother Alberto, that my charms were heavenly; but, God help me, I feel sorry for you, and from now on, in order to spare you more harm, I forgive you on condition that you tell me what the angel said next."

Brother Alberto said: "My lady, since you have forgiven me, I shall gladly tell you, but I remind you of one thing: you must not tell what I tell you to anyone in the world, otherwise you will spoil everything, you who are the most fortunate woman in the world today. The angel Gabriel told me that I was to tell you that you are so pleasing to him that often he would have come to pass the night with you if he had not thought it might frighten you. Now he sends me here with a message that he would like to come to you one night and spend some time with you; but since he is an angel and you would not be able to touch him in the form of an angel, he says that for your pleasure he would like to come as a human being, and he asks when you would have him come and in whose shape should he come, and he will come; therefore you, more than any other woman alive, should consider yourself blessed."

Lady Silly then said that it pleased her very much that the angel Gabriel was in love with her, for she loved him as well and never failed to light a cheap candle in his honor whenever she found a painting of him in church; and whenever he wished to come to her, he would be very welcome, and he would find her all alone in her room, and he could come on the condition that he would not leave her for the Virgin Mary, whom, it was said, he loved very much, and it was obviously true, because everywhere she saw him, he was always on his knees before her;[8] and besides this, she said that he could appear in whatever shape or form he wished—she would not be afraid.

"My Lady," Brother Alberto then said, "you speak wisely, and I shall arrange everything with him as you have said. And you could

---

8. Gabriel told the Virgin Mary that she was to bear the Son of God, and so the two are invariably shown together in paintings of the Annunciation, which Lisetta would often have seen in church.

do me a great favor which will cost you nothing; and the favor is this: that you allow him to come to you in my body. Let me tell you how you would be doing me a favor: he will take my soul from my body and place it in paradise, and he will enter my body, and as long as he is with you my soul will be in paradise."

Then Lady Dimwit replied: "That pleases me; I wish you to have this consolation for the beating he gave you on my account."

Brother Alberto then said: "Now arrange for him to find the door of your house open tonight so that he can come inside; since he will be arriving in the form of a man, he cannot enter unless he uses the door."

The lady replied that it would be done. Brother Alberto departed, and she was so delighted by the whole affair that, jumping for joy, she could hardly keep her skirts over her ass, and it seemed like a thousand years to her waiting for the angel Gabriel to come. Brother Alberto, who was thinking more about getting in the saddle than of being an angel that evening, began to fortify himself with sweetmeats and other delicacies so that he would not be easily thrown from his horse; and then he got permission to stay out that night and, as soon as it was dark, he went with a trusted companion to the house of a lady friend of his, which on other occasions he had used as his point of departure whenever he went to ride the mares; and from there, when the time seemed ripe to him, he went in disguise to the lady's house, and went inside; and, having changed himself into an angel with the different odds and ends he brought with him, he climbed the stairs, and entered the lady's bedroom.

When she saw this white object approaching, she threw herself on her knees in front of him, and the angel blessed her and raised her to her feet, and made a sign for her to get into bed; and she, most anxious to obey, did so immediately, and the angel lay down alongside his devout worshipper. Brother Alberto was a handsome young man with a robust, well-built body; Lady Lisetta was all fresh and soft, and she discovered that his ride was altogether different from that of her husband. He flew many times that night without his wings, which caused the lady to cry aloud with delight and, in addition, he told her many things about the glory of heaven. Then as day broke, having made another appointment to meet her, he gathered his equipment and returned to his companion, who had struck up a friendly relationship with the good woman of the house so that she would not be afraid of sleeping alone.

When the lady had finished breakfast, she went with one of her attendants to Brother Alberto's and told him the story of the angel Gabriel and of what she had heard from him about the glory of the eternal life and of how he looked, adding all sorts of incredible tales to her story. To this Brother Alberto said:

"My lady, I do not know how you were with him; I only know that last night, when he came to me and I delivered your message to him, in an instant he transported my soul to a place where there were more flowers and roses than I have ever seen before, and he left my soul in this most delightful spot until this morning at the hour of early prayer. What happened to my body I know not."

"But did I not tell you?" replied the lady. "Your body passed the entire night in my arms with the angel Gabriel inside it; and if you do not believe me, look under your left nipple, where I gave the angel such a passionate kiss that he will carry its mark for some days!"

Then Brother Alberto said: "Today I shall perform an act that I have not done for some time—I shall undress myself to see if what you say is true."

And after much more chatter, the lady returned home; and Brother Alberto, without the slightest problem, often went to visit her, disguised as an angel. One day, however, Madonna Lisetta was discussing the nature of beauty with one of her neighbors, and she, showing off and being the silly goose she was, said: "You would not talk about any other women if you know who it is that loves my beauty."

Her neighbor, anxious to hear more about this and knowing very well the kind of woman Lisetta was, replied: "Madame, you may be right; but as I do not know to whom you are referring, I cannot change my opinion so easily."

"Neighbor," replied Madonna Lisetta, who was easily excited, "he does not want it to be known, but my lover is the angel Gabriel, and he loves me more than himself, and he tells me that this is because I am the most beautiful woman that there is in the world or even in the Maremma."[9]

Her neighbor had the urge to break into laughter right then, but she held herself back in order to make her friend continue talking, and she said: "God's faith, Madame, if the angel Gabriel is your lover and he tells you this, it must really be so; but I did not realize that angels did such things."

"Neighbor," replied the lady, "that is where you are wrong; by God's wounds, he does it better than my husband, and he tells me that they do it up there as well; but since he thinks I am more beautiful than anyone in heaven, he fell in love with me and comes to be with me very often. Now do you see?"

When the neighbor had left Madonna Lisetta, it seemed to her as if a thousand years had passed before she was able to repeat what she had learned; and at a large gathering of women, she told them the whole story. These women told it to their husbands and to other

9. A small, marshy region of Tuscany.

women, who passed it on to others, and thus in less than two days it was the talk of all Venice. But among those whom this story reached were also the woman's in-laws, and they decided, without telling her a word, to find this angel and to see if he knew how to fly; and they kept watch for him for several nights. It just happened that some hint of this got back to Brother Alberto, so he went there one night to reprove the lady, and no sooner was he undressed than her in-laws, who had seen him arrive, were at the door of the bedroom ready to open it. When Brother Alberto heard this and realized what was going on, he jumped up, and seeing no other means of escape, he flung open a window which looked out on the Grand Canal and threw himself into the water.

The water was deep there, but he knew how to swim well, and so he did not hurt himself; after he swam to the other side of the canal, he immediately entered a home that was opened to him and begged the good man inside, for the love of God, to save his life, as he made up a story to explain why he was there at that hour and in the nude. The good man, moved to pity, gave him his own bed, since he had some affairs of his own to attend to, and he told him to remain there until he returned; and having locked him in, he went about his business.

When the lady's in-laws opened the door to her bedroom and entered, they found that the angel Gabriel had flown away, leaving his wings behind him; they abused the lady no end and finally, leaving her alone, all distressed, they returned to their home with the angel's equipment. In the meanwhile, at daybreak, while the good man was on the Rialto, he heard talk about how the angel Gabriel had gone to bed that night with Madonna Lisetta and had been discovered there by her in-laws, and how he had thrown himself into the canal out of fear, and how no one knew what had happened to him; immediately he realized that the man in his house was the man in question. Returning home and identifying him, after much discussion, he came to an agreement with the friar: he would not give him over to the in-laws if he would pay him fifty ducats; and this was done.

When Brother Alberto wished to leave the place, the good man told him:

"There is only one way out, if you agree to it. Today we are celebrating a festival in which men are led around dressed as bears, others dressed as wild men, and others in one costume or another, and a hunt is put on in St. Mark's Square, and with that the festival is ended; then everyone goes away, with whomever he led there, to wherever they please; and if you wish, so that no one will discover you, I am willing to lead you to wherever you like; otherwise, I don't see any way for you to escape from here without being recognized;

and the in-laws of the lady, knowing that you have hidden yourself somewhere around here, have posted guards everywhere to trap you."

Though it seemed rough to Brother Alberto to have to go in such a disguise, his fear of the lady's relatives induced him to agree, and he told the man where he would like to go and that in whatever way he might choose to lead him there, he would be happy. The man smeared him completely with honey, covered him up with feathers, put a chain around his neck and a mask on his head; in one of his hands he put a large club and in the other two great dogs which he had brought from the butcher; at the same time he sent someone to the Rialto to announce that whoever wished to see the angel Gabriel should go to St. Mark's Square. And this is what they call good old Venetian honesty!

And when this was done, he took the friar outside and had him take the lead, holding him by a chain from behind; and many bystanders kept asking: "Who is it? What is it?" Thus he led him up to the piazza where, between those who had followed him and those who had heard the announcement and had come from the Rialto, a huge crowd gathered. When he arrived there, he tied his wild man up to a column in a conspicuous and elevated spot, pretending to wait for the hunt; meanwhile, the flies and horseflies were giving Brother Alberto a great deal of trouble, for he was covered with honey. But when the good man saw that the piazza was full, pretending to unchain his wild man, he tore the mask from his face and announced:

"Ladies and gentlemen, since the pig has not come to the hunt, and since there is no hunt, I would not want you to have come in vain; therefore I should like you to see the angel Gabriel, who descends from heaven to earth to console the Venetian women by night."

When his mask was removed, Brother Alberto was instantly recognized by everybody, and everyone cried out against him and shouted the most insulting words that were ever directed at a scoundrel; besides this, one by one they all started throwing garbage in his face, keeping him occupied this way for a long time until, by chance, the news reached his brother friars; six of them came, and throwing a cloak over him, they unchained him, and in the midst of a great commotion, they led him back to their monastery, where he was locked up, and after a miserable life he is believed to have died there.

Thus a man who was thought to be good and who acted evilly, not recognized for what he really was, dared to turn himself into the angel Gabriel, and instead was converted into a wild man, and, finally, was cursed at as he deserved and made to lament in vain for the sins he had committed. May it please God that the same thing happen to all others like him!

*        *        *

## The Ninth Tale of the Fifth Day[1]

There was once in Florence a young man named Federigo, the son of Messer Filippo Alberighi, renowned above all other men in Tuscany for his prowess in arms and for his courtliness. As often happens to most gentlemen, he fell in love with a lady named Monna Giovanna, in her day considered to be one of the most beautiful and one of the most charming women that ever there was in Florence; and in order to win her love, he participated in jousts and tournaments, organized and gave feasts, and spent his money without restraint; but she, no less virtuous than beautiful, cared little for these things done on her behalf, nor did she care for him who did them. Now, as Federigo was spending far beyond his means and was taking nothing in, as easily happens he lost his wealth and became poor, with nothing but his little farm to his name (from whose revenues he lived very meagerly) and one falcon which was among the best in the world.

More in love than ever, but knowing that he would never be able to live the way he wished to in the city, he went to live at Campi, where his farm was. There he passed his time hawking whenever he could, asked nothing of anyone, and endured his poverty patiently. Now, during the time that Federigo was reduced to dire need, it happened that the husband of Monna Giovanna fell ill, and realizing death was near, he made his last will: he was very rich, and he made his son, who was growing up, his heir, and, since he had loved Monna Giovanna very much, he made her his heir should his son die without a legitimate heir; and then he died.

Monna Giovanna was now a widow, and as is the custom among our women, she went to the country with her son to spend a year on one of her possessions very close by to Federigo's farm, and it happened that this young boy became friends with Federigo and began to enjoy birds and hunting dogs; and after he had seen Federigo's falcon fly many times, it pleased him so much that he very much wished it were his own, but he did not dare to ask for it, for he could see how dear it was to Federigo. And during this time, it happened that the young boy took ill, and his mother was much grieved, for he was her only child and she loved him enormously; she would spend the entire day by his side, never ceasing to comfort him, and often asking him if there was anything he desired, begging him to tell her what it might be, for if it were possible to obtain it, she would certainly do everything possible to get it. After the young boy had heard her make this offer many times, he said:

1. Told by Dioneo. On the fifth day, in Fiammetta's reign, the friends were to tell love stories which end happily after a period of misfortune.

"Mother, if you can arrange for me to have Federigo's falcon, I think I would be well very soon."

When the lady heard this, she was taken aback for a moment, and she began to think what she should do. She knew that Federigo had loved her for a long while, in spite of the fact that he never received a single glance from her, and so, she said to herself:

"How can I send or go and ask for this falcon of his which is, as I have heard tell, the best that ever flew, and besides this, his only means of support? And how can I be so insensitive as to wish to take away from this gentleman the only pleasure which is left to him?"

And involved in these thoughts, knowing that she was certain to have the bird if she asked for it, but not knowing what to say to her son, she stood there without answering him. Finally the love she bore her son persuaded her that she should make him happy, and no matter what the consequences might be, she would not send for the bird, but rather go herself for it and bring it back to him; so she answered her son:

"My son, take comfort and think only of getting well, for I promise you that the first thing I shall do tomorrow morning is to go for it and bring it back to you."

The child was so happy that he showed some improvement that very day. The following morning, the lady, accompanied by another woman, as if going for a stroll, went to Federigo's modest house and asked for him. Since it was not the season for it, Federigo had not been hawking for some days and was in his orchard, attending to certain tasks; when he heard that Monna Giovanna was asking for him at the door, he was very surprised and happy to run there; as she saw him coming, she greeted him with feminine charm, and once Federigo had welcomed her courteously, she said:

"Greetings, Federigo!" Then she continued: "I have come to compensate you for the harm you have suffered on my account by loving me more than you needed to; and the compensation is this: I, along with this companion of mine, intend to dine with you—a simple meal—this very day."

To this Federigo humbly replied: "Madonna, I never remember having suffered any harm because of you; on the contrary: so much good have I received from you that if ever I have been worth anything, it has been because of your merit and the love I bore fore you; and your generous visit is certainly so dear to me that I would spend all over again that which I spent in the past; but you have come to a poor host."

And having said this, he received her into his home humbly, and from there he led her into his garden, and since he had no one there to keep her company, he said:

"My lady, since there is no one else, this good woman here, the wife of this workman, will keep you company while I go to set the table."

Though he was very poor, Federigo, until now, had never before realized to what extent he had wasted his wealth; but this morning, the fact that he found nothing with which he could honor the lady for the love of whom he had once entertained countless men in the past gave him cause to reflect: in great anguish, he cursed himself and his fortune and, like a man beside himself, he started running here and there, but could find neither money nor a pawnable object. The hour was late and his desire to honor the gracious lady was great, but not wishing to turn for help to others (not even to his own workman), he set his eyes upon his good falcon, perched in a small room; and since he had nowhere else to turn, he took the bird, and finding it plump, he decided that it would be a worthy food for such a lady. So, without further thought, he wrung its neck and quickly gave it to his servant girl to pluck, prepare, and place on a spit to be roasted with care; and when he had set the table with the whitest of tablecloths (a few of which he still had left), he returned, with a cheerful face, to the lady in his garden, saying that the meal he was able to prepare for her was ready.

The lady and her companion rose, went to the table together with Federigo, who waited upon them with the greatest devotion, and they ate the good falcon without knowing what it was they were eating. And having left the table and spent some time in pleasant conversation, the lady thought it time now to say what she had come to say, and so she spoke these kind words to Federigo:

"Federigo, if you recall your past life and my virtue, which you perhaps mistook for harshness and cruelty, I do not doubt at all that you will be amazed by my presumption when you hear what my main reason for coming here is; but if you had children, through whom you might have experienced the power of parental love, it seems certain to me that you would, at least in part, forgive me. But, just as you have no child, I do have one, and I cannot escape the common laws of other mothers; the force of such laws compels me to follow them, against my own will and against good manners and duty, and to ask of you a gift which I know is most precious to you; and it is naturally so, since your extreme condition has left you no other delight, no other pleasure, no other consolation; and this gift is your falcon, which my son is so taken by that if I do not bring it to him, I fear his sickness will grow so much worse that I may lose him. And therefore I beg you, not because of the love that you bear for me, which does not oblige you in the least, but because of your own nobleness, which you have shown to be greater than that of all others in practicing courtliness, that you be pleased to give it to me, so that I may say that I have saved the life of my son by means of this gift, and because of it I have placed him in your debt forever."

When he heard what the lady requested and knew that he could not oblige her since he had given her the falcon to eat, Federigo began to weep in her presence, for he could not utter a word in reply. The lady, at first, thought his tears were caused more by the sorrow of having to part with the good falcon than by anything else, and she was on the verge of telling him she no longer wished it, but she held back and waited for Federigo's reply after he stopped weeping. And he said:

"My lady, ever since it pleased God for me to place my love in you, I have felt that Fortune has been hostile to me in many things, and I have complained of her, but all this is nothing compared to what she has just done to me, and I must never be at peace with her again, thinking about how you have come here to my poor home where, while it was rich, you never deigned to come, and you requested a small gift, and Fortune worked to make it impossible for me to give it to you; and why this is so I shall tell you briefly. When I heard that you, out of your kindness, wished to dine with me, I considered it fitting and right, taking into account your excellence and your worthiness, that I should honor you, according to my possibilities, with a more precious food than that which I usually serve to other people; therefore, remembering the falcon that you requested and its value, I judged it a food worthy of you, and this very day you had it roasted and served to you as best I could; but seeing now that you desired it in another way, my sorrow in not being able to serve you is so great that I shall never be able to console myself again."

And after he had said this, he laid the feathers, the feet, and the beak of the bird before her as proof. When the lady heard and saw this, she first reproached him for having killed such a falcon to serve as a meal to a woman; but then to herself she commended the greatness of his spirit, which no poverty was able or would be able to diminish; then, having lost all hope of getting the falcon and, perhaps because of this, of improving the health of her son as well, she thanked Federigo both for the honor paid to her and for his good will, and she left in grief, and returned to her son. To his mother's extreme sorrow, either because of his disappointment that he could not have the falcon, or because his illness must have necessarily led to it, the boy passed from this life only a few days later.

After the period of her mourning and bitterness had passed, the lady was repeatedly urged by her brothers to remarry, since she was very rich and was still young; and although she did not wish to do so, they became so insistent that she remembered the merits of Federigo and his last act of generosity—that is, to have killed such a falcon to do her honor—and she said to her brothers:

"I would prefer to remain a widow, if that would please you; but if you wish me to take a husband, you may rest assured that I shall take no man but Federigo degli Alberighi."

In answer to this, making fun of her, her brothers replied:

"You foolish woman, what are you saying? How can you want him; he hasn't a penny to his name?"

To this she replied: "My brothers, I am well aware of what you say, but I would rather have a man who needs money than money that needs a man."

Her brothers, seeing that she was determined and knowing Federigo to be of noble birth, no matter how poor he was, accepted her wishes and gave her in marriage to him with all her riches; when he found himself the husband of such a great lady, whom he had loved so much and who was so wealthy besides, he managed his financial affairs with more prudence than in the past and lived with her happily the rest of his days.

*          *          *

---

## Sir Gawain and the Green Knight

*Sir Gawain and the Green Knight* is the best English example of a literary form immensely popular in the Middle Ages: the romance, sometimes called the light reading of our ancestors. A metrical romance is a narrative poem presenting, usually, knightly adventures and "courtly" love. The adventures typically involve the hero in fighting or jousting with other knights, and often also in encounters with giants or monsters. No medieval reader or listener would be surprised by the frequent occurrence of magical or supernatural elements. *Courtly love* is the modern term for the relationship between men and women usually depicted in medieval romances. Here the woman— or, rather, the lady—is sovereign; the man (the knight—but never her husband) is the humble suppliant or petitioner for her favors. (In this picture, with woman on a pedestal but effectively immobilized, and with man looking up to her but with both feet firmly on the ground, may be found an early version of a sexual stereotype which many now find irksome; it is probably more noticeable in this summary than in the poem itself.) The relationship, though usually adulterous, is carried on with careful regard for the conventions and manners of aristocratic (whence "courtly") society.

The poem's first audience, men and women of the late fourteenth century, might well have recognized both of the main plots of the story, the "Beheading Game" and the "Temptation," which also appear in earlier romances. This would more have pleased than troubled them, as originality *per se* was not so important then as now—indeed, the anonymous poet himself claims only to be repeating the story "As I heard it in hall." But many members of that first audience, as they listened or read, would also have noticed some of the original features of the poem that intrigue us as well.

To begin with, the hero, Gawain, must prove his courage not by fighting or jousting in the usual way but by accepting an exchange of blows which seems almost certain to kill him. Then, at Bercilak's castle, by another inversion, it is the lady who takes the initiative and woos; and the knight, because of his unusual situation, must resist. Thus Gawain, traditionally the model of the knightly warrior and courtly lover, cannot show his prowess in the traditional way. Indeed, he is tested in the most extreme way, for his fears and desires must be dealt with not in action but by strength of spirit alone. He is prevented, moreover, by the overall design of the double plot from knowing what is really going on until the very end of the story.

The structure of the *Gawain* narrative is also far tighter and more symmetrical than that of most romances. The story begins at King Arthur's court during a Christmas holiday and ends, almost exactly a year later, in the same place. At Bercilak's castle, the three days of hunting are matched by the three visits of the lady to Gawain's bedroom; each day follows the same pattern, beginning with the start of a hunt, continuing with a wooing scene, returning to the hunt, and concluding with evening festivities. The hunting and wooing are also bound together by the agreement between Bercilak and Gawain to exchange winnings at the end of each day.

Mood and atmosphere depend in large part on the premise that it is all a Christmas *game* (a word that recurs often in the poem). The Green Knight declares that he comes in peace, that he asks not for battle but for sport. But, as all realize, it is a grim and dangerous sport, for the Green Knight is plainly a magical being, and behind his apparently absurd challenge lie two threats: death to anyone who accepts it, disgrace to anyone who does not. Gawain's devotion to King Arthur and to the honor of the court compel him to offer himself for the deadly game, and later his high sense of personal obligation leads him to journey through many perils to find the Green Knight and receive the return stroke of the axe. His faithfulness to his word, his honor, are also at stake in the exchange of gifts at Bercilak's castle. A story that began as a Christmas entertainment has become a series of tests of knightly and Christian virtues.

Keeping to the spirit of the game, we might better appreciate the skill of the author if we try to answer some questions about the poem. What is the significance of the many parallels in it? For example, is there any broad similarity between Bercilak's third hunt—of the fox—and the lady's third visit to Gawain? Turning to the conclusion of the poem, what *is* Gawain's fault? Of what does he accuse himself in the final talk with Bercilak? Why are his chagrin and self-disgust so intense? What is Bercilak's view of the matter? Does the poet agree with Gawain or with Bercilak, or can their attitudes be reconciled?

A word about the language of the poem and our Modern English version of it: It was originally written by a contemporary of Chaucer but in a very different dialect than his, that of the English Midlands near the site of modern Birmingham. Further, except at the end of each stanza, the form depends not on rhyme but on the older device of alliteration: two or more words of every line begin with the same sound. The translation reproduces this pattern with great skill and fidelity. One result of this is the occasional use of unusual words or of ordinary words in slightly unaccustomed senses; some

of these have been glossed, while the meanings of others may be surmised
from the context or, if necessary, found in a dictionary.

The standard edition of the original poem (in Middle English) is by J. R.
R. Tolkien and E. V. Gordon, revised by Norman Davis (1967). A few of
the recent interpretations are M. Boroff, *Sir Gawain and the Green Knight,
A Stylistic and Metrical Study* (1962); Larry D. Benson, *Art and Tradition
in Sir Gawain and the Green Knight* (1965); and J. A Burrow, *A Reading of
Sir Gawain and the Green Knight* (1965). Donald R. Howard and Christian
K. Zacher, editors, *Critical Studies of Sir Gawain and the Green Knight*
(1968), is an excellent collection.

# Sir Gawain and the Green Knight[1]

## Part I

Since the siege and the assault was ceased at Troy,
The walls breached and burnt down to brands and ashes,
The knight that had knotted the nets of deceit
Was impeached for his perfidy,[2] proven most true,
It was high-born Aeneas and his haughty race                                    5
That since prevailed over provinces, and proudly reigned
Over well-nigh all the wealth of the West Isles.[3]
Great Romulus[4] to Rome repairs in haste;
With boast and with bravery builds he that city
And names it with his own name, that it now bears.                              10
Ticius to Tuscany,[5] and towers raises,
Langobard[6] in Lombardy lays out homes,
And far over the French Sea,[7] Felix Brutus
On many broad hills and high Britain he sets,[8]
                         most fair.                       15
            Where war and wrack and wonder
            By shifts have sojourned there,
            And bliss by turns with blunder
            In that land's lot had share.

And since this Britain was built by this baron great,                          20
Bold boys bred there, in broils delighting,
That did in their day many a deed most dire.
More marvels have happened in this merry land

1. Translated by Marie Borroff. Many of the notes are by E. Talbot Donaldson.          2. The
treacherous knight is either Aeneas himself or Antenor, both of whom were, according to medieval tradition, traitors to their city Troy; but Aeneas was actually tried ("impeached") by the Greeks
for his refusal to hand over to them his sister Polyxena.          3. Perhaps western Europe.          4. The
legendary founder of Rome is here given Trojan ancestry, like Aeneas.          5. A region north of
Rome; modern Florence is located in it. *Ticius:* Not otherwise known.          6. The reputed founder
of Lombardy, a region in the north centered on modern Milan.          7. The North Sea, including
the English Channel. *Felix Brutus:* Great-grandson of Aeneas and legendary founder of Britain;
not elsewhere given the name Felix (Latin "happy").          8. Establishes.

Than in any other I know, since that olden time,
But of those that here built, of British kings,                    25
King Arthur was counted most courteous of all,
Wherefore an adventure I aim to unfold,
That a marvel of might some men think it,
And one unmatched among Arthur's wonders.
If you will listen to my lay but a little while,                   30
As I heard it in hall, I shall hasten to tell
     anew.
        As it was fashioned featly
        In tale of derring-do,
        And linked in measures meetly[9]       35
        By letters tried and true.


This king lay at Camelot[1] at Christmastide;
Many good knights and gay his guests were there,
Arrayed of the Round Table rightful brothers,[2]
With feasting and fellowship and carefree mirth.                   40
There true men contended in tournaments many,
Joined there in jousting these gentle knights,
Then came to the court for carol-dancing,
For the feast was in force full fifteen days,
With all the meat and the mirth that men could devise,             45
Such gaiety and glee, glorious to hear,
Brave din by day, dancing by night.
High were their hearts in halls and chambers,
These lords and these ladies, for life was sweet.
In peerless pleasures passed they their days,                      50
The most noble knights known under Christ,
And the loveliest ladies that lived on earth ever,
And he the comeliest king, that that court holds,
For all this fair folk in their first age
                were still.        55
        Happiest of mortal kind,
        King noblest famed of will;
        You would now go far to find
        So hardy a host on hill.


While the New Year was new, but yesternight come,                  60
This fair folk at feast two-fold was served,
When the king and his company were come in together,
The chanting in chapel achieved and ended.

9. Suitably.    1. Capital of Arthur's kingdom, presumably located in southwest England or
southern Wales.    2. According to legend, the Round Table was made by Merlin, the wise
magician who had helped Arthur become King, after a dispute broke out among Arthur's knights
about precedence: it seated 100 knights. The table described in the poem is not round.

Clerics and all the court acclaimed the glad season,
Cried Noel anew, good news to men;                                          65
Then gallants gather gaily, hand-gifts to make,
Called them out clearly, claimed them by hand,
Bickered long and busily about those gifts.
Ladies laughed aloud, though losers they were,
And he that won was not angered, as well you will know.[3]                   70
All this mirth they made until meat was served;
When they had washed them worthily, they went to their seats,
The best seated above, as best it beseemed,
Guenevere the goodly queen gay in the midst
On a dais well-decked and duly arrayed                                       75
With costly silk curtains, a canopy over,
Of Toulouse and Turkestan tapestries rich,
All broidered and bordered with the best gems
Ever brought into Britain, with bright pennies
                              to pay.                                         80
            Fair queen, without a flaw,
            She glanced with eyes of grey.
            A seemlier[4] that once he saw,
            In truth, no man could say.

But Arthur would not eat till all were served;                              85
So light was his lordly heart, and a little boyish;
His life he liked lively—the less he cared
To be lying for long, or long to sit,
So busy his young blood, his brain so wild.
And also a point of pride pricked him in heart,                             90
For he nobly had willed, he would never eat
On so high a holiday, till he had heard first
Of some fair feat or fray some far-borne tale,
Of some marvel of might, that he might trust,
By champions of chivalry achieved in arms,                                  95
Or some suppliant came seeking some single knight
To join with him in jousting, in jeopardy each
To lay life for life, and leave it to fortune
To afford him on field fair hap[5] or other.
Such is the king's custom, when his court he holds                          100
At each far-famed feast amid his fair host
                              so dear.
            The stout king stands in state
            Till a wonder shall appear;
            He leads, with heart elate, 105
            High mirth in the New Year.

---

3. The dispensing of New Year's gifts seems to have involved kissing.     4. More suitable and
pleasing (queen).     5. Good luck.

So he stands there in state, the stout young king,
Talking before the high table[6] of trifles fair.
There Gawain the good knight by Guenevere sits,
With Agravain à la dure main[7] on her other side,     110
Both knights of renown, and nephews of the king.
Bishop Baldwin above begins the table,
And Yvain, son of Urien, ate with him there.
These few with the fair queen were fittingly served;
At the side-tables sat many stalwart knights.     115
Then the first course comes, with clamor of trumpets
That were bravely bedecked with bannerets bright,
With noise of new drums and the noble pipes.
Wild were the warbles that wakened that day
In strains that stirred many strong men's hearts.     120
There dainties were dealt out, dishes rare,
Choice fare to choose, on chargers so many
That scarce was there space to set before the people
The service of silver, with sundry meats,
on cloth.     125
Each fair guest freely there
Partakes, and nothing loth;[8]
Twelve dishes before each pair;
Good beer and bright wine both.

Of the service itself I need say no more,     130
For well you will know no tittle was wanting.
Another noise and a new was well-nigh at hand,
That the lord might have leave his life to nourish;
For scarce were the sweet strains still in the hall,
And the first course come to that company fair,     135
There hurtles in at the hall-door an unknown rider,
One the greatest on ground in growth of his frame:
From broad neck to buttocks so bulky and thick,
And his loins and his legs so long and so great,
Half a giant on earth I hold him to be,     140
But believe him no less than the largest of men,
And that the seemliest in his stature to see, as he rides,
For in back and in breast though his body was grim,
His waist in its width was worthily small,
And formed with every feature in fair accord     145
was he.
Great wonder grew in hall
At his hue most strange to see,

---

6. The high table is on a dais; the side tables (line 115) are on the main floor and run along the walls at a right angle to the high table.     7. Of the hard hand.     8. Not unwillingly.

> For man and gear and all
> Were green as green could be.                                     150

And in guise all of green, the gear and the man:
A coat cut close, that clung to his sides,
And a mantle to match, made with a lining
Of furs cut and fitted—the fabric was noble,
Embellished all with ermine, and his hood beside,                  155
That was loosed from his locks, and laid on his shoulders.
With trim hose and tight, the same tint of green,
His great calves were girt, and gold spurs under
He bore on silk bands that embellished his heels,
And footgear well-fashioned, for riding most fit.                  160
And all his vesture verily was verdant green;
Both the bosses[9] on his belt and other bright gems
That were richly ranged on his raiment noble
About himself and his saddle, set upon silk,
That to tell half the trifles would tax my wits,                   165
The butterflies and birds embroidered thereon
In green of the gayest, with many a gold thread.
The pendants of the breast-band, the princely crupper,[1]
And the bars of the bit were brightly enameled;
The stout stirrups were green, that steadied his feet,             170
And the bows of the saddle and the side-panels both,
That gleamed all and glinted with green gems about.
The steed he bestrides of that same green
                    so bright.
>                   A green horse great and thick;                  175
>                   A headstrong steed of might;
>                   In broidered bridle quick,
>                   Mount matched man aright.

Gay was this goodly man in guise all of green,
And the hair of his head to his horse suited;                      180
Fair flowing tresses enfold his shoulders;
A beard big as a bush on his breast hangs,
That with his heavy hair, that from his head falls,
Was evened all about above both his elbows,
That half his arms thereunder were hid in the fashion              185
Of a king's cap-à-dos,[2] that covers his throat.
The mane of that mighty horse much to it like,
Well curled and becombed, and cunningly knotted
With filaments of fine gold amid the fair green,
Here a strand of the hair, here one of gold;                       190

9. Ornamental knobs.   1. *Breast-band . . . crupper:* Parts of the horse's harness.   2. Or
*capados*, interpreted by the translator as a garment covering its wearer "from head to back."

His tail and his foretop twin in their hue,
And bound both with a band of a bright green
That was decked adown the dock[3] with dazzling stones
And tied tight at the top with a triple knot
Where many bells well burnished rang bright and clear.     195
Such a mount in his might, nor man on him riding,
None had seen, I dare swear, with sight in that hall
             so grand.
           As lightning quick and light
           He looked to all at hand;     200
           It seemed that no man might
           His deadly dints withstand.

Yet had he no helm, nor hauberk[4] neither,
Nor plate, nor appurtenance appending to arms,
Nor shaft pointed sharp, nor shield for defense,     205
But in his one hand he had a holly bob
That is goodliest in green when groves are bare,
And an ax in his other, a huge and immense,
A wicked piece of work in words to expound:
The head on its haft was an ell[5] long;     210
The spike of green steel, resplendent with gold;
The blade burnished bright, with a broad edge,
As well shaped to shear as a sharp razor;
Stout was the stave in the strong man's gripe,·
That was wound all with iron to the weapon's end,     215
With engravings in green of goodliest work.
A lace lightly about, that led to a knot,
Was looped in by lengths along the fair haft,
And tassels thereto attached in a row,
With buttons of bright green, brave to behold.     220
This horseman hurtles in, and the hall enters;
Riding to the high dais, recked he no danger;
Not a greeting he gave as the guests he o'erlooked,
Nor wasted his words, but "Where is," he said,
"The captain of this crowd? Keenly I wish     225
To see that sire with sight, and to himself say
             my say."
           He swaggered all about
           To scan the host so gay;
           He halted, as if in doubt
           Who in that hall held sway.     230

---

3. The solid part of the tail.     4. Tunic of chain mail.     5. Three or four feet long.

There were stares on all sides as the stranger spoke,
For much did they marvel what it might mean
That a horseman and a horse should have such a hue,
Grow green as the grass, and greener, it seemed,          235
Than green fused on gold more glorious by far.
All the onlookers eyed him, and edged nearer,
And awaited in wonder what he would do,
For many sights had they seen, but such a one never,
So that phantom and faerie the folk there deemed it,          240
Therefore chary of answer was many a champion bold,
And stunned at his strong words stone-still they sat
In a swooning silence in the stately hall.
As all were slipped into sleep, so slackened their speech
                    apace.          245
          Not all, I think, for dread,
          But some of courteous grace
          Let him who was their head
          Be spokesman in that place.

Then Arthur before the high dais that entrance beholds,          250
And hailed him, as behooved, for he had no fear,
And said "Fellow, in faith you have found fair welcome;
The head of this hostelry Arthur am I;
Leap lightly down, and linger, I pray,
And the tale of your intent you shall tell us after."          255
"Nay, so help me," said the other, "He that on high sits,
To tarry here any time, 'twas not mine errand;
But as the praise of you, prince, is puffed up so high,
And your court and your company are counted the best,
Stoutest under steel-gear on steeds to ride,          260
Worthiest of their works the wide world over,
And peerless to prove in passages of arms,
And courtesy here is carried to its height,
And so at this season I have sought you out.
You may be certain by the branch that I bear in hand          265
That I pass here in peace, and would part friends,
For had I come to this court on combat bent,
I have a hauberk at home, and a helm beside,
A shield and a sharp spear, shining bright,
And other weapons to wield, I ween[6] well, to boot,          270
But as I willed no war, I wore no metal.
But if you be so bold as all men believe,
You will graciously grant the game that I ask

6. Believe.

by right."
Arthur answer gave                                          275
And said, "Sir courteous knight,
If contest here you crave,
You shall not fail to fight."

"Nay, to fight, in good faith, is far from my thought;
There are about on these benches but beardless children,      280
Were I here in full arms on a haughty steed,
For measured against mine, their might is puny.
And so I call in this court for a Christmas game,
For 'tis Yule and New Year, and many young bloods about;
If any in this house such hardihood claims,                   285
Be so bold in his blood, his brain so wild,
As stoutly to strike one stroke for another,
I shall give him as my gift this gisarme[7] noble,
This ax, that is heavy enough, to handle as he likes,
And I shall bide[8] the first blow, as bare as I sit.         290
If there be one so wilful my words to assay,
Let him leap hither lightly, lay hold of this weapon;
I quitclaim it forever, keep it[9] as his own,
And I shall stand him a stroke, steady on this floor,
So you grant me the guerdon[1] to give him another,           295
                    sans[2] blame.
          In a twelvemonth and a day
          He shall have of me the same;
          Now be it seen straightway
          Who dares take up the game."                         300

If he astonished them at first, stiller were then
All that household in hall, the high and the low;
The stranger on his green steed stirred in the saddle,
And roisterously his red eyes he rolled all about,
Bent his bristling brows, that were bright green,             305
Wagged his beard as he watched who would arise.
When the court kept its counsel he coughed aloud,
And cleared his throat coolly, the clearer to speak:
"What, is this Arthur's house," said that horseman then,
"Whose fame is so fair in far realms and wide?                310
Where is now your arrogance and your awesome deeds,
Your valor and your victories and your vaunting words?
Now are the revel and renown of the Round Table
Overwhelmed with a word of one man's speech,
For all cower and quake, and no cut felt!"                    315

7. Weapon.    8. Endure.    9. I.e., let him keep it.    1. Reward.    2. Without.

With this he laughs so loud that the lord grieved;
The blood for sheer shame shot to his face,
                    and pride.
            With rage his face flushed red,
            And so did all beside.                               320
            Then the king as bold man bred
            Toward the stranger took a stride.


And said "Sir, now we see you will say but folly,
Which whoso has sought, it suits that he find.
No guest here is aghast of your great words.                     325
Give to me your gisarme, in God's own name,
And the boon you have begged shall straight be granted."
He leaps to him lightly, lays hold of his weapon;
The green fellow on foot fiercely alights.
Now has Arthur his ax, and the haft grips,                       330
And sternly stirs it about, on striking bent.
The stranger before him stood there erect,
Higher than any in the house by a head and more;
With stern look as he stood, he stroked his beard,
And with undaunted countenance drew down his coat,              335
No more moved nor dismayed for his mighty dints
Than any bold man on bench had brought him a drink
                    of wine.
            Gawain by Guenevere
            Toward the king doth now incline:
            "I beseech, before all here,
            That this melee may be mine."


"Would you grant me the grace," said Gawain to the king,
"To be gone from this bench and stand by you there,
If I without discourtesy might quit this board,                  345
And if my liege lady[3] misliked it not,
I would come to your counsel before your court noble.
For I find it not fit, as in faith it is known,
When such a boon is begged before all these knights,
Though you be tempted thereto, to take it on yourself            350
While so bold men about upon benches sit,
That no host under heaven is hardier of will,
Nor better brothers-in-arms where battle is joined;
I am the weakest, well I know, and of wit feeblest;
And the loss of my life would be least of any;                   355
That I have you for uncle is my only praise;

---

3. Lady entitled to the knight's feudal service.

My body, but for your blood, is barren of worth;
And for that this folly befits not a king,
And 'tis I that have asked it, it ought to be mine,
And if my claim be not comely let all this court judge,          360
                    in sight."
                    The court assays the claim,
                    And in counsel all unite
                    To give Gawain the game
                    And release the king outright.          365

Then the king called the knight to come to his side,
And he rose up readily, and reached him with speed,
Bows low to his lord, lays hold of the weapon,
And he releases it lightly, and lifts up his hand,
And gives him God's blessing, and graciously prays          370
That his heart and his hand may be hardy both.
"Keep, cousin," said the king, "what you cut with this day,
And if you rule it aright, then readily, I know,
You shall stand the stroke it will strike after."
Gawain goes to the guest with gisarme in hand,          375
And boldly he bides there, abashed not a whit.
Then hails he Sir Gawain, the horseman in green:
"Recount we our contract, ere you come further.
First I ask and adjure you, how you are called
That you tell me true, so that trust it I may."          380
"In good faith," said the good knight, "Gawain am I
Whose buffet befalls you, whate'er betide after,
And at this time twelvemonth take from you another
With what weapon you will, and with no man else
                    alive."          385
                    The other nods assent:
                    "Sir Gawain, as I may thrive,
                    I am wondrous well content
                    That you this dint shall drive."

"Sir Gawain," said the Green Knight, "By God, I rejoice          390
That your fist shall fetch this favor I seek,
And you have readily rehearsed, and in right terms,
Each clause of my covenant with the king your lord,
Save that you shall assure me, sir, upon oath,
That you shall seek me yourself, wheresoever you deem          395
My lodgings may lie, and look for such wages
As you have offered me here before all this host."
"What is the way there?" said Gawain, "Where do you dwell?
I heard never of your house, by Him that made me,
Nor I know you not, knight, your name nor your court.          400

But tell me truly thereof, and teach me your name,
And I shall fare forth to find you, so far as I may,
And this I say in good certain, and swear upon oath."
"That is enough in New Year, you need say no more,"
Said the knight in the green to Gawain the noble,                    405
"If I tell you true, when I have taken your knock,
And if you handily have hit, you shall hear straightway
Of my house and my home and my own name;
Then follow in my footsteps by faithful accord.
And if I spend no speech, you shall speed the better:                410
You can feast with your friends, nor further trace
                    my tracks.
              Now hold your grim tool steady
              And show us how it hacks."
              "Gladly, sir; all ready,"
              Says Gawain; he strokes the ax.

The Green Knight upon ground girds him with care:
Bows a bit with his head, and bares his flesh:
His long lovely locks he laid over his crown,
Let the naked nape for the need be shown.                            420
Gawain grips to his ax and gathers it aloft—
The left foot on the floor before him he set—
Brought it down deftly upon the bare neck,
That the shock of the sharp blow shivered the bones
And cut the flesh cleanly and clove it in twain,                     425
That the blade of bright steel bit into the ground.
The head was hewn off and fell to the floor;
Many found it at their feet, as forth it rolled;
The blood gushed from the body, bright on the green,
Yet fell not the fellow, nor faltered a whit,                        430
But stoutly he starts forth upon stiff shanks,
And as all stood staring he stretched forth his hand,
Laid hold of his head and heaved it aloft,
Then goes to the green steed, grasps the bridle,
Steps into the stirrup, bestrides his mount,                         435
And his head by the hair in his hand holds,
And as steady he sits in the stately saddle
As he had met with no mishap, nor missing were
                    his head.
              His bulk about he haled,[4]                            440
              That fearsome body that bled;
              There were many in the court that quailed
              Before all his say was said.

4. Hauled.

For the head in his hand he holds right up;
Toward the first on the dais directs he the face,                    445
And it lifted up its lids, and looked with wide eyes,
And said as much with its mouth as now you may hear:
"Sir Gawain, forget not to go as agreed,
And cease not to seek till me, sir, you find,
As you promised in the presence of these proud knights.              450
To the Green Chapel come, I charge you, to take
Such a dint as you have dealt—you have well deserved
That your neck should have a knock on New Year's morn.
The Knight of the Green Chapel I am well-known to many,
Wherefore you cannot fail to find me at last;                        455
Therefore come, or be counted a recreant[5] knight."
With a roisterous rush he flings round the reins,
Hurtles out at the hall-door, his head in his hand,
That the flint-fire flew from the flashing hooves.
Which way he went, not one of them knew                              460
Nor whence he was come in the wide world
                    so fair.
          The king and Gawain gay
          Make game of the Green Knight there,
          Yet all who saw it say                                     465
          'Twas a wonder past compare.

Though high-born Arthur at heart had wonder,
He let no sign be seen, but said aloud
To the comely queen, with courteous speech,
"Dear dame, on this day dismay you no whit;                          470
Such crafts are becoming at Christmastide,
Laughing at interludes, light songs and mirth,
Amid dancing of damsels with doughty knights.
Nevertheless of my meat now let me partake,
For I have met with a marvel, I may not deny."                       475
He glanced at Sir Gawain, and gaily he said,
"Now, sir, hang up your ax, that has hewn enough,"
And over the high dais it was hung on the wall
That men in amazement might on it look,
And tell in true terms the tale of the wonder.                      480
Then they turned toward the table, these two together,
The good king and Gawain, and made great feast,
With all dainties double, dishes rare,
With all manner of meat and minstrelsy both,
Such happiness wholly had they that day                             485

5. Cowardly.

                        in hold.
                 Now take care, Sir Gawain,
                 That your courage wax not cold
                 When you must turn again
                 To your enterprise foretold.                    490


                        *Part II*

This adventure had Arthur of handsels[6] first
When young was the year, for he yearned to hear tales;
Though they wanted for words when they went to sup,
Now are fierce deeds to follow, their fists stuffed full.
Gawain was glad to begin those games in hall,          495
But if the end be harsher, hold it no wonder,
For though men are merry in mind after much drink,
A year passes apace, and proves ever new:
First things and final conform but seldom.
And so this Yule to the young year yielded place,       500
And each season ensued at its set time;
After Christmas there came the cold cheer of Lent,
When with fish and plainer fare our flesh we reprove;
But then the world's weather with winter contends:
The keen cold lessens, the low clouds lift;            505
Fresh falls the rain in fostering showers
On the face of the fields; flowers appear.
The ground and the groves wear gowns of green;
Birds build their nests, and blithely sing
That solace of all sorrow with summer comes            510
                        ere long.
                 And blossoms day by day
                 Bloom rich and rife in throng;
                 Then every grove so gay
                 Of the greenwood rings with song.              515

And then the season of summer with the soft winds,
When Zephyr sighs low over seeds and shoots;
Glad is the green plant growing abroad,
When the dew at dawn drops from the leaves,
To get a gracious glance from the golden sun.          520
But harvest with harsher winds follows hard after,
Warns him to ripen well ere winter comes;
Drives forth the dust in the droughty season,
From the face of the fields to fly high in air.

6. Gifts to mark the New Year.

Wroth winds in the welkin[7] wrestle with the sun,                          525
The leaves launch from the linden and light on the ground,
And the grass turns to gray, that once grew green.
Then all ripens and rots that rose up at first,
And so the year moves on in yesterdays many,
And winter once more, by the world's law,                                   530
          draws nigh.
          At Michaelmas[8] the moon
          Hangs wintry pale in sky;
          Sir Gawain girds him soon
          For travails yet to try.                                          535

Till All-Hallows' Day[9] with Arthur he dwells,
And he held a high feast to honor that knight
With great revels and rich, of the Round Table.
Then ladies lovely and lords debonair
With sorrow for Sir Gawain were sore at heart;                              540
Yet they covered their care with countenance glad:
Many a mournful man made mirth for his sake.
So after supper soberly he speaks to his uncle
Of the hard hour at hand, and openly says,
"Now, liege lord of my life, my leave I take;                               545
The terms of this task too well you know—
To count the cost over concerns me nothing.
But I am bound forth betimes[1] to bear a stroke
From the grim man in green, as God may direct."
Then the first and foremost came forth in throng:                           550
Yvain and Eric and others of note,
Sir Dodinal le Sauvage, the Duke of Clarence,
Lionel and Lancelot and Lucan the good,
Sir Bors and Sir Bedivere, big men both,
And many manly knights more, with Mador de la Porte.                        555
All this courtly company comes to the king
To counsel their comrade, with care in their hearts;
There was much secret sorrow suffered that day
That one so good as Gawain must go in such wise
To bear a bitter blow, and his bright sword                                 560
          lay by.
          He said, "Why should I tarry?"
          And smiled with tranquil eye;
          "In destinies sad or merry,
          True men can but try."                                            565

He dwelt there all that day, and dressed in the morning;
Asked early for his arms, and all were brought.

7. The heavens.     8. September 29.     9. November 1.     1. Soon.

First a carpet of rare cost was cast on the floor
Where much goodly gear gleamed golden bright;
He takes his place promptly and picks up the steel,                570
Attired in a tight coat of Turkestan silk
And a kingly cap-à-dos, closed at the throat,
That was lavishly lined with a lustrous fur.
Then they set the steel shoes on his sturdy feet
And clad his calves about with comely greaves,                    575
And plate well-polished protected his knees,
Affixed with fastenings of the finest gold.
Fair cuisses enclosed, that were cunningly wrought,
His thick-thewed thighs, with thongs bound fast,
And massy chain-mail of many a steel ring                         580
He bore on his body, above the best cloth,
With brace burnished bright upon both his arms,
Good couters² and gay, and gloves of plate,
And all the goodly gear to grace him well
                 that tide.                              585
        His surcoat³ blazoned bold;
        Sharp spurs to prick with pride;
        And a brave silk band to hold
        The broadsword at his side.

When he had on his arms, his harness was rich,                    590
The least latchet or loop laden with gold;
So armored as he was, he heard a mass,
Honored God humbly at the high altar.
Then he comes to the king and his comrades-in-arms,
Takes his leave at last of lords and ladies,                      595
And they clasped and kissed him, commending him to Christ.
By then Gringolet⁴ was girt with a great saddle
That was gaily agleam with fine gilt fringe,
New-furbished for the need with nail-heads bright;
The bridle and the bars bedecked all with gold;                  600
The breast-plate, the saddlebow, the side-panels both,
The caparison and the crupper accorded in hue,
And all ranged on the red the resplendent studs
That glittered and glowed like the glorious sun.
His helm now he holds up and hastily kisses,                     605
Well-closed with iron clinches, and cushioned within;
It was high on his head, with a hasp behind,
And a covering of cloth to encase the visor,
All bound and embroidered with the best gems
On broad bands of silk, and bordered with birds,                 610

2. Armor for the elbows.    3. Cloth tunic worn over the armor.    4. Gawain's horse.

Parrots and popinjays preening their wings,
Lovebirds and love-knots as lavishly wrought
As many women had worked seven winters thereon,
                         entire.
                 The diadem costlier yet                              615
                 That crowned that comely sire,
                 With diamonds richly set,
                 That flashed as if on fire.

Then they showed forth the shield, that shone all red,
With the pentangle[5] portrayed in purest gold.                       620
About his broad neck by the baldric[6] he casts it,
That was meet for the man, and matched him well.
And why the pentangle is proper to that peerless prince
I intend now to tell, though detain me it must.
It is a sign by Solomon sagely devised                                625
To be a token of truth, by its title of old,
For it is a figure formed of five points,
And each line is linked and locked with the next
For ever and ever, and hence it is called
In all England, as I hear, the endless knot.                          630
And well may he wear it on his worthy arms,
For ever faithful five-fold in five-fold fashion
Was Gawain in good works, as gold unalloyed,
Devoid of all villainy, with virtues adorned
                         in sight.                                     635
                 On shield and coat in view
                 He bore that emblem bright,
                 As to his word most true
                 And in speech most courteous knight.

And first, he was faultless in his five senses,                       640
Nor found ever to fail in his five fingers,
And all his fealty was fixed upon the five wounds
That Christ got on the cross, as the creed tells;
And wherever this man in melee took part,
His one thought was of this, past all things else,                    645
That all his force was founded on the five joys[7]
That the high Queen of heaven had in her child.
And therefore, as I find, he fittingly had
On the inner part of his shield her image portrayed,
That when his look on it lighted, he never lost heart.                650

5. A five-pointed star, formed by five lines which are drawn without lifting the pen, supposed to
have mystical significance; as Solomon's sign (line 625), it was enclosed in a circle.    6. Belt
worn diagonally across the chest.    7. These were the annunciation to Mary that she was to bear
the Son of God, Christ's nativity, resurrection, and ascension into heaven, and the "assumption"
or bodily taking up of Mary into heaven to join Him.

The fifth of the five fives followed by this knight
Were beneficence boundless and brotherly love
And pure mind and manners, that none might impeach,
And compassion most precious—these peerless five
Were forged and made fast in him, foremost of men.                    655
Now all these five fives were confirmed in this knight,
And each linked in other, that end there was none,
And fixed to five points, whose force never failed,
Nor assembled all on a side, nor asunder either,
Nor anywhere at an end, but whole and entire                          660
However the pattern proceeded or played out its course.
And so on his shining shield shaped was the knot
Royally in red gold against red gules,[8]
That is the peerless pentangle, prized of old
                in lore.                                         665
          Now armed is Gawain gay,
          And bears his lance before,
          And soberly said good day,
          He thought forevermore.

He struck his steed with the spurs and sped on his way                670
So fast that the flint-fire flashed from the stones.
When they saw him set forth they were sore aggrieved,
And all sighed softly, and said to each other,
Fearing for their fellow, "Ill fortune it is
That you, man, must be marred, that most are worthy!                  675
His equal on this earth can hardly be found;
To have dealt more discreetly had done less harm,
And have dubbed him a duke, with all due honor.
A great leader of lords he was like to become,
And better so to have been than battered to bits,                     680
Beheaded by an elf-man,[9] for empty pride!
Who would credit that a king could be counseled so,
And caught in a cavil in a Christmas game?"
Many were the warm tears they wept from their eyes
When goodly Sir Gawain was gone from the court                        685
                that day.
          No longer he abode,
          But speedily went his way
          Over many a wandering road,
          As I heard my author say.                              690

Now he rides in his array through the realm of Logres,[1]
Sir Gawain, God knows, though it gave him small joy!

---

8. Background (gules is the heraldic name for red).     9. Supernatural being, in this case obviously not small.     1. Another name for Arthur's kingdom.

All alone must he lodge through many a long night
Where the food that he fancied was far from his plate;
He had no mate but his mount, over mountain and plain,     695
Nor man to say his mind to but almighty God,
Till he had wandered well-nigh into North Wales.
All the islands of Anglesey he holds on his left,
And follows, as he fares, the fords by the coast,
Comes over at Holy Head, and enters next     700
The Wilderness of Wirral[2]—few were within
That had great good will toward God or man.
And earnestly he asked of each mortal he met
If he had ever heard aught of a knight all green,
Or of a Green Chapel, on ground thereabouts,     705
And all said the same, and solemnly swore
They saw no such knight all solely green
                    in hue.
               Over country wild and strange
               The knight sets off anew;     710
               Often his course must change
               Ere the Chapel comes in view.

Many a cliff must he climb in country wild;
Far off from all his friends, forlorn must he ride;
At each strand or stream where the stalwart passed     715
'Twere a marvel if he met not some monstrous foe,
And that so fierce and forbidding that fight he must.
So many were the wonders he wandered among
That to tell but the tenth part would tax my wits.
Now with serpents he wars, now with savage wolves,     720
Now with wild men of the woods, that watched from the rocks,
Both with bulls and with bears, and with boars besides,
And giants that came gibbering from the jagged steeps.
Had he not borne himself bravely, and been on God's side,     725
He had met with many mishaps and mortal harms.
And if the wars were unwelcome, the winter was worse,
When the cold clear rains rushed from the clouds
And froze before they could fall to the frosty earth.
Near slain by the sleet he sleeps in his irons
More nights than enough, among naked rocks,     730
Where clattering from the crest the cold stream ran
And hung in hard icicles high overhead.
Thus in peril and pain and predicaments dire
He rides across country till Christmas Eve,

2. *North Wales . . . Wirral:* Gawain went from Camelot north to the northern coast of Wales, opposite the islands of Anglesey; there he turned east across the River Dee to the forest of Wirral, near what is now Liverpool.

our knight.                          735
And at that holy tide
He prays with all his might
That Mary may be his guide
Till a dwelling comes in sight.

By a mountain next morning he makes his way          740
Into a forest fastness, fearsome and wild;
High hills on either hand, with hoar woods below,
Oaks old and huge by the hundred together.
The hazel and the hawthorn were all intertwined
With rough raveled moss, that raggedly hung,          745
With many birds unblithe upon bare twigs
That peeped most piteously for pain of the cold.
The good knight on Gringolet glides thereunder
Through many a marsh and mire, a man all alone;
He feared for his default, should he fail to see          750
The service of that Sire that on that same night
Was born of a bright maid, to bring us His peace.
And therefore sighing he said, "I beseech of Thee, Lord,
And Mary, thou mildest mother so dear,
Some harborage where haply I might hear mass          755
And Thy matins tomorrow—meekly I ask it,
And thereto proffer and pray my pater and ave[3]
and creed."

He said his prayer with sighs,
Lamenting his misdeed;                          760
He crosses himself, and cries
On Christ in his great need.

No sooner had Sir Gawain signed himself[4] thrice
Than he was ware, in the wood, of a wondrous dwelling,
Within a moat, on a mound, bright amid boughs          765
Of many a tree great of girth that grew by the water—
A castle as comely as a knight could own,
On grounds fair and green, in a goodly park
With a palisade of palings planted about
For two miles and more, round many a fair tree.          770
The stout knight stared at that stronghold great
As it shimmered and shone amid shining leaves,
Then with helmet in hand he offers his thanks
To Jesus and Saint Julian,[5] that are gentle both,
That in courteous accord had inclined to his prayer;          775

---

3. Two prayers, the Pater Noster ("Our Father," the Lord's Prayer) and Ave Maria ("Hail, Mary").     4. Made the sign of the cross over his own chest.     5. Patron saint of hospitality.

"Now fair harbor," said he, "I humbly beseech!"
Then he pricks his proud steed with the plated spurs,
And by chance he has chosen the chief path
That brought the bold knight to the bridge's end

                        in haste.  780
            The bridge hung high in air;
            The gates were bolted fast;
            The walls well-framed to bear
            The fury of the blast.

The man on his mount remained on the bank  785
Of the deep double moat that defended the place.
The wall went in the water wondrous deep,
And a long way aloft it loomed overhead.
It was built of stone blocks to the battlements' height,
With corbels under cornices[6] in comeliest style;  790
Watch-towers trusty protected the gate,
With many a lean loophole, to look from within:
A better-made barbican the knight beheld never.
And behind it there hoved a great hall and fair:
Turrets rising in tiers, with tines[7] at their tops,  795
Spires set beside them, splendidly long,
With finials well-fashioned, as filigree fine.
Chalk-white chimneys over chambers high
Gleamed in gay array upon gables and roofs;
The pinnacles in panoply, pointing in air,  800
So vied there for his view that verily it seemed
A castle cut of paper for a king's feast.
The good knight on Gringolet thought it great luck
If he could but contrive to come there within
To keep the Christmas feast in that castle fair  805

                   and bright.
            There answered to his call
            A porter most polite;
            From his station on the wall
            He greets the errant knight.  810

"Good sir," said Gawain, "Wouldst go to inquire
If your lord would allow me to lodge here a space?"
"Peter!"[8] said the porter, "For my part, I think
So noble a knight will not want for a welcome!"
Then he bustles off briskly, and comes back straight,  815
And many servants beside, to receive him the better.
They let down the drawbridge and duly went forth

6. Ornamental projections supporting the top courses of stone.  7. *Hoved*: Arose.  8. I.e.,
"By Saint Peter!"

And kneeled down on their knees on the naked earth
To welcome this warrior as best they were able.
They proffered him passage—the portals stood wide—          820
And he beckoned them to rise, and rode over the bridge.
Men steadied his saddle as he stepped to the ground,
And there stabled his steed many stalwart folk.
Now come the knights and the noble squires
To bring him with bliss into the bright hall.          825
When his high helm was off, there hied forth a throng
Of attendants to take it, and see to its care;
They bore away his brand[9] and his blazoned shield;
Then graciously he greeted those gallants each one,
And many a noble drew near, to do the knight honor.          830
All in his armor into hall he was led,
Where fire on a fair hearth fiercely blazed.
And soon the lord himself descends from his chamber
To meet with good manners the man on his floor.
He said, "To this house you are heartily welcome:          835
What is here is wholly yours, to have in your power
                    and sway."
          "Many thanks," said Sir Gawain;
          "May Christ your pains repay!"
          The two embrace amain          840
          As men well met that day.

Gawain gazed on the host that greeted him there,
And a lusty fellow he looked, the lord of that place:
A man of massive mold, and of middle age;
Broad, bright was his beard, of a beaver's hue,          845
Strong, steady his stance, upon stalwart shanks,
His face fierce as fire, fair-spoken withal,
And well-suited he seemed in Sir Gawain's sight
To be a master of men in a mighty keep.
They pass into a parlor, where promptly the host          850
Has a servant assigned him to see to his needs,
And there came upon his call many courteous folk
That brought him to a bower where bedding was noble,
With heavy silk hangings hemmed all in gold,
Coverlets and counterpanes curiously wrought,          855
A canopy over the couch, clad all with fur,
Curtains running on cords, caught to gold rings,
Woven rugs on the walls of eastern work,
And the floor, under foot, well-furnished with the same.
With light talk and laughter they loosed from him then          860

9. Sword.

His war-dress of weight and his worthy clothes.
Robes richly wrought they brought him right soon,
To change there in chamber and choose what he would.
When he had found one he fancied, and flung it about,
Well-fashioned for his frame, with flowing skirts,                    865
His face fair and fresh as the flowers of spring,
All the good folk agreed, that gazed on him then,
His limbs arrayed royally in radiant hues,
That so comely a mortal never Christ made
                    as he.                                            870
          Whatever his place of birth,
          It seemed he well might be
          Without a peer on earth
          In martial rivalry.

A couch before the fire, where fresh coals burned,                    875
They spread for Sir Gawain splendidly now
With quilts quaintly stitched, and cushions beside,
And then a costly cloak they cast on his shoulders
Of bright silk, embroidered on borders and hems,
With furs of the finest well-furnished within,                        880
And bound about with ermine, both mantle and hood;
And he sat at that fireside in sumptuous estate
And warmed himself well, and soon he waxed merry.
Then attendants set a table upon trestles broad,
And lustrous white linen they laid thereupon,                         885
A saltcellar of silver, spoons of the same.
He washed himself well and went to his place,
Men set his fare before him in fashion most fit.
There were soups of all sorts, seasoned with skill,
Double-sized servings, and sundry fish,                               890
Some baked, some breaded, some broiled on the coals,
Some simmered, some in stews, steaming with spice,
And with sauces to sup that suited his taste.
He confesses it a feast with free words and fair;
They requite him as kindly with courteous jests,                      895
                    well-sped.
          "Tonight you fast and pray;
          Tomorrow we'll see you fed."
          The knight grows wondrous gay
          As the wine goes to his head.                               900

Then at times and by turns, as at table he sat,
They questioned him quietly, with queries discreet,
And he courteously confessed that he comes from the court,
And owns him of the brotherhood of high-famed Arthur,

The right royal ruler of the Round Table,                                    905
And the guest by their fireside is Gawain himself,
Who has happened on their house at that holy feast.
When the name of the knight was made known to the lord,
Then loudly he laughed, so elated he was,
And the men in that household made haste with joy                            910
To appear in his presence promptly that day,
That of courage ever-constant, and customs pure,
Is pattern and paragon, and praised without end:
Of all knights on earth most honored is he.
Each said solemnly aside to his brother,                                     915
"Now displays of deportment shall dazzle our eyes
And the polished pearls of impeccable speech;
The high art of eloquence is ours to pursue
Since the father of fine manners is found in our midst.
Great is God's grace, and goodly indeed,                                     920
That a guest such as Gawain he guides to us here
When men sit and sing of their Savior's birth
                              in view.
                    With command of manners pure
                    He shall each heart imbue;
                    Who shares his converse, sure,                           925
                    Shall learn love's language true."

When the knight had done dining and duly arose,
The dark was drawing on; the day nigh ended.
Chaplains in chapels and churches about                                      930
Rang the bells aright, reminding all men
Of the holy evensong of the high feast.
The lord attends alone; his fair lady sits
In a comely closet, secluded from sight.
Gawain in gay attire goes thither soon;                                      935
The lord catches his coat, and calls him by name,
And has him sit beside him, and says in good faith
No guest on God's earth would he gladlier greet.
For that Gawain thanked him; the two then embraced
And sat together soberly the service through.                                940
Then the lady, that longed to look on the knight,
Came forth from her closet with her comely maids.
The fair hues of her flesh, her face and her hair
And her body and her bearing were beyond praise,
And excelled the queen herself, as Sir Gawain thought.                       945
He goes forth to greet her with gracious intent;
Another lady led her by the left hand
That was older than she—an ancient, it seemed,

And held in high honor by all men about.
But unlike to look upon, those ladies were,                              950
For if the one was fresh, the other was faded:
Bedecked in bright red was the body of one;
Flesh hung in folds on the face of the other;
On one a high headdress, hung all with pearls;
Her bright throat and bosom fair to behold,                             955
Fresh as the first snow fallen upon hills;
A wimple[1] the other one wore round her throat;
Her swart chin well swaddled, swathed all in white;
Her forehead enfolded in flounces of silk
That framed a fair fillet,[2] of fashion ornate,                        960
And nothing bare beneath save the black brows,
The two eyes and the nose, the naked lips,
And they unsightly to see, and sorrily bleared.
A beldame, by God, she may well be deemed,
                                    of pride!                            965
            She was short and thick of waist,
            Her buttocks round and wide;
            More toothsome, to his taste,
            Was the beauty by her side.

When Gawain had gazed on that gay lady,                                 970
With leave of her lord, he politely approached;
To the elder in homage he humbly bows;
The lovelier he salutes with a light embrace.
He claims a comely kiss, and courteously he speaks;
They welcome him warmly, and straightway he asks                        975
To be received as their servant, if they so desire.
They take him between them; with talking they bring him
Beside a bright fire; bade then that spices
Be freely fetched forth, to refresh them the better,
And the good wine therewith, to warm their hearts.                      980
The lord leaps about in light-hearted mood;
Contrives entertainments and timely sports;
Takes his hood from his head and hangs it on a spear,
And offers him openly the honor thereof
Who should promote the most mirth at that Christmas feast;              985
"And I shall try for it, trust me—contend with the best,
Ere I go without my headgear by grace of my friends!"
Thus with light talk and laughter the lord makes merry
To gladden the guest he had greeted in hall
                                    that day.                            990
            At the last he called for light

---

1. A garment covering the neck and sides of the head.    2. Ornamental ribbon or headband.

SIR GAWAIN AND THE GREEN KNIGHT     1389

The company to convey;
Gawain says goodnight
And retires to bed straightway.

On the morn when each man is mindful in heart          995
That God's son was sent down to suffer our death,
No household but is blithe for His blessed sake;
So was it there on that day, with many delights.
Both a larger meals and less they were lavishly served
By doughty lads on dais, with delicate fare;           1000
The old ancient lady, highest she sits;
The lord at her left hand leaned, as I hear;
Sir Gawain in the center, beside the gay lady,
Where the food was brought first to that festive board,
And thence throughout the hall, as they held most fit,  1005
To each man was offered in order of rank.
There was meat, there was mirth, there was much joy,
That to tell all the tale would tax my wits,
Though I pained me, perchance, to paint it with care;
But yet I know that our knight and the noble lady       1010
Were accorded so closely in company there,
With the seemly solace of their secret words,
With speeches well-sped, spotless and pure,
That each prince's pastime their pleasures far
                                  outshone.              1015
        Sweet pipes beguile their cares,
        And the trumpet of martial tone;
        Each tends his affairs
        And those two tend their own.

That day and all the next, their disport was noble,     1020
And the third day, I think, pleased them no less;
The joys of St. John's Day[3] were justly praised,
And were the last of their like for those lords and ladies;
Then guests were to go in the gray morning,
Wherefore they whiled the night away with wine and
    with mirth,                                         1025
Moved to the measures of many a blithe carol;
At last, when it was late, took leave of each other,
Each one of those worthies, to wend his way.
Gawain bids goodbye to his goodly host
Who brings him to his chamber, the chimney beside,      1030
And detains him in talk, and tenders his thanks
And holds it an honor to him and his people

3. December 27.

That he has harbored in his house at that holy time
And embellished his abode with his inborn grace.
"As long as I may live, my luck is the better                    1035
That Gawain was my guest at God's own feast!"
"Noble sir," said the knight, "I cannot but think
All the honor is your own—may heaven requite it!
And your man to command I account myself here
As I am bound and beholden, and shall be, come              1040
               what may."
          The lord with all his might
          Entreats his guest to stay;
          Brief answer makes the knight:
          Next morning he must away.                1045


Then the lord of that land politely inquired
What dire affair had forced him, at that festive time,
So far from the king's court to fare forth alone
Ere the holidays wholly had ended in hall.
"In good faith," said Gawain, "you have guessed the truth:      1050
On a high errand and urgent I hastened away,
For I am summoned by myself to seek for a place—
I would I knew whither, or where it might be!
Far rather would I find it before the New Year
Than own the land of Logres, so help me our Lord!            1055
Wherefore, sir, in friendship this favor I ask,
That you say in sober earnest, if something you know
Of the Green Chapel, on ground far or near,
Or the lone knight that lives there, of like hue of green.
A certain day was set by assent of us both                    1060
To meet at that landmark, if I might last,
And from now to the New Year is nothing too long,
And I would greet the Green Knight there, would God but allow,
More gladly, by God's Son, than gain the world's wealth!
And I must set forth to search, as soon as I may;            1065
To be about the business I have but three days
And would as soon sink down dead as desist from my errand."
Then smiling said the lord, "Your search, sir, is done,
For we shall see you to that site by the set time.
Let Gawain grieve no more over the Green Chapel;            1070
You shall be in your own bed, in blissful ease,
All the forenoon, and fare forth the first of the year,
And make the goal by midmorn, to mind your affairs,
               no fear!
          Tarry till the fourth day                1075
          And ride on the first of the year.

We shall set you on your way;
It is not two miles from here."

Then Gawain was glad, and gleefully he laughed:
"Now I thank you for this, past all things else!                    1080
Now my goal is here at hand! With a glad heart I shall
Both tarry, and undertake any task you devise."
Then the host seized his arm and seated him there;
Let the ladies be brought, to delight them the better,
And in fellowship fair by the fireside they sit;                    1085
So gay waxed the good host, so giddy his words,
All waited in wonder what next he would say.
Then he stares on the stout knight, and sternly he speaks:
"You have bound yourself boldly my bidding to do—
Will you stand by that boast, and obey me this once?"               1090
"I shall do so indeed," said the doughty knight;
"While I lie in your lodging, your laws will I follow."
"As you have had," said the host, "many hardships abroad
And little sleep of late, you are lacking, I judge,
Both in nourishment needful and nightly rest;                       1095
You shall lie abed late in your lofty chamber
Tomorrow until mass, and meet then to dine
When you will, with my wife, who will sit by your side
And talk with you at table, the better to cheer
                      our guest.                                      1100
            A-hunting I will go
            While you lie late and rest."
            The knight, inclining low,
            Assents to each behest.

"And Gawain," said the good host, "agree now to this:               1105
Whatever I win in the woods I will give you at eve,
And all you have earned you must offer to me;
Swear now, sweet friend, to swap as I say,
Whether hands, in the end, be empty or better."
"By God," said Sir Gawain, "I grant it forthwith!                   1110
If you find the game good, I shall gladly take part."
"Let the bright wine be brought, and our bargain is done,"
Said the lord of that land—the two laughed together.
Then they drank and they dallied and doffed all constraint,
These lords and these ladies, as late as they chose,               1115
And then with gaiety and gallantries and graceful adieux
They talked in low tones, and tarried at parting.
With compliments comely they kiss at the last;
There were brisk lads about with blazing torches
To see them safe to bed, for soft repose                           1120

                    long due.
          Their covenants, yet awhile,
          They repeat, and pledge anew;
          That lord could well beguile
          Men's hearts, with mirth in view.                    1125


                    *Part III*

Long before daylight they left their beds;
Guests that wished to go gave word to their grooms,
And they set about briskly to bind on saddles,
Tend to their tackle, tie up trunks.
The proud lords appear, appareled to ride,              1130
Leap lightly astride, lay hold of their bridles,
Each one on his way to his worthy house.
The liege lord of the land was not the last
Arrayed there to ride, with retainers many;
He had a bite to eat when he had heard mass;            1135
With horn to the hills he hastens amain.
By the dawn of that day over the dim earth,
Master and men were mounted and ready.
Then they harnessed in couples the keen-scented hounds,
Cast wide the kennel-door and called them forth,         1140
Blew upon their bugles bold blasts three;
The dogs began to bay with a deafening din,
And they quieted them quickly and called them to heel,
A hundred brave huntsmen, as I have heard tell,
                    together.                            1145
          Men at stations meet;
          From the hounds they slip the tether;
          The echoing horns repeat,
          Clear in the merry weather.

At the clamor of the quest, the quarry trembled;         1150
Deer dashed through the dale, dazed with dread;
Hastened to the high ground, only to be
Turned back by the beaters, who boldly shouted.
They harmed not the harts, with their high heads,
Let the bucks go by, with their broad antlers,           1155
For it was counted a crime, in the close[4] season,
If a man of that demesne should molest the male deer.
The hinds were headed up, with "Hey!" and "Ware!"
The does with great din were driven to the valleys.
Then you were ware, as they went, of the whistling of arrows;   1160

4. Or closed.

At each bend under boughs the bright shafts flew
That tore the tawny hide with their tapered heads.
Ah! They bray and they bleed, on banks they die,
And ever the pack pell-mell comes panting behind;
Hunters with shrill horns hot on their heels—          1165
Like the cracking of cliffs their cries resounded.
What game got away from the gallant archers
Was promptly picked off at the posts below
When they were harried on the heights and herded to the streams:
The watchers were so wary at the waiting-stations,          1170
And the greyhounds so huge, that eagerly snatched,
And finished them off as fast as folk could see
                    with sight.
          The lord, now here, now there,
          Spurs forth in sheer delight.          1175
          And drives, with pleasures rare,
          The day to the dark night.

So the lord in the linden-wood leads the hunt
And Gawain the good knight in gay bed lies,
Lingered late alone, till daylight gleamed,          1180
Under coverlet costly, curtained about.
And as he slips into slumber, slyly there comes
A little din at his door, and the latch lifted,
And he holds up his heavy head out of the clothes;
A corner of the curtain he caught back a little          1185
And waited there warily, to see what befell.
Lo! it was the lady, loveliest to behold,
That drew the door behind her deftly and still
And was bound for his bed—abashed was the knight,
And laid his head low again in likeness of sleep;          1190
And she stepped stealthily, and stole to his bed,
Cast aside the curtain and came within,
And set herself softly on the bedside there,
And lingered at her leisure, to look on his waking.
The fair knight lay feigning for a long while,          1195
Conning in his conscience what his case might
Mean or amount to—a marvel he thought it.
But yet he said within himself, "More seemly it were
To try her intent by talking a little."
So he started and stretched, as startled from sleep,          1200
Lifts wide his lids in likeness of wonder,
And signs himself swiftly, as safer to be,
                    with art.
          Sweetly does she speak

And kindling glances dart,                                    1205
Blent white and red on cheek
And laughing lips apart.

"Good morning, Sir Gawain," said that gay lady,
"A slack sleeper you are, to let one slip in!
Now you are taken in a trice—a truce we must make,          1210
Or I shall bind you in your bed, of that be assured."
Thus laughing lightly that lady jested.
"Good morning, good lady," said Gawain the blithe,
"Be it with me as you will; I am well content!
For I surrender myself, and sue for your grace,             1215
And that is best, I believe, and behooves me now."
Thus jested in answer that gentle knight.
"But if, lovely lady, you misliked it not,
And were pleased to permit your prisoner to rise,
I should quit this couch and accoutre me better,            1220
And be clad in more comfort for converse here."
"Nay, not so, sweet sir," said the smiling lady;
"You shall not rise from your bed; I direct you better:
I shall hem and hold you on either hand,
And keep company awhile with my captive knight.             1225
For as certain as I sit here, Sir Gawain you are,
Whom all the world worships, whereso you ride;
Your honor, your courtesy are highest acclaimed
By lords and by ladies, by all living men;
And lo! we are alone here, and left to ourselves:           1230
My lord and his liegemen are long departed,
The household asleep, my handmaids too,
The door drawn, and held by a well-driven bolt,
And since I have in this house him whom all love,
I shall while the time away with mirthful speech            1235
                    at will.
          My body is here at hand,
          Your each wish to fulfill;
          Your servant to command
          I am, and shall be still."                        1240

"In good faith," said Gawain, "my gain is the greater,
Though I am not he of whom you have heard;
To arrive at such reverence as you recount here
I am one all unworthy, and well do I know it.
By heaven, I would hold me the happiest of men             1245
If by word or by work I once might aspire
To the prize of your praise—'twere a pure joy!"
"In good faith, Sir Gawain," said that gay lady,

"The well-proven prowess that pleases all others,
Did I scant or scout[5] it, 'twere scarce becoming.        1250
But there are ladies, believe me, that had liefer far[6]
Have thee here in their hold, as I have today,
To pass an hour in pastime with pleasant words,
Assuage all their sorrows and solace their hearts,
Than much of the goodly gems and gold they possess.        1255
But laud be to the Lord of the lofty skies,
For here in my hands all hearts' desire
                    doth lie."
                Great welcome got he there
                From the lady who sat him by;        1260
                With fitting speech and fair
                The good knight makes reply.

"Madame," said the merry man, "Mary reward you!
For in good faith, I find your beneficence noble.
And the fame of fair deeds runs far and wide,        1265
But the praise you report pertains not to me,
But comes of your courtesy and kindness of heart."
"By the high Queen of heaven" (said she) "I count it not so,
For were I worth all the women in this world alive,
And all wealth and all worship were in my hands,        1270
And I should hunt high and low, a husband to take,
For the nurture I have noted in thee, knight, here,
The comeliness and courtesies and courtly mirth—
And so I had ever heard, and now hold it true—
No other on this earth should have me for wife."        1275
"You are bound to a better man," the bold knight said,
"Yet I prize the praise you have proffered me here,
And soberly your servant, my sovereign I hold you,
And acknowledge me your knight, in the name of Christ."
So they talked of this and that until 'twas nigh noon,        1280
And ever the lady languishing in likeness of love.
With feat[7] words and fair he framed his defence,
For were she never so winsome, the warrior had
The less will to woo, for the wound that his bane
                    must be.        1285
                He must bear the blinding blow,
                For such is fate's decree;
                The lady asks leave to go;
                He grants it full and free.

Then she gaily said goodbye, and glanced at him, laughing,        1290
And as she stood, she astonished him with a stern speech:

5. Mock.   6. Would much rather.   7. Fitting.

"Now may the Giver of all good words these glad hours repay!
But our guest is not Gawain—forgot is that thought."
"How so?" said the other, and asks in some haste,
For he feared he had been at fault in the forms of his speech.     1295
But she held up her hand, and made answer thus:
"So good a knight as Gawain is given out to be,
And the model of fair demeanor and manners pure,
Had he lain so long at a lady's side,
Would have claimed a kiss, by his courtesy,     1300
Through some touch or trick of phrase at some tale's end."
Said Gawain, "Good lady, I grant it at once!
I shall kiss at your command, as becomes a knight,
And more, lest you mislike, so let be, I pray."
With that she turns toward him, takes him in her arms,     1305
Leans down her lovely head, and lo! he is kissed.
They commend each other to Christ with comely words,
He sees her forth safely, in silence they part,
And then he lies no later in his lofty bed,
But calls to his chamberlain, chooses his clothes,     1310
Goes in those garments gladly to mass,
Then takes his way to table, where attendants wait,
And made merry all day, till the moon rose
                    in view
          Was never knight beset     1315
          'Twixt worthier ladies two:
          The crone and the coquette;
          Fair pastimes they pursue.

And the lord of the land rides late and long,
Hunting the barren hind[8] over the broad heath.     1320
He had slain such a sum, when the sun sank low,
Of does and other deer, as would dizzy one's wits.
Then they trooped in together in triumph at last,
And the count of the quarry quickly they take.
The lords lent a hand with their liegemen many,     1325
Picked out the plumpest and put them together
And duly dressed the deer, as the deed requires.
Some were assigned the assay of the fat:
Two fingers'-width fully they found on the leanest.
Then they slit the slot[9] open and searched out the paunch,     1330
Trimmed it with trencher-knives and tied it up tight.
They flayed the fair hide from the legs and trunk,
Then broke open the belly and laid bare the bowels,
Deftly detaching and drawing them forth.

8. Female deer that are not pregnant.     9. The hollow above the breastbone.

And next at the neck they neatly parted                                    1335
The weasand[1] from the windpipe, and cast away the guts.
At the shoulders with sharp blades they showed their skill,
Boning them from beneath, lest the sides be marred;
They breached the broad breast and broke it in twain,
And again at the gullet they begin with their knives,                       1340
Cleave down the carcass clear to the breach;
Two tender morsels they take from the throat,
Then round the inner ribs they rid off a layer
And carve out the kidney-fat, close to the spine,
Hewing down to the haunch, that all hung together,                         1345
And held it up whole, and hacked it free,
And this they named the numbles,[2] that knew such terms
                                    of art.
                    They divide the crotch in two,
                    And straightway then they start
                    To cut the backbone through                            1350
                    And cleave the trunk apart.

With hard strokes they hewed off the head and the neck,
Then swiftly from the sides they severed the chine,
And the corbie's bone[3] they cast on a branch.                            1355
Then they pierced the plump sides, impaled either one
With the hock of the hind foot, and hung it aloft,
To each person his portion most proper and fit.
On a hide of a hind the hounds they fed
With the liver and the lights,[4] the leathery paunches,                   1360
And bread soaked in blood well blended therewith.
High horns and shrill set hounds a-baying,
Then merrily with their meat they make their way home,
Blowing on their bugles many a brave blast.
Ere dark had descended, that doughty band                                   1365
Was come within the walls where Gawain waits
                                    at leisure.
                    Bliss and hearth-fire bright
                    Await the master's pleasure;
                    When the two men met that night,
                    Joy surpassed all measure.                              1370

Then the host in the hall his household assembles,
With the dames of high degree and their damsels fair.
In the presence of the people, a party he sends
To convey him his venison in view of the knight.                           1375
And in high good-humor he hails him then,

1. Esophagus.    2. Other internal organs.    3. A bit of gristle for the ravens ("corbies").
4. Lungs.

Counts over the kill, the cuts on the tallies,[5]
Holds high the hewn ribs, heavy with fat.
"What think you, sir, of this? Have I thriven well?
Have I won with my woodcraft a worthy prize?"     1380
"In good earnest," said Gawain, "this game is the finest
I have seen in seven years in the season of winter."
"And I give it to you, Gawain," said the goodly host,
"For according to our covenant, you claim it as your own."
"That is so," said Sir Gawain, "the same say I:     1385
What I worthily have won within these fair walls,
Herewith I as willingly award it to you."
He embraces his broad neck with both his arms,
And confers on him a kiss in the comeliest style.
"Have here my profit, it proved no better;     1390
Ungrudging do I grant it, were it greater far."
"Such a gift," said the good host, "I gladly accept—
Yet it might be all the better, would you but say
Where you won this same award, by your wits alone."
"That was no part of the pact; press me no further,     1395
For you have had what behooves; all other claims
                  forbear."
          With jest and compliment
          They conversed, and cast off care;
          To the table soon they went;     1400
          Fresh dainties wait them there.

And then by the chimney-side they chat at their ease;
The best wine was brought them, and bounteously served;
And after in their jesting they jointly accord
To do on the second day the deeds of the first:     1405
That the two men should trade, betide as it may,
What each had taken in, at eve when they met.
They seal the pact solemnly in sight of the court;
Their cups were filled afresh to confirm the jest;
Then at last they took their leave, for late was the hour,     1410
Each to his own bed hastening away.
Before the barnyard cock had crowed but thrice
The lord had leapt from his rest, his liegemen as well.
Both of mass and their meal they made short work:
By the dim light of dawn they were deep in the woods     1415
                  away.
          With huntsmen and with horns
          Over plains they pass that day;
          They release, amid the thorns,
          Swift hounds that run and bay.     1420

5. Notched sticks were used to count the animals taken in the hunt.

Soon some were on a scent by the side of a marsh;
When the hounds opened cry, the head of the hunt
Rallied them with rough words, raised a great noise.
The hounds that had heard it came hurrying straight
And followed along with their fellows, forty together.          1425
Then such a clamor and cry of coursing hounds
Arose, that the rocks resounded again.
Hunters exhorted them with horn and with voice;
Then all in a body bore off together
Between a mere[6] in the marsh and a menacing crag,          1430
To a rise where the rock stood rugged and steep,
And boulders lay about, that blocked their approach.
Then the company in consort closed on their prey:
They surrounded the rise and the rocks both,
For well they were aware that it waited within,          1435
The beast that the bloodhounds boldly proclaimed.
Then they beat on the bushes and bade him appear,
And he made a murderous rush in the midst of them all;
The best of all boars broke from his cover,
That had ranged long unrivaled, a renegade old,          1440
For of tough-brawned boars he was biggest far,
Most grim when he grunted—then grieved were many,
For three at the first thrust he threw to the earth,
And dashed away at once without more damage.
With "Hi!" "Hi!" and "Hey!" "Hey!" the others followed,          1445
Had horns at their lips, blew high and clear.
Merry was the music of men and of hounds
That were bound after this boar, his bloodthirsty heart
                              to quell.
              Often he stands at bay,          1450
              Then scatters the pack pell-mell;
              He hurts the hounds, and they
              Most dolefully yowl and yell.

Men then with mighty bows moved in to shoot,
Aimed at him with their arrows and often hit,          1455
But the points had no power to pierce through his hide,
And the barbs were brushed aside by his bristly brow;
Though the shank of the shaft shivered in pieces,
The head hopped away, wheresoever it struck.
But when their stubborn strokes had stung him at last,          1460
Then, foaming in his frenzy, fiercely he charges,
Hies at them headlong that hindered his flight,
And many feared for their lives, and fell back a little.
But the lord on a lively horse leads the chase;

6. Pool.

As a high-mettled huntsman his horn he blows;　　　　　1465
He sounds the assembly and sweeps through the brush,
Pursuing this wild swine till the sunlight slanted.
All day with this deed they drive forth the time
While our lone knight so lovesome lies in his bed,
Sir Gawain safe at home, in silken bower　　　　　　1470
　　　　　　　　so gay.
　　　　　　The lady, with guile in heart,
　　　　　　Came early where he lay;
　　　　　　She was at him with all her art
　　　　　　To turn his mind her way.　　　　　　1475

She comes to the curtain and coyly peeps in;
Gawain thought it good to greet her at once,
And she richly repays him with her ready words,
Settles softly at his side, and suddenly she laughs,
And with a gracious glance, she begins on him thus:　　1480
"Sir, if you be Gawain, it seems a great wonder—
A man so well-meaning, and mannerly disposed,
And cannot act in company as courtesy bids,
And if one takes the trouble to teach him, 'tis all in vain.
That lesson learned lately is lightly forgot,　　　　1485
Though I painted it as plain as my poor wit allowed."
"What lesson, dear lady?" he asked all alarmed;
"I have been much to blame, if your story be true."
"Yet my counsel was of kissing," came her answer then,
"Where favor has been found, freely to claim　　　1490
As accords with the conduct of courteous knights."
"Such freedom, I fear, might offend you much;
It were rude to request if the right were denied."
"But none can deny you," said the noble dame,　　1495
"You are stout enough to constrain with strength, if you choose,
Were any so ungracious as to grudge you aught."
"By heaven," said he, "you have answered well,
But threats never throve among those of my land,
Nor any gift not freely given, good though it be.　　1500
I am yours to command, to kiss when you please;
You may lay on as you like, and leave off at will."
　　　　　　　　With this,
　　　　　　The lady lightly bends
　　　　　　And graciously gives him a kiss;
　　　　　　The two converse as friends　　　　1505
　　　　　　Of true love's trials and bliss.

"I should like, by your leave," said the lovely lady,
"If it did not annoy you, to know for what cause

So brisk and so bold a young blood as you,                              1510
And acclaimed for all courtesies becoming a knight—
And name what knight you will, they are noblest esteemed
For loyal faith in love, in life as in story;
For to tell the tribulations of these true hearts,
Why, 'tis the very title and text of their deeds,                       1515
How bold knights for beauty have braved many a foe,
Suffered heavy sorrows out of secret love,
And then valorously avenged them on villainous churls
And made happy ever after the hearts of their ladies.
And you are the noblest knight known in your time;                      1520
No household under heaven but has heard of your fame,
And here by your side I have sat for two days
Yet never has a fair phrase fallen from your lips
Of the language of love, not one little word!
And you, that with sweet vows sway women's hearts,                      1525
Should show your winsome ways, and woo a young thing,
And teach by some tokens the craft of true love.
How! are you artless, whom all men praise?
Or do you deem me so dull, or deaf to such words?
                    Fie! Fie!                                           1530
                    In hope of pastimes new
                    I have come where none can spy;
                    Instruct me a little, do,
                    While my husband is not nearby."

"God love you, gracious lady!" said Gawain then;                        1535
"It is a pleasure surpassing, and a peerless joy,
That one so worthy as you would willingly come
And take the time and trouble to talk with your knight
And content you with his company—it comforts my heart.
But to take to myself the task of telling of love,                      1540
And touch upon its texts, and treat of its themes
To one that, I know well, wields more power
In that art, by a half, then a hundred such
As I am where I live, or am like to become,
It were folly, fair dame, in the first degree!                         1545
In all that I am able, my aim is to please,
As in honor behooves me, and am evermore
Your servant heart and soul, so save me our Lord!"
Thus she tested his temper and tried many a time,
Whatever her true intent, to entice him to sin,                         1550
But so fair was his defense that no fault appeared,
Nor evil on either hand, but only bliss
                    they knew.

They linger and laugh awhile;
She kisses the knight so true,
Takes leave in comeliest style                                    1555
And departs without more ado.

Then he rose from his rest and made ready for mass,
And then a meal was set and served, in sumptuous style;
He dallied at home all day with the dear ladies,                  1560
But the lord lingered late at his lusty sport;
Pursued his sorry swine, that swerved as he fled,
And bit asunder the backs of the best of his hounds
When they brought him to bay, till the bowmen appeared
And soon forced him forth, though he fought for dear life,        1565
So sharp were the shafts they shot at him there.
But yet the boldest drew back from his battering head,
Till at last he was so tired he could travel no more,
But in as much haste as he might, he makes his retreat
To a rise on rocky ground, by a rushing stream.                  1570
With the bank at his back he scrapes the bare earth,
The froth foams at his jaws, frightful to see.
He whets his white tusks—then weary were all
Those hunters so hardy that hoved[7] round about
Of aiming from afar, but ever they mistrust                       1575
                    his mood.
            He had hurt so many by then
            That none had hardihood
            To be torn by his tusks again,
            That was brainsick, and out for blood.                1580

Till the lord came at last on his lofty steed,
Beheld him there at bay before all his folk;
Lightly he leaps down, leaves his courser,
Bares his bright sword, and boldly advances;
Straight into the stream he strides towards his foe.              1585
The wild thing was wary of weapon and man;
His hackles rose high; so hotly he snorts
That many watched with alarm, lest the worst befall.
The boar makes for the man with a mighty bound
So that he and his hunter came headlong together                  1590
Where the water ran wildest—the worse for the beast,
For the man, when they first met, marked him with care,
Sights well the slot, slips in the blade,
Shoves it home to the hilt, and the heart shattered,
And he falls in his fury and floats down the water,               1595

---

7. Hovered.

ill-sped.
Hounds hasten by the score
To maul him, hide and head;
Men drag him in to shore
And dogs pronounce him dead.                                    1600

With many a brave blast they boast of their prize,
All hallooed in high glee, that had their wind;
The hounds bayed their best, as the bold men bade
That were charged with chief rank in that chase of renown.
Then one wise in woodcraft, and worthily skilled,              1605
Began to dress the boar in becoming style:
He severs the savage head and sets it aloft,
Then rends the body roughly right down the spine;
Takes the bowels from the belly, broils them on coals,
Blends them well with bread to bestow on the hounds.           1610
Then he breaks out the brawn in fair broad flitches,
And the innards to be eaten in order he takes.
The two sides, attached to each other all whole,
He suspended from a spar that was springy and tough;
And so with this swine they set out for home;                  1615
The boar's head was borne before the same man
That had stabbed him in the stream with his strong arm,
                    right through.
          He thought it long indeed
          Till he had the knight in view;
          At his call, he comes with speed                     1620
          To claim his payment due.

The lord laughed aloud, with many a light word,
When he greeted Sir Gawain—with good cheer he speaks.
They fetch the fair dames and the folk of the house;          1625
He brings forth the brawn, and begins the tale
Of the great length and girth, the grim rage as well,
Of the battle of the boar they beset in the wood.
The other men meetly commended his deeds
And praised well the prize of his princely sport,             1630
For the brawn of that boar, the bold knight said,
And the sides of that swine surpassed all others.
Then they handled the huge head; he owns it a wonder,
And eyes it with abhorrence, to heighten his praise.
"Now, Gawain," said the good man, "this game becomes yours    1635
By those fair terms we fixed, as you know full well."
"That is true," returned the knight, "and trust me, fair friend,
All my gains, as agreed, I shall give you forthwith."
He clasps him and kisses him in courteous style,

Then serves him with the same fare a second time.                    1640
"Now we are even," said he, "at this evening feast,
And clear is every claim incurred here to date,
                         and debt."
                    "By Saint Giles!" the host replies,
                    "You're the best I ever met!                      1645
                    If your profits are all this size,
                    We'll see you wealthy yet!"

Then attendants set tables on trestles about,
And laid them with linen; light shone forth,
Wakened along the walls in waxen torches.                            1650
The service was set and the supper brought;
Royal were the revels that rose then in hall
At that feast by the fire, with many fair sports:
Amid the meal and after, melody sweet,
Carol-dances comely and Christmas songs,                             1655
With all the mannerly mirth my tongue may describe.
And ever our gallant knight beside the gay lady;
So uncommonly kind and complaisant was she,
With sweet stolen glances, that stirred his stout heart,
That he was at his wits' end, and wondrous vexed;                    1660
But he could not in conscience her courtship repay,
Yet took pains to please her, though the plan might
                         go wrong.
                    When they to heart's delight
                    Had reveled there in throng,                     1665
                    To his chamber he calls the knight,
                    And thither they go along.

And there they dallied and drank, and deemed it good sport
To enact their play anew on New Year's Eve,
But Gawain asked again to go on the morrow,                          1670
For the time until his tryst was not two days.
The host hindered that, and urged him to stay,
And said, "On my honor, my oath here I take
That you shall get to the Green Chapel to begin your chores
By dawn on New Year's Day, if you so desire.                         1675
Wherefore lie at your leisure in your lofty bed,
And I shall hunt hereabouts, and hold to our terms,
And we shall trade winnings when once more we meet,
For I have tested you twice, and true have I found you;
Now think this tomorrow: the third pays for all;                     1680
Be we merry while we may, and mindful of joy,
For heaviness of heart can be had for the asking."

This is gravely agreed on and Gawain will stay.
They drink a last draught and with torches depart
                            to rest.                                        1685
                    To bed Sir Gawain went;
                    His sleep was of the best;
                    The lord, on his craft intent,
                    Was early up and dressed.

After mass, with his men, a morsel he takes;                              1690
Clear and crisp the morning; he calls for his mount;
The folk that were to follow him afield that day
Were high astride their horses before the hall gates.
Wondrous fair were the fields, for the frost was light;
The sun rises red amid radiant clouds,                                    1695
Sails into the sky, and sends forth his beams.
They let loose the hounds by a leafy wood;
The rocks all around re-echo to their horns;
Soon some have set off in pursuit of the fox,
Cast about with craft for a clearer scent;                               1700
A young dog yaps, and is yelled at in turn;
His fellows fall to sniffing, and follow his lead,
Running in a rabble on the right track,
And he scampers all before; they discover him soon,
And when they see him with sight they pursue him the faster,             1705
Railing at him rudely with a wrathful din.
Often he reverses over rough terrain,
Or loops back to listen in the lee of a hedge;
At last, by a little ditch, he leaps over the brush,
Comes into a clearing at a cautious pace,                                1710
Then he thought through his wiles to have thrown off the hounds
Till he was ware, as he went, of a waiting-station
Where three athwart his path threatened him at once,
                            all gray.
                    Quick as a flash he wheels                           1715
                    And darts off in dismay;
                    With hard luck at his heels
                    He is off to the wood away.

Then it was heaven on earth to hark to the hounds
When they had come on their quarry, coursing together!                   1720
Such harsh cries and howls they hurled at his head
As all the cliffs with a crash had come down at once.
Here he was hailed, when huntsmen met him;
Yonder they yelled at him, yapping and snarling;
There they cried "Thief!" and threatened his life,                       1725
And ever the harriers at his heels, that he had no rest.

Often he was menaced when he made for the open,
And often rushed in again, for Reynard was wily;
And so he leads them a merry chase, the lord and his men,
In this manner on the mountains, till midday or near,          1730
While our hero lies at home in wholesome sleep
Within the comely curtains on the cold morning.
But the lady, as love would allow her no rest,
And pursuing ever the purpose that pricked her heart,
Was awake with the dawn, and went to his chamber          1735
In a fair flowing mantle that fell to the earth,
All edged and embellished with ermines fine;
No hood on her head, but heavy with gems
Were her fillet and the fret[8] that confined her tresses;
Her face and her fair throat freely displayed;          1740
Her bosom all but bare, and her back as well.
She comes in at the chamber-door, and closes it with care,
Throws wide a window—then waits no longer,
But hails him thus airily with her artful words,
                              with cheer:          1745
            "Ah, man, how can you sleep?
            The morning is so clear!"
            Though dreams have drowned him deep,
            He cannot choose but hear.

Deep in his dreams he darkly mutters          1750
As a man may that mourns, with many grim thoughts
Of that day when destiny shall deal him his doom
When he greets his grim host at the Green Chapel
And must bow to his buffet, bating all strife.
But when he sees her at his side he summons his wits,          1755
Breaks from the black dreams, and blithely answers.
That lovely lady comes laughing sweet,
Sinks down at his side, and salutes him with a kiss.
He accords her fair welcome in courtliest style;
He sees her so glorious, so gaily attired,          1760
So faultless her features, so fair and so bright,
His heart swelled swiftly with surging joys.
They melt into mirth with many a fond smile,
And there was bliss beyond telling between those two,
                              at height.          1765
            Good were their words of greeting;
            Each joyed in other's sight;
            Great peril attends that meeting
            Should Mary forget her knight.

8. Ornamental net.

For that high-born beauty so hemmed him about,                    1770
Made so plain her meaning, the man must needs
Either take her tendered love or distastefully refuse.
His courtesy concerned him, lest crass he appear,
But more his soul's mischief, should he commit sin
And belie his loyal oath to the lord of that house.               1775
"God forbid!" said the bold knight, "That shall not befall!"
With a little fond laughter he lightly let pass
All the words of special weight that were sped his way;
"I find you much at fault," the fair one said,
"Who can be cold toward a creature so close by your side,         1780
Of all women in this world most wounded in heart,
Unless you have a sweetheart, one you hold dearer,
And allegiance to that lady so loyally knit
That you will never love another, as now I believe.
And, sir, if it be so, then say it, I beg you;                   1785
By all your heart holds dear, hide it no longer
                        with guile."
                    "Lady, by Saint John,"
                    He answers with a smile,
                    "Lover have I none,                          1790
                    Nor will have, yet awhile."

"Those words," said the woman, "are the worst of all,
But I have had my answer, and hard do I find it!
Kiss me now kindly; I can but go hence
To lament my life long like a maid lovelorn."                    1795
She inclines her head quickly and kisses the knight,
Then straightens with a sigh, and says as she stands,
"Now, dear, ere I depart, do me this pleasure:
Give me some little gift, your glove or the like,
That I may think on you, man, and mourn the less."               1800
"Now by heaven," said he, "I wish I had here
My most precious possession, to put it in your hands,
For your deeds, beyond doubt, have often deserved
A repayment far passing my power to bestow.
But a love-token, lady, were of little avail;                    1805
It is not to your honor to have at this time
A glove as a guerdon from Gawain's hand,
And I am here on an errand in unknown realms
And have no bearers with baggage with becoming gifts,
Which distresses me, madame, for your dear sake.                 1810
A man must keep within his compass: account it neither grief
                        nor slight."
                    "Nay, noblest knight alive,"

Said that beauty of body white,
"Though you be loath to give,
Yet you shall take, by right."                        1815

She reached out a rich ring, wrought all of gold,
With a splendid stone displayed on the band
That flashed before his eyes like a fiery sun;
It was worth a king's wealth, you may well believe.    1820
But he waved it away with these ready words:
"Before God, good lady, I forego all gifts;
None have I to offer, nor any will I take."
And she urged it on him eagerly, and ever he refused,
And vowed in very earnest, prevail she would not.      1825
And she sad to find it so, and said to him then,
"If my ring is refused for its rich cost—
You would not be my debtor for so dear a thing—
I shall give you my girdle;[9] you gain less thereby."
She released a knot lightly, and loosened a belt        1830
That was caught about her kirtle, the bright cloak beneath,
Of a gay green silk, with gold overwrought,
And the borders all bound with embroidery fine,
And this she presses upon him, and pleads with a smile,
Unworthy though it were, that it would not be scorned.  1835
But the man still maintains that he means to accept
Neither gold nor any gift, till by God's grace
The fate that lay before him was fully achieved.
"And be not offended, fair lady, I beg,
And give over your offer, for ever I must              1840
                    decline.
            I am grateful for favor shown
            Past all deserts of mine,
            And ever shall be your own
            True servant, rain or shine."               1845

"Now does my present displease you," she promptly inquired,
"Because it seems in your sight so simple a thing?
And belike, as it is little, it is less to praise,
But if the virtue that invests it were verily known,
It would be held, I hope, in higher esteem.            1850
For the man that possesses this piece of silk,
If he bore it on his body, belted about,
There is no hand under heaven that could hew him down,
For he could not be killed by any craft on earth."
Then the man began to muse, and mainly he thought       1855

9. Belt.

It was a pearl for his plight, the peril to come
When he gains the Green Chapel to get his reward:
Could he escape unscathed, the scheme were noble!
Then he bore with her words and withstood them no more,
And she repeated her petition and pleaded anew,                1860
And he granted it, and gladly she gave him the belt,
And besought him for her sake to conceal it well,
Lest the noble lord should know—and the knight agrees
That not a soul save themselves shall see it thenceforth
          with sight.                1865
        He thanked her with fervent heart,
        As often as ever he might;
        Three times, before they part,
        She has kissed the stalwart knight.

Then the lady took her leave, and left him there,                1870
For more mirth with that man she might not have.
When she was gone, Sir Gawain got from his bed,
Arose and arrayed him in his rich attire;
Tucked away the token the temptress had left,
Laid it reliably where he looked for it after.                1875
And then with good cheer to the chapel he goes,
Approached a priest in private, and prayed to be taught
To lead a better life and lift up his mind,
Lest he be among the lost when he must leave this world.
And shamefaced at shrift[1] he showed his misdeeds                1880
From the largest to the least, and asked the Lord's mercy,
And called on his confessor to cleanse his soul,
And he absolved him of his sins as safe and as clean
As if the dread Day of Judgment should dawn on the morrow.
And then he made merry amid the fine ladies                1885
With deft-footed dances and dalliance light,
As never until now, while the afternoon wore
          away.
        He delighted all around him,
        And all agreed, that day,                1890
        They never before had found him
        So gracious and so gay.

Now peaceful be his pasture, and love play him fair!
The host is on horseback, hunting afield;
He has finished off this fox that he followed so long:                1895
As he leapt a low hedge to look for the villain
Where he heard all the hounds in hot pursuit,

1. Confession.

Reynard comes racing out of a rough thicket,
And all the rabble in a rush, right at his heels.
The man beholds the beast, and bides his time,       1900
And bares his bright sword, and brings it down hard,
And he blenches from the blade, and backward he starts;
A hound hurries up and hinders that move,
And before the horse's feet they fell on him at once
And ripped the rascal's throat with a wrathful din.       1905
The lord soon alighted and lifted him free,
Swiftly snatched him up from the snapping jaws,
Holds him over his head, halloos with a will,
And the dogs bayed the dirge, that had done him to death.
Hunters hastened thither with horns at their lips,       1910
Sounding the assembly till they saw him at last.
When that comely company was come in together,
All that bore bugles blew them at once,
And the others all hallooed, that had no horns.
It was the merriest medley that ever a man heard,       1915
The racket that they raised for Sir Reynard's soul
                  that died.
            Their hounds they praised and fed,
            Fondling their heads with pride,
            And they took Reynard the Red       1920
            And stripped away his hide.

And then they headed homeward, for evening had come,
Blowing many a blast on their bugles bright.
The lord at long last alights at his house,
Finds fire on the hearth where the fair knight waits,       1925
Sir Gawain the good, that was glad in heart.
With the ladies, that loved him, he lingered at ease;
He wore a rich robe of blue, that reached to the earth
And a surcoat lined softly with sumptuous furs;
A hood of the same hue hung on his shoulders;       1930
With bands of bright ermine embellished were both.
He comes to meet the man amid all the folk,
And greets him good-humoredly, and gaily he says,
"I shall follow forthwith the form of our pledge
That we framed to good effect amid fresh-filled cups."       1935
He clasps him accordingly and kisses him thrice,
As amiably and as earnestly as ever he could.
"By heaven," said the host, "you have had some luck
Since you took up this trade, if the terms were good."
"Never trouble about the terms," he returned at once,       1940
"Since all that I owe here is openly paid."

"Marry!" said the other man, "mine is much less,
For I have hunted all day, and nought have I got
But this foul fox pelt, the fiend take the goods!
Which but poorly repays those precious things          1945
That you have cordially conferred, those kisses three
                    so good."
                    "Enought!" said Sir Gawain;
                    "I thank you, by the rood!"[2]
                    And how the fox was slain
                    He told him, as they stood.          1950

With minstrelsy and mirth, with all manner of meats,
They made as much merriment as any men might
(Amid laughing of ladies and light-hearted girls,
So gay grew Sir Gawain and the goodly host)          1955
Unless they had been besotted, or brainless fools.
The knight joined in jesting with that joyous folk,
Until at last it was late; ere long they must part,
And be off to their beds, as behooved them each one.
Then politely his leave of the lord of the house          1960
Our noble knight takes, and renews his thanks:
"The courtesies countless accorded me here,
Your kindness at this Christmas, may heaven's King repay!
Henceforth, if you will have me, I hold you my liege,
And so, as I have said, I must set forth tomorrow,          1965
If I may take some trusty man to teach, as you promised,
The way to the Green Chapel, that as God allows
I shall see my fate fulfilled on the first of the year."
"In good faith," said the good man, "with a good will
Every promise on my part shall be fully performed."          1970
He assigns him a servant to set him on the path,
To see him safe and sound over the snowy hills,
To follow the fastest way through forest green
                    and grove.
                    Gawain thanks him again,
                    So kind his favors prove,          1975
                    And of the ladies then
                    He takes his leave, with love.

Courteously he kissed them, with care in his heart,
And often wished them well, with warmest thanks,          1980
Which they for their part were prompt to repay.
They commend him to Christ with disconsolate sighs;
And then in that hall with the household he parts—

2. Cross.

Each man that he met, he remembered to thank
For his deeds of devotion and diligent pains,                              1985
And the trouble he had taken to tend to his needs;
And each one as woeful, that watched him depart,
As he had lived with him loyally all his life long.
By lads bearing lights he was led to his chamber
And blithely brought to his bed, to be at his rest.                        1990
How soundly he slept, I presume not to say,
For there were matters of moment his thoughts might well
                              pursue.
              Let him lie and wait;
              He has little more to do,                                     1995
              Then listen, while I relate
              How they kept their rendezvous.


## Part IV

Now the New Year draws near, and the night passes,
The day dispels the dark, by the Lord's decree;
But wild weather awoke in the world without:                               2000
The clouds in the cold sky cast down their snow
With great gusts from the north, grievous to bear.
Sleet showered aslant upon shivering beasts;
The wind warbled wild as it whipped from aloft,
And drove the drifts deep in the dales below.                              2005
Long and well he listens, that lies in his bed;
Though he lifts not his eyelids, little he sleeps;
Each crow of the cock he counts without fail.
Readily from his rest he rose before dawn,
For a lamp had been left him, that lighted his chamber.                    2010
He called to his chamberlain, who quickly appeared,
And bade him get him his gear, and gird his good steed,
And he sets about briskly to bring in his arms,
And makes ready his master in manner most fit.
First he clad him in his clothes, to keep out the cold,                    2015
And then his other harness, made handsome anew,
His plate-armor of proof, polished with pains,
The rings of his rich mail rid of their rust,
And all was fresh as at first, and for this he gave thanks
                              indeed.                                       2020
              With pride he wears each piece,
              New-furbished for his need:
              No gayer from here to Greece;
              He bids them bring his steed.

In his richest raiment he robed himself then:                        2025
His crested coat-armor, close-stitched with craft,
With stones of strange virtue on silk velvet set;
All bound with embroidery on borders and seams
And lined warmly and well with furs of the best.
Yet he left not his love-gift, the lady's girdle;                     2030
Gawain, for his own good, forgot not that:
When the bright sword was belted and bound on his haunches,
Then twice with that token he twined him about.
Sweetly did he swathe him in that swatch of silk,
That girdle of green so goodly to see,                                2035
That against the gay red showed gorgeous bright.
Yet he wore not for its wealth that wondrous girdle,
Nor pride in its pendants, though polished they were,
Though glittering gold gleamed at the tips,
But to keep himself safe when consent he must                        2040
To endure a deadly dint, and all defense
                              denied.
                    And now the bold knight came
                    Into the courtyard wide;
                    That folk of worthy fame                          2045
                    He thanks on every side.

Then was Gringolet girt, that was great and huge,
And had sojourned safe and sound, and savored his fare;
He pawed the earth in his pride, that princely steed.
The good knight draws near him and notes well his look,              2050
And says sagely to himself, and soberly swears,
"Here is a household in hall that upholds the right!
The man that maintains it, may happiness be his!
Likewise the dear lady, may love betide her!
If thus they in charity cherish a guest                              2055
That are honored here on earth, may they have His reward
That reigns high in heaven—and also you all;
And were I to live in this land but a little while,
I should willingly reward you, and well, if I might."
Then he steps into the stirrup and bestrides his mount;              2060
His shield is shown forth; on his shoulder he casts it;
Strikes the side of his steed with his steel spurs,
And he starts across the stones, nor stands any longer
                              to prance.
                    On horseback was the swain
                    That bore his spear and lance;                    2065
                    "May Christ this house maintain
                    And guard it from mischance!"

The bridge was brought down, and the broad gates
Unbarred and carried back upon both sides;     2070
He commended him[3] to Christ, and crossed over the planks;
Praised the noble porter, who prayed on his knees
That God save Sir Gawain, and bade him good day,
And went on his way alone with the man
That was to lead him ere long to that luckless place     2075
Where the dolorous dint must be dealt him at last.
Under bare boughs they ride, where steep banks rise,
Over high cliffs they climb, where cold snow clings;
The heavens held aloof, but heavy thereunder
Mist mantled the moors, moved on the slopes.     2080
Each hill had a hat, a huge cape of cloud;
Brooks bubbled and broke over broken rocks,
Flashing in freshets that waterfalls fed.
Roundabout was the road that ran through the wood
Till the sun at that season was soon to rise,     2085
             that day.
         They were on a hilltop high;
         The white snow round them lay;
         The man that rode nearby
         Now bade his master stay.     2090

"For I have seen you here safe at the set time,
And now you are not far from that notable place
That you have sought for so long with such special pains.
But this I say for certain, since I know you, sir knight,
And have your good at heart, and hold you dear—     2095
Would you heed well my words, it were worth your while—
You are rushing into risks that you reck not of:
There is a villain in yon valley, the veriest on earth,
For he is rugged and rude, and ready with fists,
And most immense in his mold of mortals alive,     2100
And his body bigger than the best four
That are in Arthur's house, Hector[4] or any.
He gets his grim way at the Green Chapel;
None passes by that place so proud in his arms
That he does not dash him down with his deadly blows,     2105
For he is heartless wholly, and heedless of right,
For be it chaplain or churl that by the Chapel rides,
Monk or mass-priest or any man else,
He would as soon strike him dead as stand on two feet.
Wherefore I say, just as certain as you sit there astride,     2110

---

3. I.e., himself.     4. Either the Trojan hero or one of Arthur's knights.

You cannot but be killed, if his counsel holds,
For he would trounce you in a trice, had you twenty lives
                    for sale.
          He has lived long in this land
          And dealt out deadly bale;                       2115
          Against his heavy hand
          Your power cannot prevail.

"And so, good Sir Gawain, let the grim man be;
Go off by some other road, in God's own name!
Leave by some other land, for the love of Christ,            2120
And I shall get me home again, and give you my word
That I shall swear by God's self and the saints above,
By heaven and by my halidom[5] and other oaths more,
To conceal this day's deed, nor say to a soul
That ever you fled for fear from any that I knew."           2125
"Many thanks!" said the other man—and demurring he speaks—
"Fair fortune befall you for your friendly words!
And conceal this day's deed I doubt not you would,
But though you never told the tale, if I turned back now,
Forsook this place for fear, and fled, as you say,           2130
I were a caitiff[6] coward; I could not be excused.
But I must to the Chapel to chance my luck
And say to that same man such words as I please,
Befall what may befall through Fortune's will
                    or whim.                     2135
          Though he be a quarrelsome knave
          With a cudgel great and grim,
          The Lord is strong to save:
          His servants trust in Him."

"Marry," said the man, "since you tell me so much,           2140
And I see you are set to seek your own harm,
If you crave a quick death, let me keep you no longer!
Put your helm on your head, your hand on your lance,
And ride the narrow road down yon rocky slope
Till it brings you to the bottom of the broad valley.        2145
Then look a little ahead, on your left hand,
And you will soon see before you that self-same Chapel,
And the man of great might that is master there.
Now goodbye in God's name, Gawain the noble!
For all the world's wealth I would not stay here,            2150
Or go with you in this wood on footstep further!"
He tarried no more to talk, but turned his bridle,

5. Holiness or, more likely, patron saints.    6. Despicable.

Hit his horse with his heels as hard as he might,
Leaves the knight alone, and off like the wind
                    goes leaping.          2155
         "By God," said Gawain then,
         "I shall not give way to weeping;
         God's will be done, amen!
         I commend me to His keeping."

He puts his heels to his horse, and picks up the path;     2160
Goes in beside a grove where the ground is steep,
Rides down the rough slope right to the valley;
And then he looked a little about him—the landscape was wild,
And not a soul to be seen, nor sign of a dwelling,
But high banks on either hand hemmed it about,     2165
With many a ragged rock and rough-hewn crag;
The skies seemed scored by the scowling peaks.
Then he halted his horse, and hoved there a space,
And sought on every side for a sight of the Chapel,
But no such place appeared, which puzzled him sore,     2170
Yet he saw some way off what seemed like a mound,
A hillock high and broad, hard by the water,
Where the stream fell in foam down the face of the steep
And bubbled as if it boiled on its bed below.
The knight urges his horse, and heads for the knoll;     2175
Leaps lightly to earth; loops well the rein
Of his steed to a stout branch, and stations him there.
He strides straight to the mound, and strolls all about,
Much wondering what it was, but no whit the wiser;
It had a hole at one end, and on either side,     2180
And was covered with coarse grass in clumps all without,
And hollow all within, like some old cave,
Or a crevice of an old crag—he could not discern
                  aright.
         "Can this be the Chapel Green?
         Alack!" said the man, "Here might     2185
         The devil himself be seen
         Saying matins[7] at black midnight!"

"Now by heaven," said he, "it is bleak hereabouts;
This prayer-house is hideous, half-covered with grass!     2190
Well may the grim man mantled in green
Hold here his orisons, in hell's own style!
Now I feel it is the Fiend, in my five wits,

7. Morning prayers.

That has tempted me to this tryst, to take my life;
This is a Chapel of mischance, may the mischief take it! 2195
As accursed a country church as I came upon ever!"
With his helm on his head, his lance in his hand,
He stalks toward the steep wall of that strange house.
Then he heard, on the hill, behind a hard rock,
Beyond the brook, from the bank, a most barbarous din: 2200
Lord! it clattered in the cliff fit to cleave it in two,
As one upon a grindstone ground a great scythe!
Lord! it whirred like a mill-wheel whirling about!
Lord! it echoed loud and long, lamentable to hear!
Then "By heaven," said the bold knight, "That business
       up there 2205
Is arranged for my arrival, or else I am much
                       misled.
              Let God work! Ah me!
              All hope of help has fled!
              Forfeit my life may be 2210
              But noise I do not dread."

Then he listened no longer, but loudly he called,
"Who has power in this place, high parley to hold?
For none greets Sir Gawain, or gives him good day;
If any would a word with him, let him walk forth 2215
And speak now or never, to speed his affairs."
"Abide," said one on the bank above over his head,
"And what I promised you once shall straightway be given."
Yet he stayed not his grindstone, nor stinted its noise,
But worked awhile at his whetting before he would rest, 2220
And then he comes around a crag, from a cave in the rocks,
Hurtling out of hiding with a hateful weapon,
A Danish ax devised for that day's deed,
With a broad blade and bright, bent in a curve,
Filed to a fine edge—four feet it measured 2225
By the length of the lace that was looped round the haft.
And in form as at first, the fellow all green,
His lordly face and his legs, his locks and his beard,
Save that firm upon two feet forward he strides,
Sets a hand on the ax-head, the haft to the earth; 2230
When he came to the cold stream, and cared not to wade,
He vaults over on his ax, and advances amain
On a broad bank of snow, overbearing and brisk
                    of mood.
              Little did the knight incline 2235

> When face to face they stood;
> Said the other man, "Friend mine,
> It seems your word holds good!"

"God love you, Sir Gawain!" said the Green Knight then,
"And well met this morning, man, at my place!      2240
And you have followed me faithfully and found me betimes,[8]
And on the business between us we both are agreed:
Twelve months ago today you took what was yours,
And you at this New Year must yield me the same.
And we have met in these mountains, remote from all eyes:      2245
There is none here to halt us or hinder our sport;
Unhasp your high helm, and have here your wages;
Make no more demur than I did myself
When you hacked off my head with one hard blow."
"No, by God," said Sir Gawain, "that granted me life,      2250
I shall grudge not the guerdon, grim though it prove;
Bestow but one stroke, and I shall stand still,
And you may lay on as you like till the last of my part
> be paid."
> He proffered, with good grace,
> His bare neck to the blade,      2255
> And feigned a cheerful face:
> He scorned to seem afraid.

Then the grim man in green gathers his strength,
Heaves high the heavy ax to hit him the blow.      2260
With all the force in his frame he fetches it aloft,
With a grimace as grim as he would grind him to bits;
Had the blow he bestowed been as big as he threatened,
A good knight and gallant had gone to his grave.
But Gawain at the great ax glanced up aside      2265
As down it descended with death-dealing force,
And his shoulders shrank a little from the sharp iron.
Abruptly the brawny man breaks off the stroke,
And then reproved with proud words that prince among knights.
"You are not Gawain the glorious," the green man said,      2270
"That never fell back on field in the face of the foe,
And now you flee for fear, and have felt no harm:
Such news of that knight I never heard yet!
I moved not a muscle when you made to strike,
Nor caviled at the cut in King Arthur's house;      2275
My head fell to my feet, yet steadfast I stood,
And you, all unharmed, are wholly dismayed—
Wherefore the better man I, by all odds,

8. In good time.

                              must be."
                    Said Gawain, "Strike once more;        2280
                    I shall neither flinch nor flee;
                    But if my head falls to the floor
                    There is no mending me!"

"But go on, man, in God's name, and get to the point!
Deliver me my destiny, and do it out of hand,                2285
For I shall stand to the stroke and stir not an inch
Till your ax has hit home—on my honor I swear it!"
"Have at thee then!" said the other, and heaves it aloft,
And glares down as grimly as he had gone mad.
He made a mighty feint, but marred not his hide;            2290
Withdrew the ax adroitly before it did damage.
Gawain gave no ground, nor glanced up aside,
But stood still as a stone, or else a stout stump
That is held in hard earth by a hundred roots.
Then merrily does he mock him, the man all in green:        2295
"So now you have your nerve again, I needs must strike;
Uphold the high knighthood that Arthur bestowed,
And keep your neck-bone clear, if this cut allows!"
Then was Gawain gripped with rage, and grimly he said,
"Why, thrash away, tyrant, I tire of your threats;          2300
You make such a scene, you must frighten yourself."
Said the green fellow, "In faith, so fiercely you speak
That I shall finish this affair, nor further grace
                              allow."
                    He stands prepared to strike          2305
                    And scowls with both lip and brow;
                    No marvel if the man mislike
                    Who can hope no rescue now.

He gathered up the grim ax and guided it well:
Let the barb at the blade's end brush the bare throat;      2310
He hammered down hard, yet harmed him no whit
Save a scratch on one side, that severed the skin;
The end of the hooked edge entered the flesh,
And a little blood lightly leapt to the earth.
And when the man beheld his own blood bright on the snow,   2315
He sprang a spear's length with feet spread wide,
Seized his high helm, and set it on his head,
Shoved before his shoulders the shield at his back,
Bares his trusty blade, and boldly he speaks—
Not since he was a babe born of his mother                  2320
Was he once in this world one-half so blithe—
"Have done with your hacking—harry me no more!

I have borne, as behooved, one blow in this place;
If you make another move I shall meet it midway
And promptly, I promise you, pay back each blow          2325
                    with brand.
            One stroke acquits me here;
            So did our covenant stand
            In Arthur's court last year—
            Wherefore, sir, hold your hand!"          2330

He lowers the long ax and leans on it there,
Sets his arms on the head, the haft on the earth,
And beholds the bold knight that bides there afoot,
How he faces him fearless, fierce in full arms,
And plies him with proud words—it pleases him well.          2335
Then once again gaily to Gawain he calls,
And in a loud voice and lusty, delivers these words:
"Bold fellow, on this field your anger forbear!
No man has made demands here in manner uncouth,
Nor done, save as duly determined at court.          2340
I owed you a hit and you have it; be happy therewith!
The rest of my rights here I freely resign.
Had I been a bit busier, a buffet, perhaps,
I could have dealt more directly, and done you some harm.
First I flourished with a feint, in frolicsome mood,          2345
And left your hide unhurt—and here I did well
By the fair terms we fixed on the first night;
And fully and faithfully you followed accord:
Gave over all your gains as a good man should.
A second feint, sir, I assigned for the morning          2350
You kissed my comely wife—each kiss you restored.
For both of these there behooved but two feigned blows
                    by right.
            True men pay what they owe;
            No danger then in sight.          2355
            You failed at the third throw,
            So take my tap, sir knight.

"For that is my belt about you, that same braided girdle,
My wife it was that wore it; I know well the tale,
And the count of your kisses and your conduct too,          2360
And the wooing of my wife—it was all my scheme!
She made trial of a man most faultless by far
Of all that ever walked over the wide earth;
As pearls to white peas, more precious and prized,
So is Gawain, in good faith, to other gay knights.          2365
Yet you lacked, sir, a little in loyalty there,

But the cause was not cunning, nor courtship either,
But that you loved your own life; the less, then, to blame."
The other stout knight in a study stood a long while,
So gripped with grim rage that his great heart shook.          2370
All the blood of his body burned in his face
As he shrank back in shame from the man's sharp speech.
The first words that fell from the fair knight's lips:
"Accursed be a cowardly and covetous heart!
In you is villainy and vice, and virtue laid low!"          2375
Then he grasps the green girdle and lets go the knot,
Hands it over in haste, and hotly he says:
"Behold there my falsehood, ill hap betide it!
Your cut taught me cowardice, care for my life,
And coveting came after, contrary both          2380
To largesse and loyalty belonging to knights.
Now am I faulty and false, that fearful was ever
Of disloyalty and lies, bad luck to them both!
                    and greed.
          I confess, knight, in this place,          2385
          Most dire is my misdeed;
          Let me gain back your good grace,
          And thereafter I shall take heed."

Then the other laughed aloud, and lightly he said,
"Such harm as I have had, I hold it quite healed.          2390
You are so fully confessed, your failings made known,
And bear the plain penance of the point of my blade,
I hold you polished as a pearl, as pure and as bright
As you had lived free of fault since first you were born.
And I give you, sir, this girdle that is gold-hemmed          2395
And green as my garments, that, Gawain, you may
Be mindful of this meeting when you mingle in throng
With nobles of renown—and known by this token
How it chanced at the Green Chapel, to chivalrous knights.
And you shall in this New Year come yet again          2400
And we shall finish out our feast in my fair hall,
                    with cheer."
          He urged the knight to stay,
          And said, "With my wife so dear
          We shall see you friends this day,
          Whose enmity touched you near."          2405

"Indeed," said the doughty knight, and doffed his high helm,
And held it in his hands as he offered his thanks,
"I have lingered long enough—may good luck be yours,
And He reward you well that all worship bestows!          2410

And commend me to that comely one, your courteous wife,
Both herself and that other, my honoured ladies,
That have trapped their true knight in their trammels so quaint.
But if a dullard should dote, deem it no wonder,
And through the wiles of a woman be wooed into sorrow,           2415
For so was Adam by one, when the world began,
And Solomon by many more, and Samson the mighty—
Delilah was his doom, and David thereafter
Was beguiled by Bathsheba, and bore much distress;
Now these were vexed by their devices—'twere a very joy          2420
Could one but learn to love, and believe them not.
For these were proud princes, most prosperous of old,
Past all lovers lucky, that languished under heaven,
                              bemused.
                    And one and all fell prey                    2425
                    To women that they had used;
                    If I be led astray,
                    Methinks I may be excused.

"But your girdle, God love you! I gladly shall take
And be pleased to possess, not for the pure gold,                2430
Nor the bright belt itself, nor the beauteous pendants,
Nor for wealth, nor worldly state, nor workmanship fine,
But a sign of excess it shall seem oftentimes
When I ride in renown, and remember with shame
The faults and the frailty of the flesh perverse,               2435
How its tenderness entices the foul taint of sin;
And so when praise and high prowess have pleased my heart,
A look at this love-lace will lower my pride.
But one thing would I learn, if you were not loath,
Since you are lord of yonder land where I have long sojourned    2440
With honor in your house—may you have His reward
That upholds all the heavens, highest on throne!
How runs your right name?—and let the rest go."
"That shall I give you gladly," said the Green Knight then;
"Bercilak de Hautdesert this barony I hold,                      2445
Through the might of Morgan le Fay,[9] that lodges at my house,
By subtleties of science and sorcerers' arts,
The mistress of Merlin, she has caught many a man,
For sweet love in secret she shared sometime
With that wizard, that knows well each one of your knights       2450
                    and you.
                    Morgan the Goddess, she,

9. Arthur's half-sister, an enchantress ("Faye," fairy) who sometimes abetted him, sometimes made trouble for him.

So styled by title true;
None holds so high degree
That her arts cannot subdue.                              2455

"She guided me in this guise to your glorious hall,
To assay, if such it were, the surfeit of pride
That is rumored of the retinue of the Round Table.
She put this shape upon me to puzzle your wits,
To afflict the fair queen, and frighten her to death       2460
With awe of that elvish man that eerily spoke
With his head in his hand before the high table.
She was with my wife at home, that old withered lady,
Your own aunt is she,[1] Arthur's half-sister,
The Duchess' daughter of Tintagel, that dear King Uther    2465
Got Arthur on after, that honored is now.
And therefore, good friend, come feast with your aunt;
Make merry in my house; my men hold you dear,
And I wish you as well, sir, with all my heart,
As any mortal man, for your matchless faith."             2470
But the knight said him nay, that he might by no means.
They clasped then and kissed, and commended each other
To the Prince of Paradise, and parted with one
                              assent.
          Gawain sets out anew;                           2475
          Toward the court his course is bent;
          And the knight all green in hue,
          Wheresoever he wished, he went.

Wild ways in the world our worthy knight rides
On Gringolet, that by grace had been granted his life.     2480
He harbored often in houses, and often abroad,
And with many valiant adventures verily he met
That I shall not take time to tell in this story.
The hurt was whole that he had had in his neck,
And the bright green belt on his body he bore,             2485
Oblique, like a baldric, bound at his side,
Below his left shoulder, laced in a knot,
In betokening of the blame he had borne for his fault;
And so to court in due course he comes safe and sound.
Bliss abounded in hall when the high-born heard            2490
That good Gawain was come; glad tidings they thought it.
The king kisses the knight, and the queen as well,
And many a comrade came to clasp him in arms,

1. Morgan was the daughter of Igraine, Duchess of Tintagel, and her husband, the Duke. Igraine conceived Arthur when his father, Uther, lay with her through one of Merlin's trickeries.

And eagerly they asked, and awesomely he told,
Confessed all his cares and discomfitures many,      2495
How it chanced at the Chapel, what cheer made the knight,
The love of the lady, the green lace at last.
The nick on his neck he naked displayed
That he got in his disgrace at the Green Knight's hands,
                            alone.      2500
              With rage in heart he speaks,
              And grieves with many a groan;
              The blood burns in his cheeks
              For shame at what must be shown.

"Behold, sir," said he, and handles the belt,      2505
"This is the blazon of the blemish that I bear on my neck;
This is the sign of sore loss that I have suffered there
For the cowardice and coveting that I came to there;
This is the badge of false faith that I was found in there,
And I must bear it on my body till I breathe my last.      2510
For one may keep a deed dark, but undo it no whit,
For where a fault is made fast, it is fixed evermore."
The king comforts the knight, and the court all together
Agree with gay laughter and gracious intent
That the lords and the ladies belonging to the Table,      2515
Each brother of that band, a baldric should have,
A belt borne oblique, of a bright green,
To be worn with one accord for that worthy's sake.
So that was taken as a token by the Table Round,
And he honored that had it, evermore after,      2520
As the best book of knighthood bids it be known.
In the old days of Arthur this happening befell;
The books of Brutus' deeds bear witness thereto
Since Brutus, the bold knight, embarked for this land
After the siege ceased at Troy and the city fared      2525
                          amiss.
              Many such, ere we were born,
              Have befallen here, ere this.
              May He that was crowned with thorn
              Bring all men to His bliss! Amen.      2530

---

# GEOFFREY CHAUCER
## 1340?–1400

Although the French produced the richest and most influential body of vernacular literature in the Middle Ages, the greatest writers of the period were an Italian, Dante, and an Englishman, Chaucer. The Florentine poet and the Londoner both wrote their most important works in the fourteenth century, the former in its early decades, the latter in its latest. In origin and background, both represent the point of view of the upper middle class or the lesser gentry, groups which were not sharply separated in the urban life of Italy and of London in the later medieval centuries. Both were active in public affairs; both on occasion were envoys of their respective governments. Dante was once responsible for widening a street in Florence, and Chaucer for a time held a post comparable to that of an under secretary of the interior in the cabinet of the United States. If Dante had sharper political convictions and a greater theoretical interest in the philosophy of government, Chaucer held a wider variety of offices—and held them longer.

Geoffrey Chaucer was born in 1340 or a few years later, the son of a London wine merchant. In 1357 he apparently became a page in the household of the Countess of Ulster, wife of Lionel, a son of King Edward III. In 1359, in military service with the English in France, he was captured by the French and ransomed with royal funds. Between 1368 and 1378 Chaucer made several journeys to France and Italy as king's envoy or courier. In 1374 he received a pension from John of Gaunt, a son of Edward III, and became comptroller of customs in the port of London; about 1385 he moved to Kent, where he was elected knight of the shire in 1386, and sat in Parliament for one term. In 1389 he became Clerk of the King's Works (under Richard II), in 1391 deputy forester of the royal forest of North Petherton in Somerset, and in 1399 pensioner of King Henry IV. He died in 1400.

His early works include *The Romance of the Rose*, a translation (probably never finished) of the *Roman de la Rose*; the *Book of the Duchess*; the *House of Fame*; the *Parliament of Fowls*—all in English verse. He also translated A *Treatise on the Astrolabe* and Boethius' *Consolation of Philosophy* into English prose. His major works are *Troilus and Criseyde*, completed about 1385; and *The Canterbury Tales*, composed largely in the 1390s but with some use of earlier material.

Both Dante and Chaucer probably lived out their lives as laymen; their view of the world is free from any bias due to a clerical vocation. Yet both were completely orthodox in religion and theology. Dante was severe with heretics and schismatics, and Chaucer was neither a Wycliffite nor a sympathizer with the Peasants' Revolt. With the partial exception of Dante's insistence on the equal status of the Holy Roman Empire and the Papacy, alike providentially sponsored, it may be said that both poets found themselves in harmony with the traditional institutions and patterns of medieval civilization. Both were keenly aware of injustices resulting from abuses of the system; each exposed rascals with enthusiasm—Dante with bitterness, Chaucer with amusement. But their denunciation of wicked rulers and their satire directed against the worldliness of bishops and abbots and the corruptness of friars and pardoners do not show either writer to be a rebel against the established institutions of Church or State. The background against which abuses are portrayed is always, implicitly or explicitly, the ideal pattern for the king or priest or monk—not some utopian or revolutionary social order which would dispense with or radically alter the patterns themselves.

On the ultimate issues of human life, as in these questions of the structure of civilization, the two greatest literary geniuses of the Middle Ages were in agreement with each other and with their fellow men. For each, God was the center of the universe, as man and his earth were the center of the cosmic order. Man's goal was union with God; if he attained it—after this short earthly life—he would spend eternity in heaven; if he missed it, then hell awaited him. For man's direction and guidance toward the good in this life and the next, there were the divinely ordained religion and its Church, and the divinely approved hierarchy of society on earth. As men of independent intelligence, of education—and of essentially middle-class origin—both Dante and Chaucer insisted that true nobility depends on intrinsic character, not the accident of birth. But the modern conceptions of political, social, and economic equality, and complete religious freedom, would have appeared to them as anarchy. They had fundamental faith in the quite different patterns of institutional hierarchy and authority.

If Dante chose the life after death as the theme of the greatest medieval poem, Chaucer chose a religious pilgrimage as the framework of the richest portrayal of medieval men and women in the earthly scene. Chaucer's pilgrims are not dead, but very much alive; they are on their way to thank St. Thomas of Canterbury for his help in keeping them in that state! Yet the twenty-nine travelers, including those described in the course of the pilgrimage, are not incomparable in number or vividness to the characters presented with similar fullness in *The Divine Comedy*. Both poets—when they wish—make the individual stand out clearly and distinctly; both—when they choose—present fully the background, the milieu, the occupational or moral setting from which the individual emerges and in terms of which he is to be estimated. Both poets sketch the portraits with extraordinary insight, discrimination, and perception of the subtle mixture of good and bad in humanity. It would be interesting to attempt the assignment of Chaucer's pilgrims to their proper places in *The Divine Comedy*—assuming that each of them dies in the condition described in the Prologue.

With the Knight, the Parson, his brother the Plowman, the Clerk of Oxford, and the Nun's Priest (who is characterized in the course of the journey) we should have no trouble. Though thoroughly human, flesh-and-blood people, these are all wholly excellent and admirable men. Moral and ethical nobility is a part of their personal and vocational perfection. They embody—not personify as abstractions—the ideal characteristics of men in their several stations in life; they are models as well as individuals. But these individuals are living men on earth. We recognize in the portrait of the Clerk, for instance, an ingredient of tacit humor hardly duplicated in Dante's presentation of the blessed. The Clerk's unique traits of temperament and taste—the concise habit of speech, the aloofness, the ardent book-collecting—might be a little irrelevant in Heaven, while eminently suited to his portrait in this world.

The scoundrels, likewise, would be easy to deal with. The Friar, the Pardoner, the Summoner, and, I fear, also the Shipman, the Reeve, the Manciple, and the Miller, would easily find their respective niches in the circles of Hell—most of them in the ten subdivisions of the eighth circle, in which those guilty of various kinds of fraud are punished. Dante might have made each of them tell his story in much the same terms as Chaucer used. He would have done it with as much gusto; indeed, his work includes parallels to most of them. But denunciation and contempt would have replaced Chaucer's detached delight in the cleverness and success of their rascality. Again, the vantage point dictates an appropriate difference of treatment; time and our earth are a different background from eternity and Hell. Both Dante's and Chaucer's portraits achieve symmetry. But Dante's are more decisive, more limited, more exclusively concentrated on ethical definition; Chaucer's have room for more mundane, personal, and morally neutral detail.

We should have great difficulty in classifying some of the others. The exquisite Prioress is doubtless destined for Heaven. But should we expect to find her, fairly soon, among the blessed in one of the three lowest spheres— the moon, Mercury, or Venus? Is she, like Piccarda, a soul whose unquestionably genuine devotion is linked with an intrinsically limited spiritual capacity—limited in a way suggested by her unmonastic fondness for pet dogs, nice clothes, and fashionable manners? Or is her sensibility an outward sign of great spiritual endowment, so that, after some time on the terraces of Purgatory, she will be found among the higher spheres of the celestial hierarchy? Dante had to decide such questions concerning his characters, and his portraits naturally show how they fit the classifications. Chaucer did not have to decide; his pilgrims still belong to the earth, and some of their portraits are executed without conclusive moral definition. The worldly, hunting Monk, a fine figure of a man—will he take his place among the avaricious or the hypocrites in Hell? Or will he purge his worldliness, like Pope Adrian, on the fifth ledge of the mountain?

In general, Chaucer shows a large "middle" group of people, confirmed perhaps in neither wickedness nor holiness, but absorbed in the things of this world. Such an absorption exposes the professed cleric, secular or monastic, to ironical satire; for the religious vocation involves renunciation of the world. This is why many of the pilgrims connected with the Church are obvious targets. But laymen also run the risk of ridicule if their absorption in worldly matters leads to excessive egotism or affectation or limitation of perspective. Thus the Sergeant of the Law, whose days are, in fact, full, *seems* even busier than he is; the Merchant apparently talks entirely about profits; and the Physician's financial astuteness is not unmixed with complacency. The Franklin's pride in his hospitality and fine table is a more attractive form of egotism—although one might hesitate to become his cook! Traits like these, casually mentioned in the Prologue, would be valuable hints as to where on the terraces of Purgatory the several pilgrims might be expected to spend some time. Meanwhile, it is just such qualities, the weaknesses, foibles, excesses, and limitations, that endow them with distinctness and poignancy in this world—in short, with individuality and personality.

It is often said that the characters in the Prologue are delineated in terms of the superlative—each of the pilgrims is the best, or worst, representative of his particular kind of human being. This is true. Yet it is also true that Chaucer finds far less to say about some than about others. He is, in fact, interested in them in different ways. Thus the Knight is described at length; occupationally, ethically, and otherwise he emerges as an individual member of a class. His son, the young Squire, is presented primarily as a fine but standard specimen of his type, the fashionable young warrior and politely cultivated "lover." And in their servant, the Yeoman, we see a yet smaller segment of the whole character: he is simply an expert woodsman. Other pilgrims, like the five Guildsmen, receive only a collective portrait; they all share in the pride of their crafts and their organized "fraternity," in the garb of which they are handsomely turned out. A few of the company are not described at all in the Prologue.

Evidently Chaucer has allowed himself a margin of freedom in his account of this imaginary company as they present themselves to the imaginary observer and fellow traveler, the poet. With the future possibilities of the pilgrimage in mind, he readily leaves a few members of the group undeveloped; one of these, the Nun's Priest, does emerge in full characterization as the tales proceed. But in the Prologue itself Chaucer gives us the fullest, the most varied, and the liveliest, panorama of men and women in medieval literature. The portraits are usually fairly complete and satisfying in themselves, though, as we have noted, some are miniatures and some large canvases, some are full face, some profile, and a few quarter face. Yet the portraits are not merely lively in themselves; they are dynamic; they prepare us for the highly dramatic relationships which develop among the pilgrims in the course of the journey.

### THE MILLER'S TALE

At the end of the General Prologue we are told that the Knight will tell the first tale. This narrative, not included in our book, is a fine example of medieval metrical romance—with important variations from the standard types. As we learn from the words between the Host and the Miller, the latter, now drunk, refuses to follow the decorous order preferred by the Host; he insists on matching the Knight right now with his tale. When he goes on to say that it will be a story of an old carpenter, his wife, and her student lover, we anticipate, rightly, that it will be the opposite of the Knight's courtly romance. Like the medieval reader, we expect a tale of amorous intrigue and trickery involving people of considerably less than noble rank, in short, a fabliau. But the carpenter's wife, Alison, has not only a husband, John, and a lover, Nicholas; there is also a would-be lover, the parish clerk, Absalom. There is thus a double triangle plot, with Alison at the apex of both triangles; and the denouement comes when one triangle crashes down on the other!

This addition to the traditional kind of fabliau plot is one part of Chaucer's vast enrichment of what must have been a fairly stereotyped narrative. In mediocre tales of this sort the plot is the thing—almost the whole thing; they are comic anecdotes. But Chaucer has lavished as much effort on characterization and depiction of scenes as one expects in the best serious literature. We get to know the clever, opportunistic, cynical Nicholas very well indeed. His rival, Absalom, is a complete contrast. He is theatrical, sentimental, and silly; his "love" songs are an amusing parody of the poetic pleas of chivalric suitors. (Nicholas is much too practical and hardheaded to go in for amorous complaints; he keeps his eye on the main chance—and he is right; he knows how to manage Alison, as Absalom does not.)

The vivid, detailed description of Alison, rich in comparisons and fresh images, would remind the medieval reader of traditional portraits of ladies in romances—by difference rather than similarity. Instead of the noble lady, a standard blonde, looking out placidly from a castle window, we have Alison, neat, washed, bright as a new coin, skipping like a colt. The personality of John, the carpenter, is similarly enlarged and deepened. Here the prototype was an old husband married to a young wife; he was jealous and suspicious. Chaucer's John is a great deal more than this. He is genuinely devoted to his wife—he dotes on her; he is fond of Nicholas, his student lodger, though he also believes in the common-sense advantages of the ordinary man (himself) over the scholar; he is attractively gullible: He embraces the plan for dealing with the flood with great gusto.

The denouement of the Miller's Tale does not satisfy the requirements of poetic justice; it does not reward the good and punish the wicked—at least, not consistently. Instead, it penalizes stupidity and vindicates cleverness. Moreover, characterization and plot sustain each other: the various individuals do the kinds of things that we are willing to believe that these kinds of people would do. And there is room for variation within the basic pattern: The ingenuity of Nicholas is duly rewarded, but when overconfidence leads him to overreach himself a bit (both metaphorically and literally), he suffers in the end. Alison's cleverness is unflawed by such excess—and she escapes.

### THE PARDONER'S TALE

The Pardoner is one of the liveliest rascals on the Canterbury pilgrimage. His rascality is so complete that it may be difficult for us to realize just what a pardoner was properly or ideally like in the fourteenth century. For one thing, a legitimate pardoner did not go about "pardoning" people for their sins. Many such men were not—and were not expected to be—priests, in the proper sense of the term, at all. Many doubtless were in what is called minor orders, extending up to subdeacon. Such men were not qualified or authorized to hear confession or grant absolution. The legitimate activity of a pardoner consisted in making available to devout persons a certificate of ecclesiastical "indulgence." The charge made for this constituted a gift or offering to God and the Church. The purchase was therefore considered a worthy act in the sight of God which might benefit the souls of the purchaser's relatives or friends if they were doing penance in purgatory (but *not* if they had been sent to hell).

No doubt there were many perfectly honest and worthy pardoners in medieval Europe. But the opportunities for personal profit are evident, and there must have been some who exploited these opportunities unscrupulously. The satiric literature of the time tells us much about bad pardoners, and Chaucer's is clearly one of them. Besides distributing indulgences of doubtful validity, he preaches in country churches, intimidating the congregation so that they will not fail to put money in the collection plate; and he makes a good profit out of fake relics. Far from being ashamed of these vices, Chaucer's Pardoner is proud of his skill in dishonesty. He tells us all about it in the Prologue to his tale.

The Pardoner's Tale itself, furthermore, is a sample of his preaching. The text of the sermon is his favorite: Covetousness is the root of evil. It is ironical, of course, that such a man should preach so regularly and strenuously against his own greatest sin. His sermon, as Chaucer gives it, is really a very old and simple story about three men who went in search of Death and found him unexpectedly. The Pardoner dramatizes the narrative with great energy and imagination. In addition, he embroiders it with brief anecdotes which are really digressions. Before he has got really started on the story, moreover, he takes time out for a ringing denunciation of gluttony (including drunkenness), gambling, and swearing—complete with examples of each.

The tale of Chanticleer and Dame Partlet is Chaucer at his best. Since the basic story, of a cock, a hen, and a fox, is rich in human implications and applications and in intrinsic humor it must have been especially congenial to the imaginative comic spirit of the mature Chaucer—and it apparently does belong to a late period in the composition of *The Canterbury Tales*. For its narrator the poet chose the genial Priest who rode with the two nuns on the pilgrimage; his good taste and inexhaustible sense of humor have been ripened by years of reading and observation of life.

The setting of the tale in the Canterbury pilgrimage contributes to its total effect. The Knight, seconded by the Host, has suddenly interrupted the Monk, who was retailing an apparently endless series of "tragedies," or tales of misfortune. This has become unendurably gloomy and dull, they protest; they want something more cheerful and entertaining! When the Monk has nothing else to offer, the Host turns to Sir John, the Priest, and bids him "Tell us a thing to make our spirits glad./Be cheerful, though the jade you ride is bad."

Thus launched, the Priest gives us a remarkable version of one of the favorite stories of the Middle Ages. For of course Chaucer did not invent the plot itself. The popular literature of Europe had long included tales of the cock's capture through his weakness for flattery, and his escape through the fox's over-weening pride. The narrative can be condensed in a paragraph or spun out to indeterminate length, according to the inclination of the narrator. The Priest, without losing sight of its identity as a moral fable, makes it many other things as well.

First, with leisurely detail and humor, he gives the cock and hen a human background. The quiet, realistic description of the circumstances of the poor widow—her narrow cottage with a small yard surrounded by a wooden fence, her three cows, three hogs, and one sheep, named Moll—reads like the beginning of a skillfully told modern short story. The implicit contrast with a great house or castle is cumulatively comic; it evokes a smile rather than a guffaw.

Then we are brought to the description of Chanticleer and his seven wives—they are part of the widow's household, indoors and outdoors. The account of the cock is at first simply "superlative," like the characterization of the Canterbury pilgrims themselves; he is initially the best imaginable cock. His regular crowing, exactly on the hour, doubtless appeared less extraordinary to Chaucer's audience than it does to us, for apparently this accuracy was commonly attributed to roosters during the medieval period. But the detailed description of his features and coloring is done in the manner of the literary portraits of heroes in romances; and the cock's comb, scalloped "like a crenelated castle wall," is a first touch of the mock-heroic. Partlet too has the virtues of highborn ladies in romances; she is courtly, discreet, and debonair. And she has held Chanticleer's firm affection since she was seven nights old!

Having been thus acquainted with the general capacities of these unusual chickens, we are now moved on to the first incident in the story itself—Chanticleer's dream. The tone here is that of ordinary, commonplace domesticity: a husband is awakened from a nightmare, which he then relates to his wife. Their further conversation is in the same vein, Partlet combining in her character both the comicstrip wife who measures her husband, reproachfully, against a standard of heroic perfection, and the more ordinary Mrs. Smith who confidently diagnoses her man's indisposition and energetically tells him what to take for it. The line "Have you no man's heart, when you have a beard?" indicates how completely the cock and hen have become a human pair.

In the matrimonial argument about the nature and significance of dreams Chaucer employs the two principal medieval theories on the subject. Doubtless he is right in assigning the physiological explanation to Partlet; women are said to be more realistic and practical than men. And we might say that her sixty-two-line speech exemplifies the feminine love of talking—if Chanticleer did not take two hundred lines to answer her! Both speeches in fact poke fun at the method of proof by citing authorities. But Chanticleer's extended monologue has a further purpose: it is structural in the development of the plot; it produces the comic irony which is at the center of the tale. For the very act of vigorously refuting Partlet and proving that dreams *do* portend danger has the effect of reassuring him. Having won the argument—to his own satisfaction and by default of rebuttal from Partlet—Chanticleer is in reality no longer disturbed about the dream. His thoughts turn exuberantly to love, and the climax of the plot is reached when he declares: "I am then so full of pure felicity/That I defy whatever sort of dream!"

Having fully established this mood in Chanticleer—having in fact characterized him in terms of superheroism—Chaucer tells us that a cunning fox has got through the hedge during the night and is now hiding in a bed of herbs in the yard, lying in wait for Chanticleer. This leads to a citation of traitors and deceivers from epic literature and an elaborate raising of the question of predestination, foreknowledge, and free will.

Next it is pointed out that Chanticleer unfortunately took his wife's advice about the dream ("Woman have many times, as wise men hold,/Offered advice that left men in the cold"), and Adam's loss of Paradise is immediately cited as a parallel. Thus we see finally that the whole situation has been presented as a kind of parody of the Fall of Man, with Chanticleer as Adam, Partlet as Eve, and the fox, now lurking but later to speak with persuasive and successful flattery, as the Serpent.

The rest of the tale is carried out in the same vein of elaborate mockery, with allusions, exclamations, and comparisons. The fox displays consummate diplomacy, Chanticleer is as naïve and susceptible as possible, and Partlet's grief is epic. The finest passage, among many excellent, is the picture of the utter confusion and uproar of men, women, beasts, and fowls when the alarm is given. At last—to provide the happy ending demanded by the Knight and the Host as well as to conform to the familiar plot of the story—comes the second reversal, when Chanticleer escapes. And in conclusion Sir John, who, for all his gift of wit and fun, is a deeply and wholesomely religious man, reminds us:

> Such is it to be reckless and unheedful
> And trust in flattery. . . .
> Think twice, and take the moral, my good men!

### CHAUCER IN MODERN ENGLISH

In this book Chaucer is presented in a Modern English version made in the twentieth century. Theodore Morrison's translation is remarkably clear, accurate, and easy to read. But, in order to get some idea of what Chaucer's original language was, we may profitably compare the first eighteen lines of the *General Prologue* in the two forms. It will be evident that changes have occurred in pronunciation, in grammatical forms, and sometimes in the use and meaning of words. Here it will be possible only to point out a few examples of these changes.

> Whan that Aprille with his shoures sote
> The droghte of Marche hath perced to the rote,
> And bathed every veyne in swich licour,
> Of which vertu engendred is the flour;
> When Zephirus eek with his swete breeth                     5
> Inspired hath in every holt and heeth
> The tendre croppes, and the yonge sonne
> Hath in the Ram his halfe cours y-ronne,
> And smale fowles maken melodye,
> That slepen al the night with open yë,                      10
> So priketh hem nature in hir corages:
> Than longen folk to goon on pilgrimages
> And palmers for to seken straunge strandes
> To ferne halwes, couthe in sondry landes;
> And specially, from every shires ende
> Of Engeland, to Caunterbury they wende,
> The holy blisful martir for to seke,
> That hem hath holpen, whan that they were seke.

In Chaucer's language (Middle English of the late fourteenth century) the letters representing the stressed vowels were pronounced about as they are in Spanish or Italian in our time. Thus the A of *Aprille* sounded like *a* in our *father*; the first *e* in *swete* (line 5) was like *a* in Modern English *late*; and the second *i* in *Inspired* (line 6) was like *i* in our *machine*. In verbs, the third person singular ends in -*th*, not -*s*, as in *hath* (line 2); and the plural ending, either -*en* or -*e*, forms a separate syllable, as in *maken* (line 9), *slepen* (line 10), and *wende* (line 16). Among the pronouns and pronominal adjectives, Chaucer's language did not have our *its*, *their*, or *them*. Instead, the corresponding forms were, respectively, *his* (line 1), *hir(e)* (line 11), and *hem* (line 18).

When differences like these occur a translator must, of course, replace the original by the modern form. Changes in the meaning or use of words may also compel a substitution. Thus Chaucer's *couthe* (line 14) has become obsolete and hence the translation has *renowned* instead; so also *corages* (line 11) becomes *hearts*, and *ferne halwes* (line 14) becomes *foreign shrines*.

It will be noted that both the original and the translation have lines regularly rhyming in couplets. Sometimes the translator has been able to keep the same rhyming words (with some difference of pronunciation) as in lines 7 and 8 and 13 and 14. In other places he has found it necessary to substitute a new rhyming pair of his own, as in lines 1 and 2 and 17 and 18—although in the first instance the translator keeps one of the original rhyming words but not the other.

The essential edition is F. N. Robinson, *The Complete Works of Geoffrey Chaucer* (1933); see also E. T. Donaldson (ed.), *Chaucer's Poetry: An Anthology for the Modern Reader* (1958). The artistic growth of the poet is sketched in Derek S. Brewer, *Chaucer* (1953). For general criticism see G. L. Kittredge, *Chaucer and His Poetry* (1915).

# The Canterbury Tales[1]

## General Prologue

As soon as April pierces to the root
The drought of March, and bathes each bud and shoot
Through every vein of sap with gentle showers
From whose engendering liquor spring the flowers;
When zephyrs[2] have breathed softly all about          5
Inspiring every wood and field to sprout,
And in the zodiac the youthful sun
His journey halfway through the Ram[3] has run;
When little birds are busy with their song
Who sleep with open eyes the whole night long          10
Life stirs their hearts and tingles in them so,
Then off as pilgrims people long to go,
And palmers[4] to set out for distant strands
And foreign shrines renowned in many lands.
And specially in England people ride          15
To Canterbury from every countryside
To visit there the blessed martyred saint[5]
Who gave them strength when they were sick and faint.
In Southwark at the Tabard[6] one spring day
It happened, as I stopped there on my way,          20
Myself a pilgrim with a heart devout

1. Selections. Translated and edited by Theodore Morrison.   2. The west wind.   3. A sign of the Zodiac (Aries); the sun is in the Ram from March 12 to April 11.   4. Pilgrims, who, originally, brought back palm leaves from the Holy Land.   5. St. Thomas à Becket, slain in Canterbury cathedral in 1170.   6. An inn at Southwark, across the river Thames from London.

Ready for Canterbury to set out,
At night came all of twenty-nine assorted
Travelers, and to that same inn resorted,
Who by a turn of fortune chanced to fall          25
In fellowship together, and they were all
Pilgrims who had it in their minds to ride
Toward Canterbury. The stable doors were wide,
The rooms were large, and we enjoyed the best,
And shortly, when the sun had gone to rest,          30
I had so talked with each that presently
I was a member of their company
And promised to rise early the next day
To start, as I shall show, upon our way.

    But none the less, while I have time and space,          35
Before this tale has gone a further pace,
I should in reason tell you the condition
Of each of them, his rank and his position,
And also what array they all were in;
And so then, with a knight I will begin.          40

    A Knight was with us, and an excellent man,
Who from the earliest moment he began
To follow his career loved chivalry,
Truth, openhandedness, and courtesy.
He was a stout man in the king's campaigns          45
And in that cause had gripped his horse's reins
In Christian lands and pagan through the earth,
None farther, and always honored for his worth.
He was on hand at Alexandria's fall.[7]
He had often sat in precedence to all          50
The nations at the banquet board in Prussia.
He had fought in Lithuania and in Russia,
No Christian knight more often; he had been
In Moorish Africa at Benmarin,
At the siege of Algeciras in Granada,          55
And sailed in many a glorious armada
In the Mediterranean, and fought as well
At Ayas and Attalia when they fell
In Armenia and on Asia Minor's coast.
Of fifteen deadly battles he could boast,          60
And in Algeria, at Tremessen,
Fought for the faith and killed three separate men
In single combat. He had done good work
Joining against another pagan Turk

---

7. In Egypt, captured in 1365 by King Peter of Cyprus.

With the king of Palathia. And he was wise,                        65
Despite his prowess, honored in men's eyes,
Meek as a girl and gentle in his ways.
He had never spoken ignobly all his days
To any man by even a rude inflection.
He was a knight in all things to perfection.                        70
He rode a good horse, but his gear was plain,
For he had lately served on a campaign.
His tunic was still spattered by the rust
Left by his coat of mail, for he had just
Returned and set out on his pilgrimage.                             75
    His son was with him, a young Squire, in age
Some twenty years as near as I could guess.
His hair curled as if taken from a press.
He was a lover and would become a knight.
In stature he was of a moderate height                              80
But powerful and wonderfully quick.
He had been in Flanders, riding in the thick
Of forays in Artois and Picardy,
And bore up well for one so young as he,
Still hoping by his exploits in such places                        85
To stand the better in his lady's graces.
He wore embroidered flowers, red and white,
And blazed like a spring meadow to the sight.
He sang or played his flute the livelong day.
He was as lusty as the month of May.                               90
His coat was short, its sleeves were long and wide.
He sat his horse well, and knew how to ride,
And how to make a song and use his lance,
And he could write and draw well, too, and dance.
So hot his love that when the moon rose pale                       95
He got no more sleep than a nightingale.
He was modest, and helped whomever he was able,
And carved as his father's squire at the table.
    But one more servant had the Knight beside,
Choosing thus simply for the time to ride:                         100
A Yeoman, in a coat and hood of green.
His peacock-feathered arrows, bright and keen,
He carried under his belt in tidy fashion.
For well-kept gear he had a yeoman's passion,
No draggled feather might his arrows show,                         105
And in his hand he held a mighty bow.
He kept his hair close-cropped, his face was brown.
He knew the lore of woodcraft up and down.
His arm was guarded from the bowstring's whip

By a bracer, gaily trimmed. He had at hip                          110
A sword and buckler, and at his other side
A dagger whose fine mounting was his pride,
Sharp-pointed as a spear. His horn he bore
In a sling of green, and on his chest he wore
A silver image of St. Christopher,                                 115
His patron, since he was a forester.
   There was also a Nun, a Prioress,
Whose smile was gentle and full of guilelessness.
"By St. Loy!"[8] was the worst oath she would say.
She sang mass well, in a becoming way,                             120
Intoning through her nose the words divine,
And she was known as Madame Eglantine.
She spoke good French, as taught at Stratford-Bow[9]
For the Parisian French she did not know.
She was schooled to eat so primly and so well                      125
That from her lips no morsel ever fell.
She wet her fingers lightly in the dish
Of sauce, for courtesy was her first wish.
With every bite she did her skillful best
To see that no drop fell upon her breast.                          130
She always wiped her upper lip so clean
That in her cup was never to be seen
A hint of grease when she had drunk her share.
She reached out for her meat with comely air.
She was a great delight, and always tried                          135
To imitate court ways, and had her pride,
Both amiable and gracious in her dealings.
As for her charity and tender feelings,
She melted at whatever was piteous.
She would weep if she but came upon a mouse                        140
Caught in a trap, if it were dead or bleeding.
Some little dogs that she took pleasure feeding
On roasted meat or milk or good wheat bread
She had, but how she wept to find one dead
Or yelping from a blow that made it smart,                         145
And all was sympathy and loving heart.
Neat was her wimple in its every plait,
Her nose well formed, her eyes as gray as slate.
Her mouth was very small and soft and red.
She had so wide a brow I think her head                            150
Was nearly a span broad, for certainly
She was not undergrown, as all could see.

8. Perhaps St. Eligius, apparently a popular saint at this time.    9. In Middlesex, near London,
where there was a nunnery.

She wore her cloak with dignity and charm,
And had her rosary about her arm,
The small beads coral and the larger green,                              155
And from them hung a brooch of golden sheen,
On it a large A and a crown above;
Beneath, "All things are subject unto love."
  A Priest accompanied her toward Canterbury,
And an attendant Nun, her secretary.                                     160
  There was a Monk, and nowhere was his peer,
A hunter, and a roving overseer.
He was a manly man, and fully able
To be an abbot. He kept a hunting stable,
And when he rode the neighborhood could hear                             165
His bridle jingling in the wind as clear
And loud as if it were a chapel bell.
Wherever he was master of a cell
The principles of good St. Benedict,[1]
For being a little old and somewhat strict,                              170
Were honored in the breach, as past their prime.
He lived by the fashion of a newer time.
He would have swapped that text for a plucked hen
Which says that hunters are not holy men,
Or a monk outside his discipline and rule                                175
Is too much like a fish outside his pool;
That is to say, a monk outside his cloister.
But such a text he deemed not worth an oyster.
I told him his opinion made me glad.
Why should he study always and go mad,                                   180
Mewed in his cell with only a book for neighbor?
Or why, as Augustine commanded, labor
And sweat his hands? How shall the world be served?
To Augustine be all such toil reserved!
And so he hunted, as was only right.                                     185
He had greyhounds as swift as birds in flight.
His taste was all for tracking down the hare,
And what his sport might cost he did not care.
His sleeves I noticed, where they met his hand,
Trimmed with gray fur, the finest in the land.                           190
His hood was fastened with a curious pin
Made of wrought gold and clasped beneath his chin,
A love knot at the tip. His head might pass,
Bald as it was, for a lump of shining glass,
And his face was glistening as if anointed.                              195

1. Monastic rules, authored by St. Maurus and St. Benedict in the sixth century A.D.

Fat as a lord he was, and well appointed.
His eyes were large, and rolled inside his head
As if they gleamed from a furnace of hot lead.
His boots were supple, his horse superbly kept.
He was a prelate to dream of while you slept.     200
He was not pale nor peaked like a ghost.
He relished a plump swan as his favorite roast.
He rode a palfrey brown as a ripe berry.
   A Friar was with us, a gay dog and a merry,
Who begged his district with a jolly air.     205
No friar in all four orders could compare
With him for gallantry; his tongue was wooing.
Many a girl was married by his doing,
And at his own cost it was often done.
He was a pillar, and a noble one,     210
To his whole order. In his neighborhood
Rich franklins[2] knew him well, who served good food,
and worthy women welcomed him to town;
For the license that his order handed down,
He said himself, conferred on him possession     215
Of more than a curate's power of confession.
Sweetly the list of frailties he heard,
Assigning penance with a pleasant word.
He was an easy man for absolution
Where he looked forward to a contribution,     220
For if to a poor order a man has given
It signifies that he has been well shriven,
And if a sinner let his purse be dented
The Friar would stake his oath he had repented.
For many men become so hard of heart     225
They cannot weep, though conscience makes them smart.
Instead of tears and prayers, then, let the sinner
Supply the poor friars with the price of dinner.
For pretty women he had more than shrift.
His cape was stuffed with many a little gift,     230
As knives and pins and suchlike. He could sing
A merry note, and pluck a tender string,
And had no rival at all in balladry.
His neck was whiter than a fleur-de-lis,[3]
And yet he could have knocked a strong man down.     235
He knew the taverns well in every town.
The barmaids and innkeepers pleased his mind
Better than beggars and lepers and their kind.

---

2. Landowners or country squires, not belonging to the nobility.   3. Lily.

In his position it was unbecoming
Among the wretched lepers to go slumming.                    240
It mocks all decency, it sews no stitch
To deal with such riffraff, but with the rich,
With sellers of victuals, that's another thing.
Wherever he saw some hope of profiting,
None so polite, so humble. He was good,                      245
The champion beggar of his brotherhood.
Should a woman have no shoes against the snow,
So pleasant was his "*In principio*"[4]
He would have her widow's mite before he went.
He took in far more than he paid in rent                     250
For his right of begging within certain bounds.
None of his brethren trespassed on his grounds!
He loved as freely as a half-grown whelp.
On arbitration-days[5] he gave great help,
For his cloak was never shiny nor threadbare                 255
Like a poor cloistered scholar's. He had an air
As if he were a doctor or a pope.
It took stout wool to make his semicope[6]
That plumped out like a bell for portliness.
He lisped a little in his rakishness                         260
To make his English sweeter on his tongue,
And twanging his harp to end some song he'd sung
His eyes would twinkle in his head as bright
As the stars twinkle on a frosty night.
Hubert this gallant Friar was by name.                       265
    Among the rest a Merchant also came.
He wore a forked beard and a beaver hat
From Flanders. High up in the saddle he sat,
In figured cloth, his boots clasped handsomely,
Delivering his opinions pompously,                           270
Always on how his gains might be increased.
At all costs he desired the sea policed
From Middleburg in Holland to Orwell.[7]
He knew the exchange rates, and the time to sell
French currency, and there was never yet                     275
A man who could have told he was in debt
So grave he seemed and hid so well his feelings
With all his shrewd engagements and close dealings.
You'd find no better man at any turn;
But what his name was I could never learn.                   280

4. "In the beginning"—the opening phrase of a famous passage in the Gospels (John 1:1–16), which the friar recites in Latin as a devotional exercise to awe the ignorant and extract their alms.    5. Days appointed for the adjustment of disputes.    6. A short cape.    7. He desired protection from piracy between Middleburg in Holland and Orwell, an English port near Harwich.

    There was an Oxford Student too, it chanced,
Already in his logic well advanced.
He rode a mount as skinny as a rake,
And he was hardly fat. For learning's sake
He let himself look hollow and sober enough.      285
He wore an outer coat of threadbare stuff,
For he had no benefice for his enjoyment
And was too unworldly for some lay employment.
He much preferred to have beside his bed
His twenty volumes bound in black or red      290
All packed with Aristotle from end to middle
Than a sumptuous wardrobe or a merry fiddle.
For though he knew what learning had to offer
There was little coin to jingle in his coffer.
Whatever he got by touching up a friend      295
On books and learning he would promptly spend
And busily pray for the soul of anybody
Who furnished him the wherewithal for study.
His scholarship was what he truly heeded.
He never spoke a word more than was needed,      300
And that was said with dignity and force,
And quick and brief. He was of grave discourse
Giving new weight to virtue by his speech,
And gladly would he learn and gladly teach.

    There was a Lawyer, cunning and discreet,      305
Who had often been to St. Paul's porch[8] to meet
His clients. He was a Sergeant of the Law,
A man deserving to be held in awe,
Or so he seemed, his manner was so wise.
He had often served as Justice of Assize      310
By the king's appointment, with a broad commission,
For his knowledge and his eminent position.
He had many a handsome gift by way of fee.
There was no buyer of land as shrewd as he.
All ownership to him became fee simple.[9]      315
His titles were never faulty by a pimple.
None was so busy as he with case and cause,
And yet he seemed much busier than he was.
In all cases and decisions he was schooled
That were of record since King William[1] ruled.      320
No one could pick a loophole or a flaw
In any lease or contract he might draw.
Each statute on the books he knew by rote.

8. A meeting place for lawyers and their clients.    9. Owned outright without legal impediments.    1. The conqueror, reigned 1066–1087.

He traveled in a plain, silk-belted coat.
    A Franklin traveled in his company.                                      325
Whiter could never daisy petal[2] be
Than was his beard. His ruddy face gave sign
He liked his morning sop of toast in wine.
He lived in comfort, as he would assure us,
For he was a true son of Epicurus[3]                                          330
Who held the opinion that the only measure
Of perfect happiness was simply pleasure.
Such hospitality did he provide,
He was St. Julian[4] to his countryside.
His bread and ale were always up to scratch.                                  335
He had a cellar none on earth could match.
There was no lack of pasties in his house,
Both fish and flesh, and that so plenteous
That where he lived it snowed of meat and drink.
With every dish of which a man can think,                                     340
After the various seasons of the year,
He changed his diet for his better cheer.
He had coops of partridges as fat as cream,
He had a fishpond stocked with pike and bream.
Woe to his cook for an unready pot                                            345
Or a sauce that wasn't seasoned and spiced hot!
A table in his hall stood on display
Prepared and covered through the livelong day.
He presided at court sessions for his bounty
And sat in Parliament often for his county.                                   350
A well-wrought dagger and a purse of silk
Hung at his belt, as white as morning milk.
He had been a sheriff and county auditor.
On earth was no such rich proprietor!
    There were five Guildsmen, in the livery                                 355
Of one august and great fraternity,
A Weaver, a Dyer, and a Carpenter,
A Tapestry-maker and a Haberdasher.
Their gear was furbished new and clean as glass.
The mountings of their knives were not of brass                               360
But silver. Their pouches were well made and neat,
And each of them, it seemed, deserved a seat
On the platform at the Guildhall, for each one
Was likely timber to make an alderman.
They had goods enough, and money to be spent,                                 365

2. The English daisy, a small white flower; not the same as the American.    3. The Greek
philosopher whose teaching (presented here in a somewhat debased form) is believed to make
pleasure the goal of life.    4. Patron saint of hospitality.

Also their wives would willingly consent
And would have been at fault if they had not.
For to be "Madamed" is a pleasant lot,
And to march in first at feasts for being well married,
And royally to have their mantles carried.       370
    For the pilgrimage these Guildsmen brought their own
Cook to boil their chicken and marrow bone
With seasoning powder and capers and sharp spice.
In judging London ale his taste was nice.
He well knew how to roast and broil and fry,       375
To mix a stew, and bake a good meat pie,
Or capon creamed with almond, rice, and egg.
Pity he had an ulcer on his leg!
    A Skipper was with us, his home far in the west.
He came from the port of Dartmouth, as I guessed.       380
He sat his carthorse pretty much at sea
In a coarse smock that joggled on his knee.
From his neck a dagger on a string hung down
Under his arm. His face was burnished brown
By the summer sun. He was a true good fellow.       385
Many a time he had tapped a wine cask mellow
Sailing from Bordeaux while the owner slept.
Too nice a point of honor he never kept.
In a sea fight, if he got the upper hand,
Drowned prisoners floated home to every land.       390
But in navigation, whether reckoning tides,
Currents, or what might threaten him besides,
Harborage, pilotage, or the moon's demeanor,
None was his like from Hull to Cartagena.[5]
He knew each harbor and the anchorage there       395
From Gotland to the Cape of Finisterre[6]
And every creek in Brittany and Spain,
And he had called his ship the *Madeleine*.
    With us came also an astute Physician.
There was none like him for a disquisition       400
On the art of medicine or surgery,
For he was grounded in astrology.
He kept his patient long in observation,
Choosing the proper hour for application
Of charms and images by intuition       405
Of magic, and the planets' best position.
For he was one who understood the laws
That rule the humors, and could tell the cause

5. A Spanish port. *Hull*: In England.     6. On the Spanish coast. *Gotland*: A Swedish island.

That brought on every human malady,
Whether of hot or cold, or moist or dry.                    410
He was a perfect medico, for sure.
The cause once known, he would prescribe the cure
For he had his druggists ready at a motion
To provide the sick man with some pill or potion—
A game of mutual aid, with each one winning.                    415
Their partnership was hardly just beginning!
He was well versed in his authorities,
Old Aesculapius, Dioscorides,
Rufus, and old Hippocrates, and Galen,
Haly, and Rhazes, and Serapion,                    420
Averroës, Bernard, Johannes Damascenus,
Avicenna, Gilbert, Gaddesden, Constantinus.[7]
He urged a moderate fare on principle,
But rich in nourishment, digestible;
Of nothing in excess would he admit.                    425
He gave but little heed to Holy Writ.
His clothes were lined with taffeta; their hue
Was all of blood red and of Persian blue,
Yet he was far from careless of expense.
He saved his fees from times of pestilence,                    430
For gold is a cordial, as physicians hold,
And so he had a special love for gold.
    A worthy woman there was from near the city
Of Bath,[8] but somewhat deaf, and more's the pity.
For weaving she possessed so great a bent                    435
She outdid the people of Ypres and of Ghent.[9]
No other woman dreamed of such a thing
As to precede her at the offering,
Or if any did, she fell in such a wrath
She dried up all the charity in Bath.                    440
She wore fine kerchiefs of old-fashioned air,
And on a Sunday morning, I could swear,
She had ten pounds of linen on her head.
Her stockings were of finest scarlet-red,
Laced tightly, and her shoes were soft and new.                    445
Bold was her face, and fair, and red in hue.
She had been an excellent woman all her life
Five men in turn had taken her to wife,
Omitting other youthful company—
But let that pass for now! Over the sea                    450

7. A list of eminent medical authorities from ancient Greece, ancient and medieval Arabic civilization, and England in the thirteenth and fourteenth centuries.    8. A town in the southwest of England.    9. Towns in Flanders famous for their cloth.

She had traveled freely; many a distant stream
She crossed, and visited Jerusalem
Three times. She had been at Rome and at Boulogne,
At the shrine of Compostella, and at Cologne.[1]
She had wandered by the way through many a scene     455
Her teeth were set with little gaps between.[2]
Easily on her ambling horse she sat.
She was well wimpled, and she wore a hat
As wide in circuit as a shield or targe.[3]
A skirt swathed up her hips, and they were large.     460
Upon her feet she wore sharp-roweled spurs.
She was a good fellow; a ready tongue was hers.
All remedies of love she knew by name,[4]
For she had all the tricks of that old game.

    There was a good man of the priests' vocation,     465
A poor town Parson of true consecration,
But he was rich in holy thought and work.
Learned he was, in the truest sense a clerk
Who meant Christ's gospel faithfully to preach
And truly his parishioners to teach.     470
He was a kind man, full of industry,
Many times tested by adversity
And always patient. If tithes[5] were in arrears,
He was loth to threaten any man with fears
Of excommunication; past a doubt     475
He would rather spread his offering about
To his poor flock, or spend his property.
To him a little meant sufficiency.
Wide was his parish, with houses far asunder,
But he would not be kept by rain or thunder,     480
If any had suffered a sickness or a blow,
From visiting the farthest, high or low
Plodding his way on foot, his staff in hand.
He was a model his flock could understand,
For first he did and afterward he taught.     485
That precept from the Gospel he had caught,
And he added as a metaphor thereto,
"If the gold rusts, what will the iron do?"
For if a priest is foul, in whom we trust,
No wonder a layman shows a little rust.     490
A priest should take to heart the shameful scene
Of shepherds filthy while the sheep are clean.

---

1. Sites of shrines much visited by pilgrims.     2. I.e., gap-toothed; in a woman considered a
sign of sexual prowess.     3. A small shield.     4. Chaucer has Ovid's *Love Cures* (*Remedia
Amoris*) in mind.     5. Payments due to the priest, usually a tenth of annual income.

By his own purity a priest should give
The example to his sheep, how they should live.
He did not rent his benefice for hire,[6]                    495
Leaving his flock to flounder in the mire,
And run to London, happiest of goals,
To sing paid masses in St. Paul's for souls,
Or as chaplain from some rich guild take his keep,
But dwelt at home and guarded well his sheep                    500
So that no wolf should make his flock miscarry.
He was a shepherd, and not a mercenary.
And though himself a man of strict vocation
He was not harsh to weak souls in temptation,
Not overbearing nor haughty in his speech,                    505
But wise and kind in all he tried to teach.
By good example and just words to turn
Sinners to heaven was his whole concern.
But should a man in truth prove obstinate,
Whoever he was, of rich or mean estate,                    510
The Parson would give him a snub to meet the case.
I doubt there was a priest in any place
His better. He did not stand on dignity
Nor affect in conscience too much nicety,
But Christ's and his disciples' words he sought                    515
To teach, and first he followed what he taught.
    There was a Plowman with him on the road,
His brother, who had forked up many a load
Of good manure. A hearty worker he,
Living in peace and perfect charity.                    520
Whether his fortune made him smart or smile,
He loved God with his whole heart all the while
And his neighbor as himself. He would undertake,
For every luckless poor man, for the sake
Of Christ to thresh and ditch and dig by the hour                    525
And with no wage, if it was in his power.
His tithes on goods and earnings he paid fair.
He wore a coarse, rough coat and rode a mare.
    There also were a Manciple, a Miller,
A Reeve, a Summoner, and a Pardoner,[7]                    530
And I—this makes our company complete.
    As tough a yokel as you care to meet
The Miller was. His big-beefed arms and thighs

---

6. I.e., rent out his appointment to a substitute.    7. *Manciple:* A steward. *Reeve:* Farm overseer. *Summoner:* He summoned people to appear before the church court (presided over by the
archdeacon), and in general acted as a kind of deputy sheriff of the court. *Pardoner:* Dispenser of
papal pardons.

Took many a ram put up as wrestling prize.
He was a thick, squat-shouldered lump of sins.                    535
No door but he could heave it off its pins
Or break it running at it with his head.
His beard was broader than a shovel, and red
As a fat sow or fox. A wart stood clear
Atop his nose, and red as a pig's ear                             540
A tuft of bristles on it. Black and wide
His nostrils were. He carried at his side
A sword and buckler. His mouth would open out
Like a great furnace, and he would sing and shout
His ballads and jokes of harlotries and crimes.                   545
He could steal corn and charge for it three times,
And yet was honest enough, as millers come,
For a miller, as they say, has a golden thumb.
In white coat and blue hood this lusty clown,
Blowing his bagpipes, brought us out of town.                     550
　　The Manciple was of a lawyers' college,
And other buyers might have used his knowledge
How to be shrewd provisioners, for whether
He bought on cash or credit, altogether
He managed that the end should be the same:                       555
He came out more than even with the game.
Now isn't it an instance of God's grace
How a man of little knowledge can keep pace
In wit with a whole school of learned men?
He had masters to the number of three times ten                   560
Who knew each twist of equity and tort;
A dozen in that very Inn of Court
Were worthy to be steward of the estate
To any of England's lords, however great,
And keep him to his income well confined                          565
And free from debt, unless he lost his mind,
Or let him scrimp, if he were mean in bounty;
They could have given help to a whole county
In any sort of case that might befall;
And yet this Manciple could cheat them all!                       570
　　The Reeve was a slender, fiery-tempered man.
He shaved as closely as a razor can.
His hair was cropped about his ears, and shorn
Above his forehead as a priest's is worn.
His legs were very long and very lean.                            575
No calf on his lank spindles could be seen.
But he knew how to keep a barn or bin,
He could play the game with auditors and win.

He knew well how to judge by drought and rain
The harvest of his seed and of his grain.                                    580
His master's cattle, swine, and poultry flock,
Horses and sheep and dairy, all his stock,
Were altogether in this Reeve's control.
And by agreement, he had given the sole
Accounting since his lord reached twenty years.                              585
No man could ever catch him in arrears.
There wasn't a bailiff, shepherd, or farmer working
But the Reeve knew all his tricks of cheating and shirking.
He would not let him draw an easy breath.
They feared him as they feared the very death.                               590
He lived in a good house on an open space,
Well shaded by green trees, a pleasant place.
He was shrewder in acquisition than his lord.
With private riches he was amply stored.
He had learned a good trade young by work and will.                          595
He was a carpenter of first-rate skill.
On a fine mount, a stallion, dappled gray,
Whose name was Scot, he rode along the way.
He wore a long blue coat hitched up and tied
As if it were a friar's, and at his side                                     600
A sword with rusty blade was hanging down.
He came from Norfolk, from nearby the town
That men call Bawdswell. As we rode the while,
The Reeve kept always hindmost in our file.
    A Summoner in our company had his place.                                 605
Red as the fiery cherubim[8] his face.
He was pocked and pimpled, and his eyes were narrow.
He was lecherous and hot as a cock sparrow.
His brows were scabby and black, and thin his beard.
His was a face that little children feared.                                  610
Brimstone or litharge bought in any quarter,
Quicksilver, ceruse, borax, oil of tartar,
No salve nor ointment that will cleanse or bite
Could cure him of his blotches, livid white,
Or the nobs and nubbins sitting on his cheeks.                               615
He loved his garlic, his onions, and his leeks.
He loved to drink the strong wine down blood-red.
Then would he bellow as if he had lost his head.
And when he had drunk enough to parch his drouth,
Nothing but Latin issued from his mouth.                                     620
He had smattered up a few terms, two or three,

---

8. An order of angels; represented with red faces in medieval art.

That he had gathered out of some decree—
No wonder; he heard law Latin all the day,
And everyone knows a parrot or a jay
Can cry out "Wat" or "Poll" as well as the pope;                     625
But give him a strange term, he began to grope.
His little store of learning was paid out,
So "*Questio quod juris*"[9] he would shout.
He was a goodhearted bastard and a kind one.
If there were better, it was hard to find one.                      630
He would let a good fellow, for a quart of wine,
The whole year round enjoy his concubine
Scot-free from summons, hearing, fine, or bail,
And on the sly he too could flush a quail.
If he liked a scoundrel, no matter for church law.                   635
He would teach him that he need not stand in awe
If the archdeacon threatened with his curse—
That is, unless his soul was in his purse,
For in his purse he would be punished well.
"The purse," he said, "is the archdeacon's hell."                   640
Of course I know he lied in what he said.
There is nothing a guilty man should so much dread
As the curse that damns his soul, when, without fail,
The church can save him, or send him off to jail.[1]
He had the young men and girls in his control                        645
Throughout the diocese; he knew the soul
Of youth, and heard their every last design.
A garland big enough to be the sign
Above an alehouse balanced on his head,
And he made a shield of a great round loaf of bread.                 650
    There was a Pardoner of Rouncivalle[2]
With him, of the blessed Mary's hospital,
But now come straight from Rome (or so said he).
Loudly he sang, "Come hither, love, to me,"
While the Summoner's counterbass trolled out profound—              655
No trumpet blew with half so vast a sound.
This Pardoner had hair as yellow as wax,
But it hung as smoothly as a hank of flax.
His locks trailed down in bunches from his head,
And he let the ends about his shoulders spread,                      660
But in thin clusters, lying one by one.

---

9. "The question is, what (part) of the law (applies)."    1. Lines 643–4 attempt to render the
sense and tone of a passage in which Chaucer says literally that a guilty man should be in dread
"because a curse will slay just as absolution saves, and he should also beware of a Significavit."
This word, according to Robinson, was the first word of a writ remanding an excommunicated
person to prison. [Translator's note.]    2. A religious house near Charing Cross, now part of
London.

Of hood, for rakishness, he would have none,
For in his wallet he kept it safely stowed.
He traveled, as he thought, in the latest mode,
Disheveled. Save for his cap, his head was bare,                665
And in his eyes he glittered like a hare.
A Veronica³ was stitched upon his cap
His wallet lay before him in his lap
Brimful of pardons from the very seat
In Rome. He had a voice like a goat's bleat.                670
He was beardless and would never have a beard.
His cheek was always smooth as if just sheared.
I think he was a gelding or a mare;
But in this trade, from Berwick down to Ware,
No pardoner could beat him in the race,                675
For in his wallet he had a pillow case
Which he represented as Our Lady's veil;
He said he had a piece of the very sail
St. Peter, when he fished in Galilee
Before Christ caught him, used upon the sea.                680
He had a latten⁴ cross embossed with stones
And in a glass he carried some pig's bones,
And with these holy relics, when he found
Some village parson grubbing his poor ground,
He would get more money in a single day                685
Than in two months would come the parson's way.
Thus with his flattery and his trumped-up stock
He made dupes of the parson and his flock.
But though his conscience was a little plastic
He was in church a noble ecclesiastic.                690
Well could he read the Scripture or saint's story,
But best of all he sang the offertory,
For he understood that when this song was sung,
Then he must preach, and sharpen up his tongue
To rake in cash, as well he knew the art,                695
And so he sang out gaily, with full heart.
Now I have set down briefly, as it was,
Our rank, our dress, our number, and the cause
That many our sundry fellowship begin
In Southwark, at this hospitable inn                700
Known as the Tabard, nor far from the Bell.
But what we did that night I ought to tell,
And after that our journey, stage by stage,

3. A reproduction of the handkerchief bearing the miraculous impression of Christ's face, said to
have been impressed on the handkerchief that St. Veronica gave him to wipe his face with on the
way to his crucifixion.    4. An alloy of copper and zinc made to resemble brass.

And the whole story of our pilgrimage.
But first, in justice, do not look askance      705
I plead, nor lay it to my ignorance
If in this matter I should use plain speech
And tell you just the words and style of each,
Reporting all their language faithfully.
For it must be known to you as well as me      710
That whoever tells a story after a man
Must follow him as closely as he can.
If he takes the tale in charge, he must be true
To every word, unless he would find new
Or else invent a thing or falsify.      715
Better some breadth of language than a lie!
He may not spare the truth to save his brother.
He might as well use one word as another.
In Holy Writ Christ spoke in a broad sense
And surely his word is without offense.      720
Plato, if his pages you can read,
Says let the word be cousin to the deed.
So I petition your indulgence for it
If I have cut the cloth just as men wore it,
Here in this tale, and shown its very weave.      725
My wits are none too sharp, you must believe.
    Our Host gave each of us a cheerful greeting
And promptly of our supper had us eating.
The victuals that he served us were his best.
The wine was potent, and we drank with zest.      730
Our Host cut such a figure, all in all,
He might have been a marshal in a hall.
He was a big man, and his eyes bulged wide.
No sturdier citizen lived in all Cheapside,[5]
Lacking no trace of manhood, bold in speech,      735
Prudent, and well versed in what life can teach,
And with all this he was a jovial man.
And so when supper ended he began
To jolly us, when all our debts were clear.
"Welcome," he said. "I have not seen this year      740
So merry a company in this tavern as now,
And I would give you pleasure if I knew how.
And just this very minute a plan has crossed
My mind that might amuse you at no cost.
    "You go to Canterbury—may the Lord      745
Speed you, and may the martyred saint reward

5. A London street.

Your journey! And to while the time away
You mean to talk and pass the time of day,
For you would be as cheerful all alone
As riding on your journey dumb as stone.          750
Therefore, if you'll abide by what I say,
Tomorrow, when you ride off on your way,
Now, by my father's soul, and he is dead,
If you don't enjoy yourselves, cut off my head!
Hold up your hands, if you accept my speech."          755
    Our counsel did not take us long to reach.
We bade him give his orders at his will.
"Well, sirs," he said, "then do not take it ill,
But hear me in good part, and for your sport.
Each one of you, to make our journey short,          760
Shall tell two stories, as we ride, I mean,
Toward Canterbury; and coming home again
Shall tell two other tales he may have heard
Of happenings that some time have occurred.
And the one of you whose stories please us most,          765
Here in this tavern, sitting by this post
Shall sup at our expense while we make merry
When we come riding home from Canterbury.
And to cheer you still the more, I too will ride
With you at my own cost, and be your guide.          770
And if anyone my judgment shall gainsay
He must pay for all we spend along the way.
If you agree, no need to stand and reason.
Tell me, and I'll be stirring in good season."
    This thing was granted, and we swore our pledge          775
To take his judgment on our pilgrimage,
His verdict on our tales, and his advice.
He was to plan a supper at a price
Agreed upon; and so we all assented
To his command, and we were well contented.          780
The wine was fetched; we drank, and went to rest.
    Next morning, when the dawn was in the east,
Up spring our Host, who acted as our cock,
And gathered us together in a flock,
And off we rode, till presently our pace          785
Had brought us to St. Thomas' watering place.
And there our Host began to check his horse.
"Good sirs," he said, "you know your promise, of course.
Shall I remind you what it was about?
If evensong and matins don't fall out,          790
We'll soon find who shall tell us the first tale.

But as I hope to drink my wine and ale,
Whoever won't accept what I decide
Pays everything we spend along the ride.
Draw lots, before we're farther from the Inn.                    795
Whoever draws the shortest shall begin.
Sir Knight," said he, "my master, choose your straw.
Come here, my lady Prioress, and draw,
And you, Sir Scholar, don't look thoughtful, man!
Pitch in now, everyone!" So all began                            800
To draw the lots, and as the luck would fall
The draw went to the Knight, which pleased us all.
And when this excellent man saw how it stood,
Ready to keep his promise, he said, "Good!
Since it appears that I must start the game,                      805
Why then, the draw is welcome, in God's name.
Now let's ride on, and listen, what I say."
And with that word we rode forth on our way,
And he, with his courteous manner and good cheer,
Began to tell his tale, as you shall hear.                       810

### Prologue to the Miller's Tale

When the Knight had finished,[6] no one, young or old,
In the whole company, but said he had told
A noble story, one that ought to be
Preserved and kept alive in memory,
Especially the gentlefolk, each one.                             5
Our good Host laughed, and swore, "The game's begun,
The ball is rolling! This is going well.
Let's see who has another tale to tell.
Come, match the Knight's tale if you can, Sir Monk!"
    The Miller, who by this time was so drunk                    10
He looked quite bloodless, and who hardly sat
His horse, he was never one to doff his hat
Or stand on courtesy for any man.
Like Pilate in the Church plays[7] he began
To bellow. "Arms and blood and bones," he swore,                 15
"I know a yarn that will even up the score,
A noble one, I'll pay off the Knight's tale!"
    Our Host could see that he was drunk on ale.
"Robin," he said, "hold on a minute, brother.
Some better man shall come first with another.                   20

6. The Knight's Tale is the first told, immediately following the General Prologue.    7. Miracle
plays represented Pilate as a braggart and loud mouth. His lines were marked by frequent alliteration.

Let's do this right. You tell yours by and by."
    "God's soul," the Miller told him, "that won't I!
Either I'll speak, or go on my own way."
    "The devil with you! Say what you have to say,"
Answered our Host. "You are a fool. Your head          25
Is overpowered."
                        "Now," the Miller said,
"Everyone listen! But first I will propound
That I am drunk, I know it by my sound.
If I can't get my words out, put the blame               30
On Southwark ale, I ask you, in God's name!
For I'll tell a golden legend and a life
Both of a carpenter and of his wife,
How a student put horns on the fellow's head."
    "Shut up and stop your racket," the Reeve said.       35
"Forget your ignorant drunken bawdiness.
It is a sin and a great foolishness
To injure any man by defamation
And to give women such a reputation.
Tell us of other things; you'll find no lack."           40
    Promptly this drunken Miller answered back:
"Oswald, my brother, true as babes are suckled,
The man who has no wife, he is no cuckold.
I don't say for this reason that you are.
There are plenty of faithful wives, both near and far,   45
Always a thousand good for every bad,
And you know this yourself, unless you're mad.
I see you are angry with my tale, but why?
You have a wife; no less, by God, do I.
But I wouldn't, for the oxen in my plow,                 50
Shoulder more than I need by thinking how
I may myself, for aught I know, be one.
I'll certainly believe that I am none.
A husband mustn't be curious, for his life,
About God's secrets or about his wife.                   55
If she gives him plenty and he's in the clover,
No need to worry about what's left over."
    The Miller, to make the best of it I can,
Refused to hold his tongue for any man,
But told his tale like any low-born clown.               60
I am sorry that I have to set it down,
And all you people, for God's love, I pray,
Whose taste is higher, do not think I say
A word with evil purpose; I must rehearse
Their stories one and all, both better and worse,        65

Or play false with my matter, that is clear.
Whoever, therefore, may not wish to hear,
Turn over the page and choose another tale;
For small and great, he'll find enough, no fail,
Of things from history, touching courtliness,    70
And virtue too, and also holiness.
If you choose wrong, don't lay it on my head.
You know the Miller couldn't be called well bred.
So with the Reeve, and many more as well,
And both of them had bawdy tales to tell.    75
Reflect a little, and don't hold me to blame.
There's no sense making earnest out of game.

## The Miller's Tale

There used to be a rich old oaf who made
His home at Oxford, a carpenter by trade,
And took in boarders. With him used to dwell
A student who had done his studies well,
But he was poor; for all that he had learned,    5
It was toward astrology his fancy turned.
He knew a number of figures and constructions
By which he could supply men with deductions
If they should ask him at a given hour
Whether to look for sunshine or for shower,    10
Or want to know whatever might befall,
Events of all sorts, I can't count them all.
  He was known as handy Nicholas,[8] this student.
Well versed in love, he knew how to be prudent,
Going about unnoticed, sly, and sure.    15
In looks no girl was ever more demure.
Lodged at this carpenter's, he lived alone;
He had a room there that he made his own,
Festooned with herbs, and he was sweet himself
As licorice or ginger. On a shelf    20
Above his bed's head, neatly stowed apart,
He kept the trappings that went with his art,
His astrolabe, his books—among the rest,
Thick ones and thin ones, lay his *Almagest*—[9]
And the counters for his abacus as well.    25
Over his cupboard a red curtain fell
And up above a pretty zither lay

8. Chaucer's word is hendë, implying, I take it, both *ready to hand* and *ingratiating*. Nicholas was a Johnny-on-the-spot and also had a way with him. [Translator's note.]   **9.** Second century treatise by Ptolemy, an astronomy textbook.

On which at night so sweetly would he play
That with the music the whole room would ring.
"Angelus to the Virgin" he would sing                                    30
And then the song that's known as "The King's Note."
Blessings were called down on his merry throat!
So this sweet scholar passed his time, his end
Being to eat and live upon his friend.
    This carpenter had newly wed a wife                35
And loved her better than he loved his life.
He was jealous, for she was eighteen in age;
He tried to keep her close as in a cage,
For she was wild and young, and old was he
And guessed that he might smack of cuckoldry.                            40
His ignorant wits had never chanced to strike
On Cato's word,[1] that man should wed his like;
Men ought to wed where their conditions point,
For youth and age are often out of joint.
But now, since he had fallen in the snare,                               45
He must, like other men, endure his care.
    Fair this young woman was, her body trim
As any mink, so graceful and so slim.
She wore a striped belt that was all of silk;
A piece-work apron, white as morning milk,                               50
About her loins and down her lap she wore.
White was her smock, her collar both before
And on the back embroidered all about
In coal-black silk, inside as well as out.
And like her collar, her white-laundered bonnet                          55
Had ribbons of the same embroidery on it.
Wide was her silken fillet, worn up high,
And for a fact she had a willing eye.
She plucked each brow into a little bow,
And each one was as black as any sloe.                                   60
She was a prettier sight to see by far
Than the blossoms of the early pear tree are,
And softer than the wool of an old wether.
Down from her belt there hung a purse of leather
With silken tassels and with studs of brass.                             65
No man so wise, wherever people pass,
Who could imagine in this world at all
A wench like her, the pretty little doll!
Far brighter was the dazzle of her hue
Than a coin struck in the Tower,[2] fresh and new.                       70

1. Dionysius Cato, the supposed author of a book of maxims employed in elementary
education.    2. The Tower of London.

As for her song, it twittered from her head
Sharp as a swallow perching on a shed.
And she could skip and sport as a young ram
Or calf will gambol, following his dam.
Her mouth was sweet as honey-ale or mead                                  75
Or apples in the hay, stored up for need.
She was as skittish as an untrained colt,
Slim as a mast and straighter than a bolt.
On her simple collar she wore a big brooch-pin
Wide as a shield's boss underneath her chin.                              80
High up along her legs she laced her shoes.
She was a pigsney, she was a primrose
For any lord to tumble in his bed
Or a good yeoman honestly to wed.
  Now sir, and again sir, this is how it was:                            85
A day came round when handy Nicholas,
While her husband was at Oseney,[3] well away,
Began to fool with this young wife, and play.
These students always have a wily head.
He caught her in between the legs, and said,                             90
"Sweetheart, unless I have my will with you
I'll die for stifled love, by all that's true,"
And held her by the haunches, hard. "I vow
I'll die unless you love me here and now,
Sure as my soul," he said, "is God's to save."                          95
  She shied just as a colt does in the trave,[4]
And turned her head hard from him, this young wife,
And said, "I will not kiss you, on my life.
Why, stop it now," she said, "stop, Nicholas,
Or I will cry out 'Help, help,' and 'Alas!'                             100
Be good enough to take your hands away."
  "Mercy," this Nicholas began to pray,
And spoke so well and poured it on so fast
She promised she would be his love at last,
And swore by Thomas à Becket, saint of Kent,                            105
That she would serve him when she could invent
Or spy out some good opportunity.
"My husband is so full of jealousy
You must be watchful and take care," she said,
"Or well I know I'll be as good as dead.                                110
You must go secretly about this business."
  "Don't give a thought to that," said Nicholas.
"A student has been wasting time at school

3. A town near Oxford.    4. A wooden frame confining a horse being shod.

If he can't make a carpenter a fool."
And so they were agreed, these two, and swore          115
To watch their chance, as I have said before.
When Nicholas had spanked her haunches neatly
And done all I have spoken of, he sweetly
Gave her a kiss, and then he took his zither
And loudly played, and sang his music with her.          120
    Now in her Christian duty, one saint's day,
To the parish church this good wife made her way,
And as she went her forehead cast a glow
As bright as noon, for she had washed it so
It glistened when she finished with her work.          125
    Serving this church there was a parish clerk
Whose name was Absolom, a ruddy man
With goose-gray eyes and curls like a great fan
That shone like gold on his neatly parted head.
His tunic was light blue and his nose red,          130
And he had patterns that had been cut through
Like the windows of St. Paul's in either shoe.
He wore above his tunic, fresh and gay,
A surplice white as a blossom on a spray.
A merry devil, as true as God can save,          135
He knew how to let blood, trim hair, and shave,
Or write a deed of land in proper phrase,
And he could dance in twenty different ways
In the Oxford fashion, and sometimes he would sing
A loud falsetto to his fiddle string          140
Or his guitar. No tavern anywhere
But he had furnished entertainment there.
Yet his speech was delicate, and for his part
He was a little squeamish toward a fart.
    This Absolom, so jolly and so gay,          145
With a censer went about on the saint's day
Censing the parish women one and all.
Many the doting look that he let fall,
And specially on this carpenter's young wife.
To look at her, he thought, was a good life,          150
She was so trim, so sweetly lecherous.
I dare say that if she had been a mouse
And he a cat, he would have made short work
Of catching her. This jolly parish clerk
Had such a heartful of love-hankerings          155
He would not take the women's offerings;
No, no, he said, it would not be polite.
    The moon, when darkness fell, shone full and bright

And Absolom was ready for love's sake
With his guitar to be up and awake,                                    160
And toward the carpenter's, brisk and amorous,
He made his way until he reached the house
A little after the cocks began to crow.
Under a casement he sang sweet and low,
"Dear lady, by your will, be kind to me,"                              165
And strummed on his guitar in harmony.
This lovelorn singing woke the carpenter
Who said to his wife, "What, Alison, don't you hear
Absolom singing under our bedroom wall?"
        "Yes, God knows, John," she answered, "I hear it all."        170
        What would you like? In this way things went on
Till jolly Absolom was woebegone
For wooing her, awake all night and day.
He combed his curls and made himself look gay.
He swore to be her slave and used all means                           175
To court her with his gifts and go-betweens.
He sang and quavered like a nightingale.
He sent her sweet spiced wine and seasoned ale,
Cakes that were piping hot, mead sweet with honey,
And since she was town-bred, he proffered money.                      180
For some are won by wealth, and some no less
By blows, and others yet by gentleness.
    Sometimes, to keep his talents in her gaze,
He acted Herod[5] in the mystery plays
High on the stage. But what can help his case?                        185
For she so loves this handy Nicholas
That Absolom is living in a bubble.
He has nothing but a laugh for all his trouble.
She leaves his earnestness for scorn to cool
And makes this Absolom her proper fool.                               190
For this is a true proverb, and no lie;
"It always happens that the nigh and sly
Will let the absent suffer." So 'tis said,
And Absolom may rage or lose his head
But just because he was farther from her sight                        195
This nearby Nicholas got in his light.
    Now hold your chin up, handy Nicholas,
For Absolom may wail and sing "Alas!"
One Saturday when the carpenter had gone
To Oseney, Nicholas and Alison                                        200
Agreed that he should use his wit and guile

---

5. A role traditionally played as a bully in the Miracle plays.

This simple jealous husband to beguile.
And if it happened that the game went right
She would sleep in his arms the livelong night,
For this was his desire and hers as well.
At once, with no more words, this Nicholas fell                    205
To working out his plan. He would not tarry,
But quietly to his room began to carry
Both food and drink to last him out a day,
Or more than one, and told her what to say                    210
If her husband asked her about Nicholas.
She must say she had no notion where he was;
She hadn't laid eyes on him all day long;
He must be sick, or something must be wrong;
No matter how her maid had called and cried                    215
He wouldn't answer, whatever might betide.
  This was the plan, and Nicholas kept away,
Shut in his room, for that whole Saturday.
He ate and slept or did as he thought best
Till Sunday, when the sun was going to rest,                    220
This carpenter began to wonder greatly
Where Nicholas was and what might ail him lately,
"Now, by St. Thomas, I begin to dread
All isn't right with Nicholas," he said.
"He hasn't, God forbid died suddenly!                    225
The world is ticklish these days, certainly.
Today I saw a corpse to church go past,
A man that I saw working Monday last!
Go up," he told his chore-boy, "call and shout,
Knock with a stone, find what it's all about                    230
And let me know."
                    The boy went up and pounded
And yelled as if his wits had been confounded.
"What, how, what's doing, Master Nicholas?
How can you sleep all day?" But all his fuss                    235
Was wasted, for he could not hear a word.
He noticed at the bottom of a board
A hole the cat used when she wished to creep
Into the room, and through it looked in deep
And finally of Nicholas caught sight.                    240
This Nicholas sat gaping there upright
As though his wits were addled by the moon
When it was new. The boy went down, and soon
Had told his master how he had seen the man.
  The carpenter, when he heard this news, began                    245
To cross himself. "Help us, St. Frideswide!

Little can we foresee what may betide!
The man's astronomy has turned his wit,
Or else he's in some agonizing fit.
I always knew that it would turn out so.　250
What God has hidden is not for men to know.
Aye, blessed is the ignorant man indeed,
Blessed is he that only knows his creed!
So fared another scholar of the sky,
For walking in the meadows once to spy　255
Upon the stars and what they might foretell,
Down in a clay-pit suddenly he fell!
He overlooked that! By St. Thomas, though,
I'm sorry for handy Nicholas. I'll go
And scold him roundly for his studying　260
If so I may, by Jesus, heaven's king!
Give me a staff, I'll pry up from the floor
While you, Robin, are heaving at the door.
He'll quit his books, I think."

                He took his stand　265
Outside the room. The boy had a strong hand
And by the hasp he heaved it off at once.
The door fell flat. With gaping countenance
This Nicholas sat studying the air
As still as stone. He was in black despair,　270
The carpenter believed, and hard about
The shoulders caught and shook him, and cried out
Rudely, "What, how! What is it? Look down at us!
Wake up, think of Christ's passion, Nicholas!
I'll sign you with the cross to keep away　275
These elves and things!" And he began to say,
Facing the quarters of the house, each side,
And on the threshold of the door outside,
The night-spell: "Jesu and St. Benedict
From every wicked thing this house protect . . ."　280
   Choosing his time, this handy Nicholas
Produced a dreadful sigh, and said, "Alas,
This world, must it be all destroyed straightway?"
   "What," asked the carpenter, "what's that you say?
Do as we do, we working men, and think　285
Of God."
   Nicholas answered, "Get me a drink,
And afterwards I'll tell you privately
Of something that concerns us, you and me.
I'll tell you only, you among all men."　290
   This carpenter went down and came again

With a draught of mighty ale, a generous quart.
As soon as each of them had drunk his part
Nicholas shut the door and made it fast
And sat down by the carpenter at last                                    295
And spoke to him. "My host," he said, "John dear,
You must swear by all that you hold sacred here
That not to any man will you betray
My confidence. What I'm about to say
Is Christ's own secret. If you tell a soul                               300
You are undone, and this will be the toll:
If you betray me, you shall go stark mad."
    "Now Christ forbid it, by His holy blood,"
Answered this simple man. "I don't go blabbing.
If I say it myself, I have no taste for gabbing.                         305
Speak up just as you like, I'll never tell,
Not wife nor child, by Him that harrowed hell."[6]
    "Now, John," said Nicholas, "this is no lie.
I have discovered through astrology,
And studying the moon that shines so bright                              310
That Monday next, a quarter through the night,
A rain will fall, and such a mad, wild spate
That Noah's flood was never half so great.
This world," he said, "in less time than an hour
Shall drown entirely in that hideous shower.                             315
Yes, every man shall drown and lose his life."
    "Alas," the carpenter answered, "for my wife!
Alas, my Alison! And shall she drown?"
For grief at this he nearly tumbled down,
And said, "But is there nothing to be done?"                             320
    "Why, happily there is, for anyone
Who will take advice," this handy Nicholas said.
"You mustn't expect to follow your own head.
For what said Solomon, whose words were true?
'Proceed by counsel, and you'll never rue.'                              325
If you will act on good advice, no fail,
I'll promise, and without a mast or sail,
To see that she's preserved, and you and I.
Haven't you heard how Noah was kept dry
When, warned by Christ beforehand, he discovered                         330
That the whole earth with water should be covered?"
    "Yes," said the carpenter, "long, long ago."
    "And then again," said Nicholas, "don't you know

6. I.e., Christ, who descended into Hell and led away Adam, Eve, the Patriarchs, John the
Baptist, and others, redeeming and releasing them. It was the subject of a number of Miracle
plays. The original story comes from the Apocryphal New Testament.

The grief they all had trying to embark
Till Noah could get his wife into the Ark?[7]                     335
That was a time when Noah, I dare say,
Would gladly have given his best black wethers away
If she could have had a ship herself alone.
And therefore do you know what must be done?
This demands haste, and with a hasty thing             340
People can't stop for talk and tarrying.
    "Start out and get into the house right off
For each of us a tub or kneading-trough,
Above all making sure that they are large,
In which we'll float away as in a barge.               345
And put in food enough to last a day.
Beyond won't matter; the flood will fall away
Early next morning. Take care not to spill
A word to your boy Robin, nor to Jill
Your maid. I cannot save her, don't ask why.           350
I will not tell God's secrets, no, not I.
Let it be enough, unless your wits are mad,
To have as good a grace as Noah had.
I'll save your wife for certain, never doubt it.
Now go along, and make good time about it.             355
    "But when you have, for her and you and me,
Brought to the house these kneading-tubs, all three,
Then you must hang them under the roof, up high,
To keep our plans from any watchful eye.
When you have done exactly as I've said,               360
And put in snug our victuals and our bread,
Also an ax to cut the ropes apart
So when the rain comes we can make our start,
And when you've broken a hole high in the gable
Facing the garden plot, above the stable,              365
To give us a free passage out, each one,
Then, soon as the great fall of rain is done,
You'll swim as merrily, I undertake,
As the white duck paddles along behind her drake.
Then I shall call, 'How, Alison! How, John!           370
Be cheerful, for the flood will soon be gone.'
And 'Master Nicholas, what ho!' you'll say.
'Good morning, I see you clearly, for it's day.'
Then we shall lord it for the rest of life
Over the world, like Noah and his wife.                375
    "But one thing I must warn you of downright.

7. A stock comedy scene in the mystery plays, of which the carpenter would have been an avid spectator. [Translator's note.]

Use every care that on that selfsame night
When we have taken ship and climbed aboard,
No one of us must speak a single word,
Nor call, nor cry, but pray with all his heart.          380
It is God's will. You must hang far apart,
You and your wife, for there must be no sin
Between you, no more in a look than in
The very deed. Go now, the plans are drawn.
Go, set to work, and may God spur you on!          385
Tomorrow night when all men are asleep
Into our kneading-troughs we three shall creep
And sit there waiting, and abide God's grace.
Go along now, this isn't the time or place
For me to talk at length or sermonize.          390
The proverb says, 'Don't waste words on the wise.'
You are so wise there is no need to teach you.
Go, save our lives—that's all that I beseech you!"
     This simple carpenter went on his way.
Many a time he said, "Alack the day,"          395
And to his wife he laid the secret bare.
She knew it better than he; she was aware
What this quaint bargain was designed to buy.
She carried on as if about to die,
And said, "Alas, go get this business done.          400
Help us escape, or we are dead, each one.
I am your true, your faithful wedded wife.
Go, my dear husband, save us, limb and life!"
     Great things, in all truth, can the emotions be!
A man can perish through credulity          405
So deep the print imagination makes.
This simple carpenter, he quails and quakes.
He really sees, according to his notion,
Noah's flood come wallowing like an ocean
To drown his Alison, his pet, his dear.          410
He weeps and wails, and gone is his good cheer,
And wretchedly he sighs. But he goes off
And gets himself a tub, a kneading-trough,
Another tub, and has them on the sly
Sent home, and there in secret hangs them high          415
Beneath the roof. He made three ladders, these
With his own hands, and stowed in bread and cheese
And a jug of good ale, plenty for a day.
Before all this was done, he sent away
His chore-boy Robin and his wench likewise          420
To London on some trumped-up enterprise,

And so on Monday, when it drew toward night,
He shut the door without a candlelight
And saw that all was just as it should be,
And shortly they went clambering up, all three.     425
They sat there still, and let a moment pass.
    "Now then, 'Our Father,' mum!" said Nicholas,
And "Mum!" said John, and "Mum!" said Alison,
And piously this carpenter went on
Saying his prayers. He sat there still and straining,     430
Trying to make out whether he heard it raining.
    The dead of sleep, for very weariness,
Fell on this carpenter, as I should guess,
At about curfew time, or little more.
His head was twisted, and that made him snore.     435
His spirit groaned in its uneasiness.
Down from his ladder slipped this Nicholas,
And Alison too, downward she softly sped
And without further word they went to bed
Where the carpenter himself slept other nights.     440
There were the revels, there were the delights!
And so this Alison and Nicholas lay
Busy about their solace and their play
Until the bell for lauds began to ring
And in the chancel friars began to sing.     445
    Now on this Monday, woebegone and glum
For love, this parish clerk, this Absolom
Was with some friends at Oseney, and while there
Inquired after John the carpenter.
A member of the cloister drew him away     450
Out of the church, and told him, "I can't say.
I haven't seen him working hereabout
Since Saturday. The abbot sent him out
For timber, I suppose. He'll often go
And stay at the granary a day or so.     455
Or else he's at his own house, possibly.
I can't for certain say where he may be."
    Absolom at once felt jolly and light,
And thought, "Time now to be awake all night,
For certainly I haven't seen him making     460
A stir about his door since day was breaking.
Don't call me a man if when I hear the cock
Begin to crow I don't slip up and knock
On the low window by his bedroom wall.
To Alison at last I'll pour out all     465
My love-pangs, for at this point I can't miss,

Whatever happens, at the least a kiss.
Some comfort, by my word, will come my way.
I've felt my mouth itch the whole livelong day,
And that's a sign of kissing at the least.                    470
I dreamed all night that I was at a feast.
So now I'll go and sleep an hour or two,
And then I'll wake and play the whole night through."
　　When the first cockcrow through the dark had come
Up rose this jolly lover Absolom                    475
And dressed up smartly. He was not remiss
About the least point. He chewed licorice
And cardamom to smell sweet, even before
He combed his hair. Beneath his tongue he bore
A sprig of Paris[8] like a truelove knot.                    480
He strolled off to the carpenter's house, and got
Beneath the window. It came so near the ground
It reached his chest. Softly, with half a sound,
He coughed, "My honeycomb, sweet Alison,
What are you doing, my sweet cinnamon?                    485
Awake, my sweetheart and my pretty bird,
Awake, and give me from your lips a word!
Little enough you care for all my woe,
How for your love I sweat wherever I go!
No wonder I sweat and faint and cannot eat                    490
More than a girl; as a lamb does for the teat
I pine. Yes, truly, I so long for love
I mourn as if I were a turtledove."
　　Said she, "You jack-fool, get away from here!
So help me God, I won't sing 'Kiss me, dear!'                    495
I love another more than you. Get on,
For Christ's sake, Absolom, or I'll throw a stone.
The devil with you! Go and let me sleep."
　　"Ah, that true love should ever have to reap
So evil a fortune," Absolom said. "A kiss,                    500
At least, if it can be no more than this,
Give me, for love of Jesus and of me."
　　"And will you go away for that?" said she.
　　"Yes, truly, sweetheart," answered Absolom.
　　"Get ready then," she said, "for here I come,"                    505
And softly said to Nicholas, "Keep still,
And in a minute you can laugh your fill."
This Absolom got down upon his knee
And said, "I am a lord of pure degree,

8. A cloverlike plant.

For after this, I hope, comes more to savor.                    510
Sweetheart, your grace, and pretty bird, your favor!"
    She undid the window quickly. "That will do,"
She said. "Be quick about it, and get through,
For fear the neighbors will look out and spy."
    Absolom wiped his mouth to make it dry.          515
The night was pitch dark, coal-black all about.
Her rear end through the window she thrust out.
He got no better or worse, did Absolom,
Than to kiss her with his mouth on the bare bum
Before he had caught on, a smacking kiss.            520
    He jumped back, thinking something was amiss.
A woman had no beard, he was well aware,
But what he felt was rough and had long hair.
    "Alas," he cried, "what have you made me do?"
"Te-hee!" she said, and banged the window to.         525
Absolom backed away a sorry pace.
    "You've bearded him!" said handy Nicholas.
"God's body, this is going fair and fit!"
    This luckless Absolom heard every bit,
And gnawed his mouth, so angry he became.           530
He said to himself, "I'll square you, all the same."
    But who now scrubs and rubs, who chafes his lips
With dust, with sand, with straw, with cloth and chips
If not this Absolom? "The devil," says he,
"Welcome my soul if I wouldn't rather be            535
Revenged than have the whole town in a sack!
Alas," he cries, "if only I'd held back!"
His hot love had become all cold and ashen.
He didn't have a curse to spare for passion
From the moment when he kissed her on the ass.      540
That was the cure to make his sickness pass!
He cried as a child does after being whipped;
He railed at love. Then quietly he slipped
Across the street to a smith who was forging out
Parts that the farmers needed round about.          545
He was busy sharpening colter[9] and plowshare
When Absolom knocked as though without a care.
    "Undo the door, Jervice, and let me come."
    "What? Who are you?"
                 "It is I, Absolom."          550
    "Absolom, is it! By Christ's precious tree,
Why are you up so early? Lord bless me,

9. A turf-cutter on a plow.

What's ailing you? Some gay girl has the power
To bring you out, God knows, at such an hour!
Yes, by St. Neot, you know well what I mean!"          555
    Absolom thought his jokes not worth a bean.
Without a word he let them all go by.
He had another kind of fish to fry
Than Jervice guessed. "Lend me this colter here
That's hot in the chimney, friend," he said. "Don't fear,    560
I'll bring it back right off when I am through.
I need it for a job I have to do."
    "Of course," said Jervice. "Why, if it were gold
Or coins in a sack, uncounted and untold,
As I'm a rightful smith, I wouldn't refuse it.          565
But, Christ's foot! how on earth do you mean to use it?"
    "Let that," said Absolom, "be as it may.
I'll let you know tomorrow or next day,"
And took the colter where the steel was cold
And slipped out with it safely in his hold            570
And softly over to the carpenter's wall.
He coughed and then he rapped the window, all
As he had done before.
                              "Who's knocking there?"
Said Alison. "It is a thief, I swear."              575
    "No, no," said he. "God knows, my sugarplum,
My bird, my darling, it's your Absolom.
I've brought a golden ring my mother gave me,
Fine and well cut, as I hope that God will save me.
It's yours, if you will let me have a kiss."          580
    Nicholas had got up to take a piss
And thought he would improve the whole affair.
This clerk, before he got away from there,
Should give *his* ass a smack; and hastily
He opened the window, and thrust out quietly,          585
Buttocks and haunches, all the way, his bum.
Up spoke this clerk, this jolly Absolom:
"Speak, for I don't know where you are, sweetheart."
    Nicholas promptly let fly with a fart
As loud as if a clap of thunder broke,              590
So great he was nearly blinded by the stroke,
And ready with his hot iron to make a pass,
Absolom caught him fairly on the ass.
    Off flew the skin, a good handbreadth of fat
Lay bare, the iron so scorched him where he sat.          595
As for the pain, he thought that he would die,
And like a madman he began to cry.

"Help! Water! Water! Help, for God's own heart!"
   At this the carpenter came to with a start.
He heard a man cry "Water!" as if mad.             600
"It's coming now," was the first thought he had.
"It's Noah's flood, alas, God be our hope!"
He sat up with his ax and chopped the rope
And down at once the whole contraption fell.
He didn't take time out to buy or sell           605
Till he hit the floor and lay there in a swoon.
   Then up jumped Nicholas and Alison
And in the street began to cry, "Help, ho!"
The neighbors all came running, high and low,
And poured into the house to see the sight.       610
The man still lay there, passed out cold and white,
For in his tumble he had broken an arm.
But he himself brought on his greatest harm,
For when he spoke he was at once outdone
By handy Nicholas and Alison            615
Who told them one and all that he was mad.
So great a fear of Noah's flood he had,
By some delusion, that in his vanity
He had bought himself these kneading-troughs, all three.
And hung them from the roof there, up above,     620
And he had pleaded with them, for God's love,
To sit there in the loft for company.
   The neighbors laughed at such a fantasy,
And round the loft began to pry and poke
And turned his whole disaster to a joke.        625
He found it was no use to say a word.
Whatever reason he offered, no one heard.
With oaths and curses people swore him down
Until he passed for mad in the whole town.
Wit, clerk, and student all stood by each other.    630
They said, "It's clear the man is crazy, brother."
Everyone had his laugh about this feud.
So Alison, the carpenter's wife, got screwed
For all the jealous watching he could try,
And Absolom, he kissed her nether eye,       635
And Nicholas got his bottom roasted well.
God save this troop! That's all I have to tell.


### Prologue to the Pardoner's Tale

"In churches," said the Pardoner, "when I preach,
I use, milords, a lofty style of speech

And ring it out as roundly as a bell,
Knowing by rote all that I have to tell.
My text is ever the same, and ever was:                                    5
*Radix malorum est cupiditas.*[1]
    "First I inform them whence I come; that done,
I then display my papal bulls, each one.
I show my license first, my body's warrant,
Sealed by the bishop, for it would be abhorrent                           10
If any man made bold, though priest or clerk,
To interrupt me in Christ's holy work.
And after that I give myself full scope.
Bulls in the name of cardinal and pope,
Of bishops and of patriarchs I show.                                      15
I say in Latin some few words or so
To spice my sermon; it flavors my appeal
And stirs my listeners to greater zeal.
Then I display my cases made of glass
Crammed to the top with rags and bones. They pass                         20
For relics with all the people in the place.
I have a shoulder bone in a metal case,
Part of a sheep owned by a holy Jew.
'Good men,' I say, 'heed what I'm telling you:
Just let this bone be dipped in any well                                   25
And if cow, calf, or sheep, or ox should swell
From eating a worm, or by a worm be stung,
Take water from this well and wash its tongue
And it is healed at once. And furthermore
Of scab and ulcers and of every sore                                      30
Shall every sheep be cured, and that straightway,
That drinks from the same well. Heed what I say:
If the good man who owns the beasts will go,
Fasting, each week, and drink before cockcrow
Out of this well, his cattle shall be brought                             35
To multiply—that holy Jew so taught
Our elders—and his property increase.
    " 'Moreover, sirs, this bone cures jealousies.
Though into a jealous madness a man fell,
Let him cook his soup in water from this well,                            40
He'll never, though for truth he knew her sin,
Suspect his wife again, though she took in
A priest, or even two of them or three.
    " 'Now here's a mitten that you all can see.
Whoever puts his hand in it shall gain,                                   45

1. The root of evil is greed.

When he sows his land, increasing crops of grain,
Be it wheat or oats, provided that he bring
His penny or so to make his offering.
　" 'There is one word of warning I must say,
Good men and women. If any here today　　　　　　　　50
Has done a sin so horrible to name
He daren't be shriven of it for the shame,
Or if any woman, young or old, is here
Who has cuckolded her husband, be it clear
They may not make an offering in that case　　　　　55
To these my relics; they have no power nor grace.
But any who is free of such dire blame,
Let him come up and offer in God's name
And I'll absolve him through the authority
That by the pope's bull has been granted me.'　　　60
　"By such hornswoggling I've won, year by year,
A hundred marks[2] since being a pardoner.
I stand in my pulpit like a true divine,
And when the people sit I preach my line
To ignorant souls, as you have heard before,　　　65
And tell skullduggeries by the hundred more.
Then I take care to stretch my neck well out
And over the people I nod and peer about
Just like a pigeon perching on a shed.
My hands fly and my tongue wags in my head　　　70
So busily that to watch me is a joy.
Avarice is the theme that I employ
In all my sermons, to make the people free
In giving pennies—especially to me.
My mind is fixed on what I stand to win　　　　　75
And not at all upon correcting sin.
I do not care, when they are in the grave,
If souls go berry-picking that I could save.
Truth is that evil purposes determine,
And many a time, the origin of a sermon:　　　　　80
Some to please people and by flattery
To gain advancement through hypocrisy,
Some for vainglory, some again for hate.
For when I daren't fight otherwise, I wait
And give him a tongue-lashing when I preach.　　　85
No man escapes or gets beyond the reach
Of my defaming tongue, supposing he
Has done a wrong to my brethren or to me.

2. Probably the equivalent of several thousand dollars in modern purchasing power.

For though I do not tell his proper name,
People will recognize him all the same.                90
By sign and circumstance I let them learn.
Thus I serve those who have done us an ill turn.
Thus I spit out my venom under hue
Of sanctity, and seem devout and true!
  "But to put my purpose briefly, I confess        95
I preach for nothing but for covetousness.
That's why my text is still and ever was
*Radix malorum est cupiditas.*
For by this text I can denounce, indeed,
The very vice I practice, which is greed.          100
But though that sin is lodged in my own heart,
I am able to make other people part
From avarice, and sorely to repent,
Though that is not my principal intent.
  "Then I bring in examples, many a one,           105
And tell them many a tale of days long done.
Plain folk love tales that come down from of old.
Such things their minds can well report and hold.
Do you think that while I have the power to preach
And take in silver and gold for what I teach       110
I shall ever live in willful poverty?
No, no, that never was my thought, certainly.
I mean to preach and beg in sundry lands.
I won't do any labor with my hands,
Nor live by making baskets. I don't intend         115
To beg for nothing; that is not my end.
I won't ape the apostles; I must eat,
I must have money, wool, and cheese, and wheat,
Though I took it from the meanest wretch's tillage
Or from the poorest widow in a village,            120
Yes, though her children starved for want. In fine,
I mean to drink the liquor of the vine
And have a jolly wench in every town.
But, in conclusion, lords, I will get down
To business: you would have me tell a tale.        125
Now that I've had a drink of corny ale,
By God, I hope the thing I'm going to tell
Is one that you'll have reason to like well.
For though myself a very sinful man,
I can tell a moral tale, indeed I can,             130
One that I use to bring the profits in
While preaching. Now be still, and I'll begin."

## The Pardoner's Tale

There was a company of young folk living
One time in Flanders, who were bent on giving
Their lives to follies and extravagances,
Brothels and taverns, where they held their dances
With lutes, harps, and guitars, diced at all hours,                    5
And also ate and drank beyond their powers,
Through which they paid the devil sacrifice
In the devil's temple with their drink and dice,
Their abominable excess and dissipation.
They swore oaths that were worthy of damnation;                       10
It was grisly to be listening when they swore.
The blessed body of our Lord they tore—
The Jews, it seemed to them, had failed to rend
His body enough—and each laughed at his friend
And fellow in sin. To encourage their pursuits                        15
Came comely dancing girls, peddlers of fruits,
Singers with harps, bawds and confectioners
Who are the very devil's officers
To kindle and blow the fire of lechery
That is the follower of gluttony.                                     20
    Witness the Bible, if licentiousness
Does not reside in wine and drunkenness!
Recall how drunken Lot, unnaturally,
With his two daughters lay unwittingly,
So drunk he had no notion what he did.[3]                            25
    Herod, the stories tell us, God forbid,
When full of liquor at his banquet board
Right at his very table gave the word
To kill the Baptist, John, though guiltless he.[4]
    Seneca says a good word, certainly.                              30
He says there is no difference he can find
Between a man who has gone out of his mind
And one who carries drinking to excess,
Only that madness outlasts drunkenness.[5]
O gluttony, first cause of mankind's fall,[6]                        35
Of our damnation the cursed original
Until Christ bought us with his blood again!
How dearly paid for by the race of men
Was this detestable iniquity!
This whole world was destroyed through gluttony.                     40
    Adam our father and his wife also

---

3. Genesis 19:33–35.    4. Matthew 14:1–11; Mark 6:14–28.    5. Seneca's *Epistles*, Epistle
lxxxiii.    6. Since the Fall was caused by man's eating the forbidden apple.

From paradise to labor and to woe
Were driven for that selfsame vice, indeed.
As long as Adam fasted—so I read—
He was in heaven; but as soon as he                              45
Devoured the fruit of that forbidden tree
Then he was driven out in sorrow and pain.
Of gluttony well ought we to complain!
Could a man know how many maladies
Follow indulgences and gluttonies                               50
He would keep his diet under stricter measure
And sit at table with more temperate pleasure.
The throat is short and tender is the mouth,
And hence men toil east, west, and north, and south,
In earth, and air, and water—alas to think—                     55
Fetching a glutton dainty meat and drink.
    This is a theme, O Paul, that you well treat:
"Meat unto belly, and belly unto meat,
God shall destroy them both," as Paul has said.[7]
When a man drinks the white wine and the red—                   60
This is a foul word, by my soul, to say,
And fouler is the deed in every way—
He makes his throat his privy through excess.
    The Apostle says, weeping for piteousness,
"There are many of whom I told you—at a loss                    65
I say it, weeping—enemies of Christ's cross,
Whose belly is their god; their end is death."[8]
O cursed belly! Sack of stinking breath
In which corruption lodges, dung abounds!
At either end of you come forth foul sounds.                    70
Great cost it is to fill you, and great pain!
These cooks, how they must grind and pound and strain
And transform substance into accident[9]
To please your cravings, though exorbitant!
From the hard bones they knock the marrow out.                  75
They'll find a use for everything, past doubt,
That down the gullet sweet and soft will glide.
The spiceries of leaf and root provide
Sauces that are concocted for delight,
To give a man a second appetite.                                80
But truly, he whom gluttonies entice
Is dead, while he continues in that vice.
    O drunken man, disfigured is your face,

7. I Corinthians 6:13.    8. Philippians 3:18–19.    9. A distinction was made in philosophy
between "substance," the real nature of a thing, and "accident," its merely sensory qualities, such
as flavor.

Sour is your breath, foul are you to embrace!
You seem to mutter through your drunken nose          85
The sound of "Samson, Samson," yet God knows
That Samson never indulged himself in wine.[1]
Your tongue is lost, you fall like a stuck swine,
And all the self-respect that you possess
Is gone, for of man's judgment, drunkenness          90
Is the very sepulcher and annihilation.
A man whom drink has under domination
Can never keep a secret in his head.
Now steer away from both the white and red,
And most of all from that white wine keep wide          95
That comes from Lepe.[2] They sell it in Cheapside
And Fish Street. It's a Spanish wine, and sly
To creep in other wines that grow nearby,
And such a vapor it has that with three drinks
It takes a man to Spain; although he thinks          100
He is home in Cheapside, he is far away
At Lepe. Then "Samson, Samson" will he say!

By God himself, who is omnipotent,
All the great exploits in the Old Testament
Were done in abstinence, I say, and prayer.          105
Look in the Bible, you may learn it there.

Attila,[3] conqueror of many a place,
Died in his sleep in shame and in disgrace
Bleeding out of his nose in drunkenness.
A captain ought to live in temperateness!          110
And more than this, I say, remember well
The injunction that was laid on Lemuel—[4]
Not Samuel, but Lemuel, I say!
Read in the Bible; in the plainest way
Wine is forbidden to judges and to kings.          115
This will suffice; no more upon these things.

Now that I've shown what gluttony will do,
Now I will warn you against gambling, too;
Gambling, the very mother of low scheming,
Of lying and forswearing and blaspheming          120
Against Christ's name, of murder and waste as well
Alike of goods and time; and, truth to tell,
With honor and renown it cannot suit
To be held a common gambler by repute.
The higher a gambler stands in power and place,          125
The more his name is lowered in disgrace.

---

1. Judges 13:4.     2. A town in Spain noted for strong wines.     3. Leader of the Hun invasion
of Europe, fifth century A.D.     4. Proverbs 31:4–7.

If a prince gambles, whatever his kingdom be,
In his whole government and policy
He is, in all the general estimation,
Considered so much less in reputation. 130
    Stilbon, who was a wise ambassador,
From Lacedaemon once to Corinth bore
A mission of alliance. When he came
It happened that he found there at a game
Of hazard all the great ones of the land, 135
And so, as quickly as it could be planned,
He stole back, saying, "I will not lose my name
Nor have my reputation put to shame
Allying you with gamblers. You may send
Other wise emissaries to gain your end, 140
For by my honor, rather than ally
My countrymen to gamblers, I will die.
For you that are so gloriously renowned
Shall never with this gambling race be bound
By will of mine or treaty I prepare." 145
Thus did this wise philosopher declare.
    Remember also how the Parthians' lord
Sent King Demetrius, as the books record,
A pair of golden dice, by this proclaiming
His scorn, because that king was known for gaming, 150
And the king of Parthia therefore held his crown
Devoid of glory, value, or renown.
Lords can discover other means of play
More suitable to while the time away.
    Now about oaths I'll say a word or two, 155
Great oaths and false oaths, as the old books do.
Great swearing is a thing abominable,
And false oaths yet more reprehensible.
Almighty God forbade swearing at all,
Matthew be witness;[5] but specially I call 160
The holy Jeremiah on this head.
"Swear thine oaths truly, do not lie," he said.
"Swear under judgment, and in righteousness."[6]
But idle swearing is a great wickedness.
Consult and see, and he that understands 165
In the first table of the Lord's commands
Will find the second of his commandments this:
"Take not the Lord's name idly or amiss."
If a man's oaths and curses are extreme,

5. Matthew 5:34.   6. Jeremiah 4:2.

Vengeance shall find his house, both roof and beam.    170
"By the precious heart of God," and "By his nails"—
"My chance is seven,[7] by Christ's blood at Hailes,
Yours five and three." "Cheat me, and if you do,
By God's arms, with this knife I'll run you through!"—
Such fruit comes from the bones, that pair of bitches:    175
Oaths broken, treachery, murder. For the riches
Of Christ's love, give up curses, without fail,
Both great and small!—Now, sirs, I'll tell my tale.
    These three young roisterers of whom I tell
Long before prime had rung from any bell    180
Were seated in a tavern at their drinking,
And as they sat, they heard a bell go clinking
Before a corpse being carried to his grave.
One of these roisterers, when he heard it, gave
An order to his boy: "Go out and try    185
To learn whose corpse is being carried by.
Get me his name, and get it right. Take heed."
    "Sir," said the boy, "there isn't any need.
I learned before you came here, by two hours.
He was, it happens, an old friend of yours,    190
And all at once, there on his bench upright
As he was sitting drunk, he was killed last night.
A sly thief, Death men call him, who deprives
All the people in this country of their lives,
Came with his spear and smiting his heart in two    195
Went on his business with no more ado.
A thousand have been slaughtered by his hand
During this plague. And, sir, before you stand
Within his presence, it should be necessary,
It seems to me, to know your adversary.    200
Be evermore prepared to meet this foe.
My mother taught me thus; that's all I know."
    "Now by St. Mary," said the innkeeper,
"This child speaks truth. Man, woman, laborer,
Servant, and child the thief has slain this year    205
In a big village a mile or more from here.
I think it is his place of habitation.
It would be wise to make some preparation
Before he brought a man into disgrace."
    "God's arms!" this roisterer said. "So that's the case!    210
Is it so dangerous with this thief to meet?
I'll look for him by every path and street,

7. My lucky number is seven. *Hailes*: An abbey in Gloucestershire, where some of Christ's blood
was believed to be preserved.

I vow it, by God's holy bones! Hear me,
Fellows of mine, we are all one, we three.
Let each of us hold up his hand to the other                               215
And each of us become his fellow's brother.
We'll slay this Death, who slaughters and betrays.
He shall be slain whose hand so many slays,
By the dignity of God, before tonight!"
   The three together set about to plight                      220
Their oaths to live and die each for the other
Just as though each had been to each born brother,
And in their drunken frenzy up they get
And toward the village off at once they set
Which the innkeeper had spoken of before,                                  225
And many were the grisly oaths they swore.
They rent Christ's precious body limb from limb—
Death shall be dead, if they lay hands on him!
   When they had hardly gone the first half mile,
Just as they were about to cross a stile,                                  230
An old man, poor and humble, met them there.
The old man greeted them with a meek air
And said, "God bless you, lords, and be your guide."
   "What's this?" the proudest of the three replied.
"Old beggar, I hope you meet with evil grace!                             235
Why are you all wrapped up except your face?
What are you doing alive so many a year?"
   The old man at these words began to peer
Into this gambler's face. "Because I can,
Though I should walk to India, find no man,"                               240
He said, "in any village or any town,
Who for my age is willing to lay down
His youth. So I must keep my old age still
For as long a time as it may be God's will.
Nor will Death take my life from me, alas!                                 245
Thus like a restless prisoner I pass
And on the ground, which is my mother's gate,
I walk and with my staff both early and late
I knock and say, 'Dear mother, let me in!
See how I vanish, flesh, and blood, and skin!                              250
Alas, when shall my bones be laid to rest?
I would exchange with you my clothing chest,
Mother, that in my chamber long has been
For an old haircloth rag to wrap me in.'
And yet she still refuses me that grace.                                   255
All white, therefore, and withered is my face.
   "But, sirs, you do yourselves no courtesy

To speak to an old man so churlishly
Unless he had wronged you either in word or deed.
As you yourselves in Holy Writ may read,　　　　　　　260
'Before an aged man whose head is hoar
Men ought to rise.'[8] I counsel you, therefore,
No harm nor wrong here to an old man do,
No more than you would have men do to you
In your old age, if you so long abide.　　　　　　　265
And God be with you, whether you walk or ride!
I must go yonder where I have to go."
　　　"No, you old beggar, by St. John, not so,"
Said another of these gamblers. "As for me,
By God, you won't get off so easily!　　　　　　　270
You spoke just now of that false traitor, Death,
Who in this land robs all our friends of breath.
Tell where he is, since you must be his spy,
Or you will suffer for it, so say I
By God and by the holy sacrament.　　　　　　　275
You are in league with him, false thief, and bent
On killing us young folk, that's clear to my mind."
　　　"If you are so impatient, sirs, to find
Death," he replied, "turn up this crooked way,
For in that grove I left him, truth to say,　　　　　　　280
Beneath a tree, and there he will abide.
No boast of yours will make him run and hide.
Do you see that oak tree? Just there you will find
This Death, and God, who bought again mankind,
Save and amend you!" So said this old man;　　　　　　　285
And promptly each of these three gamblers ran
Until he reached the tree, and there they found
Florins of fine gold, minted bright and round,
Nearly eight bushels of them, as they thought.
And after Death no longer then they sought.　　　　　　　290
Each of them was so ravished at the sight,
So fair the florins glittered and so bright,
That down they sat beside the precious hoard.
The worst of them, he uttered the first word.
　　　"Brothers," he told them, "listen to what I say.　　　　　　　295
My head is sharp, for all I joke and play.
Fortune has given us this pile of treasure
To set us up in lives of ease and pleasure.
Lightly it comes, lightly we'll make it go.
God's precious dignity! Who was to know　　　　　　　300

8. Leviticus 19:32.

We'd ever tumble on such luck today?
If we could only carry this gold away,
Home to my house, or either one of yours—
For well you know that all this gold is ours—
We'd touch the summit of felicity.                                     305
But still, by daylight that can hardly be.
People would call us thieves, too bold for stealth,
And they would have us hanged for our own wealth.
It must be done by night, that's our best plan,
As prudently and slyly as we can.                                      310
Hence my proposal is that we should all
Draw lots, and let's see where the lot will fall,
And the one of us who draws the shortest stick
Shall run back to town, and make it quick,
And bring us bread and wine here on the sly,                           315
And two of us will keep a watchful eye
Over this gold; and if he doesn't stay
Too long in town, we'll carry this gold away
By night, wherever we all agree it's best."
    One of them held the cut out in his fist                           320
And had them draw to see where it would fall,
And the cut fell on the youngest of them all.
At once he set off on his way to town,
And the very moment after he was gone
The one who urged this plan said to the other:                         325
"You know that by sworn oath you are my brother.
I'll tell you something you can profit by.
Our friend has gone, that's clear to any eye,
And here is gold, abundant as can be,
That we propose to share alike, we three.                              330
But if I worked it out, as I could do,
So that it could be shared between us two,
Wouldn't that be a favor, a friendly one?"
    The other answered, "How that can be done,
I don't quite see. He knows we have the gold.                          335
What shall we do, or what shall he be told?"
    "Will you keep the secret tucked inside your head?
And in a few words," the first scoundrel said,
"I'll tell you how to bring this end about."
    "Granted," the other told him. "Never doubt,                       340
I won't betray you, that you can believe."
    "Now," said the first, "we are two, as you pereceive,
And two of us must have more strength than one.
When he sits down, get up as if in fun
And wrestle with him. While you play this game                         345

I'll run him through the ribs. You do the same
With your dagger there, and then this gold shall be
Divided, dear friend, between you and me.
Then all that we desire we can fulfill,
And both of us can roll the dice at will."                                   350
Thus in agreement these two scoundrels fell
To slay the third, as you have heard me tell.

   The youngest, who had started off to town,
Within his heart kept rolling up and down
The beauty of those florins, new and bright.                                 355
"O Lord," he thought, "were there some way I might
Have all this treasure to myself alone,
There isn't a man who dwells beneath God's throne
Could live a life as merry as mine should be!"
And so at last the fiend, our enemy,                                         360
Put in his head that he could gain his ends
If he bought poison to kill off his friends.
Finding his life in such a sinful state,
The devil was allowed to seal his fate.
For it was altogether his intent                                             365
To kill his friends, and never to repent.
So off he set, no longer would he tarry,
Into the town, to an apothecary,
And begged for poison; he wanted it because
He meant to kill his rats; besides, there was                                370
A polecat living in his hedge, he said,
Who killed his capons; and when he went to bed
He wanted to take vengeance, if he might,
On vermin that devoured him by night.

   The apothecary answered, "You shall have                     375
A drug that as I hope the Lord will save
My soul, no living thing in all creation,
Eating or drinking of this preparation
A dose no bigger than a grain of wheat,
But promptly with his death-stroke he shall meet.                            380
Die, that he will, and in a briefer while
Than you can walk the distance of a mile,
This poison is so strong and virulent."

   Taking the poison, off the scoundrel went,
Holding it in a box, and next he ran                                         385
To the neighboring street, and borrowed from a man
Three generous flagons. He emptied out his drug
In two of them, and kept the other jug
For his own drink; he let no poison lurk
In that! And so all night he meant to work                                   390

Carrying off the gold. Such was his plan,
And when he had filled them, this accursed man
Retraced his path, still following his design,
Back to his friends with his three jugs of wine.
    But why dilate upon it any more?                              395
For just as they had planned his death before,
Just so they killed him, and with no delay.
When it was finished, one spoke up to say:
"Now let's sit down and drink, and we can bury
His body later on. First we'll be merry,"                               400
And as he said the words, he took the jug
That, as it happened, held the poisonous drug,
And drank, and gave his friend a drink as well,
And promptly they both died. But truth to tell,
In all that Avicenna[9] ever wrote                                      405
He never described in chapter, rule, or note
More marvelous signs of poisoning, I suppose,
Than appeared in these two wretches at the close.
Thus they both perished for their homicide,
And thus the traitorous poisoner also died.                             410
    O sin accursed above all cursedness,
O treacherous murder, O foul wickedness,
O gambling, lustfulness, and gluttony,
Traducer of Christ's name by blasphemy
And monstrous oaths, through habit and through pride!                   415
Alas, mankind! Ah, how may it betide
That you to your Creator, he that wrought you
And even with his precious heart's blood bought you,
So falsely and ungratefully can live?
    And now, good men, your sins may God forgive                420
And keep you specially from avarice!
My holy pardon will avail in this,
For it can heal each one of you that brings
His pennies, silver brooches, spoons, or rings.
Come, bow your head under this holy bull!                               425
You wives, come offer up your cloth or wool!
I write your names here in my roll, just so.
Into the bliss of heaven you shall go!
I will absolve you here by my high power,
You that will offer, as clean as in the hour                            430
When you were born.—Sirs, thus I preach. And now
Christ Jesus, our souls' healer, show you how
Within his pardon evermore to rest,

9. An Arab physician.

For that, I will not lie to you, is best.
    But in my tale, sirs, I forgot one thing.                    435
The relics and the pardons that I bring
Here in my pouch, no man in the whole land
Has finer, given me by the pope's own hand.
If any of you devoutly wants to offer
And have my absolution, come and proffer                          440
Whatever you have to give. Kneel down right here,
Humbly, and take my pardon, full and clear,
Or have a new, fresh pardon if you like
At the end of every mile of road we strike,
As long as you keep offering ever newly                           445
Good coins, not counterfeit, but minted truly.
Indeed it is an honor I confer
On each of you, an authentic pardoner
Going along to absolve you as you ride.
For in the country mishaps may betide—                            450
One or another of you in due course
May break his neck by falling from his horse.
Think what security it gives you all
That in this company I chanced to fall
Who can absolve you each, both low and high,                      455
When the soul, alas, shall from the body fly!
By my advice, our Host here shall begin,
For he's the man enveloped most by sin.
Come, offer first, Sir Host, and once that's done,
Then you shall kiss the relics, every one,                        460
Yes, for a penny! Come, undo your purse!
    "No, no," said he. "Then I should have Christ's curse!
I'll do nothing of the sort, for love or riches!
You'd make me kiss a piece of your old britches
And for a saintly relic make it pass                              465
Although it had the tincture of your ass.
By the cross St. Helen[1] found in the Holy Land,
I wish I had your balls here in my hand
For relics! Cut 'em off, and I'll be bound
If I don't help you carry them around.                            470
I'll have the things enshrined in a hog's turd!"
    The Pardoner did not answer; not a word,
He was so angry, could he find to say.
    "Now," said our Host, "I will not try to play
With you, nor any other angry man."                               475
    Immediately the worthy Knight began,

1. Mother of Constantine the Great; believed to have found the True Cross.

When he saw that all the people laughed, "No more,
This has gone far enough. Now as before,
Sir Pardoner, be gay, look cheerfully,
And you, Sir Host, who are so dear to me,      480
Come, kiss the Pardoner, I beg of you,
And Pardoner, draw near, and let us do
As we've been doing, let us laugh and play."
And so they kissed, and rode along their way.

### [The Knight's Interruption of the Monk's Tale]

"Stop!" cried the Knight. "No more of this, good sir!
You have said plenty, and much more, for sure,
For only a little such lugubriousness
Is plenty for a lot of folk, I guess.
I say for me it is a great displeasure,      5
When men have wealth and comfort in good measure,
To hear how they have tumbled down the slope,
And the opposite is a solace and a hope,
As when a man begins in low estate
And climbs the ladder and grows fortunate,      10
And stands there firm in his prosperity.
That is a welcome thing, it seems to me,
And of such things it would be good to tell."
"Well said," our Host declared. "By St. Paul's bell,
You speak the truth; this Monk's tongue is too loud.      15
He told how fortune covered with a cloud—
I don't know what-all; and of tragedy
You heard just now, and it's no remedy,
When things are over and done with, to complain.
Besides, as you have said, it is a pain      20
To hear of misery; it is distressing.
Sir Monk, no more, as you would have God's blessing.
This company is all one weary sigh.
Such talking isn't worth a butterfly,
For where's the amusement in it, or the game?      25
And so, Sir Monk, or Don Pierce by your name,
I beg you heartily, tell us something else.
Truly, but for the jingling of your bells
That from your bridle hang on every side,
By Heaven's King, who was born for us and died,      30
I should long since have tumbled down in sleep,
Although the mud had never been so deep,
And then you would have told your tale in vain;
For certainly, as these learned men explain,

When his audience have turned their backs away,                    35
It doesn't matter what a man may say.
I know well I shall have the essence of it
If anything is told here for our profit.
A tale of hunting, sir, pray share with us."
    "No," said the Monk, "I'll not be frivolous.                   40
Let another tell a tale, as I have told."
    Then spoke our Host, with a rude voice and bold,
And said to the Nun's Priest, "Come over here,
You priest, come hither, you Sir John, draw near!
Tell us a thing to make our spirits glad.                          45
Be cheerful, though the jade you ride is bad.
What if your horse is miserable and lean?
If he will carry you, don't care a bean!
Keep up a joyful heart, and look alive."
    "Yes, Host," he answered, "as I hope to thrive,                 50
If I weren't merry, I know I'd be reproached."
And with no more ado his tale he broached,
And this is what he told us, every one,
This precious priest, this goodly man, Sir John.


## The Nun's Priest's Tale

Once a poor widow, aging year by year,
Lived in a tiny cottage that stood near
A clump of shade trees rising in a dale.
This widow, of whom I tell you in my tale,
Since the last day that she had been a wife                         5
Had led a very patient, simple life.
She had but few possessions to content her.
By thrift and husbandry of what God sent her
She and two daughters found the means to dine.
She had no more than three well-fattened swine,                    10
As many cows, and one sheep, Moll by name.
Her bower and hall were black from the hearth-flame
Where she had eaten many a slender meal.
No dainty morsel did her palate feel
And no sharp sauce was needed with her pottage.                    15
Her table was in keeping with her cottage.
Excess had never given her disquiet.
Her only doctor was a moderate diet,
And exercise, and a heart that was contented.
If she did not dance, at least no gout prevented;                  20
No apoplexy had destroyed her head.
She never drank wine, whether white or red.

She served brown bread and milk, loaves white or black,
Singed bacon, all this with no sense of lack,
And now and then an egg or two. In short,                    25
She was a dairy woman of a sort.
    She had a yard, on the inside fenced about
With hedges, and an empty ditch without,
In which she kept a cock, called Chanticleer.
In all the realm of crowing he had no peer.                    30
His voice was merrier than the merry sound
Of the church organ grumbling out its ground
Upon a saint's day. Stouter was this cock
In crowing than the loudest abbey clock.
Of astronomy instinctively aware,                    35
He kept the sun's hours with celestial care,
For when through each fifteen degrees it moved,
He crowed so that it couldn't be improved.
His comb, like a crenelated castle wall,
Red as fine coral, stood up proud and tall.                    40
His bill was black; like polished jet it glowed,
And he was azure-legged and azure-toed.
As lilies were his nails, they were so white;
Like burnished gold his hue, it shone so bright.
This cock had in his princely sway and measure                    45
Seven hens to satisfy his every pleasure,
Who were his sisters and his sweethearts true,
Each wonderfully like him in her hue,
Of whom the fairest-feathered throat to see
Was fair Dame Partlet. Courteous was she,                    50
Discreet, and always acted debonairly.
She was sociable, and bore herself so fairly,
Since the very time that she was seven nights old,
The heart of Chanticleer was in her hold
As if she had him locked up, every limb.                    55
He loved her so that all was well with him.
It was a joy, when up the sun would spring,
To hear them both together sweetly sing,
"My love has gone to the country, far away!"
For as I understand it, in that day                    60
The animals and birds could sing and speak.
    Now as this cock, one morning at daybreak,
With each of the seven hens that he called spouse,
Sat on his perch inside the widow's house,
And next him fair Dame Partlet, in his throat                    65
This Chanticleer produced a hideous note
And groaned like a man who is having a bad dream;

And Partlet, when she heard her husband scream,
Was all aghast, and said, "Soul of my passion,
What ails you that you groan in such a fashion?                    70
You are always a sound sleeper. Fie, for shame!"
    And Chanticleer awoke and answered, "Dame,
Take no offense, I beg you, on this score.
I dreamt, by God, I was in a plight so sore
Just now, my heart still quivers from the fright.                   75
Now God see that my dream turns out all right
And keep my flesh and body from foul seizure!
I dreamed I was strutting in our yard at leisure
When there I saw, among the weeds and vines,
A beast, he was like a hound, and had designs                       80
Upon my person, and would have killed me dead.
His coat was not quite yellow, not quite red,
And both his ears and tail were tipped with black
Unlike the fur along his sides and back.
He had a small snout and a fiery eye.                               85
His look for fear still makes me almost die.
This is what made me groan, I have no doubt."
    "For shame! Fie on you, faint heart!" she burst out.
"Alas," she said, "by the great God above,
Now you have lost my heart and all my love!                         90
I cannot love a coward, as I'm blest!
Whatever any woman may protest,
We all want, could it be so, for our part,
Husbands who are wise and stout of heart,
No blabber, and no niggard, and no fool,                            95
Nor afraid of every weapon or sharp tool,
No braggart either, by the God above!
How dare you say, for shame, to your true love
That there is anything you ever feared?
Have you no man's heart, when you have a beard?                     100
Alas, and can a nightmare set you screaming?
God knows there's only vanity in dreaming!
Dreams are produced by such unseemly capers
As overeating; they come from stomach vapors
When a man's humors aren't behaving right                           105
From some excess. This dream you had tonight,
It comes straight from the superfluity
Of your red choler,[2] certain as can be,
That causes people terror in their dreams
Of darts and arrows, and fire in red streams,                      110

---

2. One of the four humors, or fluids, composing the body, according to ancient medical theory.

And of red beasts, for fear that they will bite,
Of little dogs, or of being in a fight;
As in the humor of melancholy lies
The reason why so many a sleeper cries
For fear of a black bull or a black bear                                    115
Or that black devils have him by the hair.
Through other humors also I could go
That visit many a sleeping man with woe,
But I will finish as quickly as I can.
    "Cato, that has been thought so wise a man,                             120
Didn't he tell us, 'Put no stock in dreams'?
Now, sir," she said, "when we fly down from our beams,
For God's sake, go and take a laxative!
On my salvation, as I hope to live,
I give you good advice, and no mere folly:                                  125
Purge both your choler and your melancholy!
You mustn't wait or let yourself bog down,
And since there is no druggist in this town
I shall myself prescribe for what disturbs
Your humors, and instruct you in the herbs                                  130
That will be good for you. For I shall find
Here in our yard herbs of the proper kind
For purging you both under and above.
Don't let this slip your mind, for God's own love!
Yours is a very choleric complexion.                                        135
When the sun is in the ascendant, my direction
Is to beware those humors that are hot.
Avoid excess of them; if you should not,
I'll be a penny, as a true believer,
You'll die of ague, or a tertian³ fever.                                    140
A day or so, if you do as I am urging,
You shall have worm-digestives, before purging
With fumitory or with hellebore
Or other herbs that grow here by the score;
With caper-spurge, or with the goat-tree berry                              145
Or the ground-ivy, found in your yard so merry.
Peck 'em up just as they grow, and eat 'em in!
Be cheerful, husband, by your father's kin!
Don't worry about a dream. I say no more."
    "Madame," he answered, "thanks for all your lore.                       150
But still, to speak of Cato,⁴ though his name
For wisdom has enjoyed so great a fame,
And though he counseled us there was no need

---

3. Recurring every third day.    4. In refuting Cato, Chanticleer gives a long account of authorities who have pronounced in favor of the truth of dreams.

To be afraid of dreams, by God, men read
Of many a man of more authority                                   155
Than this Don Cato could pretend to be
Who in old books declare the opposite,
And by experience they have settled it,
That dreams are omens and prefigurations
Both of good fortune and of tribulations                          160
That life and its vicissitudes present.
This question leaves no room for argument.
The very upshot makes it plain, indeed.
    "One of the greatest authors that men read
Informs us that two fellow travelers went,                        165
Once on a time, and with the best intent,
Upon a pilgrimage, and it fell out
They reached a town where there was such a rout
Of people, and so little lodging space,
They could not find even the smallest place                       170
Where they could both put up. So, for that night,
These pilgrims had to do as best they might,
And since they must, they parted company.
Each of them went off to his hostelry
And took his lodging as his luck might fall.                       175
Among plow oxen in a farmyard stall
One of them found a place, though it was rough.
His friend and fellow was lodged well enough
As his luck would have it, or his destiny
That governs all us creatures equally.                            180
And so it happened, long before the day,
He had a dream as in his bed he lay.
He dreamed that his parted friend began to call
And said, 'Alas, for in an ox's stall
This night I shall be murdered where I lie.                       185
Come to my aid, dear brother, or I die.
Come to me quickly, come in haste!' he said.
He started from his sleep, this man, for dread,
But when he had wakened, he rolled back once more
And on this dream of his he set no store.                         190
As a vain thing he dismissed it, unconcerned.
Twice as he slept that night the dream returned,
And still another and third time his friend
Came in a dream and said, 'I have met my end!
Look on my wounds! They are bloody, deep, and wide.               195
Now rise up early in the morningtide
And at the west gate of the town,' said he,
'A wagon with a load of dung you'll see.

Have it arrested boldly. Do as bidden,
For underneath you'll find my body hidden. 200
My money caused my murder, truth to tell,'
And told him each detail of how he fell,
With piteous face, and with a bloodless hue.
And do not doubt it, he found the dream was true,
For on the morrow, as soon as it was day, 205
To the place where his friend had lodged he made his way,
And no sooner did he reach this ox's stall
Than for his fellow he began to call.
    "Promptly the stableman replied, and said,
'Your friend is gone, sir. He got out of bed 210
And left the town as soon as day began.'
    "At last suspicion overtook this man.
Remembering his dreams, he would not wait,
But quickly went and found at the west gate,
Being driven to manure a farmer's land 215
As it might seem, a dung cart close at hand
That answered the description every way,
As you yourself have heard the dead man say.
And he began to shout courageously
For law and vengeance on this felony. 220
'My friend was killed this very night! He lies
Flat in this load of dung, with staring eyes.
I call on those who should keep rule and head,
The magistrates and governors here,' he said.
'Alas! Here lies my fellow, done to death!' 225
    "Why on this tale should I waste further breath?
The people sprang and flung the cart to ground
And in the middle of the dung they found
The dead man, while his murder was still new.
    "O blessed God, thou art so just and true, 230
Murder, though secret, ever thou wilt betray!
Murder will out, we see it day by day.
Murder so loathsome and abominable
To God is, who is just and reasonable,
That he will never suffer it to be 235
Concealed, though it hide a year, or two, or three.
Murder will out; to this point it comes down.
    "Promptly the magistrates who ruled that town
Have seized the driver, and put him to such pain.
And the stableman as well, that under strain 240
Of torture they were both led to confess
And hanged by the neck-bone for their wickedness.
    "Here's proof enough that dreams are things to dread!

And in the same book I have also read,
In the very chapter that comes right after this—      245
I don't speak idly, by my hope of bliss—
Two travelers who for some reason planned
To cross the ocean to a distant land
Found that the wind, by an opposing fate,
Blew contrary, and forced them both to wait      250
In a fair city by a harborside.
But one day the wind changed, toward eventide,
And blew just as it suited them instead.
Cheerfully these travelers went to bed
And planned to sail the first thing in the morning.      255
But to one of them befell a strange forewarning
And a great marvel. While asleep he lay,
He dreamed a curious dream along toward day.
He dreamed that a man appeared at his bedside
And told him not to sail, but wait and bide.      260
'Tomorrow,' he told the man, 'if you set sail,
You shall be drowned. I have told you my whole tale.'
He woke, and of this warning he had met
He told his friend, and begged him to forget
His voyage, and to wait that day and bide.      265
His friend, who was lying close at his bedside,
Began to laugh, and told him in derision,
'I am not so flabbergasted by a vision
As to put off my business for such cause.
I do not think your dream is worth two straws!      270
For dreams are but a vain absurdity.
Of apes and owls and many a mystery
People are always dreaming, in a maze
Of things that never were seen in all their days
And never shall be. But I see it's clear      275
You mean to waste your time by waiting here.
I'm sorry for that, God knows; and so good day.'
With this he took his leave and went his way.
But not the half his course had this man sailed—
I don't know why, nor what it was that failed—      280
When by an accident the hull was rent
And ship and man under the water went
In full view of the vessels alongside
That had put out with them on the same tide.
Now then, fair Partlet, whom I love so well,      285
From old examples such as these I tell
You may see that none should give too little heed
To dreams; for I say seriously, indeed,

That many a dream is too well worth our dread.
   "Yes, in St. Kenelm's life I have also read—                    290
He was the son of Cynewulf, the king
Of Mercia—how this Kenelm dreamed a thing.
One day, as the time when he was killed drew near,
He saw his murder in a dream appear.
His nurse explained his dream in each detail,                    295
And warned him to be wary without fail
Of treason; yet he was but seven years old,
And therefore any dream he could but hold
Of little weight, in heart he was so pure.
I'd give my shirt, by God, you may be sure,                    300
If you had read his story through like me!
   "Moreover, Partlet, I tell you truthfully,
Macrobius writes—and by his book we know
The African vision of great Scipio—
Confirming dreams, and holds that they may be                    305
Forewarnings of events that men shall see.
Again, I beg, look well at what is meant
By the Book of Daniel in the Old Testament,
Whether *he* held that dreams are vanity!
Read also about Joseph. You shall see                    310
That dreams, or some of them—I don't say all—
Warn us of things that afterward befall.
Think of the king of Egypt, Don Pharaoh;
Of his butler and his baker think also,
Whether they found that dreams have no result.                    315
Whoever will search through kingdoms and consult
Their histories reads many a wondrous thing
Of dreams. What about Croesus, Lydian king—
Didn't he dream he was sitting on a tree,
Which meant he would be hanged? Andromache,                    320
The woman who was once great Hector's wife,
On the day that Hector was to lose his life,
The very night before his blood was spilled
She dreamed of how her husband would be killed
If he went out to battle on that day.                    325
She warned him; but he would not heed nor stay.
In spite of her he rode out on the plain,
And by Achilles he was promptly slain.
But all that story is too long to tell,
And it is nearly day. I must not dwell                    330
Upon this matter. Briefly, in conclusion,
I say this dream will bring me to confusion
And mischief of some sort. And furthermore,

On laxatives, I say, I set no store,
For they are poisonous, I'm sure of it.                                335
I do not trust them! I like them not one bit!
    "Now let's talk cheerfully, and forget all this.
My pretty Partlet, by my hope of bliss,
In one thing God has sent me ample grace,
For when I see the beauty of your face,                                340
You are so scarlet-red about the eye,
It is enough to make my terrors die.
For just as true as *In principio*
*Mulier est hominis confusio*—[5]
And Madame, what this Latin means is this:                             345
'Woman is man's whole comfort and true bliss'—
When I feel you soft at night, and I beside you,
Although it's true, alas, I cannot ride you
Because our perch is built so narrowly,
I am then so full of pure felicity                                     350
That I defy whatever sort of dream!"
    And day being come, he flew down from the beam,
And with him his hens fluttered, one and all;
And with a "cluck, cluck" he began to call
His wives to where a kernel had been tossed.                           355
He was a prince, his fears entirely lost.
The morning had not passed the hour of prime
When he treaded Partlet for the twentieth time.
Grim as a lion he strolled to and fro,
And strutted only on his either toe.                                   360
He would not deign to set foot on the ground.
"Cluck, cluck," he said, whenever he had found
A kernel, and his wives came running all.
Thus royal as a monarch in his hall
I leave to his delights this Chanticleer,                              365
And presently the sequel you shall hear.
    After the month in which the world began,
The month of March, when God created man,[6]
Had passed, and when the season had run through
Since March began just thirty days and two,                            370
It happened that Chanticleer, in all his pride,
While his seven hens were walking by his side,
Lifted his eyes, beholding the bright sun,
Which in the sign of Taurus had then run
Twenty and one degrees and somewhat more,                              375
And knew by instinct, not by learned lore,

---

5. As sure as gospel, women is man's ruin.    6. Man was thought to have been created at the time of the spring equinox.

It was the hour of prime.[7] He raised his head
And crowed with lordly voice. "The sun," he said,
"Forty and one degrees and more in height
Has climbed the sky. Partlet, my world's delight,                    380
Hear all these birds, how happily they sing,
And see the pretty flowers, how they spring.
With solace and with joy my spirits dance!"
But suddenly he met a sore mischance,
For in the end joys ever turn to woes.                    385
Quickly the joys of earth are gone, God knows,
And could a rhetorician's art indite it,
He would be on solid ground if he should write it,
In a chronicle, as true notoriously!
Now every wise man, listen well to me.                    390
This story is as true, I undertake,
As the very book of Lancelot of the Lake
On which the women set so great a store.
Now to my matter I will turn once more.
    A sly iniquitous fox, with black-tipped ears,                    395
Who had lived in the neighboring wood for some three years,
His fated fancy swollen to a height,
Had broken through the hedges that same night
Into the yard where in his pride sublime
Chanticleer with his seven wives passed the time.                    400
Quietly in a bed of herbs he lay
Till it was past the middle of the day,
Waiting his hour on Chanticleer to fall
As gladly do these murderers, one and all,
Who lie in wait, concealed, to murder men.                    405
O murderer, lurking traitorous in your den!
O new Iscariot, second Ganelon,
False hypocrite, Greek Sinon,[8] who brought on
The utter woe of Troy and all her sorrow!
O Chanticleer, accursed be that morrow                    410
When to the yard you flew down from the beams!
That day, as you were well warned in your dreams,
Would threaten you with dire catastrophe.
But that which God foresees must come to be,
As there are certain scholars who aver.                    415
Bear witness, any true philosopher,
That in the schools there has been great altercation
Upon this question, and much disputation
By a hundred thousand scholars, man for man.

---

7. Nine.    8. Traitor at Troy. *Ganelon*: Traitor in the *Song of Roland*.

I cannot sift it down to the pure bran                                    420
As can the sacred Doctor, Augustine,
Or Boëthius, or Bishop Bradwardine,[9]
Whether God's high foreknowledge so enchains me
I needs must do a thing as it constrains me—
"Needs must"—that is, by plain necessity;                                 425
Or whether a free choice is granted me
To do it or not do it, either one,
Though God must know all things before they are done;
Or whether his foresight nowise can constrain
Except contingently, as some explain;                                     430
I will not labor such a high concern.
My tale is of a cock, as you shall learn,
Who took his wife's advice, to his own sorrow,
And walked out in the yard that fatal morrow.
Women have many times, as wise men hold,                                  435
Offered advice that left men in the cold.
A woman's counsel brought us first to woe
And out of Paradise made Adam go
Where he lived a merry life and one of ease.
But since I don't know whom I may displease                               440
By giving women's words an ill report,
Pass over it; I only spoke in sport.
There are books about it you can read or skim in,
And you'll discover what they say of women.
I'm telling you the cock's words, and not mine.                           445
Harm in no woman at all can I divine.
    Merrily bathing where the sand was dry
Lay Partlet, with her sisters all near by,
And Chanticleer, as regal as could be,
Sang merrily as the mermaid in the sea;                                   450
For the *Physiologus*[1] itself declares
That they know how to sing the merriest airs.
And so it happened that as he fixed his eye
Among the herbs upon a butterfly,
He caught sight of this fox who crouched there low.                       455
He felt no impulse then to strut or crow,
But cried "cucock!" and gave a fearful start
Like a man who has been frightened to the heart.
For instinctively, if he should chance to see
His opposite, a beast desires to flee,                                    460
Even the first time that it meets his eye.

9. *Augustine*: St. Augustine (354–430), the great Church Father. *Boëthius*: Author of the *Consolation of Philosophy* (*De consolatione philosophiae*), one of the most popular works of the Middle Ages; written in the early sixth century. *Bradwardine*: Archbishop of Canterbury in Chaucer's boyhood.    1. A collection of nature lore.

　　This Chanticleer, no sooner did he spy
The fox than promptly enough he would have fled.
But "Where are you going, kind sir?" the fox said.
"Are you afraid of me, who am your friend?          465
Truly, I'd be a devil from end to end
If I meant you any harm or villainy.
I have not come to invade your privacy.
In truth, the only reason that could bring
This visit of mine was just to hear you sing.          470
Beyond a doubt, you have as fine a voice
As any angel who makes heaven rejoice.
Also you have more feeling in your note
Than Boëthius,[2] or any tuneful throat.
Milord your father once—and may God bless          475
His soul—your noble mother too, no less,
Have been inside my house, to my great ease.
And verily sir, I should be glad to please
You also. But for singing, I declare,
As I enjoy my eyes, that precious pair,          480
Save you, I never heard a man so sing
As your father did when night was on the wing.
Straight from the heart, in truth, came all his song,
And to make his voice more resonant and strong
He would strain until he shut his either eye,          485
So loud and lordly would he make his cry,
And stand up on his tiptoes therewithal
And stretch his neck till it grew long and small.
He had such excellent discretion, too,
That whether his singing, all the region through,          490
Or his wisdom, there was no one to surpass.
I read in that old book, *Don Burnel the Ass*,[3]
Among his verses once about a cock
Hit on the leg by a priest who threw a rock
When he was young and foolish; and for this          495
He caused the priest to lose his benefice.[4]
But no comparison, in all truth, lies
Between your father, so prudent and so wise,
And this other cock, for all his subtlety.
Sing, sir! Show me, for holy charity,          500
Can you imitate your father, that wise man?"
　　Blind to all treachery, Chanticleer began
To beat his wings, like one who cannot see
The traitor, ravished by his flattery.

---

2. He was also author of a treatise on music.　　3. A twelfth-century Latin work by the English-man Nigel Wireker.　　4. By failing to wake him with his crowing.

Alas, you lords, about your court there slips            505
Many a flatterer with deceiving lips
Who can please you more abundantly, I fear,
Than he who speaks the plain truth to your ear.
Read in *Ecclesiastes*,[5] you will see
What flatterers are. Lords, heed their treachery!       510
   This Chanticleer stood tiptoe at full height.
He stretched his neck, he shut his eyelids tight,
And he began to crow a lordly note.
The fox, Don Russell, seized him by the throat
At once, and on his back bore Chanticleer               515
Off toward his den that in the grove stood near,
For no one yet had threatened to pursue.
   O destiny, that no man may eschew!
Alas, that he left his safe perch on the beams!
Alas, that Partlet took no stock in dreams!             520
And on a Friday happened this mischance!
   Venus, whose pleasures make the whole world dance,
Since Chanticleer was ever your true servant,
And of your rites with all his power observant
For pleasure rather than to multiply,                   525
Would you on Friday suffer him to die?
   Geoffrey,[6] dear master of the poet's art,
Who when your Richard perished by a dart
Made for your king an elegy so burning,
Why have I not your eloquence and learning             530
To chide, as you did, with a heart so filled,
Fridays? For on a Friday he was killed.
Then should I show you how I could complain
For Chanticleer in all his fright and pain!
   In truth, no lamentation ever rose,                535
No shriek of ladies when before its foes
Ilium fell, and Pyrrhus with drawn blade
Had seized King Priam by the beard and made
An end of him— the *Aeneid* tells the tale—[7]
Such as the hens made with their piteous wail          540
In their enclosure, seeing the dread sight
Of Chanticleer. But at the shrillest height
Shrieked Partlet. She shrieked louder than the wife
Of Hasdrubal,[8] when her husband lost his life
And the Romans burned down Carthage; for her state     545
Of torment and of frenzy was so great

---

5. This should apparently be Ecclesiasticus (a book of the Old Testament Apocrypha) 12:10 ff;
27:26.    6. Geoffrey de Vinsauf, author of a treatise on poetry, with specimens, among them an
elegy on Richard I.    7. Book II, ll. 550 ff.    8. King of Carthage (second century B.C.).

She willfully chose the fire for her part,
Leaped in, and burned herself with steadfast heart.
    Unhappy hens, you shrieked as when for pity,
While the tyrant Nero put to flames the city                550
Of Rome, rang out the shriek of senators' wives
Because their husbands had all lost their lives;
This Nero put to death these innocent men.
But I will come back to my tale again.
    Now this good widow and her two daughters heard        555
These woeful hens shriek when the crime occurred,
And sprang outdoors as quickly as they could
And saw the fox, who was making for the wood
Bearing this Chanticleer across his back.
"Help, help!" they cried. They cried, "Alas! Alack!        560
The fox, the fox!" and after him they ran,
And armed with clubs came running many a man.
Ran Coll the dog, and led a yelping band;
Ran Malkyn, with a distaff in her hand;
Ran cow and calf, and even the very hogs,                  565
By the yelping and the barking of the dogs
And men's and women's shouts so terrified
They ran till it seemed their hearts would burst inside;
They squealed like fiends in the pit, with none to still them.
The ducks quacked as if men were going to kill them.       570
The geese for very fear flew over the trees.
Out of the beehive came the swarm of bees.
Ah! Bless my soul, the noise, by all that's true,
So hideous was that Jack Straw's[9] retinue
Made never a hubbub that was half so shrill                575
Over a Fleming they were going to kill
As the clamor made that day over the fox.
They brought brass trumpets, and trumpets made of box,
Of horn, of bone, on which they blew and squeaked,
And those who were not blowing whooped and shrieked.       580
It seemed as if the very heavens would fall!
    Now hear me, you good people, one and all!
Fortune, I say, will suddenly override
Her enemy in his very hope and pride!
This cock, as on the fox's back he lay,                    585
Plucked up his courage to speak to him and say
"God be my help, sir, but I'd tell them all,
That is, if I were you, 'Plague on you fall!
Go back, proud fools! Now that I've reached the wood,
I'll eat the cock at once, for all the good                590

9. Leader of the Peasants' Revolt of 1381, caused in part by the competition in labor of immigrating Flemings.

Your noise can do. Here Chanticleer shall stay.' "
   "Fine!" said the fox. "I'll do just what you say."
But the cock, as he was speaking, suddenly
Out of his jaws lurched expeditiously,
And flew at once high up into a tree.                595
And when the fox saw that the cock was free,
"Alas," he said, "alas, O Chanticleer!
Inasmuch as I have given you cause for fear
By seizing you and bearing you away,
I have done you wrong, I am prepared to say.     600
But, sir, I did it with no ill intent.
Come down, and I shall tell you what I meant.
So help me God, it's truth I'll offer you!"
   "No, no," said he. "We're both fools, through and through.
But curse my blood and bones for the chief dunce    605
If you deceive me oftener than once!
You shall never again by flattery persuade me
To sing and wink my eyes, by him that made me.
For he that willfully winks when he should see,
God never bless him with prosperity!"          610
   "Ah," said the fox, "with mischief may God greet
The man ungoverned, rash, and indiscreet
Who babbles when to hold his tongue were needful!"
   Such is it to be reckless and unheedful
And trust in flattery. But you who hold       615
That this is a mere trifle I have told,
Concerning only a fox, or a cock and hen,
Think twice, and take the moral, my good men!
For truly, of whatever is written, all
Is written for our doctrine, says St. Paul.[1]    620
Then take the fruit, and let the chaff lie still.
Now, gracious God, if it should be your will,
As my Lord teaches, make us all good men
And bring us to your holy bliss! Amen.

---

# EVERYMAN

Drama scarcely attained the status of a dominant literary form in the Middle
Ages, although in the later centuries of the period it was popular, fairly
abundant, and varied in character. It began with the impersonation or dramatization of passages from the liturgy of the Resurrection and the Nativity of
Christ. "Produced" at first in the Latin language and inside a church, it was
later moved outside and Latin was replaced with vernacular languages of

1. Romans 15:4.

several European peoples. By the fourteenth century, if not earlier, whole
"cycles" of short plays were performed on certain feast days of the Church,
especially Corpus Christi. A complete sequence began with the revolt of
Satan and his followers against God and ended with the Last Judgment;
inside these limits, some forty "one-act" pieces presented the important events
in the divine plan for the history of mankind. The content of these plays was
based very closely on the narrative of the Bible; hence the name *miracle*
plays—that is, dealing with things wonderful to man.

About the time when the miracle plays had reached their fullest development, another kind of dramatic composition emerged, also religious in
nature and purpose. As the miracle plays dramatize the liturgy and certain
Biblical events, so the *morality* plays dramatize the content of a typical hom-
ily or sermon. By common consent, *Everyman* is regarded as the best of this
kind of drama. We do not know the author's name, but the play belongs to
the fifteenth century; it may owe something to a Dutch piece on the same
theme. Whereas miracle plays were produced in a long sequence, with
"amateur" casts drawn from more or less suitable craft guilds (for example,
the carpenters might present the building of Noah's ark and the subsequent
flood), morality plays may have been acted by professional or semiprofes-
sional companies. Nothing is actually known about the original productions
of *Everyman*; it is well suited, however, to outdoor performance. Its com-
parative length, along with the large part of the title character, favors the
possibility of some degree of professionalism in the cast.

The modern reader may find it profitable to compare *Everyman* with such
different kinds of drama as Greek tragedy, Marlowe's *Doctor Faustus*, or
MacLeish's modern play, *J.B.* In its brevity, simplicity, and concentration
on a single theme and situation, it recalls especially the shorter plays of the
ancient Greeks. Its topic has much in common with that of Marlowe's play—
man facing death, in the light of his past life—but the decisive choice and
consequent ending are different. The role assigned to deity is both like and
unlike that in MacLeish's adaptation of the story of Job in his play.

As in most morality plays, the characters are personifications of abstractions, or generalizations. Everyman himself of course represents all humanity. But we should not assume in advance that "abstract" characters make a
dull play. In the first place, dramatizing the characters gives them actuality;
the actors must be flesh and blood. Then, in *Everyman*, the situations, the
talk, and the behavior of the various characters are thoroughly realistic as
well as representative of their respective generalized significance. For example, Good Fellowship does and says just about what a single boon companion would be likely to say and do under the same circumstances. Good
Deeds is not a static figure: we see her first bound to the earth (the floor of
the stage) by Everyman's sins; when he scourges himself in penance, she
rises joyfully to accompany him. The author's ingenuity is notable in the
character Goods (Riches): Goods is offstage when Everyman calls him; the
audience hears but does not see him at first as he explains that he lies there
in corners, trussed and piled up, locked in chests, stuffed in bags! Surely he
must have got a laugh when he did come on stage. And of course God, who
instigates the action by sending Death to call Everyman to his account, is
no abstraction. He was probably a voice off-stage rather than an actor—but
a very effective character none the less.

Together with the rapidly moving plot, free from extraneous matter, it is the rightness of its words that makes *Everyman* a success. God speaks with an unfailing simplicity and directness:

> Charyte they do all clene forgete.
> I hoped well that every man
> In my glory shulde make his mansyon;
> And thereto I had them all electe. . . .
> They be so combred with worldly ryches
> That nedes on them I must do iustyce. . . .

He does not need the modern author's humor or triviality. Yet humor is not absent from the play. Cousin, asked by Everyman to go with him at the summons of Death, exclaims: "No, by Our Lady! I have the crampe in my to[e]"; and later, Beauty replies to the same effect: "I crosse out all this! Adewe, by Saynt Iohan!/I take my cap in my lappe, and am gone." There is irony in Good Fellowship's farewell verse: "For you I wyll remembre that partynge is mournynge." Best of all, perhaps, are the short speeches, scattered throughout the earlier parts of the play especially, which express Everyman's disappointment in his friends and consequent disillusion. One example must suffice. After a long colloquy with Goods, that character asks Everyman, "What! wenest thou that I am thyne?" Reversal, necessary prelude to re-orientation, is condensed in Everyman's brief reply: "I had went [believed] so."

A good selection of miracle plays, morality plays, and other medieval drama is contained in Joseph Quincy Adams, *Chief Pre-Shakespearean Dramas* (1924). On the medieval theater and staging see Richard Southern, *The Medieval Theatre in the Round; A Study of the Staging of the Castle of Perseverance and Other Matters* (1957). For a recent survey of the whole matter, see Hardin Craig, *English Religious Drama* (1955). For an interesting fresh approach, see the chapter on "The Mystery Cycle" in John Speirs, *Medieval English Poetry: The Non-Chaucerian Tradition* (1958).

# Everyman[1]

## Dramatis Personae

| | |
|---|---|
| MESSENGER | KNOWLEDGE |
| GOD | CONFESSION |
| DEATH | BEAUTY |
| EVERYMAN | STRENGTH |
| FELLOWSHIP | DISCRETION |
| KINDRED | FIVE-WITS |
| COUSIN | ANGEL |
| GOODS | DOCTOR |
| GOOD DEEDS | |

---

1. Modernized text and notes by E. Talbot Donaldson.

HERE BEGINNETH A TREATISE HOW THE HIGH FATHER OF
HEAVEN SENDETH DEATH TO SUMMON EVERY CREATURE
TO COME AND GIVE ACCOUNT OF THEIR LIVES IN THIS
WORLD, AND IS IN MANNER OF A MORAL PLAY

[*Enter* MESSENGER.]

MESSENGER. I pray you all give your audience,
    And hear this matter with reverence,
    By figure[2] a moral play,
    *The Summoning of Everyman* called it is,
    That of our lives and ending shows        5
    How transitory we be all day.[3]
    The matter is wonder precious,
    But the intent of it is more gracious
    And sweet to bear away.
    The story saith: Man, in the beginning        10
    Look well, and take good heed to the ending,
    Be you never so gay.
    You think sin in the beginning full sweet,
    Which in the end causeth the soul to weep,
    When the body lieth in clay.        15
    Here shall you see how fellowship and jollity,
    Both strength, pleasure, and beauty,
    Will fade from thee as flower in May.
    For ye shall hear how our Heaven-King
    Calleth Everyman to a general reckoning.        20
    Give audience and hear what he doth say.
    [*Exit* MESSENGER.—*Enter* GOD.]

GOD. I perceive, here in my majesty,
    How that all creatures be to me unkind,[4]
    Living without dread in worldly prosperity.
    Of ghostly[5] sight the people be so blind,        25
    Drowned in sin, they know me not for their God.
    In worldly riches is all their mind:
    They fear not of my righteousness the sharp rod;
    My law that I showed when I for them died
    They forget clean, and shedding of my blood red.        30
    I hanged between two,[6] it cannot be denied:
    To get them life I suffered to be dead.
    I healed their feet, with thorns hurt was my head.
    I could do no more than I did, truly—
    And now I see the people do clean forsake me.        35
    They use the seven deadly sins damnable,

2. In form.    3. Always.    4. Thoughtless.    5. Spiritual.    6. The two thieves between
whom Christ was crucified.

As pride, coveitise,[7] wrath, and lechery
Now in the world be made commendable.
And thus they leave of angels the heavenly company.
Every man liveth so after his own pleasure,      40
And yet of their life they be nothing sure.
I see the more that I them forbear,
The worse they be from year to year:
All that liveth appaireth[8] fast.
Therefore I will, in all the haste,      45
Have a reckoning of every man's person.
For, and I leave the people thus alone
In their life and wicked tempests,
Verily they will become much worse than beasts;
For now one would by envy another up eat.      50
Charity do they all clean forgeet.
I hoped well that every man
In my glory should make his mansion,
And thereto I had them all elect.[9]
But now I see, like traitors deject,[1]      55
They thank me not for the pleasure that I to them meant,
Nor yet for their being that I them have lent.
I proffered the people great multitude of mercy,
And few there be that asketh it heartily.
They be so cumbered with worldly riches      60
That needs on them I must do justice—
On every man living without fear.
Where art thou, Death, thou mighty messenger?
     [*Enter* DEATH.]
DEATH. Almighty God, I am here at your will,
Your commandment to fulfill.      65
GOD. Go thou to Everyman,
     And show him, in my name,
     A pilgrimage he must on him take,
     Which he in no wise may escape;
     And that he bring with him a sure reckoning      70
     Without delay or any tarrying.
DEATH. Lord, I will in the world go run over all,
     And cruelly out-search both great and small.
     [*Exit* GOD.]
     Everyman will I beset that liveth beastly
     Out of God's laws, and dreadeth not folly.      75
     He that loveth riches I will strike with my dart,
     His sight to blind, and from heaven to depart—[2]

7. Avarice.     8. Degenerates.     9. Chosen.     1. Abased.     2. Separate.

Except that Almsdeeds be his good friend—
In hell for to dwell, world without end.
Lo, yonder I see Everyman walking:                                    80
Full little he thinketh on my coming;
His mind is on fleshly lusts and his treasure,
And great pain it shall cause him to endure
Before the Lord, Heaven-King.
    [*Enter* EVERYMAN.]
Everyman, stand still! Whither art thou going                         85
Thus gaily? Hast thou thy Maker forgeet?
EVERYMAN. Why askest thou?
Why wouldest thou weet?[3]
DEATH. Yea, sir, I will show you:
In great haste I am sent to thee                                       90
From God out of his majesty.
EVERYMAN. What! sent to me?
DEATH. Yea, certainly.
Though thou have forgot him here,
He thinketh on thee in the heavenly sphere,                           95
As, ere we depart, thou shalt know.
EVERYMAN. What desireth God of me?
DEATH. That shall I show thee:
A reckoning he will needs have
Without any longer respite.                                          100
EVERYMAN. To give a reckoning longer leisure I crave.
This blind[4] matter troubleth my wit.
DEATH. On thee thou must take a long journay:
Therefore thy book of count with thee thou bring,
For turn again thou cannot by no way.                                105
And look thou be sure of thy reckoning,
For before God thou shalt answer and shew
Thy many bad deeds and good but a few—
How thou hast spent thy life and in what wise,
Before the Chief Lord of Paradise.                                   110
Have ado that we were in that way,[5]
For weet thou well thou shalt make none attornay.[6]
EVERYMAN. Full unready I am such reckoning to give.
I know thee not. What messenger art thou?
DEATH. I am Death that no man dreadeth,[7]                           115
For every man I 'rest, and no man spareth;
For it is God's commandment
That all to me should be obedient.
EVERYMAN. O Death, thou comest when I had thee least in mind.

3. Know.   4. Unexpected.   5. Let's get started at once.   6. None to appear in your stead.   7. That fears nobody.

In thy power it lieth me to save:                              120
Yet of my good will I give thee, if thou will be kind,
Yea, a thousand pound shalt thou have—
And defer this matter till another day.
DEATH. Everyman, it may not be, by no way.
I set nought by gold, silver, nor riches,                      125
Nor by pope, emperor, king, duke, nor princes,
For, and I would receive gifts great,
All the world I might get.
But my custom is clean contrary:
I give thee no respite. Come hence and not tarry!              130
EVERYMAN. Alas, shall I have no longer respite?
I may say Death giveth no warning.
To think on thee it maketh my heart sick,
For all unready is my book of reckoning.
But twelve year and I might have a biding,[8]                  135
My counting-book I would make so clear
That my reckoning I should not need to fear.
Wherefore, Death, I pray thee, for God's mercy,
Spare me till I be provided of remedy.
DEATH. Thee availeth not to cry, weep, and pray;               140
But haste thee lightly[9] that thou were gone that journay,
And prove thy friends, if thou can.
For weet thou well the tide abideth no man,
And in the world each living creature
For Adam's sin must die of nature.[1]                          145
EVERYMAN. Death, if I should this pilgrimage take
And my reckoning surely make,
Show me, for saint[2] charity,
Should I not come again shortly?
DEATH. No, Everyman. And thou be once there,                   150
Thou mayst never more come here,
Trust me verily.
EVERYMAN. O gracious God in the high seat celestial,
Have mercy on me in this most need!
Shall I have no company from this vale terrestrial             155
Of mine acquaintance that way me to lead?
DEATH. Yea, if any be so hardy
That would go with thee and bear thee company.
Hie thee that thou were gone to God's magnificence,
Thy reckoning to give before his presence.                     160
What, weenest[3] thou thy life is given thee,
And thy worldly goods also?

8. If I might have a delay for just twelve years.   9. Quickly.   1. Naturally.   2. Holy.
3. Suppose.

EVERYMAN. I had weened so, verily.

DEATH. Nay, nay, it was but lent thee.
   For as soon as thou art go,                 165
   Another a while shall have it and then go therefro,
   Even as thou hast done.
   Everyman, thou art mad! Thou hast thy wits[4] five,
   And here on earth will not amend thy life!
   For suddenly I do come.               170

EVERYMAN. O wretched caitiff! Whither shall I flee
   That I might 'scape this endless sorrow?
   Now, gentle Death, spare me till tomorrow,
   That I may amend me
   With good advisement.[5]              175

DEATH. Nay, thereto I will not consent,
   Nor no man will I respite,
   But to the heart suddenly I shall smite,
   Without any advisement.
   And now out of thy sight I will me hie:      180
   See thou make thee ready shortly,
   For thou mayst say this is the day
   That no man living may 'scape away.
    [*Exit* DEATH.]

EVERYMAN. Alas, I may well weep with sighs deep:
   Now have I no manner of company         185
   To help me in my journey and me to keep.
   And also my writing[6] is full unready—
   How shall I do now for to excuse me?
   I would to God I had never be geet![7]
   To my soul a full great profit it had be.     190
   For now I fear pains huge and great.
   The time passeth: Lord, help, that all wrought!
   For though I mourn, it availeth nought.
   The day passeth and is almost ago:
   I wot[8] not well what for to do.        195
   To whom were I best my complaint to make?
   What and I to Fellowship thereof spake,
   And showed him of this sudden chance?
   For in him is all mine affiance,[9]
   We have in the world so many a day      200
   Be good friends in sport and play.
   I see him yonder, certainly.
   I trust that he will bear me company.
   Therefore to him will I speak to ease my sorrow.

---

4. Senses.   5. Preparation.   6. Ledger.   7. Been begotten.   8. Know.   9. Trust.

[*Enter* FELLOWSHIP.]

Well met, good Fellowship, and good morrow!                    205

FELLOWSHIP. Everyman, good morrow, by this day!
  Sir, why lookest thou so piteously?
  If anything be amiss, I pray thee me say,
  That I may help to remedy.

EVERYMAN. Yea, good Fellowship, yea:                            210
  I am in great jeopardy.

FELLOWSHIP. My true friend, show to me your mind.
  I will not forsake thee to my life's end
  In the way of good company.

EVERYMAN. That was well spoken, and lovingly!                   215

FELLOWSHIP. Sir, I must needs know your heaviness.
  I have pity to see you in any distress.
  If any have you wronged, ye shall revenged be,
  Though I on the ground be slain for thee,
  Though that I know before that I should die.                  220

EVERYMAN. Verily, Fellowship, gramercy.[1]

FELLOWSHIP. Tush! by thy thanks I set not a stree.[2]
  Show me your grief and say no more.

EVERYMAN. If I my heart should to you break,[3]
  And then you to turn your mind fro me,                        225
  And would not me comfort when ye hear me speak,
  Then should I ten times sorrier be.

FELLOWSHIP. Sir, I say as I will do, indeed.

EVERYMAN. Then be you a good friend at need.
  I have found you true herebefore.                             230

FELLOWSHIP. And so ye shall evermore.
  For, in faith, and thou go to hell,
  I will not forsake thee by the way.

EVERYMAN. Ye speak like a good friend. I believe you well.
  I shall deserve[4] it, and I may.                             235

FELLOWSHIP. I speak of no deserving, by this day!
  For he that will say and nothing do
  Is not worthy with good company to go.
  Therefore show me the grief of your mind,
  As to your friend most loving and kind.                       240

EVERYMAN. I shall show you how it is:
  Commanded I am to go a journay,
  A long way, hard and dangerous,
  And give a strait[5] count, without delay,
  Before the high judge Adonai.[6]                              245
  Wherefore I pray you bear me company,

1. Many thanks.   2. Straw.   3. Disclose.   4. Repay.   5. Strict.   6. God.

As ye have promised, in this journay.
FELLOWSHIP. This is matter indeed! Promise is duty—
    But, and I should take such a voyage on me,
    I know it well, it should be to my pain.                          250
    Also it maketh me afeard, certain.
    But let us take counsel here, as well as we can—
    For your words would fear a strong man.
EVERYMAN. Why, ye said if I had need,
    Ye would me never forsake, quick ne dead,                          255
    Though it were to hell, truly.
FELLOWSHIP. So I said, certainly.
    But such pleasures[7] be set aside, the sooth to say.
    And also, if we took such a journay,
    When should we again come?                                         260
EVERYMAN. Nay, never again, till the day of doom.
FELLOWSHIP. In faith, then will not I come there!
    Who hath you these tidings brought?
EVERYMAN. Indeed, Death was with me here.
FELLOWSHIP. Now by God that all hath bought,[8]                       265
    If Death were the messenger,
    For no man that is living today
    I will not go that loath journay—
    Not for the father that begat me!
EVERYMAN. Ye promised otherwise, pardie.[9]                           270
FELLOWSHIP. I wot well I said so, truly.
    And yet, if thou wilt eat and drink and make good cheer,
    Or haunt to women the lusty company,
    I would not forsake you while the day is clear,
    Trust me verily!                                                   275
EVERYMAN. Yea, thereto ye would be ready—
    To go to mirth, solace,[1] and play:
    Your mind to folly will sooner apply
    Than to bear me company in my long journay.
FELLOWSHIP. Now in good faith, I will not that way.                   280
    But, and thou will murder or any man kill,
    In that I will help thee with a good will.
EVERYMAN. O that is simple[2] advice, indeed!
    Gentle fellow, help me in my necessity:
    We have loved long, and now I need—                                285
    And now, gentle Fellowship, remember me!
FELLOWSHIP. Whether ye have loved me or no,
    By Saint John, I will not with thee go!
EVERYMAN. Yet I pray thee take the labor and do so much for me,

7. Jokes.   8. Redeemed.   9. By God.   1. Pleasure.   2. Foolish.

To bring me forward,[3] for saint charity,                     290
And comfort me till I come without the town.
FELLOWSHIP. Nay, and thou would give me a new gown,
    I will not a foot with thee go.
    But, and thou had tarried, I would not have left thee so.
    And as now, God speed thee in thy journay!                     295
    For from thee I will depart as fast as I may.
EVERYMAN. Whither away, Fellowship? Will thou forsake me?
FELLOWSHIP. Yea, by my fay! To God I betake[4] thee.
EVERYMAN. Farewell, good Fellowship! For thee my heart is sore.
    Adieu forever—I shall see thee no more                     300
FELLOWSHIP. In faith, Everyman, farewell now at the ending:
    For you I will remember that parting is mourning.
        [*Exit* FELLOWSHIP.]
EVERYMAN. Alack, shall we thus depart[5] indeed—
    Ah, Lady, help!—without any more comfort?
    Lo, Fellowship forsaketh me in my most need!                     305
    For help in this world whither shall I resort?
    Fellowship herebefore with me would merry make,
    And now little sorrow for me doth he take.
    It is said, "In prosperity men friends may find
    Which in adversity be full unkind."                     310
    Now whither for succor shall I flee,
    Sith[6] that Fellowship hath forsaken me?
    To my kinsmen I will, truly,
    Praying them to help me in my necessity.
    I believe that they will do so,                     315
    For kind will creep where it may not go.[7]
    I will go 'say[8]—for yonder I see them—
    Where[9] be ye now my friends and kinsmen.
        [*Enter* KINDRED *and* COUSIN.]
KINDRED. Here be we now at your commandment:
    Cousin, I pray you show us your intent                     320
    In any wise, and not spare.
COUSIN. Yea, Everyman, and to us declare
    If ye be disposed to go anywhither.
    For, weet you well, we will live and die togither.
KINDRED. In wealth and woe we will with you hold,                     325
    For over his kin a man may be bold.
EVERYMAN. Gramercy, my friends and kinsmen kind.
    Now shall I show you the grief of my mind.
    I was commanded by a messenger
    That is a high king's chief officer:                     330

---

3. Escort me.   4. Commend.   5. Part.   6. Since.   7. For kinship will creep where it
cannot walk (i.e., kinsmen will suffer hardship for one another).   8. Assay.   9. Whether.

. He bade me go a pilgrimage, to my pain—
  And I know well I shall never come again.
  Also I must give a reckoning strait,
  For I have a great enemy that hath me in wait,[1]
  Which intendeth me to hinder.                                    335
KINDRED. What account is that which ye must render?
  That would I know.
EVERYMAN. Of all my works I must show
  How I have lived and my days spent;
  Also of ill deeds that I have used                              340
  In my time sith life was me lent,
  And of all virtues that I have refused.
  Therefore I pray you go thither with me
  To help me make mine account, for saint charity.
COUSIN. What, to go thither? Is that the matter?                     345
  Nay, Everyman, I had liefer fast[2] bread and water
  All this five year and more!
EVERYMAN. Alas, that ever I was bore!
  For now shall I never be merry
  If that you forsake me.                                         350
KINDRED. Ah, sir, what? Ye be a merry man:
  Take good heart to you and make no moan.
  But one thing I warn you, by Saint Anne,
  As for me, ye shall go alone.
EVERYMAN. My Cousin, will you not with me go?                        355
COUSIN. No, by Our Lady! I have the cramp in my toe:
  Trust not to me. For, so God me speed,
  I will deceive you in your most need.
KINDRED. It availeth you not us to 'tice.[3]
  Ye shall have my maid with all my heart:                        360
  She loveth to go to feasts, there to be nice,[4]
  And to dance, and abroad to start.[5]
  I will give her leave to help you in that journey,
  If that you and she may agree.
EVERYMAN. Now show me the very effect of your mind:                  365
  Will you go with me or abide behind?
KINDRED. Abide behind? Yea, that will I and I may!
  Therefore farewell till another day.
    [*Exit* KINDRED.]
EVERYMAN. How should I be merry or glad?
  For fair promises men to me make,                               370
  But when I have most need they me forsake.
  I am deceived. That maketh me sad.

---

1. Satan lies in ambush for me.  2. Rather fast on.  3. Entice.  4. Wanton.  5. To go gadding about.

COUSIN. Cousin Everyman, farewell now,
    For verily I will not go with you;
    Also of mine own an unready reckoning                                    375
    I have to account—therefore I make tarrying.
    Now God keep thee, for now I go.
        [*Exit* COUSIN.]
EVERYMAN. Ah, Jesus, is all come hereto?
    Lo, fair words maketh fools fain:[6]
    They promise and nothing will do, certain.                                    380
    My kinsmen promised me faithfully
    For to abide with me steadfastly,
    And now fast away do they flee.
    Even so Fellowship promised me.
    What friend were best me of to provide?                                    385
    I lose my time here longer to abide.
    Yet in my mind a thing there is:
    All my life I have loved riches;
    If that my Good[7] now help me might,
    He would make my heart full light.                                    390
    I will speak to him in this distress.
    Where art thou, my Goods and riches?
GOODS. [*Within*] Who calleth me? Everyman? What, hast thou
    haste?
    And in chests I am locked so fast—                                    395
    Also sacked in bags—thou mayst see with thine eye
    I cannot stir, in packs low where I lie.
    What would ye have? Lightly[8] me say.
EVERYMAN. Come hither, Good, in all the haste thou may,
    For of counsel I must desire thee.                                    400
        [*Enter* GOODS.]
GOODS. Sir, and ye in the world have sorrow or adversity,
    That can I help you to remedy shortly.
EVERYMAN. It is another disease[9] that grieveth me:
    In this world it is not, I tell thee so.
    I am sent for another way to go,                                    405
    To give a strait count general
    Before the highest Jupiter of all.
    And all my life I have had joy and pleasure in thee:
    Therefore I pray thee go with me,
    For peradventure, thou mayst before God Almighty                                    410
    My reckoning help to clean and purify.
    For it is said ever among[1]
    That money maketh all right that is wrong.

6. Glad.    7. Goods.    8. Quickly.    9. Distress.    1. Now and then.

GOODS. Nay, Everyman, I sing another song:
   I follow no man in such voyages.                      415
   For, and I went with thee,
   Thou shouldest fare much the worse for me;
   For because on me thou did set thy mind,
   Thy reckoning I have made blotted and blind,[2]
   That thine account thou cannot make truly—       420
   And that hast thou for the love of me.
EVERYMAN. That would grieve me full sore,
   When I should come to that fearful answer.
   Up, let us go thither together.
GOODS. Nay, not so, I am too brittle, I may not endure.   425
   I will follow no man one foot, be ye sure.
EVERYMAN. Alas, I have thee loved and had great pleasure
   All my life-days on good and treasure.
GOODS. That is to thy damnation, without leasing,[3]
   For my love is contrary to the love everlasting.      430
   But if thou had me loved moderately during,
   As to the poor to give part of me,
   Then shouldest thou not in this dolor be,
   Nor in this great sorrow and care.
EVERYMAN. Lo, now was I deceived ere I was ware,     435
   And all I may wite[4] misspending of time.
GOODS. What, weenest[5] thou that I am thine?
EVERYMAN. I had weened so.
GOODS. Nay, Everyman, I say no.
   As for a while I was lent thee;                440
   A season thou hast had me in prosperity.
   My condition is man's soul to kill;
   If I save one, a thousand I do spill.
   Weenest thou that I will follow thee?
   Nay, from this world, not verily.             445
EVERYMAN. I had weened otherwise.
GOODS. Therefore to thy soul Good is a thief;
   For when thou art dead, this is my guise—[6]
   Another to deceive in the same wise
   As I have done thee, and all to his soul's repreef.[7]   450
EVERYMAN. O false Good, cursed thou be,
   Thou traitor to God, that hast deceived me
   And caught me in thy snare!
GOODS. Marry, thou brought thyself in care,[8]
   Whereof I am glad:                    455
   I must needs laugh, I cannot be sad.

2. Illegible.   3. Lie.   4. Blame   on.   5. Suppose.   6. Custom.   7. Shame.
8. Sorrow.

EVERYMAN. Ah, Good, thou hast had long my heartly[9] love;
   I gave thee that which should be the Lord's above.
   But wilt thou not go with me, indeed?
   I pray thee truth to say.                 460
GOODS. No, so God me speed!
   Therefore farewell and have good day.
     [*Exit* GOODS.]
EVERYMAN. Oh, to whom shall I make my moan
   For to go with me in that heavy journay?
   First Fellowship said he would with me gone:     465
   His words were very pleasant and gay,
   But afterward he left me alone.
   Then spake I to my kinsmen, all in despair,
   And also they gave me words fair—
   They lacked no fair speaking,           470
   But all forsake me in the ending.
   Then went I to my Goods that I loved best,
   In hope to have comfort; but there had I least,
   For my Goods sharply did me tell
   That he bringeth many into hell.         475
   Then of myself I was ashamed,
   And so I am worthy to be blamed:
   Thus may I well myself hate.
   Of whom shall I now counsel take?
   I think that I shall never speed         480
   Till that I go to my Good Deed.
   But alas, she is so weak
   That she can neither go[1] nor speak.
   Yet will I venture[2] on her now.
   My Good Deeds, where be you?         485
GOOD DEEDS. [*speaking from the ground*] Here I lie, cold in the
    ground:
   Thy sins hath me sore bound
   That I cannot stear.[3]
EVERYMAN. O Good Deeds, I stand in fear:
   I must you pray of counsel,          490
   For help now should come right well.
GOOD DEEDS. Everyman, I have understanding
   That ye be summoned, account to make,
   Before Messiah of Jer'salem King.
   And you do by me, that journey with you will I take.     495
EVERYMAN. Therefore I come to you my moan to make.
   I pray you that ye will go with me.

9. Sincere.   1. Walk.   2. Gamble.   3. Stir.

GOOD DEEDS. I would full fain, but I cannot stand, verily.
EVERYMAN. Why, is there anything on you fall?
GOOD DEEDS. Yea, sir, I may thank you of all:                        500
   If ye had perfectly cheered me,
   Your book of count full ready had be.
     [GOOD DEEDS *shows him the account book.*]
   Look, the books of your works and deeds eke,[4]
   As how they lie under the feet,
   To your soul's heaviness.                        505
EVERYMAN. Our Lord Jesus help me!
   For one letter here I cannot see.
GOOD DEEDS. There is a blind reckoning in time of distress!
EVERYMAN. Good Deeds, I pray you help me in this need,
   Or else I am forever damned indeed.                        510
   Therefore help me to make reckoning
   Before the Redeemer of all thing
   That King is and was and every shall.
GOOD DEEDS. Everyman, I am sorry of your fall
   And fain would help you and I were able.                        515
EVERYMAN. Good Deeds, your counsel I pray you give me.
GOOD DEEDS. That shall I do verily,
   Though that on my feet I may not go;
   I have a sister that shall with you also,
   Called Knowledge, which shall with you abide                        520
   To help you to make that dreadful reckoning.
     [*Enter* KNOWLEDGE.]
KNOWLEDGE. Everyman, I will go with thee and be thy guide,
   In thy most need to go by thy side.
EVERYMAN. In good condition I am now in everything,
   And am whole content with this good thing,                        525
   Thanked be God my Creator.
GOOD DEEDS. And when she hath brought you there
   Where thou shalt heal thee of thy smart,[5]
   Then go you with your reckoning and your Good Deeds together
   For to make you joyful at heart                        530
   Before the blessed Trinity.
EVERYMAN. My Good Deeds, gramercy!
   I am well content, certainly,
   With your words sweet.
KNOWLEDGE. Now go we together lovingly                        535
   To Confession, that cleansing river.
EVERYMAN. For joy I weep—I would we were there!
   But I pray you give me cognition,

4. Also.    5. Pain.

Where dwelleth that holy man Confession?

KNOWLEDGE. In the House of Salvation:  540

    We shall find him in that place

    That shall us comfort, by God's grace.

       [KNOWLEDGE *leads* EVERYMAN *to* CONFESSION.]

    Lo, this is Confession: kneel down and ask mercy,

    For he is in good conceit[6] with God Almighty.

EVERYMAN. *[Kneeling]* O glorious fountain that all uncleanness doth

    clarify,[7]  545

    Wash from me the spots of vice unclean,

That on me no sin may be seen.

    I come with Knowledge for my redemption,

    Redempt with heart and full contrition,

    For I am commanded a pilgrimage to take  550

    And great accounts before God to make.

    Now I pray you, Shrift, mother of Salvation,

    Help my Good Deeds for my piteous exclamation.

CONFESSION. I know your sorrow well, Everyman:

    Because with Knowledge ye come to me,  555

    I will you comfort as well as I can,

    And a precious jewel I will give thee,

    Called Penance, voider of adversity.

    Therewith shall your body chastised be—

    With abstinence and perseverance in God's service.  560

    Here shall you receive that scourge of me,

    Which is penance strong that ye must endure,

    To remember thy Saviour was scourged for thee

    With sharp scourges, and suffered it patiently.

    So must thou ere thou 'scape that painful pilgrimage.  565

    Knowledge, keep him in this voyage,

    And by that time Good Deeds will be with thee.

    But in any wise be secure of mercy—

    For your time draweth fast—and ye will saved be.

    Ask God mercy and he will grant, truly.  570

    When with the scourge of penance man doth him bind,

    The oil of forgiveness then shall he find.

EVERYMAN. Thanked be God for his gracious work,

    For now I will my penance begin.

    This hath rejoiced and lighted my heart,  575

    Though the knots[8] be painful and hard within.

KNOWLEDGE. Everyman, look your penance that ye fulfill,

    What pain that ever it to you be;

    And Knowledge shall give you counsel at will

---

6. Esteem.   7. Purify.   8. Knots on the scourge (whip) of penance. *Within*: To my senses.

How your account ye shall make clearly.                        580
EVERYMAN. O eternal God, O heavenly figure,
  O way of righteousness, O goodly vision,
  Which descended down in a virgin pure
  Because he would every man redeem,
  Which Adam forfeited by his disobedience;                   585
  O blessed Godhead, elect and high Divine,
  Forgive my grievous offense!
  Here I cry thee mercy in this presence:
  O ghostly Treasure, O Ransomer and Redeemer,
  Of all the world Hope and Conduiter,⁹                       590
  Mirror of joy, Foundator of mercy,
  Which enlumineth heaven and earth thereby,
  Hear by clamorous complaint, though it late be;
  Receive my prayers, of thy benignity.
  Though I be a sinner most abominable,                       595
  Yet let my name be written in Moses' table.¹
  O Mary, pray to the Maker of all thing
  Me for to help at my ending,
  And save me from the power of my enemy,
  For Death assaileth me strongly.                            600
  And lady, that I may by mean of thy prayer
  Of your Son's glory to be partner—
  By the means of his passion I it crave.
  I beseech you help my soul to save.
  Knowledge, give me the scourge of penance:                  605
  My flesh therewith shall give acquittance.²
  I will now begin, if God give me grace.
KNOWLEDGE. Everyman, God give you time and space!³
  Thus I bequeath you in the hands of our Saviour:
  Now may you make your reckoning sure.                       610
EVERYMAN. In the name of the Holy Trinity
  My body sore punished shall be:
  Take this, body, for the sin of the flesh!
  Also⁴ thou delightest to go gay and fresh,
  And in the way of damnation thou did me bring,              615
  Therefore suffer now strokes of punishing!
  Now of penance I will wade the water clear,
  To save me from purgatory, that sharp fire.
GOOD DEEDS. I thank God, now can I walk and go,
  And am delivered of my sickness and woe.                    620
  Therefore with Everyman I will go, and not spare:
  His good works I will help him to declare.

9. Guide.   1. Tablet on which are recorded those who have been baptized and have done penance.   2. Satisfaction for sins.   3. Opportunity.   4. As.

KNOWLEDGE. Now Everyman, be merry and glad:
    Your Good Deeds cometh now, ye may not be sad.
    Now is your Good Deeds whole and sound, 625
    Going upright upon the ground.
EVERYMAN. My heart is light, and shall be evermore.
    Now will I smite faster than I did before.
GOOD DEEDS. Everyman, pilgrim, my special friend,
    Blessed be thou without end! 630
    For thee is preparate the eternal glory.
    Ye have me made whole and sound:
    Therefore I will bide by thee in every stound. 5
EVERYMAN. Welcome, my Good Deeds! Now I hear thy voice,
    I weep for very sweetness of love. 635
KNOWLEDGE. Be no more sad, but ever rejoice:
    God seeth thy living in this throne above.
    Put on this garment to thy behove, 6
    Which is wet with your tears—
    Or else before God you may it miss 640
    When ye to your journey's end come shall.
EVERYMAN. Gentle Knowledge, what do ye it call?
KNOWLEDGE. It is a garment of sorrow;
    From pain it will you borrow: 7
    Contrition it is 645
    That getteth forgiveness;
    It pleaseth God passing 8 well.
GOOD DEEDS. Everyman, will you wear it for your heal? 9
EVERYMAN. Now blessed be Jesu, Mary's son,
    For now have I on true contrition. 650
    And let us go now without tarrying.
    Good Deeds, have we clear our reckoning?
GOOD DEEDS. Yea, indeed, I have it here.
EVERYMAN. Then I trust we need not fear.
    Now friends, let us now part in twain. 655
KNOWLEDGE. Nay, Everyman, that will we not, certain.
GOOD DEEDS. Yet must thou lead with thee
    Three persons of great might.
EVERYMAN. Who should they be?
GOOD DEEDS. Discretion and Strength they hight, 1 660
    And thy Beauty may not abide behind.
KNOWLEDGE. Also ye must call to mind
    Your Five-Wits as for your counselors.
GOOD DEEDS. You must have them ready at all hours.
EVERYMAN. How shall I get them hither? 665

5. Trial.   6. Advantage.   7. Redeem.   8. Surpassingly.   9. Welfare.   1. Are called.

KNOWLEDGE. You must call them all togither,
   And they will be here incontinent.[2]
EVERYMAN. My friends, come hither and be present,
   Discretion, Strength, my Five-Wits, and Beauty!
     [*They enter.*]
BEAUTY. Here at your will we be all ready.              670
   What will ye that we should do?
GOOD DEEDS. That ye would with Everyman go
   And help him in his pilgrimage.
   Advise you: will ye with him or not in that voyage?
STRENGTH. We will bring him all thither,             675
   To his help and comfort, ye may believe me.
DISCRETION. So will we go with him all togither.
EVERYMAN. Almighty God, loved might thou be!
   I give thee laud that I have hither brought        680
   Strength, Discretion, Beauty, and Five-Wits—lack I nought—
   And my Good Deeds, with Knowledge clear,
   All be in my company at my will here:
   I desire no more to my business.
STRENGTH. And I, Strength, will by you stand in distress,
   Though thou would in battle fight on the ground.     685
FIVE-WITS. And though it were through the world round,
   We will not depart for sweet ne sour.
BEAUTY. No more will I, until death's hour,
   Whatsoever thereof befall.
DISCRETION. Everyman, advise you first of all:        690
   Go with a good advisement[3] and deliberation.
   We all give you virtuous monition[4]
   That all shall be well.
EVERYMAN. My friends, hearken what I will tell;
   I pray God reward you in his heaven-sphere;      695
   Now hearken all that be here,
   For I will make my testament,
   Here before you all present:
   In alms half my good I will give with my hands twain,
   In the way of charity with good intent;        700
   And the other half, still[5] shall remain,
   I 'queath to be returned there it ought to be.
   This I do in despite of the fiend of hell,
   To go quit out of his perel,[6]
   Ever after and this day.              705
KNOWLEDGE. Everyman, hearken what I say:
   Go to Priesthood, I you advise,

2. At once.   3. Preparation.   4. Confident prediction.   5. Which still.   6. In order to
go free from danger from him.

And receive of him, in any wise,
The holy sacrament and ointment[7] togither;
Then shortly see ye turn again hither:                    710
We will all abide you here.
FIVE-WITS. Yea, Everyman, hie you that ye ready were.
    There is no emperor, king, duke, ne baron,
    That of God hath commission
    As hath the least priest in the world being:          715
    For the blessed sacraments pure and bening[8]
    He beareth the keys, and thereof hath the cure[9]
    For man's redemption—it is every sure—
    Which God for our souls' medicine
    Gave us out of his heart with great pine,[1]          720
    Here in this transitory life for thee and me.
    The blessed sacraments seven there be:
    Baptism, confirmation, with priesthood[2] good,
    And the sacrament of God's precious flesh and blood,
    Marriage, the holy extreme unction, and penance:      725
    These seven be good to have in remembrance,
    Gracious sacraments of high divinity.
EVERYMAN. Fain would I receive that holy body,
    And meekly to my ghostly[3] father I will go.
FIVE-WITS. Everyman, that is the best that ye can do:     730
    God will you to salvation bring.
    For priesthood exceedeth all other thing:
    To us Holy Scripture they do teach,
    And converteth man from sin, heaven to reach;
    God hath to them more power given                     735
    Than to any angel that is in heaven.
    With five words[4] he may consecrate
    God's body in flesh and blood to make,
    And handleth his Maker between his hands.
    The priest bindeth and unbindeth all bands,[5]        740
    Both in earth and in heaven.
    Thou ministers[6] all the sacraments seven;
    Though we kiss thy feet, thou were worthy;
    Thou art surgeon that cureth sin deadly;
    No remedy we find under God                           745
    But all only priesthood.[7]

7. Extreme unction.    8. Benign.    9. Care.    1. Torment.    2. Ordination.    3. Spiritual.    4. "For this is my body," spoken by the priest when he offers the wafer at communion.
5. A reference to the power of the keys, inherited by the priesthood from St. Peter, who received
it from Christ (Matthew 16: 19) with the promise that whatever St. Peter bound or loosed on
earth would be bound or loosed in heaven.    6. Administers.    7. Except from priesthood alone.

Everyman, God gave priests that dignity
And setteth them in his stead among us to be.
Thus be they above angels in degree.
   [*Exit* EVERYMAN.]
KNOWLEDGE. If priests be good, it is so, surely.            750
   But when Jesu hanged on the cross with great smart,[8]
   There he.gave out of his blessed heart
   The same sacrament in great torment,
   He sold them not to us, that Lord omnipotent:
   Therefore Saint Peter the Apostle doth say         755
   That Jesu's curse hath all they
   Which God their Saviour do buy or sell,[9]
   Or they for any money do take or tell[1]
   Sinful priests giveth the sinners example bad:
   Their children sitteth by other men's fires, I have heard;   760
   And some haunteth women's company
   With unclean life, as lusts of lechery.
   These be with sin made blind.
FIVE-WITS. I trust to God no such may we find.
   Therefore let us priesthood honor,         765
   And follow their doctrine for our souls' succor.
   We be their sheep and they shepherds be
   By whom we all be kept in surety.
   Peace, for yonder I see Everyman come,
   Which hath made true satisfaction.         770
GOOD DEEDS. Methink it is he indeed.
   [*Re-enter* EVERYMAN.]
EVERYMAN. Now Jesu be your alder speed![2]
   I have received the sacrament for my redemption,
   And then mine extreme unction.
   Blessed be all they that counseled me to take it!   775
   And now, friends, let us go without longer respite.
   I thank God that ye have tarried so long.
   Now set each of you on this rood[3] your hond
   And shortly follow me:
   I go before there[4] I would be. God be our guide!   780
STRENGTH. Everyman, we will not from you go
   Till ye have done this voyage long.
DISCRETION. I, Discretion, will bide by you also.
KNOWLEDGE. And though this pilgrimage be never so strong,
   I will never part you fro.         785

8. Pain.   9. To give or receive money for the sacraments is simony, named after Simon, who wished to buy the gift of the Holy Ghost and was cursed by St. Peter.   1. Or who, for any sacrament, take or count out money.   2. The prosperer of you all.   3. Cross.   4. Where.

STRENGTH. Everyman, I will be as sure by thee
   As ever I did by Judas Maccabee.[5]
EVERYMAN. Alas, I am so faint I may not stand—
   My limbs under me doth fold!
   Friends, let us not turn again to this land,          790
   Not for all the world's gold.
   For into this cave must I creep
   And turn to earth, and there to sleep.
BEAUTY. What, into this grave, alas?
EVERYMAN. Yea, there shall ye consume, more and lass.[6]    795
BEAUTY. And what, should I smother here?
EVERYMAN. Yea, by my faith, and nevermore appear.
   In this world live no more we shall,
   But in heaven before the highest Lord of all.
BEAUTY. I cross out all this! Adieu, by Saint John—      800
   I take my tape in my lap and am gone.[7]
EVERYMAN. What, Beauty, whither will ye?
BEAUTY. Peace, I am deaf—I look not behind me,
   Not and thou wouldest give me all the gold in thy chest.
   [*Exit* BEAUTY.]
EVERYMAN. Alas, whereto may I trust?             805
   Beauty goeth fast away fro me—
   She promised with me to live and die!
STRENGTH. Everyman, I will thee also forsake and deny.
   Thy game liketh me not at all.
EVERYMAN. Why then, ye will forsake me all?       810
   Sweet Strength, tarry a little space.
STRENGTH. Nay, sir, by the rood of grace,
   I will hie me from thee fast,
   Though thou weep till thy heart tobrast.[8]
EVERYMAN. Ye would ever bide by me, ye said.      815
STRENGTH. Yea, I have you far enough conveyed!
   Ye be old enough, I understand,
   Your pilgrimage to take on hand:
   I repent me that I hither came.
EVERYMAN. Strength, you to displease I am to blame,    820
   Yet promise is debt, this ye well wot.[9]
STRENGTH. In faith, I care not:
   Thou art but a fool to complain:
   You spend your speech and waste your brain.
   Go, thrust thee into the ground.            825
   [*Exit* STRENGTH.]

---

5. Judas Maccabaeus was an enormously powerful warrior in the defense of Israel against the Syrians in late Old Testament times.   6. Decay, all of you.   7. I tuck my skirts in my belt and am off.   8. Break.   9. Know.

EVERYMAN. I had weened[1] surer I should you have found.
   He that trusteth in his Strength
   She him deceiveth at the length.
   Both Strength and Beauty forsaketh me—
   Yet they promised me fair and lovingly.                              830
DISCRETION. Everyman, I will after Strength be gone:
   As for me, I will leave you alone.
EVERYMAN. Why Discretion, will ye forsake me?
DISCRETION. Yea, in faith, I will go from thee.
   For when Strength goeth before,                                     835
   I follow after evermore.
EVERYMAN. Yet I pray thee, for the love of the Trinity,
   Look in my grave once piteously.
DISCRETION. Nay, so nigh will I not come.
   Farewell everyone!                                                  840
     [*Exit* DISCRETION.]
EVERYMAN. Of all thing faileth save God alone—
   Beauty, Strength, and Discretion.
   For when Death bloweth his blast
   They all run fro me full fast.
FIVE-WITS. Everyman, my leave now of thee I take.                          845
   I will follow the other, for here I thee forsake.
EVERYMAN. Alas, then may I wail and weep,
   For I took you for my best friend.
FIVE-WITS. I will no longer thee keep.
   Now farewell, and there an end!                                     850
     [*Exit* FIVE-WITS.]
EVERYMAN. O Jesu, help, all hath forsaken me!
GOOD DEEDS. Nay, Everyman, I will bide with thee:
   I will not forsake thee indeed;
   Thou shalt find me a good friend at need.                           854
EVERYMAN. Gramercy, Good Deeds! Now may I true friends see.
   They have forsaken me every one—
   I loved them better than my Good Deeds alone.
   Knowledge, will ye forsake me also?
KNOWLEDGE. Yea, Everyman, when ye to Death shall go,
   But not yet, for no manner of danger.                               860
EVERYMAN. Gramercy, Knowledge, with all my heart!
KNOWLEDGE. Nay, yet will I not from hence depart
   Till I see where ye shall become.
EVERYMAN. Methink, alas, that I must be gone
   To make my reckoning and my debts pay,                              865
   For I see my time is nigh spent away.

1. Supposed.

Take example, all ye that this do hear or see,
How they that I best loved do forsake me,
Except my Good Deeds that bideth truly.
GOOD DEEDS. All earthly things is but vanity.                        870
    Beauty, Strength, and Discretion do man forsake,
    Foolish friends and kinsmen that fair spake—
    All fleeth save Good Deeds, and that am I.
EVERYMAN. Have mercy on me, God most mighty,
    And stand by me, thou mother and maid, holy Mary!     875
GOOD DEEDS. Fear not: I will speak for thee.
EVERYMAN. Here I cry God mercy!
GOOD DEEDS. Short our end, and 'minish our pain.[2]
    Let us go, and never come again.
EVERYMAN. Into thy hands, Lord, my soul I commend:      880
    Receive it, Lord, that it be not lost.
    As thou me boughtest,[3] so me defend,
    And save me from the fiend's boast,
    That I may appear with that blessed host
    That shall be saved at the day of doom.                        885
    *In manus tuas*, of mights most,
    Forever *commendo spiritum meum*.[4]
        [EVERYMAN *and* GOOD DEEDS *descend into the grave.*]
KNOWLEDGE. Now hath he suffered that we all shall endure,
    The Good Deeds shall make all sure.
    Now hath he made ending,                                        890
    Methinketh that I hear angels sing
    And make great joy and melody
    Where Everyman's soul received shall be.
ANGEL. [*Within*] Come, excellent elect spouse to Jesu![5]
    Here above thou shalt go                                        895
    Because of thy singular virtue.
    Now the soul is taken the body fro,
    Thy reckoning is crystal clear:
    Now shalt thou into the heavenly sphere—
    Unto the which all ye shall come                                900
    That liveth well before the day of doom.
        [*Enter* DOCTOR.[6]]
DOCTOR. This memorial men may have in mind:
    Ye hearers, take it of worth, old and young,
    And forsake Pride, for he deceiveth you in the end.
    And remember Beauty, Five-Wits, Strength, and Discretion,  905
    They all at the last do Everyman forsake,

2. Make our dying quick and diminish our pain.    3. Redeemed.    4. "Into thy hands, O greatest of powers, I commend my spirit forever."    5. Man's soul is often referred to as the bride of Jesus.    6. The learned theologian who explains the meaning of the play. *Memorial:* Reminder.

Save his Good Deeds there doth he take—
But beware, for and they be small,
Before God he hath no help at all—
None excuse may be there for Everyman.                          910
Alas, how shall he do than?[7]
For after death amends may no man make,
For then mercy and pity doth him forsake.
If his reckoning be not clear when he doth come,
God will say, *"Ite, maledicti, in ignem eternum!"*[8]              915
And he that hath his account whole and sound,
High in heaven he shall be crowned,
Unto which place God bring us all thither,
That we may live body and soul togither.
Thereto help, the Trinity!                                      920
Amen say ye, for saint charity.

7. Then.    8. "Depart, ye cursed, into everlasting fire."

# Masterpieces of the
# Renaissance

As with other terms that have currency in cultural history (for instance, *Romanticism*), the usefulness of the term *Renaissance* depends on its keeping a certain degree of elasticity. The literal meaning of the word—"rebirth"—suggests that one impulse toward the great intellectual and artistic achievements of the period came from the example of ancient culture, or even better, from a certain vision that the artists and intellectuals of the Renaissance possessed of the world of antiquity which was "reborn" through their work. Especially in the more mature phase of the Renaissance, men were aware of having brought about a vigorous renewal, which they openly associated with the cult of antiquity. The restoration of ancient canons was regarded as a glorious achievement to be set beside the thrilling discoveries of their own age. "Today," Rabelais writes through his Gargantua,

> the old sciences are revived, knowledge is systematized, discipline reestablished. The learned languages are restored: Greek, without which a man would be ashamed to consider himself educated; Hebrew, Chaldean, and Latin. Printing is now in use, an art so accurate and elegant that it betrays the divine inspiration of its discovery, which I have lived to witness. Alas! Conversely, I was not spared the horror of such diabolic works as gunpowder and artillery.

Machiavelli, whose infatuation with antiquity is as typical a trait as his better-advertised political realism, in the opening of his *Discourses on the First Ten Books of Livy* (1513–21) suggests that rulers should be as keen on the imitation of ancient "virtues" as are artists, lawyers, and the scientists: "The civil laws are nothing but decisions given by the ancient jurisconsults. . . . And what is the science of medicine, but the experience of ancient physicians, which their successors have taken for their guide?"

Elasticity should likewise be maintained in regard to the chronological span of the Renaissance as a "movement" extending through varying periods of years, and as including phases and traits of the epoch that is otherwise known as the Middle Ages (and vice versa). The peak of the Renaissance can be shown to have occurred at different times in different countries, the "movement" having had its inception in Italy, where its impact was at first most remarkable in the visual arts, while in England, for instance, it developed later and its main achievements were in literature, particularly the drama. The meaning of the term has also, in the course of time, widened considerably: nowadays it conveys, to say the least, a general notion of artistic creativity, of extraordinary zest for life and knowledge, of sensory delight in opulence and magnificence, of spectacular individual achievement, thus extending far beyond the literal meaning of rebirth and the strict idea of a revival and imitation of antiquity.

Even, however, in its stricter sense, the term continues to have its function. The degree to which European intellectuals of the period possessed and were possessed by the writings of the ancient world is difficult for the average modern reader to realize. For these writers references to classical mythology, philosophy, and literature are not ornaments or affectations; along with references to the Scriptures they are part, and a major part, of their mental equipment and way of thinking. When Erasmus through his "Folly" speaks in a cluster of classical allusions, or when Machiavelli writes to a friend: "I will get up before daylight, prepare my birdlime, and go out with a bundle of cages on my back, so that I look like Geta when he came back from the harbor with the books of Amphitryo," the words have by no means the sound of erudite self-gratification which they might have nowadays; they are wholly natural, familiar, unassuming.

When we are overcome by sudden emotion, our first exclamations are likely to be in the language most familiar to us—our dialect, if we happen to have one. Montaigne relates of himself that when once his father unexpectedly fell back in his arms in a swoon, the first words he uttered under the emotion of that experience were in Latin. Similarly Benvenuto Cellini, the Italian sculptor, goldsmith, and autobiographer, talking to his patron and expressing admiration of a Greek statue, establishes with the ancient artist an immediate contact, a proud familiarity:

> I cried to the Duke: "My lord, this is a statue in Greek marble, and it is a miracle of beauty. . . . If your Excellency permits, I should like to restore it—head and arms and feet. . . . It is certainly not my business to patch up statues, that being the trade of botchers, who do it in all conscience villainously ill; yet the art displayed by this great master of antiquity cries out to me to help him."

The men who, starting at about the middle of the fourteenth century, gave new impulse to this emulation of the classics are often referred to as humanists. The word in that sense is related to what we call the humanities, and the humanities at that time were Latin and Greek. Every cultivated person wrote and spoke Latin, with the result that a Western community of intellectuals could exist, a spiritual "republic of letters" above individual nations. There was also a considerable amount of individual contact among humanists. In glancing at the biographies of the authors included in this section, the extensiveness of their travels may strike us as a remarkable or even surprising fact, considering the hardships and slowness of traveling during those centuries.

The archetype of the modern "man of letters" is often said to be Petrarch—the first author in this section—who anticipated certain ideals of the high Renaissance: a lofty conception of the literary art, a taste for the good life, a basic pacifism, and a strong sense of the memories and glories of antiquity.

In this last respect, what should be emphasized is the imaginative quality, the visionary impulse with which the men of letters of the period looked at those memories—the same vision and imagination with which they regarded such contemporary heroes as the great navigators and astronomers. The Renaissance view of the cultural monuments of antiquity was far from being that of the philologist and the antiquarian; indeed, familiarity was facilitated by the very lack of a scientific sense of history. We find the visionary and imaginative element not only in the creations of poets and dramatists (Shakespeare's Romans, to give an obvious example) but also in the works of political writers: as when Machiavelli describes himself entering, through his reading, the

> ancient courts of ancient men, where, being lovingly received, I feed on that food which alone is mine, and which I was born for; I am not ashamed to speak with them and to ask the reasons for their actions, and they courteously answer me. For . . . hours I feel no boredom and forget every worry; I do not fear poverty, and death does not terrify me. I give myself completely over to the ancients.

Imitation of antiquity acquires, in Machiavelli and many others, a special quality; between mere "academic" imitation and the Renaissance approach there is as much difference as between the impulse to learn and the impulse to *be*.

The vision of an ancient age of glorious intellectual achievement which is "now" brought to life again, implies of course, however roughly, the idea of an intervening "middle" time, by comparison ignorant and dark. The hackneyed notion that the "light" of the Renaissance broke through a long "night" of the Middle Ages may be vastly inaccurate, yet it is inevitable to remember that this view was not devised by subsequent "enlightened" centuries but held by the men of the Renaissance themselves. In his genealogy of giants from Grangousier to Gargantua to Pantagruel, Rabelais conveniently represents the generations of modern learning with their varying degrees of enlightenment; this is what Gargantua writes to his son:

> My late father Grangousier, of blessed memory, made every effort that I might achieve mental, moral and technical excellence. . . . But you can realize that conditions were not as favorable to learning as they are to-day. Nor had I such gifted teachers as you. We were still in the dark ages; we still walked in the shadow of the dark clouds of ignorance; we suffered the calamitous consequences of the destruction of good literature by the Goths. Now, by God's grace, light and dignity have been restored to letters, and I have lived to see it.

Definitions of the Renaissance must also in one way or another include the idea that the period was characterized by preoccupation with this life rather than with the life beyond. The contrast of an ideal Medieval Man, whose mode of action is basically oriented toward the thought of the afterlife—and who therefore conceives of his days on earth as transient and preparatory—with an ideal Renaissance Man, possessing and cherishing earthly interests so concrete and self-sufficient that the very realization of the ephemeral

quality of life is to him nothing but an added spur to its immediate enjoyment—this is a useful contrast even though it represents an enormous oversimplification of the facts.

The same emphasis on the immediate and tangible is reflected in the
earthly, amoral, and esthetic character of what we may call the Renaissance
code of behavior. According to this "code," human action is judged not in
terms of right and wrong, of good and evil (as it is judged when life is viewed
as a moral "test," with reward or punishment in the afterlife), but in terms
of its present concrete validity and effectiveness, of the delight it affords, of
its memorability and its beauty. In that sense a good deal that is typical of
the Renaissance, from architecture to poetry, from sculpture to rhetoric,
may be related to a taste for the harmonious and the memorable, for the
spectacular effect, for the successful striking of a pose. Individual human
action, seeking as it were in itself its own reward, finds justification in its
formal appropriateness; in its being a well-rounded achievement, perfect of
its kind; in the zest and gusto with which it is, here and now, performed;
and, finally, in its proving worthy of remaining as a testimony to the per-
former's power on earth.

A convenient way to illustrate this emphasis is to consider certain words
especially expressive of the interests of the period—"virtue," "fame," "glory."
"Virtue," particularly in its Italian form, virtù, is to be understood in a wide
sense. As we may see even now in some relics of its older meanings, the
word (from the Latin vir, "man") connotes active power—the intrinsic force
and ability of a person or thing (the "virtue" of a law or of a medicine)—and
hence, also, technical skill (the capacity of the "virtuoso"). The Machiavellian prince's "virtues," therefore, are not necessarily goodness, temperance,
clemency, and the like; they are whatever forces and skills may help him in
the efficient management and preservation of his princely powers. The
idealistic, intangible part of the prince's success is consigned to such concepts as "fame" and "glory," but even in this case the dimension within
which human action is considered is still an earthly one. These concepts
connote the hero's success and reputation with his contemporaries, or look
forward to splendid recognition from posterity, on earth.

In this sense (though completely pure examples of such an attitude are
rare) the purpose of life is the unrestrained and self-sufficient practice of
one's "virtue," the competent and delighted exercise of one's skill. At the
same time, there is no reason to forget that such virtues and skills are God's
gift to man. The world view of even some of the most clearly earthbound
Renaissance men was hardly godless; Machiavelli, Cellini, Rabelais take for
granted the presence of God in their own and in their heroes' lives:

> . . . we have before our eyes extraordinary and unexampled means
> prepared by God. The sea has been divided. A cloud has guided you
> on your way. The rock has given forth water. Manna has fallen. Every-
> thing has united to make you great. The rest is for you to do. God does
> not intend to do everything, lest he deprive us of our free will and the
> share of glory that belongs to us. (Machiavelli.)

> According to the Pythagorean system, Gargantua would, with his tutor,
> recapitulate briefly all that he had read, seen, learned, done, and

assimilated in the course of the day. Then they prayed to God the Creator, doing Him worship and confirming their faith in Him, glorifying Him for His immense goodness, vouchsafing thanks for all the mighty past, and imploring His divine clemency for all the future. And so they retired to rest. (Rabelais.)

I found that all the bronze my furnace contained had been exhausted in the head of this figure [of the statue of Perseus]. It was a miracle to observe that not one fragment remained in the orifice of the channel, and that nothing was wanting to the statue. In my great astonishment I seemed to see in this the hand of God arranging and controlling all. (Cellini.)

Yet there is no doubt that if we compare the attitudes of these authors with the view of the world and of the value of human action which emerges from the major literary work of the Middle Ages, the *Divine Comedy*, and with the manner in which human action is there seen within a grand extra-temporal design, the presence of God in the Renaissance writers cited above cannot help appearing marginal and perfunctory.

In any attempt to discuss the religious temper of the Renaissance, we should not lose sight of certain basic historical facts: the Papacy was not only a spiritual power, but a political and military one as well; furthermore, the European Renaissance was a period of violent religious strife. The consequences of the Protestant Reformation (Lutheranism, Zwinglianism, Calvinism) were not only theological and ideological debates, but also armed conflict and bloodshed, as is apparent from the biographies of several of the writers presented here (Erasmus, Rabelais, Montaigne). It is also apparent that the position of the intellectual generally was not one of militant partisanship or, conversely, of retreat to an "ivory tower," but rather was characterized by wisdom and attempts at conciliation.

Much about the religious temper of the age is expressed in its art, particularly in Italian painting, where Renaissance Madonnas often make it difficult, as the saying goes, to recite a properly devout Hail Mary—serving as celebrations of earthly beauty rather than exhortations to contrite thoughts and mystical hope of salvation. Castiglione in the first pages of the *Courtier* pays homage to the memory of the late lord of Montefeltro, in whose palace at Urbino the book's personages hold their lofty debate on the idea of a perfect gentleman (an earlier Montefeltro appears in Dante's Hell, another in Dante's Purgatory); but Castiglione praises him only for his achievements as a man of arms and a promoter of the arts. There is no thought of either the salvation or the damnation of his soul (though the general tone of the work would seem to imply his salvation); he is exalted instead for military victories, and even more warmly, for having built a splendid palace—the tangible symbol of his earthly glory, for it is both the mark of political and social power and a work of art.

Thus the popular view which associates the idea of the Renaissance especially with the flourishing of the arts is correct. The leaders of the period saw in a work of art the clearest instance of beautiful, harmonious, and self-justified performance. To create such a work became the valuable occupation par excellence, the most satisfactory display of *virtù*. The Renaissance view of antiquity exemplifies this attitude: the artists and intellectuals of the period not only drew on antiquity for certain practices and forms but also found there a recognition of the place of the arts among outstanding modes of human action. In this way, the concepts of "fame" and "glory" became particularly associated with the art of poetry because the Renaissance drew from antiquity the idea of the poet as celebrator of high deeds, the "dispenser of glory."

There is, then, an important part of the Renaissance mind which sees terrestrial life as positive fulfillment. This is especially clear where there is a close association between the practical and the intellectual, as in the exercise of political power, the act of scientific discovery, the creation of works of art. The Renaissance assumption is that there are things highly worth doing, within a strictly temporal pattern. By doing them, man proves his privileged position in Creation and therefore incidentally follows God's intent. The often cited phrase "the dignity of man" describes this positive, strongly affirmed awareness of the intellectual and physical "virtues" of the human being, and of his place in Creation.

It is important, however, to see this fact about the Renaissance in the light of another phenomenon: where there is a singularly high capacity for feeling the delight of earthly achievement, there is a possibility that its ultimate worth will also be questioned profoundly. What (the Renaissance mind usually seems to ask at some point) is the purpose of all this activity? What meaningful relation does it bear to any all-inclusive, cosmic pattern? The Renaissance coincided with, and perhaps to some extent occasioned, a loss of firm belief in the final unity and the final intelligibility of the universe, such belief as underlies, for example, the *Divine Comedy*, enabling Dante to say in Paradise:

> I saw within Its depth how It conceives
>     all things in a single volume bound by Love,
>     of which the universe is the scattered leaves;
> Substance, accident, and their relation
>     so fused that all I say could do no more
>     than yield a glimpse of that bright revelation.

Once the notion of this grand unity of design has lost its authority, certainty about the final value of human actions is no longer to be found. For some minds, indeed, the sense of void becomes so strong as to paralyze all aspiration to power or thirst for knowledge or delight in beauty; the resulting attitude we may call Renaissance melancholy, whether it be openly shown (as by some characters in Elizabethan drama) or provide an undercurrent of sadness, or incite to ironical forms of compromise, to some sort of wise adjustment (as in Erasmus or Montaigne.) The legend of Faust— "Doctor" Faustus—a great amasser of knowledge doomed to frustration by his perception of the vanity of science, for which he finds at one point desperate substitutes in pseudoscience and the devil's arts, is one illustration of this sense of vanity. Shakespeare's *Hamlet* is another, a play in which the very word "thought" seems to acquire a troubled connotation: "the pale cast of thought," "thought and affliction, passion, hell itself." In these instances, the intellectual excitement of understanding, the zest and pride of achievement through what chiefly constitutes man's "dignity," his intellect, seem not so much lost as directly inverted.

Thus while on one, and perhaps the better-known, side of the picture man's intellect in Renaissance literature enthusiastically expatiates over the realms of knowledge and unveils the mysteries of the universe, on the other it is beset by puzzling doubts and a profound mistrust of its own powers. Man's moral nature is seen as only a little lower than the angels', but also scarcely above the beasts'. Earthly power—a favorite theme because Renaissance literature was so largely produced in the courts or with a vivid sense of courtly ideas—is the crown of human aspirations ("How sweet a thing it is to wear a crown, / Within whose circuit is Elysium") but it is also the death's head ("Imperious Caesar, dead and turn'd to clay, / Might stop a hole to keep the wind away").

Much of Renaissance literature takes its character and strength from the tensions generated by this simultaneous exaltation and pessimism about the human condition.

## FURTHER READING

Richard L. DeMolen, ed., *The Meaning of Renaissance and Reformation* (1974), is a collection of essays by experts on the Renaissance and Reformation, with maps and illustrations. Paul Oskar Kristeller's lecture series on the Renaissance is now a paperback, *Renaissance Thought: The Classic, Scholastic, and Humanist Strains* (1961). A solid, well-written general historical and cultural presentation is Eugene F. Rice, Jr.'s *The Foundations of Early Modern Europe, 1460–1559* (1970), with illustrations, facsimiles, maps, bibliographic references. Lewis W. Spitz gives a reliable historical presentation of the period, taking into account literary and artistic trends in *The Renaissance and Reformation Movements* (1971).

# FRANCIS PETRARCH
## 1304–1374

Francesco Petrarca (forty years younger than Dante) was born at Arezzo on July 13, 1304. His father, like Dante, was exiled from Florence for political reasons and in 1312 moved with his family to Avignon with hopes of employment at the Papal court, which had been transferred there in 1309 by a Pope of French nationality—Clement V (Bertrand de Got). Following his father's wish, Petrarch studied law at Montpellier and Bologna for a brief period. A highly cultivated man of the world, on his return to Avignon he was well received by the brilliant and refined society that moved around the Papal court. It was in Avignon, in the church of St. Clare, on April 6, 1327, that he saw for the first time Laura, who would become the object and image of his love poetry. Soon after this momentous event, he began to travel widely (France, Flanders, Germany), not only on diplomatic missions but also, and perhaps more relevantly, as a man of letters and humanist in search of manuscripts from classical antiquity.

In 1338 he made his first trip to Rome, a twofold spiritual capital for him as a classical scholar and as a Christian. Later that same year, at his home in Vaucluse near Avignon, Petrarch attempted to revive the ancient ideal of spiritually active relaxation, or *otium*. He was so imbued with the idea of a renovation of classical antiquity that he expected his major glory as a poet from the work he began at this time—*Africa*, an epic poem in Latin hexameters which has for its central figure Scipio Africanus, conceived by the poet as the model of the valiant and pious Roman hero. No less characteristic of his devotion to classical ideals is the fact that when in 1340 he received invitations from both Paris and Rome to be crowned poet laureate, he chose Rome, and received the crown in the Capitol.

There was in his life, as in Dante's, a pattern of moral dissipation followed by spiritual conflict and repentance. This conflict, which is reflected in Petrarch's autobiographical treatise in Latin, *Secretum*, may have been enhanced by his brother Gherardo's decision to enter a monastery and by the news of Laura's death by plague, which he received in 1348 while traveling in Italy. She died on April 6, the very day of the month on which he had first seen her, and the day of Christ's passion as well. Thus Laura remained an image of exclusively spiritual love, in contrast to Petrarch's more earthly attachments, evidenced by the birth of two illegitimate children, Giovanni, in 1337, and Francesca, in 1343.

As a pilgrim on his way to Rome for the Papal Jubilee of 1350, Petrarch stopped at Florence as a guest of Boccaccio, the great Florentine storyteller and fellow humanist. Most of the years between 1353 and 1361 he spent in Milan, where he was entrusted by the ruling Visconti family with various diplomatic missions (to Venice, to Prague, to the king of France). He alternated such duties with intense literary work, including a complete edition of his lyric poetry in Italian, letters and treatises in Latin, and progress on his great unfinished *terza rima* allegory, *The Triumphs*. To avoid the plague, in 1361 he moved to Padua, spending much of his time in a nearby country house in the Euganean hills at Arquà, now called Arquà Petrarca. He died there in 1374, on the eve of his seventieth birthday, working until the very end on the refinement and ordering of his work and on the careful creation of what we would call today his "public image," polishing for posterity with exquisite care his poems and letters (the letter was then an established literary form). Even accidental events in his life seem to have been inspired by his taste for the harmonious and well-rounded gesture. He even came within a few hours of reaching the "perfect" life span, three score and ten, and frequently used April 6, as in sonnet 3, to symbolize his own drama of passion.

If we compare Petrarch to the standard image of Medieval Man, what first strikes us as new is the self-centered quality of his work. A comparison between him and Dante points to this quality, and the contrast is made sharper by certain analogies in their situations. Both illustrate the same basic motif, the quest for salvation. But while Dante as hero of the quest focused dramatically on himself only on a few enormously effective and severe occasions (his first exchange with Beatrice in *Purgatory* XXX, for example), Petrarch was continuously at work on his personal drama, its lights and shades, its subtle modulations of feeling.

A different way of getting at the distinction between Renaissance Man and Medieval Man may be found in Petrarch's conception of the literary profession and the status of the poet. His attitude toward classical antiquity makes him "the first writer of the Renaissance," rather than a writer of the Middle Ages. As a self-aware man of letters he modeled his work on classical examples—the texts which, as a humanistic scholar, he had sometimes helped rediscover and bring back to life. In 1333 at Liège, for example, he found a manuscript of Cicero's oration *Pro Archia*, a Roman "defense of poetry," celebrating the role of artist and thinker as creators of value, legislators of virtuous behavior, and dispensers of fame: the program to which Petrarch was to devote his life. It would be difficult to overestimate his importance for European culture in establishing that model of the poet, scholar, and member of the "republic of letters" which remains today an ideal of Western civilization.

But however important this aspect of his work may have been, the prevailing Petrarchan image in literary history is the drama of his love for Laura, both in life and in death. Of course there would be no drama in that love without an element of the tragic—his sense of its sinfulness and vanity. Thus he sounds a "medieval" note, but in a new context: that of the ever-changing, ambiguous attractions of mortal beauty and earthly values. One even surmises that these values might have been less attractive to him had they not kept the taint of vanity, for without it they would have afforded a less rich and complex life. Thus he sings in sonnet 61, "Blest Be the Day," of his first encounter with Laura, the source of his torment. Even though calling him a romantic may stretch the meaning of the term to the point of uselessness, we can say that his definition of love as sorrow has had a yet wider influence than those striking verbal inventions which inspired European poetry for a century and more before degenerating into "Petrarchism," the arsenal of tired conceits, witticisms, and hyperboles on which much popular twentieth-century songwriting still draws.

Another essential part of Petrarch's drama is the death of his lady and her role as mediator between the penitent poet and Divine Grace. Here again, the inevitable comparison with Dante makes the differences between the two poets stand clear. The shift in tone between Petrarch's poems for Laura "in life" and the ones for her "in death" is less relevant than the similarity of the two sections of the *Canzoniere* (*Song Book*). A sensuous quality pervades both groups of poems, suggesting an earthly relationship even when the beloved lady is dead. Thus the poet, in sonnet 300, envies the earth "folding her in invisible embrace," and in sonnet 292, also written after Laura's death, the larger part of the octave is devoted to the living lady's physical appearance. In other sonnets Laura herself, in heaven, refers to her mortal body as her "beautiful veil." In sonnet 333 the poet implores her to come to him at the moment of his death and guide him to "the blessed place." His poetry has made the world know and love her, and the implication is that he has thus become worthy of her succor. Hence Petrarch is not only a repentant sinner, but also a literary master turning autobiography and confession into art. However strong his sense of the vanity and fallaciousness of human attachments, he seems to have no doubt about the validity of one particular manifestation of *virtù*: the sensuous, expert handling of words, the poetic art itself.

A thorough account of Petrarch's life with many quotations from his writing may be found in Morris Bishop, *Petrarch and His World* (1963). Two other worthwhile biographical studies are J. H. Whitfield, *Petrarch and the Renaissance* (1943; 1966), and Ernest Hatch Wilkins, *Life of Petrarch* (1961).

## It Was the Morning[1]

It was the morning of that blessèd day[2]
Whereon the Sun in pity veiled his glare
For the Lord's agony, that, unaware,
I fell a captive, Lady, to the sway

Of your swift eyes: that seemed no time to stay                    5
The strokes of Love: I stepped into the snare
Secure, with no suspicion: then, and there
I found my cue in man's most tragic play.

Love caught me naked to his shaft, his sheaf,
The entrance for his ambush and surprise                           10
Against the heart wide open through the eyes,[3]

---

1. *Era 'l giorno ch'al sol si scoloraro*, sonnet 3. Translated by Joseph Auslander.    2. Elsewhere (sonnet 211) Petrarch gives the date as April 6, 1327, a Monday. Here too the day is apparently intended to be the day of Christ's death (April 6) rather than Good Friday, 1327.    3. The image of the eyes as the gateway to the heart had been a poetic commonplace since pre-Dante days.

The constant gate and fountain of my grief:
How craven so to strike me stricken so,[4]
Yet from you fully armed conceal his bow!


## Blest Be the Day[5]

Blest be the day, and blest the month and year,
Season[6] and hour and very moment blest,
The lovely land and place[7] where first possessed
By two pure eyes I found me prisoner;

And blest the first sweet pain, the first most dear,          5
Which burnt my heart when Love came in as guest;
And blest the bow, the shafts which shook my breast,
And even the wounds which Love delivered there.

Blest be the words and voices which filled grove
And glen with echoes of my lady's name;                     10
The sighs, the tears, the fierce despair of love;

And blest the sonnet-sources of my fame;
And blest that thought of thoughts which is her own,
Of her, her only, of herself alone!


## Father in Heaven[8]

Father in heaven, after each lost day,
Each night spent raving with that fierce desire
Which in my heart has kindled into fire
Seeing your acts adorned for my dismay;

Grant henceforth that I turn, within your light[9]           5
To another life and deeds more truly fair,
So having spread to no avail the snare
My bitter foe[1] might hold it in despite.

The eleventh year,[2] my Lord, has now come round
Since I was yoked beneath the heavy trace                   10
That on the meekest weighs most cruelly.

---

**4.** With grief on commemorating Christ's Passion.   **5.** *Benedetto sia 'l giorno e 'l mese e l'anno,*
sonnet 61. Translated by Joseph Auslander.   **6.** Spring. *Hour:* "Upon the first hour" (sonnet
211), sunrise.   **7.** The Church of Saint Clare at Avignon.   **8.** *Padre del ciel, dopo i perduti
giorni,* sonnet 62. Translated by Vernard Bergonzi.   **9.** The light of grace.   **1.** The Devil,
not Love as some commentators have thought.   **2.** 1327.

Pity the abject plight where I am found;
Return my straying thoughts to a nobler place;
Show them this day you were on Calvary.

## She Used To Let Her Golden Hair Fly Free[3]

She used to let her golden hair fly free
For the wind to toy and tangle and molest;
Her eyes were brighter than the radiant west.
(Seldom they shine so now.) I used to see

Pity look out of those deep eyes on me.       5
("It was false pity," you would now protest.)
I had love's tinder heaped within my breast;
What wonder that the flame burned furiously?

She did not walk in any mortal way,
But with angelic progress; when she spoke,       10
Unearthly voices sang in unison.

She seemed divine among the dreary folk
Of earth. You say she is not so today?
Well, though the bow's unbent, the wound bleeds on.

## The Eyes That Drew from Me[4]

The eyes that drew from me such fervent praise,
The arms and hands and feet and countenance
Which made me a stranger in my own romance
And set me apart from the well-trodden ways;

The gleaming golden curly hair, the rays       5
Flashing from a smiling angel's glance
Which moved the world in paradisal dance,
Are grains of dust, insensibilities.

And I live on, but in grief and self-contempt,
Left here without the light I loved so much,       10
In a great tempest and with shrouds unkempt.

---

3. *Erano i capei d'oro a l'aura sparsi*, sonnet 90. Tranlsated by Morris Bishop.    4. *Gli occhi di ch'io parlai sì caldamente*, sonnet 292. Translated by Edwin Morgan. All the poems in the canon from number 267 on were written to commemorate Laura. She died at Avignon on April 6, 1348.

No more love songs, then, I have done with such;
My old skill now runs thin at each attempt,
And tears are heard within the harp I touch.[5]


## Great Is My Envy of You[6]

Great is my envy of you, earth, in your greed
Folding her in invisible embrace,
Denying me the look of the sweet face
Where I found peace from all my strife at need!
Great is my envy of heaven which can lead                    5
And lock within itself in avarice
That spirit from its lovely biding-place
And leave so many others here to bleed!

Great is my envy of those souls whose reward
Is the gentle heaven of her company,                          10
Which I so fiercely sought beneath these skies!

Great is my envy of death whose curt hard sword
Carried her whom I called my life away;
Me he disdains, and mocks me from her eyes!


## Go, Grieving Rimes of Mine[7]

Go, grieving rimes of mine, to that hard stone
Whereunder lies my darling, lies my dear,
And cry to her to speak from heaven's sphere.
Her mortal part with grass is overgrown.

Tell her, I'm sick of living; that I'm blown                  5
By winds of grief from the course I ought to steer,
That praise of her is all my purpose here
And all my business; that of her alone

Do I go telling, that how she lived and died
And lives again in immortality,                               10
All men may know, and love my Laura's grace.

Oh, may she deign to stand at my bedside
When I come to die; and may she call to me
And draw me to her in the blessèd place!

---

5. Cf. Job 30:31.   6. *Quanta invidia io ti porto, avara terra*, sonnet 300. Translated by Edwin Morgan.   7. *Ite, rime dolenti, al duro sasso*, sonnet 333. Translated by Morris Bishop.

# DESIDERIUS ERASMUS
## 1466–1536

Erasmus was born around 1466, apparently in Rotterdam, to a physician's daughter and a father who later became a priest; in any event, he later referred to himself as Desiderius Erasmus Roterodamus. He received his early schooling under humanistic masters who fostered his love of good literature. After both his parents died, Erasmus's guardians sent him to the Augustinian canons at Steyn, although his desire had been to enter a university. He was ordained a priest on April 25, 1492. Erasmus's humanistic aspirations found an outlet in 1494 when he became Latin secretary to Henry of Bergen, bishop of Cambrai, through whose help he entered the college of Montaigu at the University of Paris in 1495. College discipline was very strict, but in the following year, with lodgings in town, he received pupils. One of his pupils, William Blount, Baron Mountjoy, accompanied him on his first trip to England in 1499–1500, where he met Thomas More and the English theologian John Colet; the latter encouraged him toward serious religious study and a direct scholarly approach to the early Church Fathers.

In the following years Erasmus traveled on the continent; his first collection of *Adages* (short sayings from classical authors) appeared in Paris in 1500, and his *Handbook of the Christian Knight*, a plea for a return to primitive Christian simplicity, was published at Antwerp in 1504. After a second visit to England in 1505–06, during which he met Warham, the archbishop of Canterbury, a chance to act as tutor to the son of Henry VII's physician, Boeri, enabled him to fulfill the humanist's aspiration to visit Italy. He spent time at the universities of Turin (where he received a doctorate of theology) and Bologna, visited Padua and Florence, and conversed with high church dignitaries in Rome. In Venice, the great humanistic printer Aldus Manutius became a friend and published an enlarged collection of *Adages*. In 1509 Erasmus returned to England, where in the same year he wrote *The Praise of Folly*. During this third and longest stay in England (until 1514) he lectured in Greek and divinity at Cambridge. Erasmus offers the highest illustration of the learned cosmopolitan humanist endeavoring to conciliate humanistic learning and religious piety. After leaving England in 1514, he continued to travel on the continent, finally making his most permanent home in Basel, a center whose cultural importance cannot be overestimated, especially as the seat of the printing house of Frobenius, whose general editor Erasmus became. In 1529 religious disturbances and the victories of the Swiss Protestants caused him to move to Freiburg in the Breisgau, the German university town in the Black Forest. His attitude toward the Protestant reformers (Luther in Germany, Zwingli in Switzerland) was typical: having tried to promote an impartial arbitration of the question between Luther and the Roman church, he was alienated by excesses on both sides. The shattering news of Thomas More's execution in England in 1535 reached him in Freiburg. He returned to Basel that same year and died there in July 1536.

Though his literary works and pamphlets, his editions of the Church Fathers, and his Latin edition of the New Testament (based on the Greek), and especially his letters (about three thousand of them) gave an important perspective on the cultural life of the period, Erasmus's most famous work remains *The Praise of Folly*. Its popularity is partly due to its dramatic and elegant literary form, partly to the fact that it deals in a wise, temperate way with perennial concerns, as pressing now as they were then: the power (and arrogance) of the human intellect, the worth (and futility) of knowledge, and above all the folly (and wisdom) of man's behavior.

To present these issues concretely, Erasmus uses an oratorical and theatrical approach. He takes for his speaker a feminine figure, Folly, placing her in front of an audience of whom she herself makes us aware: "as soon as I began to speak to this great audience, all faces suddenly brightened." We see her gesture, point to her public, call for their attention: "I am almost out of breath." "But why not speak to you more openly . . . ?" "You applaud! I was sure that you were not so wise, or rather so foolish—no, so wise." The general tone of speech balances between the jocose and the serious, the erudite and the foolish. In this way, she also throws light upon the audience—a congenial one, we feel, made up of people to whom the cultured allusions with which her speech is studded are so familiar that they appreciate the comic twists performed upon them, as they appreciate, more generally, the satire on conventional oratory which her monologue contains. "I see that you are expecting a peroration," she admits in the end, "but you are certainly foolish if you think that I can remember any part of such a hodgepodge of words as I have poured out." Her attitude toward her audience is thus not adversary but convivial. The butts of her polemic—the passionless Stoics—constitute a third party, and rather than address such people, she enlists her audience's support in rejecting them: "I ask you, if it were put to a vote, what city would choose such a person as mayor?"

This is the "play" as it is presented to us. But of course it is actually a "play within a play," performed for Erasmus and *his* audience, i.e., ourselves. From his vantage point backstage, he uses Folly as an ambiguous mouthpiece. In fact, by showing her to be foolish, light-headed, and rambling, he throws into sharper focus the truths she expresses; he secures the advantage of her directness and "innocence" while granting her the full support of his own erudition and wit. The apparent surface frivolity calls on us to expect an undercover depth and complexity, to read between the lines, and we may best measure that complexity by asking, What does Folly stand for? Does she stand for carefree living? For a way of life not hostile to the passions? For foolishness? For self-abandonment? For naïveté? For imagination? Is she simply the lighthearted creation of a great scholar in a frivolous moment, deploring the vanity of intellectual knowledge and the scholar's austere and solitary life in favor of instinct, intuition, good fellowship, "innocence"? Or does she embody a paradoxical "wisdom" to be found at the end of a long and perhaps finally frustrating accumulation of learning? Our answer to such questions must be at least as equivocal as the attitude of the work itself.

Clearly, the issue of knowledge versus ignorance underlies *The Praise of Folly*. What "Folly" says may often seem to be a debunking of the former in favor of the latter, but—and this is the function of the "play"—the attitude ultimately suggested is one neither of "barbaric" rebellion nor of unrelieved satiety and desperation. Erasmus's position, whether overtly or between the lines, is that of noble and wise compromise: a serene acceptance of the limitations of knowledge rather than a "melancholic" rejection of its value followed by a desperate gesture of rebellion. The attitude proposed, in other words, is a far cry from that of a dissatisfied intellectual who finds the mind has not given him satisfactory answers and who therefore embraces folly as Faust embraces the diabolical. On the other hand, the author's "praise" of folly is certainly not feigned or *mainly* ironical. His point of view is not that of the sophisticate who takes a frivolous delight in masquerading, let us say, as a shepherd. When a man like Erasmus implies that possibly fools are really wiser than we are (an implication that underlies many a passage in the book), his attitude toward the "fool" includes understanding, affection, and a real question about value. The balance of irony is maintained in both directions; the wisdom of compromise and the wise man's sense of limits guide the performance from backstage.

What has been said about the value of knowledge can be extended to the value of life: the world is a stage, and the forces ruling its actors may be irrational or not understandable, but it is in accordance with nature that we should go on playing our roles. Folly is imagination, inventiveness, and therefore make-believe; "everything is pretense." But at the same time, "this play is performed in no other way"; "true prudence . . . consists in not desiring more wisdom than is proper to mortals." This is "to act the play of life."

Acceptance of life as a play, as a pageant, opens a vision of true human reality, Erasmus feels, whereas the wisdom of the Stoics (who stand for pure intellectualism) produces "a marble imitation of a man" from which one shudders away "as from a ghost." Folly's far preferable prescription is "a timely mixture of ignorance, thoughtlessness, forgetfulness of evil, hope of good, and a dash of delight."

A good introduction to Erasmus is Richard L. DeMolen, ed., *Erasmus of Rotterdam. A Quincentennial Symposium* (1971), with brief essays by leading scholars, notes, selected bibliography, and a brief chronology of Erasmus's life. A more specialized collection of essays is provided by T. A. Dorey, ed., *Erasmus* (1970). George Faludy's modern biography, *Erasmus of Rotterdam* (1970), is intended for the general reader. Kathleen Williams, ed., *Twentieth Century Interpretations of "The Praise of Folly": A Collection of Critical Essays* (1969) is recommended.

# The Praise of Folly[1]

## I. *Folly Herself*

*Folly Speaks:*
    No matter what is ordinarily said about me (and I am not ignorant of how bad the name of Folly sounds, even to the biggest fools), I

1. Abridged. Translated by Leonard F. Dean.

am still the one, the only one I may say, whose influence makes Gods and men cheerful. A convincing proof of this is that as soon as I began to speak to this great audience, all faces suddenly brightened with a new and unusual gaiety, all frowns disappeared, and you applauded hilariously. Now you seem intoxicated with nectar, and also with nepenthe,[2] like the gods of Homer; whereas a moment ago you were sad and careworn, as if you had just come out of the cave of Trophonius.[3] Just as a new and youthful color reappears everywhere when the sun first shows its beautiful, golden face to the earth, or when spring breathes softly after a hard winter, so your faces changed at the sight of me. And thus what great orators can hardly accomplish with long and elaborate speeches, namely the banishment of care, I have done with my appearance alone.

. . . Since my ancestry is not known to many, I will undertake to describe it, with the Muses' kind assistance. My father was neither Chaos, Orcus, Saturn, Japetus, nor any other of that obsolete and senile set of gods; on the contrary he was Plutus,[4] the real father of men and gods, despite the opinion of Hesiod,[5] Homer, and Jove himself. Now, as always, one nod from Plutus turns everything sacred or profane upside down. By his decision wars, peace, empires, plans, judgments, assemblies, marriages, treaties, pacts, laws, arts, sports, solemnities (I am almost out of breath)—in short, all public and private affairs are governed. Without his help, all the poets' multitude of gods, even, I may boldly say, the chief ones, either would not exist or would have to live leanly at home. Not even Pallas can help the person who arouses Plutus' anger, but with his favor one can laugh at Jove's thunderbolts. What a magnificent father! He did not beget me out of his head, as Jupiter did that grim and gloomy Pallas, but from Youth, the best-looking as well as the gayest of all the nymphs. Nor was this done dully in wedlock, in the way that lame blacksmith[6] was conceived, but more pleasantly in passion, as old Homer puts it. It should also be clearly understood that I was not born of Aristophanes' worn-out and weak-eyed Plutus, but of the unimpaired Plutus, hot with youth and still hotter with nectar which by chance he had drunk straight and freely at a party of the gods.

Next, if you want to know the place of my birth (since the place where one first squalled is nowadays considered a mark of nobility), I was born neither in wandering Delos,[7] nor on the foaming sea,[8] nor "in deep caves," but in the Fortunate Isles themselves, where all

---

2. Legendary drug causing oblivion.    3. Seat of a particularly awesome oracle.    4. God of wealth and abundance. In Aristophanes' play by that name, to which Erasmus refers later in the paragraph, he is shown in decrepit age; ordinarily he is represented as a boy with a cornucopia. 5. Greek didactic poet of the eighth century B.C., cited here because he was author of the *Theogony* (about the generation and genealogy of the gods).    6. Hephaestus (Vulcan).    7. Birthplace of Apollo.    8. From which Venus emerged. "*In deep caves*": A Homeric expression. *Fortunate Isles*: The mythical and remote islands where, according to Greek tradition, some favorites of the gods dwelt in immortality and bliss.

things grow "without plowing or planting." There where there is no
labor, no old age, and no sickness; where not a daffodil, mallow,
onion, bean, or any other ordinary thing is to be seen; but where
nose and eyes are equally delighted by moly, panacea, nepenthes,
sweet marjoram, ambrosia, lotus, rose, violet, hyacinth, and the gardens of Adonis. Being born amidst these pleasant things, I did not
begin life crying, but from the first laughed good-naturedly at my
mother. I certainly need not envy Jove for being suckled by a she-
goat, for I was nursed at the breasts of two charming nymphs—
Drunkenness, offspring of Bacchus, and Ignorance, daughter of Pan.
Both of them you see here with my other attendants and followers.
If you ask the names of the others, I must answer in Greek. The
haughty one over there is Philantia (Self-love). The one with laughing eyes who is clapping her hands is Kolakia (Flattery). This drowsy
one is Lethe (Forgetfulness). She leaning on her elbows with folded
hands is Misoponia (Laziness). She with the perfume and wreath of
roses is Hedone (Pleasure). This wild-eyed one is Anoia (Madness).
The smooth-skinned and shapely one is Tryphe (Sensuality). And
you see those two gods playing with the girls; well, one is Comus
(Intemperance) and the other is Negretos Hypnos (Sound Sleep).
With the help of these faithful servants I gain control of all things,
even dictating to dictators.

## II. The Powers and Pleasures of Folly

. . . Now, that it may not seem that I call myself a goddess without good cause, let me tell you of the range of my influence and of
my benefits to men and gods. If to be a god is simply to aid men, as
someone has wisely said, and if they have been deservedly deified
who have shown mankind the uses of wine or grain, why am I not
justly called the Alpha[9] of gods, I who have all alone given all things
to all men.

First, what is more dear and precious than life itself? And by whose
aid but mine is life conceived? It is not the spear of "potently-sired"
Pallas nor the shield of "cloud-controlling" Jove that propagates and
multiplies mankind. Even the father of gods and the king of men,
he who shakes Olympus with a nod, must lay aside the three-pronged
thunderer and that Titanic manner with which when he pleases he
terrifies the gods, and like a poor actor assume another character, if
he wishes to do what he is forever doing, namely, begetting children.
The Stoics[1] assert that they are almost god-like. But give me one

9. First letter of the Greek alphabet; hence, "beginning," "origin."    1. Stoicism originated in
the Stoa Poikile ("painted porch"), a building in the market place in Athens where the philosopher
Zeno lectured in the fourth century B.C., and later was perhaps the main type of philosophy of
the Roman elite. It became known during the Renaissance especially through Seneca. Erasmus
here makes the Stoics the butts of Folly's irony on account of their supposedly godlike disregard
of the passions.

who is three, four, or six hundred times a Stoic, and if on this occasion he does not remove his beard, the sign of wisdom (in common with goats), at least he will shed his gravity, stop frowning, abandon his rock-bound principles and for a while be a silly fool. In short, the wise man must send for me if he wants to be a father. But why not speak to you more openly, as I usually do? I ask whether the head, the face, the breast, the hand, or the ear—each an honorable part—creates gods and men? I think not, but instead the job is done by that foolish, even ridiculous part which cannot be named without laughter. This is the sacred fountain from which all things rise, more certainly than from the Pythagorean tetrad.[2]

What man, I ask you, would stick his head into the halter of marriage if, following the practice of the wise, he first weighed the inconveniences of that life? Or what woman would ever embrace her husband if she foresaw or considered the dangers of childbirth and the drudgery of motherhood? Now since you owe your life to the marriage-bed, and marriage itself to my follower Madness, you can see how completely indebted you are to me. Moreover, would a woman who had experienced that travail once ever repeat it without the influence of my Forgetfulness? And Venus herself, no matter what Lucretius says,[3] cannot deny that her work would be weak and inconclusive without my help. Hence from my ridiculous and crazy game are produced supercilious philosophers, their present-day successors, vulgarly called monks, kings in purple robes, pious priests, thrice-holy popes, and finally all the gods invented by the poets, so numerous that spacious Olympus is crowded.

That the conception of life is due to me is a small matter when I can show you that I am responsible for everything agreeable. Would life without pleasure be life at all? You applaud! I was sure that you were not so wise, or rather so foolish—no, so wise, as to think otherwise. As a matter of fact, even the Stoics do not really dislike pleasure; they carefully pretend to and they loudly denounce it in public, but only in order to deter others and thus have it all to themselves. Just let them explain to me what part of life is not sad, troublesome, graceless, flat, and distressing without a dash of pleasure, or in other words, folly. This is very adequately proved by Sophocles,[4] a person insufficiently appreciated, who has left this pretty eulogy of me: "Ignorance is bliss." . . .

If someone should unmask the actors in the middle of a scene on the stage and show their real faces to the audience, would he not

---

2. According to the numerical conception of the universe of Pythagoras (sixth century B.C.) and his followers, the first four numbers (the "tetrad"—one, two, three, and four, adding up to the ideal number, ten) signified the root of all being.     3. In the opening lines of his poem *On the Nature of Things*, Lucretius (99?–55 B.C.) invokes Venus because "all living things" are conceived through her.     4. See his *Ajax*, ll. 554–555: ". . . life is sweetest before the feelings are awake—until one learns to know joy and pain."     5. Mythical mountain, home of the Muses.

spoil the whole play? And would not everyone think he deserved to
be driven out of the theater with brickbats as a crazy man? For at
once a new order of things would suddenly arise. He who played the
woman is now seen to be a man; the juvenile is revealed to be old;
he who a little before was a king is suddenly a slave; and he who was
a god now appears as a little man. Truly, to destroy the illusion is to
upset the whole play. The masks and costumes are precisely what
hold the eyes of the spectators. Now what else is our whole life but
a kind of stage play through which men pass in various disguises,
each one going on to play his part until he is led off by the director?
And often the same actor is ordered back in a different costume, so
that he who played the king in purple, now acts the slave in rags.
Thus everything is pretense; yet this play is performed in no other
way.

What if some wise man, dropped from heaven, should suddenly
confront me at this point and exclaim that the person whom everyone has looked up to as a god and ruler is not even a man, because
he is led sheeplike by his passions; that he is the meanest slave because
he voluntarily serves so many and such foul masters? Or what if this
wise man should instruct someone mourning his parent's death to
laugh, on the grounds that the parent had at last really begun to
live—our life here being in one way nothing but a kind of death?
And what if he should entitle another who was glorying in ancestry,
ignoble and illegitimate, because he was so far from virtue, the only
source of nobility? And what if he should speak of all others in the
same way? What, I ask, would he gain by it except to be regarded as
dangerously insane by everyone? Just as nothing is more foolish than
unseasonable wisdom, so nothing is more imprudent than bull-headed
prudence. And he is indeed perverse who does not accommodate
himself to the way of the world, who will not follow the crowd, who
does not at least remember the rule of good fellowship, drink or
begone, and who demands that the play shall no longer be a play.
True prudence, on the contrary, consists in not desiring more wisdom than is proper to mortals, and in being willing to wink at the
doings of the crowd or to go along with it sociably. But that, they
say, is folly itself. I shall certainly not deny it; yet they must in turn
admit that it is also to act the play of life.

I hesitate to speak about the next point. But why should I be silent
about what is truer than truth? For so great an undertaking, however,
it would probably be wise to call the Muses from Helicon;[5] the poets
usually invoke them on the slightest pretext. Therefore, stand by for
a moment, daughters of Jove, while I show that one cannot acquire
that widely advertised wisdom, which the wise call the secret of hap-

5. Mythical mountain, home of the Muses.

piness, unless one follows the leadership of Folly. First, everyone admits that all the emotions belong to folly. Indeed a fool and a wise man are distinguished by the fact that emotions control the former, and reason the latter. Now the Stoics would purge the wise man of all strong emotions, as if they were diseases; yet these emotions serve not only as a guide and teacher to those who are hastening toward the portal of wisdom, but also as a stimulus in all virtuous actions, as exhorters to good deeds. Of course that superstoic, Seneca, strongly denies this and strips the wise of absolutely every emotion; yet in so doing he leaves something that is not a man at all, but rather a new kind of god or sub-god who never existed and never will. To put it bluntly, he makes a marble imitation of a man, stupid, and altogether alien to every human feeling.

If this is the way they want it, let them keep their wise man. They can love him without any rivals and live with him in Plato's republic or, if they prefer, in the realm of Ideas, or in the gardens of Tantalus.[6] Who would not shudder at such a man and flee from him as from a ghost? He would be insensible to every natural feeling, no more moved by love or pity than if he were solid flint or Marpesian stone.[7] Nothing escapes him; he never makes a mistake; like another Lynceus[8] he sees all; he evaluates everything rigidly; he excuses nothing; he alone is satisfied with himself as the only one who is really rich, sane, royal, free—in short, unique in everything, but only so in his own opinion. Desiring no friend, he is himself the friend of none. He does not hesitate to bid the gods go hang themselves. All that life holds he condemns and scorns as folly. And this animal is the perfect wise man. I ask you, if it were put to a vote, what city would choose such a person as mayor? What army would want such a general? What woman such a husband? What host such a guest? What servant such a master? Who would not rather have any man at all from the rank and file of fools? Now such a choice, being a fool, would be able to command or obey fools. He would be able to please those like himself—or nearly everyone; he would be kind to his wife, a jolly friend, a gay companion, a polished guest; finally, he would consider nothing human to be alien to him.[9] But this wise man has been boring me for some time; let us turn to other instructive topics.

Imagine, then, that a man should look down from a great height, as the poets say that Jove does. What calamities would he see in man's life. How miserable, how vile, man's birth. How laborious his

6. Plato's republic, his celestial realm of pure ideas, and the mythical garden of Tantalus in Hades (where rich fruit always evades Tantalus' grasp) are all mentioned because they are characterized by the presence of abstractions and figments.    7. From Marpessos, a mountain on the island of Paros famous for its marble.    8. A mythical figure whose eyesight was proverbially supposed to penetrate even solid objects.    9. From a proverbial phrase in Terence's *Self-Tormentor*, 1. 77: "I am a man: nothing human do I consider alien to me."

education. His childhood is subject to injuries; his youth is painful; his age a burden; his death a hard necessity. He is attacked by a host of diseases, threatened by accidents, and assaulted by misfortunes; there is nothing without some gall. There are also the multitude of evils that man does to man. Here are poverty, imprisonment, infamy, shame, tortures, plots, treachery, slander, lawsuits, fraud. But this is plainly to count the grains of sand. It is not proper for me at the moment to suggest for what offenses men have deserved these misfortunes, nor what angry god caused them to be born to such miseries. Yet will not anyone who considers these things approve the example of the Milesian virgins,[1] pitiable as it is? Recall, however, what kind of people have committed suicide because they were tired of life. Have they not been the wise or near-wise? Among them, besides Diogenes, Xenocrates, Cato, Cassius, and Brutus, there was Chiron,[2] who chose death rather than immortality. Now you begin to see, I believe, what would happen if all men became wise: there would be need for new clay and another potter like Prometheus.[3]

But by a timely mixture of ignorance, thoughtlessness, forgetfulness of evil, hope of good, and a dash of delight, I bring relief from troubles; so that men are unwilling to relinquish their lives even when their lives are ready to relinquish them. They are so far from being weary of existence, that the less reason they have for living, the more they enjoy life. Clearly it is because of my good work that you everywhere see old fellows of Nestor's[4] age, scarcely recognizable as members of the human race, babbling, silly, toothless, white-haired, bald—or better let me describe them in the words of Aristophanes: "dirty, stooped, wrinkled, bald, toothless, and toolless."[5] And yet they are so in love with life and so eager to be young that one of them dyes his white hair, another hides his baldness with a wig, another obtains false teeth from heaven knows where, another is infatuated with some young girl and is a sillier lover than any adolescent. Nowadays for one of these old sticks, these drybones, to marry a juicy young wife, and one without a dowry and sure to be enjoyed by others, is becoming the usual and proper thing. But it is even more entertaining to observe the old women, long since half-dead with age, so cadaverous that they seem to have returned from the grave; yet always saying, "It's good to be alive." They, too, are always in heat, and hire young men at a handsome fee. They carefully paint their faces, and constantly inspect themselves in the mirror; they pluck out hairs from the strangest places; they display their withered and flabby breasts; with a quavering love-song they stir a

1. Of the city of Miletus, in Asia Minor. There is an ancient tale that most of them, seemingly gone insane, hanged themselves.   2. The centaur (half man, half horse); incurably wounded and suffering great pain, he asked Zeus for relief from his own immortality.   3. He supposedly molded man out of clay.   4. The old, eloquent sage in the Homeric epic.   5. See Aristophanes, *Plutus*, 11. 266–267.

worn-out desire; they drink and go around with girls; they write love-letters. Everyone laughs at all this, and very properly, since it is the greatest folly in the world; yet the old ladies are well pleased with themselves. They are perfectly happy solely because of me. More-over, those who scorn this kind of behavior might consider whether it is not better to lead a life of pleasant folly than to look for a rafter and a rope. Anyway, it is nothing to my fools that their actions are scorned; they either feel no shame, or shrug it off easily. If a rock falls on your head, that is clearly painful; but shame, disgrace, and curses hurt only so far as they are felt. What isn't noticed isn't trou-blesome. So long as you applaud yourself, what harm are the hisses of the world? And folly is the only key to this happiness.

I seem to hear the philosophers disagreeing. This is really unhap-piness, they say, this life of folly, error, and ignorance. No, indeed; this is to be human. I cannot see why they should call this unhap-piness when it is the common lot of all to be thus born, brought up, and constituted. Nothing can be unhappy if it expresses its true nature. Or do you argue that man is to be pitied because he cannot fly with the birds, and cannot run on four legs with the animals, and is not armed with horns like a bull? It can be argued equally well that the finest horse is unhappy because it is not a grammarian and a gour-met, or that a bull is miserable because it is found wanting at the minuet. A foolish man is no more unhappy than an illiterate horse: both are true to themselves.

The casuists argue next that men are naturally imperfect, and sup-port and strengthen themselves by the peculiarly human device of study. As if it were possible that nature should be so careful in mak-ing a midge, a flower, or an herb, and then should have dozed in making man! And with the result that the sciences are needed! They were really invented by Theuth,[6] the evil genius of the human race, for the hurt of mankind. Instead of promoting man's happiness, they hinder it. They were probably even discovered for that purpose, just as letters were, according to the admirable argument of Plato's wise king.[7] In this way, studies crept in with the other trials of life, and from the same devilish source. This is shown by their name: "dae-mons," which means "those who know."

The people of the golden age lived without the advantages of learning, being guided by instinct and nature alone. What was the need of grammar when all spoke the same language, and spoke only to be understood? What use for dialectic when there was no conflict of opinion? What place for rhetoric when no one wished to get the better of another? What need for legal skill before the time of those

6. In Plato's *Phaedrus*, the name of an Egyptian god who brought the art of writing to King Thamus.    7. King Thamus argued that the invention of writing would produce only false wis-dom and destroy the power of man's memory.

evil acts which called forth our good laws? Furthermore, they were
then too religious to pry impiously into nature's secrets, to measure
the size, motion, and influence of the stars, or to seek the hidden
causes of things. They considered it a sacrilege for man to know
more than he should. They were free from the insane desire to discover what may lie beyond the stars. But as men fell slowly from the
innocence of the golden age, the arts were invented, and by evil
spirits, as I have said. At first they were few in number and were
accepted by a few people. Later, hundreds more were added by the
superstition of the Chaldeans and by the idle speculation of the Greeks.
This was a needless vexation of the spirit, when one considers that a
single grammatical system is perfectly adequate for a lifetime of torture.

Of course the arts which are nearest to common sense, that is, to
folly, are most highly esteemed. Theologians are starved, scientists
are given the cold shoulder, astrologers are laughed at, and logicians
are ignored. The doctor alone, as they say, is worth all the rest put
together. And a doctor is honored, especially among nobles, to the
degree that he is ignorant and impudent. Medicine, as now generally
practiced, is a branch of the art of flattery just as much as rhetoric is.
Lawyers rank next to doctors. Perhaps they should be placed first,
but I hesitate to join the philosophers, who unanimously laugh at
lawyers as being so many asses. Nevertheless, all affairs, both great
and small, are arbitrated by these asses. Their lands increase; while
the theologian, who has mastered a trunkful of manuscripts, lives on
beans, and wages a gallant war against lice and fleas. As those arts
are more successful which have the greatest proportion of folly, so
those people are happiest who have nothing to do with learning and
follow nature as their only guide. She is in no way wanting, except
as a man wishes to go beyond what is proper for him. Nature hates
counterfeits; the less the art, the greater the happiness.

Isn't it true that the happiest creatures are those which are least
artificial and most natural? What could be happier than the bees, or
more wonderful? They lack some of the senses, but what architect
has equalled their constructive skill, or what philosopher has framed
a republic to match theirs? Now the horse, who does have some of
the human senses and who travels around with men, suffers also
from human ills. He feels ashamed if he loses a race. While seeking
military glory, he is run through and bites the dust along with his
rider. Think, too, of the hard bit, the sharp spurs, the prison-like
stable, the whips, sticks, and straps, the rider himself—in short, all
the tragedy of servitude to which he exposes himself when he imitates men of honor and zealously seeks vengeance against the enemy.
How much more desirable except for the interference of men, is the
lot of flies and birds, who live for the moment and by the light of

nature. Everyone has noticed how a bird loses its natural beauty when it is shut up in a cage and taught to speak. In every sphere, what is natural is happier than what is falsified by art.

For these reasons I can never sufficiently praise that cock (really Pythagoras)[8] who had been all things—philosopher, man, woman, king, subject, fish, horse, frog, perhaps even a sponge—and who concluded that none is as miserable as man. All the others are content with their natural limitations; man alone is vainly ambitious. Among men, furthermore, the fools are in many respects superior to the learned and the great. Gryllus,[9] for example, proved to be considerably wiser than wise Ulysses when he chose to grunt in a sty rather than to expose himself to the dangers of a further odyssey. Homer, the father of fiction, seems to agree with this: he often observes that men are wretched, and he still oftener describes Ulysses, the pattern of wisdom, as miserable, but he never speaks in this way of Paris, Ajax, or Achilles. Obviously Ulysses was unhappy because that tricky and artful fellow never did anything without consulting the goddess of wisdom. Wouldn't you say that he was over-educated, and that he had got too far away from nature? The seekers after wisdom are the farthest from happiness. They are fools twice over: forgetting the human station to which they were born, they grasp at divinity, and imitating the Giants,[1] they use their arts as engines with which to attack nature. It follows that the least unhappy are those who approximate the naivete of the beasts and who never attempt what is beyond men.

There is no need to argue this like a Stoic logician, however, when we can prove it with a plain example. Is anyone happier than those we commonly call morons, fools, nitwits, and naturals—the most beautiful of names? This may sound absurd at first, but it is profoundly true. In the first place, these fools are free from the fear of death—and that fear is not an insignificant evil. They are free from the pangs of conscience. They are not terrified by ghosts and hobgoblins. They are not filled with vain worries and hopes. In short, they are not troubled by the thousand cares to which this life is subject. Shame, fear, ambition, envy, and love are not for them. If they were just a little dumber and more animal-like they would not even sin—or so the theologians say. Count your cares, you stupid intellectuals, and then you will begin to appreciate what I do for my followers. Remember also that they are always merry; wherever they go they bring pleasure, as if they were mercifully created by the gods

8. In the dialogue *The Dream, or the Cock*, written in the second century A.D. by the Greek satirist Lucian, the cock upholds the Pythagorean notion of transmigration of souls from one body to another by claiming that he is Pythagoras.     9. Character in a dialogue by Plutarch, changed into a pig by Circe.     1. Following the example of the Giants, or Titans, of Greek mythology who, inspired by their wronged mother Gaea (Earth), fought the Olympian gods and were defeated.

to lighten the sadness of human life.

In a world where men are mostly at odds, all are as one in their attitude toward these innocents. They are sought out and sheltered; everyone permits them to do and say what they wish with impunity. Even the wild beasts perceive their harmlessness and do not attack them. They are sacred to the gods, and especially to me; therefore do all men properly honor them. Kings cannot eat or travel or spend an hour without their fools, in whom they take the greatest delight. In fact they rather prefer them to their crabbed counsellors, whom they nevertheless support for the sake of appearances. This royal preference is easily explained, I think. Counsellors, confident in their wisdom and forced to speak the unpleasant truth, bring only problems to princes; but fools bring what rulers are always looking for— jokes and laughter.

Fools have another not insignificant virtue: they alone are candid and truthful. What is more admirable than truth? I know that Alcibiades thought that only drunkards and children speak the truth;[2] nevertheless, the merit is really mine, as is proved by a line from Euripides: A fool speaks folly.[3] Whatever a fool has in his heart is all over his face and in his speech. Now wise men have two tongues, as Euripides also remarks,[4] one for speaking the truth, and the other for saying whatever is expedient at the moment. They turn black into white, and blow hot and cold with the same breath; their words are far from what is in their hearts. Kings are unhappiest at this point it seems to me, since in the midst of their prosperity they can find no one to tell them the truth, and are obliged to have flatterers for friends. You may say that kings hate to hear the truth and avoid wise counsellors for fear that one more daring than the others will speak what is true rather than what is pleasant. By and large this is so. It is remarkable, therefore, that kings will take the truth, and a sharp truth too, from my fools. A statement which would cost a wise man his head is received from a fool with the greatest delight. Truth that is free from offensiveness does give genuine pleasure, and only fools have the power to speak it. It is for these reasons, too, that fools are taken up by women, who are naturally inclined to pleasure and frivolity. Moreover, they can explain away whatever games they indulge in with fools, even when the sport becomes serious, as good clean fun—for the sex is ingenious, especially at covering up its own lapses.

Now let's return to the subject of the happiness of fools. After a life of jollity, and with no fear of death, or sense of it, they go straight to the Elysian fields, where they entertain the pious and leisurely shades. Compare the life of a wise man with that of a fool. Put up against a fool some model of wisdom, one who lost his boyhood and

2. See Plato's *Symposium*.   3. *The Bacchanals (Bacchae)*, 1. 369.   4. The source of this reference is uncertain.

youth in the classroom, who dissipated the best part of his life in continual worry and study, and who never tasted a particle of pleasure thereafter. He is always abstemious, poor, unhappy, and crabbed; he is harsh and unjust to himself, grim and mean to others; he is pale, emaciated, sickly, sore-eyed, prematurely old and white-haired, dying before his time. Of course it really makes little difference when such a man dies. He has never lived. Well, there is your wise man for you.

Here the Stoics croak at me again. Nothing, they say, is more lamentable than madness, and pure folly is either very near madness, or more likely is the same thing. What is madness but a wandering of the wits? (But the Stoics wander the whole way.) With the Muses' help we will explode this line of reasoning. The argument is plausible, but our opponents should remember the practice of Socrates in splitting Cupids and Venuses,[5] and distinguish one kind of madness from another—at least they should if they wish to be considered sane themselves. To begin with, not every kind of madness is a calamity. Otherwise Horace would not have said, "A pleasant madness inspires me."[6] Nor would Plato have ranked the frenzy of poets, prophets, and lovers among the chief blessings of life. And the oracle would not have called the labors of Aeneas, insane.[7] Madness is really of two kinds. The first is sent up from hell by the vengeful Furies. Unloosing their snaky locks, they assault the hearts of men with hot desire for war, with insatiable greed and shameful lust, with parricide, incest, sacrilege, or any other evil of that sort. At other times the Furies pursue the guilty and conscience-stricken soul with terror and the fire of wrath. The second kind of madness is far different from this. It comes from me and is to be desired above all things. It arises whenever a cheerful confusion of the mind frees the spirit from care and at the same time anoints it with many-sided delight. It is the state of mind that Cicero desired as a defense against the evils of his age. The Greek in Horace[8] also had the right idea. He was just sufficiently mad to sit alone in the theater all day, laughing and applauding at a bare stage, because he thought that tragedies were being enacted there. Otherwise he was sane enough—pleasant with his friends, kind to his wife, and indulgent to his servants, who could uncork a bottle without his getting angry. When the care of family and physician had freed him of his disease, he protested that he had been killed rather than cured, that they had taken away his pleasures and destroyed his delightful delusions. And he was perfectly right. They were the mad ones themselves, and needed the medicine more than he did. What sense is there in regarding a for-

5. Distinguishing different types of love.     6. Horace, *Odes*, Book III, Ode iv, ll. 5–6.
7. *Aeneid*, Book VI, l. 135.     8. What follows is a paraphrase of a passage in Horace's *Epistles*, Book II, Epistle ii, ll. 128–140.

tunate delusion like his as a disease to be purged with drugs?

It is not certain that every delusion and vagary ought to be called madness. A short-sighted man who thinks a mule is an ass is not commonly considered insane, nor is one who judges popular music to be great poetry. However, we must grant that a man is pretty nearly mad if he is continually and extraordinarily deluded by both his senses and his judgment. Take, for example, a person who thinks he is listening to a symphony orchestra whenever an ass brays, or a beggar who believes himself to be Croesus. Nevertheless, when this extreme madness gives pleasure, as it usually does, it is remarkably delightful both to those who are possessed by it, and to those who look on and are not mad in exactly the same way. Indeed this kind of madness is much more common than the ordinary person realizes. One madman laughs at another; they take turns entertaining each other. And the maddest one gets the biggest laugh.

If Folly is any judge, the happiest man is the one who is the most thoroughly deluded. May he maintain that ecstasy. It comes only from me, and is so widespread that I doubt if there is one man anywhere who is consistently wise and untouched by some madness. It may be only a tendency to think a gourd is a woman; but since very few see eye to eye with him on this, he will be called mad. When a man foolishly maintains that his wife (whom he shares with many others) is a pluperfect Penelope, however, nobody calls him mad, because they see that this is a plight common to other husbands.

To this latter class belong those who sacrifice everything for hunting. They swear that the sound of the horn and the baying of the hounds fill them with indescribable joy. I understand that even the dung of the dogs smells like cinnamon to them. And what is so delightful as an animal being butchered? Bulls and oxen are of course slaughtered by commoners, but it is a crime for anyone except a gentleman to touch wild game. Bareheaded and kneeling, he performs the ceremony with a special knife (no other can be used), cutting certain parts in approved order. The silent company stands as if spellbound by some novelty, although it has seen the spectacle a thousand times. If one of them is given a piece to taste, he feels that he has risen somewhat in the ranks of nobility. They think they are living royally, whereas they are really gaining nothing from this butchering and eating of animals, except to degenerate into animals themselves.

A similar class is those who are afire with a tremendous enthusiasm for building. They change round structures into square ones, and then back into round ones again. There is no end to this, until, having built themselves into poverty, they have no house to live in, and nothing to eat. What of it? In the meantime, they have been happy.

Next to these, I believe, are those who with new and secret arts
labor to transmute the forms of things and who ransack earth and sea
for a fifth essence.[9] Lured on by hope, and begrudging neither pain
nor cost, they contrive, with marvelous ingenuity, their own delightful deception. Finally, they have spent all their money and can't
afford another furnace. Even then, however, they dream on pleasantly, urging others to experience the same happiness. When absolutely all hope is gone, they find much comfort in this last thought,
"In great things, it is enough to have tried." They complain that life
is too short for the magnitude of their undertaking.

I am not sure that gamblers should be admitted to our fellowship,
and yet some of these addicts are a foolish and ridiculous sight. At
the sound of the dice their hearts beat faster. The hope of winning
always lures them on, until their means are gone, until their ship is
split on the gaming table, which is a more deadly promontory than
Malea.[1] Now, when they have lost their shirt, they will cheat anyone
except the winner, in order to preserve their word and honor. Think,
also, of the old and half-blind fellows, who have to wear glasses to
play. When well-earned gout has tied their joints in knots, they hire
a proxy to put the dice in the box for them. A delightful affair, were
it not that the game usually degenerates into a brawl, and so belongs
to the Furies rather than to me.

A group that does belong with us beyond any doubt is made up of
those who enjoy telling and hearing monstrous lies and tall tales.
They never get enough of ghosts and goblins and the like. They are
most pleased by stories that are farthest from the truth. Such wonders
are a diversion from boredom, and they may also be very profitable,
especially for priests and pardoners.

Closely related are those who have reached the foolish but comforting belief that if they gaze on a picture of Polyphemus-Christo-
pher,[2] they will not die that day; or that whoever speaks the right
words to an image of Barbara[3] will return unharmed from battle; or
that a novena[4] to Erasmus, with proper prayers and candles, will
shortly make one rich. In St. George they have turned up another
Hercules or Hippolytus.[5] They all but adore his horse, which is piously
studded and ornamented, and they ingratiate themselves by small
gifts. To swear by St. George's brass helmets is an oath for a king.
Then, what shall I say of those who happily delude themselves with
forged pardons for their sins? They calculate the time to be spent in
Purgatory down to the year, month, day, and hour, as if from a fool-

9. A substance (in addition to the four traditional elements—earth, water, air, and fire) of which
the heavenly bodies were believed to be composed.    1. A proverbially dangerous promontory
in Greece.    2. Polyphemus is the Cyclops (one-eyed giant) in Homer's *Odyssey*; St. Christopher is also represented with only one eye.    3. St. Barbara, supposed to protect her worshipers
against fire and artillery.    4. A nine days' devotion.    5. In Greco-Roman mythology, both
fought against monsters.

proof mathematical table. There are also those who propose to get everything they desire by relying on magical charms and prayers devised by some pious impostor for the sake of his soul, or for profit. They will have wealth, honor, pleasure, plenty, good health, long life, a vigorous old age, and at last, a place next to Christ in heaven. However they don't want that seat of honor until the very last minute; celestial pleasures may come only when worldly pleasures, hung on to with tooth and nail, finally depart.

I picture a business man, a soldier, or a judge taking from all his loot one small coin as a proper expiation for the infinite evil of his life. He thinks it possible to buy up, like notes, so many perjuries, rapes, debauches, fights, murders, frauds, lies and treacheries. Having done this, he feels free to start with a clean slate on a new round of sin. How foolish also—and how happy—are those who expect something more than the highest happiness if they repeat daily the seven verses of the Psalms. These are the verses believed to have been pointed out to St. Bernard by the devil. He was a merry fellow but not very shrewd, since his tongue was loosened by the saint's trick.[6] Things like that are so foolish that I am almost ashamed of them myself; yet they are accepted not only by the laity but by the professors of theology themselves. The same thing on a larger scale occurs when sections of the country set up regional saints, and assign peculiar rites and powers to each one. One gives relief from toothache, another aids women in labor, a third recovers stolen goods, a fourth succors the shipwrecked, and still another watches over the sheep—the list is too long to finish. Some are helpful in a number of difficulties, especially the Virgin Mother, whom the common people honor more than they do the Son.

Do men ask anything but folly from these saints? Among all the gifts hanging from the walls and even from the ceilings of churches, have you ever seen one in payment for an escape from folly, or for making the giver wiser? One person has escaped from drowning. Another has lived after being run through. This fellow had the good luck or the nerve to leave the battlefield, allowing the others to fight. Another was delivered from the shadow of the gallows by the patron saint of thieves so that he could continue to relieve those who are burdened with too much wealth. This one escaped from jail. That one crossed up his doctor by surviving a fever. This man was saved by a poisoned drink, which loosened his bowels instead of killing him. His wife was not exactly pleased, since she lost both her labor and expense. Another's wagon was overturned, but he drove his horses home unharmed. That fellow's house fell on him and he lived. This one sneaked out safely when he was surprised by a husband. No one,

6. A devil had told St. Bernard that repeating seven particular verses of the Psalms would bring him the certainty of salvation; "the saint's trick" was that of proposing to recite all of the Psalms.

however, gives thanks for warding off folly. It is so pleasant not to be wise that men will seek to avoid anything rather than folly.

Why should I go farther on this sea of superstition? "If I had a hundred tongues, a hundred mouths, a voice of brass, I could not describe all the forms of folly, or list all its names."[7] The life of Christians everywhere runs over with such nonsense. Superstitions are allowed and even promoted by the priests; they do not regret anything so profitable. Imagine, in the midst of this, some insolent wise men speaking the real truth: "You will not die badly if you live well. Your sins are redeemed if to the payment of money you add tears, vigils, prayers, fastings, and hatred of evil, and if you change your whole way of living. The saints will favor you if you imitate them." A wise man who snarled out things like that would throw the world into turmoil and deprive it of happiness!

Also of our fellowship are those who while still living make elaborate funeral arrangements, even prescribing the number of candles, mourners, singers, and hired pall-bearers. They must think that their sight will be returned to them after they are dead, or that their corpses will feel ashamed at not being buried grandly. They labor as if they were planning a civic entertainment.

I must not pass over those nobodies who take enormous pride in empty titles of nobility. One will trace his family back to Aeneas, another to Brutus,[8] and a third to King Arthur. They are surrounded by busts and portraits of their ancestors. They name over their grandfathers and great-grandfathers, and have the old titles by heart. At the same time, they are not far from being senseless statues themselves, and are probably worth less than the ones they show off. My follower, Self-love, enables them to live happily, however; and there are always other fools who regard monsters like these as gods.

Of course Self-love brings joy to others too. This ape-like fellow here seems handsome enough to himself. That one drawing circles over there thinks he is another Euclid. The man with the rooster's voice considers himself a great musician. The happiest fool, however, is the dolt who glories in some talent which is really made possible by his followers. Seneca tells[9] of that double-happy rich man, for example, who had servants on hand to refresh his memory whenever he told stories. He was so weak he could hardly stand, but he was a great fighter—with the support of hired thugs.

Artists are notoriously conceited. They would rather lose the family homestead than any part of their talent. This is especially true of actors, singers, orators, and poets. The worse they are, the more insolent, pushing, and conceited they become. And the more applause

7. A variation on a passage in the *Aeneid*, Book VI, ll. 625–627, in which, however, Virgil is talking of "forms of crime" rather than of "folly."    8. The legendary founder of Britain. 9. The reference has not been traced.

they receive. The worst always please the most, because the majority of people, as I have remarked, are fools. If the poorer artist is most pleased with himself and is admired by the largest number, why should he wish to have true skill? It will cost him more; it will make him self-conscious and critical; and it will please far fewer of his audience.

I observe that races and cities are also attended by self-love. The English pride themselves on their good looks, their music, and their fine food, among other things. Noble or royal lineage is the claim of all Scots, together with argumentative skill. The French are the masters of courtesy; and the Parisians, in addition, are the only ones who understand theology.[1] The Italians have a monopoly on literature and eloquence, and they are pleased to admit that they alone are not barbarians. Happiest in this delusion are the Romans, who dream pleasantly of their ancient glories. The Venetians are content with their own nobility. The Greeks, of course, discovered the arts and possess the heroes of antiquity. Christian superstitions entertain the Turks and the other actual barbarians, who boast of their own religions. Better yet, the Jews steadfastly await the Messiah, and still hold grimly to Moses. The Spaniards scorn all other soldiers; and the Germans pride themselves on their great size and their knowledge of magic. I believe this is sufficient to convince you that the happiness of men, individually and collectively, springs from self-love.

Another source of pleasure is flattery, an extension of self-love. Instead of admiring yourself, you simply admire someone else. Nowadays flattery is condemned, but only among those who confuse the names of things with the things themselves. They think that flattery is necessarily insincere. The example of dumb animals should show them how wrong they are. What is more fawning than a dog? And yet, what is more faithful and a better friend to man? Or perhaps you prefer fierce lions, tigers, and leopards? Of course there is a harmful kind of flattery, the kind with which traitors and mockers destroy their victims; but my kind springs from kindliness and candor. It is much closer to virtue than is its opposite, surliness—or what Horace calls a heavy and awkward rudeness.[2] It raises the spirits and dispels grief; it stimulates the faint, enlivens the dull, and eases the suffering; it brings lovers together and keeps them together. It entices boys to study literature; it inspires the old. Disguised as praise, it warns and instructs princes without offense. In short, it makes everyone more pleased with himself—which is the chief part of happiness. What is more courteous than the way two mules scratch each other? There is no need to point out that flattery is important in the admired art

1. The Sorbonne, the theological faculty in Paris, was the center of theological studies in Europe.    2. Horace, *Epistles*, Book I, Epistle xviii, ll. 508.

of oratory, that it is a great part of medicine, and that it is a still greater part of poetry. It is nothing less than the sugar and spice of all human intercourse.

Still, it is a sad thing, they say, to be deceived. No; the saddest thing is not to be deceived. The notion that happiness comes from a knowledge of things as they really are is wrong. Happiness resides in opinion. Human affairs are so obscure and various that nothing can be clearly known. This was the sound conclusion of the Academics,[3] who were the least surly of the philosophers. At least if something can be truly known, it is rarely anything that adds to the pleasure of life. Anyway, man's mind is much more taken with appearances than with reality. This can be easily and surely tested by going to church. When anything serious is being said, the congregation dozes or squirms. But if the ranter—I mean the reverend—begins some old wives' tale, as often happens, everyone wakes up and strains to hear. You will also see more devotion being paid to such fabulous and poetic saints as George, Christopher, or Barbara than to Peter or Paul or even to Christ Himself. But these examples belong elsewhere.

The price of this kind of happiness is very low. Much more must be paid for substantial things, even for the least of them—grammar, for instance. It is easy enough to acquire mere opinions; nevertheless they bring greater happiness than knowledge does. The satisfaction of a man who thinks rotten kippers taste and smell like ambrosia is not affected by the fact that his neighbor cannot abide their odor. On the other hand, if the finest fish turn your stomach, their quality has no bearing on your happiness. A man who thinks his extremely ugly wife is another Venus is as well off as if she really were beautiful. Here's a person who gazes admiringly at a picture made of red lead and mud which he believes is by Apelles or Zeuxis. Isn't he happier than someone who has paid a high price for an authentic masterpiece, but who gets little pleasure from it? I know a man by my name,[4] a practical joker, who gave his new wife some imitation jewels and persuaded her that they were genuine and very valuable. Now what difference did it make to the girl? She was delighted with the glass trinkets and kept them locked in a secret place. In the meantime, the husband had saved money, had enjoyed fooling his wife, and had won her devotion as well as he would have by a more expensive present.

What difference do you see between the self-satisfied inhabitants of Plato's cave[5] who contentedly admire the shadows of things, and

3. Philosophers of Plato's school, the Academy, which later became a school of skeptics. 4. Sir Thomas More, who was a close friend of Erasmus's and on whose name Erasmus puns with *moria* (Latin for "folly").   5. The reference is to Plato's allegory in the *Republic*, Book VII, where he compares the soul in the body to a prisoner chained in a cave, his back against the light, able to see only the shadows of things outside.

the wise man who emerges from the cave and sees reality? If Lucian's Micyllus[6] could have dreamed forever his rich and golden dream, there would have been no reason for him to desire any other kind of happiness. Evidently, then, there is either no difference between a fool and a wise man, or if there is a difference, a fool has the better of it. A fool's happiness costs least—no more than a bit of illusion. In addition, it is enjoyed in the company of a great many others. The good things of life must be shared to be delightful; and who has not heard of the scarcity of wise men, if indeed any exist at all. The Greeks listed seven all told;[7] a more accurate census would do well to turn up one-half or one-third of a wise man.

Of course drink will drown your sorrows, but only for a time. The next morning they come galloping back, riding four white horses, as the saying is. Folly, on the other hand, is a spree that never ends. Its effect is complete and immediate. Without requiring any bothersome preparations, it fills the heart with joy. It is available to all, rather than to a chosen few, as with other gifts of the gods. Vintage wine is not made everywhere; beauty comes to few, and eloquence to fewer still. Not many are rich, and not many can be kings. Mars often favors neither side; Neptune drowns more than he saves. The majority are turned away from wisdom. Jove himself thunders, and the anti-Joves—Pluto, Ate, Poena, Febris,[8] and the others—are executioners rather than gods. Only I, great-hearted Folly, embrace all men equally. Nor do I come only when prayed for. If some devotion is neglected, I don't grow testy and demand expiation. I don't upset heaven and earth if I have been left at home and not invited along with the other gods to smell the sacrifices. In fact, the other gods are so hard to please that it is safer and wiser not to try to worship them, but rather to avoid them altogether. Men are sometimes like that; so thin-skinned and irritable that hands off is the best policy.

Even though all this is so, I understand that no one sacrifices to Folly or builds a temple for her. Such ingratitude, I repeat, is amazing. At the same time, I good-naturedly persuade myself that respect is not really lacking. What need have I for incense, meal, a he-goat, or a she-hog, so long as men everywhere whole-heartedly worship me in the way that preachers tell us is best? Let Diana have her human sacrifices! I am not envious when I consider that all men honor me in the truest way, that is, by taking me to their hearts and manifesting me in their lives and actions. This kind of worship of the saints is not exactly customary among Christians. Plenty of them burn little candles to the Virgin, and in the middle of the day, when

---

6. A character in Lucian's *The Dream, or the Cock* who dreams that he has taken the place of a rich man.     7. The Seven Sages listed were philosophers of the sixth century B.C., among them Thales and Solon.     8. Pluto was god of the underworld; *Ate*, goddess of revenge and discord; *Poena*, goddess of punishment; *Febris*, goddess of fever.

it does no good; but how few of them burn with zeal to imitate her in chastity, temperance, and love of heavenly things! That, after all, is the true worship, and it is by far the most pleasing to those above. Besides, why should I desire a temple, when the whole world, if I am not mistaken, is a handsome shrine to me? Nor are priests lacking—except where men are lacking. As for stone and painted images, I am not so foolish as to demand what stands in the way of worship. The stupid adore such substitutes in place of the saints themselves, who are finally crowded out altogether. The same thing would happen to me. One might say, of course, that there are as many statues to me as there are people who look foolish, even unintentionally so. What do I care if other gods are worshipped in certain places on stated days—Phoebus at Rhodes, Venus at Cyprus, Juno at Argos, Minerva at Athens, Jupiter at Olympus, Neptune at Tarentum, Priapus[9] at Lampsacus? Why should I envy them when all men eagerly offer greater sacrifices to me?

[The third section deals with "The Followers of Folly," and includes among them, in lively and paradoxical descriptions, all categories of people, from merchants to poets, from scholars to popes and cardinals; in fact, Folly concludes: "My real point has been that no man can live happily unless he has been admitted into my mysteries and enjoys my favor."]

## IV. *The Christian Fool*

. . . There is really no need for me to marshal proof[1] with so much care, when in the mystical psalms Christ himself, speaking to the Father, says perfectly plainly, "Thou knowest my foolishness."[2] It is not hard to see why fools are greatly pleasing to God. We know that great princes look with suspicion on men who are too clever, and hate them. Julius Caesar, for instance, suspected and hated Brutus and Cassius, while he did not fear the drunken Antony at all. Nero, likewise, was suspicious of Seneca, and Dionysius[3] of Plato; but all princes take pleasure in duller and simpler souls. In the same way, Christ always hates and condemns those who rely on their own wisdom. Paul testifies to this clearly enough when he says, "God has chosen the foolish things of the world,"[4] and when he says, "It has pleased God to save the world by foolishness,"[5] since it could never be redeemed by wisdom. God himself indicates this plainly when he

9. A god of procreation, son of Dionysus and Aphrodite.    1. Of the relationship between "Folly" and Christianity.    2. The quotation is from Psalm 69:5, where the speaker is not Christ, but the Psalmist.    3. Dionysius the Younger, tyrant of Syracuse, in Sicily, in the fourth century B.C.    4. "But God hath chosen the foolish things of the world to confound the wise." (I Corinthians 1:27.    5. "For after that in the wisdom of God the world by wisdom knew not God, it pleased God by the foolishness of preaching to save them that believe."

proclaims through the mouth of the prophet, "I will destroy the wisdom of the wise and I will reject the prudence of the prudent."[6] Christ also gave thanks that God had concealed the mystery of salvation from the wise, but had revealed it to babes, that is, to fools.[7] The Greek for "babes" is νηπιοισ, which is the opposite of σοφοισ, "the wise." Equally pertinent is the fact that in the Gospels Christ often attacks the scribes and Pharisees and doctors of laws, whereas he faithfully defends the ignorant multitude. What is "Woe unto you, scribes and Pharisees,"[8] except "Woe unto you that are wise"? Little children, women, and fishermen seem to delight Him most. Even among animals, those pleased Christ best which had the least slyness. He preferred to ride upon a donkey, though had He chosen He could safely have ridden upon a lion. The Holy Spirit descended in the likeness of a dove, not of an eagle or a hawk; and the Gospels frequently mention harts, fawns, and lambs. Those who are chosen for eternal life are called "sheep." No animal is more foolish, as is shown by the proverbial phrase in Aristotle, "sheepish character," which was suggested by the stupidity of the animal and is commonly used as a taunt against dull and foolish men. Nevertheless, Christ declares himself the shepherd of his flock, and even takes delight in the name of "the Lamb," as when John pointed Him out, "Behold the Lamb of God."[9] The expression also appears frequently in the book of *Revelations*.

What do these things declare except that all men, even the pious, are fools? And that Christ himself, although He possessed the wisdom of the Father,[1] became something like a fool in order to cure the folly of mankind, when He assumed the nature and being of a mortal? And that He was made "to be sin"[2] in order to redeem sinners? He did not wish to redeem them by any way except by the foolishness of the Cross, and by weak and simple apostles. These He taught to practice folly and to avoid wisdom. He incited them by the example of children, lilies, mustard-seed, and sparrows,[3] all of them foolish things, living without art or care, by the light of nature alone. Furthermore, He forbade the apostles to be concerned about how they should answer the charges of the magistrates, and He forbade them to pry into the times and seasons. They should not rely on their own wisdom, but should wholly depend upon Him. We know, likewise, that the Creator commanded men not to eat of the Tree of Knowledge, just as if knowledge were the destroyer of happiness.

6. ". . . for the wisdom of their wise men shall perish, and the understanding of their prudent men shall be hid."    7. "I thank thee, O Father, Lord of heaven and earth, because thou hast hid these things from the wise and prudent, and hast revealed them unto babes." (Matthew 11:25.)    8. Luke 11:44.    9. John 1:29, 36.    1. "But unto them which are called, both Jews and Greeks, Christ the power of God, and the wisdom of God." (I Corinthians 1:24.) 2. "For he hath made him to be sin for us, who knew no sin." (II Corinthians 5:21.)    3. For the reference to *children*, see Luke 18:17; for *lilies*, see Matthew 6:28; for *mustard-seed*, see Luke, 17:6; for *sparrows*, see Matthew 10:29.

Paul roundly condemns knowledge as that which puffs up[4] and works harm. St. Bernard is following him, I believe, when he explains that the mountain wherein Lucifer established his headquarters was "the Mount of Knowledge."

Surely we should not overlook this argument, that folly is so pleasing to the heavenly powers that forgiveness of its errors is certain; whereas nothing is forgiven to wisdom. And so it comes about that when the prudent pray to be forgiven, although they were clever enough when they sinned, they use the excuse and defense of having acted foolishly. This was the argument that Aaron used in the book of *Numbers*, if I remember correctly, to excuse his sister from punishment: "I beseech, my master, that you lay not this sin, which we have committed foolishly, to our charge."[5] Saul asked forgiveness of David by saying, "It is apparent that I have done foolishly."[6] David, in turn, speaks placatingly to the Lord: "I beseech Thee, do away the iniquity of thy servant, for I have done very foolishly."[7] It is as if he could not obtain grace by praying unless he pleaded folly and ignorance. Much stronger proof is the fact that Christ when he prayed on the Cross for His enemies, "Father, forgive them," pleaded no other excuse than ignorance, saying, "for they know not what they do."[8] In the same manner, Paul wrote to Timothy: "But therefore I have obtained the mercy of the Lord, because I acted ignorantly in unbelief."[9] What is "I acted ignorantly" except "I acted foolishly, not maliciously"? What is "But therefore I have obtained the mercy of the Lord" except "I should not have obtained it if I had not been supported by the excuse of folly"? The mystical psalmist, whom I failed to recall at the proper place, aids us: "Remember not the sins of my youth and my ignorances."[1]

Let me stop pursuing the infinite and try to summarize. The Christian religion on the whole seems to have some kinship with folly, while it has none at all with wisdom. If you want proof of this, observe first that children, old people, women, and fools take more delight than anyone else in holy and religious things; and that they are therefore ever nearest the altars, led no doubt solely by instinct. Next, you will notice that the founders of religion have prized simplicity exceedingly, and have been the bitterest foes of learning. Finally, no people seem to act more foolishly than those who have been truly possessed with Christian piety. They give away whatever is theirs; they overlook injuries, allow themselves to be cheated, make no distinction between friends and enemies, shun pleasure, and feast on

4. "Knowledge puffeth up, but charity edifieth." (I Corinthians 8:1.)    5. "And Aaron said unto Moses, Alas, my lord, I beseech thee, lay not the sin upon us, wherein we have done foolishly, and wherein we have sinned." (Numbers 12:11.)    6. ". . . behold, I have played the fool, and have erred exceedingly." (I Samuel 26:21.)    7. I Chronicles 21:8.    8. Luke 23:34.    9. ". . . but I obtained mercy, because I did it ignorantly in unbelief." (I Timothy 1:13.)    1. "Remember not the sins of my youth, nor my transgressions." (Psalms 25:7.)

hunger, vigils, tears, labors, and scorn. They disdain life, and utterly prefer death; in short, they seem to have become altogether indifferent to ordinary interests, quite as if their souls lived elsewhere and not in their bodies. What is this, if not to be mad? Considering this, we should not find it very strange that the apostles appeared to be drunk on new wine, and that Paul, in the eyes of Festus, his judge,[2] looked as if he had gone mad.

. . . Since the pious and the vulgar are so radically different, it comes about that each appears to the other to be mad. It is obvious to me, however, that the word is more correctly applied to the pious rather than to the others. This will become clearer if I briefly demonstrate, as I promised to do, that their *summum bonum* is nothing but a kind of insanity. First, let us assume that Plato was dreaming of approximately the same thing when he wrote that "the madness of lovers is the highest kind of happiness."[3] He who loves intensely no longer lives in himself but in whatever he loves, and the more he can leave himself and enter into the other, the happier he is. Now when a soul is eager to leave the body, and does not use its bodily organs normally, you call it madness and rightly so. Isn't this what is meant by the common sayings: "there's nobody home," and "to come to," and "he is himself again"? Furthermore, as the love becomes more nearly complete, the madness is greater and more delightful. What is that heavenly life, then, towards which the truly religious aspire with such devotion? Very certainly the stronger and victorious spirit will absorb the body, and it will do this the more easily because now it is in its own realm, and also because during life it has cleansed and contracted the body in preparation for this change. Then the soul will itself be marvellously absorbed by that supreme spirit, which is greater than its infinite parts. And so at last the whole man will be outside of himself; nor will he be happy for any other reason than that, being outside of himself, he shall have some ineffable portion of that supreme good which draws all things unto itself. Although this happiness becomes complete only when the soul has recovered its original body by being clothed with immortality; yet since the life of pious folk is a contemplation and a shadowing forth of that other life, they feel a glow and a foretaste of the reward to come. This is only a drop, of course, in comparison with the fountain of eternal happiness, but it far surpasses all physical pleasures, even all mortal delights rolled into one. By so much does the spiritual exceed the bodily, the invisible exceed the visible. This surely is what the prophet has promised: "Eye hath not seen, nor ear heard, neither have entered into the heart of man, the things which God hath prepared for them that love Him."[4] And this is that portion of folly which will not be

2. "For he hath made him to be sin for us, who knew no sin." (II Corinthians 5:21.)  3. For the reference to *children*, see Luke 18:17; for *lilies*, see Matthew 6:28; for *mustard-seed*, see Luke, 17:6; for *sparrows*, see Matthew 10:29.

taken away by the transformation of life, but will be perfected.

Those who are permitted to have a foretaste of this—and it comes to very few—experience something very like madness. They say things that are not quite coherent or conventional, sounds without meaning, and their expressions change suddenly. They are exuberant and melancholy, crying, laughing, and sighing by turns; in brief, they are truly beside themselves. When presently they return to themselves, they say that they do not know where they have been, whether in the body or out of it, waking or sleeping. They do not remember what they have heard, seen, said, or done; and yet mistily as in a dream, they know that they were happiest when they were out of their minds. So they are sorry to come to themselves again, and they desire nothing more than to be mad always with this kind of madness. And this is only the slightest taste of the happiness hereafter.

But indeed I have long since forgotten who I am and have run out of bounds. If anything I have said seems sharp or gossipy, remember that it is Folly and a woman who has spoken. At the same time remember the Greek proverb, "Even a foolish man will often speak a word in season." Or perhaps you think that does not hold for women? I see that you are expecting a peroration, but you are certainly foolish if you think that I can remember any part of such a hodgepodge of words as I have poured out. There is an old saying, "I hate a drinking companion with a memory." Here is a new one, "I hate an audience that remembers anything."

And so farewell. Applaud, live, drink, most distinguished worshippers of Folly.

---

# BALDESAR CASTIGLIONE
## 1487–1529

Castiglione was born in 1487 at Casatico, near Mantua. His father, Cristoforo, was a courtier, and his mother was a Gonzaga, related to the lords of Mantua. In Milan Castiglione received a humanistic education and prepared himself for the career of a courtier. As such, from 1499 to 1503 he was in the service of Francesco Gonzaga, lord of Mantua, and from 1504 to 1513 he was at Urbino in the service of Guidobaldo da Montefeltro, duke of Urbino, and later of Guidobaldo's successor, Francesco Maria della Rovere, commander of the Pope's army, whom he followed on military compaigns. In 1506 he went to England on a mission to the court of Henry VII, from whom he received, on behalf of his lord, the Order of the Garter and to whom he presented a painting by Raphael. In 1511 he took part in the siege of Mirandola under Pope Julius II (Giuliano della Rovere). As a reward for his services, he was made a count. In 1515 he was again with the Gonzagas, who made him their ambassador to Pope Leo X (Giovanni de' Medici). In Rome, his friends included Raphael and Michelangelo, and he saw Renaissance social and intellectual life at its most brilliant. He thus not only codified the ideal of the refined and "virtuous" courtier in his works, but also embodied it in his life. In 1525 Clement VII made him Papal nuncio to the court of Emperor Charles V in Spain. His premature death in Toledo in 1529 was probably caused in part by sorrow at his failure to foresee the emperor's designs as they most dramatically took shape in the storming and plundering of Rome in 1527 (the "Sack of Rome"). *The Book of the Courtier*, in which the court of Urbino is idealized, was written between 1508 and 1516 and published in 1528 in Venice.

Even from these brief data, it appears very likely that as Castiglione advanced in experience of the world, his treatise on the ideal courtly gentleman acquired a nostalgic character. Indeed, in reading selections from *The Book of the Courtier*, it is helpful to consider the description with which the book opens as a "setting," because this approach serves to suggest the theatrical atmosphere that pervades the work. We should not, however, forget that the characters whose highly mannered conversation the book records were all actual members (presented with their own names) of a courtly milieu of which Castiglione himself had been a part. These people, then, were known to him not as objects of adulation or satire (the two extremes with which we are perhaps accustomed to associate literary portrayals of the aristocracy), but rather as equals and companions whose standards were his own. Hence Castiglione's attitude contains neither flattery nor mockery; the theatrical way in which the scene is set and the characters talk (the traditional form of the Platonic dialogue acquires here the tone of what in the Renaissance was called "civil conversation") is simply the expression of a style, "artificial" in no derogatory sense, which both the characters and the author considered ideally appropriate to people of their kind and station. The speakers appear somewhat like ladies and gentlemen who have kindly consented, on some courtly occasion, to take roles in a play, except that it happens that the play is their own; they enact, so to speak, themselves. The strong element of stylization (the elaborate phrasings, the manner of repartee) is not forced by the writer on his material; we feel rather that in his formalizing process he has merely emphasized qualities inherent in the world he portrays. In this sense the book is an ideal vision of Renaissance court society at its most refined and self-conscious; of a society which had a penchant, as was observed in the general introduction (p. 1526), for the well-finished gesture, the formally perfect act of its kind—a penchant that was applied to all modes and norms of activity, conversation or dueling, art, courtship, etiquette.

Our selections are from the first of the four books (or evening conversations) into which the *Courtier* is divided. The purpose of this first book is to arrive, through the contributions of the obviously experienced speakers, at a description of the perfect courtly gentleman. Although Machiavelli too, in his description of the prince, presents something of an idealization of a type, his explicit intention is to come down to reality and practical motives, in contrast to the abstractions of preceding authors. Castiglione's attitude is different from the start. He has what we may call a Platonic turn of mind, in the sense that he intentionally and openly seeks the ideal and permanent form behind the transient and fragmentary examples. This point of view in the *Courtier* suggests, among other things, the sense of rule, of adjustment to correct norms; Castiglione's optimistic assumption is that such norms exist and can be defined, and that man can educate himself to comply with them. There is even, as the famous passage on "nonchalance" (*sprezzatura*) at the end of our second selection suggests, a sort of formalization of informality.

Considered against the background of the period with which we are concerned here, *The Book of the Courtier* persents a healthy corrective to those views of the Renaissance court, especially popularized by drama, in which that institution is the typical scene of intrigue, corruption, and violence. Castiglione codifies a moment of perfection and gentle equilibrium.

Julia Cartwright Ady's illustrated biography, *Baldassare Castiglione, the Perfect Courtier. His Life and Letters*, 2 vols. (1908), is old-fashioned but thorough. Robert W. Hanning and David Rosand, eds., *Castiglione: The Ideal and the Real in Renaissance Culture* (1983), offers several views of Castiglione. An essay on *The Courtier* is found in Joseph Anthony Mazzeo's *Renaissance and Revolution: The Remaking of European Thought* (1965).

# The Book of the Courtier[1]

## [The Setting][2]

On the slopes of the Apennines towards the Adriatic sea, almost in the centre of Italy, there lies (as everyone knows) the little city of Urbino. Although amid mountains, and less pleasing ones than perhaps some others that we see in many places, it has yet enjoyed such favour of heaven that the country round about is very fertile and rich in crops; so that besides the wholesomeness of the air, there is great abundance of everything needful for human life. But among the greatest blessings that can be attributed to it, this I believe to be the chief, that for a long time it has ever been ruled by the best of lords; although in the calamities of the universal wars of Italy, it was for a season deprived of them.[3] But without seeking further, we can give good proof of this by the glorious memory of Duke Federico,[4] who in his day was the light of Italy; nor is there lack of credible and abundant witnesses, who are still living, to his prudence, humanity, justice, liberality, unconquered courage,—and to his military discipline, which is conspicuously attested by his numerous victories, his capture of impregnable places, the sudden swiftness of his expeditions, the frequency with which he put to flight large and formidable armies by means of a very small force, and by his loss of no single battle whatever; so that we may not unreasonably compare him to many famous men of old.

1. Translated by Leonard E. Opdycke.     2. Book I, Chapters 2–4.     3. For a certain period of time, when Duke Guidobaldo, described below, had to relinquish the duchy of Urbino to Cesare Borgia, who occupied it by force.     4. Federico II (1422–1482), of the house of Monte-feltro, duke of Urbino.

Among his other praiseworthy deeds, he built on the rugged site of Urbino a palace regarded by many as the most beautiful to be found in all Italy; and he so well furnished it with everything suitable that it seemed not a palace but a city in the form of a palace; and not merely with what is ordinarily used,—such as silver vases, hangings of richest cloth-of-gold and silk, and other similar things,—but for ornament he added countless antique statues in marble and bronze, pictures most choice, and musical instruments of every sort, nor would he admit anything there that was not very rare and excellent. Then at very great cost he collected a goodly number of most excellent and rare books in Greek, Latin and Hebrew, all of which he adorned with gold and with silver, esteeming this to be the chiefest excellence of his great palace.

Following then the course of nature, and already sixty-five years old,[5] he died gloriously, as he had lived; and he left as his successor a motherless little boy of ten years, his only son Guidobaldo. Heir to the State, he seemed to be heir also to all his father's virtues, and soon his noble nature gave such promise as seemed not permissible to hope for from mortal man; so that men esteemed none among the notable deeds of Duke Federico to be greater than to have begotten such a son. But envious of so much virtue, fortune thwarted this glorious beginning with all her power; so that before Duke Guido reached the age of twenty years, he fell ill of the gout, which grew upon him with grievous pain, and in a short space of time so crippled all his members that he could neither stand upon his feet nor move; and thus one of the fairest and most promising forms in the world was distorted and spoiled in tender youth.

And not content even with this, fortune was so contrary to him in all his purposes, that he could seldom carry into effect anything that he desired; and although he was very wise of counsel and unconquered in spirit, it seemed that what he undertook, both in war and in everything else whether small or great, always ended ill for him. And proof of this is found in his many and diverse calamities, which he ever bore with such strength of mind, that his spirit was never vanquished by fortune; nay, scorning her assaults with unbroken courage, he lived in illness as if in health and in adversity as if fortunate, with perfect dignity and universal esteem; so that although he was thus infirm in body, he fought with most honourable rank[6] in the service of their Serene Highnesses the Kings of Naples, Alfonso and Ferdinand the Younger;[7] later with Pope Alexander VI,[8] and with the Venetian and Florentine signories.

---

5. Actually only sixty.　　6. As a mercenary captain or *condottiere*.　　7. Alfonso II and Ferdinand II (both of the house of Aragon), kings of Naples in the late fifteenth century.　　8. Rodrigo Borgia, pope from 1492 to 1503.

Upon the accession of Julius II[9] to the pontificate, he was made Captain of the Church;[1] at which time, following his accustomed habit, above all else he took care to fill his household with very noble and valiant gentlemen, with whom he lived most familiarly, delighting in their intercourse: wherein the pleasure he gave to others was not less than that he received from others, he being well versed in both the [learned] languages, and uniting affability and pleasantness to a knowledge of things without number. And besides this, the greatness of his spirit so set him on, that although he could not practise in person the exercises of chivalry, as he once had done, yet he took the utmost pleasure in witnessing them in others; and by his words, now correcting now praising every man according to desert, he clearly showed his judgment in those matters; wherefore, in jousts and tournaments, in riding, in the handling of every sort of weapon, as well as in pastimes, games, music,—in short, in all the exercises proper to noble cavaliers,—everyone strove so to show himself, as to merit being deemed worthy of such noble fellowship.

Thus all the hours of the day were assigned to honourable and pleasant exercises as well for the body as for the mind; but since my lord Duke was always wont by reason of his infirmity to retire to sleep very early after supper, everyone usually betook himself at that hour to the presence of my lady Duchess, Elisabetta Gonzaga;[2] where also was ever to be found my lady Emilia Pia, who was endowed with such lively wit and judgment that, as you know, it seemed as if she were the Mistress of us all, and as if everyone gained wisdom and worth from her. Here then, gentle discussions and innocent pleasantries were heard, and on the face of everyone a jocund gaiety was seen depicted, so that the house could truly be called the very abode of mirth: nor ever elsewhere, I think, was so relished, as once was here, how great sweetness may flow from dear and cherished companionship; for not to speak of the honour it was to each of us to serve such a lord as he of whom I have just spoken, there was born in the hearts of all a supreme contentment every time we came into the presence of my lady Duchess; and it seemed as if this were a chain that held us all linked in love, so that never was concord of will or cordial love between brothers greater than that which here was between us all.

The same was it among the ladies, with whom there was intercourse most free and honourable; for everyone was permitted to talk, sit, jest and laugh with whom he pleased; but such was the reverence

9. In 1503.    1. Captain in the pontiff's army.    2. Of the ruling family of Mantua, she had married Duke Guidobaldo in 1488. She is the one who presides over this courtly scene. *Emilia Pia*: sister-in-law and companion of the duchess, widow of an illegitimate son of the old duke, Federico, she wittily directs much of the conversation.

paid to the wish of my lady Duchess, that this same liberty was a very great check; nor was there anyone who did not esteem it the utmost pleasure he could have in the world, to please her, and the utmost pain to displease her. And thus, most decorous manners were here joined with greatest liberty, and games and laughter in her presence were seasoned not only with witty jests, but with gracious and sober dignity; for that modesty and loftiness which governed all the acts, words and gestures of my lady Duchess, bantering and laughing, were such that she would have been known for a lady of noblest rank by anyone who saw her even but once. And impressing herself thus upon those about her, she seemed to attune us all to her own quality and tone; accordingly every man strove to follow this pattern, taking as it were a rule of beautiful behaviour from the presence of so great and virtuous a lady; whose highest qualities I do not now purpose to recount, they not being my theme and being well known to all the world, and far more because I could not express them with either tongue or pen; and those that perhaps might have been somewhat hid, fortune, as if wondering at such rare virtue, chose to reveal through many adversities and stings of calamity, so as to give proof that in the tender breast of woman, in company with singular beauty, there may abide prudence and strength of soul, and all those virtues that even among stern men are very rare.

["*Everything He May Do or Say Shall Be Stamped with Grace*"][3]

"I am of opinion[4] that the principal and true profession of the Courtier ought to be that of arms; which I would have him follow actively above all else, and be known among others as bold and strong, and loyal to whomsoever he serves. And he will win a reputation for these good qualities by exercising them at all times and in all places, since one may never fail in this without severest censure. And just as among women, their fair fame once sullied never recovers its first lustre, so that reputation of a gentleman who bears arms, if once it be in the least tarnished with cowardice or other disgrace, remains forever infamous before the world and full of ignominy. Therefore the more our Courtier excels in this art, the more he will be worthy of praise; and yet I do not deem essential in him that perfect knowledge of things and those other qualities that befit a commander; since this would be too wide a sea, let us be content, as we have said, with perfect loyalty and unconquered courage, and that he be always seen to possess them. For the courageous are often recognized even more

---

3. From Book I, Chapters 17–26.    4. The conversational "game" through which the courtiers at Urbino are attempting to achieve a description of the perfect courtly gentleman, is in progress. The speaker at this point is Count Ludovico da Canossa (1476–1532). A relative of the writer and a friend of the painter Raphael, he was later a bishop and held many important offices, such as that of papal ambassador to England.

in small things than in great; and frequently in perils of importance and where there are many spectators, some men are to be found, who, although their hearts be dead within them, yet, moved by shame or by the presence of others, press forward almost with their eyes shut, and do their duty God knows how. While on occasions of little moment, when they think they can avoid putting themselves in danger without being detected, they are glad to keep safe. But those who, even when they do not expect to be observed or seen or recognized by anyone, show their ardour and neglect nothing, however paltry, that may be laid to their charge,—they have that strength of mind which we seek in our Courtier.

"Not that we would have him look so fierce, or go about blustering, or say that he has taken his cuirass to wife, or threaten with those grim scowls that we have often seen in Berto; because to such men as this, one might justly say that which a brave lady jestingly said in gentle company to one whom I will not name at present; who, being invited by her out of compliment to dance, refused not only that, but to listen to the music, and many other entertainments proposed to him,—saying always that such silly trifles were not his business; so that at last the lady said, 'What is your business, then?' He replied with a sour look, 'To fight.' Then the lady at once said, 'Now that you are in no war and out of fighting trim, I should think it were a good thing to have yourself well oiled, and to stow yourself with all your battle harness in a closet until you be needed, lest you grow more rusty than you are'; and so, amid much laughter from the bystanders, she left the discomfited fellow to his silly presumption.

"Therefore let the man we are seeking, be very bold, stern, and always among the first, where the enemy are to be seen; and in every other place, gentle, modest, reserved, above all things avoiding ostentation and that impudent self-praise by which men ever excite hatred and disgust in all who hear them."

Then my lord Gaspar[5] replied:

"As for me, I have known few men excellent in anything whatever, who do not praise themselves; and it seems to me that this may well be permitted them; for when anyone who feels himself to be of worth, sees that he is not known to the ignorant by his works, he is offended that his worth should lie buried, and needs must in some way hold it up to view, in order that he may not be cheated of the fame that is the true reward of worthy effort. Thus among the ancient authors, whoever carries weight seldom fails to praise himself. They indeed are insufferable who do this without desert, but such we do not presume our Courtier to be."

The Count then said:

---

5. Count Gaspar Pallavicino (1486–1511), a very young member of the court, who died only a few years afterward.

"If you heard what I said, it was impudent and indiscriminate self-praise that I censured: and as you say, we surely ought not to form a bad opinion of a brave man who praises himself modestly, nay we ought rather to regard such praise as better evidence than if it came from the mouth of others. I say, however, that he, who in praising himself runs into no error and incurs no annoyance or envy at the hands of those that heard him, is a very discreet man indeed and merits praise from others in addition to that which he bestows upon himself; because it is a very difficult matter."

Then my lord Gaspar said:

"You must teach us that."

The Count replied:

"Among the ancient authors there is no lack of those who have taught it; but to my thinking, the whole art consists in saying things in such a way that they shall not seem to be said to that end, but let fall so naturally that it was impossible not to say them, and while seeming always to avoid self-praise, yet to achieve it; but not after the manner of those boasters, who open their mouths and let the words come forth haphazard. Like one of our friends a few days ago, who, being quite run through the thigh with a spear at Pisa, said he thought it was a fly that had stung him; and another man said he kept no mirror in his room because, when angry, he became so terrible to look at, that the sight of himself would have frightened him too much."

Everyone laughed at this, but Messer Cesare Gonzaga[6] added:

"Why do you laugh? Do you not know that Alexander the Great, on hearing the opinion of a philosopher to be that there was an infinite number of worlds, began to weep, and being asked why he wept, replied, 'Because I have not yet conquered one of them'; as if he would fain have vanquished all? Does not this seem to you a greater boast than that about the fly-sting?"

Then the Count said:

"Yes, and Alexander was a greater man than he who made the other speech. But extraordinary men are surely to be pardoned when they assume much; for he who has great things to do must needs have daring to do them, and confidence in himself, and must not be abject or mean in spirit, yet very modest in speech, showing less confidence in himself than he has, lest his self-confidence lead to rashness."

The Count now paused a little, and messer Bernardo Bibbiena[7] said, laughing:

6. Considered by some the "first gentleman" at the court of Urbino. A cousin of the writer, he was a warrior, a diplomat, and a pastoral poet; he died in 1512, at thirty-seven.    7. Bernardo Dovizi da Bibbiena (1470–1520), author of a play performed at the court of Urbino, patron and friend of the painter Raphael, and later a cardinal.

"I remember what you said earlier, that this Courtier of ours must be endowed by nature with beauty of countenance and person, and with a grace that shall make him so agreeable. Grace and beauty of countenance I think I certainly possess, and this is the reason why so many ladies are ardently in love with me, as you know; but I am rather doubtful as to the beauty of my person, especially as regards these legs of mine, which seem to me decidedly less well proportioned than I should wish: as to my bust and other members, however, I am quite content. Pray, now, describe a little more in particular the sort of body that the Courtier is to have, so that I may dismiss this doubt and set my mind at rest."

After some laughter at this, the Count continued:

"Of a certainty that grace of countenance can be truly said to be yours, nor need I cite further example than this to show what manner of thing it is, for we unquestionably perceive your aspect to be most agreeable and pleasing to everyone, albeit the lineaments of it are not very delicate. Still it is of a manly cast and at the same time full of grace; and this characteristic is to be found in many different types of countenance. And of such sort I would have our Courtier's aspect; not so soft and effeminate as is sought by many, who not only curl their hair and pluck their brows, but gloss their faces with all those arts employed by the most wanton and unchaste women in the world; and in their walk, posture and every act, they seem so limp and languid that their limbs are like to fall apart; and they pronounce their words so mournfully that they appear about to expire upon the spot: and the more they find themselves with men of rank, the more they affect such tricks. Since nature has not made them women, as they seem to wish to appear and be, they should be treated not as good women but as public harlots, and driven not merely from the courts of great lords but from the society of honest men.

"Then coming to the bodily frame, I say it is enough if this be neither extremely short nor tall, for both of these conditions excite a certain contemptuous surprise, and men of either sort are gazed upon in much the same way that we gaze on monsters. Yet if we must offend in one of the two extremes, it is preferable to fall a little short of the just measure of height than to exceed it, for besides often being dull of intellect, men thus huge of body are also unfit for every exercise of agility, which thing I should much wish in the Courtier. And so I would have him well built and shapely of limb, and would have him show strength and lightness and suppleness, and know all bodily exercises that befit a man of war: whereof I think the first should be to handle every sort of weapon well on foot and on horse, to understand the advantages of each, and especially to be familiar with those weapons that are ordinarily used among gentlemen; for besides the use of them in war, where such subtlety in contrivance is perhaps not needful, there frequently arise differences between one gentle-man and another, which afterwards result in duels often fought with such weapons as happen at the moment to be within reach: thus knowledge of this kind is a very safe thing. Nor am I one of those who say that skill is forgotten in the hour of need; for he whose skill forsakes him at such a time, indeed gives token that he has already lost heart and head through fear.

"Moreover I deem it very important to know how to wrestle, for it is a great help in the use of all kinds of weapons on foot. Then, both for his own sake and for that of his friends, he must understand the quarrels and differences that may arise, and must be quick to seize an advantage, always showing courage and prudence in all things. Nor should he be too ready to fight except when honour demands it; for besides the great danger that the uncertainty of fate entails, he who rushes into such affairs recklessly and without urgent cause, merits the severest censure even though he be successful. But when he finds himself so far engaged that he cannot withdraw without reproach, he ought to be most deliberate, both in the preliminaries to the duel and in the duel itself, and always show readiness and daring. Nor must he act like some, who fritter the affair away in disputes and controversies, and who, having the choice of weapons, select those that neither cut nor pierce, and arm themselves as if they were expecting a cannonade; and thinking it enough not to be defeated, stand ever on the defensive and retreat,—showing therein their utter cowardice. And thus they make themselves a laughing-stock for boys, like those two men of Ancona who fought at Perugia not long since, and made everyone laugh who saw them."

"And who were they?" asked my lord Gaspar Pallavicino.

"Two cousins," replied messer Cesare.

Then the Count said:

"In their fighting they were as like as two brothers"; and soon continued: "Even in time of peace weapons are often used in various exercises, and gentlemen appear in public shows before the people and ladies and great lords. For this reason I would have our Courtier a perfect horseman in every kind of seat; and besides understanding horses and what pertains to riding, I would have him use all possible care and diligence to lift himself a little beyond the rest in every-thing, so that he may be ever recognized as eminent above all others. And as we read of Alcibiades that he surpassed all the nations with whom he lived, each in their particular province, so I would have this Courtier of ours excel all others, and each in that which is most their profession. And as it is the especial pride of the Italians to ride well with the rein, to govern wild horses with consummate skill, and to play at tilting and jousting,—in these things let him be among the best of the Italians. In tourneys and in the arts of defence and attack, let him shine among the best in France. In stick-throwing, bull-fighting, and in casting spears and darts, let him excel among the Spaniards. But above everything he should temper all his movements with a certain good judgment and grace, if he wishes to merit that universal favour which is so greatly prized.

"There are also many other exercises, which although not immediately dependent upon arms, yet are closely connected therewith, and greatly foster manly sturdiness; and one of the chief among these seems to me to be the chase, because it bears a certain likeness to war; and truly it is an amusement for great lords and befitting a man at court, and furthermore it is seen to have been much cultivated among the ancients. It is fitting also to know how to swim, to leap, to run, to throw stones, for besides the use that may be made of this in war, a man often has occasion to show what he can do in such matters; whence good esteem is to be won, especially with the multitude, who must be taken into account withal. Another admirable exercise, and one very befitting a man at court, is the game of tennis, in which are well shown the disposition of the body, the quickness and suppleness of every member, and all those qualities that are seen in nearly every other exercise. Nor less highly do I esteem vaulting on horse, which although it be fatiguing and difficult, makes a man very light and dexterous more than any other thing; and besides its utility, if this lightness is accompanied by grace, it is to my thinking a finer show than any of the others.

"Our Courtier having once become more than fairly expert in these exercises, I think he should leave the others on one side: such as turning summersaults, rope-walking, and the like, which savour of the mountebank and little befit a gentleman.

"But since one cannot devote himself to such fatiguing exercises continually, and since repetition becomes very tiresome and abates the admiration felt for what is rare, we must always diversify our life with various occupations. For this reason I would have our Courtier sometimes descend to quieter and more tranquil exercises, and in order to escape envy and to entertain himself agreeably with everyone, let him do whatever others do, yet never departing from praiseworthy deeds, and governing himself with that good judgment which will keep him from all folly; but let him laugh, jest, banter, frolic and dance, yet in such fashion that he shall always appear genial and discreet, and that everything he may do or say shall be stamped with grace."

Then messer Cesare Gonzaga said:

"We certainly ought on no account to hinder the course of this discussion; but if I were to keep silence, I should be neglected both of the right I have to speak and of my desire to know one thing: and let me be pardoned if I ask a question instead of contradicting; for this I think may be permitted me, after the precedent of messer Bernardo here, who in his over desire to be held comely, broke the rules of our game by asking a question instead of contradicting."[8]

Then my lady Duchess said:

"You see how one error begets many. Therefore he who transgresses and sets a bad example, like messer Bernardo, deserves to be punished not only for his own transgression but also for the others'."

Then messer Cesare replied:

"In that case, my Lady, I shall be exempt from penalty, since messer Bernardo is to be punished for his own fault as well as mine."

"Nay," said my lady Duchess, "you both ought to have double punishment: he for his own transgression and for leading you to transgress; you for your own transgression and for imitating him."

"My Lady," replied messer Cesare, "as yet I have not transgressed; so, to leave all this punishment to messer Bernardo alone, I will keep silence."

And indeed he remained silent; when my lady Emilia laughed and said:

"Say whatever you like, for under leave of my lady Duchess I pardon him that has transgressed and him that shall transgress, in so small a degree."

"I consent," continued my lady Duchess. "But take care lest perchance you fall into the mistake of thinking to gain more by being merciful than by being just; for to pardon him too easily that has transgressed is to wrong him that transgresses not. Yet I would not have my severity reproach your indulgence, and thus be the cause of our not hearing this question of messer Cesare."

And so, being given the signal by my lady Duchess and by my lady Emilia, he at once said:

"If I remember rightly, Sir Count, I think you have repeated several times this evening that the Courtier must accompany his actions, gestures, habits, in short his every movement, with grace; and this you seem to regard as an universal seasoning, without which all other properties and good qualities are of little worth. And indeed I think that in this everyone would allow himself to be persuaded easily, since from the very force of the word, it may be said that he who has grace finds grace. But since you said that this is oftentimes the gift of nature and of heaven and, even when not thus perfect, can with care and pains be made much greater,—those men who are born so fortunate and so rich in this treasure as are some we see, seem to me in this to have little need of other master; because that benign favour of heaven almost in despite of themselves leads them higher than they

8. According to the plan agreed upon at the start, one of the company began a description of the perfect courtier, and the others made their contributions by contradicting the preceding speaker.

will, and makes them not only pleasing but admirable to all the world. Therefore I do not discuss this, it not being in our power to acquire it of ourselves. But they who have received from nature only so much, that they are capable of becoming graceful by pains, industry and care,—I long to know by what art, by what training, by what method, they can acquire this grace, as well in bodily exercises (in which you esteem it to be so necessary) as also in everything else that they may do or say. Therefore, since by much praise of this quality you have aroused in all of us, I think, an ardent thirst to pursue it, you are further bound, by the charge that my lady Emilia laid upon you, to satisfy that thirst by teaching us how to attain it."

"I am not bound," said the Count, "to teach you how to become graceful, or anything else; but only to show you what manner of man a perfect Courtier ought to be. Nor would I in any case undertake the task of teaching you this perfection; especially having said a little while ago that the Courtier must know how to wrestle, vault, and do many other things, which I am sure you all know quite as well as if I, who have never learned them, were to teach you. For just as a good soldier knows how to tell the smith what fashion, shape and quality his armour ought to have, but cannot show how it is to be made or forged or tempered; so I perhaps may be able to tell you what manner of man a perfect Courtier ought to be, but cannot teach you what you must do to become one.

"Yet to comply with your request as far as is within my power,— although it is almost a proverb that grace is not to be learned,—I say that whoever would acquire grace in bodily exercises (assuming first that he be by nature not incapable), ought to begin early and learn the rudiments from the best masters. And how important this seemed to King Philip of Macedon, may be seen from the fact that he chose Aristotle, the famous philosopher and perhaps the greatest that has ever been in the world, to teach his son Alexander the first elements of letters. And of the men whom we know at the present day, consider how well and how gracefully my lord Galeazzo Sanseverino,[9] Grand Equerry of France, performs all bodily exercises; and this because in addition to the natural aptitude of person that he possesses, he has taken the utmost pains to study with good masters, and always to have about him men who excel and to select from each the best of what they know: for just as in wrestling, vaulting and in the use of many sorts of weapons, he has taken for his guide our friend messer Pietro Monte,[1] who (as you know) is the true and only master of every form of trained strength and ability,—so in riding, jousting and all else, he has ever had before his eyes the most proficient men that were known in those matters.

9. Of a famous Neapolitan family, he fought for Louis XII and Francis I of France, and died at the battle of Pavia (1525).   1. Fencing master at the court of Urbino.

"Therefore he who wishes to be a good pupil, besides performing his tasks well, must put forth every effort to resemble his master, and, if it were possible, to transform himself into his master. And when he feels that he has made some progress, it will be very profitable to observe different men of the same calling, and governing himself with that good judgment which must ever be his guide, to go about selecting now this thing from one and that thing from another. And as the bee in the green meadows is ever wont to rob the flowers among the grass, so our Courtier must steal this grace from all who seem to possess it, taking from each that part which shall most be worthy of praise; and not act like a friend of ours whom you all know, who thought he greatly resembled King Ferdinand the Younger of Aragon,[2] and made it his care to imitate the latter in nothing but a certain trick of continually raising the head and twisting one side of the mouth, which the king had contracted from some infirmity. And there are many such, who think they gain a point if only they be like a great man in some thing; and frequently they devote themselves to that which is his only fault.

"But having before now often considered whence this grace springs, laying aside those men who have it by nature, I find one universal rule concerning it, which seems to me worth more in this matter than any other in all things human that are done or said: and that is to avoid affectation to the uttermost and as it were a very sharp and dangerous rock; and, to use possibly a new word, to practise in every-thing a certain nonchalance[3] that shall conceal design and show that what is done and said is done without effort and almost without thought. From this I believe grace is in large measure derived, because everyone knows the difficulty of those things that are rare and well done, and therefore facility in them excites the highest admiration; while on the other hand, to strive and as the saying is to drag by the hair, is extremely ungraceful, and makes us esteem everything slightly, however great it be.

"Accordingly we may affirm that to be true art which does not appear to be art; nor to anything must we give greater care than to conceal art, for if it is discovered, it quite destroys our credit and brings us into small esteem. And I remember having once read that there were several very excellent orators of antiquity, who among their other devices strove to make everyone believe that they had no knowledge of letters; and hiding their knowledge they pretended that their orations were composed very simply and as if springing rather from nature and truth than from study and art; the which, if it had been detected, would have made men wary of being duped by it.

2. Ferdinand II, king of Naples from 1495 to 1496.    3. *Sprezzatura*, here translated as "non-chalance," is indeed Castiglione's own word, epitomizing the important concept of gentlemanly behavior discussed in this passage.

"Thus you see how the exhibition of art and study so intense destroys the grace in everything. Which of you is there who does not laugh when our friend messer Pierpaolo[4] dances in his peculiar way, with those capers of his,—legs stiff to the toe and head motionless, as if he were a stick, and with such intentness that he actually seems to be counting the steps? What eye so blind as not to see in this the ungracefulness of affectation,—and in many men and women who are here present, the grace of that nonchalant ease (for in the case of bodily movements many call it thus), showing by word or laugh or gesture that they have no care and are thinking more of everything else than of that, to make the onlooker think they can hardly go amiss?"

# NICCOLÒ MACHIAVELLI
## 1469–1527

The most famous and controversial political writer and theorist of his time—indeed, possibly of all times—Niccolò Machiavelli, was born in Florence on May 3, 1469. Little is known of his schooling, but it is obvious from his works that he knew the Latin and Italian writers well. He entered public life in 1494 as a clerk and from 1498 to 1512 was secretary to the second chancery of the commune of Florence, whose magistrates were in charge of internal and war affairs. During the conflict between Florence and Pisa, he dealt with military problems first-hand. Thus he had a direct experience of war and likewise of diplomacy; he was entrusted with many missions—among others, to King Louis XII of France in 1500 and in 1502 to Cesare Borgia, duke of Valentinois or "il duca Valentino," the favorite son of Pope Alexander VI. The latter's ruthless methods in crushing a conspiracy during his conquest of the Romagna region, Machiavelli described in a terse booklet *Of the Method Followed by Duke Valentino in Killing Vitellozzo Vitelli . . .* which already shows direct insight into the type of the amoral and technically efficient "prince." In 1506 Machiavelli went on a mission to Pope Julius II, whose expedition into Romagna (an old name for North-central Italy) he followed closely. From this and other missions—to Emperor Maximilian (1508) and again to the king of France (1509)—Machiavelli drew his two books of observations or *Portraits* of the affairs of those territories, written in 1508 and 1510.

Preeminently a student of politics and an acute observer of historical events, Machiavelli endeavored to apply his experience of other states to the strengthening of his own, the Florentine Republic, and busied himself in 1507 with the establishment of a Florentine militia, encountering great difficulties. When the republican regime came to an end, he lost his post and was exiled from the city proper, though forbidden to leave Florentine ter-

4. An otherwise unidentified character.

ritory. The new regime of the Medici accused him unjustly of conspiracy, and he was released only after a period of imprisonment and torture. To the period of his exile (spent near San Casciano, a few miles from Florence, where he retired with his wife, Marietta Corsini, and his five children), we owe his major works: the *Discourses on the First Ten Books of Livy* (1513– 21) and *The Prince*, written in 1513 with the hope of obtaining public office from the Medici. In 1520 Machiavelli was commissioned to write a history of Florence, which he presented in 1525 to Pope Clement VII (Giulio de' Medici). The following year, conscious of imminent dangers, he took part in the work to improve the military fortifications of Florence. The fate of the city at this point depended on the outcome of the larger struggle between Francis I of France and the Holy Roman Emperor, Charles V. Pope Clement's siding with the king of France led to the disastrous "Sack of Rome" by Charles V in 1527, and the result for Florence was the collapse of Medici domination. Machiavelli's hopes, briefly raised by the re-establishment of the republic, came to naught because he was now regarded as a Medici sympathizer. This last disappointment may have accelerated his end. He died on June 22, 1527, and was buried in the church of Santa Croce.

Though Machiavelli has a place in literary history for a short novel and two plays, one of which, *La mandragola*, first performed in the early 1520s, belongs in the upper rank of Italian comedies of intrigue, his world reputation is based on *The Prince*. This "handbook" on how to obtain and keep political power consists of twenty-six chapters. The first eleven deal with different types of dominions and the ways in which they are acquired and preserved—the early title of the whole book, in Latin, was *De principatibus* (*Of Princedoms*)—and the twelfth to fourteenth focus particularly on problems of military power. The book's astounding fame, however, is based on the final part (from chapter fifteen to the end), which deals primarily with the attributes and "virtues" of the prince himself. In other words, despite its reputation for cool, precise realism, the work presents a hypothetical type, the idealized portrait of a certain kind of man.

Manuals of this sort may be classified, in one sense, as pedagogical literature. While for their merits of form and of vivid, if stylized, characterization they can be considered works of art, their overt purpose is to codify a certain set of manners and rules of conduct; the author therefore presents himself as especially wise, an expert in the field, the "mind" offering advice to the executive "arm." Machiavelli is a clear example of this approach. His fervor, the dramatic, oratorical way he confronts his reader, the wealth and pertinence of his illustrations are all essential qualities of his pedagogical *persona*: "Either you are already a prince, or you are on the way to become one. In the first case liberality is dangerous; in the second it is very necessary to be thought liberal. Caesar was one of those. . . . Somebody may answer . . . I answer . . ." Relying on his direct knowledge of politics, he uses examples he can personally vouch for:

> Men are so simple and so subject to present needs that he who deceives in this way will always find those who will let themselves be deceived. I do not wish to keep still about one of the recent instances. Alexander VI did nothing else than deceive men, and had no other intention. . . .

The implied tone of *I know, I have seen such things myself* adds a special immediacy to Machiavelli's prose. His view of the practical world may have been an especially startling one; but the sensation caused by his work would have been far less without the rhetorical power, the drama of argumentation, which make *The Prince* a unique example of "the art of persuasion."

The view of man in Machiavelli is not at all cheerful. Indeed, the pessimistic notion that man is evil is not so much Machiavelli's conclusion about human nature as his premise; it is the point of departure of all subsequent reasoning upon the course for a ruler to follow. The very fact of its being given as a premise, however, tends to qualify it; it is not a firm philosophical judgment, but a stratagem, dictated by the facts as they are seen by a lucid observer of the here and now. The author is committed to his view of mankind not as a philosopher or as a religious man but as a practical politician. He indicates the rules of the game as his experience shows it must, under the circumstances, be played.

> A prudent . . . ruler cannot and should not observe faith when such observance is to his disadvantage and the causes that made him give his promise have vanished. If men were all good, this advice would not be good, but since men are wicked and do not keep their promises to you, you likewise do not have to keep yours to them.

A basic question in the study of Machiavelli, therefore, is: How much of a realist is he? His picture of the perfectly efficient ruler has something of the quality of an abstraction; it shows, though much less clearly than Castiglione's portrayal of the courtier, the well-known Renaissance tendency toward "perfected" form. Machiavelli's abandonment of complex actualities in favor of an ideal vision is shown most clearly at the conclusion of the book, particularly in the last chapter. This is where he offers what amounts to the greatest of his illustrations as the prince's preceptor and counselor: the ideal ruler, now technically equipped by his pedagogue, is to undertake a mission—the liberation of Machiavelli's Italy. If we regard the last chapter of *The Prince* as a culmination of Machiavelli's discussion rather than as a dissonant addition to it, we are likely to feel at that point not only that Machiavelli's realistic method is ultimately directed toward an ideal task, but also that his conception of that task, far from being based on immediate realities, is founded on cultural and poetic myths. Machiavelli's method here becomes imaginative rather than scientific. His exhortation to liberate Italy, and his final prophecy, belong to the tradition of poetic visions in which a present state of decay is lamented, and a hope of future redemption is expressed (as in Dante, *Purgatory*, Canto VI). And a very significant part of this hope is presented not in terms of technical political considerations (choice of the opportune moment, evaluation of military power), but in terms of a poetic justice for which precedents are sought in religious and ancient history and in mythology:

> . . . if it was necessary to make clear the ability of Moses that the people of Israel should be enslaved in Egypt, and to reveal Cyrus' greatness of mind that the Persians should be oppressed by the Medes, and to demonstrate the excellence of Theseus that the Athenians should be scattered, so at the present time. . . . Everything is now fully disposed for

> the work . . . if only your House adopts the methods of those I have set
> forth as examples. Moreover, we have before our eyes extraordinary and
> unexampled means prepared by God. The sea has been divided. . . .
> Manna has fallen.

Machiavelli's Italy, as he observed in the preceding chapter, is now a country "without dykes and without any wall of defence." It has suffered from
"deluges," and its present rule, a "barbarian" one, "stinks in every nostril."
Something is rotten in it, in short, as in Hamlet's Denmark. And we become
more and more detached even from the particular example, Italy, as we
recognize in the situation a pattern frequently exemplified in tragedy: the
desire for communal regeneration, for the cleansing of the city-state, the
*polis*. Of this cleansing, Italy on the one side and the imaginary prince on
the other may be taken as symbols. The envisaged redemption is identified
with antiquity and Roman virtue, while the realism of the political observer
is here drowned out by the cry of the humanist dreaming of ancient glories.

    Peter E. Bondanella focuses on the literary aspects of Machiavelli's works
in *Machiavelli and the Art of Renaissance History* (1973). J. R. Hale's biography, *Machiavelli and Renaissance Italy* (1972), places Machiavelli in a
historical perspective. A political analysis is provided by Anthony Parel in
*The Political Calculus. Essays on Machiavelli's Political Philosophy* (1972).
Roberto Ridolfi, *The Life of Niccolò Machiavelli*, translated by Cecil Grayson
(1963) is still considered the best and most accurate biobraphy. Silvia Ruffo-
Fiore's *Niccolò Machiavelli* (1982) is a useful comprehensive guide for the
beginning student.

## ["That Food Which Alone Is Mine"][1]

I am living on my farm, and since my last troubles[2] I have not been
in Florence twenty days, putting them all together. Up to now I have
been setting snares for thrushes with my own hands; I get up before
daylight, prepare my birdlime, and go out with a bundle of cages on
my back, so that I look like Geta when he came back from the harbor
with the books of Amphitryo,[3] and catch at the least two thrushes
and at the most six. So I did all of September; then this trifling
diversion, despicable and strange as it is, to my regret failed. What
my life is now I shall tell you.

    In the morning I get up with the sun and go out into a grove that
I am having cut; there I remain a couple of hours to look over the
work of the past day and kill some time with the woodmen, who

1. From a letter of December 10, 1513, to Francesco Vettori, Florentine Ambassador at Rome.
Translated by Allan H. Gilbert.    2. Machiavelli had been suspected of participation in a conspiracy led by two young friends of his, and had been imprisoned and subjected to torture before
his innocence was recognized.    3. Allusion to a popular tale in which Amphitryo, returning to
Thebes after having studied at Athens, sends forward from the harbor his servant Geta to announce
his arrival to his wife Alcmene, and loads him with his books.

always have on hand some dispute either among themselves or among their neighbors. . . .

When I leave the grove, I go to a spring, and from there into my aviary. I have a book in my pocket, either Dante or Petrarch or one of the minor poets, as Tibullus,[4] Ovid, and the like. I read about their tender passions and their loves, remember mine, and take pleasure for a while in thinking about them. Then I go along the road to the inn, talk with those who pass by, ask the news of their villages, learn various things, and note the varied tastes and different fancies of men. It gets to be dinner time, and with my troop I eat what food my poor farm and my little property permit. After dinner, I return to the inn; there I usually find the host, a butcher, a miller, and two furnace-tenders. With these fellows I sink into vulgarity for the rest of the day, playing at *cricca* and *tricche-trach*;[5] from these games come a thousand quarrels and numberless offensive and insulting words; we often dispute over a penny, and all the same are heard shouting as far as San Casciano.[6] So, involved in these trifles, I keep my brain from getting mouldy, and express the perversity of Fate, for I am willing to have her drive me along this path, to see if she will be ashamed of it.

In the evening, I return to my house, and go into my study. At the door I take off the clothes I have worn all day, mud spotted and dirty, and put on regal and courtly garments. Thus appropriately clothed, I enter into the ancient courts of ancient men,[7] where, being lovingly received, I feed on that food which alone is mine, and which I was born for; I am not ashamed to speak with them and to ask the reasons for their actions, and they courteously answer me. For four hours I feel no boredom and forget every worry; I do not fear poverty, and death does not terrify me. I give myself completely over to the ancients. And because Dante says that there is no knowledge unless one retains what one has read,[8] I have written down the profit I have gained from their conversation, and composed a little book *De principatibus*,[9] in which I go as deep as I can into reflections on this subject, debating what a principate is, what the species are, how they are gained, how they are kept, and why they are lost. If ever any of my trifles can please you, this one should not displease you; and to a prince, and especially a new prince, it ought to be welcome.

---

4. Albius Tibullus, Roman elegiac poet of the first century B.C.    5. Two popular games, the first played with cards, the second with dice thrown to regulate the movements of pawns on a chessboard.    6. Nearby village; in the region around Florence.    7. Machiavelli here refers figuratively to his study of ancient history.    8. ". . . for knowledge none can vaunt / Who retains not, although he have understood." (*Paradise*, Canto V, ll. 41–42.)    9. *Of Princedoms*; the Latin title of *The Prince*. All chapter headings are also in Latin in the original.

# The Prince[1]

## [*Princely Virtues*][2]

### ON THE THINGS FOR WHICH MEN, AND ESPECIALLY PRINCES, ARE PRAISED OR CENSURED

. . . Because I know that many have written on this topic, I fear that when I too write I shall be thought presumptuous, because, in discussing it, I break away completely from the principles laid down by my predecessors. But since it is my purpose to write something useful to an attentive reader, I think it more effective to go back to the practical truth of the subject than to depend on my fancies about it. And many have imagined republics and principalities that never have been seen or known to exist in reality. For there is such a difference between the way men live and the way they ought to live, that anybody who abandons what is for what ought to be will learn something that will ruin rather than preserve him, because anyone who determines to act in all circumstances the part of a good man must come to ruin among so many who are not good. Hence, if a prince wishes to maintain himself, he must learn how to be not good, and to use that ability or not as is required.

Leaving out of account, then, things about an imaginary prince, and considering things that are true, I say that all men, when they are spoken of, and especially princes, because they are set higher, are marked with some of the qualities that bring them either blame or praise. To wit, one man is thought liberal, another stingy (using a Tuscan word, because *avaricious* in our language is still applied to one who desires to get things through violence, but *stingy* we apply to him who refrains too much from using his own property); one is thought open-handed, another grasping; one cruel, the other compassionate; one is a breaker of faith, the other reliable; one is effeminate and cowardly, the other vigorous and spirited; one is philanthropic, the other egotistic; one is lascivious, the other chaste; one is straight-forward, the other crafty; one hard, the other easy to deal with; one is firm, the other unsettled; one is religious, the other unbelieving; and so on.

And I know that everybody will admit that it would be very praiseworthy for a prince to possess all of the above-mentioned qualities that are considered good. But since he is not able to have them or to observe them completely, because human conditions do not allow him to, it is necessary that he be prudent enough to understand how to avoid getting a bad name because he is given to those vices that will deprive him of his position. He should also, if he can, guard

---

1. Translated by Allan H. Gilbert.   2. From Chapters 15–18.

himself from those vices that will not take his place away from him, but if he cannot do it, he can with less anxiety let them go. Moreover, he should not be troubled if he gets a bad name because of vices without which it will be difficult for him to preserve his position. I say this because, if everything is considered, it will be seen that some things seem to be virtuous, but if they are put into practice will be ruinous to him; other things seem to be vices, yet if put into practice will bring the prince security and well-being.

### ON LIBERALITY AND PARSIMONY

Beginning, then, with the first of the above-mentioned qualities, I assert that it is good to be thought liberal.[3] Yet liberality, practiced in such a way that you get a reputation for it, is damaging to you, for the following reasons: If you use it wisely and as it ought to be used, it will not become known, and you will not escape being censured for the opposite vice. Hence, if you wish to have men call you liberal, it is necessary not to omit any sort of lavishness. A prince who does this will always be obliged to use up all his property in lavish actions; he will then, if he wishes to keep the name of liberal, be forced to lay heavy taxes on his people and exact money from them, and do everything he can to raise money. This will begin to make his subjects hate him, and as he grows poor he will be little esteemed by anybody. So it comes about that because of this liberality of his, with which he has damaged a large number and been of advantage to but a few, he is affected by every petty annoyance and is in peril from every slight danger. If he recognizes this and wishes to draw back, he quickly gets a bad name for stinginess.

Since, then, a prince cannot without harming himself practice this virtue of liberality to such an extent that it will be recognized, he will, if he is prudent, not care about being called stingy. As time goes on he will be thought more and more liberal, for the people will see that because of his economy his income is enough for him, that he can defend himself from those who make war against him, and that he can enter upon undertakings without burdening his people. Such a prince is in the end liberal to all those from whom he takes nothing, and they are numerous; he is stingy to those to whom he does not give, and they are few. In our times we have seen big things done only by those who have been looked on as stingy; the others have utterly failed. Pope Julius II,[4] though he made use of a reputation for liberality to attain the papacy, did not then try to maintain it, because he wished to be able to make war. The present

3. Generous, openhanded.    4. Giuliano della Rovere, elected to the papacy in 1503 at the death of Pius III, who had been successor to Alexander VI (Rodrigo Borgia). Alexander VI is discussed in the chapter "In What Way Faith Should Be Kept by Princes"; for Machiavelli's view of the character of Julius II, see the chapter "The Power of Fortune in Human Affairs  . . ."

King of France[5] has carried on great wars without laying unusually heavy taxes on his people, merely because his long economy has made provision for heavy expenditures. The present King of Spain,[6] if he had continued liberal, would not have carried on or completed so many undertakings.

Therefore a prince ought to care little about getting called stingy, if as a result he does not have to rob his subjects, is able to defend himself, does not become poor and contemptible, and is not obliged to become grasping. For this vice of stinginess is one of those that enables him to rule. Somebody may say: Caesar, by means of his liberality became emperor, and many others have come to high positions because they have been liberal and have been thought so. I answer: Either you are already prince, or you are on the way to become one. In the first case liberality is dangerous; in the second it is very necessary to be thought liberal. Caesar was one of those who wished to attain dominion over Rome. But if, when he had attained it, he had lived for a long time and had not moderated his expenses, he would have destroyed his authority. Somebody may answer: Many who have been thought very liberal have been princes and done great things with their armies. I answer: The prince spends either his own property and that of his subjects or that of others. In the first case he ought to be frugal; in the second he ought to abstain from no sort of liberality. When he marches with his army and lives on plunder, loot, and ransom, a prince controls the property of others. To him liberality is essential, for without it his soldiers would not follow him. You can be a free giver of what does not belong to you or your subjects, as were Cyrus, Caesar, and Alexander, because to spend the money of others does not decrease your reputation but adds to it. It is only the spending of your own money that hurts you.

There is nothing that eats itself up as fast as does liberality, for when you practice it you lose the power to practice it, and become poor and contemptible, or else to escape poverty you become rapacious and therefore are hated. And of all the things against which a prince must guard himself, the first is being an object of contempt and hatred. Liberality leads you to both of these. Hence there is more wisdom in keeping a name for stinginess, which produces a bad reputation without hatred, than in striving for the name of liberal, only to be forced to get the name of rapacious, which brings forth both bad reputation and hatred.

### ON CRUELTY AND PITY, AND WHETHER IT IS BETTER TO BE LOVED OR TO BE FEARED, AND VICE VERSA

Coming then to the other qualities already mentioned, I say that every prince should wish to be thought compassionate and not cruel;

5. Louis XII.    6. Ferdinand II, "the Catholic."

still, he should be careful not to make a bad use of the pity he feels. Cesare Borgia[7] was considered cruel, yet this cruelty of his pacified the Romagna, united it, and changed its condition to that of peace and loyalty. If the matter is well considered, it will be seen that Cesare was much more compassionate than the people of Florence, for in order to escape the name of cruel they allowed Pistoia to be destroyed.[8] Hence a prince ought not to be troubled by the stigma of cruelty, acquired in keeping his subjects united and faithful. By giving a very few examples of cruelty he can be more truly compassionate than those who through too much compassion allow disturbances to continue, from which arise murders or acts of plunder. Lawless acts are injurious to a large group, but the executions ordered by the prince injure a single person. The new prince, above all other princes, cannot possibly avoid the name of cruel, because new states are full of perils. Dido in Vergil puts it thus: "Hard circumstances and the newness of my realm force me to do such things, and to keep watch and ward over all my lands."[9]

All the same, he should be slow in believing and acting, and should make no one afraid of him, his procedure should be so tempered with prudence and humanity that too much confidence does not make him incautious, and too much suspicion does not make him unbearable.

All this gives rise to a question for debate: Is it better to be loved than to be feared, or the reverse? I answer that a prince should wish for both. But because it is difficult to reconcile them, I hold that it is much more secure to be feared than to be loved, if one of them must be given up. The reason for my answer is that one must say of men generally that they are ungrateful, mutable, pretenders and dissemblers, prone to avoid danger, thirsty for gain. So long as you benefit them they are all yours; as I said above, they offer you their blood, their property, their lives, their children, when the need for such things is remote. But when need comes upon you, they turn around. So if a prince has relied wholly on their words, and is lacking in other preparations, he falls. For friendships that are gained with money, and not with greatness and nobility of spirit, are deserved but not possessed, and in the nick of time one cannot avail himself of them. Men hesitate less to injure a man who makes himself loved than to injure one who makes himself feared, for their love is held by a chain of obligation, which, because of men's wickedness, is broken on every occasion for the sake of selfish profit; but their fear is secured by a dread of punishment which never fails you.

Nevertheless the prince should make himself feared in such a way

7. Son of Pope Alexander VI, and duke of Valentinois and Romagna. His skillful and merciless subjugation of the local lords of Romagna occurred during the years between 1499 and 1502. 8. By internal dissensions because the Florentines, Machiavelli contends, failed to treat the leaders of the dissenting parties with an iron hand.   9. *Aeneid*, Book I, ll. 563–564.

that, if he does not win love, he escapes hatred. This is possible, for to be feared and not to be hated can easily coexist. In fact it is always possible, if the ruler abstains from the property of his citizens and subjects, and from their women. And if, as sometimes happens, he finds that he must inflict the penalty of death, he should do it when he has proper justification and evident reason. But above all he must refrain from taking property, for men forget the death of a father more quickly than the loss of their patrimony. Further, causes for taking property are never lacking, and he who begins to live on plunder is always finding cause to seize what belongs to others. But on the contrary, reasons for taking life are rare and fail sooner.

But when a prince is with his army and has a great number of soldiers under his command, then above all he must pay no heed to being called cruel, because if he does not have that name he cannot keep his army united or ready for duty. It should be numbered among the wonderful feats of Hannibal that he led to war in foreign lands a large army, made up of countless types of men, yet never suffered from dissension, either among the soldiers or against the general, in either bad or good fortune. His success resulted from nothing else than his inhuman cruelty, which, when added to his numerous other strong qualities, made him respected and terrible in the sight of his soldiers. Yet without his cruelty his other qualities would not have been adequate. So it seems that those writers have not thought very deeply who on one side admire his accomplishment and on the other condemn the chief cause for it.

The truth that his other qualities alone would not have been adequate may be learned from Scipio,[1] a man of the most unusual powers not only in his own times but in all ages we know of. When he was in Spain his armies mutinied. This resulted from nothing other than his compassion, which had allowed his soldiers more license than befits military discipline. This fault was censured before the Senate by Fabius Maximus, and Scipio was called by him the corruptor of the Roman soldiery. The Locrians[2] were destroyed by a lieutenant of Scipio's, yet he did not avenge them or punish the disobedience of that lieutenant. This all came from his easy nature, which was so well understood that one who wished to excuse him in the Senate said there were many men who knew better how not to err than how to punish errors. This easy nature would in time have overthrown the fame and glory of Scipio if, in spite of this weakness, he had kept on in independent command. But since he was under the orders of the Senate, this bad quality was not merely concealed but was a glory to him.

Returning, then, to the debate on being loved and feared, I con-

1. Publius Cornelius Scipio Africanus the Elder (235–183 B.C.). The episode of the mutiny occurred in 206 B.C.   2. Citizens of Locri, in Sicily.

clude that since men love as they please and fear as the prince pleases, a wise prince will evidently rely on what is in his own power and not on what is in the power of another. As I have said, he need only take pains to avoid hatred.

### IN WHAT WAY FAITH SHOULD BE KEPT BY PRINCES

Everybody knows how laudable it is in a prince to keep his faith and to be an honest man and not a trickster. Nevertheless, the experience of our times shows that the princes who have done great things are the ones who have taken little account of their promises and who have known how to addle the brains of men with craft. In the end they have conquered those who have put their reliance on good faith.

You must realize, then, that there are two ways to fight. In one kind the laws are used, in the other, force. The first is suitable to man, the second to animals. But because the first often falls short, one has to turn to the second. Hence a prince must know perfectly how to act like a beast and like a man. This truth was covertly taught to princes by ancient authors, who write that Achilles and many other ancient princes were turned over for their up-bringing to Chiron the centaur,[3] that he might keep them under his tuition. To have as teacher one who is half beast and half man means nothing else than that a prince needs to know how to use the qualities of both creatures. The one without the other will not last long.

Since, then, it is necessary for a prince to understand how to make good use of the conduct of the animals, he should select among them the fox and the lion, because the lion cannot protect himself from traps, and the fox cannot protect himself from the wolves. So the prince needs to be a fox that he may know how to deal with traps, and a lion that he may frighten the wolves. Those who act like the lion alone do not understand their business. A prudent ruler, therefore, cannot and should not observe faith when such observance is to his disadvantage and the causes that made him give his promise have vanished. If men were all good, this advice would not be good, but since men are wicked and do not keep their promises to you, you likewise do not have to keep yours to them. Lawful reasons to excuse his failure to keep them will never be lacking to a prince. It would be possible to give innumerable modern examples of this and to show many treaties and promises that have been made null and void by the faithlessness of princes. And the prince who has best known how to act as a fox has come out best. But one who has this capacity must understand how to keep it covered, and be a skilful pretender and dissembler. Men are so simple and so subject to pre-

3. Reputed in myth to be the educator of many heroes, among them Achilles, Theseus, Jason, and Hercules.

sent needs that he who deceives in this way will always find those who will let themselves be deceived.

I do not wish to keep still about one of the recent instances. Alexander VI[4] did nothing else than deceive men, and had no other intention; yet he always found a subject to work on. There never was a man more effective in swearing that things were true, and the greater the oaths with which he made a promise, the less he observed it. Nonetheless his deceptions always succeeded to his wish, because he thoroughly understood this aspect of the world.

It is not necessary, then, for a prince really to have all the virtues mentioned above, but it is very necessary to seem to have them. I will even venture to say that they damage a prince who possesses them and always observes them, but if he seems to have them they are useful. I mean that he should seem compassionate, trustworthy, humane, honest, and religious, and actually be so; but yet he should have his mind so trained that, when it is necessary not to practice these virtues, he can change to the opposite, and do it skilfully. It is to be understood that a prince, especially a new prince, cannot observe all the things because of which men are considered good, because he is often obliged, if he wishes to maintain his government, to act contrary to faith, contrary to charity, contrary to humanity, contrary to religion. It is therefore necessary that he have a mind capable of turning in whatever direction the winds of Fortune and the variations of affairs require, and, as I said above, that he should not depart from what is morally right, if he can observe it, but should know how to adopt what is bad, when he is obliged to.

A prince, then, should be very careful that there does not issue from his mouth anything that is not full of the above-mentioned five qualities. To those who see and hear him he should seem all compassion, all faith, all honesty, all humanity, all religion. There is nothing more necessary to make a show of possessing than this last quality. For men in general judge more by their eyes than by their hands; everybody is fitted to see, few to understand. Everybody sees what you appear to be; few make out what you really are. And these few do not dare to oppose the opinion of the many, who have the majesty of the state to confirm their view. In the actions of all men, and especially those of princes, where there is no court to which to appeal, people think of the outcome. A prince needs only to conquer and to maintain his position. The means he has used will always be judged honorable and will be praised by everybody, because the crowd is always caught by appearance and by the outcome of events, and the crowd is all there is in the world; there is no place for the few when the many have room enough. A certain prince of the present

4. Rodrigo Borgia, father of Cesare Borgia; he was pope from 1492 to 1503.

day,[5] whom it is not good to name, preaches nothing else than peace and faith, and is wholly opposed to both of them, and both of them, if he had observed them, would many times have taken from him either his reputation or his throne.

### ["*Fortune Is a Woman*"][6]

#### THE POWER OF FORTUNE IN HUMAN AFFAIRS, AND TO WHAT EXTENT SHE SHOULD BE RELIED ON

It is not unknown to me that many have been and still are of the opinion that the affairs of this world are so under the direction of Fortune and of God that man's prudence cannot control them; in fact, that man has no resource against them. For this reason many think there is no use in sweating much over such matters, but that one might as well let Chance take control. This opinion has been the more accepted in our times, because of the great changes in the state of the world that have been and now are seen every day, beyond all human surmise. And I myself, when thinking on these things, have now and then in some measure inclined to their view. Nevertheless, because the freedom of the will should not be wholly annulled, I think it may be true that Fortune is arbiter of half of our actions, but that she still leaves the control of the other half, or about that, to us.

I liken her to one of those raging streams that, when they go mad, flood the plains, ruin the trees and the buildings, and take away the fields from one bank and put them down on the other. Everybody flees before them; everybody yields to their onrush without being able to resist anywhere. And though this is their nature, it does not cease to be true that, in calm weather, men can make some provisions against them with walls and dykes, so that, when the streams swell, their waters will go off through a canal, or their currents will not be so wild and do so much damage. The same is true of Fortune. She shows her power where there is no wise preparation for resisting her, and turns her fury where she knows that no walls and dykes have been made to hold her in. And if you consider Italy—the place where these variations occur and the cause that has set them in motion—you will see that she is a country without dykes and without any wall of defence. If, like Germany, Spain, and France, she had had a sufficient bulwark of military vigor, this flood would not have made the great changes it has, or would not have come at all.

And this, I think, is all I need to say on opposing oneself to Fortune, in general. But limiting myself more to particulars, I say that

---

5. Ferdinand II, "the Catholic," king of Spain. In refraining from mentioning him, Machiavelli apparently had in mind the good relations existing between Spain and the house of Medici.
6. Chapter 25.

a prince may be seen prospering today and falling in ruin tomorrow, though it does not appear that he has changed in his nature or any of his qualities. I believe this comes, in the first place, from the causes that have been discussed at length in preceding chapters. That is, if a prince bases himself entirely on Fortune, he will fall when she varies. I also believe that a ruler will be successful who adapts his mode of procedure to the quality of the times, and likewise that he will be unsuccessful if the times are out of accord with his procedure. Because it may be seen that in things leading to the end each has before him, namely glory and riches, men proceed differently. One acts with caution, another rashly; one with violence, another with skill; one with patience, another with its opposite; yet with these different methods each one attains his end. Still further, two cautious men will be seen, of whom one comes to his goal, the other does not. Likewise you will see two who succeed with two different methods, one of them being cautious and the other rash. These results are caused by nothing else than the nature of the times, which is or is not in harmony with the procedure of men. It also accounts for what I have mentioned, namely, that two persons, working differently, chance to arrive at the same result; and that of two who work in the same way, one attains his end, but the other does not.

On the nature of the times also depends the variability of the best method. If a man conducts himself with caution and patience, times and affairs may come around in such a way that his procedure is good, and he goes on successfully. But if times and circumstances change, he is ruined, because he does not change his method of action. There is no man so prudent as to understand how to fit himself to this condition, either because he is unable to deviate from the course to which nature inclines him, or because, having always prospered by walking in one path, he cannot persuade himself to leave it. So the cautious man, when the time comes to go at a reckless pace, does not know how to do it. Hence he comes to ruin. Yet if he could change his nature with the times and with circumstances, his fortune would not be altered.

Pope Julius II proceeded rashly in all his actions, and found the times and circumstances so harmonious with his mode of procedure that he was always so lucky as to succeed. Consider the first enterprise he engaged in, that of Bologna, while messer Giovanni Bentivogli[7] was still alive. The Venetians were not pleased with it; the King of Spain felt the same way; the Pope was debating such an enterprise with the King of France. Nevertheless, in his courage and rashness Julius personally undertook that expedition. This movement made the King of Spain and the Venetians stand irresolute and

---

7. Of the ruling family Bentivogli (the prefix *Messer* means "my lord"); the Pope undertook to dislodge him from Bologna, in 1506.

motionless, the latter for fear, and the King because of his wish to recover the entire kingdom of Naples. On the other side, the King of France was dragged behind Julius, because the King, seeing that the Pope had moved and wishing to make him a friend in order to put down the Venetians, judged he could not refuse him soldiers without doing him open injury. Julius, then, with his rash movement, attained what no other pontiff, with the utmost human prudence, would have attained. If he had waited to leave Rome until the agreements were fixed and everything arranged, as any other pontiff would have done, he would never have succeeded, for the King of France would have had a thousand excuses, and the others would have raised a thousand fears. I wish to omit his other acts, which are all of the same sort, and all succeeded perfectly. The brevity of his life did not allow him to know anything different. Yet if times had come in which it was necessary to act with caution, they would have ruined him, for he would never have deviated from the methods to which nature inclined him.

I conclude, then, that since Fortune is variable and men are set in their ways, they are successful when they are in harmony with Fortune and unsuccessful when they disagree with her. Yet I am of the opinion that it is better to be rash than over-cautious, because Fortune is a woman and, if you wish to keep her down, you must beat her and pound her. It is evident that she allows herself to be overcome by men who treat her in that way rather than by those who proceed coldly. For that reason, like a woman, she is always the friend of young men, because they are less cautious, and more courageous, and command her with more boldness.

## [The Roman Dream][8]

### AN EXHORTATION TO TAKE HOLD OF ITALY AND RESTORE HER TO LIBERTY FROM THE BARBARIANS

Having considered all the things discussed above, I have been turning over in my own mind whether at present in Italy the time is ripe for a new prince to win prestige, and whether conditions there give a wise and vigorous ruler occasion to introduce methods that will do him honor, and bring good to the mass of the people of the land. It appears to me that so many things unite for the advantage of a new prince, that I do not know of any time that has ever been more suited for this. And, as I said, if it was necessary to make clear the ability of Moses that the people of Israel should be enslaved in Egypt, and to reveal Cyrus's greatness of mind that the Persians should be oppressed by the Medes, and to demonstrate the excellence of The-

8. Chapter 26.

seus that the Athenians should be scattered, so at the present time, in order to make known the greatness of an Italian soul, Italy had to be brought down to her present position, to be more a slave than the Hebrews, more a servant than the Persians, more scattered than the Athenians; without head, without government; defeated, plundered, torn asunder, overrun; subject to every sort of disaster.

And though before this, certain persons[9] have showed signs from which it could be inferred that they were chosen by God for the redemption of Italy, nevertheless it has afterwards been seen that in the full current of action they have been cast off by Fortune. So Italy remains without life and awaits the man, whoever he may be, who is to heal her wounds, put an end to the plundering of Lombardy and the tribute laid on Tuscany and the kingdom of Naples, and cure her of those sores that have long been suppurating. She may be seen praying God to send some one to redeem her from these cruel and barbarous insults. She is evidently ready and willing to follow a banner, if only some one will raise it. Nor is there at present anyone to be seen in whom she can put more hope than in your illustrious House,[1] because its fortune and vigor, and the favor of God and of the Church, which it now governs,[2] enable it to be the leader in such a redemption. This will not be very difficult, as you will see if you will bring to mind the actions and lives of those I have named above. And though these men were striking exceptions, yet they were men, and each of them had less opportunity than the present gives; their enterprises were not more just than this, nor easier, nor was God their friend more than he is yours. Here justice is complete. "A way is just to those to whom it is necessary, and arms are holy to him who has no hope save in arms."[3] Everything is now fully disposed for the work, and when that is true an undertaking cannot be difficult, if only your House adopts the methods of those I have set forth as examples. Moreover, we have before our eyes extraordinary and unexampled means prepared by God. The sea has been divided. A cloud has guided you on your way. The rock has given forth water. Manna has fallen.[4] Everything has united to make you great. The rest is for you to do. God does not intend to do everything, lest he deprive us of our free will and the share of glory that belongs to us.

It is no wonder if no one of the above-named Italians[5] has been able to do what we hope your illustrious House can. Nor is it strange if in the many revolutions and military enterprises of Italy, the martial vigor of the land always appears to be exhausted. This is because

9. Possibly Cesare Borgia and Francesco Sforza, discussed in an earlier chapter of the book. 1. The house of Medici. The *Prince* was first meant for Giuliano de' Medici; after Giuliano's death it was dedicated to his nephew, Lorenzo, later duke of Urbino. 2. Pope Leo X was a Medici (Giovanni de' Medici). 3. Livy, *History*, Book IX, Chapter 1, paragraph 10. 4. See the allusion to Moses in the preceding paragraph. 5. Possibly a further allusion to Cesare Borgia and Francesco Sforza.

the old military customs were not good, and there has been nobody able to find new ones. Yet nothing brings so much honor to a man who rises to new power, as the new laws and new methods he discovers. These things, when they are well founded and have greatness in them, make him revered and worthy of admiration. And in Italy matter is not lacking on which to impress forms of every sort. There is great vigor in the limbs if only it is not lacking in the heads. You may see that in duels and combats between small numbers, the Italians have been much superior in force, skill, and intelligence. But when it is a matter of armies, Italians cannot be compared with foreigners. All this comes from the weakness of the heads, because those who know are not obeyed, and each man thinks he knows. Nor up to this time has there been a man able to raise himself so high, through both ability and fortune, that the others would yield to him. The result is that for the past twenty years, in all the wars that have been fought when there has been an army entirely Italian, it has always made a bad showing. Proof of this was given first at the Taro, and then at Alessandria, Capua, Genoa, Vailà, Bologna, and Mestri.[6]

If your illustrious House, then, wishes to imitate those excellent men who redeemed their countries, it is necessary, before everything else, to furnish yourself with your own army, as the true foundation of every enterprise. You cannot have more faithful, nor truer, nor better soldiers. And though every individual of these may be good, they become better as a body when they see that they are commanded by their prince, and honored and trusted by him. It is necessary, therefore, that your House should be prepared with such forces, in order that it may be able to defend itself against the foreigners with Italian courage.

And though the Swiss and the Spanish infantry are properly estimated as terribly effective, yet both have defects. Hence a third type would be able not merely to oppose them but to feel sure of overcoming them. The fact is that the Spaniards are not able to resist cavalry, and the Swiss have reason to fear infantry, when they meet any as determined in battle as themselves. For this reason it has been seen and will be seen in experience that the Spaniards are unable to resist the French cavalry, and the Swiss are overthrown by Spanish infantry. And though of this last a clear instance has not been observed, yet an approach to it appeared in the battle of Ravenna,[7] when the Spanish infantry met the German battalions, who use the same methods as the Swiss. There the Spanish, through their ability and the assistance given by their shields, got within the points of the spears from below, and slew their enemies in security, while the

6. Sites of battles occurring between the end of the fifteenth century and the year 1513.
7. Between Spaniards and French in April, 1512.

Germans could find no means of resistance. If the cavalry had not charged the Spanish, they would have annihilated the Germans. It is possible, then, for one who realizes the defects of these two types, to equip infantry in a new manner, so that it can resist cavalry and not be afraid of foot-soldiers; but to gain this end they must have weapons of the right sorts, and adopt varied methods of combat. These are some of the things which, when they are put into service as novelties, give reputation and greatness to a new ruler.[8]

This opportunity, then, should not be allowed to pass, in order that after so long a time Italy may see her redeemer. I am unable to express with what love he would be received in all the provinces that have suffered from these foreign deluges; with what thirst for vengeance, what firm faith, what piety, what tears! What gates would be shut against him? what peoples would deny him obedience? what envy would oppose itself to him? what Italian would refuse to follow him? This barbarian rule stinks in every nostril. May your illustrious House, then, undertake this charge with the spirit and the hope with which all just enterprises are taken up, in order that, beneath its ensign, our native land may be ennobled, and, under its auspices, that saying of Petrarch may come true: "Manhood[9] will take arms against fury, and the combat will be short, because in Italian hearts the ancient valor is not yet dead."

---

# FRANÇOIS RABELAIS
## 1495?–1553

The life of François Rabelais, a man of wide humanistic education in the Renaissance tradition, typifies the variety of interests of the period, for he was at various points a law student, a monk, and a practicing physician; and he knew the life of people in cities and on country estates, in monasteries and at court. Born probably about 1494–95 into a middle-class landowning family at La Devinière, near Chinon in the province of Touraine, Rabelais was the son of a successful lawyer. Apparently first drawn to a monastic career, he was trained as a novice in the Franciscan order in the monastery of La Baumette at Angers. Later, as a monk in the Franciscan monastery of Puy-Saint-Martin at Fontenay-le-Comte, he busied himself especially with the "new learning" (Greek and other humanistic studies), which was suspect to conventional theologians. In 1524 he obtained authorization from Pope Clement VII to transfer to the less strict Benedictine order. He maintained close and continuous contacts, both personal and epistolary, with prominent humanists and jurists. He probably studied law at Poitiers. Between 1527

---

8. Machiavelli was subsequently the author of a treatise on the *Art of War* (1521).    9. An etymological translation of the original *virtù* (from the Latin *vir*, "man.") The quotation is from Petrarch's *canzone* "My Italy."

and 1530 he seems to have traveled extensively, and probably to have studied medicine at the University of Paris, a supposition warranted by the fact that when in 1530 he entered the University of Montpellier as a medical student he received the degree of bachelor of medicine in two months. We know that in 1532 he was a physician in the important hospital of the Pont-du-Rhône at Lyon and practiced medicine with success.

Also in 1532, Rabelais published, under the name of Alcofibas Nasier, an anagram of his own name, the volume of *Pantagruel* which now constitutes Book II of *Gargantua and Pantagruel*. The story of Gargantua, the present Book I, appeared in 1534. In that year Rabelais traveled to Rome as personal physician to Jean du Bellay, then bishop of Paris and later a cardinal. In Rome in 1535 Rabelais obtained papal absolution for having discarded the monk's robe without authorization; later in the same year, back in France, his status became that of a lay priest. In 1537 he received his doctorate of medicine at Montpellier and gave lectures there, using the texts of the ancient Greek physicians such as Hippocrates in the original. In the following years he traveled widely and also acquired some standing at court, holding a minor post in the retinue of King Francis I. Court contacts helped him counteract the condemnations of his literary work by the theologians of the Sorbonne. The seriousness of his difficulties—arising out of accusations of heresy and leanings toward the Protestant Reformation—varied according to the protection that the court could grant him and his own success in compromising. After Book III of *Gargantua and Pantagruel* (1546) was banned, Rabelais resided for two years in voluntary exile at Metz in the Alsace. He was again in Rome in 1548, and in 1551 was appointed to the two curacies of Saint-Martin-de-Meudon and Saint-Christophe-de-Jambet, both of which he resigned early in 1553 because of ill health. The tradition is that Rabelais died in Paris, in the Rue des Jardins, probably in April of that same year. Book IV of *Gargantua and Pantagruel*, which had appeared in 1552, had also been banned; a fifth book, of dubious authenticity, appeared in 1562–64. It is evident from the above that Rabelais' life and work are both highly representative of the period in which he lived and yet conspicuously unique.

Rabelais was by no means exclusively a professional writer; indeed, his story of the giants Gargantua and Pantagruel, written piecemeal during his mature years, is not so much a traditional unified work of fiction as a summation of Rabelais' wide knowledge, of his diverse notions of the world, and of his fantasies. Its peculiar quality may be described in terms of contrasts: the supernatural and realistic in the characters and action; the solemn and comic, lofty and bawdy in the themes; and the erudite and colloquial in the style. Rabelais' heroes, as giants, move in a dimension that is entirely out of proportion to ordinary reality. They belong—with their extraordinary size, power, and longevity—to a tradition known to us through myths, through folk tales, and through biblical narrative. Yet these same fantastic characters express the feelings and attitudes of ordinary men. In fact, they seem to be presented as epitomes of what man, according to Rabelais, ought to be in a reasonable and enjoyable world.

Rabelais' view of the world, we soon realize, is also well reflected in his literary style. High and low, pedantic and farcical, ponderous and mocking, it shows a broad intellectual and moral inclusiveness, an enthusiastic open-mindedness and gusto. As we come across the learned allusion, the solemn Ciceronian phrasing, and the scholastic pedantry, all mingled with the familiar and folksy, we notice that the presence of the colloquial quality by no means destroys the impact of the erudition or necessarily gives it the tone of parody. For Rabelais attends to both with equal delight and blends them with complete success; the resulting mixture is a consistent whole, sustained throughout by the same rich manipulation of words and the same exuberant vitality. Thus Rabelais' style concretely embodies his view of the world and of man. His message, his view of the human condition, are basically cheerful; his work is usually considered to be a major monument of the Renaissance at its most satisfied and affirmative. The basic theme of drinking, the vast thirst of Rabelais' gigantic protagonists, is conveniently taken to symbolize the healthy and all-embracing sensual and intellectual appetites of the period.

A famous contemporary of Rabelais, Benvenuto Cellini (1500–1571), mentioned in our general introduction, can also be regarded as an instance of the affirmative Renaissance spirit little hampered by doubt and melancholy. In fact, Cellini is even too pure and unmeditative, too "innocent" an example. In his fully adujsted way of living, this somewhat bombastic extrovert does not ask himself about value and meaning. Rabelais, at least implicitly, does take an interest in questions of value; and he seems assured, on what may appear to us relatively scant evidence, of the basic goodness and perfectibility of man. The selections from Rabelais given here emphasize that assurance, showing, among other things, Rabelais' faith in a certain type of physical and mental education; they illustrate his conception of the ideal man fit to live in what he considered to be a new age. It will be observed in this connection that although Rabelais was, among Europeans of the period, as responsible as anyone for the popular notion of an intellectual Renaissance following the aridity and bondage of medieval scholasticism and the barbarism of the Gothic "night," his ideal man also possesses certain qualities that seem to us to be survivals of medieval codes. Rabelais' ideal man remains a kind of knight-at-arms, despite the added emphasis on the intellectual ornaments of humanism. And this is true of other Renaissance writers. For example, in the works of Castiglione, Cervantes, Shakespeare, and Ludovico Ariosto (1474–1533), author of the epic *Orlando Furioso*, the knightly ideal continues to appear, though variously twisted through irony or distorted in other ways. Rabelais' approach is very direct and hopeful; from his pages we receive the impression that a healthy, wise, gallant, and happy type of man is a concrete possibility. Give the young the right tutoring—Rabelais' implication is—do away with hampering scholasticism, let them take proper care of their bodily functions, and certain values of tolerance, *bonhommie*, and substantial well-being will finally and inevitably triumph. The sophistic, the arrogant, the hypocritical will be exposed and defeated in the most reasonable and enjoyable of worlds.

Nowhere is this pleasant view expressed more clearly than in the conception of Thélème, the supremely good place on earth, the "abbey" of Rabelais' heart and imagination, where all restrictions are banned, not because total anarchy and license are advocated but rather because for such supremely civilized "nuns" and "monks" as those of the Thélèmite order instinctive inclinations will coincide with virtue: "The only rule of the house was: DO AS THOU WILT, because men that are free, of gentle birth, well-bred and at home in civilized company possess a natural instinct that inclines them to virtue and saves them from vice. This instinct they name their honor." Such optimism is qualified, of course, by the very premise of his story. For all its realism, and in spite of the fact that some episodes are mock-heroic versions of actual and even of provincial and domestic events (the Picrochole war that precedes the establishment of the abbey of Thélème), this is still a fable, with giants as its main heroes and fantasy as its normal mode.

Much war, horror, intrigue, and injustice existed in the world as Rabelais knew it. In practical life, he muddled through by his tolerance, wisdom, and capacity for compromise (his temporary sympathy for the Protestant Reformation, in a time of raging religious conflict, stopped "this side of the stake"). But he survived also because with his literary art he invented a world fashioned according to his own aspirations. In that world, the heroes on the side of good and of justice not only win wars but also display an effective and nobly magniloquent clemency toward the vanquished. Its utopian quality again illustrates the tendency of the Renaissance mind to seek a perfect model, an exemplary, ideal form. Some important passages of the book, especially the famous letter (included in our selections) of Gargantua to Pantagruel, dated from Sir Thomas More's ideal land, Utopia, make clear that this chronicle of giants, biblical in its magnitude and in its patriarchal qualities and Renaissance in its aspiration to "achieve mental, moral and technical excellence," symbolized in its serious moments the urge to perpetuate, from father to son, the true and noble form of man and thus idealistically confirm his divine origin, his "dignity."

Mikhail Mikhailovich Bakhtin, *Rabelais and His World,* translated by Helene Iswolsky (1968), views Rabelais' satire in the racy, carnivalesque context of popular culture. Donald M. Frame's *François Rabelais: A Study* (1977), is a solid treatment intended for the general reader. Thomas M. Greene, *Rabelais: A Study in Comic Courage* (1970), gives a brief, comprehensive account of Rabelais' life and work. The general reader will find Brian Masters, *A Student's Guide to Rabelais* (1977), helpful.

# Gargantua and Pantagruel[1]

# Book I

## [Education of a Giant Humanist]

### CHAPTER 14

*How Gargantua was taught Latin by a Theologian and Sophist.*

The excellent Grangousier was rapt with admiration as he listened to his son[2] talking. Truly this lad was marvellously gifted! What a

1. Translated by Jacques Le Clercq.   2. Gargantua.

vast intelligence, what cogent understanding! Turning to the govern-
esses:

"Philip, King of Macedon," he declared, "recognized the sound
judgment of Alexander, his son, when he saw how skilfully the lad
managed his horse. This beast Bucephalus was so fierce and unruly
that it threw all its riders. It cracked one man's neck, smashed another's legs, brained a third, and crushed the jawbone of a fourth. No
one, then, dared mount it. Alexander happened to be in the hippod-
rome watching them breaking in and training the horses; he noticed
at once that the beast's frenzy came from fright at its own shadow.
He therefore made short shrift of vaulting upon its back and heading
it towards the sun. There, its shadow falling behind it, he easily
mastered it. Philip, by this token, realized the divine insight rooted
in his son's intelligence and had him most carefully reared by Aristotle, then the most renowned philosopher in Greece.

"For my part, the brief conversation I have just had with Gargantua in your presence suffices to convince me that his mind is illumined by the divine spark. How else, pray, could he have proved so
acute, so subtle, so profound and withal so serene? Give the boy
proper schooling, say I, and he will attain a supreme degree of wisdom! Accordingly, I intend to trust him to some scholar who will
instruct him to his capacity. What is more, I shall spare no cost."

The name of Master Tubal Holofernes, a great sophist and Doctor
of Theology, was proposed to Grangousier. Subsequently this savant
taught Gargantua his A B C so thoroughly that he could say it by
heart backwards. This took five years and three months. A succession
of standard texts[3] followed; the *Facet* (a treatise of puerile moral precepts), the *Ars Grammatica* of Actius Donatus, the fourth-century
grammarian; the *Theodolet* (in which Theodulus, Bishop of Syria in
the fifth century, exposed in Latin the falsity of mythology and the
truth of Holy Scripture) and the *Alanus in Parabolis* (a series of moral
quatrains by Alanus of Lille, a thirteenth-century worthy). It took
Gargantua thirteen years, six months and two weeks to master these
authorities.

It is only fair to add, however, that Gargantua, in the process,
learned to write in Gothic characters. (Printing had not yet been
invented and the young student had to write out his own texts.)

He had, therefore, to carry in front of him a tremendous writing
apparatus that weighed more than seven hundred thousand pounds.
The pencase was as large and as tall as the great columns of the
Church of St. Martin of Ainay in Lyons; the inkhorn was suspended
to it by great iron chains wide enough to hold five cubic yards of
merchandise.

---

3. The books mentioned in this chapter were actually part of the educational curriculum which
Rabelais is here satirizing.

Another book, *De Modis Significandi*—a work of speculative grammar by Thomas Aquinas, or Albert of Saxony or probably Duns Scotus—was Gargantua's next reading, together with comments by Hurtebize or Windjammer, by Fasquin or Roadheaver, by Tropdit-eux or Toomanysuch, by Gualehault or Galahad, by Jean Le Veau or John Calf, by Billonio or Lickspittle, by Brelinguandus or Time-server, and by a rabble of others. This took more than eighteen years and eleven months, but Gargantua knew the texts so well that at examinations he could recite them by heart backwards. And he could prove to his mother on his fingers' ends that *de modis significandi non erat scientia*, grammar was no science.

Next he read the *Compost* or *Popular Calendar*, and had spent sixteen years and two months at it, when suddenly, in 1420, his tutor died of the pox.

Holofernes' successor was another wheezy old pedant named Master Jobelin Bridé or Jolter Clotpoll, who read him the *Liber Deriva-tionum* or *Latin Vocabulary* of Hugutio of Pisa, thirteenth-century Bishop of Ferrara . . . the *Grecism* by Everard de Béthune, a phil-ological lexicon illustrating the Latin words derived from the Greek . . . *De Octo Partibus Orationis* or *Of the Eight Parts of Speech* . . . the *Quid Est?* or *What is it?* a school manual in the form of ques-tions and answers . . . the *Supplementum*, a collection of commen-taries . . . the *Mammotreptus*, a monkish or monkeyish commentary on the Psalter and the Saints . . . the *Libellus de Moribus in Mensa Servandis* or *Essay on Manners in Serving at Table*, a rhymed trea-tise on youthful propriety and morals by Sulpizio de Veroli . . . Seneca's *De Quatuor Virtutibus Cardinalibus* or *Of the Four Car-dinal Virtues*, a moral work by Martin de Braga, Bishop of Mondo-nedo in the sixth century . . . the *Specchio della vera Penitenza* or *Mirror of True Penitence* by Jacopo Passavanti, the Florentine monk of the sixteenth century—with its inevitable commentary! . . . a book of sermons, *Dormi Secure* or *Sleep in Peace*, a collection designed to save the preacher the pains of composing his sermons . . . and finally, other stuff of the same ilk, feather, kidney and broth. . . .

Indeed, Gargantua grew as even as any down ever smoothed, as full of matter as any goose liver ever crammed!

CHAPTER 15

*How Gargantua was put under other professors.*

At last his father realized that though Gargantua was studying most industriously and spending all his time at it, he was profiting not at all. Worse, this training had actually made the lad over into a fool, a dunce, a booby and a nincompoop.

One day Grangousier happened to complain of it to Don Philippe des Marais, Viceroy of Papeligosse, a kingdom of Cockaigne.[4] That monarch assured Grangousier that Gargantua would be better off learning nothing than studying books of the sort with pedagogues of that school. Their knowledge, said Don Philippe, was but rubbish, this wisdom flapdoodle; they succeeded merely in bastardizing noble spirits and corrupting the flower of youth.

"Upon my word, I'll prove it!" Don Philippe declared. "Take any lad of to-day with but two years' schooling. If he is not superior to your son in judgment, speech, bearing and personality, then I'm the greatest loggerhead and shallowpate from here to Brenne."[5]

This challenge pleased Grangousier mightily; he at once gave orders that a match of wits take place.

That evening, at supper, Don Philippe brought in a young page of his named Eudemon, which means "the fortunate." The lad hailed from Villegongis near St. Genou in Touraine. He was so neat, so spruce, so handsome and his hair was so beautifully combed that he looked more like an angel than like a man.

Don Philippe turned to Grangousier:

"Do you see this lad? He's not twelve years old. Let us prove, if you will, the difference between the pedantic balderdash of yesterday's wiseacres and the intelligence of our modern boys."

Grangousier was agreeable to such a test and bade the page begin the debate. Whereupon Eudemon, asking leave of the Viceroy, his master, to do so, rose, hat in hand. His face was open and frank, his lips red, his glance confident. Looking at Gargantua with youthful modesty, he proceeded to praise and commend the boy—first for his virtues and good manners, next for his knowledge, thirdly for his nobility, fourthly for his bodily excellences and, in the fifth place, exhorted him most gracefully to reverence his father in all respects, because his father was so careful to have him well brought up. Finally, Eudemon prayed Gargantua to admit him among the least of his bondsmen. He added that the only boon he craved from Heaven, at present, was to serve Gargantua in some agreeable manner. Eudemon accompanied the whole speech with gestures so appropriate, his delivery was so distinct, his voice rang so eloquent, his idiom was so elegant and he couched his phrases in such perfect Latin that he seemed rather a Tiberius Gracchus, a Cicero or an Aemilius Lepidus of old, than a youth of our own day.

Gargantua's only reaction was to burst into tears. He bawled like a sick cow, hung his head and hid his face in his cap, until there was about as much possibility of drawing a word from him as a salvo of

---

4. Rabelais probably alludes to some existing person; his method is to take real people and introduce them into his fantastic world. The kingdom of Cockaigne is the traditional imaginary land of luck and plenty.    5. An actual locality. What was said of Rabelais' characters in the preceding footnote applies also to his geography, his local lore, and the like.

farts from the rump of a dead donkey.

This so incensed his father that Grangousier vowed to slay Master Jobelin Clotpoll, but Don Philippe remonstrated with him and, by fair persuasions, soothed his ire. Grangousier thereupon ordered them to pay the pedagogue off and to get him as properly fuddled up as your finest scholar of the Sorbonne. This accomplished, let him go to the devil!

"There is this consolation!" cried Grangousier. "To-day at least, he will not cost his host much if by chance he dies in his cups like an Englishman."

When Master Jobelin Clotpoll had gone away, Grangousier asked Don Philippe's advice about a tutor for Gargantua. They finally decided to appoint Ponocrates, Eudemon's teacher, to the position; auspiciously enough, in Greek the name means "vigorous." And soon, the three were to go to Paris in order to find out what studies young men were at this period pursuing in France.

## CHAPTER 16

*How Gargantua went to Paris upon an enormous mare which*
*destroyed the oxflies of the Beauce.*

In the same season, Fayolles, fourth king of Numidia, sent Grangousier a mare from Africa. It was the hugest and most enormous mare ever seen, the strangest monster in the world; for Africa, as the saying goes, may always be relied upon to produce something wonderfully new. The beast was as big as six elephants; like Julius Caesar's charger, her feet were cloven into human toes; her ears hung down like those of the goats of Languedoc; and a little horn grew out of one buttock. Save for a few dapple-gray spots as overlay, her coat was the color of burnt sorrel, which shows that she partook of the four elements, earth, water, air and fire. Above all, she had a horrible tail. It was more or less as tall as the tower of St. Mars near Langeais; and just as square, with tufts of hair as tightly spun and woven as the beards on ears of corn.

Do you marvel at this? You have greater cause to marvel at the tails of the rams of Scythia, which weighed more than thirty pounds each, or—if Jean Thenaud speaks truthfully in his *Voyage from Angoulême to Cairo*—at those of the Syrian sheep which are so long and heavy that, to hold them up, the natives have to hitch a small cart to the beast's rump. Ha! my lusty country wenchthumpers, you've no such tails as these!

The mare Fayolles sent Grangousier was brought overseas in three Genoese carracks and a brigantine; she landed at Les Sables d'Olonne in Talmondais.

When Grangousier laid eyes upon her:

"Ah!" he exclaimed. "Here is just what my son needs to bear him to Paris! So now, in God's name, all will go well: Gargantua shall be a great scholar one of these days! Were it not for dumb brutes we should all be scholars!"

Next day, having drunk liberally, as you may imagine, Gargantua set out on his journey, accompanied by his tutor Ponocrates, the young page Eudemon and his train. And, because the weather was serene and temperate, Grangousier had a pair of dun-colored boots made for him. According to Babin and the Chinon cobblers, these are technically known as buskins.

So they travelled along the highway very merrily, living on the fat of the land and making the best of cheer, until a little beyond Orléans they came to a huge forest, about thirty-five leagues long and seventeen wide. Alas! the woods were aswarm with oxflies and hornets of all varieties, so the wretched mares, asses and horses suffered a veritable massacre. But, by means of a trick they never suspected, Gargantua's mare handsomely avenged all the outrages visited upon her kind. For suddenly, when in the heart of the forest the wasps attacked her, she swished her tail and, sweeping all about her, not only felled the stingers but uprooted all the trees. Up and down, right and left, lengthwise and athwart, here and there, over and under, before her and aback, this way and that, she mowed down the woods like so much grass. And this region, which she thus turned into fallow land, has never known tree or wasp since.

Gargantua, delighted by the spectacle, forebore to boast, merely commenting to his followers:

"*Je trouve beau ce!* I find this pleasant!"

Whence this pleasant land has been known as Beauce ever since.

However, when it came to breakfasting, they had to content themselves with their yawns; in memory of which the gentlemen of the Beauce, proverbially poor, still subsist on a diet of yawns and gaping, and find it very nourishing. Indeed, they spit all the better for it.

At last they reached Paris, where Gargantua rested two or three days, making merry with his followers and inquiring about what scholars were then in the city and what wines people drank.

✳     ✳     ✳

## CHAPTER 21

*Gargantua's education and social life under the direction of his preceptors at the Sorbonne.*

. . . Gargantua resolved with all his heart to study under the direction of Ponocrates. But the latter, wishing to learn how the lad's former teachers had wasted so much time making a crack-brained, addlepated dunce of him, decided he should do exactly as he had in the past.

Gargantua therefore arranged his schedule so as to awake usually between eight and nine o'clock, rain or shine, dark or daylight, simply because his preceptors had decided this on the strength of the Psalmist's saw: "*Vanum est vobis ante lucem surgere, it is vain for you to rise up betimes.*"[6]

Then he wriggled and writhed, wallowing in his bed and tossing about like a parched pea, the better to stimulate his vital spirits. Next, he would dress, according to the season, but he was always happy to don a long, hanging gown of heavy wool lined with fox. Next, he combed out his hair with the comb of Jacques Almain, the Sorbonne theologian, known in English as John Handy—a comb consisting of four fingers and a thumb—for his mentors maintained that to brush one's hair, wash one's face and make oneself clean were, in this world, a pure waste of time.

Next Gargantua dunged, piddled, vomited, belched, broke wind, yawned, spat, coughed, hiccoughed, sneezed and snotted himself as majestically and bountifully as an archdeacon. Next he proceeded to breakfast in order to fortify himself against the morning mist and cold. His menu consisted of splendid fried tripe, choice meats grilled on charcoal, rich hams, succulent roast venison and numerous soups and brews, with toast, cheese, parsley and chopped meat floating on the surface.

Ponocrates objected that he should not eat so soon after rising without having taken any exercise. To which he replied:

"Exercise? Good God, didn't I tumble and jounce in bed six or seven times before I got up? Surely, that is exercise enough? Pope Alexander VI did this on the advice of his Jew physician, Bonnet de Lates, and lived till the day of his death in spite of his enemies. My first masters taught me this habit, for breakfast, they said, gave man a good mind. So they started the day by drinking. It suits me perfectly and I manage to dine the better for it. Master Tubal Holofernes, who was graduated Licentiate in Paris at the head of his class, used to tell me that hasten was not enough, one must set out betimes. By the same token, the total health of mankind does not consist in drinking down and lapping up, *glub, glub, glub*, like so many ducks, but rather in falling to, early in the morning. *Unde versus*; so runs the rune:

> Lever matin n'est point bonheur
> Boire matin est le meilleur.

6. "It is vain for you to rise up early, to sit up late, to eat the bread of sorrows: for so he giveth his beloved sleep." (Psalm 127:2.)

To rise betimes is not enough,
To drink at morning, that's the stuff!

After an abundant breakfast, Gargantua repaired to church, with, in
his train, a varlet bearing a basket. The latter contained a huge bre-
viary swaddled in velvet and weighing about twelve hundred and six
pounds including the filth of thumbmarks, dogeared corners, golden
clasps and nonpareil parchment. Twenty-six, if not thirty, masses
ensued for the benefit of Gargantua and his chaplain. Under his tall
hood, this chaplain looked for all the world like a peewit . . . and
had very thoroughly antidoted his breath against possible poisons
with much syrup of the vine! Chaplain and pupil babbled the mumbo
jumbo of the litany, thumbing their rosaries so carefully that not one
single bead fell to the ground.

As he left the church, they brought him an oxcart laden with a
huge heap of paternosters, chaplets and relics from St. Claude in the
Jura, each bigger than a hatblock. Gargantua and his chaplain then
strolled in the cloisters, galleries or garden, saying more aves than
sixteen hermits.

After, Gargantua would study for a short half-hour, his eyes glued
to his book but his mind, to quote Terence's *Eunuch*, woolgathering
in the kitchen.[7] Then he proceeded to make water, filling a large
urinal to capacity, after which he sat down at table, and, being naturally phlegmatic, began his meal with a few dozen hams, smoked
tongues of beef, caviar, sausages and other like forerunners of wine.

Then four servants in turn shovelled mustard into his mouth by
the spadeful, thus preparing him to drain a horrific draught of white
wine to relieve his kidneys. Then the meal proper began with viands
to his liking, according to the season; Gargantua ceasing to eat only
when his belly had reached bursting point.

When it came to drinking, he acknowledged neither end nor rule;
for, he said, there were no limits and boundaries to swilling until the
tosspot felt the cork soles of his shoes swell up a half-foot from the
ground.

*          *          *

## CHAPTER 23

*How Ponocrates gave Gargantua such instruction that not an hour
of the day was wasted.*

When Ponocrates saw Gargantua's vicious mode of life, he determined to bring him up otherwise. But for the first few days he bore
with him, for he realized that nature cannot endure sudden and
violent changes.

7. See Terence's play *The Eunuch*, l. 816.

To begin his work the better, Ponocrates requested a learned physician of the times, Master Theodore—the name means "God-given"—to examine Gargantua thoroughly with a view to steering him on the right course. The scholar purged Gargantua canonically with Anticyrian hellebore, an herb indicated for cerebral disorders and insanity, thus cleansing his brain of its unnatural, perverse condition. Ponocrates, by the same aperient means, made the lad forget all he had learned under his former teachers, just as Timotheus[8] of old treated pupils who had already studied under other musicians. Timotheus, incidentally, used to charge this class of students double!

For Gargantua's further edification, Ponocrates made him mingle among learned men whose company fired him with a desire to emulate them, to study more profitably and to make his mark. Next, Ponocrates so arranged the lad's schedule that not a moment of the day was wasted; all his time was spent in the pursuit of learning and honest knowledge.

By this new dispensation, Gargantua awoke at about four in the morning. While the servants massaged him, he would listen to some page of Holy Scripture, read aloud in clear tones and pronounced with fitting respect for the text. A young page, a native of Basché, near Chinon, was appointed reader, as his name, Anagnostes,[9] shows. According to the purpose and argument of this lesson, Gargantua frequently turned to worship, adore, pray and reverence Almighty God, Whose majesty and wondrous wisdom were made manifest in the reading.

Next, he would repair to secret places to make excretion of his natural digestions; here his tutor repeated what had been read, expounding its more obscure and difficult features. Returning to the house, they would study the heavens. Was it the same sky they had observed the night before? Into what signs was the sun entering that day? and the moon?

After this astronomical survey, Gargantua was dressed, combed, curled, trimmed and perfumed, and, while this was being done, he heard the lessons of the day before. Then, having recited them by heart, he would argue certain practical, human and utilitarian cases based upon the principles enunciated. This part of the program sometimes took two or three hours, though usually he had exhausted it by the time he was fully clad.

Then, for three good hours, he was read or lectured to, after which they went to the Tennis Court at the Grande Bracque in the Place de l'Estrapade or to the playing fields.

On the way, they discussed various aspects of the subject previously treated. Then they would play tennis, handball and three-cor-

8. Timotheus of Miletus, famous musician of the time of Alexander the Great.    9. In Greek meaning "reader."

nered catch, exercising their bodies as vigorously as they had exercised their minds before.

All their play was free for they left off when they pleased, which
was usually when they had sweated a good bit or were otherwise
tired. They were thoroughly wiped and rubbed down, after which
they changed their shirts and walked quietly home to see if dinner
were ready. As they waited, they would go over certain points they
had retained of the lectures.

Meanwhile My Lord Appetite put in an appearance and they sat
down most opportunely to table.

At the beginning of the meal, they listened to the reading of some
agreeable chronicle of chivalry in ancient times, until Gargantua
gave the signal for wine to be served. Then, if they wished, the reading went on or they could talk merrily together. Often they discussed
the virtues, property, efficacy and nature of what was served at table:
bread, wine, water, salt, meat, fish, fruit, herbs, roots and their preparation. Thus Gargantua soon knew all the relevant passages of Pliny's *Natural History* . . . in the grammarian Athenæus'
*Deipnosophistes* or *The Banquet of the Sages*, which treats of flowers,
fruits and their various uses . . . in Dioscorides' famous medical
treatise, the bible of apothecaries . . . in the *Vocabularium* by Julius
Pollux, a grammarian and sophist of Marcus Aurelius' day, who wrote
of hunting and fishing . . . in Galen's numerous dissertations upon
alimentation . . . in the works of Porphyrius, the third-century Greek
author of a *Treatise upon Abstinence from Meat* . . . in Oppian's
two poems, *Cynegetica* which deals with venery and *Halieutica* with
angling . . . in *Of Healthy Diet* by Polybius of Cos, disciple and
son-in-law of Hippocrates . . . in Heliodorus of Emesa, Syrian Bishop
of Tricca and a celebrated novelist of the fourth century . . . in Aristotle's essays on natural history . . . in the Greek works upon animals
by Claudius Ælianus, a Roman contemporary of Heliogabalus . . .
and in various other tomes.[1] . . . Often for surer authority as they
argued, they would have the book in question brought to the table.
Gargantua so thoroughly and cogently learned and assimilated all he
heard that no physician of his times knew one-half so much as he.

They discussed the lessons they had learned that morning and
topped their meal off with quiddany, a sort of quince marmalade
and an excellent digestive. After which Gargantua picked his teeth
with a fragment of mastic,[2] washed his hands and daubed his eyes
with cool clear water, and, instead of saying grace, sang the glory of
God in noble hymns, composed in praise of divine bounty and
munificence.

1. Some of the most famous scientific treatises of antiquity are listed in Gargantua's new curriculum, which exacting as it is, reflects a less "medieval" type of learning than was embodied in his
earlier couse of study. See also the enumeration of authors on p. 1608.    2. Wood from the
mastic tree.

Presently cards were brought them and they played, not for the sake of the pastime itself but to learn a thousand new tricks and inventions all based on arithmetic.

Thus Gargantua developed a keen enthusiasm for mathematics, spending his leisure after dinner and supper every evening as pleasantly as once he had, dicing and gaming. As a result, he knew so much about its theory and practice that Cuthbert Tunstal, Bishop of Durham and secretary to King Henry VIII, a voluminous writer on the subject,[3] confessed that, beside Gargantua, he knew no more about arithmetic than he did about Old High Gothic. Nor was it arithmetic alone our hero learned, but also such sister sciences as geometry, astronomy and music.

Now the digestion of foods is a most important matter. There is the first stage which occurs in the stomach, where the viands are changed into chyle; the second, in the liver, where the chyle is transformed into blood; the third, in the habit of the body, where the blood is finally converted into the substance of each part. So, whilst Gargantua awaited the first stage of digestion, they made a thousand delightful instruments, drew geometrical figures and even applied the principles of astronomy.

After, they amused themselves singing a five-part score or improvising on a theme chosen at random. As for musical instruments, Gargantua learned to play the lute, the spinet, the harp, the nine-holed transverse or German flute, the viol and the sackbut or trombone.

Having spent an hour thus and completed his digestion, he discharged his natural excrements and then settled down again to work three hours or more at his principal study. Either he revised the morning reading, or proceeded in the text at hand or practised penmanship in the most carefully formed characters of modern Roman and ancient Gothic script.

Next, they went out with a young gentleman of Touraine, the esquire Gymnastes, who instructed Gargantua in the art of horsemanship. Having changed his clothes, he proceeded to mount a fiery Italian charger, a Flemish dray horse, a Spanish jennet, an Arab thoroughbred and a hackney. These he would put vigorously through their paces, letting them "career" or gallop a short distance at full speed, making them leap high in the air, jump ditches, clear stiles, and turn short in a ring both to the right and to the left. Next he wielded but did not break his lance, for it is arrant stupidity to boast: "I have broken ten lances in a tilt or fight." A wretched carpenter can do the same. On the contrary, the whole glory of such combat lies in besting ten enemies with one and the same lance. So with

3. Tunstal was the author of the treatise *The Art of Computation* (*De arte supputandi*, 1522).

strong, stiff, steel-tipped lance, Gargantua would force the outer door of some house, pierce an adversary's armor, beat down a tree, pick up a ring, carry off a cuirassier saddle, a hauberk or a gauntlet. And he performed these feats armed cap-à-pie.[4]

In the technique of parading his horse with prances and flourishes to a fanfare of trumpets—the ceremonial of knights as they enter the lists—he had no equal. As for the divers terms of the equine vocabulary from *giddy-up* and *cluck* to *whoa* and *grrr*, no horseman could hold a candle to him. Indeed Cesare Fieschi, the celebrated jockey of Ferrara, was a mere monkey in comparison.

He learned, too, to leap hastily and with singular dexterity from one horse to another without setting foot to the ground (the nags were circus horses or, to be technical, "desultories"). Further, lance in hand, he could leap on horseback from either side without stirrups and rule the beast at will without a bridle, for such accomplishments are highly useful in military engagements.

Another day he would practise wielding the battle-axe, which he managed so skilfully, in the nimblest thrusts, the most powerful lunges and the vast encircling sweeps of the art, that he passed knight-at-arms in the field and at all tests. Sometimes unarmed, sometimes carrying a buckler or a rolled cape of mail over his arm or a small shield over his wrist, Gargantua brandished the pike, plied the double-edged, two-handed sword, the bastard claymore used by archers, the Spanish rapier, the dagger and the poniard.

He hunted, too: stag, roebuck, bear, fallow deer, wild boar, hare, partridge, pheasant and otter . . . he played at ball, ever ready with well-aimed foot or powerful fist to send the great sphere whizzing through the air . . . he learned to wrestle and to run. . . . As for jumping, he did not go in for the various forms of running jumps, such as the three-steps-and-a-leap, the hop-step-and-jump or the German high-jump. As Gymnastes pointed out, these were quite useless in warfare. Instead, he practised the standing jumps. Starting from scratch, he could in one leap top a hedge, clear a ditch, mount six paces upon a wall and thus reach a window-ledge one lance's height from the ground.

Gargantua could swim in the deepest water, breaststroke, back and sidestroke, using his whole body or his feet alone. He could cross the breadth of the Seine or the Loire at Montsoreau, dragging his cloak along in his teeth and holding a book high and dry over the waters—thus renewing the exploit with which Plutarch credits Julius Cæsar during the Alexandrian War. Then, using one hand only, he could, with a single great pull, climb into a boat, whence a moment later he would dive headlong into the water again, sound its utmost depths,

---

4. From head to toe; *hauberk*: coat of mail.

touch bottom, explore the hollows of rocks and plunge into any pits and abysses he fancied. He would turn the boat about, managing it perfectly, bringing it swiftly or slowly upstream or down and arresting its course at a milldam. He could guide it with one hand while he plied hard about him with a great oar; he could run up a sail, hoist himself up a mast by the shrouds, dance along the yards, operate the compass, tackle the bowlines to sail close to the wind and steer the helm.

His water sports done, he would dash full speed up a mountain, then down quite as fast. He climbed trees like a cat, hopping from one to the next like a squirrel and pulling down great boughs—like the celebrated Milo of Crotona who, Pausanias[5] tells us, met his death devoured by wolves, his hands caught in the cleft of an oak he had sought to split. With two well-steeled daggers and a pair of well-tried mason's punches, he could scurry up the side of a house like a rat, then leap down again, from roof to ground, so expertly that he landed without hurt. Gargantua also cast the dart, threw the iron bar, put the stone, tossed the boar-spear, hurled the javelin, shied the halberd. He drew the bow to breaking point; he could shoulder a harquebuss—a great siege piece weighing fifty pounds—and fire it off like a crossbow. He could set a huge cannon on its carriage, hit buttmarks and other targets for horizontal shooting, or, point-blank, bring down papgays (stuffed figures of parrots on poles), clay pigeons and other vertical marks, facing them on a level or upwards, or downwards or sidewise. Like the ancient Parthians, he could even hit them as he retreated.

They would tie a cable to a high tower and let it dangle to the ground. Gargantua hoisted himself up with both hands, then slipped down again as evenly, surely and plumb as a man running along a flat meadow. Or they would set a great pole across two trees for Gargantua to hang from by his hands. He moved along the pole from tree to tree so swiftly, without setting foot on *terra firma*, that a man, running on the ground below, could not have caught him. To expand his chest and exercise his lungs, he would roar like all the devils in hell. Once indeed, I heard him call Eudemon across all Paris, from the Porte St. Victor, the gate by the University, all the way to Montmartre, a village on a hill two miles beyond the walls of the city. Stentor,[6] who cried louder than forty men, displayed no such vocal power, even at the siege of Troy.

To develop his sinews, they made him two great pigs of lead, each weighing eight hundred and five tons. These pigs (called salmons in France because the metal is shaped like this fish) Gargantua named *alteres*, an ancient Greek term for the weights used to give jumpers

---

5. Greek geographer and traveler of the second century A.D.    6. The loud-voiced herald in the *Iliad*, Book V.

their initial spring—our modern dumb-bells. Taking one in each
hand, Gargantua then performed an inimitable feat. He would raise
them high above his head and, never turning a hair, stock-still as a
statue, hold them aloft for three-quarters of an hour. He played at
Barriers or Tug-of-War with the stoutest champions. When his turn
came he took root so firmly as to defy the sturdiest to budge him.
Nor was it thus alone he emulated Milo of Crotona. Like the ancient
athlete, he could hold a pomegranate so fast in his hand that none
could wrest it from him, yet so adroitly that he did not crush it.

Having spent his time in such manly sports, he had himself washed,
rubbed down and given a change of clothes. Then he returned home
at a leisurely pace, passing through some meadow or grassy space to
examine the trees and plants. These he would compare with what
the authorities wrote of them in their books: among the Ancients,
Theophrastus, the successor of Aristotle and teacher of Menander
. . . or Palladius, whose poem *De re rustica* was translated by Pietro
Marini . . . or Dioscorides Pedanius, the Greek physician of the first
century . . . or Pliny or Nicander or Aemilius Macer, the Roman,
or Galen himself . . . Gargantua and his companions picked specimens by the handful and took them home to a younger page named
Rhizotome or Rootcutter, who watched over them and the various
small mattocks, pickaxes, hooks, hoes, pruning-knives, shears and
other botanical instruments.

At home, whilst the servants prepared dinner, our young men
repeated certain passages of what had been read. Then they sat down
to table. Here I would have you note that their dinner was simple
and frugal; they ate no more than necessary to quiet the baying of
the belly. Supper, on the contrary, was a large and copious meal;
they ate what they needed for their sustenance and nourishment.
Such indeed is the true system prescribed by the art of sound, self-
respecting physicians though a rabble of dunderhead quacks, wrangling eternally in the claptrap routine of the Arab nostrum shop of
Avicenna,[7] recommend the exact opposite. During supper, they
continued the lesson given at dinner as long as they saw fit; the rest
of the meal was spent in earnest and profitable discussion.

Having said grace, they applied their voices to sing tunefully or
they played upon harmonious instruments. Or they amused themselves with such minor pastimes as cards, dice cups and dice afforded.
Sometimes they tarried here enjoying themselves and making merry
until bedtime; they would visit learned men or such as had travelled
in foreign lands. Well into the night, before retiring, they would go
to the most exposed spot in the house, whence they examined the
face of the sky, noting the comets, if any were visible, and the var-

---

7. Arab physician and philosopher (980–1037).

ious figures, positions, aspects, oppositions and conjunctions of the heavenly bodies.

According to the Pythagorean system, Gargantua would, with his tutor, recapitulate briefly all that he had read, seen, learned, done and assimilated in the course of the day.

Then they prayed to God the Creator, doing Him worship and confirming their faith in Him, glorifying Him for His immense goodness, vouchsafing thanks for all the mighty past and imploring His divine clemency for all the future.

And so they retired to rest.

CHAPTER 24

*How Gargantua spent his time in rainy weather.*

In intemperate or rainy weather, things went on much the same as usual before dinner except that Gargantua had a fine bright fire lighted to correct the inclemency of the air. But after dinner, instead of gymnastics, they stayed indoors and, by way of apotherapy[8] or exercise amused themselves by bundling hay, splitting logs, sawing wood and threshing sheaves in the barn. Then they studied the arts of painting and sculpture. Or they revived the ancient Roman game of *Tali*, dicing as the Italian humanist Nicolaus Leonicus Thomaeus[9] wrote of it in his dialogue *Sannutus, Of the Game of Dice*, and as our good friend Janus Lascaris,[1] librarian to our sovereign king, plays at the game. In their sport, they reviewed such passages of ancient authors as mention or quote some metaphor drawn from this play.

In much the same way, they might go to watch workmen forging metals or casting pieces of ordnance. Or they might visit the lapidaries, goldsmiths and cutters of precious stones in their ateliers, the alchemists in their laboratories, the coiners at the mint, the tapestry-workers, velvet-workers and weavers at their looms, the watchmakers, looking-glass framers, printers, lutemakers, dyers and other such artisans in their workshops. Wherever they went, they would distribute gratuities, invariably investigating and learning the various inventions and industry of the trade.

Or they might attend public lectures, official convocations, oratorical performances, speeches, pleadings by eloquent attorneys and sermons by evangelical preachers—that is, such priests as wished to restore Christianity to the primitive tradition of the Gospel. Gargantua also frequented fencing halls and tested his skill at all weapons against the masters, proving to them by experience that he knew as much as they and, indeed, even more.

---

8. Physical exercise as a regime to maintain health. The terminology is from Galen (the outstanding Greek physician of the second century A.D.).      9. A Venetian, professor at Padua (died 1531).      1. André Jean de Lascaris, librarian to King Francis I and a friend of Rabelais'.

Instead of herborizing,[2] they would inspect the shops of druggists, herbalists and apothecaries, studiously examining the sundry fruits, roots, leaves, gums, seeds and exotic unguents and learning how they could be diluted or adulterated. He viewed jugglers, mountebanks and medicasters—who sold Venice treacle, a cure for all ills—carefully observing their tricks and gestures, their agile capers and smooth oratory. His favorites were those from Chauny in Picardy who are born jabberers and the readiest expounders of mealy-mouthed flimflam concerning their ability to weave ropes of sand, extract sunbeams from cucumbers and milk a he-goat into a sieve.

Returning home to supper, they would eat more sparingly than on fine days. Their meats would, by the same token, be more desiccative and extenuating so as to counteract the humidity communicated to their bodies by the necessary contiguity of the atmosphere and to nullify what harm might arise from lack of their customary exercise.

Such was Gargantua's program and so he continued from day to day, benefiting as you would expect a young man of his age and intelligence to benefit under such a system faithfully applied. To be sure, the whole thing may have seemed incredibly difficult to him at the outset, but it soon proved so light, so easy and so pleasant as to appear more like a king's pastime than the study of a schoolboy.

However, Ponocrates was careful to supply relaxation from this violent bodily and mental tension. Once a month, on some very bright serene day, they would clear out of town early in the morning, bound for the near-by villages of Gentilly, Boulogne, Montrouge, Pont-de-Charenton, Vanves or St. Cloud. There they spent the whole day enjoying themselves to their heart's content, sporting and merrymaking, drinking toast for proffered toast, playing, singing, dancing, tumbling about or loafing in some fair meadow, turning sparrows out of their nests, bagging quail and fishing for frogs and crayfish.

But though this holiday was free of books and reading, it was not spent unprofitably. Lying in the green meadow, they usually recited certain delightful lines from Virgil's *Georgics*, from Hesiod's *Works and Days* or from Politian's *Husbandry*.[3] Or they broached some savory epigram in Latin, then turned it into a French roundelay or ballade.

In their feasting, they would sometimes separate the twin elements, isolating the wine and the water in their drink by pouring the latter into a cup of ivy-wood, as Cato teaches in his *De re rustica*, and Pliny elsewhere.[4] Then they would wash the wine in a basin

---

2. Gathering herbs.    3. A poem, *Rusticus*, in the manner of Virgil's *Georgics*, by the Italian fifteenth-century poet Politian.    4. Both Cato in his book *On Farming* (*De re rustica*), CIX, and Pliny in his *Natural History* Book XVI, Chapter 63, suggest an ivy-wood cup as a means to detect water in wine.

full of water and draw it out with a funnel, as pure as ever. And they pumped the water with a syphon from one glass to another, manufacturing several sorts of automatic or self-operating devices.

## [The Abbey of Thélème]

### CHAPTER 52

*How Gargantua had the Abbey of Thélème built for the monk.*

There remained only the monk[5] to provide for. Gargantua offered him the Abbey of Seuilly: he refused. What about the Benedictine abbeys of Bourgueil or St. Florent, among the richest in France: he might have either or both?[6] Again, the offer met with a flat refusal: Friar John of the Funnels answered peremptorily that he did not seek the charge or government of monks.

"For," he explained, "how shall I govern others when I cannot possibly govern myself?" There was a pause. "But—" he hesitated. "But if you believe I have given and can give you good service, let me found an abbey after my own heart."

The notion delighted Gargantua: he forthwith offered his estate of Thélème, by the Loire, two leagues away from Port Huault. Thélème in Greek means free will, an auspicious name for Friar John's abbey. Here indeed he could institute a religious order contrary to all others.

"First," said Gargantua, "you must not build a wall around it, for all other abbeys are solidly enclosed."

"Quite so," agreed the monk, "for where there are *mures*, walls, before, and *mures*, walls, behind, we have *murmures*, murmurs of envy and plotting."

Now in certain monasteries it is a rule that if any women enter (I mean honest and chaste ones) the ground they tread upon must be swept over. Therefore it was decreed that if a monk or nun should by any chance enter Thélème, every place that religious passed through should be thoroughly disinfected.

Similarly because all monasteries and convents on earth are compassed, limited and regulated by hours, at Thélème no clock or dial of any sort should be tolerated. On the contrary, their time here would be governed by what occasions and opportunities might arise. As Gargantua sagaciously commented:

"I can conceive of no greater waste of time than to count the hours. What good comes of it? To order your life by the toll of a bell

---

5. Friar John of the Funnels, the muscular and highly unconventional monk who has had a major part in helping the party of Gargantua's father win the mock-heroic war against the arrogant Picrochole.   6. A satiric allusion to the custom of accumulating church livings.

instead of by reason or common sense is the veriest piece of asininity imaginable."

By the same token, they established the qualifications for entrance into their order. Was it not true that at present women took the veil only if they were wall-eyed, lame, hunchbacked, ill-favored, misshapen, half-witted, unreasonable or somewhat damaged? That only such men entered monasteries as were cankered, ill-bred idiots or plain nuisances?

("Incidentally," said Friar John, "if the woman is neither fair nor good, of what use is the cloth?"

"Let the clot hump her," Gargantua replied.

"I said 'cloth' not 'clot.' "

"Well, what's the answer?"

"To cover her face or her arse with!")

Accordingly, they decided to admit into the new order only such women as were beautiful, shapely, pleasing of form and nature, and such men as were handsome, athletic and personable.

Again, because men entered the convents of this world only by guile and stealth, it was decreed that no women would be in Thélème unless men were there also, and vice-versa.

Moreover, since both men in monasteries and women in convents were forced after their year of noviciate to stay there perpetually, Gargantua and Friar John decided that the Thélèmites, men or women, might come and go whenever they saw fit.

Further, since the religious usually made the triple vow of chastity, poverty and obedience, at Thélème all had full leave to marry honestly, to enjoy wealth and to live in perfect freedom.

As for the age of initiation, they stipulated that women were admissible between the ages of ten and fifteen, men between twelve and eighteen.

CHAPTER 53

*How the Abbey of Thélème was built and endowed.*

To build and furnish the abbey, Gargantua paid in cash twenty-seven hundred thousand eight hundred and thirty-one crowns in current coin of the realm, fresh from the mint, with a sheep on the obverse and the king's head on the reverse. He undertook to pay yearly, until the project was completed, sixteen hundred and sixty-nine thousand crowns, with the sum on the obverse, and as many again with the seven stars, the whole to be levied upon custom receipts.

For the foundation and maintenance of Thélème, he settled in perpetuity twenty-three hundred and sixty-nine thousand, five hundred and fourteen nobles (a coin stamped by the English kings with the rose of York), free of all tax, burden or fealty, payable yearly at the abbey gate. These privileges were all corroborated by letters patent.

The building was hexagonal; in each corner rose a great, circular tower, each identical, sixty yards in diameter. To the north, the river Loire flowed past the first tower which was named *Arctice* or Northern. East of it rose *Calaer* which means "situated in the balmy air"; then, successively, *Anatole* or Eastern; *Mesembrine* or Southern; *Hesperia* or Occidental; and the last, *Cryere* or Glacial. The distance between each tower was three hundred and twelve yards. The building was throughout six storeys high, counting the underground cellar for one. The ground floor was vaulted like a basket handle; the others, covered with Flanders mistletoe, jutting out like brackets and pendants. The roof, of finest slate, was lined with lead and bore little figures of mannikins and animals well assorted and gilt. The gutters jutted out from the walls between the casement arches; they were painted diagonally gold and blue down to the ground, where they ended in pipes which carried the water into the river below.

This building was a hundred times more magnificent than Bonnivet, Chambord or Chantilly.[7] There were nine thousand three hundred and thirty-two suites, each with a salon, a study, a dressing room, an oratory and an exit into a great hall. In the wing between each tower was a winding stairway. The steps, grouped in units of twelve between each landing, were of prophyry, of Numidian stone, of serpentine marble; they were twenty-two feet long and three fingers thick. At each landing, two splendid round antique archways admitted the light and led to an open loggia of the same dimensions. The stairway, rising to the roof, ended in a pavilion; on either side lay a great hall which in turn led to the apartments.

The wing between the towers called *Arctice* and *Cryere* contained rich libraries of Greek, Latin, Hebrew, French, Italian and Spanish volumes, grouped in their respective sections. In the centre rose a marvellous winding ramp conceived in such ample proportions that six soldiers with their lances at rest could ride up it abreast to the top of the palace. Its entry, outside the house, was an archway six fathoms wide.

Between *Anatole* and *Mesembrine* were spacious galleries with murals representing heroic feats of olden times, scenes from history and pictures of the earth. Here again were a stairway and gate as described upon the river side. On this gate, couched in great antique letters, ran the following legend.

---

7. Châteaux built in the early and middle years of the sixteenth century. By referring to actual buildings, building materials, and architectural elements, Rabelais as usual mixes realism with his fantasy.

## CHAPTER 54

*Inscription engraved on the main gate at Thélème.*

Here enter not, smug hypocrites or holy loons,
Bigots, sham-Abrahams, impostors of the cloth,
Mealy-mouthed humbugs, holier-than-thou baboons,
Lip-service lubbers, smell-feast picaroons.[8]
Else had we to admit the Goth and Ostrogoth
Precursors of the ape and others of that broth.
Hence, sneaks and mischief-makers, colporteurs of lies,
Be off to other parts to sell your merchandise.

        Being foul you would befoul
        Man, woman, beast or fowl.
        The vileness of your ways
        Would sully my sweet lays,
        Owls—And your own black cowl,
        Being foul, you would befoul.

Here enter not, defenders of dishonest pleas,
Clerks, barristers, attorneys who make freemen slaves,
Canon Law pettifoggers, censors, Pharisees,
Judges, assessors, arbitrators, referees
Who blithely doom good people to untimely graves,
The gibbet is your destination, legal knaves!
Be off: indict the rope if you should find it short,
Here there is no abuse; we do not need your court.

        Tangle, wrangle, brangle
        We loathe, from any angle.
        Our aim is joy and sport,
        Time's swift, youth's fleet, life's short.
        You, go and disentangle
        Tangle, wrangle, brangle!

Here enter not, curmudgeon, loan shark, muckworm, hunks,
Bloodsucking usurer, extortioner, pennystint, . . .
Hence, lawsuit-chasing crimps, greedy as starving punks
Tracking a patron; lickgolds, hiding cash in trunks,
Harpyclaws, crunchfists, jaundiced zealots of the mint,
Your crackling, sallow palms are itching. Skin a flint!
Heap up your hoard, O scrub-faced curs, heap up afresh,
And as you grudge and gripe and screw, God rot your flesh!

---

8. Various ways of saying "hypocritical bigots."

> Those grim and grisly faces
> Bear all the ravaged traces
> Of hidebound avarice;
> We cannot stomach this.
> Banish from all blithe places
> Those grim and grisly faces.

Here enter not, you churls, sour boors, invidious fools,
Old, jealous brabblers, scolds, neither by night nor day,
Nor grumblers, soreheads, sulkers, badgers bred in schools
Of hate; nor ghosts of malaperts; nor firebrands' ghouls
From Rhineland, Greece or Rome, fiercer than wolves at bay;
Nor you, riddled with pox, your face a Milky Way
Of scars not stars; nor you, clapstricken to the bone:
Enjoy your shameless crusts and blemishes alone.

> Honor, praise and pleasure
> Are here in goodly measure:
> Health reigns supreme because
> We follow Nature's laws.
> Ours is a triple treasure:
> Honor, praise and pleasure.

But enter here thrice welcome, men of goodly parts,
Gallants and noble gentlemen, thrice welcome be!
Here you will find an abbey after your own hearts,
Where living is esteemed the highest of the arts.
Come in your tens and hundreds, come in thousands, we
Shall clasp you to our bosoms in fond amity:
Come wise, come proud, come gay, come courteous, come mellow,
Come true sophisticate, come worldling, come, good fellow!

> Comrades, companions, friends,
> Assemble from the ends
> Of earth in this fair place
> Where all is mirth and grace.
> Felicity here blends
> Comrades, companions, friends.

Here enter, all ye loyal scholars who expound
Novel interpretations of the Holy Writ.
Here is a fort and refuge; from this favored ground
You may confound the error that is elsewhere found,
You may found a profound new faith instead of it,
Sweeping away false teachings, bit by fallacious bit.

Come unto us and make your cogent meanings heard:
Destroy the foes of God and of his Holy Word.

> The Holy Word of God
> Shall never be downtrod
> Here in this holy place,
> If all deem reason grace,
> And use for staff and rod
> The Holy Word of God.

Here enter, ladies fair of eminent degree,
Come soon with starry eyes, lips smiling, comely face,
Flowers of loveliness, angels of harmony,
Resplendent, proud yet of the rarest modesty,
Sprightly of flesh, lithe-waisted and compact of grace,
Here is your home. A gallant lord designed this place
For you, that beauty, charm and virtue might find room
Deliciously to breathe, exquisitely to bloom.

> Who makes a priceless gift
> Wins pardon without shrift.
> Donor, recipient
> Alike find rich content.
> To him your voices lift
> Who makes a priceless gift.

## CHAPTER 55

*How the monks and nuns lived at Thélème.*

In the middle of the lower court stood a magnificent alabaster
fountain, surmounted by the Three Graces holding cornucopias and
spouting water through their breasts, mouths, ears, eyes and other
orifices. The buildings above this court stood upon great pillars of
chalcedony and porphyry, forming classical arches about lengthy wide
galleries adorned with paintings and trophies of various animals: the
horns of bucks, unicorns and hippopotami, elephants' tusks and sundry other curiosities.

The ladies' quarters ran from *Arctice* all the way to the *Mesembrine* Gate; the rest of the abbey was reserved for men. In front of
this part, between the outer two towers, lay the recreational facilities:
the tilting yard, the riding school, the theatre and the natatorium
which included wonderful swimming pools on three different levels,
with every sort of equipment and myrtle water aplenty.

Near the river was the fine pleasure garden, with, in the middle,
a maze. Tennis courts and football fields spread out between the next
two towers. Close to *Cryere*, an orchard offered a mass of fruit trees

laid out in quincunxes, with, at its end, a sizy park abounding in venison.

The space between the third pair of towers was reserved for the shooting ranges: here were targets and butts for harquebuss, long bow and crossbow. The servants' quarters, one storey high, were situated outside *Hesperia*. Beyond was the falconry, managed by expert falconers and hawk trainers and annually supplied by the Cretans, Venetians and Sarmatian Poles with all manner of birds. There were priceless eagles for hunting hares, foxes and cranes. There were gerfalcons, goshawks, sakers for hunting wild geese, herons and bitterns. There were falcons, lanners, sparhawks and merlins for hunting larks and partridges. Other birds there were, too, in great quantities, so well trained that when they flew afield for their own sport they never failed to catch every bird they encountered. . . . The venery with its hounds and beagles stood a little further along towards the park.

All the halls, apartments and chambers were richly hung with tapestries varying with the season; the floors were covered with green cloth, the beds all embroidered. Each rear chamber boasted a pier-glass set in a heavy gold frame adorned with pearls. Near the exits of the ladies' halls were the perfumers and hairdressers who ministered to the gentlemen before the latter visited the ladies. These attendants furnished the ladies' rooms with rose water, orange-flower water and angelica, supplying a precious small atomizer to give forth the most exquisite aromatic perfumes.

CHAPTER 56

*How the monks and nuns of Thélème were apparelled.*

When first the abbey was founded, the ladies dressed according to their taste and pleasure. Subsequently of their own free will they modified their costume as follows.

They wore hose, of scarlet or kermes-red, reaching some three inches above the knee, the edge being exquisitely embroidered or slashed. Their garters, which matched their bracelets, came both a whit over and under the knee. Their shoes, pumps and slippers were of red, violet or crimson velvet and jagged as a lobster's claws.

Over their slips, they put on a tight tunic of pure silk camlet, and over that a taffeta farthingale or petticoat, red, white, beige, gray or of any other color. Above this farthingale went a skirt of silver taffeta, with fine gold embroidery and delicate cross-stitch work. According to the temperature, the season or the ladies' whim, these skirts might be satin, damask or velvet and, in color, orange, green, cendré, blue, canary yellow, scarlet, crimson or white, or of cloth-of-gold, cloth-of-silver, or any other choice material variously embroidered, stitched, brocaded or spangled according to the occasion for which they were worn.

Their gowns, or over-garments, were also governed by timely considerations. They might be cloth-of-gold with silver embossing or red satin with gold brocade or taffeta, white, blue, black or tawny. Or they might be silk rep, silk camlet, velvet, cloth-of-silver, cloth-of-gold or satin variously figured with gold and silver thread.

In summer, instead of these gowns, they wore lovely light smocks made of the same material, or capes, Moorish-fashion, with hoods to protect and shade their faces from the sun. These Moresco capes were of violet velvet, having raised gold stitching over silver purl or gold piping and cording, with small Indian pearls at their ends. And ever a gay colored plume, the color of their sleeves, bravely garnished with gold! In winter, their gowns were of taffeta in all the colors mentioned above, but lined with lynx, weasel, Calabrian marten, sable and other rare fur. Their beads, rings, chains and necklaces were of precious stones: carbuncles, rubies, balas rubies, diamonds, sapphires, emeralds, turquoises, garnets, agates, beryls and priceless pearls.

Their headgear also varied with the season. In winter, it was in the French fashion with a cap over the temples covered by a velvet hood with hanging veil. In spring it was in the Spanish, with laces and veils. In summer it was in the Tuscan, the hair elaborately entwined with gold chains and jewels. On Sundays and holidays, however, they followed the French mode which is more seemly and modest.

The men, too, dressed according to their personal taste. Their hose were of light wool or serge cloth, white, black, scarlet or kermes-red. Their velvet breeches were of the same hue or almost; they were embroidered or slashed to their taste. The doublet was of cloth-of-gold, cloth-of-silver, velvet, satin or damask, embroidered, panelled or slashed on one model, the points silk to match and the ornaments of fine enamelled gold.

Their cloaks and jerkins were of cloth-of-gold, cloth-of-silver, gold tissue or velvet, purfled or brocaded at pleasure; their over-garments were every whit as costly as the ladies'. Their girdles were silk, matching their doublets. Each wore on his side a handsome sword with gilt hilt and pommel; the scabbard velvet, matching his breeches, and the ferrule a wondrous example of the goldsmith's art. So too the dagger. Their caps were of black velvet, trimmed with jewels and rings and buttons of gold, with a white plume set in jauntily and parted by many rows of spangles from which hung splendent emeralds and various other stones.

Such was the sympathy between the gallants and their ladies that they matched one another's costumes every day. And in order to be sure of it, certain gentlemen were appointed to report every morning to the youths what garments their ladies planned to wear on that occasion. All here was done for the pleasure of the fair.

Handsome though the clothes were and rich the accoutrements, lads or girls wasted no time in dressing. The wardrobe masters had everything ready before their gentlemen arose and the maids were so nimble that in a trice their mistresses were apparelled from head to toe.

To facilitate matters, over a distance of half-a-league, a row of light, well-appointed cottages housed the goldsmiths, lapidaries, embroiderers, tailors, gold drawers, velvet weavers, tapestry makers and upholsterers. Here each worked at his trade, and all for the jolly friars and comely nuns of the new abbey. They received materials and stuffs from My Lord Nausiclete, famous for his ships, as the name indicates. Each year brought them seven vessels from the Pearl and Cannibal Islands or Antilles, laden with ingots of gold, raw silk, pearls and precious stones.

If pearls through age tended to lose their lustre, the jewellers, following the method of Avicenna, fed them to the roosters, and they regained their native sparkle.

CHAPTER 57

*How those of Thélème were governed in their manner of living.*

Their whole life was ordered not by law, statute or rule, but according to their free will and pleasure. They arose when they pleased. They ate, drank, worked and slept when the spirit moved them. No one awoke them, forced food or drink upon them or *made* them do anything else. Gargantua's plan called for perfect liberty. The only rule of the house was:

DO AS THOU WILT

because men that are free, of gentle birth, well-bred and at home in civilized company possess a natural instinct that inclines them to virtue and saves them from vice. This instinct they name their honor. Sometimes they may be depressed or enslaved by subjection or constraint; for we all long for forbidden fruit and covet what is denied us. But they usually apply the fine forces that tend to virtue in such a way as to shake off the yoke of servitude.

The Thélèmites, thanks to their liberty, knew the virtues of emulation. All wished to do what they saw pleased one of their number. Let some lad or maid say "Let us drink" and all of them drank, "Let us play" and all of them played, "Let us frolic in the fields" and all of them frolicked. When falconry or hawking were in order, the ladies sat high upon their saddles on fine nags, a sparhawk, lanner or merlin on one daintily gloved wrist, while the men bore other kinds of hawks.

They were so well-bred that none, man or woman, but could read, write, sing, play several instruments, speak five or six languages and readily compose verse and prose in any of them. Never had earth known knights so proud, so gallant, so adroit on horseback and on foot, so athletic, so lively, so well-trained in arms as these. Never were ladies seen so dainty, so comely, so winsome, so deft at hand-work and needlework, so skilful in feminine arts, so frank and so free as these.

Thus when the time came for a man to leave the abbey (either at his parents' request or for some other reason) he took with him one of the ladies—the particular one who had chosen him for her knight— and they were married. And though they had lived in devotion and friendship at Thélème, their marriage relations proved even more tender and agreeable. Indeed to the end of their lives they loved one another as they had on the day of their wedding. . . .

## Gargantua and Pantagruel, Book II

### [Pantagruel: Birth and Education]

#### CHAPTER 2

*Of the nativity of the most redoubtable Pantagruel.*

At the age of four hundred fourscore and forty-four years, Gargantua begat his son Pantagruel upon his wife named Badebec, daughter to the king of the dimly-seen Amaurotes in Utopia.[9] She died in the throes of childbirth. Alas! Pantagruel was so extraordinarily large and heavy that he could not possibly come to light without suffocating his mother.

If you would fully understand how he came to be christened Pantagruel, you must remember that a terrible drought raged that year throughout the land of Africa. For thirty-six months, three weeks, four days, thirteen hours and even longer, there was no drop of rain. And the sun blazed so fiercely that the whole earth was parched.

Even in the days of Elijah, the soil was no drier, for now no tree on earth bore leaf or flower. The grass had no verdure; rivers and springs ran dry; the luckless fishes, abandoned by their element, crawled on solid earth, crying and screaming most horribly. Birds fell from the air for want of moisture; wolves, foxes, harts, wild boars,

---

9. Names taken from Sir Thomas More's *Utopia*. Literally, "no place," the word *Utopia* has become synonymous with "ideal country."

fallow deer, hares, rabbits, weasels, martens, badgers and other beasts
were found dead in the fields, their mouths agape.

As for the men, their state was very piteous. You should have seen
them with their tongues dangling like a hound's after a run of six
hours. Not a few threw themselves into the wells. Others lay under
a cow's belly to enjoy the shade—these it is whom Homer calls *Alibantes*, the desiccated.[1] The whole country was at a standstill. The
strenuous efforts of mortals against the vehemence of this drought
was a horrible spectacle. It was hard enough, God knows, to save the
holy water in the churches from being wasted; but My Lords the
Cardinals and our Holy Father laid down such strict rules that no
man dared take more than a lick of it. In the churches, scores of
parched, unhappy wretches followed the priest who distributed it,
their jaws yawning for one tiny driblet. Like the rich man in *Luke*,
who cried for Lazarus to dip his fingers in water, they were tormented by a flame,[2] and would not suffer the slightest drop to be
wasted. Ah! thrice happy that year the man who had a cool, well-
plenished wine cellar underground!

In discussing the question: "Why is sea water salty?" the philosopher Aristotle, after Empedocles, supplies the following reason. When
Phoebus gave the reins of his luminous chariot[3] to Phaéton, his son,
the latter, unskilled in the art of driving, was incapable of following
the ecliptic lines between the two tropics of the sun's sphere. Accordingly, he strayed from the appointed path and came so close to earth
that he dried up all the countries under his course. He also burnished that great portion of heaven which philosophers call V*ia Lac-
tea* or the Milky Way, and good drinkers St. James' Way, since it is
the starry line that guides pilgrims to Santiago de Compostella. (On
the other hand, poets declare that it is here Juno's milk dropped
while she was suckling Hercules.)

Earth at that time was so excessively heated that it broke into an
enormous sweat which ran over the sea, making the latter salty, since
all sweat is salt. If you do not admit this last statement, then taste of
your own sweat. Or savor the perspiration of your pox-stricken friends
when they are put in sweatboxes for treatment. It is all one to me.

Practically the same thing happened the year I am speaking of.
On a certain Friday, all the people were intent upon their devotions.
A noble procession was in progress with plenty of litanies and fine
preachings. Supplications arose toward Almighty God beseeching
Him to cast His eye of mercy upon them in their affliction. Suddenly

1. The allusion to Homer is apparently mistaken, but "Alibantes"—possibly derived from the
name of Alibas, a dry river in hell—is used by other ancient writers with reference to the dead or
the very old.    2. "And he cried and said, Father Abraham, have mercy on me, and send Lazarus, that he may dip the tip of his finger in water, and cool my tongue; for I am tormented in
this flame." (Luke 16:24.)    3. The chariot of the sun.

they clearly saw some great drops of water stand out upon the ground, exactly as from a person sweating copiously.

The wretched populace began to rejoice as though here were a great blessing. Some declared that, since the air lacked all moisture, earth was supplying the deficiency. Other scientists asseverated that it was a shower of the Antipodes, as described by Seneca in *Quaestiones Naturales*, Book IV, where he treats of the Nile's source, attributing its floods to distant rains washed underground into the river. But they were thoroughly deceived. For, the procession done, when each sought to gather up this dew and drink it up by the bowlful, they found it was only pickle, far saltier than the saltiest water of the sea.

Another great mishap befell Gargantua that week. A dungchafing lout, bearing two great bags of salt and a hambone in his game-pouch, walked into poor Gargantua's mouth as the giant lay snoring. The clod spilled a quantity of salt in Gargantua's throat. Gargantua, crazy with a thirst he could not slake, angrily snapped his mouth shut. He gnashed his teeth fiercely; they ground like millstones. Later the rascal told me he was so terrified you could have stopped up his nose with a bale of hay. He fell flat on his face like a dead man, dropping the two saltbags that had tormented Gargantua. They were at once swallowed up and entombed.

My rogue vowed vengeance. Thrusting his hand in his game-pouch, he drew out a great hambone, highly salted, still covered with hair, and twenty-eight inches long. Ragefully he rammed it down Gargantua's throat. The giant, drier than ever, felt the pig's hair tickling his belly and, willy-nilly, spewed up all he had. Eighteen tumbrils could not have drawn away the rich nauseous yield. My dungchafer, hidden in the cavity of one of his teeth, was forced to take French leave in such pitiful condition that all who saw him were horrified. Gargantua, looking down, noticed this jackpudding whirling about in a great puddle.

"Here is some worm that sought to sting me in the belly," he mused, happy to have expelled him from his body.

Because he was born that very day, his father called him Pantagruel or All-Athirst, a name derived from the Greek *panta* meaning all, and the Hagarene or Saracen *gruel* meaning athirst. Gargantua inferred thereby that at his son's birth the entire universe was wholly parched. Prophetically, too, he realized that some day Pantagruel would become Supreme Lord of the Thirsty, a fact indicated even more surely by a further portent.

For while his mother Badebec was bringing him forth and the midwives stood by ready to receive him, there first issued from her belly seventy-eight salt-vendors, each leading a salt-laden mule by the halter. They were followed by nine dromedaries, bearing hams and smoked oxtongues; seven camels bearing chitterlings; twenty-five cartloads of leeks, garlic, onions and chives. This terrified some mid-wives, but others said:

"Here is good provision! As it is, we drink but lazily, instead of vigorously. This must be a good omen, since these victuals are spurs to bibbing wine!"

As they were tattling away, out pops Pantagruel, hairy as a bear! At which, prophetically, one of them exclaimed:

"God help us, he is born hair and all, straight from the arse of Satan in flight. He will do terrible wonders. If he lives, he will grow to a lusty age!"

Of Pantagruel's race are those who drink so heavily in the evening that they must rise at night to drink again, quenching the coals of fire and blistering thirst in their throats. This form of thirst is called Pantagruel, in memory of the giant.

## [Father's Letter from Home]
### CHAPTER 8

*How Pantagruel in Paris received a letter from his father Gargan-*
*tua.*

As you may suppose, Pantagruel studied very hard and profited much by his study, for his intelligence was naturally active and his memory as full as twelve casks of olives. While in Paris,[4] he received the following letter from his father:

MY BELOVED SON,

Among the gifts, graces and prerogatives with which our sovereign Creator, God Almighty, blessed and enriched humanity from the beginning, there is one that I deem supreme. By its means, though we be mortal, we can yet achieve a sort of immortality; through it, we may, in the course of our transitory lives, yet perpetuate our name and race.

To be sure, what we gain by a progeny born of lawful wedlock cannot make up for what we lost through the sin of our first parents. Adam and Eve disobeyed the commandments of the Lord their God: mortality was their punishment. By death the magnificent mould in which Man was fashioned vanished into the dust of oblivion.

However, thanks to seminal propagation, what a man loses his children revive and, where they fail, their children prevail. So it has gone, and so it shall be, from generation to generation, until the

---

4. Like his father before him, Pantagruel has been sent to Paris to study. The following letter, patterned after Ciceronian models of eloquence, summarizes Rabelais' view of an ideal education, and generally illustrates the attitude of the Renaissance intellectual elite toward culture.

Day of Judgment, when Christ shall restore to God the Father His kingdom pacified, secured and cleansed of all sin. Then all generations and corruption shall cease, for the elements will have completed their continuous transmutations. The peace humanity has craved so anxiously will have been attained; all things will have been reduced to their appointed end and period.

I therefore have reason to give thanks to God, my Saviour, for having granted me the joy of beholding my old age blossom anew in your youth. When, by His pleasure, which rules and orders everything, my soul must abandon this human habitation, I shall not believe I am dying utterly, but rather passing from one place to another. For in you my visible image will continue to live on earth; by you, I shall go on frequenting honorable men and true friends, as I was wont to do.

My associations have not been without sin, I confess. We all transgress and must continually beseech God to forgive us our trespasses. But they have been without reproach in the eyes of men.

That is why if, beside my bodily image, my soul did not likewise shine in you, you would not be accounted worthy of guarding the precious immortality of my name. In that case, the least part of me (my body) would endure. Scant satisfaction, that, when the best part (my soul, which should keep my name blessed among men) had degenerated and been bastardized. I say this not through any doubt as to your virtue, which I have already often tested, but to encourage you to go on doing ever better and profiting by your constant improvement.

My purpose is not so much to keep you absolutely on your present virtuous course as to make you rejoice that you have kept and are keeping on it. I seek to quicken your heart with resolutions for the future. To help you make and carry these out, remember that I have spared nothing. I have helped you as though my sole treasure on earth were once in my lifetime to see you well-bred and accomplished in honesty and valor as well as in knowledge and civility. Ay, I have longed to leave you after my death as a mirror of your father's personality. The reflection may not prove perfect in practice, but certainly I could not more studiously wish for its perfection.

My late father Grangousier, of blessed memory, made every effort that I might achieve mental, moral and technical excellence. The fruit of my studies and labors matched, indeed surpassed, his dearest wish. But you can realize that conditions were not as favorable to learning as they are to-day. Nor had I such gifted teachers as you. We were still in the dark ages; we still walked in the shadow of the dark clouds of ignorance; we suffered the calamitous consequences of the destruction of good literature by the Goths. Now, by God's grace, light and dignity have been restored to letters, and I have lived to see it. Indeed, I have watched such a revolution in learning that I, not erroneously reputed in my manhood the leading scholar of the century, would find it difficult to enter the bottom class in a grammar school.

I tell you all this not through boastfulness, though in writing to you I might be proud with impunity. Does not Marcus Tullius[5] authorize it in his book *Of Old Age*, and Plutarch in *How a Man May Praise Himself without Envy*? Both authors recognize that such pride is useful in fostering the spirit of emulation. No—I do it simply to give you a proof of my love and affection.

To-day, the old sciences are revived, knowledge is systematized, discipline reëstablished. The learned languages are restored: Greek, without which a man would be ashamed to consider himself educated; Hebrew, Chaldean and Latin.[6] Printing is now in use, an art so accurate, and elegant that it betrays the divine inspiration of its discovery,[7] which I have lived to witness. Alas! Conversely, I was not spared the horror of such diabolic works as gunpowder[8] and artillery.

To-day, the world is full of learned men, brilliant teachers and vast libraries: I do not believe that the ages of Plato, Cicero or Papinian[9] afforded such facilities for culture. From now on, it is unthinkable to come before the public or move in polite circles without having worshipped at Minerva's shrine. Why, the robbers, hangmen, adventurers and jockeys of to-day are infinitely better educated than the doctors and preachers of my time. More, even women and girls aspire to the glory, the heavenly manna of learning. Thus, at my advanced age, I have been forced to take up Greek. Not that I had despised it, like Cato;[1] I never had the opportunity to learn it. Now I delight in reading Plutarch's *Morals*, Plato's noble *Dialogues*, the *Monuments* of Pausanias and the *Antiquities* of Athenæus,[2] as I await the hour when it shall please God, my Creator, to call me back to His bosom.

That is why, my dear son, I urge you to spend your youth making the most of your studies and developing your moral sense. You are in Paris, which abounds in noble men upon whom to pattern yourself; you have Epistemon, an admirable tutor, who can inspire you by direct oral teaching. But I demand more of you. I insist you learn languages perfectly! Greek first, as old Quintilian prescribes;[3] then Latin; then Hebrew for the sake of the Holy Scripture; then Chaldee

5. Cicero.    6. The languages which are the instruments of classical learning are listed along with those useful for the study of the Old Testament.    7. Printing from movable type was independently invented in Europe about the middle of the fifteenth century; the idea of its divine origin was commonplace during the Renaissance.    8. Probably introduced into Europe through the Arabs, rather than invented, in the fourteenth century.    9. Jurisconsult of the time of Emperor Septimius Severus (reigned A.D. 193–211).    1. Plutarch's life of Cato is the source of the notion that he despised Greek.    2. The works of Pausanias and Athenaeus were standard sources of information on ancient geography, art, and everyday life.    3. In his *Institutio oratoria*, Book I, Chapter 1, paragraph 12, he recommends studying Greek before Latin.

and Arabic, too. Model your Greek style on Plato, your Latin on Cicero. Let no history slip your memory; cultivate cosmography, for you will find its texts helpful.

As for the liberal arts of geometry, arithmetic and music, I gave you a taste of them when you were a little lad of five or six. Proceed further in them yourself, learning as much as you can. Be sure to master all the rules of astronomy; but dismiss astrology and the divinatory art of Lullius[4] as but vanity and imposture. Of civil law, I would have you know the texts of the Code by heart, then compare them with philosophy.

A knowledge of nature is indispensable; devote yourself to this study with unflagging curiosity. Let there be no sea, river or fountain but you know the fish that dwell in it. Be familiar with all the shrubs, bushes and trees in forest or orchard, all the plants, herbs and flowers that grow on the ground, all the birds of the air, all the metals in the bowels of earth, all the precious stones in the orient and the south. In a word, be well informed in everything that concerns the physical world we live in.

Then carefully consult the works of Greek, Arabian and Latin physicians, without slighting the Jewish doctors, Talmudists and Cabbalists. By frequent exercises in dissection, acquire a perfect knowledge of that other world, which is man.

Devote a few hours a day to the study of Holy Writ. Take up the New Testament and the Epistles in Greek; then, the Old Testament in Hebrew. Strive to make your mind an inexhaustible storehouse of knowledge. For you are growing to manhood now: soon you will have to give up your studious repose to lead a life of action. You will have to learn to bear arms, to achieve knighthood, so as to defend my house and help our allies frustrate the attacks of evildoers.

Further, I wish you soon to test what profit you have gained from your education. This you can best do by public discussion and debate on all subjects against all comers, and by frequenting learned men both in Paris and elsewhere.

But remember this. As Solomon says, wisdom entereth not into a malicious soul, and science without conscience spells but destruction of the spirit. Therefore serve, love and fear God, on Him pin all your thoughts and hopes; by faith built of charity, cling to Him so closely that never a sin come between you. Hold the abuses of the world in just suspicion. Set not your heart upon vanity, for this life is a transitory thing, but the Word of God endureth forever. Be serviceable to your neighbor, love him as you do yourself. Honor your teachers. Shun the company of all men you would not wish to resemble; receive not in vain the favors God has bestowed upon you.

4. Raymond Lully, Spanish philosopher of the thirteenth century, who dabbled in magic.

When you realize that you have acquired all the knowledge Paris has to offer, come back so I may see you and give you my blessing before I die.

My son, the peace and grace of Our Lord be with you. Amen.

Your father,<br>GARGANTUA

From Utopia, the seventeenth day of September.

Having read this letter, Pantagruel, greatly encouraged, strove more ardently than ever to profit in his work. Had you seen him studying vigorously, practically and tirelessly, you would have compared his spirit moving among his books to flames blazing through a bonfire of dry branches.

CHAPTER 16

*Of the character and condition of Panurge.*[5]

Panurge was then about thirty-five years old and as fine to gild as a dagger of lead. Of medium height, neither too tall nor too short, he had an aquiline nose, shaped like the handle of a razor. He cut a very gallant figure though he was a trifle lewd by nature, and subject to a disease at that time called impecunitis, an incomparable malady.

Yet when he needed money, he knew thirty-three methods of acquiring it, the most ordinary and honorable of which was filching. He was a quarrelsome fellow, a sharper, a toper, a roisterer and a profligate, if ever there was one in the city of Paris. In every other respect, he was the best fellow in the world.

He was constantly plotting against the sergeants and the watch. Sometimes he assembled three or four sportsmen, plied them with drink until they were boozy as Knights Templars,[6] then took them up the hill to Ste. Geneviève or near the Collège de Navarre. Placing his sword on the pavement and his ear to his sword, he waited till he heard the blade shake—an infallible sign that the watch was not far off. Then he and his companions took a dung cart and rolled it down hill. Ere it was halfway down, they had fled in the opposite direction, for in less than two days Panurge knew every street and alley in Paris as well as his postprandial grace: *Deus det nobis pacem suam,* God grant us His peace.

Another time he laid down a train of gunpowder where the watch

<hr>

5. Panurge (*Pan-ourgos* in Greek, the "all-doer") is the major character in *Gargantua and Pantagruel* except for the heroes themselves: a magnification of the perennial-student type, Panurge is an imaginative and scandalous pauper, erudite and bawdy, a lover of outrageous pranks. On first meeting Pantagruel he addressed him in thirteen different languages, a couple of them invented, before discovering that they both spoke French. He has since become a permanent fixture of the young lord's retinue.    6. A medieval religious and medical order, suppressed in 1312. The original *templiers,* not capitalized, suggests a current proverbial expression.

was due to pass. Just as the troop debouched, he set fire to it, vastly delighted in observing how gracefully they took to their heels, in mortal terror that St. Anthony's fire had caught them by the legs.

The luckless Masters of Arts and theologians he persecuted more than any other class of men. When he met one, he never failed to do him some harm, either slipping a turd into his hood or pinning little foxtails or hares' ears to his back.

One day when all the theologians had been summoned to the Sorbonne to examine the articles of the faith, he made a tart of garlic, asafoetida, galbanum, castoreum[7] and steaming excrement, which he steeped and tempered in the corrupt manner of chancres and pockbiles. Very early in the morning he so theologically greased and anointed the lattices and grates of the trellised gallery of the Hall of Records that not even the devil himself had dared stay there. The worthy pedagogues pewked in public as abundantly as though they had flayed the fox. Ten or twelve died of the plague, fourteen contracted leprosy, eight came down with pestiferous ulcers, and more than twenty-eight caught the pox. But Panurge was jubilant.

Usually he carried a whip under his gown with which he mercilessly belabored such pages as he met bearing wine for their masters, in order to speed them on their way.

In his coat he had more than twenty-six little pockets and pouches which were always full. One held a pair of loaded dice and a small knife like a glover's awl to cut purses with. Another, verjuice to throw in the eyes of those who annoyed him. A third, burrs, penned with gosling or capon feathers, to stick on to the robes and bonnets of honest people. He often gave married men a fine pair of horns which they bore through the city sometimes all their lives long. To the back of the women's hoods, he liked to affix various knicknacks shaped like the sexual organ of man.

Another pocket held a lot of little packages filled with fleas and lice which he recruited from the tramps of St. Innocent's graveyard and cast with small sticks or quills down the backs of the smartest gentlewomen he could find. He did this even in church, for he never sat up in the choir, preferring to stand in the nave among the women during mass, vespers or sermon. Another pocket held a large supply of bent nails with which he would couple men and women together where they sat. This was particularly amusing when the victims wore gowns of costly sarsenet taffeta, because they ripped them to shreds as they sought to separate. Still another pocket held a squib with tinder, flints, matches, vesuvians, sulphur and other combustibles. Another, two or three burning-glasses with which he tortured and disconcerted men and women at church. For he said there was only

7. Asafoetida and galbanum are resins extracted from Persian plants; castoreum is a substance obtained from the inguinal region of the beaver; all three produce nauseous smells.

an antistrophe between *femme folle à la messe* and *molle à la fesse* or working a cunning stunt and a stunning cunt. Another pouch held needles, threads and pins for all manner of minor deviltries.

Once at the door of the Great Hall in the Palais de Justice, Panurge saw a Cordelier father getting ready to say mass before the proceedings of the day. Immediately he ran up to help the holy man don his vestments and, in the process, managed to sew his alb to his robe and shirt. Then, as the magistrates arrived for mass, Panurge withdrew. Mass done, as he reached the formula *Ite, missa est*, the wretched friar tried to take off his alb. But, at the same time, off came the robe and shirt solidly sewn to it. Our Cordelier, thus stripped to the shoulders, revealed his dangledingus to all the world—and it was no small crosier, as you may imagine. The harder he tugged, the more he exposed himself. So much so, indeed, that one of the counsellors cried:

"What is the matter? Is this good friar making an offering of his tail for us to kiss? No, by heaven, let St. Anthony's fire kiss it for us!"

From then on, an ordinance forbade the poor good fathers to disrobe before the world, the vestry-room being indicated as the only fit place for this. They were especially warned against doing so in the presence of women, lest it tempt the latter to sin through longing. When people wondered why the fathers were genitally so well-equipped, Panurge solved the problem.

"What makes the ears of asses so long?" he asked, and answering his own question: "Their dams put no caps on their ears. Alliacus,[8] Chancellor of the University and Chaplain to Charles VI, proves this in his *Suppositiones*. Similarly, what makes the whangle-tools of our holy fathers hang so low? Well, they never wear dark breeches, so their lusty organs, dangling down at liberty like a horse given head, knock against their knees like women's beads. Why are they correspondingly large? Because, with all this waggling to and fro, the humors of the body sink down into these parts. Do not the legists point out that continual agitation and continual motion are the cause of attraction?"

Another of Panurge's pouches held stone-alum, an itching-powder which he poured down the backs of those he considered the proudest and most stately ladies. Some would at once strip off their clothes then and there before the public . . . others danced like cats on hot coals or a drumstick on a tabor . . . others again rushed madly into the street and he at their heels. . . . Those inclined to disrobe, he assisted by sheltering them under his cape, as any courteous and gallant gentleman would have done.

In another pocket he had a small leather bottle full of old oil. If

8. Latinized name of Pierre d'Ailly (1350–1425).

he saw a man or woman in a handsome costume, he would grease
and stain it in the most conspicuous places. His technique here was
an art. Pretending to admire the material, he would finger it.

"Rare cloth, this, sir," or "Fine satin, upon my word!" or "Oh,
what lovely taffeta, Madame!" he would exclaim. "God give you all
your noble heart desires. You have a new suit, My Lord! And you a
new dress, My Lady. Well, you know the saying: New clothes, new
friends. God give you joy in them!"

As he spoke, his hands passed lightly over the shoulders and a long
ugly smear remained.

> So indelible a spot
> Stamped on body, soul and fame
> That the devil could not blot
> Out its testament of shame.

As he took his leave of the ladies, he would say:

"Madame, take care not to fall. You've a huge filthy hole out of
sight in front of you, there!"

In another pocket he kept euphorbium, very finely pulverized and
spread over a dainty handkerchief he had stolen from a pretty sales-
girl in the Galleries of the Sainte-Chapelle,[9] hard by the law courts
and frequented by the gallants of the day. (He filched it while removing from between her breasts a louse he had dropped there.)

When he happened to be in gentle company, he would steer the
conversation on to the subject of lace and lingerie. Then, thrusting
his hands into some lady's bosom:

"Glorious work, this. Is it Flanders or Hainault?"

Then, drawing his handkerchief:

"Just look at this kerchief, Madame. Would you say it was Fron-
tignan or Fontarabia?"

Shaking it hard under her nose, he would make her sneeze for
hours at a time. Then he would fart like a dray horse.

"Tut, tut," the lady would say. "Are you whiffling, Panurge?"

"No, Madame," he would reply gallantly, "I am merely tuning
my tail to the plain song you make with your nose."

Panurge was never without pincers, a picklock, a pelican, a jimmy,
a crook or other tools against which no chest or door could avail.
Finally, in another pocket he kept a whole battery of small goblets
which he worked with amazing skill, for his fingers were nimble and
adroit as those of Minerva or Arachne.[1] He had indeed once been
an itinerant quack, barking antidotes for poison. When he presented
a sum of money and asked for change, the changer had to be spry as

9. A shopping center in old Paris.   1. In Greek mythology the goddess Athena, being enraged
at the Lydian maid Arachne's irreverence and weaving skill, transformed her into a spider.

Argus[2] to catch Panurge spiriting away five, six or seven coins at a time, visibly, openly, manifestly, without lesion or hurt, whilst all the changer noticed was a slight draught.

CHAPTER 21

*How Panurge fell in love with a Parisienne of high degree.*

As a result of his debate with the English scholar,[3] Panurge had acquired quite a reputation in Paris. The activity of his codpiece was proportionally greater, and, to that effect, he had it pinked and slashed with ornate embroidery, after the Roman fashion. His praises became a topic of general conversation. There was even a song written to celebrate his exploits; the little children sang it as they went to fetch mustard. Best of all, he was made welcome in the most elegant circles. But it went to his head; he actually had the presumption to beleaguer one of the great ladies of the city.

Scorning the rigmarole of prefaces and preliminaries dear to such languishing, dreamy lovers as never touch meat in Lent, Panurge popped the question outright.

"Madame," he told this lofty lady, "it would prove beneficent to the commonwealth, pleasurable to your person, honorable to your progeny and necessary to me that I cover you for the propagation of my race. You may take my word for this, Madame; experience will prove it to you conclusively."

The lady, indignant, thrust him a thousand leagues away.

"You crazy knave, how dare you talk like that? Who do you think I am? Get out of here at once and never let me lay eyes upon you again. For two pins, I'd have your arms and legs sawed off!"

"Madame," he protested, "I would not care two pins if my arms and legs were sawed off, providing you and I had first fought a merry bout of spermary-snuggery. For," he showed her his long cod-piece, "here is Master Johnny Inigo, a master instrumentalist who begs to fiddle and thrum, sweep the *viola d'amore*, play the manichord, tweedle the gittern, strike the lyre, beat the drum, wind the horn and grind the organ until you feel his music throbbing in the marrow of your bones. A wily gallant, Master Johnny: he will not fail to find all the cranks, winches, wedges, pullies, nippers, clutches, teeth, springs and rigging stored in your delicate cockpit. You'll be needing no scouring or brushing up after *him*."

"Go to, scoundrel, and away! One more word out of you and I'll shout for help; I'll have my servants beat you to death."

"No, Madame," Panurge protested. "You are not as cruel as you

2. The Greek mythological figure with a hundred eyes.    3. Thaumastes, who in the previous chapters has long argued with Panurge, using both words and signs, and has been "nonplussed" by the latter's knowledge.

pretend. You cannot be or else your face is a living lie. Let earth soar upward into the firmament, let high heaven sink into the bottomless pit, let the whole concert of nature be annihilated ere your beauty and grace secrete one drop of gall or malice. They say that it is virtually impossible for man:

> To find in women beauty unallied
> With arrogance or cruelty or pride

but that holds only for vulgar beauties. Your own is so priceless, so unique, so heavenly that I vow Nature has bestowed it on you as a paragon to prove what she can do when she cares to muster all her power and science. Everything in you is honey, sugar, celestial manna. To you Paris should have awarded the golden apple, not to Venus or Juno or Minerva. For Juno possessed no such nobility, Minerva no such wisdom, Venus no such comeliness.

"O ye heavenly gods and goddesses! how happy the man whom you allow to kiss and fondle you, to cosset, nuzzle and cockle you, to thrust his prolific engine of pleasure into the pod of your quivering quim. By God, I am that man, I plainly feel it. Already she loves me her bellyful I swear; ay, Panurge is predestined to it by the nixies and fairies. Let us lose no time: come, slap-dash, helter-skelter, holus-bolus, to horse and fair riding, tantivy, hoicks!"

Whereupon he sought to embrace her; but she moved towards the window as if to call for help, so Panurge made off hastily. Yet ere retreating:

"Madame," he said, "wait for me here; I'll call your friends, don't bother!"

And he withdrew, unfeased and no less cheerful despite the rebuff.

Next day, as she arrived at church, Panurge stood waiting at the door, offered her holy water, bowed deep as she passed, then kneeled familiarly beside her:

"Madame," he declared, "you must know how madly in love with you I am. Why, I can neither piddle nor cack for love of you! I don't know how *you* feel, but, Madame, suppose I took ill from it, wouldn't you be responsible?"

"Go away, I don't care anything about it. Leave me alone to my prayers."

"One moment!" Panurge begged. "Please equivocate on '*à Beaumont le Viconte?*' or on 'Runt and Codger are fellow-muckers!' "

"I don't know what you mean!"

"Quite easy! '*A beau con le vit monte,*' 'Cunt and Rodger are mellow fuckers!' Now, pray to God that He grant whatever your noble heart desires. And oh, Madame, I beg you: give me those beads a moment."

"Here you are, stop bothering me."

She was about to take off her rosary—it was of cestrin wood with gold ornamentation—when Panurge promptly drew one of his knives and neatly cut it. Before carrying it off to pawn:

"Would you like my knife?" he asked.

"No, certainly not!"

"It's yours to grind or sheathe, Madame, body and soul, bag and baggage, tripe and guts."

But the lady was worried over the loss of her beads, so many implements to help her keep her countenance in church:

"This chattering scoundrel must be some eccentric foreigner," she mused. "He will never return my rosary. What will my dear husband say? He'll be furious! But I'll tell him a sneak thief cut it off me at church. He must believe me: I've still the end fastened on my girdle."

After dinner, Panurge went to call on her with, in his sleeve, a purse full of tokens specially struck for use in the law courts.

"Which of us is the better lover, Madame, you or I?"

"For my part I cannot hate you," she said magnanimously. "God commands us to love our neighbors."

"Aren't you in love with me?"

"I've told you repeatedly not to talk to me like that!" she insisted. "If you mention it again, I'll show you I'm not to be trifled with. Go away, I tell you. But give me back my rosary; my husband might ask me for it."

"Give you back your rosary? No, by heaven, I shall do nothing of the sort. But I'll tell you what I *will* do: I'll gladly give you another. Would you like one in beautifully enamelled gold with beads shaped like great pendulous knockers? Or like loveknots or ingots, heavy in the hand? Or ebony or broad zircons or square-cut garnets with mountings of rare turquoises, or costly topazes or priceless sapphires or precious rubies set with glittering diamonds of twenty-eight facets? No, no, that is a trumpery gift. I know of a marvellous rosary: it's made of exquisite emeralds with a mounting of speckled gray amber; at the buckle there's a Persian pearl fat as an orange . . . and the bauble costs but a paltry five-and-twenty thousand ducats. I will make you a present of it; I've heaps of cash!"

He made his tokens ring as though they were genuine, authentic golden crowns with the shining sun of France stamped upon them.

"Do you fancy a piece of violet or crimson velure, dyed in grain, or a piece of scarlet or brocaded satin? Is it your pleasure to accept chains, brooches, tiaras or rings? You have but to say the word: fifty thousand is a trifle!"

His offer made her mouth water. Yet she stood her ground.

"No, thank you, I want nothing to do with you."

"By God, I certainly want to do something with *you!* What I want will cost you nothing; you'll be out nothing when you've given it. Look, Madame," and he showed her his long codpiece. "Here is Master Johnny Scramblecunney who craves lodging."

He was about to strike root there, when she started to cry out, though none too loud. The mask of courtesy fell from Panurge's face.

"So you won't let me have a little harmless fun, eh? Not even a morsel for me, eh? A bucket of turds to you! you don't deserve the honor or pleasure of it. But by God! I'll make the dogs ride you!"

With which he beat a hasty retreat in dread of blows. (He was by nature fearful of them.)

CHAPTER 22

*How Panurge played a none too pleasant trick on the Parisienne of high degree.*

Next day was Corpus Christi, a feast on which the ladies of Paris put on their stateliest apparel. Panurge's charmer was decked out in a rich gown of crimson velvet, with a skirt of costly white velure.

The day before, Panurge scoured the town for a bitch in heat. Having found one, he tied his belt around her neck and took her home. All that day and through the night, he fed her abundantly; in the morning he killed her, plucked out that part the Greek geomancians[4] know, cut it as fine as he could, tucked it away in one of his innumerable pockets and went to the church. He was sure his lady would soon arrive to take part in the procession always held on that day.

When she entered, Panurge bowed courteously, offered her some holy water and, shortly after she had finished her petty devotions, sat down on the bench beside her. As she looked up, he passed her a paper on which he had written the following rondeau:

> Sweet lady, once, once only I expressed
> My admiration; you denied my quest,
> You drove me irremediably away
> Although I never harmed you (welladay!)
> In act or word or libel or the rest. . . .
> Granted my wooing stirred no answering zest,
> You could have been more honest, and confessed:
> "I do not wish it, friend. Leave me, I pray!"
>     Sweet lady, once,
> Once more and never again I shall protest
> Ere love's flame utterly consume my breast,

4. A species of magicians.

One boon alone I languish for: to lay
My peacock, shoveller, cockerel, popinjay
Deep in the shelter of your downy nest.
    Sweet lady, once!

While she was unfolding the paper to see what was inside, Panurge deftly sprinkled his drug all over her, spilling it impartially in the folds of her sleeves and skirt.

"Madame," he said before taking his leave, "a lover's life is not always a bed of roses. In my case I can only hope the anguished nights, the sorrows and tribulation I undergo for love of you will be deducted from my trials in purgatory. At least pray God He give me patience to bear my affliction."

Panurge had scarcely spoken when all the dogs in the church, attracted by the odor of the drug, scurried over to the lady. Big and little, large and small, one and all came up, sniffed, raised their legs, cocked their members and let fly on her dress. It was the most horrible sight imaginable.

Panurge pretended to chase them off, then bowed and retired to watch the sport from the vantage point of a chapel. Those wretched curs were squirting all over her clothes. One huge greyhound placed a paw on her shoulder to aim at her head . . . other dogs pumped in her sleeves . . . still others drenched her backside, while the puppies piddled in her shoes. . . . The women close to her sought to keep the beasts off, but with scant success. Meanwhile, holding his sides, Panurge, between guffaws of laughter, told certain lords who were next to him:

"I think that lady's in heat. Or some wolfhound covered her recently."

Seeing the dogs crowded as thick about her as about a bitch in heat, he ran off to fetch Pantagruel. On the way, he stopped to kick every dog he met, crying:

"To church with you! To your genuflexions! Follow the odor of sanctity! Be off and join your fellows at the urinarian baptism! Forward, by all the devils, be off, devil take you!"

"Master," he said breathlessly to Pantagruel, "please come and see all the dogs of the country gathered about the loveliest lady in town, and every one of them agog to scrounge her!"

Pantagruel, delighted at the novelty of it, accompanied Panurge back to church and enjoyed the fun immensely. By the time the procession began, matters had reached a crisis. There were more than six hundred thousand and fourteen dogs thronging about her and finding one thousand and one means of harassing her. Whichever way she turned, the newcomers followed the scent, dogged her heels and flooded whatever spot her dress touched. The only course

left her was to go home. As she fled through the streets, every one
stopped to watch the dogs leaping high as her neck, turning her
elegant toilette into a very toilet, as she ran on, helpless and steaming. It was impossible to give them the slip, the trail was too pungent. So they followed her to her residence.

While she hid in her room and her chambermaids burst into
laughter behind politely raised aprons, all the dogs within a radius of
a half-league came rushing up and showered so hard against the gate
as to form a stream in which ducks might very well have swum. Today this same current, now called the creek of Bièvre, flows through
the grounds of the Abbey of St. Victor and past the Gobelin dye-
works.[5] Materials steeped in its waters turn a rare scarlet thanks to
some special virtue of these pissdogs, as our learned Master Doribus
recently pointed out in a brilliant sermon. God help us, a mill could
have ground corn there, though not so much as the famous Bazacle
in Toulouse on the Garonne.

---

# MICHEL DE MONTAIGNE
## 1533–1592

Like his fellow Frenchman Rabelais, though in a different context and manner, Michel Eyquem de Montaigne was representative of his age and unique
at the same time. Though involved in the political and religious conflicts of
the day, he yet maintained an unmistakable sense of individuality and a
considerable degree of detachment. These same qualities characterize his
writing.

Montaigne was born on February 28, 1533, in the castle of Montaigne
(in the wine-rich Bordeaux region), which had been bought by his great-
grandfather and from which his family of traders derived their surname. His
father, Pierre Eyquem, was for two terms mayor of Bordeaux and had fought
in Italy under Francis I. Montaigne's inclination to tolerance and natural-
ness may have had its origin in his background and early training: his mother,
of Spanish-Jewish descent, was a Protestant, as were his brother Beauregard
and his sister Jeanne; the third of nine children, Michel himself, like his
other brothers and sisters, was raised a Catholic. His father, though no man
of learning, had unconventional ideas of upbringing: Michel, who had a
peasant nurse and peasant godparents, was awakened in the morning by the
sound of music and had Latin taught him as his mother tongue by a German
tutor. At six he went to the famous Collège de Guienne at Bordeaux; later
he studied law, probably at Toulouse. In his youth he already had first-hand
experience of court life. (At the court celebrations at Rouen for the coming
of age of Charles IX in 1560, he saw cannibals, brought from Brazil, who

---

5. The geography is correct. At the time of Rabelais' writing the celebrated dye-works were still
run by the Gobelin family. Mysterious qualities were attributed to the water of the small river
Bièvre, and urine was actually used in the industry on account of its ammonia content.

became the subject of the famous essay reprinted here.) In 1557 he was a member of the Bordeaux parliament; during that period he formed the deepest friendship of his life, with the young nobleman and fellow lawyer Étienne de la Boétie, who was to die of the plague a few years later. During his friend's last illness, Montaigne assisted him day and night despite the contagiousness of the disease. In 1565 he married Françoise de la Chassaigne, daughter of a colleague in the Bordeaux parliament, and the object of his temperate love. It is possible that disappointed political ambitions contributed to Montaigne's decision to "retire" at the age of thirty-eight to his castle of Montaigne and devote himself to meditation and writing. His stay there, however, had various interruptions. France was split between the Protestants, led by Henry of Navarre, and two Catholic factions: those faithful to the reigning kings of the house of Valois (first Charles IX and then Henry III) and the "leaguers," i.e., the followers of the house of Guise. Though his sympathies went to the unfanatical Navarre, the future founder of the Bourbon dynasty as Henry IV, Montaigne's attitude was balanced and conservative (both Henry III of Valois and Henry of Navarre bestowed honors upon him), and in 1574 Montaigne attempted to mediate an agreement between Henry and the Duke of Guise.

In 1580 he undertook a journey through Switzerland, Germany, and Italy (partly to cure his gallstones); while in Italy he received news that he had been appointed mayor of Bordeaux, an office he held competently for two terms (1581–85). Toward the end of his life he began an important friendship with the intelligent and ardently devoted Marie de Gournay, who became a kind of adopted daughter and was his literary executrix. When Henry of Navarre, who had visited him twice in his castle, became King Henry IV, Montaigne expressed his joy, though he refused Henry's offers of money; he did not live to witness in Paris, as he probably would have, the entry of the king turned Catholic ("Paris," Henry said, "is well worth a Mass"), for he died on September 13, 1592, and was buried in a church in Bordeaux.

Montaigne's major claim to fame, the *Essays*, were started as a collection of interesting quotations, observations, recordings of remarkable events, and the like, and slowly developed to their large form and bulk. Of the three books, I and II were first published in 1580; III (together with I and II revised and amplified) appeared in 1588. A posthumous edition prepared by Mlle. de Gournay, and containing some further additions, appeared in 1595. A noteworthy early English translation by John Florio was published in 1603.

Although the quality of Montaigne's *Essays* can perhaps be fully appreciated only by a direct experience of them, let us attempt to describe this unique genre and place it within the context of its time. If one accepts the common view that in the Renaissance the individual human being was exalted, and therefore a special emphasis was placed on the study of man in his "virtues" and singularities, it might be appropriate to think of Montaigne as a typical product of that new emphasis. As the inventor of the personal essay, he obviously felt that the characteristics of his individual mind and heart— all their minute aspects, variations, and even whims—were worthy of being carefully recorded. Indeed, of the writers presented in this book, Montaigne is the one who most openly speaks in his own right, clearly and unabashedly as himself. While, for instance, Erasmus adopts the ambiguous mouthpiece of "Folly" to express his views, Montaigne's characteristic and somewhat rambling prose is in the simplest and most quintessential first person. Perhaps at no other time in literature—certainly not in the nineteenth-century age of romanticism, where in spite of widespread notions about the "free" expression of individual feelings writers so often wrapped themselves in an alter ego or a heroic mask—has a writer so thoroughly attempted to present himself without in the least assuming a pose, of falling into a type. "Had my intention been to court the world's favor," Montaigne writes in the foreword to his *Essays*, "I should have trimmed myself more bravely, and stood before it in a studied attitude. I desire to be seen in my simple, natural, and everyday dress, without artifice or constraint; for it is myself I portray." And elsewhere he affirms:

> Authors communicate themselves to the world by some special and extrinsic mark; I am the first to do so by my general being, as Michel de Montaigne, not as a grammarian or a poet or a lawyer. If the world finds fault with me for speaking too much of myself, I find fault with the world for not even thinking of itself.

Yet nothing would be more erroneous than to suppose that Montaigne's focusing on his individual self implies a sense of the extraordinary importance of man, of his central place in the world, or of the special power of his understanding. As a matter of fact, the contrary is true. In the first place, in temperament Montaigne is singularly opposed to assuming an attitude of importance: one of the keynotes of his writing, and one of his premises in undertaking it, is that the subject is average, "mediocre." In describing himself he insists that he is presenting an example of the ordinary human being, for the benefit of a few intimates. He declares that he has "but a private and family end in view," and in that sense, in fact, the way he introduces himself to the reader shows a nobly elegant and perhaps vaguely ironic humbleness—not to mention a considerable degree of the artfulness he disclaims! "So, Reader, I am myself the subject of my book; it is not reasonable to expect you to waste your leisure on a matter so frivolous and empty."

And there is an even more fundamental reason why Montaigne's presentation of himself is free from any heroic posturing or intellectual pride—a reason which involves his whole view of man's place in the world. In deciding to write about himself to probe, to "essay," his own nature, the implication is that this is the only subject on which a man can speak with any degree of certainty. Actually, then, this writer whose work is the most acute exposure of an individual personality in the literature of the Renaissance, is at the same time one of the highest illustrations of man's ironic awareness of his intellectual limits.

It would be a mistake to forget, however, that Montaigne's work remains an outstanding assertion of an individuality, even though it is an assertion of doubt, contradiction, change. Here as always the quality and novelty of the work should be experienced in the actual text, in terms of "style." Montaigne's style conjoins a solid classical manner, reflected in certain elements of the syntactical structure and in the continous support of classical quotations, with the variety, the apparent disconnectedness, and the dramatic assertiveness of a man who is continuously analyzing a constantly changing subject, and—his modesty notwithstanding—a singularly attractive one.

Others form man; I describe him, and portray a particular, very ill-made one, who, if I had to fashion him anew, should indeed be very different from what he is. But now it is done. . . . The world is but a perennial see-saw. All things in it are incessantly on the swing, the earth, the rocks of the Caucasus, the Egyptian pyramids. . . . Even fixedness is nothing but a more sluggish motion. I cannot fix my object; it is befogged, and reels with a natural intoxication. . . . I do not portray the thing in itself. I portray the passage. . . .

In spite of what may often seem a leisurely gait, Montaigne is permanently on the alert, listening to the promptings of his thought, his sensibility, his imagination—and recording them. The affirmation of the fluidity of the human personality, of the universality of the flux, is therefore both the premise of his writing and the sum of his study of man; it is both his method and his result.

Thus Montaigne writes in terms of one individual, and with a fairly obvious abhorrence of any sort of classification or description of human types in the manner of conventional moralists; yet at the same time a powerfully keen observation of man in general emerges from his writings—an observation of man's nature, intellectual power, and capacity for coherent action; of his place on earth among other beings; of his place in Creation.

If we keep in mind the broad range of Renaissance literature, poised between positive and negative, enthusiasm and melancholy, we shall probably find that the general temper of Montaigne's assertions of doubt, and his consciousness of vanity, by no means imply an attitude of despair and gloom. His attitude is positive and negative in the same breath; it is a rich and fruitful sense of the relativity of everything. Thus if he examines and "essays" man's capacity to act purposefully and coherently (see the essay "Of the Inconsistency of Our Actions" among our selections), his implicit verdict is not that man's action is absolutely futile. Rather, observing the usual example—himself—and seeing that there is nothing he can say "absolutely, simply, and steadily" on the subject, he refuses to attribute to the human personality a coherence it does not possess and which, we may be tempted to surmise, would rather impoverish it. "Our actions are but a patchwork. . . . We are all made up of bits. . . . There is as much difference between us and ourselves, as between us and others." And he sustains his arguments, as usual, with a wealth of examples and anecdotes which are at once evidence of his vital curiosity about human nature and, in many instances, of his direct familiarity with antiquity: Emperor Augustus, to mention one, pleases him because his character successfully escapes an all-of-a-piece description; he has "slipped through the fingers of even the most daring critics."

A sense of relativity and a balanced outlook—rather than a desperate reversal of the optimistic view of the human situation—are apparent also from Montaigne's observation of man, and particularly of the civilized Renaissance man whom he exemplifies, in relation to his fellow human beings. In the famous essay "Of Cannibals," where a comparison is made between the behavioral codes of primitive tribes and those of "ourselves," the basic idea is not a disparagement of our civilization but a relativistic warning, for "we all call barbarism that which does not fit in with our usages." The cannibals' acts of barbarity are recognized, but the writer is "not so much concerned that we should remark on the horrible barbarity of such acts, as that, whilst rightly judging their errors, we should be so blind to our own." We do much worse, adds Montaigne, who wrote in times of violent religious strife, and we do it under the guise of piety. The enlightening sense of relativity—rather than a more extreme and totally paradoxical view of the "nobility" of savages—permits Montaigne to see and admire what he considers superior elements in the customs of the cannibals (for instance, their conception of valor and their conduct of warfare). Here, in fact, Montaigne describes and admires a code of unrewarded gallantry, of valor for valor's sake, which was not uncommonly cherished by writers of the Renaissance (Castiglione, for example). "The acquisition of the victor," writes Montaigne, "is the glory and advantage of having proved himself the superior in valour and virtue. . . . The honour of virtue consists in combating, not in beating." We may incidentally add that acceptance of this notion of pure "virtue," practiced for no material purposes—as self-rewarding as a beautiful object—appears to have been, for a writer like Montaigne, the way to preserve his admiration for the warrior's code of manly courage and valor in spite of the basically pacifist tendencies of his temperament and his revulsion from the spectacles of conflict and bloodshed witnessed in his own time.

Naturally, an even larger sense of relativity emerges from Montaigne's writing when he examines man's place in the universal frame of things, as he does, in an outstanding instance, in some famous passages of the "Apology for Raimond Sebond" (a selection from which is included in this volume). Man's notion of his privileged position in Creation is eloquently questioned: "What has induced him to believe that that wonderful motion of the heavenly vault, the eternal light of those torches rolling so proudly over his head, the awe-inspiring agitations of that infinite sea, were established, and endure through so many centuries for his service and convenience?" The tone of this whole section is particularly revealing. In many other writers a similar anxiety about man's smallness and ignorance casts a light of tragic vanity upon the human condition. Montaigne's acceptance of the situation is—to use some of our other examples as convenient points of reference—more like Erasmus than Hamlet. If he asks questions which involve, to say the very least, the whole Renaissance conception of man's "dignity," our impression is never really one of negation and gloom. While man's advantages over other beings are quietly evaluated and discredited ("this licence of thought . . . is an advantage sold to him very dearly. . . . For from it springs the principal source of . . . sin, sickness, irresolution, affliction, despair"), Montaigne maintains a balanced and often humorous tone in which even the frivolous aside of the personal essayist is not dissonant, but characteristic: "When I play with my cat, who knows but that she regards me more as a plaything than I do her?" So without raising his voice he achieves a point of view that suggests broadness and inclusiveness rather than gloom and despair. For, while his view of the "mediocrity" of man among other beings debunks any form of intellectual conceit, on the other hand an all-encompassing sense of natural fellowship in Creation is envisaged: "I have said all this to establish the resemblance to human conditions, and to bring us back and join us to the majority."

This sense of a "natural" fellowship seems to characterize not only Montaigne's veiw of man's place in Creation but also his conception of man as a moral individual in relation to other men. This can be clearly seen at the end of our final selection, where the practice of goodness—as, in other instances, that of valor—is seen as a beautiful and self-rewarding act of "virtue":

> There is . . . no goodness in which a well-born nature does not delight.
> . . . There is no small pleasure in feeling oneself preserved from the contagion of so corrupt an age, and saying to oneself, "Should any one look into my very soul, he would yet not find me guilty of the affliction or ruin of any man. . . ." These testimonies of a good conscience please; and this natural satisfaction is a great boon to us, and the only payment that will never fail us.

In conclusion—and difficult as it is to reduce Montaigne's views to short and abstract statements—we are left with the impression that here Montaigne's vision of man, and of the possibility of a good life, is nearer to hopefulness than to despair. Although his attitude is far from Rabelais' optimism and exuberance, it too is based on a balance between the "natural" and the intellectual, between instinct and reason. He belittles, at times even scornfully, the power of the human intellect, and like Erasmus he points to instinctive simplicity of mind as being more conducive to happiness and even to true knowledge; but on the other hand the whole tone of his work, its intellectual sophistication, its very bulk, and the loving manner with which he attended to it, show that his own thought was not something that "sicklied o'er" his life, but something that gave it sustenance and delight. Thus we see in him some of the basic contrasts of the Renaissance mind— the acceptance and the rejection of the intellectual dignity of man—leading not to disruption but to temperately positive results. Though his work offers anything but the abstract scheme of an ideal man, and he is not proposing a model or a formula, yet in passages like the one cited in the preceding paragraph, some kind of pattern of the truly virtuous man seems to emerge unobtrusively. And though it is not imposed upon the audience, any reader is free to think that conforming to this pattern would result in better spiritual balance in the individual and a more harmonious and sensible fellowship in society. Montaigne does not preach ("Others form man; I describe him . . . .") because his code of conduct is one which cannot be taught but only experienced. He limits himself to exemplifying it in his own wise and unheroic self.

Donald M. Frame's *Montaigne: A Biography* (1965), is a modern work by one of the leading contemporary scholars of French literature. Frame is also author of *Montaigne's Essais: A Study* (1969), a brief, clear, cogent account. Frederick Rider's *The Dialectic of Selfhood in Montaigne* (1973), assesses Montaigne's personal development and the creation of his self-image in the *Essais*.

# Essays[1]

## Of Cannibals[2]

When King Pyrrhus[3] passed over into Italy, after acknowledging
the good order that prevailed in the army that the Romans had sent
to meet him, he said, 'I know not what barbarians are these (for so
the Greeks called all foreign nations), but the disposition of this army
I see is by no means barbarous.' The Greeks said the same of the
army which Flaminius brought into their country, as did also Philip,
on viewing from an eminence the orderly distribution of the Roman
camp, in his kingdom, under Publius Sulpicius Galba.[4] Thereby we
may see how we should be on our guard against clinging to vulgar
opinions, and how we should judge things by the light of reason,
and not from common rumour.

I had living with me for a long time a man who had lived for ten
or twelve years in that other world which was discovered in our century, in that place where Villegaignon landed, which he called *Antarctic France*.[5] This discovery of an unbounded country seems to me
worthy of consideration. I do not know that I could pledge myself
that some other discovery may not be made in the future, so many
persons greater than we having been mistaken about this one. I fear
our eyes are greater than our bellies, and that we have more curiosity
than capacity. We embrace all, but we clasp only wind.

Plato introduces Solon,[6] telling how he had learned of the priests
of the city of Saïs in Egypt that, in days of old and before the Deluge,
there was a large island named Atlantis, directly at the mouth of the
Strait of Gibraltar, which contained more countries than all Asia and
Africa together; and that the kings of that region, who not only possessed that island, but had extended their dominion so far into the
mainland, that of the breadth of Africa they held as far as Egypt, and
of the length of Europe as far as Tuscany, attempted to stride even
into Asia, and to subjugate all the nations that border on the Mediterranean Sea as far as the gulf of the Greater Sea,[7] and to that end
traversed the Spains, Gaul, Italy, as far as Greece, where the Athenians stood up against them; but that some time after both the Athenians and they and their island were swallowed up by the Flood.

It is most likely that that extreme watery devastation has caused
some wonderful alterations in the habitations of the earth, as it is
thought that the sea cut off Sicily from Italy,

---

1. Translated by E. J. Trechmann.   2. Book I, Chapter 31.   3. King of Epirus, in Greece,
fought the Romans in Italy in 280 B.C.   4. Both Titus Quinctius Flaminius (mentioned earlier
in this sentence) and Publius Sulpicius Galba were Roman statesmen and generals who fought
Philip V of Macedon in the early years of the second century B.C.   5. In Brazil. Villegaignon
landed there in 1557.   6. In his *Timaeus*.   7. The Black Sea.

> These lands, 'tis said, one continent of yore
> (Such change can ages work) an earthquake tore
> Asunder; in with havoc rushed the main,
> And far Sicilia from Hesperia bore,
> And now, where leapt the parted lands in twain,
> The narrow tide pours through, 'twixt severed town and plain;
> (Virgil.)[8]

Cyprus from Syria, the island of Negropont from the mainland of Boeotia; and elsewhere joined lands which were divided, by filling up the channels between them with sand and mud:

> Swamps, sterile long, all plashy, rank and drear,
> Groan 'neath the plough, and feed whole cities near.
> (Horace.)[9]

But it does not appear very likely that that great island was the new world that we have lately discovered, for it almost touched Spain, and it would have been an incredible result of an inundation to have removed it as far back as it is, more than twelve hundred leagues; besides that our modern navigators have already almost discovered it to be no island, but a firm land holding together with the East Indies on the one hand, and on the other with the lands which lie under the two poles; or, if it is separated from them, it is by so narrow a strait and interval, that it does not on that account deserve to be called an island.

It would seem that there are movements, some natural, others diseased, in those great bodies as well as in our own. When I consider the inroads that my river, the Dordogne, is making even in my time, upon the right bank in its descent, and that in twenty years it has gained so much ground, and robbed many buildings of their foundations, I plainly see that an extraordinary disturbance is going on; for if it had always been going on at this rate, or were to do so in the future, the face of the world would be entirely altered. But rivers are subject to changes: now they overflow in one direction, now in another, now they keep within their beds. I do not speak of the sudden inundations whose causes are manifest. In Médoc, along the sea-shore, my brother the Sieur d'Arsac sees an estate of his buried beneath the sands that the sea vomits before it; the tops of several buildings are still visible; his rents and domains have been converted into very poor pasturage. The inhabitants say that the sea has been

---

8. *Aeneid*, Book III, ll. 414 ff.  9. *Art of Poetry*, ll. 65f.

for some time pushing so strongly towards them, that they have lost four leagues of land. These sands are its harbingers, and we see great dunes of moving sand, that march half a league before it, and are gaining ground.

The other testimony from antiquity, from which some infer this discovery, is in Aristotle, if at least that little book *Of Unheard-of Marvels* be his. He there relates how certain Carthaginians, having ventured across the Atlantic Sea, outside the Strait of Gibraltar, and navigated a long time, had at last discovered a large fertile island, all clothed in woods, and watered by broad and deep rivers, far remote from any mainland; and that they, and others after them, attracted by the goodness and fertility of the soil, had gone thither with their wives and children and begun to settle there. The lords of Carthage, seeing that their country was gradually becoming depopulated, expressly forbade any more to go there, on pain of death, and drove out those new settlers, fearing, it is said, lest in course of time they might multiply to such an extent as to supplant themselves and ruin their state. This narration of Aristotle no more agrees with our new-found lands than the other.

This man I had was a simple and ignorant fellow: hence the more fit to give true evidence; for your sophisticated men are more curious observers, and take in more things, but they glose[1] them; to lend weight to their interpretations and induce your belief, they cannot help altering their story a little. They never describe things as they really are, but bend them and mask them according to the point of view from which they see things, and, to make their judgements the more credible and attractive, they are not loath to add a little to their matter, and to spin out and amplify their tale. Now we need either a very truthful man, or one so simple that he has not the art of building up and giving an air of probability to fictions, and is wedded to no theory. Such was my man; and he has besides at different times brought several sailors and traders to see me, whom he had known on that voyage. So I shall content myself with his information, without troubling myself about what the cosmographers may say about it.

We need topographers who would give us an exact account of the places which they have visited. But because they have this advantage over us that they have seen Palestine, they claim to enjoy the privilege of telling us new things of all the rest of the world. I would have every man write about what he knows, and no more than he knows, not only in this but on all other subjects. For a man may have some particular knowledge or experience of the nature of a river or a fountain, who otherwise knows no more than what everybody knows. Yet

1. Gloze; gloss.

he will undertake, in order to circulate this little scrap of knowledge, to write a book on the whole science of physics. From this fault spring many great abuses.

Now, to return to my subject, from what I have heard of that nation, I can see nothing barbarous or uncivilized about it, except that we all call barbarism that which does not fit in with our usages. And indeed we have no other level of truth and reason but the example and model of the opinions and usages of the country we live in. There we always see the perfect religion, the perfect government, the perfect and accomplished manner of doing all things. Those people are wild in the sense in which we call wild the fruits that Nature has produced by herself and in her ordinary progress; whereas in truth it is those we have altered artificially and diverted from the common order, that we should rather call wild. In the first we still see, in full life and vigour, the genuine and most natural and useful virtues and properties, which we have bastardized in the latter, and only adapted to please our corrupt taste. And yet in some of the uncultivated fruits of those countries there is a delicacy of flavour that is excellent even to our taste, and rivals even our own. It is not reasonable that art should gain the point of honour over our great and powerful mother Nature. We have so overburdened the beauty and richness of her works with our inventions, that we have quite smothered her. And yet, wherever she shines in her purity, she marvellously puts to shame our vain and trivial efforts,

> Uncared, unmarked the ivy blossoms best;
> Midst desert rocks the ilex clusters still;
> And sweet the wild bird's untaught melody.
> (Propertius.)[2]

With all our efforts we are unable even to copy the nest of the smallest of little birds, its contexture, its beauty and convenience; not so much as the web of the poor spider.

All things, says Plato,[3] are produced either by Nature, or by chance, or by art: the greatest and most beautiful by one or other of the two first; the least and most imperfect by the latter.

Those nations, then, appear to me so far barbarous in this sense, that their minds have been formed to a very slight degree, and that they are still very close to their original simplicity. They are still ruled by the laws of Nature, and very little corrupted by ours; but they are still in such a state of purity, that I am sometimes vexed that they were not known earlier, at a time when there were men who could have appreciated them better than we do.

---

2. *Elegies*, Book I, Elegy ii, ll. 10 ff.   3. See his *Laws*.

I am sorry that Lycurgus[4] and Plato had no knowledge of them, for it seems to me that what we have learned by contact with those nations surpasses not only all the beautiful colours in which the poets have depicted the golden age, and all their ingenuity in inventing a happy state of man, but also the conceptions and desires of Philosophy herself. They were incapable of imagining so pure and native a simplicity, as that which we see by experience; nor could they have believed that human society could have been maintained with so little human artifice and solder. This is a nation,[5] I should say to Plato, which has no manner of traffic; no knowledge of letters; no science of numbers; no name of magistrate or statesman; no use for slaves; neither wealth nor poverty; no contracts; no successions; no partitions; no occupation but that of idleness; only a general respect of parents; no clothing; no agriculture; no metals; no use of wine or corn. The very words denoting falsehood, treachery, dissimulation, avarice, envy, detraction, pardon, unheard of. How far removed from this perfection would he find the ideal republic he imagined! *Men newly come from the hands of the gods* (Seneca).

These manners first by nature taught.    (Virgil.)[6]

For the rest, they live in a region with a very agreeable and very temperate climate, so that, according to my witnesses, a sick man is rarely seen; and they assured me that they had never seen any man shaking with palsy, or with dripping eyes, toothless or bent with age. They are settled along the sea-coast, and closed in on the land side by large and high mountains, the land between them and the sea extending for a hundred leagues or thereabouts. They have great abundance of fish and flesh, which bear no resemblance to ours, and they eat them roasted without any other preparation. The first man who brought a horse thither, although he had associated with them on several previous voyages, so horrified them in the riding posture, that they shot him dead with arrows before recognizing him. Their buildings are very long, capable of holding two or three hundred souls, covered with the bark of tall trees, the strips resting by one end on the ground, and leaning to and supporting one another at the top, after the manner of some of our barns, the coverings of which slope down to the ground and serve as sidewalls. They have a wood so hard that they can cut with it, of which they make their swords, and gridirons to roast their meat. Their beds are made of cotton tissue, suspended from the roof like those in our ships, each one having his own: for the women sleep apart from their husbands.

4. The half-legendary Spartan lawgiver (ninth century B.C.).    5. The passage beginning here is always compared with Shakespeare, *The Tempest,* Act II, Scene 1, ll. 154 ff.    6. *Georgics,* Book II, l. 20. *Seneca: Epistles,* Epistle xc.

They rise with the sun and eat immediately after rising, for the whole day: for they have no other meal. They drink nothing with that meal, like some other Eastern peoples of whom Suidas[7] tells us, who drank apart from eating; but they drink several times a day, and to excess. Their drink is made of some root, and is of the colour of our claret wines, and they only drink it warm. This beverage will keep only two or three days; it has a slightly pungent taste, is anything but heady, good for the stomach, and laxative for such as are not used to it, but a very pleasant drink for those who are. For bread they use a certain white material resembling preserved coriander. I have tried some of it: it is sweet but rather tasteless.

The whole day is spent in dancing. The younger men hunt animals with bows. Some of the women meanwhile spend their time warming their drink, which is their chief duty. One of their old men, in the morning before they begin to eat, preaches to the whole barnful of people in common, walking from one end to the other, repeating the same words several times, until he has finished the round (for the buildings are quite a hundred paces in length). He recommends only two things, valour against the enemy and love to their wives. And they never fail to stress this obligation, which forms their refrain, 'that it is they who keep their wine warm and seasoned.'

In several places, among others in my house, may be seen the formation of their beds, of their ropes, their wooden swords and bracelets, with which they cover their wrists in battle, and large canes open at one end, by the sound of which they keep the time and rhythm of their dances. They are close shaven all over, and remove the hair much more neatly than we do although their razors are only made of wood or stone. They believe the soul to be immortal, and that those who have deserved well of the gods are lodged in that part of the heaven where the sun rises, and those who are damned in the west.

They have some kind of priest and prophet, who very seldom appears among the people, having his dwelling in the mountains. On his arrival there is a great feast and a solemn assembly of several villages (each barn, as I have described it, forms a village, and they are about a French league[8] distant one from the other). This prophet speaks to them in public, exhorting them to virtue and their duty; but their whole ethical science comprises only these two articles: an unfaltering courage in war and affection to their women. This man foretells things to come, and the issue they are to expect from their enterprises; urges them to war, or holds them back; but he does so on the understanding that, where he fails to prophesy correctly, and if things turn out otherwise than he has predicted, he is cut into a thousand

7. A Byzantine lexicographer.    8. About 2.49 miles.

pieces if he is caught, and condemned for a false prophet. For that reason he who has once miscalculated is seen no more.

Divination is a gift of God, wherefore to abuse it ought to be regarded as a punishable imposture. Among the Scythians, when the prophets failed to hit the mark, they were laid, shackled hand and foot, on a little cart filled with heather and drawn by oxen, on which they were burned. They who take in hand such matters as depend on the conduct of human capacity are to be excused if they do their best. But those others who come and delude us with assurances of an extraordinary faculty that is beyond our ken, should they not be punished when they fail to carry out what they promise, and for the temerity of their imposture?

They have their wars with the nations beyond their mountains, further back on the mainland, to which they go quite naked, with no other weapons but bows or wooden swords pointed at one end, after the fashion of the tongues of our boar-spears. It is marvellous with what obstinacy they fight their battles, which never end but in massacre and bloodshed: for of routs and terrors they know not even the meaning. Each man brings back as a trophy the head of the enemy he has slain, and fixes it over the entrance to his dwelling. After treating his prisoner well for a considerable time, and giving him all that hospitality can devise, his captor convokes a great gathering of his acquaintance. He ties a cord to one of his prisoner's arms, holding him at some distance for fear of being hurt, and gives the other arm to be held in the same way by his best friend; and these two, in presence of the whole assembly, dispatch him with their swords. This done, they roast and eat him in common, and send bits of him to their absent friends. Not, as one might suppose, for nourishment, as the ancient Scythians used to do, but to signify an extreme revenge.

And that it is so, may be seen from this: having perceived that the Portuguese, who had allied themselves with their adversaries, inflicted a different kind of death on their prisoners, which was to bury them up to the waist, shoot the upper part of the bodies full of arrows, and afterwards to hang them; they imagined that these people of another world (seeing that they had sown the knowledge of a great many vices among their neighbours, and were much greater masters than themselves in every kind of wickedness) had some reason for adopting this kind of vengeance, and that it must be more painful than their own; wherefore they began to give up their old method, and followed this one.

I am not so much concerned that we should remark on the horrible barbarity of such acts, as that, whilst rightly judging their errors, we should be so blind to our own. I think there is more barbarity in eating a live than a dead man, in tearing on the rack and torturing the body of a man still full of feeling, in roasting him piecemeal and giving him to be bitten and mangled by dogs and swine (as we have not only read, but seen within fresh memory, not between old enemies, but between neighbours and fellow citizens, and, what is worse, under the cloak of piety and religion),[9] than in roasting and eating him after he is dead.

Chrysippus and Zeno, the leaders of the Stoic sect, thought indeed that there was no harm in making use of our carrion for any purpose in case of necessity, and of extracting nourishment from it. And our ancestors,[1] when besieged by Caesar in the city of Alexia, decided to relieve the famine during the siege by eating the bodies of the old men, women, and other persons incapable of fighting;

> Time was, the Gascons, as old tales relate,
> Thus fed, contended long with cruel fate.
>                                    (Juvenal.)[2]

And physicians are not afraid of using it in all sorts of ways as cures, either for inward or outward application. But no man's brain was ever so disordered that he would excuse treachery, disloyalty, cruelty, tyranny, which are our ordinary vices.

We may therefore well call those people barbarians in respect to the rules of reason, but not in respect to ourselves, who surpass them in every kind of barbarity.

Their warfare is entirely noble and generous, and is as fair and excusable as can be expected in that human disease: their only motive being a zeal for valour. They do not strive to conquer new territory, for they still enjoy that luxuriance of nature which provides them, without labour and pains, with all necessary things in such abundance, that they have no need to enlarge their borders. They are still in that happy state of not desiring more than their natural needs demand: all that is over and above it is for them superfluity.

They generally call each other, if of the same age, brothers; if younger, children; and the old men are fathers to all the others. These latter leave to their heirs in common the full and undivided possession of their property, without any but that pure title that Nature gives to her creatures, by bringing them into the world. If their neighbours cross the mountains to attack them, and gain the victory over them, the acquisition of the victor is the glory and advantage of having proved himself the superior in valour and virtue, for otherwise they have no need for the spoils of the vanquished; and so they return to their own country, where they have no want of any necessaries, nor even of that great portion, which is to know how to enjoy

---

9. The allusion is to the spectacles of religious warfare which Montaigne himself had witnessed in his time and country.    1. The Gauls.    2. *Satires*. Satire xv, ll. 93 ff.

happily their condition, and be content with it. These do the same in their turn. They ask of their prisoners no other ransom but a confession and acknowledgement of being vanquished. But you will not find one in a whole century who would not rather die than yield, either by word or look, one tittle of on invincible greatness of courage; not one who would not rather be killed and eaten than even pray to be spared. They are very liberal in their treatment of their prisoners, in order to make life the more dear to them, and usually entertain them with threats of their impending death, the torments they will suffer, the preparations made to that end, the cutting up of their limbs, and the banquet that will be made at their expense. All this is done with the sole purpose of extorting from them a weak or spiritless word, or to give them a desire to escape, in order to gain the advantage of having terrified them and shaken their firmness. For indeed, if rightly taken, therein alone lies the real victory:

> The victor's wreath no triumphs more attest
> Than when the foe's subjection is confest.
> (Claudian.)[3]

The Hungarians, very bellicose fighters, did not formerly pursue their advantage further than making their enemy cry for mercy. For, after forcing from them that confession, they let them go without hurt or ransom, except, at the most, making them pledge their word not again to take up arms against them.

We often enough gain an advantage over our enemy which is a borrowed advantage, and to which we have no real claim. To have more muscular arms and legs is the quality of a porter, not a sign of valour; skill is a dead and corporal quality: it is a stroke of fortune that causes our adversary to stumble or to be dazzled by the glare of the sun; it is a trick of art and science that makes an able fencer, who may easily be a coward and an insignificant fellow.

A man's value and estimation consists in heart and will: there lies his true honour. Valour is strength, not of legs and arms, but of heart and soul; it lies not in the goodness of our horse, or our weapons, but in our own. He who falls fighting with obstinate courage, *if his legs fail him, he fights on his knees* (Seneca).[4] He who, in spite of being in danger of imminent death, abates nothing of his assurance, who, in yielding up his soul, still fixes on his enemy a firm and scornful glance, is vanquished, not by us, but by Fortune: he is slain but not conquered.

The most valiant are sometimes the most unfortunate. Hence there are triumphant defeats that vie in glory with victories. Neither did

---

3. *Of the Sixth Consulate of Honorius*, ll. 248 ff.    4. *Of Providence*, Book II.

those four sister victories, the most glorious that the sun has ever beheld with its eyes, of Salamis, Plataea, Mycale, and Sicily,[5] ever dare to oppose their combined glories to the glory of the discomfiture of King Leonidas and his comrades at the pass of Thermopylae.[6]

What man ever hastened with a more glorious and ambitious desire to the winning, than Captain Ischolas did to the losing, of a battle? What man ever used more care and ingenuity to secure his own safety than he did to ensure his destruction? He was charged to defend a certain pass in the Peloponnesus against the Arcadians. But knowing that he was wholly unable to do so, on account of the nature of the place and the inequality of the forces, and being sure that every man who confronted the enemy must needs remain on the spot; on the other hand, deeming it unworthy both of his own virtue and magnanimity, and of the name of a Spartan, to fail in his charge, he adopted a middle course between these two extremes, which was in this manner: the youngest and most active of his band he reserved for the service and defence of their country, and sent them home; and with those whose loss would be of less account he decided to hold the pass, and with their death make the enemy purchase their entry as dear as possible. And so it fell out: for, being presently surrounded on every side by the Arcadians, after a great butchery of them he and his comrades were all put to the sword. Was ever a trophy raised to a victor that was not rather due to these vanquished men? The part that true victory plays is the struggle, not the coming off safe; and the honour of virtue consists in combating, not in beating.

To return to our narrative. Far from giving in, in spite of all they suffer, these prisoners, on the contrary, during the two or three months that they are held in captivity, bear a cheerful countenance; they urge their captors to hasten to put them to the proof, defy them, insult them, reproach them with their cowardice and the number of battles lost against their own countrymen.

I have a song composed by a prisoner, which contains this outburst: 'Come boldly, every one of you, and assemble together to dine off me, for you shall at the same time eat your fathers and grandfathers, whose flesh has served to feed and nourish this body. These muscles, this flesh and these veins are yours, poor fools that you are! can you not see that they still contain the substance of your ancestors' limbs? Relish them well, you will find that they have the flavour of your own flesh.' A fiction that by no means savours of barbarity. On the pictures which represent these prisoners being executed or at the point of death, they are seen spitting in the face of their slayers

---

5. Montaigne here refers to the famous Greek victories against the Persians and (at Himera, Sicily) against the Carthaginians in or about 480 B.C.    6. The Spartan king Leonidas' defense of the pass at Thermopylae also took place in 480 B.C., during the war against the Persians.

or making mouths at them. Indeed they never cease to challenge and defy them by word and look until the breath is out of their body. Verily here we see men who are indeed savages if we compare them with ourselves: for either they must be so in good sooth, or we; there is a wonderful distance between their character and ours.

The men there have several wives, and the higher their reputation for valour the greater is the number of their wives. It is a remarkably beautiful feature in their marriages, that the same jealousy that our wives have to keep us from the love and favors of other women, they have to an equal degree to procure it. Being more solicitous for their husbands' honour than for anything else, they use their best endeavours to have as many companions as they can, seeing that that is a proof of their husbands' worth.

Ours will cry 'miracle,' but it is not so. It is after all a proper matrimonial virtue, but of the highest order. And in the Bible, Leah, Rachel, Sarah and Jacob's wives accommodated their husbands with their fair handmaids; and Livia gratified Augustus' appetites to her own detriment; and Stratonice, the wife of King Deiotarus,[7] not only lent her husband the use of a very beautiful young chambermaid in her service, but carefully brought up her children, and gave them a shoulder in succeeding to their father's estates.

And, that it may not be supposed that all this is done through a simple and slavish obligation to follow usage, and under the weight of authority of their ancient customs, without reasoning or judgement, and because their minds are too dull to imagine any other, I must give a few proofs of their intellectual capacity. Besides the warlike song I have just cited I have another, of an amorous nature, which begins thus: 'Adder, stay; stay, adder, that thy colours may serve as a pattern for my sister to work a rich girdle to give to my love: thus shall thy beauty and disposition of thy spots be preferred for all time to all other serpents.' This first verse is the burden of the song. Now, I have enough knowledge of poetry to judge this much: that not only is there nothing barbarous in this idea, but that it is altogether Anacreontic.[8] Their language, by the way, is a soft language, with an agreeable tone, and their terminations resemble the Greek.

Three men of this nation, not knowing how dear, in tranquillity and happiness, it will one day cost them to know the corruptions of this side of the world, and that this intercourse will be the cause of their ruin, which indeed I imagine is already advanced (poor wretches, to be allured by the desire to see new things and to leave their own serene sky to come and see ours!), were at Rouen at a time when the late King Charles the Ninth was there. The King had a long talk

7. Tetrarch of Galatia, in Asia Minor.    8. Worthy of Anacreon (572?–488? B.C.), major Greek writer of amatory lyrics.

with them. They were shown our ways, our pomp, the form of a fine city. After that somebody asked their opinion, desiring to know what they most wondered at. They mentioned three things, the third of which I am sorry to have forgotten, but I still remember two. They said that in the first place they thought it very strange that so many big men with beards, strong and armed, who were about the King (they were probably thinking of the Swiss who formed his guard) should submit to obey a child, and that they did not rather choose one of their own number to command them. Secondly (they have a way of speaking of men as if they were halves of one another), that they had observed that there were men amongst us, full and gorged with all kinds of good things, and that their halves were begging at their doors, emaciated with hunger and poverty; and they thought it strange how these necessitous halves could suffer such injustice, and that they did not seize the others by the throat, or set fire to their houses.

I had a long talk with one of them; but I had an interpreter who followed my meaning so badly, and was at such a loss, in his stupidity, to take in my ideas, that I could get little satisfaction out of him. When I asked the native, 'What he gained from his superior position among his people?' (for he was a captain, and our sailors called him a king), he said it was 'to march foremost in war.' How many men did he lead? He pointed to a piece of ground, to signify as many as that space could hold: it might be four or five thousand men. Did all his authority lapse with the war? He said 'that this remained, that, when he visited the villages that were dependent on him, they made paths through their thickets, by which he might pass at his ease.' All this does not sound too ill; but hold! they don't wear trousers.

## Of the Inconsistency of Our Actions[9]

They who make a practice of comparing human actions are never so perplexed as when they try to piece them together and place them in the same light, for they commonly contradict one another so strangely that it seems impossible they should have come out of the same shop. Marius the younger[1] is now a son of Mars, now a son of Venus.[2] Some one said that Pope Boniface the Eighth entered upon his charge like a fox, behaved therein like a lion, and died like a dog. And who could believe that it was Nero, the very image of cruelty, who, when the sentence of a condemned criminal was brought to him to be signed in the usual way, exclaimed, 'Would to God that I had never learned to write!' So grieved was he in his heart to doom a man to death!

9. Book II, Chapter 1. 1. Nephew of the older and better known Marius. Montaigne's source is Plutarch's *Life of Marius*. 2. *Mars . . . Venus*: war and love.

The world is full of such examples, nay, any man may provide such an abundance of them out of his own experience, that I some-times wonder to see intelligent men at pains to sort the pieces, seeing that irresolution is, in my view, the most common and conspicuous defect of our nature: witness that famous line of Publilius the writer of low comedies,

> Poor is the plan that never can be changed.
> (Publilius Syrus.)[3]

It seems reasonable to judge a man by the most ordinary acts of his life, but in view of the natural instability of our habits and opinions, I have often thought that even good authors are wrong in obstinately attributing to us a steadfast and consistent character. They hit upon a general feature in a man and arrange and interpret all his actions in accordance with this fanciful conception; and if they are unable to twist them sufficiently, set them down to dissimulation. Augustus has escaped them, for we see in this man, throughout the course of his life, so manifest, abrupt, and continual a variety of actions, that he has slipped through the fingers of even the most daring critics, and been left undecided. I find nothing more difficult to believe than man's consistency, and nothing more easy than his inconsistency. If we examine him in detail and judge of his actions separately, bit by bit, we shall most often find this true.

Throughout ancient history it would be difficult to choose a dozen men who have steered their lives in one certain and constant course, which is the principal aim of wisdom. For, to comprise it all in one word, as an ancient writer says,[4] and to embrace all the rules of life in one, is 'to wish and not to wish always the same thing. I will not vouchsafe to add, he says, provided the wish be right; for if it be not right, it is impossible it should be always the same.' I once learned indeed that vice is no more than want of rule and moderation, and that it is consequently impossible to associate it with consistency. It is a saying attributed to Demosthenes, 'that the beginning of all virtue is consultation and deliberation; and the end and perfection, constancy.' If reason directed our course we should choose the fairest; but no one has thought of that:

> He scorns that which he sought, seeks what he scorned of late;
> He flows and ebbs, his whole life contradiction.   (Horace.)[5]

Our ordinary practice is to follow the inclinations of our appetite, to right, to left, up hill, down dale, as we are borne along by the wind

---

3. *Apothegms (Sententiae)*, l. 362.   4. Seneca, in *Epistles*, Epistle xx.   5. *Epistles*, Book I, Epistle i, ll. 98 ff.

of opportunity. We do not consider what we wish except at the moment of wishing it, and we change like that animal which takes its colour from what it is laid upon. What we have but now determined we presently alter, and soon again we retrace our steps: it is nothing but wavering and uncertainty;

> We are led as a puppet is moved by the strings.
>                                                  (Horace.)[6]

We do not go, we are carried along, like things floating, now smoothly, now perturbedly, according as the water is angry or calm;

> We see them, knowing not
> What 'tis they want, and seeking ever and ever
> A change of place, as if to drop the burden.
>                                                  (Lucretius.)[7]

Every day a new fancy; and our humours move with the changes of weather:

> So change the minds of men, like days
> That Father Jove sends down to earth,
> To alternate 'twixt wet and fine.    (Homer.)[8]

We waver between different minds; we wish nothing freely, nothing absolutely, nothing constantly. Should any man prescribe and establish definite laws and a definite policy in his own head, he would present throughout his life a shining example of even habits, an order and an unfailing relation of one action to another.

(Empedocles remarked in the inhabitants of Agrigentum this discrepancy, that they abandoned themselves to their pleasures as if they were to die on the morrow, and that they built as if they were never to die.)[9]

The reason will be easily found, as we see in the case of the younger Cato;[1] he who touches one note of the keyboard touches all: there is a harmony of sounds, all in perfect tune with each other, which is not to be mistaken. With us, on the other hand, the rule is: so many actions, so many particular judgments to be passed. The surest, in my opinion, would be to refer them to the nearest circumstances, without seeking any farther, and without drawing from them any other inferences.

It was told me, during the tumultuous times our poor State had to

---

6. *Satire*, Book II, Satire vii, l. 82.    7. *On the Nature of Things*, Book III, ll. 1057 ff.
8. *Odyssey*, Book XVIII, l. 135.    9. From the life of the fifth-century Greek philosopher Empedocles, by Diogenes Laertius.    1. The philosopher, Cato "Uticensis" (first century B.C.); to Montaigne, and also traditionally, he is an epitome of moral and intellectual integrity.

go through,[2] that a young woman who lived quite near to where I then was, had thrown herself from a high window to avoid the forcible caresses of a poor knave of a soldier who was quartered in her house; the fall did not kill her, and, repeating the attempt on her life, she would have cut her throat with a knife, but was prevented; not however without inflicting a serious wound. She herself then confessed that the soldier had done no more than importune her with gifts, entreaties, and solicitations, but that she feared he would in the end proceed to violence. And all this, her words, her mien, and the blood which testified to her virtue, in the true manner of a second Lucretia![3]

Now I have heard, as a fact, that, both before and after, she was a wench not very difficult to come by. As the tale[4] has it, 'Be as handsome and as fine a gentleman as you will, when you have failed in your pursuit, do not immediately conclude an inviolable chastity in your mistress; it does not follow that the muleteer will not find his opportunity.'

Antigonus,[5] having taken a liking to one of his soldiers, on account of his virtue and valour, ordered his physicians to attend him for a persistent internal malady which had long tormented him, and perceiving that after his cure he went much more coldly to work than before, asked him what it was that had so altered and cowed him. 'You yourself, Sire, he replied, by delivering me from the ill which made me indifferent to life.' A soldier of Lucullus,[6] having been plundered by enemies, devised a bold stroke for his revenge; when he had retrieved his loss with interest, Lucullus, whose good opinion he had gained, tried to induce him, with the best persuasions he could think of, to undertake some risky business:

> With words that might have stirred a coward's heart.
>                      (Horace.)[7]

'Employ, he replied, some wretched soldier who has been plundered;'

> Though but a rustic clown, he'll go
> Who's lost his money-belt,' he said;     (Horace.)[8]

and resolutely refused to go.

When we read that Mahomet having furiously rated Chasan, chief of his Janissaries, for allowing his line of troops to be broken by the Hungarians, and bearing himself like a coward in the battle; and that

---

2. See footnote, page 1649, and the corresponding passage in the text of "Of Cannibals." 3. The legendary, virtuous Roman who stabbed herself after being raped by King Tarquinius' son.    4. A common folk tale.    5. Macedonian king.    6. Roman general of the first century B.C.    7. *Epistles*, Book II, Epistle ii, l. 36.    8. *Epistles*, Book II, Epistle ii, ll. 39 f.

Chasan made no reply but, alone and just as he was with his weapon in his hand, rushed furiously into the first body of enemies that he met with, and was immediately overwhelmed; it was not so much a justification of his conduct as a change of mood, not so much natural prowess as a new spite.

Do not think it strange that the man who was so venturesome yesterday should prove such a poltroon on the morrow; either anger, or necessity, or company, or wine, or the sound of the trumpet had put his heart into his belly; it was not a courage thus formed by reason, but a courage stiffened by those circumstances; it was no marvel if other contrary circumstances made a new man of him.

These so supple changes and contradictions which we manifest have made some to imagine that we have two souls, others, that we have two powers which, each in its own way, accompany and stir us, the one to good, the other to evil, since so abrupt a diversity is not to be reconciled with a single subject.

Not only does the wind of accidents stir me according to its blowing, but I am also stirred and troubled by the instability of my attitude; and he who examines himself closely will seldom find himself twice in the same state. I give to my soul now one face, now another, according to the side to which I turn it. If I speak differently of myself, it is because I regard myself differently. All the contradictions are to be found in me, according as the wind turns and changes. Bashful, insolent; chaste, lascivious; talkative, taciturn; clumsy, gentle; witty, dull; peevish, sweet-tempered; mendacious, truthful; knowing, ignorant; and liberal and avaricious and prodigal: all this I see in myself in some degree, according as I veer about; and whoever will study himself very attentively will find in himself, yea, in his judgement, this discordance and unsteadiness. I can say nothing of myself absolutely, simply, and steadily, without confusion and mixture, nor in one word. *Distinguo*[9] is the most universal member of my logic.

Though I am ever inclined to speak well of what is good, and rather to interpret favourably the things that are capable of such interpretation, yet such is the strangeness of our nature that we are often driven to do good, even by vice; if it were not that well-doing is judged by the intention alone.

Therefore a courageous deed ought not to imply a valiant man: the man who is really brave will be always so, and on all occasions. If valour were a habit, and not a sudden eruption, it would make a man equally resolute for all emergencies, the same alone as in company, the same in single combat as in a battle; for let them say what they will, there is not one valour for the pavement and another for the field. As bravely would he bear sickness in his bed as a wound in

9. I distinguish; I separate into its components.

camp, nor would he fear death in his own home any more than in an assault. We should not see the same man charge with brave assurance into the breach, and afterwards worrying like a woman, over the loss of a law-suit or a son. When, though afraid of infamy, he bears up against poverty; when, though wincing at a surgeon's lancet, he stiffly faces the enemy's sword, the action is praiseworthy, but not the man.

Many Greeks, says Cicero, cannot look upon an enemy, and are brave in sickness. The Cimbrians and the Celtiberians, quite the contrary: *For nothing can be consistent that has not reason for its foundation* (Cicero).[1]

No valour could be more extreme in its kind than Alexander's; but it is of one kind only, and is not complete enough, nor universal on all occasions. Incomparable though it be, it has its blemishes. So it is that we see him so desperately disturbed by the slightest suspicions that his subjects may be plotting against his life, and carried away in his investigations to such violent and indiscriminate acts of injustice, and haunted by a fear that upsets his natural good sense. The superstition too with which he was so strongly tainted bears some likeness to pusillanimity. And the excess of his penitence for the murder of Clytus[2] is also evidence of uneven temper.

Our actions are but a patchwork (*they despise pleasure, but are cowardly in pain; they are indifferent to fame, but infamy breaks their spirit*[3]), and we try to gain honour by false pretences. Virtue will not be wooed but for her own sake, and if we sometimes borrow her mask for some other purpose, she will very soon snatch it from our face. When the soul is once steeped in it, the dye is strong and vivid, and will not go without taking the skin with it. Wherefore, to judge a man, we must long and carefully follow his traces. If constancy does not stand firm and wholly on its own foundation, *if the path of life has not been well considered and preconcerted* (Cicero);[4] if changing circumstances make him alter his pace (I should say his route, for the pace may be accelerated or retarded by them), let him go: that man will go A *vau le vent* (down the wind), as the motto of our Talebot[5] has it.

It is no wonder, says an ancient writer,[6] that chance has so great a hold over us, since we live by chance. Unless a man has directed his life as a whole to a certain fixed goal, he cannot possibly dispose his particular actions. Unless he have an image of the whole in his mind, he cannot possibly arrange the pieces. How can a painter lay

---

1. *Tusculan Disputations*, Book II, Chapter 27.　　2. Clytus, a commander in Alexander's army, was killed by him during an argument, an act which Alexander immediately and bitterly regretted, as related by Plutarch in his *Life of Alexander*, Chapters 50–52.　　3. Cicero, *Of Duties* (*De officiis*), Book I, Chapter 21.　　4. *Paradoxes*, Paradox v.　　5. Talbot, an English captain who fought in France and died there in 1453.　　6. Seneca, in *Epistles*, Epistle lxxi.

in a stock of colours, if he knows not what he is going to paint? No man draws a definite outline of his life, and we only think it out in details. The archer must first know at what he is aiming, and then accommodate his hand, his bow, the string, the arrow, and his movements, accordingly. Our plans go wrong because they have neither aim nor direction. No wind serves the ship that has no port of destination.

I cannot agree with those judges who, on the strength of seeing one of his tragedies, declared in favour of Sophocles, when accused by his son of being incapable of managing his domestic affairs. Nor do I hold with the conclusions arrived at by the Parians who were sent to reform the Milesians. Visiting the island, they remarked the best-cultivated lands and the best-kept country-houses, and made a note of their owners; and then, having called an assembly of the citizens in the town, they appointed these owners the new governors and magistrates, concluding that, being careful of their private affairs, they would be equally careful of those of the public.

We are all made up of bits, and so shapelessly and diversely put together, that every piece, at every moment, plays its own game. And there is as much difference between us and ourselves, as between us and others. *Be sure that it is very difficult to be always the same man* (Seneca).[7] Since ambition can teach a man valour, temperance, and liberality, yea and justice too; since greed can implant in the heart of a shop-apprentice, bred up in obscurity and neglect, the confidence to entrust himself, so far from the domestic hearth, to the mercy of the waves and angry Neptune in a frail bark; since it teaches also discretion and prudence; and since Venus herself can put resolution and temerity into the boy who is still under the discipline of the rod, and embolden the heart of the tender virgin in her mother's arms,

> With Love for guide,
> Alone the maid steps o'er her prostrate guards,
> And steals by night into the young man's arms;
> (Tibullus.)[8]

it is not enough for a sober understanding to judge us simply by our external actions: we must sound the innermost recesses, and observe the springs which give the swing. But since it is a high and hazardous undertaking, I would rather that fewer people meddled with it.

---

7. *Epistles*, Epistle cxx.    8. *Elegies*, Book II, Elegy i, ll. 75 ff.

## Apology for Raimond Sebond[9]

### [MAN'S PRESUMPTION AND LITTLENESS]

What does Truth[1] preach to us, when she preaches to us to fly worldly philosophy,[2] when she so often impresses upon us, That our wisdom is but folly in the sight of God;[3] That of all vain things the most vain is man; That man, who presumes on his learning, does not yet know what it is to know;[4] and That if man, who is nothing, thinks himself something, he deceives and beguiles himself?[5] These sayings of the Holy Spirit so clearly and vividly express what I wish to maintain, that I should need no other proof against men who would bow with all submission and obedience to its authority. But the others[6] would rather be whipped to their own cost, and will not suffer their reason to be combated except by itself.

Let us then for the nonce consider man alone, without outside assistance, armed only with his own weapons, and destitute of the divine grace and knowledge, which comprise all his honour, his strength and the foundation of his being. Let us see how he will hold out in this fine equipment. Let him explain to me, by the force of his reason, on what foundation he has built those great advantages he thinks he has over the other creatures. What has induced him to believe that that wonderful motion of the heavenly vault, the eternal light of those torches rolling so proudly over his head, the awe-inspiring agitations of that infinite sea, were established, and endure through so many centuries for his service and convenience?

Is it possible to imagine anything more ridiculous than that this miserable and puny creature, who is not so much as master of himself, exposed to shocks on all sides should call himself Master and Emperor of the universe, of which it is not in his power to know the smallest part, much less to command it? And that privilege which he assumes of being the only creature in this great edifice that has the capacity to know the beauty and the several parts of it, the only one who is able to give thanks to the architect, and to keep an account of the receipts and outlay of the world: who has sealed him this privilege? Let him show us his letters-patent for this great and noble charge.

Have they been granted in favour of the wise only? Then few people would be concerned. Are the fools and the wicked deserving of so extraordinary a favour, and, being the worst lot in the world, of being preferred to all the rest?

---

9. Book II, Chapter 12. A small but significant section of the very long "Apology" is reprinted here.   1. Revealed truth, the Scriptures.   2. Colossians 2:8.   3. I Corinthians 3:19.   4. I Corinthians 8:2.   5. Galatians 6:3. This and the previous passages from St. Paul were among those inscribed on the walls of Montaigne's library.   6. Those who pretend to arrive at certainty through their human means, their reason, alone.

Shall we believe the man who says this, *For whose sake shall we then say that the world has been made? Undoubtedly for those creatures that have the use of reason: these are gods and men, to whom assuredly nothing is superior?* (Balbus the Stoic, according to Cicero).[7] We could never sufficiently deride the impudence of this coupling of gods and men.

But, poor devil, what is there in him deserving of such a privilege? When we consider the incorruptible life of the heavenly bodies, their beauty, their grandeur, their continual motion by so exact a rule:

> When we gaze aloft
> Upon the skiey vaults of yon great world
> The ether, fixt high over twinkling stars,
> And into our thought there come the journeyings
> Of sun and moon;   (Lucretius.)[8]

when we consider the dominion and power those bodies have, not only over our lives and the conditions of our fortune,

> Our lives and actions on the stars depend,
>                    (Manilius.)[9]

but even over our dispositions, our judgement, our will, which they govern, impel and stir at the mercy of their influence, as our reason discovers and tells us:

> This we learn: the far, far distant stars
> Govern by silent laws; the world is ruled
> By periodic causes, and the turns of destiny
> Observed by certain signs;   (Manilius.)[1]

when we see that not only a man, not only a king, but kingdoms, empires, and all this world here below are moved according to the lightest swing of the heavenly motions:

> How great a change each little motion brings!
> So great this kingdom that it governs kings;
>                    (Manilius.)[2]

if our virtue, our vices, our talents and our knowledge, if even this dissertation of mine on the power of the stars, this comparison between them and ourselves, comes, as our reason supposes, by their means and their favour;

---

7. Quoted in Cicero's *Of the Nature of the Gods*, Book II, Chapter 53.    8. *On the Nature of Things*, Book V, ll. 1204 ff.    9. *Astronomicon*, Book III, l. 58.    1. *Astronomicon*, Book I, ll. 60 ff.    2. *Astronomicon*, Book I, l. 57, and Book IV, l. 93.

> Maddened by love, Leander swims the strait,
> A Grecian king o'erturns the walls of Troy.
> 'Tis this man's lot to give his country laws.
> Sons kill their fathers, fathers kill their sons,
> And brothers arm themselves in mutual strife.
> Not we have made these wars; 'tis Fate compels
> To bear such pains with lacerated limbs.
> And Fate it is that makes me ponder Fate;    (Manilius.)[3]

if this little portion of reason we possess has been allotted to us by heaven, how can reason make us the equal of heaven? How can it subject its essence and conditions to our knowledge? All that we see in those bodies fills us with amazement. *What apparatus, what instruments, what levers, what engines, what craftsmen were employed about so mighty a work?* (Cicero).[4]

Why do we deny them a soul, and life and reason? Have we discovered in them any stubborn, senseless stupidity, we who have no concern with them but to obey them? Shall we say that we have seen no other creature but man in possession of a reasoning mind? Why! have we seen anything comparable to the sun? Does it exist the less for our not having seen its like? Does it move the less because no other movement is to be compared with it? If what we have not seen does not exist, our knowledge is marvellously shortsighted: *How close the confines of our mind!* (Cicero).[5]

Is it not a delusion of human vanity to make the moon a celestial earth, and to imagine that there are mountains and valleys upon it, as did Anaxagoras;[6] to set up human habitations and dwellings and establish colonies upon it for our convenience, as do Plato and Plutarch,[7] and to make our earth a bright and shining star? *Amongst other infirmities of human nature is that mental blindness which not only forces man to err, but makes him hug his errors* (Seneca).[8] *The corruptible body weighs down the soul, and this earthly habitation prevents it from pondering on many things* (The Book of Wisdom, quoted by Saint Augustine).[9]

Presumption is our natural and original infirmity. The frailest and most vulnerable of all creatures is man, and at the same time the most arrogant.[1] He sees and feels himself lodged here in the mud and filth of the world, nailed and riveted to the worst, the deadest and most stagnant part of the universe, at the lowest story of the house and the most remote from the vault of heaven, with the animals of the worst condition of the three; and he goes and sets himself

---

3. *Astronomicon*, Book IV, ll. 79 ff., and l. 118.    4. *Of the Nature of the Gods*, Book I, Chapter 8.    5. *Of the Nature of the Gods*, Book I, Chapter 31.    6. According to Diogenes Laertius, *Life of Anaxagoras*, Book II, Chapter 8.    7. For the notion that the moon is inhabited, Montaigne refers to Plutarch's *Of the Face of the Moon*.    8. *Of Wrath*, Book II, Chapter 9.    9. *City of God*, Book XII, Section 15.    1. The phrase, originally Pliny's, is another of those engraved on the walls of Montaigne's library.

in imagination above the circle of the moon, and brings heaven under his feet.

With this same vanity of imagination he makes himself the equal of God, assumes to himself divine qualities, selects and separates himself from among the multitude of other creatures, carves out their shares to each of his fellows and comrades, the animals, and allots to them their portion of faculties and powers according as it seems good to him. How can he know, by the force of his understanding, the secret and internal motions of the animals? By what comparison between them and himself does he suppose them to be as stupid as he thinks?

When I play with my cat, who knows but that she regards me more as a plaything than I do her? [We amuse each other with our respective monkey-tricks; if I have my moments for beginning and refusing, so she has hers.]

Plato,[2] in his picture of the golden age under Saturn, numbers, among the chief advantages of the man of that time, his communion with the beasts, of whom inquiring and learning he knew the real attributes and differences of each of them; whereby he acquired a very perfect understanding and wisdom, and in consequence passed his life very much more happily than we are able to do. Do we need a better proof of the impudence of man where the beasts are concerned? That great author[3] opined that, in giving them their bodily shape, Nature for the most part only considered the use they could be put to in the prognostications which were drawn from them in his time.

That defect which hinders communication between us and them, why may it not as well be in ourselves as in them? It is a matter of conjecture with whom the fault lies that we do not understand one another; for we understand them no more than they do us. By the same reasoning they may regard us as beasts, as we do them.

It is no great wonder if we do not understand them for neither do we understand the Basques[4] and the Troglodytes. Yet some have boasted of understanding them, as Apollonius of Tyana, Melampus, Tiresias, Thales, and others.[5] And since it is the case that, as the cosmographers tell, there are nations that receive a dog for their king, they must needs in some way interpret its voice and actions.

We must observe the parity there is between us. We have some halfway understanding of their meaning, as the animals have of ours, in about the same degree. They cajole us, they threaten us, they

---

2. In his *Statesman*.   3. Plato, in the *Timaeus*.   4. Inhabitants of the Pyrenees region on the Bay of Biscay, known for the difficulty and peculiarity of their language. *Troglodytes:* Cave dwellers.   5. A mixture of mythical and historical figures: Apollonius of Tyana, Greek neo-Pythagorean philosopher and magician (first century A.D.); Melampus, mythical physician and sage; Tiresias, mythical blind prophet of Thebes: Thales, regarded as the first Greek philosopher (sixth century B.C.), one of the Seven Sages of Greece.

entreat us, as we do them. Moreover, it is very evident to us that
they are able fully and completely to communicate with one another,
that they understand one another, and not only those of the same
species, but also those of different species.

> Since even the speechless herds, aye, since
> The very generations of wild beasts
> Are wont dissimilar and diverse sounds
> To rouse from in them, when there's fear or pain,
> And when they burst with joys.   (Lucretius.)[6]

A horse knows that a dog is angry when it barks in a certain way,
but is not afraid when it gives voice in another way. Even in those
creatures that have no voice we may easily infer, from the mutual
services we see them rendering each other, that they have some other
means of communication; their movements speak and negotiate:

> In much the same way as the lack-speech years
> Compel young children into gesturings.   (Lucretius.)[7]

Why not? just as well as our deaf-mutes dispute, argue and tell
stories by means of signs? I have seen some so skilful and practised
in that language, that in truth they did not fall short of perfection in
making themselves understood. Lovers use their eyes to express anger,
reconciliation, entreaty, thanks, to make appointments, in short for
every purpose;

> Silence too our thought and wish betrays.
>                                     (Tasso.)[8]

What of the hands? We beg, we promise, we call, we send away,
threaten, pray, entreat, deny, refuse, question, wonder, count, confess, repent, we express fear and shame, we doubt, inform, command, incite, encourage, swear, testify, accuse, condemn, absolve,
insult, despise, challenge, we show vexation, we flatter, applaud,
bless, humiliate, mock, reconcile, recommend, exalt, welcome,
rejoice, complain, we express grief, dejection, despair, astonishment, protestation, silence, and what not, in such varied and
numerous ways, in rivalry with the tongue.

With the head we invite, we dismiss, admit, disclaim, give the lie,
welcome, honour, reverence, disdain, demand, show the door, we
cheer, lament, caress, chide, submit, defy, exhort, threaten, assure,
and inquire. What of the eye-brows? What of the shoulders? There
is no movement that does not speak an intelligible, untaught lan-

---

6. *On the Nature of Things*, Book V, ll. 1058 ff.   7. *On the Nature of Things*, Book V, ll.
1029 ff.   8. Torquato Tasso, in the pastoral drama *Aminta*, Act II, Scene 3, ll. 35–36.

guage, that is understood by all. Which shows that, seeing the variety that distinguishes the spoken languages in use, this one must rather be considered the proper and natural speech of humankind. I pass over that which a particular necessity teaches one who is taken unawares; and the finger-alphabet; and grammar and the sciences which are only practised and expressed by gestures; and the nations that Pliny tells of, who have no other language.

An ambassador of the city of Abdera, after speaking at great length to King Agis of Sparta, said to him, 'Well, Sire, what answer do you wish me to carry back to our citizens?' 'That I allowed you to say all that you would and as much as you would, without ever a word.'[9] Was not that a very speaking and intelligible silence?

After all, which of our arts do we not see in the activities of animals? Is there any organization regulated with more order, with a better distribution of charges and functions, and more consistently maintained, than that of the bees? Can we imagine that so well-ordered a disposition of activities and occupations could be carried on without reason and foresight?

> Following signs and instances like these,
> Some testify that bees possess a share
> Of the world-spirit and the mind divine.   (Virgil.)[1]

Do the swallows that we see at the return of spring, ferreting out all the corners of the houses, conduct their search without judgment? Do they choose without discrimination, out of a thousand places, that which is most commodious for their lodging? Are the birds, when they weave those beautiful and wonderful habitations of theirs, able to use a square figure rather than a round, an obtuse rather than a right angle, without knowing their properties and effects? Do they fetch, now water, now clay, without having concluded that hardness is softened by moisture? Do they line the floors of their palaces with moss or down unless they have foreseen that the tender limbs of their young will lie more softly and comfortably? Do they shelter themselves from the rainy wind and build their cabins to the east, without knowing the different properties of the winds, and without considering that one is more healthy for them than the other?

Why does the spider thicken her web in one place and slacken it in another? Why does she use now one kind of knot, now another, unless she possesses thought, deliberation and the power of inference?

We may see well enough, in most of their works, how much the animals surpass us, and how much we fall short in the art of imitat-

9. The story is told by Plutarch in *Apothegms of the Lacedaemonians.*    1. *Georgics*, Book IV, ll. 219 ff.

ing them. And yet, in our ruder performances, we are sensible of
what faculties we employ, and we know that our mind applies to
them its utmost powers; why do we not conclude the same of the
animals? Why do we ascribe to I know not what slavish instinct of
nature those works that excel anything we can do by nature or art?
Herein we unconsciously give them a very great advantage over ourselves, in making Nature, with a maternal kindness, to accompany
and lead them as it were by the hand, to all the activities and con-
veniences of their life; whilst us she abandons to chance and fortune,
and forces us to seek by art the things necessary for our preservation,
at the same time denying us the means of attaining, by any education or mental effort, to the natural skill of the animals. So that their
brutish stupidity surpasses in all their contrivances everything we are
able to do with our divine intelligence.

Truly, by this reckoning, we might with great reason call her a
very unjust stepmother; but that is not so. Our organization is not so
formless and unregulated. Nature has been universally kind to all
her creatures, and there is none that she has not very amply furnished with all the means necessary for the preservation of its being.
For those common complaints that I hear men uttering (as the licence of their opinions now lifts them up above the clouds, now brings
them down to the antipodes), that we are the only outcast animal,
bare on the bare earth, bound and tied down, with no means of
arming or covering ourselves but with others' spoils; whereas all the
other creatures have been clothed by Nature with shells, husks, bark,
hair, wool, spikes, leather, down, feathers, scales, fleece, bristles,
according to the need of their being; armed with claws, teeth, horns
for attack and defence, and has herself instructed them in what is
requisite to each, to swim, run, fly, sing, whilst man cannot even
walk or speak, nor eat, nor do anything but weep, without an
apprenticeship:

> Then again the babe,
> Like to the castaway of the raging surf,
> Lies naked on the ground, speechless, in want
> Of every help for life, when Nature first
> Hath poured him forth upon the shores of light
> With birth-pangs from within the mother's womb,
> And with a plaintive wail he fills the place,—
> As well befitting one for whom remains
> In life a journey through so many ills.
> But all the flocks and herds and all wild beasts
> Come forth and grow, nor need the little rattles,
> Nor must be treated to the humouring nurse's
> Dear broken chatter; nor seek they divers clothes
> To suit the changing skies; nor need, in fine,

> Nor arms, nor lofty ramparts, wherewithal
> Their own to guard—because the earth herself
> And Nature, artificer of the world, bring forth
> Aboundingly all things for all.   (Lucretius.)[2]

These complaints are unfounded; there is in the governance of the world a much greater equality and a more uniform relationship. Our skin is provided as abundantly as theirs with power to resist the inclemency of the weather. Witness the many nations that have not yet tried the use of clothes. Our ancient Gauls wore hardly any clothes, like our neighbours the Irish of the present day, in spite of their cold climate.

But we may judge better by ourselves: for all those parts of our person which we are pleased to expose to the wind and air are adapted to endure it, the feet, the face, the hands, the legs, the shoulders, the head, according to the demands of usage. For if there is in us a tender spot, in which we should seem to fear the cold, it should be the stomach, where digestion takes place; our fathers used to leave it uncovered, and our ladies, soft and delicate as they are, sometimes go half-covered down to the navel.

Nor are the bindings and swaddlings of infants any more necessary. The Lacedemonian mothers reared their children in all freedom to move their limbs, without any wrappings or fastenings.

Our weeping we have in common with most of the other animals; there are hardly any that do not wail and whine long after their birth, seeing that it is a natural effect of their helplessness at that age. As to the habit of eating, it is natural to us as well as to them, and comes without instruction:

> For each creature feels
> By instinct to what use to put its powers.
>                (Lucretius.)[3]

Who doubts but that a child, having acquired the strength to feed himself, is able to seek his food? And the earth yields and offers him enough for his needs, without any cultivation and artifice; and if not at all times, no more does she do it for the animals. Witness the provision we see made by the ants and other creatures, in view of the barren season of the year. Those nations we have lately discovered, so abundantly provided with meat and a natural drink, without care or trouble on their part, have now made us realize that bread is not our only sustenance, and that, without any tilling, our Mother Nature has plentifully provided us with all that we need. Nay, as seems very

---

2. *On the Nature of Things*, Book V, ll. 222 ff.    3. *On the Nature of Things*, Book V, ll. 1033 ff.

probable, more amply and richly than she does now that we have
taken to meddling with it by our contrivances:

> She first, the Earth, of own accord
> The shining grains and vineyards of all joy
> Created for mortality; herself
> Gave the sweet fruitage and the pastures glad,
> Which now to-day yet scarcely wax in size,
> Even when, aided by our toiling arms,
> We break the ox, and wear away the strength
> Of sturdy farm-hands;     (Lucretius.)[4]

the excess and unruliness of our appetite outstripping all the inventions wherewith we seek to satisfy it.

With regard to weapons, we are better provided by Nature than
most other animals; we are more able to move our limbs about and
to extract service from them, naturally and without being taught.
Those who are trained to fight naked are seen to rush into dangers
just like our own soldiers. If some of the beasts surpass us in this
advantage, we surpass many others in the same. We possess by a
natural instinct and teaching the skill to fortify our bodies and protect
them by acquired means. That this is so is proved by the example of
the elephant who sharpens and grinds the teeth which he makes use
of in warfare (for he has special teeth which he saves and employs
for this purpose only). When bulls go to battle they throw up and
scatter the dust around them; the boars whet their tusks; the ichneu-
mon, when it is about to grapple with the crocodile, fortifies its body
by coating it all over with a crust of mud, well kneaded and compressed, as with a cuirass. Why shall we not say that it is as natural
to us to arm ourselves with wood and iron?

As to speech, it is certain that, if it is not natural neither is it
necessary. Nevertheless I believe that a child brought up in complete
solitude, far from all intercourse (which would be a difficult experiment to make), would have some kind of speech to express his ideas.
And it is not to be believed that Nature has denied us this power
which she has given to many other animals; for what else but speech
is that faculty we observe in them of complaining, rejoicing, calling
to one another for succour, inviting to love, which they do by the
use of their voice?

Why should they not speak with one another? They speak to us,
and we to them: in how many different tones do we not speak to our
dogs? and they answer us. We use another language with them, than
we do in talking to birds, pigs, oxen and horses, and give them other
names; we change the idiom according to the kind.

---

4. *On the Nature of Things,* Book II, ll. 1157 ff.

> So ants amidst their sable-coloured band
> One with another mouth to mouth confer,
> Haply their way or state to understand.   (Dante.)[5]

Lactantius seems to attribute to beasts not only the power of speech but also of laughter. And the same difference of tongues which, according to the differences of countries, is found in human beings, is also found in animals of the same species. Aristotle, writing on this subject, instances the various calls of partridges, according to locality:

> The dappled birds
> Utter at other times far other cries
> Than when they fight for food, or with their prey
> Struggle and strain. And birds there are which change
> With changing weather their own raucous songs.
> (Lucretius.)[6]

But it is yet to be known what language the supposed child would speak; and what has been conjectured about it has no great probability. If any one declares to me, in opposition to this belief, that those deaf by nature do not speak, I reply that it is not only because they have not been taught to speak by ear, but more because the sense of hearing, of which they are deprived, is related to that of speech, and that they hold together by a natural tie; in such a way that the words we speak must in the first place be spoken to ourselves, and be made to strike upon our own inward ears, before being sent out to others' ears.

I have said all this to establish the resemblance to human conditions, and to bring us back and join us to the majority. We are neither superior nor inferior to the rest. All that is under heaven, says the sage, is subject to one law and one fate:

> Enshackled in the gruesome bonds of doom.
> (Lucretius.)[7]

Some difference there is; there are orders and degrees, but under the aspect of one same Nature:

> But each sole thing
> Proceeds according to its proper wont,
> And all conserve their own distinctions, based
> In Nature's fixed decree.   (Lucretius.)[8]

---

5. *Purgatory*, Canto XXVI, ll. 34 ff.   6. *On the Nature of Things*, Book V, ll. 1078 ff.
7. *On the Nature of Things*, Book V, l. 874.   8. *On the Nature of Things*, Book V, ll. 921 ff.

Man must be forced and lined up within the barriers of this organization. The poor wretch has no mind really to step over them. He is shackled and entangled, he is subjected to the same obligation as the other creatures of his order, and is of a very mediocre condition, without any real and essential prerogative and preeminence. That which he thinks and imagines himself to possess, neither has body nor can it be perceived. And if it be so that he alone of all the animals has this freedom of imagination, this licence of thought, which represents to him that which is, that which is not, that which he wills, the false and the true; it is an advantage sold to him very dearly, and of which he has very little cause to boast. For from it springs the principal source of all the ills that press upon him, sin, sickness, irresolution, affliction, despair.

## Of Repentance[9]

### ["THESE TESTIMONIES OF A GOOD CONSCIENCE"]

Others form man; I describe him, and portray a particular, very ill-made one, who, if I had to fashion him anew, should indeed be very different from what he is. But now it is done.

Now the features of my painting do not err, although they change and vary. The world is but a perennial see-saw. All things in it are incessantly on the swing, the earth, the rocks of the Caucasus, the Egyptian pyramids, both with the common movement and their own particular movement. Even fixedness is nothing but a more sluggish motion.

I cannot fix my object; it is befogged, and reels with a natural intoxication. I seize it at this point, as it is at the moment when I beguile myself with it. I do not portray the thing in itself. I portray the passage; not a passing from one age to another, or, as the people put it, from seven years to seven years,[1] but from day to day, from minute to minute. I must adapt my history to the moment. I may presently change, not only by chance, but also by intention. It is a record of diverse and changeable events, of undecided, and when the occasion arises, contradictory ideas; whether it be that I am another self, or that I grasp a subject in different circumstances and see it from a different point of view. So it may be that I contradict myself, but, as Demades[2] said, the truth I never contradict. If my mind could find a firm footing, I should not speak tentatively, I should decide; it is always in a state of apprenticeship, and on trial.

I am holding up to view a humble and lustreless life; that is all one. Moral philosophy, in any degree, may apply to an ordinary and

9. Book III, Chapter 2. The opening part of the essay is reprinted here.    1. An allusion to the popular notion that the human body is completely renewed every seven years.    2. Greek orator and politician of the fourth century B.C.

secluded life as well as to one of richer stuff; every man carries within him the entire form of the human constitution.

Authors communicate themselves to the world by some special and extrinsic mark; I am the first to do so by my general being, as Michel de Montaigne, not as a grammarian or a poet or a lawyer. If the world finds fault with me for speaking too much of myself, I find fault with the world for not even thinking of itself.

But is it reasonable that I, who am so retired in actual life, should aspire to make myself known to the public? And is it reasonable that I should show up to the world, where artifice and ceremony enjoy so much credit and authority, the crude and simple results of nature, and of a nature besides very feeble? Is it not like making a wall without stone or a similar material, thus to build a book without learning or art? The ideas of music are guided by art, mine by chance. This I have at least in conformity with rules, that no man ever treated of a subject that he knew and understood better than I do this that I have taken up; and that in this I am the most learned man alive. Secondly, that no man ever penetrated more deeply into his matter, nor more minutely analysed its parts and consequences, nor more fully and exactly reached the goal he had made it his business to set up. To accomplish it I need only bring fidelity to it; and that is here, as pure and sincere as may be found.

I speak the truth, not enough to satisfy myself, but as much as I dare to speak. And I become a little more daring as I grow older; for it would seem that custom allows this age more freedom to prate, and more indiscretion in speaking of oneself. It cannot be the case here, as I often see elsewhere, that the craftsman and his work contradict each other. 'How could a man who shows to such advantage in company write so foolish a book?' or, 'Are these learned writings the work of a man of such feeble conversation?'

When a man of ordinary conversation writes uncommon things, it means that his talent lies in the place from which he borrows them, and not in himself. A learned man is not learned at all things; but the accomplished man is accomplished in all things, even in ignorance.

Here, my book and I go hand in hand together, and keep one pace. In other cases we may commend or censure the work apart from the workman; not so here. Who touches the one touches the other. He who judges the one without knowing the other will wrong himself more than he does me; he who has come to know the work will completely satisfy me. Happy beyond my deserts if I have only this share of public approval, that intelligent persons will be made to feel that I was capable of profiting by learning, if I had any; and that I deserved more assistance from my memory!

In this place let me offer an excuse for what I often repeat, that I seldom repent, and that my conscience is satisfied with itself, not as the conscience of an angel or a horse, but as the conscience of a man; always with the addition of this refrain, not a formal or conventional refrain, but prompted by a real and natural modesty, 'that I speak as an inquirer and an ignoramus, leaving the decision purely and simply to the common and authorized beliefs.' I do not teach, I relate.

There is no vice, that is really a vice, which is not hurtful and which a sound judgement does not condemn; for its ugliness and evil consequences are so apparent that they are perhaps right who say that it is chiefly begotten of stupidity and ignorance. So hard it is to imagine that a man may know it and not hate it!

Wickedness sucks in the greater part of its own venom, and poisons itself with it.

Vice, like an ulcer in the flesh, leaves a repentance in the soul, which is always scratching itself and drawing blood. For Reason blots out all other grief and sorrow, but begets that of repentance, which is the more hard to bear since it is born from within; as the chill and heat of a fever are more acutely felt than those which are external. I regard as vices (but each according to its measure), not only those which are condemned by reason and Nature, but those too which have been created by human opinion, even false and erroneous opinion, if it is authorized by laws and custom.

There is likewise no goodness in which a well-born nature does not delight. We feel indeed a certain self-congratulation when we do a good deed, which gives us inward satisfaction, and that generous pride which accompanies a good conscience. A boldly wicked soul may perhaps arm itself with assurance; but with that complacency and satisfaction it cannot provide itself.

There is no small pleasure in feeling oneself preserved from the contagion of so corrupt an age, and saying to oneself, 'Should any one look into my very soul, he would yet not find me guilty of the affliction or ruin of any man, or of revenge or envy, of publicly offending against the laws, of innovation or disturbance, or of failing to keep my word. And whatever the licence of the times may permit or suggest to any man, I have laid hands on no Frenchman's property nor dived into his purse. I have never lived but on what is my own, either in war or peace time; and have never used another man's labour without hire.' These testimonies of a good conscience please; and this natural satisfaction is a great boon to us, and the only payment that will never fail us.

# MIGUEL DE CERVANTES

## 1547–1616

The author of Don Quixote's extravagant adventures himself had a very unusual and adventurous life. The son of an apothecary, Miguel de Cervantes Saavedra was born in 1547 in Alcalá de Henares, a university town near Madrid. Almost nothing is known of his childhood and early education. Only in 1569 is he mentioned as a favorite pupil by a Madrid humanist, Juan López. Records indicate that by the end of that year he had left Spain and was living in Rome, for a time in the service of Giulio Acquaviva, who later became a cardinal. We know that he enlisted in the Spanish fleet under the command of Don John of Austria and that he took part in the struggle of the allied forces of Christendom against the Turks. He was at the crucial Battle of Lepanto (1571), where in spite of fever he fought valiantly and received three gunshot wounds, one of which permanently impaired the use of his left hand, "for the greater glory of the right." After further military action and garrison duty at Palermo and Naples, he and his brother Rodrigo, bearing testimonials from Don John and from the viceroy of Sicily, began the journey back to Spain, where Miguel hoped to obtain a captaincy. In September 1575 their ship was captured near the Marseille coast by Barbary pirates, and the two brothers were taken as prisoners to Algiers. Cervantes's captors, considering him a person of some consequence, held him as a slave for a high ransom. He repeatedly attempted to escape, and his daring and foritude excited the admiration of Hassan Pasha, the viceroy of Algiers, who bought him for five hundred crowns after five years of captivity.

Cervantes was freed on September 15, 1580, and reached Madrid in December of that year. There his literary career began rather inauspiciously; he wrote twenty or thirty plays, with little success, and in 1585 published a pastoral romance, *Galatea*. At about this time he had a natural daughter by Ana Franca de Rojas, and during the same period married Catalina de Salazar, who was eighteen years his junior. Seeking nonliterary employment, he obtained a position in the navy, requisitioning and collecting supplies for the Invincible Armada. Irregularities in his administration, for which he was held responsible if not directly guilty, caused him to spend time in prison. In 1590 he tried unsuccessfully to obtain colonial employment in the New World. Later he served as tax collector in the province of Granada, but was dismissed from government service in 1597.

The following years of Cervantes's life are the most obscure: there is a legend that *Don Quixote* was first conceived and planned while its author was in prison in Seville. In 1604 he was in Valladolid, then the temporary capital of Spain, living in sordid surroundings with the numerous women of his family (his wife, daughter, niece, and two sisters). It was in Valladolid, in late 1604, that he obtained the official license for the publication of *Don Quixote* (Part I). The book appeared in 1605 and was a popular success. Cervantes followed the Spanish court when it returned to Madrid, where he continued to live poorly in spite of a popularity with readers that quickly made proverbial figures of his heroes. A false sequel to his book appeared, prompting him to write his own continuation, *Don Quixote*, Part II, published in 1615. His *Exemplary Tales* had appeared in 1613. He died on April 23, 1616, and was buried in the convent of the Barefooted Trinitarian nuns. *Persiles and Sigismunda*, his last novel, was published posthumously in 1617.

Although, as we have indicated, *The Ingenious Gentleman Don Quixote de la Mancha* was a popular success from the time Part I was published in 1605, it was only later recognized as an important work of literature. This delay was due partly to the fact that in a period of established and well-defined literary genres such as the epic, the tragedy, and the pastoral romance (Cervantes himself had tried his hand at some of these forms), the unconventional combination of elements in *Don Quixote* resulted in a work of considerable novelty, with the serious aspects hidden under a mocking surface.

The initial and overt purpose of the book was to satirize the romances of chivalry. In those long yarns, which had to do with the Carolingian and Arthurian legends and which were full of supernatural deeds of valor, implausible and complicated adventures, duels, and enchantments, the literature that had expressed the medieval spirit of chivalry and romance had degenerated to the same extent to which, in our day, certain conventions of romantic literature have degenerated in "pulp" fiction and film melodrama. Up to a point, then, what Cervantes set out to do was to produce a parody, a caricature of a literary type. But neither the nature of his genius nor the particular method he chose allowed him to limit himself to such a relatively simple and direct undertaking. The actual method he followed in order to expose the silliness of the romances of chivalry was to show to what extraordinary consequences they would lead a man insanely infatuated with them, once this man set out to live "now" according to their patterns of action and belief.

So what we have is not mere parody or caricature; for there is a great deal of difference between presenting a remote and more or less imaginary world, and presenting a modern man deciding to live by the standards of that world in a modern and realistic context. The first consequence is a mingling of genres. On the one hand, much of the book has the color and intonation of the world of medieval chivalry as its poets had portrayed it. The fact that that vision and that tone depend for their existence in the book on the self-deception of the hero makes them no less operative artistically, and adds, in fact, an important element of idealization. On the other hand, the chivalric world is continuously jostled by elements of contemporary life evoked by the narrator—the realities of landscape and speech, peasants and nobles, inns and highways. So the author can draw on two sources, roughly the realistic and the romantic, truth and vision, practical facts and lofty values. In this respect—having found a way to bring together concrete actuality and highly ideal values—Cervantes can be said to have fathered the modern novel.

The consequences of Cervantes's invention are more apparent when we begin to analyze a little more closely the nature of these worlds, romantic and realistic, and the kind of impact the first exerts on the second. The hero embodying the world of the romances is not, as we know, a cavalier; he is an impoverished country gentleman who embraces that code in the "modern" world. Chivalry is not directly satirized; it is simply placed in a context different from its native one. The result of that new association is a new whole, a new unity. The "code" is renovated; it is put into a different perspective, given another chance.

We should remember at this point that in the process of deterioration which the romances of chivalry had undergone, certain basically attractive ideals had become empty conventions—for instance, the ideal of love as devoted "service." In this connection, it may be especially interesting to observe that the treatment of love, and Don Quixote's conception of it, are not limited to his well-known admiration for his purely fantastic lady Dulcinea, but are also dealt with from a feminine point of view. See, as illustration, Marcela's elaborate, logical, and poetic speech (Part I, chapter 14, reprinted here) which Don Quixote warmly admires; in it the noble shepherdesss defends herself against the accusation of being "a wild beast and a basilisk" for having caused Grisóstomo's death, and proclaims her right to choose her particular kind of freedom in nature, where "these mountain trees are my company, the clear running waters in these brooks are my mirror. . . ."

No less relevant are Quixote's ideals of adventurousness, of loyalty to high concepts of valor and generosity. In the new context those values are re-examined. Cervantes may well have gained a practical sense of them in his own life while still a youth, for instance at the Battle of Lepanto (the great victory of the European coalition against the "infidels"), and as a pirate's captive. Since he began writing *Don Quixote* in his late fifties, a vantage point from which the adventures of his youth must have appeared impossibly remote, a factor of nostalgia—which could hardly have been present in a pure satire—may well have entered into his work. Furthermore, had he undertaken a direct caricature of the romance genre, the serious and noble values of chivalry could not have been made apparent except negatively, whereas in the context devised by him in *Don Quixote* they find a way to assert themselves positively as well.

The book in its development is, to a considerable extent, the story of that assertion—of the impact that Don Quixote's revitalization of the chivalric code has on a contemporary world. We must remember, of course, that there is ambiguity in the way the assertion is made; it works slowly on the reader, as his own discovery rather than as the narrator's overt suggestion. Actually, whatever attraction the chivalric world of his hero's vision may have had for Cervantes, he does not openly support Don Quixote at all. He even seems at times to go further in repudiating him than he needs to, for the hero is officially insane, and the narrator never tires of reminding us of this. One critic has described the attitude Cervantes affects toward his creature as "animosity." Nevertheless, by the very magniloquence and, often, the extraordinary coherence and beauty which the narrator allows his hero to display in his speeches in defense of his vision and his code, we are gradually led to discover for ourselves the serious and important elements these contain. For instance, Don Quixote's speech evoking the lost Golden Age and justifying the institution of knight-errantry (in Part I, chapter 12, reprinted here) is described by the narrator—after Don Quixote has delivered it—as a "futile harangue" which "Might very well have been dispensed with"; but there it is, in all of its fervor and effectiveness. Thus the narrator's so-called animosity ultimately does nothing but intensify our interest in Don Quixote and our sympathy for him. And in that process we are, as audience, simply repeating the experience many characters have on the "stage" of the book, in their relationships with him.

Generally speaking, the encounters between the ordinary world and Don Quixote are encounters between the world of reality and that of illusion, between reason and imagination, ultimately between the world in which action is prompted by material considerations and interests and a world in which action is prompted by ideal motives. Our selections illustrate these aspects of the experience. Among the first adventures are some which have most contributed to popularize the Don Quixote legend: he sees windmills and decides they are giants; country inns become castles; flocks of sheep, armies. Though the conclusions of such episodes often have the ludicrousness of slapstick comedy, there is a powerfully imposing quality about Don Quixote's insanity: his madness always has method, a commanding persistence and coherence. And there is perhaps an inevitable sense of moral grandeur in the spectacle of anyone remaining so unflinchingly faithful to his own vision. The world of "reason" may win in point of fact, but we come to wonder whether from a moral point of view Quixote is not the victor.

Furthermore, we increasingly realize that Quixote's own manner of action has greatness in itself, and not only the greatness of persistence: his purpose is to redress wrongs, to come to the aid of the afflicted, to offer generous help, to challenge danger and practice valor. And we finally feel the impact of the arguments that sustain his action—for example, in the section from Part II (the episode of the lions) in which he expounds "the meaning of valor." The ridiculousness of the situation is counterbalanced by the basic seriousness of Quixote's motives; his notion of courage for its own sake appears, and is recognized, as singularly noble, a sort of generous display of integrity in a world usually ruled by lower standards. Thus the distinction between "reason" and "madness," truth and illusion, becomes, to say the least, ambiguous. The hero's delusions are indeed exposed when they come up against hard facts, but the authority of such facts is seen to be morally questionable.

The effectiveness of Don Quixote's conduct and vision is seen most clearly in his relationship with his "squire" Sancho Panza. It would be a crude oversimplification to say that Don Quixote and Sancho represent illusion and reality, the insane code of knight-errantry versus down-to-earth practicalities. Actually Sancho—though his nature is strongly defined by such elements as his common sense, his earthy speech, his simple phrases studded with proverbs set against the hero's magniloquence—is mainly characterized in his development by the degree to which he believes in his master. He is caught in the snare of Don Quixote's vision; the seeds of the imaginative life are successfully implanted in him.

The impact of Quixote's view of life on Sancho serves therefore to illustrate one of the important qualities of the protagonist and, we may finally say, one of the important aspects of Renaissance literature: the attempt, ultimately frustrated but extremely attractive as long as it lasts, of the individual mind to produce a vision and a system of its own, in a world that often seems to have lost a universal frame of reference and a fully satisfactory sense of the value and meaning of action. What Don Quixote presents is a vision of a world which, for all its aberrant qualities, appears generally to be more colorful and more thrilling, and also, incidentally, to be inspired by more honorable rules of conduct, than the world of ordinary people, "realism," current affairs, private interests, easy jibes, and petty pranks. It is a world in which actions are performed out of a sense of their beauty and excitement, not for the sake of their usefulness. It is, again, the world as stage, animated by "folly"; in this case the lights go out at the end, an end which is "reasonable" and therefore gloomy. Sancho provides the main example of one who is exposed to that vision and absorbs that light while it lasts. How successfully he has done so is seen during Don Quixote's death scene, in which Sancho begs his master not to die but to continue the play, as has been suggested, in a new costume—that of shepherds in an Arcadian setting. But at that final point the hero is "cured" and killed, and Sancho is restored to the petty interests of the world as he can see it by his own lights, after the cord connecting him to his imaginative master is cut by the latter's "repentance" and death.

William Byron's *Cervantes: A Biography* (1978) is very thorough. The more advanced student of *Don Quixote* will find useful Howard Mancing's detailed study, *The Chivalric World of Don Quijote: Style, Structure, and Narrative Technique* (1982). Lowry Nelson, ed., *Cervantes: A Collection of Critical Essays* (1969), offers the views of eminent scholars and authors.

# Don Quixote[1]

## Part I

### ["I Know Who I Am, and Who I May Be, If I Choose"]

#### CHAPTER 1

*Which treats of the station in life and the pursuits of the famous gentleman, Don Quixote de la Mancha.*

In a village of La Mancha[2] the name of which I have no desire to recall, there lived not so long ago one of those gentlemen who always have a lance in the rack, an ancient buckler, a skinny nag, and a greyhound for the chase. A stew with more beef than mutton in it, chopped meat for his evening meal, scraps for a Saturday, lentils on Friday, and a young pigeon as a special delicacy for Sunday, went to account for three-quarters of his income. The rest of it he laid out on a broadcloth greatcoat and velvet stockings for feast days, with

---

1. Abridged. Translated by Samuel Putnam.    2. Efforts at identifying the village have proved inconclusive; La Mancha is a section of Spain south of Madrid.

slippers to match, while the other days of the week he cut a figure in a suit of the finest homespun. Living with him were a housekeeper in her forties, a niece who was not yet twenty, and a lad of the field and market place who saddled his horse for him and wielded the pruning knife.

This gentleman of ours was close on to fifty, of a robust constitution but with little flesh on his bones and a face that was lean and gaunt. He was noted for his early rising, being very fond of the hunt. They will try to tell you that his surname was Quijada or Quesada—there is some difference of opinion among those who have written on the subject—but according to the most likely conjectures we are to understand that it was really Quejana. But all this means very little so far as our story is concerned, providing that in the telling of it we do not depart one iota from the truth.

You may know, then, that the aforesaid gentleman, on those occasions when he was at leisure, which was most of the year around, was in the habit of reading books of chivalry with such pleasure and devotion as to lead him almost wholly to forget the life of a hunter and even the administration of his estate. So great was his curiosity and infatuation in this regard that he even sold many acres of tillable land in order to be able to buy and read the books that he loved, and he would carry home with him as many of them as he could obtain.

Of all those that he thus devoured none pleased him so well as the ones that had been composed by the famous Feliciano de Silva,[3] whose lucid prose style and involved conceits were as precious to him as pearls; especially when he came to read those tales of love and amorous challenges that are to be met with in many places, such a passage as the following, for example: "The reason of the unreason that afflicts my reason, in such a manner weakens my reason that I with reason lament me of your comeliness." And he was similarly affected when his eyes fell upon such lines as these: ". . . the high Heaven of your divinity divinely fortifies you with the stars and renders you deserving of that desert your greatness doth deserve."

The poor fellow used to lie awake nights in an effort to disentangle the meaning and make sense out of passages such as these, although Aristotle himself would not have been able to understand them, even if he had been resurrected for that sole purpose. He was not at ease in his mind over those wounds that Don Belianís[4] gave and received; for no matter how great the surgeons who treated him, the poor fellow must have been left with his face and his entire body covered with marks and scars. Nevertheless, he was grateful to the author for closing the book with the promise of an interminable adventure to come; many a time he was tempted to take up his pen and literally

---

3. A sixteenth-century author of romances; the quotation which follows is from his *Don Florisel de Niquea*.    4. The allusion is to a romance by Jeronimo Fernández.

finish the tale as had been promised, and he undoubtedly would have done so, and would have succeeded at it very well, if his thoughts had not been constantly occupied with other things of greater moment.

He often talked it over with the village curate, who was a learned man, a graduate of Sigüenza,[5] and they would hold long discussions as to who had been the better knight, Palmerin of England or Amadis of Gaul;[6] but Master Nicholas, the barber of the same village, was in the habit of saying that no one could come up to the Knight of Phoebus,[7] and that if anyone *could* compare with him it was Don Galaor, brother of Amadis of Gaul, for Galaor was ready for anything—he was none of your finical knights, who went around whimpering as his brother did, and in point of valor he did not lag behind him.

In short, our gentleman became so immersed in his reading that he spent whole nights from sundown to sunup and his days from dawn to dusk in poring over his books, until, finally, from so little sleeping and so much reading, his brain dried up and he went completely out of his mind. He had filled his imagination with everything that he had read, with enchantments, knightly encounters, battles, challenges, wounds, with tales of love and its torments, and all sorts of impossible things, and as a result had come to believe that all these fictitious happenings were true; they were more real to him than anything else in the world. He would remark that the Cid Ruy Díaz had been a very good knight, but there was no comparison between him and the Knight of the Flaming Sword, who with a single backward stroke had cut in half two fierce and monstrous giants. He preferred Bernardo del Carpio, who at Roncesvalles had slain Roland despite the charm[8] the latter bore, availing himself of the stratagem which Hercules employed when he strangled Antaeus, the son of Earth, in his arms.[9]

He had much good to say for Morgante[1] who, though he belonged to the haughty, overbearing race of giants, was of an affable disposition and well brought up. But, above all, he cherished an admiration for Rinaldo of Montalbán,[2] especially as he beheld him sallying forth from his castle to rob all those that crossed his path, or when he thought of him overseas stealing the image of Mohammed which, so the story has it, was all of gold. And he would have liked very well

---

5. Ironical, for Sigüenza was the seat of a minor and discredited university.    6. Heroes of two very famous romances of chivalry.    7. Or Knight of the Sun. Heroes of romances customarily adopted emblematic names and also changed them according to circumstances. See in the following paragraph the reference to the Knight of the Flaming Sword.    8. The magic gift of invulnerability.    9. The mythological Antaeus was invulnerable as long as he maintained contact with his mother, Earth; Hercules killed him while holding him raised in his arms.    1. In Pulci's *Morgante maggiore*, a comic-epic poem of the Italian Renaissance.    2. In Boiardo's *Roland in Love (Orlando innamorato)* and Ariosto's *Roland Mad (Orlando furioso)*, romantic and comic-epic poems of the Italian Renaissance. Rinaldo is Roland's cousin.

to have had his fill of kicking that traitor Galalón,[3] a privilege for which he would have given his housekeeper with his niece thrown into the bargain.

At last, when his wits were gone beyond repair, he came to conceive the strangest idea that ever occurred to any madman in this world. It now appeared to him fitting and necessary, in order to win a greater amount of honor for himself and serve his country at the same time, to become a knight-errant and roam the world on horseback, in a suit of armor; he would go in quest of adventures, by way of putting into practice all that he had read in his books; he would right every manner of wrong, placing himself in situations of the greatest peril such as would redound to the eternal glory of his name. As a reward for his valor and the might of his arm, the poor fellow could already see himself crowned Emperor of Trebizond at the very least; and so, carried away by the strange pleasure that he found in such thoughts as these, he at once set about putting his plan into effect.

The first thing he did was to burnish up some old pieces of armor, left him by his great-grandfather, which for ages had lain in a corner, moldering and forgotten. He polished and adjusted them as best he could, and then he noticed that one very important thing was lacking: there was no closed helmet, but only a morion, or visorless headpiece, with turned up brim of the kind foot soldiers wore. His ingenuity, however, enabled him to remedy this, and he proceeded to fashion out of cardboard a kind of half-helmet, which, when attached to the morion, gave the appearance of a whole one. True, when he went to see if it was strong enough to withstand a good slashing blow, he was somewhat disappointed; for when he drew his sword and gave it a couple of thrusts, he succeeded only in undoing a whole week's labor. The ease with which he had hewed it to bits disturbed him no little, and he decided to make it over. This time he placed a few strips of iron on the inside, and then, convinced that it was strong enough, refrained from putting it to any further test; instead, he adopted it then and there as the finest helmet ever made.

After this, he went out to have a look at his nag; and although the animal had more *cuartos*, or cracks, in its hoof than there are quarters in a real,[4] and more blemishes than Gonela's steed which *tantum pellis et ossa fuit*,[5] it nonetheless looked to its master like a far better horse than Alexander's Bucephalus or the Babieca of the Cid.[6] He spent all of four days in trying to think up a name for his mount; for—so he told himself—seeing that it belonged to so famous and worthy a knight, there was no reason why it should not have a name

3. Ganelon, the villain in the Charlemagne legend who betrayed the French at Roncesvalles.
4. A coin (about five cents); a *cuarto* was one eighth of a *real*.     5. Was so much skin and bones.     6. "The chief," Ruy Diaz, celebrated hero of the twelfth-century *Pocma del Cid*.

of equal renown. The kind of name he wanted was one that would
at once indicate what the nag had been before it came to belong to
a knight-errant and what its present status was; for it stood to reason
that, when the master's worldly condition changed, his horse also
ought to have a famous, high-sounding appellation, one suited to
the new order of things and the new profession that it was to follow.

After he in his memory and imagination had made up, struck out,
and discarded many names, now adding to and now subtracting from
the list, he finally hit upon "Rocinante," a name that impressed him
as being sonorous and at the same time indicative of what the steed
had been when it was but a hack, whereas now it was nothing other
than the first and foremost of all the hacks[7] in the world.

Having found a name for his horse that pleased his fancy, he then
desired to do as much for himself, and this required another week,
and by the end of that period he had made up his mind that he was
henceforth to be known as Don Quixote, which, as has been stated,
has led the authors of this veracious history to assume that his real
name must undoubtedly have been Quijada, and not Quesada as
others would have it. But remembering that the valiant Amadis was
not content to call himself that and nothing more, but added the
name of his kingdom and fatherland that he might make it famous
also, and thus came to take the name Amadis of Gaul, so our good
knight chose to add his place of origin and become "Don Quixote
de la Mancha"; for by this means, as he saw it, he was making very
plain his lineage and was conferring honor upon his country by taking its name as his own.

And so, having polished up his armor and made the morion over
into a closed helmet, and having given himself and his horse a name,
he naturally found but one thing lacking still: he must seek out a
lady of whom he could become enamored; for a knight-errant without a lady-love was like a tree without leaves or fruit, a body without
a soul.

"If," he said to himself, "as a punishment for my sins or by a
stroke of fortune I should come upon some giant hereabouts, a thing
that very commonly happens to knights-errant, and if I should slay
him in a hand-to-hand encounter or perhaps cut him in two, or,
finally, if I should vanquish and subdue him, would it not be well
to have someone to whom I may send him as a present, in order that
he, if he is living, may come in, fall upon his knees in front of my
sweet lady, and say in a humble and submissive tone of voice, 'I,
lady, am the giant Caraculiambro, lord of the island Malindrania,
who has been overcome in single combat by that knight who never
can be praised enough, Don Quixote de la Mancha, the same who

7. In Spanish, *rocin*.

sent me to present myself before your Grace that your Highness may dispose of me as you see fit'?"

Oh, how our good knight reveled in this speech, and more than ever when he came to think of the name that he should give his lady! As the story goes, there was a very good-looking farm girl who lived near by, with whom he had once been smitten, although it is generally believed that she never knew or suspected it. Her name was Aldonza Lorenzo, and it seemed to him that she was the one upon whom he should bestow the title of mistress of his thoughts. For her he wished a name that should not be incongruous with his own and that would convey the suggestion of a princess or a great lady; and, accordingly, he resolved to call her "Dulcinea del Toboso," she being a native of that place. A musical name to his ears, out of the ordinary and significant, like the others he had chosen for himself and his appurtenances.

CHAPTER 2

*Which treats of the first sally that the ingenious Don Quixote made from his native heath.*

Having, then, made all these preparations, he did not wish to lose any time in putting his plan into effect, for he could not but blame himself for what the world was losing by his delay, so many were the wrongs that were to be righted, the grievances to be redressed, the abuses to be done away with, and the duties to be performed. Accordingly, without informing anyone of his intention and without letting anyone see him, he set out one morning before daybreak on one of those very hot days in July. Donning all his armor, mounting Rocinante, adjusting his ill-contrived helmet, bracing his shield on his arm, and taking up his lance, he sallied forth by the back gate of his stable yard into the open countryside. It was with great contentment and joy that he saw how easily he had made a beginning toward the fulfillment of his desire.

No sooner was he out on the plain, however, than a terrible thought assailed him, one that all but caused him to abandon the enterprise he had undertaken. This occurred when he suddenly remembered that he had never formally been dubbed a knight, and so, in accordance with the law of knighthood, was not permitted to bear arms against one who had a right to that title. And even if he had been, as a novice knight he would have had to wear white armor, without any device on his shield, until he should have earned one by his exploits. These thoughts led him to waver in his purpose, but, madness prevailing over reason, he resolved to have himself knighted by the first person he met, as many others had done if what he had read in those books that he had at home was true. And so far as white

armor was concerned, he would scour his own the first chance that
offered until it shone whiter than any ermine. With this he became
more tranquil and continued on his way, letting his horse take whatever path it chose, for he believed that therein lay the very essence
of adventures.

And so we find our newly fledged adventurer jogging along and
talking to himself. "Undoubtedly," he is saying, "in the days to come,
when the true history of my famous deeds is published, the learned
chronicler who records them, when he comes to describe my first
sally so early in the morning, will put down something like this: 'No
sooner had the rubicund Apollo spread over the face of the broad
and spacious earth the gilded filaments of his beauteous locks, and
no sooner had the little singing birds of painted plumage greeted with
their sweet and mellifluous harmony the coming of the Dawn, who,
leaving the soft couch of her jealous spouse, now showed herself to
mortals at all the doors and balconies of the horizon that bounds La
Mancha—no sooner had this happened than the famous knight, Don
Quixote de la Mancha, forsaking his own downy bed and mounting
his famous steed, Rocinante, fared forth and began riding over the
ancient and famous Campo de Montiel.' "[8]
And this was the truth, for he was indeed riding over that stretch
of plain.

"O happy age and happy century," he went on, "in which my
famous exploits shall be published, exploits worthy of being engraved
in bronze, sculptured in marble, and depicted in paintings for the
benefit of posterity. O wise magician, whoever you be, to whom
shall fall the task of chronicling this extraordinary history of mine! I
beg of you not to forget my good Rocinante, eternal companion of
my wayfarings and my wanderings."

Then, as though he really had been in love: "O Princess Dulcinea, lady of this captive heart! Much wrong have you done me in
thus sending me forth with your reproaches and sternly commanding
me not to appear in your beauteous presence. O lady, deign to be
mindful of this your subject who endures so many woes for the love
of you."

And so he went on, stringing together absurdities, all of a kind
that his books had taught him, imitating insofar as he was able the
language of their authors. He rode slowly, and the sun came up so
swiftly and with so much heat that it would have been sufficient to
melt his brains if he had had any. He had been on the road almost
the entire day without anything happening that is worthy of being
set down here; and he was on the verge of despair, for he wished to
meet someone at once with whom he might try the valor of his good

8. Famous because it had been the scene of a battle in 1369.

right arm. Certain authors say that his first adventure was that of
Puerto Lápice, while others state that it was that of the windmills;
but in this particular instance I am in a position to affirm what I have
read in the annals of La Mancha; and that is to the effect that he
went all that day until nightfall, when he and his hack found themselves tired to death and famished. Gazing all around him to see if
he could discover some castle or shepherd's hut where he might take
shelter and attend to his pressing needs, he caught sight of an inn
not far off the road along which they were traveling, and this to him
was like a star guiding him not merely to the gates, but rather, let us
say, to the palace of redemption. Quickening his pace, he came up
to it just as night was falling.

By chance there stood in the doorway two lasses of the sort known
as "of the district"; they were on their way to Seville in the company
of some mule drivers who were spending the night in the inn. Now,
everything that this adventurer of ours thought, saw, or imagined
seemed to him to be directly out of one of the storybooks he had
read, and so, when he caught sight of the inn, it at once became a
castle with its four turrets and its pinnacles of gleaming silver, not to
speak of the drawbridge and moat and all the other things that are
commonly supposed to go with a castle. As he rode up to it, he
accordingly reined in Rocinante and sat there waiting for a dwarf to
appear upon the battlements and blow his trumpet by way of
announcing the arrival of a knight. The dwarf, however, was slow in
coming, and as Rocinante was anxious to reach the stable, Don
Quixote drew up to the door of the hostelry and surveyed the two
merry maidens, who to him were a pair of beauteous damsels or
gracious ladies taking their ease at the castle gate.

And then a swineherd came along, engaged in rounding up his
drove of hogs—for, without any apology, that is what they were. He
gave a blast on his horn to bring them together, and this at once
became for Don Quixote just what he wished it to be: some dwarf
who was heralding his coming; and so it was with a vast deal of
satisfaction that he presented himself before the ladies in question,
who, upon beholding a man in full armor like this, with lance and
buckler, were filled with fright and made as if to flee indoors. Realizing that they were afraid, Don Quixote raised his pasteboard visor
and revealed his withered, dust-covered face.

"Do not flee, your Ladyships," he said to them in a courteous
manner and gentle voice. "You need not fear that any wrong will be
done you, for it is not in accordance with the order of knighthood
which I profess to wrong anyone, much less such highborn damsels
as your appearance shows you to be."

The girls looked at him, endeavoring to scan his face, which was
half hidden by his ill-made visor. Never having heard women of

their profession called damsels before, they were unable to restrain their laughter, at which Don Quixote took offense.

"Modesty," he observed, "well becomes those with the dower of beauty, and, moreover, laughter that has not good cause is a very foolish thing. But I do not say this to be discourteous or to hurt your feelings; my only desire is to serve you."

The ladies did not understand what he was talking about, but felt more than ever like laughing at our knight's unprepossessing figure. This increased his annoyance, and there is no telling what would have happened if at that moment the innkeeper had not come out. He was very fat and very peaceably inclined; but upon sighting this grotesque personage clad in bits of armor that were quite as oddly matched as were his bridle, lance, buckler, and corselet, mine host was not at all indisposed to join the lasses in their merriment. He was suspicious, however, of all this paraphernalia and decided that it would be better to keep a civil tongue in his head.

"If, Sir Knight," he said, "your Grace desires a lodging, aside from a bed—for there is none to be had in this inn—you will find all else that you may want in great abundance."

When Don Quixote saw how humble the governor of the castle was—for he took the innkeeper and his inn to be no less than that— he replied, "For me, Sir Castellan,[9] anything will do, since

> Arms are my only ornament,
> My only rest the fight, etc."

The landlord thought that the knight had called him a castellan because he took him for one of those worthies of Castile, whereas the truth was, he was an Andalusian from the beach of Sanlúcar, no less a thief than Cacus[1] himself, and as full of tricks as a student or a page boy.

"In that case," he said,

> "Your bed will be the solid rock,
> Your sleep: to watch all night.

This being so, you may be assured of finding beneath this roof enough to keep you awake for a whole year, to say nothing of a single night."

With this, he went up to hold the stirrup for Don Quixote, who encountered much difficulty in dismounting, not having broken his fast all day long. The knight then directed his host to take good care of his steed, as it was the best piece of horseflesh in all the world. The innkeeper looked it over, and it did not impress him as being

---

9. The original, *castellano*, means both "castellan" and "Castilian."    1. In Roman mythology he stole some of the cattle of Hercules, concealing the theft by having them walk backward into his cave, but was finally discovered and slain.

half as good as Don Quixote had said it was. Having stabled the animal, he came back to see what his guest would have and found the latter being relieved of his armor by the damsels, who by now had made their peace with the new arrival. They had already removed his breastplate and backpiece but had no idea how they were going to open his gorget or get his improvised helmet off. That piece of armor had been tied on with green ribbons which it would be necessary to cut, since the knots could not be undone, but he would not hear of this, and so spent all the rest of that night with his headpiece in place, which gave him the weirdest, most laughable appearance that could be imagined.

Don Quixote fancied that these wenches who were assisting him must surely be the chatelaine and other ladies of the castle, and so proceeded to address them very gracefully and with much wit:

> Never was knight so served
> By any noble dame
> As was Don Quixote
> When from his village he came,
> With damsels to wait on his every need
> While princesses cared for his hack . . .

"By hack," he explained, "is meant my steed Rocinante, for that is his name, and mine is Don Quixote de la Mancha. I had no intention of revealing my identity until my exploits done in your service should have made me known to you; but the necessity of adapting to present circumstances that old ballad of Lancelot has led to your becoming acquainted with it prematurely. However, the time will come when your Ladyships shall command and I will obey and with the valor of my good right arm show you how eager I am to serve you."

The young women were not used to listening to speeches like this and had not a word to say, but merely asked him if he desired to eat anything.

"I could eat a bite of something, yes," replied Don Quixote. "Indeed, I feel that a little food would go very nicely just now."

He thereupon learned that, since it was Friday, there was nothing to be had in all the inn except a few portions of codfish, which in Castile is called *abadejo*, in Andalusia *bacalao*, in some places *curadillo*, and elsewhere *truchuela* or small trout. Would his Grace, then, have some small trout, seeing that was all there was that they could offer him?

"If there are enough of them," said Don Quixote, "they will take the place of a trout, for it is all one to me whether I am given in change eight reales or one piece of eight. What is more, those small trout may be like veal, which is better than beef, or like kid, which is better than goat. But however that may be, bring them on at once, for the weight and burden of arms is not to be borne without inner sustenance."

Placing the table at the door of the hostelry, in the open air, they brought the guest a portion of badly soaked and worse cooked codfish and a piece of bread as black and moldy as the suit of armor that he wore. It was a mirth-provoking sight to see him eat, for he still had his helmet on with his visor fastened, which made it impossible for him to put anything into his mouth with his hands, and so it was necessary for one of the girls to feed him. As for giving him anything to drink, that would have been out of the question if the innkeeper had not hollowed out a reed, placing one end in Don Quixote's mouth while through the other end he poured the wine. All this the knight bore very patiently rather than have them cut the ribbons of his helmet.

At this point a gelder of pigs approached the inn, announcing his arrival with four or five blasts on his horn, all of which confirmed Don Quixote in the belief that this was indeed a famous castle, for what was this if not music that they were playing for him? The fish was trout, the bread was the finest, the wenches were ladies, and the innkeeper was the castellan. He was convinced that he had been right in his resolve to sally forth and roam the world at large, but there was one thing that still distressed him greatly, and that was the fact that he had not as yet been dubbed a knight; as he saw it, he could not legitimately engage in any adventure until he had received the order of knighthood.

## CHAPTER 3

*Of the amusing manner in which Don Quixote had himself dubbed a knight.*

Wearied of his thoughts, Don Quixote lost no time over the scanty repast which the inn afforded him. When he had finished, he summoned the landlord and, taking him out to the stable, closed the doors and fell on his knees in front of him.

"Never, valiant knight," he said, "shall I arise from here until you have courteously granted me the boon I seek, one which will redound to your praise and to the good of the human race."

Seeing his guest at his feet and hearing him utter such words as these, the innkeeper could only stare at him in bewilderment, not knowing what to say or do. It was in vain that he entreated him to rise, for Don Quixote refused to do so until his request had been granted.

"I expected nothing less of your great magnificence, my lord," the latter then continued, "and so I may tell you that the boon I asked and which you have so generously conceded me is that tomorrow morning you dub me a knight. Until that time, in the chapel of this your castle, I will watch over my armor, and when morning comes, as I have said, that which I so desire shall then be done, in order that I may lawfully go to the four corners of the earth in quest of adventures and to succor the needy, which is the chivalrous duty of all knights-errant such as I who long to engage in deeds of high emprise."

The innkeeper, as we have said, was a sharp fellow. He already had a suspicion that his guest was not quite right in the head, and he was now convinced of it as he listened to such remarks as these. However, just for the sport of it, he determined to humor him; and so he went on to assure Don Quixote that he was fully justified in his request and that such a desire and purpose was only natural on the part of so distinguished a knight as his gallant bearing plainly showed him to be.

He himself, the landlord added, when he was a young man, had followed the same honorable calling. He had gone through various parts of the world seeking adventures, among the places he had visited being the Percheles of Málaga, the Isles of Riarán, the District of Seville, the Little Market Place of Segovia, the Olivera of Valencia, the Rondilla of Granada, the beach of Sanlúcar, the Horse Fountain of Cordova, the Small Taverns of Toledo, and numerous other localities[2] where his nimble feet and light fingers had found much exercise. He had done many wrongs, cheated many widows, ruined many maidens, and swindled not a few minors until he had finally come to be known in almost all the courts and tribunals that are to be found in the whole of Spain.

At last he had retired to his castle here, where he lived upon his own income and the property of others; and here it was that he received all knights-errant of whatever quality and condition, simply out of the great affection that he bore them and that they might share with him their possessions in payment of his good will. Unfortunately, in this castle there was no chapel where Don Quixote might keep watch over his arms, for the old chapel had been torn down to make way for a new one; but in case of necessity, he felt quite sure that such a vigil could be maintained anywhere, and for the present occasion the courtyard of the castle would do; and then in the morning, please God, the requisite ceremony could be performed and his guest be duly dubbed a knight, as much a knight as anyone ever was.

He then inquired if Don Quixote had any money on his person, and the latter replied that he had not a cent, for in all the storybooks

---

2. All the places mentioned were reputed to be haunts of robbers and rogues.

he had never read of knights-errant carrying any. But the innkeeper told him he was mistaken on this point: supposing the authors of those stories had not set down the fact in black and white, that was because they did not deem it necessary to speak of things as indispensable as money and a clean shirt, and one was not to assume for that reason that those knights-errant of whom the books were so full did not have any. He looked upon it as an absolute certainty that they all had well-stuffed purses, that they might be prepared for any emergency; and they also carried shirts and a little box of ointment for healing the wounds that they received.

For when they had been wounded in combat on the plains and in desert places, there was not always someone at hand to treat them, unless they had some skilled enchanter for a friend who then would succor them, bringing to them through the air, upon a cloud, some damsel or dwarf bearing a vial of water of such virtue that one had but to taste a drop of it and at once his wounds were healed and he was as sound as if he had never received any.

But even if this was not the case, knights in times past saw to it that their squires were well provided with money and other necessities, such as lint and ointment for healing purposes; and if they had no squires—which happened very rarely—they themselves carried these objects in a pair of saddlebags very cleverly attached to their horses' croups in such a manner as to be scarcely noticeable, as if they held something of greater importance than that, for among the knights-errant saddlebags as a rule were not favored. Accordingly, he would advise the novice before him, and inasmuch as the latter was soon to be his godson, he might even command him, that henceforth he should not go without money and a supply of those things that have been mentioned, as he would find that they came in useful at a time when he least expected it.

Don Quixote promised to follow his host's advice punctiliously; and so it was arranged that he should watch his armor in a large barnyard at one side of the inn. He gathered up all the pieces, placed them in a horse trough that stood near the well, and, bracing his shield on his arm, took up his lance and with stately demeanor began pacing up and down in front of the trough even as night was closing in.

The innkeeper informed his other guests of what was going on, of Don Quixote's vigil and his expectation of being dubbed a knight; and, marveling greatly at so extraordinary a variety of madness, they all went out to see for themselves and stood there watching from a distance. For a while the knight-to-be, with tranquil mien, would merely walk up and down; then, leaning on his lance, he would pause to survey his armor, gazing fixedly at it for a considerable length of time. As has been said, it was night now, but the brightness of the moon, which well might rival that of Him who lent it, was such that everything the novice knight did was plainly visible to all.

At this point one of the mule drivers who were stopping at the inn came out to water his drove, and in order to do this it was necessary to remove the armor from the trough.

As he saw the man approaching, Don Quixote cried out to him, "O bold knight, whoever you may be, who thus would dare to lay hands upon the accouterments of the most valiant man of arms that ever girded on a sword, look well what you do and desist if you do not wish to pay with your life for your insolence!"

The muleteer gave no heed to these words—it would have been better for his own sake had he done so—but, taking it up by the straps, tossed the armor some distance from him. When he beheld this, Don Quixote rolled his eyes heavenward and with his thoughts apparently upon his Dulcinea exclaimed, "Succor, O lady mine, this vassal heart in this my first encounter; let not your favor and protection fail me in the peril in which for the first time I now find myself."

With these and other similar words, he loosed his buckler, grasped his lance in both his hands, and let the mule driver have such a blow on the head that the man fell to the ground stunned; and had it been followed by another one, he would have had no need of a surgeon to treat him. Having done this, Don Quixote gathered up his armor and resumed his pacing up and down with the same calm manner as before. Not long afterward, without knowing what had happened—for the first muleteer was still lying there unconscious—another came out with the same intention of watering his mules, and he too was about to remove the armor from the trough when the knight, without saying a word or asking favor of anyone, once more adjusted his buckler and raised his lance, and if he did not break the second mule driver's head to bits, he made more than three pieces of it by dividing it into quarters. At the sound of the fracas everybody in the inn came running out, among them the innkeeper; whereupon Don Quixote again lifted his buckler and laid his hand on his sword.

"O lady of beauty," he said, "strength and vigor of this fainting heart of mine! Now is the time to turn the eyes of your greatness upon this captive knight of yours who must face so formidable an adventure."

By this time he had worked himself up to such a pitch of anger that if all the mule drivers in the world had attacked him he would not have taken one step backward. The comrades of the wounded men, seeing the plight those two were in, now began showering stones on Don Quixote, who shielded himself as best he could with his buckler, although he did not dare stir from the trough for fear of

leaving his armor unprotected. The landlord, meanwhile, kept calling for them to stop, for he had told them that this was a madman
who would be sure to go free even though he killed them all. The
knight was shouting louder than ever, calling them knaves and traitors. As for the lord of the castle, who allowed knights-errant to be
treated in this fashion, he was a lowborn villain, and if he, Don
Quixote, had but received the order of knighthood, he would make
him pay for his treachery.

"As for you others, vile and filthy rabble, I take no account of you;
you may stone me or come forward and attack me all you like; you
shall see what the reward of your folly and insolence will be."

He spoke so vigorously and was so undaunted in bearing as to
strike terror in those who would assail him; and for this reason, and
owing also to the persuasions of the innkeeper, they ceased stoning
him. He then permitted them to carry away the wounded, and went
back to watching his armor with the same tranquil, unconcerned air
that he had previously displayed.

The landlord was none too well pleased with these mad pranks on
the part of his guest and determined to confer upon him that accursed
order of knighthood before something else happened. Going up to
him, he begged Don Quixote's pardon for the insolence which, without
his knowledge, had been shown the knight by those of low degree.
They, however, had been well punished for their impudence. As he
had said, there was no chapel in this castle, but for that which remained
to be done there was no need of any. According to what he had read
of the ceremonial of the order, there was nothing to this business of
being dubbed a knight except a slap on the neck and one across the
shoulder, and that could be performed in the middle of a field as
well as anywhere else. All that was required was for the knight-to-be
to keep watch over his armor for a couple of hours, and Don Quixote
had been at it more than four. The latter believed all this and
announced that he was ready to obey and get the matter over with as
speedily as possible. Once dubbed a knight, if he were attacked one
more time, he did not think that he would leave a single person in
the castle alive, save such as he might command be spared, at the
bidding of his host and out of respect to him.

Thus warned, and fearful that it might occur, the castellan brought
out the book in which he had jotted down the hay and barley for
which the mule drivers owed him, and, accompanied by a lad bearing the butt of a candle and the two aforesaid damsels, he came up
to where Don Quixote stood and commanded him to kneel. Reading
from the account book—as if he had been saying a prayer—he raised
his hand and, with the knight's own sword, gave him a good thwack
upon the neck and another lusty one upon the shoulder, muttering
all the while between his teeth. He then directed one of the ladies to

gird on Don Quixote's sword, which she did with much gravity and composure; for it was all they could do to keep from laughing at every point of the ceremony, but the thought of the knight's prowess which they had already witnessed was sufficient to restrain their mirth.

"May God give your Grace much good fortune," said the worthy lady as she attached the blade, "and prosper you in battle."

Don Quixote thereupon inquired her name, for he desired to know to whom it was he was indebted for the favor he had just received, that he might share with her some of the honor which his strong right arm was sure to bring him. She replied very humbly that her name was Tolosa and that she was the daughter of a shoemaker, a native of Toledo who lived in the stalls of Sancho Bicnaya.[3] To this the knight replied that she would do him a very great favor if from then on she would call herself Doña Tolosa, and she promised to do so. The other girl then helped him on with his spurs, and practically the same conversation was repeated. When asked her name, she stated that it was La Molinera and added that she was the daughter of a respectable miller of Antequera. Don Quixote likewise requested her to assume the "don" and become Doña Molinera and offered to render her further services and favors.

These unheard-of ceremonies having been dispatched in great haste, Don Quixote could scarcely wait to be astride his horse and sally forth on his quest for adventures. Saddling and mounting Rocinante, he embraced his host, thanking him for the favor of having dubbed him a knight and saying such strange things that it would be quite impossible to record them here. The innkeeper, who was only too glad to be rid of him, answered with a speech that was no less flowery, though somewhat shorter, and he did not so much as ask him for the price of a lodging, so glad was he to see him go.

CHAPTER 4

*Of what happened to our knight when he sallied forth from the inn.*

Day was dawning when Don Quixote left the inn, so well satisfied with himself, so gay, so exhilarated, that the very girths of his steed all but burst with joy. But remembering the advice which his host had given him concerning the stock of necessary provisions that he should carry with him, especially money and shirts, he decided to turn back home and supply himself with whatever he needed, and with a squire as well; he had in mind a farmer who was a neighbor of his, a poor man and the father of a family but very well suited to fulfill the duties of squire to a man of arms. With this thought in mind he guided Rocinante toward the village once more, and that

---

3. An old square in Toledo.

animal, realizing that he was homeward bound, began stepping out at so lively a gait that it seemed as if his feet barely touched the ground.

The knight had not gone far when from a hedge on his right hand he heard the sound of faint moans as of someone in distress.

"Thanks be to Heaven," he at once exclaimed, "for the favor it has shown me by providing me so soon with an opportunity to fulfill the obligations that I owe to my profession, a chance to pluck the fruit of my worthy desires. Those, undoubtedly, are the cries of someone in distress, who stands in need of my favor and assistance."

Turning Rocinante's head, he rode back to the place from which the cries appeared to be coming. Entering the wood, he had gone but a few paces when he saw a mare attached to an oak, while bound to another tree was a lad of fifteen or thereabouts, naked from the waist up. It was he who was uttering the cries, and not without reason, for there in front of him was a lusty farmer with a girdle who was giving him many lashes, each one accompanied by a reproof and a command, "Hold your tongue and keep your eyes open"; and the lad was saying, "I won't do it again, sir; by God's Passion, I won't do it again. I promise you that after this I'll take better care of the flock."

When he saw what was going on, Don Quixote was very angry. "Discourteous knight," he said, "it ill becomes you to strike one who is powerless to defend himself. Mount your steed and take your lance in hand"—for there was a lance leaning against the oak to which the mare was tied—"and I will show you what a coward you are."

The farmer, seeing before him this figure all clad in armor and brandishing a lance, decided that he was as good as done for. "Sir Knight," he said, speaking very mildly, "this lad that I am punishing here is my servant; he tends a flock of sheep which I have in these parts and he is so careless that every day one of them shows up missing. And when I punish him for his carelessness or his roguery, he says it is just because I am a miser and do not want to pay him the wages that I owe him, but I swear to God and upon my soul that he lies."

"It is you who lie, base lout," said Don Quixote, "and in my presence; and by the sun that gives us light, I am minded to run you through with this lance. Pay him and say no more about it, or else, by the God who rules us, I will make an end of you and annihilate you here and now. Release him at once."

The farmer hung his head and without a word untied his servant. Don Quixote then asked the boy how much has master owed him. For nine months' work, the lad told him, at seven reales the month. The knight did a little reckoning and found that this came to sixty-three reales; whereupon he ordered the farmer to pay over the money immediately, as he valued his life. The cowardly bumpkin replied that, facing death as he was and by the oath that he had sworn—he had not sworn any oath as yet—it did not amount to as much as that; for there were three pairs of shoes which he had given the lad that were to be deducted and taken into account, and a real for two blood-lettings when his servant was ill.

"That," said Don Quixote, "is all very well; but let the shoes and the blood-lettings go for the undeserved lashings which you have given him; if he has worn out the leather of the shoes that you paid for, you have taken the hide off his body, and if the barber let a little blood for him when he was sick,[4] you have done the same when he was well; and so far as that goes, he owes you nothing."

"But the trouble is, Sir Knight, that I have no money with me. Come along home with me, Andrés, and I will pay you real for real."

"I go home with him!" cried the lad. "Never in the world! No, sir, I would not even think of it; for once he has me alone he'll flay me like a St. Bartholomew."

"He will do nothing of the sort," said Don Quixote. "It is sufficient for me to command, and he out of respect will obey. Since he has sworn to me by the order of knighthood which he has received, I shall let him go free and I will guarantee that you will be paid."

"But look, your Grace," the lad remonstrated, "my master is no knight; he has never received any order of knighthood whatsoever. He is Juan Haldudo, a rich man and a resident of Quintanar."

"That makes little difference," declared Don Quixote, "for there may well be knights among the Haldudos, all the more so in view of the fact that every man is the son of his works."

"That is true enough," said Andrés, "but this master of mine—of what works is he the son, seeing that he refuses me the pay for my sweat and labor?"

"I do not refuse you, brother Andrés," said the farmer. "Do me the favor of coming with me, and I swear to you by all the orders of knighthood that there are in this world to pay you, as I have said, real for real, and perfumed at that."

"You can dispense with the perfume," said Don Quixote; "just give him the reales and I shall be satisfied. And see to it that you keep your oath, or by the one that I myself have sworn I shall return to seek you out and chastise you, and I shall find you though you be as well hidden as a lizard. In case you would like to know who it is that is giving you this command in order that you may feel the more obliged to comply with it, I may tell you that I am the valorous Don Quixote de la Mancha, righter of wrongs and injustices; and so, God

4. Barbers were also surgeons.

be with you, and do not fail to do as you have promised, under that penalty that I have pronounced."

As he said this, he put spurs to Rocinante and was off. The farmer watched him go, and when he saw that Don Quixote was out of the wood and out of sight, he turned to his servant, Andrés.

"Come here, my son," he said. "I want to pay you what I owe you as that righter of wrongs has commanded me."

"Take my word for it," replied Andrés, "your Grace would do well to observe the command of that good knight—may he live a thousand years; for as he is valorous and a righteous judge, if you don't pay me then, by Rocque,[5] he will come back and do just what he said!"

"And I will give you my word as well," said the farmer; "but seeing that I am so fond of you, I wish to increase the debt, that I may owe you all the more." And with this he seized the lad's arm and bound him to the tree again and flogged him within an inch of his life. "There, Master Andrés, you may call on that righter of wrongs if you like and you will see whether or not he rights this one. I do not think I have quite finished with you yet, for I have a good mind to flay you alive as you feared."

Finally, however, he unbound him and told him he might go look for that judge of his to carry out the sentence that had been pronounced. Andrés left, rather down in the mouth, swearing that he would indeed go look for the brave Don Quixote de la Mancha; he would relate to him everything that had happened, point by point, and the farmer would have to pay for it seven times over. But for all that, he went away weeping, and his master stood laughing at him.

Such was the manner in which the valorous knight righted this particular wrong. Don Quixote was quite content with the way everything had turned out; it seemed to him that he had made a very fortunate and noble beginning with his deeds of chivalry, and he was very well satisfied with himself as he jogged along in the direction of his native village, talking to himself in a low voice all the while.

"Well may'st thou call thyself fortunate today, above all other women on earth, O fairest of the fair, Dulcinea del Toboso! Seeing that it has fallen to thy lot to hold subject and submissive to thine every wish and pleasure so valiant and renowned a knight as Don Quixote de la Mancha is and shall be, who, as everyone knows, yesterday received the order of knighthood and this day has righted the greatest wrong and grievance that injustice ever conceived or cruelty ever perpetrated, by snatching the lash from the hand of the merciless foeman who was so unreasonably flogging that tender child."

At this point he came to a road that forked off in four directions,

5. The origin of the oath is unknown.

and at once he thought of those crossroads where knights-errant would pause to consider which path they should take. By way of imitating them, he halted there for a while; and when he had given the subject much thought, he slackened Rocinante's rein and let the hack follow its inclination. The animal's first impulse was to make straight for its own stable. After they had gone a couple of miles or so Don Quixote caught sight of what appeared to be a great throng of people, who, as was afterward learned, were certain merchants of Toledo on their way to purchase silk at Murcia. There were six of them altogether with their sunshades, accompanied by four attendants on horseback and three mule drivers on foot.

No sooner had he sighted them than Don Quixote imagined that he was on the brink of some fresh adventure. He was eager to imitate those passages at arms of which he had read in his books, and here, so it seemed to him, was one made to order. And so, with bold and knightly bearing, he settled himself firmly in the stirrups, couched his lance, covered himself with his shield, and took up a position in the middle of the road, where he paused to wait for those other knights-errant (for such he took them to be) to come up to him. When they were near enough to see and hear plainly, Don Quixote raised his voice and made a haughty gesture.

"Let everyone," he cried, "stand where he is, unless everyone will confess that there is not in all the world a more beauteous damsel than the Empress of La Mancha, the peerless Dulcinea del Toboso."

Upon hearing these words and beholding the weird figure who uttered them, the merchants stopped short. From the knight's appearance and his speech they knew at once that they had to deal with a madman; but they were curious to know what was meant by that confession that was demanded of them, and one of their number who was somewhat of a jester and a very clever fellow raised his voice.

"Sir Knight," he said, "we do not know who this beauteous lady is of whom you speak. Show her to us, and if she is as beautiful as you say, then we will right willingly and without any compulsion confess the truth as you have asked of us."

"If I were to show her to you," replied Don Quixote, "what merit would there be in your confessing a truth so self-evident? The important thing is for you, without seeing her, to believe, confess, affirm, swear, and defend that truth. Otherwise, monstrous and arrogant creatures that you are, you shall do battle with me. Come on, then, one by one, as the order of knighthood prescribes; or all of you together, if you will have it so, as is the sorry custom of those of your breed. Come on, and I will await you here, for I am confident that my cause is just."

"Sir Knight," responded the merchant, "I beg your Grace, in the

name of all the princes here present, in order that we may not have
upon our consciences the burden of confessing a thing which we
have never seen nor heard, and one, moreover, so prejudicial to the
empresses and queens of Alcarria and Estremadura,[6] that your Grace
will show us some portrait of this lady, even though it be no larger
than a grain of wheat, for by the thread one comes to the ball of
yarn; and with this we shall remain satisfied and assured, and your
Grace will likewise be content and satisfied. The truth is, I believe
that we are already so much of your way of thinking that though it
should show her to be blind of one eye and distilling vermilion and
brimstone from the other, nevertheless, to please your Grace, we
would say in her behalf all that you desire."

"She distills nothing of the sort, infamous rabble!" shouted Don
Quixote, for his wrath was kindling now. "I tell you, she does not
distill what you say at all, but amber and civet[7] wrapped in cotton;
and she is neither one-eyed nor hunchbacked but straighter than a
spindle that comes from Guadarrama. You shall pay for the great
blasphemy which you have uttered against such a beauty as is my
lady!"

Saying this, he came on with lowered lance against the one who
had spoken, charging with such wrath and fury that if fortune had
not caused Rocinante to stumble and fall in mid-career, things would
have gone badly with the merchant and he would have paid for his
insolent gibe. As it was, Don Quixote went rolling over the plain for
some little distance, and when he tried to get to his feet, found that
he was unable to do so, being too encumbered with his lance, shield,
spurs, helmet, and the weight of that ancient suit of armor.

"Do not flee, cowardly ones," he cried even as he struggled to
rise. "Stay, cravens, for it is not my fault but that of my steed that I
am stretched out here."

One of the muleteers, who must have been an ill-natured lad,
upon hearing the poor fallen knight speak so arrogantly, could not
refrain from giving him an answer in the ribs. Going up to him, he
took the knight's lance and broke it into bits, and then with a companion proceeded to belabor him so mercilessly that in spite of his
armor they milled him like a hopper of wheat. The merchants called
to them not to lay on so hard, saying that was enough and they
should desist, but the mule driver by this time had warmed up to the
sport and would not stop until he had vented his wrath, and, snatching up the broken pieces of the lance, he began hurling them at the
wretched victim as he lay there on the ground. And through all this
tempest of sticks that rained upon him Don Quixote never once
closed his mouth nor ceased threatening Heaven and earth and these

6. Ironical, since both were known as particularly backward regions.    7. A musky substance
used as perfume, imported from Africa in cotton packings.

ruffians, for such he took them to be, who were thus mishandling him.

Finally the lad grew tired, and the merchants went their way with a good story to tell about the poor fellow who had had such a cudgeling. Finding himself alone, the knight endeavored to see if he could rise; but if this was a feat that he could not accomplish when he was sound and whole, how was he to achieve it when he had been thrashed and pounded to a pulp? Yet nonetheless he considered himself fortunate; for as he saw it, misfortunes such as this were common to knights-errant, and he put all the blame upon his horse; and if he was unable to rise, that was because his body was so bruised and battered all over.

## CHAPTER 5

*In which is continued the narrative of the misfortune that befell our knight.*

Seeing, then, that he was indeed unable to stir, he decided to fall back upon a favorite remedy of his, which was to think of some passage or other in his books; and as it happened, the one that he in his madness now recalled was the story of Baldwin and the Marquis of Mantua, when Carloto left the former wounded upon the mountainside,[8] a tale that is known to children, not unknown to young men, celebrated and believed in by the old, and, for all of that, not any truer than the miracles of Mohammed. Moreover, it impressed him as being especially suited to the straits in which he found himself; and, accordingly, with a great show of feeling, he began rolling and tossing on the ground as he feebly gasped out the lines which the wounded knight of the wood is supposed to have uttered:

> "Where art thou, lady mine,
> That thou dost not grieve for my woe?
> Either thou art disloyal,
> Or my grief thou dost not know."

He went on reciting the old ballad until he came to the following verses:

> "O noble Marquis of Mantua,
> My uncle and liege lord true!"

He had reached this point when down the road came a farmer of the same village, a neighbor of his, who had been to the mill with a load

8. The allusion is to an old ballad about Charlemagne's son Charlot (Carloto) wounding Baldwin, nephew of the Marquis of Mantua.

of wheat. Seeing a man lying there stretched out like that, he went up to him and inquired who he was and what was the trouble that caused him to utter such mournful complaints. Thinking that this must undoubtedly be his uncle, the Marquis of Mantua, Don Quixote did not answer but went on with his recitation of the ballad, giving an account of the Marquis' misfortunes and the amours of his wife and the emperor's son, exactly as the ballad has it.

The farmer was astounded at hearing all these absurdities, and after removing the knight's visor which had been battered to pieces by the blows it had received, the good man bathed the victim's face, only to discover, once the dust was off, that he knew him very well. "Señor Quijana," he said (for such must have been Don Quixote's real name when he was in his right senses and before he had given up the life of a quiet country gentleman to become a knight-errant), "who is responsible for your Grace's being in such a plight as this?"

But the knight merely went on with his ballad in response to all the questions asked of him. Perceiving that it was impossible to obtain any information from him, the farmer as best he could relieved him of his breastplate and backpiece to see if he had any wounds, but there was no blood and no mark of any sort. He then tried to lift him from the ground, and with a great deal of effort finally managed to get him astride the ass, which appeared to be the easier mount for him. Gathering up the armor, including even the splinters from the lance, he made a bundle and tied it on Rocinante's back, and, taking the horse by the reins and the ass by the halter, he started out for the village. He was worried in his mind at hearing all the foolish things that Don Quixote said, and that individual himself was far from being at ease. Unable by reason of his bruises and his soreness to sit upright on the donkey, our knight-errant kept sighing to Heaven, which led the farmer to ask him once more what it was that ailed him.

It must have been the devil himself who caused him to remember those tales that seemed to fit his own case; for at this point he forgot all about Baldwin and recalled Abindarráez, and how the governor of Antequera, Rodrigo de Narvéez, had taken him prisoner and carried him off captive to his castle. Accordingly, when the countryman turned to inquire how he was and what was troubling him, Don Quixote replied with the very same words and phrases that the captive Abindarráez used in answering Rodrigo, just as he had read in the story *Diana* of Jorge de Montemayor,[9] where it is all written down, applying them very aptly to the present circumstances as the farmer went along cursing his luck for having to listen to such a lot

9. The reference is to the tale of the love of Abindarráez, a captive Moor, for the beautiful Jarifa (mentioned in the following paragraph), contained in the second edition of *Diana*, the pastoral romance by Jorge de Montemayor.

of nonsense. Realizing that his neighbor was quite mad, he made haste to reach the village that he might not have to be annoyed any longer by Don Quixote's tiresome harangue.

"Señor Don Rodrigo de Narváez," the knight was saying, "I may inform your Grace that this beautiful Jarifa of whom I speak is not the lovely Dulcinea del Toboso, in whose behalf I have done, am doing, and shall do the most famous deeds of chivalry that ever have been or will be seen in all the world."

"But, sir," replied the farmer, "sinner that I am, cannot your Grace see that I am not Don Rodrigo de Narváez nor the Marquis of Mantua, but Pedro Alonso, your neighbor? And your Grace is neither Baldwin nor Abindarráez but a respectable gentleman by the name of Señor Quijana."

"I know who I am," said Don Quixote, "and who I may be, if I choose: not only those I have mentioned but all the Twelve Peers of France and the Nine Worthies[1] as well; for the exploits of all of them together, or separately, cannot compare with mine."

With such talk as this they reached their destination just as night was falling; but the farmer decided to wait until it was a little darker in order that the badly battered gentleman might not be seen arriving in such a condition and mounted on an ass. When he thought the proper time had come, they entered the village and proceeded to Don Quixote's house, where they found everything in confusion. The curate and the barber were there, for they were great friends of the knight, and the housekeeper was speaking to them.

"Señor Licentiate Pero Pérez," she was saying, for that was the manner in which she addressed the curate, "what does your Grace think could have happened to my master? Three days now, and not a word of him, nor the hack, nor the buckler, nor the lance, nor the suit of armor. Ah, poor me! I am as certain as I am that I was born to die that it is those cursed books of chivalry he is always reading that have turned his head; for now that I recall, I have often heard him muttering to himself that he must become a knight-errant and go through the world in search of adventures. May such books as those be consigned to Satan and Barabbas,[2] for they have sent to perdition the finest mind in all La Mancha."

The niece was of the same opinion. "I may tell you, Señor Master Nicholas," she said, for that was the barber's name, "that many times my uncle would sit reading those impious tales of misadventure for two whole days and nights at a stretch; and when he was through, he

1. In the French medieval epics the Twelve Peers (Roland, Olivier, and so on) were warriors all equal in rank forming a sort of guard of honor around Charlemagne. The Nine Worthies, in a tradition originating in France, were nine famous figures, three biblical, three classical, and three Christian (David, Hector, Alexander, Charlemagne, and so on).    2. The thief whose release, rather than that of Jesus Christ, the crowd requested when Pilate, conforming to Passover custom, was ready to have one prisoner set free.

would toss the book aside, lay his hand on his sword, and begin slashing at the walls. When he was completely exhausted, he would tell us that he had just killed four giants as big as castle towers, while the sweat that poured off him was blood from the wounds that he had received in battle. He would then drink a big jug of cold water, after which he would be very calm and peaceful, saying that the water was the most precious liquid which the wise Esquife, a great magician and his friend, had brought to him. But I blame myself for everything. I should have advised your Worships of my uncle's nonsensical actions so that you could have done something about it by burning those damnable books of his before things came to such a pass; for he has many that ought to be burned as if they were heretics."

"I agree with you," said the curate, "and before tomorrow's sun has set there shall be a public *auto da fé*, and those works shall be condemned to the flames that they may not lead some other who reads them to follow the example of my good friend."

Don Quixote and the farmer overheard all this, and it was then that the latter came to understand the nature of his neighbor's affliction.

"Open the door, your Worships," the good man cried. "Open for Sir Baldwin and the Marquis of Mantua, who comes badly wounded, and for Señor Abindarráez the Moor whom the valiant Rodrigo de Narváez, governor of Antequera, brings captive."

At the sound of his voice they all ran out, recognizing at once friend, master, and uncle, who as yet was unable to get down off the donkey's back. They all ran up to embrace him.

"Wait, all of you," said Don Quixote, "for I am sorely wounded through fault of my steed. Bear me to my couch and summon, if it be possible, the wise Urganda to treat and care for my wounds."

"There!" exclaimed the housekeeper. "Plague take it! Did not my heart tell me right as to which foot my master limped on? To bed with your Grace at once, and we will take care of you without sending for that Urganda of yours. A curse, I say, and a hundred other curses, on those books of chivalry that have brought your Grace to this."

And so they carried him off to bed, but when they went to look for his wounds, they found none at all. He told them it was all the result of a great fall he had taken with Rocinante, his horse, while engaged in combating ten giants, the hugest and most insolent that were ever heard of in all the world.

"Tut, tut," said the curate. "So there are giants in the dance now, are there? Then, by the sign of the cross, I'll have them burned before nightfall tomorrow."

They had a thousand questions to put to Don Quixote, but his only answer was that they should give him something to eat and let him sleep, for that was the most important thing of all; so they humored him in this. The curate then interrogated the farmer at great length concerning the conversation he had had with his neighbor. The peasant told him everything, all the absurd things their friend had said when he found him lying there and afterward on the way home, all of which made the licentiate more anxious than ever to do what he did the following day,[3] when he summoned Master Nicholas and went with him to Don Quixote's house.

### [Fighting the Windmills and a Choleric Biscayan]

#### CHAPTER 7

*Of the second sally of our good knight, Don Quixote de la Mancha.*

. . . After that he remained at home very tranquilly for a couple of weeks, without giving sign of any desire to repeat his former madness. During that time he had the most pleasant conversations with his two old friends, the curate and the barber, on the point he had raised to the effect that what the world needed most was knights-errant and a revival of chivalry. The curate would occasionally contradict him and again would give in, for it was only by means of this artifice that he could carry on a conversation with him at all.

In the meanwhile Don Quixote was bringing his powers of persuasion to bear upon a farmer who lived near by, a good man—if this title may be applied to one who is poor—but with very few wits in his head. The short of it is, by pleas and promises, he got the hapless rustic to agree to ride forth with him and serve him as his squire. Among other things, Don Quixote told him that he ought to be more than willing to go, because no telling what adventure might occur which would win them an island, and then he (the farmer) would be left to be the governor of it. As a result of these and other similar assurances, Sancho Panza forsook his wife and children and consented to take upon himself the duties of squire to his neighbor.

Next, Don Quixote set out to raise some money, and by selling this thing and pawning that and getting the worst of the bargain always, he finally scraped together a reasonable amount. He also asked a friend of his for the loan of a buckler and patched up his broken helmet as well as he could. He advised his squire, Sancho, of the day and hour when they were to take the road and told him to see to laying in a supply of those things that were most necessary, and, above all, not to forget the saddlebags. Sancho replied that he would see to all this and added that he was also thinking of taking

---

3. What he and the barber did was to burn most of Don Quixote's library.

along with him a very good ass that he had, as he was not much used to going on foot.

With regard to the ass, Don Quixote had to do a little thinking, trying to recall if any knight-errant had ever had a squire thus asininely mounted. He could not think of any, but nevertheless he decided to take Sancho with the intention of providing him with a nobler steed as soon as occasion offered; he had but to appropriate the horse of the first discourteous knight he met. Having furnished himself with shirts and all the other things that the innkeeper had recommended, he and Panza rode forth one night unseen by anyone and without taking leave of wife and children, housekeeper or niece. They went so far that by the time morning came they were safe from discovery had a hunt been started for them.

Mounted on his ass, Sancho Panza rode along like a patriarch, with saddlebags and flask, his mind set upon becoming governor of that island that his master had promised him. Don Quixote determined to take the same route and road over the Campo de Montiel that he had followed on his first journey; but he was not so uncomfortable this time, for it was early morning and the sun's rays fell upon them slantingly and accordingly did not tire them too much.

"Look, Sir Knight-errant," said Sancho, "your Grace should not forget that island you promised me; for no matter how big it is, I'll be able to govern it right enough."

"I would have you know, friend Sancho Panza," replied Don Quixote, "that among the knights-errant of old it was a very common custom to make their squires governors of the islands or the kingdoms that they won, and I am resolved that in my case so pleasing a usage shall not fall into desuetude. I even mean to go them one better; for they very often, perhaps most of the time, waited until their squires were old men who had had their fill of serving their masters during bad days and worse nights, whereupon they would give them the title of count, or marquis at most, of some valley or province more or less. But if you live and I live, it well may be that within a week I shall win some kingdom with others dependent upon it, and it will be the easiest thing in the world to crown you king of one of them. You need not marvel at this, for all sorts of unforeseen things happen to knights like me, and I may readily be able to give you even more than I have promised."

"In that case," said Sancho Panza, "if by one of those miracles of which your Grace was speaking I should become king, I would certainly send for Juana Gutiérrez, my old lady, to come and be my queen, and the young ones could be infantes."

"There is no doubt about it," Don Quixote assured him.

"Well, I doubt it," said Sancho, "for I think that even if God were to rain kingdoms upon the earth, no crown would sit well on the head of Mari Gutiérrez,[4] for I am telling you, sir, as a queen she is not worth two maravedis.[5] She would do better as a countess, God help her."

"Leave everything to God, Sancho," said Don Quixote, "and he will give you whatever is most fitting; but I trust you will not be so pusillanimous as to be content with anything less than the title of viceroy."

"That I will not," said Sancho Panza, "especially seeing that I have in your Grace so illustrious a master who can give me all that is suitable to me and all that I can manage."

CHAPTER 8

*Of the good fortune which the valorous Don Quixote had in the terrifying and never-before-imagined adventure of the windmills, along with other events that deserve to be suitably recorded.*

At this point they caught sight of thirty or forty windmills which were standing on the plain there, and no sooner had Don Quixote laid eyes upon them than he turned to his squire and said, "Fortune is guiding our affairs better than we could have wished; for you see there before you, friend Sancho Panza, some thirty or more lawless giants with whom I mean to do battle. I shall deprive them of their lives, and with the spoils from this encounter we shall begin to enrich ourselves; for this is righteous warfare, and it is a great service to God to remove so accursed a breed from the face of the earth."

"What giants?" said Sancho Panza.

"Those that you see there," replied his master, "those with the long arms some of which are as much as two leagues in length."

"But look, your Grace, those are not giants but windmills, and what appear to be arms are their wings which, when whirled in the breeze, cause the millstone to go."

"It is plain to be seen," said Don Quixote, "that you have had little experience in this matter of adventures. If you are afraid, go off to one side and say your prayers while I am engaging them in fierce, unequal combat."

Saying this, he gave spurs to his steed Rocinante, without paying any heed to Sancho's warning that these were truly windmills and not giants that he was riding forth to attack. Nor even when he was close upon them did he perceive what they really were, but shouted at the top of his lungs, "Do not seek to flee, cowards and vile creatures that you are, for it is but a single knight with whom you have to deal!"

---

4. Sancho's wife; she is called Juana Gutiérrez a few lines earlier.    5. Coin worth ⅓₄ real.

At that moment a little wind came up and the big wings began turning.

"Though you flourish as many arms as did the giant Briareus,"[6] said Don Quixote when he perceived this, "you still shall have to answer to me."

He thereupon commended himself with all his heart to his lady Dulcinea, beseeching her to succor him in this peril; and, being well covered with his shield and with his lance at rest, he bore down upon them at a full gallop and fell upon the first mill that stood in his way, giving a thrust at the wing, which was whirling at such a speed that his lance was broken into bits and both horse and horseman went rolling over the plain, very much battered indeed. Sancho upon his donkey came hurrying to his master's assistance as fast as he could, but when he reached the spot, the knight was unable to move, so great was the shock with which he and Rocinante had hit the ground.

"God help us!" exclaimed Sancho, "did I not tell your Grace to look well, that those were nothing but windmills, a fact which no one could fail to see unless he had other mills of the same sort in his head?"

"Be quiet, friend Sancho," said Don Quixote. "Such are the fortunes of war, which more than any other are subject to constant change. What is more, when I come to think of it, I am sure that this must be the work of that magician Frestón, the one who robbed me of my study and my books,[7] and who has thus changed the giants into windmills in order to deprive me of the glory of overcoming them, so great is the enmity that he bears me; but in the end his evil arts shall not prevail against this trusty sword of mine."

"May God's will be done," was Sancho Panza's response. And with the aid of his squire the knight was once more mounted on Rocinante, who stood there with one shoulder half out of joint. And so, speaking of the adventure that had just befallen them, they continued along the Puerto Lápice highway; for there, Don Quixote said, they could not fail to find many and varied adventures, this being a much traveled thoroughfare. The only thing was, the knight was exceedingly downcast over the loss of his lance.

"I remember," he said to his squire, "having read of a Spanish knight by the name of Diego Pérez de Vargas, who, having broken his sword in battle, tore from an oak a heavy bough or branch and with it did such feats of valor that day, and pounded so many Moors, that he came to be known as Machuca,[8] and he and his descendants from that day forth have been called Vargas y Machuca. I tell you this because I too intend to provide myself with just such a bough as

---

6. Mythological giant with a hundred arms.    7. Don Quixote had promptly attributed the ruin of his library, performed by the curate and the barber, to magical intervention.    8. Machuca, meaning "The Crusher," was the hero of a folk ballad.

the one he wielded, and with it I propose to do such exploits that you shall deem yourself fortunate to have been found worthy to come with me and behold and witness things that are almost beyond belief."

"God's will be done," said Sancho. "I believe everything that your Grace says; but straighten yourself up in the saddle a little, for you seem to be slipping down on one side, owing, no doubt, to the shaking-up that you received in your fall."

"Ah, that is the truth," replied Don Quixote, "and if I do not speak of my sufferings, it is for the reason that it is not permitted knights-errant to complain of any wound whatsoever, even though their bowels may be dropping out."

"If that is the way it is," said Sancho, "I have nothing more to say; but, God knows, it would suit me better if your Grace did complain when something hurts him. I can assure you that I mean to do so, over the least little thing that ails me—that is, unless the same rule applies to squires as well."

Don Quixote laughed long and heartily over Sancho's simplicity, telling him that he might complain as much as he liked and where and when he liked, whether he had good cause or not; for he had read nothing to the contrary in the ordinances of chivalry. Sancho then called his master's attention to the fact that it was time to eat. The knight replied that he himself had no need of food at the moment, but his squire might eat whenever he chose. Having been granted this permission, Sancho seated himself as best he could upon his beast, and, taking out from his saddlebags the provisions that he had stored there, he rode along leisurely behind his master, munching his victuals and taking a good, hearty swig now and then at the leather flask in a manner that might well have caused the biggest-bellied tavernkeeper of Málaga to envy him. Between draughts he gave not so much as a thought to any promise that his master might have made him, nor did he look upon it as any hardship, but rather as good sport, to go in quest of adventures however hazardous they might be.

The short of the matter is, they spent the night under some trees, from one of which Don Quixote tore off a withered bough to serve him as a lance, placing it in the lance head from which he had removed the broken one. He did not sleep all night long for thinking of his lady Dulcinea; for this was in accordance with what he had read in his books, of men of arms in the forest or desert places who kept a wakeful vigil, sustained by the memory of their ladies fair. Not so with Sancho, whose stomach was full, and not with chicory water. He fell into a dreamless slumber, and had not his master called him, he would not have been awakened either by the rays of the sun in his face or by the many birds who greeted the coming of the new day with their merry song.

Upon arising, he had another go at the flask, finding it somewhat more flaccid then it had been the night before, a circumstance which grieved his heart, for he could not see that they were on the way to remedying the deficiency within any very short space of time. Don Quixote did not wish any breakfast; for, as has been said, he was in the habit of nourishing himself on savorous memories. They then set out once more along the road to Puerto Lápice, and around three in the afternoon they came in sight of the pass that bears that name.

"There," said Don Quixote as his eyes fell upon it, "we may plunge our arms up to the elbow in what are known as adventures. But I must warn you that even though you see me in the greatest peril in the world, you are not to lay hand upon your sword to defend me, unless it be that those who attack me are rabble and men of low degree, in which case you may very well come to my aid; but if they be gentlemen, it is in no wise permitted by the laws of chivalry that you should assist me until you yourself shall have been dubbed a knight."

"Most certainly, sir," replied Sancho, "your Grace shall be very well obeyed in this; all the more so for the reason that I myself am of a peaceful disposition and not fond of meddling in the quarrels and feuds of others. However, when it comes to protecting my own person, I shall not take account of those laws of which you speak, seeing that all laws, human and divine, permit each one to defend himself whenever he is attacked."

"I am willing to grant you that," assented Don Quixote, "but in this matter of defending me against gentlemen you must restrain your natural impulses."

"I promise you I shall do so," said Sancho. "I will observe this precept as I would the Sabbath day."

As they were conversing in this manner, there appeared in the road in front of them two friars of the Order of St. Benedict, mounted upon dromedaries—for the she-mules they rode were certainly no smaller than that. The friars wore travelers' spectacles and carried sunshades, and behind them came a coach accompanied by four or five men on horseback and a couple of muleteers on foot. In the coach, as was afterwards learned, was a lady of Biscay, on her way to Seville to bid farewell to her husband, who had been appointed to some high post in the Indies. The religious were not of her company although they were going by the same road.

The instant Don Quixote laid eyes upon them he turned to his squire. "Either I am mistaken or this is going to be the most famous adventure that ever was seen; for those black-clad figures that you behold must be, and without any doubt are, certain enchanters who are bearing with them a captive princess in that coach, and I must do all I can to right this wrong."

"It will be worse than the windmills," declared Sancho. "Look you, sir, those are Benedictine friars and the coach must be that of some travelers. Mark well what I say and what you do, lest the devil lead you astray."

"I have already told you, Sancho," replied Don Quixote, "that you know little where the subject of adventures is concerned. What I am saying to you is the truth, as you shall now see."

With this, he rode forward and took up a position in the middle of the road along which the friars were coming, and as soon as they appeared to be within earshot he cried out to them in a loud voice, "O devilish and monstrous beings, set free at once the highborn princesses whom you bear captive in that coach, or else prepare at once to meet your death as the just punishment of your evil deeds."

The friars drew rein and sat there in astonishment, marveling as much at Don Quixote's appearance as at the words he spoke. "Sir Knight," they answered him, "we are neither devilish nor monstrous but religious of the Order of St. Benedict who are merely going our way. We know nothing of those who are in that coach, nor of any captive princesses either."

"Soft words," said Don Quixtoe, "have no effect on me. I know you for what you are, lying rabble!" And without waiting for any further parley he gave spur to Rocinante and, with lowered lance, bore down upon the first friar with such fury and intrepidity that, had not the fellow tumbled from his mule of his own accord, he would have been hurled to the ground and either killed or badly wounded. The second religious, seeing how his companion had been treated, dug his legs into his she-mule's flanks and scurried away over the countryside faster than the wind.

Seeing the friar upon the ground, Sancho Panza slipped lightly from his mount and, falling upon him, began stripping him of his habit. The two mule drivers accompanying the religious thereupon came running up and asked Sancho why he was doing this. The latter replied that the friar's garments belonged to him as legitimate spoils of the battle that his master Don Quixote had just won. The muleteers, however, were lads with no sense of humor, nor did they know what all this talk of spoils and battles was about; but, perceiving that Don Quixote had ridden off to one side to converse with those inside the coach, they pounced upon Sancho, threw him to the ground, and proceeded to pull out the hair of his beard and kick him to a pulp, after which they went off and left him stretched out there, bereft at once of breath and sense.

Without losing any time, they then assisted the friar to remount. The good brother was trembling all over from fright, and there was not a speck of color in his face, but when he found himself in the saddle once more, he quickly spurred his beast to where his companion, at some little distance, sat watching and waiting to see what the result of the encounter would be. Having no curiosity as to the final outcome of the fray, the two of them now resumed their journey, making more signs of the cross than the devil would be able to carry upon his back.

Meanwhile Don Quixote, as we have said, was speaking to the lady in the coach.

"Your beauty, my lady, may now dispose of your person as best may please you, for the arrogance of your abductors lies upon the ground, overthrown by this good arm of mine; and in order that you may not pine to know the name of your liberator, I may inform you that I am Don Quixote de la Mancha, knight-errant and adventurer and captive of the peerless and beauteous Doña Dulcinea del Toboso. In payment of the favor which you have received from me, I ask nothing other than that you return to El Toboso and on my behalf pay your respects to this lady, telling her that it was I who set you free."

One of the squires accompanying those in the coach, a Biscayan,[9] was listening to Don Quixote's words, and when he saw that the knight did not propose to let the coach proceed upon its way but was bent upon having it turn back to El Toboso, he promptly went up to him, seized his lance, and said to him in bad Castilian and worse Biscayan, "Go, *caballero*, and bad luck go with you; for by the God that created me, if you do not let this coach pass, me kill you or me no Biscayan."

Don Quixote heard him attentively enough and answered him very mildly, "If you were a *caballero*,[1] which you are not, I should already have chastised you, wretched creature, for your foolhardiness and your impudence."

"Me no *caballero*?" cried the Biscayan "Me swear to God, you lie like a Christian. If you will but lay aside your lance and unsheath your sword, you will soon see that you are carrying water to the cat![2] Biscayan on land, gentleman at sea, but a gentleman in spite of the devil, and you lie if you say otherwise."

" 'You shall see as to that presently,' said Agrajes,' " Don Quixote quoted.[3] He cast his lance to the earth, drew his sword, and, taking his buckler on his arm, attacked the Biscayan with intent to slay him. The latter, when he saw his adversary approaching, would have liked to dismount from his mule, for she was one of the worthless sort that are let for hire and he had no confidence in her; but there was no time for this, and so he had no choice but to draw his

---

9. From the Basque region in northeastern Spain.    1. *Caballero* means both "knight" and "gentleman."    2. An inversion of a proverbial phrase, "carrying the cat to the water."    3. Agrajes is a violent character in the romance *Amadis de Gaul*; his challenging phrase is the conventional opener of a fight.

own sword in turn and make the best of it. However, he was near enough to the coach to be able to snatch a cushion from it to serve him as a shield; and then they fell upon each other as though they were mortal enemies. The rest of those present sought to make peace between them but did not succeed, for the Biscayan with his disjointed phrases kept muttering that if they did not let him finish the battle then he himself would have to kill his mistress and anyone else who tried to stop him.

The lady inside the carriage, amazed by it all and trembling at what she saw, directed her coachman to drive on a little way; and there from a distance she watched the deadly combat, in the course of which the Biscayan came down with a great blow on Don Quixote's shoulder, over the top of the latter's shield, and had not the knight been clad in armor, it would have split him to the waist.

Feeling the weight of this blow, Don Quixote cried out, "O lady of my soul, Dulcinea, flower of beauty, succor this your champion who out of gratitude for your many favors finds himself in so perilous a plight!" To utter these words, lay hold of his sword, cover himself with his buckler, and attack the Biscayan was but the work of a moment; for he was now resolved to risk everything upon a single stroke.

As he saw Don Quixote approaching with so dauntless a bearing, the Biscayan was well aware of his adversary's courage and forthwith determined to imitate the example thus set him. He kept himself protected with his cushion, but he was unable to get his she-mule to budge to one side or the other, for the beast, out of sheer exhaustion and being, moreover, unused to such childish play, was incapable of taking a single step. And so, then, as has been stated, Don Quixote was approaching the wary Biscayan, his sword raised on high and with the firm resolve of cleaving his enemy in two; and the Biscayan was awaiting the knight in the same posture, cushion in front of him and with uplifted sword. All the bystanders were trembling with suspense at what would happen as a result of the terrible blows that were threatened, and the lady in the coach and her maids were making a thousand vows and offerings to all the images and shrines in Spain, praying that God would save them all and the lady's squire from this great peril that confronted them.

But the unfortunate part of the matter is that at this very point the author of the history breaks off and leaves the battle pending, excusing himself upon the ground that he has been unable to find anything else in writing concerning the exploits of Don Quixote beyond those already set forth. It is true, on the other hand, that the second author[4] of this work could not bring himself to believe that so unusual

---

4. Cervantes himself, adopting here—with tongue in cheek—a device used in the romances of chivalry to create suspense.

a chronicle would have been consigned to oblivion, nor that the learned ones of La Mancha were possessed of so little curiosity as not to be able to discover in their archives or registry offices certain papers that have to do with this famous knight. Being convinced of this, he did not despair of coming upon the end of this pleasing story. . . .

### CHAPTER 9

*In which is concluded and brought to an end the stupendous battle between the gallant Biscayan and the valiant Knight of La Mancha.*

. . . we left the valorous Biscayan and the famous Don Quixote with swords unsheathed and raised aloft, about to let fall furious slashing blows which, had they been delivered fairly and squarely, would at the very least have split them in two and laid them wide open from top to bottom like a pomegranate; and it was at this doubtful point that the pleasing chronicle came to a halt and broke off, without the author's informing us as to where the rest of it might be found.

I was deeply grieved by such a circumstance, and the pleasure I had had in reading so slight a portion was turned into annoyance as I thought of how difficult it would be to come upon the greater part which it seemed to me must still be missing. It appeared impossible and contrary to all good precedent that so worthy a knight should not have had some scribe to take upon himself the task of writing an account of these unheard-of exploits; for that was something that had happened to none of the knights-errant who, as the saying has it, had gone forth in quest of adventures, seeing that each of them had one or two chroniclers, as if ready at hand, who not only had set down their deeds, but had depicted their most trivial thoughts and amiable weaknesses, however well concealed they might be. The good knight of La Mancha surely could not have been so unfortunate as to have lacked what Platir and others like him had in abundance. And so I could not bring myself to believe that this gallant history could have remained thus lopped off and mutilated, and I could not but lay the blame upon the malignity of time, that devourer and consumer of all things, which must either have consumed it or kept it hidden.

On the other hand, I reflected that inasmuch as among the knight's books had been found such modern works as *The Disenchantments of Jealousy* and *The Nymphs and Shepherds of Henares*, his story likewise must be modern, and that even though it might not have been written down, it must remain in the memory of the good folk of his village and the surrounding ones. This thought left me somewhat confused and more than ever desirous of knowing the real and true story, the whole story, of the life and wondrous deeds of our

famous Spaniard, Don Quixote, light and mirror of the chivalry of
La Mancha, the first in our age and in these calamitous times to
devote himself to the hardships and exercises of knight-errantry and
to go about righting wrongs, succoring widows, and protecting
damsels—damsels such as those who, mounted upon their palfreys
and with riding-whip in hand, in full possession of their virginity,
were in the habit of going from mountain to mountain and from
valley to valley; for unless there were some villain, some rustic with
an ax and hood, or some monstrous giant to force them, there were
in times past maiden ladies who at the end of eighty years, during all
which time they had not slept for a single day beneath a roof, would
go to their graves as virginal as when their mothers had borne them.

If I speak of these things, it is for the reason that in this and in all
other respects our gallant Quixote is deserving of constant memory
and praise, and even I am not to be denied my share of it for my
diligence and the labor to which I put myself in searching out the
conclusion of this agreeable narrative; although if heaven, luck, and
circumstance had not aided me, the world would have had to do
without the pleasure and the pastime which anyone may enjoy who
will read this work attentively for an hour or two. The manner in
which it came about was as follows:

I was standing one day in the Alcaná, or market place, of Toledo
when a lad came up to sell some old notebooks and other papers to
a silk weaver who was there. As I am extremely fond of reading
anything, even though it be but the scraps of paper in the streets, I
followed my natural inclination and took one of the books, whereupon I at once perceived that it was written in characters which I
recognized as Arabic. I recognized them, but reading them was another
thing; and so I began looking around to see if there was any Spanish-
speaking Moor near by who would be able to read them for me. It
was not very hard to find such an interpreter, nor would it have been
even if the tongue in question had been an older and a better one.[5]
To make a long story short, chance brought a fellow my way; and
when I told him what it was I wished and placed the book in his
hands, he opened it in the middle and began reading and at once fell
to laughing. When I asked him what the cause of his laughter was,
he replied that it was a note which had been written in the margin.

I besought him to tell me the content of the note, and he, laughing still, went on, "As I told you, it is something in the margin here:
'This Dulcinea del Toboso, so often referred to, is said to have been
the best hand at salting pigs of any woman in all La Mancha.' "

No sooner had I heard the name Dulcinea del Toboso than I was
astonished and held in suspense, for at once the thought occurred to

5. I.e., the Hebrew language.

me that those notebooks must contain the history of Don Quixote. With this in mind I urged him to read me the title, and he proceeded to do so, turning the Arabic into Castilian upon the spot: *History of Don Quixote de la Mancha, Written by Cid Hamete Benengeli*[6] *Arabic Historian*. It was all I could do to conceal my satisfaction and, snatching them from the silk weaver, I bought from the lad all the papers and notebooks that he had for half a real; but if he had known or suspected how very much I wanted them, he might well have had more than six reales for them.

The Moor and I then betook ourselves to the cathedral cloister, where I requested him to translate for me into the Castilian tongue all the books that had to do with Don Quixote, adding nothing and subtracting nothing; and I offered him whatever payment he desired. He was content with two arrobas of raisins and two fanegas of wheat[7] and promised to translate them well and faithfully and with all dispatch. However, in order to facilitate matters, and also because I did not wish to let such a find as this out of my hands, I took the fellow home with me, where in a little more than a month and a half he translated the whole of the work just as you will find it set down here.

In the first of the books there was a very lifelike picture of the battle between Don Quixote and the Biscayan, the two being in precisely the same posture as described in the history, their swords upraised, the one covered by his buckler, the other with his cushion. As for the Biscayan's mule, you could see at the distance of a crossbow shot that it was one for hire. Beneath the Biscayan there was a rubric which read: "Don Sancho de Azpeitia," which must undoubtedly have been his name; while beneath the feet of Rocinante was another inscription: "Don Quixote." Rocinante was marvelously portrayed: so long and lank, so lean and flabby, so extremely consumptive-looking that one could well understand the justness and propriety with which the name of "hack" had been bestowed upon him.

Alongside Rocinante stood Sancho Panza, holding the halter of his ass, and below was the legend: "Sancho Zancas." The picture showed him with a big belly, a short body and long shanks, and that must have been where he got the names of Panza y Zancas[8] by which he is a number of times called in the course of the history. There are other small details that might be mentioned, but they are of little importance and have nothing to do with the truth of the story—and no story is bad so long as it is true.

If there is any objection to be raised against the veracity of the present one, it can be only that the author was an Arab, and that

6. Citing some ancient chronicle as the author's source and authority is very much in the tradition of the romances. *Benengeli*, incidentally, means "eggplant."   7. About 50 pounds of the first and 3 bushels of the second.   8. I.e., Paunch and Shanks.

nation is known for its lying propensities; but even though they be our enemies, it may readily be understood that they would more likely have detracted from, rather than added to, the chronicle. So it seems to me, at any rate; for whenever he might and should deploy the resources of his pen in praise of so worthy a knight, the author appears to take pains to pass over the matter in silence; all of which in my opinion is ill done and ill conceived, for it should be the duty of historians to be exact, truthful, and dispassionate, and neither interest nor fear nor rancor nor affection should swerve them from the path of truth, whose mother is history, rival of time, depository of deeds, witness of the past, exemplar and adviser to the present, and the future's counselor. In this work, I am sure, will be found all that could be desired in the way of pleasant reading; and if it is lacking in any way, I maintain that this is the fault of that hound of an author rather than of the subject.

But to come to the point, the second part, according to the translation, began as follows:

As the two valorous and enraged combatants stood there, swords upraised and poised on high, it seemed from their bold mien as if they must surely be threatening heaven, earth, and hell itself. The first to let fall a blow was the choleric Biscayan, and he came down with such force and fury that, had not his sword been deflected in mid-air, that single stroke would have sufficed to put an end to this fearful combat and to all our knight's adventures at the same time; but fortune, which was reserving him for greater things, turned aside his adversary's blade in such a manner that, even though it fell upon his left shoulder, it did him no other damage than to strip him completely of his armor on that side, carrying with it a good part of his helmet along with half an ear, the headpiece clattering to the ground with a dreadful din, leaving its wearer in a sorry state.

Heaven help me! Who could properly describe the rage that now entered the heart of our hero of La Mancha as he saw himself treated in this fashion? It may merely be said that he once more reared himself in the stirrups, laid hold of his sword with both hands, and dealt the Biscayan such a blow, over the cushion and upon the head, that, even so good a defense proving useless, it was as if a mountain had fallen upon his enemy. The latter now began bleeding through the mouth, nose, and ears; he seemed about to fall from his mule, and would have fallen, no doubt, if he had not grasped the beast about the neck, but at that moment his feet slipped from the stirrups and his arms let go, and the mule, frightened by the terrible blow, began running across the plain, hurling its rider to the earth with a few quick plunges.

Don Quixote stood watching all this very calmly. When he saw his enemy fall, he leaped from his horse, ran over very nimbly, and thrust the point of his sword into the Biscayan's eyes, calling upon him at the same time to surrender or otherwise he would cut off his head. The Biscayan was so bewildered that he was unable to utter a single word in reply, and things would have gone badly with him, so blind was Don Quixote in his rage, if the ladies of the coach, who up to then had watched the struggle in dismay, had not come up to him at this point and begged him with many blandishments to do them the very great favor of sparing their squire's life.

To which Don Quixote replied with much haughtiness and dignity, "Most certainly, lovely ladies, I shall be very happy to do that which you ask of me, but upon one conditon and understanding, and that is that this knight promise me that he will go to El Toboso and present himself in my behalf before Doña Dulcinea, in order that she may do with him as she may see fit."

Trembling and disconsolate, the ladies did not pause to discuss Don Quixote's request, but without so much as inquiring who Dulcinea might be they promised him that the squire would fulfill that which was commanded of him.

"Very well, then, trusting in your word, I will do him no further harm, even though he has well deserved it."

## CHAPTER 10

*Of the pleasing conversation that took place between Don Quixote and Sancho Panza, his squire.*

By this time Sancho Panza had got to his feet, somewhat the worse for wear as the result of the treatment he had received from the friars' lads. He had been watching the battle attentively and praying God in his heart to give the victory to his master, Don Quixote, in order that he, Sancho, might gain some island where he could go to be governor as had been promised him. Seeing now that the combat was over and the knight was returning to mount Rocinante once more, he went up to hold the stirrup for him; but first he fell on his knees in front of him and, taking his hand, kissed it and said, "May your Grace be pleased, Señor Don Quixote, to grant me the governorship of that island which you have won in this deadly affray; for however large it may be, I feel that I am indeed capable of governing it as well as any man in this world has ever done."

To which Don Quixote replied, "Be advised, brother Sancho, that this adventure and other similar ones have nothing to do with islands; they are affairs of the crossroads in which one gains nothing more than a broken head or an ear the less. Be patient, for there will be others which will not only make you a governor, but more than that."

Sancho thanked him very much and, kissing his hand again and the skirt of his cuirass, he assisted him up on Rocinante's back, after which the squire bestraddled his own mount and started jogging along behind his master, who was now going at a good clip. Without pausing for any further converse with those in the coach, the knight made for a near-by wood, with Sancho following as fast as his beast could trot; but Rocinante was making such speed that the ass and its rider were left behind, and it was necessary to call out to Don Quixote to pull up and wait for them. He did so, reining in Rocinante until the weary Sancho had drawn abreast of him.

"It strikes me, sir," said the squire as he reached his master's side, "that it would be better for us to take refuge in some church; for in view of the way you have treated that one with whom you were fighting, it would be small wonder if they did not lay the matter before the Holy Brotherhood[9] and have us arrested; and faith, if they do that, we shall have to sweat a-plenty before we come out of jail."

"Be quiet," said Don Quixote. "And where have you ever seen, or read of, a knight being brought to justice no matter how many homicides he might have committed?"

"I know nothing about omecils,"[1] replied Sancho, "nor ever in my life did I bear one to anybody; all I know is that the Holy Brotherhood has something to say about those who go around fighting on the highway, and I want nothing of it."

"Do not let it worry you," said Don Quixote, "for I will rescue you from the hands of the Chaldeans, not to speak of the Brotherhood. But answer me upon your life: have you ever seen a more valorous knight than I on all the known face of the earth? Have you ever read in the histories of any other who had more mettle in the attack, more perserverance in sustaining it, more dexterity in wounding his enemy, or more skill in overthrowing him?"

"The truth is," said Sancho, "I have never read any history whatsoever, for I do not know how to read or write; but what I would wager is that in all the days of my life I have never served a more courageous master than your Grace; I only hope your courage is not paid for in the place that I have mentioned. What I would suggest is that your Grace allow me to do something for that ear, for there is much blood coming from it, and I have here in my saddlebags some lint and a little white ointment."

"We could well dispense with all that," said Don Quixote, "if only I had remembered to bring along a vial of Fierabrás's[2] balm, a single drop of which saves time and medicines."

"What vial and what balm is that?" inquired Sancho Panza.

"It is a balm the receipt[3] for which I know by heart; with it one

9. A tribunal instituted by Ferdinand and Isabella at the end of the fifteenth century to punish highway robbers.    1. In the original, a word play on *homecidio-omecillo*. Not to bear an *ome-cillo* to anybody means not to bear a grudge; and good-natured Sancho does not.    2. Fierabrás is a giant Saracen healer in the medieval epics of the Twelve Peers (cf. footnote 1, p. 1700).

need have no fear of death nor think of dying from any wound. I shall make some of it and give it to you; and thereafter, whenever in any battle you see my body cut in two—as very often happens—all that is necessary is for you to take the part that lies on the ground, before the blood has congealed, and fit it very neatly and with great nicety upon the other part that remains in the saddle, taking care to adjust it evenly and exactly. Then you will give me but a couple of swallows of the balm of which I have told you, and you will see me sounder than an apple in no time at all."

"If that is so," said Panza, "I herewith renounce the governorship of the island you promised me and ask nothing other in payment of my many and faithful services than that your Grace give me the receipt for this wonderful potion, for I am sure that it would be worth more than two reales the ounce anywhere, and that is all I need for a life of ease and honor. But may I be so bold as to ask how much it costs to make it?"

"For less than three reales you can make something like six quarts," Don Quixote told him.

"Sinner that I am!" exclaimed Sancho. "Then why does your Grace not make some at once and teach me also?"

"Hush, my friend," said the knight, "I mean to teach you greater secrets than that and do you greater favors; but, for the present, let us look after this ear of mine, for it is hurting me more than I like."

Sancho thereupon took the lint and the ointment from his saddlebags; but when Don Quixote caught a glimpse of his helmet, he almost went out of his mind and, laying his hand upon his sword and lifting his eyes heavenward, he cried, "I make a vow to the Creator of all things and to the four holy Gospels in all their fullness of meaning that I will lead from now on the life that the great Marquis of Mantua did after he had sworn to avenge the death of his nephew Baldwin: not to eat bread of a tablecloth, not to embrace his wife, and other things which, although I am unable to recall them, we will look upon as understood—all this until I shall have wreaked an utter vengeance upon the one who has perpetrated such an outrage upon me.'

"But let me remind your Grace," said Sancho when he heard these words, "that if the knight fulfills that which was commanded of him, by going to present himself before my lady Dulcinea del Toboso, then he will have paid his debt to you and merits no further punishment at your hands, unless it be for some fresh offense."

"You have spoken very well and to the point," said Don Quixote, "and so I annul the vow I have just made insofar as it has to do with any further vengeance, but I make it and confirm it anew so far as leading the life of which I have spoken is concerned, until such time as I shall have obtained by force of arms from some other knight another headpiece as good as this. And do not think, Sancho, that I am making smoke out of straw; there is one whom I well may imitate in this matter, for the same thing happened in all literalness in the case of Mambrino's helmet which cost Sacripante so dear."[4]

"I wish," said Sancho, "that your Grace would send all such oaths to the devil, for they are very bad for the health and harmful for the conscience as well. Tell me, please; supposing that for many days to come we meet no man wearing a helmet, then what are we to do? Must you still keep your vow in spite of all the inconveniences and discomforts, such as sleeping with your clothes on, not sleeping in any town, and a thousand other penances contained in the oath of that old madman of a Marquis of Mantua, an oath which you would now revive? Mark you, sir, along all these roads you meet no men of arms but only muleteers and carters, who not only do not wear helmets but quite likely have never heard tell of them in all their livelong days."

"In that you are wrong," said Don Quixote, "for we shall not be at these crossroads for the space of two hours before we shall see more men of arms than came to Albraca to win the fair Angélica."[5] "Very well, then," said Sancho, "so be it, and pray God that all turns out for the best so that I may at last win that island that is costing me so dearly, and then let me die."

'I have already told you, Sancho, that you are to give no thought to that; should the island fail, there is the kingdom of Denmark or that of Sobradisa,[6] which would fit you like a ring on your finger, and you ought, moreover, to be happy to be on *terra firma*.[7] But let us leave all this for some other time, while you look and see if you have something in those saddlebags for us to eat, after which we will go in search of some castle where we may lodge for the night and prepare that balm of which I was telling you, for I swear to God that my ear is paining me greatly."

"I have here an onion, a little cheese, and a few crusts of bread," said Sancho, "but they are not victuals fit for a valiant knight like your grace.'

"How little you know about it!" replied Don Quixote. "I would inform you, Sancho, that it is a point of honor with knights-errant to go for a month at a time without eating, and when they do eat, it is whatever may be at hand. You would certainly know that if you had read the histories as I have. There are many of them, and in none have I found any mention of knights eating unless it was by chance or at some sumptuous banquet that was tendered them; on other days they fasted. And even though it is well understood that,

---

4. The enchanted helmet of Mambrino, a Moorish king, is stolen by Rinaldo in the fifteenth-century epic poem *Orlando Innamorato* ("Roland in Love") by Matteo Maria Boiardo. 5. Also an allusion to an episode in Boiardo's poem. 6. A nonexistent realm. 7. *Solid earth*, here also *Firm Island*, an imaginary final destination for the squires of knights-errant.

being men like us, they could not go without food entirely, any more than they could fail to satisfy the other necessities of nature, nevertheless, since they spent the greater part of their lives in forest and desert places without any cook to prepare their meals, their diet ordinarily consisted of rustic viands such as those that you now offer me. And so, Sancho my friend, do not be grieved at that which pleases me, nor seek to make the world over, nor to unhinge the institution of knight-errantry."

"Pardon me, your Grace," said Sancho, "but seeing that, as I have told you I do not know how to read or write, I am consequently not familiar with the rules of the knightly calling. Hereafter, I will stuff my saddlebags with all manner of dried fruit for your Grace, but inasmuch as I am not a knight, I shall lay in for myself a stock of fowls and other more substantial fare."

"I am not saying, Sancho, that it is incumbent upon knights-errant to eat only those fruits of which you speak; what I am saying is that their ordinary sustenance should consist of fruit and a few herbs such as are to be found in the fields and with which they are well acquainted, as am I myself."

"It is a good thing,' said Sancho, "to know those herbs, for, so far as I can see, we are going to have need of that knowledge one of these days."

With this, he brought out the articles he had mentioned, and the two of them ate in peace, and most companionably. Being desirous, however, of seeking a lodging for the night, they did not tarry long over their humble and unsavory repast. They then mounted and made what haste they could that they might arrive at a shelter before nightfall but the sun failed them, and with it went the hope of attaining their wish. As the day ended they found themselves beside some goatherds' huts, and they accordingly decided to spend the night there. Sancho was as much disappointed at their not having reached a town as his master was content with sleeping under the open sky; for it seemed to Don Quixote that every time this happened it merely provided him with yet another opportunity to establish his claim to the title of knight-errant.

*[Of Goatherds, Roaming Shepherdesses, and Unrequited Loves]*

### CHAPTER 11

*Of what happened to Don Quixote in the company of certain goat-herds.*

He was received by the herders with good grace, and Sancho having looked after Rocinante and the ass to the best of his ability, the knight, drawn by the aroma, went up to where some pieces of goat's meat were simmering in a pot over the fire. He would have liked then and there to see if they were done well enough to be transferred from pot to stomach, but he refrained in view of the fact that his hosts were already taking them off the fire. Spreading a few sheep-skins on the ground, they hastily laid their rustic board and invited the strangers to share what there was of it. There were six of them altogether who belonged to that fold, and after they had urged Don Quixote, with rude politeness, to seat himself upon a small trough which they had turned upside down for the purpose, they took their own places upon the sheep hides round about. While his master sat there, Sancho remained standing to serve him the cup, which was made of horn. When the knight perceived this, he addressed his squire as follows:

"In order, Sancho, that you may see the good that there is in knight-errantry and how speedily those who follow the profession, no matter what the nature of their service may be, come to be hon-ored and esteemed in the eyes of the world, I would have you here in the company of these good folk seat yourself at my side, that you may be even as I who am your master and natural lord, and eat fom my plate and drink from where I drink; for of knight-errantry one may be even as I who am your master and natural lord, and eat from

"Many thanks!" said Sancho, "but if it is all the same to your Grace, providing there is enough to go around, I can eat just as well, or better, standing up and alone as I can seated beside an emperor. And if the truth must be told, I enjoy much more that which I eat in my own corner without any bowings and scrapings, even though it be only bread and onions, than I do a meal of roast turkey where I have to chew slowly, drink little, be always wiping my mouth, and can neither sneeze nor cough if I feel like it, nor do any of those other things that you can when you are free and alone.

"And so, my master," he went on, "these honors that your Grace would confer upon me as your servant and a follower of knight-errantry—which I am, being your Grace's squire—I would have you convert, if you will, into other things that will be of more profit and advantage to me; for though I hereby acknowledge them as duly received, I renounce them from this time forth to the end of the world."

"But for all that," said Don Quixote, "you must sit down; for whosoever humbleth himself, him God will exalt." And, laying hold of his squire's arm, he compelled him to take a seat beside him.

The goatherds did not understand all this jargon about squires and knights-errant; they did nothing but eat, keep silent, and study their guests, who very dexterously and with much appetite were stowing away chunks of meat as big as your fist. When the meat course was finished, they laid out upon the sheepskins a great quantity of dried acorns and half a cheese, which was harder than if it had been made of mortar. The drinking horn all this while was not idle but went the rounds so often—now full, now empty, like the bucket of a water wheel—that they soon drained one of the two wine bags that were on hand. After Don Quixote had well satisfied his stomach, he took up a handful of acorns and, gazing at them attentively, fell into a soliloquy.

"Happy the age and happy those centuries to which the ancients gave the name of golden, and not because gold, which is so esteemed in this iron age of ours, was then to be had without toil, but because those who lived in that time did not know the meaning of the words 'thine' and 'mine.' In that blessed year all things were held in common, and to gain his daily sustenance no labor was required of any man save to reach forth his hand and take it from the sturdy oaks that stood liberally inviting him with their sweet and seasoned fruit. The clear-running fountains and rivers in magnificent abundance offered him palatable and transparent water for his thirst; while in the clefts of the rocks and the hollows of the trees the wise and busy honey-makers set up their republic so that any hand whatever might avail itself, fully and freely, of the fertile harvest which their fragrant toil had produced. The vigorous cork trees of their own free will and grace, without the asking, shed their broad, light bark with which men began to cover their dwellings, erected upon rude stakes merely as a protection against the inclemency of the heavens.

"All then was peace, all was concord and friendship; the crooked plowshare had not as yet grievously laid open and pried into the merciful bowels of our first mother, who without any forcing on man's part yielded her spacious fertile bosom on every hand for the satisfaction, sustenance, and delight of her first sons. Then it was that lovely and unspoiled young shepherdesses, with locks that were sometimes braided, sometimes flowing, went roaming from valley to valley and hillock to hillock with no more garments than were needed to cover decently that which modesty requires and always had required should remain covered. Nor were their adornments such as those in use today—of Tyrian purple and silk worked up in tortured patterns; a few green leaves of burdock or of ivy, and they were as splendidly and as becomingly clad as our ladies of the court with all the rare and exotic tricks of fashion that idle curiosity has taught them.

"Thoughts of love, also, in those days were set forth as simply as the simple hearts that conceived them, without any roundabout and artificial play of words by way of ornament. Fraud, deceit, and malice had not yet come to mingle with truth and plain-speaking. Justice kept its own domain, where favor and self-interest dared not trespass, dared not impair her rights, becloud, and persecute her as they now do. There was no such thing then as arbitrary judgments, for the

reason that there was no one to judge or be judged. Maidens in all
their modesty, as I have said, went where they would and unattended; whereas in this hateful age of ours none is safe, even though
she go to hide and shut herself up in some new labyrinth like that of
Crete; for in spite of all her seclusion, through chinks and crevices
or borne upon the air, the amorous plague with all its cursed impor-
tunities will find her out and lead her to her ruin.

"It was for the safety of such as these, as time went on and depravity increased, that the order of knights-errant was instituted, for the
protection of damsels, the aid of widows and orphans, and the succoring of the needy. It is to this order that I belong, my brothers, and
I thank you for the welcome and the kindly treatment that you have
accorded to me and my squire. By natural law, all living men are
obliged to show favor to knights-errant, yet without being aware of
this you have received and entertained me; and so it is with all possible good will that I acknowledge your own good will to me."

This long harangue on the part of our knight—it might very well
have been dispensed with—was all due to the acorns they had given
him, which had brought back to memory the age of gold; whereupon
the whim had seized him to indulge in this futile harangue with the
goatherds as his auditors. They listened in open-mouthed wonderment, saying not a word, and Sancho himself kept quiet and went
on munching acorns, taking occasion very frequently to pay a visit
to the second wine bag, which they had suspended from a cork tree
to keep it cool.

It took Don Quixote much longer to finish his speech than it did
to put away his supper; and when he was through, one of the goatherds addressed him.

"In order that your Grace may say with more truth that we have
received you with readiness and good will, we desire to give you
solace and contentment by having one of our comrades, who will be
here soon, sing for you. He is a very bright young fellow and deeply
in love, and what is more, you could not ask for anything better than
to hear him play the three-stringed lute."

Scarcely had he done saying this when the sound of a rebec was
heard, and shortly afterward the one who played it appeared. He was
a goodlooking youth, around twenty-two years of age. His companions asked him if he had had his supper, and when he replied that
he had, the one who had spoken to Don Quixote said to him, "Well,
then, Antonio, you can give us the pleasure of hearing you sing, in
order that this gentleman whom we have as our guest may see that
we of the woods and mountains also know something about music.
We have been telling him how clever you are, and now we want you
to show him that we were speaking the truth. And so I beg you by
all means to sit down and sing us that lovesong of yours that your

uncle the prebendary composed for you and which the villagers liked
so well."

"With great pleasure," the lad replied, and without any urging he
seated himself on the stump of an oak that had been felled and,
tuning up his rebec, soon began singing, very prettily, the following
ballad:

## The Ballad That Antonio Sang

> I know well that thou dost love me,
> My Olalla, even though
> Eyes of thine have never spoken—
> Love's mute tongues—to tell me so.
>   Since I know thou knowest my passion,
> Of thy love I am more sure:
> No love ever was unhappy
> When it was both frank and pure.
>   True it is, Olalla, sometimes
> Thou a heart of bronze hast shown,
> And it seemed to me that bosom,
> White and fair, was made of stone.
>   Yet in spite of all repulses
> And a chastity so cold,
> It appeared that I Hope's garment
> By the hem did clutch and hold.
>   For my faith I ever cherished;
> It would rise to meet the bait;
> Spurned, it never did diminish;
> Favored, it preferred to wait.
>   Love, they say, hath gentle manners:
> Thus it is it shows its face;
> Then may I take hope, Olalla,
> Trust to win a longed for grace.
>   If devotion hath the power
> Hearts to move and make them kind,
> Let the loyalty I've shown thee
> Plead my cause, be kept in mind.
>   For if thou didst note my costume,
> More than once thou must have seen,
> Worn upon a simple Monday
> Sunday's garb so bright and clean.
>   Love and brightness go together.
> Dost thou ask the reason why
> I thus deck myself on Monday?
> It is but to catch thine eye.

> I say nothing of the dances
> I have danced for thy sweet sake;
> Nor the serenades I've sung thee
> Till the first cock did awake.
>
>     Nor will I repeat my praises
> Of that beauty all can see;
> True my words but oft unwelcome—
> Certain lasses hated me.
>
>     One girl there is, I well remember—
> She's Teresa on the hill—
> Said, "You think you love an angel,
> But she is a monkey still.
>
>     "Thanks to all her many trinkets
> And her artificial hair
> And her many aids to beauty,
> Love's own self she would ensnare."
>
>     She was lying, I was angry,
> And her cousin, very bold,
> Challenged me upon my honor;
> What ensued need not be told.
>
>     Highflown words do not become me;
> I'm a plain and simple man.
> Pure the love that I would offer,
> Serving thee as best I can.
>
>     Silken are the bonds of marriage,
> When two hearts do intertwine;
> Mother Church the yoke will fasten;
> Bow your neck and I'll bow mine.
>
>     Or if not, my word I'll give thee,
> From these mountains I'll come down—
> Saint most holy be my witness—
> Wearing a Capuchin gown.

With this the goatherd brought his song to a close, and although Don Quixote begged him to sing some more, Sancho Panza would not hear of this as he was too sleepy for any more ballads.

"Your Grace," he said to his master, "would do well to find out at once where his bed is to be, for the labor that these good men have to perform all day long does not permit them to stay up all night singing."

"I understand, Sancho," replied Don Quixote. "I perceive that those visits to the wine bag call for sleep rather than music as a recompense."

"It tastes well enough to all of us, God be praised," said Sancho.

"I am not denying that," said his master; "but go ahead and settle yourself down wherever you like. As for men of my profession, they prefer to keep vigil. But all the same, Sancho, perhaps you had better look after this ear, for it is paining me more than I like."

Sancho started to do as he was commanded, but one of the goatherds, when he saw the wound, told him not to bother, that he would place a remedy upon it that would heal it in no time. Taking a few leaves of rosemary, of which there was a great deal growing thereabouts, he mashed them in his mouth and, mixing them with a little salt, laid them on the ear, with the assurance that no other medicine was needed; and this proved to be the truth.

## CHAPTER 12

*Of the story that one of the goatherds told to Don Quixote and the others.*

Just then, another lad came up, one of those who brought the goatherds their provisions from the village.

"Do you know what's happening down there, my friends?" he said.

"How should we know?" one of the men answered him.

"In that case," the lad went on, "I must tell you that the famous student and shepherd known as Grisóstomo died this morning, muttering that the cause of his death was the love he had for that bewitched lass of a Marcela, daughter of the wealthy Guillermo—you know, the one who's been going around in these parts dressed like a shepherdess."

"For love of Marcela, you say?" one of the herders spoke up.

"That is what I'm telling you," replied the other lad. "And the best part of it is that he left directions in his will that he was to be buried in the field, as if he were a Moor, and that his grave was to be at the foot of the cliff where the Cork Tree Spring is; for, according to report, and he is supposed to have said so himself, that is the place where he saw her for the first time. There were other provisions, which the clergy of the village say cannot be carried out, nor would it be proper to fulfill them, seeing that they savor of heathen practices. But Grisóstomo's good friend, the student Ambrosio, who also dresses like a shepherd, insists that everything must be done to the letter, and as a result there is great excitement in the village.

"Nevertheless, from all I can hear, they will end by doing as Ambrosio and Grisóstomo's other friends desire, and tomorrow they will bury him with great ceremony in the place that I have mentioned. I believe it is going to be something worth seeing; at any rate, I mean to see it, even though it is too far for me to be able to return to the village before nightfall."

"We will all do the same," said the other goatherds. "We will cast lots to see who stays to watch the goats."

"That is right, Pedro," said one of their number, "but it will not be necessary to go to the trouble of casting lots. I will take care of the flocks for all of us; and do not think that I am being generous or that I am not as curious as the rest of you; it is simply that I cannot walk on account of the splinter I picked up in this foot the other day."

"Well, we thank you just the same," said Pedro.

Don Quixote then asked Pedro to tell him more about the dead man and the shepherd lass; to which the latter replied that all he knew was that Grisóstomo was a rich gentleman who had lived in a near-by village. He had been a student for many years at Salamanca and then had returned to his birthplace with the reputation of being very learned and well read; he was especially noted for his knowledge of the science of the stars and what the sun and moon were doing up there in the heavens, "for he would promptly tell us when their clips was to come."

"*Eclipse*, my friend, not *clips*," said Don Quixote, "is the name applied to the darkening-over of those major luminaries."

But Pedro, not pausing for any trifles, went on with his story. "He could also tell when the year was going to be plentiful or estil—"

"*Sterile*, you mean to say, friend—"

"*Sterile* or *estil*," said Pedro, "it all comes out the same in the end. But I can tell you one thing, that his father and his friends, who believed in him, did just as he advised them and they became rich; for he would say to them, 'This year, sow barley and not wheat'; and again, 'Sow chickpeas and not barley'; or, 'This season there will be a good crop of oil[8] but the three following ones you will not get a drop.' "

"That science," Don Quixote explained, "is known as astrology."

"I don't know what it's called," said Pedro, "but he knew all this and more yet. Finally, not many months after he returned from Salamanca, he appeared one day dressed like a shepherd with crook and sheepskin jacket; for he had resolved to lay aside the long gown that he wore as a scholar, and in this he was joined by Ambrosio, a dear friend of his and the companion of his studies. I forgot to tell you that Grisóstomo was a great one for composing verses; he even wrote the carols for Christmas Eve and the plays that were performed at Corpus Christi by the lads of our village, and everyone said that they were the best ever.

"When the villagers saw the two scholars coming out dressed like shepherds, they were amazed and could not imagine what was the

---

8. Olive oil.

reason for such strange conduct on their part. It was about that time that Grisóstomo's father died and left him the heir to a large fortune, consisting of land and chattels, no small quantity of cattle, and a considerable sum of money, of all of which the young man was absolute master; and, to tell the truth, he deserved it, for he was very sociable and charitably inclined, a friend to all worthy folk, and he had a face that was like a benediction. Afterward it was learned that if he had changed his garments like this, it was only that he might be able to wander over the wastelands on the trail of that shepherdess Marcela of whom our friend was speaking, for the poor fellow had fallen in love with her. And now I should like to tell you, for it is well that you should know, just who this lass is; for it may be—indeed, there is no maybe about it—you will never hear the like in all the days of your life, though you live to be older than Sarna."

"You should say *Sarah*," Don Quixtoe corrected him; for he could not bear hearing the goatherd using the wrong words all the time.[9]

"The itch," said Pedro, "lives long enough; and if, sir, you go on interrupting me at every word, we'll never be through in a year."

"Pardon me, friend," said Don Quixote, "it was only because there is so great a difference between Sarna and Sarah that I pointed it out to you; but you have given me a very good answer, for the itch does live longer than Sarah; and so go on with your story, and I will not contradict you any more."

"I was about to say, then, my dear sir," the goatherd went on, "that in our village there was a farmer who was richer still than Grisóstomo's father. His name was Guillermo, and, over and above his great wealth, God gave him a daughter whose mother, the most highly respected woman in these parts, died in bearing her. It seems to me I can see the good lady now, with that face that rivaled the sun and moon; and I remember, above all, what a friend she was to the poor, for which reason I believe that her soul at this very moment must be enjoying God's presence in the other world.

"Grieving for the loss of so excellent a wife, Guillermo himself died, leaving his daughter Marcela, now a rich young woman, in the custody of one of her uncles, a priest who holds a benefice in our village. The girl grew up with such beauty as to remind us of her mother, beautiful as that lady had been. By the time she was fourteen or fifteen no one looked at her without giving thanks to God who had created such comeliness, and almost all were hopelessly in love with her. Her uncle kept her very closely shut up, but, for all of that, word of her great beauty spread to such an extent that by reason of it, as much as on account of the girl's wealth, her uncle

9. Actually in this case the goatherd is not really wrong, for *sarna* means "itch" and "older than the itch" was a proverbial expression.

found himself besought and importuned not only by the young men of our village, but by those for leagues around who desired to have her for a wife.

"But he, an upright Christian, although he wished to marry her off as soon as she was of age, had no desire to do so without her consent, not that he had any eye to the gain and profit which the custody of his niece's property brought him while her marriage was deferred. Indeed, this much was said in praise of the good priest in more than one circle of the village; for I would have you know, Sir Knight, that in these little places everything is discussed and becomes a subject of gossip; and you may rest assured, as I am for my part, that a priest must be more than ordinarily good if his parishioners feel bound to speak well of him, especially in the small towns."

"That is true," said Don Quixote, "but go on. I like your story very much, and you, good Pedro, tell it with very good grace."

"May the Lord's grace never fail me, for that is what counts. But to go on: Although the uncle set forth to his niece the qualities of each one in particular of the many who sought her hand, begging her to choose and marry whichever one she pleased, she never gave him any answer other than this: that she did not wish to marry at all, since being but a young girl she did not feel that she was equal to bearing the burdens of matrimony. As her reasons appeared to be proper and just, the uncle did not insist but thought he would wait until she was a little older, when she would be capable of selecting someone to her taste. For, he said, and quite right he was, parents ought not to impose a way of life upon their children against the latters' will. And then, one fine day, lo and behold, there was the finical Marcela turned shepherdess; and without paying any attention to her uncle or all those of the village who advised against it, she set out to wander through the fields with the other lasses, guarding flocks as they did.

"Well, the moment she appeared in public and her beauty was uncovered for all to see, I really cannot tell you how many rich young bachelors, gentlemen, and farmers proceeded to don a shepherd's garb and go to make love to her in the meadows. One of her suitors, as I have told you, was our deceased friend, and it is said that he did not love but adored her. But you must not think that because Marcela chose so free and easy a life, and one that offers little or no privacy, that she was thereby giving the faintest semblance of encouragement to those who would disparage her modesty and prudence; rather, so great was the vigilance with which she looked after her honor that of all those who waited upon her and solicited her favors, none could truly say that she had given him the slightest hope of attaining his desire.

"For although she does not flee nor shun the company and conversation of the shepherds, treating them in courteous and friendly fashion, the moment she discovers any intentions on their part, even though it be the just and holy one of matrimony, she hurls them from her like a catapult. As a result, she is doing more damage in this land than if a plague had fallen upon it; for her beauty and graciousness win the hearts of all who would serve her, but her disdain and the disillusionment it brings lead them in the end to despair, and then they can only call her cruel and ungrateful, along with other similar epithets that reveal all too plainly the state of mind that prompts them. If you were to stay here some time, sir, you would hear these uplands and valleys echo with the laments of those who have followed her only to be deceived.

"Not far from here is a place where there are a couple of dozen tall beeches, and there is not a one of them on whose smooth bark Marcela's name has not been engraved; and above some of these inscriptions you will find a crown, as if by this her lover meant to indicate that she deserved to wear the garland of beauty above all the women on the earth. Here a shepherd sighs and there another voices his lament. Now are to be heard amorous ballads, and again despairing ditties. One will spend all the hours of the night seated at the foot of some oak or rock without once closing his tearful eyes, and the morning sun will find him there, stupefied and lost in thought. Another, without giving truce or respite to his sights, will lie stretched upon the burning sands in the full heat of the most exhausting summer noontide, sending up his complaint to merciful Heaven.

"And, meanwhile, over this one and that one, over one and all, the beauteous Marcela triumphs and goes her own way, free and unconcerned. All those of us who know her are waiting to see how far her pride will carry her, and who will be the fortunate man who will succeed in taming this terrible creature and thus come into possession of a beauty so matchless as hers. Knowing all this that I have told you to be undoubtedly true, I can readily believe this lad's story about the cause of Grisóstomo's death. And so I advise you, sir, not to fail to be present tomorrow at his burial; it will be well worth seeing, for he has many friends, and the place is not half a league from here."

"I will make a point of it," said Don Quixote, "and I thank you for the pleasure you have given me by telling me so delightful a tale."

"Oh," said the goatherd, "I do not know the half of the things that have happened to Marcela's lovers; but it is possible that tomorrow we may meet along the way some shepherd who will tell us more. And now it would be well for you to go and sleep under cover, for the night air may not be good for your wound, though with the remedy that has been put on it there is not much to fear."

Sancho Panza, who had been sending the goatherd to the devil for talking so much, now put in a word with his master, urging him to come and sleep in Pedro's hut. Don Quixote did so; and all the rest of the night was spent by him in thinking of his lady Dulcinea, in imitation of Marcela's lovers. As for Sancho, he made himself comfortable between Rocinante and the ass and at once dropped off to sleep, not like a lovelorn swain but, rather, like a man who has had a sound kicking that day.

CHAPTER 13

*In which is brought to a close the story of the shepherdess Marcela, along with other events.*

Day had barely begun to appear upon the balconies of the east when five or six goatherds arose and went to awaken Don Quixote and tell him that if he was still of a mind to go see Grisóstomo's famous burial they would keep him company. The knight, desiring nothing better, ordered Sancho to saddle at once, which was done with much dispatch, and then they all set out forthwith.

They had not gone more than a quarter of a league when, upon crossing a footpath, they saw coming toward them six shepherds clad in black sheepskins and with garlands of cypress and bitter rosebay on their heads. Each of them carried a thick staff made of the wood of the holly, and with them came two gentlemen on horseback in handsome traveling attire, accompanied by three lads on foot. As the two parties met they greeted each other courteously, each inquiring as to the other's destination, whereupon they learned that they were all going to the burial, and so continued to ride along together.

Speaking to his companion, one of them said, "I think, Señor Vivaldo, that we are going to be well repaid for the delay it will cost us to see this famous funeral; for famous it must surely be, judging by the strange things that these shepherds have told us of the dead man and the homicidal shepherdess."

"I think so too," agreed Vivaldo. "I should be willing to delay our journey not one day, but four, for the sake of seeing it."

Don Quixote then asked them what it was they had heard of Marcela and Grisóstomo. The traveler replied that on that very morning they had fallen in with those shepherds and, seeing them so mournfully trigged out, had asked them what the occasion for it was. One of the fellows had then told them of the beauty and strange demeanor of a shepherdess by the name of Marcela, her many suitors, and the death of this Grisóstomo, to whose funeral they were bound. He related, in short, the entire story as Don Quixote had heard it from Pedro.

Changing the subject, the gentleman called Vivaldo inquired of Don Quixote what it was that led him to go armed in that manner in a land that was so peaceful.

"The calling that I profess," replied Don Quixote, "does not permit me to do otherwise. An easy pace, pleasure, and repose—those things were invented for delicate courtiers; but toil, anxiety, and arms— they are for those whom the world knows as knights-errant, of whom I, though unworthy, am the very least."

No sooner had they heard this than all of them immediately took him for a madman. By way of assuring himself further and seeing what kind of madness it was of which Don Quixote was possessed, Vivaldo now asked him what was meant by the term knights-errant.

"Have not your Worships read the annals and the histories of England that treat of the famous exploits of King Arthur, who in our Castilian balladry is always called King Artús? According to a very old tradition that is common throughout the entire realm of Great Britain, this king did not die, but by an act of enchantment was changed into a raven; and in due course of time he is to return and reign once more, recovering his kingdom and his scepter; for which reason, from that day to this, no Englishman is known to have killed one of those birds. It was, moreover, in the time of that good king that the famous order of the Knights of the Round Table was instituted; and as for the love of Sir Lancelot of the Lake and Queen Guinevere, everything took place exactly as the story has it, their confidante and go-between being the honored matron Quintañona; whence comes that charming ballad that is such a favorite with us Spaniards:

*Never was there a knight*
*So served by maid and dame*
*As the one they call Sir Lancelot*
*When from Britain he came—*

to carry on the gentle, pleasing course of his loves and noble deeds.

"From that time forth, the order of chivalry was passed on and propagated from one individual to another until it had spread through many and various parts of the world. Among those famed for their exploits was the valiant Amadis of Gaul, with all his sons and grandsons to the fifth generation; and there was also the brave Felixmarte of Hircania, and the never sufficiently praised Tirant lo Blanch; and in view of the fact that he lived in our own day, almost, we came near to seeing, hearing, and conversing with that other courageous knight, Don Belianís of Greece.

"And that, gentlemen, is what it means to be a knight-errant, and what I have been telling you of is the order of chivalry which such a knight professes, an order to which, as I have already informed you, I, although a sinner, have the honor of belonging; for I have made the same profession as have those other knights. That is why it is you find me in these wild and lonely places, riding in quest of adventure, being resolved to offer my arm and my person in the most dangerous undertaking fate may have in store for me, that I may be of aid to the weak and needy."

Listening to this speech, the travelers had some while since come to the conclusion that Don Quixote was out of his mind, and were likewise able to perceive the peculiar nature of his madness, and they wondered at it quite as much as did all those who encountered it for the first time. Being endowed with a ready wit and a merry disposition and thinking to pass the time until they reached the end of the short journey which, so he was told, awaited them before they should arrive at the mountain where the burial was to take place, Vivaldo decided to give him a further opportunity of displaying his absurdities.

"It strikes me, Sir Knight-errant," he said, "that your Grace has espoused one of the most austere professions to be found anywhere on earth—even more austere, if I am not mistaken, than that of the Carthusian monks."

"Theirs may be as austere as ours," Don Quixote replied, "but that it is as necessary I am very much inclined to doubt. For if the truth be told, the soldier who carries out his captain's order does no less than the captain who gives the order. By that I mean to say that the religious, in all peace and tranquility, pray to Heaven for earth's good, but we soldiers and knights put their prayers into execution by defending with the might of our good right arms and at the edge of the sword those things for which they pray; and we do this not under cover of a roof but under the open sky, beneath the insufferable rays of the summer sun and the biting cold of winter. Thus we become the ministers of God on earth, and our arms the means by which He executes His decrees. And just as war and all the things that have to do with it are impossible without toil, sweat, and anxiety, it follows that those who have taken upon themselves such a profession must unquestionably labor harder than do those who in peace and tranquility and at their ease pray God to favor the ones who can do little in their own behalf.

"I do not mean to say—I should not think of saying—that the state of knight-errant is as holy as that of the cloistered monk; I merely would imply, from what I myself endure, that ours is beyond a doubt the more laborious and arduous calling, more beset by hunger and thirst, more wretched, ragged, and ridden with lice. It is an absolute certainty that the knights-errant of old experienced much misfortune in the course of their lives; and if some by their might and valor came to be emperors, you may take my word for it, it cost them dearly in blood and sweat, and if those who rose to such a rank had lacked enchanters and magicians to aid them, they surely would have been cheated of their desires, deceived in their hopes and expectations."

"I agree with you on that," said the traveler, "but there is one thing among others that gives me a very bad impression of the knights-errant, and that is the fact that when they are about to enter upon some great and perilous adventure in which they are in danger of losing their lives, they never at that moment think of commending themselves to God as every good Christian is obliged to do under similar circumstances, but, rather, commend themselves to their ladies with as much fervor and devotion as if their mistresses were God himself; all of which to me smacks somewhat of paganism."

"Sir," Don Quixote answered him, "it could not by any means be otherwise; the knight-errant who did not do so would fall into disgrace, for it is the usage and custom of chivalry that the knight, before engaging in some great feat of arms, shall behold his lady in front of him and shall turn his eyes toward her, gently and lovingly, as if beseeching her favor and protection in the hazardous encounter that awaits him, and even though no one hears him, he is obliged to utter certain words between his teeth, commending himself to her with all his heart; and of this we have numerous examples in the histories. Nor is it to be assumed that he does not commend himself to God also, but the time and place for that is in the course of the undertaking."

"All the same," said the traveler, "I am not wholly clear in this matter; for I have often read of two knights-errant exchanging words until, one word leading to another, their wrath is kindled; whereupon, turning their steeds and taking a good run up the field, they whirl about and bear down upon each other at full speed, commending themselves to their ladies in the midst of it all. What commonly happens then is that one of the two topples from his horse's flanks and is run through and through with the other's lance; and his adversary would also fall to the ground if he did not cling to his horse's mane. What I do not understand is how the dead man would have had time to commend himself to God in the course of this accelerated combat. It would be better if the words he wasted in calling upon his lady as he ran toward the other knight had been spent in paying the debt that he owed as a Christian. Moreover, it is my personal opinion that not all knights-errant have ladies to whom to commend themselves, for not all of them are in love."

"That," said Don Quixote, "is impossible. I assert there can be no knight-errant without a lady; for it is as natural and proper for them to be in love as it is for the heavens to have stars, and I am quite sure that no one ever read a story in which a loveless man of arms was to be met with, for the simple reason that such a one would not be looked upon as a legitimate knight but as a bastard one who had entered the fortress of chivalry not by the main gate, but over the walls, like a robber and a thief."

"Nevertheless," said the traveler, "if my memory serves me right, I have read that Don Galaor, brother of the valorous Amadis of Gaul, never had a special lady to whom he prayed, yet he was not held in any the less esteem for that but was a very brave and famous knight."

Once again, our Don Quixote had an answer. "Sir, one swallow does not make a summer. And in any event, I happen to know that this knight was secretly very much in love. As for his habit of paying court to all the ladies that caught his fancy, that was a natural propensity on his part and one that he was unable to resist. There was, however, one particular lady whom he had made the mistress of his will and to whom he did commend himself very frequently and privately; for he prided himself upon being a reticent knight."

"Well, then," said the traveler, "if it is essential that every knight-errant be in love, it is to be presumed that your Grace is also, since you are of the profession. And unless it be that you pride yourself upon your reticence as much as did Don Galaor, then I truly, on my own behalf and in the name of all this company, beseech your Grace to tell us your lady's name, the name of the country where she resides, what her rank is, and something of the beauty of her person, that she may esteem herself fortunate in having all the world know that she is loved and served by such a knight as your Grace appears to me to be."

At this, Don Quixote heaved a deep sigh. "I cannot say," he began, "as to whether or not my sweet enemy would be pleased that all the world should know I serve her. I can only tell you, in response to the question which you have so politely put to me, that her name is Dulcinea, her place of residence El Toboso, a village of La Mancha. As to her rank, she should be at the very least a princess, seeing that she is my lady and my queen. Her beauty is superhuman, for in it are realized all the impossible and chimerical attributes that poets are accustomed to give their fair ones. Her locks are golden, her brow the Elysian Fields, her eyebrows rainbows, her eyes suns, her cheeks roses, her lips coral, her teeth pearls, her neck alabaster, her bosom marble, her hands ivory, her complexion snow-white. As for those parts which modesty keeps covered from the human sight, it is my opinion that, discreetly considered, they are only to be extolled and not compared to any other."

"We should like," said Vivaldo, "to know something as well of her lineage, her race and ancestry."

"She is not," said Don Quixote, "of the ancient Roman Curtii, Caii, or Scipios, nor of the modern Colonnas and Orsini, nor of the Moncades and Requesenses of Catalonia, nor is she of the Rebellas and Villanovas of Valencia, or the Palafoxes, Nuzas, Rocabertis, Corellas, Lunas, Alagones, Urreas, or Gurreas of Aragon, the Cerdas, Manriques, Mendozas, or Guzmanes of Castile, the Alencastros, Pallas, or Menezes of Portugal; but she is of the Tobosos of La Mancha, and although the line is a modern one, it well may give rise to the most illustrious families of the centuries to come. And let none dispute this with me, unless it be under the conditions which Zerbino has set forth in the inscription beneath Orlando's arms:

> *These let none move*
> *Who dares not with Orlando his valor prove.*"[1]

"Although my own line," replied the traveler, "is that of the Gachupins of Laredo, I should not venture to compare it with the Tobosos of La Mancha, in view of the fact that, to tell you the truth, I have never heard the name before."

"How does it come that you have never heard it!" exclaimed Don Quixote.

The others were listening most attentively to the conversation of these two, and even the goatherds and shepherds were by now aware that our knight of La Mancha was more than a little insane. Sancho Panza alone thought that all his master said was the truth, for he was well acquainted with him, having known him since birth. The only doubt in his mind had to do with the beauteous Dulcinea del Toboso, for he knew of no such princess and the name was strange to his ears, although he lived not far from that place.

They were continuing on their way, conversing in this manner, when they caught sight of some twenty shepherds coming through the gap between two high mountains, all of them clad in black woolen garments and with wreaths on their heads, some of the garlands, as was afterward learned, being of cypress, others of yew. Six of them were carrying a bier covered with a great variety of flowers and boughs.

"There they come with Grisóstomo's body," said one of the goatherds, "and the foot of the mountain yonder is where he wished to be buried."

They accordingly quickened their pace and arrived just as those carrying the bier had set it down on the ground. Four of the shepherds with sharpened picks were engaged in digging a grave alongside the barren rock. After a courteous exchange of greetings, Don Quixote and his companions turned to look at the bier. Upon it lay a corpse covered with flowers, the body of a man dressed like a shepherd and around thirty years of age. Even in death it could be seen that he had had a handsome face and had been of a jovial disposi-

---

1. From Lodovico Ariosto's *Orlando Furioso*, canto XXIV, stanza 57.

tion. Round about him upon the bier were a number of books and many papers, open and folded.

Meanwhile, those who stood gazing at the dead man and those who were digging the grave—everyone present, in fact—preserved an awed silence, until one of the pallbearers said to another, "Look well, Ambrosio, and make sure that this is the place that Grisóstomo had in mind, since you are bent upon carrying out to the letter the provisions of his will."

"This is it," replied Ambrosio; "for many times my unfortunate friend told me the story of his misadventure. He told me that it was here that he first laid eyes upon that mortal enemy of the human race, and it was here, also, that he first revealed to her his passion, for he was as honorable as he was lovelorn; and it was here, finally, at their last meeting, that she shattered his illusions and showed him her disdain, thus bringing to an end the tragedy of his wretched life. And here, in memory of his great misfortune, he wished to be laid in the bowels of eternal oblivion."

Then, turning to Don Quixote and the travelers, he went on, "This body, gentlemen, on which you now look with pitying eyes was the depository of a soul which heaven had endowed with a vast share of its riches. This is the body of Grisóstomo, who was unrivaled in wit, unequaled in courtesy, supreme in gentleness of bearing, a model of friendship, generous without stint, grave without conceit, merry without being vulgar—in short, first in all that is good and second to none in the matter of misfortunes. He loved well and was hated, he adored and was disdained; he wooed a wild beast, importuned a piece of marble, ran after the wind, cried out to loneliness, waited upon ingratitude, and his reward was to be the spoils of death midway in his life's course—a life that was brought to an end by a shepherdess whom he sought to immortalize that she might live on in the memory of mankind, as those papers that you see there would very plainly show if he had not commanded me to consign them to the flames even as his body is given to the earth."

"You," said Vivaldo, "would treat them with greater harshness and cruelty than their owner himself, for it is neither just nor fitting to carry out the will of one who commands what is contrary to all reason. It would not have been a good thing for Augustus Caesar to consent to have them execute the behests of the divine Mantuan in his last testament.[2] And so, Señor Ambrosio, while you may give the body of your friend to the earth, you ought not to give his writings to oblivion. If out of bitterness he left such an order, that does not mean that you are to obey it without using your own discretion. Rather, by granting life to these papers, you permit Marcela's cruelheartedness to live forever and serve as an example to the others in

2. Virgil (born near Mantua) had left instructions that his Roman epic, the *Aeneid*, should be burned.

the days that are to come in order that they may flee and avoid such pitfalls as these.

"I and those that have come with me know the story of this love-sick and despairing friend of yours; we know the affection that was between you, and what the occasion of his death was, and the things that he commanded be done as his life drew to a close. And from this lamentable tale anyone may see how great was Marcela's cruelty; they may behold Grisóstomo's love, the loyalty that lay in your friendship, and the end that awaits those who run headlong, with unbridled passion, down the path that doting love opens before their gaze. Last night we heard of your friend's death and learned that he was to be buried here, and out of pity and curiosity we turned aside from our journey and resolved to come see with our own eyes that which had aroused so much compassion when it was told to us. And in requital of that compassion, and the desire that has been born in us to prevent if we can a recurrence of such tragic circumstances, we beg you, O prudent Ambrosio!—or, at least, I for my part implore you—to give up your intention of burning these papers and let me carry some of them away with me."

Without waiting for the shepherd to reply he put out his hand and took a few of those that were nearest him.

"Out of courtesy, sir," said Ambrosio when he saw this, "I will consent for you to keep those that you have taken; but it is vain to think that I will refrain from burning the others."

Vivaldo, who was anxious to find out what was in the papers, opened one of them and perceived that it bore the title "Song of Despair."

Hearing this, Ambrosio said, "That is the last thing the poor fellow wrote; and in order, sir, that you may see the end to which his misfortunes brought him, read it aloud if you will, for we shall have time for it while they are digging the grave."

"That I will very willingly do," said Vivaldo.

And since all the bystanders had the same desire, they gathered around as he in a loud clear voice read the following poem.

## CHAPTER 14

*In which are set down the despairing verses of the deceased shepherd, with other unlooked-for happenings.*

## Grisóstomo's Song

*Since thou desirest that thy cruelty*
*Be spread from tongue to tongue and land to land,*
*The unrelenting sternness of thy heart*

Shall turn my bosom's hell to minstrelsy
That all men everywhere may understand
The nature of my grief and what thou art.
And as I seek my sorrows to impart,
Telling of all the things that thou hast done,
My very entrails shall speak out to brand
Thy heartlessness, thy soul to reprimand,
Where no compassion ever have I won.
Then listen well, lend an attentive ear;
This ballad that thou art about to hear
Is not contrived by art; 'tis a simple song
Such as shepherds sing each day throughout the year—
Surcease of pain for me, for thee a prong.

    Then let the roar of lion, fierce wolf's cry,
The horrid hissing of the scaly snake,
The terrifying sound of monsters strange,
Ill-omened call of crow against the sky,
The howling of the wind as it doth shake
The tossing sea where all is constant change,
Bellow of vanquished bull that cannot range
As it was wont to do, the piteous sob
Of the widowed dove as if its heart would break,
Hoot of the envied owl,[3] ever awake,
From hell's own choir the deep and mournful throb—
Let all these sounds come forth and mingle now.
For if I'm to tell my woes, why then, I vow,
I must new measures find, new modes invent,
With sound confusing sense, I may somehow
Portray the inferno where my days are spent.

    The mournful echoes of my murmurous plaint
Father Tagus[4] shall not hear as he rolls his sand,
Nor olive-bordered Betis; my lament shall be
To the tall and barren rock as I acquaint
The caves with my sorrow; the far and lonely strand
No human foot has trod shall hear from me
The story of thine inhumanity
As told with lifeless tongue but living word.
I'll tell it to the valleys near at hand
Where never shines the sun upon the land;
By venomous serpents shall my tale be heard
On the low-lying, marshy river plain.
And yet, the telling will not be in vain;
For the reverberations of my plight,

3. Envied by other birds as the only one that witnessed the Crucifixion.    4. The river Tagus.
Betis: the Guadalquivir.

*Thy matchless austerity and this my pain,*
*Through the wide world shall go, thee to indict.*
   *Disdain may kill; suspicion false or true*
*May slay all patience; deadliest of all*
*Is jealousy; while absence renders life*
*Worse than a void; Hope lends no roseate hue*
*Against forgetfulness or the dread call*
*Of death inevitable, the end of strife.*
*Yet—unheard miracle!—with sorrows rife,*
*My own existence somehow still goes on;*
*The flame of life with me doth rise and fall.*
*Jealous I am, disdained; I know the gall*
*Of those suspicions that will not be gone,*
*Which leave me not the shadow of a hope,*
*And, desperate, I will not even grope*
*But rather will endure until the end,*
*And with despair eternally I'll cope,*
*Knowing that things for me will never mend.*
   *Can one both hope and fear at the same season?*
*Would it be well to do so in any case,*
*Seeing that fear, by far, hath the better excuse?*
*Confronting jealousy, is there any reason*
*For me to close my eyes to its stern face,*
*Pretend to see it not? What is the use,*
*When its dread presence I can still deduce*
*From countless gaping wounds deep in my heart?*
*When suspicion—bitter change!—to truth gives place,*
*And truth itself, losing its virgin grace,*
*Becomes a lie, is it not wisdom's part*
*To open wide the door to frank mistrust?*
*When disdain's unveiled, to doubt is only just.*
*O ye fierce tyrants of Love's empery!*
*Shackle these hands with stout cord, if ye must.*
*My pain shall drown your triumph—woe is me!*
   *I die, in short, and since nor life nor death*
*Yields any hope, to my fancy will I cling.*
*That man is freest who is Love's bond slave:*
*I'll say this with my living-dying breath,*
*And the ancient tyrant's praises I will sing.*
*Love is the greatest blessing Heaven e'er gave.*
*What greater beauty could a lover crave*
*Than that which my fair enemy doth show*
*In soul and body and in everything?*
*E'en her forgetfulness of me doth spring*
*From my own lack of grace, that I well know.*

In spite of all the wrongs that he has wrought,
Love rules his empire justly as he ought.
Throw all to the winds and speed life's wretched span
By feeding on his self-deluding thought.
No blessing holds the future that I scan.

    Thou whose unreasonableness reason doth give
For putting an end to this tired life of mine,
From the deep heart wounds which thou mayest plainly see,
Judge if the better course be to die or live.
Gladly did I surrender my will to thine,
Gladly I suffered all thou didst to me;
And now that I'm dying, should it seem to thee
My death is worth a tear from thy bright eyes,
Pray hold it back, fair one, do not repine,
For I would have from thee no faintest sign
Of penitence, e'en though my soul thy prize.
Rather, I'd have thee laugh, be very gay,
And let my funeral be a festive day—
But I am very simple! knowing full well
That thou art bound to go thy blithesome way,
And my untimely end thy fame shall swell.

    Come, thirsting Tantalus from out Hell's pit;
Come, Sisyphus with the terrifying weight
Of that stone thou rollest; Tityus, bring
Thy vulture and thine anguish infinite;
Ixion[5] with thy wheel, be thou not late;
Come, too, ye sisters ever laboring;[6]
Come all, your griefs into my bosom fling,
And then, with lowered voices, intone a dirge,
If dirge be fitting for one so desperate,
A body without a shroud, unhappy fate!
And Hell's three-headed gateman,[7] do thou emerge
With a myriad other phantoms, monstrous swarm,
Beings infernal of fantastic form,
Raising their voices for the uncomforted
In a counterpoint of grief, harmonious storm.
What better burial for a lover dead?

    Despairing song of mine, do not complain,
Nor let our parting cause thee any pain,
For my misfortune is not wholly bad,

---

5. In Greek myth, all four are proverbial images of mortals punished by the Gods with different forms of torture: *Tantalus*, craving water and fruit which he always fails to reach; *Sisyphus*, forever vainly trying to roll a stone upward to the top of a hill; *Tityus*, having his liver devoured by a vulture; and Ixion, being bound to a revolving wheel.     6. In classical mythology the three Fates (Moerae to the Greeks, Parcae to the Romans), spinners of man's destiny.     7. Cerberus, a dog-like three-headed monster, the mythological guardian of Hell.

*Seeing her fortune's bettered by my demise.*
*Then, even in the grave, be thou not sad.*

Those who had listened to Grisóstomo's poem liked it well enough, but the one who read it remarked that it did not appear to him to conform to what had been told him of Marcela's modesty and virtue, seeing that in it the author complains of jealousy, suspicion, and absence, all to the prejudice of her good name. To this Ambrosio, as one who had known his friend's most deeply hidden thoughts, replied as follows:

"By way of satisfying, sir, the doubt that you entertain, it is well for you to know that when the unfortunate man wrote that poem, he was by his own volition absent from Marcela, to see if this would work a cure; but when the enamored one is away from his love, there is nothing that does not inspire in him fear and torment, and such was the case with Grisóstomo, for whom jealous imaginings, fears, and suspicions became a seeming reality. And so, in this respect, Marcela's reputation for virtue remains unimpaired; beyond being cruel and somewhat arrogant, and exceedingly disdainful, she could not be accused by the most envious of any other fault."

"Yes, that is so," said Vivaldo.

He was about to read another of the papers he had saved from the fire when he was stopped by a marvelous vision—for such it appeared—that suddenly met his sight; for there atop the rock beside which the grave was being hollowed out stood the shepherdess Marcela herself, more beautiful even than she was reputed to be. Those who up to then had never seen her looked on in silent admiration, while those who were accustomed to beholding her were held in as great a suspense as the ones who were gazing upon her for the first time.

No sooner had Ambrosio glimpsed her than, with a show of indignation, he called out to her, "So, fierce basilisk[8] of these mountains, have you perchance come to see if in your presence blood will flow from the wounds of this poor wretch whom you by your cruelty have deprived of life?[9] Have you come to gloat over your inhuman exploits, or would you from that height look down like another pitiless Nero upon your Rome in flames and ashes?[1] Or perhaps you would arrogantly tread under foot this poor corpse, as an ungrateful daughter did that of her father Tarquinius?[2] Tell us quickly why you have come and what it is that you want most; for I know that Grisóstomo's

8. A mythical lizard-like creature whose look and breath were supposed to be lethal.    9. According to folklore, the corpse of a murdered person was supposed to bleed in the presence of the murderer.    1. The Roman emperor Nero is supposed, in tale and proverb, to have been singing while from a tower he observed the burning of Rome in A.D. 64.    2. The inaccurate allusion is to Tullia, actually the wife of the last of the legendary kings of early Rome, Tarquinius; she let the wheel of her carriage trample over the body of her father—the previous king Servius Tullius—whom her husband Tarquinius had liquidated.

thoughts never failed to obey you in life, and though he is dead now, I will see that all those who call themselves his friends obey you likewise."

"I do not come, O Ambrosio, for any of the reasons that you have mentioned," replied Marcela. "I come to defend myself and to demonstrate how unreasonable all those persons are who blame me for their sufferings and for Grisóstomo's death. I therefore ask all present to hear me attentively. It will not take long and I shall not have to spend many words in persuading those of you who are sensible that I speak the truth.

"Heaven made me beautiful, you say, so beautiful that you are compelled to love me whether you will or no; and in return for the love that you show me, you would have it that I am obliged to love you in return. I know, with that natural understanding that God has given me, that everything beautiful is lovable; but I cannot see that it follows that the object that is loved for its beauty must love the one who loves it. Let us suppose that the lover of the beautiful were ugly and, being ugly, deserved to be shunned; it would then be highly absurd for him to say, 'I love you because you are beautiful; you must love me because I am ugly.'

"But assuming that two individuals are equally beautiful, it does not mean that their desires are the same; for not all beauty inspires love, but may sometimes merely delight the eye and leave the will intact. If it were otherwise, no one would know what he wanted, but all would wander vaguely and aimlessly with nothing upon which to settle their affections; for the number of beautiful objects being infinite, desires similarly would be boundless. I have heard it said that true love knows no division and must be voluntary and not forced. This being so, as I believe it is, then why would you compel me to surrender my will for no other reason than that you say you love me? But tell me: supposing that Heaven which made me beautiful had made me ugly instead, should I have any right to complain because you did not love me? You must remember, moreover, that I did not choose this beauty that is mine; such as it is, Heaven gave it to me of its grace, without any choice or asking on my part. As the viper is not to be blamed for the deadly poison that it bears, since that is a gift of nature, so I do not deserve to be reprehended for my comeliness of form.

"Beauty in a modest woman is like a distant fire or a sharp-edged sword: the one does not burn, the other does not cut, those who do not come near it. Honor and virtue are the adornments of the soul, without which the body is not beautiful though it may appear to be. If modesty is one of the virtues that most adorn and beautify body and soul, why should she who is loved for her beauty part with that virtue merely to satify the whim of one who solely for his own pleasure strives with all his force and energy to cause her to lose it? I was born a free being, and in order to live freely I chose the solitude of the fields; these mountain trees are my company, the clear-running waters in these brooks are my mirror, and to the trees and waters I communicate my thoughts and lend them of my beauty.

"In short, I am that distant fire, that sharp-edged sword, that does not burn or cut. Those who have been enamored by the sight of me I have disillusioned with my words; and if desire is sustained by hope, I gave none to Grisóstomo or any other, and of none of them can it be said that I killed them with my cruelty, for it was rather their own obstinacy that was to blame. And if you reproach me with the fact that his intentions were honorable and that I ought for that reason to have complied with them, I will tell you that when, on this very spot where his grave is now being dug, he revealed them to me, I replied that it was my own intention to live in perpetual solitude and that only the earth should enjoy the fruit of my retirement and the spoils of my beauty; and if he with all this plain-speaking was still stubbornly bent upon hoping against hope and sailing against the wind, is it to be wondered at if he drowned in the gulf of his own folly?

"Had I led him on, it would have been falsely; had I gratified his passion, it would have been against my own best judgment and intentions; but, though I had disillusioned him, he persisted, and though I did not hate him, he was driven to despair. Ask yourselves, then, if it is reasonable to blame me for his woes! Let him who has been truly deceived complain; let him despair who has been cheated of his promised hopes; if I have enticed any, let him speak up; if I have accepted the attentions of any, let him boast of it; but let not him to whom I have promised nothing, whom I have neither enticed nor accepted, apply to me such terms as cruel and homicidal. It has not as yet been Heaven's will to destine me to love any man, and there is no use expecting me to love of my own free choice.

"Let what I am saying now apply to each and every one of those who would have me for their own, and let it be understood from now on that if any die on account of me, he is not to be regarded as an unfortunate victim of jealousy, since she that cares for none can give to none the occasion for being jealous; nor is my plain-speaking to be taken as disdain. He who calls me a wild beast and a basilisk, let him leave me alone as something that is evil and harmful; let him who calls me ungrateful cease to wait upon me; let him who finds me strange shun my acquaintance; if I am cruel, do not run after me; in which case this wild beast, this basilisk, this strange, cruel, ungrateful creature will not run after them, seek them out, wait upon them, nor endeavor to know them in any way.

"The thing that killed Grisóstomo was his impatience and the impetuosity of his desire; so why blame my modest conduct and retiring life? If I choose to preserve my purity here in the company of the trees, how can he complain of my unwillingness to lose it who would have me keep it with other men? I, as you know, have a worldly fortune of my own and do not covet that of others. My life is a free one, and I do not wish to be subject to another in any way. I neither love nor hate anyone; I do not repel this one and allure that one; I do not play fast and loose with any. The modest conversation of these village lasses and the care of my goats is sufficient to occupy me. Those mountains there represent the bounds of my desire, and should my wishes go beyond them, it is but to contemplate the beauty of the heavens, that pathway by which the soul travels to its first dwelling place."

Saying this and without waiting for any reply, she turned her back and entered the thickest part of a near-by wood, leaving all present lost in admiration of her wit as well as her beauty. A few—those who had felt the powerful dart of her glances and bore the wounds inflicted by her lovely eyes—were of a mind to follow her, taking no heed of the plainly worded warning they had just had from her lips; whereupon Don Quixote, seeing this and thinking to himself that here was an opportunity to display his chivalry by succoring a damsel in distress, laid his hand upon the hilt of his sword and cried out, loudly and distinctly, "Let no person of whatever state or condition he may be dare to follow the beauteous Marcela under pain of incurring my furious wrath. She has shown with clear and sufficient reasons that little or no blame for Grisóstomo's death is to be attached to her; she has likewise shown how far she is from acceding to the desires of any of her suitors, and it is accordingly only just that in place of being hounded and persecuted she should be honored and esteemed by all good people in this world as the only woman in it who lives with such modesty and good intentions."

Whether it was due to Don Quixote's threats or because Ambrosio now told them that they should finish doing the things which his good friend had desired should be done, no one stirred from the spot until the burial was over and Grisóstomo's papers had been burned. As the body was laid in the grave, many tears were shed by the bystanders. Then they placed a heavy stone upon it until the slab which Ambrosio was thinking of having made should be ready, with an epitaph that was to read:

Here lies a shepherd by love betrayed,
His body cold in death,
Who with his last and faltering breath
Spoke of a faithless maid.
He died by the cruel, heartless hand
Of a coy and lovely lass,

> *Who by bringing men to so sorry a pass*
> *Love's tyranny doth expand.*

They then scattered many flowers and boughs over the top of the grave, and, expressing their condolences to the dead man's friend, Ambrosio, they all took their leave, including Vivaldo and his companions. Don Quixote now said good-by to the travelers as well, although they urged him to come with them to Seville, assuring him that he would find in every street and at every corner of that city more adventures than are to be met with anywhere else. He thanked them for the invitation and the courtesy they had shown him in offering it, but added that for the present he had no desire to visit Seville, not until he should have rid these mountains of the robbers and bandits of which they were said to be full.

Seeing that his mind was made up, the travelers did not urge him further but, bidding him another farewell, left him and continued on their way; and the reader may be sure that in the course of their journey they did not fail to discuss the story of Marcela and Grisóstomo as well as Don Quixotes madness. As for the good knight himself, he was resolved to go seek the shepherdess and offer her any service that lay in his power; but things did not turn out the way he expected. . . .

### [Fighting the Sheep]

#### CHAPTER 18

*In which is set forth the conversation that Sancho Panza had with his master, Don Quixote, along with other adventures deserving of record.*

. . . Don Quixote caught sight down the road of a large cloud of dust that was drawing nearer.

"This, O Sancho," he said, turning to his squire, "is the day when you shall see the boon that fate has in store for me; this, I repeat, is the day when, as well as on any other, shall be displayed the valor of my good right arm. On this day I shall perform deeds that will be written down in the book of fame for all centuries to come. Do you see that dust cloud rising there, Sancho? That is the dust stirred up by a vast army marching in this direction and composed of many nations."

"At that rate," said Sancho, "there must be two of them, for there is another one just like it on the other side."

Don Quixote turned to look and saw that this was so. He was overjoyed by the thought that these were indeed two armies about to meet and clash in the middle of the broad plain; for at every hour

and every moment his imagination was filled with battles, enchantments, nonsensical adventures, tales of love, amorous challenges,
and the like, such as he had read of in the books of chivalry, and
every word he uttered, every thought that crossed his mind, every act
he performed, had to do with such things as these. The dust clouds
he had sighted were raised by two large droves of sheep coming along
the road in opposite directions, which by reason of the dust were not
visible until they were close at hand, but Don Quixote insisted so
earnestly that they were armies that Sancho came to believe it.

"Sir," he said, "what are we to do?"

"What are we to do?" echoed his master. "Favor and aid the weak
and needy. I would inform you, Sancho, that the one coming toward
us is led and commanded by the great emperor Alifanfarón, lord of
the great isle of Trapobana. This other one at my back is that of his
enemy, the king of the Garamantas, Pentapolín of the Rolled-up
Sleeve, for he always goes into battle with his right arm bare."

"But why are they such enemies?" Sancho asked.

"Because," said Don Quixote, "this Alifanfarón is a terrible pagan
and in love with Pentapolín's daughter, who is a very beautiful and
gracious lady and a Christian, for which reason her father does not
wish to give her to the pagan king unless the latter first abjures the
law of the false prophet, Mohammed, and adopts the faith that is
Pentapolín's own."

"Then, by my beard," said Sancho, "if Pentapolín isn't right, and
I am going to aid him all I can."

"In that," said Don Quixote, "you will only be doing your duty;
for to engage in battles of this sort you need not have been dubbed a
knight."

"I can understand that," said Sancho, "but where are we going to
put this ass so that we will be certain of finding him after the fray is
over? As for going into battle on such a mount, I do not think that
has been done up to now."

"That is true enough," said Don Quixote. "What you had best do
with him is to turn him loose and run the risk of losing him; for after
we emerge the victors we shall have so many horses that even Rocinante will be in danger of being exchanged for another. But listen
closely to what I am about to tell you, for I wish to give you an
account of the principal knights that are accompanying these two
armies; and in order that you may be the better able to see and take
note of them, let us retire to that hillock over there which will afford
us a very good view."

They then stationed themselves upon a slight elevation from which
they would have been able to see very well the two droves of sheep
that Don Quixote took to be armies if it had not been for the blinding
clouds of dust. In spite of this, however, the worthy gentleman con-

trived to behold in his imagination what he did not see and what did not exist in reality.

Raising his voice, he went on to explain, "That knight in the gilded armor that you see there, bearing upon his shield a crowned lion crouched at the feet of a damsel, is the valiant Laurcalco, lord of the Silver Bridge; the other with the golden flowers on his armor, and on his shield three crowns argent on an azure field, is the dread Micocolembo, grand duke of Quirocia. And that one on Micocolembo's right hand, with the limbs of a giant, is the ever undaunted Brandabarbarán de Boliche, lord of the three Arabias. He goes armored in a serpent's skin and has for shield a door which, so report has it, is one of those from the temple that Samson pulled down, that time when he avenged himself on his enemies with his own death.

"But turn your eyes in this direction, and you will behold at the head of the other army the ever victorious, never vanquished Timonel de Carcajona, prince of New Biscay, who comes with quartered arms—azure, vert, argent, and or—and who has upon his shield a cat or on a field tawny, with the inscription *Miau*, which is the beginning of his lady's name; for she, so it is said, is the peerless Miulina, daughter of Alfeñquén, duke of Algarve. And that one over there, who weights down and presses the loins of that powerful charger, in a suit of snow-white armor with a white shield that bears no device whatever—he is a novice knight of the French nation, called Pierres Papin, lord of the baronies of Utrique. As for him you see digging his iron spurs into the flanks of that fleet-footed zebra courser and whose arms are vairs azure, he is the mighty duke of Nervia, Espartafilardo of the Wood, who has for device upon his shield an asparagus plant with a motto in Castilian that says '*Rastrea mi suerte.*' "[3]

In this manner he went on naming any number of imaginary knights on either side, describing on the spur of the moment their arms, colors, devices, and mottoes; for he was completely carried away by his imagination and by this unheard-of madness that had laid hold of him.

Without pausing, he went on, "This squadron in front of us is composed of men of various nations. There are those who drink the sweet waters of the famous Xanthus; woodsmen who tread the Massilian plain; those that sift the fine gold nuggets of Arabia Felix; those that are so fortunate as to dwell on the banks of the clear-running Thermodon, famed for their coolness; those who in many and diverse ways drain the golden Pactolus; Numidians, whose word is never to be trusted; Persians, with their famous bows and arrows; Medes and Parthians, who fight as they flee; Scythians, as cruel as they are fair

---

3. Probably a pun on *rastrear*: the meaning of the motto may be either "On Fortune's track" or "My Fortune creeps."

of skin; Ethiopians, with their pierced lips; and an infinite number of other nationalities whose visages I see and recognize although I cannot recall their names.

"In this other squadron come those that drink from the crystal currents of the olive-bearing Betis; those that smooth and polish their faces with the liquid of the ever rich and gilded Tagus; those that enjoy the beneficial waters of the divine Genil; those that roam the Tartessian plains with their abundant pasturage; those that disport themselves in the Elysian meadows of Jerez; the men of La Mancha, rich and crowned with golden ears of corn; others clad in iron garments, ancient relics of the Gothic race; those that bathe in the Pisuerga, noted for the mildness of its current; those that feed their herds in the wide-spreading pasture lands along the banks of the winding Guadiana, celebrated for its underground course;[4] those that shiver from the cold of the wooded Pyrenees or dwell amid the white peaks of the lofty Apennines—in short, all those whom Europe holds within its girth."

So help me God! How many provinces, how many nations did he not mention by name, giving to each one with marvelous readiness its proper attributes; for he was wholly absorbed and filled to the brim with what he had read in those lying books of his! Sancho Panza hung on his words, saying nothing, merely turning his head from time to time to have a look at those knights and giants that his master was pointing out to him; but he was unable to discover any of them.

"Sir," he said, "may I go to the devil if I see a single man, giant, or knight of all those that your Grace is talking about. Who knows? Maybe it is another spell, like last night."[5]

"How can you say that?" replied Don Quixote. "Can you not hear the neighing of the horses, the sound of trumpets, the roll of drums?"

"I hear nothing," said Sancho, "except the bleating of sheep."

And this, of course, was the truth; for the flocks were drawing near.

"The trouble is, Sancho," said Don Quixote, "you are so afraid that you cannot see or hear properly; for one of the effects of fear is to disturb the senses and cause things to appear other than what they are. If you are so craven as all that, go off to one side and leave me alone, and I without your help will assure the victory to that side to which I lend my aid."

Saying this, he put spurs to Rocinante and, with his lance at rest, darted down the hillside like a flash of lightning.

As he did so, Sancho called after him, "Come back, your Grace, Señor Don Quixote; I vow to God those are sheep that you are charg-

---

4. The Guadiana does run underground part of the way through La Mancha.   5. The inn where they had spent the previous night had been pronounced by Don Quixote an enchanted castle.

ing. Come back! O wretched father that bore me! What madness is this? Look you, there are no giants, nor knights, nor cats, nor shields either quartered or whole, nor vairs azure or bedeviled. What is this you are doing, O sinner that I am in God's sight?"

But all this did not cause Don Quixote to turn back. Instead, he rode on, crying out at the top of his voice, "Ho, knights, those of you who follow and fight under the banners of the valiant Pentapolín of the Rolled-up Sleeves; follow me, all of you, and you shall see how easily I give you revenge on your enemy, Alifanfarón of Trapobana."

With these words he charged into the middle of the flock of sheep and began spearing at them with as much courage and boldness as if they had been his mortal enemies. The shepherds and herdsmen who were with the animals called to him to stop; but seeing it was no use, they unloosed their slings and saluted his ears with stones as big as your fist.

Don Quixote paid no attention to the missiles and, dashing about here and there, kept crying, "Where are you, haughty Alifanfarón? Come out to me; for here is a solitary knight who desires in single combat to test your strength and deprive you of your life, as a punishment for that which you have done to the valorous Pentapolín Garamanta."

At that instant a pebble from the brook struck him in the side and buried a couple of ribs in his body. Believing himself dead or badly wounded, and remembering his potion, he took out his vial, placed it to his mouth, and began to swallow the balm; but before he had had what he thought was enough, there came another almond, which struck him in the hand, crushing the tin vial and carrying away with it a couple of grinders from his mouth, as well as badly mashing two of his fingers. As a result of these blows the poor knight tumbled from his horse. Believing that they had killed him, the shepherds hastily collected their flock and, picking up the dead beasts, of which there were more than seven, they went off down the road without more ado.

Sancho all this time was standing on the slope observing the insane things that his master was doing; and as he plucked savagely at his beard he cursed the hour and minute when luck had brought them together. But when he saw him lying there on the ground and perceived that the shepherds were gone, he went down the hill and came up to him, finding him in very bad shape though not unconscious.

"Didn't I tell you, Señor Don Quixote," he said, "that you should come back, that those were not armies you were charging but flocks of sheep?"

"This," said Don Quixote, "is the work of that thieving magician, my enemy, who thus counterfeits things and causes them to disappear. You must know, Sancho, that it is very easy for them to make us assume any appearance that they choose; and so it is that malign one who persecutes me, envious of the glory he saw me about to achieve in this battle, changed the squadrons of the foe into flocks of sheep. If you do not believe me, I beseech you on my life to do one thing for me, that you may be undeceived and discover for yourself that what I say is true. Mount your ass and follow them quietly, and when you have gone a short way from here, you will see them become their former selves once more; they will no longer be sheep but men exactly as I described them to you in the first place. But do not go now, for I need your kind assistance; come over here and have a look and tell me how many grinders are missing, for it feels as if I did not have a single one left."

## ["To Right Wrongs and Come to the Aid of the Wretched"]

### CHAPTER 22

*Of how Don Quixote freed many unfortunate ones who, much
against their will, were being taken where they did not wish to go.*

Cid Hamete Benengeli, the Arabic and Manchegan[6] author, in the course of this most grave, high-sounding, minute, delightful, and imaginative history, informs us that, following the remarks that were exchanged between Don Quixote de la Mancha and Sancho Panza, his squire, . . . the knight looked up and saw coming toward them down the road which they were following a dozen or so men on foot, strung together by their necks like beads on an iron chain and all of them wearing handcuffs. They were accompanied by two men on horseback and two on foot, the former carrying wheel-lock muskets while the other two were armed with swords and javelins.

"That," said Sancho as soon as he saw them, "is a chain of galley slaves, people on their way to the galleys where by order of the king they are forced to labor."

"What do you mean by 'forced'?" asked Don Quixote. "Is it possible that the king uses force on anyone?"

"I did not say that," replied Sancho. "What I did say was that these are folks who have been condemned for their crimes to forced labor in the galleys for his Majesty the King."

"The short of it is," said the knight, "whichever way you put it, these people are being taken there by force and not of their own free will."

"That is the way it is," said Sancho.

6. Of La Mancha.

"Well, in that case," said his master, "now is the time for me to fulfill the duties of my calling, which is to right wrongs and come to the aid of the wretched."

"But take note, your Grace," said Sancho, "that justice, that is to say, the king himself, is not using any force upon, or doing any wrong to, people like these, but is merely punishing them for the crimes they have committed."

The chain of galley slaves had come up to them by this time, whereupon Don Quixote very courteously requested the guards to inform him of the reason or reasons why they were conducting these people in such a manner as this. One of the men on horseback then replied that the men were prisoners who had been condemned by his Majesty to serve in the galleys, whither they were bound, and that was all there was to be said about it and all that he, Don Quixote, need know.

"Nevertheless," said the latter, "I should like to inquire of each one of them, individually, the cause of his misfortune." And he went on speaking so very politely in an effort to persuade them to tell him what he wanted to know that the other mounted guard finally said, "Although we have here the record and certificate of sentence of each one of these wretches, we have not the time to get them out and read them to you; and so your Grace may come over and ask the prisoners themselves, and they will tell you if they choose, and you may be sure that they will, for these fellows take a delight in their knavish exploits and in boasting of them afterward."

With this permission, even though he would have done so if it had not been granted him, Don Quixote went up to the chain of prisoners and asked the first whom he encountered what sins had brought him to so sorry a plight. The man replied that it was for being a lover that he found himself in that line.

"For that and nothing more?" said Don Quixote. "And do they, then, send lovers to the galleys? If so, I should have been rowing there long ago."

"But it was not the kind of love that your Grace has in mind," the prisoner went on. "I loved a wash basket full of white linen so well and hugged it so tightly that, if they had not taken it away from me by force, I would never of my own choice have let go of it to this very minute. I was caught in the act, there was no need to torture me, the case was soon disposed of, and they supplied me with a hundred lashes across the shoulders and, in addition, a three-year stretch in the *gurapas*, and that's all there is to tell."

"What are *gurapas*?" asked Don Quixote.

"*Gurapas* are the galleys," replied the prisoner. He was a lad of around twenty-four and stated that he was a native of Piedrahita.

The knight then put the same question to a second man, who

appeared to be very downcast and melancholy and did not have a word to say. The first man answered for him.

"This one, sir," he said, "is going as a canary—I mean, as a musician and singer."

"How is that?" Don Quixote wanted to know. "Do musicians and singers go to the galleys too?"

"Yes, sir; and there is nothing worse than singing when you're in trouble."

"On the contrary," said Don Quixote, "I have heard it said that he who sings frightens away his sorrows."

"It is just the opposite," said the prisoner; "for he who sings once weeps all his life long."

"I do not understand," said the knight.

One of the guards then explained. "Sir Knight, with this *non sancta*[7] tribe, to sing when you're in trouble means to confess under torture. This singer was put to the torture and confessed his crime, which was that of being a *cuatrero*, or cattle thief, and as a result of his confession he was condemned to six years in the galleys in addition to two hundred lashes which he took on his shoulders; and so it is he is always downcast and moody, for the other thieves, those back where he came from and the ones here, mistreat, snub, ridicule, and despise him for having confessed and for not having had the courage to deny his guilt. They are in the habit of saying that the word no has the same number of letters as the word *sí*, and that a culprit is in luck when his life or death depends on his own tongue and not that of witnesses or upon evidence; and, in my opinion, they are not very far wrong."

"And I," said Don Quixote, "feel the same way about it." He then went on to a third prisoner and repeated his question.

The fellow answered at once, quite unconcernedly. "I'm going to my ladies, the *gurapas*, for five years, for the lack of five ducats."

"I would gladly give twenty," said Don Quixote, "to get you out of this."

"That," said the prisoner, "reminds me of the man in the middle of the ocean who has money and is dying of hunger because there is no place to buy what he needs. I say this for the reason that if I had had, at the right time, those twenty ducats your Grace is now offering me, I'd have greased the notary's quill and freshened up the attorney's wit with them, and I'd now be living in the middle of Zocodover Square in Toledo instead of being here on this highway coupled like a greyhound. But God is great; patience, and that's enough of it."

Don Quixote went on to a fourth prisoner, a venerable-looking

7. Unholy.

old fellow with a white beard that fell over his bosom. When asked how he came to be there, this one began weeping and made no reply, but a fifth comrade spoke up in his behalf.

"This worthy man," he said, "is on his way to the galleys after having made the usual rounds clad in a robe of state and on horse-back."[8]

"That means, I take it," said Sancho, "that he has been put to shame in public."

"That is it," said the prisoner, "and the offense for which he is being punished is that of having been an ear broker, or, better, a body broker. By that I mean to say, in short, that the gentleman is a pimp, and besides, he has his points as a sorcerer."

"If that point had not been thrown in," said Don Quixote, "he would not deserve, for merely being a pimp, to have to row in the galleys, but rather should be the general and give orders there. For the office of pimp is not an indifferent one; it is a function to be performed by persons of discretion and is most necessary in a well-ordered state; it is a profession that should be followed only by the wellborn, and there should, moreover, be a superviser or examiner as in the case of other offices, and the number of practitioners should be fixed by law as is done with brokers on the exchange. In that way many evils would be averted that arise when this office is filled and this calling practiced by stupid folk and those with little sense, such as silly women and pages or mountebanks with few years and less experience to their credit, who, on the most pressing occasions, when it is necessary to use one's wits, let the crumbs freeze between their hand and their mouth and do not know which is their right hand and which is the left.

"I would go on and give reasons why it is fitting to choose carefully those who are to fulfill so necessary a state function, but this is not the place for it. One of these days I will speak of the matter to someone who is able to do something about it. I will say here only that the pain I felt at seeing those white hairs and this venerable countenance in such a plight, and all for his having been a pimp, has been offset for me by the additional information you have given me, to the effect that he is a sorcerer as well; for I am convinced that there are no sorcerers in the world who can move and compel the will, as some simple-minded persons think, but that our will is free and no herb or charm can force it.[9] All that certain foolish women and cunning tricksters do is to compound a few mixtures and poisons with which they deprive men of their senses while pretending that

---

8. After having been flogged in public, with all the ceremony that accompanied that punishment.    9. Here Don Quixote despises charms and love potions though often elsewhere, in his own vision of himself as a knight-errant, he accepts enchantments and spells as part of his world of fantasy.

they have the power to make them loved, although, as I have just said, one cannot affect another's will in that manner."

"That is so," said the worthy old man; "but the truth is, sir, I am not guilty on the sorcery charge. As for being a pimp, that is something I cannot deny. I never thought there was any harm in it, however, my only desire being that everyone should enjoy himself and live in peace and quiet, without any quarrels or troubles. But these good intentions on my part cannot prevent me from going where I do not want to go, to a place from which I do not expect to return; for my years are heavy upon me and an affection of the urine that I have will not give me a moment's rest."

With this, he began weeping once more, and Sancho was so touched by it that he took a four-real piece from his bosom and gave it to him as an act of charity.

Don Quixote then went on and asked another what his offense was. The fellow answered him, not with less, but with much more, briskness than the preceding one had shown.

"I am here," he said, "for the reason that I carried a joke too far with a couple of cousins-german of mine and a couple of others who were not mine, and I ended by jesting with all of them to such an extent that the devil himself would never be able to straighten out the relationship. They proved everything on me, there was no one to show me favor, I had no money, I came near swinging for it, they sentenced me to the galleys for six years, and I accepted the sentence as the punishment that was due me. I am young yet, and if I live long enough, everything will come out all right. If, Sir Knight, your Grace has anything with which to aid these poor creatures that you see before you, God will reward you in Heaven, and we here on earth will make it a point to ask God in our prayers to grant you long life and good health, as long and as good as your amiable presence deserves."

This man was dressed as a student, and one of the guards told Don Quixote that he was a great talker and a very fine Latinist.

Back of these came a man around thirty years of age and of very good appearance, except that when he looked at you his eyes were seen to be a little crossed. He was shackled in a different manner from the others, for he dragged behind a chain so huge that it was wrapped all around his body, with two rings at the throat, one of which was attached to the chain while the other was fastened to what is known as a keep-friend or friend's foot, from which two irons hung down to his waist, ending in handcuffs secured by a heavy padlock in such a manner that he could neither raise his hands to his mouth nor lower his head to reach his hands.

When Don Quixote asked why this man was so much more heavily chained than the others, the guard replied that it was because he had more crimes against him than all the others put together, and he was so bold and cunning that, even though they had him chained like this, they were by no means sure of him but feared that he might escape from them.

"What crimes could he have committed," asked the knight, "if he has merited a punishment no greater than that of being sent to the galleys?"

"He is being sent there for ten years," replied the guard, "and that is equivalent to civil death. I need tell you no more than that this good man is the famous Ginés de Pasamonte, otherwise known as Ginesillo de Parapilla."

"Señor Commissary," spoke up the prisoner at this point, "go easy there and let us not be so free with names and surnames. My just name is Ginés and not Ginesillo; and Pasamonte, not Parapilla as you make it out to be, is my family name. Let each one mind his own affairs and he will have his hands full."

"Speak a little more respectfully, you big thief, you," said the commissary, "unless you want me to make you be quiet in a way you won't like."

"Man goes as God pleases, that is plain to be seen," replied the galley slave, "but someday someone will know whether my name is Ginesillo de Parapilla or not."

"But, you liar, isn't that what they call you?"

"Yes," said Ginés, "they do call me that; but I'll put a stop to it, or else I'll skin their you-know-what. And you, sir, if you have anything to give us, give it and may God go with you, for I am tired of all this prying into other people's lives. If you want to know anything about my life, know that I am Ginés de Pasamonte whose life story has been written down by these fingers that you see here."

"He speaks the truth," said the commissary, "for he has himself written his story, as big as you please, and has left the book in the prison, having pawned it for two hundred reales."

"And I mean to redeem it," said Ginés, "even if it costs me two hundred ducats."

"Is it as good as that?" inquired Don Quixote.

"It is so good," replied Ginés, "that it will cast into the shade *Lazarillo de Tormes*[1] and all others of that sort that have been or will be written. What I would tell you is that it deals with facts, and facts so interesting and amusing that no lies could equal them."

"And what is the title of the book?" asked Don Quixote.

"*The Life of Ginés de Pasamonte.*"

"Is it finished?"

"How could it be finished," said Ginés, "when my life is not fin-

1. A picaresque or rogue novel, published anonymously about the middle of the fifteenth century.

ished as yet? What I have written thus far is an account of what happened to me from the time I was born up to the last time that they sent me to the galleys."

"Then you have been there before?"

"In the service of God and the king I was there four years, and I know what the biscuit and the cowhide are like. I don't mind going very much, for there I will have a chance to finish my book. I still have many things to say, and in the Spanish galleys I shall have all the leisure that I need, though I don't need much, since I know by heart what it is I want to write."

"You seem to be a clever fellow," said Don Quixote.

"And an unfortunate one," said Ginés; "for misfortunes always pursue men of genius."

"They pursue rogues," said the commissary.

"I have told you to go easy, Señor Commissary," said Pasamonte, "for their Lordships did not give you that staff in order that you might mistreat us poor devils with it, but they intended that you should guide and conduct us in accordance with his Majesty's command. Otherwise, by the life of— But enough. It may be that someday the stains made in the inn will come out in the wash. Meanwhile, let everyone hold his tongue, behave well, and speak better, and let us be on our way. We've had enough of this foolishness."

At this point the commissary raised his staff as if to let Pasamonte have it in answer to his threats, but Don Quixote placed himself between them and begged the officer not to abuse the man; for it was not to be wondered at if one who had his hands so bound should be a trifle free with his tongue. With this, he turned and addressed them all.

"From all that you have told me, my dearest brothers," he said, "one thing stands out clearly for me, and that is the fact that, even though it is a punishment for offenses which you have committed, the penalty you are about to pay is not greatly to your liking and you are going to the galleys very much against your own will and desire. It may be that the lack of spirit which one of you displayed under torture, the lack of money on the part of another, the lack of influential friends, or, finally, warped judgment on the part of the magistrate, was the thing that led to your downfall; and, as a result, justice was not done you. All of which presents itself to my mind in such a fashion that I am at this moment engaged in trying to persuade and even force myself to show you what the purpose was for which Heaven sent me into this world, why it was it led me to adopt the calling of knighthood which I profess and take the knightly vow to favor the needy and aid those who are oppressed by the powerful.

"However, knowing as I do that it is not the part of prudence to do by foul means what can be accomplished by fair ones, I propose to ask these gentlemen, your guards, and the commissary to be so good as to unshackle you and permit you to go in peace. There will be no dearth of others to serve his Majesty under more propitious circumstances; and it does not appear to me to be just to make slaves of those whom God created as free men. What is more, gentlemen of the guard, these poor fellows have committed no offense against you. Up there, each of us will have to answer for his own sins; for God in Heaven will not fail to punish the evil and reward the good; and it is not good for self-respecting men to be executioners of their fellow-men in something that does not concern them. And so, I ask this of you, gently and quietly, in order that, if you comply with my request, I shall have reason to thank you; and if you do not do so of your own accord, then this lance and this sword and the valor of my arm shall compel you to do it by force."

"A fine lot of foolishness!" exclaimed the commissary. "So he comes out at last with this nonsense! He would have us let the prisoners of the king go free, as if we had any authority to do so or he any right to command it! Be on your way, sir, at once; straighten that basin that you have on your head, and do not go looking for three feet on a cat."[2]

"You," replied Don Quixote, "are the cat and the rat and the rascal!" And, saying this, he charged the commissary so quickly that the latter had no chance to defend himself but fell to the ground badly wounded by the lance blow. The other guards were astounded by this unexpected occurrence; but, recovering their self-possession, those on horseback drew their swords, those on foot leveled their javelins, and all bore down on Don Quixote, who stood waiting for them very calmly. Things undoubtedly would have gone badly for him if the galley slaves, seeing an opportunity to gain their freedom, had not succeeded in breaking the chain that linked them together. Such was the confusion that the guards, now running to fall upon the prisoners and now attacking Don Quixote, who in turn was attacking them, accomplished nothing that was of any use.

Sancho for his part aided Ginés de Pasamonte to free himself, and that individual was the first to drop his chains and leap out onto the field, where, attacking the fallen commissary, he took away that officer's sword and musket; and as he stood there, aiming first at one and then at another, though without firing, the plain was soon cleared of guards, for they had taken to their heels, fleeing at once Pasamonte's weapon and the stones which the galley slaves, freed now, were hurling at them. Sancho, meanwhile, was very much disturbed over this unfortunate event, as he felt sure that the fugitives would report the matter to the Holy Brotherhood, which, to the ringing of

2. Looking for the impossible ("five feet" in the more usual form of the proverb).

the alarm bell, would come out to search for the guilty parties. He said as much to his master, telling him that they should leave at once and go into hiding in the near-by mountains.

"That is all very well," said Don Quixote, "but I know what had best be done now." He then summoned all the prisoners, who, running riot, had by this time despoiled the commissary of everything that he had, down to his skin, and as they gathered around to hear what he had to say, he addressed them as follows:

"It is fitting that those who are wellborn should give thanks for the benefits they have received, and one of the sins with which God is most offended is that of ingratitude. I say this, gentlemen, for the reason that you have seen and had manifest proof of what you owe to me; and now that you are free of the yoke which I have removed from about your necks, it is my will and desire that you should set out and proceed to the city of El Toboso and there present yourselves before the lady Dulcinea del Toboso and say to her that her champion, the Knight of the Mournful Countenance, has sent you; and then you will relate to her, point by point, the whole of this famous adventure which has won you your longed-for freedom. Having done that, you may go where you like, and may good luck go with you."

To this Ginés de Pasamonte replied in behalf of all of them, "It is absolutely impossible, your Grace, our liberator, for us to do what you have commanded. We cannot go down the highway all together but must separate and go singly, each in his own direction, endeavoring to hide ourselves in the bowels of the earth in order not to be found by the Holy Brotherhood, which undoubtedly will come out to search for us. What your Grace can do, and it is right that you should do so, is to change this service and toll that you require of us in connection with the lady Dulcinea del Toboso into a certain number of Credos and Hail Marys which we will say for your Grace's intention, as this is something that can be accomplished by day or night, fleeing or resting, in peace or in war. To imagine, on the other hand, that we are going to return to the fleshpots of Egypt, by which I mean, take up our chains again by setting out along the highway for El Toboso, is to believe that it is night now instead of ten o'clock in the morning and is to ask of us something that is the same as asking pears of the elm tree."

"Then by all that's holy!" exclaimed Don Quixote, whose wrath was now aroused, "you, Don Son of a Whore, Don Ginesillo de Parapilla, or whatever your name is, you shall go alone, your tail between your legs and the whole chain on your back."

Pasamonte, who was by no means a long-suffering individual, was by this time convinced that Don Quixote was not quite right in the head, seeing that he had been guilty of such a folly as that of desiring to free them; and so, when he heard himself insulted in this manner, he merely gave the wink to his companions and, going off to one side, began raining so many stones upon the knight that the latter was wholly unable to protect himself with his buckler, while poor Rocinante paid no more attention to the spur than if he had been made of brass. As for Sancho, he took refuge behind his donkey as a protection against the cloud and shower of rocks that was falling on both of them, but Don Quixote was not able to shield himself so well, and there is no telling how many struck his body, with such force as to unhorse and bring him to the ground.

No sooner had he fallen than the student was upon him. Seizing the basin from the knight's head, he struck him three or four blows with it across the shoulders and banged it against the ground an equal number of times until it was fairly shattered to bits. They then stripped Don Quixote of the doublet which he wore over his armor, and would have taken his hose as well, if his greaves had not prevented them from doing so, and made off with Sancho's greatcoat, leaving him naked; after which, dividing the rest of the battle spoils amongst themselves, each of them went his own way, being a good deal more concerned with eluding the dreaded Holy Brotherhood than they were with burdening themselves with a chain or going to present themselves before the lady Dulcinea del Toboso.

They were left alone now—the ass and Rocinante, Sancho and Don Quixote: the ass, crestfallen and pensive, wagging its ears now and then, being under the impression that the hurricane of stones that had raged about them was not yet over; Rocinante, stretched alongside his master, for the hack also had been felled by a stone; Sancho, naked and fearful of the Holy Brotherhood; and Don Quixote, making wry faces at seeing himself so mishandled by those to whom he had done so much good.

["Set Free at Once that Lovely Lady . . ."]

### CHAPTER 52[3]

*Of the quarrel that Don Quixote had with the goatherd, together with the rare adventure of the penitents, which the knight by the sweat of his brow brought to a happy conclusion.*

All those who had listened to it were greatly pleased with the goatherd's story, especially the canon,[4] who was more than usually

---

3. Last chapter of Part I. Through various devices, including the use of Don Quixote's own belief in enchantments and spells, the curate and the barber have persuaded the knight to let himself be taken home in an ox cart.    4. A canon from Toledo who has joined Don Quixote and his guardians on the way; conversing about chivalry with the knight, he has had cause to be "astonished at Don Quixote's well-reasoned nonsense." Eugenio, a very literate goatherd met on the way, has just told them the story of his unhappy love for Leandra: the girl, instead of choosing one of her local suitors, had eloped with a flashy and crooked soldier; robbed and abandoned by him, she had been put by her father in a convent.

interested in noting the manner in which it had been told. Far from
being a mere rustic herdsman, the narrator seemed rather a cultured
city dweller; and the canon accordingly remarked that the curate had
been quite right in saying that the mountain groves bred men of
learning. They all now offered their services to Eugenio, and Don
Quixote was the most generous of any in this regard.

"Most assuredly, brother goatherd," he said, "if it were possible
for me to undertake any adventure just now, I would set out at once
to aid you and would take Leandra out of that convent, where she is
undoubtedly being held against her will, in spite of the abbess and
all the others who might try to prevent me, after which I would place
her in your hands to do with as you liked, with due respect, however,
for the laws of chivalry, which command that no violence be offered
to any damsel. But I trust in God, Our Lord, that the power of one
malicious enchanter is not so great that another magician may not
prove still more powerful, and then I promise you my favor and my
aid, as my calling obliges me to do, since it is none other than that
of succoring the weak and those who are in distress."

The goatherd stared at him, observing in some astonishment the
knight's unprepossessing appearance.

"Sir," he said, turning to the barber who sat beside him, "who is
this man who looks so strange and talks in this way?"

"Who should it be," the barber replied, "if not the famous Don
Quixote de la Mancha, righter of wrongs, avenger of injustices, protector of damsels, terror of giants, and champion of battles?"

"That," said the goatherd, "sounds to me like the sort of thing you
read of in books of chivalry, where they do all those things that your
Grace has mentioned in connection with this man. But if you ask
me, either your Grace is joking or this worthy gentleman must have
a number of rooms to let inside his head."

"You are the greatest villain that ever was!" cried Don Quixote
when he heard this. "It is you who are the empty one; I am fuller
than the bitch that bore you ever was." Saying this, he snatched up
a loaf of bread that was lying beside him and hurled it straight in the
goatherd's face with such force as to flatten the man's nose. Upon
finding himself thus mistreated in earnest, Eugenio, who did not
understand this kind of joke, forgot all about the carpet, the tablecloth, and the other diners and leaped upon Don Quixote. Seizing
him by the throat with both hands, he would no doubt have strangled him if Sancho Panza, who now came running up, had not
grasped him by the shoulders and flung him backward over the table,
smashing plates and cups and spilling and scattering all the food and
drink that was there. Thus freed of his assailant, Don Quixote then
threw himself upon the shepherd, who, with bleeding face and very
much battered by Sancho's feet, was creeping about on his hands

and knees in search of a table knife with which to exact a sanguinary vengeance, a purpose which the canon and the curate prevented him from carrying out. The barber, however, so contrived it that the goatherd came down on top of his opponent, upon whom he now showered so many blows that the poor knight's countenance was soon as bloody as his own.

As all this went on, the canon and the curate were laughing fit to burst, the troopers[5] were dancing with glee, and they all hissed on the pair as men do at a dog fight. Sancho Panza alone was in despair, being unable to free himself of one of the canon's servants who held him back from going to his master's aid. And then, just as they were all enjoying themselves hugely, with the exception of the two who were mauling each other, the note of a trumpet fell upon their ears, a sound so mournful that it caused them all to turn their heads in the direction from which it came. The one who was most excited by it was Don Quixote; who, very much against his will and more than a little bruised, was lying pinned beneath the goatherd.

"Brother Demon," he now said to the shepherd, "for you could not possibly be anything but a demon, seeing that you have shown a strength and valor greater than mine, I request you to call a truce for no more than an hour; for the doleful sound of that trumpet that we hear seems to me to be some new adventure that is calling me."

Tired of mauling and being mauled, the goatherd let him up at once. As he rose to his feet and turned his head in the direction of the sound, Don Quixote then saw, coming down the slope of a hill, a large number of persons clad in white after the fashion of penitents; for, as it happened, the clouds that year had denied their moisture to the earth, and in all the villages of that district processions for prayer and penance were being organized with the purpose of beseeching God to have mercy and send rain. With this object in view, the good folk from a near-by town were making a pilgrimage to a devout hermit who dwelt on these slopes. Upon beholding the strange costumes that the penitents wore, without pausing to think how many times he had seen them before, Don Quixote imagined that this must be some adventure or other, and that it was for him alone as a knight-errant to undertake it. He was strengthened in this belief by the sight of a covered image that they bore, as it seemed to him this must be some highborn lady whom these scoundrelly and discourteous brigands were forcibly carrying off; and no sooner did this idea occur to him than he made for Rocinante, who was grazing not far away.

Taking the bridle and his buckler from off the saddletree, he had

---

5. Law officers from the Holy Brotherhood. They had wanted to arrest Don Quixote on account of his having attempted the liberation of the galley slaves but had been persuaded not to do so, considering the knight's state of insanity.

the bridle adjusted in no time, and then, asking Sancho for his sword, he climbed into the saddle, braced his shield upon his arm, and cried out to those present, "And now, valorous company, you shall see how important it is to have in the world those who follow the profession of knight-errantry. You have but to watch how I shall set at liberty that worthy lady who there goes captive, and then you may tell me whether or not such knights are to be esteemed."

As he said this, he dug his legs into Rocinante's flanks, since he had no spurs, and at a fast trot (for nowhere in this veracious history are we ever told that the hack ran full speed) he bore down on the penitents in spite of all that the canon, the curate, and the barber could do to restrain him—their efforts were as vain as were the pleadings of his squire.

"Where are you bound for, Señor Don Quixote?" Sancho called after him. "What evil spirits in your bosom spur you on to go against our Catholic faith? Plague take me, can't you see that's a procession of penitents and that lady they're carrying on the litter is the most blessed image of the Immaculate Virgin? Look well what you're doing, my master, for this time it may be said that you really do not know."

His exertions were in vain, however, for his master was so bent upon having it out with the sheeted figures and freeing the lady clad in mourning that he did not hear a word, nor would he have turned back if he had, though the king himself might have commanded it. Having reached the procession, he reined in Rocinante, who by this time was wanting a little rest, and in a hoarse, excited voice he shouted, "You who go there with your faces covered, out of shame, it may be, listen well to what I have to say to you."

The first to come to a halt were those who carried the image; and then one of the four clerics who were intoning the litanies, upon beholding Don Quixote's weird figure, his bony nag, and other amusing appurtenances, spoke up in reply.

"Brother, if you have something to say to us, say it quickly, for these brethren are engaged in macerating their flesh, and we cannot stop to hear anything, nor is it fitting that we should, unless it is capable of being said in a couple of words."

"I will say it to you in one word," Don Quixote answered, "and that word is the following: 'Set free at once that lovely lady whose tears and mournful countenance show plainly that you are carrying her away against her will and that you have done her some shameful wrong. I will not consent to your going one step farther until you shall have given her the freedom that should be hers.' "

Hearing these words, they all thought that Don Quixote must be some madman or other and began laughing heartily; but their laughter proved to be gunpowder to his wrath, and without saying another word he drew his sword and fell upon the litter. One of those who bore the image, leaving his share of the burden to his companions, then sallied forth to meet the knight, flourishing a forked stick that he used to support the Virgin while he was resting; and upon this stick he now received a mighty slash that Don Quixote dealt him, one that shattered it in two, but with the piece about a third long that remained in his hand he came down on the shoulder of his opponent's sword arm, left unprotected by the buckler, with so much force that the poor fellow sank to the ground sorely battered and bruised.

Sancho Panza, who was puffing along close behind his master, upon seeing him fall cried out to the attacker not to deal another blow, as this was an unfortunate knight who was under a magic spell but who had never in all the days of his life done any harm to anyone. But the thing that stopped the rustic was not Sancho's words; it was, rather, the sight of Don Quixote lying there without moving hand or foot. And so, thinking that he had killed him, he hastily girded up his tunic and took to his heels across the countryside like a deer.

By this time all of Don Quixote's companions had come running up to where he lay; and the penitents, when they observed this, and especially when they caught sight of the officers of the Brotherhood with their crossbows, at once rallied around the image, where they raised their hoods and grasped their whips as the priests raised their tapers aloft in expectations of an assault; for they were resolved to defend themselves and even, if possible, to take the offensive against their assailants, but, as luck would have it, things turned out better than they had hoped. Sancho, meanwhile, believing Don Quixote to be dead, had flung himself across his master's body and was weeping and wailing in the most lugubrious and, at the same time, the most laughable fashion that could be imagined; and the curate had discovered among those who marched in the procession another curate whom he knew, their recognition of each other serving to allay the fears of all parties concerned. The first curate then gave the second a very brief account of who Don Quixote was, whereupon all the penitents came up to see if the poor knight was dead. And as they did so, they heard Sancho Panza speaking with tears in his eyes.

"O flower of chivalry,"[6] he was saying, "the course of whose well-spent years has been brought to an end by a single blow of a club! O honor of your line, honor and glory of all La Mancha and of all the world, which, with you absent from it, will be full of evil-doers who will not fear being punished for their deeds! O master more generous than all the Alexanders, who after only eight months of service presented me with the best island that the sea washes and surrounds!

6. Note how Sancho has absorbed some of his master's speech mannerisms.

Humble with the proud, haughty with the humble, brave in facing dangers, long-suffering under outrages, in love without reason, imitator of the good, scourge of the wicked, enemy of the mean—in a word, a knight-errant, which is all there is to say."

At the sound of Sancho's cries and moans, Don Quixote revived, and the first thing he said was, "He who lives apart from thee, O fairest Dulcinea, is subject to greater woes than those I now endure. Friend Sancho, help me onto that enchanted cart, as I am in no condition to sit in Rocinante's saddle with this shoulder of mine knocked to pieces the way it is."

"That I will gladly do, my master," replied Sancho, "and we will go back to my village in the company of these gentlemen who are concerned for your welfare, and there we will arrange for another sally and one, let us hope, that will bring us more profit and fame than this one has."

"Well spoken, Sancho," said Don Quixote, "for it will be an act of great prudence to wait until the present evil influence of the stars has passed."

The canon, the curate, and the barber all assured him that he would be wise in doing this; and so, much amused by Sancho Panza's simplicity, they placed Don Quixote upon the cart as before, while the procession of penitents re-formed and continued on its way. The goatherd took leave of all of them, and the curate paid the troopers what was coming to them, since they did not wish to go any farther. The canon requested the priest to inform him of the outcome of Don Quixote's madness, as to whether it yielded to treatment or not; and with this he begged permission to resume his journey. In short, the party broke up and separated, leaving only the curate and the barber, Don Quixote and Panza, and the good Rocinante, who looked upon everything that he had seen with the same resignation as his master. Yoking his oxen, the carter made the knight comfortable upon a bale of hay, and then at his customary slow pace proceeded to follow the road that the curate directed him to take. At the end of the six days they reached Don Quixote's village, making their entrance at noon of a Sunday, when the square was filled with a crowd of people through which the cart had to pass.

They all came running to see who it was, and when they recognized their townsman, they were vastly astonished. One lad sped to bring the news to the knight's housekeeper and his niece, telling them that their master had returned lean and jaundiced and lying stretched out upon a bale of hay on an ox-cart. It was pitiful to hear the good ladies' screams, to behold the way in which they beat their breasts, and to listen to the curses which they once more heaped upon those damnable books of chivalry, and this demonstration increased as they saw Don Quixote coming through the doorway.

At news of the knight's return, Sancho Panza's wife had hurried to the scene, for she had some while since learned that her husband had accompanied him as his squire; and now, as soon as she laid eyes upon her man, the first question she asked was if all was well with the ass, to which Sancho replied that the beast was better off then his master.

"Thank God," she exclaimed, "for all his blessings! But tell me now, my dear, what have you brought me from all your squirings? A new cloak to wear? Or shoes for the young ones?"

"I've brought you nothing of the sort, good wife," said Sancho, "but other things of greater value and importance."

"I'm glad to hear that," she replied. "Show me those things of greater value and importance, my dear. I'd like a sight of them just to cheer this heart of mine which has been so sad and unhappy all the centuries that you've been gone."

"I will show them to you at home, wife," said Sancho. "For the present be satisfied that if, God willing, we set out on another journey in search of adventures, you will see me in no time a count or the governor of an island, and not one of those around here, but the best that is to be had."

"I hope to Heaven it's true, my husband, for we certainly need it. But tell me, what is all this about islands? I don't understand."

"Honey," replied Sancho, "is not for the mouth of an ass. You will find out in good time, woman; and you're going to be surprised to hear yourself called 'my Ladyship' by all your vassals."

"What's this you are saying, Sancho, about ladyships, islands, and vassals?" Juana Panza insisted on knowing—for such was the name of Sancho's wife, although they were not blood relatives, it being the custom in La Mancha for wives to take their husbands' surnames.

"Do not be in such a hurry to know all this, Juana," he said. "It is enough that I am telling you the truth. Sew up your mouth, then; for all I will say, in passing, is that there is nothing in the world that is more pleasant than being a respected man, squire to a knight-errant who goes in search of adventures. It is true that most of the adventures you meet with do not come out the way you'd like them to, for ninety-nine out of a hundred will prove to be all twisted and crosswise. I know that from experience, for I've come out of some of them blanketed and out of others beaten to a pulp. But, all the same, it's a fine thing to go along waiting for what will happen next, crossing mountains, making your way through woods, climbing over cliffs, visiting castles, and putting up at inns free of charge, and the devil take the maravedi that is to pay."

Such was the conversation that took place between Sancho Panza and Juana Panza, his wife, as Don Quixote's housekeeper and niece were taking him in, stripping him, and stretching him out on his old-time bed. He gazed at them blankly, being unable to make out where he was. The curate charged the niece to take great care to see that her uncle was comfortable and to keep close watch over him so that he would not slip away from them another time. He then told them of what it had been necessary to do in order to get him home, at which they once more screamed to Heaven and began cursing the books of chivalry all over again, praying God to plunge the authors of such lying nonsense into the center of the bottomless pit. In short, they scarcely knew what to do, for they were very much afraid that their master and uncle would give them the slip once more, the moment he was a little better, and it turned out just the way they feared it might.

# Don Quixote

## Part II

### ["Put into a Book"]

#### CHAPTER 3

*Of the laughable conversation that took place between Don Qui-*
*xote, Sancho Panza, and the bachelor Sansón Carrasco.*

Don Quixote remained in a thoughtful mood as he waited for the bachelor Carrasco,[7] from whom he hoped to hear the news as to how he had been put into a book, as Sancho had said. He could not bring himself to believe that any such history existed, since the blood of the enemies he had slain was not yet dry on the blade of his sword; and here they were trying to tell him that his high deeds of chivalry were already circulating in printed form. But, for that matter, he imagined that some sage, either friend or enemy, must have seen to the printing of them through the art of magic. If the chronicler was a friend, he must have undertaken the task in order to magnify and exalt Don Quixote's exploits above the most notable ones achieved by knights-errant of old. If an enemy, his purpose would have been to make them out as nothing at all, by debasing them below the mean-est acts ever recorded of any mean squire. The only thing was, the knight reflected, the exploits of squires never were set down in writ-ing. If it was true that such a history existed, being about a knight-errant, then it must be eloquent and lofty in tone, a splendid and distinguished piece of work and veracious in its details.

---

7. The bachelor of arts Sansón Carrasco, an important new character who appears at the begin-ning of Part II and will play a considerable role in the story with his attempts at "curing" Don Quixote (the first one a failure, the second one a success; see our following selections). Just now he has been telling Sancho about a book relating the adventures of Don Quixote and his squire, by which the two have been made famous; the book is, of course, *Don Quixote*, Part I.

This consoled him somewhat, although he was a bit put out at the thought that the author was a Moor, if the appellation "Cid" was to be taken as an indication,[8] and from the Moors you could never hope for any word of truth, seeing that they are all of them cheats, forgers, and schemers. He feared lest his love should not have been treated with becoming modesty but rather in a way that would reflect upon the virtue of his lady Dulcinea del Toboso. He hoped that his fidelity had been made clear, and the respect he had always shown her, and that something had been said as to how he had spurned queens, empresses, and damsels of every rank while keeping a rein upon those impulses that are natural to a man. He was still wrapped up in these and many other similar thoughts when Sancho returned with Carrasco.

Don Quixote received the bachelor very amiably. The latter, although his name was Sansón, or Samson, was not very big so far as bodily size went, but he was a great joker, with a sallow complexion and a ready wit. He was going on twenty-four and had a round face, a snub nose, and a large mouth, all of which showed him to be of a mischievous disposition and fond of jests and witticisms. This became apparent when, as soon as he saw Don Quixote, he fell upon his knees and addressed the knight as follows:

"O mighty Don Quixote de la Mancha, give me your hands; for by the habit of St. Peter that I wear[9]—though I have received but the first four orders—your Grace is one of the most famous knights-errant that ever have been or ever will be anywhere on this earth. Blessings upon Cid Hamete Benengeli who wrote down the history of your great achievements, and upon that curious-minded one who was at pains to have it translated from the Arabic into our Castilian vulgate for the universal entertainment of the people."

Don Quixote bade him rise. "Is it true, then," he asked, "that there is a book about me and that it was some Moorish sage who composed it?"

"By way of showing you how true it is," replied Sansón, "I may tell you that it is my belief that there are in existence today more than twelve thousand copies of that history. If you do not believe me, you have but to make inquiries in Portugal, Barcelona, and Valencia, where editions have been brought out, and there is even a report to the effect that one edition was printed at Antwerp. In short, I feel certain that there will soon not be a nation that does not know it or a language into which it has not been translated."

"One of the things," remarked Don Quixote, "that should give most satisfaction to a virtuous and eminent man is to see his good name spread abroad during his own lifetime, by means of the print-

8. The allusion is to Cid Hamete Benengeli; the word *cid*, "chief," is of Arabic derivation.
9. The dress of one of the minor clerical orders.

ing press, through translations into the languages of the various peoples. I have said 'good name,' for if he has any other kind, his fate is worse than death."

"If it is a matter of good name and good reputation," said the bachelor, "your Grace bears off the palm from all the knights-errant in the world; for the Moor in his tongue and the Christian in his have most vividly depicted you Grace's gallantry, your courage in facing dangers, your patience in adversity and suffering, whether the suffering be due to wounds or to misfortunes of another sort, and your virtue and continence in love, in connection with that platonic relationship that exists between your Grace and my lady Doña Dulcinea del Toboso."

At this point Sancho spoke up. "Never in my life," he said, "have I heard my lady Dulcinea called 'Doña,' but only 'la Señora Dulcinea del Toboso'; so on that point, already, the history is wrong."

"That is not important," said Carrasco.

"No, certainly not," Don Quixote agreed. "But tell me, Señor Bachelor, what adventures of mine as set down in this book have made the deepest impression?"

"As to that," the bachelor answered, "opinions differ, for it is a matter of individual taste. There are some who are very fond of the adventure of the windmills—those windmills which to your Grace appeared to be so many Briareuses and giants. Others like the episode at the fulling mill. One relishes the story of the two armies which took on the appearance of droves of sheep, while another fancies the tale of the dead man whom they were taking to Segovia for burial. One will assert that the freeing of the galley slaves is the best of all, and yet another will maintain that nothing can come up to the Benedictine giants and the encounter with the valiant Biscayan."

Again Sancho interrupted him. "Tell me, Señor Bachelor," he said, "does the book say anything about the adventure with the Yanguesans, that time our good Rocinante took it into his head to go looking for tidbits in the sea?"

"The sage," replied Sansón, "has left nothing in the inkwell. He has told everything and to the point, even to the capers which the worthy Sancho cut as they tossed him in the blanket."

"I cut no capers in the blanket," objected Sancho, "but I did in the air, and more than I liked."

"I imagine," said Don Quixote, "that there is no history in the world, dealing with humankind, that does not have its ups and downs, and this is particularly true of those that have to do with deeds of chivalry, for they can never be filled with happy incidents alone."

"Nevertheless," the bachelor went on, "there are some who have read the book who say that they would have been glad if the authors had forgotten a few of the innumerable cudgelings which Señor Don Quixote received in the course of his various encounters."

"But that is where the truth of the story comes in," Sancho protested.

"For all of that," observed Don Quixote, "they might well have said nothing about them; for there is no need of recording those events that do not alter the veracity of the chronicle, when they tend only to lessen the reader's respect for the hero. You may be sure that Aeneas was not as pious as Vergil would have us believe, nor was Ulysses as wise as Homer depicts him."

"That is true enough," replied Sansón, "but it is one thing to write as a poet and another as a historian. The former may narrate or sing of things not as they were but as they should have been; the latter must describe them not as they should have been but as they were, without adding to or detracting from the truth in any degree whatsoever."

"Well," said Sancho, "if this Moorish gentleman is bent upon telling the truth, I have no doubt that among my master's thrashings my own will be found; for they never took the measure of his Grace's shoulders without measuring my whole body. But I don't wonder at that; for as my master himself says, when there's an ache in the head the members have to share it."

"You are a sly fox, Sancho," said Don Quixote. "My word, but you can remember things well enough when you choose to do so!"

"Even if I wanted to forget the whacks they gave me," Sancho answered him, "the welts on my ribs wouldn't let me, for they are still fresh."

"Be quiet, Sancho," his master admonished him, "and do not interrupt the bachelor. I beg him to go on and tell me what is said of me in this book."

"And what it says about me, too," put in Sancho, "for I have heard that I am one of the main presonages in it—"

"*Personages*, not *presonages*, Sancho my friend," said Sansón.

"So we have another one who catches you up on everything you say," was Sancho's retort. "If we go on at this rate, we'll never be through in a lifetime."

"My God put a curse on *my* life," the bachelor told him, "if you are not the second most important person in the story; and there are some who would rather listen to you talk than to anyone else in the book. It is true, there are those who say that you are too gullible in believing it to be the truth that you could become the governor of that island that was offered you by Señor Don Quixote, here present."

"There is still sun on the top of the wall," said Don Quixote, "and when Sancho is a little older, with the experience that the years bring, he will be wiser and better fitted to be a governor than he is at the present time."

"By God, master," said Sancho, "the island that I couldn't govern right now I'd never be able to govern if I lived to be as old as Methuselah. The trouble is, I don't know where that island we are talking about is located; it is not due to any lack of noddle on my part."

"Leave it to God, Sancho," was Don Quixote's advice, "and everything will come out all right, perhaps even better than you think; for not a leaf on the tree stirs except by His will."

"Yes," said Sansón, "if it be God's will, Sancho will not lack a thousand islands to govern, not to speak of one island alone."

"I have seen governors around here," said Sancho, "that are not to be compared to the sole of my shoe, and yet they call them 'your Lordship' and serve them on silver plate."

"Those are not the same kind of governors," Sansón informed him. "Their task is a good deal easier. The ones that govern islands must at least know grammar."

"I could make out well enough with the *gram*," replied Sancho, "but with the *mar* I want nothing to do, for I don't understand it at all. But leaving this business of the governorship in God's hands—for He will send me wherever I can best serve Him—I will tell you, Señor Bachelor Sansón Carrasco, that I am very much pleased that the author of the history should have spoken of me in such a way as does not offend me; for, upon the word of a faithful squire, if he had said anything about me that was not becoming to an old Christian, the deaf would have heard of it."

"That would be to work miracles," said Sansón.

"Miracles or no miracles," was the answer, "let everyone take care as to what he says or writes about people and not be setting down the first thing that pops into his head."

"One of the faults that is found with the book," continued the bachelor, "is that the author has inserted in it a story entitled *The One Who Was Too Curious for His Own Good*. It is not that the story in itself is a bad one or badly written; it is simply that it is out of place there, having nothing to do with the story of his Grace, Señor Don Quixote."[1]

"I will bet you," said Sancho, "that the son of a dog has mixed the cabbages with the baskets."[3]

"And I will say right now," declared Don Quixote, "that the author of this book was not a sage but some ignorant prattler who at haphazard and without any method set about the writing of it, being

1. The story, a tragic tale about a jealousy-ridden husband, occupies several chapters of Part I. Here, as elsewhere in this chapter, Cervantes echoes criticism currently aimed at his book.
2. Has jumbled together things of different kinds.

content to let things turn out as they might. In the same manner, Orbaneja,[3] the painter of Ubeda, when asked what he was painting would reply, 'Whatever it turns out to be.' Sometimes it would be a cock, in which case he would have to write alongside it, in Gothic letters, 'This is a cock.' And so it must be with my story, which will need a commentary to make it understandable."

"No," replied Sansón, "that it will not; for it is so clearly written that none can fail to understand it. Little children leaf through it, young people read it, adults appreciate it, and the aged sing its praises. In short, it is so thumbed and read and so well known to persons of every walk in life that no sooner do folks see some skinny nag than they at once cry, 'There goes Rocinante!' Those that like it best of all are the pages; for there is no lord's antechamber where a *Don Quixote* is not to be found. If one lays it down, another will pick it up; one will pounce upon it, and another will beg for it. It affords the pleasantest and least harmful reading of any book that has been published up to now. In the whole of it there is not to be found an indecent word or a thought that is other than Catholic."

"To write in any other manner," observed Don Quixote, "would be to write lies and not the truth. Those historians who make use of falsehoods ought to be burned like the makers of counterfeit money. I do not know what could have led the author to introduce stories and episodes that are foreign to the subject matter when he had so much to write about in describing my adventures. He must, undoubtedly, have been inspired by the old saying, 'With straw or with hay . . .'[4] For, in truth, all he had to do was to record my thoughts, my sighs, my tears, my lofty purposes, and my undertakings, and he would have had a volume bigger or at least as big as that which the works of El Tostado[5] would make. To sum the matter up, Señor Bachelor, it is my opinion that, in composing histories or books of any sort, a great deal of judgment and ripe understanding is called for. To say and write witty and amusing things is the mark of great genius. The cleverest character in a comedy is the clown, since he who would make himself out to be a simpleton cannot be one. History is a near-sacred thing, for it must be true, and where the truth is, there is God. And yet there are those who compose books and toss them out into the world as if they were no more than fritters."

"There is no book so bad," opined the bachelor, "that there is not some good in it."

"Doubtless that is so," replied Don Quixote, "but it very often

3. This painter is known only through the present allusion in *Don Quixote*.    4. The proverb concludes either "the mattress is filled" or "I fill my belly."    5. Alonso de Madrigal, biship of Avila, a prolific author of devotional works.

happens that those who have won in advance a great and well-deserved reputation for their writings, lose it in whole or in part when they give their works to the printer."

"The reason for it," said Sansón, "is that, printed works being read at leisure, their faults are the more readily apparent, and the greater the reputation of the author the more closely are they scrutinized. Men famous for their genius, great poets, illustrious historians, are almost always envied by those who take a special delight in criticizing the writings of others without having produced anything of their own."

"That is not to be wondered at," said Don Quixote, "for there are many theologians who are not good enough for the pulpit but who are very good indeed when it comes to detecting the faults or excesses of those who preach."

"All of this is very true, Señor Don Quixote," replied Carrasco, "but, all the same, I could wish that these self-appointed censors were a bit more forbearing and less hypercritical; I wish they would pay a little less attention to the spots on the bright sun of the work that occasions their fault-finding. For if *aliquando bonus dormitat Homerus*,[6] let them consider how much of his time he spent awake, shedding the light of his genius with a minimum of shade. It well may be that what to them seems a flaw is but one of those moles which sometimes add to the beauty of a face. In any event, I insist that he who has a book printed runs a very great risk, inasmuch as it is an utter impossibility to write it in such a manner that it will please all who read it."

"This book about me must have pleased very few," remarked Don Quixote.

"Quite the contrary," said Sansón, "for just as *stultorum infinitus est numerus*,[7] so the number of those who have enjoyed this history is likewise infinite. Some, to be sure, have complained of the author's forgetfulness, seeing that he neglected to make it plain who the thief was who stole Sancho's gray;[8] for it is not stated there, but merely implied, that the ass was stolen; and, a little further on, we find the knight mounted on the same beast, although it has not made its reappearance in the story. They also say that the author forgot to tell us what Sancho did with those hundred crowns that he found in the valise on the Sierra Morena, as nothing more is said of them and there are many who would like to know how he disposed of the money or how he spent it. This is one of the serious omissions to be found in the work."

To this Sancho replied, "I, Señor Sansón, do not feel like giving any account or accounting just now; for I feel a little weak in my

6. "Good Homer sometimes nods too." (Horace, *Art of Poetry*, l. 359.)   7. "Infinite is the number of fools." (Ecclesiasticus 1:15.)   8. In Part I, Chapter 23.

stomach, and if I don't do something about it by taking a few swigs of the old stuff, I'll be sitting on St. Lucy's thorn.[9] I have some of it at home, and my old woman is waiting for me. After I've had my dinner, I'll come back and answer any questions your Grace or anybody else wants to ask me, whether it's about the loss of the ass or the spending of the hundred crowns."

And without waiting for a reply or saying another word, he went on home. Don Quixote urged the bachelor to stay and take potluck with him, and Sansón accepted the invitation and remained. In addition to the knight's ordinary fare, they had a couple of pigeons, and at table their talk was of chivalry and feats of arms.

[A Victorious Duel]

CHAPTER 12

*Of the strange adventure that befell the valiant Don Quixote with the fearless Knight of the Mirrors.*[1]

The night following the encounter with Death was spent by Don Quixote and his squire beneath some tall and shady trees,[2] the knight having been persuaded to eat a little from the stock of provisions carried by the gray.

"Sir," said Sancho, in the course of their repast, "how foolish I'd have been if I had chosen the spoils from your Grace's first adventure rather than the foals from the three mares.[3] Truly, truly, a sparrow in the hand is worth more than a vulture on the wing."

"And yet, Sancho," replied Don Quixote, "if you had but let me attack them as I wished to do, you would at least have had as spoils the Empress's gold crown and Cupid's painted wings;[4] for I should have taken them whether or no and placed them in your hands."

"The crowns and scepters of stage emperors," remarked Sancho, "were never known to be of pure gold; they are always of tinsel or tinplate."

"That is the truth," said Don Quixote, "for it is only right that the accessories of a drama should be fictitious and not real, like the play

---

9. I shall be weak and exhausted.    1. He will duly earn this title only in Chapter 15. In between, the author will be referring to him as the Knight of the Wood.    2. Don Quixote and his squire are now in the woody region around El Toboso, Dulcinea's town. Sancho has been sent to look for his knight's lady and has saved the day by pretending to see the beautiful damsel in a "village wench, and not a pretty one at that, for she was round-faced and snub-nosed." But by his imaginative lie he has succeeded, as he had planned, in setting in motion Don Quixote's belief in spells and enchantments: enemy magicians, envious of him, have hidden his lady's splendor only from his sight. While the knight was still under the shock of this experience, further along their way he and his squire have met a group of itinerant players dressed in their proper costumes for a religious play, *The Parliament of Death*.    3. Don Quixote has promised them to Sancho as a reward for bringing news of Dulcinea. The following sentence is a proverb roughly corresponding to "a bird in the hand is worth two in the bush."    4. The Empress and Cupid were among the characters in *The Parliament of Death*.

itself. Speaking of that, Sancho, I would have you lc    kindly upon
the art of the theater and, as a consequence, upon those who write
the pieces and perform in them, for they all render a service of great
value to the State by holding up a mirror for us at each step that we
take, wherein we may observe, vividly depicted, all the varied aspects
of human life; and I may add that there is nothing that shows us
more clearly, by similitude, what we are and what we ought to be
than do plays and players.

"Tell me, have you not seen some comedy in which kings,
emperors, pontiffs, knights, ladies, and numerous other characters
are introduced? One plays the ruffian, another the cheat, this one a
merchant and that one a soldier, while yet another is the fool who is
not so foolish as he appears, and still another the one of whom love
has made a fool. Yet when the play is over and they have taken off
their players' garments, all the actors are once more equal."

"Yes," replied Sancho, "I have seen all that."

"Well," continued Don Quixote, "the same thing happens in the
comedy that we call life, where some play the part of emperors,
others that of pontiffs—in short, all the characters that a drama may
have—but when it is all over, that is to say, when life is done, death
takes from each the garb that differentiates him, and all at last are
equal in the grave."

"It is a fine comparison," Sancho admitted, "though not so new
but that I have heard it many times before. It reminds me of that
other one, about the game of chess. So long as the game lasts, each
piece has its special qualities, but when it is over they are all mixed
and jumbled together and put into a bag, which is to the chess pieces
what the grave is to life."

"Every day, Sancho," said Don Quixote, "you are becoming less
stupid and more sensible."

"It must be that some of your Grace's good sense is sticking to
me," was Sancho's answer. "I am like a piece of land that of itself is
dry and barren, but if you scatter manure over it and cultivate it, it
will bear good fruit. By this I mean to say that your Grace's conversation is the manure that has been cast upon the barren land of my
dry wit; the time that I spend in your service, associating with you,
does the cultivating; and as a result of it all, I hope to bring forth
blessed fruits by not departing, slipping, or sliding, from those paths
of good breeding which your Grace has marked out for me in my
parched understanding."

Don Quixote had to laugh at this affected speech of Sancho's, but
he could not help perceiving that what the squire had said about his
improvement was true enough; for every now and then the servant
would speak in a manner that astonished his master. It must be
admitted, however, that most of the time when he tried to use fine

language, he would tumble from the mountain of his simple-mind-edness into the abyss of his ignorance. It was when he was quoting old saws and sayings, whether or not they had anything to do with the subject under discussion, that he was at his best, displaying upon such occasions a prodigious memory, as will already have been seen and noted in the course of this history.

With such talk as this they spent a good part of the night. Then Sancho felt a desire to draw down the curtains of his eyes, as he was in the habit of saying when he wished to sleep, and, unsaddling his mount, he turned him loose to graze at will on the abundant grass. If he did not remove Rocinante's saddle, this was due to his master's express command; for when they had taken the field and were not sleeping under a roof, the hack was under no circumstances to be stripped. This was in accordance with an old and established custom which knights-errant faithfully observed: the bridle and saddlebow might be removed, but beware of touching the saddle itself! Guided by this precept, Sancho now gave Rocinante the same freedom that the ass enjoyed.

The close friendship that existed between the two animals was a most unusual one, so remarkable indeed that it has become a tradition handed down from father to son, and the author of this veracious chronicle even wrote a number of special chapters on the subject, although, in order to preserve the decency and decorum that are fitting in so heroic an account, he chose to omit them in the final version. But he forgets himself once in a while and goes on to tell us how the two beasts when they were together would hasten to scratch each other, and how, when they were tired and their bellies were full, Rocinante would lay his long neck over that of the ass—it extended more than a half a yard on the other side—and the pair would then stand there gazing pensively at the ground for as much as three whole days at a time, or at least until someone came for them or hunger compelled them to seek nourishment.

I may tell you that I have heard it said that the author of this history, in one of his writings, has compared the friendship of Roci-nante and the gray to that of Nisus and Euryalus and that of Pylades and Orestes;[5] and if this be true, it shows for the edification of all what great friends these two peace-loving animals were, and should be enough to make men ashamed, who are so inept at preserving friendship with one another. For this reason it has been said:

> There is no friend for friend,
> Reeds to lances turn . . .[6]

---

5. Famous examples of friendship in Virgil's *Aeneid* and in Greek tradition and drama.    6. From a popular ballad.

And there was the other poet who sang:

Between friend and friend the bug . . .[7]

Let no one think that the author has gone out of his way in comparing the friendship of animals with that of men; for human beings
have received valuable lessons from the beasts and have learned many
important things from them. From the stork they have learned the
use of clysters; the dog has taught them the salutary effects of vom-
iting as well as a lesson in gratitude; the cranes have taught them
vigilance, the ants foresight, the elephants modesty, and the horse
loyalty.[8]

Sancho had at last fallen asleep at the foot of a cork tree, while
Don Quixote was slumbering beneath a sturdy oak. Very little time
had passed when the knight was awakened by a noise behind him,
and, starting up, he began looking about him and listening to see if
he could make out where it came from. Then he caught sight of two
men on horseback, one of whom, slipping down from the saddle,
said to the other, "Dismount, my friend, and unbridle the horses;
for there seems to be plenty of grass around here for them and sufficient silence and solitude for my amorous thoughts."

Saying this, he stretched himself out on the ground, and as he
flung himself down the armor that he wore made such a noise that
Don Quixote knew at once, for a certainty, that he must be a knight-
errant. Going over to Sancho, who was still sleeping, he shook him
by the arm and with no little effort managed to get him awake.

"Brother Sancho," he said to him in a low voice, "we have an
adventure on our hands."

"God give us a good one," said Sancho. "And where, my master,
may her Ladyship, Mistress Adventure, be?"

"Where, Sancho?" replied Don Quixote. "Turn your eyes and
look, and you will see stretched out over there a knight-errant who,
so far as I can make out, is not any too happy; for I saw him fling
himself from his horse to the ground with a certain show of despondency, and as he fell his armor rattled."

"Well," said Sancho, "and how does you Grace make this out to
be an adventure?"

"I would not say," the knight answered him, "that this is an
adventure in itself, but rather the beginning of one, for that is the
way they start. But listen; he seems to be tuning a lute or guitar, and
from the way he is spitting and clearing his throat he must be getting
ready to sing something."

"Faith, so he is," said Sancho. "He must be some lovesick knight."

7. The Spanish "a bug in the eye" implies keeping a watchful eye on somebody.    8. All folk-
loristic beliefs about the "virtues" of animals.

"There are no knights-errant that are not lovesick," Don Quixote informed him. "Let us listen to him, and the thread of his song will lead us to the yarn-ball of his thoughts; for out of the abundance of the heart the mouth speaketh."

Sancho would have liked to reply to his master, but the voice of the Knight of the Wood, which was neither very good nor very bad, kept him from it; and as the two of them listened attentively, they heard the following:

### Sonnet

Show me, O lady, the pattern of thy will,
That mine may take that very form and shape;
For my will in thine own I fain would drape,
Each slightest wish of thine I would fulfill.
If thou wouldst have me silence this dead ill
Of which I'm dying now, prepare the crape!
Or if I must another manner ape,
Then let Love's self display his rhyming skill.
Of opposites I am made, that's manifest:
In part soft wax, in part hard-diamond fire;
Yet to Love's laws my heart I do adjust,
And, hard or soft, I offer thee this breast:
Print or engrave there what thou may'st desire,
And I'll preserve it in eternal trust.[9]

With an *Ay!* that appeared to be wrung from the very depths of his heart, the Knight of the Wood brought his song to a close, and then after a brief pause began speaking in a grief-stricken voice that was piteous to hear.

"O most beautiful and most ungrateful woman in all the world!" he cried, "how is it possible, O most serene Casildea de Vandalia,[1] for you to permit this captive knight of yours to waste away and perish in constant wanderings, amid rude toils and bitter hardships? Is it not enough that I have compelled all the knights of Navarre, all those of León, all the Tartessians and Castilians, and, finally, all those of La Mancha, to confess that there is no beauty anywhere that can rival yours?"

"That is not so!" cried Don Quixote at this point. "I am of La Mancha, and I have never confessed, I never could nor would confess a thing so prejudicial to the beauty of my lady. The knight whom you see there, Sancho, is raving; but let us listen and perhaps he will tell us more."

9. The poem intentionally follows affected conventions of the time.      1. The Knight of the Wood's counterpart to Don Quixote's Dulcinea del Tobooso.

"That he will," replied Sancho, "for at the rate he is carrying on, he is good for a month at a stretch."

This did not prove to be the case, however; for when the Knight of the Wood heard voices near him, he cut short his lamentations and rose to his feet.

"Who goes there?" he called in a loud but courteous tone. "What kind of people are you? Are you, perchance, numbered among the happy or among the afflicted?"

"Among the afflicted," was Don Quixote's response.

"Then come to me," said the one of the Wood, "and, in doing so, know that you come to sorrow's self and the very essence of affliction."

Upon receiving so gentle and courteous an answer, Don Quixote and Sancho as well went over to him, whereupon the sorrowing one took the Manchegan's arm.

"Sit down here, Sir Knight," he continued, "for in order to know that you are one of those who follow the profession of knight-errantry, it is enough for me to have found you in this place where solitude and serenity keep you company, such a spot being the natural bed and proper dwelling of wandering men of arms."

"A knight I am," replied Don Quixote, "and of the profession that you mention; and though sorrows, troubles, and misfortunes have made my heart their abode, this does not mean that compassion for the woes of others has been banished from it. From your song a while ago I gather that your misfortunes are due to love—the love you bear that ungrateful fair one whom you named in your lamentations."

As they conversed in this manner, they sat together upon the hard earth, very peaceably and companionably, as if at daybreak they were not going to break each other's heads.

"Sir Knight," inquired the one of the Wood, "are you by any chance in love?"

"By mischance I am," said Don Quixote, "although the ills that come from well-placed affection should be looked upon as favors rather than as misfortunes."

"That is the truth," the Knight of the Wood agreed, "if it were not that the loved one's scorn disturbs our reason and understanding; for when it is excessive scorn appears as vengeance."

"I was never scorned by my lady," said Don Quixote.

"No, certainly not," said Sancho, who was standing near by, "for my lady is gentle as a ewe lamb and soft as butter."

"Is he your squire?" asked the one of the Wood.

"He is," replied Don Quixote.

"I never saw a squire," said the one of the Wood, "who dared to speak while his master was talking. At least, there is mine over there;

he is as big as your father, and it cannot be proved that he has ever opened his lips while I was conversing."

"Well, upon my word," said Sancho, "I have spoken, and I will speak in front of any other as good—but never mind; it only makes it worse to stir it."

The Knight of the Wood's squire now seized Sancho's arm. "Come along," he said, "let the two of us go where we can talk all we like, squire fashion, and leave these gentlemen our masters to come to lance blows as they tell each other the story of their loves; for you may rest assured, daybreak will find them still at it."

"Let us, by all means," said Sancho, "and I will tell your Grace who I am, so that you may be able to see for yourself whether or not I am to be numbered among the dozen most talkative squires."

With this, the pair went off to one side, and there then took place between them a conversation that was as droll as the one between their masters was solemn.

### CHAPTER 13

*In which is continued the adventure of the Knight of the Wood, together with the shrewd, highly original, and amicable conversation that took place between the two squires.*

The knights and the squires had now separated, the latter to tell their life stories, the former to talk of their loves; but the history first relates the conversation of the servants and then goes on to report that of the masters. We are told that, after they had gone some little distance from where the others were, the one who served the Knight of the Wood began speaking to Sancho as follows:

"It is a hard life that we lead and live, *Señor mio*, those of us who are squires to knights-errant. It is certainly true that we eat our bread in the sweat of our faces, which is one of the curses that God put upon our first parents."[2]

"It might also be said," added Sancho, "that we eat it in the chill of our bodies, for who endures more heat and cold than we wretched ones who wait upon these wandering men of arms? It would not be so bad if we did eat once in a while, for troubles are less where there is bread; but as it is, we sometimes go for a day or two without breaking our fast, unless we feed on the wind that blows."

"But all this," said the other, "may very well be put up with, by reason of the hope we have of being rewarded; for it a knight is not too unlucky, his squire after a little while will find himself the governor of some fine island or prosperous earldom."

"I," replied Sancho, "have told my master that I would be satisfied

2. Cf. Genesis 3:19.

with the governorship of an island, and he is so noble and so generous that he has promised it to me on many different occasions."

"In return for my services," said the Squire of the Wood, "I'd be content with a canonry. My master has already appointed me to one—and what a canonry!"

"Then he must be a churchly knight," said Sancho, "and in a position to grant favors of that sort to his faithful squire; but mine is a layman, pure and simple, although, as I recall, certain shrewd and, as I see it, scheming persons did advise him to try to become an archbishop. However, he did not want to be anything but an emperor. And there I was, all the time trembling for fear he would take it into his head to enter the Church, since I was not educated enough to hold any benefices. For I may as well tell your Grace that, though I look like a man, I am no more than a beast where holy orders are concerned."

"That is where you are making a mistake," the Squire of the Wood assured him. "Not all island governments are desirable. Some of them are misshapen bits of land, some are poor, others are gloomy, and, in short, the best of them lays a heavy burden of care and trouble upon the shoulders of the unfortunate one to whose lot it falls. It would be far better if we who follow this cursed trade were to go back to our homes and there engage in pleasanter occupations, such as hunting or fishing, for example; for where is there in this world a squire so poor that he does not have a hack, a couple of greyhounds, and a fishing rod to provide him with sport in his own village?"

"I don't lack any of those," replied Sancho. "It is true, I have no hack, but I do have an ass that is worth twice as much as my master's horse. God send me a bad Easter, and let it be the next one that comes, if I would make a trade, even though he gave me four fanegas[3] of barley to boot. Your Grace will laugh at the price I put on my gray—for that is the color of the beast. As to greyhounds, I shan't want for them, as there are plenty and to spare in my village. And, anyway, there is more pleasure in hunting when someone else pays for it."

"Really and truly, Sir Squire," said the one of the Wood, "I have made up my mind and resolved to have no more to do with the mad whims of these knights; I intend to retire to my village and bring up my little ones—I have three of them, and they are like oriental pearls."

"I have two of them," said Sancho, "that might be presented to the Pope in person, especially one of my girls that I am bringing up to be a countess, God willing, in spite of what her mother says."

"And how old is this young lady that is destined to be a countess?"

3. About 1.6 bushels.

"Fifteen," replied Sancho, "or a couple of years more or less. But she is tall as a lance, fresh as an April morning, and strong as a porter."

"Those," remarked the one of the Wood, "are qualifications that fit her to be not merely a countess but a nymph of the verdant wild-wood. O whore's daughter of a whore! What strength the she-rogue must have!"

Sancho was a bit put out by this. "She is not a whore," he said, "nor was her mother before her, nor will either of them ever be, please God, so long as I live. And you might speak more courteously. For one who has been brought up among knights-errant, who are the soul of courtesy, those words are not very becoming."

"Oh, how little your Grace knows about compliments, Sir Squire!" the one of the Wood exclaimed. "Are you not aware that when some knight gives a good lance thrust to the bull in the plaza, or when a person does anything remarkably well, it is the custom for the crowd to cry out, 'Well done, whoreson rascal!' and that what appears to be vituperation in such a case is in reality high praise? Sir, I would bid you disown those sons or daughters who do nothing to cause such praise to be bestowed upon their parents."

"I would indeed disown them if they didn't," replied Sancho, "and so your Grace may go ahead and call me, my children, and my wife all the whores in the world if you like, for everything that they say and do deserves the very highest praise. And in order that I may see them all again, I pray God to deliver me from mortal sin, or, what amounts to the same thing, from this dangerous calling of squire, seeing that I have fallen into it a second time, decoyed and deceived by a purse of a hundred ducats that I found one day in the heart of the Sierra Morena.[4] The devil is always holding up a bag full of doubloons in front of my eyes, here, there—no, not here, but there—everywhere, until it seems to me at every step I take that I am touching it with my hand, hugging it, carrying it off home with me, investing it, drawing an income from it, and living on it like a prince. And while I am thinking such thoughts, all the hardships I have to put up with serving this crackbrained master of mine, who is more of a madman than a knight, seem to me light and easy to bear."

"That," observed the Squire of the Wood, "is why it is they say that avarice bursts the bag. But, speaking of madmen, there is no greater one in all this world than my master; for he is one of those of whom it is said, 'The cares of others kill the ass.' Because another knight has lost his senses, he has to play mad too[5] and go hunting for that which, when he finds it, may fly up in his snout."

---

4. When Don Quixote retired there in Part I, Chapter 23.    5. In the Sierra Morena, Don Quixote had decided to imitate Amadis de Gaul and Ariosto's Roland "by playing the part of a desperate and raving madman" as a consequence of love (Part I, Chapter 25).

"Is he in love, maybe?"

"Yes, with a certain Casildea de Vandalia, the rawest[6] and best-roasted lady to be found anywhere on earth; but her rawness is not the foot he limps on, for he has other and greater schemes rumbling in his bowels, as you will hear tell before many hours have gone by."

"There is no road so smooth," said Sancho, "that it does not have some hole or rut to make you stumble. In other houses they cook horse beans, in mine they boil them by the kettleful.[7] Madness has more companions and attendants than good sense does. But if it is true what they say, that company in trouble brings relief, I may take comfort from your Grace, since you serve a master as foolish as my own."

"Foolish but brave," the one of the Wood corrected him, "and more of a rogue than anything else."

"That is not true of my master," replied Sancho. "I can assure you there is nothing of the rogue about him; he is as open and above-board as a wine pitcher and would not harm anyone but does good to all. There is no malice in his make-up, and a child could make him believe it was night at midday. For that very reason I love him with all my heart and cannot bring myself to leave him, no matter how many foolish things he does."

"But, nevertheless, good sir and brother," said the Squire of the Wood, "with the blind leading the blind, both are in danger of falling into the pit. It would be better for us to get out of all this as quickly as we can and return to our old haunts; for those that go seeking adventures do not always find good ones."

Sancho kept clearing his throat from time to time, and his saliva seemed rather viscous and dry; seeing which, the woodland squire said to him, "It looks to me as if we have been talking so much that our tongues are cleaving to our palates, but I have a loosener over there, hanging from the bow of my saddle, and a pretty good one it is." With this, he got up and went over to his horse and came back a moment later with a big flask of wine and a meat pie half a yard in diameter. This is no exaggeration, for the pasty in question was made of a hutch-rabbit of such a size that Sancho took it to be a goat, or at the very least a kid.

"And are you in the habit of carrying this with you, Señor?" he asked.

"What do you think?" replied the other. "Am I by any chance one of your wood-and-water[8] squires? I carry better rations on the flanks of my horse than a general does when he takes the field."

Sancho ate without any urging, gulping down mouthfuls that were like the knots on a tether, as they sat there in the dark.

---

6. The original has a pun on *crudo*, meaning both "raw" and "cruel."   7. Meaning that his misfortunes always come in large quantities.   8. Of low quality.

"You are a squire of the right sort," he said, "loyal and true, and you live in grand style as shown by this feast, which I would almost say was produced by magic. You are not like me, poor wretch, who have in my saddlebags only a morsel of cheese so hard you could crack a giant's skull with it, three or four dozen carob beans, and a few nuts. For this I have my master to thank, who believes in observing the rule that knights-errant should nourish and sustain themselves on nothing but dried fruits and the herbs of the field."

"Upon my word, brother," said the other squire, "my stomach was not made for thistles, wild pears, and woodland herbs. Let our masters observe those knightly laws and traditions and eat what their rules prescribe; I carry a hamper of food and a flask on my saddle-bow, whether they like it or not. And speaking of that flask, how I love it! There is scarcely a minute in the day that I'm not hugging and kissing it, over and over again."

As he said this, he placed the wine bag in Sancho's hands, who put it to his mouth, threw his head back, and sat there gazing up at the stars for a quarter of an hour. Then, when he had finished drinking, he let his head loll on one side and heaved a deep sigh.

"The whoreson rascal!" he exclaimed, "that's a fine vintage for you!"

"There!" cried the Squire of the Wood, as he heard the epithet Sancho had used, "do you see how you have praised this wine by calling it 'whoreson'?"

"I grant you," replied Sancho, "that it is no insult to call anyone a son of a whore so long as you really do mean to praise him. But tell me, sir, in the name of what you love most, is this the wine of Ciudad Real?"[9]

"What a winetaster you are! It comes from nowhere else, and it's a few years old, at that."

"Leave it to me," said Sancho, "and never fear, I'll show you how much I know about it. Would you believe me, Sir Squire, I have such a great natural instinct in this matter of wines that I have but to smell a vintage and I will tell you the country where it was grown, from what kind of grapes, what it tastes like, and how good it is, and everything that has to do with it. There is nothing so unusual about this, however, seeing that on my father's side were two of the best winetasters La Mancha has known in many a year, in proof of which, listen to the story of what happened to them.

"The two were given a sample of wine from a certain vat and asked to state its condition and quality and determine whether it was good or bad. One of them tasted it with the tip of his tongue while the other merely brought it up to his nose. The first man said that it

---

9. The main town in La Mancha and the center of a wine region.

tasted of iron, the second that it smelled of Cordovan leather. The owner insisted that the vat was clean and that there could be nothing in the wine to give it a flavor of leather or of iron, but, nevertheless, the two famous winetasters stood their ground. Time went by, and when they came to clean out the vat they found in it a small key attached to a leather strap. And so your Grace may see for yourself whether or not one who comes of that kind of stock has a right to give his opinion in such cases."

"And for that very reason," said the Squire of the Wood, "I maintain that we ought to stop going about in search of adventures. Seeing that we have loaves, let us not go looking for cakes, but return to our cottages, for God will find us there if He so wills."

"I mean to stay with my master," Sancho replied, "until he reaches Saragossa, but after that we will come to an understanding."

The short of the matter is, the two worthy squires talked so much and drank so much that sleep had to tie their tongues and moderate their thirst, since to quench the latter was impossible. Clinging to the wine flask, which was almost empty by now, and with half-chewed morsels of food in their mouths, they both slept peacefully; and we shall leave them there as we go on to relate what took place between the Knight of the Wood and the Knight of the Mournful Countenance.

## CHAPTER 14

*Wherein is continued the adventure of the Knight of the Wood.*

In the course of the long conversation that took place between Don Quixote and the Knight of the Wood, the history informs us that the latter addressed the following remarks to the Manchegan:

"In short, Sir Knight, I would have you know that my destiny, or, more properly speaking, my own free choice, has led me to fall in love with the peerless Casildea de Vandalia. I call her peerless for the reason that she has no equal as regards either her bodily proportions or her very great beauty. This Casildea, then, of whom I am telling you, repaid my worthy affections and honorable intentions by forcing me, as Hercules was forced by his stepmother, to incur many and diverse perils;[1] and each time as I overcame one of them she would promise me that with the next one I should have that which I desired; but instead my labors have continued, forming a chain whose links I am no longer able to count, nor can I say which will be the last one, that shall mark the beginning of the realization of my hopes.

"One time she sent me forth to challenge that famous giantess of

1. Son of Zeus and Alcmena, Hercules was persecuted by Zeus' wife Hera.

Seville, known as La Giralda,[2] who is as strong and brave as if made of brass, and who without moving from the spot where she stands is the most changeable and fickle woman in the world. I came, I saw, I conquered her, I made her stand still and point in one direction only, and for more than a week nothing but north winds blew. Then, there was that other time when Casildea sent me to lift those ancient stones, the mighty Bulls of Guisando,[3] an enterprise that had better have been entrusted to porters than to knights. On another occasion she commanded me to hurl myself down into the Cabra chasm[4]— an unheard-of and terribly dangerous undertaking—and bring her back a detailed account of what lay concealed in that deep and gloomy pit. I rendered La Giralda motionless, I lifted the Bulls of Guisando, and I threw myself into the abyss and brought to light what was hidden in its depths; yet my hopes are dead—how dead!—while her commands and her scorn are as lively as can be.

"Finally, she commanded me to ride through all the provinces of Spain and compel all the knights-errant whom I met with to confess that she is the most beautiful woman now living and that I am the most enamored man of arms that is to be found anywhere in the world. In fulfillment of this behest I have already traveled over the greater part of these realms and have vanquished many knights who have dared to contradict me. But the one whom I am proudest to have overcome in single combat is that famous gentleman, Don Quixote de la Mancha; for I made him confess that my Casildea is more beautiful than his Dulcinea, and by achieving such a conquest I reckon that I have conquered all the others on the face of the earth, seeing that this same Don Quixote had himself routed them. Accordingly, when I vanquished him, his fame, glory, and honor passed over and were transferred to my person.

> The brighter is the conquered one's lost crown,
> The greater is the conqueror's renown.[5]

Thus, the innumerable exploits of the said Don Quixote are now set down to my account and are indeed my own."

Don Quixote was astounded as he listened to the Knight of the Wood, and was about to tell him any number of times that he lied; the words were on the tip of his tongue, but he held them back as best he could, thinking that he would bring the other to confess with his own lips that what he had said was a lie. And so it was quite calmly that he now replied to him.

---

2. Actually a statue on the Moorish belfry of the cathedral at Seville.    3. Statues representing animals and supposedly marking a place where Caesar defeated Pompey. (Cf. the use of Caesar's famous words a few lines above.)    4. Possibly an ancient mine in the Sierra de Cabra near Cordova.    5. From the *Araucana*, a poem by Alonso de Ercilla y Zúñiga on the Spanish struggle against the Araucanian Indians of Chile.

"Sir Knight," he began, "as to the assertion that your Grace has conquered most of the knights-errant in Spain and even in all the world, I have nothing to say, but that you have vanquished Don Quixote de la Mancha, I am inclined to doubt. It may be that it was someone else who resembled him, ahtough there are very few that

"What do you mean?" replied the one of the Wood. "I swear by the heavens above that I did fight with Don Quixote and that I overcame him and forced him to yield. He is a tall man, with a dried-up face, long, lean legs, graying hair, an eagle-like nose somewhat hooked, and a big, black, drooping mustache. He takes the field under the name of the Knight of the Mournful Countenance, he has for squire a peasant named Sancho Panza, and he rides a famous steed called Rocinante. Lastly, the lady of his heart is a certain Dulcinea del Toboso, once upon a time known as Aldonza Lorenzo, just as my own lady, whose name is Casildea and who is an Andalusian by birth, is called by me Casildea de Vandalia. If all this is not sufficient to show that I speak the truth, here is my sword which shall make incredulity itself believe."

"Calm yourself, Sir Knight," replied Don Quixote, "and listen to what I have to say to you. You must know that this Don Quixote of whom you speak is the best friend that I have in the world, so great a friend that I may say that I feel toward him as I do toward my own self; and from all that you have told me, the very definite and accurate details that you have given me, I cannot doubt that he is the one whom you have conquered. On the other hand, the sight of my eyes and the touch of my hands assure me that he could not possibly be the one, unless some enchanter who is his enemy—for he has many, and one in particular who delights in persecuting him—may have assumed the knight's form and then permitted himself to be routed, by way of defrauding Don Quixote of the fame which his high deeds of chivalry have earned for him throughout the known world. To show you how true this may be, I will inform you that not more than a couple of days ago those same enemy magicians transformed the figure and person of the beauteous Dulcinea del Toboso into a low and mean village lass, and it is possible that they have done something of the same sort to the knight who is her lover. And if all this does not suffice to convince you of the truth of what I say, here is Don Quixote himself who will maintain it by force of arms, on foot or on horseback, or in any way you like."

Saying this, he rose and laid hold of his sword, and waited to see what the Knight of the Wood's decision would be. That worthy now replied in a voice as calm as the one Don Quixote had used.

"Pledges," he said, "do not distress one who is sure of his ability to pay. He who was able to overcome you when you were transformed, Señor Don Quixote, may hope to bring you to your knees when you are your own proper self. But inasmuch as it is not fitting that knights should perform their feats of arms in the darkness, like ruffians and highwaymen, let us wait until it is day in order that the sun may behold what we do. And the condition governing our encounter shall be that the one who is vanquished must submit to the will of his conqueror and perform all those things that are commanded of him, provided they are such as are in keeping with the state of knighthood."

"With that condition and understanding," said Don Quixote, "I shall be satisfied."

With this, they went off to where their squires were, only to find them snoring away as hard as when sleep had first overtaken them. Awakening the pair, they ordered them to look to the horses; for as soon as the sun was up the two knights meant to stage an arduous and bloody single-handed combat. At this news Sancho was astonished and terrified, since, as a result of what the other squire had told him of the Knight of the Wood's prowess, he was led to fear for his master's safety. Nevertheless, he and his friend now went to seek the mounts without saying a word, and they found the animals all together, for by this time the two horses and the ass had smelled one another out. On the way the Squire of the Wood turned to Sancho and addressed him as follows:

"I must inform you, brother, that it is the custom of the fighters of Andalusia, when they are godfathers in any combat, not to remain idly by, with folded hands, while their godsons fight it out. I tell you this by way of warning you that while our masters are settling matters, we, too, shall have to come to blows and hack each other to bits."

"The custom, Sir Squire," replied Sancho, "may be all very well among the fighters and ruffians that you mention, but with the squires of knights-errant it is not to be thought of. At least, I have never heard my master speak of any such custom, and he knows all the laws of chivalry by heart. But granting that it is true and that there is a law which states in so many words that squires must fight while their masters do, I have no intention of obeying it but rather will pay whatever penalty is laid on peaceable-minded ones like myself, for I am sure it cannot be more than a couple of pounds of wax,[6] and that would be less expensive than the lint which it would take to heal my head—I can already see it split in two. What's more, it's out of the question for me to fight since I have no sword nor did I ever in my life carry one."

"That," said the one of the Wood, "is something that is easily

---

6. In some confraternities, penalties were paid in wax, presumably to make church candles.

remedied. I have here two linen bags of the same size. You take one and I'll take the other and we will fight that way, on equal terms."

"So be it, by all means," said Sancho, "for that will simply knock the dust out of us without wounding us."

"But that's not the way it's to be," said the other squire. "Inside the bags, to keep the wind from blowing them away, we will put a half-dozen nice smooth pebbles of the same weight, and so we'll be able to give each other a good pounding without doing ourselves any real harm or damage."

"Body of my father!" cried Sancho, "just look, will you, at the marten and sable and wads of carded cotton that he's stuffing into those bags so that we won't get our heads cracked or our bones crushed to a pulp. But I am telling you, *Señor mio*, that even though you fill them with silken pellets, I don't mean to fight. Let our masters fight and make the best of it, but as for us, let us drink and live; for time will see to ending our lives without any help on our part by way of bringing them to a close before they have reached their proper season and fall from ripeness."

"Nevertheless," replied the Squire of the Wood, "fight we must, if only for half an hour."

"No," Sancho insisted, "that I will not do. I will not be so impolite or so ungrateful as to pick any quarrel however slight with one whose food and drink I've shared. And, moreover, who in the devil could bring himself to fight in cold blood, when he's not angry or vexed in any way?"

"I can take care of that, right enough," said the one of the Wood. "Before we begin, I will come up to your Grace as nicely as you please and give you three or four punches that will stretch you out at my feet; and that will surely be enough to awaken your anger, even though it's sleeping sounder than a dormouse."

"And I," said Sancho, "have another idea that's every bit as good as yours. I will take a big club, and before your Grace has had a chance to awaken my anger I will put yours to sleep with such mighty whacks that if it wakes at all it will be in the other world; for it is known there that I am not the man to let my face be mussed by anyone, and let each look out for the arrow.[7] But the best thing to do would be to leave one's anger to its slumbers, for no one knows the heart of any other, he who comes for wool may go back shorn, and God bless peace and curse all strife. If a hunted cat when surrounded and cornered turns into a lion, God knows what I who am a man might not become. And so from this time forth I am warning you, Sir Squire, that all the harm and damage that may result from our quarrel will be upon your head."

7. A proverbial expression from archery: let each one take care of his own arrow. Other obviously proverbial expressions follow, as is typical of Sancho's speech.

"Very well," the one of the Wood replied, "God will send the dawn and we shall make out somehow."

At that moment gay-colored birds of all sorts began warbling in the trees and with their merry and varied songs appeared to be greeting and welcoming the fresh-dawning day, which already at the gates and on the balconies of the east was revealing its beautiful face as it shook out from its hair an infinite number of liquid pearls. Bathed in this gentle moisture, the grass seemed to shed a pearly spray, the willows distilled a savory manna, the fountains laughed, the brooks murmured, the woods were glad, and the meadows put on their finest raiment. The first thing that Sancho Panza beheld, as soon as it was light enough to tell one object from another, was the Squire of the Wood's nose, which was so big as to cast into the shade all the rest of his body. In addition to being of enormous size, it is said to have been hooked in the middle and all covered with warts of a mulberry hue, like eggplant; it hung down for a couple of inches below his mouth, and the size, color, warts, and shape of this organ gave his face so ugly an appearance that Sancho began trembling hand and foot like a child with convulsions and made up his mind then and there that he would take a couple of hundred punches before he would let his anger be awakened to a point where he would fight with this monster.

Don Quixote in the meanwhile was surveying his opponent, who had already adjusted and closed his helmet so that it was impossible to make out what he looked like. It was apparent, however, that he was not very tall and was stockily built. Over his armor he wore a coat of some kind or other made of what appeared to be the finest cloth of gold, all bespangled with glittering mirrors that resembled little moons and that gave him a most gallant and festive air, while above his helmet were a large number of waving plumes, green, white, and yellow in color. His lance, which was leaning against a tree, was very long and stout and had a steel point of more than a palm in length. Don Quixote took all this in, and from what he observed concluded that his opponent must be of tremendous strength, but he was not for this reason filled with fear as Sancho Panza was. Rather, he proceeded to address the Knight of the Mirrors,[8] quite boldly and in a highbred manner.

"Sir Knight," he said, "if in your eagerness to fight you have not lost your courtesy, I would beg you to be so good as to raise your visor a little in order that I may see if your face is as handsome as your trappings."

"Whether you come out of this emprise the victor or the vanquished, Sir Knight," he of the Mirrors replied, "there will be ample

8. See note 1, page 1773.

time and opportunity for you to have a sight of me. If I do not now gratify your desire, it is because it seems to me that I should be doing a very great wrong to the beauteous Casildea de Vandalia by wasting the time it would take me to raise my visor before having forced you to confess that I am right in my contention, with which you are well acquainted."

"Well, then," said Don Quixote, "while we are mounting our steeds you might at least inform me if I am that knight of La Mancha whom you say you conquered."

"To that our[9] answer," said he of the Mirrors, "is that you are as like the knight I overcame as one egg is like another; but since you assert that you are persecuted by enchanters, I should not venture to state positively that you are the one in question."

"All of which," said Don Quixote, "is sufficient to convince me that you are laboring under a misapprehension; but in order to relieve you of it once and for all, let them bring our steeds, and in less time than you would spend in lifting your visor, if God, my lady, and my arm give me strength, I will see your face and you shall see that I am not the vanquished knight you take me to be."

With this, they cut short their conversation and mounted, and, turning Rocinante around, Don Quixote began measuring off the proper length of field for a run against his opponent as he of the Mirrors did the same. But the Knight of La Mancha had not gone twenty paces when he heard his adversary calling to him, whereupon each of them turned halfway and he of the Mirrors spoke.

"I must remind you, Sir Knight," he said, "of the condition under which we fight, which is that the vanquished, as I have said before, shall place himself wholly at the disposition of the victor."

"I am aware of that," replied Don Quixote, "not forgetting the provision that the behest laid upon the vanquished shall not exceed the bounds of chivalry."

"Agreed," said the Knight of the Mirrors.

At that moment Don Quixote caught sight of the other squire's weird nose and was as greatly astonished by it as Sancho had been. Indeed, he took the fellow for some monster, or some new kind of human being wholly unlike those that people this world. As he saw his master riding away down the field preparatory to the tilt, Sancho was alarmed; for he did not like to be left alone with the big-nosed individual, fearing that one powerful swipe of that protuberance against his own nose would end the battle so far as he was concerned and he would be lying stretched out on the ground, from fear if not from the force of the blow.

He accordingly ran after the knight, clinging to one of Rocinante's

---

9. Note the dignified, "majestic" plural form.

stirrup straps, and when he thought it was time for Don Quixote to whirl about and bear down upon his opponent, he called to him and said, "*Señor mio*, I beg your Grace, before you turn for the charge, to help me up into that cork tree yonder where I can watch the encounter which your Grace is going to have with this knight better than I can from the ground and in a way that is much more to my liking."

"I rather think, Sancho," said Don Quixote, "that what you wish to do is to mount a platform where you can see the bulls without any danger to yourself."

"The truth of the matter is," Sancho admitted, "the monstrous nose on that squire has given me such a fright that I don't dare stay near him."

"It is indeed of such a sort," his master assured him, "that if I were not the person I am, I myself should be frightened. And so, come, I will help you up."

While Don Quixote tarried to see Sancho ensconced in the cork tree, the Knight of the Mirrors measured as much ground as seemed to him necessary and then, assuming that his adversary had done the same, without waiting for sound of trumpet or any other signal, he wheeled his horse, which was no swifter nor any more impressive-looking than Rocinante, and bore down upon his enemy at a mild trot; but when he saw that the Manchegan was busy helping his squire, he reined in his mount and came to a stop midway in his course, for which his horse was extremely grateful, being no longer able to stir a single step. To Don Quixote, on the other hand, it seemed as if his enemy was flying, and digging his spurs with all his might into Rocinante's lean flanks he caused that animal to run a bit for the first and only time, according to the history, for on all other occasions a simple trot had represented his utmost speed. And so it was that, with an unheard-of-fury, the Knight of the Mournful Countenance came down upon the Knight of the Mirrors as the latter sat there sinking his spurs all the way up to the buttons without being able to persuade his horse to budge a single inch from the spot where he had come to a sudden standstill.

It was at this fortunate moment, while his adversary was in such a predicament, that Don Quixote fell upon him, quite unmindful of the fact that the other knight was having trouble with his mount and either was unable or did not have time to put his lance at rest. The upshot of it was, he encountered him with such force that, much against his will, the Knight of the Mirrors went rolling over his horse's flanks and tumbled to the ground, where as a result of his terrific fall he lay as if dead, without moving hand or foot.

No sooner did Sancho perceive what had happened than he slipped down from the cork tree and ran up as fast as he could to where his master was. Dismounting from Rocinante, Don Quixote now stood over the Knight of the Mirrors, and undoing the helmet straps to see if the man was dead, or to give him air in case he was alive, he beheld—who can say what he beheld without creating astonishment, wonder, and amazement in those who hear the tale? The history tells us that it was the very countenance, form, aspect, physiognomy, effigy, and image of the bachelor Sansón Carrasco!

"Come, Sancho," he cried in a loud voice, "and see what is to be seen but is not to be believed. Hasten, my son, and learn what magic can do and how great is the power of wizards and enchanters."

Sancho came, and the moment his eyes fell on the bachelor Carrasco's face he began crossing and blessing himself a countless number of times. Meanwhile, the overthrown knight gave no signs of life.

"If you ask me, master," said Sancho, "I would say that the best thing for your Grace to do is to run his sword down the mouth of this one who appears to be the bachelor Carrasco; maybe by so doing you would be killing one of your enemies, the enchanters."

"That is not a bad idea," replied Don Quixote, "for the fewer enemies the better." And, drawing his sword, he was about to act upon Sancho's advice and counsel when the Knight of the Mirrors' squire came up to them, now minus the nose which had made him so ugly.

"Look well what you are doing, Don Quixote!" he cried. "The one who lies there at your feet is your Grace's friend, the bachelor Sansón Carrasco, and I am his squire."

"And where is your nose?" inquired Sancho, who was surprised to see him without that deformity.

"Here in my pocket," was the reply. And, thrusting his hand into his coat, he drew out a nose of varnished pasteboard of the make that has been described. Studying him more and more closely, Sancho finally exclaimed, in a voice that was filled with amazement, "Holy Mary preserve me! And is this not my neighbor and crony, Tomé Cecial?"

"That is who I am!" replied the de-nosed squire, "your good friend Tomé Cecial, Sancho Panza. I will tell you presently of the means and snares and falsehoods that brought me here. But, for the present, I beg and entreat your master not to lay hands on, mistreat, wound, or slay the Knight of the Mirrors whom he now has at his feet; for without any doubt it is the rash and ill-advised bachelor Sansón Carrasco, our fellow villager."

The Knight of the Mirrors now recovered consciousness, and, seeing this, Don Quixote at once placed the naked point of his sword above the face of the vanquished one.

"Dead you are, knight," he said, "unless you confess that the peerless Dulcinea del Toboso is more beautiful than your Casildea de Vandalia. And what is more, you will have to promise that, should you survive this encounter and the fall you have had, you will go to the city of El Toboso and present yourself to her in my behalf, that she may do with you as she may see fit. And in case she leaves you free to follow your own will, you are to return to seek me out—the trail of my exploits will serve as a guide to bring you wherever I may be—and tell me all that has taken place between you and her. These conditions are in conformity with those that we arranged before our combat and they do not go beyond the bounds of knight-errantry."

"I confess," said the fallen knight, "that the tattered and filthy shoe of the lady Dulcinea del Toboso is of greater worth than the badly combed if clean beard of Casildea, and I promise to go to her presence and return to yours and to give you a complete and detailed account concerning anything you may wish to know."

"Another thing," added Don Quixote, "that you will have to confess and believe is that the knight you conquered was not and could not have been Don Quixote de la Mancha, but was some other that resembled him, just as I am convinced that you, though you appear to be the bachelor Sansón Carrasco, are another person in his form and likeness who has been put here by my enemies to induce me to restrain and moderate the impetuosity of my wrath and make a gentle use of my glorious victory."

"I confess, think, and feel as you feel, think, and believe," replied the lamed knight. "Permit me to rise, I beg of you, if the jolt I received in my fall will let me do so, for I am in very bad shape."

Don Quixote and Tomé Cecial the squire now helped him to his feet. As for Sancho, he could not take his eyes off Tomé but kept asking him one question after another, and although the answers he received afforded clear enough proof that the man was really his fellow townsman, the fear that had been aroused in him by his master's words—about the enchanters' having transformed the Knight of the Mirrors into the bachelor Sansón Carrasco—prevented him from believing the truth that was apparent to his eyes. The short of it is, both master and servant were left with this delusion as the other illerrant knight and his squire, in no pleasant state of mind, took their departure with the object of looking for some village where they might be able to apply poultices and splints to the bachelor's battered ribs.

Don Quixote and Sancho then resumed their journey along the road to Saragossa, and here for the time being the history leaves them in order to give an account of who the Knight of the Mirrors and his long-nosed squire really were.

*Wherein is told and revealed who the Knight of the Mirrors and his squire were.*

Don Quixote went off very happy, self-satisfied, and vainglorious at having achieved a victory over so valiant a knight as he imagined the one of the Mirrors to be, from whose knightly word he hoped to learn whether or not the spell which had been put upon his lady was still in effect; for, unless he chose to forfeit his honor, the vanquished contender must of necessity return and give an account of what had happened in the course of his interview with her. But Don Quixote was of one mind, the Knight of the Mirrors of another, for, as has been stated, the latter's only thought at the moment was to find some village where plasters were available.

The history goes on to state that when the bachelor Sansón Carrasco advised Don Quixote to resume his feats of chivalry, after having desisted from them for a while, this action was taken as the result of a conference which he had held with the curate and the barber as to the means to be adopted in persuading the knight to remain quietly at home and cease agitating himself over his unfortunate adventures. It had been Carrasco's suggestion, to which they had unanimously agreed, that they let Don Quixote sally forth, since it appeared to be impossible to prevent his doing so, and that Sansón should then take to the road as a knight-errant and pick a quarrel and do battle with him. There would be no difficulty about finding a pretext, and then the bachelor knight would overcome him (which was looked upon as easy of accomplishment), having first entered into a pact to the effect that the vanquished should remain at the mercy and bidding of his conqueror. The behest in this case was to be that the fallen one should return to his village and home and not leave it for the space of two years or until further orders were given him, it being a certainty that, once having been overcome, Don Quixote would fulfill the agreement, in order not to contravene or fail to obey the laws of chivalry. And it was possible that in the course of his seclusion he would forget his fancies, or they would at least have an opportunity to seek some suitable cure for his madness.

Sansón agreed to undertake this, and Tomé Cecial, Sancho's friend and neighbor, a merry but featherbrained chap, offered to go along as squire. Sansón then proceeded to arm himself in the manner that has been described, while Tomé disguised his nose with the aforementioned mask so that his crony would not recognize him when they met. Thus equipped, they followed the same route as Don Quixote and had almost caught up with him by the time he had the adventure with the Cart of Death. They finally overtook him in the wood, where those events occurred with which the attentive reader is already familiar; and if it had not been for the knight's extraordinary fancies, which led him to believe that the bachelor was not the bachelor, the said bachelor might have been prevented from ever attaining his degree of licentiate, as a result of having found no nests where he thought to find birds.

Seeing how ill they had succeeded in their undertaking and what an end they had reached, Tomé Cecial now addressed his master.

"Surely, Señor Sansón Carrasco," he said, "we have had our deserts. It is easy enough to plan and embark upon an enterprise, but most of the time it's hard to get out of it. Don Quixote is a madman and we are sane, yet he goes away sound and laughing while your Grace is left here, battered and sorrowful. I wish you would tell me now who is the crazier: the one who is so because he cannot help it, or he who turns crazy of his own free will?"

"The difference between the two," replied Sansón, "lies in this: that the one who cannot help being crazy will be so always, whereas the one who is a madman by choice can leave off being one whenever he so desires."

"Well," said Tomé Cecial, "since that is the way it is, and since I chose to be crazy when I became your Grace's squire, by the same reasoning I now choose to stop being insane and to return to my home."

"That is your affair," said Sansón, "but to imagine that I am going back before I have given Don Quixote a good thrashing is senseless; and what will urge me on now is not any desire to see him recover his wits, but rather a thirst for vengeance; for with the terrible pain that I have in my ribs, you can't expect me to feel very charitable."

Conversing in this manner they kept on until they reached a village where it was their luck to find a bonesetter to take care of poor Sansón. Tomé Cecial then left him and returned home, while the bachelor meditated plans for revenge. The history has more to say of him in due time, but for the present it goes on to make merry with Don Quixote.

## CHAPTER 16

*Of what happened to Don Quixote upon his meeting with a prudent gentleman of La Mancha.*

With that feeling of happiness and vainglorious self-satisfaction that has been mentioned, Don Quixote continued on his way, imagining himself to be, as a result of the victory he had just achieved, the most valiant knight-errant of the age. Whatever adventures might befall him from then on he regarded as already accomplished and brought to a fortunate conclusion. He thought little now of enchanters and enchantments and was unmindful of the innumerable beatings he

had received in the course of his knightly wanderings, of the volley
of pebbles that had knocked out half his teeth, of the ungratefulness
of the galley slaves and the audacity of the Yanguesans whose poles
had fallen upon his body like rain. In short, he told himself, if he
could but find the means, manner, or way of freeing his lady Dulcinea of the spell that had been put upon her, he would not envy
the greatest good fortune that the most fortunate of knights-errant in
ages past had ever by any possibility attained.

He was still wholly wrapped up in these thoughts when Sancho
spoke to him.

"Isn't it strange, sir, that I can still see in front of my eyes the huge
and monstrous nose of my old crony, Tomé Cecial?"

"And do you by any chance believe, Sancho, that the Knight of
the Mirrors was the bachelor Sansón Carrasco and that his squire
was your friend Tomé?"

"I don't know what to say to that," replied Sancho. "All I know is
that the things he told me about my home, my wife and young ones,
could not have come from anybody else; and the face, too, once you
took the nose away, was the same as Tomé Cecial's, which I have
seen many times in our village, right next door to my own house,
and the tone of voice was the same also."

"Let us reason the matter out, Sancho," said Don Quixote. "Look
at it this way: how can it be thought that the bachelor Sansón Carrasco would come as a knight-errant, equipped with offensive and
defensive armor, to contend with me? Am I, perchance, his enemy?
Have I given him any occasion to cherish a grudge against me? Am
I a rival of his? Or can it be jealousy of the fame I have acquired that
has led him to take up the profession of arms?"

"Well, then, sir," Sancho answered him, "how are we to explain
the fact that the knight was so like the bachelor and his squire like
my friend? And if this was a magic spell, as your Grace has said, was
there no other pair in the world whose likeness they might have
taken?"

"It is all a scheme and a plot," replied Don Quixote, "on the part
of those wicked magicians who are persecuting me and who, foreseeing that I would be the victor in the combat, saw to it that the conquered knight should display the face of my friend the bachelor, so
that the affection which I bear him would come between my fallen
enemy and the edge of my sword and might of my arm, to temper
the righteous indignation of my heart. In that way, he who had sought
by falsehood and deceits to take my life, would be left to go on living.
As proof of all this, Sancho, experience, which neither lies nor
deceives, has already taught you how easy it is for enchanters to
change one countenance into another, making the beautiful ugly
and the ugly beautiful. It was not two days ago that you beheld the

peerless Dulcinea's beauty and elegance in its entirety and natural form, while I saw only the repulsive features of a low and ignorant peasant girl with cataracts over her eyes and a foul smell in her mouth. And if the perverse enchanter was bold enough to effect so vile a transformation as this, there is certainly no cause for wonderment at what he has done in the case of Sansón Carrasco and your friend, all by way of snatching my glorious victory out of my hands. But in spite of it all, I find consolation in the fact that, whatever the shape he may have chosen to assume, I have laid my enemy low."

"God knows what the truth of it all may be," was Sancho's comment. Knowing as he did that Dulcinea's transformation had been due to his own scheming and plotting, he was not taken in by his master's delusions. He was at a loss for a reply, however, lest he say something that would reveal his own trickery.

As they were carrying on this conversation, they were overtaken by a man who, following the same road, was coming along behind them. He was mounted on a handsome flea-bitten mare and wore a hooded greatcoat of fine green cloth trimmed in tawny velvet and a cap of the same material, while the trappings of his steed, which was accoutered for the field, were green and mulberry in hue, his saddle being of the *jineta* mode.[1] From his broad green and gold shoulder strap there dangled a Moorish cutlass, and his half-boots were of the same make as the baldric. His spurs were not gilded but were covered with highly polished green lacquer, so that harmonizing as they did with the rest of his apparel, they seemed more appropriate than if they had been of purest gold. As he came up, he greeted the pair courteously and, spurring his mare, was about to ride on past when Don Quixote called to him.

"Gallant sir," he said, "If your Grace is going our way and is not in a hurry, it would be a favor to us if we might travel together."

"The truth is," replied the stranger, "I should not have ridden past you if I had not been afraid that the company of my mare would excite your horse."

"In that case, sir," Sancho spoke up, "you may as well rein in, for this horse of ours is the most virtuous and well mannered of any that there is. Never on such an occasion has he done anything that was not right—the only time he did misbehave, my master and I suffered for it aplenty. And so, I say again, your Grace may slow up if you like; for even if you offered him your mare on a couple of platters, he'd never try to mount her."

With this, the other traveler drew rein, being greatly astonished at Don Quixote's face and figure. For the knight was now riding along without his helmet, which was carried by Sancho like a piece of

1. A saddle with a high pummel and short stirrups.

luggage on the back of his gray, in front of the packsaddle. If the green-clad gentleman stared hard at his new-found companion, the latter returned his gaze with an even greater intensity. He impressed Don Quixote as being a man of good judgment, around fifty years of age, with hair that was slightly graying and an aquiline nose, while the expression of his countenance was half humorous, half serious. In short, both his person and his accouterments indicated that he was an individual of some worth.

As for the man in green's impression of Don Quixote de la Mancha, he was thinking that he had never before seen any human being that resembled this one. He could not but marvel at the knight's long neck, his tall frame, and the leanness and the sallowness of his face, as well as his armor and his grave bearing, the whole constituting a sight such as had not been seen for many a day in those parts. Don Quixote in turn was quite conscious of the attentiveness with which the traveler was studying him and could tell from the man's astonished look how curious he was; and so, being very courteous and fond of pleasing everyone, he proceeded to anticipate any questions that might be asked him.

"I am aware," he said, "that my appearance must strike your Grace as being very strange and out of the ordinary, and for that reason I am not surprised at your wonderment. But your Grace will cease to wonder when I tell you, as I am telling you now, that I am a knight, one of those

> Of whom it is folks say,
> They to adventures go.

I have left my native heath, mortgaged my estate, given up my comfortable life, and cast myself into fortune's arms for her to do with me what she will. It has been my desire to revive a knight-errantry that is now dead, and for some time past, stumbling here and falling there, now throwing myself down headlong and then rising up once more, I have been able in good part to carry out my design by succoring widows, protecting damsels, and aiding the fallen, the orphans, and the young, all of which is the proper and natural duty of knights-errant. As a result, owing to my many valiant and Christian exploits, I have been deemed worthy of visiting in printed form nearly all the nations of the world. Thirty thousand copies of my history have been published, and, unless Heaven forbid, they will print thirty million of them.

"In short, to put it all into a few words, or even one, I will tell you that I am Don Quixote de la Mancha, otherwise known as the Knight of the Mournful Countenance. Granted that self-praise is degrading, there still are times when I must praise myself, that is to say, when there is no one else present to speak in my behalf. And so, good sir, neither this steed nor this lance nor this buckler nor this squire of mine, nor all the armor that I wear and arms I carry, nor the sallowness of my complexion, nor my leanness and gauntness, should any longer astonish you, now that you know who I am and what the profession is that I follow."

Having thus spoken, Don Quixote fell silent, and the man in green was so slow in replying that it seemed as if he was at a loss for words. Finally, however, after a considerable while, he brought himself to the point of speaking.

"You were correct, Sir Knight," he said, "about my astonishment and my curiosity, but you have not succeeded in removing the wonderment that the sight of you has aroused in me. You say that, knowing who you are, I should not wonder any more, but such is not the case, for I am now more amazed than ever. How can it be that there are knights-errant in the world today and that histories of them are actually printed? I find it hard to convince myself that at the present time there is anyone on earth who goes about aiding widows, protecting damsels, defending the honor of wives, and succoring orphans, and I should never have believed it had I not beheld your Grace with my own eyes. Thank Heaven for that book that your Grace tells me has been published concerning your true and exalted deeds of chivalry, as it should cast into oblivion all the innumerable stories of fictitious knights-errant with which the world is filled, greatly to the detriment of good morals and the prejudice and discredit of legitimate histories."

"As to whether the stories of knights-errant are fictitious or not," observed Don Quixote, "there is much that remains to be said."

"Why," replied the gentleman in green, "is there anyone who can doubt that such tales are false?"

"I doubt it," was the knight's answer, "but let the matter rest there. If our journey lasts long enough, I trust with God's help to be able to show your Grace that you are wrong in going along with those who hold it to be a certainty that they are not true."

From this last remark the traveler was led to suspect that Don Quixote must be some kind of crackbrain, and he was waiting for him to confirm the impression by further observations of the same sort; but before they could get off on another subject, the knight, seeing that he had given an account of his own station in life, turned to the stranger and politely inquired who his companion might be.

"I, Sir Knight of the Mournful Countenance," replied the one in the green-colored greatcoat, "am a gentleman, and a native of the village where, please God, we are going to dine today. I am more than moderately rich, and my name is Don Diego de Miranda. I spend my life with my wife and children and with my friends. My occupations are hunting and fishing, though I keep neither falcon nor hounds but only a tame partridge[2] and a bold ferret or two. I am the owner of about six dozen books, some of them in Spanish, others in Latin, including both histories and devotional works. As for books of chivalry, they have not as yet crossed the threshold of my door. My own preference is for profane rather than devotional writings, such as afford an innocent amusement, charming us by their style and arousing and holding our interest by their inventiveness, although I must say there are very few of that sort to be found in Spain.

"Sometimes," the man in green continued, "I dine with my friends and neighbors, and I often invite them to my house. My meals are wholesome and well prepared and there is always plenty to eat. I do not care for gossip, nor will I permit it in my presence. I am not lynx-eyed and do not pry into the lives and doings of others. I hear mass every day and share my substance with the poor, but make no parade of my good works lest hypocrisy and vainglory, those enemies that so imperceptibly take possession of the most modest heart, should find their way into mine. I try to make peace between those who are at strife. I am the devoted servant of Our Lady, and my trust is in the infinite mercy of God Our Savior."

Sancho had listened most attentively to the gentleman's account of his mode of life, and inasmuch as it seemed to him that this was a good and holy way to live and that the one who followed such a pattern ought to be able to work miracles, he now jumped down from his gray's back and, running over to seize the stranger's right stirrup, began kissing the feet of the man in green with a show of devotion that bordered on tears.

"Why are you doing that, brother?" the gentleman asked him. "What is the meaning of these kisses?"

"Let me kiss your feet," Sancho insisted, "for if I am not mistaken, your Grace is the first saint riding *jineta* fashion that I have seen in all the days of my life."

"I am not a saint," the gentleman assured him, "but a great sinner. It is you, brother, who are the saint; for you must be a good man, judging by the simplicity of heart that you show."

Sancho then went back to his packsaddle, having evoked a laugh from the depths of his master's melancholy and given Don Diego fresh cause for astonishment.

Don Quixote thereupon inquired of the newcomer how many children he had, remarking as he did so that the ancient philosophers, who were without a true knowledge of God, believed that mankind's greatest good lay in the gifts of nature, in those of fortune, and in having many friends and many and worthy sons.

2. Used as a decoy.

"I, Señor Don Quixote," replied the gentleman, "have a son without whom I should, perhaps, be happier than I am. It is not that he is bad, but rather that he is not as good as I should like him to be. He is eighteen years old, and for six of those years he has been at Salamanca studying the Greek and Latin languages. When I desired him to pass on to other branches of learning, I found him so immersed in the science of Poetry (if it can be called such) that it was not possible to interest him in the Law, which I wanted him to study, nor in Theology, the queen of them all. My wish was that he might be an honor to his family; for in this age in which we are living our monarchs are in the habit of highly rewarding those forms of learning that are good and virtuous, since learning without virtue is like pearls on a dunghill. But he spends the whole day trying to decide whether such and such a verse of Homer's *Iliad* is well conceived or not, whether or not Martial is immodest in a certain epigram, whether certain lines of Vergil are to be understood in this way or in that. In short, he spends all of his time with the books written by those poets whom I have mentioned and with those of Horace, Persius, Juvenal, and Tibullus. As for our own moderns, he sets little store by them, and yet, for all his disdain of Spanish poetry, he is at this moment racking his brains in an effort to compose a gloss on a quatrian that was sent him from Salamanca and which, I fancy, is for some literary tournament."

To all this Don Quixote made the following answer:

"Children, sir, are out of their parents' bowels and so are to be loved whether they be good or bad, just as we love those that gave us life. It is for parents to bring up their offspring, from the time they are infants, in the paths of virtue, good breeding, proper conduct, and Christian morality, in order that, when they are grown, they may be a staff to the old age of the ones that bore them and an honor to their own posterity. As to compelling them to study a particular branch of learning, I am not so sure as to that, though there may be no harm in trying to persuade them to do so. But where there is no need to study *pane lucrando*[3]—where Heaven has provided them with parents that can supply their daily bread—I should be in favor of permitting them to follow that course to which they are most inclined; and although poetry may be more pleasurable than useful, it is not one of those pursuits that bring dishonor upon those who engage in them.

"Poetry in my opinion, my dear sir," he went on, "is a young and tender maid of surpassing beauty, who has many other damsels (that is to say, the other disciplines) whose duty it is to bedeck, embellish, and adorn her. She may call upon all of them for service, and all of

---

3. Earning one's bread.

them in turn depend upon her nod. She is not one to be rudely handled, nor dragged through the streets, nor exposed at street corners, in the market place, or in the private nooks of palaces. She is fashioned through an alchemy of such power that he who knows how to make use of it will be able to convert her into the purest gold of inestimable price. Possessing her, he must keep her within bounds and not permit her to run wild in bawdy satires or soulless sonnets. She is not to be put up for sale in any manner, unless it be in the form of heroic poems, pity-inspiring tragedies, or pleasing and ingenious comedies. Let mountebanks keep hands off her, and the ignorant mob as well, which is incapable of recognizing or appreciating the treasures that are locked within her. And do not think, sir, that I apply that term 'mob' solely to plebeians and those of low estate; for anyone who is ignorant, whether he be lord or prince, may, and should, be included in the vulgar herd.

"But," Don Quixote continued, "he who possesses the gift of poetry and who makes the use of it that I have indicated, shall become famous and his name shall be honored among all the civilized nations of the world. You have stated, sir, that your son does not greatly care for poetry written in our Spanish tongue, and in that I am inclined to think he is somewhat mistaken. My reason for saying so is this: the great Homer did not write in Latin, for the reason that he was a Greek, and Vergil did not write in Greek since he was a Latin. In a word, all the poets of antiquity wrote in the language which they had imbibed with their mother's milk and did not go searching after foreign ones to express their loftiest conceptions. This being so, it would be well if the same custom were to be adopted by all nations, the German poet being no longer looked down upon because he writes in German, nor the Castilian or the Basque for employing his native speech.

"As for your son, I fancy, sir, that his quarrel is not so much with Spanish poetry as with those poets who have no other tongue or discipline at their command such as would help to awaken their natural gift; and yet, here, too, he may be wrong. There is an opinion, and a true one, to the effect that 'the poet is born,' that is to say, it is as a poet that he comes forth from his mother's womb, and with the propensity that has been bestowed upon him by Heaven, without study or artifice, he produces those compositions that attest the truth of the line: '*Est deus in nobis*,' etc.[4] I further maintain that the born poet who is aided by art will have a great advantage over the one who by art alone would become a poet, the reason being that art does not go beyond, but merely perfects, nature; and so it is

---

4. "There is a god in us." (Ovid, *Fasti*, VI, 5.)

that, by combining nature with art and art with nature, the finished poet is produced.

"In conclusion, then, my dear sir, my advice to you would be to let your son go where his star beckons him; for being a good student as he must be, and having already successfully mounted the first step on the stairway of learning, which is that of languages, he will be able to continue of his own accord to the very peak of humane letters, an accomplishment that is altogether becoming in a gentleman, one that adorns, honors, and distinguishes him as much as the miter does the bishop or his flowing robe the learned jurisconsult. Your Grace well may reprove your son, should he compose satires that reflect upon the honor of other persons; in that case, punish him and tear them up. But should he compose discourses in the manner of Horace, in which he reprehends vice in general as that poet so elegantly does, then praise him by all means; for it is permitted the poet to write verses in which he inveighs against envy and the other vices as well, and to lash out at the vicious without, however, designating any particular individual. On the other hand, there are poets who for the sake of uttering something malicious would run the risk of being banished to the shores of Pontus.[5]

"If the poet be chaste where his own manners are concerned, he would likewise be modest in his verses, for the pen is the tongue of the mind, and whatever thoughts are engendered there are bound to appear in his writings. When kings and princes behold the marvelous art of poetry as practiced by prudent, virtuous, and serious-minded subjects of their realm, they honor, esteem, and reward those persons and crown them with the leaves of the tree that is never struck by lightning[6]—as if to show that those who are crowned and adorned with such wreaths are not to be assailed by anyone."

The gentleman in the green-colored greatcoat was vastly astonished by this speech of Don Quixote's and was rapidly altering the opinion he had previously held, to the effect that his companion was but a crackbrain. In the middle of the long discourse, which was not greatly to his liking, Sancho had left the highway to go seek a little milk from some shepherds who were draining the udders of their ewes near by. Extremely well pleased with the knight's sound sense and excellent reasoning, the gentleman was about to resume the conversation when, raising his head, Don Quixote caught sight of a cart flying royal flags that was coming toward them down the road and, thinking it must be a fresh adventure, began calling to Sancho in a loud voice to bring him his helmet. Whereupon Sancho hastily left the shepherds and spurred his gray until he was once more along-

---

5. As Ovid was by Augustus in A.D. 8.     6. The laurel tree.

side his master, who was now about to encounter a dreadful and
bewildering ordeal.

["*For I Well Know the Meaning of Valor*"]

### CHAPTER 17

*Wherein Don Quixote's unimaginable courage reaches its highest
point, together with the adventure of the lions and its happy
ending.*

The history relates that, when Don Quixote called to Sancho to
bring him his helmet, the squire was busy buying some curds from
the shepherds and, flustered by his master's great haste, did not know
what to do with them or how to carry them. Having already paid for
the curds, he did not care to lose them, and so he decided to put
them into the headpiece, and, acting upon this happy inspiration,
he returned to see what was wanted of him.

"Give me that helmet," said the knight; "for either I know little
about adventures or here is one where I am going to need my armor."

Upon hearing this, the gentleman in the green-colored greatcoat
looked around in all directions but could see nothing except the cart
that was approaching them, decked out with two or three flags which
indicated that the vehicle in question must be conveying his Majesty's property. He remarked as much to Don Quixote, but the latter
paid no attention, for he was always convinced that whatever happened to him meant adventures and more adventures.

"Forewarned is forearmed," he said. "I lose nothing by being prepared, knowing as I do that I have enemies both visible and invisible
and cannot tell when or where or in what form they will attack me."

Turning to Sancho, he asked for his helmet again, and as there
was no time to shake out the curds, the squire had to hand it to him
as it was. Don Quixote took it and, without noticing what was in it,
hastily clapped it on his head; and forthwith, as a result of the pressure on the curds, the whey began running down all over his face
and beard, at which he was very much startled.

"What is this, Sancho?" he cried. "I think my head must be softening or my brains melting, or else I am sweating from head to foot.
If sweat it be, I assure you it is not from fear, though I can well
believe that the adventure which now awaits me is a terrible one
indeed. Give me something with which to wipe my face, if you have
anything, for this perspiration is so abundant that it blinds me."

Sancho said nothing but gave him a cloth and at the same time
gave thanks to God that his master had not discovered what the trouble was. Don Quixote wiped his face and then took off his helmet to
see what it was that made his head feel so cool. Catching sight of

of that watery white mass, he lifted it to his nose and smelled it.

"By the life of my lady Dulcinea del Toboso!" he exclaimed. "Those are curds that you have put there, you treacherous, brazen, ill-mannered squire!"

To this Sancho replied, very calmly and with a straight face, "If they are curds, give them to me, your Grace, so that I can eat them. But no, let the devil eat them, for he must be the one who did it. Do you think I would be so bold as to soil your Grace's helmet? Upon my word, master, by the understanding that God has given me, I, too, must have enchanters who are persecuting me as your Grace's creature and one of his members, and they are the ones who put that filthy mess there to make you lose your patience and your temper and cause you to whack my ribs as you are in the habit of doing. Well, this time, I must say, they have missed the mark; for I trust my master's good sense to tell him that I have neither curds nor milk nor anything of the kind, and if I did have, I'd put it in my stomach and not in that helmet."

"That may very well be," said Don Quixote.

Don Diego was observing all this and was more astonished than ever, especially when, after he had wiped his head, face, beard, and helmet, Don Quixote once more donned the piece of armor and, settling himself in the stirrups, proceeded to adjust his sword and fix his lance.

"Come what may, here I stand, ready to take on Satan himself in person!" shouted the knight.

The cart with the flags had come up to them by this time, accompanied only by a driver riding one of the mules and a man seated up in front.

"Where are you going, brothers?" Don Quixote called out as he placed himself in the path of the cart. "What conveyance is this, what do you carry in it, and what is the meaning of those flags?"

"The cart is mine," replied the driver, "and in it are two fierce lions in cages which the governor of Oran is sending to court as a present for his Majesty. The flags are those of our lord the King, as a sign that his property goes here."

"And are the lions large?" inquired Don Quixote.

It was the man sitting at the door of the cage who answered him. "The largest," he said, "that ever were sent from Africa to Spain. I am the lionkeeper and I have brought back others, but never any like these. They are male and female. The male is in this first cage, the female in the one behind. They are hungry right now, for they have had nothing to eat today; and so we'd be obliged if your Grace would get out of the way, for we must hasten on to the place where we are to feed them."

"Lion whelps against me?" said Don Quixote with a slight smile.

"Lion whelps against me? And at such an hour? Then, by God, those gentlemen who sent them shall see whether I am the man to be frightened by lions. Get down, my good fellow, and since you are the lionkeeper, open the cages and turn those beasts out for me; and in the middle of this plain I will teach them who Don Quixote de la Mancha is, notwithstanding and in spite of the enchanters who are responsible for their being here."

"So," said the gentleman to himself as he heard this, "our worthy knight has revealed himself. It must indeed be true that the curds have softened his skull and mellowed his brains."

At this point Sancho approached him. "For God's sake, sir," he said, "do something to keep my master from fighting those lions. For if he does, they're going to tear us all to bits."

"Is your master, then, so insane," the gentleman asked, "that you fear and believe he means to tackle those fierce animals?"

"It is not that he is insane," replied Sancho, "but, rather, fool-hardy."

"Very well," said the gentleman, "I will put a stop to it." And going up to Don Quixote, who was still urging the lionkeeper to open the cages, he said, "Sir Knight, knights-errant should undertake only those adventures that afford some hope of a successful outcome, not those that are utterly hopeless to begin with; for valor when it turns to temerity has in it more of madness than of bravery. Moreover, these lions have no thought of attacking your Grace but are a present to his Majesty, and it would not be well to detain them or interfere with their journey."

"My dear sir," answered Don Quixote, "you had best go mind your tame partridge and that bold ferret of yours and let each one attend to his own business. This is my affair, and I know whether these gentlemen, the lions, have come to attack me or not." He then turned to the lionkeeper. "I swear, Sir Rascal, if you do not open those cages at once, I'll pin you to the cart with this lance!"

Perceiving how determined the armed phantom was, the driver now spoke up. "Good sir," he said, "will your Grace please be so kind as to let me unhitch the mules and take them to a safe place before you turn those lions loose? For if they kill them for me, I am ruined for life, since the mules and cart are all the property I own."

"O man of little faith!" said Don Quixote. "Get down and unhitch your mules if you like, but you will soon see that it was quite unnecessary and that you might have spared yourself the trouble."

The driver did so, in great haste, as the lionkeeper began shouting, "I want you all to witness that I am being compelled against my will to open the cages and turn the lions out, and I further warn this gentleman that he will be responsible for all the harm and damage the beasts may do, plus my wages and my fees. You other gentlemen take cover before I open the doors; I am sure they will not do any harm to me."

Once more Don Diego sought to persuade his companion not to commit such an act of madness, as it was tempting God to undertake anything so foolish as that; but Don Quixote's only answer was that he knew what he was doing. And when the gentleman in green insisted that he was sure the knight was laboring under a delusion and ought to consider the matter well, the latter cut him short.

"Well, then, sir," he said, "if your Grace does not care to be a spectator at what you believe is going to turn out to be a tragedy, all you have to do is to spur your flea-bitten mare and seek safety."

Hearing this, Sancho with tears in his eyes again begged him to give up the undertaking, in comparison with which the adventure of the windmills and the dreadful one at the fulling mills—indeed, all the exploits his master had ever in the course of his life undertaken— were but bread and cakes.

"Look, sir," Sancho went on, "there is no enchantment here nor anything of the sort. Through the bars and chinks of that cage I have seen a real lion's claw, and judging by the size of it, the lion that it belongs to is bigger than a mountain."

"Fear, at any rate," said Don Quixote, "will make him look bigger to you than half the world. Retire, Sancho, and leave me, and if I die here, you know our ancient pact: you are to repair to Dulcinea— I say no more."

To this he added other remarks that took away any hope they had that he might not go through with his insane plan. The gentleman in the green-colored greatcoat was of a mind to resist him but saw that he was no match for the knight in the matter of arms. Then, too, it did not seem to him the part of wisdom to fight it out with a madman; for Don Quixote now impressed him as being quite mad in every way. Accordingly, while the knight was repeating his threats to the lionkeeper, Don Diego spurred his mare, Sancho his gray, and the driver his mules, all of them seeking to put as great a distance as possible between themselves and the cart before the lions broke loose.

Sancho already was bewailing his master's death, which he was convinced was bound to come from the lions' claws, and at the same time he cursed his fate and called it an unlucky hour in which he had taken it into his head to serve such a one. But despite his tears and lamentations, he did not leave off thrashing his gray in an effort to leave the cart behind them. When the lionkeeper saw that those who had fled were a good distance away, he once more entreated and warned Don Quixote as he had warned and entreated him before, but the answer he received was that he might save his breath as it would do him no good and he had best hurry and obey. In the space of time that it took the keeper to open the first cage, Don Quixote considered the question as to whether it would be well to give battle on foot or on horseback. He finally decided that he would do better on foot, as he feared that Rocinante would become frightened at sight of the lions; and so, leaping down from his horse, he fixed his lance, braced his buckler, and drew his sword, and then advanced with marvelous daring and great resoluteness until he stood directly in front of the cart, meanwhile commending himself to God with all his heart and then to his lady Dulcinea.

Upon reaching this point, the reader should know, the author of our veracious history indulges in the following exclamatory passage:

"O great-souled Don Quixote de la Mancha, thou whose courage is beyond all praise, mirror wherein all the valiant of the world may behold themselves, a new and second Don Manuel de León,[7] once the glory and the honor of Spanish knighthood! With what words shall I relate thy terrifying exploit, how render it credible to the ages that are to come? What eulogies do not belong to thee of right, even though they consist of hyperbole piled upon hyperbole? On foot and singlehanded, intrepid and with greathearted valor, armed but with a sword, and not one of the keen-edged Little Dog[8] make, and with a shield that was not of gleaming and polished steel, thou didst stand and wait for the two fiercest lions that ever the African forests bred! Thy deeds shall be thy praise, O valorous Manchegan; I leave them to speak for thee, since words fail me with which to extol them."

Here the author leaves off his exclamations and resumes the thread of the story.

Seeing Don Quixote posed there before him and perceiving that, unless he wished to incur the bold knight's indignation there was nothing for him to do but release the male lion, the keeper now opened the first cage, and it could be seen at once how extraordinarily big and horribly ugly the beast was. The first thing the recumbent animal did was to turn round, put out a claw, and stretch himself all over. Then he opened his mouth and yawned very slowly, after which he put out a tongue that was nearly two palms in length and with it licked the dust out of his eyes and washed his face. Having done this, he stuck his head outside the cage and gazed about him in all directions. His eyes were now like live coals and his appearance and demeanor were such as to strike terror in temerity itself. But Don Quixote merely stared at him attentively, waiting for him to descend from the cart so that they could come to grips, for the knight was determined to hack the brute to pieces, such was the extent of his unheard-of madness.

The lion, however, proved to be courteous rather than arrogant

7. Don Manuel Ponce de León, a paragon of gallantry and courtesy, belonging to the time of Ferdinand and Isabella.    8. The trademark of a famous armorer of Toledo and Saragossa.

and was in no mood for childish bravado. After having gazed first in one direction and then in another, as has been said, he turned his back and presented his hind parts to Don Quixote and then very calmly and peaceably lay down and stretched himself out once more in his cage. At this, Don Quixote ordered the keeper to stir him up with a stick in order to irritate him and drive him out.

"That I will not do," the keeper replied, "for if I stir him, I will be the first one he will tear to bits. Be satisfied with what you have already accomplished, Sir Knight, which leaves nothing more to be said on the score of valor, and do not go tempting your fortune a second time. The door was open and the lion could have gone out if he had chosen; since he has not done so up to now, that means he will stay where he is all day long. Your Grace's stoutheartedness has been well established; for no brave fighter, as I see it, is obliged to do more than challenge his enemy and wait for him in the field; his adversary, if he does not come, is the one who is disgraced and the one who awaits him gains the crown of victory."

"That is the truth," said Don Quixote. "Shut the door, my friend, and bear me witness as best you can with regard to what you have seen me do here. I would have you certify: that you opened the door for the lion, that I waited for him and he did not come out, that I continued to wait and still he stayed there, and finally went back and lay down. I am under no further obligation. Away with enchantments, and God uphold the right, the truth, and true chivalry! So close the door, as I have told you, while I signal to the fugitives in order that they who were not present may hear of this exploit from your lips."

The keeper did as he was commanded, and Don Quixote, taking the cloth with which he had dried his face after the rain of curds, fastened it to the point of his lance and began summoning the runaways, who, all in a body with the gentleman in green bringing up the rear, were still fleeing and turning around to look back at every step. Sancho was the first to see the white cloth.

"May they slay me," he said, "if my master hasn't conquered those fierce beasts, for he's calling to us."

They all stopped and made sure that the one who was doing the signaling was indeed Don Quixote, and then, losing some of their fear, they little by little made their way back to a point where they could distinctly hear what the knight was saying. At last they returned to the cart, and as they drew near Don Quixote spoke to the driver.

"You may come back, brother, hitch your mules, and continue your journey. And you, Sancho, may give each of them two gold crowns to recompense them for the delay they have suffered on my account."

"That I will, right enough," said Sancho. "But what has become of the lions? Are they dead or alive?"

The keeper thereupon, in leisurely fashion and in full detail, proceeded to tell them how the encounter had ended, taking pains to stress to the best of his ability the valor displayed by Don Quixote, at sight of whom the lion had been so cowed that he was unwilling to leave his cage, though the door had been left open quite a while. The fellow went on to state that the knight had wanted him to stir the lion up and force him out, but had finally been convinced that this would be tempting God and so, much to his displeasure and against his will, had permitted the door to be closed.

"What do you think of that, Sancho?" asked Don Quixote. "Are there any spells that can withstand true gallantry? The enchanters may take my luck away, but to deprive me of my strength and courage is an impossibility."

Sancho then bestowed the crowns, the driver hitched his mules, and the lionkeeper kissed Don Quixote's hands for the favor received, promising that, when he reached the court, he would relate this brave exploit to the king himself.

"In that case," replied Don Quixote, "if his Majesty by any chance should inquire who it was that performed it, you are to say that it was the Knight of the Lions; for that is the name by which I wish to be known from now on, thus changing, exchanging, altering, and converting the one I have previously borne, that of Knight of the Mournful Countenance; in which respect I am but following the old custom of knights-errant, who changed their names whenever they liked or found it convenient to do so."

With this, the cart continued on its way, and Don Quixote, Sancho, and the gentleman in the green-colored greatcoat likewise resumed their journey. During all this time Don Diego de Miranda had not uttered a word but was wholly taken up with observing what Don Quixote did and listening to what he had to say. The knight impressed him as being a crazy sane man and an insane one on the verge of sanity. The gentleman did not happen to be familiar with the first part of our history, but if he had read it he would have ceased to wonder at such talk and conduct, for he would then have known what kind of madness this was. Remaining as he did in ignorance of his companion's malady, he took him now for a sensible individual and now for a madman, since what Don Quixote said was coherent, elegantly phrased, and to the point, whereas his actions were nonsensical, foolhardy, and downright silly. What greater madness could there be, Don Diego asked himself, than to don a helmet filled with curds and then persuade oneself that enchanters were softening one's cranium? What could be more rashly absurd than to wish to fight lions by sheer strength alone? He was roused from these thoughts, this inward soliloquy, by the sound of Don Quixote's voice.

"Undoubtedly, Señor Don Diego de Miranda, your Grace must take me for a fool and a madman, am I not right? And it would be small wonder if such were the case, seeing that my deeds give evidence of nothing else. But, nevertheless, I would advise your Grace that I am neither so mad nor so lacking in wit as I must appear to you to be. A gaily caparisoned knight giving a fortunate lance thrust to a fierce bull in the middle of a great square makes a pleasing appearance in the eyes of his king. The same is true of a knight clad in shining armor as he paces the lists in front of the ladies in some joyous tournament. It is true of all those knights who, by means of military exercises or what appear to be such, divert and entertain and, if one may say so, honor the courts of princes. But the best showing of all is made by a knight-errant who, traversing deserts and solitudes, crossroads, forests, and mountains, goes seeking dangerous adventures with the intention of bringing them to a happy and successful conclusion, and solely for the purpose of winning a glorious and enduring renown.

"More impressive, I repeat, is the knight-errant succoring a widow in some unpopulated place than a courtly man of arms making love to a damsel in the city. All knights have their special callings: let the courtier wait upon the ladies and lend luster by his liveries to his sovereign's palace; let him nourish impoverished gentlemen with the splendid fare of his table; let him give tourneys and show himself truly great, generous, and magnificent and a good Christian above all, thus fulfilling his particular obligations. But the knight-errant's case is different.

"Let the latter seek out the nooks and corners of the world; let him enter into the most intricate of labyrinths; let him attempt the impossible at every step; let him endure on desolate highlands the burning rays of the midsummer sun and in winter the harsh inclemencies of wind and frost; let no lions inspire him with fear, no monsters frighten him, no dragons terrify him, for to seek them out, attack them, and conquer them all is his chief and legitimate occupation. Accordingly, I whose lot it is to be numbered among the knights-errant cannot fail to attempt anything that appears to me to fall within the scope of my duties, just as I attacked those lions a while ago even though I knew it to be an exceedingly rash thing to do, for that was a matter that directly concerned me.

"For I well know the meaning of valor: namely, a virtue that lies between the two extremes of cowardice on the one hand and temerity on the other. It is, nonethelss, better for the brave man to carry his bravery to the point of rashness than for him to sink into cowardice. Even as it is easier for the prodigal to become a generous man than it is for the miser, so is it easier for the foolhardy to become truly brave than it is for the coward to attain valor. And in this matter of adventures, you may believe me, Señor Don Diego, it is better to lose by a card too many than a card too few, and 'Such and such a knight is temerarious and overbold' sounds better to the ear than 'That knight is timid and a coward.' "

"I must assure you, Señor Don Quixote," replied Don Diego, "that everything your Grace has said and done will stand the test of reason; and it is my opinion that if the laws and ordinances of knight-errantry were to be lost, they would be found again in your Grace's bosom, which is their depository and storehouse. But it is growing late; let us hasten to my village and my home, where your Grace shall rest from your recent exertions; for if the body is not tired the spirit may be, and that sometimes results in bodily fatigue."

"I accept your offer as a great favor and an honor, Señor Don Diego," was the knight's reply. And, by spurring their mounts more than they had up to then, they arrived at the village around two in the afternoon and came to the house that was occupied by Don Diego, whom Don Quixote had dubbed the Knight of the Green-colored Greatcoat.

## [Last Duel]

### CHAPTER 64

*Which treats of the adventure that caused Don Quixote the most sorrow of all those that have thus far befallen him.*

. . . One morning, as Don Quixote went for a ride along the beach,[9] clad in full armor—for, as he was fond of saying, that was his only ornament, his only rest the fight, and, accordingly, he was never without it for a moment—he saw approaching him a horseman similarly arrayed from head to foot and with a brightly shining moon blazoned upon his shield.

As soon as he had come within earshot the stranger cried out to Don Quixote in a loud voice. "O illustrious knight, the never to be sufficiently praised Don Quixote de la Mancha, I am the Knight of the White Moon whose incomparable exploits you will perhaps recall. I come to contend with you and try the might of my arm, with the purpose of having you acknowledge and confess that my lady, whoever she may be, is beyond comparison more beautiful than your own Dulcinea del Toboso. If you will admit the truth of this fully and freely, you will escape death and I shall be spared the trouble of

9. Don Quixote and Sancho, after numberless encounters and experiences (of which the most prominent have been Don Quixote's descent into the cave of Montesinos, and the residence at the castle of the playful ducal couple who give Sancho the "governorship of an island" for ten days), are now in Barcelona. Famous as they are, they meet the viceroy and the nobles; their host is Don Antonio Moreno, "a gentleman of wealth and discernment who was fond of amusing himself in an innocent and kindly way."

inflicting it upon you. On the other hand, if you choose to fight and I should overcome you, I ask no other satisfaction than that, laying down your arms and seeking no further adventures, you retire to your own village for the space of a year, during which time you are not to lay hand to sword but are to dwell peacefully and tranquilly, enjoying a beneficial rest that shall redound to the betterment of your worldly fortunes and the salvation of your soul. But if you are the victor, then my head shall be at your disposal, my arms and steed shall be the spoils, and the fame of my exploits shall go to increase your own renown. Consider well which is the better course and let me have your answer at once, for today is all the time I have for the dispatching of this business."

Don Quixote was amazed at the knight's arrogance as well as at the nature of the challenge, but it was with a calm and stern demeanor that he replied to him.

"Knight of the White Moon," he said, "of whose exploits up to now I have never heard, I will venture to take an oath that you have not once laid eyes upon the illustrious Dulcinea; for I am quite certain that if you had beheld her you would not be staking your all upon such an issue, since the sight of her would have convinced you that there never has been, and never can be, any beauty to compare with hers. I do not say that you lie, I simply say that you are mistaken; and so I accept your challenge with the conditions you have laid down, and at once, before this day you have fixed upon shall have ended. The only exception I make is with regard to the fame of your deeds being added to my renown, since I do not know what the character of your exploits has been and am quite content with my own, such as they are. Take, then, whichever side of the field you like, and I will take up my position, and may St. Peter bless what God may give."

Now, as it happened, the Knight of the White Moon was seen by some of the townspeople, who informed the viceroy that he was there, talking to Don Quixote de la Mancha. Believing this to be a new adventure arranged by Don Antonio Moreno or some other gentleman of the place, the viceroy at once hastened down to the beach, accompanied by a large retinue, including Don Antonio, and they arrived just as Don Quixote was wheeling Rocinante to measure off the necessary stretch of field. When the viceroy perceived that they were about to engage in combat, he at once interposed and inquired of them what it was that impelled them thus to do battle all of a sudden.

The Knight of the White Moon replied that it was a matter of beauty and precedence and briefly repeated what he had said to Don Quixote, explaining the terms to which both parties had agreed. The viceroy then went up to Don Antonio and asked him if he knew any such knight as this or if it was some joke that they were playing, but the answer that he received left him more puzzled than ever; for Don Antonio did not know who the knight was, nor could he say as to whether this was a real encounter or not. The viceroy, accordingly, was doubtful about letting them proceed, but inasmuch as he could not bring himself to believe that it was anything more than a jest, he withdrew to one side, saying, "Sir Knights, if there is nothing for it but to confess or die, and if Señor Don Quixote's mind is made up and your Grace, the Knight of the White Moon, is even more firmly resolved, then fall to it in the name of God and may He bestow the victory."

The Knight of the White Moon thanked the viceroy most courteously and in well-chosen words for the permission which had been granted them, and Don Quixote did the same, whereupon the latter, commending himself with all his heart to Heaven and to his lady Dulcinea, as was his custom at the beginning of a fray, fell back a little farther down the field as he saw his adversary doing the same. And then, without blare of trumpet or other warlike instrument to give them the signal for the attack, both at the same instant wheeled their steeds about and returned for the charge. Being mounted upon the swifter horse, the Knight of the White Moon met Don Quixote two-thirds of the way and with such tremendous force that, without touching his opponent with his lance (which, it seemed, he deliberately held aloft) he brought both Rocinante and his rider to the ground in an exceedingly perilous fall. At once the victor leaped down and placed his lance at Don Quixote's visor.

"You are vanquished, O knight! Nay, more, you are dead unless you make confession in accordance with the conditions governing our encounter."

Stunned and battered, Don Quixote did not so much as raise his visor but in a faint, wan voice, as if speaking from the grave, he said, "Dulcinea del Toboso is the most beautiful woman in the world and I the most unhappy knight upon the face of this earth. It is not right that my weakness should serve to defraud the truth. Drive home your lance, O knight, and take my life since you already have deprived me of my honor."

"That I most certainly shall not do," said the one of the White Moon. "Let the fame of my lady Dulcinea del Toboso's beauty live on undiminished. As for me, I shall be content if the great Don Quixote will retire to his village for a year or until such a time as I may specify, as was agreed upon between us before joining battle."

The viceroy, Don Antonio, and all the many others who were present heard this, and they also heard Don Quixote's response, which was to the effect that, seeing nothing was asked of him that was prejudicial to Dulcinea, he would fulfill all the other conditions like

a true and punctilious knight. The one of the White Moon thereupon turned and with a bow to the viceroy rode back to the city at a
mild canter. The viceroy promptly dispatched Don Antonio to follow him and make every effort to find out who he was; and, in the
meanwhile, they lifted Don Quixote up and uncovered his face,
which held no sign of color and was bathed in perspiration. Rocinante, however, was in so sorry a state that he was unable to stir for
the present.

Brokenhearted over the turn that events had taken, Sancho did
not know what to say or do. It seemed to him that all this was something that was happening in a dream and that everything was the
result of magic. He saw his master surrender, heard him consent not
to take up arms again for a year to come as the light of his glorious
exploits faded into darkness. At the same time his own hopes, based
upon the fresh promises that had been made him, were whirled away
like smoke before the wind. He feared that Rocinante was maimed
for life, his master's bones permanently dislocated—it would have
been a bit of luck if his madness also had been jolted out of him.[1]

Finally, in a hand litter which the viceroy had them bring, they
bore the knight back to town. The viceroy himself then returned, for
he was very anxious to ascertain who the Knight of the White Moon
was who had left Don Quixote in so lamentable a condition.

CHAPTER 65

*Wherein is revealed who the Knight of the White Moon was.*

The Knight of the White Moon was followed not only by Don
Antonio Moreno, but by a throng of small boys as well, who kept
after him until the doors of one of the city's hostelries had closed
behind him. A squire came out to meet him and remove his armor,
for which purpose the victor proceeded to shut himself up in a lower
room, in the company of Don Antonio, who had also entered the
inn and whose bread would not bake until he had learned the knight's
identity. Perceiving that the gentleman had no intention of leaving
him, he of the White Moon then spoke.

"Sir," he said, "I am well aware that you have come to find out
who I am; and, seeing that there is no denying you the information
that you seek, while my servant here is removing my armor I will
tell you the exact truth of the matter. I would have you know, sir,
that I am the bachelor Sansón Carrasco from the same village as
Don Quixote de la Mancha, whose madness and absurdities inspire
pity in all of us who know him and in none more than me. And so,
being convinced that his salvation lay in his returning home for a

---

1. The original has an untranslatable pun on *deslocado*, which means "out of joint" ("dislocated")
and also "cured of madness" (from *loco*, "mad").

period of rest in his own house, I formed a plan for bringing him back.

"It was three months ago that I took to the road as a knight-errant, calling myself the Knight of the Mirrors, with the object of fighting and overcoming him without doing him any harm, intending first to lay down the condition that the vanquished was to yield to the victor's will. What I meant to ask of him—for I looked upon him as conquered from the start—was that he should return to his village and not leave it for a whole year, in the course of which time he might be cured. Fate, however, ordained things otherwise; for he was the one who conquered me and overthrew me from my horse, and thus my plan came to naught. He continued on his wanderings, and I went home, defeated, humiliated, and bruised from my fall, which was quite a dangerous one. But I did not for this reason give up the idea of hunting him up once more and vanquishing him as you have seen me do today.

"Since he is the soul of honor when it comes to observing the ordinances of knight-errantry, there is not the slightest doubt that he will keep the promise he has given me and fulfill his obligations. And that, sir, is all that I need to tell you concerning what has happened. I beg you not to disclose my secret or reveal my identity to Don Quixote, in order that my well-intentioned scheme may be carried out and a man of excellent judgment be brought back to his senses—for a sensible man he would be, once rid of the follies of chivalry."

"My dear sir," exclaimed Don Antonio, "may God forgive you for the wrong you have done the world by seeking to deprive it of its most charming madman! Do you not see that the benefit accomplished by restoring Don Quixote to his senses can never equal the pleasure which others derive from his vagaries? But it is my opinion that all the trouble to which the Señor Bachelor has put himself will not suffice to cure a man who is so hopelessly insane; and if it were not uncharitable, I would say let Don Quixote never be cured, since with his return to health we lose not only his own drolleries but also those of his squire, Sancho Panza, for either of the two is capable of turning melancholy itself into joy and merriment. Nevertheless, I will keep silent and tell him nothing, that I may see whether or not I am right in my suspicion that Señor Carrasco's efforts will prove to have been of no avail."

The bachelor replied that, all in all, things looked very favorable and he hoped for a fortunate outcome. With this, he took his leave of Don Antonio, after offering to render him any service that he could; and, having had his armor tied up and placed upon a mule's back, he rode out of the city that same day on the same horse on which he had gone into battle, returning to his native province without anything happening to him that is worthy of being set down in this veracious chronicle.

[Homecoming and Death]

CHAPTER 73

*Of the omens that Don Quixote encountered upon entering his village, with other incidents that embellish and lend credence to this great history.*

As they entered the village, Cid Hamete informs us, Don Quixote caught sight of two lads on the communal threshing floor who were engaged in a dispute.

"Don't let it worry you, Periquillo," one of them was saying to the other; "you'll never lay eyes on it again as long as you live."

Hearing this, Don Quixote turned to Sancho "Did you mark what that boy said, my friend?" he asked. " 'You'll never lay eyes on it[2] again . . .' "

"Well," replied Sancho, "what difference does it make what he said?"

"What difference?" said Don Quixote. "Don't you see that, applied to the one I love, it means I shall never again see Dulcinea."

Sancho was about to answer him when his attention was distracted by a hare that came flying across the fields pursued by a large number of hunters with their greyhounds. The frightened animal took refuge by huddling down beneath the donkey, whereupon Sancho reached out his hand and caught it and presented it to his master.

"*Malum signum, malum signum,*"[3] the knight was muttering to himself. "A hare flees, the hounds pursue it, Dulcinea appears not."

"It is very strange to hear your Grace talk like that," said Sancho. "Let us suppose that this hare *is* Dulcinea del Toboso and the hounds pursuing it are those wicked enchanters that transformed her into a peasant lass; she flees, I catch her and turn her over to your Grace, you hold her in your arms and caress her. Is that a bad sign? What ill omen can you find in it?"

The two lads who had been quarreling now came up to have a look at the hare, and Sancho asked them what their dispute was about. To this the one who had uttered the words "You'll never lay eyes on it again as long as you live," replied that he had taken a cricket cage from the other boy and had no intention of returning it ever. Sancho then brought out from his pocket four cuartos and gave

2. The same as "her" in the original, since the reference is to a cricket cage, denoted in Spanish by a feminine noun; hence the Don's inference concerning Dulcinea.    3. A bad sign. Meeting a hare is considered an ill omen.

them to the lad in exchange for the cage, which he placed in Don Quixote's hands.

"There, master," he said, "these omens are broken and destroyed, and to my way of thinking, even though I may be a dunce, they have no more to do with what is going to happen to us than the clouds of yesteryear. If I am not mistaken, I have heard our curate say that sensible persons of the Christian faith should pay no heed to such foolish things, and you yourself in the past have given me to understand that all those Christians who are guided by omens are fools. But there is no need to waste a lot of words on the subject; come, let us go on and enter our village."

The hunters at this point came up and asked for the hare, and Don Quixote gave it to them. Continuing on their way, the returning pair encountered the curate and the bachelor Carrrasco, who were strolling in a small meadow on the outskirts of the town as they read their breviaries. And here it should be mentioned that Sancho Panza, by way of sumpter cloth, had thrown over his gray and the bundle of armor it bore the flame-covered buckram robe in which they had dressed the squire at the duke's castle, on the night that witnessed Altisidora's[4] resurrection; and he had also fitted the miter over the donkey's head, the result being the weirdest transformation and the most bizarrely appareled ass that ever were seen in this world. The curate and the bachelor recognized the pair at once and came forward to receive them with open arms. Don Quixote dismounted and gave them both a warm embrace; meanwhile, the small boys (boys are like lynxes in that nothing escapes them), having spied the ass's miter, ran up for a closer view.

"Come, lads," they cried, "and see Sancho Panza's ass trigged out finer than Mingo,[5] and Don Quixote's beast is skinnier than ever!"

Finally, surrounded by the urchins and accompanied by the curate and the bachelor, they entered the village and made their way to Don Quixote's house, where they found the housekeeper and the niece standing in the doorway, for the news of their return had preceded them. Teresa Panza, Sancho's wife, had also heard of it, and, half naked and disheveled, dragging her daughter Sanchica by the hand, she hastened to greet her husband and was disappointed when she saw him, for he did not look to her as well fitted out as a governor ought to be.

"How does it come, my husband," she said, "that you return like this, tramping and footsore? You look more like a vagabond than you do like a governor."

"Be quiet, Teresa," Sancho admonished her, "for very often there

---

4. Altisidora was a girl in the duke's castle where Quixote and Sancho were guests for a time; she dramatically pretended to be in love with Don Quixote.   5. The allusion is to the opening lines of a fifteenth-century satire, *Mingo Revulgo*.

are stakes where there is no bacon. Come on home with me and you will hear marvels. I am bringing money with me, which is the thing that matters, money earned by my own efforts and without harm to anyone."

"You just bring along the money, my good husband," said Teresa, "and whether you got it here or there, or by whatever means, you will not be introducing any new custom into the world."

Sanchica then embraced her father and asked him if he had brought her anything, for she had been looking forward to his coming as to the showers in May. And so, with his wife holding him by the hand while his daughter kept one arm about his waist and at the same time led the gray, Sancho went home, leaving Don Quixote under his own roof in the company of niece and housekeeper, the curate and the barber.

Without regard to time or season, the knight at once drew his guests to one side and in a few words informed them of how he had been overcome in battle and had given his promise not to leave his village for a year, a promise that he meant to observe most scrupulously, without violating it in the slightest degree, as every knight-errant was obliged to do by the laws of chivalry. He accordingly meant to spend that year as a shepherd,[6] he said, amid the solitude of the fields, where he might give free rein to his amorous fancies as he practiced the virtues of the pastoral life; and he further begged them, if they were not too greatly occupied and more urgent matters did not prevent their doing so, to consent to be his companions. He would purchase a flock sufficiently large to justify their calling themselves shepherds; and, moreover, he would have them know, the most important thing of all had been taken care of, for he had hit upon names that would suit them marvelously well. When the curate asked him what these names were, Don Quixote replied that he himself would be known as "the shepherd Quixotiz," the bachelor as "the shepherd Carrascón," the curate as "the shepherd Curiambro," and Sancho Panza as "the shepherd Pancino."

Both his listeners were dismayed at the new form which his madness had assumed. However, in order that he might not go faring forth from the village on another of his expeditions (for they hoped that in the course of the year he would be cured), they decided to fall in with his new plan and approve it as being a wise one, and they even agreed to be his companions in the calling he proposed to adopt.

"What's more," remarked Sansón Carrasco, "I am a very famous poet, as everyone knows, and at every turn I will be composing pas-

---

6. Since the knight-errant's life has been forbidden him by his defeat, Don Quixote for a time plans to live according to another and no less "literary" code, that of the pastoral. In the following paragraphs the author, especially through the bachelor Carrasco, refers humorously to some of the conventions of pastoral literature.

toral or courtly verses or whatever may come to mind, by way of a
diversion for us as we wander in those lonely places; but what is most
necessary of all, my dear sirs, is that each one of us should choose
the name of the shepherd lass to whom he means to dedicate his
songs, so that we may not leave a tree, however hard its bark may
be, where their names are not inscribed and engraved as is the custom with lovelorn shepherds."

"That is exactly what we should do," replied Don Quixote,
"although, for my part, I am relieved of the necessity of looking for
an imaginary shepherdess, seeing that I have the peerless Dulcinea
del Toboso, glory of these brookside regions, adornment of these
meadows, beauty's mainstay, cream of the Graces—in short, one to
whom all praise is well becoming however hyperbolical it may be."

"That is right," said the curate, "but we will seek out some shepherd maids that are easily handled, who if they do not square with
us will fit in the corners."

"And," added Sansón Carrasco, "if we run out of names we will
give them those that we find printed in books the world over: such as
Fílida, Amarilis, Diana, Flérida, Galatea, and Belisarda; for since
these are for sale in the market place, we can buy them and make
them our own. If my lady, or, rather, my shepherdess, should be
chance be called Ana, I will celebrate her charms under the name
of Anarda; if she is Francisca, she will become Francenia; if Lucía,
Luscinda; for it all amounts to the same thing. And Sancho Panza,
if he enters this confraternity, may compose verses to his wife, Teresa
Panza, under the name of Teresaina."

Don Quixote had to laugh at this, and the curate then went on to
heap extravagant praise upon him for his noble resolution which did
him so much credit, and once again he offered to keep the knight
company whenever he could spare the time from the duties of his
office. With this, they took their leave of him, advising and beseeching him to take care of his health and to eat plentifully of the proper
food.

As fate would have it, the niece and the housekeeper had overheard the conversation of the three men, and as soon as the visitors
had left they both descended upon Don Quixote.

"What is the meaning of this, my uncle? Here we were thinking
your Grace had come home to lead a quiet and respectable life, and
do you mean to tell us you are going to get yourself involved in fresh
complications—

> Young shepherd, thou who comest here,
> Young shepherd, thou who goest there . . .[7]

---

7. From a ballad.

For, to tell the truth, the barley is too hard now to make shepherds' pipes of it."[8]

"And how," said the housekeeper, "is your Grace going to stand the midday heat in summer, the winter cold, the howling of the wolves out there in the fields? You certainly cannot endure it. That is an occupation for robust men, cut out and bred for such a calling almost from their swaddling clothes. Setting one evil over against another, it is better to be a knight-errant than a shepherd. Look, sir, take my advice, for I am not stuffed with bread and wine when I give it to you but am fasting and am going on fifty years of age: stay at home, attend to your affairs, go often to confession, be charitable to the poor, and let it be upon my soul if any harm comes to you as a result of it."

"Be quiet, daughters," said Don Quixote. "I know very well what I must do. Take me up to bed, for I do not feel very well; and you may be sure of one thing: whether I am a knight-errant now or a shepherd to be, I never will fail to look after your needs as you will see when the time comes."

And good daughters that they unquestionably were, the housekeeper and the niece helped him up to bed, where they gave him something to eat and made him as comfortable as they could.

## CHAPTER 74

*Of how Don Quixote fell sick, of the will that he made, and of the manner of his death.*

Inasmuch as nothing that is human is eternal but is ever declining from its beginning to its close, this being especially true of the lives of men, and since Don Quixote was not endowed by Heaven with the privilege of staying the downward course of things, his own end came when he was least expecting it. Whether it was owing to melancholy occasioned by the defeat he had suffered, or was, simply, the will of Heaven which had so ordained it, he was taken with a fever that kept him in bed for a week, during which time his friends, the curate, the bachelor, and the barber, visited him frequently, while Sancho Panza, his faithful squire, never left his bedside.

Believing that the knight's condition was due to sorrow over his downfall and disappointment at not having been able to accomplish the disenchantment and liberation of Dulcinea, Sancho and the others endeavored to cheer him up in every possible way. The bachelor urged him to take heart and get up from bed that he might begin his pastoral life, adding that he himself had already composed an eco-logue that would cast in the shade all that Sannazaro[9] had ever writ-

8. A proverb.   9. The Italian poet Jacopo Sannazaro (1456?–1530), whose *Arcadia* is one of the milestones in the pastoral tradition.

ten, and had purchased with his own money from a herdsman of Quintanar two fine dogs to guard the flock, one of them named Barcino and the other Butrón. All this, however, did not serve to relieve Don Quixote's sadness; whereupon his friends called in the doctor, who took his pulse and was not very well satisfied with it. In any case, the physician told them, they should attend to the health of his soul as that of his body was in grave danger.

Don Quixote received this news calmly enough, but not so his housekeeper, niece, and squire, who began weeping bitterly, as if he were already lying dead in front of them. It was the doctor's opinion that melancholy and depression were putting an end to his patient's life. The knight then requested them to leave him alone as he wished to sleep a little, and they complied. He slept for more than six hours at a stretch, as the saying is, and so soundly that the housekeeper and niece thought he would never wake.

At last he did, however, and at once cried out in a loud voice, "Blessed be Almighty God who has given me so many blessings! Truly His mercy is boundless and is not limited or restrained by the sins of men."

The niece listened carefully to what her uncle said, and it seemed to her that he was speaking more rationally than was his wont, at least during his illness.

"Sir," she said to him, "what does your Grace mean? Has something occurred that we know nothing about? What is this talk of mercy and sins?"

"The mercy that I speak of," replied Don Quixote, "is that which God is showing me at this moment—in spite of my sins, as I have said. My mind now is clear, unencumbered by those misty shadows of ignorance that were cast over it by my bitter and continual reading of those hateful books of chivalry. I see through all the nonsense and fraud contained in them, and my only regret is that my disillusionment has come so late, leaving me no time to make any sort of amends by reading those that are the light of the soul. I find myself, niece, at the point of death, and I would die in such a way as not to leave the impression of a life so bad that I shall be remembered as a madman; for even though I have been one, I do not wish to confirm it on my deathbed. And so, my dear, call in my good friends: the curate, the bachelor Sansón Carrasco, and Master Nicholas the barber; for I want to confess my sins and make my last will and testament."

The niece, however, was relieved of this errand, for the three of them came in just then.

"I have good news for you, kind sirs," said Don Quixote the moment he saw them. "I am no longer Don Quixote de la Mancha but Alonso Quijano, whose mode of life won for him the name of 'Good.' I am the enemy of Amadis of Gaul and all his innumerable progeny; for those profane stories dealing with knight-errantry are odious to me, and I realize how foolish I was and the danger I courted in reading them; but I am in my right senses now and I abominate them."

Hearing this, they all three were convinced that some new kind of madness must have laid hold of him.

"Why, Señor Don Quixote!" exclaimed Sansón. "What makes you talk like that, just when we have received news that my lady Dulcinea is disenchanted? And just when we are on the verge of becoming shepherds so that we may spend the rest of our lives in singing like a lot of princes, why does your Grace choose to turn hermit? Say no more, in Heaven's name, but be sensible and forget these idle tales."

"Tales of that kind," said Don Quixote, "have been the truth for me in the past, and to my detriment, but with Heaven's aid I trust to turn them to my profit now that I am dying. For I feel, gentlemen, that death is very near; so, leave all jesting aside and bring me a confessor for my sins and a notary to draw up my will. In such straits as these a man cannot trifle with his soul. Accordingly, while the Señor Curate is hearing my confession, let the notary be summoned."

Amazed at his words, they gazed at one another in some perplexity, yet they could not but believe him. One of the signs that led them to think he was dying was this quick return from madness to sanity and all the additional things he had to say, so well reasoned and well put and so becoming in a Christian that none of them could any longer doubt that he was in full possession of his faculties. Sending the others out of the room, the curate stayed behind to confess him, and before long the bachelor returned with the notary and Sancho Panza, who had been informed of his master's condition, and who, finding the housekeeper and the niece in tears, began weeping with them. When the confession was over, the curate came out.

"It is true enough," he said, "that Alonso Quijano the Good is dying, and it is also true that he is a sane man. It would be well for us to go in now while he makes his will."

At this news the housekeeper, niece, and the good squire Sancho Panza were so overcome with emotion that the tears burst forth from their eyes and their bosoms heaved with sobs; for, as has been stated more than once, whether Don Quixote was plain Alonso Quijano the Good or Don Quixote de la Mancha, he was always of a kindly and pleasant disposition and for this reason was beloved not only by the members of his household but by all who knew him.

The notary had entered along with the others, and as soon as the preamble had been attended to and the dying man had commended his soul to his Maker with all those Christian formalities that are called for in such a case, they came to the matter of bequests, with Don Quixote dictating as follows:

"ITEM. With regard to Sancho Panza, whom, in my madness, I appointed to be my squire, and who has in his possession a certain sum of money belonging to me: inasmuch as there has been a standing account between us, of debits and credits, it is my will that he shall not be asked to give any accounting whatsoever of this sum, but if any be left over after he has had payment for what I owe him, the balance, which will amount to very little, shall be his, and much good may it do him. If when I was mad I was responsible for his being given the governorship of an island, now that I am of sound mind I would present him with a kingdom if it were in my power, for his simplicity of mind and loyal conduct merit no less."

At this point he turned to Sancho. "Forgive me, my friend," he said, "for having caused you to appear as mad as I by leading you to fall into the same error, that of believing that there are still knights-errant in the world."

"Ah, master," cried Sancho through his tears, "don't die, your Grace, but take my advice and go on living for many years to come; for the greatest madness that a man can be guilty of in this life is to die without good reason, without anyone's killing him, slain only by the hands of melancholy. Look you, don't be lazy but get up from this bed and let us go out into the fields clad as shepherds as we agreed to do. Who knows but behind some bush we may come upon the lady Dulcinea, as disenchanted as you could wish. If it is because of worry over your defeat that you are dying, put the blame on me by saying that the reason for your being overthrown was that I had not properly fastened Rocinante's girth. For the matter of that, your Grace knows from reading your books of chivalry that it is a common thing for certain knights to overthrow others, and he who is vanquished today will be the victor tomorrow."

"That is right," said Sansón, "the worthy Sancho speaks the truth."

"Not so fast, gentlemen," said Don Quixote. "In last year's nests there are no birds this year. I was mad and now I am sane; I was Don Quixote de la Mancha, and now I am, as I have said, Alonso Quijano the Good. May my repentance and the truth I now speak restore to me the place I once held in your esteem. And now, let the notary proceed:

"ITEM. I bequeath my entire estate, without reservation, to my niece Antonia Quijana, here present, after the necessary deductions shall have been made from the most available portion of it to satisfy the bequests that I have stipulated. The first payment shall be to my housekeeper for the wages due her, with twenty ducats over to buy her a dress. And I hereby appoint the Señor Curate and the Señor

Bachelor Sansón Carrasco to be my executors.

"ITEM. It is my will that if my niece Antonia Quijana should see fit to marry, it shall be to a man who does not know what books of chivalry are; and if it shall be established that he is acquainted with such books and my niece still insists on marrying him, then she shall lose all that I have bequeathed her and my executors shall apply her portion to works of charity as they may see fit.

"ITEM. I entreat the aforementioned gentlemen, my executors, if by good fortune they should come to know the author who is said to have composed a history now going the rounds under the title of *Second Part of the Exploits of Don Quixote de la Mancha*, to beg his forgiveness in my behalf, as earnestly as they can, since it was I who unthinkingly led him to set down so many and such great absurdities as are to be found in it; for I leave this life with a feeling of remorse at having provided him with the occasion for putting them into writing."

The will ended here, and Don Quixote, stretching himself at length in the bed, fainted away. They all were alarmed at this and hastened to aid him. The same thing happened very frequently in the course of the three days of life that remained to him after he had made his will. The household was in a state of excitement, but with it all the niece continued to eat her meals, the housekeeper had her drink, and Sancho Panza was in good spirits; for this business of inheriting property effaces or mitigates the sorrow which the heir ought to feel and causes him to forget.

Death came at last for Don Quixote, after he had received all the sacraments and once more, with many forceful arguments, had expressed his abomination of books of chivalry. The notary who was present remarked that in none of those books had he read of any knight-errant dying in his own bed so peacefully and in so Christian a manner. And thus, amid the tears and lamentations of those present, he gave up the ghost; that is to say, he died. Perceiving that their friend was no more, the curate asked the notary to be a witness to the fact that Alonso Quijano the Good, commonly known as Don Quixote, was truly dead, this being necessary in order that some author other than Cid Hamete Benengeli might not have the opportunity of falsely resurrecting him and writing endless histories of his exploits.

Such was the end of the Ingenious Gentleman of La Mancha, whose birthplace Cid Hamete was unwilling to designate exactly in order that all the towns and villages of La Mancha might contend among themselves for the right to adopt him and claim him as their own, just as the seven cities of Greece did in the case of Homer. The lamentations of Sancho and those of Don Quixote's niece and his housekeeper, as well as the original epitaphs that were composed for his tomb, will not be recorded here, but mention may be made of the verses by Sansón Carrasco:

> Here lies a gentleman bold
> Who was so very brave
> He went to lengths untold,
> And on the brink of the grave
> Death had on him no hold.
> By the world he set small store—
> He frightened it to the core—
> Yet somehow, by Fate's plan,
> Though he'd lived a crazy man,
> When he died he was sane once more.

---

# CHRISTOPHER MARLOWE
## 1564–1593

The data we have on Christopher Marlowe's life are haunting and fragmentary; there seems to be no doubt that he entertained unorthodox religious views, that he had a violent temper, and that he engaged in some sort of spying activities for Queen Elizabeth. Born in Canterbury on February 6, 1564, the son of a shoemaker, Marlowe studied at the King's School in his native city and from 1581 on a scholarship at Corpus Christi College (then Benet College), Cambridge, where he received his B. A. in 1584 and his M. A. in 1587. There was some opposition to the granting of his degree but the Queen's Privy Council intervened in his favor, a fact which has been used to support the hypothesis that Marlowe was already affiliated with the Queen's secret service (a diplomatic and intelligence operation). After Cambridge he lived in London, where little is known about his life; we obviously do know of his connections with the theatrical world and of his four great dramatic successes between 1587 and 1593, *Tamburlaine the Great*, *The Jew of Malta*, *Edward II*, and *Dr. Faustus* (c. 1592–93). Besides the plays Marlowe also wrote a mythological poem, "Hero and Leander," and translations of the Latin poets Ovid and Lucan.

Marlowe was accused of atheism and treason by a one-time friend and fellow-playwright, Thomas Kyd. He was involved in a bloody brawl with an innkeeper named William Bradley, and at 29, in an inn at Deptford, was stabbed to death by one Ingram Frizer in an argument over the bill; Frizer was pardoned on the grounds that he had acted in self-defense.

Of the plays which make him one of the most prominent Elizabethan dramatists, *Dr. Faustus* is still the most famous, probably because the legend of Faust has occupied an important place in literature since the Renaissance. Like Don Juan, Faust is one of the characters to whom authors have returned again and again as to convenient epitomes of certain traits and aspirations. The human story of Faust has been varied and adapted to suit the intellectual needs of various times, much as both ancient and modern poets have used the heroes of Greek mythology for their own purposes.

Marlowe's Dr. Faustus powerfully exemplifies the intellectual aspirations of the Renaissance, but he is haunted by a sense of their vanity and sinfulness. Whereas the tension of opposites produces in other instances some sort of compromise, and often fruitful results, here the outcome of inner conflict is tragedy and ruin. In our gallery of Renaissance heroes Dr. Faustus represents an extreme cause, almost the reverse of Rabelais's exuberant and satisfied sensualist-scholar; to him the fruit of knowledge is not the confirmation of man's dignity and divine nature, but despair and destruction.

The popular tendency to identify Faust with magic and witchcraft, suffering a final punishment for having followed the unorthodox and sinful black arts, is of course justified. But such a simple scheme, while it may have been the whole "point" of earlier versions of the story, does not account for the obviously larger and deeper implications we discern in Marlow's tragedy. With this in mind, it may be particularly illuminating to ask ourselves what Dr. Faustus's knowledge and aspirations are. We then realize that both in the hero's initial phase, where he expresses his satiety and dissatisfaction with man's accumulated knowledge, and in the later one, where he embraces magic and the devil's arts, he is actually concerned with the proudest intellectual values of the Renaissance. Such well-known attitudes as excitement in discovery and delight in intellectual and physical power are expressed with an unmatched imaginative and metric splendor: "Faustus, these books, thy wit, and our experience/Shall make all nations to canonize us." Yet they are also presented as temptations of the devil.

In this light, the progression by which Dr. Faustus, scientist and scholar, arrives at his decision to "sell his soul to the devil" is not clear-cut. We can, of course, trace the route he travels, the crucial episode of which is his decision to give himself to the arts of Mephistopheles. As the play opens, Dr. Faustus is presented in his study, feeling the vanity of his intellectual pursuits. These studies are, to him, vain and dusty; but in his enumeration of them we recognize the very culture on which many intellectuals of the time would have securely counted: Greek philosophy and physics, the laws of the Roman empire, the Vulgate version of the Scriptures. Yet, in the opening monologue of Marlowe's play Faustus reviews and discards these pillars of humanistic culture and turns to the "metaphysics of magicians." He has tried, as it were, to cure his thirst for knowledge and power by orthodox means, but the cure, as far as he is concerned, has failed. He then turns to less usual and less reputable means to satisfy himself, somewhat in the same way that a patient dissatisfied with physicians turns to a brilliant "quack." Magic, he hopes, will "resolve" him "of all ambiguities."

But if we ask ourselves what magic promises Dr. Faustus, we come to the realization that what it promises is a more colorful and adventurous side of that same Renaissance body of values to which his discarded studies and books also belong. In this second phase, Dr. Faustus can exercise his fertile imagination and his instinctive longing for beauty and power—the "magic" of the period. Instead of plodding through the traditional texts he can imagine thrilling voyages, the "Venetian argosies," and express his desire for vast earthly conquest: "I'll join the hills that bind the Afric shore/And make that country continent to Spain,/And both contributory to my crown. . . ." This imperial dream is more than once expressed with references to antiquity, as a new vision of ancient myth ("from America the golden fleece"; "Instead of Troy shall Wittenberg be sacked"). Similarly, he sees in the image of Helen the supreme figuration of beauty and aspires to it as to a culminating fulfillment of his desires.

Such aspirations and visions, doomed to a catastrophic end, give the figure of Dr. Faustus a heroic stature, as we can clearly see by comparing him to the Scholars. The Scholars hold the position which the Chorus in Greek tragedy often does—middle-of-the-road, conformist, prudent; in contrast Dr. Faustus seems to possess the grandeur of some of Dante's damned. He lives for higher stakes and falls harder; there is greatness in the very extent of his final hopelessness. In the end it becomes clear, as we have suggested, that the sense of doom has presided over both phases, both means, fair and foul, of Faustus's search for knowledge. Not only his "magic" visions but his whole past come back to haunt him, and at this point we no longer have the lyric beauty of the Helen passage, but the panting, colloquial, extraordinarily effective monologue in which all Faustus's science, all his knowledge, are desperately rejected: "O would I had never seen Wittenberg, never read book. And what wonders I have done all Germany can witness, yea all the world, for which Faustus hath lost both Germany and the world, yea heaven itself. . . ."

Marlowe's *Dr. Faustus*, then, is considerably more interesting to the modern reader than the simple story of how a necromancer lost his soul by dabbling with magic. The nature of the hero's despair cuts deeper than that; as a Renaissance character he embodies a more deeply earned dissatisfaction. Here is more than ordinary "melancholy"; the drama seems to suggest that the seeds of damnation are implicit in some of the most cherished and proud pursuits and attitudes of the period; their depiction as devilish temptations is a concrete way of symbolizing their comprehensively damning nature. In this light, the play becomes one of the most contemporary statements we have of man's terror at the daring of his own thought and the need for "limits" that Montaigne so eloquently expounds.

Frederick S. Boas, *Christopher Marlowe: A Biographical and Critical Study* (1940), is the standard account of Marlowe's life and literary career. A helpful anthology of criticism is *Twentieth Century Interpretations of Doctor Faustus* (1969), edited by Willard Farnham. Harry Levin's *The Overreacher: A Study of Christopher Marlowe* (1952) stresses the dramatist's modern spirit. A. L. Rowes provides a very readable account of Marlowe's life in *Christopher Marlowe: A Biography* (1964).

# The Tragical History
## of the Life and Death of Doctor Faustus

### *Dramatis Personae*

DR. JOHN FAUSTUS, *of the University of Wittenberg*

CHORUS

WAGNER, *his servant*

GOOD ANGEL *and* BAD ANGEL

VALDES *and* CORNELIUS, *magicians and friends of* FAUSTUS

THREE SCHOLARS, *students at the university*

LUCIFER, MEPHISTOPHILIS, *and* BELZEBUB, *devils*

ROBIN *and* DICK, *rustic clowns*

THE SEVEN DEADLY SINS

POPE ADRIAN

RAYMOND, *King of Hungary*

BRUNO, *a rival Pope, appointed by the* EMPEROR

CARDINALS OF FRANCE *and* PADUA

ARCHBISHOP OF RHEIMS

MARTINO, FREDERICK, *and* BENVOLIO, *gentlemen at the* EMPEROR'S *court*

CAROLUS (CHARLES) THE FIFTH, EMPEROR

DUKE OF SAXONY

DUKE *and* DUCHESS OF VANHOLT

HORSE-COURSER

CARTER

HOSTESS *of a tavern*

OLD MAN

SPIRITS *of* DARIUS, ALEXANDER *and his* PARAMOUR, *and* HELEN OF TROY

ATTENDANTS, MONKS *and* FRIARS, SOLDIERS, PIPER, *two* CUPIDS

## Act 1

[*Enter* CHORUS.[1]]

CHO. Not marching in the fields of Trasimene
Where Mars did mate[2] the warlike Carthagens,
Nor sporting in the dalliance of love
In courts of kings where state[3] is overturned,
Nor in the pomp of proud audacious deeds          5
Intends our Muse to vaunt his heavenly verse:
Only this, gentles, we must now perform,
The form of Faustus' fortunes good or bad.
And so to patient judgments we appeal
And speak for Faustus in his infancy.          10
Now is he born, his parents base of stock,
In Germany within a town called Rhode;
At riper years to Wittenberg[4] he went
Whereas[5] his kinsmen chiefly brought him up;
So much he profits in divinity,          15
The fruitful plot of scholarism graced,[6]
That shortly he was graced with Doctor's name,
Excelling all whose sweet delight disputes[7]
In th' heavenly matters of theology,

1. A single actor who recited a prologue to an act or a whole play, and occasionally delivered an epilogue. 2. Join with. The battle of Lake Trasimene (217 B.C.) was one of the Carthaginian leader Hannibal's great victories. 3. Political power. 4. The famous university where Martin Luther studied, as did Shakespeare's Hamlet and Horatio. *Rhode:* Roda. 5. Where. 6. Grazed. In the next line it refers to the Cambridge word for permission to proceed to a degree. 7. The usual academic exercises were disputations, which took the place of examinations.

Till, swollen with cunning,[8] of a self-conceit,                          20
His waxen wings did mount above his reach
And melting, heavens conspired his overthrow.[9]
For, falling to a devilish exercise
And glutted more with learning's golden gifts,
He surfeits upon curséd necromancy;                                        25
Nothing so sweet as magic is to him,
Which he prefers before his chiefest bliss[1]—
And this the man that in his study sits.
    [*Draws the curtain*[2] *and exit.*]

SCENE 1

    [FAUSTUS *in his study.*]
FAUST. Settle thy studies, Faustus, and begin
    To sound the depth of that thou wilt profess.
    Having commenced, be a divine in show,
    Yet level[3] at the end of every art
    And live and die in Aristotle's works:                               5
    Sweet Analytics,[4] 'tis thou hast ravished me!        [*Reads.*]
    *Bene disserere est finis logicis*—
    Is to dispute well logic's chiefest end?
    Affords this art no greater miracle?
    Then read no more; thou hast attained the end.                        10
    A greater subject fitteth Faustus' wit:
    Bid ον χαì μὴ oν[5] farewell, Galen come,
    Seeing *ubi desinit philosophus, ibi incipit medicus;*[6]
    Be a physician, Faustus, heap up gold
    And be eternized for some wondrous cure.         [*Reads.*]   15
    *Summum bonum medicinae sanitas*—[7]
    The end of physic is our bodies' health:
    Why, Faustus, hast thou not attained that end?
    Is not thy common talk sound aphorisms?[8]
    Are not thy bills hung up as monuments                               20
    Whereby whole cities have escaped the plague
    And thousand desperate maladies been cured?
    Yet art thou still but Faustus, and a man.
    Couldst thou make men to live eternally
    Or, being dead, raise them to life again,                            25

---

8. Learning.   9. In Greek myth Icarus flew too near the sun on wings of feathers and wax; the wax melted and he fell into the sea and was drowned.   1. The salvation of his soul.   2. The curtain to the inner stage which serves here as Faustus' study. *Draws:* Draws apart.   3. Aim. *Commenced:* Graduated, i.e., received the doctor's degree. *In show:* In external appearance. 4. A treatise on logic by Aristotle. The Latin: "To carry on a disputation well is the purpose of logic."   5. "Being and not being," i.e., philosophy. *Galen:* The ancient authority on medicine (2nd century A.D.).   6. "Where the philosopher leaves off the physical begins."   7. "Good health is the object of medicine" (or "physic").   8. I.e., reliable medical pronouncements. *Bills:* Prescriptions.

Then this profession were to be esteemed.
Physic, farewell. Where is Justinian?[9]          [*Reads.*]
*Si una eademque res legatur duobus,*
*Alter rem, alter valorem rei, etc.*[1]—
A pretty case of paltry legacies!                                    30
*Exhaereditare filium non potest pater nisi*[2]
Such is the subject of the Institute
And universal body of the law.
This study fits a mercenary drudge
Who aims at nothing but external trash,                              35
Too servile and illiberal for me.
When all is done, divinity is best.
Jerome's Bible,[3] Faustus, view it well:          [*Reads.*]
*Stipendium peccati mors est*—Ha! *Stipendium, etc.*
The reward of sin is death? That's hard.                            40
*Si pecasse negamus, fallimur, et nulla est in nobis veritas*[4]—
If we say that we have no sin
We deceive ourselves, and there's no truth in us.
Why then belike
We must sin and so consequently die,                               45
Aye, we must die an everlasting death.
What doctrine call you this, *Che sera, sera.*
What will be, shall be? Divinity, adieu!
These metaphysics of magicians
And necromantic books are heavenly:                                50
Lines, circles, sings, letters, and characters—
Aye, these are those that Faustus most desires.
O what a world of profit and delight,
Of power, of honor, of omnipotence,
Is promised to the studious artisan!                               55
All things that move between the quiet[5] poles
Shall be at my command. Emperors and kings
Are but obeyed in their several provinces,
Nor can they raise the wind or rend the clouds;
But his dominion that exceeds in this                              60
Stretcheth as far as doth the mind of man.
A sound magician is a demigod:
Here tire my brains to gain a deity!
Wagner!
     [*Enter* WAGNER.]

---

9. Roman emperor and authority on law (483–565), author of the *Institutes.*     1. "If something is bequeathed to two persons, one shall have the thing itself, the other something of equal value."     2. "A father cannot disinherit his son unless."     3. The Latin translation, or "Vulgate," of St. Jerome (ca. 340–420). The Latin (Romans 6:23) is translated in line 40.     4. I John 1:8, translated in the next two lines.     5. Unmoving. *Artisan*: A master of the occult arts.

Commend me to my dearest friends, 65
The German Valdes and Cornelius;
Request them earnestly to visit me.
WAG. I will, sir.        [*Exit.*]
FAUST. Their conference will be a greater help to me
Than all my labors, plod I ne'er so fast. 70
[*Enter the* GOOD ANGEL *and the* BAD ANGEL.]
G. ANG. O Faustus, lay that damnéd book aside
And gaze not on it, lest it tempt thy soul
And heap God's heavy wrath upon thy head.
Read, read the Scriptures! That is blasphemy.
B. ANG. Go forward, Faustus, in that famous art 75
Wherein all nature's treasury is contained:
Be thou on earth, as Jove[6] is in the sky,
Lord and commander of these elements.
[*Exeunt* ANGELS.]
FAUST. How am I glutted with conceit[7] of this!
Shall I make spirits fetch me what I please, 80
Resolve me of all ambiguities,
Perform what desperate enterprise I will?
I'll have them fly to India[8] for gold,
Ransack the ocean for orient pearl,
And search all corners of the new-found world 85
For pleasant fruits and princely delicates;
I'll have them read me strange philosophy
And tell the secrets of all foreign kings;
I'll have them wall all Germany with brass
And make swift Rhine circle fair Wittenberg; 90
I'll have them fill the public schools[9] with silk
Wherewith the students shall be bravely clad;
I'll levy soldiers with the coin they bring,
And chase the Prince of Parma[1] from our land
And reign sole king of all our provinces; 95
Yea, stranger engines for the brunt of war
Than was the fiery keel[2] at Antwerp's bridge
I'll make my servile spirits to invent!
[*Enter* VALDES *and* CORNELIUS.]
Come, German Valdes and Cornelius,
And make me blest with your sage conference. 100
Valdes, sweet Valdes and Cornelius,

---

6. God (a common substitution in Elizabethan drama).    7. Filled with the idea.    8. "India" could mean the West Indies, America, or Ophir (in the east).    9. The university lecture rooms.    1. The Duke of Parma was the Spanish governor general of the Low Countries from 1579 to 1592.    2. The burning ship sent by the Netherlanders in 1585 against the barrier on the river Scheldt which Parma had built as a part of the blockade of Antwerp.

Know that your words have won me at the last
To practice magic and concealéd arts;
Yet not your words only, but mine own fantasy
That will receive no object,[3] for my head                               105
But ruminates on necromantic skill.
Philosophy is odious and obscure,
Both law and physic are for petty wits,
Divinity is basest of the three,
Unpleasant, harsh, contemptible, and vile;                                110
'Tis magic, magic, that hath ravished me!
Then, gentle friends, aid me in this attempt,
And I, that have with concise syllogisms
Graveled[4] the pastors of the German church,
And made the flowering pride of Wittenberg                                115
Swarm to my problems[5] as the infernal spirits
On sweet Musaeus when he came to hell,
Will be as cunning as Agrippa[6] was
Whose shadows made all Europe honor him.
VALD. Faustus, these books, thy wit, and our experience                   120
  Shall make all nations to canonize us.
  As Indian Moors[7] obey their Spanish lords
  So shall the spirits of every element
  Be always serviceable to us three:
  Like lions shall they guard us when we please,                          125
  Like Almain rutters[8] with their horsemen's staves,
  Or Lapland giants trotting by our sides;
  Sometimes like women, or unwedded maids,
  Shadowing more beauty in their airy brows
  Then in the white breasts of the queen of love;                         130
  From Venice shall they drag huge argosies
  And from America the golden fleece
  That yearly stuffs old Philip's[9] treasury,
  If learned Faustus will be resolute.
FAUST. Valdes, as resolute am I in this                                   135
  As thou to live; therefore object it not.
CORN. The miracles that magic will perform
  Will make thee vow to study nothing else.
  He that is grounded in astrology,
  Enriched with tongues, well seen[1] in minerals,                        140
  Hath all the principles magic doth require.

3. That will pay no attention to physical reality.    4. Confounded.    5. Lectures in logic and
mathematics.    6. Cornelius Agrippa, German author of *The Vanity and Uncertainty of Arts
and Sciences*, popularly supposed to have the power of calling up shades ("shadows") of the dead.
*Musaeus*: Mythical singer, son of Orpheus; it was, however, the latter who charmed the denizens
of hell with his music.    7. I.e., dark-skinned American Indians.    8. German horsemen.
9. Philip II, king of Spain.    1. Expert.

Then doubt not, Faustus, but to be renowned
And more frequented for this mystery
Than heretofore the Delphian oracle.[2]
The spirits tell me they can dry the sea              145
And fetch the treasure of all foreign wrecks—
Aye, all the wealth that our forefathers hid
Within the massy entrails of the earth.
Then tell me, Faustus, what shall we three want?
FAUST. Nothing, Cornelius. O this cheers my soul!      150
   Come, show me some demonstrations magical
   That I may conjure in some lusty[3] grove
   And have these joys in full possession.
VALD. Then haste thee to some solitary grove
   And bear wise Bacon's and Albanus'[4] works,       155
   The Hebrew Psalter and New Testamant;
   And whatsoever else is requisite
   We will inform thee ere our conference cease.
CORN. Valdes, first let him know the words of art,
   And then, all other ceremonies learned,           160
   Faustus may try his cunning by himself.
VALD. First I'll instruct thee in the rudiments,
   And then wilt thou be perfecter than I.
FAUST. Then come and dine with me, and after meat
   We'll canvass every quiddity[5] thereof;          165
   For ere I sleep I'll try what I can do:
   This night I'll conjure though I die therefore.       [*Exeunt.*]

SCENE 2

[*Enter two* SCHOLARS.]

1 SCH. I wonder what's become of Faustus, that was wont to
   make our schools ring with *sic probo*.[6]
2 SCH. That shall we presently know; here comes his boy.[7]
     [*Enter* WAGNER *carrying wine*.]
1 SCH. How now, sirrah; where's thy master?
WAG. God in heaven knows.                        5
2 SCH. Why, dost not thou know then?
WAG. Yes, I know; but that follows not.
1 SCH. Go to, sirrah; leave your jesting and tell us where he is.
WAG. That follows not by force of argument, which you, being
   licentiate,[8] should stand upon; therefore acknowledge your    10
   error and be attentive.

---

2. The oracle of Apollo at Delphi, much frequented in antiquity. *Mystery:* Craft.    3. Flourishing, beautiful.    4. Pietro d'Albano, 13th-century alchemist. *Bacon:* Roger Bacon, the medieval friar and scientist, popularly throught a magician.    5. Essential feature.    6. "Thus I prove," a phrase in scholastic disputation.    7. Poor student earning his keep.    8. I.e., graduate students.

2 SCH. Then you will not tell us?

WAG. You are deceived, for I will tell you. Yet if you were not
    dunces you would never ask me such a question, for is he not
    *corpus naturale,* and is not that *mobile?*[9] Then wherefore     15
    should you ask me such a question? But that I am by nature
    phlegmatic, slow to wrath and prone to lechery (to love, I
    would say), it were not for you to come within forty foot of
    the place of execution,[1] although I do not doubt to see you
    both hanged the next sessions. Thus having triumphed over    20
    you, I will set my countenance like a precisian,[2] and begin
    to speak thus: Truly, my dear brethren, my master is within
    at dinner with Valdes and Cornelius, as this wine, if it could
    speak, would inform your worships; and so the Lord bless you,
    preserve you, and keep you, my dear brethren.    [*Exit.*]

1 SCH. O Faustus, then I fear that which I have long suspected,
    That thou art fallen into that damnéd art
    For which they two are infamous throughout the world.

2 SCH. Were he a stranger, not allied to me,
    The danger of his soul would make me mourn.    30
    But come, let us go and inform the Rector,[3]
    It may be his grave counsel may reclaim him.

1 SCH. I fear me nothing will reclaim him now.

2 SCH. Yet let us see what we can do. [*Exeunt.*]

SCENE 3

    [*Enter* FAUSTUS *to conjure.*]

FAUST. Now that the gloomy shadow of the night,
    Longing to view Orion's drizzling look,[4]
    Leaps from the antarctic world unto the sky
    And dims the welkin with her pitchy breath,
    Faustus, begin thine incantations    5
    And try if devils will obey thy hest,
    Seeing thou has prayed and sacrificed to them.
    Within this circle is Jehovah's name
       [*He draws the circle*[5] *on the ground.*]
    Forward and backward anagrammatized,
    The breviated names of holy saints,    10
    Figures of every adjunct[6] to the heavens
    And characters of signs[7] and erring stars,

---

9. *Corpus naturale et mobile* (natural, movable matter) was a scholastic definition of the subject matter of physics. Wagner is here parodying the language of learning he hears around the university.    1. I.e., the dining room.    2. A Puritan. The rest of his speech is in the style of the Puritans.    3. Head of a German university.    4. Orion appears at the beginning of winter.    5. Within which the spirits rise.    6. Heavenly body, thought to be joined to the solid firmament.    7. Signs of the zodiac and the planets. *Erring:* Wandering.

By which the spirits are enforced to rise.
Then fear not, Faustus, but be resolute
And try the uttermost magic can perform.          [*Thunder.*]    15
*Sint mihi dei Acherontis propitii! Valeat numen triplex*
*Jehovae! Ignei aerii aquatici terreni spiritus, salvete! Orientis*
*princeps Lucifer Belzebub, inferni ardentis monarcha, et De-*
*mogorgon, propitiamus vos, ut appareat et surgat Mephistophi-*
*lis!*[8]                                                         20
     [FAUSTUS *pauses. Thunder still.*]
*Quid tu moraris?*[9] *Per Iehovam, Gehennam et consecratam*
*aquam quam nunc spargo, signumque crucis quod nunc facio,*
*et per vota nostra, ipse nunc surgat nobis dicatus Mephistophi-*
*lis!*
     [MEPHISTOPHILIS *in the shape of a dragon rises from the earth*
     *outside the circle.*]
I charge thee to return and change thy shape;                    25
Thou art too ugly to attend on me.
Go, and return an old Franciscan friar;
That holy shape becomes a devil best.          [*Exit* MEPH.]
I see there's virtue in my heavenly words:
Who would not be proficient in this art?                         30
How pliant is this Mephistophilis,
Full of obedience and humility!
Such is the force of magic and my spells.
Now, Faustus, thou art conjurer laureate
That canst command great Mephistophilis:                         35
*Quin redis, Mephistophilis, fratris imagine!*[1]
     [*Re-enter* MEPHISTOPHILIS *like a Friar.*]
MEPH. Now, Faustus, what wouldst thou have me do?
FAUST. I charge thee wait upon me whilst I live
     To do whatever Faustus shall command,
     Be it be make the moon drop from her sphere                 40
     Or the ocean to overwhelm the world.
MEPH. I am a servant to great Lucifer
     And may not follow thee without his leave:
     No more than he commands must we perform.
FAUST. Did not he charge thee to appear to me?                   45
MEPH. No, I came now hither of my own accord.
FAUST. Did not my conjuring speeches raise thee?
     Speak!

8. "May the gods of the lower regions favor me! Goodbye to the Trinity! Hail, spirits of fire, air,
water, and earth! Prince of the East, Belzebub, monarch of burning hell, and Demogorgon, we
pray to you that Mephistophilis may appear and rise."    9. Nothing has happened, so Faustus
asks, "What are you waiting for?" and continues to conjure: "By Jehovah, Gehenna, and the holy
water which I now sprinkle, and the sign of the cross which I now make, and by our vows, way
Mephistophilis himself now rise to serve us."    1. "Return, Mephistophilis, in the shape of a
friar."

MEPH. That was the cause, but yet *per accidens*,[2]
    For when we hear one rack the name of God,        50
    Abjure the Scriptures and his Saviour Christ,
    We fly in hope to get his glorious soul;
    Nor will we come unless he use such means
    Whereby he is in danger to be damned;
    Therefore the shortest cut for conjuring        55
    Is stoutly to abjure the Trinity
    And pray devoutly to the prince of hell.
FAUST. So I have done, and hold this principle,
    There is no chief but only Belzebub
    To whom Faustus doth dedicate himself.        60
    This word "damnation" terrifies not me
    For I confound hell in Elysium;
    My ghost be with the old philosphers![3]
    But leaving these vain trifles of men's souls—
    Tell me, what is that Lucifer thy lord?        65
MEPH. Arch-regent and commander of all spirits.
FAUST. Was not that Lucifer an angel once?
MEPH. Yes, Faustus, and most dearly loved of God.
FAUST. How comes it, then, that he is prince of devils?        70
MEPH. O, by aspiring pride and insolence,
    For which God threw him from the face of heaven.
FAUST. And what are you that live with Lucifer?
MEPH. Unhappy spirits that fell with Lucifer,
    Conspired against our God with Lucifer,        75
    And are forever damned with Lucifer.
FAUST. Where are you damned?
MEPH. In hell.
FAUST. How comes it, then, that thou art out of hell?
MEPH. Why, this is hell, nor am I out of it:        80
    Thinkst thou that I who saw the face of God
    And tasted the eternal joys of heaven
    Am not tormented with ten thousand hells
    In being deprived of everlasting bliss?
    O Faustus, leave these frivolous demands        85
    Which strike a terror to my fainting soul!
FAUST. What, is great Mephistophilis so passionate[4]
    For being deprivéd of the joys of heaven?
    Learn thou of Faustus' manly fortitude
    And scorn those joys thou never shalt possess.        90
    Go, bear these tidings to great Lucifer:

2. By the immediate, not ultimate, cause. *Rack*: Torture (by anagrammatizing).   3. I.e., I regard heaven and hell indifferently; if the old (pre-Christian) philosophers are damned, let me be damned with them.   4. Overcome by emotion.

Seeing Faustus hath incurred eternal death
By desperate thoughts against Jove's deity,
Say he surrenders up to him his soul
So he will spare him four and twenty years,                    95
Letting him live in all voluptuousness,
Having thee ever to attend on me:
To give me whatsoever I shall ask,
To tell me whatsoever I demand,
To slay mine enemies and aid my friends,                      100
And always be obedient to my will.
Go, and return to mighty Lucifer,
And meet me in my study at midnight
And then resolve me of thy master's mind.[5]
MEPH. I will, Faustus.                    [*Exit.*]            105
FAUST. Had I as many souls as there be stars
I'd give them all for Mephistophilis!
By him I'll be great emperor of the world,
And make a bridge through the moving air
To pass the ocean with a band of men;                         110
I'll join the hills that bind the Afric shore
And make that country continent to Spain,
And both contributory to my crown;
The Emperor[6] shall not live but by my leave,
Nor any potentate of Germany.                                 115
Now that I have obtained what I desire
I'll live in speculation[7] of this art
Till Mephistophilis return again.        [*Exit.*]

### SCENE 4

[*Enter* WAGNER *and the* CLOWN (ROBIN.)[8]]
WAG. Come hither, sirrah boy.
CLOWN. Boy! O disgrace to my person! Zounds, boy in your face!
   You have seen many boys with such pickadevaunts,[9] I am sure.
WAG. Sirrah, hast thou no comings in?[1]
CLOWN. Yes, and goings out too; you may see, sir.              5
WAG. Alas, poor slave. See how poverty jests in his nakedness: the
   villain's out of service, and so hungry that I know he would
   give his soul to the devil for a shoulder of mutton, though it
   were blood-raw.
CLOWN. Not so, neither; I had need to have it well-roasted, and   10
   good sauce to it, if I pay so dear, I can tell you.

---

5. Give me his decision.    6. The Holy Roman Emperor.    7. Contemplation.    8. Not a
court jester (as in some of Shakespeare's plays), but the older-fasioned stock character, a rustic
buffoon. The name "Robin" has been interpolated by later editors of the text.    9. Beards. *Zounds*:
An oath ("God's wounds").    1. Income, but the Clown then puns on the literal meaning.

WAG. Sirrah, wilt thou be my man and wait on me? And I will
    make thee go like *Qui mihi discipulus.*[2]

CLOWN. What, in verse?

WAG. No, slave, in beaten silk and staves-acre.[3]                    15

CLOWN. Staves-acre! that's good to kill vermin. Then, belike, if
    I serve you I shall be lousy.

WAG. Why, so thou shalt be, whether thou dost it or no; for, sirrah,
    if thou dost not presently bind thyself to me for seven years, I'll
    turn all the lice about thee into familiars and make                    20
    them tear thee in pieces.

CLOWN. Nay, sir, you may save yourself a labor, for they are as
    familiar with me as if they paid for their meat and drink, I can
    tell you.

WAG. Well, sirrah, leave your jesting and take these guilders.[4]                    25

CLOWN. Yes, marry, sir, and I thank you, too.

WAG. So, now thou art to be at an hour's warning whenever and
    wheresoever the devil shall fetch thee.

CLOWN. Here, take your guilders again, I'll none of 'em.

WAG. Not I, thou art pressed;[5] prepare thyself, for I will presently                    30
    raise up two devils to carry thee away. Banio! Belecher!

CLOWN. Belcher? And Belcher come here I'll belch him. I am not
    afraid of a devil.

    [*Enter two* DEVILS, *and the* CLOWN *runs up and down crying.*]

WAG. How now, sir! Will you serve me now?

CLOWN. Aye, good Wagner, take away the devils then.                    35

WAG. Spirits, away!                    [DEVILS *exeunt.*]
            Now, sirrah, follow me.

CLOWN. I will, sir. But hark you, master, will you teach me this
    conjuring occupation?

WAG. Aye, sirrah, I'll teach thee to turn thyself to a dog, or a cat,
    or a mouse, or a rat, or anything.                    40

CLOWN. A dog, or a cat, or a mouse, or a rat! O brave[6] Wagner!

WAG. Villain, call me Master Wagner; and see that you walk atten-
    tively, and let your right eye be always diametrally fixed upon my
    left heel, that thou mayst *quasi vestigiis nostris insistere.*[7]

CLOWN. Well, sir, I warrant you.                    [*Exeunt.*]                    45

## Act II

### SCENE 1

    [*Enter* FAUSTUS *in his study.*]

FAUST. Now, Fasutus, must thou needs be damned,
    Canst not be saved.

---

2. "You who are my pupil."    3. A kind of delphinium used for killing vermin.    4. Coins.
5. Impressed, i.e., hired.    6. Marvelous, wonderful.    7. A pedantic way of saying "follow
my footsteps."

What boots[8] it, then, to think of God or heaven?
Away with such vain fancies, and despair—
Despair in God and trust in Belzebub.                                    5
Now go not backward, no, be resolute!
Why waverest? Something soundeth in mine ears:
"Abjure this magic, turn to God again!"
Aye, and Faustus will turn to God again.
To God? He loves thee not;                                               10
The God thou servest is thine own appetite,
Wherein is fixed the love of Belzebub.
To him I'll build an altar and a church
And offer lukewarm blood of newborn babes.
        [*Enter* GOOD ANGEL *and* BAD ANGEL.]
G. ANG. Sweet Faustus, leave that execrable art.                         15
B. ANG. Go forward, Faustus, in that famous art.
FAUST. Contrition, prayer, repentance—what of them?
G. ANG. O they are means to bring thee unto heaven!
B. ANG. Rather illusions, fruits of lunacy,
    That makes men foolish that do use them most.                        20
G. ANG. Sweet Faustus, think of heaven and heavenly things.
B. ANG. No, Faustus, think of honor and of wealth.
        [*Exeunt* ANGELS.]
FAUST. Of wealth!
    Why, the signiory of Emden[9] shall be mine.
    When Mephistophilis shall stand by me                                25
    What power can hurt me? Faustus, thou art safe;
    Cast no more doubts. Come, Mephistophilis,
    And bring glad tidings from great Lucifer.
    Is't not midnight? Come, Mephistophilis!
    *Veni, veni, Mephistophile!*[1]                                      30
        [*Enter* MEPHISTOPHILIS.]
    Now tell me what saith Lucifer, thy lord?
MEPH. That I shall wait on Faustus whilst I live,
    So he will buy my service with his soul.
FAUST. Already Faustus hath hazarded that for thee.
MEPH. But, Faustus, thou must bequeath it solemnly                       35
    And write a deed of gift with thine own blood,
    For that security craves Lucifer.
    If thou deny it, I must back to hell.
FAUST. Stay, Mephistophilis, and tell me what good
    Will my soul do thy lord?
MEPH.                        Enlarge his kingdom.                         40
FAUST. Is that the reason why he tempts us thus?

8. Avails.    9. A wealthy German trade center.    1. "Come, come Mephistophilis!"

MEPH. *Solamen miseris socios habuisse doloris.*[2]

FAUST. Why, have you any pain that tortures others?

MEPH. As great as have the human souls of men.
    But tell me, Faustus, shall I have thy soul? 45
    And I will be thy slave, and wait on thee,
    And give thee more than thou hast wit to ask.

FAUST. Aye, Mephistophilis, I'll give it him.

MEPH. Then, Faustus, stab thine arm courageously,
    And bind thy soul that at some certain day 50
    Great Lucifer may claim it as his own,
    And then be thou as great as Lucifer.

FAUST. Lo, Mephistophilis, for love of thee
      [*Stabbing his arm.*]
    I cut mine arm, and with my proper[3] blood
    Assure my soul to be great Lucifer's. 55
    Chief lord and regent of perpetual night,
    View here the blood that trickles from mine arm
    And let it be propitious for my wish!

MEPH. But, Faustus,
    Write it in manner of a deed of gift. 60

FAUST. Aye, so I do. [*Writes.*] But, Mephistophilis,
    My blood congeals and I can write no more.

MEPH. I'll fetch thee fire to dissolve it straight.       [*Exit.*]

FAUST. What might the staying of my blood portend?
    Is it unwilling I should write this bill?[4] 65
    Why streams it not, that I may write afresh?
    "Faustus gives to thee his soul"—ah, there it stayed.
    Why shouldst thou not? Is not thy soul thine own?
    Then write again: "Faustus gives to thee his soul."
      [*Enter* MEPHISTOPHILIS *with a chafer*[5] *of fire.*]

MEPH. See, Faustus, here is fire; set it on. 70

FAUST. So: now the blood begins to clear again;
    Now will I make an end immediately.     [*Writes.*]

MEPH. [*aside*] What will not I do to obtain his soul!

FAUST. *Consummatum est*[6]—this bill is ended;
    And Faustus hath bequeathed his soul to Lucifer. 75
    But what is this inscription on mine arm?
    *"Homo, fuge!"*[7] Whither should I fly?
    If unto God, he'll throw me down to hell.
    My senses are deceived; here's nothing writ.
    O yes, I see it plain: even here is writ 80
    *"Homo, fuge!"* Yet shall not Faustus fly.

---

2. "Misery loves company."  3. Own.  4. Contract.  5. A portable grate.  6. "It is finished." A blasphemy, as these are the words of Christ on the Cross (see John 19:30).  7. "Man, fly!"

MEPH. I'll fetch him somewhat to delight his mind.        [*Exit.*]
　　[*Re-enter* MEPHISTOPHILIS *with* DEVILS, *giving crowns and rich
　　apparel to* FAUSTUS, *and dance, and then depart.*]
FAUST. What means this show?
　　Speak, Mephistophilis.
MEPH. Nothing, Faustus, but to delight thy mind                    85
　　And let thee see what magic can perform.
FAUST. But may I arise such spirits when I please?
MEPH. Aye, Faustus, and do greater things than these.
FAUST. Then, Mephistophilis, receive this scroll,
　　A deed of gift of body and of soul;                              90
　　But yet conditionally that thou perform
　　All covenant-articles between us both.
MEPH. Faustus, I swear by hell and Lucifer
　　To effect all promises between us made.
FAUST. Then hear me read it, Mephistophilis.        [*Reads.*]      95
　　"On these conditions following:
　　First, that Faustus may be a spirit in form and substance.
　　Secondly, that Mephistophilis shall be his servant and at his com-
　　mand.
　　Thirdly, that Mephistophilis shall do for him, and bring him      100
　　whatsoever.
　　Fourthly, that he shall be in his chamber or house invisible.
　　Lastly, that he shall appear to the said John Faustus at all
　　times, in what form or shape soever he please.
　　I, John Faustus of Wittenberg, Doctor, by these presents do       105
　　give both body and soul to Lucifer, Prince of the East, and his
　　minister Mephistophilis, and furthermore grant unto them,
　　that four and twenty years being expired, the articles above
　　written inviolate, full power to fetch or carry the said John
　　Faustus, body and soul, flesh, blood, or goods, into their        110
　　habitation wheresoever.
　　　　　　　　　　　　By me John Faustus."
MEPH. Speak, Faustus, do you deliver this as your deed?
FAUST. Aye, take it, and the devil give thee good of it.
MEPH. Now, Faustus, ask what thou wilt.                             115
FAUST. First will I question with thee about hell.
　　Tell me, where is the place that men call hell?
MEPH. Under the heavens.
FAUST.　　　　　　　　Aye, but whereabout?
MEPH. Within the bowels of these elements,
　　Where we are tortured and remain forever.                        120
　　Hell hath no limits, nor is circumscribed
　　In one self place, for where we are is hell,
　　And where hell is there must we ever be;

And, to be short, when all the world dissolves
And every creature shall be purified,                                    125
All places shall be hell that is not heaven.
FAUST. I think hell's a fable.
MEPH. Aye, think so, till experience change thy mind.
FAUST. Why, thinkst thou that Faustus shall be damned?
MEPH. Aye, of necessity, for here's the scroll                           130
  In which thou hast given thy soul to Lucifer.
FAUST. Aye, and body too; but what of that?
  Thinkst thou that Faustus is so fond[8] to imagine
  That after this life there is any pain?
  No, these are trifles and mere old wives' tales.                       135
MEPH. But I am an instance to prove the contrary,
  For I tell thee I am damned and now in hell.
FAUST. Nay, and this be hell I'll willingly be damned.
  What, sleeping, eating, walking, and disputing?
  But leaving off this, let me have a wife,                              140
  The fairest maid in Germany,
  For I am wanton and lascivious
  And cannot live without a wife.
MEPH. I prithee, Faustus, talk not of a wife.[9]
FAUST. Nay, sweet Mephistophilis, fetch me one, for I will have  145
  one.
MEPH. Well, thou shalt have a wife. Sit there till I come.      [*Exit.*]
  [*Re-enter* MEPHISTOPHILIS *with a* DEVIL *dressed like a woman,
  with fireworks.*]
FAUST. What sight is this?
MEPH. Now Faustus, how dost thou like thy wife?
FAUST. Here's a hot whore indeed! No, I'll no wife.                      150
MEPH. Marriage is but a ceremonial toy,
  And if thou lovest me, think no more of it.
  I'll cull thee out the fairest courtesans
  And bring them every morning to thy bed;
  She whom thine eye shall like thy heart shall have,                    155
  Were she as chaste as was Penelope,
  As wise as Saba,[1] or as beautiful
  As was bright Lucifer before his fall.
  Hold, take this book: peruse it thoroughly.
  The iterating of these lines brings gold,                              160
  The framing of this circle on the ground
  Brings whirlwinds, tempests, thunder, and lightning;
  Pronounce this thrice devoutly to thyself
  And men in harness shall appear to thee,

---

8. Foolish.  9. Mephistophilis cannot produce a wife for Faustus because marriage is a
sacrament.  1. Queen of Sheba. *Penelope:* Wife of Ulysses, famed for chastity and fidelity.

Ready to execute what thou desirest. 165

FAUST. Thanks, Mephistophilis, yet fain would I have a book
wherein I might behold all spells and incantations, that I
might raise up spirits when I please.

MEPH. Here they are in this book. *[There turn to them.]*

FAUST. Now would I have a book where I might see all characters 170
and planets of the heavens, that I might know their motions
and dispositions.

MEPH. Here they are too. *[Turn to them.]*

FAUST. Nay, let me have one book more, and then I have done,
wherein I might see all plants, herbs, and trees that grow upon 175
the earth.

MEPH. Here they be.

FAUST. O thou art deceived!

MEPH. Tut, I warrant thee. *[Turn to them.]*
 *[Exeunt.*[2]*]*

SCENE 2

*[Enter* FAUSTUS *in his study and* MEPHISTOPHILIS.*]*

FAUST. When I behold the heavens then I repent
And curse thee, wicked Mephistophilis,
Because thou hast deprived me of those joys.

MEPH. 'Twas thine own seeking, Faustus, thank thyself.
But thinkest thou heaven is such a glorious thing? 5
I tell thee, Faustus, it is not half so fair
As thou or any man that breathes on earth.

FAUST. How provest thou that?

MEPH. 'Twas made for man; then he's more excellent.

FAUST. If heaven was made for man 'twas made for me. 10
I will renounce this magic and repent.
 *[Enter* GOOD ANGEL *and* BAD ANGEL.*]*

G. ANG. Faustus, repent; yet God will pity thee.

B. ANG. Thou art a spirit; God cannot pity thee.

FAUST. Who buzzeth in mine ears I am a spirit?[3]
Be I a devil, yet God may pity me. 15
Yea, God will pity me, if I repent.

B. ANG. Aye, but Faustus never shall repent.
 *[Exeunt* ANGELS.*]*

FAUST. My heart is hardened; I cannot repent.
Scarce can I name salvation, faith, or heaven,
But fearful echoes thunder in mine ears: 20
"Faustus, thou are damned!" Then guns and knives,

---

2. After this a comic scene has been lost from the text. In it, apparently the Clown stole one of
Faustus' conjuring books and left Wagner's service. He then became an hostler at an inn.
3. Evil spirit, devil.

Swords, poison, halters, and envenomed steel
Are laid before me to dispatch myself,
And long ere this I should have done the deed
Had not sweet pleasure conquered deep despair.                    25
Have I not made blind Homer sing to me
Of Alexander's[4] love and Oenon's death,
And hath not he that built the walls of Thebes
With ravishing sound of his melodious harp[5]
Made music with my Mephistophilis?                    30
Why should I die, then, or basely despair?
I am resolved Faustus shall not repent.
Come, Mephistophilis, let us dispute again
And reason of divine astrology.
Speak, are there many spheres above the moon?                    35
Are all celestial bodies but one globe
As is the substance of this centric earth?

MEPH. As are the elements, such are the heavens,
Even from the moon unto the empyreal orb,
Mutually folded in each other's spheres,                    40
And jointly move upon one axletree
Whose termine[6] is termed the world's wide pole;
Nor are the names of Saturn, Mars, or Jupiter
Feigned, but are erring stars.

FAUST. But tell me, have they all one motion, both *situ et tem-*    45
*pore?*[7]

MEPH. All move from east to west in four and twenty hours upon
the poles of the world, but differ in their motions upon the
poles of the zodiac.

FAUST. These slender questions Wagner can decide.                    50
Hath Mephistophilis no greater skill?
Who knows not the double motion of the planets?
That the first is finished in a natural day;
The second thus, Saturn in thirty years, Jupiter in twelve, Mars
in four, the Sun, Venus, and Mercury in a year, the moon in    55
twenty-eight days. These are freshmen's suppositions. But tell
me, hath every sphere a dominion or *intelligentia?*

MEPH. Aye.

FAUST. How many heavens or spheres are there?

MEPH. Nine; the seven planets, the firmament, and the empyreal    60
heaven.

FAUST. But is there not *coelum igneum, et crystallinum?*[8]

4. Another name for Paris, the lover of Oenone; later he deserted her and abducted Helen,
causing the Trojan War. Oenone refused to heal the wounds Paris received in battle, and when
he died of them she killed herself in remorse.    5. I.e., the legendary musician Amphion.
6. End.    7. In position and time.    8. The "heaven of fire" and the "crystalline sphere,"
introduced by some of the old authorities to explain the precession of the equinoxes.

MEPH. No, Faustus, they be but fables.

FAUST. Resolve me then in this one question: why are not conjunctions, oppositions, aspects, eclipses, all at one time, but in 65
  some years we have more, in some less?

MEPH. *Per inequalem motum respectu totius.*[9]

FAUST. Well, I am answered. Tell me, who made the world?

MEPH. I will not.

FAUST. Sweet Mephistophilis, tell me. 70

MEPH. Move me not, Faustus.

FAUST. Villain, have I not bound thee to tell me anything?

MEPH. Aye, that is not against our kingdom; this is.
  Thou art damned; think thou of hell.

FAUST. Think, Faustus, upon God that made the world! 75

MEPH. Remember this!      [*Exit.*]

FAUST. Aye, go, accursèd spirit, to ugly hell;
  'Tis thou has damned distressèd Faustus' soul.
  Is't too late?
      [*Enter* GOOD ANGEL *and* BAD ANGEL.]

B. ANG. Too late. 80

G. ANG. Never too late, if Faustus will repent.

B. ANG. If thou repent, devils will tear thee in pieces.

G. ANG. Repent, and they shall never raze thy skin.
      [*Exeunt* ANGELS.]

FAUST. O Christ, my Saviour! my Saviour!
  Help to save distressèd Faustus' soul. 85
      [*Enter* LUCIFER, BELZEBUB, *and* MEPHISTOPHILIS.]

LUC. Christ cannot save thy soul, for he is just;
  There's none but I have interest in the same.

FAUST. O what art thou that lookst so terrible?

LUC. I am Lucifer,
  And this is my companion prince in hell. 90

FAUST. O Faustus, they are come to fetch thy soul!

BEL. We are come to tell thee thou dost injure us.

LUC. Thou call'st on Christ, contrary to thy promise.

BEL. Thou shouldst not think on God.

LUC. Think on the devil. 95

BEL. And his dam too.[1]

FAUST. Nor will I henceforth. Pardon me in this,
  And Faustus vows never to look to heaven,
  Never to name God or pray to him,
  To burn his Scriptures, slay his ministers, 100
  And make my spirits pull his churches down.

---

9. "Because of their unequal velocities within the system."      1. "The devil and his dam" was a
common colloquial expression.

LUC. So shalt thou show thyself an obedient servant, and we will
 highly gratify thee for it.

BEL. Faustus, we are come from hell in person to show thee some
 pastime. Sit down, and thou shalt behold the Seven Deadly  105
 Sins appear to thee in their own proper shapes and likeness.

FAUST. That sight will be as pleasant to me as Paradise was to
 Adam, the first day of his creation.

LUC. Talk not of Paradise or Creation, but mark the show. Go,
 Mephistophilis, fetch them in.  110

 [*Enter the* SEVEN DEADLY SINS, *led by a piper.*]

 Now, Faustus, question them of their names and dispositions.

FAUST. That shall I soon. What art thou, the first?

PRIDE. I am Pride. I disdain to have any parents. I am like to
 Ovid's flea:[2] I can creep into every corner of a wench; sometimes like a periwig I sit upon her brow; next like a necklace  115
 I hang about her neck; then like a fan of feathers I kiss her
 lips; and then turning myself to a wrought smock[3] do what I list.
 But fie, what a smell is here! I'll not speak another word
 except the ground be perfumed and covered with cloth of
 arras.  120

FAUST. Thou art a proud knave indeed. What art thou, the
 second?

COVET I am Covetousness, begotten of an old churl in a leather
 bag; and, might I now obtain my wish, this house, you and
 all, should turn to gold, that I might lock you safe into my  125
 chest. O my sweet gold!

FAUST. And what art thou, the third?

ENVY. I am Envy, begotten of a chimney-sweeper and an oyster-
 wife. I cannot read, and therefore wish all books were burned.
 I am lean with seeing others eat. O that there would come a  130
 famine over all the world, that all might die, and I live alone;
 then thou shouldst see how fat I'd be! But must thou sit and
 I stand? Come down, with a vengeance!

FAUST. Out, envious wretch! But what art thou, the fourth?

WRATH. I am Wrath. I had neither father nor mother; I leapt  135
 out of a lion's mouth when I was scarce an hour old, and ever
 since have run up and down the world with these case of
 rapiers, wounding myself when I could get none to fight withal.
 I was born in hell; and look to it, for some of you shall be my
 father.  140

FAUST. And what art thou, the fifth?

GLUT. I am Gluttony. My parents are all dead, and the devil a
 penny they have left me but a small pension, and that buys

2. A salacious medieval poem *Carmen de Pulice* ("The Flea") was attributed to Ovid.   3. A
decorated or ornamented petticoat.

me thirty meals a day and ten bevers—a small trifle to suffice
nature. I come of a royal pedigree: my father was a gammon[4]     145
of bacon, and my mother was a hogshead of claret wine. My
godfathers were these: Peter Pickle-herring and Martin Martle-
mas-beef. But my godmother, O, she was a jolly gentlewoman,
and well beloved in every good town and city: her name was
mistress Margery March-beer. Now, Faustus, thou hast heard     150
all my progeny; wilt thou bid me to supper?

FAUST. Not I. Thou wilt eat up all my victuals.

GLUT. Then the devil choke thee!

FAUST. Choke thyself, glutton. What art thou, the sixth?

SLOTH. Heigh ho! I am Sloth. I was begotten on a sunny bank,     155
where I have lain ever since, and you have done me great injury
to bring me from thence; let me be carried thither again by
Gluttony and Lechery. Heigh ho! I'll not speak word more for
a king's ransom.

FAUST. And what are you, mistress minx, the seventh and last?     160

LECHERY. Who, I, sir? I am one that loves an inch of raw mutton[5] better than an ell of fried stockfish, and the first letter
of my name begins with Lechery.

LUC. Away, to hell, away! On, piper!
　　[Exeunt the SINS.]

FAUST. O how this sight doth delight my soul!     165

LUC. Tut, Faustus, in hell is all manner of delight.

FAUST. O might I see hell and return again safe, how happy were
I then!

LUC. Faustus, thou shalt. At midnight I will send for thee. In
meantime peruse this book, and view it throughly, and thou     170
shalt turn thyself into what shape thou wilt.

FAUST. Thanks, mighty Lucifer; this will I keep as chary as my
life.

LUC. Now Faustus, farewell.

FAUST. Farewell, great Lucifer. Come, Mephistophilis.     175
　　[Exeunt OMNES.]

## SCENE 3

　　[Enter the CLOWN (ROBIN).]

ROBIN. What, Dick, look to the horses there till I come again.
I have gotten one of Dr. Faustus' conjuring books, and now
we'll have such knavery as 't passes.
　　[Enter DICK.]

DICK. What, Robin, you must come away and walk the horses.

ROBIN. I walk the horses! I scorn 't, faith: I have other matters     5

4. The lower side of pork, including the leg. *Bevers*: Snacks.　5. Here, the penis. *Ell*: 45 inches;
*stockfish*: dried cod.

in hand; let the horses walk themselves and they will. "A *per
se*[6] a; t, h, e, the; o *per se* o; deny orgon, gorgon." Keep further
from me, O thou illiterate and unlearned hostler.

DICK. 'Snails,[7] what has thou got there? a book? Why, thou canst
not tell ne'er a word on 't.                                    10

ROBIN. That thou shalt see presently. Keep out of the circle, I
say, lest I send you into the ostry[8] with a vengence.

DICK. That's like, faith! You had best leave your foolery, for an
my master come, he'll conjure you, faith.

ROBIN. My master conjure me! I'll tell thee what; an my master   15
come here, I'll clap as fair a pair of horns on 's head as e'er
thou sawest in thy life.[9]

DICK. Thou needst not do that, for my mistress hath done it.

ROBIN. Aye, there be of us here have waded as deep into matters
as other men, if they were disposed to talk.                    20

DICK. A plague take you! I thought you did not sneak up and
down after her for nothing. But I prithee tell me in good sadness, Robin, is that a conjuring book?

ROBIN. Do but speak what thou 't have me do, and I'll do 't. If
thou 't dance naked, put off thy clothes, and I'll conjure about  25
thee presently. Or if thou 't but to the tavern with me, I'll give
thee white wine, red wine, claret wine, sack, muscadine, mal-
mesey, and whippincrust,[1] hold-belly-hold, and we'll not pay
one penny for it.

DICK. O brave! Prithee let's to it presently, for I am as dry as
a dog.                                                          30

ROBIN. Come then, let's away.          [*Exeunt.*]

## Act III

[*Enter* CHORUS.]

CHO. Learned Faustus,
    To find the secrets of astonomy
    Graven in the book of Jove's high firmament,
    Did mount himself to scale Olympus' top.
    Where sitting in a chariot burning bright              5
    Drawn by the strength of yokéd dragons' necks,
    He views the clouds, the planets, and the stars,
    The tropics, zones, and quarters of the sky
    From the bright circle of the hornéd moon
    Even to the height of *Primum Mobile;*[2]             10

---

6. "A by itself," a method of reading the letters of the alphabet taught to children. Robin's semi-
literacy is being satirized. *Deny orgon, gorgon:* A prody of Faustus' invocation of Demogorgon in
I.iii.    7. I.e., God's nails (on the Cross).    8. Stable.    9. A wife's infidelity was supposed
to cause her husband to grow horns.    1. Robin's pronunciation of "hippocras," a spiced wine.
2. The outermost sphere, the empyrean.

And whirling round with this circumference
Within the concave compass of the pole,
From east to west his dragons swiftly glide
And in eight days did bring him home again.
Not long he stayed within his quiet house　　　　　15
To rest his bones after his weary toil
But new exploits do hale him out again;
And mounted then upon a dragon's back
That with his wings did part the subtle air,
He now is gone to prove cosmography[3]　　　　　20
That measures coasts and kingdoms of the earth:
And, as I guess, will first arrive at Rome
To see the Pope and manner of his court
And take some part of holy Peter's feast,
The which this day is highly solemnized.　　　　　25
　　[*Exit.*]

## SCENE 1

[*Enter* FAUSTUS *and* MEPHISTOPHILIS.]

FAUST. Having now, my good Mephistophilis,
Passed with delight the stately town of Trier[4]
Environed round with airy mountain tops,
With walls of flint and deep-entrenchéd lakes,[5]
Not to be won by any conquering prince;　　　　　5
From Paris next coasting the realm of France,
We saw the river Maine fall into Rhine,
Whose banks are set with groves of fruitful vines;
Then up to Naples, rich Campania,
With buildings fair and gorgeous to the eye,　　　　　10
Whose streets straight forth and paved with finest brick
Quarter the town in four equivalents
There saw we learned Maro's[6] golden tomb,
The way he cut, an English mile in length,
Through a rock of stone in one night's space.　　　　　15
From thence to Venice, Padua, and the rest,
In midst of which a sumptuous temple[7] stands
That threats the stars with her aspiring top,
Whose frame is paved with sundry colored stones
And roofed aloft with curious work in gold.　　　　　20
Thus hitherto hath Faustus spent his time.
But tell me now, what resting place is this?

---

3. I.e., to test the accuracy of maps.　　4. Treves (in Prussia).　　5. Moats.　　6. Virgil's. In medieval legend the Roman poet Virgil was considered a magician, and a tunnel ("way") on the promontory of Posilippo at Naples, near his tomb, was accredited to his magical powers.　　7. St. Mark's in Venice.

Hast thou, as erst I did command,
Conducted me within the walls of Rome?
MEPH. I have, my Faustus, and for proof thereof 25
This is the goodly palace of the Pope,
And 'cause we are no common guests
I choose his privy chamber for our use.
FAUST. I hope his Holiness will bid us welcome.
MEPH. All's one, for we'll be bold with his vension. 30
But not, my Faustus, that thou mayst perceive
What Rome contains for to delight thine eyes,
Know that this city stands upon seven hills
That underprop the groundwork of the same;
Just through the midst runs flowing Tiber's stream, 35
With winding banks that cut it in two parts,
Over the which four stately bridges lean
That make safe passage to each part of Rome.
Upon the bridge called Ponte Angelo
Erected is a castle passing strong, 40
Where thou shalt see such store of ordnance
As that the double cannons forged of brass
Do match the number of the days contained
Within the compass of one complete year;
Besides the gates and high pyramides[8] 45
That Julius Caesar brought from Africa.
FAUST. Now by the kingdoms of infernal rule,
Of Styx, Acheron, and the fiery lake
Of ever-burning Phlegethon,[9] I swear
That I do long to see the monuments 50
And situation of bright-splendent Rome.
Come, therefore, let's away.
MEPH. Nay, stay, my Faustus; I know you'd see the Pope
And take some part of holy Peter's feast,
The which in state and high solemnity 55
This day is held through Rome and Italy
In honor of the Pope's triumphant victory.
FAUST. Sweet Mephistophilis, thou pleasest me;
Whilst I am here on earth let me be cloyed
With all things that delight the heart of man. 60
My four and twenty years of liberty
I'll spend in pleasure and in dalliance,
That Faustus' name, whilst this bright frame doth stand,
May be admiréd through the furthest land.
MEPH. 'Tis well said, Faustus; come then, stand by me 65

8. *Py-rám-i-des*, a singular noun, meaning an obelisk.    9. Classical names for rivers of the underworld.

And thou shalt see them come immediately.

FAUST. Nay, stay, my gentle Mephistophilis,
And grant me my request, and then I go.
Thou knowst, within the compass of eight days
We viewed the face of heaven, of earth, of hell;                    70
So high our dragons soared into the air
That, looking down, the earth appeared to me
No bigger than my hand in quantity.
There did we view the kingdoms of the world,
And what might please mine eye I there beheld.                      75
Then in this show let me an actor be,
That this proud Pope may Faustus' cunning see.

MEPH. Let it be so, my Faustus, but first stay
And view their triumphs[1] as they pass this way
And then devise what best contents thy mind,                        80
By cunning of thine art to cross the Pope
Or dash the pride of this solemnity,
To make his monks and abbots stand like apes
And point like antics[2] at his triple crown,
To beat the beads about the friars' pates                          85
Or clap huge horns upon the cardinals' heads,
Or any villainy thou canst devise,
And I'll perform it, Faustus. Hark, they come!
This day shall make thee be admired in Rome.
     [Enter the CARDINALS and BISHOPS, some bearing crosiers,
     some the pillars; MONKS and FRIARS singing their proces-
     sion; then the POPE and RAYMOND, King of Hungary,
     with BRUNO[3] led in chains.]

POPE. Cast down our footstool.

RAY.                              Saxon Bruno, stoop,                90
Whilst on thy back his Holiness ascends
St. Peter's chair and state pontifical.

BRUNO. Proud Lucifer, that state belongs to me;
But thus I fall, to Peter, not to thee.

POPE. To me and Peter shalt thou groveling lie                     95
And crouch before the papal dignity.
Sound trumpets, then, for thus St. Peter's heir
From Bruno's back ascends St. Peter's chair.
     [A flourish while he ascends.]
Thus as the gods creep on with feet of wool
Long ere with iron hands they punish men,                          100
So shall our sleeping vengeance now arise
And smite with death thy hated enterprise.

---

1. Parades.    2. Grotesque figures.    3. Like Raymond, fictitious; he is the German pretender
to the papal throne over whom the Pope has just triumphed (line 57).

Lord Cardinals of France and Padua,
Go forthwith to our holy consistory
And read among the statutes decretal                                105
What, by the holy council held at Trent,[4]
The sacred synod hath decreed for him
That doth assume the papal government
Without election and a true consent.
Away and bring us word with speed.                                 110

1 CARD. We go, my lord.        [*Exeunt* CARDINALS.]

POPE. Lord Raymond—

FAUST. Go, haste thee, gentle Mephistophilis,
Follow the cardinals to the consistory,
And as they turn their superstitious books,                        115
Strike them with sloth and drowsy idleness
And make them sleep so sound that in their shapes
Thyself and I may parley with this Pope,
This proud confronter of the Emperor,[5]
And in despite of all his holiness                                 120
Restore this Bruno to his liberty
And bear him to the states of Germany.

MEPH. Faustus, I go.

FAUST                    Dispatch it soon.
The Pope shall curse that Faustus came to Rome.

    [*Exeunt* FAUSTUS *and* MEPHISTOPHILIS.]

BRUNO. Pope Adrian, let me have some right of law;               125
I was elected by the Emperor.

POPE. We will depose the Emperor for that deed
And curse the people that submit to him;
Both he and thou shalt stand excommunicate
And interdict from church's privilege                              130
And all society of holy men.
He grows too proud in his authority,
Lifting his lofty head above the clouds,
And like a steeple overpeers the church,
But we'll pull down his haughty insolence.                         135
And as Pope Alexander,[6] our progenitor,
Trod on the neck of German Frederick,
Adding this golden sentence to our praise,
That Peter's heirs should tread on emperors
And walk upon the dreadful adder's back,                           140
Treading the lion and the dragon down,
And fearless spurn the killing basilisk;

4. 1545–1563.    5. Holy Roman Emperor. Faustus refers to the conflict between the Pope and the Emperor; the former was victorious and captured the Emperor's choice for Pope, "Saxon Bruno."    6. Alexander III (1159–81) compelled the Emperor Frederick Barbarossa to submit to him.

So will we quell that haughty schismatic,
And by authority apostolical
Depose him from his regal government.                                    145
BRUNO. Pope Julius swore to princely Sigismond,
    For him and the succeeding popes of Rome,
    To hold the emperors their lawful lords.
POPE. Pope Julius did abuse the church's rights,
    And therefore none of his decrees can stand.                        150
    Is not all power on earth bestowed on us?
    And therefore though we would we cannot err.
    Behold this silver belt, whereto is fixed
    Seven golden keys fast sealed with seven seals
    In token of our sevenfold power from heaven,                        155
    To bind or loose, lock fast, condemn, or judge,
    Resign or seal, or whatso pleaseth us.
    Then he and thou and all the world shall stoop,
    Or be assuréd of our dreadful curse
    To light as heavy as the pains of hell.                             160
        [*Enter* FAUSTUS *and* MEPHISTOPHILIS *like cardinals.*]
MEPH. Now tell me, Faustus, are we not fitted well?
FAUST. Yes, Mephistophilis, and two such cardinals
    Ne'er served a holy pope as we shall do.
    But whilst they sleep within the consistory
    Let us salute his reverend Fatherhood.                              165
RAY. Behold, my lord, the cardinals are returned.
POPE. Welcome, grave fathers, answer presently;[7]
    What have our holy council there decreed
    Concerning Bruno and the Emperor
    In quittance of their late conspiracy                               170
    Against our state and papal dignity?
FAUST. Most sacred patron of the church of Rome,
    By full consent of all the synod
    Of priests and prelates it is thus decreed:
    That Bruno and the German Emperor                                   175
    Be held as lollards[8] and bold schismatics
    And proud disturbers of the church's peace.
    And if that Bruno by his own assent,
    Without enforcement of the German peers,
    Did seek to wear the triple diadem                                  180
    And by your death to climb St. Peter's chair,
    The statutes decretal have thus decreed:
    He shall be straight condemned of heresy

7. Immediately.    8. Protestants, usually English followers of Wycliffe, 14th-century religious
reformer.

And on a pile of fagots burned to death.

POPE. It is enough. Here, take him to your charge        185
    And bear him straight to Ponte Angelo,
    And in the strongest tower enclose him fast.
    Tomorrow, sitting in our consistory
    With all our college of grave cardinals,
    We will determine of his life or death.        190
    Here, take his triple crown along with you
    And leave it in the church's treasury.
    Make haste again, my good lord cardinals,
    And take our blessing apostolical.

MEPH. So, so. Was never devil thus blessed before!        195

FAUST. Away, sweet Mephistophilis, be gone;
    The cardinals will be plagued for this anon.
        [*Exeunt* FAUSTUS *and* MEPHISTOPHILIS *with* BRUNO.]

POPE. Go presently and bring a banquet forth,
    That we may solemnize St. Peter's feast
    And with Lord Raymond, King of Hungary,        200
    Drink to our late and happy victory.        [*Exeunt.*]


### SCENE 2

[*The banquet is brought in, and then enter* FAUSTUS *and*
    MEPHISTOPHILIS *in their own shapes.*]

MEPH. Now Faustus, come prepare thyself for mirth;
    The sleepy cardinals are hard at hand
    To censure Bruno, that is posted hence
    And on a proud-paced steed as swift as thought
    Flies o'er the Alps to fruitful Germany,        5
    There to salute the woeful Emperor.

FAUST. The Pope will curse them for their sloth today
    That slept both Bruno and his crown away.
    But now, that Faustus may delight his mind
    And by their folly make some merriment,        10
    Sweet Mephistophilis, so charm me here
    That I may walk invisible to all
    And do whate'er I please unseen of any.

MEPH. Faustus, thou shalt; then kneel down presently,

            Whilst on thy head I lay my hand        15
            And charm thee with this magic wand.
            First wear this girdle, then appear
            Invisible to all are here.
            The planets seven, the gloomy air,
            Hell, and the Furies' forkéd hair,        20

Pluto's blue fire and Hecate's[9] tree
With magic spells so compass thee
That no eye may thy body see.

So, Faustus, now, for all their holiness,
   Do what thou wilt thou shalt not be discerned.                    25
FAUST. Thanks, Mephistophilis. Now friars, take heed
   Lest Faustus make your shaven crowns to bleed.
MEPH. Faustus, no more; see where the cardinals come.
   [*Enter* POPE *and all the lords, with* KING RAYMOND *and
   the* ARCHBISHOP OF RHEIMS. *Enter the two* CARDINALS
   *with a book.*]
POPE. Welcome, lord cardinals; come, sit down.
   Lord Raymond, take your seat. Friars, attend,                     30
   And see that all things be in readiness
   As best beseems this solemn festival.
1 CARD. First may it please your sacred holiness
   To view the sentence of the reverend synod
   Concerning Bruno and the Emperor.                                 35
POPE. What needs this question? Did I not tell you
   Tomorrow we would sit i' th' consistory
   And there determine of his punishment?
   You brought us word, even now, it was decreed
   That Bruno and the curséd Emperor                                 40
   Were by the holy council both condemned
   For loathéd lollards and base schismatics;
   Then wherefore would you have me view that book?
1 CARD. Your Grace mistakes; you gave us no such charge.
RAY. Deny it not; we all are witnesses                              45
   That Bruno here was late delivered you,
   With his rich triple crown to be reserved
   And put into the church's treasury.
BOTH CARD. By holy Paul we saw them not.
POPE. By Peter, you shall die                                       50
   Unless you bring them forth immediately.
   Hale them to prison! Lade their limbs with gyves![1]
   False prelates, for this hateful treachery,
   Cursed be your souls to hellish misery.          [*Exeunt* CARDINALS.]
FAUST. So they are safe. Now, Faustus, to the feast;                55
   The Pope had never such a frolic guest.
POPE. Lord Archbishop of Rheims, sit down with us.
ARCH. I thank your Holiness.

---

9. Goddess of magic and witchcraft, whose name the Elizabethans pronounced *Héc-at.* "Tree"
may be a mistake for "three," since she was often represented as a triple goddess—of heaven,
earth, and hell.  1. I.e., load their limbs with prisoners' shackles.

FAUST. Fall to! The devil choke you an you spare!

POPE. Who's that spoke? Friars, look about.                               60
   Lord Raymond, pray fall to. I am beholden
   To the Bishop of Milan for this so rare a present.

FAUST. I thank you, sir.
    [FAUSTUS *snatches the meat from the* POPE.]

POPE. How now! Who snatched the meat from me? Villains,
   why speak you not?                                          65

FRIAR. Here's nobody, if it like your Holiness.

POPE. My good Lord Archbishop, here's a most dainty dish
   Was sent me from a cardinal in France.

FAUST. I'll have that, too.
    [FAUSTUS *snatches the dish from the* POPE.]

POPE. What lollards do attend our Holiness                                70
   That we receive such great indignity?
   Fetch me some wine.

FAUST. Aye, pray do, for Faustus is adry.

POPE. Lord Raymond, I drink unto your Grace.

FAUST. I pledge your Grace.                                               75
    [FAUSTUS *snatches the cup from the* POPE.]

POPE. My wine gone, too? Ye lubbers, look about
   And find the man that doth this villainy,
   Or by my sanctitude you all shall die.
   I pray, my lords, have patience at this troublesome banquet.

ARCH. Please your Holiness, I think it be some ghost crept out of    80
   purgatory and now is come unto your Holiness for his pardon.

POPE. It may be so;
   Go then, command our priests to sing a dirge
   To lay the fury of this same troublesome ghost.
   Once again, my lord, fall to.                                   85
    [*The* POPE *crosses himself.*]

FAUST. How now!
   Must every bit be spicéd with a cross?
   Well, use that trick no more, I would advise you.
    [*The* POPE *crosses himself.*]
   Well, there's the second time; aware the third;
   I give you fair warning.                                        90
    [*The* POPE *crosses himself again.*]
   Nay then, take that!
    [FAUSTUS *hits the* POPE *a box on the ear.*]

POPE. O, I am slain! Help me, my lords!
   O come and help to bear my body hence!
   Damned be his soul forever for this deed.
    [*Exeunt the* POPE *and his train.*]

MEPH. Now Faustus, what will you do now? For I can tell you          95 you'll be cursed with bell, book, and candle.[2]

FAUST. Bell, book, and candle; candle, book, and bell
    Forward and backward, to curse Faustus to hell!
        [*Enter all the* FRIARS *with bell, book, and candle to sing the*
        *dirge.*]

FRIAR. Come, brethren, let's about our business with good devo-
    tion.                                                                        100
        [ALL *sing this:*]
    Curséd be he that stole away his Holiness' meat from the
    table—*maledicat dominus!*[3]
    Curséd be he that struck his Holiness a blow on the face—          105
    *maledicat dominus!*
    Curséd be he that took Friar Sandelo a blow on the face—
    *maledicat dominus!*
    Curséd be he that disturbeth our holy dirge—*maledicat domi-*
    *nus!*
    Curséd be he that took away his Holiness' wine—*maledicat*
    *dominus! Et omnes sancti!*[4] Amen.                                 110
        [FAUSTUS *and* MEPHISTOPHILIS *beat the* FRIARS, *and fling*
        *fireworks among them, and so exeunt.*]

### SCENE 3

[*Enter* CLOWN (ROBIN) *and* DICK *with a cup.*]

DICK. Sirrah Robin, we were best look that your devil can answer
    the stealing of this same cup, for the vintner's boy follows us
    at the hard heels.

ROBIN. 'Tis no matter, let him come! An he follow us I'll so con-
    jure him as he was never conjured in his life, I warrant him.         5
    Let me see the cup.
        [*Enter* VINTNER.]

DICK. Here 'tis. Yonder he comes. Now, Robin, now or never
    show thy cunning.

VINT. O, are you here? I am glad I have found you. You are a
    couple of fine companions! Pray, where's the cup you stole           10
    from the tavern?

ROBIN. How, how? We steal a cup? Take heed what you say! We
    look not like cup-stealers, I can tell you.

VINT. Never deny it, for I know you have it, and I'll search you.

ROBIN. Search me? Aye, and spare not. Hold the cup, Dick!            15
    Come, come; search me, search me.

VINT. Come on, sirrah, let me search you now.

DICK. Aye, aye, do; do. Hold the cup, Robin. I fear not your
    searching. We scorn to steal your cups, I can tell you.

2. The traditional paraphernalia for cursing and excommunication.   3. "May the Lord curse
him!"   4. And all the saints (also curse him).

VINT. Never outface me for the matter, for sure the cup is be-
    tween you two.                                                    20
ROBIN. Nay, there you lie. 'Tis beyond us both.
VINT. A plague take you! I thought 'twas your knavery to take it
    away. Come, give it me again.
ROBIN. Aye, much! When, can you tell?[5] Dick, make me a circle,
    and stand close at my back and stir not for thy life. Vintner,    25
    you shall have your cup anon. Say nothing, Dick. O *per se* O;
    Demogorgon, Belcher and Mephistophilis!
        [*Enter* MEPHISTOPHILIS.]
MEPH. Monarch of hell, under whose black survey
    Great potentates do kneel with awful fear,                        30
    Upon whose altars thousand souls do lie,
    How am I vexéd with these villains' charms!
    From Constantinople am I hither brought
    Only for pleasure of these damnéd slaves.     [*Exit* VINTNER.]
ROBIN. By Lady, sir, you have had a shrewd journey of it; will it     35
    please you to take a shoulder of mutton to supper and a tester[6]
    in your purse, and go back again?
DICK. Aye, I pray you heartily, sir; for we called you but in jest,
    I promise you.
MEPH. To purge the rashness of this curséd deed,                      40
    First be thou turnéd to this ugly shape:
    For apish deeds transforméd to an ape.
ROBIN. O brave! an ape! I pray, sir, let me have the carrying of
    him about to show some tricks.
MEPH. And so thou shalt. Be thou transformed to a dog and            45
    carry him upon thy back. Away! Be gone!
ROBIN. A dog! That's excellent! Let the maids look well to their
    porridge pots, for I'll into the kitchen presently. Come, Dick,
    come.
        [*Exit* ROBIN *and* DICK.]
MEPH. Now with the flames of ever-burning fire                        50
    I'll wing myself and forthwith fly amain
    Unto my Faustus, to the Great Turk's court.          [*Exit.*]


## Act IV

    [*Enter* CHORUS.]
CHO. When Faustus had with pleasure ta'en the view
    Of rarest things and royal courts of kings,
    He stayed his course and so returnéd home,
    Where such as bear his absence but with grief,

---

5. A common Elizabethan scornful retort.     6. Sixpence.

I mean his friends and nearest companións,                    5
Did gratulate his safety with kind words,
And in their conference of what befell
Touching his journey through the world and air,
They put forth questions of astrology
Which Faustus answered with such learned skill          10
As they admired and wondered at his wit.
Now is his fame spread forth in every land:
Amongst the rest the Emperor is one,
Carolus the Fifth,[7] at whose palace now
Faustus is feasted 'mongst his noblemen.                 15
What there he did in trial of his art
I leave untold, your eyes shall see performed.        [*Exit.*]

SCENE 1

[*Enter* MARTINO *and* FREDERICK *at several doors.*[8]]
MART. What ho! Officers, gentlemen!
    Hie to the presence to attend the Emperor.
    Good Frederick, see the rooms be voided straight;
    His Majesty is coming to the hall.
    Go back, and see the state in readiness.                5
FRED. But where is Bruno, our elected Pope,
    That on a fury's back came post from Rome?
    Will not his Grace consort the Emperor?
MART. O yes, and with him comes the German conjurer,
    The learned Faustus, fame of Wittenberg,             10
    The wonder of the world for magic art;
    And he intends to show great Carolus
    The race of all his stout progenitors
    And bring in presence of his majesty
    The royal shapes and warlike semblances             15
    Of Alexander and his beauteous paramour.[9]
FRED. Where is Benvolio?
MART. Fast asleep, I warrant you;
    He took his rouse with stoups[1] of Rhenish wine
    So kindly yesternight to Bruno's health               20
    That all this day the sluggard keeps his bed.
FRED. See, see; his window's ope; we'll call to him.
MART. What ho, Benvolio!
        [*Enter* BENVOLIO *above at a window, in his nightcap,
        buttoning.*]
BENV. What a devil ail you two?

---

7. Emperor Charles V (1519–56).    8. At different entrances.    9. Alexander the Great and his mistress Thais.    1. Drank many full glasses.

MART. Speak softly, sir, lest the devil hear you;                    25
    For Faustus at the court is late arrived
    And at his heels a thousand furies wait
    To accomplish whatsoever the Doctor please.
BENV. What of this?
MART. Come, leave thy chamber first and thou shalt see          30
    This conjurer perform such rare exploits
    Before the Pope[2] and royal Emperor
    As never yet was seen in Germany.
BENV. Has not the Pope enough of conjuring yet?
    He was upon the devil's back late enough,                    35
    And if he be so far in love with him
    I would he would post home to Rome with him again.
FRED. Speak, wilt thou come and see this sport?
BENV. Not I.
MART. Wilt thou stand in thy window and see it, then?          40
BENV. Aye, and I fall not asleep i' th' meantime.
MART. The Emperor is at hand, who comes to see
    What wonders by black spells may compassed be.
BENV. Well, go you to the Emperor. I am content for this once to
    thrust my head out a window, for they say if a man be drunk    45
    overnight the devil cannot hurt him in the morning. If that be
    true, I have a charm in my head shall control him as well as the
    conjurer, I warrant you.
      [*Exit* MARTINO *and* FREDERICK.]

SCENE 2

    [*A sennet. Enter* CHARLES THE GERMAN EMPEROR, BRUNO,
    *the* DUKE OF SAXONY, FAUSTUS, MEPHISTOPHILIS, FRED-
    ERICK, MARTINO *and* ATTENDANTS. BENVOLIO *remains at
    his window.*]
EMP. Wonder of men, renowned magician,
    Thrice-learned Faustus, welcome to our court.
    This deed of thine, in setting Bruno free
    From his and our professéd enemy,
    Shall add more excellence unto thine art                     5
    Than if by powerful necromantic spells
    Thou couldst command the world's obedience.
    Forever be beloved of Carolus;
    And if this Bruno thou hast late redeemed
    In peace possess the triple diadem                           10
    And sit in Peter's chair despite of chance,
    Thou shalt be famous through all Italy
    And honored of the German Emperor.

2. Bruno.

FAUST. These gracious words, most royal Carolus,
    Shall make poor Faustus to his utmost power 15
    Both love and serve the German Emperor
    And lay his life at holy Bruno's feet.
    For proof whereof, if so your Grace be pleased,
    The Doctor stands prepared by power of art
    To cast his magic charms that shall pierce through 20
    The ebon gates of ever-burning hell
    And hale the stubborn furies from their caves
    To compass whatsoe'er your Grace commands.
BENV. [aside] Blood! He speaks terribly, but for all that I do not
    greatly believe him. He looks as like a conjurer as the Pope 25
    to a costermonger.
EMP. Then Faustus, as thou late didst promise us,
    We would behold that famous conqueror,
    Great Alexander and his paramour,
    In their true shapes and state majestical, 30
    That we may wonder at their excellence.
FAUST. Your Majesty shall see them presently.
    Mephistophilis, away!
    And with a solemn noise of trumpets' sound
    Present before this royal Emperor 35
    Great Alexander and his beauteous paramour.
MEPH. Faustus, I will.       [Exit.]
BENV. [aside] Well, master Doctor, an your devils come not away
    quickly, you shall have me asleep presently. Zounds, I could eat
    myself for anger to think I have been such an ass all this while 40
    to stand gaping after the devil's governor, and can see nothing.
FAUST. [aside] I'll make you feel something anon if my art
    fail me not.—
    My lord, I must forewarn your Majesty
    That when my spirits present the royal shapes 45
    Of Alexander and his paramour,
    Your Grace demand no questions of the King,
    But in dumb silence let them come and go.
EMP. Be it as Faustus please; we are content.
BENV. [aside] Aye, Aye, and I am content, too. And thou bring 50
    Alexander and his paramour before the Emperor, I'll be Ac-
    taeon[3] and turn myself into a stag.
FAUST. [aside] And I'll play Diana and send you the horns pres-
    ently.
        [Sennet. Enter at one door the emperor ALEXANDER, at the
        other DARIUS. They meet; DARIUS is thrown down; ALEX-

---

3. The hunter of classical legend who happened to see the goddess Diana bathing. In punishment
he was changed into a stag and pursued by his own hounds.

ANDER *kills him, takes off his crown and, offering to go out, his* PARAMOUR *meets him; he embraceth her and sets* DARIUS' *crown upon her head and, coming back, both salute the* EMPEROR, *who, leaving his state,*[4] *offers to embrace them, which* FAUSTUS *seeing, suddenly stays him. Then trumpets cease and music sounds.*]

FAUST. My gracious lord, you do forget yourself;  55
    These are but shadows, not substantial.

EMP. O pardon me; my thoughts are ravished so
    With sight of this renownéd Emperor
    That in mine arms I would have compassed him.
    But Faustus, since I may not speak to them  60
    To satisfy my longing thoughts at full,
    Let me this tell thee: I have heard it said
    That this fair lady, whilst she lived on earth,
    Had on her neck a little wart or mole.
    How may I prove that saying to be true?  65

FAUST. Your Majesty may boldly go and see.

EMP. Faustus, I see it plain;
    And in this sight thou better pleasest me
    Than if I gained another monarchy.

FAUST. Away, be gone!    [*Exit* SHOW.]  70
    See, see, my gracious lord, what strange beast is yon, that
    thrusts its head out at the window!

EMP. O wondrous sight! See, Duke of Saxony, two spreading
    horns most strangely fastened upon the head of young Ben-  75
    volio.

SAX. What, is he asleep, or dead?

FAUST. He sleeps, my lord, but dreams not of his horns.

EMP. This sport is excellent. We'll call and wake him. What ho!
    Benvolio!

BENV. A plague upon you! Let me sleep a while.  80

EMP. I blame thee not to sleep, much, having such a head of thine
    own.

SAX. Look up, Benvolio. 'Tis the Emperor calls.

BENV. The Emperor! Where? O zounds, my head!

EMP. Nay, and thy horns hold 'tis no matter for thy head, for  85
    that's armed sufficiently.

FAUST. Why, how now, sir knight! What, hanged by the horns?
    This is most horrible. Fie, fie! Pull in your head, for shame!
    Let not all the world wonder at you.

BENV. Zounds, Doctor, is this your villainy?  90

FAUST. O, say not so, sir. The Doctor has no skill,
    No art, no cunning to present these lords

4. Throne.

Or bring before this royal Emperor
The mighty monarch, warlike Alexander?
If Faustus do it, you are straight resolved                     95
In bold Actaeon's shape to turn a stag?
And therefore, my lord, so please your Majesty,
I'll raise a kennel of hounds shall hunt him so
As all his footmanship shall scarce prevail
To keep his carcass from their bloody fangs.                    100
Ho, Belimote, Argiron, Asterote!

BENV. Hold, hold! Zounds, he'll raise up a kennel of devils, I
     think, anon. Good my lord, entreat for me. 'Sblood, I am never
     able to endure these torments.

EMP. Then good master Doctor,                                    105
     Let me entreat you to remove his horns;
     He has done penance now sufficiently.

FAUST. My gracious lord, not so much for injury done to me, as
     to delight your Majesty with some mirth, hath Faustus justly
     requited this injurious knight; which, being all I desire, I am    110
     content to remove his horns.—Mephistophilis, transform him.
     —And hereafter, sir, look you speak well of scholars.

BENV. [aside] Speak well of ye! 'Sblood, and scholars be such
     cuckoldmakers to clap horns of honest men's heads o' this or-
     der, I'll ne'er trust smooth faces and small ruffs[5] more. But an   115
     I be not revenged for this, would I might be turned to a gaping
     oyster and drink nothing but salt water!

EMP. Come, Faustus. While the Emperor lives,
     In recompense of this thy high desert,
     Thou shalt command the state of Germany                    120
     And live beloved of mighty Carolus.          [Exeunt OMNES.]

### SCENE 3

[Enter BENVOLIO, MARTINO, FREDERICK, and SOLDIERS.]

MART. Nay, sweet Benvolio, let us sway thy thoughts
     From this attempt against the conjurer.

BENV. Away! You love me not to urge me thus.
     Shall I let slip so great an injury
     When every servile groom jests at my wrongs                 5
     And in their rustic gambols proudly say,
     "Benvolio's head was graced with horns today"?
     O, may these eyelids never close again
     Till with my sword I have that conjurer slain.
     If you will aid me in this enterprise,                       10
     Then draw your weapons and be resolute;

5. Scholars were often smooth-shaven and did not wear the large "ruffs" (collars) of courtiers. But
Faustus has a beard; see the next scene.

If not, depart. Here will Benvolio die,
But Faustus' death shall quit[6] my infamy.
FRED. Nay, we will stay with thee, betide what may,
And kill that Doctor if he come this way.                          15
BENV. Then gentle Frederick, hie thee to the grove
And place our servants and our followers
Close in an ambush there behind the trees.
By this I know the conjurer is near;
I saw him kneel and kiss the Emperor's hand                        20
And take his leave laden with rich rewards.
Then, soldiers, boldly fight. If Faustus die,
Take you the wealth, leave us the victory.
FRED. Come, soldiers, follow me unto the grove;
Who kills him shall have gold and endless love.                    25
    [*Exit* FREDERICK *with the* SOLDIERS.]
BENV. My head is lighter than it was by th' horns,
But yet my heart's more ponderous than my head
And pants until I see that conjurer dead.
MART. Where shall we place ourselves, Benvolio?
BENV. Here will we stay to bide the first assault.                 30
O, were that damnéd hell-hound but in place
Thou soon shouldst see me quit my foul disgrace.
    [*Enter* FREDERICK.]
FRED. Close, close! The hated conjurer is at hand
And all alone comes walking in his gown;
Be ready then and strike the peasant down.                         35
BENV. Mine be that honor then. Now, sword, strike home!
For horns he gave I'll have his head anon.
    [*Enter* FAUSTUS *wearing a false head.*]
MART. See, see, he comes.
BENV.                        No words; this blow ends all;
Hell take his soul, his body thus must fall.
FAUST. O!                                                          40
FRED. Groan you, master Doctor?
BENV. Break may his heart with groans. Dear Frederick, see
Thus will I end his griefs immediately.
    [*Cuts off the false head.*]
MART. Strike with a willing hand! His head is off.
BENV. The devil's dead; the furies now may laugh.                  45
FRED. Was this that stern aspect, that awful frown,
Made the grim monarch of infernal spirits
Tremble and quake at his commanding charms?
MART. Was this that damnéd head whose art conspired

6. Avenge.

Benvolio's shame before the Emperor?                                    50
BENV. Aye, that's the head, and here the body lies
  Justly rewarded for his villainies.
FRED. Come, let's devise how we may add more shame
  To the black scandal of his hated name.
BENV. First, on his head, in quittance of my wrongs,                    55
  I'll nail huge forkéd horns and let them hang
  Within the window where he yoked me first,
  That all the world may see my just revenge.
MART. What use shall we put his beard to?
BENV. We'll sell it to a chimney-sweeper; it will wear out ten          60
  birchen brooms, I warrant you.
FRED. What shall his eyes do?
BENV. We'll pull out his eyes, and they shall serve for buttons to
  his lips to keep his tongue from catching cold.
MART. An excellent policy. And now, sirs, having divided him,          65
  what shall the body do?
     [FAUSTUS *rises.*]
BENV. Zounds, the devil's alive again!
FRED. Give him his head, for God's sake!
FAUST. Nay, keep it. Faustus will have heads and hands,
  Aye, all your hearts, to recompense this deed.                   70
  Knew you not, traitors, I am limited
  For four and twenty years to breathe on earth?
  And had you cut my body with your swords
  Or hewed this flesh and bones as small as sand,
  Yet in a minute had my spirit returned                           75
  And I had breathed a man made free from harm.
  But wherefore do I dally my revenge?
  Asteroth, Belimoth, Mephistophilis!
     [*Enter* MEPHISTOPHILIS *and other* DEVILS.]
  Go, horse these traitors on your fiery backs
  And mount aloft with them as high as heaven,                     80
  Then pitch them headlong to the lowest hell.
  Yet stay, the world shall see their misery,
  And hell shall after plague their treachery.
  Go, Belimoth, and take this caitiff hence
  And hurl him in some lake of mud and dirt;                       85
  Take thou this other, drag him through the woods
  Amongst the pricking thorns and sharpest briars,
  Whilst with my gentle Mephistophilis
  This traitor flies unto some steepy rock
  That rolling down may break the villain's bones                  90
  As he intended to dismember me.
  Fly hence, dispatch my charge immediately.

FRED. Pity us, gentle Faustus; save our lives!
FAUST. Away!
FRED. He must needs go that the devil drives.                    95
                    [*Exeunt* SPIRITS *with the* KNIGHTS.]
        [*Enter the ambushed* SOLDIERS.]
1 SOLD. Come, sirs, prepare yourselves in readiness;
    Make haste to help these noble gentlemen;
    I heard them parley with the conjurer.
2 SOLD. See where he comes; dispatch, and kill the slave!
FAUST. What's here? An ambush to betray my life?                    100
    Then, Faustus, try thy skill. Base peasants, stand!
    For lo, these trees remove at my command
    And stand as bulwarks 'rwixt yourselves and me
    To shield me from your hated treachery;
    Yet to encounter this, your weak attempt,                    105
    Behold an army comes incontinent.[7]
        [FAUSTUS *strikes the door, and enter a* DEVIL *playing on a
        drum; after him another bearing an ensign, and divers
        with weapons;* MEPHISTOPHILIS *with fireworks. They set
        upon the* SOLDIERS *and drive them out. Exeunt.*]

                    SCENE 4

    [*Enter at several doors* BENVOLIO, FREDERICK, *and* MAR-
    TINO, *their heads and faces bloody and besmeared with
    mud and dirt, all having horns on their heads.*]
MART. What ho, Benvolio!
BENV. Here! What, Frederick, ho!
FRED. O help me, gentle friend. Where is Martino?
MART. Dear Frederick, here—
    Half smothered in a lake of mud and dirt                    5
    Through which the furies dragged me by the heels.
FRED. Martino, see! Benvolio's horns again.
MART. O misery! How now, Benvolio!
BENV. Defend me, heaven! Shall I be haunted still?
MART. Nay, fear not, man; we have no power to kill.                    10
BENV. My friends transforméd thus! O hellish spite!
    Your heads are all set with horns.
FRED. You hit it right;
    It is your own you mean; feel on your head.
BENV. Zounds, horns again!                    15
MART. Nay, chafe not, man; we are all sped.[8]
BENV. What devil attends this damned magician
    That spite of spite our wrongs are doubléd?

———————
7. Immediately.    8. Don't fret, man, we are all done for.

FRED. What may we do that we may hide our shames?
BENV. If we should follow him to work revenge,                     20
   He'd join long asses' ears to those huge horns
   And make us laughingstocks to all the world.
MART. What shall we then do, dear Benvolio?
BENV. I have a castle joining near these woods,
   And thither we'll repair and live obscure                   25
   Till time shall alter this our brutish shapes.
   Sith black disgrace hath thus eclipsed our fame,
   We'll rather die with grief than live with shame.

                                  [*Exeunt* OMNES.]

### SCENE 5

[*Enter* FAUSTUS *and the* HORSE-COURSER.[9]]
HOR. I beseech your Worship, accept of these forty dollars.[1]
FAUST. Friend, thou canst not buy so good a horse for so small a
   price. I have no great need to sell him, but if thou likest him for
   ten dollars more, take him, because I see thou hast a good
   mind to him.                                                  5
HOR. I beseech you, sir, accept of this; I am a very poor man and
   have lost very much of late by horseflesh, and this bargain will
   set me up again.
FAUST. Well, I will not stand with thee; give me the money. Now,
   sirrah, I must tell you that you may ride him o'er hedge and     10
   ditch and spare him not; but—do you hear?—in any case ride
   him not into the water.
HOR. How, sir, not into the water? Why, will he not drink of all
   waters?
FAUST. Yes, he will drink of all waters, but ride him not into      15
   the water; o'er hedge and ditch or where thou wilt, but not into
   the water. Go bid the hostler deliver him unto you, and remember
   what I say.
HOR. I warrant you, sir. O joyful day! Now am I a made man for-
   ever.                                                          20
    [*Exit.*]
FAUST. What art thou, Faustus, but a man condemned to die?
   Thy fatal time draws to a final end;
   Despair doth drive distrust into my thoughts.
   Confound these passions with a quiet sleep.
   Tush, Christ did call the thief upon the cross;[2]               25
   Then rest thee, Faustus, quiet in conceit.

---

9. Horse-trader, traditionally a sharp bargainer or a cheat.    1. Common German coins; the
word originally comes from the German *Joachimsthaler*.    2. In Luke 23:, 39–43 one of the two
thieves crucified with Jesus is promised Paradise. *In conceit*: In mind.

*[He sits to sleep in his chair.]*

*[Enter the* HORSE-COURSER *wet.]*

HOR. O, what a cozening Doctor was this! I riding my horse into
the water, thinking some hidden mystery had been in the horse,
I had nothing under me but a little straw, and had much ado
to escape drowning. Well, I'll go rouse him and make him give    30
me my forty dollars again. Ho! sirrah Doctor, you cozening
scab! Master Doctor, awake and arise, and give me my money
again, for your horse is turned to a bottle[3] of hay. Master Doctor—

*[He pulls off his leg.]*

Alas, I am undone! What shall I do? I have pulled off his leg.    35

FAUST. O help! Help! The villain hath murdered me!

HOR. Murder or not murder, now he has but one leg I'll outrun
him and cast this leg into some ditch or other.

*[Exit.]*

FAUST. Stop him, stop him, stop him! Ha ha ha! Faustus hath his
leg again, and the horse-courser a bundle of hay for his forty    40
dollars.

*[Enter* WAGNER.*]*

FAUST. How now, Wagner! What news with thee?

WAG. If it please you, the Duke of Vanholt doth earnestly entreat
your company and hath sent some of his men to attend you
with provision fit for your journey.                              45

FAUST. The Duke of Vanholt's an honorable gentleman, and one
to whom I must be no niggard of my cunning. Come, away!

## SCENE 6

*[Enter* ROBIN, DICK, HORSE-COURSER, *and a* CARTER.*]*

CART. Come, my masters, I'll bring you to the best beer in Europe—What ho, Hostess!—Where be these whores?[4]

*[Enter* HOSTESS.*]*

HOST. How now! What lack you? What, my old guests, welcome.

ROBIN. Sirrah Dick, dost thou know why I stand so mute?

DICK. No, Robin, why is 't?                                        5

ROBIN. I am eighteen pence on the score,[5] but say nothing; see if
she have forgotten me.

HOST. Who's this that stands so solemnly by himself? What, my
old guest!

ROBIN. O, hostess, how do you do? I hope my score stands still.    10

HOST. Aye, there's no doubt of that, for methinks you make no
haste to wipe it out.

DICK. Why, hostess, I say, fetch us some beer.

3. Bundle.    4. I.e., the hostess and maids of the inn.    5. Charged, not paid for.

HOST. You shall presently; look up into th' hall. There, ho!
   [*Exit.*]

DICK. Come, sirs; what shall we do now till mine hostess comes?   15

CART. Marry, sir, I'll tell you the bravest tale how a conjurer
   served me. You know Dr. Faustus?

HOR. Aye, a plague take him! Here's some on 's have cause to
   know him. Did he conjure thee too?

CART. I'll tell you how he served me. As I was going to Witten-   20
   berg t' other day, he met me and asked me what he should give
   me for as much hay as he could eat. Now, sir, I, thinking that
   a little would serve his turn, bade him take as much as he
   would for three farthings. So he presently gave me my money
   and fell to eating; and, as I am a cursen man, he never left   25
   eating till he had eat up all my load of hay.

ALL. O monstrous; eat a whole load of hay!

ROBIN. Yes, yes; that may be, for I have heard of one that has eat
   a load of logs.[6]

HOR. Now, sirs, you shall hear now villainously he served me. I   30
   went to him yesterday to buy a horse of him, and he would by
   no means sell him under forty dollars. So, sir, because I knew
   him to be such a horse as would run over hedge and ditch and
   never tire, I gave him his money. So, when I had my horse, Dr.
   Faustus bade me ride him night and day and spare him no
   time; "But," quoth he, "in any case ride him not into the wa-   35
   ter." Now sir, I thinking the horse had had some quality that
   he would not have me know of, what did I but ride him into
   a great river, and when I came just in the midst my horse vanished away and I sat straddling upon a bottle of hay.   40

ALL. O brave Doctor!

HOR. But you shall hear how bravely I served him for it. I went
   me home to his house, and there I found him asleep; I kept a
   hallowing and whooping in his ears, but all could not wake
   him. I seeing that, took him by the leg and never rested pull-   45
   ing till I had pulled me his leg quite off, and now 'tis at home
   in mine hostry.[7]

DICK. And has the Doctor but one leg then? That's excellent, for
   one of his devils turned me into the likeness of an ape's face.

CART. Some more drink, hostess!   50

ROBIN. Hark you, we'll into another room and drink awhile, and
   then we'll go seek out the Doctor.
   [*Exeunt* OMNES.]

---

6. Comic expression for being drunk—to carry a jag (or load) of logs.   7. Inn.

SCENE 7

[*Enter the* DUKE OF VANHOLT, *his* DUCHESS, FAUSTUS, *and*
MEPHISTOPHILIS.]

DUKE. Thanks, master Doctor, for these pleasant sights; nor know
I how sufficiently to recompense your great deserts in erecting
that enhanted castle in the air, the sight whereof so delighted
me as nothing in the world could please me more.

FAUST. I do think myself, my good lord, highly recompensed that    5
it pleaseth your Grace to think but well of that which Faustus
hath performed. But gracious lady, it may be that you have
taken no pleasure in those sights; therefore I pray you tell me
what is the thing you most desire to have; be it in the world
it shall be yours. I have heard that great-bellied women do long 10
for things that are rare and dainty.

DUCH. True, master Doctor, and since I find you so kind, I will
make known unto you what my heart desires to have; and were
it now summer, as it is January, a dead time of winter, I would
request no better meat than a dish of ripe grapes.                15

FAUST. This is but a small matter.—Go, Mephistophilis, away!—
    [*Exit* MEPHISTOPHILIS.]
Madam, I will do more than this for your content.
    [*Enter* MEPHISTOPHILIS *again with the grapes.*]
Here, now taste ye these; they should be good, for they come
from a far country, I can tell you.

DUKE. This makes me wonder more than all the rest, that at this   20
time of year, when every tree is barren of his fruit, from whence
you had these ripe grapes.

FAUST. Please it your Grace, the year is divided into two circles
over the whole world, so that when it is winter with us, in the
contrary circle it is likewise summer with them, as in India,     25
Saba and such countries that lie far east, where they have
fruit twice a year. From whence, by means of a swift spirit that
I have, I had these grapes brought as you see.

DUCH. And trust me they are the sweetest grapes that e'er I tasted.
    [*The* CLOWNS *bounce*[8] *at the gate within.*]

DUKE. What rude disturbers have we at the gate?                    30
Go pacify their fury, set it ope,
And then demand of them what they would have.
    [*They knock again and call out to talk with* FAUSTUS.]

A SERVANT. Why, how now, masters, what a coil[9] is there!
What is the reason you disturb the Duke?

DICK. We have no reason for it, therefore a fig[1] for him!        35

---

8. Bang.    9. Disturbance.    1. An obscene gesture, implying contempt.

SERV. Why, saucy varlets! Dare you be so bold?

HOR. I hope, sir, we have wit enough to be more bold than welcome.

SERV. It appears so; Pray be bold elsewhere
And trouble not the Duke.        40

DUKE. What would they have?

SERV. They all cry out to speak with Dr. Faustus.

CART. Aye, and we will speak with him.

DUKE. Will you, sir? Commit² the rascals!

DICK. Commit with us? He were as good commit with his father   45
as commit with us.

FAUST. I do beseech your Grace, let them come in;
They are good subject for a merriment.

DUKE. Do as thou wilt, Faustus; I give thee leave.

FAUST. I thank your Grace.

> [*Enter* ROBIN, DICK, CARTER, *and* HORSE-COURSER.]
>                      Why, how now, my good friends?     50

'Faith you are too outrageous; but come near,
I have procured your pardons. Welcome all!

ROBIN. Nay, sir, we will be welcome for our money, and we will
pay for what we take. What ho! Give 's half a dozen of beer
here, and be hanged.        55

FAUST. Nay, hark you, can you tell me where you are?

CART. Aye, marry, can I; we are under heaven.

SERV. Aye, but, sir saucebox, know you in what place?

HOR. Aye, aye, the house is good enough to drink in. Zounds, fill
us some beer, or we'll break all the barrels in the house and   60
dash out all your brains with your bottles.

FAUST. Be not so furious; come, you shall have beer.
My lord, beseech you give me leave awhile;
I'll gage my credit 'twill content your Grace.

DUKE. With all my heart, kind Doctor, please thyself;     65
Our servants and our court's at thy command.

FAUST. I humbly thank your Grace. Then fetch some beer.

HOR. Aye, marry, there spake a doctor indeed; and, faith, I'll
drink a health to thy wooden leg for that word.

FAUST. My wooden leg! What dost thou mean by that?     70

CART. Ha ha ha, dost hear him, Dick? He has forgot his leg.

HOR. Aye, he does not stand much upon that.

FAUST. No, faith, not much upon a wooden leg.

CART. Good lord, that flesh and blood should be so frail with
your worship! Do you not remember a horse-courser you sold   75
a horse to?

FAUST. Yes, I remember I sold one a horse.

---

2. Put in jail. Dick puns on its other meaning ("commit adultery"), from the Ten Commandments.

CART. And do you remember you bid he should not ride him into the water?

FAUST. Yes, I do very well remember that.                        80

CART. And do you remember nothing of your leg?

FAUST. No, in good sooth.

CART. Then I pray remember your courtesy.

FAUST. I thank you, sir.

CART. 'Tis not so much worth. I pray you tell me one thing.      85

FAUST. What's that?

CART. Be both of your legs bedfellows every night together?

FAUST. Wouldst thou make a colossus³ of me, that thou askest me such questions?

CART. No, truly, sir, I would make nothing of you, but I would     90
fain know that.

    [*Enter* HOSTESS *with drink.*]

FAUST. Then I assure thee certainly they are.

CART. I thank you; I am fully satisfied.

FAUST. But wherefore dost thou ask?

CART. For nothing, sir; but methinks you should have a wooden     95
bedfellow to one of 'em.

HOR. Why, do you hear, sir, did not I pull off one of your legs when you were asleep?

FAUST. But I have it again now I am awake; look you here, sir.

ALL. O horrible! Had the doctor three legs?                       100

CART. Do you remember, sir, how you cozened me and eat up my load of——

    [FAUSTUS *charms him dumb.*]

DICK. Do you remember how you made me wear an ape's——

HOR. You whoreson conjuring scab, do you remember how you cozened me of a ho——                                               105

ROBIN. Ha' you forgotten me? You think to carry it away with your hey-pass and your re-pass;⁴ do you remember the dog's fa——

    [*Exeunt* CLOWNS.]

HOST. Who pays for the ale? Hear you, master Doctor, now you have sent away my guests, I pray who shall pay me for my         110
a——

    [*Exit* HOSTESS.]

DUCH. My lord,
  We are much beholding to this learned man.

DUKE. So are we, madam, which we will recompense
  With all the love and kindness that we may;                  115
  His artful sport drives all sad thoughts away.        [*Exeunt.*]

---

3. The huge statue which stood at the entrance to the harbor at Rhodes; boats sailed between its legs, and Dr. Faustus is suggesting that the clowns are making his legs as important.    4. Traditional exclamations of a conjurer.

## Act V

### SCENE 1

[*Thunder and lightning. Enter* DEVILS *with covered dishes;* MEPHISTOPHILIS *leads them into* FAUSTUS' *study. Then enter* WAGNER.]

WAG. I think my master means to die shortly;
    He has made his will and given me his wealth,
    His house, his goods, and store of golden plate,
    Besides two thousand ducats ready coined.
    And yet I wonder, for if death were nigh                          5
    He would not banquet and carouse and swill
    Amongst the students as even now he doth,
    Who are at supper with such belly-cheer
    As Wagner ne'er beheld in all his life.
    See where they come; belike the feast is ended.    [*Exit.*]    10
        [*Enter* FAUSTUS *and* MEPHISTOPHILIS *with two or three* SCHOLARS.]

1 SCH. Master Doctor Faustus, since our conference about fair
    ladies, which was the beautifullest in all the world, we have de-
    termined with ourselves that Helen of Greece was the ad-
    mirablest lady that ever lived. Therefore, master Doctor, if
    you will do us that favor as to let us see that peerless dame of    15
    Greece whom all the world admires for majesty, we should
    think ourselves much beholding unto you.

FAUST. Gentlemen,
    For that I know your friendship is unfeigned,
    And Faustus' custom is not to deny                                20
    The just requests of those that wish him well,
    You shall behold that peerless dame of Greece,
    No otherways for pomp and majesty
    Than when Sir Paris crossed the seas with her
    And brought the spoils to rich Dardania.[5]                      25
    Be silent, then, for danger is in words.
        [*Music sounds, and* HELEN *passeth over the stage.*]

2 SCH. Too simple is my wit to tell her praise
    Whom all the world admires for majesty.

3 SCH. No marvel though the angry Greeks pursued
    With ten years' war the rape of such a queen                     30
    Whose heavenly beauty passeth all compare.

1 SCH. Since we have seen the pride of Nature's works

---

5. Troy.

And only paragon of excellence,
Let us depart, and for this glorious deed
Happy and blest be Faustus evermore.                            35
FAUST. Gentlemen, farewell; the same I wish to you.
                                        [*Exeunt* SCHOLARS.]
        [*Enter an* OLD MAN.]
OLD MAN. O gentle Faustus, leave this damnéd art,
    This magic, that will charm thy soul to hell
    And quite bereave[6] thee of salvation.
    Though thou hast now offended like a man,                   40
    Do not persevere in it like a devil.
    Yet, yet, thou hast an amiable soul
    If sin by custom grow not into nature;
    Then, Faustus, will repentance come too late;
    Then thou art banished from the sight of heaven.            45
    No mortal can express the pains of hell.
    It may be this my exhortation
    Seems harsh and all unpleasant; let it not;
    For, gentle son, I speak it not in wrath
    Or envy of thee, but in tender love                         50
    And pity of thy future misery,
    And so have hope that this my kind rebuke,
    Checking thy body, may amend thy soul.
FAUST. Where are thou, Faustus? Wretch, what hast thou done?
    Damned art thou, Faustus, damned! Despair and die.          55
        [MEPHISTOPHILIS *gives him a dagger.*]
    Hell claims his right, and with a roaring voice
    Says, "Faustus, come; thine hour is almost come!"
    And Faustus now will come to do thee right.
OLD MAN. O stay, good Faustus, stay thy desperate steps!
    I see an angel hovers o'er thy head                         60
    And with a vial full of precious grace
    Offers to pour the same into thy soul:
    Then call for mercy and avoid despair.
FAUST. Ah my sweet friend, I feel thy words
    To comfort my distresséd soul.                              65
    Leave me awhile to ponder on my sins.
OLD MAN. Faustus, I leave thee, but with grief of heart,
    Fearing the ruin of thy hopeless soul.          [*Exit.*]
FAUST. Accurséd Faustus, where is mercy now?
    I do repent and yet I do despair:                           70
    Hell strives with grace for conquest in my breast.
    What shall I do to shun the snares of death?

6. Deprive.

MEPH. Thou traitor, Faustus, I arrest thy soul
    For disobedience to my sovereign lord.
    Revolt, or I'll in piecemeal tear thy flesh.                    75
FAUST. I do repent I e'er offended him.
    Sweet Mephistophilis, entreat thy lord
    To pardon my unjust presumption,
    And with my blood again I will confirm
    The former vow I made to Lucifer.                              80
MEPH. Do it then, Faustus, with unfeignéd heart
    Lest greater danger do attend thy drift.
FAUST. Torment, sweet friend, that base and aged man
    That durst dissuade me from thy Lucifer,
    With greatest torments that our hell affords.                  85
MEPH. His faith is great; I cannot touch his soul;
    But what I may afflict his body with
    I will attempt, which is but little worth.
FAUST. One thing, good servant, let me crave of thee
    To glut the longing of my heart's desire:                     90
    That I might have unto my paramour
    That heavenly Helen which I saw of late,
    Whose sweet embracings may extinguish clear
    These thoughts that do dissuade me from my vow,
    And keep mine oath I made to Lucifer.                         95
MEPH. This, or what else my Faustus shall desire
    Shall be performed in twinkling of an eye.
        [*Enter* HELEN *again, passing over between two* CUPIDS.]
FAUST. Was this the face that launched a thousand ships
    And burnt the topless[7] towers of Ilium?
    Sweet Helen, make me immortal with a kiss.                    100
    Her lips sucks forth my soul—see where it flies!
    Come, Helen, come, give me my soul again.
    Here will I dwell, for heaven is in these lips
    And all is dross that is not Helena.
        [*Enter* OLD MAN *and stands watching* FAUSTUS.]
    I will be Paris, and for love of thee                          105
    Instead of Troy shall Wittenberg be sacked,
    And I will combat with weak Menelaus
    And wear thy colors on my pluméd crest;
    Yea, I will wound Achilles in the heel
    And then return to Helen for a kiss.                           110
    O thou art fairer than the evening air
    Clad in the beauty of a thousand stars!
    Brighter art thou than flaming Jupiter

---

7. So high they seemed to have no tops.

When he appeared to hapless Semele,[8]
More lovely than the monarch of the sky                         115
In wanton Arethusa's[9] azured arms,
And none but thou shalt be my paramour!
    [*Exeunt* ALL *except the* OLD MAN.]
OLD MAN. Accurséd Faustus, miserable man,
  That from thy soul exclud'st the grace of heaven
  And fliest the throne of his tribunal seat.                      120
    [*Enter the* DEVILS *to torment him.*]
Satan begins to sift me with his pride.[1]
As in this furnace God shall try my faith,
My faith, vile hell, shall triumph over thee!
Ambitious fiends, see how the heavens smiles
At your repulse, and laughs your state to scorn.               125
Hence, hell! for hence I fly unto my God.          [*Exeunt.*]

SCENE 2

    [*Thunder. Enter* LUCIFER, BELZEBUB, *and* MEPHISTOPHI-
    LIS.]
LUC. Thus from infernal Dis[2] do we ascend
  To view the subjects of our monarchy,
  Those souls which sin seals the black sons of hell.
  'Mong which as chief, Faustus, we come to thee,
  Bringing with us lasting damnation                              5
  To wait upon thy soul; the time is come
  Which makes it forfeit.
MEPH.                            And this gloomy night
  Here in this room will wretched Faustus be.
BEL. And here we'll stay
  To mark him how he doth demean himself.                        10
MEPH. How should he but with desperate lunacy?
  Fond worldling, now his heart-blood dries with grief,
  His conscience kills it, and his laboring brain
  Begets a world of idle fantasies
  To overreach the devil, but all in vain.                       15
  His store of pleasure must be sauced with pain.
  He and his servant Wagner are at hand;
  Both come from drawing Faustus' latest will.
  See where they come!
    [*Enter* FAUSTUS *and* WAGNER.]
FAUST. Say, Wagner, thou has perused my will;                  20

8. A Theban girl, loved by Jupiter and destroyed by the fire of his lightning when he appeared to
her in his full splendor.     9. The nymph of a fountain, as well as the fountain itself; no classical
myth, however, records her love affair with Jupiter, the "monarch of the sky."     1. To test me
with his strength.     2. The underworld.

How dost thou like it?

WAG.　　　　　　　Sir, so wondrous well
　As in all humble duty I do yield
　My life and lasting service for your love.
　　[*Enter the* SCHOLARS.]

FAUST. Gramercies, Wagner.—Welcome, gentlemen.

1 SCH. Now, worthy Faustus, methinks your looks are changed.　25

FAUST. Ah, gentlemen!

2 SCH. What ails Faustus?

FAUST. Ah, my sweet chamber-fellow, had I lived with thee, then
　had I lived still, but now must die eternally. Look, sirs! Comes
　he not? Comes he not?　30

1 SCH. O my dear Faustus, what imports this fear?

2 SCH. Is all our pleasure turned to melancholy?

3 SCH. He is not well with being over-solitary.

2 SCH. If it be so, we'll have physicians, and Faustus shall be
　cured.　35

3 SCH. 'Tis but a surfeit,[3] sir; fear nothing.

FAUST. A surfeit of deadly sin that hath damned both body and
　soul.

2 SCH. Yet, Faustus, look up to heaven: remember God's mercies
　are infinite.　40

FAUST. But Faustus' offense can ne'er be pardoned; the Serpent
　that tempted Eve may be saved, but not Faustus. Ah, gentle-
　men, hear me with patience, and tremble not at my speeches.
　Though my heart pants and quivers to remember that I have
　been a student here these thirty years, O would I had never seen
　Wittenberg, never read book! And what wonders I have done　45
　all Germany can witness, yea all the world, for which Faustus
　hath lost both Germany and the world, yea heaven itself—
　heaven the seat of God, the throne of the blessed, the kingdom
　of joy, and must remain in hell forever, hell, ah hell, forever!
　Sweet friends, what shall become of Faustus, being in hell　50
　forever?

3 SCH. Yet, Faustus, call on God.

FAUST. On God, whom Faustus hath abjured? on God, whom
　Faustus hath blasphemed? Ah, my God, I would weep, but　55
　the devil draws in my tears! Gush forth, blood, instead of tears,
　yea life and soul! O he stays my tongue; I would lift up my
　hands but, see, they hold 'em, they hold 'em!

ALL. Who, Faustus?

FAUST. Why, Lucifer and Mephistophilis.　60

---

3. Indigestion; the effects of overindulgence.

Ah, gentlemen, I gave them my soul for my cunning.

ALL. God forbid!

FAUST. God forbade it indeed, but Faustus hath done it: for vain
   pleasure of four and twenty years hath Faustus lost eternal joy
   and felicity. I writ them a bill with mine own blood; the date   65
   is expired, this is the time, and he will fetch me.

1 SCH. Why did not Faustus tell us of this before, that divines
   might have prayed for thee?

FAUST. Oft have I thought to have done so, but the devil threatened to tear me in pieces if I named God, to fetch both body   70
   and soul if I once gave ear to divinity; and now 'tis too late.
   Gentlemen, away, lest you perish with me!

2 SCH. O what may we do to save Faustus?

FAUST. Talk not of me, but save yourselves and depart.

3 SCH. God will strengthen me: I will stay with Faustus.   75

1 SCH. Tempt not God, sweet friend, but let us into the next
   room, and there pray for him.

FAUST. Aye, pray for me, pray for me! And what noise soever ye
   hear, come not unto me, for nothing can rescue me.

2 SCH. Pray thou, and we will pray that God may have mercy   80
   upon thee.

FAUST. Gentlemen, farewell. If I live till morning I'll visit you;
   if not, Faustus is gone to hell.

ALL. Faustus, farewell.                    [*Exeunt* SCHOLARS.]

MEPH. Aye, Faustus, now hast thou no hope of heaven;   85
   Therefore despair, think only upon hell,
   For that must be thy mansion, there to dwell.

FAUST. O thou bewitching fiend, 'twas thy temptation
   Hath robbed me of eternal happiness.

MEPH. I do confess it, Faustus, and rejoice.   90
   'Twas I, that when thou wert i' the way to heaven
   Damned up thy passage; when thou tookest the book
   To view the scriptures, then I turned the leaves
   And led thine eye.
   What, weepst thou? 'tis too late. Despair, farewell!   95
   Fools that will laugh on earth must weep in hell.   [*Exit.*]
   [*Enter the* GOOD ANGEL *and the* BAD ANGEL *at several
   doors.*]

G. ANG. Ah Faustus, if thou hadst given ear to me,
   Innumerable joys had followed thee,
   But thou didst love the world.

B. ANG.                          Gave ear to me
   And now must taste hell's pains perpetually.   100

G. ANG. O what will all thy riches, pleasures, pomps

Avail thee now?
B. ANG.                Nothing but vex thee more,
  To want in hell, that had on earth such store.
    [*Music while the throne descends.*[4]]
G. ANG. O, thou hast lost celestial happiness,
  Pleasures unspeakable, bliss without end.                105
  Hadst thou affected sweet divinity
  Hell or the devil had had no power on thee.
  Hadst thou kept on that way, Faustus, behold
  In what resplendent glory thou hadst sit
  In yonder throne, like those bright shining saints,                110
  And triumphed over hell; that hast thou lost.
  And now, poor soul, must thy good angel leave thee;
  The jaws of hell are open to receive thee.
    [*Exit. Hell is discovered.*]
B. ANG. Now Faustus, let thine eyes with horror stare
  Into that vast perpetual torture-house.                115
  There are the furies, tossing damnéd souls
  On burning forks; their bodies boil in lead.
  There are live quarters[5] broiling on the coals
  That ne'er can die; this ever-burning chair
  Is for o'ertortured souls to rest them in;                120
  These that are fed with sops of flaming fire
  Were gluttons and loved only delicates
  And laughed to see the poor starve at their gates.
  But yet all these are nothing; thou shalt see
  Ten thousand tortures that more horrid be.                125
FAUST. O, I have seen enough to torture me.
B. ANG. Nay, thou must feel them, taste the smart of all;
  He that loves pleasure must for pleasure fall.
  And so I leave thee, Faustus, till anon;
  Then wilt thou tumble in confusión.[6]                130
    [*Exit. The clock strikes eleven.*]
FAUST. Ah, Faustus,
  Now hast thou but one bare hour to live
  And then thou must be damned perpetually!
  Stand still, you ever-moving spheres of heaven,
  That time may cease and midnight never come;                135
  Fair Nature's eye, rise, rise again, and make
  Perpetual day; or let this hour be but
  A year, a month, a week, a natural day,
  That Faustus may repent and save his soul!

---

**4.** A throne suspended by ropes descended to the stage near the end of many Elizabethan plays and was an expected theatrical display. Here the throne clearly symbolizes heaven, as the next speech shows.   **5.** Bodies.   **6.** Destruction, perdition.

*O lente lente currite noctis equi.*[7]                              140
The stars move still, time runs, the clock will strike,
The devil will come, and Faustus must be damned.
O, I'll leap up to my God! Who pulls me down?
See, see, where Christ's blood streams in the firmament!—
One drop would save my soul—half a drop! ah, my Christ!     145
Rend not my heart for naming of my Christ;
Yet will I call on him—O, spare me, Lucifer!
Where is it now? 'Tis gone; and see where God
Stretcheth out his arm and bends his ireful brows.
Mountains and hills, come, come and fall on me               150
And hide me from the heavy wrath of God,
No, no—
Then will I headlong run into the earth:
Earth, gape! O no, it will not harbor me.
You stars that reigned at my nativity,                       155
Whose influence hath allotted death and hell,
Now draw up Faustus like a foggy mist
Into the entrails of yon laboring clouds
That when they vomit forth into the air,
My limbs may issue from their smoky mouths,                  160
So that my soul may but ascend to heaven.
    [*The watch strikes.*]
Ah, half the hour is past; 'twill all be past anon.
O God,
If thou wilt not have mercy on my soul,
Yet for Christ's sake whose blood hath ransomed me           165
Impose some end to my incessant pain:
Let Faustus live in hell a thousand years,
A hundred thousand, and at last be saved!
O, no end is limited to damnéd souls!
Why wert thou not a creature wanting soul?                   170
Or why is this immortal that thou hast?
Ah, Pythagoras' *metempsychosis*[8]—were that true,
This soul should fly from me, and I be changed
Unto some brutish beast. All beasts are happy,
For when they die                                            175
Their souls are soon dissolved in elements,
But mine must live still[9] to be plagued in hell.
Cursed be the parents that engendered me!
No, Faustus, curse thyself, curse Lucifer
That hath deprived thee of the joys of heaven.               180
    [*The clock strikes twelve.*]

7. "Slowly, slowly run, O horses of the night," adapted from a line in Ovid's *Amores*.
8. Pythagoras' doctrine of the transmigration of souls.   9. Always.

It strikes, it strikes! Now, body, turn to air
Or Lucifer will bear thee quick[1] to hell!
    [*Thunder and lightning.*]
O soul, be changed to little water drops
And fall into the ocean, ne'er be found.
My God, my God, look not so fierce on me!                                    185
    [*Enter* DEVILS.]
Adders and serpents, let me breathe awhile!
Ugly hell, gape not—come not, Lucifer—
I'll burn my books—ah, Mephistophilis!
    [*Exeunt* DEVILS *with* FAUSTUS.]

SCENE 3

    [*Enter the* SCHOLARS.]
1 SCH. Come, gentlemen, let us go visit Faustus,
    For such a dreadful night was never seen
    Since first the world's creation did begin,
    Such fearful shrieks and cries were never heard.
    Pray heaven the Doctor have escaped the danger.                          5
2 SCH. O, help us heaven! See, here are Faustus' limbs
    All torn asunder by the hand of death.
3 SCH. The devils whom Faustus served have torn him thus;
    For 'twixt the hours of twelve and one, methought
    I heard him shriek and call aloud for help.                             10
    At which self[2] time the house seemed all on fire
    With dreadful horror of these damnéd fiends.
2 SCH. Well, gentlemen, though Faustus' end be such
    As every Christian heart laments to think on,
    Yet for he was a scholar once admired                                   15
    For wondrous knowledge in our German schools,
    We'll give his mangled limbs due burial;
    And all the students, clothed in mourning black,
    Shall wait upon his heavy[3] funeral.                          [*Exeunt.*]
    [*Enter* CHORUS.]
CHO. Cut is the branch that might have grown full straight,                  20
    And burnéd is Apollo's laurel bough[4]
    That sometime grew within this learnéd man.
    Faustus is gone: regard his hellish fall,
    Whose fiendful fortune may exhort the wise
    Only to wonder at[5] unlawful things                                    25

---

1. Alive.    2. Same, exact.    3. Tragic, sorrowful.    4. Symbol of wisdom and learning; Apollo
was the god of divination.    5. To be content with observing with awe. *Fiendful fortune*: Devilish fate.

Whose deepness doth entice such forward wits
To practice more than heavenly power permits.

[*Exit.*]
1604, 1616

---

# WILLIAM SHAKESPEARE
## 1564–1616

When William Shakespeare was born in April 1564 at Stratford-on-Avon in Warwickshire, Stratford was a rural community with a population of less than two thousand, of which his father, John Shakespeare, was a prominent and prosperous member. Little is known of Shakespeare's early life beyond conjecture or legend; he probably received the education offered by the good local grammar school, with emphasis on Latin; at eighteen he married a farmer's daughter, Anne Hathaway, seven or eight years his senior; there are baptismal records of their children, Susanna (1583) and the twins Hamnet and Judith (1585). After a gap of seven years, records show Shakespeare in 1592 already a successful and many-talented playwright in London; in 1594 he was a sharer in a prominent players' company of which the Lord Chamberlain was patron and the famous actors Burbage and Kempe were members, while literary distinction of a type that was then more highly respected came from successful poems ("Venus and Adonis," 1593; "The Rape of Lucrece," 1594). By 1596, of his now best-known plays he had written *The Taming of the Shrew, Richard III, Romeo and Juliet,* and *The Merchant of Venice;* in 1597–98, with the two parts of *Henry IV* he added Falstaff to his growing list of famous characters.

The Chamberlain's men had been playing at the Theater, north of the city of London, and later at the Curtain; in 1598 the Theater was demolished, and the Globe, a large playhouse south of the Thames, was built, Shakespeare sharing in the expenses. Increased prosperity had brought social advancement: in 1596 the College of Heralds had sanctioned Shakespeare's claim to a gentleman's station by recognizing the family's coat of arms; in the same period he had bought New Place, a large house in his home town. In 1599, *Henry V,* the last of the plays centering on the Lancastrian kings, was followed by the first of the great Roman tragedies, *Julius Caesar.* The major plays belong to the following period; this is a usual dating of the most famous: *Hamlet,* 1601; *Othello,* 1603–4; *King Lear,* 1605; *Macbeth,* 1606; *Antony and Cleopatra,* 1607; *The Tempest,* 1611. Queen Elizabeth had favored the players, and her successor, James I, directly patronized them; the Lord Chamberlain's company thus became the King's Men. In 1608, besides the Globe, they acquired an enclosed playhouse in Blackfriars, in the city of London, for winter entertainment. At about that time Shakespeare seems to have retired from the stage, and certainly from then on he wrote fewer plays. He lived most of the time at Stratford until his death there on April 23, 1616.

Shakespeare's plays constitute the most important body of dramatic work in the history of literature, and no character in literature is more familiar to world audiences than Hamlet. He belongs to the world also in the sense that some of the influential interpretations of his character have been developed outside the country and language of his origin, the most famous being the one offered by Goethe in *Wilhelm Meister*. The unparalleled reputation of the work may also have certain nonliterary causes. For instance, it is a play whose central role is singularly cherished by actors in all languages as the test of stardom; and, conversely, audiences sometimes content themselves with a rather vague notion of the work as a whole and concentrate on the attractively problematical and eloquent hero, and on the actor impersonating him, waiting for his famous soliloquies as a certain type of operagoer waits for the next aria of his favorite singer. But along with the impact of the protagonist, there are other and deeper reasons why the world should naturally have given *Hamlet* its leading place in the common patrimony of literature. Though it is a drama that concerns personages of superior station, and the conflicts and problems associated with men of high degree, it reveals these problems in terms of a particular family, presenting an individual and domestic dimension along with a public one—the pattern of family conflict within the larger pattern of the *polis*—like the plays of antiquity that deal with the Theban myth, such as *Oedipus* and *Antigone*.

This public dimension of *Hamlet* helps us see it, for our present purposes, in relation to the literature of the Renaissance. For the framework within which the characters are presented and come into conflict is a court. In spite of the Danish locale and the relatively remote period of the action, it is a plainly Renaissance court exhibiting the structure of interests to which Machiavelli's *Prince* has potently drawn our attention. There is a ruler holding power, and much of the action is related to questions concerning the nature of that power—the way in which he had acquired it and the ways in which it can be preserved. Moreover, there is a courtly structure: the King has several courtiers around him, among whom Hamlet, the heir apparent, is only the most prominent.

We have seen some of the forms of the Renaissance court pattern in earlier selections—in Castiglione, Rabelais, Machiavelli. The court, the ruling nucleus of the community, was also an arena for conflicts of interest and of wit, a setting for the cultivation and codification of aristocratic virtues (valor, physical and intellectual brilliance, "courtesy"). The positive view of human achievement on earth, so prominent in the Renaissance, was given in courtly life its characteristic setting and testing ground. And as we have observed, the negative view (melancholy, sense of void and purposelessness) also emerged there.

Examining *Hamlet*, we soon realize that its temper belongs more to the negative than to the positive Renaissance outlook. Certain outstanding forms of human endeavor (the establishment of earthly power, the display of gallantry, the confident attempt of the mind to acquire knowledge and to inspire purposeful action), which elsewhere are presented as highly worthwhile, or are at least soberly discussed in terms of their value and limits, seem to be caught here in a condition of disorder and imbued with a sense of vanity and void.

The way in which the state and the court of Denmark are presented in *Hamlet* is significant: they are shown in images of disease and rottenness. And here again, excessive stress on the protagonist himself must be avoided. His position as denouncer of the prevailing decadence, and the major basis for his denunciation—the murder of his father, which leads to his desire to obtain revenge and purify the court by destroying the present king—are central elements in the play; but they are not the *whole* play. The public situation is indicated, and Marcellus has pronounced his famous "Something is rotten . . ." before Hamlet has talked to the Ghost and learned the Ghost's version of events. Moreover, the sense of outside dangers and internal disruption everywhere transcends the personal story of Hamlet, of his revenge, of Claudius's crime; these are rather the signs of the breakdown, portents of a general situation. In this sense, we may tentatively say that the general theme of the play has to do with a kingdom, a society, a *polis*, going to pieces—or even more, with its realization that it has already gone to pieces. Concomitant with this is a sense of the vanity of those forms of human endeavor and power of which the kingdom and the court are symbols.

The tone Shakespeare wants to establish is evident from the opening scenes: the night air is full of dread premonitions; sentinels turn their eyes toward the threatening outside world; meanwhile, the Ghost has already made his appearance, a sinister omen. The kingdom, as we proceed, is presented in terms that are an almost point by point reversal of the ideal. Claudius, the *pater patriae* and *pater familias*, whether we believe the Ghost's indictment or not (Hamlet does not necessarily, and some of his famous indecision has been attributed to his seeking evidence of the Ghost's truthfulness before acting), has by marrying the Queen committed an act that by Elizabethan standards is incestuous. There is an overwhelming sense of disintegration in the body of the state, evident in the first court assembly and in all subsequent ones: in their various ways the two courtiers, Hamlet and Laertes, are strangers, contemplating departure; they offer, around their king, a picture quite unlike that of the conventional paladins, supports of the throne, in a well-manned and well-mannered court. (In Rabelais's "kingdom," when Grangousier is ruler, the pattern is also a courtly and knightly one, but the young heir, Gargantua, who is like Hamlet a university student, readily abandons his studies to answer the fatherland's call; here the direction is reversed.)

On the other hand, as in all late and decadent phases of a social or artistic structure (the court in a sense is both), we have semblance instead of substance, ornate and empty façades, of which the more enlightened members of the group are mockingly aware. Thus Polonius, who after Hamlet is the major figure in the king's retinue, is presented satirically in his empty formalities of speech and conventional norms of behavior. And there are numerous instances (Osric is one) of manners being replaced by mannerisms. Hence the way courtly life is depicted in the play suggests always the hollow, the fractured, the crooked. The traditional forms and institutions of gentle living, and all the pomp and solemnity, are marred by corruption and distortion. Courtship and love are reduced to Hamlet's mockery of a "civil conversation" in the play scene, his phrases presenting not Castiglione's Platonic loftiness and the repartee of "gentilesse," but punning undercurrents of bawdiness. The theater, a traditional institution of court life, is "politically" used by the hero as a device to expose the king's crime. There are elements of macabre caricature in Shakespeare's treatment of the solemn theme of death (see, for instance, the manner of Polonius's death, which is a sort of sarcastic version of a cloak-and-dagger scene; or the effect of the clownish gravediggers' talk). Finally, the arms tournament, the typical occasion for the display of courtiers' gallantry in front of their king, is here turned by the scheming of the king himself into the play's conclusive scene of carnage. And the person who, on the king's behalf, invites Hamlet to that feast is Osric, the "waterfly," the caricature of the hollow courtier.

This sense of corruption and decadence dominates the temper of the play and obviously qualifies the character of Hamlet, his indecision, his sense of vanity and disenchantment with the world in which he lives. In Hamlet the relation between thought and deed, intent and realization, is confused in the same way that the norms and institutions which would regulate the life of a well-ordered court have been deprived of their original purpose and beauty. He and the king are "mighty opposites," and it can be argued that against Hamlet's indecision and negativism the king presents a more positive scheme of action, at least in the purely Machiavellian sense, at the level of practical power politics. But even this conclusion will prove only partly true. There are indeed moments in which all that the king seems to wish for himself is to forget the past and rule honorably. He advises Hamlet not to mourn his father excessively, for melancholy is not in accord with "nature." On various occasions the king shows a high and competent conception of his office: a culminating instance is the courageous and cunning way in which he confronts and handles Laertes's wrath. The point can be made that since his life is obviously threatened by Hamlet (who was seeking to kill him when by mistake he killed Polonius instead), the king acts within a legitimate pattern of politics in wanting to have Hamlet liquidated. But this argument cannot be carried so far as to demonstrate that he represents a fully positive attitude toward life and the world, even in the strictly amoral terms of political technique. For in fact his action in corroded by an element alien to that technique—the vexations of his own conscience. In spite of his energy and his extrovert qualities he too becomes part of the negative picture of disruption and lacks concentration of purpose. The images of decay and putrescence that characterize his court extend to his own speech: his "offense," in his own words, "smells to heaven."

To conclude, *Hamlet* as a Renaissance tragedy presents a world particularly "out of joint," a world which, having long ago lost the sense of a grand extratemporal design which was so important to the medieval man (to Hamlet the thought of the afterlife is even more puzzling and dark than that of this life), looks with an even greater sense of disenchantment at the circle of temporal action symbolized by the kingdom and the court. These could have offered certain codes of conduct and objects of allegiance that would have given individual action a purposeful meaning. But now their order has been destroyed. Ideals that once had power and freshness have lost their vigor under the impact of satiety, doubt, and melancholy.

Since communal values are so degraded, it is natural to ask in the end whether some alternative attempt at a settlement could be imagined, with Hamlet—like other Renaissance heroes—adopting an individual code of conduct, however extravagant. On the whole, Hamlet seems too steeped in his own hopelessness, and in the courtly mechanism to which he inevitably belongs, to be able to find personal intellectual and moral compromise or his own version of total escape or total dream; for his "antic disposition" is a strategy, his "folly" is politically motivated. Still, the tone of his brooding and often moralizing speech, his melancholy and dissatisfaction, his very desire for revenge do seem to imply an aspiration toward some form of moral beauty, a nostalgia for a world—as the king his father's must have been—of clean allegiances and respected codes of honor. One thing worth examining in this connection is Hamlet's attitude toward Fortinbras. Fortinbras is a marginal character, but our attention is emphatically drawn to him both at the very opening and at the very close of the play. There is no doubt that while in the play certain positive virtues—such as friendship, loyalty, and truthfulness—are represented by the very prominent Horatio, who will live on to give a true report of Hamlet, in Fortinbras the ideals of gallant knighthood, which in the present court have been so corrupted and lost, seem to be presented at their purest. And he has, of course, Hamlet's "dying voice." Earlier, in act 4, scene 4, Hamlet has seen Fortinbras move with his army toward an enterprise characterized by the flimsiness of its material rewards. In a world where all matter seems corrupt, Hamlet's qualified sympathy for that gratuitous display of honor for honor's sake, of valor "even for an eggshell," of death braved "for a fantasy," calls to mind some of the serious aspects of the Quixotic code.

A biography placing Shakespeare in his social context is M. C. Bradbrook, *Shakespeare the Poet in His World* (1978), while E. K. Chambers, *William Shakespeare, A Study of Facts and Problems*, 2 vols., (1930), is considered the most fully documented biography. The student will find several views in *Shakespeare: Modern Essays in Criticism* (1957), edited by Leonard F. Dean. More advanced interpretations and critical methods are presented in Paul Gottschalk, *The Meanings of Hamlet. Modes of Literary Interpretation Since Bradley* (1972). Another valuable work is Harry Levin, *The Question of Hamlet* (1959).

# Hamlet, Prince of Denmark

## Characters

| | |
|---|---|
| CLAUDIUS, *king of Denmark* | VOLTIMAND, |
| HAMLET, *son to the late, and* | CORNELIUS, |
| *nephew to the present king* | ROSENCRANTZ, |
| POLONIUS, *lord chamberlain* | GUILDENSTERN, } *courtiers* |
| HORATIO, *friend to Hamlet* | OSRIC, |
| LAERTES, *son of Polonius* | GENTLEMAN, |

PRIEST
MARCELLUS, ⎫
BERNARDO, ⎬ *officers*
FRANCISCO, *a soldier*
REYNALDO, *servant to Polonius*
PLAYERS
TWO CLOWNS, *grave-diggers*
FORTINBRAS, *prince of Norway*
CAPTAIN

ENGLISH AMBASSADORS
GERTRUDE, *queen of Denmark,*
    *and mother to Hamlet*
OPHELIA, *daughter of Polonius*
LORDS, LADIES, OFFICERS, SOL-
    DIERS, SAILORS, MESSEN-
    GERS, *and* OTHER
ATTENDANTS
GHOST OF HAMLET'S FATHER

SCENE—*Denmark.*

## Act I

### SCENE 1—*Elsinore. A platform before the castle.*

[FRANCISCO *at his post. Enter to him* BERNARDO.]
BERNARDO. Who's there?
FRANCISCO. Nay, answer me: stand, and unfold yourself.
BERNARDO. Long live the king!
FRANCISCO. Bernardo?
BERNARDO. He.                                                                              5
FRANCISCO. You come most carefully upon your hour.
BERNARDO. 'Tis now struck twelve; get thee to bed, Francisco.
FRANCISCO. For this relief much thanks: 'tis bitter cold,
    And I am sick at heart.
BERNARDO. Have you had quiet guard?
FRANCISCO.                              Not a mouse stirring.     10
BERNARDO. Well, good night.
    If you do meet Horatio and Marcellus,
    The rivals[1] of my watch, bid them make haste.
FRANCISCO. I think I hear them. Stand, ho! Who is there?
    [*Enter* HORATIO *and* MARCELLUS.]
HORATIO. Friends to this ground.
MARCELLUS.                        And liegemen to the Dane.[2]   15
FRANCISCO. Give you good night.
MARCELLUS.                        O, farewell, honest soldier:
    Who hath relieved you?
FRANCISCO.                  Bernardo hath my place.
    Give you good night.                              [*Exit.*]
MARCELLUS.              Holla! Bernardo!
BERNARDO.                                    Say,
    What, is Horatio there?
HORATIO.                    A piece of him.
BERNARDO. Welcome, Horatio; welcome, good Marcellus.         20

1. Partners.   2. The king of Denmark.

MARCELLUS. What, has this thing appear'd again to-night?

BERNARDO. I have seen nothing.

MARCELLUS. Horatio says 'tis but our fantasy,
   And will not let belief take hold of him
   Touching this dreaded sight, twice seen of us:                           25
   Therefore I have entreated him along
   With us to watch the minutes of this night,
   That if again this apparition come,
   He may approve our eyes[3] and speak to it.

HORATIO. Tush, tush, 'twill not appear.

BERNARDO.                                         Sit down a while;                    30
   And let us once again assail your ears,
   That are so fortified against our story,
   What we have two nights seen.

HORATIO.                                         Well, sit we down,
   And let us hear Bernardo speak of this.

BERNARDO. Last night of all,                                                          35
   When yond same star that's westward from the pole
   Had made his course to illume that part of heaven
   Where now it burns, Marcellus and myself,
   The bell then beating one,—
      [*Enter* GHOST.]

MARCELLUS. Peace, break thee off; look, where it comes again!                         40

BERNARDO. In the same figure, like the king that's dead.

MARCELLUS. Thou art a scholar; speak to it, Horatio.

BERNARDO. Looks it not like the king? mark it, Horatio.

HORATIO. Most like it: it harrows me with fear and wonder.

BERNARDO. It would be spoke to.

MARCELLUS.                                         Question it, Horatio.               45

HORATIO. What are thou, that usurp'st this time of night,
   Together with that fair and warlike form
   In which the majesty of buried Denmark
   Did sometimes[4] march? by heaven I charge thee, speak!

MARCELLUS. It is offended.

BERNARDO.                                         See, it stalks away!                 50

HORATIO. Stay! speak, speak! I charge thee, speak!
      [*Exit* GHOST.]

MARCELLUS. 'Tis gone, and will not answer.

BERNARDO. How now, Horatio! you tremble and look pale:
   Is not this something more than fantasy?
   What think you on't?                                                          55

HORATIO. Before my God, I might not this believe
   Without the sensible and true avouch

---

3. Confirm what we saw.     4. Formerly. *Denmark*: The king of Denmark.

Of mine own eyes.

MARCELLUS.　　　　Is it not like the king?

HORATIO. As thou art to thyself:

Such was the very armor he had on　　　　　　　60
When he the ambitious Norway[5] combated;
So frown'd he once, when, in an angry parle,[6]
He smote the sledded Polacks on the ice.
'Tis strange.

MARCELLUS. Thus twice before, and jump[7] at this dead hour,　　65
With martial stalk hath he gone by our watch.

HORATIO. In what particular thought to work I know not;
But, in the gross and scope of my opinion,[8]
This bodes some strange eruption to our state.

MARCELLUS. Good now, sit down, and tell me, he that knows,　　70
Why this same strict and most observant watch
So nightly toils the subject[9] of the land,
And why such daily cast of brazen cannon,
And foreign mart for implements of war;
Why such impress of shipwrights,[1] whose sore task　　75
Does not divide the Sunday from the week;
What might be toward,[2] that this sweaty haste
Doth make the night joint-laborer with the day:
Who is't that can inform me?

HORATIO.　　　　　　　That can I;

At least the whisper goes so. Our last king,　　　80
Whose image even but now appear'd to us,
Was, as you know, by Fortinbras of Norway,
Thereto prick'd on by a most emulate pride,
Dared to the combat; in which our valiant Hamlet—
For so this side of our known world esteem'd him—　　85
Did slay this Fortinbras; who by a seal'd compact
Well ratified by law and heraldry,[3]
Did forfeit, with his life, all those his lands
Which he stood seized of, to the conqueror:
Against the which, a moiety competent[4]　　　90
Was gagèd by our king; which had return'd
To the inheritance of Fortinbras,
Had he been vanquisher; as, by the same covenant
And carriage[5] of the article design'd,
His fell to Hamlet. Now, sir, young Fortinbras,　　95
Of unimprovèd[6] metal hot and full,

5. The king of Norway (the elder Fortinbras).　6. Parley. *Sledded:* Who travel in sledges.
7. Just.　8. Taking a general view.　9. Makes the people (the subjects) toil.　1. Forcing
of ship carpenters into service. *Mart:* Trading.　2. Impending.　3. Duly ratified and proclaimed through heralds.　4. Adequate part. *Seized:* Possessed. *Gagèd:* Pledged.
5. Purport.　6. Unused. *Skirts:* Outskirts, border regions.

Hath in the skirts of Norway here and there
Shark'd up a list of lawless resolutes,
For food and diet, to some enterprise
That hath a stomach in't:[7] which is no other— 100
As it doth well appear unto our state—
But to recover of us, by strong hand
And terms compulsatory, those foresaid lands
So by his father lost: and this, I take it,
Is the main motive of our preparations, 105
The source of this oar watch and the chief head
Of this post-haste and romage[8] in the land.
BERNARDO. I think it be no other but e'en so:
Well may it sort,[9] that this portentous figure
Comes armèd through our watch, so like the king 110
That was and is the question of these wars.
HORATIO. A mote it is to trouble the mind's eye.
In the most high and palmy state of Rome,
A little ere the mightiest Julius fell,
The graves stood tenantless, and the sheeted dead 115
Did squeak and gibber in the Roman streets:
As stars with trains of fire and dews of blood,
Disasters in the sun; and the moist star,[1]
Upon whose influence Neptune's empire stands,[2]
Was sick almost to doomsday with eclipse: 120
And even the like precurse[3] of fierce events,
As harbingers preceding still the fates
And prologue to the omen coming on,
Have heaven and earth together demonstrated
Unto our climatures[4] and countrymen. 125
    [*Re-enter* GHOST.]
But soft, behold! lo, where it comes again!
I'll cross it, though it blast me. Stay, illusion!
If thou hast any sound, or use of voice,
Speak to me:
If there be any good thing to be done, 130
That may to thee do ease and grace to me,
Speak to me:
If thou art privy to thy country's fate,
Which, happily, foreknowing may avoid,
O, speak! 135
Or if thou hast uphoarded in thy life
Extorted treasure in the womb of earth,
For which, they say, you spirits oft walk in death,

---

7. Calls for courage.   8. Bustle. *Head*: Origin, cause.   9. Happen.   1. The moon. *Disasters*: Ill omens.   2. The moon regulates the sea tides.   3. Foreboding.   4. Regions.

Speak of it: stay, and speak! [*The cock crows.*] Stop it, Marcellus.
MARCELLUS. Shall I strike at it with my partisan?                    140
HORATIO. Do, if it will not stand.
BERNARDO.                              'Tis here!
HORATIO.                                        'Tis here!
MARCELLUS. 'Tis gone!                              [*Exit* GHOST.]
We do it wrong, being so majestical,
   To offer it the show of violence;
   For it is, as the air, invulnerable,                    145
   And our vain blows malicious mockery.
BERNARDO. It was about to speak, when the cock crew.
HORATIO. And then it started like a guilty thing
   Upon a fearful summons. I have heard
   The cock, that is the trumpet to the morn,                    150
   Doth with his lofty and shrill-sounding throat
   Awake the god of day, and at his warning,
   Whether in sea or fire, in earth or air,
   The extravagant[5] and erring spirit hies
   To his confine: and of the truth herein                    155
   This present object made probation.[6]
MARCELLUS. It faded on the crowing of the cock.
   Some say that ever 'gainst[7] that season comes
   Wherein our Saviour's birth is celebrated,
   The bird of dawning singeth all night long:                    160
   And then, they say, no spirit dare stir abroad,
   The nights are wholesome, then no planets strike,
   No fairy takes[8] nor witch hath power to charm,
   So hallow'd and so gracious[9] is the time.
HORATIO. So have I heard and do in part believe it.                    165
   But look, the morn, in russet mantle clad,
   Walks o'er the dew of yon high eastward hill:
   Break we our watch up; and by my advice,
   Let us impart what we have seen to-night
   Unto young Hamlet; for, upon my life,                    170
   This spirit, dumb to us, will speak to him:
   Do you consent we shall acquaint him with it,
   As needful in our loves, fitting our duty?
MARCELLUS. Let's do't, I pray; and I this morning know
   Where we shall find him most conveniently.                    175
   [*Exeunt.*]

---

5. Wandering out of its confines.    6. Gave proof.    7. Just before.    8. Bewitches. *Strike:*
Exercise evil influence (compare "moon struck").    9. Full of blessing.

SCENE 2—A *room of state in the castle.*

[*Flourish. Enter the* KING, QUEEN, HAMLET, POLONIUS, LAERTES,
VOLTIMAND, CORNELIUS, LORDS, *and* ATTENDANTS.]

KING. Though yet of Hamlet our dear brother's death
The memory be green, and that it us befitted
To bear our hearts in grief and our whole kingdom
To be contracted in one brow of woe,
Yet so far hath discretion[1] fought with nature                5
That we with wisest sorrow think on him,
Together with remembrance of ourselves.
Therefore our sometime sister, now our queen,
The imperial jointress to this warlike state,
Have we, as 'twere with a defeated joy,—                        10
With an auspicious and a dropping eye,
With mirth in funeral and with dirge in marriage,
In equal scale weighing delight and dole,—
Taken to wife: nor have we herein barr'd[2]
Your better wisdoms, which have freely gone                     15
With this affair along. For all, our thanks.
Now follows, that you know, young Fortinbras,
Holding a weak supposal of our worth,
Or thinking by our late dear brother's death
Our state to be disjoint and out of frame,                      20
Colleaguèd with this dream[3] of his advantage,
He hath not fail'd to pester us with message,
Importing the surrender of those lands
Lost by his father, with all bonds of law,
To our most valiant brother. So much for him.                   25
Now for ourself, and for this time of meeting:
Thus much the business is: we have here writ
To Norway, uncle of young Fortinbras,—
Who, impotent and bed-rid, scarcely hears
Of this his nephew's purpose,—to suppress                       30
His further gait[4] herein; in that the levies,
The lists and full proportions,[5] are all made
Out of his subject:[6] and we here dispatch
You, good Cornelius, and you, Voltimand,
For bearers of this greeting to old Norway,                     35
Giving to you no further personal power
To business with the king more than the scope

---

1. Restraint (here, on grief).    2. Ignored. *Dole:* Grief.    3. Combined with this fantastic
notion.    4. Proceeding.    5. Amounts of forces and supplies.    6. Subjects, people.

Of these delated[7] articles allow.

Farewell, and let your haste commend your duty.

CORNELIUS. ⎱ In that all things will we show our duty.                    40
VOLTIMAND. ⎰

KING. We doubt it nothing: heartily farewell.

[*Exeunt* VOLTIMAND *and* CORNELIUS.]

And now, Laertes, what's the news with you?

You told us of some suit; what is't, Laertes?

You cannot speak of reason to the Dane,[8]

And lose your voice: what wouldst thou beg, Laertes,                    45

That shall not be my offer, not thy asking?

The head is not more native to[9] the heart,

The hand more instrumental to the mouth,

Than is the throne of Denmark to thy father.

What wouldst thou have, Laertes?

LAERTES.                                    My dread lord,                    50

Your leave and favor to return to France,

From whence though willingly I came to Denmark,

To show my duty in your coronation,

Yet now, I must confess, that duty done,

My thoughts and wishes bend again toward France                    55

And bow them to your gracious leave and pardon.

KING. Have you your father's leave? What says Polonius?

POLONIUS. He hath, my lord, wrung from me my slow leave

By laborsome petition, and at last

Upon his will I seal'd my hard consent:                    60

I do beseech you, give him leave to go.

KING. Take thy fair hour, Laertes; time be thine,

And thy best graces spend it at thy will!

But now, my cousin Hamlet, and my son,—

HAMLET. [*Aside*] A little more than kin, and less than kind.                    65

KING. How is it that the clouds still hang on you?

HAMLET. Not so, my lord; I am too much i' the sun.[1]

QUEEN. Good Hamlet, cast thy nighted color off,

And let thine eye look like a friend on Denmark.

Do not for ever with thy vailèd[2] lids                    70

Seek for thy noble father in the dust:

Thou know'st 'tis common; all that lives must die,

Passing through nature to eternity.

HAMLET. Aye, madam, it is common.

QUEEN.                                    If it be,

Why seems it so particular with thee?                    75

---

7. Detailed.    8. King of Denmark.    9. Naturally bound to.    1. The cue to Hamlet's irony is given by the King's "my cousin . . . my son." Hemlet is punning on "son."    2. Downcast.

HAMLET. Seems, madam! nay, it is; I know not 'seems.'
   'Tis not alone my inky cloak, good mother,
   Nor customary suits of solemn black,
   Nor windy suspiration of forced breath,
   No, nor the fruitful river in the eye,                80
   Nor the dejected havior of the visage,
   Together with all forms, moods, shapes of grief,
   That can denote me truly: these indeed seem,
   For they are actions that a man might play:
   But I have that within which passeth show;        85
   These but the trappings and the suits of woe.
KING. 'Tis sweet and commendable in your nature, Hamlet,
   To give these mourning duties to your father:
   But, you must know, your father lost a father,
   That father lost, lost his, and the survivor bound     90
   In filial obligation for some term
   To do obsequious[3] sorrow: but to persevere
   In obstinate condolement is a course
   Of impious stubborness; 'tis unmanly grief:
   It shows a will most incorrect[4] to heaven,        95
   A heart unfortified, a mind impatient,
   An understanding simple and unschool'd:
   For what we know must be and is as common
   As any the most vulgar thing to sense,
   Why should we in our peevish opposition        100
   Take it to heart? Fie! 'tis a fault to heaven,
   A fault against the dead, a fault to nature,
   To reason most absurd, whose common theme
   Is death of fathers, and who still hath cried,
   From the first corse till he that died to-day,      105
   'This must be so.' We pray you, throw to earth
   This unprevailing[5] woe, and think of us
   As of a father: for let the world take note,
   You are the most immediate to our throne,
   And with no less nobility of love            110
   Than that which dearest father bears his son
   Do I impart toward you. For your intent
   In going back to school in Wittenberg,[6]
   It is most retrograde[7] to our desire:
   And we beseech you, bend you to remain       115
   Here in the cheer and comfort of our eye,
   Our chiefest courtier, cousin and our son.

---

3. Dutiful, especially concerning funeral rites (obsequies).    4. Not subdued.    5. Useless.
6. The seat of a university; at the peak of fame in Shakespeare's time because of its connection
with Martin Luther.    7. Opposed.

QUEEN. Let not thy mother lose her prayers, Hamlet:
  I pray thee, stay with us; go not to Wittenberg.
HAMLET. I shall in all my best obey you, madam.                    120
KING. Why, 'tis a loving and a fair reply:
  Be as ourself in Denmark. Madam, come;
  This gentle and unforced accord of Hamlet
  Sits smiling to my heart: in grace whereof,
  No jocund health that Denmark drinks to-day,               125
  But the great cannon to the clouds shall tell,
  And the king's rouse the heaven shall bruit[8] again,
  Re-speaking earthly thunder. Come away.
    [*Flourish. Exeunt all but* HAMLET.]
HAMLET. O, that this too too sullied flesh would melt,
  Thaw and resolve itself into a dew!                         130
  Or that the Everlasting had not fix'd
  His canon[9] 'gainst self-slaughter! O God! God!
  How weary, stale, flat and unprofitable
  Seem to me all the uses of this world!
  Fie on't! ah fie! 'tis an unweeded garden,                  135
  That grows to seed; things rank and gross in nature
  Possess it merely. That it should come to this!
  But two months dead! nay, not so much, not two:
  So excellent a king; that was, to this,
  Hyperion[1] to a satyr: so loving to my mother,            140
  That he might not beteem[2] the winds of heaven
  Visit her face too roughly. Heaven and earth!
  Must I remember? why, she would hang on him,
  As if increase of appetite had grown
  By what it fed on: and yet, within a month—                 145
  Let me not think on't—Frailty, thy name is woman!—
  A little month, or ere those shoes were old
  With which she follow'd my poor father's body,
  Like Niobe,[3] all tears:—why she, even she,—
  O God! a beast that wants discourse of reason[4]           150
  Would have mourn'd longer,—married with my uncle,
  My father's brother, but no more like my father
  Than I to Hercules: within a month;
  Ere yet the salt of most unrighteous tears
  Had left the flushing in her gallèd[5] eyes,               155
  She married. O, most wicked speed, to post
  With such dexterity to incestuous sheets![6]

8. Proclaim, echo. *Rouse*: Carousal, revel.  9. Law.  1. The sun god.  2. Allow.  3. A
proud mother who boasted of having more children than Leto; her seven sons and seven daughters
were slain by Apollo and Artemis, children of Leto. The grieving Niobe was changed by Zeus
into a continually weeping stone.  4. Lacks the reasoning faculty.  5. Inflamed.
6. According to principles which Hamlet accepts, marrying one's brother's widow is incest.

It is not, nor it cannot come to good:
But break, my heart, for I must hold my tongue!
   [*Enter* HORATIO, MARCELLUS, *and* BERNARDO.]
HORATIO. Hail to your lordship!
HAMLET.                              I am glad to see you well:    160
  Horatio,—or I do forget myself.
HORATIO. The same, my lord, and your poor servant ever.
HAMLET. Sir, my good friend; I'll change[7] that name with you:
  And what make you from Wittenberg, Horatio?
  Marcellus?    165
MARCELLUS. My good lord?
HAMLET. I am very glad to see you. [*To* BARNARDO] Good even, sir.
  But what, in faith, make you from Wittenberg?
HORATIO. A truant disposition, good my lord.
HAMLET. I would not hear your enemy say so,    170
  Nor shall you do my ear that violence,
  To make it truster of your own report
  Against yourself: I know you are no truant.
  But what is your affair in Elsinore?
  We'll teach you to drink deep ere you depart.    175
HORATIO. My lord, I came to see your father's funeral.
HAMLET. I pray thee, do not mock me, fellow-student;
  I think it was to see my mother's wedding.
HORATIO. Indeed, my lord, it follow'd hard upon.
HAMLET. Thrift, thrift, Horatio! the funeral baked-meats    180
  Did coldly furnish forth the marriage tables.
  Would I had met my dearest[8] foe in heaven
  Or ever I had seen that day, Horatio!
  My father!—methinks I see my father.
HORATIO. O where, my lord?
HAMLET.                              In my mind's eye, Horatio.    185
HORATIO. I saw him once; he was a goodly king.
HAMLET. He was a man, take him for all in all,
  I shall not look upon his like again.
HORATIO. My lord, I think I saw him yesternight.
HAMLET. Saw? who?    190
HORATIO. My lord, the king your father.
HAMLET.                              The king my father!
HORATIO. Season your admiration[9] for a while
  With an attent ear, till I may deliver,
  Upon the witness of these gentlemen,
  This marvel to you.
HAMLET.                              For God's love, let me hear.    195

---

7. Exchange.    8. Bitterest.    9. Restrain your astonishment.

HORATIO. Two nights together had these gentlemen,
　　Marcellus and Bernardo, on their watch,
　　In the dead vast and middle of the night,
　　Been thus encounter'd. A figure like your father,
　　Armed at point exactly, cap-a-pe,[1]　　　　　　　　　　200
　　Appears before them, and with solemn march
　　Goes slow and stately by them: thrice he walk'd
　　By their oppress'd and fear-surprisèd eyes,
　　Within his truncheon's length; whilst they, distill'd
　　Almost to jelly with the act of fear,　　　　　　　　　205
　　Stand dumb, and speak not to him. This to me
　　In dreadful secrecy impart they did;
　　And I with them the third night kept the watch:
　　Where, as they had deliver'd, both in time,
　　Form of the thing, each word made true and good,　　210
　　The apparition comes: I knew your father;
　　These hands were not more like.
HAMLET.　　　　　　　　　　　　　But where was this?
MARCELLUS. My lord, upon the platform where we watch'd.
HAMLET. Did you not speak to it?
HORATIO.　　　　　　　　　　My lord, I did.
　　But answer made it none: yet once methought　　　　215
　　It lifted up its head and did address
　　Itself to motion, like as it would speak:
　　But even then the morning cock crew loud,
　　And at the sound it shrunk in haste away
　　And vanish'd from our sight.
HAMLET.　　　　　　　　　　　　'Tis very strange.　　220
HORATIO. As I do live, my honor'd lord, 'tis true,
　　And we did think it writ down in our duty
　　To let you know of it.
HAMLET. Indeed, indeed, sirs, but this troubles me.
　　Hold you the watch to-night?
MARCELLUS. ⎱
BERNARDO. ⎰　　　　　　　We do, my lord.　　　　225
HAMLET. Arm'd, say you?
MARCELLUS. ⎱
BERNARDO. ⎰　　　　　　Arm'd, my lord.
HAMLET.　　　　　　　　　　　　From top to toe?
MARCELLUS. ⎱
BERNARDO. ⎰ My lord, from head to foot.
HAMLET. Then saw you not his face?
HORATIO. O, yes, my lord; he wore his beaver[2] up.　　230

1. From head to foot. *At point*: Completely.　2. Visor.

HAMLET. What, look'd he frowningly?

HORATIO. A countenance more in sorrow than in anger.

HAMLET. Pale, or red?

HORATIO. Nay, very pale.

HAMLET.                          And fix'd his eyes upon you?

HORATIO. Most constantly.

HAMLET.                          I would I had been there.                    235

HORATIO. It would have much amazed you.

HAMLET. Very like, very like. Stay'd it long?

HORATIO. While one with moderate haste might tell[3] a hundred.

MARCELLUS. ⎱
BERNARDO.  ⎰ Longer, longer.

HORATIO. Not when I saw't.

HAMLET.                          His beard was grizzled?[4] no?            240

HORATIO. It was, as I have seen it in his life,
  A sable silver'd.[5]

HAMLET.                    I will watch to-night;
  Perchance 'twill walk again.

HORATIO.                          I warrant it will.

HAMLET. If it assume my noble father's person,
  I'll speak to it, though hell itself should gape
  And bid me hold my peace. I pray you all,                               245
  If you have hitherto conceal'd this sight,
  Let it be tenable in your silence still,[6]
  And whatsoever else shall hap to-night,
  Give it an understanding, but no tongue:
  I will requite your loves. So fare you well:
  Upon the platform, 'twixt eleven and twelve,                           250
  I'll visit you.

ALL.                    Our duty to your honor.

HAMLET. Your loves, as mine to you: farewell.

  [*Exeunt all but* HAMLET.]

  My father's spirit in arms! all is not well;                           255
  I doubt[7] some foul play: would the night were come!
  Till then sit still, my soul: foul deeds will rise,
  Though all the earth o'erwhelm them, to men's eyes.

  [*Exit.*]

SCENE 3—*A room in Polonius's house.*

  [*Enter* LAERTES *and* OPHELIA.]

LAERTES. My necessaries are embark'd: farewell:
  And, sister, as the winds give benefit
  And convoy[8] is assistant, do not sleep,

3. Count.    4. Gray.    5. Black and white.    6. Consider it still a secret.    7. Suspect.
8. Conveyance, means of transport.

But let me hear from you.

OPHELIA.                          Do you doubt that?

LAERTES. For Hamlet, and the trifling of his favor,                    5
Hold it a fashion,[9] and a toy in blood,
A violet in the youth of primy[1] nature,
Forward, not permanent, sweet, not lasting,
The perfume and suppliance of a minute;
No more.

OPHELIA. No more but so?

LAERTES. Think it no more:                                             10
For nature crescent[2] does not grow alone
In thews and bulk; but, as this temple[3] waxes,
The inward service of the mind and soul
Grows wide withal. Perhaps he loves you now;
And now no soil nor cautel[4] doth besmirch                            15
The virtue of his will: but you must fear,
His greatness weigh'd,[5] his will is not his own;
For he himself is subject to his birth:
He may not, as unvalued persons do,
Carve for himself, for on his choice depends                          20
The safety and health of this whole state,
And therefore must his choice be circumscribed
Unto the voice and yielding[6] of that body
Whereof he is the head. Then if he says he loves you,
It fits your wisdom so far to believe it                               25
As he in his particular act and place
May give his saying deed; which is no further
Than the main voice of Denmark goes withal.[7]
Then weigh what loss your honor may sustain,
If with too credent ear you list his songs,                           30
Or lose your heart, or your chaste treasure open
To his unmaster'd importunity.
Fear it Ophelia, fear it, my dear sister,
And keep you in the rear of your affection,
Out of the shot and danger of desire.                                 35
The chariest maid is prodigal enough,
If she unmask her beauty to the moon:
Virtue itself 'scapes not calumnious strokes:
The canker galls the infants of the spring
Too oft before their buttons be disclosed,                            40
And in the morn and liquid dew of youth
Contagious blastments[8] are most imminent.

9. A passing mood.   1. Early, young. *Forward:* Early.   2. Growing.   3. The body.
4. No foul or deceitful thoughts. *Will:* Desire.   5. When you consider his rank.
6. Assent.   7. Goes along with, agrees. *Main:* Powerful.   8. Blights.

Be wary then; best safety lies in fear:
Youth to itself rebels, though none else near.

OPHELIA. I shall the effect of this good lesson keep,                45
As watchman to my heart. But, good my brother,
Do not, as some ungracious pastors do,
Show me the steep and thorny way to heaven,
Whilst, like a puff'd and reckless libertine,
Himself the primrose path of dalliance treads          50
And recks not his own rede.[9]

LAERTES.                                      O, fear me not.
I stay too long; but here my father comes.
    [*Enter* POLONIUS.]
A double blessing is a double grace;
Occasion smiles upon a second leave.

POLONIUS. Yet here, Laertes! Aboard, aboard, for shame!          55
The wind sits in the shoulder of your sail,
And you are stay'd for. There; my blessing with thee!
And these few precepts in thy memory
See thou charàcter.[1] Give thy thoughts no tongue,
Nor any unproportion'd thought his act.                60
Be thou familiar, but by no means vulgar.
Those friends thou hast, and their adoption tried,
Grapple them to thy soul with hoops of steel,
But do not dull thy palm[2] with entertainment
Of each new-hatch'd unfledged comrade. Beware          65
Of entrance to a quarrel; but being in,
Bear't, that the opposèd may beware of thee.
Give every man thy ear, but few thy voice:
Take each man's censure,[3] but reserve thy judgment.
Costly thy habit as thy purse can buy,                 70
But not express'd in fancy; rich, not gaudy:
For the apparel oft proclaims the man;
And they in France of the best rank and station
Are of a most select and generous chief[4] in that.
Neither a borrower nor a lender be:                    75
For loan oft loses both itself and friend,
And borrowing dulls the edge of husbandry.[5]
This above all: to thine own self be true,
And it must follow, as the night the day,
Thou canst not then be false to any man.               80
Farewell: my blessing season[6] this in thee!

LAERTES. Most humbly do I take my leave, my lord.

9. Does not follow his own advice.   1. Engrave in your memory. *Unproportion'd*:
Unsuitable.   2. Make the palm of your hand callous (by indiscriminate handshaking).
3. Opinion.   4. Chiefly.   5. Thriftiness.   6. Ripen.

POLONIUS. The time invites you; go, your servants tend.[7]

LAERTES. Farewell, Ophelia, and remember well
What I have said to you.

OPHELIA.                    'Tis in my memory lock'd,                    85
And you yourself shall keep the key of it.

LAERTES. Farewell.                              [*Exit.*]

POLONIUS.              What is't, Ophelia, he hath said to you?

OPHELIA. So please you, something touching the Lord Hamlet.

POLONIUS. Marry, well bethought:
'Tis told me, he hath very oft of late                    90
Given private time to you, and you yourself
Have of your audience been most free and bounteous:
If it be so—as so 'tis put on me,
And that in way of caution—I must tell you,
You do not understand yourself so clearly                    95
As it behoves my daughter and your honor.
What is between you? give me up the truth.

OPHELIA. He hath, my lord, of late made many tenders
Of his affection to me.

POLONIUS. Affection! pooh! you speak like a green girl,                    100
Unsifted[8] in such perilous circumstance.
Do you believe his tenders, as you call them?

OPHELIA. I do not know, my lord, what I should think.

POLONIUS. Marry, I'll teach you: think yourself a baby,
That you have ta'en these tenders for true pay,                    105
Which are not sterling. Tender yourself[9] more dearly;
Or—not to crack the wind of the poor phrase,
Running it thus—you'll tender me a fool.[1]

OPHELIA. My lord, he hath importuned me with love
In honorable fashion.                    110

POLONIUS. Aye, fashion you may call it; go to, go to.

OPHELIA. And hath given countenance[2] to his speech, my lord,
With almost all the holy vows of heaven.

POLONIUS. Aye, springes to catch woodcocks. I do know,
When the blood burns, how prodigal the soul                    115
Lends the tongue vows: these blazes, daughter,
Giving more light than heat, extinct in both,
Even in their promise, as it is a-making,
You must not take for fire. From this time
Be something scanter of your maiden presence;                    120
Set your entreatments[3] at a higher rate
Than a command to parley. For Lord Hamlet,
Believe so much in him, that he is young,

---

7. Wait.    8. Untested.    9. Regard yourself.    1. You'll furnish me with a fool (a foolish daughter).    2. Authority.    3. Conversation, company.

And with a larger tether may he walk
Than may be given you: in few, Ophelia,                        125
Do not believe his vows; for they are brokers,
Not of that dye which their investments⁴ show,
But mere implorators of unholy suits,
Breathing like sanctified and pious bawds,
The better to beguile. This is for all:                        130
I would not, in plain terms, from this time forth,
Have you so slander any moment⁵ leisure,
As to give words or talk with the Lord Hamlet.
Look to't, I charge you: come your ways.
OPHELIA. I shall obey, my lord.                                 135
    [*Exeunt.*]


SCENE 4—*The platform.*

[*Enter* HAMLET, HORATIO, *and* MARCELLUS.]
HAMLET. The air bites shrewdly; it is very cold.
HORATIO. It is a nipping and an eager⁶ air.
HAMLET. What hour now?
HORATIO.                     I think it lacks of twelve.
MARCELLUS. No, it is struck.
HORATIO. Indeed? I heard it not: it then draws near the season    5
    Wherein the spirit held his wont to walk.
    [*A flourish of trumpets, and ordnance shot off within.*]
    What doth this mean, my lord?
HAMLET. The king doth wake to-night, and takes his rouse,
    Keeps wassail, and the swaggering up-spring⁷ reels;
    And as he drains his draughts of Rhenish⁸ down,              10
    The kettle-drum and trumpet thus bray out
    The triumph of his pledge.⁹
HORATIO.                     Is it a custom?
HAMLET. Aye, marry, is't:
    But to my mind, though I am native here
    And to the manner born, it is a custom                      15
    More honor'd in the breach than the observance.
    This heavy-headed revel east and west
    Makes us traduced and tax'd of other nations:
    They clepe¹ us drunkards, and with swinish phrase
    Soil our addition;² and indeed it takes                     20
    From our achievements, though perform'd at height,³

---

4. Clothes. *Brokers:* Procurers, panders.   5. Use badly any momentary.   6. Sharp.   7. Wild
dance.   8. Rhine   wine.   9. His   drinking   exploits.   1. Call.   *Tax'd:*   Blamed.
2. Reputation, title added as a distinction.   3. Done in the best possible manner. *Attribute:*
Reputation.

The pith and marrow of our attribute.
So, oft it chances in particular men,
That for some vicious mole of nature in them,
As, in their birth,—wherein they are not guilty, 25
Since nature cannot choose his origin,—
By the o'ergrowth of some complexion,[4]
Oft breaking down the pales and forts of reason,
Or by some habit that too much o'er-leavens[5]
The form of plausive manners, that these men,— 30
Carrying, I say, the stamp of one defect,
Being nature's livery, or fortune's star,—
Their virtues else—[6]be they as pure as grace,
As infinite as man may undergo—
Shall in the general censure take corruption 35
From that particular fault: the dram of evil
Doth all the noble substance often dout
To his own scandal.
      [*Enter* GHOST.]
HORATIO.                    Look, my lord it comes!
HAMLET. Angels and ministers of grace defend us!
Be thou a spirit of health or goblin damn'd, 40
Bring with thee airs from heaven or blasts from hell,
Be thy intents wicked or charitable,
Thou comest in such a questionable shape
That I will speak to thee: I'll call thee Hamlet,
King, father, royal Dane: O, answer me! 45
Let me not burst in ignorance; but tell
Why thy canonized bones, hearsèd in death,
Have burst their cerements; why the sepulchre,
Wherein we saw thee quietly inurn'd,
Hath oped his ponderous and marble jaws, 50
To cast thee up again. What may this mean,
That thou, dead corse, again, in complete steel,
Revisit'st thus the glimpses of the moon,
Making night hideous; and we fools of nature
So horridly to shake our disposition 55
With thoughts beyond the reaches of our souls?
Say, why is this? Wherefore? what should we do?
      [GHOST *beckons* HAMLET.]
HORATIO. It beckons you to go away with it,
As if it some impartment did desire

4. Excess in one side of their temperament.   5. Modifies, as yeast changes dough. *Plausive:*
Agreeable.   6. The rest of their qualities.   7. To its own harm. *Dout:* Extinguish, nullify.

    To you alone.
MARCELLUS. Look, with what courteous action                    60
    It waves you to a more removèd ground:
    But do not go with it.
HORATIO.                      No, by no means.
HAMLET. It will not speak; then I will follow it.
HORATIO. Do not, my lord.
HAMLET.                            Why, what should be the fear?
    I do not set my life at a pin's fee;                       65
    And for my soul, what can it do to that,
    Being a thing immortal as itself?
    It waves me forth again: I'll follow it.
HORATIO. What if it tempt you toward the flood, my lord,
    Or to the dreadful summit of the cliff                     70
    That beetles o'er[8] his base into the sea,
    And there assume some other horrible form,
    Which might deprive your sovereignty of reason
    And draw you into madness? think of it:
    The very place puts toys[9] of desperation,                75
    Without more motive, into every brain
    That looks so many fathoms to the sea
    And hears it roar beneath.
HAMLET.                            It waves me still.
    Go on; I'll follow thee.
MARCELLUS. You shall not go, my lord.
HAMLET.                            Hold off your hands.        80
HORATIO. Be ruled; you shall not go.
HAMLET.                            My fate cries out,
    And makes each petty artery in this body
    As hardy as the Nemean lion's nerve.[1]
    Still am I call'd, unhand me, gentlemen;
    By heaven, I'll make a ghost of him that lets[2] me:       85
    I say, away! Go on; I'll follow thee.
        [*Exeunt* GHOST *and* HAMLET.]
HORATIO. He waxes desperate with imagination.
MARCELLUS. Let's follow; 'tis not fit thus to obey him.
HORATIO. Have after. To what issue will this come?
MARCELLUS. Something is rotten in the state of Denmark.       90
HORATIO. Heaven will direct it.
MARCELLUS.                        Nay, let's follow him.
        [*Exeunt.*]

8. Juts over.  9. Fancies.  1. Sinew, muscle. *Nemean lion*: Slain by Hercules as one of his
twelve labors.  2. Hinders.

SCENE 5—*Another part of the platform.*

[*Enter* GHOST *and* HAMLET.]

HAMLET. Whither wilt thou lead me? speak; I'll go no further.

GHOST. Mark me.

HAMLET.                    I will.

GHOST.                         My hour is almost come,
   When I to sulphurous and tormenting flames[3]
   Must render up myself.

HAMLET.                         Alas, poor ghost!

GHOST. Pity me not, but lend thy serious hearing                    5
   To what I shall unfold.

HAMLET.                         Speak; I am bound to hear.

GHOST. So art thou to revenge, when thou shalt hear.

HAMLET. What?

GHOST. I am thy father's spirit;
   Doom'd for a certain term to walk the night,                    10
   And for the day confined to fast in fires,
   Till the foul crimes done in my days of nature
   Are burnt and purged away. But that I am forbid
   To tell the secrets of my prison-house,
   I could a tale unfold whose lightest word                    15
   Would harrow up thy soul, freeze thy young blood,
   Make thy two eyes, like stars, start from their spheres,[4]
   Thy knotted and combined locks to part
   And each particular hair to stand on end,
   Like quills upon the fretful porpentine:[5]                    20
   But this eternal blazon[6] must not be
   To ears of flesh and blood. List, list, O, list!
   If thou didst ever thy dear father love—

HAMLET. O God!

GHOST. Revenge his foul and most unnatural murder.                    25

HAMLET.                                   Murder!

GHOST. Murder most foul, as in the best it is,
   But this most foul, strange, and unnatural.

HAMLET. Haste me to know't, that I, with wings as swift
   As meditation or the thoughts of love,                    30
   May sweep to my revenge.

GHOST.                         I find thee apt;
   And duller shouldst thou be than the fat weed
   That roots itself in ease on Lethe[7] wharf,
   Wouldst thou not stir in this. Now, Hamlet, hear:

---

3. Of purgatory.   4. Transparent revolving shells in each of which, according to Ptolemaic astronomy, a planet or other heavenly body was placed.   5. Porcupine.   6. Publication of the secrets of the other world (i.e., of eternity).   7. The river of forgetfulness in Hades.

'Tis given out that, sleeping in my orchard,                    35
A serpent stung me; so the whole ear of Denmark
Is by a forgèd process of my death
Rankly abused: but know, thou noble youth,
The serpent that did sting thy father's life
Now wears his crown.

HAMLET.                        O my prophetic soul!              40
My uncle!

GHOST. Aye, that incestuous, that adulterate beast,
With witchcraft of his wit, with traitorous gifts,—
O wicked wit and gifts, that have the power
So to seduce!—won to his shameful lust              45
The will of my most seeming-virtuous queen:
O Hamlet, what a falling-off was there!
From me, whose love was of that dignity
That it went hand in hand even with the vow
I made to her in marriage; and to decline              50
Upon a wretch, whose natural gifts were poor
To those of mine!
But virtue, as it never will be moved,
Though lewdness court it in a shape of heaven,[8]
So lust, though to a radiant angel link'd,              55
Will sate itself in a celestial bed
And prey on garbage.
But, soft! methinks I scent the morning air;
Brief let me be. Sleeping within my orchard,
My custom always of the afternoon,              60
Upon my secure hour thy uncle stole,
With juice of cursed hebenon[9] in a vial,
And in the porches of my ears did pour
The leperous distilment; whose effect
Holds such an enmity with blood of man              65
That swift as quicksilver it courses through
The natural gates and alleys of the body;
And with a sudden vigor it doth posset[1]
And curd, like eager droppings into milk,
The thin and wholesome blood: so did it mine;              70
And a most instant tetter bark'd about,[2]
Most lazar-like, with vile and loathsome crust,
All my smooth body.
Thus was I, sleeping, by a brother's hand
Of life, of crown, of queen, at once dispatch'd:              75

8. A heavenly, angelic form.   9. Henbane, a very poisonous herb.   1. Coagulate. *Eager:*
Sour.   2. The skin immediately became thick like the bark of a tree. *Lazar-like:* Leper-like
(from the beggar Lazarus, "full of sores," in Luke 16:20).

Cut off even in the blossoms of my sin,
Unhousel'd, disappointed, unaneled;[3]
No reckoning made, but sent to my account
With all my imperfections on my head:
O, horrible! O, horrible! most horrible!                    80
If thou hast nature in thee, bear it not;
Let not the royal bed of Denmark be
A couch for luxury and damned incest.
But, howsoever thou pursuest this act,
Taint not thy mind, nor let thy soul contrive              85
Against thy mother aught: leave her to heaven,
And to those thorns that in her bosom lodge,
To prick and sting her. Fare thee well at once!
The glow-worm shows the matin to be near,
And 'gins to pale his uneffectual fire:                    90
Adieu, adieu, adieu! remember me.                   [*Exit.*]

HAMLET. O all you host of heaven! O earth! what else?
And shall I couple hell? O, fie! Hold, hold, my heart;
And you, my sinews, grow not instant old,
But bear me stiffly up. Remember thee!                     95
Aye, thou poor ghost, while memory holds a seat
In this distracted globe.[4] Remember thee!
Yea, from the table[5] of my memory
I'll wipe away all trivial fond records,
All saws of books, all forms, all pressures past,          100
That youth and observation copied there:
And thy commandment all alone shall live
Within the book and volume of my brain,
Unmix'd with baser matter: yes, by heaven!
O most pernicious woman!                                   105
O villain, villain, smiling, damnèd villain!
My tables,—meet it is I set it down,
That one may smile, and smile, and be a villain;
At least I'm sure it may be so in Denmark.        [*Writing.*]
So, uncle, there you are. Now to my word;                  110
It is 'Adieu, adieu! remember me.'
I have sworn't.

HORATIO.     } [*Within*] My lord, my lord!
MARCELLUS.   }

     [*Enter* HORATIO *and* MARCELLUS.]

MARCELLUS.                          Lord Hamlet!

HORATIO.                            Heaven
     secure him!

---

3. Without sacrament, unprepared, without extreme unction.    4. Head.    5. Writing tablet.
The word is used in the same sense in l. 107.

HAMLET. So be it!

MARCELLUS. Illo,[6] ho, ho, my lord!                                          115

HAMLET. Hillo, ho, ho, boy! come, bird, come.

MARCELLUS. How is't, my noble lord?

HORATIO.                              What news, my lord?

HAMLET. O, wonderful!

HORATIO. Good my lord, tell it.

HAMLET.                          No; you will reveal it.

HORATIO. Not I, my lord, by heaven.

MARCELLUS.                          Nor I, my lord.                            120

HAMLET. How say you, then; would heart of man once think it?
　　But you'll be secret?

HORATIO.       ⎫          Aye, by heaven, my lord.
MARCELLUS.  ⎭

HAMLET. There's ne'er a villain dwelling in all Denmark
　　But he's an arrant knave.

HORATIO. There needs no ghost, my lord, come from the grave     125
　　To tell us this.

HAMLET.                    Why, right; you are i' the right;
　　And so, without more circumstance[7] at all,
　　I hold it fit that we shake hands and part:
　　You, as your business and desire shall point you;
　　For every man hath business and desire,                          130
　　Such as it is; and for my own poor part,
　　Look you, I'll go pray.

HORATIO. These are but wild and whirling words, my lord.

HAMLET. I'm sorry they offend you, heartily;
　　Yes, faith, heartily.

HORATIO.                    There's no offense, my lord.            135

HAMLET. Yes, by Saint Patrick, but there is, Horatio,
　　And much offense too. Touching this vision here,
　　It is an honest[8] ghost, that let me tell you:
　　For your desire to know what is between us,
　　O'ermaster't as you may. And now, good friends,                  140
　　As you are friends, scholars and soldiers,
　　Give me one poor request.

HORATIO.                          What is't, my lord? we will.

HAMLET. Never make known what you have seen tonight.

MARCELLUS. ⎫
HORATIO.   ⎭ My lord, we will not.

HAMLET.                              Nay, but swear't.

HORATIO.                                        In faith,

---

6. A falconer's call.    7. Ceremony.    8. Genuine.

My lord, not I.

MARCELLUS.                    Nor I, my lord, in faith.                    145

HAMLET. Upon my sword.

MARCELLUS.                    We have sworn, my lord, already.

HAMLET. Indeed, upon my sword, indeed.

GHOST. [*Beneath*]                              Swear.

HAMLET. Ah, ha, boy! say'st thou so? art thou there, true-penny?[9]
   Come on: you hear this fellow in the cellarage:
   Consent to swear.

HORATIO.                    Propose the oath, my lord.                    150

HAMLET. Never to speak of this that you have seen,
   Swear by my sword.

GHOST. [*Beneath*] Swear.

HAMLET. Hic et ubique?[1] then we'll shift our ground.
   Come hither, gentlemen,                              155
   And lay your hands again upon my sword:
   Never to speak of this that you have heard,
   Swear by my sword.

GHOST. [*Beneath*] Swear.

HAMLET. Well said, old mole! canst work i' the earth so fast?    160
   A worthy pioner![2] Once more remove, good friends.

HORATIO. O day and night, but this is wondrous strange!

HAMLET. And therefore as a stranger give it welcome.
   There are more things in heaven and earth, Horatio,
   Than are dreamt of in your philosophy.                    165
   But come;
   Here, as before, never, so help you mercy,
   How strange or odd soe'er I bear myself,
   As I perchance hereafter shall think meet
   To put an antic[3] disposition on,                    170
   That you, at such times seeing me, never shall,
   With arms encumber'd[4] thus, or this head-shake,
   Or by pronouncing of some doubtful phrase,
   As 'Well, well, we know,' or 'We could, an if we would,'
   Or 'If we list to speak,' or 'There be, an if they might,'    175
   Or such ambiguous giving out, to note
   That you know aught of me: this not to do,
   So grace and mercy at your most need help you,
   Swear.

GHOST. [*Beneath*] Swear.                              180

HAMLET. Rest, rest, perturbed spirit!          [*They swear.*]
   So, gentlemen,

---

9. Honest fellow.   1. Here and everywhere.   2. Miner.   3. Odd, fantastic.   4. Folded.

With all my love I do commend[5] me to you:
And what so poor a man as Hamlet is
May do, to express his love and friending to you,                185
God willing, shall not lack. Let us go in together;
And still your fingers on your lips, I pray.
The time is out of joint: O cursed spite,
That ever I was born to set it right!
Nay, come, let's go together.                                    190
    [*Exeunt.*]

## Act II

### SCENE 1—A *room in Polonius's house.*

[*Enter* POLONIUS *and* REYNALDO.]

POLONIUS. Give him this money and these notes, Reynaldo.

REYNALDO. I will, my lord.

POLONIUS. You shall do marvelous wisely, good Reynaldo,
  Before you visit him, to make inquire
  Of his behavior.

REYNALDO.      My lord, I did intend it.                5

POLONIUS. Marry, well said, very well said. Look you, sir,
  Inquire me first what Danskers are in Paris,
  And how, and who, what means, and where they keep,[6]
  What company, at what expense, and finding
  By this encompassment[7] and drift of question             10
  That they do know my son, come you more nearer
  Than your particular demands will touch it:
  Take you, as 'twere, some distant knowledge of him,
  As thus, 'I know his father and his friends,
  And in part him:' do you mark this, Reynaldo?             15

REYNALDO. Aye, very well, my lord.

POLONIUS. 'And in part him; but,' you may say, 'not well:
  But if 't be he I mean, he's very wild,
  Addicted so and so;' and there put on him
  What forgeries you please; marry, none so rank             20
  As may dishonor him; take heed of that;
  But, sir, such wanton, wild and usual slips
  As are companions noted and most known
  To youth and liberty.

REYNALDO.      As gaming, my lord.

POLONIUS. Aye, or drinking, fencing, swearing, quarreling,     25
  Drabbing:[8] you may go so far.

REYNALDO. My lord, that would dishonor him.

---

5. Entrust.   6. Dwell. *Danskers:* Danes.   7. Roundabout way.   8. Whoring.

POLONIUS. Faith, no; as you may season it in the charge.[9]
  You must not put another scandal on him,
  That he is open to incontinency;                                30
  That's not my meaning: but breathe his faults so quaintly[1]
  That they may seem the taints of liberty,
  The flash and outbreak of a fiery mind,
  A savageness in unreclaimèd blood,
  Of general assault.[2]
REYNALDO.                    But, my good lord,—              35
POLONIUS. Wherefore should you do this?
REYNALDO.                          Aye, my lord,
  I would know that.
POLONIUS.            Marry, sir, here's my drift,
  And I believe it is a fetch of warrant:[3]
  You laying these slight sullies on my son,
  As 'twere a thing a little soil'd i' the working,           40
  Mark you,
  Your party in converse, him you would sound,
  Having ever seen in the prenominate[4] crimes
  The youth you breathe of guilty, be assured
  He closes with you in this consequence;[5]                   45
  'Good sir,' or so, or 'friend,' or 'gentleman,'
  According to the phrase or the addition[6]
  Of man and country.
REYNALDO.            Very good, my lord.                      48
POLONIUS. And then, sir, does he this—he does—what was I about
  to say? By the mass, I was about to say something: where did I
  leave?
REYNALDO. At 'closes in the consequence,' at 'friend or so,' and
  'gentleman.'
POLONIUS. At 'closes in the consequence,' aye, marry;        49
  He closes with you thus: 'I know the gentleman;
  I saw him yesterday, or t' other day,
  Or then, or then, with such, or such, and, as you say,
  There was a' gaming, there o'ertook in 's rouse,[7]
  There falling out at tennis': or perchance,
  'I saw him enter such a house of sale,'                      55
  Videlicet,[8] a brothel, or so forth.
  See you now;
  Your bait of falsehood takes this carp of truth:
  And thus do we of wisdom and of reach,[9]

9. Qualify it in making the accusation.  1. Delicately, skillfully. *Incontinency*: Extreme
sensuality.    2. Assailing all men. *Unreclaimèd*: Untamed.    3. Allowable stratagem.
4. Aforementioned. *Having ever*: If he has ever.    5. You may be sure he will agree in this
conclusion.    6. Title.    7. Intoxicated in his reveling.    8. Namely.    9. Wise and far-
sighted.

With windlasses and with assays of bias,[1]                    60
By indirections find directions out:
So, by my former lecture and advice,
Shall you my son. You have me, have you not?
REYNALDO. My lord, I have.
POLONIUS.                          God be wi' ye; fare ye well.
REYNALDO. Good my lord!                                        65
POLONIUS. Observe his inclination in yourself.[2]
REYNALDO. I shall, my lord.
POLONIUS. And let him ply his music.
REYNALDO.                          Well, my lord.
POLONIUS. Farewell!                          [*Exit* REYNALDO.]
     [*Enter* OPHELIA.]
How now, Ophelia! what's the matter?                          70
OPHELIA. O, my lord, I have been so affrighted!
POLONIUS. With what, i' the name of God?
OPHELIA. My lord, as I was sewing in my closet,[3]
     Lord Hamlet, with his doublet all unbraced,
     No hat upon his head, his stockings foul'd,              75
     Ungarter'd and down-gyvèd[4] to his ankle;
     Pale as his shirt, his knees knocking each other,
     And with a look so piteous in purport
     As if he had been loosèd out of hell
     To speak of horrors, he comes before me.                 80
POLONIUS. Mad for thy love?
OPHELIA.                          My lord, I do not know,
     But truly I do fear it.
POLONIUS.                          What said he?
OPHELIA. He took me by the wrist and held me hard;
     Then goes he to the length of all his arm,
     And with his other hand thus o'er his brow,              85
     He falls to such perusal of my face
     As he would draw it. Long stay'd he so;
     At last, a little shaking of mine arm,
     And thrice his head thus waving up and down,
     He raised a sigh so piteous and profound                90
     As it did seem to shatter all his bulk
     And end his being: that done, he lets me go:
     And with his head over his shoulder turn'd,
     He seem'd to find his way without his eyes;
     For out o' doors he went without their help,             95
     And to the last bended their light on me.

1. Sending the ball indirectly (in bowling), devious attacks. *Windlasses:* Winding ways, roundabout courses.   2. Ways of procedure by yourself.   3. Private room. *Doublet:* Jacket.
4. Pulled down like fetters on a prisoner's leg.

POLONIUS. Come, go with me: I will go seek the king.
  This is the very ecstasy of love;
  Whose violent property fordoes itself[5]
  And leads the will to desperate undertakings          100
  As oft as any passion under heaven
  That does afflict our natures. I am sorry.
  What, have you given him any hard words of late?
OPHELIA. No, my good lord, but, as you did command,
  I did repel his letters and denied                    105
  His access to me.
POLONIUS.           That hath made him mad.
  I am sorry that with better heed and judgment
  I had not quoted[6] him: I fear'd he did but trifle
  And meant to wreck thee; but beshrew my jealousy![7]
  By heaven, it is as proper to our age                 110
  To cast beyond ourselves[8] in our opinions
  As it is common for the younger sort
  To lack discretion. Come, go we to the king:
  This must be known; which, being kept close, might move
  More grief to hide than hate to utter love.[9]        115
  Come.                                      [*Exeunt.*]

SCENE 2—*A room in the castle.*

[*Flourish. Enter* KING, QUEEN, ROSENCRANTZ, GUILDENSTERN,
  *and* ATTENDANTS.]
KING. Welcome, dear Rosencrantz and Guildenstern!
  Moreover that we much did long to see you,
  The need we have to use you did provoke
  Our hasty sending. Something have you heard
  Of Hamlet's transformation; so call it,               5
  Sith[1] nor the exterior nor the inward man
  Resembles that it was. What it should be,
  More than his father's death, that thus hath put him
  So much from the understanding of himself,
  I cannot dream of: I entreat you both,                10
  That, being of so young days brought up with him
  And sith so neighbor'd to his youth, and behavior,
  That you vouchsafe your rest[2] here in our court
  Some little time: so by your companies
  To draw him on to pleasures, and to gather            15
  So much as from occasion you may glean,
  Whether aught to us unknown afflicts him thus,

---

5. Which, when violent, destroys itself. *Ecstasy:* Madness. 6. Noted. 7. Curse my
suspicion. 8. Overshoot, go too far. 9. If Hamlet's love is revealed. *To hide:* If kept
hidden. 1. Since. 2. Consent to stay.

That open'd[3] lies within our remedy.

QUEEN. Good gentlemen, he hath much talk'd of you,
And sure I am two men there are not living 20
To whom he more adheres.[4] If it will please you
To show us so much gentry[5] and good will
As to expend your time with us awhile
For the supply and profit of our hope,
Your visitation shall receive such thanks 25
As fits a king's remembrance.

ROSENCRANTZ.                    Both your majesties
Might, by the sovereign power you have of us,
Put your dread pleasures more into[6] command
Than to entreaty.

GUILDENSTERN.          But we both obey,
And here give up ourselves, in the full bent[7] 30
To lay our service freely at your feet,
To be commanded.

KING. Thanks, Rosencrantz and gentle Guildenstern.

QUEEN. Thanks, Guildenstern and gentle Rosencrantz:
And I beseech you instantly to visit 35
My too much changed son. Go, some of you,
And bring these gentlemen where Hamlet is.

GUILDENSTERN. Heavens make our presence and our practices
Pleasant and helpful to him!

QUEEN.                    Aye, amen!
        [*Exeunt* ROSENCRANTZ, GUILDENSTERN, *and some* ATTEN-
        DANTS.—*Enter* POLONIUS.]

POLONIUS. The ambassadors from Norway, my good lord, 40
Are joyfully return'd.

KING. Thou still[8] hast been the father of good news.

POLONIUS. Have I, my lord? I assure my good liege,
I hold my duty as I hold my soul,
Both to my God and to my gracious king: 45
And I do think, or else this brain of mine
Hunts not the trail of policy so sure
As it hath used to do, that I have found
The very cause of Hamlet's lunacy.

KING. O, speak of that; that do I long to hear. 50

POLONIUS. Give first admittance to the ambassadors;
My news shall be the fruit[9] to that great feast.

KING. Thyself do grace[1] to them, and bring them in.
        [*Exit* POLONIUS.]
He tells me, my dear Gertrude, he hath found

3. Once revealed.    4. Is more attached.    5. Courtesy.    6. Give your sovereign wishes the
form of.    7. Bent (as a bow) to the limit.    8. Always.    9. Dessert.    1. Honor.

The head and source of all your son's distemper.            55
QUEEN. I doubt it is no other but the main;
    His father's death and our o'erhasty marriage.
KING. Well, we shall sift him.
        [*Re-enter* POLONIUS, *with* VOLTIMAND *and* CORNELIUS.]
                                Welcome, my good friends!
    Say, Voltimand, what from our brother Norway?
VOLTIMAND. Most fair return of greetings and desires.          60
    Upon our first,[2] he sent out to suppress
    His nephew's levies, which to him appear'd
    To be a preparation 'gainst the Polack,
    But better look'd into, he truly found
    It was against your highness: whereat grieved,            65
    That so his sickness, age and impotence
    Was falsely borne in hand,[3] sends out arrests
    On Fortinbras; which he, in brief, obeys,
    Receives rebuke from Norway, and in fine[4]
    Makes vow before his uncle never more                     70
    To give the assay[5] of arms against your majesty.
    Whereon old Norway, overcome with joy,
    Gives him three thousand crowns in annual fee
    And his commission to employ those soldiers,
    So levied as before, against the Polack:                  75
    With an entreaty, herein further shown,          [*Giving a paper.*]
    That it might please you to give quiet pass
    Through your dominions for this enterprise,
    On such regards of safety and allowance
    As therein are set down.
KING.                        It likes us well,                80
    And at our more consider'd time we'll read,
    Answer, and think upon this business.
    Meantime we thank you for your well-took labor:
    Go to your rest; at night we'll feast together:
    Most welcome home!
        [*Exeunt* VOLTIMAND *and* CORNELIUS.]
POLONIUS.                    This business is well ended.
    My liege, and madam, to expostulate
    What majesty should be, what duty is,
    Why day is day, night night, and time is time,
    Were nothing but to waste night, day and time.
    Therefore, since brevity is the soul of wit              90
    And tediousness the limbs and outward flourishes,
    I will be brief. Your noble son is mad:

2. As soon as we made the request.    3. Deceived, deluded.    4. Finally.    5. Test.

Mad call I it; for, to define true madness,
What is 't but to be nothing else but mad?
But let that go.
QUEEN.                 More matter, with less art.                          95
POLONIUS. Madam, I swear I use no art at all.
   That he is mad, 'tis true: 'tis true 'tis pity,
   And pity 'tis 'tis true: a foolish figure;[6]
   But farewell it, for I will use no art.
   Mad let us grant him then: and now remains            100
   That we find out the cause of this effect,
   Or rather say, the cause of this defect,
   For this effect defective comes by cause:
   Thus it remains and the remainder thus.
   Perpend.[7]                                                              105
   I have a daughter,—have while she is mine,—
   Who in her duty and obedience, mark,
   Hath given me this: now gather and surmise.           108
      [*Reads.*]
   'To the celestial, and my soul's idol, the most beautified Ophe-
      lia,'—
   That's an ill phrase, a vile phrase; 'beautified' is a vile phrase;
   but you shall hear. Thus:
      [*Reads.*]
   'In her excellent white bosom, these,' &c.
QUEEN. Came this from Hamlet to her?
POLONIUS. Good madam, stay awhile; I will be faithful.
      [*Reads.*]
                  'Doubt thou the stars are fire;
                     Doubt that the sun doth move;
                  Doubt truth to be a liar;
                     But never doubt I love.
   'O dear Ophelia, I am ill at these numbers;[8] I have not art to
reckon my groans: but that I love thee best, O most best, believe
it. Adieu.
                        'Thine evermore, most dear lady, whilst this
                              machine is to him,[9] HAMLET.'
   This in obedience hath my daughter shown me;        109
   And more above,[1] hath his solicitings,
   As they fell out by time, by means and place,
   All given to mine ear.
KING.                       But how hath she
   Received his love?
POLONIUS.                    What do you think of me?
KING. As of a man faithful and honorable.

6. Of speech.   7. Consider.   8. Verses.   9. Body is attached.   1. Moreover.

POLONIUS. I would fain prove so. But what might you think,                    115
    When I had seen this hot love on the wing,—
    As I perceived it, I must tell you that,
    Before my daughter told me,—what might you,
    Or my dear majesty your queen here, think,
    If I had play'd the desk or table-book,[2]
    Or given my heart a winking, mute and dumb,                    120
    Or look'd upon this love with idle sight;
    What might you think? No, I went round[3] to work,
    And my young mistress thus I did bespeak:
    'Lord Hamlet is a prince, out of thy star;[4]                    125
    This must not be:' and then I prescripts gave her,
    That she should lock herself from his resort,
    Admit no messengers, receive no tokens.
    Which done, she took the fruits of my advice;
    And he repulsed, a short tale to make,                    130
    Fell into a sadness, then into a fast,
    Thence to a watch, thence into a weakness,
    Thence to a lightness,[5] and by this declension
    Into the madness wherein now he raves
    And all we mourn for.                    135
KING. Do you think this?
QUEEN.               It may be, very like.
POLONIUS. Hath there been such a time, I'd fain know that,
    That I have positively said ' 'tis so,'
    When it proved otherwise?
KING.               Not that I know.
POLONIUS. [*Pointing to his head and shoulder*] Take this, from
    this, if this be otherwise:                    140
    If circumstances lead me, I will find
    Where truth is hid, though it were hid indeed
    Within the center.[6]
KING.           How may we try it further?
POLONIUS. You know, sometimes he walks for hours together
    Here in the lobby.
QUEEN.           So he does, indeed.                    145
POLONIUS. At such a time I'll loose my daughter to him:
    Be you and I behind an arras then;
    Mark the encounter: if he love her not,
    And be not from his reason fall'n thereon,[7]
    Let me be no assistant for a state,                    150
    But keep a farm and carters.

---

2. If I had acted as a desk or notebook (in keeping the matter secret). *Given my heart a winking:*
Shut my heart's eye.   3. Straight.   4. Sphere.   5. Lightheadedness. *Watch:* Insomnia.
6. Of the earth.   7. For that reason.

KING.                    We will try it.

QUEEN. But look where sadly the poor wretch comes reading.

POLONIUS. Away, I do beseech you, both away:
   I'll board him presently.[8]

   [*Exeunt* KING, QUEEN, *and* ATTENDANTS. —*Enter* HAMLET,
   *reading.*]

   O, give me leave: how does my good Lord Hamlet?                    155

HAMLET. Well, God-a-mercy.

POLONIUS. Do you know me, my lord?

HAMLET. Excellent well; you are a fishmonger.[9]

POLONIUS. Not I, my lord.

HAMLET. Then I would you were so honest a man.

POLONIUS. Honest, my lord!

HAMLET. Aye, sir; to be honest, as this world goes, is to be one man
   picked out of ten thousand.

POLONIUS. That's very true, my lord.

HAMLET. For if the sun breed maggots in a dead dog, being a good
   kissing carrion[1]— Have you a daughter?

POLONIUS. I have, my lord.

HAMLET. Let her not walk i' the sun: conception is a blessing; but
   as your daughter may conceive,—friend, look to 't.

POLONIUS [*Aside*] How say you by that? Still harping on my daughter: yet he knew me not at first; he said I was a fishmonger: he
   is far gone: and truly in my youth I suffered much extremity for
   love; very near this. I'll speak to him again.—What do you read,
   my lord?

HAMLET. Words, words, words.

POLONIUS. What is the matter,[2] my lord?

HAMLET. Between who?

POLONIUS. I mean, the matter that you read, my lord.

HAMLET. Slanders, sir: for the satirical rogue says here that old men
   have gray beards, that their faces are wrinkled, their eyes purging
   thick amber and plum-tree gum, and that they have a plentiful
   lack of wit, together with most weak hams: all which, sir, though
   I most powerfully and potently believe, yet I hold it not honesty
   to have it thus set down; for yourself, sir, shall grow old as I am,
   if like a crab you could go backward.

POLONIUS. [*Aside*] Though this be madness, yet there is method
   in 't.—Will you walk out of the air, my lord?

HAMLET. Into my grave.

POLONIUS. Indeed, that's out of the air.                    [*Aside*]

---

8. Approach him at once.    9. Seller of fish, but also slang for procurer.    1. Good bit of flesh
for kissing.    2. The subject matter of the book; Hamlet responds as if he referred to the subject
of a quarrel.

How pregnant sometimes his replies are! a happiness[3] that often madness hits on, which reason and sanity could not so prosperously be delivered of. I will leave him, and suddenly contrive the means of meeting between him and my daughter.—My honorable lord, I will most humbly take my leave of you.

HAMLET. You cannot, sir, take from me any thing that I will more willingly part withal: except my life, except my life, except my life.

POLONIUS. Fare you well, my lord.

HAMLET. These tedious old fools.

[*Re-enter* ROSENCRANTZ *and* GUILDENSTERN.]

POLONIUS. You go to seek the Lord Hamlet; there he is.

ROSENCRANTZ [*To* POLONIUS] God save you, sir!

[*Exit* POLONIUS.]

GUILDENSTERN. My honored lord!

ROSENCRANTZ. My most dear lord!

HAMLET. My excellent good friends! How dost thou, Guildenstern? Ah, Rosencrantz! Good lads, how do you both?

ROSENCRANTZ. As the indifferent[4] children of the earth.

GUILDENSTERN. Happy, in that we are not over-happy; On Fortune's cap we are not the very button.[5]

HAMLET. Nor the soles of her shoe?

ROSENCRANTZ. Neither, my lord.

HAMLET. Then you live about her waist, or in the middle of her favors?

GUILDENSTERN. Faith, her privates[6] we.

HAMLET. In the secret parts of Fortune? O, most true; she is a strumpet. What's the news?

ROSENCRANTZ. None, my lord, but that the world's grown honest.

HAMLET. Then is doomsday near: but your news is not true. Let me question more in particular: what have you, my good friends, deserved at the hands of Fortune, that she sends you to prison hither?

GUILDENSTERN. Prison, my lord!

HAMLET. Denmark's a prison.

ROSENCRANTZ. Then is the world one.

HAMLET. A goodly one; in which there are many confines, wards[7] and dungeons, Denmark being one o' the worst.

ROSENCRANTZ. We think not so, my lord.

HAMLET. Why, then, 'tis none to you; for there is nothing either good or bad, but thinking makes it so: to me it is a prison.

ROSENCRANTZ. Why, then your ambition makes it one; 'tis too narrow for your mind.

3. Aptness of expression. 4. Average. 5. Top. 6. Ordinary men (with obvious play on the sexual term "private parts"). 7. Cells. *Confines:* Places of confinement.

HAMLET. O God, I could be bounded in a nut-shell and count myself
a king of infinite space, were it not that I have bad dreams.

GUILDENSTERN. Which dreams indeed are ambition; for the very substance of the ambitious is merely the shadow of a dream.

HAMLET. A dream itself is but a shadow.

ROSENCRANTZ. Truly, and I hold ambition of so airy and light a quality that it is but a shadow's shadow.

HAMLET. Then are our beggars bodies, and our monarchs and outstretched heroes the beggars' shadows. Shall we to the court? for,
by my fay, I cannot reason.

ROSENCRANTZ. ⎫
GUILDENSTERN. ⎬ We'll wait upon you.

HAMLET. No such matter: I will not sort you[8] with the rest of my
servants; for, to speak to you like an honest man, I am most dreadfully attended. But, in the beaten way of friendship, what make
you at Elsinore?

ROSENCRANTZ. To visit you, my lord; no other occasion.

HAMLET. Beggar that I am, I am even poor in thanks; but I thank
you: and sure, dear friends, my thanks are too dear a halfpenny.[9]
Were you not sent for? Is it your own inclining? Is it a free visitation? Come, deal justly[1] with me: come, come; nay, speak.

GUILDENSTERN. What should we say, my lord?

HAMLET. Why, any thing, but to the purpose. You were sent for; and
there is a kind of confession in your looks, which your modesties
have not craft enough to color: I know the good king and queen
have sent for you.

ROSENCRANTZ. To what end, my lord?

HAMLET. That you must teach me. But let me conjure you, by the
rights of our fellowship, by the consonancy of our youth, by the
obligation of our ever-preserved love, and by what more dear a
better proposer[2] could charge you withal, be even and direct with
me, whether you were sent for, or no.

ROSENCRANTZ. [Aside to GUILDENSTERN] What say you?

HAMLET. [Aside] Nay then, I have an eye of[3] you.—If you love me,
hold not off.

GUILDENSTERN. My lord, we were sent for.

HAMLET. I will tell you why; so shall my anticipation prevent your
discovery,[4] and your secrecy to the king and queen moult no feather.
I have of late—but wherefore I know not—lost all my mirth, for-
gone all custom of exercises; and indeed it goes so heavily with my
disposition that this goodly frame, the earth, seems to me a sterile
promontory; this most excellent canopy, the air, look you, this
brave o'erhanging firmament, this majestical roof fretted[5] with

8. Put you together.   9. If priced at a halfpenny.   1. Honestly.   2. Speaker.   3. On.
4. Precede your disclosure.   5. Adorned.

golden fire, why, it appears no other thing to me than a foul and pestilent congregation of vapors. What a piece of work is a man! how noble in reason! how infinite in faculty! in form and moving how expressed[6] and admirable! in action how like an angel! in apprehension how like a god! the beauty of the world! the paragon of animals! And yet, to me, what is this quintessence of dust? man delights not me; no, nor woman neither, though by your smiling you seem to say so.

ROSENCRANTZ. My lord, there was no such stuff in my thoughts.

HAMLET. Why did you laugh then, when I said 'man delights not me'?

ROSENCRANTZ. To think, my lord, if you delight not in man, what lenten entertainment the players shall receive from you: we coted[7] them on the way; and hither are they coming, to offer you service.

HAMLET. He that plays the king shall be welcome; his majesty shall have tribute of me; the adventurous knight shall use his foil and target; the lover shall not sigh gratis; the humorous[8] man shall end his part in peace; the clown shall make those laugh whose lungs are tickle o' the sere,[9] and the lady shall say her mind freely, or the blank verse shall halt for 't. What players are they?

ROSENCRANTZ. Even those you were wont to take such delight in, the tragedians of the city.

HAMLET. How chances it they travel? their residence, both in reputation and profit, was better both ways.

ROSENCRANTZ. I think their inhibition comes by means of the late innovation.[1]

HAMLET. Do they hold the same estimation they did when I was in the city? are they so followed?

ROSENCRANTZ. No, indeed, are they not.

HAMLET. How comes it? do they grow rusty?

ROSENCRANTZ. Nay, their endeavor keeps in the wonted pace: but there is, sir, an eyrie of children, little eyases,[2] that cry out on the top of question[3] and are most tyrannically clapped for 't: these are now the fashion, and so berattle[4] the common stages—so they call them—that many wearing rapiers are afraid of goose-quills,[5] and dare scarce come thither.

HAMLET. What, are they children? who maintains 'em? how are they escoted? Will they pursue the quality[6] no longer than they can sing? will they not say afterwards, if they should grow themselves to common players—as it is most like, if their means are no bet-

6. Perfect.   7. Overtook.   8. Eccentric, whimsical.   9. Ready to shoot off at a touch. 1. The introduction of "an eyrie of children," as Rosencrantz explains in his subsequent replies to Hamlet. *Inhibition:* Prohibition.   2. Nest of children, nestling hawks.   3. Above others on matter of dispute.   4. Berate.   5. Gentlemen are afraid of pens (i.e., of poets satirizing the "common stages").   6. Profession of acting. *Escoted:* Financially supported.

ter,—their writers do them wrong, to make them exclaim against their own succession?[7]

ROSENCRANTZ. Faith, there has been much to-do on both sides, and the nation holds it no sin to tarre[8] them to controversy: there was for a while no money bid for argument unless the poet and the player went to cuffs in the question.[9]

HAMLET. Is 't possible?

GUILDENSTERN. O, there has been much throwing about of brains.

HAMLET. Do the boys carry it away?[1]

ROSENCRANTZ. Aye, that they do, my lord; Hercules and his load too.[2]

HAMLET. It is not very strange; for my uncle is king of Denmark, and those that would make mows[3] at him while my father lived, give twenty, forty, fifty, a hundred ducats a-piece, for his picture in little. 'Sblood, there is something in this more than natural, if philosophy could find it out.

[*Flourish of trumpets within.*]

GUILDENSTERN. There are the players.

HAMLET. Gentlemen, you are welcome to Elsinore. Your hands, come then: the appurtenance of welcome is fashion and cere-mony: let me comply with you in this garb, lest my extent[4] to the players, which, I tell you, must show fairly outwards, should more appear like entertainment[5] than yours. You are welcome: but my uncle-father and aunt-mother are deceived.

GUILDENSTERN. In what, my dear lord?

HAMLET. I am but mad north-north-west: when the wind is southerly I know a hawk from a handsaw.[6]

[*Re-enter* POLONIUS.]

POLONIUS. Well be with you, gentlemen!

HAMLET. Hark you, Guildenstern; and you too: at each ear a hearer: that great baby you see there is not yet out of his swaddling clouts.[7]

ROSENCRANTZ. Happily he's the second time come to them; for they say an old man is twice a child.

HAMLET. I will prophesy he comes to tell me of the players; mark it. You say right, sir: o' Monday morning; 'twas so, indeed.[8]

POLONIUS. My lord, I have news to tell you.

HAMLET. My lord, I have news to tell you. When Roscius[9] was an actor in Rome,—

POLONIUS. The actors are come hither, my lord.

---

7. Recite satiric pieces against what they are themselves likely to become, common players. 8. Incite.   9. No offer to buy a plot for a play if it did not contain a quarrel between poet and player on that subject.   1. Win out.   2. The sign in front of the Globe theater showing Hercules bearing the world on his shoulders.   3. Faces, grimaces.   4. Welcoming behavior. *Garb:* Style.   5. Welcome.   6. A hawk from a heron, as well as a kind of ax from a handsaw.   7. Clothes.   8. Hamlet, for Polonius' sake, pretends he is deep in talk with Rosencrantz.   9. A famous Roman comic actor.

HAMLET. Buz, buz![1]

POLONIUS. Upon my honor,—

HAMLET. Then came each actor on his ass,—

POLONIUS. The best actors in the world, either for tragedy, comedy, history, pastoral, pastoral-comical, historical-postoral, tragical-historical, tragical-comical-historical-pastoral, scene individable, or poem unlimited:[2] Seneca cannot be too heavy, nor Plautus too light. For the law of writ and the liberty,[3] these are the only men.

HAMLET. O Jephthah,[4] judge of Israel, what a treasure hadst thou!

POLONIUS. What a treasure had he, my lord?

HAMLET. Why,

> 'One fair daughter, and no more,
>     The which he lovèd passing well.'[5]

POLONIUS. [Aside] Still on my daughter.

HAMLET. Am I not i' the right, old Jephthah?

POLONIUS. If you call me Jephthah, my lord, I have a daughter that I love passing well.

HAMLET. Nay, that follows not.

POLONIUS. What follows, then, my lord?

HAMLET. Why,

> 'As by lot, God wot.'

and then you know,

> 'It came to pass, as most like it was,'—

the first row of the pious chanson will show you more; for look, where my abridgment[6] comes.

[Enter four or five PLAYERS.]

You are welcome, masters; welcome, all. I am glad to see thee well. Welcome, good friends. O, my old friend! Why thy face is valanced[7] since I saw thee last; comest thou to beard me in Denmark? What, my young lady and mistress! By'r lady, your ladyship is nearer to heaven than when I saw you last, by the altitude of a chopine. Pray God, your voice, like a piece of uncurrent[8] gold, be not cracked within the ring.[9] Masters, you are all welcome. We'll e'en to 't like French falconers, fly at any thing we see: we'll have a speech straight: come, give us a taste of your quality; come, a passionate speech.

FIRST PLAYER. What speech, my good lord?

HAMLET. I heard thee speak me a speech once, but it was never acted; or, if it was, not above once; for the play, I remember, pleased not the million; 'twas caviare to the general:[1] but it was—as I received

1. An expression used to stop the teller of a stale story.    2. Plays which do, and plays which do not, observe the unities of time, place, and action.    3. A possible meaning is, "For both written and extemporized plays." Seneca: Roman writer of tragedies (c.4 B.C.–A.D. 65). Plautus: Roman writer of comedies (c. 254–184 B.C.).    4. Who was compelled to sacrifice a dearly beloved daughter (Judges 11).    5. From an old ballad about Jephthah.    6. I.e., the players interrupting him. Row . . . chanson: Stanza . . . song.    7. Draped (with a beard).    8. Unfit for currency. Chopine: A thick-soled shoe.    9. A pun on the "ring" of the voice and the "ring" around the king's head on a coin.    1. A delicacy wasted on the general public.

it, and others, whose judgments in such matters cried in the top
of mine[2]—an excellent play, well digested in the scenes, set down
with as much modesty as cunning. I remember, one said there
were no sallets[3] in the lines to make the matter savory, nor no
matter in the phrase that might indict the author of affection; but
called it an honest method, as wholesome as sweet, and by very
much more handsome than fine.[4] One speech in it I chiefly loved:
'twas Æneas' tale to Dido;[5] and thereabout of it especially, where
he speaks of Priam's slaughter: if it live in your memory, begin at
this line; let me see, let me see;

'The rugged Pyrrhus, like th' Hyrcanian beast,'[6]—        156
It is not so: it begins with 'Pyrrhus.'
'The rugged Pyrrhus, he whose sable arms,
Black as his purpose, did the night resemble
When he lay couched in the ominous horse,[7]              160
Hath now this dread and black complexion smear'd
With heraldry more dismal: head to foot
Now is he total gules; horridly trick'd[8]
With the blood of fathers, mothers, daughters, sons,
Baked and impasted with the parching streets,            165
That lend a tyrannous[9] and a damned light
To their lord's murder: roasted in wrath and fire,
And thus o'er-sizèd[1] with coagulate gore,
With eyes like carbuncles, the hellish Pyrrhus
Old grandsire Priam seeks.'                              170
So, proceed you.

POLONIUS. 'Fore God, my lord, well spoken, with good accent and
good discretion.

FIRST PLAYER.                'Anon he finds him
Striking too short at Greeks; his antique sword,
Rebellious to his arm, lies where it falls,
Repugnant to command: unequal match'd,                   175
Pyrrhus at Priam drives; in rage strikes wide;
But with the whiff and wind of his fell sword
The unnerved father falls. Then senseless Ilium,[2]
Seeming to feel this blow, with flaming top               180
Stoops to his base, and with a hideous crash
Takes prisoner Pyrrhus' ear: for, lo! his sword,
Which was declining on the milky head
Of reverend Priam seem'd i' the air to stick:

---

2. Were louder (more authoritative than) mine.   3. Salads (i.e., relish, spicy passages). *Affection*: Affectation.   4. More elegant than showy.   5. The story of the fall of Troy, told by Aeneas to queen Dido. Priam was the king of Troy.   6. Tiger. *Pyrrhus*: Achilles' son (also called Neoptolemus).   7. The wooden horse in which Greek warriors were smuggled into Troy.   8. Adorned. *Gules*: Heraldic term for red.   9. Savage.   1. Glued over.   2. Troy's citadel.

So, as a painted tyrant, Pyrrhus stood,                               185
And like a neutral to his will and matter,
Did nothing.
But as we often see, against some storm,
A silence in the heavens, the rack[3] stand still,
The bold winds speechless and the orb below                           190
As hush as death, anon the dreadful thunder
Doth rend the region, so after Pyrrhus' pause
Aroused vengeance sets him new a-work;
And never did the Cyclops'[4] hammers fall
On Mars's armor, forged for proof eterne,                             195
With less remorse than Pyrrhus' bleeding sword
Now falls on Priam.
Out, thou strumpet, Fortune! All you gods,
In general synod take away her power,
Break all the spokes and fellies from her wheel,                      200
And bowl the round nave[5] down the hill of heaven
As low as to the fiends!

POLONIUS. This is too long.

HAMLET. It shall to the barbier's, with your beard. Prithee, say on:
he's for a jig[6] or a tale of bawdry, or he sleeps: say on: come to
Hecuba.

FIRST PLAYER. 'But who, O, who had seen the mobled[7] queen—'

HAMLET. 'The mobled queen'?

POLONIUS. That's good; 'mobled queen' is good.                        205

FIRST PLAYER. 'Run barefoot up and down, threatening the flames
With bisson rheum; a clout[8] upon that head
Where late the diadem stood; and for a robe,
About her lank and all o'er-teemèd loins,[9]
A blanket, in the alarm of fear caught up:                            210
Who this had seen, with tongue in venom steep'd
'Gainst Fortune's state[1] would treason have pronounced:
But if the gods themselves did see her then,
When she saw Pyrrhus make malicious sport
In mincing with his sword her husband's limbs,                        215
The instant burst of clamor that she made,
Unless things mortal move them[2] not at all,
Would have made milch the burning eyes of heaven[3]
And passion in the gods.'                                             219

POLONIUS. Look, whether he has not turned his color and has tears
in 's eyes. Prithee, no more.

---

3. Clouds. *Against:* Just before.     4. The gigantic workmen of Hephaestus (Vulcan), god of
blacksmiths and fire.    5. Hub. *Fellies:* Rims.     6. Ludicrous sung dialogue, short farce.
7. Muffled.    8. Cloth. *Bisson rheum:* Blinding moisture, tears.     9. Worn out by
childbearing.    1. Government.    2. The gods.    3. The stars. *Milch:* Moist (milk-giving).

HAMLET. 'Tis well; I'll have thee speak out the rest of this soon. Good
my lord, will you see the players well bestowed?[4] Do you hear, let
them be well used, for they are the abstracts and brief chronicles
of the time: after your death you were better have a bad epitaph
than their ill report while you live.

POLONIUS. My lord, I will use them according to their desert.

HAMLET. God's bodykins,[5] man, much better: use every man after
his desert, and who shall 'scape whipping? Use them after your
own honor and dignity: the less they deserve, the more merit is in
your bounty. Take them in.

POLONIUS. Come, sirs.

HAMLET. Follow him, friends: we'll hear a play to-morrow. [*Exit*
POLONIUS *with all the* PLAYERS *but the first.*] Dost thou hear me,
old friend; can you play the Murder of Gonzago?

FIRST PLAYER. Aye, my lord.

HAMLET. We'll ha 't to-morrow night. You could, for a need, study
a speech of some dozen or sixteen lines, which I would set down
and insert in 't, could you not?

FIRST PLAYER. Aye, my lord.

HAMLET. Very well. Follow that lord; and look you mock him not.
[*Exit* FIRST PLAYER.] My good friends, I'll leave you till night: you
are welcome to Elsinore.

ROSENCRANTZ. Good my lord!

HAMLET. Aye, so, God be wi' ye! [*Exeunt* ROSENCRANTZ *and* GUIL-
DENSTERN.] Now I am alone.                                           220
O, what a rogue and peasant slave am I!
Is it not monstrous that this player here,
But in a fiction, in a dream of passion,
Could force his soul so to his own conceit
That from her[6] working all his visage wann'd;                    225
Tears in his eyes, distraction in 's aspect,
A broken voice, and his whole function[7] suiting
With forms to his conceit? and all for nothing!
For Hecuba![8]
What's Hecuba to him, or he to Hecuba,                              230
That he should weep for her? What would he do,
Had he the motive and the cue for passion
That I have? He would drown the stage with tears
And cleave the general air with horrid speech,
Make mad the guilty and appal the free,                            235
Confound the ignorant, and amaze indeed

---

**4.** Taken care of, lodged.    **5.** By God's little body.    **6.** His soul's. *Conceit:* Imagination,
conception of the role played.    **7.** Bodily action.    **8.** Queen of Troy, Priam's wife.

The very faculties of eyes and ears.
Yet I,
A dull and muddy-mettled rascal, peak,[9]
Like John-a-dreams, unpregnant of my cause,[1]                    240
And can say nothing; no, not for a king,
Upon whose property and most dear life
A damn'd defeat was made. Am I a coward?
Who calls me villain? breaks my pate across?
Plucks off my beard, and blows it in my face?                    245
Tweaks me by the nose? gives me the lie i' the throat,
As deep as to the lungs? who does me this?
Ha!
'Swounds, I should take it: for it cannot be
But I am pigeon-liver'd and lack gall                    250
To make oppression bitter, or ere this
I should have fatted all the region kites[2]
With this slave's offal: bloody, bawdy villain!
Remorseless, treacherous, lecherous, kindless[3] villain!
O, vengeance!                    255
Why, what an ass am I! This is most brave,
That I, the son of a dear father murder'd,
Prompted to my revenge by heaven and hell,
Must, like a whore, unpack my heart with words,
And fall a-cursing, like a very drab,                    260
A scullion!
Fie upon 't! About,[4] my brain! Hum, I have heard
That guilty creatures, sitting at a play,
Have by the very cunning of the scene
Been struck so to the soul that presently                    265
They have proclaim'd their malefactions;
For murder, though it have no tongue, will speak
With most miraculous organ. I'll have these players
Play something like the murder of my father
Before mine uncle: I'll observe his looks;                    270
I'll tent him to the quick: if he but blench,[5]
I know my course. The spirit that I have seen
May be the devil; and the devil hath power
To assume a pleasing shape; yea, and perhaps
Out of my weakness and my melancholy,                    275
As he is very potent with such spirits,
Abuses me to damn me. I'll have grounds

---

9. Mope. *Muddy-mettled*: of poor metal (spirit, temper), dull-spirited.    1. Not really conscious
of my cause, unquickened by it. *John-a-dreams*: A dreamy, abset-minded character.    2. Kites
(hawks) of the air.    3. Unnatural.    4. To work!    5. Flinch. *Tent*: Probe.

More relative[6] than this. The play's the thing
Wherein I'll catch the conscience of the king.
   [*Exit.*]

## Act III

### SCENE 1—*A room in the castle.*

[*Enter* KING, QUEEN, POLONIUS, OPHELIA, ROSENCRANTZ, *and*
   GUILDENSTERN.]

KING. And can you, by no drift of circumstance,[7]
   Get from him why he puts on this confusion,
   Grating so harshly all his days of quiet
   With turbulent and dangerous lunacy?

ROSENCRANTZ. He does confess he feels himself distracted,                5
   But from what cause he will by no means speak.

GUILDENSTERN. Nor do we find him forward to be sounded;
   But, with a crafty madness, keeps aloof,
   When we would bring him on to some confession
   Of his true state.

QUEEN                       Did he receive you well?                      10

ROSENCRANTZ. Most like a gentleman.

GUILDENSTERN. But with much forcing of his disposition.

ROSENCRANTZ. Niggard of question, but of our demands
   Most free in his reply.

QUEEN.                     Did you assay[8] him
   To any pastime?                                                        15

ROSENCRANTZ. Madam, it so fell out that certain players
   We o'er-raught[9] on the way: of these we told him,
   And there did seem in him a kind of joy
   To hear of it: they are about the court,
   And, as I think, they have already order                              20
   This night to play before him.

POLONIUS.                          'Tis most true:
   And he beseech'd me to entreat your majesties
   To hear and see the matter.

KING. With all my heart; and it doth much content me
   To hear him so inclined.                                              25
   Good gentlemen, give him a further edge,[1]
   And drive his purpose on to these delights.

ROSENCRANTZ. We shall, my lord.
   [*Exeunt* ROSENCRANTZ *and* GUILDENSTERN.]

KING.                          Sweet Gertrude, leave us too;
   For we have closely[2] sent for Hamlet hither,
   That he, as 'twere by accident, may here                             30

6. Relevant.   7. Turn of talk, or roundabout way.   8. Try to attract him.   9. Overtook.
1. Incitement.   2. Privately.

   Affront[3] Ophelia:
Her father and myself, lawful espials,
Will so bestow[4] ourselves that, seeing unseen,
We may of their encounter frankly judge,
And gather by him, as he is behaved,           35
If 't be the affliction of his love or no
That thus he suffers for.

QUEEN.               I shall obey you:
   And for your part, Ophelia, I do wish
   That your good beauties be the happy cause
   Of Hamlet's wildness: so shall I hope your virtues    40
   Will bring him to his wonted way again,
   To both your honors.

OPHELIA.           Madam, I wish it may.    [*Exit* QUEEN.]

POLONIUS. Ophelia, walk you here. Gracious, so please you,
   We will bestow ourselves. [*To* OPHELIA] Read on this book;
   That show of such an exercise may color[5]         45
   Your loneliness. We are oft to blame in this,—
   'Tis too much proved—that with devotion's visage
   And pious action we do sugar o'er
   The devil himself.

KING. [*Aside*]        O, 'tis too true!
   How smart a lash that speech doth give my conscience!    50
   The harlot's cheek, beautied with plastering art,
   Is not more ugly to the thing that helps it
   Than is my deed to my most painted word:
   O heavy burthen!

POLONIUS. I hear him coming: let's withdraw, my lord.    55
   [*Exeunt* KING *and* POLONIUS. —*Enter Hamlet.*]

HAMLET. To be, or not to be: that is the question:
   Whether 'tis nobler in the mind to suffer
   The slings and arrows of outrageous fortune,
   Or to take arms against a sea of troubles,
   And by opposing end them. To die: to sleep;         60
   No more; and by a sleep to say we end
   The heart-ache, and the thousand natural shocks
   That flesh is heir to, 'tis a consummation[6]
   Devoutly to be wish'd. To die, to sleep;
   To sleep: perchance to dream: aye, there's the rub;[7]    65
   For in that sleep of death what dreams may come,
   When we have shuffled off this mortal coil,[8]
   Must give us pause: there's the respect

---

3. Confront.   4. Place. *Espials:* Spies.   5. Excuse.   6. Final settlement.   7. The impediment (a bowling term).   8. Have rid ourselves of the turmoil of mortal life. *Respect:* Consideration.

That makes calamity of so long life[9];
For who would bear the whips and scorns of time,                    70
The oppressor's wrong, the proud man's contumely,
The pangs of despised love, the law's delay,
The insolence of office, and the spurns
That patient merit of the unworthy takes,
When he himself might his quietus make                             75
With a bare bodkin? who would fardels[1] bear,
To grunt and sweat under a weary life,
But that the dread of something after death,
The undiscover'd country from whose bourn[2]
No traveler returns, puzzles the will,                             80
And makes us rather bear those ills we have
Than fly to others that we know not of?
Thus conscience does make cowards of us all,
And thus the native hue of resolution
Is sicklied o'er the pale cast of thought,                         85
And enterprises of great pitch[3] and moment
With this regard their currents turn awry
And lose the name of action. Soft you now!
The fair Ophelia! Nymph, in thy orisons[4]
Be all my sins remember'd.
OPHELIA.                               Good my lord,               90
How does your honor for this many a day?
HAMLET. I humbly thank you: well, well, well.
OPHELIA. My lord, I have remembrances of yours,
That I have longed to re-deliver;
I pray you, now receive them.
HAMLET.                               No, not I;                   95
I never gave you aught.
OPHELIA. My honor'd lord, you know right well you did;
And with them words of so sweet breath composed
As made the things more rich: their perfume lost,
Take these again; for to the noble mind
Rich gifts wax poor when givers prove unkind.                     101
There, my lord.
HAMLET. Ha, ha! are you honest?
OPHELIA. My lord?
HAMLET. Are you fair?
OPHELIA. What means your lordship?
HAMLET. That if you be honest and fair, your honesty should admit
no discourse to your beauty.

---

9. So long-lived.   1. Burdens. *Bodkin:* Poniard, dagger.   2. Boundary.   3. Height.
4. Prayers.

OPHELIA. Could beauty, my lord, have better commerce[5] than with honesty?

HAMLET. Aye, truly; for the power of beauty will sooner transform honesty from what it is to a bawd than the force of honesty can translate beauty into his[6] likeness: this was sometime a paradox, but now the time gives it proof. I did love you once.

OPHELIA. Indeed, my lord, you made me believe so.

HAMLET. You should not have believed me; for virtue cannot so inoculate our old stock, but we shall relish[7] of it: I loved you not.

OPHELIA. I was the more deceived.

HAMLET. Get thee to a nunnery: why wouldst thou be a breeder of sinners? I am myself indifferent honest; but yet I could accuse me of such things that it were better my mother had not borne me: I am very proud, revengeful, ambitious; with more offenses at my beck than I have thoughts to put them in, imagination to give them shape, or time to act them in. What should such fellows as I do crawling between heaven and earth! We are arrant knaves all; believe none of us. Go thy ways to a nunnery. Where's your father?

OPHELIA. At home, my lord.

HAMLET. Let the doors be shut upon him, that he may play the fool no where but in 's own house. Farewell.

OPHELIA. O, help him, you sweet heavens!

HAMLET. If thou dost marry, I'll give thee this plague for thy dowry: be thou as chaste as ice, as pure as snow, thou shalt not escape calumny. Get thee to a nunnery, go: farewell. Or, if thou wilt needs marry, marry a fool; for wise men know well enough what monsters[8] you make of them. To a nunnery, go; and quickly too. Farewell.

OPHELIA. O heavenly powers, restore him!

HAMLET. I have heard of your paintings too, well enough; God hath given you one face, and you make yourselves another: you jig, you amble, and you lisp, and nick-name God's creatures, and make your wantonness your ignorance.[9] Go to, I'll no more on 't; it hath made me mad. I say, we will have no more marriages: those that are married already, all but one, shall live; the rest shall keep as they are. To a nunnery, go.

    [*Exit.*]

OPHELIA. O, what a noble mind is here o'erthrown!      102
    The courtier's soldier's scholar's, eye, tongue, sword:
    The expectancy and rose of the fair state,
    The glass of fashion and the mould of form.[1]      105

---

5. Intercourse.  6. Its.  7. Have a flavor of, smack of. *Inoculate:* Graft.  8. Cuckolds bear imaginary horns and "a horned man's a monster" (*Othello*, Act IV, Scene 1).  9. Misname (out of affectation) the most natural things, and pretend that this is due to ignorance instead of affectation.  1. The mirror of fashion and the model of behavior.

The observed of all observers, quite, quite down!
And I, of ladies most deject and wretched,
That suck'd the honey of his music vows,
Now see that noble and most sovereign reason,
Like sweet bells jangled, out of tune and harsh;                                110
That unmatch'd form and feature of blown youth
Blasted with ecstasy:[2] O, woe is me,
To have seen what I have seen, see what I see!
    [*Re-enter* KING *and* POLONIUS.]
KING. Love! his affections do not that way tend;
    Nor what he spake, though it lack'd form a little,                                115
    Was not like madness. There's something in his soul
    O'er which his melancholy sits on brood,
    And I do doubt[3] the hatch and the disclose
    Will be some danger: which for to prevent,
    I have in quick determination                                120
    Thus set it down:—he shall with speed to England,
    For the demand of our neglected tribute:
    Haply the seas and countries different
    With variable objects shall expel
    This something-settled matter in his heart,                                125
    Whereon his brains still beating puts him thus
    From fashion of himself.[4] What think you on 't?
POLONIUS. It shall do well: but yet do I believe
    The origin and commencement of his grief
    Sprung from neglected love. How now, Ophelia!                                130
    You need not tell us what Lord Hamlet said;
    We heard it all. My lord, do as you please;
    But, if you hold it fit, after the play,
    Let his queen mother all alone entreat him
    To show his grief: let her be round[5] with him;                                135
    And I'll be placed, so please you, in the ear
    Of all their conference. If she find him not,
    To England send him, or confine him where
    Your wisdom best shall think.
KING.                                          It shall be so:
    Madness in great ones must not unwatch'd go.                                140
    [*Exeunt.*]


SCENE 2—*A hall in the castle.*

    [*Enter* HAMLET *and* PLAYERS.]
HAMLET. Speak the speech, I pray you, as I pronounced it to you,
    trippingly on the tongue: but if you mouth it, as many of your

2. Madness.   3. Fear.   4. Makes him behave unusually.   5. Direct.

players do, I had as lief the town-crier spoke my lines. Nor do not saw the air too much with your hand, thus; but use all gently: for in the very torrent, tempest, and, as I may say, whirlwind of your passion, you must acquire and beget a temperance that may give it smoothness. O, it offends me to the soul to hear a robustious periwig-pated fellow tear a passion to tatters, to very rags, to split the ears of the groundlings,[6] who, for the most part, are capable of nothing but inexplicable dumb-shows and noise: I would have such a fellow whipped for o'er doing Termagant;[7] it out-herods Herod: pray you, avoid it.

FIRST PLAYER. I warrant your honor.

HAMLET. Be not too tame neither, but let your own discretion be your tutor: suit the action to the word, the word to the action; with this special observance, that you o'erstep not the modesty[8] of nature: for anything so overdone is from the purpose of playing, whose end, both at the first and now, was and is, to hold, as 'twere, the mirror up to nature; to show virtue her own feature,[9] scorn her own image, and the very age and body of the time his form and pressure.[1] Now this overdone or come tardy off, though it make the unskillful laugh, cannot but make the judicious grieve; the censure of the which one must in your allowance o'erweigh a whole theater of others. O, there be players that I have seen play, and heard others praise, and that highly, not to speak it profanely,[2] that neither having the accent of Christians nor the gait of Christian, pagan, nor man, have so strutted and bellowed, that I have thought some of nature's journeymen had made men, and not made them well, they imitated humanity so abominably.

FIRST PLAYER. I hope we have reformed that indifferently[3] with us, sir.

HAMLET. O, reform it altogether. And let those that play your clowns speak no more than is set down for them: for there be of them that will themselves laugh, to set on some quantity of barren[4] spectators to laugh too, though in the mean time some necessary question of the play be then to be considered: that's villainous, and shows a most pitiful ambition in the fool that uses it. Go, make you ready.

[*Exeunt* PLAYERS. —*Enter* POLONIUS, ROSENCRANTZ, *and* GUILDENSTERN.]

How now, my lord! will the king hear this piece of work?

POLONIUS. And the queen too, and that presently.

HAMLET. Bid the players make haste.

6. Spectators in the pit, where admission was cheapest.    7. God of the Mohammedans in old romances and morality plays. He was portrayed as being noisy and excitable.    8. Moderation. 9. Form.    1. Impress, shape. *His:* Its    2. Hamlet refers apologetically to his following words, where he compares the creation of men to the work of "journeymen," or laborers.    3. Pretty well.    4. Silly.

[*Exit* POLONIUS]
Will you two help to hasten them?

ROSENCRANTZ. }
GUILDENSTERN. }   We will, my lord.

[*Exeunt* ROSENCRANTZ *and* GUILDENSTERN.]

HAMLET. What ho! Horatio!

[*Enter* HORATIO.]

HORATIO. Here, sweet lord, at your service.                    5

HAMLET. Horatio, thou art e'en as just a man
    As e'er my conversation coped withal.[5]

HORATIO. O, my dear lord,—

HAMLET.                              Nay, do not think I flatter;
    For what advancement may I hope from thee,
    That no revenue hast but thy good spirits,                 10
    To feed and clothe thee? Why should the poor be flatter'd?
    No, let the candied tongue lick absurd pomp,
    And crook the pregnant hinges of the knee
    Where thrift may follow fawning.[6] Dost thou hear?
    Since my dear soul was mistress of her choice,             15
    And could of men distinguish, her election
    Hath seal'd thee for herself: for thou hast been
    As one, in suffering all, that suffers nothing;
    A man that fortune's buffets and rewards
    Hast ta'en with equal thanks: and blest are those          20
    Whose blood and judgment[7] are so well commingled
    That they are not a pipe for fortune's finger
    To sound what stop she please.[8] Give me that man
    That is not passion's slave, and I will wear him
    In my heart's core, aye, in my heart of heart,             25
    As I do thee. Something too much of this.
    There is a play to-night before the king;
    One scene of it comes near the circumstance
    Which I have told thee of my father's death:
    I prithee, when thou sees that act a-foot,                 30
    Even with the very comment of thy soul[9]
    Observe my uncle: if he occulted guilt
    Do not itself unkennel in one speech
    It is a damned ghost that we have seen,
    And my imaginations are as foul                            35
    As Vulcan's stithy.[1] Give him heedful note;
    For I mine eyes will rivet to his face,

---

5. As I ever associated with.    6. Material profit may be derived from cringing. *Pregnant hinges:*
Supple joints.    7. Passion and reason.    8. For Fortune to put her finger on any windhole
she may please of the pipe.    9. With all your powers of observation.    1. Smithy.

And after we will both our judgments join
In censure of his seeming.[2]

HORATIO.                          Well, my lord:
If he steal aught the whilst this play is playing,                    40
And 'scape detecting. I will pay the theft.

HAMLET. They are coming to the play: I must be idle:[3]
Get you a place.

> [*Danish march. A flourish. Enter* KING, QUEEN, POLONIUS,
> OPHELIA, ROSENCRANTZ, GUILDENSTERN, *and other* LORDS *atten-*
> *dant, with the* GUARD *carrying torches.*]

KING. How fares our cousin Hamlet?

HAMLET. Excellent, i' faith; of the chameleon's dish: I eat the air,[4]
promise-crammed: you cannot feed capons so.

KING. I have nothing with this answer, Hamlet; these words are not
mine.[5]

HAMLET. No, nor mine now. [*To* POLONIUS] My lord, you played
once i' the university, you say?

POLONIUS. That did I, my lord, and was accounted a good actor.

HAMLET. What did you enact?

POLONIUS. I did enact Julius Cæsar: I was killed i' the Capitol; Brutus
killed me.

HAMLET. It was a brute part of him to kill so capital a calf there. Be
the players ready?

ROSENCRANTZ. Aye, my lord; they stay upon your patience.

QUEEN. Come hither, my dear Hamlet, sit by me.

HAMLET. No, good mother, here's metal more attractive.

POLONIUS. [*To the* KING] O, ho! do you mark that?

HAMLET. Lady, shall I lie in your lap?

> [*Lying down at* OPHELIA's *feet.*]

OPHELIA. No, my lord.

HAMLET. I mean, my head upon your lap?

OPHELIA. Aye, my lord.

HAMLET. Do you think I meant country matters?

OPHELIA. I think nothing, my lord.

HAMLET. That's a fair thought to lie between maids' legs.

OPHELIA. What is, my lord?

HAMLET. Nothing.

OPHELIA. You are merry, my lord.

HAMLET. Who, I?

OPHELIA. Aye, my lord.

HAMLET. O God, your only jig-maker.[6] What should a man do but
be merry? for, look you, how cheerfully my mother looks, and my
father died within 's two hours.

---

2. To judge his behavior.   3. Crazy.   4. The chameleon was supposed to feed on air.
5. Have nothing to do with my question.   6. Maker of comic songs.

OPHELIA. Nay, 'tis twice two months, my lord.

HAMLET. So long? Nay then, let the devil wear black, for I'll have a
suit of sables. O heavens! die two months ago, and not forgotten
yet? Then there's hope a great man's memory may outlive his life
half a year: but, by 'r lady, he must build churches then; or else
shall he suffer not thinking on, with the hobby-horse,[7] whose epitaph is, 'For, O, for, O, the hobby-horse is forgot.'

[*Hautboys play. The dumb-show enters. —Enter a King and a
Queen very lovingly; the Queen embracing him and he her.
She kneels, and makes show of protestation unto him. He takes
her up, and declines his head upon her neck; lays him down
upon a bank of flowers: she, seeing him asleep, leaves him.
Anon comes in a fellow, takes off his crown, kisses it, and pours
poison in the King's ears, and exits. The Queen returns; finds
the King dead, and makes passionate action. The Poisoner, with
some two or three Mutes comes in again, seeming to lament
with her. The dead body is carried away. The Poisoner woos
the Queen with gifts: she seems loath and unwilling awhile, but
in the end accepts his love. —Exeunt.*]

OPHELIA. What means this, my lord?

HAMLET. Marry, this is miching mallecho;[8] it means mischief.

OPHELIA. Belike this show imports the argument of the play.

[*Enter* PROLOGUE.]

HAMLET. We shall know by this fellow: the players cannot keep counsel;[9] they'll tell all.

OPHELIA. Will he tell us what this show meant?

HAMLET. Aye, or any show that you'll show him: be not you ashamed
to show, he'll not shame to tell you what it means.

OPHELIA. You are naught,[1] you are naught: I'll mark the play.

PROLOGUE. For us, and for our tragedy,
    Here stooping to your clemency,
    We beg your hearing patiently.

HAMLET. Is this a prologue, or the posy[2] of a ring?

OPHELIA. 'Tis brief, my lord.

HAMLET. As woman's love.

[*Enter two* PLAYERS, KING *and* QUEEN.]

PLAYER KING. Full thirty times hath Phœbus' cart[3] gone round      44
    Neptune's salt wash and Tellus' orbed ground,
    And thirty dozen moons with borrowed sheen
    About the world have times twelve thirties been,
    Since love our hearts and Hymen did our hands
    Unite commutual in most sacred bands.

PLAYER QUEEN. So many journeys may the sun and moon            50

---

7. A figure in the old May-day games and Morris dances.    8. Sneaking misdeed.    9. A
secret.    1. Naughty, improper.    2. Motto, inscription.    3. The chariot of the sun.

Make us again count o'er ere love be done!
But, woe is me, you are so sick of late,
So far from cheer and from your former state,
That I distrust you.[4] Yet, though I distrust,
Discomfort you, my lord, if nothing must:     55
For women's fear and love holds quantity,[5]
In neither aught, or in extremity.
Now, what my love is, proof hath made you know,
And as my love is sized, my fear is so:
Where love is great, the littlest doubts are fear,     60
Where little fears grow great, great love grows there.
PLAYER KING. Faith, I must leave thee, love, and shortly too;
My operant powers their functions leave[6] to do:
And thou shalt live in this fair world behind,
Honor'd, beloved; and haply as one as kind     65
For husband shalt thou—
PLAYER QUEEN.         O, confound the rest!
Such love must needs be treason in my breast:
In second husband let me be accurst!
None wed the second but who kill'd the first.
HAMLET. [*Aside*] Wormwood, wormwood.     70
PLAYER QUEEN. The instances that second marriage move
Are base respects of thrift,[7] but none of love:
A second time I kill my husband dead,
When second husband kisses me in bed.
PLAYER KING. I do believe you think what now you speak,     75
But what we do determine oft we break.
Purpose is but the slave to memory,
Of violent birth but poor validity:
Which now, like fruit unripe, sticks on the tree,
But fall unshaken when they mellow be.     80
Most necessary 'tis that we forget
To pay ourselves what to ourselves is debt:
What to ourselves in passion we propose,
The passion ending, both the purpose lose.
The violence of either grief or joy     85
Their own enactures[8] with themselves destroy:
Where joy most revels, grief doth most lament;
Grief joys, joy grieves, on slender accident.
This world is not for aye, nor 'tis not strange
That even our loves should with our fortunes change,     90
For 'tis a question left us yet to prove,
Whether love lead fortune or else fortune love.

---

4. I am worried about you.    5. Maintain mutual balance.    6. Cease.    7. Considerations of material profit. *Instances*: Motives.    8. Actual performances.

The great man down, you mark his favorite flies;
The poor advanced makes friends of enemies:
And hitherto doth love on fortune tend;                    95
For who not needs shall never lack a friend,
And who in want a hollow friend doth try
Directly seasons⁹ him his enemy.
But, orderly to end where I begun,
Our wills and fates do so contrary run,                    100
That our devices still are overthrown,
Our thoughts are ours, their ends none of our own:
So think thou wilt no second husband wed,
But die thy thoughts when thy first lord is dead.

PLAYER QUEEN. Nor earth to me give food nor heaven light!    105
Sport and repose lock from me day and night!
To desperation turn my trust and hope!
An anchor's cheer¹ in prison be my scope!
Each opposite, that blanks² the face of joy,
Meet what I would have well and it destroy!                 110
Both here and hence pursue me lasting strife,
If, once a widow, ever I be wife!

HAMLET. If she should break it now!

PLAYER KING. 'Tis deeply sworn. Sweet, leave me here a while;
My spirits grow dull, and fain I would beguile             115
The tedious day with sleep.                        [*Sleeps.*]

PLAYER QUEEN.                        Sleep rock thy brain;
And never come mischance between us twain!          [*Exit.*]

HAMLET. Madam, how like you this play?

QUEEN. The lady doth protest too much, methinks.

HAMLET. O, but she'll keep her word.

KING. Have you heard the argument?³ Is there no offense in 't?

HAMLET. No, no, they do but jest, poison in jest; no offense i' the world.

KING. What do you call the play?

HAMLET. The Mouse-Trap. Marry, how? Tropically.⁴ This play is the image of a murder done in Vienna: Gonzago is the duke's name; his wife, Baptista: you shall see anon; 'tis a knavish piece of work; but what o' that? your majesty, and we that have free souls, it touches us not: let the galled jade wince, our withers are unwrung.⁵

[*Enter* LUCIANUS.]

This is one Lucianus, nephew to the king.

OPHELIA. You are as good as a chorus, my lord.

9. Matures.   1. Hermit's, or anchoite's fare.   2. Makes pale.   3. Plot of the play in outline.   4. By a trope, figuratively.   5. Not wrenched. *Galled jade:* Injured horse. *Withers:* The part between the shoulders of a horse.

HAMLET. I could interpret[6] between you and your love, if I could see the puppets dallying.

OPHELIA. You are keen, my lord, you are keen.

HAMLET. It would cost you a groaning to take off my edge.

OPHELIA. Still better and worse.

HAMLET. So you must take your husbands. Begin, murderer; pox, leave thy damnable faces, and begin. Come: the croaking raven doth bellow for revenge.

LUCIANUS. Thoughts black, hands apt, drugs fit, and time agreeing;
    Confederate[7] season, else no creature seeing;
    Thou mixture rank, of midnight weeds collected,         120
    With Hecate's[8] ban thrice blasted, thrice infected,
    Thy natural magic and dire property,
    On wholesome life usurp immediately.              123
    [*Pours the poison into the sleeper's ear.*]

HAMLET. He poisons him i' the garden for his estate. His name's Gonzago: the story is extant, and written in very choice Italian: you shall see anon how the murderer gets the love of Gonzago's wife.

OPHELIA. The king rises.

HAMLET. What, frighted with false fire![9]

QUEEN. How fares my lord?

POLONIUS. Give o'er the play.

KING. Give me some light. Away!

POLONIUS. Lights, lights, lights!

    [*Exeunt all but* HAMLET *and* HORATIO.]

HAMLET. Why, let the stricken deer go weep,
        The hart ungalled play;
      For some must watch, while some must sleep:
        Thus runs the world away.
Would not this, sir, and a forest of feathers—if the rest of my fortunes turn Turk with me[1]—with two Provincial roses on my razed shoes, get me a fellowship in a cry[2] of players, sir?

HORATIO. Half a share.

HAMLET. A whole one, I.
      For thou dost know, O Damon dear,
        This realm dismantled was
      Of Jove himself; and now reigns here
        A very, very—pajock.[3]

HORATIO. You might have rhymed.[4]

HAMLET. O good Horatio, I'll take the ghost's word for a thousand pound. Didst perceive?

---

6. Act as interpreter (regular feature in puppet shows).   7. Favorable.   8. Goddess of witchcraft.   9. Blank shot.   1. Betray me (like a Christian turning Mohammedan). (term generally used with pack of hounds). *Forest of feathers . . . razed shoes:* Occasionally, parts of an actor's apparel.   3. Peacock.   4. "Ass" would have rhymed.

HORATIO. Very well, my lord.

HAMLET. Upon the talk of the poisoning?

HORATIO. I did very well note him.

HAMLET. Ah, ha! Come, some music! come, the recorders!
>      For if the king like not the comedy,
>      Why then, belike, he likes it not, perdy.
  Come, some music!

  [*Re-enter* ROSENCRANTZ *and* GUILDENSTERN.]

GUILDENSTERN. Good my lord, vouchsafe me a word with you.

HAMLET. Sir, a whole history.

GUILDENSTERN. The king, sir—

HAMLET. Aye, sir, what of him?

GUILDENSTERN. Is in his retirement marvelous distempered.

HAMLET. With drink, sir?

GUILDENSTERN. No, my lord, rather with choler.[5]

HAMLET. Your wisdom should show itself more richer to signify this
  to the doctor; for, for me to put him to his purgation would perhaps plunge him into far more choler.

GUILDENSTERN. Good my lord, put your discourse into some frame,
  and start not so wildly from my affair.

HAMLET. I am tame, sir: pronounce.

GUILDENSTERN. The queen, your mother, in most great affliction of
  spirit, hath sent me to you.

HAMLET. You are welcome.

GUILDENSTERN. Nay, good my lord, this courtesy is not of the right
  breed. If it shall please you to make me a wholesome[6] answer, I
  will do your mother's commandment: if not, your pardon and my
  return shall be the end of my business.

HAMLET. Sir, I cannot.

GUILDENSTERN. What, my lord?

HAMLET. Make you a wholesome answer; my wit's diseased: but, sir,
  such answer as I can make, you shall command; or rather, as you
  say, my mother: therefore no more, but to the matter: my mother,
  you say,—

ROSENCRANTZ. Then thus she says; your behavior hath struck her
  into amazement and admiration.[7]

HAMLET. O wonderful son, that can so astonish a mother! But is
  there no sequel at the heels of this mother's admiration? Impart.

ROSENCRANTZ. She desires to speak with you in her closet, ere you
  go to bed.

HAMLET. We shall obey, were she ten times our mother. Have you
  any further trade with us?

ROSENCRANTZ. My lord, you once did love me.

---

5. Bile, anger.    6. Sensible.    7. Confusion and surprise.

HAMLET. So I do still, by these pickers and stealers.[8]

ROSENCRANTZ. Good my lord, what is your cause of distemper? you do surely bar the door upon your own liberty, if you deny your griefs to your friend.

HAMLET. Sir, I lack advancement.[9]

ROSENCRANTZ. How can that be, when you have the voice of the king himself for your succession in Denmark?

HAMLET. Aye, sir, but 'while the grass grows,'[1]—the proverb is something musty.

[Re-enter PLAYERS *with recorders.*]

O, the recorders! let me see one. To withdraw[2] with you:—why do you go about to recover the wind of me,[3] as if you would drive me into a toil?

GUILDENSTERN. O, my lord, if my duty be too bold, my love is too unmannerly.

HAMLET. I do not well understand that. Will you play upon this pipe?

GUILDENSTERN. My lord, I cannot.

HAMLET. I pray you.

GUILDENSTERN. Believe me, I cannot.

HAMLET. I do beseech you.

GUILDENSTERN. I know no touch of it, my lord.

HAMLET. It is as easy as lying: govern these ventages[4] with your fingers and thumb, give it breath with your mouth, and it will discourse most eloquent music. Look you, these are the stops.

GUILDENSTERN. But these cannot I command to any utterance of harmony; I have not the skill.

HAMLET. Why, look you now, how unworthy a thing you make of me! You would play upon me; you would seem to know my stops; you would pluck out the heart of my mystery; you would sound me from my lowest note to the top of my compass: and there is much music, excellent voice, in this little organ; yet cannot you make it speak. 'Sblood, do you think I am easier to be played on than a pipe? Call me what instrument you will, though you can fret[5] me, yet you cannot play upon me.

[Re-enter POLONIUS.]

God bless you, sir!

POLONIUS. My lord, the queen would speak with you, and presently.

HAMLET. Do you see yonder cloud that's almost in shape of a camel?

POLONIUS. By the mass, and 'tis like a camel, indeed.

HAMLET. Methinks it is like a weasel.

POLONIUS. It is backed like a weasel.

---

8. The hands.     9. Hamlet pretends that the cause of his "distemper" is frustrated ambition.
1. The proverb ends, "oft starves the silly steed."     2. Retire (talk in private).     3. Get to windward of me. *Toil:* Snare.     4. Windholes.     5. Vex, with a pun on "frets" meaning the ridges placed across the finger board of a guitar to regulate the fingering.

HAMLET. Or like a whale?

POLONIUS. Very like a whale.

HAMLET. Then I will come to my mother by and by. They fool me
to the top of my bent.[6] I will come by and by.

POLONIUS. I will say so. [*Exit* POLONIUS.]

HAMLET. 'By and by' is easily said. Leave me, friends.

    [*Exeunt all but* HAMLET.]

    'Tis now the very witching time of night, 124

    When churchyards yawn, and hell itself breathes out

    Contagion to this world: now could I drink hot blood,

    And do such bitter business as the day

    Would quake to look on. Soft! now to my mother.

    O heart, lose not thy nature; let not ever

    The soul of Nero[7] enter this firm bosom: 130

    Let me be cruel, not unnatural:

    I will speak daggers to her, but use none;

    My tongue and soul in this be hypocrites;

    How in my words soever she be shent,

    To give them seals[8] never, my soul, consent! 135

    [*Exit.*]


### SCENE 3—*A room in the castle.*

[*Enter* KING, ROSENCRANTZ, *and* GUILDENSTERN.]

KING. I like him not, nor stands it safe with us

    To let his madness range. Therefore prepare you;

    I your commission will forthwith dispatch,

    And he to England shall along with you:

    The terms of our estate[9] may not endure 5

    Hazard so near us as doth hourly grow

    Out of his lunacies.

GUILDENSTERN.        We will ourselves provide:

    Most holy and religious fear it is

    To keep those many many bodies safe

    That live and feed upon your majesty. 10

ROSENCRANTZ. The single and peculiar[1] life is bound

    With all the strength and armor of the mind

    To keep itself from noyance; but much more

    That spirit upon whose weal depends and rests

    The lives of many. The cease[2] of majesty 15

    Dies not alone, but like a gulf doth draw

    What 's near it with it; it is a massy wheel,

---

6. Straining, tension (as of a bow).   7. This Roman emperor was the murderer of his mother.
8. Ratify them by action. *Shent:* Reproached.   9. My position as king.   1. Individual.
2. Decease, extinction.

Fix'd on the summit of the highest mount,
To whose huge spokes ten thousand lesser things
Are mortised[3] and adjoin'd; which, when it falls,                    20
Each small annexment, petty consequence,
Attends the boisterous ruin. Never alone
Did the king sigh, but with a general groan.
KING. Arm you, I pray you, to this speedy voyage,
For we will fetters put about this fear,                                25
Which now goes too free-footed.
ROSENCRANTZ. ⎱
GUILDENSTERN. ⎰ We will haste us.
     [*Exeunt* ROSENCRANTZ *and* GUILDENSTERN. —*Enter* POLONIUS.]
POLONIUS. My lord, he's going to his mother's closet:
Behind the arras I'll convey myself,
To hear the process: I'll warrant she'll tax him home:[4]
And, as you said, and wisely was it said                              30
'Tis meet that some more audience than a mother,
Since nature makes them partial, should o'erhear
The speech, of vantage.[5] Fare you well, my liege:
I'll call upon you ere you go to bed,
And tell you what I know.
KING.                            Thanks, dear my lord.                 35
     [*Exit* POLONIUS.]
O, my offense is rank, it smells to heaven;
It hath the primal eldest curse[6] upon 't,
A brother's murder. Pray can I not,
Though inclination be as sharp as will:
My stronger guilt defeats my strong intent,                           40
And like a man to double business bound,
I stand in pause where I shall first begin,
And both neglect. What if this cursed hand
Were thicker than itself with brother's blood,
Is there not rain enough in the sweet heavens                         45
To wash it white as snow? Whereto serves mercy
But to confront the visage of offense?[7]
And what's in prayer but this twofold force,
To be forestalled ere we come to fall,
Or pardon'd being down? Then I'll look up;                            50
My fault is past. But O, what form of prayer
Can serve my turn? 'Forgive me my foul murder?'
That cannot be, since I am still possess'd
Of those effects for which I did the murder,

---

3. Fastened.    4. Take him to task thoroughly.    5. From a vantage point.    6. Cain's.
7. Guilt.

My crown, mine own ambition and my queen.                           55
May one be pardon'd and retain the offense?[8]
In the corrupted currents of this world
Offense's gilded hand may shove by justice,
And oft 'tis seen the wicked prize itself
Buys out the law:[9] but 'tis not so above;                         60
There is no shuffling, there the action lies
In his[1] true nature, and we ourselves compell'd
Even to the teeth and forehead of our faults
To give in evidence. What then? what rests?[2]
Try what repentance can: what can it not?                           65
Yet what can it when one can not repent?
O wretched state! O bosom black as death!
O limèd soul, that struggling to be free
Art more engaged! Help, angels! make assay![3]
Bow, stubborn knees, and, heart with strings of steel,             70
Be soft as sinews of the new-born babe!
All may be well.
     [*Retires and kneels. —Enter* HAMLET.]
HAMLET. Now might I do it pat,[4] now he is praying
     And now I'll do 't: and so he goes to heaven:
     And so am I revenged. That would be scann'd;[5]               75
     A villain kills my father; and for that,
     I, his sole son, do this same villain send
     To heaven.
     O, this is hire and salary, not revenge.
     He took my father grossly, full of bread,                    80
     With all his crimes broad blown, as flush as May;
     And how his audit[6] stands who knows save heaven?
     But in our circumstance and course of thought,
     'Tis heavy with him: and am I then revenged,
     To take him in the purging of his soul,                      85
     When he is fit and season'd[7] for his passage?
     No.
     Up, sword, and know thou a more horrid hent:[8]
     When he is drunk asleep, or in his rage,
     Or, in the incestuous pleasure of his bed;                   90
     At game, a-swearing, or about some act
     That has no relish of salvation in 't;
     Then trip him, that his heels may kick at heaven
     And that his soul may be as damn'd and black

8. The things obtained through the offense.   9. The wealth unduly acquired is used for bribery.   1. Its.   2. What remains?   3. Make the attempt! (addressed by the King to himself). *Limèd*: Caught as with birdlime.   4. Conveniently.   5. Would have to be considered carefully.   6. Account. *Broad blown:* In full bloom.   7. Ripe, ready.   8. Grip.

As hell, whereto it goes. My mother stays:                            95
This physic but prolongs thy sickly days.                        [*Exit.*]
KING. [*Rising*] My words fly up, my thoughts remain below:
Words without thoughts never to heaven go.                       [*Exit.*]


SCENE 4—*The Queen's closet.*

[*Enter* QUEEN *and* POLONIUS.]
POLONIUS. He will come straight. Look you lay home to him:
Tell him his pranks have been too broad⁹ to bear with,
And that your grace hath screen'd and stood between
Much heat and him. I'll sconce me even here.
Pray you, be round¹ with him.
HAMLET. [*Within*]                    Mother, mother, mother!     5
QUEEN. I'll warrant you; fear me not. Withdraw,
I hear him coming.
[POLONIUS *hides behind the arras. —Enter* HAMLET.]
HAMLET. Now, mother, what's the matter?
QUEEN. Hamlet, thou hast thy father much offended.
HAMLET. Mother, you have my father much offended.            10
QUEEN. Come, come, you answer with an idle tongue.
HAMLET. Go, go, you question with a wicked tongue.
QUEEN. Why, how now, Hamlet!
HAMLET.                        What's the matter now?
QUEEN. Have you forgot me?
HAMLET.                        No, by the rood,² not so:
You are the queen, your husband's brother's wife;
And—would it were not so!—you are my mother.                 15
QUEEN. Nay, then, I'll set those to you that can speak.
HAMLET. Come, come, and sit you down; you shall not budge:
You go not till I set you up a glass³
Where you may see the inmost part of you.                     20
QUEEN. What wilt thou do? thou wilt not murder me?
Help, help, ho!
POLONIUS. [*Behind*] What, ho! help, help, help!
HAMLET. [*Drawing*] How now! a rat? Dead, for a ducat, dead!
[*Makes a pass through the arras.*]
POLONIUS. [*Behind*] O, I am slain!            [*Falls and dies.*]
QUEEN.                        O me, what hast thou done?
HAMLET. Nay, I know not: is it the king?                      25
QUEEN. O, what a rash and bloody deed is this!
HAMLET. A bloody deed! almost as bad, good mother,
As kill a king, and marry with his brother.

9. Unrestrained. *Lay home:* Give him a stern lesson.   1. Straightforward.   2. Cross.
3. Mirror.

QUEEN. As kill a king!

HAMLET.                              Aye, lady, 'twas my word.

[*Lifts up the arras and discovers* POLONIUS.]

Thou wretched, rash, intruding fool, farewell!                    30
I took thee for thy better: take thy fortune;
Thou find'st to be too busy[4] is some danger.
Leave wringing of your hands: peace! sit you down,
And let me wring your heart: for so I shall,
If it be made of penetrable stuff;                               35
If damned custom have not brass'd it so,
That it be proof and bulwark against sense.[5]

QUEEN. What have I done, that thou darest wag thy tongue
In noise so rude against me?

HAMLET.                              Such an act
That blurs the grace and blush of modesty,                        40
Calls virtue hypocrite, takes off the rose
From the fair forehead of an innocent love,
And sets a blister there; makes marriage vows
As false as dicers' oaths: O, such a deed
As from the body of contraction[6] plucks                        45
The very soul, and sweet religion makes
A rhapsody of words: heaven's face doth glow;[7]
With tristful visage, as against the doom,[8]
Is thought-sick at the act.                                      50
Is thought-sick at the act.

QUEEN. Aye me, what act,
That roars so loud and thunders in the index?[9]

HAMLET. Look here, upon this picture, and on this,
The counterfeit presentment[1] of two brothers.
See what a grace was seated on this brow;                        55
Hyperion's curls, the front of Jove himself,
An eye like Mars, to threaten and command;
A station[2] like the herald Mercury
New-lighted on a heaven-kissing hill;
A combination and a form indeed,                                 60
Where every god did seem to set his seal
To give the world assurance of a man:
This was your husband. Look you now, what follows:
Here is your husband; like a mildew'd ear,[3]
Blasting his wholesome brother. Have you eyes?                   65
Could you on this fair mountain leave to feed,
And batten[4] on this moor? Ha! have you eyes?

---

4. Too much of a busybody.   5. Feeling.   6. Duty to the marriage contract.   7. Blush
with shame.   8. Doomsday. *Tristful:* Sad.   9. Prologue, table of contents.   1. Portrait.
2. Posture.   3. Ear of corn.   4. Gorge, fatten. *Leave:* Cease.

You cannot call it love, for at your age
The hey-day in the blood is tame, it's humble,
And waits upon[5] the judgment: and what judgment          70
Would step from this to this? Sense[6] sure you have,
Else could you not have motion: but sure that sense
Is apoplex'd: for madness would not err,
Nor sense to ecstasy[7] was ne'er so thrall'd
But it reserved some quantity of choice,                   75
To serve in such a difference. What devil was 't
That thus hath cozen'd you at hoodman-blind?[8]
Eyes without feeling, feeling without sight,
Ears without hands or eyes, smelling sans[9] all,
Or but a sickly part of one true sense                     80
Could not so mope.[1]
O shame! where is thy blush? Rebellious hell,
If thou canst mutine in a matron's bones,
To flaming youth let virtue be as wax
And melt in her own fire: proclaim no shame                85
When the compulsive ardor gives the charge,[2]
Since frost itself as actively doth burn,
And reason panders[3] will.
QUEEN.                        O Hamlet, speak no more:
Thou turn'st mine eyes into my very soul,
And there I see such black and grained spots               90
As will not leave their tinct.[4]
HAMLET.                        Nay, but to live
In the rank sweat of an enseamèd[5] bed,
Stew'd in corruption, honeying and making love
Over the nasty sty,—
QUEEN.                        O, speak to me no more;
These words like daggers enter in my ears;                 95
No more, sweet Hamlet!
HAMLET.                        A murderer and a villain;
A slave that is not twentieth part the tithe[6]
Of your precedent lord; a vice of kings;
A cutpurse[7] of the empire and the rule,
That from a shelf the precious diadem stole                100
And put it in his pocket!
QUEEN.                        No more!
HAMLET. A king of shreds and patches—
     [*Enter* GHOST.]

5. Is subordinated to.   6. Sensibility, feeling.   7. Madness.   8. Blindman's bluff. *Coz-
en'd*: Tricked.   9. Without.   1. Be stupid.   2. Attacks.   3. Becomes subservient to.
4. Lose their color. *Grained*: Dyed in.   5. Greasy.   6. Tenth.   7. Pickpocket. *Vice*: Clown
(from the custom in the old morality plays of having a buffoon take the part of Vice, or of a
particular vice).

Save me, and hover o'er me with your wings,
You heavenly guards! What would your gracious figure?
QUEEN. Alas, he's mad!                                                    105
HAMLET. Do you not come your tardy son to chide,
   That, lapsed in time and passion, lets go by
   The important acting of your dread command?
   O, say!
GHOST. Do not forget: this visitation                                    110
   Is but to whet thy almost blunted purpose.
   But look, amazement on thy mother sits:
   O, step between her and her fighting soul:
   Conceit[8] in weakest bodies strongest works:
   Speak to her, Hamlet.
HAMLET.                    How is it with you, lady?                      115
QUEEN. Alas, how is 't with you,
   That you do bend your eye on vacancy
   And with the incorporal air do hold discourse?
   Forth at your eyes your spirits wildly peep;
   And, as the sleeping soldiers in the alarm,                           120
   Your bedded hairs, like life in excrements,[9]
   Start up and stand on end. O gentle son,
   Upon the heat and flame of thy distemper
   Sprinkle cool patience. Whereon do you look?
HAMLET. On him, on him! Look you how pale he glares!                     125
   His form and cause conjoin'd, preaching to stones,
   Would make them capable.[1] Do not look upon me,
   Lest with this piteous action you convert
   My stern effects:[2] then what I have to do
   Will want true color; tears perchance for[3] blood.                   130
QUEEN. To whom do you speak this?
HAMLET.                              Do you see nothing there?
QUEEN. Nothing at all; yet all that is I see.
HAMLET. Nor did you nothing hear?
QUEEN.                             No, nothing but ourselves.
HAMLET. Why, look you there! look, how it steals away!
   My father, in his habit as he lived!                                  135
   Look, where he goes, even now, out at the portal!
       [*Exit* GHOST.]
QUEEN. This is the very coinage of your brain:
   This bodiless creation ecstasy[4]
   Is very cunning in.
HAMLET.               Ecstasy!
   My pulse, as yours, doth temperately keep time,

8. Imagination.   9. Outgrowths. *Alarm:* Call to arms.   1. Capable of feeling.   2. You make
me change my purpose.   3. Instead of.   4. Madness.

And makes as healthful music: it is not madness
That I have utter'd: bring me to the test,
And I the matter will re-word, which madness
Would gambol from. Mother, for love of grace,
Lay not that flattering unction to your soul,                    145
That not your trespass but my madness speaks:
It will but skin and film the ulcerous place,
Whiles rank corruption, mining all within,
Infects unseen. Confess yourself to heaven;
Repent what's past, avoid what is to come,                       150
And do not spread the compost on the weeds,
To make them ranker. Forgive me this my virtue,
For in the fatness of these pursy[5] times
Virtue itself of vice must pardon beg.
Yea, curb[6] and woo for leave to do him good.                   155
QUEEN. O Hamlet, thou hast cleft my heart in twain.
HAMLET. O, throw away the worser part of it,
And live the purer with the other half.
Good night: but go not to my uncle's bed;
Assume a virtue, if you have it not.                             160
That monster, custom, who all sense doth eat,
Of habits devil, is angel yet in this,
That to the use of actions fair and good
He likewise gives a frock or livery,
That aptly[7] is put on. Refrain to-night,                      165
And that shall lend a kind of easiness
To the next abstinence; the next more easy;
For use almost can change the stamp[8] of nature,
And either curb the devil, or throw him out
With wondrous potency. Once more, good night:                   170
And when you are desirous to be blest,
I'll blessing beg of you. For this same lord,
    [*Pointing to* POLONIUS.]
I do repent: but heaven hath pleased it so,
To punish me with this, and this with me,
That I must be their scourge and minister.                      175
I will bestow[9] him, and will answer well
The death I gave him. So, again, good night.
I must be cruel, only to be kind:
Thus bad begins, and worse remains behind.
One word more, good lady.
QUEEN.                        What shall I do?                   180
HAMLET. Not this, by no means, that I bid you do:

5. Swollen from pampering.    6. Bow.    7. Easily.    8. Cast, form. *Use:* Habit.    9. Stow away. *Minister:* Agent of punishment.

Let the bloat[1] king tempt you again to bed;
Pinch wanton on your cheek, call you his mouse;
And let him, for a pair of reechy[2] kisses,
Or paddling in your neck with his damn'd fingers,                    185
Make you to ravel all this matter out,
That I essentially am not in madness,
But mad in craft.[3] 'Twere good you let him know;
For who, that's but a queen, fair, sober, wise,
Would from a paddock, from a bat, a gib,[4]                          190
Such dear concernings hide? who would do so?
No, in despite of sense and secrecy,
Unpeg the basket on the house's top,
Let the birds fly, and like the famous ape,[5]
To try conclusions, in the basket creep                             195
And break your own neck down.

QUEEN. Be thou assured, if words be made of breath
And breath of life, I have no life to breathe
What thou hast said to me.

HAMLET. I must to England; you know that?

QUEEN.                                        Alack,                 200
I had forgot: 'tis so concluded on.

HAMLET. There's letters seal'd: and my two schoolfellows,
Whom I will trust as I will adders fang'd,
They bear the mandate; they must sweep my way,
And marshal[6] me to knavery. Let it work;                          205
For 'tis the sport to have the enginer[7]
Hoist with his own petar:[8] and 't shall go hard
But I will delve one yard below their mines,
And blow them at the moon: I, 'tis most sweet
When in one line two crafts directly meet.                          210
This man shall set me packing:
I'll lug the guts into the neighbor room.
Mother, good night. Indeed this counselor
Is now most still, most secret and most grave,[9]
Who was in life a foolish prating knave.                            215
Come, sir, to draw toward an end with you.
Good night, mother.

[*Exeunt severally;* HAMLET *dragging in* POLONIUS.]

---

1. Bloated with drink.   2. Fetid.   3. Simulation.   4. Tomcat. *Paddock*: Toad. *Concern-ings*: Matters with which one is closely concerned.   5. The ape in the unidentified animal fable to which Hamlet alludes; apparently the animal saw birds fly out of a basket and drew the conclusion that by placing himself in a basket he could fly too.   6. Lead.   7. Military engineer.
8. Petard, a variety of bomb. *Hoist*: Blow up.   9. Hamlet is punning on the word.

## Act IV

SCENE 1—*A room in the castle.*

[*Enter* KING, QUEEN, ROSENCRANTZ, *and* GUILDENSTERN]

KING. There's matter in these sighs, these profound heaves:
　　You must translate: 'tis fit we understand them.
　　Where is your son?
QUEEN. Bestow this place on us[1] a little while.
　　[*Exeunt* ROSENCRANTZ *and* GUILDENSTERN.]
　　Ah, mine own lord, what have I seen to-night!                    5
KING. What, Gertrude? How does Hamlet?
QUEEN. Mad as the sea and wind, when both contend
　　Which is the mightier: in his lawless fit,
　　Behind the arras hearing something stir,
　　Whips out his rapier, cries 'A rat, a rat!'                    10
　　And in this brainish apprehension[2] kills
　　The unseen good old man.
KING.　　　　　　　　　　O heavy deed!
　　It had been so with us, had we been there:
　　His liberty is full of threats to all,
　　To you yourself, to us, to every one.                    15
　　Alas, how shall this bloody deed be answer'd?
　　It will be laid to us, whose providence
　　Should have kept short,[3] restrain'd and out of haunt,
　　This mad young man: but so much was our love,
　　We would not understand what was most fit,                    20
　　But, like the owner of a foul disease,
　　To keep it from divulging, let it feed
　　Even on the pith of life. Where is he gone?
QUEEN. To draw apart the body he hath kill'd:
　　O'er whom his very madness, like some ore[4]                    25
　　Among a mineral of metals base,
　　Shows itself pure; he weeps for what is done.
KING. O Gertrude, come away!
　　The sun no sooner shall the mountains touch,
　　But we will ship him hence: and this vile deed                    30
　　We must, with all our majesty and skill,
　　Both countenance[5] and excuse. Ho, Guildenstern!
　　[*Re-enter* ROSENCRANTZ *and* GUILDENSTERN.]
　　Friends both, go join you with some further aid:
　　Hamlet in madness hath Polonius slain,
　　And from his mother's closet hath he dragg'd him:                    35

1. Leave　us　alone.　2. Imaginary　notion.　3. Under　close　watch.　4. Gold.
5. Recognize.

Go seek him out; speak fair, and bring the body
Into the chapel. I pray you, haste in this.
　　　[*Exeunt* ROSENCRANTZ *and* GUILDENSTERN.]
Come, Gertrude, we'll call up our wisest friends;
And let them know, both what we mean to do,
And what's untimely done. . . . 　　　　　　　　　　　　　40
Whose whisper o'er the world's diameter
As level as the cannon to his blank[6]
Transports his poison'd shot, may miss our name
And hit the woundless air. O, come away!
My soul is full of discord and dismay. 　　　　　　　　　[*Exeunt.*]


SCENE 2—*Another room in the castle.*

　　　[*Enter* HAMLET.]
HAMLET. Safely stowed.
ROSENCRANTZ.
GUILDENSTERN. } [*Within*] Hamlet! Lord Hamlet!
HAMLET. But soft, what noise? who calls on Hamlet?
　　O, here they come.
　　　[*Enter* ROSENCRANTZ *and* GUILDENSTERN.]
ROSENCRANTZ. What have you done, my lord, with the dead body?
HAMLET. Compounded[7] it with dust, whereto 'tis kin. 　　　　　6
ROSENCRANTZ. Tell us where 'tis, that we may take it thence
　　And bear it to the chapel.
HAMLET. Do not believe it.
ROSENCRANTZ. Believe what?
HAMLET. That I can keep your counsel and not mine own. Besides,
　　to be demanded of a sponge! what replication[8] should be made by
　　the son of a king?
ROSENCRANTZ. Take you me for a sponge, my lord?
HAMLET. Aye, sir; that soaks up the king's countenance,[9] his rewards,
　　his authorities. But such officers do the king best service in the
　　end: he keeps them, like an ape, in the corner of his jaw; first
　　mouthed, to be last swallowed: when he needs what you have
　　gleaned, it is but squeezing you, and sponge, you shall be dry
　　again.
ROSENCRANTZ. I understand you not, my lord.
HAMLET. I am glad of it: a knavish speech sleeps in a foolish ear.
ROSENCRANTZ. My lord, you must tell us where the body is, and go
　　with us to the king.
HAMLET. The body is with the king, but the king is not with the body.
　　The king is a thing—

6. His target.　　7. Mixed.　　8. Formal reply. *Demanded:* Questioned by.　　9. Favor.

GUILDENSTERN. A thing, my lord?

HAMLET. Of nothing: bring me to him. Hide fox, and all after.[1]

    [*Exeunt.*]

SCENE 3—*Another room in the castle.*

    [*Enter* KING, *attended.*]

KING. I have sent to seek him, and to find the body.

  How dangerous is it that this man goes loose!

  Yet must not we put the strong law on him:

  He's loved of the distracted multitude,

  Who like not in their judgment, but their eyes;      5

  And where 'tis so, the offender's scourge[2] is weigh'd,

  But never the offense. To bear[3] all smooth and even,

  This sudden sending away must seem

  Deliberate pause:[4] diseases desperate grown

  By desperate appliance[5] are relieved,      10

  Or not at all.

    [*Enter* ROSENCRANTZ.]

            How now! what hath befall'n?

ROSENCRANTZ. Where the dead body is bestow'd, my lord,

  We cannot get from him.

KING.                 But where is he?      13

ROSENCRANTZ. Without, my lord; guarded, to know your pleasure.

KING. Bring him before us.

ROSENCRANTZ. Ho, Guildenstern! bring in my lord.

    [*Enter* HAMLET *and* GUILDENSTERN.]

KING. Now, Hamlet, where's Polonius?

HAMLET. At supper.

KING. At supper! where?

HAMLET. Not where he eats, but where he is eaten: a certain convocation of public worms are e'en at him. Your worm is your only emperor for diet:[6] we fat all creatures else to fat us, and we fat ourselves for maggots: your fat king and your lean beggar is but variable service,[7] two dishes, but to one table: that's the end.

KING. Alas, alas!

HAMLET. A man may fish with the worm that hath eat of a king, and eat of the fish that hath fed of that worm.

KING. What dost thou mean by this?

HAMLET. Nothing but to show you how a king may go a progress[8] through the guts of a beggar.

---

1. The name of a children's game.   2. Punishment.   3. Conduct.   4. The result of careful arrangement.   5. Treatment.   6. Possibly a punning reference to the Diet (assembly) of the Holy Roman Empire at Worms.   7. I.e., the service varies, not the food.   8. Royal state journey.

KING. Where is Polonius?

HAMLET. In heaven; send thither to see: if your messenger find him
not there, seek him i' the other place yourself. But indeed, if you
find him not within this month, you shall nose⁹ him as you go up
the stairs into the lobby.

KING. Go seek him there.          [*To some* ATTENDANTS.]

HAMLET. He will stay till you come.       [*Exeunt* ATTENDANTS.]

KING. Hamlet, this deed, for thine especial safety,          14
    Which we do tender,¹ as we dearly grieve
    For that which thou hast done, must send thee hence
    With fiery quickness: therefore prepare thyself;
    The bark is ready and the wind at help,
    The associates tend, and every thing is bent
    For England.

HAMLET.          For England?

KING.                  Aye, Hamlet.

HAMLET.                       Good.     20

KING. So is it, if thou knew'st our purposes.

HAMLET. I see a cherub that sees them. But, come; for England!
    Farewell, dear mother.

KING. Thy loving father, Hamlet.

HAMLET. My mother: father and mother is man and wife; man and
wife is one flesh, and so, my mother. Come, for England!
    [*Exit.*]

KING. Follow him at foot;² tempt him with speed aboard;      21
    Delay it not; I'll have him hence to-night:
    Away! for every thing is seal'd and done
    That else leans on³ the affair: pray you, make haste.
    [*Exeunt* ROSENCRANTZ *and* GUILDENSTERN.]
    And, England,⁴ if my love thou hold'st at aught—      25
    As my great power thereof may give thee sense,⁵
    Since yet thy cicatrice looks raw and red
    After the Danish sword, and thy free awe
    Pays homage to us—thou mayst not coldly set⁶
    Our sovereign process; which imports at full,      30
    By letters conjuring⁷ to that effect,
    The present death of Hamlet. Do it, England;
    For like the hectic⁸ in my blood he rages,
    And thou must cure me; till I know 'tis done,
    Howe'er my haps, my joys were ne'er begun.      35
    [*Exit.*]

---

9. Smell.    1. Care for.    2. At his heels.    3. Pertains to.    4. The king of England.
5. Make you feel.    6. Regard with indifference.    7. Enjoining.    8. Fever.

SCENE 4—A *plain in Denmark.*

[*Enter* FORTINBRAS, *a* CAPTAIN *and* SOLDIERS, *marching.*]

FORTINBRAS. Go, captain, from me greet the Danish king;
Tell him that by his license Fortinbras
Craves the conveyance[9] of a promised march
Over his kingdom. You know the rendezvous.
If that his majesty would aught with us,                                        5
We shall express our duty in his eye;[1]
And let him know so.

CAPTAIN.                              I will do 't, my lord.

FORTINBRAS. Go softly on.

[*Exeunt* FORTINBRAS *and* SOLDIERS. —*Enter* HAMLET, ROSEN-
CRANTZ, GUILDENSTERN, *and others.*]

HAMLET. Good sir, whose powers[2] are these?

CAPTAIN. They are of Norway, sir.                                            10

HAMLET. How purposed, sir, I pray you?

CAPTAIN. Against some part of Poland.

HAMLET. Who commands them, sir?

CAPTAIN. The nephew to Old Norway, Fortinbras.

HAMLET. Goes it against the main[3] of Poland, sir,                            15
Or for some frontier?

CAPTAIN. Truly to speak, and with no addition,
We go to gain a little patch of ground
That hath in it no profit but the name.
To pay five ducats, five, I would not farm it;                                 20
Nor will it yield to Norway or the Pole
A ranker rate, should it be sold in fee.[4]

HAMLET. Why, then the Polack never will defend it.

CAPTAIN. Yes, it is already garrison'd.

HAMLET. Two thousand souls and twenty thousand ducats                          25
Will not debate the question of this straw:
This is the imposthume[5] of much wealth and peace,
That inward breaks, and shows no cause without
Why the man dies. I humbly thank you, sir.

CAPTAIN. God be wi' you, sir.                                    [*Exit.*]

ROSENCRANTZ.                    Will 't please you go, my lord?        30

HAMLET. I'll be with you straight. Go a little before.

[*Exeunt all but* HAMLET.]

How all occasions do inform against[6] me,
And spur my dull revenge! What is a man,
If his chief good and market[7] of his time
Be but to sleep and feed? a beast, no more.                                    35

---

9. Convoy.   1. Presence.   2. Armed forces.   3. The whole of.   4. For absolute possession. *Ranker:* Higher.   5. Ulcer.   6. Denounce.   7. Payment for, reward.

Sure, he that made us with such large discourse,[8]
Looking before and after, gave us not
That capability and god-like reason
To fust[9] in us unused. Now, whether it be
Bestial oblivion, or some craven scruple                    40
Of thinking too precisely on the event,[1]—
A thought which, quarter'd, hath but one part wisdom
And ever three parts coward,—I do not know
Why yet I live to say 'this thing's to do,'
Sith[2] I have cause, and will, and strength, and means,       45
To do 't. Examples gross as earth exhort me:
Witness this army, of such mass and charge,[3]
Led by a delicate and tender prince,
Whose spirit with divine ambition puff'd
Makes mouths[4] at the invisible event,                       50
Exposing what is mortal and unsure
To all that fortune, death and danger dare,
Even for an egg-shell. Rightly to be great
Is not to stir without great argument,
But greatly to find quarrel in a straw                       55
When honor's at the stake. How stand I then,
That have a father kill'd, a mother stain'd,
Excitements of my reason and my blood,
And let all sleep, while to my shame I see
The imminent death of twenty thousand men,                   60
That for a fantasy and trick[5] of fame
Go to their graves like beds, fight for a plot
Whereon the numbers cannot try the cause,[6]
Which is not tomb enough and continent
To hide the slain? O, from this time forth,                  65
My thoughts be bloody, or be nothing worth!        [*Exit.*]

SCENE 5—*Elsinore. A room in the castle.*

[*Enter* QUEEN, HORATIO, *and a* GENTLEMAN.]
QUEEN. I will not speak with her.
GENTLEMAN. She is importunate, indeed distract:
    Her mood will needs be pitied.
QUEEN.                                    What would she have?
GENTLEMAN. She speaks much of her father, says she hears
    There's tricks i' the world, and hems and beats her heart,   5
    Spurns enviously at straws;[7] speaks things in doubt,

8. Reasoning power.   9. Become moldy, taste of the cask.   1. Outcome.   2. Since.
3. Cost.   4. Makes faces.   5. Trifle of.   6. So small that it cannot hold the men who fight
for it. *Continent:* Container.   7. Gets angry at trifles.

That carry but half sense: her speech is nothing,
Yet the unshapèd use of it doth move
The hearers to collection; they aim[8] at it,
And botch the words up fit to their own thoughts;                    10
Which, as her winks and nods and gestures yield them,
Indeed would make one think there might be thought,
Though nothing sure, yet much unhappily.
HORATIO. 'Twere good she were spoken with, for she may strew
      Dangerous conjectures in ill-breeding minds.[9]              15
QUEEN. Let her come in.                         [Exit GENTLEMAN.]
      [Aside] To my sick soul, as sin's true nature is,
      Each toy seems prologue to some great amiss:[1]
      So full of artless jealousy is guilt,
      It spills itself in fearing to be spilt.                        20
            [Re-enter GENTLEMAN, with OPHELIA.
OPHELIA. Where is the beauteous majesty of Denmark?
QUEEN. How now, Ophelia!
OPHELIA. [Sings] How should I your true love know
                  From another one?
                  By his cockle hat and staff                         25
                  And his sandal shoon.[2]
QUEEN. Alas, sweet lady, what imports this song?
OPHELIA. Say you? nay, pray you, mark.
      [Sings] He is dead and gone, lady,
                  He is dead and gone;                                30
            At his head a grass-green turf,
                  At his heels a stone.
      Oh, oh!
QUEEN.          Nay, but Ophelia,—
OPHELIA.                            Pray you, mark.
      [Sings] White his shroud as the mountain snow,—               35
            [Enter KING.]
QUEEN. Alas, look here, my lord.
OPHELIA. [Sings]    Larded[3] with sweet flowers;
                  Which bewept to the grave did go
                  With true-love showers.                            39
KING. How do you, pretty lady?
OPHELIA. Well, God 'ild you![4] They say the owl was a baker's daugh-
      ter. Lord, we know what we are, but know not what we may be.[5]
      God be at your table!
KING. Conceit upon her father.

---

8. Guess. *Collection*: Gathering up her words and trying to make sense of them. *Botch*: Patch.
9. Minds breeding evil thoughts. 1. Misfortune. *Toy*: Trifle. *Jealousy*: Uncontrolled
suspicion. 2. Typical signs of pilgrims traveling to places of devotion. *Shoon*: Shoes.
3. Garnished. 4. God yield (i.e., repay) you. 5. An allusion to a folk tale about a baker's
daughter changed into an owl for having show a little charity to the Lord.

OPHELIA. Pray you, let's have no words of this; but when they ask
    you what it means, say you this:
    [*Sings*] To-morrow is Saint Valentine's day          40
          All in the morning betime,
        And I a maid at your window,
          To be your Valentine.
        Then up he rose, and donn'd his clothes,
          And dupp'd[6] the chamber-door;          45
        Let in the maid, that out a maid
          Never departed more.
KING. Pretty Ophelia!
OPHELIA. Indeed, la, without an oath, I'll make an end on 't:
    [*Sings*] By Gis[7] and by Saint Charity,          50
          Alack, and fie for shame!
        Young men will do 't, if they come to 't;
          By cock, they are to blame.
        Quoth she, before you tumbled me,
          You promised me to wed.          55
  He answers:
        So would I ha' done, by yonder sun,
          An thou hadst not come to my bed.        58
KING. How long hath she been thus?
OPHELIA. I hope all will be well. We must be patient: but I cannot
  choose but weep, to think they should lay him i' the cold ground.
  My brother shall know of it: and so I thank you for your good
  counsel. Come, my coach! Good night, ladies; good night, sweet
  ladies; good night, good night.
    [*Exit.*]
KING. Follow her close; give her good watch, I pray you.
    [*Exit* HORATIO.]
  O, this is the poison of deep grief; it springs        59
All from her father's death. O Gertrude, Gertrude,
When sorrows come, they come not single spies,
But in battalions! First, her father slain:
Next, your son gone; and he most violent author
Of his own just remove: the people muddied,[8]
Thick and unwholesome in their thoughts and whispers,      65
For good Polonius' death; and we have done but greenly,
In hugger-mugger[9] to inter him: poor Ophelia
Divided from herself and her fair judgment,
Without the which we are pictures, or mere beasts:
Last, and as much containing as all these,        70
Her brother is in secret come from France,

6. Opened.    7. By Jesus.    8. Confused, their thoughts made turbid (as water by mud).
9. Hasty secrecy. *Greenly*: Foolishly.

Feeds on his wonder,[1] keeps himself in clouds,
And wants[2] not buzzers to infect his ear
With pestilent speeches of his father's death;
Wherein necessity, of matter beggar'd,[3]　　　　　　　　75
Will nothing stick our person to arraign[4]
In ear and ear. O my dear Gertrude, this,
Like to a murdering-piece,[5] in many places
Gives me superfluous death.　　　　　　　　[*A noise within.*]

QUEEN.　　　　　　　　　　Alack, what noise is this?

KING. Where are my Switzers?[6] Let them guard the door.　　　80

　　　[*Enter another* GENTLEMAN.]

What is the matter?

GENTLEMAN.　　　　　　Save yourself, my lord:
　The ocean, overpeering of his list,[7]
　Eats not the flats with more impetuous haste
　Than young Laertes, in a riotous head,[8]
　O'erbears your officers. The rabble call him lord;　　　85
　And, as the world were now but to begin,
　Antiquity forgot, custom not known,
　The ratifiers and props of every word,
　They cry 'Choose we; Laertes shall be king!'
　Caps, hands and tongues applaud it to the clouds,　　　90
　'Laertes shall be king, Laertes king!'

QUEEN. How cheerfully on the false trail they cry!
　O, this is counter,[9] you false Danish dogs! 　　[*Noise within.*]

KING. The doors are broke.

　　　[*Enter* LAERTES, *armed;* DANES *following.*]

LAERTES. Where is this king? Sirs, stand you all without.　　95

DANES. No, let's come in.

LAERTES.　　　　　　　　I pray you, give me leave.

DANES. We will, we will.　　　[*They retire without the door.*]

LAERTES. I thank you: keep the door. O thou vile king,
　Give me my father!

QUEEN.　　　　　　Calmly, good Laertes.

LAERTES. That drop of blood that's calm proclaims me bastard;　　100
　Cries cuckold to my father; brands the harlot
　Even here, between the chaste unsmirched brows
　Of my true mother.

KING.　　　　　　What is the cause, Laertes,
　That thy rebellion looks so giant-like?
　Let him go, Gertrude; do not fear[1] our person:　　　105

---

1. Broods, keeps wondering.　2. Lacks.　3. The necessity to build up a story without the materials for doing so.　4. Will not hesitate to accuse me.　5. A variety of cannon which scattered its shot in many directions.　6. Swiss guards.　7. Overflowing above the high-water mark.　8. Group of rebels.　9. Following the scent in the wrong direction.　1. Fear for.

There's such divinity doth hedge a king,
That treason can but peep to what it would,[2]
Acts little of his will. Tell me, Laertes,
Why thou art thus incensed: let him go, Gertrude:
Speak, man.                                                    110

LAERTES. Where is my father?

KING.                                  Dead.

QUEEN.                                          But not by him.

KING. Let him demand his fill.

LAERTES. How came he dead? I'll not be juggled with:
To hell, allegiance! vows, to the blackest devil!
Conscience and grace, to the profoundest pit             115
I dare damnation: to this point I stand,
That both the worlds I give to negligence,[3]
Let come what comes; only I'll be revenged
Most throughly for my father.

KING.                                  Who shall stay you?

LAERTES. My will, not all the world:                     120
And for my means, I'll husband them so well,
They shall go far with little.

KING.                                  Good Laertes,
If you desire to know the certainty
Of your dear father's death, is 't writ in your revenge
That, swoopstake,[4] you will draw both friend and foe,   125
Winner and loser?

LAERTES. None but his enemies.

KING.                                  Will you know them then?

LAERTES. To his good friends thus wide I'll ope my arms;
And, like the kind life-rendering pelican,[5]
Repast them with my blood.

KING.                                  Why, now you speak     130
Like a good child and a true gentleman.
That I am guiltless of your father's death,
And am most sensibly in grief for it,
It shall as level to your judgment pierce
As day does to your eye.

DANES. [*Within*]               Let her come in.             135

LAERTES. How now! what noise is that?

        [*Re-enter* OPHELIA.]

O heat, dry up my brains! tears seven times salt,
Burn out the sense and virtue[6] of mine eye!

2. Look from a distance at what it desires. *His*: Its.    3. I don't care what may happen to me in
either this world or the next.    4. Without making any distinction, as the winner takes the whole
stake in a card game.    5. The mythical pelican is supposed to feed its young with its own
blood.    6. Power, faculty.

By heaven, thy madness shall be paid with weight,
Till our scale turn the beam. O rose of May!                    140
Dear maid, kind sister, sweet Ophelia!
O heavens! is 't possible a young maid's wits
Should be as mortal as an old man's life?
Nature is fine in love, and where 'tis fine[7]
It sends some precious instance of itself                       145
After the thing it loves.

OPHELIA. [*Sings*] They bore him barefaced on the bier:
          Hey non nonny, nonny, hey nonny:
          And in his grave rain'd many a tear,—
Fare you well, my dove!                                         150

LAERTES. Hadst thou thy wits, and didst persuade revenge,
It could not move thus.

OPHELIA. [*Sings*] You must sing down a-down,
          An you call him a-down-a.                   154
O, how the wheel[8] becomes it! It is the false steward, that stole his
master's daughter.

LAERTES. This nothing's more than matter.[9]

OPHELIA. There's rosemary, that's for remembrance: pray you, love,
remember: and there is pansies,[1] that's for thoughts.

LAERTES. A document[2] in madness; thoughts and remembrance
fitted.

OPHELIA. There's fennel for you, and columbines: there's rue[3] for
you: and here's some for me: we may call it herbs of grace o Sundays: O, you must wear your rue with a difference. There's a daisy:
I would give you some violets,[4] but they withered all when my
father died: they say he made a good end,—
   [*Sings*] For bonnie sweet Robin is all my joy.        155

LAERTES. Thought and affliction, passion, hell itself,
She turns to favor[5] and to prettiness.

OPHELIA. [*Sings*] And will he not come again?
        And will he not come again?
          No, no, he is dead,                          160
          Go to thy death-bed,
        He never will come again.
        His beard was as white as snow,
        All flaxen was his poll:
          He is gone, he is gone,                       165
          And we cast away moan:
        God ha' mercy on his soul!

---

7. Refined. *Instance:* Sample, token.    8. Ballads were often sung to the motion of a spinning
wheel. *The false steward:* An allusion to an unknown folk ballad.    9. This nonsense is more
indicative than sane speech.    1. The symbol of thought.    2. Lesson.    3. Emblem of sorrow and repentence (compare the verb "rue"). *Fennel:* Emblem of flattery. *Columbines:* Emblem
of cuckoldom.    4. For faithfulness.    5. Charm.

And of all Christian souls, I pray God. God be wi' you.
   [*Exit.*]
LAERTES. Do you see this, O God?
KING. Laertes, I must commune with your grief,          170
   Or you deny me right. Go but apart,
   Make choice of whom your wisest friends you will.
   And they shall hear and judge 'twixt you and me:
   If by direct or by collateral hand
   They find us touched,[6] we will our kingdom give,     175
   Our crown, our life, and all that we call ours,
   To you in satisfaction; but if not,
   Be you content to lend your patience to us,
   And we shall jointly labor with your soul
   To give it due content.
LAERTES.                 Let this be so;          180
   His means of death, his obscure funeral,
   No trophy, sword, nor hatchment[7] o'er his bones,
   No noble rite nor formal ostentation,
   Cry to be heard, as 'twere from heaven to earth,
   That I must call 't in question.
KING                 So you shall;        185
   And where the offense is let the great axe fall.
   I pray you, go with me.                 [*Exeunt.*]


SCENE 6—*Another room in the castle.*

   [*Enter* HORATIO *and a* SERVANT.]
HORATIO. What are they that would speak with me?
SERVANT. Sea-faring men, sir: they say they have letters for you.
HORATIO. Let them come in.            [*Exit* SERVANT.]
   I do not know from what part of the world
   I should be greeted, if not from Lord Hamlet.
   [*Enter* SAILORS.]
FIRST SAILOR. God bless you, sir.
HORATIO. Let him bless thee too.
FIRST SAILOR. He shall, sir, an 't please him.
   There's a letter for you, sir; it comes from the ambassador that was
   bound for England; if your name be Horatio, as I am let to know
   it is.
HORATIO. [*Reads*] 'Horatio, when thou shalt have overlooked[8] this,
   give these fellows some means to the king: they have letters for
   him. Ere we were two days old at sea, a pirate of very warlike
   appointment give us chase. Finding ourselves too slow of sail, we

---

6. Involved (in the murder). *Collateral:* Indirect.    7. Coat of arms.    8. Read over.

put on a compelled valor, and in the grapple I boarded them: on the instant they got clear of our ship; so I alone became their prisoner. They have dealt with me like thieves of mercy:[9] but they knew what they did; I am to do a good turn for them. Let the king have the letters I have sent; and repair thou to me with as much speed as thou wouldst fly death. I have words to speak in thine ear will make thee dumb; yet are they much too light for the bore[1] of the matter. These good fellows will bring thee where I am. Rosencrantz and Guildenstern hold their course for England: of them I have much to tell thee. Farewell.

> 'He that thou knowest thine, HAMLET.'

Come, I will make you way for these your letters;
And do 't the speedier, that you may direct me
To him from whom you brought them.                [*Exeunt.*]

SCENE 7—*Another room in the castle.*

[*Enter* KING *and* LAERTES.]

KING. Now must your conscience my acquittance seal,
    And you must put me in your heart for friend,
    Sith you have heard, and with a knowing ear,
    That he which hath your noble father slain
    Pursued my life.
LAERTES.                It well appears: but tell me            5
    Why you proceeded not against these feats,
    So crimeful and so capital in nature,
    As by your safety, wisdom, all things else,
    You mainly[2] were stirr'd up.
KING.                          O, for two special reasons,
    Which may to you perhaps seem much unsinew'd,[3]            10
    But yet to me they're strong. The queen his mother
    Lives almost by his looks; and for myself—
    My virtue or my plague, be it either which—
    She's so conjunctive[4] to my life and soul,
    That, as the star moves not but in his sphere,            15
    I could not but my her. The other motive,
    Why to a public count I might not go,
    Is the great love the general gender[5] bear him;
    Who, dipping all his faults in their affection,
    Would, like the spring that turneth wood to stone,        20
    Convert his gyves[6] to graces; so that my arrows,
    Too slightly timber'd for so loud a wind,
    Would have reverted to my bow again
    And not where I had aim'd them.

9. Merciful.  1. Caliber, i.e., importance.  2. Powerfully.  3. Weak.  4. Closely joined.  5. Common people. *Count:* Accounting, trial.  6. Fetters.

LAERTES.  And so have I a noble father lost;                    25
   A sister driven into desperate terms,
   Whose worth, if praises may go back again,
   Stood challenger on mount of[7] all the age
   For her perfections: but my revenge will come.
KING.  Break not your sleeps for that: you must not think      30
   That we are made of stuff so flat and dull
   That we can let our beard be shook with danger
   And think it pastime. You shortly shall hear more:
   I loved your father, and we love ourself;
   And that, I hope, will teach you to imagine—            35
     [*Enter a* MESSENGER, *with letters.*]
   How now! what news?
MESSENGER.                    Letters, my lord, from Hamlet:
   This to your majesty; this to the queen.
KING.  From Hamlet! who brought them?
MESSENGER.  Sailors, my lord, they say; I saw them not:
   They were given me by Claudio; he received them
   Of him that brought them.
KING.                         Laertes, you shall hear them.    41
   Leave us.                        [*Exit* MESSENGER.]
   [*Reads*] 'High and mighty, you shall know I am set naked on your
   kingdom. To-morrow shall I beg leave to see your kingly eyes:
   when I shall, first asking your pardon thereunto, recount the occa-
   sion of my sudden and more strange return.    HAMLET.'
   What should this mean? Are all the rest come back?         42
   Or is it some abuse, and no such thing?[8]
LAERTES.  Know you the hand?
KING.  'Tis Hamlet's character.[9] 'Naked'!                     45
   And in a postscript here, he says 'alone.'
   Can you advise me?
LAERTES.  I'm lost in it, my lord. But let him come;
   It warms the very sickness in my heart,
   That I shall live and tell him to his teeth,                50
   'Thus diddest thou.'
KING.                        If it be so, Laertes,—
   As how should it be so? how otherwise?—
   Will you be ruled by me?
LAERTES.                        Aye, my lord;
   So you will not o'errule me to a peace.
KING.  To thine own peace. If he be now return'd,              55
   As checking[1] at his voyage, and that he means
   No more to undertake it, I will work him

---

7. Above. *Go back*: I.e., to what she was before her madness.    8. A delusion, not a reality.
9. Handwriting.    1. Changing the course of, refusing to continue.

To an exploit now ripe in my device,
Under the which he shall not choose but fall:
And for his death no wind of blame shall breathe;                    60
But even his mother shall uncharge the practice,[2]
And call it accident.

LAERTES.                    My lord, I will be ruled;
    The rather, if you could devise it so
    That I might be the organ.[3]

KING.                    It falls right.
    You have been talk'd of since your travel much,                  65
    And that in Hamlet's hearing, for a quality
    Wherein, they say, you shine; your sum of parts[4]
    Did not together pluck such envy from him,
    As did that one, and that in my regard
    Of the unworthiest siege.[5]

LAERTES.                    What part is that, my lord?              70

KING. A very riband in the cap of youth,
    Yet needful too; for youth no less becomes[6]
    The light and careless livery that it wears
    Than settled age his sables and his weeds,[7]
    Importing health and graveness. Two months since                75
    Here was a gentleman of Normandy:—
    I've seen myself, and served against, the French,
    And they can well on horseback: but this gallant
    Had witchcraft in 't; he grew unto his seat,
    And to such wondrous doing brought this horse                    80
    As had he been incorpsed and demi-natured[8]
    With the brave beast: so far he topp'd my thought
    That I, in forgery of shapes and tricks,[9]
    Come short of what he did.

LAERTES.                    A Norman was 't?

KING. A Norman.                                                      85

LAERTES. Upon my life, Lamord.

KING.                    The very same.

LAERTES. I know him well: he is the brooch[1] indeed
    And gem of all the nation.

KING. He made confession of you,
    And gave you such a masterly report,                             90
    For art and exercise in your defense,[2]
    And for your rapier most especial,
    That he cried out, 'twould be a sight indeed

---

2. Not recognize it as a plot.    3. Instrument.    4. The sum of your gifts.    5. Seat, i.e.,
rank.    6. Is the appropriate age for. *Riband*: Ribbon, ornament.    7. Furs (also meaning
"blacks," dark colors) and robes.    8. Incorporated and split his nature in two.    9. In imagining methods and skills of horsemanship.    1. Ornament.    2. Report of your mastery in the
theory and practice of fencing.

If one could match you: the scrimers[3] of their nation,
He swore, had neither motion, guard, nor eye,                    95
If you opposed them. Sir, this report of his
Did Hamlet so unvenom with his envy
That he could nothing do but wish and beg
Your sudden coming o'er, to play with him.
Now, out of this—

LAERTES.                    What out of this, my lord?          100

KING. Laertes, was your father dear to you?
  Or are you like the painting of a sorrow,
  A face without a heart?

LAERTES.                         Why ask you this?

KING. Not that I think you did not love your father,
  But that I know love is begun by time,                         105
  And that I see, in passages of proof,[4]
  Time qualifies the spark and fire of it.
  There lives within the very flame of love
  A kind of wick or snuff[5] that will abate it;
  And nothing is at a like goodness still,                       110
  For goodness, growing to a plurisy,[6]
  Dies in his own too much: that we would do
  We should do when we would; for this 'would' changes
  And hath abatements and delays as many
  As there are tongues, are hands, are accidents,                115
  And then this 'should' is like a spendthrift sigh,
  That hurts by easing.[7] But, to the quick o' the ulcer:
  Hamlet comes back: what would you undertake,
  To show yourself your father's son in deed
  More than in words?

LAERTES.                    To cut his throat i' the church.     120

KING. No place indeed should murder sanctuarize;
  Revenge should have no bounds. But, good Laertes,
  Will you do this, keep close within your chamber.
  Hamlet return'd shall know you are come home:
  We'll put on[8] those shall praise your excellence            125
  And set a double varnish on the fame
  The Frenchman gave you; bring you in fine together
  And wager on your heads: he, being remiss,[9]
  Most generous and free from all contriving,
  Will not peruse[1] the foils, so that with ease,             130
  Or with a little shuffling, you may choose

---

3. Fencers.    4. Instances which prove it. *Qualifies*: Weakens.    5. Charred part of the wick.
6. Excess of blood. *Still*: Constantly.    7. A sigh which gives relief but is harmful (according to
an old notion that it draws blood from the heart).    8. Instigate.    9. Careless. *In fine*:
Finally.    1. Examine closely.

A sword unbated, and in a pass of practice[2]
Requite him for your father.

LAERTES.                    I will do 't;
  And for that purpose I'll anoint my sword.
  I bought an unction of a mountebank,[3]                135
  So mortal that but dip a knife in it,
  Where it draws blood no cataplasm[4] so rare,
  Collected from all simples[5] that have virtue
  Under the moon, can save the thing from death
  That is but scratch'd withal: I'll touch my point      140
  With this contagion, that, if I gall[6] him slightly,
  It may be death.

KING.             Let's further think of this;
  Weigh what convenience both of time and means
  May fit us to our shape:[7] if this should fail,
  And that our drift look through[8] our bad performance,    145
  'Twere better not assay'd: therefore this project
  Should have a back or second, that might hold
  If this did blast in proof.[9] Soft! let me see:
  We'll make a solemn wager on your cunnings:
  I ha 't:                                       150
  When in your motion you are hot and dry—
  As make your bouts more violent to that end—
  And that he calls for drink, I'll have prepared him
  A chalice for the nonce;[1] whereon but sipping,
  If he by chance escape your venom'd stuck,[2]        155
  Our purpose may hold there. But stay, what noise?

      [*Enter* QUEEN.]

  How now, sweet queen!

QUEEN. One woe doth tread upon another's heel,
  So fast they follow: your sister's drown'd, Laertes.

LAERTES. Drown'd! O, where?                         160

QUEEN. There is a willow grows aslant[3] a brook,
  That shows his hoar leaves in the glassy stream;
  There with fantastic garlands did she come
  Of crow-flowers, nettles, daisies, and long purples,
  That liberal shepherds give a grosser name,           165
  But our cold maids do dead men's fingers call them:
  There, on the pendent boughs her coronet weeds
  Clambering to hang, an envious sliver[4] broke;
  When down her weedy trophies and herself

---

2. Treacherous thrust. *Unbated:* Not blunted (as a rapier for exercise ordinarily would be).
3. Ointment of a peddler of quack medicines.  4. Plaster.  5. Healing herbs.
6. Scratch.  7. Plan.  8. Our design should show through.   9. Burst (like a new firearm)
once it is put to the test.  1. For that particular occasion.  2. Thrust.  3. Across.
4. Malicious bough.

Fell in the weeping brook. Her clothes spread wide,                    170
And mermaid-like a while they bore her up:
Which time she chanted snatches of old tunes,
As one incapable of[5] her own distress,
Or like a creature native and indued[6]
Unto that element: but long it could not be                           175
Till that her garments, heavy with their drink,
Pull'd the poor wretch from her melodious lay
To muddy death.
LAERTES.                    Alas, then she is drown'd!
QUEEN. Drown'd, drown'd.
LAERTES. Too much of water hast thou, poor Ophelia,                    180
And therefore I forbid my tears: but yet
It is our trick;[7] nature her custom holds,
Let shame say what it will: when these are gone,
The woman[8] will be out. Adieu, my lord:
I have a speech of fire that fain would blaze,                         185
But that this folly douts[9] it.                          [*Exit.*]
KING.                              Let's follow, Gertrude:
How much I had to do to calm his rage!
Now fear I this will give it start again;
Therefore let's follow.                                  [*Exeunt.*]

## Act V

### SCENE 1—*A churchyard.*

[*Enter two* CLOWNS, *with spades, &c.*]
FIRST CLOWN. Is she to be buried in Christian burial that willfully
    seeks her own salvation?
SECOND CLOWN. I tell thee she is; and therefore make her grave straight:
    the crowner[1] hath sat on her, and finds it Christian burial.
FIRST CLOWN. How can that be, unless she drowned herself in her
    own defense?
SECOND CLOWN. Why, 'tis found so.
FIRST CLOWN. It must be 'se offendendo;'[2] it cannot be else. For here
    lies the point: if I drown myself wittingly, it argues an act: and an
    act hath three branches; it is, to act, to do, to perform: argal,[3] she
    drowned herself wittingly.
SECOND CLOWN. Nay, but hear you, goodman delver.
FIRST CLOWN. Give me leave. Here lies the water; good: here stands
    the man; good: if the man go to this water and drown himself, it
    is, will he, nill he,[4] he goes; mark you that; but if the water come

5. Insensitive to.    6. Adapted, in harmony with.    7. Peculiar trait.    8. The softer qualities, the woman in me.    9. Extinguishes.    1. Coroner. *Straight:* Right away.    2. The
Clown's blunder for *se defendendo,* "in self-defense."    3. Blunder for *ergo,* "therefore."
4. Willy-nilly.

to him and drown him, he drowns not himself: argal, he that is not guilty of his own death shortens not his own life.

SECOND CLOWN. But is this law?

FIRST CLOWN. Aye, marry, is 't; crowner's quest[5] law.

SECOND CLOWN. Will you ha' the truth on 't? If this had not been a gentlewoman, she should have been buried out o' Christian burial.

FIRST CLOWN. Why, there thou say'st: and the more pity that great folk should have countenance[6] in this world to drown or hang themselves, more than their even Christian.[7] Come, my spade. There is no ancient gentlemen but gardeners, ditchers and gravemakers: they hold up Adam's profession.

SECOND CLOWN. Was he a gentleman?

FIRST CLOWN. A' was the first that ever bore arms.

SECOND CLOWN. Why, he had none.

FIRST CLOWN. What, art a heathen? How dost thou understand the Scripture? The Scripture says Adam digged: could he dig without arms? I'll put another question to thee: if thou answerest me not to the purpose, confess thyself—

SECOND CLOWN. Go to.

FIRST CLOWN. What is he that builds stronger than either the mason, the shipwright, or the carpenter?

SECOND CLOWN. The gallows-maker; for that frame outlives a thousand tenants.

FIRST CLOWN. I like thy wit well, in good faith: the gallows does well; but how does it well? it does well to those that do ill: now, thou dost ill to say the gallows is built stronger than the church: argal, the gallows may do well to thee. To 't again, come.

SECOND CLOWN. 'Who builds stronger than a mason, a shipwright, or a carpenter?'

FIRST CLOWN. Aye, tell me that, and unyoke.[8]

SECOND CLOWN. Marry, now I can tell.

FIRST CLOWN. To 't.

SECOND CLOWN. Mass, I cannot tell.

[*Enter* HAMLET *and* HORATIO, *afar off.*]

FIRST CLOWN. Cudgel thy brains no more about it, for your dull ass will not mend his pace with beating, and when you are asked this question next, say 'a grave-maker:' the houses that he makes last till doomsday. Go, get thee to Yaughan; fetch me a stoup[9] of liquor.

[*Exit* SECOND CLOWN.—FIRST CLOWN *digs and sings.*]

In youth, when I did love, did love,
　　Methought it was very sweet,

5. Inquest.　6. Sanction.　7. Fellow Christian.　8. Call it a day.　9. Mug. *Yaughan:* Apparently a tavern-keeper's name.

To contract, O, the time, for-a my behove,[1]
   O, methought, there-a was nothing-a meet.[2]

HAMLET. Has this fellow no feeling of his business that he sings at grave-making?

HORATIO. Custom hath made it in him a property of easiness.[3]

HAMLET. 'Tis e'en so: the hand of little employment hath the daintier[4] sense.

FIRST CLOWN. [*Sings*] But age, with his stealing steps,
              Hath clow'd me in his clutch,
              And hath shipped me intil[5] the land,
              As if I had never been such.

[*Throws up a skull.*]

HAMLET. That skull had a tongue in it, and could sing once: how the knave jowls[6] it to the ground, as if it were Cain's jaw-bone, that did the first murder! It might be the pate of a politician,[7] which this ass now o'er-reaches;[8] one that would circumvent God, might it not?

HORATIO. It might, my lord.

HAMLET. Or of a courtier, which could say, 'Good morrow, sweet lord! How dost thou, sweet lord?' This might be my lord such-a-one, that praised my lord such-a-one's horse, when he meant to beg it; might it not?

HORATIO. Aye, my lord.

HAMLET. Why, e'en so: and now my Lady Worm's; chapless, and knocked about the mazzard[9] with a sexton's spade: here's fine revolution, an we had the trick[1] to see 't. Did these bones cost no more the breeding, but to play at loggats[2] with 'em? mine ache to think on 't.

FIRST CLOWN. [*Sings*] A pick-axe, and a spade, a spade,
              For a shrouding sheet:
              O, a pit of clay for to be made
              For such a guest is meet.

[*Throws up another skull.*]

HAMLET. There's another: why may not that be the skull of a lawyer? Where be his quiddities now, his quillets, his cases, his tenures,[3] and his tricks? why does he suffer this rude knave now to knock him about the sconce with a dirty shovel, and will not tell him of his action of battery?[4] Hum! This fellow might be in 's time a great buyer of land, with his statutes, his recognizances,[5] his fines, his

---

1. Profit. *Contract:* Shorten.   2. Fitting.   3. Has made it a matter of indifference to him.
4. Finer sensitivity. *Of little employment:* Which does little labor.   5. Into.   6. Knocks.
7. The word has a pejorative sense. *First murder:* Possible an allusion to the legend according to which Cain slew Abel with an ass's jawbone.   8. Outwits.   9. Pate. *Chapless:* The lower jawbone missing.   1. Faculty.   2. A game resembling bowls.   3. Real-estate holdings. *Quiddities:* Subtle definitions. *Quillets:* Quibbles.   4. Assault. *Sconce:* Head.   5. Varieties of bonds. Following are legal terms relating to the transfer of estates.

double vouchers, his recoveries: is this the fine[6] of his fines and the recovery of his recoveries, to have his fine pate full of fine dirt? will his vouchers vouch him no more of his purchases, and double ones too, than the length and breadth of a pair of indentures? The very conveyances[7] of his lands will hardly lie in this box; and must the inheritor himself have no more, ha?

HORATIO. Not a jot more, my lord.

HAMLET. Is not parchment made of sheep-skins?

HORATIO. Aye, my lord, and of calf-skins too.

HAMLET. They are sheep and calves which seek out assurance[8] in that. I will speak to this fellow. Whose grave's this, sirrah?

FIRST CLOWN. Mine, sir.

[*Sings*] O, a pit of clay for to be made
    For such a guest is meet.

HAMLET. I think it be thine indeed, for thou liest in 't.

FIRST CLOWN. You lie out on 't, sir, and therefore 'tis not yours: for my part, I do not lie in 't, and yet it is mine.

HAMLET. Thou dost lie in 't, to be in 't and say it is thine: 'tis for the dead, not for the quick;[9] therefore thou liest.

FIRST CLOWN. 'Tis a quick lie, sir; 'twill away again, from me to you.

HAMLET. What man dost thou dig it for?

FIRST CLOWN. For no man, sir.

HAMLET. What woman then?

FIRST CLOWN. For none neither.

HAMLET. Who is to be buried in 't?

FIRST CLOWN. One that was a woman, sir; but, rest her soul, she's dead.

HAMLET. How absolute the knave is! we must speak by the card,[1] or equivocation will undo us. By the Lord, Horatio, these three years I have taken note of it; the age is grown so picked that the toe of the peasant comes so near the heel of the courtier, he galls his kibe.[3] How long hast thou been a grave-maker?

FIRST CLOWN. Of all the days i' the year, I came to 't that day that our last King Hamlet o'ercame Fortinbras.

HAMLET. How long is that since?

FIRST CLOWN. Cannot you tell that? every fool can tell that: it was that very day that young Hamlet was born: he that is mad, and sent into England.

HAMLET. Aye, marry, why was he sent into England?

FIRST CLOWN. Why, because a' was mad; a' shall recover his wits there: or, if a' do not, 'tis no great matter there.

6. End. Hamlet is punning on the legal and nonlegal meanings of the word.   7. Deeds. *Indentures:* Contracts drawn in duplicate on the same piece of parchment, the two copies separated by an "indented" line.   8. Security; another pun, since the word is also a legal term. 9. Living.   1. By the chart, i.e., exactness. *Absolute:* Positive.   2. Choice, fastidious. 3. Hurts the chilblain on the courtier's heel.

HAMLET. Why?

FIRST CLOWN. 'Twill not be seen in him there; there the men are as mad as he.

HAMLET. How came he mad?

FIRST CLOWN. Very strangely, they say.

HAMLET. How 'strangely'?

FIRST CLOWN. Faith, e'en with losing his wits.

HAMLET. Upon what ground?

FIRST CLOWN. Why, here in Denmark: I have been sexton here, man and boy, thirty years.

HAMLET. How long will a man lie i' the earth ere he rot?

FIRST CLOWN. I' faith, if a' be not rotten before a' die—as we have many pocky corses now-a-days, that will scarce hold the laying in[4]—a' will last you some eight year or nine year: a tanner will last you nine year.

HAMLET. Why he more than another?

FIRST CLOWN. Why, sir, his hide is so tanned with his trade that a' will keep out water a great while; and your water is a sore decayer of your whoreson dead body. Here's a skull now: this skull has lain in the earth three and twenty years.

HAMLET. Whose was it?

FIRST CLOWN. A whoreson mad fellow's it was: whose do you think it was?

HAMLET. Nay, I know not.

FIRST CLOWN. A pestilence on him for a mad rogue! a' poured a flagon of Rhenish on my head once. This same skull, sir, was Yorick's skull, the king's jester.

HAMLET. This?

FIRST CLOWN. E'en that.

HAMLET. Let me see. [*Takes the skull.*] Alas, poor Yorick! I knew him, Horatio: a fellow of infinite jest, of most excellent fancy: he hath borne me on his back a thousand times; and now how abhorred in my imagination it is! my gorge rises at it. Here hung those lips that I have kissed I know not how oft. Where be your gibes now? your gambols? your songs? your flashes of merriment, that were wont to set the table on a roar? Not one now, to mock your own grinning? quite chop-fallen?[6] Now get you to my lady's chamber, and tell her, let her paint an inch thick, to this favor[7] she must come; make her laugh at that. Prithee, Horatio, tell me one thing.

HORATIO. What's that, my lord?

HAMLET. Dost thou think Alexander looked o' this fashion i' the earth?

HORATIO. E'en so.

HAMLET. And smelt so? pah!                              [*Puts down the skull.*]

4. Hold together till they are buried. *Pocky:* With marks of disease (from "pox").   5. Rhine wine.   6. The lower jaw fallen down, hence dejected.   7. Appearance.

HORATIO. E'en so, my lord.

HAMLET. To what base uses we may return, Horatio! Why may not imagination trace the noble dust of Alexander, till he find it stopping a bung-hole?

HORATIO. 'Twere to consider too curiously, to consider so.

HAMLET. No, faith, not a jot; but to follow him thither with modesty enough[8] and likelihood to lead it: as thus: Alexander died, Alexander was buried, Alexander returneth into dust; the dust is earth; of earth we make loam; and why of that loam, whereto he was converted, might they not stop a beer-barrel?

> Imperious Caesar, dead and turn'd to clay,    1
> Might stop a hole to keep the wind away:
> O, that that earth, which kept the world in awe,
> Should patch a wall to expel the winter's flaw!

But soft! but soft! aside: here comes the king.    5

[*Enter* PRIESTS *&c, in procession; the Corpse of Ophelia,* LAERTES *and* MOURNERS *following;* KING, QUEEN, *their trains, &c.*]

The queen, the courtiers: who is this they follow?
And with such maimèd rites?[9] This doth betoken
The corse they follow did with desperate hand
Fordo its own life: 'twas of some estate.[1]
Couch we awhile, and mark.    10

[*Retiring with* HORATIO.]

LAERTES. What ceremony else?

HAMLET. That is Laertes, a very noble youth: mark.

LAERTES. What ceremony else?

FIRST PRIEST. Her obsequies have been as far enlarged
As we have warranty: her death was doubtful;    15
And, but that great command o'ersways the order[2]
She should in ground unsanctified have lodged
Till the last trumpet; for[3] charitable prayers,
Shards, flints and pebbles should be thrown on her:
Yet here she is allow'd her virgin crants,    20
Her maiden strewments and the bringing home[4]
Of bell and burial.

LAERTES. Must there no more be done?

FIRST PRIEST.                    No more be done:
We should profane the service of the dead
To sing a requiem and such rest to her    25
As to peace-parted souls.

LAERTES.              Lay her i' the earth:

---

8. Without exaggeration.   9. Incomplete, mutilated ritual.   1. Rank. *Fordo:* Destroy. 2. The king's command prevails against ordinary rules. *Doubtful:* Of uncertain cause (i.e., accident or suicide).   3. Instead of.   4. Laying to rest. *Crants:* Garland. *Strewments:* Strewing of the grave with flowers.

And from her fair and unpolluted flesh
May violets spring! I tell thee, churlish priest,
A ministering angel shall my sister be,
When thou liest howling.
HAMLET.                              What, the fair Ophelia!                30
QUEEN. [*Scattering flowers*] Sweets to the sweet: farewell!
  I hoped thou shouldst have been my Hamlet's wife;
  I thought thy bride-bed to have deck'd, sweet maid,
  And not have strew'd thy grave.
LAERTES.                              O, treble woe
  Fall ten times treble on that cursed head                           35
  Whose wicked deed thy most ingenious sense
  Deprived thee of! Hold off the earth a while,
  Till I have caught her once more in mine arms.
      [*Leaps into the grave.*]
  Now pile your dust upon the quick and dead,
  Till of this flat a mountain you have made                          40
  To o'ertop old Pelion[5] or the skyish head
  Of blue Olympus.
HAMLET. [*Advancing*] What is he whose grief
  Bears such an emphasis? whose phrase of sorrow
  Conjures the wandering stars and makes them stand                   45
  Like wonder-wounded hearers? This is I,
  Hamlet the Dane.                            [*Leaps into the grave.*]
LAERTES. The devil take thy soul!            [*Grappling with him.*]
HAMLET.                              Thou pray'st not well.
  I prithee, take thy fingers from my throat;
  For, though I am not splenitive[6] and rash,                        50
  Yet have I in me something dangerous,
  Which let thy wisdom fear. Hold off thy hand.
KING. Pluck them asunder.
QUEEN.                              Hamlet, Hamlet!
ALL.                                          Gentlemen,—
HORATIO. Good my lord, be quiet.
      [*The* ATTENDANTS *part them, and they come out of the grave.*]
HAMLET. Why, I will fight with him upon this theme                    55
  Until my eyelids will no longer wag.
QUEEN. O my son, what theme?
HAMLET. I loved Ophelia: forty thousand brothers
  Could not, with all their quantity of love,
  Make up my sum. What wilt thou do for her?                          60
KING. O, he is mad, Laertes.
QUEEN. For love of God, forbear him.

5. The mountain upon which the Aloadae, two rebellious giants in Greek mythology, piled up
Mount Ossa in their attempt to reach Olympus.   6. Easily moved to anger.

HAMLET. 'Swounds, show me what thou 'lt do:
    Woo't weep? woo't fight? woo't fast? woo't tear thyself?
    Woo't drink up eisel?[7] eat a crocodile?               65
    I'll do't. Dost thou come here to whine?
    To outface me with leaping in her grave?
    Be buried quick with her, and so will I:
    And, if thou prate of mountains, let them throw
    Millions of acres on us, till our ground,           70
    Singeing his pate against the burning zone,
    Make Ossa like a wart! Nay, an thou 'lt mouth,
    I'll rant as well as thou.
QUEEN.                    This is mere madness:
    And thus a while the fit will work on him;
    Anon, as patient as the female dove           75
    When that her golden couplets are disclosed,[8]
    His silence will sit dropping.
HAMLET.                 Hear you, sir;
    What is the reason that you use me thus?
    I loved you ever: but it is no matter;
    Let Hercules himself do what he may,           80
    The cat will mew, and dog will have his day.      [Exit.]
KING. I pray thee, good Horatio, wait upon him.
    [Exit HORATIO.]
    [To LAERTES] Strengthen your patience in our last night's speech;
    We'll put the matter to the present push.[9]
    Good Gertrude, set some watch over your son.     85
    This grave shall have a living monument:
    An hour of quiet shortly shall we see;
    Till then, in patience our proceeding be.      [Exeunt.]


SCENE 2—A *hall in the castle*.

    [*Enter* HAMLET *and* HORATIO.]
HAMLET. So much for this, sir: now shall you see the other;
    You do remember all the circumstance?
HORATIO. Remember it, my lord?
HAMLET. Sir, in my heart there was a kind of fighting,
    That would not let me sleep: methought I lay     5
    Worse than the mutines in the bilboes.[1] Rashly,
    And praised be rashness for it, let us know,
    Our indiscretion sometime serves us well

---

7. Vinegar (the bitter drink given to Christ). *Woo't:* Wilt thou.    8. Twins are hatched.
9. We will push the matter on immediately.    1. Mutineers in iron fetters.

When our deep plots do pall;[2] and that should learn us
There's a divinity that shapes our ends,                              10
Rough-hew them how we will.
HORATIO.                                    That is most certain.
HAMLET. Up from my cabin,
    My sea-gown scarf'd about me, in the dark
    Groped I to find out them; had my desire,
    Finger'd their packet, and in fine withdrew               15
    To mine own room again; making so bold,
    My fears forgetting manners, to unseal
    Their grand commission; where I found, Horatio,—
    O royal knavery!—an exact command,
    Larded with many several sorts of reasons,                20
    Importing[3] Denmark's health and England's too,
    With, ho! such bugs and goblins in my life,
    That, on the supervise, no leisure bated,[4]
    No, not to stay the grinding of the axe,
    My head should be struck off.
HORATIO.                                    Is't possible?                 25
HAMLET. Here's the commission: read it at more leisure.
    But wilt thou hear now how I did proceed?
HORATIO. I beseech you.
HAMLET. Being thus be-netted round with villainies,—
    Ere I could make a prologue to my brains,                 30
    They had begun the play,—I sat me down;
    Devised a new commission; wrote it fair:
    I once did hold it, as our statists[5] do,
    A baseness to write fair, and labor'd much
    How to forget that learning; but, sir, now                35
    It did me yeoman's service:[6] wilt thou know
    The effect of what I wrote?
HORATIO.                               Aye, good my lord.
HAMLET. An earnest conjuration from the king,
    As England was his faithful tributary,
    As love between them like the palm might flourish,        40
    As peace should still her wheaten garland wear
    And stand a comma[7] 'tween their amities,
    And many such-like 'As'es[8] of great charge,
    That, on the view and knowing of these contents,
    Without debatement further, more or less,                 45
    He should the bearers put to sudden death,

---

2. Become useless.    3. Concerning.    4. As soon as the message was read, with no time sub-
tracted for leisure. *Bugs:* Bugbears.    5. Statesmen.    6. Excellent service.    7. Connecting
element.    8. A pun on "as" and "ass," which extends to the following *of great charge,* signifying
both "moral weight," and "ass's burden."

Not shriving-time[9] allow'd.

HORATIO.                      How was this seal'd?

HAMLET. Why, even in that was heaven ordinant.
  I had my father's signet in my purse,
  Which was the model of that Danish seal:                 50
  Folded the writ up in the form of the other;
  Subscribed it; gave 't the impression;[2] placed it sefely,
  The changeling never known. Now, the next day
  Was our sea-fight; and what to this was sequent
  Thou know'st already.                               55

HORATIO. So Guildenstern and Rosencrantz go to 't.

HAMLET. Why, man, they did make love to this employment;
  They are not near my conscience; their defeat
  Does by their own insinuation[3] grow:
  'Tis dangerous when the baser nature comes           60
  Between the pass and fell[4]-incensèd points
  Of mighty opposites.

HORATIO.                 Why, what a king is this!

HAMLET. Does it not, think'st thee, stand me now upon[5]—
  He that hath kill'd my king, and whored my mother;
  Popp'd in between the election and my hopes;          65
  Thrown out his angle for my proper life,[6]
  And with such cozenage—is't not perfect conscience,
  To quit[7] him with this arm? and is't not to be damn'd,
  To let this canker of our nature come
  In further evil?                            70

HORATIO. It must be shortly known to him from England
  What is the issue of the business there.

HAMLET. It will be short: the interim is mine;
  And a man's life's no more than to say 'One.'
  But I am very sorry, good Horatio,               75
  That to Laertes I forgot myself;
  For, by the image of my cause, I see
  The portraiture of his: I'll court his favors:
  But, sure, the bravery[8] of his grief did put me
  Into a towering passion.

HORATIO.               Peace! who comes here?      80

     [*Enter* OSRIC.]

OSRIC. Your lordship is right welcome back to Denmark.

HAMLET. I humbly thank you, sir. Dost know this waterfly?

HORATIO. No, my good lord.

HAMLET. Thy state is the more gracious, for 'tis a vice to know him.

9. Time for confession and absolution.   1. Ordaining.   2. Of the seal.   3. Meddling. *Defeat:* Destruction.   4. Fiercely. *Pass:* Thrust. *Baser:* Lower in rank than the King and Prince Hamlet.   5. Is it not my duty now?   6. Angling line for my own life.   7. Pay back. 8. Ostentation, bravado.

He hath much land, and fertile: let a beast be lord of beasts, and
his crib shall stand at the king's mess: 'tis a chough,[9] but, as I say,
spacious in the possession of dirt.

OSRIC. Sweet lord, if your lordship were at leisure, I should impart a
thing to you from his majesty.

HAMLET. I will receive it, sir, with all diligence of spirit. Put your
bonnet to his right use; 'tis for the head.

OSRIC. I thank your lordship, it is very hot.

HAMLET. No, believe me, 'tis very cold; the wind is northerly.

OSRIC. It is indifferent[1] cold, my lord, indeed.

HAMLET. But yet methinks it is very sultry and hot, or my complexion—

OSRIC. Exceedingly, my lord; it is very sultry, as 'twere,—I cannot
tell how. But, my lord, his majesty bade me signify to you that he
has laid a great wager on your head: sir, this is the matter—

HAMLET. I beseech you, remember—

 [HAMLET *moves him to put on his hat.*]

OSRIC. Nay, good my lord; for mine ease, in good faith. Sir, here is
newly come to court Laertes; believe me, an absolute gentleman,
full of most excellent differences, of very soft society and great
showing:[2] indeed, to speak feelingly of him, he is the card or calendar of gentry, for you shall find in him the continent of[3] what part
a gentleman would see.

HAMLET. Sir, his definement suffers no perdition[4] in you; though, I
know, to divide him inventorially would dizzy the arithmetic[5] of
memory, and yet but yaw neither,[6] in respect of his quick sail. But
in the verity of extolment,[7] I take him to be a soul of great article,
and his infusion of such dearth and rareness, as, to make true
diction of him, his semblable is his mirror, and who else would
trace him, his umbrage,[8] nothing more.

OSRIC. Your lordship speaks most infallibly of him.

HAMLET. The concernancy, sir? why do we wrap the gentleman[9] in
our more rawer breath?

OSRIC. Sir?

HORATIO. Is 't not possible to understand in another tongue?[1] You
will do 't, sir, really.

HAMLET. What imports the nomination of this gentleman?

OSRIC. Of Laertes?

HORATIO. His purse is empty already; all's golden words are spent.

---

9. Jackdaw. *Mess:* Table.    1. Fairly.    2. Agreeable company, and handsome in appearance.
*Differences:* Distinctions.    3. Container. *Card or calendar of gentry:* Chart and model of gentlemanly manners. *What part:* Whatever quality.    4. Loss. *Definement:* Definition.
5. Arithmetical power. *Inventorially:* Make an inventory of his virtues.    6. And yet would only
be able to steer unsteadily (unable to catch up with the "sail" of Laertes' virtues).    7. To prize
Laertes truthfully. *Article:* Importance. *Infusion:* The virtues fused into him.    8. Keep pace
with him, his shadow.    9. Laertes. *Concernancy:* Meaning.    1. In a less affected jargon; or,
in the same jargon when spoken by another (i.e., Hamlet's) tongue.

HAMLET. Of him, sir.

OSRIC. I know you are not ignorant—

HAMLET. I would you did, sir; yet, in faith, if you did, it would not much approve me.[2] Well, sir?

OSRIC. You are not ignorant of what excellence Laertes is—

HAMLET. I dare not confess that, lest I should compare with him in excellence; but, to know a man well, were to know himself.[3]

OSRIC. I mean, sir, for his weapon; but in the imputation laid on him by them, in his meed he's unfellowed.[4]

HAMLET. What's his weapon?

OSRIC. Rapier and dagger.

HAMLET. That's two of his weapons: but, well.

OSRIC. The king, sir, hath wagered with him six Barbary horses: against the which he has imponed, as I take it, six French rapiers and poniards, with their assigns,[5] as girdle, hanger, and so: three of the carriages, in faith, are very dear to fancy, very responsive[6] to the hilts, most delicate carriages, and of very liberal conceit.[7]

HAMLET. What call you the carriages?

HORATIO. I knew you must be edified by the margent[8] ere you had done.

OSRIC. The carriages, sir, are the hangers.

HAMLET. The phrase would be more germane to the matter if we could carry a cannon by our sides:[9] I would it might be hangers till then. But, on: six Barbary horses against six French swords, their assigns, and three liberal-conceited carriages; that's the French bet against the Danish. Why is this 'imponed,' as you call it?

OSRIC. The king, sir, hath laid, sir, that in a dozen passes between yourself and him, he shall not exceed you three hits: he hath laid on twelve for nine; and it would come to immediate trial, if your lordship would vouchasfe the answer.[1]

HAMLET. How if I answer 'no'?

OSRIC. I mean, my lord, the opposition of your person in trial.

HAMLET. Sir, I will walk here in the hall: if it please his majesty, it is the breathing time[2] of day with me; let the foils be brought, the gentleman willing, and the king hold his purpose, I will win for him an I can; if not, I will gain nothing but my shame and the odd hits.

OSRIC. Shall I redeliver you e'en so?[3]

HAMLET. To this effect, sir, after what flourish your nature will.

---

2. Be to my credit.    3. To know others one has to know oneself.    4. In the reputation given him by his weapons, his merit is unparalleled.    5. Appendages. *Imponed:* Wagered. 6. Corresponding, closely matched. *Carriages:* Ornamented straps by which the rapiers hung from the belt. *Very dear to fancy:* Agreeable to the taste.    7. Elegant design.    8. Instructed by the marginal note.    9. Hamlet is playfully criticizing Osric's affected application of the term "carriage," more properly used to mean "gun carriage."    1. "The passage is of no importance; it is sufficient that there was a wager." [Samuel Johnson.]    2. Time for exercise.    3. Is that the reply you want me to carry back?

OSRIC. I commend my duty to your lordship.

HAMLET. Yours, yours. [*Exit* OSRIC.] He does well to commend it himself; there are no tongues else for's turn.

HORATIO. This lapwing[4] runs away with the shell on his head.

HAMLET. He did comply[5] with his dug before he sucked it. Thus has he—and many more of the same breed that I know the drossy[6] age dotes on—only got the tune of the time and outward habit of encounter; a kind of yesty collection, which carries them through and through the most fond and winnowed opinions; and do but blow them to their trial, the bubbles are out.

[*Enter a* LORD.]

LORD. My lord, his majesty commended him[8] to you by young Osric, who brings back to him, that you attend him in the hall: he sends to know if your pleasure hold to play with Laertes, or that you will take longer time.

HAMLET. I am constant to my purposes; they follow the king's pleasure: if his fitness speaks, mine is ready; now or whensoever, provided I be so able as now.

LORD. The king and queen and all are coming down.

HAMLET. In happy time.

LORD. The queen desires you to use some gentle entertainment[9] to Laertes before you fall to play.

HAMLET. She well instructs me.                    [*Exit* LORD.]

HORATIO. You will lose this wager, my lord.

HAMLET. I do not think so; since he went into France, I have been in continual practice; I shall win at the odds. But thou wouldst not think how ill all's here about my heart: but it is no matter.

HORATIO. Nay, good my lord,—

HAMLET. It is but foolery; but it is such a kind of gaingiving[1] as would perhaps trouble a woman.

HORATIO. If your mind dislike anything, obey it. I will forestall their repair[2] hither, and say you are not fit.

HAMLET. Not a whit; we defy augury: there is special providence in the fall of a sparrow. If it be now, 'tis not to come; if it be not to come, it will be now; if it be not now, yet it will come: the readiness is all; since no man has aught of what he leaves, what is't to leave betimes?[3] Let be.

[*Enter* KING, QUEEN, LAERTES, *and* LORDS, OSRIC *and other* ATTENDANTS *with foils and gauntlets; a table and flagons of wine on it.*]

KING. Come, Hamlet, come, and take this hand from me.

---

4. A bird supposedly able to run as soon as it is out of its shell.   5. Use ceremony.
6. Degenerate. *Yesty:* Foamy.   7. Makes them pass the test of the most refined judgment.
8. Sent his regards.   9. Kind word of greeting.   1. Misgiving.   2. Coming.   3. What is wrong with dying early (leaving "betimes") since man knows nothing of life ("what he leaves")?

[*The* KING *puts* LAERTES' *hand into* HAMLET'S.]

HAMLET. Give me your pardon, sir: I've done you wrong;     81
  But pardon't, as you are a gentleman.
  This presence[4] knows,
  And you must needs have heard, how I am punish'd
  With sore distraction. What I have done,     85
  That might your nature, honor and exception[5]
  Roughly awake, I here proclaim was madness.
  Was't Hamlet wrong'd Laertes? Never Hamlet:
  If Hamlet from himself be ta'en away,
  And when he's not himself does wrong Laertes,     90
  Then Hamlet does it not, Hamlet denies it.
  Who does it then? His madness: if't be so,
  Hamlet is of the faction that is wrong'd;
  His madness is poor Hamlet's enemy.
  Sir, in this audience,     95
  Let my disclaiming from a purposed evil
  Free me so far in your most generous thoughts,
  That I have shot mine arrow o'er the house,
  And hurt my brother.

LAERTES.                I am satisfied in nature,
  Whose motive, in this case, should stir me most     100
  To my revenge: but in my terms of honor[6]
  I stand aloof, and will no reconcilement,
  Till by some elder masters of known honor
  I have a voice and precedent[7] of peace,
  To keep my name ungored.[8] But till that time     105
  I do receive your offer'd love like love
  And will not wrong it.

HAMLET.                I embrace it freely,
  And will this brother's wager frankly play.
  Give us the foils. Come on.

LAERTES.                Come, one for me.

HAMLET. I'll be your foil,[9] Laertes: in mine ignorance     110
  Your skill shall, like a star i' the darkest night,
  Stick fiery off[1] indeed.

LAERTES.                You mock me, sir.

HAMLET. No, by this hand.

KING. Give them the foils, young Osric. Cousin Hamlet,
  You know the wager?

HAMLET.                Very well, my lord;     115

---

4. Audience.    5. Objection.    6. Laertes answers separately each of the two points brought up by Hamlet in line 86; "nature" is Laertes' natural feeling toward his father, and "honor" the code of honor with its conventional rules.    7. Competent opinion based on precedent. 8. Unwounded.    9. A pun, since the word means both "rapier" and "a thing which sets off another to advantage" (as gold leaf under a jewel).    1. Stand out brilliantly.

Your grace has laid the odds o' the weaker side.
KING. I do not fear it; I have seen you both:
  But since he is better'd, we have therefore odds.
LAERTES. This is too heavy; let me see another.
HAMLET. This likes me well. These foils have all a length?    120
     [*They prepare to play.*]
OSRIC. Aye, my good lord.
KING. Set me the stoups[2] of wine upon that table.
  If Hamlet give the first or second hit,
  Or quit in answer of the third exchange,[3]
  Let all the battlements their ordnance fire;    125
  The king shall drink to Hamlet's better breath;
  And in the cup an union[4] shall he throw,
  Richer than that which four successive kings
  In Denmark's crown have worn. Give me the cups;
  And let the kettle[5] to the trumpet speak,    130
  The trumpet to the cannoneer without,
  The cannons to the heavens, the heaven to earth,
  'Now the king drinks to Hamlet.' Come, begin;
  And you, the judges, bear a wary eye.
HAMLET. Come on, sir.
LAERTES.              Come, my lord.         [*They play.*]
HAMLET.                     One.
LAERTES.                        No.
HAMLET.                             Judgment.
OSRIC. A hit, a very palpable hit.
LEARTES.                   Well; again.    136
KING. Stay; give me drink. Hamlet, this pearl is thine;
  Here's to thy health.
    [*Trumpets sound, and cannon shot off within.*]
                Give him the cup.
HAMLET. I'll play this bout first; set it by awhile.
  Come. [*They play.*] Another hit; what say you?    140
LAERTES. A touch, a touch, I do confess.
KING. Our son shall win.
QUEEN.              He's fat[6] and scant of breath.
  Here, Hamlet, take my napkin,[7] rub thy brows:
  The queen carouses to thy fortune, Hamlet.
HAMLET. Good madam!
KING.            Gertrude, do not drink.    145
QUEEN. I will, my lord; I pray you, pardon me.
KING. [*Aside*] It is the poison'd cup; it is too late.
QUEEN. Come, let me wipe thy face.

2. Cups.   3. Requite, or repay (by scoring a hit) on the third bout.   4. A large pearl.
5. Kettledrum.   6. Sweaty, or soft, because out of training.   7. Handkerchief.

LAERTES. My lord, I'll hit him now.

KING.                                    I do not think't.

LAERTES. [*Aside*] And yet it is almost against my conscience.        150

HAMLET. Come, for the third, Laertes: you but dally;
    I pray you, pass with your best violence;
    I am afeard you make a wanton[8] of me.

LAERTES. Say you so? come on.                        [*They play.*]

OSRIC. Nothing, neither way.                                    155

LAERTES. Have at you now!

    [LAERTES *wounds* HAMLET; *then, in scuffling, they change rapiers,*
    *and* HAMLET *wounds* LAERTES.]

KING.                        Part them; they are incensed.

HAMLET. Nay, come, again.                        [*The* QUEEN *falls.*]

OSRIC.                        Look to the queen there, ho!

HORATIO. They bleed on both sides. How is it, my lord?

OSRIC. How is't, Laertes?

LAERTES. Why, as a woodcock to mine own springe,[9] Osric;        160
    I am justly kill'd with mine own treachery.

HAMLET.                                How does the queen?

KING. She swounds to see them bleed.

QUEEN. No, no, the drink, the drink,—O my dear Hamlet,—
    The drink, the drink! I am poison'd.            [*Dies.*]

HAMLET. O villainy! Ho! let the door be lock'd:            165
    Treachery! seek it out.                        [LAERTES *falls.*]

LAERTES. It is here, Hamlet: Hamlet, thou art slain;
    No medicine in the world can do thee good,
    In thee there is not half an hour of life;
    The treacherous instrument is in thy hand,            170
    Unbated and envenom'd: the foul practice[1]
    Hath turn'd itself on me; lo, here I lie,
    Never to rise again: thy mother's poison'd:
    I can no more: the king, the king's to blame.

HAMLET. The point envenom'd too!                        175
    Then, venom, to thy work.                [*Stabs the* KING.]

ALL. Treason! treason!

KING. O, yet defend me, friends; I am but hurt.

HAMLET. Here, thou incestuous, murderous, damned Dane,
    Drink off this potion: is thy union here?            180
    Follow my mother.                        [KING *dies.*]

LAERTES.                        He is justly served;
    It is a poison temper'd[2] by himself.
    Exchange forgiveness with me, noble Hamlet:
    Mine and my father's death come not upon thee,

8. Weakling, spoiled child.   9. Snare.   1. Plot.   2. Compounded.

Nor thine on me!                                      185
        [*Dies.*]
HAMLET. Heaven make thee free of it! I follow thee.
    I am dead, Horatio. Wretched queen, adieu!
    You that look pale and tremble at this chance,
    That are but mutes or audience to this act,
    Had I but time—as this fell sergeant, death,       190
    Is strict in his arrest—O, I could tell you—
    But let it be. Horatio, I am dead;
    Thou livest; report me and my cause aright
    To the unsatisfied.
HORATIO.                    Never believe it:
    I am more an antique Roman than a Dane:            195
    Here's yet some liquor left.
HAMLET.                        As thou'rt a man,
    Give me the cup: let go; by heaven, I'll have 't.
    O good Horatio, what a wounded name,
    Things standing thus unknown, shall live behind me!
    If thou didst ever hold me in thy heart,           200
    Absent thee from felicity a while,
    And in this harsh world draw thy breath in pain,
    To tell my story.        [*March afar off, and shot within.*]
                    What warlike noise is this?
OSRIC. Young Fortinbras, with conquest come from Poland,
    To the ambassadors of England gives                205
    This warlike volley.
HAMLET.              O, I die, Horatio;
    The potent poison quite o'er-crows[3] my spirit:
    I cannot live to hear the news from England;
    But I do prophesy the election lights
    On Fortinbras: he has my dying voice;              210
    So tell him, with the occurrents, more and less,
    Which have solicited.[4] The rest is silence.    [*Dies.*]
HORATIO. Now cracks a noble heart. Good night sweet prince,
    And flights of angels sing thee to thy rest;    [*March within.*]
    Why does the drum come hither?                      215
        [*Enter* FORTINBRAS, *and the* ENGLISH AMBASSADORS, *with drum,
        colors, and* ATTENDANTS.]
FORTINBRAS. Where is this sight?
HORATIO.                        What is it you would see?
    If aught of woe or wonder, cease your search.
FORTINBRAS. This quarry cries on havoc.[5] O proud death,
    What feast is toward[6] in thine eternal cell,

3. Overcomes.    4. Which have brought all this about. *Occurrents:* Occurrences.    5. This
heap of corpses proclaims a carnage.    6. Imminent.

    That thou so many princes at a shot                    220
    So bloodily hast struck?
FIRST AMBASSADOR.           The sight is dismal;
    And our affairs from England come too late:
    The ears are senseless that should give us hearing,
    To tell him his commandment is fulfill'd,
    That Rosencrantz and Guildenstern are dead:           225
    Where should we have our thanks?
HORATIO.                 Not from his mouth
    Had it the ability of life to thank you:
    He never gave commandment for their death.
    But since, so jump upon[7] this bloody question,
    You from the Polack wars, and you from England      230
    Are here arrived, give order that these bodies
    High on a stage be placed to the view;
    And let me speak to the yet unknowing world
    How these things came about; so shall you hear
    Of carnal, bloody and unnatural acts,              235
    Of accidental judgments, casual slaughters,
    Of deaths put on[8] by cunning and forced cause,
    And, in this upshot, purposes mistook
    Fall'n on the inventors' heads: all this can I
    Truly deliver.
FORTINBRAS.       Let us haste to hear it,           240
    And call the noblest to the audience.
    For me, with sorrow I embrace my fortune:
    I have some rights of memory[9] in this kingdom,
    Which now to claim my vantage doth invite me.
HORATIO. Of that I shall have also cause to speak,      245
    And from his mouth whose voice will draw on more[1]:
    But let this same be presently perform'd,
    Even while men's minds are wild; lest more mischance
    On[2] plots and errors happen.
FORTINBRAS. Let four captains
    Bear Hamlet, like a soldier, to the stage;          250
    For he was likely, had he been put on,[3]
    To have proved most royally: and, for his passage,[4]
    The soldiers' music and the rites of war
    Speak loudly for him.
    Take up the bodies: such a sight as this          255

---

7. So immediately upon.   8. Prompted. *Casual*: Chance.   9. Still remembered. *Vantage*:
Advantageous position, opportunity.   1. More voices.   2. Following on.   3. Tried (as a
king).   4. Death.

Becomes the field, but here shows much amiss.
Go, bid the soldiers shoot.
> [*A dead march. Exeunt, bearing off the bodies: after which a
> peal of ordnance is shot off.*]

---

# JOHN DONNE
## 1572–1631

John Donne was born in London in 1572 in a Catholic family and attended
Oxford, Cambridge, and Lincoln's Inn (law school) without obtaining degrees
or becoming a lawyer. His intellectual energy, his voracious reading, his
wide traveling (including expeditions to Cadiz and to the Azores with Raleigh
and Essex) combined to prepare him for a brilliant career at court. In 1598
he was appointed private secretary to the Lord Keeper, Sir Thomas Egerton;
but a couple of years later he destroyed his prospects of advancement by
secretly marrying Ann More, the sixteen-year-old niece of Lady Egerton.
When, after long inner debate, Donne left the Catholic Church and joined
the Church of England, his decision bore no trace of opportunism. In 1615
he took sacred orders and was appointed Dean of St. Paul's in 1621. He died
in 1631 a few weeks after having preached what is known as his own death
sermon. His collected *Songs and Sonnets* were first published two years after
his death.

The revaluation of Donne's poetry has been one of the crucial experiences
in the history of poetic taste in our century. And there seems to be no doubt
that his place among the most effective and original poets in any language
is now firmly assured. The main reasons for this, as even the newest of
readers probably perceives at once, can be summarized under two large
headings: the poet's "tone of voice," the feeling of lively, vibrantly "spoken"
language; and the use of varied, "startling" situations and images, especially
in the sense that elements supposedly belonging to diverse areas of knowledge and sensibility are put together, with the result of stirring imagination
and reason, senses and mind.

In our present context, briefly trying to elaborate on those two aspects of
Donne's genius, we can see that they fit quite well within some of the definitions of the Renaissance that we have been using. If we say that Donne
gathers images and situations from many different areas of knowledge and
human experience—which in Donne's case, as we have indicated, were of
extraordinary breadth and variety—our emphasis is not on the scattered
diversity of his objects and themes, but on his power and effectiveness in
combining them; his "startling" associations are his way of encompassing
large segments of that knowledge and experience, and of giving them poetic
shape and impact. So Donne's poetic voice is that of a man who has absorbed
with intelligence and gusto the culture of a time of great historical and psychological upheaval and of equally great intellectual enrichment.

His mode of expression, his poetic manner, is correspondingly varied and authoritative. In Donne at his best, we first of all find the famous, irresistible openings—"I wonder, by my troth, what thou and I/Did, till we loved"; "For God's sake hold your tongue, and let me love"; "Death, be not proud, though some have called thee/Mighty and dreadful"—and then the characteristic developments, unpredictable yet logical, studded with images which for all their seeming oddity will prove wholly functional. For instance, in the opening of his song, "Go and catch a falling star," he uses six different images, all of them appropriate and interesting, to express the idea of impossibility. But this is no mere display of bravura and wit; it is a cultivated, incisive, and attractive way of making a point.

Indeed, behind the speaking voice of Donne's best poems we can easily imagine a character in a drama, convincingly and imaginatively addressing his interlocutors. To do so he draws from such diverse sources as theology, myth, the sciences, folklore, geography, war, court litigation. Donne studied the law, traveled quite extensively, was a man of the world who experienced the beginnings of a courtier's career with its implications of intellectual brilliance and sensual pleasures; his daring secret marriage to an aristocratic girl, though socially and professionally ruinous to him, was based on deep, lasting, fully requited love; and of course he ended his life on the pulpit as one of the most powerful preachers of all time. The situations, the language, the metaphors of his worldly and sacred poems are rooted in experience and are perfectly plausible in his human and cultural circumstances; he is eminently fit to use them as instruments of his rhetoric—the rhetoric of a man very much alive in an age of discovery and controversy, of ever widening physical and intellectual perspectives.

Donne's method of conciliating disparate objects and concepts to make important points about the human condition applies to his worldly as well as to his religious poems. In fact, a distinction between the two types seems irrelevant on that score. As our selections will indicate, the same poetic and intellectual vigor is found in the first category—where the major theme is love—as in the second—where the main themes are death and resurrection. The effectiveness of both depends on love and death never being handled as abstractions but as events contemplated and discussed anew against the background of concrete human reality, tested against the variety of experience. Random examples—the lovers in "The Canonization": "Soldiers find wars, and lawyers find out still/Litigious men, which quarrels move,/Though she and I do love"; or the dead in Holy Sonnet 7: "All whom war, dearth, age, agues, tyrannies/Despair, law, chance hath slain . . ."

In poems like "The Good-Morrow" or "The Canonization" the idea of lovers discovering in their intimacy and in their exchange of looks the universal and the eternal—a situation which in itself is potentially a cliché—is wholly renovated through the poet's vision and skill. Holy Sonnets 7 and 10—undoubtedly two of the most beautiful devotional poems in world literature—perform a similar operation on the orthodox idea of death as awakening to eternal life. In both cases the poet is a believer whose faith is poetically (i.e., intelligently) realized, expressed, made perceptible.

R. C. Bald, *John Donne. A Life* (1970), gives the reader a thorough biography; more advanced students will find a detailed stylistic study of Donne's poetry and prose in Astley Cooper Partridge, *John Donne. Language and Style* (1978). Helpful studies of Donne include Peter Amadeus Fiore, ed., *Just So Much Honor: Essays Commemorating the Four-Hundredth Anniversary of the Birth of John Donne* (1972), William Zunder, *The Poetry of John Donne: Literature and Culture in the Elizabethan and Jacobean Period* (1982), and Helen Gardner, ed., *John Donne: A Collection of Critical Essays* (1962).

## The Good-Morrow

I wonder, by my troth, what thou and I
Did, 'till we loved? Were we not weaned till then,
But sucked on country pleasures, childishly?
Or snorted we in the seven sleepers' den?[1]
'Twas so; But this, all pleasures fancies be.     5
If ever any beauty I did see,
Which I desired, and got, 'twas but a dream of thee.

And now good morrow to our waking souls,
Which watch not one another out of fear;
For love all love of other sights controls,     10
And makes one little room an everywhere.
Let sea-discoverers to new worlds have gone,
Let maps to other,[2] worlds on worlds have shown,
Let us possess one world; each hath one, and is one.

My face in thine eye, thine in mine appears,     15
And true plain hearts do in the faces rest;
Where can we find two better hemispheres
Without sharp North, without declining West?
Whatever dies was not mixed equally;[3]
If our two loves be one, or thou and I     20
Love so alike that none do slacken, none can die.

1633

## Song

Go and catch a falling star,
    Get with child a mandrake root,

---

1. Both Christian and Mohammedan authors recite the legend of seven youths of Ephesus, who hid in a cave from the persecutions of Decius, and slept there for 187 years.   2. I.e., let us concede that maps to other investigators have shown, etc. ("other" is an archaic plural form). 3. Scholastic philosophy taught that when the elements were imperfectly ("not equally") mixed, matter was mortal and mutable; but when they were perfectly mixed, it was undying and unchanging.

Tell me where all past years are,
   Or who cleft the Devil's foot,
Teach me to hear mermaids singing,                            5
Or to keep off envy's stinging,
     And find
     What wind
Serves to advance an honest mind.

If thou beest born to strange sights,                       10
   Things invisible to see,
Ride ten thousand days and nights,
   Till age snow white hairs on thee,
Thou, when thou return'st, wilt tell me
All strange wonders that befell thee,                     15
     And swear
     No where
Lives a woman true, and fair.

If thou find'st one, let me know,
   Such a pilgrimage were sweet;                           20
Yet do not, I would not go,
   Though at next door we might meet;
Though she were true when you met her.
And last till you write your letter,
     Yet she                                   25
     Will be
False, ere I come, to two, or three.

                              1633

## The Indifferent

I can love both fair and brown,[4]
Her whom abundance melts, and her whom want betrays,
Her who loves loneness best, and her who masks and plays,
Her whom the country formed, and whom the town,
Her who believes, and her who tries,                       5
Her who still weeps with spongy eyes,
And her who is dry cork, and never cries;
I can love her, and her, and you, and you,
I can love any, so she be not true.

Will no other vice content you?                         10
Will it not serve your turn to do as did your mothers?

---

4. Both blonde and brunette.

Or have you all old vices spent, and now would find out others?
Or doth a fear that men are true torment you?
O we are not, be not you so;
Let me, and do you, twenty know.
Rob me, but bind me not, and let me go.                            15
Must I, who came to travail thorough you[5]
Grow your fixed subject, because you are true?

Venus heard me sigh this song,
And by love's sweetest part, variety, she swore,                   20
She heard not this till now; and that it should be so no more.
She went, examined, and returned ere long,
And said, Alas, some two or three
Poor heretics in love there be,
Which think to 'stablish dangerous constancy.                      25
But I have told them, Since you will be true,
You shall be true to them who are false to you.

                                                    1633


## The Canonization

For God's sake hold your tongue, and let me love,
    Or chide my palsy, or my gout,
My five gray hairs, or ruined fortune, flout,
    With wealth your state, your mind with arts improve,
        Take you a course,[6] get you a place,                     5
        Observe His Honor, or His Grace,
Or the King's real, or his stamped face[7]
    Contemplate; what you will, approve,[8]
    So you will let me love.

Alas, alas, who's injured by my love?                              10
    What merchant's ships have my sighs drowned?
Who says my tears have overflowed his ground?
    When did my colds a forward spring remove?
        When did the heats which my veins fill
        Add one man to the plaguy bill?[9]                         15
Soldiers find wars, and lawyers find out still
    Litigious men, which quarrels move,
    Though she and I do love.

5. Through.    6. A direction (for life). *Place:* An appointment, at court or elsewhere.    7. On coins.    8. Test, put to proof.    9. Deaths from the hot-weather plague were recorded, by parish, in weekly lists.

Call us what you will, we are made such by love;
   Call her one, me another fly,                                    20
We're tapers[1] too, and at our own cost die,
    And we in us find the eagle and the dove.[2]
      The phoenix riddle hath more wit
      By us: we two being one, are it.
So, to one neutral thing both sexes fit.                               25
  We die and rise the same, and prove
  Mysterious by this love.

We can die by it, if not live by love,
   And if unfit for tombs and hearse
Our legend be, it will be fit for verse;                              30
    And if no piece of chronicle we prove,
      We'll build in sonnets pretty rooms;
      As well a well-wrought urn becomes
The greatest ashes, as half-acre tombs,
   And by these hymns, all shall approve                         35
   Us canonized for love:

And thus invoke us: You whom reverend love
   Made one another's hermitage;
You, to whom love was peace, that now is rage;
    Who did the whole world's soul contract, and drove        40
      Into the glasses of your eyes
      (So made such mirrors, and such spies,
That they did all to you epitomize)
    Countries, towns, courts: Beg from above
    A pattern of your love!                                       45

               1633

## The Apparition

When by thy scorn, O murderess, I am dead,
  And that thou thinkst thee free
  From all solicitation from me,
Then shall my ghost come to thy bed,
And thee, feigned vestal, in worse arms shall see;                    5
Then thy sick taper will begin to wink,

---

1. Like the "fly," a symbol of transitory life, we are burned up in "tapers," which consume
themselves.   2. Symbols of earthly wisdom (strength) and heavenly meekness (purity), the latter
paradoxically more powerful than the former. The phoenix, in general mythology, was a fabulous
Arabian bird, only one of which existed at any one time. After living a thousand years, it lit its
own funeral pyre, jumped in, and sang its funeral song at it was consumed—then rose triumphantly from its ashes, a new bird.

And he whose thou art then, being tired before,
Will, if thou stir, or pinch to wake him, think
   Thou call'st for more,
An in false sleep will from thee shrink,             10
And then, poor aspen[3] wretch, neglected thou
Bathed in a cold quicksilver sweat[4] wilt lie
   A verier ghost than I;
What I will say, I will not tell thee now,
Lest that preserve thee; and since my love is spent,   15
I had rather thou shouldst painfully repent,
Than by my threatenings rest still innocent.

                            1633

## The Funeral

Whoever comes to shroud me, do not harm
   Nor question much
That subtle wreath of hair which crowns my arm;
The mystery, the sign you must not touch,
   For 'tis my outward soul,               5
Viceroy to that, which then to heaven being gone,
   Will leave this to control,
And keep these limbs, her provinces, from dissolution.

For if the sinewy thread my brain lets fall
   Through every part                  10
Can tie those parts and make me one of all;
These hairs, which upward grew, and strength and art
   Have from a better brain,
Can better do it: except she meant that I
   By this should know my pain,          15
As prisoners then are manacled, when they're condemned to die.

Whate'er she meant by it, bury it with me,
   For since I am
Love's martyr, it might breed idolatry,
If into others' hands these relics came;        ·20
   As 'twas humility
To afford to it all that a soul can do,
   So 'tis some bravery,
That since you would save none of me, I bury some of you.

                            1633

---

3. Aspen leaves flutter in the slightest breeze.    4. Sweating in terror; quicksilver (mercury) was
a stock prescription for venereal disease.

# Holy Sonnets

## 7

At the round earth's imagined corners, blow
Your trumpets, angels;[5] and arise, arise
From death, you numberless infinities
Of souls, and to your scattered bodies go;
All whom the flood did, and fire shall, o'erthrow,      5
All whom war, dearth, age, agues, tyrannies,
Despair, law, chance hath slain, and you whose eyes
Shall behold God, and never taste death's woe.
But let them sleep, Lord, and me mourn a space;
For, if above all these, my sins abound,      10
'Tis late to ask abundance of Thy grace
When we are there. Here on this lowly ground,
Teach me how to repent; for that's as good
As if Thou hadst sealed my pardon with Thy blood.

          1633

## 10

Death, be not proud, though some have callèd thee
Mighty and dreadful, for thou art not so;
For those whom thou think'st thou dost overthrow
Die not, poor Death, nor yet canst thou kill me.
From rest and sleep, which but thy pictures be,      5
Much pleasure; then from thee much more must flow,
And soonest our best men with thee do go,
Rest of their bones, and soul's delivery.
Thou art slave to fate, chance, kings, and desperate men
And dost with poison, war, and sickness dwell,      10
And poppy or charms can make us sleep as well,
And better than thy stroke; why swell'st[6] thou then?
One short sleep past, we wake eternally
And death shall be no more; Death, thou shalt die.

          1633

---

5. Donne may have been thinking of the angels on old maps, who blow their trumpets to the four points of the compass. See also Revelation 7:1.     6. Puff up with pride.

# JOHN MILTON
## 1608–1674

The quality of Milton's literary achievement places him, however late, still within the broad span of the Renaissance. His intellectual inclinations and the support of a learned and artistic father combined to make him, already in early life, a most accomplished exemplar of the Renaissance scholar and literary artist. Concomitant with this achievement, and inseparable from it, are Milton's views and activities as a reformed Christian humanist.

Milton was born in London on December 9, 1608. Encouraged by his father—a well-to-do notary, private banker, and distinguished musician—he was educated both at home by tutors and at excellent schools (St. Paul's in London and Christ's College, Cambridge). He took his B. A. in 1629 and his M. A. in 1632. Milton decided against taking holy orders and retired to his father's estate at Horton, near Windsor, where he rounded out his prodigiously vast education and reading. His view of education included science and the new discoveries, while his splendid knowledge of ancient languages, including Hebrew, permitted him to maintain a constant, deep familiarity with both the pagan classics and the Scriptures, in their original texts. As a young student at Cambridge he exchanged letters in Latin verse with a friend. His early poetry culminated in the splendid elegy *Lycidas* (1637), commemorating a dead classmate. In 1638–39, now a highly educated man in his early thirties, he traveled on the continent, especially in Italy, where he conversed with prominent intellectuals, including scientists like Galileo, and wrote sonnets in Italian. Rumors of political trouble at home hastened his return to England.

The following twenty years were the period of Milton's involvement in doctrinal and governmental controversy. The major events of this period of his life are the writing of *Areopagitica* (1664, an eloquent defense of the right to print without a license) and his appointment as Latin Secretary to Cromwell's Council of State; Milton's writings in English and Latin defending the execution of King Charles I also belong to this period. The restoration of the monarchy brought him difficulties, brief imprisonment, and loss of property. Milton's first wife, Mary Powell (who left him shortly after their marriage in 1642 and later returned to him) died in 1652. His second wife died in childbirth in 1658. In 1663 he married Elizabeth Minshull, who outlived him. Totally blind from 1651 on, the poet now attended to his major tasks: *Paradise Lost* was published in 1667; *Paradise Regained* and *Samson Agonistes* followed in 1671. In his late years Milton had passages of the Hebrew Bible read to him every morning. He died in 1674.

Quite understandably, then, the apex of Milton's career as a poet (his long commitment to public life does not directly concern us here) was ultimately represented by a monumental exercise in the grandest and most authoritative of the classic genres—the epic poem. His choice of subject matter is obviously significant as well. Milton, as a Protestant heroic poet reflecting a trend toward an individual humanistic relationship to the Scriptures, undertook an epic dramatization and a free poetic reappropriation of the story of man's first disobedience.

Naturally, Milton believed in the superiority of his epic material to that of his ancient and medieval predecessors. Book IX of *Paradise Lost*—which, with the opening and conclusion of the poem, constitutes our selection from Milton—repeatedly illustrates this point. Mythological reference often provides support for action and characterization: Eve's divine touch and "goddesslike deport" not only recall but surpass those of the goddess Diana; and as she goes to work in the fields she is equated with the major Roman goddesses of agriculture. The fatal spot where she will be tempted is "more delicious" than the gardens of Adonis or of King Alcinous, both of which possess high mythological and epic credentials; to them, with full awareness of his higher theme, Milton adds a garden taken from Scriptural tradition. Even the serpent is lovelier than those sung by Ovid, and Eve's animals are "more duteous" than were Circe's pigs in the *Odyssey*. Indeed, in the proemium to Book IX and in the invocation to this muse (Urania, to be sure, not the Virgin Mary as in the poem of the Roman Catholic Counter-Reformation, Tasso's *Jerusalem Delivered*), Milton has declared his material to be "not less but more heroic" than the high points of the *Iliad* and the *Aeneid*, implying that his purpose is nobler than Homer's or Virgil's, not to mention that of the medieval chivalric poets with their "mastery to dissect/With long and tedious havoc fabled knights/In battles feigned. . . ."

Milton's battle, or drama, is not "feigned" for the preeminent reason that it is the basic inner drama of Christian mankind. Man is fallen, yet his fall is the precondition to human life as we know it, and it contains the promise of redemption; it is a happy fault, a *felix culpa*. So the subject of Milton's epic is not only the fall, of course, but also the transgressors' discovery and acceptance of their new mortal status, implying moral awareness and hope along with corruptibility and guilt.

Our major selection from *Paradise Lost* is the key moment in the action, the temptation and fall. Here Milton faced, among other problems, that of describing the fundamentally evil in ambiguously attractive terms. Without ever abandoning his grand manner or relenting in his highly literate sense of style, he handles blank verse with beautifully appropriate variety and mobility: passages like lines 71 ff. or 1067–1080 speak for themselves. In some of his most felicitous moments Milton strikes a balance between sustained epic tone and quick, effective notation. Take, for example, some of the varying images of the Satanic serpent: "Stupidly good, of enmity disarmed," "his head/crested aloft, and carbuncle his eyes"; or observe the rapid effectiveness of the fatal act: "Forth reaching to the fruit, she plucked, she eat."

The two main stages in the dramatic sequence of events are the serpent successfully tempting Eve, and Even convincing Adam to join her in the new knowledge. The dramatic situation demanded masterful handling, equal to its complexity and variety. For instance, Adam sins out of loyalty, out of chivalrous trust in his wife; and the poet does not shun such stagy lines as ". . . for with thee/Certain my resolution is to die," while Eve's rhetoric matches Adam's, in a lighter vein: "On my experience, Adam, freely taste, / And fear of death deliver to the winds." In all possible ways, the exchange of argumentation is given dramatic substance and vitality.

Milton was well acquainted with the arts of rhetoric and eloquence; and the story of the fall is largely told in terms of the use and misuse of those arts. From the serpent, Eve is not only taught evil action but also evil counseling, verbal cunning, sophistry. While before the tempter's success her speech was only externally twisted by an occasional pun or conceit, after the fall her rhetorical art becomes internally perverse, in perfect correspondence with the "distemper" in her now corrupt body.

On the other hand, new dimensions are added as the protagonists are now bound by "earthly" love and by mutual rancor and misery and also by the knowledge of a new delight, however condemnable; a line like "as with new wine intoxicated both" must work, so to speak, positively and negatively, strike a note at once joyful and ominous. Earthly attachments, however corrupt, must be poetically perceptible, as in the pivotal consummation passage (lines 1034–1045). Hence the variety in Milton's use not only of his stylistic and prosodic instrument but also of his wide range of cultural reference, as when he adopts exotic imagery suggested by the new geographic discoveries in the comparison between the transgressors and "th'American, so girt/With feathered cincture, naked else and wild. . . ."

In brief, Milton is fully recognizable as a Renaissance literary artist: his service to his God is inseparable from his service to poetry, to the cultivated and esthetically beautiful handling of language fit to encompass and express a wide range of human experience. The work for which he had prepared himself through all of his life, a Biblical epic in the grand classic manner, is also a crowning product of ripe, autumnal Renaissance culture.

Douglas Bush, *John Milton: A Sketch of His Life and Writings* (1964; 1967), provides a brief account of Milton's life. The standard modern biography is William Riley Parker, *Milton: A Biography*, 2 vols. (1981), Louis Lohr Martz, ed., *Milton: A Collection of Critical Essays* (1966), and Marjorie H. Nicolson, *John Milton: A Reader's Guide to His Poetry* (1975), will give the reader insight into his work.

## Paradise Lost[1]

### Book I

#### ["THIS GREAT ARGUMENT"]

Of man's first disobedience, and the fruit[2]
Of that forbidden tree whose mortal taste[3]
Brought death into the world, and all our woe,
With loss of Eden, till one greater Man[4]
Restore us, and regain the blissful seat,                              5
Sing, Heavenly Muse,[5] that, on the secret top

1. Abridged.    2. The apple itself, and also the consequences of Adam and Eve's disobedience.    3. The tasting of which brought mortality into the world.    4. Christ.    5. The opening invocation to the Muse who will inspire ("sing" to) the poet is a regular feature of epic poems. Milton's "Heavenly Muse," elsewhere in the poem (the first line of Book VII), is given

Of Oreb, or of Sinai,[6] didst inspire
That shepherd who first taught the chosen seed
In the beginning how the Heavens and Earth
Rose out of Chaos: or, if Sion hill                                    10
Delight thee more, and Siloa's brook that flowed
Fast by the oracle of God,[7] I thence
Invoke thy aid to my adventurous[8] song,
That with no middle flight intends to soar
Above th' Aonian mount,[9] while it pursues                            15
Things unattempted yet in prose or rhyme.
And chiefly thou, O Spirit,[1] that dost prefer
Before all temples th' upright heart and pure,
Instruct me, for thou know'st; thou from the first
Wast present, and, with mighty wings outspread,                       20
Dovelike sat'st brooding[2] on the vast abyss,
And mad'st it pregnant: what in me is dark
Illumine; what is low, raise and support;
That, to the height of this great argument,[3]
I may assert[4] Eternal Providence,                                   25
And justify the ways of God to men.[5]

## Book IX

### THE ARGUMENT

Satan, having compassed the Earth, with meditated guile returns as
a mist by night into Paradise; enters into the serpent sleeping. Adam
and Eve in the morning go forth to their labors, which Eve proposes
to divide in several places, each laboring apart: Adam consents not,
alleging the danger lest that enemy of whom they were forewarned

the name of the mythological Urania; in another passage (see Book IX, line 21), she is given the
adjective "celestial." Both words—of Greek and Latin derivation, respectively—mean "heavenly."
Clearly (see following lines), and typically, in Milton's "Heavenly Muse" pagan elements and
images are adopted and given new substance within the framework of Judeo-Christian culture and
beliefs.     6. The names Oreb and Sinai designate the mountain where God spoke to Moses
("that shepherd"), who in Genesis taught the Hebrew people ("the chosen seed") the story of the
Creation.     7. The names of biblical localities suggested here as haunts for Milton's muse are
emblematic of his certainty about the higher nature of his theme in comparison with the epic
subjects of pagan antiquity. The fact that "Siloa's brook" is flowing by the Temple ("the oracle of
God") suggests the holy nature of Milton's subject. Typically also, the geographical symbology is
patterned on a similar situation in Greek myth (see note 9 below).     8. Perilous, as the poet is
daring something new (see line 16).     9. Helicon, the Greek mountain that was the seat of the
nine Muses. A spring (Aganippe) giving poetic power, and an altar of Zeus, were part of that
landscape.     1. Described in Milton's Latin treatise on Christian doctrine as "that impulse or
voice of God by which the prophets were inspired," the "Spirit" is a further source of inspiration
over and above the "Heavenly Muse:" the poet asks not for song, but for knowledge ("instruct
me"), and identifies the "Spirit" with the Spirit of God that "moved upon the face of the waters"
in the opening lines of Genesis.     2. As a bird hatching eggs; the image is pursued in the "pregnant" of the following line. *Dovelike*: The traditional figuration of the Holy Spirit (e.g., Luke 3:
22: ". . . the Holy Ghost descended in a bodily shape like a dove . . ."). 3. Subject, theme.
4. Champion, vindicate.     5. Demonstrate to man the justice of "the ways of God," i.e., of the
course of God's providence.

should attempt her found alone. Eve, loath to be thought not cir-
cumspect or firm enough, urges her going apart, the rather desirous
to make trial of her strength; Adam at last yields. The serpent finds
her alone: his subtle approach, first gazing, then speaking, with much
flattery extolling Eve above all other creatures. Eve, wondering to
hear the serpent speak, asks how he attained to human speech and
such understanding not till now; the serpent answers that by tasting
of a certain tree in the garden he attained both to speech and reason,
till then void of both. Eve requires him to bring her to that tree, and
finds it to be the Tree of Knowledge forbidden: the serpent, now
grown bolder, with many wiles and arguments induces her at length
to eat. She, pleased with the taste, deliberates a while whether to
impart thereof to Adam or not; at last brings him of the fruit; relates
what persuaded her to eat thereof. Adam, at first amazed, but perceiving her lost, resolves, through vehemence of love, to perish with
her, and, extenuating the trespass, eats also of the fruit. The effects
thereof in them both; they seek to cover their nakedness; then fall to
variance and accusation of one another.


No more of talk where God or angel guest[6]
With man, as with his friend, familiar used
To sit indulgent, and with him partake
Rural repast, permitting him the while
Venial[7] discourse unblamed. I now must change                    5
Those notes to tragic; foul distrust, and breach
Disloyal, on the part of man, revolt
And disobedience; on the part of Heaven,
Now alienated, distance and distaste,
Anger and just rebuke, and judgment given,                    10
That brought into this world a world of woe,
Sin and her shadow Death, and Misery,
Death's harbinger. Sad task! yet argument
Not less but more heroic than the wrath
Of stern Achilles on his foe pursued                    15
Thrice fugitive about Troy wall;[8] or rage
Of Turnus for Lavinia disespoused;[9]
Or Neptune's ire, or Juno's, that so long
Perplexed the Greek, and Cytherea's son:[1]

6. Raphael, the "affable archangel," who in preceding books (V–VIII) has sat with Adam sharing
"rural repast" and discoursing on such highly relevant matters as Lucifer's fall, the Creation, the
structure of the universe. To him, Adam has told of the warning he has received from God not to
touch the Tree of Knowledge.    7. Unblemished.    8. Achilles, whose "wrath" is the subject
announced in the first line of the *Iliad*, at the end of that epic will chase his enemy, the Trojan
Hector, three times around the walls of Troy before killing him.    9. In Virgil's *Aeneid*, Lavinia,
fated to be Aeneas' wife, had earlier been promised to king Turnus.    1. In the *Odyssey*, Poseidon (Neptune) is the god hostile to Odysseus ("the Greek"); in the *Aeneid*, the hero is persecuted
by the wrath of the goddess Juno who had quarrelled with Aeneas' mother, Venus (Cytherea).

If answerable style I can obtain                                    20
Of my celestial Patroness,[2] who deigns
Her nightly visitation unimplored,
And dictates to me slumbering, or inspires
Easy my unpremeditated verse,[3]
Since first this subject for heroic song                            25
Pleased me,[4] long choosing and beginning late,
Not sedulous by nature to indite
War, hitherto the only argument
Heroic deemed, chief mastery to dissect[5]
With long and tedious havoc fabled knights                          30
In battles feigned (the better fortitude
Of patience and heroic martyrdom
Unsung), or to describe races and games,[6]
Or tilting furniture, emblazoned shields,
Impresses[7] quaint, caparisons and steeds,                         35
Bases and tinsel trappings, gorgeous knights
At joust and tournament; then marshaled feast
Served up in hall with sewers and seneschals:[8]
The skill of artifice or office mean;
Not that which justly gives heroic name                             40
To person or to poem. Me, of these
Nor skilled nor studious, higher argument
Remains, sufficient of itself to raise
That name, unless an age too late, or cold
Climate,[9] or years, damp my intended wing                         45
Depressed; and much they may if all be mine,
Not hers who brings it nightly to my ear.
    The sun was sunk, and after him the star
Of Hesperus, whose office is to bring
Twilight upon the Earth, short arbiter                              50
'Twixt day and night, and now from end to end
Night's hemisphere had veiled the horizon round,
When Satan, who late fled before the threats
Of Gabriel out of Eden,[1] now improved
In meditated fraud and malice, bent                                 55

2. Urania, originally the Muse of Astronomy; to Milton, in a wider sense, the source of "celestial" inspiration. *Answerable*: Suitable.    3. In other passages of the poem, Milton refers to inspiration coming to him at night or at early dawn, with spontaneous ("unpremeditated") ease.    4. The choice of his present heroic theme had occurred early, as had the rejection of the kind of subject matter described in the subsequent lines.    5. To analyze, but also to cut up: a possible allusion to the abundance of bloody battle wounds described in classical epics.    6. There are long descriptions of games in the *Iliad* (Book XXIII) and in the *Aeneid* (Book V).    7. Fancy emblems on shields. *Tilting furniture*: The paraphernalia of arms tournaments. *Bases*: Skirts worn by knights on horseback.    8. Attendants at meals and stewards in noble households.    9. The notion that nordic climates "damp" (i.e., benumb) human wit was accepted by Milton and is as old as Aristotle. *That name*: That of epic poet. *An age too late*: A time no longer fit for epic poetry.    1. As described in the conclusion of Book IV.

On man's destruction, mauger[2] what might hap
Of heavier on himself, fearless returned.
By night he fled, and at midnight returned
From compassing the Earth—cautious of day
Since Uriel, regent of the sun, descried                    60
His entrance, and forewarned the Cherubim
That kept their watch.[3] Thence, full of anguish, driven,
The space of seven continued nights he rode
With darkness; thrice the equinoctial line
He circled, four times crossed the car of Night            65
From pole to pole, traversing each colure;[4]
On the eighth returned, and on the coast averse[5]
From entrance or cherubic watch by stealth
Found unsuspected way. There was a place                    70
(Now not, though sin, not time, first wrought the change)
Where Tigris,[6] at the foot of Paradise,
Into a gulf shot under ground, till part
Rose up a fountain by the Tree of Life.
In with the river sunk, and with it rose,                  75
Satan, involved in rising mist; then sought
Where to lie hid. Sea he had searched and land
From Eden over Pontus, and the pool
Maeotis, up beyond the river Ob;[7]
Downward as far antarctic; and, in length,                 80
West from Orontes to the ocean barred
At Darien,[8] thence to the land where flows
Ganges and Indus.[9] Thus the orb he roamed
With narrow search, and with inspection deep
Considered every creature, which of all                    85
Most opportune might serve his wiles, and found
The serpent subtlest beast of all the field.[1]
Him, after long debate, irresolute
Of thoughts revolved, his final sentence[2] chose
Fit vessel, fittest imp[3] of fraud, in whom               90
To enter, and his dark suggestions hide
From sharpest sight; for in the wily snake
Whatever sleights none would suspicious mark,

2. In spite of.   3. The angel Uriel, possibly because the name means "fire of God," according to a tradition used by Milton is the "Regent" of the sun and of heat; in Book IV, it was he who, "gliding . . . on a sun-beam," had come to Gabriel, ("the Cherubim") and warned him against Satan entering Eden.   4. Satan manages always to stay on the dark side of the earth by circling it three times along the equator ("the equinoctial line") and twice on each of the two "colures," i.e., the two circles of longitude which intersect at the poles.   5. The side opposite to the gate guarded by Gabriel.   6. Cf. the river which "went out of Eden to water the garden" in Genesis 2:10.   7. Siberian river flowing into the Arctic Ocean. *Pontus:* The Black Sea. *Maeotis:* The Sea of Azov.   8. The Isthmus of Panama. *Orontes:* A river in Syria.   9. Rivers in India. 1. Cf. Genesis 3:1.   2. Decision.   3. Offspring, with a devilish connotation.

As from his wit and native subtlety
Proceeding, which, in other beasts observed,                    95
Doubt[4] might beget of diabolic power
Active within beyond the sense of brute.
Thus he resolved, but first from inward grief
His bursting passion into plaints thus poured:
   "O Earth, how like to Heaven, if not preferred
More justly, seat worthier of Gods, as built                    100
With second thought, reforming what was old!
For what God, after better, worse would build?
Terrestrial Heaven, danced round by other Heavens,
That shine, yet bear their bright officious[5] lamps,
Light above light, for thee alone, as seems,                    105
In thee concent'ring all their precious beams
Of sacred influence! As God in Heaven
Is center, yet extends to all, so thou
Cent'ring receiv'st from all those orbs; in thee,
Not in themselves, all their known virtue appears,             110
Productive in herb, plant, and nobler birth
Of creatures animate with gradual life
Of growth, sense, reason, all summed up in man.[6]
With what delight could I have walked thee round,
If I could joy in aught; sweet interchange                      115
Of hill and valley, rivers, woods, and plains,
Now land, now sea, and shores with forest crowned,
Rocks, dens, and caves! But I in none of these
Find place or refuge; and the more I see
Pleasures about me, so much more I feel                         120
Torment within me, as from the hateful siege[7]
Of contraries; all good to me becomes
Bane,[8] and in Heaven much worse would be my state.
But neither here seek I, no, nor in Heaven,
To dwell, unless by mastering Heaven's Supreme;                 125
Nor hope to be myself less miserable
By what I seek, but others to make such
As I, though thereby worse to me redound.
For only in destroying I find ease
To my relentless thoughts, and him[9] destroyed,               130
Or won to what may work his utter loss,
For whom all this was made, all this[1] will soon
Follow, as to him linked in weal or woe:

---

4. Suspicion.  5. Performing their function.  6. What Adam has called (in Book V, 509)
"the scale of Nature" ascends from the vegetable order (pure growth), to the animal (sensation),
to the human (the two, plus reason).  7. Seat, place.  8. Poison.  9. Man.  1. All of
created nature.

In woe then, that destruction wide may range!
To me shall be the glory sole among                                    135
The infernal Powers, in one day to have marred
What he, Almighty styled, six nights and days
Continued making, and who knows how long
Before had been contriving? though perhaps
Not longer than since I in one night freed                             140
From servitude inglorious well-nigh half
Th' angelic name,[2] and thinner left the throng
Of his adorers. He, to be avenged,
And to repair his numbers thus impaired,
Whether such virtue,[3] spent of old, now failed                       145
More angels to create (if they at least
Are his created),[4] or to spite us more,
Determined to advance into our room
A creature formed of earth, and him endow,
Exalted from so base original,                                         150
With heavenly spoils, our spoils. What he decreed
He effected; man he made, and for him built
Magnificent this World, and Earth his seat,
Him lord pronounced, and, O indignity!
Subjected to his service angel-wings                                   155
And flaming ministers, to watch and tend
Their earthy charge. Of these the vigilance
I dread, and to elude, thus wrapt in mist
Of midnight vapor, glide obscure, and pry
In every bush and brake, where hap may find                            160
The serpent sleeping, in whose mazy folds
To hide me, and the dark intent I bring.
O foul descent! that I, who erst contended
With Gods to sit the highest, am now constrained
Into a beast, and, mixed with bestial slime,                           165
This essence[5] to incarnate and imbrute,
That to the height of deity aspired!
But what will not ambition and revenge
Descend to? Who aspires must down as low
As high he soared, obnoxious,[6] first or last,                        170
To basest things. Revenge, at first though sweet,
Bitter ere long back on itself recoils.
Let it; I reck not, so it light well aimed,
Since higher[7] I fall short, on him who next

---

2. Family, clan.    3. Power, force.    4. Inciting the angels to rebellion, Satan has pretended
that they are not God's creation, but "self-begot" (Book V, 860).    5. The supernatural substance of which he considers himself to be made.    6. Exposed to.    7. Against God. *I reck
not:* I don't mind.

Provokes my envy, this new favorite      175
Of Heaven, this man of clay, son of despite,
Whom, us the more to spite, his Maker raised
From dust: spite then with spite is best repaid."
    So saying, through each thicket, dank or dry,
Like a black mist low-creeping, he held on      180
His midnight search, where soonest he might find
The serpent. Him fast sleeping soon he found,
In labyrinth of many a round self-rolled,
His head the midst, well stored with subtle wiles:
Not yet in horrid shade or dismal den,      185
Nor nocent[8] yet, but on the grassy herb,
Fearless, unfeared, he slept. In at his mouth
The devil entered, and his brutal sense,
In heart or head, possessing soon inspired
With act intelligential;[9] but his sleep      190
Disturbed not, waiting close[1] th' approach of morn.
    Now, whenas sacred light began to dawn
In Eden on the humid flowers, that breathed
Their morning incense, when all things that breathe
From th' Earth's great altar send up silent praise      195
To the Creator, and his nostrils fill
With grateful smell, forth came the human pair,
And joined their vocal worship to the choir
Of creatures wanting[2] voice; that done, partake
The season, prime for sweetest scents and airs;      200
Then cómmune how that day they best may ply
Their growing work; for much their work outgrew
The hands' dispatch of two gardening so wide:
And Eve first to her husband thus began:
    "Adam, well may we labor still[3] to dress      205
This garden, still to tend plant, herb, and flower,
Our pleasant task enjoined; but, till more hands
Aid us, the work under our labor grows,
Luxurious by restraint: what we by day
Lop overgrown, or prune, or prop, or bind,      210
One night or two with wanton growth derides,
Tending to wild. Thou, therefore, now advise,
Or hear what to my mind first thoughts present.
Let us divide our labors; thou where choice
Leads thee, or where most needs, whether to wind      215
The woodbine round this arbor, or direct
The clasping ivy where to climb; while I

8. Harmful.     9. Intellectual activity.     1. Hidden.     2. Lacking.     3. Constantly.

In yonder spring[4] of roses intermixed
With myrtle find what to redress till noon.
For, while so near each other thus all day                    220
Our task we choose, what wonder if so near
Looks intervene and smiles, or objects new
Casual discourse draw on, which intermits
Our day's work, brought to little, though begun
Early, and th' hour of supper comes unearned!"                    225
    To whom mild answer Adam thus returned:
"Sole Eve, associate sole, to me beyond
Compare above all living creatures dear!
Well hast thou motioned,[5] well thy thoughts employed
How we might best fulfil the work which here                    230
God hath assigned us, nor of me shalt pass
Unpraised; for nothing lovelier can be found
In woman than to study household good,
And good works in her husband to promote.
Yet not so strictly hath our Lord imposed                    235
Labor as to debar us when we need
Refreshment, whether food or talk between,
Food of the mind, or this sweet intercourse
Of looks and smiles; for smiles from reason flow,
To brute denied, and are of love the food,                    240
Love, not the lowest end[6] of human life.
For not to irksome toil, but to delight,
He made us, and delight to reason joined.
These paths and bowers doubt not but our joint hands
Will keep from wilderness[7] with ease, as wide.                    245
As we need walk, till younger hands ere long
Assist us. But, if much converse perhaps
Thee satiate, to short absence I could yield;
For solitude sometimes is best society,
And short retirement urges sweet return.                    250
But other doubt possesses me, lest harm
Befall thee, severed from me; for thou know'st
What hath been warned us, what malicious foe,
Envying our happiness, and of his own
Despairing, seeks to work us woe and shame                    255
By sly assault, and somewhere nigh at hand
Watches, no doubt, with greedy hope to find
His wish and best adventage, us asunder,
Hopeless to circumvent us joined, where each
To other speedy aid might lend at need.                    260

4. Thicket, grove.   5. Suggested.   6. Object.   7. Wildness.

Whether his first design be to withdraw
Our fealty from God, or to disturb
Conjugal love, than which perhaps no bliss
Enjoyed by us excites his envy more;
Or this, or worse,[8] leave not the faithful side                    265
That gave thee being, still shades thee and protects.
The wife, where danger or dishonor lurks,
Safest and seemliest by her husband stays,
Who guards her, or with her the worst endures."
    To whom the virgin[9] majesty of Eve,                          270
As one who loves, and some unkindness meets,
With sweet austere composure thus replied:
    "Offspring of Heaven and Earth, and all Earth's lord!
That such an enemy we have, who seeks
Our ruin, both by thee informed I learn,                          275
And from the parting angel[1] overheard,
As in a shady nook I stood behind,
Just then returned at shut of evening flowers.
But that thou shouldst my firmness therefore doubt
To God or thee, because we have a foe                             280
May tempt it, I expected not to hear.
His violence thou fear'st not, being such
As we, not capable of death or pain,
Can either not receive, or can repel.
His fraud is, then, thy fear; which plain infers                  285
Thy equal fear that my firm faith and love
Can by his fraud be shaken or seduced:
Thoughts, which how found they harbor in thy breast,
Adam, misthought of her to thee so dear?"[2]
    To whom, with healing words, Adam replied:                    290
"Daughter of God and man, immortal Eve,
For such thou art, from sin and blame entire;[3]
Not diffident of thee do I dissuade
Thy absence from my sight, but to avoid
Th' attempt itself, intended by our foe.                          295
For he who tempts, though in vain, at least asperses[4]
The tempted with dishonor foul, supposed
Not incorruptible of faith,[5] not proof
Against temptation. Thou thyself with scorn
And anger wouldst resent the offered wrong,                       300
Though ineffectual found; misdeem not, then,
If such affront I labor to avert

8. Whether his design be this, or something even worse.    9. Pure, sinless.    1. Raphael.
2. A misjudgment ("misthought") of me ("of her to thee so dear").    3. Intact.    4. Literally,
"sprinkles."    5. Faithfulness, loyalty.

From thee alone, which on us both at once
The enemy, though bold, will hardly dare;
Or, daring, first on me th' assault shall light.                    305
Nor thou his malice and false guile contemn—
Subtle he needs must be who could seduce
Angels—nor think superfluous others' aid.
I from the influence of thy looks receive
Access in every virtue;[6] in thy sight                    310
More wise, more watchful, stronger, if need were
Of outward strength; while shame, thou looking on,
Shame to be overcome or overreached,[7]
Would utmost vigor raise, and raised unite.
Why shouldst not thou like sense[8] within thee feel                    315
When I am present, and thy trial choose
With me, best witness of thy virtue tried?"
     So spake domestic Adam in his care
And matrimonial love; but Eve, who thought
Less[9] áttributed to her faith sincere,                    320
Thus her reply with accent sweet renewed:
     "If this be our condition, thus to dwell
In narrow circuit straitened1 by a foe,
Subtle or violent, we not endued[2]
Single with like defence wherever met,                    325
How are we happy, still in fear of harm?
But harm precedes not sin: only our foe
Tempting affronts us with his foul esteem
Of our integrity: his foul esteem
Sticks no dishonor on our front,[3] but turns                    330
Foul on himself; then wherefore shunned or feared
By us, who rather double honor gain
From his surmise proved false, find peace within,
Favor from Heaven, our witness, from th' event?
And what is faith, love, virtue, unassayed                    335
Alone, without exterior help sustained?[4]
Let us not then suspect our happy state
Left so imperfect by the Maker wise
As not secure to single or combined.
Frail is our happiness, if this be so;                    340
And Eden were no Eden, thus exposed."
     To whom thus Adam fervently replied:
"O woman, best are all things as the will
Of God ordained them; his creating hand
Nothing imperfect or deficient left                    345

6. Increased  strength.   7. Outdone.   8. Sensation.   9. Less   than   she   deserves.
1. Confined.   2. Endowed.   3. Brow.   4. Without being put to test by outside forces.

Of all that he created, much less man,
Or aught that might his happy state secure,
Secure from outward force. Within himself
The danger lies, yet lies within his power;
Against his will he can receive no harm.      350
But God left free the will; for what obeys
Reason is free; and reason he made right,
But bid her well beware, and still erect,[5]
Lest, by some fair appearing good surprised,
She dictate false, and misinform the will      355
To do what God expressly hath forbid.
Not then mistrust, but tender love, enjoins
That I should mind[6] thee oft; and mind thou me.
Firm we subsist, yet possible to swerve,
Since reason not impossibly may meet      360
Some specious object by the foe suborned,[7]
And fall into deception unaware,
Not keeping strictest watch, as she was warned.
Seek not temptation, then, which to avoid
Were better, and most likely if from me      365
Thou sever not: trial will come unsought.
Wouldst thou approve[8] thy constancy, approve
First thy obedience; th' other who can know,
Not seeing thee attempted, who attest?
But if thou think trial unsought may find      370
Us both securer[9] than thus warned thou seem'st,
Go; for thy stay, not free, absents thee more.
Go in thy native innocence; rely
On what thou hast of virtue; summon all;
For God towards thee hath done his part: do thine."      375
    So spake the patriarch of mankind; but Eve
Persisted; yet submiss,[1] though last, replied:
    "With thy permission, then, and thus forewarned,
Chiefly by what thy own last reasoning words
Touched only, that our trial, when least sought,      380
May find us both perhaps far less prepared,
The willinger I go, nor much expect
A foe so proud will first the weaker seek;
So bent, the more shall shame him his repulse."
Thus saying, from her husband's hand her hand      385

---

5. On the alert against temptation, since God has "created Man free and able enough to have withstood his Temper" (Book III, The Argument).   6. Remind.   7. Procured for treacherous purposes.   8. Give proof, test.   9. Less careful, less alert to danger.   1. Submissive. Eve's submissiveness, however, is qualified by Adam's reluctant tone as he agree to her go; and by the fact that it is she who speaks the final words of their dialogue.

Soft she withdrew, and like a wood nymph light,
Oread or dryad, or of Delia's train,[2]
Betook her to the groves, but Delia's self
In gait surpassed and goddesslike deport,
Though not as she with bow and quiver armed,                    390
But with such gardening tools as art yet rude,
Guiltless of fire[3] had formed, or angels brought.
To Pales, or Pomona, thus adorned,
Likest she seemed, Pomona when she fled
Vertumnus, or to Ceres in her prime,                    395
Yet virgin of Proserpina from Jove.[4]
Her long with ardent look his eye pursued
Delighted, but desiring more her stay.
Oft he to her his charge of quick return
Repeated; she to him as oft engaged                    400
To be returned by noon amid the bower,
And all things in best order to invite
Noontide repast, or afternoon's repose.
O much deceived, much failing, hapless Eve,
Of[5] thy presumed return! Event perverse!                    405
Thou never from that hour in Paradise
Found'st either sweet repast, or sound repose;
Such ambush hid among sweet flowers and shades
Waited with hellish rancor imminent[6]
To intercept thy way, or send thee back                    410
Despoiled of innocence, of faith, of bliss.
For now, and since first break of dawn, the fiend,
Mere serpent in appearance, forth was come,
And on his quest, where likeliest he might find
The only two of mankind, but in them                    415
The whole included race, his purposed prey.
In bower and field he sought, where any tuft
Of grove or garden-plot more[7] pleasant lay,
Their tendance[7] or plantation for delight;
By fountain or by shady rivulet                    420
He sought them both, but wished his hap might find
Eve separate; he wished, but not with hope
Of what so seldom chanced; when to his wish,

---

2. In Greek mythology, the Oreads were nymphs of the mountains, the Dryads of the woods; Delia (i.e., born on the island of Delos) is the goddess Diana (Artemis), the huntress with her train of nymphs.    3. The producing of fire will become necessary only after the Fall. (Cf. Book X, 1070–1082.)    4. In pratical-minded Roman mythology, Pales and Pomona are deities who preside over flocks and fruit, respectively; Ceres is the goddess of agriculture in general. Both Pomona and Ceres are presented here in virginal youth, Pomona fleeing from her suitor Vertumnus (another agricultural deity), and Ceres before the time when Jupiter made her the mother of Proserpina.    5. About.    6. Ominously ready.    7. Particularly.    8. A spot which they tended.

Beyond his hope, Eve separate he spies,
Veiled in a cloud of fragrance, where she stood,                    425
Half spied, so thick the roses bushing round
About her glowed, oft stooping to support
Each flower of slender stalk, whose head though gay
Carnation, purple, azure, or specked with gold,
Hung drooping unsustained, them she upstays                    430
Gently with myrtle band, mindless the while
Herself, though fairest unsupported flower,
From her best prop so far, and storm so nigh.
Nearer he drew, and many a walk traversed
Of stateliest covert, cedar, pine, or palm;                    435
Then voluble[9] and bold, now hid, now seen
Among thick-woven arborets[1] and flowers
Embordered on each bank,[2] the hand of Eve:
Spot more delicious than those gardens feigned[3]
Or of revived Adonis, or renowned                    440
Alcinous,[4] host of old Laertes' son,
Or that, not mystic, where the sapient king[5]
Held dalliance with his fair Egyptian spouse.
Much he the place admired, the person more.
As one who long in populous city pent,                    445
Where houses thick and sewers annoy[6] the air,
Forth issuing on a summer's morn to breathe
Among the pleasant villages and farms
Adjoined, from each thing met conceives delight,
The smell of grain, or tedded[7] grass, or kine,                    450
Or dairy, each rural sight, each rural sound:
If chance[8] with nymphlike step fair virgin pass,
What pleasing seemed, for her[9] now pleases more,
She most, and in her look sums[1] all delight.
Such pleasure took the serpent to behold                    455
This flowery plat,[2] the sweet recess of Eve
Thus early, thus alone; her heavenly form
Angelic, but more soft, and feminine,
Her graceful innocence, her every air
Of gesture or least action overawed                    460
His malice, and with rapine[3] sweet bereaved

---

9. Rolling.    1. Shrubbery.    2. Forming a border on each side of a walk. *Hand:*
Handiwork.    3. Imagined by the poets (cf. line 31 above).    4. King of the Phaeacians and
host to Odysseus, son of Laertes. His perpetually flowering garden is described in Book VII of the
*Odyssey. Of revived Adonis:* The mythical garden where Aphrodite (Venus) nursed her lover
Adonis, wounded by a boar. The most famous description of the garden, certainly known to
Milton, is in Book III of Spenser's *Faerie Queene.*    5. Solomon. *Not mystic:* Not mythical like
the previous "feigned" gardens of pagan antiquity. *Egyptian spouse:* Pharaoh's daughter (cf. I
*Kings,* 3:1 and *Song of Solomon,* 6:2).    6. Make noisome, pollute.    7. Spread out for
drying.    8. If it should happen that.    9. Because of her.    1. Rounds out and brings to
perfection.    2. Plot.    3. Theft.

His fierceness of the fierce intent it brought:
That space the evil one abstracted[4] stood
From his own evil, and for the time remained
Stupidly good, of enmity disarmed,                                    465
Of guile, of hate, of envy, of revenge.
But the hot Hell that always in him burns,
Though in mid Heaven, soon ended his delight,
And tortures him now more, the more he sees
Of pleasure not for him ordained: then soon                          470
Fierce hate he recollects, and all his thoughts
Of mischief, gratulating,[5] thus excites:
     "Thoughts, whither have ye led me? with what sweet
Compulsion thus transported to forget
What hither brought us? hate, not love, nor hope                     475
Of Paradise for Hell, hope here to taste
Of pleasure, but all pleasure to destroy,
Save what[6] is in destroying; other joy
To me is lost. Then let me not let pass
Occasion which now smiles; behold alone                              480
The woman, opportune to all attempts,[7]
Her husband, for I view far round, not nigh,
Whose higher intellectual more I shun,
And strength, of courage haughty, and of limb
Heroic built, though of terrestrial mold.[8]                         485
Foe not informidable, exempt from wound,[9]
I not; so much hath Hell debased, and pain
Enfeebled me, to what I was in Heaven.
She fair, divinely fair, fit love for gods,
Not terrible, though terror be in love                               490
And beauty, not approached by stronger hate,[1]
Hate stronger, under show of love well feigned,
The way which to her ruin now I tend."
     So spake the enemy of mankind, enclosed
In serpent, inmate bad, and toward Eve                               495
Addressed his way, not with indented wave,[2]
Prone on the ground, as since, but on his rear,
Circular base of rising folds, that towered
Fold above fold a surging maze; his head
Crested aloft, and carbuncle[3] his eyes;                            500
With burnished neck of verdant gold, erect
Amidst his circling spires,[4] that on the grass

---

4. Drawn off, separated.   5. Rejoicing.   6. Whatever pleasure.   7. In the appropriate situation for Satan's attempts on her.   8. Formed of earth.   9. See line 283 above.   1. If not
approached, and counteracted, by hate.   2. Zigzagging.   3. Fiery red.   4. Coils, loops.
*Redundant:* In great abundance.

Floated redundant. Pleasing was his shape,
And lovely; never since of serpent kind
Lovelier, not those that in Illyria changed                          505
Hermione and Cadmus,[5] or the god
In Epidaurus; nor to which transformed
Ammonian Jove, or Capitoline was seen,
He with Olympias, this with her who bore
Scipio, the height of Rome.[6] With tract oblique                    510
At first, as one who sought access, but feared
To interrupt, sidelong he works his way.
As when a ship by skillful steersman wrought
Nigh river's mouth or foreland, where the wind
Veers oft, as oft so steers, and shifts her sail:                    515
So varied he, and of his tortuous train
Curled many a wanton wreath in sight of Eve,
To lure her eye: she busied heard the sound
Of rustling leaves, but minded not, as used
To such disport before her through the field,                        520
From every beast, more duteous at her call,
Than at Circean call the herd disguised.[7]
He bolder now, uncalled before her stood:
But as in gaze admiring; oft he bowed
His turret[8] crest, and sleek enameled neck,                        525
Fawning, and licked the ground whereon she trod.
His gentle dumb expression turned at length
The eye of Eve to mark his play: he, glad
Of her attention gained, with serpent tongue
Organic, or impulse of vocal air,[9]                                 530
His fraudulent temptation thus began.
     "Wonder not, sovereign mistress, if perhaps
Thou canst, who art sole wonder; much less arm
Thy looks, the heaven of mildness, with disdain,
Displeased that I approach thee thus, and gaze                       535
Insatiate, I thus single, nor have feared
Thy awful brow, more awful thus retired.

5. Cadmus, the founder of Thebes, and his wife Harmonia (Herminoe), according to their story
as told by Ovid (*Metamorphoses* IV, 562–602), were transformed into snakes when they retired to
Illyria after much family tragedy. *Epidaurus*: The place in Greece where Aesculapius, the god of
medicine, had his major temple, and appeared to worshippers in the form of an erect, flashy-eyed
serpent (again as in Ovid, *Metamorphoses* XV, 622–744.     6. According to hero-deifying legends, Jupiter (Jove), in his personification as Jupiter Ammon (a mingling of Greco-Roman and
Egyptian cults), loved the Princess Olympias and became the father of Alexander the Great. As
the Capitoline Jupiter (worshipped in the major Roman temple on the Capitol), he fathered
Scipio, the supreme hero (the "height") of Rome's African wars. In both cases, the father-god
appeared in the form of a snake.     7. The enchantress Circe, in Book X of the *Odyssey*, is
surrounded by subjected beasts, and transforms some of the hero's companions into swine.
8. Towering.     9. Producing a voice either by using his serpent's ("organic") tongue, or by some
more direct impulse on the air.

Fairest resemblance of thy Maker fair,
Thee all things living gaze on, all things thine
By gift, and thy celestial beauty adore                           540
With ravishment beheld, there best beheld
Where universally admired: but here
In this enclosure wild, these beasts among,
Beholders rude, and shallow[1] to discern
Half what in thee is fair, one man except,                        545
Who sees thee? (and what is one?) who shouldst be seen
A goddess among gods, adored and served
By angels numberless, thy daily train."
    So glozed the tempter, and his proem[2] tuned;
Into the heart of Eve his words made way,                         550
Though at the voice much marveling: at length,
Not unamazed, she thus in answer spake.
"What may this mean? Language of man pronounced
By tongue of brute, and human sense expressed?
The first at least of these I thought denied                      555
To beasts, whom God on their creation-day
Created mute to all articulate sound;
The latter I demur, for in their looks
Much reason, and in their actions oft appears.[3]
Thee, serpent, subtlest beast of all the field                    560
I knew, but not with human voice endued:
Redouble then this miracle, and say,
How cam'st thou speakable of mute,[4] and how
To me so friendly grown above the rest
Of brutal kind, that daily are in sight?                          565
Say, for such wonder claims attention due."
    To whom the guileful tempter thus replied:
"Empress of this fair world, resplendent Eve!
Easy to me it is to tell thee all
What thou command'st and right thou shouldst be obeyed:           570
I was at first as other beasts that graze
The trodden herb, of abject thoughts and low,
As was my food, nor aught but food discerned
Or sex, and apprehended nothing high:
Till on a day, roving the field, I chanced                        575
A goodly tree far distant to behold
Loaden with fruit of fairest colors mixed,
Ruddy and gold; I nearer drew to gaze;

---

1. Mentally inadequate.    2. Preamble, introduction. *Glozed:* Flattered.    3. Eve, well
acquainted with animals, which are "duteous at her call" (line 521 above), questions the notion
("I demur") that they are wholly deprived of "human sense" and "reason."    4. How did you
acquire speech after being dumb.

When from the boughs a savory odor blown,
Grateful to appetite, more pleased my sense         580
Than smell of sweetest fennel, or the teats
Of ewe or goat dropping with milk[5] at even,
Unsucked of lamb or kid, that tend their play.
To satisfy the sharp desire I had
Of tasting those fair apples, I resolved         585
Not to defer: hunger and thirst at once,
Powerful persuaders, quickened at the scent
Of that alluring fruit, urged me so keen.
About the mossy trunk I wound me soon,
For, high from ground, the branches would require     590
Thy utmost reach, or Adam's: rould the tree
All other beasts that saw, with like desire
Longing and envying stood, but could not reach.
Amid the tree now got, where plenty hung
Tempting so nigh, to pluck and eat my fill         595
I spared not; for such pleasure till that hour
At feed or fountain never had I found.
Sated at length, ere long I might perceive
Strange alteration in me, to degree
Of reason[6] in my inward powers, and speech        600
Wanted not long,[7] though to this shape retained.
Thenceforth to speculations high or deep
I turned my thoughts, and with capacious mind
Considered all things visible in Heaven,
Or Earth, or middle,[8] all things fair and good:     605
But all that fair[9] and good in thy divine
Semblance, and in thy beauty's heavenly ray
United I beheld: no fair to thine
Equivalent or second, which compelled
Me thus, though importune perhaps, to come       610
And gaze, and worship thee of right declared
Sovereign of creatures, universal dame."[1]
    So talked the spirited[2] sly snake: and Eve
Yet more amazed, unwary thus replied:
    "Serpent, thy overpraising leaves in doubt      615
The virtue of that fruit, in thee first proved.
But say, where grows the tree, from hence how far?
For many are the trees of God that grow
In Paradise, and various, yet unknown
To us; in such abundance lies our choice,      620

5. According to old folklore, snakes were fond of fennel, which was supposed to sharpen their eyesight, and of goat's milk.   6. To the point of acquiring the faculty of reason.   7. The faculty of speech soon followed. *Retained:* Restrained, kept to his outward appearance.   8. The air.   9. Fairness, beauty.   1. Mistress of this world.   2. Possessed by an evil spirit.

As leaves a greater store of fruit untouched,
Still hanging incorruptible, till men
Grow up to their provision, and more hands
Help to disburden Nature of her bearth."[3]
 To whom the wily adder, blithe and glad:                    625
"Empress, the way is ready, and not long,
Beyond a row of myrtles, on a flat,
Fast by a fountain, one small thicket past
Of blowing[4] myrrh and balm: if thou accept
My conduct, I can bring thee thither soon."                    630
 "Lead then," said Eve. He leading swiftly rolled
In tangles, and made intricate seem straight,
To mischief swift. Hope elevates, and joy
Brightens his crest; as when a wandering fire
Compact of unctuous vapor,[5] which the night                    635
Condenses, and the cold environs round,
Kindled through agitation to a flame
(Which oft, they say, some evil spirit attends),
Hovering and blazing with delusive light,
Misleads th' amazed night-wanderer from his way                    640
To bogs and mires, and oft through pond or pool,
There swallowed up and lost, from succor far:
So glistered the dire snake, and into fraud
Led Eve our credulous mother, to the tree
Of prohibition,[6] root of all our woe:                    645
Which when she saw, thus to her guide she spake:
 "Serpent, we might have spared our coming hither,
Fruitless to me, though fruit be here to excess,
The credit of whose virtue rest with thee;[7]
Wondrous indeed, if cause of such effects!                    650
But of this tree we may not taste nor touch:
God so commanded, and left that command
Sole daughter of his voice;[8] the rest, we live
Law to ourselves; our reason is our law."
 To whom the tempter guilefully replied:                    655
"Indeed? Hath God then said that of the fruit
Of all these garden trees ye shall not eat,
Yet lords declared of all in Earth or air?"
 To whom thus Eve, yet sinless: "Of the fruit
Of each tree in the garden we may eat,                    660

---

3. Products. 4. Blossoming. 5. Composed of greasy vapor. *Wandering fire*: Will-o'-the-wisp. 6. The forbidden Tree of Knowledge. 7. Since the forbidden tree is as good as fruitless to Eve, the only proof of its power ("virtue") will remain with the Serpent. 8. God's command, elsewhere described (Book IV, 433) as "one easy prohibition," in its present form is the translation of a Hebrew phrase. *The rest*: For the rest.

But of the fruit of this fair tree amidst
The garden, God hath said, 'Ye shall not eat
Thereof, nor shall yet touch it, lest ye die.' "
   She scarce had said, though brief, when now more bold,
The tempter, but with show of zeal and love                    665
To man, and indignation at his wrong,
New part[9] puts on, and as to passion moved,
Fluctuates[1] disturbed, yet comely, and in act
Raised,[2] as of some great matter to begin.
As when of old some orator renowned                            670
In Athens or free Rome, where eloquence
Flourished, since mute, to some great cause addressed,
Stood in himself collected, while each part,[3]
Motion, each act, won audience ere the tongue,
Sometimes in height began, as no delay                         675
Of preface brooking,[4] through his zeal of right.
So standing, moving, or to height upgrown
The tempter all impassioned thus began:
   "O sacred, wise, and wisdom-giving plant,
Mother of science![5] now I feel thy power                     680
Within me clear, not only to discern
Things in their causes, but to trace the ways
Of highest agents, deemed however wise.
Queen of this universe! do not believe
Those rigid threats of death. Ye shall not die;                685
How should ye? By the fruit? it gives you life
To knowledge;[6] by the Threatener? look on me,
Me who have touched and tasted, yet both live,
And life more perfect have attained than Fate
Meant me, by venturing higher than my lot.                     690
Shall that be shut to man, which to the beast
Is open? Or will God incense his ire
For such a petty trespass, and not praise
Rather your dauntless virtue, whom the pain
Of death denounced, whatever thing death be,                   695
Deterred not from achieving what might lead
To happier life, knowledge of good and evil?
Of good, how just! Of evil, if what is evil
Be real, why not known, since easier shunned?
God therefore cannot hurt ye, and be just;                     700
Not just, not God; not feared then, nor obeyed:

9. A new role, as of an actor in drama.     1. Undulates with his body.     2. Assuming the
orator's posture.     3. Of the body.     4. Plunging into the middle of the subject (*in medias res*),
without any preamble.     5. Knowledge.     6. Life as well as knowledge.

Your fear itself of death removes the fear.[7]
Why then was this forbid? Why but to awe,
Why but to keep ye low and ignorant,
His worshipers? He knows that in the day                    705
Ye eat thereof, your eyes that seem so clear,
Yet are but dim, shall perfectly be then
Opened and cleared, and ye shall be as gods,
Knowing both good and evil, as they know.
That ye should be as gods, since I as man,                    710
Internal man,[8] is but proportion meet,
I, of brute, human; ye, of human, gods.
So ye shall die perhaps, by putting off
Human, to put on gods:[9] death to be wished,
Though threatened, which no worse than this can bring.        715
And what are gods that man may not become
As they, participating godlike food?
The gods are first, and that advantage use
On our belief, that all from them proceeds.
I question it; for this fair Earth I see,                    720
Warmed by the sun, producing every kind,
Them nothing: If they[1] all things, who enclosed
Knowledge of good ane evil in this tree,
That whoso eats thereof forthwith attains
Wisdom without their leave? And wherein lies                 725
Th' offense, that man should thus attain to know?
What can your knowledge hurt him, or this tree
Impart against his will if all be his?
Or is it envy, and can envy dwell
In heavenly breasts? These, these, and many more            730
Causes import[2] your need of this fair fruit.
Goddess humane, reach then, and freely taste!"
      He ended, and his words, replete with guile,
Into her heart too easy entrance won:
Fixed on the fruit she gazed, which to behold                735
Might tempt alone, and in her ears the sound
Yet rung of his persuasive words, impregned[3]
With reason, to her seeming, and with truth;
Meanwhile the hour of noon drew on, and waked
An eager appetite, raised by the smell                      740
So savory of that fruit, which with desire,

7. The Serpent's captious argument is that God is by definition just; but since a death-giving God would not be just, he would not be God; consequently, he would not have to be feared and obeyed.    8. Cf. "inward," line 600 above. The Serpent has acquired human faculties although his outer form has remained unchanged.    9. *Human . . . gods:* Humanity . . . divinity.
1. If they produced.    2. Imply, indicate.    3. Impregnated, filled.

Inclinable now grown to touch or taste,
Solicited her longing eye; yet first
Pausing a while, thus to herself she mused:
  "Great are thy virtues, doubtless, best of fruits,     745
Though kept from man, and worthy to be admired,
Whose taste, too long forborn, at first essay
Gave elocution to the mute, and taught
The tongue not made for speech to speak thy praise:
Thy praise he also who forbids thy use,      750
Conceals not from us, naming thee the Tree
Of Knowledge, knowledge both of good and evil;
Forbids us then to taste; but his forbidding
Commends thee more, while it infers[5] the good
By thee communicated, and our want:      755
For good unknown, sure is not had, or had
And yet unknown, is as not had at all.
In plain[6] then, what forbids he but to know?
Forbids us good, forbids us to be wise!
Such prohibitions bind not.[7] But if Death     760
Bind us with after-bands, what profits then
Our inward freedom?[8] In the day we eat
Of this fair fruit, our doom is, we shall die.
How dies the serpent? He hath eaten and lives,
And knows, and speaks, and reasons, and discerns,   765
Irrational till then. For us alone
Was death invented? Or to us denied
This intellectual food, for beasts reserved?
For beasts it seems: yet that one beast which first
Hath tasted, envies not, but brings with joy    770
The good befallen him, author unsuspect,[9]
Friendly to man, far from deceit or guile.
What fear I then, rather what know to fear
Under this ignorance of good and evil,[1]
Of God or death, of law or penalty?      775
Here grows the cure of all, this fruit divine,
Fair to the eye, inviting to the taste,
Of virtue[2] to make wise: what hinders then
To reach, and feed at once both body and mind?"
  So saying, her rash hand in evil hour,     780

---

4. Favorably disposed. 5. Implies. 6. In plain words. 7. Eve, who has learned from the Serpent the art of sophistical argument, claims that God himself, by naming the Tree, has indicated to man the "good" in it; but a "good unknown" is as nothing; besides, forbidding the experience of the Tree of Knowledge is forbidding man "to be wise;" hence the prohibition is not binding. 8. Death would constitute a later bond ("after-bands"), after God has granted man his free will ("inward freedom"). 9. An unsuspectable authority on the subject. 1. Having no knowledge of good and evil, Eve doesn't know what is to be feared. 2. With the power.

Forth reaching to the fruit, she plucked, she eat.[3]
Earth felt the wound, and Nature from her seat
Sighing through all her works gave signs of woe,[4]
That all was lost. Back to the thicket slunk
The guilty serpent, and well might, for Eve                    785
Intent now wholly on her taste, naught else
Regarded; such delight till then, as seemed,
In fruit she never tasted, whether true
Or fancied so, through expectation high
Of knowledge; nor was godhead from her thought.[5]            790
Greedily she engorged without restraint,
And knew not eating death:[6] satiate at length,
And heightened as with wine, jocund and boon,[7]
Thus to herself she pleasingly began:
    "O sovereign, virtuous, precious of all trees            795
In Paradise! of operation blest
To sapience,[8] hitherto obscured, infamed,
And thy fair fruit let hang, as to no end
Created; but henceforth my early care,
Not without song each morning, and due praise                800
Shall tend thee, and the fertile burden ease
Of thy full branches offered free to all;
Till dieted by thee I grow mature
In knowledge, as the gods who all things know;
Though others envy what they cannot give:                     805
For had the gift been theirs, it had not here
Thus grown.[9] Experience, next to thee I owe,
Best guide; not following thee I had remained
In ignorance; thou open'st Wisdom's way,
And giv'st access, though secret she retire.                  810
And I perhaps am secret; Heaven is high,
High and remote to see from thence distinct
Each thing on Earth; and other care perhaps
May have diverted from continual watch
Our great Forbidder, safe[1] with all his spies               815
About him. But to Adam in what sort[2]
Shall I appear? Shall I to him make known
As yet my change, and give him to partake
Full happiness with me, or rather not,
But keep the odds[3] of knowledge in my power                 820

3. Ate.    4. Natural "signs," omens, metaphorically given as—and punning with—the "sighs" of Nature; forebodings of disaster.    5. She thought of acquiring divinity.    6. That she was eating death.    7. Cheerful.    8. Endowed with the power to give wisdom. *Infamed*: Made infamous.    9. For Satan's argument (here adopted by Eve) about "the gods" not having created the forbidden tree, and their consequent envy, see lines 720–730 above.    1. Not dangerous. 2. Manner.    3. Advantage.

Without copartner? so to add what wants
In female sex, the more to draw his love,
And render me more equal, and perhaps,
A thing not undesirable, sometime
Superior: for, inferior, who is free?                                   825
This may be well: but what if God have seen
And death ensue? Then I shall be no more,
And Adam, wedded to another Eve,
Shall live with her enjoying, I extinct;
A death to think. Confirmed then I resolve,                             830
Adam shall share with me in bliss or woe:
So dear I love him, that with him all deaths
I could endure, without him live no life."[4]
     So saying, from the tree her step she turned,
But first low reverence done, as to the power                           835
That dwelt within, whose presence had infused
Into the plant sciental[5] sap, derived
From nectar, drink of gods. Adam the while
Waiting desirous her return, had wove
Of choicest flowers a garland to adorn                                  840
Her tresses, and her rural labors crown,
As reapers oft are wont their harvest queen.
Great joy he promised to his thoughts, and new
Solace in her return, so long delayed:
Yet oft his heart, divine of[6] something ill,                         845
Misgave him; he the faltering measure[7] felt;
And forth to meet her went, the way she took
That morn when first they parted. By the Tree
Of Knowledge he must pass; there he her met,
Scarce from the tree returning; in her hand                            850
A bough of fairest fruit that downy smiled,
New gathered, and ambrosial smell diffused.
To him she hastened, in her face excuse
Came prologue, and apology to prompt,[8]
Which with bland words at will she thus addressed:                     855
     "Hast thou not wondered, Adam, at my stay?

---

4. In the crucial lines 817–833, Eve's thoughts are shown moving through three stages: first, the idea of not sharing her knowledge with Adam, so as to enhance her own power, with the gratuitous notion that lesser power equates no freedom at all (817–820); then, jealously at the thought of her own possible death, and Adam "wedded to another Eve" (820–825); finally, with an opportune resurgence of "love," the resolve to be with Adam "in bliss or woe," i.e., to make him her partner in sin. Thus the passage is centrally representative of Milton's characterization of Eve in her relation to Adam, and possibly of some of the poet's own conceptions of femininity in general. Cf., in this same Book, such other characterizing passages as 377–384 above, 869–885 and 1155–1161 below.    5. Infusing knowledge.    6. Divining, foreseeing.    7. Irregularity of heartbeats.    8. A pleading expression on her face came as an introduction (the "prologue" to a play) to prepare for ("prompt" is also a theatrical term) the formal "apology."

Thee I have missed, and thought it long, deprived
Thy presence, agony of love till now
Not felt, nor shall be twice; for never more
Mean I to try, what rash untried I sought,                         860
The pain of absence from thy sight. But strange
Hath been the cause, and wonderful to hear:
This tree is not as we are told, a tree
Of danger tasted,[9] nor to evil unknown
Opening the way, but of divine effect                              865
To open eyes, and make them gods who taste;
And hath been tasted such.[1] The serpent wise,
Or not restrained as we, or not obeying,
Hath eaten of the fruit, and is become,
Not dead, as we are threatened, but thenceforth                    870
Endued with human voice and human sense,
Reasoning to admiration,[2] and with me
Persuasively hath so prevailed, that I
Have also tasted, and have also found
Th' effects to correspond, opener mine eyes                        875
Dim erst, dilated spirits, ampler heart,
And growing up to godhead; which for thee
Chiefly I sought, without thee can despise.
For bliss, as thou hast part, to me is bliss,
Tedious, unshared with thee, and odious soon.                      880
Thou therefore also taste, that equal lot
May join us, equal joy, as equal love;
Lest, thou not tasting, different degree[3]
Disjoin us, and I then too late renounce
Deity for thee, when Fate will not permit."[4]                     885
     Thus Eve with countenance blithe her story told;
But in her cheek distemper[5] flushing glowed.
On th' other side, Adam, soon as he heard
The fatal trespass done by Eve, amazed,
Astonied[6] stood and blank, while horror chill                    890
Ran through his veins, and all his joints relaxed;[7]
From his slack hand the garland wreathed for Eve
Down dropped, and all the faded roses shed.
Speechless he stood and pale, till thus at length
First to himself he inward silence broke:                          895
     "O fairest of creation, last and best
Of all God's works, creature in whom excelled
Whatever can to sight or thought be formed,

---

9. When tasted.    1. Has been proved by tasting.    2. Admirably.    3. A difference in rank
between us.    4. Cf., and contrast, lines, 825–833 above.    5. Disharmony in the body's
"humours"; disease.    6. Stunned.    7. Slackened.

Holy, divine, good, amiable, or sweet!
How art thou lost, how on a sudden lost,                    900
Defaced, deflowered, and now to death devote?[8]
Rather how hast thou yielded to transgress
The strict forbiddance, how to violate
The sacred fruit forbidden! Some cursèd fraud
Of enemy hath beguiled thee, yet unknown,[9]             905
And me with thee hath ruined, for with thee
Certain my resolution is to die.
How can I live without thee, how forgo
Thy sweet converse and love so dearly joined,
To live again in these wild woods forlorn?               910
Should God create another Eve, and I
Another rib afford, yet loss of thee
Would never from my heart; no, no! I feel
The link of nature draw me: flesh of flesh,
Bone of my bone thou art, and from thy state            915
Mine never shall be parted, bliss or woe."
    So having said, as one from sad dismay
Recomforted, and after thoughts disturbed
Submitting to what seemed remediless,
Thus in calm mood his words to Eve he turned:            920
    "Bold deed thou hast presumed, adventurous Eve
And peril great provoked, who thus hath dared
Had it been only coveting to eye
That sacred fruit, sacred to abstinence,
Much more to taste it, under ban to touch.               925
But past who can recall, or done undo?
Not God omnipotent, nor Fate! Yet so
Perhaps thou shalt not die, perhaps the fact
Is not so heinous now, foretasted fruit,
Profaned first by the serpent, by him first              930
Made common and unhallowed ere our taste,
Nor yet on him found deadly; he yet lives,
Lives, as thou saidst, and gains to live as man
Higher degree of life: inducement strong
To us, as likely, tasting, to attain                     935
Proportional[1] ascent, which cannot be
But to be gods, or angels, demigods.
Nor can I think that God, Creator wise,
Though threatening, will in earnest so destroy
Us his prime creatures, dignified so high,               940
Set over all his works, which in our fall,

8. Doomed.   9. Refers to "enemy."   1. Proportionate to our human status (cf. the Serpent's
argument, lines 710–12 above).

For us created, needs with us must fail,
Dependent made; so God shall uncreate,
Be frustrate, do, undo, and labor lose;
Not well conceived of God,[2] who, though his power                  945
Creation could repeat, yet would be loath
Us to abolish, lest the adversary
Triúmph and say: 'Fickle their state whom God
Most favors; who can please him long? Me first
He ruined, now mankind; whom will he next?'                         950
Matter of scorn, not to be given the foe.
However, I with thee have fixed my lot.
Certain[3] to undergo like doom: if death
Consort with thee, death is to me as life;
So forcible within my heart I feel                                  955
The bond of nature draw me to my own,
My own in thee, for what thou art is mine;
Our state cannot be severed; we are one,
One flesh; to lose thee were to lose myself."
    So Adam, and thus Eve to him replied:                          960
"O glorius trial of exceeding love,
Illustrious evidence, example high!
Engaging me to emulate; but short
Of thy perfection, how shall I attain,
Adam? from whose dear side I boast me sprung,                      965
And gladly of our union hear thee speak,
One heart, one soul in both; whereof good proof
This day affords, declaring thee resolved,
Rather than death or aught than death more dread
Shall separate us, linked in love so dear,                         970
To undergo with me one guilt, one crime,
If any be, of tasting this fair fruit;
Whose virtue (for of good still good proceeds,
Direct, or by occasion)[4] hath presented
This happy trial of thy love, which else                           975
So eminently never had been known.
Were it I thought death menaced would ensue
This my attempt, I would sustain alone
The worst, and not persuade thee, rather die
Deserted, than oblige[5] thee with a fact                          980
Pernicious to thy peace, chiefly assured
Remarkably so late of thy so true,
So faithful love unequaled; but I feel
Far otherwise th' event;[6] not death, but life

2. That would be a wrong conception of God.   3. Resolved.   4. Indirectly.   5. Involve
(Adam in her guilty action).   6. The eventual consequence of her transgression.

Augmented, opened eyes, new hopes, new joys,                    985
Taste so divine, that what of sweet before
Hath touched my sense, flat seems to this, and harsh.
On my experience, Adam, freely taste,
And fear of death deliver to the winds."
    So saying, she embraced him, and for joy                    990
Tenderly wept, much won that he his love
Had so ennobled, as of choice to incur
Divine displeasure for her sake, or death.
In recompense (for such compliance bad
Such recompense best merits), from the bough                   995
She gave him of that fair enticing fruit
With liberal hand; he scrupled not to eat,
Against his better knowledge, not deceived,[7]
But fondly overcome with female charm.
Earth trembled from her entrails, as again                     1000
In pangs, and Nature gave a second groan.
Sky lowered, and muttering thunder, some sad drops
Wept at completing of the mortal sin
Original; while Adam took no thought,
Eating his fill, nor Eve to iterate                            1005
Her former trespass feared, the more to soothe
Him with her loved society; that now
As with new wine intoxicated both,
They swim in mirth, and fancy that they feel
Divinity within them breeding wings                            1010
Wherewith to scorn the Earth. But that false fruit
Far other operation first displayed,
Carnal desire inflaming; he on Eve
Began to cast lascivious eyes, she him
As wantonly repaid; in lust they burn,                         1015
Till Adam thus 'gan Eve to dalliance move:
    "Eve, now I see thou art exact of taste,[8]
And elegant, of sapience[9] no small part,
Since to each meaning savor we apply,
And palate call judicious. I the praise                        1020
Yield thee, so well this day thou hast purveyed.
Much pleasure we have lost, while we abstained
From this delightful fruit, nor known till now
True relish, tasting; if such pleasure be
In things to us forbidden, it might be wished,                 1025

---

7. Adam, unlike Eve, acts in full consciousness, not having been "deceived" by the Serpent.
8. Of exacting taste.    9. In both meanings of the word ("wisdom" and "taste") originating in
the Latin *sapere*, as does "savour," similarly played on in the next line. *Elegant:* Choosy, refined.

For[1] this one tree had been forbidden ten.
But come; so well refreshed, now let us play,
As meet is, after such delicious fare;
For never did thy beauty, since the day
I saw thee first and wedded thee, adorned                    1030
With all perfections, so enflame my sense
With ardor to enjoy thee, fairer now
Than ever, bounty of this virtuous[2] tree."
    So said he, and forbore not glance or toy[3]
Of[4] amorous intent, well understood                        1035
Of Eve, whose eye darted contagious fire.
Her hand he seized, and to a shady bank,
Thick overhead with verdant roof embowered
He led her, nothing loath; flowers were the couch,
Pansies, and violets, and asphodel,                          1040
And hyacinth, Earth's freshest, softest lap.
There they their fill of love and love's disport
Took largely, of their mutual guilt the seal,
The solace of their sin, till dewy sleep
Oppressed them, wearied with their amorous play.             1045
    Soon as the force of that fallacious fruit,
That with exhilarating vapor bland
About their spirits had played, and inmost powers
Made err, was now exhaled, and grosser sleep
Bred of unkindly fumes,[5] with conscious dreams             1050
Encumbered, now had left them, up they rose
As from unrest, and each the other viewing,
Soon found their eyes how opened, and their minds
How darkened. Innocence, that as a veil
Had shadowed them from knowing ill, was gone;                1055
Just confidence, and native righteousness,
And honor from about them, naked left
To guilty Shame; he covered, but his robe
Uncovered more.[6] So rose the Danite strong,
Herculean Samson, from the harlot-lap                        1060
Of Philistean Dalilah, and waked
Shorn of his strength;[7] they destitute and bare
Of all their virtue. Silent, and in face
Confounded, long they sat, as strucken mute;
Till Adam, though not less than Eve abashed,                 1065
At length gave utterance to these words constrained:

1. Instead of.    2. Endowed with special power (the "virtue" of lines 651 and 778 above).
3. Toying, playing.    4. By.    5. Unnatural exhalations.    6. Shame (personified) covered
them, but his cover ("robe") only made them aware of their nakedness ("uncovered more").
7. For the story of Samson betrayed by his wife Delilah see Judges 16:4–20. *Danite*: Of the tribe
of Dan.

"O Eve, in evil hour thou didst give ear
To that false worm,[8] of whomsoever taught
To counterfeit man's voice, true in our fall,
False in our promised rising; since our eyes          1070
Opened we find indeed, and find we know
Both good and evil, good lost, and evil got:
Bad fruit of knowledge, if this be to know,
Which leaves us naked thus, of honor void,
Of innocence, of faith, of purity,          1075
Our wonted ornaments now soiled and stained,
And in our faces evident the signs
Of foul concupiscence; whence evil store,[9]
Even shame, the last[1] of evils; of the first
Be sure then. How shall I behold the face          1080
Henceforth of God or angel, erst with joy
And rapture so oft beheld? Those heavenly shapes
Will dazzle now this earthly[2] with their blaze
Insufferably bright. O might I here
In solitude live savage, in some glade          1085
Obscured, where highest woods, impenetrable
To star or sunlight, spread their umbrage broad,
And brown[3] as evening! Cover me, ye pines,
Ye cedars, with innumerable boughs
Hide me, where I may never see them[4] more!          1090
But let us now, as in[5] bad plight, devise
What best may for the present serve to hide
The parts of each from other, that seem most
To shame obnoxious,[6] and unseemliest seen;
Some tree whose broad smooth leaves together sewed,          1095
And girded on our loins, may cover round
Those middle parts, that this newcomer, Shame,
There sit not, and reproach us as unclean."
    So counseled he, and both together went
Into the thickest wood; there soon they chose          1100
The figtree,[7] not that kind for fruit renowned,
But such as at this day, to Indians known,
In Malabar or Deccan[8] spreads her arms
Branching so broad and long, that in the ground
The bended twigs take root, and daughters grow          1105
About the mother tree, a pillared shade
High overarched, and echoing walks between;

8. The Serpent, now disparaged.    9. An abundance of evils.    1. Extreme, ultimate.
2. Adam's now earthly nature and senses.    3. Dark.    4. The "heavenly shapes" of line
1082.    5. As we are in.    6. Exposed to.    7. Identified as the banyan or Indian fig tree, also
classified in botany as *Ficus religiosa*.    8. Regions in southern India.

There oft the Indian herdsman, shunning heat,
Shelters in cool, and tends his pasturing herds
At loopholes cut through thickest shade. Those leaves 1110
They gathered, broad as Amazonian targe,[9]
And with what skill they had, together sewed,
To gird their waist; vain covering, if to hide
Their guilt and dreaded shame! O how unlike
To that first naked glory! Such of late 1115
Columbus found th' American, so girt
With feathered cincture,[1] naked else and wild
Among the trees on isles and woody shores.
Thus fenced, and, as they thought, their shame in part
Covered, but not at rest or ease of mind, 1120
They sat them down to weep; nor only tears
Rained at their eyes, but high winds worse within
Began to rise, high passions, anger, hate,
Mistrust, suspicion, discord, and shook sore
Their inward state of mind, calm region once 1125
And full of peace, now tossed and turbulent:
For Understanding ruled not, and the Will
Heard not her lore, both in subjection now
To sensual Appetite, who, from beneath
Usurping over sovereign Reason, claimed 1130
Superior sway.[2] From thus distempered breast,
Adam, estranged in look and altered style,
Speech intermitted thus to Eve renewed:
   "Would thou hadst hearkened to my words, and stayed
With me, as I besought thee, when that strange 1135
Desire of wandering, this unhappy morn,
I know not whence possessed thee! we had then
Remained still happy, not as now, despoiled
Of all our good, shamed, naked, miserable.
Let none henceforth seek needless cause to approve 1140
The faith they owe;[3] when earnestly they seek
Such proof, conclude, they then begin to fail."
   To whom, soon moved with touch of blame, thus Eve:
"What words have passed thy lips, Adam severe?
Imput'st thou that to my default, or will 1145
Of wandering, as thou call'st it, which who knows
But might as ill have happened, thou being by,

---

9. Cf. "target": the shield of the Amazons, women warriors in Greco-Roman myth (and memorably in Virgil's *Aeneid*). Actually, the leaf of the "Indian fig tree" is small; Milton's inaccurate notion comes from contemporary sources he knew, and goes back to antiquity.   1. Belt. 2. The victory of "sensual Appetite" over "Reason," both here personified (cf. line 113 above, and note 37) and over man's free will (cf. line 351 ff.), man's distinguishing traits, is of course, in brief abstract, the very history of the Fall.   3. Own. *Approve:* Prove by testing.

Or to thyself perhaps? Hadst thou been there,
Or here th' attempt, thou couldst not have discerned
Fraud in the serpent, speaking as he spake;        1150
No gound of enmity between us known,
Why he should mean me ill, or seek to harm?
Was I to have never parted from thy side?
As good have grown there still a lifeless rib.
Being as I am, why didst not thou, the head,        1155
Command me absolutely not to go,
Going into such danger, as thou saidst?
Too facile then, thou didst not much gainsay,
Nay, didst permit, approve, and fair dismiss.
Hadst thou been firm and fixed in thy dissent,        1160
Neither had I transgressed, nor thou with me."[4]
    To whom, then first incensed, Adam replied:
"Is this the love, is this the recompense
Of mine to thee, ingrateful Eve, expressed[5]
Immutable when thou were lost, not I,        1165
Who might have lived and joyed immortal bliss,
Yet willingly chose rather death with thee?
And am I now upbraided as the cause
Of thy transgressing? not enough severe,
It seems, in thy restraint![6] What could I more?        1170
I warned thee, I admonished thee, foretold
The danger, and the lurking enemy
That lay in wait; beyond this had been force,
And force upon free will hath here no place.
But confidence then bore thee on, secure        1175
Either to meet no danger, or to find
Matter of glorious trial; and perhaps
I also erred in overmuch admiring
What seemed in thee so perfect, that I thought
No evil durst attempt thee! but I rue        1180
That error now, which is become my crime,
And thou th' accuser. Thus it shall befall
Him who, to worth in women overtrusting,
Lets her will rule; restraint she will not brook,[7]
And, left to herself, if evil thence ensue,        1185
She first his weak indulgence will accuse."
    Thus they in mutual accusation spent

---

4. The notion of man's authority over woman—recognized by Milton's Eve (e.g., in Book IV, 442–443: "my guide / and head") and echoing St. Paul ("the head of the woman is the man," I Corinthians, 10:13) is here used by her to make Adam her equal in guilt, accusing him of indulgence in letting her go ("too facile").   **5.** Demonstrated, proved.   **6.** In restraining Eve.   **7.** Put up with.

The fruitless hours, but neither self-condemning;
And of their vain contést appeared no end.

### Book X.

THE ARGUMENT.

Man's transgression known, the guardian Angels forsake Paradise,
and return up the Heaven to approve their vigilance, and are approved;
God declaring that the entrance of Satan could not be by them prevented. He sends his Son to judge the transgressors; who descends,
and gives sentence accordingly; then, in pity, clothes them both, and
reascends. Sin and Death, sitting till then at the gates of Hell, by
wondrous sympathy feeling the success of Satan in this new World,
and the sin by Man there committed, resolve to sit no longer confined in Hell, but to follow Satan, their sire, up to the place of Man:
to make the way easier from Hell to this World to and fro, they pave
a broad highway or bridge over Chaos, according to the track that
Satan first made; then, preparing for Earth, they meet him, proud of
his success, returning to Hell; their mutual gratulation. Satan arrives
at Pandemonium; in full assembly relates, with boasting, his success
against Man; instead of applause is entertained with a general hiss by
all his audience, transformed, with himself also, suddenly into Serpents, according to his doom given in Paradise; then, deluded with
a show of the Forbidden Tree springing up before them, they, greedily reaching to take of the fruit, chew dust and bitter ashes. The
proceedings of Sin and Death: God foretells the final victory of his
Son over them, and the renewing of all things; but, for the present,
commands his Angels to make several alterations in the Heavens and
Elements. Adam, more and more perceiving his fallen condition,
heavily bewails,[8] rejects the condolement of Eve; she persists, and at
lenght appeases him: then, to evade the curse likely to fall on their
offspring, proposes to Adam violent ways; which he approves not,
but, conceiving better hope, puts her in mind of the late promise
made them, that her seed should be revenged on the Serpent, and
exhorts her, with him, to seek peace of the offended Deity by repentance and supplication.

[ACCEPTANCE, RECONCILIATION, HOPE]

Be it so, for I submit; his doom is fair,[9]
That dust I am and shall to dust return.                    770

8. Our selection starts toward the end of Adam's long lamentation.    9. In his inner debate,
Adam has just been arguing to himself that God created man "of choice his own, / and of his own
to serve him"; hence in the same way as reward "was of his [God's] grace," so punishment "justly
is at his will," therefore acceptable.

O welcome hour whenever! Why delays
His hand to execute what his decree
Fixed on this day? Why do I overlive?
Why am I mocked with death, and lengthened out
To deathless pain? How gladly would I meet                        775
Mortality, my sentence, and be earth
Insensible! how glad would lay me down
As in my mother's lap![1] There I should rest
And sleep secure; his dreadful voice no more
Would thunder in my ears; no fear of worse                        780
To me and to my offspring would torment me
With cruel expectation. Yet one doubt
Pursues me still, lest all I cannot die;
Lest that pure breath of life, the spirit of man
Which God inspired, cannot together perish                        785
With this corporeal clod; then, in the grave,
Or in some other dismal place, who knows
But I shall die a living death? O thought
Horrid, if true![2] Yet why? It was but breath
Of life that sinned; what dies but what had life                  790
And sin? the body properly hath neither.
All of me then shall die: let this appease
The doubt, since human reach no further knows.
For though the Lord of all be infinite,
Is his wrath also? Be it, man is not so,                          795
But mortal doomed. How can he exercise
Wrath without end on man whom death must end?
Can he make deathless death? That were to make
Strange contradiction, which to God himself
Impossible is held, as argument                                   800
Of weakness, nor of power.[3] Will he draw out,
For anger's sake, finite to infinte
In punished man, to satisfy his rigor
Satisfied never? That were to extend
His sentence beyond dust and Nature's law;                        805
By which all causes else according still
To the reception of their matter act,

---

1. The reference is to the earth (in Book XI, line 536, Michael, addressing Adam, calls the earth "thy Mother's lap"), and is in part probably an echo of Job 3.   2. Adam's fear at first is that the body ("corporeal clod") may not die with the soul (the God-inspired [i.e., inbreathed] "Spirit of Man"), causing a "living death" in the grave.   3. Adam corrects himself, arguing (as Milton did in his theological writings) that since only the spirit ("breath of life") sinned, it shall die with the body (and, implicitly, await resurrection). Otherwise, according to the same theological line of thinking, there would be "strange contradiction," an inadmissable sign of weakness in God.

Not to th' extent of their own sphere.[4] But say
That death be not one stroke, as I supposed,
Bereaving sense,[5] but endless misery                              810
From this day onward, which I feel begun
Both in me and without[6] me, and so last
To perpetuity—Ay me! that fear
Comes thundering back with dreadful revolution
On my defenseless head! Both death and I                           815
Am[7] found eternal, and incorporate both:
Nor I on my part single; in me all
Posterity stands cursed. Fair patrimony
That I must leave ye, sons! O, were I able
To waste it all myself, and leave ye none!                         820
So disinherited, how would ye bless
Me, now your curse! Ah, why should all mankind
For one man's fault thus guiltless be condemned,
If guiltless? But from me what can proceed,
But all corrupt, both mind and will depraved,                      825
Not to do only, but to will the same
With me? How can they then acquitted stand
In sight of God?[8] Him, after all disputes,
Forced I absolve. All my evasions vain
And reasonings, though through mazes, lead me still                830
But to my own conviction: first and last
On me, me only, as the source and spring
Of all corruption, all the blame lights due;
So might the wrath! Fond[9] wish! Couldst thou support
That burden, heavier than the earth to bear;                       835
Than all the world much heavier, though divided
With that bad woman? Thus, what thou desir'st,
And what thou fear'st, alike destroys all hope[1]
Of refuge, and concludes thee[2] miserable
Beyond all past example[3] and future;                             840
To Satan only like, both crime and doom.[4]

---

4. According to "Nature's law," the power of all agents, God excepted ("all causes else"), cannot be exercised to its utmost ("the extent of their own sphere"), but is limited by the capacity for "reception" that the object of that power possesses. Consequently, man cannot suffer further punishment beyond death.    5. Removing all sensory powers.    6. Outside.    7. The verb in the singular form stresses Adam's concentration on himself, and on the fact that he and Death are now united in one body ("incorporate").    8. Inheriting Adam's original sin, his descendents, like him ("with me"), are going to act sinfully by their own free will.    9. Foolish.    1. Actually, by his desperate self-accusation, and by wanting to assume, alone, the burden of guilt, Adam is shown to be already on the way to full repentance and to his own regeneration.    2. Demonstrates that you are.    3. That of the fallen angels.    4. The comparison is clearly invalid, Adam's remorse and repentent despair being opposite to Satan's choice, as seen for instance in Book IV, 109–110: "Farewell Remorse: all good to me is lost; / Evil be now my Good. . ."

O Conscience! into what abyss of fears
And horrors hast thou driven me; out of which
I find no way, from deep to deeper plunged!"
   Thus Adam to himself lamented loud                                845
Through the still night, not now, as ere man fell,
Wholesome and cool and mild, but with black air
Accompanied, with damps and dreadful gloom;
Which to his evil conscience represented
All things with double terror. On the ground                        850
Outstretched he lay, on the cold ground, and oft
Cursed his creation; Death as oft accused
Of tardy execution, since denounced
The day of his offense. "Why comes not Death,"
Said he, "with one thrice-acceptable stroke                          855
To end me? Shall Truth fail to keep her word,
Justice divine not hasten to be just?
But Death comes not at call; Justice divine
Mends not her slowest pace for prayers or cries.
O woods, O fountains, hillocks, dales, and bowers!                   860
With other echo late I taught your shades
To answer, and resound far other song."
Whom thus afflicted when sad Eve beheld,
Desolate where she sat, approaching nigh,
Soft words to his fierce passion she essayed;                        865
But her with stern regard he thus repelled:
   "Out of my sight, thou serpent! that name best
Befits thee, with him leagued, thyself as false
And hateful: nothing wants, but that thy shape,
Like his, and color serpentine, may show                            870
Thy inward fraud, to warn all creatures from thee
Henceforth; lest that too heavenly form, pretended[5]
To hellish falsehood, snare them. But for thee
I had persisted happy, had not thy pride
And wandering vanity, when least was safe,                          875
Rejected my forewarning, and disdained
Not to be trusted, longing to be seen
Though by the devil himself, him overweening
To overreach,[6] but, with the serpent meeting,
Fooled and beguiled; by him thou, I by thee,                        880
To trust thee from my side, imagined wise,
Constant, mature, proof against all assaults;
And understood not all was but a show
Rather than solid virtue, all but a rib

---

5. Put up as a screen.     6. Overestimating your power to outwit him.

Crooked by nature—bent, as now appears,                    885
More to the part siníster—from me drawn;
Well if thrown out, as supernumerary
To my just number found![7] Oh, why did God,
Creator wise, that peopled highest Heaven
With spirits masculine, create at last                    890
This novelty on earth, this fair defect
Of nature, and not fill the world at once
With men, as angels, without feminine;
Or find some other way to generate
Mankind?[8] This mischief had not then befallen,                    895
And more that shall befall—innumerable
Disturbances on earth through female snares,
And strait conjunction with this sex. For either
He never shall find out fit mate, but such
As some misfortune brings him, or mistake;                    900
Or whom he wishes most shall seldom gain,
Through her perverseness, but shall see her gained
By a far worse, or, if she love, withheld
By parents, or his happiest choice too late
Shall meet, already linked[9] and wedlock-bound                    905
To a fell[1] adversary, his hate or shame:
Which infinite calamity shall cause
To human life, and household peace confound."
    He added not, and from her turned; but Eve,
Not so repulsed, with tears that ceased not flowing,                    910
And tresses all disordered, at his feet
Fell humble, and, embracing them, besought
His peace, and thus proceeded in her plaint:
    "Forsake me not thus, Adam! witness Heaven
What love sincere and reverence in my heart                    915
I bear thee, and unweeting[2] have offended,
Unhappily deceived! Thy suppliant[3]
I beg, and clasp thy knees; beereave me not,
Whereon I live, thy gentle looks, thy aid,
Thy counsel in this uttermost distress,                    920
My only strength and stay: forlorn of thee,
Whither shall I betake me, where subsist?
While yet we live, scarce one short hour perhaps,
Between us two let there be peace; both joining,

7. Folklore has it that the rib from which Eve was created was an extra thirteenth rib on Adam's left (Latin *sinister*) side. Note double meaning of "sinister."   8. Adam's frenzied speech belongs to a tradition of anti-feminist rhetoric that goes back to antiquity. Lines 888–895, in particular, seem to echo lines 617–620 of the tragedy *Hippolytus* by Euripides, one of Milton's favorite poets.   9. When *he* is already linked.   1. Fierce, bitter.   2. Unknowingly.   3. As thy suppliant.

As joined in injuries, one enmity                                925
Against a foe by doom express assigned us,
That cruel serpent. On me exercise not
Thy hatred for this misery befallen;
On me already lost, me than thyself
More miserable. Both have sinned, but thou                       930
Against God only; I against God and thee,
And to the place of judgment will return,
There with my cries importune Heaven, that all
The sentence, from thy head removed, may light
On me, sole cause to thee of all this woe,                       935
Me, me only, just object of his ire."
     She ended weeping; and her lowly plight,
Immovable till peace obtained from fault
Acknowledged and deplored, in Adam wrought
Commiseration.[4] Soon his heart relented                        940
Towards her, his life so late and sole delight,
Now at his feet submissive in distress,
Creature so fair his reconcilement seeking,
His counsel, whom she had displeased, his aid;
As one disarmed, his anger all he lost,                          945
And thus with peaceful words upraised her soon:
     "Unwary, and too desirous, as before,
So now, of what thou know'st not,[5] who desir'st
The punishment all on thyself! Alas!
Bear thine own first, ill able to sustain                        950
His full wrath, whose thou feel'st as yet least part,[6]
And my displeasure bear'st so ill. If prayers
Could alter high decrees, I to that place
Would speed before thee, and be louder heard,
That on my head all might be visited,                            955
Thy frailty and infirmer sex forgiven,
To me committed, and by me exposed.[7]
But rise; let us no more contend, nor blame
Each other, blamed enough elsewhere,[8] but strive
In offices of love, how we may lighten                           960
Each other's burden in our share of woe;
Since this day's death denounced, if aught I see,

---

4. Adam was at first untouched ("immutable") by Eve's humble attitude ("lowly plight"); what
brings "peace" and "reconcilement" between them is her admission and deploration of her own
guilt.    5. Once more ("as before / so now") Eve is "too desirous" of the unknown; but her
situation and her tone are now totally different and so are Adam's, whose "counsel" and "aid" she
has sought.    6. Eve would not be able to bear the weight of God's full wrath, of which she has
until now experienced only the smallest part.    7. In the present atmosphere of reconciliation,
Adam seems to accept Eve's earlier charge (cf. Book IX, lines 1158–1161, and note 228): now he
blames himself for having "exposed" her to temptation.    8. At the place of judgment (cf. lines
932 and 953 above, 1098–1099 below).

Will prove no sudden, but a slow-paced evil,
A long day's dying to augment our pain,
And to our seed (O hapless seed!) derived."[9]                                965
    To whom thus Eve, recovering heart, replied:—
"Adam, by sad experiment I know
How little weight my words with thee can find,
Found so erroneous, thence by just event
Found so unfortunate. Nevertheless,                                        970
Restored by thee, vile as I am, to place
Of new acceptance, hopeful to regain
Thy love, the sole contentment of my heart,
Living or dying from thee I will not hide
What thoughts in my unquiet breast are risen,                              975
Tending to some relief of our extremes,
Or end, though sharp and sad, yet tolerable,
As in our evils,[1] and of easier choice.
If care of our descent[2] perplex us most,
Which must be born to certain woe, devoured                                980
By Death at last (and miserable it is
To be to others cause of misery,
Our own begotten, and of our loins to bring
Into this cursed world a woeful race,
That, after wretched life, must be at last                                 985
Food for so foul a monster), in thy power
It lies, yet ere conception, to prevent
The race unblest, to being yet unbegot.[3]
Childless thou art; childless remain. So Death
Shall be deceived his glut,[4] and with us two                             990
Be forced to satisfy his ravenous maw.
But, if thou judge it hard and difficult,
Conversing, looking, loving, to abstain
From love's due rites, nuptial embraces sweet,
And with desire to languish without hope
Before the present object[5] languishing
With like desire—which would be misery                                     995
And torment less than none of what we dread—
Then, both our selves and seed at once to free
From what we fear for both, let us make short;                             1000
Let us seek Death, or, he not found, supply
With our own hands his office on ourselves.
Why stand we longer shivering under fears
That show no end but death, and have the power,

9. Transmitted.   1. We being in such evils.   2. Descendants, lineage.   3. To forestall,
by abstinence, the birth of descendants.   4. Shall be cheated of its fill,   5. Eve herself, object
of Adam's love, and now in his presence.

Of many ways to die the shortest choosing                                    1005
Destruction with destruction to destroy?"[6]
   She ended here, or vehement despair
Broke off the rest; so much of death her thoughts
Had entertained as dyed her cheeks with pale.
But Adam, with such counsel nothing swayed,                                    1010
To better hopes his more attentive mind
Laboring had raised, and thus to Eve replied:—
   "Eve, thy contempt of life and pleasure seems
To argue in thee something more sublime
And excellent than what thy mind contemns:                                    1015
But self-distruction therefore sought refutes
That excellence thought in thee, and implies
Not thy contempt, but anguish and regret
For loss of life and pleasure overloved.[7]
Or, if thou covet death, as utmost end                                    1020
Of misery, so thinking to evade
The penalty pronounced, doubt not but God
Hath wiselier armed his vengeful ire than so
To be forestalled. Much more I fear lest death
So snatched will not exempt us from the pain                                    1025
We are by doom to pay; rather such acts
Of contumacy will provoke the Highest
To make death in us live. Then let us seek
Some safer resolution—which methinks
I have in view, calling to mind with heed                                    1030
Part of our sentence,[8] that thy seed shall bruise
The Serpent's head. Piteous amends! unless
Be meant whom I conjecture,[9] our grand foe,
Satan, who in the Serpent hath contrived
Against us this deceit. To crush his head                                    1035
Would be revenge indeed—which will be lost
By death brought on ourselves, or childless days
Resolved as thou proposest; so our foe
Shall scape his punishment ordained, and we
Instead shall double ours upon our heads,                                    1040

6. Destroy "destruction" (i.e., Death's power to destroy future mankind) by destroying ourselves now.    7. I.e., the suicide project excludes ("refutes") the idea that Eve be contemptuous of life and pleasure in view of "something more sublime;" it rather implies "anguish and regret" at the thought of losing those goods.    8. In lines 163–208 of this Book X (cf. The Argument), the Lord "gives sentence" on the Serpent and on the transgressors. The references in the following lines are to that passage (which in turn is quite literally based on Genesis, XXX), particularly to lines 179–181: "Between thee and the Woman I will put / Enmity, and between thine and her seed; / Her seed shall bruise thy head, thou bruise his heel."    9. The notion that Satan spoke through the Serpent was not at first given to Man (lines 170–171 of this Book: "Concerned not Man. . . . / Nor altered his offense"); Adam is late in coming to that conclusion ("I conjecture"); and on it he bases his following eloquent argument in favor of survival, hope, procreation, activity.

No more be mentioned, then, of violence
Against ourselves, and wilful barrenness
That cuts us off from hope, and savors only
Rancor and pride, impatience and despite,
Reluctance[1] against God and his just yoke                          1045
Laid on our necks. Remember with what mild
And gracious temper he both heard and judged,
Without wrath or reviling. We expected
Immediate dissolution, which we thought
Was meant by death that day; when, lo! to thee                       1050
Pains only in child-bearing were foretold,
And bringing forth, soon recompensed with joy,
Fruit of thy womb. On me the curse aslope
Glanced on the ground.[2] With labor I must earn
My bread; what harm: Idleness had been worse;                        1055
My labor will sustain me; and, lest cold
Or heat should injure us, his timely care
Hath, unbesought, provided, and his hands
Clothed us unworthy, pitying while he judged.
How much more, if we pray him, will his ear                          1060
Be open, and his heart to pity incline,
And teach us further by what means to shun
The inclement seasons, rain, ice, hail, and snow!
Which now the sky, with various face, begins
To show us in this mountain,[3] while the winds                      1065
Blow moist and keen, shattering the graceful locks
Of these fair spreading trees; which bids us seek
Some better shroud, some better warmth to cherish
Our limbs benumbed—ere this diurnal star[4]
Leave cold the night, now[5] we his gathered beams                   1070
Reflected may with matter sere foment,[6]
Or by collision of two bodies grind
The air attrite to fire;[7] as late the clouds,

1. Resistance, opposition.    2. I.e., the curse descending ("aslope") on Adam took an oblique course ("glanced") toward the ground. Thus Adam is not only accepting the Lord's sentence (lines 201–202 and 205 of this Book: "Curs'd is the ground for thy sake; thou in sorrow / Shalt eat thereof all the days of thy life; / . . . . In the sweat of thy face thou shalt eat bread. . . ."), but turning it into a project for an active life after the Fall.    3. In his description of "delicious Paradise" in Book IV, lines 132–158, Milton situates it on a high plateau at the top of a "steep wilderness" which denies access to the "enclosure green" and its "insuperable height of loftiest shade, / Cedar, and pine, and fir, and branching palm, / A sylvan scene, and, as the ranks ascend / Shade above shade, a woody theater / Of stateliest view . . . ," where "gentle gales / . . . dispense / Native perfumes, and whisper whence they stole / Those balmy spoils." That stately and blissful order is now disrupted, and after the radical alterations in the heavens and in the elements which God has commanded, Adam is preparing to cope with the hardships and the challenges of his mortal state in a time-conditioned universe of season changes, dawns and sunsets, heat and ice, and shattering winds.    4. The day-star, the sun.    5. "Seek" how.    6. Heat, warm.    7. The implied belief is that rubbing two "bodies" (as two flints) against each other, the air thus "attrite" (i.e., "ground" down by the attrition) turns into fire.

Justling, or pushed with winds, rude in their shock,
Tine[8] the slant lightning, whose thwart flame, driven down,                    1075
Kindles the gummy bark of fir or pine,
And sends a comfortable heat from far,
Which might supply the Sun. Such fire to use,
And what may else be remedy or cure
To evils which our own misdeeds have wrought,                    1080
He will instruct us praying,[9] and of grace
Beseeching him; so as we need not fear
To pass commodiously this life, sustained
By him with many comforts, till we end
In dust, our final rest and native home.                    1085
What better can we do than, to the place
Repairing where he judged us, prostrate fall
Before him reverent, and there confess
Humbly our faults, and pardon beg, with tears
Watering the ground, and with our sighs the air                    1090
Frequenting,[1] sent from hearts contrite, in sign
Of sorrow unfeigned and humiliation meek?
Undoubtedly he will relent, and turn
From his displeasure, in whose look serene,
When angry most he seemed and most severe,                    1095
What else but favor, grace, and mercy shone?"
    So spake our Father penitent; nor Eve
Felt less remorse. They, forthwith to the place
Repairing where he judged them, prostrate fell
Before him reverent, and both confessed                    110
Humbly their faults, and pardon begged, with tears
Watering the ground, and with their sighs the air
Frequenting, sent from hearts contrite, in sign
Of sorrow unfeigned and humiliation meek.

## Book XII

### ["THE WORLD WAS ALL BEFORE THEM"]

    After God's acceptance of the transgressors' prayers, and the decree
that "they must no longer abide in Paradise" (Book XI, The Argument), Michael the Archangel, with a band of Cherubim, has been
sent "to dispossess them." After Eve's lamentation and his own
pleading, Adam has submitted; Michael has led him up to a high
hill where, in a mixture of prophecy and instruction, he has set
"before him in vision" the future of mankind, from Cain and Abel

---

8. Kindle. That fire was produced by lightning is one of the ancient theories about its origin on
earth. *Thwart*: Passing across the sky.     9. If we pray to him.     1. Filling.

through Noah (end of Book XI) and the Prophets, thus coming "by degrees to explain who that Seed of Woman shall be which was promised Adam and Eve in the Fall: his incarnation, death, resurrection, and ascension; the state of the Church till his second coming" (Book XII, The Argument). Toward the close of his speech, Michael has recommended the exercise of the basic Christian virtues, culminating in love, "By name to come called Charity, the soul / Of all the rest: then will thou not be loath / To leave this Paradise, but shalt possess / A Paradise within thee, happier far" (lines 584–587). Michael has just ended his long speech.]

. . . He ended, and they both descend the hill.
Descended, Adam to the bower where Eve
Lay sleeping[2] ran before, but found her waked;
And thus with words not sad she him received:
        "Whence thou return'st and whither went'st, I know;        610
For God is also in sleep, and dreams[3] advise,
Which he hath sent propitious, some great good
Presaging, since, with sorrow and heart's distress
Wearied, I fell asleep. But now lead on;
In me is no delay; with thee to go        615
Is to stay here; without thee here to stay
Is to go hence unwilling; thou to me
Art all things under Heaven, all places thou,
Who for my willful crime art banished hence.
This further consolation yet secure        620
I carry hence: though all by me is lost,
Such favor I unworthy am vouchsafed,
By me the Promised Seed shall all restore."
        So spake our mother Eve; and Adam heard
Well pleased, but answered not; for now too nigh        625
Th' archangel stood, and from the other hill[4]
To their fixed station, all in bright array,
The cherubim descended; on the ground
Gliding meteorous, as evening mist
Risen from a river o'er the marish[5] glides,        630
And gathers ground fast at the laborer's heel
Homeward returning. High in front advanced,[6]
The brandished sword of God before them blazed,

---

**2.** Michael has just said to Adam (lines 594–597): ". . . Go, waken Eve; / Her also I with gentle dreams have calmed, / Portending good, and all her spirits composed / To meek submission. . ."
**3.** The fact that Adam was granted a "vision" and Eve a "dream" may symbolize a difference in the mode of perception between man and woman; at any rate, both are God's revelations.
**4.** The hill which Michael had indicated to Adam in lines 590–592: ". . . and, see! the guards, / By me encamped on yonder hill, expect / Their motion, at whose front a flaming sword, / In signal of remove, waves fiercely round." **5.** Marsh. **6.** Raised high, carried like a banner.

Fierce as a comet; which with torrid heat,
And vapor as the Libyan air adust,[7]                                    635
Began to parch that temperate clime; whereat
In either hand the hastening angel caught
Our lingering parents, and to th' eastern gate[8]
Led them direct, and down the cliff as fast
To the subjected[9] plain; then disappeared.                            640
They, looking back, all th' eastern side beheld
Of Paradise, so late their happy seat,[1]
Waved over by that flaming brand;[2] the gate
With dreadful faces thronged and fiery arms.
Some natural tears they dropped, but wiped them soon;                   645
The world was all before them, where to choose
Their place of rest,[3] and Providence their guide.
They, hand in hand, with wandering steps and slow,
Through Eden took their solitary way.

7. Burned up, as the air of the Sahara Desert in Libya.    8. Milton describes "the eastern gate"
of Eden, guarded by Gabriel, in Book IV, lines 543 ff.: "It was a rock / Of alabaster, piled up to
the clouds, / Conspicuous far, winding with one ascent / Accessible from Earth, one entrance
high; / The rest was craggy cliff. . ."    9. Lying below.    1. Abode.    2. The word "brand,"
here in its meaning of "sword," also conveys the image of "burning," "flaming."    3. Not, of
course, a place of repose, but their new, earthly abode.

# A Note on Translation

Reading literature in translation is a pleasure on which it is fruitless to frown. The purist may insist that we ought always read in the original languages, and we know ideally that this is true. But it is a counsel of perfection, quite impractical even for the purist, since no one in a lifetime can master all the languages whose literatures it would be a joy to explore. Master languages as fast as we may, we shall always have to read to some extent in translation, and this means we must be alert to what we are about: if in reading a work of literature in translation we are not reading the "original," what precisely are we reading? This is a question of great complexity, to which justice cannot be done in a brief note, but the following sketch of some of the considerations may be helpful.

One of the memorable scenes of ancient literature is the meeting of Hector and Andromache in Book VI of Homer's *Iliad*. Hector, leader and mainstay of the armies defending Troy, is implored by his wife Andromache to withdraw within the city walls and carry on the defense from there, where his life will not be constantly at hazard. In Homer's text her opening words to him are these: δαιμόνιε, φθίσει σε τὸ σὸν μένος (daimonie, phthisei se to son menos). How should they be translated into English?

Here is how they have actually been translated into English by capable translators, at various periods, in verse and prose.

1. George Chapman, 1598

> O noblest in desire,
> Thy mind, inflamed with others' good, will set thy self on fire.

2. John Dryden, 1693

> Thy dauntless heart (which I foresee too late),
> Too daring man, will urge thee to thy fate.

3. Alexander Pope, 1715

> Too daring Prince! . . .
> For sure such courage length of life denies,
> And thou must fall, thy virtue's sacrifice.

4. William Cowper, 1791

> Thy own great courage will cut short thy days,
> My noble Hector. . . .

5. Lang, Leaf, and Myers, 1883 (prose)

> Dear my lord, this thy hardihood will undo thee. . . .

6. A. T. Murray, 1924 (prose, Loeb Library)

> Ah, my husband, this prowess of thine will be thy doom. . . .

7. E. V. Rieu, 1950 (prose)

> "Hector," she said, "you are possessed. This bravery of yours will be your end."

8. I. A. Richards, 1950 (prose)

> "Strange man," she said, "your courage will be your destruction."

9. Richmond Lattimore, 1951

> Dearest,
> Your own great strength will be your death. . . .

From these strikingly different renderings of the same six words, certain facts about the nature of translation begin to emerge. We notice, for one thing, that Homer's word μένος (menos) is diversified by the translators into "mind," "dauntless heart," "such courage," "great courage," "hardihood," "prowess," "bravery," "courage," and "great strength." The word has in fact all these possibilities. Used of things, it normally means "force"; of animals, "fierceness" or "brute strength" or (in the case of horses) "mettle"; of men, "passion" or "spirit" or even "purpose." Homer's application of it in the present case points our attention equally—whatever particular sense we may imagine Andromache to have uppermost—to Hector's force, strength, fierceness in battle, spirited heart and mind. But since English has no matching term of like inclusiveness, the passage as the translators give it to us reflects this lack and we find one attribute singled out to the exclusion of the rest.

Here then is the first and most crucial fact about any work of literature read in translation. It cannot escape the linguistic characteristics of the language into which it is turned: the grammatical, syntactical, lexical, and phonetic boundaries which constitute collectively the individuality or "genius" of that language. A Greek play or a Russian novel in English will be governed first of all by the resources of the English language, resources which are certain to be in every instance very different, as the efforts with μένος show, from those of the original.

Turning from μένος to δαιμόνιε (daimonie) in Homer's clause, we encounter a second crucial fact about translations. Nobody knows exactly what shade of meaning δαιμόνιε had for Homer. In later writers the word normally suggests divinity, something miraculous, wondrous; but in Homer it appears as a vocative of address for both chieftain and commoner, man and wife. The coloring one gives it must therefore be determined either by the way one thinks a Greek wife of Homer's era might actually address her husband (a subject on which we have no information whatever), or in the way one thinks it suitable for a hero's wife to address her husband in an epic poem, that is to say, a highly stylized and formal work. In general, the translators of our century will be seen to have abandoned formality in order to stress the intimacy, the wifeliness, and, especially in Lattimore's case, a certain chiding tenderness, in Andromache's appeal: (6) "Ah, my husband," (7) "Hector" (with perhaps a hint, in "you are possessed," of the alarmed distaste with which wives have so often viewed their husbands' bellicose moods), (8) "Strange man," (9) "Dearest." On the other hand, the older translators have obviously removed Andromache to an epic or heroic distance from her beloved, whence she sees and kindles to his selfless courage, acknowledging, even in the moment of pleading with him to be otherwise, his moral grandeur and the tragic destiny this too certainly implies: (1) "O noblest in desire, . . . inflamed by others' good"; (2) "Thy dauntless heart (which I foresee too late), / Too daring man"; (3) "Too daring Prince! . . . / And thou must fall, thy virtue's sacrifice"; (4) "My noble Hector." Even the less specific "Dear my lord" of Lang, Leaf, and Myers looks in the same direction because of its echo of the speech of countless Shakespearean men and women who have shared this powerful moral sense: "Dear my lord, make me acquainted with your cause of grief"; "Perseverance, dear my lord, keeps honor bright"; etc.

   The fact about translation which emerges from all this is that just as the translated work reflects the individuality of the language it is turned into, so it reflects the individuality of the age in which it is made, and the age will permeate it everywhere like yeast in dough. We think of one kind of permeation when we think of the governing verse forms and attitudes toward verse at a given epoch. In Chapman's time, experiments seeking an "heroic" verse form for English were widespread, and accordingly he tries a "four-teener" couplet (two rhymed lines of seven stresses each) in his *Iliad* and a pentameter couplet in his *Odyssey*. When Dryden and Pope wrote, a closed pentameter couplet had become established as the heroic form *par excellence*. By Cowper's day, thanks largely to the prestige of *Paradise Lost*, the couplet had gone out of fashion for narrative poetry in favor of blank verse. Our age, inclining to prose and in verse to proselike informalities and relaxations, has, predictably, produced half a dozen excellent prose translations of the *Iliad*, but only two in verse (Lattimore's and that of Robert Fitzgerald), both relying on rhythms that are much of the time closer to the verse of William Carlos Williams and some of the prose of novelists like Faulkner than to the swift firm tread of Homer's Greek. For if it is true that what we translate from a given work is what, wearing the spectacles of our time, we see in it, it is also true that we see in it what we have the power to translate.

   Of course there are other effects of the translator's epoch on his translation besides those exercised by contemporary taste in verse and verse forms. Chapman writes in a great age of poetic metaphor and therefore almost instinctively translates his understanding of Homer's verb φθίσει (phthisei, "to cause to wane, consume, waste, pine") into metaphorical terms of flame, presenting his Hector to us as a man of burning generosity who will be consumed by his very ardor. This is a conception rooted in large part in the psychology of the Elizabethans, who had the habit of speaking of the soul as "fire," of one of the four temperaments as "fiery," of even the more material bodily processes, like digestion, as if they were carried on by the heat of fire ("concoction," "decoction"). It is rooted too in that characteristic Renaissance élan so unforgettably expressed in characters like Tamburlaine and Dr. Faustus, the former of whom exclaims to the stars above:

> . . . I, the chiefest lamp of all the earth,
> First rising in the East with mild aspect,
> But fixèd now in the meridian line,
> Will send up fire to your turning spheres,
> And cause the sun to borrow light of you. . . .

Pope and Dryden, by contrast, write to audiences for whom strong metaphor has become suspect. They therefore reject the fire image (which we must recall is not present in the Greek) in favor of a form of speech more congenial to their age, the *sententia* or aphorism, and give it extra vitality by making it the scene of a miniature drama: in Dryden's case, the hero's dauntless heart "urges" him (in the double sense of physical as well as moral pressure) to his fate; in Pope's, the hero's courage, like a judge, "denies" continuance of life, with the consequence that he "falls"—and here Pope's second line suggests analogy to the sacrificial animal—the victim of his own essential nature, of what he is.

To pose even more graphically the pressures that a translator's period brings, consider the following lines from Hector's reply to Andromache's appeal that he withdraw, first in Chapman's Elizabethan version, then in Lattimore's twentieth-century one:

Chapman, 1598:

> The spirit I did first breathe
> Did never teach    me that—much less since the contempt of death
> Was settled in me, and my mind knew what a Worthy was,
> Whose office is to lead in fight and give no danger pass
> Without improvement. In this fire must Hector's trial shine.
> Here must his country, father, friends be in him made divine.

Lattimore, 1951:

> and the spirit will not let me, since I have learned to be valiant and
> to fight always among the foremost ranks of the Trojans, winning for
> my own self great glory, and for my father.

If one may exaggerate to make a necessary point, the world of Henry V and Othello suddenly gives way here to our own, a world whose discomfort with any form of heroic self-assertion is remarkably mirrored in the burial of Homer's key terms (*spirit, valiant, fight, foremost, glory*)—five out of twenty-two words in the original, five out of thirty-six in the translation—in a cushioning huddle of harmless sounds.

Besides the two factors so far mentioned, language and period, as affecting the character of a translation, there is inevitably a third—the translator, with a particular degree of talent, a personal way of regarding the work to be translated, a special hierarchy of values, moral, esthetic, metaphysical (which may or may not be summed up in a "world view"), and a unique style or lack of it. But this influence all readers are likely to bear in mind, and it needs no laboring here. That, for example, two translators of Hamlet, one a Freudian, the other a Jungian, will produce impressively different translations is obvious from the fact that when Freudian and Jungian argue about the play in English they often seem to have different plays in mind.

We can now return to the question from which we started. After all allowances have been made for language, age, and individual translator, is anything of the original left? What, in short, does the reader of translations read? Let it be said at once that in utility prose—prose whose function is mainly referential—the reader who reads a translation reads everything that matters. "*Nicht Rauchen*," "*Défense de Fumer*," and "*No Smoking*," posted in a railway car, make their point, and the differences between them in sound and form have no significance for us in that context. Since the prose of a treatise and of most fiction is preponderantly referential, we rightly feel, when we have paid close attention to Cervantes or Montaigne or Machiavelli or Tolstoy in a good English translation, that we have had roughly the same experience as a native Spaniard, Frenchman, Italian, or Russian. But "roughly" is the correct word; for good prose points iconically *to* itself as well as referentially beyond itself, and everything that it points to in itself in the original (rhythms, sounds, idioms, word play, etc.) must alter radically in being translated. The best analogy is to imagine a Van Gogh painting reproduced in the medium of tempera, etching, or engraving: the "picture" remains, but the intricate interanimation of volumes with colorings with brushstrokes has disappeared.

When we move on to poetry, even in its longer narrative and dramatic forms—plays like *Oedipus*, poems like the *Iliad* or the *Divine Comedy*—our situation as English readers worsens appreciably, as the many unlike versions of Andromache's appeal to Hector make very clear. But, again, only appreciably. True, this is the point at which the fact that a translation is *always* an interpretation explodes irresistibly on our attention; but if it is the best translation of its time, like John Ciardi's translation of the *Divine Comedy* for our time, the result will be not only a sensitive interpretation but also a work with intrinsic interest in its own right—at very best, a true work of art, a new poem. It is only when the shorter, primarily lyrical forms of poetry are presented that the reader of translations faces insuperable disadvantage. In these forms, the referential aspect of language has a tendency to disappear into, or, more often, draw its real meaning and accreditation from, the iconic aspect. Let us look for just a moment at a brief poem by Federico García Lorca and its English translation (by Stephen Spender and J. L. Gili):

> *Alto pinar!*
> *Cuatro palomas por el aire van.*
>
> *Cuatro palomas*
> *vuelan y tornan.*
> *Llevan heridas*
> *sus cuatro sombras.*
>
> *Bajo pinar!*
> *Cuatro palomas en la tierra están.*

> Above the pine trees:
> Four pigeons go through the air.
>
> Four pigeons
> fly and turn round.
> They carry wounded
> their four shadows.
>
> Below the pine trees:
> Four pigeons lie on the earth.

In this translation the referential sense of the English words follows with remarkable exactness the referential sense of the Spanish words they replace. But the life of Lorca's poem does not lie in that sense. It lies in such matters as the abruptness, like an intake of breath at a sudden revelation, of the two exclamatory lines (1 and 7), which then exhale musically in images of flight and death; or as the echoings of *palomas* in *heridas* and *sombras*, bringing together (as in fact the hunter's gun has done) these unrelated nouns and the unrelated experiences they stand for in a sequence that seems, momentarily, to have all the logic of a tragic action, in which *doves* become *wounds* become *shadows*; or as the external and internal rhyming among the five verbs, as though all motion must (as in fact it must) end with *están*.

Since none of this can be brought over into another tongue (least of all Lorca's rhythms), the translator must decide between leaving a reader to wonder why Lorca is a poet to be bothered about at all, and making a new but true poem, whose merit will almost certainly be in inverse ratio to its likeness to the original. Samuel Johnson made such a poem in translating Horace's famous *Diffugere nives*, and so did A. E. Housman. If we juxtapose the last two stanzas of each translation, and the corresponding Latin, we can see at a glance that each has the consistency and inner life of a genuine poem, and that neither of them (even if we consider only what is obvious to the eye, the line-lengths) is very close to Horace.

> *Cum semel occideris, et de te splendida Minos*
> > *fecerit arbitria,*
> *non, Torquate, genus, non te facundia, non te*
> > *restituet pietas.*
>
> *Infernis neque enim tenebris Diana pudicum*
> > *liberat Hippolytum*
> *nec Lethaea valet Theseus abrumpere caro*
> > *vincula Pirithoo.*

Johnson:

> Not you, Torquatus, boast of Rome,
> When Minos once has fixed your doom,
> Or eloquence, or splendid birth,
> Or virtue, shall restore to earth.
> Hippolytus, unjustly slain,
> Diana calls to life in vain;

Nor can the might of Theseus rend
The chains of hell that hold his friend.

Housman:

When thou descendest once the shades among,
    The stern assize and equal judgment o'er,
Not thy long lineage nor thy golden tongue,
    No, nor thy righteousness, shall friend thee more.

Night holds Hippolytus the pure of stain,
    Diana steads him nothing, he must stay;
And Theseus leaves Pirithous in the chain
    The love of comrades cannot take away.

The truth of the matter is that when the translator of short poems chooses to be literal, most or all of the poetry is lost; and when the translator succeeds in forging a new poetry, most or all of the original author is lost. Since there is no way out of this dilemma, we have always been sparing, in this anthology, in our use of short poems in translation, the sole exceptions at the present time being a modest selection from one lyric poet of each of the four major European languages: Petrarch, Baudelaire, Rilke, and Lorca.

We may assure ourselves, then, that the reading of literature in translation is not the disaster it has sometimes been represented. It is true that, however good the translation, we remain at a remove from the original, the remove becoming closest to impassable in the genre of the lyric poem. But with this exception, it is obvious that translation brings us closer by far to the work than we could be if we did not read it at all, or read it with a defective knowledge of the language. "To a thousand cavils," said Samuel Johnson, "one answer is sufficient; the purpose of a writer is to be read, and the criticism which would destroy the power of pleasing must be blown aside." Johnson was defending Pope's Homer for those marks of its own time and place that make it the great interpretation it is; but Johnson's exhilarating common sense applies equally to the problem we are considering here. Literature is to be read, and the criticism that would destroy the reader's power to make some form of contact with much of the world's great writing must indeed be blown aside.

Maynard Mack

# Index